DISC 1

Chapter 1: What Is Psychology?
Early Psychological Perspectives: *Identify terms/Puzzle* • Modern Psychological Perspectives: *Identify terms/Puzzle* • Fields Within Psychology: *Identify terms/Puzzle* • Careers in Psychology: *Identify terms/Puzzle*

Chapter 2: Research Methods
Research Methods: *Identify terms/Puzzle* • Effects of Marijuana on Memory: Hypothetical Study: *Identify terms/Puzzle/movie;* Darley et al. Study: *Identify terms/Puzzle* • Experimental Designs: *Identify terms/Puzzle* • Measures of Central Tendency: *Interactive activity*

Chapter 3: Biological Bases of Behavior
Neuron Structure & Function: *Animation*/Interactive activity/ Puzzle/Interactive virtual reality* • Conduction of Information Within Neurons*: Action Potential (AP)/Resting Potential/AP: Na⁺ Ions/AP: Na⁺ & K⁺ Ions/AP: Tetrodotoxin (TTX)/Postsynaptic Potentials: *Animations* • Communication Between Neurons*: Cholinergic Synapse/Release of ACh/AChE Inactivates ACh/AChE Inhibitors/Nicotine Mimics ACh/Curare Blocks Receptors: *Animations* • Brain Structure & Function: *Interactive activities/ Puzzle/Interactive virtual 3D brain* • Cerebral Cortex Structure & Function: *Interactive activities/Puzzle*

Chapter 4: Sensation & Perception
Anatomy of the Eye, Structure: *Interactive activity/Puzzle/Interactive virtual reality eye;* Retina: *Animation;* Retina, Fovea, & Blind Spot: *Animation;* Color Vision, Trichromatic & Opponent Process Theories: *Interactive activities* • Visual Perception: Size Constancy: *Animation;* Size Constancy Illusions: *Animation;* Müller-Lyer & Ponzo Illusions: *Interactive activities;* Size Constancy, Normal & Illusory: *Interactive virtual reality;* Ames Room: *Animation/Interactive virtual reality;* Moon Illusion: *Animation* • Gestalt Principles of Visual Perception: *Identify terms/Puzzle*

Chapter 5: Consciousness
Circadian Rhythms: Owls & Larks: *Interactive activity;* Stages of Sleep: *Interactive activity* • Psychoactive Drugs: Opiate Narcotics/ CNS Depressants/CNS Stimulants/Hallucinogens: *Animations;* Understanding Addiction: *Video*

Chapter 6: Learning
Classical Conditioning: Watch Sam Learn*/Before Conditioning/ During Conditioning/After Conditioning: *Animations* • Factors in Classical Conditioning: Watch Sam Learn More*/Generalization/ Discrimination/Extinction/Spontaneous Recovery: *Animations* • Classical Conditioning of Fear: Watch the Baby Learn*/Before Conditioning/During Conditioning/After Conditioning: *Animations* • Operant Conditioning, Reinforcement & Punishment: *Identify terms/Puzzle* • Successive Approximations, Shaping: *Interactive activity*

DISC 2

Chapter 7: Memory
Three Memory Stores: *Identify terms/Puzzle* • Mechanisms & Processes of Memory: *Identify terms/Puzzle* • Improving Memory: Using Mnemonics/Three Stores View: *Animations;* Neural Networks & Memory: *Video*

Chapter 8: Language & Thought
Kinds of Critical Thinking: *Identify terms/Puzzle* • Strategies & Obstacles in Problem Solving: Solving Well-Structured & Ill-Structured Problems/Hindrances to Problem Solving: Mental Set: *Interactive activities* • Judgment & Decision Making: Gambler's Fallacy: *Interactive activity*

Chapter 9: Intelligence
Factor Theories: *Identify terms/Puzzle* • Multiple Intelligences: *Identify terms; Puzzle* • Triarchic Theory: *Identify terms/Puzzle* • Culture & Intelligence: The "Chitling" Test/Cattell's Culture-Fair Intelligence Test: *Interactive activities;* Normal Distribution of IQs: *Animation* • Gender & Intelligence: Mental Rotation/Embedded-Figures Test: *Interactive activities*

Chapter 10: Physical & Cognitive Development
Theories of Cognitive Development: *Identify terms/Puzzle* • Cognitive Development During Infancy: Object Permanence, Absent & Present: *Animations* • Cognitive Development During Childhood: Conservation, Difficulties & Success: *Animations* • Cognitive Development During Adolescence: Abstract Reasoning, Difficulties & Success: *Animations*

Chapter 11: Social Development
Personality Development, Erikson's Theory: *Identify terms/Puzzle* • Moral Development, Kohlberg's Theory: *Identify terms/Puzzle*

Chapter 12: Motivation & Emotion
Theories of Motivation: *Identify terms/Puzzle;* Hunger: Sensitivity to External Cues/Psychosocial Response to Orgasm: *Interactive activities* • Theories of Emotion: *Identify terms/Puzzle;* Schacter & Singer's Theory: *Animation* • Expressions of Emotions: Facial Expressions/Cultural & Emotional Expressions/Genuine & False Smiles: *Interactive activities*

Chapter 13: Social Psychology: Personal Perspectives
Attribution Theory: *Identify terms/Puzzle* • Attraction, Liking, & Loving, Factors & Theories: *Identify terms/Puzzle* • Sternberg's Triangular Theory of Love/Triangular Love Scale: *Interactive activities*

Chapter 14: Social Psychology: Interpersonal & Group Perspectives
Conformity: Asch Experiment Simulation: *Interactive activity* • Compliance: *Identify terms/Puzzle* • Prosocial Behavior: *Identify terms/Puzzle;* Support Groups: *Video*

Chapter 15: Personality
Personality Theories: *Identify terms/Puzzle* • Freud's Structure of Personality: *Identify terms/Puzzle* • Defense Mechanisms: *Identify terms/Puzzle* • Stages of Psychosexual Development: *Identify terms/ Puzzle* • The Big Five Personality Traits: *Identify terms/Puzzle;* Big Five Demonstration: *Interactive activity*

Chapter 16: Psychological Disorders
The Five Axes of DSM-IV: *Identify terms/Puzzle* • Diagnosing Anxiety, Mood, & Schizophrenic Disorders: *Interactive activities* • Depression: *Video/Identify terms/Puzzle* • Schizophrenia: *Video*

Chapter 17: Psychotherapy
Psychotherapies & Pharmacotherapies: *Identify terms/Puzzles*

Chapter 18: Health, Stress, & Coping
Stress & Coping: Social Readjustment Rating Scale/Hassles Rating Scale/Type-A Versus Type-B • Behavior: *Interactive activities* • Health & Stress: *Video*

You can also check your mastery of the material by taking the self-tests and answering the critical thinking questions at the end of every chapter.

* In Spanish & English

www.wadsworth.com

www.wadsworth.com is the World Wide Web site for Wadsworth and is your direct source to dozens of online resources.

At *www.wadsworth.com* you can find out about supplements, demonstration software, and student resources. You can also send email to many of our authors and preview new publications and exciting new technologies.

www.wadsworth.com
Changing the way the world learns®

ROBERT J. STERNBERG

YALE UNIVERSITY

With contributions by
JOSEPHINE F. WILSON
WITTENBERG UNIVERSITY

THOMSON ™

WADSWORTH

Australia • Canada • Mexico • Singapore • Spain
United Kingdom • United States

THOMSON

WADSWORTH

Psychology Editor: *Vicki Knight*
Development Editor: *Penelope Sky*
Assistant Editor: *Jennifer Wilkinson*
Editorial Assistant: *Monica Sarmiento*
Technology Project Manager: *Darin Derstine*
Marketing Manager: *Lori Grebe*
Marketing Assistant: *Laurel Anderson*
Advertising Project Manager: *Brian Chaffee*
Project Manager, Editorial Production: *Kirk Bomont*
Print/Media Buyer: *Karen Hunt*

Permissions Editor: *Joohee Lee*
Art Editor: *Lisa Torri*
Photo Researcher: *Linda Rill*
Copy Editor: *Carol Reitz*
Illustrator: *Precision Graphics*
Cover Image: *Judith Larzelere*
Cover Printer: *Transcontinental Printing/Interglobe*
Compositor: *Graphic World, Inc.*
Printer: *Transcontinental Printing/Interglobe*

For more information about our products, contact us at:
Thomson Learning Academic Resource Center
1-800-423-0563
For permission to use material from this text, contact us by:
Phone: 1-800-730-2214
Fax: 1-800-730-2215
Web: http://www.thomsonrights.com

Library of Congress Control Number: 2003108944

Student Edition: ISBN 0-534-61812-X

Instructor's Edition: ISBN 0-534-61820-0

Wadsworth/Thomson Learning
10 Davis Drive
Belmont, CA 94002-3098
USA

Asia
Thomson Learning
5 Shenton Way #01-01
UIC Building
Singapore 068808

Australia/New Zealand
Thomson Learning
102 Dodds Street
Southbank, Victoria 3006
Australia

Canada
Nelson
1120 Birchmount Road
Toronto, Ontario M1K 5G4
Canada

Europe/Middle East/Africa
Thomson Learning
High Holborn House
50/51 Bedford Row
London WC1R 4LR
United Kingdom

Latin America
Thomson Learning
Seneca, 53
Colonia Polanco
11560 Mexico D.F.
Mexico

Spain/Portugal
Paraninfo
Calle/Magallanes, 25
28015 Madrid, Spain

Robert J. Sternberg is IBM Professor of Psychology and Education in the department of psychology at Yale University; director of the Yale Center for the Psychology of Abilities, Competences, and Expertise; and president of the American Psychological Association. He graduated summa cum laude, Phi Beta Kappa, from Yale in 1972, receiving honors with exceptional distinction in psychology. He received his PhD in psychology from Stanford University in 1975, and holds four honorary doctorates.

Sternberg is a fellow of the American Psychological Association, the American Psychological Society, the Connecticut Psychological Association, the American Academy of Arts and Sciences, the American Association for the Advancement of Science, and the Society of Experimental Psychologists. His many awards include several from APA: the Early Career Award; the Boyd R. McCandless Award of the Division of Developmental Psychology (7); the Farnsworth Award of the Division of Psychology and the Arts (10); and the E. L. Thorndike Award for Career Achievement in Educational Psychology of the Division of Educational Psychology (15). He also received the James McKeen Cattell Award from APS.

Sternberg has served as president of four divisions of APA. He has been editor of the Psychological Bulletin and is currently editor of the APA Review of Books: Contemporary Psychology. He has written or edited roughly 950 refereed publications, most in the fields of intelligence, creativity, wisdom, styles of thinking, and love.

One of Sternberg's great passions is teaching the introductory psychology course, as he has done almost every year since 1980. He has edited a book on the teaching of introductory psychology and been a featured speaker on the subject at many conferences; he frequently contributes to Teaching of Psychology. This textbook grew out of Sternberg's desire to share with students his enthusiasm and passion for the introductory course.

Sternberg has two children, Seth and Sara, and is married to Elena L. Grigorenko.

CONTENTS IN BRIEF

CONTENTS

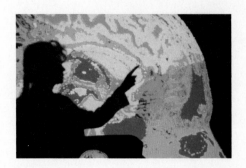

CHAPTER 9
INTELLIGENCE   324

IN THE LAB OF RICHARD HAIER
Watching Intelligence and Consciousness   337

FEATURE BOXES

UNIFYING PSYCHOLOGY

A PERSONAL JOURNEY

My interest in introductory psychology began years ago, when I took the course and got a C in it. My work was so mediocre that one day the teacher commented that "there is a famous Sternberg in psychology [Saul Sternberg, a cognitive psychologist now at the University of Pennsylvania], and it looks like there won't be another one." Yet somehow I went on to graduate from college with honors, with exceptional distinction in psychology. I then earned a PhD in psychology from Stanford, and eventually became president of the American Psychological Association. I have taught psychology for many years, in a way that I hope enables every student to excel.

Many years ago, when my career had just begun, another psychologist at Yale asked me to collaborate on an introductory psychology text that would have an evolutionary approach. Committed then (and now) to this perspective, I agreed. Unfortunately, the collaboration ended when my colleague and I discovered that each of us meant something different by "evolution"—she meant biological evolution and I meant intellectual evolution. Some years later, I wrote the first edition of this book, focusing on the evolution of ideas.

The second edition of *Psychology* represented progress in my own thinking by integrating the evolution of organisms and ideas. We can be grateful that humans have evolved biologically to the point where our thinking can evolve as well.

The third edition of *Psychology* reflected the further development of my thinking, particularly as it pertains to teaching. Students need to understand the fundamental flow of ideas—from the mind to the lab to the everyday world and back again.

The fourth edition of *Psychology* offers new pedagogical features and emphasizes the theme of unity in psychological science.

THE FOURTH EDITION

The goal of *Psychology*, Fourth Edition, is to teach students to think about psychology the way psychologists do. That is, I want them to learn its processes as well as its content. To demonstrate this relationship, biological, cognitive, developmental, social-psychological, and clinical approaches are discussed throughout, both independently and in terms of their interactions. Psychology advances as a scientific discipline because psychologists integrate ideas from diverse perspectives.

The main theme of this edition is that psychology as a discipline unites many diverse specialties and perspectives. It arose out of my mission as president of the American Psychological Association—to promote the unity of psychology as a whole.

POINTS OF CONTINUITY

The fourth edition of *Psychology* retains the most successful features of the third edition.

- Psychology is presented as both a natural science and a social science, and their interactions are explored.
- How organisms and ideas develop is emphasized, resulting in a text that is fully rather than partially evolutionary in its approach.
- Multicultural and cross-cultural information helps students understand that various perspectives are an integral part of psychology.
- "Psychology in Everyday Life" boxes show practical ways of applying psychology to everyday life.
- The glossary captures key terms and definitions in one place.
- An appendix illustrates statistical methods by showing students how to survey their classmates and analyze the data.

GENERAL CHANGES IN THIS EDITION

I have made a number of substantial improvements in this revision.

New title I dropped the subtitle *In Search of the Human Mind* because for some professors it implied an acceptance of Cartesian dualism, in which mind and body are separate. The book is not intended to promote this particular position, so the subtitle was viewed as misleading by some.

Reading level Students will find this edition much easier to read than its predecessors. The level of the previous editions seemed higher in part because some sentences were simply too long and convoluted. I have reviewed every sentence to ensure readability. Additional examples add interest and promote retention of the material under discussion.

Currency   This is the most extensively updated edition yet, with about 1000 new references—roughly 50 per chapter—most of them from 2000 and later. Students will learn about the latest theories and research. Classical references remain, however, because students need to understand not only what psychology is today but how it has developed.

New box   To extend the main theme of the book, every chapter now includes a box called "Unifying Psychology" to show how psychologists from various disciplines would approach the same topic. The topics themselves are compelling—"The Effects of Sleep Deprivation," "Treatment for Addicted Women," "Learning a Second Language," "Fear and Shyness," "The Social Contagion of Bulimia," "Snipers: The Criminal Mind," and many others.

"In the Lab" box   In this feature, which appears in every chapter, practicing psychologists explain how they conduct research, usually by describing particular experiments. Half the essays are new; those that have been retained are thoroughly updated. Professional biographies of the researchers have been added.

Concept Checks   Self-quizzes are one of the best ways for students to make sure they understand what they have been studying. I have added three multiple-choice questions at the end of every main section to ensure that students comprehend the material. Answers are at the end of the chapter.

Critical thinking   As in the third edition, "Think About It" questions are included at the end of each chapter (suggested answers have been moved to the back of the book). Because critical thinking requires a knowledge base that is both broad and deep, 10 multiple-choice "Knowledge Check" questions have been added to the chapter-ending features.

Chapter summaries   In the previous editions, chapter summaries reiterated the main points of the chapter without making clear what questions they addressed. Consequently, the questions that follow the main text heads in this edition reappear in the summaries, to help students recognize the subject of each section.

Highlighted definitions   The in-text key terms and definitions are now set in blue type so students can find them easily when they review the chapters.

Icons indicating evolutionary and cultural content   Passages that focus on evolution are marked with a small circled "E"; cross-cultural content with a "C."

Web resources   At the end of every chapter, students will find annotated URLs for excellent sites that are of particular relevance to the subjects they have just been reading about. They will also have access to InfoTrac College Edition, an online library of complete articles from a wide variety of journals. They will be directed to the Wadsworth Web site, where they will find many features that are specific to this text and available nowhere else, including tutorials and quizzes.

CD correlations   Another chapter-ending feature is a list of the corresponding topics on the accompanying CD, *Unifying Psychology*. Students can move smoothly from one medium to another as they study the subjects that are included in both places, but with different kinds of pedagogy.

CHAPTER-BY-CHAPTER CHANGES

CHAPTER 1
- New coverage of female and minority contributions to psychology
- Abbreviated material on the very early history of psychology, which is not of much interest to many modern students (e.g., detailed discussion of Hippocrates)
- New material on the importance of theory to psychology
- Simplified section on Skinner highlights major concepts
- New material on molecular genetics
- New discussion of forensic psychology, political psychology, and positive psychology

CHAPTER 2
- Ethics section expanded to increase coverage of IRBs
- Reorganized material on experimental methods and causal inference
- New examples of experimental methods
- New cultural material (for example, children who may not do well in school may be gifted interpreters for their non-English-speaking parents, based on Valdes's work)
- Expanded section on critical thinking

CHAPTER 3
- Additional material on spinal-cord injury
- More material on Phineas Gage, a case that seems to interest all students
- New table on neurotransmitters
- Section on specific neurotransmitters moved to follow the discussion of nerve conduction in general

- Emphasis that the terms "left-brained" and "right-brained" are metaphorical rather than scientific
- New material on fMRI
- New section distinguishing evolutionary psychology from biological evolution

CHAPTER 4
- Addition of optimal foraging theory as an example of how evolution shapes our interactions with the environment
- New material on the deterioration with age of eye functioning; includes macular degeneration
- New material on the role of perception in mate choice
- Expanded discussion of how the opponent-process and trichromatic theories of color vision can be reconciled

CHAPTER 5
- Further coverage of the hallucinogenic drug Ecstasy
- New section on the Stroop effect
- New material on priming and unconscious stereotypes
- New section on blindsight
- Updated table on common dreams of college students
- New material on the reliability of courtroom testimony by witnesses who have been hypnotized
- New material on the relation of thinking to drinking

CHAPTER 6
- Reorganized to improve comprehension
- New material on the concrete shaping of behavior
- New material on how behavioral interventions can reduce aggression

CHAPTER 7
- New section on autobiographical memory
- New section on memory distortions
- New material on eyewitness testimony
- Updating to reflect Baddeley's expanded theory of working memory
- New material on the functioning of the amygdala

CHAPTER 8
- New material on brain mechanisms in children's language learning
- New material on children's learning of language across cultures
- New discussion of Clark's principles of conventionality and contrast
- New discussion of the sunk-cost fallacy
- New discussion of the "take-the-best" heuristic
- New discussion of the false-consensus effect

CHAPTER 9
- Update on work relating working memory to general intelligence
- Update on new physiological work on the relation of brain size to IQ
- Update on evolutionary theories of intelligence
- Enhanced material relating culture to intelligence
- Updated discussion of emotional intelligence
- Additional material on teaching for intelligence
- Update on the effects of the environment on intellectual skills

CHAPTER 10
- New material on the effects of the environment on cognitive development, including family variables
- Clarified exposition of Piaget's theory
- New material on concept development
- New material on the theory of mind

CHAPTER 11
- New material on the fundamental nature of socioemotional development, including the notion of critical periods
- New material on extended families and their effects
- New material on positive and negative emotions in emotional development
- New material on the effects of labeling and self-fulfilling prophecy
- New material on sex differences in psychosexual development
- New material on the effects of caregiving on socio-emotional development
- New material on the NICHD Study of Early Child Care
- New material on resilience

CHAPTER 12
- New obesity statistics from the CDC
- Discussion of a study on the effects of media images on dieters and non-dieters
- New statistics on changes in sexual behavior with age
- New material on sexual jealousy in men and women
- New material on men's and women's perceptions of date rape
- New research showing that people living in miserable circumstances can find happiness
- New research showing that trained professionals (including psychologists) can detect lying
- New section on death and dying

CHAPTER 13
- Three new concept-summary tables
- New research showing that likeability affects memory

- New research linking self-perception theory to PMS
- New research on self-handicapping in women with regard to math
- New material on self-serving bias
- New research on how impressions of negative relatives generalize across their families
- New research showing that confirmation bias is stronger when information is presented sequentially instead of all at once
- New research showing that self-fulfilling prophecy occurs at organizational levels as well as individually
- New material on impression formation in family members of criminals
- New research showing that chickens, like humans, respond most favorably to attractive human faces!
- New material on the effects of equity in relationships

CHAPTER 14
- New material on Nisbett's recent work on Eastern versus Western ways of thinking and interacting
- New material on students in classrooms and social loafing
- New material on Wood and Eagly's (2002) theory of sex differences in conformity and adaptive behavior
- New material on studies of conformity in the United States and Japan
- New discussion of a study comparing how children in the United States and Japan relate to other children (for example, with regard to exclusionary behavior in social groups)
- New section on evil and hatred, considering work by Staub, Baumeister, and others

CHAPTER 15
- New discussion of the relationship between culture and personality
- Addition of relational theories
- Revised discussion of the humanistic approach, to make it evaluative rather than pejorative
- New material on the use of Eysenck's theory to predict health outcomes
- New material on the influence of culture on whether achievement is viewed as primarily individual or group-based
- New material on relational theories as an extension of object-relations theories
- New material showing that smokers who score high on neuroticism tend to be more susceptible to heart disease
- New material on Saucier and Goldberg's extension of the Big Five
- New biological material showing that asymmetries in ear-drum temperatures predict individual differences in personality and behavior

CHAPTER 16
- New discussion of the affective model of self-esteem as it pertains to mental health
- Clarification of the diasthesis-stress model
- Clarification that the DSM is continually under revision
- New examples of compulsions
- New explanation of the two main forms of bipolar disorder, and of its treatment
- Updated statistics on suicide and related phenomena
- New discussion of attempted suicide
- New material on evolutionary interpretations of schizophrenia
- New material on the affective theory of self-esteem
- Updated statistics on suicide
- Evidence that stress increases the likelihood of schizophrenia symptoms in susceptible people
- Discussion of an evolutionary view of schizophrenia

CHAPTER 17
- Discussion of Torrey and Miller study showing that mental illness has been widespread for at least 250 years
- Mention of new SSRI drugs
- Note that benzodiazapines affect driving much as alcohol does
- Discussion of religious cults and charismatic groups administering "psychotherapy"
- Further data on the success of 12-step programs as therapy
- Inclusion of A. Lazarus on the importance of temperamental compatibility to success in marriage
- New material on the effects of deinstitutionalization
- New note that the name of a type of therapy does not necessarily describe what actually happens in sessions
- New explanation that the effectiveness of a certain kind of therapy depends in part on the client's personality

CHAPTER 18
- Added material on the effects of stress on health and marital adjustment
- Added material on Type A personality
- Added material on patients' preference for patient-centered medical practitioners
- New statistics on hospital admissions and their causes
- New material on SARS
- Updating of Holmes-Rahe SRRS stressor statistics
- Updated data on causes of death

ANCILLARIES

Instructor's Resource Manual *Prepared by Benjamin R. Walker, Georgetown University.* The Instructor's Resource Manual contains a resource integration guide, learning objectives, brief chapter outlines, detailed chapter outlines with additional activities and discussion topics, additional lecture topics, Internet activities, InfoTrac search terms and exercises, additional readings, video suggestions, annotated Web links, and approximately 10 projects/written assignments to enhance critical thinking in every chapter of the book. (0-534-61814-6)

Test Bank *Prepared by Melvyn B. King, State University of New York, Cortland, and Debra E. Clark.* For every chapter of the text, the Test Bank contains approximately 180 multiple-choice items (two-thirds conceptual, one-third factual), and approximately 45 essay questions (several based on the new "Unifying Psychology" boxes). Fifteen multiple-choice items per chapter, marked with "WWW," are available as online student quizzes. (0-534-61815-4). The Test Bank is also available in ExamView® electronic format. (0-534-61816-2).

Multimedia Manager *Prepared by Lonnie Yandell, Belmont University.* This one-stop lecture tool makes it easy to assemble, edit, publish, and deliver custom lectures for your course, using Microsoft® PowerPoint®. The Multimedia Manager lets you combine text-specific lecture outlines, art, video, animations from the CD-ROM, and Web features with your own material—culminating in a powerful, personalized, media-enhanced presentation. (0-534-61817-0)

Study Guide *Prepared by Jada Kearns, Valencia Community College, East Campus.* Each chapter of the Study Guide contains a chapter review, learning objectives, and multiple-choice and fill-in questions for each main-text section. Other features include "Can You Put It All Together?" a section with matching, labeling, and short-answer questions, "Think About It," a section with one creative, one analytical, and one practical essay question, and a "Progress Test" that offers multiple-choice questions that cover the entire text chapter. (0-534-61813-8)

WebTutor Advantage on WebCT and Blackboard WebTutor Advantage is a complete course management system and communication tool. Ready to use as soon as you log in, WebTutor is pre-loaded with text-specific content organized by chapter, including animations, video clips, practice quizzes, and more. Customize in any way you choose—from up-loading images and text to adding Web links and your own materials. Conduct virtual office hours, post syllabi and other course content, set up threaded discussions, and track student progress with quizzes. Robust communication tools include a course calendar, asynchronous discussion, real-time chat, a whiteboard, and an integrated email system, making it easy for you to connect with your students and for your students to stay involved in the course. WebTutor Advantage features expand your course beyond the classroom, and include real-time access to:

> *Study tools:* chapter outlines, summaries, learning objectives, glossary flashcards with audio, practice quizzes, InfoTrac® College Edition exercises, and Web links.
>
> *Audiovisual aids:* lab simulations, animations, and videos that make difficult concepts less intimidating.
>
> *Engaging interactive content:* assessments and learning games that encourage mastery. (WebCT: 0-534-61819-7; Blackboard: 0-534-61818-9)

MyCourse 2.1 This versatile course management system lets you quickly create a course-specific Web site. MyCourse includes pre- and post-test quizzes prepared by James Haugh, Rowan University. It allows you to attach or load your syllabus, assign your own materials, track and report student progress, create individual performance grade books, and more. MyCourse requires no pincodes. Contact your Thomson representative if you are interested in using this useful tool. Not available separately.

Unifying Psychology CD-ROM This text-specific CD contains more than 150 modules, including videos, animations, virtual reality reviews, matching, unit quizzing, and interactive activities. The two-CD set includes:

- Quizzes prepared by Chris Hakala, Western New England College, and critical thinking questions for each chapter, all of which can be emailed or printed.
- 34 pairs of interactive "Identify/Puzzle" modules, in which definition screens ("Identify") are followed by Jeopardy-like puzzle screens ("Puzzle").
- 43 QuickTime animations, mostly rendered in 3D. Sixteen animations include a Spanish language audio tract.
- 7 QuickTime Virtual Reality interactive movies. In these, students can manipulate and explore objects in 3D space—for example, a neuron or a brain.
- 37 interactive activities, including sections on the parts of a research study, descriptive statistics, parts of the neuron, brain structure and function, structure and function of the eye, visual perception, and more.

ACKNOWLEDGMENTS

I am grateful to the following colleagues whose helpful comments in prerevision and manuscript reviews, in this and previous editions, were of considerable benefit:

FOURTH EDITION

Mary Beth Ahlum, Nebraska Wesleyan University
Ronald Baenninger, Temple University
Carol Batt, Sacred Heart University
Patricia Berretty, Fordham University
Amy Bohmann, Texas Lutheran University
Jennifer Butler, Wittenberg University
Robert Caldwell, Michigan State University
James Calhoun, University of Georgia
Jodi DeLuca, Embry-Riddle Aeronautical University
Kim Dielmann, University of Central Arkansas
Kenneth Elliot, University of Maine at Augusta
James Forbes, Angelo State University
Sandra Frankmann, University of Southern Colorado
Nelson Freedman, Queen's University
Stephen Guastello, Marquette University
Mark Hartlaub, Texas A & M University—Corpus Christie
Anthony Hermann, Kalamazoo College
G. Christian Jernstedt, Dartmouth College
David McDonald, University of Missouri
Paul Merritt, The George Washington University
Dianne Moran, Benedictine University
Teresa Polenski, West Liberty State College
Paula Shear, University of Cincinnati
Benjamin Walker, Georgetown University
Nancy Woolf, University of California, Los Angeles

THIRD EDITION

Ronald Baenninger, Temple University
Nan Bernstein Ratner, University of Maryland, College Park
Ellen Berscheid, University of Minnesota
John Borkowski, University of Notre Dame
Donald M. Burke, Minot State University
George A. Cicala, University of Delaware
David E. Clement, University of South Carolina
Dennis Cogan, Texas Tech University
Paul T. Costa, National Institute on Aging
Lawrence Fehr, Widener University
Michela Gallagher, Johns Hopkins University
Gary Gargano, St. Joseph's University
Thomas Gerstenberger, SUNY Potsdam
Harvey J. Ginsburg, Southwest Texas State University
Gary Greenberg, Wichita State University
R. W. Kamphaus, University of Georgia
Matthew Kinslow, Eastern Kentucky University

Karen Kopera-Frye, University of Akron
Stephen A. Maisto, Syracuse University
Arthur Markman, University of Texas, Austin
Johnmarshall Reeve, University of Iowa
Brian Oppy, California State University, Chico
Jesse E. Purdy, Southwestern University
Michael Raulin, State University of New York, Buffalo
Russell Revlin, University of California, Santa Barbara
Bret Roark, Oklahoma Baptist University
Henry Roediger, Washington University
Thomas Rowe, University of Wisconsin–Stevens Point
Juan Salinas, University of Texas, Austin
Thomas R. Scott, University of Delaware
Jerome Sehulster, University of Connecticut, Stamford
Robert S. Siegler, Carnegie Mellon University
Pawan Sinha, University of Wisconsin, Madison
Steven Smith, Texas A & M University
Shelley Taylor, University of California, Los Angeles
William Van Ornum, Marist College
Nancy J. Woolf, University of California, Los Angeles
Michael Zarate, University of Texas, El Paso

SECOND EDITION

David Baker, University of North Texas
James Butler, James Madison University
James F. Calhoun, University of Georgia
Mary Camac, Roanoke Universty
Jeffrey L. Charvat, University of Missouri
Michael L. Chase, Quincy University
Stephen L. Chew, Stanford University
Scott D. Churchill, University of Dallas
Thaddeus M. Cowan, Kansas State University
Robert H. I. Dale, Butler University
Jeanne Dugas, Columbus College
Michael B. Ehlert, Brigham Young University
Gloria J. Emmett, University of North Texas
Donald Evans, Drake University
Paul Finn, St. Anselm University
Mary Ann Fischer, Indiana University Northwest
Kathleen A. Flannery, St. Anselm College
Dwight Fultz, Bemidji State University
Grace Galliano, Kennesaw State College
Pryor Hale, Piedmont Virginia Community College
George Hertl, Northwest Mississippi Community College
Mark Hoyert, Indiana University Northwest
Kriss Klassen, North Idaho College
Mike Knight, University of Central Oklahoma
Lester Krames, University of Toronto
Theresa Lee, University of Michigan
Zella Luria, Tufts University
Leonard S. Mark, Miami University of Ohio
Carolyn Meyer, Lake Sumter Community College
David I. Mostofsky, Boston University
Cynthia O'Dell, Indiana University Northwest
Marites F. Pinon, Southwest Texas State University

Michael Renner, West Chester University
Gloria Scheff, Broward Community College
Peggy Skinner, South Plains College
Holly R. Straub, University of South Dakota
Holly A. Taylor, Tufts University
Donna Thompson, Midland College
Spencer Thompson, University of Texas—Permian Basin
Frank J. Vattano, Colorado State University
Matthew Westra, Longview Community College
Judith Wheat, James Madison University
Burrton G. Woodruff, Butler University
Diana Younger, University of Texas—Permian Basin
Andrea Zabel, Midland College
Martha S. Zlokovich, Southeast Missouri State University

I also thank a number of people who worked together as a team to produce this textbook. Vicki Knight, the acquisitions editor, watched it closely in every phase of its development. Penelope Sky, the developmental editor, spent countless hours going over each chapter in detail to make sure it was the best it could possibly be. Project manager Kirk Bomont did a masterful job of shepherding the project from the time the book went into production through to publication, missing none of the many, many details. Carol Reitz, the copyeditor, carefully polished each chapter to ensure its readability and to correct any errors that had been missed in earlier stages. Lisa Torri, the art coordinator, improved the look of the figures considerably. Linda Rill, the photo researcher, found many fresh and exciting images that enhance both the visual appeal and the pedagogical value of the text. Art director Vernon Boes expertly coordinated and oversaw the development of the fresh new interior and cover designs. Jeanne Calabrese, the designer, created a more exciting look for the book than it had in any previous edition. Brian Chaffee, advertising project manager, and Lori Grebe, marketing manager, worked hard and enthusiastically to develop superior marketing and advertising for this fourth edition. Alex Isgut, my administrative assistant, provided invaluable help in preparing the manuscript for the publishing team. Special appreciation goes to Josephine F. Wilson, who contributed the great new feature, Unifying Psychology, that appears in every chapter.

I especially thank my introductory psychology students for putting up with me over the years as I tried out materials in class. My undergraduate advisor, Endel Tulving, and my graduate advisor, Gordon Bower, both profoundly affected how I think about psychology, as did Wendell Garner, a faculty mentor at Yale.

I thank my group of collaborators at the PACE Center at Yale for the support they have always given me. Without them, I could never have accomplished even a small fraction of the work I have done.

Finally, I deeply thank my wife, Elena Grigorenko, for putting up with and supporting me while I was writing this revision.

Robert J. Sternberg

CHAPTER 1

WHAT IS PSYCHOLOGY?

The school psychologist entered the elementary-school classroom. I froze, paralyzed by test anxiety that had led to low scores in the past. She passed out some booklets. When she loudly said, "Go," I didn't. I couldn't. While my classmates were busily working, I sat there, still frozen, gaping at the test. I had to know what was wrong with me. That's how I first became interested in intelligence and mental abilities, which I later came to know were aspects of psychology. Anxiety during test-taking is also part of that field of study. So are concerns about the culture-fairness of tests. Because of this experience, I decided to study psychology and become a psychologist. How about you? What interests you about psychology? And what is psychology, anyway?

PSYCHOLOGY AS A NATURAL SCIENCE AND A SOCIAL SCIENCE

What is psychology? What do psychologists study? How is psychology different from other ways of studying mental processes and behavior?

Psychology is the study of mental processes, behavior, and the relationship between them. Mental processes include skills like learning, reasoning, emotion, and motivation. To study psychology is to learn how humans and other organisms think, understand, learn, perceive, feel, act, and interact with others. It is to learn, for example, why some people, like me as a child, experience anxiety when taking tests. Although people are the predominant focus of psychological theory and research, psychologists study a broad array of organisms, from single-celled creatures to mammals. Sometimes these studies are ends in themselves, as when one wishes to understand the relative intelligence of different species of nonhuman animals (Zentall, 2000). Other times they are ways to investigate structures and phenomena that would be impossible, impractical, or unethical to study in humans. For example, the study of the physiology (such as the functioning of the eye or of nerve cells) and behavior (such as responses to various kinds of rewards) of nonhuman animals offers possible analogies with human physiology and behavior. Because psychology encompasses human and social issues as well as biological and physiological ones, it is categorized as both a natural and a social science.

As a *natural science*, psychology is concerned with the laws of nature. As a *social science*, psychology involves the study of the laws of the thoughts, feelings, and behaviors of humans and other organisms. Some psychologists deal more with the natural–scientific aspects of psychology. An example is the brain and its relation to behavior. Other psychologists deal more with the social–scientific aspects of psychology. An example is how people interact in groups. Often, though, it is difficult to distinguish between the two aspects of psychology because nature interacts bidirectionally with all living organisms. For example, climate affects the way people act. But people also have acted on the environment in ways that affect the climate, such as creating the rising temperatures of the greenhouse effect. Many natural scientists study human behavior. *Geneticists* study the influence of genes (as well as the environment) on behavior, and *physiologists* study physical and biochemical influences on behavior.

Psychologists and other scientists view these various ways of understanding behavior as complementary because they contribute to each other. Thus, psychology possesses a certain fundamental unity despite differences in particular approaches. Psychologists profit from insights into human behavior offered by other disciplines as well. Important examples are biology and computer science. Psychology shares a focus on human behavior with other social–scientific disciplines, such as sociology and anthropology. The fields overlap considerably in both what they study and how they study it. Consider the family. The focus of psychology is generally on the individual, whether alone or in interaction with others and the environment. *Psychologists* might study how the family affects the development of the child, or how the behavior of the child affects the family. *Sociologists* generally inves-

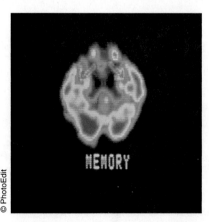

Psychology is both a natural and a social science. Psychologists may study the neural basis for memory. They may also study ways to help children learn and recall information.

tigate larger aggregates of individuals, such as occupational, societal, economic, or ethnic groups. The sociologist might therefore be interested in how economic factors affect the cohesion of the family unit. *Cultural anthropologists* seek to gain insight into various cultures. Thus, a cultural anthropologist might be interested in how family units differ from one culture to another. *Physical anthropologists* study human evolution from simpler organisms. They might be interested in comparing the human family unit with a group of birds or monkeys.

Nonscientists also study human behavior. We can learn what people are like and how they act by reading poems or novels, historical analyses, or religious works. Works of art such as paintings and sculptures can also provide insight into human behavior. The difference between the psychological approach to mental processes and behavior and the approach of the humanities is psychology's emphasis on scientific theory and methodology. Science provides a unique set of methods for validating and sometimes replacing old ideas with new and (usually) better ones. These methods are the subject of the next chapter.

This chapter is concerned with the general shape and development of the field of psychology. We examine its history, the roots of contemporary psychology, by getting to know a little about the people and ideas that have shaped the field. Looking back may not seem like the best way to begin, but the advantage of this approach is its recognition that the way we view the present is shaped, in part, by the past. One key theme of the historical view is that ideas evolve in a cyclical way. Recent research (discussed in Chapter 18) has begun to show the ways in which psychological stress can impair immune system functioning and even lead to physical illness (Kiecolt-Glaser, McGuire, Robles, & Glaser, 2002a, 2002b; McGuire, Kiecolt-Glaser, & Glaser, 2002; Stowell, Kiecolt-Glaser, & Glaser, 2001). The idea that the mind affects the body was accepted by the ancient Greeks, but it was not at all popular with many psychologists during the first half of the 20th century. These psychologists were seeking to establish psychology's credentials as a science. The concept has come up again at the turn of this new century because modern scientific studies have provided evidence for it. We will look at the evolution of some of the core ideas of psychology throughout this book.

One reason for the cyclical development of ideas is that philosophers, psychologists, and others often propose and believe strongly in one set of ideas for a while, until a contrasting set comes to light. The most attractive or reasonable elements in each are melded into a new arrangement, which then gains acceptance. This integrated view then serves as the springboard for a new collection of ideas and eventually yet another melding of ideas.

✓ CONCEPT CHECK 1

1. Psychologists study
   a. only mental processes.
   b. only behavior.
   c. both mental processes and behavior.
   d. neither mental processes nor behavior.
2. Psychology is best conceived of as
   a. a natural science only.
   b. a social science only.
   c. a natural and a social science.
   d. neither a natural nor a social science.
3. The religious rituals of native inhabitants of a preindustrial tribe in Papua New Guinea are most likely to be studied by a
   a. sociologist.
   b. cultural anthropologist.
   c. physical anthropologist.
   d. cognitive psychologist.

KEY THEMES IN THE EVOLUTION OF PSYCHOLOGICAL IDEAS

How do you think ideas evolve over time?

Georg Hegel (1770–1831), a German philosopher, referred to the evolution of thought as a **dialectic,** a continuing intellectual dialogue in which thinkers strive for increased understanding. First, thinkers strive to reach the truth by positing an initial **thesis,** or statement of opinion. Other thinkers soon propose an **antithesis,** an opinion that takes a somewhat different perspective and often contradicts the original thesis. Eventually, another thinker suggests a **synthesis,** the selective combining of the two opinions (Hegel, 1807/1931). This synthesized statement may then be considered a new thesis, for which an antithesis may then arise. This sequence continues as the evolutionary process of developing thought moves onward. An example of the dialectical process in psychology is the attitudes of researchers of intelligence about the roles of nature (biology) and nurture

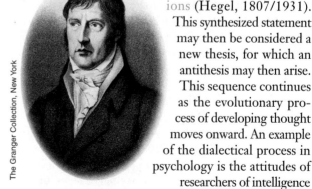

The Granger Collection, New York

Georg Hegel is known for introducing the concept of the dialectic.

TABLE 1.1
CONCEPT REVIEW

Historical Dialectic of Psychology

Thesis (Original Statement)	Antithesis (Opposing Statement)	Synthesis (Integrative Statement)
Opinion		
Scientific problems are best solved by rational thought (e.g., Descartes).	Scientific problems are best solved by empirical observations (e.g., Locke).	Scientific problems are best solved by combining rational thought and empirical observations (e.g., Kant).
Example		
Language development is guided by behavior is operating on the environment (e.g., Skinner).	Language development is guided by an innate language-acquisition device (e.g., Chomsky).	Language development is guided by responses to environmental stimuli interacting with an innate language-acquisition device (e.g., Bloom).

(environment) in human development. Early in the 20th century, researchers very much emphasized the role of biological factors (*thesis*). By the 1960s and 1970s, there was a heavy emphasis on environment as opposed to biology (*antithesis*). But by the end of the century, most researchers realized that both nature and nurture matter a great deal (*synthesis*). The dialectical process is not entirely linear; scientists may find new problems with long-established theses. They also may find that long-discarded theses have new relevance. This dialectical evolution of thought is a primary characteristic of science and contributes to reaching scientific goals (see Table 1.1).

Dialectical progression depends on permitting current theses to be challenged by alternative, contrasting, and sometimes even *radically* divergent antitheses. These challenges then may lead to syntheses of features of several old ideas. Western critical tradition is often traced back to the Greek philosopher Thales (624–545 B.C.), who invited his students to improve on his thinking—not an easy stance for any teacher to take. In addition, Thales did not hesitate to profit from knowledge accumulated in other parts of the world. During his travels around the Mediterranean, he learned a great deal about subjects such as astronomy and geometry from the Egyptians and others. Today, when we criticize the ideas of our predecessors, we accept Thales's invitation to make progress by building upon or springing away from old ideas.

Note that even when we reject outdated ideas, they still move us forward. They serve as valuable springboards for new ways of looking at things. They are theses to our innovative antitheses. What are some early views that have been used as springboards for current thinking?

This book presents four major themes:

1. Are the mind and body separate entities or are they united?
2. To what extent can we understand psychological phenomena by learning about biology, and to what extent must we understand such phenomena by studying behavior?
3. To what extent is our developed set of skills the result of innate capabilities and to what extent are skills acquired through experience?
4. To what extent do skills and knowledge hold true across domains (such as linguistic, mathematical, and artistic processing), and to what extent are they specific to such domains? (Knowledge and skills that are general across domains are referred to as *domain general*; knowledge and skills that are specific to individual domains are called *domain specific*.)

✓ CONCEPT CHECK 2

1. Suppose you first believe that people are generally good; then you come to believe that they are usually bad; finally you realize that most people have both good and bad qualities. This sequence of thought represents a
   a. thesis.
   b. antithesis.

    ✗ c. synthesis.
    – d. dialectic.
2. An important theme in psychology is the extent to which
   – a. behavior is specific to domains rather than general across domains.
    b. psychology is really the same thing as sociology.
    c. psychology is really the same thing as anthropology.
    d. human minds are really no different than those of one-celled organisms.
3. Memory can be profitably studied
    a. only by psychologists who are interested in the functioning of the brain.
    b. only by psychologists who are interested in strategies for learning and later recalling information.
   – c. by psychologists with a wide range of interests and specializations.
    d. only by people who have very good memories.

THE EARLY HISTORY OF PSYCHOLOGY

What were some of the early recorded ideas about the nature of the human mind?

Where and when did the formal study of psychology begin? Arguably, historical records do not accurately trace the earliest efforts to understand the ways in which we humans think, feel, and act. In fact, contemporary historians recognize that much of what we know—or think we know—about the past is not accurate. Rather, it reflects the biases and prejudices of those who have written the accounts of history. All of us are shaped by the social context in which we live and view the world. We are guided by the thoughts of those persons who preceded us and of those who surround us.

© Historians are not immune to the influences of the society in which they are writing their historical records. Because the historical documents that have reached us were written primarily by Europeans, these records tend to highlight the contributions of Europeans and to downplay or ignore altogether the contributions of Asians, Africans, Latinos, Middle Easterners, and others.

In this chapter, we trace our roots only as far back as ancient Greece. Actually, many highly sophisticated civilizations, such as the Egyptians, Phoenicians, and Hebrews, predated European civilization by centuries. Many technological advances occurred outside of Europe millennia before Europeans either imported them or invented them independently.

Centuries later the seeds of such intellectual endeavor reached the northern shores of the Mediterranean, where they took root and grew. Some of our earliest records of the attempt to understand human psychology are found in Greek literature. Around the eighth century B.C., the blind poet Homer wove his psychological insights into his epic poems about Greek history, the *Iliad* and the *Odyssey*. Indeed, psychology derives its name from the ancient Greek myth of *Psyche*. Psyche's name was synonymous with the vital "breath of life"—the soul—believed to leave the body at death. Today psychologists look for sophisticated understandings of human behavior that go beyond just attributing them to "the soul." The names of psychological disorders have Greek or Latin roots; for example, the term *schizophrenia* derives from the Greek root *skhizo-*, "to split."

600–300 B.C.: ANCIENT GREECE AND ROME

ROOTS OF PSYCHOLOGY IN PHILOSOPHY AND PHYSIOLOGY

Psychology is rooted in two different approaches to human behavior. The first is **philosophy,** a means of exploring and understanding the general nature of many aspects of the world. Philosophy is pursued primarily through **introspection,** the self-examination of inner ideas and experiences. The second approach is **physiology,** the scientific study of living organisms and of life-sustaining functions and processes, primarily through observation. Actually, in ancient Greece, these two fields did not differ much. Both used the philosophical approach of introspective contemplation and speculation as a means of seeking to understand the nature of the body and the mind—how each works and how they interact. In ancient Greece, philosophers and physiologists believed that understanding could be reached without having or even pursuing supporting observations.

HIPPOCRATES, PLATO, AND ARISTOTLE: THOUGHT, OBSERVATION, AND EXPERIMENTATION

The Greek physician (and philosopher) Hippocrates (ca. 460–377 B.C.), commonly known as the father of medicine, left his mark on both physiology and philosophy. What sharply distinguished Hippocrates from archaic Greek philosophers and physicians was his unorthodox idea that disease is not a punishment

At the School of Athens, rationalist Plato disagreed with empiricist Aristotle regarding the path to knowledge. (Raphael Raffaello Sanzio, The School of Athens)

this conclusion by observing that when either side of the head was injured, spasms were observed in the opposite side of the body (D. N. Robinson, 1995).

Two younger contemporaries of Hippocrates also considered the location of the mind to be within the body. Plato (ca. 428–348 B.C.) agreed that the mind resides within the brain. His student Aristotle (384–322 B.C.) located the mind within the heart. These two philosophers profoundly affected modern thinking in psychology and in many other fields. Plato and Aristotle differed in their views of mind and body because of their differing views about the nature of reality. According to Plato, reality resides not in the concrete objects we recognize but in the ideal, abstract forms that these objects represent. These abstract forms exist in a timeless dimension of pure abstract thought. For example, reality is not inherent in any particular chair we see or touch; rather, it is in the eternal abstract *idea* of a chair that exists in our minds. We reach truth not through our senses but through our thoughts.

Aristotle, in contrast, believed that reality lies *only* in the concrete world of objects. To Aristotle (a naturalist and a biologist as well as a philosopher), Plato's abstract forms—such as the idea of a chair—are only derivations of concrete objects. Aristotle rejected mind–body dualism. He believed the mind (or soul) does not exist in its own right; it is merely an illusory by-product of anatomical and physiological activity. Thus, for Aristotle, the study of the mind and the study of the body are one and the same. We can understand the mind only by understanding the body.

Today we would call Aristotle an **empiricist,** a person who believes that we acquire knowledge through **empirical methods,** obtaining evidence through experience, observation, and experimentation. The Aristotelian view is associated with the empirical methods by which we conduct research—in laboratories or in the field—on how people think and behave. Aristotelians tend to *induce* general principles or tendencies based on observations of many specific instances of a phenomenon. For example, empiricists might induce principles of how to learn about psychology from observations of psychology students engaged in learning.

For Plato, however, empirical methods have little merit because true reality lies in the abstract forms, not in the imperfect copies of reality that we see in the world outside our minds. Observations of these imperfect, unreal objects and actions would be irrelevant to the pursuit of truth. Instead, Plato suggested a

sent by the gods. He also anticipated modern psychology by speculating that biological malfunctions rather than demons cause mental illness. He thereby turned away from divine intervention as a cause of human behavior.

Hippocrates also used what were then unorthodox methods—empirical observations—to study medicine. He was particularly interested in discovering the source of the mind. He saw the mind as a separate, distinct entity that controlled the body. The philosophical belief that the mind is qualitatively different from the body is termed **mind–body dualism.** According to this view, the body is composed of physical substance, whereas the mind is ethereal. Hippocrates proposed that the mind resides in the brain. He induced

rationalist approach that asserts that knowledge is most effectively acquired through logical methods, using philosophical analysis to understand the world and people's relationships to it.

Aristotle's view, then, leads directly to empirical psychological research. In contrast, Plato's view foreshadows theorizing that might not be grounded in extensive empirical observation. Each approach has merit. Rationalist theories with no connection to observations may have little connection to everyday events, but mountains of observational data without an organizing theoretical framework can be puzzling. Consider an example. Scores on intelligence tests have been rising ever since records started being kept early in the 20th century (Flynn, 1987; Resing & Nijland, 2002; Truscott & Frank, 2001). On average, people of your generation score higher on tests of intelligence than did people of your parents' generation. This observation is fascinating. But without a theory to explain it, we are left in the dark. Is the increase a result of better nutrition (Martorell, 1998), the spread of technology (Greenfield, 1997), better parental practices (Williams, 1998), or something else? Or does the increase suggest that intelligence tests do not really measure intelligence but something else (Flynn, 1987)? Without an adequate theory to explain the finding, it is difficult to know just what to make of the phenomenon of rising scores on tests of intelligence.

Plato and Aristotle also had divergent views about the origin of ideas. On the one hand, Aristotle believed that ideas are acquired from experience. Plato, on the other hand, believed that ideas are innate and need only to be dug out from the sometimes hidden nooks and crannies of the mind.

1300–1600: THE RENAISSANCE AND THE BIRTH OF MODERN SCIENCE

Science as we know it was born during the Renaissance, when direct observation was established as the basis of knowledge. Many contemporary scientists seek to synthesize theory and observation. Theory should guide and give meaning to our observations, yet our theories should be formed, modified, and perhaps even discarded as a result of our observations. For example, if psychologists want to understand how people

learn, it helps to start off with a theory, which may be based, in part, on informal observations. But it also helps to let observations be a guide in modifying the theory or discarding it entirely if the observations indicate that the theory is wrong. As you will see, the development of psychology as a science today depends on a continual interaction between theory and data. During the beginnings of the modern period, however, many thinkers, such as Descartes and Locke, emphasized either theory or data rather than their interaction.

1600–1850: THE EARLY MODERN PERIOD

The French philosopher René Descartes (1596–1650) continued the dialectic of theory versus data in the 17th century (see Table 1.1 on page 4). Descartes agreed with Plato's rationalist belief that the introspective, reflective method is superior to empirical methods for finding truth. Also like Plato, Descartes (1662/1972) espoused the ideas of *mind–body dualism*, believing that the mind and the body are separate and qualitatively different, and of innate (versus acquired) knowledge. According to Descartes, the dualistic nature of humans is what separates us from nonhuman animals.

In contrast, the British empiricist philosopher John Locke (1632–1704) believed that humans are born without knowledge, and they must therefore seek knowledge through empirical observation (J. Locke, 1690/1961).

Locke's term for this human condition is *tabula rasa*, which means "blank slate" in Latin. Experience "writes" knowledge upon us (see Table 1.1).

In the 18th century, the debates about dualism versus **monism** (the belief that mind and body are one) and empiricism versus rationalism reached a peak. German philosopher Immanuel Kant (1724–1804) began the process of dialectical synthesis for these questions (see Table 1.1). Kant (1781/1987) believed that the quest for understanding mental processes requires both

René Descartes (1596–1650)

Archives of the History of American Psychology, University of Akron, Akron, Ohio

John Locke (1632–1704)

Archives of the History of American Psychology, University of Akron, Akron, Ohio

Immanuel Kant synthesized monism and dualism as well as rationalism and empiricism.

The Granger Collection, New York

rationalism and empiricism working together. According to Kant's synthesis, understanding requires both experience-based knowledge (thesis) and innate concepts (antithesis). Examples are knowledge of the concepts of time and causality, which permit us to profit from our experiences. In this way, understanding evolves through both nature (innate concepts) and nurture (knowledge gained through experience).

✓CONCEPT CHECK 3

1. The earliest study of psychological concepts occurred
   a. before ancient Greece.
   b. in ancient Greece.
   c. during the Renaissance.
   d. at the beginning of the 20th century.
2. Descartes believed
   a. in the unity of the mind and the body.
   b. in mind–body dualism.
   c. that science and philosophy are futile enterprises.
   d. in the superiority of empiricism over rationalism.
3. Immanuel Kant's philosophy
   a. was largely rationalist.
   b. was largely empiricist.
   c. integrated rationalism and empiricism.
   d. rejected both rationalism and empiricism.

EARLY PSYCHOLOGICAL APPROACHES TO BEHAVIOR

What were the earliest major psychological approaches to understanding behavior?

The issues confronted by philosophers, physicians, and psychologists have always been intertwined. Perhaps for this reason, when psychology was starting out as a field in the late 1800s, it was viewed by some as a branch of philosophy and by others as a branch of medicine. Gradually, the psychological branches of philosophy and medicine diverged from the two parent disciplines. Psychology was increasingly seen as a distinct, unified, scientific discipline that focuses on the study of mind and behavior. "In the Lab" researcher Ludy Benjamin describes how he and his associates have gone about tracing how the public image of psychology evolved during the 20th century.

The evolution of key themes in psychology provides evidence for the idea that psychology has inspired a wide variety of intellectual perspectives on how the mind should be studied. The predominant early psychological perspectives (summarized in Table 1.2) are discussed in this section. As you read, notice how different perspectives build on and react to those perspectives that came before them. The cyclical, dialectical process that appears throughout the early history of psychology also threads through modern psychology. This process starts with approaches that focus on mental structures and continues with approaches that focus on mental functions or mental associations.

STRUCTURALISM: TAKING INVENTORY OF THE MIND

In **structuralism,** the first major school of thought in psychology, the goal was to understand the mind by analyzing its elements, such as particular sensations or thoughts (see Chapter 4). When structuralism was the dominant school of psychological thought, scientists in other fields were similarly analyzing the basic elements of matter. For example, chemists analyzed substances by looking at their constituent chemical elements. Although structuralism is no longer a dynamic force, it is important for having taken the first steps toward making psychology a systematic, empirical science and for establishing some of its dialectics, such as between molecular and global analyses of behavior.

A forerunner to structuralism was the perspective of German psychologist Wilhelm Wundt (1832–1920). Wundt was no great success in school, failing time and again and frequently subjected to the ridicule of

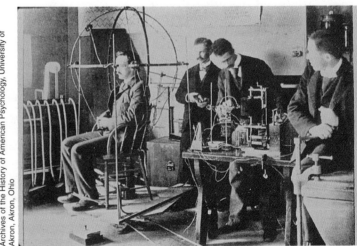

Wilhelm Wundt (1832–1920) established the first laboratory for psychological experimentation.

Archives of the History of American Psychology, University of Akron, Akron, Ohio

IN THE LAB OF LUDY T. BENJAMIN, JR.

UNDERSTANDING THE PUBLIC IMAGE OF PSYCHOLOGY

I am interested in what the general public knows about psychology. As a historian of psychology, I study the past, in part to make sense of the present. Surveys today, including those by my colleagues and me, tell us that the public doesn't know much about the kind of psychology described in this textbook. I want to understand why that is.

Before the first American psychology laboratories were founded in the 1880s, a popular psychology was already embraced by the American public. There were psychological practitioners who called themselves mesmerists, spiritualists, mental healers, and psychologists (Benjamin & Baker, 2004). "Having your head examined" was big business in the 19th century. The phrase referred to the work of the phrenologist, who measured the bumps and indentations on the skull to help someone choose a suitable career or perhaps a marital partner. Psychology was also equated with psychic phenomena, such as extrasensory perception and mind reading. This sort of popular psychology had existed for centuries, and that it thrives today is evident in the popularity of self-help books, "reality" television programs, magazines, movies, and musical forms such as rap and country music ("Call me Cleopatra, I'm the Queen of Denial"). Psychologists today are often dismayed by the misconceptions people hold about their field. In truth, the public has never understood scientific psychology very well (Benjamin, 1986). As indicated, most people have believed in their own brand of psychology for a long time and are not going to give it up just because some scientists say they should (Wood, Jones, & Benjamin, 1986).

I think of "public image" as having two broad dimensions. *Understanding* refers to what people believe to be

Ludy Benjamin, Jr. holds an endowed chair and endowed professorship in the department of psychology at Texas A&M University, where he has taught for 23 years. Trained as an experimental psychologist, his principal area of scholarship today is the history of American psychology, especially its applications and public image. He has written 14 books and more than 100 articles, most of them on historical subjects. When not practicing psychology he enjoys traveling with his wife, reading American history, fishing, and watching baseball.

true about psychology. *Popularity* refers to how the public feels about psychology and psychologists. The former is a cognitive dimension; the latter is an affective or emotional one. Public understanding can be measured against the body of scientific knowledge. Popularity is not about right or wrong answers but about where psychology falls on a continuum of disliking to liking. We assess these two dimensions in a number of different ways.

In our work we have surveyed the entries about psychology in encyclopedias published between 1880 and 1940 (Benjamin, Bryant, Campbell, Luttrell, & Holtz, 1997). We have analyzed the content of popular magazines devoted to psychology, magazines that began publication in the 1920s, a decade of dramatic social change in America that fostered, understandably, a strong interest in psychology. More than 40 different popular psychology magazines have been published in the United States during the past 80 years, and we are studying them across time to understand how the portrayal of popular psychology has changed in response to changes in American society. Unlike the encyclopedia entries, which were usually written by psychologists, the magazine articles were written by non-psychologists who offered their own versions of popular psychology that

typically promised the readers "health, happiness, and success" (Benjamin & Bryant, 1997). We have also studied popular psychology books, books written by psychologists for public consumption, psychology museums and expositions, psychology newspaper columns, and psychological applications (Benjamin & Nielsen-Gammon, 1999) in pursuit of answers.

Our research, and the work of others, has shown that the American public has an insatiable appetite for psychology in many popular forms but is largely uninformed about its nature and processes. This is partly because so few psychologists write for popular consumption (such writing is often frowned upon by academic psychologists). Furthermore, we have found that when psychologists write for the public, they do not often satisfy their audience. The public wants definite answers, certainty. They want what psychologist Leigh Shaffer has called "recipe knowledge"; that is, people want to know the five steps that will ensure that their children grow up to be happy or the seven keys to a successful marriage. As a science, psychology doesn't work that way. And psychological scientists can't (and ethically won't) write that way. So it is no surprise to find that most people learn about psychology from non-

continued

psychologists, and consequently their knowledge is quite poor. Yet our surveys show that their liking for psychology and psychologists is quite high.

Why do I study the public image of psychology? Partly out of sheer fascination and intellectual curiosity. But there is a more important purpose. I believe that the science and practice of psychology have much to offer the public. Consider just the mental health venue. At some time, almost everyone will know someone who could benefit from high-quality mental health services. The better informed the public is about psychological science and the legitimately trained psychologists who practice it, the better their chances are for effective and long-lasting treatment. A better understanding of public image can thus help the field of psychology better serve those who need its services (Benjamin & Baker, 2004).

others. However, Wundt's stunning career shows that school performance does not always predict career success. Wundt defied low expectations for himself. He also defied many conventional beliefs to become the individual some psychologists consider to be the "founder" of modern psychology. In general, many of the very creative psychologists who change the field are people who go their own way. They fight for what they believe in even if many others disagree with them (R. J. Sternberg, 2003a, 2003b).

Wundt believed that psychology should focus on immediate and direct, as opposed to *mediated* or interpreted, conscious experience. Suppose that you look at a green, grassy lawn. To Wundt, the concepts of *lawn* and even *grass* would be irrelevant. Even your awareness of looking at a grassy lawn would not have particularly interested Wundt. These conceptually mediated experiences are too far removed from the mental elements of your experience. You infer these mental elements from the more important (to Wundt) immediate experience of seeing narrow, vertical, spiky, green protrusions of varying lengths and widths, amassed closely together on a two-dimensional surface. It was to these elementary sensations that Wundt gave his attention.

For Wundt, the optimal method by which a person could be trained to analyze these sensory experiences was a form of self-observation called *introspection*. This method involves looking inward at pieces of information passing through consciousness—a form of

TABLE 1.2
CONCEPT REVIEW

Early Psychological Perspectives. To this day, psychological research continues to reflect its roots in structuralism (focusing on basic psychological structures) and in functionalism (focusing on the processes of thinking and feeling).

Perspective	Key Emphases	Key Methods of Acquiring Information	Key Thinkers Instrumental in Development of Perspective	Key Criticisms
Structuralism	The nature of consciousness; analysis of consciousness into its constituent components (elementary sensations)	Introspection (self-observation)	Wilhelm Wundt, Edward Titchener	Too many elementary sensations; lack of means for understanding the processes of thought; lack of application to the world outside the structuralist's laboratory; rigid use of introspective techniques
Functionalism (and its offshoot, pragmatism)	Mental operations; practical uses of consciousness; the total relationship of the organism to its environment	Whatever works best, including any and all methods of collecting data	William James, John Dewey	Too many definitions of the term *function*; overly flexible use of too many different techniques, resulting in lack of experimental coherence; overemphasis on applications of psychology; insufficient study of fundamental issues
Associationism	Mental connections between two events or ideas, which lead to forms of learning	Empirical strategies, applied to self-observation and to animal studies	Hermann Ebbinghaus, Edward Lee Thorndike, Ivan Pavlov	Overly simplistic; does not explain cognition, emotion, or many other psychological processes

self-observation. Wundt and his associates tried to train observers to be as objective as possible in making their observations.

Wundt's student Edward Titchener (1867–1927) went to Cornell University after studying with Wundt. Titchener was a full-blown structuralist with views generally similar but by no means identical to Wundt's. Like Wundt, Titchener (1910) believed that all consciousness could be reduced to elementary states.

After using strict structuralist principles in his teaching, research, and writings, however, Titchener changed his mind toward the end of his life. Like others, he recognized the problem that structuralism proposed too many elementary sensations. The number of such sensations could increase without end. Structuralism also provided no means for understanding processes of thought. Furthermore, it probably was too rigidly tied to a single methodology: introspection.

Titchener's change of mind illustrates an important point about scientists in general and psychologists in particular. Outstanding scientists do not necessarily adopt a particular viewpoint and then stick with it for the rest of their lives. They allow their thinking to evolve, and they often change their views during this evolutionary process. This process gave rise to the next major school of thought in psychology: functionalism.

FUNCTIONALISM: WHY WE DO WHAT WE DO

The roots of structuralism are in Germany, but its countermovement, functionalism, originated in the United States—the first U.S.-born movement in psychology. **Functionalism** focuses on active psychological processes rather than on passive psychological structures or elements. The key difference between structuralists and functionalists was not the answers they found but the fundamentally different questions they asked. Whereas structuralists asked, What are the elementary contents, the structures, of the human mind?, functionalists asked, What do people *do*, and *why* do they do it?

Another way of viewing the difference between structuralism and functionalism is that structuralists considered humans and other organisms as largely passive in analyzing incoming sensations. Functionalists, in contrast, viewed humans and others as more actively engaged in processing their sensations and formulating their actions. American culture, which emphasizes initiative, enterprise, and people's ability to shape their environment, may have contributed to this more active kind of psychology.

Functionalists were unified by the kinds of questions they asked, but they were not necessarily unified by the answers they found or by the methods they used for finding those answers. We might even suggest that they were unified in believing that they could use a diversity of methods, as long as each method helped to answer the particular question being probed.

Ⓔ Functionalists' openness to diverse methodologies broadened the scope of psychological methods. Among the various approaches used by functionalists was experimentation on nonhuman animals. This approach was perhaps prompted by Charles Darwin's (1809–1882) revolutionary idea that living individuals are the product of a long history in which organisms have adapted to their environments. Darwin's theory is unique in its usefulness in an astonishingly wide variety of disciplines.

A leader in the functionalist movement was William James (1842–1910), whose chief contribution to the field of psychology was a single book, his landmark *Principles of Psychology* (1890b). James demonstrated that one truly influential work, as well as the reputation of its author, can help shape a field. James is particularly well known for his pragmatic theorizing about consciousness. He emphasized that the function of consciousness is to enable people to adapt to the environment. It gives people choices for operating within that environment. James was a leader in guiding functionalism toward *pragmatism*, a view of science and psychology that asserts that knowledge is validated by its usefulness.

Functionalism, like structuralism, did not survive as an organized school of thought. The term *function* lacked clear definition as applied to psychology. The result was that the school did not hold together. But the influence of functionalism remains widespread today in psychological specializations that stress the flexibility of research methods or the practical usefulness of potential results as a basis for choosing problems to study. The influence of functionalism is particularly apparent in a related strand of thought, associationism.

William James (1842–1910)

Culver Pictures, Inc.

ASSOCIATIONISM: EARLY IDEAS ABOUT LEARNING

Associationism, like functionalism, was less a rigid school of psychology than an influential way of thinking. In general, associationists are mainly interested in the middle- to higher-level mental processes, such as those of learning. This focus on rather high-level mental processes is the opposite of Wundt's insistence on studying elementary sensations.

Associationism examines how events or ideas can become associated in the mind, thereby resulting in a form of learning. For example, with repetition, concepts such as *thesis*, *antithesis*, and *synthesis* will become linked in your mind because they are presented together so often that they become inextricably associated. You will thereby learn that the dialectical process involves a thesis, an antithesis, and a synthesis. Learning and remembering thus depend on mental association.

An influential associationist, the German experimenter Hermann Ebbinghaus (1850–1909) was the first experimenter to apply associationist principles systematically. Ebbinghaus prided himself on using much more rigorous experimental techniques (such as counting his errors and recording his response times) than Wundt used during introspection. But Ebbinghaus used himself as his only experimental participant. In particular, Ebbinghaus used his self-observations to study and quantify the relationship between *rehearsal*—conscious repetition—and recollection of material. Interestingly, Ebbinghaus had no university appointment, no formal laboratory, no formal mentor, and none of the usual trappings of academe. He worked alone, yet he made what then was a groundbreaking experimental discovery. He found that frequent repetition fixes mental associations more firmly in memory and, by extension, that repetition aids in learning (see Chapter 6). In other words, his work was the first to show formally that the age-old saw "Practice makes perfect" truly is supported by psychological research. Great contributions do not require academic positions or complicated equipment.

Ebbinghaus's ideas were elaborated by Edwin Guthrie (1886–1959), who observed nonhuman animals instead of himself. Guthrie proposed that two observed events (a stimulus and a response) become associated through their close *temporal contiguity*—their occurring very close together in time. The stimulus events and the response behaviors become linked because they continually occur at about the same time. In contrast, Edward Lee Thorndike (1874–1949) held that "satisfaction," rather than Guthrie's temporal contiguity, is the key to forming associations. Thorndike (1905) called this principle the **law of effect:** Over time the actions ("the *effect*") for which an organism is rewarded ("the *satisfaction*") are strengthened and are therefore more likely to occur again in the future. In contrast, actions that are followed by punishment tend to be weakened and are thus less likely to occur in the future.

In considering the methods of Ebbinghaus, Guthrie, and Thorndike, we see that the associationists followed the functionalist tradition of using various methods in their research. In fact, the work of Thorndike can be traced directly back to the work of his functionalist mentor, William James. James even encouraged Thorndike to conduct his experiments on nonhuman animals. He offered Thorndike his

own house as the locale for some of Thorndike's earliest studies of nonhuman animals learning to run through mazes.

Associationism in its strictest form has not survived. The school of thought was overly simplistic and did not explain cognition, emotion, or many other psychological processes. Nevertheless, associationism made a contribution to contemporary thinking in psychology and has been linked to many other theoretical viewpoints. Traveling backward in time, we can trace its principles directly to Locke's view that the mind and the body are two aspects of the same unified phenomenon, a view rooted in Aristotle's ideas. Traveling forward in time, subsequent views, such as behaviorism, described in the next section, were founded on associationism. Clearly, it is difficult to categorize associationism as belonging strictly to one era.

✓ CONCEPT CHECK 4

1. Structuralism is most associated with
   a. Titchener.
   b. James.
   c. Thorndike.
   d. Ebbinghaus.
2. Functionalists emphasized the study of
   a. the structure of objects in the world.
   b. how objects are associated with one another.
   c. what people do and why they do it.
   d. nonhuman animals rather than humans.
3. If you are repeatedly rewarded for doing something, you will continue to do it. This statement represents the
   a. law of association.
   b. law of effect.
   c. law of reward.
   d. law of functions.

PSYCHOLOGY IN THE 20TH CENTURY

What were the main perspectives of the 20th century on psychological thought?

Perspectives of the 20th century built on earlier viewpoints. At the same time, they added new layers of sophistication. In fact, the history of psychology during the first half of the 20th century was characterized by a series of competing perspectives (see Table 1.3). Each new view gave rise to a countering school of thought. At

TABLE 1.3
CONCEPT REVIEW

Modern Psychological Perspectives. The various psychological perspectives offer complementary insights into the human psyche.

Perspective and Its Key Developers	Key Emphasis	Key Methods of Investigation	Key Criticisms
Behaviorism • John Watson • B. F. Skinner	Observable behavior	Experimental; strong focus on animal subjects	Ignores or does not address any internal causes of behavior; does not allow for social (observational) learning; doesn't explain many aspects of human behavior (e.g., the acquisition and use of language or the enjoyment and appreciation of music or other arts).
Gestalt psychology abundance • Max Wertheimer • Kurt Koffka • Wolfgang Köhler	Holistic concepts, not merely as additive sums of the parts but as emergent phenomena in their own right	Experimentation and observation (more emphasis on observing holistic data than on controlling variables)	Little data relative to the of theory; lack of experimental control; lack of precise definitions and use of circular thinking.
Cognitivism • Herbert Simon • George Miller • Ulric Neisser	Understanding how people think; how knowledge is learned, structured, stored, and used	Experimentation and naturalistic observation, primarily of humans and of other primates	Emotions, social interactions, and other aspects of human behavior are not investigated as enthusiastically as more obviously cognitive aspects of behavior; naturalistic observations reduce scientific rigor and control.
Biological psychology • Roger Sperry • Eric Kandel	Biological interactions of the body and the mind, particularly the workings of the brain and nervous system	Experimentation; studies on humans and animals; neurophysiological and neurochemical examination of brains	Not all aspects of human behavior are now subject to investigation via biopsychological study; many aspects of human behavior may not now ethically be studied in humans, and animal investigations may not always generalize to humans.
Evolutionary psychology • Leda Cosmides • David Buss	Evolutionary bases of human behavior	Plausible inference; experimentation; survey methodology	Views are difficult to falsify empirically; speculative quality.
Psychodynamic psychology • Sigmund Freud	Personality development; psychotherapy; uncovering unconscious experience	Psychoanalysis, based on clinical case studies	Overemphasis on sexuality; over-reliance on case-study research; overly comprehensive; not easily subject to scientific investigation; overly theory driven.
Humanistic psychology • Abraham Maslow • Carl Rogers	Free will and self-actualization of human potential; conscious rather than unconscious experience	Clinical practice and case-study observations; holistic rather than analytic approach	Theories not particularly comprehensive; limited research base.

the heart of the differences among these perspectives lay some of the central themes or questions first examined by the Greeks. In the first half of the 20th century, the human mind was viewed somewhat rigidly by fairly strict schools of psychology. By the second half, however, efforts were made to integrate approaches. At the end of the 20th century, the idea that one school of psychological thought would emerge as *the* explanation of all human behavior and mental life had itself evolved into a more inclusive and integrative view. The view

Mary Whiton Calkins (1863–1930) may be considered a forerunner of cognitivism. In 1913, she wrote an article criticizing Watson's behaviorist approach to psychology and suggested that the study of the human mind was essential.

of behavior and mental states as a mix of biological, psychological, and social factors had gained momentum. Before all this could happen, however, the central themes of psychology were intensely debated. New perspectives emerged frequently.

An important 20th-century contribution was the idea that the primary subject matter of psychology ought to be the self. In her self-psychology, Mary Whiton Calkins (1863-1930) argued both that the self should be the focus of psychological investigation and that the self must be studied in its social context. Although Calkins was to become the first female president of both the American Psychological Association and the American Philosophical Association, she could not attain a PhD because graduate study was limited to men only. She attended classes at Clark and Harvard universities, but as a nondegree student and only at the sufferance of her professors. At Harvard, four men dropped out of a class to protest her attendance. The early history of psychology is dominated by white men because women and members of many minority groups had to fight even to be able to sit in on classes in which they were not allowed to enroll.

FROM ASSOCIATIONISM TO BEHAVIORISM

IVAN PAVLOV AND CLASSICALLY CONDITIONED LEARNING

Some contemporaries of Thorndike used animal experiments to probe stimulus–response relationships in ways that differed from those of Thorndike and his fellow associationists. In Russia, Nobel Prize–winning physiologist Ivan Pavlov (1849–1936) studied involuntary learning behavior. He began with the observation that dogs salivated in response to the sight of the lab technician who fed them before the dogs even saw whether the techni-

Ivan Pavlov (1849–1936)

cian had food. To Pavlov, this response indicated **classically conditioned learning,** whereby an originally neutral stimulus comes to be associated with a stimulus that already produces a particular physiological or emotional response. Pavlov (1955) believed that the dogs had no conscious control over this form of learning. In the dogs' minds, some type of involuntary learning was linking the technician with the food.

BEHAVIORISM: A SEARCH FOR RIGOR AND REDUCTION

Behaviorism is a theoretical outlook that emphasizes the idea that psychology should be scrupulously objective: Psychology should focus only on the relationship between observable behavior, on the one hand, and environmental events or stimuli, on the other. Behaviorism was born as a reaction against the focus found in both structuralism and functionalism, as well as in psychodynamic theorizing (discussed below), on personal, subjective mental states. According to strict, "radical" behaviorists, any conjectures about internal thoughts and ways of thinking are nothing more than speculation. Although such conjectures might belong within the domain of philosophy, they have no place in psychology.

JOHN WATSON AND RADICAL BEHAVIORISM

The individual usually acknowledged as the founder of radical behaviorism is American psychologist John Watson (1878–1958). Watson had no use for internal mental contents or mechanisms. His radical conception of behaviorism stated that any behavior can be shaped and controlled. This view is dramatized in a famous challenge:

> Give me a dozen healthy infants, well-formed, and my own specified world to bring them up in, and I'll guarantee to take any one at random and train him to become any type of specialist I might select—doctor, lawyer, artist, merchant-chief and yes, even beggarman and thief—regardless of his talents, penchants, tendencies, abilities, vocations, and race of his ancestors. (J. B. Watson, 1930, p. 104)

John Watson (1878–1958)

Some psychologists disagreed with Watson's behaviorist view. In a debate between Watson and psychologist William McDougall (1871–1938), McDougall said:

> I come into this hall and see a man on this platform scraping the guts of a cat with hairs from the tail of a

horse; and, sitting silently in attitudes of rapt attention, are a thousand persons who presently break out into wild applause. How will the Behaviorist explain these strange incidents: How explain the fact that the vibrations emitted by the cat-gut stimulate all the thousand into absolute silence and quiescence; and the further fact that the cessation of the stimulus seems to be a stimulus to the most frantic activity? (J. B. Watson & McDougall, 1929, p. 63)

Behaviorism differed from earlier movements in psychology in its emphasis on nonhuman animal rather than human research participants. Historically, much behavioristic work has been (and still is) conducted with laboratory animals such as rats and pigeons. Watson himself preferred animal subjects. He believed that it was easier with these animal subjects to ensure behavioral control and to establish stimulus–response relationships while at the same time minimizing external interference. Indeed, from his point of view, the simpler the organism's emotional and physiological makeup, the less the researcher needs to worry about any of the interference that can plague psychological research with humans as participants.

An American behavioral psychologist who tried to connect the involuntary learning studied by Pavlov with the voluntary learning studied by Watson and Thorndike was Clark Hull (1884–1952). Hull's work was ignored for a decade before its importance was recognized (Hilgard, 1987). Hull (1952) was particularly influential for his belief that the laws of behavior could be *quantified*—expressed in terms of numerical quantities—like the laws in other scientific disciplines such as physics.

SKINNER'S EXPERIMENTAL ANALYSIS OF BEHAVIOR

In modern times, radical behaviorism has seemed almost synonymous with the work of one of its most radical proponents, B. F. Skinner (1904–1990). Skinner, unlike Watson, was not an S–R (stimulus–response) psychologist (Skinner, 1953; Viney, 1993). Skinner (1953) distinguished between two kinds of learned behavior. *Respondent* behavior, the kind studied by Pavlov, is involuntary. It is elicited by a definite stimulus (such as food or even the sight of a lab technician). *Operant* behavior, on the other hand, is largely voluntary. It cannot be simply and certainly elicited. The probability of an operant behavior occurring can be increased, however, if it is followed by an event referred to as a *reinforcer*. The reinforcer increases the likelihood that the operant behavior will occur again under similar circumstances (see Chapter 6).

Suppose we train a rat to press a lever or bar. We reinforce the bar-press

B. F. Skinner (1904–1990)

© Christopher Johnson/Stock Boston

with food only when a light comes on above the bar. Soon the rat learns to press the bar when the light comes on. According to Skinner, the light does not directly elicit the response; rather, it enables the rat to discriminate a reinforcing situation from a nonreinforcing one. The rat thereby learns a new class of behaviors.

The radical behaviorist approach, by ignoring internal states, effectively limits itself. It has difficulty explaining many aspects of behavior, such as the acquisition and use of language and the enjoyment and appreciation of music or other arts. But in evaluating behaviorism we must remember that even critics agree that the overt behavior of a research participant is the object of study most accessible to observation. Despite many criticisms, such as those of the Gestalt psychologists considered next, behaviorism has had a great impact on the development of psychology as a rigorous science grounded in empirical evidence.

GESTALT PSYCHOLOGY: THE WHOLE IS DIFFERENT FROM THE SUM OF ITS PARTS

Of the many critics of behaviorism, Gestalt psychologists have been among the most vocal. Actually, this movement was not only a reaction against the early behaviorist tendency to break down behaviors into stimulus–response units. It also was a reaction against the structuralist tendency to analyze mental processes by studying elementary sensations. According to **Gestalt psychology**, psychological phenomena are best understood when viewed as organized, structured wholes—that is, *holistically*—not when they are analyzed into myriad component elements. The Gestalt movement originated in Germany, the fount of structuralism. It spread to the United States, the fount of behaviorism, and to other countries. Gestalt psychology is usually traced back to the work of German psychologist Max Wertheimer (1880–1943). He collaborated with compatriots Kurt Koffka (1886–1941) and Wolfgang Köhler (1887–1968) to form the new school of psychology.

The maxim "The whole is different from the sum of its parts" aptly sums up the Gestalt approach. The Gestaltists applied this framework to many areas in psychology. For example, they proposed that problem solving cannot be explained simply in terms of automatic responses to stimuli or to elementary sensations. Instead, new insights often emerge in problem solving. People can devise entirely new ways of seeing problems, ways that are not merely recombinations of old ways of perceiving them.

What two images do you see in this Gestalt reversible figure?

logical phenomena is to combine the holistic strategies tracing back to the Gestalt approach with more analytic strategies originating with associationist and behaviorist approaches. Cognitivists use both of these strategies.

COGNITIVISM: HOW WE THINK AS A KEY TO HOW WE BEHAVE

Cognitivism emphasizes the importance of thought as a basis for understanding much of human behavior. Such behavior can be understood if we first analyze how people think. The cognitivist movement began during the 1960s. Early cognitivists (e.g., G. A. Miller, Galanter, & Pribram, 1960) argued that traditional behaviorist accounts of behavior are inadequate because they ignore how people think. Subsequently, Allen Newell and Herbert Simon (1972) proposed detailed models of human thinking and problem solving from the most basic levels to the most complex (such as playing chess). Ulric Neisser's (b. 1928) book *Cognitive Psychology* (1967) was especially critical in bringing cognitivism to prominence. Neisser defined *cognitive psychology* as the study of how people learn, structure, store, and use knowledge. Jean Piaget was central in applying a cognitive approach to the study of child development.

The Gestalt perspective has been criticized on several grounds. It generated little data relative to the abundance of theory it provided. Studies conducted under the Gestalt approach tended to lack careful experimental controls, and the approach often used imprecise definitions of terms and even occasionally circular thinking. For example, an insight was viewed as a sudden "aha" experience, which in turn was viewed as an insight. But many psychologists now believe that the most fruitful approach to understanding psycho-

The approach of the early cognitivists tended to emphasize exclusively *serial processing*, or step-by-step processing of information. In solving a math problem, for example, the problem solver might be seen as first reading the problem, then formulating a relevant equation, then solving the equation, and so on. Some cognitivists continue to emphasize serial processing

In Sunday on La Grande Jatte *(ca. 1885), Georges Seurat demonstrated the Gestalt principle of the whole being different from the sum of its parts. See from the detail how the painting comprises only dots of paint.*

(e.g., J. R. Anderson, 1983, 1993, 2002; Anderson & Betz, 2001; Anderson, Budiu, & Reder, 2001; Newell, 1990; Sohn & Anderson, 2001), either alone or in combination with *parallel processing*, in which multiple mental processes are viewed as occurring all at once (e.g., Hinton, Plaut, & Shallice, 2000; McClelland, 2000, 2001; McLeod, Shallice, & Plaut, 2000; Plaut, 2001; Plaut & Gonerman, 2000; Seidenberg, 1993). Parallel processing might occur in the way we respond to many aspects of a great painting simultaneously. We see it, consider it, and may have an emotional response to it all at the same time.

The cognitive approach has been applied in a variety of areas of psychology, including thinking (R. J. Sternberg & Ben-Zeev, 2001), emotion (Detweiler-Bedell & Salovey, 2002; Salovey, 2001; Salovey, Mayer, & Caruso, 2002), daydreaming and imagination (Beck, 2002a; J. L. Singer, 1998; D. J. Singer & Singer, 2001), and the treatment of various psychological difficulties, such as anxiety, stress, and depression (Beck, 2002b; Krefetz, Steer, Gulab, & Beck, 2002; Pretzer, Beck, & Newman, 2002; Sanderson, Beck, & McGinn, 2002). In the functionalist tradition, cognitive psychologists use a variety of methods to pursue their goal of understanding human thought. Such methods include the study of reaction times, the study of people's subjective reports as they solve problems, and the formulation and implementation of computer simulations.

In the 1960s cognitivism was just coming of age, and today it is still popular. Many fields within psychology have adopted a cognitive perspective. At the same time, it is important to remember that many aspects of behavior, such as emotion and social interaction, probably cannot be reduced simply to cognitive processing. Like all perspectives, the cognitivist way of seeing things may someday fade in importance. At such time, it will yield to other ways of seeing things. The dominant perspective of the future and even some of the psychological phenomena it seeks to explain may be unimaginable today. Psychology is a dynamic science precisely because it is ever-evolving in its perspectives on the puzzles of why people act the way they do. Of course, human behavior itself changes. This fact has motivated biological psychologists in general, and evolutionary psychologists in particular, to understand just how behavior may have evolved and may still be evolving.

BIOLOGICAL PSYCHOLOGY: THE MIND AND THE BODY RECONCILED?

One of the most dynamic areas in psychology today is a field that yields exhilarating discoveries almost daily. **Biological psychology** attempts to understand be-havior by carefully studying anatomy and physiology, especially of the brain (*neurobiology*). Its roots go back to Hippocrates, who observed that the brain seems to control many other parts of the body. By definition, biological psychology (also called *psychobiology*) assumes that mental processes and the body are interrelated and perhaps indistinguishable. Certainly, the study of each one can yield information about the other. Psychobiology is not really an organized school of thought grounded in a particular place and time. Rather, it is an affirmation of biological theorizing and experimentation as desirable bases for studying psychological problems.

One psychobiological approach is to determine which specific regions of the brain are responsible for the origination, learning, and expression of particular behaviors, feelings, or kinds of thoughts. For example, Nobel Prize–winning American researcher Roger Sperry tried to determine what kinds of thinking occur in each half of the brain. Neuroscientists are isolating with great precision the locations in the brain where various cognitive operations take place (e.g., Bunge, Ochsner, Desmond, Glover, & Gabrieli, 2001; Canli, Sivers, Whitfield, Gotlib, & Gabrieli, 2002; Golby, Gabrieli, Chiao, & Eberhardt, 2001; Golby, Poldrack, et al., 2001; Kandel, 1991; Posner, 2000, 2001, 2002; Rypma, Prabhakaran, Desmond, J., & Gabrieli, 2001; Stebbins, et al., 2002; Tulving et al., 1994). Today, moreover, many psychological disorders, which once were studied and treated exclusively by psychological means, are being understood and treated, at least in part, by biological means.

Behavioral genetics attributes behavior and underlying traits in part to the influence of particular combinations of genes as expressed in a given environment. A behavioral geneticist might attempt to identify, for example, genetic elements that contribute to intelligence, creativity, or mental illness, as well as their relationships to environmental influences (Petrill, 2002).

An even newer field is *molecular genetics*. Molecular geneticists try to find the genes that contribute to mental processes and behavior. Robert Plomin and his colleagues have found possible links between genes and intelligence, although the work is still in its early stages. These and other insights into our minds and bodies— and the interactions between the two—fascinate scientists and laypeople alike (e.g., Kosslyn & Plomin, 2001; Petrill, 2002; Plomin, 2001, 2002; Plomin & Colledge, 2001; Plomin, Owen, & McGuffin, 1994). Several investigators have also found specific sites on human chromosomes that appear to be linked to difficulties in reading (Grigorenko, 2001; Grigorenko et al., 1997). A successful endeavor in molecular genetics is the Human Geonome Project, which has created a first draft of the sequence of the human genome. This work is still being refined and expanded.

The **biopsychosocial approach** to psychology understands the individual in terms of the various psychological, social, and biological factors that contribute to behavior. It is most often applied in health psychology, but it really applies in all areas of psychology. This approach suggests that thought and behavior cannot be fully understood through any single view or perspective.

(E)

EVOLUTIONARY PSYCHOLOGY: UNDERSTANDING THE ADAPTIVE VALUE OF CERTAIN BEHAVIORS

In his theory of natural selection and evolution, Charles Darwin (1859) sought to understand how behaviors such as facial expressions, mating rituals, and even emotions might have evolved from or be related to those in other species. Today, psychologists building on the integrative work of Darwin have created a new and exciting field, evolutionary psychology (Buss, 1995, 2001a, 2001b; Buss & Kenrick, 1998; Cosmides & Tooby, 1987, 2002; Dennett, 1995; D. P. Schmitt, Shackelford, & Buss, 2001; R. J. Sternberg & Kaufman, 2002; R. Wright, 1994). The goal of **evolutionary psychology** is to explain behavior in terms of organisms' evolved adaptations to a constantly changing environmental landscape. For example, certain gender differences between women and men are explained in terms of the different challenges the two genders have faced over evolutionary time. Men and women might have adapted differently to meet these challenges. Successful individuals were more likely to survive long enough to reproduce. They would then pass their genes (hereditary material) on to subsequent generations. As a result, individuals of the present epoch are likely still to show in their behavior the adaptations that worked for extended periods of time in the distant past. It is important to realize that, at least at the present time, evolutionary explanations

The Granger Collection, New York

Sigmund Freud (1856–1939) developed the first and most influential psychodynamic theory. His daughter, Anna Freud (1895–1982), also became an influential psychodynamic psychologist.

often have a speculative quality to them; they may not be directly confirmable or disconfirmable empirically.

PSYCHODYNAMIC PSYCHOLOGY: CONSCIOUS BEHAVIOR AS THE TIP OF THE ICEBERG

One of the oldest, most controversial, stimulating, and influential schools of psychology developed from the observations made in the clinical practice of a *neurologist* (a physician who treats disorders of the brain and nervous system). The neurologist was Sigmund Freud (1856–1839). He incorporated many ideas from biology into his psychological theories. When many people think of psychology, they think of Freud's views of human motivations and behavior. Freud's **psychodynamic theory** emphasizes the importance of conflicting unconscious mental processes. It also underscores the importance of early childhood experiences as influences on adult personality. **Psychoanalysis** is the kind of psychological treatment based on Freud's theory of motivations and behavior (discussed in Chapter 17).

In his theory of psychoanalysis, Freud (1949) proposed two levels of awareness of reality. The *conscious* is composed of mental states, such as memories, of which we are aware. But it is just the tip of the iceberg. According to Freud, the motivation for many of our actions is often outside our awareness. The *unconscious* is composed of mental states of which we are unaware or to which we do not normally have access. The unconscious and conscious minds operate according to different governing principles. For example, the individual who vehemently opposes pornography at a conscious level may be attracted to it at an unconscious level.

In addition, Freud proposed three mental structures (the id, the ego, and the superego, discussed in Chapter 15), each operating according to different principles and serving different functions. Freud also posited a multistage theory of development that emphasizes the important role of early childhood experiences in the development of personality—and, when problems arise in this development, mental disorder.

Several valid criticisms have been leveled against psychoanalysis. It probably overemphasized sexual explanations of phenomena. It also relied too much on case-study research, and some of the case studies may have been interpreted in ways that overstated their fit to Freud's ideas. These ideas also have not been subjected to as much rigorous empirical testing as would be ideal. In recent years, however, more empirical research has been done to test the theory (e.g., J. Weinberger & Westen, 2001; Westen & Gabbard, 2002a, 2002b). In any case, Freud contributed greatly to the development of psychological theory. His insights have shown us the rich material that can be available through case-study research (see Chapter 2).

Freud's is not the only version of psychodynamic theory. Several of Freud's disciples rebelled and formulated their own versions of the theory. These more recent psychodynamic theorists are often called "neo-Freudians." Their views differ from Freud's in many and varied respects. One of the main differences is the neo-Freudians' greater emphasis on conscious as opposed to unconscious processing. Another main difference is the neo-Freudians' belief in the profound influence key human relationships (such as those with our parents) can have on how we come to view the world. Freud's theories, as well as those of the neo-Freudians, are discussed in detail in Chapters 15 and 17.

HUMANISTIC PSYCHOLOGY: FREE WILL AND THE IMPORTANCE OF HUMAN POTENTIAL

During the 1950s, one response to psychodynamic theory in America (behaviorism was another) was the humanistic-psychology movement. Recall that psychodynamic psychology tends to see humans as being somewhat at the mercy of developmental events in their individual lives. In contrast, **humanistic psychology** emphasizes free will and the importance of human potential as well as holistic rather than analytic approaches to psychological phenomena. It also emphasizes conscious experience in personal development rather than unconscious experience. An *analytic* approach, such as Freud's, aims to break down a construct like personality into its constituent components. A *holistic* approach to personality theory, however, seeks to avoid dividing the personality into smaller elements. It argues that the essence

Abraham Maslow (1908–1970)

of the construct is lost through such divisions. These hallmarks of the Renaissance-era humanistic movement (from which modern humanism takes its name) thus contrast with the more deterministic view of Freud, according to which we are subject to a host of conflicting unconscious impulses.

A leading humanistic psychologist, Abraham Maslow (1908–1970) proposed that all people possess an innate drive for *self-actualization* (Maslow, 1970). People seek to *actualize* (make real through action) their potential as creatively as they can. Maslow believed that people differ in the extent to which they succeed in self-actualizing. Those who succeed have in common an objective view of reality and an acceptance of their nature, including both their strengths and their limitations. They also share a commitment to their work, a need for autonomy coupled with empathy for humankind, resistance to blind conformity, and a drive to be creative in their work and in their lives in general.

Carl Rogers (1902–1987), another humanistic psychologist, followed Maslow's emphasis on self-actualization. But Rogers (1961a) stressed the dependence of self-actualization on the relationship between mother and child. He believed that if the mother meets the child's need for unconditional love, then the child will probably develop in a well-adjusted way. Rogers argued that we need this love, which he termed *unconditional positive regard*, in infancy and childhood. Many of the problems we have as adults are due to lack of regard.

The humanistic approach has made a valuable contribution to our understanding of human nature. At the same time, its theories tend to be somewhat less comprehensive than those of some alternative approaches. Moreover, the research base supporting this approach is limited.

To conclude, a wide variety of approaches have been used to understand the nature of the human mind. By understanding these approaches, students of psychology can both learn from their predecessors and hope to avoid their mistakes. Psychology students also can better understand the diversity of approaches that continue to be applied within the fields that exist in contemporary psychology.

Carl Rogers (1902–1987)

PSYCHOLOGY IN EVERYDAY LIFE:

PSYCHOLOGY AND SOCIAL ACTION

The history of psychology is filled with examples of how psychology has been used to make a difference in people's lives. There are many examples of the interaction between psychology and social policy.

In the United States, ability and achievement testing have a profound impact on us for better or for worse. The testing industry is a multimillion-dollar business that affects people's lives from early childhood through adulthood. Tests are used for military recruitment and placement, school-based decisions, evaluation of job performance, and assessment of people's personal suitability for work in jobs that require great discretion, such as in intelligence agencies. Indeed, the tragedy of September 11, 2001, has made tests for selecting individuals for key jobs, such as in the airline and security industries, even more important.

Today many attorneys hire psychologists to serve as jury consultants in order to select juries that are most likely to render a favorable verdict for their clients. These consultants sometimes have proven to be accurate in their assessments of how potential jurors will vote. This accuracy is astonishing, given that the decisions must be made before the case is even presented to the future jury. In the famous O. J. Simpson criminal trial, the defense relied heavily on jury consultants, whereas the prosecution scorned their advice. Simpson was acquitted.

A third area in which psychology interacts with social action is in framing messages so that they have maximum persuasive effect. Some such work is done in commercial advertising, but other work of this kind looks at how people can be convinced to avoid various forms of risky behavior, such as those that might lead to AIDS. For example, it has been found that celebrities with AIDS, such as Magic Johnson, the former basketball player, can be useful sources of messages against risky behaviors if the people who hear the messages have some emotional involvement with these celebrities (W. J. Brown & Basil, 1995; see Devos-Comby & Salovey, 2002).

A fourth area in which psychology has had a profound influence on social policy is in the design of programs to help disadvantaged children achieve their maximum potential. Beginning in the 1960s, the United States started a massive series of intervention programs under the label "Head Start" to help children, especially disadvantaged children, reach their full potential. These programs are still going strong today.

Some of the most important work on psychology and social policy has been done by Kenneth Clark, a social psychologist and former president of the American Psychological Association. In collaboration with his wife Mamie, Clark developed the "doll test." African-American children of early school age viewed four dolls that were identical except that two were Black and two were White. The children were asked to identify the racial identity of each doll and also to state which doll was best, which was nice, which was bad, and which they would prefer to play with (see Clark, 1988). The Clarks found that most African-American children, based

Archives of the History of American Psychology, University of Akron, Akron, Ohio

Social psychologist Kenneth Clark devoted a major portion of his career to studying how schools could be improved in ways that serve minority children.

on these questions, preferred the White to the Black dolls. As a result of this research, Clark concluded that racism in the United States was having a negative effect on the psychological development of African-American children. Clark particularly challenged school segregation as a major cause of the damage to these children. His work was cited in the landmark 1954 Supreme Court decision, *Brown v. Board of Education,* which declared school segregation to be unconstitutional.

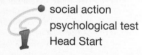

social action
psychological test
Head Start

PSYCHOLOGY AS A FIELD OF STUDY

What are the principal specialized fields within psychology? What are some career opportunities in these fields?

The previous section was a sprint through the often cyclical history of psychology. This section is another sprint, this time through the territory that the discipline of psychology has come to cover. This territory is easily as vast and varied as the history of psychology might lead you to expect. A psychological **perspective** centers on a particular set of theories and beliefs based on the philosophical strands described early in this chapter. In contrast, a **field** is a domain of study centered on a set of topics that have a common core of related phenomena.

There are many fields within psychology. The names of these fields suggest the scope of their topics: educational psychology, personality psychology, developmental psychology, social psychology, and so on. Certainly, investigators within some fields are believers in one or more perspectives that define the field. For example, biological psychologists take a biological viewpoint. Still, a given field can encompass a multitude of perspectives. Among *clinical psychologists*—those who treat clients with psychological problems—you will find psychoanalysts, behaviorists, cognitivists, and

others. Each of the main fields of psychology may have several subfields. Developmental psychology includes the study of infancy, social development, cognitive development, physical development, adolescence, and adulthood and aging, to name only a few of the subfields in this one area. These fields and subfields will become more familiar as you move through the chapters of this text; in many cases they serve as the topics of chapters. One of the most useful ways of understanding these different fields is to look at the questions with which they concern themselves. Many different terms are used to describe these fields, but most of them reflect simple commonsense notions of how to divide the field. So they should be easy to learn.

PSYCHOBIOLOGY Also termed *biological* or *physiological psychology*, this field deals with the biological structures and processes underlying thought, feeling, motivation, and behavior. In some cases biological psychologists may work at the level of the biochemistry of cells, or they may work on understanding the physical effects of emotions or on how the eye's structure affects perception. Some questions of interest to psychologists working in this area might be:

What neurochemicals are active in the brain when a person feels depressed?

What happens in the brain when we experience physical pleasure?

What brain structures are invoked when people perceive three-dimensional objects?

How does the brain receive messages from and send messages to the limbs?

COGNITIVE PSYCHOLOGY This field deals with how people perceive, learn, remember, and think about information. Cognitive psychologists study how people use language, think, solve problems, and make decisions. Those working in this field might be concerned with:

How do people perceive depth?

Why do people remember some facts but forget others?

How do people think when they play chess or solve everyday problems?

What is insight? How is insight different from creativity?

DEVELOPMENTAL PSYCHOLOGY This field is the study of how people develop over time through the processes of maturation and learning. As mentioned earlier, developmental psychologists may focus on particular ages (infancy, childhood, adolescence, adulthood, and aging). They also tend to focus on an aspect of development such as mental abilities or social skills such as peer relations. A developmental psychologist might wonder:

Are certain kinds of substance-abuse prevention messages likely to be particularly effective with an adolescent audience?

How do children form attachments to their parents?

How do people acquire an understanding of what others expect of them in social interactions?

At what age does it begin to be more difficult for a child to learn a second language?

NEUROPSYCHOLOGY This field is concerned with the bases of behavior in the human nervous system, with special emphasis on the brain. It is one of the most rapidly developing fields in psychology today. Neuropsychologists study the biological bases of perception, learning, memory, emotion, motivation, and other phenomena. They might ask:

What neural circuitry is responsible for learning?

What parts of the brain are activated when we feel anger?

What are the differences between the brains of people with and without autism?

SOCIAL PSYCHOLOGY This field is concerned with how people interact, both as individuals and in groups. The field encompasses work on attraction, prejudice, persuasion, and conformity, to name just a few areas of research. Social psychologists might ask:

What situations encourage people to be violent or cruel?

What makes a message persuasive?

Do opposites attract?

How do people form stereotypes and prejudices?

PERSONALITY PSYCHOLOGY This field focuses on the personal dispositions that lead people to behave as they do, and also on how these dispositions interact with situations to affect behavior. Personality psychologists may be concerned with trying to pinpoint or measure personality traits. They may be seeking answers to these questions:

Why do some people seem nervous and tense, even in apparently safe settings, whereas other people are easygoing and relaxed?

What makes some people highly conscientious and others less so?

How much does personality change over time?

CLINICAL PSYCHOLOGY This field deals with understanding and treating abnormal behavior. Clinical psychologists may offer therapy or do research on particular disorders or kinds of treatment. Questions they might be concerned with include:

What behavior is just a little out of the ordinary, and what behavior is truly abnormal?

How could a person lose touch with reality and with rational thought?

What causes people to engage in behavior that they themselves consider inappropriate and even abnormal and would like to stop if they could?

What sorts of experiences seem linked to depression? Anxiety?

Notice that both physiological and clinical psychologists may be interested in depression. A biological psychologist is perhaps seeking biochemical clues to this disorder, while the clinician may be using therapeutic techniques to discover the roots of an individual's feelings of depression. Similarly, a social psychologist, a personality psychologist, and a clinical psychologist may all be concerned with substance abuse, but from different angles. The social psychologist may be interested in social situations that contribute to drug use. The personality psychologist might be interested in personality types at risk for substance abuse. A clinical psychologist might be interested in what makes an effective treatment program. There is often considerable overlap. A clinical psychologist studying the problems of adolescence, for example, is also likely to have a great deal of interest and background in developmental psychology.

Although the fields of psychology described above are the main ones covered in this book, they are by no means the only ones. New specialties of psychology are constantly evolving as old ones fade, although specialties rarely die out altogether.

- *Cultural psychology* extends the study of psychological topics to all cultures. Through it, mechanisms of mind and behavior can be studied and compared in multiple cultures. Researchers in cultural psychology endeavor to understand how culture and ethnicity affect human behavior. For example, do people of certain cultural groups show more of a predisposition to violence than people of other groups, and why?
- *Health psychology* seeks to understand the reciprocal interaction between the psychological processes of the mind and the physical health of the body. For example, does a positive attitude in and of itself help people recover from physical illnesses?
- *Educational psychology* uses psychology to develop and improve curricula, school administration, and classroom teaching practices.

- *School psychology* uses psychology to diagnose psychologically based problems of children in school and to recommend, where possible, means of correcting or at least coping with these problems.
- *Organizational psychology* applies psychology to understanding organizations and to making decisions about employees and hiring in institutional settings, such as workplaces and businesses.
- *Engineering psychology* deals with human–machine systems and how instruments such as computers and automobile dashboards can be made more user-friendly.
- *Forensic psychology* applies psychology to issues that arise in the legal profession, such as the validity of eyewitness testimony, jury decision making, and the relevance of psychological disorders to legal guilt or innocence.
- *Political psychology* applies the methods of psychology, especially social psychology, to political issues, such as voter behavior in elections, behavior of political leaders, and mass political movements.
- *Positive psychology*, a very new field, studies valued human experiences, such as well-being, contentment, hope, optimism, and happiness.

Positive psychology is a good example of how a new field can develop. Some psychologists believed that psychology was concentrating too much on the negative aspects of human behavior, such as psychological disorders and stress. So they created a movement to focus on the positive phenomena psychology deals with, such as happiness and hope (Gillham, 2000; Seligman & Csikszentmihalyi, 2000; Snyder & Lopez, 2002). New fields like positive psychology can appear at any time. Some last; others do not. The future of positive psychology, like other new fields, thus remains uncertain (see Lazarus, in press). Only time will tell.

When reading about some of the fields and specialties within psychology, you may find yourself drawn to consider a career in psychology. Table 1.4 lists some of the specific career paths available to psychology majors and describes the typical duties, education required, and work settings for various fields. A more detailed description of some of these careers, as well as others within psychology, can be found in *Career Paths in Psychology* (R. J. Sternberg, 1997a).

The list of careers within psychology is not static. As psychology is applied to more and more other disciplines, new specialties within psychology are appearing almost every year. Recent examples of this growth are health psychology and forensic psychology. With aging populations in many countries, gerontological psychology—the psychological study of the elderly—though not new, has become of more interest than ever before. Within just a few years' time, other specialties, as yet unheard of, may well have appeared. Psychology frequently draws on and contributes to other academic disciplines, which in turn continually stimulate and rejuvenate psychological thought. Just as psychological thought has evolved from diverse ideas in its past, it continues to develop through intersection and interaction with diverse fields and sources of information in the present. It will continue to develop in this way in the future. At the same time, the methods of investigation it uses will continue to develop. Old and new methods alike are discussed in Chapter 2.

✓CONCEPT CHECK 6

1. An engineering psychologist is most likely to study how people interact with
   a. other people.
   b. trains.
   c. animals.
   d. computer keyboards.
2. The psychologist most likely to treat patients in a private practice is a(n)
   a. organizational psychologist.
   b. clinical psychologist.
   c. cultural psychologist.
   d. evolutionary psychologist.
3. A forensic psychologist studies applications of psychology to
   a. infants.
   b. young children.
   c. computers.
   d. law.

TABLE 1.4

Career Options for Psychologists. The study of psychology can prove valuable for any career path. Here are some of the options available to persons who pursue degrees in psychology.

Career	Typical Training	Job Description
Academic psychologist	PhD	Works in a college or university teaching and conducting research; advises students, assists in educational administration
Clinical psychologist	PhD, EdD, or PsyD	Diagnoses and treats patients for psychological problems; teaches, trains, and conducts research in a hospital, clinic, college, or university
Counseling psychologist	MA, EdD, or PhD	Counsels people about their problems, conflicts, or choices; often works in a school, office, hospital, or clinic
Engineering or human-factors psychologist	PhD	May work in an industrial setting; designs machines and workplace environments to maximize productivity and safety; often works with engineers and designers
Industrial or organizational psychologist	MA or PhD	Works in a business or industrial setting to help with hiring and firing, testing, interviewing, and placement; assists in developing more hospitable and effective workplaces
Consumer psychologist	MA or PhD	Works in a business, consulting, or advertising firm to generate ads that will sell products; supervises testing of ads and determines consumer preferences
Military psychologist	PhD	Works in the armed forces to deal with the interface between psychology and military life; involved in testing, counseling, designing, and implementing new procedures and requirements
Psychometrician	MA or PhD	Creates psychological tests, including aptitude, achievement, personality, attitude, and vocational preference tests; collects and analyzes test data
School psychologist	MA, EdD, or PhD	Works in a school setting to test and counsel students; identifies children with perceptual and learning disabilities, as well as gifted children
Consulting psychologist	MA, EdD, or PhD	Works for a consulting firm on a special for-hire basis to perform any of the various aforementioned services

ETHICAL BEHAVIOR

Consider this dilemma: A runaway trolley is racing down a track toward five people who will surely be killed unless you pull a switch that diverts the trolley to another track where one person will be killed. Do you pull the switch and save five people instead of one? Consider another dilemma: You stand with others on a footbridge above the track and see the runaway trolley racing toward five people who will surely be killed unless you push the large person next to you onto the track to stop the trolley. Again, do you sacrifice one person in order to save five others?

These famous dilemmas have received much attention by psychologists and philosophers who study moral judgments. The first is called the "trolley dilemma." Most people say they would pull the switch to divert the trolley, letting one person die to save five others. The second scenario is called the "footbridge dilemma." In this situation, most people say they would not kill one person to save five others. How do we explain the reasoning that it is acceptable to sacrifice one person in the trolley dilemma but not in the footbridge dilemma? **Cognitive psychologists** study people's responses to dilemmas like these to learn more

about thinking and decision-making processes. One thing they've discovered is that the very few people who decide they would push the person off the bridge take twice as long to make up their minds as the people who decide they wouldn't do it.

Physiological psychologists and **cognitive neuroscientists** have studied the brain activity of people in the process of considering these dilemmas. Using special imaging techniques, Jonathan Cohen and his colleagues examined nine subjects who were asked to solve 60 different dilemmas. When thinking about the trolley dilemma, they tended to use areas in their frontal lobes that are associated with complex reasoning. The same subjects showed significant activity in the areas of their brains that are associated with emotions when they thought about personally shoving the person off the footbridge (Greene, Sommerville, Nystrom, Darley, & Cohen, 2001).

Developmental psychologists examine reasoning ability in people of all ages. According to Kohlberg (see Chapter 11), moral judgment develops and improves throughout adulthood. Research by *social psychologists* demonstrates that other people can influence

our moral judgment. In Chapter 14 you will learn that the influence of authority figures and people in groups can lead us to make decisions we might not have arrived at if left alone.

Moral development requires that we develop a set of ethical values that guide our behavior. Because **clinical psychologists** often learn very private details about their patients' lives, they must adhere to the strictest code of ethics regarding their own behavior. Matters such as confidentiality (not divulging private information) and how to behave towards people who may be emotionally unstable are taught to students preparing to become clinical psychologists. Much research has been devoted to studying the best way to teach ethical standards and moral judgments to graduate students (Cellucci & Heffer, 2002). Having them consider and discuss ethical dilemmas and case studies of ethical situations that arise in clinical practice is an excellent way to guide them in applying the ethical standards of our profession. The valuable contributions of physiological, cognitive, developmental, social, and clinical psychologists complement one another to benefit the study and teaching of ethics.

SUMMARY

PSYCHOLOGY AS A NATURAL SCIENCE AND A SOCIAL SCIENCE 2

What is psychology? What do psychologists study? How is psychology different from other ways of studying mental processes and behavior?

1. *Psychology* is the study of mental processes, behavior, and the relationship between them.
2. Psychology is both a natural science and a social science.

KEY THEMES IN THE EVOLUTION OF PSYCHOLOGICAL IDEAS 3

How do you think ideas evolve over time?

3. By studying views on certain issues in philosophy and physiology, as they have evolved over time, we can trace the history of the foundations of psychology. Some of the most important questions in the history of psychology are whether the mind and body are one or are two separate phenomena, to

what extent psychology should focus on each of biology and behavior, to what extent behavior is a function of innate factors and to what extent it is a function of environmental factors, and the extent to which behavior is general or specific across domains.

4. A *dialectic* is a search for truth through the resolution of opposites; first a *thesis* is proposed, then a countering *antithesis*, and eventually a unifying *synthesis*. One such dialectic in psychology relates to the role of theory in scientific research. Should research be wholly guided by theory, performed without regard to theory, or performed with both a theory in mind and a recognition that results may not fit into the proposed theoretical framework?

THE EARLY HISTORY OF PSYCHOLOGY 5

What were some of the early recorded ideas about the nature of the human mind?

5. Psychology traces its roots back to archaic Greece. In fact, the word *psychology* (the study of the mind and behavior) is derived from the Greek word *psyche*, which means soul or breath of life.

6. The Greek physician Hippocrates believed that the mind resided in the brain. He espoused an *empirical* approach to learning how the body works.

7. The work of the ancient Greek philosophers Plato and Aristotle aptly demonstrates the nature of dialectics. The issues raised in their work are still argued today. Plato emphasized the supreme power of the mind and thought, which made him a *rationalist*. Plato believed that knowledge is innate; that the search for truth can best be achieved through intellectual reflection; and that the mind and body are qualitatively different and separate, a concept known as *mind–body dualism*. Aristotle emphasized the world we can see and touch as the route to reality, truth, and knowledge, which made him an *empiricist*. In contrast to Plato, Aristotle believed that knowledge is learned through interactions with and direct observation of the environment. He also presaged *monism*, the view that the mind and body are essentially one.

8. During the Renaissance (1300–1600), science as we know it was born. Thinkers began to depend less on faith and more on empirical observation for proof of theories.

9. René Descartes, a rationalist philosopher, believed in mind–body dualism. In opposition, the British empiricist school of philosophers (1600–1850), including John Locke, believed in the continuity and interdependence of mind and body.

10. Immanuel Kant sought to synthesize questions about innate versus acquired sources of knowledge. Kant's work in philosophy helped to establish psychology as a discrete discipline, separate from both philosophy and medicine.

EARLY PSYCHOLOGICAL APPROACHES TO BEHAVIOR 8

What were the earliest major psychological approaches to understanding behavior?

11. Over time, psychologists have approached the study of the mind and behavior from different perspectives as manifested in different schools of thought. These perspectives, from functionalism through cognitivism, have often been in part reactions to what came before them. Modern perspectives in psychology are viewed, generally speaking, as those that originated in the 20th century. New theories continue to evolve dialectically.

12. Structuralism was the first strictly psychological school of thought. *Structuralists* sought to analyze consciousness into its constituent components of elementary sensations, using *introspection*, a reflective self-observation technique. Structuralism emphasized the role of experience in behavior.

13. *Functionalists*, in reaction to structuralism, sought to understand what people do and why. Many functionalists were pragmatists, who looked at the applications of knowledge to practice.

14. *Associationism* examined how events or ideas become associated with one another in the mind to result in a form of learning. Associationism emphasized the role of experience over innate factors in behavior.

PSYCHOLOGY IN THE 20TH CENTURY 12

What were the main perspectives of the 20th century on psychological thought?

15. An offshoot of associationism, *behaviorism*, was a reaction to structuralism and is based on the belief that the science of psychology should deal only with observable behavior.

16. *Gestalt psychology* is based on the notion that the whole is often more meaningful than the sum of its parts. This perspective developed partly as a reaction against the extreme analytic perspectives of both structuralists and behaviorists.

17. *Cognitivism* is the belief that much of human behavior can be understood in terms of how people think. Some cognitivists emphasize the importance of innate factors in behavior, whereas others emphasize the role of environmental factors.

18. *Biological psychology* studies the ways in which human anatomy and physiology (especially of the nervous system, including the brain) interact with human behavior. Biological researchers emphasize the importance of the biological bases of behavior.

19. *Evolutionary psychology* seeks explanations of how behavior might have been adaptive for our ancestors in the environments they confronted.

20. The basis of *psychodynamic psychology* is the view that many of the thoughts and feelings that motivate our behavior are unconscious, and that there is a continual tension among internal mental structures.

21. *Humanistic psychology* studies how people consciously actualize, or realize through action, their own great inner potential.

What are the principal specialized fields within psychology? What are some career opportunities in these fields?

22. Many different *fields* appear under the umbrella of psychology. Some of the main fields are psychobiology, cognitive psychology, social psychology, personality psychology, clinical psychology, and developmental psychology. Some fields, such as clinical psychology, accommodate a variety of *perspectives* (cognitive, psychoanalytic, humanistic, and others). New specialties are constantly evolving. The various fields in psychology have given rise to diverse career opportunities.

23. Psychologists in different specializations may study the same problem. But depending on the perspectives they use, they may organize information differently and use different methods of inquiry—in effect, approaching the same issue from different angles.

KEY TERMS

antithesis 3
contradicts thesis
associationism 11
ideas become associated
behavioral genetics 17
behavior influenced by genes
behaviorism 14
observable behavior
biological psychology 17
understand behavior by studying brain
biopsychosocial approach 18
understand behavior by bio, psych, and social
classically conditioned learning 14
Pavlov's dogs
cognitivism 16
importance of thought
dialectic 3
thesis, antithesis synthesis → thesis, ...
empirical methods 6
evidence through experience and observation
knowledge based on fact

empiricist 6
based on fact
evolutionary psychology 18
organism's adaptation to environment
field 21
topics w/ a common core
functionalism 11
what people do and why
Gestalt psychology 15
"whole different from sum"
humanistic psychology 19
free will
introspection 5
inner ideas and experiences
law of effect 12
actions are rewarded
mind–body dualism 6
separate entities
monism 7
mind and body are one

perspective 21
centers on set of theories
philosophy 5
> roots of psychology
physiology 5
psychoanalysis 18
based on theories of motivation & behavior
psychodynamic theory 18
conflicting unconscious
psychology 2
study of mental processes/behavior
rationalist 7
vs. empiricist
structuralism 8
analyze elements of mind
synthesis 3
combines 2 opinions
thesis 3
opinion

ANSWERS TO CONCEPT CHECKS

Concept Check 1
1. c   2. c   3. b

Concept Check 2
1. d   2. a   3. c

Concept Check 3
1. a   2. b   3. c

Concept Check 4
1. a   2. c   3. b

Concept Check 5
1. d   2. b   3. b

Concept Check 6
1. d   2. b   3. d.

1. Which of the following terms is not relevant to the dialectic?
   a. thesis
   b. prosthesis
   c. antithesis
   d. synthesis
2. ____was an important empiricist philosopher.
   a. Plato
   b. René Descartes
   c. John Locke
   d. Immanuel Kant
3. According to mind–body dualism, the mind
   a. is important but the body is not.
   b. is not important but the body is.
   c. and the body are very similar, differing only quantitatively.
   d. and the body differ in kind.
4. A structuralist would be likely to use ___ as a primary method of studying psychological phenomena.
   a. biological analysis
   b. introspection
   c. spiritualism
   d. rationalism
5. Functionalism
   a. involved a tightly knit set of methods that all functionalists used.
   b. has had virtually no influence on current thinking in psychology.
   c. is the school of thought associated with William James.
   d. is still a major school of psychology.
6. Associationism
   a. equally emphasizes the role of innate factors and the environment.
   b. emphasizes the role of the environment over innate factors.

   c. emphasizes the role of innate factors over the environment.
   d. does not speak to the role of innate factors versus the environment.
7. A radical behaviorist
   a. believes in the great psychological importance of mental states and studies them carefully.
   b. believes in the great psychological importance of mental states but does not study them.
   c. believes that mental states play only a minor role in human functioning.
   d. rejects the study of mental states as a part of psychology.
8. A cognitivist is likely to devote the most attention to the study of
   a. thought.
   b. motivation.
   c. emotion.
   d. the soul.
9. Carl Rogers was a _____ psychologist.
   a. psychodynamic
   b. cognitivist
   c. radical behaviorist
   d. humanist
10. A health psychologist is most likely to believe that the state of the
   a. mind affects the body but not vice versa.
   b. body affects the mind but not vice versa.
   c. body is independent of the state of the mind.
   d. mind and the body mutually affect each other.

Answers
1. b   2. c   3. d   4. b   5. c   6. b   7. d   8. a
9. d   10. d

THINK ABOUT IT

1. If you were to accept Thales's invitation to participate in the critical tradition, what perspectives and ideas in this chapter would you criticize? Critique at least one of the views that has been described in this chapter.
2. Choose an early school of thought and a current one. In what ways did the older one pave the way for the newer one? (List both similarities and differences.)

3. Quickly jot down a description of your sensations as you believe a structuralist would describe them introspectively.
4. In *Walden Two*, B. F. Skinner (1948) describes a utopia in which behaviorist principles are applied to all aspects of life for people of all ages. Choose one of the schools of thought described in this chapter and briefly describe a utopian community being governed by psychologists with that viewpoint.

5. In your everyday life you confront many new situations. Describe a situation in which your theory of the nature of the situation (which may be entirely idiosyncratic) largely guided your responses.

6. What is one thing that your psychology professor—or the author of this book—could do to apply the notion of the dialectic to your current psychology course. Give a specific example of how you might apply this notion.

WEB RESOURCES

For a chapter tutorial quiz, direct links to Internet sites, and other useful features, visit the book-specific website at http://psychology.wadsworth.com/sternberg4e. You can also connect directly to the following sites:

American Psychological Association
http://www.apa.org
This official Web site of the American Psychological Association is loaded with helpful links to APA divisions, general resources for teachers and students of psychology, and links to APA publications, such as the APA Monitor. Some articles from the Monitor are also available on the Website.

American Psychological Society
http://www.psychologicalscience.org
This is the official Web site of the American Psychological Society.

For additional readings on many of the topics covered in this chapter, check out InfoTrac College Edition at **www.infotrac-college.com/ wadsworth.**

CD-ROM: UNIFYING PSYCHOLOGY

Disk One
Psychological Perspectives: The 1850s and Beyond
Fields Within Psychology
Careers in Psychology
Chapter Quiz
Critical Thinking Questions

CHAPTER 2

RESEARCH METHODS

Nearly all of us consider ourselves at least somewhat expert at observing and understanding behavior. You may have heard talk-show guests offer tips about love and how you can improve your love life. He or she might say, "Two of the best predictors of happiness in a relationship are how you feel about your partner and how your partner feels about you." Hearing that, you may wonder why psychologists even bother to study such obvious and commonsensical "facts" about human behavior. Interestingly, this statement, that happiness in a relationship is best measured by the feelings of the two people involved, shows why psychologists do bother—because psychological research has demonstrated that "obvious" statement to be wrong (R. J. Sternberg & Barnes, 1985).

Many of us have used a self-help program: to stop smoking, to improve our love life, to start exercising, to overcome depression, to lose weight, and so on. How do self-help programs work? Many of them emphasize that focusing on our goals can help us attain them. The idea is that if we want to be rich, or professionally successful, or successful in love, we should visualize our goal and think frequently about it. Shelley Taylor and her colleagues (S. Taylor, Pham, Rivkin, & Armor, 1998) did a series of studies to test this idea. They had people focus on the goals they wished to attain, on the processes of attaining those goals, or on nothing in particular. She found that the best way to attain one's goals is by focusing on the *means*, not the end.

People in different cultures may have very different ideas about what kinds of goals they should seek. Consider the following anecdote:

> Once upon a time, an anthropologist was telling an English folk-fable to a gathering of the Bemba of Rhodesia. She glowingly described "a young prince who climbed glass mountains, crossed chasms, and fought dragons, all to obtain the hand of a maiden he loved." The Bemba were plainly bewildered, but remained silent. Finally an old chief spoke up, voicing the feelings of all present in the simplest of questions: "Why not take another girl?" he asked.
> —M. M. Hunt, *The Natural History of Love*

Psychology does not just restate what everyone knows. It is more precise and thoughtful than common sense. Some findings do confirm what we already suspected, but many surprise us. In fact, psychologists, like other scientists, expect to be surprised.

CHARACTERISTICS OF SCIENTIFIC FINDINGS

What are the main characteristics of scientific findings?

Scientists use particular methods as they strive to find the truth. These methods ensure that the information (data) they gather and the theories they develop are verifiable, made public, and built on other verified findings. Of course, scientists cannot guarantee such standards. But by using the methods described in this chapter, researchers seek to achieve them to the best of their abilities, given their frailties, biases, and cultural identities (see Table 2.1).

SCIENTIFIC FINDINGS ARE VERIFIABLE

Scientific findings are **verifiable;** that is, they can be confirmed. When one scientist conducts an experiment and draws conclusions, other scientists must be able to **replicate** the experiment—to use the original methods and produce the same results. Suppose you want to investigate why, in the middle of a test, you cannot remember something you studied earlier. You suspect anxiety about running out of time caused the problem.

To test your hypothesis, you must devise a procedure that will produce reliable and valid results. If your results are **reliable,** then you and others can count on your procedure to produce the same results time after time.

Reliability is necessary but not sufficient. Suppose that a researcher investigated the effects of anxiety about time on test performance. This researcher compared students' test performance in a room in which a clock ticked loudly with test performance in a room without a clock. Suppose the results of this procedure were tested again and again and reliably showed that test takers in the room without the clock performed better than students in the other room. But the investigation might not have shown what it was purported to show. Maybe the difference was due to the test takers' irritation with the noisy clock rather than to anxiety about time. The results of the procedure might be reliable, but the interpretation that those results confirmed the effects of anxiety might not be **valid,** or assessing what a procedure is supposed to measure. Additional research would have to determine whether it was anxiety about time, irritation, or some other factor that caused the difference in performance.

The test-taking example shows why scientific findings must be *accurately reported*. Accurate reporting allows both the initial researcher and later researchers to assess the reliability and the validity of their results.

TABLE 2.1
CONCEPT REVIEW

Three Characteristics of Valid Scientific Research. Scientists use various methods for obtaining data and formulating theories, which have these three characteristics.

Characteristics Prized by Scientists	Reason for Prizing the Characteristic
Verifiable results	Evaluating the research findings determines whether they are reliable and the resulting interpretations valid.
Public disclosure	Carefully reviewed findings published in scientific journals inform scientists about existing research, so they may evaluate and build on it.
Cumulative effects	Science is moved forward by scientists building on past research.

SCIENTIFIC FINDINGS ARE PUBLIC

Science is *public*. No matter how many interesting research studies are conducted, the results do not fully benefit science and society until they are made public, usually in scientific journals.

Scientists have at least three reasons to write about their results. First, the process of writing has helped many scientists interpret their own results. It also has clarified the directions in which their experiments led (D. J. Bem, 2000; Eisenberg, 2000; R. J. Sternberg, in press-a). For example, Sir Isaac Newton made discoveries about prisms while he was writing about his studies of light (Gorman, 1992).

Second, referees (people who evaluate articles submitted to scientific journals) and editors (people who decide which articles should be published in scientific journals) assess the relative scientific merits of the articles submitted for publication (R. J. Sternberg, 2000). They evaluate the ideas, the research methods, and the interpretations presented in the articles (Grigorenko, 2000; Reis, 2000; Salovey, 2000; R. A. Smith, 2000; Tesser, 2000).

Third, the publication of compelling results permits readers to learn about findings that might lead to further research or to relevant applications in their own fields. Fellow scientists have the opportunity to read, pause, reread, reflect, mull over details, and analyze the research, as well as to consider possible applications. Once the scientific merits of the findings have been evaluated, reporters in the nonscientific media may consider broader publication of the findings. These implications are based on *news value*—general appeal and popular interest. (Note that scientific value and news value often differ.)

This public aspect of science affected the writing of this book and could help you read it. The information in the book was investigated, documented, and supported in the many sources that are cited in the text. The last name of the author and the year in which the source was published appear in parentheses after the statement the research supports (see the Gorman citation above). Citations show that the claims in a work are based on published and accepted data. Citations also publicly credit other researchers. Finally, citations are a source of more information for readers. You may look up the citations in the References section at the back of this textbook. They will lead you to the original study, which in turn will include references to earlier research findings.

SCIENTIFIC FINDINGS ARE CUMULATIVE

In addition to being verifiable, scientific research is *cumulative*. Even revolutionary scientists who invent new ways of looking at problems build on past work, perhaps using it as a basis for what not to do. When Albert Einstein changed the way scientists view physics, he built on the foundation of Newtonian physics. Without Isaac Newton's earlier work, Einstein never could have formulated his theories of relativity. Whether scientists embrace or reject the work of their intellectual ancestors, they profit from it. In designing experiments for your hypothetical study of the factors that affect test performance, you would profit from your predecessors' work. You also would benefit from reading widely about other research on attention, memory, thinking, the effects of emotions on performance, and the ways in which physiological stress affects thinking. Where possible, scientists prefer simple explanations that account for as many different findings as possible.

Having discussed some of the major characteristics of scientific work, we can look at some common misconceptions about it.

WHAT SCIENTIFIC RESEARCH IS NOT

Scientific thinking examines one's assumptions. An example is the hypothesis that the anxiety-producing presence of the clock and not its ticking affects test scores. So, when we consider what science is, it is helpful to examine our assumptions about it. Some may turn out to be misconceptions.

ARE SCIENTIFIC FINDINGS ALL OBVIOUS?

Folk wisdom often guides people in their everyday lives. The most common form of folk wisdom is the proverb, or wise saying. Are proverbs really useful guides to living? Robert Epstein (1997) pointed out that the problem with proverbs is that they so often recommend contradictory courses of action: "Absence makes the heart grow fonder" and "Out of sight, out of mind"; "Haste makes waste" and "He who hesitates is lost." Epstein decided to examine some key proverbs to determine whether they are supported by research.

Consider the proverb "Confession is good for the soul." Generally research supports this notion. People who self-disclose are likely to have better mental and physical health than people who do not (Pennebaker, 1997). The research shows that self-disclosure is not uniformly helpful, however. Some kinds of disclosure, such as to individuals who are likely to be judgmental, may backfire (Kelly, 1999). Another proverb is "All work and no play makes Jack a dull boy." Research suggests that long working hours can slow down reaction times and reduce alertness (Knauth, 1996). In contrast, leisure activities tend to improve mood, relieve stress, and even boost the functioning of the immune system (Tinsley, Hinson, Tinsley, & Holt, 1993).

In sum, proverbs are a mixed bag. Sometimes they can be supported, sometimes not, and sometimes they are verified to be true under certain circumstances and not others. An advantage of psychology over conventional wisdom is that it seeks answers not merely from people's beliefs but from scientific research on human behavior.

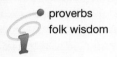

proverbs
folk wisdom

MISCONCEPTION 1: SCIENTIFIC FINDINGS ARE VALID FOREVER
Fact: Scientists are products of their times
Scientific accounts are not always correct. In fact, they are often wrong, or at least incomplete. Today we view many of the beliefs of 19th-century and even early 20th-century psychology—such as the belief that thinking is always accompanied by some form of talking to oneself (J. B. Watson, 1930)—as quaint and curious. In the future, many of the views we hold dear today also will seem outdated and peculiar. To be of value, science must be dynamic and constantly evolving as new theories continually replace old ones. But this evolution does not always occur in an idealized manner.

MISCONCEPTION 2: SCIENTIFIC RESEARCH IS ALWAYS CONDUCTED IN A CERTAIN WAY
Fact: The scientific process must suit the situation
Scientists in general and psychologists in particular do not always use the orderly, linear, scientific methods they may have learned in school. Almost all scientists make false starts from time to time. They have to reconsider *why* they are doing *what* they are doing, or even what they should have done in the first place. Sometimes they have to revise their original hypotheses or fine-tune their research procedures in order to get them to work. Sometimes research that starts off being about one thing ends up being about something else. For example, studies of why children fail in school may begin by studying the children's abilities. But they end up also studying their motivations, personalities, and environments, which may surface as more important to success than ability.

MISCONCEPTION 3: SCIENTIFIC RESEARCH IS ALWAYS PERFECTLY OBJECTIVE
Fact: Scientists are influenced by human values
Scientists sometimes fail to reach their goal of being completely objective in deciding what to study, how to study it, and how to interpret their findings. Like their fellow humans, they can rationalize when they fall prey to errors in thinking. For example, people who show **confirmation bias** tend to confirm rather than to refute existing beliefs (D. F. Halpern, 1995; Oakhill & Garnham, 1993; R. J. Sternberg & Ben-Zeev, 2001; Wason & Johnson-Laird, 1972). When viewing new evidence, scientists, like anyone else, may look for an interpretation that best fits what they already believe (T. S. Kuhn, 1970). For this and other reasons, scientists should actively seek to **disconfirm,** or refute, what they believe (Popper, 1959): Science often advances most effectively when studies are designed not to show just which ideas are useful but also which ones are not.

Values—preconceptions about what is valuable—also affect the way we do research. They influence what topics we deem worthy of study, how we believe these topics should be studied, and how we interpret the results. As human life expectancies have lengthened and populations in various countries thus have increased in average age, the study of aging has become more valuable to many people—hence increased attention has been devoted to it.

As we are seeing, scientific values include objectivity, empirical testing of theories, accuracy, honesty, public sharing of information, and openness to question and to verification. When these values are set aside, the effects can be disastrous. For example, the occasional cases in which companies have hidden research or not fully tested for potentially disastrous side effects of drugs have resulted in catastrophic results for the human guinea pigs who unwittingly took them. Fenphen was a combination of drugs many people used to lose weight. Taken singly, the drugs were relatively harmless but ineffective in promoting weight loss. Taken together, the drugs promoted weight loss but also damage to the heart! Sometimes it is not even obvious that a drug is involved, as in the case of nicotine, a potentially deadly component of tobacco. Many of its harmful effects were known to officers of certain cigarette manufacturing companies well before information about these effects became public. A realistic aspiration is to recognize our values and try to keep them from biasing or otherwise interfering with the way we study human behavior.

© Nathan Benn/Corbis

Expecting that children in an environment like this will have a difficult time learning may result in a confirmation bias—a tendency to focus on information that confirms one's beliefs. It is better when studies are designed not just to show which ideas are useful, but also to show which are not.

MISCONCEPTION 4: SCIENCE IS MERELY A COLLECTION OF FACTS
Fact: Scientific interpretation makes facts meaningful
One cultural value that can color our view of science is that we tend to emphasize products (such as facts) above processes (such as the pursuit of knowledge and understanding). This emphasis leads to what may be the most important misconception about science—that it is merely a collection of facts. Facts become part of the scientific enterprise only when they are presented in the context of a **theory**, a statement of some general principles explaining particular events. Theories are not opinions; rather, they are analyses of the relationships among facts. Science is not merely descriptive but also explanatory. Without theories, we still might be able to describe behavior or at least to make some discrete observations about it. But we would not really understand it. In looking at human behavior, we would be able to investigate and find answers to *what* is happening but not to *why*, and possibly not even to *how* it is happening.

Theories also play an important role in guiding observations and experimentation. For example, people typically think of illusions as problematical. Shelley Taylor and Jonathan Brown (1988) formulated a theory that postulated the reverse. They argued that certain illusions actually may help preserve rather than damage psychological well-being by increasing motivation. Even if you are under 6 feet tall and overweight, you

could still become a professional basketball player. Their theory provided the impetus for them to review the literature and find that the available data in fact supported their theory. Their theory guided their thinking, determined what they were looking for, and led them to an important discovery.

Thus far we have described the characteristics of science, including some of the erroneous assumptions made about it. Let us now begin to consider how scientists think about the topics they study, and how they study those topics.

✓ CONCEPT CHECK 1
1. If you repeat an experiment someone else has done and you get the same results, you have _____ the investigator's results.
   - a. replicated
   - b. elucidated
   - c. publicized
   - d. appropriated
2. Scientists
   - a. do not even try to be objective.
   - b. try to be objective but do not always succeed.
   - c. are objective without even trying to be.
   - d. are always objective.
3. Sometimes investigators' prior beliefs influence the results they obtain in their scientific work. The investigators fall victims to
   - a. replication.
   - b. disconfirmation bias.
   - c. elucidation.
   - d. confirmation bias.

IN THE LAB OF WILLIAM J. RAY

STUDYING BEHAVIOR AND EXPERIENCE

Some years ago I noticed that our students not only did not look forward to our courses on research methods but actually dreaded taking them. That concerned me on a number of levels. First, my colleagues and I found research exciting and were always willing to ask questions about how the world works and especially how psychology could help to explain its processes. But we evidently were not communicating the fun of doing science. Second, given the variety of information confronting us every day in articles, political statements, and infomercials, it seemed important to me that all of us think about what we are told and how we evaluate it. Even if students never perform research, it is critical that they become informed consumers of information and know how to evaluate what they read. Third, science plays a pervasive role in our society and often is the touchstone for making large-scale governmental and corporate decisions as to which programs to implement. Thus, it is imperative that citizens understand scientific language. Finally, psychological science is meaningful not only for society but also for ourselves. It is one of the few areas in which we study not only our visible behavior but also our internal experiences.

Studying ourselves reveals many opportunities and problems for performing science, as well as challenges. Studying ourselves makes it more difficult to know how we know what we know, and how we know

William J. Ray received his PhD from Vanderbilt University in 1971, with an emphasis in psychophysiology and clinical psychology. He was a Fellow in Medical Psychology at the University of California Medical Center in San Francisco before joining the faculty at Penn State University, where he is a professor of psychology. His research connects clinical psychology and cognitive neuroscience, with an emphasis on motor processes, physiological concomitants of clinical processes, and the nature of dissociation and hypnosis. He currently has an active brain imaging collaboration at the University of Konstanz, Germany.

what we don't know. For these reasons, I have continued to think and write about science throughout my career. In my textbook for undergraduate students, *Methods Toward a Science of Behavior and Experience* (2003), I show that science has influenced Western civilization for at least the last 500 years. Its hallmark, the scientific method, lets us know when we are wrong. Anyone can claim that something is true. We watch politicians and advertisers do this every day. Throughout history, leaders have asked us to rely on their authority rather than test what they say. "What do you mean the earth is not the center of the universe?" and "The earth is not flat?" authorities once demanded. Today, science is the best method we have for testing our assumptions about the world and ourselves.

In my research as a clinical psychologist, I sought to understand how individuals experienced their cognitive and emotional processes (Borkovec, Stöber, & Ray, 1998; Ray, 1996). I learned early on that just

asking people what they were experiencing did not produce the absolute answers for which I was looking. I turned to psychophysiological methods of measuring brain activity and cardiovascular functions, to understand what was happening on another level of processing (Ray & Cole, 1985; Stern, Ray, & Quigley, 2001). Sometimes I have sought to determine if one technique or another might be useful. For example, several years ago we asked if chaos techniques might help us understand physiological processes that others had considered random (Elbert et al., 1994). Recently, we asked if behavioral therapy for anxiety disorders changed the physiological processes of the brain and heart. We also asked more basic questions about simple movement responses (Ray, Slobounow, & Simon, 2000). The critical finding is that the brain reflects not only our movements but also our intention to move. Movement preparations actually play a more critical role in determining how the brain executes a movement than the actual movement itself.

Psychologists are particularly well equipped to study expectations and plans. How we feel internally is another area we study, using a variety of techniques. Colleagues in Europe joined us in asking if hypnosis influences the experience of simple pain processes. EEG scans demonstrated that hypnotic suggestions influence the emotional experience of pain, which appears around a quarter of a second after the painful event occurs, but not the initial sensory experience, which occurs much more quickly (Ray, Keil, Mikuteit, Bongartz, & Elbert, 2002). Such research can help us create therapies to treat the negative experience of pain. From a scientific standpoint, having colleagues in other countries is not only fun but helps us see which psychological processes are universal and which are characteristic only of one's own culture.

Doing science is not unlike the task of a detective who sorts through different sets of clues hoping to discover how a particular situation occurred. The scientist has an advantage over the detective, in that experiments can recreate the situation as many times as necessary. By changing different factors, we discover which ones influence the processes we are studying. The key, of course, is that experimental designs and procedures help us to rule out factors that are not involved and consider alternative explanations for the results.

Finally, psychological scientists perform a service for society by agreeing to share their findings with society through the publication of the information learned in research. In learning research methods, you have the opportunity to continue this tradition and to answer critical questions of importance to you. Even if you choose a different career path than that of a scientist, you can use your knowledge of research procedures to aid society as an informed consumer.

HOW SCIENTISTS SOLVE PROBLEMS

How do you think scientists approach problem solving?

Scientists have methods for finding the solutions to a variety of problems. But today's solutions frequently become tomorrow's new problems. Consider a question: Do women prefer men with a more masculine face or a more feminine face? Some people might guess that women prefer a more masculine face; others might guess the opposite. But neither option is correct. Some scientists tackled the tricky problem of how to answer this question. According to one report (Penton-Voak et al., 1999), whether a woman prefers a more masculine or a more feminine face depends on the stage she is in with respect to her menstrual cycle. Women near ovulation and hence more likely to conceive prefer faces that are more masculine. Women far from ovulation and hence less likely to conceive prefer more feminine faces. So one problem is solved. But others are raised. Why would women prefer different kinds of faces at different times in their menstrual cycle? An evolutionary interpretation might be that during ovulation women look for the man most likely to produce the best possible offspring (which, in evolutionary terms, means those offspring most likely to survive). But is a man with a masculine face really more likely to contribute to producing the best possible offspring? Do men have similar time-bound preferences for women? And the list of questions goes on.

Much problem solving proceeds in the same way as in this example. Solving one scientific problem or answering one question raises a set of other problems or questions. Questions and answers proceed forward in a dialectical fashion (see Chapter 1). However, not all people may find dialectical thinking in science, or anything else, equally comfortable. Peng and Nisbett (1999, 2000) have shown that Westerners are less likely naturally to engage in dialectical thinking than Easterners, such as Chinese people.

IDENTIFYING THE PROBLEM

"Is there any point to which you would wish to draw my attention?"

"To the curious incident of the dog in the night-time."

"The dog did nothing in the night-time."

"That was the curious incident," remarked Sherlock Holmes.

—Sir Arthur Conan Doyle, "Silver Blaze," *The Memoirs of Sherlock Holmes*

The first step in problem solving is to select what to study: to identify the problem (Bransford & Stein, 1993; Galotti, 2002; R. J. Sternberg & Ben-Zeev, 2001). Some problems are more deserving of attention than others. Harriet Zuckerman (1983) and other sociologists who study science have claimed that a major distinction between greater and lesser scientists is their taste in problems. Greater scientists identify and study more significant problems.

No one way of coming up with ideas works for everyone. If you are having difficulty thinking of ideas for your own studies, try simply watching people, including yourself. You are bound to find puzzles that intrigue you. For example, as I write this paragraph, I am sitting on a train. The person in front of me not only has pushed back his seat as far as it will go, but also has broken the mechanism on the seat in order to push it back even farther, so that the seat back is practically in my face. Why are people sometimes so inconsiderate? Why would someone actually break something just to make himself a bit more comfortable at someone else's expense?

One of the best ways to generate ideas is to become broadly educated. Many of the best problem identifiers are people who bring ideas from one field to bear on research in another. Nobel Prize–winning cognitive psychologist Herbert Simon dramatically influenced psychology by introducing ideas from computer science, such as comparing and contrasting how humans and computers solve problems. Other people have contributed ideas from far-flung disciplines to various areas of psychology as well. Psychologist Margaret Floy Washburn brought her extensive knowledge of animal behavior to bear on questions of human sensation and movement (Furumoto & Scarborough, 1986; Hilgard, 1987). Psychologist Kenneth Clark imported ideas from sociology to help understand certain problems of African American children in schools (Clark, 1992; Klineberg, Clark, Clark, & Samelson, 1997; see also Pickren & Tomes, 2002; see Chapter 1). And psychologist George Miller (1990) used ideas from linguistics to reach his remarkable insights into memory.

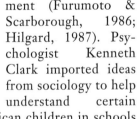

Margaret Floy Washburn was the first woman to receive her PhD and the first female president of the American Psychological Association.

DEFINING THE PROBLEM

Once we identify the existence of a problem, we have to define its nature. When defining a scientific problem, researchers use an **operational definition,** a means of specifying exactly how to test or measure the particular phenomenon being studied. Operational definitions allow researchers to communicate how they conducted an experiment and how they came to particular conclusions.

For example, Laurel Furumoto and Elizabeth Scarborough (1986) were interested in investigating the ways in which early female psychologists contributed to the field. They needed to find some way to narrow their focus to particular early female psychologists whose contributions they could investigate. Thus, they operationally defined the object of their study as the contributions to psychology made by "the 22 women who identified themselves as psychologists in the first edition of *American Men of Science*" (p. 35). The authors acknowledged that their investigation, by definition, did not include the work done by many other women who contributed significantly to the early development of psychology. Because these two researchers clarified their operational definition, other psychologists and historians who read about Furumoto and Scarborough's findings are able to interpret them in light of their own definition.

One reason operational definitions are so important is that psychology often makes use of the **hypothetical construct,** an abstract concept that is not itself directly measurable or observable but that gives rise to measurable phenomena and patterns of data. For example, psychologists infer the existence of the hypothetical construct of *conscientiousness* based on test scores and on particular kinds of behavior. Constructs are often the centerpieces of psychological theories.

Much of scientific research depends on how a problem is identified and defined. Most of us have much more experience in solving problems than we do in identifying and defining them (Bruer, 1993). To become good scientists, we need both kinds of experience. I am interested in the problem of why humans commit genocide, in which they attempt to destroy entire targeted populations. But where would I begin (see Chapter 14)? Different psychologists have different ideas. With a psycholinguist analysis of the concept of genocide (Moshman, 2001, in press)? With the study of hate (R. J. Sternberg, in press-b)? With the study of evil (Baumeister & Campbell, 1999; Berkowitz, 1999; A. G. Miller, 1999; Staub, 1999)? With the study of violence (Muehlenhard & Kimes, 1999)? Where one begins may have a large effect on where one ends. Hence, it is important to make sure that one properly identifies the problem one wishes to study.

FORMULATING HYPOTHESES

Once you have figured out the problem you wish to study, you may formulate hypotheses (Galotti, 2002; R. J. Sternberg & Grigorenko, in press). For example, British psychologist Michael Howe and his colleagues (Howe, 1999, 2001; Howe, Davidson, & Sloboda, 1999), building upon work by K. Anders Ericsson (1996, 2000, 2002) and others, hypothesized that the main difference between experts and novices in a field such as music or art is the amount of time they devote to *deliberate practice*—practice that focuses on a goal and is directed toward correcting errors. Reviewing the literature in a wide variety of fields, they found that, consistent with their expectations, deliberate practice seemed to be an excellent predictor of the level of expertise a person obtains in a given endeavor. Their results were surprising because many people had assumed that differences in levels of attained expertise were due largely to differences in people's inborn levels of talent. Although these results do not rule out the importance of innate differences, they suggest that

A study designed to test the hypothesis that the best predictor of expertise is the amount of time devoted to deliberate practice found that this was the case. Experts tend to spend more time practicing in a systematic way.

dedicated effort may play a larger role in expertise than previously had been believed. Often psychologists not only formulate hypotheses but also revise them. For example, some psychologists have come to believe that although deliberate practice is important, it interacts with abilities to produce expert behavior (e.g., R. J. Sternberg, 1996b, 1998a).

CONSTRUCTING A PROBLEM-SOLVING STRATEGY

After you have determined what problem you wish to solve and you have some hypotheses about the solution, you still need to figure out how to test your ideas (Nisbett, 1993). No single strategy is ideal for addressing every problem. Instead, the optimal strategy depends on both the problem and the investigator's personal taste in problem-solving methods.

Robert Cialdini (1993) became interested in how he and other people are suckered into buying things they do not really want. Cialdini decided on a strategy of *participant observation*, whereby the person studying a phenomenon participates in it. For a 3-year period, Cialdini answered newspaper ads for sales trainees in advertising, public-relations firms, and fund-raising organizations. While feigning to be in training for sales, he learned the techniques that organizations use for persuading people to buy products and services that people do not necessarily want. Had Cialdini not been willing to become a participant in sales training, it is unlikely that the organizations would have told him their secrets. Cialdini's distinctive strategy provided the basis for his comprehensive model of influence.

Studies also show that expert problem solvers (and better students) tend to devote more of their mental resources to *global* (big picture) planning than do novice problem solvers. Novices (and poorer students) tend to allocate more time to *local* (detail-oriented) strategy planning than do experts (Larkin, McDermott, Simon, & Simon, 1980; R. J. Sternberg, 1981a). Better students usually spend more time than poorer students deciding how to solve a problem and less time actually solving it (Bloom & Broder, 1950). By spending more time in advance deciding what to do, good students are less likely to fall prey to false starts, winding paths, and all kinds of other errors. By allocating more of their mental resources to planning on a large scale, they are able to save time and energy and to avoid frustration. Similarly, when you conduct scientific research, it makes good sense to anticipate potential problems before you start.

MONITORING AND EVALUATING PROBLEM SOLVING

You need to monitor your problem solving while you are in the process of solving a problem. In other words, you have to ask yourself whether you are moving toward a solution of the problem you set out to study. It is for this reason that scientists often conduct *pilot studies*, small-scale studies to determine whether the effects they expect to see actually can be produced. The investigators do not proceed to their full-scale investigation until they have some confidence that they are likely to get the results they expect. In studies of the effects of rewards on behavior, for example, psychologists might wish to do pilot studies with different kinds of potential rewards in order to find just which ones their participants actually believe to be rewarding.

When you are done with your problem solving, you need to evaluate your solution (Bereiter, 2002; Bryson, Bereiter, Scardamalia, & Joram, 1991; D. F. Halpern, 1995; Perkins, 1995a, 2002; Stanovich, 1994, 1996, 2002; Stanovich & West, 2002). Some of the evaluation may occur right away; the rest may occur a bit later, or even much later. As suggested, very few scientific questions—particularly questions about how people behave—are ever resolved once and for all. Rather, we reach an answer that seems right at a given time or that is the best or most nearly complete one we are able to find. Later we may realize that the answer was incomplete or even incorrect. To a large extent, success in scientific problem solving depends on the researcher's ability to profit from feedback, both self-generated and from others.

✓CONCEPT CHECK 2

1. If you solve a problem but it is not the one you should have solved, you have failed in the process of
   a. monitoring your problem solving.
   b. constructing a strategy for problem solving.

   c. formulating hypotheses.
   d. identifying the problem to be solved.
2. In good scientific research, guiding hypotheses are
   a. almost always found to be supported.
   b. almost never found to be supported.
   c. sometimes found to be supported and sometimes not.
   d. typically never even tested by the research.
3. In his research on influence, Cialdini used a strategy of
   a. anecdotal observation.
   b. participant observation.
   c. monitoring.
   d. problem identification.

THE GOALS OF SCIENTIFIC RESEARCH

What do scientists seek to accomplish in their work?

Thus far we have addressed the *what* and the *how* of scientific research. We still must discuss the *why*. Why do scientists do what they do? What are their goals? In addition to the broad goal of advancing scientific thought, the four main goals are description, explanation, prediction, and control. (See Table 2.2 for a summary.)

DESCRIPTION

In psychology, **description** means simply characterizing what and how people think, feel, or act in response to various situations. Before we can begin to explain or to predict behavior, we need to describe it. At first

---

TABLE 2.2
CONCEPT REVIEW

Four Primary Goals of Psychological Research. Psychologists seek to achieve one or more of the following goals in their research.

Goal	Questions Psychologists Ask When Trying to Reach This Goal
Description	What happens?
	When and where does it happen?
	How does it happen?
Explanation	Why does it happen?
Prediction	What will happen next?
Control	How can we influence this behavior or intervene in this situation?

description might seem trivial. Why do scientists need to describe behavior that people easily can see for themselves? Indeed, descriptive research often starts with people watching, and then wondering. Many of the most interesting ideas in psychology, such as Freud's, emanated from observing and describing behavior.

Various studies have shown certain sex differences, on average, in abilities (A. R. Halpern, 1986, 1989; D. F. Halpern, 1997). One such difference is that women show better spatial-location memory than men (Silverman & Eals, 1992) (see Figure 2.1). They may find it easier to remember where they saw something. Men, however, show better spatial-rotation ability than women (Silverman & Eals, 1992). They can more quickly and accurately state whether a given object is a rotated version of another object or is a mirror image of the first object. Thus, research can tell us at a descriptive level that both men and women show certain superiorities with respect to aspects of spatial ability. But why? To explain this phenomenon, we need to probe further.

EXPLANATION

Explanation addresses why people think, feel, or act as they do. If psychology were only descriptive, people would almost certainly become disillusioned with it. Ideally, theories in psychology should also be explanatory. Theories need to answer the *why* as well as the *what* and the *how* of psychological functioning that are revealed by descriptive studies.

Let us return to the question of spatial ability. Why might men be superior in one aspect and women in another? One explanation is an evolutionary one. Over the course of many generations, women may have developed superior spatial-location memory to aid them in gathering food. In times past (and in some places, present), gathering was their primary role in bringing food to the table. Men may have developed superior spatial-rotation ability to aid them in hunting. They needed to be able to estimate trajectories of moving objects. Although we cannot be certain these explanations are correct, they give a plausible account of how sex differences might have emerged (Buss, 1995; Silverman & Eals, 1992). They do not

FIGURE 2.1.

Spatial-rotation and spatial-location tasks. Women tend to perform better in spatial-location tasks. After memorizing the diagram at the top, they tend to be better at recalling what object appeared in the cell marked with an X (in this case, a banana). Men tend to be better at spatial-rotation tasks. They are better able to say what a given object would look like if rotated into various spatial orientations.

provide the only possible accounts, but they do make sense in terms of likely adaptations to the environment over many generations of human evolution. Bear in mind, however, that few explanations are definitive. As psychologists learn more and gather more data, their interpretations will be elaborated, modified, and perhaps replaced altogether by others that better fit the new information.

One of the most important explanatory studies in psychology was conducted by Rescorla and Wagner (1972; see Chapter 6). Their data suggested that learning in animals (and by implication in humans) could be explained by higher-order thinking processes that many scientists previously doubted even existed in laboratory animals.

PREDICTION

Psychologists often try to predict the outcomes of their research. **Prediction** is a declaration about the future based on observation, experience, or reasoning that can be very important in practice as well as in theory. For example, given the sex differences we have described, we could predict that men and women might prefer to play different video games. In one game, people shoot at fast attacking invaders from another planet. In another game, people need to remember where in an imaginary jungle they have seen various creatures. We might predict that, on average, men would do better on the first task, women on the second. We could give men and women both tasks and see whether, in fact, our prediction is supported by the data. Keep in mind, however, that recent evidence indicates that average sex differences in abilities may be decreasing over time (R. Feingold, 1988; A. R. Halpern, 1989; D. F. Halpern, 2000).

Predictive information can be a double-edged sword. It can help predict behavior but, if overvalued, it can lead to erroneous judgments. Sometimes it even can *affect* the outcomes it was originally supposed to only *predict*. Researchers tested this notion in one context by telling teachers that particular students in their classes were likely to be "late bloomers"—students whose performance was likely to start poorly and then improve (Rosenthal & Jacobson, 1968). Later on, the students who had been thus identified did indeed improve scholastically. The teachers had been deceived, however. In reality, the "late bloomers" had been selected at random. They were initially no different in measured abilities from any of the other students. Although the teachers could not recall that they had treated the "late bloomers" differently, the teachers' expectations clearly affected their students. The results suggest that a prediction can become a *self-fulfilling prophecy*. The very fact of predicting something about

someone can make that prediction come true. Although the Rosenthal–Jacobson study had some flaws (Elashoff & Snow, 1971; R. E. Snow, 1995), the phenomenon of the self-fulfilling prophecy seems fairly common (Tauber, 1997; Weinstein, 2002). We must be careful in making predictions, especially pessimistic ones, about people's behavior because the predictions may bring about that very behavior. Prediction, therefore, can end up not only anticipating but also exerting some control over future behavior.

CONTROL

In seeking **control** of behavior, psychologists always need to think in terms of helping people gain command of their own destinies rather than taking that power away from them. Many of us would like to be able to eliminate some of our bad habits or improve ourselves in other ways. Control of behavior is what enables us to change it. Many people seek **psychotherapy**, a remedial intervention that uses the principles of psychology to treat a mental or emotional disorder, in order to take charge of their lives.

People can control not only their behavior but also their minds. Such control is a major goal of efforts to improve intellectual abilities, which are not fixed but rather flexible and modifiable. Many educational programs are designed to help students develop their thinking skills (Bransford, Brophy, & Williams, 2000; Bransford, Brown, & Cocking, 1999; Bransford, Zech, Schwartz, Barron, & Vye, 2000; Costa, 2000; Detterman & Sternberg, 1993; Kozulin & Rand, 2000; Perkins, 2002; Ritchhart & Perkins, 2000; R. J. Sternberg & Grigorenko, in press; W. Williams et al., 1996). When these programs are successful, they help students to take better control of their intellectual functioning and to develop and use their abilities more effectively.

The goals of science, then, as they apply to psychological theory, research, and practice, help us describe, explain, predict, and control thoughts and actions. These achievements are not mutually exclusive, and psychologists usually combine them in their work.

✓ CONCEPT CHECK 3

1. You believe that you have a pretty good idea of how people will do in a course on the basis of a test you give before you begin teaching. Your main focus is on
   a. description.
   b. explanation.

c. prediction.

d. control.

2. At the conclusion of a study, you think you have a really good idea of why people behave the way they do in certain situations. Your main focus is on

a. description.

b. explanation.

c. prediction.

d. control.

3. You have devised a series of steps that have helped people lose weight successfully. Your main focus is on

a. description.

b. explanation.

c. prediction.

d. control.

RESEARCH METHODS IN PSYCHOLOGY

How would you expect psychologists to conduct research?

So far in this chapter we have alluded to various reasons and ways that psychologists study problems. Now let's explore the specific research methodologies they use. This section covers some of the ways psychologists study the problems that interest them: (1) naturalistic observation; (2) case studies; (3) tests, questionnaires, and surveys; and (4) experiments. These research methods are summarized in Table 2.3. In every form of research, empirical *data* are gathered by one means or another and analyzed.

NATURALISTIC OBSERVATION

Naturalistic observation, also known as *field study*, involves going into the community to observe and record the behavior of people engaged in the normal activities of their daily lives. Naturalistic observation is particularly useful when the phenomenon being studied is strongly affected by the context in which it occurs. It includes the participant observation done by Cialdini (1993), whose work on persuasion was described earlier in this chapter. Shirley Heath and her colleagues used naturalistic observation to study identity formation in inner-city youth (Heath & McLaughlin, 1993; Roach et al., 1999). In particular, Heath and her associates studied how organizations in which youngsters participate after school sometimes

Jane Goodall uses naturalistic observations to study the behavior of chimpanzes.

provide a sense of identity and purpose that the children are not able to find in class. Children who engaged in organized, socially constructive after-school activities showed better adjustment than children who did not.

Other research has shown that children of diverse cultures who may not do particularly well at school may nevertheless be gifted interpreters outside of school. They may have parents who do not speak English, and they effectively interpret what their parents say, in the parents' native language, to other people who speak only English (Valdes, 2002). Naturalistic observation thus revealed that children who lack academic skills may have highly developed and useful cultural skills that serve both them and their families well in the families' interactions in the everyday world. This work has provided rich insights about identity formation that would be hard to obtain from laboratory experiments.

Naturalistic observation has several potential advantages, including the usually wide applicability of the results. A potential disadvantage of this method is the uncontrolled complexity of what is observed (and hence the difficulty of isolating causes of behavior). Another is the possibility that the presence of an observer may influence the behavior being observed.

Sometimes it may not be possible directly to observe those you would like to observe. In this event, another method may be called for: the case study.

CASE STUDIES

In a **case study,** a psychologist conducts an intensive investigation of a person or group in order to draw general conclusions about behavior. Case studies are conducted in a variety of psychological pursuits. They are particularly useful when the phenomenon being studied is relatively rare, as in studies of highly creative people or of people with unusual psychological disorders. In **clinical** work, psychologists offer therapy

TABLE 2.3
CONCEPT REVIEW

Research Methods. To achieve their goals, psychologists use various methods of investigation.

Method	Description	Form of Data Obtained	Advantages	Disadvantages
Naturalistic observations	Observations of real-life situations	Qualitative	1. Wide applicability of results 2. Understanding of behavior in natural contexts	1. Loss of experimental control 2. Presence of observer may influence observed behavior
Case studies	Intensive studies of single individuals, which draw general conclusions about behavior	Qualitative	Highly detailed information, including the historical context	1. Small sample size compromises ability to generalize information 2. Reliability can be limited
Tests, questionnaires, and surveys	Samples of behavior, beliefs, or abilities obtained at a particular time and place	Quantitative or qualitative ("soft data," descriptive, practical)	1. Ease of administration 2. Ease of scoring and statistical analysis	1. May not be able to generalize results 2. Discrepancies between real-life behavior and test behavior
Experiments	Studies of cause-and-effect relationships through the manipulation of variables	Quantitative ("hard data," statistical, verifiable by replication)	1. Precise control of independent variables 2. Usually, large numbers of participants allow results to be generalized	1. Usually, less intensive study of individuals 2. Ability to generalize to real-world behavior is sometimes limited

Case studies, such as those developed in psychotherapy, are intensive investigations of a single individual or set of individuals. Though they provide highly detailed information, their findings are not readily generalizable.

© Michael Newman/PhotoEdit

directly to clients and case studies are essential for understanding problems that people face both individually and collectively.

One of the better-known writings in the field of marriage and family therapy (see Chapter 17 on psychotherapy) is Robert Weiss's (1975) analysis of marital separation. Called a *monograph* because it is written about one topic in depth, the report drew almost exclusively on case-study observations. Weiss's style was to find commonalities that suggested why marriages fail. A recurrent theme in some of the accounts was that the marriage was wrong from the start. Often case studies are used in conjunction with other kinds of evidence to establish a point. For example, David Lykken (1998) drew upon varied evidence to make the point that the results of polygraph (lie-detector) tests are highly questionable and can have disastrous results for both individuals and society. One of the case studies Lykken presented involved Mack Coker, who worked for a company that was experiencing thefts. First Coker lost his job because he failed a polygraph test even though no other evidence was offered to support the suspicion that he was guilty of the thefts. He then became subject to vicious rumors in his community. Coker eventually got his job back, but many others are not so lucky.

Case-study methodology provides highly detailed information, including information about the historical contexts of behavior. It provides a rich, three-dimensional portrait of the person and the circumstances for his or her behavior. A disadvantage of the method is that the sample size typically is small, which makes it hard to generalize the results. Moreover, the reliability of the information can be limited, given that it is obtained in very particular settings.

Other variables, such as abilities and attitudes, evolve over many years, and may be studied through tests, questionnaires, and surveys.

TESTS, QUESTIONNAIRES, AND SURVEYS

Early in the 20th century, French psychologist Alfred Binet was commissioned to develop a test to distinguish children who were genuinely mentally deficient from those who were capable of scholastic achievement but who had behavior problems that interfered. A **test** is a procedure used to measure an attribute at a particular time and in a particular place. Examiners almost invariably key test responses as either right or wrong, or at least as better (more accurate, more appropriate, more creative, and so on) or worse. Tests are used in many kinds of psychological studies. Scores vary not only across people but also across time for a given person. Test results may vary because of an actual change in what is being measured or because of various factors that may affect performance at the time of testing, such as ill health or ambient noise. Thus, tests can only approximate a person's true abilities, personality, or other traits.

Interpreting test scores may seem to be a cut-and-dried affair, but it rarely is. Consider an example. Individuals who have reading disabilities can function intellectually at a normal level but cannot read rapidly or fluently (Gayan & Olson, 2001; R. J. Sternberg & Spear-Swerling, 1999; Torgesen, 2002). These individuals often are given extra time on certain tests in order to perform at their intellectual level. In the past, the scores of students who took college-admissions tests with additional time were flagged so that college-admissions officers would know that the test was taken under nonstandard conditions. In 2002 the publishers of the SAT and the ACT announced that such score flagging would be discontinued because they viewed it as prejudicial to the students whose scores were sin-

gled out. Does the test score mean the same when it is achieved with extra time? Does the score when the test is taken in Braille mean the same as a non-Braille test? What if the test is taken by someone whose native language is not English or who had limited educational opportunities? Clearly, interpreting test scores is far from straightforward.

Psychologists also use two other methods in their research. In a **survey,** the researcher seeks people's responses to questions provided in a **questionnaire.** Questionnaires are frequently used to inquire into people's health practices, such as their eating, drinking, or smoking habits. Surveys and questionnaires are particularly useful when one wishes to obtain a large amount of information in a relatively short time.

Unlike tests, surveys and questionnaires do not have right or wrong answers. They typically measure beliefs and opinions rather than abilities or knowledge. You might want to determine college students' attitudes toward campus regulations about alcohol, to gather their opinions about the usefulness of survey data, or to determine whether they mind responding to questionnaires. Questionnaire and survey data are notorious for lending themselves to multiple interpretations. In politics, the identical survey data may be interpreted in entirely different ways by opposing political parties. For example, survey data indicated that President George W. Bush's popularity dipped in 2002, after a series of corporate accounting scandals, relative to 2001, after his response to the terrorist attacks of September 11, 2001. But what does the decline in popularity mean? Some Republicans interpreted the data as showing that Bush had the courage to stay his course despite some people's objection to what he was doing. At the same time, many Democrats interpreted the data as showing that Republican candidates would be easier to defeat in the 2002 congressional elections. Thus, interpreting survey data is a complex process. Nonetheless, questionnaires and surveys are handy tools for quantifying beliefs and opinions.

An advantage of tests, questionnaires, and surveys is that they tend to be easily administered, scored, and analyzed. A disadvantage is that unless the sample is fairly large and representative, it may be difficult to generalize the results to people who were not directly tested or surveyed. Sometimes, moreover, there are discrepancies between what people say or do in tests, questionnaires, and surveys, and how they actually behave.

EXPERIMENTS

An **experiment** is, in the scientific sense, an investigation into cause–effect relationships through the control and manipulation of variables. **Experimental**

methods let researchers investigate cause–effect relationships by controlling or carefully manipulating particular variables to note their effects on other variables. Experiments are not always practical because people sometimes behave differently in research settings. But experiments can be done in real-world settings as well as in laboratories.

Consider an example. Daniel Simons and Daniel Levin (1998; see also Mitroff, Simons, & Franconeri, 2002; Simons, Chabris, Schnur, & Levin, 2002) studied people's ability to detect changes during a real-world interaction. An experimenter approached 15 pedestrians on the Cornell University campus and asked for directions to a nearby building. After the experimenter and the pedestrian had been talking for 10 to 15 seconds, two other experimenters carrying a door rudely passed between them. As the door passed by, the first experimenter grabbed the back of the door, and the experimenter who had been carrying the part of the door that had been grabbed stayed behind and continued the inquiry. The two experimenters thus switched roles. The two experimenters wore different clothing, differed in height by about 5 centimeters (about 2 inches), and had clearly distinguishable voices. After the pedestrian finished giving directions, the experimenter asked the pedestrian whether he or she had noticed anything unusual when the door had passed. Only 7 of the 15 pedestrians noticed the switch. People were most likely to notice if they were from the same social group as the experimenters. The experimental results show that people can exhibit "blindness" even to events that happen right in front of their eyes.

Variables are characteristics of a situation, person, or phenomenon that may fluctuate across situations, persons, or phenomena. Experiments are particularly useful when it is possible to manipulate and thus gain control of the variables whose effects one wishes to study. Experimenters carefully manipulate one or more variables to note the effects on other variables. An experiment is a way to test ideas about human behavior (or anything else) by constructing a set of operations to test these ideas. The construction of this set of operations is called *operationalization*.

Suppose you conduct an experiment in which students are given challenging mathematics problems that require serious effort to solve. You want to see the effect of encouragement on the students' performance. So you tell some of the students that they can expect to do very well, whereas you give other students no encouragement at all. What are the elements of this experiment?

There are basically two kinds of variables in any given experiment. **Independent variables** are aspects of an investigation that are individually *manipulated*, or carefully regulated, by the experimenter while other aspects of the investigation are held constant (i.e., not subject to variation). **Dependent variables** are outcome responses whose values depend on how one or more independent variables influence or affect the participants in the experiment. When you tell some student research participants that they will do very well on a task, but you do not say anything to other participants, the independent variable is the amount of information that the students are given about their expected task performance. The dependent variable is how well both groups actually perform the task—that is, their score on the math test.

Experiments often involve two different types of *conditions*, or aspects of an experimental design. The conditions typically represent different manipulations of the independent variable. In the **experimental condition** (or *treatment condition*), participants are exposed to a carefully prescribed set of circumstances. For example, some participants are told that they will do very well on a task. In the **control condition**, the participants receive an alternative treatment. In this experiment, other participants are not told anything about how they will do on the task. The goal of the experiment is to see whether the participants who are told that they will succeed actually perform better than those who are told nothing.

In fact, this particular manipulation can make a large difference in test scores. Claude Steele and Joshua Aronson (1995) found that African American children performed better on ability tests when they were told that the particular test showed comparable performance for African American and Caucasian groups. Similarly, Wendy Walsh (1997) found that when women were told that there would be no gender differences on a difficult mathematical problem-solving test, the women outperformed the men. But when the women were told that there typically were gender differences on the test, the men outperformed the women.

Two kinds of groups of participants are usually used: one for the experimental condition and the other for the control condition. The *control group* may receive some alternative (and usually irrelevant) treatment or no treatment at all. The results for the control group are included as a standard of comparison against which to judge the results of the *experimental group*(s) and also to control for irrelevant, confounding variables. Sometimes there is more than one control group. Without a control group, it is usually hard to draw any conclusions at all. For example, if you told all of the participants that they would do well on a task they were about to be given, then you would have no way of isolating, and hence of knowing, the effect of telling them what kind of performance to expect. Ideally, the inclusion of the control group or groups leads to just one interpretation of the results. It can be difficult to reach this ideal in practice, however. Without any control groups at all, causal inference is impossible.

Controlled experiments have several advantages. For one thing, they allow precise control of independent variables. For another, if they involve large numbers of participants, they may yield generalizable results. The method also has disadvantages. First, individuals usually are not studied intensively, as they might be in case studies. Second, the ability to generalize to real-world behavior is limited if what people do in the lab or other experimental setting does not match what they do in their everyday lives.

EVALUATING AND INTERPRETING RESEARCH DATA

REPRESENTATIVE SAMPLES

A problem in all research, regardless of design, is that we can almost never be certain that our inferences are correct. The reason is that we can never be absolutely sure that a difference between group results is not caused by chance fluctuations in the data. The only way to be sure of our results is to test the entire population of people in whom we are interested. Unfortunately, that is rarely practical or even possible. So we may settle for testing what we believe to be a **representative sample,** a subset of the population carefully chosen to represent the proportionate diversity of the population as a whole. We may obtain representation by having a wholly **random sample,** which is a sample in which every person in a population has an equal chance of being selected.

As you might imagine, some portions of the total population are more readily accessible to researchers than others, so they may be overrepresented in research. In addition, there may be other reasons some people are under- or overrepresented in research samples. Women and persons of color are often understudied, whereas men, Caucasians, and college students are often overrepresented in research.

It is common for cross-cultural researchers to use *samples of convenience* (also called "bunch" or "grab" samples). These samples are people, such as college sophomores, who are immediately available but who are not necessarily most relevant for what the researchers want to test (Lonner & Berry, 1986). This strategy is not restricted to research across cultures. Countless millions of students in U.S. colleges and universities have been included in samples over the years. It is very common, for example, for researchers to solicit the participation of several hundred students from an introductory psychology class. Are such groups representative of any population of interest? If so, what population do they represent?

STATISTICAL ANALYSIS

When we test participants, we are really interested in the results not only for them but also for the population as a whole (e.g., all humans, all mothers, all college students). Because the whole population is not tested, we use **sample statistics,** numbers that characterize the sample we have tested with regard to the attributes under investigation. Sample statistics are intended to serve as estimates of **population parameters,** numbers that characterize everyone we conceivably might test who fit our desired description. Actual population parameters are unknowable unless we have the whole population to test, and we almost never do. It is for this reason that we need to use sam-

Is this a random sample? A good deal of psychological research has been done on college students, a sample of convenience; consequently, they are overrepresented in research.

ples to estimate the characteristics of the population. (See the Statistical Appendix for more details on statistical issues and procedures.)

Because sample statistics are only estimates of population parameters, they vary to some degree from one sample to another. In general, researchers seek to include as large a proportion of the population as possible in the research sample. Although constraints of time and other resources limit the sizes of the samples researchers can actually test, proportionately larger samples help to average out random errors.

Statistical analysis helps researchers minimize errors in two ways. First, it helps ensure the accurate and consistent *description* of a sample from a population (for example, the average annual salaries reported by sampled 30-year-olds). Second, it provides a consistent basis for the *inference* of characteristics of an entire population based on the characteristics of only a sample. Suppose that the average annual salaries of college graduates in the sample were much higher than the annual salaries of those who did not graduate. We might infer that, for the whole population, having graduated from college is associated with the potential to earn higher annual salaries. We cannot be sure that going to college caused the increased earnings potential. Possibly, people who go to college have higher earnings potential for some other reason than college per se, such as coming from a wealthier family background. Clearly, it is easier to be certain of the accuracy of the descriptions than it is to be certain of the accuracy of the inferences.

To increase the accuracy of our inferences, we use specially devised *inferential statistics*, which allow us to draw reasoned conclusions based on the implications of the descriptive data. Inferential statistics can help us decide whether the difference between a treatment group and a control group (or other group) is likely to be true of the population as a whole, or whether the difference is likely to be caused by chance fluctuations in the data. We use the concept of **statistical significance**, a probability level agreed on by convention that helps us decide how likely it is that a result would be obtained if only chance factors were in operation. To determine whether a result is statistically significant, we measure the probability that an obtained result would have been obtained if only chance were at work. If that probability reaches a particular preset point (usually 5% down to 1%), we consider the result statistically significant.

For example, we could determine whether clients in psychotherapy for a specified period of time improved more during this period than did individuals with comparable problems who did not receive psychotherapy. If the analysis of our experiment revealed that there was only a 5% chance that the results we found would have been obtained if only chance had

been at work, then we could say that our results were statistically significant at the "0.05 level." If our results showed a 0.01 level of significance, there would be only a 1% chance that our findings would have been obtained if only chance factors were at work. If clients in psychotherapy showed greater improvement than those without therapy, at a rate that was statistically significant at the 0.01 level, it means there was only a 1% chance that such unusual results would have been obtained if only chance factors were affecting the outcomes of the psychotherapy. The smaller the probability level, the greater is the level of statistical significance for the result. In fact, research overwhelmingly suggests that clients view themselves as having improved through psychotherapy (Seligman, 1995).

There are two important points to consider. First, although we can set our probability level as low as we want, we can never be absolutely certain that a difference is not due to the operation of chance factors. We can be 99% confident (with a 0.01 level of significance) but never 100% confident (with a 0.00 level). Second, we can never prove beyond doubt the **null hypothesis** of *no* difference or relationship between the performance of two or more groups. That is, we cannot prove that a particular variable has no effect or that there is no difference between two different groups of participants or among two or more different conditions. Suppose a psychologist compares two kinds of psychotherapy and finds that the difference in average effects is not significant. The psychologist cannot therefore conclude with certainty that the two forms of psychotherapy are equally effective. Our inability to prove the null hypothesis applies whether we use the kind of controlled experimental design we have discussed here or the quasi-experimental design to which we now turn. It always is possible that, with a larger sample or with more careful measurements, a difference could emerge.

✓CONCEPT CHECK 4

1. In an experimental study, one group is taught by a new and innovative method and the other group is taught by a standard method. The second group serves as a(n) _____ group in this study, helping to determine whether the innovative method results in superior learning outcomes.
   a. experimental
   b. normalization
   c. control
   d. treatment

2. A psychologist moves to Alaska for a year to record her observations of Yup'ik Eskimo cultural customs and compare these customs with those of majority-group Alaskans in major cities. She is most likely using the method of
   a. a controlled experiment.
   b. a case study.
   c. correlational résearch.
   d. naturalistic observation.
3. A psychologist varies the amount of light in different rooms in which a social interaction takes place. The amount of light serves as a(n)
   a. independent variable.
   b. dependent variable.
   c. fixed variable.
   d. interaction variable.

CAUSAL INFERENCE IN PSYCHOLOGICAL RESEARCH

How do you think scientists draw causal inferences from their research?

As we have seen, both the problem studied and the personal stylistic preferences of the investigator influence the researcher's choice of method. One remaining issue also influences this choice. A major goal of psychological research is to draw **causal inferences,** which are conjectures about cause–effect relationships regarding behavior that seek to explain what causes a person to behave in a certain way. We might ask whether a particular independent variable (e.g., whether people are told that they will do well on a task) is responsible for

Advertisers want us to make the causal inference that their product has caused an athlete-spokesperson's success. But correlation is not causation.

certain variation in a given dependent variable (e.g., the number of items answered correctly on a mathematical problem-solving task). What circumstances enable investigators to draw conclusions about causality? In other words, what do we need in a research study to be able to conclude that "so-and-so" causes "such-and-such"?

As you may suspect, when it comes to human behavior it is not always possible to detect a clear causal relationship between independent and dependent variables. One reason is that our ability to draw causal inferences depends not only on the question we ask in our research but also on how the research is designed. **Design** refers to how a given set of variables are chosen and interrelated as well as how participants are assigned to conditions.

In speaking of controlled experiments, we used the strictest definition for *experiment*. Now we can broaden the definition to apply to investigations not as highly controlled by the experimenter. Loosely speaking, an experiment studies the effect of some variables on other variables. Now we explore three ways in which to design experimental research, including the strict, narrow definition used here and two other types of experimental design. Three major kinds of designs in psychological research are controlled experimental, quasi-experimental, and correlational. The kinds and degrees of causal inference that can be drawn from each differ. (See Table 2.4 for a summary of the similarities and differences among these designs.)

CONTROLLED AND QUASI-EXPERIMENTAL DESIGNS

In a true **controlled experimental design,** the experimenter carefully manipulates or controls one or more independent variables in order to see the effect on the dependent variable or variables. To be sure the treatment is producing the effect (and not some other variables or even random variation), the experimenter often includes one or more control groups that do not receive the experimental treatment. Participants must be randomly assigned to the experimental and the control groups. *Random assignment* is important because it ensures that later differences between the results for each group are not due to prior differences in the participants themselves.

Suppose that we wish to study the effect on students' learning of two methods of teaching introductory psychology. Ideally, we would establish two completely comparable colleges, with virtually identical instructors, to which we might randomly assign two groups of students. We then would offer the two groups of students different courses taught by different methods. This

TABLE 2.4
CONCEPT REVIEW

Experimental Designs. Psychologists draw different conclusions from their research, depending on the type of research design they use to study a given phenomenon.

Type of Design	Definition	Advantages	Disadvantages
Controlled experimental	Experimenter manipulates one or more independent variables and observes the effects on the dependent variable or variables; participants are randomly assigned to control or treatment conditions.	Permits causal inference regarding the treatment variable or variables.	Might not apply to settings outside the laboratory; a sample may not truly represent the entire population of interest. May involve ethical concerns.
Quasi-experimental	Similar to experimental design, but participants are not randomly assigned; in some cases, there is no control group.	May be more convenient in some situations; may be permissible where ethical considerations prohibit random assignment of participants; may be conducted in a naturalistic setting, yielding more richly textured data. In the case of correlational data, the entire population (e.g., all voters) may sometimes be available for study.	Does not permit causal inferences regarding the treatment variable or variables. Also, sample data may not apply to the entire population.
Correlational	Researchers just observe the degree of association between two or more attributes that occur naturally. Researchers do not manipulate variables or randomly assign participants to groups.		

controlled experiment could never actually be done, however. Instead, we are likely to use a more convenient design. Students who already are enrolled in one college might serve as experimental participants (they receive the independent variable, the new curriculum). Students enrolled in a similar college might serve as control participants (they do not receive the new curriculum). In this case, participants are not randomly assigned to groups, so the design is not a true controlled experimental design. Although a **quasi-experimental design** has many features of a controlled experimental design, it does not ensure the random assignment of participants to the treatment and the control groups. The study still uses the experimental method. Variables are manipulated, and cause–effect relationships are still sought. Nonetheless, the quasi-experimental design is less precise and less experimenter-controlled than is a true experimental design. For this reason, we cannot draw a definite causal conclusion from a quasi-experimental design.

In the curriculum study, we cannot draw causal conclusions. Instead of the difference in results be-

tween the two college groups being caused by the experimental curriculum, it is possible that some of the difference is caused by preexisting differences in the kinds of students who attend the two colleges or in other aspects of the two environments. There are statistical methods for trying to control for differences between groups after the fact. However, we can never be certain that we are controlling for all relevant differences, and so nonrandom assignment of participants to groups precludes firm causal inferences.

Another form of quasi-experimental design uses a group that receives an experimental treatment but no control group. A researcher might have students take a preliminary test (*pretest*) on their knowledge of introductory psychology. At the end of the course, the students take a concluding test (*posttest*) similar in content to the pretest. The purpose of the experiment is to measure student achievement and curriculum effectiveness.

This pretest–posttest quasi-experimental design is commonly used in research on curricula. Its use is surprising because no one can conclude that the curriculum caused any of the gains that might be observed. Why not? Perhaps students matured from pretest to posttest, independently of the curriculum, and thus scored higher on the posttest. They also might have learned something about psychology outside of class that helped them improve. Perhaps even the very experience of taking the pretest enabled them to do better the second time around. The test information had become familiar, and the students therefore knew what to expect. A parallel control group that received the pretest and the posttest without the curriculum (or better, with a curriculum on some other topic) would counter these alternative explanations. Without the use of a control group, however, no clear conclusions can be drawn.

Quasi-experimental designs are less scientifically desirable than controlled experimental designs, but they are often unavoidable. In naturalistic observational settings that cannot be controlled by experimenters, we sometimes have to take what we are given or else take nothing at all. We gain the advantage of the naturalistic setting but lose control.

Sometimes the limitations on research are ethical constraints. Suppose we wish to study the effects of long-term alcohol addiction on psychological health. Then we are ethically bound to accept in the alcoholic group those who already have chosen to drink excessively and in the control group those who already have chosen not to do so. We cannot randomly assign people to one group or the other and then insist that those assigned to the drinking group become chronic alcoholics! Thus, quasi-experimental designs are used when controlled experimental designs simply are not feasible or ethically appropriate. But sometimes even quasi-experimental designs are not feasible, in which case we may use correlational designs.

CORRELATIONAL DESIGNS

Correlational methods assess the degree of relationship between two or more variables or attributes and are therefore often used instead of experimental methods. Correlational methods generally are not useful for establishing causal direction. In a pure **correlational design,** researchers merely observe the degree of association between two (or more) *attributes,* which are characteristics of the participants, of the setting, or of the situation. The attributes typically already occur naturally in the group or groups under study. In correlational designs, researchers do not directly manipulate the variables themselves. Also, they do not randomly assign participants to groups. Instead, researchers usually observe participants in naturally preexisting groups, such as particular students in two or more classrooms, or particular employees in two or more work settings. Like quasi-experimental designs,

a correlational study is less scientifically desirable than a strict controlled experimental investigation, but frequently it is all we have. As is the case with quasi-experimental designs, correlational designs generally do not permit us to infer causation.

Consider the finding that boys are more likely to be hyperactive than girls (Shaywitz et al., 1990; Willcutt & Pennington, 2000). What does this correlation mean? At first glance, it suggests that being male leads one to become hyperactive. But is it being male per se that causes the relationship? Might parents treat boys differently from girls, or might male friends interact differently? The correlation itself does not tell us what actually *causes* the relationship.

When two attributes show some degree of statistical relationship to one another, they are *correlated.* **Correlation** is a degree of statistical relationship between two attributes, which usually is expressed as a number on a scale that ranges from −1 to 0 to 1. A correlation of −1 indicates a perfect **negative (inverse) correlation,** in which increases in the value of one attribute are associated with decreases in the value of another attribute, such as the number of equal slices of a pizza eaten in relation to the number of slices that remain. A correlation equal to 0 indicates no relationship at all. For instance, we would expect a 0 correlation between the frequency of eating pizza for dinner and undergraduate grade-point average. A correlation of 1 indicates a perfect **positive correlation,** in which increases (or decreases) in the value of one attribute are associated with increases (or decreases) in the value of another attribute. An example of a correlation of 1 is the number of equal pepperoni slices consumed in relation to the amount of pepperoni pizza you eat. Numbers between 0 and 1 indicate some intermediate degree of positive correlation (e.g., 0.7, 0.23, 0.01); numbers between 0 and −1 indicate some intermediate degree of negative correlation (e.g., −0.03, −0.2, −0.75). The closer a correlation is to being perfect (either 1 or −1), the stronger the relationship between the two items. A correlation close to 0 indicates a weak relationship. A correlation of −0.75, for example, indicates a stronger relationship between two variables than does a correlation of 0.25. Perfect correlations of 1 and −1 are extremely rare. Usually, if two variables are correlated, it is in some intermediate degree, such as the correlation between number of years of education and future income. Figure 2.2 shows how a positive correlation is represented in graphic form.

It is important to note that for each kind of correlation, the direction of causality, if any, is not known. We might give people a test of depression and a test of self-esteem to determine whether the traits are related. Both self-esteem and depression are preexisting variables over which experimenters have no control.

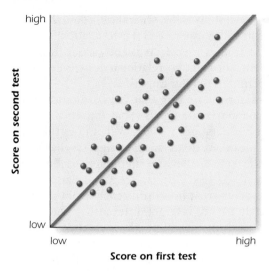

FIGURE 2.2

Graphic Representation of a Correlation. This graph shows a positive correlation between a pair of variables.

Suppose that we find a *correlation* between self-esteem and depression. We might expect it to be negative (inverse) in some degree, and it is. Those who have high self-esteem tend to be less depressed, and those with low self-esteem are more depressed. This correlation might mean that low self-esteem causes depression. Or it might mean that depression causes low self-esteem. Or it might even mean that both depression and low self-esteem depend on some third overarching variable, which we have not yet identified (e.g., rejection in childhood).

To conclude, then, correlational designs are useful to see whether relationships exist, but they cannot be used to specify exactly how a relationship works or what might cause it. The fact that the number of home electrical appliances is an excellent predictor of the use of contraceptives in Taiwanese households (Li, 1975; Stanovich, 1996) almost certainly does not imply a direct causal link between having electrical appliances and using contraception!

✓ CONCEPT CHECK 5

1. In a study of people's reactions to advertisements, research participants are assigned to groups randomly. Random assignment is part of the _____ the study.
   a. results of
   b. hypothesis for
   c. theory underlying
   d. design of

2. A psychologist finds that children in Mrs. Jones's class do better on a particular test than children in Mrs. Smith's class. He concludes that Mrs. Jones is a better teacher than Mrs. Smith. His causal inference is _____ because the design involved here is _____.
   a. right, experimental.
   b. right, quasi-experimental.
   c. wrong, quasi-experimental.
   d. wrong, correlational.

3. Two variables have a correlation of −1. Knowing the value of one variable, one can
   a. predict the value of the other variable with certainty.
   b. not predict the value of the other variable at all.
   c. predict the value of the other variable with some but not complete certainty.
   d. not know the extent to which one can predict the value of the other variable.

CRITICAL THINKING IN PSYCHOLOGICAL RESEARCH

How do you think critical thinking is relevant to psychological research?

THE NATURE OF CRITICAL THINKING

Critical thinking is the conscious direction of mental processes toward representing and processing information, usually in order to find thoughtful solutions to problems, make judgments or decisions, or reason. Critical thinking is essential in psychology.

Critical thinking involves both dispositions and abilities (Ennis, 1987). *Dispositions* are how you decide to approach a problem or decision. *Abilities* are how well you approach the problem or decision. Examples of dispositions are seeking reasons for what you believe, trying to be well informed in making decisions, looking for alternative options in making decisions, being open-minded, and being sensitive to the feelings, knowledge, and viewpoints of others. Abilities are skills for solving problems. Relevant abilities include focusing on the question at hand, analyzing arguments, deciding whether a conclusion follows from the data, asking questions relevant to the problem or decision upon which you are focused, and making generalizations from past experience.

Consider an example. You find yourself thinking negatively about a group of people. You start to wonder whether your thoughts reflect critical thinking or express a prejudice. How might you decide? With respect to dispositions, you can start by asking yourself whether you have good reasons for feeling the way you do. You might also seek information about the group. With respect to abilities, you might analyze the arguments for and against your beliefs and then decide whether the conclusions you have reached follow from the data. Critical thinking can help us overcome prejudices by making us aware of the flaws in our thinking.

When people draw the wrong conclusions from psychological (or any other kind of) research, it often is because of a failure in critical thinking. Suppose that Dr. Schlotz is convinced that speaking to plants in a soothing tone of voice helps them grow. He has 20 plants. At the beginning of a 30-day period, he carefully measures the height of each plant. Then, each day for 30 days, he speaks to them soothingly. At the end of 30 days, he compares their heights to their heights at the beginning of the 30 days. He finds that all of them have grown at least somewhat and that the difference in height is statistically significant. He concludes that talking to the plants really did help them grow.

Schlotz has shown poor critical thinking. He did not look for alternative explanations before deciding that the plants grew because he talked to them. Other factors might have caused them to grow, such as watering them, exposing them to sunlight, or just leaving them to follow their normal course of growth. If he had analyzed his argument carefully, he would have realized that his conclusion did not follow from his data. To support his conclusion, he would have needed a control group of plants. Plants would be randomly assigned to groups, and all would be treated exactly the same except that one group of plants would be talked to soothingly and the other would not. Schlotz might well have obtained a different result had he thought more critically about his experiment.

FALLACIES THAT PREVENT CRITICAL THINKING

When people do not think critically, they often fall into traps by committing one or more of the following informal logical fallacies.

- *Irrelevant conclusion.* We commit this fallacy when our conclusion is irrelevant to the line of reasoning that led to it. For example, Tom reads an experiment by Dr. Bailey. Tom is very upset that Dr. Bailey withheld food from rats so that they would run mazes in order to seek a food reward. Asked about the experiment, Tom criticizes its results as invalid because he "would never trust the results of someone who starves animals."

- *Composition.* We commit this fallacy when we reason that what is true of parts of a whole is necessarily true of the whole itself. In fact, elements (such as members of a team) may interact in ways (such as poor teamwork) that render untrue for the whole what is true for each part. For example, Jeannette reads an experiment by a team of five researchers led by Dr. Hawthorne, whom Jeannette greatly respects. Later Jeannette is asked what she thinks of the particular team of researchers that produced the article. Jeannette comments that "it is a great team," figuring that any team with Hawthorne on it must be great.

- *Personalization.* If you see yourself as the cause of some event for which you were not primarily responsible, you have committed the fallacy of personalization. Taking personally a statement that is not directed toward you is also inappropriate. For example, Mrs. Dittman criticizes a particular statistic as yielding questionable results. Mrs. Fleming has used that statistic in her research. She decides that Dittman is criticizing her personally and attacks Dittman as ignorant and incompetent.

- *False cause.* The fallacy of false cause is committed when someone concludes from the fact that two events happened in rapid succession, or have tended to happen together, that the first event caused the second. For example, one day Jack wears his fraternity T-shirt and the results of his experiment are positive. A couple of weeks later Jack is again wearing his T-shirt and his results again work out. Jack decides that it is probably a good idea to wear his fraternity T-shirt on days when he will find out whether his results have worked out.

- *Ad hominem argument.* This kind of argument is directed "to the man" rather than the position of the person. One attempts to attack an individual personally in order to undermine the person's position. For example, Mr. Faver has been asked to comment on the research of Mr. Dunn. Faver has never liked Dunn and sees his chance to get back at what he perceives as injustices Dunn has committed toward him. Faver remarks that Dunn received his degree at a university that is not very well known and therefore people really should not trust Dunn's results.

When people fail to apply critical thinking to problems—scientific or otherwise—they are likely to fall into traps that jeopardize the quality of their thinking. I have argued that even smart people can do stupid things (R. J. Sternberg, 2002). There are four traps into which smart people frequently fall. The first, *egocentrism*, occurs when an individual starts to view the world as centered around him or her. The person thinks that the important point is satisfying his or her ego rather

Critical thinking helps keep us alert to the informal fallacies to which we are all prone. For example, these two candidates seem to be blaming each other, a classic ad hominem argument in which one tries to undermine the other's position simply by saying that he or she is wrong, rather than offering evidence.

✓CONCEPT CHECK 6

1. Critical thinking is _____ appropriate in addressing psychological problems.
   a. never
   b. rarely
   c. often
   d. always
2. Daryl believes that because each member of the Blue Fins swimming team is outstanding, the team is outstanding as well. Daryl is best described as committing the fallacy of
   a. composition.
   b. false cause.
   c. personalization.
   d. irrelevant conclusion.
3. A disposition is best described as a(n) _____ problem solving.
   a. attitude toward
   b. ability for
   c. disliking for
   d. synonym of

than doing what is best. The second trap is *omniscience*. The person starts to think he or she "knows it all." The third trap is *omnipotence*, or feeling that one is all-powerful. And the fourth trap is *invulnerability*, or believing that no matter what one does, probably no one will be able to find out; or even if someone finds out, it will not matter because one has disguised one's tracks. Business executives can fall into these traps. High-level executives of major corporations severely mismanaged their companies in the late 1990s, often taking money for themselves that rightfully belonged to shareholders. This mismanagement set the stage for the sharp decline in the stock market in 2002.

These traps can also occur in science. For many years, Soviet scientists believed in *Lysenkoism*, the notion that acquired traits (such as becoming overweight by eating too much) could be inherited. In other words, if you eat too much and become obese, you may pass on your acquired obesity to your children. In fact, acquired traits cannot be inherited. A whole scientific edifice was built in the former Soviet Union around this myth. Instead of thinking critically, followers of this theory fell into traps in their thinking, perhaps believing that neither Lysenko nor they could do wrong. Scientists need to pay careful attention to critical thinking in their work to make sure they do not fall into the same traps anyone else can fall into in everyday life. The important point is to be on guard for these fallacies and to catch ourselves when we make them. In this way, we improve both our thinking and the conclusions we draw from it.

One more important issue remains before we leave this introductory discussion of psychological research methods and practices: researcher ethics.

RESEARCH ETHICS

What ethical issues confront psychologists?

A number of ethical issues arise in psychological research (as well as in medical and other research). Some of the main ones involve deception, pain, confidentiality, and research on animals.

DECEPTION, INFORMED CONSENT, AND DEBRIEFING

Sometimes, in order for research to work, participants must be kept unaware of the purpose of the research until it is completed. The deception involved in the Rosenthal–Jacobson study discussed earlier probably would be considered benign. In some cases, however, psychologists have used extreme forms of deception. Stanley Milgram (1974) led participants to believe that they were delivering painful electric shocks to another person, when in fact they were not. At the time Milgram carried out his studies, researchers were generally not required to obtain advance approval of their plans before conducting a psychological investigation. Another ethical issue arises when researchers pay participants to indulge in a vice, as when researchers pay alcoholics to drink in order to study their drinking behavior (Jacob, Krahn, & Leonard, 1991). Today deception is permitted in research only when the benefits clearly outweigh the costs.

There are two key methods for making sure that research participants are protected. First, before participants begin their involvement in a study, they are required to give *informed consent* to participating in the research. The individuals are told what kinds of tasks they may be expected to perform and what kinds of situations they may expect to encounter, with specific qualifications for the use of deception (see Chapter 17 for more on informed consent). Second, after the research is completed, the participants are fully *debriefed* about the research. They are told the exact nature of the experiment, informed about any deception that may have been involved, and given the reason for the deception. Minor deception is usually permitted if the value of the proposed research seems to justify it. But the deception must be necessary for the purpose of the experiment and it must be fully explained afterward.

PAIN

In the past it was not uncommon for experiments to involve mild electric shocks to participants. These shocks were slightly painful but not harmful. Studies sometimes have had the potential for causing psychological damage because many experiments are stressful. How stressful a study is often depends on the individual as much as on the experiment. What is difficult for one person may be relaxing for another and neutral for yet another. Still, researchers generally try to anticipate and to minimize distress (unless distress itself is the construct under study). Institutions generally do not permit studies that are likely to cause any long-lasting pain or harm. If participating in a study might cause short-term pain or stress, participants must be fully informed in advance about possible consequences via the informed-consent procedure. Moreover, informed consent requires that participants be told that they are free to leave the experiment at any time without fear of any negative repercussions. Thus, if participants thought that they could tolerate the conditions of an experiment beforehand but then found in the course of it that they could not, they could leave at once.

CONFIDENTIALITY

The large majority of psychology experiments are conducted on an anonymous basis; participants' names are not associated with their data. Occasionally, however, complete anonymity is not possible. For example, if an experimenter wants to compare students' scores on some standardized test of ability to their freshman grades in college, the experimenter needs to have some means of identifying individual students. Even when participants cannot be anonymous, experimenters go to great lengths to ensure that their names are known only to the experimenters. Confidentiality can be a particularly important issue when researchers are studying basic characteristics, such as health status. One needs to guarantee that information about people's health will not later be used against them, such as in employment situations.

RESEARCH WITH NONHUMAN ANIMALS

Ethical issues become murky when nonhuman animals—such as rats, pigeons, rabbits, dogs, or even simple multicelled organisms—are involved instead of people. Nonhuman animals cannot sign informed-consent forms. Most institutions vigorously attempt to ensure that animals are protected and that they have all they require in terms of food, shelter, and freedom from harm or discomfort. Furthermore, in recent years, government has increasingly regulated scientific research and the appropriate treatment of animals. However, nonhuman animals sometimes still are exposed to painful or even harmful procedures. In such cases, institutions attempt to weigh

Research with nonhuman animals enables us to study questions that could not be addressed in research with humans.

© James L. Amos/Corbis

the potential benefits of the research to humans against the potential harm to the animals.

Questions about how to guard animal rights are not easily answered. On the one hand, no scrupulous researcher actively wishes to cause harm to animals. On the other hand, some of our most important discoveries in both medicine and psychology have come from research in which laboratory animals were sacrificed in order to advance our knowledge about and our ability to help humans. Given the choice of testing new drugs that may be beneficial but whose side effects are unknown first on laboratory animals or first on people, society has opted for testing on laboratory animals. Those whose lives have been saved by such testing, or who have had relatives whose lives have been saved, understand first hand why the testing has been approved by society. Review boards and policy-makers attempt to weigh the costs and benefits involved in all research, whether it employs human or animal participants. Still, the controversy over the use of animal participants is far from over.

THE ROLE OF INSTITUTIONAL REVIEW BOARDS (IRBs)

All institutions that conduct research with human or nonhuman animal subjects must have *institutional review boards (IRBs)* that approve the research before it is conducted. Although the U.S. government requires approval only for studies that are government funded, most institutions these days require approval for all studies, regardless of where funding comes from, if any. Today it is considered a serious violation of ethical standards to conduct research without prior approval or a waiver from the IRB indicating that the research is outside its jurisdiction. Investigators who violate IRB rules are likely to have not only the offending research shut down but also all the research they are doing. In cases of flagrant violations,

the government has shut down all research at universities where violations have occurred, although such cases are rare. The bottom line is that researchers must get their research approved, which always involves getting informed consent when human participants are involved.

The next chapter, concerning the biological bases of behavior, looks at how psychology intersects with one particular but very broad-ranging field, biology. We turn our focus to the body, the source of all biological and psychological activity. We also consider the evolutionary bases of behavioral adaptations to the environment. We further examine how the nervous system works as well as how the body's functioning affects and interacts with mental processes.

✓ CONCEPT CHECK 7

1. Before doing psychological research with human participants, investigators _____ must obtain informed consent.
   a. always
   b. usually
   c. sometimes
   d. never
2. Debriefing
   a. typically occurs before a study.
   b. usually happens during a study.
   c. most often occurs at the end of a study.
   d. usually does not occur in psychological research.
3. When testing nonhuman animals such as dogs, researchers _____ must adhere to strict ethical guidelines.
   a. always
   b. usually
   c. sometimes
   d. never

USING ANIMALS IN RESEARCH

Nonhuman animals have been important to psychological research since it began. They have been used in experiments that are highly significant to our understanding of taste, vision, hearing, feeding, learning, and emotion. In the early 1900s, Karl Lashley conducted the first studies of the effects of brain injury, using rats as subjects. Ivan Pavlov won a Nobel Prize in 1904 for his research on salivary responses in dogs, which led to his discovery of a type of learning called classical conditioning. Georg Von Bekesy won a Nobel Prize in 1961 for his 1928 discovery of the mechanism underlying pitch perception, which was based on his studies of frogs' inner ears. Eric Kandel won the Nobel Prize in 2000 for his research on learning in the sea slug.

Today, *physiological* or *biological psychologists* use animals to study behavior. For example, scientists eliminate or "knock out" a particular gene in a mouse or rat and then study the effect of its absence on the animal's behavior. The knock-out technique helps us understand the biological bases of drug addiction and of such psychological disorders as depression, anxiety, autism, and schizophrenia. Because physiological and biological psychologists study the brain activity that underlies behavior by altering those processes in the lab, nonhuman animals are sometimes the best and only choice for use as research subjects. However, other kinds of psychologists study animals without altering their physiology.

Animals are important in our everyday lives, and psychologists like to study how they affect our well-being. You've undoubtedly seen a person with a visual or physical disability with a service dog. These specially trained dogs act as eyes for the blind, ears for the deaf, and hands for people with physical disabilities, and in many cases they also improve their owners' psychological well-being. *Rehabilitation psychologists* and *health psychologists* have studied the benefits of animal–human contact for people with disabilities. Owners of service dogs report that they have more fun and are more independent because of their dogs. They experience improved psychosocial functioning, reduced loneliness, increased participation in their communities, and more social contact (Camp, 2001). The social contact may be due to the fact that strangers are more likely to stop and talk to a child or adult with a disability who has a dog than to a person with a disability who is alone (Innes, 2000; Mader, Hart, & Bergin, 1989; McNicholas & Collis, 2000). *Applied behavioral psychologists* study how to improve the training of puppies that are being raised as service dogs (Koda, 2001). Poorly trained puppies cannot be of help to people with disabilities.

Developmental psychologists have examined the effects of service dogs on the psychological well-being and self-esteem of children who use wheelchairs. Bonnie Mader and her colleagues studied friendly social acknowledgments such as smiles,

nods, and comments offered to wheelchair-bound children with and without service dogs on school playgrounds and in shopping malls (Mader, Hart, & Bergin, 1989). Children who had dogs received significantly more positive attention from schoolmates and strangers than did children without dogs, who tended to be ignored or overlooked.

Developmental psychologist Andreas Hergovich and colleagues have demonstrated that dogs can improve the behavior of children without disabilities. They observed first-grade children when a dog was present in their classroom for 3 months, and compared it to the behavior of first-grade children who did not have a dog in the classroom (Hergovich, Monshi, Semmler, & Zieglmayer, 2002). Children whose school days were shared with a dog developed better empathy with other dogs and with different kinds of animals. They also showed more sensitivity toward the needs of others and were less aggressive than the children who had not had a dog in the classroom. This study demonstrated that familiarity with a dog can positively affect the social and cognitive development of children.

Research by biological, physiological, rehabilitation, health, applied behavioral, and developmental psychologists has increased our awareness of the value to our lives of nonhuman animals. Such research has given us crucial information about human biological, developmental, and social processes.

SUMMARY

1. Although much of what we learn from studying psychology is obvious, many psychological results are surprising.
2. Results that would seem surprising before we know what they are often seem more obvious after we become aware of them.

CHARACTERISTICS OF SCIENTIFIC FINDINGS 32

What are the main characteristics of scientific findings?

3. In a scientific discipline, (a) ideas are accurately reported and can be *verified*, (b) researchers report findings *publicly* in scientific journals, and (c) work is cumulative with respect to past research.
4. It is important to recognize some misconceptions about science. Science (a) is not always correct, (b) does not always follow the orderly progression of steps students learned as "the scientific method," (c) is not always completely objective and value-free because it is practiced by human beings, and (d) is not merely a collection of facts.

HOW SCIENTISTS SOLVE PROBLEMS 37

How do you think scientists approach problem solving?

5. Scientific problem solving is a thought process. Typically it occurs in steps: (a) identifying the problem, (b) defining the problem, (c) formulating hypotheses, (d) constructing a strategy for problem solving, and (e) monitoring and evaluating problem solving. The evaluation of the solution often leads to the recognition of a new challenge and thus the repetition of the process. The steps of the process are not necessarily executed exactly in this order. Some problems are redefined as the process goes along or as new strategies are tried as old ones fail.

THE GOALS OF SCIENTIFIC RESEARCH 40

What do scientists seek to accomplish in their work?

6. When a problem is addressed, the goals of psychological research are: (a) *description*, (b) *explanation*, (c) *prediction*, and (d) *control*.

RESEARCH METHODS IN PSYCHOLOGY 43

How would you expect psychologists to conduct research?

7. Psychologists employ research methods such as (a) *naturalistic observation;* (b) *case studies;* (c) *tests, questionnaires,* and *surveys;* and (d) *experiments.*
8. An experiment is a carefully supervised investigation in which a researcher studies cause–effect relationships by manipulating one or more *independent variables* in order to observe their effects on one or more *dependent variables.* An experiment should include at least one *control group* to ensure that differences in results are caused by the *experimental treatment* and not by irrelevant group differences.
9. Because we generally cannot conduct studies on whole populations, we use *sample statistics* (numbers that characterize the sample we have tested with regard to the attributes under investigation) as estimates of the *population parameters* (numbers that would characterize everyone we conceivably might test who would fit our desired description). The use of sample statistics is based on the assumption that the researcher has found a *representative sample* or a *random sample* of the population under study.
10. Although we are never able to prove the *null hypothesis* (which states that there is no difference between two groups under study), we can demonstrate that a particular difference has reached a level of *statistical significance*—that is, one unlikely to have occurred if the null hypothesis (of no difference) were true.

CAUSAL INFERENCE IN PSYCHOLOGICAL RESEARCH 49

How do you think scientists draw causal inferences from their research?

11. Psychological researchers try to draw *causal inferences* or conjectures about cause–effect relationships. *Controlled experimental designs* are better suited to drawing such inferences than are *quasi-experimental designs*, which lack at least one experimental characteristic (usually random assignment of participants to groups), or *correlational designs*, which show associations between variables but not which variables cause which other ones.
12. *Correlation* is the degree of statistical relationship between two variables. Correlation does not imply causation.

How do you think critical thinking is relevant
to psychological research?

13. *Critical thinking* is of great importance to psychological research. When people do not think critically, they are likely to commit informal fallacies, such as irrelevant conclusion, composition, personalization, false cause, and ad hominem argument.

What ethical issues confront psychologists?

14. Scientists, including psychologists, must use ethical research procedures. Most questions about ethics center on whether participants—human or animal—are treated fairly. Research institutions today have standard policies that require informed consent by and debriefing of human participants. Most institutions have also set up institutional review boards to study and approve proposed research. Some government agencies monitor research practices, especially as they pertain to animals.

KEY TERMS

case study 43
intensive study of a person
causal inferences 49
what causes person to behave in certain way
clinical 43
therapy directly to clients
confirmation bias 34
tend to confirm existing beliefs
control 42
helping people command their destinies
control condition 46
controlled experimental design 49
manipulate indep. var. to see effect on dep. var.
correlation 51
statistical relationship
correlational design 51
degree of association
correlational methods 51
assess degree of relationship
critical thinking 52
reasoning
dependent variables 46
affected by indep. var.
description 40
design 49
how experiment is set up
disconfirm 34
refute

experiment 45
investigation
experimental condition 46
experimental methods 45
manipulating variables
explanation 41
why
hypothetical construct 38
not directly measurable
independent variables 46
manipulated
naturalistic observation 43
field study
negative (inverse) correlation 51
↑ in one causes ↓ in other
null hypothesis 48
no relationship
operational definition 38
specify exactly how to test
population parameters 47
characterize everyone that could be tested
positive correlation 51
↑ in one causes ↑ in other
prediction 42
what you think will happen
psychotherapy 42
uses psychology to treat disorders
quasi-experimental design 50
groups not assigned randomly
results not as reliable

questionnaire 45
random sample 47
equal chance of being selected
reliable 32
same results every time
replicate 32
do same thing again
representative sample 47
carefully chosen to represent whole
sample statistics 47
characterize sample used
statistical significance 48
probability how likely is result if only chance factors
survey 45
test 45
theory 35
statement that explains something
valid 32
true
variables 46
verifiable 32
can be confirmed

ANSWERS TO CONCEPT CHECKS

Concept Check 1

1. a   2. b   3. d

Concept Check 2

1. d   2. c   3. b

Concept Check 3

1. c   2. b   3. d

Concept Check 4

1. c   2. d   3. a

Concept Check 5

1. d   2. c   3. a

Concept Check 6

1. d   2. a   3. a

Concept Check 7

1. a   2. c   3. a

1. Which of the following is *not* typically a characteristic of scientific findings?
   a. verifiable
   b. public
   c. cumulative
   d. certain
2. Which of the following is *not* one of the steps psychologists typically use in solving problems?
   a. identifying the problem
   b. defining the problem
   c. logically proving the correctness of their findings
   d. formulating hypotheses
3. Which of the following is *not* typically a goal of scientific research?
   a. description
   b. mystification
   c. explanation
   d. prediction
4. Which of the following is *not* a method used in psychological research?
   a. extrasensory perception
   b. naturalistic observation
   c. case studies
   d. experiments
5. A result that is significant at the 0.05 level
   a. occurs 5% of the time.
   b. would occur only 5% of the time if only chance factors were at work.
   c. occurs as much as 5% of the time if systematic factors are at work.
   d. fails to occur 5% of the time.
6. Deception in psychological research
   a. is routinely approved by institutional review boards.
   b. is allowed by institutional review boards only when the benefits clearly outweight the costs.

c. is never allowed in psychological research.
   d. is a part of most psychological research.
7. Which of the following statements is most likely to result from a correlational study?
   a. People in Group A performed better than people in Group B.
   b. All of the participants showed the same effect.
   c. Increases in scores on Test A were associated with increases in scores on Test B.
   d. Participants showed no improvement.
8. A particular study looked at the effects of number of hours of darkness per day on levels of depression. In this study, level of depression was a(n)
   a. dependent variable.
   b. independent variable.
   c. random variable.
   d. fixed variable.
9. An example of an *ad hominen* argument is:
   a. He is not a reliable person so don't trust his conclusion.
   b. His conclusion is an overgeneralization.
   c. His conclusion does not follow from his data.
   d. His conclusion is not causal.
10. In a survey, all members of a population had an equal chance of being selected. The sample chosen was
   a. equivalent.
   b. systematic.
   c. biased.
   d. random.

Answers

1. d 2. c 3. b 4. a 5. b 6. b 7. c 8. a
9. a 10. d

THINK ABOUT IT

1. For what kinds of psychological phenomena is *control* a suitable goal? What kinds of psychological phenomena should be off-limits in terms of control? (If you answer "none" to any question, tell why you say so.)
2. If you were in charge of an institutional review board deciding which experiments should be permitted, what questions about the experiments would you ask the researcher?
3. Describe the steps you would take if you were systematically to observe members of an unfamiliar culture with the goal of learning what their customs are and why they have those customs.
4. If psychologists from a distant planet were to observe television programs, what conclusions would they draw about our culture?

5. What is a challenging problem you have solved in your personal life? Compare the steps you took in solving your problem with the steps of the problem-solving process described in this chapter.

6. Why should all psychological interventions in schools and communities have control groups of some kind?

7. Why do researchers and psychotherapists both need to think scientifically?

WEB RESOURCES

For a chapter tutorial quiz, direct links to Internet sites, and other useful features, visit the book-specific website at http://psychology.wadsworth.com/sternberg4e. You can also connect directly to the following sites:

American Psychological Society: Psychological Research on the Net
http://psych.hanover.edu/research/exponnet.html
Here you'll find links to experiments on topics related to psychology. Some allow you to participate in an experimental procedure, so you can get a sense of what it feels like to be a research subject.

The Junk Science Homepage
http://www.junkscience.com/
According to text at this site, "junk science is bad science used by personal injury lawyers to shake down deep-pocket businesses, the 'food police' and environmental Chicken Littles to fuel wacky social agendas . . ." —you get the idea. This site is devoted to debunking erroneous reports of science in the media; it's a great place to find examples of correlation misinterpreted as causation.

Office of Research Integrity
http://ori.dhhs.gov/
Anyone who needs a comprehensive, up-to-date overview of ethical concerns in research from the perspective of the U.S. government should consider visiting this site. Although the Office of Research Integrity (OPI) deals with research sponsored by the U.S. Public Health Service, it also offers links to related offices and resources in many other agencies.

For additional readings on many of the topics covered in this chapter, check out InfoTrac College Edition at **www.infotrac-college.com/ wadsworth.**

CD-ROM: UNIFYING PSYCHOLOGY

Disk One
Research Methods in Psychology
Causal Inference in Psychological Research
Descriptive Statistics
Chapter Quiz
Critical Thinking Questions

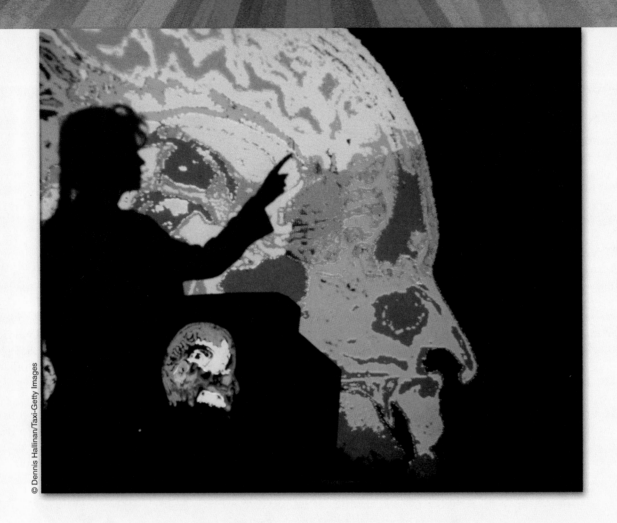

CHAPTER 3

BIOLOGICAL BASES
OF BEHAVIOR

D r. P. was a musician of distinction. . . . "What seems to be the matter?" I asked him at length.

"Nothing that I know of," he replied with a smile, "but people seem to think there's something wrong with my eyes."

"But you don't recognise any visual problems?"

"No, not directly, but I occasionally make mistakes."

It was while examining his reflexes—a trifle abnormal on the left side—that the first bizarre experience occurred. I had taken off his left shoe and scratched the sole of his foot with a key—a frivolous-seeming but essential test of a reflex—and then, excusing myself to screw my ophthalmoscope together, left him to put on the shoe himself. To my surprise, a minute later, he had not done this.

"Can I help?" I asked.

"Help what? Help whom?"

"Help you put on your shoe."

"Ach," he said, "I had forgotten the shoe," adding sotto voce, "The shoe? The shoe?" He seemed baffled.

"Your shoe," I repeated. "Perhaps you'd put it on?"

He continued to look downwards, though not at the shoe, with an intense but misplaced concentration. Finally his gaze settled on his foot. . . . "My eyes," he explained, and put a hand to his foot, "This is my shoe, no?"

"No, it is not. That is your foot. There is your shoe."

"Ah! I thought that was my foot."

—*Oliver Sacks,* The Man Who Mistook His Wife for a Hat. *Reprinted with permission of Simon & Schuster. Copyright © 1990, 1981, 1983, 1984, 1985 by Oliver Sacks.*

At the core of our thinking, feeling, and acting is the nervous system. The **nervous system** is the physiological network of intercommunicating cells that forms the basis of our ability to perceive, adapt to, and interact with the world (Gazzaniga, 2000; Gazzaniga, Ivry, & Mangun, 1998). It is the means by which humans and other vertebrates receive, process, and respond to messages from the environment and from inside their bodies (Pinker, 1999; Rugg, 1997). According to neurologist Oliver Sacks, Dr. P's strange perceptions and behavior were rooted in a disruption in his brain caused by a tumor or other brain disease. Because of the seamless way the nervous system processes information and executes commands, its work is often seen most clearly when something goes awry. Dr. P. is an example. We take for granted that we know the difference between our feet and our shoes until the ability to do so vanishes. Then we recognize the highly integrated communication system on which our perceptions depend.

Our discussion of the nervous system takes a functional approach. We are concerned not only with anatomical structures but also with what they do and why. We often compare the functions of our physiological communication systems to such machines as telephones and computers. However, nothing we can create even approaches the complexity, subtlety, and sophistication of the communication systems within our bodies.

In discussing the nervous system, we first consider its structures and subsystems. Then we examine how information moves both within cells and among them. Finally we examine the **brain**, the supreme organ of the nervous system, which most directly controls our thoughts, emotions, and motivations. (Frackowiak, Friston, Frith, Dolan, & Mazziotta, 1997; Gloor, 1997; Rockland, 2000; Shepherd, 1998). We pay special attention to the cerebral cortex, which controls many of our thought processes.

© RF/Corbis

The feedback our nervous system provides about body position helps make this feat possible.

THE ORGANIZATION OF THE NERVOUS SYSTEM

How is the nervous system organized?

THE CENTRAL NERVOUS SYSTEM (CNS)

The nervous system consists of two main parts, the central nervous system and the peripheral nervous system (see Figure 3.1). The **central nervous system (CNS)** has two parts: the brain and the spinal cord. Both parts are encased in bone and further buffered from shocks and minor injuries by fluid, which is secreted constantly in the brain. *Cerebrospinal fluid* circulates throughout the brain and the spinal cord. The clear, colorless fluid probably does not provide nourishment, which is furnished by the rich blood supply going to the CNS. But this fluid may help the CNS dispose of waste products. The CNS controls our senses and motor abilities as well as our reflexes and mental activity.

THE BRAIN AND SPINAL CORD

The brain responds to information it receives from elsewhere in the body. Communication within the brain is two-way; the brain both receives information

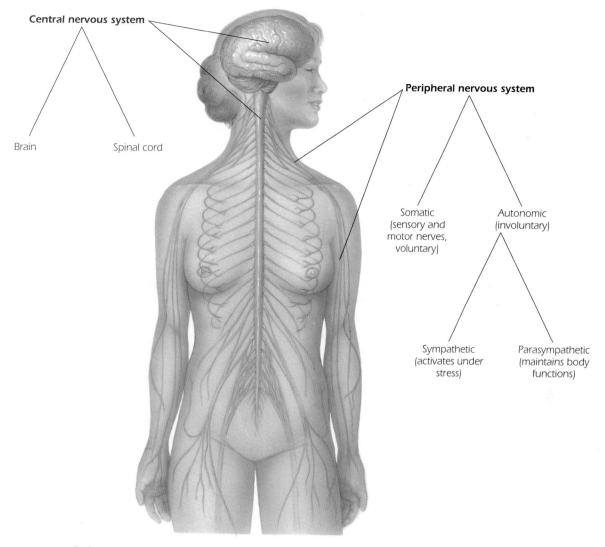

Central nervous system

Brain   Spinal cord

Peripheral nervous system

Somatic
(sensory and
motor nerves,
voluntary)

Autonomic
(involuntary)

Sympathetic
(activates under
stress)

Parasympathetic
(maintains body
functions)

FIGURE 3.1

Divisions of the Nervous System. The central nervous system (CNS), protected by bone, comprises the brain and spinal cord. The peripheral nervous system (PNS), not protected by bone, comprises the nerves of the autonomic and somatic systems. The autonomic system transmits messages between the brain and internal organs, and the somatic system transmits messages between the brain and the sensory and motor nerves, which are linked to the skeletal muscles.

and processes it. And then the brain forwards the information with instructions on how to proceed.

Consider the events that take place on a football field during a game. A quarterback gets ready to pass the ball to a teammate. The quarterback is running. The teammate is running. An opponent is moving toward the quarterback to try to tackle him. The teammate is distracted by a different opponent. Other players are constantly in motion. The complexity of the system seems overwhelming. Yet the game goes on and has a sensible and coherent outcome. Similarly, the brain and all the elements of the nervous system are able to work together in a coherent fashion, despite the astonishing complexity of the system as a

whole. This complexity makes the events on a football field look like child's play.

Within the brain, a network of individual cells called **neurons** receives information and transmits it to the spinal cord (Bear, Connors, & Paradiso, 1996; N. Carlson, 2000a; Shepherd, 1991, 1999; Uylings, 2002). The **spinal cord** is a slender, roughly cylindrical rope of interconnected fibers, about the diameter of your little finger, enclosed within the spinal column, that transmits information from sensory neurons to the brain and from the brain to motor neurons. It starts at the brain and ends at the lower end of the back (see Figure 3.2). The arms, hands, legs, and feet are required to do important work almost constantly, and

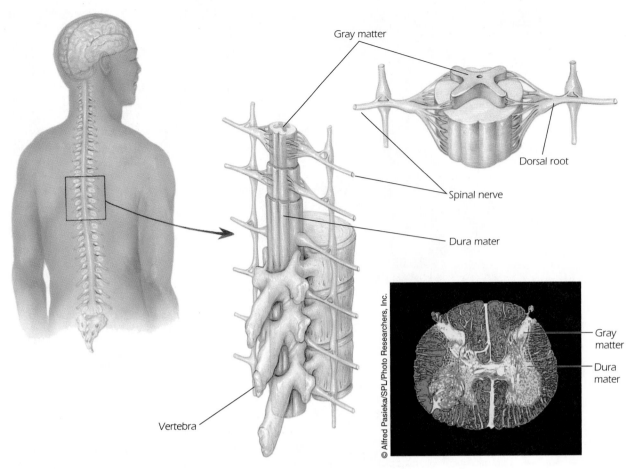

Gray matter

Dorsal root

Spinal nerve

Dura mater

Gray matter

Dura mater

© Alfred Pasieka/SPL/Photo Researchers, Inc.

Vertebra

FIGURE 3.2

The Structure of the Spinal Column. The spinal cord and its connecting nerves are protected by dura mater and vertebrae.

controlling them requires many neurons. One of the two bulges in the spinal cord contains the neurons that control the sensations and movement of the arms and hands. The other contains the neurons that control the legs and feet. Past the bulges, the cord tapers gradually to a point lower in the back.

One function of the spinal cord is to collect information from the peripheral nervous system and transmit it to the brain and back again. This two-way communication involves two kinds of neurons. **Sensory afferents** receive electrochemical information from outlying neurons in the eyes, ears, and skin, and transmit it back up through the spinal cord to the brain. An *afferent* of any kind is a neuron that brings information into a structure. **Motor efferents** transmit such information as movements of the large and small muscles either from the brain through the spinal cord to the muscles (for voluntary movements) or directly from the spinal cord to the muscles (in the case of reflexes). They thus control bodily responses. More generally, an *efferent* is a neuron that carries information away from a structure.

Disorders of the spinal cord can seriously affect a person's health and mental well-being. For example, *paraplegia* is a loss of sensation and muscle control in the legs caused by damage to the spinal cord above the areas that control the legs. Even more serious is *quadriplegia*, a loss of sensation and control of the muscles in the arms and legs caused by damage to the spinal cord higher up—above the level that controls the arms. Christopher Reeve, an actor who once played Superman in a series of movies, became quadriplegic after a serious fall from a horse. He has become a major supporter of research on recovery of function after spinal-cord injury. He has recovered some sensation in parts of his body, such as his left leg and parts of his left arm, but he needs a ventilator to breathe and cannot move any part of his body below the shoulders. Promising treatments for spinal-cord injuries are being found through research on stem cells.

SPINAL REFLEXES

The spinal cord plays a crucial role in routing sensory and motor information to and from the brain. Under

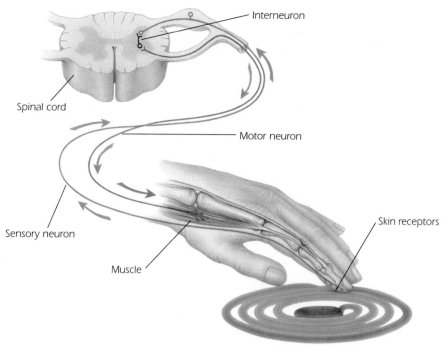

FIGURE 3.3

Spinal Reflex. Reflexes enable us to remove ourselves immediately from danger by avoiding the time it would take for a message to go to and from the brain. In this example, the interneuron in the spinal column intercepts the "extreme heat" message from the sensory neuron and directs the motor neurons to contract the hand muscles, thereby pulling the hand away from the burner.

Labels: Interneuron, Spinal cord, Motor neuron, Sensory neuron, Muscle, Skin receptors

some circumstances, however, the spinal cord transmits a message directly from sensory afferent neurons to motor efferent neurons, without routing it through the brain first. The reaction to this direct connection is a **reflex,** which is a much faster automatic physiological response to an external stimulus than a voluntary response (see Figure 3.3). For example, it takes only about 50 milliseconds from the time the patellar tendon in your knee is tapped until your calf and foot jerk forward. In comparison, it requires many hundreds of milliseconds for you to move your knee in response to being told to do so. Indeed, 50 milliseconds is such a short time that normally you are not even aware of it. If you press the button on a stopwatch twice as rapidly as you can, once to start the watch and once to stop it, you can never be as fast as 50 milliseconds.

Quick reflexes are adaptive. They allow the body to respond immediately to sensory information, without waiting for the information to route through the brain. When you cut yourself, you reflexively withdraw from whatever causes the damage. Reflexes help us avoid pain. Even more important, they minimize tissue damage from potentially harmful stimuli such as fire. Thus, in both functional and evolutionary terms, our reflexes help us survive.

The reflex response shows that the spinal cord has the power to act alone; yet it also demonstrates the brain's essential role in our conscious feelings of pain, pleasure, pressure, and temperature. Suppose that a traumatic accident severed your spinal cord at the neck. Your spinal cord would not be able to receive or send messages from or to your brain. You therefore would be quadriplegic, paralyzed and without sensa-

tion below your neck. This is not to say, however, that you could not move at all. Your intact spinal reflexes would still jerk your hand away from a hot stove. You would not be consciously aware of pain because your brain would not get the sensory information via your spinal cord. And you could not intentionally move your hand away from an impending danger. This situation gives an interesting twist to the mind–body dilemma: When the brain is disconnected from the spinal cord, events that happen in the body below the break cannot be processed by the mind. In sum, the body is an exceptionally well-organized system. Lower levels in the hierarchy of command are capable of responding to stimuli without the intervention of the brain. But the higher levels are essential for full physical interaction with the external world.

THE PERIPHERAL NERVOUS SYSTEM (PNS)

Below the CNS in the hierarchy of command is the **peripheral nervous system (PNS),** which comprises all of the neurons *except* those in the brain and spinal cord. The PNS even includes the neurons of the face and head that are not a part of the CNS. *Peripheral* has two meanings. The first is "auxiliary," or supportive, because the PNS assists the CNS. The second is "away from the center" because the peripheral neurons are outside the CNS. The primary function of the PNS is to relay information between the CNS and the afferents and efferents. The PNS connects with afferents in our external sensory organs—such as skin, ears, and eyes—and with our internal body parts—like the stomach and the muscles. It also connects with efferents in other parts of the body, including those that produce movement (such as the arms and legs).

THE SOMATIC AND AUTONOMIC NERVOUS SYSTEMS

The PNS has two main parts: the somatic nervous system and the autonomic nervous system. The **somatic nervous system** is in charge of quick, deliberate movements by our roughly 400 skeletal muscles. *Skeletal muscles* are attached directly to bones. They allow us to walk, type, wave, swim—in short, to move. The skeletal muscles are sometimes referred to as *striated muscles* because under a microscope they can be seen to have striations, or stripes. In general, we have voluntary control over the muscles served by the somatic system. These muscles usually can respond quickly to whatever the CNS asks of it. For example, we can jump out of the way of an oncoming bicycle.

The **autonomic nervous system** controls the movement of our *nonskeletal muscles.* These muscles are the striated cardiac (heart) muscles and the *smooth muscles*, which are not striated. The smooth muscles include those of the blood vessels and the internal body organs, such as the muscles of the digestive tract. We have little or no voluntary control over these muscles. We are usually not even aware of their functioning. In fact, *autonomic* means "self-regulating"; this system does not need our conscious attention in order to function.

To illustrate the two systems, suppose that you are using a word processor. You control the striated muscular movements of your hands and fingers as they press the keys. But you do not direct the smooth muscles of your stomach, which may be digesting your dinner. In general, the responses of the autonomic nervous system are more sustained and less rapid than those of the somatic nervous system.

THE SYMPATHETIC AND PARASYMPATHETIC NERVOUS SYSTEMS

The autonomic nervous system is further divided into two intercommunicating parts: the sympathetic nervous system and the parasympathetic nervous system (see Figure 3.4). Both systems are involved with your *metabolism*—the processes by which your body captures, stores, and uses energy and material resources from food and eliminates waste. The **sympathetic nervous system** is concerned primarily with *catabolism*—the metabolic processes that *use* the energy and other resources from the reserves stored in the body. The **parasympathetic nervous system** is concerned primarily with *anabolism*—the metabolic processes that *store* energy.

In general, the sympathetic nervous system is activated by situations that require arousal and alertness. Then the system increases heart rate and diverts blood flow to muscles for exercise or emergency. The parasympathetic nervous system promotes the activity of the digestive system and slows heart rate. It thereby calms the body and stores energy. Thus, the sympathetic and parasympathetic systems work in tandem. Yet they may also work in opposition. If you have a heated argument right after dinner, your sympathetic system will be stirred up, readying you for a fight. Unfortunately, it will also end up warring with your parasympathetic system, which will try to conserve energy in order to digest your food. You may end up feeling drained, tired, and even sick to your stomach.

Now let us consider the most basic unit of the nervous system, the neuron.

✓CONCEPT CHECK 1

1. An afferent is a kind of
   a. neuron.
   b. spinal reflex.
   c. muscle.
   d. sensory information.
2. Spinal reflexes are _____ voluntary responses.
   a. always slower than
   b. equal in speed to
   c. always faster than
   d. sometimes slower than and sometimes faster than
3. The somatic nervous system controls
   a. primarily striated muscles.
   b. primarily smooth muscles.
   c. both striated and smooth muscles in equal degree.
   d. neither striated nor smooth muscles.

NERVOUS SYSTEM CELLS AND FUNCTIONS

What are neurons, and how do they communicate?

NEURONS

To understand how the entire nervous system processes information, we first need to examine the structure of the cells—*neurons*—that make up the nervous system. The three main types of neurons are sensory neurons, motor neurons, and interneurons.

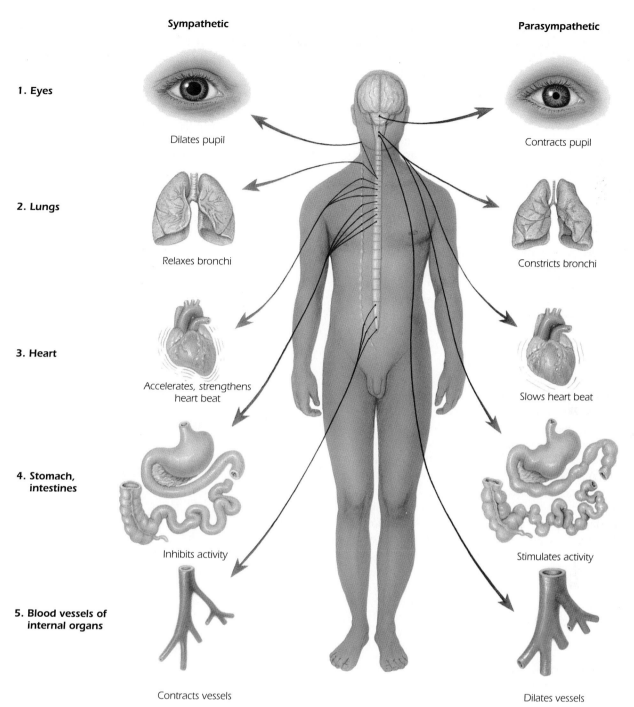

Sympathetic

Parasympathetic

1. Eyes

Dilates pupil

Contracts pupil

2. Lungs

Relaxes bronchi

Constricts bronchi

3. Heart

Accelerates, strengthens heart beat

Slows heart beat

4. Stomach, intestines

Inhibits activity

Stimulates activity

5. Blood vessels of internal organs

Contracts vessels

Dilates vessels

FIGURE 3.4

The Autonomic Nervous System. Note how the two parts of the autonomic system, the sympathetic and parasympathetic systems, complement each other as they regulate the functions of the organs.

THREE TYPES OF NEURONS

Sensory neurons receive information from the environment. They connect with *receptor cells* that detect physical or chemical changes in the skin, ears, tongue, eyes, nose, muscles, joints, and internal organs. Sensory neurons carry information away from the sensory receptor cells and *toward* the spinal cord or brain. **Motor neurons** carry information *away* from the spinal cord and the brain and toward the body parts that are supposed to respond to the information in some way. Motor neurons and sensory neurons are part of both the PNS and the CNS. For example, through the autonomic nervous system, motor and sensory neurons send information to and from the intestines. Through the somatic nervous system, they send information to and from the toe muscles.

Interneurons serve as intermediaries between sensory and motor neurons. They are neither afferent (originating from another source) nor efferent (projecting to another structure). They *receive* signals from either sensory neurons or other interneurons. They *send* signals either to other interneurons or to motor neurons. In complex organisms such as humans, the large majority of neurons are interneurons. In the spinal reflex discussed earlier, an interneuron located in the spinal cord might act as an intermediary between neurons. In essence it could carry the messages, "Burning hand on stove!" from the incoming sensory neuron and "Move that hand!" to the outgoing motor neuron. Another interneuron sends the incoming message via the spinal cord to the brain. It interprets this message as pain and determines what to do about the situation.

THE ANATOMY OF THE NEURON

Neurons vary in their structure, but almost all have four basic parts: a soma, or cell body; dendrites; an axon; and terminal buttons (see Figure 3.5). We discuss each part in turn, as well as the synapse, the important gap between neurons through which messages are transmitted (N. Carlson, 2000b; Maass & Markram, 2002; Nicholls, Martin, Wallace, & Kuffler, 1992; Rosenzweig, Leiman, & Breedlove, 1996).

The soma, or body of the neuron, is responsible for the life of the cell because it contains the *nucleus*, which performs metabolic and reproductive functions for the cell. The dendrites (branchlike parts of the neuron at the end of the soma) and the soma receive communications from other cells via distinctive receptors on their external membranes.

The axon is a long, thin tube, which can divide and branch many times at its *terminus* (end). The axon responds to the information received by the dendrites and soma. The information is transmitted through the neuron until it reaches a synapse, where it can be transmitted to other neurons through the release of chemicals (see Figure 3.6). A bundle of axons is called a nerve.

Axons are of two basic kinds, in approximately equal proportions. The key distinction is the presence or absence of *myelin*, a white fatty substance. One kind of axon is *myelinated*. It is surrounded by a myelin sheath, which insulates and protects the axon from electrochemical interference from other neurons in the area. The myelin sheath also speeds up the conduction of information along the axon. The speed of transmission in myelinated axons can reach more than 100 meters per second (or about 224 miles per hour). Myelin is not distributed continuously along the axon but rather in segments that are separated by gaps, or nodes of Ranvier. A balanced diet in infancy, one that includes fat, is important for proper development of the myelin sheath. Degeneration of the myelin sheath results in the tangled communication among neurons associated with multiple sclerosis (MS). Progressive loss of motor function follows. Why the myelin deteriorates is unknown. The second kind of axon lacks the myelin coat altogether. Typically, these axons are thinner and shorter than the myelinated ones. As a result, they do not need the fast conduction velocity of a long myelinated axon. In unmyelinated axons, conduction is much slower,

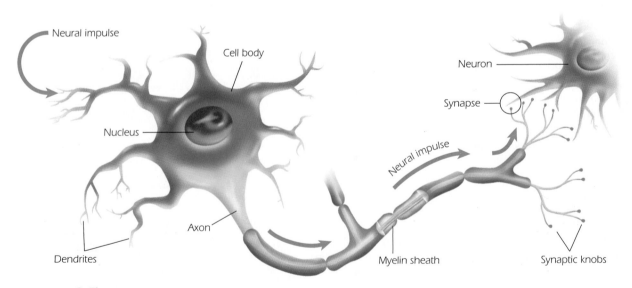

FIGURE 3.5

Neurons. The shape of a neuron is determined by its function. Each neuron, however, has the same structure: soma, dendrites, axon, and terminal buttons.

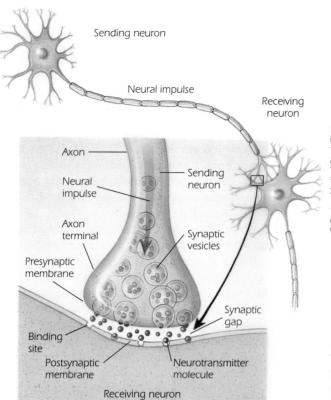

Sending neuron

Neural impulse

Receiving neuron

Axon

Neural impulse

Sending neuron

Axon terminal

Synaptic vesicles

Presynaptic membrane

Binding site

Synaptic gap

Postsynaptic membrane

Neurotransmitter molecule

Receiving neuron

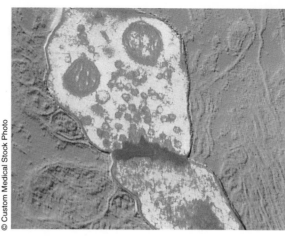

© Custom Medical Stock Photo

FIGURE 3.6

The Synapse. Neurons relay electrochemical messages by releasing neurotransmitters that cross the synapse to the dendrites of the receiving neurons. This electron micrograph shows how densely packed the neurons are.

sometimes only 5 meters per second (though most of us would be lucky to be able to run that fast).

Conduction speeds up as the diameter of the axon increases. Motor neurons that supply quick and constant power to arms and legs, for example, are generally thick and myelinated. Neurons to the stomach muscles are mostly small in diameter and unmyelinated because the digestive process usually does not require speed. Thus, form follows function. At the end of the neuron are the **terminal buttons,** small knobby structures that play an important part in interneuronal communication. For the most part, neurons are irreplaceable, at least in adults. Once the neuron's soma dies, the neuron is gone forever. As long as the soma lives, however, the remaining stumps of damaged but living neurons can sometimes regenerate new axons, more successfully in the PNS than in the CNS. As a result, damage to the CNS is much more serious than to the PNS because of the lower probability of full recovery.

Neuron size is more difficult to quantify in absolute terms. The soma's diameter ranges from about 5 to 100 microns (thousandths of a millimeter, or millionths of a meter). Dendrites, too, are relatively small, generally a few hundred microns long. Axons can vary considerably in length. Some are as short as a few hundred microns (in fact, some neurons in the eye have virtually indistinguishable axons). The axons of some of the longer motor neurons, however, can extend

very far. They can stretch all the way from the head to the base of the spinal cord, and from the spinal cord to the fingers and the toes. In relative terms, visualize an orange attached to a long wire stretching the length of more than 200 football fields (roughly 14 miles).

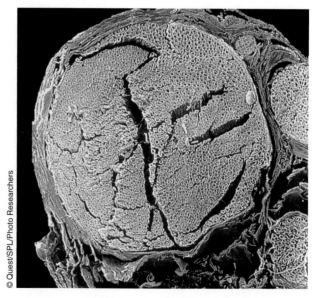

© Quest/SPL/Photo Researchers

This photomicrograph shows the myelin sheath and nodes of Ranvier, the terminal buttons, and the glial cells of a neuron.

Neurons are not the only kind of cell in the nervous system. In fact, they make up only about 10% of the cells in the CNS, where they are supported by the all-purpose glial cells (also termed *neuroglia*). **Glial cells** function as a kind of glue to hold the CNS together by keeping the neurons in their proper places, at optimal distances from one another and from other structures (Noctor et al., 2002; Uylings, 2002). Thus, glial cells help ensure that signals do not get crossed. Some of the glial cells also assist in forming the myelin sheath. In fact, the nodes of Ranvier in the sheath are actually the gaps between glial cells.

Glial cells nourish and support healthy neurons. They also destroy and eliminate neurons that have died through injury or age. The dead neurons are then often replaced with new glial cells. Destruction of glial cells by disease can result in serious breakdowns in communication within the nervous system. Messages become scrambled as they cross through uncharted territory: As the disease progresses and the insulating myelin sheaths deteriorate, dead neurons and other waste accumulate and clutter the neural landscape. Inadequate nourishment then impedes normal cell function and repair of damaged tissue.

The two kinds of neuronal communication are intraneuronal (within the neuron) and interneuronal (between neurons). We consider intraneuronal communication first.

Communication within the neuron is *electrochemical*— through the interactions of chemicals that have positive or negative electrical charges. Each neuron contains electrically charged chemical particles called *ions*. Suppose the concentrations of the ions inside and outside the neuron always remained in a *static equilibrium*, a perfect balance. Then intraneuronal communication would never occur. In living organisms, however, change is constant. Ongoing electrical activity within the body stimulates changes in the concentrations of ions inside and outside the neuron that affect its functioning (see Figure 3.7).

Because of the tremendous amount of fluctuating electrical activity going on every moment, our neurons must be somewhat selective in reacting. If neurons reacted to every slight fluctuation, utter chaos would result. To avoid pandemonium, electrical charges at most levels of intensity and frequency produce virtually no effect at all. Once a charge reaches or surpasses a certain level, however, the neuron reacts. At or above a neuron's **threshold of excitation**, a brief change occurs in the electrochemical balance inside and outside the neuron. The specific threshold of excitation that is required for a given neuron's action potential differs for the various kinds of neurons. When an **action potential** occurs, the neuron "fires." It carries impulses, or messages, through the axon from one end to the other. Action potentials are *all or*

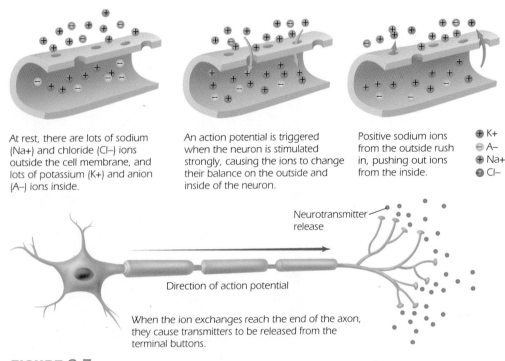

At rest, there are lots of sodium (Na+) and chloride (Cl–) ions outside the cell membrane, and lots of potassium (K+) and anion (A–) ions inside.

An action potential is triggered when the neuron is stimulated strongly, causing the ions to change their balance on the outside and inside of the neuron.

Positive sodium ions from the outside rush in, pushing out ions from the inside.

⊕ K+
⊖ A–
⊕ Na+
⊖ Cl–

Neurotransmitter release

Direction of action potential

When the ion exchanges reach the end of the axon, they cause transmitters to be released from the terminal buttons.

FIGURE 3.7

Neural Impulse. The neural impulse depends on the alternating flow of sodium and potassium ions.

none. Either the electrical charge is strong enough to generate an action potential, or it is not. Once the threshold is reached, the charge will travel all the way down the axon without losing strength.

You might compare the firing of a neuron to a sneeze. To generate a sneeze, the membranes of your nose must be tickled beyond a certain point by some outside irritant. If you are like most people, once that tickle threshold has been crossed, you will definitely sneeze. It is an all-or-none process. Similarly, a neuron will definitely fire once its threshold of excitation has been reached.

What exactly happens during the conduction of a neural impulse? Initially, the neuron is at rest; it has a potential of −70 millivolts. When the neuron is stimulated and an action potential occurs, the voltage changes and becomes positive (see Figure 3.8). Gates that allow sodium to enter the axon open, with the result that positively charged sodium ions start to flow into the axon. As the action potential peaks, the sodium gates close, but different gates open and allow potassium ions to flow outward. This process can be repeated many times. The sodium gates open, and sodium ions flow into the axon. The potassium gates then begin to open, and the sodium gates close. Potassium flows outward. Finally, the potassium gates close. At the end of this complex process, the neuron returns to its initial potential of −70 millivolts. The whole process of conduction involves changes in the balance of sodium and potassium ions.

Now suppose that the neuron has just fired. Another strong electrical charge has reached the axon. Will the neuron fire? It will not. As long as the dynamic equilibrium of the ions inside and outside the neuron has not yet returned to normal after firing, the neuron cannot reach its action potential again. During the **absolute refractory phase,** no matter how strong the stimulus may be, the neuron cannot fire again. After the absolute refractory phase, some of the dynamic equilibrium of ions begins to return to normal. During the **relative refractory phase,** the neuron can fire but only in response to a stronger stimulus than would typically be necessary. Finally, when the equilibrium is normal, the neuron regains its usual sensitivity. Functionally, the refractory phases prevent the organism from the overstimulation of individual neurons.

Consider the sneezing analogy again. A few sneezes are helpful. But if they were to continue without interruption, the negative effects gradually would start to outweigh the positive effects of clearing irritating particles from the nasal cavity.

To summarize, information is transmitted within a neuron through the propagation of all-or-none action potentials along the axon. The potentials are set off by an electrical current at or beyond the neuron's threshold of excitation. This process sets in motion a complex electrochemical reaction that transmits the message down the neuron. Propagation of impulses is especially rapid in myelinated axons.

NEURAL TRANSMISSION

Internal communication is essential for each neuron to function effectively. But the work of each individual neuron would be useless if there were no way for neurons to communicate with one another. Interneuronal communication begins with the terminal buttons. The terminal buttons of the axon do not directly touch the dendrites of the next neuron; rather, the synapse, which is between the terminal buttons of one neuron's axon and the dendrites of the next neuron (see Figure 3.6), is important for sending messages. The terminal buttons on the axon of the presynaptic neuron sending the message release a neurotransmitter. A **neurotransmitter** is a chemical messenger that carries information from one neuron to others. Each neuron is equipped to release just one neurotransmitter (Cooper, Bloom, & Roth, 1996; Wurtman, 1999). This substance travels across the synaptic gap to the receptor sites of either the receiving dendrites or the soma of the postsynaptic neuron. The neurotransmitter then reaches one or more (usually more) neurons and continues the line of communication. Several kinds of neurotransmitters operate at any given synapse (as

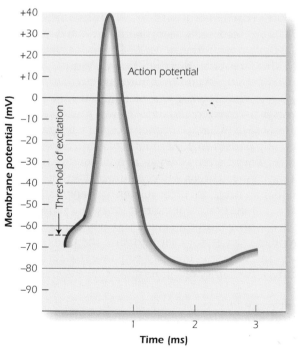

FIGURE 3.8

Action Potential. When electrochemical stimulation reaches a neuron's threshold of excitation, the neuron generates an action potential. During an action potential, ions swiftly cross the membrane of the neuron.

described in the next section). The receptor sites on the postsynaptic neuron are specialized. Each kind is affected by only a certain kind of neurotransmitter.

Stated simply, here is the sequence of interneuronal communication (see Figure 3.9):

1. One neuron ("Neuron A") releases a neurotransmitter from its terminal buttons.
2. The neurotransmitter crosses the synapse and reaches the receptors in the dendrites (or soma) of another neuron ("Neuron B").
3. The dendrites of Neuron B are stimulated by the neurotransmitters Neuron B receives from Neuron A until Neuron B reaches its own distinctive threshold of excitation. The effects of these neurotransmitters are additive, growing as their quantities increase.
4. At Neuron B's threshold of excitation, the action potential travels down its axon.
5. When Neuron B's action potential reaches Neuron B's terminal buttons, Neuron B releases its own neurotransmitter into the next synapse (perhaps with Neuron C), and so on.

Any given synapse usually has numerous, often hundreds, of connections among neurons. Dendritic trees branch out to receive messages from many axons (see Figure 3.10). Furthermore, the receiving mem-

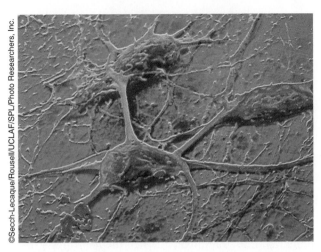

FIGURE 3.10

Dendrites. Dendrites are the primary structures by which neurons receive communications from other cells. They do this via distinctive receptors on their external membranes. The multibranched dendrites resemble tree branches and are named for the Greek word for "tree."

branes of each postsynaptic neuron have numerous receptor sites for neurotransmitters. Neurotransmitters and receptors operate like keys and keyholes. Each receptor has a different shape, like a keyhole, and the distinctive shape of a given chemical is like a key. When the shape of the key matches the shape of the keyhole, the receptor responds.

EXCITATORY AND INHIBITORY MESSAGES

Different receptor sites respond distinctively to the messages of neurotransmitters. The message received is either of excitation or inhibition. Many receptors are *excited* by the neurotransmitters they contact in the synapse. They thereby *increase* the likelihood that the postsynaptic (receiving) neurons will reach their own threshold of excitation. Other receptors, however, are actually *inhibited* by the neurotransmitters they receive. They thereby *decrease* the probability that the postsynaptic neurons will reach their threshold of excitation. That is, for a given neurotransmitter, certain receptor sites on some neurons may be excited, and certain other receptor sites on other neurons may be inhibited. Excitatory receptors on the postsynaptic neurons excite the neuron's response to neurotransmitters. Inhibitory receptors inhibit the response.

REUPTAKE

What happens to unused transmitter chemicals? In reuptake, excess neurotransmitters are reabsorbed by the terminal buttons. The next cell is thereby spared overstimulation. The neuron that released the substance can then store it for future use. The second, less common mechanism is *enzymatic deactivation*. This

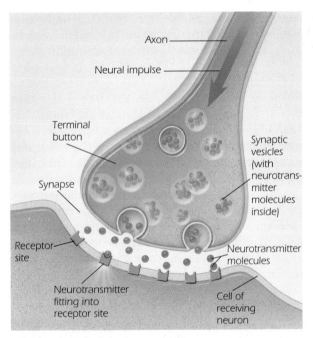

FIGURE 3.9

Neural Transmission. A neural impulse flows from the axon of a neuron to the axon's terminal buttons, instigating the release of neurotransmitter substances, which bind to specific receptor sites that provide a fit to them. The relationship is like a key opening only a specific kind of lock.

SYNAPTIC BASES FOR LEARNING AND MEMORY

As an undergraduate student in 1963–1964, I worked with Dr. James McGaugh, who had just made a major scientific discovery about long-term memory: It could be improved or weakened during the time it takes to form. Memory is therefore an ongoing process rather than a single event, and it can be studied from a physiological perspective. Previously, most researchers tried to determine what parts of the brain are related to various types of memory, usually by destroying brain regions in laboratory animals. Now we could ask, What happens in the brain when a memory is formed? I decided to work on this problem and, while I've made some progress, I haven't completely solved it, nor has any other researcher, but we are getting there. My work shows that, like the early brain organization that results from developmental experience, much adult memory involves changes in the synapses through which neurons communicate.

Rats raised in challenging, object-rich environments are called EC ("environmental complexity") rats. A rat raised with others in an ordinary cage is an SC ("social cage") rat. One raised alone is an IC ("individual cage") rat. My research was initially stimulated by the following findings:

1. Synapses in rats' visual cortices changed when the rats first saw patterns.
2. Regions of EC rats' cerebral cortices grew larger than those of SC rats.
3. EC rats performed better than SC or IC rats on complex behavioral tasks such as maze learning.

As a graduate student, I was fortunate to be exposed to molecular biology by Arthur Yuwiler, and to brain anatomy by Shawn Schapiro and Arnold Scheibel. As a professor with my first lab group, I used electron microscopy, the "gold standard" for

William T. Greenough, *Professor of Psychology at the University of Illinois, Urbana-Champaign, where he has taught since 1968, is an authority on the effects of experience (including physical exercise) and learning on the structure and function of the mammalian brain. His work in the 1970s and 1980s on the effects on the brain of being raised in a complex environment revolutionized thinking about brain plasticity; it is the primary basis for the current belief that memory involves formation and modification of synapses. He received his BA degree from the University of Oregon and MA and PhD degrees from UCLA.*

anatomical research, to study synapses in rats. We also used an optical microscope to study whole nerve cells. We found that the dendrites, the parts of neurons that receive most synaptic input, were most extensive in the visual cortices of EC rats. EC rats also had larger synapses than SC or IC rats in the visual cortex. We hypothesized that this was a result of their greater opportunity for learning. Later we confirmed that there were more synapses per neuron in the visual cortices of EC rats, and this is probably the more important correlate of long-term memory.

When we examined other types of brain tissue, we found that EC rats had more blood vessels and more supportive glial cells in the visual cortex than other rats. This indicated that *plasticity*, the ability of cells to change in response to how they are used, is a fairly general property of brain tissues and not a special property of neurons. We also found that dendritic fields expanded in animals trained on mazes or taught such motor skills as how to reach into a tube for food. When we put a single opaque contact lens on a rat for maze learning, or trained only one forepaw to reach for food, the neuronal changes were appropriately lateralized to one side of the brain. This indicated that they arose specifically from the training.

To make sure that the neuronal changes reflected *learning* rather than simple activity, we compared rats that had learned motor skills on a difficult elevated obstacle course with others that had merely exercised in an activity wheel or on a treadmill without learning much. We found that the learners formed additional synapses with no increase in blood vessels, and that the exercisers formed additional blood vessels with no increase in synapses. Thus, synapse formation was associated with learning and blood vessel formation was associated with stamina, the capacity for sustained activity.

Research Methods Are Key to Success

Electron microscopy is one of many technical procedures I have learned. It is important to master whatever methods are necessary to answer critical research questions, and not be limited to the techniques you already know well. Training in psychology provides an enormous advantage by emphasizing rigorous experimental methods, balanced research designs, and appropriate statistical analyses—areas that may receive less attention in other fields. Some disciplines, particularly the biological sciences, provide valuable measurement techniques that can be used in psychological research.

process uses *enzymes*—proteins that *catalyze*, or bring about, chemical reactions—to break apart the neurotransmitter or neuromodulator and thereby make it inactive.

An additional kind of mechanism also may affect interneuronal processing. An *autoreceptor* sometimes can be found at the tip of the axon of the presynaptic neuron. An autoreceptor is sensitive to the neurotransmitter released by the axon. It appears that some of the transmitter substance can make its way back to the autoreceptor and provide feedback to it. This feedback possibly reduces further release of the neurotransmitter (Kalsner, 1990).

NEUROTRANSMITTERS AND NEUROMODULATORS

Although scientists already know about hundreds of chemicals involved in neurotransmission, it seems likely that we have yet to identify all of them. Medical and psychological researchers are working to discover and understand these chemicals and how they interact with drugs, foods, moods, abilities, and perceptions. Although we know quite a bit about the mechanics of communication in neurons, we still know relatively little about how the nervous system's chemical activity relates to psychological states. However, we have gained some insight into how several chemicals affect our psychological functioning. See Table 3.1 for a list of some major neurotransmitters and their functions.

The key neurotransmitters are often termed *classical neurotransmitters* because they were among the first to be discovered. They include **acetylcholine (ACh),** which is synthesized from the choline in our diet (found in large quantities in milk, eggs, liver, and peanuts, and often classified as part of the Vitamin-B complex). Also included are dopamine, epinephrine, and norepinephrine, which are synthesized from dietary tyrosine (found in large quantities in milk, eggs, cornmeal, and soybeans). Finally, the neurotransmitters include serotonin, which is synthesized from dietary tryptophan (found in relatively large quantities in milk, eggs, and soybeans). These classical neurotransmitters account for only a small fraction of the transmission sites in the brain. The most common neurotransmitters are excitatory amino acids, glutamate, and gamma-aminobutyric acid (GABA) (discussed below).

Acetylcholine excites the neuronal **receptors,** which are protein molecules in the postsynaptic membrane that receive the neurotransmitters. Because ACh has been found in the hippocampus, an area known to be involved in memory (Squire, 1987), acetylcholine is believed to be involved in memory function. Researchers are currently trying to find out whether ACh is somehow blocked from action in the brains of persons who have *Alzheimer's disease*, which causes devastating loss of memory. ACh is also found in various sites throughout the body. It can excite the PNS to contract the skeletal muscles, leading to movement, or it can inhibit the neurons in the muscles of the heart.

Dopamine (DA) seems to influence such important activities as movement, attention, and learning. Although most receptors for dopamine are inhibitory, some are excitatory. In persons with *Parkinson's disease*, a particular group of neurons that produce dopamine degenerates, causing tremors, rigidity of limbs, and difficulty in maintaining balance. Neurons synthesize dopamine through enzyme actions. One enzyme adds a chemical ingredient to tyrosine to form L-dopa. Then

TABLE 3.1
CONCEPT REVIEW

Some Major Neurotransmitters

Transmitter	Function
Acetylcholine (ACh)	Excites the neuronal receptors; involved in memory function; can excite the peripheral nervous system to contract the skeletal muscles, leading to movement; can inhibit the neurons in the muscles of the heart. Action may be blocked in persons who have Alzheimer's disease.
Dopamine (DA)	Influences movement, attention, and learning; involved in pleasurable responses. Deficit associated with Parkinson's disease; excess associated with schizophrenia.
Serotonin (5-HT)	Relates to arousal and sleep as well as to regulation of mood, appetite, and sensitivity to pain; can inhibit dreaming and produce anxiety.
Gamma-aminobutyric acid (GABA)	Has direct inhibitory effects on axons, thereby increasing the threshold of excitation. Imbalances in the amino acid neurotransmitters, including GABA, have been linked to seizures, Huntington's chorea (an inherited neurological disorder), and the fatal effects of tetanus, a serious bacterially caused disease characterized by painful muscular contractions.

another enzyme removes a different chemical constituent from L-dopa to form dopamine. There is no easy way to get dopamine to the brain, but physicians have been able to give Parkinson's sufferers synthetic L-dopa. This substance is rapidly converted by the remaining dopamine-producing neurons to produce more dopamine. Unfortunately, it also is possible to get too much of a good neurotransmitter: Schizophrenia appears to be associated with too much dopamine. Drugs used to treat schizophrenia often inhibit dopamine production (Wurtman, 1999). Similarly, overdoses of L-dopa in the treatment of Parkinson's disease can result in overproduction of dopamine, which can lead to symptoms of schizophrenia. Further synthesis of tyrosine produces norepinephrine and epinephrine, which appear to be involved in the regulation of alertness.

Serotonin (5-HT) appears to be related to arousal and sleep as well as to regulation of mood, appetite, and sensitivity to pain (Rockland, 2000). Although serotonin has an excitatory effect on a few receptor sites, it is usually an inhibitory neurotransmitter, and its behavioral outcomes are generally inhibitory as well. Among other actions, serotonin inhibits dreaming. The mood-altering drug lysergic acid diethylamide (LSD) inhibits the actions of serotonin. LSD can accumulate in the brain and overstimulate neurons, leading to feelings of well-being but also to hallucinations—in effect, waking dreams. Serotonin also can produce anxiety. Mice that lack certain serotonin receptors (and hence are unable to process serotonin) show reduced anxiety. They are hyperactive during their entire life span (Brunner, Buhot, Hen, & Hofer, 1999).

Other primary neurotransmitters are glutamate (glutamic acid), aspartate, glycine, and gamma-aminobutyric acid (GABA), which is synthesized from glutamate by the simple removal of one chemical constituent. These neurotransmitters are particularly interesting because they appear to have both a particular effect when acting on specific neuronal receptor sites and general neuromodulating effects. For example, glutamate seems to have direct excitatory effects on the axons of postsynaptic neurons; it thereby lowers the threshold of excitation. GABA seems to have direct inhibitory effects on axons; it thereby increases the threshold of excitation. Imbalances in the amino-acid neurotransmitters, as this group is called, have been linked to seizures, Huntington's chorea (an inherited neurological disorder), and the fatal effects of tetanus, a serious bacterially caused disease characterized by painful muscular contractions.

Although many neurotransmitters pass through brain tissue, a *blood–brain barrier* prevents most other substances from entering the brain. The purpose of this barrier is to prevent potential toxins from destroying brain tissue. In the process of evolution, organisms that have such a barrier have an advantage over other organisms without the barrier in their potential to survive and reproduce.

To make matters even more complicated, the terminal buttons of some neurons also release chemical substances besides neurotransmitters. **Neuromodulators** enhance or diminish the responsivity of the postsynaptic neuron, either by directly affecting the axon or by affecting the sensitivity of the receptor sites.

To summarize, many presynaptic neurons release neurotransmitters and neuromodulators into the synapse. Some postsynaptic receptors are excited and others are inhibited. Furthermore, the degree of excitation or inhibition is influenced by the actions of the neuromodulators, which either enhance or diminish the responsivity of the postsynaptic neurons. In order for the postsynaptic neuron to fire, the overall balance of excitatory and inhibitory responses must reach the neuron's threshold level of excitation. When you think about all that is involved in getting one neuron to fire, it seems a miracle that any of us can think at all. But, in fact, the time it takes for a given message to cross the synapse can be as brief as half a millisecond or as long as a second or more. As you process the words on this page, many thousands of interacting neurons are working to help you understand just what it is that the text is telling you about these neurons.

This description of neurotransmission and neurotransmitters may seem complex, but it drastically oversimplifies the intricacies of the neuronal communication that constantly takes place in the nervous system, especially in the brain, to which we turn next.

✓ CONCEPT CHECK 2

1. Which of the following is *not* a type of neuron?
   a. sensory neuron
   b. motor neuron
   c. interneuron
   d. intraneuron
2. The space across which neurotransmitters cross is called the
   a. terminal button.
   b. axon.
   c. synapse.
   d. dendrite.
3. A neuron has just fired and is completely unable to fire again. Most likely it is in the _____ refractory period.
   a. absolute
   b. relative
   c. compensated
   d. final

THE STRUCTURES AND FUNCTIONS OF THE BRAIN

How do you think the brain and its various parts function to produce feelings, thoughts, and behaviors?

The brain has three major regions: hindbrain, midbrain, and forebrain (see Figure 3.11). These labels do not reflect exact locations in an adult's or even a child's head. Rather, the terms come from the front-to-back physical order of these parts in a developing embryo's nervous system. This system is formed from the *neural tube*, a primitive structure that develops into the brain and the spinal cord. The **hindbrain** is near the back of the neck; the **midbrain** is between the forebrain and the hindbrain; and the **forebrain** is near what becomes the face (see Figure 3.12a). The remainder of the neural tube becomes the spinal cord (see Figure 3.12b). During development, the relative orientations change. The forebrain becomes almost a cap on top of the midbrain and hindbrain. Nonetheless, the terms are used to designate areas of the fully developed brain. Figure 3.12 shows the changing locations and relationships of the hindbrain,

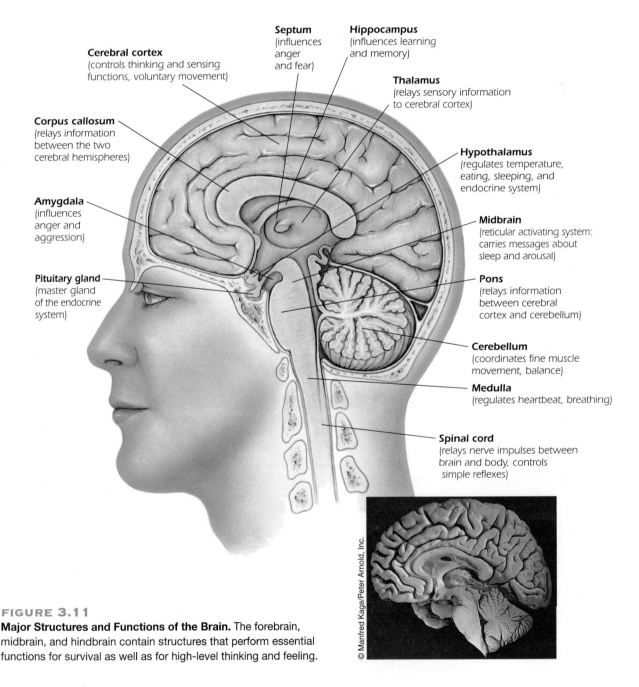

Cerebral cortex
(controls thinking and sensing functions, voluntary movement)

Septum
(influences anger and fear)

Hippocampus
(influences learning and memory)

Thalamus
(relays sensory information to cerebral cortex)

Corpus callosum
(relays information between the two cerebral hemispheres)

Hypothalamus
(regulates temperature, eating, sleeping, and endocrine system)

Amygdala
(influences anger and aggression)

Midbrain
(reticular activating system: carries messages about sleep and arousal)

Pituitary gland
(master gland of the endocrine system)

Pons
(relays information between cerebral cortex and cerebellum)

Cerebellum
(coordinates fine muscle movement, balance)

Medulla
(regulates heartbeat, breathing)

Spinal cord
(relays nerve impulses between brain and body, controls simple reflexes)

© Manfred Kage/Peter Arnold, Inc.

FIGURE 3.11

Major Structures and Functions of the Brain. The forebrain, midbrain, and hindbrain contain structures that perform essential functions for survival as well as for high-level thinking and feeling.

the midbrain, and the forebrain over the course of development.

We now consider each of these major regions in turn, starting from the hindbrain and working our way roughly upward and forward.

THE HINDBRAIN

The hindbrain is the site of some of the most primitive and basic functions that the brain controls. It comprises the medulla oblongata, the pons, and the cerebellum. The **medulla oblongata** is an elongated structure at the point where the spinal cord enters the skull and joins with the brain. It helps to keep us alive by entirely controlling the heart rate and largely controlling breathing, swallowing, and digestion. The medulla is also where neurons from the right side of the body cross over to the left side of the brain, and neurons from the left side of the body cross over to the right side of the brain. The **pons** serves as a kind of relay station, containing neurons that pass signals from one part of the brain to another. *Pons* means "bridge," which reflects the fact that many axons in the pons cross from one side of the brain to the other side. The pons also contains neurons that serve parts of the head and face. The **cerebellum** controls bodily coordination, balance, and muscle tone. If the cerebellum is damaged, movement becomes jerky and disjointed, posing a challenge to the midbrain function. Recent evidence suggests that the cerebellum also plays a role in higher-order functions.

THE MIDBRAIN

The midbrain is less important in mammals than in nonmammals, where it is the main source of control for visual and auditory information. In mammals these

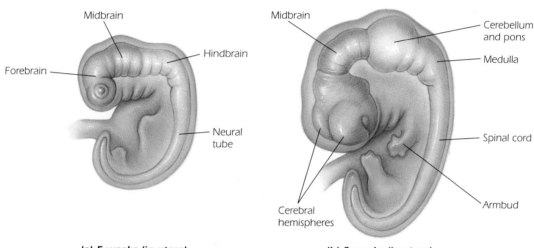

(a) 5 weeks (in utero)

(b) 8 weeks (in utero)

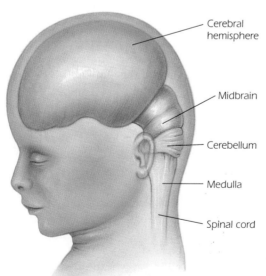

(c) 7 months (in utero)

FIGURE 3.12

Neural Development. Over the course of embryonic and fetal development the brain becomes more highly specialized; the locations and relative positions of the hindbrain, midbrain, and forebrain change from conception to full term.

TABLE 3.2
CONCEPT REVIEW

The Three Major Regions of the Brain. The brain has three major regions, each with distinct structures and functions.

Region of the Brain	Major Structures Within the Regions	Functions of the Structures
Hindbrain	• **Cerebellum** • **Pons** (contains part of the RAS) • **Medulla oblongata**	• Essential to balance, coordination, and muscle tone • Involved in consciousness (sleep, arousal); bridges neural transmissions from one part of the brain to another; involved with facial nerves • Juncture at which nerves cross from one side of the body to the opposite side of the brain; involved in cardiorespiratory function, digestion, and swallowing
Midbrain	• **Superior colliculi** (on top) • **Inferior colliculi** (below) • **Reticular activating system** (extends into the hindbrain) • **Gray matter, red nucleus, substantia nigra, ventral region**	• Involved in vision (especially visual reflexes) • Involved in hearing • Important in controlling consciousness (sleep, arousal), attention, cardiorespiratory function, and movement • Important in controlling movement

Forebrain	• **Cerebral cortex** (outer layer of the cerebral hemispheres)
	
	• **Limbic system**
	  Hippocampus
	  Amygdala
	  Septum
	• **Thalamus**
	
	• **Hypothalamus** (sometimes viewed as part of the limbic system)
		• Receives and processes sensory information, thinking, and other cognitive processing; plans and sends motor information
		• Learning, emotions, and motivation
		  Learning and memory
		  Anger and aggression
		  Anger and fear
		• Primary relay station for sensory information coming into the brain; transmits information to the correct regions of the cerebral cortex
		• Controls the endocrine system (described later in this chapter); controls the autonomic nervous system; regulates internal temperature, appetite, thirst, and other key functions; involved in regulation of behavior related to species survival; plays a role in controlling consciousness (see reticular activating system); involved in emotions, sexual response, pleasure, pain, and stress reactions

functions are mostly taken over by the forebrain. But the midbrain does help to control eye movements and coordination. Table 3.2 lists several structures and functions of the midbrain.

By far the most important structure of the midbrain is the reticular activating system (RAS), a network of neurons essential to the regulation of sleep, wakefulness, arousal, and even attention, to some extent, as well as to such vital functions as heart rate and breathing (see Figure 3.13). The RAS actually extends into the hindbrain and includes the medulla and pons.

The midbrain, the hindbrain, and the thalamus and hypothalamus, both located in the forebrain, form the brainstem, which connects the brain to the spinal cord. Brainstem function is central to life. Electrical stimulation of the brain can cause confrontational or avoidance responses (Bandler & Shipley, 1994; Rockland, 2000).

Physicians determine brain death on the basis of brainstem function. Even more central to our experience of life is the functioning of the forebrain.

THE FOREBRAIN

The forebrain is the region located toward the top and front of the brain (see Table 3.2 and Figure 3.11). The largest area of the brain, it has four parts: the limbic system, the thalamus, the hypothalamus (often viewed as part of the limbic system), and the cerebral cortex. The most complex mental processing takes place here.

THE LIMBIC SYSTEM

The limbic system is important to emotion, motivation, and learning. Animals such as fish and reptiles, which have relatively undeveloped limbic systems, respond to the environment almost exclusively by instinct. Mammals, especially humans, have more developed limbic systems, which seem to allow us to suppress instinctive responses (such as the impulse to strike someone who accidentally causes us pain). Our limbic systems make us better able to adapt our behavior flexibly in response to our changing environment.

The limbic system involves three central interconnected cerebral structures: the hippocampus, the amygdala, and the septum. The **hippocampus** plays an essential role in memory formation (N. J. Cohen & Eichenbaum, 1993; Dusek & Eichenbaum, 1997; Eichenbaum, 1997, 1999; Gluck, 1996; McClelland, McNaughton, & O'Reilly, 1995; Schacter & Tulving, 1994). People who have suffered damage to or removal of the hippocampus can still recall existing memories (for example, they can recognize old friends and places), but they are unable to form new memories after the time of the brain damage. You could converse with such a person every day for a year, and each time the two of you met you would be entirely unfamiliar (Squire, 1987). Disruption in the hippocampus appears to result in deficits in declarative memory (i.e., memory for facts) but not in procedural memory (i.e., memory for courses of action) (Rockland, 2000; Squire, 1992). The 2000 film *Memento* is about a man who is trying to hunt down the man who raped and killed his wife. But he lost his long-term memory and thus needs external aids to try to keep track of what he has done and what he has left to do.

Below the hippocampus is the **amygdala**, which plays a role in emotions, including anger and aggression (Canli, Sivers, Whitfield, Gotlib, & Gabrieli, 2002). The **septum** is involved in anger and fear (Frackowiak et al., 1997; Gloor, 1997; Rockland, 2000; Stefannaci, 1999). Monkeys that have lesions (damage) in some areas of the limbic system seem to lack inhibition and are easily enraged (Adolphs, Tranel, Damasio, & Damasio, 1994; Frackowiak et al., 1997). Monkeys with damage to other areas of the limbic system cannot be provoked to anger even when attacked. Their hostility seems to have been erased. The amygdala also may be involved in long-term storage of

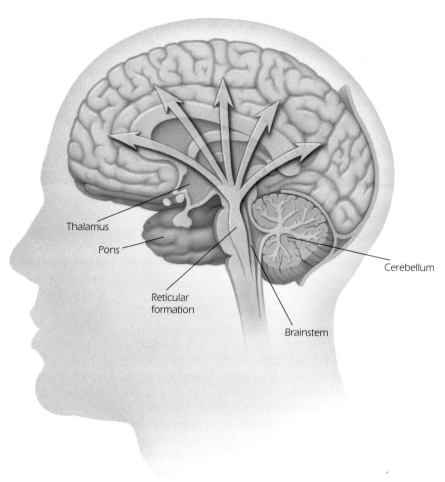

FIGURE 3.13

Reticular Activating System. The reticular activating system is important in regulating sleep and waking and arousal in general.

memories carried out in other parts of the brain (Bianchin, Mello, Souza, Medina, & Izquierdo, 1999).

THE THALAMUS

The **thalamus** is a two-lobed structure near the center of the brain, at about the level of the eyes, just beneath the cerebral cortex. The thalamus relays the incoming sensory information to the appropriate region of the cortex through *projection fibers*, neurons that extend from one part of the brain to another. To accommodate all the information that must be sorted out, the thalamus is divided into groups of neurons with similar functions, called *nuclei*. The nuclei receive sensory information and project it to the cerebral cortex. For example, the lateral geniculate nucleus receives information from the visual-receptor neurons via the optic nerves. It then projects the information to the visual cortex, permitting us to see. The thalamus also helps control sleep and waking. Both the thalamus and the reticular activating system are essential to our conscious awareness and control. Malfunction of the thalamus can result in pain, tremor, amnesia, impairment of language, and disruption in the sleeping–waking cycle (Rockland, 2000; Steriade, Jones, & McCormick, 1997).

The **basal ganglia** constitute a set of structures close to the thalamus and hypothalamus that are involved in control of movements as well as in judgments and decisions that require minimal amounts of thought. In conditions where the basal ganglia deteriorate, such as Parkinson's and Huntington's diseases, individuals show diverse symptoms. These include impaired movement, attention disorders, and memory and thinking deficits.

THE HYPOTHALAMUS

The **hypothalamus,** located at the base of the forebrain beneath the thalamus, is roughly the size of a kidney bean and controls water balance in the tissues and bloodstream as well as many other functions of the autonomic nervous system (see Table 3.2 for more information). The hypothalamus, which interacts with and is often viewed as part of the limbic system, also regulates behavior related to species survival: fighting, feeding, fleeing, and mating. It makes sense, therefore, that the hypothalamus is also active in regulating emotions and reactions to stress. Mild electrical stimulation in particular areas of the hypothalamus causes pleasurable sensations. Stimulation in nearby areas causes sensations of pain.

THE CEREBRAL CORTEX AND HEMISPHERES

The *cerebral cortex* forms the outer layer of the right and left halves of the brain, the cerebral hemispheres (Davidson & Hugdahl, 1995; Gazzaniga, 1995; Gazzaniga & Hutsler, 1999; Hellige, 1993, 1995; Levy, 2000; Mangun et al., 1994). The cerebral hemispheres and the cerebral cortex together make up the **cerebrum,** that essential part of the human brain that sets us apart from other members of the animal kingdom by allowing us a greater range of psychological functioning and, in particular, thought.

The **cerebral cortex** is a 2-millimeter-deep layer of tissue that covers the surface of the brain, much as the bark of a tree wraps around the trunk. In humans, the cerebral cortex is highly *convoluted*, containing many folds. If it were smoothed out, it would cover about 2 square feet. The cortex makes up 80% of the human brain. The cerebral cortex is responsible for our ability to plan, coordinate thoughts and actions, perceive visual and sound patterns, use language, and in general think.

The surface of the cerebral cortex is grayish because it contains the gray neurons that process the incoming and outgoing information. The cerebral cortex is sometimes referred to as the *gray matter* of the brain. In contrast, the underlying *white matter* of the brain's interior contains mostly white neurons, which conduct information. The white matter is made up of axons that are covered with myelin. The gray matter is composed of axons that are not so covered. Both the white and the gray matter are essential to cognitive abilities such as reasoning and decision making.

The cerebral cortex is actually the outer layer of the two rounded halves of the brain, the left and right **cerebral hemispheres.** Although the two hemispheres look similar, they function quite differently. The left hemisphere is specialized for some kinds of activity, the right for other kinds. Much information is transmitted from one side of the body (e.g., the left) to the part of the brain on the opposite side (e.g., the right) (see Figure 3.14). Note that not all information transmission is *contralateral*, occurring or appearing on the opposite side. Some same-side, or *ipsilateral*, transmission occurs as well.

Despite this general tendency for contralateral specialization, the hemispheres do communicate with each other. The **corpus callosum,** a dense body of nerve fibers, connects the two cerebral hemispheres (see Figure 3.15). Once information has reached one hemisphere, the corpus callosum allows it to travel across to the other hemisphere without difficulty. Research shows that when the corpus callosum is severed, cognitive functioning, such as learning and memory performance, is impaired (Jha, Kroll, Baynes, & Gazzaniga, 1997).

How did psychologists find out that the two hemispheres have different responsibilities?

THE HEMISPHERES OF THE BRAIN

Paul Broca (1824–1880) was a major figure in the study of hemispheric specialization. At a meeting of the French Society of Anthropology in 1861, Broca noted that a patient of his with *aphasia*, a loss of speech as a result of brain damage, was later shown to have a lesion in the left hemisphere of the brain. Despite an initially cool response to his ideas, Broca was soon involved in a heated controversy. The issue under dispute was whether functions, particularly speech, are indeed localized in particular areas of the brain rather than generalized over the entire brain. By 1864 Broca was convinced that the left hemisphere of the brain is critical for speech. Others before him had proposed this view, and the idea has held up over time. **Broca's area,** a structure in the left frontal lobe, is involved in the movements of the mouth needed for speech. It is also involved in our ability to speak grammatically. Curiously, although peo-

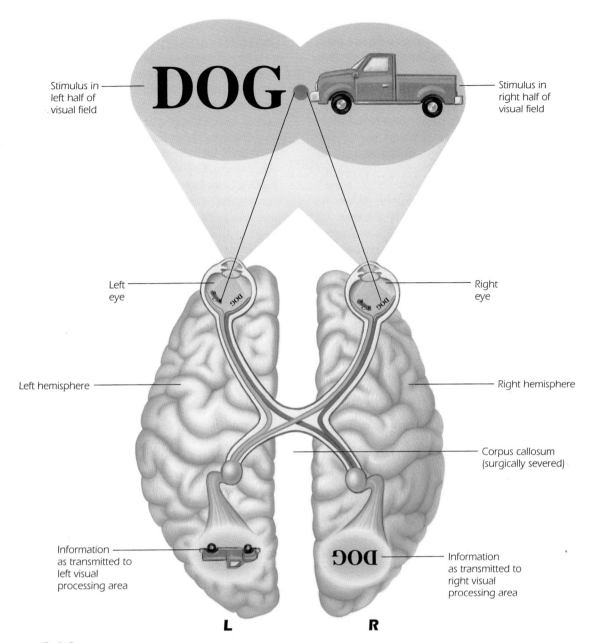

Stimulus in left half of visual field

Stimulus in right half of visual field

Left eye

Right eye

Left hemisphere

Right hemisphere

Corpus callosum (surgically severed)

Information as transmitted to left visual processing area

Information as transmitted to right visual processing area

L

R

FIGURE 3.14

Visual Input to a Split Brain. Input received from the left visual field reaches the right side of each eye and is transmitted to the right hemisphere of the brain. Input received from the right visual field reaches the left side of each eye and is transmitted to the left hemisphere of the brain. Typically, information is shared between the two hemispheres. In split-brain patients, however, the corpus callosum that connects the two hemispheres has been severed, so that information is not shared. Thus, information can be presented by an experimenter to one hemisphere without its being shared by the other hemisphere.

ple with lesions in Broca's area cannot speak fluently, they can use their voices to sing or shout.

Another important early researcher, German neurologist Carl Wernicke (1848–1905), studied language-deficient patients who could speak but whose speech made no sense. He also traced language-comprehension ability to the left hemisphere, though to a different precise location in the temporal lobe of the brain, now known as **Wernicke's area** (see Figure 3.21 p. 91).

It appears that roughly 90% of the adult population has language functions predominantly localized within the left hemisphere. More than 95% of right-handers and about 70% of left-handers have left-hemisphere dominance for language (Gazzaniga & Hutsler, 1999). For most people, the right hemisphere is largely "mute," in the sense that it has little grammatical or phonetic understanding (Levy, 2000). But it does have very good knowledge of the meanings of words and is involved in practical language use. People with damage to the right hemisphere tend to have trouble following conversations or stories, making inferences from context, and understanding metaphorical or humorous speech (Levy, 2000).

Other researchers continued in this tradition. Some studied problems such as *apraxia*, the inability to perform movements upon request. Others studied *agnosia*, the inability to recognize familiar objects, often faces. In addition to Broca's and Wernicke's case-study research and postmortem examination of brains, researchers (e.g., Penfield & Roberts, 1959) have used techniques such as stimulation by electrodes to map specific functions to particular areas. For example, following the stimulation of the speech area, people experience temporary aphasia.

SPLIT-BRAIN STUDIES

The individual most responsible for modern theory and research on hemispheric specialization is Nobel Prize–winning American psychologist Roger Sperry.

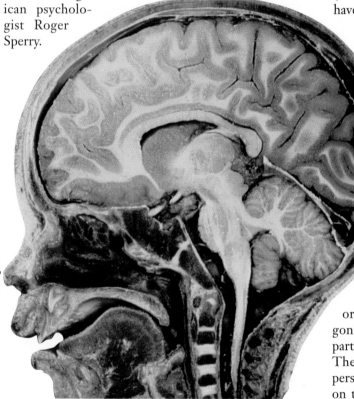

FIGURE 3.15

Corpus Callosum. This dense network of fibers, shown from the base of the brain, provides a fundamental communication link between the two cerebral hemispheres.

Sperry (1964a, 1964b) argued that each hemisphere behaves in many respects like a separate brain. In a classic experiment that supports this contention, Sperry and his colleagues severed a cat's corpus callosum (Sperry, 1964a). They then showed that information presented visually to one cerebral hemisphere of the cat was not recognizable to the other hemisphere.

Some of the most interesting information about how the human brain works, and especially about the roles of the hemispheres, has emerged from studies of humans who have epilepsy. Surgeons have severed the corpus callosum to prevent epileptic seizures from spreading from one hemisphere to the other. The operation greatly lessened the severity of the seizures, and it also resulted in a loss of communication between the two hemispheres. It is as if the person had two separate specialized brains processing different information and performing separate functions.

People who have undergone such operations are termed *split-brain* patients. Although they behave normally in many respects, in a few ways their behavior is bizarre. Instances have been reported of a person's left hand struggling against the right hand to accomplish a task such as putting on pants. One patient, angry at his wife, reached to strike her with his left hand while his right hand tried to protect her by stopping the left (Gazzaniga, 1970). Split-brain patients almost literally have two separate minds of their own.

Split-brain research reveals fascinating possibilities about the ways we think. Many investigators have argued that language is completely localized in the left hemisphere and that *visuospatial* ability, skills involving visual and spatial orientation and perception, is localized in the right hemisphere (Farah, 1988a, 1988b; Gazzaniga, 1985; Zaidel, 1983). For example, the ability to understand this sentence would be localized in the left hemisphere. But the ability to imagine what a car would look like if it were rotated 180 degrees would be localized in the right hemisphere.

Jerre Levy (one of Sperry's students) and colleagues (Levy, Trevarthen, & Sperry, 1972) probed the link between the cerebral hemispheres and visuospatial versus language-oriented tasks, using participants who had undergone split-brain surgery. In one kind of study, the participant is asked to focus on the center of a screen. Then a *chimeric face*, made up of the left side of one person's face and the right side of another's, is flashed on the screen. The participant is asked to identify what he or she saw, either verbally or by pointing to one of several normal (not chimeric) faces (see Figure 3.16). Typically, split-brain patients are unaware that they saw conflicting information in the two halves

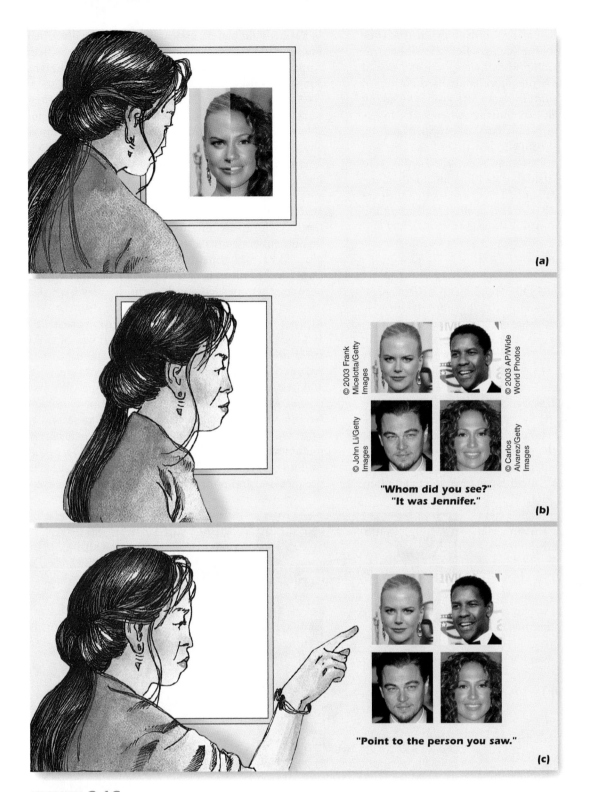

FIGURE 3.16
Chimeric Faces. Research on split-brain patients reveals that each hemisphere of the brain processes images and other information distinctively. (a) A composite photograph of two different faces is flashed before a split-brain participant. (b) When shown a group of photographs and asked to pick out the person shown in the composite, the participant will say it is the face from the right half of the composite. (c) When asked to point out which one the participant originally saw, she will indicate the picture from the left side of the composite. (After Levy, Trevarthen, & Sperry, 1972)

of the picture. When using words, they say that they saw the right half of the picture. Because of the contralateral association between hemisphere and side of the body, the left hemisphere controls their verbal processing of visual information—their speaking about what they saw. In contrast, when asked to use their fingers to point to what they saw, participants choose the image from the left half of the picture. This finding indicates that the right hemisphere appears to control spatial processing, including pointing out visual information. Thus, the task that the participants are asked to perform is crucial in determining what image they think was shown.

HEMISPHERIC SPECIALIZATION

Do the two sides of the brain really have such distinct functions? Additional split-brain research (Gazzaniga, 1985; Gazzaniga & LeDoux, 1978) supports the view that visuospatial processing occurs primarily in the right hemisphere and language processing primarily in the left hemisphere. Some researchers, however, hold that the right hemisphere may have some role in language processing. Michael Gazzaniga (1985; Gazzaniga, Ivry, & Mangun, 1998) has argued that the brain, especially the right hemisphere, is organized into relatively independent functioning units that work in parallel. According to Gazzaniga, the many discrete units of the mind operate relatively independently, often outside of conscious awareness. While these independent and often subconscious operations are taking place, the left hemisphere tries to interpret them. Even when the left hemisphere perceives that the individual is behaving in a way that does not intrinsically make any particular sense, it still finds a way to assign some meaning to that behavior. For example, a person who senselessly attacks someone who is helpless may justify his or her behavior as giving the person what he or she deserves.

Some biopsychological researchers have tried to determine whether the two hemispheres think differently. Levy (1974) found some evidence that the left hemisphere tends to process information _analytically_ (piece by piece, usually in a sequence) and the right hemisphere _holistically_ (as a whole, all at once). In another study, Schiffer, Zaidel, Bogen, and Chasan-Taber (1998) found that the right hemisphere

of a split-brain patient appeared to be more disturbed than the left by childhood memories of being bullied. At present, the precise distinctions between the right and left hemispheres have not been firmly established. As always, alternative scientific interpretations of the same data make science both frustrating and exciting.

You need to be aware of outrageous claims that are sometimes made about hemispheric specialization. You might hear someone referred to as a "right-brain" or a "left-brain" individual, often in reference to whether the person is more holistic ("right brain") or analytic ("left brain") in his or her approach to problems. Such expressions are purely metaphorical and do not represent any biological reality. Except for people who have extremely serious brain damage, everyone uses both hemispheres and the interaction between them in accomplishing most everyday tasks.

© SEEING AND HEARING IN JAPANESE SCHOOLS

Cross-cultural research offers yet another way of looking at how visuospatial and sound-based language symbols are localized in the brain. In school, Japanese children study two forms of written language. The first is _kanji_, which is based on Chinese ideographs and conveys an entire idea within each symbol. The second is _kana_, which is based on phonetic syllables and can be used for writing foreign words (see Figure 3.17). In the 1970s, Japanese researchers started wondering whether the pictorial and phonetic forms might be processed

FIGURE 3.17

Pictures versus Symbols. Japanese schoolchildren study two forms of written language: _kanji_ and _kana_. _Kanji_ is based on Chinese ideographs and conveys an entire idea within each symbol; _kana_ is based on phonetic syllables. In the 1970s, Japanese researchers studied whether the pictorial and phonetic forms are processed differently in the two hemispheres of the brain. Some concluded that the phonetic-based _kana_ is processed in the left hemisphere, while the picture-based _kanji_ is processed in both hemispheres.

differently in the two hemispheres of the brain. Some concluded that the phonetic-based *kana* are processed entirely in the left hemisphere, while the picture-based *kanji* are processed in both the left and the right hemispheres (Shibazaki, 1983; Shimada & Otsuka, 1981; Sibitani, 1980; Tsunoda, 1979). To explore and understand the diverse abilities and functions of the human brain, researchers must also study the rich diversity of the human community.

THE FOUR LOBES OF THE BRAIN

Hemispheric specialization is only one way to view the various parts of the cortex. Another way divides it into four *lobes*: frontal, parietal, temporal, and occipital (shown in Figure 3.21, p. 91). These lobes are not distinct units. Rather, they are arbitrary anatomical regions named for the bones of the skull lying directly over them. We are able to distinguish some local specializations among the lobes, but they also interact. Roughly speaking, the frontal lobe is the location of higher thought processes, such as abstract reasoning and motor processing. *Somatosensory* processing of sensations in the skin and muscles of the body takes place in the **parietal lobe.** Auditory processing is in the **temporal lobe.** Visual processing occurs in the **occipital lobe.**

Sensory processing occurs in the **projection areas,** where the neurons that contain sensory information from the eyes, ears, lips, tongue, nose, and skin senses go to the thalamus. Then, from the thalamus, they are projected to the appropriate area in the relevant lobe. Similarly, the projection areas relay motor information downward through the spinal cord, via the PNS, to the appropriate muscles to direct their movement. What happens when sensory information reaches the lobes of the brain? Consider first what happens in the frontal lobe.

THE FRONTAL LOBE

The frontal lobe is located toward the front of the head. It contains the **primary motor cortex,** which specializes in the planning, control, and execution of movement, particularly movement involving any kind of delayed response. If your motor cortex were electrically stimulated, you would react by moving a corresponding body part, depending on where the stimulation occurred.

Control of body movements is contralateral and originates in the primary motor cortex. A similar inverse mapping occurs from top to bottom. The lower extremities of the body are represented on the upper side of the motor cortex, toward the top of the head, and the upper part of the body is represented on the lower side of the motor cortex. Information that goes to neighboring parts of the body comes from neigh-boring parts of the motor cortex. Thus, the motor cortex can be mapped to show where and in what proportions different parts of the body are represented in the brain. Such a map is often called a *homunculus,* which means "little person" (see Figure 3.18). Motor functioning works in conjunction with sensory functioning, largely controlled by the parietal lobe.

THE PARIETAL LOBE

The three other lobes are farther away from the front of the head. These lobes specialize in various kinds of sensory and perceptual activity. In the parietal lobe, for example, the **primary somatosensory cortex** receives information from the senses about pressure, texture, temperature, and pain. It is located right behind the frontal lobe's primary motor cortex. If your somatosensory cortex were electrically stimulated, you would probably report feeling as if you had been touched. The parietal lobe is also involved in attention. As with the primary motor cortex in the frontal lobe, a homunculus of the somatosensory cortex maps the parts of the body from which it receives information (see Figure 3.19).

From looking at the motor and sensory homunculi, you can see that the relation of function to form applies in the development of the motor and somatosensory cortex regions. The more we need sensitivity and fine control in a particular body part, the larger the area of cortex that is generally devoted to that part. It appears that the brain has evolved such that its form relates to its function, including the auditory function considered next.

THE TEMPORAL LOBE

The region of the cerebral cortex that pertains to hearing is in the temporal lobe, just above the ear. This lobe performs the complex auditory analysis needed in understanding speech and in listening to music. Damage to parts of the temporal lobe can cause impaired comprehension of speech, in particular, and of language, in general.

The temporal lobe is specialized. Some parts are sensitive to sounds of higher pitch, others to sounds of lower pitch. The auditory region, like other regions we have discussed, is primarily contralateral. Processing on one side of the auditory cortex depends mostly on sensory information from the ear on the opposite side. However, both sides of the auditory area have at least some representation from each ear. If your auditory cortex were stimulated electrically, you would report hearing some sort of sound. Hearing must also be coordinated with vision, which is controlled in the brain by the occipital lobe. Otherwise, you would be unable to understand movies, television, or even everyday conversations where you combine auditory and visual cues.

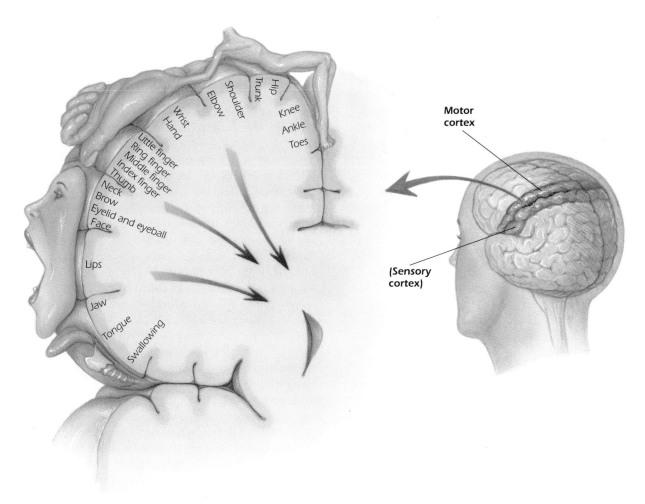

FIGURE 3.18
Homunculus of the Motor Cortex. The proportion of information received from the body's parts and sent to them can be mapped in the motor cortex of the frontal lobe.

THE OCCIPITAL LOBE

The visual region of the cerebral cortex is primarily in the occipital lobe, at the back of the head. Some neurons that carry visual information travel ipsilaterally from the left eye to the left cerebral hemisphere and from the right eye to the right cerebral hemisphere. Other neural fibers cross over the **optic chiasma**, a structure in which roughly half of the information from each eye crosses over to reach cortical areas in the contralateral hemisphere (see Figure 3.20). In particular, neurons go from the left side of the visual field for each eye to the right side of the visual cortex. Complementarily, the neurons from the right side of each eye's visual field go to the left side of the visual cortex. Electrical stimulation of the visual cortex results in the perception of random patterns of light, as when you close your eyes and gently rub your eyelids. (See Figure 3.21 for views of the cortical locations of the various lobes.)

THE ASSOCIATION AREAS

The interconnections among our senses, body movements, and thought processes are among the most complex that the brain handles. It therefore is not surprising that a great deal of the brain is devoted to handling associations among various areas and functions. **Association areas** process sensory information more elaborately than do the primary sensory areas of the brain (Van Hoesen, 1993). They are not part of the somatosensory, motor, auditory, or visual cortices.

It used to be thought that the association areas are primarily responsible for linking the activity of the sensory and motor cortices, although we now know this to be incorrect. In humans, these areas comprise roughly 75% of the cerebral cortex, although in most other animals the association areas are much smaller. More than 50% of the cortex in the primate brain is used for visual processing. Thus, the association cor-

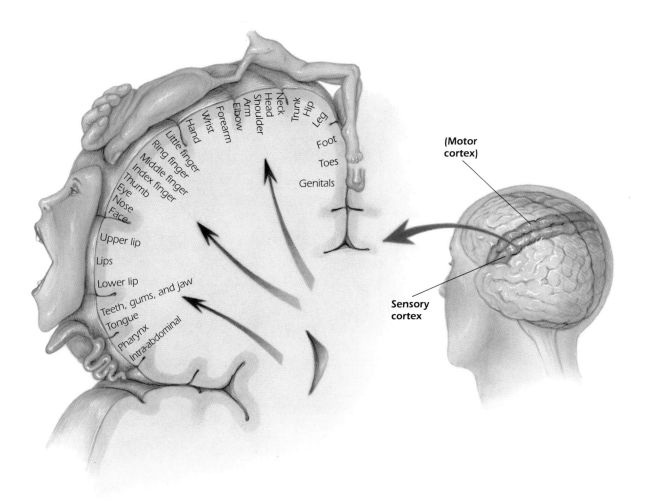

FIGURE 3.19

Homunculus of the Somatosensory Cortex. The proportion of sensory information received from the parts of the body can be mapped in the somatosensory cortex of the parietal lobe.

tex adjacent to the primary visual cortex is responsive to visual information. But it does not "associate" visual and motor information. Moreover, input to the association areas does not come exclusively from primary sensory areas of the cortex. It can come from sensory areas of the thalamus, too (Diamond, 1979, 1983). There does not appear to be any one area of the brain that "associates." Association functions are diffused throughout the brain.

The association area in the frontal lobe seems to be crucial to problem solving, planning, judgment, and personality. In a situation that calls for escape from danger, for example, people with damaged frontal lobes know that they ought to run away. Paradoxically, however, they may stand still, incapable of initiating flight. Broca's and Wernicke's speech areas, mentioned earlier in this chapter, are also located in association areas. Although their roles in thinking are not completely understood, these parts of the brain

definitely seem to be where a variety of intellectual abilities are seated.

Given all its activities, it may not surprise you to learn that although the brain typically makes up only 2.5% (one-fortieth) of the weight of an adult human body, it uses about 20% (one-fifth) of the circulating blood, 20% of the available *glucose* (the blood sugar that supplies the body with energy), and 20% of the available oxygen.

THE CASE OF PHINEAS GAGE

What we learn about the parts of the brain may seem very abstract, and it can be hard to see how the brain's various parts work together. But the brain does work as a unified whole. Nowhere is this seen more clearly than in cases of serious brain damage. Consider Phineas Gage, one of the most famous cases in neuropsychology (see Zillmer & Spiers, 2001).

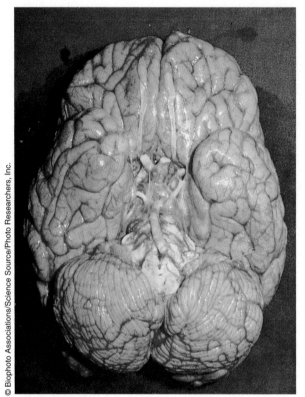

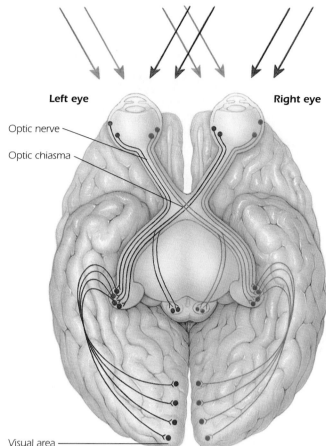

Left eye **Right eye**

Optic nerve

Optic chiasma

Visual area

FIGURE 3.20

Optic Nerves and Optic Chiasma. Some nerve fibers carry visual information ipsilaterally from each eye to each cerebral hemisphere; other fibers cross the optic chiasma and carry visual information contralaterally to the opposite hemisphere.

Gage was a railroad employee in Vermont. As he and his team were blasting through rocks, an explosion occurred. A long metal bar shot out and passed through Gage's head. The bar entered under his left cheek and exited at the top of the skull. So powerful was the blast that the bar ended up 30 meters away from Gage. One would expect such a blow to be fatal, but it wasn't. Although Gage was knocked over, he was able to get up and actually walk away from the scene of the accident. After battling the immediate physical effects of the blow, Gage appeared on the surface to have fully recovered. He had not, however.

Before the injury, Gage was relatively mature, shrewd, and clever. Although not particularly well educated, he was able to make plans and execute them. The head injury led to fairly dramatic changes in his behavior. Gage's doctor noted that whatever balance had existed between his intellect and his emotions seemed to have vanished. Gage became childish, impatient, obstinate, impulsive, and capricious, as well as profane in his language. He would make a grand plan,

only quickly to change to another grand plan. His friends observed the changes in behavior and felt that he was no longer acting like himself.

As a result of the changes in his personality, Gage was unable to regain his former position as a foreman. According to his doctor, he went to work for Phineas Barnum's Museum in New York (which exhibited people who had highly unusual physical traits), worked in a livery stable in New Hampshire, and cared for horses in Chile. His health then began to fail him, and he died in 1860.

A team of researchers (H. Damasio, Grabowski, Frank, Galaburda, & Damasio, 1994) tried to plot the trajectory of the metal bar in order to determine the kinds of brain damage that led to the observed changes in behavior. They suggested that the rod penetrated the front half of a portion of the frontal cortex as well as other parts of the brain. This portion of the frontal cortex controls planning, among other things. So the changes in Gage's behavior could be linked directly to specific parts of the brain.

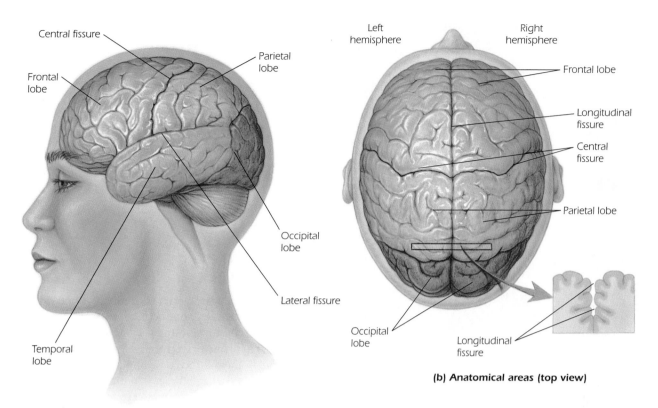

(a) Anatomical areas (left lateral view)

(b) Anatomical areas (top view)

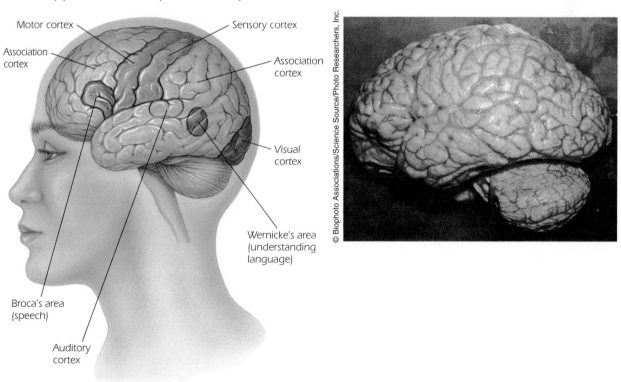

(c) Functional areas

FIGURE 3.21

Lobes of the Cerebral Cortex. The cortex is divided into the frontal, parietal, temporal, and occipital lobes. The lobes have specific functions but also interact to perform complex processes.

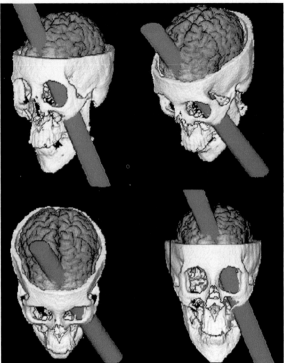

From Damasio, HJ., Grabowski T., Frank R., Galaburda AM, Damasio AR: The return of Phineas Gage: Clues about the brain from a famous patient. *Science*, 264:1102-1105, 1994. Department of Neurology and Image Analysis Facility, University of Iowa. Reproduced by permission of Dr. Hanna Damasio.

Phineas Gage contributed greatly to the history of psychology by permitting investigators to examine his brain and its functioning.

What we see as fairly unified behavioral patterns thus can be traced to individual parts of the brain and their interactions. The brain is the basis of almost all of the kinds of human behavior that psychology studies. Cases such as that of Phineas Gage remind us how extraordinary it is that an organ can have so many different parts that work together in a marvelously unified and generally adaptive way.

✓ CONCEPT CHECK 3

1. Which of the following is *not* a region of the brain?
   a. hindbrain
   b. midbrain
   c. sidebrain
   d. forebrain
2. The hippocampus is part of the
   a. limbic system.
   b. endocrine system.
   c. hindbrain.
   d. cerebellum.
3. Which of the following is *not* a lobe of the brain?
   a. temporal
   b. occipital
   c. frontal
   d. dorsal

STUDYING THE LIVING BRAIN

How can scientists study the brain in action?

It is now possible to watch the brain at work (Buckner, 2000; Posner & Raichle, 1994; B. R. Rosen, Buckner, & Dale, 1998). New research methods are greatly expanding our understanding of where brain functions are located and how they are interrelated. In the Psychology in Everyday Life box, "Seeing inside the Brain," you will learn about some of these methods.

THE ELECTROENCEPHALOGRAM (EEG)

The electrical activity of the entire living brain can be measured by the **electroencephalogram,** which sums the effects of brain activity over large areas that contain many neurons. Electrodes establish contact between the brain and the recording device. In humans, electrodes are attached directly to the scalp. In laboratory animals, microelectrodes are inserted into the brain. In either case, the minute quantifiable fluctuations of electrical activity picked up by the electrodes are amplified. They then are displayed on a computer screen as fluctuating waves. The wave patterns indicate different levels and kinds of brain activity (see Figure 3.22).

EEGs are particularly helpful for studying mental functioning, especially as it is affected by sleep, awareness, and brain disease. For example, there appears to be an overall decrease in cortical activation as measured by EEG after an individual performs various cognitive tasks (M. E. Smith, McEvoy, & Gevins, 1999). This result suggests that once a task becomes familiar, the brain no longer needs to process it as actively. EEGs also support the notion of hemispheric localization. More activity occurs in the left hemisphere during a verbal task, more in the right hemisphere during a spatial task (Kosslyn, 1988; Springer & Deutsch, 1985). Different EEG patterns also have been found in different people's emotional responses to faces (Pizzagalli, Koenig, Regard, & Lehmann, 1999).

EEG measurement is problematic, however, because it is registered as a *hash recording*. The electrical activity of many large areas is measured at once, so it is hard to sort out the exact origins of particular wave forms. For this reason, investigators have turned to **event-related potentials (ERPs),** which are measured by averaging wave forms on successive EEG recordings. In other words, an ERP is an EEG recording of a specific stimulus event in which at least some of the electrical interference has been averaged out of the data (see Figure 3.23). Event-related potentials have been used to map which parts of the brain are

PSYCHOLOGY IN EVERYDAY LIFE

SEEING INSIDE THE BRAIN

When Marta Koopmans hit a crack in the pavement in the dark and was thrown from her bike, the doctors at the emergency room were concerned about a possible head injury. She had been riding without a helmet and admitted she had "blacked out a little" for what she thought was a minute or two. She had a serious cut that required stitches above her left eye.

Brain trauma can cause swelling of the brain or bleeding in the *dura mater,* the tough membrane that is the outermost covering of the brain and spinal cord, that can put pressure on the brain. Either can result in brain damage. For centuries, the only means available for seeing the brain was through surgery or autopsy. As valuable as such studies have been and continue to be, scientists are not content merely to study the state of dead brains. As Marta's example illustrates, an organ characterized by constant dynamic activity seems to cry out for methods to study it *in vivo* (within living organisms) and noninvasively. Contemporary microscopic and biochemical techniques developed in the last half-century allow scientists to study dissected portions of the brain at increasingly precise levels of detail. The images these methods provide can help doctors pinpoint problems and injuries and also have enabled researchers to understand more about the areas of the brain where certain mental functions, such as listening to music or thinking about a math problem, take place.

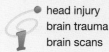
head injury
brain trauma
brain scans

---

active and to what degree, in response to familiar and unfamiliar stimuli. Helen Neville (1998) used ERPs to study people who were born deaf. She discovered that their brains are organized differently from those of hearing people. In particular, visual ERPs are substantially larger in the deaf. Her results suggest that parts of the brain that are used for auditory processing in hearing people are used for expanded visual processing in deaf people.

Despite many intriguing findings, the EEG and the ERP provide only a limited understanding of various structures of the brain. We need some way of getting a picture of a living, functioning person's working brain. Fortunately, advances in technology make it possible to observe brain function with little discomfort to the patient. The photos and illustrations in this section show several of the many ways of viewing the brain.

X RAYS AND ANGIOGRAMS

Neuroscientists are psychologists and other kinds of scientists who study the nervous system. Since early in the past century, they have been able to take snapshots of the living brain. The first technique to be developed uses *X rays*, a type of electromagnetic radiation that can pass through solids. An X ray yields a two-dimensional picture that shows the varying densities of the structures that have been scanned. Unfortunately, however, most areas of the brain have roughly

© Richard T. Nowitz/Corbis

FIGURE 3.22

Electroencephalograms (EEGs). EEGs record electrical activity and translate the data into wave patterns.

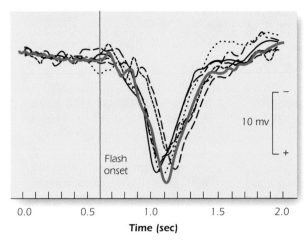

FIGURE 3.23

Event-Related Potential (ERP). An ERP is a series of EEG recordings in which the variability of electrical interference has been averaged out of the data. The colored line in the graph is averaged from the many recordings shown with it.

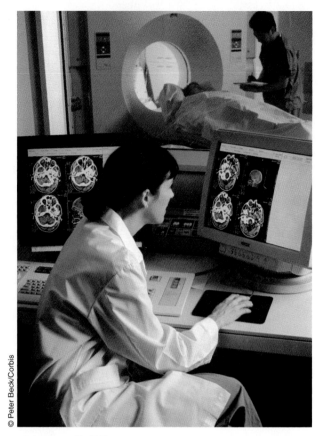

© Peter Beck/Corbis

FIGURE 3.24

CAT Scan. A lab technician gives a patient a CAT scan.

the same density, so X rays of the head are useful for showing skull fractures but little else of concern to psychologists.

Angiograms are a kind of X rays that provide some visual contrast when special dyes are injected into the blood vessels. Angiograms are most frequently used to study heart functioning. They also often are used to assess *vascular* diseases (diseases of the blood vessels, which may lead to strokes), to locate particular kinds of brain tumors, and to indicate which parts of the brain are active when people perform different kinds of listening, speaking, or movement tasks (see Figure 3.25a). Thus, by focusing mostly on blood vessels, angiograms provide dynamic information about the living brain.

BRAIN SCANS

As you might infer from the brain's extraordinary use of the nutrients and oxygen in the blood, any disturbance in the blood supply is dangerous. Whether due to clots, narrowed vessels, or hemorrhage, a reduction in the blood supply to the brain can cause a cerebral accident, a stroke. A stroke, in turn, immediately alters consciousness. If the blood supply is impaired for any length of time, the deprived tissue begins to die. The potentially devastating implications of a stroke depend on its duration and the area that is affected.

When clinicians and researchers try to detect strokes or other physiological bases for disorders, they often use a highly sophisticated X ray–based technique for viewing the brain: the **computerized axial tomogram (CAT)** or *CAT scan*, which generates a cross-sectional image of the brain. In this procedure, a

patient lies on a table with his or her head in the middle of a doughnut-shaped ring (see Figure 3.24). The ring takes X rays as it rotates 360 degrees around the patient's head. Thus, small amounts of X rays penetrate the head from many angles. Opposite the sources of the X rays in the ring are detectors that record the amount of X-ray radiation reaching them. This amount is determined by the density of tissue at various locations in the head. The more dense the tissue, the smaller the amount of X-ray radiation that reaches the detectors. A computer then analyzes the amount of radiation that reaches each of the detectors to construct a three-dimensional X ray of a cross-section of the brain. The result is far more revealing than pictures taken from a single position only (see Figure 3.25b). CAT scans are often used to detect blood clots, tumors, or brain diseases. They are also used by neuropsychologists to study how particular types and locations of brain damage affect behavior.

Magnetic resonance imaging (MRI) resembles a CAT scanner and reveals much of the same information using a magnetic field instead of radiation. Its pictures are clearer and more detailed. With the patient lying down, an extremely strong magnetic field is

(a) Angiogram (X ray)

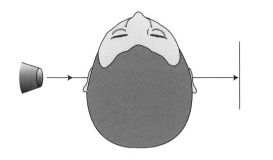

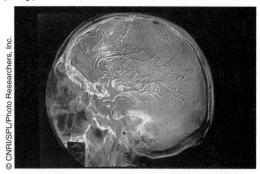

© CNRI/SPL/Photo Researchers, Inc.

(b) CAT scan

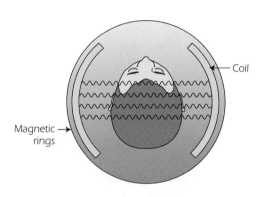

3

2

1

1

Detectors 2

3

Moving
X-ray
source

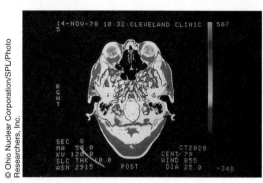

© Ohio Nuclear Corporation/SPL/Photo Researchers, Inc.

(c) MRI

Coil

Magnetic
rings

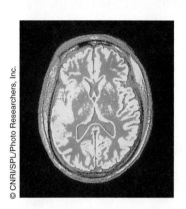

© CNRI/SPL/Photo Researchers, Inc.

(d) PET scan

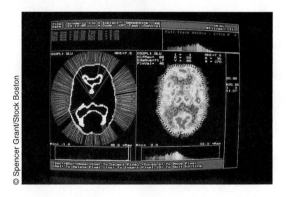

© Spencer Grant/Stock Boston

FIGURE 3.25

Images of the Brain. Researchers and physicians use various techniques to identify and diagnose the structures and processes of the brain. (a) A brain angiogram highlights the blood vessels of the brain. (b) CAT-scan images show a three-dimensional view of brain structures. (c) A rotating series of MRI scans show a clearer three-dimensional picture of brain structures than do CAT scans. (d) PET scans permit the study of brain physiology.

passed through the part of the body being studied. This field changes the orbits of nuclear particles in the molecules of the body. The bursts of energy associated with these changes are registered over time and analyzed by computer. Different molecules react differently to the magnetic field as a result of their composition and environments. The computer then generates a highly precise, three-dimensional picture based on the molecular variations (see Figure 3.25c).

Several types of MRI scans are available (Malonek & Grinvald, 1996; Ugurbil, 1999). Structural MRI looks at static anatomical images. Functional MRI (also called fMRI) measures changes in the magnetic state of the blood as a function of its degree of oxygenation (Gabrieli et al., 1996; Ogawa, Lee, Nayak, & Glynn, 1990). Functional MRI has been used to identify regions of brain activity in many areas, such as vision (Engel et al., 1994), movement (S. G. Kim et al., 1993), language (McCarthy, Blamire, Rothman, Gruetter, & Shulman, 1993), attention (J. D. Cohen et al., 1994), and memory (Gabrieli et al., 1996; Squire et al., 1992; Tulving et al., 1994). For example, fMRI has shown that the lateral prefontal cortex is essential for working memory (see Chapter 7), which is used to process information that is actively in use at a given time (McCarthy et al., 1994).

The development of fMRI techniques has generated great excitement among psychologists. It is now possible to specify with some precision where in the brain mental activity takes place. These techniques thus provide a wonderful opportunity to link the psychological and biological study of the brain with the psychological study of mental processes. It is important to realize, however, that simply identifying where in the brain a certain process occurs is not the same as understanding it. Psychologists also seek to understand *how* the brain works in producing these processes, and how certain ones connect to others, such as learning to memory or anger to aggression.

Another breakthrough is positron emission tomography (PET), a scan that enables us to see the brain in action by tracing radioactive glucose (Buckner et al., 1996; Raichle, 1998, 1999). A mildly radioactive form of glucose is injected and absorbed. The amount of glucose absorbed by the brain indicates the degree to which a given cell is metabolically active. While the irradiated glucose is going to the person's brain, the person's head is placed in a ring similar to that of the CAT scanner, and a beam of X rays is passed through it. The radioactive substance is detected by the scanners. A computer then determines which portions of the brain have absorbed the most radioactive glucose, and thereby pinpoints the areas that are the most active (see Figure 3.25d). PET scans have been used to show which parts of the brain are active in such tasks as listening to music, playing computer games, speaking, and moving parts of the body (see Figure 3.26). They also have shown that dreaming during certain

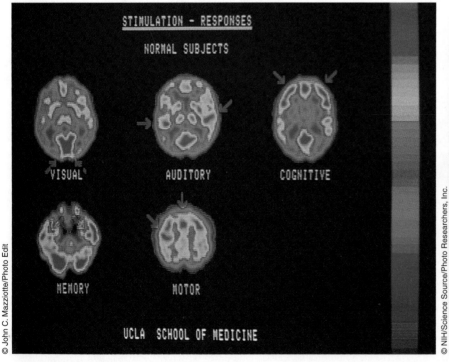
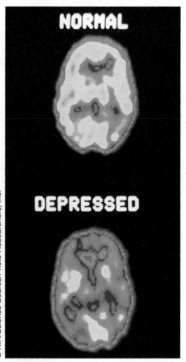

FIGURE 3.26

PET Scan Images. Images from PET scans show different metabolic processes in reaction to different activities and stimuli as well as different mental states.

stages of sleep engages areas of the brain that are involved in language processing and other aspects of cognition (Gottschalk et al., 1991). Because the PET scan shows the physiological functioning of the brain, not just its anatomical structure, this technique offers dynamic insights into the brain that were previously offered only by cruder techniques, such as the EEG and the angiogram. PET scanning has been used in many psychological studies that attempt to localize function. For example, it has shown that attention to features of stimuli such as color, form, and movement occurs in a particular area of the brain called the extrastriate visual cortex (Corbetta, Miezin, Dobmeyer, Shulman, & Petersen, 1991; Corbetta, Miezin, Shulman, & Petersen, 1993).

Optical imaging is a newer technique that uses fiber-optic light and a special camera attached to a surgical microscope. The many imaging techniques that are becoming available shed new light on the brain, both literally and metaphorically.

✓CONCEPT CHECK 4

1. The medulla oblongata is most involved in control of
   a. movement of the hands.
   b. heart rate.
   c. liver function.
   d. learning and memory.
2. The nerve fibers that connect the left and right hemispheres of the brain are jointly referred to as the
   a. corpus callosum.
   b. corpus delicti.
   c. habeas corpus.
   d. corpus cortex.
3. The visual region of the cerebral cortex is primarily located in the _____ lobe.
   a. frontal
   b. parietal
   c. temporal
   d. occipital

THE ENDOCRINE SYSTEM

What are the basic elements of the endocrine system, and how does it function?

Under most circumstances, the nervous system does an excellent job of communicating sensory information to our brains and motor information from our brains to our muscles. It is particularly effective in transmitting specific information speedily, so that we can respond immediately to the environment. Sometimes, however, our bodies use an alternative mode of communication, the **endocrine system,** which regulates aspects of growth, reproduction, metabolism, and behavior. "Endocrine" means *secreting or releasing inside*. The endocrine system operates by means of **glands,** groups of cells that release chemical substances directly into the bloodstream, which carries them to the target organ or organs. The hypothalamus plays an important role in regulating the endocrine system.

Our bodies also have an *exocrine system*, in which some glands excrete substances, such as tears or sweat, through *ducts* to the outside of the body.

HORMONES

Hormones, the chemical substances secreted by endocrine-system glands, foster the growth and proliferation of cells. Hormones also play an important part in growth and general development, especially sexual development. In some cases, hormones affect the way a receptive cell functions. Hormones perform their work either by interacting with receptors on the surfaces of target cells or by entering target cells directly and interacting with specialized receptor molecules inside them. Some parallels exist between neurotransmitters and hormones. Hormones are chemical substances that operate within a communications network. They are secreted by one set of cells (the glands) and then communicate a message to another set of cells (the target organ or organs). The specific actions of the chemicals are largely determined by the nature of the receptors that receive the chemicals. For example, the same hormones that speed the heart can slow the digestive organs. Thus, hormones, like neurotransmitters, play a key role in internal communication. Indeed, some transmitters in the nervous system also serve as hormones in the bloodstream.

The whole endocrine system largely operates without our conscious control, and hormones are released reflexively. A stimulus from either inside or outside the body brings about a change in neural activity, which prompts secretion of one or more hormones. The body monitors the levels of a given hormone and the activities that it affects through a *negative-feedback loop*, diagrammed in Figure 3.27. When the particular hormonal function has been accomplished or the hormone levels in the bloodstream have reached a target level, a message is sent to the brain and the secretion stops.

ENDOCRINE GLANDS

Some of the major endocrine glands are shown in Figure 3.28.

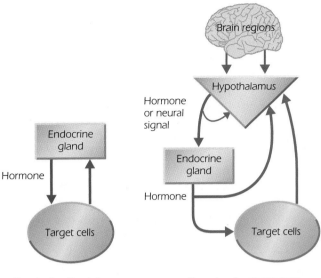

Simple feedback loop

Complex feedback loop

FIGURE 3.27

Negative-Feedback Loop. Through a negative-feedback loop, an endocrine gland monitors the levels of hormones in the bloodstream. If the monitoring processes yield negative responses (feedback), indicating the need for a higher level of a given hormone, the hormone secretion continues.

© AP/Wide World Photos

In 1998 Mark McGwire used a legal form of anabolic steroids to build his muscle mass and thus improve his hitting. He stopped using the preparation in 1999 because he believed it set a bad example for young athletes.

THE ADRENAL SYSTEM

Each of the adrenal glands, which are located above the kidneys, consists of two parts. The first is the *adrenal medulla*, the inner part of an anatomical structure. The second is the *adrenal cortex*, the outer part. These glands are very important to mood, energy level, and reaction to stress. The **adrenal medulla** secretes two hormones: epinephrine (also called "adrenaline") and norepinephrine (also called "noradrenaline"). In the nervous system, epinephrine and norepinephrine can serve as neurotransmitters, and they serve as hormones in the bloodstream. As a neurotransmitter, norepinephrine plays a more important role than epinephrine, affecting wakefulness, for example. When the two substances function as hormones, epinephrine and norepinephrine are intimately involved in sudden arousal reactions, such as increased heart rate and blood pressure and reduced flow of blood to the digestive system. Such reactions can lead to a *fight-or-flight response:* The surge of energy you feel in response to a crisis that requires confrontation or escape comes from adrenal arousal.

The **adrenal cortex** alone produces more than 50 hormones that perform various functions, many of them vital to physiological survival or to sexual differentiation and reproductive function. Disturbing the complex balance of hormones can lead to unwanted consequences. For example, high doses of anabolic steroids—synthetic forms of the male sex hormones produced in the adrenal cortex—have been linked to extreme aggression, severe mood swings, and mental instability, as well as to sterility and other physiological damage or disease (Pope & Katz, 1988). Home-run star Mark McGwire dosed himself with a commercially available preparation that was legal for use in baseball but not in most other sports during the 1998 season in order to increase his muscle mass and fitness. He set a home-run record. In the 1999 season, he stopped using the preparation because he did not want to set a bad example for younger people. Nevertheless, he had a splendid season. Whatever caused him to be a home-run star, it was not the drug.

THE THYROID AND PITUITARY GLANDS

The **thyroid gland**, located at the front of the throat, regulates the metabolic rate of cells. The hormone produced by the thyroid, *thyroxine*, increases metabolic rate. Overproduction of thyroxine leads to *hyperthyroidism*, a condition associated with high blood pressure, weight loss, and muscular weakness. Not enough thyroxine causes *hypothyroidism*, associated with slowed metabolism and consequent weight gain and sluggishness. When physicians are confronted by patients who feel fatigued or depressed, they may check the patients' thyroid function before making a referral for psychological counseling.

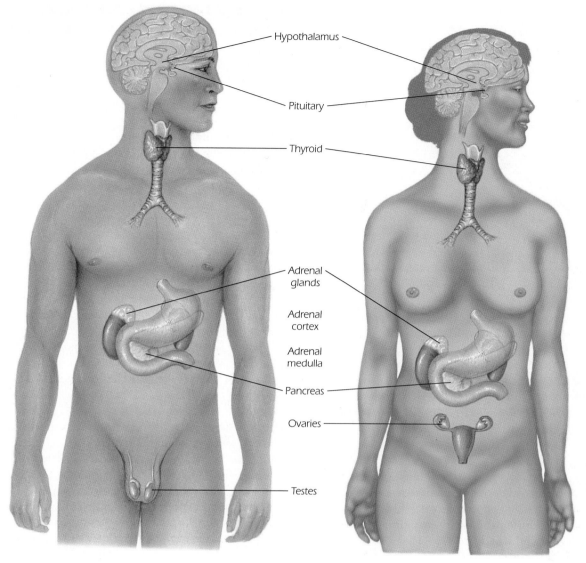

Hypothalamus

Pituitary

Thyroid

Adrenal glands

Adrenal cortex

Adrenal medulla

Pancreas

Ovaries

Testes

FIGURE 3.28

Major Endocrine Glands of the Body. The adrenal glands, thyroid gland, and pituitary gland are among the most important endocrine glands, but other glands also have important physiological functions.

The **pituitary gland,** sometimes called the master gland, affects growth and regulates other endocrine glands. Many other endocrine glands release their hormones in response to hormones released by the pituitary. The pituitary itself is controlled by the hypothalamus (in the forebrain). The pituitary gland (located above the mouth and underneath the hypothalamus, to which it is attached) releases hormones that affect other physiological functions both directly and indirectly.

The pituitary also provides a direct link between the endocrine system and the nervous system. When the nervous system signals a stressful situation to the brain, neurons in the hypothalamus stimulate it to act on the pituitary. In response, the pituitary secretes *adrenocorticotropic hormone (ACTH),* our primary stress hormone. The bloodstream carries ACTH to various other organs, most notably the adrenal glands. They secrete, among other hormones, the fight-or-flight hormones epinephrine and norepinephrine. This action loop is diagrammed in Figure 3.29.

As we have seen, the endocrine system activates responses in the body via hormones in the bloodstream. The endocrine system is in some ways self-directing, but it is also subject to control by the nervous system via the hypothalamus. Nonetheless, both the endocrine system and the nervous system

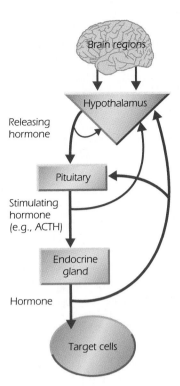

FIGURE 3.29
Action Loop. The physiological interaction of the pituitary gland and the hypothalamus provides a crucial link between the nervous system and the endocrine system.

EVOLUTION, GENETICS, AND HERITABILITY

How is evolutionary theory relevant to psychology?

To understand the influence of biology on psychologists' thinking, we need to understand the influence of evolutionary theory and genetics on biologists' thinking.

Ⓔ EVOLUTIONARY THEORY

NATURAL SELECTION

Evolutionary theory describes the ways our bodies and behaviors change across many generations. The idea is usually credited to English naturalist Charles Darwin (1809–1882). In *The Origin of Species* (1859), Darwin proposed the notion of **natural selection,** a mechanism by which organisms have developed and changed, based on what is commonly called the "survival of the fittest." In this view, organisms show a great deal of biological variation. Variation is due in part to **mutation,** which occurs when the genetic message that would normally be passed from parent to offspring is altered, resulting in a new organism with a genetic code not predictable from the genetic code of the parents. At a given time, some individuals are better able to adapt to their environmental conditions than others, so they have an advantage for survival and will

are integral parts of the fabulous network of the human body. Both play important roles (not yet fully understood) in defining the elusive relationship of mental processes to the body.

✓CONCEPT CHECK 5

1. The chemical substances in hormones are
   a. always the same as those in neurotransmitters.
   b. sometimes the same as those in neurotransmitters.
   c. never the same as those in neurotransmitters.
   d. still unknown.
2. Anabolic steroids are highly related chemically to
   a. female sex hormones.
   b. male sex hormones.
   c. Vitamin K.
   d. selenium.
3. ACTH is primarily a _____ hormone.
   a. stress-related
   b. weight-producing
   c. weight-reducing
   d. sex

Charles Darwin (1809–1882) was the father of evolutionary theory.

eventually produce a larger number of viable offspring. Over generations, their progeny will become prevalent. These individuals will have been "selected" by nature for survival—hence the term *natural selection.* On average, those individuals that are not as well able to adapt will reproduce less successfully, where reproductive success is viewed in terms of the number of viable offspring that will themselves eventually be able to reproduce. It is important to remember that as environmental conditions change, so does the potential adaptability of each individual organism. Adaptability can be assessed only in relation to a particular set of environmental conditions.

For example, during the Industrial Revolution in late 19th-century England, a particular dark-colored moth became more prevalent than a related light-colored moth. Why? Industrial pollution had blackened the forests and improved the darker moth's camouflage against predators such as birds. The light-colored moth was too visible to survive. More recently, however, with restrictions on air pollution, the light moth is making a comeback. Thus, natural selection is a constantly shifting process. It is influenced not only by an organism's biology but also by the interaction of that biology with environmental conditions.

How have Darwin's ideas about natural selection influenced psychology and the study of behavior? As we have evolved, more of our behavior has come under voluntary control by the brain. Our actions are more self-directed and less instinctual than those of other animals whose brains are less developed (Pinker, 1998). Thus, biopsychologists study the nervous system to pinpoint its influence on our moods, feelings, drives, thought processes, and behavior. Others in fields related to psychology have also attempted to apply evolutionary principles of natural selection to human behavior using very different approaches. It is important to remember that, from an evolutionary standpoint, the adaptive success of an organism depends on its fit in an environmental niche. Suppose, for example, there were major climatic changes in the world. The organisms that survive would be able to adjust to the changes, whether or not they are complex in the sense of having well-evolved brains or anything else.

Evolutionary theory is important not only for the concept of natural selection but also for its embodiment of the philosophy of *functionalism,* discussed in Chapter 1. Just as early functionalists in psychology sought to understand why *people* behave as they do, functionalists who have studied evolution have sought to explain why *organisms* change and evolve as they do. What purpose does a particular evolutionary change serve for the affected organism? According to evolutionary theory as it was originally posed, evolution through natural selection has been gradual. Recently, however, some theorists have proposed an alternative

viewpoint: *punctuated equilibrium.* According to this perspective, organisms remain relatively stable for long periods of time, with relatively brief periods (on an evolutionary scale) of rapid change (e.g., Gould, 1981, 2002a, 2002b). The late Stephen Jay Gould and others have agreed with Darwin that natural selection is the key to evolution. They have disagreed with him about the timing of evolutionary processes.

EVOLUTION AND PSYCHOLOGY

Evolutionary theory provides a wonderful, unified framework for integrating diverse psychological phenomena (Buss, 2001a, 2001b; Palmer & Palmer, 2002; Pinker, 1998). Just as we seek to understand the evolution of ideas in order to appreciate how psychologists and others have come to think the way they do (see Chapter 2), we also can seek to comprehend the evolution of organisms in order to appreciate how they have come to be the way they are.

It is important to distinguish between biological evolution and evolutionary psychology. *Biological evolution* refers to how the processes of natural selection and mutation have resulted in the kinds of organisms that are alive today. *Evolutionary psychology* applies ideas from the theory of evolution to psychology. The evidence for biological evolution, especially fossil remains, is generally much better developed than the evidence that has been offered for evolutionary psychology. But evolutionary psychology is a relatively new field, and so we need more time to develop a large base of evidence for its various claims.

Sometimes evolutionary theory helps us understand phenomena that are difficult to explain in any other way. Leda Cosmides (1989) found that in a certain type of reasoning task, people do better if the content pertains to people being cheated than if it is about other things. Why would people be at an advantage when the problem deals with cheating behavior? Because, according to Cosmides, we have evolved in a way that makes us particularly sensitive to cheating. Our ancestors who were not sensitive to being cheated were at a disadvantage in adapting to their environments. By letting themselves be taken advantage of, they had fewer opportunities to reproduce. They may have let themselves be cheated out of reproductive opportunities or perhaps the food they needed to stay alive to reach the point when they could reproduce. Whatever the case, people who were good "cheater detectors" were at an adaptive advantage. They were more likely to have been our ancestors than those who were poor cheater detectors.

This book contains many references both to the evolution of organisms and to the evolution of ideas. Is there any relationship between the two kinds of evolution? Richard Dawkins (1989) has speculated that essentially the same laws of evolution that apply to organisms may apply to cultural artifacts, including ideas.

And other psychologists have suggested that ideas may evolve along the lines of a mechanism whereby the "fittest" survive. In other words, those ideas last that are best adapted to the cultural milieu in which they are proposed and diffused (D. T. Campbell, 1960; Lumsden, 1998; Perkins, 1995b; Simonton, 1995, 1999). On the one hand, we need to recognize that ideas are not living organisms in the same way that people are. On the other hand, we also recognize that ideas, like organisms, can fit more or less well into an environmental niche. Their fit does not render them true, however. Cultures have accepted, over the years, many ideas that are demonstrably false, such as the idea in Europe in times past that a mysterious (and, in fact, nonexistent) substance called phlogiston causes fire. Why do we say "God bless you!" when someone sneezes? Because once people believed that a devil could enter the nose when one inhaled after a sneeze. We are trying to prevent that devil from entering, or at least encourage it to be sneezed out subsequently. Evolutionary theory does not provide any kind of code of truth or ethics. Neither organisms nor ideas that fit a given environment are in any real sense better than others in an absolute sense. Rather, they are simply organisms or ideas that are well adapted to a given time or place.

Although evolution provides a useful framework for understanding many psychological phenomena, we need to be careful not to push this or any other framework too far. We can end up in a position where we take whatever phenomenon we observe and then, after the fact, construct an evolutionary "explanation" for it, just as we would have if we had found the opposite phenomenon. In such cases, evolutionary interpretations cannot be refuted because they are created after the fact to account for whatever is found. The evolutionary framework, like all others, is useful if we realize that it can provide a way of understanding some phenomena. But it is no more a cure-all than is any other single framework. No one framework will provide the answers to all the questions we might ask in psychology.

GENETICS

A final topic in our consideration of the biological bases of behavior is even more minute than the neurons described earlier. Inside each cell our **genes** provide the basic physiological building blocks for the hereditary transmission of our **biological traits**—the distinctive characteristics or behavior patterns that are genetically determined. We receive our genes, and hence our traits, from our parents at the time of our conception. Although no one doubts that genes influence behavior, the degree to which they exert this influence is a matter of ongoing research and debate in

the field of psychology. **Behavioral genetics** is the branch of psychology that attempts to discover the extent to which behavior and mental processes are genetically influenced. *Molecular genetics* seeks to identify just what genes have this influence.

MENDEL'S PEAS

Modern genetic theory dates back to the research of an Austrian monk and botanist, Gregor Mendel (1822–1884), who performed breeding experiments on common varieties of the garden pea. Mendel observed some interesting effects in the inheritance of attributes of the pea. For example, if true-breeding tall pea plants (ones that always produce tall offspring) are crossed with true-breeding dwarf pea plants (ones that always produce small offspring), the offspring of the tall and the dwarf plants will always be tall. Mendel referred to the stronger attribute that appeared in this first generation of offspring as the **dominant trait** (here, tallness). He called the weaker trait, which did not appear, the **recessive trait** (here, dwarfism).

In order to understand Mendel's work, you need to understand two other concepts. A **genotype** is the pair of genes on a given chromosome pair. Chromosomes are inherited, and therefore they are not subject to environmental influence or prenatal trauma, except in cases of genetic mutation. A **phenotype**, in contrast, is the expression of an inherited trait, based on the dominant trait in the genotype and also subject to environmental influence. The phenotype, then, is what you potentially can observe. The genotype is what lies beneath it.

Mendel discovered that, if you interbreed all the tall members of the first generation of offspring, the second generation of offspring will have both tall and short plants, in a ratio of about three tall plants to every one short plant. How can we account for this odd result? Today we know it is due to genes.

To make this example simple, suppose that the height of a plant is controlled by exactly two genes, one from each parent. Both inherited genes may be for tallness, both may be for dwarfism, or one may be for tallness and one for dwarfism. If we represent tallness by T and dwarfism by d, then the possible genotypes for height in the plant are TT, Td, dT, and dd. Now we need to know just one principle: Whenever a dominant gene is paired with a recessive gene, even though both genes are present in the offspring, the phenotype will be the dominant trait. Mendel determined that tallness was dominant because a plant with TT, Td, or dT gene combinations shows up as tall. In contrast, only a plant with a dd gene combination shows up as short.

Now we can account for Mendel's results in the heights of his pea plants in different generations. In the first generation, all offspring were *hybrids*, meaning that they contained mixed gene patterns (Td and dT). Because tallness (T) is the dominant trait, all offspring appeared tall. The second generation of offspring, however, had equal numbers of TT, Td, dT, and dd offspring. In this generation, three of the genotypes (TT, Td, dT) produce the phenotype of tall plants, and only one of the genotypes (dd) produces the phenotype of a short plant. (See Figure 3.30 for a chart of Mendel's results.)

HUMAN GENOTYPES AND PHENOTYPES

In humans, the expression of a single genotype can give rise to a fairly wide range of phenotypes because the science of genetics is not as simple as we have just described. For example, a person's height is largely genetically controlled, but a range of actual phenotypic heights may be reached, depending on factors such as nutrition, hormones, and immune-system efficiency. Thus, the expression of even traits that are genetically based is not completely controlled by genetics. Genes do help to determine phenotypes, but so do other influences, such as the environment.

The environment that is ideal for one genotype may not be ideal for another. For example, the ideal environment for the white moth is different from the ideal environment for the gray moth. Which set of genes (those for whiteness or those for grayness) will thrive will depend on the environment in which the set of genes is expressed. The sickle-cell anemia trait conveys an advantage to humans who live in malaria-prone regions because it makes it harder for the malaria parasite to infect the body. But this same trait can cause health problems, especially for someone who lives at high altitudes (where the mosquitoes that cause malaria are not to be found). Thus, whether the sickle-cell trait is advantageous or not depends on the environment in which the individual lives.

Consider a psychological trait, such as musical ability. A child is born, say, with a set of genes that provides the basis to develop tremendous musical talent. But will the child ever develop this talent? Will the child ever become a first-rate musician? If the child is brought up in a home where musical instruction is valued, perhaps the child will fulfill such a potential. But even given these opportunities, other factors will come into play. Sheer persistence and luck may influence whether the individual's talent is recognized by the music world. Now suppose the child is brought up in a home where music is frowned upon. Perhaps musical expression is contrary to the family's religion, or perhaps the parents view music as a frivolous pursuit. In such cases, no one may even know that the child had the potential to be a great musician, including the child. The potential is left unexpressed. Similarly, a child who is brought up and passes through adulthood in a preliterate culture may have a genetic potential for reading, but it will forever remain unexpressed. No individual differences in reading skills will be expressed in that culture because there is no reading.

True–breeding dwarf pea plant (dd)

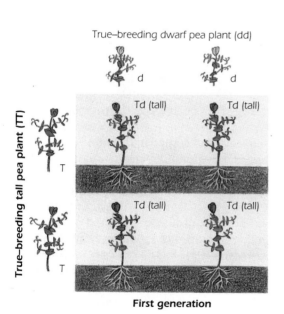

First generation

Hybrid tall pea plant (Td)

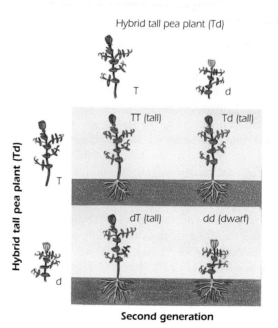

Second generation

FIGURE 3.30

Genetic Chart of Pea Traits. By studying the characteristics of successive generations of peas, Gregor Mendel (1822–1884) discovered the fundamental process of genetic inheritance.

THE HUMAN GENOME PROJECT

Efforts are under way to do *genetic mapping*, which is the determination of the location as well as the chemical sequence of specific genes located on specific chromosomes. A 15-year international project called the *Human Genome Project* preliminarily mapped the entire human genome, or the configuration of genes on chromosomes. But even with this success, it is important to remember that the result is not total prediction of behavior. Behavior is also affected by the environment and the interaction of the genes with the environment.

The information gleaned from the Human Genome Project already is allowing scientists to better understand the genes that cause or contribute to diseases. It ultimately will help scientists devise more effective pharmaceutical treatments for some diseases. The information also may enable us to better understand how people are similar to and different from one another genetically. Some people are concerned about possible unethical uses of the database. But any scientific discovery ultimately can be used for good or ill, and it is the responsibility of a society to turn scientific knowledge to helpful rather than harmful uses.

HERITABILITY

It is possible to measure genetic influence, but only in a limited way. Heritability is the extent to which variation among individuals is caused by genetics. It is important, however, to distinguish genetic influence on a trait from the heritability of that trait. For example, height is highly heritable because who will be taller and who will be shorter can be predicted on the basis of inheritance from parents. If there is little or no variability among individuals in a trait, then the trait is genetic but not heritable. The fact that we are born with two hands is genetic but is not reflected in measures of heritability because almost everyone is born with two hands and thus there is little variability.

This distinction becomes particularly important for traits that a given society may value highly, such as intelligence. In concentrating on individual differences among people, we can forget the ways in which people are highly similar genetically and the ways that have made it possible for them to be intelligent as a species. One of the most impressive human attributes is the ability to speak. It is made possible through a variety of complex genetic (as well as environmental) mechanisms. But because virtually all humans speak, we are unlikely to find a test of the ability to speak on a test of intelligence. Nor is the ability to speak reflected in measures of heritability, precisely because almost everyone has it.

In interpreting measures of heritability, you need to keep several things in mind (Plomin, DeFries, Craig, & McGuffin, 2003; Plomin, DeFries, McClearn, & Rutter, 1997; R. J. Sternberg & Grigorenko, 1999; Wahlsten & Gottlieb, 1997). First, heritability is always estimated with respect to a given trait in a given population at a given time. It does not apply to single individuals. How heritable a trait is estimated to be will depend in part on the source of variation in the trait in the population. For example, in a society that forces children to write with their right hand, the heritability of observed handedness in writing will be quite low. However, it could be high in some other society that had no environmental pressure to write with the right hand. We need also to remember that even highly heritable traits can be subject to environmental modification. Although height is highly heritable, heights have increased substantially in recent generations due to better nutrition. Human intelligence, as measured by conventional tests of abilities, also increased during most of the years of the 20th century, despite some level of heritability of intelligence (see Neisser, 1998). Note that these increases could not have been due to some kind of biological evolutionary process because biological evolution in humans works on a scale of thousands of years, not of a hundred! Finally, we need to remember that relatively few traits are controlled by a single gene. Rather, traits are often caused by multiple genes. We will never find "the" gene for intelligence, for example, because no single gene controls intelligence. Moreover, genes interact, in part through their relations to chromosomes.

CHROMOSOMES

Chromosomes are rod-shaped bodies that contain many genes. Different species have different numbers of chromosomes, which come in pairs. Humans, for example, have 23 pairs of chromosomes, for a total of 46. Most cells of our bodies have each of these 23 pairs of chromosomes. One of each pair was received at conception from the mother and one from the father, so that half of each person's heredity can be traced to each parent.

Chromosomes are composed, in part, of deoxyribonucleic acid (DNA), the biological material that provides the mechanism for transmission of genetic information. Chromosomes govern everything from our eye color to our blood type and sex. Two specific chromosomes are crucial in determining sex: the X and Y chromosomes, which appear as the 23rd pair in each set. Females receive an X chromosome from both parents. Their sex-chromosome pairing is thus XX. Males receive an X chromosome from their mothers and a Y chromosome from their fathers. Their sex-

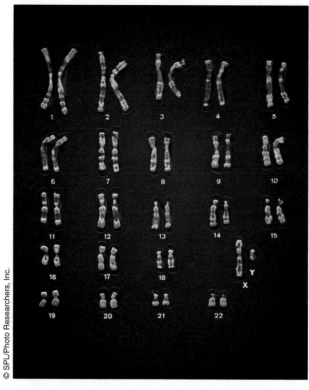

Humans have 23 pairs of chromosomes, including the pair that determines each person's gender.

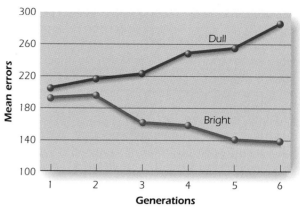

FIGURE 3.31

Selective Breeding in Rats. Successive generations of rats were bred for their ability to run particular mazes. This ability did not generalize to other aspects of intelligence—or even to other kinds of mazes. (After W. R. Thompson, 1954)

astonishingly specific. Even changes in the nature of the maze eliminated the significant difference in maze-running ability between groups. Clearly, the relationship of genes to environment—in this case, the maze—is more complex than we might have thought.

chromosome pairing is thus XY. Can we influence the hereditary material that passes from one generation to another? People have tried to.

SELECTIVE BREEDING

If we can breed for height in peas, we might expect that we could breed for other traits as well. Indeed, race horses often become breeding studs after they are retired. Their owners command high prices for granting the opportunity to mate mares with them. In fact, many sophisticated reproductive options (e.g., artificial insemination, in vitro fertilization, surrogacy) are in use among animal breeders. If we can breed racing ability, can we also breed learning ability, emotionality, resistance to alcohol dependency, or even intelligence? All of these selective breeding experiments have actually been done. Here, we focus on an experiment involving the breeding of rats for intelligence.

Various rats were tested for their ability to run a maze and then were bred in successive generations to be more or less able to run the maze (Tryon, 1940). The results were mixed. On the one hand, it was possible to breed rats that were more or less able to run the maze, as you can see in Figure 3.31. On the other hand, the rats' abilities turned out to be

✓ CONCEPT CHECK 6

1. A phenotype is influenced by
   a. genes only.
   b. environment only.
   c. genes and environment.
   d. neither genes nor environment.
2. If there were almost no genetic variation in a particular trait that itself showed variability, then the heritability of that trait would probably be
   a. very low.
   b. very high.
   c. moderate.
   d. unknown.
3. If everyone in a given population wrote with their right hand, one could conclude
   a. that there is no influence of genes on handedness.
   b. nothing about genetic influences on handedness because people may have been forced to write with their right hand.
   c. that genes are the primary determinant of the hand with which people write.
   d. that the effects of genes cannot be overcome.

NATURE AND NURTURE

Are heredity and environment opposing forces?

The best way to conduct a controlled experimental investigation of genetic influences on underlying traits and on behavior in the environment is by looking at genetically identical twins. Identical twins show similarities in intelligence and other characteristics, even if they have been raised separately in different environments.

This is not to say, however, that our genes unalterably determine everything about us. There is no question that our upbringing, our parents' personalities, our schooling, our physical surroundings—in short, our environments—greatly affect who we become. How much? We have no clear answer to this question. In fact, throughout this book, in discussions of mental disorders, personality, cognitive abilities, and temperament, you will read of efforts to try to uncover the relative contributions of nature and nurture—of the degree to which who we are is determined by our environment and genetics. Today nature and nurture are seen as interacting rather than in opposition. For example, one may have a genetic predisposition to anxiety by being genetically predisposed to be more easily arousable (Kalin, 1993). But the environment one lives in, including one's neighborhood, economic situation, family life, and social network, may play a big role in how this genetic predisposition plays out (Plomin, DeFries, McClearn, & Rutter, 1997).

The respective roles of nature and nurture can be seen in the development of intelligence (discussed further in Chapter 9). Suppose a child has genes that make him or her likely to be intelligent. The person's phenotypic intelligence will depend not only on those genes but also on how they are expressed in the environment. For example, if the child is severely maltreated and is raised in a closet, the child most likely will never see the potential of those genes expressed. Moreover, behavior that is considered intelligent in one culture may not be considered intelligent in another culture (R. J. Sternberg, 1996b). So how intelligent the individual will be viewed in a particular culture will depend upon what kinds of behavior that culture values (Gardner, 1983).

Another example of how nature and nurture may interact is in the expression of *handedness*, the preference a person shows for using the right hand, the left hand, or both as in the case of ambidextrous individuals. Substantial evidence supports a genetic basis for handedness. But genetic factors alone cannot adequately account for variations in handedness across cultures (J. W. Berry, Poortinga, Segall, & Dasen, 1992). Although left-handedness apparently occurs in 5% to 10% of individuals in populations that do not restrict the use of either hand, socialization processes in some societies use selective pressures to force the use of the right hand and not the left, as mentioned earlier. In some of these right-selective societies, the left hand is often used to achieve personal cleanliness, and therefore it is associated with dirtiness. Thus, cultural factors may influence rates of handedness.

Intelligence (see Chapter 9) and many other traits appear to be greatly affected by a highly complex and incompletely understood interaction of genetic and environmental factors. Even sensation and perception, the topics of the next chapter, represent a complex interaction between genes and environment.

FETAL ALCOHOL SYNDROME

During the prenatal stage of human brain development, 250,000 new neurons are formed per minute. Glial cells then move the newly created neurons to their appropriate places in the brain and body. Obviously, anything that interferes with the rapid development of the nervous system can severely affect mental and motor abilities. Alcohol is one substance that can wreak havoc on the developing nervous system. When a pregnant woman consumes large amounts of alcohol early in her pregnancy, the development of her unborn baby's brain may well be impaired.

Pediatricians were the first investigators to document the effects of alcohol on the developing brain (Clarren & Smith, 1978). Naming the condition "fetal alcohol syndrome (FAS)," they observed that babies born to alcoholic mothers were smaller than normal at birth and less responsive than the babies of mothers who did not drink during pregnancy. Many psychologists have since studied infants who have fetal alcohol syndrome. In addition to deficiencies in their growth, these babies have behavioral problems that include irritability, short attention spans, poor motor coordination, and perceptual disorders. Psychologists in many different fields conduct research on children with FAS.

Biological psychologists have studied fetal alcohol syndrome induced in laboratory animals in order to understand the effects of alcohol on the developing human nervous system. For example, Daniel Savage has worked with other *behavioral neuroscientists* to determine what blood alcohol levels in pregnant rats are associated with low birth weight, abnormal development of the hippocampus, and impaired spatial learning ability in their pups (Savage, Becher, de la Torre, & Sutherland, 2001). Other biological psychologists have examined the effects of prenatal exposure to alcohol on the social behavior of adolescent rats. Rats whose mothers were given alcohol throughout their pregnancies showed abnormal interactions with other rats, compared to control rats of the same age. Rats with fetal alcohol syndrome exhibited more anogenital sniffing, chasing, hopping, and darting than control rats, behaviors that are similar to symptoms of hyperactivity in humans (Lugo, Marino, Cronise, & Kelly, 2003). Inappropriate social and sexual behavior have been observed in both humans and other animals with FAS (Kelly, Day, & Streissguth, 2000).

Biological psychologists have also studied the effects of prenatal exposure to alcohol in other species. Psychophysicist Joseph Bilotta and his colleagues immersed the larvae of zebrafish in alcohol solutions. The development of the eyes was affected and, consequently, the zebrafish had impaired vision (Bilotta, Saszik, Givin, Hardesty, & Sutherland, 2002). Mary Schneider and her colleagues studied 63 infant macaque monkeys whose mothers had been given alcohol early or late in pregnancy, or throughout, or not at all. Early prenatal exposure to alcohol had detrimental effects on the baby monkeys' motor coordination and orientation to stimuli (Schneider, Moore, & Becker, 2001).

Developmental psychologists examine the effects of fetal alcohol syndrome on children's physical, social, and cognitive development. Nancy Day and her colleagues studied the physical development of teenagers who had prenatal exposure to alcohol. Height, weight, and head circumference were significantly reduced in 14-year-old children whose mothers drank from moderately to very heavily during pregnancy (Day et al., 2002).

Clinical psychologists treat children and adults with FAS, which is associated with a number of psychological disorders, including depression and bipolar disorder (O'Connor et al., 2002). Individuals with fetal alcohol syndrome also have been found to have poor attachment to their mothers or other caretakers, significantly more negative affect (depression or bad mood), and poor tolerance for frustration (O'Connor, Kogan, & Findlay, 2002). *Clinical neuropsychologists* have tested children to determine the extent of the cognitive and motor disabilities that result from fetal brain damage. Their tests revealed that these children have deficits in both visual and verbal memory (Kaemingk, Mulvaney, & Halverson, 2003). Children with FAS also show impaired gross and fine motor skills; the ability to make their movements in a specified period of time is also impaired (Wass, Simmons, Thomas, & Riley, 2002). The corpus callosum is smaller than in children in control groups; this impedes the ability to perform tasks that require transferring information from one cerebral hemisphere to the other (Roebuck, Mattson, & Riley, 2002).

It is clear from research by biological psychologists, behavioral neuroscientists, developmental psychologists, clinical psychologists, and clinical neuropsychologists that prenatal exposure to alcohol affects physical growth, motor development, cognitive ability, and social adjustment during childhood.

1. Biological psychology is the study of how biology affects behavior. Examination of the nervous and endocrine systems—in particular, the brain—helps psychologists answer questions about the interaction of mind and body.

THE ORGANIZATION OF THE NERVOUS SYSTEM 64

How is the nervous system organized?

2. The *nervous system* is divided into two main parts: the *central nervous system*, consisting of the brain and the *spinal cord*, and the *peripheral nervous system*, consisting of the rest of the nervous system (e.g., the nerves in the face, legs, arms, and viscera).

3. *Afferents* are structures that receive something; afferent neurons receive sensory information (e.g., sensations in the eyes, ears, and skin) from the outlying nerves of the body and transmit that information back up through the spinal cord to the brain. *Efferents* transmit motor information (e.g., movements of the large and small muscles) from the spinal cord (and usually from the brain) about how the body should act in response to the information it receives.

4. A *reflex* is an automatic, involuntary response to stimulation that does not require input from the brain. The brain, however, assigns conscious meaning to stimuli that elicit reflexes.

5. The peripheral nervous system is divided into two parts: the *somatic nervous system*, which controls the voluntary movements of skeletal muscles, and the *autonomic nervous system*, which controls the involuntary cardiac and smooth muscles.

6. The autonomic nervous system is further divided into two parts: the *sympathetic nervous system* and the *parasympathetic nervous system*. The former is concerned primarily with expending energy, especially in situations that require arousal and alertness. The latter is involved in storing energy.

NERVOUS SYSTEM CELLS AND FUNCTIONS 68

What are neurons, and how do they communicate?

7. A *neuron* is an individual nerve cell. *Nerves* are bunches of neurons. The three functional types of neurons are *sensory neurons*, by which the CNS receives information from the environment; *motor neurons*, which carry information away from the CNS toward the environment; and *interneurons*, which transmit information between sensory and motor neurons.

8. The *soma* (cell body) of a neuron is responsible for the life of the nerve cell. The branchlike *dendrites* are the means by which neurons receive messages, either from bodily receptors or from other neurons. *Axons* are the means by which neurons transmit messages. Some axons are covered with a white, fatty substance termed *myelin*, which increases the speed and accuracy of transmitting information down the neuron. Axons often branch at their ends. *Terminal buttons* are knobs at the end of each branch of an axon; each of these buttons releases a chemical *neurotransmitter*. The small gap between the terminal buttons of one neuron and the dendrites of the next neuron is the *synapse*.

9. *Glial cells* serve as supportive structures for the neurons, holding them in place, isolating them from the rest of the body, and getting rid of dead neurons and other waste.

10. A rapid increase in the membrane potential (electrical charge) of a neuron, followed by a quick decrease, is an *action potential*. It provides the means by which intraneuronal communication takes place. Action potentials are all or none, occurring only if the electrical charge of the neuron has reached a *threshold of excitation*.

11. After a neuron fires, it goes through an *absolute refractory phase*, during which it absolutely cannot fire again, and a brief subsequent *relative refractory phase*, during which its susceptibility to firing is diminished.

12. The effects of *neurotransmitters* on the receptors located on the dendrites of postsynaptic neurons can be either excitatory (stimulating the likelihood of firing) or inhibitory (suppressing the likelihood of firing).

13. An excess of neurotransmitters at the synapse can be absorbed by *reuptake* back into the terminal buttons or by enzymatic deactivation, whereby the transmitter substance is chemically decomposed.

14. The classical neurotransmitters include *acetylcholine (ACh)*, *dopamine (DA)*, and *serotonin*. Newer neurotransmitters include glutamate and gamma-aminobutyric acid (GABA).

How do you think the brain and its various parts function to produce feelings, thoughts, and behaviors?

15. In the *hindbrain*, the *medulla oblongata* controls the heart rate and largely controls breathing, swallowing, and digestion. The medulla oblongata also routes the sensory and motor neurons contralaterally from one side of the body to the opposite side of the brain. The *pons* contains nerve cells that pass signals from one part of the brain to another. The *cerebellum* controls bodily coordination.

16. The *midbrain* is involved in eye movements and coordination. Its relative importance is greater in animals that have less complex brains. The *reticular activating system*, which is responsible for arousal and sleep, extends from the midbrain to the hindbrain. The midbrain, the hindbrain, and part of the forebrain together make up the *brainstem*; its good health is vital to human survival.

17. In the *forebrain*, the *thalamus* serves as a relay station for input to the cerebral cortex. The *hypothalamus*, which controls the autonomic nervous system and the endocrine system, is involved in activities such as regulating temperature, eating, and drinking. The *limbic system*, also in the forebrain, is involved in emotion, motivation, and learning; in particular, the *hippocampus* is involved in memory.

18. The highly convoluted *cerebral cortex* surrounds the interior of the brain. It is the source of humans' ability to reason, think abstractly, and plan ahead.

19. The cerebral cortex covers the left and right *hemispheres* of the brain, which are connected by the *corpus callosum*. In general, each hemisphere contralaterally controls the opposite side of the body.

20. Based on split-brain research, many investigators believe that the two hemispheres are specialized (perform different functions). In most people, the left hemisphere seems to control language; the right hemisphere seems to control certain aspects of spatial and visual processing. The two hemispheres may process information differently.

21. Another way to divide the brain is into four lobes. Roughly speaking, higher thought and motor processing occur in the *frontal lobe*, sensory processing in the *parietal lobe*, auditory processing in the *temporal lobe*, and visual processing in the *occipital lobe*.

22. The *primary motor cortex*, in the frontal lobe, governs the planning, control, and execution of movement. The *primary somatosensory cortex*, in the parietal lobe, is responsible for the sensations in our muscles and skin.

23. *Association areas* process sensory information more elaborately than do the primary sensory areas of the brain.

How can scientists study the brain in action?

24. *Electroencephalograms (EEGs)* measure and record electrical activity in the brain. Because many processes are measured at once with EEG techniques, wave forms are often averaged to increase the stability of the readings. Averaged wave forms are referred to as *event-related potentials (ERPs)*.

25. X-ray pictures of the brain are taken by passing electromagnetic radiation through the tissues of the head. *Angiograms* are X-ray pictures taken after the injection of special dyes that increase the visibility of specific structures, such as blood vessels.

26. A *computerized axial tomogram (CAT scan)* uses computer analysis of X-ray pictures taken from a variety of locations to construct a more revealing picture of the brain than is possible with X-ray pictures taken from a stationary device.

27. *Magnetic resonance imaging (MRI)* provides pictures of the brain by creating a very strong magnetic field that changes the orbits of nuclear particles, which emit energy bursts; these bursts are picked up by the scan.

28. *Positron emission tomography (PET scan)* enables psychologists, physicians, and other scientists to see the brain in action. X rays trace the passage of an injected radioactive substance through various parts of the brain.

What are the basic elements of the endocrine system, and how does it function?

29. The *endocrine system* is the means by which *glands* secrete their products directly into the bloodstream. The secretions of the endocrine system are *hormones*, and their release is regulated by a negative-feedback loop (which feeds information back to the gland regarding the level of a hormone in the bloodstream).

30. One of the major endocrine glands is the *adrenal medulla*, which secretes epinephrine and norepinephrine. Both hormones increase heart rate and blood pressure and also reduce the flow of blood to the digestive system.

31. The nervous and endocrine systems are to some extent parallel, in that both are communications systems and both use chemical substances as messengers: neurotransmitters and hormones, respectively. The brain also has some control over the endocrine system, just as hormones can influence the brain.

EVOLUTION, GENETICS, AND HERITABILITY 100

How is evolutionary theory relevant to psychology?

32. Darwin's view of *natural selection* holds that individuals tend to have reproductive success as a function of their ability to adapt to the environment, with more adaptable individuals producing, on average, a larger number of viable offspring. The concept of natural selection has been applied to ideas as well as to organisms, although this application remains speculative.

33. A *mutation* occurs when the genetic message that would normally be passed on from parents to offspring is altered, resulting in a new organism with a genetic code not predictable from the genetic material of the parents.

34. Punctuated equilibrium is the view that evolutionary change proceeds in bursts rather than through smooth, gradual transitions.

35. *Genes* are the biological units that are the basis of the hereditary transmission of traits. Genes are located on *chromosomes*, which come in pairs. Humans have 23 chromosome pairs; the 23rd is responsible for determining sex.

36. A *genotype* is the genetic code for a trait. A *phenotype* is the actual visible expression of the trait in offspring. A given genotype may produce a variety of phenotypes.

37. *Heritability* is a measure of the genetic contribution to individual differences in a trait. Heritability is distinct from modifiability and can vary across time and place.

NATURE AND NURTURE 106

Are heredity and environment opposing forces?

38. Nature and nurture work together to produce organisms that are adapted to their environments.

KEY TERMS

absolute refractory phase 73
neuron cannot fire
acetylcholine (ACh) 76
memory
action potential 72
fires neuron
adrenal cortex 98
produces over 50 hormones
adrenal medulla 98
secretes epinephrine & norepinephrine
amygdala 81
w. limbic system, anger/agression
angiograms 94
x-rays w/ dye
association areas 88
process info more elaborately
autonomic nervous system 68
controls involuntary (heart)
axon 70
part of nerve
basal ganglia 82
control movements, in forebrain
behavioral genetics 102
genetic influence on behavior
biological traits 102
characteristics ~ genetically determined
brain 64
supreme in Nervous System
brainstem 80
hindbrain, midbrain, thal, hypothal
Broca's area 82
left frontal, needed for speech
central nervous system (CNS) 64
brain & spinal cord
cerebellum 79
hindbrain, coordination
cerebral cortex 82
covers surface of brain
cerebral hemispheres (left and right) 82 *2 sides of brain*
cerebrum 82
allows for thought
chromosomes 104
contain genes
computerized axial tomogram (CAT) 94 *cross-sectional x-ray*
corpus callosum 82
connects hemispheres
dendrites 70
recieve communication
deoxyribonucleic acid (DNA) 104

dominant trait 102
dopamine (DA) 76
neurotransmitter, movement
electroencephalogram (EEG) 92
endocrine system 97
regulates through hormones
event-related potential (ERP) 92
average EEGs
forebrain 78
thal, hypothal, limbic
frontal lobe 87
higher thought
genes 102
genotypes 102
glands 97
release chemicals into bloodstream
glial cells 72
hold CNS together
heritability 104
variation caused by genetics
hindbrain 78
medulla oblongata, pons, cerebellum
hippocampus 81
memory, in limbic system
hormones 97
chemicals from endocrine sys.
hypothalamus 82
controls water balance & autonomic
interneurons 70
intermediaries
limbic system 80
in forebrain, hippocamp, amyg, septum
magnetic resonance imaging (MRI) 94
medulla oblongata 79
hindbrain, controls heart rate/breathing
midbrain 78
RAS
motor efferents 66
brain to motor functions
motor neurons 69
away from periph.
mutation 100
genetic message altered
myelin sheath 70
insulates and protects
natural selection 100
nerves 70
bundle of axons

nervous system 64
network of communicating cells
neuromodulators 76
enhance/diminish responsivity of post-synaptic
neurons 65
receive & transmit info
neurotransmitter 73
chemicals comes into gaps
nodes of Ranvier 70
occipital lobe 87
vision
optic chiasma 88
info from eyes cross
parasympathetic nervous system 68
anabolism
parietal lobe 87
somatosensory
peripheral nervous system (PNS) 67
supports CNS
phenotype 102
expressed trait
pituitary gland 99
"master" gland
pons 79
"bridge" relay station
positron emission tomography (PET) 96 *traces radioactive glucose*
primary motor cortex 87
movement, frontal lobe
primary somatosensory cortex 87
in parietal lobe
projection areas 87
sensory info goes to thalamus, then to appropriate area
receptors 76
receive neurotransmitters
recessive trait 102
not shown
reflexes 67
skip brain
relative refractory phase 73
only fires if stronger stimulus
reticular activating system (RAS) 80
midbrain, regulates sleep
reuptake 74
neurotransmitters reabsorbed
sensory afferents 66
senses → spinal cord → brain
sensory neurons 69
info from environment
septum 81
in limbic system, anger/fear
serotonin 77
neurotransmitter, sleep & mood

ANSWERS TO CONCEPT CHECKS

Concept Check 1

1. a   2. c   3. a

Concept Check 2

1. d   2. c   3. a

Concept Check 3

1. c   2. a   3. d

Concept Check 4

1. b   2. a   3. d

Concept Check 5

1. b   2. b   3. a

Concept Check 6

1. c   2. a   3. b

KNOWLEDGE CHECK

1. The sympathetic nervous system is concerned primarily with regulation of how the body
   a. stores energy.
   b. uses energy.
   c. feels emotions.
   d. understands emotions.
2. The nucleus is found in the _____ of the neuron.
   a. dendrites
   b. axon
   c. synapse
   d. soma
3. The gates of the neuron that open and close with action potentials involve a balance between
   a. carbon and oxygen.
   b. sodium and potassium.
   c. magnesium and manganese.
   d. iron and zinc.
4. The process by which neurotransmitters are removed from a synapse and return to a neuron is called
   a. enzymatic deactivation.
   b. neuromodulation.
   c. reuptake.
   d. inhibition.
5. Which of the following is *not* a neurotransmitter?
   a. dopamine
   b. serotonin
   c. lysine
   d. acetylcholine
6. William Greenough has shown that early brain development involves changes in the number and structure of the
   a. synapses.
   b. somas.
   c. axons.
   d. dendrites.
7. The hippocampus is essential in
   a. memory formation.
   b. feelings of rage.
   c. feelings of happiness.
   d. complex problem solving.
8. Language processing is typically
   a. localized primarily in the right hemisphere.
   b. localized primarily in the left hemisphere.
   c. equally distributed across both hemispheres.
   d. outside either hemisphere.
9. A technique that assesses changes in the magnetic state of the blood as a function of the blood's degree of oxygenation is the
   a. CAT scan.
   b. angiogram.
   c. fMRI.
   d. PET scan.

10. Humans have _____ pairs of chromosomes.
    a. 16
    b. 23
    c. 32
    d. 46

Answers
1. b   2. d   3. b   4. c   5. c   6. a   7. a   8. b
9. c   10. b

THINK ABOUT IT

1. What ethical issues would be involved in tinkering with humans' genetic material?
2. Compare and contrast the ways in which people you know respond to new information that casts doubt onto existing beliefs. How might people improve their ways of responding?
3. If you were designing the human brain, what, if anything, would you do differently to render humans more adaptive to their environments?
4. Imagine beings who evolved on another planet and who differed from humans in ways that led them never to have wars. What differences in brain structure might be associated with such a course of evolution?
5. Karl Spencer Lashley, a pioneering neuropsychologist in the study of brain localization, suffered from migraine headaches, the specific nature of which still puzzles neuropsychologists. Many scientists have personal reasons for their intense curiosity about particular psychological phenomena or special fields of study. What aspect of human behavior particularly puzzles you? Which area or areas of the brain might you wish to study to find out about that behavior? Why?
6. What is a circumstance in which you find it particularly difficult to think as clearly or as insightfully as you would like? If you were a biological psychologist trying to determine the physiological factors that contribute to this circumstance, how might you investigate these factors?

WEB RESOURCES

For a chapter tutorial quiz, direct links to Internet sites, and other useful features, visit the book-specific website at http://psychology.wadsworth.com/sternberg4e. You can also connect directly to the following sites:

Brain Facts and Figures
http://faculty.washington.edu/chudler/introb.html
Here you'll find handy facts and figures about the brain, as well as general information about other features of the nervous system, including neurons, spinal cord, and sensory apparatus.

The Whole Brain Atlas
http://www.med.harvard.edu/AANLIB/home.html
This site offers an extensive guide to the brain, including an atlas of normal brain structure, a list of the top 100 brain structures, and a quiz that lets you test your knowledge of brain structure.

Basic Neural Processes
http://psych.hanover.edu/Krantz/neurotut.html
The undergraduate-level tutorials at this site will help you review basic neural functions. Then you can test yourself with the interactive quizzing.

For additional readings on many of the topics covered in this chapter, check out InfoTrac College Edition at **www.infotrac-college.com/wadsworth.**

Disk One
Cellular Structures and Functions
The Brain: Structure and Function
Chapter Quiz
Critical Thinking Questions

© Robb Kendrick/AuroraPhotos

SENSATION AND PERCEPTION

Where Am I?

She could see nothing. . . . It was not black, but . . . gray . . . like a night cloud reflecting the city lights of Moscow, featureless, but somehow textured. She could hear nothing, not the rumble of traffic, not the mechanical sounds of running water or slamming doors. . . . She turned her head, but the view remained the same, a gray blankness, like the inside of a cloud, or a ball of cotton, or—

She breathed. The air had no smell, no taste, neither moist nor dry, not even a temperature that she could discern. She spoke . . . but incredibly she heard nothing. . . .

Is this hell?

—*Tom Clancy*, The Cardinal of the Kremlin

Not hell, but sensory deprivation. In Tom Clancy's novel *The Cardinal of the Kremlin*, Svetlana Vaneyeva has been purposely deprived of all sensory stimulation to force a confession from her. First she panics, later she hallucinates, and eventually she confesses everything. Sensory deprivation can have such effects on people but, interestingly, it is also used for relaxation and stress reduction. The paradoxical effects of sensory deprivation illustrate the importance both of sensations from the world around us and of occasionally being free of some sensations. Psychologists study sensation because our thoughts, feelings, and actions are largely a reaction to what our senses do—or do not—take in. Without your senses, you would have no contact whatsoever with the world outside yourself.

Generally speaking, psychologists define a **sensation** as a message our brains receive from a sensory receptor that has been stimulated. A **sense** is a physical system that receives a particular kind of physical stimulation and translates it into an electrochemical message the brain can understand (see Reid, 2000). You might collect through your eyes and nose information about a steaming, circular, flat, tangy-smelling, red and white object. You translate this information and send it racing to your brain by means of sensory neurons. You have yet to make sense of the sensations.

Your brain organizes, integrates, processes, and interprets the sensory information, so that you say, "Ah! Pizza for dinner!" This high-level processing of information is *perception,* which takes up roughly where sensation leaves off. **Perception** is the set of cognitive processes through which we interpret the messages our senses provide. It synthesizes sensations and assigns meaning to them by taking into account our expectations, our prior experiences, and sometimes our culture. The distinction between sensation and perception is not clear-cut, however. When a background noise (e.g., a fan or other motor noise) is so constant that we get used to it, for example, we may say that we don't hear it any more.

Many psychologists are intrigued by the extent to which the brain's structures and processes are affected by culture. The more closely a psychological phenomenon is tied to strictly physiological processes, the less variability we find among humans, regardless of culture. Conversely, the more closely a phenomenon is tied to the environment and to social processes, the more cultural variation we are likely to find (Poortinga, Kop, & van de Vijver, 1990). For example, there is likely to be more variation in the way people across cultures *perceive* distant points of light in the sky than in the way they *sense* them. People in two different cultures might have the same sensory experience when they look at the moon. But the moon may be perceived as a desolate wasteland by us and as the home of distant gods by someone from another culture.

In another example of cultural differences in perception, Richard Nisbett and his colleagues have found that East Asians tend to be more holistic in their thinking and Westerners more analytic. Thus, East Asians may tend to perceive objects in terms of their entirety, whereas Westerners may perceive them in terms of their parts. East Asians also tend to find it easier to engage in dialectical thinking than do Westerners (see Chapter 1) (Ji, Nisbett, & Su, 2001; Nisbett, Peng, Choi, & Norenzayan, 2001; Nisbett & Norenzayan, 2002; Norenzayan & Nisbett, 2002). Westerners tend to see statements as true or not true, whereas Easterners may attempt to view truth or falsity as a function of the context in which the statement is made. Westerns often see events as good or bad. Nisbett cites an Eastern story in which an apparently good event happens. But in the long run it results in a bad consequence. Then, in the longer run, this bad consequence has a good outcome. But, in the still longer run, this good outcome leads to bad results.

And the story goes on indefinitely, with seemingly good outcomes turning bad and seemingly bad outcomes turning good. The point is that, from the Eastern point of view, there is no easy and clear way to label an event good or bad.

(E) Consider the adaptive value of sensory processing from an evolutionary standpoint. We are sensitive to only a small range of the various kinds of stimulation in our environment. For example, our eyes cannot detect most wavelengths in the electromagnetic spectrum. Similarly, our ears cannot hear very high and very low frequencies. Are there advantages to not being able to detect certain stimuli? Yes—we are protected from drowning in a sea of irrelevant stimulation. At the same time, we must be able to detect certain forms of stimulation. An organism that could not feel pain would be in grave danger of damage to bodily tissue. As another example, after a while, we stop noticing stimuli that are constant in the environment. The adaptive advantage is that we thereby are more ready to detect changes, including ones that are potentially hazardous. We may become more alert to a car (driven, perhaps, by an intoxicated driver) that is suddenly rushing toward us. In short, we have evolved ways of tuning in to the most relevant information in our surroundings and of detecting changes from constant levels of this information. These adaptations optimize our fit to our environments.

(E) There is another important way in which evolution shapes our interaction with the environment. Members of different species see different objects in their environments. Members of the same species may see different objects at different periods of history. One of the main necessities they search for is food. According to *optimal foraging theory*, evolution directs members of various species to become optimal foragers (Greenberg & Haraway, 2002; Mellgren, 1998). So, members of several species might look at a garden and perceive different objects that meet their needs, depending on whether they eat vegetables, insects, worms, grubs, or whatever.

In this chapter we learn how our senses convey light, color, sound, taste, scent, pressure, temperature, pain, balance, and motion. We also learn how visual sensations are converted into perceptions. Before we examine each sense individually, however, we should explore two areas relevant to the study of all kinds of sensation and perception. First we investigate how the senses are studied and measured, and then we probe some biological properties common to all our senses.

PSYCHOPHYSICS

What are the relationships between various forms of physical stimulation and the psychological sensations they produce?

Psychophysics is the systematic study of the relationship between the *physical* stimulation of a sense organ and the *psychological* sensations produced by that stimulation. A psychophysical experiment, for example, might measure the relationship between the rate at which a neon light flashes and your ability to detect individual flashes.

Measurements of psychophysical relationships can be put to many practical uses. When you have your vision checked, the eye doctor determines how large the letters must be for you to see them clearly. The audiologist who checks your hearing determines how faint a tone you can hear. Psychophysics is also relevant in human factors and engineering psychology, as in the design of instrument panels. How brightly lit should an automobile's dashboard gauges be in order to be visible but not distracting at night? You want to see the gauges, not be blinded by them! In the development of products, consumer psychologists tackle questions such as how strong a perfume can be without becoming overpowering. A woman wearing perfume may want a man to be attracted to

Computer software makers must take psychophysics into account when they design the complex functions of games such as this one. They must design the visual images on the screen to be optimally detectable.

TABLE 4.1

Absolute Sense Thresholds. Here are some approximations of the absolute thresholds for the senses. (From Galanter, Eugene [1962]. Contemporary psychophysics. In R. Brown, et al. (Eds.), *New Directions in Psychology,* New York: Holt, Rinehart & Winston, p. 97. Reprinted by permission.)

Sense	Minimum Stimulus
Vision	A candle flame seen at 30 miles on a dark, clear night
Hearing	The tick of a watch 20 feet away under quiet conditions
Taste	One teaspoon of sugar in 2 gallons of water
Smell	One drop of perfume diffused into the entire air volume of six rooms
Touch	The wing of a fly falling on your cheek from a distance of 1 centimeter

her scent; she does not want him to reel over! All of these answers can be found with psychophysical techniques. Psychophysics also deals with basic problems related to perception: detection, measurement error, and discrimination (Coren, Ward, & Enns, 1994; Galanter, 2000; Geschieder, 1997).

THRESHOLDS

Detection is awareness of the presence of a sensory stimulus. In sensory-detection studies, researchers ask how much light, sound, taste, or other sensory stimulation is needed in order for our senses minimally to detect it (Galanter, 2000). The hypothetical minimum amount of physical energy of a given kind—scent, sound, pressure, and so on—that an individual can detect is the **absolute threshold** for that kind of energy. We cannot sense the stimulus below the absolute-threshold level, but we can consistently sense it above that level. Table 4.1 lists some approximations of the absolute thresholds of different senses.

An experimenter can determine an absolute threshold by starting with an extremely weak stimulus, such as a faint beep, and asking the participant to detect it. The beep should be so weak that detection is impossible. The experimenter then increases the stimulus intensity until the person hears the beep. In theory, the dividing line between when the person can and cannot hear the stimulus is the absolute threshold for detecting that sort of sound. In practice, however, factors such as fatigue, distractions, or a cold can affect when people begin to notice the stimulus. To account for such differences, psychologists operationally define (that is, define in terms of measurement operations; see Chapter 2) the absolute threshold *as the level*

at which a stimulus is first detected 50% of the time (see Figure 4.1).

The traditional method of determining an absolute threshold does not fully take into account factors that can distort sensory measurements, such as a person's patterns of guessing, response bias, and background noise. For example, when a signal, such as a doorbell, is very faint, we sometimes cannot be sure whether we hear anything or not. Some people are inclined to guess "yes," saying they heard the bell. Others say they heard the bell only when they are quite confident of having heard it, responding "no" otherwise. This predisposition to guess one way or another is *response bias*. A further confounding problem is background noise. Sometimes people truly think they hear a signal but actually they are just picking up background sounds in the environment or even within themselves.

SIGNAL-DETECTION ANALYSIS

A more systematic way of measuring detection takes into account distortions of the measurement process. This method, *signal-detection analysis*, provides both an important approach to psychophysics and ingenious insights into the processes of decision making. The key advantage of this method is that it allows the experimenter to separate out true sensitivity to a stimulus from distorting factors like response bias and background noise.

According to **signal-detection theory (SDT)**, four combinations of stimulus and response are possi-

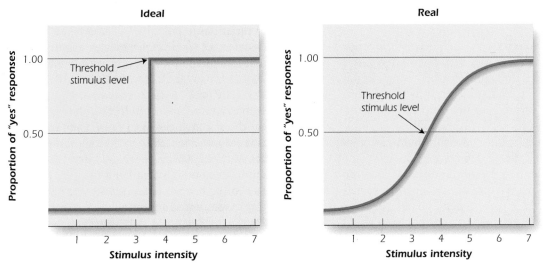

FIGURE 4.1

Ideal and Real Absolute Thresholds. Because it is virtually impossible to identify an ideal absolute threshold, psychologists define absolute threshold as the level of stimulation that an individual can detect.

ble. Suppose you are asked to detect the faint flicker of a light. One possibility is a *hit:* The *signal,* or stimulus (in this case the flicker of the light), is present and your response is to detect it correctly. A second possibility is a *miss:* The light flickers, but you do not detect it. A third possibility is a *false alarm:* The light does not flicker, but you think you see it flicker. The fourth possibility is a *correct rejection:* The light does not flicker, and you do not think that it does. Table 4.2 summarizes these combinations of stimuli and responses. Thus, SDT allows for hits and misses, like traditional psychophysical threshold measurement. But it also allows for false alarms and correct rejections (Colman, 2001; Green & Swets, 1966; Swets, Tanner, & Birdsall, 1961).

According to SDT, we do not merely *report* objectively whether we *do* or *do not* detect a signal. Rather, we *decide*—taking into account the background noise, emotional context, and personal expectations—*how likely* it is that a sensation has been caused by a signal. For example, you might detect (and be frightened by) a slight creaking noise when you are home alone late at night. You might not detect that very same stimulus if you were at home during the day with other people around. Psychologists compare the percentages of responses that fall into the four categories. They then use these figures to determine whether people have a response bias toward giving more "yes" or more "no" answers in guessing situations. Knowing about any response bias or other distorting effects can help researchers reach more nearly correct threshold measurements.

TABLE 4.2

Outcomes of a Signal-Detection Experiment. Signal-detection theory allows for four possible combinations of stimulus and response, thereby allowing psychologists to consider the expectations of the person sensing the stimulus.

	Response	
Signal	**"Yes, present"**	**"No, absent"**
Light present	Hit	Miss
Light absent	False alarm	Correct rejection

DISCRIMINATING AMONG STIMULI

Being able to detect a single stimulus is certainly crucial in many circumstances. Often, however, the problem is not how strong or intense a stimulus must be in order for a person to detect it, but rather how easily one stimulus can be distinguished from another. This psychophysics problem involves discrimination: the ability to ascertain the difference between one stimulus and another. In your everyday life you might need to discern in a poorly lit room whether two socks are the same color. Or in listening to a concert, you might observe that an instrument is out of tune and that its notes are not in harmony with those of other instruments.

THE JUST NOTICEABLE DIFFERENCE

The minimum amount of difference that can be detected between two sensory stimuli is the **difference threshold,** or the **just noticeable difference (jnd).** Just as our absolute thresholds for detecting stimuli vary, so do our responses to differences between stimuli. The resulting variation causes measurement error. For this reason, psychologists average data from multiple trials that measure difference thresholds. In practical terms, the operational definition of the jnd is the difference between two stimuli that can be detected 50% of the time. In a typical jnd experiment, a participant makes many comparisons between pairs of stimuli that vary in only one respect. You could be asked to lay your hand on two otherwise identical surfaces that might differ in temperature. You would then have to say whether the two surfaces feel as though they are the same temperature. The difference that you could detect exactly 50% of the time would be your jnd for temperature.

Sensory-difference thresholds are important in everyday life and even in some professions. A coffee taster must be able to taste and smell the differences among blends, grinds, and roasts of bean. Musicians must be able to hear whether their instruments are just a fraction of a pitch off-key. Diamond graders must be able to distinguish diamonds that differ only slightly in color.

If one bucket has 2 ounces more water in it than the other, will the difference be noticeable?

No single jnd applies to all senses equally. In addition to variations in jnd's from person to person, the human species as a whole varies in its responses to different types and magnitudes of sensory stimulation.

WEBER'S LAW

Ernst Weber, a German physiologist, first noticed in 1834 that the change needed to cause a jnd increases proportionately with increases in the magnitude of the stimulus (Murray, 2000). Weber noted that a jnd is not a constant fixed amount but rather a constant proportion of the stimulus. According to **Weber's law,** the greater the magnitude of the stimulus, the larger a difference needs to be in order to be detected.

The relative amount of change needed for a given type of stimulus to produce a jnd is termed the *Weber fraction*. The actual fraction varies for different sensory experiences. The Weber fraction for weights is about 0.02. For example, for a 10-pound bag, you would just notice a difference of as little as a fifth of a pound, 2% of 10 pounds. For the 10-ounce bag, you would need a difference of only a fifth of an ounce. However, for a 50-pound bag, you would need a difference of 1 pound in order to detect the difference. We are much better able to detect differences in amounts of electric shock (low Weber fraction of 0.01) than differences in taste (high Weber fraction of 0.2). Table 4.3 shows Weber fractions for a variety of sensory stimulation. The smaller the fraction, the more sensitive we are to differences in that sensory *modality* (e.g., vision or hearing). The higher the fraction, the less sensitive we are. Although Weber fractions differ across sensory modalities, there are many similarities among them. We consider these similarities next.

TABLE 4.3

Weber Fractions for Various Types of Stimuli.
Because people show different degrees of sensitivity to distinct kinds of sensations, the Weber fractions for various kinds of stimuli differ. (After Teghtsoonian, 1971)

Stimulus	Weber Fraction
Electric shock	0.01
Heaviness	0.02
Length	0.03
Vibration (fingertip)	0.04
Loudness	0.05
Odor	0.05
Brightness	0.08
Taste (salt)	0.2

© Owen Franken/Stock, Boston

BIOLOGICAL PROPERTIES COMMON TO ALL SENSES

How do we sense physical stimuli?

RECEIVING AND CONVEYING SENSORY INFORMATION

Every sensation—whether it is the color of a lawn, the smell of a rose, or a breeze felt on our skin—starts when a sensory organ is stimulated. This stimulation occurs at specialized **receptor cells** that have evolved to detect particular kinds of energy, such as mechanical, electromagnetic, or chemical energy. Each receptor cell receives messages from a specific area of the external world.

When sensory receptors in our eyes, ears, or other sense organs are stimulated by a form of energy, they must relay that information in electrochemical form to the brain. Because the information is not initially electrochemical, the sensory receptors must first convert, or **transduce,** this energy received from the environment into the form of energy that is meaningful to the nervous system (Colman, 2001). Although the task of transduction is common to all the senses, the method for achieving it is different for each sense. Each sense has a set of specialized receptors for transducing its own kind of stimulus energy.

A bright red floodlight does not look the same as a dim blue night light. The trill of a flute does not sound like the wail of an electric guitar. **Sensory coding** is a physiological form of communication through which sensory receptors convey a range of information about stimuli throughout the nervous system. Receptors and neurons use an electrochemical language to convey shades of meaning in their messages.

Each sensory stimulus has two important properties. The first is *intensity*, the amount of physical energy that is transduced by a sensory receptor and then sensed by the brain (such as the spiciness we taste in a food). The second is *quality*, the nature of the stimulus that reaches a sensory receptor and is then sensed in the brain (for example, whether the food is salty or sweet). Sensory neurons encode the physical properties of a stimulus by means of special *patterns* of action potentials that specifically identify those properties to the brain. One way to measure the firing patterns of individual neurons is **single-cell recording,** a recording of one neuron in the brain. Single-cell recording lets researchers determine exactly which kinds of stimuli activate which kinds of neurons. Once researchers know which neurons are active, they look for firing patterns.

Single-cell recording techniques have vastly increased our knowledge about how neurons perform sensory coding, especially regarding stimulus intensity. Two factors determine stimulus intensity: the neuron's *rate of firing*, how many times the neuron fires within a given period, and the neuron's *firing-pattern regularity*. The less intense the stimulus, the less frequently and the less regularly the neuron will fire. The more intense the stimulus, the more frequently and the more regularly the neuron will fire. (See Figure 4.2 for an illustration of patterns of neural rates of firing.)

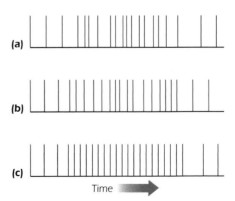

FIGURE 4.2

Neural Rates of Firing. Neurons fire at varying rates according to the types of stimuli that prompt the neural activity. Responses of three different neurons are shown.

One of the most important functions of the senses is in sexual attraction. Humans and other animals use their senses to decide on suitable sexual partners. We are most attracted to individuals who are attractive in the way they look, sound, feel, and smell. We may spend time making ourselves look more attractive, or trying to sound a certain way, or putting on cologne, all in an effort to increase our attractiveness. Thus, the senses are functional not only for adapting to the environment but also in creating the conditions for our progeny to do the same.

SENSORY ADAPTATION

As explained above, our senses are designed to detect *changes* in stimulus energy. From a functional and evolutionary standpoint, this reaction reflects our need to pay attention to what is new and strange in order to determine whether it is—literally or figuratively—friend or foe. When stimulus energy changes, the receptor cells fire more vigorously and thus alert the brain to the change. A physiological mechanism, sensory adaptation, helps us adjust to changes in stimuli.

Sensory adaptation is a temporary physiological response to a sensed change in the environment. It encompasses both the temporary gradual decrease in sensitivity that occurs when a sensory system is stimulated for a period of time and the temporary increase in sensitivity that occurs when a sensory system is not stimulated for a period of time. Because adaptation is generally not subject to conscious manipulation or control, it does not usually depend on previous experience with the given change (e.g., changes in temperature or other changes in intensity). For example, without any conscious effort, our vision adapts to changes in light intensity (to darkness or to increased brightness). Similarly, our sense of smell, or olfaction, adapts to having a particular odor in the environment. A smell that is intolerable at first may be barely detectable after a few minutes (Dalton & Wysocki, 1996). You need no training or previous experience to make these sensory adaptations. You will make the adaptation (e.g., to bad smells) about the same way the first time and every time thereafter. (There is, however, some decrement due to aging in our visual ability to adjust to darkness.) The degree of sensory adaptation required relates directly to the intensity of the stimulus in the environment, not to the number of times you were previously exposed to the stimulus or to the length of time between your last exposure and your present one. Furthermore, when the environment returns to its former state, your physiological mechanisms for adaptation return to their former states.

If you have adapted to a stimulus, such as cold ocean water on your body, then you will eventually find that the water does not seem as cold as it originally did. You have thus shifted to a new adaptation level (Helson,

Water that at first seems cold later seems warmer as you adapt to the temperature.

1964). The **adaptation level** is the reference level of sensory stimulation against which an individual may judge new stimuli or changes in existing stimuli (Keith, 2000). Once your body has adapted to the cold water, an ice cube will feel less cold to you than before you went swimming. Conversely, hot sand will feel hotter. As soon as you get out of the water and spend some time sunning on the sand, however, your body will reach a new adaptation level for this warmer temperature. Regardless of how many times you repeat this process, or how long you wait between jumping into or out of the water, your body will go through approximately the same adaptation response that it went through the very first time you adapted to the change in temperature. Furthermore, you generally have little conscious control over how quickly your body adapts to the change in temperature, or to other types of changes, such as in levels of light.

✓CONCEPT CHECK 2

1. Which of the following is an example of sensory adaptation?
   a. You enter Schmooville. At first it smells terrible, and after a while it smells even worse.
   b. You enter Schmooville. At first it smells terrible, but after a while it does not smell anymore.

c. You lose your sense of smell entirely.

d. Upon leaving Schmooville, you notice a new odor you have never smelled before.

2. Receptor cells detect
   a. only electromagnetic energy.
   b. only electromechanical energy.
   c. no kind of energy.
   d. various kinds of energy.

3. Transduction makes
   a. one language understandable in terms of the words of another.
   b. various forms of energy interpretable by the nervous system.
   c. one color into another color.
   d. a false alarm into a signal.

VISION

What are the sensory and perceptual mechanisms that enable us to see?

Have you ever awakened to utter darkness? You get out of bed and stumble over the shoes you left out in the middle of the floor. The light switch on the wall—somehow, it seems not to be there when you cannot see it. You appreciate your vision then in a way that you cannot when you see well, and in a way that a blind person might like to be able to do. To understand how vision is possible, we need to know something about light, about the structure of the eye, and about how the eye interacts with light to enable us to see. We consider each of these topics in turn.

Light is the form of electromagnetic energy that the receptors of our eyes are distinctively designed to receive. Our eyes detect only a very narrow band of the electromagnetic spectrum of radiation. The **electromagnetic spectrum** is a range of energy of varying wavelengths (see Figure 4.3). Human eyes are receptive to only the narrow wavelength range from about 350 to 750 *nanometers* (nm; billionths of a meter). White light, such as the light from the sun, consists of all of the visible wavelengths combined. Other visible wavelengths of light are seen as different colors. Other species differ from humans in what they can see. Some nonhuman animals can see electromagnetic radiation that is invisible to us. Humans cannot see wavelengths in the infrared and ultraviolet bands of the spectrum as bees can see. The ability to detect different wavelengths depends on contextual factors also. For example, sensitivity is reduced in the presence of a bright, uniform background (A. W. Freeman & Badcock, 1999).

THE FUNCTIONAL ORGANIZATION OF THE EYE

The **cornea** is a curved exterior lens that gathers and focuses the entering light. The cornea is actually a specialized region of the *sclera* of the eye (the external rubbery layer that holds in the gelatinous substance of the eye). The entire sclera, and particularly the cornea, is very sensitive to touch. When a foreign substance comes in contact with the sclera, your body almost instantaneously initiates a series of protective responses, as you know from having had dust, lashes, or any other particles touch your eye.

Light beams enter the eye via the cornea, which bulges slightly to form a clear, dome-shaped window, as illustrated in Figure 4.4. Upon penetrating the cornea, the light beam passes through the **pupil**, which is a hole in the center of a circular muscle called the **iris.** The iris reflects certain light beams outward and away from the eye to give our eyes their distinctive colors. When the light coming into the eye is very bright, the iris reflexively causes the pupil to constrict and limit the amount of light entering the eye. The pupil can reach a diameter as small as 2 millimeters. When light is dim, the pupil becomes dilated to as large as 8 millimeters to collect more light. (The 4-fold increase in diameter equals about a 16-fold increase in area, so the eyes are actually quite adaptive.) As we age, however, our pupils become less able to dilate. This decreased ability leads to more difficulty seeing in dim light. Slower pupillary reflexes also make it harder for older persons to adapt to rapid changes in light and dark, such as those encountered driving at night on a busy two-way street.

After light enters the pupil, the curved interior **lens** of the eye causes light to bend as it passes through it. Because the curvature of the cornea does most of the gross *refraction* (bending of light waves), the lens does mostly fine tuning. It adjusts its own amount of curvature to get the focus just right. The process by which the lens changes its curvature to focus on objects at different distances is termed **accommodation.** Figure 4.4 shows how the changes in the curvature of the cornea and the lens adjust the focus of objects at different distances. A flatter lens bends the light less and focuses more distant objects, whereas a more curved lens focuses closer objects more clearly.

Figure 4.5 shows the anatomy of the entire eye, including the cornea and the lens. In general, the functioning of the eye deteriorates with age. Starting at about age 50, many people find that their visual acuity for seeing patterns decreases (Sekuler & Sekuler, 2000). Certain disorders of the eye can also impair vision. In macular degeneration, the cells of the retina that transduce light start to degenerate and thus lose their ability to contribute properly to vision

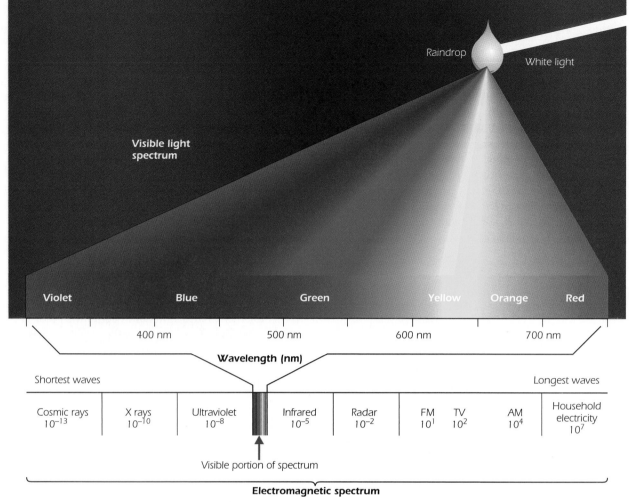

FIGURE 4.3
Electromagnetic Spectrum. Within the wide range of the electromagnetic spectrum, humans can detect only a narrow band of wavelengths of light.

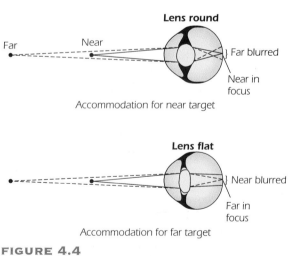

FIGURE 4.4
How the Eye Focuses Visual Images. The cornea and lens refract light through the pupil to focus the light on the retina at the back of the eye.

(G. S. Rubin, 2000; G. Rubin et al., 1997; Wahl, 2000; Wahl, Schilling, Oswald, & Heyl, 1999). In glaucoma, interior pressure starts to degrade the performance of the eye.

THE RETINA
The refracted light focuses on the **retina,** a network of neurons that extends over most of the back (posterior) surface of the interior of the eye. The retina is where electromagnetic light energy is transduced into neural electrochemical impulses (Blake, 2000). Although the retina is only about as thick as a single page in this book, it nevertheless consists of three main layers of neural tissue (see Figure 4.5).

The first layer of neuronal tissue—closest to the front, outward-facing surface of the eye—is the layer of **ganglion cells,** whose axons constitute the **optic nerve.** The second layer consists of three kinds of in-

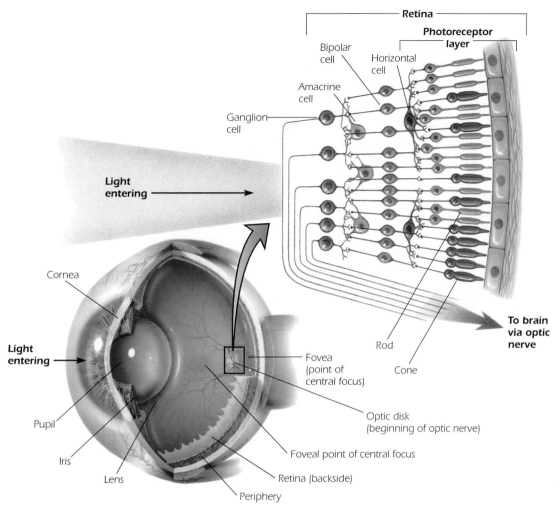

FIGURE 4.5

Anatomy of the Eye. The light refracted through the cornea and lens onto the retina stimulates the sensory receptors in the retina. The receptors, the rods and cones, sense the wavelength (color) of the light and transduce its electromagnetic energy to electrochemical energy. The optic nerve carries the neural impulses to the visual cortex.

terneuron cells. **Amacrine cells** and **horizontal cells** make single lateral connections among adjacent areas of the retina in the middle layer of cells. **Bipolar cells** make dual connections forward and outward to the ganglion cells, as well as backward and inward to the third layer of retinal cells.

The third layer of the retina contains the **photoreceptors,** which transduce light energy into electrochemical energy. This energy then can be transmitted by neurons to the brain. The transmission enables the eye to detect visual stimulation. Ironically, the photoreceptor cells are the retinal cells farthest from the light source. Light must pass through the other two layers first. Messages are then passed back outward toward the front of your eye before they travel to the brain. There are two kinds of photoreceptors. The **rods** are long and thin photoreceptors.

They are more highly concentrated in the periphery of the retina than in the foveal region of the retina, where vision is most acute. The **cones** are short and thick photoreceptors. They are more highly concentrated in the foveal region of the retina than in the periphery. The **fovea** is a small, thin region of the retina, the size of the head of a pin, that is most directly in the line of sight. In fact, when you look straight at an object, your eyes rotate so that the image falls directly onto the fovea. The visual receptive field of the fovea is approximately as big as the size of a grape held at arm's length.

Each cone in the fovea typically has its own ganglion cell, but the rods on the *periphery* (outer boundary area) of the retina share ganglion cells with other rods. Thus, each ganglion cell gathering information from the periphery gathers information from many rods. But each ganglion cell in the fovea gathers information from only one cone, perhaps because of the more complex function of cones in the processing of color.

Each eye contains roughly 120 million rods and 8 million cones. Rods and cones differ not only in shape (see Figure 4.6) but also in their compositions, locations, and responses to light. Within the rods and cones are **photopigments**, chemical substances that react to light. The photopigments start the complex transduction process that transforms physical electromagnetic energy into an electrochemical neural impulse that can be understood by the brain.

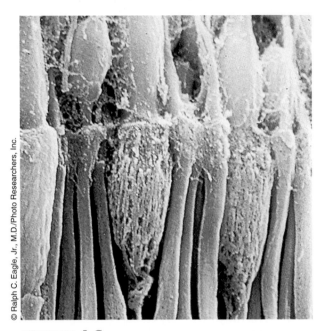

© Ralph C. Eagle, Jr., M.D./Photo Researchers, Inc.

FIGURE 4.6
Photoreceptors. An electron microscope photo of photoreceptors shows the distinct shape and length of the rods and the cones.

FROM THE EYE TO THE BRAIN

The rods, cones, and photopigments within them could not do their work without being hooked up to the brain (Sandell, 2000). The neurochemical messages processed by the rods and cones of the retina travel via the bipolar cells to the ganglion cells (see Goodale, 2000). As noted earlier, the axons of the ganglion cells in the eye collectively form the optic nerve for that eye. The optic nerves of the two eyes join at the base of the brain to form the optic chiasma. At this point, the ganglion cells from the inward, or nasal, part of the retina—the part closer to your nose—cross through the optic chiasma and go to the opposite hemisphere of the brain. The ganglion cells from the outward, or temporal, area of the retina, closer to your temple, go to the hemisphere on the

same side of the body (see Figure 4.7). The lens of each eye naturally inverts the image of the world as it projects the image onto the retina. In this way, the message sent to your brain is literally upside down and backward.

After being routed via the optic chiasma, the ganglion cells go to the thalamus. From the thalamus, neurons carry information to the primary visual cortex in the occipital lobe of the brain. The visual cortex contains several processing areas. Each area handles different kinds of visual information relating to intensity and quality, including color, location, depth, pattern, and form. Let us consider in more detail how the cortex processes color information through the workings of the rods and the cones.

HOW WE SEE: RODS AND CONES

We have two separate visual systems. One, responsible for vision in dim light, depends on the rods. The other, responsible for vision in brighter light, depends on the cones (Durgin, 2000).

Critical evidence for the separate functioning of these two systems comes from people who lack either rods or cones. Such people are rare, but they were first studied by German physiologist J. A. von Kries. Von Kries (1895) found that people with no (or nonfunctioning) rods suffer from night blindness. From twilight onward, they cannot see without artificial light. Individuals without functioning cones, in contrast, exhibit day, or bright light, blindness. Whereas they can see relatively well in dim light, they find normal sunlight or bright artificial light painful. They have very poor visual *acuity* (keenness of sensation) in such light. People without working cones are also completely color-blind because the cones receive color but the rods do not. It is for this reason that, for all of us, objects that are dimly lit appear only in various shades of gray (see Figure 4.8). Our night vision is *achromatic*, or lacking color.

The **blind spot** is the small area on the retina where the optic nerve pushes aside photoreceptors to exit the eye. Because you lack photoreceptors in the blind spot, you are unable to see any images that happen to be projected onto that spot. You are not normally aware of the blind spot, in part because the spot one eye cannot see is in the normal visual field of the other eye. Your brain thus uses the complete information from one eye to compensate for the blind spot in the other eye (see Figure 4.9).

Figure 4.10 depicts much of the information we have covered so far about the retina. In particular, it shows the effectiveness of the rods and the cones at different visual angles. Your day vision, as you have probably already noticed, is better when you look at objects directly in front of you rather than off to the

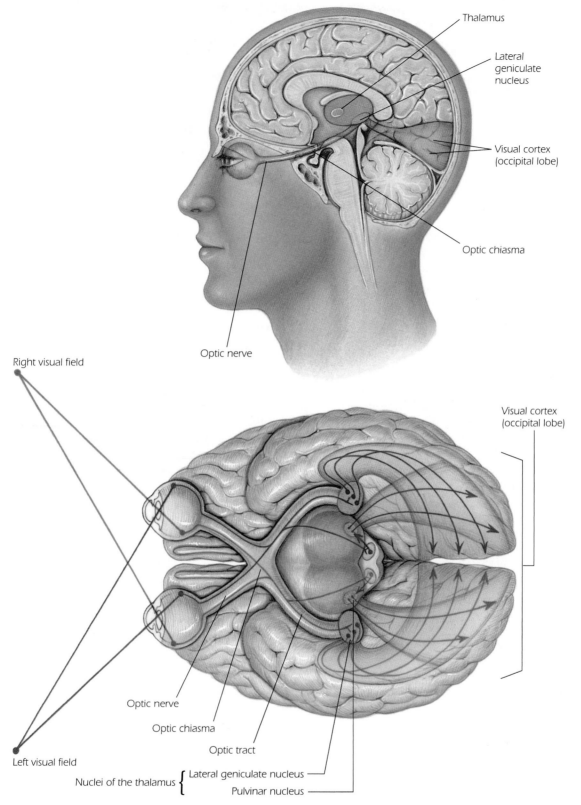

Thalamus

Lateral
geniculate
nucleus

Visual cortex
(occipital lobe)

Optic chiasma

Optic nerve

Right visual field

Visual cortex
(occipital lobe)

Optic nerve

Optic chiasma

Optic tract

Left visual field

Nuclei of the thalamus { Lateral geniculate nucleus

Pulvinar nucleus

FIGURE 4.7

Neural Pathways from the Eye to the Brain. From the photoreceptors in the retina, the ganglion cells travel to the optic nerve of each eye. The impulses from each side of the eye then route via the optic nerve through the optic chiasma to the thalamus. The thalamus organizes the visual information and sends it to the visual cortex in the occipital lobe.

FIGURE 4.8

Colorful Cones and Monochromatic Rods. (a) During the day, in bright light, our cones enable us to see vivid colors. (b) As the sun sets, limiting the amount of light, our rods enable us to see the same image but in monochromatic shades—that is, in shades of gray.

side. Your rod-based night vision is better for objects in your peripheral vision than in your central line of vision (see Figure 4.11). Thus, at night, you can see a star more clearly if you look just to the side of it. One star may appear to us as brighter than another. How do we detect brightness and differences in brightness?

SEEING BY LIGHT AND DARKNESS

Light has the physical dimensions of intensity and *wavelength* (the distance from the crest of one light wave to the crest of the next wave). It also has the corresponding psychological dimensions of brightness and color. These properties result from how our bodies and minds process the physical information we take in through our receptors. The physically quantifiable amount of light that reaches our eyes from an object

is termed the *retinal illuminance. Brightness*, however, does not refer to an actual quantifiable light intensity. Rather, it references our *impression* of light intensity based on light-wave *amplitude* or "height." Brightness is thus a psychological phenomenon rather than a physical quantity (see Figure 4.12). Our sensation of brightness is not directly related to the actual intensity of light reflected by an object. Rather, the relationship is curvilinear. An increase of one physical unit has less impact as the intensity of the light increases. (We saw this principle earlier in the discussion of psychophysics.)

We sense brightness partly because of the physical structure of the eye. In particular, perceived brightness depends in part on the retinal location of the image of a stimulus. As mentioned previously, our senses help us adapt to environmental changes. When you walk from a dark room into bright sun-

(a)

(b)

FIGURE 4.9

Blind Spot. To find your blind spot, hold this page about 12 inches from your face and close your right eye. Staring at the cross in the upper right corner, gradually move the page toward and away from your face until the circle on the left disappears. You can do the same to the cross and the bar until the bar seems solid.

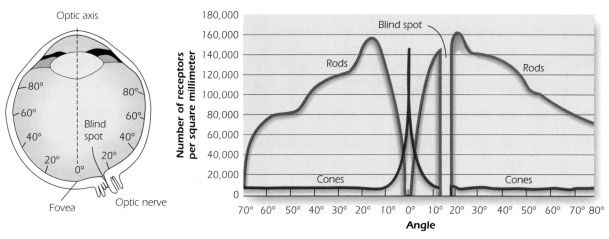

FIGURE 4.10
Retina of the Eye. In the fovea, the center of the retina, the concentration of cones is greater. In the periphery of the retina, the concentration of rods is greater. Why are these photoreceptors distributed as they are?

FIGURE 4.11
Visual Acuity. In dim light, look directly at these converging lines and mark with your finger where the lines begin to blur together. Then look slightly to the side and again mark where the lines begin to blur. Which condition showed greater acuity? Why?

light, you probably have to squint. You may even have to close your eyes for a moment. Your eyes are experiencing *light adaptation*—adjustment to an increase in light intensity. Similarly, when you go from the bright outdoors into a dim or dark room, at first you will have difficulty seeing anything at all. It may

take 30 minutes, or even longer, for your eyes to adapt fully. You are experiencing dark adaptation, an adjustment to a decrease in light intensity. Interestingly, in dark adaptation, although your pupil area may increase by a factor of about 16, your visual sensitivity to light may increase by a factor of as much as 100,000. The time course of dark adaptation, as measured by absolute thresholds, does not progress uniformly. The oddly shaped curve in Figure 4.13 shows this nonuniform progress. What might generate this curve for the time course of dark adaptation?

A discontinuity in a curve often suggests that two or more processes underlie the function it represents. The two mechanisms in Figure 4.13 are the cones and the rods. Because these mechanisms enter the process of dark adaptation at different times, they generate an irregular curve.

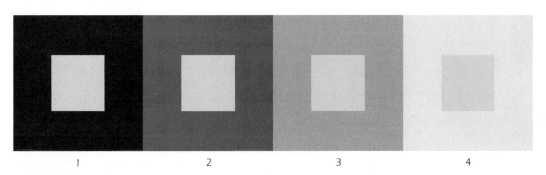

FIGURE 4.12
Brightness as a Psychological Phenomenon. Which gray area in the center appears to be brightest? Why?

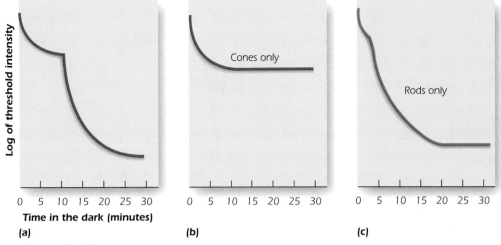

FIGURE 4.13

Dark Adaptation Curve. After participants have adapted to a bright light, they are placed in darkness and become increasingly sensitive to light. The sharp break in the curve at about 10 minutes is known as the rod-cone break.

HOW WE SEE COLOR

Look at Figure 4.14. Can you see the shapes embedded in the circles? If so, you probably have normal color vision. Some people who are wholly or partially color-blind do not see red or green. Rather, they may see either or both colors as shades of gray. Before we address color-blindness and its causes, we should look at how a person with normal vision senses color.

HUE, SATURATION, AND BRIGHTNESS

Wavelength produces the first property of color—hue. **Hue** corresponds closely to what we call "color." People with normal color vision see light waves of a variety of hues within the visible electromagnetic spectrum. The shortest wavelengths we can see are violet (starting at a wavelength of about 350 nm). The longest are red (up to a wavelength of about 750 nm). Colors are not inherent in the objects we see as colored. They are not even inherent in the light reflected from objects. Rather, colors are a reaction of our nervous systems to particular wavelengths of the visible spectrum. The sensation of color, then, depends on the interaction between light and the nervous system.

A second property of color, also determined by spectral wavelength, is saturation. *Saturation* refers to how vivid, vibrant, or rich the hue appears. A highly saturated hue seems to be bursting with color, with no hint of paleness. A weakly saturated one seems to be washed out. The third property of color, *brightness*, was described earlier in terms of the way we see visible light. Brightness is caused by the amplitude of the light wave. It refers to the amount of light that we see emanating from the hue. (See Figure 4.15 for illustrations of these properties.)

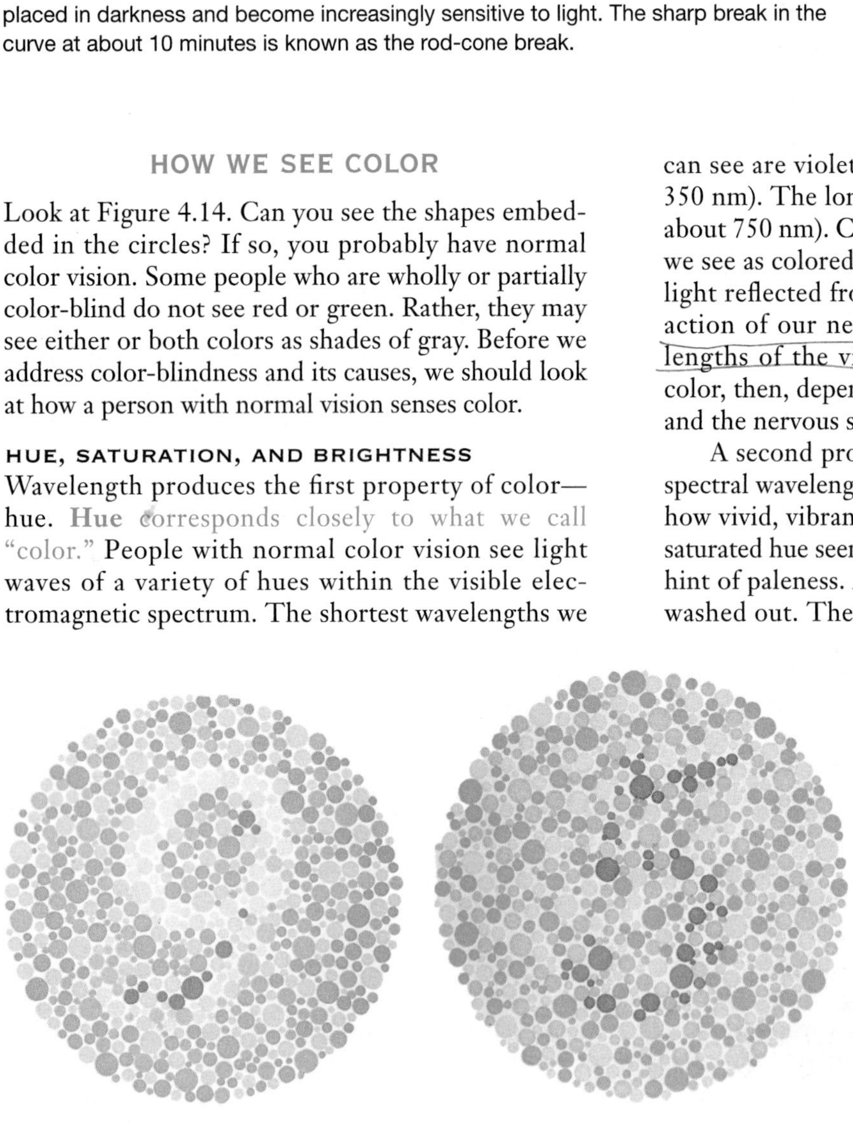

RELATIONSHIPS AMONG COLORS

The colors we see correspond to spectrum intensities that increase from violet to red. Yet, psychologically, violet and red do not appear to be as different from each other as, say, violet and green, or red and green. Somehow, the way that we perceive colors to be related

FIGURE 4.14

Psychophysical Tests for Color-Blindness. What shapes can you see when you look at these circles? These and other psychophysical tests are used to diagnose red-green color-blindness.

(a)

(b)

© Brand X/Alamy Images

(c)

FIGURE 4.15

The Three Properties of Color. The image on the left in each row is an untouched real-life photo. In the right column, (a) shows brightness; (b) shows saturation; and (c) shows hue.

psychologically is not the way they are related in terms of physical wavelengths (see Figure 4.3).

Within the visible spectrum, we see approximately 150 hues. Given that hues can also have brightness and saturation, we can discriminate more than 7 million colors of varying hue, intensity, and brightness. It turns out that these hues can be mixed to produce other hues in two ways.

Colors can be mixed either additively or subtractively. These two processes work differently and they also result in different colors. We obtain an **additive color mixture** when light waves of varying wavelengths are mixed or blended, as when spotlights of different colors are aimed toward one point. Each light wave *adds* its wavelength to the color mixture. The resulting sum of the wavelengths is what we see. Figure 4.16a shows what happens when red light, blue light, and green light are mixed in different combinations. The additive mixture of all three colors, or indeed of all colors, of light produces white light.

Subtractive color mixture is the remaining wavelengths of light that are reflected from an object after other wavelengths of light have been absorbed by that object. To most people, this is the more familiar kind of mixture. Most colored objects do not generate light; rather, they reflect it. That is, an apple appears red to us not because it generates red light but because it absorbs all wavelengths other than red. It thereby subtracts those colors from our sight and reflects only red light. Therefore, when light-reflecting colors (such as those in paint pigments) are mixed, the combination of pigments *absorbs* or *subtracts* from our vision more wavelengths of light than each pigment does individually. The more light that is subtracted,

the darker the result looks. Figure 4.16b shows what happens when pigments that are yellow, *cyan* (greenish blue as a pigment but deep blue when used as an additive color), and *magenta* (purplish red) are subtractively mixed together. In summary, mix together (additively) all the different hues of light, and you get the white appearance of streaming sunlight. Mix together (subtractively) all the different hues on a painter's palette, and you get the appearance of black or near-black paint.

THEORIES OF COLOR VISION

A theory of color vision must address the question of how we can see more than 150 hues and millions of colors that differ in saturation and brightness as well as in hue (Coren et al., 1994; Kaiser & Boynton, 1996; Shevell, 2000a, 2000b). Almost certainly, we could not have a different kind of receptor for each conceivable hue.

TRICHROMATIC THEORY. This theory was originally proposed by Thomas Young (1901/1948) and revived by Hermann von Helmholtz (1909/1962) (see R. S. Turner, 2000a). Young and Helmholtz worked solely from behavioral data rather than studying the anatomy of the eye. Their theory is based on our understanding of the notion of *primary colors* (red, green, and blue), which can combine additively to form all other colors. If primary colors can generate all the different hues, then perhaps different receptors are somehow attuned to each of the primary colors. Imagine that there are just three kinds of receptors, one especially sensitive to red, one to green, and one to blue. Each receptor is a different type of cone (functioning through a different

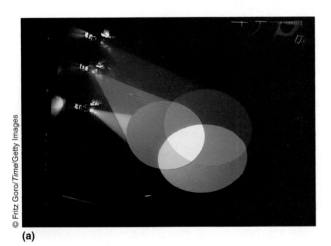

(a)

(b)

FIGURE 4.16

Color Mixtures. (a) Additive color mixtures combine lights; when all light colors are mixed together, the result is white. (b) Subtractive color mixtures combine pigments, such as those in paints or crayons; when the three primary pigments are mixed together, the result is black.

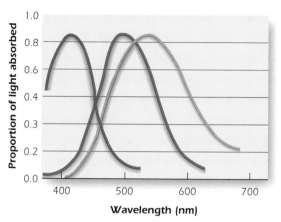

FIGURE 4.17

Trichromatic Theory. According to the trichromatic theory, our cones are particularly receptive to light of specific wavelengths. Each cone absorbs light waves that are either short, medium, or long. Light of relatively short wavelength is violet or blue, light of medium wavelength is green or yellow, and light of relatively long wavelength is orange or red. (After Wald & Brown, 1965)

kind of photopigment). The idea, then, is that one photopigment is activated primarily on exposure to what we see as red, one to what we see as green, and one to what we see as blue. We see the full range of colors by the combination and the amount of activation of the pigments by which each of the three kinds of cones operates. Figure 4.17 shows how cones respond to different wavelengths of light. The Young–Helmholtz theory is known as the **trichromatic theory of color vision.**

Support for the trichromatic theory can be found by studying people whose cones are defective. Most people who have such defects are only selectively color-blind. They can see some colors, but not others. The trichromatic theory suggests that people who are selectively color-blind will have trouble seeing red, or green, or blue, or combinations of these three hues. This prediction is, in fact, confirmed by empirical observations (C. H. Graham & Hsia, 1954). Further supporting the trichromatic theory is the discovery of genes that direct the cones to produce red-, green-, or blue-sensitive pigments (Nathans, Thomas, & Hogness, 1986).

OPPONENT-PROCESS THEORY. The other major theory is the **opponent-process theory of color vision,** according to which there are opposing processes in human vision, each of which contrasts one color with another. This theory was proposed originally by psychophysiologist Ewald Hering (1878/1964) (see R. S. Turner, 2000b) and later formalized by Leo Hurvich and Dorothea Jameson (1957). It specifies two sets of two opposed colors—

four colors altogether. The four opposed colors are blue and yellow, and red and green. Hurvich and Jameson also counted black and white as a third opposing set of achromatic primaries that are perceived in much the same way as the other opposing pairs.

Hering noted that we virtually never combine the opposing primaries, referring, say, to a yellowish blue or a reddish green. Hering suggested that a single neuron handles both colors in an opponent color pair. The activity of the neuron either increases or decreases, depending on which color in the pair is presented. For example, the activity of a red–green opponent-pair neuron would increase with exposure to red and decrease with exposure to green. If you detected red at a particular point on your retina, you would be physiologically unable to detect green at that same point. Thus, you could not see greenish red. Red–green and yellow–blue neurons interact to produce sensations of other colors.

Both psychological and physiological evidence supports the opponent-process theory. When people select what they think are the essential colors, they choose the four primaries postulated by the opponent-process theory. Furthermore, neurophysiological excitation of a red receptor does seem to inhibit the sensation of green, and vice versa. The same applies for blue and yellow (Hurvich & Jameson, 1957). Opponent-process theory also accounts for afterimages (see Figure 4.18). If you stare at a colored picture for a long time and then look away at a white blank space, you will see an afterimage of the same picture in different colors. The colors of the afterimage are the opponent colors of opponent-process theory.

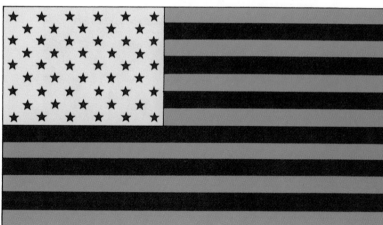

FIGURE 4.18

Afterimages. Stare at the center of this flag for about 30 seconds and then look at a blank white page. What do you see? How does the opponent-process theory explain the afterimage that you see?

The trichromatic and opponent-process theories both appear to be correct, but at different levels of analysis. The two theories may be reconciled, at least to some extent. The trichromatic theory accounts for aspects of color vision at the level of receptors. The opponent-process theory accounts for aspects of color vision at the higher level of the ganglia. The trichromatic theory is correct with regard to the existence of three types of cones in the retina. But this theory does not explain complementary colors and afterimages. To understand these phenomena, we need to turn to opponent-process theory. Thus, each of the two theories seems to capture different aspects of the phenomenon of color vision (Hurvich, 1981).

VISUAL PERCEPTION

Sensation receives psychological meaning through perception, but sometimes the meaning it receives is illusory. Optical illusions occur when visual images prompt distortions of visual perceptions (Gregory, 1998, 2000). For example, humans have been pondering for millennia the optical illusions that were used in the construction of the Parthenon (see Figure 4.19). What factors affect perception and whether we see optical illusions?

Picture yourself walking across campus to your psychology class. Suppose that a student is standing just outside the door as you approach. As you get closer to the door, the amount of retinal space devoted to the student increases. Yet, despite this clear sensory evidence that the student is becoming larger, you know that the student has remained the same size. Why? Your classmate's unchanging size is an example of perceptual constancy. Perceptual constancy is the perception that stimuli remain the same even when immediate sensations of the stimuli change. There are several kinds of perceptual constancies (Gillam, 2000).

Size constancy is the perception that an object remains the same size despite changes in the size of the proximal stimulus on the retina. The size of an image on the retina depends directly on the distance of that object from the eye. That is, the same object at two different distances projects different-sized images onto the retina. Size constancy is illustrated nicely by *Le Moulin de la Galette*, a painting by French Impressionist Pierre-Auguste Renoir (1841–1919) (shown in Figure 4.20). The characters in the background are much smaller than the ones in the foreground. But we are not led to believe that the background characters are extremely small in stature or that the foreground characters are extremely tall. We observe that the persons in the foreground of the Renoir painting are of roughly the same height with respect to the bench as those in the background. Hence, the bench provides contextual information that tells us that all the people are roughly the same height. We perceive all the characters as being about the same size because of size constancy.

Size constancy is learned through experience. A classic example of how experience helps us interpret perceptions comes from C. Turnbull's (1961) ethnographic account of the pygmies of the Iturbi Forest. A pygmy once accompanied Turnbull out of the for-

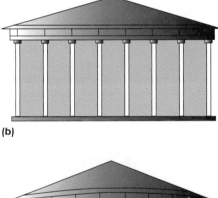

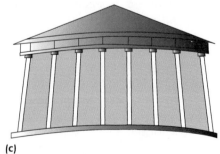

(a)

FIGURE 4.19

The Parthenon. Ictinus and Callicrates, designers of the Parthenon (a), were keenly aware of optical illusions—that is, how the immense facade would appear to people standing at its base. To make the facade look rectilinear (b), they raised the center of the base to offset the illusion (c).

(b)

(c)

FIGURE 4.20

The Role of Size Constancy in Art. French Impressionist Pierre-Auguste Renoir's *Le Moulin de la Gallette* relies on our perception of size constancy to know that the people in the background are similar in size to those in the foreground.

est. At one point, the two saw some cows grazing in the distance. Although most pygmies frequently have seen cows at close range in the forest, few have ever seen cows at a distance. Much to Turnbull's surprise, his travel companion thought that he was looking at ants.

Our ability to use size constancy can be fooled when we experience novel stimuli, such as the distorted room shown in Figure 4.21. In this room, called an *Ames room* after its inventor, our perceptions of sizes are distorted by the odd proportions of the room.

The contextual clues we normally use to make judgments of size constancy do not work here.

Illusions can be striking when our perceptual apparatus is fooled by the very same information that usually helps us to experience size constancy. For example, in the **Ponzo illusion,** we perceive the top line and the top log as being longer than the bottom line and the bottom log, respectively (see Figure 4.22). In fact, the top and bottom figures are the same length. We misperceive because in the real three-dimensional world, the top line and log would appear larger. This effect stems from the depth cue provided by the converging lines.

In the **Müller–Lyer illusion,** we tend to view two equally long line segments as being different lengths (see Figure 4.23). In particular, the vertical line segments in (a) and (c) appear shorter than those in (b) and (d), even though all are the same length. Psychologists are not certain why such a simple illusion occurs. One explanation is that the diagonal lines at the ends of the vertical segments in the first pair serve as implicit depth cues similar to the ones we would see in our perceptions of the exterior and interior of a building (Coren & Girgus, 1978; Gregory, 1966).

When you consider illusions, remember that they are relatively rare occurrences in our lives and often have to be carefully contrived to work. Most of the time our perceptual apparatus enables us to perceive properties of objects, such as size, in ways that are surprisingly accurate, despite potential distortions (such as fog or rain). Our perceptual apparatus also enables us to perceive shape constancy.

Shape constancy refers to our perceiving an object as retaining its shape even when the shape it casts on the retina changes. In Figure 4.24, you see a rectangular door and door frame. The door is closed,

  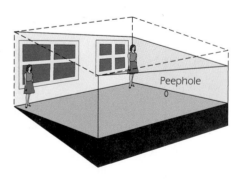

FIGURE 4.21

Perceptual Constancy. When we view the boy and the dog through a hole in the wall, we perceive impossible relative sizes. When we see a sketch of the room, however, we see that its shape is actually distorted. This kind of room, named after its inventor, is called an Ames room.

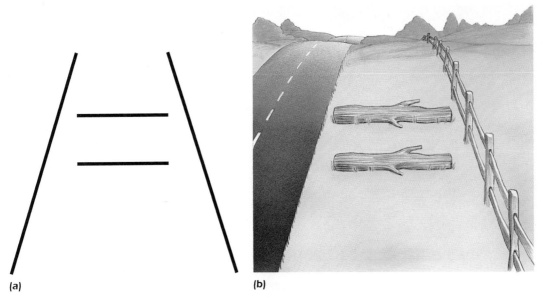

(a) (b)

FIGURE 4.22
The Ponzo Illusion. These two figures show that depth cues can lead to perceptual errors. In (a), which of the two horizontal lines is longest? In (b), which log is longest? To check your answers, measure the lines and the logs.

slightly opened, or half-opened. Of course, the door does not seem to take on a different shape in each panel. It would be odd, indeed, if we perceived a door to be changing shape as we opened it. Yet, the shape of the image of the door is different in each panel. Moreover, the image of the door on the retina changes as we open the door.

Lightness constancy refers to our perception that an object is evenly illuminated despite differences in the actual amount of light that reaches our eyes. In fact, we are remarkably capable of compensating for differences in the actual amount of light that is reflected at a given moment. Observe how Jan Vermeer used lightness constancy to advantage in his

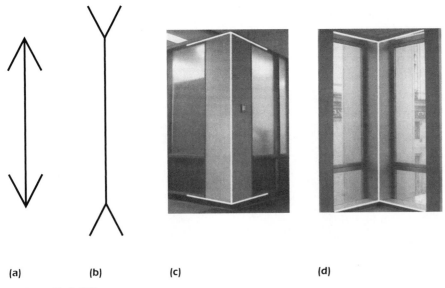

(a) (b) (c) (d)

FIGURE 4.23
Müller–Lyer Illusion. Which of the line segments (a or b, c or d) is longer? Measure them. The principle of depth constancy may lead us to perceive the inward-facing angles as being larger, as if they represent the "far" corner of the room instead of the "near" corner of the wall.

painting *Woman Holding a Balance*, shown in Figure 4.25. The wall in the background is illuminated by a brilliant ray of light, as is part of the face of the woman weighing gold. Nonetheless, we see the whole wall as blue and the gold-weigher's face as white, even though the shadings of light on the wall and her face are varied. Art provides one of the best ways of studying perceptual constancies (Kubovy, 2000). Similarly, if you observe this page with different shading caused by different amounts of background illumination, the page will always appear white and of roughly the same shade.

An interesting way of viewing perception and the phenomena associated with it is to consider evolutionary theory. That is, how does perceptual constancy aid us in surviving and being able to reproduce? We are indeed more adaptive because of the way our brains work to create the constancies described here. In fact, we would not survive long in this world if we were unable to experience perceptual constancies. You could not even have located this book on your desk if you were incapable of perceptual constancy. You certainly could not have opened the book and positioned it for reading. Without such constancy, you could not recognize the book as the same object despite changes in retinal illumination with changes in room lighting. Furthermore, you would not recognize the book as a single object after changes in the shape of its image on the retina caused by changes in its position on the desk. Without perceptual constancies, you would be lost in the world and your survival would be at risk.

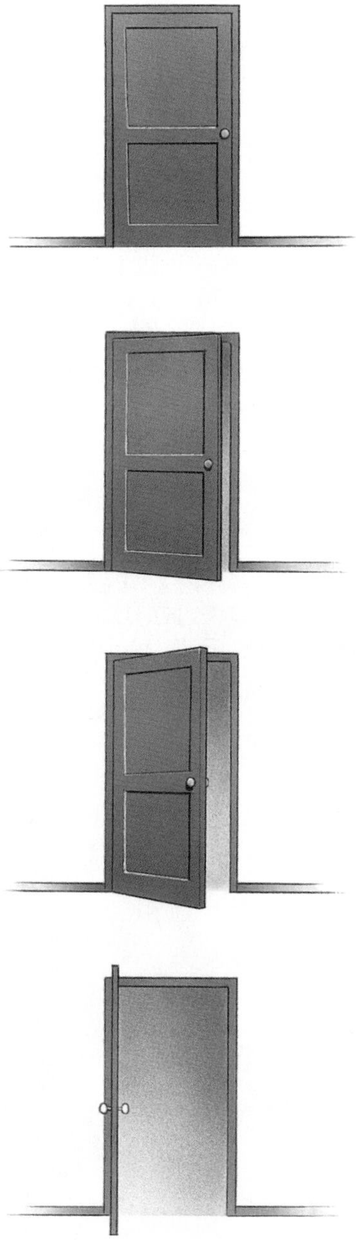

FIGURE 4.24
Shape Constancy. When we look at a door, we perceive it always to have the same shape, even though our sensations of the shape change as the door opens and closes. (From James J. Gibson, "Shape Constancy Illusion—Door" from *The Ecological Approach to Visual Perception.* Copyright © 1979 James J. Gibson. Reprinted by permission.)

FIGURE 4.25
Lightness Constancy. In *Woman Holding a Balance*, painted about 1657, Dutch artist Jan Vermeer uses the principles of lightness constancy to manipulate our perception of the woman and the room. We perceive his use of highlighting and shadowing as changes in illumination, not as changes in the perceived lightness of the room.

Another important survival skill, for both humans and nonhuman animals, is the ability to perceive depth, which we discuss next.

DEPTH PERCEPTION

Before you read this section, look at the engraving by William Hogarth in Figure 4.26. List the perceptual cues in Hogarth's picture that are consistent with other such cues and those that are not consistent with other cues. (For example, consider the sign hanging in front of the building.)

As you move, you constantly look around and visually orient yourself in three-dimensional space. As you look forward into the distance, you look into the third dimension of *depth*, or distance from a surface (usually using your own body as that reference surface). Whenever you transport your body, reach for or manipulate objects, or otherwise position yourself in your three-dimensional world, you must make judgments regarding depth.

You even make judgments about depth and distances that extend beyond the range of your body's reach. When you drive, you judge depth to assess the distance of an approaching automobile. When you de-

cide to call out to a friend walking down the street, you determine how loudly to call according to how far away you perceive your friend to be. If you decide to jump into water, you use depth cues to ascertain whether you are about to land with a thud in shallow water or to plunge freely into deep water.

As can happen with size constancies, we can also be taken in by optical illusions of depth. An everyday example is our belief that two-dimensional representations actually have depth when we enjoy television and movies. Generally, depth cues are either monocular (one-eyed) or binocular (two-eyed). We consider each of these kinds of cues in turn.

MONOCULAR DEPTH CUES

One way of judging depth is through monocular depth cues, which can be represented in just two dimensions, as in a picture. These depth cues are called "monocular" because one eye is sufficient to perceive them, in contrast to depth cues (considered later), which require two eyes. Refer to Figure 4.27, *The Annunciation*, which illustrates the following monocular depth cues.

FIGURE 4.26

False Perspective. At first, the engraving of English artist William Hogarth (1697–1764) seems realistic, but closer inspection reveals conflicting perceptual cues. As Hogarth explained, "Whoever makes a design, without the knowledge of perspective, will be liable to such absurdities as are shown in this print."

FIGURE 4.27

Monocular Depth Cues in Art. Giovanni di Paolo's *The Annunciation,* painted in 1481, illustrates monocular depth cues: relative size, texture gradient, interposition, linear perspective, location in the picture plane, and aerial perspective.

Relative size is the perception that objects farther away (such as the rear tiles on the floor or the trees in the background) are smaller. The farther away an object is, the smaller its image is on the retina. When you look down from an ascending airplane, automobiles look like toys. People, if you can still see them, look like midgets. Our ability to perceive depth using relative size as a cue is related to our ability to perceive size constancy.

Texture gradient is a change in both the relative sizes of objects and the densities in the distribution of objects—distances among particles, components, or objects—when viewed at different distances. Consider the floor tiles again. At a distance, the floor tiles appear much more densely packed than when viewed from up close.

Interposition occurs when an object perceived to be closer partially blocks the view of an object perceived to be farther away. The blocking object, such as the angel in Figure 4.27, is perceived to be in front of the blocked object, in this case the columns and the wall.

Linear perspective helps us make judgments about distance based on the perception that parallel lines appear to converge as they move farther away. Examples are the lines along the sides of the corridor walls in Figure 4.27 and the rails of a railroad track as you stand on it. In some pictures, the lines extend all the way toward the horizon, where we can see the so-called vanishing point. At the *vanishing point*, the lines appear to converge, become indistinguishable, and then disappear entirely at the horizon.

Location in the picture plane indicates depth, in that objects farther from the horizon are more distant. When the objects we look at are below the horizon, the objects that are higher in the picture plane appear to be more distant. An example is the location of the door at the end of the corridor, compared with the figures of Mary and the angel kneeling in the cubicle to the foreground. When the objects we look at are above the horizon, higher objects appear to be closer. In other words, the closer the object is to the plane of the horizon, the farther it is perceived to be from the viewer. Try noticing this phenomenon for yourself. Either look out the window or draw a horizon and then draw two birds, one higher and one lower in the picture plane. Then notice which bird appears to be closer to you.

Aerial perspective lets us use the relative distribution of moisture and dust particles in the atmosphere as a means of judging distance. Objects closer to us are relatively unaffected by these particles and therefore appear clearly. But, at increasing distances, larger numbers of these particles make objects appear hazier and less distinct. Notice how clear the two figures in the foreground appear in comparison to the mountains visible through the doorway at the end of the corridor. The effect of aerial perspective is particularly dramatic on foggy, smoggy, or otherwise hazy days. On such days, objects can appear farther away than they actually are because of the unusually high concentration of water droplets or dust particles in the air. On a particularly clear day, objects may appear closer than they actually are because of the near-absence of water and dust particles. A mountain range that is a day's drive away may look as though it can be reached in a couple of hours.

Glance back at Hogarth's *False Perspective* in Figure 4.26 and your list of perceptual cues and miscues. How many cues did you miss before that you can find now? One final monocular depth cue is not shown clearly in either *The Annunciation* or Hogarth's engraving: motion parallax.

Motion parallax is the apparent difference in the speed and direction of objects when seen from a moving viewpoint. Because motion parallax is the result of movement, it cannot be shown in a two-dimensional, static picture. You have observed the phenomenon before, however. Imagine being in a moving train and watching the passing scenery through a side window. Motion creates parallax as you move from one point to another and observe stationary distant objects from changing points of view. If you look through the window and fixate on one given point in the scene, objects closer to you than that point will appear to be moving in the direction opposite to the one you are traveling. In contrast, objects beyond the fixation point will appear to be moving in the same direction as you are. You thereby obtain a depth cue by ascertaining which objects are moving in which direction. Moreover, the objects that are closer to you (either before or after your focal point) appear to be moving (toward you or with you) more quickly than do objects that are farther away (see Figure 4.28).

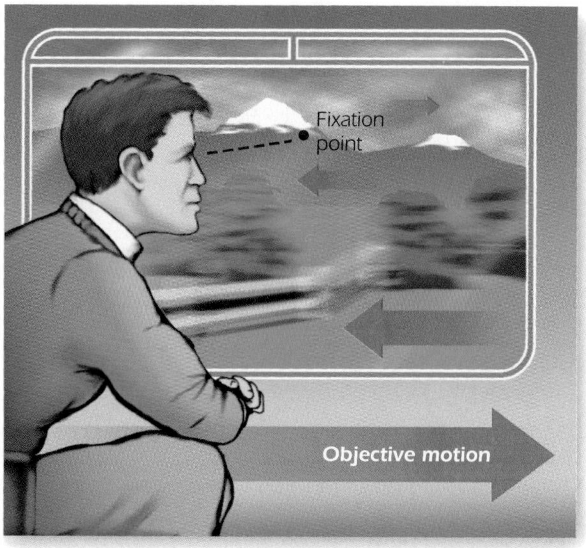

FIGURE 4.28

Effects of Motion Parallax. When we are moving through a (relatively) stationary environment, the objects we see will appear to move in the direction opposite to the direction of our own actual movement.

Binocular depth cues, unlike monocular cues, are based on disparities in perception between the two eyes. Table 4.4 summarizes some of the monocular and binocular cues used in perceiving depth.

BINOCULAR DEPTH CUES

Binocular depth cues capitalize on the fact that each eye views a scene from a slightly different angle. This disparity of viewing angles provides information about depth. The term for three-dimensional perception of the world through the use of binocular (two-eyed) vision is *stereopsis*. With stereo sound, you hear slightly different sounds coming to each ear. You then fuse those sounds to form realistic auditory perceptions. With stereopsis, you receive slightly different visual images in each eye. You then fuse those two images to form realistic visual perceptions. You rely on this fusion of the images from both eyes to give you a coherent visual representation of what you are viewing. Not all parts of a visual image actually fuse, although you are not normally aware of seeing two images. Under extraordinary circumstances, such as after a serious blow to the head, your eyes may temporarily go out of alignment. You may then become uncomfortably aware of *diplopia*, or double vision. Now consider two binocular depth cues.

Binocular convergence is the use of two eyes in coordination to perceive depth. Your two eyes are in slightly different places on your face. As a result, when you rotate your eyes so that an image of an object that is in front of you falls directly on each fovea, each eye must turn inward slightly to register the same image. The closer the object you are trying to see, the more your eyes must turn inward (see Figure 4.29). The brain receives neural information from the eye muscles about the convergence of the eyes, and it assumes that the more the eyes converge, the closer the perceived object must be.

Because the two eyes are in different places, each has a slightly different view of the world (see Figure 4.29). Binocular disparity is the slight discrepancy in the viewpoints of the two eyes. Because of this discrepancy, the brain must integrate two slightly different sets of information from each of the optic nerves to make decisions about depth as well as about height and width. The closer an object is to us, the greater the disparity is between each eye's view of the object. You can test these differing perspectives by holding your finger about an inch from the tip of your nose. Look at it first with one eye covered, then with the other eye covered. Your finger will appear to jump back and forth. Now do the same for an object 20 feet away, then 100 yards

---

TABLE 4.4
CONCEPT REVIEW

Monocular and Binocular Cues for Depth Perception. Various perceptual cues help us perceive the three-dimensional world. We can observe some of these cues with only one eye and others with both eyes.

Cues for Depth Perception	Appears Closer	Appears Farther Away
Monocular Depth Cues		
Relative size	Bigger.	Smaller.
Texture gradients	Larger grains, farther apart.	Smaller grains, closer together.
Interposition	Partially obscures other object.	Is partially obscured by other object.
Linear perspective	Apparently parallel lines seem to diverge.	Apparently parallel lines seem to converge.
Location in the picture plane	Above the horizon, objects are higher in the picture plane; below the horizon, objects are lower in the picture plane.	Above the horizon, objects are lower in the picture plane; below the horizon, objects are higher in the picture plane.
Aerial perspective	Images seem crisper, more clearly delineated.	Images seem fuzzier, less clearly delineated.
Motion parallax	Objects closer than the fixation point appear to be moving in the direction opposite to your direction.	Objects beyond the fixation point appear to be moving in the same direction as you.
Binocular Depth Cues		
Binocular convergence	Eyes feel a tug inward toward nose.	Eyes relax outward toward ears.
Binocular disparity	Huge discrepancy between image seen by left eye and image seen by right eye.	Minuscule discrepancy between image seen by left eye and image seen by right eye.

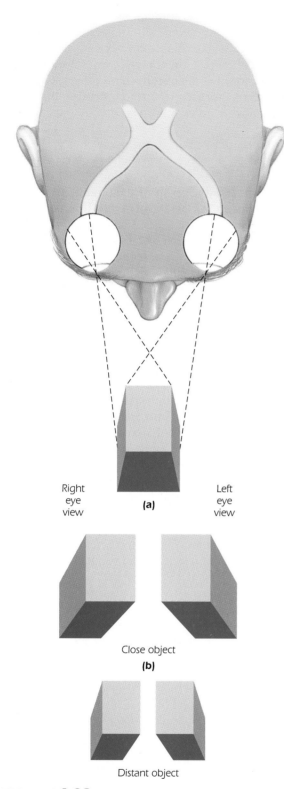

Right eye view

(a)

Left eye view

Close object

(b)

Distant object

FIGURE 4.29

Binocular Convergence and Disparity. To focus on an object, our eyes converge; that is, they adjust to have the image fall on each retina (a). Because our eyes are separated, they see a slightly different angle of the object. This disparity in the view from each eye is greater for objects that are closer to us (b). Our brains use the convergence and disparity information as depth cues.

away. The apparent jumping, which indicates the amount of binocular disparity, will decrease with distance. If something is amiss in our depth perception, we are seriously impaired in our ability to function in a three-dimensional world.

Another aspect of vision seems to be at least as important as depth perception and appears to be far less complex at first glance: form perception.

FORM PERCEPTION

Form perception enables us to distinguish one form from another. Principles of form recognition are important in understanding both human and machine-based perception, such as recognizing fingerprints or faces. Two of the main attributes of form are size and shape. How, exactly, do we perceive them? Let's consider the Gestalt and the feature-detector approaches to form perception.

GESTALT APPROACH

The **Gestalt approach** is based on the notion that the whole is different from the sum of its individual parts (see Chapter 2). Gestalt principles are particularly relevant to understanding how we perceive an assembly of forms. They account for much of our ability perceptually to organize the world (Palmer, 1992). One of the key Gestalt ideas is that of figure and ground.

When you walk into a familiar room, you perceive that some objects stand out, such as faces in photographs or posters. Other things fade into the background, like undecorated walls and floors. A **figure** is any object perceived as being highlighted almost always against, or in contrast to, some kind of receding, unhighlighted (back)**ground.** This is known as the **figure–ground** concept. Figure 4.30 shows **reversible figures,** in which each of a given pair of adjacent or even interconnecting figures can be seen as either figure or ground. In one, you can see a white vase against a black background. In the other, two silhouetted faces gaze at each other against the ground of a white screen. Note, however, that it is impossible to see both sets of objects at the same time. One important use of figure–ground is in camouflage: Soldiers wearing camouflage uniforms hope to blend in with the background—that is, to make it more difficult for the enemy to distinguish figure from ground.

Table 4.5 summarizes and defines some of the Gestalt principles of form perception, including figure–ground perception (see Figure 4.31; see also Palmer, 2000):

- *Proximity.* Elements that are close to one another are grouped together.
- *Similarity.* Elements that resemble one another are grouped together.

FIGURE 4.30

A Gestalt Gift. The figure shows a reversible figure–ground picture. One way of perceiving the picture brings one object to the fore as the figure, and another way of perceiving the picture brings out a different figure and relegates the former foreground to the background. Is this a light vase against a dark ground or the light-silhouetted profiles of Queen Elizabeth II and Prince Philip against the background? The vase was a gift to the queen on her silver jubilee.

- *Closure.* Gaps in what otherwise would be viewed as a continuous border are ignored.
- *Good continuation.* Those segments of intersecting lines that would form a continuous line with minimal change in direction are grouped together.
- *Symmetry.* Elements are grouped together so as to form figures that are mirror images on either side of a central axis.
- *Common movement.* Elements that are moving in the same direction and at the same velocity are grouped together.

The Gestalt principles of form perception are remarkably simple, but they characterize much of our perceptual organization. It is important to realize, however, that these principles are descriptive rather than explanatory. The Gestalt perspective cannot be categorized as taking either a top-down or a bottom-up approach. In a **top-down approach,** one views perception as involving complex problem solving. In a **bottom-up approach,** one views perception as involving simpler and lower-level processes such as responses to retinal stimulation. Merely labeling a phenomenon does not, in itself, account for how the phenomenon occurs. One contemporary approach to form perception better explains how we perceive forms.

FEATURE-DETECTOR APPROACH

The **feature-detector approach** attempts to link the perception of form to the functioning of neurons in the brain. It is the result of the pioneering work of Nobel laureates David Hubel and Torsten Wiesel (1979). The approach is based on observing the activity of the brain in which specific neurons of the visual cortex respond to specific features detected by photoreceptors. Using single-cell recording techniques with nonhuman animals, Hubel and Wiesel carefully traced the route of electrochemical transmission of information from the receptors in the retina, through the ganglion cells and the thalamic nucleus cells, to the visual cortex. Their research showed that specific neurons of the visual cortex respond to varying stimuli that are presented to the particular retinal regions connected to these neurons. Each individual cortical neuron, therefore, can be mapped to a specific receptive field on the retina. The researchers found a disproportionately large amount of the visual cortex devoted to neurons mapped to receptive fields in the foveal region of the retina.

Surprisingly, most of the cells in the cortex do not respond simply to spots of light but rather to "specifically oriented line segments" (Hubel & Wiesel, 1979, p. 9). What's more, these cells vary in the degree of complexity of the stimuli to which they respond. In general, the size of the receptive field increases as the stimulus proceeds through the visual system to higher levels in the cortex. The complexity of the stimulus required to prompt a response also increases. More specifically, Hubel and Wiesel isolated three kinds of visual cortex neurons: simple cells, complex cells, and hypercomplex cells (see Figure 4.32 on page 144).

Primitive cortical cells chiefly relay information to the appropriate *simple cells,* which then fire in response to lines in the receptive field. Each of these cells seems to be most excited by lines in particular parts of the receptive field. These lines have particular widths and are oriented at a particular optimal angle. The simple cells feed into complex cells. Each *complex cell* fires in response to lines of specific orientations anywhere in the receptive field of that cell's group of simple cells. Complex cells appear to be insensitive to the particular type of light–dark contrasts of a line segment, as long as the segment is oriented

TABLE 4.5
CONCEPT REVIEW

Some Gestalt Principles of Form Perception. Gestalt psychologists proposed a number of principles regarding how we perceive form.

Gestalt Principles	Principle	Figure Illustrating the Principle
Figure–ground	When we perceive a visual field, some objects (figures) seem prominent and other aspects of the field recede into the background (ground).	Figure 4.30 shows a reversible figure–ground picture. One way of perceiving the picture brings one object to the fore as the figure. Another way of perceiving the picture brings out a different figure, relegating the former foreground to the background.
Proximity	When we perceive an assortment of objects, we tend to see those that are close to each other as forming a group.	Figure 4.31a shows six circles, which we tend to see in groups rather than as six separate circles.
Similarity	We group objects on the basis of their similarity.	Figure 4.31b shows four rows of letters. We see alternating rows of Xs and Os.
Good continuation	We tend to perceive smoothly flowing or continuous forms rather than disrupted or discontinuous ones.	Figure 4.31c shows crossed lines, which we perceive as a straight line bisecting a curved line, rather than as two angles, one atop the other.
Closure	We tend perceptually to close up or complete objects that are not, in fact, complete.	Figure 4.31d shows only disjointed, jumbled line segments, which we close up perceptually in order to see a triangle and a circle.
Symmetry	We tend to perceive separate forms that are mirror images at the center as single forms, based on limited sensory information.	Figure 4.31e shows two triangles and two hemispheres, which we perceive as a diamond and a circle each split into two symmetrical parts.

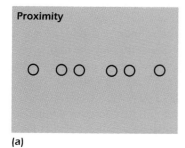

(a)

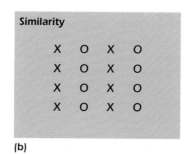

(b)

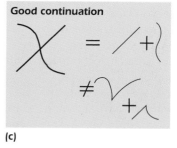

(c)

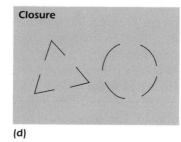

(d)

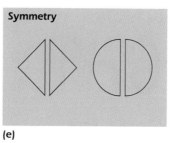

(e)

FIGURE 4.31

Gestalt Principles of Visual Perception. The Gestalt principles of proximity, similarity, good continuation, closure, and symmetry aid in our perception.

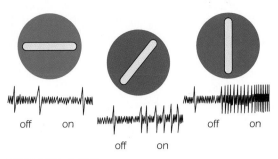

FIGURE 4.32

Feature Detectors. David Hubel and Torsten Wiesel discovered that cells in our visual cortex become activated only when they detect the sensation of line segments or particular orientations. The illustrations show the firing pattern of a cell sensitive to vertical lines.

appropriately. *Hypercomplex cells*, which respond to certain lengths of stimulus lines, may provide the basis for perceiving patterns.

PATTERN RECOGNITION

The forms we perceive fall into patterns, such as letters, numbers, or faces. But although it is relatively easy to specify the features of a letter or number, it is much more difficult to specify completely the features of a face. What you may take for granted—for example, the ability to recognize the face of your friend—is not something everyone does easily.

How do you know the letter A when you see it? You may be thinking it is an A because it looks like an A. What makes it an A instead of an H? Just how difficult it is to answer this question becomes apparent when you look at Figure 4.33, in which two identical perceptual forms evoke different letter names. What subjectively feels to us like a simple process of pattern recognition is almost certainly quite complex.

How do we connect what we sense in the environment to what we have stored in our minds? What explanations account for how we connect what we

THE CAT

FIGURE 4.33

Pattern Recognition. When you read these words, you probably see a capital H and a capital A in the middle of each respective word. Look more closely at them though. Do any features differentiate the two letters? If not, why did you perceive them as different? (After Selfridge, 1959)

perceive with what we know? Two main approaches to pattern recognition are template matching and feature matching. The **template-matching theory** posits that we have templates or prototypes stored in our minds. They are the best examples of each of the patterns we might potentially recognize. We recognize a pattern by matching it to the template that best fits what we see (Selfridge & Neisser, 1960). We see examples of template matching in our everyday lives. Fingerprints are matched in this way. Similarly, machines rapidly process imprinted numerals on checks by comparing them to templates. The theory of template matching has some obvious difficulties, however—for example, its inability to explain our perception of the words in Figure 4.33.

Plausible explanations of pattern recognition that fit the Hubel and Wiesel findings are **feature-matching theories,** according to which we attempt to match features of an observed pattern to features stored in memory. One such feature-matching model is Oliver Selfridge's (1959) "pandemonium" model, which is based on the notion that metaphorical "demons" with specific duties receive and analyze the features of a stimulus (see Figure 4.34).

We can compare Selfridge's model with Hubel and Wiesel's description of the hierarchically arranged visual system. Selfridge's model describes "image demons" (much like the subcortical parts of the visual system) that pass on a retinal image to "feature demons." The feature demons behave like the simple and complex cells described by Hubel and Wiesel. Selfridge did not specify exactly what such features might be. But Hubel and Wiesel's feature detectors respond to such details as orientation of lines, angles of intersecting lines, and shapes.

At this point, the parallel ends because Hubel and Wiesel left it to future research to trace the higher levels of cortical processing. Selfridge's model goes on, however. It suggests that at a higher level are "cognitive [thinking] demons." They "shout out" possible patterns stored in memory that conform to one or more of the features processed by the feature demons. A "decision demon" listens to the pandemonium of the shouting cognitive demons and decides what has been seen. The decision is based on which demon is shouting the most frequently (i.e., which has the most matching features).

Although Selfridge's pandemonium model specifies neither what the elementary features are exactly nor how to go about determining what they might be, Hubel and Wiesel supplied some of the missing information, based on how the brain really works. However, no one would argue that lines of various lengths and orientations can account for the richness of all our visual perception.

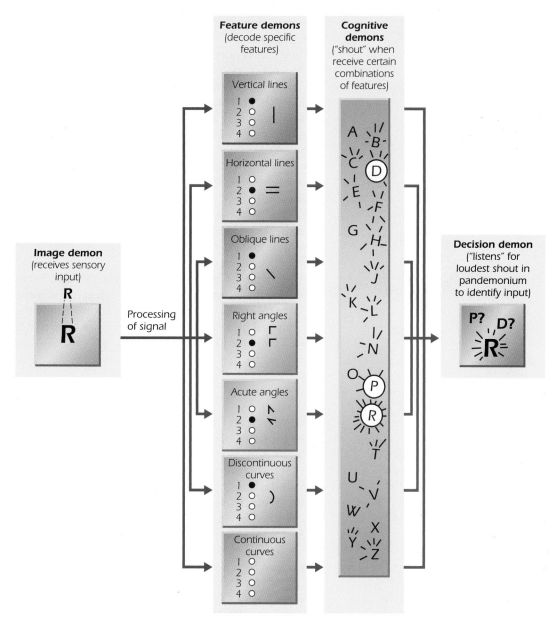

FIGURE 4.34
Pandemonium. According to the feature-matching model, we recognize patterns by matching observed features already stored in our memory. We recognize the patterns for which we have found the greatest number of matches. (After Selfridge, 1959)

Irving Biederman (1987) proposed a more comprehensive set of elementary components. They are called *geons* and are hypothesized to be variations on the shape of a cylinder. Figure 4.35 shows how a small number of geons can be used to build up basic shapes and objects. A small set of geons with as few as 36 elements can generate many three-geon objects. The perceptual system can build up a representation of what it sees by combining geons. Other theorists have taken a similar tack (e.g., Guzman, 1971; Marr, 1982).

Thus, it seems within our grasp to construct a feature-matching theory that specifies the simple features that together make up complex objects. As of yet, however, no theory is definitive.

PROBLEMS FOR THEORIES OF PATTERN PERCEPTION.
Neither template nor feature theories can account for some remaining problems. For example, current models do not fully explain the influence of the environment on cognition. These *context effects* were

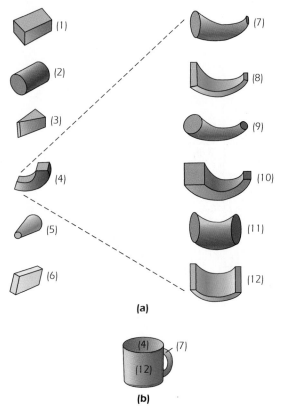

(a)

(b)

FIGURE 4.35

Geons. Irving Biederman amplified feature-matching theory by proposing a set of elementary shapes (a) that can be combined to become more sophisticated objects (b). (From "Biederman's Geons" in "Geons" by I. Biederman from Computer Vision, Graphics, and Image Processing, 1985, No. 32. Copyright © 1985 Academic Press, Inc. Reprinted by permission.)

letters that do not form words. This effect again demonstrates top-down, higher-order processing. The first report of this effect dates back to James McKeen Cattell (1886). He observed that it takes people substantially longer to read unrelated letters than to read letters that form a word. Gerald Reicher (1969) and Daniel Wheeler (1970) further demonstrated this effect, and so it is sometimes called the "Reicher–Wheeler effect."

To summarize, neither the template-matching nor the feature-matching approach can explain all of the phenomena we encounter in the study of form and pattern perception. Still, given the complexity of the form-perception process, it is impressive that we understand as much as we do. A comprehensive theory eludes our grasp.

In addition to explaining how we perceive forms and patterns, another challenge for perceptual theories is to explain movement. How do we know when the forms and patterns we see are moving and when they are standing still?

MOTION PERCEPTION

As we perceive motion, we make inferences about the forms and patterns of what we see. In one experiment, Gunner Johanssen (1975) attached a small light bulb to each of the major joints of a person's body and then filmed the person walking and performing various actions. He showed experimental participants only the lights and not the person. When they saw just a single frame—a still—they did not know what they were seeing. But even two frames of the film—a mere 1/10-second of viewing time—were sufficient for most people to see a person walking. The same paradigm with lights attached to both men and women revealed that people often judge the sex of a moving figure by the patterns of motion (Cutting, Proffitt, & Kozlowski, 1978; Runeson & Frykholm, 1986).

Our perception of motion does not depend exclusively on the movement of the object we observe. Recent research suggests that moving stimuli of higher visual contrast appear to be moving faster than stimuli of lower contrast, even when they are not actually moving faster (Gegenfurtner, Mayser, & Sharpe, 1999).

Stroboscopic motion (termed "apparent motion" in the descriptions of Gestalt psychology in Chapter 2) is the perception of motion produced by a stroboscope—an instrument that intermittently flashes an alternating pair of lights against a dark background. If the lights are flashed at an appropriate distance apart and at appropriately timed intervals (within milliseconds), it appears that a solitary light has moved. If

demonstrated in Figure 4.33 when we perceived THE CAT correctly even though what we perceived as two different letters are actually physically identical. Clearly, some top-down, higher-order processes must be at work for us to be able to read two identical stimuli as being different letters.

In one demonstration of context effects, people were asked to identify objects after they had viewed them in either an appropriate or an inappropriate context (Palmer, 1975). Research participants might have viewed a scene of a kitchen followed by stimuli such as a loaf of bread, a mailbox, and a drum. Objects that were appropriate to the established context, such as the loaf of bread in this example, were recognized more rapidly than objects inappropriate to the established context.

Perhaps even more striking is a context effect known as the *word-superiority effect.* You read letters more easily when they are embedded in words than when they are presented either in isolation or with

the time interval is too short, the lights appear to flash simultaneously. If the interval is too long, the lights appear to flash in succession, and the observer does not sense the apparent motion. Given just the right timing, the experience of apparent motion indicates that the viewer actually perceives motion and does not merely make an inference from two static states (Wertheimer, 1912).

Movies and cartoons use the principle of stroboscopic motion. Movies are merely rapidly displayed sequences of individual frames, or single still pictures, shown at the rate of 24 frames per second. We see the same effect in neon signs that appear to be cascades of flowing lights. The apparently moving lights are in fact rapid linear sequences of individual bulbs flashing on and off.

In sum, we have visual perception of many different kinds of things. The cerebral cortex contains separate neural pathways for processing different aspects of the same stimuli (De Yoe & Van Essen, 1988; Köhler, Kapur, Moscovitch, Winocur, & Houle, 1995). They are termed the "what" and the "where" pathways. The "what" pathway descends from the primary visual cortex in the occipital lobe toward the temporal lobes. It is mainly responsible for processing the color, shape, and identity of visual stimuli. The "where" pathway ascends from the occipital lobe toward the parietal lobe. It is responsible for processing location and motion information. Thus, feature information feeds into at least two systems for identifying objects and events in the environment.

DEFICITS IN PERCEPTION

Severe deficits in visual perception, as mentioned in Chapter 3, are referred to collectively as *agnosias*. Although people with *visual-object agnosia* can sense all parts of the visual field, the objects they see do not mean anything to them. One agnosic patient, upon seeing a pair of eyeglasses, noted first that there was a circle, then that there was another circle, then that there was a crossbar. He finally guessed that he was looking at a bicycle, which does indeed comprise two circles and a crossbar (Luria, 1973). In *prosopagnosia*, people have a severe deficit in their ability to recognize human faces. Yet, they may be able to recognize other kinds of faces, such as those of farm animals. This disorder is a hot topic of research in perception (Farah, Levinson, & Klein, 1995; Farah, Wilson, Drain, & Tanaka, 1995; Haxby et al., 1996).

Although most of us rely on vision as our primary means of sensing the world around us, our life experiences would be diminished if we were deprived of our other senses. Chief among them is our sense of hearing.

HEARING

How do we hear stimuli in the environment?

The ability to hear sounds can be both a blessing and a curse. It enables us to hear what goes on in the world around us. At the same time, we often wish we could turn down the volume, or eliminate many sounds altogether. To understand hearing, you need to know about the structures and processes that permit us to hear. They include the nature of sound, the functional organization of the ear, and the distinctive interactions between sound and the ear.

SOUND WAVES

Sound results from mechanical pressure on the air. When you pluck the string of a guitar or clap your hands together, you are pushing on air molecules. The disrupted air molecules momentarily collide with other air molecules, which then collide with still other air molecules, resulting in a three-dimensional wave of mechanical energy. The air particles themselves do not move much. The wave of pressure is what covers the distance. Compare this effect to a line of cars waiting at a stoplight. Along comes a speeder who fails to stop in time. He rear-ends the last car in line. That car then hits the car in front of it, and so on. The mechanical pressure spreads in a wave forward through the line of cars. But the car that started the wave does not move much at all. You can observe the same phenomenon with billiard balls.

We are accustomed to thinking of sound as traveling through air. But it can also result from mechanical pressure applied to another medium, such as water. If there is no medium, such as in an airless vacuum, there is no sound. For sound to occur, there must be some particles through which the pressure wave can pass. Therefore, in a vacuum you can see light but not hear sound.

Sound also travels much more slowly than light. You see a distant lightning bolt before you hear the thunder, even though the lightning and thunder occur almost simultaneously. In addition, the speed of sound depends on the density of the medium. Somewhat surprisingly, sound generally moves more quickly through more densely packed molecules. This is not completely counterintuitive if you remember the car-crash analogy. The more densely packed the cars, the more rapidly the wave of crashing cars proceeds. Sound travels approximately 340 meters per second (750 miles per hour) in air. But it travels 1,360 meters per second (3,000 miles per hour) in water, which is why sounds are amplified under water.

Sound waves have three physical properties that affect how we sense them and process them psychologically. The first two are familiar: amplitude and wavelength. Sound **amplitude** (intensity) corresponds to our sensation of loudness. The higher the amplitude, the louder the sound. The usual unit of measurement for the intensity of sound is the *decibel (dB)*. The absolute threshold for normal human hearing is 0 decibels. Sound that is comfortably audible to humans ranges from about 50 to 100 decibels in amplitude. Table 4.6 lists the decibel levels of various common sounds.

Sound waves also vary in frequency, which produces our sensation of **pitch,** how high or low a tone sounds. Frequency is conventionally measured as the number of *cycles* (crest-to-crest progressions of sound waves) per second rather than in terms of wavelengths. A frequency of one cycle per second is called 1 *hertz (Hz)*, after the German physicist Heinrich Hertz. Humans can generally hear sound waves in the range from about 20 to 20,000 Hz. For us to sense sounds above 20,000 Hz, they must have increasingly higher amplitude. Many other animals, however, can hear sound waves of much higher frequencies. Frequency and wavelength are inversely related. A short wavelength will crest over and over again more frequently than will a long one within the same space or time interval. Thus, a high-pitched sound has a high frequency and a short wavelength. A low-pitched

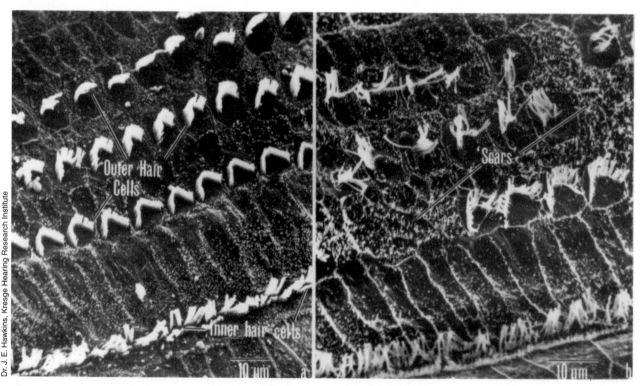

This electron micrograph shows healthy and scarred hair cells, which were damaged by prolonged exposure to loud noises.

TABLE 4.6
Decibel Table. This table shows the intensities of some common sounds and indicates how dangerous to our receptors certain levels of sound can become.

Decibel Level	Example	Time to Damage Hearing Without Ear Protection
0	Lowest sound audible to human ear (threshold)	
30	Quiet library, soft whisper	
40	Quiet office, living room, bedroom away from traffic	
50	Light traffic at a distance, refrigerator, gentle breeze	
60	Air conditioner at 20 feet, conversation	
70	Busy traffic, noisy restaurant (constant exposure)	Critical level begins with constant exposure
80	Subway, heavy city traffic, alarm clock 2 feet away, factory noise	More than 8 hours
90	Truck traffic, noisy appliances, shop tools, lawn mower	Less than 8 hours
100	Chain saw, boiler shop, pneumatic drill	2 hours
120	Rock concert in front of speakers, sandblasting, thunderclap	Immediate danger
140	Gunshot blast, jet plane	Any exposure is dangerous
180	Spacecraft launch	Hearing loss inevitable

sound has a low frequency and a long wavelength (see Figure 4.36).

The third property of sound is timbre (pronounced "tamber"). **Timbre** is the quality of sound that allows us to tell the difference between an A flat played on a piano and an A flat played on a harmonica. It corresponds to the visual sensation of color saturation. When you play a note on a musical instrument, you generate a complex series of tones. The single tone that the note produces is the *fundamental frequency*. But at the same time, the instrument produces distinctive tones, or *harmonics*, that are multiples higher than the fundamental frequency. Different musical instruments produce different harmonics that result in the distinctive sounds of the instruments. When additional sound waves are irregular and unrelated, we hear *noise*—confusing, nonsensical, and often unpleasant combinations of sounds. Figure 4.37 shows the contrast between the pleasant sounds of harmonics and the random dispersal of noise.

What are the parts of the ear that work together to enable us to hear noise, or anything else?

THE FUNCTIONAL ORGANIZATION OF THE EAR

When sound waves enter the ear, they pass through three regions (Ehret & Romand, 1997; Wickesberg, 2000): the outer ear, the middle ear, and the inner ear

© Ted Streshinsky/Corbis

People who use power tools or work in other loud environments, from construction sites to rock concerts, now frequently use protective earphones.

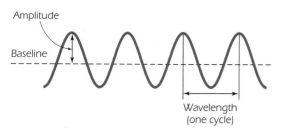

(a) Long-wavelength (low-frequency) sound

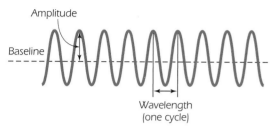

(b) Short-wavelength (high-frequency) sound

FIGURE 4.36

Properties of Sound Waves. What we sense of sound consists of waves of compressed air. Sound waves are measured in amplitude (what we sense as loudness) and frequency (what we sense as pitch).

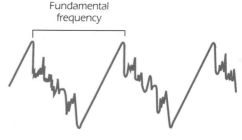

(a) A single note played on a piano

(b) Explosion (noise)

FIGURE 4.37

Sound Waves: Music versus an Explosion. As you look at these two sets of sound waves, how do you explain the differences in our sensation of a single note played on a piano versus an explosion?

(see Figure 4.38a). The **pinna,** the visible outer part of the ear, collects sound waves. From the pinna, the sound waves move down the auditory canal toward the **eardrum** (also termed the *tympanum*), a physiological structure of the outer ear that vibrates in response to the sound waves. The higher the frequency of the sound, the faster the vibrations of the eardrum.

The eardrum vibrations pass into the middle ear, where a sequence of three tiny bones passes them to the inner ear. The three bones—the *malleus, incus,* and *stapes*—normally amplify the vibrations transmitted by the eardrum and then transmit them to the cochlea. For extremely intense sounds that could damage the inner ear, the angle of the stapes against the inner ear changes. The new angle decreases the vibration and thereby protects the ear. This adjustment is another adaptive function of our physiology.

The stapes normally rests on the **oval window,** the first part of the inner ear. As Figure 4.38b shows, the oval window is at one end of the **cochlea,** the coiled and channeled main structure of the inner ear. Three fluid-filled canals run the entire length of the cochlea. The fluid-filled canals are separated by membranes. One of them is the **basilar membrane.** On the basilar membrane are thousands of **hair cells,** which function as our auditory receptors. The vibration of the stapes moves specialized hairlike appendages, or offshoots, of the hair cells. The hair cells transduce the mechanical

energy into electrochemical energy. It then is transmitted via the sensory neurons to the brain.

FROM THE EAR TO THE BRAIN

The axons of the sensory neurons form the *acoustic nerve* (also called the auditory nerve; see Figures 4.38 and 4.39). The specific route of information conveyed along the acoustic nerve is complex. It involves relay stops first in the medulla oblongata and then in the midbrain. The information is finally relayed through the thalamus to the auditory cortex in the temporal lobes of the brain. The cortex seems to map out the relationships among frequencies of the auditory field in a way that roughly approximates the way the visual cortex maps out spatial relationships in the visual field. Also, although the contralateral connections are the strongest ones, some information from both ears reaches both cerebral hemispheres. In the brain, the auditory cortex is connected to the areas for language perception and production (see Kiang, 2000).

HOW WE HEAR

Just as we can see only intermediate wavelengths of the full electromagnetic spectrum, we are most sensitive to sounds in the middle range of audible frequencies. They roughly correspond to the range of human

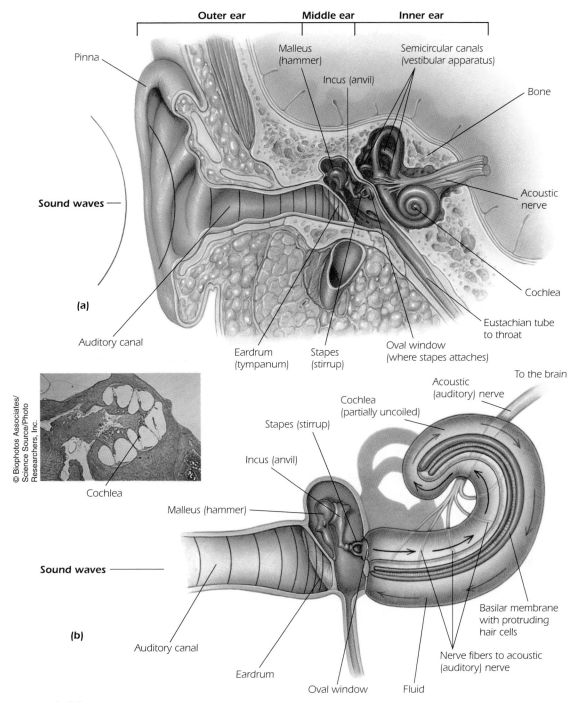

FIGURE 4.38

Anatomy of the Ear. The ear has three parts: the outer, middle, and inner ear. The inner ear contains the cochlea (see detail and photograph), which includes the auditory receptors as well as the vestibular system.

Ⓔ voices. Consistent with our discussions of psychophysics and evolutionary adaptability, we are especially sensitive to changes in sounds, such as changes in pitch. The major theories of how we sense pitch are place theory, frequency theory, and duplicity theory.

PLACE THEORY

Helmholtz (1863/1930), whose ideas on color were noted in our discussion of vision, proposed a theory of how we hear called place theory. **Place theory** posits that we hear each pitch as a function of the location in

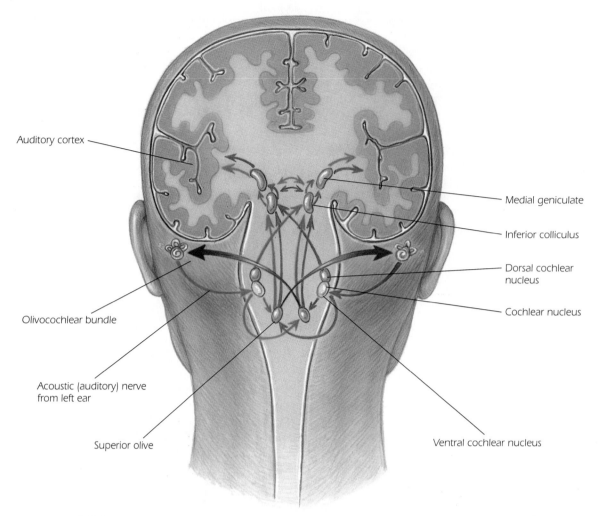

Auditory cortex

Medial geniculate

Inferior colliculus

Dorsal cochlear nucleus

Cochlear nucleus

Olivocochlear bundle

Acoustic (auditory) nerve from left ear

Superior olive

Ventral cochlear nucleus

FIGURE 4.39

Neural Pathways from the Ear to the Brain. The auditory receptors on the basilar membrane of the cochlea join to form the acoustic nerve, which routes through the medulla oblongata to the thalamus. The thalamus organizes the electrochemical impulses and sends them to regions of the auditory cortex in the temporal lobes.

the basilar membrane that is stimulated. The hair cells at different places on the basilar membrane vibrate in response to different pitches. In the process they excite different neurons. Each neuron is therefore sensitive to the specific frequencies that originally stimulated the basilar membrane. In fact, prolonged exposure to a very loud sound of a particular frequency damages the hair cells at a specific spot on the basilar membrane and causes hearing loss for sounds of that pitch.

Georg von Békésy's (1960) Nobel Prize–winning research led him to similar conclusions. He cut tiny holes in the cochleas of guinea pigs. As pitches of different frequencies were played, he observed the guinea pigs' basilar membranes with a microscope. Low-frequency tones stimulated the hair cells at the wider end of the basilar membrane (farthest

from the oval window). High-frequency tones stimulated the cells at the narrower end (closest to the oval window). Unfortunately, not everything Békésy saw fit in perfectly with place theory. Low-frequency tones also stimulated the cells along the whole basilar membrane. Even tones of intermediate frequencies sometimes stimulated wide areas of the membrane.

FREQUENCY THEORY

Frequency theory suggests that the basilar membrane reproduces the vibrations that enter the ear. According to this theory, the basilar membrane triggers neural impulses at the same frequency as the original sound wave (E. G. Wever, 1970). The pitch we sense is a result of the frequency of the impulses that enter the auditory nerve connecting the ear with the brain. For example, a tone of 500 Hz produces 500 bursts of electrical responses per second in the auditory nerve.

Frequency theory handles well certain phenomena that place theory does not fully explain. An example is the broader stimulation associated with low-frequency tones. However, frequency theory cannot account for pitches at the high end of the frequency scale. The problem for frequency theory is that a single neuron can conduct a maximum of only about 1,000 impulses per second (corresponding to a 1,000-Hz sound), but humans can hear frequencies of up to 20,000 Hz. We are not capable of a high enough rate of neuronal conduction to mirror the vibrations of high-frequency pitches. So once again, one theory does not provide all the answers.

According to the **volley principle**, auditory neurons are able to cooperate (E. G. Wever, 1970). That is, neurons can fire not just singly but in alternating groups. While one neuron is resting, a neighboring neuron can fire. This neighbor can cooperate similarly with other neurons as well. Thus, although no one neuron can fire at a fast enough rate to simulate the vibrations of the higher frequencies, a group of neurons can. Think of a group of rifle-wielding sharpshooters, each of whom must reload after each shot. If the sharpshooters cooperate so that some of them fire while others reload, the group can fire volleys much faster than can any one sharpshooter alone.

DUPLICITY THEORY

The most widely accepted current view on the hearing of pitch is **duplicity theory,** according to which both place and frequency play some role in hearing pitch. The details of duplicity theory have not yet been worked out, however. We saw a similar dialectic in vision research with the trichromatic and opponent-process theories of color vision. Theories that incorporate elements of competing theories are popular ways of resolving problems because they use the best features of each of the competitors (Kalmar & Sternberg, 1988). The final word in theories of pitch has yet to be heard. Psychologists have more definitive ideas, however, about how people locate sounds.

LOCATING SOUNDS

How do we determine where sounds are coming from? The key is that we have two ears roughly 6 inches apart on opposite sides of the head. When a sound comes from our right, it travels a shorter distance to reach the right ear than the left ear. Granted, the time difference between arrival at the right and left ears can be minuscule, but it is enough for us to sense and process. In fact, we can detect

time differences as brief as 10 microseconds (Durlach & Colburn, 1978). Another way we process location is by comparing the differences in the intensities of the sounds that reach our ears. The farther ear receives a sound of lesser intensity than the closer ear because our head absorbs some of the sound going to the farther ear. It seems that the *time-difference method* works best for low-frequency sounds. In contrast, the *intensity-difference method* works best for high-frequency sounds (see Figure 4.40).

What if a sound comes from a source equidistant from our ears, so that it arrives at both ears simultaneously? Then we are easily confused. When you hear a sound and are not able to pinpoint its location, you probably (and almost unconsciously) rotate your head in order to receive two slightly different messages in your ears. Then, using either the time- or intensity-difference method, you locate the source of the sound.

Hearing, together with seeing, provides us with much of our input from the outside world. But if we could only see and hear, we miss many pleasures, like tasting a delicious chocolate cake, smelling a freshly baked pizza, or feeling a massage. Other senses are important to our enjoyment of life and sometimes, as in the case of pain, to our survival.

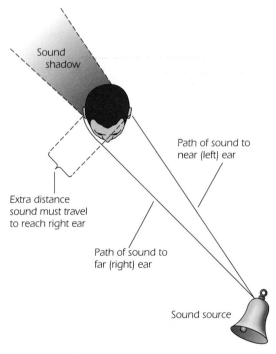

FIGURE 4.40
Determining the Source of a Sound. We locate the source of a sound by using two methods: We infer that the sound is coming from the direction of the ear that either heard the sound first or sensed the greater volume.

TASTE

How do we experience stimuli through our sense of taste?

We are able to see and hear things that occur at some distance from our bodies. To do so, we transduce the energy waves that we receive from those things into the electrochemical energy of neural transmission. In contrast, to use our sense of taste we must come into physical contact with the particular chemical makeup of the things we eat. In fact, what we taste has already entered our bodies. Just how does this highly intimate sensory system work? To answer this question, we explore the physical and psychological properties of taste and the anatomy in the tongue.

PHYSICAL AND PSYCHOLOGICAL PROPERTIES OF TASTE

For us to experience taste, a stimulus must contain chemical molecules that can dissolve in saliva, and we must have sufficient saliva in our mouths to dissolve them. In these chemicals, we detect the four primary psychological qualities of saltiness, bitterness, sweetness, and sourness (Bartoshuk, 1988). Sweet tastes typically come from *organic molecules*, which contain varying amounts of carbon, hydrogen, and oxygen. Bitter-tasting substances tend to contain some amount of nitrogen. Sour substances are usually acidic. And salty-tasting substances tend to have molecules that break down into electrically charged particles (ions) in water. Other tastes are produced by combinations of the four primary tastes, much as colors can be produced by a combination of the three primary colors. For example, a grapefruit is both sour and bitter and sometimes also sweet.

Our sensitivity to taste changes as we age. Children are hypersensitive to taste, as you may have noticed. The total number of taste buds on the tongue, however, decreases as we grow older, so we have decreased sensitivity to tastes. Although most people's absolute thresholds for taste are fairly low, the jnd's for taste are rather high. They have Weber fractions ranging from 0.1 to 1.0. These relatively high jnd thresholds mean that, in order for us to perceive differences in intensities, we must add at least 10% more taste, and possibly 100% more, depending on the flavor! Taste is probably our least finely tuned sensory system.

ANATOMY OF THE TONGUE

As substances enter the mouth they land on the tongue, where they are detected by one or more of roughly 10,000 **taste buds,** or **papillae,** clusters that contain taste-receptor cells located inside the small visible protrusions on the tongue (see E. T. Rolls, 1997; Schiffman, 2000; Scott, 2000). Taste buds are clustered all over the tongue and also in the back of the throat (see Figure 4.41). The cells within the taste buds last only about 10 days, and then they typically are replaced (Pfaffman, 1978). In the center of each taste bud is a pore, out of which grow microvilli (extremely small, fingerlike projections) that sample chemicals from food and drink.

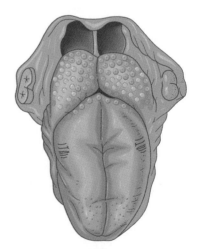

FIGURE 4.41

The Tongue and Our Sense of Taste. Taste buds cluster around tiny bumps on the tongue called papillae. The three types of papillae are circumvallate papillae, foliate papillae, and fungiform papillae. The taste buds located in each of the types of papillae show somewhat different levels of sensitivity to each of the four basic tastes. (Adopted from Bartoshuk, 1993)

Contact with these chemicals activates the taste buds, thereby beginning the transduction process. The receptors for taste (and for smell) transduce chemical energy into electrochemical energy. They then send the message about the chemicals through the electrochemical system of neuronal conduction. Sensitivity to the various tastes is distributed unevenly across the tongue. The pattern of distribution is complex, so it is not possible completely to localize a particular taste to a particular portion of the tongue (Bartoshuk, 1993).

The most widely accepted theory of taste (Pfaffman, 1974) posits that although each sensory receptor on the tongue does not respond uniquely to a single taste, different receptors do respond more strongly to certain taste sensations than to others. It appears that taste buds interact to produce the wide variety of tastes that we sense.

Three nerves carry information from the taste bud receptors on different regions of the tongue to the medulla oblongata. From there, the information is transmitted first to the thalamus and then to an area of the cortex. The area is near where areas of the face are mapped, primarily in the parietal lobe and also in the temporal lobe (see Figure 4.42). Some of the gustatory (taste) information, however, gets sidetracked from the thalamus to the nearby hypothalamus and to parts of the limbic system.

Thus far, we have indicated that taste embraces only four fundamental sensations. What about all the other nuances of flavor we enjoy? Much of what we refer to as the distinctive flavor of food is actually its aroma (see Figure 4.43).

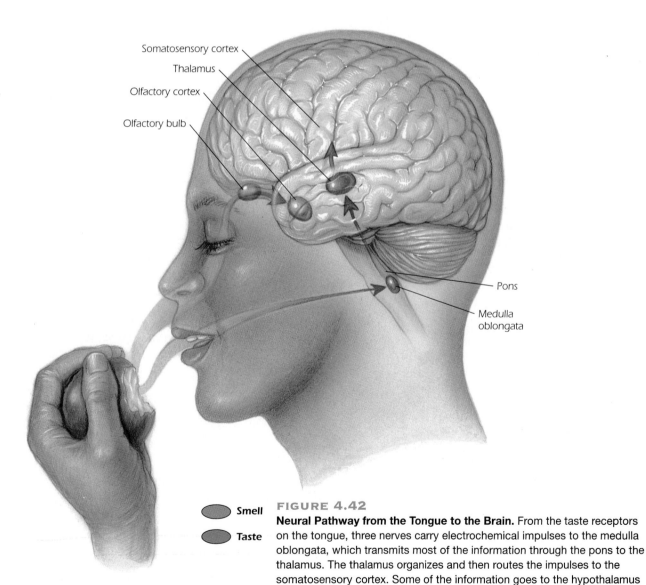

Somatosensory cortex
Thalamus
Olfactory cortex
Olfactory bulb

Pons
Medulla oblongata

Smell
Taste

FIGURE 4.42

Neural Pathway from the Tongue to the Brain. From the taste receptors on the tongue, three nerves carry electrochemical impulses to the medulla oblongata, which transmits most of the information through the pons to the thalamus. The thalamus organizes and then routes the impulses to the somatosensory cortex. Some of the information goes to the hypothalamus and to parts of the limbic system.

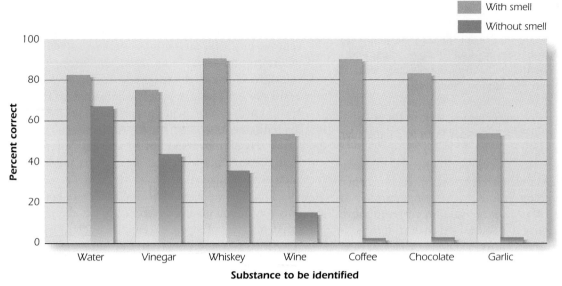

FIGURE 4.43

The Importance of Smell to Perceived Taste. Many foods are much less easy to identify when they cannot be smelled.

With smell

Without smell

✓ CONCEPT CHECK 5

1. Taste buds are also called
   a. papillae.
   b. microvilli.
   c. microneurons.
   d. papillomas.
2. Taste buds for sweet tastes are
   a. almost all in front of the tongue.
   b. almost all in back of the tongue.
   c. almost all on the sides of the tongue.
   d. distributed throughout the tongue.
3. According to Pfaffman,
   a. all receptors respond equally to all tastes.
   b. each receptor responds to only a single taste.
   c. different receptors respond more strongly to certain taste sensations than to others.
   d. receptors do not respond to the various tastes.

SMELL

How do we detect odors?

Many of us discover the importance of smell when we have a bad cold. Our food seems tasteless because our nasal passages are blocked. Two foods that are equally sweet but smell quite different (and hence are described casually as "tasting" different) may taste the same un-

less we can also smell them. The temperature of food can also affect our sensation of smell because heat tends to release aromas. For some of us, color and texture are also important to our enjoyment of food and drink.

As is the case with vision and hearing, humans depend on their sense of smell for survival and for information gathering, but not nearly as much as do other animals. In fact, humans have only 10 million smell receptors, whereas dogs have about 200 million. Nonetheless, odors and fragrances interact powerfully with our emotions, instantaneously calling up memories of past times and places.

Odors are important not only for our enjoyment of food and fragrance but for other reasons as well. Because the human nose is not particularly sensitive, machines have been created that can sniff out drugs and explosives. Sometimes trained dogs are used for these purposes because their sensitivity to odors so far exceeds ours.

PHYSICAL AND PSYCHOLOGICAL PROPERTIES IN THE SENSE OF SMELL

The sense of smell, **olfaction**, enhances our ability to savor food and also functions on its own, independent of taste. Like taste, smell is a chemically activated sense (Doty, 2000). Airborne molecules that can dissolve in either water or fat are candidates for sensation by our olfactory system.

Once our olfactory system detects scent-bearing molecules, we sense the odor. Researchers have tried to define *primary smells* that parallel the basic psycho-

DO IDEAS EVOLVE AS ORGANISMS DO?

We know that organisms evolve. Ideas also evolve. Is there any relationship between the two? Richard Dawkins (1989) has speculated that essentially the same laws of evolution that apply to organisms may apply to cultural artifacts, including ideas. Other psychologists have suggested that ideas may evolve along the lines of a mechanism whereby the "fittest" survive—namely, those that are best adapted to the cultural milieu in which they are proposed and diffused (D. T. Campbell, 1960; Perkins, 1995b; Simonton, 1995, 1999). On the one hand, we need to recognize that ideas are not living organisms in the same way that we are. On the other hand, ideas, like organisms, can fit more or less well into an environ-

mental niche. Their fit does not render them true, however. Cultures have accepted, over the years, many ideas that are demonstrably false, such as the idea that a mysterious (and, in fact, nonexistent) substance called phlogiston causes fire. Evolutionary theory does not provide any kind of code of truth or ethics. Neither organisms nor ideas that fit a given environment are in any real sense *better* than others in an absolute sense. Rather, they are simply the organisms or ideas that are well adapted to a given time or place.

Consider the notion that we love the taste of pizza, coconut, peaches, or whatever food we happen to love. For generation after generation, the idea that we love certain kinds of tastes and

dislike others has remained with us. We all speak this way, despite the fact that it is, strictly speaking, incorrect. What we love is the smell. There are only four basic tastes—sweet, sour, bitter, and salty—and this fact has been known for a long time. Most of what we refer to as taste is really smell. So why doesn't the idea of "how foods taste" go away? Because we perceive flavors as tastes, not as scents. Many wrong ideas survive even after society, or at least scientists, know they are wrong. You must be especially careful before accepting what you are told.

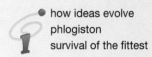

how ideas evolve
phlogiston
survival of the fittest

---

logical qualities of the other sense systems we have studied. One such attempt divided odors into flowery, foul, fruity, burnt, resinous, and spicy, leaving room for combinations (Henning, 1915). The relationships and differences among odors, however, have proven very hard to define systematically. To get an idea of the problem, think of five things you enjoy smelling. Now, describe those aromas without using any similes (i.e., "it smells like . . . "). Our vocabulary for aromas is limited unless we compare or contrast one odor with another. Thus, although we know that smell is active in our psychological functioning in the recall of memories, there is still no satisfactory way of characterizing what we sense when we detect an odor.

Absolute thresholds for smell are difficult to study because the nasal receptors are somewhat inaccessible. In addition, different substances have different thresholds for detection, as do the smell receptors of different people. In fact, some people are *odor-blind*, unable to detect one or more specific scents. It is also extremely difficult to control the concentrations of odors and to eliminate interference from body, clothing, and environmental odors.

The olfactory system seems to be more sensitive than the gustatory (taste) system in discriminating between stimuli. Weber fractions for jnd's in odor inten-

sity can be as low as 0.05. In other words, differences in scent intensity of only 5% can be detected about half the time (Cain, 1977).

One of the most interesting topics in the study of smell is **pheromones**, chemical substances secreted by nonhuman animals. Pheromones trigger specific kinds of reactions in other animals, usually of the same species. These reactions include mutual identification of parent and child, sexual signals, territorial-boundary markers, and both limits on and prompts toward aggression. There is some disagreement about whether pheromones operate in the human species in a way that triggers sexual attraction (Gangestad & Thornhill, 1998; Quadagno, 1987).

Research shows that people react psychologically to odors. For example, within the first few weeks of life, breast-fed infants can identify their mothers by scent (Cernoch & Porter, 1985). Women who have at least weekly contact with male underarm secretions (e.g., through intimate contact) appear to have more regularly timed menstrual cycles. And women who have regular contact with other women (or with their underarm secretions) tend to have synchronized menstrual cycles (W. B. Cutler et al., 1986). The link between odor and sexual attraction is less clear. But women seem to find male odors more attractive than other men do. In any case, women seem more sensitive to odors (in absolute terms) and more responsive to odors (in terms of their self-reports and other behavior) than men. Scents can also evoke distant memories, including the emotions associated with the remembered events.

FROM THE NOSE TO THE BRAIN

Airborne scent molecules rise into the nose by the force of a person's inhalation (see Figure 4.44). They pass up through the nasal cavity to a point below and behind the eyes. Here they encounter the **olfactory epithelium** (the "smell skin") in the nasal *mucosa*, the membranes that secrete protective mucus. The particles contact the olfactory receptor cells that detect odors and initiate the transduction of the chemical energy of the odors into the electrochemical energy needed for neural transmission. Smell receptors can fully regenerate in adult mammals. It is a good thing they do because they die after 4 to 8 weeks.

The receptors in the olfactory epithelium are unique among sensory systems in that their axons actually penetrate the skull and combine directly to form each of the two olfactory nerves. Each olfactory nerve terminates at one of the two **olfactory bulbs,** where its neurons communicate with other neurons in complex arrangements. From an olfactory bulb, smell impulses primarily bypass the thalamus (unlike other sensory neurons). They go eventually into the olfactory cortex in the temporal lobe or to the limbic system (especially the hypothalamus). The hypothalamus and the limbic system may be involved in whether we accept or reject a food based on its aroma.

✓**CONCEPT CHECK 6**

1. In comparison with dogs, humans have
   a. a much less sensitive sense of smell.
   b. a much more sensitive sense of smell.
   c. a comparable sense of smell.
   d. a variable sense of smell: Many humans are better, but many are worse.
2. The olfactory nerves terminate at the olfactory
   a. knobs.
   b. bulbs.

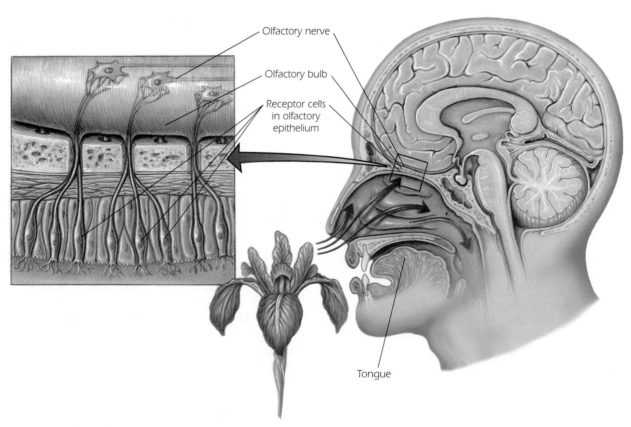

FIGURE 4.44
Nasal Cavity. Airborne molecules are inhaled into the nasal cavity. Receptor cells in the olfactory epithelium transduce the chemical energy of smell into the electrochemical energy of the nervous system.

Olfactory nerve

Olfactory bulb

Receptor cells in olfactory epithelium

Tongue

c. neurons.
d. locus.
3. We are able to smell airborne molecules that dissolve in
   a. water only.
   b. fat only.
   c. either water or fat.
   d. neither water nor fat.

THE SKIN SENSES

What is the sense of touch?

Many talk-show hosts and perfume sellers suggest that odor plays a powerful role in our sexual and other interpersonal behavior. Although psychologists may question this conclusion, few of them doubt that touch plays such a role.

Often we call the sense of touch the fifth sense. It is intimately connected with the skin, our largest bodily organ. The term *touch*, however, insufficiently characterizes the various sensations of pressure, temperature, and pain. A better term may be the *skin senses* because we receive so many sensations through the skin. The formal term for the various means by which we become sensitive to pressure, temperature, and pain stimulation directly on the skin is the *haptic senses*.

Thus far, we have discussed the ways in which our sensory systems respond to sensory information that reaches us from outside our bodies. These *exteroceptive* systems receive external stimulation. In addition, we have *interoceptive* systems, which receive stimulation from within our bodies, such as feeling flushed, feeling a stomachache, feeling dizzy, or feeling how our bodies are positioned in space. Some also refer to interoception as *proprioception* (receiving information about your own body). The haptic senses largely include exteroceptive systems, but some senses, such as the sense of pain, can offer us proprioceptive information as well.

Touch is very important to humans. Although researchers clearly would not severely deprive human infants of touch, medical professionals and developmental psychologists have noticed that tactile stimulation seems to enhance the physiological stability of preterm infants. It also promotes weight gain, a crucial factor in the health and vitality of infants. Studies of children from Romanian orphanages have shown that absence of touch is associated with disorders in attachment of children to their parents (Cassidy & Shaver, 1999; Chisholm et al., 1995; see Chapter 11

for a discussion of attachment). Some research on adults shows positive effects of touch as well. For example, touching or stroking a pet seems to lower the heart rate of the person doing the petting.

PHYSICAL AND PSYCHOLOGICAL PROPERTIES OF THE SKIN SENSES

Our skin can respond to a variety of external stimuli. The way we sense these physical stimuli results in a psychological interpretation of the sensation as pain, warmth, and so on. Objects pressed against the skin change its shape and cause the sensation of pressure. When even a single tiny hair on our skin is displaced, we feel pressure from its movement. The temperature of an object against the skin results in a sensation of warmth or cold. Slight electrical stimulation of our skin usually causes a sensation of pressure and perhaps of temperature. Too much of any kind of stimulation generally results in pain. Intense stimulation from inside the body, or tissue damage either inside or outside the body, can lead to the sensation of pain as well. The bodily response that culminates in pain often begins with sensations detected in the skin.

ANATOMY OF THE SKIN

We can feel through our skin because sensory receptors permeate its layers (see Figure 4.45). Our skin has different kinds of sensory receptors for touch, pain, pressure, and temperature. Our specialized receptors for touch have distinctive globular ("corpuscular") swellings at their dendritic endings. These corpuscular cells are located at different skin layers. They are sensitive to different types of touch (pinpoint surface pressure, broad-region surface pressure, deep pressure, movement, and vibration). Imagine being blindfolded and then touched by three different objects. Each has a 1-inch-square surface that is pressed against your skin: a cube of absorbent cotton, a stiff brush, and a polished metal cube. Even with the blindfold on, you can probably tell the difference. If the brush or other object is vibrated, even if it is not moved otherwise, you can detect the vibration, too. Our skin also contains specialized sensory receptors called **free nerve endings** that register pain and temperature and notice when a hair follicle is bent. These receptors are noncorpuscular. They lack the globular swellings of touch receptors. Sensations travel from them and eventually reach the brain.

FROM THE SKIN TO THE BRAIN

From the skin, two kinds of sensory neurons travel to the spinal cord, where they pass impulses to other neurons that travel to the brain. One kind of neuron is myelinated, the other unmyelinated. The fast-

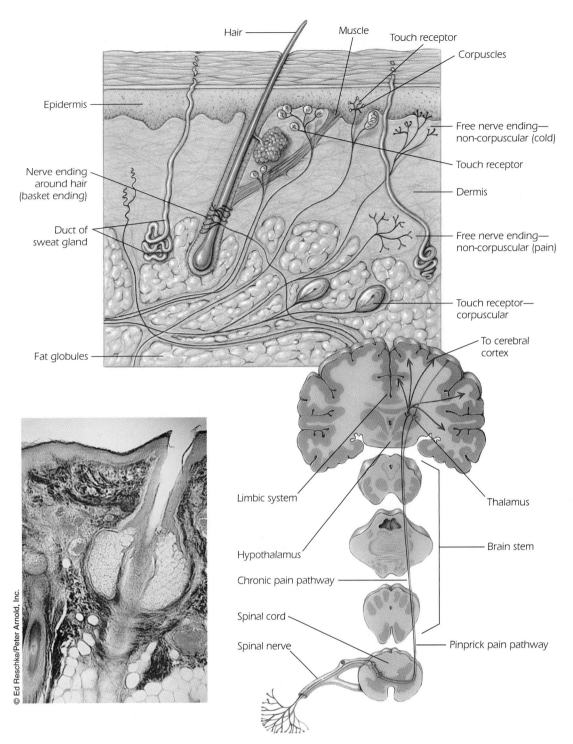

FIGURE 4.45

Skin Receptors. Our skin contains sensory receptors for pain, pressure, and temperature. Each receptor serves a different function and provides distinctive sensory information. (See the magnified photo.) As we saw in the discussion of reflexes in Chapter 3, if the receptors detect a sudden, strong feeling of pain (or pressure or extreme temperature), the neural impulse normally sent to the brain may be rerouted at the spine to create a sudden muscular movement that removes the body from the source of the pain. If the strong pain continues, the neural impulses it creates go directly to the cerebral cortex; the sensation of chronic pain is routed through the limbic system to the cortex.

conducting myelinated neurons usually travel over relatively long distances to reach the spinal cord. The slow-conducting unmyelinated neurons usually have to travel only short distances to reach the spinal cord. When the sensory neurons reach the spinal cord, the two kinds of neurons take different routes, through two different kinds of nerves in the spinal cord.

The first kind of spinal-cord nerve collects information from the myelinated neurons. It ascends the spinal cord, crosses over to the other half of the brain at the medulla oblongata, goes to the thalamus, and then to the somatosensory cortex. This kind of nerve responds mostly to the senses of pressure and movement.

The second kind of spinal-cord nerve collects information from the unmyelinated sensory neurons. These neurons can also make local connections with motor effector neurons to produce reflexive reactions. This kind of nerve provides information to the brain about pain, temperature, and pressure. The nerve travels up the spinal cord and then divides into two bundles at the medulla oblongata. One bundle conveys information about diffuse, dull, or burning pain. The other bundle carries information about localized, sharp, or piercing pain. Both bundles cross over contralaterally. Thus, pain in the right side of the body is related to activity in the left side of the brain, and vice versa. The nerve bundles stop at the thalamus and the limbic system, which are important for emotion and memory. They then go to the somatosensory cortex. We sense temperature, pressure, pain, and movement information that travels this route less precisely than we sense sensations that travel the faster route. Let us consider how we process these various kinds of information.

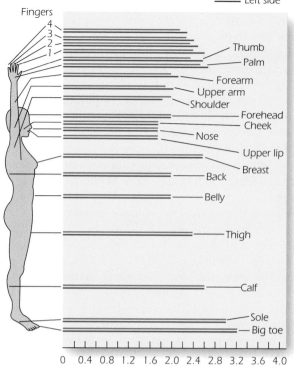

FIGURE 4.46

Absolute Thresholds for Pressure. Different regions of the body have differing degrees of sensitivity to pressure. How would an evolutionary psychologist explain the varying amounts of sensitivity? (From "Average Absolute Thresholds for Different Regions of the Female and Male Skin" from Weinstein and Kenshalo, *The Skin Senses,* Copyright © 1968. Reprinted courtesy of Charles C. Thomas, Publishers, Ltd., Springfield, IL.)

PRESSURE, TEMPERATURE, AND PAIN

The skin sense of pressure allows us to feel physical stimuli that contact the exterior of the body. We are able to sense the weight, vibration, and location of pressure. Our absolute thresholds for pressure differ widely across various parts of the body (see Figure 4.46). For example, the cheek is more sensitive than the palm of the hand (Weinstein, 1968). Researchers test absolute thresholds by touching different locations on the skin with a small bristle or vibrating stimulus, using varying amounts of force.

Maintaining a consistent body temperature is essential to our survival. Two kinds of nerve fibers

The pressure receptors in their skin enable these children to sense touching and being touched.

(bundles of neurons) in the skin enable us to sense warmth and cold via their patterns of firing. *Cold fibers,* as you might imagine, respond to cooling of the skin by increasing their rate of firing. *Warm fibers* respond analogously to warming of the skin (in the range of 95°–115° Fahrenheit [35°–46° Celsius]; Hensel, 1981). The two types of fibers are not equally distributed across the body. Even in a small patch of skin, different portions may be differentially responsive to cold and warmth.

Because the two types of fibers are highly responsive to changes in temperature, what we sense as cold or warm depends on our adaptation level. When we start off cold, what we sense as warm may be quite a bit colder than what we sense as warm when we start off hot. Consequently, it is difficult to quantify absolute thresholds in measuring temperature. Research thus has focused largely on adaptation and, to a lesser extent, on jnd's. When our skin is at a normal temperature, we can detect greater warmth of 0.72° Fahrenheit (0.4° Celsius) and increased coolness of 0.27° Fahrenheit (0.15° Celsius; Kenshalo, Nafe, & Brooks, 1961).

Intense stimulation, as well as any resulting damage to tissues, can lead to pain. When tissue is damaged, it releases a neurotransmitter, which starts an impulse on its way to the central nervous system.

Different parts of the body are unequally susceptible to pain (Gatchel & Turk, 1996; Mogil, 2000; Turk & Okifuji, 2000; Wall & Melzack, 1999). The back of the knee, for example, is much more susceptible than the sole of the foot. Moreover, people differ widely in their apparent sensitivity to pain. In extreme cases, some individuals feel no pain at all (see Sternbach, 1963). Although such insensitivity might seem to be an ideal state, such people may die early from accidental injury. For instance, they might lose an enormous amount of blood before even noticing they had been injured, particularly in cases of internal bleeding. People who are insensitive to pain also may not realize how sensitive others are. Pain is unpleasant, but it serves a functional, evolutionary purpose. It prompts us to remove ourselves from dangerous or stressful situations or to seek a quick remedy for injuries. Stomachache, earache, intestinal cramps, injured joints or bones, and other proprioceptive pain (i.e., pain that arises from within the body) alert us to internal assaults. This information may at least help us to avoid future insults to our systems, even if we cannot escape the immediate one.

It is important to recognize, however, that factors beyond the individual's sensory physiology seem to affect how much pain a person experiences. Cultural influences, personal expectations, and adaptation levels play a role. The needs, beliefs, expectations, and practices characteristic of one culture may serve to either raise or lower thresholds in contrast with other cultures. For example, Asians report more pain than Caucasians and other groups in response to having their ears pierced (V. J. Thomas & Rose, 1991).

✓CONCEPT CHECK 7

1. Our feeling a stomachache is an example of
   a. proprioception.
   b. exteroception.
   c. introspection.
   d. extraversion.

2. Pain serves an adaptive function because it leads us to
   a. remember how lucky we are when we do not feel pain.
   b. avoid stimuli that can cause tissue damage.
   c. kill our prey in a way that does not cause it pain.
   d. seek stimulation through small amounts of pain.
3. Human bodies have
   a. warm fibers but not cool fibers.
   b. cool fibers but not warm fibers.
   c. both warm fibers and cool fibers.
   d. neither warm fibers nor cool fibers.

THE BODY SENSES

How do we experience and maintain movement, balance, and equilibrium?

Pain is not the only proprioceptive sense that serves us. You probably do not remember when you learned to walk. But that moment was a triumphant one for your sense of kinesthesis and your vestibular sense, or equilibrium. These senses help us to move, stand upright, and generally feel physically and spatially oriented. We typically are not even aware of them. Our lack of awareness does not imply that these senses are unimportant, however. If you question the importance of the body senses, try spinning yourself around and around, as you probably did when you were a child. Then see whether you can walk a straight line. Now let us consider the two body senses of kinesthesis and equilibrium.

KINESTHESIS

Kinesthesis is the sense that helps us ascertain our skeletal movements and positioning (Gandevia, 1996; L. A. Jones, 2000; Prochazka, 1996): Where are the various parts of our body in relation to one another? How (if at all) are they moving? Kinesthetic receptors are in the muscles, tendons, joints, and skin. When these receptors detect changes in positions via pressure, they transduce this mechanical energy into neural energy. This energy in turn codes information about the speed of the change, the angle of the bones, and the tension of the muscles. The information is sent up the spinal cord, where it eventually reaches the brain. It is shifted contralaterally in the brain to the somatosensory cortex and to the cerebellum, which is responsible for automatic processes and motor coordination (see Chapter 3).

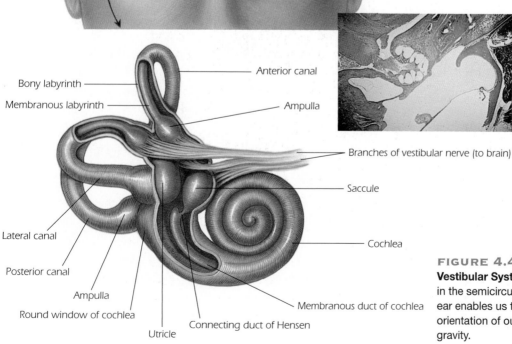

The kinesthetic receptors in this girl's skeletal muscles combine with her vestibular sense to make her aware of the swiftly changing position of her body as she leaps through space.

THE VESTIBULAR SENSE

The **vestibular sense** is, roughly speaking, the sense of balance or equilibrium. It is determined by the orientation of the head in relation to the source of gravity, as well as by the movement and acceleration of our bodies through space. We tend to be unaware of our vestibular sense unless it is overstimulated. Overstimulation might occur, for example, on a bumpy airplane flight or on a carnival ride that is a bit too wild. You probably know the results: dizziness and nausea. Video games and virtual reality simulations can also cause a form of motion sickness known as cybersickness. Research on reducing these unwanted effects is the subject of the In the Lab box.

The receptors for equilibrium are located in the inner ear (see Figure 4.47). The **vestibular system** comprises the vestibular sacs and semicircular canals. Both contain a fluid that moves when the head rotates. The movement in turn causes the hair cells inside the sacs and canals to bend. This mechanical energy is then transduced into electrochemical impulses in the nerves. The impulses travel through the auditory nerve to the cerebellum and the cortex of the brain. They carry information about the rate of acceleration of the head as well as about its direction of movement and its relative orientation. Motion sickness can result when the brain has to integrate incompatible information from various sensory systems. For example, picture yourself riding in a moving vehicle. You are unable to see outside (like a young child in a car or a below-deck passenger on a boat). You see only the inside of the vehicle, which is not

Bony labyrinth
Membranous labyrinth
Anterior canal
Ampulla
Branches of vestibular nerve (to brain)
Saccule
Cochlea
Lateral canal
Posterior canal
Ampulla
Round window of cochlea
Membranous duct of cochlea
Connecting duct of Hensen
Utricle

FIGURE 4.47
Vestibular System. Movement of fluid in the semicircular canals in the inner ear enables us to sense shifts in the orientation of our head in relation to gravity.

IN THE LAB OF JAMES G. MAY

VIRTUAL REALITY AND CYBERSICKNESS

Computer technology can provide us with virtual environments (VE) within which we may become immersed. VE works interactively with the participant by sensing head movements and translating the visual scene on the display screen in the direction opposite of head movement. This arrangement mimics what happens in the real world. If you turn your head to the right, your view of the world shifts to the left. This produces the illusion of "presence" in the virtual world. The current applications of VE range from dynamic video games to simulations for practicing driving, flying, and surgical techniques. VE is also used in constructing architectural plans. But even brief exposure to this technology may produce the severe side effect *cybersickness* (Kennedy, Lanham, Drexler, Massey, & Lilienthal, 1997).

Cybersickness resembles other forms of motion sickness or MS (e.g., car sickness, sea sickness, air sickness), but it is produced visually, without significant bodily motion. There are three current theories of how MS comes about. According to *sensory conflict theory* (Benson, 1984), we become sick whenever a comparator in the brain gets mixed messages from our sensory systems. For example, below deck on a ship, your vestibular system confirms that you are moving, but because you are moving with the ship your eyes do not sense it. If you are seated in a stationary chair in an IMAX theater, the vestibular system senses little motion, but the visual display gives the illusion of movement. This illusion

is called *vection* (Dichgans & Brandt, 1973), and it is produced whenever a moving scene fills all or most of your visual field of view.

The *postural instability theory* (Stoffregan & Smart, 1998) argues that conditions that challenge your postural stability lead to MS if you attempt to maintain your balance. So, standing or walking on a ship's deck is more likely to provoke MS than is lying down in your bunk. When you experience vection, your body sways to compensate for the illusion.

The third theory of MS etiology, the *eye movement hypothesis* (Ebenholtz, Cohen, & Linder, 1994), notes that most situations that lead to MS elicit reflexive eye movements. Look at the X below and turn your head to the left and right:

X

While your head moved, your eyes remained stationary, right? Wrong!! Your eyes had to rotate in their sockets at precisely same velocity as your head moved, and in the opposite direction. This is termed the *vestibulo-ocular reflex* (VOR). Head movements lead to eye movements. When you view a moving scene that fills your whole visual field, another eye movement pat-

tern, *optokinetic nystagmus* (OKN), is often elicited. In this situation, your eyes smoothly pursue a moving feature in the scene and then abruptly snap back to the center of the field. So, full-field visual stimulation can also cause eye movements. But how can eye movements lead to MS? Ebenholtz and colleagues argue that certain eye movement patterns send signals to the comparator and ultimately to the vagus nerve, which triggers vomiting.

Treisman (1977) suggested that MS occurs when we fool a basic adaptive mechanism that is aimed at avoiding toxic substances. He notes that the ingestion of neurotoxins results in sensory and motor disruptions that give rise to disorientation and trigger the emetic response, which rids the body of the toxic substance. As stated above, actual and apparent motion also give rise to sensory and motor disruptions.

So which of these factors, or combination of factors, is the true cause of MS? We have carried out experiments in our lab in which we have manipulated each variable (sensory conflict, eye movement, postural stability) to determine its role in the production of MS. In one

James G. May is Research Professor Emeritus in the Psychology Department at the University of New Orleans. His honors include the LSU Foundation Distinguished Faculty Fellowship Award, the UNO Alumni Association Career Achievement Award for Excellence in Research, the Fulbright Senior Research Fellowship, the Fogarty Senior International Scholarship, and the Villere Chair for Research in Neuroscience.

experiment, we elicited vection and OKN with a large striped drum that rotated around seated subjects. We suppressed OKN by providing a fixation point to prevent this reflex, and we restricted the field of view to prevent vection. Preventing OKN and vection both reduced MS (Flanagan, May, & Dobie, 2002). Preventing OKN also reduced vection, and preventing vection reduced OKN amplitude. One explanation is that OKN gives rise to vection, which in turn produces MS.

In another study (Flanagan, May, & Dobie, in press), we had subjects view a large-screen movie (that produced eye movements and vection) while standing on a "wiggle" board (that produced postural instability).

We suppressed eye movements with fixation, removed the wiggle board to promote postural stability, and turned off the movie to remove vection. The results indicated that vection was most provocative of MS, but that eye movements and postural stability also contributed. MS was greatest when all three factors were present. We interpreted this result to mean that there may be many ways of stimulating an adaptive mechanism that has evolved to trigger the emetic response, as shown in the figure:

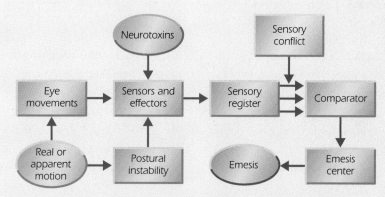

Summary of how multiple factors can trigger the adaptive emetic reflex.

moving, but your body still feels vestibular and kinesthetic movements. As you might guess, we generally feel better when our visual information agrees with our vestibular and kinesthetic information. Often reading while riding in a car makes us nauseous because of such disagreement.

Vestibular sensations are welcomed by more than just sensation-seekers who crave speed and motion. The countless rocking chairs that have been used for ages attest to the lulling effects of vestibular stimulation. Perhaps you have gone for a drive or for a walk when troubled, seeking to be soothed.

We are tremendously lucky to have the resources of our sensory and perceptual systems available to us. When they are damaged or lacking, life as we know it is radically different. Our senses are our gateways to thoughts, feelings, and ideas. They provide bridges from the external world, through our bodies, to our minds. Consciousness, considered in the next chapter, enables us to keep track of our sensations and perceptions.

✓ **CONCEPT CHECK 8**

1. Motion sickness can result from an upset to the _____ system.
   a. olfactory
   b. digestive
   c. vestibular
   d. gustatory
2. The sense that helps us ascertain our skeletal movements and positioning is the
   a. olfactory.
   b. gustatory.
   c. fractal.
   d. kinesthetic.
3. Kinesthetic information travels, in large part, to the _____
   a. cerebellum.
   b. pons.
   c. thalamus.
   d. hippocampus.

PERCEIVING SYMMETRY

The principles of perception may seem dry and dusty to some people, but when they are applied to the real world, they are anything but. Consider, for example, the Gestalt principle of symmetry.

Mate choice is based in part on perceptions of bodily symmetry in a variety of species, including (but not limited to) scorpion flies, swallows, lizards, fruit flies, and humans (Gangestad, Thornhill, & Yeo, 1994; Palmer & Palmer, 2002). All vertebrates are bilaterally symmetrical, in that the left and right sides of the body are mirror images of each other. High levels of symmetry tend to be associated with greater physical attractiveness. *Psychobiologists* and *ethological psychologists* have observed that male animals of various species make displays in order to attract females. The Archibold's bowerbird, a native of Papua New Guinea, builds a hut and platform of twigs for courtship purposes (not as a nest), and then searches for bird of paradise feathers with which to decorate its bower. Symmetrical arrangements are most attractive to female bowerbirds (Kubovy, 2000). Similarly, the more symmetrical the plumage of male peacocks, the more the females find them attractive. More generally, the perception of symmetry appears to have adaptive value, in that the more symmetrical organisms tend to be viewed as more attractive, which in turn leads to greater reproductive potential (Kubovy, 2000).

Research by *social psychologists* indicates that symmetry shapes the preferences of humans, too. For example, women rate symmetrical male faces as most attractive (Koehler, Rhodes, & Simmons, 2002). *Evolutionary psychologists* propose that people associate symmetry with health, and we tend to be attracted to healthy potential sex partners (Fink & Penton-Voak, 2002; Palmer & Palmer, 2002). *Developmental psychologists* have discovered that babies who are 5 to 8 months old spend more time gazing at symmetrical than at asymmetrical faces (Rhodes, Geddes, Jeffery, Dziurawiec, & Clark, 2002). These findings strongly suggest that the cross-species preference for symmetry may have a biological basis.

Social psychologist Pierre Gosselin and his colleagues have studied the responses of children and adults to symmetrical and asymmetrical smiles. They found that smiles that communicate enjoyment are more symmetrical than phony smiles (Gosselin, Perron, Legault, & Campanella, 2002). In another experiment, Maiko Nakamura (2002) discovered that asymmetrical facial expressions signal anxiety. Thus, symmetrical expressions indicate a pleasant mood and asymmetrical expressions may indicate distress. The ability to recognize emotions from facial expressions not only is important for survival but also is considered, by *cognitive psychologists,* to be a measure of emotional intelligence (Elfenbein, Marsh, & Ambady, 2002).

Perceptual psychologists who have studied the role of symmetry in object identification and artistic esthetics have found that it gives us cues about the orientation of an object and aids in our recognition of it (Large, McMullen, & Hamm, 2003; Parovel & Vezzani, 2002). They have also found that we prefer symmetry in art. When college art and non-art students were asked to make constructions, the art students most frequently made them symmetrical. In the same study, both groups showed a preference for symmetry when asked to rate seven different arrays (Washburn & Humphrey, 2001). Symmetry in a Japanese Zen rock garden heightens its visual appeal (Van Tonder, Lyons, & Ejima, 2002).

Studying the perception of symmetry lets psychologists analyze complex pattern recognition in people of all ages. Developmental psychologists Marc Bornstein and Sharon Krinsky (1985) studied 72 four-month-old infants. Their research demonstrated that babies perceive symmetry best when it is oriented vertically, just as adults do. Most important, Bornstein and Krinsky's (1985) research indicated that very young infants are able to perceive whole patterns.

Andrew Herbert and his colleagues (2002) examined the perception of symmetry in 40 people ranging from 19 to 80 years old. Like

continued

the babies in Bornstein and Krinsky's experiment, adults detect symmetry best when it is oriented along a vertical axis rather than along a horizontal or oblique (45 degrees from vertical) one. The ability to detect symmetry declined significantly for people over the age of 60, and the performance of people older than 70 was much worse than of people 60 to 70 years old (Herbert, Overbury, Singh, & Faubert, 2002). Thus, research by a variety of specialists has demonstrated that perceptual processing declines with age (Faubert, 2002).

The Gestalt principle of symmetry has been studied by psychologists from many different specialty areas. Psychobiologists, ethological psychologists, and evolutionary psychologists have examined the biological roots of a preference for symmetry. Social, developmental, and perceptual psychologists have investigated human preferences for symmetry. Research from these diverse specialties suggests that symmetry may be preferred because it indicates health or good humor or because it is more visually appealing.

SUMMARY

1. A *sensation* is a message that the brain receives from a sense. A *sense* is a physical system that collects information and transduces it from one form of energy into the brain's electrochemical energy.
2. *Perception* is the set of processes by which we recognize, organize, and make sense of stimuli in our environment.

PSYCHOPHYSICS 117

What are the relationships between various forms of physical stimulation and the psychological sensations they produce?

3. *Psychophysics* is the study of the relationship between physical stimulation and its psychological effects.
4. *Detection* refers to the ability to sense a stimulus. The minimal amount of physical energy of a given kind that can be sensed (detected) exactly 50% of the time is operationally defined as the *absolute threshold*.
5. *Signal-detection theory (SDT)* analyzes responses in terms of hits (true positive responses), misses (false negatives), false alarms (false positives), and correct rejections (true negatives). SDT is also used for explaining how we determine the likelihood that a sensation is caused by a particular signal.

6. *Discrimination* involves ascertaining the difference between one stimulus and another. The *just noticeable difference (jnd)* is the minimum amount of difference that can be detected between two stimuli 50% of the time. The jnd provides a way of measuring the *difference threshold*.
7. *Weber's law* states that a jnd is a constant proportion of the stimulus. The Weber fraction is a measure of the ratio of change in stimulus intensity to intensity.

BIOLOGICAL PROPERTIES COMMON TO ALL SENSES 121

How do we sense physical stimuli?

8. All of the senses share particular biological properties, such as psychophysical thresholds, *transduction, sensory coding,* and *sensory adaptation*.
9. Each sense has specialized sensory *receptor cells*, which take in a particular form of energy and transduce it so that sensory neurons can transmit the sensed information to the brain. Impulses from most sensory receptors go via the sensory neurons to the thalamus, which then relays information to the cerebral cortex.
10. The contralateral shift enables sensory neurons from the left side of the body to cross over to the right hemisphere of the brain, and vice versa.

11. Through sensory coding, sensory receptors convey a range of information, such as intensity (amplitude) and quality (e.g., wavelength) of a stimulus. Sensory neurons encode these physical aspects through neural firing, which can be measured by *single-cell recording*. Stimulus intensity is coded by rate of firing and firing-pattern regularity.

12. When our senses detect changes in energy, receptor cells fire vigorously to alert the brain. *Sensory adaptation* is the temporary physiological response to a change in the environment; it varies according to the intensity of the change in the stimulus.

VISION 123

What are the sensory and perceptual mechanisms that enable us to see?

13. We can see because the receptors of our eyes receive and transduce the electromagnetic radiant energy of a very small portion of the *electromagnetic spectrum* of light.

14. The black round opening in the center of the *iris* is the *pupil*, which dilates or contracts in response to the amount of light that enters it. The *lens* of the eye refracts light and focuses it on the retina, enabling us to see objects clearly at varying distances from us. The *retina* transduces the electromagnetic radiant energy in light into electrochemical impulses.

15. People have two separate visual systems; one is used primarily for vision in the dark (*rods*) and the other primarily for vision in light (*cones*).

16. Brightness is our impression of light intensity. It is a psychological, rather than a physical, phenomenon.

17. Three properties of color are *hue*, which is what we usually call as "color"; saturation, which is the vividness, vibrancy, or richness of a color; and brightness, reflected from the color.

18. The *trichromatic theory of color vision* posits that we see color through the actions and interactions of cone receptors for three primary colors: red, green, and blue.

19. The *opponent-process theory of color vision* states that we see color through the opposing actions of receptors for red versus green and blue versus yellow.

20. Perceptual constancies result when our perceptions of objects tend to remain constant even as the stimuli registered by the sensory apparatus change. Examples are size, shape, and lightness constancies. Two *size-constancy* illusions are the *Ponzo illusion* and the *Müller–Lyer illusion*, both related to the way we interpret monocular depth cues. *Shape constancy*, too, may be tied to our interpretation of depth cues (e.g., in the observation that parallel lines appear to converge as they recede into the distance). *Lightness constancy* appears to be affected by context cues.

21. Depth perception is made possible in part by *monocular depth cues*, which can be noted by just a single eye. Examples of monocular depth cues are relative size, texture gradients, interposition, linear perspective, location in the picture plane, aerial perspective, and motion parallax. Artists manipulate many of these cues to create illusions of depth on two-dimensional surfaces.

22. *Binocular depth cues*, those used by the two eyes in conjunction, also facilitate space perception. *Binocular convergence* cues depend on the degree to which our two eyes must turn inward toward each other as objects get closer to us. *Binocular disparity* cues capitalize on the fact that each of the two eyes receives a slightly different image of the viewed object.

23. According to the *Gestalt approach*, the whole is different from the sum of its parts. Gestalt principles of form perception—such as *figure–ground*, proximity, similarity, closure, good continuation, and symmetry—characterize how we perceptually group together objects and parts of objects.

24. According to the *feature-detector approach* to form perception, cortical neurons can be linked to specific receptive fields on the retina. Differing cortical neurons respond to different kinds of forms, such as line segments or edges in various spatial orientations. Visual perception seems to depend on three levels of complexity in the cortical neurons; each successive level of complexity seems to be further removed from the incoming information received by the sensory receptors.

25. Two of the main theoretical approaches to pattern perception are *template matching*, according to which we recognize a pattern by matching it to a corresponding form (prototype) in our minds, and *feature matching*, according to which we recognize a pattern by comparing the features of the pattern to features stored in our memories. Neither the template-based nor the feature-based model of pattern perception, however, can fully account for context effects or influences of the situation in which perception occurs.

26. *Stroboscopic motion* is the appearance of motion produced by the precisely timed intermittent and alternating flashing of two lights positioned at precise locations against a dark background.

27. Various deficits in visual perception fall into the category of agnosias.

HEARING 147

How do we hear stimuli in the environment?

28. The *cochlea*, the main structure of the inner ear, has within it the *basilar membrane*. The *hair cells* of the basilar membrane transduce the mechanical energy of sound waves into electrochemical energy that can be processed by the brain.

29. According to *place theory*, we hear each pitch as a function of the location that it stimulates in the inner ear. According to *frequency theory*, the vibrations in the inner ear reproduce the vibrations of the sounds that enter the ear. According to the *volley principle*, neurons cooperate in reproducing these vibrations. *Duplicity theory* holds that both place and frequency contribute to hearing.

30. There are two methods for locating the source of a sound: The time-difference method works best for low-frequency sounds, and the intensity-difference method works best for high-frequency sounds.

TASTE 154

How do we experience stimuli through our sense of taste?

31. We are able to taste because of interactions between chemical substances and our *taste buds*, sensory receptors on our tongues. According to a widely accepted theory of taste, the various sensory receptors in the tongue are differentially sensitive to various combinations of the four primary tastes: sweet, sour, bitter, and salty.

SMELL 156

How do we detect odors?

32. We are able to smell because of interactions between chemical substances and sensory receptors in our nasal cavities.

THE SKIN SENSES 159

What is the sense of touch?

33. Some skin-sense nerves respond to the sense of pressure and movement; others convey two kinds of pain information (one dull, the other sharp) as well as temperature and pressure information.

34. Cold and warm nerve fibers in the skin enable us to sense temperature through their patterns of firing. Our response to temperature depends on our existing adaptation level.

35. Pain results when damaged tissue stimulates the release of a neurotransmitter, which sends an impulse to the central nervous system. Different parts of the body have differing sensitivities to pain. People also differ in their sensitivity to pain.

THE BODY SENSES 162

How do we experience and maintain movement, balance, and equilibrium?

36. *Kinesthesis* is the sense whereby we ascertain whether we are moving or stationary, where our body parts are, and how (if at all) the parts are moving. The receptors for kinesthesis are in the muscles, tendons, joints, and skin.

37. Receptors of the *vestibular system*, located in the inner ear, allow us to maintain our balance, or equilibrium. Inputs from the vestibular, kinesthetic, and visual systems converge in the cerebral cortex.

KEY TERMS

ANSWERS TO CONCEPT CHECKS

Concept Check 1

1. c 2. a 3. a

Concept Check 2

1. b 2. b 3. b

Concept Check 3

1. c 2. c 3. a

Concept Check 4

1. d 2. b 3. c

Concept Check 5

1. a 2. d 3. c

Concept Check 6

1. a 2. b 3. c

Concept Check 7

1. a 2. b 3. a

Concept Check 8

1. c 2. d 3. a

1. Nisbett and his colleagues have found that East Asians are
   a. more holistic than Westerners in their perceptions.
   b. less holistic than Westerners in their perceptions.
   c. more holistic in their perceptions than Middle Easterners.
   d. less holistic in their perceptions than Middle Easterners.

2. A just noticeable difference between two stimuli can be detected _____ of the time.
   a. 0%
   b. 50%
   c. 99%
   d. 100%

3. The proportion of false alarms is _____ the proportion of hits.
   a. always greater than
   b. always less than
   c. always equal to
   d. either less than or greater than

4. The concentration of cones in the fovea is typically _____ the concentration of rods.
   a. less than
   b. equal to
   c. greater than
   d. without relation to

5. Elements that resemble each other are grouped together. In Gestalt psychology, this statement represents the principle of
   a. similarity.
   b. good continuation.
   c. symmetry.
   d. closure.

6. The process by which the lens changes its curvature to focus on objects at different distances is called
   a. assimilation.
   b. accommodation.
   c. refraction.
   d. adaptation.

7. According to _____ theory, the hair cells at different places on the basilar membrane vibrate in response to different pitches.
   a. volley theory
   b. frequency theory
   c. place theory
   d. dual-process

8. The different timbres of different musical instruments result in large part from differences in the _____ the instruments produce.
   a. melodics
   b. pitches
   c. decibels
   d. harmonics

9. The way foods taste is probably due at least as much to our _____ sense as to our gustatory sense.
   a. olfactory
   b. vestibular
   c. kinesthetic
   d. auditory

10. Which of the following is *not* a monocular depth cue?
    a. relative size
    b. interposition
    c. linear perspective
    d. disparity

Answers
1. a   2. b   3. d   4. c   5. a   6. b   7. c   8. d
9. a   10. d

1. What are the main limitations of template-matching theories of visual perception?
2. Why are objects closer than they visually appear on a foggy day?
3. Hubel and Wiesel noted that their discoveries and their research were possible because of the technologies available to them. What current technology do you find not only pleasant but also important to your ability to perform a task you do often? How would your life be different without that technology? (It does not have to be a complex or "high-tech" item.)
4. Try eating your next meal (or a snack) with your eyes closed. Briefly describe how the other senses work together to help you avoid ingesting bad food.
5. In what ways have you noticed that smells affect the way you feel about particular people, particular kinds of food, and particular situations or settings?
6. If you had to memorize a long list of terms and definitions, would you be better off trying to remember them by seeing them (e.g., reading printed flashcards) or by hearing them (e.g., having someone drill you by saying the words aloud)? Do you seem to be able to remember material better if it is presented visually (e.g., in a book) or vocally (e.g., in a lecture)? How do you tailor your studying to your sensory preferences?

WEB RESOURCES

For a chapter tutorial quiz, direct links to Internet sites, and other useful features, visit the book-specific website at http://psychology.wadsworth.com/sternberg4e. You can also connect directly to the following sites:

Seeing, Hearing, and Smelling the World
http://www.hhmi.org/senses
This fascinating site sponsored by the Howard Hughes Medical Institute allows you to explore the senses, and it provides information about the brain's role in perception and illusions.

Psychological Science on the Net
http://www.psychologicalscience.com/Psychology_
Topics/Sensation_-_Perception/Demos/
This site contains links to much information on perception and many demonstrations.

IllusionWorks
http://psylux.psych.tu-dresden.de/i1/kaw/
diverses%20Material/www.illusionworks.com/
html/illusionworks.html
IllusionWorks bills itself as "the most comprehensive collection of optical and sensory illusions on the World Wide Web." At both introductory and advanced levels, this is an excellent source of some of the strangest and most thought-provoking illusions ever created.

For additional readings on many of the topics covered in this chapter, check out InfoTrac College Edition at **www.infotrac-college.com/ wadsworth.**

Disk One
Vision
Visual Perception
Chapter Quiz
Critical Thinking Questions

CHAPTER 5

CONSCIOUSNESS

Milkman slipped into Sweet's bed and slept the night in her perfect arms. It was a warm dreamy sleep all about flying, sailing high over the earth. But not with arms stretched out like airplane wings, nor shot forward like Superman in a horizontal dive, but floating, cruising, in the relaxed position of a man flying on a couch reading a newspaper. Part of his flight was over the dark sea, but it didn't frighten him because he knew he could not fall. He was alone in the sky, but somebody was applauding him, watching him and applauding. He couldn't see who it was.

When he awoke the next morning and set about seeing to the repair of his car, he couldn't shake the dream, and didn't really want to. In Solomon's store he found Omar and Solomon shaking sacks of okra into peck baskets and he still felt the sense of lightness and power that flying had given him.

—*Toni Morrison*, Song of Solomon. Reprinted by permission of International Creative Management, Inc. Copyright © 1977 Alfred A. Knopf, Inc.

Nobel Prize winner Toni Morrison frequently explores consciousness from a literary perspective. In the opening excerpt, the protagonist in her novel illustrates how an altered state of consciousness, such as dreaming, can affect waking experiences. Psychologists, too, observe that our conscious awareness of the world, and even of ourselves, often changes from moment to moment, influenced both by our sensations of the world around us and by our inner thoughts and feelings.

Consciousness is one's awareness of both internal and external stimuli and of oneself. It includes awareness of one's states of mind (internal stimuli), features of the environment, such as lights and noises (external stimuli), and the fact of personal existence (oneself). In discussing consciousness, we consider the role of attention, levels of consciousness, sleep and dreams, hypnosis and meditation, and the effects of drugs.

The history of the world is none other than the progress of the consciousness of freedom.
—Georg Hegel, *Philosophy of History*

PAYING ATTENTION

How do we manage to pay attention to some things in the environment and to tune out others?

Consciousness might be overwhelming if we were unable to limit our experience of stimuli in the environment by focusing our attention. **Attention** is the link between the enormous amount of information that assails our senses and the limited amount that we actually perceive. It enables us to perceive things we need to be aware of and to ignore others (Pashler, 1998). As you read these words, you are probably paying attention to the words (figure) on the text page and disregarding all the other visual sensations (ground) reaching your retina. If you paid attention to all the sensory information available to you at any one time, you would never be able to concentrate on the important and ignore the unimportant. You may be vaguely aware of the ways your skin is being touched by your clothes, of the ambient sounds surrounding you, or even of some internal cues such as hunger or fatigue. What allows you to dismiss most of this sensory information and concentrate on reading? Pay attention and find out.

Attention involves mostly the interaction of diverse areas of the brain, with no specialized areas fully responsible for specific attentional functions (Cohen, Romero, Servan-Schreiber, & Farah, 1994; Farah, 1994). Certain areas of the brain do appear to be partly responsible for certain kinds of attentional processing, however (Farah, 2001; Polk & Farah, 2002; Polk et al., 2002). Michael Posner (1995, 2001) has

Attention is what enables us to focus on some stimuli and block out others. However, sometimes our attention may wander.

suggested that the frontal lobe tends to be activated during tasks that require attention to verbal stimuli. The parietal lobe tends to be activated during tasks that require attention to visual and spatial stimuli (see Albright, Kandel, & Posner, 2000; Fan, McCandliss, Sommer, Raz, & Posner, 2002).

SELECTIVE ATTENTION

Suppose you are at a banquet. It is just your luck to be seated next to this year's winner of the "Most Boring Conversationalist" award. As you are talking to this blatherer, who happens to be on your right, you become aware of the conversation of the two guests sitting on your left. Their exchange is much more interesting. So you find yourself trying to keep up the semblance of a conversation with the bore on your right while tuning in to the dialogue on your left.

THE COCKTAIL PARTY PHENOMENON

This vignette illustrates a naturalistic experiment in **selective attention**, in which you attempt to track one message and ignore another. This phenomenon inspired the research of E. Colin Cherry (1953) on the **cocktail party phenomenon**, in which we follow one conversation despite the distraction of other conversations.

Cherry did not actually do his research at cocktail parties. Rather, he investigated conversations in a carefully controlled setting. In an experimental task called *shadowing*, each of the ears listens to a different message and the listener is required to repeat the message that goes to one of the ears as soon as possible after hearing it. Think of a detective "shadowing" a suspect. In *dichotic presentation* each ear receives a different message. When the two ears receive the same message, it is called *binaural presentation*.

Cherry's research prompted additional work in this area. Anne Treisman (1964a, 1964b) noted that although people who shadowed the message presented to one ear heard almost nothing of the message presented to the other ear, they were not totally ignorant of the unattended message. They could hear, for example, if the voice was replaced by a tone or if a man's voice was replaced by a woman's. If the unattended message was identical to the attended one, every research participant noticed it, even if one of the messages was temporally out of synchronization with the other. When this delay effect was studied systematically, people typically recognized the two messages to be the same. In particular, they recognized the relationship between messages when the shadowed message was either as much as 4.5 seconds ahead of the unattended one or as far as 1.5 seconds behind (Treisman, 1964a, 1964b). In other words, it is easier to recognize the unattended message when it follows, rather than precedes, the attended one. Treisman also observed that some people who were fluently bilingual noticed the identity of messages if the unattended message was the translated version of the attended one.

MINDLESSNESS

A construct related to selective attention is *mindfulness* (Langer, 1989, 1997, 2000, 2002; Moldoveanu & Langer, 2002), which is paying deliberate attention to the immediate situation at hand. Lack of mindfulness is *mindlessness*. Ellen Langer (1989) gave an example of mindlessness. In 1982, a pilot and copilot went

© Paul Barton/Corbis

Have you ever thought you heard someone call your name in a crowded room? Selective attention is involved in the cocktail party phenomenon.

through a routine checklist prior to takeoff, mindlessly noting that the anti-icer was "off"—as it should be under most circumstances, but not under the icy conditions for which they were preparing. The flight ended in a crash that killed 74 passengers. Fortunately for most of us, our mindlessness usually has far less fatal consequences, as when we put a carton of milk in the cupboard rather than in the refrigerator. Attention is generally a purposeful application of our consciousness. But it also operates automatically and at different levels.

Selective attention can be influenced by various psychological disorders. People with obsessive-compulsive disorder (see Chapter 16) tend to be preoccupied with thoughts they cannot get out of their minds and behaviors they are unable to control. They show decreased ability selectively to attend to stimuli they want to focus on and to screen out other stimuli they wish to ignore (Clayton, Richards, & Edwards, 1999).

Theories of selective attention differ primarily in whether or not they propose that we somehow filter, and thus sort out, competing stimuli. Theories that propose a filter disagree about when filtering occurs and what it affects.

THE STROOP EFFECT

Much of the research on selective attention has focused on auditory processing. However, selective attention can also be studied visually. One of the tasks most frequently used for this purpose was formulated by John Ridley Stroop (1935), for whom the effect is named. You can try it: Quickly read aloud

IN THE LAB OF ELLEN LANGER

Before the airport in Provincetown, Massachusetts, was renovated, a large glass wall overlooked the runway. While waiting for a friend to arrive, I asked the woman at the check-in counter when the flight from Boston was expected. She said it should be on time. There was no one else at the gate or in the surrounding area, and I was less than 2 feet from the check-in counter when the plane arrived in full view. Rather than lean over and say, "Here's your plane," she announced the arrival over the public address system, filling the empty room with information that was relevant only to me. I have often noticed smart people not paying attention to available information.

In my work, I have focused on understanding how *mindlessness* comes about and how pervasive it may be. When we are mindless, we do not consciously process new information. Instead of mindfully attending to change and novelty, we regard things as if they are holding still and treat the present as though it is an exact replica of the past. In our experiments, we've found that mindlessness comes about in two ways: through repetition of information or as the result of a single exposure to information.

The first type is most familiar. For example, most of us have had the experience of driving and then realizing, because of the surprising distance we have come, that we made part of the trip on "automatic pilot," as we sometimes call mindless,

Professor Langer received her PhD from Yale University in Social and Clinical Psychology and taught at The Graduate Center of CUNY before joining the faculty at Harvard in 1977. She has received a Guggenheim Fellowship, the APA Award for Distinguished Contributions to Psychology in the Public Interest, and AAPP's Award for Distinguished Contributions of Basic Science for Applications in Psychology. More than 150 research articles and 11 books (including Mindfulness, *which has been translated into 13 languages) describe Professor Langer's research on decision making, health, deviance, aging, perceived control and art. Her recent work analyzes and extends each of these subjects in terms of her theory of mindfulness.*

repetitive behavior. Another example of mindlessness induced by repetition is learning something—like riding a bike home—by practicing it so that it becomes "second nature" to us. We learn the new skill so well that we don't have to think about practicing it. The problem is that if we've been successful, it won't occur to us to think about it even in situations that require us to be mindful. We expect the route to be the same because we ride it automatically and we may not even notice a new way that may be shorter and more scenic, or a new hole in the pavement that would have been good to avoid.

The second way mindlessness sets in is that we hear or read something and accept it without question. Most of what we know about the world and ourselves we have learned mindlessly. I'm particularly fond of recalling my own mindlessness, which I wrote about in *The Power of Mindful Learning* (1997). At a friend's house the dinner table was set with the fork on

the right side of the plate. I felt that a natural law had been violated because I had been taught that the fork goes on the left side! I knew this was ridiculous. Who cares where the fork is placed? It is actually easier for right-handed people to reach it on the right. When I was a child, my mother simply told me that the fork goes on the left. I became trapped in a behavior without any awareness that the way I learned the information would determine how I used it in the future. Whether we become mindless through behaving repetitively over time or on our initial acceptance of information, we unwittingly lock ourselves into a single way of understanding that information.

When we are mindful, we actively draw novel distinctions, not relying on distinctions drawn in the past. This makes us sensitive to context and perspective. When we are mindless, our behavior is governed by rule and routine. Our understanding has frozen and we are oblivious to sutble changes that would lead us to act differently, if only we were aware of them. In contrast, when we are mindful, our behavior may be guided rather than governed by rules and routines, and we are sensitive to the ways the situation has changed. Thus, if we're biking mindfully, we avert the danger not yet arisen by paying attention, and avoid the new pothole.

Having established the difference between mindlessness and mindfulness, the next step was to assess the costs of being mindless. While pursuing this inquiry, I was also conducting research on the importance of perceived control with elderly people in nursing homes. I was quick to ask myself about mindlessness with respect to this population. Were the elderly suffering because of mindlessness? After all, the older we get, the more we are exposed to repetition and the more "perspective-free" facts we learn. We can perceive that we have control only if we are mindful. If an elderly person were experiencing excessive mindlessness, would encouraging mindfulness help? In several experimental investigations in nursing homes, we found that having residents attend to novelty

increased their mindfulness, which had clear health benefits, not the least among them increased longevity.

Over 25 years of research has revealed that mindlessness may be very costly. In studies conducted in hospitals, schools, and businesses, we have found that an increase in mindfulness results in an increase in competence, health and longevity, positive affect, creativity, charisma, and reduced burnout, to name a few of the findings (Langer 1989, 1997). We have found ways of increasing mindfulness and ways of preventing mindlessness, but breaking an established pattern of mindlessness is more difficult and how to do it most successfully requires more investigation.

The newest work on the topic explores mindful creativity. The argument is that we should be mindful almost all of the time. To know what that feels like, I suggest beginning a *new* sustained activity like painting, writing, photography, or playing a musical instrument. Many of us are afraid to try new things because our mind-sets about such things were established through repeated evaluation, mis-

takes, talent, assessments, and social comparisons. I chose to start painting. I removed each of the mindless roadblocks that stood in my way. I'd paint without knowing what I was doing, then think about my experience, and then conduct experiments, on art or music, for example, to see if what I experienced could be generalized to others. Indeed it was.

Then I conducted conceptual replications to see if there were broader principles at work. For example, while painting, I made a "mistake" accidentally. Surprisingly, the painting was improved. It occurred to me that mistakes are a result of mindlessly following a rigid plan conceived in the past, and thus mistakes may be seen as an opportunity to alert us to the present. If we go forward mindfully, rather than try to reverse the error, we can take advantage of all the information in the present, including the "mistake." The research that followed supported this view and is discussed in my new book *Mindful Creativity* (Langer, 2003).

---

the following words: *brown, blue, green, red, purple.* Easy, isn't it? Now quickly name aloud the colors shown in part (a) of Figure 5.1. The ink matches the name of the color word. This task, too, is easy. Now look at part (c) of the figure, in which the colors of the inks differ from the color names that are printed with them. Again name the ink colors you see, out loud, as quickly as possible.

You probably found the last task very difficult: Your understanding of the written words interferes with naming the color of the ink. The **Stroop effect** demonstrates the psychological difficulty of selectively attending to the color of the ink and trying

to ignore the word it forms. One reason the Stroop test may be particularly difficult is that, for you and most other adults, reading is an automatic process, not readily subject to your conscious control (MacLeod, 1991, 1996). You find it difficult to ignore what you read and concentrate on the color of the ink. An alternative explanation is that the output of a response occurs when the mental pathways for producing the response are activated sufficiently (MacLeod, 1991). In the Stroop test, the name of the written color activates a cortical pathway for saying the word. In contrast, the name of the color the word is written in activates a pathway for naming

(a) Read through this list of color names as quickly as possible. Read from right to left across each line.

Red	Yellow	**Blue**	Green
Blue	Red	**Green**	Yellow
Yellow	**Green**	Red	**Blue**

(b) Name each of these color patches as quickly as possible. Name from left to right across each line.

(c) Name as quickly as possible the color of ink in which each word is printed. Name from left to right across each line.

Red	**Blue**	Green	**Yellow**
Yellow	Red	**Blue**	**Green**
Blue	**Yellow**	**Green**	**Red**

FIGURE 5.1
The Stroop Effect. If you are like most people, you will find it more difficult to perform task (c) than either task (a) or task (b).

the color. But the activity of the first pathway interferes with the latter. In this situation, it takes longer to gather sufficient strength of activation to produce the color-naming response and not the word-reading response.

What do you think explains why you attend to some things and not to others? Why do you think you sometimes find it difficult to focus your attention?

FILTER THEORIES

An early theory of selective attention, proposed by Donald Broadbent (1958), suggested that we filter information right after it is registered at the sensory level. Thus, we filter out irrelevant stimuli almost as soon as we sense them, and so they never receive any top-down, higher-order processing. Subsequent research, however, indicated that Broadbent's model must be wrong. For example, participants in shadowing studies hear one particular stimulus in the unattended ear regardless of when it occurs: the sound of their own name (Moray, 1959). If we are able to recognize our own names in this way, then some higher-level processing of the information must be occurring and reaching the supposedly unattended ear. If such processing were not occurring, we would not recognize the familiar sounds. That is, if the incoming in-

formation were filtered out at the level of sensation, we would never perceive it at all.

This kind of finding led some investigators to propose a theory that places the filter later in the perceptual process, after some top-down, higher-order conceptual analysis of input has taken place (Deutsch & Deutsch, 1963; D. A. Norman, 1968). This later filtering would allow us to recognize the meaning of information that enters the unattended ear (such as the sound of our own names).

An alternative to both of these theories suggests that a filter may take the form of a signal-attenuating mechanism rather than a signal-blocking mechanism (Treisman, 1964b). Information is not totally blocked out at any level; it is just weakened. We receive some of the information that is transmitted, but in a degraded form. What gets through is determined by whether the information is more likely to be important (such as our names) or unimportant (such as idle prattle).

ATTENTIONAL RESOURCE THEORIES

Theorists have moved away from the notion of filters and toward attentional resources. The idea is that we have a fixed amount of attention, which we can allocate according to what the task requires. Our single pool of attentional resources can be divided up, say, among multiple tasks (Kahneman, 1973). Suppose that you were dividing your total attention among the acts of talking to a friend, surfing the Internet, and thinking about an upcoming exam. The amount of attention you could devote to each task would depend on how you allocated your single pool of attentional resources. In the *single-pool model*, allocating attention to one task always takes away attention from all other tasks.

This model now appears to be oversimplified because we are much better at dividing our attention when the competing stimuli are in different perceptual modalities (e.g., one requires seeing, the other hearing). Multiple-pool resource models specify that at least some attentional resources may be specific to the modality in which a task is presented. Thus, it is more likely that two visual tasks will interfere with each other than that a visual task will interfere with an auditory one. Competition for attentional resources also can occur as a result of overlap in the content type. For example, speech heard on a radio is more likely to interfere with your reading than instrumental music.

In sum, current models of selective attention emphasize that we bring to bear multiple attentional resources, using more than one sensory modality, on tasks that require divided attention.

✓ CONCEPT CHECK 1

1. John is talking to a group of people and seems to be engaged with them, but secretly he is listening to another conversation occurring nearby. John's behavior exemplifies what is called in psychology the _____ phenomenon.
   a. party eavesdropping
   b. cocktail party
   c. timeshare
   d. multitask
2. The Broadbent model of selective attention is best characterized as having _____ filter.
   a. an early
   b. a late
   c. an intermediate
   d. no
3. Ellen's mind is on a fight she had yesterday with her boyfriend and unfortunately she locks herself out of her car. Ellen's behavior is an example of _____
   a. mindfulness.
   b. mindlessness.
   c. mind blindness.
   d. mind storm.

LEVELS OF CONSCIOUSNESS

What is consciousness, and what forms does it take?

According to British philosopher John Locke (1632–1704), a major function of consciousness is to help us form a sense of personal identity by linking past and present events to ourselves. Consciousness is the means by which we define who we are. British philosopher David Hume (1711–1776), in contrast, believed that our sense of personal identity is a myth. It is not something we can empirically establish through any of our senses. All consciousness can do is reveal a succession of states of the world. It can never connect them. An analogy is the successive frames of a film strip. We provide the connections between what are really large numbers of rapidly moving static frames. We only imagine them to be linked together.

Psychological interest in levels of consciousness has waxed and waned over the years. Behaviorists would not give the subject any attention at all, whereas psychodynamic theorists saw it as one of the most fundamental issues in psychology.

A contemporary philosopher, Daniel Dennett (1995), believes, like Locke, that we have a sense of identity. Dennett (1997, 2001) believes our sense of identity stems not from high-level consciousness, but from low-level processing. Basing his notions on Darwin's (1859) theory of evolution, Dennett argues that our senses of self and of intentionality (what we want to do) are products of countless simple processes going on within us simultaneously.

Whether or not consciousness establishes a sense of personal identity, it clearly serves two main purposes: monitoring and controlling (Kihlstrom, 1984; Kihlstrom, Mulvaney, Tobias, & Tobis, 2000). By *monitoring*, the individual keeps track of internal mental processes, personal behavior, and the environment to maintain self-awareness in relation to the surrounding environment. If you feel depressed and try to figure out what is bothering you, you are monitoring your thinking. By *controlling*, the individual plans what to do based on the information received from the monitoring process. If you realize you are depressed because you have not had any fun all week, and you then decide it is time to do something fun, you are controlling your thinking and behavior. These two functions seem to operate, in one way or another, at various levels of consciousness. Normally, we see ourselves as being at a fully conscious level of awareness. Sometimes people seek to achieve a "higher" level of consciousness through practices like meditation and drug use. Other levels of consciousness exist as well (Lambie & Marcel, 2002). One way of classifying them is as either preconscious or subconscious.

THE PRECONSCIOUS LEVEL

The **preconscious** level of consciousness contains information that could easily become conscious but that is not continuously available. For example, if prompted, you can remember what your bedroom looks like. But obviously you are not always thinking about your bedroom. Also stored at the preconscious level are *automatic behaviors*—those that require no conscious decisions about which muscles to move or which actions to take. Examples are dialing a familiar telephone number and driving a car to a familiar place.

TIP-OF-THE-TONGUE PHENOMENON

Perhaps our most common experience of preconsciousness is the *tip-of-the-tongue phenomenon*, which occurs when we are trying to remember something we already know but cannot quite retrieve. If a man needs a new wallet, he might try to remember the name of the store where he bought the wallet he has. But the store is not one he patronizes frequently, and the name does not immediately come to mind. He remembers the name of the store begins with a "C." An image of a cow comes into his mind. Eventually he remembers the name of the store is "Cowley's." This phenomenon indicates that particular preconscious information, though not fully accessible, is still available in conscious thinking.

SUBLIMINAL PERCEPTION

Researchers have demonstrated preconscious processing (Marcel, 1983). Research participants were shown words for just 10 milliseconds. The rate of presentation was so rapid that observers were generally unaware that they had even seen a word. When the research participants were shown a second word for a longer period of time, this new word was recognized more quickly if it was related to the first word than if it was unrelated. For example, *doctor* and *nurse* were considered to be related words, whereas *doctor* and *oven* were considered unrelated. Some kind of recognition of the rapidly presented word must have taken place; the recognition was clearly preconscious. This *subliminal perception*, a preconscious processing of information that is thus below the level of conscious awareness of that information, suggests that people have the ability to detect information without being aware they are doing so. However, situations in which subliminal perception occurs appear to be quite limited.

The effects of subliminal perception are small. Krosnick, Betz, Jussim, and Lynn (1992) studied the ef-

fects of a subliminal intervention on attitudes. Participants were shown slides designed to arouse either positive emotions (e.g., a bride and groom) or negative emotions (e.g., a skull). The exposure times of the slides were extremely brief, however—only 13/1000 second. Participants then viewed a series of slides showing an individual engaged in ordinary, everyday activities. The question was whether the subliminally presented slides would affect people's attitudes toward the individual in the slides. Krosnick and his colleagues obtained small but statistically significant effects. Their data suggested that the subliminal intervention had some effect in the expected direction, but that the effect was a small one (see also Bizer & Krosnick, 2001).

One effect that appears to be totally absent is for subliminal tapes. Indeed, a careful study of such tapes renders it questionable whether they really contain any subliminal messages at all. Even if the messages are there but well-hidden, they do not work (Greenwald, Spangenberg, Pratkanis, & Eskenazi, 1991). Many users of these tapes believe they work, however. Available data suggest that any effect they have is likely to be a *placebo effect*, whereby people's belief in the efficacy of an intervention, rather than the intervention itself, results in an improvement in behavior, health, or whatever else the intervention is supposed to affect.

BLINDSIGHT

Another example of information processing that is outside of conscious awareness is **blindsight,** a phenomenon by which individuals can see but are unaware that they are seeing (Sahraie et al., 1997; Scharli, Harman, & Hogben, 1999; Weiskrantz, Warrington, Sanders, & Marshall, 1974). This phenomenon is observed in individuals who have damage to the primary visual cortex, but whose optic nerve fibers from the eyes nevertheless are still hooked up with those parts of the brain that handle visual information. When asked whether they see an object, these patients will say no. But they can nevertheless give information about it, such as what shape or color it is. Thus, they have information about an object that they are certain they cannot see.

To summarize, automatic behaviors, tip-of-the-tongue phenomena, subliminal perception, blindsight, and other forms of preconscious knowledge generally are outside the view of our conscious minds. We engage in them without being fully aware of doing so.

THE SUBCONSCIOUS LEVEL

Unlike information stored at the preconscious level, information stored at the **subconscious** or **unconscious** level is not easily accessible. The subconscious level involves less awareness than full consciousness and is either synonymous with the unconscious level

PSYCHOLOGY IN EVERYDAY LIFE

NEAR-DEATH EXPERIENCE

In a near-death experience, an individual either comes extremely close to dying or is actually believed to be dead and then is revived before permanent brain death occurs. During this time, some people undergo unusual psychological experiences.

Near-death experiences have been reported in writings throughout history and in the lore of cultures as disparate as those of the ancient Greeks, Buddhists, and North American Indians. A variety of researchers have reviewed accounts of people who claim to have had near-death experiences (e.g., Blackmore, 1993, 1999; Serdahely, 1990; Zaleski, 1987). A large number of people of differing ages and cultural backgrounds report similar near-death sensations. They often feel peace or intense joy. Some feel that they have left their bodies or have looked at them from the outside. They often report traveling through a

dark tunnel and seeing a brilliant light at the end of it. Some speak of reunions with deceased friends or relatives, and others report contact with a being that encourages them to return to life. Some report rapidly reviewing many or all of the events of their lives.

Not all people who have the near-death experience are equally likely to experience all of these phenomena. The frequency and intensity of these experiences tend to be greatest for people who are ill, lowest for people who have attempted suicide, and in between for accident victims. Interestingly, few people have reported any negative experiences.

Although there are many explanations for near-death experiences, recent thinking has converged on events produced by the brain (Blackmore, 1993, 1999; Persinger, 1999, 2001; Persinger & Richards,

1995). For example, the experience of seeing or walking through a tunnel may result from activation of the medial occipital cortexes due to insufficient blood supply, which then causes contrast between the peripheral and central visual fields, or the experiencing of a tunnel. Although such explanations are plausible, they have yet to be verified, and so near-death experience remains something of a mystery. Perhaps the most interesting news to come out of the research is that people who have such experiences typically say that their lives have changed for the better. They are less afraid of death, more appreciative of what they have, and more determined to live their lives to the fullest.

 near-death experiences
brain death

(according to many theorists) or slightly more accessible to consciousness than the unconscious level (according to a few theorists). For our purposes, we make no distinction. In general, however, the term *unconscious* is usually preferred by followers of Sigmund Freud, the founder of psychoanalysis.

According to Freud, material that we find too anxiety-provoking to handle at a conscious level is often *repressed*—that is, never admitted to consciousness. Repressing the material keeps it from distressing us. Freud believed that many of our most important memories and impulses are unconscious, but they still have a profound effect on our behavior. For example, people who experienced rejection by one of their parents (or both) are more likely to be extremely sensitive to rejection in all areas of life than are individuals who had no such early experience. However, the people who experienced rejection may be unaware of why they are more sensitive to it. Their unawareness derives from their repression of the original feelings of rejection. The process of repres-

sion is open to debate, however. Even its existence has not been conclusively documented.

ALTERED STATES OF CONSCIOUSNESS

There are many different states of consciousness. What constitutes a "normal" state and what constitutes an "altered" state are a matter of some debate. One way to view "altered states" is as those other than our normal, waking state. In an altered state of consciousness, such as sleep and dreaming (discussed below), awareness is somehow changed from our normal, waking state. Each state of consciousness involves qualitative changes in our alertness and awareness.

Altered states of consciousness have several common characteristics (Martindale, 1981). First, cognitive processes may be more shallow or uncritical than usual. For example, during sleep, you accept unrealistic dream events as being real, although you would never accept those events as realistic while awake. Second, perceptions of self and of the world may change from what they are during wakefulness. Under the influence of hallucinogenic drugs, objects may appear to take on bizarre forms. Even objects that do not exist may be clearly perceived. Third, normal inhibitions and control over behavior may weaken. People under the influence of alcohol may do things they normally would not do in a sober state. The remainder of this chapter looks at consciousness through the lens of altered states of consciousness. We will consider sleep and dreaming, hypnosis, meditation, and chemically induced altered states.

✓CONCEPT CHECK 2

1. The tip-of-the tongue phenomenon is an example of the _____ in action.
   a. conscious
   b. preconscious
   c. unconscious
   d. deconscious
2. An Internet advertiser flashes a message very briefly on your computer screen in the hope of persuading you to buy the product. You are not even aware of having seen anything. The advertiser is trying to take advantage of _____ perception.
   a. subterfuge
   b. subterranean
   c. sublime
   d. subliminal
3. The term *unconscious* is roughly synonymous with the term
   a. *conscious.*
   b. *preconscious.*
   c. *subconscious.*
   d. *deconscious.*

SLEEP

Why do we sleep? What mechanisms are involved in producing sleep?

The cycle of sleep and waking is one of the most basic in humans as well as other animals. In humans, the part of the brain most relevant to sleep is the reticular formation (see Chapter 3). In particular, the *ascending reticular activating system* contributes to the alternating cycle of sleep and wakefulness. Other areas of the brain are involved as well, however, so that this one area cannot be seen as "responsible for" sleep. Neurotransmitters, including norepinephrine, dopamine, and GABA, are involved in sleep. Their exact roles re-

main to be determined, however (B. E. Jones, 1994). Thus, there is no one neurotransmitter that is responsible for sleep.

WHY DO WE SLEEP?

During sleep, people become relatively, but not totally, unaware of external sources of stimulation (Antrobus, 1991). Despite centuries of inquiry, scientists have yet to reach a consensus about exactly why people need to sleep (Borbely & Tononi, 2001). Two possibilities, which are not mutually exclusive, are a preservation and protection theory and a restorative theory. Although scientists do not know why we sleep, they do know that healthful sleep is one of the best predictors of longevity (Dement & Vaughan, 1999).

Ⓔ PRESERVATION AND PROTECTION

One view is that sleep serves an adaptive function. It protects the individual during that portion of the 24-hour day in which being awake, and hence roaming around, would place the individual at greatest risk. Animals do not require 24 hours to feed themselves and meet other necessities. From the standpoint of adaptation, therefore, they are best off staying out of harm's way.

There is some evidence to support this theory (Allison & Cicchetti, 1976; Webb, 1982). The amount of time various species sleep tends to vary with two important factors. The first is the amount of time they require to find the food they need to stay alive. The second is how well they can hide themselves when they sleep. Moreover, they sleep at times that maximize their safety, given their physical capacities and their habits. For example, animals that tend to be prey for other animals guided primarily by vision tend to sleep during the day (when they would most likely be seen if they were roaming about) and in hidden places.

According to the preservation and protection theory of sleep, day-sleeping animals maximize their safety by remaining hidden and asleep during the hours when their predators are awake.

RESTORATION

A second view is that we sleep to restore depleted resources and dissipate accumulated wastes. In other words, the restoration view of sleep is that it may have chemical causes. Psychologists study the restoration view of why people sleep by searching specifically for sleep-causing chemicals produced in our bodies. Several substances seem to be associated with sleep, although none of them has been shown conclusively to cause sleep.

One experiment was designed to see whether chemicals in the brains of sleep-deprived goats would induce sleep in rats (Pappenheimer, Koski, Fencl, Karnovsky, & Krueger, 1975). One group of goats was deprived of sleep for several days. A control group was allowed to sleep normally. Then cerebrospinal fluid (see Chapter 3) from each group of goats was injected into rats. Rats injected with fluid from the first group of goats slept more than did rats that received fluid from the control group. What was in the sleep-deprived goats' cerebrospinal fluid that caused the rats to sleep more? It was a small peptide made up of five amino acids, including muramic acid. This amino acid was recognized to be the sleep-producing compound that may have built up in the central nervous systems of the sleep-deprived goats. A second sleep-producing compound is sleep-promoting substance, or SPS (Inoue, Uchizono, & Nagasaki, 1982). A third is DSIP (delta-sleep–inducing peptide; Schroeder-Helmert, 1985). There may be many more.

CIRCADIAN RHYTHMS

Circadian rhythms are biological cycles that last about 24 hours in humans and other species. In humans, circadian rhythms vary with age and individual and cultural factors.

Usually infants alternate frequently between sleep and wakefulness. They sleep for a total of about 17 hours each day. Within the first 6 months, however, their sleep patterns change to about two short naps and one long stretch of sleep at night. They are then totaling about 13 hours per day. By 5 to 7 years of age, most of us have adopted what is basically an adult pattern of sleep (Berger, 1980). We sleep about 8 hours each night and remain awake about 16 hours each day. Regardless of the average, the actual range of sleep needed varies widely across individuals. Some people require as little as an hour of sleep each day, and others need 10 to 12 hours. Studies of long sleepers (people who regularly

sleep more than 9.5 hours per day) and short sleepers (who regularly sleep less than 4.4 hours per day) show no differences in their average health. People differ not only in how much they sleep but also in when they prefer to sleep. Research has shown that our intuitions are correct that people differ in the time of day when they are most alert and aroused—that there are "day people" and "night people" (B. Wallace, 1993). Culture can also affect people's circadian rhythms. People's sleep schedules can be affected by a variable as simple as the typical hour for dinner. For example, in the United States, dinner time is 3 to 5 hours earlier than it is in Spain.

THE EFFECT OF DAYLIGHT ON SLEEP CYCLES

Despite individual and cultural differences, the usual sleeping–waking pattern for most people roughly corresponds to our planet's cycle of darkness and light. Humans experience physiological changes that can be measured according to their daily rhythm. Such changes include a lowering of body temperature at night and changes in hormone levels. The rhythm is controlled by the hypothalamus (Ralph, Foster, Davis, & Menaker, 1990).

Several investigators have studied circadian rhythms (see Hobson, 1989, 2001; R. A. Wever, 1979). Participants in one study lived in a specially built underground environment in which they were deprived of all cues that are normally used for telling the time

French geologist Michel Siffre was shielded from all time cues in this underground cavern for 6 months. When people have no external time cues, their natural circadian rhythms shift from a 24-hour day to a 25-hour day. When they return to a normal environment, their circadian rhythms return to a 24-hour day, cued by clocks and the daily cycle of the sun.

Michel Siffre, © National Geographic Society–Getty Images

of day. These cues include the rising and setting of the sun, clocks, scheduled activities, and so on (R. A. Wever, 1979). For one month, these participants were told that they could create their own schedules. They could sleep whenever they wished. But they were discouraged from napping so that they would get on a regular sleeping–waking cycle.

The results were striking and have since been replicated many times (e.g., Mistlberger & Rusak, 1999; Welsh, 1993). As people acclimated to an environment without time cues, their subjective days became longer, averaging about 25 hours. Typically, they went to bed a little bit later each night that they spent in isolation. Eventually, they drifted toward a point where they were spending slightly more awake time than they had when there were time cues. The difference could, of course, have been due in part to the departure from the normal activities of their daily lives. Participants showed stable individual rhythms. The rhythms differed somewhat from person to person, however. When returned to the normal environment, the participants reestablished a 24-hour cycle.

Anything that changes our circadian rhythm can interfere with sleep. Many of us have experienced *jet lag*, which is a disturbance in circadian rhythm caused by altering the light–dark cycle too rapidly or too slowly when we travel through time zones. Even if you have never flown out of your own time zone, you may have experienced a mild case of jet lag when you have changed to and from daylight savings time. Think about how you feel that first Sunday morning after setting your clocks forward an hour in the spring.

It sometimes is easier to adjust one's circadian rhythm when flying in one direction rather than another. Suppose someone travels from Los Angeles to New York. When it is 8:00 P.M. for native New Yorkers, it is only 5:00 P.M. for native Californians. The westerners therefore may be less tired than the easterners. One study found that visiting teams in basketball performed 4 points better, on average, when they traveled west to east rather than east to west, thereby almost nullifying the home-court advantage of the home team (Steenland & Deddens, 1997). The reason for the difference may be, at least in part, that people tend to have a natural sleeping–waking cycle of 25 rather than 24 hours, so that it is easier for them to have to go to sleep later than to go to sleep earlier.

NEUROCHEMICAL INFLUENCES ON SLEEP CYCLES

Sleeping–waking cycles appear to be controlled in part by the pineal gland, which also secretes certain sleep-producing substances. *Melatonin*, a natural hormone secreted by the pineal gland, is one of several chemicals that appears to play an important role in regulating waking–sleeping cycles (Lewy, Ahmed, Jackson, & Sack, 1992; Reppert, Weaver, Rivkees, & Stopa, 1988). Small doses of melatonin—as little as a fraction of a milligram—appear to be capable of restarting the bodily clock and, especially, helping travelers who cross time zones to adjust to the changes in the clock (Arendt, Aldhous, & Wright, 1988; Tzischinsky, Pal, Epstein, Dagan, & Lavie, 1992). Melatonin supplements are now available without a prescription. People who take such supplements need to exercise caution, however, because there can be some side effects (such as drowsiness in the morning). The long-term effects of high dosages are unknown. *Tryptophan*, an amino acid that is a precursor to the neurotransmitter serotonin, also has sleep-inducing properties. Light also affects the sleeping–waking cycle. For example, bright lights have been used to help people get over jet lag (D. Dawson, Lack, & Morris, 1993). Computer software is now available to calculate the optimal amounts of bright light to use for different flight paths. Such software makes it possible to individualize the level of light to an actual trip (Houpt, Boulos, & Moore-Ede, 1996).

Although some chemicals that *can* cause sleep have indeed been found, the view that sleep actually *is* induced chemically has not been conclusively supported. Indeed, the restoration view presumably would predict that people who are more active on a given day would sleep more than when they are not active. A related prediction would be that people who are active in general would sleep more. But these predictions have not been upheld. Researchers have thus sought other ways to study why we sleep, such as looking at the effects of not sleeping.

Athletes who travel to competitions in different time zones must adjust their sleep schedules to maintain peak performance.

SLEEP DEPRIVATION

In sleep-deprivation experiments (e.g., Borbely, 1986; Dement, 1976), research participants usually have few problems after the first sleepless night. They appear to be relaxed and cheerful. They have more difficulty staying awake during the second night, however, and usually are severely tired by 3:00 A.M. of the next day. If they are given long test problems to solve, they will fall asleep but will often deny having done so.

After three nights without sleep, the participants appear tense. They become increasingly apathetic and are irritable when disturbed. Although they may follow the instructions of the experimenter, they do so with little energy. Their moods swing wildly. They often are unable to stay awake without special intervention. By this time, periods of *microsleep* are observed: People stop what they are doing for several seconds and stare into space. During these periods, their EEGs (electroencephalograms; see Chapter 3) show brain-wave patterns typical of sleep. People deprived of sleep for this long may start to experience visual **illusions,** distorted perceptions of objects and other external stimuli. They may also succumb to **hallucinations,** or perceptions of sensory stimuli in the absence of any actual corresponding external sensory input from the physical world. They commonly experience auditory hallucinations, such as hearing voices in the sound of running water.

Things really start to fall apart after four days without sleep. Research participants typically become paranoid, sometimes believing the experimenters are plotting against them. It is possible to keep sleep-deprived people awake for longer than four days, but prolonged sleep deprivation is clearly serious business and of questionable ethical justification.

Although research has not determined conclusively why we need to sleep, studies of circadian rhythms help us understand when and how much most people need to sleep.

STAGES OF SLEEP

When studying circadian rhythms and other aspects of our sleeping–waking cycles, psychologists often examine people's brain-wave patterns using electroencephalograms (EEGs). EEG recordings of the brain activity of sleeping people (see Figure 5.2) have shown that sleep occurs in stages common to almost everyone, although EEG patterns vary slightly as a function of a person's age (Landolt & Borbely, 2001). During relaxed wakefulness, we exhibit an *alpha-wave* EEG pattern. As we doze, the alpha-wave rhythm of the EEG gives way to smaller, more rapid, irregular waves. This pattern characterizes *Stage 1* sleep, a transitional state between wakefulness and sleep. If we are

brought back to full consciousness from Stage 1 sleep, we may observe that our thoughts during this period did not make much sense, even though we may have felt fully or almost fully awake.

In *Stage 2* sleep, the stage in which we spend more than half of our sleeping time, the EEG pattern changes again. EEG waves are larger and overlap with *sleep spindles* (bursts of rapid EEG waves) and occasionally with *K-complexes* (large, slow waves). Muscle tension is markedly lower in Stage 2 than in the waking state.

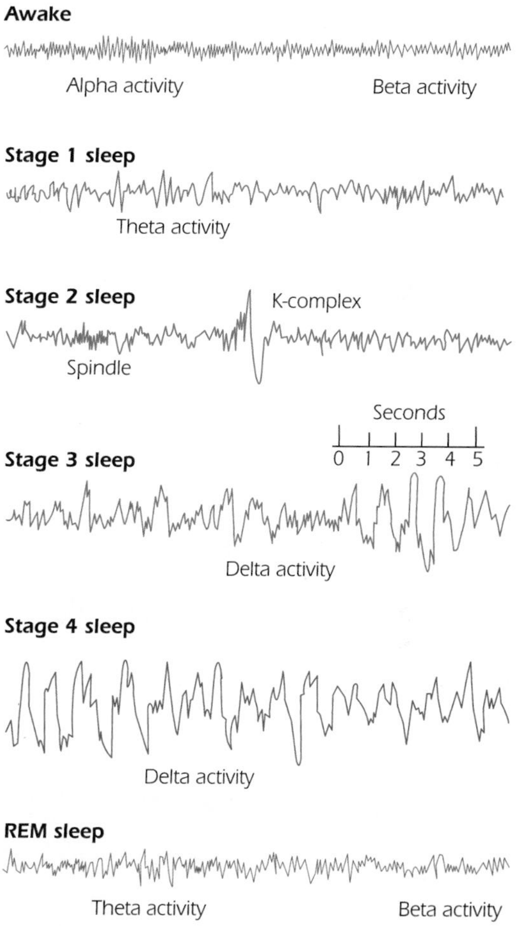

FIGURE 5.2

EEG Patterns in the Stages of Sleep. These EEG patterns illustrate changes in brain waves, which reflect changes in consciousness during REM sleep and during the four stages of N-REM sleep. (a) Alpha waves typify relaxed wakefulness. (b) More rapid, irregular brain waves typify Stage 1 of N-REM sleep. (c) During Stage 2, large, slow waves are occasionally interrupted by bursts of rapid brain waves. (d) During Stages 3 and 4, extremely large, slow brain waves (delta waves) predominate. When delta waves are 20% to 50% of all EEG waves, the sleeper is in Stage 3, whereas when delta waves are more than 50% of all EEG waves, the sleeper is in Stage 4. (e) During REM sleep, the brain waves look very much like those of the awake brain.

In the next stages, the EEG pattern changes to *delta waves*, which are larger and slower than alpha waves. Delta waves characterize *delta sleep*, or deep sleep, which comprises both Stages 3 and 4. The distinction between Stages 3 and 4 is the proportion of delta waves. When delta waves represent 20% to 50% of the EEG waves, the sleeper is in *Stage 3*. When delta waves represent more than 50% of the EEG waves, the sleeper is in *Stage 4*.

The first four stages of sleep, sometimes associated with dreaming, make up **N-REM sleep**, which is non–rapid eye movement sleep. During these four stages, as the name "N-REM" implies, our eyes are not moving very much. During the next stage, however, our eyes roll around in their sockets (Kleitman, 1963). If sleepers are awakened during this eye-rolling stage of sleep, they usually report being in the midst of a dream (Dement & Kleitman, 1957).

This fifth stage has become known as **REM sleep,** the distinctive kind of sleep that is characterized by rapid eye movements (REMs) and is frequently—though not exclusively—associated with dreaming. Fosse, Stickgold, and Hobson (2001) investigated emotions experienced during dreaming in REM sleep. They found that emotions were reported 74% of the time, with roughly balanced proportions of positive and negative emotions. A total of 86% of the reports were of at least two emotions. Joy was most frequently experienced, followed by surprise, anger, anxiety/fear, and sadness. Levels of anxiety and fear were significantly less intense than those of other emotions.

Dreaming frequently occurs during N-REM sleep. Dreams from N-REM sleep, however, are generally less clearly remembered upon waking than are dreams from REM sleep. Because dreaming can be associated with both REM and N-REM sleep, some investigators believe the difference is exaggerated (Antrobus, 2001). But other investigators argue that the distinction between REM and N-REM sleep is quite clear (Hobson, Pace-Schott, & Stickgold, 2000). EEG patterns become extremely active during REM sleep, which begins about an hour after Stage 1. The EEG of REM sleep somewhat resembles the EEG of the awake brain (see Figure 5.2). REM sleep is both the most like wakefulness in EEG patterns and yet the hardest from which to wake people. For this reason, REM sleep is sometimes called "paradoxical sleep." This term is also used because at the same time that the brain is very active, the body's capacity for movement is greatly diminished.

The stages of N-REM and REM sleep alternate throughout the night, roughly in 90-minute cycles. As the night progresses, the duration and sequence of the sleep stages may vary, as shown in Figure 5.3.

SLEEP DISORDERS

Although circadian rhythms and sleep cycles normally vary somewhat from person to person, extreme variations from the normal sleep patterns can wreak havoc on a person's life. Sleep disorders that cause problems for many people include: inability to sleep, known as *insomnia;* sudden uncontrollable sleep, called *narcolepsy;* breathing difficulties during sleep, or *sleep apnea;* talking in one's sleep, called *somniloquy;* and sleepwalking, also termed *somnambulism.*

INSOMNIA

Insomnia afflicts millions and is characterized by various disturbances of sleep. They include difficulty falling asleep, waking up during the night and being unable to go back to sleep, and waking up too early in the morning. These symptoms may vary in intensity and duration. People may experience temporary insomnia because of stress. They may suffer prolonged bouts of insomnia because of poor sleeping habits. Somewhat surprisingly, most people who suffer from insomnia usually sleep for at least a few hours, although they may not be aware of having slept. Laboratory studies have shown that insomniacs usually overestimate the amount of time it takes them to fall asleep.

Although almost everybody has trouble

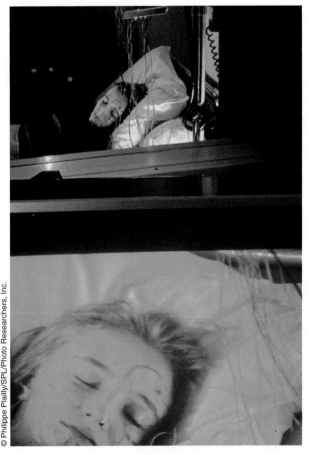

Sleep researchers monitor the patterns of brain-wave activity throughout the sleep cycles of research participants.

© Philippe Plailly/SPL/Photo Researchers, Inc.

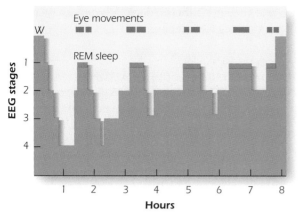

Sequences of States and Stages of Sleep. The sequence of REM and N-REM stages of sleep cycles alternates throughout the night. The repetitions of the REM stage are identified in red. (From Hartmann, *The Biology of Dreaming*, 1967. Courtesy of Charles C. Thomas, Publishers, Ltd., Springfield, IL.)

About 15% of adults experience insomnia, which encompasses a number of sleep disturbances.

falling asleep occasionally, in one survey, 6% of adult respondents said that they had sought medical attention because of sleeplessness. Roughly 15% of adults report serious insomnia. Another 15% report milder levels of insomnia or occasional insomnia (Bootzin, Manger, Perlis, Salvio, & Wyatt, 1993). Insomnia and most other sleep disorders are more common among women and the elderly (Borbely, 1986; Mellinger, Balter, & Uhlenhuth, 1985). Sleeping pills may help temporarily, but their side effects are troublesome. They often eventually intensify the insomnia. Prescription sleeping pills interfere with the natural sleep cycle, usually decreasing REM sleep. Moreover, seda-

tives often continue to work during the day, impairing cognitive and motor functions while the user is awake. Sedatives are also habit-forming, and people who rely on them may find it hard to sleep without taking medicine. For all of these reasons, physicians often recommend that their patients take the steps listed in Table 5.1 to avoid the need to take medicine (Borbely, 1986).

Some people believe they suffer from insomnia when they do not. What they are showing is a form of pseudo-insomnia, or *sleep state misperception*. Many of us have had the experience of thinking that we are awake for hours. We then check the clock, only to discover that we had tossed and turned for a much shorter time than we thought. Others have had the experience of being certain that they did not sleep all night. Then someone who observed them says they actually slept for

TABLE 5.1

How to Get a Good Night's Sleep. The following recommendations have been suggested by numerous experts in the field of sleep research. (After Atkinson, Atkinson, Smith, & Bem, 1993)

Do	Don't
Set a regular bedtime.	Change your schedule on the weekends.
Get up at the same time every morning.	Have caffeine 5–6 hours before bedtime.
Drink alcohol only in moderation.	Eat heavily just before bedtime.
Try warm milk or a *light* snack before bedtime.	Take sleeping pills; they can disrupt sleep cycles and leave you hung over.
Establish a relaxing evening ritual, such as reading before bed.	Attempt to wear yourself out with exercise before bedtime or when sleep won't come.
Exercise regularly.	
Stay in bed and try to relax if you're having problems sleeping.	

several hours. In each case, people believe their sleep is severely disrupted when, at worst, it is only mildly disrupted. Indeed, 5% of individuals who go to insomnia clinics may suffer from pseudo-insomnia (Hauri, 1994).

NARCOLEPSY

In contrast to insomnia, **narcolepsy** is a disturbance in the pattern of wakefulness and sleep in which the narcoleptic experiences an uncontrollable urge to fall asleep periodically during the day. The afflicted individual loses consciousness for brief periods of time (usually 10 or 15 minutes). The narcoleptic can be in grave danger if the attacks occur while driving or engaged in activities in which sudden sleep might be hazardous. Narcolepsy actually is more accurately described as a disorder of the waking state than as a sleep disorder. Nevertheless, narcoleptics frequently experience disturbed nighttime sleep as well. Narcoleptics usually fall into REM sleep immediately, whereas a person with normal sleep patterns rarely (if ever) does so. This observation has led some scientists to suggest that, for narcoleptics, REM sleep may be insufficiently differentiated from the waking state. Narcolepsy affects 1 or 2 people in every 1,000 (Borbely, 1986). Although the cause of narcolepsy is unknown, the disorder seems to run in families and so may be inherited. Fortunately, medication can usually control the symptoms of this disorder.

SLEEP APNEA

Another disorder with unknown etiology and possible hereditary involvement is **sleep apnea,** a breathing disorder that occurs when the sleeper repeatedly (perhaps hundreds of times per night) stops breathing. The episodes usually last only a few seconds, but they may last as long as 2 minutes in severe cases. Sleep apnea is potentially dangerous because it deprives the body of oxygen. It most often afflicts overweight men over 40 years of age. A study of long-haul truck drivers found that men with disordered breathing during sleep were twice as likely to have accidents on the road as men with normal breathing during sleep (Stoohs, Guilleminault, Itoi, & Dement, 1994). Sleep apnea also seems to be associated with alcohol consumption. The disorder is difficult to treat in adults, although weight loss sometimes helps.

Sleep apnea occurs frequently in prematurely born infants. Infants generally outgrow the disorder, but it may be life threatening if the breathing patterns of infants at risk are not closely monitored. It has also been suggested that there may be a link between sudden infant death syndrome (SIDS) and sleep apnea. Maternal smoking has been linked to SIDS, as has the baby's sleeping on its stomach (J. A. Taylor & Sanderson, 1995). It is therefore particularly important that parents not expose their baby to smoke (even in utero) and also that they place their baby in a position other than on the stomach for sleeping.

SLEEPWALKING

In **somnambulism** (sleepwalking), the sleepwalker is able to see, walk, and perhaps even talk, but usually cannot remember the episodes. For many years, scientists believed that sleepwalkers were merely acting out their dreams. In fact, however, sleepwalking usually begins during Stage 3 or Stage 4 of N-REM sleep. It typically is not accompanied by dreaming. If the sleepwalking episode is short, sleepwalkers may stay in the deep sleep of Stages 3 and 4. If the episode is lengthy, EEG patterns begin to resemble either those of Stage 1 of N-REM sleep or those of the waking state.

Sleepwalking varies in severity. Some people may simply sit up in bed, mutter a few words, and then lie down again. Such episodes are no cause for concern. Other people may get out of bed, get dressed, walk around, and even leave their homes. Although sleepwalkers' eyes are open (usually with a rigid facial expression) and they can see, their perception is often impaired. They can injure themselves by mistaking one object for another, such as a window for a door.

Most sleepwalkers do not remember their episodes of sleepwalking when they awaken the next morning. They may even be surprised to find themselves asleep in some place other than their beds. Scientists have not found a cause or a cure for sleepwalking. However, sleepwalking is known to be more common in children than in adults. It usually disappears as children grow older.

✓CONCEPT CHECK 3

1. Almost every day Jade awakes at roughly 7:00 A.M. Her pattern of sleeping and waking is an example of a _____ rhythm.
   a. circadian
   b. contemporaneous
   c. contraceptive
   d. diluvian
2. Dreaming _____ occurs during N-REM sleep.
   a. only
   b. almost always
   c. occasionally
   d. never
3. Max sometimes stops breathing for brief periods of time as many as 100 times a night. He most likely suffers from
   a. narcolepsy.
   b. somnambulism.
   c. sleep apnea.
   d. naloxone.

DREAMS

Why do we dream? What are some of the main theories of dreaming?

People have always been fascinated with dreams. Dreams have been used to predict the outcomes of battles. They even have caused people to change religions. Indeed, dreams fill our heads with fantastic ideas—sometimes pleasant, sometimes frightening. Some people have experienced breakthrough insights or other creative ideas while dreaming or in a dreamlike state of mind. What is it about dreaming that may facilitate such breakthroughs?

All of us have dreams every night, whether or not we remember them (Ornstein, 1986). Dreams often occur in the form of strange fantasies that we accept as true while we sleep yet would dismiss if we were awake (Antrobus & Conroy, 1999). Common dream themes among college students are listed in Table 5.2.

Mary Whiton Calkins was one of the earliest American investigators of dreaming. She and her advisor, Edmund Sanford, collected dreams of college students. On the basis of 375 dreams studied, they concluded that people averaged four dreams per night. Calkins also argued that there is a close relationship between dreaming and waking life. She believed that dreams draw on the persons, places, and happenings of everyday life (Furumoto, 1980).

Why do we dream? There are several views. Perhaps the best-known theory of dreaming was proposed by Sigmund Freud (1900/1954). According to Freud, dreams allow us to express our unconscious wishes in a disguised way. Freud called dreams the "royal road to the unconscious" because they are one of the few ways we have of allowing the contents of the unconscious to be expressed. However, he also postulated that the contents of the unconscious would be so threatening if expressed directly and clearly that we might awaken every time we dreamed. Thus, according to Freud, we dream in symbols that both express and disguise our unconscious wishes. Because these wishes are disguised, they do not shock us into wakefulness. The empirical support for this theory is weak.

Other theorists have suggested that dreams represent everyday concerns expressed in a language that is peculiar to dreams (Foulkes, 1990, 1996, 1999) or even that dreams have no particular meaning at all (F. Crick & Mitchison, 1983, 1995)—that they represent a kind of mental housekeeping that has no deep psychological meaning whatsoever.

TABLE 5.2 **Common Dreams of College Students, in percent** (Data from Schneider & Domhoff, 2003)	Men	Women
Who and What We Dream About		
Animals	6	4
Familiar characters	45	58
Friends	31	37
Groups	31	28
Men	67	48
Women	37	52
Acts of aggression	59	51
Aggression is physical	50	34
Dreamer is aggressor	40	33
Dreamer is victim	60	67
Acts of friendliness	41	49
Dreamer befriends others	50	47
Dreamer achieves success	51	42
Bodily misfortune	29	35
Negative emotions	80	80
Where Our Dreams Are Set		
Indoors	48	61
Outdoors	52	39
Familiar place	62	79
Unfamiliar place	38	21
Percentage of Dreams with at Least One		
Act of aggression	47	44
Act of friendliness	38	42
Act of sexuality	12	4
Misfortune	36	33
Success	15	8
Failure	15	10

If dreams do indeed have meaning, the disguises of dream content are sometimes rather thin (Dement, 1976; Dement & Vaughan, 1999). In a study of the dreams of people who were deprived of liquid, many dreams were found to involve liquid consumption (p. 69): "Just as the bell went off, somebody raised a glass and said something about a toast. I don't think I had a glass."

Some theorists take a cognitive perspective on dreaming. In particular, a *problem-solving view* of dreaming suggests that dreams provide a way for us to work out our problems (Cartwright, 1977, 1993;

Cartwright & Lamberg, 1992; Cartwright, Newell, & Mercer, 2001). For example, women going through a divorce are likely to dream about problems related to divorce. In fact, women who dream about divorce-related problems seem better able when they are awake to cope with the problems of divorce than are those who do not frequently dream about it (Cartwright, 1991).

According to the **activation–synthesis hypothesis,** dreams are the result of subjective organization and interpretation (synthesis) of neural activity (activation) that takes place during sleep (Hobson, 2001; McCarley & Hobson, 1981). Robert W. McCarley and J. Allan Hobson believe that we accept bizarre occurrences in dreams because of changes in brain physiology. That is, just as our brains work to organize sensory information during wakefulness, our brains also strive to organize sensory information during sleep. The brain may interpret the neural activity that occurs during dreaming. That activity, in turn, blocks motor commands as a sensation of our being chased. Our sleeping brains may interpret neural activity in the vestibular system (which controls balance; see Chapter 4) as the sensation of floating, flying, or falling.

The biological purpose or reasons for dreaming may someday be discovered. It is unlikely that scientists will ever devise a definitive model for interpreting dreams or for decoding the contents of dreams. Dreams are highly personal. To say that you could predict why people dream what they dream, you would have to be able to predict the content of a specific dream at a particular time (Hobson, 1989). Such prediction is not likely to occur.

Sigmund Freud and Carl Jung looked for universal symbols that would have the same meanings in every person's dreams. But people freely interpret their own dreams within the context of their current lives and past memories. They draw conclusions that seem appropriate to them. Some people find analyzing their dreams merely entertaining. Others believe the messages they find in their dreams are useful in solving the problems of waking life. Occasionally, dreams can be terrifying. Certain kinds of antidepressants that keep the serotonin system active can deprive people of dreaming and lead to a state of distress.

Nightmares are anxiety-arousing dreams that may awaken the dreamer. Sometimes we seem to wake up in order to avoid some threat in the nightmare. People who have nightmares often remember them if asked to recount them immediately after waking. Nightmares tend to increase during times of stress. Some people, however, seem to be more susceptible to them than others. Children are more susceptible, on average, than are adults. Nightmares generally re-

Daydreaming can help us to creatively contemplate the information we have been studying.

quire no special action, except when they are unusually severe or common or when the same nightmare repeats again and again.

Night terrors are sudden awakenings from N-REM sleep that are accompanied by feelings of intense fright or panic. These awakenings are characterized by intense arousal of the autonomic nervous system. A common symptom is greatly accelerated heart rate. People can experience night terrors at any age, but they are especially common in children from 3 to 8 years old. Often people wake up suddenly and may scream or sit upright. They usually do not remember any specific, coherent nightmare. They may, nevertheless, recall a frightening image or thought. People who experience night terrors may find that their sense of panic quickly fades. They then are able fairly rapidly to fall back asleep.

No discussion of dreaming is complete without mentioning daydreaming. **Daydreaming** is a state of consciousness somewhere between waking and sleeping that permits a shift in focus from external events toward internal thoughts and images (see J. L. Singer, 1998; J. A. Singer, Singer, & Zittel, 2000). Daydreaming can be useful in cognitive processes that involve the generation of creative ideas (D. G. Singer & Singer, 2001). It also can be disruptive, however. Anyone who has ever been questioned in class while daydreaming has learned firsthand how aggravating and even embarrassing this disruption can be.

✓ CONCEPT CHECK 4

1. Sigmund Freud referred to dreaming as the
   a. key to the kingdom.
   b. place where the rubber hits to road.
   c. royal road to the unconscious.
   d. height of the sublime.
2. Night terrors are awakenings from
   a. N-REM sleep.
   b. REM sleep.
   c. delta waves.
   d. theta waves.
3. The idea that dreams are the result of the subjective interpretation of neural activity is referred to as the
   a. activation–synthesis hypothesis.
   b. mental-garbage theory.
   c. physiological activation hypothesis.
   d. deactivation–analysis hypothesis.

HYPNOSIS AND MEDITATION

What is hypnosis and why does it occur?
What is meditation and how is it produced?

Most (but not all) psychologists view **hypnosis** as an altered state of consciousness that usually involves deep relaxation and extreme sensitivity to suggestion. It appears to bear some resemblance to sleep. Hypnotized people may imagine that they see or hear things when they are prompted to do so (Bowers, 1976). They may also receive a **posthypnotic suggestion**, an instruction given during hypnosis that is to be implemented after the subject wakens. Participants often have no recollection of receiving the instruction or even being hypnotized (Ruch, 1975). Hypnotized persons also may not sense things that they otherwise would sense. For example, a person may not feel pain when dipping an arm into very cold water. Hypnotized persons may be induced to remember things they had seemingly forgotten.

Many psychologists wonder whether hypnotism is a genuine psychological phenomenon. Historically, even the man credited with introducing hypnotism, Franz Anton Mesmer (1734–1815), did not fully understand the phenomenon. Mesmer came to be viewed as a fraud, largely because he made claims for his techniques that he could not scientifically support (see Figure 5.4).

Since Mesmer's time, scientists have continued to investigate hypnotism. The **simulating paradigm** is a research technique for determining the true effects of a psychological treatment in which one group of participants is subjected to the treatment (hypnotized) and another group (a control group) is not (Orne, 1959). The control participants are then asked to behave as though they had received the treatment (in this case, been hypnotized). People must then try to distinguish between the behavior of the treatment group and the behavior of the control group.

© National Library of Medicine/Peter Arnold, Inc.

FIGURE 5.4

Mesmerism. Franz Anton Mesmer, one of the first to experiment with hypnotism, believed that animal magnetism could cure illnesses. His patients would sit around the "magnetized" tub, wrap themselves with cord, and hold onto bent iron bars. "Magnetizers," Mesmer's helpers, would rub the patients' afflicted parts to hasten the cure. Mesmer and his method were discredited.

As it turns out, simulators are able to mimic some, but not all, of the behavior of hypnotized participants (Gray, Bowers, & Fenz, 1970). Also, hypnotized participants in simulation experiments provide very different reports than do simulators of their subjective experiences. Simulating participants report themselves as actively faking. Hypnotized participants, in contrast, report the behavior as more or less just happening to them. Simulating participants try to figure out what the hypnotist expects from them. Hypnotized participants instead claim to be uninfluenced by the experimenter's expectations of them (Orne, 1959). Thus, hypnotized people do not appear to be faking (Kinnunen, Zamansky, & Block, 1994; Spanos, Burgess, Roncon, Wallace-Capretta, & Cross, 1993; Spanos, Burgess, Wallace-Capretta, & Ouaida, 1996).

THEORIES OF HYPNOSIS

If we accept the phenomenon of hypnosis as genuine, we still need to determine exactly what goes on during hypnosis. We discuss here only the more credible theories. One theory holds that hypnosis is a form of deep relaxation (Edmonston, 1981, 1991). This theory builds on the idea of hypnosis as a form of sleep, as suggested earlier by Ivan Pavlov, a Russian physiologist (see also Chapter 6). We now know that EEG patterns shown during hypnosis are different from EEG patterns shown during sleep. Nevertheless, there may still be a close connection between hypnosis and the deep relaxation that sometimes precedes or resembles sleep.

A second theory suggests that hypnosis is an *epiphenomenon*, something that exists only as a secondary outcome of another phenomenon. Two psychologists who have taken this position are Theodore Barber (1979, 1986) and Nicholas Spanos (1986; Spanos & Coe, 1992). According to this view, hypnosis is largely a form of role-playing in response to experimenter demands. In attempting to meet the expectations of the experimenter, a person may act in particular ways.

The view of hypnosis as an epiphenomenon seems similar to the view that the behavior of hypnotized people is merely a sham, but the two ideas are not the same. According to the epiphenomenal view, the person in a hypnosis situation becomes so genuinely caught up in the role that he or she unwittingly plays the role of a hypnotized person for a brief time. Advocates of this position point out that individuals can successfully fake many of the phenomena attributed to hypnosis. More recently, it has become increasingly apparent that many of the memories seemingly miraculously retrieved under hypnosis are instead after-the-fact constructions that come from the suggestions of the hypnotist (McConkey, 1992; see also Chapter 7).

In other words, hypnosis did not result in people's being able to perform an astounding feat of memory. Rather they constructed memories that they believed to be ones the hypnotist wanted them to construct.

Perhaps the most widely accepted view among scientists who believe that hypnosis is a genuine phenomenon was developed by Ernest Hilgard. According to his **neodissociative theory,** some individuals can separate one part of their conscious minds from another part (*dissociation*) (Hilgard, 1977, 1992a, 1992b, 1994). In one part of the mind, the individual responds to the hypnotist's commands. In the other part of the mind, the individual becomes a hidden observer who simultaneously observes and monitors the events and actions taking place. These events and actions include some of those that the hypnotized participant appears not to be processing in the part of the conscious mind that is engaging in the actions (Hilgard, 1977, 1994).

For example, psychologists have found that while participants respond to a hypnotist's suggestion that they feel no pain and behave in ways that seem to show they are not in pain, they nevertheless are also able to describe how the pain feels. In other experiments, participants can be made to write down messages while

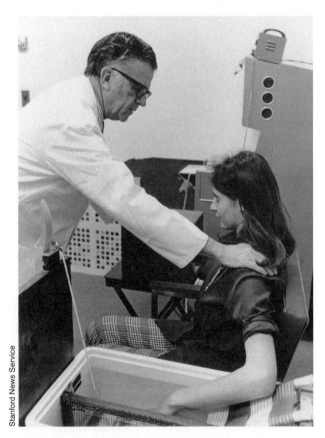

Hypnotists are able to induce a state of deep relaxation in susceptible individuals. Here, Ernest Hilgard conducts an experiment to determine the effects of hypnosis.

unaware that they are doing so because they are actively engaged in another task at the same time (see Kihlstrom, 1985; Knox, Crutchfield, & Hilgard, 1975; Zamansky & Bartis, 1985). Thus, it seems that part of the person's consciousness is unself-consciously involved in the hypnosis. At the same time, another part observes and thereby knows, at some level, what is taking place.

People differ in their susceptibility to hypnosis (Bowers, 1998; Hilgard, 1965; Oakman, Woody, & Bowers, 1996). Some people readily become deeply hypnotized, others do not. Still others appear to be relatively invulnerable to hypnotism. Four factors are hypothesized to influence whether an individual can be easily hypnotized: (1) social factors that lead the individual to cooperate and to try to conform to the wishes of the hypnotist; (2) the skill of the hypnotist and the individual's relationship with the hypnotist; (3) the effectiveness of the procedure for inducing hypnosis; and (4) what, exactly, the individual is being asked to do (Barber, 1999a, 1999b, 2000). It is not surprising that hypnosis is more successful as a clinical treatment with highly suggestible individuals.

HYPNOSIS AND MEMORY

Some psychologists have become convinced that hypnosis can be used to dredge up old memories of events that otherwise seem to be forgotten, even memories of past lives! In one study, a third of the hypnotized college students who were instructed to remember events from previous lives were able to do so (Spanos, DuBreuil, & Gabora, 1991). While they were recalling these past lives, they were asked questions about their lives and surrounding events. Their recall cast serious doubt on the validity of their assertions. One student, for example, recalled his life as Julius Caesar in A.D. 50, when he was emperor of Rome. In fact, Caesar died in 44 B.C. and was never crowned emperor of Rome.

Evidence suggests that at least some recall may be inadvertently induced by hypnotists (L. S. Newman & Baumeister, 1994). Hypnotists' questions about events during reported abductions by extraterrestrial aliens often contain suggestions that are picked up by the hypnotized individual and "recalled" as having happened. An example is being asked whether one was injected with a needle by the extraterrestrials and then "remembering" that one was indeed injected (Fiore, 1989).

Some recollections under hypnosis may be correct (Geiselman, Fisher, MacKinnon, & Holland, 1985). But the current weight of the evidence is that memories under hypnosis need to be viewed with skepticism. Corroborating evidence for these recollections is needed before they are accepted as true

memories. Hypnosis not only seems to be questionable as a technique for inducing recall of memories from the intermediate and distant past. It also is dubious as a technique for inducing recall of very recent memories. When memory for recently learned stories was compared for participants who either were or were not hypnotized, the hypnotized participants actually showed worse recall of the stories than did the nonhypnotized participants (Muzur, Fabbro, Clarici, Braun, & Bava, 1998).

At times, courts have allowed testimony from individuals who are under hypnosis, allegedly to improve their recall of past events. Research suggests that the testimony of such people is less reliable than that of people who are not hypnotized (Karlin & Orne, 1997), possibly because the people under hypnosis are so suggestible they may pick up clues about what they are expected to say.

In sum, the verdict on hypnosis is not yet in. Today, hypnosis is used in clinical settings to control smoking and to treat a variety of health-related problems, such as asthma, high blood pressure, and migraine headaches. The effects of hypnosis, however, appear to be temporary. For this reason, hypnotism generally is used in conjunction with other therapeutic techniques. Still, hypnosis appears to be more effective than other treatment techniques, whether in relieving pain or in changing behavior. Although persuasive evidence suggests that hypnosis is more than a crass simulation, psychologists have not reached consensus regarding what hypnosis is or even whether it is a genuine phenomenon.

MEDITATION

Meditation is a state of awareness that depends on techniques for altering consciousness through contemplation. It functions by "a shift away from the active, outward-oriented, linear mode and toward the receptive and quiescent mode, and often, a shift from an external focus of attention to an internal one" (Ornstein, 1977, p. 159). In its emphasis on receptivity and quiescence, meditation bears some resemblance to hypnotism. Brain-wave patterns as well as external perceptions can be altered during meditation. Meditation is viewed as slightly exotic in many Western cultures but is a normal part of life in some Eastern cultures.

Concentrative meditation is a form of contemplation in which the meditator focuses on an object or thought. The individual attempts to remove all else from consciousness. Concentrative meditation is performed in various ways. For example, meditators might focus on the whole process of breathing. They might think about the movement of the air as it reaches the nose, permeates the lungs, remains in the

Meditation and yoga can relax people and improve their mental health.

lungs, and then is finally expelled. The idea is to focus on a simple, repetitive, and rhythmic activity.

In Zen meditation, the meditator might contemplate the answer to a *koan*—a riddle or paradox, such as What is the sound of one hand clapping? or What is the size of the real you? These questions have no logical answers, which is just the point. You can think about the questions time and again without coming to a conclusion.

Opening-up meditation is the second of the two main forms of contemplation, in which the meditator integrates meditation with the events of everyday life, seeking to expand awareness of everyday events rather than to separate meditation from mundane existence. Yoga can take an opening-up form as well as a concentrative one. In one form of opening-up yoga, the individual learns to observe himself or herself as though another person. In another form of opening-up meditation, the person performs everyday actions slightly differently from the customary way. The goal is to become more aware of the routine of life.

What actually happens during meditation? What value, if any, is in the various forms of meditation? In general, respiration, heart rate, blood pressure, and muscle tension decrease (D. H. Shapiro & Giber, 1978; R. K. Wallace & Benson, 1972). Some evidence indicates that meditation can help patients who have bronchial asthma (Honsberger & Wilson, 1973). It also can decrease blood pressure in patients who are hypertensive (H. Benson, 1977). It may reduce insomnia in some people (Woolfolk, Carr-Kaffashan, McNulty, & Lehrer, 1976) and symptoms of psychiatric syndromes in others (Glueck & Stroebel, 1975). It also helps reduce addictive behavior (Marlatt, 2002), anxiety (M. E. Taylor, 2002), and irritable bowel syndrome (Keefer & Blanchard, 2002). EEG studies suggest that concentrative meditation tends to produce an accumulation of alpha waves. This is the type of brain wave associated with a state of relaxation and the beginning stages of sleep (Fenwick, 1987). Thus, concentrative meditation seems to relax people, which is of value in its own right. In addition, many practitioners of meditation believe that it enhances their overall consciousness. They think it moves them toward a more enlightened state of consciousness. (Users of various drugs also sometimes seek a similar state, more often than not with negative, and sometimes even life-threatening, results.)

✓**CONCEPT CHECK 5**

1. A technique used to discover whether someone is faking hypnosis is called
   a. posthypnotic suggestion.
   b. hypnotherapy.
   c. the simulating paradigm.
   d. hypno-staging.
2. An important component of neodissociative theory is the
   a. hidden observer.
   b. epiphenomena.
   c. posthypnotic suggestion.
   d. activation by synthesis.

3. A meditator who focuses on his or her pattern of breathing is probably engaging in
   a. opening-up mediation.
   b. concentrative meditation.
   c. koanic breathing.
   d. closing-down meditation.

PSYCHOACTIVE DRUGS

What are the main psychoactive drugs, and what are their psychological consequences?

Drugs introduced into the body may destroy bacteria, ease pain, or alter consciousness. In this chapter we are concerned only with **psychoactive** drugs, which produce a significant effect on behavior, mood, and consciousness. Psychoactive drugs can be classified into four basic categories (Seymour & Smith, 1987): narcotics, central nervous system depressants, central nervous system stimulants, and hallucinogens. (See Table 5.3 for a summary of drugs in each category.) It is important to realize that different kinds of drugs can be used in combination, such as a "speedball," which combines a stimulant (cocaine) with a narcotic (heroin). The use of such combinations is more likely to be seriously toxic or deadly than is the use of single drugs.

With all the problems associated with psychoactive drug use, you may wonder why anybody uses drugs. The answers are as varied as people themselves. Some people take drugs to experiment, feeling confident that they are personally immune to addiction or that they will not get addicted in the short amount of time they plan to take the drugs. Others feel so unhappy in their daily lives that the risks seem worth it.

TABLE 5.3
CONCEPT REVIEW

Four Basic Categories of Drugs. Psychoactive drugs can be sorted into four basic categories, each of which produces distinctive psychoactive effects.

Category	Effect	Drugs
Narcotics	Produce numbness or stupor, relieve pain	• Opium and its natural derivatives: morphine, heroin, and codeine • Opioids (synthetic narcotics): meperidine (Demerol®), propoxyphene (Darvon®), oxycodone (Percodan®), methadone

CNS depressants ("downers")	Slow (depress) the operation of the central nervous system	• Alcohol
		• Sedatives
		  Barbiturates: secobarbital (Seconal®), phenobarbital (Dilantin®)
		  Tranquilizers (benzodiazepines): chlorpromazine (Thorazine®), chlordiazepoxide (Librium®), diazepam (Valium®), alprazolam (Xanax®)
		• Methaqualone (Quaalude®)
		• Chloral hydrate

CNS stimulants ("uppers")	Excite (stimulate) the operation of the central nervous system	• Caffeine (found in coffee, teas, cola drinks, chocolate) • Amphetamines: amphetamine (Benzedrine®), dextroamphetamine (Dexedrine®), methamphetamine (Methedrine®) • Cocaine • Nicotine (commonly found in tobacco)
Hallucinogens (psychedelics, psychotomimetics)	Induce alterations of consciousnessn	• LSD • Mescaline • Marijuana • Hashish • Phencyclidine (PCP) • MDMA (ecstasy) • Psilocybin ("magic" mushrooms)

NARCOTICS

Narcotic, from the Greek term for "numbness," originally referred only to *opium* and to drugs derived from opium. Derivatives include drugs such as heroin, morphine, and codeine. Narcotics can be either naturally or synthetically produced to create the numbing, stuporous effects of opium. They also can lead to addiction. Narcotics derived from the opium poppy pod are **opiates. Opioids** are synthetically produced drugs that have similar chemical structure and effects as opiates. Examples are meperidine and methadone. When used illegally, opiates and opioids are usually injected intravenously, smoked, or inhaled. When used medically, they are either swallowed or injected intravenously. Narcotics are potent analgesics that lead to a reduction in pain and an overall sense of well-being.

DRUG ACTIONS

Narcotics are highly addictive. They are usually either regulated by prescription or banned outright. Narcotics are sometimes prescribed for very brief periods to reduce postsurgical pain. In very low doses, they can relieve diarrhea. Narcotics have a constipating effect because they also depress other physiological systems, including metabolic processes.

Narcotics primarily affect the functioning of the brain and the bowel. They bring about pain relief, relaxation, and sleepiness. They help to suppress coughs (hence their use in *codeine* prescription cough medicines) and also can stimulate vomiting. Users typically notice an impaired ability to concentrate and a sense of mental fuzziness or cloudiness. For these reasons, driving under the influence of narcotics is extremely dangerous. Doing cognitively intensive work (such as studying) while under their influence is likely to be unproductive. Side effects of narcotics include contraction of the pupils, sweating, nausea, and depressed breathing.

TOLERANCE AND DEPENDENCY

Another danger of narcotic use over time is the possibility of an eventual **overdose,** in which the user ingests a life-threatening or lethal dose of drugs. Prolonged use of psychoactive drugs leads to **tolerance,** in which individuals progressively experience fewer effects for a given amount of the drug. Tolerance often prompts drug users to take increasing amounts of a given drug to achieve the same desired effect. Actually, most narcotics users find that the euphoria they felt when they initially used the drug disappears after prolonged use. They must continue to use drugs to keep from feeling ill from withdrawal from them.

Dependency occurs because, like many other drugs, narcotics mimic neurotransmitters in the way they act at synapses (see Chapter 3 and Figure 5.5). The molecular composition of opiates resembles that

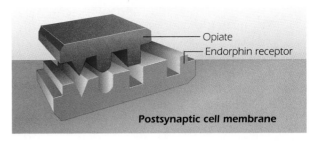

FIGURE 5.5
Molecular Similarity of Opiates and Endorphins. Opiates and endorphins have similar structures, which is why narcotics easily fit the receptor sites for endorphins.

of endorphins, which are *endogenous morphines*, the body's natural painkilling neurotransmitters (see also Chapter 18). Initial use of narcotics prompts pain relief and some of the euphoria that normally accompanies the natural release of endorphins. Prolonged use of narcotics apparently causes a drop in the body's natural production of particular endorphins. As a drug replaces the body's natural painkillers, people can develop *drug dependence*, a state in which an individual must continue to use a drug to satisfy intense physical, mental, or emotional cravings for the drug. In the past, it was common to distinguish between physical dependence, in which a person continues to use a drug to avoid physical symptoms, and psychological dependence, in which a person continues to use a drug to avoid mental or emotional symptoms. Today, however, many psychologists believe that the distinction between the two kinds of dependence is so fuzzy as to be useless (Koob & Bloom, 1988; Ray & Ksir, 1990). Dependence increases and tolerance develops because more narcotic is needed to do the job that the body gradually ceases to perform. **Withdrawal** symptoms are the temporary discomforts that result from a decreased dosage or a complete discontinuation of a psychoactive drug. A former user undergoing withdrawal may experience symptoms much like a severe case of intestinal flu, accompanied by extreme depression or anxiety. During withdrawal, the drug user's physiology and mental processes must adjust to the loss of the drug. Typical narcotic withdrawal symptoms are chills, sweating, intense stomach cramps, diarrhea, headache, and repeated vomiting. These symptoms may occur separately or in combinations.

TREATMENT OF NARCOTIC ABUSE

Once a user has formed narcotic dependence, the form of treatment differs for *acute toxicity* (the damage done from a particular overdose) versus *chronic toxicity* (the damage done by long-term drug addiction). Acute toxicity is often treated with naloxone or related drugs. Naloxone (as well as a related drug, naltrexone) occupies opiate receptors in the brain better than the opiates themselves occupy those sites; thus, it blocks all effects of narcotics (see Figure 5.6). In fact, naloxone has such a strong affinity for the endorphin receptors in the brain that it actually displaces molecules of narcotics already in these receptors and then moves into the receptors itself. Naloxone is not addictive, however. Even though it binds to receptors, it does not activate them. Naloxone can be a lifesaving drug for someone who has overdosed on opiates, but its effects are short-lived. Thus, it is a poor long-term treatment for drug addiction.

Maintenance and detoxification are the primary methods of treating chronic toxicity caused by prolonged drug addiction. *Maintenance* controls an addict's use of the drug. In a maintenance program, the addict is still given the drug or a substitute, but in a controlled manner. The goal is to substitute a more controllable, less lethal, addiction—a goal considered controversial by many. *Detoxification* seeks to break the addiction both by weaning an addict off the drug to break the habit and by restoring good health habits. In narcotic detoxification, methadone often is substituted for the narcotic (typically heroin). Methadone binds to endorphin receptor sites (see panel (b) in Figure 5.6) and reduces the heroin cravings and withdrawal symptoms of addicted persons. After the substitution, gradually decreasing dosages are administered to the patient until he or she is drug-free. Unfortunately, the usefulness of methadone is limited because it is itself addictive.

CENTRAL NERVOUS SYSTEM DEPRESSANTS

DRUG ACTIONS

Central nervous system (CNS) depressant drugs are a highly addictive class of psychoactive drugs (e.g., alcohol and the sedatives) that slow the operation of the CNS. They are often prescribed in low doses to

FIGURE 5.6

Molecular Similarity of Opiates, Methadone, and Naloxone. The nonnarcotic drug naloxone fits the receptor sites for endorphins so well that it can push out opiates and block them from reentering those sites, as shown in panel (c). Hence, naloxone can be used as effective temporary treatment for narcotic overdose, although its effects are short-lived. For long-term treatment, methadone is often substituted for heroin. It also fits the endorphin receptor sites, as shown in panel (b), and can reduce heroin cravings and withdrawal symptoms.

(a) Heroin / Opioid receptor / Neuron membrane

(b) Methadone

(c) Heroin / Naloxone

© Robert E. Daemmrich/Stone-Getty Images

Although party-goers often drink alcohol to relax and reduce inhibitions, prolonged or excessive drinking can cause stupor, damage to the brain and nervous system, and sometimes death. Is this person having fun yet?

reduce anxiety and in relatively high doses to combat insomnia. Alcohol is readily available for purchase by adults in most countries around the world. Sedatives are usually prescribed (Nishino, Mignot, & Dement, 2001). CNS depressants can be ingested orally or injected. They usually elevate mood, reduce anxiety and guilt, and relax normal inhibitions. However, such drugs may cause people to become intoxicated—that is, stupefied by toxins in the depressants. The individuals may also find themselves susceptible to sudden shifts in mood. Their sense of relaxation and euphoria quickly can give way to *increased* anxiety and irritability. High doses of depressants can cause slow reflexes, unsteady gait, slurred speech, and impaired judgment. Overdoses can slow physiological responses so much that they cause death.

ALCOHOL ABUSE AND TREATMENT

Alcohol is the most well known and widely used CNS depressant. It is the natural result of the fermentation of fruits and grains. Alcohol is so widely promoted and consumed that people tend to ignore the fact that it is an addictive psychoactive drug.

Alcohol's effects vary with the amount consumed, the rate of consumption, and an individual's body weight, tolerance, and metabolism. Someone who sips a drink over the course of an evening is less likely to become intoxicated than someone who gulps it. Furthermore, a 300-pound person is typically less affected than a 100-pound person by the same amount of alcohol. A frequent drinker usually builds up a tolerance (similar to narcotics tolerance), however, and this tolerance can lead to increased consumption.

When concentrations of alcohol in the blood are around 0.03% to 0.05%, people often feel relaxed and uninhibited, and they have a general sense of well-being. At a blood-alcohol level of 0.10%, sensorimotor functioning is markedly impaired. Many states consider people to be legally drunk at this level. Some states use a lower level of 0.08%. People may exhibit slurred speech and grow angry, sullen, or morose. At a concentration of 0.20%, people show grave dysfunction. With concentrations of 0.40% or higher, there is a serious risk of death.

Most dosages of alcohol decrease the effectiveness of the neurotransmitter *dopamine* (see Chapter 3), thus reducing motor abilities and attention. Alcohol also appears to interfere with the activities of other neurotransmitters (Hittner, 1997). At first, alcohol often seems to increase people's level of arousal, apparently because it first depresses the effects of synapses that release inhibitory neurotransmitters in the brain. People initially may feel more excited because inhibitory activity is slowed and excitatory transmissions predominate. Soon, however, alcohol depresses the effects of excitatory synapses as well, causing a general decrease in sen-

sorimotor functioning. Interestingly, it has been found that there are strong expectancy effects for alcohol consumption, which is sometimes called the "think-drink" phenomenon. The effects one gets from alcohol are very much determined by the effects one expects to get (Stacy, Widaman, & Marlatt, 1990). If one drinks a substance that one believes to be alcoholic but that is not, one will experience some signs of inebriation. If one drinks a substance that one believes is not alcoholic but that is, one will feel fewer signs of inebriation.

Larimer, Anderson, Baer, and Marlatt (2000) did a study of drinking among residents of fraternities, sororities, and residence halls. They found that men who lived in a fraternity were likely to consume more alcohol than men who lived in a residence hall, with more negative consequences, even after controlling for family history, expectancies, and history of drinking in high school. A history of alcohol problems in the family produced negative consequences only for men, not for women. The results for women were quite different. Residence in a sorority was actually found to moderate the negative consequences of drinking. Heavy drinkers among women in residence halls reported more negative consequences than did heavy drinkers in sororities.

In a separate study, Blume, Marlatt, and Schmaling (2000) found reduced higher-order cognitive functioning among heavy drinkers in college. This finding suggests a possible explanation for people who become heavy drinkers. They may lack the cognitive skills to anticipate the long-term consequences of heavy drinking.

Alcoholism is the tendency to abuse alcohol to a degree that leads to social, cognitive, or occupational dysfunction. It is one of the most common afflictions in the United States. Alcoholics have great difficulty abstaining from alcohol and controlling their drinking once they start. Roughly two-thirds of adults in the United States report that they use alcohol. An estimated 10% of these people have problems related to alcohol use. An estimated 90% of all assaults, 50%–60% of all homicides, and more than 50% of rapes and sexual attacks on children are alcohol related. The costs to society of alcohol abuse are probably double those of all other types of drug abuse combined (Segal, 1988).

Chronic alcoholics may sustain permanent damage to the nervous system, pancreas, liver, and brain cells. Heavy drinking can also lead to suppression of the immune system, nutritional deficits, and general failure to be careful about health matters. These problems can eventually result in other unfortunate consequences, including increased risk of cancer (Herity, Moriarty, Daly, Dunn, & Bourke, 1982; Heuch, Kvale, Jacobsen, & Bjelke, 1983). For these and other reasons, alcoholics generally have their life expectancy shortened by an average of 10 to 12 years. Alcoholics also may experience blackouts, loss of memory, cardiac arrest, psychosis, and alcohol-induced death. They are at risk for *Korsakoff's syndrome*, a brain disorder in which learning and other cognitive functions are impaired. Alcohol use by pregnant women, even in moderate amounts, can result in *fetal alcohol syndrome*. This illness may produce permanent mental retardation, as well as facial deformities, in the children who must endure this toxic prenatal environment.

The National Institute on Alcohol Abuse and Alcoholism has developed a list of seven questions for self-diagnosis of alcoholism (see Table 5.4). A "yes" answer to even one question may suggest that alcohol is a problem. Affirmative answers to several questions should be taken as an indication that you may be an alcoholic. Most of these questions boil down to a central issue: Is your use of alcohol creating problems in other areas of your life?

Heavy drinkers experience withdrawal symptoms when they stop drinking alcohol. In withdrawal from chronic intoxication, symptoms may be severe, including convulsions, hallucinations, tremors, agitation, and even death (Seymour & Smith, 1987). Chronic alcoholism can be treated through medical intervention, through a peer counseling program such as Alcoholics Anonymous, through therapy that combines cognitive and behavioral change (Parks, Marlatt, & Anderson, 2001), or through a combination of treatments.

In withdrawal from acute intoxication, typical symptoms are headache, loss of appetite, nausea, and shakiness—in short, a hangover. Detoxification from a hangover is simply a matter of time. As time passes, the body metabolizes the alcohol and the symptoms dissipate. Drinking coffee does not reduce the effects of alcohol. Instead, it creates a wide-awake, stimulated drunk. Drinking a lot of nonalcoholic liquids can help, as can moderate exercise. Drinking more alcohol to reduce the effect of a hangover does little good. Moreover, it can lead to increased alcohol dependence.

TRANQUILIZERS AND BARBITURATES

Sedatives depress the CNS and are used for calming anxiety and relieving insomnia (see Table 5.3; see also Chapter 17). The most widely used sedative drugs are **barbiturates,** which are prescribed to reduce anxiety through physiological inhibition of arousal. When used properly, barbiturates are effective sedatives. In low doses, barbiturates calm the user. Higher dosages inhibit neurons in arousal centers in the brain, causing sleep. Still higher dosages can cause respiratory failure. As is true of nearly all psychoactive drugs, the addictive properties of barbiturates encourage rampant abuse. Chronic use leads to increased tolerance, so that the user takes more and more of the drug to achieve the same effect. Increased dosages can misfire in several ways, however. The user may fall asleep or be groggy in situations that demand full attention. Accidents can lead to injury or even death. The user may also ingest a lethal dosage in a desperate attempt to fall asleep.

Following the development of tranquilizers (benzodiazepines, listed in Table 5.3), physicians shifted away from prescribing barbiturates as sedatives and moved toward prescribing them primarily as sleep inducers. **Tranquilizers,** another class of the sedative drugs used for combating anxiety, are considered to be safer than barbiturates because of the lower dosages required and the reduced likelihood of drowsiness and respiratory difficulties. The potential for addiction remains a problem, however. Even so, they are among the more commonly prescribed drugs in the United States (Seymour & Smith, 1987). Clearly, the potential for abuse exists.

TABLE 5.4
Are You an Alcoholic? If you answer yes to any of these questions, developed by the National Institute on Alcohol Abuse and Alcoholism, alcohol may be a problem in your life. If you answer yes to several of the questions, you may be an alcoholic.

If You Can Answer Yes to Even One of These Questions, Consider Seeking Advice About Your Use of Alcohol

1. Has someone close to you sometimes expressed concern about your drinking?
2. When faced with a problem, do you often turn to alcohol for relief?
3. Are you sometimes unable to meet home or work responsibilities because of drinking?
4. Have you ever required medical attention as a result of drinking?
5. Have you ever experienced a blackout—a total loss of memory while still awake—when drinking?
6. Have you ever come in conflict with the law in connection with your drinking?
7. Have you often failed to keep the promises you have made to yourself about controlling or cutting out your drinking?

Treatment for addiction or overdose varies according to the sedative drug. Both psychological and physiological dependence must be addressed. Chronic toxicity may be treated through a counseling and support program or, in the case of barbiturates, through maintenance via gradual phenobarbital substitution. Whereas withdrawal from narcotic drugs is extremely uncomfortable but usually not life-threatening, withdrawal from sedative drugs can be both painful and life-threatening. Withdrawal symptoms can include anxiety, tremors, nightmares, insomnia, nausea, vomiting, fever, seizures, and delirium (Seymour & Smith, 1987).

CENTRAL NERVOUS SYSTEM STIMULANTS

DRUG ACTIONS

Stimulants, like the other drugs we have considered, have been around for centuries. Central nervous system (CNS) stimulants are drugs (e.g., caffeine, amphetamines, cocaine, and nicotine) that arouse and excite the central nervous system. They do so either by stimulating the heart or by inhibiting the actions of natural compounds that depress brain activity. (In other words, they act as "double-negatives" on brain stimulation; see Table 5.3.) Short-term effects of relatively low doses include increased stamina and alertness, reduced appetite, exuberance, and euphoria. Larger doses may cause anxiety and irritability. Problems with tolerance and addiction are linked with long-term use; problems with sensitization are tied to intermittent use. Illegal stimulants, most notably cocaine, have overtaken narcotics as a drug problem in the United States.

CAFFEINE

Caffeine, a mild stimulant, is found in a number of drinks that come close to being "national drinks"—coffee in the United States, tea in the United Kingdom, *guarana* in Brazil, *maté* in Argentina. It creates fewer problems than the other drugs in this category. Chocolate and cola drinks are also sources of caffeine. An ounce of coffee typically contains 11–29 mg of caffeine, whereas tea typically contains 5–17 mg. Cola and other soft drinks vary widely in their caffeine content, depending on the brand.

Caffeine increases neural activity, stimulating ten-

Caffeine in coffee is a powerful stimulant.

© Norris Blake/Visuals Unlimited

sion in the heart and skeletal muscles. Caffeine stimulates the CNS partly by suppressing the effects of *adenosine*, a naturally occurring depressant (inhibitory chemical) in the brain. High doses of caffeine can cause anxiety, nervousness, irritability, tremulousness, muscle twitching, insomnia, rapid heart beat, hyperventilation, increased urination, and gastrointestinal disturbances. Very high doses of caffeine can increase blood pressure and possibly contribute to coronary heart disease (Lane & Williams, 1987; D. Shapiro, Lane, & Henry, 1986). It appears, though, that caffeine is dangerous for most people only in very large amounts. Someone who drinks seven or eight cups of coffee a day may be at risk, but someone who drinks a cup or two a day is not.

Although caffeine is addictive, caffeine addiction is not a major societal problem. However, the indications of addiction are similar to those of other, more destructive drugs. These indications include compulsive behavior, loss of control, and continued drug use despite adverse consequences (Seymour & Smith, 1987). Some people, for example, continue to ingest high doses of caffeine despite symptoms such as noticeable increases in heart rate, nervousness, and difficulties sleeping at night after drinking coffee or tea. Symptoms of withdrawal from caffeine include lethargy, irritability, difficulties in working, constipation, and headache.

AMPHETAMINES

Amphetamines are a type of synthetic CNS stimulant that increases body temperature, heart rate, and endurance. They are usually either swallowed or injected. They are sometimes used by people whose jobs require long hours and sustained attention. They are also used in some diet pills to reduce appetite. In the brain, amphetamines stimulate the release of neurotransmitters such as *norepinephrine* and *dopamine* (see Chapter 3) into brain synapses. The result is a euphoric "high" and increasing alertness. Amphetamines may further increase the levels of these neurotransmitters by preventing their reuptake from the synaptic gaps (Ray & Ksir, 1990). The resulting higher-than-normal concentrations of these neurotransmitters lead to increased arousal and motor activity. When amphetamines are taken over long periods of time, the levels of serotonin and other neurotransmitters in the brain may start to decrease. The result can be damage to the neural communication system within the brain.

As is true of many other drugs, the prolonged use of amphetamines creates tolerance and a resulting need for higher doses. In sufficiently large doses, amphetamines can produce odd behavior, such as repetitive searching and examining, prolonged staring at objects, chewing, and moving an object back and forth (Groves & Rebec, 1988). Overdoses produce intoxication, paranoia, confusion, and hallucinations. They also may lead to death from respiratory failure or wild fluctuations in body temperature. Withdrawal symptoms include extreme fatigue and depression. Rare or occasional use of amphetamines seems to produce the paradoxical phenomenon of *sensitization*, in which an intermittent user of a drug demonstrates heightened sensitivity to low doses of the drug.

COCAINE

Cocaine is probably the most powerful natural stimulant. It was used in religious ceremonies by the Incas in pre-Columbian times. For centuries, South Americans have chewed the leaves of the coca plant to increase their physical stamina in their rugged environment. Cocaine, commonly known as "coke," is highly addictive, especially when smoked in the form of "crack." Physiologically, cocaine increases body temperature and constricts peripheral blood vessels. It also produces spurious feelings of increased mental ability and can produce great excitement. If consumed in sufficient quantity, cocaine can cause hallucinations and seizures. Like amphetamines, cocaine appears to increase the transmission of *norepinephrine* and *dopamine* across synapses and to inhibit the reuptake of both these neurotransmitters and of *serotonin*. Increased concentrations of these neurotransmitters result in the heightened arousal and motor activity associated with amphetamines. Initially at least, cocaine also seems to stimulate acute sexual arousal. But prolonged use diminishes sexual arousability and performance (Wade & Cirese, 1991). Prolonged use also leads to lower levels of neurotransmitters and difficulties in neural transmission similar to those associated with prolonged amphetamine use.

Recovering cocaine addicts crave the drug intensely. Their prolonged use has diminished their natural brain-stimulant mechanisms, and as a result, they feel great anxiety, loss of control, depression, and lethargy.

TOBACCO

Tobacco is a plant product that contains *nicotine*, a CNS stimulant. It is legally available to adults in a variety of forms. Nevertheless, stop-smoking campaigns have emerged from widespread publicity about the health dangers of tobacco. Studies have also found harmful effects from inhaling *secondary smoke*, exhaled by smokers or otherwise released into the air by burning tobacco. The result has been increasingly restrictive laws prohibiting smoking in public places. Laws also restrict the accessibility of tobacco to young people. Still, even preadolescent children often can obtain tobacco products.

The tobacco leaf is grown throughout the world. It is usually smoked, but it is also often chewed. Nicotine is absorbed through the respiratory tract as well as the oral and nasal mucosa and the gastrointestinal

The nicotine in tobacco is one of the most addictive drugs known.

Coca leaves processed into cocaine become highly addictive.

tract. Most of the inhaled nicotine is absorbed by the lungs. Nicotine activates nicotinic receptors located on nerve cells and on skeletal muscles. These receptors use *acetylcholine*. Their activation thereby increases the neurotransmission of acetylcholine.

Tobacco has complex effects on the body. It can increase respiration, heart rate, and blood pressure, but decrease appetite. Intoxication is characterized by euphoria, light-headedness, giddiness, dizziness, and a tingling sensation in the extremities (Seymour & Smith, 1987). Tolerance and dependence develop relatively quickly. As a result, the intoxication effect is typically experienced only by newcomers to smoking. People who habitually use tobacco usually stabilize at some point that becomes a maintenance dosage for them.

Tobacco is now believed to be among the most addictive substances in existence. Fully 9 out of 10 people who start smoking become addicted (compared with 1 in 6 people who try crack cocaine and 1 in 10 people who experiment with alcohol). In 1996, the Food and Drug Administration recommended that nicotine be classified as a controlled substance. Smoking by pregnant women has been linked to both premature birth and low birth weight, grave risk factors for newborns. Most of the long-term adverse effects of tobacco occur after prolonged use. They include heart disease, cancers of various sorts (especially lung and mouth cancers), gum disease, eating disorders, emphysema, gastrointestinal disease, and brittle bones. Secondary smoke has been linked with many of these ailments as well. Nicotine is highly poisonous and is even used as a potent insecticide. Tobacco smoke contains other potentially harmful by-products in addition to nicotine, including tar, carbon monoxide, and hydrogen cyanide. During the 1980s, 5 million people are believed to have died because of tobacco use. In comparison, 1 million died from alcohol-related causes and 350,000 died from other addictions. Actually, nearly all of the stimulant drugs discussed here can cause death if taken in sufficient quantities. Abuse can and should be treated before it is too late.

TREATMENT OF STIMULANT ABUSE

Acute toxicity from stimulants must be treated medically. The exact treatment depends on the drug that was taken. For example, a massive amphetamine overdose may call for inducing bowel movements in people who are conscious. It may require stomach pumping in individuals who have lost consciousness. Overdoses of cocaine may be treated with tranquilizers and may require hospitalization.

The most common treatment for chronic addiction to stimulants is individual or group psychotherapy. Stimulant abusers need to find ways to stay off drugs. Education about the dangers of cocaine abuse and attendance at support groups are, for now, the best methods of overcoming cocaine addiction. Organizations dedicated to helping people get off drugs include Narcotics Anonymous, which helps with stimulant abuse as well, and Cocaine Anonymous.

Drug-substitution therapy is generally not used except for nicotine. For acute nicotine withdrawal, nicotine gum and epidermal patches appear to be effective when used in combination with some other form of therapy. Without additional supportive treatment, users run the risk of becoming addicted to the substitute. Stop-smoking programs (such as those offered by the American Lung Association) use a wide array of techniques, including hypnosis, acupuncture, *aversion therapy* (overdosing people with smoke or nicotine to render it repulsive), group support, and education. (See Chapter 17 for more information on these treatments.)

Finally, let's consider the remaining major class of psychoactive drugs: hallucinogens.

HALLUCINOGENS

DRUG ACTIONS

Hallucinogenic drugs are a type of psychoactive drug (e.g., mescaline and LSD) that alter consciousness by inducing hallucinations. They also affect the way the drug takers perceive both their inner worlds and their external environments. *Hallucinations* are experiences of sensory stimulation in the absence of any actual corresponding external sensory input. These drugs are often termed *psychotomimetics* (and are also known as "psychedelics") because some clinicians believe these drugs mimic the effects produced by psychosis. Others suggest that these hallucinations differ in kind from those produced by psychosis (see Table 5.3).

People react in very different ways to hallucinogenic drugs. Their reactions appear to be determined partly by situational factors. Physiologically, most hallucinogenic drugs, such as LSD, work by interfering with the transmission of *serotonin* in the brain (Jacobs, 1987). Serotonin-releasing neuronal systems begin in the brainstem (see Chapter 3) and progress to nearly all parts of the brain. The fact that hallucinations can seem so real on so many different sensory levels may be connected to this widespread cerebral interference. Some suggest that a way to think of this mechanism is that serotonin normally blocks us from dreaming when we are awake. So the inhibition of serotonin during wakefulness allows the hallucinations associated with dreams to occur. Serotonin interference is not characteristic of marijuana, mescaline, or phencyclidine (PCP), however. The mechanisms of action for these hallucinogens are still uncertain; however, stimulation of norepinephrine neurotransmission may be a factor.

LSD

The hallucinogenic effects of *lysergic acid diethylamide* (LSD, first synthesized in 1938) were discovered in 1943, when a chemist at Sandoz Pharmaceuticals in Switzerland accidentally ingested some. LSD typically causes physical symptoms such as dizziness, creeping or tingling of the skin, nausea, and tremors. It also can cause perceptual symptoms such as hallucinations and an altered sense of time. Affective (emotional) symptoms include rapid mood swings ranging from severe depression to extreme agitation and anxiety. Finally, cognitive symptoms can involve the feeling of having learned things that would have been impossible to learn without the drug (Groves & Rebec, 1988; Jacobs & Trulson, 1979).

LSD can cause people to become anxious at their inability to control the drug experience or "trip." The most dangerous time in a bad reaction to LSD occurs during hallucinations. Users may try to flee the hallucinations, which can put them into physical danger. Even LSD users who enjoy the experience can be at risk for dangerous behavior. Occasionally, users who forgot they had ingested LSD or people who were given the drug without their knowledge panic. They feel afraid the hallucinations will go on forever.

MARIJUANA

The most commonly used hallucinogen, *marijuana*, is produced from the dried leaves and flowers of the cannabis plant. *Hashish* is a stronger form of marijuana made from a concentrated resin derived from the plant's flowers. Most users of marijuana or hashish either smoke the drug or ingest it as an ingredient in food.

People under the influence of marijuana typically experience a disconnected flow of ideas and altered perceptions of space and time. Some people become extremely talkative, others inarticulate. Users may experience intense food cravings and may become impulsive. Very high doses can even lead to hallucinations, although typical use of the drug does not.

Even moderate use of marijuana appears to impair some short-term learning and memory processes (C. F. Darley, Tinklenberg, Roth, Hollister, & Atkinson, 1973; Sullivan, 2000). There is disagreement about the long-term effects of marijuana use (Gunderson, Vosburg, & Hart, 2002). Some investigators claim that it damages nerve cells and the reproductive system. Other researchers have failed to replicate such findings (V. Rubin & Comitas, 1974) or have argued that the beneficial effects of marijuana for pain relief outweigh any potential negative effects.

PHENCYCLIDINE

Phencyclidine (PCP) is popular among adolescents in some communities because of its modest price and easy accessibility. PCP somehow profoundly alters the rela-

Marijuana is used by many people for relaxation, but it has adverse effects on memory and some other cognitive processes.

tionship between the body's physical experiences and the mind's perceptual experiences. It causes extreme cognitive and perceptual distortions. Its effects work particularly on receptors that play a role in learning. Thus, PCP has great potential for causing serious cognitive deficits. Users should be medically treated as soon as possible.

MDMA (ECSTASY)

Another popular drug with similar effects is MDMA, known commonly by its street name, ecstasy. (The technical name for the drug is 3-4 methylenedioxymethamphetamine.) The use of ecstasy can cause psychological difficulties such as confusion, depression, problems in sleeping, and intense anxiety. It also can cause physical symptoms such as muscle tension, involuntary clenching of the teeth, nausea, blurred vision, increased heart rate and blood pressure, and liver damage.

TREATMENT OF HALLUCINOGEN ABUSE

Acute overdoses of hallucinogens are normally treated by a therapist attempting to talk to the user. The goal is to reduce anxiety reactions and to make the user feel as comfortable as possible ("talking the user down"). Tranquilizers are sometimes used. A final alternative is antipsychotic drugs. Chronic use of hallucinogens can lead to prolonged psychotic reactions, severe and sometimes life-threatening depression, a worsening of pre-existing psychiatric problems, and flashbacks of past drug experiences without further ingestion of the drug (Seymour & Smith, 1987). Scientists do not understand how flashbacks occur. They have not yet found any physiological mechanism that can account for them.

In sum, consciousness is our means of monitoring and evaluating the environment. Through consciousness, we come to experience the world in our own terms. Altered states of consciousness enrich our lives. Some of them, such as sleep, seem to be necessary to our survival. Other altered states, however, are produced by substances that may have considerable addictive potential. Whatever the reasons for taking addictive psychoactive drugs, people need to learn that the harmful outcomes generally outweigh any perceived benefits. Learning is the topic of the next chapter.

✓CONCEPT CHECK 6

1. Opioids, unlike opiates, are
   a. natural.
   b. synthetic.
   c. analytic.
   d. nonaddictive.
2. A drug used to combat drug addiction is
   a. acetylcholine.
   b. epinephrine.
   c. laetrile.
   d. naloxone.
3. Caffeine is
   a. habit-forming but not addictive.
   b. never habit-forming or addictive.
   c. potentially addictive.
   d. a depressant.

UNIFYING PSYCHOLOGY

THE EFFECTS OF SLEEP DEPRIVATION

Most of what we know about sleep is based on the results of research conducted by **psychophysiologists.** Psychophysiologists are psychologists who study behavior and emotion by measuring such physiological responses as heart and respiration rates, muscle activity, electrical skin responses, and electrical activity in the brain. Their research helps us understand changes in brain activity in people who have been deprived of sleep or engaged in intense physical exertion.

Research conducted by psychophysiologists has revealed that sleep deprivation alters normal sleep rhythms during the following night, when subjects experience increased REM sleep and less deep sleep. This result is very different from the change in sleep patterns observed in runners after they race for 20 miles or farther. The night after an extremely strenuous race, runners spend less time in REM sleep and more time in deep sleep, especially

in Stage 4 (Torsvall, Akerstedt, & Lindbeck, 1984).

Psychophysiologists have examined the effects of sleep deprivation on brain activity, but not its effect on behavior. Fortunately, health psychologists, developmental psychologists, cognitive psychologists, clinical psychologists, and neuropsychologists also conduct research on the effects of sleep deprivation. For example, **health psychologists** study the relationship between sleep deprivation and traffic accidents. **Developmental psychologists** examine the effects of sleep deprivation on children's temperament, cognitive development, and academic achievement. **Cognitive psychologists** concentrate on how sleep deprivation affects attention, thinking, memory, and language skills in children and adults. **Clinical psychologists** focus on the relationship between sleep deprivation and behavioral problems in clinical populations, such as people with

asthma, sleep apnea, attention-deficit/ hyperactivity disorder, schizophrenia, or autism. **Neuropsychologists** measure brain functioning in people who are sleep-deprived.

Avi Sadeh and his colleagues at Tel Aviv University recently examined the cognitive and behavioral effects of sleep deprivation in 135 healthy children in the second, fourth, and sixth grades (Sadeh, Gruber, & Raviv, 2002). To assess cognitive functioning, Sadeh and his colleagues used neuropsychological tests that included a continuous performance test (in which a child watched pictures of animals that were continually shown on a computer monitor and pressed a key as quickly as possible whenever a cat appeared) and a symbol-digit substitution test (in which a child was shown nine pairs of symbols and digits on the computer monitor and typed in corresponding digits).

continued

Sadeh and his fellow investigators also used the Child Behavior Checklist, an assessment instrument developed by clinical psychologists to measure behavioral problems in the children.

Each child's sleep was monitored for five nights with a device that measured movement. The researchers calculated the number of hours the children slept and the number of times they awakened. Children who slept for fewer hours and who woke up more often performed less well than the other children on tests that required high levels of cognitive functioning, particularly the symbol-digit substitu-tion test and the continuous perfor-mance test. This was especially true for the second-graders, the youngest children in the study, whose cognitive performance was seriously disrupted by a lack of sleep.

According to Sadeh and his col-leagues, sleep deprivation was also associated with behavior problems. Children who woke up at least three times per night, or spent at least 10% of the night awake, had significantly higher scores on assessments of be-havior problems. They were observed to be significantly more delinquent and to think in significantly more disordered ways than children who slept well during the test period. Using neuropsychological and clinical tests, these cognitive psychologists were able to demonstrate a relationship be-tween sleep deprivation and cognitive and behavioral problems in children (Sadeh, Gruber, & Raviv, 2002).

Taken as a whole, research con-ducted by psychophysiologists and physiological, health, developmental, cognitive, and clinical psychologists has conclusively determined that sleep deprivation affects brain activity, cog-nition, mood, and behavior in adults and children.

SUMMARY

PAYING ATTENTION 176

How do we manage to pay attention to some things in the environment and to tune out others?

1. *Attention* is the link between the enormous amount of information that assails our senses and the limited amount that we actually perceive.
2. People use *selective attention* to track one message and simultaneously ignore others (such as in the *cocktail party phenomenon* or in shadowing).
3. Two theories of selective attention are filter theo-ries, according to which information is selectively blocked out or attenuated as it passes from one level of processing to the next, and attentional re-source theories, according to which people have a fixed amount of attentional resources (perhaps modulated by sensory modalities) that they allo-cate according to the perceived requirements of a given task.

LEVELS OF CONSCIOUSNESS 181

What is consciousness, and what forms does it take?

4. *Consciousness* is a stream of thought or awareness—the state of mind by which we compare possibili-ties for what we might perceive, and then select some of these possibilities and reject others.

5. Some of the functions of consciousness are to aid in our species' survival, to keep track of (monitor and evaluate) the environment, to sift important from unimportant information, and to facilitate memory and planning.
6. John Locke believed that consciousness is essen-tial to establishing a sense of personal identity.
7. Consciousness occurs on multiple levels. The *pre-conscious* level is immediately prior to or just out-side of consciousness. The *unconscious* level is deeper, and we normally can gain access to it only with great difficulty or via dreams.

SLEEP 184

Why do we sleep? What mechanisms are involved in producing sleep?

8. Scientists have isolated several chemical sleep substances in our bodies, although it has not been verified that any of these is fully responsible for our normal sleep.
9. In the absence of typical environmental cues, peo-ple seem to settle on a daily, or *circadian, rhythm* of about 25 hours.
10. If people are deprived of sleep for several days, they show increasingly severe maladaptive symp-toms. By the fourth day of deprivation, they often

show signs of psychopathology, such as paranoid delusions of persecution.

11. There are two basic kinds of sleep: *REM sleep* and *non-REM (N-REM) sleep*. The former is characterized by rapid eye movements and is usually accompanied by dreaming. N-REM sleep is customarily divided into a series of four stages of successively deeper sleep and is seldom accompanied by dreaming.

12. *Insomnia* is a condition in which an individual has trouble falling asleep, wakes up during the night, or wakes up too early in the morning. *Narcolepsy* is a syndrome characterized by the strong impulse to sleep during the day or when it is otherwise undesirable to do so. *Sleep apnea* is a syndrome in which oxygen intake is temporarily impaired during sleep. *Somnambulism* (sleepwalking) most often occurs in children. Contrary to popular belief, somnambulists are typically not dreaming while they are engaging in wakeful-seeming behaviors in their sleep.

DREAMS 191

Why do we dream? What are some of the main theories of dreaming?

13. Several theories of dreaming have been proposed. According to Freud, dreams express the hidden wishes of the unconscious. Another view is that dreams represent a kind of mental housekeeping. A cognitive view holds that we work out our daily problems through dreams. According to McCarley and Hobson's *activation–synthesis hypothesis*, dreams represent our subjective interpretation of nocturnal brain activity.

14. *Nightmares* are anxiety-arousing dreams that may lead to a person's waking up, sometimes seemingly to avoid some threat that emerges in the nightmares. *Night terrors* are sudden awakenings from N-REM sleep that are accompanied by feelings of intense fright or panic.

HYPNOSIS AND MEDITATION 193

What is hypnosis and why does it occur? What is meditation and how is it produced?

15. *Hypnosis* is an altered state of consciousness in which a person becomes extremely sensitive to, and often compliant with, the communications of the hypnotist. The hypnotized person accepts distortions of reality that would not be accepted in the normal waking state of consciousness.

16. Some psychologists question whether hypnotism is a genuine psychological phenomenon; they suggest instead that it is an epiphenomenon, in which research participants respond to demands, pleasing the hypnotist by doing what he or she says to do.

17. A *posthypnotic suggestion* is a means by which hypnotized people can be asked to do something—typically something that they would not normally do or might have difficulty doing—after the hypnotic trance is removed.

18. Various theories of hypnosis have been proposed. One theory views it as a form of deep relaxation. Another theory considers hypnosis as genuine involvement in a play-acted role. A third views it as a form of split consciousness; that is, a hidden observer in the person observes what is going on, as though from the outside, at the same time that the person responds to hypnotic suggestions.

19. *Meditation* is a set of techniques to alter one's state of consciousness by shifting away from an active, linear mode of thinking toward a more receptive and quiescent mode. Meditation generally decreases respiration, heart rate, blood pressure, and muscle tension.

20. Two main kinds of meditation are *concentrative*, in which the meditator focuses on an object or thought and attempts to remove all else from consciousness, and *opening-up*, in which the meditator attempts to integrate meditation with, rather than separate it from, other activities.

PSYCHOACTIVE DRUGS 197

What are the main psychoactive drugs, and what are their psychological consequences?

21. A person's current state of consciousness can be altered by four kinds of *psychoactive* drugs: narcotics, CNS (central nervous system) depressants, CNS stimulants, and hallucinogens.

22. *Narcotics*, including natural *opiates* and synthetic *opioids*, produce some degree of numbness, stupor, often a feeling of well-being, or freedom from pain.

23. *Tolerance* is a lessening of the effects of a drug with prolonged use, which can lead users to take larger amounts of the drug. *Withdrawal* is the temporary discomfort, which may be severe, following discontinuation of a psychoactive drug.

24. *Depressants*, including alcohol and *sedative* drugs, slow the operation of the central nervous system. In contrast, *stimulants*, including *caffeine*, *nicotine*, *cocaine*, and *amphetamines*, speed up the operation of the central nervous system.

25. *Hallucinogens*, including LSD, marijuana, PCP, and ecstasy, produce distorted perceptions of reality.

KEY TERMS

activation–synthesis hypothesis 192
dreams are our interpretation of nocturnal brain activity
amphetamines 202
CNS stimulant
attention 176
into that we actually perceive
barbiturates 201
↓ anxiety, inhibit arousal
blindsight 182
see but unaware
caffeine 202
CNS stimulant
central nervous system (CNS)
  depressant 199 *slow CNS*
central nervous system (CNS)
  stimulant 202 *speed CNS*
circadian rhythm 185 *24 hr biological cycles*
cocaine 203 *CNS stimulant*
cocktail party phenomenon 176
selective attention
concentrative meditation 195
focus on object or thought
consciousness 176
awareness of stimuli
daydreaming 192
shift from external to internal

hallucinations 187
seeing something that is not there
hallucinogenic 204
induce hallucinations
hypnosis 193
altered state of consciousness, deep relaxation
illusions 187
distorted perceptions
insomnia 188
disturbances of sleep
intoxicated 200
stupefied by toxins in depressants
meditation 195
alter consciousness through contemplation
narcolepsy 190
fall asleep during day
narcotic 198
derived from opium
neodissociative theory 194
separate minds during hypnosis
N-REM sleep 188
non-rapid eye movement, 4 stages
opening-up meditation 196
everyday life
opiates 198
narcotic
opioids 198
synthetic
overdose 198
lethal dose
posthypnotic suggestion 193
hypnotized people do something after hypnosis is removed

preconscious 182 *not readily available*
could become conscious
psychoactive 197
drugs affect mood and behavior
REM sleep 188
rapid eye movement, dreaming
sedatives 201
depress CNS
selective attention 177
track one message, ignore another
simulating paradigm 193
one group hypnotized, other not
sleep apnea 190
stop breathing
somnambulism 190
sleep walking
Stroop effect 179
color test
subconscious 182
not easily accessible
tobacco 203
CNS stimulant
tolerance 198
drugs have less effect
tranquilizers 201
CNS depressants
unconscious 182
same as subconscious
withdrawal 198
discomforts from decreased drug use

ANSWERS TO CONCEPT CHECKS

Concept Check 1

1. b   2. a   3. b

Concept Check 2

1. b   2. d   3. c

Concept Check 3

1. a   2. c   3. c

Concept Check 4

1. c   2. a   3. a

Concept Check 5

1. c   2. a   3 b

Concept Check 6

1. b   2. d   3. c

KNOWLEDGE CHECK

1. Attentional resource theories are characterized by
   a. an early filter.
   b. a late filter.
   c. an attenuating filter.
   d. no filter.
2. Automatic behaviors are viewed as being stored at the
   a. conscious level.
   b. preconscious level.
   c. unconscious level.
   d. exconscious level.
3. Sleep keeps organisms out of harm's way, according to the
   a. preservation and protection theory.
   b. predator escape theory.
   c. restorative theory.
   d. circadian rhythm theory.
4. During relaxed wakefulness, people's brain waves show a(n) _____ pattern.
   a. alpha
   b. beta
   c. delta
   d. theta

5. Beatrice has an illness that makes it dangerous for her to drive because she is susceptible to falling asleep at the wheel. Beatrice most likely has
   a. somnambulism.
   b. sleep apnea.
   c. epilepsy.
   d. narcolepsy.
6. Posthypnotic suggestions are intended to be implemented
   a. before an individual is hypnotized.
   b. after a person is hypnotized but before the individual wakes up.
   c. after a hypnotized person wakes up.
   d. at any time, but only if they are agreeable to the individual to whom the suggestions were made.
7. Over time, a given narcotic has less effect due to the development of drug
   a. tolerance.
   b. habituation.
   c. adaptation.
   d. alleviation.

8. Which of the following is *not* typically a withdrawal symptom?
   a. chills
   b. sweating
   c. stomach cramps
   d. heart murmur
9. Alcohol interferes with the effectiveness of the neurotransmitter
   a. choline.
   b. arginine.
   c. lysine.
   d. dopamine.
10. Long-term toxicity effects are referred to as
    a. acute.
    b. chronic.
    c. obtuse.
    d. scaline.

Answers
1. d   2. b   3. a   4. a   5. d   6. c   7. a   8. d
9. d   10. b

THINK ABOUT IT

1. What are your normal sleep patterns? How do you react when your normal patterns are interrupted?
2. Why might meditation improve psychological well-being in some people?
3. What effect does divided attention have on your work, for example, if you listen to music and work at the same time?
4. Why is hypnosis used in some psychotherapeutic contexts?

5. How should society regulate the sale, purchase, possession, and use of psychoactive drugs? How should society respond to individuals who abuse such drugs but who do not directly harm others with their drug use?
6. What factors do you believe lead people to abuse psychoactive drugs? What do you believe can be done to help people to avoid becoming involved in the abuse of these drugs?

For a chapter tutorial quiz, direct links to Internet sites, and other useful features, visit the book-specific website at http://psychology.wadsworth.com/sternberg4e. You can also connect directly to the following sites:

Sleepnet
http://www.sleepnet.com
This site attempts to link all Internet sleep resources. Included are links to information about sleep disorders, sleep deprivation, dreaming, and many other topics.

Circadian Learning Center
http://www.circadian.com/learning_center/
Are you sleepy all the time? Do you have trouble concentrating? At this circadian learning center you will learn more about how circadian rhythms, your biological clock, and sleep habits affect you throughout the day.

States of Consciousness
http://www.psywww.com/asc/asc.html
PsychWeb, the superb site hosted by Russ Dewey of Georgia Southern University, contains a fine collection of scientifically sound guides to three topics that too often provoke nonsensical claims: hypnosis, out-of-body experiences, and dreaming.

For additional readings on many of the topics covered in this chapter, check out InfoTrac College Edition at **www.infotrac-college.com/wadsworth.**

CD-ROM: UNIFYING PSYCHOLOGY

Disk One
Sleep
Drug-Induced Alterations in Consciousness
Chapter Quiz
Critical Thinking Questions

© Peter Beck/Corbis

LEARNING

Personally, I'm always ready to learn, although I do not always
like being taught.

—*Winston Churchill*

Psychologists generally define **learning** as any relatively permanent change in the behavior, thoughts, and feelings of an organism—human or other animal—that results from prior experience. The study of learning is an active field in psychology (Domjan & Krause, 2002) because learning is one of the most basic psychological processes: Without it, you would be a creature of instinct and nothing more. From an evolutionary point of view, learning plays an important role in the adaptation of the individual to the environment. If all behavior were instinctive or otherwise preprogrammed, organisms might come to be very well adapted to a given fixed set of environmental circumstances. But unless they were able to learn, to adapt to changes in these circumstances, changes in the environment might wreak havoc. Learning is what enables individuals, as well as species, to remain flexible and to adapt to the ever-changing circumstances in which they find themselves (see Domjan, 2000b; T. D. Johnston & Pietrewica, 1985).

Interest in learning extends all the way back to the Greek philosophers. In the Platonic dialogue, *Meno*, Plato pondered whether we are born with virtue or learn it from our environments. Plato, of course, believed that our concepts are inborn. Psychologists, however, are interested in doing more than pondering. They typically do research to test their views about learning. One type of learning that they have studied is classical conditioning.

CLASSICAL CONDITIONING

What is classical conditioning and how does it occur?

It is beyond a doubt that all our knowledge begins with experience.
—Immanuel Kant, *The Critique of Pure Reason*

Does the aroma of particular foods make your mouth water? Does the sound of barking or growling dogs make your heart pound? Each of these common responses results from **classical conditioning,** the learning process in which an originally neutral stimulus, such as the food or the dogs, becomes associated with a particular physiological or emotional response that the stimulus did not originally produce (Gormezano, 2000). In classical conditioning, the originally neutral stimulus is paired with a stimulus that originally produced this response or, in many cases, a similar or related response. The pleasurable experience of eating chocolate chip cookies may become associated with the smell of chocolate or the sight of cookies in general. This association may cause you to feel hungry or at least your mouth to water when you walk by a bakery.

The mechanisms of classical conditioning were originally studied by Ivan Pavlov (1849-1936). Pavlov accidentally noticed a phenomenon of learning while he was studying digestive processes in dogs. A meticulous investigator, Pavlov conscientiously avoided allowing extraneous factors to interfere with his research on digestion. However, one particularly annoying factor continually hampered his work. He had devised a means of collecting and measuring the amount of saliva a dog produced when it smelled food (meat powder, in this case; see Figure 6.1). The dogs would start salivating even *before* they smelled the powder, in response to the sight of the lab technician or even to the sound of the lab technician's footsteps. At first, Pavlov (1928) tried to invent ways to keep this irritating phenomenon from interfering with his important research on digestion. But happily for psychology, Pavlov was open to new discoveries. He was able to see the startling implications that any number of other scientists conducting the same research might well have let pass. As Louis Pasteur once said, "Chance favors only the prepared mind."

Pavlov realized that some kind of associative learning must have taken place. The response (the salivation) that was originally connected to receiving the food was now being elicited by stimuli associated with the food. This form of learning has come to be called *classical conditioning,* or *Pavlovian conditioning.* Having made his serendipitous discovery, Pavlov set out to study classical conditioning systematically. First, he needed to show that dogs would naturally and spontaneously salivate at the sight or other sensation of food but would not naturally salivate in response to a nonfood stimulus, such as a buzzer. He experimentally confirmed that a dog, indeed, would salivate in response to meat powder placed on its tongue. But it would not salivate in response to the sound of the buzzer alone.

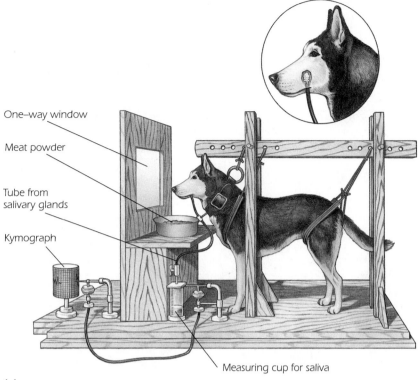

One–way window

Meat powder

Tube from
salivary glands

Kymograph

Measuring cup for saliva

(a)

© Bettmann/Corbis

(b)

FIGURE 6.1

Pavlov's Apparatus. Ivan Pavlov used specialized equipment to measure the amount of saliva that dogs produced when they smelled food. After using a buzzer in his first experiments, he investigated whether other cues could be manipulated systematically to prompt associative learning in dogs. His creative testing of alternative stimuli is an example of the scientific method at work.

Once the original pattern of stimuli and responses was established, Pavlov started the second phase of the experiment. He sounded the buzzer and then immediately placed the meat powder on the dog's tongue. After he repeated this procedure a number of times, he sounded the buzzer without the meat powder following it. The dog still salivated. It had been conditioned to respond to the originally neutral stimulus of the buzzer through the pairing of the buzzer with the food. Figure 6.2 illustrates this experiment. What are the components of this conditioning process?

FIGURE 6.2

Pavlov's Classic Experiment. Before the experiment, the sound yielded no response from the dog. Tasting the food (US) made the dog salivate (UR). During the experiment, Pavlov paired the sound (CS) with the food (US) to prompt the dog to salivate (UR). After many repetitions, the sound (CS alone) prompted salivation (CR).

THE COMPONENTS AND TIMING OF CLASSICAL CONDITIONING

Although the stimuli and responses used in classical conditioning can vary, the basic structure of the paradigm does not. To create a classical conditioning experiment, you would proceed as follows:

1. Start with an **unconditioned stimulus (US)** (such as Pavlov's meat powder) that elicits an automatic, unlearned physiological or emotional response.
2. The **unconditioned response (UR)** is your participant's automatic, unlearned physiological response to this stimulus. (For Pavlov's dogs the unconditioned response was salivation.)
3. Choose a stimulus (like the buzzer Pavlov used) that is originally neutral. This stimulus will become the **conditioned stimulus (CS)** when paired with the unconditioned stimulus.
4. Pair your CS and your US so that they are associated. Eventually, the CS alone will elicit the **conditioned response (CR),** a learned pattern of

behavior that is typically similar or identical to the UR. (In Pavlov's studies, the salivation response came to be elicited from the buzzer.)

Stand-up comics, actors, musicians, ventriloquists, dancers, and magicians all appreciate the value of timing. Psychologists involved in classical conditioning, too, have observed the importance of timing.

The effects of timing in classical conditioning are shown in Figure 6.3. Panel (a) shows the standard classical conditioning paradigm. The onset of the CS occurs immediately before the onset of the US. For example, a child starts to learn that every time his or her father comes home from work with a certain kind of a smile, the child soon will receive a present. The child learns to associate that smile with an upcoming present. In this example, the unconditioned stimulus is the present. The conditioned stimulus is the smile shown by the father. The unconditioned response is the happiness the child experiences upon receiving the present. The conditioned response is the happiness the child experiences upon seeing the father's smile. What happens if this classical timing is changed?

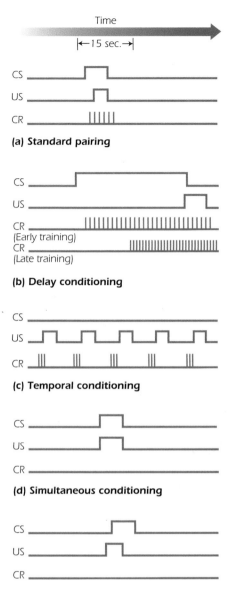

FIGURE 6.3

Some Common Pavlovian Conditioning Procedures.
Various classical conditioning procedures yield different outcomes. The stimulus starts when the line rises and stops when it falls.

Panel (b) shows **delay conditioning**, which introduces a long delay between the onset of the CS and the onset of the US. **Trace conditioning** is similar to delay conditioning, except that the CS is terminated for a while before the US begins. In the example of the child and the father applied to trace conditioning, the father would come home from work with a smile. Then the smile would vanish. And at some point thereafter, the child would receive a present. What is the result of delay or trace conditioning? Initially, conditioning re-

sults are similar to those for the standard paradigm. Eventually, however, the animal learns that there will be a long delay from the onset of the CS to the onset of the US. The result is that the CR does not appear until the CS has been in effect for some time.

In **temporal conditioning**, shown in panel (c), the CS is given at fixed time intervals between US presentations. The animal thereby learns that the US— say, food—will occur at a given fixed time. The result is that the animal begins to show a CR right before the presentation of the US. In effect, it has learned that when a certain amount of time has passed, the food will be presented. In our example, the child might learn that his or her father will give a present every 7 days. Thus, the 7-day interval serves as the conditioned stimulus for learning when the present will be forthcoming.

Two other kinds of conditioning are *simultaneous conditioning*, in which the conditioned and unconditioned stimuli occur at the same time, and *backward conditioning*, in which the conditioned stimulus occurs *after* the unconditioned stimulus. Both kinds of conditioning are typically ineffective as means of producing learning.

CONTINGENCY: WHY CONDITIONING WORKS

Psychologists—and most other scientists—are rarely satisfied with merely noting their observations of phenomena. Many of the most intriguing investigations attempt to discover why particular phenomena occur. Several explanations have been proposed to explain why classical conditioning takes place.

An obvious explanation is *temporal contiguity*. According to this notion, the mere proximity in time between the CS and the US is sufficient to explain conditioning. Simple contiguity is necessary for learning. If too long a time passes between the offset of the CS and the onset of the US, conditioning will not take place. It is by no means sufficient for learning to take place because the organism will not associate one stimulus (the CS) with the other (the US).

A now classic study by Robert Rescorla (1967) suggests that more than just temporal contiguity is needed for conditioning to take place. Conditioning also requires **contingency,** the dependent relationship between the occurrence of an unconditioned stimulus and the occurrence of a conditioned stimulus. Rescorla designed an experiment to test the notion that contingency analysis underlies classical conditioning. In the experiment, the CS was a tone and the US was a painful shock. Rescorla conducted the experiment with four different groups of dogs. In all four groups, he was looking to see whether the physiological and emotional responses of pain and fear (the URs) would become associated with the tone (thereby becoming CRs). These were the four conditions:

- *Condition A: CS consistently preceding US.* The dogs received the standard pairing of the CS with the US. In other words, shock consistently followed the presentation of a tone. The prediction was that classical conditioning would take place as usual.
- *Condition B: CS unlinked from US.* The dogs received the same number of CSs and USs as in Condition A, but they were explicitly unlinked. In other words, the CS was disassociated from the US; they were never presented together. Thus, the CS (tone) predicted the *absence* of the US (shock).
- *Condition C: Random association between CS and US* (a control group). The dogs again received the same number of CSs and USs, but now the association between the US and the CS was random. Sometimes the CS (the tone) predicted the US (the shock). Other times it did not. Any pairings that occurred were strictly by chance. Thus, the CS was a worthless predictor of the US.
- *Condition D: Random association between CS and US, except in cases of long delay.* The CS and the US were again paired only at random, with one exception. Whenever the random pairing indicated delivery of the US (shock) more than 30 seconds after the most recent CS (tone), the US was canceled. Thus, the US never occurred more than 30 seconds after the CS. The number of accidental pairings between the US and the CS was the same in Group D as in Group C. Nevertheless, the shock was more likely to occur within 30 seconds following the tone than to occur in the absence of the tone. Thus, the animals should learn to associate shock with the tone because there is a contingency, albeit an imperfect one.

The results of Rescorla's experiment confirmed the contingency point of view. Fear conditioning took place in Conditions A and D, where there was a positive contingency between the tone and the shock. No conditioning took place in Group C. In this group, although the tone and the shock were sometimes paired, the pairing was random and hence not contingent. In Group B, the tone actually became an inhibitor of fear. The dogs learned to associate the tone with safety. Thus, they learned a *negative contingency*, whereby the CS (a tone) predicted the absence of the US (a shock).

In his experiment, Rescorla showed that contingency rather than contiguity seems to establish classical conditioning. He suggested that the mechanism underlying classical conditioning is more cognitive

than would seem possible for such a simple form of learning—a view accepted by many learning theorists today for nonhuman animals (Capaldi, 2000; Pearce, 1997; W. A. Roberts, 1998) and also for humans (Roediger & Meade, 2000). In other words, classical conditioning is more sophisticated and thoughtful in terms of the functioning of the mind than it previously had appeared to be. According to Rescorla, humans and other animals try to make sense of the stimuli in their environments that affect them. The initial presentation of the US is unexpected and is therefore surprising. This element of surprise sets the stage for optimal learning in order to make subsequent presentations of the US more predictable and thus less surprising. The environment thereby becomes more comprehensible. When a CS contingently predicts the occurrence of the US, learning occurs easily and rapidly. More generally, animals appear to have some kind of mental representation of both the conditioned and the unconditioned stimuli (Domjan, 1997; Roitblat & von Fersen, 1992; Rescorla, 1988).

The results of Rescorla's experiment apply to humans. Suppose that every time you see a certain friend who lives in your dormitory, he has something nice to say about you. He might comment, for example, about the way you look, about the way you think, or about the way you act. Soon you may find yourself having a warmly positive feeling the moment you see this individual, before he even says anything. The friend represents a contingency for you. His presence predicts a positive remark soon to be made.

A cognitive interpretation of classical conditioning is bolstered by a phenomenon first observed by Leon Kamin (1969). Suppose you condition a rat to behave in a certain way whenever it hears a particular sound. The sound thus becomes a reliable conditioned stimulus that leads to a particular conditioned response. Then you begin to pair a light with the sound: Anytime the rat hears the sound, it also sees the light. The question now is, Does the rat become conditioned to the light? The answer is no. The prior conditioning to the sound, in effect, *blocks* conditioning to the light. A cognitive interpretation of this **blocking effect** (the failure of a second CS to become classically conditioned because the first CS blocks the second one in eliciting a CR) is that the rat has already become able to predict the unconditioned stimulus (such as a shock) via the sound. The light is completely redundant. Because the light provides no new predictive information, conditioning to it does not occur.

In sum, humans and other animals learn not simply because two stimuli happen to occur close together in time. For learning to occur, the first stimulus must somehow predict the second. Temporal proximity, in which one stimulus does not predict the other, by itself will not establish systematic learning.

IN THE LAB OF BRUCE W. TUCKMAN

HOW CAN WE HELP STUDENTS GET BETTER GRADES?

As a result of my research on enhancing students' academic engagement and performance in college, I had begun to suspect that many students who performed poorly actually had study skills and knew self-regulation strategies, but simply didn't use them. Low achievers did not seem to spend the necessary time and effort to absorb the information they were learning in their classes.

I had come to the conclusion from my own work and others' that achievement required aptitude and motivation, and that motivation required attitude, strategy, and drive. In my research I had been able to improve both attitude and strategy, but had not found a way to increase drive. I began to think about what might finally motivate a student to learn, or at least to move information from short- to long-term memory. And then it hit me: *tests*! As much as we all dread them, tests motivate us because they put us in a situation in which, if we want to achieve success or avoid failure, we have to learn material in such a way as to be able to recall it. In this way, tests provide an incentive to learn.

I had to find a way to test the hypothesis that tests prompted better achievement. Positive results would also imply that students already knew appropriate learning skills and strategies.

I was teaching a large lecture course that had a number of sections, all of which covered the same material, used the same textbook, and included the same examinations. This was ideal, since I felt that academic motivation and performance could be studied only in real classes involving real grades, rather than in a laboratory, where

Bruce W. Tuckman is Professor of Educational Psychology and Director of the Academic Learning Lab, a technology-based student assistance center at Ohio State University (http://ALL.successcenter.ohio-state.edu). Formerly, he was dean, professor, and coordinator of the educational psychology program at Florida State University, dean and professor at CUNY, and professor and director of educational research at Rutgers. He earned his PhD in psychology from Princeton University in 1963 (working under Robert Gagne). His best-known work includes Conducting Educational Research (5 editions), Theories and Applications of Educational Psychology (3 editions), Learning and Motivation Strategies: Your Guide to Success (2002), and stages of group development (forming, storming, norming, performing). His current work deals with the application of learning and motivation strategies to academic success, including ways of overcoming procrastination.

student behavior would not have the same consequences. I constructed a series of studies in which I manipulated a variable in the environment and studied its effects, instead of examining outcomes after the fact, where it is difficult to draw conclusions about cause and effect.

Frequent Testing versus Homework

In experiments it is necessary to control variables other than those you are studying. I needed something to which I could compare frequent testing to see if it led to higher grades. I decided to use required homework. The assignment was to outline each chapter in the textbook by identifying the 20 most important concepts and provide an original description and example of each. This would (a) teach the students the study skill of developing this type of outline, and (b) require that they spend about as much time as students in the testing condition who were given a test on each chapter.

I did essentially the same study three times:

1. On a 5-week segment of the 15-week course, in which I also included a third group that got neither tests nor homework;
2. On the whole course, where I included only tests and homework conditions and required all students to keep a log of time spent on coursework, which I then used to compare the results for high-, middle-, and low-GPA students;
3. On exactly the same group as in the second set of conditions, I used a scale I had developed to measure students' tendency to procrastinate. I compared results for high, middle, and low procrastinators.

The Results

In all three studies, students in the frequent testing condition earned higher grades than students in the homework condition (and in the control condition in the first experi-

continued

ment). The difference ranged from a whole grade (a B compared to a C) to a third of a grade (a B− compared to a C+).

What was considerably more dramatic and revealing were the results for students at different GPA levels and different degrees of procrastination. Students with high (3.6–4.0) or middle (2.9–3.5) GPAs showed no differences in examination grades in the frequent tests and homework conditions. However, students with low GPAs (2.0–2.8) who were given frequent tests averaged B− on the grade scale across the three tests, whereas those who did homework averaged only a C−,

a difference of 10% on a 100-point scale. In fact, the low-GPA students who were tested frequently outscored the middle-GPA students in both homework and frequent testing conditions. This implies that GPA is a function more of motivation than of ability, because when the motivation of low GPA students is increased sufficiently the ability they demonstrate is superior to that of middle-GPA students. Although the difference was not huge, it shows that low-GPA students are not working up to their potential, and that professors can get more out of them if they test more often.

For procrastination level, the findings were even more dramatic. High procrastinators in the frequent test condition not only outscored high procrastinators in the homework condition (by over a full grade), they also outscored both middle and low procrastinators in both homework and test conditions.

The overall results clearly showed that frequent tests worked better than homework in improving achievement. So, even if your professors don't give many tests, create them for yourself on a regular basis to ensure that you are getting what you learn into long-term memory.

RATES OF CONDITIONING

Pavlov had long established that classical conditioning takes place over a series of learning trials, not all at once (although exceptions to this rule are described later in this chapter). Rescorla and his colleague, Allan Wagner, observed the process of learning over successive learning trials. Then, building on the suggested mechanism of contingency, they proposed a quantitative theory to specify precisely the rate at which learning takes place (Rescorla & Wagner, 1972; A. R. Wagner & Rescorla, 1972). This theory is still in active use today (Brandon, Vogel, & Wagner, 2000; Myers, Vogel, Shin, & Wagner, 2001; A. R. Wagner & Brandon, 2001).

Rescorla and Wagner (1972) found that learning tends to increase at a rate that actually *slows down* as the amount of learning increases (see also Rescorla, 2001). In this pattern of *negative acceleration*, a gradual reduction in the amount of increase occurs over successive conditioning trials. The more learning that has taken place, the slower the pace of the subsequent learning. If you think about your own learning curve—when learning a new sport, for example—you will probably recognize this phenomenon. Rescorla and Wagner reasoned that, as learning progresses, the relative unpredictability of the US declines. As the US becomes more predictable, there is less need to notice the contingent relationship between the US and the CS. According to this theory, if we were to graph the trials linking the US and the CS, the curve would start to rise quickly, then taper off, and eventually reach an *asymptote*, the most stable level of response, where the degree of learning peaks. This pattern is shown in the idealized learning curve of Figure 6.4.

Consider again the example of the friend who always says something nice about you. Most of your learning occurs after the first few remarks. Suppose the friend maintains his behavior. You then may find that the increase in your positive feelings starts to slow down as no new learning is taking place, at least with respect to the friend's offering of compliments. Eventually, you reach an asymptote in your response.

Rescorla and Wagner further noted that successful conditioning depends on at least two variables.

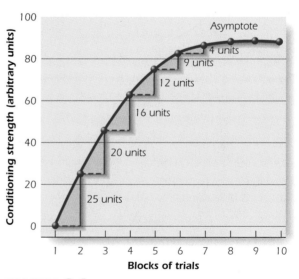

FIGURE 6.4

Idealized Learning Curve. According to Robert Rescorla, the rate of learning slows down as the amount of learning increases, until eventually learning peaks at a stable level.

The first is the salience of the stimuli. The second is the maximum level of conditioning that can be achieved for a given US. As the *salience*—the degree of conspicuousness or obviousness—increases, so does the rate of learning. For example, a strong *emetic* (chemical that causes vomiting) is likely to be a very salient US. In contrast, a barely noticeable electric shock is likely to be much less salient and to result in a slower *rate* of learning. In addition, according to the theory, different USs support different maximum levels of conditioning. A strong emetic is likely to lead to a higher stable level of learning than is a very weak shock. Thus, the second variable is the particular *maximum* stable level of learning (shown on a graph as the distinctive asymptote of the learning curve) that can be achieved for a given CS-US pairing. If we were to plot curves graphing the trials that link the US and the CS for different stimuli, each stimulus would have a distinctive curve. Some of these curves would yield higher asymptotes than others.

THE PHASES OF CLASSICAL CONDITIONING

ACQUISITION

The *rate* of learning typically *decreases* over learning trials. However, the *probability* of a given performance reflecting learning—that is, the likelihood of the occurrence of a CR—*increases* over learning trials. If students nod their heads in agreement when a teacher shows a certain behavior, the teacher's learning will be reflected by the fact that the behavior probably will become more likely. During the **acquisition** phase, the CR strengthens and the occurrence of the response increases in likelihood. Eventually, as shown in the work of Rescorla and others, the CR reaches its asymptote—its most stable probability of occurrence.

EXTINCTION

Suppose that the CS was presented in the absence of the US. For example, a buzzer that previously had preceded shock would no longer precede shock. Gradually, the probability of the occurrence of the CR would decrease, eventually approaching zero. This phase of learning is the **extinction** phase. The curve and asymptote for extinction would show a decrease in the number of responses over time, with the response level eventually reaching zero. There is some evidence that extinction tends to occur less rapidly than does acquisition (Rescorla, 2002a).

SPONTANEOUS RECOVERY

The term *extinction* may be somewhat misleading. A casual observer of an extinguished CR might assume that because the CR was extinguished, it was gone forever, as if the CR had never existed at all. That is not quite the case. The CR may be extinguished, but the memory of the learning has not been completely erased. The behavior can still be elicited. In fact, an interesting phenomenon occurs after an individual is given a series of extinction trials and is then allowed to rest. Surprisingly, a resumption of extinction trials after the rest period will result in a higher level of responding than had occurred just before it. This phenomenon is **spontaneous recovery,** in which a CR reappears without any environmental prompting. The individual seems to recover some level of responding spontaneously during the rest period, even though the CS was already absent before the rest.

New views of extinction suggest that it is relatively context-specific. If the conditioned response of an animal is extinguished in one context (e.g., a particular maze), it may not be extinguished in a novel context (e.g., a completely different maze or another environment). Thus, extinction appears to involve the inhibition of a particular learned response in a particular context rather than true forgetting (Bouton, 1991, 1993).

Consider again your friend who pays you compliments. You have now been conditioned to react favorably immediately upon seeing him. You have reached asymptotic response. But then your friend has a personal crisis that makes him bitter toward you and others. You continue to see him, but he no longer pays you compliments. Over time, the positive response you once felt upon seeing him starts to fade. You are experiencing extinction. Eventually the two of you drift apart. When you see him, you feel pretty much nothing at all. The positive response you once had has been completely extinguished. Then he changes dormitories and you stop seeing him altogether. In fact, you do not see him again until graduation, when you see him only in the distance. Upon seeing him again after all this time, you are surprised to experience a bit of the positive feeling you once felt toward him. You now realize that your positive feelings never disappeared entirely. You have experienced spontaneous recovery of your learned feelings toward him.

Note that in spontaneous recovery, the CS is presented again without the US. Spontaneous recovery is related to another phenomenon, savings. *Savings* occurs when, for a period of time, the CS and the US are not linked and then the CS is presented again in the presence of the US. When the CS is again paired with the US, even if only briefly, the CR returns to levels approaching those at the asymptote (stable peak of the learning curve) of the acquisition phase (see Rescorla, 2002b). The phenomenon is called "savings" because when learning occurs again, time is saved in reaching the earlier level of learning.

Table 6.1 presents the phases of classical conditioning.

TABLE 6.1
CONCEPT REVIEW

Phases of Classical Conditioning. Once a learner acquires a CR, if the CS and the US are uncoupled, the CR may be extinguished. Even if the CR is extinguished, however, the learner may still experience spontaneous recovery or savings of the CR.

Phase	Explanation	Example
Acquisition	The probability of a CR increases as the CS is paired with the US.	Each time your phone has rung, it has been your new beloved calling to tell you how delightful this evening will be. Your heart flutters joyously in response. As the morning progresses, your heart starts to flutter just on hearing the phone ring.
Extinction	The probability of a CR decreases as the CS and the US are uncoupled, with only one or the other being presented at any one time.	Your phone continues to ring, but your beloved is in a long meeting, so now your calls are from a salesperson, a wrong-number caller, and several people who want you to do things you do not want to do. Your heart stops fluttering at the sound of the ring.
Spontaneous recovery	After a brief period of rest following extinction, the CS spontaneously prompts the CR.	Your phone service is temporarily out of order. After service is restored, your heart flutters at the first ring.
Savings	When the CS is paired with the US again, even briefly, the CR returns to levels approaching those at the peak of the acquisition phase.	Your beloved's meeting ends, and your phone begins to ring again with frequent calls from your beloved. Once again, your heart flutters when you hear the phone ring.

THE LEVELS AND FEATURES OF CLASSICAL CONDITIONING

He who is bitten by the snake fears the lizard.
—Bugandan proverb

A man who has been tossed by a buffalo, when he sees a black ox, thinks it's another buffalo.
—Kenyan proverb

Up to now, we have discussed only what is sometimes referred to as **first-order conditioning**, whereby a CS is linked directly with a US. Suppose, however, that we have conditioned a fear response to the sound of a tone. Now we pair the flash of a light with the tone. Right before the tone, a light comes on. In this case, we might link the CR (the emotion of fear), which is already linked to the first CS (the tone), to the second CS (the light) as well. When a second CS is linked to a first one, the resulting conditioning is *second-order conditioning*. In theory, conditioning can proceed up to any level of **higher-order conditioning**, where a CS is not directly linked with a US but rather is linked to an established CS. Conditioning beyond the first order tends to be rather unstable, however, and relatively more susceptible to extinction than is first-order conditioning.

STIMULUS GENERALIZATION

As the proverbs suggest, conditioning occurs in association not only with the exact CS but also with stimuli that are similar to it. Slightly changing the frequency, or pitch, of a tone that is a CS will have only a barely perceptible effect on the CR, if any at all. The more the frequency of the tone is changed, however, the less the tone will elicit the CR. **Stimulus generalization** is a response to the observed similarity of a new stimulus to the CS that increases the likelihood that the CR will occur following presentation of the new CS. Stimulus generalization thus results in an expansion of the range of stimuli that produce the CR, such that stimuli that resemble the CS can also elicit the CR.

A famous experiment involving stimulus generalization was conducted by John B. Watson (see Chapter 1) and Rosalie Rayner (1920). Their study examined generalization of conditioned fear in an 11-month-old infant who has come to be called "Little Albert." Initially, Little Albert was not afraid of a live white rat. Watson and Rayner paired the presentation of the white rat with the presentation of a loud and startling noise that did evoke fear in Little Albert. After just seven pairings of the rat with the noise, the rat came to elicit fear. Then, five days later, Watson and Rayner exposed Little Albert to other similar

John Watson and Rosalie Raynor with Little Albert before they conditioned him to fear the rat. Watson and Raynor's proof that fears can be conditioned is a good example of stimulus generalization. Today such an experiment would be considered unethical.

stimuli, including a white rabbit, a white dog, and a white fur coat, among other things. The fear response generalized to these other white, furry things and even to Watson's whitening hair.

Unfortunately, Little Albert's mother removed him from the hospital setting where the research was conducted before Watson and Rayner had an opportunity to extinguish the fears they had created. We thus have no idea what eventually happened to Little Albert. Perhaps the fears were gradually extinguished over time as Little Albert learned that not all white, furry things are dangerous. Perhaps Little Albert remained phobic of white, furry things for the rest of his life. Watson and Rayner were criticized in later years for failing to ensure that Little Albert's fear was extinguished. But at the time, the stringent institutional review of experiments that now exists was not required. As a result, such fiascoes may have happened more often than we can know.

STIMULUS DISCRIMINATION

As the observed difference between a new stimulus and the original CS increases, it becomes increasingly less likely that the CR will occur. This mechanism, whereby the CR becomes less probable as the new stimulus increasingly differs from the old one, is **stimulus discrimination**. Discrimination requires the ability to ascertain the difference between one stimulus and another. The more different the new stimulus is from the old one, the lower the probability of the

new stimulus eliciting the CR. In discrimination-learning experiments, the experimenter helps produce learning by reinforcing responses to one stimulus but not to another similar stimulus or perhaps a set of similar stimuli.

For example, the proverbial Bugandan who fears lizards, which somewhat resemble snakes, would be less likely to be afraid of a long, thin, but furry mammal, such as a weasel or a mink. He or she would be even less likely to fear pigs, elephants, or buffalo. The fabled Kenyan who fears both the buffalo and the black ox might feel mildly anxious at the sight of a pig or an elephant. However, he or she would be fearless at the sight of a snake, a lizard, or a weasel. Thus, for the snake-shy Bugandan, the fine gradations of discrimination center on the stimulus's similarity to the snake; for the buffalo-fearing Kenyan, being able to discriminate among animals that resemble the buffalo determines his likelihood of experiencing fear.

PREPAREDNESS

An interesting follow-up to this story is that although fears may be learned, predispositions to have certain fears may be innate. In particular, research suggests that rhesus monkeys do not innately fear snakes. They do have an apparent predisposition to fear snakes, however (Cook & Mineka, 1990). Organisms appear to have a *preparedness* to learn. They learn some associations more easily than others (Seligman, 1971). For example, phobias of some things, such as spiders and snakes, are much more common than phobias of objects like flowers and rain. Many investigators believe that these differences in preparedness reflect evolutionary programming: Spiders and snakes *are* more likely to be dangerous to humans than are flowers and rain.

STIMULUS AND RESPONSE: A QUALITATIVE RELATIONSHIP

Up to now, we have described conditioned and unconditioned stimuli that bear only an arbitrary relationship to each other—for example, a tone and an electric shock. Does the nature of the CS and the US ever make any difference? Apparently, it does, although this relationship was not appreciated until the 1960s. In fact, the discovery of a relationship we now consider "obvious" was not at all obvious prior to its discovery. Psychologists used to think that the nature of the association between the CS and the US was irrelevant to the rate at which conditioning would take place.

In an experiment by John Garcia and Robert Koelling (1966), whenever a group of experimental rats licked a drinking spout, the rats tasted some flavored solution, heard a clicking sound, and saw a flash of light. That is, whenever the rats licked the spout, they sensed three conditioned stimuli: the taste of a flavored solution, the sound of a click, and the sight of a flash of light. After they licked the spout, some of the rats were mildly poisoned and other rats were shocked. Following a number of learning trials for both the poisoned rats and the shocked rats, a new procedure was introduced: The CS of the flavoring was separated from the combined CS of the sound and the light. Thus, for each group of rats, on one day, when the rats licked the spout, the rats tasted the flavored solution without seeing the light or hearing the noise. On another day, when the rats licked the spout, they saw the light and heard the noise. But they tasted only regular tap water instead of the flavored solution.

John Garcia found that conditioning can occur after only a single learning trial. His work on taste aversion was not at first accepted by fellow psychologists because it ran counter to what was then known about learning.

The critical finding was that for the rats that were exposed to poison as the US, taste was a more effective CS than was the combination of light and noise. In contrast, when electric shock was the US, the bright, noisy water was a more effective CS than was the flavored solution. In other words, there was a natural association between taste and poison, on the one hand, and between electric shock and the combination of light and sound, on the other (see Figure 6.5). As we will see in the next section, the most effective timing of the stimulus is also influenced by the type of physiological response. In general, rate of learning is not fixed across all possible stimuli and responses. It can depend on the nature of both the stimulus and the response (Domjan, 2000a).

Garcia and Koelling's finding of a relationship between the CS and the US surprised the scientific community, given the then-prevalent view that the choice of CS was arbitrary. Garcia had yet another surprise for fellow psychologists that was even more counterintuitive to the prevailing perspective. Conditioning could occur after only a single learning trial. Garcia found that if rats were subsequently poisoned, they demonstrated a CR to the flavored solution after just one exposure to it. Because his finding so strongly conflicted with the prevailing views, Garcia had a great deal of difficulty getting his research published. People just did not believe—and did not want to believe—Garcia's results, precisely because his results differed sharply from what people thought they knew about learning. Variations of Garcia's initial experiment have shown the effect to be replicable (e.g., Garcia & Garcia y Robertson, 1985; Gustavson, Kelly, Sweeny, & Garcia, 1976).

CONDITIONED EMOTIONAL RESPONSES

We have discussed classical conditioning theory primarily in the context of experiments with animals, but its principles are relevant to the lives of humans as well. Consider just a few examples: fear and other conditioned emotional reactions, neuroses, and addictions. An understanding of these phenomena

Modality of CS	Modality of US	Classical-Conditioning Response
Taste	Poisoning	Easily paired; apparent predisposition to classical conditioning
Light and noise (click)	Poisoning	Not easily paired; apparent resistance to classical conditioning
Taste	Electric shock	Not easily paired; apparent resistance to classical conditioning
Light and noise (click)	Electric shock	Easily paired; apparent predisposition to classical conditioning

FIGURE 6.5

Sickening Tastes and Shocking Sights and Sounds. John Garcia and Robert Koelling surprised the scientific community when they found that some pairs of stimuli and responses were more easily formed than were others. Taste was a more effective CS for learning a CR to poisoning, and a pairing of bright light and noise was a more effective CS for learning a CR to electric shock.

This child is afraid of a toy turtle, perhaps because of conditioning of which his parents are not even aware.

already has led to some treatments and may lead to others.

Fear, a distinct feeling about a particular object or situation, and *anxiety*, a more generalized feeling about a situation or experience, are both emotions that we can become conditioned to feel. Classical conditioning also accounts for many of our other emotional responses. When it does, the outcomes are called **conditioned emotional responses,** or CERs, which are classically conditioned feelings that an individual experiences in association with particular stimulus events. Such responses are linked to distinctive physiological reactions. Partly because of their potent physiological associations, emotional responses appear to be very susceptible to classical conditioning. For example, most of us have experienced the *Garcia effect*. This effect occurs when we avoid eating a particular food because its taste and perhaps its associated smell remind us of a past unpleasant association. This association therefore disgusts us and may make our stomachs feel queasy as well.

CERs need not be negative. Suppose you see your loved one approaching. You may feel joyful, tingling from head to toe, because of previous pleasurable experiences with that individual. Television advertisers are experts in classically conditioning our positive emotions. They know how to use classical conditioning to appeal to our appetites for food and for sexual gratification. Their appeals lead us to associate satisfaction with new cars, perfumes, cosmetics, and foods of every shape, texture, and color. Just what are you expected to learn about a product by hearing the high-pitched acceleration of a flashy red car as a sexy driver zips around a narrow road on a cliff overlooking the ocean?

The *process* of becoming conditioned to experience particular emotions appears to be universal.

However, the *content* of the conditioning can vary widely across both individuals and cultures. In U.S. culture, total silence means rapt attention. Thus, many U.S. students and instructors have learned to feel annoyed when other people talk during lectures. If you whisper to your neighbor during a lecture, you are not likely to be rewarded. You are more likely to be punished. Students and educators elsewhere may respond differently. In India, it is fairly common for students to talk among themselves during lectures. The Indian professor typically interprets classroom chatter as an affirmation that he or she is stimulating students to talk about the topic. In fact, for many Indian instructors, silence in the classroom may be a classically conditioned stimulus that might arouse in them a fear that the students may have lost interest in the lecture (W. Lonner, personal communication, December 1993). Instructors thus may actually reward students who whisper or chatter while the instructors are lecturing. In sum, classical conditioning can arouse either positive or negative feelings, as shown in work by Ivan Pavlov.

In addition to discovering and investigating classical conditioning in dogs, Pavlov explored how dogs reacted to an unusual *discrimination-learning procedure.* In his procedure, subjects learned to recognize the differences between at least two stimuli. At the start of the procedure, one neutral stimulus was linked to an unconditioned stimulus, whereas another neutral stimulus was not. In one experiment, a picture of a circle was accompanied by food, whereas a picture of an ellipse was not (Pavlov, 1928). Over repeated trials, Pavlov changed the conditioned stimuli, gradually making the circle more like the ellipse and the ellipse still more like the circle. Eventually, the two stimuli became virtually indistinguishable. Pavlov observed that the dogs subjected to this conditioning procedure became extremely agitated, barking and howling and attempting to escape from the situation. Pavlov referred to this conditioning procedure as having induced an *experimental neurosis,* a maladjustment in behavior or cognitive processing in which the discriminative stimulus is so ambiguous that it is virtually impossible to discern whether a particular response is appropriate or inappropriate. What at first seems like a clear choice becomes less and less clear, leading to conflict on the part of the learner.

It is possible that some disorders (maladjustments in living) develop as a result of a classical conditioning procedure similar to the one Pavlov used in his laboratory. Pavlov's idea that his discoveries about experimental neurosis in animals apply to humans is not as widely accepted as are his discoveries about classical conditioning overall. Still, it is easy to see how such disorders might develop.

Sometimes it is difficult to tell which stimuli are associated with which responses. Some people make us feel both excited with passion and frustrated with anger. Some situations strike fear in our hearts, yet thrill us with the possibility of tremendous rewards. In each case, it is not clear whether the relevant stimulus is aversive or delightful, with the result that we find ourselves agitated when exposed to it. Like Pavlov's dogs, we may be experiencing a neurosis induced through classical conditioning.

We can also become addicted to harmful substances through the mechanisms of classical conditioning as well as other mechanisms. Addictions are persistent, habitual, or compulsive physiological or at least psychological dependencies on one or more psychoactive drugs. Addictions are extremely complex, which is one reason they are so hard to break (see Chapter 5). At least in part, however, addictions appear to be classically conditioned. Consider the consumption of alcoholic beverages. Many people find the state of intoxication induced by the alcohol to be pleasant, so that this state (or the emotion associated with the anticipation of it) becomes the US. Unfortunately, over time, it takes more and more of a given drug to produce the same effect. This phenomenon tends to lead to drug abuse. The need for more of the substance to produce the same effect, however, is partly driven by the environmental context. If the user abuses a drug in a novel environment, the amount needed may decrease greatly. The result is that the usual amount has a much larger effect, resulting in a major overdose and potential death of the user.

Classical conditioning also has important implications for treating addictions. Simply to stop drinking—or to stop smoking, to consider another addiction—will not break the addiction (B. Schwartz, 1989). Extinction does not result from simple discontinuation of the CS. Rather, the addict has to stop the pairing of the CS with the US. Effective procedures for overcoming addictions break this association (see Chapter 17).

One way of overcoming addictions is through the procedure of counterconditioning. Counterconditioning is a technique in which the positive association between a given US and a given CS is replaced with a negative one by the substitution of a new US that has a different UR. For example, some specific drugs can cause violently aversive reactions when combined with the consumption of alcohol (or of tobacco). The idea is that the addict is thereby counterconditioned to avoid rather than to seek out the addictive substance. A less aggressive procedure is to elicit extinction simply by removing the desirable properties of the addictive substance. The recovering addict might start drinking nonalcoholic beer or smoking cigarettes that have little or no nicotine. In such cases, the idea is to achieve extinction by stopping the association between the CS and the US. Regardless of the procedure, the strategy involves using principles of learning to fight the addiction.

THE BIOLOGICAL BASES OF CLASSICAL CONDITIONING

Many investigators take a biological approach to understanding learning (e.g., Dubnau & Tully, 1998; Greenough & Black, 2000; Kolb & Whishaw, 2001; Rosenzweig, Leiman, & Breedlove, 1999). The neurobiological basis of classical conditioning has been studied extensively in *Aplysia*, a type of sea snail. Recent work suggests that the gill-withdrawal reflex in this sea animal exhibits the principles of classical conditioning, including second-order conditioning (Hawkins, Greene, & Kandel, 1998). What mechanism underlies this learning? Research suggests that increases in the sensitivity of the synapse, referred to as *potentiation*, occur at the sensory-motor neuron synapses and may partly account for the classical conditioning of the gill-withdrawal reflex in *Aplysia* (Bao, Kandel, & Hawkins, 1998). In other words, conditioning can be linked directly to neural events. Moreover, many of the molecular and structural changes that accompany potentiation at the synapse have been determined in *Aplysia* (Bailey, Alberini, Ghirardi, & Kandel, 1994).

Clearly, classical conditioning has many practical applications. An entirely different type of conditioning also offers a vast array of practical applications. This alternative means of associative learning—operant conditioning—holds similar potential for improving people's lives when it is understood and applied appropriately.

✓CONCEPT CHECK 1

1. Suppose that once, when you were with a friend, you received a really bad piece of news. Now, every time you see the friend, you feel uncomfortable. Your friend is serving as a(n)
   a. unconditioned stimulus.
   b. conditioned stimulus.
   c. unconditioned response.
   d. conditioned response.
2. According to Rescorla, conditioning is a function of
   a. temporal contiguity.
   b. luck.
   c. motivation.
   d. contingency.
3. The joy you feel at the approach of a loved one is a(n)
   a. conditioned emotional response.
   b. unconditioned emotional response.
   c. conditioned emotional stimulus.
   d. unconditioned emotional stimulus.

OPERANT CONDITIONING

What is operant conditioning and how does it occur?

He who learns and runs away will live to learn another day.
—Edward Lee Thorndike

In **operant conditioning** (or *instrumental conditioning*), learning occurs as a result of stimuli that either strengthen (through reinforcement) or weaken (through punishment or lack of reinforcement) the likelihood of a given behavioral response. The organism operates on the environment to create reinforcement: Behavior is *emitted*, meaning that it is executed voluntarily rather than executed largely in response to a particular stimulus. Much everyday learning occurs through random trial-and-error reactions to the environment. Operant conditioning is the kind of learning that takes place in such situations.

Suppose that there is a vending machine on your dormitory floor. On the machine is a sign saying "1 dollar" for a can of soda. You put in a dollar's worth of change. Nothing comes out. You trying shaking the machine. Still nothing happens. There is a number to call to get a refund, but you do not want to bother. You leave the machine feeling angry. A week later, you are thirsty. You pass by the machine. You decide to give it one more try. In goes your dollar. Out comes nothing. You mutter something under your breath. Then you go to a local convenience store. You never use the soda machine again. You have learned something about the machine, not through classical conditioning but through operant conditioning. This kind of learning was first demonstrated in a very different context.

The study of operant conditioning is usually viewed as originating with Edward Lee Thorndike. Through experiments with cats in *puzzle boxes*, which present cats with problems to solve, Thorndike (1898, 1911) discovered this distinct type of learning. Consider the hungry cat in the puzzle box shown in Figure 6.6. The door to the puzzle box is held tightly shut by a simple latch. The door opens easily when a fastening device located inside the cage is triggered, usually by a button, a loop, or a string. The cat inside the cage can see a delicious-looking piece of fish in a dish just outside the cage. The cat first tries to reach the fish by extending its paws through the slats. Then it starts scratching, bumping, and jumping around the cage. Eventually, it accidentally releases the latch, simply through trial and error. When the latch gives way, the door to the cage opens. The cat then runs to get the fish. Later the cat is placed in the cage again. Now the whole procedure is repeated. This time the scratching and jumping around do not last very long.

FIGURE 6.6

Thorndike's Puzzle Box. Edward Lee Thorndike's puzzle box demonstrates operant conditioning—that is, how an animal (including a human) can learn a behavior by interacting with its environment. In this case, the cat in the box learns how to release the latch, so it can get out of the box and eat the fish.

As Thorndike (1898) explained, "After many trials, the cat will, when put in the box, immediately claw the button or loop in a definite way" to release the latch. This action opens the cage so the cat can get the fish.

LAW OF EFFECT

It is a process of selection among reactions . . . by eliminating the unsuitable reaction directly by discomfort, and also by positively selecting the suitable one by pleasure. . . . It is of tremendous usefulness.
—Edward Lee Thorndike

Thorndike proposed a behavioristic principle to account for operant conditioning, which he called the *law of effect*. Occasionally, our actions result in a reward that has pleasurable consequences. At other times, our actions result in a punishment that has aversive consequences. The law of effect states that over time those actions ("the effect") that are rewarded ("the satisfaction") are strengthened. They therefore are more likely to occur again. In contrast, actions that are punished tend to be weakened. They therefore are less likely to occur in the future.

The main difference between classical and operant conditioning is the role of the individual. In classical conditioning, the individual has less control over what happens during learning. Behavior is *elicited*. The experimenter or the environment controls the reinforcement schedule—for example, by repeatedly pairing a CS with a US. In operant conditioning, in contrast, the individual has more control. As noted earlier, the individual operates on the environment to create reinforcement. Behavior is thus *emitted*. In classical conditioning, the crucial relationship for conditioning is between the

CS and the US. In operant conditioning, the crucial relationship is between an emitted behavior and the environmental circumstances that it creates.

In operant conditioning, acquisition occurs because certain emitted behaviors are reinforced. Extinction occurs when these behaviors stop being reinforced. Behavior can become generalized if a wider and wider range of behavior is reinforced. Discrimination can result if the range of behavior that is reinforced becomes increasingly narrow. The laws of operant conditioning have been elucidated through the experimental analysis of behavior.

EXPERIMENTAL ANALYSIS OF BEHAVIOR

Possibly the most influential of the modern behaviorists was B. F. Skinner, who developed the theory and methods for what he called the *experimental analysis of behavior*. For Skinner (1974), this meant that all behavior should be studied and analyzed in terms of specific behaviors emitted as a function of environmental contingencies. Skinner particularly prized the observation of nonhuman animal behavior as a means of understanding behavior in humans. Containers in which an animal undergoes conditioning experiments are often called **Skinner boxes** in his honor.

Skinner believed that the principles of conditioning can be applied widely in life. He focused on the reinforcement contingencies that produce various patterns of behavior, regardless of what might go on inside the head. By defining the problem of understanding human behavior totally in terms of emitted behavior as a function of environmental contingencies, Skinner created a mission for the field of psychology that was extremely influential. He believed

A researcher does an experiment in which he is conditioning a white rat using an operant-conditioning paradigm.

this mission was highly relevant to people's everyday lives.

Operant conditioning is of great importance in our lives, literally from the day we are born. Parents reward some actions and punish others, exploiting the laws of operant conditioning to socialize their children. In this way, parents hope to strengthen their children's adaptive behavior and weaken their maladaptive behavior. The same mechanisms are used in school. Some kinds of behavior are rewarded by nods, approbation, or good grades. Other behaviors result in punishments, such as isolation from other students and trips to the principal's office. Operant conditioning, like classical conditioning, can be sensitive to the context in which it takes place. It is also subject to the kind of occasion setting described earlier for classical conditioning (Colwill & Delamater, 1995).

REINFORCEMENT

In the study of operant conditioning, the term *operant* refers to a kind of behavior that operates on or has some effect on the world. Operants include asking for help, drinking a glass of water, threatening to hurt someone, and kissing your lover. Operant conditioning results in either an increase or a decrease in the probability that these operant behaviors will be performed again.

A **reinforcer** is a stimulus that increases the probability that a given operant behavior associated with the stimulus (which usually has occurred immediately or almost immediately before the reinforcing stimulus) will be repeated. Reinforcers can be either positive or negative.

A **positive reinforcer** is a reward, a pleasant stimulus that follows an operant and strengthens the associated response. An example of a positive reinforcer (for most of us) is a smile or a compliment from a teacher after we give a correct answer. Another example is a candy bar released by a vending machine after we put in the required change. When a positive reinforcer occurs soon after an operant response, we get **positive reinforcement**.

A **negative reinforcer** is a (usually unpleasant) stimulus whose removal or cessation increases the probability that the type of behavior that preceded it will be repeated in the same type of situation. **Negative reinforcement** is the process whereby the removal of the unpleasant stimulus results in an increased probability of response. Consider an example: the removal of electric shock. It would serve as a negative reinforcement if the reward of its removal increased the probability that the type of behavior that preceded it would be repeated in the same type of situation. If putting up an umbrella stops cold rainwater from trickling down the back of your neck, you might be more likely to open your umbrella in the future because you have been negatively reinforced for doing so.

PUNISHMENT

> Do not call to a dog with a whip in your hand.
> —Zulu proverb

Unlike the various forms of reinforcement, which increase the probability of an operant response, **punishment** is a process that *decreases* the probability of an operant response. (It should not be confused with negative reinforcement, which *increases* the likelihood of a response.) **Positive punishment** is the application of an unpleasant stimulus. Examples of positive punishment include hitting, humiliating, or laughing at someone. **Negative punishment** (also sometimes called a *penalty*) is the removal of a pleasant stimulus. Examples are being restricted from enjoyable activities such as television viewing and social interactions with friends.

One way of looking at the difference between reinforcement and punishment is that reinforcement encourages and to some extent controls behavior, whereas punishment blocks behavior. Reinforcement has fairly predictable consequences, whereas punishment does not. Punishment is thus a less effective way of controlling behavior than is reinforcement.

Punishment must be used with care because it can sometimes lead to unintended consequences (Bongiovanni, 1977). First, a person may find a way to circumvent the punishment without reducing or otherwise changing the operant behavior. Second, punishment can increase the likelihood of aggressive behavior on the part of the person being punished; that is, the person being punished may imitate the punishing behavior in other interactions. The stereotypical example of this pattern is when the boss yells at the parent, the parent goes home and screams at the child, the child wails at the dog, and the dog snarls at the cat. Third, the punished person may be injured. Punishment becomes child abuse when the child is damaged, physically or psychologically—an unfortunately common occurrence. Fourth, sufficiently severe punishment may result in extreme fear of the punishing person and context. Then the punished individual may be incapable of changing the behavior that is being punished. For example, screaming at a child who scored poorly on a test because of test anxiety is more likely to increase than to reduce the child's anxiety. Fifth, even if the behavior is changed, the change may damage the punished person's self-esteem. This cost may be greater in the long run than was the cost of the operant behavior that prompted the punishment.

Behaviorists have studied how to make reinforcement and punishment more effective in producing behavioral change. To correct errant behavior, punishment works best under the following circumstances (Parke & Walters, 1967; G. C. Walters & Grusec, 1977), which are useful for parents:

1. Make alternative responses available to replace those that are being punished. A Kenyan proverb suggests the intuitive wisdom of this strategy: "When you take a knife away from a child, give him a piece of wood instead."
2. Complement the punishment technique by using positive reinforcement to foster the desired alternative behavior.
3. Make sure that the individual being punished knows exactly what behavior is being punished and why.
4. Implement the punishment immediately after the undesirable behavior.
5. Administer a punishment that is sufficiently intense to stop the undesirable behavior but is no greater and of no longer duration than necessary.
6. Try to ensure that it is impossible to escape punishment if the behavior is demonstrated.
7. Use negative punishment or penalties—removal of pleasant stimuli—rather than physical or emotional pain as a punisher.
8. Take advantage of the natural predilection to escape from and to avoid punishment. Use punishment in situations in which the desired alternative behavior involves escape from or avoidance of a dangerous situation (e.g., teaching a child to seek escape from dangerous places or to avoid dangerous objects).

Punishment can be used in operant conditioning. In **aversive conditioning**, the individual is encouraged to avoid a particular behavior or setting as a consequence of punishment in association with the given behavior or setting. The goal of aversive conditioning is avoidance learning. In **avoidance learning,** an individual learns to refrain from a particular behavior or keep away from a particular stimulus. For example, rats can learn to avoid a particular behavior (such as scratching at a door latch) by being aversively conditioned (such as through shocks) to avoid that behavior. Or children can learn not to touch hot burners if they are accidentally burned by them. Note that the aversive conditioning that leads to avoidance learning may also lead to some classical conditioning. In the case of rats that learn to avoid scratching at a latch, the rats also may learn (through classical conditioning) to fear the latch or even the area near the latch. Operant conditioning through the use of punishment leads to the behavioral outcome of avoidance. The classical conditioning that may accompany it leads to the emotional and physiological response of fear. Thus, the two forms of learning may interact complementarily to strengthen the outcome.

DISCRIMINATING BETWEEN REINFORCEMENT AND PUNISHMENT

To summarize, reinforcement *increases* the probability of some future response. Punishment *decreases* the probability. Reinforcement can involve the presentation of a rewarding stimulus (positive reinforcement) or the removal of an aversive stimulus (negative reinforcement). Punishment can involve the presentation of an aversive stimulus (positive punishment) or the removal of a rewarding one (negative punishment, or penalty). In other words, both forms of reinforcement (positive and negative) teach the person what to do, whereas both forms of punishment teach the learner what *not* to do. Table 6.2 summarizes these differences.

Thus far, we have discussed reinforcement without explicitly discussing the problem of what makes a stimulus reinforcing, both in general and in particular circumstances. David Premack studied this problem.

THE PREMACK PRINCIPLE

In 1959, Premack offered children a choice of two activities: playing with a pinball machine or eating candy. Not surprisingly, some children preferred one activity while others preferred the alternative activity. For the children who preferred to eat candy, giving them candy as a reinforcer increased their rate of playing with the pinball machine. For the children who preferred to play with the pinball machine, using pinball-machine playing as a reinforcer increased the amount of candy they ate. Thus, the more preferred activity, whichever it was, served to reinforce the less preferred one.

This research led to what is termed the **Premack principle:** (1) More preferred activities reinforce less preferred ones, and (2) the specific degree of prefer-

A scholar is rewarded with a diploma and a hug from his mother.

Spanking is an ineffective and—many psychologists and others believe—inhumane form of punishment.

TABLE 6.2
CONCEPT REVIEW

Summary of Operant Conditioning. For a given operant behavior, reinforcement increases the probability of it recurring in the future. Punishment reduces the likelihood that it will be repeated in the future. How might you use these principles to shape others' behavior?

Operant-Conditioning Technique	Stimulus Presented in the Environment as an Outcome of Operant Behavior	Effect of Stimulus on Operant Behavior
Positive reinforcement	Presentation of *positive reinforcer*—a pleasant stimulus that is introduced following desired behavior	Strengthens and increases the likelihood of the operant behavior
Negative reinforcement	Presentation of *negative reinforcer*—an unpleasant stimulus that is removed following desired behavior	Strengthens and increases the likelihood of the operant behavior
Positive punishment	Presentation of unpleasant stimulus	Weakens and decreases the likelihood of the operant behavior
Negative punishment (penalty)	Removal of pleasant stimulus	Weakens and decreases the likelihood of the operant behavior

ence is determined by the individual who holds the preference. According to Premack, all individuals have a reinforcement hierarchy. Reinforcers higher in the hierarchy are more likely to trigger operant behaviors than are reinforcers lower in the hierarchy. Moreover, activities higher in the hierarchy reinforce activities that are lower in the hierarchy. Using this principle, we can reinforce someone's operant behavior by offering as a reward something the person prefers more than the activity we wish to reinforce. Thus, candy will reinforce playing a pinball machine if candy is the preferred stimulus. Playing pinball will reinforce eating candy if playing the pinball machine is the preferred stimulus.

PRIMARY AND SECONDARY REINFORCERS

Primary reinforcers are those stimuli that are immediately rewarding, such as food, sexual pleasure, and other immediately satisfying or enjoyable rewards. As you may recall from our earlier discussion of the levels of classical conditioning (p. 000), second-order conditioning sometimes develops based on first-order conditioning. Similarly, **secondary reinforcers** are rewarding stimuli that are less immediately satisfying and perhaps also less tangible than primary reinforcers. They include money, good grades, and high-status objects that may gain reinforcing value through association with primary reinforcers. Thus, when a primary reinforcer is not immediately available or is inconvenient to administer, secondary reinforcers can fill in the gap.

A common type of secondary reinforcer used extensively in operant conditioning is the *token*, a tangible object (such as a metal disc) that has no intrinsic worth but that can be exchanged for something valuable to the person whose behavior is subject to operant conditioning. *Token economies*, or systems in which token-based reinforcement is used to change behavior, have shown some success in facilitating language development and behavioral control in autistic persons, who are otherwise out of touch with their environments (Lovaas, 1968, 1977). Researchers and clinicians have become interested in using similar reward systems with normal children. A danger of such systems, however, is that under some circumstances they can undermine children's natural interest in performing the behaviors that are being reinforced (Eisenberger & Cameron, 1996; Lepper, Greene, & Nisbett, 1973).

STIMULUS GENERALIZATION AND DISCRIMINATION

Stimulus generalization and stimulus discrimination can apply in operant conditioning as well as in classical conditioning. The basic ideas are the same, although the implementations are different.

In the context of operant conditioning, *stimulus generalization* results when an operant that occurs with one discriminative stimulus spreads to another. Suppose a child is reinforced for pleasing her first-grade teacher. She is likely to continue to act in ways to please that teacher. Then, the next year, the child is reinforced for pleasing her second-grade teacher. It is likely that in the subsequent year, she will wish to please her third-grade teacher because she has learned that pleasing teachers, in general, results in reinforcement.

Stimulus discrimination results when an operant that occurs with one discriminative stimulus does not spread to another discriminative stimulus, even though that other stimulus may be similar. To continue our example, suppose that originally the child seeks to please her third-grade teacher. But the third-grade teacher does not seem to care. He does not reward the child for acting in pleasing ways. Eventually, the child makes a discrimination between the effects of her behavior on her third-grade teacher and the effects on her first two teachers, and she stops acting so as to please the third-grade teacher.

Animals of all kinds—human and nonhuman—can be trained to make subtle generalizations and discriminations among stimuli. In one research project, pigeons were taught to peck a key when a slide of a painting was presented. The pigeons received different reinforcements depending on the artist of the painting. Half the pigeons were reinforced for pressing the key when a painting by French-Impressionist Claude Monet flashed on the screen. The other half of the pigeons were reinforced when a painting by Spanish-Cubist Pablo Picasso was shown. When shown new paintings by Monet or Picasso, the pigeons generalized only to the artist for whom they were taught to peck (either Monet or Picasso) and not to the other artist. They were able to make relatively fine discriminations among painters. They even were able to generalize to other paintings of the same kind, such as from Monet to Renoir (another Impressionist) or from Picasso to Matisse (another Cubist) (Watanabe, Sakamoto, & Wakita, 1995).

PHYSIOLOGICAL CONSIDERATIONS IN REINFORCEMENT

Most of the reinforcers we consider, and the large majority of reinforcers that have been studied in the laboratory, are either objects or activities. However, research suggests that the brain itself offers even more fundamental reinforcement. Reinforcement can come through direct stimulation of specific regions of the brain. About five decades ago, James Olds and Peter Milner (1954) were investigating rat brains by using microelectrodes. During their studies of mammal brains, Olds and Milner implanted an electrode in an area of the brain near the hypothalamus. Much to the surprise of these investigators, the animals sought the electrical stimulation. When the rats were given a chance to press a bar that would stimulate this same area of the brain, the rats pressed at phenomenal rates, in excess of 2,000 times per hour for as long as 15 to 20 hours. Indeed, the rats kept pressing until they collapsed through sheer exhaustion. Subsequent research has shown that similar behavior can be generated in other species. Moreover, whereas the stimulation in this research was pleasurable, stimulation in other areas of the brain can be aversive and thus punishing. In short, it is possible to produce learning not only through reactions to external objects and activities, but also through reactions to direct internal stimulation of the brain.

The physiological processes of learning continue to be a dynamic area of psychological research. Other physiological factors internal to the individual also influence learning (see Table 6.3).

THE GRADIENT OF REINFORCEMENT: EFFECTS OF DELAYS

An important consideration in establishing, maintaining, or extinguishing operant conditioning is the gradient of reinforcement, which is the length of time between the operant response and the reinforcement that affects the strength of the conditioning. This gradient is important both for establishing and for suppressing behavior. For example, one of the difficulties people face when trying to stop smoking is that the positive reinforcement for smoking comes soon after they light up the cigarette. The punishment, in contrast, is not certain and, in any case, is usually per-

---

TABLE 6.3
Physiological Considerations in Learning. Physiological conditions can affect the rate and level of learning.

Physiological Considerations	Examples
Behavioral predispositions	It is much easier to train a seal to perform stunts such as leaping into and out of the water than to train a kangaroo to do so.
Maturational considerations	It is easier to toilet train a 30-month-old child than an 18-month-old because the 30-month-old is maturationally ready for bowel and bladder control.
Trauma and acute physiological factors	An injured leg might hamper one's ability to jump over a hurdle. Also, fatigue and other temporary physiological conditions affect performance and the conditioning experience. The effects of physiological need (e.g., hunger) on the salience of stimuli (e.g., food) are well known.

ceived as occurring far in the future. Similarly, in the age of casual sexual relationships and AIDS, most people know that they should use condoms for protection against the deadly disease. Yet many do not use them. The immediate reinforcements of not using condoms (e.g., not wishing to interrupt the flow of sexual communion) take psychological precedence over the perception of a less immediate and less predictable danger. Even very intelligent people engage in dangerous behaviors such as smoking and unprotected intercourse because reinforcement can be so strong that it overpowers rational thinking.

The effectiveness of reinforcement generally declines rapidly with the passage of time because the link between the reinforcement and the behavior it reinforces rapidly becomes less clear. The father who tells the child that she will be sorry for her misbehavior when her mother comes home is reducing the effect of the punishment by having the child wait for hours. Similarly, it is ineffective to reward children for desirable behavior long after the behavior occurs. Immediate reinforcement produces far more potent results. The principle applies to all species.

SHAPING BEHAVIOR

Sometimes, of course, we wish to create a behavior, not suppress one. We may wish to teach an elephant to stand on a small platform or encourage a significant other to do the laundry. How can we create behavior when we cannot realistically expect it to occur by chance? **Shaping** is a means of operant conditioning for behavior that is unlikely to be generated spontaneously. It works through a series of **successive approximations** (the stimulation of a sequence of operant behaviors to be reinforced during shaping of a desired behavior). Shaping is used for training animals in circuses, aquatic shows, and the like. To shape a behavior, you first reward a crude approximation of the behavior of interest. Once that rather rudimentary behavior has been established, you begin to look for a somewhat closer approximation to the desired behavior. You then reward only those closer approximations. You continue with this procedure until the desired behavior is reached.

Parents use shaping on their children all the time. For example, parents usually expect their children to show certain table manners. The parents do not expect children to know these table manners all at once, however. At first, the parents may reward their children just for keeping their places at the table reasonably neat. Then the parents may expect the children to learn properly to use each of the pieces of silverware. By raising the stakes for what kinds of behavior they will reinforce, parents try to shape behavior that will generally be acceptable.

To a large extent, you can shape your own behavior. Suppose you are trying to break a bad habit, such as

When we think of trained animals, we usually think of the amazing stunts they perform at circuses and other shows. More commonly, trained animals perform important—and perhaps even heroic—work. Working with his guide dog, this man hiked the entire Appalachian Trail.

watching too much television. You might first decide that this is a behavior you sincerely want to change. Next you might want to keep a daily log. You start with your initial level of television watching, recording the number of hours you now watch per day. Suppose you wish to cut the amount in half. Then you will want to record how many hours you watch TV each day and reward yourself when you decrease the number of hours by a certain amount. You gradually decrease the number of hours per day, rewarding yourself when you watch less and neither rewarding nor punishing yourself when you fail to meet your daily goal. When you are down to the number of hours you wanted to reach, don't immediately assume you will stay at that number of hours. Keep your log going for a while to ensure that you maintain the new level of behavior. You can use similar techniques for changing other behaviors, such as quitting smoking or eating less.

EXTINCTION

As applied to operant conditioning, **extinction** is the gradual weakening and eventual disappearance of an operant because a reinforcer no longer follows that operant. Behavior that once brought a food pellet to a rat may no longer bring the food pellet. Often the behavior increases before there is a decrease in that behavior. Parents of infants often have to decide how to extinguish crying behavior in their infants. Newborns cry periodically during the night in order to be fed. The parents typically get up, feed the infant, and then go back to sleep. But after some months, the crying behavior of the infant may continue past the point where it is desirable for either infant or parents. The infant has reached a point where he or she could sleep through much or all of the night but has become accustomed to frequent feedings. The parents typically decide at some point to stop going in to feed the infant. At first, the infant is likely to cry more. But eventually, when reinforcement is not forthcoming, the infant cries less.

Infants differ in the amount of resistance they show to extinction. Some may stop crying after just a few nights. Others may cry for a week or more. In this case resistance to extinction is a burden to the parents and to the infant as well. But in other cases resistance to extinction may be viewed as a blessing rather than a burden. Parents typically try to instill in their children a prosocial set of values, such as honesty, sincerity, and the desire to help others in need. But, inevitably, there are times in their children's lives when these values are challenged. At these times, honesty, sincerity, and the desire to help others do not seem to be paying off. Parents hope that the values and behaviors they have taught their children will resist extinction—that they will endure despite times when they do not seem to pay off.

© David Young-Wolff/PhotoEdit

A parent might use punishment to teach this child not to climb in such a dangerous place.

SCHEDULES OF REINFORCEMENT

When and how regularly reinforcement is given affect its effectiveness in producing a desired behavior. The child who always receives a dollar for reading a book may cease to value the dollar as a reward. When we think of reinforcement, we need to think of it as a phenomenon that can be administered on various **schedules of reinforcement,** patterns of operant conditioning that determine the timing of reinforcement following the operant behavior.

Up to now, we have assumed **continuous reinforcement,** whereby a reinforcement always and invariably follows a particular operant behavior. A continuous schedule of reinforcement is fairly easy to establish in a laboratory. It is rare in everyday life, however. Usually we are much more likely to encounter a schedule of **partial reinforcement** (also termed *intermittent reinforcement*), whereby a given type of operant response is rewarded some of the time but not all of the time. Partial reinforcement schedules are of two types: ratio schedules and interval schedules. In a **ratio schedule,** a proportion (ratio) of operant responses are reinforced, regardless of the amount of time that elapses between responses. In an **interval schedule,** reinforcement is given for the first response after a certain amount of time has passed, regardless of how many operant responses occur during that time.

RATIO SCHEDULES

There are two basic types of ratio schedules. In a **fixed-ratio reinforcement** schedule, reinforcement always occurs after a certain number of operant responses, regardless of the amount of time it takes to reach that number of responses. Many factory workers and cottage-industry artisans get *piecework wages*, meaning that they get paid a flat rate for completing a set number of tasks or crafting a set number of products. In a **variable-ratio reinforcement** schedule, reinforcement occurs, *on average*, after a certain number of operant responses. The specific number of responses that precede reinforcement changes from one reinforcement to the next, however. The classic real-world example of a variable-ratio reinforcement schedule is the slot machine. Gamblers are reinforced by winning coins or tokens after a varying number of pulls on the handle, with each machine set to require a certain number of pulls, on average, before it "pays off."

INTERVAL SCHEDULES

Just as there are fixed- and variable-ratio schedules, so there are fixed- and variable-interval reinforcement schedules. In a **fixed-interval reinforcement** schedule, reinforcement always occurs for the first response after the passage of a fixed amount of time, regardless of how many operant responses take place during that time interval. Many aspects of our lives are tied to fixed-interval reinforcements. In most salaried and wage-based jobs, workers are reinforced with paychecks at regular intervals. Similarly, you may study your school assignments in anticipation of fixed-interval reinforcement, such as high grades on final examinations. In a **variable-interval reinforcement** schedule, reinforcement occurs for the first response after the passage of an average interval of time, regardless of how many operant responses take place after that time interval. In this type of reinforcement, the specific amount of time preceding reinforcement changes from one reinforcement to the next. For example, in some countries that are undergoing economic turmoil, workers are supposed to be paid on a fixed-interval schedule but actually are paid on a variable-interval schedule. The workers are eventually paid the amount they are owed, but the paychecks are not nearly as regular as they are supposed to be.

EFFECTIVENESS OF REINFORCEMENT SCHEDULES

What effects can we expect from the four kinds of partial-reinforcement schedules? How do they compare with one another and with a continuous-reinforcement

schedule? Perhaps the most important point is that partial reinforcement is generally more effective than continuous reinforcement at maintaining a long-term change in behavior. If we want to establish or maintain a long-lasting behavior, we will be more successful if we partially reinforce it. This result seems paradoxical. Why should partial reinforcement be more effective than continuous reinforcement in maintaining behavior? With continuous reinforcement, cessation of reinforcement is obvious and easy to recognize. When people notice that a vending machine (which supplies continuous reinforcement for depositing money) has stopped dispensing the items, individual purchasers stop depositing their quarters into the machine almost immediately. With partial reinforcement, it is often difficult to distinguish the cessation of reinforcement from what may be merely a prolonged interval within a partial-reinforcement schedule. For example, people often do not immediately stop putting their quarters into a slot machine for gambling, even when the machine has not provided any reinforcement for quite a while.

Figure 6.7 shows the different patterns of behavior that tend to be produced by the various schedules of reinforcement. These patterns appear to apply to all organisms, including humans. Although the rate of

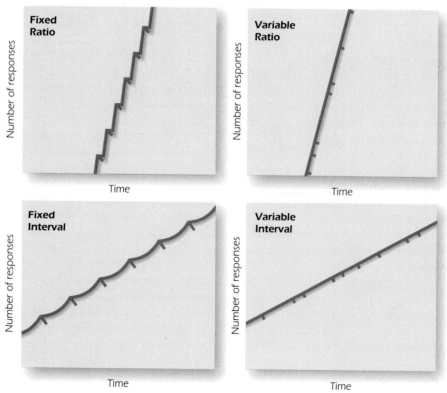

FIGURE 6.7

Typical Patterns of Response to Reinforcement. Each kind of reinforcement schedule leads to a different pattern of response. Steeper curves represent higher response rates. In general, variable schedules lead to more stable patterns of response (straight lines) than fixed schedules (zigzag lines). Ratio schedules produce higher levels of response than interval schedules.

PSYCHOLOGY IN EVERYDAY LIFE

LEARNED HELPLESSNESS

Alas, humans are not invulnerable to learned helplessness, which appears to be a fairly pervasive phenomenon. We try something; we fail. Maybe we try again and fail again. Soon we have learned to believe that we cannot perform that task or master that skill, so we never try again. The child who fails in school, the adult who fails on the job, the lover who fails to sustain a lasting romantic relationship—all of these people are susceptible to learned helplessness. Our conditioning may tell us that we cannot succeed. Some people stop accepting challenges because they feel sure that they cannot cope with them.

It is worthwhile to analyze our own behavior in terms of learned helpless-ness. In my own case, I was only a middling French student and was becoming convinced that I simply did not have the ability to learn a foreign language adequately. One day my French teacher confirmed my impression by telling me that she could tell from the kinds of mistakes I made that I had little foreign-language learning ability. I stopped even trying hard in the course, which just reinforced the futility of my efforts. I was convinced I was unable to master foreign languages, and I never took another foreign-language course during my school years.

As an adult, my work required me to learn Spanish, and I learned it quite easily because it was taught by a method that better fit my learning style than the way I had been taught French. I realized that I had incorrectly learned to feel helpless about my language-learning skills. With dedication and a style of teaching that fit my needs, I could learn a new language.

Ask yourself whether there are opportunities you are missing out on just because you have convinced yourself that you cannot take advantage of them. You may find, as I did, that you really can do "impossible" things if you only set your mind to it.

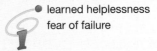

learned helplessness
fear of failure

---

extinction is greater for continuous reinforcement, the onset of the operant behavior is also faster for this schedule. In other words, on this schedule, behavior starts quickly and stops quickly. For the intermittent-reinforcement schedules, ratio schedules generally produce more operant behavior than do interval schedules. Put in another way, fixed-ratio schedules produce higher rates of operant behavior than do fixed-interval schedules, just as variable-ratio sched-ules produce higher rates than do variable-interval schedules. Note that for the fixed schedules, the oper-ant ceases for a time after each reinforcement. Vari-able schedules maintain a more constant rate of responding.

In everyday life, reinforcement schedules may be complex, with the ratio or interval of reinforcement changing with the times and the circumstances. More-over, what starts out as one kind of schedule may change to another (e.g., variable ratio to variable interval).

LEARNED HELPLESSNESS

Some types of conditioning, particularly punishment, may lead to a far more serious consequence: the phe-nomenon of learned helplessness. **Learned helpless-ness** occurs when an individual is conditioned to emit no behavior to escape aversive conditions. In a classic experiment, Martin Seligman and S. F. Maier (Seligman, 1975; Seligman & Maier, 1967) placed dogs in a cham-ber where they received painful (but not harmful) elec-tric shocks. The dogs were unable to escape the shocks. Later the chamber was divided into two parts. The dogs could then escape the shock simply by jumping over a barrier that separated the electrified part from the non-electrified part. Because the dogs had previously learned that they could not escape, however, they made no ef-fort to escape. Instead, they just whined.

In contrast, consider the behavior of a second group of dogs, which did not have the previous experi-ence of being unable to escape. These dogs were placed in the cage and the shock was turned on. At first, the dogs ran around frantically. Eventually they saw the barrier and jumped over it, escaping the shock. On sub-sequent trials, when the shock was turned on, they quickly jumped over the barrier, minimizing the time that they felt pain. It is evident the first group of dogs' feelings of helplessness rendered them unable to learn.

OPERANT VERSUS CLASSICAL CONDITIONING

By now, you may be feeling greatly challenged by the similarities and differences between classical and operant conditioning. At this point, it may be helpful to summarize briefly the features of each, as we have done in Table 6.4. Note that classical conditioning is largely passive. Operant conditioning, in contrast, is largely active. For example, Pavlov's dogs did not have to perform any overt behavior in order to be conditioned. Skinner's rats and pigeons did have to perform behavior to be reinforced.

Up to this point, we have described conditioning in terms of the observable changes that occur as a result of learning. What we learn is not always immediately evident, however. In 1930, Edward Tolman and C. H. Honzik performed an elegant experiment to illustrate an instance in which performance may not be a clear reflection of learning. This work occurred long before other researchers acknowledged that internal mechanisms affect conditioning. The investigators were interested in the ability of rats to learn a maze. Rats were divided into three groups:

Group 1. The rats had to learn the maze. Their reward for getting from the start box to the end box was food. Eventually, these rats learned to run the maze without making any wrong turns or following blind alleys.

Group 2. The rats were also placed in the maze. However, they received no reinforcement for successfully getting to the end box. Although their performance improved over time, they continued to make more errors than did the Group 1 rats.

These results are hardly surprising. We would expect the rewarded group to have more incentive to learn.

Group 3. The rats received no reward for 10 days of learning trials. On the 11th day, however, food was placed in the end box. With just one reinforcement, the learning of these rats improved dramatically. At this point, they ran the maze about as well as the rats in Group 1.

The Tolman and Honzik experiment shows the effects of **latent learning**, conditioning or acquired knowledge that is not presently reflected in performance. It seems that the unrewarded rats learned the route even though it was not reflected in their performance. Once they were given a reward, they displayed their learning, as shown by the fact that just one rewarded trial enormously boosted their performance. The key to the performance of the Group 3 rats was that they were given the opportunity to display that they had learned something.

What exactly were the rats learning in Tolman and Honzik's experiment? It seems unlikely that they were learning simply "turn right here, turn left there." Rather, Tolman argued that the rats were learning a **cognitive map**, an internal cognitive representation of a pattern—in this case, the maze. With this argument, Tolman became one of the earliest cognitive theorists to argue for the importance not only of

---

TABLE 6.4
CONCEPT REVIEW

Comparison of Classical and Operant Conditioning. Although classical and operant conditioning are processes of association by which individuals learn behavior, they differ in several key ways.

Characteristics	Classical (or Pavlovian)	Operant (or Instrumental)
Key relationship	Environment's CS and Environment's US	Organism's operant and environment's contingencies (reinforcement or punishment)
Organism's role	Elicited behavior: little or no control over learning situation Largely passive	Emitted behavior: more control over learning situation Largely active
Sequence of events	Initiation of conditioning: CS→US→UR	Operant→reinforcer→increased response rate
	Peak of acquisition phase: CS→CR	Operant →punishment→decreased response rate
Schedules of conditioning	Standard classical conditioning, delay conditioning, trace conditioning, temporal conditioning	Continuous reinforcement, fixed ratios, variable ratios, fixed intervals, and variable intervals of reinforcement
Extinction techniques	Uncouple the CS from the US; repeatedly presenting the CS in the absence of the US	Uncouple the operant behavior from the reinforcer or punishment; repeatedly fail to reinforce or to punish the operant behavior

behavior but also of the mental representations that give rise to the behavior.

Note that the work of Tolman was a beginning of a cognitive tradition for understanding learning, rather than being strictly in the behaviorist tradition. Tolman's work thus provides a bridge between strictly behaviorist approaches and the more cognitive approaches to learning considered in subsequent chapters.

> Wise men learn by others' mistakes, fools by their own.
> —Henry George Bohn

> When you follow in the path of your father, you learn to walk like him.
> —Ashanti proverb

All of the research discussed so far has involved learning through classical or operant conditioning. In our everyday lives, however, not all of our learning derives from direct participation. Consider the effect on a child of seeing an older sibling punished for something that she herself did just the day before or the effect on a drug addict of seeing a fellow addict die of an overdose of drugs.

✓ CONCEPT CHECK 2

1. You leave the key in your car and then open the car door. An annoying buzzer sounds until you withdraw the key from its keyhole. You learn to take your key out of the keyhole before opening the car door to leave. This anecdote is an example of
   a. positive reinforcement.
   b. negative reinforcement.
   c. positive punishment.
   d. negative punishment.

   key in door → buzzer
   take key out → no buzzer

2. Little Jackie likes fruit, but she likes candy even more. According to the Premack principle,
   a. fruit can be used to reinforce candy.
   b. candy can be used reinforce fruit.
   c. either fruit or candy can be used to reinforce the other.
   d. neither fruit nor candy can be used to reinforce the other.

3. You are in a relationship with someone who is inconsistent. Sometimes he or she is very nice, other times not at all. Yet you keep going back for more. You are being
   a. continuously reinforced.
   b. partially reinforced.
   c. positively punished.
   d. negatively punished.

OTHER KINDS OF LEARNING

What is social learning and how does it take place? What is the focus of systems views of learning?

SOCIAL LEARNING

Social learning, sometimes called *observational* or *vicarious learning,* is learning that occurs by observing the behavior of others as well as the environmental outcomes of their behavior. Is there empirical evidence for this kind of learning?

Albert Bandura (1965, 1969) and his colleagues performed numerous experiments demonstrating that vicarious social learning is an effective way of learning. In a typical study, preschool children were shown a film. This film featured an adult who punched, kicked, and threw things at an inflatable punching doll, also called a Bobo doll. The adult even hit the doll with a hammer. The film ended in different ways depending on the group to which a particular child viewer was assigned. For one group, the adult model was rewarded for the aggressive behavior. For a second group, the adult model was punished. And for a third (control) group, the adult model was neither rewarded nor punished. After the film, the children were allowed to play with a Bobo doll. Those children who had seen the adult model rewarded for aggressive behavior were more likely than the controls to behave aggressively with the doll. In contrast, those children who had observed the adult model punished were less likely than the controls to behave aggressively with the doll. Clearly, observational learning had taken place.

Other studies have shown that reinforcement contingencies are not needed for social learning to take place. In another experiment (Bandura, Ross, & Ross, 1963), preschool children watched an adult model either sit quietly next to the Bobo doll or attack it. No rewards or punishments went to the adult. When children were later left alone with the doll, those who had observed aggressive behavior were more likely to behave aggressively.

What conditions are necessary for observational learning to occur? There appear to be four of them (Bandura, 1977b):

1. *Attention* to the behavior on which the learning might be based.
2. *Retention* of the observed scene when the opportunity arises later to exploit the learning.
3. *Motivation* to reproduce the observed behavior.
4. *Potential reproduction* of the behavior; in other words, you need to be able to do what you saw being done.

Also, generalization and discrimination play important roles in the effectiveness of learning and in the applicability of learning to a particular context.

Each of these four conditions has several contributing factors. These factors enhance the salience of a model, although they are not necessary for social learning to take place:

- The model stands out in contrast to other competing models.
- The model is liked and respected by the observer (or by others in the environment).
- The observer perceives a similarity between herself or himself and the model.
- The model's behavior is reinforced.

Observational learning is not limited to scenes with Bobo dolls, of course. Many children, as well as adults, spend countless hours watching violent behavior on television. Considerable evidence supports the contention that exposure to violent activity on television leads to aggressive behavior (e.g., Friedrich-Cofer & Huston, 1986; Huesmann, Lagerspetz, & Eron, 1984; Parke, Berkowitz, Leyens, West, & Sebastian, 1977). Fortunately, it is possible to design intervention programs to reduce such aggression (Eron et al., 2002; D. Henry et al., 2000). One of the most effective ways of combating aggression is to set norms, in classrooms and elsewhere, that make aggressive behavior unacceptable. Aggression then may cease to be reinforced and, when necessary, may be punished.

Observational learning not only is important in identifying behavior that is typically considered to be undesirable, such as highly aggressive behavior. It also is useful in identifying and establishing who we are. For example, gender identification and gender-role development (discussed in Chapter 11) clearly rely heavily on observational learning. Children's observations of same-sex parents, as well as of same-sex peers, are particularly influential (S. K. Thompson, 1975).

In sum, observational learning is important to both children and adults. We are not always aware of its occurrence, but it is always consequential for us—whether beneficial or harmful. Those of us who are loath to practice what we preach especially need to be aware: Children are more likely to learn and remember by imitating what we practice than by listening to what we preach.

SYSTEMS VIEWS OF LEARNING

It is important to understand not only how conditioning is represented cognitively, but also how it occurs in natural contexts. Michael Domjan (1997) has noted that many animal-learning theorists seek to understand how animals learn within the context of an adaptive behavior system. *Systems views* place learning in the context of the animal's natural history. They re-

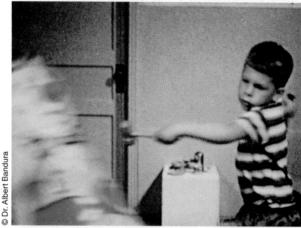

In numerous experiments, Albert Bandura showed that children learn to imitate the behavior of others. By observing a movie of a woman behaving aggressively toward a Bobo doll, this boy and girl learned to punch the doll.

quire us to examine the organism's individual experiences, its evolutionary history, its genetics, and its physiological states. Examples of this approach are an analysis of foraging behavior in rats (Timberlake, 1993) and an analysis of animal responses to predators (Fanselow & Lester, 1988).

One study of Norway rats examined social influences on food choices. The investigators found that prior association with a rat eating a certain diet tended to influence the Norway rats to choose the diet preferred by the rat with which they had been grouped (Galef & Whiskin, 1998; Galef, Whiskin, & Bielavska, 1997). Thus, the Norway rats were affected by social influences, a topic discussed in Chapter 14. Once they began the new diet, it was made successively more unpalatable. For example, the amount of cayenne flavoring in a cayenne-pepper-flavored diet was increased until the food became unpalatable. Under these circumstances, the rats *decreasingly* chose the cayenne-pepper-flavored food. In sum, the rats were socially influenced up to a point, but then palatability took over as the more important factor in their food choices. This study shows how complex a system of variables can be involved in a behavior as basic as food choice. Both biologically based and social factors as well as food availability, of course, can influence what an organism decides to eat at a given time.

Another example of the importance of context is shown by work on *hierarchical learning*. Researchers provided rats with two types of trials (R. T. Ross, 1983; R. T. Ross & Holland, 1981). In the first type, rats received a presentation of a light for 5 seconds followed by a 5-second delay. This delay was followed by a 5-second tone and then food was delivered. In the second type of trial, the rat received the 5-second tone followed by no food. The two types of trials were randomly distributed during a day's session. The researchers found that the rats came to respond to the tone, but only in the presence of the light. They argued that the light "set the occasion" for the tone-food relationship. They suggested that this kind of occasion-setting represented a new form of learning, one that is cognitive in nature and affected by the contextual setting in which the learning takes place (P. C. Holland, 1992; Rescorla, 1985).

Organisms need not only to learn but also to recall later what they learned. We discuss recall and other forms of memory in the next chapter.

✓ CONCEPT CHECK 3

1. Social learning does *not* require _____ observed behavior.
   a. attention to
   b. retention of
   c. motivation to reproduce
   d. understanding the meaning of
2. Social learning is also called
   a. observational learning.
   b. latent learning.
   c. conditioned learning.
   d. unconditioned learning.
3. Systems views may place learning in the context of
   a. all available reinforcers.
   b. evolutionary history.
   c. all available punishers.
   d. both reinforcers and punishers.

UNIFYING PSYCHOLOGY

TREATMENT FOR ADDICTED WOMEN

Drug addiction often leads to devastating losses: of employment, of contact with family, of control, and perhaps of freedom, with incarceration. Even more tragic are the short- and long-term effects on children of having a drug-addicted parent. Psychologists in many different fields are working to understand how addiction develops and to find lasting treatments for it.

Health psychologists study who becomes addicted, the drugs they use, and the outcome of different treatments. For example, Conrad Wong and his colleagues (2002) have examined differences between male and female cocaine addicts. They found that more female than male addicts in their study were unemployed and lived on government assistance with their children. In addition, the female addicts were more likely than men to test positive for cocaine upon admission into a treatment program, and men were more likely to test positive for sedatives, alcohol, and marijuana. According to Wong's study, men and women showed equal improvement after being treated for their addictions (Wong, Badger, Sigmon, & Higgins, 2002).

Experimental psychologists apply learning principles to the treatment of drug addiction. Stephen Higgins and his colleagues (2000) have developed a treatment program based on operant conditioning principles. In their experiment, 70 cocaine addicts were placed in two groups. Both groups received rewards (vouchers to use at a retail store) for participating in the program. However, one group's rewards were contingent on passing a cocaine test, whereas the other group was rewarded simply for participating in the

continued

program. A year later, the addicts whose rewards were contingent on passing a drug test were significantly more recovered from their addiction than addicts who were rewarded for mere participation in the program (Higgins, Wong, Badger, Ogden, & Dantona, 2000).

Forensic psychologists, who study psychology and the law, have examined a number of topics related to drug addiction, including the effects of jail on addicts, the use of courts to enforce treatment, and the types of crimes associated with addicts. Drug addiction is also studied by **clinical** and **counseling psychologists,** who typically focus on treatment. For example, Anita Steele (2002) has examined the effects of music therapy. Clinical psychologists Christine Timko and Rudolf Moos (Timko, Moos, Finney, & Moos, 1994) studied 515 recovering alcoholics who either received no treatment, only attended Alcoholics Anonymous (AA) meetings, were treated in residential facilities, or had outpatient psychotherapeutic treatment. They were followed for one year to determine the effect of treatment on their drinking. Those who received no treatment improved somewhat, but those in the three treatment groups improved more. The greatest improvement was seen in the alcoholics who had received inpatient treatment and who also attended AA meetings on an ongoing basis.

Because alcohol and other drugs affect the nervous system, **biological psychologists** study how addictions develop and examine the associated neuronal processes. In a recent study, a team of biological psychologists and psychopharmacologists headed by Thomas Gomez tested rhesus monkeys that were addicted to sedatives to determine which doses they preferred. The monkeys were allowed to barpress on two levers, which were associated with different doses of a sedative. The monkeys barpressed at higher rates for high doses of sedatives than for low doses. All addictive drugs show this response pattern: The highest doses produce the highest barpressing rates in addicted people, confirming that addiction must be fed with greater and greater amounts of the drug, whatever it is.

Researchers from all areas of psychology are involved in studying and treating drug addiction. Experimental, clinical, and biological psychologists all use many of the learning principles described in this chapter, including classical and operant conditioning. Together with health, developmental, social, personality, and forensic psychologists, they are improving our understanding of the development, the occurrence, and the treatment of drug addiction.

SUMMARY

1. An organism (including a human) *learns* when it makes a relatively permanent change in its behavior, thoughts, or feelings as a result of experience.
2. Learning serves an important evolutionary function by enabling organisms to adapt to ever-changing environments.

CLASSICAL CONDITIONING 214

What is classical conditioning and how does it occur?

3. Pavlov identified *classical conditioning* when he was trying to conduct experiments on digestion. After noting that his dog drooled when it anticipated meat powder, he realized that he could condition or teach the dog to have the same reaction to a sound, something that it would not do otherwise.
4. *Classical conditioning* teaches an organism to pair a neutral stimulus with a stimulus that produces an unconditioned physiological or emotional response.
5. The dog's salivation in response to the meat powder was the *unconditioned response (UR)*, the meat powder was the *unconditioned stimulus (US)*, the buzzer (an originally neutral stimulus) became the *conditioned stimulus (CS)*, and the salivation (originally the UR) in response to the buzzer became the *conditioned response (CR)*.
6. In the standard classical conditioning paradigm, the CS precedes the onset of the US by a brief interval of time. Other timing arrangements are *delay conditioning, temporal conditioning,* and *trace conditioning*.
7. Temporal contiguity appears not to be sufficient for classical conditioning to occur; rather, for conditioning, a *contingency* must be established between the stimulus and the response.
8. If we plotted the rate of learning, the curve would rise quickly but then level off at the asymptote. The rate of learning shows a negative acceleration over time.

9. The probability of learning is highest in the *acquisition* phase. If the US is not presented in conjunction with the CS, the learned response is *extinguished*. However, the learned behavior will *spontaneously recover* if the CS is presented once again. If the US is presented once again with the CS, then *savings* will occur and the CR will be almost as strong as during the asymptote.

10. In *first-order conditioning*, a CS is linked to a US. In second-order conditioning, a second CS is linked to the first CS, and so on analogously for *higher-order conditioning*.

11. When we show a CR to a stimulus that is similar to the CS, we experience *stimulus generalization*. However, when the new stimulus increasingly differs from the CS, to the point where we are unlikely to show the CR, we experience *stimulus discrimination*.

12. We seem to be predisposed toward making some associations and not others. For example, for rats that were exposed to poison as the US, taste was a more effective CS than was the combination of light.

13. Classical conditioning applies to more than just animal experimentation. Many of our *conditioned emotional responses*—such as fear, anxiety, or even joy—are linked to distinctive physiological feelings. When we experience conflicting stimuli, we may experience a neurosis. *Addictions* also appear to be partly classically conditioned, although they can be broken by *counterconditioning*.

14. Many of the effects of conditioning can be traced to changes that occur at neuronal synapses.

OPERANT CONDITIONING 227

What is operant conditioning and how does it occur?

15. *Operant conditioning* is learning produced by the active behavior (an *operant*) of an individual. According to the law of effect, operant actions that are rewarded will tend to be strengthened and thus will be more likely to occur in the future, whereas operant actions that are punished will tend to be weakened and thus will be less likely to occur in the future.

16. B. F. Skinner believed that all behavior should be studied and analyzed into specific emitted behaviors emanating from environmental contingencies.

17. A *reinforcer* is a stimulus that increases the probability that the operant associated with it will happen again. A *positive reinforcer* is a reward that strengthens an associated response; *positive reinforcement* pairs the positive reinforcer with an operant. A *negative reinforcer* is an unpleasant stimulus, relief from which also strengthens an associated response; *negative reinforcement* pairs an operant with the discontinuation of an unpleasant stimulus.

18. *Punishment* is a process that decreases the probability of a response. *Positive punishment* provides an unpleasant stimulus that is introduced after an undesired response. *Negative punishment* is the removal of a desired stimulus. Punishment differs from negative reinforcement, which increases the probability of a response. Punishment should be administered carefully because it can have unintended consequences.

19. *Avoidance learning* occurs when an individual learns to stay away from something. Under some circumstances, avoidance learning can occur after just a single trial of *aversive conditioning*.

20. According to the *Premack principle*, more-preferred activities can serve to reinforce less-preferred activities.

21. When *primary reinforcers* (e.g., food or sexual pleasure) are not available, *secondary reinforcers* (e.g., money, gifts, or good grades) can provide reinforcement if they are associated with primary reinforcers.

22. Stimulus generalization and stimulus discrimination influence the breadth of learning that takes place in operant conditioning.

23. Reinforcement can be administered directly to the brain. Reinforcement to some areas of the brains of animals can cause them to seek repeated stimulation until they drop from exhaustion.

24. The *gradient of reinforcement* refers to the fact that the longer the time interval is between the operant behavior and the reinforcement, the weaker the effect of the reinforcement will be.

25. When *shaping* behavior, such as training an animal or changing a person's behavior, one uses the method of successive approximations to reinforce operant behaviors that are successively closer to the desired behavior.

26. Operant conditioning is extinguished when an operant that once was reinforced stops being reinforced.

27. In operant conditioning, behavior can be *reinforced continuously* or *partially*. Partial reinforcement has four forms: *fixed-ratio reinforcement*, *variable-ratio reinforcement*, *fixed-interval reinforcement*, and *variable-interval reinforcement*.

28. Animals or people display *learned helplessness* when they feel there is no way to escape a painful or aversive stimulus. The original experimental demonstration of this phenomenon was with dogs that learned that they could not escape electric shocks. People often display this behavior when they have repeated failures.

29. We do not always display in our behavior what we have learned; this nonobservable learning is termed *latent learning*. Edward Tolman showed that mental representations, such as are provided by a *cognitive map*, are the foundation for behavior.

OTHER KINDS OF LEARNING 233

What is social learning and how does it take place? What is the focus of systems views of learning?

30. When we watch the behavior of others and the outcomes of that behavior, we learn the behavior vicariously; we engage in *social learning*. A classic example of this kind of social learning is shown in Bandura's experiment with children who watched and mimicked aggressive behavior with a Bobo doll.

31. *Social learning* is important because it helps us identify desired behavior and establish our identities.

32. *Systems views* place learning in the context of the animal's natural history

KEY TERMS

acquisition 221
addictions 226
aversive conditioning 229
avoidance learning 229
blocking effect 218
classical conditioning 214
cognitive map 237
conditioned emotional responses 225
conditioned response (CR) 216
conditioned stimulus (CS) 216
contingency 217
continuous reinforcement 233
counterconditioning 226
delay conditioning 217
extinction 221
first-order conditioning 222
fixed-interval reinforcement 234
fixed-ratio reinforcement 234

gradient of reinforcement 232
higher-order conditioning 222
interval schedule 234
latent learning 237
learned helplessness 236
learning 214
negative punishment 229
negative reinforcement 228
negative reinforcer 228
operant conditioning 227
partial reinforcement 234
positive punishment 229
positive reinforcement 228
positive reinforcer 228
Premack principle 230
primary reinforcers 231
punishment 229
ratio schedule 234

reinforcer 228
schedules of reinforcement 234
secondary reinforcers 231
shaping 233
Skinner boxes 228
social learning 238
spontaneous recovery 221
stimulus discrimination 223
stimulus generalization 222
successive approximations 233
temporal conditioning 217
trace conditioning 217
unconditioned response (UR) 216
unconditioned stimulus (US) 216
variable-interval reinforcement 235
variable-ratio reinforcement 235

ANSWERS TO CONCEPT CHECKS

Concept Check 1

1. b   2. d   3. a

Concept Check 2

1. b   2. b   3. b

Concept Check 3

1. d   2. a   3. b

1. In trace conditioning, the CS is terminated
   a. before the onset of the US.
   b. during the US.
   c. slightly after the completion of the US.
   d. well after the completion of the US.

2. In the idealized learning curve, the amount of learning that takes place between Trials 7 and 8 is _____ the amount of learning that takes place between Trials 3 and 4.
   a. less than
   b. equal to
   c. more than
   d. undefined with respect to

3. You thought you got over your ex-boyfriend or ex-girlfriend. Then, after not seeing him or her for several years, you indeed see him or her and are surprised to feel your heart race. You are experiencing
   a. savings.
   b. extinction.
   c. spontaneous recovery.
   d. latent learning.

4. Second-order conditioning is typically _____ first-order conditioning.
   a. weaker than
   b. equal in strength to
   c. stronger than
   d. of unpredictable strength with regard to

5. A child who at first is afraid of furry animals is now starting to show fear of other kinds of animals as well. The child may be showing
   a. stimulus discrimination.
   b. stimulus generalization.
   c. response discrimination.
   d. response generalization.

6. John Garcia surprised many learning theorists by showing that learning could take place after
   a. zero trials.
   b. one trial.
   c. two trials.
   d. three trials.

7. A penalty is the same as a(n)
   a. negative reinforcement.
   b. positive punishment.
   c. negative punishment.
   d. absence of reinforcement.

8. Food is an example of a _____ reinforcer.
   a. null
   b. primary
   c. secondary
   d. tertiary

9. Trained elephants in circuses have undergone many learning trials through a series of
   a. counterconditioning trials.
   b. extinction trials.
   c. feedback-free learning intervals.
   d. successive approximations.

10. Tolman called the internal representations that organisms use to guide their behavior
    a. images.
    b. propositions.
    c. mentrons.
    d. cognitive maps.

Answers
1. a 2. a 3. c 4. a 5. b 6. b 7. c 8. b
9. d 10. d

THINK ABOUT IT

1. In what kinds of situations does learning tend to be advantageous? In what kinds of situations might learning be disadvantageous?

2. What are the main similarities and differences between classical and operant conditioning?

3. Prescribe a counterconditioning program for a specific phobia or addiction.

4. Suppose you worked for a company and wanted people to buy a particular product you believe they need. How could you use some of the principles of conditioning to encourage people to buy this product?

5. What is something (a skill, a task, or an achievement) that you think is worthwhile but that you feel a sense of learned helplessness about successfully accomplishing? How could you design a conditioning program for yourself to overcome your learned helplessness?

6. Given the powerful effects of social learning, how might the medium of television be used as a medium for *lowering* the rate of violent crimes in our society?

For a chapter tutorial quiz, direct links to Internet sites, and other useful features, visit the book-specific website at http://psychology.wadsworth.com/sternberg4e. You can also connect directly to the following sites:

Positive Reinforcement: A Self-Instructional Exercise
http://psych.athabascau.ca/html/prtut/reinpair.htm
This site contains exercises that teach positive reinforcement. It offers a great opportunity for learning basic behavioral principles.

B. F. Skinner Foundation
http://www.bfskinner.org/index.asp
This is the B.F. Skinner Foundation home page.

Classical Conditioning
http://www.as.wvu.edu/~sbb/comm221/chapters/pavlov.htm
By now we should know what Pavlov's dogs do when they hear a bell, but do we know what an average teacher does when a bell rings? Monitor the hall, of course! Learn more about how classical conditioning can influence your actions.

 For additional readings on many of the topics covered in this chapter, check out InfoTrac College Edition at **www.infotrac-college.com/wadsworth.**

CD-ROM: UNIFYING PSYCHOLOGY

Disk One
Classical Conditioning
Operant Conditioning
Chapter Quiz
Critical Thinking Questions

CHAPTER 7

MEMORY

No Passenger was known to flee—
That lodged a night in memory—
That wily—subterranean Inn
Contrives that none go out again—
—*Emily Dickinson*, Poem 1406*

*Reprinted by permission of the publishers and the Trustees of Amherst College from *The Poems of Emily Dickinson*, Ralph W. Franklin, ed., Cambridge, Mass., The Belknap Press of Harvard University Press. Copyright © 1998 by the President and Fellows of Harvard College. Copyright © 1951, 1955, 1979 by the President and Fellows of Harvard College.

Do you remember where you live? What if you didn't? We use our memories almost constantly—to remember phone numbers, people's faces, names of people we once knew, and even where we live. Sometimes a sound or an odor can bring back the memory of an experience we had many years before, complete with a recollection or even a reexperiencing of the feelings we had at the time.

Sometimes what we need to remember is material we intentionally learned. Many of us have had the experience of memorizing large amounts of information for a test, only to discover that we seem to have forgotten it a short time later. Sometimes we do not even seem to remember the information long enough to recall it when we take the test. These phenomena illustrate two points.

First, at times we memorize or think we are memorizing material. But unless we process the information in a way that renders it memorable, we later may remember nothing of what we memorized (or thought we memorized). This issue is addressed in the section on long-term memory. Second, if we wish to memorize material for the long term, the conventional study techniques many college students use may not be adequate. This issue is addressed throughout the chapter and especially in the discussions of encoding specificity and mnemonics. In addition, we consider the answers to several important questions about memory: What, exactly, is memory? How does memory work? Are there different kinds of memory? How is each kind of memory organized? How are different kinds of memories related? How can we measure memory, and how can we improve it? To answer these questions, we first explore what memory is and how it is measured.

A major theme of this chapter is that when we remember things, we are constructing an account of the past. We are not just dredging up information from some mental storage bin. Because memory involves constructive processing, it can play tricks on us. In one commentary, President Ronald Reagan reminisced on his role in World War II. Unfortunately, what he was remembering was a role he had played in a movie rather than anything he actually did in the war. Perhaps he was beginning to show symptoms of the Alzheimer's disease with which he was later diagnosed; or perhaps his memory simply failed him, as memory sometimes fails us all. In any case, there is no guarantee that what people remember actually happened or is even close to anything that happened.

HOW TO STUDY MEMORY

How can we assess people's memories?

Memory is the process by which past experience and learning can be used in the present. We draw upon our memory of the past to help us understand the present (Tulving, 2000b; Tulving & Craik, 2000).

In studying memory, researchers have devised tasks that require research participants to remember arbitrary information, such as numerals, in different ways. Because this chapter includes many references to these tasks, it is useful to have an *advance organizer*—an explicit basis for organizing the information to be given—so that you will know how memory is studied. Our advance organizer describes the main tasks that are used in memory research. Refer back to this description of memory tasks if you forget some of the details about their purposes.

RECALL AND RECOGNITION

Memory tasks can involve recall, recognition, or a combination of the two. For a task that requires **recall memory**, you would be asked to produce facts, words, or other items from memory. Fill-in-the-blank tests require that you recall items from memory. For example, "Who is the author of this textbook?" is a recall question (if you don't peek at the answer). In a task that requires **recognition memory,** you would have to recognize (not produce) a previously learned fact, word, or other item from memory and select it. Multiple-choice and true-false tests typically involve recognition, although they may require other processes, such as reasoning, as well. The question "Is Robert J. Sternberg the author of this textbook?" requires you to recognize whether the given information is correct. If you are told to "Fill in the missing letters in the last name of the author of this book—"S_e_n_e_g," then you are being asked to recall the letters, but you are given some of them, which may help you recognize the author's name. This last task, combining elements of both recall and recognition, is sometimes called cued recall. In **cued recall,** you must recall something by using a cue, or prompt, provided by an experimenter or other individual.

The types of recall tasks typically used in experiments are serial recall, free recall, and paired-associates recall. In each kind of task, items may be presented orally or in writing. In **serial recall,** you are presented with a list of items and asked to repeat the items in the exact order in which they were presented (see Crowder & Green, 2000). Occasionally, research participants are asked to repeat the list they heard, but backward, as on the Wechsler intelligence scales (see Chapter 9). Serial recall can be done with other kinds of stimuli besides digits, of course, such as letters or words.

In **free recall,** you are presented with a list of items and asked to repeat them in any order you prefer. When there are multiple trials, items are usually presented in a different random order on each trial.

In **paired-associates recall,** you are presented with a list of paired (and often related) items, which you are asked to store in memory. Then, you are presented with one item in each pair and asked to provide the mate. Suppose you learn the list of pairs *time-city, mist-home, switch-paper, credit-day, fist-cloud, number-branch.* When you are later given the stimulus *switch,* you will be expected to say *paper.* Again, the task may be presented either in a single-recall trial or in multiple trials.

In each of these tasks, you need to produce an item from memory. In a recognition memory task, however, the experimenter produces an item. Your job is to indicate whether it is one that you have learned in the context of the experiment. Suppose you receive the list *time, city, mist, home, switch.* You are asked later whether the word *switch* appeared on the list. The paired-associates recall task may be viewed as a form of cued recall (Lockhart, 2000) because the experimenter provides a cue, or prompt, and the research participant uses that cue to bolster recall.

Although there are exceptions, recognition memory is usually much better than recall. Lionel Standing, Jerry Conezio, and Ralph Haber (1970) found that people could recognize almost 2,000 pictures in a recognition-memory task. Recall from Chapter 6 the discussion of the relationship between learning and performance. Your performance on a memory task often seems to indicate different levels of learning, depending on whether you were asked to recall or simply to recognize what you had learned. (For this reason, you may prefer multiple-choice over fill-in-the-blank questions when you are less confident of your knowledge in a particular subject.)

Typically, research participants are aware that they are performing a memory task, but not an implicit-memory task.

EXPLICIT VERSUS IMPLICIT MEMORY TASKS

Each of the preceding tasks involves **explicit memory,** a form of memory in which an individual consciously acts to recall or recognize particular information—for example, words from a list seen earlier. Psychologists also find it useful to understand the phenomenon of **implicit memory,** in which an individual recalls or recognizes information without consciously being aware of doing so (Graf & Schacter, 1985; Schacter, 2000; Schacter, Chiu, & Ochsner, 1993; Tulving, 2000a). Every day you engage in many tasks that involve your recollection of information with no awareness of being engaged in recall. As you read this book, for example, you are remembering the meanings of particular words, some of the psychological concepts you read about in earlier chapters, and even how to read, without being aware of doing these things.

Memory researchers also distinguish between procedural and declarative memories. **Procedural memory** is a recognition and awareness of how to perform particular tasks, skills, or procedures—"knowing how" skills, such as how to ride a bicycle (Rempel-Clower, Zola, Squire, & Amaral, 1996; Squire, Knowlton, & Musen, 1993). **Declarative memory,** in contrast, is a recognition and understanding of factual information—"knowing that," such as the terms in a psychology textbook.

In the laboratory, experimenters sometimes investigate implicit memory by studying people's performance on word-completion tasks. In a *word-completion task,* the research participant is presented with a word fragment, such as the first three letters of a word. The participant then is asked to complete it with the first word that comes to mind. Suppose that you were asked to supply the missing five letters to fill in these blanks and form a word: *imp_ _ _ _ _.* Because you had recently seen the word *implicit,* you would be more likely to provide the five letters *l-i-c-i-t* for the blanks than would someone who had not recently been exposed to the word. In general, research participants perform better when the word is one they have seen recently. Even though they have not been explicitly instructed to remember the list, their improved performance on the word-completion tasks shows they may have remembered implicitly.

Implicit memory encompasses several phenomena. For example, memory for how to do things—*procedural memory*—is typically implicit. When you ride a bicycle, you are not typically aware of recalling how to mount, how to steer, how to use the brakes, and so on. You just do it. The same is true when you write a paper for a course. You are not aware, typically, of recalling a set of procedures: First I need a title, then I need an opening sentence, then I need to make sure that sentence has a subject and a verb and that it ends with a period, and so on. Again, you just do it. Another typically implicit memory phenomenon is priming, the activation of one or more existing memories by a stimulus. In the example above, you probably filled in the blanks to make the word *implicit* because you had recently seen this word.

Memories appear to be of several types, not just one. What are the types of memories? You are likely to remember your parents' names forever. When you are introduced to someone new at a party, however, you may forget that person's name almost immediately. Why and how do we remember some things and not others? To understand, it is necessary to learn about different types of memory as well as how information is placed into, retained in, and later extracted from memory.

© Rich Beauchesne/*Portsmouth Herald*

Hitting a ball with a bat requires encoding, storing, and retrieving procedural knowledge. If he hasn't stored this knowledge, the boy must work hard to remember how to move his muscles in the right ways at the right times. With a little rehearsal, however, he will master the skills so well that he will remember them the rest of his life.

✓ CONCEPT CHECK 1

1. The question "Did the word *priming* occur in the material you have read so far?" measures _____ memory.
   a. recall
   b. recognition
   c. paired-associates
   d. priming
2. The question "What is the first name of the president of the country?" measures _____ memory.
   a. implicit
   b. procedural
   c. duplicit
   d. explicit
3. Knowing how to boot up a computer requires you to draw primarily on _____ memory.
   a. declarative
   b. designated
   c. procedural
   d. prorated

THE MULTIPLE-STORE MODEL OF MEMORY

What are the stores of memory in the "standard" memory model?

The prevailing model of memory was originally proposed by Richard C. Atkinson and Richard Shiffrin (1968), who conceptualized three memory stores (functional storage locations): (1) a small store of brief, fleeting sensory memories; (2) a somewhat larger but still limited store of actively conscious memories; and (3) a store of information that is of virtually limitless capacity, which requires effective retrieval to bring into active memory. This metaphor is not the only way to conceptualize memory, and alternative models are discussed later in the chapter, but many psychologists still use variants of the Atkinson-Shiffrin model.

The **sensory store** has the shortest duration for memory storage. The **short-term store,** or short-term memory (STM), has a modest capacity and a duration for storing information of only seconds.

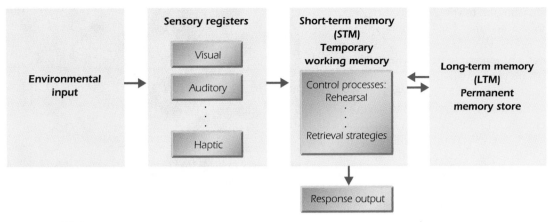

FIGURE 7.1
The Three-Stores View. In Richard Atkinson and Richard Shiffrin's model of memory, information flows from sensory to short-term to long-term memory stores. Their metaphor for memory long served as the basis for research on memory processes. (From "The Control of Short-term Memory" by Atkinson & Shiffrin, August 1971, Scientific American.)

The **long-term store,** or long-term memory (LTM), can store information for very long periods of time, perhaps even indefinitely (Bahrick, 2000).

These three stores are not distinct physiological structures. Rather, they are hypothetical constructs that embrace sets of processes. For example, the processes used for long-term memory are thought to be somewhat different from those used for short-term memory. Figure 7.1 shows a simple information-processing model of these stores, which typifies models proposed in the 1960s and 1970s (e.g., R. C. Atkinson & Shiffrin, 1971).

ENCODING, STORAGE, AND RETRIEVAL

All three memory stores process information similarly. They encode, store, and retrieve it (Tulving, 2000b; Tulving & Craik, 2000). **Encoding** is a process by which a physical, sensory input, such as a word, a sound, or even an odor, is transformed into a representation that can be stored in memory. **Storage** is the moving of encoded information into a memory store and the maintenance of the information. **Retrieval** is the recovery of information from a memory store and the moving of the information into consciousness for use in active cognitive processing. Encoding, storage, and retrieval are sequential stages. First we take in information. Then we hold it for a while. Later we pull it out. The three processes interact and are interdependent. For example, when you study, you need first to encode information and then to store it. When you are tested, you need to retrieve some of that information. How well you retrieve the information depends on how well you encoded and then stored it (Brown & Craik, 2000).

The three stages of memory can be illustrated with reference to Figure 7.2. Suppose that you see a photo of this animal while you are leafing through a magazine. You are in a hurry and do not have time to read the accompanying article. You find the creature difficult to fathom. Later you go back to the magazine and learn that the animal is a large African mammal that feeds on insects, especially ants and termites: an *aardvark.* You have heard of this animal before but have never actually seen one, either in life or in a picture. Now, knowing what the animal is, you find yourself encoding such features as the powerful claws, large ears, and heavy tail. You also encode the animal's name. You do not make any particular effort to remember what an aardvark looks like. But the visual information has been stored in your memory because the verbal

FIGURE 7.2
What is this?

label has made it meaningful to you. Several years later, on a visit to a zoo, you see an animal and immediately recognize it as an aardvark. You have retrieved from memory the representation you stored earlier without even being fully aware you were doing so.

The example of the aardvark illustrates an interesting property of memory—namely, that having a verbal label (such as a name) to attach to something can often help us make sense of that something. In this case, the verbal label helped us organize information about an animal shown in a picture. Verbal labels also can help us encode, store, and retrieve information that is presented in text. See if you can figure out what is going on in this passage:

> The procedure is actually quite simple. First you arrange items into different groups. Of course one pile may be sufficient depending on how much there is to do. If you have to go somewhere else due to lack of facilities, that is the next step; otherwise, you are pretty well set. It is important not to overdo things. That is, it is better to do too few things at once than too many. In the short run this may not seem important, but complications can easily arise. A mistake can be expensive as well. At first, the whole procedure will seem complicated. Soon, however, it will become just another facet of life. It is difficult to foresee any end to the necessity for this task in the immediate future, but then one can never tell. After the procedure is completed, one arranges the materials into different groups again. Then they can be put into their appropriate places. Eventually they will be used once more and the whole cycle will then have to be repeated. However, that is part of life.

If you are given the title "Washing Clothes," this procedure is considerably easier to recall and understand than it is without the title (Bransford & Johnson, 1972, cited in Bransford, 1979, pp. 134-135). The verbal label helps us to encode, and therefore to remember, a passage that otherwise seems incomprehensible.

Now that we have mapped out an overview of memory processes and the three memory stores, we can more deeply probe each memory store, starting with the sensory store.

SENSORY MEMORY

The sensory store, which is the initial repository of much information that eventually enters the short- and long-term stores, may have at least two forms: the *iconic* store for visual memories and the *echoic* store for auditory memories. There may also be sensory stores for other sensory modalities (such as olfaction and taste), although the existence of such stores is speculative at the present time.

Excellent evidence indicates the existence of the iconic store (so called because information is believed

The persistence of visual memory is what makes "writing" with a sparkler possible.

to be stored in the form of *icons*, visual images that represent something). Visual information appears to enter our memory system through an **iconic store** that holds the information for very short periods of time. George Sperling (1960) showed people 12 letters in a 3 × 4 grid for 50 milliseconds. Participants then were asked via a tone to report the items in one row of the grid. Sperling found that people can hold about eight items in iconic memory after a tenth of a second. Most of the information is gone after half a second and almost all of it is gone after a whole second. In the normal course of events, this information may be either transferred to another store or erased if other information is superimposed on it. If you have ever "written" your name with a lighted sparkler on the Fourth of July, you have experienced the persistence of a visual memory; that is, you have briefly "seen" your name, even though the sparkler left no physical trace. This *visual persistence* is an example of the type of information held in the iconic store.

SHORT-TERM MEMORY

Our short-term store holds information for seconds and occasionally for as long as a minute or two. Even though you might look at something you remember after a day as involving only recall over the short term, for psychologists the short-term store is responsible for the storage of information for only much briefer periods of time (up to a couple of minutes). Originally, the capacity of short-term memory was thought to be about seven items (G. A. Miller, 1956). However, the capacity limit may be closer to three to five items than it is to seven (Cowan, 2001). When you look up a phone number and try to remember it long enough to enter it, you are using the short-term store. Why do we forget such simple information so easily? How can we keep ourselves from forgetting it? In discussing the

When you need to remember the number the operator just gave you, you use short-term memory encoding strategies.

short-term store, we consider next the encoding, storage, and retrieval of information.

ENCODING INFORMATION

When you need to remember a phone number, you may repeat it back to yourself, perhaps several times. What you are trying to do is encode the information into your short-term memory. What kind of code do you use? A landmark experiment by R. Conrad (1964) successfully addressed this question. Conrad presented research participants visually with several series of six letters at the rate of 0.75 second per letter. The letters used in the various lists were B, C, F, M, N, P, S, T, V, and X. Participants had to write down each list of six letters, in the order given, immediately after the letters were presented. Conrad was interested particularly in the kinds of recall errors people made. The pattern of errors was clear. Even though the letters were presented *visually*, errors tended to be based on *acoustic confusability*. In other words, people substituted letters that sounded like the correct letters. They were likely to confuse F for S, T for C, B for V, P for B, and so on. In an experiment based on acoustically similar and dissimilar words versus semantically similar and dissimilar words (words that have similar or different meanings), Alan Baddeley (1966) clinched the argument that short-term storage relies primarily on an acoustic rather than a *semantic code*. Information can also be stored over the short term in other forms, however, such as visual images (Baddeley, 1992) or a semantic code (Shulman, 1970).

REHEARSAL

Why doesn't information retained in the short-term store remain there indefinitely? How do we keep it and how do we lose it? Although psychologists may disagree about how we forget information from the short-term store, they have reached fairly widespread consensus on how we retain it. **Rehearsal** is one strategy we use for keeping material in short-term memory, or for moving it into long-term memory, by repeating it over and over. Rehearsal can be of two types. In *maintenance rehearsal*, one merely repeats words over and over to oneself, without giving much thought to the words. In *elaborative rehearsal*, one reflects mindfully on the words and their meanings as one repeats them. One might form interactive images that relate the words to each other (e.g., if two words are *table* and *food*, by imagining food sitting on a table).

Rehearsal comes naturally to almost all of us as adults—so much so that we may believe we have always done it. We have not. The major difference between the memory of younger and older children (as well as adults) is not in the basic mechanisms but in learned strategies, such as rehearsal (Flavell & Wellman, 1977). In particular, younger children, and especially preschoolers, lack *metamemory skills*—that is, understanding and control of their own memory abilities (Koriat & Goldsmith, 1996; Metcalfe, 2000; T. O. Nelson & Narens, 1994; B.L. Schwartz & Metcalfe, 1994).

Older children and adults understand that to retain words in the short-term store they need to rehearse; younger children do not understand this fact. Another consideration is that for rehearsal to be effective, the person must be actively engaged in trying to encode and store the information; mere repeated exposure to words does not constitute effective rehearsal (Tulving, 1966).

INTERFERENCE

Rehearsal strategies enable us to retain information. What leads us to forget? Why do we forget a phone number or the names of people at a party after a brief period of time? Several theories have been proposed to explain why we forget information from the short-term store. The two most well-known theories are interference theory and decay theory. **Interference** refers to information that competes with the information an individual is trying to store in memory, thereby causing the individual to forget that information. **Decay** refers to forgetting that occurs as a result of the passage of time.

One of the most famous experimental paradigms in the study of human memory is called the Brown-Peterson paradigm after its originators, John Brown (1958) and Lloyd Peterson and Margaret Peterson (1959). Both the Brown and the Peterson and Peterson studies were taken as evidence for the existence of a short-term store and also for the interference theory of forgetting. According to the **interference theory**, information is forgotten because it is displaced by competing information, which disrupts and displaces the information that the individual had tried to store in memory originally.

The Petersons asked their research participants to recall strings of three letters, called *trigrams*. Items were given at intervals of 3, 6, 9, 12, 15, or 18 seconds after the last letter was presented. The Petersons used only consonants, so that the trigrams would not be easily pronounceable—for example, "K-B-F." Figure 7.3 shows the percentages of correct recalls after the various intervals of time. Why does recall decline so rapidly? Because after the oral presentation of each trigram, the Petersons asked their participants to count backward by threes from a three-digit number given immediately after the trigram. The purpose of having the participants count backward was to prevent them from rehearsing during the *retention interval*, which is the time between the presentation of the last letter and the start of the recall phase of the experimental trial. Clearly, the trigram is almost completely forgotten after just 18 seconds if participants are not allowed to rehearse it.

At least two kinds of interference figure prominently in memory theory and research. **Retroactive interference** (or retroactive inhibition) occurs when interfering information is presented *after* the information that is to be remembered. An example of retroactive interference would be studying for a psychology test, then studying for a biology test, and then taking the psychology test. One might find, to one's dismay,

that biology facts kept coming to mind but psychology facts did not! **Proactive interference** (or proactive inhibition) occurs when the interfering information is presented *before* the information that is to be remembered. (See Figure 7.4.) An example of proactive interference would be studying for a biology test, then studying for a psychology test, then taking the psychology test. One might find, in this case, that studying for the biology test interfered with one's recall of the material for the psychology test.

DECAY

Decay theory asserts that information is forgotten because it gradually disappears over time, rather than because it is displaced by other information. Whereas interference theory views one piece of information as knocking out another, decay theory views the original piece as gradually disappearing unless something is done to keep it intact. There is some evidence for decay theory (Reitman, 1974).

Decay theory is hard to test because it is difficult to prevent research participants from intentionally or even inadvertently rehearsing, and thereby retaining the given information. If participants are prevented from rehearsing, however, the possibility of interference arises. The task used to prevent rehearsal may interfere retroactively with the original memory (Reitman, 1971, 1974). Try, for example, not to think of white elephants as you read the next page. When you are instructed not to think about them, it is actually quite difficult not to, even if you try to follow the instructions.

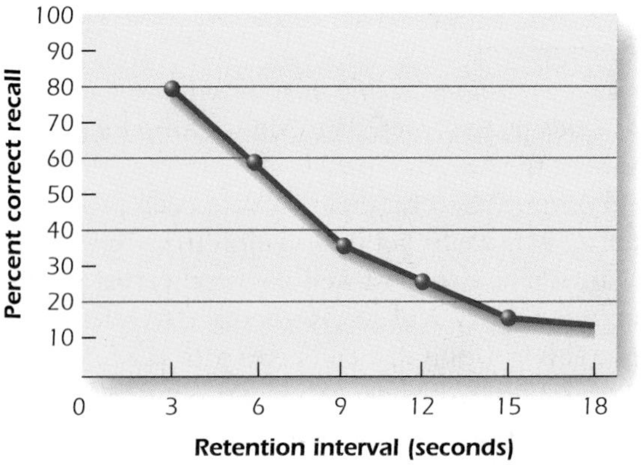

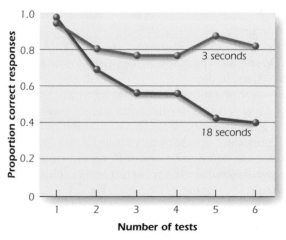

FIGURE 7.3

Percentage of Recall from Short-Term Memory. In the study by Lloyd Peterson and Margaret Peterson, research participants could not use rehearsal to keep information in short-term memory. As a consequence, their ability to recall three consonants (a trigram) rapidly declined as the delay between presentation and recall increased from 3 to 18 seconds. Some have suggested that retroactive interference may cause the rapid decline in recall.

FIGURE 7.4

Proactive Interference and Short-Term Memory. Geoffrey Keppel and Benton Underwood (1962) demonstrated that proactive interference also affects recall, as shown by the decline in recall after increasing numbers of trigrams were presented. The effect of proactive interference intensified over increasingly long retention intervals.

To conclude, evidence exists for both interference and decay in the short-term store. The evidence for decay is not airtight, but it is certainly suggestive. The evidence for interference is rather strong, but at present it is unclear to what extent the interference is retroactive, proactive, or both.

We have discussed how information gets encoded into short-term memory, how it can be kept there, and how it may be lost. But what about the information that is kept in short-term memory? How much can we hold? How can we retrieve it?

THE CAPACITY OF THE SHORT-TERM STORE

Try to remember this string of 21 digits: 101001000100001000100. It is extremely difficult to hold so many single digits in short-term memory. Now try chunking the digits into larger units, such as 10, 100, 1000, 10000, 1000, and 100. You will probably find you can easily reproduce the 21 digits as six items. In a classic article, George Miller (1956) noted that our short-term memory capacity appears to be about seven items, plus or minus two. An item can be something as simple as a digit or something more complex, such as a word. Remembering more complex units, or **chunks,** which are collections of separate items into a single grouping, effectively increases the amount of total information we can hold. This increase holds despite the seven-item limit.

Of course, our seven-item capacity can be limited still further by any delay or interference in recall. Cognitive psychologists have sought a way to measure the degree to which delay and interference can limit this seven-item capacity. One method for estimating the capacity of the short-term store under delay or interference conditions draws inferences from a mathematical function. This function, called a **serial-position curve,** represents the probability that each of a series of given items will be recalled, given the order in which the items were presented in a list, or their respective *serial positions.*

Say the following list of words once to yourself and then, immediately thereafter, try to recall all the words in any order, without looking back at them: *table, cloud, book, tree, shirt, cat, light, bench, chalk.* If you are like most people, you will find that your recall of words is different for items in different parts of the list. Typically, recall is best for items at and near the end of the list, second best for items near the beginning of the list, and poorest for items in the middle of the list. A typical serial-position curve is shown in Figure 7.5. Superior recall of words that occur at or near the end of a list of words is a **recency effect.** Superior recall of words that occur at or near the beginning of a list of words is a **primacy effect.** Recall of words from the beginning and middle of the list is due primarily to the effects of the long-term store, consid-

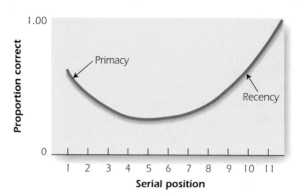

FIGURE 7.5

Serial-Position Curve. Most people recall items at the end of a list (greatest recall) and at the beginning of a list (second greatest recall) much more easily than items in the middle of a list (least recall).

ered later in this chapter, and recall of words from the end of the list is due primarily to the effects of the short-term store. The recency effect is attributable to the participants' dumping out the newest and hence most easily recallable contents of their short-term store just as soon as they are given the signal to recall. The serial-position curve, incidentally, makes sense in terms of interference theory. Words at the end of the list are subject to proactive but not to retroactive interference. Words at the beginning of the list are subject to retroactive but not to proactive interference. And words in the middle of the list are subject to both. Thus, recall would be expected to be poorest in the middle of the list, as indeed it is.

Another way of broadening our understanding of short-term memory is to consider the cultures within which people are immersed. Rumjahn Hoosain and others have shown that Hong Kong undergraduates have a mean digit span of 9.9; that is, they can store 9.9 numerals in their short-term memory. This span is more than two digits greater than the span reported for speakers of several Western languages. Before we infer any far-reaching conclusions about the arithmetical abilities of Asians, however, it may be important to consider a property of the Chinese language. Readers can read numerals more quickly in Mandarin than in German. And speakers can pronounce numbers in Cantonese more rapidly than in English (M. H. Bond, 1986; Hoosain & Salili, 1987). The linguistic differences may affect encoding.

RETRIEVAL

Once we encode and store information in the short-term store, how do we retrieve that information? A classic series of experiments on this issue was done by Saul Sternberg (1966). The phenomenon he studied is short-term **memory scanning,** whereby an individual checks what is contained usually in short-term memory.

Sternberg's basic paradigm was simple. He gave participants a short list that contained from one to six digits. Participants were expected to be able to hold the list in short-term storage. After a brief pause, a test digit was flashed on a screen and participants had to say whether this digit had appeared in the set they had been asked to memorize.

Psychologists use information-processing models to specify the stages a person must go through when undertaking a task such as the one Sternberg proposed. In the case of retrieval from the short-term memory store, a fundamental question is whether items are retrieved all at once or sequentially. If we retrieve the items sequentially, the question then arises, Do we retrieve all of the items, regardless of the task, or do we stop retrieving them as soon as an item seems to accomplish the task?

Parallel processing refers to cognitive manipulation of multiple operations simultaneously, so that the items stored in short-term memory are retrieved all at once, not one at a time. **Serial processing** refers to the cognitive manipulation of operations in which each operation is executed one at a time in a series. In the digit-recall task, the digits would be retrieved in succession, rather than all at once. If information processing is serial, then there are two ways to gain access to the stimuli: exhaustive and self-terminating processing.

Exhaustive serial processing implies that the individual seeks to retrieve an item stored in memory by checking the item being sought against *all* of the possible items that are presented, even if a match is found partway through the list. *Self-terminating serial processing* implies that the individual seeks to retrieve a particular item stored in memory by checking each of the presented items against the item being sought until the individual reaches the item being sought. The person checks the test digit against only those digits that are needed in order to make a response.

Sternberg (1966) found that his data supported an exhaustive serial processing model of comparisons and that comparisons took roughly 38 milliseconds (0.038 second) each. Subsequent research, however, has presented alternative interpretations of the data (e.g., Townsend, 1971).

LONG-TERM MEMORY

When we talk about memory in our everyday interactions, we are usually talking about the long-term store, which is where we keep memories over long periods of time, sometimes indefinitely. How do we get information from the short-term store to the long-term store? One method is by rehearsing. Another is by deliberately attempting to understand information. Perhaps an even more important way that we accomplish this transfer is by making connections or associations between the new information and what we already know and understand—by integrating the new data into our existing stored information. As we did for the short-term store, we will examine the three processes of encoding, storage, and retrieval in the long-term store.

FORMS OF ENCODING IN LONG-TERM MEMORY

Information in the long-term store seems to be primarily *semantically encoded*—that is, encoded by the meanings of words. We can also hold visual and acoustic information in the long-term store, however. Thus, there is considerable flexibility in the way we store information in long-term memory. One way to show semantic encoding is to use test words that bear a semantic relationship to other test words. William Bousfield (1953) had research participants learn a list of 60 words that included 15 animals, 15 professions, 15 vegetables, and 15 names of people. The words were presented in a random order, so that members of the various categories were thoroughly mixed. After participants heard the words, they were asked to recall the items in any order they wished. Bousfield then analyzed the order of output of the recalled words. The participants recalled successive words from the same category more frequently than would be expected by chance. It thus appears that people were remembering words by grouping them into categories.

Encoding can also be achieved visually. Nancy Frost (1972) presented participants with 16 drawings of objects, including four items of clothing, four animals, four vehicles, and four items of furniture. Frost manipulated not only the semantic category but also the visual category. The drawings differed in visual orientation, with four angled to the left, four angled to the right, four horizontal, and four vertical. Items were presented in random order, and participants were asked to recall them freely. Participants' output orders of items showed effects of both semantic and visual categories, suggesting that people were encoding visually as well as semantically. Even acoustic information can be encoded in the long-term store (T. O. Nelson & Rothbart, 1972).

We store memories both verbally and visually in complementary ways (Paivio, 1971, 1986). The form of representation depends on both the form of presentation (verbal or nonverbal) and the imagery of the stimuli to be remembered. Some words are highly concrete and also high in imagery value, such as *bluejay*, *lemon*, *radio*, and *pencil*. They lend themselves to visual representation, even if presented verbally. In contrast, words like *truth*, *kindness*, and *joy* are less likely to be stored visually, simply because we have no images that we more or less uniformly associate with these words.

ENCODING MEANING

What about the meaning underlying a relationship among concepts? John Anderson and Gordon Bower (1973) proposed a *propositional* view, according to which both images and verbal statements are stored in terms of their *deep meanings*—that is, as propositions, not as specific images or statements. Herbert Clark and William Chase (1972) asked their study participants to compare verbal representations of situations (e.g., "The star is above the plus") with pictorial representations of the same situations (i.e., a picture of a star above the plus). Half the time the verbal and pictorial representations corresponded, and half the time they did not (e.g., the picture showed a plus above a star rather than the star above the plus). Clark and Chase found that people were able to do such comparisons very efficiently. On the basis of their data, Clark and Chase proposed a fairly simple model of how both the verbal form of the statement and the pictorial form could be encoded into a deeper propositional form. Colin MacLeod, Earl Hunt, and Nancy Mathews (1978) obtained persuasive evidence suggesting that we can use either a propositional or an imaginal representation.

As these studies show, we seem to encode information in memory by using both propositional and imaginal representations. *Dual-trace theory* captures these two kinds of representations, although other theories explain them in different ways. When do we use each kind of representation?

REPRESENTING IMAGES

Stephen Kosslyn has done a number of experiments to demonstrate the use of imaginal representations in memory. In one of the more interesting experiments (Kosslyn, Ball, & Reiser, 1978), research participants were shown a map of an imaginary island, which you can see in Figure 7.6. The participants studied the map until they could reproduce it accurately from memory, placing the locations of the six objects on the map no more than a quarter of an inch from their correct positions. Once the memorization phase of the experiment was completed, the critical phase began.

Research participants were instructed that, upon hearing the name of an object read to them, they should follow a series of steps. In particular, they should picture the map, mentally scan directly to the mentioned object, and press a key as soon as they arrived at the location of the named object. This procedure was repeated several times, with the participants mentally moving between various pairs of objects on successive trials. The experimenter kept track of the response times on each trial: how long it took to scan from one object to the next. An almost perfect linear relationship was found between the dis-

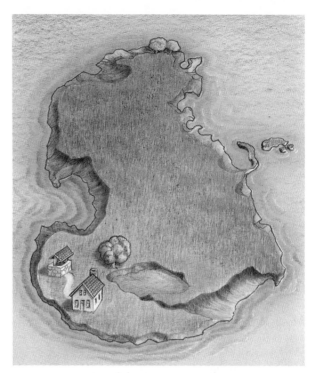

FIGURE 7.6

Image-Based Encoding in Long-Term Memory. This map of an imaginary island shows six target objects, including a hut, a tree, and a lake. Research participants learned to draw such maps from memory, accurately placing each of the six objects within one-quarter inch of their correct locations. (From "Visual Images Preserve Metric Spatial Information" by Kosslyn et al., *Journal of Experimental Psychology*, No. 4, pp. 47-60, 1978. Copyright © 1978 by the American Psychological Association. Reprinted with permission.)

tance separating successive pairs of objects in the mental map and the amount of time it took people to press the button. In other words, people seem to have encoded the map in the form of an image and actually to have scanned that image as needed.

Kosslyn (Kosslyn & Koenig, 1992) has also found some intriguing effects of image size. Look at the rabbit and the honeybee in Figure 7.7. Now close your eyes and picture them both in your mind. Now imagine only the honeybee. Determine the color of its head. Do you notice that you have to take time to zoom in to "see" its features in detail? Now look at the rabbit and the elephant. Close your eyes and picture them both in your mind. Now look only at the elephant. Imagine walking toward the elephant, watching it as it gets closer to you. Do you find there comes a point when you can no longer see all of the elephant? Most people find that the image of the elephant seems to overflow the size of their image space, as it would literally.

FIGURE 7.7
Image Size. Participants in Stephen Kosslyn's study tested their mental imagery limits by picturing the rabbit first with the honeybee and then with the elephant. They had to zoom in to see details of the honeybee, but the image of the elephant overflowed their mental image space as they imagined approaching it.

People also may use mental images to store geographical information in memory (Stevens & Coupe, 1978). For example, many people have stored a rough map of the United States. Which city is farther west: Reno, Nevada, or San Diego, California? Most people believe San Diego is west of Reno. Their map looks something like the one in Figure 7.8a. Actually,

however, Reno is west of San Diego, as shown on the correct map in Figure 7.8b. The kinds of errors people make in this task suggest they use imaginal representations.

We rely heavily on our long-term store, in which we keep the information we need to function in our daily lives. We have seen how we encode information, but how do we store it?

STORING AND FORGETTING
Many factors affect our ability to store or to forget information, including the pace at which the information is learned, rehearsal strategies, organization, and both retroactive and proactive interference.

TIME AND PACE DURING LEARNING. Suppose you have to study vocabulary words for a French test. You have 240 vocabulary words to learn, and you can allocate 4 hours to study. You could budget your time in several ways. One would be to study each word once for 1 minute. Another would be to study each word twice for 30 seconds each time. What strategy will help you remember the words best?

If your 4 hours are available all in one block of time, it does not matter which strategy you use. According to the **total-time hypothesis,** the degree to which a person is able to learn information by storing it in memory depends on the total amount of time spent studying the material in a given session, rather than on the way in which the time is apportioned within a given session.

If you distribute your time across a series of sessions, however, it becomes another matter. The temporal pacing of learning can affect the storage or

(a)

(b)

FIGURE 7.8
Accuracy of Images in Stored Memory. Most people believe San Diego, California, is west of Reno, Nevada, so their mental map looks something like the one in panel (a). Actually, Reno is west of San Diego, as shown in panel (b).

forgetting of information. Harry Bahrick and Elizabeth Phelps (1987) found an important principle of memory while studying people's long-term recall of Spanish vocabulary words learned 8 years earlier. People tend to learn better when they acquire knowledge via **distributed learning,** which is spaced across sessions over time, rather than via **massed learning,** which is crammed together all at once. The greater the distribution of learning trials over time, the more people remember. This principle is important to remember when you study.

No matter how you divide your study time, one of the strategies you will probably use to memorize class information is rehearsal. Does the quality of your rehearsal also affect the effectiveness of your memory?

ELABORATION. In the discussion of short-term memory, we saw that rehearsal clearly helps maintain information in memory. Rehearsal also seems to facilitate the transfer of information from short-term to long-term memory. How you rehearse the information, though, influences how well you retain it. Going back to the example of studying Spanish vocabulary words, you could simply repeat the items over and over again, or you could elaborate the items in a way that makes them more meaningful to you. That is, you could relate the items to what you already know or connect them to one another and thereby make them more memorable. (Recall the effects of chunking, in which a person can chunk many smaller units of information into larger units of integrated information in order to remember the information more easily.) Elaborating information during rehearsal is better than merely repeating it. Elaboration can greatly increase the effectiveness of the rehearsal, especially when one studies for a test. One way to elaborate information is to organize it.

ORGANIZING INFORMATION:
SEMANTIC AND EPISODIC MEMORY
How do we organize information in memory? Probably the most illuminating studies addressing this question have looked at information in **semantic memory,** which is our general world knowledge, our memory for facts that are not unique to us and that are not recalled in any particular temporal context (Tulving, 1972). For example, my knowledge that the long, cylindrical object outside my window is a tree trunk and that Napoleon was a French general are examples of information stored in my semantic memory. Semantic memory is different from **episodic memory,** the

memory of personally experienced events or episodes. This is the kind of memory we use when we learn meaningless lists of words. If I need to remember that I saw Hector Gonzalez in the lunchroom yesterday, I must draw on an episodic memory. However, if I need to remember the name of the person I now see in the lunchroom again today ("Hector Gonzalez"), I must draw on a semantic memory. No particular time tag is associated with the name of that individual as being Hector. But there is a time tag associated with my having seen him at lunch yesterday. It is not clear that semantic and episodic memories are two distinct systems, although they do appear to function, at times, in different ways.

Semantic memory operates on **concepts,** ideas to which various characteristics may be attached and to which other ideas may be connected. People mentally organize concepts in some way. Thus, researchers have tried to make memory processing more readily understood by envisioning an organizational structure of memory. Psychologists often use the term **schema** to describe a cognitive framework for organizing associated concepts, including information and ideas, based on previous experiences. For example, a schema for having lunch at a nice restaurant might associate all the events you have personally experienced about lunch at such a restaurant. It might also include what you have learned from other people and other information sources regarding lunch. The schema might include events like entering through the door, having a host or hostess seat you, having your water glass filled up, being handed a menu, being told the day's specials, and so forth.

INTERFERENCE
We have seen that interference affects short-term memory. It also plays an important role in long-term memory. Recall that *retroactive interference* is caused by activity that occurs *after* we try to store something in memory but before we try to retrieve it. In contrast, *proactive interference* occurs when the interfering material occurs *before* the learning of the material.

In other situations, prior learning can cause *positive transfer*; that is, old information facilitates greater ease of learning and remembering new information. For example, the prior experience of learning to drive a standard-shift car may offer positive transfer when we are learning to drive an automatic-shift car. Most of the skills and knowledge of the former aid in learning the latter. Often prior learning helps in some ways and hurts in others. When it hurts, it results in

Prior learning can help us learn new things more easily, but sometimes negative transfer occurs. Using training wheels to learn to ride a bike may make learning to ride without them more difficult.

© Gale Zucker/Stock, Boston

semantic vs. episodic
~general   personal
~ concepts

negative transfer; that is, old information interferes with learning and remembering new material. Someone who has learned first to drive a standard-shift car may put his or her foot on the brake in an effort to shift gears, nearly putting everyone in the front seat through the windshield.

Once we learn to drive a standard shift, we will probably remember the skill for years, maybe for the rest of our life. The remarkable duration of long-term memory suggests these questions: How much information can we hold in the long-term store? How long does it last?

CAPACITY

Psychologists do not know the capacity of long-term storage, nor do they know how they would find out. They can design experiments to tax the limits of the short-term store. But they do not know how to tax the limits of the long-term store and thereby find out its capacity. Some theorists have suggested that the capacity of the long-term store is infinite, at least in practical terms (Hintzman, 1978).

The question of how long information lasts in the long-term store is not easy to answer either. At present, psychologists have no proof that there is an absolute outer limit to how long information can be stored. It appears to be quite a while, though.

Harry Bahrick, Phyllis Bahrick, and Roy Wittlinger (1975) conducted a relevant study on memory for names and faces. They tested research participants' memories for names and photographs of their high-school classmates. Even after 25 years, people tended to recognize names as belonging to classmates rather than to outsiders. Recognition memory for matching names to graduation photos was quite high.

As you might expect, recall of names showed a higher rate of forgetting. Names appear to be harder to retrieve than faces. What, in general, makes some memories harder to retrieve than others? Let's now consider retrieval of information from memory.

RETRIEVAL

But this mysterious power that binds our life together has its own vagaries and interruptions. It sometimes occurs that Memory has a personality of its own, and volunteers or refuses its information at its will, not at mine.
—Ralph Waldo Emerson, *Natural History of Intellect*

If, as some people believe, nothing is ever lost from long-term memory, then why do we sometimes have trouble remembering things? It is important to distinguish between **availability,** or existence of given information in long-term memory, **and accessibility,** or ease of gaining access to information that has been stored in long-term memory.

The difference between availability and accessibility of memories is particularly important in a phenomenon that has become one of the most controversial in psychology: the recovery of repressed memories, particularly adults' memories of sexual abuse suffered as children. The main controversy is whether the phenomenon is a genuine one and, if so, how frequently it occurs.

Sexual abuse of children has always been with us. For the most part, such abuse has been considered to be more or less rare. Some books have been published—largely for the mass market rather than for psychologists—arguing that such abuse is much more common than anyone thought. According to these books, the reason so little abuse has been reported is that many victims repress their memories of it; in other words, memories are available but largely inaccessible. Using a variety of techniques, some therapists have claimed that they are able to help clients recover these repressed memories. But the validity of at least some of these memories remains in serious doubt (Bowers & Farvolden, 1996; Ceci & Loftus, 1994; Joslyn, Loftus, McNoughton, & Powers, 2001; Lindsay & Read, 1994; Loftus, 2001; Loftus & Ketcham, 1991; Pennebaker & Memon, 1996; Thomas & Loftus, 2002).

Studies of retrieval from the long-term store date back to Hermann Ebbinghaus (1902, 1885/1964), who tested his own memory using nonsense syllables, which should have made it possible to study pure recall phenomena without the influence of prior associations and meanings. There are two problems with this logic, however. The first is that people sometimes make up their own associations. The second is that, arguably, we should be interested in how people learn material of the kind they actually need to recall in their everyday lives, not just material they will never have any occasion to learn.

CUE EFFECTIVENESS AND ENCODING SPECIFICITY. The way information is presented can make a difference in how likely a person is to recall it. Associations, or cues of any kind, can substantially aid recall, especially if they are meaningful to the individual. Timo Mantyla (1986) found that when research participants created their own retrieval cues, they were able to remember, almost without errors, lists of 500 and even 600 words. For each word on a list, the participants were asked to generate another word (the cue). The cue was to be, at least for them, an appropriate description or property of the target word. Later, they were given a list of their cue words. They were then asked to recall the target word. Mantyla found that cues were most helpful when they were both *compatible* with the target word and *distinctive*, in that they would not tend to generate a large number of related words. For example, if you are given the word *coat*, then *jacket* might be both compatible and distinctive as a cue. If you came up with the word *wool* as a cue, however, it might make you think of many words, such as *fabric* and *sheep*, that are not the target word.

The associations we assign to material we remember are not always generated entirely by the material itself. External contexts may also affect our ability to recall information. We appear to be better able to recall information when we are in the same context we were in when we learned the material. For example, we are likely to do better on a test if we are tested in the same room in which we learn material than if we are tested in a different room. In one experiment, 16 underwater divers were asked to learn a list of 40 unrelated words, either while they were on shore or while they were 20 feet beneath the surface (Godden & Baddeley, 1975). Later the divers were asked to recall the words either when in the same environment as where they had learned them or in the other environment. Recall was better when it occurred in the same place as the learning.

In another study (Butler & Rovee-Collier, 1989), researchers found that even infants demonstrate context effects on memory. When given an opportunity to kick a mobile in the same context as that in which they first had learned to kick it or in a different context, they kicked more strongly in the same context.

Even our moods and states of consciousness may provide a context for encoding and later retrieving memories. That is, we may retrieve those objects or events that we encode during a particular mood or state of consciousness more readily when we are in the same state again (Baddeley, 1989; G. H. Bower, 1983). Baddeley (1989) suggested that a factor in maintaining depression may be that the depressed person can more readily retrieve memories of previous sad experiences, which may contribute to continuing the depression. (For other cognitive views of depression, see Chapter 17.) If psychologists or others can intervene to prevent this vicious cycle, the person may begin to feel happier. This happiness may in turn lead to the retrieval of happier memories, thus further relieving the depression, and so on. Perhaps the folk wisdom to "think happy thoughts" is not entirely unfounded.

The results of the various retrieval experiments suggest that the way in which items are encoded has a strong effect on the way they are retrieved and how well they are retrieved. Endel Tulving and Donald Thomson (1973) have referred to this relationship as **encoding specificity,** which is the specific way of representing information that is placed into memory as it affects the specific way in which the information may be retrieved later. In sum, retrieval interacts strongly with encoding. If you study for a test and want to recall the information well at the time of testing, organize the information you are studying in a way that will help you to recall it.

THE CONSTRUCTIVE NATURE OF MEMORY

It appears that we recall meaningful information more readily than meaningless information, and that sometimes we even create the meaning that we later recall. In fact, it appears that memory is not just **reconstructive,** whereby the individual stores in memory some information about events or facts exactly as the events or facts took place. It is also **constructive,** whereby the individual actually builds memories based on experience and expectations (Grant & Ceci, 2000). Existing schemas may affect the way in which new information is stored.

Frederick Bartlett (1932) was an early researcher interested in whether memory for material is affected by culturally based understandings. Bartlett had research

When Simon Rodia built the Watts Towers in East Los Angeles, he used fragments of real objects, arranging them according to his own preexisting ideas. Similarly, we construct our memories from fragments of realistic events, according to our own preexisting schemas.

FLASHBULB MEMORIES

An important factor that seems to increase the likelihood that we will recall a particular experience over other experiences is the emotional intensity of that experience. Unfortunately, such intensity does not ensure the accuracy of our recall either. An oft-studied form of vivid memory is the **flashbulb memory,** a recollection of an event that is so emotionally powerful that it is highly vivid and richly detailed. It is as if the memory were indelibly preserved on film (R. Brown & Kulik, 1977).

Memories of the assassination of President John F. Kennedy, of the attack on Pearl Harbor, and of the destruction of the twin towers in New York on September 11, 2001, have been cited as examples of flashbulb memories. Flashbulb memories may be preferentially recalled because their recall is mediated by the hormones that are released in response to arousal.

Thus, experiencing strong emotion when viewing important events may enhance later recall of these events. People feel certain of their memories of the events, and the vividness and detailed texture of their memories seem to support their accuracy. It turns out, however, that these remembered events are often recalled inaccurately (Schacter, 1996).

flashbulb memories
hormones and memory
emotional memories

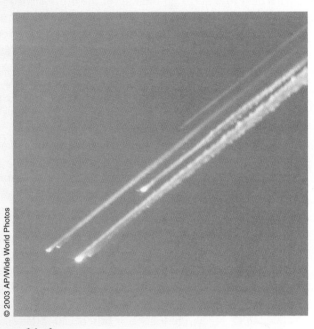

© 2001 AP/Wide World Photos

© 2003 AP/Wide World Photos

Two events likely to result in flashbulb memories are the attack on the twin towers of the former World Trade Center in New York and the tragedy of the destruction of the space shuttle Columbia.

participants in Great Britain learn what was to them a strange and difficult-to-understand North American Indian legend called "The War of the Ghosts." The text in its entirety is printed in Figure 7.9a. He found that people distorted their recall to make the story more understandable. In other words, their prior knowledge and expectations had a substantial effect on their recall. Bartlett suggested that people bring into a memory task their already existing schemas, which affect the way they recall what they learn. This result has recently been replicated (Bergman & Roediger, 1999). Figure 7.9b shows a typical student's recall of "The War of the Ghosts."

Some later cross-cultural work (Tripathi, 1979) also illustrates the importance of schemas as a framework for constructive memory. Children from India were asked to read several stories from *The Panchatantra,* a collection of ancient Hindi fables and folk tales. The stories contain quaint names and unusual settings that are unfamiliar to contemporary Indian

(a) Original Indian myth

The War of the Ghosts

One night two young men from Egulac went down to the river to hunt seals, and while they were there it became foggy and calm. Then they heard war-cries, and they thought: "Maybe this is a war-party." They escaped to the shore, and hid behind a log. Now canoes came up, and they heard the noise of paddles, and saw one canoe coming up to them. There were five men in the canoe, and they said:

"What do you think? We wish to take you along. We are going up the river to make war on the people."

One of the young men said, " I have no arrows."

"Arrows are in the canoe," they said.

"I will not go along. I might be killed. My relatives do not know where I have gone. But you," he said, turning to the other, "may go with them."

So one of the young men went, but the other returned home.

And the warriors went on up the river to a town on the other side of Kalama. The people came down to the water, and they began to fight, and many were killed. But presently the young man heard one of the warriors say: "Quick, let us go home; that Indian has been hit." Now he thought: "Oh, they are ghosts." He did not feel sick, but they said he had been shot.

So the canoes went back to Egulac, and the young man went ashore to his house, and made a fire. And he told everybody and said: "Behold I accompanied the ghosts, and we went to fight. Many of our fellows were killed, and many of those who attacked us were killed. They said I was hit, and I did not feel sick."

He told it all, and then he became quiet. When the sun rose he fell down. Something black came out of his mouth. His face became contorted. The people jumped up and cried.

He was dead.

(b) Typical recall by a student in England

The War of the Ghosts

Two men from Edulac went fishing. While thus occupied by the river they heard a noise in the distance.

"It sounds like a cry," said one, and presently there appeared some in canoes who invited them to join the party of their adventure. One of the young men refused to go, on the ground of family ties, but the other offered to go.

"But there are no arrows," he said.

"The arrows are in the boat," was the reply.

He thereupon took his place, while his friend returned home. The party paddled up the river to Kaloma, and began to land on the banks of the river. The enemy came rushing upon them, and some sharp fighting ensued. Presently someone was injured, and the cry was raised that the enemy were ghosts.

The party returned down the stream, and the young man arrived home feeling none the worse for his experience. The next morning at dawn he endeavoured to recount his adventures. While he was talking something black issued from his mouth. Suddenly he uttered a cry and fell down. His friends gathered round him.

But he was dead.

FIGURE 7.9

Bartlett's Legend. Read the legend quickly. Then move it out of view and write everything you can recall. Turn back to the legend and compare what you wrote with what you read. (From Bartlett, Sir Frederic C., "The War of the Ghosts" from *Remembering*, p. 65. Copyright Cambridge University Press. Reprinted by permission of the publisher.)

schoolchildren. Subsequently, the children were asked to recall the stories. Over time, the children added words and sentences not originally presented in the stories. Their reconstructions generally modified the stories from unfamiliar to more familiar forms, as well as from complex to simple forms.

When we are recalling a given experience, we often associate the degree to which the remembered experience seems vivid and richly detailed with the degree to which we are accurately remembering the experience. Ulric Neisser (1982) and others have questioned that relationship. Apparently, we cannot distinguish constructive from reconstructive memory based on the vividness of our recall.

AUTOBIOGRAPHICAL MEMORY

Autobiographical memory is what we remember of our own history. Autobiographical memory is constructive: You do not remember exactly what happened but instead your reconstruction of what happened. Our autobiographical memories are usually quite good, although they can be distorted. They are differentially good for different periods of life. David Rubin (1982, 1996) has found that middle-aged adults often remember events from their youthful and early-adult periods better than they remember events from their more recent past.

One way of studying autobiographical memory is through diary studies. In such studies, individuals, often researchers, keep detailed autobiographies (e.g., Linton, 1982; Wagenaar, 1986). Linton, for example, kept a diary for 6 years, recording at least two experiences per day on index cards. Then, each month, she chose two cards at random and tried to recall the events on the cards as well as their dates. She further rated each memory for its salience and its emotional content. Surprisingly, her rate of forgetting events was linear, not curvilinear as is usually the case. In other words, a typical memory curve shows substantial forgetting over short time intervals, and then a slowing in the rate of forgetting over longer time intervals. Linton's forgetting curve, however, did not show any such pattern. Her rate of forgetting was about the same over the entire 6-year period. She also found little relationship between her ratings of the salience and emotionality of memories, on the one hand, and their memorability, on the other. Thus, she surprised herself in what she did and did not remember.

In another study of autobiographical memory, Sehulster (1989) attempted to recall information about performances he attended at the Metropolitan Opera over a period of 25 years. A total of 284 performances were the data for the study. Sehulster's results were more in line with traditional expectations. His memory was best for the operas he had seen near the beginning and end of the 25-year period (serial-position effect). He also recalled more important performances better than less important ones.

MEMORY DISTORTIONS

People sometimes find that their memories are distorted (Ayers & Reder, 1998; Balota et al., 1999; Garry, Manning, Loftus, & Sherman, 1996; Goff & Roediger, 1998; Heaps & Nash, 1999; M. K. Johnson & Raye, 1998; Norman & Schacter, 1997; Roediger & McDermott, 2000a; Schacter, 1995; Schacter & Curran, 2000). For example, just saying something has happened to you makes you more likely to think it really happened, whether it did or not (Ackil & Zaragoza, 1998). According to Schacter (2001), distortions tend to occur in seven specific ways (which Schacter refers to as the "seven sins of memory"). Here are the "seven sins" and some examples of them from Schacter and elsewhere:

1. *Transience.* Memory fades quickly. Although many people know that actress Winona Ryder was convicted of felony theft for shoplifting clothing, they do not remember exactly where they found it out. At one time they could have said, but they no longer can.
2. *Absent-mindedness.* People sometimes brush their teeth after already having brushed them, or they enter a room looking for something, only to discover that they have forgotten what they were seeking.
3. *Blocking.* People think of something that they know they should remember, but they can't. It's as though the information is on the tip of their tongue, but they cannot retrieve it. People may see someone they know but the name escapes them, or they may try to think of a synonym for a word, knowing there is an obvious synonym but being unable to recall it.
4. *Misattribution.* People often cannot remember where they heard what they heard or read something. Sometimes people also think they see things they do not see or hear things they do not hear. For example, eyewitness testimony is sometimes clouded by what we think makes sense that we should have seen, rather than what we actually saw.
5. *Suggestibility.* People are susceptible to suggestion, so if it is suggested to them that they saw something, they may think they remember seeing it. For example, in Holland, when asked whether they had seen a television film of a plane crashing into an apartment building, many people said they had seen it. In fact, there was no such film.
6. *Bias.* People are often biased in their recall. People who are currently experiencing chronic pain are more likely to remember pain in their past, whether or not they actually experienced it, whereas people who are not experiencing such pain are less likely to recall pain in the past, again with little regard to their actual past experience.
7. *Persistence.* People sometimes remember as consequential things that, in a broad context, are inconsequential. Someone with many successes but one notable failure may remember the single failure better than the many successes.

What are some of the specific ways in which memory distortions are studied? One is through eyewitness accounts.

EYEWITNESS ACCOUNTS

A survey of U.S. prosecutors estimated that about 77,000 suspects are arrested each year after being identified by eyewitnesses (Dolan, 1995). Studies of more than 1,000 known wrongful convictions have pointed to errors in eyewitness identification as being "the single largest factor leading to those false convictions" (Wells, 1993, p. 554). What proportion of eyewitness identifications are mistaken? The answer to that question varies widely ("from as low as a few percent to greater than 90%"; Wells, 1993, p. 554), but even the most conservative estimates suggest frightening possibilities.

Consider the story of Timothy. In 1986, Timothy was convicted of brutally murdering a mother and her two young daughters (Dolan, 1995). He was then sentenced to die. For 2 years and 4 months, Timothy lived on death row. Although the physical evidence did not point to Timothy, eyewitness testimony placed him near the scene of the crime at the time of the murder. Subsequently, it was discovered that a man who looked like Timothy was a frequent visitor to the neighborhood of the murder victims. Timothy was given a second trial and was acquitted.

Experiments by Elizabeth Loftus and her colleagues (e.g., Loftus, 1975, 1977) have demonstrated that eyewitness accounts are highly susceptible to distortion. In one study, Elizabeth Loftus, David Miller, and Helen Burns (1978) showed people a series of 30 slides. In them, someone drove a red car down a street, stopped at a stop sign, turned right, and then knocked down a pedestrian crossing at a crosswalk. As soon as the people finished seeing the slides, they had to answer a series of 20 questions about the accident. One of the questions contained information that was either consistent or inconsistent with what they had been shown. Half of the research participants were asked: "Did another car pass the red car while it was stopped at the stop sign?" The other half of the participants were asked the same question, except with the word *yield* replacing *stop*. In other words, the information in the question given to this second group was inconsistent with what the people had seen.

Later, after an unrelated activity, all people were shown two slides and asked which they had seen before. One had a stop sign and the other a yield sign. Accuracy on this task was 34% better for people who had received the consistent question (stop sign) than for people who had the inconsistent question (yield sign). Although this distortion may be due to phenomena other than just constructive memory, it does show that we can easily be led to construct a memory that differs from what really happened.

Loftus (e.g., Loftus & Ketcham, 1991) has been instrumental in pointing to the possibility of wrongful conviction when eyewitness testimony is used as the sole or even the primary basis for convicting accused persons of crimes. She further has noted that eyewitness testimony is often a powerful determinant of whether a jury will convict an accused person. The effect is particularly pronounced if eyewitnesses appear highly confident of their testimony, even if they can provide few perceptual details or offer apparently conflicting responses. People sometimes even think they remember things simply because they have imagined or thought about them. Indeed, having people repeatedly imagine doing something increases their confidence that they actually have done what they only have imagined doing (Goff & Roediger, 1998). It has been estimated that as many as 10,000 people per year

Eyewitness testimony is of variable quality, depending on such factors as the recency of a remembered event and the amount of attention paid to the event at the time it occurred.

may be convicted wrongfully on the basis of mistaken eyewitness testimony (Cutler & Penrod, 1995; Loftus & Ketcham, 1991).

John Brigham, Roy Malpass, and others (e.g., Bothwell, Brigham, & Malpass, 1989; Brigham & Malpass, 1985; Shapiro & Penrod, 1986) have pointed out that eyewitness accounts are particularly weak for identifying persons of a race other than the race of the witness. Astonishingly, even infants seem to be influenced by post-event information when recalling an experience, as shown through their behavior in operant-conditioning experiments (Rovee-Collier, Borza, Adler, & Boller, 1993). Not everyone views eyewitness testimony with such skepticism, however (e.g., see McKenna, Treadway, & McCloskey, 1992; Zaragoza, McCloskey, & Jamis, 1987). The validity of such testimony is still open to question.

A study that suggests how easy it is for people to manufacture memories was conducted by Henry Roediger III and Kathleen McDermott (1995). These investigators asked people to memorize lists of words with extremely high associates to target words, such as *sleep*. Thus, words like *dream* and *bed* appeared on the list to be memorized, but *sleep* did not appear. To the researchers' surprise, people were as likely to remember having heard the nonpresented word (*sleep*) as they were to remember the words actually presented on the list! People can believe they have heard something they have not heard with the same confidence they remember something they actually have heard. This result has been replicated multiple times (McDermott, 1996; Schacter, Verfaellie, & Pradere, 1996).

Why are people so weak in distinguishing what they have heard from what they have not heard? One

IN THE LAB OF HENRY L. ROEDIGER III
AND KATHLEEN B. McDERMOTT

REMEMBERING EVENTS THAT NEVER HAPPENED

In the 1990s controversy swirled around the topic of false memories. How could people vividly recall events that either had not occurred or had occurred quite differently from the way in which they were remembered? A gulf existed between laboratory research on human memory, which often employed straightforward tests such as word lists, and studies of false memory that were often conducted with very different paradigms. (See the section on "The Constructive Nature of Memory.") Some researchers proposed that standard laboratory paradigms examined mere reproductive memory (people simply reproduce events and don't make errors), which differed from the kinds of constructive memories that involves "filling in" information to tell a story, or what is called reconstructive memory. According to some psychologists, laboratory studies using word lists to test memory could not capture the phenomenon of false memories.

In 1993 we found a mostly forgotten paper by James Deese (published in 1959) that we thought offered a method of studying false memories in the laboratory. Deese was interested in associative factors that affect recall of word lists. He developed a set of lists, each containing 12 words that were highly associated with a word that was absent from the list. For example, *door, glass, pane, shade, ledge, sill, house, open, curtain, frame, view,* and *breeze* are all associated with *window*, which was not presented. Students who were given the lists were asked immediately after they listened to them to recall as many words as possible. Deese discovered that some (but by no means

all) of his lists led people to make predictable intrusions. Even though the word *window* was not on the list, a high proportion of people recalled it as if it were. If we could show that this was not a fluke—that the phenomenon was reliable and occurred repeatedly—we could confirm that we had found a straightforward new laboratory technique for studying false memories. Recalling a small event–the presentation of a word–that had not actually occurred was a form of false memory.

We began by conducting two experiments to test the idea that the paradigm could be used to study one type of false memories, those based on association or inference.

Henry L. Roediger III is the James S. McDonnell Distinguished University Professor and Department Chair at Washington University in St. Louis. He graduated with a BA in Psychology from Washington & Lee University in 1969 and received his PhD from Yale University in 1973. Dr. Roediger is President of the American Psychological Society. Roediger's research has centered on human learning and memory.

Kathleen McDermott is an Assistant Professor in the departments of Psychology and Radiology at Washington University in St. Louis. She received a BA from the University of Notre Dame in 1990 and a PhD from Rice University in 1996. She studies human cognition, with an emphasis on memory, using behavioral and functional neuroimaging techniques.

The results, published in 1995 in the *Journal of Experimental Psychology: Learning, Memory and Cognition,* showed that the technique was more successful than even we had hoped at the outset of our project.

The Pilot Study

The first of our two experiments was a pilot study, not a true experiment (i.e., no independent variable was manipulated). Using six of Deese's lists, we tested 36 students in an undergraduate class to see if the lists would lead to false recall and false recognition. Each of the 12 words in each list was read once, and the entire list was recalled immediately after. Students were warned against guessing—we asked them to write down only words that they were sure they had heard. After all six lists had been presented and the recalled words written, the students took a final recognition test in which printed list items were mixed in with words that had not been presented. The students had to decide whether or not each word on the final list had appeared on an earlier one. Most of the "lure" (new) items were unrelated to the words on the six lists, but the six key absent words, like *window*, were also included.

On 40% of the trials, students recalled a word like *window* that was implied by the words on the list but had not actually been presented! After all the lists were recalled, the recognition test was given. False recognition was even more frequent: Students reported that 84% of the critical words like *window* had been presented in the list! This was nearly the same level as for words that had actually been presented (86%). The students were not guessing randomly because the error rate for unrelated words on the recognition test was only 2%.

The Second Experiment
Now confident that the technique worked, we conducted a more careful experiment on a new group of 30 students. We wanted to use a larger set of materials, so we developed 24 lists that we thought might provoke high levels of false recall and false recognition. We made the lists a bit longer—15 words instead of 12—to make the phenomenon stronger. We read 16 lists aloud and saved 8 other lists to be used in the recognition test as lure or distractor items. After hearing 8 lists, students recalled as many words as they could; after the next 8 lists they solved arithmetic problems. The reason for this manipulation was to examine the possible effect of recalling the first lists on students' performance on the later recognition test; that is, would the initial test increase later false recognition? The math test after 8 lists kept students busy and prevented them from rehearsing the list.

For the 8 lists that were recalled, students reported the critical missing item 55% of the time. The probability of false recall was about the same as the probability that they would correctly recall a word that had actually been presented! These high levels of false recall occurred immediately after the presentation, despite the emphatic warning against guessing.

After studying the 16 lists, students received another recognition test that covered all the words they had tried to remember. False recognition was again quite high—77% as compared to 72% correct recognition of words that actually were studied. Further, prior false recall boosted false recognition by a few percentage points. Participants in these experiments also report their errors with very high confidence. They are not just guessing; they seemed to be remembering.

Implications
Our method of studying false memory, the Deese-Roediger-McDermott (or DRM) paradigm, is now widely used for many purposes. One exciting avenue of current research is the study of individual differences among people. The paradigm measures the tendency to make incorrect associative inferences, and some people show the phenomenon more than others. Similar errors represent one of the tricks that memory can play and are probably common in everyday life (Roediger & McDermott, 2000b; Roediger & Gallo, in press).

possibility is a *source-monitoring error*, which occurs when a person attributes a memory derived from one source to another source. Research by Marcia Johnson and her colleagues (Johnson, 1996; Johnson, Hashtroudi, & Lindsay, 1993; Lindsay & Johnson, 1991; Mitchell & Johnson, 2000) suggests that people frequently have difficulties in *source monitoring*, or figuring out the origins of a memory. They may believe they read an article in a prestigious newspaper, such as the *New York Times*, when in fact they saw it in a tabloid on a supermarket shelf while waiting to check out. When people hear a list of words that does not contain a word that is highly associated with the other words, they may believe that their recall of that central word is from the list rather than from their minds.

In general, then, people are remarkably susceptible to making mistakes and, in general, to imagining that they have seen things they have not seen (Loftus, 1998). Wells (1993) has shown how lineups can lead to faulty conclusions. Eyewitnesses assume that the perpetrator is in the lineup, but this is not always the case. When the perpetrator of a staged crime was not in a lineup, participants were likely to name someone other than the perpetrator as the guilty person, simply so that they could recognize *someone* in the lineup as having committed the crime. The identities of the non-perpetrators in the lineup also can affect judgments (Wells, Luus, & Windschitl, 1994). In other words, whether a given person is identified as a perpetrator can be influenced simply by who the others in the lineup are. In choosing the "distractor" individuals, therefore, police inadvertently affect the likelihood of whether or not an identification occurs and also whether a false identification is likely to occur.

© Darama/Corbis

Children's testimony in legal situations is generally considered to be less reliable than that of adults and must be interpreted with great care.

CHILDREN'S MEMORIES

Children's recollections are particularly susceptible to distortion, especially when the children are asked leading questions, as in a courtroom setting. Stephen Ceci and Maggie Bruck (1993, 1995) have reviewed the literature on children's eyewitness testimony and come to some conclusions. First, the younger the child is, the less reliable his or her testimony can be expected to be. In particular, children of preschool age are much more susceptible to suggestive questioning that tries to steer them to a certain response than are children of school age or adults. Second, when a questioner is coercive or even just seems to want a particular answer, children can be quite susceptible to providing what the adult seems to want to hear. Given the pressures in court cases, such forms of questioning may be unfortunately prevalent. Third, children may believe that they recall observing things that others have said they observed. In other words, they hear a story about something that took place. They then believe that they have observed what allegedly took place. Perhaps even more than eyewitness testimony from adults, the testimony of children must be interpreted with great caution.

Steps can be taken to make eyewitness identification more reliable. Investigators can use methods that reduce potential biases, reduce the pressure to choose a suspect from a limited set of options, and ensure that each member of an array of suspects fits the description given by the eyewitness (Wells, 1993). In addition, some psychologists (e.g., Loftus, 1993a, 1993b) and many defense attorneys believe that jurors should be advised that confidence does not imply validity. The degree to which the eyewitness feels confident of her or his identification does not necessarily correspond to the degree to which the eyewitness accurately identifies the defendant as being the culprit. At the same time, some psychologists (e.g., Egeth, 1993; Yuille, 1993) and many prosecutors believe that the existing evidence, based largely on simulated eyewitness studies rather than on actual eyewitness accounts, is not strong enough to risk attacking the credibility of eyewitness testimony when such testimony might send a true criminal to prison. Still others (e.g., Bekerian, 1993; described also in LaFraniere, 1992) suggest that there are no typical eyewitnesses. Conclusions based on an average case should not necessarily be applied to all cases.

Thus far, we have discussed several ways that psychologists disagree about some of the specific mechanisms of memory within the context of the three-store model of memory. Next we consider whether there is a plausible alternative way to view what we know about memory.

✓CONCEPT CHECK 2

1. When you keep repeating a phone number to yourself in order to remember it, you are _____ the phone number.
   a. rehearsing
   b. retrieving
   c. reintegrating
   d. recoding
2. Research suggests that, on average, children's testimony in court, based on memory, is
   a. more reliable than that of adults.
   b. about as reliable as that of adults.
   c. less reliable than that of adults.
   d. of unknown reliability in comparison with that of adults.
3. You are asked to recall the list 8, 2, 5, 3, 9, 1, 7 immediately after hearing it. The serial-position effect suggests that your recall will be best for the digit
   a. 8.   b. 2.   c. 3.   d. 7.

ALTERNATIVE MODELS OF MEMORY

What are alternatives to the traditional model of memory?

In previous chapters, we have seen how different psychologists interpret identical data in different ways. Memory is another area in which what we know can be interpreted in more than one way (Roediger, 1980).

LEVELS-OF-PROCESSING MODEL

Craik and Lockhart (1972) proposed that rather than being in separate stores, memories are saved along a continuum. In this *levels-of-processing framework*, storage varies along the dimension depth of encoding. In other words, items can be encoded at a theoretically infinite number of levels of processing, with no distinct boundaries between one level and the next. Craik and Lockhart found that they could manipulate the alleged level of processing to which a word was encoded by the kind of question they asked when a word was presented. For example, asking whether the word was presented in all capital letters would result in a relatively superficial level of encoding. In contrast, asking the meaning of the presented word would result in a deeper level of encoding.

This framework has an immediate, practical application. As you study, the more elaborately and diversely you encode material, the more you are likely to recall it later (Craik & Brown, 2000). Just looking at material again and again in the same way is less productive for learning the material than is asking yourself meaningful questions about the material and finding more than one way to learn it. Suppose you wish to learn that the Spanish word *caballo* means "horse." You might elaborate your encoding of the word by forming an image of a horse riding in a cab (the "cab-" in *caballo*). Then, when you see the word *horse*, you may be reminded of the image, which in turn will help you produce the word. The more elaborate and diverse encoding helps you to retrieve the meaning of the word when you need it.

BADDELEY'S MODEL

Some psychologists (e.g., Baddeley, 1990a, 1990b, 2000a, 2000b; Baddeley & Hitch, 1994; J. Cantor & Engle, 1993; Daneman & Tardif, 1987; Engle, 1994; E. E. Smith & Jonides, 1995; Squire & Knowlton, 2000) view short-term and long-term memory from yet a different perspective. Table 7.1 contrasts the traditional Atkinson-Shiffrin model with this alternative perspective. Note the semantic distinctions, the differences in metaphorical representation, and the differences in emphasis for each view. The key feature of the alternative view is the emphasis on **working memory**, which is the currently active portion of long-term memory that moves elements of information into and out of short-term memory.

Working memory consists of three main elements: the phonological loop, the visuospatial sketchpad, and the central executive. The *phonological loop* briefly holds inner speech for both verbal comprehension and acoustic rehearsal (without which acoustic information decays after about 2 seconds). The *visuospatial sketchpad* briefly holds some visual images. The *central executive* coordinates attentional activities and governs responses. Baddeley also has proposed that a number of other "subsidiary slave systems" probably perform other cognitive or perceptual tasks. Recently, Baddeley (2000a) has added another component to working memory: the episodic buffer. The **episodic buffer** is a limited-capacity system that is capable of binding information from the subsidiary systems and from long-term memory into a unitary episodic representation. That is, this component integrates information from different parts of working memory so that they make sense to us.

Some support for a distinction between working memory and long-term memory comes from neuropsychological research. Neuropsychological studies have shown abundant evidence of a brief memory buffer (used for remembering information temporarily) that is distinct from long-term memory. Furthermore, some promising new research using PET techniques (see Chapter 3) has found evidence for distinct brain areas involved in the different aspects of working memory. The phonological loop, which maintains speech-related information, appears to involve bilateral activation of the frontal and parietal lobes (Cabeza & Nyberg, 1997). Interestingly, the visuospatial sketchpad appears to activate slightly different areas, depending on the length of the retention interval. Shorter intervals activate areas of the occipital and right frontal lobes, whereas longer intervals activate areas of the parietal and left frontal lobes (Haxby et al., 1995). Finally, the central executive functions appear to involve activation mostly in the frontal lobes (Roberts, Robbins, & Weiskrantz, 1996). Although these findings are

TABLE 7.1
CONCEPT REVIEW

Traditional versus Nontraditional Views of Memory. The traditional three-stores view differs from a contemporary alternative view in terms of the choice of terms, of metaphors, and of emphasis.

	Traditional Three-Stores View	Baddeley's Model
Terminology	*Working memory* is another name for short-term memory, which is distinct from long-term memory.	*Working memory* (active memory) is the part of long-term memory that comprises all the knowledge of facts and procedures that has been recently activated in memory, including the brief, fleeting short-term memory and its contents.
Relationships of stores	Short-term memory is distinct from long-term memory, perhaps either alongside it or hierarchically linked to it.	Short-term memory, working memory, and long-term memory are concentric spheres, in which working memory contains only the most recently activated portion of long-term memory, and short-term memory contains only a very small, fleeting portion of working memory.
Movement of information	Information moves directly from long-term memory to short-term memory, and then back; it is never in both locations at once.	Information remains within long-term memory; when activated, information moves into long-term memory's specialized working memory, which would actively move information into and out of the short-term memory store contained within it.
Emphasis	Distinction between long- and short-term memory.	Role of activation in moving information into working memory and the role of working memory in memory processes.

*See Baddeley, 1990a, 1990b; J. Cantor & Engle, 1993; Daneman & Tardif, 1987; Engle, 1994; Engle, Carullo, & Collins, 1992.

interesting and exciting, they should be taken as somewhat speculative until more research has been done to confirm them.

PARALLEL-PROCESSING MODEL

Based partly on the use of computer models of memory processes, including simulations of memory used in artificial intelligence, many cognitive psychologists now prefer a *parallel-processing model* to describe many phenomena of memory, particularly working memory as the activated portion of long-term memory. This view implies that working memory contains the simultaneously activated (parallel), yet perhaps widely distributed, portions of long-term memory. Thus, the new metaphor also broadens the debate between serial and parallel processes in memory function, encompassing the use of long-term memory in addition to the ramifications for short-term memory discussed earlier.

✓CONCEPT CHECK 3

1. Levels-of-processing theory assumes _____ memory stores.
   a. 2
   b. 3
   c. 10
   d. no separate

2. In Baddeley's model, working memory is the _____ part of long-term memory.
   a. active
   b. deepest
   c. shallowest
   d. inactive

3. In the parallel-processing model, multiple events occur
   a. in slow succession.
   b. in rapid succession.
   c. at the same time.
   d. only once.

EXTREMES OF MEMORY

Some people have exceptional memories. They may remember either poorly or extremely well. Let's consider both extremes.

MEMORY DEFICIENCIES: AMNESIA

We usually take for granted the ability to remember, much as we do the ability to breathe. However, just as we become more aware of the importance of air when we do not have enough to breathe, we are less likely to take memory for granted when we observe people who have serious memory deficiencies.

Amnesia is loss of explicit memory (Squire, 1999). Amnesia victims perform extremely poorly on many explicit memory tasks, but they show normal or almost normal performance on word-completion tasks that involve implicit memory (Baddeley, 1989). When asked whether they have previously seen the word they just completed, however, they are unlikely to remember the specific experience of having seen it. Amnesia victims also show paradoxical performance in tasks that involve *procedural memory* versus those that involve *declarative memory*. For example, amnesia victims may perform extremely poorly on traditional tasks that require recall or recognition memory of declarative knowledge. However, they may demonstrate improvement in performance due to learning when engaged in tasks that require procedural memory, such as solving puzzles, learning to read mirror writing, or mastering motor skills (Baddeley, 1989).

Psychologists study amnesia patients in part to gain insight into normal memory function. One of the general insights gained by studying amnesia victims is that the ability to reflect consciously on prior experience, which is required for tasks that involve explicit memory of declarative knowledge, seems to differ from the ability to demonstrate remembered learning in an apparently automatic way, without conscious recollection of the learning (Baddeley, 1989).

One of the most famous cases of amnesia is H. M., reported by William Scoville and Brenda Milner (1957; Milner, Corkin, & Teuber, 1968). Following an experimental surgical treatment for uncontrollable epilepsy, H. M. suffered severe anterograde amnesia, the inability explicitly to recall events that occurred *after* whatever trauma caused the memory loss. However, H. M. had full recollection of events that had occurred before his operation. Although his postsurgical IQ was 112, which is above average, his score on the memory test was 67, which is far below average (see Chapter 9). Moreover, shortly after taking a test from the memory scale, he could not remember that he had taken it. If he had been given the test again, it would have been as though he were taking it for the first time. H. M. once remarked on his situation: "Every day is alone in itself, whatever enjoyment I've had, and whatever sorrow I've had" (Scoville & Milner, p. 217). H. M. all but lost his ability to form new explicit memories, so he lived suspended in an eternal present.

> Without [memory] all life and thought [are] an unrelated succession. As gravity holds matter from flying off into space, so memory gives stability to knowledge; it is the cohesion which keeps things from falling into a lump, or flowing in waves.
> —Ralph Waldo Emerson, *Natural History of Intellect*

Retrograde amnesia is the inability explicitly to recall events that occurred *before* the trauma that caused the memory loss. W. Ritchie Russell and P. W. Nathan (1946) reported on a 22-year-old greens keeper who suffered serious memory loss following a motorcycle accident. By 10 weeks after the accident, however, he had recovered his explicit memory for most events, starting with the events in the most distant past and gradually progressing up to more recent ones. Eventually, he was able explicitly to recall everything that had happened up to a few minutes prior to the accident. As is often the case, he was never able to recall the events that occurred immediately before the trauma.

Yet another form of amnesia is one that all of us experience: infantile amnesia, the inability to recall events that happened during the early development of the brain. Generally, we can remember little or nothing that happened to us before the age of about 5 years. It is extremely rare for someone to have any memories before the age of 3 years. Reports of childhood memories usually involve significant events, such as the birth of a sibling or the death of a parent (see Fivush & Hamond, 1991). Presumably, these emotional memories last because they make a very strong impression. They are not always accurate, though (Schacter, 1996).

People with various forms of amnesia show reduced memory functioning. Some people, however, show exceptionally high levels of memory functioning; among them are mnemonists.

OUTSTANDING MEMORIES: MNEMONISTS

A mnemonist is a person who uses memory-enhancing techniques to greatly improve his or her memory or who has a distinctive sensory or cognitive ability to remember information, particularly information that is highly concrete or can be visualized readily. The mnemonist's ability shows us what we might long to have, especially when, as students, we wish we had photographic memories for material we need to remember when taking exams.

Perhaps the most famous of mnemonists was "S.," a man described by Alexander Luria, a celebrated Russian psychologist. Luria (1968) reported that one day a man employed as a newspaper reporter appeared in his laboratory. He asked to have his memory tested. Luria tested him and discovered that the man's memory appeared to have virtually no limits. S. could reproduce series of words of any length whatsoever, regardless of how long ago the items had been presented to him. Luria studied S. over a period of 30 years. He found that even when his retention was measured 15 or 16 years after a session in which S. had learned words, S. could still reproduce the words.

What was S.'s trick? How did he remember so much? Apparently, he relied heavily on visual imagery. He converted material that he needed to remember into visual images. For example, he reported that when asked to remember the word *green*, he visualized a green flowerpot, whereas for the word *red*, he visualized a man in a red shirt coming toward him. Even numbers called up images. The number *1* was a proud, well-built man, and so on. S.'s heavy reliance on imagery created difficulty for him when he tried to remember abstract concepts, such as *infinity* or *nothing*, which did not lend themselves well to visual images.

His excellent memory caused S. other problems as well. He could not forget things even when he wanted to. At times, images would come into his consciousness and interfere with his ability to concentrate and even to carry on a conversation. Eventually, S. became a professional entertainer, dazzling audiences with his memory feats. His career choice reflected not his desire to entertain, but rather his inability to succeed in other pursuits.

(E) The story of S. is a good example of how memory and all other cognitive functions represent an evolutionary compromise. Often, as we improve in one function, other functioning can suffer as a result. S.'s superior memory interfered with his ability to adapt in other spheres of life. Similarly, in the physical domain, someone who builds up an extraordinarily muscular frame may lose agility. In eons past, such a person might have had an advantage in some forms of hand-to-hand combat, but might have had some difficulty making a quick escape in the face of overwhelming odds against a stronger, possibly nonhuman predator. Thus, when we complain about being forgetful or even less strong than we might like to be, we should remember that our minds and physiques represent evolutionary compromises. These compro-

mises may not optimize any one function, but they may optimize (or close to it) a delicate balance of functions.

Another mnemonist, S. F., studied by K. Anders Ericsson, William Chase, and Steve Faloon (1980), remembered long strings of numbers by segmenting them into groups of three or four digits each, and encoding them as running times for different races. An experienced long-distance runner himself, S. F. was familiar with the times that would be plausible for different races. S. F. did not enter the laboratory as a mnemonist. Rather, he was selected to represent the average college student in terms of intelligence and memory ability. S. F.'s original memory for a string of numbers was about seven digits, average for a college student. After 200 practice sessions distributed over a 2 years, S. F. had increased his memory for digits more than 10-fold. He could recall up to about 80 digits. His memory was only average, however, when the experimenters intentionally gave him sequences of digits that could not be translated into running times. The work with S. F. by Ericsson and his colleagues suggests that a person with a fairly typical memory ability can be converted into one with quite an extraordinary memory, at least in some domains, with a great amount of concerted practice.

Exceptional mnemonists offer some insight into the processes of memory. Mnemonists generally recode arbitrary, abstract, meaningless information into more meaningful or sensorially concrete information. The recoding aids recall from long-term memory, as we saw earlier. Next we consider how to use mnemonic devices to improve our own memory abilities. These devices rely on similar kinds of recodings that add meaning to otherwise meaningless information. Although most people will never perform at the level of these extraordinary mnemonists, we can all improve our memories by using mnemonics.

Most of the time, we try to improve our *retrospective memory*—that is, our memory for the past. But at times we also try to improve our *prospective memory*—that is, our memory for things we need to do or remember in the future. For example, we may need to remember to call someone, to buy cereal at the supermarket, or to finish a homework assignment due the next day. We use a number of strategies to improve our prospective memory, such as keeping a list, asking someone to remind us to do something, and tying a string or band around our finger to remind us. Curiously, research suggests that having to do something regularly on a certain day does not necessarily improve prospective memory for doing that thing, but being monetarily reinforced for doing the thing does tend to improve prospective memory (Meacham, 1982; Meacham & Singer, 1977).

You can use mnemonic devices to improve your learning of new material. **Mnemonic devices** are specific techniques for aiding in the memorization of isolated items by adding meaning or imagery to an otherwise arbitrary listing of items that may be difficult to remember. Of the many mnemonic devices available, the ones described here rely on organizing information into meaningful chunks: acronyms, interactive images, the method of loci, the pegword system, acrostics, categorical clustering, and the keyword system.

Acronyms are another type of memory device in which a set of letters forms a word or phrase, with each letter standing for a certain other word or concept (e.g., USA, IQ, and laser). You could try to remember the names of these mnemonic devices by using the acronym I AM PACK: **I**nteractive images, **A**cronyms, **M**ethod of loci, **P**egwords, **A**crostics, **C**ategories, and **K**eywords.

When using **interactive images** to enhance memory, you link isolated words by creating visual representations for the words and then picturing interactions among the items. If you needed to remember a list of unrelated words such as *aardvark*, *table*, *pencil*, and *book*, you could imagine an *aardvark* sitting on a *table* holding a *pencil* in its claws and writing in a *book*.

The **method of loci** consists of visualizing a familiar area with distinctive landmarks that can be linked (via interactive images) with items to be remembered. You then mentally walk past each of the landmarks and visualize an image incorporating a new word and a landmark. For example, you could envision an *aardvark* digging at the roots of a familiar tree, a *table* sitting on a familiar sidewalk, and a *pencil*-shaped statue in the center of a familiar fountain. To remember the list, you take your mental walk and pick up the words you have linked to each of the landmarks.

With a **pegword system**, a familiar list of items is linked (via interactive images) with unfamiliar items on a new list. You might take advantage of this nursery rhyme: "One is a bun, two is a shoe, three is a tree, four is a door." Then you imagine, say, an aardvark ready to be eaten on a bun, a shoe resting on a table, a tree that has pencils for branches, and a large book serving as a door, complete with doorknob and hinges.

Acrostics are the initial letters of a series of items that are used to form a sentence, such that the sentence prompts the recall of the initial letters, and the letters prompt the recall of each of the items. Music students use the acrostic "**E**very **G**ood **B**oy **D**oes **F**ine" to memorize the notes on the lines of the treble clef.

In **categorical clustering**, various items are grouped into categories to facilitate recall of the items. If you need to remember to buy apples, milk, grapes, yogurt, Swiss cheese, and grapefruit, try to memorize the items by categories: *fruits*—apples, grapes, grapefruit; *dairy products*—milk, yogurt, Swiss cheese.

A **keyword system** for learning isolated words in a foreign language forms an interactive image that links the sound and meaning of the foreign word to the sound and meaning of a familiar word. To learn that the French word for *butter* is *beurre*, you might note that *beurre* sounds like *bear*. Next, you associate the keyword *bear* with butter in an image or sentence, such as a bear eating a stick of butter. Later, *bear* provides a retrieval cue for *beurre*.

Of the many mnemonic devices available, the ones described here rely on two general principles of effective recall that we covered earlier. Categorical clustering, acronyms, and acrostics involve organizing information into meaningful chunks, which we have seen can help with both short-term and long-term memory. Storing memory as visual images can help with retrieval from long-term memory. It is the basis of the mnemonic techniques of interactive images, the pegword system, the method of loci, and the keyword system. What happens in the brain when we store memories?

✓CONCEPT CHECK 4

1. Mr. Phillips has amnesia as a result of a head injury. He cannot remember events that have occurred since the head injury. He suffers from _____ amnesia.
   a. retrograde
   b. anterograde
   c. proprioceptive
   d. childhood

2. Mrs. Dunning also has amnesia as a result of a head injury. She cannot remember events that occurred prior to the head injury. She suffers from _____ amnesia.
   a. retrograde
   b. anterograde
   c. proprioceptive
   d. childhood

3. Research suggests that _____ can be trained to be mnemonists.
   a. only people of very high IQ
   b. only people who are born with exceptional memory skills
   c. fairly ordinary people
   d. younger but not older people

THE BIOLOGICAL UNDERPINNINGS OF MEMORY

What are the neural and other mechanisms underlying memory functioning?

Psychologists have been able to locate many cerebral structures involved in memory, such as the hippocampus (Buckner, 2000; Markowitsch, 2000; Squire, 1987; R. F. Thompson, 2000; R. F. Thompson & Krupa, 1994). The amygdala interacts with other structures of the brain in memory storage (McGaugh, Cahill, & Roozendaal, 1996). A great deal of our information on the brain structures involved in memory came from the study of people who had sustained some sort of brain damage. Memory is volatile. It may be disturbed by a blow to the head, a disturbance in consciousness, or any number of other injuries to, or pathologies of, the brain. Studies of brain-injured patients are informative because they offer distinctive insights not previously observed in people with normal brain function, such as the insights into declarative versus procedural knowledge gained through the study of amnesia victims. In addition, although studies of brain-injured people do not necessarily provide conclusive evidence regarding localization of function, they may still indicate that a particular structure at least participates in a given function (Kosslyn & Koenig, 1995).

Some studies show preliminary findings regarding the specific structures involved in various kinds of memory, such as procedural versus declarative memory. In particular, procedural memory seems to depend on the basal ganglia (Mishkin & Petri, 1984). However, the hippocampus seems to play a crucial role in complex learning (McCormick & Thompson, 1984; Nyberg & Cabeza, 2000), particularly the encoding of declarative information (Kolb & Whishaw, 1990; Zola & Squire, 2000; Zola-Morgan & Squire, 1990). The hippocampus also appears to be involved in the consolidation of encoded information in long-term store, perhaps as a means of cross-referencing information stored in different parts of the brain (Squire, Cohen, & Nadel, 1984). The amygdala also seems to play an important role in memory consolidation, especially where emotional experience is involved (Cahill, Babinsky, Markowitsch, & McGaugh, 1995; Cahill & McGaugh, 1996; LeDoux, 1996; McGaugh, 1999; Packard, Cahill, & McGaugh, 1994; Roozendaal, Cahill, & McGaugh, 1996). In addition, the cerebral cortex appears to play a minor but important role in long-term memory, particularly declarative memory (Zola-Morgan & Squire, 1990). Another form of memory is the classically conditioned response, in which the cerebellum is important (R. F. Thompson, 1987). For example, when dogs are classically conditioned to salivate at the

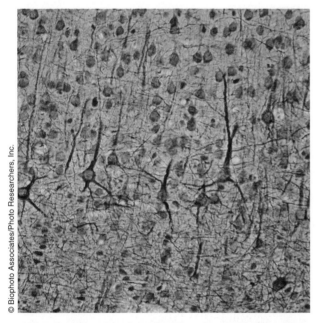 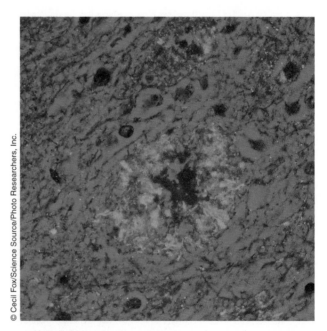

Alzheimer's plaques can be seen in these photomicrographs. Such accretions may interfere with memory. Alzheimer's patients show severe loss of the brain tissue that secretes acetylcholine, a neurotransmitter that seems to enhance neural transmission associated with memory.

sight of those who bring them food, we can expect activation in the cerebellum.

NEUROCHEMISTRY

In addition to these preliminary insights into whatever macro-level structures of memory may exist, we are beginning to understand the micro-level structure of memory. We know that some neurotransmitters enhance memory storage, and other neurotransmitters disrupt memory storage. Both serotonin and acetylcholine seem to enhance neural transmission associated with memory, and noradrenaline may also do so. Moreover, high concentrations of acetylcholine have been found in the hippocampus of normal persons (Squire, 1987), but low concentrations are found in victims of Alzheimer's disease—a disorder that causes severe memory loss. In fact, Alzheimer's patients show severe loss of the brain tissue that secretes acetylcholine. Despite intensive research in this area, scientists have yet to pin down the specific causes of Alzheimer's disease, although they are getting closer to understanding this serious disease.

Memory tests may be given to assess whether an individual has Alzheimer's disease, although definitive diagnosis is possible only through analysis of brain tissue (which shows plaques and tangles in case of disease). In one test (Buschke et al., 1999), individuals see a sheet of paper that contains four words, each belonging to a different category. The examiner says the category name for one of the words, and the individual must point to the appropriate word. For example, if the category is animal, the individual might point to a picture of a cow. A few minutes after the words have been presented, individuals make an attempt to recall all the words they saw. If they cannot recall a word, they are given the category to which the word belongs. Some individuals cannot remember the words, even when prompted with the categories. Alzheimer's patients score much worse on this test than do other individuals.

Researchers have been better able to track down the cause of another form of memory dysfunction, alcohol consumption, which disrupts the activity of serotonin, thereby impairing the formation of memories (Weingartner, Rudorfer, Buchsbaum, & Linnoila, 1983).

How might neurotransmitters affect memory? Consider acetylcholine. Some evidence suggests that this neurotransmitter may cause dendritic changes. During memory formation, there is a breakdown of the protein called MAP-2 (a microtubule-associated protein that normally stabilizes dendrite structure and regulates branching of the dendrites). This breakdown occurs particularly in the cortical and hippocampal pyramidal cells that contain receptors to acetylcholine (Woolf, 1998). A relationship between dendrite structure and acetylcholine is also apparent in experiments with transgenic mice (mice that have genes taken from other organisms). Transgenic mice that have too much acetycholinesterase (the protein that breaks down acetylcholine) show poor spatial memory as adults. Their cortical dendrite branches are no further developed than those of normal 5-week-old mice (Beeri et al., 1997).

NEUROPHYSIOLOGY

The neurophysiology of memory is somewhat different from the neurophysiology of learning because the changes that accompany long-term memory storage have to endure longer than the changes in synaptic effectiveness that occur in learning could possibly last. After all, memories can endure for a person's entire lifetime. Relatively permanent structural alterations can occur in dendrites that correlate with memory consolidation or other mental abilities in mammals. A type of neuron that appears to be important for memory is called a *pyramidal neuron*, which has a cell body shaped like a pyramid and generally has a long axon (see Chapter 3). The large pyramidal cells in the cerebral cortex and hippocampus appear to be critical in memory.

The dendrites of these large cells become increasingly structured over the life span, with alterations and additions occurring mainly at the outermost branches. One key structural element underlying the shape and branching pattern of the dendrite is the *microtubule* (extremely small tubelike structure) and the proteins associated with it. Microtubules transport materials to and from the cell body. Ultimately, memory-related changes in dendritic structure affect the number and distribution of synapses, which in turn affect overall patterns of neural activity. Thus, we might become conscious of a particular memory when certain synapses are activated. Alternatively, it may be that various states of excitation can develop in dendritic microtubules. Perhaps it is this excitatory phenomenon that is the basis of consciousness and conscious recall (Hameroff, 1994; Hameroff & Penrose, 1995; Penrose, 1994).

Although we have learned a great deal about how memory works in this chapter, much remains unknown. As researchers engage in increasingly sophisticated studies of the cognitive and physiological mechanisms of memory, we will understand memory much more profoundly. We are also rapidly approaching the day when we can use physiological means to help people who have pathological deficits of memory. Perhaps we will even be able to expand our normal memory capacities through neuropsychological interventions, such as pills that improve memory. For now, however, we must be content to use mnemonic devices and other external aids to enhance our memories.

One of the key ways we remember information is by using language. Language aids memory by offering us external aids such as written lists and by making isolated bits of information meaningful through the organization of the information and the use of mnemonic devices such as acrostics and acronyms.

Clearly, there are many systems of memory. As you have seen in this chapter, different investigators emphasize different systems. Schacter (2000) has proposed that there are five memory systems in all: episodic, semantic, perceptual (i.e., recognizing things on the basis of their form and structure), procedural, and working. This proposal may be as accurate as any we have, although there are differences in language, at times, in speaking of these systems. The many facets and uses of language are topics for the next chapter.

✓ CONCEPT CHECK 5

1. Procedural memory seems to depend especially on the
   a. amygdala.
   b. septum.
   c. basal ganglia.
   d. cerebellum.
2. Alcohol consumption disrupts the regulation of _____ and thus may disrupt the formation of memories.
   a. acetylcholine
   b. epinephrine
   c. norepinephrine
   d. serotonin
3. A type of neuron that seems to be especially important for memory is the _____ neuron.
   a. triangular
   b. quadrangular
   c. pyramidal
   d. hexagonal

UNIFYING PSYCHOLOGY

PSYCHOGENIC AMNESIA

D.B. is an elderly gentleman who suffered brain damage as a result of partial suffocation. He does not remember his personal past before the brain damage, but his memory for events that were not directly related to him, such as those in the news, is largely intact (Klein, Loftus, & Kihlstrom, 2002). In other words, D.B.'s episodic memory is impaired, but his semantic memory was spared. Psychologists in a variety of specialties are very interested in studying cases like D.B.'s because they inform us about how memories are stored and retrieved, the relationship between consciousness and memories, and the underlying brain processes.

D.B.'s case is very similar to a phenomenon known as psychogenic amnesia, a memory disorder caused by stress or a traumatic experience that is characterized by episodic memory loss.

People who have psychogenic amnesia remember little or nothing about their own pasts. In some cases, they may forget only the events associated with the traumatic event, such as a rape or a combat experience. For example, *clinical psychologist* Eliezer Witztum and his colleagues have reported that psychogenic amnesia is a core symptom of posttraumatic stress disorder in war veterans (Witztum, Maragalit, & van der Hart, 2002). (You will learn more about posttraumatic stress disorder in Chapter 16.) Clinical psychologists who treat people with psychogenic amnesia may use intensive psychotherapy and hypnosis to help them process suppressed experiences. However, research by *experimental psychologist* Theo Dekkers and his colleagues has indicated that most people who experience trauma do not develop psychogenic amnesia (Dekkers, Wessel, & Roefs, 2003).

Forensic psychologists also conduct research on psychogenic amnesia because criminal offenders sometimes claim memory loss when questioned about a crime (Cima, Merckelbach, Nijman, Knauer, & Hollnack, 2002). In these cases, forensic or clinical psychologists may be called to court to testify about whether the suspect truly does suffer from psychogenic amnesia. The psychologist interviews the suspect and uses a series of sophisticated tests to determine whether or not the suspect is being untruthful (malingering).

Not all criminal suspects who claim to have impaired memory are lying. The combination of strong emotions and drug or alcohol use can disorder the storage of memory for current events. In *The Man Who Mistook His Wife for a Hat,* Oliver Sacks, a *neurologist,*

continued

describes the case of a young man named Donald, who did not remember killing his girlfriend in a fit of rage until he was involved in a bicycle wreck. His frontal lobes were injured so that they no longer repressed the horrific memory of the event, and it began to haunt him (Sacks, 1985). Because psychogenic amnesia is so rare, however, most people who commit crimes and claim amnesia are malingering.

Criminals are certainly motivated to lie and deny any memory of the crime. **Experimental forensic psychologist** Susanna Bylin tested 76 college students to determine how feigning memory impairment affects the recall of genuine memories (Bylin & Christianson, 2002). All the students read a story about a violent crime that they'd supposedly committed, and half were asked to fake memory impairment during an interview. The students were then interviewed a second time, and all were asked to recall the

crime truthfully. The subjects who faked memory impairment during the first interview now made more mistakes in recalling the details of the crime in a free-recall or open-ended questioning format, but their answers were perfect in a multiple-choice format that let them recognize the details (Bylin & Christianson, 2002). Thus, the act of lying about a past incident can interfere with the retrieval of facts.

Personality psychologists and **cognitive neuroscientists** have also studied people with psychogenic amnesia. For example, personality psychologists who examined the characteristics of suspects who claimed memory loss found that psychogenic amnesia was associated with such personality factors as introversion and excellent impulse control (Gudjonsson, Hannesdottir, & Petursson, 1999). **Clinical neuropsychologist** Hans Markowitsch and a team of neuroscientists reported the test results of two men who had severe,

persistent psychogenic amnesia of unknown cause (Kessler, Markowitsch, Huber, Kalbe, Weber-Luxenberger, & Kock, 1997; Markowitsch, Calabrese, Fink, & Durwen, 1997). MRI scans and EEG tests indicated no evidence of brain damage, and neuropsychological tests revealed that the men were of average to high intelligence and had excellent short-term memories. A PET scan of one man showed a disturbance in the functioning of an area of the frontal lobe that is associated with the retrieval of episodic memory (Markowitsch et al., 1997).

The phenomenon of psychogenic amnesia is not well understood. Reports of experimental and case studies of people who have the disorder are slowly adding to our knowledge of this baffling impairment. Piece by piece, the puzzle is being solved by many kinds of psychologists, working from different perspectives toward the same goal.

SUMMARY

1. *Memory* is the process by which past experience and learning can be used in the present.
2. Four of the main kinds of tasks used to study memory are: (a) *serial recall*, in which a person needs to remember items according to the order in which they are presented; (b) *free recall*, in which the person can remember items in any order; (c) *paired-associates recall*, in which a person needs to remember the second member of two paired words; and (d) *recognition*, in which a person must indicate whether a presented word is one that has been learned previously. Cued recall has aspects of both recall and recognition tasks.
3. Memory researchers study *explicit memory*, in which people are asked to make a conscious recollection, as well as *implicit memory*, in which task

performance is characterized by a recollection that we are not conscious of making. *Declarative memory* is memory for static knowledge, whereas *procedural memory* is memory for how to do things.

4. In a model proposed by Richard Atkinson and Richard Shiffrin, memory is thought to involve three stores: (a) a *sensory store*, capable of holding relatively limited amounts of information for very brief periods of time; (b) a *short-term store*, capable of holding small amounts of information for somewhat longer periods of time; and (c) a *long-term store*, capable of storing large amounts of information virtually indefinitely.

5. Three operations occur in all three of the suggested memory stores: (a) *encoding*, by which information is placed into the store; (b) *storage*, by which information is maintained in the store; and (c) *retrieval*, by which information is pulled from the store into consciousness.

6. The *iconic store* refers to visual sensory memory.

7. Encoding of information in the *short-term store* appears to be largely, though not exclusively, acoustic, as shown by the susceptibility of information in the short-term store to acoustic confusability—that is, errors based on sounds of words.

8. We retain information mainly by *rehearsal*.

9. Two of the main theories of forgetting are (a) *interference theory*, which hypothesizes that information is forgotten when a new memory trace competes with an old one, and (b) *decay theory*, which postulates that information is lost when it remains unused for a long period of time. These theories apply to both short-term and long-term memory.

10. Interference theory distinguishes between (a) *retroactive interference*, caused by activity that occurs *after* we learn the stimulus material to be recalled, and (b) *proactive interference*, caused by activity that occurs *before* we learn the stimulus material to be recalled.

11. The capacity of the short-term store is about seven plus or minus two items. We often form *chunks* of bits of information if the items are lengthy or complex.

12. The *serial-position curve* shows our level of learning as a function of where a particular item appears in a list. The curve typically shows elevated recall at the beginning (*primacy effect*) and the end (*recency effect*) of a list, although experimental conditions can be constructed to reduce or eliminate these effects.

13. Processing of information in the short-term store may be in the form of either (a) *parallel processing*, which refers to multiple operations occurring simultaneously, or (b) *serial processing*, which refers to just a single operation occurring at a given time.

14. *Serial processing* can be characterized as either (a) exhaustive, implying that a person always checks all information on a list, or (b) self-terminating, implying that a person checks only that information on a list that is necessary for a particular comparison to be made.

15. Information in the long-term store appears to be encoded primarily in a semantic form, so that confusions tend to be in terms of the meanings rather than the sounds of words.

16. Theorists disagree about whether all information in the long-term store is encoded in terms of propositions (the meaning underlying a particular relationship among concepts or things) or in terms of both propositions and images (mental pictures).

17. We tend to remember better when we acquire knowledge through *distributed learning* (learning that is spaced over time) rather than through *massed learning* (learning that occurs within a short period of time). To learn material gradually over the term of a course is an example of distributed learning, whereas to cram for an examination is an example of massed learning.

18. How we *rehearse* information influences how well we retain it. If we elaborate the items—that is, if we relate them or connect them to something we already know—then we are far more likely to remember them.

19. Some theorists distinguish between (a) *semantic memory*, our memory for facts not recalled in any particular temporal context, and (b) *episodic memory*, our memory for facts that have some kind of temporal tag associated with them. Our memory for the meaning of a word is normally semantic; we do not remember when or where we learned that meaning. In contrast, our memory for the words on a list to be learned is normally episodic; we are likely to recall words from some list just learned and not from other lists that may be in the long-term store.

20. An item is *available* in memory if it is there to be retrieved. An item is *accessible* to the extent that it is available and easily retrieved.

21. *Encoding specificity* refers to the fact that what is recalled depends largely on what is encoded: How information is encoded at the time of learning greatly affects how it is later recalled. The context and the category of information also influence how we encode information.

22. Memory appears to be not only *reconstructive* (a direct reproduction of what was learned) but also *constructive* (influenced by attitudes and past knowledge). Constructive memories can present special problems if they interfere with eyewitness testimony in court.

ALTERNATIVE MODELS OF MEMORY 269

What are alternatives to the traditional model of memory?

23. Some theorists conceive of memory not in terms of fixed stores but rather a potentially infinite number of levels of processing.

24. *Working memory* usually is defined as part of long-term memory and also comprises short-term memory. From this perspective, working memory holds only the most recently activated portion of long-term memory, and it moves these activated elements into and out of short-term memory. Instead of this view, some psychologists define working memory as being the same as short-term memory.

EXTREMES OF MEMORY 271

What is exceptional memory, and what are its causes?

25. Severe loss of memory is referred to as *amnesia*. *Anterograde amnesia* refers to difficulty in explicitly remembering events that occur after the time of trauma, whereas *retrograde amnesia* refers to severe difficulty in explicitly remembering events that occur before the time of trauma. *Infantile amnesia* is our inability to remember events that occurred to us before about age 5.

26. A *mnemonist* relies on special techniques, such as imagery, for greatly improving his or her memory; anyone can use these techniques.

27. *Mnemonic devices* are used to improve recall. Examples of such devices are *categorical clustering*, *acronyms*, *acrostics*, *interactive imagery*, and *keywords*.

THE BIOLOGICAL UNDERPINNINGS OF MEMORY 274

What are the neural and other mechanisms underlying memory functioning?

28. Although they have yet to identify particular locations for particular memories, researchers have been able to learn a great deal about the specific structures of the brain that are involved in memory. In addition, researchers are investigating the biochemistry of neural processes involved in memory, such as the role of specific neurotransmitters (e.g., serotonin and acetylcholine) and hormones.

KEY TERMS

accessibility 260
acronyms 273
acrostics 273
amnesia 271
anterograde amnesia 271
availability 260
categorical clustering 273
chunk 255
concepts 259
constructive memory 261
cued recall 249
decay 253
decay theory 254
declarative memory 249
distributed learning 259
encoding 251
encoding specificity 261
episodic buffer 269
episodic memory 259
explicit memory 249
flashbulb memory 262

free recall 249
iconic store 252
implicit memory 249
infantile amnesia 271
interactive images 273
interference 253
interference theory 254
keyword system 273
long-term store 251
massed learning 259
memory 248
memory scanning 255
method of loci 273
mnemonic devices 273
mnemonist 271
paired-associates recall 249
parallel processing 256
pegword system 273
primacy effect 255
priming 250
proactive interference 254

procedural memory 249
recall memory 248
recency effect 255
recognition memory 248
reconstructive memory 261
rehearsal 253
retrieval 251
retroactive interference 254
retrograde amnesia 271
schema 259
semantic memory 259
sensory store 250
serial-position curve 255
serial processing 256
serial recall 249
short-term store 250
storage 251
total-time hypothesis 258
working memory 269

Concept Check 1

1. b   2. d   3. c

Concept Check 2

1. a   2. c   3. d

Concept Check 3

1. d   2. a   3. c

Concept Check 4

1. b   2. a   3. c

Concept Check 5

1. c   2. d   3. c

KNOWLEDGE CHECK

1. Visual sensory memory is also called _____ memory.
   a. echoic
   b. iconic
   c. short-term
   d. ocular
2. Which of the following is *not* part of Baddeley's model of working memory?
   a. the phonological loop
   b. the visuospatial sketchpad
   c. the central executive
   d. the levels of processing
3. Which of the following stores is *not* part of the Atkinson-Shiffrin model?
   a. sensory storage
   b. short-term storage
   c. intermediate-term storage
   d. long-term storage
4. Repressed memories have
   a. definitively been shown never to occur.
   b. definitively been shown to occur frequently.
   c. definitively been shown to occur relatively rarely.
   d. not been definitively shown to occur or not to occur.
5. The primacy effect in the serial-position curve is attributable to the effects of
   a. short-term memory.
   b. long-term memory.
   c. implicit memory.
   d. procedural memory.

6. You study for a French test. Then you study for a Spanish test. Now you are taking the Spanish test. Your studying for the French test may lead to
   a. proactive interference.
   b. retroactive interference.
   c. reactive interference.
   d. inactive interference.
7. Research shows that cramming the night before an examination is an ineffective way of studying because it produces _____ learning.
   a. distributed
   b. implicit
   c. delayed
   d. massed
8. Bartlett's experiment was a demonstration of the extent to which memory is
   a. constructive.
   b. deconstructive.
   c. reconstructive.
   d. instructive.
9. Your recall of your earliest experience is an example of _____ memory.
   a. semantic
   b. procedural
   c. episodic
   d. implicit
10. In general, interactive imagery has _____ on memory.
    a. a positive effect
    b. a negative effect
    c. no effect
    d. a variable effect

Answers
1. b   2. d   3. c   4. d   5. b   6. a   7. d   8. a
9. c   10. a

THINK ABOUT IT

1. How did the Atkinson-Shiffrin model shape both the questions asked about memory and the methods used to find answers to those questions?
2. It is often said that Alzheimer's patients eventually lose their personalities and their distinctive identities when they lose their memories. How does your memory serve as the basis for your unique personality and identity?
3. Why might people sometimes think they remember events that in fact never have happened?
4. Describe one means by which a researcher could study the relationship between perception and memory.
5. Cognitive psychologists frequently study patterns of errors when they investigate how a particular cognitive process works. What is a pattern of errors in memory tasks you have performed?
6. What have you learned that has led to both positive transfer and negative transfer when you were learning something else? Explain the effects of each.

WEB RESOURCES

For a chapter tutorial quiz, direct links to Internet sites, and other useful features, visit the book-specific website at http://psychology.wadsworth.com/sternberg4e. You can also connect directly to the following sites:

Amnesia and Cognition Unit
http://w3.arizona.edu/~amcog/
This site is maintained by the amnesia research group at the University of Arizona, and describes ongoing research into the effects on memory function of aging and brain injury.

Memory Improvement and Training
http://www.selfgrowth.com/memory.html
This site is part of Self-Improvement Online. It provides links to recommended Web sites that focus on memory improvement and training.

Human Memory
http://www.cc.gatech.edu/classes/cs6751_97_winter/ Topics/human-cap/memory.html
This large site contains general information on memory, including memory types and short- and long-term memory.

 For additional readings on many of the topics covered in this chapter, check out InfoTrac College Edition at **www.infotrac-college.com/ wadsworth.**

CD-ROM: UNIFYING PSYCHOLOGY

Disk Two
The Atkinson-Schiffrin Model of Memory
Improving Memory
Chapter Quiz
Critical Thinking Questions

© 2002 AP/Wide World Photos

CHAPTER **8**

LANGUAGE AND THOUGHT

I n *Through the Looking Glass*, Humpty Dumpty points out that there is only one day in a year when people receive birthday presents but 364 days when they can receive unbirthday presents. He remarks:

"There's glory for you!"

"I don't know what you mean by 'glory,'" Alice said.

Humpty Dumpty smiled contemptuously. "Of course you don't—till I tell you. I meant 'there's a nice knockdown argument for you.'"

"But 'glory' doesn't mean 'a nice knockdown argument,'" Alice objected.

"When I use a word," Humpty Dumpty said in rather a scornful tone, "it means just what I choose it to mean—neither more nor less."

"The question is," said Alice, "whether you can make words mean so many different things."

"The question is," said Humpty Dumpty, "which is to be master— that's all."

—*Lewis Carroll*, Through the Looking Glass

Language is an organized way to combine words in order to communicate. To be meaningful, words and other features of language must be at least somewhat common to us all. So Humpty Dumpty's thinking is unusual because much of our thinking is reflected in language.

The first part of this chapter reviews some of what psychologists know about language. The second part reviews some of what we know about how thought uses language. Both language and thought build upon complex long-term memories. So it makes sense that this chapter follows the chapter on memory.

THE NATURE OF LANGUAGE

What characteristics define language?

Although there is some disagreement about what qualities define language, many psychologists accept six properties as distinctive (e.g., R. Brown, 1965; H. H. Clark & Clark, 1977; Glucksberg & Danks, 1975). Some psychologists also add a seventh property.

1. **Language is communicative.** Despite being the most obvious feature of language, communication is the most important. The notion that I can express what I am thinking and feeling so that you can understand my thoughts and feelings is the basis for all uses of language.

2. **Language is arbitrary.** Human language involves a shared system of *arbitrary symbolic reference*, symbols (images, sounds, or objects that represent or suggest other things) that are selected arbitrarily as a means of representing particular things, ideas, processes, relationships, and descriptions. A particular combination of letters or sounds may be meaningful to us. But the particular symbols do not themselves lead to the meaning of the word. Shakespeare aptly described the arbitrary nature of language when he wrote: "What's in a name? That which we call a rose, by any other name would smell as sweet" (*Romeo and Juliet*, Act 2, Scene 2). With the rare exception of *onomatopoeia*, in which a word sounds like what it describes (e.g., *buzz, hiss, hum*), the sound combination is arbitrary. For example, the word for *tree* in Spanish is *arbol*. Neither the English nor the Spanish word is particularly evocative of anything intrinsic about a tree.

3. **Language is meaningfully structured or rule governed.** Structure makes this shared system of communication possible. Particular patterns of sounds and of letters form meaningful words. In turn, particular patterns of words form meaningful sentences, paragraphs, and discourse. Although individual languages vary in organization, all require some sort of structure. For example, adding *-s* to an English-language singular noun typically converts that noun into its plural form.

4. **Language has multiple levels.** Any meaningful utterance can be analyzed at more than one level. Particular patterns of words can have more than one meaning. An illustration is a sign in a New York drugstore: "We dispense with accuracy" (Lederer, 1987, p. 63). A basic idea can be expressed by more than one pattern of words. "The student chewed the pencil" is fundamentally the same as "The pencil was chewed by the student."

5. **Language is productive.** We can produce an infinite number of unique sentences and other meaningful combinations of words. Language is inherently creative precisely because none of us can have heard all the sentences we are capable of producing. Moreover, every language has the potential to express any idea that can be expressed in any other language. The ease, clarity, and succinctness of expression of a particular idea, however, vary greatly from one language to the next. "I lost the key" is often said as "Se me olividó la llave" ("The key was lost to me") in Spanish. The Spanish expression may seem awkward to an English speaker. But it also differs in connotation; the passive voice seems to remove some of the responsibility from the person who lost the key.

6. **Language is dynamic.** It constantly evolves. New words, phrases, and meanings make their way into common use every day.

An additional property sometimes added to this list is that a first language is spontaneously acquired. Children learn to speak their first language without any special effort, through their interactions with parents and peers.

Although we can list the properties of language, it is important always to keep in mind what the main purpose of language is. Language lets us construct a mental representation of a situation so we can understand the situation and communicate about it (Budwig, 1995; Zwaan & Radvansky, 1998). Ultimately, language is primarily about use, not just about a set of properties.

How does language, and especially these characteristics of language, relate to the brain?

✓CONCEPT CHECK 1

1. Which of the following is *not* one of the key properties of all languages?
   a. meaningfully structured
   b. productive
   c. arbitrary
   d. written

2. To say that language is dynamic is to say that it is
   a. constantly evolving.
   b. different in different places.
   c. a source of energy.
   d. lacking in rules.

3. The number of possible sentences in the English language is
   a. in the thousands.
   b. in the millions.
   c. in the trillions.
   d. infinite.

LANGUAGE AND THE BRAIN

What brain mechanisms underlie language?

Researchers interested in the brain's role in language have devised increasingly sophisticated techniques to study the brain. Some of our earliest insights into brain localization are related to an association between certain language deficits and specific organic damage to the brain. These relationships were first explored systematically by Paul Broca and Carl Wernicke (see Chapters 2 and 3). Broca's aphasia and Wernicke's aphasia are particularly well documented instances in which brain lesions affect speech (see Chapter 3). Since the time of Broca and Wernicke, doctors and researchers have found that lesions in certain areas of the brain are often associated with specific observed language deficits in patients who are brain-injured.

Researchers also investigate brain localization of linguistic function via other methods, such as evaluating the effects on linguistic function caused by electrical stimulation of the brain (e.g., Ojemann, 1982; Ojemann & Mateer, 1979). Stimulating certain places in the brain seems to have discrete effects on particu-

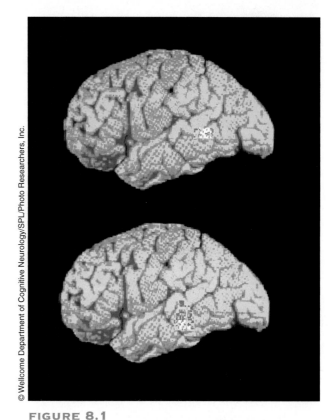

© Wellcome Department of Cognitive Neurology/SPL/Photo Researchers, Inc.

FIGURE 8.1

PET Scans of Brain Activity During Speech. For all right-handed and most left-handed people, the left hemisphere is responsible for syntactical aspects of linguistic processing and is clearly essential to speech. The areas shown in red are activated during speech.

lar linguistic functions (such as the naming of objects) across repeated, successive trials. Across individuals, however, these particular localizations of function vary widely. Yet another avenue of research involves studying the metabolic activity of the brain and the flow of blood in the brain while a person performs various verbal tasks. Figure 8.1 shows brain scans relevant to the production of language.

Relying mainly upon lesion studies, scientists have been able to identify many locations of the brain that are involved in both normal language activities and disruptions in language. For example, we can broadly generalize that many linguistic functions are located primarily in the areas identified by Broca and Wernicke, although it is now believed that damage to Wernicke's area, in the back area of the cortex, reduces linguistic function more than does damage to Broca's area, closer to the front of the brain (Kolb & Whishaw, 1990). Also, lesion studies have shown that linguistic function is governed by a much larger area of the posterior cortex than just the area identified by Wernicke, and that other areas of the cortex also play a role, such as association-cortex areas in the left hemisphere, a portion of the left

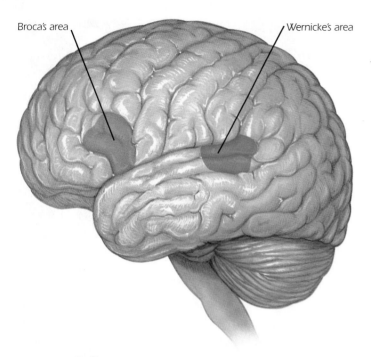

Broca's area   Wernicke's area

FIGURE 8.2
Areas of the Brain Responsible for Language. Broca's area and Wernicke's area are particularly important in language processing.

temporal cortex, and some subcortical structures. Studies of brain metabolism have contributed to research on the location of language functions in the brain. For example, preliminary metabolic and blood-flow studies of the brain (e.g., Petersen, Fox, Posner, Mintun, & Raichle, 1988) have indicated that more areas of the brain are involved in linguistic function than we would have determined without having these studies available (see Figure 8.2).

HEMISPHERIC DIFFERENCES IN PROCESSING

In addition to being more widespread than early researchers might have thought, language functions seem to be differentially specialized in the hemispheres of the brain. The various methods of studying the brain support the view that for all right-handed individuals and most left-handed persons, the left hemisphere of the brain is clearly implicated in syntactical aspects of linguistic processing. It is clearly essential to speech (Cabeza & Nyberg, 1997). The left

© Shaywitz et al., 1995, Nature, 373, 607–609. Courtesy of NMR Research/Yale Medical School

LEFT   FRONT   LEFT   FRONT
WOMEN   MEN

MRI scans showed that women use right and left hemispheres to process language; men use only left.

hemisphere also seems to be essential to the ability to write. The right hemisphere is capable of quite a bit of auditory comprehension, particularly semantic processing and some reading comprehension. The right hemisphere also seems to be important in several subtle nuances of linguistic comprehension and expression, such as understanding and expressing vocal inflection and gesture. It also is involved in comprehending metaphors and other nonliteral aspects of language, such as those used in jokes and sarcasm (Kolb & Whishaw, 1990). Damage to the major left-hemisphere areas responsible for language functioning can sometimes lead to enhanced involvement of other areas as language functioning recovers. In such cases, it is as if previously dormant or overshadowed areas take over the duties left vacant (Cappa et al., 1997; Weiller et al., 1996).

There is some evidence that the brain mechanisms responsible for language learning in children are different from those responsible for language use in adults (Stiles, Bates, Thal, Trauner, & Reilly, 1998). In general, the left hemisphere seems to be better at processing well-practiced routines in behavior and the right hemisphere at dealing with novel stimuli (Mills, Coffey-Corina, & Neville, 1997). A possibly related finding is that individuals who have learned language as adults show more right-hemisphere involvement (Neville, 1995), perhaps because language remains somewhat more novel for them. This finding points out that one cannot precisely map linguistic or other kinds of functioning in hemispheres in a way that works for everyone. Rather, the mappings differ somewhat from one person to another (Zurif, 1995).

SEX DIFFERENCES

From her studies of brain-injured men and women, Doreen Kimura (1987) observed some intriguing sex differences in linguistic function. The men she studied seemed to show more left-hemisphere dominance for language than the women showed. Women showed more bilateral, symmetrical patterns of language. Furthermore, the brain locations associated with aphasia differed in men and women. Most aphasic women showed lesions in the anterior region, although some had lesions in the temporal region. In contrast, aphasic men showed a more varied pattern of lesions. Men also were more likely to show lesions in posterior regions (toward the back of the head) than in anterior regions (more toward the front of the head).

One interpretation of Kimura's findings is that the role of the posterior region in language use may be different for women than for men. Another interpretation is that because women show less lateralization of language, their brains may be better able than men's to compensate for any possible loss of function due to lesions in the left posterior hemisphere. Women compensate by making increased use of the right posterior hemisphere. The possibility that there also may be subcortical sex differences in linguistic function further complicates the interpretation of Kimura's findings.

Related evidence from another lab suggests that men and women appear to process some aspects of language differently (Shaywitz et al., 1995). In an fMRI (functional magnetic resonance imaging) study of men and women, participants were asked to perform one of four tasks: (1) indicate whether a pair of letters are identical; (2) indicate whether two words have the same meaning; (3) indicate whether two words rhyme; and (4) compare the lengths of two lines (a control task). The researchers found that when both male and female participants were performing the letter-recognition and word-meaning tasks, they showed activation in the left temporal lobe of the brain. When they were performing the rhyming task, however, men and women showed a difference. Only the inferior (lower) frontal region of the left hemisphere was activated in men. The inferior frontal region of both the left and right hemispheres was activated in women. These results suggested that men localize their processing in these tasks more than women.

✓CONCEPT CHECK 2

1. Language processing is dealt with in
   a. Wernicke's area but not Broca's area.
   b. Broca's area but not Wernicke's area.
   c. both Wernicke's and Broca's areas.
   d. neither Wernicke's nor Broca's area.
2. Lesion studies to localize language processing rely on
   a. EEG measurements.
   b. fMRI measurements.
   c. assessments of the results of damage to the brain.
   d. assessments of intact brain functioning.

3. Which of the following is a function of the right hemisphere in most people?
   a. understanding spoken language
   b. understanding written language
   c. understanding vocal expression and gesture
   d. producing written language

ASPECTS OF LANGUAGE

What are the different aspects of language and its use?

How do we study this vehicle that lets us engage in flights of communication with our fellow humans? The smallest distinguishable unit of all possible human speech sounds is the *phone*, of which there are more than 100. No known language uses all of the possible phones, however. Each distinct language uses only a subset of these possibilities. **Phonemes** are the particular speech sounds the users of a given language can identify. In English, phonemes are generally identifiable as vowel or consonant sounds, such as the *b*, *i*, and *t* sounds in *bit*. Linguists sometimes travel to remote villages to observe, record, and analyze other languages, some of which are becoming extinct as members leave tribal areas for more urban areas (e.g., Ladefoged & Maddieson, 1996).

A **morpheme** is the smallest unit of sound that denotes meaning in a particular language. The word *talked* has two morphemes: *talk* and the suffix *-ed*. Thus, some morphemes are words and others are word-building components, such as suffixes.

Linguists use the term **lexicon** to describe the entire set of morphemes in a given language or in a given person's linguistic repertoire. The average English-speaking high school graduate has a lexicon of about 60,000 root morphemes. Most college students have lexicons about twice that large (G. A. Miller, 1990). By combining morphemes, most adult English speakers have a **vocabulary**, or repertoire of words, in the hundreds of thousands of words. For example, by affixing just a few morphemes to the root content morpheme *study*, we get *student, studious, studied, studying,* and *studies.*

For linguists, after the analysis of phonemes, morphemes, and the lexicon, the next level is **syntax**, which refers to the way users of a particular language put words together in sentences. Linguists consider the study of syntax to be fundamental to understanding the structure of a language.

The final and most comprehensive level of linguistic analysis is **discourse**, which encompasses language

IN THE LAB OF MORTON GERNSBACHER

WATCHING THE BRAIN PROCESS LANGUAGE

When I was in graduate school, I sat in on an undergraduate cognition course to see how one of the best teachers in the department inspired excitement about cognitive psychology. On the first day, the professor began by posing the following challenge: Imagine that you have been sent to some faraway planet on a mission to discern the workings of a mysterious structure (what on Earth we would call a building). However, you are prohibited from entering the structure. How can you figure out what goes on inside?

With guidance, the students arrived at such recommendations as to carefully observe what is taken into the structure and what is taken out, and from those observations infer what must go on inside. Thus, if you saw sheet metal, rubber, and glass going in and automobiles coming out, you would probably infer something different than if denim, thread, and zippers entered the structure and jeans came out.

At this point, the professor skillfully introduced some rudimentary concepts of experimental design. If clever enough, one can manipulate certain aspects of the input to the structure while controlling as many extraneous variables as possible, and then measure the output qualitatively or quantitatively. Students suggested other covert techniques. For example, you could sneak in at night when activity had ceased, ob-

Professor Gernsbacher earned her PhD from the University of Texas at Austin in 1983. She is the Sir Frederic C. Bartlett Professor of Psychology at the University of Wisconsin—Madison. She has received a National Institutes of Health Research Career Development Award and Senior Research Fellowship, a Fulbright Research Scholar Award, a James McKeen Cattell Fellowship, and a Professional Opportunities for Women Award from the National Science Foundation. She has served as chair of the board of Scientific Affairs and as president of APA Division 3 (experimental psychology). Dr. Gernsbacher's research explores the cognitive processes that underlie language comprehension.

tain a blueprint of the structure, or even bomb a section to see how the output was affected (a method similar to one used in U.S. military reconnaissance). These approaches resemble the techniques of neuro-anatomical inquiry: postmortem analyses, structural brain imaging, and lesion studies. However, as the professor pointed out, none of these approaches would reveal the structure at work. And indeed, over 20 years ago, when I sat in on this class, the opportunity to see the brain *at work* eluded psycholinguists like me.

Times have changed, and our ability to answer questions such as how we comprehend and produce language is enhanced by our ability to watch the brain at work. Using brain imaging such as functional magnetic resonance imaging (fMRI), we can watch that mysterious structure in our heads while it engages in psycholinguistic

processes. In the first experiment I conducted using fMRI, my goal was to observe the brain at work while it processed coherent discourse (D. A. Robertson et al., 2000). To do so, we manipulated a very subtle marker of discourse coherence: the English definite article "the."

In languages that use an article system, the definite article signals repeated reference, which typically signals coherence. For example, in the sentences *A student was reading a textbook* and *A student was becoming bored,* the indefinite article *a* makes it unclear whether the student who was reading the textbook was also the student who was becoming bored. However, if we substitute the definite article *the* for the indefinite article *a—The student was reading a textbook. The student was becoming bored*—the dismal situation becomes clear. In fact, *the* can signal co-reference even when the noun it modifies is only a synonym of the previous noun (e.g., *A student was becoming bored. The clod skipped ahead in the textbook without reading the material inside the box*).

In our fMRI experiment, we presented several series of sentences that contained only indefinite articles. The beginning of one such series follows:

A grandmother sat at a table.
A young child played in a backyard.
A mother talked on a telephone.
A husband drove a tractor.
A grandchild walked up to a door.
A little boy pouted and acted bored.
A grandmother promised to bake cookies.
A wife looked out at a field.
A family was worried about some crops.

We also presented the same sentences after replacing the indefinite articles with the definite article:

The grandmother sat at the table.
The young child played in the backyard.
The mother talked on the telephone.
The husband drove the tractor.
The grandchild walked up to the door.
The little boy pouted and acted bored.
The grandmother promised to bake cookies.
The wife looked out at the field.
The family was worried about the crops.

Although the psycholinguist in me wanted to compare these two conditions directly, the medical physicists I consulted did not believe that such a subtle comparison would lead to observable differences in brain activity. Given their skepticism, and to conform to the fMRI literature of the time, we also included a "loose" contrast condition, in which we replaced the letters of each sentence with nonletter characters while retaining interword spacing and string length—for example, < `<^#%} |<- |*))#~/ <>*{+ -*^ ~ ?)*(-. This combination of "tight" and "loose" contrast conditions turned out to be very fruitful.

In the loose condition, we observed that contrasting sentences with nonletter strings led to robust activity in the left hemisphere, the region of the brain that had historically been considered to do the work of language comprehension. However, our tight condition, which contrasted sentences that contained only definite articles with sentences that contained only indefinite articles, revealed virtually no changes in left-hemisphere activation. Instead, differential activation was observed in frontal regions not previously assumed to underlie language comprehension, particularly the right superior and medial frontal gyri.

Could we have arrived at the same conclusions without functional imaging data? Granted, this experiment was not as memorable as Blakemore, Wolpert, and Frith's (2000) study in which they used fMRI data to explain why tickling yourself is never as ticklish as someone else tickling you. But our study was a landmark in demonstrating that functional images might explain how we understand a thousand words. A thousand coherent words.

use beyond the sentence, as in conversation, paragraphs, articles, chapters, and entire books. The goal of discourse is generally to communicate some message or meaning. The paragraph you are reading, for example, is part of the discourse in a chapter designed to teach you about language and thought.

You probably do not remember the moment words first came alive to you, but your parents surely do. In fact, one of the greatest joys of being a parent is to watch a child discovering that words have meanings.

SEMANTICS

Semantics is the study of the meanings of words. Linguists, philosophers, and psychologists have long contemplated just what the word *meaning* means, and they have proposed several theories over the years. The fundamental unit of symbolic knowledge is the **concept,** an idea about something that provides a means of understanding the world (Aguilar & Medin, 1999; Barsalou, 2000; Bruner, Goodnow, & Austin, 1956; Coley, Medin, Proffitt, Lynch, & Atran, 1999; Fodor, 1994; Hampton, 1997b, 1999; Mayer, 2000). Thus, the concept or idea of a dog is evoked by the word *dog*.

According to Clark (1993, 1995), two principles underlying word meanings are the *principle of conventionality* and the *principle of contrast*. The first states that meanings of words are determined by conventions; words mean what conventions make them mean. According to the second principle, different words have different meanings. The point of having different words is precisely to have them symbolize things that are at least slightly different.

Componential theory, also termed *definitional theory,* claims that we can understand the meaning of a word or concept by disassembling it into a set of basic elements. These elements, called *defining features,* are essential elements of meaning that are singly necessary and jointly sufficient to define a word (or concept; J. J. Katz, 1972; J. J. Katz & Fodor, 1963). Consider the word *bachelor.* A bachelor can be viewed as having three components: male, unmarried, and adult. Because the components are each singly necessary, even the absence of one component makes the word inapplicable. An unmarried male who is not an adult is not a bachelor.

The **prototype theory** claims that we understand a word or concept through a prototype, which is the best representation of a given concept and which comprises a set of *characteristic features* that tend to be typical of most examples of the concept (Rosch, 1978; Rosch & Mervis, 1975; see also E. E. Smith, 1995; E. E. Smith & Medin, 1981). Whereas a defining feature is possessed by every instance of a concept, a characteristic feature need not be. Instead, many or most instances possess a characteristic feature. Thus, the ability to fly is typical of birds. But it is not a defining feature of a bird because some birds, such as ostriches, cannot fly. A robin seems more prototypically birdlike than an ostrich. Why? Because a robin has many features that match most people's prototype of a bird, including the fact that, unlike the ostrich, it can fly. Both defining and characteristic features are important to the meanings of most concepts (Hampton, 1997a; E. E. Smith, Osherson, Rips, & Keane, 1999; Wisniewski, 1997, 2000).

Some theorists (e.g., Erickson & Kruschke, 1998; B. H. Ross & Makin, 1999; B. H. Ross & Spalding, 1994; E. E. Smith, Patalano, & Jonides, 1998) have suggested that instead of using a single prototype for deriving the meaning of a concept, we use several *exemplars,* which are typical representatives of a particular concept or class of objects (Estes, 1994; Murphy, 1993; Ross, 2000). In considering birds, we might think not only of the prototypical songbird, which is small, flies, builds nests, sings, and so on, but also of exemplars for birds of prey, for large flightless birds, for medium-sized waterfowl, and so on. If we have multiple exemplars, when we see a bird, we can more flexibly match this instance to an appropriate exemplar than to a single prototype.

To understand concepts fully, we also have to understand their roles in sentences—that is, their syntactic usage.

The penguin, left, has all the defining features of a bird, but it has fewer of the characteristic features than the bird above. For example, the penguin does not fly.

SYNTAX

As mentioned earlier, an important part of the psychology of language is *syntax*, the systematic structure through which words can be combined and sequenced to make meaningful phrases and sentences. Syntax includes the grammar of phrases and sentences.

Psycholinguists—psychologists who study language—use the term **grammar** to refer to regular patterns that relate to the functions and relationships of words in a sentence. Grammar is as broad as the level of discourse and as narrow as the pronunciation and meaning of individual words. In your English courses, you may have been introduced to **prescriptive grammar,** which is the rules that dictate the preferred use of written and spoken language. For example, in standard English, it is grammatically correct to say, "The student loves the book," not "The student love the book." Of greater interest to psycholinguists is **descriptive grammar,** language rules that relate to the structures, functions, and relationships of words in a sentence (Pinker, 1994). There are several kinds of descriptive grammars (Maratsos, 1998).

Phrase-structure grammars, also termed *surface-structure grammars*, analyze sentences in terms of the superficial sequence of words in sentences, regardless of differences or similarities in meaning. Basically, any sentence in the English language can be analyzed according to a phrase-structure grammar. Consider these two sentences:

1. Susie greedily ate the hungry crocodile.
2. The hungry crocodile was eaten greedily by Susie.

A phrase-structure grammar would not show any particular relationship at all between sentences 1 and 2. Yet in terms of meaning, the two sentences differ only in voice. The first sentence expresses ideas in the active voice, the second in the passive voice. The underlying meaning of the two sentences is the same, so the structural difference between the two sentences centers on *attitude*—that is, the stance that the speaker is taking toward the events or items being described.

Transformational grammar, pioneered by linguist Noam Chomsky, focuses on the operations used to *transform* deep structures into surface structures. Chomsky (1957) proposed that sentences can be ana-

Noam Chomsky proposed a highly influential theory of transformational grammar.

Donna Coveny/MIT

lyzed at two different levels. The first is a surface-structure level, as is done with phrase-structure grammars. The second is a **deep-structure level,** described as the underlying meaning of a sentence that gives rise, through transformations, to alternative surface structures. The two sentences about Susie and the crocodile have the same deep-structural representations, even though their surface-level phrase-structural representations are quite different. Chomsky posited a way to derive surface structures from deep structures and to interrelate different surface structures. Not all psychologists agree with all aspects of Chomsky's theories. Many particularly disagree with his emphasis on syntax (form) over semantics (meaning) (e.g., Bock, Loebell, & Morey, 1992; Garrett, 1992; Jackendoff, 1991). In any case, syntax is only part of the story of meaning; we also need to look at pragmatics.

PRAGMATICS

Traditionally, linguistic studies have focused on how people understand language at the phoneme, morpheme, word, and sentence levels, giving little attention to the broader range of discourse. Psycholinguistic research has followed suit. In recent decades, however, students of language have become increasingly interested in **pragmatics,** the study of how people use language, and **sociolinguistics,** the study of how people use language in the context of social interaction.

Some sociolinguists also study the ways in which people use nonlinguistic elements in conversational contexts. Sociolinguists and psycholinguists would be interested in your use of gestures and vocal inflections. They would also observe your use of *proxemics*, the relative distancing and positioning of you and your fellow conversants. For example, how far away are you from the person to whom you are speaking, and where is the listener relative to you—directly in front, off a bit to the side? Under most circumstances, you naturally change your language patterns and nonlinguistic elements to fit different contexts, such as on a first date versus in a classroom.

SCRIPTS

Maxims and turn-taking strategies may help guide us through almost any conversational context. For example, we are expected to wait for a person to finish what he or she is saying before we take our turn. To communicate effectively in some situations, however, the parties must have a shared understanding about the situation they are discussing. Some researchers suggest that, in such cases, we may use scripts to help us fill in the gaps that often arise in actual conversations. Roger Schank and Robert Abelson (1977, p. 41) defined a **script** as a predetermined, stereotyped sequence of actions that defines a well-known situation. Two common examples of scripts are going to a doctor's office and going to a fast-food restaurant. In the latter case, typical elements of the script are entering, standing in line, ordering, paying, and sitting down to eat.

Various empirical studies have tested the validity of the script notion. Gordon Bower, John Black, and Terrence Turner (1979) presented research participants with various brief stories describing common situations. The participants were then asked either to recall as much as they could of each story or to discern which of several sentences had been included in the stories. The critical result was that people showed a significant tendency to recall elements and sentences that were not actually in the stories. Rather, they were parts of the scripts that the stories represented. That is, scripts seem to guide what people recall and recognize (see also Brewer, 1999).

SLIPS OF THE TONGUE

Until now, this chapter has focused on how people use—or at least attempt to use—language correctly. It is only fair, in a discussion of pragmatics, to talk about how people use language incorrectly. One of the most obvious errors is **slips of the tongue,** inadvertent errors in what is said. Among the first psychologists to study slips of the tongue was Sigmund Freud. In fact, his description of this phenomenon led us to call particular kinds of such errors *Freudian slips,* which are those slips that seem to reveal repressed motivations and sentiments. For example, a businessperson might encounter a rival and say "I'm glad to beat you" instead of "I'm glad to meet you."

In contrast to the psychoanalytic view, psycholinguists and other cognitive psychologists are intrigued by slips of the tongue because of what the errors may tell us about how language is produced. We have a mental plan for what we are going to say. Sometimes, however, this plan is disrupted when our articulatory mechanism does not cooperate with our cognitive one. Slips of the tongue may be taken to indicate that the language of thought differs from ordinary language (Fodor, 1975). We have the idea right, but its expression comes out wrong. We may not even be aware of the slip until it is pointed out to us because in the language of the mind, the idea is right.

Slips of the tongue may be fortuitously opportune, creating **spoonerisms,** in which a reversal of the initial sounds of two words produces two entirely different words, usually with a humorous outcome. Spoonerisms are named after the Reverend William Spooner, who was famous for reversals. One of his choicest slips was "You have hissed all my mystery lectures." As you might have guessed, many slips of the tongue provide insights not only into how people use language but also into how they think.

THE RELATION OF LANGUAGE TO THOUGHT

Almost everything written about language implies that thought and language interact. The language we hear and read shapes our thoughts. At the same time, our thoughts shape what we say and write. For example, hate mongers tend to dehumanize their targets by referring to them with derogatory words, such as *insect* or *vermin.* Such language is designed to instill negative thoughts and feelings toward the victims (Sternberg, in press-b). Studies comparing and contrasting different languages and the expressions within them are one way to explore how language and thought are intertwined.

Ⓒ LINGUISTIC RELATIVITY

> "This rain is very strong," I said in Chinyanja. The word I used for rain, *mpemera,* was very precise. It meant the sweeping rain driven into the veranda by the wind.
> —Paul Theroux, *My Secret History*

Different languages use different lexicons and syntactical structures that reflect the physical and cultural environments in which the languages arose and developed. The Garo of Burma distinguish among many kinds of rice because they are a rice-growing culture. Nomadic Arabs have more than 20 words for camels. These peoples clearly conceptualize rice and camels more specifically and in more complex ways than do people outside their cultural groups. The question is whether, as a result of these linguistic differences, the Garo and nomadic Arabs *think* about rice and camels differently from the ways we do. There is some evidence that word learning may occur, in part, as a result of infants' mental differentiation among various kinds of concepts (Carey, 1994; Xu & Carey, 1995, 1996). So it might make sense that infants who encounter different kinds of objects, as a function of the culture in which they grow up, make different kinds of mental differentiations.

The syntactical structures of languages differ, too. Almost all languages communicate actions, agents of actions, and objects of actions (Gerrig & Banaji, 1994). What differs across languages is the range of grammatical inflections and other markings that speakers are obliged to include as key elements of a sentence. For example, in English, we indicate whether an action took place in the past by using the past-tense verb form (e.g., walk*ed*). In Spanish and German, the verb must also indicate whether the agent of action was singular or plural and is being referred to in the first, second, or third person. Do these and other differences in obligatory syntactical structures influence—perhaps even constrain—the users of these languages to think about things differently?

Linguistic relativity theory asserts that the language you speak influences the way you think and the cognitive systems you develop. Consequently, people who speak different languages think quite differently. The Garo may develop more cognitive categories for rice than English speakers do. The Garo conception of rice may be more complex and variegated. Thus, language does, at least in part, shape thought (Lucy, 1997).

The linguistic relativity hypothesis is sometimes referred to as the *Sapir-Whorf hypothesis,* after the two men who most assertively propagated it. Edward Sapir (1941/1964) said that "we see and hear and otherwise experience very largely as we do because the language habits of our community predispose certain choices of interpretation" (p. 69). Benjamin Lee Whorf (1956) expressed the idea even more strongly:

> We dissect nature along lines laid down by our native languages. The categories and types that we isolate from the world of phenomena we do not find there because they stare every observer in the face; on the contrary, the world is presented in a kaleidoscopic flux of impressions which has to be organized by our minds—and this means largely by the linguistic systems in our minds. (p. 213)

The Sapir-Whorf hypothesis has been one of the most widely mentioned ideas in the social and behavioral sciences (Lonner, 1989). However, some of its implications appear to have reached mythical proportions. For example, it would make sense, in terms of the Sapir-Whorf hypothesis, for Eskimos to have many words for snow. These multiple words would allow them to think about snow in the many ways that they encounter it in their environment. Many social scientists have, in fact, warmly accepted and gladly propagated the notion that Eskimos have a multitude of words for the single English one. In direct refutation of the myth, however, anthropologist Laura Martin (1986) has shown that Eskimos do *not* have numerous words for snow. According to G. K. Pullum (1991), "no one who knows anything about Eskimo (or more accurately, about the Inuit and Yupik families of related languages spoken from Siberia to Greenland) has ever said they do" (p. 160).

THE LIMITS OF LINGUISTIC RELATIVITY

Thus, it appears that we must exercise caution in our interpretation of linguistic relativity when we consider nouns such as *rice* and *camel*. In fact, such relativity becomes even more interesting when we go beyond nouns to look at other syntactical elements of language. For example, Spanish has two forms of the verb *to be: ser* and *estar.* They are used in different

contexts (see Sera, 1992). In general, *ser* is used for permanent or at least long-term states of being. I might say "Soy profesor," which uses the first-person singular form of *ser* to communicate that I am a professor. *Estar* is used for temporary states of being. I would say "Estoy escribiendo," using the first-person singular form of *estar,* to express that I am temporarily engaged in writing. The psychological question is whether native Spanish speakers have a more differentiated sense of the temporary and the permanent than do native English speakers, who use the same verb form to express both senses of *to be.* Thus far, based on the existing literature in linguistic relativity and cross-cultural analyses, we do not know.

Curt Hoffman, Ivy Lau, and David Johnson (1986) came up with an intriguing experiment designed to assess the possible effects of linguistic relativity. In Chinese, a single term, *sh ì gù,* describes a person who is "worldly, experienced, socially skillful, devoted to his or her family, and somewhat reserved" (p. 1098). English clearly has no comparable term to embrace all these characteristics. Hoffman and colleagues composed passages in English and in Chinese describing various characters, including the *sh ì gù* character. The researchers then asked individuals who were bilingual in Chinese and English to read the passages either in Chinese or in English. The individuals were further asked to rate various statements in terms of the likelihood that they would be true of the characters. Their results seemed to support the notion of linguistic relativity. The research participants were more likely to rate the statements in accord with the *sh ì gù* stereotype when they had read the passages in Chinese than when they had read them in English. Similarly, when participants were asked to write their own impressions of the characters, their descriptions conformed more closely to the *sh ì gù* stereotype if they had read the passages in Chinese. These authors did not suggest that it would be impossible for English speakers to comprehend the *sh ì gù* stereotype, but rather that having that stereotype readily accessible facilitates its use.

Children who speak different languages may or may not think differently, but they certainly learn to use languages differently (Bhatia & Ritchie, 1999; deHouwer, 1998; Khubchandani, 1997; Pearson, Fernandez, Lewedeg, & Oller, 1997). Children who learn Mandarin Chinese tend to use more verbs than nouns, whereas children acquiring English or Italian tend to use more nouns than verbs (Tardif, 1996; Tardif, Shatz, & Naigles, 1997). Korean-speaking children use verbs earlier than English-speaking children do, whereas English-speaking children acquire large naming vocabularies earlier than Korean-speaking children do (Gopnik & Choi, 1995; Gopnik, Choi, & Baumberger, 1996).

Some research addresses linguistic universals, characteristic patterns of language that apply across all the languages of various cultures. Much of this research has used color names. At first glance, color words seem to be an ideal focus of research because they provide an especially convenient way of testing the hypothesis. People in every culture can be expected to be exposed, at least potentially, to roughly same range of colors. Yet it turns out that languages name colors quite differently (Berlin & Kay, 1969; Kay, 1975). It appears that people see colors in particular, and the world in general, in pretty much the same way, regardless of the language they use (Davies, 1998; Davies & Corbett, 1997). There thus appear to be some universals. But do people see the world in the same way, regardless of their level of cognitive and linguistic development? Let us consider next how language develops.

✓CONCEPT CHECK 3

1. Prototype theory claims that meaning can be understood largely in terms of
   a. defining features.
   b. characteristic features.
   c. explicit features.
   d. implicit features.
2. According to the linguistic relativity hypothesis,
   a. language influences thought.
   b. thought influences language.
   c. languages all express exactly the same concepts.
   d. the deep-structural grammar of all languages is the same.
3. Young language learners of Mandarin Chinese use
   a. more nouns than verbs.
   b. more verbs than nouns.
   c. equal numbers of nouns and verbs.
   d. first more nouns, than fewer nouns than verbs.

LANGUAGE ACQUISITION

How do people acquire language?

STAGES OF LANGUAGE ACQUISITION

During our earliest years, we go from listening and responding to language to being able to produce it ourselves. All people seem to accomplish this feat in just about the same way, by following the same sequence of steps. Humans progress through the following stages to acquire their primary language:

1. Prenatal responsivity to human voices
2. Postnatal cooing, which comprises all possible phones
3. Babbling, which comprises only the distinct phonemes that characterize the primary language of the infant
4. One-word utterances (holophrasic speech)
5. Two-word utterances
6. Telegraphic speech
7. Basic adult sentence structure, which is present by about age 4

From day one, infants appear to be programmed to tune into their linguistic environment with the specific goal of acquiring language (Fodor, 1997; Marcus, 1998; Pinker, 1999; Plunkett, 1998). Infants clearly have remarkably acute language-learning abilities, even from an early age (Marcus, Vijayan, Bandi Rao, & Vishton, 1999; Pinker, 1997, 1999). They are highly attuned to environmental opportunities to learn language. From infancy, children listen to and try to imitate the speech sounds they hear (Kuhl & Meltzoff, 1997).

PRENATAL INFLUENCES

Some studies suggest that language acquisition begins before birth. Fetuses can hear their mothers' voices in the watery prenatal environment, and within days after birth newborns show clear preferences for their mothers' voices over the voices of other women (DeCasper & Fifer, 1980). They also seem to prefer hearing their mother read stories they heard her read *in utero* to stories she never read aloud before their birth (DeCasper & Spence, 1986). The results of these studies seem to show that newborns already have gained some familiarity with their mothers' voices. They are being prepared to pay attention to them after birth. Interestingly, infants prefer to listen to someone speaking in their native language over a nonnative language, possibly focusing on the rhythmic structure as their means of identification (Bertoncini, 1993; Mehler, Dupoux, Nazzi, & Dehaene-Lambertz, 1996). After birth, in addition to responding preferentially to their mothers' voices, newborns seem to move in synchrony with the speech of the caregivers who interact with them (T. M. Field, 1978; J. A. Martin, 1981; Schaffer, 1977; C. E. Snow, 1977). Furthermore, the emotional expression of infants responds to and matches that of their caregivers (Fogel, 1992).

Perhaps because they heard their mother's voice from within the womb, newborns tend to prefer it to others' voices, and they seem to move in response to the speech of caregivers.

COOING AND BABBLING

Infants also produce sounds of their own. Most obviously, the communicative act of crying—whether intentional or not—works well to get attention or food, or to signal distress in general. In terms of language acquisition, however, it is the cooing of infants that most intrigues linguists. **Cooing** is infant vocalization that explores all the phones humans can possibly produce. The cooing of infants around the world, including deaf infants, is practically identical.

During the cooing stage, hearing infants can discriminate among all phones, not just the phonemes characteristic of their own language. Both Japanese and American infants can discriminate the /l/ from the /r/ phone (Eimas, 1985). As infants move into the next stage (babbling), however, they gradually lose their ability to distinguish the phones. By 1 year of age, Japanese infants—for whom the distinction does not make a phonemic difference—can no longer make this discrimination (Eimas, 1985).

At the babbling stage, deaf infants no longer vocalize. Moreover, the sounds produced by hearing infants change. **Babbling** is the infant's preferential

production of only those distinct phonemes characteristic of the babbler's own language (J. L. Locke, 1994; Petitto & Marentette, 1991). Thus, although the cooing of infants around the world is essentially the same, infant babbling reflects the language the infant is acquiring. The ability of the infant to perceive as well as to produce nonphonemic phones recedes during this stage.

HOLOPHRASTIC SPEECH

Eventually, that first magnificent word is uttered, followed shortly by one or two more, and soon even more. The infant uses these one-word utterances—termed *holophrases*—to convey intentions, desires, and demands (Ingram, 1999). Usually the words are nouns that describe familiar objects that the child observes (e.g., *car, book, ball, baby, nose*) or wants (e.g., *Mama, Dada, juice, cookie*). By 18 months of age, children typically have vocabularies of 3 to 100 words (Siegler, 1986). But this vocabulary cannot encompass everything the child wishes to describe. As a result, the child deftly overextends the meanings of words in his or her existing lexicon to cover things and ideas for which a new word is lacking. For example, the general term for any man may be "Dada"—which can be distressing to a new father in a public setting—and the general term for any kind of four-legged animal may be "doggie." This overapplication of the meaning of a given word is called **overextension error**.

Why do overextension errors occur? A *feature hypothesis* suggests that children form definitions that include too few features (E. V. Clark, 1973). Thus, a child might refer to a cat as a dog because of a mental rule that if an animal has four legs, it is a "doggie." An alternative *functional hypothesis* (K. Nelson, 1973) suggests that children base their initial use of words on the important purposes (functions) of the concepts that the words represent, and then they make overextension errors because of their confusion about the functions of the objects being identified. Lamps give light, and blankets make us warm. A dog and a cat both do similar things and serve as pets. So a child is likely to confuse them. Although the functional hypothesis has usually been viewed as an alternative to the feature hypothesis, it seems entirely possible that both mechanisms are at work. As is often the case, perhaps neither position is completely right. The truth as best we can know it is a synthesis of both views.

TELEGRAPHIC SPEECH

Gradually, by about $2\frac{1}{2}$ years of age, children begin to combine single words to produce utterances. Thus begins an understanding of syntax. These early syntactical communications lead to **telegraphic speech**, which is more like a telegram than a conversation because articles, prepositions, and other functional morphemes are left out. Examples are "Up Mama" to indicate that the child wants to be picked up, and "Daddy cup" to point out a drinking glass. In fact, the term *telegraphic speech* describes three-word utterances and even slightly longer ones if they characteristically omit some function morphemes. Vocabulary expands rapidly, more than tripling from about 300 words at about age 2 to about 1,000 words at about age 3 (Bloom, 2000).

Children in the first grade in the United States have more than 10,000 words in their vocabularies. By the third grade, they are at about 20,000. And by the fifth grade, they have reached about 40,000, or half of their eventual adult level (Anglin, 1993). By combining morphemes, most adult English speakers have a vocabulary of hundreds of thousands of words. Vocabulary is built up slowly, through many diverse exposures to words and clues about their meanings (Akhtar & Montague, 1999; Hoff & Naigles, 1999; Woodward & Markman, 1998).

Almost incredibly, by age 4 children acquire the foundations of adult syntax and language structure. By age 5, most children also can understand and produce quite complex and uncommon sentences. By age 10, children's language is fundamentally the same as that of adults. The aspects of language that are difficult for children at this point—things like dealing with passives, ambiguity, and abstractions—are also difficult for adults. In the next section we look at some explanations of the processes that allow humans to acquire language.

One of children's most impressive accomplishments is learning to read. At a minimum, reading involves language, memory, thinking, and intelligence, as well as perception (Adams, 1990, 1999; Adams,

Treiman, & Pressley, 1997). The ability to read is fundamental to our everyday lives, and people who have *dyslexia*—difficulty in deciphering, reading, and comprehending text—can suffer greatly in a society that puts a high premium on fluent reading (Galaburda, 1999; National Research Council, 1998; Neisen & Hynd, 2000; Spear-Swerling & Sternberg, 1996; R. J. Sternberg & Grigorenko, 1999; R. J. Sternberg & Spear-Swerling, 1999; Torgesen, 1997). The various kinds of dyslexia and the causes suggested for it go beyond the scope of this textbook, but it has been suggested that problems in phonological processing, and thus in word identification, pose "the major stumbling block in learning to read" (Pollatsek & Rayner, 1989, p. 403; see also Rayner & Pollatsek, 2000).

EXPLANATIONS OF LANGUAGE ACQUISITION

A major theme in psychology and in this book is whether nature or nurture molds who we are and what we do. This debate continually resurfaces in new forms, particularly in regard to language acquisition. On the one hand, exposure to language—nurture—influences language development. On the other hand, there appears to be a biologically determined window of opportunity for learning language, which suggests that we are "wired" for language by nature.

IMITATION

Even amateur observers notice that children's speech patterns and vocabulary reflect those in their environment. In fact, parents of very young children go to great lengths to make it easy for children to attend to and understand what they are saying. Almost without thinking, parents and other adults tend to use a higher pitch than usual, to exaggerate the *vocal inflection* of their speech (i.e., more extreme raising and lowering of pitch and volume). They also use simpler sentence constructions when speaking with infants and young children. This characteristic form of speech has been called *motherese*, but it is perhaps more accurately termed *child-directed speech*. The goal of parents who use such speech is successfully to communicate with their infants (Acredolo & Goodwyn, 1998). Not all parents use such speech, however, and their children still develop clear, accurate speech.

Infants seem to prefer listening to child-directed speech over other forms of adult speech (Fernald, 1985). The exaggerations seem to gain and hold infants' attention, to communicate emotional information, and to signal when to take turns in vocalizing. Across cultures, many parents use this kind of speech,

A teacher instructs a child on the basics of reading.

tailoring it to particular circumstances: using rising intonations to gain attention; falling intonations to comfort; and brief, discontinuous, rapid-fire explosions of speech to warn against prohibited behavior (Fernald et al., 1989).

Parents even seem to model the correct format for verbal interactions. Early caregiver-child interactions are characterized by *verbal turn-taking*. The caregiver says something and then uses vocal inflection to cue the infant to respond. The infant babbles, sneezes, burps, or otherwise makes some audible response. The caregiver accepts whatever noises the infant makes as valid communicative utterances and replies. The infant further responds to the cue, and so on. Parents work hard to understand children's early utterances. One or two words, such as *ma* or *pa*, might be used for conveying an entire array of concepts. As the child grows older and more sophisticated and acquires more language, parents gradually provide less linguistic support. They demand increasingly sophisticated utterances from the child. It is as if they initially provide scaffolding from which the child can construct an edifice of language. As the child's language develops, the parents gradually remove the scaffolding.

The mechanism of imitation is appealing in its simplicity. Unfortunately, it does not explain many aspects of language acquisition. For example, if imitation is the primary mechanism, why do children universally begin talking in one-word utterances, then two-word and other telegraphic utterances, and later complete sentences? Why don't they start out with complete sentences? The most compelling argument against imitation alone is overregularization. In this phenomenon, which commonly occurs during language acquisition, the novice speaker has gained an understanding of how a language usually works and overapplies the general rules to exceptional cases in which the rule does not apply. Instead of imitating the parent's sentence, "The mice fell down the hole, and they ran home," the young child might overregularize the irregular forms and say, "The mouses falled down the hole, and they runned home." An alternative explanation of language acquisition is thus needed.

CONDITIONING

The proposed alternative mechanism of conditioning is exquisitely simple. Children hear utterances and associate them with particular objects and events in their environment. They then produce those utterances and are rewarded by their parents and others for having spoken. Initially, their utterances are not perfect, but through successive approximations, they come to speak just as well as native adult speakers of their language. The progression from babbling to one-word utterances to more complex speech seems to support

the notion that children begin with simple associations. Their output gradually increases in complexity and in the degree to which they approximate adult speech.

As with imitation, the simplicity of the proposed conditioning mechanism does not fully explain actual language acquisition. For one thing, parents are much more likely to respond to the truth or falsity of the child's statement than to its relative pronunciational or grammatical correctness (R. Brown, Cazden, & Bellugi, 1969). If parents did respond to the grammatical correctness of children's speech, their responses might explain why children eventually stop overregularizing their speech but not why they ever begin doing so. Perhaps the most compelling contradiction relates to productivity. Children constantly employ novel utterances, for which they have never previously been rewarded and which they have never heard. Children consistently apply the words and language structures they already know to novel situations and contexts for which they have never before received reinforcement. Clearly, some other process or predisposition must be involved in children's acquisition of language.

CRITICAL PERIODS

If neither nature nor nurture alone adequately explains all aspects of language acquisition, just how might nature facilitate nurture in the process? Noam Chomsky (1965, 1972) proposed a **language-acquisition device (LAD),** a hypothetical construct of an innate human predisposition to acquire language (see also Gilger, 1996; Pinker, 1994; Stromswold, 1998, 2000). That is, we seem to be mentally prewired or biologically preconfigured to acquire language. In fact, there seems to be a **critical period** for acquiring language, a time of rapid development, during which a particular ability must be developed if it is ever to be adequate (Stromswold, 2000). No one knows exactly why critical periods occur. Newport (1991) suggested that young children might have an advantage in language learning because limitations in their perceptual and memory abilities render them more likely to process smaller chunks of speech information. These smaller chunks, she has suggested, make it easier for them to see the structure of language. This view by no means has unanimous support, however (Rohde & Plaut, 1999), nor does any other for the existence of critical periods. During such periods, the environment plays a crucial role. For example, the cooing and babbling stages seem to be critical to acquiring a native speaker's discrimination and production of the distinctive phonemes of a particular language. During this period, the child's linguistic context must provide those distinctive phonemes.

Evidence for a general critical period in language development comes from studies of "wild children." In 1970, a social worker in California discovered that a woman and her husband had kept their 13-year-old daughter locked up in nearly total isolation during her childhood. The girl, Genie, could neither speak nor stand erect. Unclothed, she had been tied to a child's potty seat for her entire childhood. She was able to move only her hands and feet. At night Genie was put into a sort of straitjacket and placed in a crib with wire mesh sides. A covering turned it into a cage. If Genie made any kind of noise, her father beat her. The father communicated with her only through growling (Rymer, 1993). After Genie was discovered, attempts were made to teach her basic skills (Curtiss, 1977), including language, but Genie never was able to produce sentences of more than two or three words. Moreover, the sentences lacked basic elements of grammar. Cases such as Genie's suggest that if language is not acquired by a certain age, it may never be acquired. At the same time, given the traumatic environment in which Genie was raised, her case presents many confounding variables. It is hard to know whether her later failure to acquire language was truly a result only of her lack of exposure to language during childhood.

Oral reading can help children improve their reading skills.

There seems to be a critical period for acquiring a native understanding of syntax. Despite 30 years of signing, people who acquired American Sign Language (ASL) later in childhood understood the distinctive syntax of ASL less profoundly than did those who had learned it earlier.

There seems to be a critical period for acquiring a native understanding of syntax, too. Perhaps the greatest support for this view comes from studies of adult users of American Sign Language (ASL). Among adults who have signed for 30 years or more, researchers could differentiate among those who acquired ASL before age 4, between ages 4 and 6, and after age 12. Despite 30 years of signing, those who acquired ASL later in childhood showed less profound understanding of the distinctive syntax of ASL (Meier, 1991; Newport, 1990). Studies of linguistically isolated children seem to provide additional support for a critical interaction of physiological maturation and environmental support. Those who are rescued at younger ages seem to acquire more sophisticated language structures than those who are rescued later.

In any case, there do not appear to be critical periods for second-language acquisition (Birdsong, 1999), except possibly for the acquisition of native accent. Adults may appear to have a harder time learning second languages because their native language remains dominant, whereas young children, who typically need to attend school in the new language, may have to switch dominant languages and thus learn the new language to a higher level of mastery (Jia & Aaronson, 1999).

Given the complex neurophysiology of other aspects of human perception and thought, it is not unreasonable to consider that we may be predisposed to acquire language. Several observations support this notion. For example, human speech perception is quite remarkable. In addition to noting our rapid phonemic specialization (mentioned in regard to babbling), consider our amazing ability to discern from a continuous flow of auditory stimuli the distinct places where one word ends and another word begins. Note also that all children within a broad normal range of abilities and environments seem to acquire language at an incredibly rapid rate.

Innate processes work with the environment in the acquisition of language. Acquiring language really involves a natural endowment modified by the environment (Bates & Goodman, 1999; MacWhinney, 1999; Wexler, 1996). For example, the social environment, in which infants use their social capacities to interact with others, is one source of information for language acquisition (Carpenter, Nagell, & Tomasello, 1998; Snow, 1999; Tomasello, 1999). Thus, the study of language acquisition now centers on discovering what abilities are innately given, and how these abilities are tempered by the child's environment—a process aptly termed "innately guided learning" (see Elman et al., 1996; Jusczyk, 1997). Environmental differences can lead to sex differences in the use of language. For example, young girls are more likely to ask for help than are young boys (Thompson, 1999), a reflection of social sex-role influences.

(E) EVOLUTIONARY PROCESSES

Some theorists, including Noam Chomsky (1980) and Steven Pinker (1994, 1997, 2002), have argued that the pattern of language acquisition must be innate. Moreover, because it follows a common path across many cultures (Pinker, 1994), it appears to be an evolutionary adaptation. Children all around the world pass through the same stages of language acquisition. They also generate combinations of words that adults would never produce (an argument against imitation). In addition, they acquire more or less correct syntax despite infrequent correction of errors by parents and other adults. Even children of relatively low intelligence acquire language. Although Pinker and others do not deny the role of the environment in language acquisition, they believe that evolutionary processes have set us up to acquire language in a certain way, which proceeds except in cases of severe environmental deprivation.

Thus, it seems that neither nature nor nurture alone determines language acquisition. An alternative postulate, *hypothesis testing*, also suggests an integration of nature and nurture: Children acquire language by mentally forming tentative hypotheses about language and then testing these hypotheses in the environment. Dan Slobin (1971, 1985) suggested that the way in which children implement this process follows several operating principles. In forming hypotheses, young children look for and attend to patterns of changes in the forms of words. They also note morphemic inflections that signal changes in meaning, especially suffixes. And they observe sequences of morphemes, including both affixes and the roots of words in sentences.

In addition, children learn to avoid exceptions to the general patterns they observe and to avoid interrupting or rearranging the noun phrase and the verb phrase in sentences. Children seem to follow these same general patterns of hypothesis testing regardless of the language they acquire or the context in which they acquire it. Some psychologists thus believe that children must be naturally predisposed to hypothesis testing. Although

not all linguists support the hypothesis-testing view, the phenomena of overregularization (using and sometimes overapplying rules) and of language productivity (creating novel utterances based on some kind of understanding of how to do so) seem to support it.

The bottom line, therefore, is that the old debate of nature versus nurture does not well represent the current state of knowledge. Nature and nurture always interact in language development, in both humans and nonhuman animals.

✓ CONCEPT CHECK 4

1. Cooing involves an infant's production of
   a. the same number of sounds as in babbling.
   b. fewer sounds than in babbling.
   c. more sounds than in babbling.
   d. sounds that differ totally from those in babbling.
2. Holophrastic speech involves
   a. no words at all.
   b. one-word utterances.
   c. utterances of three to five words.
   d. disconnected sentences.
3. Chomsky believes that language acquisition can be explained in part through
   a. an innate language-acquisition device.
   b. classical conditioning.
   c. instrumental conditioning.
   d. social learning.

DO ANIMALS USE LANGUAGE?

What is the evidence for and against language use by nonhuman animals?

The philosopher René Descartes suggested that language is what qualitatively distinguishes human beings from other species. Was he right? Before we get into the particulars of language in nonhuman species, we should emphasize the distinction between communication and language. Few would doubt that nonhuman animals communicate in one way or another. What is at issue is whether they do so through what reasonably can be called a language. Whereas *language* is an organized means of combining words in order to communicate, *communication* more broadly encompasses not only the exchange of thoughts and feelings

Chimpanzees show language-like skills, but it is unclear whether they actually demonstrate language.

through language but also nonverbal expression. Examples are gestures, glances, distancing, and other contextual cues.

Primates—especially chimpanzees—offer our most promising insights into nonhuman language. Jane Goodall, the well-known investigator of chimpanzees in the wild, has studied diverse aspects of chimp behavior. One is vocalizations. Goodall considers many of them to be clearly communicative, though not necessarily indicative of language. For example, chimps have a specific cry to indicate that they are about to be attacked. They have another for calling their fellow chimps together. Nonetheless, their repertoire of communicative vocalizations seems to be small, nonproductive (new utterances are not produced), limited in structure, lacking in structural complexity, and relatively nonarbitrary. It also is not spontaneously acquired. The chimps' communications thus do not satisfy our criteria for a language.

By using sign language, R. Allen and Beatrice Gardner were able to teach their tame chimp, Washoe, basic language skills beyond the stages a human toddler could reach (R. Brown, 1973). Subsequently, David Premack (1971) had even greater success with his chimpanzee, Sarah. She acquired a vocabulary of more than 100 words of various parts of speech and showed at least rudimentary linguistic skills.

A less positive view of the linguistic capabilities of chimpanzees was taken by Herbert Terrace (1979),

who raised a chimp named Nim Chimpsky—a takeoff on Noam Chomsky, the eminent linguist. Over several years, Nim made more than 19,000 multiple-sign utterances in a slightly modified version of American Sign Language. Most of his utterances consisted of two-word combinations.

Terrace's careful analysis of these utterances, however, revealed that the large majority of them were repetitions of what Nim had seen. Terrace concluded that, despite what appeared to be impressive accomplishments, Nim did not show even the rudiments of syntactic expression. The chimp could produce single- or even multiple-word utterances, but not in a syntactically organized way. For example, Nim would alternate signing "Give Nim banana," "Banana give Nim," and "Banana Nim give," showing no preference for the grammatically correct form. Moreover, Terrace studied films that showed other chimpanzees supposedly producing language. He came to the same conclusion for them that he had reached for Nim. His position, then, is that although chimpanzees can understand and produce utterances, they do not have linguistic competence in the same sense that even very young humans do. Their communications lack structure and particularly multiplicity of structure.

Susan Savage-Rumbaugh and her colleagues (Savage-Rumbaugh, McDonald, Sevcik, Hopkins, & Rubert, 1986; Savage-Rumbaugh et al., 1993) have found the best evidence yet for language use among chimpanzees. Their pygmy chimpanzees spontaneously combined the visual symbols (such as red triangles and blue squares) of an artificial language the researchers taught them. They even appear to have understood some of the language spoken to them. One pygmy chimp in particular seemed to possess remarkable skill, even possibly demonstrating a primitive grasp of language structure (Greenfield & Savage-Rumbaugh, 1990). It may be that the difference in results across groups of investigators is due to the particular kind of chimp tested or to the procedures used. The chimp's language may not have all the properties of language described at this beginning of the chapter. For example, the language used by the chimps is not spontaneously acquired. Rather, they learn it only through very deliberate and systematic programs of instruction. At this point, we just cannot be sure whether the chimps truly show the full range of language abilities.

Whether nonhuman species can use language, it seems almost certain that the language facility of humans far exceeds that of other species we have studied. Noam Chomsky (1991) has eloquently stated the key question regarding nonhuman language:

> If an animal had a capacity as biologically advantageous as language but somehow hadn't used it until now, it would be an evolutionary miracle, like finding an island of humans who could be taught to fly.

✓ CONCEPT CHECK 5

1. Descartes believed that
   a. all animals have some form of language.
   b. primates have language; other animals do not.
   c. only humans have language.
   d. humans know many languages but are aware only of their knowledge of one.
2. Terrace concluded that his chimp, Nim Chimpsky,
   a. could not understand or produce utterances.
   b. understood and produced utterances but did not have linguistic competence in the sense that humans do.
   c. had language abilities comparable to those of human infants.
   d. had language abilities comparable to those of children in middle childhood, but could not show these competencies in conventional psychological research.
3. Susan Savage-Rumbaugh believes that chimpanzees
   a. cannot understand or produce utterances.
   b. have rudimentary language skills.

   c. have language abilities comparable to those of human infants.
   d. have language abilities comparable to those of children in middle childhood, but cannot show these competencies in conventional psychological research.

THE NATURE OF THOUGHT

How would you define *thought*?

Thinking is the representation and processing of information in the mind with words, images, mental maps, concepts, and other elements. Because thinking is so important to almost everything we do, it is one of the most active areas of investigation in psychological research (J. R. Anderson, 1993; Hunt, 1999; Reed, 2000; Simon, 1999). **Critical thinking** is the conscious direction of mental processes toward representing and processing information, usually in order to find thoughtful solutions to problems. In noncritical thinking, we routinely follow customary thought patterns, without consciously directing them. Critical thinking may be directed to *analysis*, which involves breaking down wholes into component elements. It complements *synthesis*, which involves integrating component parts into wholes. Critical thought may also generate many different ideas, in which case it is known as *divergent thinking*. Or it may focus on one idea from an assortment of possible ideas, in which case it is called *convergent thinking*. Analysis and synthesis can be complementary processes, as can divergent and convergent thinking (see Table 8.1). Thinking processes probably occur both serially—one after another (J. R. Anderson, 1993; Newell & Simon, 1972; R. J. Sternberg, 1977)—and in parallel, with multiple processes occurring at the same time (Elman et al., 1996; Hinton & Shallice, 1991; McLeod, Plunkett, & Rolls, 1998; Plaut, McClelland, Seidenberg, & Patterson, 1996; Plaut & Shallice, 1994; Smolensky, 1999). Good thinking involves recognition that the solution of a life problem can depend on when the problem is encountered (Sternberg, 1999a). For example, an adult may have a glass of wine to relieve stress. This solution would not be appropriate for a young child.

Psychologists have studied thinking in terms of four domains of inquiry: problem solving, judgment and decision making, reasoning, and creativity. The goal of **problem solving** is to move from a problem

TABLE 8.1
CONCEPT REVIEW

Kinds of Critical Thinking. Critical thinking can be expressed in terms of analysis and synthesis, and in terms of divergent and convergent thinking.

Kind of Thinking	Description	Example
Analysis	Breaks down large, complex concepts or processes into smaller, simpler forms	Suppose that you are preparing to write a term paper. You might break the whole big project into smaller steps: (1) choose a topic, (2) research the topic, (3) write a first draft, (4) revise, and so on.
Synthesis	Combines two or more concepts or processes into a more complex form	In writing a psychology term paper, you might combine examples from your literature or history class to show how poor judgment affected various literary or historical figures, and then integrate the examples with psychological theories of decision making and judgment.
Divergent thinking	Generates diverse alternative solutions to a problem	To discover a topic for your paper, you might come up with as many ideas as possible in order to find one that can be investigated and reported within a single semester.
Convergent thinking	Proceeds from various possible alternatives to converge on a single, best answer	From the many ideas you generated, you converge on a single research topic.

situation (e.g., not having enough money to buy a new car) to a solution, overcoming obstacles along the way. The goal of **judgment and decision making** is to select from among choices or to evaluate opportunities (e.g., choosing the used car that you like the most for the amount of money you have). The goal of **reasoning** is to draw conclusions from evidence (e.g., reading consumer-oriented statistics to find out the reliability, economy, and safety of various cars). The goal of **creativity** is to produce something original and valuable (e.g., a fuel-efficient engine design, a distinctive marketing idea for the car, or a story to tell your parents about why you need a car). Accordingly, the next part of the chapter is divided into four parts, each corresponding to one domain of inquiry.

✓CONCEPT CHECK 6

1. Critical thinking is
   a. neither conscious nor unconscious.
   b. always conscious.
   c. always unconscious.
   d. either conscious or unconscious.

2. Problem solving always involves
   a. difficult choices.
   b. creativity.
   c. incubation.
   d. overcoming one or more obstacles.

3. Creativity involves producing something that is
   a. neither original nor valuable.
   b. original, but not necessarily valuable.
   c. valuable, but not necessarily original.
   d. both original and valuable.

STRATEGIES AND OBSTACLES IN PROBLEM SOLVING

How do you solve problems? What difficulties do you encounter?

We engage in problem solving when we need to overcome obstacles in order to answer a question or achieve a goal (Holyoak, 1995). Successful problem solving may occasionally involve tolerating some ambiguity regarding how best to proceed.

In fact, cognitive psychologists often categorize problems according to whether there are clear paths to a solution. **Well-structured problems** are problems for which a clear path to the solution is known, although it may still be very difficult to implement (such as: How do you find the area of a parallelogram?). **Ill-structured problems** are those problems for which a clear path to the solution is not known (such as: How do you succeed in the career of your choice?). Of course, in the real world, these two categories may overlap. We next consider each of these kinds of problems in turn.

SOLVING WELL-STRUCTURED PROBLEMS: HEURISTICS AND ALGORITHMS

Heuristics are informal, intuitive, and speculative strategies used to solve well-structured problems that sometimes work and sometimes do not (Fischhoff, 1999; Holyoak, 1990; Korf, 1999). You might try several routes to get to your early morning class in order to find the fastest one, so that you can sleep as late as possible. Here you are employing a simple *trial-and-error heuristic*. In contrast to heuristics, **algorithms** are formal paths for reaching a solution that involve one or more successive processes that usually lead to a correct solution. An algorithm to find a book on your book shelf is to start with the first book at the left corner on the top shelf and then to proceed left to right, top to bottom, until you find the book.

Why would anyone ever use a heuristic, which does *not* guarantee a solution, instead of an algorithm, which does? For one thing, often there is no obvious algorithm for solving a problem. In chess, for example, it is usually not obvious what algorithm, if any, would guarantee a win. Later in this chapter, we discuss judgment and decision making, for which we may be able to apply heuristics in some situations, but for which it is rare to find a surefire algorithm. For another thing, it may be that an available algorithm would take so long to execute that it just is not practical to use it. One algorithm for cracking a safe would be to try all possible combinations. But this strategy is generally not practical for the safecracker in a hurry!

© Many problems can be solved in more than one way. Often the way we view a problem is shaped by our cultural context. Suppose that you want to sail from one island to another. If you are a Westerner, you will probably plan to use charts and navigational equipment. Some natives in the South Pacific would probably scoff at such technicalities, however; they might be puzzled by the idea of "going to" another island. Instead, they use the concept of the "moving island" to navigate vast expanses of ocean (Gladwin, 1970). In their view, each island is adrift, floating along in the ocean. To get from one floating island to another, they do not "go" anywhere in the usual sense. Rather, they sit in their small boats and watch the changes in the currents and the color of the water. They then "catch" the island as *it* drifts by. As these approaches indicate, many problems may be solved in various ways, and some may seem more obvious to us than others. When the apparently obvious means of solving a problem does not seem to be working, it may be valuable to view the problem from a different perspective. Sometimes the means to solving a problem are not obvious because the problem is ill structured.

SOLVING ILL-STRUCTURED PROBLEMS: INSIGHT

Before reading on, treat yourself to a little quiz (R. J. Sternberg, 1986a). Be sure to try both of the following problems before you read about their solutions:

1. Figure 8.3 shows nine dots arrayed in three rows of three. Your task is to connect all nine dots. You must never lift your pencil off the page, you must not go through a dot more than once, and you must not use more than four straight line segments.
2. A woman was putting some finishing touches on her house and realized she needed something she did not have. She went to the hardware store and asked the clerk, "How much will 150 cost me?" The clerk answered, "They are 75 cents apiece, so 150 will cost you $2.25." What did the woman buy?

FIGURE 8.3

The Nine-Dot Problem. Can you connect all nine dots without lifting your pencil from the paper and using just four straight lines? Psychologists study how we use insight to solve this and other ill-structured problems.

Both of these are *ill-structured* problems that require **insight,** novel reconceptualization of the problem in order to reach a solution. Insight provides a distinctive and apparently sudden understanding of a problem or a sudden realization of a strategy that aids in solving a problem. Insight often involves reconceptualizing a problem or a strategy for its solution in a totally new way. To solve each of the problems above, you need to see it differently from the way you would probably see it at first (J. E. Davidson, 1995). Frequently, an insight emerges through the detection and combination of relevant old and new information. Insight can be involved in solving well-structured problems. But it is more often associated with the rocky and twisting path to a solution that characterizes ill-structured problems. Although insights may feel sudden, they are often the result of much prior thought and hard work, without which the insight would never have occurred.

To understand insightful problem solving, it is useful to know the solutions to the two preceding insight problems. The solution to problem 1, the nine-dot problem, is shown in Figure 8.4. Most people find the problem extremely difficult and many never solve it. One hindrance is the common assumption that the lines must remain within the confines of the square implicitly formed by the nine dots. In fact, the problem can be solved only by going outside those confines.

In problem 2, the woman might have been buying house numbers. Her house number is 150. So she needs three numerals, for a total cost of $2.25. From this point of view, the problem can be solved only if it is recognized that the "150" in the problem refers to

the three separate digits, rather than to the number 150. "House numbers" is not the only possible answer, however. The woman might have been buying boxes of nails; one box (of 50 nails) would cost 75 cents, and 150 nails (three boxes) would cost $2.25. With the solution involving nails, the problem can be solved only if we realize that the units have changed from nails to boxes of nails. Whether the problem is defined as one of house numbers or of nails (or something else bought in quantity), the terms of the problem are not what they originally appear to be. Sometimes problems that appear to be about one thing really turn out to be about another, as was the case here.

A PSYCHOLOGICAL PERSPECTIVE ON INSIGHT

Insight problems have intrigued psychologists for decades. According to the Gestaltists (see Chapter 1), insight problems require problem solvers to go beyond associations among various parts in order to perceive the problem as a whole. Gestalt psychologist Max Wertheimer distinguished two kinds of thinking. *Productive thinking* (Wertheimer, 1945/1959) goes beyond the bounds of existing associations identified by the thinker. *Reproductive thinking* makes use of existing associations involving what the thinker already knows. According to Wertheimer, insightful, productive thinking differs fundamentally from associational, reproductive thinking. It does not just extend associationistic thinking to novel kinds of problems. In solving the preceding insight problems, you had to break away from your existing associations. You needed to see each problem in an entirely new light. Productive thinking also can be applied to well-structured problems, as shown in Figures 8.5 and 8.7. (Before looking at Figure 8.7, try to solve the problem in Figure 8.5.)

Wertheimer's Gestaltist colleague, Wolfgang Köhler (1927), studied insight by observing a chimpanzee confined in a cage with two sticks. Outside the cage, out of his reach and out of the reach of either stick, was a banana. After trying to grab the banana with his hand and each stick, the chimp started to tinker with the sticks. Suddenly he realized that the sticks could be attached to each other to form a new tool, a long pole that he could use to roll the banana into range. In Köhler's view, the chimp's behavior illustrated insight. It showed that insight is a special process, involving thinking that differs from normal information processing. (Figure 8.6 shows a chimp engaged in a similar insight task.)

Gestalt psychologists described many other examples of insight and speculated on a few ways in which insight might occur. It might result from extended unconscious leaps in thinking, greatly accelerated mental processing, or some kind of short-circuiting of

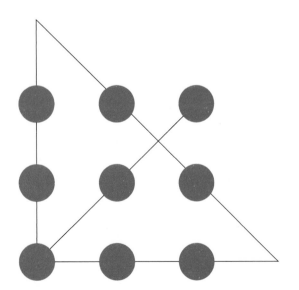

FIGURE 8.4

Solution to the Nine-Dot Problem. How did you approach the task of solving this problem?

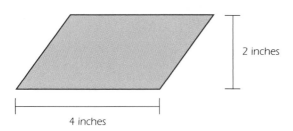

2 inches

4 inches

FIGURE 8.5
Area of Parallelogram Problem. What is the area of this parallelogram? According to Gestaltist Max Wertheimer, to figure it out you will need to engage in productive thinking, not reproductive thinking.

normal reasoning processes (see Perkins, 1981). Unfortunately, the Gestaltists did not provide convincing evidence for any of these views, nor did they define just what insight is (see Weisberg, 1992).

Insights can startle us with their brilliance but still be wrong. Many great insights have seemed right at the time but were later proved at least partly wrong. The physical principles proposed by Sir Isaac Newton represented brilliant insights. But they were later shown by Albert Einstein to be based on an incomplete understanding of the nature of the physical universe. No matter how convinced we may be of the validity of our own or someone else's insights, we need to be open to the possibility that they may later be found incorrect. On the other hand, we should not dismiss our insights just because they seem improba-

ble at first glance. Figure 8.8 shows the different artistic insights of two landscape painters.

HINDRANCES TO PROBLEM SOLVING

Hindrances to problem solving, such as mental sets and fixation as well as functional fixedness, can occur singly or in combination. Each sheds light on our problem-solving processes and potential blind spots.

MENTAL SETS AND FIXATION

Many insight problems are hard to solve because we tend to bring to the new problem a particular **mental set,** a frame of mind in which a problem solver is predisposed to think of a problem or a situation in a particular way (sometimes termed *entrenchment*). Mental sets often lead problem solvers to focus or fixate on strategies that work most of the time but not always. A mental set may be helpful in solving some (or perhaps even most) problems. But it still may not work in solving a particular problem. For example, in the nine-dot problem, we may fixate on strategies that involve drawing lines within the implicit square surrounding the dots. In the house-numbers problem, we may fixate on strategies that involve 150 items.

Abraham Luchins (1942) exquisitely demonstrated the phenomenon of a mental set in what he called "water-jar" problems. Participants are asked how to measure a certain amount of water into jars that each hold a different amount of water. The jars do not have graduated measurements on their sides.

FIGURE 8.6
A Chimpanzee Demonstrates Insight. In one of Wolfgang Köhler's experiments, a chimp demonstrated insightful problem solving to retrieve bananas hanging from the top of the enclosure. According to Gestaltists, insightful problem solving is a special process that differs from ordinary information processing.

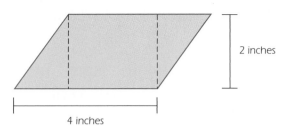

2 inches

4 inches

FIGURE 8.7

Solution to Area of Parallelogram Problem. To solve the problem posed by Wertheimer, you may have to reframe it in terms of the lines shown in this figure. Once the problem is reframed, you can see that it is similar to finding the area of a rectangle.

Table 8.2 shows the problems used by Luchins. You are to use the jars to obtain the required amounts of water (measured in numbers of cups) in the last column. Columns A, B, and C show the capacity of each jar. The first problem, for example, requires you to get 20 cups of water from just two of the jars, a 29-cup one (Jar A) and a 3-cup one (Jar B). The problem is easy. Just fill Jar A and then empty out 9 cups from this jar by taking out 3 cups three times using Jar B. Problem 2 is not too hard either. Fill Jar B with 127 cups, then empty out 21 cups using Jar A, and then empty out 6 cups using Jar C twice. Now try the rest of the problems yourself.

If you are like many people, you will have found a formula that works for all but one of the remaining problems (Which one?). You fill up Jar B, then pour out the amount of water you can put into Jar A, and

TABLE 8.2

The Water-Jar Problems. What is the most effective way of measuring out the correct amounts of water using Jars A, B, and C? *(From Luchins, A. S., "Water Jar Problems" from "Mechanization in Problem Solving: The Effect of Einstellung," Psychological Monographs, Vol. 54, No. 6, 1942, p. 1. Reprinted by permission of the author.)*

Problem Number	Jars and Their Capacities			Required Amount (Cups)
	A	**B**	**C**	
1	29	3		20
2	21	127	3	100
3	14	163	25	99
4	18	43	10	5
5	9	42	6	21
6	20	59	4	31
7	23	49	3	20
8	15	39	3	18
9	28	76	3	25
10	18	48	4	22
11	14	36	8	6

then twice pour out of it the amount of water you can put into Jar C. The formula, therefore, is $B - A - 2C$ (see Figure 8.9). However, problems 7 through 11 can be solved in a much simpler way, using just two

Cesanne, Paul, *Mont Saint-Victorie*, 1902-04. Philadelphia Museum of Art, George W. Elkins Collection, # E1936-1-1.

© Scala/Art Resource, NY

FIGURE 8.8

Examples of Insight in Art. Excellent examples of insights are Claude Lorrain's awareness of the natural beauty of landscapes in *Il Tramonto* (*The Sunset,* left) and Paul Cezanne's observations of diffuse, warm light in *Mont Saint-Victoire Seen from Les Lauves* (right). Each artist selected key relevant visual elements from the vast array of visual information.

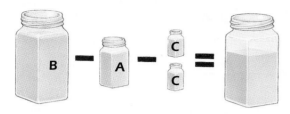

FIGURE 8.9

Luchin's Water-Jar Solution. This is an algorithm for solving most of the water-jar problems shown in Table 8.2. Is there an easier way to solve some of them? (From Luchins, 1942)

of the jars. For example, problem 7 can be solved by A − C, problem 8 by A + C, and problem 9 by A − C but *not* by B − A − 2C. Problem 10 can be solved by A + C and problem 11 by A − C. People who are given problems 1 through 6 to solve generally continue to try to use the B − A − 2C formula to solve problems 7 through 11. However, people who go from problem 2 immediately to problem 7 generally see the simpler formula. They have no established mental set to interfere with seeing things in a new and simpler way.

FUNCTIONAL FIXEDNESS

Functional fixedness prevents us from using old tools in novel ways to solve new problems. Overcoming functional fixedness is what first allowed people to use a reshaped coat hanger to get into a locked car, and it is what first allowed thieves to pick simple spring-door locks with a credit card. It is also what might allow you to think of an introductory psychology textbook as a resource for criminal ideas!

Ⓒ Functional fixedness may be influenced by cultural context in a way that might surprise Westerners. Some early writers hypothesized that there are higher and lower levels of mental development across cultures that might influence the depth or quality of cognitive processes. French anthropologist Claude Levi-Strauss (1966; see also Cole & Scribner, 1974) rejected this highly ethnocentric hypothesis. Instead, he maintained that the human mind works in essentially the same way across cultures and across time. The only difference between the thought systems in nonindustrialized and industrialized societies might be in the strategies people use. Levi-Strauss noted that scientific thinkers and problem solvers in nonindustrialized societies are generally *bricoleurs* (jacks-of-all-trades). A *bricoleur* has a bag of tools that can be used to fix all sorts of things. In contrast, the expert in an industrialized society might be effective only within a narrow area of expertise. One extension of this line of thinking is

that persons who live in nonindustrialized societies may be less subject to functional fixedness than their industrialized counterparts.

TRANSFER

Transfer is prior learning that may help or hinder problem solving (Detterman & Sternberg, 1993; Gentile, 2000; Gick & Holyoak, 1980, 1983). For example, when you learn a second language, your knowledge of the first language can help because it may share many of the same word roots and grammatical principles. But as you try to recall words in the new language, words from the old language may keep popping into your mind, hindering your recall. In this sense, transfer can be a form of functional fixedness. If you allow yourself to apply or transfer knowledge from one domain to another, however, you can expand on your own experiences ("I know I passed that store near the end of the bike race, so if I just retrace my steps starting at the finish line, I'll find it"). One of the best ways for people to transfer is to see meaningful analogies between what they are learning and something they already know (Ben-Zeev, 1996; Blessing & Ross, 1996; Gentner, 2000; Gentner & Markman, 1997).

INCUBATION

Sometimes we get stuck on a problem that requires insight that just does not seem to come to us. **Incubation** is a process by which a problem solver stops focusing conscious attention on solving the problem

Sometimes we get stuck on a problem. The insight needed to solve it just won't come. In such cases, it may be best to allow the problem to incubate for a while, as time permits.

for a while and lets the work continue. During incubation, you do not consciously think about the problem. Although no one knows exactly why incubation works, some researchers believe it is because as time passes, new stimuli—both internal and external—may activate new perspectives on the problem, weakening the effects of old mental sets (Bastik, 1982; Yaniv & Meyer, 1987). People who are prepared to receive relevant new information from the environment are particularly likely to incubate successfully (Seifert, Meyer, Davidson, Patalano, & Yaniv, 1995).

When you sit down to write a paper for a course and you find that you just cannot seem to organize your ideas effectively, it may help to let the problem incubate for a while. A few days later, you may come across some new ideas or otherwise find that what seemed like an insoluble problem is now more easily solved. Using this strategy means, of course, that you need to start thinking about the paper far enough in advance of the deadline so that you have time for incubation.

EXPERTISE

If the various strategies for solving problems are available to all of us, why can experts solve problems in their field more effectively than novices can?

Studies have shown that much of what distinguishes experts from novices is the extent and organization of their knowledge base. William Chase and Herbert Simon (1973), following up on work by Adrian de Groot (1965), set out to determine what distinguishes expert from novice chess players. They had players at both levels briefly view a display of a chessboard and then recall the positions of the chess pieces. In general, the experts did better than the novices—but only if the positions of the pieces on the board made sense in terms of an actual game. If the pieces were randomly distributed, experts did not recall their positions any better than the novices.

According to Chase and Simon, the key difference was that chess experts could call on their knowledge of tens of thousands of board positions, each of which they could remember as an integrated, organized chunk of information. For a random pattern, however, knowledge offered experts no advantage over novices. Both groups had to try to memorize the interrelationships among the many positions.

After the Chase and Simon work, other investigators conducted extensive studies of large numbers of experts in different domains (e.g., see Chi, Glaser, & Farr, 1988; Ericsson, 1996, 1999; Ericsson, Krampe, & Tesch-Römer, 1993; Sloboda, Davidson, Howe, & Moore, 1996; R. J. Sternberg & Frensch, 1991). Although several characteristics distinguished experts from novices, what most clearly differentiated the two groups was the amount of existing knowledge and how well it was organized. It also has been found that deliberate, systematic practice is one of the best ways to become an expert in a wide variety of endeavors (Ericsson, 1996), although such practice is more effective if supplemented by a talent for the endeavor one pursues (Shiffrin, 1996; Wagner & Stanovich, 1996). Micheline Chi and her colleagues (e.g., Chi, Feltovich, & Glaser, 1981) asked people to sort physics problems into groups of problems that "belonged together." Chi found that the experts tended to sort by the underlying principles of the physics involved, whereas novices tended to sort the problems by surface features, such as whether they involved pulleys. Alan Lesgold and his colleagues studied radiologists and found additional differences between experts and novices (Lesgold, 1988; Lesgold et al., 1988). For example, experts tend to spend more time than novices in representing problems, and they are better at using new evidence.

Whereas problem solving involves inventing or discovering strategies in order to answer complex questions, other forms of thinking may involve choosing among or evaluating opportunities. The next section deals with how we make these choices and judgments.

✓ CONCEPT CHECK 7

1. The nine-dot problem is an example of a(n) _____ problem
   a. well-defined
   b. ill-defined
   c. partially defined
   d. fully defined
2. While incubating a problem, people
   a. consciously work hard and continuously on the problem.
   b. consciously work on the problem at fixed intervals.
   c. consciously work on the problem at variable intervals.
   d. do not consciously work on the problem.
3. Chase and Simon found that the main difference between experts and novices was with respect to
   a. knowledge.
   b. critical thinking.
   c. creativity.
   d. family background.

MAKING JUDGMENTS AND DECISIONS

Can you describe the processes by which you arrive at a judgment or decision?

In the course of our everyday lives, we are constantly making judgments and decisions. One of the most important decisions you have made is whether or where to go to college. Once in college, you need to choose your courses and, eventually, your major field of study. You make decisions about friends, about how to relate to your parents, and about how to spend money. How do you go about making these decisions?

DECISION THEORY

The earliest models of decision theory assumed that decision makers operate in ideal circumstances and make optimal decisions. Although we now consider these assumptions unrealistic, a great deal of economic research has been and still is based on this model. Subsequent models of decision making have recognized that we may not face ideal circumstances but that we nevertheless strive to make optimal decisions.

According to *utility-maximization theory*, the goal of human action is to maximize pleasure (*positive utility*) and to minimize pain (*negative utility*). Utility-maximization theorists suggest that we can predict what people will do by assuming that they will seek the highest possible utility. In other words, they make the decision that maximizes pleasure and minimizes pain. Suppose that you are deciding whether to buy a desktop computer. You do not like the fact that this model is not portable. This can be viewed as a negative utility. At the same time, you like the large screen and the rapid processing speed. These factors are positive utilities. Whether you buy the desktop computer will depend on whether the positive utilities outweigh the negative ones in your mind.

It is certainly appealing to come up with objective, mathematical models for decision making. In practice, though, it is very difficult to assign objective utilities to decisions. Models based on such assignments are likely to produce inaccurate representations of reality. As a result, cognitive psychologists interested in decision theory introduced *subjective-utility theory*. This theory acknowledges that each individual may have a distinct understanding of the various utilities for a given action, based on the idiosyncratic hopes, fears, and other subjective motivations of the individual. For example, being turned down for a date may be extremely negative for one person but only slightly negative for another.

SATISFICING

Principles of economics are often based on the notion that decision makers have unlimited rationality and use it in making their decisions. The decision makers decide what criterion to maximize or minimize. Then they make the optimal decision for doing so. Even in the 1950s, however, some psychologists were beginning to recognize that we do not always make ideal decisions. Rather, we are usually influenced by subjective considerations. Thus, we are not entirely rational in making decisions.

The best-known challenge came from Herbert Simon (1957), who went on to win the Nobel Prize in economics. Simon did not suggest that we are irrational. Rather, we exhibit **bounded rationality,** the limits within which humans demonstrate reasoned behavior. Simon proposed one of the most typical decision-making strategies: satisficing. In **satisficing,** the decision maker considers options one by one and immediately selects the first option that appears to be satisfactory. This option is just good enough. We do not consider all of the possible options and then carefully compute which of the entire universe of options will maximize gains and minimize losses. We consider the minimum number of options in order to arrive at a decision that we believe will satisfy our minimum requirements. You may use satisficing when you consider topics for a term paper. Of the countless possible topics, you may think about a few. You then settle on the first satisfactory or even pretty good topic you think of, without continuing your exploration.

The progression from fully rational models of decision making to models of bounded rationality involved the increasing recognition that people are not perfect decision makers. We make decisions in less than ideal circumstances, given inadequate or incomplete information. We use limited objectivity and rationality. Often we are even willing to settle for the first acceptable option that becomes available, fully aware that others may be better.

What additional human frailties have researchers discovered in their study of decision making?

HEURISTICS AND BIASES

In the 1970s, Amos Tversky and Daniel Kahneman found even more evidence for the boundaries of human rationality. Daniel Kahneman won the 2002 Nobel Prize in economics for this work, and had Tversky still lived, he almost certainly would have shared the prize with Kahneman. Tversky, Kahneman, and their colleagues investigated the heuristics and biases we often use when making decisions and other judgments (see Dawes, 2000; Gigerenzer, 1996; Shafir & Tversky,

1995). Some of these—such as representativeness, availability, and other phenomena—are described next.

REPRESENTATIVENESS

Before you read a definition of representativeness, try to solve this problem (Kahneman & Tversky, 1971):

> All the families that have exactly six children in a particular city were surveyed. In 72 of the families, the exact order of births of boys (B) and girls (G) was G B G B B G. What is your estimate of the number of families surveyed in which the exact order of births was B G B B B B?

Most people estimate the number of families with the B G B B B B birth pattern to be less than 72. Actually the best estimate of the number of families with this birth order is 72, the same as for the G B G B B G birth order. The expected number for the second pattern would be the same because the sex for each birth is independent (at least, theoretically) of the sex for every other birth. For any one birth, the chances of a boy (or a girl) are one out of two. Thus, any particular pattern of births is equally likely, even B B B B B B or G G G G G G.

Why do people believe some birth orders are more likely than others? Kahneman and Tversky suggested that it is because they use the **representativeness heuristic,** a judgment about the probability of an uncertain event according to (1) how obviously the event is similar to or representative of the population from which it is derived, and (2) the degree to which the event reflects the salient features of the process by which it is generated (such as randomness) (see also Fischhoff, 1999; Johnson-Laird, 2000). People believe that the first birth order is more likely. First, it is more representative of the number of females and males in the population. Second, it looks more random than the second birth order. In fact, of course, either order is equally likely to occur by chance.

Similarly, when asked to judge the probability of flips of a coin yielding the sequence H T H H T H, people will judge it as higher than when they are asked to judge the sequence H H H H T H. If you expect a sequence to be random, you tend to view one that "looks random" as likely to occur. Indeed, people often comment that the ordering of numbers in a table of random numbers "doesn't look random." People underestimate the number of runs of the same number that will appear wholly by chance.

To fully understand the representativeness heuristic, it helps to understand the concept of **base rate,** the prevalence of an event or characteristic within its population of events or characteristics. People often ignore base-rate information, but it is important to effective judgment and decision making. In many occupations, the use of base-rate information and the representativeness heuristic are essential for adequate job performance. A doctor who is told that a 10-year-old girl is suffering chest pains is much less likely to worry about an incipient heart attack than if the patient were a 50-year-old man. Why? Because the base rate of heart attacks is much higher in 50-year-old men than in 10-year-old girls. It is also easier to recall people of roughly 50 who have had heart attacks. Such instances are more available, which leads us to the next heuristic. People can be taught how to use base rates to improve their decision making (Gigerenzer, 1996; Koehler, 1996).

AVAILABILITY

Fewer than 1 in 250,000 plane flights has even the most minor accident; fewer than 1 in 1.6 million scheduled flights end in fatalities (L. Krantz, 1992); the odds were 1 in 2.2 million of being killed in an airplane crash in 1988 (Shook & Shook, 1991). Although the chances of dying during a car trip (however brief) are low, more than 1 in 125 Americans will die in car-related accidents (L. Krantz, 1992). Intoxicated 18-year-old men driving without seat belts are 1,000 times more likely to die in a car crash than sober 40-year-old drivers, either male or female, who wear their seat belts (Shook & Shook, 1991).

Which of these accidents has the higher base rate? How do the availability and unavailability of information influence our perceptions and decisions?

Why is it that so many more people are afraid of flying in airplanes than of riding in cars, despite the fact that the probability of being injured or dying in a car crash is much higher? One reason is the **availability heuristic** (Tversky & Kahneman, 1973), an intuitive strategy for making judgments or inferences, or for solving problems, based on the ease with which particular examples or ideas may be called to mind (see Fischhoff, 1999; R. J. Sternberg, 2000). This heuristic does not necessarily take into account the degree to which they are relevant. Newspapers and television give much more play to plane crashes than to car accidents. It is usually easier to call to mind grim instances of plane crashes. Hence, unequal coverage may be one reason (of many) that people tend to fear riding in planes more than in cars. Similarly, politicians spend a lot of time raising money to buy advertising. They know that the media exposure that makes their names more readily available to voters than the names of their competitors can be critical to their winning.

OTHER DECISION-MAKING AND JUDGMENT PHENOMENA

There are other oddities in people's judgments (see Osherson, 1995). One is **overconfidence,** an excessive valuation of skills, knowledge, or judgment. Baruch Fischhoff, Paul Slovic, and Sarah Lichtenstein (1977) gave people 200 two-alternative statements, such as "*Absinthe* is (a) a liqueur, (b) a precious stone." People were asked to choose the correct answer and to give the probability that their answer was correct. They were strangely overconfident. When people were 100% confident of their answers, they were right only 80% of the time! (Absinthe is a licorice-flavored liqueur.) Kahneman and Tversky (1979) asked people to complete statements such as "I feel 98% certain that the number of nuclear plants operating in the world in 1980 was more than _____ but less than _____." People were often wrong, even when they were certain they were correct. Nearly one-third of the time, the correct answer was outside the range that people gave (in this case, exactly 189 nuclear plants were operating at that time). In general, people are overconfident of their judgments (Carlson, 1995; Griffin & Tversky, 1992; Kahneman & Tversky, 1996). Due to overconfidence, people often do things that are dangerous or bad for them. One example of overconfidence is a belief held by many smokers. They think that although other people may get lung cancer and heart disease, they themselves are not likely to be afflicted. It is not clear why we tend to be overconfident in our judgments. One simple explanation is that we prefer not to think about being wrong (Fischhoff, 1988).

Another common error is the **gambler's fallacy,** the false belief that when a sequence of coincidental events occur in a nonrandom pattern, subsequent events are more likely to deviate from the pattern than to continue in it. Actually, the probability of each event continues to be exactly the same at each occurrence. Thus, the gambler who loses in five successive bets may believe that a win is more likely the sixth time. In truth, of course, the gambler is no more likely to win on the sixth bet than on the first—or on the 1,001st!

A common error in judgment is the *sunk-cost fallacy* (Dupuy, 1998, 1999; Nozick, 1993), which is the decision to continue to invest in something simply because one has already invested in it and hopes to recover the investment. Suppose your car is a lemon. You have already invested thousands of dollars to buy it and get it fixed. Now you are facing another major repair. You have no reason to believe that this additional repair will be the last. You think how much money you have spent on repairs, and you reason that you need to do the additional repair, rather than buy a different car, to justify the amount you already have spent. You have just fallen prey to the sunk-cost fallacy. The problem is that you already have lost the money on those repairs. Throwing more money into the car will not get the spent money back. Your best bet may well be to view the money already spent on repairs as a "sunk cost" and to buy a different car. Similarly, suppose you go on a vacation, which you intend to last two weeks. You are having a miserable time. Should you go home a week early? You decide against it, so as to justify the investment you already have made in the vacation. Again, you have committed the sunk-cost fallacy.

Much of the research on judgment and decision making has focused on the errors people make. As Jonathan Cohen (1981) and Gilbert Harman (1995) have pointed out, however, people do act rationally in many instances. Moreover, heuristics do not always lead us astray. Sometimes they are amazingly simple ways of drawing sound conclusions. Gerd Gigerenzer and his colleagues (Gigerenzer & Goldstein, 1996; Gigerenzer, Todd, & the ABC Research Group, 1999) have shown that a simple heuristic, *take the best*, can be amazingly effective in decision situations. The rule is simple. Identify the single most important criterion to you for making a decision. In choosing a new automobile, for example, the most important factor might be good gas mileage, safety, or appearance. Gigerenzer and his colleagues have shown that this heuristic, which may seem on the surface to be inadequate, often leads to very good decisions—even better decisions, in many cases, than far more complicated heuristics. Thus, heuristics can be used for good as well as for bad decision making. Indeed, when we take people's goals into account, heuristics often are amazingly effective (J. Evans & Over, 1996).

1. Gerald votes for a particular candidate because that candidate's name is the one he has heard the most. Gerald is using the
   a. availability heuristic.
   b. representativeness heuristic.
   c. base-rate heuristic.
   d. overconfident heuristic.
2. In satisficing, one
   a. optimizes on the available options.
   b. ignores advice.
   c. picks the first minimally acceptable option.
   d. picks all satisfactory options.
3. In gambler's fallacy, one believes that if flipping a coin has yielded seven heads, then the most likely outcome of the eighth flip is
   a. heads again.
   b. tails.
   c. either heads or tails, both of which are equally likely.
   d. unknown.

REASONING

Can you describe how you reason?

We have seen that making judgments and decisions involves evaluating opportunities and selecting one. A related kind of thinking is reasoning. **Reasoning** is drawing conclusions from evidence (Wason & Johnson-Laird, 1972). **Deductive reasoning** is the process of drawing logically certain conclusions from evidence. It involves one or more general **premises,** statements of fact or assertions of belief on which a deductively reasoned argument may be based, to reach a logically certain, specific conclusion. In contrast, **inductive reasoning** is the process of drawing uncertain conclusions based on specific facts or observations (Holyoak & Thagard, 1995). Inductive reasoning permits the reasoner to draw well-founded or probable conclusions but not logically certain conclusions. One kind of inductive reasoning is the causal inference, through which the reasoner tries to determine the cause or causes of certain events (Cheng, 1997, 1999; Cheng & Holyoak, 1995; Koslowski, 1996; Spellman, 1997).

Some theorists believe that we have two systems of reasoning: one is largely logical and the other is largely experiential (e.g., Sloman, 1996, 1999). Moreover, even when people are trying to be rational, their preconceptions can have a strong effect on their reasoning (Bassok, Wu, & Olseth, 1995). An example of the workings of the associative system is the *false-consensus effect,* whereby people believe that their own behavior and judgments are more reflective of the norm and more appropriate than are those of other people (Ross, Greene, & House, 1977). A person who has an opinion on an issue believes that it is likely to be shared and thought correct by others. Of course, there is some diagnostic value in one's own opinions, as it is quite possible that others do indeed believe the same thing (Dawes & Mulford, 1996; Krueger, 1998). But on the whole, assuming that others' views are the same as our own, simply because they are our own, is a questionable practice.

In any case, people do not show the same reasoning skill in all domains. They might be strong verbal reasoners but not so strong in mathematical reasoning (Frensch & Buchner, 1999).

DEDUCTIVE REASONING

Deductive reasoning is the process of starting with what is already known and reaching a new conclusion. **Syllogisms** are deductive arguments that permit one to draw conclusions on the basis of two premises, each of which contains two terms and at least one of which is common to both premises. Although it is possible to specify rules for solving syllogisms, some psychologists believe that problem solvers do not use formal rules, but rather model the problems by imagining concrete terms (Johnson-Laird, 1999). For example, they might think of the following syllogism in terms of psychology students, pianists, and athletes:

All psychology students are pianists.

All pianists are athletes.

Therefore, all psychology students are athletes.

Various theories have been proposed for how people solve syllogisms. The theory of Philip Johnson-Laird and Mark Steedman (1978; see also Johnson-Laird & Byrne, 1991) is based on the notion that people solve syllogisms using mental models (Johnson-Laird, 1988, 1997; Johnson-Laird et al., Johnson-Laird et al., 1999). They manipulate in their minds actual exemplars of elements of the syllogisms. In this way, they try to figure out what the correct solution should be (Garcia-Madruga, Moreno, Carriedo, & Gutierrez, 2000; Johnson-Laird & Savary, 1999). In contrast, Lance Rips (1994, 1995, 1999) has suggested that we use a set of mental rules for combining premises.

A different approach to deductive reasoning has been suggested by Leda Cosmides (1989; Cosmides & Tooby, 1992, 1996). According to Cosmides, psychologists should take an evolutionary view of cognition. They should consider what kinds of thinking skills would provide a naturally selective advantage for humans in adapting to our environment across evolutionary time. To gain insight into human cognition, we should look to see what kinds of adaptations would have been most useful to hunters and gatherers during the millions of years before the relatively recent development of agriculture and the very recent development of industrialized societies.

Cosmides has suggested that one distinctive adaptation of hunters and gatherers was in the area of social exchange, such as a barter or sale. Two kinds of inferences that people should be well equipped to make are those related to cost-benefit relationships and those related to the detection of cheating. You will reason better if a problem involves detecting you are being cheated than if it involves, say, a procedure for washing clothes. The idea is that people in earlier times who were not skilled in assessing the costs and benefits of a deal or in determining when they were being cheated would have been at a disadvantage in adaptation. They thus would have been less likely to have descendants. Over a series of nine experiments, Cosmides found that the predictions of her social-exchange theory better fit the data from people's performance on deductive-reasoning tasks than did the predictions of other theories.

Deductive reasoning with abstract terms is practiced and rewarded in some cultures but not others. Individuals in some cultures may find such problems confusing and rather pointless (Cole, Gay, Glick, & Sharp, 1971; Luria, 1976).

"Alas, Adso, you have too much faith in syllogisms! What we have, once again, is simply the question. . . ."

I was upset. I had always believed logic was a universal weapon, and now I realized how its validity depended on the way it was employed.
—Umberto Eco, *The Name of the Rose*

INDUCTIVE REASONING

In inductive reasoning, the reasoner cannot reach a logically certain conclusion but can determine the strength, or probability, of a conclusion (Johnson-Laird, 2000; Thagard, 1999). Suppose that you are not given a neat set of premises from which to draw a conclusion. Instead, you are given a set of observations. For example, you notice that everyone enrolled in your introductory psychology course is on the dean's list (or honor roll). You could inductively reason that everyone who enrolls in introductory psychology is an excellent student. However, unless you can observe the grade-point averages of everyone who ever has taken or will take introductory psychology, you will be unable to prove your conclusion. Furthermore, a single poor student will disprove your conclusion. Still, after many observations, you might conclude that you had made enough observations to make an inductive inference.

In this situation and others that require reasoning, you were not given clearly stated premises or obvious relationships among the elements by which you could deduce a surefire conclusion. You simply cannot deduce a logically valid conclusion. You need to use an alternative kind of reasoning. Inductive reasoning involves reasoning from specific facts or observations to a general conclusion (Bisanz, Bisanz, & Korpan, 1994). You may try to remember where you placed your lost keys on the basis of plausible inferences. Examples would be where you usually put them, where you have recently been, and so forth. None of these considerations guarantees a solution to the problem, but your inductive reasoning may help you find the keys. We cannot reasonably leap from saying "All observed instances of X are Y" to "Therefore, all X are Y."

An evolutionary view of how our reasoning abilities have developed emphasizes social exchange. In some cultures, the Western model of deductive reasoning with abstract terms is not practiced or rewarded.

Suppose that a child has seen many kinds of birds flying in the sky. She may reasonably conclude "All birds fly." When she visits the zoo and encounters penguins and ostriches for the first time, however, she can see that her inductive conclusion is false. Like other empiricists, she can thereby find that her inductive conclusions, based on many observations, can be disproved by just one contradictory observation. Furthermore, regardless of the number of observations or the soundness of the reasoning, no inductively based conclusions can be proved. They can only be supported, to a greater or lesser degree, by available evidence. Thus, the inductive reasoner must state any conclusions about a hypothesis in terms of likelihoods. Examples are "There is a good chance of rain tomorrow" and "There is a 99% probability that these findings are not a result of random variability."

Suppose that Jason had a particular mental model of a college campus. His rule was "People on college campuses are either students or professors." Later Jason had a few encounters with administrative personnel, librarians, service personnel, and others on campus who are neither students nor professors. He then realized that he had to modify his rule. His new rule became "People on college campuses are students, professors, or paid staff members."

It seems that despite our occasional lapses and distortions, we often reason pretty well. Still, even the most enlightened reasoning cannot create something from what appears to be nothing. To do that, we need creativity.

✓ CONCEPT CHECK 9

1. Syllogisms require
   a. primarily deductive reasoning.
   b. primarily inductive reasoning.
   c. an equal combination of inductive and deductive reasoning.
   d. neither inductive nor deductive reasoning.
2. According to Cosmides, evolution has resulted in our having a well-developed ability to detect
   a. logical inconsistencies.
   b. cheaters.
   c. main ideas but not details.
   d. facial expressions.
3. Inductive problems have
   a. no logically certain conclusion.
   b. one logically certain conclusion.
   c. multiple but not infinite logically certain conclusions.
   d. infinite logically certain conclusions.

CREATIVITY

What is creativity, and what are the characteristics of many creative people?

Creativity is the process of producing something that is both original and valuable in some way (Boden, 1999; Collins & Amabile, 1999; Csikszentmihalyi, 1999a, 2000; Runco, 2000). The *something* could be a theory, a dance, a chemical, a process or procedure, or almost anything else (Figure 8.10).

Just what does it mean to be *original?* Almost everything we do is based on the work of those who have come before us. Creative individuals learn from the techniques, styles, and ideas of their predecessors. But they analyze or synthesize this information in a novel, unconventional, and valuable way (Ward, Smith, & Finke, 1999; Weisberg, 1999). Value is another important idea in the definition of creativity. What makes something valuable is that it is significant, useful, or worthwhile in some way, to some segment of the population or some field of endeavor. Sometimes people do not appreciate the value of the creative work until long after the creator dies.

Some creative products are modestly creative; others are revolutionary (T. S. Kuhn, 1970; R. J. Sternberg, 1999c; R. J. Sternberg, Kaufman, & Pretz, 2001, 2002). Hence, when we speak of creative work, we should remember that it ranges from the mundane to the extraordinary.

CHARACTERISTICS OF CREATIVE THINKING

Although we have yet to develop a method for detecting highly creative individuals at a glance, psychologists have found that they seem to share a few intrinsic characteristics. Psychologists who take a *psychometric* approach, such as Joy P. Guilford (1950), have emphasized performance on tasks involving specific aspects of creativity, such as *divergent production* of a diverse assortment of appropriate responses to a problem, question, or task. For example, coming up with ideas for a term paper involves divergent production.

Creativity may vary in its manifestation at different points in life. Howard Gardner (1993a; Policastro & Gardner, 1999), using case studies, has suggested that an individual's earlier contributions tend to be more radically creative and later ones more integrative with past work. It also seems that differing forms of literary creativity surface at different ages. A survey of 420 literary creators across both cultures and vast

FIGURE 8.10

Creativity in Art. Highly creative individuals, such as Vincent van Gogh, whose *Landscape with Cypress and Star* is on the right, often lead a revolutionary movement away from the contemporary mode, illustrated by the Impressionist painting *Le Moulin de la Galette,* by Pierre-Auguste Renoir, shown on the left.

expanses of time supports the notion that people write more creative poetry during their youth but better prose when they are older (Simonton, 1975). These data suggest that powerful poetry draws on the idealism, romanticism, passionate love, and whimsical moods that often accompany youth. But outstanding prose requires the depth, wisdom, and understanding of age.

INTERNAL AND EXTERNAL FACTORS

Teresa Amabile and others (e.g., Amabile, 1996; Collins & Amabile, 1999; Hennessey & Amabile, 1988) have noted the importance of motivation. They distinguish *intrinsic motivation*, which is internal, from *extrinsic motivation*, which is external. For example, intrinsic motivators might include sheer enjoyment of the creative process or personal desire to solve a problem, whereas extrinsic motivators might include desire for fame or fortune. According to Amabile, the former is essential to creativity, but the latter may actually impede creativity.

Some researchers focus on the importance of external factors in influencing creativity (e.g., Csikszentmihalyi, 1996, 1999b; Feldman, 1999). According to Mihaly Csikszentmihalyi (1988, p. 325), "we cannot study creativity by isolating individuals and their works from the social and historical milieu in which their actions are carried out. . . . [W]hat we call creative is never the result of individual action alone."

Dean Simonton (1988, 1999) goes beyond the immediate social, intellectual, and cultural context to embrace the entire sweep of history. In Simonton's view, multiple internal and external factors contribute to highly creative work. Thus, a highly creative individual must be the right person, exploring the right ideas, in the right social, cultural, and historical setting. Who knows what Einstein would have contributed had he lived during the Middle Ages?

These contextual considerations may be the reason so few women gained recognition in art and science until recently. Until the latter half of the 19th century, few women were encouraged—or even permitted—to nurture their intellects. Most were expected to nurture others instead. Even women who were educated or who developed their talents were discouraged from using them. For example, Felix Mendelssohn's older sister, Fanny, was viewed by some as being a finer musician and composer than her brother—or was considered at least comparable in talent. Yet her family, including Felix, would not permit her to publish her compositions under her own name. They also would not allow her to perform in public (Forbes, 1990). Once society allowed women to be productive outside of the family, outstanding women came to the fore. Examples are writers, such as Maya Angelou, Nelly Bly, the Brontë sisters, Emily Dickinson, Toni Morrison, Gertrude Stein, Alice Walker, and Virginia Woolf. Painters include Frida Kahlo and Georgia O'Keeffe. Still

INCREASING CREATIVITY

Most researchers believe that anyone can become more creative by working at it. Quite a few also believe that many more of us could become exceptionally creative if we wished. You could increase your own creativity by taking these steps:

1. Find something you love to do. People do their most creative work when they are excited about what they are doing.
2. Listen to feedback, but do not mindlessly follow the crowd. Creative people forge their own paths; at the same time they profit from others' advice.
3. Deeply believe in the value and importance of your creative work; do not let others discourage you or dissuade you from pursuing your work. On the other hand, you should monitor and criticize your own work, seeking always to improve it.
4. Carefully choose the problems or subjects on which you will focus your creative attention. Remember the importance of problem selection and definition. Find problems that appeal to your own sense of aesthetics. Creative people often generate ideas that are undervalued, underappreciated, and even scorned by their contemporaries.
5. Use the processes that characterize insight as well as divergent-thinking processes. At the same time, realize that creative work always takes tradition into account, even if only to challenge it.
6. Choose associates who will encourage you to take sensible risks, to go against convention, and to try new ideas and methods.
7. Acquire as much knowledge as possible in your field of endeavor. In this way, you can avoid "reinventing the wheel" or producing the same old stuff being produced by others. Then try to go beyond the boundaries of this knowledge.
8. Commit yourself deeply to your creative endeavor.

There is some consensus that each of the preceding suggestions may play a role in creative productivity. However, many psychologists and other researchers might dispute one or more of these factors, and many creative individuals deviate from this general pattern. In fact, we might say that as a group, creative people are characterized by their deviations. There are many other factors in the study of creativity about which psychologists have not reached consensus.

One additional factor seems to show a consistent relationship to creativity: above-average intelligence. Surprisingly, beyond a given level of intelligence, further increases in intelligence do not necessarily correlate with increases in creativity. Thus, to be creative, an individual must be bright but not necessarily brilliant.

enhancing creativity
creativity and productivity
creative intelligence

---

others are poet and politician Sojourner Truth and scientists Rachel Carson (biology), Marie Curie (physics and chemistry), Rosalind Franklin (DNA structure), Sophie Germain (mathematics and physics), Margaret Mead (anthropology), and Helen Taussig (medicine), among countless others.

Robert Sternberg and Todd Lubart (1995, 1996, 1999) have synthesized several approaches to creativity by suggesting that multiple individual and environmental factors must converge for creativity to occur. In addition to having a suitable environmental context, the creative individual must possess adequate knowledge, intellectual processes, personality variables, and motivation as well as an intellectual style to facilitate creativity. Sternberg and Lubart call their theory the *investment theory of creativity*. The idea is that the creative individual buys low and sells high. That is, the creative individual focuses attention on an idea that is undervalued by contemporaries ("buys low") and then develops it into a meaningful, significant contribution. Once other people are convinced of the worth of his or her idea, the creator moves on to the next idea ("sells high"). Creativity is viewed as an attitude toward life that can be taught (Sternberg, 1999c; R. J. Sternberg & Williams, 1997). The Psychology in Everyday Life box, "Increasing Creativity," describes some of the steps you can take to foster your own creativity.

Ⓔ EVOLUTIONARY INFLUENCES

David Perkins (1995b) and Dean Simonton (1995, 1998) have suggested that evolutionary principles may be applied, at least to some extent, to the understanding of human creativity (see also Cziko, 1998). According to these investigators (see also D. T. Campbell, 1960), new ideas are generated more or less at random, like genetic mutations. But ideas, like mutations, undergo a selection process. Most serve no particularly useful purpose and are quickly discarded. But a few ideas may be not only novel but also useful, and they are selected by a society as valuable. They then become a part of our way of thinking, much as useful mutations can become part of our genetic makeup. Genetics, in combination with environment, contributes to creativity but also to intelligence, as discussed in the next chapter.

✓CONCEPT CHECK 10

1. According to Amabile, _____ especially important to encouraging creativity.
   a. intrinsic motivation is
   b. extrinsic motivation is
   c. intrinsic and extrinsic motivation both are equally and
   d. neither intrinsic nor extrinsic motivation is
2. Howard Gardner has suggested that earlier contributions by creative individuals tend to be _____ later contributions.
   a. more radically creative than
   b. less radically creative than
   c. equally creative as
   d. more appreciated than
3. Mihaly Csikszentmihalyi has argued that to understand creativity, we must also consider
   a. wisdom.
   b. age of the individual.
   c. environmental context of the individual.
   d. IQ of the individual.

UNIFYING PSYCHOLOGY

LEARNING A SECOND LANGUAGE

Nadia was born in Moscow and moved to England when she was 3 years old. She spoke Russian at home but acquired English as a second language very quickly in nursery school. During the next 60 years, she continued to speak Russian with family members and English with her friends and colleagues. Shortly before her 65th birthday, Nadia suffered a stroke that was caused by a blocked artery in her right frontal lobe. From then on she could speak Russian only.

How can a person lose the ability to speak a familiar language? Research by *clinical neuropsychologists* has demonstrated that language is typically processed by Broca's area on the left side of the brain. If a second language is learned before the age of 4, as in Nadia's case, it is processed in a second Broca's area in the opposite hemisphere. Thus, Nadia's loss of English indicated that the stroke damaged Broca's area in her right hemisphere. When a second language is learned later in life, however, it is

processed in Broca's area in the left hemisphere. One area of the brain is thus processing two languages, which probably explains why it is so hard to master a second language in high school or in adulthood.

Some *cognitive psychologists* who study language acquisition look at the role of verbal working memory in learning a second language, whereas others study the relationship between the written and oral components of the new language. Languages in which written symbols correspond directly to a spoken phoneme, such as Italian or Finnish, are more easily learned than languages in which many different written symbols correspond to a single phoneme, as in the case of the English "f," which can be represented as "f," "gh," or "ph" in writing (Lundberg, 2002). Languages in which the written symbols do not represent individual phonemes, like Chinese, Japanese, and Korean, are the most difficult to learn.

Developmental psychologists have examined how a first language

can impede the acquisition of a second language during adulthood. For example, German subjects were found to be more like American subjects in their sensitivity to the phoneme "r," whereas Japanese subjects did not respond to "r" sounds (Iverson, Kuhl, Akahane-Yamada, Diesch, Tohkura, Kettermann, & Siebert, 2003). The Japanese subjects did not learn "r" in early childhood and were therefore unable to process it later in adulthood.

As hard as it is for ordinary high school and college students to learn a second language, students with learning disabilities have an even more difficult time. *Educational psychologists, developmental psychologists,* and *neuropsychologists* have attempted to get to the root of this difficulty in order to help students with learning disabilities. In a study of 6-month-old babies, those who had a family history of dyslexia, a language-based reading disorder, showed abnormal brain responses to nonsense syllables,

continued

LEARNING A SECOND LANGUAGE

compared to other babies (Leppaenen, Richardson, Ulla, Eklund, Guttorm, Aro, & Lyytinen, 2002). This experiment demonstrates that, even before they begin to speak, babies who are at risk for reading problems process sounds differently from babies who are not at risk. EEG recordings help clinical and educational psychologists determine which components of auditory language are improperly processed in people with dyslexia. The recordings can then be used to design individual training programs for dyslexic students who are learning a second language (Kujala & Naeaetaenen, 2001).

Applied cognitive psychologists have studied the effectiveness of computer programs in teaching a second language. In fact, a large network of psychologists conduct research on computer-assisted language learning (CALL). Paul Allum (2002) compared the acquisition of a second language by 26 students who were taught by a classroom teacher to the acquisition of the same language by 28 students who used CALL. On most measures of language mastery, the CALL students learned the second language as well as the students who were taught in a traditional classroom. However, over long periods of time, students who used CALL lost their motivation to learn the second language, whereas students who were taught in class did not.

Research by clinical neuropsychologists has helped us understand how language is processed in the brain. Cognitive psychologists study the learning process involved in the acquisition of a second language, and developmental psychologists examine the acquisition of a second language by children and adults. Educational psychologists and applied cognitive psychologists examine normal and faulty language acquisition, such as language learning in children with dyslexia. Together, these different types of psychologists have helped us to understand how a second language is learned.

SUMMARY

1. *Language* is the use of an organized means of combining words in order to communicate.

THE NATURE OF LANGUAGE 284
What characteristics define language?

2. There are at least six properties of language: (a) Language permits us to communicate with one or more persons who share our language. (b) Language creates an arbitrary relationship between a symbol and its referent—an idea, a thing, a process, a relationship, or a description. (c) Language has a structure; only particularly patterned arrangements of symbols have meaning. Different arrangements yield different meanings. (d) The structure of language can be analyzed at more than one level (e.g., phonemic and morphemic). (e) Despite having the limits of a structure, language users can produce novel utterances; the possibilities for creating new utterances are virtually limitless. (f) Languages constantly evolve. In addition, a first language typically is acquired spontaneously.

LANGUAGE AND THE BRAIN 285
What brain mechanisms underlie language?

3. Several linguistic functions in the brain have been localized, largely from observations of what happens when a particular area of the brain is injured or is electrically stimulated.

ASPECTS OF LANGUAGE 287
What are the different aspects of language and its use?

4. The smallest semantically meaningful unit in a language is a *morpheme*.
5. *Semantics* is the study of the meanings of words.
6. Several alternative theories of meaning exist. The three main alternatives are the *componential theory* (meaning can be understood in terms of components, or basic elements, of a word), the *prototype theory* (meaning is inherent in "best examples" of a concept), and the *exemplar theory* (meaning is inherent in our use of exemplars of a concept).
7. *Syntax* is the study of linguistic structure at the sentence level.

8. Alternative kinds of grammars have been proposed to understand the structure of sentences: (a) *Phrase-structure grammars* analyze sentences in terms of the order in which words appear in phrases and sentences; and (b) *transformational grammars* analyze sentences in terms of deep (propositional meaning) structures that underlie surface (word-sequence) structures.

9. *Pragmatics* is the study of how language is used.

10. *Sociolinguists*, who study the relationship between social behavior and language, have observed that people engage in various strategies to signal turn-taking in conversations.

11. In order to communicate effectively, parties must have a shared understanding about the situation being discussed; these shared understandings are called *scripts*.

12. *Slips of the tongue* are inadvertent semantic or articulation errors in things we say.

13. *Linguistic relativity theory* asserts that cognitive differences resulting from a given language cause people who speak that language to perceive the world uniquely.

14. *Linguistic universals* are properties of language that are common across all languages.

LANGUAGE ACQUISITION 294

How do people acquire language?

15. Humans seem to progress through the following stages in acquiring language: (a) prenatal responsivity to human voices; (b) postnatal *cooing*, which comprises all possible phones; (c) *babbling*, which comprises only the distinct phonemes that characterize the primary language of the infant; (d) one-word utterances; (e) two-word utterances; (f) *telegraphic speech*; and (g) basic adult sentence structure (present by about age 4).

16. During language acquisition, children engage in *overextensions*, in which they extend the meaning of a word to encompass more concepts than the word is intended to include.

17. Neither nature alone nor nurture alone can account for human language acquisition. The mechanism of hypothesis testing suggests an integration of nature and nurture: Children acquire language by mentally forming tentative hypotheses about language and then testing these hypotheses in the environment. They are guided in the formation of these hypotheses by an innate *language-acquisition device (LAD)*, which facilitates language acquisition.

DO ANIMALS USE LANGUAGE? 299

What is the evidence for and against language use by nonhuman animals?

18. Animals can clearly communicate with one another, although debate exists over whether this communication constitutes animal language—that is, communication that exhibits all the properties found in human language.

THE NATURE OF THOUGHT 301

How would you define *thought*?

19. Thinking involves the processing of mental representations.

20. *Problem solving* involves mental work to overcome obstacles that stand in the way of answering a question.

STRATEGIES AND OBSTACLES IN PROBLEM SOLVING 302

How do you solve problems? What difficulties do you encounter?

21. Problems with well-defined paths to solution are referred to as *well-structured*.

22. *Ill-structured problems* are problems for which there is no clear, readily available path to solution.

23. *Heuristics* are informal, intuitive, speculative strategies for solving problems; they sometimes work and sometimes do not. Heuristics are often contrasted with *algorithms*, which are formal paths to an accurate solution.

24. *Insightful* problem solving involves the subjective feeling of a sudden realization of the solution to a problem.

25. *Mental set* refers to the use of a strategy that has worked in the past but does not necessarily work for a particular problem that needs to be solved in the present. A particular type of mental set is *functional fixedness*, which is the inability to see that something that is known to have a particular use may also be used for performing other functions.

26. *Incubation*, which follows a period of intensive work on a problem, involves laying a problem to rest for a while and then returning to it, so that subconscious work can continue on the problem while consciously the problem is being ignored.

27. Experts differ from novices in both the amount and the organization of knowledge that they bring to bear on problem solving in the domain of their expertise.

28. *Utility-maximization theory* assumes that the goal of human action is to seek pleasure and to avoid pain. A refined form of this theory is *subjective-utility theory*, which acknowledges that utilities cannot always be objectified.
29. *Satisficing* involves selecting the first acceptable alternative that comes to mind.
30. A person who uses the *representativeness heuristic* judges the probability of an uncertain event by the degree to which that event is essentially similar to the population from which it derives and by the degree to which it reflects the salient features of the processes by which it is generated.
31. A person who uses the *availability heuristic* makes judgments on the basis of how easily she or he is able to call to mind what are perceived as relevant instances of a phenomenon.
32. People often exhibit *overconfidence*, judging that the probability of their correctness in reaching a solution to a problem is substantially higher than it actually is.
33. The *gambler's fallacy* is the false belief that a person's luck is bound to change, just by the nature of things.

34. *Reasoning* is the process of drawing conclusions from evidence.
35. *Deductive reasoning* is involved when a person seeks to determine whether one or more logically certain conclusions can be drawn from a set of *premises*.
36. *Inductive reasoning* involves reasoning from specific facts or observations to reach a general conclusion that may explain the specific facts. Such reasoning is used when it is not possible to draw a logically certain conclusion from a set of premises.

37. Creativity involves producing something that is both original and valuable.
38. Many factors characterize highly creative individuals, such as extremely high motivation to be creative in a particular field of endeavor and nonconformity in questioning conventions.

KEY TERMS

ANSWERS TO CONCEPT CHECKS

Concept Check 1

1. d   2. a   3. d

Concept Check 2

1. c   2. c   3. c

Concept Check 3

1. b   2. a   3. b

Concept Check 4

1. c   2. b   3. a

Concept Check 5

1. c   2. b   3. b

Concept Check 6

1. b   2. d   3. d

Concept Check 7

1. b   2. d   3. a

Concept Check 8

1. a   2. c   3. b

Concept Check 9

1. a   2. b   3. a

Concept Check 10

1. a   2. a   3. c

KNOWLEDGE CHECK

1. Research on language in chimpanzees yields the conclusion that
   a. chimpanzees definitely have language skills.
   b. chimpanzees definitely do not have language skills.
   c. chimpanzees may have language skills.
   d. it is impossible to know whether chimpanzees have language skills.
2. For most people, linguistic processing occurs
   a. primarily in the right hemisphere.
   b. primarily in the left hemisphere.
   c. equally in both hemispheres.
   d. in neither hemisphere.
3. The word *predestined* has _____ morpheme(s).
   a. one
   b. two
   c. three
   d. four
4. The componential theory can
   a. more easily account for the meaning of *bachelor* than for the meaning of *game*.
   b. more easily account for the meaning of *game* than for the meaning of *bachelor*.
   c. account for the meanings of *bachelor* and of *game* equally well.
   d. not account for the meaning of either *bachelor* or *game*.
5. The sequence of events you go through when you boot up a computer is an example of a
   a. spoonerism.
   b. slip.
   c. pragmatic.
   d. script.
6. "Down Dada" is an example of
   a. cooing.
   b. babbling.
   c. mewing.
   d. telegraphic speech.
7. If you toss a coin and get five heads in a row, it seems less likely than your getting the pattern heads-tails-tails-heads-tails, even though both patterns are equally likely. The latter pattern seems more likely than the former because of the _____ heuristic.
   a. representativeness
   b. availability
   c. satisficing
   d. base-rate
8. You have had a string of bad luck, and now you are sure your luck will change because you could not possibly continue to have bad luck. You are most likely exhibiting
   a. the representativeness heuristic.
   b. the availability heuristic.
   c. the base-rate fallacy.
   d. the gambler's fallacy.

9. How do deductive reasoning and inductive reasoning compare?
   a. Both can yield logically certain conclusions.
   b. Deductive reasoning can yield a logically certain conclusion; inductive reasoning cannot.
   c. Inductive reasoning can yield a logically certain conclusion; deductive reasoning cannot.
   d. Neither can yield a logically certain conclusion.

10. The work of Teresa Amabile suggests that _____ motivation is especially important for creativity.
    a. effectance
    b. causal
    c. intrinsic
    d. extrinsic

Answers
1. c   2. b   3. c   4. a   5. d   6. d   7. a   8. d
9. b   10. c

THINK ABOUT IT

1. Many language lovers enjoy the dynamic quality of language and relish each new nuance of meaning and change of form that arises. In contrast, others believe that to cherish a language is to preserve it exactly as it is at present—or even exactly as it was at some time in the past. Give the pros and cons of both welcoming and resisting change in language.

2. If we assume that some animals can be taught rudimentary language or language-like skills, what distinguishes humans from other animals?

3. What steps can nonnatives take when studying another culture to understand the breadth and depth of that culture with minimal distortion from their own biases?

4. How do advertisers (and other propagandists) use invalid reasoning to influence people? Give some specific examples of ads you have seen or experiences you have had with salespersons or other persuaders.

5. If you were the head of a problem-solving team and your team members seemed to be running into a block in their approach to the problem being addressed, what would you have the team members do to get around the block?

6. What is a particularly challenging ill-structured problem that you now face (or have recently faced)? What strategies do you find (or did you find) most helpful in confronting this problem?

WEB RESOURCES

For a chapter tutorial quiz, direct links to Internet sites, and other useful features, visit the book-specific website at http://psychology.wadsworth.com/sternberg4e. You can also connect directly to the following sites:

Dyslexia: The Gift
http://www.dyslexia.com
This is a wonderful introduction to the reading disabilities collectively known as dyslexia. It includes basic information, suggestions for adapting to dyslexia-related problems, and links to related Web sites.

The Language of Thought Hypothesis
http://www.hbcollege.com/psych/atkinson/student/links/ch09.html
This extensive page contains much information on language and thought.

Judgment and Decision-Making Experiments
http://psych.fullerton.edu/mbirnbaum/exp.htm
Michael Birnbaum (California State University, Fullerton) presents continuing and completed online experiments that illustrate how people make decisions.

For additional readings on many of the topics covered in this chapter, check out InfoTrac College Edition at **www.infotrac-college.com/wadsworth.**

Disk Two
The Nature of Thought
Strategies and Obstacles in Problem Solving
Judgment and Decision Making
Chapter Quiz
Critical Thinking Questions

CHAPTER 9

INTELLIGENCE

Two sophomores are hiking in the woods. One of them "aced" her freshman-year courses, getting straight A's. Her college entrance test scores had been phenomenal and she was admitted to college with a special scholarship reserved for the brightest entering students. The other student barely made it through her freshman year. Her college entrance test scores were marginal and she just squeaked by even getting into college. Nonetheless, people say of her that she is shrewd and clever—her teachers call her "street smart." As the friends are hiking, they encounter a huge, ferocious, obviously hungry grizzly bear. Its next meal has just come into sight and they are it. The first student calculates that the grizzly bear will overtake them in 27.3 seconds. At that point, she panics, realizing there is no escape. She faces her friend, the fear of death in her eyes. To her amazement, she observes that her friend is not scared at all. To the contrary, her friend is quickly but calmly taking off her hiking boots and putting on jogging shoes. "What do you think you're doing?" the first hiker says to her companion. "You'll never be able to outrun that grizzly bear." "That's true," says the companion, "but all I have to do is outrun you."

Both students in this obviously fictional story are intelligent. But it is clear that they are intelligent in different ways. Indeed, the story raises the issue of just what it means to be intelligent. Although the first student would typically be labeled intelligent, the second student would come out of the crisis alive. The story shows how intelligence is goal-directed adaptive behavior. Actually, there are perhaps as many definitions of intelligence as there are intelligence researchers and theoreticians. Much research is dedicated to trying to answer such questions as What is intelligence? and How can we even find out what it is? (Mackintosh, 1998; R. J. Sternberg, 2000).

It is clear that intelligence draws on many of the skills that we have already discussed, including perceptual, learning, memory-based, language-based, and thinking skills. The nature of intelligence is not some abstract academic issue of interest only in psychology courses. Many children in the United States and in other countries take tests of intelligence. The results of these tests are used for academic placement, admissions to special academic programs, and high-stakes decisions about a child's future. Tests that are not called "intelligence tests" but that contain problems similar to those on intelligence tests are used for admission to colleges, universities, graduate schools, and professional schools in the United States and elsewhere. With some societies so heavily invested in the use of these tests, it is crucial that we understand what intelligence is (Ramey & Ramey, 2000; Ramey, Ramey, & Lanzi, 2001). In the opening story, suppose the second sophomore is intelligent but the type of intelligence she has is not measured by conventional tests. Then we may be missing out on one or more important aspects of intelligence when we make crucial decisions about children's futures. So what, then, is intelligence?

DEFINITIONS OF INTELLIGENCE

How have experts and others defined intelligence?

In 1921, 14 famous psychologists made explicit their implicit views on the nature of intelligence (see "Intelligence and its measurement: A symposium," 1921). Although their responses varied, two important themes were clear: Intelligence comprises (1) the ability to learn from experience and (2) ability to adapt to the surrounding environment. The ability to learn from experience implies, for example, that smart people learn from their mistakes. They do not keep making the same ones again and again. Adaptation to the environment means that being smart goes beyond getting high scores on tests. It includes how you perform in school, handle a job, get along with other people, and manage your life in general.

Sixty-five years after the initial symposium, 24 different experts were asked to give their views on the nature of intelligence (R. J. Sternberg & Detterman, 1986). They noted the standard themes of learning from experience and adapting to the environment. However, contemporary experts put more emphasis on the role of *metacognition*, people's understanding and control of their own thinking processes (during problem solving, reasoning, and decision making). Contemporary experts also emphasized the role of culture in intelligence. They pointed out that what is considered intelligent in one society may be considered stupid in another. In the study of intelligence, the questions scientists ask in large part determine the answers.

Some psychologists, including Edwin Boring (1923), have been content to define intelligence as whatever it is that the tests measure. Unfortunately, this definition is circular: It implies that the nature of intelligence is what is tested, but what is tested must necessarily be determined by the nature of intelligence. Moreover, all tests do not measure the same thing. Different tests measure somewhat different constructs (Daniel, 1997, 2000; Kaufman, 2000; Kaufman & Lichtenberger, 1998), so it is not feasible to define intelligence by what tests test.

To understand current thinking about intelligence, we must go back to the late 19th and early 20th centuries to peek at the work of two intellectual giants: Francis Galton and Alfred Binet. These men started largely opposing traditions for measuring intelligence and to some extent for understanding it: Galton the psychophysical tradition, Binet the judgmental. Galton and Binet did not agree about much, but they did agree that it is possible to understand and to measure intelligence scientifically (N. Brody, 2000).

Ⓔ FRANCIS GALTON: MEASURING PSYCHOPHYSICAL PERFORMANCE

Charles Darwin's *The Origin of Species* (1859) profoundly affected many areas of scientific endeavor. One was the investigation of human intelligence and its development. Darwin suggested that human capabilities exist in some sense on a continuum with those of lower animals. Hence, they can be understood through scientific investigations like those conducted on animals. By studying individual human development, he argued, we might better understand the evolution of the human species and vice versa.

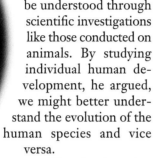

Sir Francis Galton formulated a psychophysical test of intelligence.

The development of intelligence is one of the crowning achievements of evolution, but it is difficult to track across species. Stanley Coren (1994) noted that when we compare the intelligence of different kinds of dogs, we compare in terms of what we value in dogs. But what we value in dogs may be only a limited aspect of what is truly adaptive for them. And it may not be what is truly most adaptive for the dogs in their lives, apart from our wants and preferences. In short, comparisons of intelligence across species are fraught with hazards because what leads to successful adaptation in different species may vary markedly (Zentall, 2000).

Sir Francis Galton (Darwin's cousin) was probably the first to explore the implications of *The Origin of Species* for the study of intelligence. Galton's (1883) theory emphasized basic psychophysical skills, such as how quickly you could move your arm over a span of 50 centimeters. Galton was also a believer in *eugenics*, the notion that organisms (including humans) can be carefully bred to increase the overall intelligence (or other abilities) of the population. Severe misuses of these notions in Nazi Germany make eugenics a highly questionable practice. James McKeen Cattell (1890) brought many of Galton's ideas from England to the United States.

ALFRED BINET: MEASURING JUDGMENT

In 1904, the Minister of Public Instruction in Paris named a commission to find a means to differentiate mentally "defective" children from those who were unsuccessful in school for other reasons. The commission was to ensure that no child suspected of retardation was placed in a special class without first being given an examination. The test was to certify "that because of the state of his intelligence, he was unable to profit, in an average measure, from the instruction given in the ordinary schools" (Binet & Simon, 1916, p. 9).

Alfred Binet's test of intelligence emphasized judgment.

Alfred Binet and his collaborator, Theodore Simon, devised tests to meet this requirement. Thus, theory and research in the tradition of Binet grew out of practical educational concerns. In contrast, the theory and research in the tradition of Galton and Cattell grew out of purely scientific concerns.

Helen Keller was blind and deaf and performed poorly on psychophysical tests of intelligence. She was thought to be retarded until she learned to use sign language and eventually to speak. Alfred Binet cited her as an example to stress the limitations of early psychophysical measures of intelligence.

Binet and Simon's definition of intelligence and their ways of measuring it differed substantially from Galton's and Cattell's, whose tests they dismissed as "wasted time." To Binet and Simon (1916), the core of intelligence is "judgment, otherwise called good sense, practical sense, initiative, the faculty of adapting one's self to circumstances. To judge well, to comprehend well, to reason well, these are the essential activities of intelligence" (pp. 42–43). Binet cited the example of the blind, deaf Helen Keller as someone whose scores on psychophysical tests would be notably inferior and yet who could be expected to perform at a very high level on tests of judgment. How might the core qualities of intelligence be measured?

MENTAL AGE AND THE INTELLIGENCE QUOTIENT

To this day, schools usually segregate children according to their physical, or chronological, age. In conjunction with his theory of intelligence based on judgment, Binet suggested that we might assess children's intelligence on the basis of their mental age, a score that indicates the chronological age of persons who typically perform at the same level of intelligence as a test taker. If, for example, someone's performance on a test is at a level comparable to that of an average 12-year-old, then the person's mental age is 12, regardless of the chronological age. Suppose that José is 10 years old but his performance on a test of intelligence is equal to that of the average 12-year-old. His mental age would be 12. Mental age also conveniently might suggest an appropriate grade placement in school.

William Stern, a German psychologist, noted that mental age is not useful for comparing levels of intelligence in children who have different chronological ages. Stern (1912) suggested instead that we measure intelligence by using an intelligence quotient (IQ): mental age (MA) divided by chronological age (CA), multiplied by 100. This ratio can be expressed mathematically:

$$IQ = (MA/CA) \times 100$$

Thus, if Anita's mental age of 5 equals her chronological age of 5, then her intelligence is average and her IQ is 100 because (5/5)(100) = 100. People whose mental age equals their chronological age always have IQs of 100 because the numerator of the equation equals the denominator, giving a quotient of 1. Subsequent investigators have suggested further modifications of the IQ. As a result, Stern's particular conception of intelligence expressed in terms of a ratio of mental age to chronological age, multiplied by 100, is now termed a **ratio IQ.**

Unfortunately, the concept of mental age proved to be a weak link in the measurement of intelligence,

even when used for calculating a ratio IQ. Increases in measured mental age slow down at about the age of 16 years. Compare what you knew and how you thought when you were 8 years old with what you knew and how you thought when you reached 12 years old. Quite a difference! Now think about someone who is 30 years old. Do you imagine that person's knowledge and thought processes are very different from what they will be at age 45? It makes sense to say that an 8-year-old who performs at the level of a 12-year-old has an IQ of 150. But it makes no sense at all to say that a 30-year-old who performs at the level of a 45-year-old has an IQ of 150. The intellectual performance of a typical 45-year-old differs only minimally from that of a typical 30-year-old. Indeed, in older age, scores on some kinds of mental tests actually may start to decrease. When we measure across the whole life span, it seems ineffective to base the calculation of intelligence on mental age.

INTELLIGENCE TESTS

In a strange way, tests of intelligence have influenced the definition of intelligence. These tests and the numerical results they produce frequently stand in for what intelligence is. Intelligence becomes a score. As we will see when we discuss modern models of intelligence (p. 334), this is perhaps too simplistic. Tests of intelligence measure various kinds of cognitive skills (Daniel, 1997, 2000; Kaufman, 2000). These tests are based largely on the notion that intelligence is a function of judgments of a fairly academic kind. You may recognize the names of some of the tests but wonder what they are like.

THE STANFORD-BINET INTELLIGENCE SCALES

Binet and Simon's original intelligence test calculated mental age only. The next major developer of intelligence tests—Lewis Terman, a professor of psychology at Stanford University—used ratio IQs to compare intelligence across different individuals. Terman rewrote Binet and Simon's test in English. He also added some items and restructured the scoring so that it reflected ratio IQs instead of mental age. He thereby constructed the earliest version of what has come to be called the Stanford-Binet Intelligence Scales (Terman & Merrill, 1937, 1973; R. L. Thorndike, Hagen, & Sattler, 1986). A *scale*, used in this sense, is a standard of measurement that puts people (or anything else) in order from highest to lowest. The Stanford-Binet scales measure a variety of skills. But they may not do justice to the wide range of judgmental and other skills that, according to Binet, constitute intelligence.

A downward extension of the Stanford-Binet, the Bayley Scales of Infant Development are frequently used to measure intelligence in infants. Infant intelligence is discussed further in the next chapter.

David Wechsler constructed an alternative set of scales. They have become the preeminent scales of this type for measuring intelligence.

THE WECHSLER SCALES

The Wechsler intelligence scales include the third edition of the Wechsler Adult Intelligence Scale (WAIS-III), the third edition of the Wechsler Intelligence Scale for Children (WISC-III), and the Wechsler Preschool and Primary Scale of Intelligence (WPPSI). The Wechsler tests yield three scores: verbal, performance, and overall. The verbal score is based on tests such as vocabulary and verbal similarities, in which the test taker has to say how two things are similar. The vocabulary test measures knowledge of word meanings. The similarities test measures verbal reasoning skills. The performance score is based on tests of a different kind. Picture completion, for example, requires identifying a missing part in a picture of an object. In picture arrangement, a scrambled set of cartoonlike pictures is rearranged into an order that tells a coherent story. Picture completion measures perceptual speed and acuity. Picture arrangement measures a person's ability to plan and understand how to organize events into a coherent structure. The overall score is a combination of the verbal and the performance scores. Figure 9.1 shows the types of items in each of the Wechsler adult-scale subtests.

Like Binet, Wechsler (1974) recognized that intelligence goes beyond what his own test measures. We use our intelligence to relate to people, to do our jobs effectively, and to manage our lives in general. In fact, intelligence tests predict performance in a variety of real-world pursuits, such as education (R. Mayer, 2000) and the work force (Schmidt, Ones, & Hunter, 1992; R. K. Wagner, 1997).

APTITUDE AND ACHIEVEMENT TESTS

Galton and Binet, and later Terman and Wechsler, were enormously influential in starting a tradition of testing for intelligence. Today hundreds of intelligence tests are in everyday use. Some of them, like the Stanford-Binet and the Wechsler, are administered to people individually by highly trained psychologists. Others are group tests, which can be administered to large numbers of people at the same time by someone with no extensive training.

Not all tests of cognitive performance assess intelligence. Some cognitively oriented tests measure *aptitudes*, potentials to accomplish something, to attain a level of expertise in a task or a set of tasks, or to acquire knowledge in a given domain or a set of domains, such as music, sports, or fine eye–hand coordination. These aptitudes may or may not involve intelligence.

You are probably familiar with another widely used test that includes content often considered to reflect intelligence: the Scholastic Assessment Test (SAT), administered by the College Board. The SAT contains items such as those shown in Table 9.1. Formerly titled the Scholastic Aptitude Test and then the Scholastic Achievement Test, the SAT was renamed to acknowledge that it measures both **aptitude,** an accomplishment or an attained level of expertise on performance of a task, and **achievement,** an acquired base of knowledge in a domain or a set of domains. In order to bring the test further in line with the kinds of achievements required by schools, a newly constructed SAT includes

On both the WAIS-III for adults (left) and the Wechsler Intelligence Scale for Children (WISC-III) (right), test takers are asked to arrange simple cartoonlike pictures into a logical narrative sequence. In the WISC-III, the sequences involve fewer pictures and simpler stories than in the WAIS-III.

Content area	Explanation of tasks/questions	Example of a possible task/question
Verbal scale		
Comprehension	Answer questions of social knowledge	What does it mean when people say, "A stitch in time saves nine"? Why are convicted criminals put into prison?
Vocabulary	Define the meaning of a word	What does **persistent** mean? What does **archaeology** mean?
Information	Supply generally known information	Who is Vladimir Putin? What are six New England states?
Similarities	Explain how two things or concepts are similar	In what ways are an ostrich and a penguin alike? In what ways are a lamp and a heater alike?
Arithmetic	Solve simple arithmetical-word problems	If Paul has $14.43, and he buys two sandwiches, which cost $5.23 each, how much change will he receive?
Digit span	Listen to a series of digits (numbers), then repeat the numbers either forward or backward or both	Repeat these numbers backward: "9, 1, 8, 3, 6."
Performance Scale		
Object assembly	Put together a puzzle by combining pieces to form a particular common object	Put together these pieces to make something. 
Block design	Use patterned blocks to form a design that looks identical to a design shown by the examiner	Assemble the blocks on the left to make the design on the right. 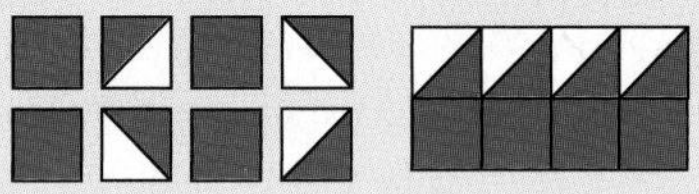
Picture completion	Tell what is missing from each picture	What is missing from this picture? 
Picture arrangement	Put a set of cartoonlike pictures into a chronological order, so they tell a coherent story	Arrange these pictures in an order that tells a story, and then tell what is happening in the story. 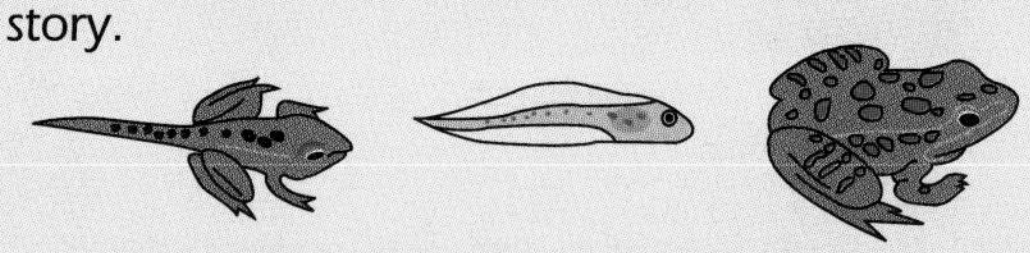
Digit symbol	When given a key matching particular symbols to particular numerals, copy a sequence of symbols, transcribing from symbols to numerals, using the key	Look carefully at the key. In the blanks, write the correct numeral for the symbol below each symbol.

FIGURE 9.1

The Wechsler Adult Intelligence Scale–III (WAIS-III). The Wechsler scales are based on deviation IQs. Items shown here are typical but are not found on the actual test.

TABLE 9.1
CONCEPT REVIEW

The SAT. The test assesses not only aptitude but also achievement. Which of the following questions or types of questions more clearly assess achievement and which more clearly test aptitude?

Content Area	Explanation of Task/Question	Example Task/Question
	Verbal	
Vocabulary	Show knowledge of words and their definitions.	Choose the word or set of words that best fits into the whole sentence.
Comprehension	Demonstrate understanding of a text passage.	Correctly answer multiple-choice questions about a text passage.
	Quantitative	
Quantitative skills	Make calculations involving arithmetic, algebra, geometry, and so on	Choose the correct answer from among several possible answers.

a writing section in addition to the traditional verbal and mathematical sections.

SCORE DISTRIBUTIONS

NORMAL DISTRIBUTIONS. Subsequent measurements of IQ have focused on the way intelligence is believed to be distributed within the human population at a given age or range of ages. In large human populations, measurement values often show a roughly normal distribution. In a **normal distribution,** a lot of people score near the middle of a score distribution. The measured values rapidly decline in number on either side of the middle. They then tail off more slowly as scores become more extreme. Like other measurements of large populations, IQ scores at a given age or range of ages show a roughly normal distribution. Figure 9.2 shows a picture of a normal distribution as it applies to IQ. One question that arises is: What is the "middle" of a distribution? This question can be answered in several different ways.

MEASURES OF CENTRAL TENDENCY. One way of thinking about the middle of a distribution is in terms of the **median,** the middle score or other measurement

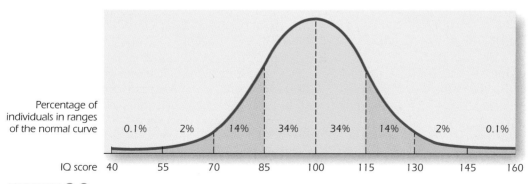

Percentage of individuals in ranges of the normal curve

0.1%   2%   14%   34%   34%   14%   2%   0.1%

IQ score   40   55   70   85   100   115   130   145   160

FIGURE 9.2

Normal Distribution of IQs. Normal distributions result from many measurements of large populations. Most college students have IQ scores above the middle of the range. Does this mean that most college students are smarter than most people who never attended college? Why, or why not?

value (100 on IQ tests) within a distribution of values. In a normal distribution, the median is the same as the **mean,** the average score within a distribution of values, computed by adding all the scores and dividing the sum by the number of scores. In a normal distribution, the median is also the same as the **mode,** the most frequently obtained score or other measurement value.

DEVIATION IQS. Scores on many psychological tests—including intelligence tests—are commonly calculated such that the average score is set to 100. In a normal distribution of IQ scores for a large population, roughly two-thirds of the scores are set to fall between 85 and 115, and about 95% of the scores to fall between 70 and 130. Such **deviation IQs,** based on standardized deviations from the average score, are not, strictly speaking, IQs because no quotient is involved. They thus contrast with ratio IQs, which are derived from an actual quotient (mental age divided by chronological age).

Designing a suitable test of intelligence requires a lot of careful planning and trial-and-error testing. The next section describes some of the *psychometric*—psychological measurement—properties of psychological tests and some of the ways in which test developers work to create the most suitable tests possible.

✓ CONCEPT CHECK 1

1. In their conceptions of intelligence, many experts emphasize
   a. the ability to learn from experience and adapt to the environment.
   b. scores on achievement tests.
   c. the ability to learn from experience and develop wisdom.
   d. adaptation to the environment and wisdom.
2. Binet's view of intelligence emphasized the importance of
   a. speed of thinking.
   b. psychophysical skills.
   c. emotional regulation.
   d. judgment.
3. If John receives an average score on a test of intelligence, his score is
   a. 50.
   b. 80.
   c. 100.
   d. 500.

ASSESSMENT ISSUES

How can intelligence be assessed?
What kinds of problems may be encountered
during the assessment process?

The usefulness of tests of intelligence depends on how well the tests are constructed. Any *assessment instrument* (i.e., way of measuring intelligence or anything else) needs to measure what it is supposed to measure and do so accurately. It is important to determine that the results of a test mean what they are supposed to mean. Recall, for example, Galton's and Cattell's psychophysically based tests of intelligence. They failed to measure adequately what they were supposed to measure. The first step in test construction is to decide what to measure and how. Next the test constructor must figure out what kinds of test items will assess the psychological characteristics he or she wishes to measure. Then the test constructor is ready to evaluate the quality of the test.

Three critical properties of tests are validity, reliability, and standardization (Anastasi & Urbina, 1997; Millsap, 1994).

VALIDITY

Validity is the extent to which a given form of measurement assesses what it is supposed to measure. For example, a test of musical aptitude is valid to the extent that it predicts success in musical endeavors. Several kinds of validity exist (Anastasi & Urbina, 1997; Messick, 1995; Moss, 1994).

One particularly important kind is **predictive validity,** which is the extent to which a test or other measurement predicts some kind of performance outcome (the criterion performance) measured well after the test has been taken. For example, the SAT is designed to predict freshman grades in college. The closer the relationship between the SAT scores and the students' performance in college, the more predictively valid the test is said to be.

In assessing the predictive validity of a test, we must be careful about the inferences we make. Consider a finding by Herrnstein and Murray (1994). These researchers reported that natural forces in the environment have created what they call a "cognitive elite." These are people with higher IQs who tend to end up in high-prestige, high-paying, cognitively rewarding jobs. In contrast, according to these researchers, people with lower IQs tend to end up in lower-prestige, low-paying, less cognitively rewarding jobs. The authors view this finding as evidence that cognitively rewarding jobs require high IQs. They also view it as support for the predictive validity of conventional ability tests.

We must be careful, however, about using data on group differences to draw conclusions. The tests themselves were used to select people for the access routes to the highly demanding jobs. This selection process may improve the correlation between test scores and being in demanding jobs. If one does not do well on those tests, it is very difficult to become, say, a lawyer, a doctor, or an academic scholar. Admission to graduate programs in these areas requires the individual to do well on an abilities-based admissions test. People who do not test well may have great difficulty gaining the access routes to these occupations. Using the tests as we do guarantees that there will be some correlation between the test scores and occupational placement. In the same way, selecting tall people to play on basketball teams guarantees a correlation between height and entrance into the world of professional basketball players (see R. J. Sternberg, 1995b, 1995c, 1996b). Other arguments have been advanced against Herrnstein and Murray's arguments as well (see, e.g., Fraser, 1995; Jacoby & Glauberman, 1995). Some of these arguments have been well-reasoned, others less so. The point is that one must be careful in accepting causal explanations (e.g., high IQ causes greater success; low IQ causes lesser success) that may not *fully* reflect the causal factors involved in a given situation.

RELIABILITY

Whereas validity assesses how well a test measures what it is supposed to measure, **reliability** indicates the dependability of a measurement instrument (e.g., a test). It indicates the extent to which the instrument consistently assesses the outcome being measured. High reliability is indicated, for example, when the people who score relatively well (or poorly) in one administration of a test also score relatively well (or poorly) in a second administration of the test.

A test can be reliable and yet invalid if it consistently measures something that is irrelevant to what the test is supposed to measure. It would be possible to develop a reliable measure of the length of college applicants' index fingers. But we would not expect any significant validity of this measure in predicting performance in college. Both reliability and validity are important in test construction.

STANDARDIZATION AND NORMS

Most tests are standardized before they are administered. **Standardization** ensures that the conditions for taking tests are the same for all test takers. For example, all students who take a test should have a quiet place to work. To ensure that the test-taking conditions are the same for all test takers, environmental distractors (such as interruptions) should be kept to a minimum. In addition, the instructions given before and during the test should be uniform. The amount of time available for making responses also should be identical, and the materials available should be consistent across test sessions.

A test that has been standardized can be administered to an enormous number of individuals. Thus, it is possible to determine scaled scores based on the scores of a large number of test takers. **Normative scores** (sometimes called simply **norms**) are the scaled equivalents of **raw scores** (the actual numbers of points achieved by test takers on a given test) that reflect the relative levels of performance of many test takers. Norms are useful for helping interpreters of scores relate the scores of one group to those of another group. For example, statewide norms on an achievement test can tell a principal whether the students in her school are performing above, at, or below the state average.

Test developers can use any scale they choose. IQ, for example, is a standard score that centers on a score of 100. Raw scores on various subscales are also typically converted into standardized equivalents with a mean of 100. Having the same mean facilitates comparisons among individuals. The College Board uses a different standard scale for the SAT, with an average of 500 and a standard deviation of 100. The range is from a low of 200 to a high of 800. The tests that yield these scores are based on experts' conceptions of what should be measured.

✓CONCEPT CHECK 2

1. A psychologist evaluates the extent to which a test measures the same thing consistently each time it is given. The psychologist is assessing
   a. validity.
   b. reliability.
   c. bias.
   d. norms.
2. A valid test
   a. measures only one thing.
   b. is always totally objective.
   c. must be timed.
   d. measures what it is supposed to measure.
3. Standardization of a test requires that the
   a. conditions under which various people take a test are roughly the same.
   b. test be given without a time limit.
   c. test be given to everyone in a quiet room.
   d. test scores be converted to scores with a mean of 100.

THEORIES OF THE NATURE OF INTELLIGENCE

What are the major theories of the nature of intelligence?

PSYCHOMETRIC MODELS: INTELLIGENCE AS A MEASUREMENT-BASED MAP OF THE MIND

The view of intelligence as a map of the mind dates back at least to the 1800s, when phrenology was in vogue. During the first half of the 20th century, the idea that intelligence is something to be mapped dominated theory and research. The psychologist who studied intelligence was both an explorer and a cartographer, seeking to chart the innermost regions of the mind. Like other explorers, those psychologists needed tools. In the case of research on intelligence, a useful tool appeared to be **factor analysis.** This method of statistical analysis allows an investigator to infer distinct hypothetical constructs, elements, or structures (called factors) that underlie a phenomenon. Some intelligence researchers believe that these factors form the basis of individual differences in test performance. The actual factors derived, of course, depend on the particular questions being asked and the tasks being evaluated. This approach continues to be used actively today (e.g., J. B. Carroll, 1993; see N. Brody, 2000; Embretson & McCollam, 2000).

Among the many competing psychometric theories, the main ones have focused on a single general factor that dominates intelligence (Jensen, 1998; R. J. Sternberg & Grigorenko, 2002), many equally important abilities that make up intelligence, or a hierarchy of abilities that contribute to intelligence. Figure 9.3 contrasts three of these theories.

CHARLES SPEARMAN: THE *G* FACTOR

Charles Spearman is usually credited with inventing factor analysis. Using factor-analytic studies, Spearman (1927) concluded that intelligence could be understood in terms of both a single general factor (called *g*), which pervades performance on all

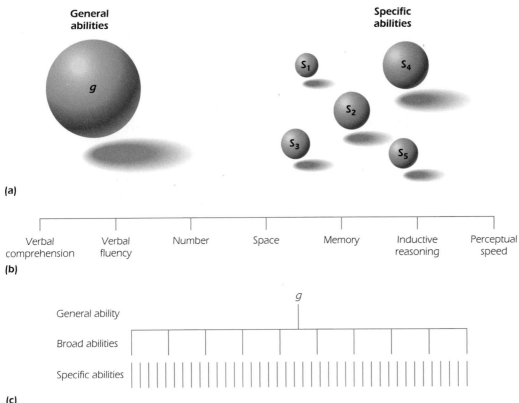

FIGURE 9.3
Some Psychometric Models of Intelligence. Although Spearman (a), Thurstone (b), and Carroll (c) all used factor analysis to determine the elements of intelligence, they reached different conclusions. Which model most simply, yet comprehensively, describes the structure of intelligence as you understand it? How do these models add to your understanding?

tests of mental ability, and a set of specific factors (called *s*), each involved in performance on only a single type of mental-ability test. (A specific ability might be arithmetic computation.) In Spearman's view, the specific factors are of only casual interest because of their narrow applicability. The general factor provides the key to understanding intelligence. Spearman believed that *g* derives from individual differences in mental energy. The belief in a general factor of intelligence persists among many contemporary psychologists (e.g., Demetriou, 2002; Detterman, 2002; Humphreys & Stark, 2002; Jensen, 1998, 2002; Kyllonen, 2002; Petrill, 2002). Other psychologists furiously debate just how general the "general factor" is (Berg & Klaczynski, 2002; Grigorenko, 2002; Naglieri & Das, 2002; Stankov, 2002; R. J. Sternberg, 1999, 2002; Wahlsten, 2002).

LOUIS THURSTONE: PRIMARY MENTAL ABILITIES

In contrast to Spearman, Louis Thurstone (1938) concluded that the core of intelligence resides not in one single factor but in seven factors of equal importance. He referred to these factors as primary mental abilities. According to Thurstone, the primary mental abilities and typical measures of them are: (1) verbal comprehension—vocabulary tests; (2) verbal fluency—tests that require the test taker to think of as many words as possible that begin with a given letter, in a limited amount of time; (3) inductive reasoning—tests such as analogies and number-series completion tasks; (4) spatial visualization—tests that require mental rotation of pictures of objects; (5) number—computation and simple mathematical problem-solving tests; (6) memory—picture and word-recall tests; and (7) perceptual speed—tests that require the test taker to recognize small differences in pictures or to cross out the A's in strings of various letters.

RAYMOND CATTELL AND JOHN CARROLL: HIERARCHICAL MODELS

A more parsimonious way of handling multiple factors is with a hierarchical model of intelligence. Two models of this sort are those of Raymond Cattell and John Carroll.

The model developed by R. Cattell (1971) proposes that general intelligence comprises two major factors: fluid intelligence and crystallized intelligence. **Fluid intelligence** represents speed, flexibility, and skill in the acquisition of new information, or the grasping of new relationships and abstractions regarding known information. These skills are required in inductive reasoning tests such as analogies and series completions. **Crystallized intelligence** represents

cumulated knowledge over the life span of the individual. This knowledge is measured in tests of vocabulary, of general information, and of achievement. Subsumed within these two major factors are more specific factors. The Kaufman Adolescent and Adult Intelligence Test is based on this model.

J. B. Carroll (1993) has proposed a more detailed hierarchical model, based on a reanalysis of many data sets from studies. At the top of the hierarchy is general ability; in the middle of the hierarchy are various broad abilities (including learning and memory processes and the effortless production of many ideas). At the bottom of the hierarchy are many narrow, specific abilities, such as spelling ability and reasoning speed. But how does one actually produce ideas, or spell, or reason? Computational models address this question.

COMPUTATIONAL MODELS: INTELLIGENCE AS INFORMATION PROCESSING

Unlike the psychometric models, which map the *structure* of human intelligence, computational models strongly emphasize the *processes* underlying intelligent behavior. Theorists who use these models are interested in studying how people engage in **information processing**—that is, operations by which people mentally manipulate what they learn and know about the world. Studies of information processing differ primarily in the complexity of the processes being studied. One way to study the relationship between intelligence and information processing is to examine simple information processing, in which an individual has to make a very simple decision as rapidly as possible. An example is deciding which of two line segments is longer.

SIMPLE INFORMATION PROCESSING

Ian Deary and Laura Stough (1996) have proposed that a low-level psychophysical measure, inspection time, may provide us with insights into the fundamental nature of intelligence (see also Deary, 2000). The basic idea is that individual differences in intelligence may derive, in part, from differences in the rate of intake and processing of simple stimulus information. In the inspection-time task, a person looks at two vertical lines with different lengths. The person simply has to say which line is longer. Inspection time is the length of stimulus presentation an individual needs in order to discriminate which of the two lines is longer. Investigators have found that more intelligent individuals can discriminate the lengths of the lines with shorter stimulus duration (inspection) times. In other words, smarter people process information more rapidly.

COMPLEX INFORMATION PROCESSING

Another computational approach considers the complex information processing that occurs in tasks such as making analogies, solving series problems (e.g., completing a numerical or figural series), and understanding syllogisms (Lohman, 2000; Pellegrino & Glaser, 1980; R. E. Snow, 1980; R. J. Sternberg, 1977, 1984). With this approach, psychologists study what makes some people more intelligent processors of information than others. Psychologists take the kinds of tasks used on conventional intelligence tests and try to isolate the information-processing components used to perform the tasks. Examples of such processes are translating sensory input into a mental representation, transforming one conceptual representation into another, and translating a conceptual representation into a motor output.

In general, more intelligent people take longer during global planning—encoding the problem (or set of problems) and formulating a general strategy for attacking it. But they take less time for local planning—forming and implementing strategies for the details of the task (R. J. Sternberg, 1981a, 1982). The advantage of spending more time on global planning is the increased likelihood that the overall strategy will be correct. For example, the brighter person might spend more time researching and planning a term paper but less time actually writing it. This same differential in time allocation has been shown in other tasks as well, including solving physics problems (Larkin, McDermott, Simon, & Simon, 1980).

Recent work suggests that a critical component of intelligence may be working memory. Indeed, Kyllonen (2002) and Kyllonen and Christal (1990) have argued that intelligence may be little more than working memory! Daneman and Carpenter (1983) had participants read sets of passages and then try to remember the last word of each passage. Recall was highly correlated with verbal ability. Turner and Engle (1989) had participants perform a variety of working-memory tasks. In one task, the participants saw a set of simple arithmetic problems, each followed by a word or a digit. Here is an example: Is $(3 \times 5) - 6 = 7$? TABLE. The participants saw sets of two to six problems and solved each one. Then they tried to recall the words that followed the problems. The number of words recalled was highly correlated with measured intelligence. Thus, it appears that the ability to store and manipulate information in working memory may be an important aspect of intelligence, though probably not all there is to it.

In sum, information-processing investigators study differences at the level of hypothesized mental processes. Biological investigators work in a complementary way, seeking to understand the origins of such differences in the functioning of the brain.

BIOLOGICAL MODELS: INTELLIGENCE AS A PHYSIOLOGICAL PHENOMENON

Biological approaches seek to understand intelligence by directly studying the brain and its functioning (Jerison, 2000; Vernon, Wickett, Bazana, & Stelmack, 2000). As suggested in previous chapters, early studies were not very successful. As tools for studying the brain have become more sophisticated, however, we are beginning to see the possibility of finding physiological indications of intelligence. Some researchers (e.g., Matarazzo, 1992) believe that we eventually will have clinically useful psychophysiological indices of intelligence. Widely applicable indices will be much longer in coming, though. It may be possible in the future to use psychophysiological measurements to assess individuals for characteristics such as mental retardation.

Another biological approach examines the genetic influences on intelligence. The methods for studying heritability and some of the findings those methods have yielded are discussed later in this chapter (p. 349).

ELECTROPHYSIOLOGICAL EVIDENCE

Laboratory research has found that complex patterns of electrical activity in the brain, which are prompted by specific stimuli, correlate with scores on IQ tests (Barrett & Eysenck, 1992; Caryl, 1994). Also, several studies suggest that the speed of conduction of neural impulses may correlate with intelligence as measured by IQ tests (e.g., McGarry-Roberts, Stelmack, & Campbell, 1992; Reed & Jensen, 1992; P. A. Vernon & Mori, 1992; Vernon et al., 2000), although the evidence is mixed. Some investigators (e.g., Jensen, 1997; P. A. Vernon & Mori, 1992; Vernon et al., 2000) suggest that this research supports a view that intelligence is based on neural efficiency.

METABOLIC EVIDENCE

Additional support for neural efficiency as a measure of intelligence can be found from studies of how the brain metabolizes glucose, a simple sugar required for brain activity, during mental activities. (This process is revealed in PET scans; see Chapter 3.) Richard Haier (see In the Lab) and his colleagues (Haier, Siegel, Tang, Abel, & Buchsbaum, 1992) cite other research that supports their own findings that higher intelligence correlates with reduced levels of glucose metabolism during problem-solving tasks. In other words, smarter brains consume less sugar (meaning that they expend less effort) than do less smart brains doing the same task. Furthermore, Haier and colleagues found that cerebral efficiency increases as a result of learning in a relatively complex task involving visuospatial manipulations (like in the computer game Tetris). As a result of practice, more intelligent individuals show

IN THE LAB OF RICHARD HAIER

WATCHING INTELLIGENCE AND CONSCIOUSNESS

Understanding why some people learn faster, remember more, and think better than other people is one of the oldest and most important challenges in psychology. Intelligence researchers have developed a number of potential explanations of these individual differences. Another fundamental problem, how attention and awareness work, has led to new interest in consciousness research. Surely, answers to both questions have something to do with the brain. We have been studying some aspects of these problems, using the functional brain imaging technology of positron emission tomography (PET), and we are testing ideas about how both may have similar answers.

Where in the brain does intelligence reside? We asked this question in 1988, when we published the results of the first experiment that used PET scans to study abstract reasoning in normal volunteers. PET was then a new and expensive tool. Few psychologists had access to the complex equipment; consequently, few theories included explicit hypotheses about the relevance to intelligence of specific brain areas. We were surprised to find *inverse* correlations between cortical glucose metabolic rate (GMR) in several areas and scores on tests of reasoning. The individuals with the highest test scores on a problem-solving measure of general intelligence (the Raven's Advanced Progressive Matrices) showed the lowest brain activation during actual reasoning. We interpreted this as

Richard J. Haier received his PhD in psychology from Johns Hopkins University in 1975. He was a staff fellow at the National Institute of Mental Health in the Laboratory of Psychology and Psychopathology until 1979, when he joined the faculty of the psychiatry department in the medical school at Brown University. In 1984 he moved to the College of Medicine at the University of California, Irvine, where he is a professor of psychology in the Department of Pediatrics. Dr. Haier's brain imaging research is currently funded by the National Institute of Child Health and Development.

evidence that intelligence is related to the efficiency of brain activity rather than to greater activation of a specific area.

In our next study, we wanted to find out whether the brain becomes more efficient with learning. Do you remember the first time you drove a car? You were thinking about each move you made. It would have been hard to talk about current events with the person in the passenger seat. Now that you are an experienced driver, you can converse in the midst of heavy traffic. Is your brain working harder today when you drive on a freeway than it did the first time you drove around an empty parking lot? We scanned the brains of people who were playing the visuospatial game Tetris for the first time, and then again after 50 days of practice. We found lower GMR after practice, which supported our hypothesis that efficient brain activity is linked to proficiency. Moreover, the subjects with the highest scores on the reasoning test also showed the greatest decreases in GMR with practice, suggesting that high intelligence

leads to brain efficiency that increases with practice.

Interestingly, we have found *increased* GMR in mildly retarded people and in people with Down syndrome, which suggests brain inefficiency or, perhaps, compensatory neural activity. One of our latest studies indicates that intelligent people may process cognitive information differently in posterior brain pathways than less intelligent people, so the issue of where intelligence resides is still unsettled. Ultimately, the answer may have to do with the connections among several areas rather than activity in only one area.

During our studies of brain efficiency, Michael Alkire, a medical school resident in anesthesiology (now a faculty member), asked me to help him use PET scans to learn where anesthetic drugs worked in the brain. Since these drugs switch consciousness off and on, we used them to manipulate consciousness in volunteers during PET scanning. In a series of papers that address

continued

what brain areas are affected by anesthetic drugs, we have described what we believe to be relevant neurocircuitry for consciousness. We are now seeking to discover whether there are individual differences in consciousness that may be related to individual differences in intelligence. We are looking for overlap in the respective neurocircuits, as revealed by functional imaging.

At the beginning of the 21st century, the brain is no longer an unknowable black box. Psychologists are using some of the most advanced technology, including PET and functional MRI, to help answer some of the oldest questions. Each imaging study provides new empirical observations, which contribute to new theories, which in turn suggest more specific hypotheses. This is an exciting time in the field of intelligence, as we can now design behavioral, cognitive, and pharmacological experiments that probe the deepest recesses of the human brain—and actually watch what happens.

lower cerebral glucose metabolism overall. But they also demonstrate more specifically localized metabolism of glucose. In most areas of their brains, smarter persons show less glucose metabolism, but in selected areas of their brains (thought to be important to the task at hand), they show higher levels of glucose metabolism. Thus, more intelligent people may have learned how to use their brains more efficiently.

BRAIN SIZE

One line of research looks at the relationship between brain size and intelligence (see Jerison, 2000, 2002; Vernon et al., 2000). The evidence suggests that, for humans, the statistical relationship is modest but significant. It is difficult to know what to make of this relationship, however, because greater brain size may cause greater intelligence, greater intelligence may cause greater brain size, or both may be dependent on some third factor. Moreover, how efficiently the brain is used is probably more important than its size. For example, on average, men have larger brains than women, but women have better connections, through the corpus callosum, between the two hemispheres. So it is not clear which sex would have, on average, an advantage—probably neither. It is important to note that the relationship between brain size and intelligence does not hold across species (Jerison, 2000). Rather, there seems to be a relationship between intelligence and brain size relative to the rough general size of the organism.

Ⓔ EVOLUTIONARY THEORY

Some theorists have tried to understand intelligence in terms of how it has evolved over the eons (e.g., Bjorklund & Kipp, 2002; Bradshaw, 2002; Byrne, 2002; Corballis, 2002; J. B. Grossman & Kaufman, 2002; Pinker, 1997). The basic idea in these models is that we are intelligent in the ways we are because it was important for our distant ancestors to acquire certain skills. According to Cosmides and Tooby (2002), we are particularly skilled at detecting cheating because people in the past who were not sensitive to cheaters did not live to have children, or they had fewer children. If a hunter-gatherer of long ago made a bad bargain, he or she might be left with-

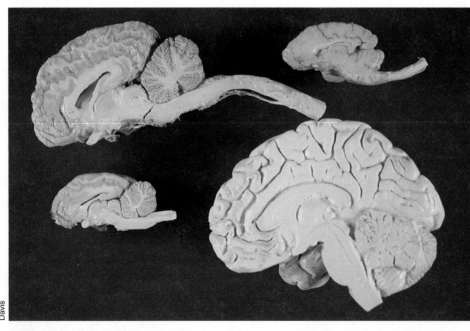

Mammalian brains are larger and more powerful than those of nonmammals. Clockwise from top left: horse, dog, human, sheep.

Photo by David Hines, courtesy of Sharon L. Cummings, PhD, University of California, Davis

out enough food to survive a long, hard winter. Evolutionary approaches stress the continuity of intelligence over long stretches of time and, in some theories, across species.

CULTURAL AND CONTEXTUAL MODELS: INTELLIGENCE AS A CULTURAL CONSTRUCT

We have seen how the psychometric, computational, and biological models view intelligence as residing inside the head. In contrast, **contextualist** theorists of intelligence focus largely on the context in which an individual is observed. They suggest that intelligence cannot be understood—let alone measured—outside the real-world context of the individual (Serpell, 2000; Suzuki & Valencia, 1997). These theorists study how intelligence relates to the external world. They view intelligence as so inextricably linked to culture that it is something that a culture creates, at least in part. The purpose of this creation is to define the nature of adaptive performance in the culture and to account for why some people perform better than others on the tasks that the culture happens to value (see Suzuki & Valencia, 1997). Stated another way, societies label as "intelligent" behavior that they happen to value.

To a member of the Kpelle tribe in Africa, categories are functional, not hierarchical. Cultural differences may affect performance on intelligence tests by people of different backgrounds.

Courtesy of Dr. Michael Cole

ⓒ CULTURAL INFLUENCES ON PERCEIVED INTELLIGENCE

People in different cultures may have quite different ideas of what it means to be smart. One of the more interesting cross-cultural studies of intelligence was performed by Michael Cole and his colleagues (M. Cole, Gay, Glick, & Sharp, 1971; Glick, 1975). They asked adult members of the Kpelle tribe in Africa to sort terms. In Western culture, when adults are given a sorting task on an intelligence test, intelligent people typically sort hierarchically. For example, they may place names of different kinds of fish together and then the word "fish" over that, with the name "animal" over "fish" as well as "birds," and so on. Less intelligent Westerners typically sort functionally. They might sort "fish" with "eat" because we eat fish, or "clothes" with "wear" because we wear clothes.

Members of the Kpelle tribe generally sorted functionally even after investigators tried indirectly to encourage them to sort hierarchically. Finally, in desperation, one of the experimenters directly asked one of the Kpelle to show how a foolish person would do the task. When asked to sort in this way, the Kpelle had no trouble at all sorting hierarchically. He and the others had been able to sort this way all along. They just had not done so because they viewed it as foolish. Moreover, they probably considered the questioners unintelligent for asking such foolish questions. Why would they view functional sorting as intelligent? In ordinary life, we normally think functionally. When we think of a fish, we think of catching or eating it. When we think of clothes, we think of wearing them. In Western schooling, however, we learn what is expected of us on tests. The Kpelle did not have Western schooling. They had not been exposed to intelligence testing. As a result, they solved the problems the way Western adults might do in their everyday lives but not on an intelligence test.

The Kpelle people are not the only ones who might question Western understandings of intelligence. Work by Robert Serpell (1993, 1994) in Zambia shows that Zambians also have conceptions of intelligence quite different from those of North Americans, and research has found many other such differences around the world (Berry, 1974; R. J. Sternberg & Kaufman, 1998). Similarly, research has revealed that rural Kenyans have four different words associated with intelligence (Grigorenko et al., 2001; R. J. Sternberg et al., 2002). Only one of the four words refers to academic skills. The other three have to do with obedience and respect toward elders, social skills, good judgment in everyday situations, and, in general, everyday competencies.

Implicit theories differ in Taiwan as well. There is evidence that Chinese people in Taiwan include both interpersonal and intrapersonal (self-understanding) skills as part of their conception of intelligence (Yang & Sternberg, 1999). What might be considered a comprehensive assessment of intelligence could differ from one culture to another (R. J. Sternberg & Kaufman, 1998).

Even within our own society, different groups can have different notions of intelligence. Okagaki and Sternberg (1993) found that Anglo American and Asian American parents in a school district in San Jose, California, tended to emphasize cognitive skills more and to emphasize social skills less in their ideas of what it means to have a smart child. Latino American parents showed the opposite pattern. However, teachers in the school adhered to a conception of intelligence that was closer to that of the Anglo American and Asian American parents. As a result, they tended to view the Latino American children as less intelligent. In short, groups have a fairly fixed idea of intelligence, and they are often ready to assume that their belief is correct not only for themselves but for everyone else as well.

A study by Seymour Sarason and John Doris (1979) provides a close-to-home example of the effects of cultural differences on intelligence, particularly on intelligence tests. These researchers tracked the IQ scores of immigrant Italian Americans. Less than a century ago, first-generation Italian American children had a median IQ of 87, which is in the low average range. Some social commentators and intelligence researchers of the day pointed to heredity and other nonenvironmental factors as the basis for the low IQs. A leading researcher, Henry Goddard, pronounced that 79% of immigrant Italians were "feeble-minded." He also asserted that about 80% of immigrant Hungarians and Russians similarly lacked intelligence (Eysenck & Kamin, 1981). Goddard (1917) associated moral decadence with this deficit in intelligence. He recommended that the intelligence tests he used be administered to all immigrants. And, he declared that all potential immigrants with low scores should be selectively excluded from entering the United States.

Today, Italian American students who take IQ tests show slightly above-average IQs; other immigrant groups that Goddard denigrated have shown similar "amazing" increases (Ceci, 1996). Even the most fervent hereditarians would be unlikely to attribute such remarkable gains in so few generations to heredity. Cultural assimilation, including integrated education and adoption of American definitions of intelligence, seems a much more plausible explanation.

Ⓒ CULTURE-FAIR TESTING

A **culture-fair test** is equally appropriate for members of all cultures and comprises items that are equally fair to everyone. Performance on tests that have been labeled "culture fair" in fact seems to be influenced by cultural factors. Examples are years of schooling and academic achievements (e.g., Ceci, 1996). One must be careful when drawing conclusions about group differences in intelligence (Greenfield, 1997; Loehlin, 2000). Developing culture-fair tests based on each culture's own definition of intelligence may be an unrealistic goal. But it is possible to provide culture-relevant tests. **Culture-relevant tests** require skills and knowledge that are relevant to the cultural experiences of the test takers. The content and procedures are appropriate to the cultural norms of the test takers. For example, 14-year-old boys performed poorly on a task when it was presented in terms of baking cupcakes. But they performed well when the task was framed in terms of charging batteries (Ceci & Bronfenbrenner, 1985). Brazilian maids had no difficulty with proportional reasoning when hypothetically purchasing food. But they had great difficulty with it when hypothetically purchasing medicinal herbs (Schliemann & Magalhües, 1990). Brazilian children whose poverty had forced them to become street vendors showed no difficulty in performing complex arithmetic computations when selling things. But they had great difficulty performing similar calculations in a classroom (Carraher, Carraher, & Schliemann, 1985; Ceci & Roazzi, 1994; Nuñes, 1994).

SYSTEMS MODELS OF INTELLIGENCE

Two contemporary theories of intelligence attempt to encompass both our internal and our external worlds. They view intelligence as a complex system (J. E. Davidson & Downing, 2000; R. J. Sternberg, 1990b). Artificial-intelligence models, which are used in the attempt to create intelligent computer programs (see Schank & Towle, 2000), also view intelligence in terms of a systems model.

HOWARD GARDNER: MULTIPLE INTELLIGENCES

Howard Gardner (1983, 1993b, 1999) does not view intelligence as a single construct. Instead of speaking of multiple abilities that together constitute intelligence, like some other theorists, Gardner proposed a **theory of multiple intelligences,** in which eight distinct intelligences function somewhat independently but may interact to produce intelligent behavior. The types of intelligence are linguistic, logical-mathematical, spatial, musical, bodily-kinesthetic, interpersonal, intrapersonal, and naturalist (see Table 9.2 on p. 342). Gardner

According to Howard Gardner's theory of multiple intelligences, the girl on the left is using her spatial intelligence and the musicians on the right are using their musical intelligence.

(1999) also speculated on the possible existence of existential and spiritual intelligences. Each intelligence is a separate system of functioning. Nevertheless, these systems can interact to produce intelligent performance. For example, novelists rely heavily on linguistic intelligence but might use logical-mathematical intelligence in plotting story lines or checking for logical inconsistencies. Measuring intelligences separately may produce a profile of skills that is broader than would be obtained from, say, measuring verbal and mathematical abilities alone. This profile could then be used to facilitate educational and career decisions.

To identify particular intelligences, Gardner used converging operations, gathering evidence from multiple sources and types of data. The evidence includes (but is not limited to) the distinctive effects of localized brain damage on specific kinds of intelligences, distinctive patterns of development in each kind of intelligence across the life span, exceptional individuals (from both ends of the spectrum), and evolutionary history.

Gardner's view of the mind is *modular*. Modularity theorists believe that different abilities can be isolated as they emanate from distinct portions or modules of the brain. Thus, a major task of existing and future research on intelligence is to isolate the portions of the brain responsible for each of the intelligences. Gardner has speculated about some of these relevant portions, but hard evidence for the existence of separate intelligences has yet to be produced.

There may be multiple kinds of intelligence beyond those suggested by Gardner. Peter Salovey and John Mayer (1990; see also J. Mayer, Salovey, & Caruso, 2000) have proposed **emotional intelligence.** It is defined as "the ability to perceive and express emotion, assimilate emotion in thought, understand and reason with emotion, and regulate emotion in the self and others" (p. 396). There is good evidence for the existence of some kind of emotional intelligence (Ciarrochi, Forgas, & Mayer, 2001; J. D. Mayer & Salovey, 1997; Salovey & Sluyter, 1997), although the findings are mixed (Davies, Stankov, & Roberts, 1998). The concept has become popularized in recent years (Goleman, 1995, 1998). Research also shows that personality variables are related to intelligence (Ackerman, 1996).

Researchers have proposed the notion of *social intelligence*, used in interacting effectively with other people (N. Cantor & Kihlstrom, 1987b; M. E. Ford, 1994; Kihlstrom & Cantor, 2000). Still other investigators have suggested a concept of *practical intelligence*, or the ability to function effectively in everyday life (R. J. Sternberg et al., 2000; R. K. Wagner, 2000). Clearly, our concepts of intelligence are becoming much broader than they were just a few years ago. At the same time, not all psychologists accept these broader conceptions.

ROBERT J. STERNBERG: THE TRIARCHIC THEORY

Whereas Gardner emphasizes the separateness of various types of intelligence, I tend to emphasize the extent to which they work together in my triarchic theory of successful intelligence (R. J. Sternberg, 1985a,

TABLE 9.2
CONCEPT REVIEW

Gardner's Eight Intelligences. On which of Howard Gardner's eight intelligences do you show the greatest ability? In what contexts can you use your intelligences most effectively? (After H. Gardner, 1983, 1993b, 1999)

Type of Intelligence	Tasks Reflecting This Type of Intelligence
Linguistic intelligence	Reading, writing, understanding spoken words
Logical-mathematical intelligence	Solving math problems, balancing a checkbook, doing a mathematical proof, logical reasoning
Spatial intelligence	Getting from one place to another, reading a map, packing suitcases in the trunk of a car
Musical intelligence	Singing, composing, playing a musical instrument, appreciating musical structure
Bodily-kinesthetic intelligence	Dancing, athletics
Interpersonal intelligence	Understanding another person's behavior, motives, or emotions
Intrapersonal intelligence	Understanding who we are, what makes us tick, and how we can change ourselves
Naturalist intelligence	Understanding patterns in the natural world

1988b, 1996b, 1999). Successful intelligence is the ability to succeed in life according to your own definition of success within your own environment. In the **triarchic theory of intelligence,** successful intelligence comprises three aspects, which deal with the relationship of intelligence to the internal world, to experience, and to the external world. Intelligence draws on three kinds of information-processing components. *Metacomponents* are executive processes used to plan, monitor, and evaluate problem solving. *Performance components* are lower-order processes used for implementing the commands of the metacomponents. *Knowledge-acquisition components* are the processes used for learning how to solve the problems in the first place. The components are highly interdependent.

Suppose you are asked to write a term paper. To do well you need all three types of components. You use metacomponents to decide on a topic, plan the paper, monitor the writing, and evaluate how well your finished product accomplishes your goals. You use knowledge-acquisition components to conduct research on the topic. You also use performance components for the actual writing. In practice, the three kinds of components do not function in isolation. Before beginning to write, you first have to decide on a topic and then do some research. Similarly, your ideas might change as you gather new information. It may turn out there just is not enough information on particular aspects of the chosen topic, forcing you to shift your emphasis. Your plans also may change if some aspects of the writing go more smoothly than others.

The three kinds of components all contribute to three relatively distinct aspects of intelligence, as shown in Figure 9.4. In this "triarchy" of intelligence, analytical abilities are used to analyze, evaluate, critique, or judge, as when you decide whether a certain argument you or someone else has made is logical. A metacomponent, such as planning, might be used analytically to devise a strategy for solving a geometry problem. Creative abilities are used to create, invent, discover, and imagine. Examples are when you come up with new ideas for

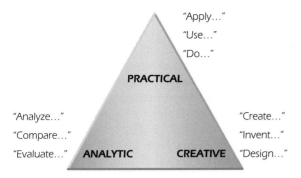

FIGURE 9.4
Sternberg's Triarchic Theory of Intelligence. According to this theory, intelligence comprises analytical, creative, and practical abilities. In analytical thinking, we try to solve a familiar problem by manipulating its elements or the relationships among them. In creative thinking, we try to solve a new kind of problem that requires us to think about it in a new way. In practical thinking, we try to solve a problem by applying everyday knowledge.

a paper topic or an idea for a scientific experiment. The metacomponent of planning might be used here to help design a building. Practical abilities are used to apply, utilize, and implement ideas in the real world. An example is when you decide that your psychology professor would probably rather read a term paper on a psychology topic than on the geological formation of the Himalayas. Mapping a route for climbing the Himalayas could be a practical use of the metacomponent of planning. Research suggests that the three types of abilities—analytical, creative, and practical—are statistically relatively independent (R. J. Sternberg, 1985a; R. J. Sternberg et al., 2000; R. J. Sternberg, Castejón, Prieto, Hautamäki, & Grigorenko, 2001; R. J. Sternberg, Grigorenko, Ferrari, & Clinkenbeard, 1999; R. J. Sternberg & Lubart, 1995).

Practical abilities serve three functions in real-world contexts: adapting to our existing environments, shaping our existing environments to create new environments, and selecting new environments. You use adaptation when you learn the ropes in a new environment and try to figure out how to succeed in it. When you started college, you probably tried to figure out the explicit and implicit rules of college life. You also needed to learn how you could use them to succeed in the new environment. You further shaped your environment by deciding what courses to take and what activities to pursue. You even might have tried to shape the behavior of those around you. Finally, if you were unable either to adapt yourself or to shape your environment to suit you, you might have considered selecting another environment. In this case, you might have thought about transferring to another college.

According to the triarchic theory, we may apply our intelligence to many kinds of problems. Some people may be better at abstract, academic problems, whereas others may be better at concrete, practical problems. The theory does not define an intelligent person as someone who necessarily excels in all aspects of intelligence. Rather, intelligent persons know their own strengths and weaknesses. They find ways to capitalize on their strengths and either compensate for or correct their weaknesses. For example, a person who is strong in psychology but not in physics might choose as a physics project to create a physics aptitude test (as I did when I took physics!). The point is to make the most of your strengths and to find ways to improve upon, or at least to live comfortably with, your weaknesses.

In a recent comprehensive study testing the validity of the triarchic theory and its usefulness in improving performance, we predicted that students who were taught triarchically would learn social studies and science better than students who were taught in a way that just emphasized memory or that just emphasized critical thinking (Sternberg, Torff, & Grigorenko, 1998). Fourth-grade students learned a social-studies unit in a way that emphasized one of these three kinds of learning strategies (memory, critical-thinking, or triarchic). Eighth-grade students learned science in one of the three ways. In the triarchic condition, students were invited not just to memorize material, but to analyze and evaluate it (analytical), create and go beyond what was in the text (creative), and apply what they learned (practical). We found that students in the triarchic condition in general outscored students in the other two conditions on tests of achievement, even when the tests of achievement assessed just memory-based learning. Indeed, without regard to how the students were assessed, the triarchically-taught students at both grade levels did as well as or better than did the students in the other two groups.

✓CONCEPT CHECK 3

1. Which of the following is *not* one of Thurstone's primary mental abilities?
   a. verbal comprehension
   b. spatial visualization
   c. musical ability
   d. memory
2. Cultural differences in conceptions of intelligence
   a. are almost never found.
   b. are rare.

c. are common.

d. cannot be assessed.

3. Gardner's theory of multiple intelligences is based on the idea of _____ the intelligences.

a. high dependence among

b. modularity of

c. similarity of

d. cultural relativity

GROUP DIFFERENCES

How do groups differ on various tests of intelligence?

Cultural and societal analyses of intelligence make it particularly important to consider carefully the meaning of group differences in measured IQs (Fischer et al., 1996; Loehlin, 2000). On average, African Americans score somewhat lower than Caucasians on standardized tests of intelligence (Herrnstein & Murray, 1994). But remember, Italian American scores used to be considerably lower than they are now. Test scores of African Americans have been increasing over time, just like scores for other groups. Available evidence suggests an environmental explanation for these group differences (Mackintosh, 1998; Nisbett, 1995), although opinions vary. Moreover, differences between groups in societal outcomes, such as the likelihood of graduating from high school or going on welfare, cannot really be attributed simply to differences in IQs, as some people have tried to do. When IQ is removed as a source of group differences, African Americans are still considerably more likely than Caucasians to be born out of wedlock, be born into poverty, and be underweight at birth (Herrnstein & Murray, 1994; see R. J. Sternberg, 1996b). Group differences may thus stem from several factors, many of which change over time. The result is that group differences are not immutable. A group that scores, on average, lower than another group at one given time may score, on average, lower, the same, or even higher at another time.

SEX DIFFERENCES

Males and females score about the same on cognitive-ability tests, although differences have been noted on specific ability tests. Analyses of trends over time suggest that sex differences in scores on these cognitive-ability tests have been shrinking (Feingold, 1988). Nevertheless, some differences appear to remain. In particular, males, on average, tend to score higher on tasks that require visual and spatial working memory, motor skills that are involved in aiming at a target, and certain aspects of mathematical performance. Females tend to score higher on tasks that require rapid access to phonological and semantic information in long-term memory, production and comprehension of complex prose, fine motor skills, and perceptual speed (D. F. Halpern, 1997). These differences refer only to averages. Many individuals of one sex do better than individuals of the other sex regardless of the particular skill measured by a given test. In any case, these score differences are not easy to interpret. In the past, teachers have tended to believe that boys are smarter than girls, but one recent study found no difference in teachers' beliefs about the overall intelligence of boys versus girls (Furnham & Budhani, 2002).

Claude Steele (1997) found that when boys and girls take difficult mathematical tests, boys often do better. But when the two groups are told in advance that a particular test will show no difference, on average, the boys' and girls' scores converge, with girls' scores increasing and boys' actually decreasing.

SOCIALLY DEFINED RACIAL/ETHNIC GROUP DIFFERENCES

I refer to racial and ethnic groups as "socially defined" because race and ethnicity are constructed culturally, not biologically. Societies have different definitions of what constitute racial and ethnic groups. For example, South Africans recognize two groups of "colored" and "black" people that would be lumped into a single category in the United States. We in the United States sometimes refer to "hispanic Americans," but Puerto Rican Americans, Mexican Americans, Dominican Americans, and members of other groups are distinct in many ways.

A group difference that has received considerable study is between African Americans and Whites. As mentioned earlier, African Americans tend to score lower than white Americans on conventional tests of intelligence. The available evidence is largely consistent with an environmental explanation (Nisbett, 1995). One study looked at the offspring of American servicemen and German women during the Allied occupation of Germany after World War II. It revealed no significant difference between the IQs of children of African American and children of white servicemen (Eyferth, 1961). This suggests that with similar environments, the children of the two groups of servicemen performed equally on tests of intelligence. Another study found that children adopted by white families obtained higher IQ scores than children adopted by African American families, again suggesting that environmental factors contribute to the difference between the two groups (E. G. J. Moore, 1986). One way of studying group differences has been transracial adoption studies. In studies of families in which white parents have adopted African American children (Scarr & Weinberg, 1976; Scarr, Weinberg, & Waldman, 1993; R. A. Weinberg, Scarr, & Waldman, 1992), the results have been difficult to interpret. In these and other studies, both white and African American children who were adopted showed decreased IQs in a 10-year follow-up on their performance.

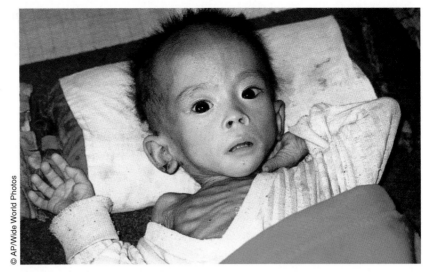

Famine can impair a child's mental as well as physical development.

ENVIRONMENTAL DIFFERENCES

There are a number of mechanisms by which environmental factors such as poverty, malnutrition, and illness might affect intelligence (R. J. Sternberg et al., 2000). One mechanism is resources. Children who are poor often do not have the resources in the home and school that are enjoyed by children in more affluent environments. Another mechanism is attention to and concentration on the skills taught in school. Children who are undernourished or ill may find it hard to concentrate. They may therefore profit less from instruction. A third mechanism is the system of rewards in the environment. Children who grow up in economically deprived environments may note that those who are most rewarded are not necessarily those who do well in school. Rather, they may be those who earn the money they need to survive. It is unlikely that any one mechanism fully explains the effects of all these variables. It is also important to realize that whatever the mechanisms are, they can start *in utero*, not just after birth. For example, fetal alcohol syndrome leads to lowered IQ and has its initial effects prenatally, before the child even enters the world.

✓CONCEPT CHECK 4

1. Men tend, on average, to score higher than women on tests of
   a. memory.
   b. spatial working memory.
   c. social intelligence.
   d. fine hand coordination.

2. Women tend, on average, to score higher than men on tests of
   a. rapid access to semantic information in memory.
   b. spatial visualization.
   c. long-term memory.
   d. logical reasoning.
3. Research on group differences suggests that most of them are due
   a. only to heredity.
   b. only to environmental effects.
   c. primarily to heredity.
   d. primarily to environmental effects.

EXTREMES OF INTELLIGENCE

What constitute extremes of intelligence? What do they tell us about human potentials?

Every theory of intelligence must address the issue of extremes. Although most of us fall within the broad middle range of intellectual abilities, there are, of course, people at both the upper and the lower extremes. Different theorists conceive of the extremes in different ways. People at the upper extreme are usually labeled intellectually gifted. Those at the lower extreme may be labeled mentally retarded.

Psychologists differ in how they define the intellectually gifted (Callahan, 2000; Winner, 1997). Some use an exclusively IQ-based criterion. Many programs for the gifted screen largely on the basis of scores on conventional intelligence tests, taking children in perhaps the top 1% (IQs of roughly 135 or above) or 2% (IQs of roughly 132 or above) for their programs. Others supplement IQ with other criteria, such as school or career achievements or other measures of gifted performance.

Probably the best-known studies of gifted individuals were done by Lewis Terman. He conducted a *longitudinal study* that followed particular individuals throughout their life spans (Terman, 1925; Terman & Oden, 1959). The study has continued since Terman's death. In his sample of the gifted, Terman included children from California under age 11 with IQs over 140 as well as children in the 11- to 14-year age bracket with slightly lower IQs. The mean IQ of the 643 research participants selected was 151. Only 22 of these participants had IQs lower than 140.

The accomplishments in later life of the selected group were extraordinary by any criteria. Thirty-one

By the time she was 10 years old, Romanian-American artist Alexandra Nechita was selling her paintings for as much as $30,000 per canvas. Many museums feature her work.

© AP/Wide World Photos

men were listed in *Who's Who in America*. There were numerous highly successful businessmen as well as individuals who excelled in other professions. The sex bias is obvious. Most of the women became housewives, so it is impossible to make any meaningful comparison between the men (none of whom were reported to have become househusbands) and the women. As with all correlational data, it would be difficult to assign a causal role to IQ in accounting for the accomplishments of the individuals in the study. Many factors other than IQ could have contributed to the success of Terman's sample. Among the most important of them are family socioeconomic status and the educational level attained by these individuals.

Today many, if not most, psychologists look to more than IQ to identify the intellectually gifted. (See R. J. Sternberg & Davidson, 1986, and Winner, 1996, for descriptions of a variety of theories of giftedness.) Joseph Renzulli (1986) believes that high motivation, or commitment to tasks, and high creativity are important to giftedness, in addition to above-average (though not necessarily outstanding) intelligence. Perhaps some gifted people are good at just one thing, but they find a way of capitalizing on that thing to make the most of their capabilities (R. J. Sternberg, 1985a). All of these theorists agree that there is more to giftedness than a high IQ. Indeed, I argue that people can be creatively or practically gifted and not even show up as particularly distinguished on an IQ test.

In one set of studies, high school students from all around the United States and some other countries were identified in terms of analytical, creative, and practical giftedness (R. J. Sternberg, 1997b; R. J. Sternberg & Clinkenbeard, 1995; R. J. Sternberg et al., 1996). Many students were gifted in only one kind of ability. The students were taught a college-level course that emphasized the analytical, creative, or practical form of instruction. Some students were in an instructional condition that matched their abilities. Other students were taught in a way that mismatched their abilities. Students' achievement was also evaluated in all three ways. We found that students achieved at higher levels when they were taught in a style that matched their strength (see also Grigorenko, Jarvin, & Sternberg, 2002).

These findings raise a potentially important issue. Research suggests that intelligence tests are not biased in a narrow statistical sense: They do not tend, on average, falsely to predict criterion performance for particular groups (Mackintosh, 1998). For example, lower intelligence test scores tend to be associated with lower school achievement for people from a variety of groups. But if intelligence tests measure the somewhat narrow set of skills that schools tend to value, then there is a possibility that both the predictor (such as an intelligence test) and the criterion (such as school grades) have the same bias. Statistical analyses would fail to detect bias because both the predictor and the criterion that is predicted share the same bias. The bias is not in the predictor (the test) per se, but in the entire system of prediction (the test, the measure of achievement, and their interrelation). Perhaps if intelligence tests and schools both valued creative and practical abilities as well as analytical abilities, children now identified as relatively lacking in intelligence would be viewed as more intelligent.

In sum, the tendency today is to look beyond IQ to identify intellectually gifted individuals. There are many ways to be gifted. Scores on conventional intelligence tests represent only one of these ways. Indeed, some of the most gifted adult contributors to society, such as Albert Einstein and Thomas Edison, were not top performers either on tests or in school during their early years. Einstein did not even speak until he was 3 years old!

MENTAL RETARDATION

Mental retardation refers to low levels of measured intelligence, including low *adaptive competence*, or ability to get along in the everyday world (Detterman, Gabriel, & Ruthsatz, 2000; Detterman & Thompson,

1997). Simple enough. Much less simple is determining who we should label as being mentally retarded. Different viewpoints lead to different conclusions.

THE ROLE OF ADAPTIVE COMPETENCE

The American Association on Mental Retardation (1992) includes within its definition two components: low IQ and low adaptive competence. In other words, to be labeled as retarded, an individual not only has to perform poorly on an intelligence test but also must show problems adapting to the environment. A child whose performance was normal in every way except for low IQ would not, by this definition, be classified as mentally retarded. Table 9.3 lists some of the ways in which particular IQ scores are related to adaptive life skills, which are judged in a variety of domains, such as communication (as in talking to someone or writing a letter), self-care (as in dressing oneself or using the toilet), home living (as in preparing meals), and social interaction (as in meeting the expectations of others).

It is not always easy to assess adaptive competence, as the following example shows (Edgerton, 1967). A man who was regarded as mentally retarded because he had scored low on tests of intelligence was

---

TABLE 9.3

Levels of Mental Retardation. Contemporary views of mental retardation deemphasize IQ scores and more strongly underscore the ability of the individual to show the skills needed for adapting to the requirements of self-care and to societal expectations.

Degree of Retardation	Range of Typical IQ Scores	Adaptive Life Skills	Living Requirements
Mild (≈85% of retarded persons; about 2% of general population)	50–70	With adequate training and appropriate environmental support: • Academic skills at or below the sixth-grade level • Social and vocation-related skills	Independent living and occupational success can be achieved.
Moderate (≈10% of retarded persons; 0.1% of the general population)	35–55	• Academic tasks at or below the fourth-grade level if given special education • Unskilled or possibly highly routinized semiskilled vocational activities • Many personal self-maintenance activities	Sheltered home and work environments, in which supervision and guidance are readily available, often work well.
Severe (≈4% of retarded persons; ≈0.003% of the general population)	20–40	• Speech, or at least some manner of communication, possible • Simple tasks required for personal self-maintenance (including toileting) • Possibly some limited vocational activity	Some custodial services may be required, in addition to a carefully controlled environment.
Profound (<2% of retarded persons)	Below 25	• Limited motor development and little or no speech • Some self-maintenance activities (not including toileting) possible.	Constant supervision and assistance in a custodial setting are required.

unable to tell time—an indication of some kind of cognitive deficit. He used a clever compensatory strategy, however. He wore a nonfunctional watch. Whenever he wanted to know the time, he stopped, looked at his watch, and pretended to notice that it did not work. Then he asked a stranger who had observed his behavior to tell him the correct time. How should we assess this man's adaptive competence—in terms of his strategy for determining the time or his inability to tell time by looking at a watch? Was the man mentally retarded? If you think so, why?

COGNITIVE BASES OF MENTAL RETARDATION

Edward Zigler (1982; see also Hodapp, 1994) suggested that some mentally retarded individuals simply develop mentally at a slower rate than individuals with normal intelligence. Most investigators, however, look not only at quantitative differences in rates of development but also at qualitative differences in performance. A key qualitative difference is metacognitive skill. There is fairly widespread agreement that mentally retarded individuals have difficulties with the executive processes of cognition, such as planning, monitoring, and evaluating their strategies for task performance (Campione, Brown, & Ferrara, 1982). An example is planning to rehearse lists of words they are asked to memorize (A. L. Brown, Campione, Bray, & Wilcox, 1973). To what extent might such difficulties be based on hereditary factors and to what extent on environmental factors?

HEREDITARY AND ENVIRONMENTAL IMPAIRMENTS OF INTELLIGENCE

Both environmental and hereditary factors may contribute to retardation (Grigorenko, 2000; R. J. Sternberg & Grigorenko, 1997). Environmental influences before birth may cause permanent retardation. For example, retardation may result from a mother's inadequate nutrition or ingestion of toxins such as alcohol during the infant's prenatal development (Grantham-McGregor, Ani, & Fernald, 2001; Mayes & Fahy, 2001; Olson, 1994). Among the other environmental factors that can harm intelligence are low social and economic status (Ogbu & Stern, 2001; Seifer, 2001), high levels of pollutants (Bellinger & Adams, 2001), inadequate care in the family, divorce (Fiese, 2001; Guidubaldi & Duckworth, 2001), infectious diseases (Alcock & Bundy, 2001), high levels of radiation (Grigorenko, 2001), and inadequate schooling (Christian, Bachnan, & Morrison, 2001). Physical trauma can injure the brain to cause mental retardation.

Although we do not understand the subtle influences of heredity on intelligence very well, we do know of several genetic syndromes that clearly cause mental retardation. Down's syndrome, once called "mongolism," results from extra material on one of

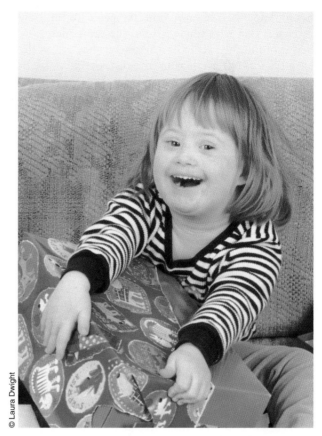

© Laura Dwight

Down's syndrome results in mental retardation as well as an unusual physical appearance.

the chromosomes that disrupts the normal biochemical messages and results in retardation. The chromosomal irregularity also causes the distinctive physical appearance characteristic of this syndrome, such as atypical facial features, short stature, and unusual bodily proportions.

Sometimes hereditary factors interact with environmental ones to produce mental retardation. Although we cannot yet prevent the inheritance of diseases, we can try to block their contribution to retardation. For example, we now know how to minimize the likelihood of mental retardation in persons who have phenylketonuria (PKU), a rare hereditary disease. Children with PKU do not produce an enzyme that is needed to properly metabolize the amino acid phenylalanine. As a result, it is essential that PKU be quickly discovered after birth. If it is not and the infant consumes foods that contain complete proteins or other sources of phenylalanine, by-products of this amino acid will accumulate in the bloodstream. These by-products cause progressively severe brain damage and permanent retardation. In PKU, the interactive roles of nature and nurture are clear. A child who is fed a diet low in phenylalanine from birth may grow up with normal or near-normal intelligence.

1. Individuals with PKU
   a. are always severely mentally retarded.
   b. are unable properly to metabolize phenylalanine.
   c. cannot be identified until around the age of 5.
   d. almost always die in infancy.
2. Ingestion of alcohol by pregnant mothers
   a. lowers the IQs of the mothers.
   b. is toxic to their unborn infants.
   c. should be limited to no more than two drinks per day.
   d. has positive effects on the coronary health of their unborn infants.
3. Mental retardation is often defined in terms of
   a. low IQ only.
   b. low adaptive competence only.
   c. both low IQ and low adaptive competence.
   d. either low IQ or low adaptive competence.

THE HERITABILITY OF INTELLIGENCE

To what extent is intelligence inherited?

The ancient nature–nurture controversy continues in regard to intelligence (R. J. Sternberg & Grigorenko, 1997). However, today the large majority of psychologists and *behavior geneticists*—those who study the effects of genes on behavior—believe that differences in intelligence result from a combination of hereditary and environmental factors (Grigorenko, 2000; Loehlin, Horn, & Willerman, 1997; Plomin, 1997; R. J. Sternberg & Grigorenko, 1999; Wahlsten & Gottlieb, 1997). The degree to which heredity contributes to intelligence is often expressed in terms of a **heritability coefficient,** which is a number on a scale from 0 to 1. A coefficient of 0 means that heredity has no influence on variation among people. A coefficient of 1 means that heredity is the only influence on such variation. This coefficient can be applied to intelligence or to any other trait, such as height or weight.

It is important to remember that the coefficient indicates variation in measured intelligence. The heritability coefficient can tell us only about genetic effects that result in individual differences among people. It tells us nothing about genetic effects when there are no, or only trivial, differences. For example, both how tall you are and how many fingers you have

at birth are in large part genetically preprogrammed. But we can use the coefficient of heritability only to assess genetic effects on height, where there are large individual differences. We cannot use the coefficient to understand number of fingers at birth because there is so little variation across people.

Heritability tells us nothing about the *modifiability* of intelligence. A trait can be heritable and yet modifiable. For example, height is highly heritable. It has a heritability coefficient greater than 0.9 in most populations. Yet heights of Europeans and North Americans increased by more than 5 centimeters between 1920 and 1970 (Van Wieringen, 1978).

Many attributes of corn, including its height, are highly heritable. But if one batch of corn seeds were planted in the fertile fields of Iowa and a similar batch in the Mojave Desert, the seeds planted in Iowa undoubtedly would grow taller and thrive better, regardless of the heritability of the attributes of the corn. In this case, environment would largely determine how well the corn grew (Lewontin, 1975).

Current estimates of the heritability coefficient of intelligence are based almost exclusively on performance on standard tests of intelligence. The estimates can be no better than the tests, and we have already seen that the tests define intelligence somewhat narrowly. How can we estimate the heritability of intelligence, or at least that portion of it measured by the conventional tests? Several methods have been used. The main ones are studies of separated identical twins, studies of identical versus fraternal twins, and studies of adopted children (Mackintosh, 1998; R. J. Sternberg & Grigorenko, 1997).

TWIN STUDIES

SEPARATED IDENTICAL TWINS

Identical twins have identical genes. No one knows exactly why identical twinning occurs, but we do know that identical twins result when a sperm fertilizes an egg and the newly formed embryo splits in two. The result is two embryos with identical genes. Suppose that identical twins are born and then one twin is immediately whisked away to a new environment, chosen at random, so that no relationship exists between the environments in which the twins are raised. They have identical genes, but any similarity between their environments would be due only to chance. If we had many such separated twin pairs, we could study them to estimate the contribution of heredity to individual differences in intelligence. We could correlate the measured intelligence of each individual with that of his or her identical twin. The twins have in common all their heredity but none of their environment (except any aspects that might be similar due to chance).

© Thomas K. Wanstal/The Image Works

These identical twins were separated at birth. When they were reunited at 31 years old, they were both firefighters who discovered further striking similarities in habits and interests.

Although, of course, purposely creating such a group of separated twins is unethical, circumstances have resulted in twins being separated at birth and raised separately. In studies of twins reared apart, the various estimates tend to fall within roughly the same heritability-coefficient range of 0.6 to 0.8 (e.g., Bouchard & McGue, 1981; Juel-Nielsen, 1965; H. H. Newman, Freeman, & Holzinger, 1937; Shields, 1962).

These relatively high figures must be interpreted with some caution, however. In many cases, the twins were not actually separated at birth but at a later time, so they had a shared environment for at least a while. In other cases, it is clear that the environments were not truly random. Placement authorities tend to place children in environments relatively similar to those they are leaving. This tendency may inflate the apparent contribution of heredity to variation in measured intelligence. Variation that is actually environmental is included in the correlation that is supposed to represent only the effect of heredity.

IDENTICAL VERSUS FRATERNAL TWINS

Another way to estimate heritability is to compare the correlations of IQs for identical versus fraternal twins. The idea is that, whereas identical twins have identical genes, fraternal twins share only as many genes as any brother or sister. On average, fraternal twins have only 50% of their genes in common. To the extent that the identical and fraternal twin pairs share similar environments due to age, we should not get environmental differences due merely to variations in age among sibling pairs. If environments are nearly the same for both twins, then differences in the correlations of intelligence scores between fraternal and identical twins should be attributable to heredity.

© Roy Morsch/Corbis

© Laura Dwight

Identical twins (left) share all of their genes in common. Fraternal twins (above) share only half. Identical twins typically are more similar in measured levels of intelligence than are fraternal twins.

IMPROVING INTELLIGENCE

At one time, it was believed that intelligence was fixed and that we are stuck with the level we have at birth. Today, many researchers believe that intelligence and the thinking skills associated with it are malleable, that they can be shaped and even increased through various kinds of interventions (Bransford & Stein, 1993; Detterman & Sternberg, 1982; Grotzer & Perkins, 2000; D. F. Halpern, 1996; R. Mayer, 2000; Perkins & Grotzer, 1997; R. J. Sternberg, 1996b). For example, the Head Start program was initiated in the 1960s to give preschoolers an edge on intellectual abilities and accomplishments when they started school. Long-term follow-up studies have indicated that by mid-adolescence, children who participated in the program were more than a grade ahead of matched controls who were not in the program (Lazar & Darlington, 1982; Zigler & Berman, 1983). Children in the program also scored higher on tests of scholastic achievement, were less likely to need remedial attention, and were less likely to show behavioral problems. Although such measures are not truly measures of intelligence, they show strong positive correlations with intelligence tests. Other programs have also shown some success in environments outside of the family home (e.g., Adams, 1986).

Support for the importance of home environment was found by Robert Bradley and Bettye Caldwell (1984) in regard to the development of intelligence in young children. These researchers found that several factors in the home environment before children start school may be linked to high IQ scores: emotional and verbal responsivity of the primary caregiver and the caregiver's involvement with the child, avoidance of restriction and punishment, organization of the physical environment and activity schedule, provision of appropriate play materials, and opportunities for variety in daily stimulation. Furthermore, Bradley and Caldwell found that these factors more effectively predicted IQs than did socioeconomic status or family-structure variables. Note, however, that the Bradley–Caldwell study pertained to preschool children. Children's IQ scores do not begin to predict adult IQ scores well until about age 4. Before age 7, the scores are not very stable (Bloom, 1964).

Perhaps the best evidence for the modifiability of intelligence comes from research by James Flynn (1987; see also Neisser, 1998). This research suggests that ever since record keeping began early in the 20th century, IQ scores have been increasing roughly 9 points per generation (every 30 years). This result is sometimes referred to as the *Flynn effect*. From any point of view, this increase is large. No one knows exactly why such large increases have occurred, although the explanation must be environmental because the period of time involved is too brief for genetic mutations to have had an effect. If psychologists were able to understand the cause of the increase, they might be able to apply what they learned to increasing the intellectual skills of individuals within a given generation.

Altogether, evidence now indicates that environment, motivation, and training can profoundly affect intellectual skills. Heredity may set some kind of upper limit on how intelligent a person can become. We now know that for any attribute that is partly genetic, there is a **reaction range,** the broad limits within which a particular attribute can be expressed in various possible ways, given the inherited potential for expression of the attribute in a particular individual. Thus, each person's intelligence can be developed further within this broad range of potential intelligence. We have no reason to believe that we now reach the upper limits in the development of our intellectual skills. On the contrary, the evidence suggests that, although we cannot work miracles, we can do quite a bit to become more intelligent.

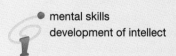

mental skills
development of intellect

According to a review by Thomas Bouchard and Matthew McGue (1981), these data lead to a heritability estimate of about 0.75, a high level. More recent estimates are similar, though quite variable (Mackintosh, 1998).

These data may be affected by the fact that fraternal twins often do not share environments to the same extent that identical ones do. If the fraternal twins are not of the same sex, their environments are even less similar. Parents tend to treat identical twins more nearly alike than they do fraternal twins, sometimes even dressing them the same way. Moreover, the twins themselves are likely to respond differently if they are identical, perhaps seeking agreement with each other. Thus, once again, the contribution of environment may be underestimated to some extent.

ADOPTION STUDIES

Yet another way to examine the influence of heredity versus environment in intelligence is by comparing the correlations between the IQs of adopted children with those of their biological parents, on the one hand, and their adoptive parents, on the other. Biological parents provide adopted children with their genes, and adoptive parents provide the environments. So, to the extent that heredity matters, the higher correlation should be with the intelligence of the biological rather than the adoptive parents. To the extent that environment matters, the higher correlation should be with the intelligence of the adoptive rather than the biological parents. In some families, it is also possible to compare the IQs of the adopted children with the IQs of either biological or adoptive siblings.

Many psychologists who have studied intelligence as measured by IQ believe the heritability coefficient of intelligence is about 0.5 in children and somewhat higher in adults (Mackintosh, 1998; Plomin, 1997), for whom the early effects of the child-rearing environment have receded. However, no one coefficient of heritability applies to all populations under all circumstances. Indeed, changes in distributions of genes or in environments can change the estimates. Moreover, even if a trait shows a high heritability coefficient, we could not say that it cannot be developed. We can thus see how better environments can lead to growth, physical as well as intellectual. This possibility of making the most of our intelligence brings us to the topic explored in the Psychology in Everyday Life box on p. 351, "Improving Intelligence."

> ## ✓ CONCEPT CHECK 6
>
> 1. Which of the following *cannot be* a coefficient of heritability?
>   a. 0.25
>   b. 0
>   c. 1.0
>   d. −1.0
> 2. Identical twins raised apart are useful in heritability studies because they have
>   a. the same genes but different environments.
>   b. the same environments but different genes.
>   c. the same genes and the same environments.
>   d. different genes and different environments.
> 3. Intelligence as measured by intelligence tests is
>   a. almost entirely heritable.
>   b. partially heritable.
>   c. not heritable at all.
>   d. heritable only in cases of mental retardation.

UNIFYING PSYCHOLOGY

AUTISTIC SAVANT SYNDROME

Vaughn's IQ is below the normal range. Yet, when given a random date, he can correctly tell you within 5 seconds the corresponding day of the week. He outperformed a university mathematics professor on a test that required them to figure out the rules that govern the relationship between a series of letters and numbers. The professor made errors when first presented with new problems, but Vaughn made no mistakes on any test (Pring & Hermelin, 2002). Gabriel has an IQ in the mental-retardation range and is nearly blind; he uses binoculars to see the world around him. But he can accurately and artistically paint a scene he just observed in astonishing detail. Gabriel works entirely from memory (Hermelin, Pring, Buhler, Wolff, & Heaton, 1999).

Autism, which is also known as pervasive developmental disorder (see Chapter 16), is characterized by a severe disturbance of communication, social, and cognitive skills, and is often associated with mental retardation. Despite intellectual and social impairments, though, a statistically small number of people with autism have talents that would not be expected of someone with limited cognitive and perceptual abilities. Both Vaughn and Gabriel have been diagnosed as autistic, and both are considered to be mentally retarded. Vaughn, the calendar calculator, has never been trained in math, and Gabriel, the artistic prodigy, knows nothing about art theory. Yet both have amazing abilities and, therefore, are classified as *autistic savants.* (A *savant* is an individual who demonstrates a special ability or skill beyond what would normally be expected for that person.)

In the autistic savant syndrome, a person with intellectual impairment and severe developmental disability

continued

displays an exceptional skill (Miller, 1999). Some examples are the ability to perform unusual calendar calculations, mastery of several languages, amazing feats of memory, and creative talent.

Cognitive psychologists have examined the mental strategies used by autistic savants who demonstrate superior calendar calculation ability. Linda Pring and her colleagues have found that autistic savants appear to show flexibility in their reasoning when presented with new mathematical problems (Pring & Hermelin, 2002). Even with very limited intellectual capabilities, calendar savants can organize, transform, and reconstruct information.

Educational and *developmental psychologists* have studied calendar calculators to determine whether they rely on rote memory skills or actually perform calculations to arrive at the correct day of the week for the dates

they are given. In one study, tests that assessed mental and written math skills showed that all 10 autistic-savant participants used arithmetic calculations (Cowan, O'Connor, & Samella, 2003; O'Connor, Cowan, & Samella, 2000). Despite having IQs that ranged from 50 to 97, these individuals do possess a mathematical intelligence that is essentially normal. *Neuropsychologists* look for evidence of brain damage and dysfunction when they test autistic savants. Notable characteristics are repetitive thoughts, behaviors that are compulsive and ritualistic (that is, always done the same way), extreme concentration on one topic to the exclusion of others, and unusual attention to detail (Hou, Miller, Cummings, Goldberg, Mychack, Bottino, & Benson, 2000). They have discovered that the frontal lobe and the basal ganglia appear to be involved in the syndrome. Brain-imaging techniques have shown that activation dur-

ing visual-spatial tests in many areas of the brain is similar in autistic savants and healthy controls. However, several prefrontal cortical areas were activated in the brains of control subjects only (Ring, Baron-Cohen, Wheelwright, Williams, Brammer, Andrew, & Bullmore, 1999).

Educational, rehabilitation, and clinical psychologists help autistic savants learn to take care of themselves and become relatively self-sufficient (Barnes & Earnshaw, 1995; Miller, 1998). Special abilities must not be allowed to dominate the savant's life to the point of interfering with other life skills. Education and rehabilitation are necessary to the development of appropriate behavior. Clinical psychologists work with autistic savants who have extreme adjustment problems. Psychologists in many specialties attempt to understand autistic savants and help them cope with the demands of everyday life.

SUMMARY

DEFINITIONS OF INTELLIGENCE 326
How have experts and others defined intelligence?

1. Two common themes that run through the definitions of *intelligence* proposed by many experts are the ability to learn from experience and the ability to adapt to the environment.
2. Two traditions in the study of intelligence are those of Francis Galton and Alfred Binet. The tradition of Galton emphasizes psychophysical acuity; that of Binet emphasizes judgment.
3. *Mental age* refers to a person's level of intelligence as compared with the "average" person of a given chronological age. Because of conceptual and statistical problems, the mental age construct is rarely used in testing today.

4. The intelligence quotient (IQ) originally represented the *ratio* of mental age to chronological age, multiplied by 100. It was intended to provide a measure of a person's intelligence relative to his or her age-mates.
5. Two of the most widely used individually administered intelligence tests are the Stanford-Binet Intelligence Scales and the Wechsler Adult Intelligence Scale-III (as well as the third edition of the Wechsler Intelligence Scale for Children).
6. The Bayley Scales of Infant Development are a downward extension of the Stanford-Binet scales.
7. Today IQ scores are typically computed so as to have a *median* (middle score) of 100. IQ scores based on deviations from the average score are called *deviation IQs*.

How can intelligence be assessed? What kinds of problems may be encountered during the assessment process?

8. Test *validity* refers to the extent to which a test measures what it is supposed to measure.

9. Test *reliability* refers to the dependability of the measurement of a test.

10. Test *standardization* refers to the process of ensuring that the conditions for taking the test are the same for all test takers. *Normative scores* are standardized scores that represent a translation of *raw scores* into scaled equivalents that reflect the relative performance of individual test takers, thereby permitting comparison.

THEORIES OF THE NATURE OF INTELLIGENCE 334

What are the major theories of the nature of intelligence?

11. One approach to intelligence, the psychometric model, involves the use of *factor analysis*, a statistical technique that may enable the user to identify latent sources of individual differences in performance on tests. Some of the main factor models of the mind are the two-factor model of Spearman, the primary-mental-abilities model of Thurstone, and the hierarchical models of Cattell and Carroll. (fluid and crystallization)

12. An alternative approach to intelligence, the computational model, involves the analysis of *information processing*—the mental manipulation of symbols. Information-processing theorists have sought to understand intelligence in terms of constructs such as speed of lexical access or of components of reasoning and problem solving.

13. A third approach is the biological model, which involves sophisticated means of viewing certain kinds of activity within the brain. The evolutionary approach derives from the attempt to understand biological bases of intelligence.

14. A fourth approach to understanding intelligence (based on an anthropological model) is a contextual model, in which intelligence is viewed as wholly or partly determined by cultural values. *Contextual* theorists differ in the extent to which they believe that the meaning of intelligence differs from one culture to another.

15. What is considered to be intelligent behavior is to some extent culturally relative. The same behavior that is considered to be intelligent in one culture may be considered unintelligent in another culture.

16. Because members of different cultures have different ideas about what constitutes intelligent behavior, it is difficult, perhaps impossible, to create a test of intelligence that is *culture-fair*—that is, equally fair for members of different cultures. Tests may be *culture-relevant*, however.

17. A fifth approach to understanding intelligence is based on a systems model. Gardner's *theory of multiple intelligences* specifies that intelligence is not a unitary construct, but rather that there are multiple intelligences, each relatively independent of the others. Sternberg's *triarchic theory of intelligence* conceives of intelligence in terms of information-processing components, which are applied to experience to serve the functions of adaptation to the environment, shaping of the environment, and selection of new environments.

GROUP DIFFERENCES 344

How do groups differ on various tests of intelligence?

18. Different groups perform, on average, at different levels on conventional tests of intelligence. The full set of reasons for the differences remains elusive.

EXTREMES OF INTELLIGENCE 345

What constitute extremes of intelligence? What do they tell us about human potentials?

19. Intellectual giftedness refers to a very high level of intelligence and is often believed to involve more than just IQ—for example, high creativity and high motivation.

20. The American Association on Mental Retardation includes in its definition of *mental retardation* two components: low IQ and low adaptive competence, or how a person gets along in the world.

21. Mental retardation appears typically to be caused by both hereditary and environmental factors, often in interaction.

22. Down's syndrome results from the presence of extra chromosomal material, and it usually results in some degree of mental retardation.

To what extent is intelligence inherited?

23. The heritability of intelligence refers to the proportion of individual-differences variation in intelligence tests that is inherited within a given population. Heritability can differ both across populations and within populations, and across different times and places. Heritability measures only those genetic effects that produce individual differences.

24. Heritability can be estimated in several ways. Three of the most common are studies of separated identical twins, comparisons of identical versus fraternal twins, and adoption studies that compare IQs of adopted versus biological siblings raised by a given set of parents with IQs of both the biological and the adoptive parents.

KEY TERMS

achievement 329
aptitude 329
contextualist 339
crystallized intelligence 335
culture-fair test 340
culture-relevant test 340
deviation IQs 332
emotional intelligence 341
factor analysis 334
fluid intelligence 335

heritability coefficient 349
information processing 335
intelligence 326
mean 332
median 331
mental age 328
mental retardation 347
mode 332
normal distribution 331
normative scores (norms) 333

predictive validity 332
ratio IQ 328
raw score 333
reaction range 351
reliability 333
standardization 333
theory of multiple intelligences 340
triarchic theory of intelligence 342
validity 332

ANSWERS TO CONCEPT CHECKS

Concept Check 1

1. a   2. d   3. c

Concept Check 2

1. b   2. d   3. a

Concept Check 3

1. c   2. c   3. b

Concept Check 4

1. b   2. a   3. d

Concept Check 5

1. b   2. b   3. c

Concept Check 6

1. d   2. a   3. b

KNOWLEDGE CHECK

1. Charles Spearman's theory had at its base the notion of
   a. primary mental abilities.
   b. multiple intelligences.
   c. a general factor of intelligence.
   d. triarchic abilities.

2. The notion that "intelligence is what intelligence tests test" is first associated with
   a. Arthur Jensen.
   b. Raymond Cattell.
   c. Edwin Boring.
   d. Howard Gardner.

3. John, who is 10 years old, performs on a traditional IQ test at the level of a 12-year old. We could say that John's _____ age is _____.
   a. mental, 10
   b. mental, 12
   c. chronological, 120
   d. chronological, 12
4. Three children have IQs of 100, 104, and 104. The mode of the distribution is the same as
   a. the median but not the mean.
   b. the mean but not the median.
   c. both the median and the mean.
   d. neither the median nor the mode.
5. The Wechsler Adult Intelligence Scale (WAIS-III) does *not* yield a _____ score.
   a. verbal
   b. performance
   c. mathematical
   d. total
6. Crystallized intelligence might be measured by a test of
   a. spatial visualization.
   b. abstract reasoning.
   c. memory for faces.
   d. vocabulary.
7. In rural Kenya, conceptions of intelligence
   a. are limited to academic skills.
   b. are limited to practical skills.
   c. emphasize academic skills but include practical skills.
   d. emphasize practical skills but include academic skills.
8. According to Joseph Renzulli, a high level of _____ is *not* a necessary component of giftedness.
   a. interpersonal skill
   b. creativity
   c. ability
   d. task commitment
9. The fact that intelligence is heritable in some degree means that it
   a. cannot be modifiable.
   b. may or may not be modifiable.
   c. must be modifiable.
   d. may be modifiable, but only *in utero*.
10. A test is *valid* if it measures
    a. what it is supposed to measure.
    b. the same thing consistently.
    c. without bias.
    d. in a standardized way.

Answers
1. c   2. c   3. b   4. a   5. c   6. d   7. d   8. a
9. b   10. a

THINK ABOUT IT

1. Does it make sense to speak of "overachievers"? Why or why not?
2. To what extent are people's achievements—including your own—an accurate reflection of their aptitudes? What factors beside aptitudes affect achievement?
3. Create a test question that assesses a particular skill or topic. Tailor that question to the following persons: (a) a 9-year-old homeless boy who supports himself by whatever means he finds available, (b) a 20-year-old college student, and (c) a 70-year-old retired plumber.
4. Many museums now include child-oriented experiences and exhibits. Think of an exhibit you have visited or heard about. How might you enhance the learning experience of a 10-year-old to help the child profit from the exhibit?
5. Are there things you could do to increase your own abilities? If so, what?
6. Are there aspects of your abilities that you could use better? If so, how might you better use them?

For a chapter tutorial quiz, direct links to Internet sites, and other useful features, visit the book-specific web-site at http://psychology.wadsworth.com/sternberg4e. You can also connect directly to the following sites:

The ARC Home Page
http://TheArc.org/
The official home page of the Association for Retarded Citizens of the United States includes links to local and state home pages, questions and answers regarding mental retardation, and related Web sites.

ETSnet
http://www.ets.org
The official Web site of the Educational Testing Service contains information on the SAT, GRE, and other standardized tests.

ERIC Clearinghouse on Assessment and Evaluation
http://ericae.net/
The most comprehensive set of links to sites on psychological testing and assessment on the Web is available here. A recent addition is the full-text library of more than 250 scholarly and professional books and articles about assessment.

For additional readings on many of the topics covered in this chapter, check out InfoTrac College Edition at **www.infotrac-college.com/ wadsworth.**

CD-ROM: UNIFYING PSYCHOLOGY

Disk Two
The Nature of Intelligence
Culture and Intelligence
Gender and Intelligence
Chapter Quiz
Critical Thinking Questions

© Ronnie Kaufman/Corbis

CHAPTER 10

PHYSICAL AND COGNITIVE DEVELOPMENT

The baby, assailed by eyes, ears, nose, skin, and entrails at once, feels that all is one great blooming, buzzing confusion.
—*William James*, Principles of Psychology

Does a baby really start life thinking that all is one blooming, buzzing confusion? Psychologists are interested in how our physical, mental, and social abilities develop from birth onward because each plays a big role in who we become. The 2-year-old, 10-year-old, and 25-year-old have different physical, mental, and social abilities as a result of their differing points in development as well as their unique life experiences. **Developmental psychology** is the study of the differences and similarities among people of different ages and of the qualitative and quantitative psychological changes that occur across the life span. Developmental psychologists are interested in all aspects of the developing person. Psychologists who study physical development want to know what physical changes occur over time as well as what aspects remain relatively the same. **Cognitive development** is the study of how mental skills accumulate and change with increasing physiological maturity and experience. Psychologists who study cognitive development want to know how and why people think and behave as they do at different times in their lives. Psychologists who study social development are interested in the ways we interact with other people throughout our lives.

This chapter focuses on physical and cognitive development. Because much of our social development depends on cognitive outcomes, we will cover social development in the next chapter, the first of a trio of chapters on social psychology.

An obvious feature of human development is our dependence on other human beings. In Western (but not all) societies, children live with their parents for many years and also go to school for many years. A newly licensed physician, for example, may have had 20 years of schooling or more. Westerners are accustomed to a long period of dependence on parents and other adults. But this extended dependence is unique among species. Why, if humans are so smart, do they take so long to become independent?

In some non-Western cultures, children are expected to show independence from their parents at an earlier age than is true in the West. Some countries allow or tolerate child labor, which is not permitted in the United States.

(E) In terms of evolution, longer periods of dependence are associated with greater cognitive abilities. Most species have a high proportion of day-to-day behavior that is instinctive. Because their behavior is programmed, it does not need to be taught to younger individuals by older ones. Humans have greater ability to adapt successfully to diverse environmental challenges. But the cost of this greater flexibility is a longer period of learning how to use the talents we have. With age, we learn more and more about how to adapt successfully.

At first glance, it might seem that differences across the life span are due only to **growth,** quantitative linear increases in physical, cognitive, and social skills. Development involves much more than growth, however. **Development** also encompasses qualitative changes in complexity, often accompanied by quantitative increases in size or amount.

Social development depends, to some extent, on a person's level of cognitive development. Similarly, the person's cognitive development is dependent, in part, on his or her level of physical development. There are many connections between physical and cognitive growth and development. Our first task is to clarify the basic questions researchers confront when they study physical and cognitive development.

BASIC QUESTIONS IN THE STUDY OF PHYSICAL AND COGNITIVE DEVELOPMENT

What are some basic questions we need to answer about cognitive development?

Five broad questions stand out:

1. What are the newborn's physical and cognitive abilities?
2. At what ages do infants, children, and adults first demonstrate various competencies, and what do these competencies tell us about the individual as a whole? Here, we wish to know whether there are critical periods for the acquisition of these competencies. If some skills are to be learned at all, they must be learned in critical periods (e.g., learning to speak a second language without an accent that reflects one's first language). Answers to this question are averages and do not necessarily apply to each individual.
3. What are the relative roles of maturation (nature) and learning (nurture) in physical and cognitive development?
4. To what extent is development stagelike or discontinuous, and to what extent is it a smooth, uninterrupted, gradual progression?
5. To what extent is development domain general, and to what extent is it domain specific? For example, does verbal development occur at the same rate as mathematical development in a given individual, or does development in these two domains occur at different rates?

The last three questions have been subjects of great controversy among developmental psychologists. Often the questions are phrased to suggest an either-or answer, such as: Which is more important, nature or nurture? (see Bouchard, 1997; Grigorenko, 1999; Loehlin, Horn, & Willerman, 1997; Plomin, 1999; Plomin, DeFries, Craig, & McGuffin, 2003; Plomin, Fulker, Corley, & DeFries, 1997; Scarr, 1997; R. J. Sternberg & Grigorenko, 1997; R. J. Sternberg & Okagaki, 1989). Simplistic questions evoke simplistic answers. Unfortunately, development—like so many other aspects of psychology—is not that simple. The questions we ask and the ways we define problems determine how we go about seeking answers and whether we will find them. If we are to understand human development, we must phrase our questions in ways that encourage us to find realistic—and therefore possibly complex—answers.

Consider an example of such complexity. Although we usually think of children being influenced by their environment, it is important as well to remember that children influence their environment, especially in the context of their families and friends (Goodnow, 1999). To some extent, children create their own opportunities through their influence on the environment. For example, a child might get music or art lessons, not because the parents decide on them, but rather because the child insists on having them. In this way, the child's musical, artistic, or other development emanates from the child's own influence on the environment in which he or she lives. Interestingly, it appears to be nonshared environments rather than shared environments within families that most affect cognitive development (J. R. Harris, 1995; Plomin, 1999; Plomin et al., 2003; Plomin, Fulker, Corley, & DeFries, 1997). When siblings grow up in the same family, what seems to matter most for their development is not the common aspects of the environment that the siblings share, but those aspects of the environment that are unique to each sibling, such as the idiosyncratic ways the parents treat each of the siblings and their own relationships with particular friends. Individual differences between children, therefore, appear to be due in part to differences in environments even within the same family of origin (Bjorklund, 2000). Although the emphasis in this chapter is on individual cognition, it is important to keep in mind that much of cognition is collaborative (Rogoff, 1998).

MATURATION AND LEARNING

Two main aspects of development are maturation and learning (see Bornstein, 1999). **Maturation** is any relatively permanent change that occurs strictly as a result of the biological processes of growing older. **Learning** is any relatively permanent change in thought or behavior that results from experience (see Chapter 6). Maturation is preprogrammed. It will happen regardless of the environment. For example, an infant's ability to suck appears and then disappears at predetermined ages, almost regardless of environmental influences. In contrast, learning takes place only if the individual has particular experiences. Recognizing your own name when it is spoken is almost exclusively a function of learning. It will not happen if you never hear your name spoken.

Maturation and learning typically interact. It often is difficult to separate their effects. For example, one should not assume that reflexes (discussed below) are wholly preprogrammed biologically. Esther Thelen (1995) has studied the stepping reflex, which once was assumed to be preprogrammed. Instead, it may be the

Maturation results in major changes—physically, intellectually, emotionally, and socially.

result of gene–environment interaction (Bornstein, 1999; Plomin, 1999; Plomin & Rutter, 1998).

The stepping reflex is a well-coordinated, step-like pattern of movement of an infant held upright with the feet resting on a supporting surface. The reflex disappears mysteriously within the first few months after birth and then reappears when the child starts to stand and walk. Thelen has suggested that the reflex disappears because rapid gains in body fat make the infant unable to show the reflex, which actually is still available. The infant's legs just are too heavy. When the baby fat disappears, the infant once again exhibits the reflex. Thelen showed this phenomenon in a simple way. She submerged the legs of infants who appear to have lost the stepping reflex in water, which reduces their weight. Then they again exhibited the reflex.

Fundamentally, the maturation versus learning question is one form of the age-old philosophical and psychological debate over nature versus nurture. Today, almost all psychologists believe that maturation and learning interact to influence development. We may be born with a particular genetic predisposition, such as the capacity to play a musical instrument. But the extent to which our performance develops will depend greatly on the environment. One environment might bring out skills that another might not. A child with extraordinary musical talent might never discover it if raised in a nonmusical home.

Another controversy is about how we interpret our data. Does development occur in a series of discrete stages or in a single, continuous, gradual progression (Amsel & Renninger, 1997; Bennett, 1999)?

CONTINUITY VERSUS DISCONTINUITY

If development occurs continuously, then it does not have clearly delineated, discrete stages. But what, exactly, is a stage? John Flavell (1971) has suggested four key criteria.

First, a stage implies *qualitative* changes. As children grow older, they improve not only at doing what they already did but also at learning new things. A child at a particular stage can think and reason only in particular ways. The ability to think and reason in those ways develops during that stage and not before. For example, according to the late Swiss theorist Jean Piaget (1954), young children tend to see things strictly from their own points of view (thereby exhibiting *egocentrism*). Later they see things in a qualitatively different way, from the points of view of many people, including themselves.

Second, a stage implies that a number of different new skills appear simultaneously. Verbal, mathematical, spatial, and other skills all develop in synchrony. These skills also develop early. By 5 months of age, infants have sensitivity to pictorial depth cues such as perspective, size, and interposition (Kellman, 1995; Liben, 2002; see Chapter 4).

Third, the transitions between stages are fairly abrupt. New abilities appear in a sudden surge rather than in tiny steps spread out over time. For instance, the abilities to solve analogies (and thus see complex relationships) between words (lawyer : doctor : : client : patient) and between numbers (3 : 9 : : 11 : 33) occur at about the same time.

Fourth and finally, in a new stage, the child does not just add a skill here and a skill there. Rather, he or she reorganizes large amounts of information at the same time. The child comes to see the world in a new way. For example, the child begins to understand the points of view of both peers and adults at roughly the same time.

Stages occur in an invariable sequence (Beilin, 1971, 1994; Kurtines & Greif, 1974; see also Beilin & Fireman, 2000). Children almost always creep on their bellies before they crawl on their hands and knees. They generally do both before they walk. Children also seem to develop language in an invariably sequenced progression (see Chapter 8). Language is critical to their development because it provides a major symbol system through which they will understand the world (DeLoache, 2002).

Given these criteria, does development actually exhibit stagelike properties? As with so many questions in psychology, the answer depends on whom you ask. Piaget (1969, 1972) strongly believed in discontinuous phases in development. Charles Brainerd (1978) remained unconvinced. He believes that too many findings do not meet the criteria for classifying development into discrete stages. Learning theories also do not posit stages of development. And, even theorists who propose discontinuous stages recognize that development is rarely straightforward. Piaget (1972) conceded that achievements within a given stage do not appear to occur all at once for every task in every domain. For example, children are able to recognize that the number of countable items remains the same even though their appearance changes before they can recognize that volume stays the same despite changes in appearance.

Such variations in a single child's abilities are argued about in the third major controversy: whether development is domain general or domain specific.

DOMAIN GENERALITY AND DOMAIN SPECIFICITY

Throughout the first half of the 20th century, theories of cognitive development emphasized *domain generality*, the notion that comparable skill development tends to occur in multiple areas simultaneously. Examples of domains are the verbal domain (words, sentences, paragraph), the mathematical domain, the artistic domain, and so forth. If memory ability were general, for instance, then children would develop the ability to remember verbal material such as letters at the same time they develop the ability to remember mathematical material such as numbers. Some contemporary researchers continue to study domain-general processes of development. They point to several ways in which children's information processing becomes generally more sophisticated with age (Demetriou & Papadopoulos, in press).

Since the 1970s, however, theorists have placed more emphasis on *domain specificity*, the notion that skill development can occur in specific areas without comparable development in others (Frensch & Buchner, 1999). Much of this emphasis can be traced back to studies of chess masters (mentioned in Chapters 7 and 8). This work showed that experts recall chessboard positions better than do chess novices, but only if the positions they need to remember make sense in terms of their prior experience (Chase & Simon, 1973; de Groot, 1965). Chess masters have better memories only within their domain of expertise. They are superior only if what they need to remember fits their schemas for that domain.

This finding has been replicated not only with experts and novices but also with adults and children. Countless experiments have shown that adults remember better than children do (see Keil, 1989). The domain in which memory is tested can affect this finding, however. Children who were experts at chess performed better than adults at remembering chessboard positions (Chi, 1978). The children's memory is not better overall, but it is superior in their domains of expertise (see Figure 10.1). Thus, children's conceptual development appears to be largely (although not entirely) domain specific. But, the procedures by which children acquire concepts may be rather general. They look for ways to link novel objects in the environment to what they already know (Waxman, 2002). If they encounter a new animal that looks like their pet dog, they may conclude that the new animal is a dog. Of course, it may or may not actually be a dog.

We probably pose an unanswerable question if we ask whether development as a whole is domain general or domain specific. It appears to be both. Those who argue for domain generality have to explain why development is not uniform across content domains within a given stage. Those who argue for domain specificity are hard pressed to account for obvious uniformities in children's development, starting with those we observe at birth.

Of the five key questions about development, the second has prompted the most speculation and research. At what ages do infants, children, and adults demonstrate various kinds of thought and behavior? When there are serious problems in children's development, we need to know the normal progression of developmental milestones and the

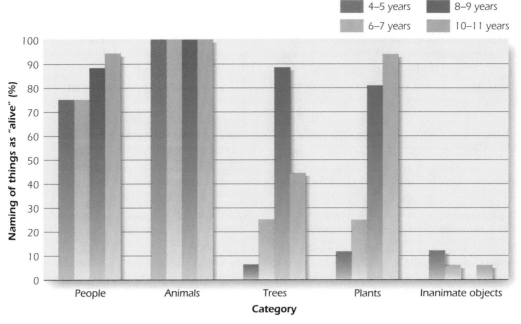

FIGURE 10.1

The Domain of Biological Knowledge. Development influences children's biological knowledge. When D. D. Richards and Robert Siegler asked children to name things that are alive, the responses depended on the children's level of development. Children of all ages recognized that inanimate objects are not alive. However, only "animals" were uniformly recognized as alive by children of the various ages studied. (After data from Richards & Siegler, 1984)

normal age ranges for these milestones. Researchers and theorists also need data about the basic accomplishments of different ages in order to construct theories of what underlies such achievements.

METHODOLOGICAL ISSUES

The research methods discussed in Chapter 2 are all used to study development. But, because a key component of development is time, two types of studies dominate. In **cross-sectional studies,** researchers investigate a diverse sample of people of various ages at the same time. In contrast, **longitudinal studies** follow one particular group of individuals for many years (e.g., Bayley & Oden, 1955). Suppose we are interested in changes in the function of working memory with age. A cross-sectional study might simultaneously look at groups of 30-year-olds, 50-year-olds, and 70-year-olds to compare their working memories. A longitudinal study, in contrast, would follow one group of people over time, first testing them when they are 30, then when they are 50, and finally when they are 70. Longitudinal studies are obviously much harder to do than cross-sectional ones and hence much less common in the psychological literature.

It is misleading to say that one or the other kind of study is more likely to indicate abilities accurately because each type has its limitations. Cross-sectional studies are susceptible to **cohort effects,** which are the distinctive effects of a particular group of participants who have lived through a particular time period. It would be pointless to compare the cognitive performances of current 80-year-olds and current 30-year-olds, for example, because their cohorts were influenced by different educational systems, opportunities, values, and hardships. For instance, many of those who served in the Gulf War or the war in Afghanistan found their lives forever changed by the experience. Earlier, many people who grew up during the Great Depression had to drop out of school to support their families, regardless of how well they performed in school.

Longitudinal studies are not perfect either. For one thing, they are susceptible to systematic "dropout." Over time, people inevitably disappear from the study sample. Some move away. Others decide that they no longer want to participate. Still others die before the study is completed. Unfortunately, neither those who drop out nor those who remain are a random sample of the group as a whole. In a study of abilities, however, those with lower abilities may be less likely to continue in the study because they feel embarrassed or otherwise unmotivated. Perhaps people who die young, or those who move frequently and thus disappear, are cognitively different from those who live longer or those whose lives are more stable. Today, many researchers believe that both cross-sectional and longitudinal designs are necessary, used separately and together, to reach accurate conclusions about cognitive development.

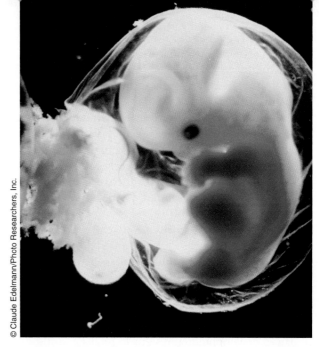

Development starts in the womb well before a baby is even born.

✓ CONCEPT CHECK 1

1. People born in 1985 will have different experiences, on average, from those born in 1965. This difference is sometimes called a _____ effect.
   a. cross-sectional
   b. longitudinal
   c. cohort
   d. cross-validated
2. Which of the following is *not* a characteristic of stage theories?
   a. qualitative changes between stages
   b. a number of different skills appear simultaneously
   c. transitions between stages are fairly abrupt
   d. order of stages varies between children
3. When one speaks of *nature* and *nurture*, *nature* refers to
   a. maturation.
   b. learning.
   c. *memory*.
   d. environment.

PHYSICAL AND NEURAL DEVELOPMENT

How do developmental changes in the brain and body affect cognitive development?

PRENATAL DEVELOPMENT

All humans start as a single cell formed by the union of just one sperm and one egg. This single cell contains all of the genetic information that, in combination with environmental forces, makes the person develop into the particular adult he or she becomes.

Some students believe that genes and environment work independently. They argue that genetic or other biological forces somehow determine the brain's capacity. On the contrary, brain development is *not* rigidly determined by genetic programming (M. H. Johnson, 1999; C. A. Nelson & Bloom, 1997). During the pre-

natal period and afterward, the neural circuits in the cerebral cortex are constantly being modified in reaction to the input they receive from the environment.

Our brain structures are not uniquely human. What differentiates the human brain from the brains of other animals is its greater volume, particularly in the cerebral cortex, and its much slower and more extended development after birth. This rate of development renders us more open to influences in our interactions with the environment than are other organisms (M. H. Johnson, 1997). Interestingly, it is not the addition of neurons that is critical in early neural development, but rather the elimination of neurons (called *neural pruning*) and the strengthening of connections between neurons (Casey, Giedd, & Thomas, 2000). Neonates are born with too many neurons. In the pruning stage, those that will not serve a useful purpose wither and die. Neural development is partially biologically driven and partially environmentally driven.

The time of life before birth is called the *prenatal* period. It is commonly divided into three stages. The first, *germinal* stage lasts for only about two weeks after conception. The main accomplishment of this time is that the fertilized egg becomes firmly implanted in the uterus of the mother. The second, *embryonic* stage lasts from about the third to the eighth week after conception. During this stage, the central nervous system starts to form. Major organs, such as the heart, and parts of the body, such as the arms, legs, eyes, and ears, also begin to develop. The embryo becomes recognizable as human. During the *fetal* stage, which lasts from about nine weeks after conception until birth, the fetus develops to the point of being able to sustain its own life. Muscular formation proceeds rapidly, as does development of the brain. By around 40 weeks (9 months), the fetus is typically ready for birth.

The importance of the prenatal period to later development can hardly be overstated. Good health and nutrition on the part of the mother are essential. Toxins ingested by the mother can severely damage the developing fetus. For example, drinking alcohol is strongly discouraged because of the risk of fetal alcohol syndrome, a group of disorders that include impaired motor development, permanent and irreparable mental retardation, facial deformities, deformed limbs, and malformed genitals (Julien, 1995). At one time it was thought that moderate drinking during pregnancy was safe, but the current recommendation is that expectant mothers ingest no alcohol whatsoever. Even small amounts of drinking have been linked to impaired development and signs of fetal alcohol syndrome (Hunt, Streissguth, Kerr, & Olsen, 1995). Such links are inferred from large samples; they may or may not emerge in individual cases. Learning disabilities and behavioral problems can also result from alcohol consumption during pregnancy (Streissguth et al., 1984; Streissguth, Sampson, & Barr, 1989). Exposure to drugs (Griffith, Azuma, & Chasnoff, 1994; Lester et al., 1991) as well as dangerous chemicals in the environment, such as PCBs (polychlorinated biphenyls), can adversely affect development after birth (Jacobson, Jacobson, & Humphrey, 1990; Jacobson, Jacobson, Padgett, Brunitt, & Billings, 1992).

Now let's look at what a healthy newborn can do.

THE NEWBORN'S CAPABILITIES

Our views regarding the capabilities of the neonate, or newborn, have changed radically over time. Aristotle and the 17th-century English philosopher John Locke believed that the newborn's mind is a *tabula rasa*, a blank slate, on which experiences will be written. In contrast to these proponents of *nurture*—the role of the environment in learning—Plato argued that learning brings into consciousness what we already know. In the 18th century, Jean-Jacques Rousseau advocated the *nativist* position—that our nature dictates our course of development. According to this view, whether we will become friendly or antagonistic, open-minded or closed-minded, and any of a number of other things depends on our heredity.

PERCEPTUAL ABILITIES

Just what can newborns do? To start with, newborns are very nearsighted. For roughly the first month of life, the infant's eyes cannot accommodate to distances that vary from about 19 centimeters. This is the ap-

Is this infant seeing "one great blooming, buzzing confusion," as William James put it, or already scanning the environment deliberately? The more sophisticated we become in our observations of infants, the more we are amazed by their capabilities.

proximate distance from the infant to the mother's face during feeding (see also Chapter 4). Images that are closer or farther than the optimal 19 centimeters are blurred (Teller & Movshon, 1986). Thus, infants cannot see small objects well, but they can see large ones close up. During early infancy, the lens of the eye reaches approximately normal flexibility with respect to accommodation.

Infants seem to have a set of inborn rules that guide the way they scan the environment (Haith, 1979, 1994). For example, they scan the environment broadly but stop and explore in depth if they see an edge. The edge is more likely than an uninterrupted surface to contain interesting information.

Infants also prefer to look at objects characterized by a high degree of complexity. For example, they prefer many narrow stripes to a few wide ones. They also prefer visual contours (e.g., edges and patterns rather than solid regions of color), curved contours rather than straight ones, high contrast between light and dark (e.g., black and white rather than gray), and frequent movements (see Banks & Salapatek, 1983). Conveniently, every parent offers a highly stimulating object that perfectly matches these criteria: a human face. In one study, infants as young as 4 days of age were shown three different patterns: a standard face, a face with its features scrambled, and a bull's-eye (Fantz, 1958, 1961). The babies showed a small but consistent preference for the standard face over the scrambled one. They also very much preferred both faces to the bull's-eye. Some researchers have suggested that infants' preference for faces might be a built-in biological imperative. Others question this notion.

Hearing, like seeing, is important to humans. Hearing skills even precede birth. Although fetuses can hear, the amniotic fluid may be an impediment. Nevertheless, their hearing is pretty good. In one study, expectant mothers read aloud Dr. Seuss's *The Cat in the Hat* once a day during the final six weeks of pregnancy. After birth, their infants listened to a recording of the mother reading either that story or an unfamiliar one. The infants exposed in utero to Dr. Seuss showed recognition of *The Cat in the Hat* (through sucking behavior) but not of the unfamiliar story (DeCasper & Spence, 1986).

Within just a few days after birth, any residual amniotic fluid has drained or evaporated from their ear canals. Infants then can hear voices and even distinguish musical notes just one tone apart. Neonates preferentially attend to the human voice. They particularly respond to the child-directed speech sometimes called "motherese." This is the speech many adults use to communicate with infants. Newborns also respond to the "clicks, kisses, and clucks" often used by caregivers (Blass, 1990). Newborns seem to have an almost reflexive response for imitating a caregiver's smile, pout, open-mouthed expression of surprise, or tongue protrusion (e.g., T. G. R. Bower, 1989; Field, 1989;

Meltzoff & Moore, 1989; Reissland, 1988). Newborns seem custom-designed to elicit and encourage the attention—perhaps even the love—of their caregivers. These caregiver responses derive from the infants' preprogrammed reflexes and their sometimes unpredictable but delightful behavior, such as smiling at unexpected moments.

REFLEXES

In normal infants, many reflexes are present at or before birth. Some, such as the breathing reflex, stay with us. Others, such as the rooting reflex, disappear during infancy. Table 10.1 lists some of the key reflexes that physicians and psychologists look for in normal infants. Deviations from the broad normal range may indicate damage to the central nervous system. In the *orienting reflex*, a series of preprogrammed responses are prompted by a sudden change in the environment. This orienting reflex never disappears. When a bright light flashes, we pay attention to it reflexively.

Developmental psychologists are interested not only in reflexes but also in motor behavior more generally.

TABLE 10.1

Reflexes Present in Newborns. Infants are born equipped with the reflexes they need for basic physiological survival. They can elicit help, affection, and care from their parents and subsequently develop conscious control of their bodies.

Reflex	Stimulus for Reflex	Infant's Response	Adaptive Function
Rooting (birth to around 1 year)	Gentle touch on cheek	Turns toward the source of the stroking	Turns the infant's head toward the nipple for feeding
Sucking (present at birth)	Insertion of a nipple or finger into the infant's mouth	Sucks on the object	Draws out the fluid from a nipple
Swallowing (present at birth)	Putting fluid in contact with the back of the mouth (e.g., through a nipple)	Swallows the fluid	Ingests milk
Eliminating (present at birth)	Digestion	Urinates and defecates	Removes waste products from infant
Crying (present at birth)	Hunger or pain	Cries	Gets the attention of a caregiver; lays down the neural pathways for more subtle psychological reasons for crying
Breathing (starts at full-term birth)	Birth or pat on back	Inhales and exhales	Oxygenates the blood
Eyeblink (present at birth)	Puff of air or bright light in eye	Closes eyes	Protects eye from foreign matter
Withdrawal (present at birth)	An aversive stimulus, such as a pinprick	Flexes the legs, cries; may flex the arms or twist the body, depending on the location of the stimulus	Protects the infant from the stimulus and gets the attention of the caregiver, who can offer further protection

The Bayley Scales of Mental and Motor Development (Revised) (Bayley, 1993) specify the ages at which various motor tasks, involving movements of the muscles, are typically accomplished (see Table 10.2). Some psychologists have devoted their careers to determining what skills (e.g., walking) and task performances (e.g., using thumb and forefinger to grasp a small object) can be expected to develop when. Perhaps the most notable of these psychologists was Arnold Gesell (1928; Gesell & Ilg, 1949). He meticulously specified a calendar of expected childhood accomplishments in several domains, including motor skills and language achievements.

As with most reflexes, the ages at which children develop particular motor skills bear little relationship to their cognitive development or their future intelligence. The exception is when the development of these skills is very retarded. Examples are if particular 6-month-olds cannot lift their heads, 18-month-olds cannot crawl, or 4-year-olds cannot walk—and these children have no known motoric

TABLE 10.2

Landmarks of Motor Development. Although the ages at which infants achieve various psychomotor tasks may differ from one individual to another, the sequence rarely varies.

Age	Motor Behavior	Hand–Eye Coordination
1 Month	• Prefers to lie on back • Cannot hold head erect; head sags forward • Keeps hands in tight fists	• Looks at object directly in line of vision • Grasps reflexively if object is placed in hand • Eyes begin to work together
2–3 Months	• When lying on stomach, can lift head 45 degrees and extend legs • Head-bobbing gradually disappears; may hold head erect	• Follows objects visually within limited range • Looks at object but can grasp only by reflex
4 Months	• Can roll from back to side • When lying on stomach, can lift head 90 degrees, arms and legs lift and extend • Can sit propped up for 10–15 minutes	• Follows objects with eyes through an arc of 180 degrees • When presented with object, may touch or grasp it • Brings any grasped object to mouth
5–6 Months	• Can roll from back to stomach • May "bounce" when held standing	• Grasps small object using palmar grasp; little use of thumb or forefingers • Scratches at tiny objects but cannot pick them up • May hold own bottle with one or two hands
7–8 Months	• When lying on back, can lift feet to mouth • Can sit erect for a few minutes • May crawl • Can stand supporting full body weight on feet—if held up	• Can grasp a small object, or may transfer it from hand to hand • Likes banging objects to make noise
9–10 Months	• Creeps on hands and knees • Can sit indefinitely • Can pull self to standing position and may "cruise" by moving feet • By 10 months may be able to sit down from standing position	• Pokes at objects with forefinger • Can play pat-a-cake • May uncover hidden toy hidden
11 Months	• Pulls self actively to feet and "cruises" along table or crib • May stand momentarily without support • Can walk if one hand is held; may take a few steps alone	• Can grasp small objects in a pincer grasp; can grasp larger objects using thumb opposition • May try to stack two blocks
12 Months	• Can get up without help and may take several steps alone • Can creep up stairs on hands and knees • May squat or stoop without losing balance • Can throw ball	• Helps turn pages of book • Can stack two blocks • Enjoys putting objects into containers and taking them out

reason for the impairment. These infants may have serious impairments of the nervous system. Such impairments can have grave implications for cognitive development. In addition, although particular motor accomplishments do not directly correlate with particular cognitive changes, they do alter the way the child can interact with the environment. These interactions may facilitate cognitive development, discussed shortly.

ADOLESCENCE AND ADULTHOOD

BECOMING PHYSICALLY MATURE

Up to about the age of 10, boys and girls grow at the same rates. Then, from about 10 to 12 years of age, girls grow more quickly. They become taller than their male counterparts. Boys show a comparable growth spurt at 12 to 14 or 15 years of age. At this time, they often become taller, on average, than girls. By age 16, growth for both boys and girls has slowed considerably.

Somewhere between the ages of 11 and 13, on average, children enter **puberty,** the stage of development when they become capable of reproduction. Girls experience the growth of breasts and appearance of pubic hair and usually have their first menstruation, called **menarche.** Boys experience the appearance of pubic hair, enlargement of the genitals, and their first ejaculation of sperm. Sexual maturity occurs at earlier ages today than it did in times past. In 1890, menarche usually occurred around the age of $14\frac{1}{2}$. By 1995, it typically occurred around the age of $12\frac{1}{2}$. Moreover, today the interval between menarche and marriage is longer than it was in the past. In 1890, the average age of marriage for a woman was roughly 22. Today, it is roughly 25 (Guttmacher Institute, 2000).

At puberty, the difference between two kinds of sexual characteristics becomes important. *Primary sex characteristics* make sexual reproduction possible. For girls, the characteristics include the vagina, uterus, fallopian tubes, and ovaries. For boys, they include the penis, scrotum, testes, prostate gland (which manufactures seminal fluid), and seminal vesicles. *Secondary sex characteristics* are sex-stereotypical but not associated directly with reproduction. Examples are enlarged breasts for women and notable deepening of the voice in men.

Although girls become capable of reproduction before adolescence, their reproductive systems are immature until about the age of 15 (Garn, 1980). As a result, when younger girls become pregnant, their infants are at increased risk of premature birth as well as low birth weight.

Early menarche can pose problems of adjustment for girls. Girls who attain menarche earlier are likely to have their first sexual experience at an earlier age, to get lower grades, and to engage in more counter-normative behavior than are girls who have menarche at a more typical age (Stattin & Magnusson, 1990). Girls who have difficulties prior to puberty and who also reach puberty early are more likely to get drunk, to steal from classmates, to get into fights, and to show other antisocial behavior (Caspi & Moffitt, 1991).

Growth in height typically ends by mid to late adolescence. Increase in weight is a typical but not necessary occurrence through the middle-aged years and can put a person's health at risk. Exercise becomes more and more important to maintain cardiovascular fitness and muscle mass. (People should be sensible in their exercising to avoid needless injuries.) Women experience an additional physical change with age: **menopause,** the end of the menstrual cycle. The average age of menopause in the West is 51 (C. Bailey, 1991), although there is considerable variation. Men's reproductive capacities also change. Men typically experience decreased sperm counts during their later years.

In adulthood, many physical changes take place. As people grow older, their reaction times tend to slow down. Moreover, their sensitivity to visual contrasts decreases, which can lead to problems with climbing up and down stairs because they have difficulty seeing where one stair ends and the next begins. As people age, dark adaptation takes longer, and they may also develop visual problems such as cataracts, which block their vision. Often, they experience hearing loss, particularly for sounds at high frequencies. Many older adults need, but do not have, hearing aids.

Older adults may also be treated as though they are less competent than younger people, which leads them to feel as though they are incompetent and then even to behave less competently. *Ageism*, or prejudice against older people, is common in many societies and can result in older people being marginalized. In most of Europe, Canada, and many other societies, individuals are forced to retire at the age of 65, which may give them the feeling that their ability to be useful has decreased greatly. Thus, older people must confront many problems, only some of which are caused by physical changes.

NEURAL DEVELOPMENT

The physiological development of the brain is crucial to all other aspects of development (M. H. Johnson, 1999). At birth, the brain stem is almost fully developed, but the cerebral cortex is still largely immature (see Chapter 3). The areas of the brain that develop most rapidly after birth are the sensory and motor cortexes. Subsequently, the association areas that relate to problem solving, reasoning, memory, and language development grow most rapidly. This pattern of neural development parallels the physical and cognitive development detailed in this chapter.

Neural interconnections become increasingly complex during the first 2 years after birth. After that, the rate of neural growth and development declines dramatically. In fact, 90% of neural growth is complete by age 6 years. Between our peak of neural development in early adulthood and about age 80, we typically lose about 5% of our brain weight. Nonetheless, neural connections continue to increase as long as we remain mentally active. These connections help to compensate for our cell loss (Coleman & Flood, 1986).

A study (Thatcher, Walker, & Giudice, 1987) of the EEG patterns of 577 people ranging in age from 2 months to early adulthood shows different patterns in each of the cerebral hemispheres. In the right hemisphere, which often is associated with holistic processing of information, continuous, gradual changes in EEG patterns occur with age. In the left hemisphere, which typically is associated with analytic processing of information, there appear to be abrupt shifts in the EEG patterns, at least up through early adulthood (see Figure 10.2). Thus, different kinds of cognitive processing may show different developmental progressions. Possibly, development results in part from changes in the electrical activity in the frontal lobe of the brain, the part most associated with problem solving (Case, 1992b; Thatcher, 1992). Other sources of development must be involved as well, however, because the frontal lobe does not develop fully until late in childhood. (See Chapter 3 for more on EEGs and other aspects of physiological psychology.)

In considering these various changes, we must realize that just as the brain can affect cognitive functioning, so can cognitive functioning affect the brain.

The brain is remodeled, to some extent, as a function of the experiences we have and how we interpret them (M. H. Johnson, 1999).

Now let's consider some basic questions about cognitive development.

COGNITIVE DEVELOPMENT

What are the major mechanisms and milestones of cognitive development?

While infants develop physically, they are also developing mentally. One of the first indicators of an infant's cognitive development is a preference for novelty. Infants learn the rules for how physical events occur by paying attention to novel stimuli (Baillargeon, 2002). This preference is associated with the *moderate-discrepancy hypothesis*, according to which infants prefer stimuli that are moderately discrepant, or different, from what they already know (McCall, Kennedy, & Appelbaum, 1977).

The preference for novelty explains why infants learn about things only when they are ready. They do not waste their time attending to familiar things or to things so new that they are overwhelming. Indeed, infants who prefer some degree of novelty often are more intelligent than those who do not (M. H. Bornstein & Sigman, 1986; M. Lewis & Brooks-Gunn, 1981). Joseph Fagan (1984, 1985; Fagan & Montie, 1988) and Marc Bornstein (1989) have found that infants who show stronger preferences for novelty at ages 2 to 6 months are more likely to have high scores on intelligence tests at ages 2 to 7 years. Thus, new methods of

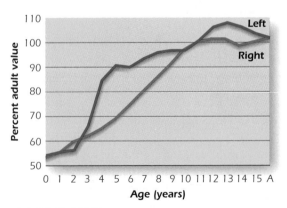

FIGURE 10.2

Developmental Changes in EEG Patterns. This graph shows increasing electrical activity in both cerebral hemispheres. Note that development is discontinuous in the left hemisphere, showing bursts and plateaus, and continuous in the right hemisphere. (After Thatcher, Walker, & Giudice, 1987)

measuring intelligence in infants show that infant intelligence may predict later intelligence (Colombo, 1993; McCall & Carriger, 1993; Rose & Feldman, 1995).

No single theory has yet explained all aspects of cognitive development (see Table 10.3 on page 379). For example, it is difficult to explain in the context of a single theory how both perceptual skills and mathematical skills develop. The theories discussed below represent psychological theorists' best attempts to account for the development of human cognition. These theories are representative of a conversation that has been going on for hundreds of years between rationalists and empiricists (see Chapter 1). Some theories, such as Piaget's, take a rationalist stance, emphasizing inborn potentials and how they unfold over the course of the lifetime. Others, such as Vygotsky's, take a more empirical stance, emphasizing the role of experience. The ongoing conversation challenges researchers to develop and improve their theories in response to the inadequacies pointed out by those who hold other positions.

We now turn to the cognitive-developmental work of Jean Piaget and the "neo-Piagetians," Lev Vygotsky, and the cognitive theorists. After looking at these theorists' work, we briefly summarize how each would respond to the questions that opened this chapter. For a brief outline of how each theory describes the characteristic progression of cognitive development, refer back to Table 10.1 as you read.

Jean Piaget (1896–1980) learned a great deal about how children think by observing them and attending in detail to apparent errors in their reasoning.

JEAN PIAGET

We cannot overestimate the importance of Swiss psychologist Jean Piaget to developmental research (L. Smith, 2002). His theory is generally considered to provide the most comprehensive account of cognitive development. Although aspects of Piaget's theory have been questioned, and in some details disconfirmed, it is still highly influential. Indeed, the contribution of his theory is shown more by its influence on later theory and research than by its accuracy.

Through his repeated observations of children, including his own, Piaget concluded that coherent logical systems underlie children's thought. These systems, he believed, differ in kind from those that adults use. If we are to understand development, we must identify these systems and their distinctive characteristics.

We first consider some of Piaget's general principles of development and then look at the stages of development he proposed.

EQUILIBRATION, ASSIMILATION, AND ACCOMMODATION

Piaget believed that the function of cognitive development in general and intelligence in particular is to aid in adaptation to the environment. Piaget (1972) proposed that both intelligence and its manifestations

become differentiated with age. Piaget believed that development occurs in stages that evolve through **equilibration,** a process of cognitive development during which children seek a balance (equilibrium) between what the environment offers in an encounter and what the child brings to it. Equilibration involves two processes: assimilation and accommodation.

In some situations, the child's existing ways of thinking, or *schemas*, are adequate for confronting and adapting to the challenges of the environment. The child is in a state of equilibrium. At other times, however, information that does not fit with the child's existing schemas creates cognitive disequilibrium. The imbalance comes from shortcomings in thinking as the child encounters new challenges. Thus, disequilibrium is more likely to occur during stage transitions. The child attempts to restore equilibrium through **assimilation,** the process of regaining cognitive equilibrium by incorporating new information into existing schemas. For example, a very young child, seeing a cat for the first time, might call it a "doggie," thinking that all pets are "doggies." Piaget suggested that the child would make use of **accommodation,** the process of responding to cognitively disequilibrating information about the environment by modifying relevant schemas. The old schemas are adapted to fit the new information and reestablish equilibrium. An older child, rec-

EIll Anderson/Photo Researchers, Inc.

ognizing that the cat does not fit the schema for dogs, might create a modified conceptual schema in which cats and dogs are viewed as distinct kinds of pets. Together, the processes of assimilation and accommodation produce a more sophisticated level of thought than was previously possible. In addition, these processes reestablish equilibrium and offer the individual greater adaptability.

STAGES OF DEVELOPMENT

According to Piaget, the equilibrative processes of assimilation and accommodation account for all the changes associated with cognitive development. Although Piaget posited that these processes continue throughout childhood, he also considered development to involve discrete stages. In particular, Piaget (1969, 1972) divided cognitive development into four main stages: the sensorimotor, the preoperational, the concrete-operational, and the formal-operational.

THE SENSORIMOTOR STAGE: BIRTH TO 2 YEARS. During the **sensorimotor stage**, the child builds on reflexes and develops the first mental representations of things that are not perceptible at the moment. In the first month after birth, the infant responds primarily reflexively. The infant has schemas for sucking, grasping, and orienting toward noises and other novel stimuli. According to Piaget, as infants adapt to their environments, they gradually modify these reflexive schemas to accomplish purposeful action. During the next few months, infants repeat interesting effects they produce, such as gurgling.

From ages 4 to 12 months, new actions involve repetitive behavior. Now, however, the outcomes also may involve objects other than the child's own body. The infant might play with a ball or a mobile and watch what it does, again and again. Still, even these actions are largely a means of capitalizing on interesting events that happen by chance.

From 12 to 18 months, infants actively search for novel ways of relating to objects. They no longer wait for interesting things to happen by chance. Rather, they make them happen. Although infants repeat actions, they may modify them to achieve some desired effect. An example is getting a mobile to swing in a preferred way. During this time, infants continue to experiment with the objects in their environments, just to see what *might* happen.

Children in this stage have surprisingly good memories. A 3-month-old who encounters a mobile twice within three days will better recall five to seven days later how kicking the mobile affects it than if the mobile had been seen only once before (Rovee-Collier, Evancio, & Earley, 1995).

Throughout these early phases of cognitive development, infants focus on what they can immediately perceive through their senses. They do not conceive of anything that is not immediately perceptible to them. According to Piaget, infants do not have a sense of **object permanence,** the cognitive realization that objects exist even when they are not currently being perceived. Before about 9 months of age, infants who observe an object being hidden from view will not look for it. A 4-month-old who watches you hide a rattle beneath a blanket will not try to find the rattle. A 9-month-old will (see Figure 10.3).

A sense of object permanence requires mental representation of an object. By 18 to 24 months of age, in fact, children begin to show signs of **representational thought,** thinking that involves mental images of tangible objects or other forms of representation (such as propositions; see Chapter 7). At the end of

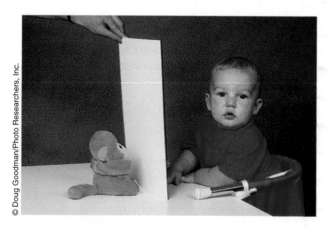

FIGURE 10.3

Object Permanence. Before about 9 months of age, infants do not realize that objects exist even when they cannot be seen or heard. Thus, once the turquoise monkey is out of sight, it no longer exists, so the infant loses all interest in it. An older infant would look for the monkey behind the screen.

the sensorimotor stage, which is a transition to the preoperational stage, children start to be able to think about objects and people who are not immediately perceptible.

THE PREOPERATIONAL STAGE: 2 TO 7 YEARS.

During the **preoperational stage,** the child develops language and concepts about physical objects. At first, communication is largely egocentric. A conversation may seem to have no coherence at all. Very young children say what is on their minds, pretty much without regard to what anyone else has said. As children develop, however, they increasingly take into account what others have said when forming their own comments and replies.

In a study of representational thinking, Judith DeLoache (1987) showed a scale model of a room to children 30 and 36 months of age (see also DeLoache, Kolstad, & Anderson, 1991). They were then shown a small toy being hidden in the scale model of the room. Next, the children were asked to find the toy in a life-sized version of that room. So, for example, the children might see the experimenter hiding "Little Snoopy" in the scale version of the room. Then they would be asked to find "Little Snoopy" in the full-sized room. At age 30 months ($2\frac{1}{2}$ years), children showed an error rate higher than 80%. At age 36 months (3 years), children showed an error rate less than 30%.

Why did the younger children have difficulty with the task? A control condition showed that the problem was not memory. The children did remember where the object was hidden in the model. Continued research suggested that the problem was not exactly a difference in representational thinking either, as Piaget's theory would suggest. Rather, it appears that the younger children found the scale model particularly interesting in its own right, not just as a representation of what would occur in a full-sized room. The older children, less interested in the scale model in its own right, were more willing to see it as representative of the more interesting larger room (DeLoache, 1991, 1995).

As children grow older, they become less egocentric. Here, **egocentrism** refers to a cognitive characteristic (not a personality trait) in which children's mental representations reflect only their own point of view and experiences. Preoperational children find it difficult to grasp the viewpoints of others. They cannot imagine how a scene, say, of a mountain range, would look when viewed from another perspective (e.g., from the top versus the bottom of the mountain range). Piaget viewed this early characteristic as indicative of a broader trend in which children of all ages become increasingly aware of the outer world and of how others perceive it. (The effect of egocentrism on the child's interpersonal interactions is discussed in Chapter 11.)

Many developmental changes occur during the preoperational stage. Children's active, intentional experimentation with language and with objects leads to tremendous increases in conceptual and language development. These developments help to pave the way for the next stage of cognitive development.

THE CONCRETE-OPERATIONAL STAGE: 7 TO 12 YEARS.

During the stage of **concrete operations,** children can mentally manipulate internal representations of objects. For example, they can imagine a top spinning without actually seeing it revolve. However, they can perform mental operations only in regard to tangible things.

Initially, children rely on their immediate perceptions of how things appear to be. Gradually, they begin to formulate internal rules for how the world works. Eventually, they use these rules, rather than appearances alone, to guide their reasoning. The change from preoperational thought to the representational thought of the concrete-operational stage is dramatically seen in Piaget's classic experiments (1952, 1954, 1969) on conservation.

The best-known experiment uses two beakers to demonstrate *conservation of liquid quantity* (see Figure 10.4). The experimenter shows the child two short, stout beakers with liquid in them. The experimenter has the child verify that the two beakers contain the same amounts of liquid. Then, as the child watches, the experimenter pours the liquid from one beaker into a third beaker. It is taller and thinner than the other two. The liquid in its narrower tube rises to a higher level than in the other still-full shorter beaker. The child is asked whether the amounts of liquid in the two full beakers are the same or different. He or she says that there is now more liquid in the taller, thinner beaker because the liquid in that beaker reaches a perceptibly higher point. The preoperational child does not conceive that the amount is conserved despite the change in appearance. The concrete-operational child, in contrast, says that the beakers contain the same amount of liquid, reflecting the child's internal schemas regarding the conservation of matter. The child can now manipulate internal images, mentally conserving the notion of amount and concluding that despite different physical appearances, the quantities are identical. Moreover, concrete-operational thinking is *reversible*. If the experimenter poured the liquid back into the small beaker, the concrete-operational child would still recognize it as the same amount. Remember, however, that the operations are concrete. In other words, the mental operations act on mental representations of actual physical events.

THE FORMAL-OPERATIONAL STAGE: 11 YEARS AND BEYOND.

During the **formal-operational stage** of cognitive development, children become able to manipulate abstract ideas and formal relationships (Inhelder & Piaget, 1958). They also create systematic mental representations of situations they confront.

According to Piaget (1972), during the formal-operational stage, people first become able to conceive of *second-order relationships*—that is, relations between relationships. Children realize not only that they have parents (first-order relationships) but also that all children have parents (second-order relationships; I am to

FIGURE 10.4

Conservation of Liquid Quantity. This young boy is partici-pating in the classic Piagetian liquid conservation task.

my parents as other children are to their parents). Eventually, they are able to see second-order relationships in the mathematical domain as well. Examples are being able to draw a parallel between the inverse relationships of addition and subtraction, on the one hand, and multiplication and division, on the other. They can now see not only how two individual objects are related but also how two sets of objects are related (as in reasoning by analogy; see Table 10.1 for a sum-mary of Piaget's stages). Formal-operational children are much more systematic in abstract situations than are concrete-operational children. Suppose that an in-dividual is asked to state all possible orderings of the numbers 1, 2, 3, and 4. A concrete-operational child is likely to list the permutations in a haphazard fashion. A formal-operational child is likely to be systematic, listing them, for example, as 1, 2, 3, 4; then 1, 2, 4, 3; then 1, 3, 2, 4; then 1, 3, 4, 2; and so forth.

In sum, Piaget's theory of cognitive development involves stages that occur in a fixed order. The stages occur at roughly the same ages for different children. Each stage builds on the preceding one. Piaget also believed that progress through the stages is irre-versible. A child who enters a new stage never re-gresses. Other theorists disagree with this view. For example, observations of some elderly persons seem to discredit the view that regression never occurs. In-deed, in evaluating Piaget's theory, we find several areas in which theorists and researchers disagree with his conclusions.

EVALUATIONS OF PIAGET'S THEORY

Piaget contributed enormously to our understanding of cognitive development. His major contribution was in prompting us to view children in a new light and to ponder the way they think. Those who have followed him have profited from his work and his insights. At the same time, their investigations have led them to ques-tion many of his conclusions and even some of his ob-servations. To gain a richer perspective on Piaget's place in the field of developmental psychology, we must con-sider a few of the major criticisms of his theory.

First, Piaget's methodology was largely clinical (R. M. Thomas, 2000). The almost exclusive use of natural-observational methodology may have limited the validity of the conclusions Piaget reached. Second, as suggested earlier, many theorists question Piaget's fundamental assumption that development occurs in discontinuous stages. They believe that development is at least partly continuous (e.g., Brainerd, 1978; Z. Chen & Siegler, 2000; Siegler, 1998; Siegler & Chen, 1998). Third, theorists have questioned Piaget's view of what causes children difficulty in particular tasks (as discussed later in this chapter). Fourth, theo-rists have questioned Piaget's estimates of the ages at which particular accomplishments can first be made.

In general, the trend has been toward demonstrating that children can do things earlier than Piaget had thought (Ahn, Kalish, Medin, & Gelman, 1995; Baillargeon, 1987; R. Gelman & Baillargeon, 1983; Huttenlocher, Newcombe, & Sandberg, 1994; Oakes & Cohen, 1995). For example, infants as young as $3\frac{1}{2}$ months, if tested appropriately, have behaved as though they can remember things they cannot see, showing signs of object permanence (Baillargeon & DeVos, 1991). Fifth, Piaget's work focused mainly on children in Western cultures. It is difficult to know whether his findings would apply to children elsewhere. The sequence of the early Piagetian stages seems to be confirmed by cross-cultural research. But the specific age ranges hypothesized for the stages may vary across cultures. There is also some question whether adults, even in advanced societies, typically display formal reasoning (Byrnes, 1988; D. Kuhn, Garcia-Mila, Zohar, & Andersen, 1995).

Most cross-cultural psychologists attribute disparities in achievement to environmental, experiential differences rather than to heredity. Some have questioned the universality of Piaget's later stages. For example, in some non-Western cultures, neither adolescents nor adults seem to demonstrate the cognitive characteristics of Piaget's stage of formal operations. Some adults do not even demonstrate mastery of the relatively symbolic aspects of concrete operations (see Dasen & Heron, 1981). In 1972, Piaget modified his own theory. He acknowledged that the stage of formal operations may be in large part a product of an individual's domain-specific expertise, based on experience. Maturational processes would still matter, but not as much as Piaget had previously claimed. Some theorists draw on Piaget's ideas but believe that cognitive development does not take the exact form proposed.

NEO-PIAGETIAN THEORISTS

Some theorists who do not fully accept Piaget's theory have modified and built upon it (e.g., Case, 1999; Case & Okamoto, 1996; Demetriou, Efklides, & Platsidou, 1993; Fischer & Grannott, 1995; Halford, 1995). Although each neo-Piagetian researcher is different, most (1) accept Piaget's broad notion of distinct stages of cognitive development; (2) concentrate on the scientific or logical aspects of cognitive development (often observing children engage in much the same tasks as those used by Piaget); and (3) believe that cognitive development occurs through some sort of equilibration. Of the many neo-Piagetian theorists, we briefly consider here only a few—namely, those who propose a fifth stage of development beyond formal operations: dialectical thinking.

Several psychologists, such as Deirdre Kramer (1990), Gisela Labouvie-Vief (1980, 1990), Juan Pascual-Leone (1984, 1990), and Klaus Riegel (1973), have asserted that the stage of formal operations is followed by a fifth stage that occurs during adolescence. In **postformal thinking**, individuals recognize the constant unfolding and evolution of thought (the dialectic originally proposed by philosopher Georg Hegel). In this stage, individuals can mentally manipulate various options for decisions and alternative answers to questions. As described earlier, through **dialectical thinking**, we progress through a thesis and a subsequent antithesis and then achieve synthesis, which serves as the new thesis for the continuing evolution of thought. For example, at one point in the history of psychology, psychologists thought that most of human development is controlled by heredity. Then they thought it was mostly controlled by environment. Now they recognize that it is controlled by both influences operating together and in interaction. In thinking dialectically, we recognize that humans seldom find final, correct answers to the important questions in life. Postformal, or dialectical thought, allows adults to accommodate the vagaries and inconsistencies of everyday situations, in which simple, unambiguous answers are rarely available. With postformal thinking, we choose among alternatives, recognizing that other options may offer benefits not obtainable from the one we choose.

Lev Vygotsky developed an alternative theory of cognitive development.

LEV VYGOTSKY

Cognitive-developmental theorist Lev Vygotsky died of tuberculosis in 1934 at age 37. Despite his youth, the importance of this Russian psychologist's work has increased in recent years. Today, Vygotsky's stature in developmental psychology is comparable to Piaget's. Piaget dominated developmental psychology in the 1960s and 1970s. Vygotsky was rediscovered in the late 1970s and 1980s and continues to be highly influential (Rowe & Wertsch, 2002). Although Vygotsky had many fertile ideas, two are particularly important for us to consider here: internalization and the zone of proximal development.

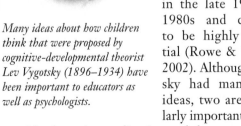

Archives of the History of American Psychology, University of Akron, Akron, Ohio

Many ideas about how children think that were proposed by cognitive-developmental theorist Lev Vygotsky (1896–1934) have been important to educators as well as psychologists.

IN THE LAB OF SUSAN GELMAN

STUDYING EARLY COGNITIVE DEVELOPMENT

Most children ask a lot of questions from a young age. Some of their questions are so deep they have also occupied the minds of scientists and philosophers—for example: Where do babies come from? What is God? What makes boys different from girls? What are the stars made of? Such questions show that children work hard to understand the larger world and how they fit into it.

In my research, I try to uncover the rudimentary theories that children construct about the world, especially in relation to biological categories (Where do babies come from? and What makes boys different from girls?). All of us (indeed, all animals) have to organize our experiences into categories. We couldn't survive if every object we came across seemed wholly new and different from everything we had experienced before. If we have a category for *fruit,* we will probably not be thrown by seeing a new kind of fruit. We sort the things we perceive so automatically that we're usually not even aware of doing it.

It was once believed that children think about categories in qualitatively different ways from adults—that they can't even form categories in the same sense. In my own work, I have challenged this notion. I have found that children form categories from a young age and, most importantly, draw extensive inferences on the basis of knowing to what category something belongs. In some respects,

Susan A. Gelman is the Frederick G. L. Huetwell Professor of Psychology at the University of Michigan and the author of more than a hundred publications on language and cognitive development, including The Essential Child (*Oxford University Press, 2003*). Her honors and awards include a J. S. Guggenheim Fellowship, an APA Distinguished Scientific Award for Early Career Contribution to Psychology, and a Boyd McCandless Young Scientist Award from Division 7 of the APA. She serves on the editorial boards of several journals. Professor Gelman's research has been funded by the National Institutes of Child Health and Human Development, the National Science Foundation, and the Spencer Foundation.

young children seem even more aware of categories and their boundaries than adults. What most distinguishes my work from that of others who came to different conclusions is that my colleagues and I use new kinds of experimental tasks to reveal how children understand their world.

In a typical experiment, I present the child with a set of questions in a gamelike format, questions that (unbeknownst to the child) are aimed at revealing a specific issue. For example, in one series of studies, I reexamined Piaget's claim that children's categories are based strictly on superficial cues, such as the size, shape, or color of an object. I wondered whether children—like scientists—appreciate that categorization is not always based on appearance. We asked our questions indirectly, focusing on categories with which children have a great deal of experience: animals, both human and nonhuman.

The children we studied were all preschoolers, in some cases no more than $2\frac{1}{2}$ years old. We presented them with sets of three pictures that posed a conflict between appearance and reality—for example, a stegosaurus (a dinosaur), a pterodactyl (a dinosaur that looked like a bird), and a blue jay (bird). After they were told what kind of animal each item depicted, the children were asked to make an inference about a biological property—for example, whether the pterodactyl would have the same kind of blood as a stegosaurus or a blue jay. The results showed that very young children made inferences on the basis of category membership (for example, generalizing from the stegosaurus to the pterodactyl) rather than outward appearances (generalizing from the blue jay to the pterodactyl).

In another set of studies, we probed children's beliefs about the sources of category differences.

Having found that children do expect categories to capture important properties that are more than superficial appearances (such as internal parts and typical behaviors), we asked how malleable or flexible they consider such properties to be. For example, are the typical properties that a cow displays (mooing, straight tail) due to fixed inborn potential, or can they be modified by environmental conditions? We asked young children what sound, for example, a cow would make if it had been raised by pigs: Would it moo or would it oink? Despite the messages often given in children's fiction (e.g., the movie *Babe* or Dr. Seuss's *Horton Hatches an Egg*), preschool children emphasized an animal's nature over its nurture, reporting that animals have inborn properties that emerge even under unfavorable environmental conditions.

There are three general motivations for doing this work. The first is scientific. I think we have an excellent opportunity to discover general cognitive biases by studying how beliefs form in early childhood. I hope that some day my studies of children's categorization will help explain why people form stereotypes and how to reduce stereotyping in adults and children. The second motivation is practical. I believe that the more we understand the complexities of young children's thought processes, the better we can educate and parent them. The final motivation is purely selfish. It is fascinating—and great fun—to listen to children as they try to answer important questions. I have enormous respect for the intellectual work that preschool children do when thinking about the questions I pose in my experiments. I am also amused by the many charming things children tell me along the way.

INTERNALIZATION, OR DEVELOPMENT FROM THE OUTSIDE IN

Granting that environments can foster or impede development, Piaget emphasized the biological, and hence the maturational, aspect of development. In contrast to this inside-out approach, Vygotsky (1962, 1978) emphasized the role of the environment in children's intellectual development. His first significant contribution to cognitive psychology was to posit that development proceeds largely from the outside in, in a process called **internalization,** which involves absorbing information in terms of its context. Thus, social rather than biological influences are key in Vygotsky's theory.

Every day, at home, in school, and on the street, children listen to what people say and how they say it. They also watch what people do and how they do it. For example, they see how their parents treat service people—teachers and gas station attendants, waitpersons, store clerks. They internalize what they see, making it their own. They re-create within themselves the conversations and other interactions in their world. According to Vygotsky, then, much of a child's learning occurs through interactions within an environment, which largely determine what the child internalizes.

THE ZONE OF PROXIMAL DEVELOPMENT

Vygotsky's (1962, 1978) second major contribution to educational and developmental psychology is the **zone of proximal development,** or **ZPD** (sometimes termed the *zone of potential development*), the range between the developed abilities that a child clearly shows and the abilities that the child might acquire, given the appropriate environment. When we observe children, what we typically see are the abilities they have developed through the interaction of heredity and environment. We are truly interested in what children are capable of doing, however. We wish to know what their potential would be if they were freed from the confines of an environment that is never truly optimal. Before Vygotsky, people were unclear about how to measure this latent capacity.

Vygotsky argued that we need to reconsider not only how we think about children's cognitive abilities but also how we measure them. Typically, we test children in a *static assessment environment*, in which an examiner asks a series of questions, neither helping nor revealing whether the test taker has answered them correctly or incorrectly. Vygotsky recommended that we test differently. In a *dynamic assessment environment*, when the child gives a wrong answer, the examiner offers a sequence of guided hints to facilitate problem solving. In other words, the examiner serves as both teacher and tester. The examiner is particularly interested in the child's ability to use hints. This ability is the basis for measuring the ZPD because it indicates the extent to which the child can expand beyond the abilities observable at the time of testing. Several tests have been created to measure the ZPD (e.g., A. L. Brown & French, 1979; Campione, 1989; Campione & Brown, 1990; Grigorenko & Sternberg, 1998). The best known is Israeli psychologist Reuven Feuerstein's (1979) Learning Potential Assessment Device.

The ZPD is one of the more exciting concepts in cognitive-developmental psychology because it enables us to see beyond a child's observed performance. Moreover, combining testing and teaching appeals to many professionals. Educators, psychologists, and other researchers have been captivated by Vygotsky's notion that we can facilitate children's cognitive development.

Feuerstein (1980) has extended Vygotsky's work by highlighting the role of parents in facilitating their children's learning, through *mediated learning experiences*, or MLE. An adult uses these experiences to introduce a child to an interesting environment (such as a museum) or task (such as how to cook). The adult also enhances the child's ability to learn by interpreting the experience through language the child understands. An alternative to MLE is *direct instruction*, in which the adult gives the child specific information. Although mediation may come from adults or other children, mediation by adults tends to be more effective. Adults better understand how children learn than other children do (Rogoff, 1990). As a result, adults typically can construct better learning experiences (Rogoff, Mistry, Goncu, & Mosler, 1993).

The power of Piaget and Vygotsky lies in their interest in probing beneath the surface to try to understand why children behave and respond as they do. As with most significant contributions to science, the ideas of Vygotsky and of Piaget are evaluated largely by how much they prompt us to extend our knowledge. Less important is the extent to which they represent a complete, final understanding of a concept. Perhaps the most we can ask of a theory is to be worthy of further exploration. We now explore the information-processing theories of cognitive development.

COGNITIVE THEORIES

Cognitive theorists seek to understand how people perform mental operations, particularly when solving challenging problems (Halford, 2002; Klahr & MacWhinney, 1998). They do not claim to provide as comprehensive an explanation of cognitive development as Piaget's. But they do consider the entire range of mental processes used by people of all ages. Any mental activity that involves noticing, taking in, mentally manipulating, storing, combining, retrieving, or acting on information falls within the range of cognitive theory.

Cognitive research offers several advantages over alternative approaches. First, it allows more precise analyses of the mental processes underlying cognition. Second, it pays more specific attention to the question of exactly how change occurs. Third, it applies well to learning in specific areas, such as reading and arithmetic. Cognitive analysis enables the investigator to model quite precisely how students are learning and thinking in these areas (Siegler, 1998).

When we turn the focus of cognitive theory to the topic of cognitive development, we ask how our processes, strategies, or ways of representing and organizing information change over time. If there are changes, what might cause them? Let us consider several domains of cognition.

PERCEPTUAL UNDERSTANDING

To learn about the world, infants need to know how to pay attention to particular stimuli. They seem to be surprisingly competent in doing so.

These perceptual abilities develop rapidly. They enable babies to learn a great deal. In one study, children as young as 4 months were shown two movies (Spelke, 1976). In one, a woman played and said "peek-a-boo." In the other, a hand holding a stick rhythmically struck a wooden block. The catch was that the babies were shown the film either with its own soundtrack or with the other movie's. The children spent more time looking at the film if the sound corresponded to the actions. In other words, even at 4 months, children can match visual and auditory stimuli. This skill is important to all of us. We make sense of the world by integrating sensory inputs.

Cognitive researchers are also interested in the skills of older children, such as how they distinguish appearance and reality (Flavell, 1999; Flavell, Green, & Flavell, 2000). For example, children of 4 and 5 years of age were shown imitation objects, such as a sponge that looked exactly like a rock (Flavell, Flavell, & Green, 1983). The researchers encouraged the children to become thoroughly familiar with the objects. The children then had to answer questions about them. Afterward, the children were asked to view the objects through a blue plastic sheet and to say what color they were. They also were asked to make size judgments while viewing the objects through a magnifying glass. The children were fully aware that they were viewing the objects through intermediaries.

The children's errors were of two fundamental kinds. On the one hand, when asked to report the reality (the way the object actually was), the children would sometimes report the appearance (the way the object looked). On the other hand, when asked to report the appearance of the objects, they would sometimes report the reality. In other words, they did not yet clearly perceive the distinction between appearance and reality (Flavell, Green, & Flavell, 1995). Older children do make this distinction. For example, they are likely to recognize that a monster toy is harmless even if it does have a scary appearance.

MEMORY

As you might expect, memory is better in older children than in younger children (see Kail, 1990; Schneider, 2002). The way we organize information plays a powerful role in memory and its development (see Chapter 7). In particular, when we are knowledgeable about an area

TABLE 10.3
CONCEPT REVIEW

Typical Milestones in Cognitive Development. Various theories are complementary regarding how cognition develops from birth through adolescence.

Theorists	Birth to 1 Year	1–2 Years	2–4 Years	4–6 Years	6–8 Years	8–10 Years	10–12 Years	12–16 Years
Bayley, Gesell	Sensorimotor alertness and abilities; social imitation; verbal and motor imitation		Persistence; verbal labeling, compre-hension, fluency, and syntax	Abstract reasoning ability emerges. Cognitive abilities increase (e.g., manipulation of language, emergence of reading and writing skills, quantitative skills).				
Piaget	Sensorimotor: builds on reflexive actions and acts to maintain or repeat interesting sensations. Major accomplishment: object permanence.		Preoperational: intentional experimentation on physical objects; increasingly thoughtful planning; internal representations of physical objects. Major accomplishments: language and conceptual development.			Concrete operations: increasingly sophisticated mental manipulations of the internal represen-tations of concrete objects. Major accomplishment: conservation of quantity.		Formal operations: abstract thought and logical reasoning. Major accom-plishment: systematic abstract reasoning.
Fifth-stage theorists (e.g., Pascual-Leone, Riegel)	Sensorimotor, per Piaget		Preoperational, per Piaget			Concrete operations, see Piaget.		Formal operations, per Piaget, followed by postformal thinking; the ability to handle ambiguities and contradictions in solving problems
Vygotsky	Increasing internalization and increasing abilities within the zone of proximal development							
Cognitive theorists (e.g., Flavell, Siegler)	Increasingly sophisticated encoding, combination, knowledge acquisition, self-monitoring, use of feedback. Increasing ability to distinguish appearances from reality. Increasing verbal fluency and comprehension. Increasing grasp of quantity. Increasing knowledge of and control over memory. Increasing control over strategies for solving problems. Increasing ability to reason deductively and inductively.							

and can organize many small bits of information into larger chunks, we can more easily recall the information we need in that area.

Some fascinating research has focused on the strategies children use in regard to memory.

In trying to learn new material, young children are more likely to resort to very simple strategies, such as rote repetition, whereas older children are more likely to use elaborative rehearsal strategies, such as visual imagery and semantic categorization

© Laura Dwight

Children use strategies to make easy and habitual a task that may initially be difficult and require effort.

(Alexander & Schwanenflugel, 1994; Hasselhorn, 1990).

Several factors affect whether children remember material over the long term (Bauer, 2002). First, when children need to remember things in order, it helps if the order makes sense (e.g., events in their temporal sequence) rather than if it is arbitrary (e.g., a string of random numbers). Second, repeated experience with the to-be-remembered material helps. Third, participation in events to be recalled enhances their recall. Finally, reminders of previously experienced events help children recall those events over a period of time. One particular line of memory-development research has sparked great interest: metamemory, which involves understanding memory abilities and ways to enhance them (Flavell, 1976, 1981; Flavell & Wellman, 1977; T. O. Nelson, 1996). Metamemory is a special case of *metacognition*, or understanding and control of one's own cognitive functioning (T. O. Nelson, 1999). For example, preschool children seriously overestimate their ability to recall information. They rarely use rehearsal strategies when asked to recall items.

They seem not to know many memory-enhancing strategies, and even when they do know strategies, they do not always use them. When trained to use rehearsal strategies in one task, most young children do not transfer that approach to other tasks (Flavell & Wellman, 1977). Children's metamemory skills do improve with age. Generally, metamemory is not a particularly good predictor of memory skills (Flavell, 1985; Flavell & Wellman, 1977). More generally, children's knowledge about their minds and mental states increases dramatically between the ages of 2 and 5 years (Astington, 1993; B. Bower, 1993; Perner, 1999).

© Cross-cultural comparisons of Western and non-Western children support the thesis that culture, experience, and environmental demands affect the use of memory-enhancing strategies. For example, Western children, who generally have more formal schooling than non-Western children, have much more practice using rehearsal strategies for remembering isolated bits of information. In contrast, Guatemalan children and Australian aboriginal children generally have many more opportunities to become adept at using memory-enhancing strategies that rely on spatial location and arrangements of objects (Kearins, 1981; Rogoff, 1986).

VERBAL COMPREHENSION AND FLUENCY

In Chapter 8 we discussed language acquisition in detail, so we summarize it only briefly here. Recall that *verbal comprehension* is the ability to comprehend written and spoken language, such as words, sentences, and paragraphs. *Verbal fluency* is the ability to produce such materials. In general, children's verbal comprehension increases with age (e.g., Hunt, Lunneberg, & Lewis, 1975; Keating & Bobbitt, 1978; K. Nelson, 1999). Older children also demonstrate greater verbal fluency than do younger children (e.g., Siegler, 1998; Sincoff & Sternberg, 1988). Children also develop the ability to generate useful strategies.

In *comprehension monitoring*, the individual observes whether the information being processed is understood, or contains internal contradictions or other problematic features that require attention (E. M. Markman, 1977, 1979, 1992). In a typical experiment, children between the ages of 8 and 11 years heard passages that contained contradictory information. This description of how to make the desert Baked Alaska is an example:

> To make it they put the ice cream in a very hot oven. The ice cream in Baked Alaska melts when it gets that hot. Then they take the ice cream out of the oven and serve it right away. When they make Baked Alaska, the ice cream stays firm and does not melt. (E. M. Markman, 1979, p. 656)

Note that the passage contains a blatant internal contradiction, saying both that the ice cream melts and that it does not. Almost half of the young children who read this passage did not notice the contradiction at all. Even when they were warned in advance about problems with the story, many of the youngest children still did not detect the inconsistency. Thus, young children are not very successful at comprehension monitoring, even when cued to be aware of inconsistencies in the text they read. Some young children also find quantitative problems to be a challenge.

QUANTITATIVE SKILLS

The ability to count objects—and thereby to conserve number—is one of the earliest indications of children's quantitative skills and their conceptions of number. Piagetian descriptions of the numerical abilities of young children have generally underestimated those abilities (Bryant & Nuñes, 2002; R. Gelman & Gallistel, 1978; Siegler, 1996; Wynn, 1995). They conclude that many 2- and 3-year-olds may not be able to count more than three or four items. Nevertheless, they can differentiate when making judgments about unknown quantities. For example, toddlers may not be able to count to 100, but they know that 100 cookies are more than 20 cookies. Thus, even very young children have rudimentary counting abilities not considered in Piagetian accounts. Moreover, Brazilian street vendors between the ages of 9 and 15 who could not solve certain mathematics problems in school could solve problems that were formally identical if they were presented in terms of their own sales activities on the streets (Carraher, Schliemann, & Carraher, 1988; Nuñes, Schliemann, & Carraher, 1993). Such activities require active problem solving.

PROBLEM SOLVING

Many psychologists study problem solving in children. Here, we focus on one particularly interesting line of research: balance-scale problems (Inhelder & Piaget, 1958; Siegler, 1976, 1978, 1996). In the balance-scale task, children see a balance scale with four equally spaced pegs on each side. The arms of the scale can fall to the left or right, or they can remain even, depending on the distribution of weights. The child's

task is to predict which (if either) side of the balance scale will descend if a lever that holds the scale motionless is released (see Figure 10.5).

At first, children consider only the number of weights, not their distance from the fulcrum. As they grow older, they use more complex rules. These rules take into account more information than is present in the problem situation (e.g., discerning a relationship between the distance from the fulcrum to the weight). Using information is also important in deductive reasoning (Siegler, 1976).

In general, children are less able to formulate and solve scientific problems than are adults, often because, as in the balance-scale task, they see situations too simplistically (Kuhn, 2002; Wilkening & Huber, 2002). For example, children are less likely than adults to formulate strategies that enable them to identify what causes what. As a result, their experiments often have multiple interpretations of the data (Klahr, Fay, & Dunbar, 1993; Kuhn, Schauble, & Garcia-Mila, 1992). They also often do not conduct all the experimentation they need to reach a conclusion (Klahr, Fay, & Dunbar, 1993; Kuhn, Garcia-Mila, Zohar, & Andersen, 1995).

INDUCTIVE REASONING

Inductive reasoning involves inferring general principles from specific observations (Goswami, 2002). It does not lead to a single, logically certain solution to a problem, but only to solutions that have different levels of plausibility (see Chapter 8).

Induction often involves categorization, which occurs when a child decides that a particular object can be classified as being of one kind and not other kinds. Categorization helps children make sense of and organize experience (Quinn, 2002). Children as young as 3 years seem to induce some general principles from specific observations, particularly those that pertain to categories for animals (S. A. Gelman, 1985; S. A. Gelman & Markman, 1987; S. A. Gelman & Wellman, 1991). For example, preschoolers were able to induce principles that correctly attribute the cause of phenomena such as growth to natural processes

(a)

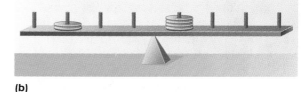

(b)

FIGURE 10.5

Balance-Scale Problems. Balance-scale problems similar to these are used in some particularly interesting studies of how problem-solving skills develop. Which way do you predict these scales will tip?

rather than to human intervention (S. A. Gelman & Kremer, 1991). Preschoolers also were able to reason correctly that a blackbird is more likely to behave like a flamingo than like a bat because blackbirds and flamingos are both birds (S. A. Gelman & Markman, 1987). Note that in this example preschoolers are going against their perception that blackbirds look more like bats than like flamingos, basing their judgment instead on the fact that bats are not birds (although the effect is admittedly strongest when the term *bird* is used in regard to both the flamingo and the blackbird). In addition, a supportive context for induction, in which the outcomes of the induction make intuitive sense to the child, can greatly enhance children's ability to induce appropriate principles (Keil, 1989, 1999).

Although the purpose of words is largely to express meaning—for example, to indicate a dog by the use of the word *dog* or a flamingo by the use of the word *flamingo*—there is some evidence that the process is not wholly one-directional. Sometimes children use words whose meanings they do not understand and then only gradually acquire the correct meaning after they have started to use the words (Kessler Shaw, 1999). K. Nelson (1999) refers to this phenomenon as "use without meaning."

The distinction between animate and inanimate objects arises in infancy (S. A. Gelman & Opfer, 2002). Gelman and Opfer (2002) have suggested that a particularly important distinction for children is between animate and inanimate objects (see also Keil, 1989). For one thing, this distinction is fundamental to our lives. We need to know that inanimate objects will not suddenly rise up and attack us or become friends with us. Superstitions result when people believe that inanimate objects have the properties of animate ones. For another thing, understanding this

distinction helps us understand general principles of cognitive development. It has been found that the distinction between animate and inanimate objects has neurophysiological correlates (Caramazza & Shelton, 1998) and that it is cross-culturally uniform (Atran, 1999). Children use both feature cues (e.g., the object possesses a face) and dynamic cues (e.g., the object can move on its own) to decide whether objects are animate or inanimate.

To summarize these findings, it once again appears that early developmental psychologists may have underestimated the cognitive capabilities of young children. Nonetheless, there does appear to be a trend as we get older toward increasing sophistication in inducing general principles from specific information. Children also increasing rely on more subtle features of the information on which such inductions are based.

THEORY OF MIND

An important aspect of cognitive development is the acquisition of a **theory of mind**—that is, an implicit set of ideas about the existence of mental states, such as feelings and beliefs, and about how the mind operates (Flavell, 1999; Keil, 1999; Perner, 1998, 1999; Wellman, 2002). Precursors to a theory of mind first occur in infancy. For example, infants seem to recognize that people's goals are reflected in their actions, as when infants grab an object in order to hold it (Woodward & Somerville, 2000). But their understanding is limited. Although researchers argue about exactly when youngsters first develop a coherent theory of mind, many believe it typically emerges between the ages of 2 and 4. Before children have such a theory, they may not realize that what people think differs from what is really true. As a result, they may not realize that people's beliefs can be false. As children grow older, their theory of mind becomes more sophisticated. Consider an example (Perner, 1999, p. 207): "Maxi puts his chocolate into the cupboard. He goes out to play. While he is outside he can't see that his mother comes and transfers the chocolate from the cupboard into the table drawer. She then leaves to visit a friend. When Maxi comes home to get his chocolate, where will he look for it?" Children younger than 3 years typically give the wrong answer, believing that Maxi will search for the chocolate in the drawer where it actually is. By age 3, some children start to get the problem right. By 4 years of age, most children solve the problem correctly, although even some 5- and 6-year-olds still make errors (Ruffman, Perner, Naito, Parkin, & Clements, 1998). Autistic children seem to lack or have a seriously defective theory of mind (Baron-Cohen, Leslie, & Frith, 1985; Perner, 1999).

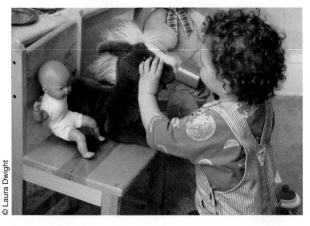

Infants and toddlers often cannot distinguish between animate and inanimate objects.

TABLE 10.4
CONCEPT REVIEW

Theories of Cognitive Development. The theories presented in this chapter address the issues of nature versus nurture, continuity versus discontinuity, domain generality versus domain specificity, and the developmental process.

Theory	Nature or Nurture?	Continuous or Discontinuous (Stages)?	Domain General or Domain Specific?	Process by Which Development Occurs?
Piaget	Biological maturation is crucial; environment plays a secondary but important role.	Discontinuous; development occurs in four stages.	Development largely occurs simultaneously across domains, although some domains may show change slightly ahead of others.	Equilibrative processes of assimilation and accommodation
Neo-Piagetians	May emphasize role of the environment somewhat more than Piaget did.	Discontinuous; may add a fifth stage; may question the ages for particular stages suggested by Piaget.	Same as Piaget	Same as Piaget
Vygotsky	Social and physical environments play crucial roles; maturational readiness may provide the broad parameters (zone of proximal development) within which the social environment determines development.	Continuous	The zone of proximal development may apply to many domains, but the environment may provide sufficient support for development only in specific domains.	Internalization results from interactions between the individual and the environment, occurring within the individual's zone of proximal development.
Cognitive theorists	Nature provides the physiological structures and functions (e.g., memory capacity), and nurture provides the environmental supports that allow the individual to make the most of existing structures and functions.	Continuous	Some theorists have been interested in processes that generalize across all domains; others have focused their research and theories on specific domains.	Internal changes in cognitive processing from physiological maturation, environmental events, and the individual's own shaping of cognitive processes.

Piagetian, neo-Piagetian, Vygotskyan, and information-processing theories are all influential. They are not mutually exclusive, however. Some have been pursued simultaneously, some have evolved as reactions to others, and some are offshoots of others. Table 10.4 summarizes some of the relationships among these theories. Theories of cognitive development and of other important issues in psychology all contribute to the ongoing dialectical process of understanding how and why we think, feel, and behave as we do.

1. Which of the following is *not* a stage in Piaget's theory of cognitive development?
   a. sensorimotor
   b. preoperational
   c. concrete operations
   d. postoperational
2. Central to Vygotsky's theory of cognitive development is the notion of
   a. internalization.
   b. externalization.
   c. assimilation.
   d. a fifth stage of thinking.
3. When children fail to detect contradictions in texts, they show a failure of
   a. verbal fluency.
   b. comprehension monitoring.
   c. lexical decoding.
   d. decoding.

DEVELOPMENT THROUGH ADULTHOOD

What kinds of development occur in adults?

Thus far, we have focused primarily on cognitive development in children. Psychological development, however, does not stop at adolescence. Many psychologists study **life-span development,** the changes that occur over the course of a lifetime.

Fluid intelligence tends to decline with age, and other cognitive abilities also seem to decrease in many individuals. For example, performance on many information-processing tasks appears to slow down, particularly on complex tasks (Bashore, Osman, & Hefley, 1989; Cerella, 1985; Poon, 1987; Schaie, 1989, 1995, 1996). Similarly, for older adults, performance on some problem-solving tasks appears to be less effective (Denny, 1980). Even brief training, however, seems to improve their scores on problem-solving tasks (Willis, 1985).

When we hear about the devastating memory losses associated with aging, such as those that accompany Alzheimer's disease, we may think that dementia is widespread among the elderly. In fact, devastating memory loss is uncommon even among the oldest of us (see Figure 10.6). The elderly population as a whole shows much more diversity in abilities than does the population of young adults.

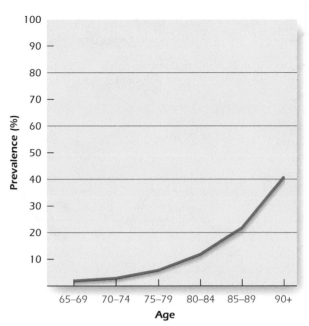

FIGURE 10.6

Prevalance of Dementia. Studies conducted in Japan, Australia, New Zealand, the United Kingdom, Sweden, and Denmark show that the actual rate of dementia (such as that caused by Alzheimer's disease) does not match our assumptions about memory loss among the elderly until people reach very late adulthood. (After data from Preston, 1986)

Evidence of intellectual decline has come under question (Berg, 2000; Schaie, 1974, 1995, 1996). For one thing, not all cognitive abilities decline. Some investigators (Schaie & Willis, 1986) have found that particular learning abilities seem to increase. Others (Graf, 1990; Labouvie-Vief & Schell, 1982; Perlmutter, 1983) have found that the ability to learn and remember meaningful skills and information shows little decline. Decreases in a single domain, such as memory, do not necessarily imply decreases in another. For example, although short-term memory performance seems to decline (Hultsch & Dixon, 1990; West, 1986), long-term memory (Bahrick, Bahrick, & Wuttlinger, 1975) and recognition memory (Schonfield & Robertson, 1966) remain quite good. In sum, older adults develop practical strategies to retain relatively high levels of functioning (Berg, Meegan, & Deviney, 1998; Berg, Strough, Calderone, Sansone, & Weir, 1998; R. J. Sternberg, Grigorenko, & Oh, 2001). They also can draw upon practical knowledge that younger people may not have (Berg, 2000; Colonia-Willner, 1998; Torff & Sternberg, 2001).

Although the debate continues about intellectual decline with age, positions have converged somewhat. Three basic principles of cognitive development in adulthood have been suggested (Baltes, 1997; Dixon &

PSYCHOLOGY IN EVERYDAY LIFE

USE IT OR LOSE IT

Is cognitive growth never-ending? Do scores on cognitive-abilities tests increase indefinitely? Available data suggest not. There is a difference between *fluid intelligence*—the ability to perform mental operations—and *crystallized intelligence*—knowledge tied to a particular cultural and historical milieu (see Chapter 9).

Although crystallized intelligence is often higher for older adults, fluid intelligence is often higher for younger adults (Horn, 1994; Horn & Cattell, 1966). In general, crystallized cognitive abilities seem to increase throughout the life span, whereas fluid cognitive abilities seem to increase through the 20s, 30s, or even 40s, and slowly decrease thereafter (Salthouse, 1996).

The rate and extent of decline vary widely (Mackintosh, 1998). However, the greatest decline in fluid abilities appears to occur, on average, during the last 10 years of a person's life. Moreover, there are enormous individual differences in the rate of decline. Some people show steep declines in intelligence; others show hardly any at all.

The lesson appears to be that brain power is like muscle power: Use it or lose it. The best way to prevent loss of intelligence is to use what you have continuously.

cognitive development
fluid intelligence

Baltes, 1986). First, although fluid abilities and other aspects of information processing may decline in late adulthood, this decline is balanced by stabilization and even increases in well-practiced and pragmatic aspects of mental functioning (Horn & Hofer, 1992; Salthouse, 1992, 1996). Thus, when adults lose some of their speed and physiology-related efficiency in information processing, they often compensate with other knowledge-based skills (see Salthouse & Somberg, 1982). Second, despite the age-related decline in cognition, sufficient reserve capacity allows at least temporary increases in performance, especially if the older adult is motivated to perform well. Third, other investigators (Baltes & Willis, 1979) have further argued that throughout the life span, there is considerable **plasticity** of abilities, which means none of us is stuck at a particular level of performance. Each of us can improve.

Recall, for example, the characteristics of postformal thought described by some of the neo-Piagetian fifth-stage theorists. Those who support the notion of postformal thought indicate several ways in which older adults may show a kind of thinking that differs qualitatively from that of adolescents and perhaps even of young adults. Although older adults generally do not demonstrate the same speed of information processing as younger adults, they may show instead the benefits of taking time to consider alternatives and to reflect on experience before making judgments—a skill often viewed as *wisdom* (Baltes, Lindenberger, & Staudinger, 1998; Baltes & Staudinger, 2000; R. J. Sternberg, 1998a). According to one theory, wise people use their intelligence not just to further their own ends but also to advance the common good (R. J.

Sternberg, 1998a). They balance their own interests with the interests of other people and the interests of institutions, such as their community or country.

In this chapter we have considered different theories about cognitive development. Can we find any unifying principles that transcend a particular theory? In other words, regardless of the particular approach—Piagetian, Vygotskyan, or cognitive—what basic principles underlie the study of cognitive development and tie its various aspects together?

As we review the data, we find some possible answers (Lutz & Sternberg, 1999; R. J. Sternberg & Powell, 1983). First, over the course of development we gain more control over our own thinking and learning. As we grow older, we become capable of increasingly complex interactions between thought and behavior. Second, we engage in more thorough information processing with age. Older children encode more information from problems than do younger children. They are therefore more likely to solve problems correctly. Third, we become able to comprehend ideas of greater and greater complexity over the course of development. Finally, over time we develop increasing flexibility in using strategies or other information. We become less likely to use information in a single context, and we learn to apply it in more and more contexts. We may even gain greater wisdom—insight into ourselves and the world around us (Baltes & Staudinger, 2000; R. J. Sternberg, 1990b, 1998a). These conclusions are confirmed by a wide variety of theoretical and experimental approaches.

Will the diverse perspectives on social development, the subject of the next chapter, similarly yield numerous conclusions?

UNIFYING PSYCHOLOGY

CONJOINED TWINS

Psychologists from many fields study twins, and their research tells us a lot about the development of emotions, individual differences, and the biology of sensation and perception. For example, *developmental psychologist* Nancy Segal (1999, 2001) has examined suicide behavior, bereavement, intelligence (IQ), brain differences, behavior problems, job satisfaction, and cooperation and competition in twins, as well as olfactory sensation and perception, spatial and mathematical reasoning, and reading and spelling disabilities. Other kinds of psychologists have studied language patterns, athletic skills, and health psychology in twins.

Conjoined twins are identical twins who do not achieve complete physical separation during embryonic development. About 200 pairs are born alive every year; fewer than half survive until their first birthday. Most conjoined twins (about 75%) are joined at the chest. Others are joined at the head, abdomen, or pelvis. For most, separation is impossible because they share vital organs. However, twins who cannot be separated adapt to being tethered to another human being. Many conjoined pairs live full, satisfying lives well into old age.

The phenomenon of conjoined twins was brought to public attention with the 2002 news coverage of the

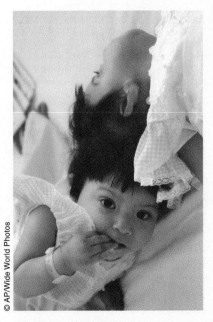

The Alvarez twins before separation.

Maria Teresa and Maria de Jesus with their parents after surgery.

continued

successful surgical separation of 1-year-old Maria Teresa and Maria de Jesus Alvarez, who were joined at the head. Less than 5% of all conjoined twins are joined in this manner, so very few surgeons are trained to perform the risky procedure necessary to separate them. Maria Teresa and Maria de Jesus, born in Guatemala, were flown with their parents to the United States to undergo separation by neurosurgeons in Los Angeles. Although they shared a skull, blood vessels, and protective tissue, each girl has a complete brain. Surgeons were able to cut through the skull and separate the girls successfully, without damaging their brains. After the two little Marias recu-perated for 5 months, the family returned to Guatemala, where the girls will undergo more surgeries to stretch their scalps to cover the surgical sites so they can grow full heads of hair.

Lori and Reba Schappell are 40-year-old Pennsylvania twins who are also joined at the skull. Like the Alvarez twins, they have completely separate brains. Surgery to separate them would be extremely risky because they are joined at the left side of their skulls and many blood vessels serve both brains. Although they are genetically identical, Reba has spina bifida and is 4 inches shorter than Lori, who pulls her around on a wheeled stool. The women have adapted well

Lori and Reba Schappell.

to life together and insist that they are happy and productive. Lori is more assertive and outgoing than Reba, who is musically gifted and ambitious. During the 6 years when Lori worked at a hospital laundry, Reba went to work with her. Today, Reba is pursuing a country-music career. She

has performed in the United States, Europe, and Asia, with Lori dancing along beside her singing sister. Lori hopes to have a husband and children. The sisters clearly have distinct personalities and separate goals, even though they are together every minute and have the same genes. They have accepted their fate and dream of their future.

Conjoined twins are particularly interesting to researchers because they help psychologists learn about the development of self-identity, personality, and motivation in people who have been forced to coexist (Smith, 1988). **Psychophysiologists** Gene Sackett and Anneliese Korner (1993) have studied sleep patterns in conjoined twins and found that the sleep state of one does not influence the other's. In the field of skin sensation and kinesthesia, **sensory psychologist** Craig Murray (2001) has studied the "boundary" that separates the bodies of conjoined twins. Because in some areas their skin and muscles overlap, conjoined twins often experience their bodies as one. These and other kinds of findings prompt **personality** and **clinical psychologists** to ponder the meaning of self and identity.

SUMMARY

BASIC QUESTIONS IN THE STUDY OF PHYSICAL AND COGNITIVE DEVELOPMENT 361

What are some basic questions we need to answer about cognitive development?

1. *Learning* refers to any relatively permanent change in thought or behavior as a result of experience; *maturation* refers to any relatively perma-nent change in thought or behavior that occurs simply as a result of aging, without regard to particular experiences.

2. Today, almost all psychologists believe that both maturation and learning play a role in cognitive development and, moreover, that the two processes interact.

3. Two criteria proposed for determining that cognitive development occurs in discontinuous stages

are that development occurs in an invariant sequence and that each stage involves a distinctive set of thinking skills.

4. Much of children's conceptual development appears to be domain specific—occurring at different rates in different domains—although some appears to be domain general—occurring in all domains at about the same rate.

5. Researchers use both *cross-sectional* and *longitudinal* designs in the study of development.

PHYSICAL AND NEURAL DEVELOPMENT 366

How do developmental changes in the brain and body affect cognitive development?

6. Infants possess many more physical and perceptual capacities than was once believed to be the case.

7. Reflexes are an important mechanism whereby infants adapt to their environments.

8. Neural networks of the brain show their greatest growth during the first 6 years of a child's life. The brain areas that develop most rapidly are the sensory and motor cortexes, followed by the association areas related to problem solving, reasoning, memory, and language development. Studies suggest, however, that development throughout the brain is not uniform. EEG patterns indicate that while the right cerebral hemisphere undergoes continuous, gradual changes, the left hemisphere shows more abrupt, discontinuous changes.

COGNITIVE DEVELOPMENT 371

What are the major mechanisms and milestones of cognitive development?

9. Jean Piaget proposed that cognitive development occurs largely through two processes of *equilibration: assimilation*, whereby the child incorporates new information into existing cognitive schemas, and *accommodation*, whereby the child attempts to modify cognitive schemas to fit relevant aspects of the new environment.

10. Piaget posited four stages of cognitive development: the *sensorimotor stage*, in roughly the first 2 years of life; the *preoperational stage*, from roughly 2 to 7 years of age; the *concrete-operational stage*, from roughly 7 to 12 years of age; and the *formal-operational stage*, from 11 or 12 years onward.

11. As children grow older, they become less *egocentric*—that is, less focused on themselves—and more able to see things from the perspectives of others.

12. At the end of the sensorimotor stage, children start to develop *representational thought*—cognitions about people and objects that the child cannot see, hear, or otherwise perceive.

13. Children start to show conservation in the concrete-operational stage. They can recognize that two quantities remain the same despite transformations that may change their appearance.

14. Despite the valuable contribution of Piaget's theory to our understanding of cognitive development, most scholars now believe that it inadequately estimates the ages at which children first become able to perform various tasks.

15. Some theorists have posited a fifth stage beyond Piaget's original four. The *postformal* stage might involve a tendency toward dialectical thinking. In *dialectical thinking*, beliefs tend to incorporate disparate, sometimes seemingly contradictory elements, with the recognition that many problems have no one right answer.

16. Lev Vygotsky's theory of cognitive development stresses the importance of (a) *internalization*, whereby we incorporate into ourselves the knowledge we gain from social contexts, and (b) the *zone of proximal development*, which is the range between a child's existing undeveloped potential ability and the child's actual developed ability.

17. Reuven Feuerstein has emphasized the importance of mediated learning experiences, whereby an adult interprets, or mediates, for the child the potential opportunities for learning offered by experiences in the environment.

18. *Cognitive theorists* seek to understand cognitive development in terms of how children at different ages process information. Some theorists formulate general theories of how information processing works, and others study information processing within specific domains.

19. Over the course of development, children learn to engage in comprehension monitoring—the tracking of their own understanding of what they read and learn, more generally.

20. Young children appear to fail on some transitive-inference problems, apparently due not to a lack of reasoning ability but rather to a lack of memory of the terms and relations in the problems.

DEVELOPMENT THROUGH ADULTHOOD 384

What kinds of development occur in adults?

21. It appears that although some cognitive abilities, such as fluid abilities—involved in thinking flexibly and in novel ways—start to decline at some point in later adulthood, the decline is balanced

by stability and perhaps increases in other abilities, such as crystallized abilities—represented by the accumulation of knowledge.

22. Some principles of cognitive development appear to transcend specific theories or perspectives. With age, people develop more sophisticated thinking strategies, their information processing becomes more thorough, their ability to comprehend more complex ideas develops, and they become increasingly flexible in their uses of strategies for problem solving.

KEY TERMS

accommodation 372
assimilation 372
cognitive development 360
cognitive theorists 379
cohort effects 364
concrete operations 374
cross-sectional studies 364
development 360
developmental psychology 360
dialectical thinking 377
egocentrism 374
equilibration 372

fetal alcohol syndrome 367
formal-operational stage 375
growth 360
internalization 378
learning 361
life-span development 384
longitudinal studies 364
maturation 361
menarche 370
menopause 370
metamemory 380
motor 368

neonate 367
object permanence 373
plasticity 385
postformal thinking 377
preoperational stage 373
puberty 370
representational thought 373
sensorimotor stage 373
theory of mind 382
zone of proximal development
(ZPD) 378

ANSWERS TO CONCEPT CHECKS

Concept Check 1

1. c   2. d   3. a

Concept Check 2

1. d   2. a   3. d

Concept Check 3

1. d   2. a   3. b

Concept Check 4

1. b   2. d   3. a

KNOWLEDGE CHECK

1. If development is domain general, then advances in verbal abilities will occur _____ advances in mathematical abilities.
   a. together with
   b. preceding
   c. following
   d. in no particular relation to

2. Which of the following is *not* a stage of life during the prenatal period?
   a. germinal
   b. embryonic
   c. emergenic
   d. fetal

3. Which of the following is *not* a reflex in the newborn?
   a. rooting
   b. grabbing
   c. crying
   d. withdrawal

4. Infants prefer discrepancies that are
   a. extremely small.
   b. moderate.

c. fairly large.

d. extremely large.

5. Little Billy realizes that the furry animal in front of him is not a dog but rather a cat. He modifies his relevant schemas using

a. accommodation.

b. assimilation.

c. internalization.

d. externalization.

6. Object permanence occurs during which of the following Piagetian stages?

a. sensorimotor

b. preoperational

c. concrete-operational

d. formal-operational

7. The zone of proximal development is a cornerstone of _____ theory of cognitive development.

a. Watson's

b. Piaget's

c. Vygotsky's

d. Markman's

8. Understanding and control of one's own cognition are called

a. hypercognition.

b. supercognition.

c. megacognition.

d. metacognition.

9. Piaget generally _____ young children's quantitative skills.

a. underestimated

b. correctly estimated

c. overestimated

d. avoided studying

10. Dementia is _____ in people of age 75.

a. almost never found

b. relatively uncommon

c. quite common

d. extremely common

Answers

1. a   2. c   3. b   4. b   5. a   6. a   7. c   8. d

9. a   10. b

THINK ABOUT IT

1. What steps should researchers take to avoid confusing their own limitations as investigators with the cognitive limitations of children?

2. How does Piaget's notion of equilibration through assimilation and accommodation compare with Vygotsky's concept of the zone of proximal development?

3. What might you suggest as a possible fifth stage of cognitive development?

4. What skills might a child in a remote village in Kenya have that a child in a city in a highly developed country might not have?

5. How have you developed cognitively in the past 3 years? In what ways do you think differently?

6. What principal aspects of your parents' or your teachers' behavior have you internalized over the years?

For a chapter tutorial quiz, direct links to Internet sites, and other useful features, visit the book-specific website at http://psychology.wadsworth.com/sternberg4e. You can also connect directly to the following sites:

PBS: The Whole Child
http://www.pbs.org/wholechild/
Coordinated with the videotape series of the same name, this Public Broadcasting System site offers a broad collection of information for parents, caregivers, and others about the developing child from birth through age 5. The resources here—in English and Spanish—include an interactive timeline of developmental milestones, reading lists, and a guide to other online sites about child development.

Administration on Aging: Information on Older Americans
http://www.aoa.gov/
The U.S. Department of Health and Human Service provides a content-rich site devoted to all aspect of aging; it includes one of the best available guides to online information about older Americans.

For additional readings on many of the topics covered in this chapter, check out InfoTrac College Edition at **www.infotrac-college.com/ wadsworth.**

CD-ROM: UNIFYING PSYCHOLOGY

Disk Two
Theories of Cognitive Development
Cognitive Development during Infancy
Cognitive Development during Childhood
Cognitive Development during Adolescence
Chapter Quiz
Critical Thinking Questions

CHAPTER 11

SOCIAL DEVELOPMENT

I do not remember having ever told a lie, . . . either to my teachers or to my school-mates. I used to be very shy and avoided all company. My books and my lessons were my sole companions. To be at school at the stroke of the hour and to run back home as soon as school closed, that was my daily habit. I literally ran back, because I could not bear to talk to anybody. I was even afraid lest anyone should poke fun at me.

—*Mohandas Gandhi*, Autobiography

In the preceding chapter we looked at how we develop physically and how we think. Many of the changes associated with cognitive development affect how we feel about ourselves and our relationships with others. The opening vignette reveals that Gandhi's thinking obviously affected the way he felt. His thinking made him fear how others would react to him. As another example, 4-year-olds may be cognitively unable to consider others' points of view.

In this chapter we look at **social development,** the process by which we learn to understand ourselves and to interact successfully with other people. We start with infancy because early development sets the stage for the development that comes later, both in childhood and beyond (Shonkoff & Phillips, 2000). But there is no good evidence for "critical periods" in socioemotional development needed for normal brain development (R. A. Thompson, 2002; R. A. Thompson & Nelson, 2001). Thus, socioemotional development appears to be different from, say, language development, where a critical period seems to exist for normal first-language acquisition (see Chapter 10). Moreover, barring abuse or neglect, most children experience normal socioemotional development (Shonkoff & Phillips, 2000). The brain is very flexible and can adapt to a wide variety of caregiving situations (Hann, Huffman, Lederhendler, & Meinecke, 1998). The effects of care do not originate with the primary caregiver only, but with everyone in the environment who provides care, such as parents, older siblings, and extended family (Howes, 1999). Different cultures have different caregiving emphases (Fitzgerald et al., 1999; Mistry & Saraswathi, 2003). In some cultures, such as in Zaire, the extended family may be as important as the nuclear family in providing child care (Morelli & Tronick, 1991).

Even in the United States, extended families can be critical to care, both positively and negatively. In January 2003, one infant died and two were seriously neglected and abused by their mother's cousin, who had kept the children while the mother was in prison (Purdy, Jacobs, & Jones, 2003). This extended-family care obviously went horribly wrong. In other cases, however, extended-family care may be critical to a child's survival and positive development. Many of us were brought up by grandparents, aunts and uncles, or others who enabled us to thrive when our parents were unavailable.

Fifty years ago, the difference between the nuclear family and the extended family was clear, and the nature of the nuclear family was clear, too. The nuclear family typically was viewed as a married man and woman, often with one or more children. The extended family was made up of relatives beyond that nucleus. Today, these strict boundaries no longer apply. A nuclear family may also consist of two men plus children or two women plus children. Moreover, some families are blended, including children from prior relationships. In many families, the parents are not married, have no intention of marrying, and view their unmarried state as perfectly acceptable for themselves and their children. In sum, today we need to be inclusive in the way we view families.

Social development encompasses our emotional and moral experience as well as our personalities and our relationships with others. Each of these aspects is an area of study in itself, so together they certainly cover a lot of psychological territory. They are so closely interrelated, however, that it is often quite difficult to distinguish them. For example, is the relationship of an infant or a young child to its primary caregiver an emotion (love), a personality trait (dependence), or an interpersonal interaction (attachment)? Is our treatment of someone we love based on our sense of what is right and wrong, our ideas about how to interact with others, our behavioral predispositions, or a general tendency to feel certain ways but not others? Psychologists who study social development often consider numerous aspects of development when they investigate a particular psychological phenomenon (see Figure 11.1).

EMOTIONAL DEVELOPMENT

How and why do we develop emotions?

Emotional development is an important part of a child's development as a whole (Cummings, Braungart-Rieker, & Du Rocher-Schudlich, 2003; Galambos & Costigan, 2003). An **emotion** is a subjective, conscious experience accompanied by bodily arousal and typical facial expressions, such as a smile. Thus, an emotion has a cognitive component (the subjective, conscious experience), a physiological component (the bodily arousal), and a behavioral component (the facial expression).

The cognitive component is that how we think affects how we feel. The physiological component is that the brain and nervous system affect how we feel. For example, emotional activity in the prefrontal cortex functions differently in each hemisphere (see Chapter 3). Right prefrontal activity is associated primarily with negative affect, left prefrontal activity primarily with positive affect (R. J. Davidson, 1994a; R. J. Davidson & Slagter, 2000). The behavioral component is that our emotions both affect how we behave and are affected by how we behave. We will discuss emotions themselves in more detail in the next chapter. Here our focus is on how and when they develop.

Anguished desolation

Interpersonal enjoyment

Shyness and sociability

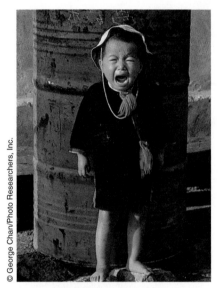

Correction by authority figures

FIGURE 11.1
Emotional Development. Children develop emotionally through a wide range of experience.

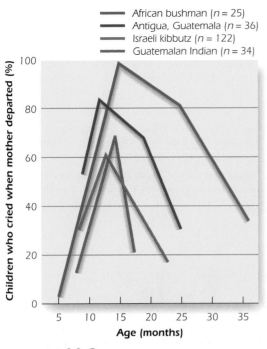

African bushman (*n* = 25)
Antigua, Guatemala (*n* = 36)
Israeli kibbutz (*n* = 122)
Guatemalan Indian (*n* = 34)

Children who cried when mother departed (%)

Age (months)

© Laura Dwight

FIGURE 11.2

Separation Anxiety. At approximately 8 months of age, an infant starts to show separation anxiety—a fear of being parted from the mother or other familiar adults. Despite the universality of separation anxiety, some cross-cultural differences affect its intensity, age of onset, and duration. (After Kagan, 1984)

Researchers are in surprising agreement about when emotions develop (Brazelton, 1983; Izard, 1991; Izard, Kagan, & Zajonc, 1984; Sroufe, 1979). Some of our earliest and most basic emotions appear to be common across cultures. They also occur at roughly the same ages as children develop (see Figure 11.2). Although infants develop emotions at roughly the same ages, infant boys seem to express emotions somewhat differently from infant girls (L. R. Brody, 1996). Six-month-old boys displayed more positive emotions (e.g., happiness) than did girls, but also displayed more negative emotions (e.g., anger) (M. K. Weinberg, 1992). Boys also cry more when they feel frustrated and take longer to recover when they are distressed than do girls (Kohnstamm, 1989).

It is a long road from the emotional world of the infant to the emotional world of the adult. The stages along the way are summarized in Table 11.1.

STAGES OF EMOTIONAL DEVELOPMENT

Some investigators believe that a child's response to stimuli can be represented by a curved shape, like a hill or an inverted U (Kagan, Kearsley, & Zelazo, 1978; see Figure 11.3). This view is based on a discrepancy hypothesis proposed by Jerome Kagan. On first being presented with an unfamiliar stimulus, a child may

show no particular emotional reaction. If something happens to violate the child's expectations, an emotional reaction ensues. This reaction is represented by the upward arc of the curve. Finally, when the child has either assimilated the experience into existing expectations or accommodated existing schemas by forming new expectations (see Chapter 10), the situation no longer provokes much interest or emotion. This lessened reaction is represented by the downward arc of the curve.

Children handle emotions differently at different times in their development. For example, the presence of a stranger can cause *stranger anxiety*. A 6-month-old confronted by a stranger may look away or become fussy. But an 18-month-old is more likely to use self-soothing and distraction to cope with the stranger anxiety (Mangelsdorf, Shapiro, & Marzolf, 1995). (See also the discussion of attachment on pp. 407–411 of this chapter.)

THEORIES OF EMOTIONAL DEVELOPMENT

There are several different theories of emotional development. **Differentiation theory** posits that when we are born, we are in a generalized state of arousal that gradually becomes differentiated into various emotions (Sroufe, 1979, 1996). Just as cognitive abilities become specialized over time, so do emotions.

Stage 4: 6 to 12 years—Industry versus inferiority. Children must develop a sense of capability. Those who do not develop this sense feel incompetent and have low self-worth. They may feel unable to do much of anything well. The child who successfully passes through this stage develops a sense of *competence*.

Stage 5: Adolescence—Identity versus role confusion. Adolescents try to figure out who they are, what they value, and who they will grow up to become. They try to integrate intellectual, social, sexual, ethical, and other aspects of themselves into a unified self-identity. Those who succeed develop a sense of *fidelity* to themselves. Those who do not remain confused about who they are and what to do with their lives.

Stage 6: Early adulthood—Intimacy versus isolation. Young adults usually try to commit themselves to loving, intimate relationships. The person who succeeds learns how to *love* in a giving and unselfish way. The person who fails develops a sense of isolation and may fail to connect intimately with significant others.

Stage 7: Middle adulthood—Generativity versus stagnation. Adults try to contribute to the next generation through ideas, products, or child raising, singly or together. Such productivity is termed *generativity*. Adults who do not pass through this stage become stagnant and probably self-centered as well. Their lives leave no lasting mark.

Stage 8: Old age—Integrity versus despair. We try to make sense of our lives and of our choices. When the elderly do not feel as though a particular important decision was right, they must come to terms with their mistake. Adults who succeed in this stage gain the *wisdom* of old age. Adults who fail may feel a sense of despair.

Table 11.2 summarizes the stages of Erikson's theory.

Do Erikson's stages actually exist? It is hard to say. No one has yet proposed a test that would clearly disconfirm the model. Certainly, many people experience conflicts at the ages Erikson specified. Whether these conflicts are their primary ones is an open question. One drawback is that the theory does not address cultural generality. For example, does generativity, so valued in the West, really characterize every human life? Are the intimate relationships so prized in our early adulthood characteristic of everyone's life? If we cannot accept past mistakes, must we fall into permanent despair? No theory of psychosocial development can account for every person in every culture. But, Erikson's theory does a

---

TABLE 11.2
CONCEPT REVIEW

Erikson's Theory of Psychosocial Development

Stage	Ages	Result of Successful Passage
1: Trust versus mistrust	Birth–1 year	Hopeful attitude toward life
2: Autonomy versus shame and doubt	1–3 years	Sense of control and mastery
3: Initiative versus guilt	3–6 years	Sense of purpose in life
4: Industry versus inferiority	6–12 years	Sense of competence
5: Identity versus role confusion	Adolescence	Sense of fidelity to oneself
6: Intimacy versus isolation	Early adulthood	Unselfish love
7: Generativity versus stagnation	Middle adulthood	Feeling of productivity
8: Integrity versus despair	Late adulthood	Wisdom

commendable job of defining some of the major personal conflicts Westerners experience.

JAMES MARCIA: THE ACHIEVEMENT OF PERSONAL IDENTITY

Erikson's theory deals with attempts to form and re-form identity. James Marcia (1966, 1980) proposed four kinds of identities that can emerge from conflicts and the process of decision making. (Note that these identities add another dimension to Erikson's theory, not a separate series of stages.) The identities Marcia described are *identity achievement, foreclosure, diffusion,* and *moratorium* (see Table 11.3). People who have reached identity achievement move beyond Erikson's stage of identity development. But those with any of the other three identities are blocked from progressing further.

As an example of how psychological theories reflect and are even determined by the times, Marcia added a fifth identity during the time of the Vietnam War. *Alienated achievement* characterizes the individual who considers the values of mainstream society to be inappropriate, or even morally bankrupt, and rejects identification with that society.

Like most theories, Marcia's may be culturally bound. It has not generated much evidence that either confirms or disconfirms it. Still, it provides an interesting way of viewing identity development. The category into which each of us falls is likely to affect both how others see us and how we see ourselves.

A DEVELOPING SENSE OF SELF: SELF-CONCEPT

Self-concept is how an individual views herself or himself. Self-concept may or may not be realistic or reflect how the person is perceived by others. A more specific, culturally relevant definition includes our senses of *independence* and *interdependence,* the feeling of belonging and collectivity (see, e.g., Markus & Kitayama, 1991). Culture determines how independence and interdependence combine to characterize a particular individual. In some Asian countries, including China and Japan, individuals are socialized to be interdependent and collectivistic. Most Western societies, however, tend to foster independence and emphasize individualism. Misunderstandings can arise between people of different cultures when their priorities conflict. An adolescent from an individualistic culture may have trouble understanding why an adolescent from a collectivistic culture places so much emphasis on pleasing parents and other family members.

TABLE 11.3
CONCEPT REVIEW

Marcia's Achievement of Personal Identity. You can assess your personal identity by asking yourself the two key questions in this table. (This matrix does not show the possible fifth identity, alienated achievement.)

		Do You Make Commitments?	
		Yes	*No*
Have You Actively Searched for Identity?	*Yes*	You have reached *identity achievement*, and you now have a firm and relatively secure sense of who you are. You have made conscious and purposeful commitments to your occupation, religion, beliefs about gender roles, and so on. You have considered others' views, beliefs, and values in achieving your identity, but you have achieved your own resolution.	Your identity is in *moratorium*, and you have reached an identity crisis or turning point. You are not clearly committed to society and do not yet have a clear sense of who you are, but you are actively trying to reach that point.
	No	Your identity is in *foreclosure*. You have committed yourself to an occupation and various ideological positions, but you show little evidence of self-construction. By adopting the attitudes of others, without serious searching and questioning, you have foreclosed on the possibility of arriving at your own unique identity.	You are experiencing *identity diffusion*, or lack of direction. You are unconcerned about political, religious, moral, and occupational issues. You go your own way, not worrying about what others are doing.

Most research in developmental psychology emphasizes self-understanding, which is mainly cognitive, and self-esteem, which is mainly emotional.

SELF-UNDERSTANDING

How we comprehend our personal characteristics and social roles contributes to our **self-understanding,** or how we understand ourselves as individuals. William Damon and Daniel Hart (1982, 1992) developed an integrative model of the development of self-understanding. According to their model, the self has four aspects. The *physical self* is the person's name, body, and material possessions. The *active self* includes actual and potential behaviors. The *social self* encompasses relationships with others. The *psychological self* takes into account feelings, thoughts, beliefs, and personality.

Different aspects of the self take precedence at different ages. The earliest signs of self-awareness are related to the physical self (see Bertenthal & Fischer, 1978; L. E. Levine, 1983). During the first year, infants become aware of the babies they see in the mirror and recognize the sound of their own names. Toddlers learn to say their own names. They also develop a sense of gender identity and know how old they are. They clearly recognize their own possessions: "Mine!" A sense of mastery also emerges during the preschool years (Kagan, 1981). Two-year-olds are clearly frustrated when they cannot succeed at doing something. When they do succeed, they are obviously pleased with themselves (recall Erikson's stages of autonomy versus shame and doubt and of initiative versus guilt). Lev Vygotsky (1934/1962) pointed out that at 3 to 4 years of age, children begin to differentiate between the speech they direct toward themselves (e.g., while playing alone) and the speech they direct toward others. Eventually, inner-directed speech becomes silent thought. Despite these accomplishments, preschool-aged children largely emphasize their physical selves. What they look like is the same as who they are.

During the elementary school years, children increasingly focus on their active selves. They emphasize what they can *do*—dance, play soccer, get good grades. In early adolescence, children concentrate on their social selves, paying special attention to peer relationships. In late adolescence, teens turn their attention to their psychological selves and consider their beliefs, values, thoughts, and attitudes. They try to understand who they "really" are. Damon and Hart's model, like many others, stops with

adolescence. But it is generally agreed that development of the self continues throughout adulthood, as shown in Erikson's models.

The Damon and Hart model involves *successive differentiation.* As we develop, our self-concepts become more differentiated. In addition, just as we become more aware of how we differ from other people, we also come to realize more and more how we are connected to others. These connections are through culture and society, through the organizations we participate in, and through our choices. Note that Damon and Hart's research was based on American children. Children in other cultures may emphasize their social selves over their personal selves. In the West, we may think of ourselves as psychologically well adjusted at home but not at work, or vice versa. Such differences in self-perception can lead to a complex picture of self-esteem.

SELF-ESTEEM

Self-esteem is the value we place on ourselves. According to Susan Harter (1990), as we explore our abilities and learn more skills, our self-esteem becomes more differentiated. We may think highly of ourselves in one area but not in another.

Harter's differentiation hypothesis posits that between the ages of 4 and 7, children can make reliable judgments about themselves in four personal domains: cognitive competence, physical competence, social competence, and behavioral conduct (Harter & Pike, 1984). The younger the children are, however, the more likely their self-evaluations will show a *halo effect,* in which a high rating in one capacity leads to a high rating in others.

Between the ages of 8 and 12, the four domains of the early years are further differentiated into five separate areas of self-esteem. Harter categorizes them as scholastic (rather than cognitive) competence, athletic (rather than physical) competence, peer acceptance (rather than social competence), behavioral conduct, and physical appearance. During adolescence, even more areas of self-esteem emerge, including close friendship, romantic appeal, and job competence.

By adulthood, 11 areas of competency emerge as aspects of self-worth: intelligence, sense of humor, job competence, morality, athletic ability, physical appearance, sociability, intimacy, nurturance, adequacy as a provider, and household management (Messer & Harter, 1985). According

© Chris Rogers/Rainbow

Where does self-esteem come from? There is evidence that both internal evaluation and others' judgments play a role in how we see ourselves.

IN THE LAB OF CAROL S. DWECK

CAN PRAISING CHILDREN'S INTELLIGENCE BE HARMFUL?

Most of us are eager to make children feel good about themselves. Praising their intelligence lavishly is often a method of choice. In one survey we conducted, 85% of parents said that it was necessary to praise children's intelligence to make them feel good about themselves. We tested whether this was true, and found that it is not (Mueller & Dweck, 1998; cf. Kamins & Dweck, 1999). The initial good feelings created by praise gave way to a drop in self-esteem, motivation, and performance as soon as the children encountered something difficult.

For many years I've studied the effects of children's beliefs on their performance. Over and over I've found that many children, no matter how bright, are extremely vulnerable when they hit difficulty. They denigrate their abilities, they lose interest in the task, and their performance falls off—dramatically. Why is this? My research has shown that such children often believe that their intelligence is fixed at a certain level, and they are overly concerned about it. They worry about how high it is, they worry that a challenging task might make them look dumb and, when they are having a hard time, they worry that they *are* dumb (see Dweck, 1999).

In contrast, many other students are eager to be challenged and are resilient in the face of obstacles. They often believe that their intelligence is something they can cultivate over time, through their efforts. Thus, they worry less about looking smart right now and more about enhancing their intellectual abilities over the long run.

Well, we thought, couldn't praising their intelligence make children more obsessed with it, just the way vulnerable children are? Doesn't praising intelligence, even after a job well done, convey to children that their intelligence is a fixed thing that can be

Carol S. Dweck received her PhD in psychology from Yale University in 1972 and is a professor of psychology at Columbia University. She is a leading researcher in the area of motivation, having pioneered the study on how students' self-beliefs and goals influence their learning and academic achievement. Her recent books include Motivation and Self-Regulation Across the Life Span *(with Jutta Heckhausen), and* Self-Theories: Their Role in Motivation, Personality and Development, *which has been translated into several languages. In recognition of her contributions she was recently elected to the American Academy of Arts and Sciences.*

judged on the basis of their performance? Claudia Mueller and I (Mueller & Dweck, 1998) designed a series of studies to test this idea. Upper grade school children worked on a set of ten conceptual problems from a nonverbal IQ test. They all did fairly well on the first set and were complimented for doing so. One-third of the children were praised for their intelligence (e.g., "You got 8 right. That's a really good score. You must be smart at this!"); one-third were praised for their effort (e.g., You got 8 right, . . . You must have worked really hard!"), and one-third were simply praised for their performance (e.g., You got 8 right, That's a really good score.")

The children who were praised for their intelligence had the biggest smiles, but they were short-lived, for we then gave everyone a set of ten *very* difficult problems. After experiencing these difficult problems, the children who had been praised for their intelligence rated themselves as dumb, lost interest in the task, and performed significantly worse than children in the other two groups, even when the problems became easier again. They even lied about their scores when asked to write (anonymously) about the task to a child in

another school. In contrast, the children who had been praised for their effort enjoyed the challenging problems and performed better than children in both of the other groups. The findings were so strong that we repeated the study over and over just to confirm them, and found the same thing each time (see Kamins & Dweck for related work with younger children).

Do these findings mean we should praise children less or be less excited about their triumphs? Not really. They simply mean that we should praise the *process* children engaged in (e.g., the effort they put forth, the strategy they used, the learning they acquired) and not focus on what their performance indicates about their intelligence.

By putting it to a rigorous test, our research has helped overturn a common-sense but misguided practice. These studies are part of a broader program of research that views socialization as a teaching process and that examines the lessons children learn from the practices followed by parents and teachers. In using praise, adults may often be teaching children lessons that produce unintended results.

to William James (1890b), overall self-esteem is more than the average of our perceived competencies. Instead, we consider the importance of each competency and form a weighted average. Suppose a boy does not think much of his physical abilities but also does not care much about physical competence. His overall self-esteem might be quite high. A boy who highly values physical competence would have lower self-esteem if he felt he was not athletic.

An alternative view (Cooley, 1982) is that self-esteem is largely determined by other people's social judgments. As we absorb others' evaluations, they eventually become our own. Evidence supports a synthesis of the two positions (Harter, 1985). On the one hand, we do make internal evaluations, and we do not view all the areas in which we evaluate ourselves as equally important. On the other hand, others' judgments affect our self-perceptions. Once again, we find that theoretical positions that seem to be opposed may be more complementary than contradictory. A synthesis can include the best aspects of both the thesis and its antithesis.

Generally, our perceptions of our abilities become both more modest and more accurate as we age (Eccles, Wigfield, Harold, & Blumenfeld, 1993; Frey & Ruble, 1987; Phillips & Zimmerman, 1990; Stipek, 1984). Problems arise, however, when a child's self-perceptions are too modest and therefore inaccurate. Teachers and parents cannot neglect the importance of self-perceptions. They affect how children handle their lives at school and outside it (Phillips, 1984, 1987). Children who think they have low abilities have motivational problems, especially older children (Rholes, Jones, & Wade, 1980). Children who underestimate their abilities seek out less challenging tasks than children who are more realistic (see Harter, 1983). In addition, children who seriously underestimate themselves expect little of themselves, believe that respected adults also take a dim view of their abilities, and are reluctant to sustain effort in difficult tasks. They also are more anxious about being evaluated than are other children (Phillips & Zimmerman, 1990).

GENDER DIFFERENCES IN SELF-ESTEEM

Research has suggested that gender affects self-perceptions of competence, as determined by the difference between children's self-evaluations and their achievement-test scores. One study showed that in the third and fifth grades, gender differences are not apparent. But at the ninth-grade level, virtually all those who mistakenly believe they are incompetent in particular academic areas are girls (Phillips & Zimmerman, 1990). Other investigators (e.g., Entwistle & Baker, 1983) have found differences as early as the first grade, again with more girls than boys doubting their competence in particular subjects.

The American Association of University Women (AAUW) Education Foundation (1992) found that girls who enter school roughly equal in abilities and self-esteem tend to leave school deficient in mathematical ability and in self-esteem, as compared with boys. What causes this change? Research has shown that girls receive less attention from teachers and that curricula emphasize achievements of boys almost exclusively (C. Nelson, 1990; Sadker & Sadker, 1984). It appears also that early adolescence is a particularly difficult time for girls. Researchers Annie Rogers and Carol Gilligan (1988) found that girls are extremely self-confident until the age of 11 or 12, when they become increasingly conflicted about themselves and their roles in the world. In later adolescence, girls often cope with negative body image, low self-esteem, and depression. Some researchers point to social inequality as the source of adolescent turmoil in girls (AAUW, 1992). They therefore recommend changes in educational policy.

Some of the differences in boys' and girls' self-esteem may develop because of gender-related messages they receive in school (Martin, Ruble, & Szkrybalo, 2002; Ruble & Martin, 1998). The power structure is usually male-dominated. In some elementary schools, the only male member of the faculty may be the principal. Teachers also often pay more attention to boys than to girls, perhaps because of the teachers' own socialization. The result is that girls become more and more likely to underachieve academically as they get older (Eccles et al., 1993; Eccles, Wigfield, & Schiefele, 1998).

Our self-evaluations become more complex, more differentiated, and more psychological and abstract across the life span. In childhood and adolescence, we increasingly consider what others think and say about us. We also become more concerned about how they behave toward us. We may even internalize what we perceive others to believe about us. In adulthood, we continue to consider our perceptions of how others feel about us. But we also measure ourselves against our own internalized criteria. We give more weight to some aspects of ourselves than to others. One characteristic that may affect how others feel about us is our temperament.

TEMPERAMENT

Some people get angry easily but get over it quickly. Others are slow to anger but have more difficulty recovering. Still others rarely get angry at all. Differences such as these are a matter of temperament—the individual tendency to feel a given emotion with a particular intensity and duration. Temperament is relatively consistent across situations and over time (Kagan, 2001; Rothbart & Bates, 1998). Caspi, Elder, and Herbener (1990) studied consistency of tempera-

ment in a project conducted in Berkeley, California. They found that children 8, 9, and 10 years of age who were ill-tempered were also ill-tempered at age 30. Moreover, they tended to show a variety of maladaptive personality characteristics as well as relatively poor performance at work. Temperament involves both emotional and self-regulatory aspects. A shy child, for example, may be fearful in response to others—an emotional response—but

Children can show a wide variety of emotions, such as anger, patience, and contemplativeness.

also inhibited in dealing with them—a matter of self-regulation (Kagan, 1998). Temperament is shaped by genetic as well as environmental factors (Caspi, 1998; Kagan, Snidman, & Arcus, 1998; Lerner, 2002). It influences the development of personality and therefore of relationships (Thompson, 1999).

Some of the best-known and most highly regarded work on temperament was done by A. Thomas and Stella Chess, who conducted a longitudinal study of children from birth until adolescence (e.g., A. Thomas & Chess, 1977, 1987; A. Thomas, Chess, & Birch, 1970). The study found three types of temperament in babies. *Easy babies* constituted roughly 40% of the sample. They were playful, adaptable, and regular in their eating and other bodily functions. They were interested in novel situations and responded moderately to them. *Difficult babies* constituted 10% of the sample. They were irritable and not very adaptable. They avoided unfamiliar situations and reacted intensely to them. *Slow-to-warm-up babies* constituted 15% of the sample. They had relatively low activity levels and showed minimal responses to novelty. They disliked new situations and needed more time than other babies to adapt to them. Unfortunately, more than one in every three babies, the

remaining 35%, could not be classified according to these criteria. Nevertheless, the categories have proven helpful in understanding temperament.

To what extent do differences in infant temperament remain stable throughout development? Several studies (Kagan & Moss, 1962; Kagan, Reznick, Clarke, Snidman, & Garcia-Coll, 1984) have found consistency in temperament over time. In one study, children identified as either highly inhibited or essentially fearless at 21 months showed similar patterns at age 4. In particular, three-fourths of the inhibited children remained inhibited. None of the children who had been fearless became inhibited. Calkins and Fox (1994) also found that inhibited behavior in childhood was predicted by temperamental characteristics during infancy.

HOW TEMPERAMENT AFFECTS SOCIAL DEVELOPMENT

At first glance, temperament research seems only to state the obvious. Is it really surprising that two categories of babies are "easy" and "difficult"? Can categorizing children really change the way we look at them? Yes. In fact, Thomas and Chess's work profoundly changed the way we view the *person–environment interaction*. Prior to the work of Thomas and Chess, countless books were written to tell parents how to create a good environment for children, in general. The Thomas and Chess findings, however, suggested that we ought to ask: Which environment is best for this particular baby? Clearly, no two people are the same at any age, and the right nurturing atmosphere is different for different babies. This conclusion was the true gift of the research by Thomas and Chess.

EVALUATING THE INFLUENCE OF TEMPERAMENT

The idea that environment should be matched to temperament has not been universally accepted (e.g., Kagan, 1982; Wasserman, Di Basio, Bond, Young, & Collett, 1990). Thomas and Chess suggested that difficult children are essentially unmodifiable. They believed that attempts by parents to change them would only increase their resistance. According to the researchers, parents of these children need patience more than anything else. But consider some of the implications of this notion. One is that some babies are, in a sense, preferable to others. The terms *easy* and *difficult* reflect value judgments, and the danger in using them is that parents might think that their "difficult" children are inferior. Moreover, grave dangers are associated with the risk of self-fulfilling prophecies. Once people rightly or wrongly assign the "difficult" label, they may treat the child accordingly. Eventually the child may fulfill the prophecy by behaving according to expectations. Even worse, the misbehaving child may then become vulnerable to abuse (Starr, Dietrich, Fischoff, Ceresnie, & Zweier, 1984).

A second implication is that parents should not blame themselves for their children's temperaments. Parents are responsible for guiding and sometimes even controlling their children's behavior. But they are not necessarily the causes of that behavior. From an (E) evolutionary point of view, there is no one "better" type of person. The adaptive value of different attributes differs from time to time, place to place, and person to person. In fact, few people have a single type of temperament. Genes that might have committed people to one type only would have lost out evolutionarily to genes that provided a more flexible personality (Trivers, 1971; Wright, 1994). In personality and temperament, as in other attributes, the flexible individual has the greatest advantage.

PSYCHOSEXUAL DEVELOPMENT AND THEORIES OF GENDER TYPING

During **psychosexual development,** children increasingly identify with a particular gender. On average, more rapid psychosexual development tends to be advantageous for boys but not for girls (Ge, Conger, & Elder, 2001). But children of either sex who develop rapidly may experience more stress if they are not prepared for and able to understand their own rate of development (J. M. Williams & Dunlop, 1999). During development, juvenile perceptions about sexuality change. Although adolescence is obviously a period of rapid psychological and sexual growth, most developmental psychologists believe that psychosexual identity begins to develop much earlier. In fact, most children form gender identifications by the age of 2 or 3 (R. F. Thompson, 1975). **Gender typing** is the process of assuming the roles and associations related to the social and psychological definitions of male or female. Until they are about 7, most children view sex roles rigidly. Soon they develop **gender constancy,** the recognition that gender is stable and cannot be altered by changing superficial characteristics or behaviors. For example, they understand that carrying a purse does not change a man into a woman.

BIOLOGICAL AND SOCIOBIOLOGICAL THEORIES

Biological theories of sex-role acquisition (e.g., Benbow & Stanley, 1980) hold that boys and girls acquire different sex roles because they are genetically predisposed to do so. Sociobiological theorists (Kenrick & Trost, 1993) (E) hold that evolution determines or at least guides social behavior, including behavior associated with sex roles (Buss, 1996). Obviously, many sexual characteristics are biologically based. Men and women are indisputably physically different. Still, men are often perceived to be more dominant than women or more likely to be interested in sports. Are such beliefs correct? If so, are these patterns of behavior biological? Or do they result from *socialization,* the process by which we learn how to feel, think, and act by observing and imitating parents, siblings, peers, and other role models?

SOCIAL-LEARNING THEORY

Social-learning theory attributes psychosexual development to role modeling and the prospect of external rewards (Bandura, 1977b). In this view, gender typing is no different from other kinds of social learning. Adults and peers reward boys for behavior they consider masculine and punish boys if they stray from the gender-appropriate role. Girls are similarly rewarded for emulating female role models and punished for deviating from the social norm. Thus, each generation repeats the sex-role patterns of the past, with modifications that reflect the times.

Social (also called observational) learning is clearly important in establishing gender identity. Parents bolster their children's social observations by encouraging gender-specific behaviors. For example, parents are more likely to encourage independence, competitiveness, and achievement in boys, and sensitivity, empathy, and trustworthiness in girls (Archer & Lloyd, 1985; Block, 1980, 1983; A. C. Huston, Carpenter, Atwater, & Johnson, 1986). Whereas boys are encouraged to act on their own, girls are encouraged to request help and to help others (A. C. Huston, 1983).

Both girls and boys may behave in ways that are stereotypically "feminine" or "masculine" in western cultures. Just as often, they may not.

The most important period of gender-role development is during high school, college, and early adulthood. At that time, young adults consciously look for models. The role-modeling function of a respected adult is often more important than the knowledge he or she may wish to impart. In gender identity as in other areas of life, role modeling is not only an abstract psychological idea but also an active process by which we develop our unique identities. Who we become depends partly on our schemas.

SCHEMA THEORY

Sandra Bem (1981, 1993) proposed a cognitively based **schema theory,** which holds that we mentally organize information into systems (i.e., *schemas*) that help us make sense of our experiences and shape our interactions. Gender schemas differ for boys and girls and for men and women. We acquire sex roles by following our gender-appropriate schemas. Individuals socially construct their concepts about gender with the help of those around them (Beall & Sternberg,

1993, 1995; Eagly, Beall, & Sternberg, in press). We acquire our schemas through interactions with the environment. But these interactions in turn affect how others respond to us. For example, a man who learns that toughness is part of being "male" may be tough toward others, who may respond unsympathetically. In general, schema theory focuses on concepts that individuals may incorporate into their schemas rather than on the development of an integrated, global concept of gender.

CONCLUSIONS ABOUT GENDER-ROLE DEVELOPMENT

Gender theories typically treat masculinity and femininity as opposite ends of a continuum. But it is important to point out that these extremes are by no means universally accepted. Some theorists do not see masculinity and femininity as mutually exclusive constructs (e.g., S. L. Bem, 1981). They suggest that someone can be both masculine and feminine simultaneously. Some have argued that theories of gender typing should incorporate the concept of *androgyny*, which applies both to someone who has many masculine and feminine qualities and to someone for whom stereotypically masculine and feminine behaviors are simply not very relevant. Using schema theory, we would say that an androgynous person does not have very strong sex-based schemas. This individual acts in ways that seem appropriate to the situation, regardless of stereotypical expectations about how members of each gender should act.

Although nature determines anatomical differences, our schemas for boys and girls influence the way we perceive our children. They also affect how our children respond to us. Quite simply, there is no foolproof way to separate the effects of biology from the effects of the environment.

We have been focusing on *intrapersonal development*, which occurs within, as exemplified by emotional and personality development. Next we consider the relationship between our *interpersonal* interactions and our individual development.

✓ CONCEPT CHECK 2

1. According to Erikson, the very first challenge infants face is that of
   a. autonomy versus shame and doubt.
   b. trust versus mistrust.
   c. initiative versus guilt.
   d. shame versus inferiority.

2. Which of the following is *not* one of the temperaments in Chess and Thomas's theory?
   a. easy
   b. difficult
   c. fast to warm up
   d. slow to warm up

3. According to social-learning theory, boys often act in stereotypical "male" ways because they are
   a. hard-wired to do so.
   b. rewarded for doing so.
   c. forced to do so.
   d. punished if they do anything else.

INTERPERSONAL DEVELOPMENT

How do we develop interpersonal skills?

Throughout childhood and adolescence we are increasingly aware of others and consider their perspectives more and more. In this section, we consider the ways we interact directly with others, starting with our parents and progressing outward into the wider community.

ATTACHMENT

Attachment is a strong and relatively long-lasting emotional tie (Bowlby, 1969). Our first attachment begins to form at birth (earlier, according to some mothers) and is usually fully established within several years. Mary Ainsworth and her colleagues (Ainsworth, Bell, & Stayton, 1971; Ainsworth, Blehar, Waters, & Wall, 1978) studied attachment by using a research paradigm known as the **strange situation,** in which a child is separated and then reunited with a caregiver. The paradigm capitalizes on **separation anxiety,** a child's generalized fear of being separated from a primary caregiver or other familiar adult. In this paradigm, the research participants are usually a child 12 to 18 months old and the toddler's mother. They enter a room that contains a variety of toys. The mother puts the infant down and sits in a chair. A few minutes later, an unfamiliar woman enters. She talks to the mother and then tries to play with the child. While the stranger is trying to engage the child, the mother quietly walks out, leaving her purse on the chair to indicate that she will be back. An observer positioned behind a one-way mirror records the child's reactions to the mother's return. Still later, the mother leaves again, but this time the child is

FIGURE 11.4

Strange Situation. Researchers observe the attachment of children to their mothers by noting how each child reacts to the "strange situation," the mother's departure and return.

left alone, without the strange woman. The mother returns once more, and the observer again records the child's reactions (see Figure 11.4). The features of the greatest interest are the child's reaction upon separation from the mother and then the child's reaction upon reunion with the mother.

Ainsworth noticed that children's reactions tend to fit one of three patterns: avoidant, secure, and resistant. In the **avoidant attachment pattern** ("Type A"), the child generally ignores the mother and shows minimal distress when she leaves. If the child does show distress, the stranger is about as effective as the mother in providing comfort. In the **secure attachment pattern** ("Type B"), the child generally shows preferential interest in the mother but not excessive dependence on her. The child shows some distress when the mother leaves but can be cuddled and calmed when she returns. The secure child is friendly with the stranger but shows an obvious preference for the mother. In the **resistant attachment pattern** ("Type C"), the child generally shows ambivalence toward the mother, seeking both to gain and to resist physical contact when she returns after a short time. For example, the child might first run to the mother but then wiggle away from her embrace.

A *disorganized attachment pattern* (Main & Solomon, 1990) has also been proposed, which is related to the avoidant and resistant patterns. When babies with this attachment pattern are reunited with their mothers, they seem confused and disoriented, as though they are not sure what is happening to them.

Attachment research originally focused on the role of the mother in the life of the infant. It later turned to the role of the father and others as well (Coley, 2001; Ricks, 1985). Infants do become attached to fathers, protesting separations from about 7 months of age (Lamb, 1977a, 1977b, 1979, 1996). At home, infants approach their fathers, smile at them, and seek contact with them. Fathers who feed their 3-month-old babies can show the same sensitivity to cues as do mothers. But fathers rarely use this skill. They usually yield the feeding function to the mother (Parke & Sawin, 1980; Parke & Tinsley, 1987).

When the father substitutes for the mother in the strange situation, the child uses the father as a haven. Children prefer fathers to a strange woman as well. In addition, infants who are cared for by their fathers while their mothers are at work are more likely to show secure attachment than are infants who are cared for outside the home (Belsky & Rovine, 1988).

Fathers seem to provide a different kind of care from mothers. They tend to be more active in playing with their children (Clarke-Stewart, Perlmutter, & Friedman, 1988; Parke, 1981, 1996). They also engage

Fathers have become much more involved in child care than they were in times past.

in more novel games (Lamb, 1977b). One study found that two-thirds of toddlers prefer playing with their fathers to playing with their mothers (Clarke-Stewart, 1978). Also, the relationship between toddlers and their fathers may be more instrumental in helping the infants to widen their social contacts and to interact sociably with persons outside their families (Bridges, Connell, & Belsky, 1988).

Caregiving has lasting biological as well as socio-emotional effects. If the early experiences of an infant with respect to caregiving are stressful or if the mother is seriously depressed, such experiences can have lasting effects on the development of the child's neuro-biological functioning (Dawson & Ashman, 2000; Gunnar, 2000; Gunnar & Davis, 2003; Thompson, Easterbrooks, & Padilla-Walker, 2003). Similar effects are associated with lower socioeconomic status of the family (DiPietro, Costigan, Shupe, Pressman, & Johnson, 1999), presumably because mothers experience more stress in such environments. Poverty and sometimes physical danger associated with some low-income neighborhoods are stressors on parents and children alike (Duncan & Brooks-Gunn, 1997; Fitzgerald, Zucker, & Yang, 1995; Zucker et al., 2000). Interestingly, a child whose stress level is low is less

likely to stress the mother (Gunnar, 2000). This reciprocal effect shows that development is a system, not a simple linear process (Sameroff, 2000).

EVALUATING ATTACHMENT THEORY

Just how much credence can we give to attachment theory, as measured by the strange situation? Researchers differ in their views. Some are skeptical (e.g., Kagan, 1986). The strange situation has a number of possible limitations. First, an infant's attachment pattern appears not to be highly stable. In one study, roughly half of the infants classified one way at age 12 months were classified another way at 18 months (R. A. Thompson, Lamb, & Estes, 1982). Second, the strange situation may measure temperament at least as much as attachment. Highly independent infants might be classified as avoidant. Likewise, infants who are upset by almost any new situation, regardless of whether it involves the mother, might be classified as ambivalent or resistant. Third, the experiment itself is brief, typically lasting only 6 to 8 minutes. How much can we tell about infants, or anyone, in such a short time? Fourth, the implied value judgments in the terms used for classification are open to question. Finally, societal norms and cultural mores can also affect attachment patterns (Colin, 1996; R. A. Thompson, 1998). Thus, the attachment patterns that are valued in one culture may be less valued in another.

Socioeconomic status and environment also seem to play roles in attachment patterns. Ainsworth worked primarily with American middle-class children from stable homes during the 1970s. She found that about 20% to 25% of children were avoidant, roughly 65% were secure, and approximately 12% were resistant. Different patterns appear among children in other cultural and socioeconomic contexts, however. Children in nonstable, nonintact American families of lower socioeconomic status are more likely to be considered avoidant or resistant (Egeland & Sroufe, 1981; Vaughn, Gove, & Egeland, 1980). Studies of other cultures have shown more avoidant children in Western Europe and more resistant children in Israel and Japan (Bretherton & Waters, 1985; Miyake, Chen, & Campos, 1985; Morelli, Rogoff, Oppenheim, & Goldsmith, 1992). German children are more likely to show avoidant attachment behavior, but they are encouraged to be independent at an early age. Why should we categorize such an independent pattern as somehow less than secure? Clearly, values regarding attachment patterns differ across cultures (R. A. Thompson, 1998).

Do attachment patterns have any long-term consequences? If so, what are they? John Bowlby (1951, 1969) claimed that an infant's attachment pattern has long-term effects on the child's development. Evidence supports this claim. For example, infants who are securely attached at age 12 to 18 months approach

© Bill Lai/Rainbow

Attachment does not end in childhood; it is crucial to the establishment of intimacy. One of the main purposes of intimate relationships is to give adults comfort in times of need.

problems at age 2 with greater interest and enthusiasm than do avoidant or resistant children (Matas, Arend, & Sroufe, 1978). Similarly, securely attached children in nursery school tend to be more active, more sought out by other children, and rated by their teachers as more eager to learn (Waters, Wippman, & Sroufe, 1979). In other words, secure attachment in infancy predicts advantages in both cognitive and social adaptation later on.

ADULT ATTACHMENT

Attachment does not end in childhood. Robert Weiss (1982) observed that adults, like children, tend to attach themselves to others. Attachment is crucial to the establishment of intimacy. Indeed, intimate relationships give adults someone to comfort them in times of need. Intimate relationships also provide them with something resembling the closeness they once had with a childhood attachment figure. We still lack sufficient hard data to assert unequivocally that the quality of our early attachments to our parents affects the quality of our attachments as adults. But some evidence suggests this relationship (Feeney & Noller, 1990; Hazan & Shaver, 1994; Main, Kaplan, & Cassidy, 1985; Scharfe & Bartholomew, 1994).

Adults who have secure styles of attachment tend to be comfortable about, and to speak freely about, their relationship with their parents. People with a resistant style appear to be ambivalent about, and sometimes anxiously preoccupied with, these relationships. People with an avoidant style tend to try to dissociate themselves from feelings of attachment toward their parents, thereby avoiding anxiety about their relationship (Dozier & Kobak, 1992).

ATTACHMENT GONE AWRY

Children become attached to both mothers and fathers. Members of the family or extended family can help compensate for an infant's inadequate attachment to the mother (Parke & Asher, 1983). But what happens when children are deprived of love and warmth from both father and mother? Do attachment processes fail to form or go utterly awry? No scientist would conduct an experiment that purposely exposes children to inadequate or distorted attachment. However, two methods enable researchers to examine such situations. One is the unfortunate instance in which naturalistic observation of extremely deprived children is possible. The other is controlled experimentation with animals.

In one case of extreme deprivation, a girl named Genie was isolated in a small room (Curtiss, 1977), as discussed in Chapter 8. From roughly ages 2 to 13, she was strapped to a potty chair. Genie's only contact with humans was when a family member entered the room to give her food. When found at age 13, Genie could not walk, talk, stand up straight, or eat solid food. Nor was she toilet-trained. Eventually, Genie did learn to speak a bit. But she never progressed beyond the level of a 4- to 5-year-old. Initially, Genie showed exciting improvements. An onslaught of social scientists and social workers of all kinds then descended on her. Genie now lives in an institution for retarded adults (Angier, 1993; Rymer, 1993). We must be wary of the conclusions we reach based on anecdotal evidence, however rich the case material. But we can reasonably conclude that Genie was severely and permanently harmed by her lack of contact with loving, caring humans.

The other kind of research, controlled experimentation with animals, enables researchers to study attachment processes more directly (Harlow, 1958, 1962; Harlow & Harlow, 1965, 1966). In a series of experiments, Harry Harlow, Margaret Harlow, and other researchers raised infant monkeys with either or both of two substitute mothers. One was a wire mesh cylinder, the other a cylinder covered with soft terrycloth. Either "mother" could be set up with a bottle providing milk. Even when only the wire mother could provide milk, however, the monkeys still clung to the cloth mother. Their behavior suggests that comfort through physical contact was more important than nourishment. The monkeys also showed other signs of attachment to the cloth mother but not to the wire mother. When a frightening, noisy, bear-monster doll was placed next to the monkeys, those raised with the cloth mother would run to it and cling. But later they would investigate the monster. The monkeys raised with the wire mother, however, just clutched themselves and rocked back and forth (see Figure 11.5).

On the one hand, the cloth mother but not the wire mother fostered attachment and security. On the other, ultimately neither surrogate proved adequate for fostering normal social development. Monkeys reared with either of the surrogate mothers were socially and sexually incompetent. Females who them-

FIGURE 11.5

"Mother Love" in Primates. Harry Harlow's revolutionary research on the importance of "contact comfort" revealed that infant rhesus monkeys would become attached to—and seek comfort from—a cloth "mother" rather than a wire "mother." Even when the wire mother provided milk and the cloth mother did not, the infants clung to the cloth mother. (After Harlow Primate Lab, University of Wisconsin)

selves later had children were poor mothers. Live, interactive attachment processes, therefore, appear to be crucial for the development of later social and familial competence, both in humans and in animals.

As you think about this research, keep in mind that standards for experimentation with nonhuman animals are higher today than they were in the 1950s and 1960s, when Harlow's work was done. If the research had been conducted more recently, stricter controls on the well-being of the animals probably would have been implemented.

In sum, attachment is an essential part of development, and it continues to play a role throughout our lives. Although the patterns themselves may not yet be understood fully, their influence is clear. In addition to the quality of attachment patterns, other aspects of the child–parent relationship are important to the development of later social competence. See the Psychology in Everyday Life box, "Parenting Styles," to learn how different ways of expressing parental authority can affect how children see themselves in relation to others.

An entirely different avenue of research suggests that being away from parents for a portion of the day

may also affect children's social competence. Children who attend child-care programs tend to be more likely to interact spontaneously with other children than do those who do not attend. Participation in child care is not unequivocally beneficial, however, as the next section explains.

EFFECTS OF CHILD CARE ON CHILDREN'S DEVELOPMENT

Given the importance of both the child's attachment to the parents and parental style, how does child care affect the social development of children of various ages? In the United States, an estimated three-fourths of mothers with children ages 6 to 17 work outside the home. Almost 58% of mothers with children younger than 6 years do so (H. A. Scarr, 1994). Overall, more than half of infants under the age of 12 months are routinely receiving care from someone other than their mothers (National Institute of Child Health and Human Development, 1996). Roughly 61% of children 4 years of age and younger have participated in some kind of regularly scheduled child care (Fitzgerald, Mann, Cabrera, & Wong, 2003, citing a 1999 National

We know that large differences exist in how parents bring up their children, differences not only across individuals but also across levels of education and socioeconomic status. For example, parents with lower levels of education and socioeconomic status are more likely to value obedience to authority and are more likely to use physical punishment. Parents with higher socioeconomic status and education levels are more likely to explain their actions and to let children make decisions for themselves (M. L. Kohn, 1976).

Research by Diana Baumrind (1971, 1978) suggests that parental styles of caring for children can be viewed in terms of three categories: authoritarian, permissive, and authoritative. Authoritarian mothers and fathers exhibit a style of parenting in which they tend to be firm, punitive, and generally unsympathetic to their children. These parents believe in the importance of their authority, and they value their children's obedience. They see children as willful and in need of disciplining to meet parental standards. Authoritarian parents are somewhat detached from their children and tend to be sparing with praise. Permissive mothers and fathers exhibit a style of parenting in which they tend to give their children a great deal of freedom, possibly more than the children can handle. These parents tend to be

lax in discipline and to let children make their own decisions about many things that other parents might find inappropriate. Authoritative mothers and fathers exhibit a style of parenting in which they tend to encourage and support responsibility and reasoning in their children, explain their reasoning for what they do, and establish firm limits within which they encourage children to be independent, and which they enforce firmly but with understanding. The actual situation is a bit more complicated than one with only three styles of parenting. A father's parenting style may differ from the mother's so that there is no consistent style within the family. In extended families, grandparents or other relatives may become involved in child care, resulting in even greater mixtures.

© Research on 186 cultures (Rohner & Rohner, 1981) showed that the authoritative parenting style seemed to be the most common. Nonetheless, there are wide variations in the nurturance and control exhibited by parents, and cultural expressions of nurturance and control may differ greatly. Japanese mothers, whose interactions tend to foster warm and close relationships with their children, may exert firm behavioral control over their children by merely suggesting indirectly how the child's behavior may affect the quality of the relationship

(Azuma, 1986). Japanese mothers are also likely to respond in a more animated fashion when infants are attending to them. American parents, in contrast, are more responsive when infants look at objects rather than at them (Bornstein, Tal, & Tamis-LeMonda, 1991; Bornstein, Toda, Azuma, Tamis-LeMonda, & Ogino, 1990). Puerto Rican mothers tend to be more likely physically to restrain infants and to give them direct commands than are parents from the mainland United States (Harwood, Scholmerich, & Schulze, 2000).

As you might expect, different parental styles lead to varying outcomes for the children (Baumrind, 1971, 1978, 1991). Children of authoritarian parents tend to be unfriendly, distrustful of others, and somewhat withdrawn in their social relationships. Children of permissive parents tend to be immature and dependent, seeking aid for even minor difficulties. They also tend to be unhappy in their lives in general. Children of authoritative parents seem to be the most well adapted. They tend to be friendly, generally cooperative, and relatively independent, showing a sense of responsibility in their social relations with others.

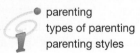

parenting
types of parenting
parenting styles

Household Survey). Included in these figures are 44% of infants under 1 year of age, 53% of 1-year-olds, and 57% of 2-year-olds. It is important to understand the effects of child care.

The National Institute of Health and Human Development (NICHD) Study of Early Child Care was designed to evaluate the effects of caregivers other than parents on a broad range of outcomes for children, including cognitive as well as social ones. The study took an ecological approach to understanding child development in the context of the environment in which

children grow up (Bronfenbrenner & Morris, 1998). There were 10 different data-collection sites across the United States. The study found that mothers with higher incomes and families that were dependent on the mother's income were more likely to place their children in care at an earlier age. Generally, more positive child-care outcomes were associated with smaller groups, higher adult-child ratios, and caregivers who hold less authoritarian beliefs about raising children. Safe, clean, and stimulating environments also helped (National Institute of Child Health and Human

Day care may take place in a licensed caregiver's home, or in a formal school-like setting.

Development Early Child Care Research Network, 1994, 1996, 1997, 2000).

A summary of five studies of children's responses to the strange situation revealed that 74% of infants who participated in child care fewer than 20 hours per week were securely attached. In contrast, 57% of infants who participated in child care more than 20 hours per week were securely attached (Belsky & Rovine, 1988). As noted earlier, one can debate the merits of determining attachment based on the strange situation. Nevertheless, it appears that increased participation in child care is associated with a decreased likelihood of being securely attached. The majority of infants in the studies were still securely attached, however.

Other factors influence the outcomes of infants' participation in child care. A mother's stress level will affect her behavior toward her child and can even have an effect on unborn infants. Mothers who experience more stress are more likely to have fetuses with higher heart rates and lower birth weights (Huizink, de Medina, Mulder, Visser, & Buitelaar, 2000; Wadhwa, Sandman, & Garite, 2001). For example, mothers who work part-time rather than full-time may feel less stress (L. W. Hoffman, 1989). Moreover, mothers who can cope more successfully with their employment are more likely to have securely attached infants (Belsky & Rovine, 1988). Another stress reducer for mothers is the participation of fathers in child care and in household chores (L. W. Hoffman, 1989).

An extensive body of research (Andersson, 1989; Belsky, 1990; Clarke-Stewart, 1989, 1993; T. M. Field, 1990; Gottfried & Gottfried, 1988; L. W. Hoffman, 1989) regarding preschoolers and school-aged children yields mixed results. Some research indicates the benefits of early child care, such as sociability and greater academic success (Andersson, 1989; T. M. Field, 1990). Other research indicates some drawbacks of early child care, such as increased aggressive behavior and increased desire for approval by peers. But these patterns appeared only when specific efforts to curb such behaviors were not implemented in the child-care setting (Clarke-Stewart, 1989, 1993).

Perhaps the most useful lesson from this research is the importance of evaluating and considering the quality of the specific child-care program. Children in high-quality daycare are better self-regulated, more task-oriented, more considerate, less distracting toward other children, and less hostile than children in low-quality daycare (Howes, 1990). Many factors influence the quality of the program, but the single most important is the amount and quality of the attention given to children. As you might expect, caregivers are better able to provide more high-quality attention to each child when they are in charge of fewer children. Individual attention is particularly important for infants and toddlers. In addition, the professional qualifications of the caregivers (S. Scarr, Phillips, & McCartney, 1990) and the stability of the center's work force affect the quality of the program. These facts are especially understandable when one considers that annual turnover of 50% is the average for these poorly paid professionals (Wingert & Kantrowitz, 1990). Highly qualified professionals who are motivated to remain in the program can provide child-centered activities that are appropriately challenging to children's needs. Such activities involve open-ended, creative, hands-on exploration of a wide array of materials. What seems to matter most is not whether children are in a child-care program but, if they are, which child-care program they are in.

Some child-care programs are federally subsidized and, to some extent, organized. An example is Head Start, a federally funded program for improving the cognitive and social development of children from low-income families. Roughly 10% of the funding is for Early Head Start, a program for infants and toddlers (Jerald, 2000; Raikes & Love, 2002). Head Start does not have a single curriculum, but rather varies somewhat across sites (Fenichel & Mann, 2001). The program appears to have a modestly positive influence on development—in particular, with respect to cognitive and language skills and reduced levels of aggression. It had no effect on toddlers' emotional regulation or interactions with parents (Commissioner's Office of Research and Evaluation, 2001a, 2001b, 2001c).

At any age, an important determinant of successful development is **resilience,** the ability of an individual to function well in the face of adversity (Cummings, Braungart-Rieker, & DuRocher-Schudlich, 2003). The development of resilience is fostered by good child care, whether inside or outside the home. Characteristics of resilient children are good intellectual functioning, sociability, self-confidence, an easy-going disposition, and a belief in one's ability to do what needs to be done (Masten, 1999, 2001; Masten & Coatsworth, 1998; Perkins & Borden, 2003). Resilience is not necessarily equal across domains. Children may be resilient with respect, say, to problems with other children, but not with respect to problems with parents, or vice versa (Luthar & Cushing, 1999; Luthar, Cicchetti, & Becker, 2000).

An additional consideration in evaluating high-quality child-care programs must be the kinds of social relationships and social behaviors the caregivers encourage among the children.

PEER INTERACTIONS: FRIENDSHIP AND PLAY

An important aspect of interpersonal development is learning how to interact with peers and to form friendships. Indeed, social rejection by peer groups is one of the best predictors of school failure and dropout (Rubin, Bukowski, & Parker, 1998; Rubin, Coplan, Nelson, Cheah, & Lagace-Seguin, 1999). Relationships with peers during childhood are of course important for a child's well-being. But they also matter for the well-being of the adult that the child will become. A. F. Newcomb, Bukowski, and Pattee (1993) have referred to children as falling into distinct categories: *popular* (sociable, well-liked), *rejected* (usually because they are either aggressive or withdrawn), *controversial* (social but often aggressive as well, so that they are liked by some but disliked by others), and *neglected* (usually less sociable and less aggressive than peers, and seldom mentioned by other children in their peer group).

Children interact more with peers as they grow older. Infants are likely to cry if they see or hear another infant crying. By about 3 or 4 months, they reach toward and even touch one another when they can (Vandell & Mueller, 1980). They also often smile at one another. But until 1 year of age, their exchanges usually are limited to one overture followed by one response. During the next couple of years, play interactions increase. By age 2, children would rather play near each other than by themselves. By ages 4 to 5, they prefer some playmates to others, and start to refer to each other as friends. Thus, at this age, true friendship is starting (Hartup & Stevens, 1999; Ladd, 1999). Children learn gradually to cooperate, share, and play with one another. Friendships appear to teach children conflict-resolution techniques. Indeed, friends are more likely than nonfriends to resolve conflicts effectively (Hartup, 1996; A. F. Newcomb & Bagwell, 1995). Preschoolers show stable friendship patterns, often keeping the same friend for more than a year (Howes, 1988).

Play continues to be at the center of friendships during most of childhood (Gottman, 1983, 1986; Howes, 1988). According to John Gottman (1983), friends of ages 3 to 9 increasingly share thoughts and feelings, exchange information, establish common ground, resolve conflicts, deliberately please each other, and confide intimate details about themselves. These qualities also characterize friendships among adults.

Although parents may be in the background, they contribute to children's friendships in three ways (Parke & O'Neil, 1997, 1998). First, they can serve as interactive partners who help their youngsters acquire the skills they need to make friends. Second, they can serve as coaches and educators in teaching their children to get along with others. Third, they can facilitate their children's social interactions with other youngsters.

GENDER DIFFERENCES IN FRIENDSHIPS

During childhood and adolescence, the friendships of boys and of girls pass through different stages. Children of both sexes seem to prefer same-sex friends throughout this period. Moreover, early friendships usually center on shared activities and other interests. The interests and activities of girls and boys differ, however. Boys are more likely to be involved in groups and competitive activities. Girls are more likely to prefer cooperative activities involving just two people.

Adolescent girls' friendships progress through three stages (Douvan & Adelson, 1966). From roughly ages 11 to 13, the emphasis is on joint activities. A friend is someone with whom to do fun things. From roughly ages 14 to 16, friendships pass through an emotional stage. Girls share secrets, especially about other friends, both male and female. Trust is a critical element of friendship at this stage. Across the life span, in fact, women show greater emotional closeness and shared intimacies in their friendships than do men (Berndt, 1982, 1986; K. H. Rubin, 1980). This pattern may be changing, however, as young men and women, particularly the well-educated, now show fewer differences regarding self-disclosure (Peplau, 1983). In late adolescence (age 17 years and beyond), the emphasis shifts to compatibility, shared personalities, and shared interests.

In contrast, boys' friendships are oriented toward joint activities throughout adolescence. For boys, achievement and autonomy are important not only in their development as individuals but also in their friendships. Perhaps as a result, adult men typically report having far fewer close friends than do women.

CHANGES IN SOCIAL AWARENESS IN ADOLESCENCE

Adolescents are well able to consider the thoughts and feelings of friends and others in their interpersonal relationships. But they still show forms of egocentrism, much as younger children do (Elkind, 1967, 1985). A common form of egocentrism in adolescents is the *personal fable*, in which adolescents believe that they—as

Although adolescents can consider the thoughts and feelings of others in interpersonal relationships, they may still think egocentrically by believing they are invincible.

opposed to other persons—are somehow uniquely destined for fame and fortune. They also exhibit an *invincibility fallacy*, by which they believe that they are not vulnerable to the kinds of ill fortune that can befall others. Adolescents are at great risk for dangers ranging from automobile accidents to AIDS because of their belief in their own invincibility. They also often believe in what is known as an *imaginary audience*, the unfounded belief that other people are constantly watching or otherwise paying attention to, as well as judging, them.

Whatever our age and sex, we need to have someone (or ones) in whom we can confide. We need a person on whom we can depend for support, and to whom we are important, special, and needed as givers of support and as recipients of revealing self-disclosures. Across the life span, we improve in our skill at showing friendship toward our friends, a skill that helps us cultivate the special relationship that, for some people, becomes marriage, our next topic.

MARRIAGE AND THE FAMILY

Marriage provides an opportunity for serious intimacy. Most people get married sooner or later. For some people, the institution may be unsuitable because of their individual personalities. In recent years, the trend for those who decide to marry has been to do so later. More and more people have postponed marriage into their late 20s, early 30s, or even later (Sporakowski, 1988). The reasons for postponement include the increasing need and desire of women to support themselves in the work force, the increasing acceptability of being single for longer periods of time, and the tendency even among the earlier married to postpone childbearing.

Satisfaction in marriage tends to be greatest in the early years. It then often falls during child raising. Typically, it increases again in the later years. By this time, children grow older and often start their own lives away from their original families. Thus, the **empty-nest syndrome,** whereby parents adjust to having their children grow up and move out of the family home, can be partially offset by their own newfound happiness with each other.

What makes a happy marriage? According to Gottman (1994), the key is the way a couple resolves the conflicts that are inevitable in any marriage. Gottman has found that three styles can succeed for resolving conflict. In a *validating marriage*, couples compromise often and develop relatively calm ways of resolving conflicts. In a *conflict-avoiding marriage*, couples agree to disagree and avoid conflicts to the extent possible. In a *volatile marriage*, couples have frequent conflicts, some of them very antagonistic. Any one of these styles can work, as long as the number of positive moments the couple has together is at least five times greater than the number of negative moments. Four types of behavior destroy a marriage, according to Gottman. The first is attacking the partner's personality or character rather than his or her particular behavior. A second is showing contempt for a partner. Third is being defensive in response to constructive criticism. Finally, the fourth is stonewalling—failing to respond at all to the concerns of the partner.

Clifford Notarius and Howard Markman (1993) have suggested that one really negative act can erase the effects of 20 acts of kindness. Moreover, it is not the differences between partners that cause problems. Rather, it is how the differences are handled. Notarius and Markman found that they can predict with more than 90% accuracy whether a couple will stay married solely on the basis of how the couple handles conflict. They have devised a questionnaire that assesses conflict-resolution skills. It includes statements such as "I sometimes nag at my partner to get him/her to talk" and "It is very easy for me to get angry at my partner" (Notarius & Markman, 1993, p. 41). "True" answers to these statements tend to be associated with marital unhappiness.

THE WORLD OF WORK

Marriage and family responsibilities are part of many adults' lives. Work is another responsibility. Work provides a way to achieve the money necessary to survive. It also provides the satisfaction that comes from a job well done. As we discuss in the next chapter, individuals tend to be satisfied with their work if it meets two conditions. First, they want it to be *intrinsically rewarding*, or enjoyable in itself. Second, they look for it to be *extrinsically rewarding*, compensating the person in various ways, including financially, for the work.

According to Donald Super (1985), career development has five main stages. In the *growth stage*, from ages 0 to 14, the individual learns about and acquires the ability to pursue a vocation. In the *exploration stage*, from roughly ages 15 to 24, the individual makes a tentative vocational choice and may enter a first job. In the *establishment stage*, from roughly ages 25 to 44, the individual seeks entry into a permanent occupation. In the *maintenance stage*, from roughly 45 to 65, the individual is usually established in the occupation and continues in it. Finally, in the *decline stage*, from roughly age 65 to death, the individual adapts to the notion of leaving and then ultimately retires from the work force. Whereas 30 years ago, this pattern applied almost exclusively to men, today it applies to large numbers of men and women alike. Moreover, the ages at which the stages occur can change over time. Today many people remain in the workplace longer. Some stay with the same jobs for many years. Others retire and find new jobs, often ones that are less demanding than the ones they had held before.

✓ CONCEPT CHECK 3

1. Which of the following is *not* an attachment pattern that emerges from Ainsworth's strange-situation paradigm?
   a. acquiescent
   b. resistant
   c. avoidant
   d. secure
2. Attachment patterns are
   a. identical across all cultures.
   b. identical across Western cultures.
   c. identical across Eastern cultures.
   d. different across cultures, even within a given hemisphere.
3. Many adolescents believe that others are constantly watching them. These others are referred to as
   a. a virtual audience.
   b. an imaginary audience.
   c. fictitious spectators.
   d. factitious spectators.

MORAL DEVELOPMENT

What are the stages in the development of moral reasoning? How, if at all, do they differ between men and women?

As children shift away from a more egocentric orientation toward life, they are better able to understand others' points of view and to formulate moral standards (Eisenberg & Fabes, 1998; Harter, 1998). Children view strictly moral issues as different from social issues (Bersoff & Miller, 1993; Helwig, 1995). They recognize that issues of morality tend to be universal. Social conventions, in contrast, vary from one culture to another. For example, children as young as 6 years of age believe it is wrong to steal. But they recognize that children in other countries play different games (Turiel, 1998). They probably learn these distinctions through interactions with family and community members (Nucci & Weber, 1995). Parents are delegated by society to serve as authorities in moral matters. Even teenagers who reject many aspects of their parents' teachings recognize the parents' societally designated role as moral authorities (Smetana, 1995, 1997; Smetana & Asquith, 1994).

In every generation, young people as well as older ones face moral quandaries. Some moral dilemmas, such as those regarding sex and alcohol, seem to change little over time. But others do change. Some of today's issues are unique. Whereas World War II was widely considered by the U.S. population to be a moral war, there was more disagreement about the 2003 war in Iraq. Thirty years ago, many people questioned the morality of the war in Vietnam. Today, many children face moral dilemmas about designer drugs that did not even exist 30 years ago. And scandals in various churches have led some people to wonder whether organized religion really can provide them the comfort they once thought it could. In any era, moral development is crucial to all of us. The issues may change. But the need to confront moral dilemmas does not.

Theories of moral development must address a number of questions. How do children of different ages perceive their moral responsibilities to others and to themselves? How do these perceptions change, and why? Two major views of moral development are those of Lawrence Kohlberg and of Carol Gilligan. Kohlberg has proposed a model that emphasizes conceptions of justice. Gilligan has argued that Kohlberg's model may apply to men but that it does not apply as well to women, for whom caring is often more important than some abstract concept of justice.

KOHLBERG'S MODEL

HEINZ'S DILEMMA

Kohlberg developed a number of scenarios to assess children's moral development. One of the most famous involves a man, Heinz, who is faced with a serious moral dilemma:

> In Europe, a woman was near death from a rare form of cancer. The doctors thought that one drug might save her: a form of radium a druggist in the same town had recently discovered. The drug was expensive to make, but the druggist was also charging ten times his cost; having paid $400 for the radium, he charged $4,000 for a small dose. The sick woman's husband, Heinz, went to everyone he knew to borrow the money, but he could collect only $2,000. He begged the druggist to sell it more cheaply or to let him pay the balance later, but the druggist refused. So, having tried every legal means, Heinz desperately considered breaking into the drugstore to steal the drug for his wife. (Adapted from Kohlberg, 1963, 1984)

Suppose that you are Heinz. Should you steal the drug? Why or why not? These and similar scenario-related questions form the basis for measuring the development of moral reasoning according to Lawrence Kohlberg's influential model (see Table 11.4).

According to Kohlberg, your answers will depend on your level of moral reasoning. Such reasoning passes through six specific stages, embedded within three general levels. Your solutions do not determine your stage of moral reasoning. Rather, the kinds of reasons you give to justify either stealing or not stealing the drug determine your moral stage. Your ability to produce various kinds of reasons depends critically on your ability to take on other perspectives—to see your actions as others see them (Turiel, 1998).

LEVELS IN KOHLBERG'S MODEL

Level I (ages 7–10) represents **preconventional morality,** in which moral reasoning is guided by *punishments* and *rewards.* In the first stage of this level, *punishment* and *obedience* guide reasoning. Stage 1 children think that it is right to avoid breaking rules because punishment may follow. Obedience to authority is desirable for its own sake. This stage is egocentric in that children do not really consider others' interests. Children simply assume that the perspective of authority figures is correct because the authority figures will punish the children otherwise.

In Stage 2 of preconventional morality, children's orientation shifts to *individualism* and *exchange.* Stage 2 children follow rules, but only when it is to their benefit. Children serve their own interests, but they recognize that other people may have different interests. They therefore strike deals to meet everyone's interests. In this stage of the first level, what children consider to be morally right depends on whatever they will be rewarded for doing.

Level II (ages 10–16 or beyond) involves **conventional morality,** in which moral reasoning is guided by *mutual interpersonal expectations* and *interpersonal conformity.* Upon reaching this level, the individual moves into Stage 3, in which societal rules have become internalized. The individual conforms because it is right to do so. Stage 3 children live up to what others who are important in their lives expect of them. To be good is to have good motives behind their actions and to show concern for other people. They live by the Golden Rule, doing unto others what they would have done unto them. In this stage, children want to maintain rules and authority systems that support conventionally appropriate behavior. They recognize that the needs of the group take primacy over their individual interests.

In Stage 4 of the second level, teens become oriented toward *conscience.* They recognize the importance of the *social system.* In general, they obey laws and fulfill their duties, except in extreme cases when those duties conflict with higher social obligations. Right consists of contributing to and maintaining the society or institutions of which they are a part. They need to think of the consequences if everyone behaves as they do. In this stage, teens distinguish the point of view of society from agreements between individuals. Even if two people agree that something is right, the

TABLE 11.4
CONCEPT REVIEW

Kohlberg's Theory of Development of Moral Reasoning. How did you respond to the dilemma? How did you reach your answer?

Level/Stage	Basis for Reasoning	Why You (as Heinz) Should Steal	Why You (as Heinz) Should Not Steal
Level I: Preconventional Morality (Ages 7–10)			
Stage 1 Do not get caught.	Egocentric consideration of whether a behavior leads to punishment or to reward. "Might makes right," so we should obey authority.	If you do not steal the drug, your wife will be very angry with you, which would be painful. She might even die.	If you were caught you would be punished, and your wife would not get the drug.
Stage 2 What is in it for me?	Give-and-take exchanges guide behavior. Recognition that others have their own interests. Tries to strike deals that serve both parties.	The druggist is making it impossible to make a deal that will work for everyone, forcing you to find another solution. If you can get away with stealing the drug, your wife will be very happy.	If you cannot work out a deal with the druggist, then work out a deal with your wife. She knows that it would not be reasonable to expect you to figure out how to steal the drug without getting caught. Besides, she might die even with the drug, so you would go to jail for no reason.
Level II: Conventional Morality (Ages 10–16 and Usually Beyond)			
Stage 3 I am being good/nice.	Rules of behavior become internalized. Individuals perceive themselves as behaving in ways that are good, appropriate, or nice. They conform to particular behaviors to please others.	Good people take care of the people they love. Even if it means breaking the law, to be a good person you must steal the drug for your wife. People will think you are very kind to your wife.	Good people do not steal. Even if it means that your wife will die, you must not steal. If you do, people will think you are a bad person, but if you don't, they will think you are a good person.
Stage 4 Preserve the social order.	Societal rules form the basis of moral reasoning, which is guided by conscience and respect for the social system.	You must steal the drug because when you married you promised to do all you could to ensure your wife's well-being. Not to steal the drug would be to break your promise.	You must not steal the drug because stealing violates the rules and laws of society.
Level III: Postconventional Morality (Ages 16 and Beyond)			
Stage 5 What ensures the rights and well-being of each person?	Social contracts and individual rights form the basis of moral reasoning.	You must steal the drug because the individual's right to live exceeds society's right to impose property laws.	You must not steal the drug because the life of one individual should not cause you to act in ways that rupture the fabric of society. If you steal, you ultimately harm everyone, including your wife.
Stage 6 What is best from the point of view of each person involved?	Universal principles of justice guide moral reasoning.	You should steal the drug because the principle of preserving life takes precedence over the law against stealing. Even the druggist would be better off because he would not be a party to your wife's death. If you were caught, your case might bring attention to the problems of paying for expensive drugs, so others might benefit even if your wife did not.	You should not steal the drug because your feelings for your wife should not take precedence over the well-being of others. If you steal the drug, others who need it may be deprived. The druggist may even raise the price of the drug.

Stage 4 individual may still consider it wrong from the standpoint of society as a whole.

Level III (ages 16 and beyond) comprises post-conventional morality, which recognizes the importance of *social contracts* and *individual rights*. A person who reaches this level moves on to Stage 5. People hold a wide variety of values and opinions, most of which are essentially relative. But the values should be upheld because they are part of a social contract to which people have agreed. Individuals also have a few values and rights, such as the rights of life and liberty. These should be protected and safeguarded regardless of the opinion of the majority of individuals or authority figures in a given society. (Interestingly, this assertion is in itself a moral judgment.) Persons in Stage 5 define right in terms of a sense of obligation to the law. People need to abide by laws to protect everyone and bring about the greatest good for the greatest number of people. Sometimes, however, moral and legal points of view conflict, with no easy resolution. Only about one-fifth of adolescents reach Stage 5.

In Stage 6, which Kohlberg believed few people reach, individuals are oriented toward *universal principles of justice*. They believe that it is right to follow universal ethical principles, which they have chosen after considerable thoughtful reflection. Most laws and social agreements are valid because they follow such principles. But if laws violate these principles, Stage 6 individuals believe that they must act according to their own principles. They seek to uphold universal principles. They are personally committed to these principles, whether others adhere to them or not.

Developmental changes in moral development seem to level off in early adulthood, but college education seems to facilitate continued development. For those who attend college, the onset of the plateau occurs later and generally at a higher level than for those who do not attend college (Rest & Thoma, 1985; see also Finger, Borduin, & Baumstark, 1992; see Figure 11.6).

EVALUATION OF KOHLBERG'S MODEL
Responses to Kohlberg's model are decidedly mixed. Some research has been supportive. Other psychologists also have found that complexity of moral reasoning increases with age roughly along the lines Kohlberg suggested (e.g., Rest, 1983). Moreover, research with members of other cultures in places such as Turkey (Nisan & Kohlberg, 1982) and Israel (Snarey, Reimer, & Kohlberg, 1985a, 1985b) has been rather supportive of Kohlberg's theory.

Despite this supporting evidence, however, Kohlberg's theory has been highly controversial. First, the theory has been criticized because Kohlberg's moral dilemmas do not adequately represent situations commonly confronted by children and adoles-

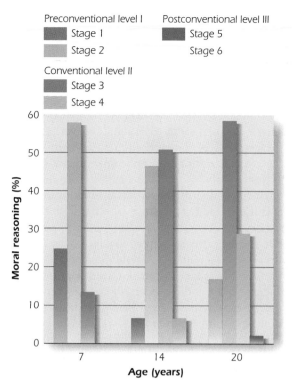

FIGURE 11.6
Developmental Changes in Moral Reasoning.
Preconventional reasoning sharply decreases and postconventional reasoning slightly increases across the span of childhood and adolescence. Stage 6 is extremely rare, representing an ideal, not a common occurrence. (After Colby, Kohlberg, Gibbs, & Liberman, 1983)

cents (Yussen, 1977). Second, Kohlberg's scoring is very subjective. Furthermore, interview-based scoring is difficult, and Kohlberg's highly detailed criteria complicate matters even further.

A third criticism is about the fixed-stage progression that Kohlberg's theory postulates (Kurtines & Greif, 1974). For one thing, people's responses may differ depending on which scenario is used for the assessment. Some people may skip stages (Holstein, 1976). Others may regress to earlier stages (Kohlberg & Kramer, 1969). For example, students who had previously gone beyond Stage 2 were in some cases found to return to it in college. Perhaps this regression was caused by the highly competitive nature of the environment. Kohlberg argued that such students still understood higher levels of morality, even if they did not act on them. Indeed, adults placed in a sufficiently harsh environment may sometimes regress to cope with the challenges they face. Still, regressions suggest that development may not be unidirectional, even if it occurs loosely in stages.

As the preceding criticism implies, a fourth criticism concerns the tenuous relationship between thought and action (Kurtines & Greif, 1974). Sometimes an individual understands a given level of moral reasoning and even may answer test questions accordingly. But he or she may behave in a way that does not reflect this level. The test of morality perhaps shows how well the test taker plays the game rather than whether the test taker actually behaves according to moral principles. Kohlberg never claimed that understanding was tantamount to action, however. In general, research suggests that the measured moral stage does predict behavior, but only imperfectly (Blasi, 1980; Rest, 1983).

Finally, Kohlberg's theory has been criticized because it was based on the study of a small sample of white, middle-class, American boys under 17 years of age. Do the findings really apply to people who do not fit into all of these categories? John Snarey (1985) has reviewed more than 45 cross-cultural studies of Kohlberg's theory and has generally found support for Kohlberg's view. Nonetheless, Snarey points out some cultural limitations in the range of stages and in the applicability of all of Kohlberg's stages across cultures. Even Snarey's studies in collaboration with Kohlberg revealed some cross-cultural differences. In particular, the communal kibbutz lifestyle of Israel encourages greater emphasis on community and collective happiness than is found in the individualistic lifestyle of the United States (Snarey et al., 1985b).

Since Snarey's review, other researchers have similarly found that the theory has some cross-cultural support, within limits (e.g., studies in South Africa [Maqsud & Rouhani, 1990], Iceland [Keller, Eckensberger, & von Rosen, 1989], and Poland [Niemczynski, Czyzowska, Pourkos, & Mirski, 1988]). In China, the first three stages apply well, but the last three stages are less well supported and require modification to work within traditional Chinese thought (Ma, 1988). In fact, probably no universal stages of morality can apply without modification across cultures. Still, Kohlberg's theory has shown some strength in this area, as previously noted.

Carol Gilligan, a student of Kohlberg's, had been coding interviews of moral dilemmas when she began to notice that many of the women's responses did not fit neatly into Kohlberg's categories. In fact, many of their apparent responses seemed to reflect an entirely different approach to moral dilemmas. In 1977, Gilligan proposed an alternative view of moral development in women.

GILLIGAN'S ALTERNATIVE MODEL

According to Gilligan (1982; Gilligan, Hamner, & Lyons, 1990), women and men tend to differ in their understanding of morality. Men tend to focus on principles such as justice and respect for the rights of others. Women tend to see morality more in terms of caring and compassion. They are more concerned about general human welfare and the relationships that contribute to it. Women focus on the special obligations of their close relationships. They resolve moral issues with sensitivity to the social context. Whereas men are more likely to be competitive, women are more likely to be cooperative. Gilligan proposed that women pass through three basic levels of morality, although not all women reach the third level. The first level involves the individual's concern only for herself. The second involves self-sacrifice, in which concern for others predominates. And the third level involves integrating responsibilities to both self and others.

Other researchers (e.g., Baumrind, 1986; J. C. Gibbs, Arnold, Ahlborn, & Cheesman, 1984) have found similar sex differences with responses to moral dilemmas. Gilligan and J. Attanucci (1988) have since confirmed these differences. L. Walker (1989) replicated Gilligan and Attanucci's procedures, using a larger sample, and found that most men and women, as well as girls and boys, considered both caring and justice in their responses to moral dilemmas. Although women were more likely than men to express a caring orientation, however, girls were not more likely than boys to do so. Support for Gilligan's model is mixed, however. For example, some research has found that men and women perform at comparable levels on Kohlberg's moral dilemmas (Rest, 1986; Walker, 1984), suggesting that Gilligan's claim of sex differences may not hold up under empirical scrutiny. Perhaps a synthesis of both perspectives will eventually be proposed.

✓ **CONCEPT CHECK 4**

1. In Heinz's problem, one's stage of moral development is evaluated as a function of
   a. the processes one uses in solving the problem.
   b. what one recommends Heinz do to acquire the drug.
   c. the complexity of one's response.
   d. the number of morality-based words in one's response.
2. Cross-cultural support for Kohlberg's model would best be described as
   a. nonexistent.
   b. limited.
   c. abundant.
   d. conclusive.
3. Gilligan emphasizes the importance of _____ in the moral development of women.
   a. justice
   b. equality
   c. care
   d. trust

DEATH AND DYING

How do we cope with death and bereavement?

Sooner or later, people reach the end of life. People in different cultures, and even within a given culture, have different ideas about what it means to die. For some people, death is more a beginning than an end. For many Christians, Jews, and Muslims, death means a transition to an afterlife. For many Hindus and Buddhists, death is a transition to reincarnation. Others, including religious individuals, may view death as a completion of life, with no kind of life after death.

There are cultural differences in the way people view dying. R. L. Steele (1992) studied ideas about death among Mayan people. The Mayans come to terms with death much more readily than do people in many other parts of the world. They announce that their time has come and that their life will soon be over. They then excuse themselves, separating themselves from others. They do not accept food or water. Rather, they lie down and wait to die.

People's attitudes toward death depend in part on their religious or personal beliefs and also on events that happen to be transpiring in the time and place they live. In the year 2000, for example, almost 460,000 people in the United States and its dependencies had died of AIDS (http://www.cdc.gov/hiv/stats/hasrsupp81/table2.htm). The World Health Organization estimated that, by the end of 2002, 42 million people around the world were living with AIDS (http://www.elca.org/dcs/aidsintheworld.html). Most of them will die with the disease. For these people, death is a threat every day of their lives. In 1999 alone, 2.6 million people worldwide died of AIDS. There are other threats as well. SARS, severe acute respiratory syndrome, poses a new threat. As of April 21, 2003, SARS had reportedly infected 3,461 people and killed 170 people around the world (http://www.wired.com/news/medtech/0,1286,58552,00.html). These figures are almost certainly underestimates because some countries have grossly underreported cases of the illness. At this time, SARS is on the way to becoming a potential global epidemic. In many areas of the world, wars are a constant reality. In several parts of Africa, wars are ongoing and show no sign of abating. The 2003 war in Iraq killed numerous Iraqis. These are anything but quiet times.

When an individual comes to terms with the nearness of death, he or she may go through a series of stages to cope with issues regarding the end of life.

Elisabeth Kübler-Ross (1969) studied end-of-life issues. Her views were based on interviews with several hundred individuals who were on the verge of death. She suggested that people often go through these five stages:

Stage 1: Denial. In this stage, people find it difficult to confront the end of life. They may think that a doctor's diagnosis is wrong, that signs of serious illness are actually of minor consequence, or that what is happening to them cannot really be happening.

Stage 2: Anger. In this stage, people feel a combination of anger and resentment. They may think that what is happening to them is not fair, that it is someone else's fault, or that they have been unfairly singled out. The anger may be directed against other people, against objects, or even against God.

Stage 3: Bargaining. In this stage, people try to bargain for more time. They may ask God to spare them this one time. Or they may offer something to God in exchange for a longer life. When the death is viewed as caused by another individual—whether or not the view is correct—they may try to bargain with that individual.

Stage 4: Depression. In this stage, people feel despair that all is lost. They may think that whatever they do from that time on makes no difference to anyone, least of all themselves. They may be reluctant to see other people.

Stage 5: Acceptance. In this stage, people experience a transition to a feeling of calmness and peace. They come to accept their fate and the fact that there is nothing they can do about it.

This model does not capture the full complexity of the experience of dying, of course. Not everyone necessarily goes through all the stages. Some people may feel depressed until the end, and others may try to bargain right up to the last moment. The model also seems to apply more to younger people who are dying than to older ones. The latter may be more likely to feel that they have fully experienced their lives and hence may be more accepting of their fate. Finally, the empirical evidence in favor of this theory is rather modest.

Dying affects not only the individual whose life is at an end but also all the people around that individual. Loved ones often experience grief and then a period of bereavement, in which they feel a longing for the one who has passed away. Bereavement can be seen as passing through three stages (Lindemann, 1991):

Stage 1: Shock. This period typically lasts about three weeks, although it may be shorter or considerably longer. The individual can hardly accept what has happened. He or she feels intense longing for the departed individual. The bereaved may experience a sense of denial and disbelief that the death could have happened. He or she also feels disoriented, as though nothing in life seems quite right.

Stage 2: Periodic turmoil. This stage can last from three weeks to a year. The bereaved individual generally copes, but goes through periods of upheaval. During these times, the individual reflects on the deceased and his or her relations with the deceased. What could have been different? Did the death really have to happen? Sometimes the bereaved may have brief periods of imagining that the deceased is still alive.

Stage 3: Acceptance. After about a year, the bereaved comes to accept the death. He or she may think about the deceased only infrequently. If a parent has died, the child accepts that he or she now must forge through life without the presence and perhaps guidance of that parent. If it is a spouse, the individual may start to think about the possibility of a new relationship. If it is a child who has died, the individual may think about having another child.

Death and dying usually are hard on everyone affected, not just the deceased. But the cycle of life goes on. Those left behind often find meaning in their remembrance of and love for the person who has left them.

In conclusion, social development is a lifelong process that encompasses emotional, personality, interpersonal, and moral development. It is inextricably intertwined with the environment, which largely dictates what people consider appropriate for a child. We have seen this interweaving in many of the research studies discussed in this chapter, such as the work on attachment patterns in children, in which proportions of the various attachment patterns differ across countries. Social development is also clearly linked to cognitive development. A child cognitively processes the perceptions and conceptions that influence his or her socialization. Tables 11.5, 11.6, and 11.7 summarize the key aspects of social development in infants, children, and adults, respectively.

✓**CONCEPT CHECK 5**

1. Different cultures have _____ views of death and dying.
   a. essentially identical
   b. very similar but not identical
   c. quite different
   d. totally different and nonoverlapping
2. In Kübler-Ross's theory, the final stage is
   a. anger.
   b. bargaining.
   c. acceptance.
   d. denial.
3. According to Lindemann, the first stage of bereavement involves
   a. shock.
   b. denial.
   c. anger.
   d. acceptance.

TABLE 11.5
CONCEPT REVIEW

Social Development: Birth to Age 3. The first 3 years of a child's life are surprisingly eventful in terms of social development.

Aspect of Development (Theorist)	Age (Months)							
	0–1	1–2 2–3	3–6	6–9	9–12	12–18	18–36
Emotional (Sroufe)	Undifferentiated emotions; insensitivity to others' emotions	Social smile develops; facial expressions reflect others; smiles in response to things	Highly positive emotions; smiles and laughs with caregivers	Participates in emotional exchanges; begins to show anger	Communicates emotional states effectively; focuses on caregivers; possessive; fears strangers	Explores wider world beyond caregivers; attaches securely; fears strangers less	Differentiates from others, including self-concept; ambivalent impulses to assert independence and seek reassurance
Personality (Erikson)	Trust versus mistrust					Autonomy versus shame and doubt	
Attachment (Ainsworth)	Preattachment; nondifferentiated responses to people	Attachment in the making; responds more to familiars than to strangers; increasingly seeks contact with primary caregivers; anxious around strangers		Clear-cut attachment; prefers primary caregivers; differentiated response to strangers; separation anxiety			Mature relationships
Self-understanding (Damon and Hart)	Emerging self-awareness; focuses on the physical self					Understands own gender, age, and possessions; emerging feelings of mastery	
Self-esteem (Harter)	Undifferentiated self-concept and evaluations of self-worth						
Friendships (Vandell, Mueller)	May cry if another infant cries		May smile at another infant; may reach toward and even touch another infant			Interactions and positive affect increase; frequent playmates may be recognized with positive affect	
Moral (Piaget, Kohlberg)	Premoral						

TABLE 11.6
CONCEPT REVIEW

Social Development: Preschool through Adolescence. From preschool through adolescence, the child undergoes tremendous changes in social development.

Aspect of Development (Theorist)	Age (Years)							
	3–5	5–7	7–9	9–11	11–13	13–15	15–17	17+
Emotional (Sroufe)	Social smile; festivities important; fears of unknown and strangers		Less distinctive events also important; fears include fantastic creatures or unrealistic beliefs		Happiness comes from school and after-school activities, peer relationships		Happiness comes from relationships, self-improvement, recreation, and travel	
	Anger becomes focused	Anger includes consideration of others' intentions						
Personality (Erikson)	Initiative versus guilt	Industry versus inferiority			Identity versus role confusion			
Self-understanding (Damon and Hart)	Emerging self-awareness based on physical self; differentiates inner-directed versus other-directed speech	Self-understanding based on active self, on personal achievements and skills			Self-understanding based on social self and peer relations		Self-understanding based on psychological self and personal beliefs, thoughts, attitudes, and values	
Self-esteem (Harter)	Self-esteem based on cognitive, physical, and social competence, and on behavioral conduct		Self-esteem based on scholastic and athletic competence, peer social acceptance, behavioral conduct, and physical appearance		Self-esteem based on job, scholastic, and athletic competence; close friendship; romantic appeal; peer social acceptance; behavioral conduct; and physical appearance			
Play interactions (Parten)	Play becomes increasingly social and interactive with peers							
Friendships (Gottman)	Prefer same-sex friends; friendships center on shared activities; boys more attracted to competitive activities, autonomy, and achievement; girls more likely to prefer a cooperative friend, emotional closeness, and shared confidences						Boys do not show much change in forming friendships; girls increasingly emphasize shared personalities, interests, compatibility, turn their attention to boys	
Moral (Kohlberg)			Preconventional morality		Conventional morality		Possible postconventional morality	

TABLE 11.7
CONCEPT REVIEW

Social Development: Adulthood. Psychologists have developed theories of personality, identity, self-esteem, life structure, and morality for all three stages of adulthood.

Aspect of Development (Theorist)	Early Adulthood	Middle Adulthood	Late Adulthood
Personality (Erikson)	Intimacy versus isolation	Generativity versus stagnation	Integrity versus despair
Identity (Marcia)	Identity achievement, foreclosure, identity diffusion, or moratorium (or alienated achievement)		
Self-esteem (Harter)	Self-esteem based on intelligence, sense of humor, job competence, morality, athletic ability, physical appearance, sociability, intimate relationships, nurturance, adequacy as a provider, and household management		
Life structure (Levinson)	Evaluates the nature of the world and one's place in it; eventually establishes family and career; attempts to build a better life	Evaluates accomplishments to date; sometimes changes marital status, career, or attitudes; begins to consider retirement and old age	Is aware of changing physical and mental abilities; must stay connected to family, friends, interests; comes to terms with mortality
Moral (Kohlberg)	Conventional morality (and, in rare cases, postconventional morality)		

UNIFYING PSYCHOLOGY

FACIAL DISFIGUREMENT AND SOCIAL DEVELOPMENT

Some children are born with disfigured faces, and some suffer facial damage during childhood. In children who are born with Apert Syndrome, the skull and face are deformed. The skull is flat and very tall, the eyes are set widely apart, and the nose and upper jaw are sunk into the face. Because the jaws and throat are malformed, children with Apert's Syndrome often have abnormal voices and severe speech problems (Shipster, Hearst, Dockrell, Kilby, & Hayward, 2002). Other causes of facial disfigurement are prominent birthmarks, drastic injury, severe burns, and medical conditions that

scar the face. In every case, the disfigurement adversely affects the child's social development. Researchers in many areas of psychology have studied the effects of facial disfigurement and have developed models of psychological support.

Children who grow up with facial disfigurement are exposed to hurtful comments and even rejection by other children. This naturally results in diminished self-esteem and self-confidence, as research by developmental psychologists and social psychologists has shown. **Developmental psychologist** David Crystal and his colleagues com-

pared the reactions of 175 American and 257 Japanese 5th and 11th graders to children with facial disfigurement (Crystal, Watanabe, & Chen, 2000). The Japanese students were more likely than American students to express positive and inclusive attitudes toward the disfigurement, although children in both groups were not comfortable actually interacting with an affected child.

Research by **social psychologists** indicates that adults also express negative attitudes toward people with facial disfigurement. When college students and trained personnel

continued

FACIAL DISFIGUREMENT AND SOCIAL DEVELOPMENT

recruiters were asked to judge mock job candidates who had physical disabilities, facial disfigurement, or no obvious physical problems, they rated the applicants with facial disfigurement most negatively (Stevenage & McKay, 1999). Social psychologists Vicky Houston and Ray Bull planted confederates on a suburban commuter train. Some had normal faces, and others had faces disfigured by a large birthmark, a narrow scar, or a bruise. The other passengers avoided sitting next to a person with a disfiguring birthmark, but they readily sat next to someone with a normal, scarred, or bruised face (Houston & Bull, 1994). Thus, disfigured individuals are undoubtedly correct in believing that other people avoid them.

Self-esteem enables us to enter into relationships with others. Research by **clinical psychologists** has demonstrated that, due to low self-esteem, people with facial disfigurement often experience social anxiety, which keeps them from interacting normally with others, especially strangers (Cole, 2001). Clinical psychologist Gerry Kent has studied the social and psychological consequences of facial disfigurement caused by skin problems, burns, and cleft palate (Kent, 2000; Kent & Keohane, 2001; Thompson & Kent, 2001). His studies have shown that these conditions have a negative impact on the person's quality of life, especially people who are most fearful of critical evaluations. His research also indicates that the most effective psychotherapy for people with facial disfigurement focuses on teaching social skills so that clients can manage social interactions, and coping strategies so they can control the destructive thought processes that further undermine their self-esteem and self-confidence.

Health psychologists have investigated the impact of facial disfigurement on social functioning. Patients who feel stigmatized by their disfigurement (that is, ostracized or excluded by others) are more likely to experience psychological distress, such as depression, even to the point of becoming disabled and unable to work and take care of themselves (Richards, Fortune, Griffiths, & Main, 2001).

The effects of facial disfigurement are also investigated by **forensic psychologists,** who concentrate on disfigurement that results from accidents. Forensic psychologists Donna Long and Spencer DeVault (1990) have examined the impact of facial disfigurement in adolescent accident victims and found devastating psychological consequences. The adverse effects they identify are used in personal injury suits to calculate monetary compensation for future loss due to the nature of the injuries.

Human faces play an important role in communication, especially of emotion, and therefore in emotional bonding. Many people with disfigured faces are deprived of this mode of communication and, as a result, feel isolated and depressed. Developmental, social, clinical, health, and forensic psychologists have enabled us to understand the unfortunate consequences of facial disfigurement. Clinical and health psychologists are working to develop therapeutic and educational programs to help affected people feel more accepted by others.

SUMMARY

1. *Social development* encompasses four areas of personal growth: emotional development, personality development, interpersonal development, and moral development.

EMOTIONAL DEVELOPMENT 395

How and why do we develop emotions?

2. Infants change from being egocentric, with limited emotional expression, to being fully functioning, independent, empathic, and responsive explorers of the world around them.

3. Researchers do not agree about how people develop *emotions*. Sroufe posits that we are born with one general form of emotional arousal, which later differentiates into various specific emotions *(differentiation theory)*. Others (e.g., Izard) say that *discrete emotions* are generated by specific neural patterns in our brains.

4. A *cognitive-evolutionary theory* of emotional development posits that we can understand how human emotions develop by understanding the adaptive needs emotions serve.

PERSONALITY DEVELOPMENT 398

What changes occur in personality over time, and why do they occur?

5. Erikson's theory of *psychosocial development* was originally considered revolutionary because it

traces development all the way through adulthood instead of stopping at adolescence. The theory comprises eight stages. Those who successfully complete the stages develop hope, will, purpose, competence, fidelity, love, care, and wisdom.

6. Your sense of identity can be categorized, according to Marcia, as being in a state of *identity achievement* if you have made your own decisions and have a firm sense of who you are, *foreclosure* if you have chosen your path with little thought, *moratorium* if you are still seeking an identity, *identity diffusion* if you lack direction or commitment, or *alienated achievement* if you have decided to opt out of society.

7. *Self-concept* consists of self-understanding, which is your definition of who you are, and self-esteem, which is your sense of self-worth.

8. According to Damon and Hart, *self-understanding* involves different aspects of the self, such as physical attributes, behavior, social relationships, and inner psyche. According to Harter, *self-esteem* is based on self-judgments about worth in various domains of differing importance. Older children see themselves as functioning in more domains than do younger children. By adulthood, people function in 11 different domains. People also base their self-esteem on other people's judgments of them.

9. Children who underestimate their abilities tend to have more problems in school and social life than children who do not. Girls are more likely than boys to underestimate their abilities.

10. *Temperament* refers to individual differences in the intensity and duration of emotions. According to A. Thomas and Chess, babies may be easy, difficult, or slow to warm up. Temperament must be taken into account when looking for the best fit between a person and his or her environment.

11. *Psychosexual development* is the growth of self-perceptions about sexuality and gender identifications. *Gender typing* is the acquisition of specific gender-related roles.

12. Our perceptions of sex roles and gender identification may be acquired through socialization, genetic predisposition, evolution, role modeling, or cognitive schemas.

INTERPERSONAL DEVELOPMENT 407
How do we develop interpersonal skills?

13. *Attachment* is the long-lasting emotional tie that results from bonding. It does not end in childhood, and indeed patterns of childhood attachment seem to be repeated in adult life, especially in romantic relationships.

14. *Strange-situation* research examines attachment patterns by studying how children react when left alone in an unfamiliar room with an unknown person and then when their mother returns. According to attachment patterns, *avoidant* children seem distant emotionally in the strange situation; *secure* children are more outgoing but need comforting; and *resistant* children seem both aloof and in need of closeness. These labels seem to be culturally bound.

15. Infants can become attached to fathers and other caregivers, just as they do to mothers. Fathers play more games with young children than do mothers.

16. Young humans and animals that are deprived of natural nurturing and attachment do not grow up to be fully functional adults.

17. Parental disciplinary style affects the development of social skills in children. *Authoritarian* (very strict) parents tend to raise unfriendly and distrustful children. *Permissive* parents tend to raise immature and dependent children. *Authoritative* parents, who provide more of a balance, tend to raise well-adjusted children. The authoritative style is the most common across cultures.

18. Child care is a controversial issue. Research results on its effects are somewhat contradictory, although the majority of studies indicate that good-quality child care does children little harm and may offer some benefits. The most important consideration for parents, therefore, is the quality of the program they choose.

19. Learning how to make friends is important to a child's development. Theories of friendship development point to interacting effectively, exchanging information, establishing common ground, resolving conflicts, showing positive reciprocal regard, and engaging in free self-disclosure as steps in learning how to be a friend. Girls' and boys' friendship patterns differ somewhat, with girls placing a greater emphasis on compatible feelings and outlooks, and boys on compatible activities.

20. Studies of couples show that several types of marriages can be successful. Unsuccessful marriages are characterized by personal attacks, contempt, defensiveness, and stonewalling.

21. People are most satisfied in their work when it is both intrinsically and extrinsically rewarding. People pass through several different stages of career development, including growth, exploration, establishment, maintenance, and decline.

What are the stages in the development of moral reasoning? How, if at all, do they differ in men and women?

22. Kohlberg's stage theory of moral development and reasoning is widely accepted, although it has detractors. In the *preconventional morality* level, children behave to avoid punishment and to seek self-interest; in the *conventional morality* level, older children and adolescents behave according to family and social rules; and in the *postconventional morality* level, adults behave according to shifting social needs but also according to universal ethical requirements.

23. Some evidence supports Kohlberg's theory, but on the whole, support is mixed.

24. Gilligan has suggested alternative stages of moral development for women, involving an orientation toward caring relationships more than an abstract notion of justice. This theory has little empirical evidence to support it.

DEATH AND DYING 421

How do we cope with death and bereavement?

25. All of us must confront our own deaths and those of others. Kübler-Ross has proposed a theory of the stages people go through in confronting death.

KEY TERMS

attachment 407
authoritarian parents 412
authoritative parents 412
avoidant attachment pattern 408
cognitive-evolutionary theory 397
conventional morality 417
differentiation theory 396
discrete-emotions theory 397
emotion 395
empty-nest syndrome 415

gender constancy 405
gender typing 405
permissive parents 412
postconventional morality 419
preconventional morality 417
psychosexual development 405
psychosocial theory 398
resilience 414
resistant attachment pattern 408
schema theory 406

secure attachment pattern 408
self-concept 400
self-esteem 401
self-understanding 401
separation anxiety 407
social development 394
social-learning theory 405
strange situation 407
temperament 403

ANSWERS TO CONCEPT CHECKS

Concept Check 1

1. d   2. c   3. d

Concept Check 2

1. b   2. c   3. b

Concept Check 3

1. a   2. d   3. b

Concept Check 4

1. a   2. b   3. c

Concept Check 5

1. c   2. c   3. a

KNOWLEDGE CHECK

1. The "strange situation" can be used to assess children's
   a. attachment style.
   b. temperament.
   c. emotional profile.
   d. intelligent quotient.
2. A parent who is domineering and insists on high levels of obedience from his or her children is best described as
   a. authoritative.
   b. authoritarian.
   c. permissive.
   d. resistant.
3. Erikson's theory characterizes social development
   a. in infancy.
   b. through early childhood.
   c. through adolescence.
   d. until old age.
4. Successful passage through Erikson's stage of initiative versus guilt engenders a sense of _____ in life.
   a. purpose
   b. autonomy
   c. trust
   d. competence
5. A child with a resistant attachment pattern shows _____ toward the mother.
   a. unwavering trust
   b. serious anger toward
   c. ambivalence
   d. little compassion
6. People in Stage 6 of Kohlberg's theory make moral decisions on the basis of
   a. universal principles of justice.
   b. social contracts.
   c. rewards and punishment.
   d. conventional morality.
7. An androgynous person is _____ in gender-role orientation.
   a. strongly masculine
   b. strongly feminine
   c. both strongly masculine and strongly feminine
   d. neither strongly masculine nor strongly feminine
8. Carol Gilligan views Kohlberg's theory as too
   a. male-oriented.
   b. female-oriented.
   c. oriented toward youngsters.
   d. oriented toward the elderly.
9. The empty-nest syndrome occurs when
   a. a parent dies.
   b. an infant dies of sudden infant death syndrome.
   c. children go away from home to live on their own.
   d. parents divorce.
10. Jack, a teenager, believes he is uniquely destined for fame and fortune. He is experiencing a(n)
    a. runaway emotion.
    b. personal fable.
    c. invincibility.
    d. imaginary audience.

Answers
1. a 2. b 3. d 4. a 5. c 6. a 7. d 8. a
9. c 10. b

THINK ABOUT IT

1. Describe a moral dilemma and tell how someone at Kohlberg's postconventional level of morality might respond to the dilemma. Give the rationale for the individual's response.
2. How do the development of the self-concept and interpersonal development interact?
3. Design an experience that would help children broaden their views about the range of behaviors that are appropriate for boys and for girls, helping them avoid being narrowly constrained by rigid sex-role stereotypes.
4. Suggest some criteria to be used in assessing the quality of child care for children less than 5 years of age.
5. How do your emotions influence your behavior?
6. Give examples of your own sex-role development. In what ways do you conform to traditional gender roles, and in what ways have you departed from traditional gender roles?

WEB RESOURCES

For a chapter tutorial quiz, direct links to Internet sites, and other useful features, visit the book-specific website at http://psychology.wadsworth.com/sternberg4e. You can also connect directly to the following sites:

Teen Advice Online
http://www.teenadvice.org/
This interesting non-academic site is run by teens. Their mission is to "provide support for teenage problems through a network of peers from around the world."

The Nurture Assumption
http://home.att.net/~xchar/tna/
This site is maintained by *Seeing Both Sides* author Judith Rich Harris to further explain the controversial book that highlights her belief in the importance of peers and the relative unimportance of parenting styles.

For additional readings on many of the topics covered in this chapter, check out InfoTrac College Edition at **www.infotrac-college.com/ wadsworth.**

Disk Two
Personality Development
A Developing Sense of Self
Moral Development
Chapter Quiz
Critical Thinking Questions

CHAPTER 12

MOTIVATION AND EMOTION

> "If at first you don't succeed, try, try again."
>
> "Where there's a will there's a way."

Many proverbs emphasize the importance of motivation and initiative to success. But what is motivation, and how important is it? How is it related to emotions? We consider such questions in this chapter.

The ways we describe our motivations and our emotions are intuitively similar: "I *feel* like having a hamburger," "I *feel* like dancing." Both motivations and emotions cause us to move or be moved. Both arise within us in response to events or thoughts. We often feel them as physiological sensations: "When I heard his footsteps behind me again, I panicked—I started shaking, my heart pounded, my throat shut, my palms sweated, and I froze." Motivation and emotion are inextricably linked.

A **motive** is an impulse, desire, or need that leads to an action. **Motivation** consists of processes that give behavior its energy and direction. Psychologists study *why* and *how* we are motivated to act (King & Emmons, 2000; Stricker, 2000; Weiner, 2000). They ask four questions (Houston, 1985): First, in what *directions* do our actions move us? That is, what attracts us and what repels us? Second, what motivates us to *initiate* or start taking action to pursue a particular goal? Why do some people initiate action, while others contemplate acting but never actually go ahead and do it? Third, how *intensely* do we pursue our actions? Fourth, why do some people *persist* for longer periods of time in the things that motivate them, whereas others flit from one pursuit to another? Early theories of motivation focused on its evolutionary and biological aspects, chiefly instincts and drives.

EARLY THEORIES OF MOTIVATION

How did early theorists view motivation?

INSTINCT THEORY

Instinctive behavior has three main characteristics. First, it is *inherited*. We are born with all the instincts we will ever have. Thus, the desire for sexual union or the fear of a predator is innate, not learned. Second, it is *species-specific*. For example, salmon return upriver to their birthplace, but tuna do not. Bees do a certain kind of dance, but grasshoppers do not. Third, instinctive behavior is *stereotyped*. We engage in it automatically in response to a particular stimulus. We run from a ferocious predator without waiting to think about it, and fortunately so. Charles Darwin (1859, 1965) was a major proponent of the instinctual point of view. He believed that much behavior is inherited, species-specific, and automatic. From an evolutionary point of view, instinctive behavior is key not only to individual survival but also to survival of the species. Without instincts that motivate copulatory behavior, mammals would likely be doomed.

William James, the father of much of modern psychological thinking, was one of many psychologists who studied instincts. James suggested a list of 20 physical instincts, such as sucking and locomotion.

He proposed an additional 17 mental instincts (James, 1890a), which included cleanliness, curiosity, fearfulness, jealousy, parental love, and sociability. A generation later, William McDougall (1908) proposed a larger list, including the desire for food, the desire to have sex, the desire to dominate, and the desire to make things. The inventory of proposed instincts gradually grew to 10,000 (Bernard, 1924). Whereas James believed that instincts are *important* in behavior, McDougall argued that they are *necessary* for behavior. Without them, we would be totally passive, unmoved to action by anything.

Like some other early psychological theories, instinct theory became ponderous, cumbersome, and circular (Kuo, 1921). Behaviors were explained by instincts, which in turn were explained by the behaviors. For example, maternal behavior might be "explained" by a mothering instinct, which in turn would be "explained" by the behavior it supposedly generated. The problems with instincts led people to lose interest in them as a basis for theorizing. Theorists sought new ways to explain motivation. As the aesthetic appeal of instinct theory waned, drive theory became increasingly attractive.

DRIVE THEORY

Drive theory derives many of its principles, and many of its backers, from learning theory. The theory was first put forward by Robert Woodworth (1918), but

Clark Hull proposed the best-known version. Hull (1943, 1952) believed that we have a number of basic physiological needs: for food, water, sleep, and so on. To survive, we must satisfy all these needs. A drive is a hypothetical composite source of energy that all animals try to reduce. To reduce drive, we eat, drink, sleep, and otherwise satisfy our needs.

Like instinct theory, drive theory fell out of favor because its underlying assumptions proved not to be particularly well founded (R. W. White, 1959). The theory seemed to work better for simple needs, like hunger and thirst, than for more complex needs, as are found in complex social behavior. Empirical support for the theory simply was inadequate. As drive paradigms began to yield diminishing returns, other paradigms appeared more fruitful. So researchers studying motivation moved on.

✓ **CONCEPT CHECK 1**

1. Instincts are *not*
   a. inherited.
   b. species-specific.
   c. stereotypic.
   d. learned from experience.
2. Which of the following did *not* propose sets of instincts?
   a. William James
   b. John Watson
   c. Charles Darwin
   d. William McDougall
3. According to drive theory, animals try to
   a. reduce drive.
   b. increase drive.
   c. maintain a constant level of drive.
   d. vary drive levels continuously.

CONTEMPORARY THEORIES OF MOTIVATION

Why has motivation been studied by modern psychologists? What methods do they use?

PHYSIOLOGICAL APPROACHES

What prompted psychologists to explore the relationship between the central nervous system and the psychological and behavioral phenomena of motivation? Actually, the physiological approach gained support almost by accident. Researcher James Olds misplaced an electrode in a portion of a rat's brain. When the electrode stimulated that portion, the rat acted in ways suggesting that it wanted more stimulation. Olds and Peter Milner (1954) designed an experiment to test this possibility. When electrodes were planted to stimulate the limbic system, rats spent more than three-quarters of their time pressing a bar to repeat the stimulation. Olds had inadvertently discovered a "pleasure center" in the brain. Other researchers showed that cats would do whatever they could to *avoid* electrical stimulation in a different part of the brain (Delgado, Roberts, & Miller, 1954). We consider three theories for understanding the relationship between motivation and brain physiology: arousal theory, opponent-process theory, and homeostatic-regulation theory.

AROUSAL THEORY

Suppose that three students with equal intelligence and knowledge of a subject are about to take an important test. The first student does not care about either the test or doing well on it. The second student wants to do well but is not anxious about his performance. He knows that even if he did poorly, his life would not be changed inalterably. The third student is extremely nervous about the test. She believes that her grade will largely determine her future. Which student do you think is likely to do best on the test?

These three students have varying amounts of **arousal**—a state of alertness caused by the activity of the central nervous system, including the brain. The relationship between level of arousal and efficiency of performance is graphed in Figure 12.1. The inverted U-shape illustrates the *Yerkes–Dodson law* (Yerkes & Dodson, 1908), which states that organisms will perform most efficiently with a moderate level of arousal. According to this law, the second student, who is both motivated and relaxed, will do best. People generally also feel best when their level of arousal is moderate (Berlyne, 1967). At low levels of arousal, we feel bored, listless, and unmotivated. At high levels, we are tense or fearful.

The optimal level of arousal appears to vary with the task and with the individual. For relatively simple tasks, the optimal level of arousal is moderately high. For difficult tasks, the optimal level of arousal is moderately low (Bexton, Heron, & Scott, 1954; Broadhurst, 1957). If we need to do something that is fairly repetitive and mindless, a high level of arousal may motivate us to be efficient. If we have to perform a complex task, however, a low level of arousal may help us avoid anxiety, which would hamper our ability to start work.

OPPONENT-PROCESS THEORY

The *opponent-process theory*, proposed by Richard Solomon (1980; Solomon & Corbit, 1974), addresses how emotional experience is related to substance

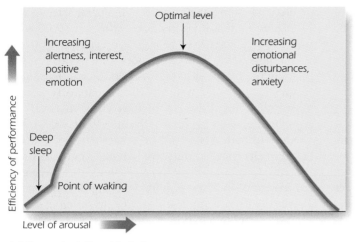

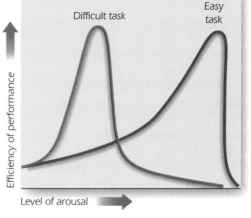

(a) General relationship between performance and arousal level

(b) Relationship between performance and arousal level on difficult vs. easy tasks

FIGURE 12.1

The Yerkes–Dodson Law. In the relationship between arousal and performance, performance is at its peak when arousal is moderate, and performance levels are lower at both the low and high extremes of arousal. (After Yerkes & Dodson, 1908)

addiction. (This theory has nothing to do with the opponent-process theory of color vision.) What happens when we acquire and then try to get rid of a motivation? As we see Figure 12.2, we start at a neutral state, a *baseline*, in which we have not felt the motivation to act (e.g., to drink coffee), and thus the stimulus (coffee) is irrelevant to us. Then we drink the first cup of coffee and feel the "high" because of the positive effect of the stimulus—often a chemical—on neural receptors. Regardless of the source, however, we have an *acquired motivation* to seek out more of the stimulus.

According to Solomon, mammalian brains always seek emotional neutrality sooner or later. In other words, when a motivational source impels us to feel emotions, whether positive or negative, we come under the influence of an opposing motivational force— an *opponent process*— that acts to bring us back to the neutral baseline. Notice in Figure 12.2 that our emotional state first rises substantially but then falls. It starts to go down when the opponent process begins to

The tendency of the body is toward a state of equilibrium. According to opponent-process theory, the pleasant buzz we at first get from just one cup of coffee will eventually be diminished by the body's efforts to counterbalance the jittery feeling, leaving us needing more coffee over time to produce the same effect.

oppose the original process. Maybe we enjoyed the coffee buzz to start with, but then found that it made us too jittery to think straight. In other words, what was initially pleasurable becomes less so. Eventually, the effect of the stimulus wears off, and we reach a *steady state* of response. The original motivating force stops because the stimulus no longer elevates us above the baseline. In the coffee example, the body may have metabolized all the caffeine.

After we use the stimulus for a long time, its effect is quite different from what it was originally, as the figure shows. Once we *habituate* to the stimulus (see Chapters 4, 5, and 6), it no longer gives us a boost. Maybe one cup of coffee no longer makes us jittery. Now it only arouses us to the "barely awake" level. Unfortunately, the opponent process, which was slow to start, is also slow to stop. When the effect of the stimulus wears off, the effect of the opponent process remains, and so we quickly go into a state of *withdrawal*. We now feel worse

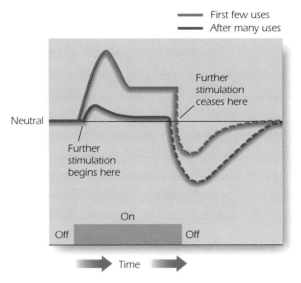

Legend:
— First few uses
— After many uses

Neutral

Further stimulation begins here

Further stimulation ceases here

On
Off   Off

Time

FIGURE 12.2

Acquired Motivation. At the beginning of physiological addiction, the addictive stimulus elevates us above our neutral baseline level of response. If we stop using the addictive substance, we first drop below our neutral baseline level and then return to it. Once we are addicted, however, our responses to the substance act only to keep us at a steady-state, neutral level of response. If we then stop using the addictive substance, our responses fall below the neutral level for a longer time, an experience called withdrawal. (From "Acquired Motivation" by R. Solomon & Corbit, *Psychological Review*, No. 81, pp. 119-145, 1974. Copyright © 1974 by the American Psychological Association. Reprinted by permission.)

than we did before: irritable, headachy, tired, and sad. We may then seek additional stimulation to relieve the withdrawal symptoms. Ironically, what starts off as a habit to achieve a high becomes a habit to avoid a low. We may drink coffee to avoid withdrawal symptoms. Fortunately, if we are able to ride out the withdrawal, the symptoms will eventually disappear.

Arousal theory explains why we seek to explore and to master our environments, and opponent-process theory explains why we are motivated to seek substances to which we are addicted. But, neither theory satisfactorily addresses why we eat, drink, or satisfy our other basic physiological needs. We need yet another theory to explain these motivations.

HOMEOSTATIC-REGULATION THEORY

Consider a typical sequence of morning behaviors. You wake up. You feel hungry and thirsty. You eat and drink. You begin your morning activities. After a while, you begin to feel hungry and thirsty again. Maybe you just grab a drink. The hunger intensifies. Finally, you eat again. **Homeostatic regulation** is the tendency of the body to maintain a state of equilibrium. When the body lacks something, it sends signals to the brain that

prompt the individual to seek the missing resource. When the body is satiated, it sends signals to stop obtaining that resource. We regulate the need for nourishment, as well as the control of body temperature, through homeostatic systems. These systems operate via a **negative-feedback loop**, a physiological mechanism for monitoring the level of a particular resource. The loop finds a way to increase a resource when levels are low and to decrease the resource when levels are high (see Chapter 3). The systems work to close up the difference between the actual and ideal states. Most people stop eating when they no longer feel hungry, stop drinking when they no longer feel thirsty, and stop sleeping when they no longer feel tired.

Homeostatic regulation is not limited to the body. In most home heating systems, when the thermostat records temperatures below the preferred setting, the heater turns on. It stays on until the thermostat reaches the set point—the desired temperature. Then the heater turns off.

In the body, negative feedback is graduated rather than all or none. Suppose that you have had a very active day and arrive at dinner famished. At first, you eat and drink rapidly. But then you slow down as you receive feedback indicating that your needs are satisfied (L. Spitzer & Rodin, 1981). The body signals well before you have finished the meal that you are reaching satiation. If you eat quickly, however, the signal is overrun. This is why one dieting tactic is to eat more slowly so as to give the body time to signal satiety and avoid overeating.

Homeostatic regulation sounds similar to drive theory, but the emphases are different. Drive theory focuses on avoiding deficits. Homeostatic-regulation theory emphasizes the need to maintain equilibrium. Both deficits and surpluses are to be avoided. Table 12.1 briefly summarizes the physiological approaches to motivation.

Although we may not fully understand all the mechanisms that prompt us to satisfy our physiological needs, we do not question our motivation to satisfy those needs. What else motivates human behavior?

CLINICAL APPROACHES

Clinical researchers consider physiological needs. But they focus on aspects of the personality and on case studies rather than on physiological data. People are motivated differently. For example, some will stand for hours in all kinds of weather to buy a ticket to a concert that others would not accept money to attend.

HENRY MURRAY: THEORY OF NEEDS

Henry Murray (1938) believed that needs are based in human physiology. He suggested that they can be understood in terms of the brain and that they form the

TABLE 12.1
CONCEPT REVIEW

Physiological Approaches to Motivation. Three theories of motivation are based on physiology.

Theory	Explanation
Arousal theory (Yerkes–Dodson law)	When we are moderately aroused, we feel relaxed and motivated and we perform at optimum level. When we are minimally aroused, we feel bored, and anxious or tense when we are highly aroused.
Opponent-process theory (Solomon)	We seek emotional neutrality. When our emotions are aroused, an opposing motive brings us back to the neutral baseline.
Homeostatic-regulation theory	We try to maintain a state of physical equilibrium. When the brain senses that the stomach is empty, it signals the body to seek food; when it senses that the stomach is full, it signals the body to stop eating.

core of a person's personality. Some of the 20 needs that Murray posited have prompted a great deal of research, which is a measure of his importance in the field. For example, much research has been done on Murray's constructs of the need for affiliation and the need for power. People who rank high in the need for affiliation

© Bob Krist/Corbis

The prospect of fame can be a strong motivator. Some of these American Idol hopefuls camped in line overnight to be sure they would get in to audition for the show.

like to form close connections with other people and to be members of groups. They avoid arguments (Exline, 1962) and competitive games (Terhune, 1968). They also tend to become anxious when they feel they are being evaluated (D. Byrne, 1961).

People who rank high in the need for power seek to control others (Burger, 1992). They try to make the world conform to their own image. In groups, they want to be recognized (Winter, 1973) and to be visible to the general public (McClelland & Teague, 1975). People who rank high in the need for power tend to be aggressive, and they are likely to choose occupations in which they can influence others (Winter, 1992, 1993; Winter & Stewart, 1978).

Murray also proposed that we each have a need for achievement. This need has been extensively investigated by many other researchers, as we see next.

DAVID MCCLELLAND: NEED FOR ACHIEVEMENT THEORY

David McClelland and his colleagues have been particularly interested in the need for achievement (McClelland, 1961; McClelland, Atkinson, Clark, & Lowell, 1953; McClelland & Koestner, 1992; McClelland, Koestner, & Weinberger, 1992; McClelland & Winter, 1969). According to McClelland (1985), people who rank high in the need for achievement seek out moderately challenging tasks, persist at them, and are especially likely to pursue success in their occupations. Many entrepreneurs have a high need for achievement. They seek tasks in which they are likely both to succeed and to surpass themselves. These people do not waste time on tasks so challenging that they have little probability of accomplishing them, nor on tasks so easy that they pose no challenge at all.

People are especially likely to develop a high need for achievement if they have been pressured by their

Some girls believe that they should be passive bystanders in a world of active men, but in the West, this belief has become much less common than in the past.

parents (McClelland & Franz, 1992). Research has shown that our perception of reality, rather than reality per se, is a powerful predictor of how we react to demands for achievement, especially when we are children (Phillips, 1984). In other words, people are motivated not by pressures that objectively exist, but rather by their perceptions of these pressures. For example, a guitarist in a successful band may struggle to become as good as he perceives his musical role model to be, despite his own objective success.

GENDER DIFFERENCES. Unfortunately, girls more often perceive themselves to be less competent than boys do, particularly as they grow older. As a result, they may expect less of themselves than boys do (Phillips & Zimmerman, 1990). In particular, girls, unlike boys, may feel unable to succeed in a competitive environment (Spence & Helmreich, 1983). This effect appears to emerge as early as kindergarten (Frey & Ruble, 1987).

ⓒ **CULTURAL DIFFERENCES.** The achievement motive, which involves surpassing an internalized standard of excellence, is present in every culture and has been the focus of dozens of cross-cultural studies (Maehr & Nicholls, 1980; Markus & Kitayama, 1991, 1994). Because a higher need for achievement may be linked to increased productivity, programs in various cultures have been designed to foster the achievement motive in workers and managers. In one project, investigators assessed the effectiveness of attempts by Indian business owners to encourage their employees to emulate the level of the achievement motive attained by many Western businessmen and women. The Indian employees participated in an intense series of seminars designed to teach them to become achievement-oriented. The project was modestly successful (McClelland & Winter, 1969).

One of numerous studies of the achievement motive in China found that Chinese parents place great emphasis on achievement. But their focus is different from that of American parents (Ho, 1986). Whereas American children are motivated to achieve in order to be independent, Chinese children are motivated to please the family and the community.

The difference between American and Chinese children points out the importance of the distinction made by Harry Triandis (1990, 1994) and others between individualistic and collectivistic cultures. Individualistic cultures, such as the United States and Great Britain, stress individuality and the achievement of personal goals. Collectivistic cultures like China, Japan, and Venezuela emphasize meeting the needs of the group. In general, collectivistic cultures (comprising about 70% of the world's population) have lower rates of crime, alcoholism, and suicide than individualistic cultures. Apparently, feeling oneself to be an integral part of a group reduces the stress that leads to these maladaptive patterns of behavior.

ABRAHAM MASLOW: HIERARCHY OF NEEDS
Abraham Maslow (1943, 1954, 1970) viewed needs as a hierarchy (see Figure 12.3). Once we have satisfied needs at lower levels, we seek to satisfy needs at higher levels of the hierarchy.

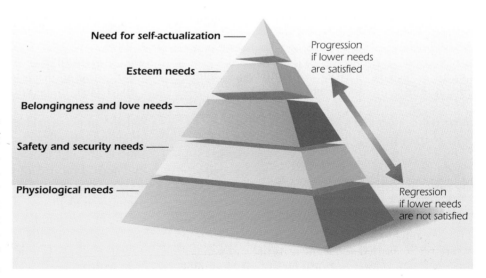

Need for self-actualization

Esteem needs

Belongingness and love needs

Safety and security needs

Physiological needs

Progression if lower needs are satisfied

Regression if lower needs are not satisfied

FIGURE 12.3

Maslow's Hierarchy of Needs. According to Abraham Maslow, we must satisfy our basic needs before we strive to meet the higher-level needs.

TABLE 12.2
CONCEPT REVIEW

Clinical Approaches to Motivation. Clinical psychologists have suggested that needs are the basis of our personalities, that we need to achieve, and that needs can be categorized into different levels.

Theory	Explanation
Theory of needs (Murray)	Needs form the core of our personalities and include needs for affiliation, power, and achievement.
Need for achievement (McClelland)	The need to achieve motivates us to be productive. People who intensely need to achieve seek out moderately difficult tasks because they are most likely to succeed at them while still being challenged.
Hierarchy of needs (Maslow)	We have five levels of needs: physiological, safety, belonging, self-esteem, and self-actualization. We must fulfill the needs at one level before we can proceed to the next.

At the first level are our basic survival or *physiological* needs for food, water, and oxygen. Even in affluent countries many people live in poverty and struggle daily to meet these most basic needs. The second-level needs for *safety and security* are for shelter and protection. At the third level is the need to *belong,* to feel that other people love and care about us and to be part of a meaningful group such as a family. The normal bond between children and parents shows how important this need is. At the fourth level is the need for *self-esteem,* to feel worthwhile. The highest-level need is for *self-actualization,* to fulfill our own potential.

Maslow's hierarchy is not rigid. However the hierarchy is conceived, though, the empirical evidence in favor of this theory of motivation is weak.

Table 12.2 summarizes the clinical approaches to motivation.

COGNITIVE APPROACHES

Cognitive theorists are especially interested in how thinking affects motivation and behavior.

INTRINSIC AND EXTRINSIC MOTIVATORS

Psychologists frequently describe motivation as either intrinsic or extrinsic. **Intrinsic motivators** are rewards that come from within, such as the desire to satisfy curiosity because to do so is enjoyable. **Extrinsic motivators** are rewards that come from the outside. We can act for intrinsic reasons, extrinsic reasons, or both. We might study hard in a given subject because we are really excited about the material and want to learn it (intrinsic motivation). Or we might simply want to get an A in the course (extrinsic motivation). Or both factors may be important to us.

Many extrinsic rewards ensure that people accomplish what is in society's interests. Our system of education focuses on grades, diplomas, and other pieces of paper that attest to what we have and have not accomplished. These extrinsic rewards reflect how society acknowledges the value of completing an educational program. How much weight do we as individuals give to extrinsic rewards?

People do their most creative work when they are intrinsically motivated (Amabile, 1983, 1985, 1996, 2001; Kurtzberg & Amabile, 2001; see also R. J. Sternberg & Lubart, 1995, 1996). The most creative writers, artists, scientists, and workers in any other field are almost invariably people who have worked largely for enjoyment. This is not to say that they were oblivious to extrinsic rewards. But they did what they did for the love of their work. The money, fame, or other extrinsic rewards were secondary. In fact, extrinsic motivators can sometimes undermine intrinsic motivation (Deci, Koestner, & Ryan, 1999a, 1999b; Henderlong & Lepper, 2002; Iyengar & Lepper, 2000; Lepper, 1998; Lepper & Henderlong, 2000; Lepper, Henderlong, & Gingras, 1999).

Janet Spence and Robert Helmreich (1983) studied the motivational patterns and achievements of thousands of college students, scientists, pilots, businesspeople, and athletes. They concluded that intrinsic motivation usually produces high achievement. Extrinsic motivation often does not. Spence and Helmreich identified and assessed three facets of intrinsic motivation: the quest for mastery, the drive to work, and competitiveness. They found that, despite similar abilities, people oriented toward mastery and hard work typically achieve more. Those who are *most* competitive, thereby showing more extrinsic orientation, often achieve *less.* People motivated by a desire

A father might encourage his daughter to build a sand castle, simply for the sheer joy of constructing it.

for mastery and the drive to work achieved more if they were not also highly competitive.

Edward Deci and his colleagues (Deci, Koestner, & Ryan, 1999a, 1999b; Deci & Ryan, 1995, 2002a, 2002b; Deci, Vallerand, Pelletier, & Ryan, 1991; Rigby, Deci, Patrick, & Ryan, 1992; Vallerand, Fortier, & Guay, 1997) have suggested that people need to feel competent, autonomous, and securely and satisfyingly connected to other people. According to Deci, we are all powerfully motivated to meet these three innate needs. (See the In the Lab box, "The Ups and Downs of Intrinsic Motivation.")

We also actively seek self-determination rather than determination by outside forces (deCharms, 1968). We tend to be unhappy when we feel controlled, whether by another person or by a substance, as in the case of addiction. We are motivated to be in charge of our own destiny.

The Western emphasis on self-determination helps explain our responses to extrinsic and intrinsic motivation. Intrinsically motivated activities satisfy both our need for competence and our need for autonomy. In contrast, many extrinsically motivated activities undermine our sense of autonomy. Then we attribute our behavior to sources outside ourselves. In such cases, lack of control may lead us to feel less competent.

CHARACTERISTICS OF EFFECTIVE REWARDS

Fortunately, not all extrinsic rewards have negative effects. Four critical factors seem to determine whether an extrinsic motivator will undermine intrinsic motivation (Cameron, Banko, & Pierce, 2001; Cameron & Pierce, 1994, 2002; Eisenberger & Armeli, 1997; Eisenberger & Cameron, 1996; Eisenberger, Haskins, & Gambleton, 1999; Eisenberger & Rhoades, 2001). The first factor is *expectancy*. The extrinsic reward will undermine intrinsic motivation only if the individual expects to receive the award for performing the tasks. The second factor is the *relevance* of the reward. The reward must be important to the individual. Suppose you are told that you will receive a spool of thread as a reward for performing a task. A spool of thread is not of any interest to you, yet you are interested in doing the task. The nominal reward will probably not undermine your intrinsic motivation. Indeed, you may even forget about it (R. Ross, 1975). The third factor is whether the extrinsic reward is *tangible* (e.g., a certificate, money, candy, a grade). Tangible rewards tend to undermine intrinsic motivation, but intangible ones—such as praise or a smile—do not (Deci, 1971, 1972; Deci, Koestner, & Ryan, 1999a, 1999b; Reeve & Deci, 1996; Swann & Pittman, 1977). The fourth and final factor is whether the reward is *contingent* on performance. Rewards that are contingent tend to undermine intrinsic motivation. Rewards that are noncontingent do not depend either on a task being performed, or, if it is performed, on its being performed well. Hence they do not tend to undermine intrinsic motivation (Deci, Koestner, & Ryan, 1999a).

EXPLANATORY STYLE

One of the best ways to remain intrinsically motivated is to adopt what Martin Seligman (1991, 2002a, 2002b) refers to as an *optimistic explanatory style*. People with such a style tend to attribute their successes to their own abilities and their failures to the environment. They motivate themselves by telling themselves that they can overcome external obstacles. People with a *pessimistic explanatory style*, in contrast, attribute their successes to the environment and their failures to their own lack of ability. They have greater difficulty motivating themselves. They believe that they lack the ability to succeed and hence it is scarcely worth trying (Peterson, Maier, & Seligman, 1993).

CURIOSITY AND CHALLENGE

What makes us curious about some things and not others? We tend to be curious about things that are moderately novel and moderately complex (Berlyne, 1960; Heyduk & Bahrick, 1977; Loewenstein, 1994). This makes sense. If something is totally familiar to us, we ignore it. We have nothing to learn from it or about it. Similarly, if something is wholly novel, we have no basis for understanding it. Something that is novel but within our realm of understanding piques our interest. We become curious and want to explore it.

Even in everyday activities, we seek some degree of intrinsic motivation and challenge. We and our fellow primates like to be active, to observe and explore our surroundings, and to gain mastery over our environments (R. W. White, 1959).

IN THE LAB OF EDWARD L. DECI

THE UPS AND DOWNS OF INTRINSIC MOTIVATION

Think for a moment about an activity that you love, something you happily do for no reward other than the interest and enjoyment you experience while doing it. It could be skateboarding, reading, or playing an instrument. Psychologists would describe you as intrinsically motivated when you do the activity: The motivation is within you and is self-sustaining. Intrinsic motivation contrasts with extrinsic motivation, in which your behavior is directed toward attaining a desired outcome, such as earning money, avoiding a reprimand, or winning a prize.

Now imagine that your uncle wants to encourage you to engage in your favorite activity—let's say it's playing softball—so he offers you $20 for each game your team wins. How do you suppose the extrinsic reward will affect your intrinsic motivation for softball? That is exactly the question I set out to answer in an experiment more than 30 years ago (Deci, 1971). I had college students come into the laboratory one at a time, and I asked them to work on four interesting building-block puzzles. I already knew the puzzles were intrinsically interesting because I had pilot-tested them with several other students. I treated all the participants in the study exactly the same, except for one detail. I told half that they would earn a dollar for each puzzle they solved, but I said nothing about money to the other half.

All the students worked on the same puzzles, but only half of them

Edward L. Deci received a PhD in social psychology from Carnegie Mellon University and was an interdisciplinary post-doctoral fellow at Stanford University. He has been on the psychology faculty at the University of Rochester since 1970. Throughout his career he has done research on human motivation and freedom, beginning with the work on intrinsic motivation. Together with Richard M. Ryan, he has developed self-determination theory, an organismic dialectical theory of human motivation that addresses issues such as the healthy development of personality, effective functioning in the social world, and the support of human autonomy among all people.

earned rewards for each one they solved. Subsequently, they all had an opportunity to work on more puzzles, but this time there were no rewards for anyone. The idea was to see how much time, if any, they would choose to spend on the puzzles when there was no reason for doing them other than their interest in the task itself. If the rewards had enhanced the participants' intrinsic motivation, the rewarded group would spend more free-play time working on the puzzles than the non-rewarded group, but if the rewards had undermined intrinsic motivation, the rewarded group would spend less time on the puzzles.

In fact, the results showed that the previously rewarded group did spend significantly less time on the puzzles, indicating that the extrinsic rewards were undermining their intrinsic motivation. Since that study, in more than 100 experiments using participants of different ages, different tasks, and different types of re-

wards, it has been confirmed that tangible extrinsic rewards do, indeed, undermine intrinsic motivation.

Many years ago, Richard Ryan and I proposed that the reason rewards undermine intrinsic motivation is that people come to view the rewards, rather than the activity, as the reason for performing the behavior. In other words, the rewards control their behavior. Ryan and his colleagues subsequently suggested that although rewards often feel controlling, it should be possible to use them in a way that is experienced as positive feedback or appreciation for a job well done. The researchers did an experiment to test this and found that when the language and style used to administer tangible rewards seemed controlling, the rewards were undermining, but when the language and style supported participants' initiative and acknowledged their good performance, the rewards were not detrimental (Ryan, Mims, & Koestner, 1983).

Ryan, our associates, and I then headed into schools and work organizations. We used questionnaires to investigate the same phenomena we had observed in the lab. We began by focusing on the degree to which different elementary-school teachers were oriented toward controlling students' behavior (e.g., by using rewards as controls) versus supporting students' autonomy. We found that students whose teachers were *autonomy supportive* reported more intrinsic motivation for learning and had higher self-esteem than students whose teachers were controlling, thus indicating that the autonomy-supportive teachers used rewards in ways that were less controlling and provided more information (Deci, Schwartz, Sheinman, & Ryan, 1981).

We then moved on to a major multinational corporation. We found that subordinates of managers who were oriented toward supporting employees' autonomy felt less pressured, had a higher level of trust, and were more satisfied with their jobs than subordinates of managers who were more controlling (Deci, Connell, & Ryan, 1989).

It seems, then, that the same effects we produced in the laboratory do occur outside it. That is, the use of rewards to motivate or control behavior tends to undermine intrinsic motivation and related feelings such as satisfaction and trust. But when those who administer rewards build and maintain meaningful relationships with the people they reward, and do not use the rewards to control their behavior, the rewards are less likely to be detrimental.

© Don Mason/Corbis

© Brooklyn Production/Corbis

Primates of all species appear to show curiosity, exploring their surroundings for the sheer joy of doing so. For example, monkeys will learn to perform tasks, such as opening latches, just to have something to do. (From Harlow, Harlow, & Meyer, 1950)

SELF-EFFICACY THEORY

How does our sense of competence affect the likelihood that we will attain our particular goal? Self-efficacy, our belief in our own competence to master the environment and reach personal goals, comes from a number of sources. They include direct experience, our interpretation of others' experiences, what people say we can do, and our assessment of our own emotional or motivational state. If we have a high degree of self-efficacy, we are likely to attain the outcomes we desire (Bandura, 1977a, 1986, 1995, 1996, 2002; Fernandez-Ballesteros, Diez-Nicolas, Caprara, Barbaranella, &

Bandura, 2002). There are no guarantees, however: Certain kinds of environments (e.g., dysfunctional families or repressive dictatorships) can make achievement difficult, regardless of self-efficacy.

Our sense of self-efficacy can lead to self-fulfilling prophecies. When we believe we are able to do something, we are more likely to devote the effort and resources to it and therefore to achieve the goal. One success leads to another. We see ourselves as continually successful in attaining the outcomes we desire. In contrast, if we have a low sense of self-efficacy, we probably believe that we are unable to succeed. As a result, we may not even try. The result, of course, is failure, which leads to the expectation of future failure. This expectation then becomes the basis for more failure.

One way to enhance our self-efficacy in reaching goals is to set realistic, highly specific goals and to devise plans for achieving them. If you have a goal of doing well in this course, for example, try telling yourself that you can do it and then make a concrete, specific plan for studying. Psychological theorists have long recognized that setting goals can be effective both in motivating people and in helping them get done what they need to get done (Ames, 1992; Dweck, 1992, 2002; Grant & Dweck, 2001; E. A. Locke & Latham, 1985, 1990; Tolman, 1932, 1959). Goals help us to focus our attention, mobilize our resources, and develop ways of getting things done, even in the face of obstacles.

The importance of goals has been demonstrated particularly well in studies that compare children who have learning versus performance goals. Carol Dweck (1999) has distinguished between goals that empha-size learning new information (learning goals) and those that emphasize showing oneself to be smart, regardless of whether one is really learning much (performance goals). Children who emphasize learning goals tend to be more willing to take on difficult challenges than children who emphasize performance goals. Moreover, when they encounter very challenging tasks, children who focus on learning are much less likely to become frustrated and fall apart than children who emphasize performance goals.

In sum, cognitive theories emphasize the role of thought processes in motivating behavior (see Table 12.3). They complement the other kinds of approaches, each offering a partial explanation of a complex behavior. Physiological, clinical, and cognitive theories all have strengths and weaknesses, generally working well to explain some motivations but not others.

Next we consider two primary motivations that are more complex than they may seem at first: hunger and sexual desire. As you read, consider how each theory discussed so far might explain why people become hungry and why they like to have sex.

✓ CONCEPT CHECK 2

1. According to arousal theory, on average, performance is optimized when arousal level is
   a. high.
   b. moderate.
   c. low.
   d. variable.

TABLE 12.3
CONCEPT REVIEW

Cognitive Approaches to Motivation. Cognitive psychologists have proposed that we respond to internal and external motivators, that we are motivated by curiosity and control, and that we are motivated by our belief in ourselves.

Approach	Description
Intrinsic and extrinsic motivators	Our interests motivate us intrinsically; rewards or threats of punishment motivate us extrinsically. Usually our behaviors are the result of a combination of intrinsic and extrinsic motivations, although we are most creative when we are mainly motivated intrinsically.
Curiosity, challenge, and control	We are most curious about things that are moderately new and complex because they challenge us without boring or confusing us. We can become totally absorbed in a task (Maslow). We always seek to understand and control our environments, to be competent (White, deCharms), and to be part of a group (Deci).
Self-efficacy theory (Bandura)	Our beliefs about whether we can reach a goal greatly influence our ability actually to attain it.

2. According to Solomon's opponent-process theory, the opponent process starts
   a. before the acquisition process.
   b. at the same time as the acquisition process.
   c. after the acquisition process.
   d. either before or after the acquisition process.
3. David McClelland is best known for his study of
   a. achievement motivation.
   b. self-actualization.
   c. intrinsic motivation.
   d. explanatory style.

BIOLOGICAL BASES OF MOTIVATION

What are the biological bases of motivation?

HUNGER

Scientists used to think that the regulation of hunger was very simple. They believed that we feel hunger when our stomach contracts (Cannon & Washburn, 1912). However, research has shown that this view is false. Both in rats (C. T. Morgan & Morgan, 1940) and in humans (M. I. Grossman & Stein, 1948), if the nerve responsible for carrying messages between the stomach and the brain is severed, organisms still feel hunger. Moreover, even after people's stomachs are surgically removed for medical reasons, the individuals continue to feel hunger (Janowitz, 1967; Wangensteen & Carlson, 1931). Clearly, there is more to hunger than just an empty feeling in the stomach.

Of course, the stomach participates in the regulation of hunger (McHugh & Moran, 1985). In all mammals, the stomach empties at a constant rate. For humans, the rate is slightly more than 2 calories per minute. Caloric content and not the volume of food determines how quickly the food leaves the stomach. A large bowl of lettuce with no dressing may leave you feeling hungry more quickly than a small piece of cake because the stomach empties itself of the lower-calorie lettuce more quickly. As the stomach contracts, we feel more and more hungry. Usually, we start to feel hunger when the stomach is roughly 60% empty. We feel very hungry when the stomach is 90% empty (Sepple & Read, 1989).

The stomach is not the only organ responsible for hunger. One of the most important organs in the body, the brain, is certainly involved in hunger.

THE ROLE OF THE BRAIN IN HUNGER

The brain, particularly the hypothalamus, is very important in regulating hunger (see Figure 3.11, p. 78, for the location of the hypothalamus). An animal that has a lesion in the ventromedial hypothalamus (VMH) will overeat and eventually become obese (Hetherington & Ranson, 1940; Teitelbaum, 1961; but see Valenstein, 1973; see Figure 12.4). The VMH, therefore, appears to regulate hunger. In particular, it serves as a source of negative feedback. When the organism is satiated, the VMH signals that it is time to stop eating. In animals with a destroyed VMH, the satiation signal never is sent.

Lesions in the lateral hypothalamus (LH) have exactly the opposite effect of VMH destruction (Anand & Brobeck, 1951). An animal that has a lesion in the LH simply does not eat. It eventually starves and then dies. Thus, the LH serves as an on switch for eating, and the VMH is an off switch.

THEORIES OF HUNGER REGULATION

In order for the VMH and LH to regulate eating behavior, they need information from the body. What signals hunger or satiety (fullness)? Two major hypotheses present possible explanations that may not be mutually exclusive. According to the *glucostatic hypothesis*, levels

© Richard Howard

FIGURE 12.4

Obese Rat. When a lesion is created in the ventromedial hypothalamus (VMH) of a rat brain, the rat becomes obese. Lesion studies led researchers to conclude that the VMH is involved in feelings of hunger.

of *glucose* (a simple body sugar) in the blood signal the body regarding the need for food (M. I. Friedman & Stricker, 1976). A person will feel hungry when the level of glucose falls below a certain point. The term *glucostatic* refers to the stability of glucose levels in the body and the brain.

Some findings cannot be accounted for by the glucostatic hypothesis (Cotman & McGaugh, 1980). As a result, an alternative explanation has emerged for understanding hunger. The *lipostatic hypothesis* suggests that the levels of *lipids* (fats) in the blood signal the body regarding the need for food. As the proportion of fats in the body decreases, hunger increases (Hoebel & Teitelbaum, 1966). According to this theory, eating is a way of maintaining adequate reserves of energy via body weight. Indeed, the body monitors these signs of fat cells on a fairly constant basis (Faust, Johnson, & Hirsch, 1977a, 1977b). When body fat gets too low, people eat. When it gets too high, they stop eating (Keesey, Boyle, Kemnitz, & Mitchell, 1976; Keesey & Powley, 1975).

A hormone called *leptin* may be involved in food-seeking behavior. Obesity may result when leptin fails to regulate hunger (Figlewicz et al., 1996; Rohner-Jeanrenaud, Cusin, Sainsbury, Zahrzewska, & Jeanrenaud, 1996; Tomaszuk, Simpson, & Williams, 1996; White & Martin, 1997). The lipostatic hypothesis led Richard Keesey, Terry Powley, and their colleagues to formulate their own theory. According to **set-point theory,** each person has a preset body weight that is biologically determined. The set point is established either at birth or within the first few years following birth, based on fat cells in the body, which may increase but not decrease in number over the life span (Grilo & Pogue-Geile,

1991; Keesey, 1980). People who have more fat cells tend to have greater body weight. The size of the fat cells varies with weight. When the person eats less, the size of the cells shrinks. The person feels hungry. When the person eats more, the size of the cells increases. The person feels full.

Set-point theory predicts that losing weight is very difficult because the tendency of the body is always to return to the set point, at which the fat cells are a normal size. If we diet, our bodies respond as though we were in a prolonged state of starvation. They store as much food energy as possible. Thus, the less we eat, the more our bodies work to help us overcome our starved condition. They struggle to keep us as fat as possible despite our low caloric intake.

Overeating for a long time can raise the set point (Keesey & Powley, 1986). Statistics on weight loss seem to support set-point theory. More than 90% of weight-losing dieters eventually gain the weight back. Certain research (Safer, 1991; Seraganian, 1993) indicates that combining exercise and a low-fat, low-calorie diet may be more effective in achieving weight loss than dietary restrictions alone. Both should be part of the treatment of obesity.

See Table 12.4 for a summary of the hunger-regulating theories.

OBESITY AND DIETING

People often are highly motivated to lose weight and yet fail. What factors lead to success or failure in losing weight, especially when one starts off as obese?

To be considered obese, a person must be at least 20% over the normal range for a given height and weight (see Chapter 18). According to the CDC Be-

---

TABLE 12.4
CONCEPT REVIEW

Theories of Hunger Regulation. Three prominent theories are based on the level of glucose in the blood, the level of fats in the blood, and the number of fat cells in the body.

Theory	Explanation
Glucostatic hypothesis	The VMH and LH monitor the level of glucose in the blood to determine the need for food.
Lipostatic hypothesis	The VMH and LH monitor the level of lipids (fats) in the blood to determine the need for food.
Set-point theory	We each have a preset body weight, determined by the number of fat cells in the body. The fat cells expand when we gain weight and contract when we lose weight. When we try to lose weight, it is difficult to get below the set point; our bodies interpret the diet as starvation and respond by storing as much food as possible. If we gain weight over time, the set point can increase.

havioral Risk Factor Surveillance System (BRFSS), about 20% of the U.S. population was obese in the year 2000. The numbers varied by geographic area, with the lowest overall rate in the mountain states (17% in Colorado and Wyoming) and the highest in the south-central states (23% in Kentucky and Tennessee). Of course, the figures depend on how we define obesity and how samples are obtained. The American Obesity Association estimates that 30.5% of the population is obese. In both cases, obesity is defined as a body mass index greater than 30.

The body mass index (BMI) is a measure of body fat based on height and weight. In general, underweight is viewed as a BMI under 18.5, normal weight as a BMI of between 18.5 and 24.9, overweight as a BMI of 25 to 29.9, and obesity as a BMI of 30 or higher (http://nhlbisupport.com/bmi/, 2003).

Many obese people, plus more who do not meet the definition of obesity, subject themselves to diets. Dieting often fails, however, because people become more susceptible to binge eating when they are dieting than when they are not (Polivy & Herman, 1983, 1985, 1993, 2002a, 2002b; Urbszat, Herman, & Polivy, 2002). When they experience anxiety, depression, stress, alcohol, high-calorie foods, or other factors, dieters seem to drop the restraints that have kept them from eating. Many start to binge (Polivy, Herman, & McFarlane, 1994). Those who are not dieting do not exhibit comparable behavior. This finding seems to give further support to set-point theory.

Polivy, Herman, and McFarlane (1994) have shown how attempts to diet or otherwise control weight through restrained eating can backfire. They classified a group of 96 college women as either restrained eaters (trying to control their weight by regulating food intake) or unrestrained eaters. Members of one group of participants were told they would have to give a speech about their abilities. Members of a second group were told they would be asked about their perceptions of fabrics on the basis of how the fabrics felt when touched. The goal of the manipulation was to introduce feelings of anxiety in the first group but not in the second. Earlier, participants had been asked to take part in a study of taste perception. In this study, they were allowed to eat as many cookies as they wished before passing judgment on their taste. Restrained eaters increased their consumption of cookies when they were anxious. In contrast, unrestrained eaters decreased their consumption. These results suggest that restrained eaters are susceptible to binge eating when confronted with the normal anxieties of life. Unrestrained eaters are actually likely to decrease food consumption when they feel anxious.

Media images also affect eating patterns. Mills, Polivy, Herman, and Tiggeman (2002) studied the effects of idealized body images on self-image in both habitual dieters and nondieters. They found that the dieters' ideal body sizes were smaller after they were exposed to idealized body images. So, restrained eaters are particularly susceptible to fantasies about thinness generated by the media.

Research (Brownell & Rodin, 1994; Brownell & Wadden, 1992; Lissner et al., 1991) also suggests that fluctuations in weight are more damaging to health than being overweight. In other words, you may do yourself more harm by engaging in a constant cycle of losing and regaining weight than by doing nothing about your weight.

Other factors seem to contribute to obesity as well. For example, we tend to eat more when presented with a wide variety of foods (Rolls, 1979; Rolls, Rowe, & Rolls, 1982). We also tend to eat more in the company of others (S. L. Berry, Beatty, & Klesges, 1985; deCastro & Brewer, 1992).

© CULTURAL FACTORS IN THE PERCEPTION OF OBESITY

Some cultural psychologists emphasize external factors in explaining wide individual differences in weight. Differences can be observed across both cultures and time. In Samoa, Fiji, Tonga, and other Pacific islands, it is not uncommon for men and women to weigh more than 300 pounds. In contrast, in Japan, very heavy people, such as well-fed Sumo wrestlers, clearly stand out in a crowd as violating societal norms. In the United States, J. Fuchs and his colleagues (1990) noted the relative infrequency of obesity among the Amish and attributed it to the healthful lifestyle in that culture.

Norms and expectations about what is considered an ideal weight also can be observed across time by viewing the historical collections in an art museum. In many masterworks by European artists, the bodies of nude women are quite ample by modern European or American standards. The contemporary trend toward ever more slender physiques is shown in the increasing prominence of slim models in popular women's magazines in various countries (Silverstein, Peterson, & Perdue, 1986). Perhaps people are motivated to satisfy their self-esteem or affiliation needs by achieving their culture's definition of the ideal weight.

ANOREXIA NERVOSA AND BULIMIA

Being overweight is a serious problem for many people. But some people tend to be chronically underweight, either because they metabolize food very quickly and inefficiently or because they have a hormonal imbalance. Instead of being motivated to eat to live, they are motivated to avoid eating and thus risk illness and even death. It is estimated that roughly 7 million girls and women, and about 1 million boys and men, suffer from eating disorders. About 10% report onset at age 10 or earlier. In contrast, 33% report

This woman fortunately recovered from anorexia, which can be life-threatening.

onset between the ages of 11 and 15, and 43% between the ages of 16 and 20. With treatment, about 60% of individuals with anorexia or other eating disorders recover fully. Another 20% recover partially (http://womensissues.about.com/library/bleatingdisorderstats.htm, 2003).

A small number of underweight people suffer from **anorexia nervosa,** an eating disorder in which a person undereats potentially to the point of starvation because of the extremely distorted belief that she (usually) or he is overweight. People who suffer from anorexia perceive themselves to be fat, so they put themselves on severe diets (Heilbrun & Witt, 1990). They are diagnosed as anorexic when they weigh less than 85% of their normal body weight, but they remain intensely afraid of becoming fat (DSM-IV, 1994). Somewhere between 0.5% and 3.7% of females suffer from anorexia during their lifetime. Between 10% and 25% of females who suffer from anorexia will die from it (http://womensissues.about.com/library/bleatingdisorderstats.htm, 2003).

The vast majority (95%) of anorexics are females between ages 15 and 30 (Gilbert & DeBlassie, 1984). The high value that American society places on slimness helps explain why mainly young women suffer from this disorder. Anorexia can also affect men, though, in whom it may be disguised as athleticism. Interestingly, the incidence of anorexia has increased in other societies as well, such as Denmark and Japan (Nielsen, 1990; Suematsu, Ishikawa, Kuboki, & Ito, 1985).

No one knows what causes anorexia. Some evidence indicates that the roots of the disorder may be in dysfunctional family relationships (Bruch, 1973), particularly those in which perfectionism and control are highly valued. Other evidence indicates that the roots may be physiological (Gwirtsman & Germer, 1981). The treatments of the disorder reflect the possible causes. Anorexics may undergo psychotherapy, drug treatment, and in severe cases, hospitalization to treat the psychological and physical problems (F. E. Martin, 1985).

More common than anorexia is *bulimia*, a disorder characterized by eating binges followed by vomiting or other means of purging, such as the use of laxatives. This disorder, like anorexia, occurs primarily in adolescence and young adulthood. Bulimia, too, is far more common in women than in men, and it is especially prevalent in adolescent girls (Striegel-Moore, Silberstein, & Rodin, 1993). It is estimated that between 1.1% and 4.2% of women suffer from bulimia at some point in their lifetime. As many as 19% of American college women are bulimic at some time during their college career (http://womensissues.about.com/library/bleatingdisorderstats.htm, 2003). Like anorexia, bulimia is difficult to treat. Also like anorexia, though, it usually can be treated successfully with psychotherapy and, where appropriate, drugs.

Concerns over body image may be a reflection of a larger preoccupation of many Western societies—sex.

SEX

How much do people think about sex anyway? According to Michael, Gagnon, Laumann, and Kolatu (1994), people think about sex a lot, especially men. As many as 54% of men and 19% of women think about it at least once a day.

The age of first sexual activity has increased over the last decade. In 1991, 57% of men and 51% of women had had sexual intercourse during their high school years. By 1999, this percentage had decreased to 52% of men and 48% of women. Men are more likely than women to report having had more than four partners (19% versus 13%). Among girls 15 to 19 years of age, 69% reported their first experience as being voluntary, 24% as voluntary but unwanted, and 7% as nonvoluntary. About two out of three sexually active girls aged 15 to 19 reported using contraception, but not every time, which raises questions about the effectiveness of using contraception (http://www.kff.org/content/2001/20011211a/TeenSexualActivity.pdf).

Sexual motivation obviously differs in key respects from hunger motivation. Although very few people try to make themselves hungry or thirsty, most do seek sexual arousal. People also tend to enjoy sex-

ual arousal more than they enjoy hunger. Perhaps the key difference relates to individual survival. People can survive without sexual gratification, but they cannot survive without food or water. You might therefore conclude that sexual motivation is in a category wholly different from hunger. In at least one sense, this conclusion is incorrect. Sexual motivation is as important to the ultimate survival of humanity as is hunger motivation. If people did not satisfy their sexual wants, humanity would disappear just as certainly as it would from starvation.

The hypothalamus, which plays a role in hunger motivation, is also important in sexual motivation. The role it plays, however, is indirect. The hypothalamus stimulates the pituitary gland, which in turn releases hormones that influence the production of sex hormones (see Chapter 3). The two main kinds of sex hormones are androgens and estrogens. Both males and females have both hormones. However, androgens predominate in the male, estrogens in the female. Without these hormones, sexual desire disappears—abruptly in many species, but only gradually among most humans (Money, Wiedeking, Walker, & Gain, 1976).

Sexual desire serves an important evolutionary function because it is key to the survival of many kinds of organisms. David Buss (1994) suggested that men and women have rather different sexual strategies. A man can impregnate several women in relatively short succession. So a man's optimal strategy for spreading and perpetuating his genes might lead him, evolutionarily, to have relatively low standards. In theory, and too often in practice, a man can impregnate a woman and quickly be gone. A woman can become pregnant no more often than once every 9 to 12 months. Perhaps, therefore, women can be expected evolutionarily to have higher standards. If a woman chooses the wrong man, she is left with the consequences—not only pregnancy and childbirth, but usually the responsibility of raising the child as well. According to Buss (2001, 2003; Shackelford, Buss, & Bennett, 2002), men are more likely to display sexual jealousy, and women tend to be more jealous about emotional infidelity. This view is by no means universally accepted, however. There is some evidence that the effect may be due to the forced-choice response format used with research participants, in which one must pick an answer even if none fits well (DeSteno, Bartlett, Braverman, & Salovey, 2002).

SEXUAL SCRIPTS AND SOCIAL NORMS

Sexual desire is always accompanied by cognitive processing. One may feel strongly attracted to someone, but even blind attraction is accompanied by thoughts of how desirable the person is. One way to describe the cognitive processes that accompany sexual response is in terms of *sexual scripts*, mental representa-

Passionately kissing in public may satisfy a sexual script but may also sometimes violate a social norm.

tions of how sequences of sexual events should be enacted (Gagnon, 1973; Gagnon, Giami, Michaels, & Colomby, 2001; W. H. Simon & Gagnon, 1986). Most of us—whether or not we have ever engaged in sexual intercourse—probably could describe some kind of sexual script. We find the scripts in racy novels, romantic television shows, and sexy movies. Most of us have many sexual scripts to choose from, depending on the person we are with—or whether we are with another person at all. Although the desire for sexual consummation is largely physiological, scripts also reflect social influences.

An example of a sexual script gone bad is *date rape*, which occurs when someone is forced to have sexual intercourse in the context of a social engagement. Date rape is most likely to occur when a man believes in a sexual script in which his role is to overcome resistance, in whatever way, on the part of a woman. If the woman has a script in which she believes she should offer token resistance and then give in, date rape is even more likely. According to Murnen, Peroit, and Byrne (1989), more than half of college women report having experienced unwanted sexual activity. Clearly, both men and women need to recognize the adverse consequences of the maladaptive sexual scripts that condone or even encourage date rape.

There are sex differences in perceptions of what constitutes date rape (Humphreys, 2001). Women are

more likely than men to emphasize the importance of consent in sexual encounters, although students who have had sexual intercourse are less likely to emphasize consent than those who have not. Men must understand the importance of consent better than they evidently do.

Ⓒ Every society attempts to regulate the sexual behavior of its members. All societies impose a taboo against *incest*—sexual contact between biologically related members of an immediate family. Similarly, most societies attempt to regulate sexual behavior through cultural norms. They involve modesty, masturbation, premarital intercourse, marital intercourse, extramarital intercourse, and homosexuality, among other things. For example, norms of modesty determine the regions of the male and the female body that should be covered or exposed, decorated or unadorned. Although the specific regions that are to be covered or exposed differ widely, all cultures seem to impose some standards of modesty.

HOMOSEXUALITY

Ⓒ In American culture, most sexual scripts are heterosexual. But homosexual scripts are also common. Homosexuality is a tendency to direct sexual desire toward members of the same sex. Thus, people with a primarily homosexual orientation are motivated to seek sexual partners of the same rather than the opposite sex. Although we speak of homosexuality and heterosexuality as though the two are discrete and mutually exclusive, perhaps it is best to consider them as points on a continuum. At one end are people who are exclusively homosexual. At the other end are those who are exclusively heterosexual. Many others fall in between. People who direct their sexual desire to members of both sexes are bisexual. Some researchers have found that about

10% of men and a slightly smaller proportion of women identify themselves as having predominantly homosexual orientations (e.g., see Fay, Turner, Klassen, & Gagnon, 1989; S. M. Rogers & Turner, 1991).

The Kinsey Institute reports a variety of statistics on the prevalence of homosexuality (http://www.indiana.edu/~kinsey/resources/bib-homoprev.html). In one study, 6% of U.S. men and about 3.5% of U.S. women reported sexual contact with someone of the same sex or with members of both sexes in the past 5 years. But 21% of U.S. men and 18% of U.S. women reported some homosexual behavior or attraction since the age of 15.

An article by Sell, Wells, and Wypij (1995) reported data on both homosexual attraction and homosexual behavior. They reported 6.2% of U.S. men and 3.6% of U.S. women with "sexual contact with someone of the same sex only or with both sexes in the previous 5 years" and 20.8% of U.S. men and 17.8% of U.S. women with some homosexual behavior or some homosexual attraction since age 15. The percentage of U.S. respondents who reported sexual contact only with others of the same sex in the past 5 years was less than 1%.

What causes homosexuality or bisexuality—or heterosexuality, for that matter? Various explanations exist, some more scientific than others (Biery, 1990). Of the several theories proposed (see Table 12.5), the most evidence seems to support a biological explanation, although the verdict is by no means in (R. Byrne, 1995). Until quite recently, many psychiatrists and psychologists believed that homosexuality was a form of mental illness. However, no inherent association between maladjustment or psychopathology and homosexuality has been found (Hooker, 1993).

Hewitt (1998) has proposed that homosexual individuals can be classified into five types: (1) *open preferential homosexuals*, who know they sexually prefer members of the same sex and are open about it; (2) *repressed preferential homosexuals*, who are reluctant to admit to themselves or to others that their sexual preference is homosexual; (3) *bisexuals*, whose sexual preference extends to both sexes; (4) *experimental homosexuals*, who try out homosexuality as an experiment but do not regularly engage in it; and (5) *situational homosexuals*, who choose homosexual partners because the situation encourages or demands it (usually due to unavailability of partners of the opposite sex).

If there is a biological basis for homosexuality, then whether this predisposition is actually expressed in behavior may well depend on social learning and other environmental factors. Daryl J. Bem (1996, 2000a,

Many gay people take pride in their sexual preference and actively display their support for their freedom of choice to do so.

TABLE 12.5
CONCEPT REVIEW

Homosexual Versus Heterosexual Orientation. Over the years, psychologists have posited various reasons for sexual orientation. Most recently, biological reasons seem to be the most plausible, but additional research in this area is sorely needed.

Reason	Related Motivational Theory	Description	Critique
Biological	Physiological	Sexual orientation is, in part, a result of biological processes.	There is some support for this view. A small region of the hypothalamus may be less than half as large in homosexual men as in heterosexual men (LeVay, 1991). If one of a pair of genetically identical male twins is homosexual, the other is almost three times more likely to have the same orientation as in nonidentical twin pairs (J. M. Bailey & Pillard, 1991).
Parenting	Clinical	Homosexuals had weak fathers or dominant mothers.	Not well supported by data. There are far too many exceptions to this generalization, and it is not widely accepted today.
Arrested development	Freudian	Homosexuals become fixated in a homosexual phase of psychosexual development.	This view implies that everyone passes through a homosexual phase. There is no empirical evidence for this point of view.
Personal choice	Cognitive, self-determination, control	We simply choose our sexual orientations.	Whatever attracts one person to another is rarely a matter of conscious choice.
Social learning	Cognitive, extrinsic motivation	Homosexuals were rewarded for homosexual leanings and punished for heterosexual ones.	Mainstream U.S. society (among others) does not reward homosexual orientation, and few children are likely to be exposed to overtly homosexual role models. Of those who are, about the same proportion become heterosexual or homosexual as in the mainstream population.
Gender nonconformity	Cognitive	Members of the same sex are seen as more exotic and hence more attractive than members of the opposite sex.	Evidence is very preliminary.

2000b) has suggested that homosexual behavior results when a child views members of the same sex as more unfamiliar and exotic than members of the opposite sex. In this view, the exotic becomes erotic. The child soon becomes attracted to members of the same sex.

We view homosexuality and sexual orientation according to our culture's prescriptions and taboos (Wade & Cirese, 1991). We are unlikely to find a single cause for homosexual orientation. A combination of factors probably leads people one way or another.

As we have just seen, what at first may seem like a simple matter of satisfying a physiological need, whether for food or for sex, may be complex. It can be affected by a tangle of different motivational processes, all interacting at once. In the next half of the chapter, we will see that our emotions are also complex.

✓ **CONCEPT CHECK 3**

1. A lesion in the lateral hypothalamus can lead an animal to
   a. overeat.
   b. starve.
   c. sleep for long periods of time.
   d. be unable to sleep.
2. According to set-point theory, each person has a preset body weight that is
   a. biologically determined.
   b. environmentally determined.
   c. determined by both biology and environment.
   d. determined by neither biology nor environment.
3. Anorexics
   a. are equally likely to be male or female.
   b. are more likely to be male.
   c. are more likely to be female.
   d. show no pattern with regard to sex.

EMOTIONS AND THEIR CHARACTERISTICS

What are the major emotions and how do they function?

An **emotion** is a positive or negative state of arousal in reaction to a perceived or remembered event or object (see J. G. Carlson & Hatfield, 1992). For example, happiness and sadness may affect us physically by changing our heart rate, blood pressure, and other indices. Emotion is a major focus of psychological research today (Keltner & Ekman, 2000; Oatley, 2000; Rosenberg & Ekman, 2000). A motivation is typically to do something (or occasionally not to do something); an emotion is typically not directed toward a particular action.

Emotions can be preprogrammed genetically or learned. They are manifested in various ways, including facial expressions, tones of voice, and actions. Furthermore, they can be caused either by stimuli impinging on us from the outside or by things that happen within our body (Ekman & Davidson, 1994). For example, the way you react to misplacing your car keys may depend on whether you have just had a large cup of coffee or a large meal. Emotion and motivation are very closely linked. Often, it is difficult to distinguish between them. In general, for motives the stimulus is unobserved, whereas for emotions it often is apparent. Motives are also more likely to occur cyclically (e.g., recurring hunger) than are emotions. Motives are further experienced as desires to attain something, whereas emotions are experienced as feelings that are not linked to any particular attainment. Just what are the major emotions?

Happiness, fear, anger, sadness, and disgust are the five emotions most often regarded as basic to all humans. Happiness is generally viewed as a positive emotion, whereas fear, anger, sadness, and disgust are considered negative emotions. Sometimes, disgust is not viewed as basic but rather as a combination of fear and anxiety. As we will see, these emotions have emerged as universal. They are experienced and recognized readily in diverse cultures. Some would add the emotions surprise (which is much less commonly recognized across cultures), guilt (a private sense of culpability), and shame (public humiliation). See Figure 12.5 for an illustration of the various shadings of emotions. The five most widely recognized emotions have been researched more than most others.

FIGURE 12.5

Plutchik's Emotion Wheel. Robert Plutchik posits eight basic emotions, which occur in four opposing pairs. Adjacent emotions combine to create a composite emotion (e.g., joy combined with acceptance yields love). (From R. Plutchik, "A Language for the Emotions," *Psychology Today,* February 1980. Reprinted with permission from Psychology Today Magazine. Copyright © 1980 Sussex Publishers, Inc.)

HAPPINESS

Happiness, the feeling of joy or at least contentment, is usually considered a fundamental emotion. When people describe what they experience when they feel *happy*, they say that they feel a warm inner glow, or feel like smiling, or feel a sense of well-being, of harmony and peace. Not everyone defines *happiness* in exactly the same way, though. For some people, happiness is achieved with pleasure, almost without regard to the cost. For others, happiness is essentially the absence of problems (Bradburn, 1969; Bradburn & Capovitz, 1965).

Although we tend to think of happiness as a temporary state, it may also have some enduring aspects. When people rate their happiness, the mean is about 6 on a 10-point scale (Wesman & Ricks, 1966). Moreover, the ratings of a given person are remarkably constant from one day to the next. Married people generally tend to be happier than never-married people, and except in very poor countries, personal wealth is not a predictor of happiness (Crawford Solberg, Diener, Wirtz, Lucas, & Oishi, 2002; Diener & Biswas-Diener, 2002; Diener, Lucas, & Oishi, 2002; D. Myers & Diener, 1995).

There may also be differences across cultures. In a study of happiness in 13 countries, the proportion of people who described themselves as "very happy" varied from one country to the next. The percentages ranged from a low of 34% in South Korea to a high of 52% in Italy (Hastings & Hastings, 1982). The difference is obviously substantial.

Even people in relatively miserable life circumstances can find happiness. Biswas-Diener and Diener (2001) interviewed 83 people who lived in the slums of Calcutta, India. The participants completed measures of subjective well-being and were asked to recall events that had made them happy. The participants were divided into three groups. One group lived in slum housing, a second consisted of sex workers, and the third was homeless people. Although the average rating of general life satisfaction was slightly negative, the average ratings of satisfaction for specific life domains were positive. Thus, the slum dwellers of Calcutta were generally less happy with their lives than people in more affluent comparison groups, but they were more satisfied than might have been anticipated on the basis of their objectively poor circumstances. In part, the authors suggested, this result might reflect India's strong emphasis on social relationships.

© Robbie Jack/Corbis

Intense anger may be felt within an intimate relationship, such as close friendship, as well as between antagonists.

FEAR AND ANXIETY

Fear is an emotion characterized by being afraid of a specific threat of danger or harm, focused on a particular object or experience. From an evolutionary point of view, fear serves a protective function. It motivates us to avoid or to flee from threats that might cause us harm. **Anxiety** is a generalized feeling of dread or apprehension that is not focused on or directed toward any particular object or event. Thus, the difference between fear and anxiety is in the identification of the cause of distress. In fear, we can point to the cause. In anxiety, we cannot. When anxious, we feel apprehensive without knowing exactly why. In addition, anxiety is generally more pervasive and diffuse and it tends to last longer. Anxiety can arise out of fear. What may be an objective fear at one time can give way to a generalized anxiety later on. Although almost everyone feels simple anxiety at one time or another, anxiety disorders are more serious (see Chapter 16).

ANGER

Anger is the belief that one's misfortune is controlled by people or events outside one's control. It is most often felt when a person believes that the misfortune is intentionally inflicted. We are most likely to be angry at another person when we perceive that we have suffered unjustified and intentional insult or injury (Averill, 1983). If we think that someone's behavior is accidental, unavoidable, or justified, we are much less likely to become angry. Typically, we believe that we are likely to feel anger toward those we dislike or detest. In fact, we are most likely to feel anger toward the people closest to us. Consider some (rounded) percentages. About 29% of our overt expressions of anger are directed toward people we love, 24% toward people we like, 25% toward acquaintances, and only 8% toward people we actively dislike (Averill, 1980, 1983). Only 13% of our expressions of anger are directed toward strangers. Anger is often associated with increases in heart rate, blood pressure, or both.

At one time, the prevailing belief was that the best way to rid oneself of anger is to express it and get it out of one's system. Recent research shows this advice to be incorrect. Expressing the anger often increases it and may lead to poor health, problems in interpersonal relationships, and even more anger as the anger feeds on itself (Deffenbacher, 1994; Tavris, 1989; R. B. Williams, 1989). The advice to count to 10— or 100—before sounding off is generally wise.

SADNESS AND GRIEF

Sadness is a relatively brief emotion of sorrow. *Grief* is a sharp, deep, and usually relatively long-lasting emotion of great sorrow, often associated with a loss. Sadness and grief tend to be caused by an involuntary, often permanent, loss or separation. Some typical causes are making a mistake, doing something to hurt others, and being forced to do something against your will (Izard, 1977). Although virtually no one enjoys sadness, it can have an adaptive function. For one thing, it can encourage people to change their lives (Izard, 1977; Tomkins, 1963). If we feel sad that we hurt another person, for example, we may be motivated to make amends. Sadness can also be a cue for other people to help us. When others see that we are sad, they may come to our aid, even if we have not explicitly said how we feel. Feeling very sad, especially for a long period of time, can lead to depression.

DISGUST

Disgust is a response to objects, experiences, or behavior deemed to be repulsive due to their nature, origin, or social history (see Rozin & Fallon, 1987; Rozin, Haidt, McCauley, Dunlop, & Ashmore, 1999). Disgust serves an adaptive purpose by motivating us to remove ourselves from what might be harmful, such as putrid meat or other contaminated food or other substances. This definition of disgust as a form of rejection is supported by experimentation and other methods of analysis (Rozin, 1996; Rozin, Millman, & Nemeroff, 1986). Disgust has a psychological origin. Things that may seem disgusting in one culture (such as eating termites or cockroaches) may not seem disgusting in another.

ARE SOME EMOTIONS BASIC?

Not all psychologists believe that the five emotions described here, or any other emotions, can be viewed as truly basic in any meaningful sense. Phillip Shaver and his colleagues have pointed out that emotions considered basic by one culture may not be considered basic by another, or may not even be experienced as emotions at all (P. Shaver, Schwartz, Krison, & O'Connor, 1987; P. Shaver, Wu, & Schwartz, 1992). For example, a basic emotion in the People's Republic of China, "sad love," involves feelings of unrequited love combined with infatuation and sorrow. This is not even considered a single emotion in the United States. Moreover, it is not clear that some emotions considered "basic" in some theories, such as disgust, are so considered by the people who experience them. Clearly, the question of whether any emotions are truly basic remains open. One way in which it can be addressed is through an evolutionary perspective.

THE EVOLUTIONARY VALUE OF EMOTIONS

Emotions have both a *physiological aspect*, in which we physically register emotions in distinctive ways, and a *cognitive aspect*, in which we interpret how we feel. Both aspects are essential to our survival. From an evolutionary perspective, there may be good reasons for emotions (Plutchik, 1983, 2003). Emotions such as anger and fear can help prepare us to behave in particular ways in a given situation. Anger can prepare us to fight an aggressor whom we have a pretty good chance of defeating. Fear can prepare us to flee from an aggressor who might conquer us. Survival depends on knowing when to fight a beatable foe and when to flee from an unbeatable enemy. Disgust can also aid survival, steering us away from poisonous substances. Judicious reliance on emotional reactions to danger may mean the difference between life and death.

Consider, too, the love parents feel for their children. Obviously, this love brings happiness to both parents and children. From the perspective of evolutionary survival, however, the love that bonds parents and children has another purpose. It helps ensure that the parent will watch over the child's safety, health, and survival as long as the child remains dependent on

The similarity of facial expressions across cultures exemplifies the communicative function of emotion. We can "read" expressions to learn what others are feeling.

Emotions have evolutionary value. The love that bonds parents and offspring helps ensure that the parent will watch over the child's safety.

the parent. Perhaps what parents exhibit in caring for their children is **emotional intelligence,** the ability to perceive emotion accurately, appraise it realistically, and express it appropriately. Emotional intelligence generates feelings when they facilitate thought and regulates them to promote emotional and intellectual growth (J. D. Mayer & Salovey, 1995). The concept of emotional intelligence (mentioned also in Chapter 9) was introduced by Salovey and Mayer (J. D. Mayer & Salovey, 1993; J. D. Mayer, Salovey, & Caruso, 2000; Salovey & Mayer, 1990; Salovey, Mayer, & Caruso, 2002; Salovey & Pizarro, 2003) and popularized and expanded upon by Goleman (1995).

There is good evidence, although it is not conclusive, for the existence of emotional intelligence. J. D. Mayer and Gehr (1996) found that understanding the emotions of characters in a variety of situations correlates with SAT scores, with empathy, and with emotional openness. At the same time, Davies, Stankov, and Roberts (1998) argued that the emotional-intelligence construct does not hold together psychologically. Full validation of the construct, therefore, appears to be needed, which in turn requires sophisticated measurement tools and techniques.

✓CONCEPT CHECK 4

1. Fear differs from anxiety in that it is a reaction to a
   a. person rather than a thing.
   b. thing rather than a person.
   c. diffuse danger.
   d. specific danger.

2. Disgust serves an adaptive purpose by removing us from things that are
   a. unpleasant.
   b. unknown.
   c. contaminated.
   d. useless.

3. Emotions have
   a. a cognitive aspect but not a physiological aspect.
   b. a physiological aspect but not a cognitive aspect.
   c. both a physiological aspect and a cognitive aspect.
   d. neither a cognitive aspect nor a physiological aspect.

MEASURING EMOTIONS

How are emotions measured?

How do we know when people feel emotion and how much of an emotion they experience? One way of finding out is simply to ask them. **Self-report measures** require people to state their responses to questions about their psychological processes and behaviors. Often, researchers find it difficult to quantify people's spontaneous self-reported expressions. So alternative self-report measures have been devised.

A **Likert scale** asks respondents to choose which of several options best describes the extent to which they are experiencing an emotion (or anything else). For example, people might be given a set of statements, such as "I feel tense," and be asked to rate each statement. Different scales might be used. On a 4-point scale, 0 might mean that they do not feel tense at all, 1 that they feel slightly tense, 2 that they feel moderately tense, and 3 that they feel very tense (see, e.g., Spielberger, Gorsuch, & Lushene, 1983). A person's feelings of anxiety would then be the average (or sum) of the numbers checked for the various self-report items.

Various psychophysiological measures also register emotion. They include heart rate, respiration rate, blood pressure, and galvanic skin response (GSR), which tracks the electrical conductivity of the skin. Conductivity increases with perspiration, so a person under emotional stress will perspire and thus have an increased GSR. This physiological fact, and the belief that the body cannot lie, are the bases for the art, and perhaps science, of lie detection. They are discussed in the Psychology in Everyday Life box, "Detecting Lies."

One controversial measure that has been used to ferret out emotions is the so-called lie detector—the polygraph. A **polygraph** assesses the accuracy of self-report measures by tracking various physiological processes, such as reactivity of heart rate, GSR, and respiration. The idea, of course, is to provide an objective measure of whether people are feeling emotional stress. In fact, because the polygraph measures only stress reactions, which also register for reasons other than lying, it does not catch falsehoods made by people who feel no stress when they are lying.

In a common format for polygraph testing, the operator asks a series of questions and compares psychophysiological responses to innocuous questions ("In what city were you born?")

with responses to potentially threatening questions ("Did you murder your professor?"). A more effective format involves questions that assess whether a person possesses information that only a guilty person would know (Bashore & Rapp, 1993).

How accurate are polygraphs? The results of controlled studies are not encouraging. Although professional interpreters of polygraphs have been found to be correct in identifying guilty parties 76% of the time, they have also labeled as guilty 37% of the innocent people they tested (Kleinmuntz & Szucko, 1984). A review of more than 250 studies of the validity of interpretation of polygraph results shows similar findings (Saxe, Dougherty, & Cross, 1985; see also Ben-Shakhar & Furedy,

1990). Thus, these studies suggest that interpreters of results are fairly good at recognizing guilty parties but also classify disturbing numbers of innocent people as guilty. In the language of signal-detection theory (see Chapter 4), the hit rate is high but so is the rate of false alarms.

Results such as these indicate that polygraph tests, as they are now interpreted, are far from reliable, and some scientists question whether they are reliable at all (Lykken, 1998). At present, polygraph results should be interpreted only with the greatest of caution.

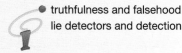

truthfulness and falsehood
lie detectors and detection

THE PHYSICAL APPEARANCE OF EMOTIONS

Expressing emotion enables us to communicate our feelings to other people and also regulates how other people respond to us (Izard, 1989, 1991, 1993). For example, mothers respond in different ways depending on their babies' expressions (Huebner & Izard, 1988). Facial expressions play a big role in the expression of emotion.

The similarity of facial expressions across cultures exemplifies the communicative function of emotion. Researchers studied the ability of tribal New Guineans to recognize facial expressions in photographs of Westerners (Ekman & Friesen, 1975). Both adults and children were quite accurate in recognizing expressions of happiness, sadness, anger, disgust, surprise, and fear. Americans also were fairly accurate in recognizing New Guinean expressions. In all cases, accuracy was greatest for happiness and lowest for fear. Ekman (1984, 1992a, 1992b) extended this work by showing identical photographs to people in the United States, Brazil, Chile, Argentina, and Japan. Once again, the consensus across cultures was remarkable, although there is some dispute over the interpretation of the results (Ekman, 1994; J. A. Russell, 1994). As in the study in New Guinea, agreement was greatest for happiness and lowest for fear.

The high level of agreement across cultures suggests that facial expressions for emotions may be an innate

part of our physiological makeup. In the case of the New Guineans, at least, the tribe members had had virtually no contact with Westerners. Yet their facial expressions and judgments of facial expressions were very similar to those of people in the United States (see Figure 12.6).

THE FACIAL-FEEDBACK HYPOTHESIS

It might seem that the expression of emotion follows the experience of that emotion. Silvan Tomkins (1962, 1963) has taken the opposite point of view. He has put forward the **facial-feedback hypothesis**, which proposes that we feel emotion as a result of feedback from the face. In other words, the facial expression of an emotion leads to the experiencing of that emotion.

A strong version of the facial-feedback hypothesis suggests that simply manipulating your face to show a certain emotion leads you to feel that emotion. Thus, smiling makes you happy; puckering up your face in disgust makes you feel disgusted. The data on the strong version of the facial-feedback hypothesis are mixed. Creating a facial expression does appear to produce particular changes in psychophysiological reactions (see Figure 12.7). But it is unclear whether or not these changes are the same as experiencing the emotion itself (Ekman, Levenson, & Friesen, 1983; Levenson, Ekman, & Friesen, 1990; Tourangeau & Ellsworth, 1979).

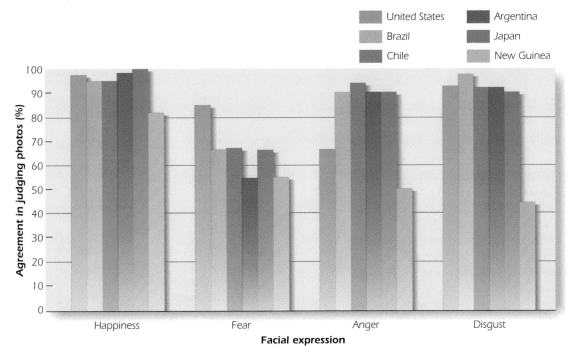

FIGURE 12.6

Cultural Agreement Regarding Facial Expressions. Cross-cultural similarity of facial expressions of emotions appears highest for happiness and disgust and lowest for anger and fear. The greatest discrepancy with others was shown by New Guineans, who had not had extensive contact with other cultural groups. (From *Unmasking the Face,* 2nd Edition, by Ekman & Friesen. Copyright © 1984. Reprinted by permission of the author.)

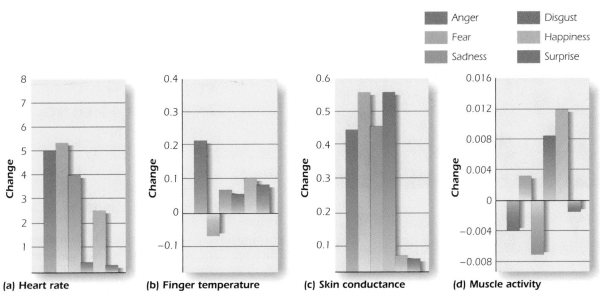

FIGURE 12.7

Physiological Changes Caused by Facial Expression. Some evidence indicates that when we deliberately change our facial expressions to show particular emotions, our bodies respond through physiological changes in heart rate, circulation (as shown in finger temperature), sweating (as shown in skin conductance), and muscle activity. (From Levenson, Ekman, & Friesen, 1990. Reprinted by permission of the author.)

A less extreme version of the facial-feedback hypothesis suggests that facial feedback can affect the intensity of an emotion but does not actually produce an emotion. The weaker version of the hypothesis has received fairly uniform support (e.g., M. Zuckerman, Klorman, Larrance, & Speigel, 1981).

SEEING THROUGH A FALSE FRONT

It is possible to detect insincere facial expressions of emotion and to tell from facial expressions when people are lying (Ekman, 1992a, 1992b, 2001; Ekman, Friesen, & O'Sullivan, 1988; Ekman, O'Sullivan, & Frank, 1999; Etcoff, Ekman, Magee, & Frank, 2000). Genuine expressions of emotions tend to involve the features symmetrically. False ones are likely to be asymmetrical (see Figure 12.8). In addition, if lying is accompanied by emotion in the liar, we may be able to detect the lie on the basis of facial expressions. If a person actually believes his or her own lies, however, it is very difficult to figure out whether the truth is being told.

Experienced liars, such as criminals, may be able to convey deceptively honest-looking expressions. Of the people who are supposed to be skillful in detecting lies (police officers, employees of the Federal Bureau of Investigation, and members of the Secret Service), Secret Service members seem to be the most able to detect the emotional expressions that identify people as liars (Ekman, 1992a, 1992b). But the picture is more complex.

Ekman, O'Sullivan, and Frank (1999) noted that most people cannot tell from facial and body cues when others are lying. Oddly, such poor performance is typical not only of lay people but also, as noted above, of most professionals whose job involves lie detection. But the situation is far from hopeless. In this study, federal officers, federal judges, law-enforcement officers, clinical psychologists, and academic psychologists all had relatively high accuracy in judging videotapes of people who were either lying or telling the truth about their opinions. This study was the first to demonstrate that trained psychologists do better than average in detecting liars.

✓ **CONCEPT CHECK 5**

1. Results from studies of the validity of polygraph testing are
   a. highly encouraging.
   b. fairly encouraging.
   c. slightly encouraging.
   d. not encouraging.
2. People, on average, seem to be most accurate in assessing faces for _____ and least accurate for _____.
   a. happiness . . . fear
   b. fear . . . happiness
   c. disgust . . . sadness
   d. sadness . . . disgust
3. The group that appears to have the greatest accuracy in detecting deception is the
   a. Secret Service.
   b. FBI.
   c. CIA.
   d. Royal Canadian Mounted Police.

APPROACHES TO UNDERSTANDING EMOTIONS

What are the major approaches to understanding emotion?

The approaches to understanding human emotions are diverse. Many of their aspects are complementary rather than contradictory. Each approach offers insight into how and why we feel as we do.

EARLY PSYCHOPHYSIOLOGICAL APPROACHES

Today, psychophysiological studies involve cutting-edge technologies, state-of-the-art methodologies, and dynamic revolutions in theoretical understand-

Ekman, P., Friesen, W. V., & O'Sullivan, M. (1988). Smiles: "Genuine" and "Fake" Journal of Personality and Social Psychology, 54, 414–420. Reprinted by permission of Paul Ekman.

FIGURE 12.8

Sincere Smiles. Which smile is genuine? (After Ekman, Friesen, & O'Sullivan, 1988)

ings. Oddly, psychophysiological approaches to understanding emotions are also the oldest approaches. Ancient Greek and Roman physicians believed that emotional states could be understood in terms of the physiology of the body. Thus, they foreshadowed the modern psychophysiological approach.

William James (1890a) proposed the earliest modern theory of emotion. Because a Danish physiologist, Carl Lange, had a similar theory, the point of view that they jointly proposed is often called the James–Lange theory of emotion. The James–Lange theory turned common notions about emotion on their heads. The commonsense view of emotion is that we perceive some event in the environment, and then that event evokes some kind of emotion within us. James and Lange proposed exactly the reverse (Lange & James, 1922). After we sense the events in the environment, we experience bodily changes in reaction to them. Those physiological changes produce the emotion, rather than the other way around.

Ironically, James's son-in-law, Walter Cannon (1929), became the foremost critic of the James–Lange theory. Cannon argued that the James–Lange theory could not be right. First, different emotions are associated with identical psychophysiological states within the body. Fear and excitement, for example, both cause a similar adrenaline rush. The identical psychophysiolog-

ical states could not cause the different emotions. Second, Cannon argued, the organs of the body are not very sensitive. They could never provide the subtle differentiating information that we need in order to experience one emotion as different from another. Moreover, many organs typically react slowly, but we often feel emotions immediately after we perceive a stimulus. Third, if researchers produce the changes in the body associated with a given set of emotions in the absence of the normal provoking stimuli, then we do not feel the emotion that corresponds to those physical reactions. For example, exposing people to onions and making them cry does not make them feel sad. Cannon proposed that the thalamus, and not bodily reactions (such as crying or clenching your fist), controls emotional behavior. Philip Bard (1934) later elaborated on this view, and so it is sometimes called the Cannon–Bard theory of emotion.

There is merit in both positions. Cannon was correct in recognizing the importance of the brain in emotional experience. Several parts of the limbic system, such as the hypothalamus and the amygdala, have been closely linked with emotional experience (see Chapter 3). James and Lange were also correct in asserting that people feel emotions in part by observing changes in the functioning of their bodies. (See Figure 12.9 for a comparison of these theories.) Just what is going on inside their bodies?

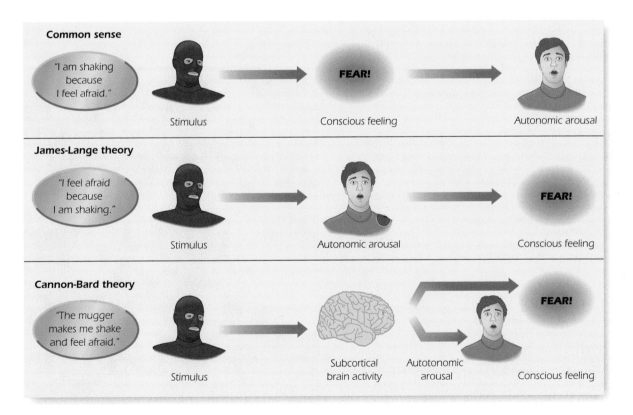

FIGURE 12.9

Psychophysiological Theories of Emotion. Various theories account differently for the physiological, affective, and cognitive components of emotions. Each theory accounts for some, but not all, emotional phenomena.

MODERN PSYCHOPHYSIOLOGICAL APPROACHES

THE CENTRAL NERVOUS SYSTEM

Joseph LeDoux (1986, 1992, 1993, 1995; LeDoux, Romanski, & Xagoraris, 1989) has suggested that arousal of the autonomic nervous system (see Chapter 3) may not be all or none, as it is typically thought to be. Rather, there may be multiple patterns of ANS arousal and different emotions may correspond to different patterns of ANS activity. Other investigators (Cacioppo & Berntson, 1999; Cacioppo & Gardner, 1999; Cacioppo & Petty, 1983; Ekman, Levenson, & Friesen, 1983; Smith, Cacioppo, Larsen, & Chartrand, 2003) have also suggested that different emotions may be characterized by different patterns of physiological response.

THE ENDOCRINE SYSTEM

In contrast, others (Henry & Stephens, 1977) have emphasized the role of the *endocrine system* in emotion. They have argued that different emotions can be linked to varying relative concentrations of hormones. For example, anger seems to be associated with increased levels of norepinephrine (noradrenaline). Fear is associated with increased levels of epinephrine (adrenaline), depression with increases in adrenocorticotropic hormone levels (see Chapter 3). Elation, in contrast, is marked by decreases in ACTH and other hormones. Aggression is associated with increased levels of testosterone (Floody, 1983). What is exciting about this approach is the linking of moods and emotions with concentrations of hormones. The approach does not establish causality, however. Changes in hormone concentrations might cause the emotion. Or the emotions might cause the changes in hormone concentrations. Or both may be dependent on other factors. Conceivably, one of these other factors might be cognitions.

COGNITIVE APPROACHES

Cognitive approaches emphasize the role of cognition in evoking emotion. Stanley Schachter and Jerome Singer (1962) designed an experiment to show that how we label arousal seems to determine the emotions we experience. They then developed a theory to account for their data. The **two-component theory of emotion** specifies two components: physiological arousal and labeling. *Physiological arousal* can be caused by any number of things, such as drugs or situational stimuli (e.g., a sudden surprise). The emotion we feel, according to Schachter and Singer, depends on the second component—how we *label* that physiological arousal. Thus, people who are aroused and who believe that the appropriate emotion is happiness will

feel happy. People who are aroused and who believe that the appropriate emotion is anger will feel anger. All that distinguishes the different emotions is how we label our arousal, which is the same in every case.

As a result of follow-up research, we now know that Schachter and Singer were not completely correct (see, e.g., Leventhal & Tomarken, 1986; G. D. Marshall & Zimbardo, 1979). For example, as previously mentioned, physiological differences exist in the kinds of arousal experienced for different emotions. Still, the classic work of Schachter and Singer instigated a great deal of important theory and research, including work by Richard Lazarus and Robert Zajonc.

TEMPORAL-SEQUENCE THEORIES

Do cognitions precede emotions or are they simultaneous? Magda Arnold (1960, 1970) proposed that our thinking about a situation in part leads us to feel emotions. Her point of view was championed and elaborated upon by Richard Lazarus (1977, 1984, 1991, 1993, 2000, 2001; R. S. Lazarus, Kanner, & Folkman, 1980). According to Lazarus, we appraise a situation in stages. First, in *primary appraisal*, we determine the potential consequences of what is about to happen. For example, is the scruffy, dirty person approaching us about to ask us for money, rob us, or start up a conversation? Second, we have to engage in *secondary appraisal*, meaning that we have to decide what to do. Given our decision about the character approaching

According to Lazarus and Zajonc, how we appraise a situation determines how we feel about it. What do you suppose this child thinks about the swan? The answer is a clue to how he feels.

us, how should we act? We may need to *reappraise* the situation, as events develop. According to Lazarus, each of our appraisals of a situation determines what emotion or emotions we feel. Thus, cognition precedes emotion.

In contrast, Robert Zajonc (1980, 1984, 1998, 2002; Zajonc, Pietromonaco, & Bargh, 1982) has argued that cognition and emotion are separate. He believes that emotion is basic. It does not require prior cognition. In fact, he and others argue that emotions preceded thinking in evolutionary history. He believes it does not make sense that cognitions would have to precede emotions now. Lower animals know to fear predators and to attack potential food without going through complex thought processes. Zajonc therefore believes that we humans often know how we feel long before we know what we think about a situation.

© ### CULTURAL APPROACHES

Batja Mesquita and Nico Frijda (1992) conducted an extensive review of the anthropological literature and developed a cross-cultural theoretical framework for understanding emotion, based in part on theories by others (such as Lazarus). In their view, when we seek to understand emotions, we must consider the following components: *antecedent events* (events that came before the emotional reaction), *event coding* (interpretation of the event), *appraisal* (evaluation of the event and its possible outcomes), *physiological reaction pattern* (emotion-related changes in the body), *action readiness* (preparedness to respond to the emotion-arousing event), *emotional behavior* (actions following the experience of the emotion), and *regulation* (degree to which the individual tries to make the emotion reaction stronger or weaker). Each element may be influenced by cultural context.

James Russell (1991) has suggested an alternative cross-cultural approach. Russell, too, conducted an extensive review of ethnographic literature, but from a slightly different angle. He studied the way people categorize emotions in terms of (1) the words they use to describe their emotions, (2) the words they assign to given facial expressions of emotions, and (3) the dimensions. The dimensions are pairs of characteristics, such as aroused/unaroused, positive/negative, dominant/

submissive, that people use in judging the categories of emotions. Russell drew two conclusions. First, not all people sort their emotions according to the basic categories used by English speakers and other speakers of Indo-European languages. That is, not all cultures recognize the same basic emotions. Other cultures may include additional emotions. Second, despite these cross-cultural differences, many similarities exist across cultures in the emotions people identify, particularly in regard to those associated with certain facial expressions (e.g., Ekman, 1971, 1993; Ekman & Oster, 1979) and vocal expressions (e.g., Bezooijen, Otto, & Heenan, 1983). Although the range of expression for emotions and the boundaries between what come to be called various emotions may differ, there appears to be a great deal of overlap in the ways distinctive cultures describe human emotions.

Motivation and emotion are linked very closely to the social contexts in which they are exhibited. These contexts are considered in the next chapter.

✓CONCEPT CHECK 6

1. The James–Lange theory of emotion states that
   a. emotions produce physiological changes.
   b. physiological changes produce emotions.
   c. emotions are independent of physiological changes.
   d. emotions and physiological changes are mutually interdependent.
2. According to Joseph LeDoux,
   a. different patterns of ANS arousal correspond to different emotions.
   b. the endocrine system causes emotions.
   c. emotions are wholly physiological.
   d. emotions can be divided into two components.
3. According to Robert Zajonc,
   a. cognition depends on emotion.
   b. emotion depends on cognition.
   c. emotions and cognitions are mutually interdependent.
   d. cognition and emotion are relatively independent systems.

FEAR AND SHYNESS

Shyness is a personality trait characterized by avoidance of other people and social withdrawal. Have you ever known someone who was painfully shy? Think of your first day in day care, nursery school, or kindergarten. Did some children cry and cling to their mothers, afraid to join the strangers? What makes some people so shy? Many different types of psychologists have studied shyness.

People who are shy are easily frightened. *Psychologists who study emotion* seek to understand the relationship between fear and shyness, often using nonhuman animals as subjects. Behavioral neuroscientists Ned Kalin and Steven Shelton have studied fear in baby monkeys. The monkeys show fear in different ways, depending on the nature of the threatening stimulus. When left alone, a baby monkey cries. When a stranger is present but does not make eye contact, the baby monkey freezes to avoid detection. When the stranger does make eye contact, however, the monkey bares its teeth and makes threatening gestures (Kalin & Shelton, 1989). Thus, a baby monkey shows fear when exposed to a stranger and will try to avoid detection by that stranger if at all possible. When forced to face the stranger who makes eye contact, the baby monkey will try to defend itself. This research has demonstrated that the frontal lobes, the amygdala, and the hypothalamus play important roles in the regulation and expression of fear (Bakshi, Shelton, & Kalin, 2000; Kalin, Shelton, Davidson, & Kelley, 2001). As you learned in Chapter 3, the frontal lobes organize responses to stimuli, the amygdala regulates fear and aggressive responses, and the hypothalamus controls the response to stress.

Evolutionary psychologists suggest that many human behaviors developed to help us survive and reproduce. Such defensive characteristics as fear of strangers and resistance to threatening stimuli promote survival because they keep us safe (Gilbert, 2002). Thus, the shy temperament might have evolved as one way of promoting reproduction.

Personality psychologists attempt to determine whether or not shyness contributes to problems in personality and behavioral adjustment (Calkins & Fox, 2002). For example, research by personality psychologist Frances Vertue (2003) suggests that shyness limits the ability of a shy individual to initiate relationships with others, which increases social anxiety in that individual.

Psychophysiologists have demonstrated that infants exhibit signs of shyness by the age of 6 months. Fox (1989) found that babies who were born with the highest heart rate variability were at 5 months most responsive to positive stimuli ("peek-a-boo") and negative stimuli (physical restraint). At 14 months, these babies were more sociable and spent less time clinging to their mothers than babies who were less reactive at birth and at 5 months of age (Fox, 1989). Thus, shyness may be predicted by lower heart rate variability. In another study, 6-month-old infants who had significantly more activity in the right cerebral hemisphere than in the left showed more fear and withdrawal behavior than other children (Buss, Schumacher, Dolski, Kalin, Goldsmith, & Davidson, 2003).

Learning psychologists who have examined the role of social learning in inhibited or shy children have determined that anxiety is characteristic of their families (Dadds, 2002). Children with highly anxious parents are most likely to be shy and may develop such behaviors as social withdrawal and avoidance of others to reduce their overall level of anxiety.

Although shy people withdraw socially and often experience social anxiety and isolation, *clinical psychologists* do not regard social withdrawal as a sign of clinical disorder (Rubin, Burgess, Kennedy, & Stewart, 2003). However, they have identified a form of severe shyness in some children called "childhood anxiety disorder" (Albano, Chorpita, & Barlow, 2003). In a study conducted by Denise Chavira and her colleagues, 49% of highly shy children were diagnosed as having psychologi-

cal disorders, such social phobia or an avoidant personality disorder (Chavira, Stein, & Melcarne, 2002). Children with social phobia have an overwhelming fear of being in social situations where they will scrutinized by others, such as when they are asked to speak up in class or make a presentation in front of the class. Those with an avoidant personality disorder will avoid situations where negative criticism is possible because they view themselves as inept or unattractive.

Developmental psychologists have examined the effects of shyness and social withdrawal on early childhood development. Some developmental psychologists have studied the effects of shyness on social development (Rubin, Burgess, & Coplan, 2002); others have examined the role of shyness in early personality development (Calkins & Fox, 2002). Developmental psychologist Irmela Florin studied the ability of children with high social anxiety to interpret facial expressions. Socially anxious and nonanxious children were shown photographs of human faces with neutral, joyful, angry, disgusted, and sad expressions. The socially anxious children reported that they saw signs of emotion on the neutral faces, whereas the nonanxious children did not (Melfsen & Florin, 2002). Regarding neutral faces as threatening may increase the levels of fear and social withdrawal in extremely shy children.

Shyness and fear of strangers appear to be related to underlying biological and perceptual processes, as research by behavioral neuroscientists, evolutionary psychologists, psychophysiologists, and development psychologists has revealed. The relationship between the emotion of fear and shyness has been explored by learning, personality, and clinical psychologists. For shy people, the fear of strangers or the fear of evaluation by others compels them to avoid the social spotlight and withdraw from the company of others.

1. The study of *motivation* considers questions of direction, initiation, intensity, and persistence.

EARLY THEORIES OF MOTIVATION 434

How did early theorists view motivation?

2. Darwin, James, and McDougall saw motivations as instincts. Their theories eventually became too complex and obscure to be useful.

3. Drive theory replaced instinct theory. According to Hull, a *drive* is a composite source of energy that animals and humans try to reduce. Drive theory was discredited because motivation can exist without physiological needs and can even be biologically maladaptive.

CONTEMPORARY THEORIES OF MOTIVATION 435

Why has motivation been studied by modern psychologists? What methods do they use?

4. Physiological approaches to motivation (arousal, opponent-process, and homeostatic-regulation theories) study how motivation relates to the brain.

5. According to the Yerkes–Dodson law, people perform most efficiently and creatively when their level of *arousal* is moderate. The optimal level of arousal varies with both task demands and personal characteristics. High levels are helpful for simple tasks; lower levels are better for complex tasks.

6. *Opponent-process theory*, proposed by Solomon, explains how an addictive drug or stimulus, started in order to achieve a high, becomes a habit to avoid a low. When we feel the effects of a motivational source, we experience an opposing force—slower to start, slower to terminate—that tends to bring us back to baseline.

7. *Homeostatic regulation* is the tendency of the body to maintain equilibrium. A *negative-feedback loop* operates like a thermostat, telling us when we need food, drink, or sex and when those needs are satisfied.

8. Clinical approaches to motivation (e.g., Murray's theory of needs) emphasize personality theory. McClelland studied three needs that emerge from Murray's theory: achievement, power, and affiliation. A highly influential theory is Maslow's hierarchy of needs. These needs are physiological, safety and security, belonging and love, self-esteem, and self-actualization.

9. Cognitive approaches show that people are most creative when they are intrinsically motivated; *extrinsic motivators* tend to undermine *intrinsic motivators*. In addition, moderately novel phenomena are more motivating than are either totally familiar or wholly novel ones. We also need to feel in control of our environment.

10. Ultimately, motivation may lie in our belief about whether or not we can attain a goal (*self-efficacy theory*).

BIOLOGICAL BASES OF MOTIVATION 445

What are the biological bases of motivation?

11. The brain is essential to the experience of hunger. The ventromedial hypothalamus (VMH) serves as an off switch for eating; the lateral hypothalamus (LH) serves as an on switch.

12. The glucostatic hypothesis holds that levels of glucose in the body signal the hypothalamus about the need for food. An alternative (perhaps complementary) explanation is the lipostatic hypothesis, which posits that the brain detects when lipids drop below a certain homeostatic level and hunger increases.

13. According to *set-point theory*, weight is biologically determined at birth by the number of fat cells. Losing weight is difficult because the body interprets dieting as starvation and so resists efforts to shrink the fat cells.

14. Sexual motivation is rooted in the hypothalamus, which stimulates the pituitary gland to release hormones that influence the production of androgens and estrogens.

15. Human sexual behavior is controlled partly by sexual scripts.

16. There are various theories of *homosexuality*. Current views tend to emphasize the role of biological factors.

EMOTIONS AND THEIR CHARACTERISTICS 452

What are the major emotions and how do they function?

17. Distinct from but closely linked to motivation is *emotion*, the predisposition to respond experientially, physiologically, and behaviorally to certain

internal and external variables. Current theories suggest the importance of the autonomic nervous system in emotional arousal.

18. Emotions serve an evolutionary function. For example, they may lead us to fight or to flee in the face of an attack, depending upon how the danger is perceived and which course of action is more likely to lead to survival.

19. The major emotions are happiness (joy), fear and *anxiety*, anger, sadness and grief, and disgust. They can be charted to show relationships among them.

20. *Emotional intelligence* is involved in the control and regulation of emotions.

MEASURING EMOTIONS 455
How are emotions measured?

21. We can measure emotional experience through *self-reporting*, psychophysiological means, or both. The *polygraph* is not a highly reliable measure of veracity.

22. Expressing emotion enables us to communicate feelings, regulates how others respond to us, facilitates social interaction, and encourages prosocial behavior.

23. The *facial-feedback hypothesis* holds (a) in its strong form, that the facial expression of an emotion leads to the experience of that emotion, or (b) in its weak form, that the facial expression affects an emotion's intensity. Facial expressions can also

help us to detect to some extent when someone is lying, particularly if the person doing the detecting has been trained to do so.

APPROACHES TO UNDERSTANDING EMOTIONS 458
What are the major approaches to understanding emotion?

24. The James–Lange theory claims that bodily changes lead to emotion, rather than the reverse. Cannon and Bard disagreed, proposing that the brain controls emotional behavior.

25. Cognitive theories differ in details and sometimes in substance, but they all hold that emotion and cognition are linked closely. According to the Schachter–Singer *two-component theory of emotion*, we distinguish one emotion from another strictly by how we label our physiological arousal.

26. Emotions and cognitions are linked, but we do not yet know which comes first. Lazarus believes that cognition precedes emotion, but Zajonc does not.

27. Cross-cultural studies analyze emotions in terms of antecedent events, event coding, appraisal, physiological response patterns, action readiness, emotional behavior, and regulation. Although not all people categorize emotions in the same way, many similarities still exist across cultures in the ways that people express and identify emotions.

KEY TERMS

anorexia nervosa 448
anxiety 453
arousal 435
bisexual 450
drive 435
emotion 452
emotional intelligence 455
extrinsic motivators 440

facial-feedback hypothesis 456
homeostatic regulation 437
homosexuality 450
intrinsic motivators 440
Likert scale 455
motivation 434
motive 434
negative-feedback loop 437

polygraph 456
self-efficacy 443
self-report measures 455
set-point theory 446
two-component theory
  of emotion 459

ANSWERS TO CONCEPT CHECKS

Concept Check 1

1. d   2. b   3. a

Concept Check 2

1. b   2. c   3. a

Concept Check 3

1. b   2. a   3. c

Concept Check 4

1. d   2. c   3. c

Concept Check 5

1. d   2. a   3. a

Concept Check 6

1. b   2. a   3. d

KNOWLEDGE CHECK

1. An impulse, desire, or need that leads to an action is a(n)
   a. motive.
   b. emotion.
   c. drive.
   d. instinct.
2. On difficult tasks, _____ level of arousal is associated with greater success.
   a. no
   b. a relatively low
   c. a relatively high
   d. a maximum
3. Opponent-process theory involves _____ motivational process(es).
   a. one
   b. two
   c. three
   d. four
4. In Maslow's need hierarchy, the highest level is the need for
   a. security.
   b. belongingness.
   c. self-actualization.
   d. esteem.
5. Extrinsic motivators come from
   a. inside the individual.
   b. outside the individual.
   c. both inside and outside the individual.
   d. neither inside nor outside the individual.
6. Self-efficacy is
   a. self-esteem.
   b. goal-directedness.
   c. the ability to get tasks done.
   d. a belief in one's own competence.

7. An emotion that is *not* considered to be basic is
   a. sadness.
   b. anxiety.
   c. anger.
   d. happiness.
8. Emotional intelligence does *not* involve the ability to _____ emotion.
   a. accurately perceive
   b. appraise
   c. express
   d. repress
9. A Likert scale is a type of
   a. self-report measure.
   b. heart-rate indicator.
   c. indicator of galvanic skin response.
   d. measure of weight.
10. According to the two-component theory of emotion, the emotion we experience depends on
    a. how we label physiological arousal.
    b. how much physiological arousal we experience.
    c. the interaction of the brain with the endocrine system.
    d. physiological arousal but not labeling.

Answers

1. a   2. b   3. b   4. c   5. b   6. d   7. b   8. d
9. a   10. a

THINK ABOUT IT

1. Why is disgust a key emotion from an evolutionary standpoint?
2. Why are negative-feedback loops important to the homeostatic regulation of temperature in the body?
3. What strategies could you use to help a child increase his or her motivation to do homework?
4. How might you expect people's motivation to succeed economically to vary across cultures?
5. What goal can you set for yourself that would satisfy your need for achievement and that would enhance your sense of competence, autonomy, and self-efficacy? Devise a specific plan for reaching your goal, including the specific subtasks and subgoals you would need to accomplish it.
6. When advertisers want you to buy their products or services, they seek to tap into some of the fundamental human emotions. Describe a recent advertisement you have seen or heard and explain how the advertiser was trying to manipulate your fundamental emotions to persuade you to buy the advertised product or service.

WEB RESOURCES

For a chapter tutorial quiz, direct links to Internet sites, and other useful features, visit the book-specific website at http://psychology.wadsworth.com/sternberg4e. You can also connect directly to the following sites:

Center for Eating Disorders
http://www.eating-disorders.com/
This informative site provides helpful information about eating disorders and other health-related issues. What do we know about the history of eating disorders? How is distorted body image related to eating disorders? What's the relationship between exercise and eating disorders? Find out here!

Obesity Research News
http://www.obesity-news.com/
This site contains a vast array of information about obesity research and weight loss drugs.

Theories of Emotion
http://www.abacon.com/psychsite/motivation_act2.html
At this interactive site you can take a quiz to find out how well you've mastered the differences among the James-Lange, Cannon-Bard, Schachter and Singer's theories emotion.

Go Ask Alice!
http://www.alice.columbia.edu/
Alice! from Columbia University's Health Education Program, is one of the longest-standing and most popular sources of frank information on the Net. Geared especially to undergraduate students, the site offers direct answers to questions about relationships, sexuality and sexual health, alcohol and drug consumption, emotional health, and general health.

For additional readings on many of the topics covered in this chapter, check out InfoTrac College Edition at **www.infotrac-college.com/ wadsworth.**

Disk Two
Motivation
Emotion
Chapter Quiz
Critical Thinking Questions

CHAPTER 13

SOCIAL PSYCHOLOGY: PERSONAL PERSPECTIVES

The presence of others, other people, excite and rattle him, force him into an endless, frenzied, social chatter, a veritable delirium of identity-making and -seeking; the presence of plants, a quiet garden, the nonhuman order, making no social demands upon him, allow this identity-delirium to relax, to subside.

—*Oliver Sacks*, The Man Who Mistook His Wife for a Hat*

Reprinted with permission of Simon & Schuster from The Man Who Mistook His Wife for a Hat and Other Clinical Tales *by Oliver Sacks. Copyright © 1970, 1981, 1983, 1984, 1985 by Oliver Sacks.*

The man who mistook his wife for a hat, in Oliver Sacks's tale, could not tolerate the presence of others. Most of us not only tolerate others but even seek them out. **Social psychology** is the study of how others affect our thoughts, feelings, and behaviors, even if their presence is only implied or imagined.

THE NATURE OF SOCIAL PSYCHOLOGY

What is social psychology?

First, social psychologists study cognition, emotion, and behavior, and how they are influenced by thoughts and emotions. For example, we can look at a car salesman trying to persuade us to buy a car as a multifaceted phenomenon. The salesman tries to convince us cognitively, with rational arguments that the car is a good buy. He tries to make us long for the car, to develop an emotional desire for it. Ultimately, his behavior leads to one of two behaviors on our part. Either we buy or we do not buy. Our decision is partly based on how effective the salesman has been in the art of persuasion.

Second, social psychologists consider how behavior is affected by either the presence or the idea of other people. For example, we may be attracted to someone and we might consider becoming further involved except for our fear of being rejected. The other person need not even be physically present for us to react as though he or she were there.

Third, social psychologists usually take a process-oriented, or *functionalist,* approach (see Chapter 1). They look not only at *what* people do but also at *how* and *why* they do it. Why do we want friends and how do we choose them? Why do we need to communicate and how do we do so?

Because social psychology addresses such compelling questions, we will take two chapters to study this field. This chapter addresses social cognition. **Social cognition** refers to the thoughts and beliefs we have about ourselves and other people. Social cognition is based on how we perceive and interpret information from other people, either directly or indirectly (see Fazio & Olson, 2003; Fiske, 1995; Fiske & Taylor, 1991; Lewis & Carpendale, 2002; Operario & Fiske, 1999). What do we think about ourselves? What do we think about other people? How are our thoughts and feelings influenced by our interactions? Whereas objects typically remain stable (e.g., the lamp on my desk just stays there until I move it, in one of two states—off or on), people constantly change, so our ideas about them are inevitably more complex and richer than our ideas about objects (see Bond & Kenny, 2002; Kenny, 1994; Kenny & DePaulo, 1993).

One of the most common examples of persuasion is selling. The seller tries to persuade the customer to buy.

© ePhoto/Alamy

Social cognition includes such topics as emotion, motivation, and personality. But it focuses on thought processes in social interactions. It deals with (1) the ways we think and feel about others and about ourselves, and (2) the ways we behave because of those thoughts and feelings. Our personal perspectives govern why and how we form and change our attitudes. They also affect how we perceive ourselves in relation to how we think others perceive us. They influence how we internally explain our own behavior and the behavior of others. And our perspectives can direct why and how we are attracted to, like, and even love other people. What these topics have in common is that internal, personal processes influence and are influenced by our interactions with other people.

We believe social relationships are of paramount importance in our lives. In fact, people who have close social relationships live longer and have better health than people who do not (Berscheid & Reis, 1998). Relationships are also important because it is so difficult for humans to survive independently of one another (Berscheid, 1999; Berscheid & Collins, 2000; Reis, Collins, & Berscheid, 2000). Each person we encounter may help or harm us. Perhaps this is why humans are characterized as the most social creatures in the animal kingdom. Moreover, it appears that over evolutionary time we have been "hard-wired" with biological equipment that facilitates our interactions with others. Early humans who could not get along with others for the purposes of defense, food gathering, and reproduction did not survive to contribute to our evolutionary heritage (Reis, Collins, & Berscheid, 2000).

✓CONCEPT CHECK 1

1. Social psychology as studied today *least* deals with
   a. cognitions.
   b. emotions.
   c. behavior.
   d. single cells.
2. A functionalist approach to social psychology emphasizes
   a. structures.
   b. processes.
   c. emotions.
   d. motivations.
3. The thoughts and beliefs we have about ourselves and other people are referred to as
   a. social cognition.
   b. interpersonal attraction.
   c. cognitive dissonance.
   d. reactance.

ATTITUDES

What are attitudes? How do they change?

Attitude has a variety of popular definitions. To psychologists, an **attitude** is a learned, stable, and relatively enduring evaluation of a person, object, or idea, which can affect behavior (Allport, 1935; Eagly & Chaiken, 1992, 1998; Petty & Cacioppo, 1981). This definition makes several points. First, we are not born with attitudes. We acquire them through our experiences, especially in our interactions with others. Second, attitudes tend to be stable and relatively enduring. Indeed, when attitudes come under strong attack, people often become more (not less) convinced that their attitudes are correct (Tormala & Petty, 2002). Third, attitudes are evaluative. They are a means by which we judge things positively or negatively, and in varying degrees. Some issues may not concern us much one way or the other. Other issues may engender strong opinions, which can be influenced by emotions (Fabrigar & Petty, 1999; Petty, DeSteno, & Rucker, 2001). Finally, attitudes can influence our behavior, causing us to act—to vote, protest, work, make friends, and so on.

Psychologists once believed that understanding people's attitudes toward things would help them predict behavior accurately. But it turned out not to be so simple. Sometimes attitudes do predict behavior, but other times they do not (Berscheid, 1999).

Some psychologists view attitudes as having cognitive, behavioral, *and* affective components. Your attitude toward someone or something depends on what you think and feel about the person or thing. It also depends on how you act toward the person or thing on the basis of your thoughts and feelings (D. Katz & Stotland, 1959). Attitudes are clearly central to our individual psychology.

Suppose you meet Jacques, who is from France. You have always had a good impression of France. You like French food and admire French culture. What you have learned makes you think the country is highly civilized and pleasant. You are eager to get to know Jacques. Indeed, your attitude toward France has already colored your attitude toward him. If Jacques had come from a country you were not interested in, you might not have been so eager to get to know him.

Why do we have attitudes? According to Daniel Katz (1960), attitudes serve at least four functions. They can (1) help us get what we want and avoid what we do not want, (2) help us avoid internal conflicts and anxieties, (3) help us understand and integrate complex sources of information, and (4) reflect our deeply held values. Suppose you have a very positive attitude toward politicians who deeply care about the poor. In terms of Katz's model, the attitude may (1) influence the way you vote and even for whom you campaign so that you are more likely to get a politician you want elected; (2) make you feel that you are doing something positive for the poor and thus relieve internal anxieties that you are not paying attention to them; (3) help you find a simple way to act upon your complex feelings about assisting people who are unfortunate; and (4) reflect your deeply held value that the unfortunate deserve society's care.

ATTITUDE FORMATION

Where do attitudes come from? We are not born with particular attitudes. Moreover, specific attitudes do not naturally unfold during our physiological maturation. Thus, we are left with various forms of learning theory to explain attitude formation. Three kinds of learning can contribute to this process: classical conditioning, operant conditioning, and observational learning (see Chapter 6).

The *classical-conditioning* view is that we learn attitudes when a concept or object toward which we have no particular attitude (an unconditioned stimulus) is paired with a concept or object toward which we already have an attitude (a conditioned stimulus; Staats & Staats, 1958). For example, if we eat a food we like while reading, then we are likely to develop a favorable attitude toward the views presented in the text (Janis, Kaye, & Kirschner, 1965). In another study, participants liked a television commercial more when it was embedded in a television program that was upbeat than when it was embedded in a program that was sad (Mathur & Chattopadhyay, 1991).

In *operant conditioning*, rewards can strengthen positive associations and punishments can strengthen negative associations (e.g., Insko, 1965). Rewarded attitudes are likely to be maintained. Those that are punished are more likely to be changed or discarded. Suppose you are rewarded for showing positive attitudes toward the political party in power (e.g., by being praised) and punished for showing negative attitudes (e.g., by being thrown in jail, which happens in some countries). You are then more likely to develop positive than negative attitudes toward the ruling party. As dissident movements around the world make clear, however, this is not the only way attitudes are learned or changed.

In *observational learning* (see Chapter 6), children acquire many of their attitudes by observing the attitudes that are voiced and acted out by the important adults and children in their environments. In addition, children learn attitudes from television and other media.

Attitudes form in complex ways, and are influenced both by upbringing and by the nature of a particular situation. This photograph was taken during an antiwar demonstration in early 2003.

One set of attitudes learned from the media pertains to the roles of men and women in society. Some stereotypes portrayed on television are not as extreme as they once were. But they persist around the world (Furnham & Skae, 1997; Mwangi, 1996). Other stereotypes die hard. Recent research on British television found that sexual stereotypes, in particular, are actually worse now than they were, and they are more extreme on British television than on Serbian television (Skoric & Furnham, 2002). In general, children's television programs show more male roles than female roles. Men are more likely to be shown as the doers who make things happen and who are rewarded for their actions. Women are more likely to be the recipients of actions. The women who do take action are more likely than men to be punished for their activity (Basow, 1986, 1992). On action-adventure shows, 85% of the major characters are men. Of the leading characters on prime-time television, 65% to 75% are white men. Occupational and familial roles strongly reinforce gender and racial stereotypes. Even when viewers selectively choose programs that minimize stereotypes, commercials still provide a whopping dose of stereotyped roles for viewers to observe (Gilly, 1988). Women are more often shown as preoccupied with their appearance, household chores, and their families. Men are usually shown working, playing, or being nurtured by women. Even music videos show conventional male–female stereotypes (Gan, Zillmann, & Mitrook, 1997; Signorielli, McLeod, & Healy, 1994). On a more positive note, when programs are designed to diminish sex-role stereotypes, both children (Eisenstock, 1984) and adults (Reep & Dambrot, 1988) express fewer stereotyped views.

Another obvious source of observational learning is found in the home: the people who live there. Examine your parents' attitudes about religion, politics, and other social issues. How do they compare and contrast with your own? Young people are often surprised—sometimes unpleasantly—to realize how many of their own attitudes have been absorbed from their families. In more ways than one, education begins at home.

Each of the three kinds of social learning contributes to the ways in which we form our attitudes. How can we change the attitudes we have already formed?

ATTITUDE CHANGE

Have you ever noticed an attitude in yourself that you wanted to change? What about the attitudes held by people with whom you interact? Have you ever wanted to change the attitudes of other people? If you did want to change someone's attitudes, how might you go about doing so? Probably by persuading the person to think differently. Easier said than done, you say. Nonetheless, advertisers, politicians, political activists, charitable organizations, and any number of other people spend a lot of time, money, and effort trying to figure out how to change people's attitudes. Governments are also very interested in issues relating to attitude change.

Scientists do not conduct research in isolation from society. Attitude research is a good example of the interaction between contemporary societal issues and psychological research. The origins of this research date back to World War II. The Japanese radio broadcaster "Tokyo Rose" was trying to break the morale of U.S. troops overseas. She broadcast innuendoes about unfaithful spouses, unconcerned citizens at home, and treacherous political and military leaders. Various German-American "friendship organizations" were attempting to drum up support for Hitler in the United States. Were such measures turning both soldiers and civilians against the war effort? How could the U.S. government counter the influence of such propaganda? Government officials needed to know how to make the American people resistant to influences that might seek to change people's attitudes in ways that could harm the war effort.

At the same time, U.S. government officials wanted to institute their own propaganda campaign. Their goal was to change the attitudes of anyone who might not fully support the war effort. Suddenly, attitude research, which had been dormant, sprang to life. Scientists sought to understand people's attitudes more fully and to figure out how and why people change their attitudes.

© Bettmann/Corbis

Government interest in attitudes and attitude change surges during wartime. As this World War II poster indicates, propaganda is developed to influence attitudes.

Many individuals and organizations work to change your attitudes. So, you may wish to learn when to accept and when to resist such efforts. For example, how can you more effectively resist attempts to change your attitudes by persons who do not necessarily have your best interests at heart? By examining various kinds of persuasive communications, researchers have discovered some variables that are likely to influence attitude change. These variables can be categorized into three groups: (1) characteristics of the recipient of the attitude-change message (e.g., the recipient's motivation and expertise), (2) characteristics of the message itself (e.g., balance and familiarity due to repetition), and (3) characteristics of the source of the message (e.g., credibility and likability). Understanding these variables helps us evaluate and, when appropriate, resist attempts to persuade us to change our attitudes.

THE RECIPIENT

Richard Petty and John Cacioppo (1981; Cialdini, Petty, & Cacioppo, 1981; Petty, Brinol, & Tormala, 2002; Petty, Priester, & Brinol, 2002; Petty & Wegener, 1998) have proposed that the effectiveness of various persuasive techniques depends on specific characteristics of the person who receives the persuasive message. These researchers note two routes to persuasion. The first is the *central route to persuasion*, which emphasizes thoughtful arguments related to the issue about which an attitude is being formed. When the recipient is both motivated to think about the issue and able to do so, the central route is the most effective. The second is the *peripheral route to persuasion*, which emphasizes tangential, situational features of the persuasive message, such as the appeal of the message sender, the attractiveness of the message's presentation, and rewarding features of the message or its source. The peripheral route may be more effective when the recipient is not strongly interested in the issue or is unable to consider it carefully.

The investigators found that strong arguments were always more persuasive than weak ones. This effect was even greater for those who were highly motivated to think about the issue (Cacioppo & Petty, 1986). Even good arguments may be wasted on those who are not really paying attention to them. But strong arguments were influential for those who were actively analyzing and interpreting them. Thus, when preparing to persuade others to your point of view, you should know your audience and know which route to persuasion will be most effective. As you might guess, attitude change that is reached through the central route is much more stable and enduring. Attitude change reached through the peripheral route is more volatile and subject to subsequent change in the opposite direction.

THE MESSAGE

In addition to the quality or forcefulness of the arguments, what other characteristics of your message might affect its persuasiveness? Two characteristics have prompted a great deal of research: balanced presentation of arguments and familiarity due to repeated exposure. A key question in attitude research has been whether the *balanced presentation of viewpoints*—a presentation of both favorable (pro) and unfavorable (con) perspectives on a given issue—helps or hinders the process of changing someone's attitudes. There appears to be no significant difference between the effects of one-sided and two-sided messages on attitude change in a group made up of some people predisposed to agree and other people predisposed to disagree (Lumsdaine & Janis, 1953). When listeners are exposed to both sides of an issue, however, they are more resistant to later persuasion from the opposing camp than are people who have heard only one side.

Another way to change people's attitudes is simply to expose them repeatedly to the desired attitude. On average, repeating an argument increases its effectiveness. Indeed, simply exposing people to a stimulus many times tends to increase their liking for that stimulus (Arkes, Boehm, & Xu, 1991). This is called the **mere exposure effect,** which is the positive effect on attitudes that results from repeated exposure to a message supporting the attitude, or even just exposure to the stimulus about which the attitude is being formed or modified (Monahan, Murphy, & Zajonc, 2000; Zajonc, 1968). For example, many people find that their appreciation of a piece of music, a work of art, or even a kind of food increases with repeated exposure, which is why we often call certain preferences "acquired tastes." The effect is quite robust, appearing even in patients who have schizophrenic mental illness (Marie et al., 2001).

If repetition becomes boring or annoying, however, it can backfire and decrease the likelihood of attitude change (Cacioppo & Petty, 1979, 1980). If someone keeps telling you how wonderful he is, you may simply become annoyed with him rather than impressed by his wonderful qualities. Thus, repetition is useful to make sure people get the message, but after a point it may hurt your case.

THE SOURCE

The source of the persuasive message also has characteristics that influence the effectiveness of the message in eliciting attitude change. Two key characteristics of the source are its credibility and its likability.

CREDIBILITY. People are most likely to believe a communication if the source is rated high in *credibility*—that is, in believability (Hovland & Weiss, 1951). The effect of source credibility on the recipient is greatest right after the persuasive message is perceived. Over time, the effect of the credible source decreases. For example, the power of Tiger Woods's endorsement of a product is likely to diminish in your mind with repetition and familiarity.

LIKABILITY. In the **likability effect,** people are more apt to be persuaded by messages from people they like than by messages from people they do not like (Chaiken & Eagly, 1983). This effect is especially important if you are trying to persuade people to take a position that they initially resist or otherwise find unappealing (Eagly & Chaiken, 1975, 1992). The magnitude of this effect, however, depends on the medium used to send the message (see Figure 13.1). The likability effect is greater for videotaped than for audiotaped messages. It is inconsequential in written messages. This difference probably occurs because we get a broader range of visual and auditory information from a videotape than we do from either an audiotape or written material. It is for this reason that some of the best radio announcers do not succeed when they try to switch to television. The personal impression they make diminishes when viewers not only hear them, but see them as well. The watchers discover that the celebrities do not look very different from or more believable than anyone else. There also appears to be a weak and not always consistent effect of likability on

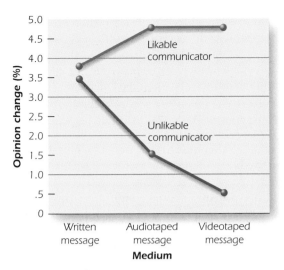

FIGURE 13.1

The Medium of the Message and the Likability of the Message Sender. The positive effect of likable message senders on attitude change is increased when audiotaped or videotaped messages are used instead of written ones. When the message sender is not likable, however, attitude change is even less likely to occur when audiotaped or videotaped messages are used.

memory. We have somewhat better memory for information from more likable sources (Eagly, Chen, Chaiken, & Shaw-Barnes, 1999).

THE LINK BETWEEN ATTITUDES AND BEHAVIOR

Implicit in the study of attitudes is the assumption that our attitudes are linked to our behavior. But, have you ever noticed a discrepancy between people's attitudes and their behavior? For example, do you always assume that the way salespeople behave toward you genuinely indicates their feelings about you?

Have you ever acted cruelly, carelessly, or unsympathetically toward someone about whom you care deeply? Clearly, our behavior does not necessarily reflect our attitudes accurately. At the least, there may be many explanations for the behavior we observe. Our beliefs and attitudes are not entirely separate from our behaviors, however. Several factors increase the likelihood that our attitudes will be reflected in our behaviors (see Brehm & Kassin, 1990; Eagly & Chaiken, 1992):

Attitude strength: Stronger attitudes are more clearly tied to behavior than weaker ones.

Amount of information and experience supporting the attitude: Attitudes based on more information and more experience are more clearly linked to behavior than attitudes based on less exposure.

Attitude specificity: Highly specific attitudes are clearly tied to behavior. For example, you are more likely to seek out the company of someone toward whom you have a very specific set of positive attitudes than someone about whom you have no strong views.

Situational factors: Your current situation may affect whether you behave in accord with your attitudes. If you win the lottery, you may find yourself contributing to charities that you had thought about contributing to before, but never did.

(c) CULTURE, TIME, AND ATTITUDE

Another factor that influences both our attitudes and our behavior is the broad cultural context in which we live. For example, the terms *monochronic* (one time) and *polychronic* (many times) have been used to describe cultural variations in the perception of time (Hall, 1966; Kaufman-Scarborough & Lindquist, 1999; M. J. Waller, Giambatista, & Zellmer-Bruhn,

Many people in the United States feel almost constantly pressured by the passing of time. In many other cultures, people have a much more relaxed attitude toward time.

1999). In a monochronic culture, time is precious, and its regulation is precise. People are more likely to have attitudes that prize time and to exhibit behavior that reflects a rigid orientation toward time. In contrast, in a polychronic culture, people place much less emphasis on the clock. The measurement of time is much more fluid. People may behave in ways that in a monochronic culture might be considered tardy or even irresponsible (because of the lack of attention to time). Thus, behavior (such as being habitually late) that may engender negative attitudes in one culture might be viewed as acceptable or even desirable in another culture.

Although we live in a largely monochronic culture, it has some disadvantages. The monochronic emphasis on time has been associated with general experiences of greater life stress (Frei, Racicot, & Travagline, 1999). In a cross-cultural study (R. V. Levine & Bartlett, 1984), it even has been linked to coronary heart disease. Perhaps if we pay less attention to the time we have, we may end up having more time to live.

COGNITIVE CONSISTENCY

Imagine that you are participating in an experiment in which the experimenter asks you to perform two mind-numbingly simple tasks of eye–hand coordination. The tasks are repeatedly emptying and refilling a tray that contains spools of thread for half an hour, and then repeatedly turning an array of pegs one-quarter turn each for another half an hour. After you have performed these excruciatingly dull tasks for a full hour, the experimenter mercifully tells you that you may stop. As far as you know, that is the end of the experiment on eye–hand coordination.

Now, as is customary after a psychological experiment, the experimenter debriefs you. He explains that the purpose of the experiment was to investigate the effects of psychological mind-set on task performance. You were in the control group, so you were given no prior indication of whether the tasks would be interesting. In the experimental group, on the other hand, participants are told in advance that the tasks will be enjoyable. The experimenter goes on to tell you that the next participant, waiting outside, has been assigned to the experimental group. A research assistant will arrive soon to tell her how great the task will be.

Then the experimenter leaves the room for a moment and returns, worried because his research assistant has not yet arrived. Would you be willing to salvage the experiment by serving as a paid research assistant just for this one participant? Persuaded, you tell the next participant how much fun the experiment was. She replies that she had heard from a friend that it was a bore. You assure her, however, that it was pure entertainment. Then you depart. As you leave, a secretary in the psychology department interviews you briefly. She asks you to rate just how much fun and how interesting the experiment really was.

Have you guessed the true point of this experiment? The independent variable was not whether you were told in advance that the experiment was fun and interesting. In fact, you and all the other participants who believed you were in the "control" condition were actually in the experimental condition. In the genuine control condition, participants merely performed the boring tasks and later were asked how interesting the tasks were.

In the true experimental condition in this classic study by Leon Festinger and J. Merrill Carlsmith (1959), the "participant" waiting outside was a confederate of the experimenter. There never was any other research assistant: The plan had always been to get you to convince the next "participant" that the experiment was a delight. The crucial manipulation was the amount of money you received for saying that the experiment was interesting. The independent variable actually was that some participants were paid only $1; others were paid $20. The dependent variable was the experimental participant's rating of the interest level of the tasks when questioned by the secretary. The goal was to find out whether a relationship existed between the amount of money a person was paid for lying about the tasks and how interesting the person later reported the dull tasks to be. In other words, how did lying about tasks affect people's attitudes toward those tasks?

Participants who were paid $1 rated the boring experiment as much more interesting than did either those who were paid $20 or the control participants, as shown in Figure 13.2. This result came as a great shock to the field of psychology. The existing *incentive-motivation theory* predicted that individuals in the $20 group would have much more incentive to change their attitude toward the experiment than would individuals in the $1 group because $20 was a greater reward. Hence, this theory predicted that people in the $20 group would be more motivated to show, and actually would show, more attitude change (Hovland, Janis, & Kelley, 1953). Festinger and Carlsmith explained the counterintuitive results by suggesting that the participants' responses could be understood in terms of their efforts to achieve **cognitive consistency**, the match between a person's thoughts and behaviors. The fundamental importance of cognitive consistency was first pointed out by Fritz Heider (1958), who recognized that when people's cognitions are inconsistent, people strive to restore consistency. Cognitive consistency is extremely important to our mental well-being. Without it, we feel tense, nervous, irritable, and even at war with ourselves.

Suppose you meet someone you like a lot but then hear from others that your "new friend" is saying nasty

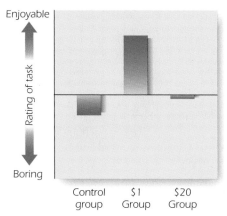

FIGURE 13.2

The Classic Festinger–Carlsmith Experiment. This graph shows the unambiguous results of Festinger and Carlsmith's experiment. To the astonishment of many psychologists, the participants who received $1 for feigning enjoyment of the task later said they had enjoyed it when asked their candid views. In contrast, the control group emphatically reasserted their extreme boredom during the task, and even the participants who received $20 for simulating enjoyment continued to assert that the task was boring.

Most smokers are aware of the hazards associated with the habit, yet do not attempt to quit. What strategies for reducing this cognitive dissonance would be most effective?

things about you behind your back. The person you liked now has become a threat to you, and you almost certainly will experience cognitive inconsistency. It is adaptive for you to feel very uncomfortable. The world no longer makes sense and your well-being is in jeopardy. Your discomfort is likely to lead you to check whether the rumors are really true and, if they are, to distance yourself from or set yourself in opposition to the false friend.

Now let's think about why people in the $1 group showed more attitude change. Two possible explanations are provided by cognitive-dissonance theory and self-perception theory.

COGNITIVE DISSONANCE THEORY

Let's reconsider the Festinger and Carlsmith experiment: The participants who were paid $20 performed an extremely boring task and then encouraged someone else to believe that the task was interesting. They were well compensated for doing so, however. They achieved cognitive consistency easily. Saying that a dull task was interesting but getting paid well for saying so allowed these participants to match their thoughts and beliefs to their behavior.

Now consider the plight of the participants who were paid $1. They not only performed a boring task but also lied about it by trying to convince someone else that it was interesting. Furthermore, they were paid poorly for their efforts. These participants may have been experiencing **cognitive dissonance,** the

disquieting perception of a mismatch among one's own attitudes.

Justification of effort—a means by which an individual rationalizes his or her expenditure of energy—is one route to reducing cognitive dissonance. Most of us need to feel that we have good, logical reasons for why we do what we do. But how could the poorly paid experimental participants justify their efforts on the task? The only apparent justification was to decide that perhaps it was not really so bad. After all, it would have been embarrassing to admit not only that they had not liked the task, but also that they had lied about it to someone else and then had been paid only a small amount of money for doing so. How much easier it must have been to decide that maybe it was all worth it. Perhaps the task was even interesting and enjoyable. Thus, these latter participants reduced cognitive dissonance by deciding that the task was perfectly acceptable. They made sense of the lies they had told the confederate by deceiving themselves and changing their attitude toward the boring task.

We now look more closely at the conditions under which cognitive dissonance occurs. Dissonance is most likely to occur when (1) you have freely chosen the action that causes the dissonance; (2) you have firmly committed yourself to that behavior, and the commitment or behavior is irrevocable; and (3) your behavior has significant consequences for other people. Suppose that a couple is very unhappily married and they have children. Both parents devoutly believe that divorce is morally wrong, especially when a couple has children.

This is a classic situation likely to generate cognitive dissonance.

In contrast, you are less likely to experience cognitive dissonance if you are forced into an action, if you still have the option of not continuing to perform the action, or if your behavior has consequences for no one but you. Someone who is coerced into marriage or who has no children to think about may have less compunction about filing for divorce. See Figure 13.3 for a look at the conditions that affect cognitive dissonance.

This interpretation of the Festinger and Carlsmith (1959) experiment is only one of several. Consider now the rather different analysis of self-perception theory, which describes another route to cognitive consistency.

SELF-PERCEPTION THEORY

If questioned about the connection between our beliefs and our behavior, most of us would probably say that our behavior is caused by our beliefs. An influential theory suggests the opposite (D. J. Bem, 1967, 1972). According to **self-perception theory,** when we are not sure of what we believe, we *infer* our beliefs *from* our behavior. We perceive our own actions much as an outside observer would. We draw conclusions about ourselves on the basis on our actions.

Consider how self-perception theory would interpret the Festinger and Carlsmith (1959) experiment. As you find yourself explaining to another participant how enjoyable the experiment was, you wonder, "Why in the world am I doing this?" If you have been paid $20, the explanation is easy: for the money. If you have

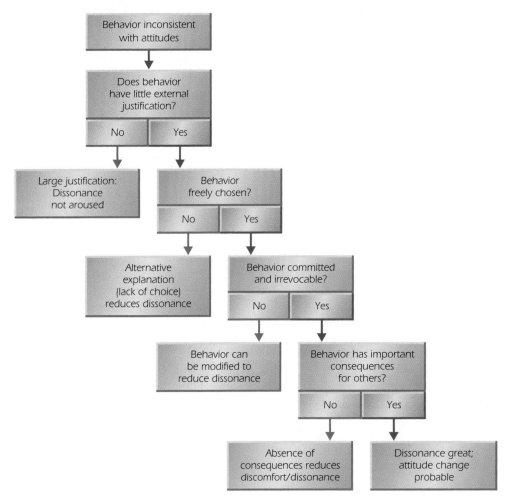

FIGURE 13.3

Qualifying Conditions for Cognitive Dissonance. In cognitive dissonance, our behavior appears inconsistent with our attitudes, so we become intellectually confused and uncomfortable. This flowchart shows the qualifying conditions for determining whether cognitive dissonance would be likely to lead to attitude change. A "no" answer means that outcomes other than attitude change would be likely. (From "Qualifying Conditions for Cognitive Dissonance" from *Introduction to Social Psychology,* R. A. Lippa. Copyright © 1990, 1994. Reprinted by permission of the author.)

been paid only $1, however, you cannot be doing it for the money. So a logical interpretation is that you must have liked the task.

Self-perception influences your attitudes in other circumstances as well. To return to an earlier example, suppose you are trying to figure out whether you want to become more involved with someone. You realize that you have been spending lots of time with the person, exchanging gifts, and spending much less time with friends. You infer on the basis of your behavior that you must really care a great deal about this person. You decide you must be ready for a deeper commitment.

Self-perception theory might seem contrary to both rationality and intuition—after all, don't you already know what you like and dislike? Not always. Suppose you "know" that you hate brussels sprouts, but you have not even tasted one for years. Now suppose that you are a guest in the home of someone you want very much to please. The only appetizer is tender brussels sprouts, marinated in a vinaigrette dressing and served icy cold with hollandaise sauce. No choice—you have to try one and appear to be pleased. After your token helping, you find yourself reaching for another. How would you explain your behavior to yourself? Would you change your view of yourself enough to like something you "knew" you did not like?

It can be advantageous to consider whether our entrenched self-perceptions may unnecessarily limit our options. People change; preferences change; fears change. According to self-perception theory, when we behave in a way that conflicts with our habitual reactions, we have a chance to look at ourselves from a fresh perspective. We may just change our self-perceptions and change how we behave.

COGNITIVE DISSONANCE VERSUS SELF-PERCEPTION. Researchers have conducted experiments to determine whether cognitive dissonance or self-perception theory better explains behavior that contradicts prior beliefs (e.g., D. J. Bem, 1967; J. Cooper, Zanna, & Taves, 1978). What are the results?

It appears that cognitive dissonance theory is a better explanation when people behave in ways that do not agree with their usual beliefs or attitudes. Suppose you have always been a staunch believer in one point of view. But a friend convinces you to attend meetings of an opposing group, which you then find persuasive. Your lack of cognitive consistency might bear out dissonance theory. Thus, cognitive dissonance theory seems to explain *attitude change* better, particularly when the change is dramatic and the original beliefs and attitudes were obvious and well defined.

Self-perception theory seems to be a clearer explanation for *attitude formation*, especially when the person's attitudes are still ambivalent (Fazio, Zanna, & Cooper, 1977). It applies better when people behave in ways that are only slightly discrepant from their normal patterns, and when attitudes are vague, uncertain, and not fully formed. If you have always avoided brussels sprouts but find yourself eating them calmly one night at dinner, self-perception theory might help you achieve cognitive consistency. Table 13.1 summarizes the two theories.

Self-perception theory has been used to explain phenomena other than attitude change (Dolinski, 2000; Reifman, 1998). Schnall, Abrahamson, and Laird (2002) argued that premenstrual syndrome (PMS) may arise from the misattribution of hormone-induced bodily changes. They found that, in fact, over a 60-day period, women who were responsive to cues from their bodies experienced significant mood changes in both positive and negative directions with their cycle. In contrast, women who were relatively unresponsive to physical cues showed no consistent cycle effects. In other words, women who were more susceptible to self-perception effects were more likely to exhibit PMS.

TABLE 13.1
CONCEPT REVIEW

Two Accounts of Why We Change our Attitudes*

Theory	Means of Attitude Change
Cognitive dissonance	We change our attitudes because of the mental discomfort we experience when they are inconsistent.
Self-perception	We form new attitudes in order to make them consistent with our behavior.

*These accounts are not mutually exclusive. We can change our attitudes for many reasons.

1. Thoughtful arguments on an issue about which an attitude is being formed reflect a _____ to persuasion.
   a. peripheral route
   b. central route
   c. circular route
   d. linear route
2. According to the mere exposure effect, listening to a piece of music over and over tends to _____ its appeal.
   a. have no effect on
   b. decrease
   c. increase
   d. first decrease and then decrease
3. Self-perception theory concerns inferring
   a. beliefs from behavior.
   b. behavior from beliefs.
   c. both beliefs and behavior from emotions.
   d. emotions from both beliefs and behavior.

ATTRIBUTIONS

What are attributions? How do they explain behavior?

One way to achieve cognitive consistency is to make an attribution—a mental explanation that points to the cause of a behavior, including the behavior of the person making the attribution. For example, to explain our newfound fondness for brussels sprouts, we may make an *attribution* in our self-perception, telling ourselves that we are among those people who like brussels sprouts, based on our observations of our own behavior. Attributions are important because they help us understand both our own behavior and the behavior of others. They can involve matters of life and death. A driver who picks up a hitchhiker attributes an outstretched thumb to the individual's need for a ride. If this attribution is wrong and the hitchhiker instead plans to rob or kill the driver, the mistaken attribution will be costly indeed.

EXPLAINING AND INTERPRETING BEHAVIOR

Attribution theories address how people explain not only their own behavior but also the behavior of others. People make attributions to themselves, others, or sit-uational variables. Their goal in doing so is to understand their social world and answer questions such as Why did I act that way? and Why did she do that?

Fritz Heider (1958) is often credited as the originator of attribution theory. He suggested that humans are inclined to observe, classify, and explain (by making causal attributions) both our own behavior and the behavior of others. We then often base our own subsequent behavior on the earlier assumptions we have made in our causal attributions. For example, people who are living through difficult circumstances, such as economic deprivation or war, often seek scapegoats on which to pin the causes of their misfortune. They seek to attribute their misfortune to external causes.

Heider pointed out that people make two basic kinds of attributions in particular. Dispositional or **personal attributions** are mental explanations that the causes of behavior are within the individual who performs the behavior. Hence, the attributions are internal (e.g., "His stubbornness got us into this argument"). **Situational attributions** are mental explanations that the causes of behavior are outside the individual who performs the behavior. These attributions are external, such as to the settings, events, or other people in the environment of the person engaging in a given behavior (e.g., "If they hadn't held the examination in that overheated room, I probably would have been more alert and gotten a better grade"). When a particular event has several possible causal attributions, we are less likely to attribute the event to any one particular cause (Morris & Larrick, 1995). People who live in a so-called culture of honor are likely to making personal attributions that result in violence, as discussed in the Psychology in Everyday Life box.

ATTRIBUTION HEURISTICS AND BIASES

Up to this point, we have described how we process the various factors that influence causal attributions almost as if humans were efficient computers, mechanistically measuring each possible factor. Actually, none of us carefully weighs every factor each time we make an attribution. Instead, we usually use *heuristics*—shortcut rules—to help us make decisions (see Chapter 8 for more on heuristics). Unfortunately, these shortcuts sometimes lead to biases and other distortions, such as in our thinking about the causes of behavior. For example, people sometimes blame others simply because it is easier to use a scapegoat than to determine the often complex causes of personal or even national misfortunes. We now turn to some of the common heuristics and biases that affect how people make their causal attributions.

PSYCHOLOGY IN EVERYDAY LIFE

THE CULTURE OF HONOR

Do you feel that if someone mistreats a member of your family, you must uphold the family honor? Whether or not you do depends partially on whether you have grown up in what has come to be called a *culture of honor.* In such a culture, people emphasize the importance of honor and social status. Aggression is viewed as necessary to preserve honor and social status. In such cultures, even minor perceived slights to the honor of an individual or a family can lead to major confrontations and even death.

Richard Nisbett and Dov Cohen (1996) have studied an area they believed, in large part, to have a culture of honor, the southern United States. As long as records have been kept, the South has led all other regions, on average, in rates of homicide. Why? Nisbett and Cohen have suggested that part of the answer lies in the self-perceived need of southerners to uphold a culture of honor.

Why should a culture of honor have emerged in the South and not in other parts of the United States? Nisbett and Cohen have speculated that the needs of early settlers in the South were somewhat different from those of settlers in other parts of the country. Southern settlers were more likely to come from migrational herding cultures with inadequate enforcement of the law. In order to protect their flocks, the herders felt a need to take the law into their own hands. Settlers in the North, in contrast, were more likely to be settled farmers and more accustomed to the rule and enforcement of law.

Nisbett and Cohen have presented evidence that southerners are more likely than northerners to agree that a person has a right to kill in order to defend his family and home. They are more likely to agree to violence, so long as it is honor-related.

In one set of experiments (Cohen, Nisbett, Bowdle, & Schwarz, 1996), white male students became involved in an encounter in a narrow hallway. An associate of the experimenters passed a given participant and did not give way, but rather bumped into him and then insulted him. The data showed that southerners were more likely than northerners, on average, to feel that their masculine reputations had been threatened. They showed more physiological signs of upset (e.g., rise in testosterone level). And subsequently, they engaged in more aggressive behavior.

The culture of honor does not apply, of course, to all people or parts of the South. Moreover, these kinds of behavior are not limited to particular individuals in the South. Members of gangs in all parts of the country can be very touchy about the kinds of "respect" shown them. People have been killed for not showing the proper "respect." Clearly, the way people react when their sense of honor is threatened is socialized by the kind of environment in which they grow up.

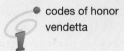

● codes of honor
  vendetta

SOCIAL DESIRABILITY. Some research has indicated that in trying to infer the dispositions of people, we tend to give undeservedly heavy weight to socially undesirable behavior (Jones & Davis, 1965). In fact, we may focus so much attention on the negative behavior that we fail to notice even highly socially desirable behavior. For example, someone who has bad manners at the dinner table may make a bad impression, despite the person's witty, insightful, thought-provoking conversation. This person may also be a kind and gentle humanitarian, but she or he may be hard-pressed to negate the effect of socially undesirable behavior in other people's minds.

THE FUNDAMENTAL ATTRIBUTION ERROR. The **fundamental attribution error** occurs when an individual overemphasizes internal causes and personal responsibility and underemphasizes external influences when observing the behavior of other people (L. Ross, 1977). This error is called "fundamental" because it appears to be so generalized and so basic. For example, if a teacher criticizes us repeatedly, we are likely to attribute the behavior to something about the teacher's nature. A person who often does favors for others is more likely to be judged as intrinsically helpful than pressured by circumstances to do favors. Middle-aged adults are less susceptible to making this error than are younger and older adults (Follett & Hess, 2002). People who are in a good mood are also more susceptible to the error than are people in a bad mood (Forgas, 1998).

Susceptibility to the fundamental attribution error varies across cultures. In certain Eastern cultures, people tend, on average, to be more aware of situational factors influencing behavior than are people in the West (Choi, Nisbett, & Norenzayan, 1999; Morris & Peng, 1994). Also, Joan Miller (1984) has found that people in India are less susceptible to the fundamental attribution error than are people in the United States.

ACTOR–OBSERVER EFFECT. Edward Jones and Richard Nisbett (1971) expanded on the notion of the fundamental attribution error. In the **actor–observer effect,** we attribute others' actions to stable characteristics, but we attribute our own actions to the momentary characteristics of the situation. In the latter, we are the actors (who must consider the relevant situational factors). In the former, we are the observers (who notice the dispositions of other people)—hence, the name of the effect (Gifford & Hine, 1997). If I kick a dog, it is because the dog was going to bite me. When someone else kicks a dog, the action shows just how mean and nasty that person really is.

The actor–observer effect may even extend to groups with which we either do or do not identify. Islam and Hewstone (1993) studied Hindu and Muslim students in Bangladesh. They found that students tended to attribute the positive behavior of members of their group to the group members' good dispositions and the bad behavior to the situation. They made the reverse attribution for members of the other group. The effect does not appear in all circumstances, however. Wolfson (1997) did not observe it among competitive swimmers, who saw their performance as highly affected by both internal and external factors.

SELF-SERVING BIASES. Another bias in our attribution processes is that we tend to be generous—to ourselves—when interpreting our own actions (S. Epstein, 1992). For example, when students study for examinations and do well, they are likely to take credit for the success. But when students study and do poorly, they are more likely to attribute the low grade to the examination ("That test was unfair!") or to the professor ("His grading is so strict!"; Whitley & Frieze, 1985). In another study of self-serving biases, Kunda (1987) found that students were aware that the divorce rate in the United States hovers close to 50%. But these same students believed that their own chances of ever personally divorcing their future spouses were only around 20%.

The occurrence of self-serving bias may differ across cultures (Markus, Kitayama, & Heiman, 1996). Markus and Kitayama (1991) have suggested, for example, that it seems to be more common among American than among Japanese students.

Self-serving biases can perform at least one constructive function in our lives: They give us necessary self-confidence. This confidence in ourselves is often a first step toward achieving the goals we value, whether in personal relationships, in school, or on the job.

Self-serving bias applies to bogus as well as real feedback. In one study, college students completed a personality inventory and then were presented with bogus results that included both positive and negative descriptions. The students were more likely to rate the positive than the negative traits as applying to themselves (MacDonald & Standing, 2002).

SELF-HANDICAPPING. In *self-handicapping,* people take actions to sabotage their own performance so that they will have excuses in case they fail to perform satisfactorily (Berglas & Jones, 1978). Uncertain of their ability to perform well, they create a situation in which

TABLE 13.2
CONCEPT REVIEW

Attribution Heuristics and Biases

Heuristic/Bias	Explanation
Social desirability	We give undeservedly heavy weight to socially undesirable behavior.
Fundamental attribution error	We overemphasize internal causes and personal responsibility when observing the behavior of other people.
Actor–observer effect	We attribute the actions of others to their stable personal characteristics, and our own actions to the momentary demands of the situation.
Self-serving biases	We tend to be generous in interpreting our own actions.
Self-handicapping	We sabotage our own performance in order to have an excuse for failing.

they *cannot* perform well. They then blame their poor performance on the situation, without acknowledging their role in creating that situation. For example, a student might not make the time to study for a test. When she does badly on it, she might attribute the failure to not being able to study. In some situations, women have been found to self-handicap in their performance on mathematics tests. Their expectations of bad performance actually interfere with their performance (Keller, 2002).

We have surveyed some of the heuristics and biases people use in making attributions (see Table 13.2). It is important to know not only the bases of attributions but also the problems and prejudices inherent in attributions. Probably no one can see a situation clearly enough to make a completely accurate attribution. Or perhaps no situation is so simple that everyone can agree on one attribution. Nevertheless, understanding heuristics and biases can help you increase the accuracy of your attributions in your daily lives. Your skill in making attributions about the causes of your own behavior and the behavior of others might be viewed as an index of interpersonal and intrapersonal intelligence, respectively (H. Gardner, 1983, 1999; see Chapter 9).

Next we consider how we perceive and interpret a wide variety of information about other people in order to form an impression of them. Note that *impression formation* is the impression you form about other people, whereas *impression management* is the impression you try to encourage others to form about you.

✓ CONCEPT CHECK 3

1. Jack is angry with his college for forcing him to learn things in which he is not interested. He has made a _____ attribution.
   a. personal
   b. situational
   c. longitudinal
   d. cross-sectional
2. The heuristic of social desirability refers to our tendency to give undeservedly heavy weight to socially _____ behavior.
   a. unusual
   b. common
   c. desirable
   d. undesirable
3. Zita tends to attribute others' mistakes to their incompetence. She is demonstrating
   a. the fundamental attribution error.
   b. self-serving bias.
   c. self-handicapping.
   d. the culture of honor.

How do we form impressions?

FORMING IMPRESSIONS

When you go to a party and meet new people, how do you decide what you think of them? An entire area of social psychology is devoted to the question of how we form impressions. **Impression formation** is the process by which we develop unified intuitive conceptions about others, based on inferences from information obtained both directly and indirectly (Hamilton & Sherman, 1996). Sometimes these impressions are based not on the person directly but on relatives. Govern and Greco (2002) had participants rate their impressions of individuals with different degrees of familial relation to someone said to be in prison. The closer the familial relation to the criminal, the more negative the rating of the person. Thus, people were being held accountable for the alleged crime of their relative. There was one interesting exception. An identical twin was rated no more negatively than an unrelated control person. So, curiously, the effect applied to all relatives except the very closest of all!

SOLOMON ASCH: A MODEL OF IMPRESSION FORMATION

Solomon Asch (1946) performed a landmark study. He presented his participants with the following list of adjectives describing a hypothetical person named Jim: "intelligent, skillful, industrious, _____, determined, practical, cautious." In the blank was one of these

© Michael Newman/PhotoEdit

Our impressions of people are based on direct and indirect information—what we have heard about them, how they look and talk, the interests and opinions they express, and so on.

TABLE 13.3

Impression Formation. Given lists of adjectives that differed by just one word, participants in the Asch experiment were asked to describe their impressions of an imaginary person. The following percentages indicate the proportion of participants, for each of the lists, who agreed that a given trait would also characterize the person described by the list of adjectives. (From "Trait Data/Impression Formation," S. E. Asch, *Journal of Abnormal and Social Psychology,* Vol. 41, 1946, pp. 258–290. Reprinted by permission of the author.)

Additional Traits	Traits Inserted Into List			
	"Warm"	"Cold"	"Polite"	"Blunt"
Generous	91%	8%	56%	58%
Wise	65	25	30	50
Happy	90	34	75	65
Good-natured	94	17	87	56
Reliable	94	99	95	100

words: *warm, cold, polite,* or *blunt.* Based on these seven adjectives, participants were asked to write descriptions of Jim and to indicate whether the adjectives *generous, wise, happy, good-natured,* and *reliable* could also describe him.

Asch interpreted the findings shown in Table 13.3 as indicating that the words *warm* and *cold* seemed to be **central traits,** characteristics that stand out in their importance to the personality and behavior of an individual (see Chapter 15). When either of these two words appeared in the blank, it had a radical effect on the sort of person Jim was perceived to be. *Polite* or *blunt* in the blank, however, had relatively little effect on impression formation.

Other investigators have criticized aspects of Asch's study. They have pointed out, for example, that the words *warm* and *cold* are social traits. In contrast, the other words in the initial list (*intelligent, skillful, industrious,* and so on) are intellectual in nature. This difference in kind may have given the social words disproportionate weight in impression formation (Zanna & Hamilton, 1972). How well the results generalize to real-world situations (their *ecological validity*) has also been questioned. Nonetheless, Asch's ideas have had a lasting influence, especially the notion of central traits around which we organize information about other personality characteristics.

HEURISTICS AND BIASES

One reason people do not form uniform impressions of other people is that almost all of us take shortcuts when we are forming impressions (Gigerenzer & Selten, 2003; Gigerenzer, Todd, & the ABC Research Group, 1999; Goldstein & Gigerenzer, 2002; Todd & Gigerenzer, 2001). Most of the time, these shortcuts save us time and give us a good enough im-

pression to help us interact with other people appropriately. Often, however, our shortcuts are altogether too short and cut out too much important information. Research suggests that the way we process information can distort our perceptions through a variety of heuristics and biases. They include the primacy effect, confirmation bias, self-fulfilling prophecy, and person-positivity bias.

THE PRIMACY EFFECT. First impressions can be powerful. In one experiment (Asch, 1946), a group of people was told that a person was "intelligent, industrious, impulsive, critical, stubborn, and envious." A second group of participants was told that the person was "envious, stubborn, critical, impulsive, industrious, and intelligent." Notice that the second list of traits is exactly the same as the first, but the words are in reverse order. Despite the similarity of the two lists, people who heard the first order—with positive traits first—formed a more positive impression than did those people who heard the second order—with negative traits first. Asch concluded that we demonstrate a *primacy effect* in our evaluations of people: First impressions can influence subsequent ones. Thus, we give more weight to the things we learn earlier than to the things we learn later. The primacy effect causes bias in judgments of abilities as well as of personality.

Schemas are one reason that the primacy effect works. As we take in new information, we try to make sense of it as quickly as possible, either by assimilating it into our existing schemas (e.g., about "people like that") or by creating new schemas to accommodate the new information. If we must create new schemas, we do it quickly, to minimize the length of time we feel the uncomfortable lack of an integrated way in which to understand the new information. As soon as we have the beginnings of a schema, we can rapidly and easily assimilate any additional information into it. If the new information is sharply discrepant from the new schema, we may modify the schema to accommodate the new information, but we leave the fundamental structure of the schema intact. We do not discard or even completely overhaul the schema once we create it. It is harder to correct an initial bad impression about abilities than to ruin an initial good one. For example, if we have a schema of someone as a good person, but he or she betrays us, then we need to create a new schema to reflect the new information.

CONFIRMATION BIAS. A second reason we tend to maintain our first impressions of people (the primacy effect) is confirmation bias. *Confirmation bias* is the human tendency to seek ways to confirm rather than to refute existing beliefs (Edwards & Smith, 1996). Our confirmation biases may lead us to seek, interpret, and even distort information in ways that verify our first impressions or preexisting beliefs about a person or a group (Yzerbyt, Rocher, & Schadron, 1996). Confirmation bias tends to be stronger when information relevant to our beliefs is presented bit by bit, sequentially, rather than all at once (Jonas, Schulz-Hardt, Frey, & Thelen, 2001). Groups as well as individuals show confirmation bias (Frey & Schulz-Hardt, 2001). We tend to notice and remember the events and behaviors that fit into our existing schemas. In contrast, we tend to ignore and forget those that do not. Thus, we have the illusion that our preconceptions are confirmed by our experiences. Our confirmation biases can lead us to distortions that reduce our appreciation of others and also distort our full understanding of the world in which we live. We may under- or overestimate the skills, abilities, and merits of the people around us as a result of our confirmation biases.

Confirmation bias can be one reason that even flagrant examples of child abuse go unnoticed. A teacher may see possible signs of physical abuse in a child. These signs may even be ones that, in most circumstances, would lead to strong suspicions of abuse. But the child happens to come from a family that is prominent in the community. Perhaps the parents have been outspoken in their criticism of child abuse. The teacher, having a strong positive impression of the behavior of the parents, may interpret the signs of child abuse as indications of a propensity of the child to have accidents. He thereby leaves the child at risk for further harm.

Why would we persist in doing something that eventually might hurt us or others? Because confirmation biases, like other heuristic shortcuts, save us time. If we took the time to get to know everyone with whom we had any contact, we would have time for little else. In our daily, transitory interactions with most people, our confirmation biases probably do us little harm. But they do save us a great deal of time. In many situations, however, we would do well to consider the powerful influence of our confirmation biases.

SELF-FULFILLING PROPHECY. Confirmation bias can lead to self-fulfilling prophecy, in which what we believe to be true becomes true, at least as we perceive it. Robert Rosenthal and Leonore Jacobson (1968) pioneered the study of self-fulfilling prophecies in their landmark investigation showing the effects of teacher expectations on student performance (see Chapter 2). Their particular study looked at positive self-fulfilling prophecies. But prophecies can be negative as well (Harris, Milich, Corbitt, Hoover, & Brady, 1992). In general, people have certain expectations of others. They then act in a way to confirm their expectations. They conclude that their original expectations were correct without acknowledging their role in making them come true.

Self-fulfilling prophecies can operate at the organizational level as well as at the individual level (Kierein & Gold, 2000). When managers believe that their organizations are doomed, their prophecies may well come true (Edwards, McKinley, & Moon, 2002).

PERSON-POSITIVITY BIAS. Person-positivity bias is the tendency to evaluate individuals more positively than groups, including groups to which we belong (Sears, 1983; Singh, 1998). Often, for example, people have a negative prejudice toward a group, but they may have a positive attitude toward a particular group member. In this case, we may be willing to take the time to form a rather elaborate schema for a particular individual we know well and with whom we interact often. Our frequent observations of an individual may so sharply conflict with our stereotype that we are forced to notice that the person defies the stereotype. Such observations would require us to make some kind of cognitive adjustment.

We still try to exert as little effort as possible, however. We try to minimize the amount of cognitive adjustment we must make. It takes less mental effort to note simply that this individual happens to deviate from the stereotype than to dismiss or to overhaul the stereotype altogether. Thus, we may have to change our views toward individuals who happen to belong to a group. When thinking about the group of people as a whole, we may still prefer to use a nice, neat stereotype. Such a stereotype works as a convenient shortcut. It replaces getting to know all the possible

TABLE 13.4
CONCEPT REVIEW

Heuristics and Biases in Impression Formation

Heuristic/Bias	Explanation
Primacy effect	We tend to be overly influenced by first impressions.
Confirmation bias	We tend to seek confirmation of what we already believe.
Self-fulfilling prophecy	What we believe is (or should be) true comes true.
Person-positivity bias	We tend to evaluate individuals more positively than the groups they belong to.

exceptions to the rule, all the varied details of the general description, and all the contextual information that might influence how we interpret a particular characteristic.

See Table 13.4 for a review of the heuristics and biases we use in forming impressions.

When people feel that they compare unfavorably to others, they may become angry or resentful.

© Bob Daemmrich/Stock, Boston

SOCIAL COMPARISON

Leon Festinger (1954), mentioned earlier in the chapter, proposed another theory about how we look at ourselves. According to **social-comparison theory,** we evaluate our abilities and accomplishments largely in comparison with the abilities and accomplishments of others, particularly in novel, uncertain, or ambiguous settings for which internal standards are not yet established (Buunk & Mussweiler, 2001; Suls & Fletcher, 1983; Suls & Miller, 1977). Our self-esteem suffers when others perform better than we do (Kulik & Gump, 1997). The realism and accuracy of our self-appraisals depend in large part on whether those with whom we compare ourselves are, in fact, appropriate bases for setting our own standards (Goethals & Darley, 1977). Suppose that Darrell, a sophomore in college, compares himself to a high school student in terms of academic accomplishments. He might thereby have an unrealistically positive image of what he has accomplished. In contrast, Melba—also a sophomore—compares herself to a graduate student. As a result, she may end up with an unrealistically negative self-image. It is important to compare ourselves to people with whom we can make appropriate comparisons.

People use a variety of techniques to maintain their self-esteem, despite unfavorable social comparisons. They may exaggerate the abilities of those who outperform them. Then they continue to see themselves as quite able even if not at the superlative level (Alicke, LoSchiavo, Zerbst, & Zhang, 1997). Or they may compare themselves to others who are substantially worse than they are (Gibbons, Benhow, & Gerrard, 1994). When feeling threatened, people may be more likely to make downward social comparisons (Gibbons et al., 2002; Wills, 1987). When people make inappropriate social comparisons, they may form overly harsh or overly accepting opinions about their own behavior.

IN THE LAB OF BERND STRAUSS

HOW IMPORTANT ARE SPECTATORS TO ATHLETES' PERFORMANCE?

A common belief among athletes, coaches, spectators, and journalists is that the presence of spectators strongly influences performance in sports. When basketball players were asked how they perform in front of an audience, 89% reported being more strongly motivated by crowd support at home games (Jurkovac, 1985). However, if we want to investigate the impact of spectators on sports performance scientifically, it is not enough to ask athletes what they think. We have to study their performances.

Results based on performance clearly indicate that assessing the impact of spectators is not as simple and straightforward as athletes and others believe. My colleagues and I took one of the first steps toward developing a more detailed analysis of this issue. First we analyzed existing research findings (e.g., Greer, 1983; Moore, & Brylinsky, 1993), looking at the variety of influences studied by other researchers (e.g., Kluger, & DeNisi, 1996). On this basis, we developed several of our own empirical studies.

One study deals with the impact of spectator cheering on performances in American Football (see detailed Strauss, 2002a). We investigated the New Yorker Hurricanes, who belong to the American Football premier league based in the German city of Kiel. We collected data from four home games in 1997 that were attended by an average of about 4,000 spectators each. Team perfor-

mance and spectator behavior were videotaped and shown to raters. The raters assessed spectator behavior ("cheering," when more than 50% of the spectators exhibited support for their team vs. "no cheering") for 15 seconds before the start of a down and during a down. The outcome of each down was given either a positive or negative rating by the head coach and one other person, based on a standardized list of items such as gaining territory, completing a touchdown, and so on.

The four games combined produced 631 downs. A statistical procedure known as *hierarchical log linear analysis* applied to the data on these downs revealed that positive effects of cheering on the home team could not be confirmed. Although the team's previous performances affected subsequent spectator behavior, spectator behavior did not affect subsequent game performance. In other words, our field study does not indicate that spectator behavior such as cheering before a down influences

Professor Strauss received his PhD in psychology from the University of Kiel, Germany, in 1992. From 1997 to 2003 he was the vice-president of the German Society of Sport Psychology. Since 1998 he has been professor of sport psychology at the University of Muenster, Germany, where he is currently dean of the faculty of psychology. He is editor-in-chief of the German Journal of Sport Psychology. Dr. Strauss's main research interests are social psychology in sports, complex problem solving, and the application of diagnosis and research methods to sports psychology.

the athletes' performances. On the other hand, athletic performance certainly influences spectator behavior: Spectators react to the performance on the field as they would to a performance on stage.

How can this be explained (see Bond, & Titus, 1993; Strauss, 2002b)? In studies using tasks that focus on stamina, speed, or power (e.g., running), it is frequently quantitative aspects (e.g., time, weight) that prove to be dominant. Such tasks reveal clear improvements in performance. These results can be contrasted with tasks that focus on the qualitative aspects of performance (e.g., errors). Such tasks often require coordination. Spectators seem to "interfere" with the attainment of optimal performance, and it tends to drop.

Many tasks require not only stamina, speed, or strength but also coordination. This is typical for team sports like soccer, handball, and American football. Whether performance improves, deteriorates, or

continued

remains unchanged seems to depend on its individual components. The presence of spectators may help improve the quantitative aspects of performance (e.g., an athlete may run more miles or sprint faster). At the same time, spectators may have a negative effect on qualitative aspects (e.g., the same athlete makes more mistakes). The final outcome may be that no spectator effects can be ascertained on such global measures of performance as the outcomes of winning or losing a match, gaining territory in football, and so forth.

Hence, if we look at the available empirical research using performance measures rather than athletes' self-reports, we can find no single study demonstrating that cheering leads to improved global performance in team sports.

✓ CONCEPT CHECK 4

1. Negative information about a person tends to do the most damage when it is presented _____ a list of information.
   a. early in
   b. in the middle of
   c. toward the end of
   d. equally distributed within
2. People have a tendency to _____ what they already believe.
   a. seek to disconfirm
   b. seek to confirm
   c. be certain of
   d. be extremely skeptical of
3. Von does not like a particular rock band. His impression of Alix, the guitar player, is likely to be _____ his impression of the band as a whole.
   a. the same as
   b. more positive than
   c. more negative than
   d. first more positive and later more negative than

ATTRACTION, LIKING, AND LOVING

What leads us to connect with others?

At the beginning of this chapter, we looked at the mental processes by which we develop and change attitudes, make attributions, and form impressions. In this section, we step back from purely internal social processing and begin to look at what happens when the initially internal notion of attraction becomes liking or loving.

Each of us needs friendship, love, and physical contact. Our perceptions of ourselves are partly shaped by our friendships, our loving relationships, and our feelings of attractiveness and attraction to others. We may even have ideal stories of what love should be, which lead us to be attracted to people who fit those stories and not attracted to those who do not (R. J. Sternberg, 1995a, 1996a, 1998c). Social psychologists ask: What is going on in the mind of a person who feels attracted to someone? Why are we more attracted—and more attractive—to one person rather than another?

Sculptors, painters, composers, writers, and philosophers have explored these same questions. While reading about the psychological perspective, bear in mind that scientific analysis of love or friendship can reveal only part of a much larger picture.

FORCES THAT INFLUENCE ATTRACTION

What forces lead to attraction in the first place, and hence to liking and loving? Some underlying variables are familiarity, arousal, proximity, physical attractiveness, and similarity (Berscheid & Reis, 1997). Recall from the discussion on persuasion that familiarity increases our liking for someone. That is, due to mere exposure, we tend to feel a stronger liking for people who are familiar. We describe the remaining four factors next.

AROUSAL

Arousal can play an important part in interpersonal attraction. The role of arousal was demonstrated in a famous and creative study (Dutton & Aron, 1974) conducted next to a scenic river with two bridges. The first bridge extended over a deep gorge. It swayed precariously from side to side when people walked across it. For most people, walking across this bridge aroused fear. The second bridge was stable, solid, and near the ground. Walking across it did not arouse anxiety.

The participants (all men) were assigned to cross one bridge or the other. As they walked across the bridge, they met either a male or a female assistant of the experimenter. The assistant asked each person

Friendship and physical attraction are only two of many kinds of close connection among human beings.

to answer a few questions and to write a brief story in response to a picture. After each participant wrote his story and then finished crossing the bridge, the research assistant gave the man his or her home phone number. The assistant remarked that the research participant should feel free to call if he would like more information about the experiment. The experimenters found that those participants who had become aroused by walking across the anxiety-evoking suspension bridge and who met a female assistant wrote stories that contained relatively high levels of sexual imagery. They were also more likely than other participants to call the assistant at home. Their arousal thus led to attraction. Of course, the fact that the participants even met the assistant was important, which leads us to discuss the importance of proximity.

PROXIMITY

We are more likely to be exposed to and to be aroused by those with whom we have the most contact. Thus, *proximity*—geographical nearness of people—can lead to increased friendship or attraction because it facilitates the likelihood of familiarity and possibly also of arousal.

Friendship patterns were investigated among military veterans and their spouses who lived in two married-student dormitories at the Massachusetts Institute of Technology (Festinger, Schachter, & Back, 1950). The researchers found that people who lived closer to each other were more likely to become friends than people who lived farther apart—even though none of the distances involved was great. Moreover, people who lived in centrally located apartments were likely to form more friendships than people who lived near the end of a floor.

PHYSICAL ATTRACTIVENESS

If you are like most people—and you are honest with yourself—physical attraction is a very important component of your attraction to people in general, at least at first. One study found that physically attractive people are judged to be kinder and stronger than people we find less attractive. They are also seen as more outgoing, nurturing, sensitive, interesting, poised, sociable, and sexually warm and responsive. They are viewed as more exciting dates and as having better characters. More attractive people also are predicted to have greater marital happiness and competence, more prestige, more social and professional success, and more general fulfillment than less attractive people (Dion, Berscheid, & Walster, 1972). These predictions, of course, are based on stereotypes rather than on facts. In collectivistic cultures such as Taiwan and South Korea, more attractive individuals are also believed to have greater concern for others and ability to relate to others (Chen, Shaffer, & Wu, 1997; Wheeler & Kim, 1997).

We treat people differently as a function of how attractive they are to us. Hatfield and Sprecher (1986) showed that attractive people have superior life outcomes. In a related vein, Langlois, Ritter, Casey, and Savin (1995) found that mothers are more affectionate and playful with attractive than with unattractive infants. But our generalized judgments based solely on physical attractiveness are often overly positive and hence mistaken (A. Feingold, 1992).

Cross-cultural studies of beauty have clearly documented that different cultures have different standards of beauty. An early review of more than 200 widely divergent cultures (C. S. Ford & Beach, 1951) found that societies differ not only in what they consider beautiful, but also in the parts of the body they emphasize in evaluating beauty (e.g., eye shape, pelvis size, overall height and weight). Berscheid and Walster (1974) supported this diversity of cultural views of attractiveness.

More may underlie human physical attractiveness than cultural preferences. In one study, the looking preferences of chickens for human faces were compared with humans' preferences. The birds and the people showed the same preferences (Ghirlanda, Jansson, & Enquist, 2002). Researchers have also investigated brain correlates of reactions to physical attractiveness. Attractive faces tended to activate the medial orbitofrontal cortex of the brain, a region that is generally involved in experiencing rewards. Moreover, responses in this region were enhanced when the faces were smiling ones (O'Doherty et al., 2003).

SIMILARITY

As you might have guessed, evidence on interpersonal attraction suggests that the more similar individuals are, the more likely they are to be attracted to each other (E. W. Burgess & Wallin, 1953; T. L. Huston & Levinger, 1978; Michinov & Monteil, 2002). Even similar attitudes and temperament (Byrne, 1971; Hatfield & Rapson, 1992), social and communication skills (Burleson & Denton, 1992), and sense of humor (Murstein & Brust, 1985) have been shown to have a positive effect on attraction. In other words, the more similar people are with respect to many variables, the more likely they are to be attracted to one another. People who are aware of this fact look for others similar to themselves (Stiles, Walz, Schroeder, Williams, & Ickes, 1996). People who are similar physically are also expected to have more successful relationships (Garcia & Khersonsky, 1997).

THEORIES OF LIKING AND INTERPERSONAL ATTRACTION

In general, we are most likely to be attracted to people whose presence we find rewarding (Clore & Byrne, 1974; Lott & Lott, 1968). The rewards we receive may be tangible, such as physical contact or gifts. Or they may be intangible, as when we feel delight in another's presence. But is there more to attraction than just being rewarded?

The **equity theory** of attraction suggests that we feel most strongly attracted to people with whom we have an equitable (fair) relationship of give and take (Walster, Walster, & Berscheid, 1978). Equity theory has important implications for relationships. The first and simplest is that, over the long term, both people in a relationship need to feel that their benefits and costs are approximately equal. A relationship starts to deteriorate when either person feels that the relationship is one-sided in terms of sacrifices or benefits. Second, when one partner feels wronged by the other, the partners must find a way to restore equity as quickly as possible. Otherwise, the relationship may be jeopardized.

A related finding is that people who were experimentally induced accidentally to hurt someone and who are unable to remedy the hurt they caused end up lowering their opinion not of themselves, but of their victim (Davis & Jones, 1960). In one study, retired Israeli men and women who had more equitable relationships were generally happier than those who had less equitable relationships. However, equity in household tasks led to greater burnout among the men than lack of equity. Apparently, men were happier when they did proportionately less housework than the women (Kulik, 2002).

According to **balance theory,** we attempt to maintain a sense of give and take (reciprocity) in a relationship. We tend to be drawn to people whose attitudes toward others are similar to our own (similarity) (F. Heider, 1958). We try to maintain our likes and dislikes in order to achieve cognitive consistency. We expect our friends to share them. Similarly, we expect our friends to share our other positive and negative attitudes. When we feel positive about something that our friends dislike (and vice versa), we feel an uncomfortable imbalance in the relationship. This imbalance tends to weaken the stability of the relationship, so we try to correct it. Maybe we change our attitude. Or we may try to change our friends' attitude. Or we may decide that the issue really is not important after all.

Consider an example of balance theory at work. Suppose you discover that your romantic partner is a member of the American Nazi Party. You probably feel very uncomfortable and even distressed. Your positive attitude toward your partner is now out of balance with your negative attitude toward Nazis. In order to maintain cognitive consistency, you are likely to find yourself (1) trying to change your partner's attitude toward the organization, (2) changing your own attitude toward it, or (3) changing your attitude toward your partner.

LOVE

Most of us distinguish between liking and loving, but we also admit that it is difficult to define the differences—not to mention the difficulty of defining the terms precisely. We assume that *love* is a deeper, stronger feeling than liking. Both are rooted in attraction, but love grows from more powerful—perhaps even instinctual—attractions than liking. People further distinguish between "loving" and being "in love" (Meyers & Berscheid, 1997). Many psychological theories have been proposed to elucidate love: what kinds have been found to exist, where it comes from, and why it exists at all.

Ⓔ THE EVOLUTIONARY VALUE OF LOVE

According to evolutionary theory, adult love is an outgrowth of three main instincts that have aided adaptation: (1) the need of the infant to be protected, (2) the desire for an adult to protect and to be protected, and (3) the sexual drive (Wilson, 1981; see also Buss, 1988a, 1988b, 1994, 2000; Buss & Kenrick, 1998; Buss & Schmitt, 1993; Shackelford, Buss, & Bennett, 2002; Wright, 1994). In the evolutionary view, the ultimate function of romantic love is to foster reproduction and thus the continuation of genes. unfortunately, however, romance generally does not last long—sometimes just long enough to commit the procreative act. If romantic love were the only force keeping couples together, children might not be raised in a way that would enable them to form attachments and to develop their

There seems to be considerable support for evolutionary theory in the universality of parental love, as shown by a contemporary photograph of an Ifugao father and child in the Philippines (left) and by Marie-Elisabeth-Louise Vigée-Lebrun's painting, Self-Portrait with Her Daughter.

potential. Couples might dissolve as soon as their romantic ardor cooled. Fortunately, companionate love—just plain strong liking—often helps a couple stay together and bring up the children, even after romantic love has cooled.

The evolutionary point of view suggests that, regardless of culture, women and men will value somewhat different things in love relationships (Buss & Schmitt, 1993; Kenrick, Groth, Trost, & Sadalla, 1993; Kenrick & Keefe, 1992; Kenrick, Li, & Butner, 2003). Women have more investment in their children because they (1) carry them during pregnancy, (2) know that the children they bear are their own, and (3) across species, tend to be more involved in bringing up the offspring. Because of their greater investment, they are particularly interested in men who have considerable resources to bring to the relationship. Men, on the other hand, (1) can impregnate many women in a short period of time, (2) generally cannot be certain the offspring is theirs (not until DNA testing becomes routine!), and (3) tend to be less involved, on average, in the offspring's upbringing. Evolutionarily, their best strategy is to find a woman who will bear the healthiest possible children. As a result, men tend to be attracted to women who show signs of good health, such as youth and beauty. The lower social status of women in almost all cultures may be responsible for observed differences between the sexes in mate preferences. For example, greater emphasis on finding a mate with resources may be simply a consequence of a woman's lesser resources. Although men and women may not look for exactly the same things in relationships, the similarities still outweigh the differences. Most people of both sexes prefer to be with someone who is physically attractive, supportive, nurturing, healthy, and so forth.

The evolutionary point of view also shows the importance of parental love. Children need nurturing adults in order to become independent and sustain themselves. Love keeps the parent attentive to the child long enough for the child to become self-sufficient. In this way, evolutionary theory is similar to attachment theory.

ATTACHMENT THEORY

Another view sees love as a reflection of the attachment patterns that we first form during infancy as we bond with our caregivers. The attachment theory of love (Hazan & Shaver, 1987, 1994; Mickelson, Kessler, & Shaver, 1997; Shaver, Collins, & Clark, 1996; Shaver & Mikulincer, 2002a, 2002b) uses the attachment concept of John Bowlby (1969) but extends it by showing that styles of adult romantic love correspond to styles of infants' attachment for their mothers (Ainsworth, 1973; see Chapter 11). The Hazan–Shaver theory distinguishes three basic types of lovers: (1) *Secure lovers* find it relatively easy to get close to others. They are comfortable depending on others and having others depend on them. They do not worry about being abandoned or about someone getting too close to them. (2) *Avoidant lovers* are uncomfortable being close to others. They find it difficult to trust others and to allow themselves to depend on others. They become nervous when anyone gets too close, and they often find that their partners in love want to become more intimate than they do. (3) *Anxious-ambivalent lovers* (analogous to infants with a resistant attachment style) find that their potential or actual partners are reluctant to get as close as the anxious-ambivalent lovers would like. Anxious-ambivalent lovers often worry that their partners do not really love them or want to stay with them. They want to merge completely with another person—a desire that sometimes scares potential or actual partners away.

An interesting implication of attachment theory is that people with different styles may respond differently to feelings of anxiety or stress. And indeed, Simpson, Rholes, and Nelligan (1992) found that when women became anxious, secure women sought and received more comfort and support from their partners. In contrast, avoidant women sought and received less comfort and support.

JOHN ALAN LEE: TYPES OF LOVE

John Alan Lee (1977, 1988) proposed six kinds of love, each with a Greek or Latin name (see Figure 13.4). The three primary types of love are *eros*, characterized by passion and desire; *ludus*, based on play; and *storge*, based in affection and friendship. The three secondary types of love are formed by combining aspects of the primary types: *agape*, a combination of eros and storge shown through altruistic, selfless adoration; *pragma*, a combination of ludus and storge with a basis in practicality; and *mania*, a combination of ludus and eros characterized by madness and possessiveness. Accord-

Agape
altruistic, seeks
little in
return

Eros
highly values physical
appearance,
intense relationship

Mania
demanding,
possessive, feels
lack of control

Storge
slow developing
relationship, lasting
commitment

Ludus
playful, many
partners

Pragma
practical needs,
such as age,
profession

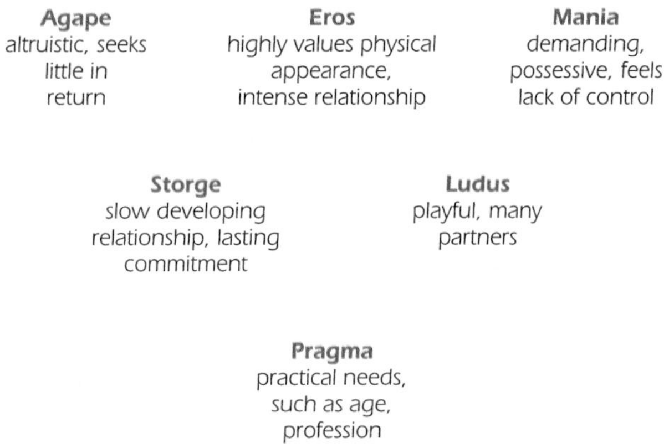

FIGURE 13.4

Lee's Six Types of Love. When John Alan Lee was formulating his three primary types of love, he looked through centuries of great literature for inspiration. (After J. A. Lee, 1977, 1988)

ing to Lee, kinds of love are like colors, and different "shades" are formed by different combinations. Support for the existence of these six kinds of love has been found in a series of investigations using questionnaires (Hendrick & Hendrick, 1986, 1992, 1997, 2002).

> My study of love began with the most successful teachers of romantic ideology for half a millennium—the great novelists. Then I turned to nonfictional observers of love, from Plato and Ovid to Andreas Cappellanus and Castiglione to the most recent psychologists. . . . It soon became obvious that no single set of statements would describe love. (J. A. Lee, 1988)

ROBERT J. STERNBERG: TRIANGULAR THEORY OF LOVE

In my own **triangular theory of love** (R. J. Sternberg, 1986b, 1998b), love has three basic components: (1) *intimacy*, feelings that promote closeness and connection; (2) *passion*, the intense desire for union with another person (Hatfield & Walster, 1981); and (3) *commitment*, the decision to maintain a relationship over the long term. Different combinations of these components yield different kinds of love, as shown in Figure 13.5. For example, intimacy and passion together yield romantic love. Combining intimacy and commitment yields companionate love, which is an enduring friendship (see also Berscheid & Walster, 1974, for a comparable distinction). The combination of passion and commitment without intimacy yields foolish (or fatuous) love; people meet, fall in love, and then commit themselves to a relationship without getting to know each other well. The triangular theory appears to come closer than many others to capturing our intuitive conceptions of love (Aron & Westbay, 1996; Barnes & Sternberg, 1997). Through the intimacy component, the theory also emphasizes the importance of communication to success in a close relationship.

Meaningful communication is probably essential for success in love relationships. For example, couples in happy marriages truly listen to each other and validate each other's points of view. Couples in unhappy marriages are less likely to listen and to cross-validate (Gottman, 1979, 1994; Gottman & Levenson, 1992). Instead, unhappy couples often *cross-complain;* each moans and whines without paying attention to what the other is saying. One complains that the other is never home. The other complains that the one spends too much money. They talk past rather than to each other.

Other factors also contribute to unsuccessful communication in couples (Gottman, 1994; Gottman & Notarius, 2002; Gottman, Notarius, Gonso, & Markman, 1976; Gottman, Swanson, & Swanson, 2002). If at least one of the partners feels hurt and ignored, thinks that the other does not see his or her point of view, neglects to focus on one problem long

FIGURE 13.5

The Triangular Theory of Love. My own triangular theory of love proposes three components: passion, intimacy, and commitment. These components are combined in different ways to produce various kinds of love. (After R. J. Sternberg, 1986b)

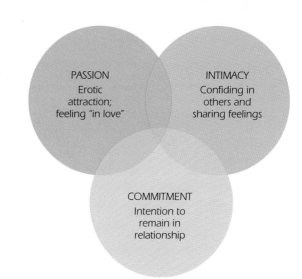

PASSION	INTIMACY	DECISION AND COMMITMENT		TYPE OF LOVE THAT RESULTS
–	–	–	=	Nonlove
+	–	–	=	Infatuated love
–	+	–	=	Liking (friendship)
–	–	+	=	Empty love
+	+	–	=	Romantic love
–	+	+	=	Companionate love
+	–	+	=	Fatuous love
+	+	+	=	Consummate (complete) love

Note: The kinds of love are typical representations; most relationships do not fit neatly within only one type. (+ = component present; – = component absent.)

enough to resolve it, frequently interrupts, and drags irrelevant issues into the discussion, then the likelihood of communication difficulties increases.

People seek others for many kinds of relationships: work associations, friendships, intimate relationships, and more. Many relationships occur in groups, the aspect of social psychology we consider in the next chapter.

✓ CONCEPT CHECK 5

1. Research suggests that people tend to be attracted to others who
   a. are unlike them.
   b. are like them.
   c. are less physically attractive than they are.
   d. live at a distance from them.
2. According to balance theory, if I like Ann but Ann likes Sue, whom I dislike, the resultant set of relationships is
   a. balanced.
   b. unbalanced.
   c. fully symmetrical.
   d. partially symmetrical.
3. Which of the following is *not* one of the three components of love in the triangular theory?
   a. intimacy
   b. passion
   c. equity
   d. commitment

FOLLOWING FADS

Think back to when you became a teenager. Like most adolescents, you probably spent a lot of time admiring yourself and as much time in self-criticism. You may have fretted about your complexion or hair or clothes. Teenagers are preoccupied with worrying about what others think of them. They want to be accepted by their peers.

One of the best ways to gain approval is to look "right" and act "right." Each generation of adolescents has its own fads. Today's fads include body piercing and black T-shirts; yesterday it was long hair and tie-dye. **Developmental psychologists** have found that following fads helps teenagers develop positive self-images and self-confidence because fitting in helps them gain ready acceptance from their peers. Developmental psychologist Richard Lerner and his colleagues have examined the relationship between teenagers' individual development and social constraints, especially those imposed by their peers (Lerner & Castellino, 2002; Lerner, De Stefanis, & Habermas, 2001). An adolescent's self-identity grows out of interactions with peers, and fads help maintain the cohesiveness of the group.

Dieting fads can be as problematic for adolescents as for adults. People trying to lose weight have followed low-fat diets, high-fat diets, high-protein diets, and grapefruit diets, among dozens of others. Some diets can be very hazardous, damaging the kidneys or heart, or causing a deficiency in vitamin B_{12}, which can produce symptoms of psychosis or dementia (Shulman, 1967). **Health psychologists** have examined the factors associated with dieting in adolescents. Due to the pressures of their peers and the media, adolescents get caught up in popular dieting strategies, especially teens who have low self-esteem and high dissatisfaction with their bodies (Ricciardelli & McCabe, 2003). Anca Codruta Rafiroiu and her colleagues surveyed 4,187 teenagers about their eating and other health habits. They found that 19.2% were extreme dieters and 43.2% dieted moderately. Extreme dieters were more likely to use alcohol, smoke tobacco and marijuana, and attempt suicide than other teens (Rafiroiu, Sargent, Parra-Medina, Drane, & Valois, 2003).

Clinical and **personality psychologists** have studied the personality profiles of people who become obsessed with food fads or vitamin supplements. They score no differently on measures of psychological well-being than people who eat normally (Lester, 1979). However, extreme dieters typically show low self-directedness on personality measures (Fassino, Abbate-Daga, Amianto, Leombruni, Boggio, & Rovera, 2002; Karwautz, Troop, Rabe-Hesketh, Collier, & Treasure, 2003; Kitagawa, Asakura, Kusumi, Denda, & Koyama, 2002). Self-directedness refers to the ability to identify one's own needs and interests and to respond to those needs and interests. Thus, extreme dieters are not in touch with their own needs and interests.

Why do rational people give up their prerogative to make their own decisions about fashion or lifestyle and follow a fad instituted by a group? **Cognitive psychologists** Saori Iwanaga and Akira Namatame (2002) have described the process a person undergoes when deciding whether or not to join a group and copy its behaviors. The group begins as a collection of individuals who eventually decide to act as one. Members must let the group as a whole make decisions for everyone, such as what to wear and how to behave. The payoffs include a sense of belonging and improved self-esteem. Iwanaga and Namatame's (2002) research indicates that following fads and being accepted into a group produce both personal stability and societal order.

Sometimes the payoffs for following a fad can be quite large, especially in the business world. **Industrial-organizational psychologists** Barry Staw and Lisa Epstein (2000) have studied the consequences for an organization of embracing a fad called total quality management (TQM). Using the popular technique did not produce more income, but the organization was regarded with more admiration, perceived to be more sensitive, and rewarded with higher ratings in management quality. In addition, chief executive officers received larger pay raises after their organizations embraced the management fad.

Fads are an unavoidable part of our lives. Social forces, especially social learning, play a large role in the adoption of a fad, as research conducted by **social psychologists** has demonstrated. In addition, research by developmental, personality, clinical, health, and industrial-organizational psychologists has contributed to our understanding of the need to fit into a group.

SUMMARY

1. Social psychologists seek to understand and explain how the presence of others (actual, imagined, or implied) affects the thoughts, feelings, and behavior of the individual.
2. *Social cognition* refers to the ways in which we perceive and interpret information from others and ourselves.

3. *Attitudes* are learned (not inborn), stable, relatively lasting evaluations of people, ideas, and things; attitudes affect our behavior.
4. Attitudes serve four functions for us: to get what we want and avoid what we do not want, to avoid internal conflicts and anxieties, to understand and integrate information, and to show our deeply held values.
5. Learning theories regarding attitude formation include classical conditioning, operant conditioning, and observational learning.
6. In attempts to change other people's attitudes, the following characteristics are important: characteristics of the recipient of the message (e.g., motivation and expertise), characteristics of the message itself (balance and familiarity due to repetition), and characteristics of the source of the message (the source's credibility and likability).
7. The links between attitudes and behavior are not always predictable and are influenced by characteristics of the attitude, of the attitude bearer, of the situation, and of the behavior.
8. One of the better-known experiments in social psychology established the theory of *cognitive dissonance*, which states that a person is uncomfortable when his or her behavior and cognitions do not mesh.
9. To ease the discomfort of cognitive dissonance, the person must justify his or her behavior. The results of a seminal experiment that studied cognitive dissonance have also been explained in other ways—by *self-perception theory*, for example.

10. *Attribution* theory deals with how we go about explaining the causes of behavior—why we do what we do and why others act as they do. In making attributions, we look for the locus (source) of the behavior, which can be *personal* or *situational*.
11. Biases and heuristics help us to make attributions but also sometimes to distort them. We give more weight to socially undesirable behavior than to its opposite. We are biased by the *fundamental attribution error*, which makes us overemphasize internal causes when viewing the behavior of others, and by the *actor–observer effect*, which expands this view to encompass our own behavior, which we explain by overemphasizing situational factors. We also use (and are used by!) self-serving biases and self-handicapping.

12. Biases and heuristics are active in *impression formation*. Due to the primacy effect, we give more weight to things we learn earlier; due to confirmation bias, we interpret new information so that it verifies beliefs we already have; due to *self-fulfilling prophecy*, we can make our expectations come true; and due to *person-positivity bias*, we evaluate individuals more positively than we do groups.
13. We often judge ourselves through *social comparisons* to others.

14. Studies show that physical attraction enhances overall attraction and liking. Other important factors underlying attraction are familiarity, arousal, proximity, and similarity.
15. Social-psychological research asks why we are attracted to some people and not to others. According to *equity theory*, attraction is a balancing act between give and take. *Cognitive-consistency* theories focus on balance.

16. Evolutionary theory deals with the genetic basis of mating behavior as well as practical, survival-of-the-species reasons for love.
17. Attachment theory describes three styles of lovers: secure, avoidant, and anxious-ambivalent.
18. According to Lee, the six types of love are eros, ludus, storge, mania, agape, and pragma.
19. Sternberg's *triangular theory of love* posits that three components—intimacy, passion, and commitment—are involved in love.

KEY TERMS

actor–observer effect 482
attitude 470
attribution 480
balance theory 490
central traits 484
cognitive consistency 476
cognitive dissonance 477

equity theory 490
fundamental attribution error 481
impression formation 483
likability effect 474
mere exposure effect 474
personal attribution 480
person-positivity bias 485

self-fulfilling prophecy 485
self-perception theory 478
situational attribution 480
social cognition 470
social-comparison theory 486
social psychology 470
triangular theory of love 492

ANSWERS TO CONCEPT CHECKS

Concept Check 1

1. d   2. b   3. a

Concept Check 2

1. b   2. c   3. a

Concept Check 3

1. b   2. d   3. a

Concept Check 4

1. a   2. b   3. b

Concept Check 5

1. b   2. b   3. c

KNOWLEDGE CHECK

1. The _____ view holds that we learn attitudes when a concept or object toward which we have no particular attitude is paired with a concept or object toward which we already have an attitude.
   a. classical-conditioning
   b. operant-conditioning
   c. observational learning
   d. transcendental learning

2. In a monochronic culture, time is viewed as
   a. fluid.
   b. continuous.
   c. precious.
   d. of no great importance.

3. The Festinger–Carlsmith (1959) experiment was famous for the researchers' claim that it demonstrated the phenomenon of
   a. self-perception.
   b. cognitive dissonance.
   c. social desirability.
   d. the fundamental attribution error.
4. When things go wrong for me, I blame the situation. When things go wrong for others, I blame them. I am demonstrating
   a. self-handicapping.
   b. confirmation bias.
   c. person-positivity bias.
   d. the actor–observer effect.
5. According to social-comparison theory, we evaluate our own abilities by comparing ourselves to
   a. ourselves.
   b. others.
   c. an ideal standard.
   d. no one in particular.
6. Dutton and Aron conducted an experiment that involved participants walking across an unstable bridge in order to demonstrate the effect on attraction of
   a. proximity.
   b. similarity.
   c. physical attractiveness.
   d. arousal.
7. According to _____ theory, people tend to feel more attracted to those with whom they have a fair relationship.
   a. equity
   b. balance
   c. attachment
   d. colors of love
8. Which of the following is *not* one of the kinds of lovers accounted for by the attachment theory of love?
   a. secure lovers
   b. anxious-ambivalent lovers
   c. avoidant lovers
   d. profound lovers
9. According to the triangular theory of love, the combination of intimacy and passion without decisive commitment is
   a. infatuated love.
   b. empty love.
   c. companionate love.
   d. romantic love.
10. A culture of honor does *not* stress
   a. social status.
   b. pacifism.
   c. aggression.
   d. honor.

Answers
1. a   2. c   3. b   4. d   5. b   6. d   7. a   8. d
9. d   10. b

THINK ABOUT IT

1. Many advertisers spend a lot of money to get celebrity endorsements of their products. Do you think that the advertisers' money is well spent? Why or why not?
2. Some investigators, such as Deborah Tannen, believe that men place more emphasis on social hierarchies than women do. Do you agree? Why or why not?
3. Describe a particular conflict you have observed, first from the perspective of one participant and then from the perspective of the other. Which heuristics and biases affected the views of each participant?
4. How would you create an advertisement for a product using the principles discussed in this chapter?
5. How could you use one or more principles of persuasion, as described in this chapter, to help elect a candidate for a student-government position?
6. Give an example of a self-handicapping behavior (e.g., drug abuse). Why and how does this example show self-handicapping?

For a chapter tutorial quiz, direct links to Internet sites, and other useful features, visit the book-specific website at http://psychology.wadsworth.com/sternberg4e. You can also connect directly to the following sites:

Social Psychology Network

www.socialpsychology.org/
This is *the* Web site for social psychology. You'll find a tremendous amount of information, including areas of study, PhD programs, and even online experiments that let you take part in actual research. The links to research include student projects on interpersonal relations, social perception, judgment, and decision making.

Racism and Psychology

http://www.apa.org/pi/oema/racism/contents.html
This American Psychological Association site offers a frank discussion of racism and stereotypes.

Y? The National Forum on People's Differences Home Page

http://www.yforum.com/index.html
Did you ever want to ask a sensitive question of someone of a different race or religion or sexual orientation—but were too embarrassed or shy? In a cyberforum with clear rules for courteous and respectful dialogue, newspaper writer and editor Philip J. Milano allows visitors to share differences openly and frankly, and to learn about aspects of the situation that are not always discussed.

For additional readings on many of the topics covered in this chapter, check out InfoTrac College Edition at **www.infotrac-college.com/ wadsworth.**

Disk Two
Attribution Theory
Attraction, Liking, and Loving
Sternberg's Triangular Theory of Love
Chapter Quiz
Critical Thinking Questions

© Susie Post/Aurora Photos

CHAPTER 14

SOCIAL PSYCHOLOGY: INTERPERSONAL AND GROUP PERSPECTIVES

O nce conform, once do what other people do because they do it, and a lethargy steals over all the finer nerves and faculty of the soul. She becomes all outer show and inward emptiness; dull, callous, and indifferent.

—Virginia Woolf

Our social interactions reveal not only how we react to others but also how they react to us. Sometimes the influence of others is obvious, as in the case of a performer who becomes animated in front of an audience. Other times it is hidden. The performer illustrates what is true for all of us: Much of our social cognition occurs in interpersonal or group contexts.

Why do smart people, when they are in a group, sometimes do stupid things (R. J. Sternberg, 2002)? How do groups of people reach consensus? What makes individuals within a group conform to a group decision they may not believe in? These are some of the questions that social psychologists attempt to answer.

Members of different cultures may respond differently to given situations (Nisbett, 2003). Be aware that most of the studies described in this chapter were conducted in the United States (Moghaddam, Taylor, & Wright, 1993; Öngel & Smith, 1994; Triandis, 1994). Many social psychologists question the generality of findings that are based on U.S. studies alone (Astatke & Serpell, 2000; M. H. Bond, 1988; M. Cole, 1999; Serpell, 2002; S. M. Stewart et al., 2000; S. M. Stewart, Bond, Kennard, Ho, & Zaman, 2002). For example, Richard Nisbett (2003) has proposed that Easterners' collectivistic ways of thinking are fundamentally different from Westerners' individualistic ways of thinking. Easterners are more likely to emphasize interdependence in their relations with others; Westerners stress independence. Although we must be careful not to overgeneralize findings from one culture to the next, many questions and problems are universal.

GROUPS

How does the presence of other people affect our beliefs and behavior?

As social psychologists define and study it, a group is a collection of individuals who *interact* with one another to accomplish work, promote interpersonal relationships, or both. A group is sometimes distinguished from a *collective*, a set of people engaged in a common activity but with minimal direct interaction. If you go to a basketball game and sit in the audience, you are part of a collective. The members of the team, however, are part of a group.

Group members typically have *roles*, or certain responsibilities; a *communication structure*, which governs who talks to whom; and a *power structure*, which reflects who wields varying amounts of influence (Forsyth, 1990, 2000; Forsyth, Zyzniewski, & Giammanco, 2002). Groups also have *norms*, or expected standards of behavior. When members depart from these norms, they may be punished by the group as a whole or by individual members.

In some groups, such as a problem-solving group in a business setting, the emphasis is likely to be on accomplishing tasks. In other groups, perhaps single parents seeking emotional support, the emphasis is likely to be on relationships among the group members.

Some groups, of course, may attend to both tasks and members' needs. As you might expect, group leaders serve two key functions: to guide the group to achieve its task-oriented goals and to facilitate the functions of mutual support and group cohesion (Bales, 1958, 1999).

Because social psychologists view interaction as the defining feature of groups, they are interested in knowing what kinds of things happen when members of a group interact. In the following sections note that group effects are complex because individual members respond to various processes in different ways, depending on their social cognitions and personalities.

SOCIAL FACILITATION AND INHIBITION

Having other people around can affect the quality of the work you do. This fact was recognized long ago by Norman Triplett (1898). He observed that bicyclists who competed against each other in a group rode faster than those who cycled alone against a clock. Similarly, children who were instructed to wind fishing reels as quickly as they could performed faster when they were with others than when they were alone. Social facilitation is a phenomenon in which the presence of other people positively influences the performance of an individual.

The presence of other people does not always improve performance, however. Anyone who has ever tried to give a speech, perform in a recital, or act in a

Although one's performance is sometimes facilitated by the presence of others, this is not always the case. Stage fright is a familiar example of social inhibition.

play in front of an audience and has been tripped up by nervousness can testify to this. **Social inhibition** is a phenomenon in which the presence of other people has a detrimental influence on an individual's performance. When does the presence (or perceived presence) of other people facilitate performance and when does it interfere?

Robert Zajonc (1965, 1980) has offered a widely accepted view of this phenomenon. According to Zajonc, the presence of other people is arousing. Arousal facilitates well-learned responses, but it inhibits new or poorly learned responses (see Figure 14.1). Thus, to predict whether facilitation or inhibition will occur, we look at the individual's experience with the particular

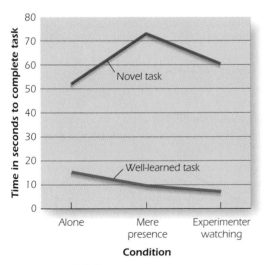

FIGURE 14.1

Social Facilitation. According to Robert Zajonc's theory of social facilitation, the mere presence of other people causes arousal. Arousal then facilitates well-learned behavior but inhibits poorly or newly learned behavior. (After Schmitt, Gilovich, Goore, & Joseph, 1986)

behavior. Suppose that Reuben is going to audition for a position in an orchestra. He has prepared for the audition by learning a new, difficult piece. Under these circumstances, the conductor's presence is likely to inhibit Reuben's playing. If Reuben had chosen a piece that he had been playing for a long time, the presence of the conductor probably would have facilitated his performance. Amazingly enough, social facilitation and inhibition apply not only to people but also to animals. Even cockroaches exhibit social facilitation in performing an easy, automatic task, but they show inhibition in performing a difficult one (Zajonc, Heingartner, & Herman, 1969). Cockroaches running toward a goal run faster in pairs than alone.

What is behind these effects? **Distraction-conflict theory** holds that the presence of others affects us through distraction (R. S. Baron, 1986; R. S. Baron, Moore, & Sanders, 1978; C. F. Bond, Atoum, & VanLeeuwen, 1996; Yoshida, 1995). In sum, general agreement exists that the presence of others can lead to either facilitation (usually of a familiar, well-learned behavior) or inhibition (usually of an unfamiliar, poorly learned behavior). Still, other explanations of exactly when and why facilitation and inhibition occur are worth considering.

SOCIAL LOAFING

What happens to our performance when we cooperate with others? Have you ever worked on a task with a group and found that you (or some of your associates) did not work as hard as you (or they) would have acting alone? For example, do you exert the same effort when you are a member of a chorus or a band as when you are singing or playing alone? As the number of people increases, the average amount of effort exerted by each individual decreases (Ringelmann, 1913). **Social loafing** is the phenomenon in which each member of a group puts forth less effort as the size of the group increases (Latané, Williams, & Harkins, 1979; Smith, Kerr, Markus, & Stasson, 2001).

Is it the actual presence of others or merely their perceived presence that causes social loafing? Part of the apparent effect might be caused by other factors, such as a lack of coordinated effort. To rule out this possibility, researchers created two kinds of groups. One kind was actual groups of two to six persons. The other kind was *pseudogroups* (Latané, Williams, & Harkins, 1979), in which participants are led to believe that they are participating with others but each person is actually alone. The participants were asked either to clap as loudly as they could or to cheer at the top of their voices.

The researchers found that people expended more effort when they were alone than when they were in groups or pseudogroups. In addition, lack of coordination contributed to a decrease in the output produced by actual groups, as opposed to pseudo-groups. As the number of people in the groups or pseudogroups increased, the amount of individual effort expended decreased, as shown in Figure 14.2. Social loafing occurs even in classrooms. When students engage in cooperative activities, there is more social loafing in large groups than in smaller ones (North, Linley, & Hargreaves, 2000).

Probably the most effective way to discourage or eliminate social loafing is to introduce evaluation apprehension. If members in a working group believe that their individual performance is being evaluated, then social loafing is reduced and social facilitation enhanced (Harkins, 1987; Harkins & Szymanski, 1987; Szymanski & Harkins, 1993). For example, social loafing is not likely to occur if an orchestra conductor can hear each musician and makes this clear. Similarly, loafing is not likely to be a problem if students involved in a group problem-solving task know that they are being watched by a teacher who will evaluate each student's contribution. Social loafing is also reduced when the task is important, when the group members expect to be punished as a whole if their performance is poor, and when the group is highly cohesive and membership is valuable to each person in it (Karau & Williams, 1993, 1997; Sheppard, 1993).

Social loafing is affected by a cultural orientation toward either *individualism* or *collectivism*. Social loafing occurs commonly in highly individualistic societies, such as the United States. It may be less common in societies that have a more collectivistic orientation, such as China and Taiwan. Studies with Chinese participants have shown that individuals work *harder* when they are in a group than when they are alone (Early, 1989; Gabrenya, Latané, & Wang, 1983; Gabrenya, Wang, & Latané, 1985).

GROUP POLARIZATION AND CONFLICT RESOLUTION

Clearly, groups influence individual behavior, making members more or less likely to act in certain ways. Groups may also influence members' attitudes. In some instances, groups choose risky alternatives. In others, they choose conservative ones. Group polarization is the exaggeration of members' initial views through the dynamic processes of group interaction (Abrams, Wetherell, Cochrane, Hogg, & Turner, 2001; Moscovici & Zavalloni, 1969; D. G. Myers & Lamm, 1976; Ohtsubo, Masuchi, & Nakanishi, 2002). For individuals who tend to take risks, being in a group exaggerates this tendency. Group members show what sometimes is called a *risky shift* in their course of action. If the members of a group individually tend toward conservatism, however, then the group as a whole tends to make a more conservative response. Group polarization has been found even when members are trying to decide merely what theme to use at their next party (Chandrashekaran, Walker, Ward, & Reingen, 1996).

Two effects appear to be responsible for group polarization. First is the effect of *new information*. In a group, people hear new arguments that support their preexisting point of view. They then become more extreme in their conviction (Burnstein & Vinokur, 1973, 1977). The more new arguments they hear, the more persuaded they become and the more extreme their attitudes.

The second effect is *movement toward the group norm.* As people meet others who share their point of view and as they receive social approval, the group begins to establish a norm. The group may gain more and more solidarity as the members' position becomes more extreme, but at the expense of rational decision making. It seems that all people who provide information and reactions are not equally effective in stimulating this process. A person will be most affected by the opinions and sentiments of members of a respected "ingroup" (J. C. Turner, 1987). Thus, Republicans are more likely to be influenced by Republicans than by Democrats in their group decision making, and vice versa.

As the phenomenon of group polarization implies, groups of people are often in conflict with one another. In addition, as your own experience has probably shown, people within groups are also often in conflict. How do people resolve these intergroup and intragroup conflicts?

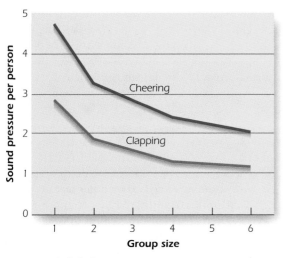

FIGURE 14.2

Social Loafing. The social-loafing phenomenon occurs even when other contributing factors are separated out (Latané et al., 1979). When people believe that increasing numbers of other people are working, they exert less individual effort—even when no one else is actually present. (From "Social Loafing," Latané et al., *Journal of Personality and Social Psychology,* Vol. 37, 1979, pp. 822-832. Copyright © 1974 by the American Psychological Association. Reprinted with permission.)

Some investigators (e.g., Kuhlman & Marshello, 1975; McClintock & Liebrand, 1988) have suggested that we have particular goals in resolving conflicts. People may have a *cooperative orientation*, seeking to maximize outcomes for themselves and others; an *individualistic orientation*, seeking to maximize outcomes for only themselves; a *competitive orientation*, seeking to maximize their own outcomes at the expense of others; or an *altruistic orientation*, seeking to maximize outcomes for only others. These goals appear to be relatively stable and valid predictors of individual behavior in situations that involve decision making (see Dehue, McClintock, & Liebrand, 1993).

GROUPTHINK

Ironically, one of the most troublesome group processes arises when there is *too little conflict*. Irving Janis has given special attention to the phenomenon of **groupthink,** which occurs when group members focus on reaching a unanimous opinion more than on other goals, including those that inspired the group to form in the first place (Frey & Schulz-Hardt, 2001; Janis, 1972; Kowert, 2002). Janis analyzed a number of foreign-policy decisions he believed reflected groupthink, including the failure to anticipate the invasion of Pearl Harbor and the appeasement of Adolf Hitler by British Prime Minister Neville Chamberlain prior to World War II.

On February 1, 2003, the space shuttle *Columbia* exploded and went plunging to Earth just minutes before it was scheduled to land in Florida. All of the astronauts aboard were killed. What caused the explosion? A seal on the left wing of the vehicle was struck by foam during liftoff and fell off the next day. It created a gap that let hot gas enter the ship during reentry. Engineers had been aware that the foam had struck the shuttle and that there was a possibility of damage. Moreover, this was not the first time that an event like this had occurred. But top NASA officials convinced themselves, wrongly, that everything would be all right. Groupthink impaired the decision-making process, resulting in a disaster. In 1986, another space shuttle, the Challenger, also exploded in space. This disaster, including the deaths of the astronauts, was also preventable. The problem, of course, is that groupthink is much more recognizable after the fact than at the time it is committed.

What conditions lead to groupthink? Janis (1972) cited three: (1) an isolated, cohesive, and homogeneous group is empowered to make decisions; (2) objective and impartial leadership is absent, within the group and outside it; and (3) high levels of stress impinge on the group decision-making process. Not all researchers agree with the importance of these three factors (Mohamed & Wiebe, 1996; Street, 1997; Tetlock, 1998). Cohesiveness, for example, appears to have inconsistent effects, although they are typically negative

if it is feared that a bad decision will become public (Turner, Pratkanis, Probasco, & Leve, 1992). Groups that are responsible for making foreign-policy decisions are excellent candidates for groupthink. They are usually like-minded. Moreover, they frequently isolate themselves from what is going on outside of their own group. They generally try to meet specific objectives and believe they cannot afford to be impartial. Also, of course, they are under great stress because the stakes involved can be very high.

SIX SYMPTOMS OF GROUPTHINK
Janis further offered six symptoms of groupthink:

1. *Closed-mindedness:* The group is not open to alternative ideas.
2. *Rationalization:* The group goes to great lengths to justify both the process and the product of its decision making, distorting reality where necessary in order to be persuasive.
3. *Squelching of dissent:* Those who disagree are ignored, criticized, and even ostracized.
4. *Formation of a "mindguard":* One person in the group appoints himself or herself the keeper of the group norm and ensures that other members stay in line.
5. *Feeling of invulnerability:* The group believes that it must be right, given the intelligence of its members and the information available to them.
6. *Sense of unanimity:* Members believe that everyone unanimously shares the opinions expressed by the group.

Groupthink results in faulty decision making because the group members examine alternatives insufficiently, examine risks inadequately, and seek information about alternatives incompletely (see Figure 14.3).

Politicians of any party may be susceptible to groupthink, which can lead to decisions that may not have the best national or international consequences.

Consider how groupthink might arise when college students decide to damage a statue on the campus of a football rival to teach a lesson to the students and faculty at the rival university. The group rationalizes that damage to a statue really is no big deal. Who cares about an old, ugly statue anyway? When one group member dissents, others quickly make him feel disloyal and cowardly. They squelch his dissent. The group's members feel invulnerable. They are going to damage the statue under the cover of darkness, and the statue is never guarded. They are sure they will not be caught. Finally, all the members agree on the course of action. This apparent feeling of unanimity convinces the group members that, far from being out of line, they are doing what needs to be done.

ANTIDOTES FOR GROUPTHINK

Janis has prescribed several antidotes for groupthink. For example, the leader of a group should encourage constructive criticism, be impartial, and ensure that members seek input from people outside the group. The group should also form subgroups that meet separately to consider alternative solutions to a single problem. It is important that the leader take responsibility for preventing spurious conformity to a group norm.

In 1997, members of the Heaven's Gate cult in California committed mass suicide in the hope of meeting up with extraterrestrials in a spaceship trailing the Hale-Bopp Comet. Although this group suicide is a striking example of conformity to a destructive group norm, similar events have occurred throughout human history, such as the suicide of more than 900 members of the Jonestown, Guyana, religious cult in 1978. Worse was the murder in 2000 of hundreds of individuals in Uganda by leaders of a cult that the individuals had joined. And now, in the 21st century, suicide bombers are killing themselves and others in carefully planned attacks.

✓CONCEPT CHECK 1

1. Social loafing predicts that individuals will tend to work less hard when they work
   a. on their own.
   b. in dyads of two people.
   c. in groups of three or four people.
   d. in large groups.
2. When a group reaches decisions that are more extreme than members would make individually, the group is showing
   a. polarization.
   b. ratiocination.
   c. coherence.
   d. conformity.
3. Which of the following is *not* a symptom of groupthink?
   a. closed-mindedness
   b. formation of a mindguard
   c. feeling of invulnerability
   d. lack of confidence in decisions

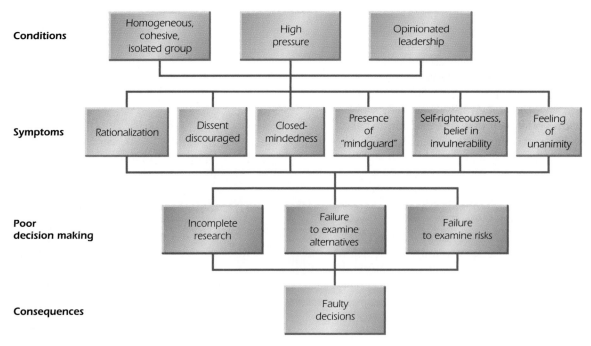

FIGURE 14.3

Janis's Groupthink. This chart summarizes the conditions, symptoms, decision-making defects, and consequences of groupthink. (After Janis, 1972)

IN THE LAB OF CLAUDE M. STEELE

THEORY AS IT EMERGES THROUGH THE BACK DOOR

The academic underperformance of minority students caught my interest when I was a faculty member at the University of Michigan. I discovered the problem while serving on a faculty committee for minority student recruitment and retention. I saw a chart that showed very clearly what has now become recognized as a national phenomenon: At each SAT level that students had when they entered Michigan, black students got lower subsequent grades than other students. I had always thought that any racial gap in grades was due to differences in how well the groups were prepared for college work, which reflected racial differences in, for example, access to education. But these data showed something different: that a racial gap in grades persisted even among students who were equally well prepared for college work, according to their SAT scores. Clearly, something other than poor preparation adversely affected the grades of black students.

Before I could decide how to address this problem, graduate student Steve Spencer and I were looking over grade data from several math classes and noticed that women underperformed in relation to men in difficult math classes (that is, got lower grades at each level of entering SAT score), but performed as well as or better than men in lower-level math classes. We checked more math classes. Same thing. The pattern seemed reliable. What caused it? Perhaps it reflected a stigma of some sort that affected

women in difficult math classes but not in easier ones. We designed an experiment to test this hunch, to see if we could reproduce the real-world pattern of performance in the laboratory.

We got women and men who were good at math to volunteer for the experiment, matched them according to skill level, and gave them either a difficult or a moderately difficult half-hour math test, one at a time, in a lab room. The same thing happened there that happened in the classroom: Women underperformed in comparison to men on the more difficult test but not on the easier one. Steve and I proceeded through a series of experiments that eventually became the basis of his dissertation; it was published in a 1999 special issue of the *Journal of Experimental Social Psychology*.

As this work was proceeding, I moved to Stanford University, where I was joined by Josh Aronson, a talented young post-doc who had just finished a PhD at Princeton. We talked a lot about the underperformance problem. Eventually we

Claude Steele is the Lucie Sterns Professor in the Social Sciences at Stanford University, where he has been on the faculty since 1991. He is past president of the Society for Personality and Social Psychology, and of the Western Psychological Association. He is a member of the National Academy of Sciences, the American Academy of Arts and Sciences, and the National Academy of Education. Thoughout his career he has been interested in how people cope with self-image threat. He has also studied addictive behaviors.

came to the idea of doing in the area of race and minority status what Steve and I were doing in the area of gender and math. We wanted to pinpoint the reason African-American students underperformed, as we had observed in the real university world. Our theory at this point was rather vague and tentative. Something in the experience of African-American students interfered with their academic performance. We settled on a working hypothesis: that the underperformance of African Americans might result, in part, from an interfering apprehension—*aroused in the situation*—about confirming, or being seen to confirm, negative stereotypes about their intellectual abilities.

If this turned out to be the case, we should see underperformance among academically strong African-American students under some conditions but not others. We should see it on a difficult task that was represented as diagnostic of intellectual ability, and thus as rele-

continued

vant to the negative group stereotype. But we should not see it when the same task was represented as nondiagnostic of ability, and thus not relevant to the negative group stereotype.

We designed a straightforward experiment, much influenced by my work with Spencer and by the experiments on race and test performance by Irwin Katz and his associates in the 1960s. We gave black and white Stanford students a very difficult verbal test, one at a time, in a lab room. We allowed half the participants to assume that the test measured verbal ability, and told the others that we were using the test to study problem solving but that it was not diagnostic of intellectual ability. Blacks who thought the test was diagnostic of ability scored a full standard deviation lower than whites, even after their scores were adjusted for individual differences in SAT scores. We reproduced in the lab the same underperformance that haunted the African-American students in real life. But when the same test was represented as nondiagnostic of ability, the black students' performances—again adjusted for SAT scores—matched the whites'.

Josh and I were pretty excited. We ran the whole study again. It replicated.

Later, Josh, Matt McGlone, and I showed that for black participants the mere act of sitting down to take a test diagnostic of ability was enough to cognitively activate negative racial stereotypes. As Josh hypothesized and his measures found, it was also enough to cause black participants to report less preference for activities associated with blackness (e.g., basketball, jazz), a phenomenon he named "stereotype avoidance."

CONFORMITY, COMPLIANCE, AND OBEDIENCE

What factors lead people to abandon their individual points of view and conform?

As we have seen, most group processes include pressure to conform. Conformity, compliance, and obedience all involve changes in one person's behavior caused by the social influence of another individual or group. **Conformity** is the process by which an individual shapes his or her behavior to make it consistent with the norms of a group. For example, when a gang member decides to wear green because other members of the gang wear green, the gang member is exhibiting conformity. **Compliance** is the process by which an individual goes along with a request made by one or more other persons. If a student who skipped a lecture asks for your notes and you give the notes to her, you are complying with the student's request. **Obedience** is the process by which an individual follows the commands of an actual or perceived authority figure. If a soldier fires on enemy troops because he is instructed to do so, he is exhibiting obedience. We consider each kind of social influence in turn. For each form of social influence, the individual may experience changes in perceptions, beliefs, attitudes, and behavior.

CONFORMITY

Solomon Asch (1951, 1956) conducted classic studies on conformity. The study participants believed that they were part of an experiment on perceptual judgment. Imagine that you are a subject in one such experiment. You sit down in a group with six other people. You are all shown a white card that has a picture of a black line and another white card that contains three black lines of different lengths. The task of each member of the group is simply to say which of the three black lines on the second card is the same length as the black line on the first card. Only one of the black lines on the second card is even remotely similar in length to the line on the first card (see Figure 14.4).

Members of the group are asked to give their judgments in order, starting with participant 1. As a participant, you expect the test to be a piece of cake. What could be easier? Unfortunately, however, participant 1 gives what appears to be the wrong answer. You are surprised. Then, to your amazement, participant 2 gives the same wrong answer. So it goes until it is your turn, as participant 6. What do you say? It is not easy to know what to say, as shown by the harried and puzzled look on the face of participant 6 from one of Asch's actual studies, seen in Figure 14.4. Of course, you do not yet realize that all the other participants are confederates who have been instructed to lie.

Asch found that most people go along with the majority, on average, in about one-third of the erroneous judgments. Not everyone conforms, of course.

FIGURE 14.4

Line Length and Normative Influence. In Solomon Asch's study, participants were shown a line (a) and then were asked to indicate which of the comparison lines (b) matched the given line. If a unanimous majority of your peers chose the first line (or third), would you claim to agree with them? (Figure 14.4a: Reprinted by permission of Solomon Asch.)

Roughly one-fourth of the participants remain true to their convictions.

Although Asch's participants frequently went along with the group, they generally did not believe the responses they announced. If participants were separated from the group and wrote down rather than orally announced their responses, then conformity to the group norm dropped by about two-thirds. Also, when Asch interviewed his participants, their responses revealed that, overwhelmingly, they did not believe the incorrect answers they had given. Rather, the participants had felt group pressure to conform.

Would a group member who deviated actually be ridiculed if he or she did not conform to the group norm? Asch (1952) reversed his initial procedure and placed one confederate among a group of genuine experimental participants. The confederate was instructed in advance to give wildly incorrect answers on certain trials. In fact, the others did laugh at the confederate. People who deviate from the group norm are not only ridiculed but also actively disliked and often rejected by the rest of the group (Schachter, 1951).

Group influences can extend to more consequential kinds of situations. Researchers asked college students to view a 1992 debate among three presidential candidates: George Bush, Bill Clinton, and Ross Perot (Fein, Goethals, & Kassin, 1998). The task was to evaluate the performance of each candidate. The student participants were divided into three conditions. In one room, a group of confederates cheered for Bush. In a second room, they cheered for Clinton. In the third room, there were no confederates and there was no cheering. The investigators found that the cheering affected evaluations of debate performance by 45 points on a 100-point scale. In other words, without realizing it, the student participants conformed to the evaluations of the cheering confederates.

Several factors seem to affect the likelihood of conformity.

GROUP SIZE

The first factor that affects the likelihood of conformity is *group size*. Asch (1955) varied the number of confederates in his line-length study from as few as 1 person to as many as 15. He found that conformity reached its highest level in groups of three to four members. Others have confirmed that, in most groups, beyond three or four members, conformity appears to level off (e.g., Latané, 1981; Tanford & Penrod, 1984). In some situations, however, larger group sizes continue to increase the likelihood of conformity. Consider, for example, the behavior of people in elevators, of a crowd gathering on a sidewalk and looking upward, and of a rioting crowd.

COHESIVENESS

A second factor that influences conformity is the *cohesiveness* of the group. In a cohesive group, the members feel very much a part of the group and are highly attracted to it. Theodore Newcomb (1943) conducted one of the best-known studies of group cohesiveness. He studied women at Bennington College, a small college in Vermont then well known for its liberal philosophy. Although the women at the college tended to come from families that were politically conservative (and well-to-do financially), the students' attitudes became increasingly liberal with each successive year at Bennington as they became more and more attached to their classmates and friends. Moreover, this liberalism remained even 20 years after graduation.

Conformity is affected simply by the *perception* of what others are doing. Researchers found that most college students tended to overestimate the extent to which their fellow students were comfortable with the amount of drinking that took place on campus (Prentice & Miller, 1996). Those students most likely to make such overestimates tended to conform in their own attitudes not to the actual perceptions of others, but to the perceived perceptions of these others.

GENDER

A third factor is *gender.* Gender-related conformity depends in part on the situation and may illustrate the influence of other factors.

Alice Eagly's (1987) *social-roles theory of gender* posits that women are generally more likely to conform than men under most circumstances. According to Eagly's view, women conform more because they perceive their gender as being of lower status, which in turn leads to feelings of reduced self-worth. Other research supports the notion that people of either gender may be more likely to conform if they feel inadequate or possess low self-esteem (Asch, 1956). Birenbaum and Kraemer (1995) found greater effects of ethnic group than of sex on feelings of competence in mathematics and language examinations. D. E. Smith and R. A. Muenchen (1995) found that age was a more powerful determinant of self-image than sex in a group of Jamaican adolescents.

More recently, Wood and Eagly (2002) have suggested that cross-cultural sex differences in human behavior, including conformity, can be understood in terms of gender-based physical specializations. Reproductive capacity is especially important. Because men are not physically compromised by becoming parents, they have economic and other social advantages women are denied. If women tend to conform more than men, it may be because society propels them into more constricting roles.

SOCIAL STATUS

As suggested by Wood and Eagly's (2002) work, a fourth factor that affects conformity is *social status.* Researchers (Dittes & Kelley, 1956) had participants engage in group discussions and then rate each other on "desirability." Then participants were told how others had rated them, except that they received phony feedback. Participants next took part in an Asch-like experiment, in which the other members of the group were the other participants. Those who had been rated "average" in desirability were more likely to conform than those rated high, low, or very low. Those who received the high, low, and very low ratings did not markedly differ from one another in conformity. The result makes sense. On the one hand, if you are high in status already, you may not need to conform because of your exalted position. On the other hand, if you are low in status, you may feel that the situation is hopeless anyway, so why bother to conform?

CULTURE

A fifth consideration is *culture.* Many researchers have tried to replicate in other cultures some of the studies on conformity and other social-psychological phenomena that have been well documented in the United States. For instance, the procedure used by Asch has been used in numerous cross-cultural studies. Although these studies have found considerable variability, a fairly clear picture has emerged: People in individualistic societies tend to conform less than do people in collectivistic societies (P. B. Smith & Bond, 1994). Actually, the extent to which people in different societies vary on many social-psychological variables can often be explained by individualism versus collectivism and the ways they influence social behavior (Han & Shavitt, 1994; Kim, Triandis, & Kagitcibasi, 1994).

Not all studies show large culture effects. One recent study looked at conformity in 1,057 4th-, 7th-, and 10th-grade boys and girls from two mid-sized cities in the United States and Japan (Killen, Crystal, & Watanabe, 2002). The students were asked why atypical, nonconforming peers were excluded from groups. Six reasons were being aggressive, having an unconventional appearance, acting like a clown, demonstrating cross-gender behavior, being a slow runner, and having a sad personality. As children grew older, they increasingly believed that the excluded

Social conformity may be resisted in some cultures and valued in others.

child should not change merely to conform enough to be accepted by the group. On average, girls were less willing than boys to exclude others, and they also were more tolerant of differences. There were very few overall effects for culture. Although most children disagreed with the decision to exclude, across age groups, they also believed that the excluded child should change in order to be accepted by the group.

UNANIMITY

A sixth variable that affects conformity is the *appearance of unanimity*. Conformity is much more likely when a group norm appears to be unanimous. Even a single dissenter can seriously diminish conformity. Asch (1951) found that if even only one of the six confederates disagreed with the group's answer in the line-length experiment, conformity was drastically reduced. Surprisingly, this effect occurred even if the dissenter offered an answer that was even further off the mark than the response of the group. Apparently, a dissenter can inoculate you against conforming to a norm established by other group members. And, the inoculation occurs even if the person does not match your point of view. Thus, another consideration in determining degree of conformity is whether you believe your views to be in the majority, in the minority, or altogether unique within the group.

Majorities exert influence through the sheer number of people who share a given point of view. Although majorities are powerful in numbers, minorities can be powerful through the style of their behavior (Moscovici, 1976, 1980). It is not just what they say, but how they say it, that determines their impact. Minorities can be powerful if they are forceful, persistent, and unflagging in support of their views. At the same time, they need to project an image of flexibility as well as open-mindedness. In other words, they need to show that they are willing to listen to the majority.

IDIOSYNCRASY

Those in the minority who wish to lead and to change the way a group is functioning first need to accumulate *idiosyncrasy credits*, commonly known as "brownie points," among group members (Estrada, Brown, & Lee, 1995; Hogg & Reid, 2001; Hollander, 1958, 1985). That is, they need to be willing to play the group's game to a great enough extent that members come to accept them as part of the group and will then listen to them when they advocate changing the group norms. In this way, a potent minority may influence the behavior—and perhaps the views—of the majority. Individuals who operate outside of group settings may also be persuasive in causing others to behave as they want them to behave.

COMPLIANCE

Do you know somebody who always seems to get his or her way? Do you ever wonder how swindlers manage to bamboozle their "marks," the persons who are the objects of their compliance-seeking techniques? Have you ever bought something just because you were wheedled into it by a salesperson? These questions address the issue of *compliance*—going along with other people's requests. Some of the most common techniques for eliciting compliance are listed in Table 14.1. Sometimes, attempts to gain compliance elicit *reactance*—the unpleasant feeling of arousal we get when we believe that our freedom of choosing from a wide range of behavior is being threatened or restricted.

Each of the techniques in Table 14.1 involves having someone you consider a peer—more or less—ask you to comply with a request. Not all requests come from peers, however. Some people who make requests of us are in positions of authority. Their authority may stem from actual or perceived greater relative power, expertise, or desirability, such as

TABLE 14.1

Techniques for Eliciting Compliance. How can you use these techniques to elicit compliance from another person? How can your knowledge of these techniques help you to resist complying with unwanted and unreasonable requests?

Technique	You Are More Likely to Gain Compliance If You . . .
Justification	Justify your request. Even when the justification is weak, you will gain compliance more readily than if you simply make the request but do not justify it.
Reciprocity	Appear to be giving the other person something, to instill a sense of obligation toward you.
Low-ball	Get the other person to commit to a deal under circumstances that you present as entirely favorable. After obtaining the person's commitment, you reveal the hidden costs or other drawbacks.
Foot in the door	Ask for compliance with a small request, which "softens up" the person for the big request.
Door in the face	Make an outlandishly large request that is almost certain to be rejected, in the hope of getting the other person to accede to a more reasonable but still substantial request.
That's not all	Offer something at a high price and then, before the other person has a chance to respond, throw in something else to sweeten the deal.
Hard to get	Convince the other person that whatever you are offering (or trying to get rid of) is very difficult to obtain.

social competence or physical attractiveness. When we agree to the requests of persons who have authority over us, we are being obedient.

OBEDIENCE

Consider what you would do in the classic experiment by Stanley Milgram. An experimenter wearing a lab coat and carrying a clipboard meets you in the laboratory and says that you are about to participate in an experiment about the effects of punishment on learning (see Chapter 6). You and another participant, Mr. Wallace (an accountant who seems average in appearance and demeanor), draw lots to determine who will be the "teacher" in the experiment and who will be the "learner." You draw the "teacher" lot, so it will be your job to teach the learner to remember a list of words. Every time Mr. Wallace makes an error in learning, you will punish him with an electric shock.

You watch the experimenter strap Mr. Wallace into a chair and roll up Mr. Wallace's sleeves. He swabs electrode paste onto Mr. Wallace's arms "to avoid blisters and burns" from the shocks (Milgram, 1974, p. 19). The experimenter now mentions that the shocks may be extremely painful. But he assures Mr. Wallace that they will "cause no permanent tissue damage" (p. 19). You are then shown the machine you will use to deliver the shocks. The forbidding-looking device has a row of levers marked in increments of 15 volts from a mere 15 volts (labeled "slight shock") to a full 450 volts (labeled "XXX," beyond the setting for "danger: severe shock"). Before you begin, the experimenter gives you what he describes as a

mild shock, so you have an idea of what the shocks are like. The shock is rather painful.

The experimenter takes Mr. Wallace into another room, and the experiment begins. You read Mr. Wallace the words through a voice connection. He must recall their paired associates (see Chapter 7). If he answers correctly, you move on to the next word. If he answers incorrectly, you tell him the correct answer and administer a shock. Each time Mr. Wallace makes a mistake, you are to increase the intensity of the shock by 15 volts. Mr. Wallace begins to make mistakes. As he makes more and more mistakes, his protestations become louder and more forceful. Eventually, there is only silence.

Would you continue administering shocks until the end—up to 450 volts? Perhaps at some point it would occur to you that something is very wrong with this experiment. You probably would not want to continue. If you tell the experimenter your concerns, he responds, "Please continue." If you protest further, he tells you, "The experiment requires that you continue." If you continue to argue, he says, "It is absolutely essential that you continue." If you still protest, he replies, "You have no other choice, you *must* go on." What would you do? Before you read on, guess how most people responded to this experiment (see Figure 14.5).

Before he conducted his experiments, Milgram expected that very few people would completely obey the commands of the experimenter and that many would refuse to obey even the early requests. As he was formulating the design for the experiment, Milgram consulted other colleagues and all had expectations similar to his (Milgram, 1974). Instead, slightly more than

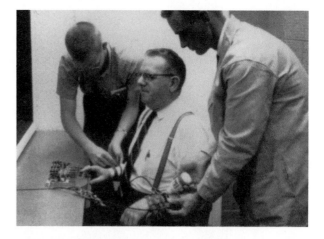
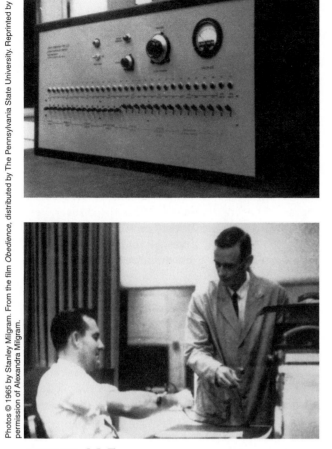

FIGURE 14.5

The Shocking Treatment of Mr. Wallace. At the upper left is the voltmeter used in Stanley Milgram's experiment to deliver shocks to Mr. Wallace. At the upper right, Mr. Wallace is being strapped into the chair. At bottom left, a participant is instructed to continue administering shocks. At bottom right, the participant refuses to continue, an unfortunately rare occurrence. (After Milgram, 1974)

two-thirds of the people tested in this procedure continued up to the maximum 450 volts. Not one person stopped administering shocks before 300 volts. This was the point at which Mr. Wallace let out an agonizing scream, absolutely refused to answer any more questions, and demanded to get out, saying that the experimenter could not hold him. The results were even more shocking than the shocks administered by the machine (see Figure 14.6).

The results so astounded Milgram that he asked members of three groups—middle-class adults with various occupations, college students, and psychiatrists—to predict what would happen. Their predictions confirmed Milgram's initial expectations that few people would demonstrate much obedience. On average, those who were surveyed estimated that the "teacher" would stop at 145 volts. Almost no one surveyed thought anyone would go up to 450 volts. The

psychiatrists estimated that "only a pathological fringe, not exceeding [1% or 2% of the participants]" would go all the way up to the end (Milgram, 1974, p. 31). Everyone was wrong.

Of course, the shock machine was fake and Mr. Wallace, a confederate of the experimenter, never felt any pain at all. Also, both lots said "teacher," so no matter which one the participant drew, he would end up administering the supposed punishments to Mr. Wallace.

As you probably have guessed, the experiment had nothing at all to do with the effect of punishment on learning. It was an experiment on obedience. The motivation for the experiment was Milgram's interest in why German soldiers during World War II obeyed the genocidal commands of their leaders. Milgram (1963, 1965, 1974) concluded that people in general are astonishingly capable of blind, mindless obedience. The

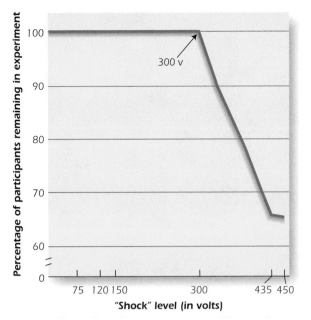

FIGURE 14.6

Milgram's Baseline Results on Voltage Levels. To Stanley Milgram's great surprise, not one participant stopped administering shocks before the reported level of 300 volts, and an alarming 65% of the participants administered the maximum level of shock. (From "Milgram's Results on Voltage Levels," from *Obedience to Authority* by Stanley Milgram. Copyright © 1974 by Stanley Milgram. Reprinted by permission of HarperCollins Publishers, Inc.)

results he obtained were even more depressing than we have indicated. In Milgram's initial study, the participants were men. Later he thought that perhaps women would be less likely to administer the maximum shock. However, when women participated in the same procedure, the same percentage (65%) went to the maximum voltage.

Milgram's results have been confirmed across both age groups and cultures (Shanab & Yahya, 1977, 1978). The effect has also been replicated with verbal rather than physical abuse (Meeus & Raaijmakers, 1995). Participants were asked verbally to abuse another person (actually, a confederate). Under the commands of an experimenter, 92% did so, no matter how abusive they were instructed to become.

Why are people so willing to obey the orders of people in authority, regardless of what the orders are (see Hofling, Brotzman, Dalrymple, Graves, & Pierce, 1966)? Milgram (1974) proposed several explanations. Whether any of them is adequate to describe the extremity of the findings is doubtful. One explanation is that experimenters use a procedure analogous to the successful foot-in-the-door technique. They start off asking for relatively little and later ask for much more. Along the way, people may become immune to the effects of what they are doing. Or they may feel committed to complying with the demands of the situation. Moreover, we are socialized to respect authority. This socialization seems to carry over to situations that require obedience.

Milgram's experimental situation demands and elicits obedience from a surprising array of people. Practically anybody placed in this situation acts in ways that no one would have thought possible. That is what is so stunning about obedience research by Milgram and others.

Some people may believe that instances of blind obedience are a thing of the past. Far from it. Massacres in the 1990s in Rwanda, Burundi, Bosnia, and Kosovo all show that obedience by soldiers and civilians alike to irrational and inhuman commands continues in full force. Recent massacres in diverse parts of the world show that nothing has changed, even in the 21st century.

The Milgram experiment raises the issue of experimental ethics. Although his participants were debriefed, it is not clear that any explanation could fully counteract the effect of realizing what the experiment was about and what their role was. There is no sure-fire way of ascertaining whether the costs to the participants justified the gains to scientific knowledge. Today, the experiment would be unlikely to be approved by an institutional review board (see "Research Ethics" in Chapter 2).

Blind obedience has led to horrible massacres in countries around the world, both in the past and in the present.

© AP/Wide World Photos

✓ CONCEPT CHECK 2

1. The process by which people shape their behavior to make it consistent with group norms is
   a. conformity.
   b. compliance.
   c. obedience.
   d. groupthink.

2. The Asch experiment showed that people are sometimes willing to conform to _____ group decisions.
   a. sound
   b. unspoken
   c. ridiculous
   d. changing

3. Psychiatrists asked how the Milgram experiments would turn out predicted total obedience in roughly _____ of the population.
   a. 1%–2%
   b. 5%–10%
   c. 10%–20%
   d. 50%–75%

© AP/Wide World Photos

PROSOCIAL BEHAVIOR

Under what circumstances do we help our fellow human beings? When are we not likely to help them?

Prosocial behavior involves societally approved actions that benefit society in general or individual members of society in particular, and that are approved by most people.

BYSTANDER INTERVENTION

In 1964, a young woman in New York City named Kitty Genovese left her night job at 3 o'clock in the morning. Before she reached home, she was repeatedly attacked for half an hour by a man who eventually killed her. Thirty-eight people who lived in her apartment complex in Queens heard her cries and screams. How many neighbors came to her aid? How many called the police? How many sought any assistance for her whatsoever? Not one. How could people listen for a long time to someone being attacked and do absolutely nothing? Bibb Latané and John Darley (1968, 1970) sought to answer this question in a series of studies on *bystander intervention* and helping behavior.

© AP/Wide World Photos

In 1964, Kitty Genovese was stabbed repeatedly while 38 adults, mostly in the large apartment building nearby, watched, listened, and did nothing to help her. After she died, only one neighbor called the authorities to report the murder.

A common view of the Genovese case was that life in the big city had hardened people to the point where they stopped caring about others. Latané and Darley suspected, however, that what happened to Kitty Genovese in New York could have happened anywhere.

In one experiment, a participant was taken into one of several small rooms. Over an intercom, the experimenter said that the participant and a small group of college students were to discuss some of their personal problems with college life. To protect confidentiality, the experimenter explained, conversations would take place via intercom. Each person would be in a separate room, and the experimenter would not be listening. Each person was to speak in turn.

During the fairly routine opening of the experiment, one of the participants admitted that he sometimes had seizures triggered by the pressures of his work. When it was his turn to speak once again, it became clear that he was suffering a seizure. He sounded as if he were in serious distress (Latané & Darley, 1970).

As you may have guessed, the apparent victim was not actually having a seizure. In fact, there were no participants other than the one in the room with the intercom. Although group sizes supposedly ranged from two (the participant and the seizure victim) to six (the participant, the seizure victim, and four strangers), in fact only the one actual participant was present. The voices of the others were all previously recorded. The dependent variables were the percentage of participants who helped the apparent seizure victim and the amount of time it took them to respond. The independent variable was the number of people that the research participants believed to be involved in the experiment. Almost 90% of the participants who thought they were the only person with whom the seizure victim was communicating left the room to get help. But as the number of persons believed to be in communication with the seizure victim increased, the likelihood of a participant's seeking help decreased, falling to less than 50% in the larger groups.

Clearly, Kitty Genovese's neighbors were not unique in being unresponsive. They illustrated what has come to be termed the **bystander effect,** the phenomenon in which the presence of increasing numbers of people presumably available to help leads to decreasing likelihood that any one person actually will help. The effect occurs in a variety of situations. Each person involved typically experiences a **diffusion of responsibility,** an implied reduction of personal responsibility to take action due to the presence of other people, particularly in considering how to respond to a crisis. Many other studies have revealed the same findings (see Latané, Nida, & Wilson, 1981).

You can witness the bystander effect on almost any highway. Cars whiz by stranded motorists, some

of whom may desperately need help. Each driver passing by is likely to think that because so many other people are on the road, certainly help must be on its way. Often it is not.

Helping behavior seems to vary as a function of place. One study looked at helping behavior in different cities and regions of the United States (R. V. Levine, Martinez, Brase, & Sorenson, 1994). Cities with the most helpful residents tended to be in the South. Those with the least helpful residents tended to be in the Northeast. The top city for helping behavior (Rochester, New York) is in the Northeast, however, as is the bottom city (Paterson, New Jersey). Population density appears to be an important underlying factor.

It is strange that the bystander effect appears even when a person's own safety is at stake. One study (Latané & Darley, 1968) asked students to fill out a questionnaire on problems of urban life. Shortly after the students began to answer the questions, smoke from a ventilator in the wall started to pour into the room. The researchers were interested in how the number of people in the room affected their decisions whether or not to report the smoke. When only one participant was in the room, half of them reported the smoke within 4 minutes, and three-quarters within 6 minutes. When there were three participants, however, only 1 of 24 reported the smoke within the first 4 minutes, and only three did so within 6 minutes. People may fail to take action even when their own safety is in jeopardy!

Why are people so passive in the face of emergencies? According to Latané and Darley (1970), the reason is that what appears to be a simple matter—seeking help—is actually more complex. Suppose you are the bystander. To seek or provide help, you must take five steps, as shown in Figure 14.7. So, there are at least five opportunities to do nothing.

THE EFFECTS OF OTHERS' ACTIONS

What factors might affect whether people help in emergencies? The characteristics of the victim, the situation, and the bystander lead either to intervention or to nonintervention (see Table 14.2). One factor is how people interpret a situation. Sometimes, nobody helps because individuals attribute other people's actions to different causes than they would attribute their own actions. In fact, their own actions are identical to those of the other people in the group (D. T. Miller & McFarland, 1987). For example, when confronted with an emergency in which you see other people taking no action, you may assume that you are the only person confused about what to do. You may believe that the other people are doing nothing because they have somehow realized that what appears to be an emergency is not one at all. Of course, the other people are making exactly the same attribution that you are.

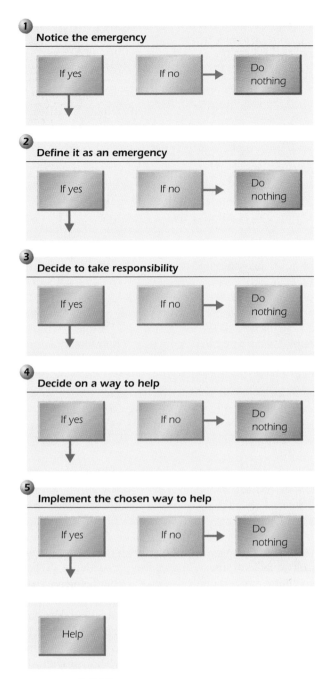

FIGURE 14.7
Latané and Darley's Five-Step Decision Model of Intervention. Before you take any action to help another person, you must take these five steps. If you fail to complete any step, you will not be able to provide helpful intervention. (After Latané & Darley, 1970)

This misattribution applies to situations that are nonemergencies as well. Very often, students in a class are afraid to ask questions because they assume that they are the only ones who do not understand what the professor is saying. In fact, each person has exactly the same anxiety. As a result, all the students end up confused but thinking that they are alone in their confusion.

The bystander effect applies even in unexpected populations. Students in a religious seminary were asked to give a talk in a university building nearby, either on the parable of the Good Samaritan—a man who exhibited extraordinary helping behavior—or on jobs that seminary students enjoy (J. M. Darley & Batson, 1973). On the way to the building, each student passed an alley in which a man was slumped over moaning, his eyes closed. Surely, if anyone would help, seminarians would, especially those thinking about the Good Samaritan. Only 40% of the students offered to help, however, and whether they were going to speak on the Good Samaritan or on their jobs had no significant impact on whether they helped. Thus, even some of those who are giving serious thought to helping behavior, and who have, in fact, pledged to devote their lives to serving others, are unlikely actually to help others in an ambiguous situation.

THE EFFECT OF TIME
Although the topic of the talk the seminarians were to give did not affect their helping behavior, another manipulation in the experiment did. Students were told that they were in a great hurry (they were already late for the talk), in a medium hurry (everything was ready to go), or not in a hurry at all (it would be a few minutes before things would even be ready). Although 63% of students who were not in a hurry helped the man in the alley, only 10% of those who were in a great hurry did. An intermediate percentage, 45%, helped in the medium-hurry condition.

ALTRUISM

By now, you may be depressed or distressed by the results of the studies on bystander intervention. **Altruism** is a generous willingness to help even when there is no discernible benefit to the helper. It often involves some sacrifice on the part of the helper. Is altruism nonexistent? Every day, parents make sacrifices for their children, firefighters rush into burning buildings, and volunteers donate their time and efforts for the well-being of other people. Altruism has also been demonstrated in experimental circumstances.

Recent studies have focused on people's motives for performing altruistic behavior. Are people motivated by empathy or by more egoistic concerns? Robert Cialdini and his associates (Cialdini, Brown, et al., 1997; Cialdini, Schaller, et al., 1987; Maner et al., 2002; Neuberg et al., 1997) have argued that empathy produces altruistic behavior. A person who responds empathetically to someone in distress feels saddened. He or she is then motivated to help in order to elevate his or her *own* mood. So, from this perspective, even empathy-based helping may be selfish. Daniel Batson

TABLE 14.2

Factors That May Influence Helping Behavior. Several characteristics of the victim, of the situation, and of the bystander may affect the likelihood that the bystander will intervene.

Factor	Effect on Likelihood of Helping Behavior
Characteristics of the Victim	
Similarity to bystander (age, sex, etc.)	Increase
Relationship to bystander (if any)	Probably increase
Bleeding or bloody	Decrease
Recognizable member of a stigmatized group	Decrease
Characteristics of the Situation	
Increasing number of bystanders	Decrease
Increasing time pressures on bystander	Decrease
Characteristics of the Bystander	
Similarity to victim (age, sex, etc.)	Increase
Relationship to victim (if any)	Probably increase
Negative responses to characteristics of the victim (e. g., prejudices, negative reactions to clothing, grooming, blood)	Decrease
Empathy	Increase
Emotionality	Probably increase
Medical expertise	Increase
Dedication to serving others	No effect
Recent thought given to being helpful	No effect
Being in a good mood	Increase

and his colleagues (Batson, 1997; Batson, Batson et al., 1989; Batson, Dyck et al., 1988) disagree with this interpretation. They found that the incidence of helping among high-empathy participants was no lower when they anticipated mood enhancement than when they did not. The researchers believe that helping behavior results from feelings of identification with the person in need of help.

Ⓔ Does altruism make sense from an evolutionary point of view? After all, one may be sacrificing one's own self-interest for the sake of others. According to George Williams (1966) and Robert Trivers (1971), it does. Williams pointed out that relationships between organisms, including humans, tend to be characterized by reciprocity. Indeed, as shown by the reciprocity technique for gaining compliance that was mentioned earlier, doing something for someone is one of the best ways to get the person to do something for you. Anatol Rapaport (1960) showed that in mutual negotiations, those who reciprocate the kind behavior of others tend to fare best. Moreover, people who are perceived as selfish often find themselves with few friends and at risk

of making enemies. This outcome is clearly not to the individual's advantage in the struggle for survival. The evolutionary view implies, however, that being *perceived* as altruistic, rather than actually being altruistic, leads to positive outcomes for the individual (R. Wright, 1994). Nevertheless, many apparently altruistic acts, such as hiding Jews during the Nazi regime in Germany (Oliner & Oliner, 1988), seem accurately characterized as genuinely altruistic.

PEACEMAKING

In recent years, a new branch of psychology has come into being—*peace psychology*—which is devoted to how psychological knowledge can be used to make peace among people, organizations, and nations (Christie, Winter, & Wagner, 2000). An entire division of the American Psychological Association, the Division of Peace Psychology, is devoted to the study of peace and its creation.

How does one bring about peace? A first step is caring about other people's points of view. If you care about only your own, you are unlikely to attain peace. A second step is actively seeking to understand other people's points of view. A third step is actively desiring to do something to resolve hostilities.

Charles Osgood, a social psychologist, has suggested a strategy for hostility reduction. Osgood (1962, 1980) called his strategy for achieving peace "Graduated and Reciprocated Initiatives in Tension Reduction" (GRIT). One first announces one's intention to seek peace and conciliation. One then makes a small and possibly unilateral step toward reducing tensions. For example, a nation might announce that the number of troops massed at the border of a country with which there are hostilities will be reduced by 10%. One then waits to see what the hostile nation (or other entity) does. If the nation responds in kind, one makes a second, more significant gesture. If the other nation does nothing, one stops making gestures. And if the other nation responds with increasing hostility, one responds in kind. Research shows that GRIT works (Lindskold, 1978, 1986).

During 2003, a strategy akin to GRIT is being used to attempt to resolve hostilities between North Korea and much of the rest of the world. Multilateral talks have been initiated without any prior commitment by North Korea. Their goal is to encourage North Korea's leaders to abandon its nuclear weapons program and its possible plans to export nuclear technology. The stakes are high, and so the world can only hope that whatever strategy is used meets with success.

✓ CONCEPT CHECK 3

1. The bystander effect illustrates _____ responsibility.
   a. incremental
   b. diffusion of
   c. concentrated
   d. total lack of
2. Before bystanders take action, they do *not* need to
   a. notice an emergency.
   b. define a situation as an emergency.
   c. decide on a way to help.
   d. be certain that their help will be successful.
3. Altruism _____ evolutionary theory.
   a. makes no sense in terms of
   b. has no relationship to
   c. always is the best course of action in terms of
   d. can be understood in terms of

ANTISOCIAL BEHAVIOR

What are the characteristics of antisocial behavior? What are its sources?

Antisocial behavior is harmful to a society or to individuals. Although we might disagree about which kinds of behaviors are antisocial or even condemned by society, we generally agree that three classes of behavior are harmful to society: prejudice, aggression, and hatred.

PREJUDICE

Prejudice is a negative attitude toward a group of people that is based on limited or distorted information about them. Note that prejudice is an attitude toward a group, not toward an individual. Unfortunately, we tend to extend many of our attitudes toward groups to the individual members of the groups as well. A negative attitude toward a group is not necessarily a prejudice. For example, if you had ample evidence that a particular group is responsible for numerous homicides, you would probably be entitled to have a negative attitude toward that group. An attitude involves prejudice when it is based on insufficient or incorrect information.

SOCIAL CATEGORIZATION AND STEREOTYPES

Social categorization is the normal human tendency to sort people into groups according to characteristics that appear to be common to their members. Across cultures, we effortlessly categorize people according to their gender, occupation, age, ethnicity, and other features (see Neto, Williams, & Widner, 1991). These

At different times different groups are victimized by prejudice, but the harm it causes is always the same.

© Catherine Karnow/Corbis

categories generally have particular defining characteristics, such as sexual characteristics or occupational requirements. In addition, we tend to formulate prototypes for various categories based on what we perceive as typical members (see Chapter 8). When such prototypes are applied to people, they are called **stereotypes,** typical perceptions of the main characteristics of a particular social category, which are usually based on the assumption that the typical example represents all others. Social categories and stereotypes help us organize our perceptions of people and provide us with speedy access to a wealth of information about new people (Sherman, Judd, & Park, 1989; Srull & Wyer, 1989). Thus, stereotypes tell us what to expect from people we do not know well. The problem with categorizing people according to stereotypes is that we often overgeneralize the characteristics of the stereotype, assuming that all the typical characteristics apply to every member of a group. Usually, they apply only to some or perhaps even most—but not all—members.

INGROUPS AND OUTGROUPS

We are less likely to overgeneralize from stereotypes when we consider our own *ingroups*—categories we think we belong to—than when we consider *outgroups*—categories we do not see ourselves as belonging to. **Outgroup homogeneity bias** is the tendency to view all members of an outgroup as alike. When we fall prey to this bias, we take stereotypical characteristics or actions that apply to only a portion of a group and infer that they apply to all or almost all of the group members (Brehm & Kassin, 1990). This bias is commonplace (Linville, 1998; Linville, Brewer, & Mackie, 1998; Vonk & van Knippenberg, 1995). For example, it may very well be that many clerics are honest, many professors are well informed, and many social workers are compassionate. However, the stereotypes do not necessarily apply to all members of these groups. Moreover, members of many other groups have the same traits that are attributed to the members of the targeted group. We also worsen the negative effects of outgroup homogeneity bias by seeking information that bolsters our sense of being dissimilar from the outgroup and similar to the ingroup (Wilder & Allen, 1978).

Another source of prejudice is **illusory correlation,** an inferred perception of a relationship between unrelated variables. It usually arises because the instances in which the variables coincide are more noticeable than the instances in which they do not coincide. For example, we are more likely to notice instances of unusual behavior in a minority population than in a majority population (D. L. Hamilton & Gifford, 1976). If a member of a minority group commits a crime, we may associate all members of that group with criminal behavior. If a member of a majority group commits the same crime, however, we may

see no such association. Indeed, newspapers sometimes identify alleged criminals by their membership in a minority group. At the same time, they say nothing about group membership if the alleged criminals are members of the majority group. Reporters may refer to a perpetrator as "black" or "hispanic," however, but they are unlikely to describe a perpetrator as "white." Thus, we may form an illusory correlation between the unusual behavior (e.g., commission of crimes) and the minority population.

Context cues also increase the likelihood that we use stereotypes. When research participants evaluated female and male leaders, they showed greater gender stereotyping and prejudicial responses toward female leaders in particular contexts (see Eagly & Johannesen-Schmidt, 2001; Eagly & Karau, 2002; Eagly, Makhijani, & Klonsky, 1992). These include (1) contexts in which the leaders' styles are considered stereotypically masculine (e.g., task oriented and directive rather than interpersonally oriented and collaborative) and (2) contexts in which women occupied roles that are male-dominated in our society (e.g., athletic coaches, manufacturing supervisors, and business managers). Outgroup versus ingroup effects also influenced the results. In particular, men were more likely than other women to evaluate women negatively.

THE PERVASIVE EFFECTS OF STEREOTYPES

Stereotypes are often activated in our thinking and affect our behavior without our awareness (Bargh, 1997; Duckworth, Bargh, Garcia, & Chaiken, 2002; Ferguson & Bargh, 2002; Greenwald & Banaji, 1995; Greenwald

Increasing the number of minority members in a particular job or profession helps ease prejudice but doesn't eliminate it.

et al., 2002; Monteith, Devine, & Zuwerink, 1993). Stereotypes and the prejudices that often accompany them can have stunning effects (Chen & Bargh, 1997). In one study, white participants were shown pictures of either black male or white male faces. The exposure to the pictures was subliminal, so the participants were not even aware that they had seen the images. Each participant who was exposed to the faces played a game with another participant who had not been exposed to the faces. Their interactions were audiotaped, and judges rated the hostility shown by each participant. The participants who had been subliminally exposed to the black faces showed more hostility in their interactions with their game partners than did the participants who had been exposed to the white faces. Presumably, the black faces had triggered stereotypes about blacks among the white participants. The hostility of the participants who had been exposed to the black faces in turn triggered hostility in their game partners.

People are often motivated to categorize and stereotype others in order to maintain their sense of power (Jost & Banaji, 1994; Operario & Fiske, 1998; Pratto, Stallworth, Sidanius, & Siers, 1997). For example, people in positions of political power may suppress or even imprison dissenters and label their behavior as criminal, insane, or both. Such labeling gives them an excuse to retain their political power and to remove threats to it.

Although social cognition plays a role in the formation of stereotypes, the fact that they are so remarkably resistant to change may be due to factors such as motivation and conformity rather than to cognitive variables (Rojahn & Pettigrew, 1992), as demonstrated in the study described next.

THE ROBBER'S CAVE STUDY

A classic experiment on prejudice was conducted in the summer of 1954 at Robber's Cave State Park in Oklahoma (Sherif, Harvey, White, Hood, & Sherif, 1961/1988). At a camp were two groups of boys, all 11 years old, white, middle class, and previously unknown to one another. No one in either group knew the other group existed. For about a week, the boys engaged in typical camp activities, such as swimming, camping, and hiking. Each group chose a name for itself, and the boys printed their groups' names on their caps and T-shirts.

After about a week, the two groups discovered each other. They also learned that an athletic tournament had been set up in which the two groups would compete. As the games took place, so did confrontations, which spread well beyond the competition. After a while, the members of the two groups became extremely antagonistic. Members of each group ransacked cabins, engaged in food fights, and stole items from the other group.

Mutual prejudice had been artificially created in the two groups. Would it be possible to reduce or eliminate this prejudice? The investigators created apparent emergencies that the boys had to resolve through cooperative efforts. In one, the water supply for the camp was lost because of a leak in a pipe. The boys were assigned to intergroup teams to inspect the pipe and find the leak. In another trial, a truck carrying boys to a campsite got trapped in the mud. Boys from the two teams had to cooperate to get the truck out. By the end of the camping season, the two groups of boys were engaged in a variety of cooperative activities and were playing together peacefully. Thus, when the boys were forced to work together, their prejudices were largely eliminated.

THEORIES OF PREJUDICE

Various theories have been proposed to account for people's prejudices. **Realistic-conflict theory** states that competition among groups for valuable, scarce resources leads to prejudice (R. A. Levine & Campbell, 1972). For example, immigrant groups may be met with hostility because they are perceived as taking jobs away from people who are already living in the country. Often the jobs the immigrants take are those that other people generally do not want—menial, laborious, and underpaid. But even the perception of job loss can cause unwarranted prejudice.

Social-identity theory suggests that people are motivated to protect their self-esteem and that prejudices increase to protect this self-esteem (Tajfel, 1982; Tajfel & Turner, 1986). People achieve self-esteem by denigrating others, believing they look good in comparison. For example, some people may have a bias against gay and lesbian people because, through their prejudice, they protect their self-esteem as heterosexuals.

A third theory is that people view prejudice within themselves the way they view their own bad habits (Devine, Evett, & Vasquez-Suson, 1995; Devine, Monteith, Zuwerink, & Elliot, 1991; Devine, Plant, Amodio, Harmon-Jones, & Vance, 2002). They are aware of their prejudice, and they know, consciously or not, that it affects their behavior. Where people differ, however, is in the extent to which they tolerate the behavior in themselves. Some people have high tolerance for their own prejudices. Others view them as unjustifiable, not as valid bases for action. For example, some people may be prejudiced against overweight individuals. They justify their bias by saying that overweight people deserve the negative reaction they get because they lack self-discipline. Although no one theory completely explains the social phenomenon of prejudice, taken together the theories suggest how prejudice might be reduced. In the Psychology in Everyday Life box, "Reducing Prejudice," we see that prejudices are fostered by ignorance.

REDUCING PREJUDICE

A good first step in reducing prejudice is to *recognize* how resistant it is to change. For example, male police officers and supervisors are often prejudiced against female members of the force (Balkin, 1988; Ott, 1989), despite clear research evidence documenting women's effectiveness as field patrol officers. One view suggests that prejudicial treatment against women and minorities will decline when their numbers increase—that is, when they are in a larger minority in their line of work. However, women already make up 51% of the U.S. population, so clearly sheer numbers alone do not reduce bias. In fact, the numeric proportion of a minority alone does not determine whether prejudicial treatment occurs. For instance, male nurses generally experience positive treatment among nurses (Ott, 1989). For negative prejudicial treatment to occur, the minority group must also be assigned a lower status within the larger social context. So to reduce bias, the perceived status of the outgroup must be raised.

The **contact hypothesis** states that prejudice will be reduced simply as a result of direct contact between social groups that are prejudiced toward each other without any regard for the context in which the contact occurs (Allport, 1954). As shown by the lasting conflicts in many desegregated school systems, however, contact alone is not sufficient to alleviate bias (N. Miller & Brewer, 1984). Rather, the quality of the contact is important to alleviating prejudice, as in the cooperative tasks in the Robber's Cave study.

For exposure to reduce prejudice between groups, it needs to meet these standards:

1. The two interacting groups must be of *equal status.*

2. The contact must involve *personal interactions* between members of the two groups.
3. The groups must engage in *cooperative activities.*
4. The social norms must *favor reduction* of prejudice.

Suppose that in a university community, members of one religious group realize that many of them are showing signs of prejudice against members of another religious group in the community. They decide to take affirmative steps to reduce the bias they have observed. The steps are more likely to be successful if they meet the four conditions. In

particular, members of the first group must see members of the second group as having equal status. Positive interactions must be established between members of the two groups, perhaps through cooperative activities, such as an interfaith organization to help the homeless. Finally, the group members must seriously want to reduce prejudice. This last idea suggests another tactic: establishing social norms that condemn intolerance.

Another consideration in reducing bias is to use *cognition.* Krystyna Rojahn and Thomas Pettigrew (1992) have suggested that we can change our own stereotypes by emphasizing any information that contradicts them. For example, we can minimize irrelevant distracting information by taking time to notice and process relevant information that contradicts the stereotype and ensure that we notice the relevance of the information that challenges the stereotype. So, by paying attention to how effective a female police officer is at gathering information and how useful her observations on the beat are, fellow officers would become less prejudiced.

Finally, one of the best ways to reduce or eliminate prejudice is to *experience* another culture directly, whether in a foreign country or in your own. Learning the language, visiting with the people, and actually living as a member of the culture can help one better understand the extent to which humans are the same all over the world.

© Mark Richards/PhotoEdit

Membership in gangs confers social identity, but at high cost. Some gang members eventually strive for reconciliation with their rivals.

racial prejudice
women and prejudice
reducing prejudice

AGGRESSION

Aggression is behavior that is intended to cause harm or injury. It is antisocial when it causes harm. In other cases, such as the effort to destroy the Nazi regime in World War II, many people believe that is necessary. Aggression should be distinguished from *assertion*, which is forceful behavior that causes neither injury nor harm, such as arguing strongly for one's point of view. The two main kinds of aggression are hostile and instrumental (R. A. Baron, 1977; Berkowitz, 1994; Feshbach, 1970; Geen, 1990). **Hostile aggression** is harmful behavior that results from an emotional outburst. It usually leads to little gain and may even result in losses for the aggressor. In fact, relationships and objects may be harmed or put at risk of harm through hostile aggression. It can injure us or others we love, or destroy property. People who frequently display hostile aggression are likely to perceive the world as a dangerous place and to respond aggressively to ambiguous stimuli (Bushman, 1996).

In contrast, **instrumental aggression** is behavior that happens to harm another person as the aggressor tries to obtain something. The behavior is often planned rather than impulsive. Assassins, bank robbers, and embezzlers are aggressive. But most of them probably feel no personal animosity toward the people they kill or injure. If they could get what they wanted another way, they might not bother to be aggressive. The 2-year-old who grabs another child's toy is showing instrumental aggression—nothing personal, she just wants the truck.

The two kinds of aggression have different causes and therefore respond to different kinds of interventions. In a given situation, however, aggressive behavior may reflect both hostile and instrumental aspects, as when an individual or group fights for land controlled by a hated enemy, or as when, in 1997, boxer Mike Tyson bit his opponent's ear in the misguided hope of gaining an advantage.

© Sean Murphy/Stone-Getty Images

Expressing hostile aggression may harm the target, but it also puts the aggressor at risk.

Some psychologists consider aggression to be a basic human motivation. Others view it as a personality trait, looking at individual differences across people (see Chapter 15). Here, we are largely interested in how social interactions contribute to aggressive behavior. First, however, we briefly consider some biological factors in human aggression.

BIOLOGICAL FACTORS

Ⓔ Although we may view aggression as undesirable, it has evolved for a reason. Aggressive responses are one means by which animals, especially males, ward off invasions of their territory by other males. They also use aggression as a means of protecting females and thereby ensuring their own future paternity. In contrast, a very nonaggressive male risks losing his territory, his paternity, and his life. In humans, the evolutionary explanation is supported by the finding that stepchildren are much more likely to be abused and killed by their stepparents than are children who are biologically related to their parents (Daly & Wilson, 1991, 1996). The same pattern holds in other species (Lore & Schultz, 1993).

Nature and nurture interact to determine the specific expression of aggression in humans (Renfrew, 1997). As in other species, the neural circuitry underlying aggressive behavior is hereditary and seems to be common across humans. Research on twins suggests that a tendency toward aggression is partly heritable (Miles & Carey, 1997). In particular, both the hypothalamus and the amygdala play an important role in stimulating or inhibiting aggressive behavior (see Chapter 3). The amygdala is influential in our emotional responses and in our responses to odors. This fact helps explain the powerful interactions between odors and emotions and between emotions and aggressive behavior. In fact, among nonhuman animals, odor plays a direct role in aggressive behavior. For example, although a male animal may attack an animal that smells like a fellow male, it will not attack an animal that smells like a female. Similarly, a mother rat may readily eat infant rats that smell strange to her. But she will not eat infant rats that she has marked with her own scent.

Aggression in nonhuman animals is subject to hormonal influence. In both male and female animals, the presence of androgens very early in development seems to influence the degree of aggressive behavior shown in adulthood. In adult animals, testosterone (a male sex hormone) seems to increase aggression in both males and females (Archer, 1991; Berman, Gladue, & Taylor, 1993; Dabbs, Karpas, Dyomina, Juechter, & Roberts, 2002; Orengo, Kunik, Ghusn, & Yudofsky, 1997). Estradiol (a female sex hormone) seems to decrease aggression in females (Albert, Jonik, & Walsh, 1991).

Hormones also may influence aggression in humans (Delgado, 1969). In institutionalized populations, men and women who have been identified as having higher levels of testosterone exhibit more aggressive behavior and are more likely to have been convicted of violent crimes. In addition, institutionalized women seem more likely to engage in aggression just prior to menstruation and less likely to do so during ovulation.

Outside of institutions, some evidence links hormones and aggression. Children who were exposed prenatally to male sex hormones, because their mothers were given a synthetic hormone to prevent miscarriage, show greater levels of aggression than their same-sex siblings (Reinisch, Ziemba-Davis, & Sanders, 1991). It is important to recall that we cannot predict causation based on correlation alone (see the Statistical Appendix, p. 000). Nonetheless, it is well documented that high doses of synthetic male sex hormones have been linked to extreme aggression, severe mood swings, and mental instability (Pope & Katz, 1988).

Among nonhuman animals, aggressive behavior is generally associated with situations such as self-defense, predation (killing a potential food source), and reproduction (winning or keeping sexual access to a mate). Among humans, although the fundamental biochemistry underlying aggression is universal, the specific circumstances that prompt the aggressive impulses and the particular expressions of aggression differ across cultures (Averill, 1993) and even across individuals. One way humans may determine which circumstances warrant, or permit, aggressive behavior is by watching others.

SOCIAL LEARNING

In social learning, people learn aggressive behavior by watching aggressive models (see Chapters 6, 11, and 12). Such learning plays a major role in aggressive behavior (Bandura, 1973, 1977a, 1983; R. A. Baron & Richardson, 1992). For example, having one or more violent parents can promote violent behavior in children (Bandura, 1973). Given the importance of social learning in contributing to violent behavior, we should pay careful attention to the kinds of role models we provide.

People who do not show high levels of aggression themselves may enjoy watching others do so, as in movies and sports (Mustonen, 1997). Watching aggressive behavior on television

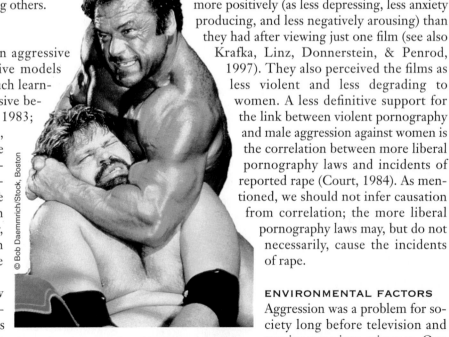

© Bob Daemmrich/Stock, Boston

Given the importance of social learning as a contributing factor in violent behavior, we should pay attention to the kinds of role models we provide.

also influences aggressive behavior. Children play more aggressively immediately after they watch violent shows on television (Liebert & Baron, 1972; see Chapter 6). Similarly, watching violent films made juvenile delinquents more aggressive, especially those who were initially the most aggressive (Parke et al., 1977). Significant correlations exist between the amount of television violence children watch and the children's aggression as rated by peers (Huesmann, Lagerspetz, & Eron, 1984; Huesmann & Miller, 1994). Moreover, these correlations appear across four countries: Australia, Finland, Poland, and the United States. In short, watching violence teaches children how to engage in violence and *desensitizes* them to its devastating consequences.

It is not only children who can become desensitized. Many studies have shown that prolonged exposure to violence desensitizes adult viewers as well. They become less affected when later they view a brawl, whether on television or in real life (Rule & Ferguson, 1986). David Linz, Edward Donnerstein, and Steven Penrod (1984) concluded that repeated exposure to filmed violence lowered their emotional reactions to the material and resulted in participants rating the films less offensive by the last day of viewing.

Violent pornography is a particular form of aggression against women. Men are more aggressive toward women after they watch pornographic films that display sexual violence (Donnerstein & Berkowitz, 1981). In addition, Linz, Donnerstein, and Penrod (1988) found that after viewing five sexually violent films in 10 days, men evaluated the films more positively (as less depressing, less anxiety producing, and less negatively arousing) than they had after viewing just one film (see also Krafka, Linz, Donnerstein, & Penrod, 1997). They also perceived the films as less violent and less degrading to women. A less definitive support for the link between violent pornography and male aggression against women is the correlation between more liberal pornography laws and incidents of reported rape (Court, 1984). As mentioned, we should not infer causation from correlation; the more liberal pornography laws may, but do not necessarily, cause the incidents of rape.

ENVIRONMENTAL FACTORS

Aggression was a problem for society long before television and movies came into existence. One factor that leads to aggression is *aggression* itself. Although some

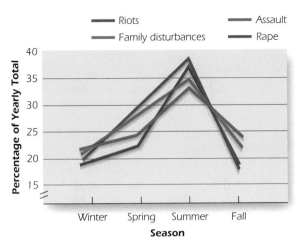

FIGURE 14.8

Temperature and Aggression. Although the link between high heat and aggression is only correlational (and we therefore cannot draw any causal conclusions from it), the correlation is robust. (From C. A. Anderson, "Temperature and Aggression," *Psychological Bulletin,* Vol. 106, 1989, pp. 74–96. Reprinted by permission of the author.)

religions may teach us to turn the other cheek, in practice people are more likely to meet aggression with a counterattack (Borden, Bowen, & Taylor, 1971; Ohbuchi & Kambara, 1985). Often, groups end up with a chicken-and-egg problem. In 1999, a group of Serbs attacked a group of Kosovars. The Kosovars later attacked the Serbs. The Serbs originally claimed they were provoked, and the Kosovars made the same claim. Often, it is hard to tell where the aggression began, and it is difficult to stop.

Hostile aggression is often provoked by physical *pain* (Berkowitz, 1993; Berkowitz, Cochran, & Embree, 1981; Ulrich & Azrin, 1962). If you are hurt by someone, even if accidentally, you may respond aggressively. If an aggressive act leads to a decrease in pain, aggression becomes even more likely (Azrin, 1967).

Discomfort is another reason for aggressive behavior. People become more aggressive when they are exposed to bad smells (Rotton, Barry, Frey, & Soler, 1978), cigarette smoke, and air pollution (Rotton & Frey, 1985). Exposure to heat above 80° F (27° C) also increases aggression (R. A. Baron & Bell, 1975; Bell & Baron, 1976). Indeed, increased feelings of discomfort may be a reason cities that have higher average temperatures also have higher average rates of violent crime than cities that have more moderate temperatures (C. A. Anderson, 1987). As Figure 14.8 shows, violent crimes occur more commonly on hotter days, in hotter seasons, in hotter years, and in hotter regions (C. A. Anderson, 1989).

Another influence on aggression is *frustration*. Indeed, classic research (e.g., Dollard, Miller, Doob, Mowrer, & Sears, 1939) has viewed frustration as a necessary and sufficient condition for aggression. Although a clear empirical link exists between frustration and aggression (Barker, Dembo, & Lewin, 1941), we now know that frustration does not *always* lead to aggression. Strong frustrations that seem to have arbitrary causes are quite likely to lead to aggression. Mild frustrations are less likely to lead to aggression, however, especially if they are viewed as having a reasonable cause (R. A. Baron, 1977; R. A. Baron, Neuman, & Geddes, 1999). Suppose that the light at an intersection turns green, but you cannot move because you are blocked by the car in front of you. Whether you react aggressively will probably depend on why the car in front of you is stopped. Your reaction will be different if the people in the car are engaged in a conversation than if the driver has suffered a heart attack.

We also know that individualistic cultures experience more aggressive behavior than collectivistic cultures (Oatley, 1993). Furthermore, individualistic societies themselves vary in the extent to which they accept and promote aggression (DeAngelis, 1992; Montagu, 1976). Even in collectivistic cultures, aggression may be promoted. For example, aggression is viewed as a desirable trait for women among the island dwellers of Margarita, Venezuela (H. B. K. Cook, 1992).

Another cultural factor that contributes to aggression is a *culture of honor*. According to R. E. Nisbett and D. Cohen (1996), southerners in the United States are sometimes more likely to respond aggressively and even violently to perceived insults than are northerners because they are more likely to feel their sense of honor has been violated. (Recall the Psychology in Everyday Life box in Chapter 13.)

DEINDIVIDUATION

What enables some of us to *dehumanize* others, to make victims feel as if they are less than human and deserving of poor treatment? Every once in a while, you read in the newspaper or see on television that fans at a sports event—such as a European soccer match—lost control and rioted, trampling and mutilating people and destroying everything in their path. How does a group become an out-of-control mob? At the end of the 19th century, Gustave Le Bon (1896) attempted to analyze the factors that lead to the mass hysteria of mob behavior. Le Bon contended that people in a crowd are more susceptible to mob behavior because they feel anonymous and invulnerable. They act more like wild animals than like humans, becoming highly impulsive and unreasoning.

Perhaps mob behavior can be understood in terms of **deindividuation,** the loss of a sense of individual identity. Because of deindividuation we lose the controls that prevent us from behaving in ways that violate social norms and even our personal moral beliefs.

In a study whose findings jolted the scientific community, the basement of a building that housed the Stanford University Psychology Department was converted into a "jail" (Zimbardo, 1972). Male volunteers were arbitrarily assigned to be either "prisoners" or "guards." Phil Zimbardo used a number of techniques to deindividuate members of both groups. The prisoners wore uniforms and nylon stocking caps and were referred to by serial numbers instead of by their names. Guards wore uniforms as well as mirrored sunglasses to hide their eyes, and they carried clubs.

What started off as a simulation became a nightmare. Prisoners started to act like prisoners, and guards truly acted like guards. The guards harassed and derided the prisoners. They frequently inflicted cruel treatment for little or no apparent reason. The prisoners soon staged a revolt, which was crushed. Prisoners became morose, depressed, and lethargic, and some had mental breakdowns. The experiment was terminated when it became obvious that it was of control.

Note that Zimbardo had assigned people arbitrarily to groups. Once deindividuated, we can act in ways we would never have thought possible, whether on the giving or the receiving end of hostile aggression.

REDUCING AGGRESSION
On the basis of deindividuation studies, we could guess that some forms of aggression might be minimized by fostering people's sense of their own individual identities as humans and their awareness of the humanity of their fellow humans. As Table 14.3 shows, some effective methods for reducing aggression are based both on these principles and on social learning.

Group behavior can be mindless, inappropriate, and even disastrous if all members yield their individual thoughts, beliefs, and actions to the apparent consensus of the group. Mob lynchings in the United States and elsewhere have attested to this fact. Yet, when even a single individual shows the initiative and takes positive action, other members of the group may be motivated to reconsider their own beliefs and behavior. The personal characteristics that enable us to stand up for what we believe, despite group pressure to the contrary, are considered in the next chapter.

EVIL AND HATRED
The Milgram experiments suggest that we can be surprisingly obedient, at least under unusual circumstances. But do they suggest something more—that evil and even hatred are more prevalent than we once thought?

Opinions differ as to what the Milgram (1974) experiments establish about human nature. Leonard Berkowitz (1999) has suggested that they are often given more validity than they deserve, that, in fact, the results of true terrorism—massacres and genocide—do not correspond well to the results of the Milgram experiments. Berkowitz believes that individual factors are substantially more important and situational factors substantially less important than Milgram would have us believe (see also J. M. Darley, 1992, 1998). For example, the sadism exhibited in the Nazi death camps far exceeded what was seen in the Milgram experiments. Berkowitz notes that no one issued orders that infants should be thrown into the air as shooting targets or hurled into fires alive (Arendt, as cited in Blass, 1993). At the same time, the causes of evil behavior during the Holocaust were probably numerous and complex, and it is not likely that any one theory will fully account for all of them. Clearly, though, to understand a phenomenon such as the Holocaust we have to dig past the psychological levels revealed by the Milgram experiments.

Both Ervin Staub (1989, 1999a, 1999b, 2000) and Roy Baumeister (1996; Baumeister & Campbell, 1999) have speculated about the nature of evil and its

TABLE 14.3
Methods for Reducing Aggression. Of the many methods for reducing aggression that have been proposed, these are most effective.

Method	Description
Observing nonaggressive models	Watching nonaggressive models can increase the likelihood of choosing alternatives to aggressive behavior.
Generating incompatible responses	One of the most successful techniques: empathy, humor, and other unexpected responses can defuse aggression.
Using cognitive strategies	Stopping to think raises alternatives to aggression in frustrating or threatening situations. Awareness of individual people as fellow humans and of their humanity reduces deindividuation. Awareness of the reasons for someone's behavior can reduce anger, frustration, and hostility.

relationship to mass murder, although they have taken different approaches. Staub (1996a) suggested that the evolution of evil starts when basic human needs are not met and destructive behaviors are developed to satisfy them. He believes that certain conditions tend to precipitate terrorism, massacres, and genocide, including the evolution of collective violence, the devaluation of a cultural group, an obedient orientation to authority, and the belief that aggression is defensive. People who are powerless are particularly susceptible to mass murder, especially when bystanders merely watch passively (Staub, 1999b). Staub (1989, 1996b) also suggested that perpetrators tend to think in terms of evening a score. They explain their violence toward others as a response to the character, intentions, or actions of their victims. As their aggression continues, they increasingly devalue their victims. They may appropriate a kind of "moral exclusion," believing that the standards and values that apply to everyone else no longer apply to them (see also Bodenhausen & Moreno, 2000; Macrae, Bodenhausen, Milne, Thorn, & Castelli, 1997; Opotow, 1990, for related views). Moral exclusion lets the object of hatred be seen not as like oneself but as "other," existing on the opposite side of a sturdy wall that separates good from bad. Even worse, as people engage in actions inspired by hate, they and the larger society progress along a continuum of destruction. The perpetrators, the institutions that define them, and ultimately society as a whole can change in ways that facilitate further hatred and atrocities (Staub, 1995).

The target group may view itself in terms of even stronger negative stereotypes than those ascribed to it by the more powerful group (Judd, Park, Brauer, Ryan, & Kraus, 1995). And, oddly enough, both groups may make a cognitive effort to justify a system that perpetuates the negative stereotyping of the less powerful group (Jost & Banaji, 1994). In fact, stereotypes may be built into society simply because systems deal with groups as well as with individuals. If a stereotyped attribute can be associated with a particular group, it may seem reasonable to base public policy on it (Maurer, Park, & Judd, 1996). Such policies may endure because people with strong stereotypical views avoid the intergroup contact that might change their minds, and they don't view the effects of such contact as positive (Pettigrew, 1998). Evidence suggests that stereotypes are often inaccurate, especially when they are used to stigmatize outgroups (Judd & Park, 1993).

Baumeister and Campbell (1999) argued that evil behavior may stem from the urge to alleviate boredom. Staub and Baumeister disagree on a fundamental detail: Staub thinks that individuals who perpetrate evil have low self-esteem, whereas in Baumeister's view their self-esteem is high.

Baumeister (1996) has proposed four roots of evil and violence. The first is an ideological belief that in a dispute one's own side is good and the other side is evil—and we hate the enemy because it is evil. This is the root of religious and political hatreds. The second source of evil is the desire for revenge when one has suffered injustices and humiliations, individually or as part of a group, especially when the ego has been threatened. The third root is greed, lust, ambition, and other forms of self-interest that are aroused when a rival gets between us and what we want. The fourth root of evil is sadism, which is associated with brutality more than with hatred.

Baumeister (1996) has further emphasized how the perpetrator and the recipient can perceive the same negative incident in different ways. In one study (Baumeister, Stillwell, & Wotman, 1990), participants provided autobiographical accounts of incidents in which they were either victims or perpetrators of events that aroused anger. In general, the perpetrator depicted the provocative behavior as meaningful and comprehensible, whereas the victim described it as arbitrary, gratuitous, or incomprehensible. Victims also tended to emphasize the long-term effects of negative behavior, whereas perpetrators saw the incident as closed and thus without lasting implications. Victims tended to see the event as one link in a chain of provocation, whereas perpetrators tended to see it as an isolated incident, and often viewed the victim's response as an unjustified overreaction.

More empirical evidence that perpetrators and victims perceive events differently comes from the work of Mikula, Athenstaedt, Heschgl, and Heimgartner (1998). In four studies, they asked both perpetrators and recipients about their reactions to particular negative events in close interpersonal relationships. Recipients regarded the events as more unjust, and they attributed more responsibility and blame to the perpetrators than did the perpetrators themselves. A strong relationship helped minimize the effects of negative incidents. Mikula and colleagues also found that women tended to respond more accusingly than men when they were in the role of recipient, and more defensively than men when they were in the role of perpetrator.

Bandura (1999; Bandura, Barbaranelli, Caprara, & Pastorelli, 1996; Bandura, Underwood, & Fromson, 1975) has suggested that the moral disengagement that leads to inhumanity stems from a series of variables: cognitively restructuring inhumane behavior into allegedly benign or worthy conduct, which requires moral justification; sanitizing language; disavowing accountability through the diffusion of responsibility; disregarding or minimizing the injurious effects of one's actions; and attributing blame to the victims themselves, who are simultaneously dehumanized. Often, when the responsibility is so diffused that those involved in evil activities feel relatively innocent, members of legitimate enterprises may be co-opted into working with them.

Finally, I have proposed what I call a "duplex" theory because it has two parts: hatred and the stories that give rise to it (R. J. Sternberg, in press-c). A "storyteller" may describe the targeted object as aggressor, enemy of God, traitor, virus, garbage, and so forth. The resulting hatred has three components: (1) negation of intimacy, whereby we perceive hated individuals or groups as less than human; (2) passion, whereby we experience the strong desire to either fight or flee from the hated object; and (3) commitment, whereby we develop a cognitive account of why the hated object is the way it is, insisting that it was this way in the past and is likely to remain this way. According to the duplex theory, the components of hatred are related to those of love (R. J. Sternberg, 1998b). The same things that are expressed positively in love are expressed negatively in hatred.

I believe that a potential solution to the problem of hate is to use our intelligence and experience for the common good (R. J. Sternberg, 1998a).

✓ CONCEPT CHECK 4

1. According to social-identity theory, prejudice helps people
   a. protect their self-esteem.
   b. understand other people's social identities.
   c. understand how they are better than other people.
   d. hide the fact that they are inferior to other people.
2. Instrumental aggression is aimed at
   a. groups, not individuals.
   b. causing harm for its own sake.
   c. obtaining valued resources.
   d. hiding hostile aggression.
3. Which of the following is *not* a component of Sternberg's theory of hate?
   a. negation of intimacy
   b. passion
   c. anger
   d. commitment

UNIFYING PSYCHOLOGY

THE SOCIAL CONTAGION OF BULIMIA

When Katie arrived at college she was unhappy with her appearance. Although she wasn't overweight, she had an athletic, muscular build and a large, solid frame. Her body fat was minimal, but that didn't prevent Katie from wishing she were thinner. She quickly made friends with the women who lived on her floor in the residence hall, and soon learned about their weight control "techniques." Katie's roommate and several other women claimed that they could eat all they wanted in the dining hall if they just vomited it all back up after the meal. At first, Katie was disgusted by the idea, but the act became second nature to her after a few weeks. During her sophomore year, Katie made an appointment with the counseling psychologist in the university health center. She was worried because she

could not hold anything down. She no longer had to stick her finger down her throat to make herself vomit. Everything she ate came right up again. The vomiting seemed out of control.

Anyone who has walked through a bathroom in a women's residence hall or sorority house is typically overwhelmed by the odor of vomit. Why do some people devote themselves to doing something that most of us find revolting? The answer is quite simple: They have an eating disorder called *bulimia.* People with bulimia eat large quantities of food and then purge, removing the food from the digestive track, usually by vomiting. Psychologists from many fields have studied the development of bulimia.

Two *social psychologists,* Catherine Sanderson and John Darley, have examined the social norm of thinness in

women and have attempted to relate it to the development of bulimia. They studied the responses of 120 college women to a survey that asked them to compare themselves to other women. The study revealed that most of the women thought they were not as thin as other women, that they wanted to be thinner, and that they exercised more frequently than other women. The investigators also found that college women who felt that their bodies were inconsistent with the thinness norm were most likely to develop an eating disorder (Sanderson, Darley, & Messinger, 2002).

In a study conducted in two sororities, social psychologist Christian Crandall (1988) examined the role of social pressure in the development of the binge eating associated with

continued

bulimia. In both sororities, group norms influenced the observed level of bingeing. In one sorority, the most popular women were the ones who binged the most. In the other sorority, the most popular women neither binged too much nor too little, but they still binged moderately. Crandall also discovered that in both sororities a woman's binge eating style closely resembled that of her friends. The results of Crandall's study demonstrated that social pressure to binge eat encouraged the development of bulimia in sorority women.

Research conducted by **developmental psychologists** focuses on how eating behaviors develop in adolescents. Tracy Dunkley, Eleanor Wertheim, and Susan Paxton (2001) have studied 577 girls aged 13 to 17. Their findings indicate that adolescents who express the most dissatisfaction with their bodies and develop eating disorders have friends and parents who support a thin ideal and encourage dieting. Dunkley's team has also shown that television

and magazine contents that endorse thinness were implicated in the development of bulimia. A team of developmental psychologists headed by James Clopton has confirmed that media and peer influences, together with body dissatisfaction, contribute to the development of bulimia (Young, McFatter, & Clopton, 2001). Other developmental psychologists have identified peer and parental encouragement of weight loss as another important predictor of bulimia (Vincent & McCabe, 2000; Tyrka, Graber, & Brooks-Gunn, 2000).

Clinical and **counseling psychologists** are involved in the treatment and assessment of bulimia. Martin Heesacker and his colleagues compared the incidence of eating disorders in American and Israeli college women. They found that more American women had eating disorders and expressed more body dissatisfaction than Israeli women (Heesacker, Samson, & Shir, 2000). Other clinical psychologists have examined the role of such personality variables as non-

conformity, self-esteem, and family influence in order to better treat bulimia and other eating disorders (Twamley & Davis, 1999).

Health psychologists are concerned with the prevention of eating disorders. They use data collected by social psychologists, developmental psychologists, and counseling and clinical psychologists to develop prevention programs that can be used in schools and community programs. For example, because dieting has been identified as a causal factor for bulimia and other eating disorders, a large-scale campaign that promotes a reduction in dieting might help prevent such disorders (Bryn, 2001; French & Jeffery, 1994). Research by psychologists in many areas indicates that social norms play a powerful role in the development of bulimia. Prevention programs must target and change prevailing social standards if they are to combat bulimia and other eating disorders.

SUMMARY

GROUPS 502

How does the presence of other people affect our beliefs and behavior?

1. Researchers who study the social psychology of *groups* seek to understand and explain how groups reach consensus and how individuals perform in a group. Groups differ in the emphasis they give to task functions versus relationships among members of the group.

2. *Social-facilitation* theory and *distraction-conflict theory* offer explanations for how the presence of others affects our performance.

3. *Social loafing* occurs in groups and can be discouraged through evaluation apprehension.

4. Groups often become *polarized*. New arguments confirm old beliefs, and social norms emerge. In-group members are especially influential.

5. The resolution of intergroup and intragroup conflicts may be viewed in terms of the reasons people resolve conflicts and the strategies they use to resolve conflicts.

6. *Groupthink* occurs when a closely knit group cares more about consensus than about honest interaction. Stress, biased leadership, and isolation compound the problem. To counter groupthink, the group needs a subgroup structure, outside input, and strong leadership.

7. People yield to social pressure by conforming, complying, and obeying.
8. Solomon Asch's studies showed that a member of a group may conform publicly or privately. People who deviate from the norm often are rejected by the group. Factors that affect *conformity* include group size, cohesiveness of the group, gender, social status, culture, the appearance of unanimity, and idiosyncrasy. Majorities encourage conformity through their large numbers; minorities, if persistent, also can influence opinion.
9. *Compliance* is encouraged through such techniques as justification, reciprocity, low-ball, foot in the door, door in the face, that's not all, and hard to get.
10. Stanley Milgram's experiments on *obedience* showed that most participants were willing to inflict excruciating pain on others when "under orders" to do so. Other research has replicated Milgram's surprising findings.

11. *Prosocial behavior* involves societally approved actions that benefit society in general or individual members of society in particular, and that are approved of by most people.
12. According to the *bystander effect*, the presence of others diffuses responsibility and discourages helping behavior. Also important are the characteristics of the victim, the bystander, and the situation.
13. *Altruism* is selfless sacrifice. Psychologists agree that it exists but disagree about how to define it.

14. Peacemaking can be guided by strategies derived from psychology, such as GRIT.

15. *Antisocial behavior* is harmful to a society or to individuals.
16. *Prejudice* is based on faulty evidence, which in turn often is based on *social categorization* and on *stereotypes*. The Robber's Cave experiment showed how prejudice can be overcome by cooperative activities.
17. Prejudice may develop when groups compete for scarce resources *(realistic-conflict theory)* or when people seek to increase their own self-esteem and boost the esteem of their ingroup *(social-identity theory)*. To reduce prejudice, groups must recognize that it exists, work cooperatively together, use information to counter the stereotypes, and, if possible, experience other cultures.
18. *Aggression* is antisocial behavior that harms another; it may be *hostile* or *instrumental*. Hormones may lead to aggression. People learn aggressive behavior when they see it modeled, such as on television and in the movies. Violent pornography is a strong example of modeling aggressive behavior. Pain, discomfort, and frustration also can promote aggressive behavior.
19. A group can become an unruly mob. When *deindividuation* occurs, people behave in ways they would not behave if they were alone.
20. Aggression can be reduced if we as individuals maximize our own identities as humans and our awareness of others as fellow humans.
21. Psychologists have proposed theories of hate and evil in an attempt to account for phenomena such as terrorism, massacres, and genocides.

KEY TERMS

ANSWERS TO CONCEPT CHECKS

Concept Check 1

1. d   2. a   3. d

Concept Check 2

1. a   2. c   3. a

Concept Check 3

1. b   2. d   3. d

Concept Check 4

1. a   2. c   3. c

KNOWLEDGE CHECK

1. A group differs from a collective in that members of a group
   a. are more numerous.
   b. know each other.
   c. like each other.
   d. interact with each other.

2. Norman Triplett discovered that bicyclists who compete with each other _____ bicyclists who cycled alone against a clock.
   a. were happier than
   b. were sadder than
   c. cycled faster than
   d. cycled slower than

3. Distraction-conflict theory holds that the presence of others
   a. is helpful.
   b. can be distracting.
   c. is distracting if one is in conflict with the others.
   d. causes internal conflict in people.

4. Individuals in collectivistic cultures seem to show _____ social loafing than individuals in individualistic cultures.
   a. the same
   b. more
   c. less
   d. first more and then less

5. Which of the following is *not* a condition of groupthink?
   a. homogeneous, cohesive, isolated group
   b. need for an immediate decision
   c. minimal pressure
   d. opinionated leadership

6. Making an outlandishly large request in the hope of softening up a target is known as the _____ technique.
   a. low-ball
   b. foot-in-the-door
   c. hard-to-get
   d. door-in-the-face

7. In the principal Milgram experiment, the percentage of participants who administered the maximum shock was about
   a. 5%.
   b. 25%.
   c. 65%.
   d. 95%.

8. An inferred perception of a relationship between unrelated variables is a(n)
   a. illusory correlation.
   b. dysfunctional correlation.
   c. notorious relation.
   d. codified relation.

9. The loss of a sense of individual identity, resulting in fewer social controls, is called
   a. disidentification.
   b. misidentification.
   c. misindividuation.
   d. deindividuation.

10. According to Staub, people are particularly susceptible to mass murder when they
    a. are powerless and when bystanders passively watch in the wings.
    b. become indifferent to everyone except themselves.
    c. themselves are mass killers.
    d. admit to serious inherent flaws.

Answers

1. d   2. c   3. b   4. c   5. c   6. d   7. c   8. a
9. d   10. a

THINK ABOUT IT

1. What criteria would you propose for determining whether behavior derives from motives that are truly altruistic?
2. Some developmental psychologists have noticed that people who demonstrate a high degree of conformity to their peers during adolescence are more likely to have shown a high degree of obedience to their parents during childhood. What do you believe is the relationship between conformity and obedience, if any?
3. How might a working group avoid the ill effects of groupthink?

4. How might you help people avoid falling prey to some of the strategies for gaining compliance described in this chapter?
5. Imagine that you wished to reduce the likelihood of your own aggression or the aggression of another person. What would you do?
6. Which compliance-seeking strategy is the most likely to be effective in gaining your own compliance? Why?

WEB RESOURCES

For a chapter tutorial quiz, direct links to Internet sites, and other useful features, visit the book-specific website at http://psychology.wadsworth.com/sternberg4e. You can also connect directly to the following sites:

Attraction
http://www.psychology.org/links/Environment_
Behavior_Relationships/Attraction/
This site contains information on love, attraction, and liking.

For additional readings on many of the topics covered in this chapter, check out InfoTrac College Edition at **www.infotrac-college.com/ wadsworth.**

Disk Two
Conformity
Compliance
Prosocial Behavior
Chapter Quiz
Critical Thinking Questions

© Steve McCurry/Magnum Photos

CHAPTER 15

PERSONALITY

Optimists expect things to go their way, and generally believe that good rather than bad things will happen to them. . . . Pessimists expect things not to go their way, and tend to anticipate bad outcomes. Moreover, casual observation suggests that these individual differences are relatively stable across time and context.

—*Scheier & Carver* (1985, pp. 219–220)

Bart and Bert are brothers, but to a casual observer they appear to have little in common. Bart is outgoing and sociable. He loves spending time with other people and going to parties. Bert is quiet, withdrawn, even reclusive. He prefers to be by himself and is almost never seen at parties. How can two brothers be so different? This is essentially the same question psychologists ask about the intriguing phenomenon of personality—enduring dispositional characteristics that together explain a person's behavior. For example, are optimism and pessimism personality traits or just passing states of mind? Personality researchers seek to answer questions such as this one. Researchers have several ways to study personality. Some psychologists conduct intensive studies of individual personalities over long periods. Others use a wide array of techniques for assessing individual personalities at a single point in time. Still others carry out empirical studies of isolated aspects or common dimensions of personality across individuals.

© Culture influences the way personality functions. For example, the culture we live in determines whether we think of achievement as primarily individual- or group-based, and whether we set career and life goals individually or as part of a group (Heine et al., 2001; Pervin, 2003; Salili, 1994).

Various theories for understanding personality can be classified according to the major approaches to psychology discussed in Chapter 1. Some approaches emphasize the importance of early experience to the development of personality. Some emphasize the importance of highly stable personal characteristics that vary little over time. Some approaches have generated a great deal of research and rigorous testing of their ideas. What, then, are these particular approaches to understanding personality? Most personality psychologists agree on the importance of using certain criteria to evaluate each approach:

What was it about Rosa Parks's personality that gave her the courage to challenge segregation on city buses? What were the roots of her courage?

> *Importance to and influence on the field of psychology:* How have the development of theory and research in the field been affected by this approach at various times?

> *Testability:* Has the approach given rise to empirically testable propositions and have these been tested?

> *Comprehensiveness:* To what extent does the approach give a reasonably complete account of the phenomena it sets out to describe or explain?

> *Parsimony:* Does the approach explain a large number of phenomena with a relatively small number of psychological constructs?

> *Usefulness to applications in assessment and psychotherapy:* Is the approach useful to clinicians and other practitioners?

In this chapter, we consider the principal approaches to personality theory: psychodynamic, humanistic, cognitive-behavioral, trait, and biological. The theories within a given approach, despite their variations, share common elements, as you will see in the concept review tables.

PSYCHODYNAMIC APPROACHES

Why is Freud's theory of personality both influential and controversial?

COMMON COMPONENTS

While the scientific community of a hundred years ago excitedly investigated certain laws of physics (thermodynamics, in particular), psychodynamic psychologists were developing theories that recognized the importance of the *dynamic processes* underlying personality. Psychodynamic theorists view each of us as a complex system of *diverse sources of psychic energy*, each of which pushes us in a somewhat different direction. As we observe someone's behavior, we are watching the moment-by-moment convergence of these multidirectional energies. For example, a child whose mother returns to work may be affected, positively or negatively, by many factors that may push his or her personality development in different directions. If her mother has made her feel loved and valued, she may continue to develop a sense of security and emotional stability. But if her mother has not instilled feelings of security, the child may feel abandoned and unloved. At the same time, she may come to admire and model her mother's commitment to her work and to a fulfilling professional career. It is always both the set of events and the constellation of feelings and thoughts surrounding them that shape personality.

Many psychodynamic theories are based on data from observations of patients in clinical settings, who typically do not lend themselves readily to controlled observation or rigorous experimentation. Typically, a psychoanalyst keeps detailed notes about a patient and then, where appropriate, writes up the notes as a case study, using a pseudonym for the patient to keep his or her identity confidential.

CONFLICT

Conflict is an important factor in psychodynamic theories. Different energy sources propel us in conflicting directions. The resulting behavior usually cannot satisfy all our diverse psychic drives at once. Psychodynamic theorists also observe conflict between individuals and their society. For example, internal psychic energy may prompt a person to achieve material fulfillment in ways that society prohibits, such as through stealing.

BIOLOGY AND ADAPTATION

Biological drives (especially sexual ones) play a key role in psychodynamic theories. Sigmund Freud, the first great psychodynamic thinker, viewed his theory as *biological* in nature, in part because it was influenced by Charles Darwin's theory of evolution through natural selection. Psychodynamic theories study how we constantly seek to adapt to our environment, even though we may not always succeed in our efforts. In trying to adapt to the environment, for example, we may ignore serious problems we urgently need to solve, such as a highly conflicted relationship. The attempt to adapt can backfire.

Psychodynamic theorists emphasize the ways in which early childhood experiences influence personality development and the moment-to-moment dynamics of adapting to external environments while responding to internal forces.

The biological and developmental characteristics of psychodynamic theories suggest another key feature of Freud's theory. **Determinism** is the belief that our behavior is ruled by forces over which we have little or no control. Freud believed that behavior is strongly influenced by often uncontrollable forces—sexual and aggressive drives in particular. Later psychodynamic theorists, the **neo-Freudians,** reacted against Freud's emphasis on instincts and determinism, and generally viewed people as having more control over their own behavior.

THE UNCONSCIOUS

Another variable that influences our actions is the *unconscious*, an aspect of the mind of which we are usually unaware. Although theorists differ about its exact nature, they all credit the unconscious with a function. The idea that much of our behavior is motivated by forces we do not consciously comprehend pervades all psychodynamic theories, although Freud emphasized it most heavily. For example, Freud argued that when we lose something, it is often because we unconsciously wish to forget the person we associate with it.

SIGMUND FREUD: PSYCHOANALYSIS

Sigmund Freud is considered one of the greatest thinkers of the 20th century. His psychoanalytic theory is sometimes thought to be the most well known in all of psychology. When it was proposed, its ideas were strikingly original and influential. Today, many of its concepts are part of everyday language (e.g., the "Oedipal complex"), and we may even forget they originated with Freud. Many aspects of the theory remain empirically unproven, however.

THE STRUCTURE OF PERSONALITY

As we saw in Chapter 5, Freud (1917/1963b) believed that the mind exists on two basic levels: conscious and unconscious. In addition to conscious thought (of which we are aware) and unconscious thought (of which we are unaware), Freud suggested the existence

Sigmund Freud (with his psychoanalyst daughter Anna) is the primary theorist of the psychodynamic paradigm. Many consider him to be the seminal thinker in the psychology of personality. Anna Freud made important contributions to child psychology.

of *preconscious* thought, which we can bring into awareness more readily than unconscious thought. Most of our memories reside in our preconscious. Freud (1933/1964a) also believed that the mind has three basic structures: the id, the ego, and the superego. The id is largely unconscious, and the ego and superego are partly conscious and partly unconscious.

THE ID. At the most primitive level, the **id** is the personality structure that serves as the unconscious, instinctual, and irrational source of primitive impulses. The id functions by means of **primary-process thought**, which is irrational, instinct-driven, and unrealistic. We engage in primary-process thought as infants and also later in our dreams. For example, a baby does not care that she is in a plane or a museum or a concert hall or a lecture—if she is hungry, she cries. Her behavior is appropriate—at her age. At a later age, of course, it would not be.

This mode of thought accepts both content and forms that would be unacceptable when we are thinking logically. The content of primary-process thought allows us to imagine consummating sexual desires that we would never satisfy in everyday life. Another expression of primary-process thought is Freudian slips of the tongue (see Chapter 8). In addition to the important functions of expressing wishes through dreams, primary-process thinking provides us with a

wellspring of creativity with its novel and even surprising imaginative connections.

Primary-process thinking is unacceptable to consciousness. It may include blatant contradictions, for instance. In a dream, you may be fully engaged in events and at the same time observing those events as a detached nonparticipant. In conscious thought, you would need to view yourself as either participating or not participating.

Freud addressed the paradoxical nature of dreams by distinguishing between their **manifest content,** the stream of events that pass through the mind during a dream, and their **latent content,** the repressed impulses and other unconscious material in dreams that give rise to the manifest content. Freud believed that our thoughts during dreaming disguise unacceptable impulses. Many elements of dreams are symbolic (e.g., a box can symbolize the womb). The manifest content of a dream might be to flee from a wild animal, but the latent content might be the need to seek protection from savage impulses. We also disguise unacceptable thoughts through *condensation*, whereby several unacceptable thoughts or impulses are combined into a single dream image.

According to Freudian theory, dreams fulfill some of the wishes that we are unable to satisfy in our conscious lives. Wish fulfillment via dreams is only one of many ways we immediately gratify the impulses of the id. Immediate gratification transforms the psychic energy of the id's impulses into internal tension and conflict. The id operates by means of the **pleasure principle,** which involves irrationally pursuing immediate gratification, regardless of external realities.

THE EGO. The **ego** is a personality structure that is largely conscious and realistic in responding to events in the world. In contrast to the id, the ego operates on the basis of the **reality principle,** which responds to the real world as it is perceived to be, rather than as the person may want or believe it should be. The ego tries to find realistic ways to gratify the id's impulses. For example, the id may be behind the idea "I want a big piece of cake!" while the ego may lead one to choose only a small piece.

Each person's ego develops from the id during infancy. Throughout life, the ego remains in contact with the id as well as with the external world. The ego relies on **secondary-process thought,** which is rational and reality-based, helping the thinker make sense of the world and act sensibly. As you read, trying to make sense of this discussion, you are engaging in secondary-process thought.

THE SUPEREGO. Freud's third structure of personality, the **superego,** is both conscious and unconscious; it is irrational, based on the rules and prohibitions we have internalized from interactions with our parents and other authority figures. It comprises all our internalized representations of the norms and values of society. The superego emerges later than the id and the ego—at around 3 to 5 years of age. To some extent, the superego is an internalized representation of the authority figures that tell us what we can and cannot do. It is based on the norms and values of society.

The superego operates by means of the **idealistic principle,** which guides a person's actions as dictated by internalized authority figures without regard for rationality or even external reality. Whereas the ego is largely rational in its thinking, the superego is not. The superego checks whether we are conforming to our internalized moral authority, not whether we are behaving rationally. For example, if we are interested in having a sexual relationship with someone forbidden to us, the superego will tell us to abandon the fantasy. The id, however, may hold sway, and we may pursue the relationship after all.

The superego has two parts: the conscience and the ego ideal. Roughly speaking, the *conscience* arises from experiences of being punished for unacceptable behavior. The *ego ideal* stems from experiences of being rewarded for praiseworthy behavior. In other words, the conscience focuses on prohibited or questionable behaviors. The ego ideal focuses on socially (or morally) valued behaviors. Thus, the superego presents a third factor that the ego must contend with when trying to decide on behavior. The relationships among the id, the ego, and the superego are shown in Table 15.1.

DEFENSE MECHANISMS

The id, ego, and superego are the structures of personality, and they form the basis for personality development and expression. How they are expressed has a good deal to do with how we cope with the conflicts that arise among the three structures. The id's strong impulses and the superego's strong prohibitions often pose problems for the ego. Freud and his daughter Anna (see A. Freud, 1946) suggested that in response to these problems, we use **defense mechanisms** to protect the ego from anxiety associated with the conflicting urges and prohibitions of the id and the superego. The eight main defense mechanisms are denial, repression, projection, displacement, sublimation, reaction formation, rationalization, and regression. In the short term, they may help us bear the discomfort of having to deal with problems we do not wish to face. In the long term, however, they can be maladaptive because they prevent us from solving these problems.

1. *Denial* occurs when the mind defends itself from thinking about unpleasant, unwanted, or threatening situations. It may also screen out anxiety-provoking physical sensations. For instance, alcoholics may deny all the obvious signs of alcoholism. Adolescents deny that their unsafe sex practices may lead to sexually transmitted diseases. Or someone with a possibly cancerous mole may "forget" noticing it and not seek medical attention.
2. *Repression* is the internal counterpart to denial. We *unknowingly* exclude from consciousness any unacceptable and potentially dangerous impulses. A woman may be afraid of intimate contact with men because she was sexually molested as a child.

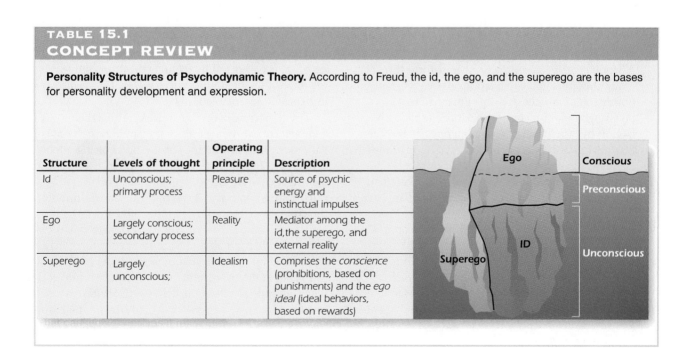

TABLE 15.1
CONCEPT REVIEW

Personality Structures of Psychodynamic Theory. According to Freud, the id, the ego, and the superego are the bases for personality development and expression.

Structure	Levels of thought	Operating principle	Description
Id	Unconscious; primary process	Pleasure	Source of psychic energy and instinctual impulses
Ego	Largely conscious; secondary process	Reality	Mediator among the id, the superego, and external reality
Superego	Largely unconscious;	Idealism	Comprises the *conscience* (prohibitions, based on punishments) and the *ego ideal* (ideal behaviors, based on rewards)

She has repressed some of her memories of the experience, however, and therefore cannot relate it to her fear of sexual intimacy.

3. *Projection* is the defense mechanism that leads us to attribute our thoughts or impulses to another person. Projection allows us to be aware of the thought or impulse but not to claim it as our own, whereas repression keeps the thought out of our consciousness altogether. Projection is at work when a person becomes obsessed with thoughts of a partner's infidelity as a way of defending against his or her own unacceptable sexual impulses toward others.

4. *Displacement* allows us to redirect an impulse away from the person who prompts it toward a safe substitute. A boy who has been punished unfairly by his father would like to strike back vengefully. However, his ego recognizes that he cannot attack such a threatening figure. So he becomes a bully and attacks helpless classmates.

5. *Sublimation* is the process by which we redirect socially unacceptable impulses, transforming their psychic energy into acceptable and even admirable behavioral expressions. A composer or other artist may rechannel sexual energy into creations that are valued by society. Sublimation is considered to be the only one of the defense mechanisms that is positive and adaptive.

6. *Reaction formation* is the defense mechanism that transforms an unacceptable impulse or thought into its opposite. By unconsciously convincing ourselves that we think or feel exactly the opposite of what we actually do unconsciously think or feel, we protect our positive views of ourselves. We may be inwardly jealous of a neighbor's new luxury car and wish we had one like it, but consciously we decide that spending so much on a mere car is incredibly superficial and materialistic.

7. Through *rationalization*, we can transform threatening thoughts and explanations of behavior into nonthreatening ones. A woman married to a compulsive gambler may rationalize her husband's behavior by attributing it to his concern for the financial well-being of the family. She may also apply this defense mechanism to her own behavior.

8. When *regression* occurs, we revert to thinking and behaving in ways that are characteristic of an earlier stage of socioemotional development. When a newborn is added to the family, for example, older siblings may start acting more babyish to attract the attention that has been diverted to the newborn. Adults, too, may revert to childish behaviors when they do not get what they want. In this way, we ward off the anxiety or pain that we are experiencing in our present stage of development (see Chapter 11).

STAGES OF PERSONALITY DEVELOPMENT

Freud (1905/1964b) believed in the biological bases of personality. He proposed that psychosexual development (see gender- and sexuality-based development in Chapter 11) begins at birth and continues through adulthood. According to Freud, the four major stages of development are oral, anal, phallic, and genital. A set of personality characteristics is associated with each stage. The **oral stage** typically occurs during the first 2 years of life, when an infant explores sucking and other oral activity, learning that this behavior provides pleasure as well as nourishment. The **anal stage** typically occurs between the ages of 2 and 4 years, when the child is potty trained and learns to derive pleasure from urination and especially defecation. The **phallic stage** typically begins at about 4 years of age and continues until about age 6, during which time children discover that genital stimulation feels good.

The phallic stage can give rise to the **Oedipal conflict,** in which the child starts to have romantic feelings for the parent of the opposite sex and thus feels jealous of and competitive with the parent of the same sex. In particular, boys desire their mothers but fear the wrath of their fathers. The conflict is named for the Greek myth in which Oedipus, who had long been separated from his parents and therefore did not recognize them, killed his father and married his mother. Girls may desire their fathers but worry about the wrath of their mothers (sometimes called the **Electra conflict,** after the Greek myth in which Electra despised her mother for having cheated on and killed her husband). Freud believed that the Oedipus and Electra complexes were the bases for the development of gender identity in childhood.

According to Freud, the Oedipal and Electra conflicts cause great turmoil in children. To resolve the conflict, children must accept the sexual unattainability of their parents. The feelings they directed toward the opposite-sex parent become *sublimated*—redirected in a socially acceptable fashion.

In the **latency stage,** children repress their sexual feelings toward their parents and sublimate their sexual energy into productive endeavors. During adolescence, the feelings that children once experienced toward the parent of the opposite sex are directed toward a contemporary of the opposite sex. Ultimately, the child enters into the **genital stage,** when the individual develops a mature relationship with a partner. For Freud, personality development is more or less completed by the end of adolescence. But, according to Freud, at any point during psychosexual development, an individual might become **fixated,** unable to resolve the relevant issues of the current stage and therefore unable to progress to the next stage. Fixations arise when individuals experience substantial dissatisfaction or discomfort at a stage of development. Fixation in a given stage of development means that the individual shows the characteristics of that stage in adulthood. (See Table 15.2.)

EVALUATING FREUD'S THEORY

Freud's theory was groundbreaking. But it generated heated debate that continues to this day. Some psychologists are concerned about the population upon which Freud based many of his conclusions. Many of Freud's ideas came from observations of patients in his clinical neurological practice. Because one is inevitably closely involved professionally with one's patients, there is a risk of bias in developing theories from these patients. Most of the patients were women referred to Freud because of *hysterical symptoms*—physical complaints for which no medical causes could be found.

Freud's case-study approach was both intensive and qualitative. It was *intensive* in the sense that Freud subjected each case to penetrating scrutiny. His analyses were *qualitative* because he made no effort to quantify anything about them.

Many psychologists think that Freud placed too much emphasis on sex as the basis of a general theory of development. Freud's theory clearly reflects the particular context of his times, as evidenced by his traditional views of female sex roles and sexual orienta-

tion, as well as his heavy emphasis on the role of sexual repression in normal adult feelings, thoughts, and behavior. Some of Freud's followers developed theories that are less sexually oriented, in part as a reaction to Freud's emphasis.

THE NEO-FREUDIANS

Freud's work inspired many to follow him and many to oppose him. The sheer abundance of theories that can be viewed as reactions to different aspects of Freud's indicates the immense influence of his work. In this way, Freud resembles Jean Piaget (see Chapter 10), whose enormous influences also prompted many psychologists to create their own theories (see, e.g., Berg & Sternberg, 1992).

The neo-Freudians emphasized the importance of continued interaction with others and the world to the development of personality throughout the life span. Indeed, Henry Stack Sullivan (1953) believed that all of personality develops through interpersonal interactions. Most neo-Freudians, however, took a less extreme position.

ALFRED ADLER: INDIVIDUAL PSYCHOLOGY

Alfred Adler was one of Freud's earliest students. He was also one of the first to break with Freud, disagreeing with many of his views. For example, Adler did

---

TABLE 15.2

Freud's Examples of Psychosexual Fixation. Freud posited that a set of personality characteristics were associated with each stage of psychosexual development. Fixation in a given stage results in the individual showing those characteristics in adulthood. (After Freud, 1905/1964b)

State	Characteristics Associated with Fixation
Oral (birth to age 2)	Displays many activities centered around the mouth: excessive eating, drinking, smoking, talking
Oral eroticism	Sucking and eating predominate; cheerful, dependent, and needy; expects to be taken care of by others
Oral sadism	Biting and chewing predominate; tends to be cynical and cruel
Anal (ages 2 to 4)	Displays any activities suggestive of the anal stage
Anal-retentive	Excessively neat, clean, meticulous, and obsessive
Anal-expulsive	Moody, sarcastic, biting, and often aggressive; untidy in personal habits
Phallic (age 4 to middle childhood)	Overly preoccupied with self; often vain and arrogant; unrealistic level of self-confidence and self-absorption
Latency (middle childhood)	Demonstrates sexual sublimation and repression
Genital (adolescence through adulthood)	Adopts traditional sex roles and heterosexual orientation

Alfred Adler (1870–1937) believed that all psychological phenomena are directed toward the goal of superiority. His "inferiority complex" is often used to describe people whose personalities center on feelings of inferiority.

not accept Freud's view that people are victimized by competing and largely instinctual inner forces. Adler believed that all psychological phenomena within the individual are unified and consistent. Although we may seem to behave inconsistently or unpredictably, our behaviors can be understood as being consistently directed toward a single goal: *superiority.*

According to Adler, personality develops in large part from the energy of striving for superiority by attempting to become as competent as possible in everything we do. Olympic athletes and famous musicians are outstanding examples of people who achieve superiority, but all of us strive for it. This striving for superiority gives meaning and coherence to our actions. Unfortunately, however, some of us feel that we cannot become superior. We develop what Adler termed an **inferiority complex** when we organize our thoughts, emotions, and behavior on the basis of perceived mistakes and shortcomings.

Adler also proposed that our actions are largely shaped by our *expectations for the future,* through the goals we set, rather than by our past experiences and development, which Freud had emphasized. Adler referred to these expectations as *fictions.* Thus, in his view we are motivated not by what is actually true but rather by our *subjective perceptions.* If a man believes that his coworkers are putting him down behind his

back, he is likely to act in ways that reflect his belief, whether or not it has any factual basis.

Finally, Adler believed in the importance of birth order. He suggested that first-borns are more likely than later-borns to strive toward and reach high levels of achievement.

CARL JUNG: ANALYTICAL PSYCHOLOGY

Like Freud, Carl Jung, a Swiss psychologist, believed that the mind consists of conscious and unconscious parts. Jung was originally close to Freud, but when his ideas went in a different direction, Freud terminated their association. Jung theorized that the unconscious was quite different from what Freud had suggested. Jung referred to the first layer of the unconscious as the **personal unconscious,** which stores each person's unique experiences and repressed memories. He believed that the contents of the personal unconscious are organized in **complexes,** clusters of independently functioning, emotionally tinged unconscious thoughts. Jung's addition of another layer to the unconscious was what distinguished him as radically different from Freud.

Jung's second layer of the mind is the **collective unconscious,** which contains memories and

Carl Jung (1875–1961) believed that the unconscious comprises both a personal unconscious, distinct to each individual, and a collective unconscious, which stores universal personality archetypes that are common to everyone.

behavioral predispositions inherited from common ancestors in the distant human past. People across space and time tend to interpret and use experiences in similar ways because of archetypes, universal inherited human tendencies to perceive and act on things in particular ways. Archetypes in the collective unconscious are roughly analogous to complexes in the personal unconscious, except that complexes are individual and archetypes are shared. To Jung, the fact that myths, legends, religions, and even cultural customs are similar across cultures is evidence for the existence of archetypes within the collective unconscious.

Jung believed that certain personal archetypes have evolved in ways that make them particularly important in our lives:

Persona: The part of our personality that we show the world; the part that we are willing to share with others.

Shadow: The darker part of us, the things about ourselves we view as frightening, hateful, and even evil; the part of us that we hide not only from others but also from our conscious awareness.

Anima: The side of a man's personality that shows tenderness, caring, compassion, and warmth toward others, and yet that tends to be irrational and emotional.

Animus: The practical, competent side of a woman's personality that tends to be rational and logical.

General archetypes in our collective unconscious include the great mother, the wise old man, and the hero. Many of these archetypes play major roles in fairy tales. Jung posited that men often try to hide their anima because it contradicts their idealized image of what men should be. A man might learn never to cry or might avoid taking care of children, assuming that women are more nurturing.

According to Jung, archetypes play a role in our interpersonal relationships. For example, the relationship between a man and a woman calls into play the archetypes in each individual's collective unconscious. The anima helps the man understand his female companion, just as the animus helps the woman understand her male companion. However, we may fall in love with our idealization of a man or a woman, based on archetypes in the collective unconscious, rather than with the other person as he or she really is. In fact, people do seem to look for ideals in their relationships (R. J. Sternberg & Barnes, 1985; see Chapter 13), although it is not at all clear that the ideals derive from any collective unconscious. Jung believed that the self, the whole of the personality, including

FIGURE 15.1

Mandala. The mandala (Sanskrit for "circle") is used as an object of meditation, and was viewed by Carl Jung as a symbol of the search for inner unity.

both conscious and unconscious elements, strives for unity among often opposing parts of the personality (see Figure 15.1).

KAREN HORNEY: PSYCHOANALYTIC THEORY

Although Karen Horney trained in the psychoanalytic tradition, she later broke with Freud in several key respects. A major contribution was her recognition that Freud's view of personality development was male-oriented and that his concepts of female development were inadequate (Horney, 1937, 1939). Perhaps most fundamentally, Horney believed that *cultural* rather than biological variables are the fundamental basis for the development of personality. She argued that the psychological differences between men and women are not the result of biology or anatomy, but rather of cultural expectations for each gender. She believed that what women really want are the privileges that the culture gives only to men (Horney, 1939). Indeed, her own career was delayed until a German university was willing to admit women to study medicine.

The essential concept in Horney's theory is *basic anxiety* (Horney, 1950), a feeling of isolation and helplessness in a world conceived of as potentially hostile due to the competitiveness of modern culture. As a result of this competitive climate, we have particularly strong needs for affection, which are not easily met by

Karen Horney (1885–1952) believed that the female personality reflects the desire for privileges that culture gives only to men (Horney, 1939).

Object-relations theory emphasizes the attachment between parent and infant as crucial to personality development, particularly affecting the ability to form close relationships with others.

society. Horney (1937) suggested that we can protect ourselves from the discomfort of basic anxiety in three ways. We can allay it by *showing affection and submissiveness*, which moves us toward other people. We can be aggressive, *striving for power, prestige, or possession*, which moves us against other people. Finally, we can allay anxiety by *withdrawing from people* and avoiding them altogether.

OBJECT-RELATIONS THEORIES

A contemporary extension of psychodynamic theory is **object-relations theory**, which holds that people relate to one another and conceptualize their relationships largely in terms of their investment in other people or *objects*. These concepts are mental representations of fundamental sources of sustenance and comfort, such as the mother, the father, friends, and teachers. In object-relations theory, *investments* in other people are more than just outlets for satisfying our instincts. Some object relations are primary and provide structure for the self. For example, a child may be invested in receiving affection and attention from a rejecting classmate because the child had a rejecting relationship with his or her parents. According to

object-relations theorists, people who develop successful object relations generally become emotionally stable, whereas those who do not are at risk for mental disorders (Blatt, Auerbach, & Levy, 1997; Kernberg, 1975; Klein, 1975; Kohut, 1984; Oberlechner, 2002; see also Goldstein, 2001). Secure adults are able to talk openly about their relationships with their parents, for instance (Main et al., 1985).

Whereas Freud particularly emphasized the Oedipal conflict, which arises around the age of 6, object-relations theorists look back even further, especially to the infant's attachment to the mother (see the discussion of attachment theory in Chapter 11). Thus, maladaptive behavior in later life can be caused by unsuccessful early attachment or an environment that provides harsh and inconsistent treatment of the young child (Ainsworth, 1989; Herman, Perry, & Van der Kolk, 1989). In an extension of object-relations theory, *relational theories* view the need for relatedness as central to healthy adaptation (Aron, 1996). According to these theories, we even modify our personalities in order to maintain and develop close ties with people who are important to us.

Object-relations theory, then, differs from classical psychodynamic theory in three main ways

(Horner, 1991; Hughes, 1989). First, whereas Freud emphasized the fear of the father that develops during the Oedipal period, object-relations theorists emphasize the attachment to the mother that develops during the first 2 years (as studied by Bowlby, 1958). Second, whereas Freud emphasized impulse gratification and the role of the unconscious in achieving it, object-relations theorists emphasize the need for attachment in human relationships, in adulthood as well as in childhood. Third, whereas Freud viewed the nature of female development as problematic and difficult to understand, object-relations theorists view male development as being somewhat puzzling (Chodorow, 1978, 1992; Dinnerstein, 1976; Sagan, 1988). These theorists believe that infants of both sexes initially identify with the mother, who, according to Bowlby, is the first figure to which the infant is attached. Boys, but not girls, need to break away from this attachment to reidentify with the father. It remains an open question whether the tendency to identify initially with the mother is biologically programmed or simply a cultural convention (Chodorow, 1992).

EVALUATING THE PSYCHODYNAMIC APPROACH

Table 15.3 comparatively evaluates psychodynamic research as a whole, using the criteria specified at the outset of this chapter. As the table shows, psychodynamic theories have been highly influential but have fostered relatively little experimental research because they are most often concerned with the uniqueness of individuals and because it has been difficult to make empirically testable predictions. Most research is relatively limited in scope. Psychodynamic theories vary in their comprehensiveness. Freud's is rather comprehensive, but others are less so. Theorists have produced extensive approaches and techniques.

Some theorists believe that psychodynamic theories are too deterministic and fatalistic in their approach to human nature. Nevertheless, the approach remains active today, and many psychologists use it in their research (Westen, 1992, 1998; Westen & Gabbard, 1999). In the next section, we consider humanistic theories of personality, which in many respects represent a rebellion against the psychodynamic point of view.

TABLE 15.3
CONCEPT REVIEW

Psychodynamic Theories: A Critical Evaluation. Psychodynamic theories get high marks for influencing psychology, as well as for comprehensiveness.

Criteria	Psychodynamic Approaches
Importance to and influence in psychology	Freud, the first major psychodynamic theorist, remains the most influential thinker in personality psychology. Many clinical psychologists (especially psychiatrists) today adhere to Freudian or neo-Freudian perspectives.
Testability of its propositions	Theories do not rate high for testability. Relatively small number of experiments, none of which studied the theories as a whole or fully compared and contrasted them. Case studies are open to many interpretations; research has proven to be nondefinitive.
Comprehensiveness	Reasonably complete account of personality phenomena. Freud's theory is comprehensive, as are Adler's and Erikson's, but many other neo-Freudian theories (e.g., Horney) are much less so. Although Jung's theory is relatively comprehensive, it is in part mystical. All the theories are derived from work with patients who presented adjustment problems and so are more descriptive of the structures and processes underlying extraordinary problems than of those of normal people with milder, more usual problems.
Parsimony	Less parsimonious than some theories, but the number of constructs is not excessive.
Usefulness to applications in assessment and psychotherapy	The TAT, Rorschach, and other projective tests have arisen from these theories.

THE HUMANISTIC APPROACH

How are the values of humanism expressed in humanistic psychology's view of personality?

The humanistic tradition in philosophy dates back to the ancient Greeks. It reflects a philosophical approach centered on the unique character of humans and their relationship to the natural world, on human interactions, on human concerns, and on secular human values. Humanism emphasizes the individual's potential for growth and change. Unlike other living organisms, humans are future-oriented and purposeful in their actions. To a large extent, we can create our own lives and determine our own destinies. We do not allow ourselves to be shaped by inexplicable forces outside our conscious control. One aspect of the humanists' nondeterministic perspective is a heavy emphasis on the role of conscious rather than unconscious experience. We consider two major humanistic theorists: Abraham Maslow and Carl Rogers.

ABRAHAM MASLOW: HOLISTIC-DYNAMIC THEORY

In Abraham Maslow's theory of motivation, which is based upon a hypothetical hierarchy of needs, the need for self-actualization is the highest level (see Chapter 12 for a full description of the hierarchy). Maslow (1970) believed that self-actualized people are free of mental illness. They have experienced love and have a true sense of their self-worth and value. They accept both themselves and others unconditionally and accept what the world brings to them. They have a keen perception of reality and can discern genuineness in others, shunning phoniness in themselves. They are neutral and ethical in their dealings with others. As they face the events in their lives, they see problems for what they are, rather than in relation to themselves and their own needs. They are able to be alone without feeling lonely, and they can map out their own paths. They have constructed their own system of beliefs and values and do not need others to agree with them in order to hold true to what they stand for. They appreciate and enjoy life and live it to its fullest.

CARL ROGERS: SELF THEORY

Carl Rogers's person-centered approach to personality strongly emphasizes the self and our perception of it. Rogers's *self theory* focuses on how the individual defines reality and personality, rather than on an external, objective view. Each person's conception of self begins in infancy and continues to develop throughout the life span. This *self-concept* comprises all the aspects of the self that the person perceives, whether or not the perceptions are accurate or shared by others. In addition, each of us has an *ideal self*, the personal characteristics that we would like to embody. A major contribution of Rogers (see the photograph on p. 615) was the recognition that the greater the similarity between the self-concept and the ideal self, the better adjusted the person is (C. R. Rogers, 1959, 1980; C. R. Rogers & Russell, 2002). Rogers (1978) argued that we tend to become more and more complex as we try to fulfill our potential. To Rogers, we have within us the power to make ourselves whatever we want to be, if only we choose to use this power.

Rogers (1961b, 1980) suggested that all people strive to be *fully functioning*, which is similar to Maslow's notion of the self-actualized person. According to Rogers, fully functioning persons have five characteristics:

1. They will constantly grow and evolve.
2. They will be open to experience, avoid defensiveness, and accept experiences as opportunities for learning.
3. They will trust themselves, and, although they will seek guidance from other people, they will make their own decisions rather than strictly following what others suggest.
4. They will have harmonious relations with other people and will realize that they do not need to be

well liked by everyone. Achieving unconditional acceptance from at least some others will free them from the need to be well liked by all.

5. They will live fully in the present rather than dwell on the past or live only for the future.

Note that a major difference between Rogers and Freud is that, for Rogers (as well as for Maslow) development is life-long. It does not stop in adolescence, but rather continues even into old age. Moreover, according to Rogers, people have a considerable amount of control over their development. For Freud, this is not true: Development is largely biologically controlled and outside a person's conscious control.

Both Maslow's and Rogers's descriptions of self-actualization may represent an ideal toward which we strive rather than a state that many of us are likely to reach. Few, if any, people meet all the criteria for self-actualization. Many people, however, have satisfied at least some of these criteria, for at least some of the time. These criteria are worthy of our strivings, even if we do fulfill them all.

EVALUATING THE HUMANISTIC APPROACH

Table 15.4 summarizes the humanistic approach in terms of the five criteria we used for evaluating the psychodynamic approach. The humanistic approach may not fully explain personality and its development.

It often seems to characterize the personality we can potentially achieve more than the one we actually have. Nonetheless, humanists encourage us to move beyond narrow views of ourselves in order to realize more of our great human potential. And they do have a concern with understanding and assessing personality, today as well as in the past (Fischer, 2002).

✓ CONCEPT CHECK 2

1. Humanism emphasizes
   a. reciprocal determinism.
   b. the relation of the anima to the animus.
   c. the potential of the individual for growth and change.
   d. cognitive change as a basis for behavioral change.
2. Carl Rogers proposed
   a. self theory.
   b. a hierarchy of motivations.
   c. the existence of a shadow side to personality.
   d. the dominance of the internal locus of control.
3. According to Maslow, self-actualized persons
   a. have conquered their repressions.
   b. never use defense mechanisms of any kind.
   c. accept themselves unconditionally.
   d. judge themselves by their behavior.

TABLE 15.4
CONCEPT REVIEW

Humanistic Theories: A Critical Evaluation. Humanistic messages are relevant to our experience today.

Criteria	Humanistic Approaches
Importance to and influence in psychology	Have generated relatively little controlled empirical research; messages continue to be important, however: focus on individuals, personal choices, opportunities to control fate, striving toward self-actualization.
Testability of its propositions	Almost untestable; predictions seldom operationally defined with enough precision to generate experiments.
Comprehensiveness	Although theories deal with some aspects of human nature (e.g., need for self-actualization or individual potential), they leave much unsaid; theories lack comprehensiveness.
Parsimony	Reasonably parsimonious; do not have many terms or overwhelming constructs.
Usefulness to applications in assessment and psychotherapy	Tend to be averse to assessment because tests focus on assigning labels to the client rather than on the person's evolving potential.

THE COGNITIVE-BEHAVIORAL APPROACH

What is distinctive about the cognitive-behavioral approach?

Cognitive-behavioral approaches to personality look at how people think, how they behave, and how their thought and behavior interact.

ANTECEDENTS

Behaviorists seek to understand personality in terms of the way people act. They also emphasize observable behavior, explaining it in terms of environmental contingencies.

B. F. Skinner (1974) saw people as having different personalities because they have been subjected to different environmental contingencies and schedules of reinforcement. Skinner did not deny that internal states might exist. He simply believed that they cannot be studied and therefore are not appropriate objects of psychological theory.

If we develop our personalities through patterns of reinforcement contingencies in the environment, then how do apparently maladjusted personalities develop? In the Skinnerian view, one way is by reinforcing antisocial behaviors, such as giving extra attention to a disruptive student. Another way is by punishing prosocial behaviors, such as disciplining a child for truthfully confessing to accidentally breaking a dish.

Behavioral psychologists, therefore, have tended to emphasize how people respond to the various contingencies of their environments. For example, they might understand the causes of depression in terms of low levels of reinforcing events. Not much happens in these people's lives that makes them happy. In contrast, cognitive psychologists are concerned with mental processes. Cognitive-behavioral psychologists are concerned with the link between mind and behavior.

JULIAN ROTTER: SOCIAL-LEARNING THEORY

Although Julian Rotter (b. 1916) is behaviorally oriented, he does not believe that behavior depends solely on external stimuli and reinforcements. Rather, what is important is the meaning that the person assigns to external experiences. If a person consistently behaves in a certain way because he or she consistently interprets situations in that way, then the mental inclination is part of the person's personality (Rotter, 1966, 1990; Rotter & Hochreich, 1975). Rotter, unlike Skinner, is interested in cognitive aspects of personality as well as behavioral ones.

Courtesy of Dr. Julian Rotter

Julian Rotter (b. 1916) believes that the importance of events lies in the meaning that we assign to them more than in external stimuli or reinforcers.

Rotter's focus on the individual's perceptions of the environment leads naturally to the most widely cited aspect of his theory. People with an **internal locus of control** believe that the causes of behavioral consequences originate within the individual. Internals tend to take personal responsibility for what happens to them. If such a person were laid off during an economic recession, he or she would still probably feel personally responsible for losing the job. At the extreme, an internal person misattributes causality to internal rather than to external causes.

In contrast, people with an **external locus of control** tend to believe that the causes of behavioral consequences originate in the environment. At the extreme, an external consistently would misattribute causality to external rather than to internal causes. Such a person who was fired due to incompetence or lack of effort would be likely to think that other factors (the boss's prejudice, coworkers' conspiracies, etc.) caused the termination. Thus, internals believe that they control their own fate, whereas externals tend to see fate as controlled by luck, by others, or by destiny. Thousands of studies, including some cross-cultural studies (Dyal, 1984), have focused on Rotter's theory and his *Internal–External (I–E) Control Scale* and have provided good support.

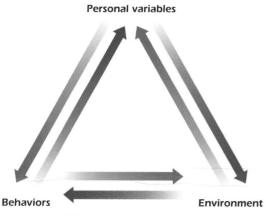

FIGURE 15.2
Reciprocal Determinism. In Albert Bandura's social-cognitive theory, personal variables, behaviors, and the environment reciprocally interact.

ALBERT BANDURA: SOCIAL-COGNITIVE THEORY

Albert Bandura's theory is truly a cognitive-behavioral one because it addresses the *interaction* between how we think and how we act. Bandura's (1986) model of **reciprocal determinism** attributes human functioning to the interactions of behaviors, personal variables, and the environment (see Figure 15.2). For example, your decision to go to college is affected by *personal variables*, such as motivation and the ability to succeed. This decision is also affected by *environmental events*, such as parental encouragement and access to funds. The result is *behavior*—going to college—which in turn affects the opportunities you have later in life, and which may affect personal variables as well, such as your level of happiness.

A crucial personal variable in personality is our set of beliefs in our own *self-efficacy*—that is, our feelings of competence to do things. Feelings of self-efficacy seem actually to lead to our being better able to do those things (Bandura, 1986; Zimmerman, Bandura, & Martinez-Pons, 1992; see Chapter 12). If I tell myself I cannot do something, then I often will not even try it, with the result that I will never really learn how to do it. If I go ahead and try to do the thing, while constantly telling myself that I will not succeed, then my negative expectations may get in the way of what I do, resulting in a negative self-fulfilling prophecy. Self-efficacy is an excellent predictor of success in many realms (Bandura, 1986, 2001).

EVALUATING COGNITIVE-BEHAVIORAL THEORIES

Table 15.5 offers a brief evaluation of the cognitive-behavioral approach. This approach to personality is particularly useful in therapy for achieving behavioral

TABLE 15.5
CONCEPT REVIEW

Cognitive-Behavioral Theories: A Critical Evaluation. Cognitive-behavioral theories have inspired a great deal of research interest, partly because their propositions are highly testable.

Criteria	Cognitive-Behavioral Approaches
Importance to and influence in psychology	Have generated much research by personality theorists and others.
Testability of its propositions	More testable than psychodynamic or humanistic approaches; strong data.
Comprehensiveness	Less comprehensive than other views, these theories do not specify the dimensions on which people differ; they say less than other theories about the structure of personality.
Parsimony	These theories rate high on parsimony, especially Bandura's because he adhered so closely to his data; Rotter's theory is only slightly less parsimonious.
Usefulness to applications in assessment and psychotherapy	Rotter's locus of control and interpersonal trust scales are widely used, but they measure only narrow bands of personality. Cognitive-behavioral theories have generated many different methods of psychotherapy (see Chapter 17) and are very influential in health psychology (see Chapter 18).

change, perhaps because of its emphasis on conscious rather than unconscious function. It is much easier for us to gain access to and to change things about which we are conscious. If our behaviors and our thoughts fall outside of our awareness and cannot be made conscious except with great difficulty, then we are hard-pressed to change them. By concentrating on what we are aware of, the cognitive-behavioral approach enables us to implement change more directly and, many would argue, more effectively as well.

Because cognitive-behavioral theories focus on the interactions between how people think and how they behave, however, the theories do not specify any distinctive traits that characterize people and how they differ.

✓ **CONCEPT CHECK 3**

1. A student has failed a test and berates herself for her having done such a poor job. She is most likely an
   a. external.
   b. internal.
   c. extravert.
   d. introvert.
2. Reciprocal determinism emphasizes the inter-relationship between
   a. motivation and personality.
   b. mind and body.
   c. time and space.
   d. how we think and how we act.
3. Cognitive-behavioral theories
   a. are not really testable.
   b. are testable but have not generated much research.
   c. are testable and have generated some studies.
   d. are testable and have generated a lot of research.

THE TRAIT-BASED APPROACH

Do our personalities reflect distinguishable, consistent traits?

Traits are a person's stable characteristics. Is there one set of traits from which all our personalities emerge, or does each person possess different traits? One of the deans of personality theory, Gordon Allport, believed that much of personality is characterized by personal dispositions, traits that are unique to each individual (Allport, 1937, 1961). Although Allport also mentioned *common traits* (which are shared across individuals), he believed that much of what makes each of us who we are can be found in the personal dispositions rather than in the common traits.

Allport also believed that each person's various traits differ in their importance for the person. Some people possess a cardinal trait, which is so salient in an individual's personality and so dominant in the person's behavior that almost everything the person does somehow relates back to this trait (Allport, 1961). Although not everyone has a cardinal trait, all people do have central traits—the 5 to 10 most salient traits in a person's disposition that affect much of the person's behavior. In addition, all people have secondary traits—personality traits that have some bearing on a person's behavior but are not particularly central.

Other theorists believe that all people have essentially the same set of traits and that people differ only in the extent to which they manifest each trait. Some of these theories try to specify the whole range of personality, suggesting a list of traits believed to characterize fully what people are like. Other theories deal with just a single trait, but in great depth.

HANS EYSENCK: THREE DIMENSIONS OF PERSONALITY

The simplicity of Eysenck's theory is one reason some researchers have accepted it. Another reason is the extensive research base that backs up the theory. Hans Eysenck (1952, 1981) argued that personality comprises three major traits: extroversion, neuroticism, and psychoticism. Extroversion characterizes people who are sociable, expansive, lively, and oriented toward having fun. Introversion, in contrast, characterizes people who are quiet, reserved, and generally unsociable. People characterized by neuroticism are nervous, emotionally unstable, moody, tense, and irritable, and they frequently worry. Emotionally stable people tend to be less fretful, more uniform in their behavior, and less subject to sudden mood swings. People characterized by psychoticism are solitary, are detached from others in their interpersonal relationships, lack feelings, and especially lack caring, empathy, and sensitivity (see Figure 15.3 and the Psychology in Everyday Life box, "Psychoticisms in Everyday Life"). Research suggests that the personality traits in Eysenck's theory can be predictive of health outcomes. For example, smokers who also score high on Eysenck's neuroticism scale are particularly susceptible to heart disease (Marusic, Gudjonsson, Eysenck, & Starc, 1999).

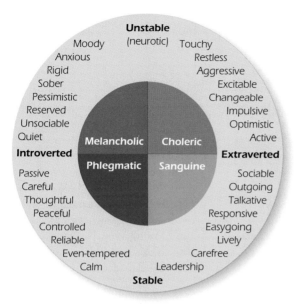

Moody
Anxious
Rigid
Sober
Pessimistic
Reserved
Unsociable
Quiet

Unstable
(neurotic)

Touchy
Restless
Aggressive
Excitable
Changeable
Impulsive
Optimistic
Active

Introverted

Melancholic | **Choleric**

Extraverted

Phlegmatic | **Sanguine**

Passive
Careful
Thoughtful
Peaceful
Controlled
Reliable
Even-tempered
Calm

Sociable
Outgoing
Talkative
Responsive
Easygoing
Lively
Carefree
Leadership

Stable

FIGURE 15.3

Eysenck's Personality Dimensions. This chart illustrates two of the three personality dimensions described by Hans Eysenck. (His third dimension, psychoticism, is not shown.)

THE BIG FIVE PERSONALITY TRAITS

As you may have noticed, many theorists, even those with different approaches, mention some of the same key personality characteristics (termed *traits, factors,* etc.). The **Big Five** theory of personality recognizes five personality traits: neuroticism, extroversion, openness, agreeableness, and conscientiousness.

1. *Neuroticism:* characterized by nervousness, emotional instability, moodiness, tension, irritability, and a tendency to worry.
2. *Extroversion:* characterized by sociability, expansiveness, liveliness, an orientation toward fun, and an interest in interacting with other people.
3. *Openness:* characterized by imaginativeness, intelligence, curiosity, and aesthetic sensitivity.
4. *Agreeableness:* characterized by a pleasant disposition, a charitable nature, empathy toward others, and friendliness.
5. *Conscientiousness:* characterized by reliability, hard work, punctuality, and a concern about doing things right.

The Big Five theory is based on analyses of the main kinds of terms people use to describe personality. It is probably the most widely accepted of the current theories. It is also well supported. The traits were first proposed by Warren Norman (1963) but have since been championed by many other investigators (e.g., Costa & McCrae, 1992a, 1992b, 1995; Costa & Widiger, 2002a, 2002b; Goldberg & Saucier, 1995; McCrae & Costa, 1997; Saucier & Goldberg, 2002).

Sometimes different names are used to refer to the same personality traits.

A number of studies have found supporting evidence for the Big Five, in both children and adults, and in countries around the world, including Australia, China, Germany, Israel, Japan, and South Korea (J. A. Johnson & Ostendorf, 1993; McCrae, Costa, & Yik, 1996; Montag & Levin, 1994; Noller, Law, & Comrey, 1987; Ostendorf & Angleitner, 1994; Piedmont & Chae, 1997; Wiggins, 1996; Wiggins & Trapnell, 1997; J. Yang et al., 2002). Moreover, these traits appear to endure throughout the entire life span, even up to the mid-90s, the highest ages that have been studied (Costa & McCrae, 1988). Some traits appear to be associated with personal feelings of well-being—in particular, openness to experience, agreeableness, and extroversion (Magnus, Diener, Fujita, & Pavot, 1993; McCrae, 1996; McCrae & Costa, 1991). Others, such as neuroticism, are associated with poorer life adjustment (Ormel & Wohlfarth, 1991). High scores on extroversion, and especially the aspect related to positive emotions, predict positive mood in everyday life (Velting & Liebert, 1997).

Some studies have looked at the relationship between Eysenck's theory and the Big Five theory (also called *five-factor theory*). One study found that people high in psychoticism tend to be low in agreeableness and that people low in psychoticism tend to be high in conscientiousness (Goldberg & Rosolack, 1994). Another study showed that low scores on neuroticism tend to be associated with high scores on extroversion (in both Eysenck's model and five-factor theory; Draycott & Kline, 1995).

Not all trait theorists agree with five-factor theory, of course. Block (1995) and Hogan (1996) have argued that the evidence suggests more about the way people perceive personality traits than about actual people, a point that itself has been disputed (Costa & McCrae, 1995). Moreover, there may be personality traits beyond these five. Saucier and Goldberg (1998) have suggested personality clusters related to Fashionableness, Sensuality/Seductiveness, Beauty, Masculinity, Frugality, Humor, Wealth, Prejudice, Folksiness, Cunning, and Luck, which are themselves related to Big Five traits. At present, the Big Five is probably the most widely accepted trait theory available.

EVALUATING TRAIT THEORIES

Psychologist Walter Mischel (1968) questioned trait theories. He argued that although traits might correlate highly from one paper-and-pencil measure to another, their correlations with any meaningful kinds of behavior are low, usually around 0.30. It turns out, however, that behavior across situations is no more

PSYCHOTICISMS IN EVERYDAY LIFE

Every so often we hear about people we would rather not get to know: sexual predators, serial killers, terrorist bombers, and the like. Do they have any personality characteristics in common?

According to Hans Eysenck (1975), most such people have very high levels of what he refers to as *psychoticism,* a predisposition to psychosis (see also Liebert & Liebert, 1998, from which this summary is drawn). People who are very high in psychoticism tend to be solitary and care little about others. They also tend to be troublesome and

do not fit in with society. They have a tendency to be cruel and inhumane as well as insensitive. They lack empathy, or genuine feelings for others. They also tend to be high in sensation seeking. They are apt to be hostile toward others and to behave aggressively. They may be eccentric and favor odd or unusual things or patterns of behavior. They are often foolhardy and disregard obvious danger. In social situations, they tend to be rude and may enjoy embarrassing or otherwise upsetting people. They are likely to be oppositional to accepted social cus-

toms and to avoid close personal interactions. They are also impulsive (Roger & Morris, 1991) and have problems in school (Furnham & Medhurst, 1995). These people are usually not religious (White, Joseph, & Neil, 1993), tending to show little or no church attendance or personal prayer (Lewis & Maltby, 1995; Maltby, 1995). They are also likely to be susceptible to drug use and risky sexual practices (Fontaine, 1994).

psychotic behavior
antisocial personality

---

highly correlated than are scores on personality traits. Studies of the cross-situational consistency of behavior have found correlations ranging from −0.11 to 0.47 (Funder, Kolar, & Blackman, 1995; Funder & Ozer, 1983; Sneed, McCrae, & Funder, 1998). Thus, these correlations center at about 0.20—if anything, a bit lower than is found with personality traits. The modest correlations for personality traits may therefore reflect limitations not in trait theory, but simply in how consistent human beings are in their feelings and behaviors. Behavior seems to be less consistent that some die-hard trait theorists might like to believe.

Mischel was not stating that higher correlations are impossible or that they are never obtained. For example, he noted that correlations were often higher for intelligence as a predictor of behavior. Still, the correlations in the personality literature were so low that he questioned whether the idea of personality traits had any basis at all. Mischel (1968; Mischel & Peake, 1983) suggested that personality theorists should concentrate on the relationships between situations and behavior, rather than on hypothetically stable traits, which, he claimed, had little effect on behavior. Today, Mischel's critique is considered less relevant than it once was (Westen, 1995). For one thing, new trait theories have been more successful than many earlier ones in predicting various kinds of behavior (Funder, 2000). For another thing, it is often difficult to separate the effects of personality traits from those of situations (Funder, 2001). Also, psychologists have recognized the importance of how personality interacts with situations.

Theorists differ in how strongly they emphasize the lifelong stability of traits. Some hold that personality traits are largely inborn and stable across the life span, whereas others believe that traits develop and change somewhat, although a predisposition to develop particular traits may exist at birth. Table 15.6 summarizes the trait-based approach to personality.

✓CONCEPT CHECK 4

1. According to Allport, the maximum number of cardinal traits per person is
   a. 0.
   b. 1.
   c. 3.
   d. 10.
2. Jason is creative but withdrawn from other people. He also does not care much about others. He exhibits what Eysenck calls
   a. neuroticism.
   b. extroversion.
   c. psychoticism.
   d. conscientiousness.
3. Which of the following is *not* one of the Big Five personality traits?
   a. psychoticism
   b. openness
   c. extroversion
   d. agreeableness

TABLE 15.6
CONCEPT REVIEW

Trait Theories: A Critical Evaluation. Because they are based in factor-analytical techniques, trait theories are highly testable and have generated a great many empirical studies.

Criteria	Trait-Based Approaches
Importance to and influence in psychology	Have generated much empirical research.
Testability of its propositions	Highly testable: Most theories make fairly precise predictions, especially compared with psychodynamic or humanistic theories.
Comprehensiveness	Those theories that focus on personality as a whole are comprehensive; those that focus on specific traits clearly are not. Trait theorists say less than others about the development of personality traits.
Parsimony	Depends on the theory: Eysenck's and the Big Five are extremely parsimonious.
Usefulness to applications in assessment and psychotherapy	Many trait theories have generated personality tests. They have generated far fewer therapeutic techniques than other theories; trait theorists focus more on static characteristics and less on dynamic processes.

THE BIOLOGICAL APPROACH

What is the role of biology in determining personality?

Some investigators take a biological approach to studying personality. Robert Plomin (Plomin & Colledge, 2001; Plomin & Crabbe, 2000; Plomin & McGuffin, 2003) has been interested in observing how both heredity and environment influence the developmental changes in our personalities, whether normal or abnormal. In Plomin's view, just as our physiological growth is influenced by heredity within an environmental framework, so are the growth of our personalities and their associated traits.

PERSONALITY, TEMPERAMENT, AND HERITABILITY

Research (e.g., Bouchard & Loehlin, 2001; Loehlin, 1992a, 1992b; Loehlin, McCrae, Costa, & John, 1998; Plomin, 1994, 1995, 2001) indicates that both nature and nurture, usually in interaction, contribute to the development of our distinctive personality traits

(T. F. Lee, 1993; Lyon & Gorner, 1995). Studies comparing identical twins raised apart as well as identical versus fraternal twins (see Chapter 9) have shown that about half of the individual-differences variation in many personality traits, as well as in intelligence, is inherited (Bouchard, 1997; Bouchard, Lykken, McGue, Segal, & Tellegen, 1990; Loehlin, 1992a, 1992b; Loehlin, Horn, & Willerman, 1997; Plomin, DeFries, McClearn, & Rutter, 1997). However, heritability may differ somewhat as a function of the particular trait as well as of the population in which it is studied. Heritability also varies as a function of age, with effects increasing as people grow older (McGue, Bouchard, Iacono, & Lykken, 1993).

Curiously, though, even certain kinds of attitudes, such as religious orientation, and of behavior, such as watching television in childhood and divorcing in adulthood, show substantial heritability (McGue et al., 1993; Plomin et al., 1997). How could television-watching behavior be heritable, given that TV was not widely available before the 1950s? How could divorce be heritable, when to this day it is not even permitted in some societies? Clearly, it is not the behavior itself that is inherited, but rather the personal predispositions that can lead to it.

Recall from Chapter 12 that *temperament* is an individual's tendency to feel a given emotion with a particular intensity and duration. Work by Jerome Kagan (1994, 2003) and others has suggested that temperament may be, in part, heritable. Babies show marked differences in temperament immediately after birth. Although these differences may be caused in part by differences in intrauterine environments, it seems likely that genetics also plays a role.

Interestingly, the variation in traits that is environmental is mostly *within* rather than *between* families (Dunn & Plomin, 1990). In other words, differences in the way children are treated within families (e.g., earlier-born versus later-born siblings) are more important than differences between families. We still have much to learn, however, about just what these differences are.

BIOLOGICAL CORRELATES OF DISPOSITION AND TEMPERAMENT

Some researchers look for direct biological causes or correlates of personality dispositions. One group of studies links aspects of personality to genes. For example, hyperactivity in childhood has been linked to a gene that serves as a transporter for dopamine (Cook et al., 1995). Moreover, a dopamine receptor gene has been linked to the trait of novelty seeking (Ebstein et al., 1996). Another group of studies links aspects of personality to the brain (R. J. Davidson & Sutton, 1995). Behavioral inhibition—the tendency to experience strong negative affect or to feel inhibited in the face of threats—has been linked to greater left-hemisphere activation of the prefrontal cortex (Sutton & Davidson, 1997; see also R. J. Davidson, 1994b).

Some researchers have attempted to integrate the biological and trait approaches. Buss (1994, 1995, 2001, 2003) has suggested that the Big Five theory is useful because it represents the results of evolutionary adaptations. According to this point of view, each of the five traits represents a different kind of adaptation. For example, extroversion represents the tendency to bond with others. Agreeableness indicates an individual's willingness to cooperate with others. Neuroticism shows a lack of facility in handling stress. Openness to experience signals the tendency to be an innovative problem solver. Conscientiousness predicts the tendency to be reliable. This evolutionary interpretation is speculative, however. Moreover, trait theories deal largely with individual differences, whereas evolutionary theory deals mostly with human commonalities. It is not clear how much the study of the one is likely to illuminate the other.

Another interesting line of research relates behavior associated with personality dimensions to asymmetries in temperatures in the two tympanic membranes, or eardrums (Boyce et al., 2002). In 4-year-old children, temperature differences across the two eardrums were associated with individual differences in behavior and socioemotional difficulties. Warmer left eardrums were associated with warmer personality and affectively positive behaviors, whereas warmer right eardrums were related to problematic, affectively negative personality and behaviors. These findings suggest that asymmetries in tympanic-membrane temperatures could be associated with behavior problems that signal risk for abnormal development.

EVALUATING THE BIOLOGICAL APPROACH

One advantage of the biological approach is that it relates personality directly to the brain and other structures. But it by no means answers all questions. So far, it has not helped us identify just what the personality traits are. It tends to be stronger on specific findings than on an overarching theoretical framework. It seems most useful when it is tied in, one way or another, with some other approach. For example, biological indices may be related to scores on personality tests, or to temperamental variables, or to behaviors. The approach thus combines well with other approaches in helping us understand the nature and functioning of personality.

Table 15.7 summarizes the biological approach to personality.

✓ CONCEPT CHECK 5

1. The tendency to divorce is
   a. not subject to heritability analysis.
   b. not heritable.
   c. somewhat heritable.
   d. perfectly heritable.
2. Heritability of traits tends to
   a. stay the same across the life span.
   b. increase with age.
   c. decrease with age.
   d. first increase and then decrease with age.
3. Variation in traits is
   a. more within than between families.
   b. more between than within families.
   c. about the same within and between families.
   d. not comparable between and within families.

TABLE 15.7
CONCEPT REVIEW

Biological Theories: A Critical Evaluation. Biological theories rate high in testability, which can result in more empirical research.

Criteria	Biological Approaches
Importance to and influence in psychology	Have generated some empirical research.
Testability of its propositions	Testable; most theories make empirically testable predictions.
Comprehensiveness	These theories tend to focus on specific aspects of personality and, hence, are generally not comprehensive.
Parsimony	These theories generally are quite parsimonious.
Usefulness to applications in assessment and psychotherapy	Biological theories have not yet generated viable personality tests. Many biological therapies are available, but they do not derive from biologically based theories of personality.

INTERACTIONIST PERSPECTIVES

How might personality result from the interaction of environmental, biological, and other factors?

An *interactionist perspective* emphasizes how personal and situational characteristics work together. Interactionist perspectives are not limited to trait theories. Indeed, Rotter's, Bandura's, and other theorists' approaches can be viewed as broadly interactionist. In fact, even Mischel, who originally took the strictly cognitive-behavioral approach, now views personality from an interactionist perspective.

The basic idea is simple: Correlations among traits, or between traits and behaviors, depend on the kinds of situations the particular person encounters. To relate extroversion to happiness, for example, the interactionist would suggest that extroverts will be happy if they are in constant interactions with other people but will be unhappy if stranded on a desert island by themselves. From the interactionist point of view, then, the correlation between personality traits and various kinds of behavior, or even between one trait and another, is me-

diated by situations. Thus, whereas a trait theorist might look only at the trait, and a behaviorist might look only at the situation, the interactionist would look at the interaction between the personality trait and the situation (Bowers, 1973; Endler & Magnusson, 1976).

One interactionist idea is Mark Snyder's construct of *self-monitoring*, the degree to which people monitor and change their behavior in response to situational demands (Snyder, 1979, 1983; Cremer, Snyder, & Dewitte, 2001; Gangestad & Snyder, 2000). High self-monitors behave very differently depending on with whom they are associating. Such a person might act one way in the presence of a professor but in a totally different way when the professor is not there. Low self-monitors are more consistent in their behavior, acting much the same with everyone. If we wanted to look at consistency of behavior across situations, we would want to know about people's tendency to monitor themselves.

Another concept that examines how people react to various kinds of situations is the construct of *sensation seeking*, which is a generalized preference for relatively higher versus lower levels of sensory stimulation (M. Zuckerman, 1998, 2002; M. Zuckerman & Kuhlman, 2000). People who are high in sensation seeking tend to show four main attributions. First, they tend to seek thrills, such as skydiving and bungee jumping. Second, they tend to seek new experiences, such as trav-

TABLE 15.8
CONCEPT REVIEW

Five Major Personality Paradigms. The major personality paradigms are psychodynamic, humanistic, cognitive-behavioral, trait, and biological theories.

	Paradigm				
	Psychodynamic	**Humanistic**	**Cognitive-Behavioral-**	**Trait**	**Biological**
Major Theorists	Freud, Adler, Jung, Horney	Rogers, Maslow	Rotter, Bandura, Mischel (also interactionists)	Eysenck	David Buss, Marvin Zuckerman
Basis for Personality	Conflicting sources of psychic energy	The distinctive human ability to act purposefully and to shape our own destiny by being future-oriented	The interactions between thought and the environment, which influence behavior	Stable sources of individual differences that characterize an individual, based on an interaction of nature and nurture	Evolutionary adaptations/biological attributes (e.g., hormonal influences)
Key Features of Personality Theory	(a) Developmental changes across the life span; early childhood experiences profoundly influencing adult personality (b) *Deterministic* view of personality as largely governed by forces over which the individual has little control (c) Importance of unconscious processes in shaping personality and behavior	*Nondeterministic* view of personality as subject to the conscious control of the individual	(a) How individuals think about and give meaning to stimuli and to their own behavior shapes personality and affects behavior (b) People need to feel that they are competent in controlling their environment.	Some theorists hold that everyone has the same set of traits, but that individuals differ in the degree to which they manifest that trait. Other theorists hold that each individual has a different set of traits.	Biological theorists believe that personality is best explained by brain-based individual differences. These theorists may study the brain or mechanisms of the transmission of traits from one generation to the other.
Basis for Theory Development	Case studies of individuals seeking help for psychological problems	Humanistic philosophy, personal experiences, and clinical practice	Experimental findings, as well as the development and use of personality tests	Trait theorists often use correlational methods and factor analysis to analyze their data.	Biological theorists use a wide variety of methods, including brain scans and studies of people's genetic profiles.

eling to exotic places or trying out unusual foods. Third, they tend to be uninhibited and thus are more likely to engage in alcohol use or sexual activity. Finally, they tend to be highly susceptible to boredom and often seek to break out of what they perceive as the monotony of life. People with higher levels of sensation seeking are more at risk for substance abuse and other problems in school and at work (Horvath & Zuckerman, 1993; Zuckerman, 1990). In general, people tend to have greater success with partners who match them in sensation-seeking level (Schroth, 1991). Sensation seeking is supposed to have both biological and environmentally socialized aspects.

In conclusion, interactionists build on the trait-based approach by asserting that the predictive validity of personality measures for behavior can be moderated by the kinds of situations in which the behavior takes place, as well as by possible differences in intraindividual consistency in a given trait.

Table 15.8, on p. 556, summarizes the major approaches to personality we have covered in this chapter.

✓CONCEPT CHECK 6

1. Interactionist perspectives on personality emphasize the interaction between
   a. one person and another.
   b. nature and nurture.
   c. persons and situations.
   d. conscious and unconscious processes.
2. Ellen, a high self-monitor,
   a. behaves differently in different situations.
   b. understands exactly why she does what she does.
   c. is careful never to make mistakes.
   d. is highly susceptible to heart attacks.
3. High sensation-seekers are _____ to use alcohol _____ low sensation-seekers.
   a. less likely . . . than
   b. as likely . . . as
   c. more likely . . . than
   d. more likely early in the day, less likely later in the day . . . than

---

MEASURING PERSONALITY

How is personality measured?

PROJECTIVE TESTS

Many assessment techniques based on psychodynamic theory have emerged from attempts to probe the unconscious. Projective tests assess how people project

unconscious conflicts in their responses to examination. Many projective tests are used to assess constructs from psychodynamic theory; we describe only some here.

THE RORSCHACH INKBLOT TEST

In 1921, Hermann Rorschach devised the *Rorschach Inkblot Test*, which is still widely used. Originally, Rorschach viewed his test as potentially useful for diagnosing psychopathology, but today it is used much more commonly for assessing personality across a broad spectrum of individuals. Those who use the test believe it provides a means for exploring patients' needs, conflicts, and desires (Erdberg, 1990; Exner, 1978, 1985; D. Rapaport, Gill, & Schafer, 1968).

The test consists of 10 symmetrical inkblot designs, each printed on a separate card. Five of the blots are in black, white, and shades of gray, and the other five are in color. One Rorschach card is shown in Figure 15.4. Rorschach intentionally created the inkblots to be nonrepresentational. Although they do not look like anything in particular, people see things such as other people, insects, bats, and plants in them. People typically see several things in a single design. The examiner carefully records how the client describes each blot. Psychologists who use the Rorschach believe that people project themselves into the designs. Their answers reveal aspects of their psychological makeup.

Although many scoring systems have been devised for the Rorschach, the most widely used at present is John Exner's "Comprehensive System," which takes into account four factors: the *location, determinants, content,* and *popularity* of the responses (Exner, 1974, 1978, 1985, 1999; Meyer et al., 2002; Viglione & Exner, 1983).

THE THEMATIC APPERCEPTION TEST (TAT)

Another widely used psychodynamic assessment tool is the **Thematic Apperception Test (TAT)** (C. D. Morgan & Murray, 1935; H. A. Murray, 1943b). In administering the TAT, the examiner presents a series of ambiguous but realistic pictures. People allegedly project their feelings into these pictures when they suggest what has led up to the depicted scene, what is happening in it, and what will happen next. *Apperception* refers to this projection of personal associations into the usual stimulus. Henry Murray (1943c) suggested that the examiner must consider six things when scoring the TAT: (1) the hero of the story; (2) the hero's motives, actions, and feelings; (3) the forces in the hero's environment that act on the hero; (4) the outcomes of the story; (5) the types of environmental stimuli that impinge on the people in the story; and (6) the interests and sentiments that appear in the story (see Figure 15.5).

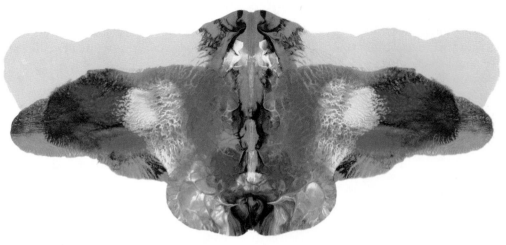

FIGURE 15.4
Rorschach Inkblot Test. What do you see?

The TAT may be scored for different kinds of motivation (see Chapter 12), such as achievement motivation (J. W. Atkinson, 1958; McClelland et al., 1953) and power motivation (Veroff, 1957; Winter, 1973, 1998, 2002). It can also be used to assess a person's use of defense mechanisms (Stewart, 1982; Stewart & Healy, 1985; Stewart, Sokol, Healy, & Chester, 1986).

FIGURE 15.5
Thematic Apperception Test (TAT). In the Thematic Apperception Test, illustrations of ambiguous situations are used to prompt test takers to project their own personalities into the scene.

On what bases can we appraise the various instruments used to assess people in psychodynamic terms? Some clinicians (e.g., Spangler, 1992; Stewart, 1982; Stewart & Healy, 1989) take projective tests such as the Rorschach and the TAT very seriously. Others believe that these tests lead clinicians to faulty decisions (Mischel, 1977, 1986). They believe that clinicians interpret test data based on what they would like to see in the data, not on what is actually implicit in the test data (see, e.g., L. J. Chapman & Chapman, 1969; Dawes, 1994). The subjective nature of scoring for projective tests has led many psychologists to use objective personality tests.

OBJECTIVE PERSONALITY TESTS

Objective personality tests are administered using a uniform standardized (i.e., objective) procedure for scoring the assessment instruments. Two popular tests that fall into this category are the NEO Five-Factor Inventory and the revised *Minnesota Multiphasic Personality Inventory*, or *MMPI-2* (Butcher, Dahlström, Graham, Tellegen, & Kaemmer, 1989; Butcher & Williams, 1992).

The NEO Personality Inventory Revised (NEO-PI-R; Costa & McCrae, 1992c) is a successor to an earlier instrument, the NEO-PI (Costa & McCrae, 1985). The NEO-PI-R contains 240 items that measure the five factors of the Big Five theory (neuroticism, extroversion, openness, agreeableness, and conscientiousness). It is a self-report inventory, requiring individuals to indicate whether certain statements characterize them.

The most widely used objective test for assessing personality as it reflects on abnormal behavior is

IN THE LAB OF LAURA KING

WRITING AS SELF-DISCLOSURE AND SELF-CONSTRUCTION

One of my key formative experiences was having a mother who was an avid soap opera watcher (some might say *addict,* but I won't). I vividly remember sitting on the living room floor while my mother set up her ironing board so she could watch "The Love of Life," "The Secret Storm," "All My Children," "As the World Turns," and "Guiding Light" while she kept up with her chores. She'd iron and quietly weep as another woman suffering from amnesia stayed married to the villain even though she was really in love with the hero. One thing you learn from watching soaps is that everyone will someday suffer amnesia or hysterical blindness, or spend time in a wheelchair. (Indeed, as a child I once memorized the number of steps between all the important landmarks in our house, in preparation for my own inevitable stint with blindness.) Another thing you learn from soaps is that everyone has a secret, something they are keeping to themselves behind a mysterious facial expression just before the commercial break. Terrible secrets lurk in the human mind, to be blurted out at the most inappropriate moment (to optimize the drama) or to be converted into some inexplicable symptom that will subside only when the truth comes out.

Although I eventually weaned myself of my own addiction to soaps (mostly), I maintained an interest in hidden secrets and their effects on people's lives. In graduate school, I discovered the work of Jamie Pennebaker (1997), who had

done fascinating work on how writing about traumatic life events affects psychological and physical well-being. The design of the experiments was quite straightforward. Participants were randomly assigned to write about their most traumatic life events. A control group wrote about a more neutral topic, such as their plans for the day. Everyone wrote for about 20 minutes each day for three or four days. One of the fascinating aspects of these studies was that no one in the trauma group ever had nothing to write about. Many people wrote about truly devastating tragedies that they had not previously disclosed. Not surprisingly, they felt increased distress immediately after writing. The surprising finding, however, was that weeks later, those who wrote about trauma showed significantly lower physical illness than those in the control group, and often showed enhanced psychological well-being as well. This finding has been replicated using a variety of different participants and focusing on a variety

of health outcomes, including enhanced immune-system function and self-assessed physical illnesses. Students who wrote about the major transition of coming to college even showed higher first-year grade-point averages. This work fascinated me. I loved the elegance of the science as well as the portrait of humanity it revealed. We all need to share some secret. If we could put our secret traumas into words, we could free ourselves from emotional burdens and enjoy our lives more.

But life isn't a soap opera, is it? Although it may be true that good drama requires negative events, I began to wonder about the good things that happen to us: Are they completely irrelevant to a psychological understanding of humanity? As a graduate student, I primarily studied people's goals and hopes and dreams—some very positive aspects of human life. In this work, we found that having personally valued goals and dreams toward which to strive was associated with

continued

Laura King received her PhD in personality psychology from the University of California, Davis, in 1991. She taught at Southern Methodist University before moving to the University of Missouri in 2001. Her research has focused on how our daily goals affect our thoughts, mood, behavior, and well-being, and their implications for the future. Dr. King has also examined peoples' stories about important life experiences, which indicate their level of happiness and maturity, and how individuals create good lives despite challenging circumstances. In general, her research reflects an enduring interest in what is good and healthy in people.

enhanced psychological and physical health. I began to think about these life goals as the "happy endings" we all write for our life stories. In later work, I have asked people to share the stories of their life transitions—from parents whose children turned out to have Down syndrome to gay men and lesbians in the process of coming out. In so many of these stories, my students and I observed the capacity of individuals to find enormous meaning in potentially negative life events—and to transform these events into positive life experiences. I began to wonder if these aspects of life might not also be worth examination.

I started to tinker with Pennebaker's original technique. In one study (King & Miner, 2000), we randomly assigned participants to three groups. In one they wrote about trauma, in one they were given a control topic, and in one they were told to think for just a moment about a trauma and then to write only about its positive aspects: How did it help them become stronger, better people? In every other way, our research design was the same as Pennebaker's. We found that people who wrote only about the positive aspects of a traumatic life event showed the same health benefits as those who simply described the trauma. This study allowed us to show that dwelling only on the negatives of life was related to health benefits—and that refocusing on the positive was associated with benefits as well. Still, as provocative as these results were, it's important to notice that, in this first study, we continued to focus on trauma as a starting point. Would it be possible to obtain health benefits by writing about a topic that had nothing to do with trauma? In a follow-up study (King, 2001), we again had participants write about trauma, or a control topic, or their best possible future selves—their life dreams. People in the third group showed enhanced positive affect after writing, compared to those in the other groups. In addition, they demonstrated health benefits identical to those that followed writing about a traumatic event. Finally, individuals who wrote about their life dreams—their most cherished self wishes—for 20 minutes each day also showed persistent increases in overall psychological well-being.

These findings challenge the idea that focusing on negative life events is central to obtaining health benefits from writing. Although expressing our deepest thoughts and feelings is key to the benefits of writing, the contents needn't be traumatic or negative. Our results demonstrate that examining the most hopeful aspects of our lives through writing can also bestow benefits upon us.

In my work, I have begun to more fully appreciate the actual act of storytelling that occurs when people participate in writing studies. They are doing more than simply describing an experience—they are writing and revising their life stories. Henry Murray once said, "The history of the organism is the organism." Part of that history is the person's unique life story as he or she understands it. Personality psychologists who focus on the narratives people construct about their lives have come to recognize that the life story is a central component of identity—that this story in many ways is the self (e.g., McAdams, 1993). A person who puts experience into words is constructing the story that is, or may become, his or her very self.

Personality psychology is, simply, the scientific study of the person. My work excites me because it gives me a chance to encounter people's stories, the little bits of meaning that convey so much about each person's capacity to cope, to thrive, to hope, and to learn lessons from life. Although I can't get my ironing done while I do it, in many ways encountering people through their life stories is just as addictive as watching the grand TV dramas of my childhood.

the Minnesota Multiphasic Personality Inventory (MMPI) (Hathaway & McKinley, 1943, 1983). This test is not strictly based on psychodynamic theory or any other theory. Rather, the scales of the test are, for the most part, empirically derived. In fact, psychologists with a variety of perspectives have contributed to its continuing development. The MMPI consists of 550 items covering a wide range of topics. Test takers answer each of the items, such as the following, as either *true* or *false* (Hathaway & McKinley, 1951, p. 28):

I often feel as if things are not real.　　T　　F

Someone has it in for me.　　T　　F

Scale	Abbreviation	Possible Interpretations
VALIDITY SCALES		
Question	?	Corresponds to number of items left unanswered
Lie	L	Lies or is highly conventional
Frequency	F	Exaggerates complaints or answers items haphazardly
Correction	K	Denies problems
CLINICAL SCALES		
Hypochondriasis	Hs	Has bodily concerns and complaints
Depression	D	Is depressed, guilty; has feelings of guilt and helplessness
Hysteria	Hy	Reacts to stress by developing physical symptoms; lacks insight
Psychopathic deviate	Pd	Is immoral, in conflict with the law; has stormy relationships
Masculinity/ femininity	Mf	Shows interests and behavior patterns considered stereotypical of the opposite gender
Paranoia	Pa	Is suspicious and resentful, highly cynical about human nature
Psychasthenia	Pt	Is anxious, worried, high-strung
Schizophrenia	Sc	Is confused, disorganized, disoriented; has bizzare ideas
Hypomania	Ma	Is energetic, restless, active, easily bored
Social introversion	Si	Is introverted, timid, shy; lacks self-confidence

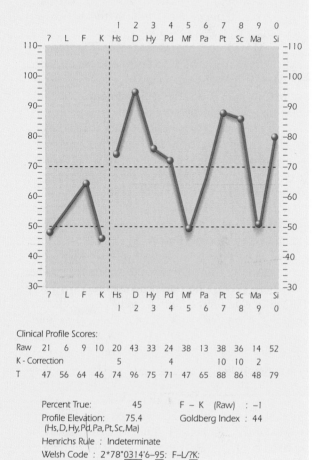

THE MINNESOTA REPORT   Page 3
for the Minnesota Multiphasic Personality Inventory : Adult System
By James N. Butcher, Ph.D.
CLINICAL PROFILE

Client No. : 987654321   Gender : Female
Setting : Mental Health Inpatient   Age : 45
Report Date : 28-APR-89

Clinical Profile Scores:

	?	L	F	K	Hs	D	Hy	Pd	Mf	Pa	Pt	Sc	Ma	Si
Raw	21	6	9	10	20	43	33	24	38	13	38	36	14	52
K - Correction					5			4			10	10	2	
T	47	56	64	46	74	96	75	71	47	65	88	86	48	79

Percent True: 45   F – K   (Raw)   : –1
Profile Elevation: 75.4   Goldberg Index : 44
(Hs, D, Hy, Pd, Pa, Pt, Sc, Ma)
Henrichs Rule : Indeterminate
Welsh Code : 2*78"0314'6–95: F–L/?K:

FIGURE 15.6

The MMPI Profile with an Interpretation. This graph shows the profile of a client's responses to the MMPI. Each column indicates a separate dimension measured by the scale. The left column indicates measures of validity, such as whether the person is believed to be lying (L); the right column indicates dimensions of personality. (From Minnesota Multiphasic Personality Inventory [MMPI]. Copyright © The University of Minnesota 1943 [renewed 1970]. This report 1983. Reprinted by permission of the University of Minnesota Press.)

As shown in Figure 15.6, the MMPI contains 4 validity scales and 10 clinical scales. The *validity scales* are designed to assess the extent to which the clinician can have confidence in the results for the other scales. For example, the lie scale (L) measures the tendency of the test takers to try to present themselves in a way that is excessively favorable. The *clinical scales* measure 10 different forms of abnormal

behavior. A person with a high score on scale 6, paranoia, tends to have suspicious or grandiose ideas.

The MMPI has several strengths. First, the test is objectively scored, which avoids the subjectivities of scoring and interpretation that characterize projective tests. Second, the scale has been widely used, so a wealth of data is available for interpretation and comparison of scores and score profiles. The data suggest the scale is useful not only for understanding personality disorders (Kolotkin, Revis, Kirkley & Janick, 1987), but also for making predictions about health and welfare. For example, high scores on the depression scale are predictive of an individual's later contracting cancer (Persky, Kempthorne-Rawson, & Shekele, 1987). Third, it contains several validity scales, which help the clinician assess the extent to which the results are credible. Fourth, the scale covers a range of abnormal behavior.

The MMPI also has some faults. The primary drawback is that it is hard to know how to interpret responses. When test takers are asked merely to answer *true* or *false* to a series of statements, they may find themselves interpreting the statements in ways that give a particular impression rather than straightforwardly. Moreover, although the MMPI may adequately assess people's impressions of what they are like or of what they do with their time, their responses do not necessarily correspond to what they really like to do (see Helmes & Reddon, 1993). A later version of the MMPI (MMPI-2) was developed to deal with some of these concerns (Butcher et al., 1989).

The MMPI has been used extensively with ethnic minorities in the United States and elsewhere (Butcher & Pancheri, 1976). Clinicians who use the MMPI with ethnic minorities in the United States must make certain adjustments (R. L. Greene, 1987). The main reason is that ethnic and racial groups were not included—or were drastically underrepresented—in the original standardization sample used to develop the norms for the test (Butcher & Williams, 1992; J. R. Graham, 1990). When the MMPI is used cross-culturally, other problems also must be considered. For instance, if the test is used in non–English-speaking countries, it must be carefully translated. Furthermore, people in other cultural contexts may not be as familiar with the very concept of testing devices, so they may either approach the task indifferently or misunderstand what is expected of them in order to perform the task (Lonner, 1990).

SELF-HELP TESTS

One can walk into the self-help section of any bookstore or pick up any of the hundreds of self-help magazines available in stores and find tests designed to measure a broad variety of personality traits. You should be highly skeptical both of the tests and of the results they produce. The tests are not standardized and have not been shown to possess satisfactory reliability or validity. Their purpose is commercial—to sell books or magazines—not to provide an accurate assessment of personality. The quizzes may be fun to take and enjoyable to reflect upon. But you should not view the results as scientifically valid.

The theories and approaches in this chapter have focused on personality traits as they apply to the normal range of behavior. Many psychologists interested in personality, especially those who treat patients, are interested particularly in abnormal personalities, which we examine in the next chapter.

✓CONCEPT CHECK 7

1. The Exner system for scoring the Rorschach test does *not* make use of
   a. location.
   b. determinants.
   c. content.
   d. depth.
2. What does the "A" in TAT stand for?
   a. application
   b. apperception
   c. avocation
   d. anomie
3. Which of the following is *not* a scale on the MMPI?
   a. psychopathic deviate
   b. agreeableness
   c. hysteria
   d. depression

THE PSYCHOLOGY OF NONCONFORMISTS

Cyrus was different from most other students on his campus. Although most of the men wore their hair short and neat, his was an unkempt mass of dreadlocks that hung nearly to his waist. His clothes were different too, and so was his taste in music. Like most nonconformists, Cyrus didn't care what others thought of him. He wasn't at all interested in being popular or accepted by any particular group of students. Compared to most young people, who spend their adolescent years obsessed with fitting in, Cyrus was a bit of an oddball.

But was Cyrus really just odd, or was he psychologically disturbed? Was he especially gifted or creative? Personality, clinical, counseling, developmental, educational, and social psychologists have all studied nonconformists in an attempt to understand their personalities, motivations, and behavior.

Research conducted by *personality psychologists* focuses on determining what personality characteristics are associated with nonconformity. Gary Davis and Sylvia Rimm (1977) found that creative people show high levels of nonconformity as well as high levels of self-confidence, playfulness, and good humor. In a large study of intellectual nonconformists who had dropped out of the University of California at Berkeley in the late 1960s, David Whittaker discovered that they preferred the creative arts, fine arts, and humanities to other courses of study. On a personality test known as the Omnibus Personality Inventory, the nonconformists scored higher on such personality variables as complexity, impulse expression, autonomy, and aestheticism than the more conforming

students who had not dropped out of college (Whittaker, 1971; Whittaker & Watts, 1969). The nonconformists scored much lower on practical outlook, however.

For *clinical psychologists,* the line between nonconformist behavior and symptoms of a psychological disorder is not always distinct. Some clinicians think that eccentric behaviors may signal a personality or adjustment disorder. On the other hand, clinical psychologists who are humanistically oriented (i.e., they encourage the development of individuality as defined by the client) are less likely to label nonconformist behaviors as abnormal (Rubenstein, 2001). For the most part, nonconformists do not have more psychological problems than other people, although in a study of visits to a university counseling center they were found to seek counseling more often (Sedlacek, Walters, & Valente, 1985). In a clinical study of adolescent boys undergoing psychological treatment in a wilderness-based residential program, those who were classified as nonconformists were more angry, resentful, immature, and narcissistic than boys who were more emotionally disturbed (McCord, 1995).

Developmental and *educational psychologists* have examined the impact of nonconformists in school settings. They have found that responses to nonconformist behavior may be culturally determined. Developmental psychologist Hans-Peter Landfeldt (1992) surveyed 246 junior high school teachers in Germany and Korea and found that teachers identified three types of problem behavior: antisocial-aggressive, withdrawn, and

nonconformist. Antisocial-aggressive and withdrawn behaviors were rated as problematic by both German and Korean teachers. However, only Korean teachers rated nonconformist behavior as problematic; German teachers found it totally acceptable (Landfeldt, 1992).

Many educational psychologists have looked at the characteristics of the nonconformist college subculture that were first identified by Clark and Trow (1966). Nonconformist students are not very interested in social activities, and they are not motivated by intellectual or career pursuits. They also express hostility toward people at all levels of authority in the college or university administration (Fiore & Sedlacek, 1972). Students in the nonconformist subculture also tend to be politically liberal rather than conservative (Wilder, McKeegan, & Midkiff, 2000).

Social psychologists have studied what other people think of nonconformists. For example, Susan Basow and Joanna Willis studied the reactions of 118 college students to videos of a young Caucasian woman with and without body hair. The students rated the young version with body hair as more nonconformist, unsociable, independent, unfriendly, and immoral than the version without body hair (Basow & Willis, 2001). Thus, other people's perceptions of nonconformists mirror some of the findings of personality psychologists. Research by clinical, counseling, developmental, and educational psychologists has confirmed that nonconformists also tend to be more hostile, artistic or aesthetically oriented, creative, and liberal than conformists.

1. *Personality* can be evaluated in terms of several criteria. Five criteria are important in psychology: importance to psychology and influence on the field, testability, comprehensiveness in accounting for psychological phenomena, parsimony, and usefulness to applied fields.

PSYCHODYNAMIC APPROACHES 537

Why is Freud's theory of personality both influential and controversial?

2. Freud created the seminal psychodynamic theory of personality, which emphasizes dynamic, biologically oriented processes. The theory also emphasizes how early development influences a person's adaptability to environments.

3. Freud's theory underscores the role of the unconscious in the life of the mind. Freud described three components of the mind: the *id* (which is largely instinctual and impulsive and seeks immediate gratification of sexual and aggressive wishes), the *ego* (which is rational and seeks to satisfy the id in ways that adapt effectively to the real world), and the *superego* (which is irrational and seeks to avoid the punishment associated with internalized moral strictures). The id operates on the basis of the *pleasure principle*, the ego on the basis of the *reality principle*, and the superego on the basis of the *idealistic principle*.

4. Eight of Freud's *defense mechanisms* are denial, repression, projection, displacement, sublimation, reaction formation, rationalization, and regression. Freud believed people used these mechanisms to protect themselves from unacceptable thoughts and impulses.

5. Freud's theory was based largely on his case studies of individual patients in his neurological/psychoanalytic practice. He also made extensive use of dream analysis, distinguishing between the *manifest content* and the *latent content* of dreams.

6. *Neo-Freudians*—such as Adler, Jung, and Horney—originally based their theories on Freud's but then developed their own psychodynamic ideas. Most neo-Freudian theories are less deterministic than Freud's and they give more consideration to the continuing development of the personality after childhood, as well as to the broader social context within which the individual's personality operates. In particular, Alfred Adler contributed the notion of the *inferiority complex;* Carl Jung, the notion of various layers of the unconscious, such as the *personal unconscious* and the *collective unconscious;* and Karen Horney, the importance of basic anxiety in leading people to feelings of isolation.

7. More contemporary psychodynamic theories include *object-relations theories*, which consider how people conceptualize their relationships with other people.

8. Psychodynamic theories have been criticized largely because of their lack of empirical support.

THE HUMANISTIC APPROACH 546

How are the values of humanism expressed in humanistic psychology's view of personality?

9. *Humanistic* theory opposes the psychodynamic approach by emphasizing individual responsibility and an appreciation of human experience.

10. Maslow emphasized the importance of self-actualization in the development of a healthy personality.

11. Rogers's *person-centered approach* to personality may be termed *self* theory. Rogers identified the self-concept (the aspects of the self that an individual perceives herself or himself to embody) and the ideal self (the aspects of the self that the person wishes to embody) and emphasized the importance of modifying one or the other so that they match as closely as possible.

12. Humanistic theories have not been as influential as other personality theories, but their strength is the emphasis they place on the value of each individual human being.

THE COGNITIVE-BEHAVIORAL APPROACH 548

What is distinctive about the cognitive-behavioral approach?

13. Skinner and other strict behaviorists have attempted to explain personality exclusively in terms of emitted behavior that results from environmental contingencies, without reverting to mentalistic descriptions.

14. Rotter used a cognitive-behavioral approach to explain personality. Rotter has emphasized the personality dimension of perceived *internal* versus *external locus of control*.

15. Bandura, also a cognitive-behavior theorist, has emphasized *reciprocal determinism*, the interaction of behaviors, personal variables, and the environment. Perceived self-efficacy is a key aspect of personality.

16. Cognitive-behavioral theories have spawned a wealth of empirical research and clinical assessment applications, partly due to the ease of testing such theories. Their parsimony varies from one theory to the next, and they are not known for great comprehensiveness.

Do our personalities reflect distinguishable, consistent traits?

17. *Traits* are stable sources of individual differences that characterize a person.
18. Gordon Allport underscored the importance of conscious awareness of experience, in stark contrast to the Freudian emphasis on the role of the unconscious. Allport posited that some individuals have *cardinal traits*, which are so central that they explain almost all behavior of the individual. In addition, all people have both *central traits* (highly salient characteristics) and *secondary traits* (less salient characteristics). Their behavior is usually explained by their central traits, but in some situations their secondary traits also play a role. Other theorists have modified Allport's idiographic approach.
19. Hans Eysenck posited that personality comprises the traits of *extroversion, neuroticism,* and *psychoticism;* others have preferred the widely investigated *Big Five* (neuroticism, extroversion, openness, agreeableness, and conscientiousness) theory.
20. Walter Mischel has criticized trait theories for inadequately considering situational factors that affect behavior. Recent advances in personality theory and measurement have tended to blunt the force of Mischel's criticism.

THE BIOLOGICAL APPROACH 553

What is the role of biology in determining personality?

21. Both nature and nurture influence personality traits, and different theorists give differing emphasis to one or the other.

22. Some theorists link personality traits to brain functioning.

INTERACTIONIST PERSPECTIVES 555

How might personality result from the interaction of environmental, biological, and other factors?

23. Some contemporary theorists emphasize an interactionist perspective, which focuses on the interaction between the individual's personality and the given situation. An example of such a notion is Mark Snyder's construct of self-monitoring, by which people are more or less consistent in their behavior according to their perceptions of what others would like to see and hear. Another example is Marvin Zuckerman's construct of sensation seeking.

MEASURING PERSONALITY 557

How is personality measured?

24. *Projective tests,* which encourage individuals to project their unconscious characteristics and conflicts in responses to open-ended questions, are a product of the psychodynamic tradition. Two projective tests are the Rorschach Inkblot Test and the *Thematic Apperception Test (TAT).*
25. *Objective tests* of personality are named for their objective methods of scoring, as opposed to the subjective ratings testers must make for projective tests. Two of the most widely used objective tests are the NEO-PI-R and the MMPI-2.

KEY TERMS

anal stage 540
archetypes 543
Big Five 551
cardinal trait 550
central traits 550
collective unconscious 542
complexes 542
defense mechanisms 539
determinism 537
ego 538
Electra conflict 540
external locus of control 548
extroversion 550
fixated 540
genital stage 540
humanism 546

id 538
idealistic principle 539
inferiority complex 542
internal locus of control 548
latency 540
latent content 538
manifest content 538
neo-Freudians 537
neuroticism 550
object-relations theory 544
objective personality tests 558
Oedipal conflict 540
oral stage 540
person-centered approach 546
personal dispositions 550
personal unconscious 542

personality 536
phallic stage 540
pleasure principle 538
primary-process thought 538
projective tests 557
psychoticism 550
reality principle 538
reciprocal determinism 549
secondary-process thought 533
secondary traits 550
self 543
superego 538
Thematic Apperception Test
   (TAT) 551
traits 550

ANSWERS TO CONCEPT CHECKS

Concept Check 1

1. a   2. c   3. b

Concept Check 2

1. c   2. a   3. c

Concept Check 3

1. b   2. d   3. d

Concept Check 4

1. b   2. c   3. a

Concept Check 5

1. c   2. b   3. a

Concept Check 6

1. c   2. a   3. c

Concept Check 7

1. d   2. b   3. b

KNOWLEDGE CHECK

1. Which of the following is *not* a neo-Freudian?
   a. Adler
   b. Horney
   c. Jung
   d. Rotter
2. According to Freud, the id thinks in terms of ____ process thinking.
   a. primary
   b. secondary
   c. tertiary
   d. complex
3. Which defense mechanism involves transforming an unacceptable impulse into its opposite?
   a. sublimation
   b. reaction formation
   c. displacement
   d. repression
4. Which of the following is *not* one of Freud's stages of psychosexual development?
   a. oral
   b. anal
   c. vaginal
   d. phallic
5. The term *archetype* was central to the theory of
   a. Freud.
   b. Jung.
   c. Adler.
   d. Horney.
6. A theory that stresses how people relate to one another is
   a. self theory.
   b. Freudian theory.
   c. object-relations theory.
   d. cognitive-behavior theory.
7. Skinner believed that people's personalities differ primarily as a function of
   a. innate personality traits.
   b. acquired personality traits.
   c. chance.
   d. environmental contingencies.
8. Allport believed that _____ personality trait(s) is(are) common across people.
   a. all
   b. more than one but not all
   c. one
   d. no
9. A person who is nervous and emotionally unstable is best characterized as
   a. neurotic.
   b. psychotic.
   c. surgent.
   d. introverted.
10. Babies show marked differences in temperament
    a. soon after birth.
    b. after about 1 year.
    c. after about 2 years.
    d. after about 3 years.

Answers

1. d   2. a   3. b   4. c   5. b   6. c   7. d   8. b
9. a   10. a

THINK ABOUT IT

1. Of the various theories of personality proposed in this chapter, which seems to you to be most reasonable; that is, which explains personality most effectively? Why?
2. In what ways do both humanistic and cognitive-behavioral theories view personality similarly to the psychodynamic perspective? How do these two theories differ from the psychodynamic perspective?
3. Picture yourself as a medically trained neurologist living in Victorian Vienna. Many of your patients are women, and a number of them come to ask you to relieve their hysterical symptoms (i.e., physical complaints for which you can find no medical explanations). How might you help your patients and what theory might you propose to explain the underlying cause of their ailments?
4. What are several ways in which you can ensure that your significant other or your child (hypothetical or real) feels sure of your unconditional positive regard?
5. What do you consider to be the essential personality characteristics, based on yourself and on the people you know?
6. In what ways might your self-schemas be limiting your flexibility? What can you do to increase your flexibility?

WEB RESOURCES

For a chapter tutorial quiz, direct links to Internet sites, and other useful features, visit the book-specific website at http://psychology.wadsworth.com/sternberg4e. You can also connect directly to the following sites:

Personality Theories
http://www.ship.edu/~cgboeree/perscontents.html
This site is an "electronic textbook" for courses in personality theories. Simply click on the names in a list of more than 15 personality theorists to read about their theories.

The Personality Project
http://pmc.psych.nwu.edu/
Why do people differ? This detailed site provides further insight into personality research as well as a variety of further links to academic and non-academic Web pages.

Great Ideas in Personality
http://www.personalityresearch.org/
Personality psychologist G. Scott Acton of Northwestern University demonstrates that scientific research programs in personality generate broad and compelling ideas about what it is to be human. He examines 12 research perspectives, including behaviorism, behavioral genetics, and sociobiology, and backs them up with extensive links to relevant print and online resources.

For additional readings on many of the topics covered in this chapter, check out InfoTrac College Edition at **www.infotrac-college.com/wadsworth.**

CD-ROM: UNIFYING PSYCHOLOGY

Disk Two
The Nature of Personality
Psychodynamic Approaches

The Trait-Based Approach
Chapter Quiz
Critical Thinking Questions

© Jana Leon/Stone-Getty Images

PSYCHOLOGICAL DISORDERS

For as long as I can remember I was frighteningly, although often wonderfully, beholden to moods. Intensely emotional as a child, mercurial as a young girl, first severely depressed as an adolescent, and then unrelentingly caught up in the cycles of manic-depressive illness by the time I began my professional life, I became, both by necessity and intellectual inclination, a student of moods.

—*Kay Jamison**

*From the Prologue to *An Unquiet Mind: A Memoir of Moods and Madness*, by Kay Jamison, Vintage Books (Random House), 1995.

WHAT BEHAVIOR
IS ABNORMAL?

How do we distinguish abnormal from normal behavior?

What makes behavior abnormal? An individual exhibits a **psychological disorder** if (1) the individual shows a clinically significant behavior or psychological syndrome that is associated with present distress or disability or with an increased risk of suffering death, pain, disability, or an important loss of freedom; (2) the syndrome is not merely an expectable and culturally sanctioned response to a particular event, such as the death of a loved one; and (3) the syndrome is not a deliberate response to particular conditions, such as poverty, conflicts with society, or prejudice.

Behavior is not classified as abnormal simply because it is unusual. For example, behavior most people would *not* consider abnormal may still be statistically unusual, such as winning a Nobel Prize, saving a child from a burning building, or earning a graduate degree in nuclear engineering. Behavior that is not abnormal may still be nonadaptive, such as habitually getting too little sleep.

The behavior of people who are labeled abnormal may challenge other people and even disrupt their lives. It is nevertheless important to act with respect and compassion toward people who have psychological disorders. As we come to understand the causes better, we may more clearly understand how to help such people lead happy and productive lives that are minimally or not at all disruptive to others.

This chapter is concerned with people who have problems that are maladaptive for an individual's everyday functioning and sometimes even survival. In some cases, psychological distress becomes maladaptive only when it reaches a certain degree over an extended period of time. Mild and temporary bouts with depression can signal that something is amiss and needs to be corrected. The symptoms that characterize these low periods, unpleasant though they may be, do not compare in intensity or duration to those experienced by people who suffer from clinical depression. Thus, you should not be concerned if some of the symptoms described in this chapter are familiar to you.

As you might expect, whether a particular behavior is statistically unusual or considered maladaptive varies across cultural contexts. Behavior that is quite common and acceptable in one culture may be considered highly unusual and unacceptable in another. For example, many people in modern Western cultures who hear about the rituals of Yoruba or Eskimo *shamans* (religious leaders who use magic to bring about therapeutic effects for individuals or for the cultural group as a whole) might consider the shamans' behavior abnormal. The Yorubas and the Eskimos, though, clearly distinguish between the shamans' behavior and that of people whose delusional actions are abnormal and inappropriate (Cuellar & Paniagua, 2000; Davison & Neale, 2001; Matsumoto, 1994, 1996, 2001; Suzuki, Meller, & Ponterotto, 1996). People in other cultures might find abnormal some behaviors that are common in American culture, such as the ritual of watching *Monday Night Football*.

As these examples suggest, the context influences which kinds of behavior are labeled abnormal regardless of their statistical frequency or relative adaptiveness. Political dissidents are sometimes labeled insane in countries under totalitarian rule. In Nazi-occupied Europe, many heroic individuals who hid Jewish families were considered demented. The labels used by mental-health practitioners are also sometimes open to question. Once someone's behavior has been diagnosed as indicating mental illness and the person has been hospitalized, subsequent normal behavior may be interpreted largely in terms of the identified mental illness (Rosenhan, 1973).

Distorted perception and cognition may be appropriate and even normal under some circumstances. In fact, Shelley Taylor and Jonathon Brown (1988) argue that some degree of perceptual and cognitive distortion is good for our mental health. According to an affective model of self-esteem, self-esteem forms early in life in response to relational and temperamental factors, and people with high self-esteem people are better able to promote, protect, and restore their feelings of self-worth than are people with low self-esteem (Bernichon, Cook, & Brown, 2003; Brown, Dutton, & Cook, 2001; Heimpel, Wood, Marshall, & Brown, 2002). Assume that you and I are normal, mentally healthy, and well adjusted. According to Taylor and Brown (1988), one reason for our mental health is that we distort our perceptions of reality through self-serving biases that inflate our positive evaluations of ourselves. We also tend to inflate our importance and our ability to control our actions and even our environments, and we view our present reality and future prospects far more optimistically than the objective reality justifies. These self-serving distortions may enhance our self-esteem, boost our happiness, and increase our ability to do productive, creative work.

HISTORICAL VIEWS

Today, we study abnormal behavior as part of psychology and psychiatry. It was not always so. In ancient times, people considered abnormal behavior an aspect

In the past, people believed that demons caused psychological disorders and were largely external, subject only to exorcism. Today, we see the demons as largely internal, requiring psychological treatment.

of *demonology*. They believed the afflicted person was possessed by a supernatural force, often an evil demon. Treatment included *exorcism*, which did not always leave the possessed individual completely whole, physically or mentally.

The first challenge to the demonological view occurred in the 5th century B.C., when Hippocrates proposed that illnesses had physiological causes and that people with mental illnesses suffered from some kind of pathology of the brain. Although Hippocrates was incorrect in his appraisal of specific physiological causes of abnormal behavior (which he believed to be imbalances in the four humors—yellow bile, black bile, phlegm, and blood), he changed history by recognizing the importance of scientific rather than supernatural explanations of abnormality.

Unfortunately, ideas that were widely accepted at one time receded from public consciousness when the political and intellectual climate opposed scientific explorations and embraced metaphysical ones. Demonic explanations of abnormal behavior came back into favor periodically after Hippocrates. During the Middle Ages, many Europeans believed that people who acted oddly—some were probably mentally ill—were witches. Suspected witches were subjected to horrendous tortures to rid them of evil spirits. In many instances they were killed. By the time of the Renaissance, mentally ill Europeans were hospitalized rather than executed, but their treatment was still far from humane or therapeutic, and many people still considered them witches.

A famous instance of assigning demonic causes to abnormal behavior took place in the 1690s, near Salem, Massachusetts, when eight girls began to act strangely, hallucinating and convulsing, but doctors could find nothing wrong with them. The girls claimed to have been bewitched, and the resulting hysteria spread rapidly, resulting in the execution of 20 townsfolk (J. W. Davidson & Lytle, 1986). At the height of the witchcraft frenzy, a prominent Harvard-educated minister, Cotton Mather, published a work considered to offer scientific proof of the work of the devil in Salem. More reasonable explanations for the strange behavior of the accused have evolved since. Many scientists now believe that the girls' behavior may have been due in part to poisoning from the cereal-grain fungus *ergot*, which contains a precursor to lysergic acid diethylamide—LSD (Caporael, 1976, 2003). Eating food made from contaminated flour can cause hallucinations similar to those experienced by the girls in Salem.

MODERN THEORETICAL PERSPECTIVES

Demonic interpretations of abnormal behavior fell from favor as other explanations were offered. Modern theoretical approaches closely parallel the broad views of personality. Each approach has shaped research, with different kinds of studies reflecting the various theoretical perspectives. The theoretical perspective a therapist brings to bear upon therapy can affect the way the therapist conceptualizes symptoms, as well as his or her choice of treatments. Because we examined the standard approaches in the preceding chapter, they are reviewed only briefly here as they apply specifically to abnormal personality.

THE PSYCHODYNAMIC APPROACH

According to the psychodynamic perspective, abnormal behavior is largely a result of intrapsychic conflict. Recall that, according to Sigmund Freud, internal conflict affects much of what we feel, think, say, and do. Because the id is governed by the pleasure principle, the ego by the reality principle, and the superego by the idealistic principle, personality depends on which psychic force dominates. A person in whom the id dominates will be relatively unrestrained, uninhibited, and perhaps impulsive. A person in whom the ego is stronger is likely to be more restrained, more reality oriented, and more rational. A person dominated by the superego will be virtually immobilized by strictures against any behavior that is considered morally questionable in any way, even when the behavior is essential to the person's effective functioning in the social world (e.g., shaking hands with a person whose moral behavior is viewed as questionable). For example, a person who has an overactive superego may feel "dirty" and hence compelled to wash his or her hands hundreds of times a day.

THE HUMANISTIC APPROACH

According to the humanistic approach to abnormal behavior, problems arise if we experience conditional rather than unconditional positive regard from significant others, and especially parents, early in life. Problems also may arise if we are overly sensitive to other people's judgments or are unable to accept our own nature. Often, the two problems are linked. People who have low self-regard or are overly critical of themselves may not have received sufficient unconditional positive regard from parents or other significant persons.

THE BEHAVIORAL APPROACH

According to the behavioral perspective, abnormal behavior is the result of either classical or instrumental conditioning gone awry. A phobia, for example, might arise from an accidental pairing, perhaps repeatedly, of punishment with an object or set of objects that normally would not stimulate fear (see Chapter 6). Recall Watson and Rayner's experiment in which Little Albert experienced conditioned fear as a result of being exposed to a neutral stimulus (a white rat) paired with a frightening stimulus (a loud bang). According to this view, the phobic person has acquired a set of responses that are involuntary and nonadaptive. Behavioral theorists would then use behavioral principles to try to counteract the detrimental effect of the conditioning (see Chapter 17).

THE COGNITIVE APPROACH

According to the cognitive perspective, abnormal behavior is the result of distorted thinking. The distortions may be in the processes of thinking, its contents, or both. For example, depression tends to occur in people who minimize their own accomplishments or believe that they will fail no matter what they do. People who irrationally believe that all snakes can harm them are likely to develop a phobia about snakes. The phobic label simply describes a syndrome that involves distorted or erroneous thought. Therapy is directed at changing the processes or the contents of the phobic person's thoughts.

THE BIOLOGICAL APPROACH

The biological approach holds that abnormal behavior is caused by underlying abnormalities in the nervous system, particularly in the brain. Often, physiological signs indicate problems in neuronal transmission (see Chapter 3). For example, abnormal behavior may result from a shortage or surplus of a neurotransmitter or from problems in its passage or reuptake. Thera-

pists with this point of view often treat psychological problems with drugs and other types of biological interventions, such as diets or changes in sleep patterns.

THE BIOPSYCHOSOCIAL APPROACH

The biopsychosocial approach emphasizes the interaction of biological, psychological, and social factors. Most psychologists recognize that biological factors interact with the environment. A now-popular theory of abnormal behavior is **diathesis-stress theory,** according to which people have different genetic vulnerabilities to particular psychological disorders, and that as stress increases, the disorder is more likely to appear (*diathesis* means "predisposition"). The disorder to which the person is vulnerable develops if the person experiences so much stress that he or she is unable to cope with the environment. This theory has been applied most successfully to schizophrenia (Harding, Zubin, & Strauss, 1992; Zubin, Magaziner, & Steinhauer, 1983; Zubin & Spring, 1977), although it is relevant to other disorders as well. Because this approach includes several others, it will not be considered separately in relation to the major disorders we consider in this chapter.

Different approaches address different levels of a problem with respect to its etiology, or cause, and treatment. It is important to realize that disorders may have multiple causes. Thus, in considering different perspectives on disorders, recognize that they are not necessarily mutually exclusive. Treatment will be described in some detail in Chapter 17. In the next section, we examine how clinicians with varying perspectives agree on how to classify and diagnose mental disorders.

✓ CONCEPT CHECK 1

1. Abnormal behavior is *not*, in general,
   a. a deliberate response to prejudice.
   b. clinically significant.
   c. labeled as abnormal.
   d. culturally universal.
2. A biological explanation of the Salem witch fiasco traces the accusations to the effect of
   a. ergot.
   b. hashish.
   c. mescaline.
   d. mushrooms.
3. Which of the following is *not* a major approach for understanding abnormal behavior?
   a. biopsychosocial
   b. cognitive
   c. biological
   d. hermeneutic

CLASSIFYING AND DIAGNOSING PSYCHOLOGICAL DISORDERS

What criteria do clinicians use to classify and diagnose various mental disorders?

By the middle of the 20th century, clinicians began to reach formal consensus regarding psychological diagnoses. Part of diagnosis is classification. In 1948, the World Health Organization published the first *International Classification of Diseases (ICD)*, and 4 years later the American Psychiatric Association published the first edition of its *Diagnostic and Statistical Manual (DSM)*. The ICD-10 (1992) and DSM-IV (1994) are the current editions of these diagnostic manuals and they are closely coordinated. The current version of the DSM, like the ICD, is descriptive and *atheoretical*, which means that it is not grounded in any particular approach. It is based on primarily clinical experience, although rigorously obtained empirical evidence is also taken into account. The DSM lists the symptoms necessary for making a diagnosis in many categories, without seeking to assess the causes of the disorders. Thus, the classification system is based wholly on observable symptoms, which makes it useful to psychologists and psychiatrists with a wide variety of theoretical orientations (see Table 16.1). The system is continually evalu-

---

TABLE 16.1

DSM-IV, or Diagnostic and Statistical Manual, Volume 4. This summary of the five axes of the DSM-IV system of classifying mental disorders illustrates the major considerations in diagnoses.

Axis I **Clinical Syndromes**	*Axis II* **Personality Disorders**
• Disorders usually first diagnosed in infancy, childhood, or adolescence	• Antisocial
• Delirium, dementia, amnesic and other cognitive disorders	• Avoidant
• Substance-related disorders	• Borderline
• Schizophrenia and other psychotic disorders	• Dependent
• Mood disorders	• Histrionic
• Anxiety disorders	• Narcissistic
• Somatoform disorders	• Obsessive–compulsive
• Factitious disorder	• Paranoid
• Dissociative disorders	• Schizoid
• Sexual and gender-identity disorders	• Schizotypal
• Eating disorders	
• Sleep disorders	*Axis III* **Mental Retardation**
• Impulse control disorders not elsewhere classified	
• Adjustment disorders	• General medical conditions

Axis IV
Psychosocial and Environmental Problems

- Problems with primary support group (childhood, adult, parent–child). Specify: _____
- Problems related to the social environment. Specify: _____
- Educational problem. Specify: _____
- Occupational problem. Specify: _____
- Housing problem. Specify: _____
- Economic problem. Specify: _____
- Problems with access to health care services. Specify: _____
- Problems related to interaction with the legal system/crime. Specify: _____
- Other psychosocial problem. Specify: _____

Continued

Axis V

Global Assessment of Functioning Scale (GAF Scale)

Consider psychological, social, and occupational functioning on a hypothetical continuum of mental health/illness. Do not include impairment in functioning due to physical (or environmental) limitations.

Code

100	Superior functioning in a wide range of activities
90	Absent or minimal symptoms, good functioning in all areas
80	No more than slight impairment in social, occupational, or school functioning
70	Some mild symptoms or some difficulty in social, occupational, or school functioning
60	Moderate symptoms or moderate difficulty in functioning
50	Serious symptoms or any serious impairment in functioning
40	Some impairment in reality testing or communication or major impairment in several areas
30	Behavior is considerably influenced by delusions or hallucinations, or serious impairment in communication, or judgment, or inability to function in almost all areas
20	Some danger of hurting self or others or occasionally fails to maintain minimal personal hygiene, or gross impairment in communication
10	Persistent danger of severely hurting self or others (e.g., recurrent violence), or persistent inability to maintain minimal personal hygiene
0	Inadequate information

ated and revised (Regier, First, Marshall, & Narrow, 2002; Regier, Narrow, First, & Marshall, 2002).

THE FIVE AXES OF DSM-IV

In DSM-IV, individuals are diagnosed on each of five *axes*, or dimensions. The major classifications are on Axes I and II. Axes III, IV, and V are used to note other conditions that may be important to diagnosis and treatment, as well as the severity of the presenting disorder.

AXIS I Axis I addresses clinical syndromes and contains the major disorders such as schizophrenia; anxiety disorders; disorders usually diagnosed in infancy, childhood, or adolescence; somatoform disorders; and sexual disorders. We will describe the first three in detail. *Somatoform disorders* center on a person's relationship with her or his own body. They have relatively rare bodily symptoms or complaints for which no physiological basis can be found. In *sexual disorders*, sexual behaviors either distress the individual or others or cause difficulty in other aspects of life. The various sexual disorders can be mild or severe and of brief or long duration.

Axis I also includes various other disorders, such as *delirium* (a confused, disordered state of mind often involving perceptual distortions), *amnesia* (memory loss), *dementia* (general deterioration in cognitive abilities that especially affects memory and judgment, due to physiological changes in the brain—for example, Alzheimer's disease, stroke, or head trauma), and other cognitive disorders, which are discussed in Chapters 5, 7, 8, and 10. In addition, Axis I includes eating disorders (discussed in Chapters 12 and 18), sleeping disorders (see Chapter 5), and substance-related disorders (see Chapter 5).

AXIS II Axis II addresses primarily *personality disorders,* which are long-standing disturbances of personality that disrupt a person's functioning. The major personality disorders are described in this chapter. The disorders in Axis II may coexist with those in Axis I, and a person may receive diagnoses on both axes—for instance, a phobia and a narcissistic personality disorder. Axis II also addresses mental retardation.

AXIS III Axis III addresses mental retardation and physical abnormal conditions. Although such disorders can be neurological, they can also include asthma, diabetes, heart problems, and physical handicaps. Physical disorders are included because they may interact with or precipitate psychological conditions. For example, fearing an asthmatic attack may provoke one.

AXIS IV Axis IV addresses the severity of psychosocial stressors, such as extreme poverty or conflict with the law. The diagnostician uses the information from the other axes and from the patient's (or client's) existing situation and history to determine the level of psychological stress that he or she is experiencing.

AXIS V Axis V represents a global assessment of the person's level of functioning. A code of 90 indicates minimal symptoms and a code of 1 maximal danger—for example, someone who is extremely violent and is viewed as likely to cause harm to others.

A MULTIAXIAL DIAGNOSIS

The goal of using five separate axes instead of a summary diagnosis is to provide as comprehensive a portrait of abnormal functioning as possible. Consider the case of Thomas, a 15-year-old who is extremely anxious. He is sweating when he enters the psychologist's office. He is diagnosed along Axis I as having an anxiety disorder. He is also observed to have an academic skill disorder: He has difficulty in mathematics and performs 3 years behind grade level, even though his overall intelligence is in the normal range. Along Axis II, Thomas is noted as having a paranoid personality disorder. In comparing separate diagnoses, the therapist considers the possibility that the anxiety disorder, the personality disorder, and the problem in mathematics are related.

Along Axis III, it is noted that Thomas had mild head trauma from an automobile accident when he was 2. It is unclear whether the head injury is related to the diagnosed difficulties, but this information might prove useful in later decisions about diagnosis and treatment. On Axis IV, Thomas is coded as currently under severe stress. His parents are going through a divorce and each wants the other to take custody. The parents have long shown little interest in Thomas, and this neglect is coming out in the divorce proceedings as well. Finally, on Axis V, Thomas receives a global assessment rating of 55 based on moderate symptoms, including anxiety and occasional panic attacks, especially when he needs to use mathematics and when he suspects others of plotting against him. His anxiety is interfering with his schoolwork and with his ability to form friendships, and he is becoming something of a target for other children. Each axis has given different but complementary information about Thomas's psychological problems.

EVALUATING DSM-IV

Any diagnostic system is potentially problematic, including DSM-IV. First, because the system is atheoretical, it describes syndromes but gives us no real insight into the causes of the abnormal behavior. A second problem is its subjectivity. Although the DSM-IV and the ICD-10 permit "clinicians to reach the same diagnosis in a remarkably high proportion

A disabling physical handicap may be associated with depression.

of cases" (Sartorius et al., 1993b, p. xvi; see also Maj, Gaebel, Lopez-Ibor, & Sartorius, 2002), reliable agreement among clinicians certainly is not perfect. A third problem, common to any diagnostic system, is "mapping" behavior onto descriptive categories. A diagnostician translates or maps observed behavior onto the symptoms expressed in DSM-IV and then maps those symptoms onto a diagnosis. DSM-IV is the product of outstanding efforts to achieve specificity and clarity in translating symptoms into diagnoses, but practitioners still need to map the behavior they observe onto the symptoms in the DSM.

PREVALENCE, INCIDENCE, COMORBIDITY, AND CONCORDANCE

Because it is impossible to specify every possible type of behavior, ambiguity is a potential problem in any classification system. For example, when do the quantity and character of antisocial acts lead a clinician to label someone as having an antisocial personality disorder? DSM-IV gives guidelines, but ultimately the clinician's judgment is the key to the diagnosis. Despite the lack of a single perfect method, various forms of assessment used together give clinicians a wide variety of information that they integrate and interpret on the basis of their professional expertise. Psychologists are interested in several key concepts.

First, psychologists are interested in prevalence. *Prevalence* is how often a given disorder occurs in the population. This statistic is important in assessing the extent to which a given disorder is common.

Second, they are interested in *incidence*, which is the number of new cases of a disorder that were diagnosed during a certain period of time. This information is important when it is suspected that some factor newly introduced into the environment (e.g., war, a chemical agent, soaring crime) has increased or decreased the extent to which a disorder occurs in the general population.

Third, psychologists are interested in *comorbidity*, which is the extent to which the presenting symptoms of different disorders overlap. Anxiety and depression, for example, show a substantial degree of comorbidity. About half of people who receive one diagnosis qualify for the second as well (Kessler, 1995).

Finally, *concordance* is the degree to which various family members (often identical twins) show the same characteristic (which for our purposes is a particular psychological disorder). Concordance helps us determine the extent to which a disorder runs in families.

As we shall see, the picture presented by prevalence, incidence, comorbidity, and concordance figures is useful in considering the causes and treatment of mental disorders.

ANXIETY DISORDERS

When does anxiety become a disorder? What different kinds of anxiety disorders do people experience?

Anxiety is a general feeling of dread or apprehension. **Anxiety disorders** are characterized primarily by *anxiety* that is so intense or so frequent that it causes serious problems. Common symptoms are tension, nervousness, distress, and uncomfortable arousal of varying levels of intensity; excessive worry; and somatic (bodily) symptoms associated with high arousal of the autonomic nervous system (Christophersen & Mortweet, 2001; DiTomasso & Gosch, 2002).

TYPES OF ANXIETY DISORDERS

DSM-IV divides anxiety disorders into five main categories: phobias, panic disorder, generalized anxiety disorder, stress disorders (posttraumatic stress disorder and acute stress disorder), and obsessive–compulsive disorder. These forms of anxiety disorders differ in their frequencies within the population. Anxiety disorders usually first appear in the late teens or early 20s (Yonkers, Warshaw, Massion, & Keller, 1996). They are more common in people who are divorced, separated, or unemployed (Wittchen, Zhao, Kessler, & Eaton, 1994). Phobias and panic disorder are more common in women, and obsessive–compulsive disorder is more common in men (J. K. Myers et al., 1984; Steiner,

In his painting "The Cry" (sometimes translated as "The Scream"), Edvard Munch (1863–1944) captured the terror often felt by people with anxiety disorders.

Eriksson, & Yonkers, 2000; Yonkers & Kidner, 2002). In particular, J. K. Myers and his colleagues found that, within the general population, 8% of women but only 3.5% of men are phobic. All five disorders share several common symptoms that characterize them as anxiety disorders.

PHOBIAS

Phobias are characterized by exaggerated, persistent, irrational, and disruptive fears of a particular object, event, or setting, or of a general kind of object, event, or setting. A fear is classified as a phobia either when it is substantially greater than what seems justified or when it has no basis in reality. People with phobias are aware that their fears are irrational and they would like to overcome them, but they have a great deal of difficulty doing so. Phobias can be specific, social, or complex.

Specific phobias are characterized by marked, persistent, irrational fears of objects, places, or conditions, such as spiders, snakes, rats, high places, and darkness (Antony & Swinson, 2000b). About 11% of the population reports having a specific phobia at some time (Robins & Regier, 1991).

Social phobias are characterized by extreme fear of being embarrassed, criticized, or otherwise negatively evaluated, which leads to avoidance of groups and any situations associated with being criticized, embarrassed, or subject to ridicule (Antony & Swinson, 2000a). Slightly less than 3% of the population reports having such a phobia at some time (Robins & Regier, 1991).

Agoraphobia is characterized by an intense fear of open spaces or of being in public places from which it might be difficult to escape in the event of a panic attack. Agoraphobia accounts for 60% of all phobias. The majority of agoraphobics are women, and the disorder usually begins to develop in adolescence or early adulthood. Extreme agoraphobics are unable to leave their homes, although some will go out if accompanied by someone they trust

Common phobias are of lightning, spiders, and snakes.

(Hollander, Simeon, & Gorman, 1994). Consider the following case:

> Mrs. Reiss is a 48-year-old woman who recently was referred to a psychiatric clinic by her general practitioner because of her fears of going out alone. She has had these fears for 6 years, but they have intensified during the past 2 years. As a result, she has not gone out of her house unescorted. Her symptoms first appeared after an argument with her husband. She proceeded to go out to the mailbox and was then overwhelmed with feelings of dizziness and anxiety. She had to struggle back to the house. Her symptoms abated for a few years, but reappeared with greater intensity after she learned that her sister had ovarian cancer. Her symptoms often were exacerbated by frequent arguments with her husband. She began to feel increasingly apprehensive and fearful upon leaving the front door. If she did leave, she began getting panicky and dizzy after a few minutes on the street. Her heart pounded and she would start perspiring. At this point, she would turn back to her house to alleviate the anxiety. When accompanied by her husband or one of her children, she felt uneasy, but was usually able to enter crowded areas for short periods of time. (After Greenberg, Szmukler, & Tantam, 1986, pp. 148–149)

About 5% of the population reports experiencing agoraphobia at some time (Robins & Regier, 1991).

PANIC DISORDER

Panic disorder is characterized by brief, abrupt, and unprovoked recurrent episodes of intense and uncontrollable anxiety (Shear et al., 2002). The person suddenly feels apprehensive or even terrified, experiencing difficulty breathing, heart palpitations, dizziness, sweating, and trembling. People with this disorder may fear losing control of themselves, going crazy, or dying. They may fear they are having a heart attack. People with panic disorder are susceptible to agoraphobia. In fact, panic attacks often lead to agoraphobia, as in the case above. Panic disorders afflict about 1.5% of the U.S. population (McGinn & Sanderson, 1995).

GENERALIZED ANXIETY DISORDER (GAD)

Generalized anxiety disorder (GAD) is characterized by general, persistent, constant, and often debilitating levels of anxiety (Andrews et al., 2003). Unlike phobias, it does not have specific triggers. The anxiety is accompanied by physiological symptoms typical of a hyperactive autonomic nervous system that can last from six months to many years. The cause is difficult to identify. A person who has this disorder commonly experiences physical symptoms, as described in this example:

> A 67-year-old woman was referred to a psychiatric clinic for treatment of an anxiety state. At the interview she appeared to be tense; she sat upright and rigid in her chair and answered questions politely. She admitted that for most of her life she had been a great worrier. She said, "I'm inclined to look ahead and expect the worst to happen. I find it hard to relax, especially while lying in bed. My worst fears come to mind." In her more anxious moments, she has experienced palpitations of the heart, and often has had difficulty falling asleep due to her brooding thoughts. Although she has experienced a persistent and chronic anxiety, she has been unable to trace her anxiety to any particular problem. (After Fottrell, 1983, p. 149)

About 5% of people report experiencing this disorder at some point in their lives (Robins & Regier, 1991).

STRESS DISORDERS

Stress disorders are characterized by an extreme reaction to a highly stressful event or situation, such as rape or combat. They often are linked to adjustment disorders (see Chapter 18). Two variations are posttraumatic stress disorder and acute stress disorder.

In **posttraumatic stress disorder (PTSD)**, a person experiences a psychological reenactment of a past traumatic event while consciously engaged in other activities. He or she may experience flashbacks so strong that the person believes the event is recurring. The event may be military combat, a natural disaster, or a serious accident. Some individuals are so plagued by these recurrences that they become apathetic and detached (Bryant & Harvey, 2000). People with PTSD tend to avoid stimuli that remind them of the original trauma and often startle easily.

In **acute stress disorder**, a traumatic event results in a mental disturbance that lasts fewer than 4 weeks (Bryant & Harvey, 2000). In some respects, it is like a PTSD that resolves itself in a short period of

People who participate in military combat may later suffer from posttraumatic stress disorder (PTSD).

time. People may experience a sense of detachment from the physical and social worlds, distortions or other changes in perceptions, and disturbances of memory.

OBSESSIVE–COMPULSIVE DISORDER

Obsessive–compulsive disorder is characterized by unwanted, persistent thoughts and irresistible impulses to perform a ritual to relieve anxiety that may be caused by those or other thoughts (Greisberg & McKay, 2003).

An **obsession** is an unwanted, persistent thought, image, or impulse that cannot be suppressed. One woman obsessively thought that her children were being kidnapped.

A **compulsion** is an irresistible impulse to perform a relatively meaningless act repeatedly and in a stereotypical fashion so as to reduce anxiety. Compulsive persons are often aware of the absurdity of their behavior and yet are unable to stop it. Some may wash their hands several hundred times a day. Other common compulsions are counting things to make sure they are all there, checking the placement of objects, and checking that appliances are turned off. In addition to being time-consuming, compulsions can be detrimental to a person's well-being. Consider this case:

> Ruth Langley was 30 years old when she sought help from a therapist after experiencing long-standing fears of contamination. She stated that she became intensely uncomfortable with any dirt on herself or in her immediate environment. After noticing any dirt, she felt compelled to carry out elaborate and time-consuming cleaning procedures. This usually involved thoroughly washing her hands and arms. Moreover, if she found dirt in her apartment, she was compelled to scrub her apartment methodically, in addition to showering in a very regimented manner. Her cleaning rituals have severely restricted her life. She now washes her hands at least four or five times an hour, showers six or seven times a day, and thoroughly cleans her apartment at least twice a day. (After G. R. Leon, 1974, pp. 129–130)

About 2.5% of the U.S. population is affected by obsessive–compulsive disorder.

SYMPTOMS OF ANXIETY DISORDERS

Anxiety disorders create mood, cognitive, somatic, and motor symptoms. *Mood symptoms* include feelings of tension, apprehension, and sometimes panic. Often, people who experience mood symptoms do not know why they feel the way they do. They may have a sense of foreboding or even of doom but not know why. Sometimes anxious persons become depressed, if only because they do not see any way to alleviate their symptoms.

Cognitive symptoms may include spending a lot of time trying to figure out why various mood symptoms are occurring. When unable to identify the causes, the individual may feel frustrated. Often, thinking about the problem actually worsens it, making it hard for the person to concentrate on other things.

Typical *somatic symptoms* are sweating, hyperventilation, high pulse rate or blood pressure, and muscle tension. All of these symptoms are characteristic of a high level of autonomic nervous system arousal (see Chapter 3). These primary symptoms may lead to secondary ones. For example, hyperventilation may lead to lightheadedness or breathlessness. Muscular tension can lead to headaches or muscle spasms. High blood pressure can cause strokes and cardiac problems. People who suffer anxiety disorders vary widely in the extent to which they experience somatic symptoms and also in the kinds of somatic symptoms they experience. Some express their anxiety in headaches, others in stomachaches, and so on.

Typical *motor symptoms* are restlessness, fidgeting, and various kinds of movements that seem to have no particular purpose, such as pacing, finger tapping, tics, and the like. People are often unaware that they are doing these things. They may pace around a room while others are seated, not realizing how their behavior is being perceived.

WHEN DOES ANXIETY BECOME A DISORDER?

What distinguishes the normal anxiety that everyone occasionally experiences from debilitating anxiety? Generally, three factors must be considered:

1. *Level of anxiety:* It is one thing to have a slight, occasional fear of elevators, especially overcrowded, rickety-looking ones; it is another thing to be unable to use any elevators at all even to get to a job at the top of a building.
2. *Source of anxiety:* It is normal to feel somewhat anxious before an important event, such as a final examination, a first date, or an important speech (see Figure 16.1), but it is not normal to feel that same level of anxiety constantly when there are no precipitating stressful events.
3. *Consequences of the anxiety:* If the anxiety leads to serious maladaptive results, such as the loss of a job because of an inability to leave home, the consequences are sufficiently severe for a clinician to classify the person as having an anxiety disorder.

© CULTURAL INFLUENCES

One cause of anxiety may be the stress brought on by modern society. This cultural factor is suggested by the higher prevalence of anxiety disorders in technologically advanced societies (Carson & Butcher, 1992). The particular manifestations of symptoms

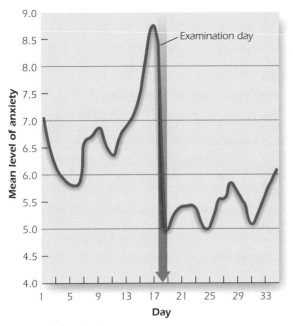

FIGURE 16.1

Situational Anxiety. In normal individuals, levels of anxiety are related to a specific situation, such as a major examination. (From "Anxiety and Exams" by N. Bolger, *Journal of Personality and Social Psychology,* Vol. 59, No. 3, p. 531, 1990. Copyright © 1990 by the American Psychological Association. Reprinted with permission.)

and the grouping of symptoms into diagnosed disorders also vary across cultures, even modern ones. In Japan, *taijin-kyofusho* (fear of humans) is a common manifestation of anxiety (Kirmayer, 1991). This condition affects mainly men, and their symptoms include staring inappropriately, emitting offensive odors or flatulence, and blushing easily. The Japanese condition of *taijin-kyofusho* is significantly related to the Western condition of social phobia (Kleinknecht, Dinnel, Tanouye, & Lonner, 1993) and to the Latin-American condition of *susto*, characterized by extreme anxiety, restlessness, and fear of black magic and the evil eye (*mal ojo*). Each complex of symptoms reflects the characteristics and values of the respective culture.

Quite a different anxiety disorder has been observed in Islamic societies, in which the obsessive–compulsive syndrome of *Waswas* has been linked to the ritual of cleansing and prayer. According to W. Pfeiffer (1982), the syndrome "relates to ritual cleanliness and to the validity of the ritual procedures, which are particularly important in Islam. Thus, the sufferer of *Waswas* finds it hard to terminate the ablutions because he is afraid that he is not yet clean enough to carry out his prayers in a lawful manner" (p. 213). Why do sufferers of *Waswas* or any other syndrome experience such debilitating symptoms?

EXPLANATIONS OF ANXIETY DISORDERS

As you might expect, different theoretical approaches lead to alternative explanations of the origin of anxiety disorders. As usual, these explanations are not necessarily mutually exclusive and may even be wholly compatible, in that disorders may have multiple causes that coexist at different levels of analysis. Researchers seldom find a single cause of a psychological phenomenon. Instead, as each of several factors comes to light, new insights contribute to an increasingly detailed picture of the phenomenon.

PSYCHODYNAMIC EXPLANATIONS

The psychodynamic emphasis is on internal conflict. Freud distinguished among three types of anxiety and believed that each requires a distinct explanation. The first, *objective anxiety*, derives from threats in the external world. Included here are anxiety about realistic financial problems, failure in work or in personal relationships, serious illnesses, and the like. This kind of anxiety corresponds to *fear*. Freud maintained that this kind of anxiety is not linked to abnormal behavior because the threat that causes the anxiety is real.

The second and third types of anxiety stem from battles between the id and the superego. *Moral anxiety* derives from fear of punishment by the superego, which arises from internal conflict over the expression of impulses from the id. *After* the impulses of the id have won out and are expressed, the person experiences moral anxiety. For example, a poorly qualified, dull candidate might attempt to win an election by smearing an opponent. Later, this person might experience some degree of moral anxiety. By giving in to impulses to succeed at the other person's expense, the candidate creates internal conflict.

Neurotic anxiety derives from a person's fear that the superego (with the aid of the ego) will not be able to control the id and that the person may not be able to avoid engaging in unacceptable behavior. A person may be afraid to go out on a date for fear of acting in an unacceptable way and thereby losing the possibility of a relationship. Note that neurotic anxiety occurs *before* the impulses of the id have been expressed, while the superego is still restraining its expression.

Freud believed that phobias occur when anxiety is focused on one or more particular objects; these objects represent conflict at a symbolic level. For example, a phobia of snakes might symbolically represent sexual conflict, whereby the snake serves as a phallic symbol to focus the anxiety. Freud believed that many anxieties originate in sexual conflicts. In contrast, many neo-Freudians believed that other important conflicts, such as those centering on feelings of inferiority (Alfred Adler) or attachment, could also lead to anxiety. In any case, the evidence for psychodynamic interpretations of anxiety is relatively weak.

HUMANISTIC EXPLANATIONS

One humanistic explanation for anxiety disorders is that the person experiences a discrepancy between the perceived self and the idealized self; the resulting feelings of failure cause the anxiety. Anxious people tend to indicate more of a discrepancy than confident people (C. R. Rogers, 1961b). Anxious people also exhibit poorer social skills than nonanxious people (Fischetti, Curran, & Wessberg, 1977), which may further reduce their confidence in themselves.

BEHAVIORAL EXPLANATIONS

The emphasis in behavioral theory is on conditioned fears and observational learning. Many behavioral (or learning) theorists view anxiety as classically conditioned. According to this thinking, a fear response has been paired with a stimulus that was previously neutral and is now fear-producing (see Chapter 6). For example, someone might have a neutral or slightly favorable attitude toward dogs. Then the person is seriously bitten by a dog. Through classical conditioning, the person becomes anxious in the presence of dogs or possibly even at the thought of dogs. As it turns out, about 44% of people with social phobia can identify a traumatic conditioning experience that they believe has contributed to their problem (Stemberger, Turner, Beidel, & Calhoun, 1995).

According to classical learning theory, the unpleasant experience would have to happen to the individual who experiences the anxiety in order for conditioning to occur. According to contemporary forms of learning theory, however, it is possible to experience *vicarious conditioning* (Bandura & Rosenthal, 1966). Simply through observational learning (see Chapters 11 and 15), we can be conditioned to experience anxiety. For example, most of us have not contracted acquired immune deficiency syndrome (AIDS). By observing the effects of AIDS, however, we could become anxious and even phobic about the possibility of contracting AIDS, solely through vicariously conditioning.

Operant conditioning can also play a role in the development of anxiety disorders. Consider compulsive behavior. Suppose that you have an irrational fear of bacteria. Washing your hands makes you feel temporarily safer. You are thereby reinforced for the hand-washing behavior, but soon the fear returns. You have learned that hand washing helps alleviate anxiety, so you wash your hands again. You feel better, but not for long. You have learned to engage in the compulsive behavior because it temporarily alleviates anxiety, as a result of operant conditioning.

COGNITIVE EXPLANATIONS

Cognitive explanations emphasize automatic self-defeating thoughts. Suppose a woman wants to ask a man out to lunch, but the thought of actually picking up the phone and calling him makes her sweat with anxiety. She starts thinking, "I know I'm going to fail. I know he's going to put me down. I'd really like to invite him, but I just can't stand being rejected again." These kinds of thoughts produce anxiety, causing people to be unable to do some of the things that they would like to do (Beck, Emery, & Greenberg, 1985; Sanderson, Beck, & McGinn, 2002; Sookman, Pinard, & Beck, 2001). The thoughts are likely to become *automatic*—mental patterns that people fall into effortlessly without being aware of them (Beck, 1976). Often, such thoughts are the beginning of a self-defeating cycle. Someone who expects rejection may feel spurned when receiving neutral cues or may find repudiation even in positive things that another person says. Thus, anxiety disorders tend to be self-propagating. In general, the thoughts are not about what is happening at the moment, but about what is expected to happen (Albano, Chorpita, & Barlow, 2003; Barlow, 1988; Barlow, Raffa, & Cohen, 2002).

BIOLOGICAL EXPLANATIONS

Several biological explanations for anxiety disorders have been proposed. One suggests that inhibitory neurons that serve to reduce neurological activity may function improperly. For example, insufficient levels of the neurotransmitter GABA (gamma-aminobutyric acid) lower activity in the inhibitory neurons and thereby increase brain activity; the result is a high level of arousal, which may be experienced as anxiety (Lloyd, Fletcher, & Minchin, 1992). Drugs that decrease GABA activity lead to increased anxiety (Insell, 1986). Various tranquilizers, such as diazepam (Valium), increase GABA activity and thereby decrease anxiety (Bertilsson, 1978; Enna & DeFranz, 1980; Haefely, 1977). These drugs are highly addictive. There also appears to be a link between a gene that controls the brain's ability to use serotonin and anxiety-related behavior (Lesch et al., 1996; Stein & Uhde, 1995). Research suggests that anxiety disorders often run in families (Andreasen, 2001; Andreasen & Black, 1991), perhaps because many brain and behavior patterns in general tend, to some extent, to run in families (White, Andreasen, & Nopoulos, 2002).

✓ CONCEPT CHECK 3

1. Which of the following is *not* a kind of anxiety disorder?
   a. phobia
   b. major depression
   c. panic disorder
   d. stress disorder

2. An intense fear of open spaces is called
   a. claustrophobia.
   b. panic disorder.
   c. agoraphobia.
   d. acrophobia.
3. An unwanted, persistent thought is a(n)
   a. compulsion.
   b. phobia.
   c. obsession.
   d. anxiety.

MOOD DISORDERS

How do mood disorders differ from
the highs and lows we all experience?

Mood disorders involve extremely sad, low-energy moods or swings between extremely high and extremely low moods. They disrupt physical, cognitive, and social processes. The two most prevalent mood disorders are major depression (sometimes called unipolar depression) and bipolar disorder (also called manic depression). Each disorder impairs function; these disorders are more than transitory high or low moods.

Depression is relatively common. Almost 23% of men and 36% of women have reported experiencing a period of at least two weeks when they have felt very sad and blue. However, for only 4% of the men and 9% of the women would the symptoms be classified as severe enough to merit a diagnosis of clinical depression (Robins & Regier, 1991). Thus, depression is more common in women than in men (Shumaker & Hill, 1991) and particularly in married women (Paykel, 1991).

Depression is more likely to occur in people of low socioeconomic status (SES) than in those of high SES (Hirschfeld & Cross, 1982). The higher frequencies in women and in persons of lower SES suggest that situational factors may be involved. Susan Nolen-Hoeksema (1990, 2002; Nolen-Hoeksema & Girgus, 1994; Nolen-Hoeksema & Jackson, 2001) has found that men tend to deal with depression by trying to distract themselves, but women are more

© Richard M. Abarno/Corbis

Axis IV of the DSM addresses psychosocial stressors that may contribute to mental disorder, such as poverty, trouble with the law, and family upheaval.

likely to ruminate on the causes and effects, a practice that may leave them even more depressed. Depression is further associated with lack of social support or failing social relationships (T. O. Harris, 1992; Henderson, 1992).

Bipolar disorder, on the other hand, afflicts men and women of all socioeconomic classes equally (Krauthammer & Klerman, 1979; MacKinnon, Jamison, & De Paulo, 1997; Robins et al., 1984). Bipolar disorder is much rarer than unipolar depression (occurring in roughly 1.0% to 1.5% of the population), and it appears to run in families (suggesting possible genetic and physiological components). Some people initially diagnosed with depression are later identified as suffering from bipolar disorder (Bowden, 1993; Winokur, Coryell, Keller, Endicott, & Leon, 1995).

MAJOR DEPRESSION

People with **major depression** have persistent feelings of sadness, discouragement, and hopelessness that last for at least six weeks (McDermut, Zimmerman, & Chelminski, 2003). It may seem to them that nothing is right with their lives. Famous people who have been reported to suffer from depression are William Styron, the writer; Mike Wallace, the newsman; Winston Churchill, the statesman; and Abraham Lincoln, the 16th president of the United States. Typical cognitive symptoms of depression are low self-esteem, loss of motivation, and pessimism. Depressed people often generalize, so that a single failure, or an event that they interpret as indicating a failure, is assumed to foreshadow worse things to come. They often have very low energy; their body movements and even speech may slow down. A typical somatic symptom is difficulty sleeping, so that the person may have trouble falling asleep or may sleep most of the time.

The reason I hadn't washed my clothes or my hair was because it seemed so silly.

I saw the days of the year stretching ahead like a series of bright, white boxes, and separating one box from another was sleep, like a black shade. Only for me, the long perspective of shades that set off one box from the next had suddenly snapped up, and I could see day after day after day glaring ahead of me like a white, broad, infinitely desolate avenue.

It seemed silly to wash one day when I would only have to wash again the next.

It made me tired just to think of it.

I wanted to do everything once and for all and be through with it. (Sylvia Plath, *The Bell Jar*)

The various types and origins of depression are listed in Table 16.2. Clinicians distinguish between external, environmental variables and internal, physiological variables, and whether depression is the principal disorder or a symptom of another clinical disorder. It is essential to determine the cause of the depression in order to treat it (see Chapter 17). Some kinds of depression are linked to phases of life, as shown in Table 16.2.

Recent research suggests that depression in many cases is linked to the absence of sunlight. **Seasonal affective disorder (SAD)** is a form of depression that typically occurs during the winter months or near them. The fact that this form of depression is more common in the extreme north—where the winter sun may shine for just a few hours a day, if at all—suggests a link to available ambient light. Indeed, light therapy is used to treat this form of depression (Lewy, Sack, Miller, & Hoban, 1987; Rohan, Sigmon, & Dorhofer, 2003; Stastny et al., 2003). SAD appears to be related to irregularities in the body's production of melatonin, which is se-

creted by the pineal gland and is implicated in the sleeping–waking cycle.

Ⓒ A large cross-national study involving more than 40,000 participants in Western and non-Western countries concluded that major depression occurs across a broad range of cultures and that recent generations are at an increased risk of depression (Cross-National Collaborative Group, 1992). These findings take on added significance because the scientists who conducted the study claim that it is the first to use standard diagnostic criteria across all societies.

Seasonal affective disorder (SAD) is associated with the prolonged absence of sunlight that is characteristic of winter in many places.

TABLE 16.2
Origins of Depression. Clinicians often classify depression according to its origins.

Type	Description	Cause
Exogenous depression	A reaction to external (environmental) factors	Conflict with a partner, stress on the job, failure to achieve a goal, and so on
Endogenous depression	A reaction to internal (physiological) factors, such as imbalance of particular neurotransmitters	Chronic depression, without regard to what is going on externally; may stem from a family history of depression
Primary depression	Has depression as the main medical problem	Someone is depressed over the breakup of a relationship and feels unable to get out of bed as a result
Secondary depression	Caused by another disorder	Someone is injured and therefore bedridden and becomes depressed because of the physical limitations
Involutional depression	Associated with advanced age	Consequences associated with age, such as realizing that it is too late in life to achieve certain goals that were set earlier
Postpartum depression	Occurs after childbirth and can last anywhere from a few weeks to a year	Stress is usually the primary cause; other causes might be hormonal changes, changes in neurotransmitters, and fatigue; external locus of control, anxiety, and hostility; and lack of spousal and other social support
Seasonal affective disorder (SAD)	Typically occurs during winter months	A lack of available ambient light; irregularities in melatonin production

BIPOLAR DISORDER

In **bipolar disorder,** or manic-depressive disorder, the individual experiences extreme mood swings. Well-known people who suffer from bipolar disorder are actors Patty Duke and Carrie Fisher, and Kay Jamison, a psychiatrist at James Hopkins University who has written extensively about the disorder (Jamison, 2000; Simpson & Jamison, 1999). The most prominent symptom is **mania,** an elevated mood in which a person feels highly energetic and often grandiose. DSM-IV distinguishes between two forms of bipolar disorder. Bipolar Disorder I is characterized by an elated mania and sometimes by intermittent depression. In Bipolar Disorder II, the mania tends to be anxious and irritable, and mood swings are more frequent than in Bipolar Disorder I.

Manic people may believe there is no limit to what they can do, and they may act accordingly. One person suddenly decided to climb Mount McKinley equipped with only a cotton jacket and a pocketknife. Manic individuals often have trouble focusing their attention and may move from one activity to another in rapid succession. Occasionally, the manic person suffers from **delusions,** false beliefs that contradict known facts. Delusions reflect distorted thought processes. Manic individuals may spend money wildly, start nu-merous projects they cannot finish, or become hyper-sexual. Consequently, they may end up bankrupt, fired from their jobs, or divorced. They may have a greatly reduced need for sleep and tend to be immune from the fatigue that would hit most people after very strenuous periods of activity (see Figure 16.2).

EXPLANATIONS OF MOOD DISORDERS

Most of the explanations in this section are of major depression, not of bipolar depression. Research has shown that they are different disorders and require different treatment (see Chapter 17). Bipolar disorder is definitely not unipolar depression with a dash of mania. Its origins appear to be primarily biological. In contrast, major depression has multiple possible causes.

PSYCHODYNAMIC EXPLANATIONS

Psychodynamic explanations of depression emphasize feelings of loss. The psychodynamic interpretation begins with an analogy that Freud observed between depression and mourning (S. Freud, 1917/1957). He noticed that in both cases there is a sense of strong and possibly overwhelming sorrow, and that people in mourning frequently become depressed. He suggested

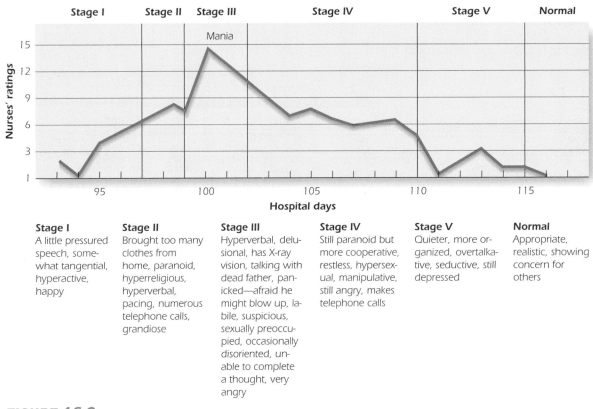

FIGURE 16.2

Stages of a Manic Episode. Case-study research often provides insight not easily available through laboratory studies, as shown in this longitudinal analysis of nurses' ratings of behavior in a patient hospitalized for mania. (After Carlson & Goodwin, 1973)

that when we lose someone we love through any termination of a relationship, we often have ambivalent feelings about the person we have lost. We may feel angry that the person has left us, although we may even realize that it is irrational to feel angry with someone who died involuntarily. According to Freud, when we lose an object of our love, we incorporate aspects of the person in a fruitless effort to regain at least parts of the relationship. At first glance, it seems as though this process should minimize our sense of loss and reduce depressive symptoms, but Freud saw a downside to incorporation: If we are angry toward the lost person, and we have incorporated aspects of that person, then we may become angry with ourselves.

Freud suggested that anger turned inward is the source of depression and that the precipitating event is the process of loss. As is typical of Freudian conceptualization, the emphasis is on losses that occurred during early childhood, although Freud acknowledged that losses at any time could cause depression.

HUMANISTIC EXPLANATIONS

Humanistic theorists have been less specific about depression than others, but one significant theory was proposed by Viktor Frankl (1959). Frankl drew largely on his own experience in Nazi concentration camps during World War II. He observed that of those individuals who were not put to death, the greatest difference between those who survived mentally intact and those who did not seemed to be their ability to find meaning in their suffering and to relate the experience to their spiritual lives. Generalizing from this experience, Frankl suggested that depression results from a lack of purpose in living. In this view, people who are depressed will improve if they can find meaning in their lives.

BEHAVIORAL EXPLANATIONS

Behavioral explanations of depression emphasize lack of rewards. The basic theory states that depressed people receive fewer rewards than do people who are not depressed (Ferster, 1973; A. A. Lazarus, 1968; Lewinsohn, 1974). In other words, fewer things make a depressed person happy and more things make a depressed person unhappy. The low level of energy and activity seen in depressed people is consistent with this explanation. Receiving little reinforcement, the depressed person has little incentive to act. A vicious cycle then ensues, whereby the individual withdraws from the kinds of activities that would provide rewards, further deepening the depression.

Depression may be self-sustaining, especially if other people actually give a depressed person fewer rewards. One study found that when nondepressed people were interacting with depressed people, the nondepressed people smiled less, were generally less

Depression can be catching, affecting family members as well as the person who suffers from the disorder directly.

pleasant, and made more negative comments than they did when interacting with other nondepressed people (Gotlib & Robinson, 1982). Other investigations have also shown that we are less pleasant toward depressed persons than toward people who are not depressed, perhaps because the low mood of the depressed person is contagious ("You bring me down") and leaves the interacting partner at least temporarily drained as well (Coyne, 1976a; Gotlib & Robinson, 1982).

Evidence also shows that when depressed people actually receive the same amount of reward or punishment as those who are not depressed, they think that they are receiving fewer rewards and more punishments (R. E. Nelson & Craighead, 1977). Their perception of the treatment they receive is more negative than the treatment they actually receive. Depressed people also appear to give themselves fewer rewards and more punishments for their own behavior (Rehm, 1977). This finding holds true whether we look at the general population or at people who are hospitalized for depression (Lobitz & Post, 1979; R. E. Nelson & Craighead, 1977, 1981).

Recall that women are more likely to be depressed than men. We cannot yet rule out the possibility that the higher frequency of depression in women may be due in part to hormonal differences, but a more intriguing, though still speculative, possibility is that learned helplessness (see Chapter 6) may contribute to the higher rate in women (Matlin, 1993; Seligman,

1974; Strickland, 1992). According to this view, women's social roles are more likely to lead them to feel depressed. Women traditionally have been forced into roles in which they have less control over the outcomes that affect them than do men. This lack of control may cause them to depend financially and emotionally on others, usually men. This dependence may lead to a form of learned helplessness. Both frustration and helplessness are linked to depression.

COGNITIVE EXPLANATIONS

Cognitive explanations of depression emphasize errors in thinking and misattributions. Inappropriate attributions and inferences directly contribute to depression, according to Aaron Beck (1967, 1985, 1991, 1997, 2002a; Brown & Beck, 2002), whose theory is probably the most prominent among contemporary cognitive theories of depression. Beck suggests that depressed people are particularly susceptible to one or more of five logical errors that lead them to view things negatively:

1. *Arbitrary inference* is drawing a conclusion even though there is little or no evidence to support it.
2. *Selective abstraction* is focusing on an insignificant detail of a situation while ignoring the more important features.
3. *Overgeneralization* is drawing global conclusions about ability on the basis of a single fact or episode.
4. *Magnification and minimization* are gross errors of evaluation—magnifying small, unfavorable events and minimizing large, favorable events.
5. *Personalization* involves taking personal responsibility for situational events.

According to a model of *hopelessness depression* (Abramson, Metalsky, & Alloy, 1989), a series of negative events can lead a person to feel hopeless about the future. Hopelessness sparks depression, which in turn sparks both more negative events and feelings of hopelessness. The cycle thus continues.

BIOLOGICAL EXPLANATIONS

Biological explanations suggest that abnormally low levels of neurotransmitters such as norepinephrine and serotonin may be linked to depression. One theory focuses on norepinephrine, the other on serotonin imbalance. Both theories focus on ways in which particular drugs reduce depression (see Chapter 17).

Certain monoamine neurotransmitters are thought to play a part in depression, including norepinephrine, dopamine, and serotonin. GABA and acetylcholine also may play a role. In particular, research suggests that people with depression or bipolar disorder may have reduced levels of serotonin and norepinephrine, especially in the hypothalamus (Malone & Mann, 1993;

McBride, Brown, Demeo, & Keilp, 1994). Sadness and helplessness have been found to be associated with changes in blood flow in the cerebrum and, in particular, in the frontal-temporal areas of the cortex (Cummings, 1993; George, Ring, & Costa, 1991). It is important to remember, however, that such associations do not reveal the causes of depression. The changes may result from, rather than cause, clinical depression.

Research suggests that the causes of bipolar disorder may be primarily biological. The causes of major depression may be partly biological. Genetic factors seem to influence the development of both mood disorders (Kelsoe, 2003; Plomin & McGuffin, 2003; Rieder, Kaufmann, & Knowles, 1994; Zubenko, Hughes, Stiffler, Zubenko, & Kaplan, 2002), although bipolar disorder seems to be more strongly genetically based (Gershon & Nurnberger, 1995; Kelsoe, 2003). One theory of bipolar disorder postulates that the manic phase is caused by an excess of norepinephrine (Bunney, Goodwin, & Murphy, 1972; Schildkraut, 1965). Urinary levels of norepinephrine decrease during the depressive phase (Bunney, Murphy, Goodwin, & Borge, 1970). Lithium, Lamictal, Depakote, Neurontin, and numerous other drugs are used to treat bipolar disorder. As mentioned earlier, the biological explanation of bipolar disorder is further supported by genetic studies showing substantially higher genetic transmission of bipolar than of major depressive disorders.

SUICIDE

Severe depression often precedes suicide or suicide attempts, as described in this example:

> Mr. Wrigley was referred by his general practitioner for an outpatient assessment after suicidal thoughts resulting from depression. Mr. Wrigley recently had been forced to retire as a hospital porter because of a series of strokes that made lifting heavy equipment impossible. He felt "completely changed" after this incident. He would burst into tears over seemingly trivial events. He had to force himself to eat because he had no appetite, and his sleeping periods became shorter and shorter. His social interactions decreased, and he became more isolated and withdrawn. Mr. Wrigley reported that he made an attempt on his life while having tea with his daughter and wife. He picked up a knife from the table as if to stab himself. He was restrained by his wife, then burst into tears sobbing, "I'm sorry, I'm sorry." (After M. Greenberg et al., 1986, pp. 16–17)

Suicide is self-inflicted death that represents an intentional, direct, and conscious effort to end one's life (Comer, 2002; Shneidman, 2001). Suicide is in the top 10 causes of death in many countries (Comer, 2002; Diekstra, 1996). Whether in the top 10 or not, however, it is a major mental-health problem (de Wilde,

Suicide threats should be taken very seriously. Many people who commit suicide have revealed their intention in one way or another.

attempts is three times as great for women as for men. At least one reason for the difference is that men are likely to shoot or hang themselves, whereas women are likely to take drugs, such as sleeping pills. Clearly, shooting and hanging are more lethal than an overdose of pills.

Other demographic factors also play a role. Men who are divorced are three times more likely to kill themselves than are married men. Men and women at all socioeconomic levels commit suicide, but professionals (e.g., psychologists, psychiatrists, attorneys, and physicians) are especially likely to do so. Finally, although suicide ranks only eighth as a cause of death among adults, it ranks third after accidents and homicides as a cause of death among people between the ages of 15 and 24. Among these young adults, whites are twice as likely as blacks to kill themselves (Bingham, Bennion, Oppenshaw, & Adams, 1994; Garland & Zigler, 1994).

If you know someone who expresses suicidal thought, you should encourage the individual, in the strongest possible terms, to seek professional counseling. You should not try to counsel the person yourself because counseling requires professional skills and judgment. If the person does not respond to your urging, you may wish to consult a college official or counselor in order to find out how best to ensure that the individual is helped.

THE MOTIVES FOR SUICIDE

The two main motivations for suicide appear to be surcease and manipulation. People who seek *surcease*, or cessation, have given up on life and see death as the only solution to their problems. Slightly more than half of suicides appear to be this kind. People seeking surcease are usually depressed, hopeless, and certain that they want their lives to end.

In contrast, those who view suicide as a means of *manipulation* use it to shape the world according to their desires. They may view suicide as a way to inflict revenge on a lover who has rejected them, to gain the attention of those who have ignored them, to hurt those who have hurt them, or to have the last word in an argument. Many of those who attempt suicide in this manner are not fully committed to dying but rather are using suicide as a call for attention and help (see Myth 2 in the Psychology in Everyday Life box). Roughly 13% of suicide attempts are this kind. Unless they receive help, people who attempt manipulative suicide often try again and may continue until they succeed.

Psychological disorders are the main risk factor for suicide attempts. The disorders most likely to lead to such attempts are mood disorders, substance-abuse disorders, personality disorders, and schizophrenia (*Risk Factors for Suicide: Summary of a Workshop*, 2001).

Kienhorst, & Diekstra, 2001). It is estimated that more than 700,000 people in the world commit suicide each year; roughly 31,000 are in the United States (Phillips, Liu, & Zhang, 1999). Many Western countries have suicide rates of 20 or more per 100,000 people; in fact, Western cultures seem to have the highest rates of suicide (Carson & Butcher, 1992), perhaps an outcome of their high rates of depression. In contrast, some cultures (e.g., the aborigines of Australia) have no known incidence of suicide whatsoever. The rate of suicide also rises in old age (particularly among white men), reaching a rate of more than 25 per 100,000 for people between the ages of 75 and 84.

Attempted suicide is referred to as *parasuicide* (Welch, 2001). Although we are not certain of the number of people who attempt suicide, estimates range between 250,000 and 600,000 per year in the United States. Many attempts probably go unrecorded. These estimates imply that for every successful suicide, there are probably more than 10 unsuccessful attempts. Many people who try once and fail will then try again and may continue until they succeed.

Men are much more likely to succeed in committing suicide than women. Although the suicide rate for men is almost four times that for women, the rate of

MOOD DISORDERS 587

MYTHS ABOUT SUICIDE

Suicide has inspired several myths (Fremouw, Perczel, & Ellis, 1990; Pokorny, 1968; Shneidman, 1973). It is useful to know about these myths so that you can help depressed individuals who are contemplating suicide. If you think someone who considers suicide cannot be talked out of it, you already believe the first myth.

Myth 1: All people who commit suicide have definitely decided that they want to die. In fact, many of those who commit suicide are not certain that they want to die. They often gamble that someone will save them. For example, a person who is attempting suicide may take pills and then call and tell someone. If the other person does not answer the call, or if that person does not follow through quickly in response to the call, the suicide attempt may succeed.

Myth 2: People who talk about committing suicide do not actually go ahead and do it. In fact, almost 8 out of 10 people who commit suicide have

given some warning that they were about to attempt it. Often, they have given several warnings.

Myth 3: Suicide occurs more often among the wealthy. In fact, suicide is about equally prevalent at all levels of the socioeconomic spectrum.

Myth 4: People who commit suicide are always depressed beforehand. Although depression is linked with suicide, some people who take their lives show no signs of depression at all. People with terminal illnesses, for example, may commit suicide not because they are depressed but to spare loved ones the suffering of having to care for them, or because they have made peace with death and have decided that its time has come.

Myth 5: People who commit suicide are crazy. Although suicide is linked to depression, relatively few people who commit suicide are truly out of touch with reality.

Myth 6: The risk of suicide ends when a person's mood improves follow-

ing a major depression or a previous suicidal crisis. In fact, most suicides occur while an individual is still depressed but has begun to show some recovery. Often, people who are severely depressed are unable to gather the energy to commit suicide, so it is more likely to occur when they are beginning to feel better and can do something about fulfilling their wish to die.

Myth 7: Suicide is influenced by the cosmos—sunspots, phases of the moon, the position of the planets, and so on. No evidence supports any of these beliefs.

Myth 8: Asking people whether they are considering killing themselves will put the idea into their heads. Therapists have a responsibility to inquire about suicidal ideation. Their professional inquiries do not generate such ideation.

suicidal ideation
suicide and depression
suicide prevention

✓CONCEPT CHECK 4

1. SAD is a form of depression that typically occurs during the
   a. summer.
   b. autumn.
   c. winter.
   d. spring.
2. People with bipolar disorder alternate between depression and
   a. schizophrenia.
   b. anxiety.
   c. repression.
   d. mania.
3. Psychodynamic explanations of depression emphasize
   a. low rates of reinforcement.
   b. feelings of loss.
   c. cognitive errors.
   d. reuptake of serotonin.

SCHIZOPHRENIC DISORDERS

What are the main symptoms of schizophrenia? What causes it?

Schizophrenia is a class of disorders marked by disturbances of perception, cognition, emotion, and motor behavior. Perceptual symptoms include hallucinations, the perception of things that aren't there. Cognitive symptoms include delusions, beliefs that have no objective basis. Emotional symptoms include flat affect (blunted expression of emotions) and inappropriate affect. These symptoms are sometimes characterized as negative or positive. *Negative symptoms* include deficits in behavior, such as affective flattening, language problems, apathy, and social isolation. *Positive symptoms* include behaviors not normally experienced, such as delusions, hallucinations, and bizarre behavior. People with schizophrenia exhibit *psychotic behavior,* meaning that they lose contact with reality and experience irrational ideas and distorted perceptions. Consider the next passage:

> [Rose] had her first psychotic break when she was fifteen. She had been coming home moody and tearful, then quietly beaming, then she stopped coming home. . . .
>
> Dinner was filled with all of our starts and stops and Rose's desperate efforts to control herself. She could barely eat and hummed the McDonald's theme song over and over again, pausing only to spill her juice down the front of her smock and begin weeping. My father looked at my mother and handed Rose his napkin. She dabbed at herself, listlessly, but the tears stopped.
>
> "I want to go to bed. I want to go to bed and be in my head. I want to go to bed and be in my bed and in my head and just wear red. For red is the color that my baby wore and once more, it's true, yes, it is, it's true. Please don't wear red tonight, ohh, ohh, please don't wear red tonight, for red is the color—" (Amy Bloom, "Silver Water")

To be diagnosed as having schizophrenia, an individual must show (1) impairment in areas such as work, social relations, and self-care; (2) at least two cognitive, affective, or motor symptoms; and (3) persistence of symptoms for at least 6 months.

The prognosis for persons who have schizophrenia is not particularly encouraging. Schizophrenia typically involves a series of acute episodes with intermittent periods of remission. In many cases, the individual's ability to function during remission declines with each successive acute episode. The consensus among psychologists is that once people have a full-fledged episode of schizophrenia, they are rarely completely rid of the disorder. Despite disagreement about this prognosis, many psychologists believe that many of the symptoms may be treated with psychotherapy and drugs (Dixon, Lehman, & Levine, 1995; Kasper & Resinger, 2003; Sartorius, Shapiro, & Jablonsky, 1974; S. C. Schulz, 1995; Tandon & Jibson, 2003).

The disorder tends to run in families. A review of several studies on the genetic transmission of schizophrenia found that a relative of a person with schizophrenia is 10 times more likely than a nonrelative to develop the disorder (Docherty & Gottesman, 2000; Gottesman, 1991, 1994; Gottesman, McGuffin, & Farmer, 1987; Gottesman & Reilly, 2003). Among schizophrenics, the prevalence rates are 44% for identical twins, 12% for fraternal twins, 7% for siblings, 9% for children, and 3% for grandchildren (see Figure 16.3). Schizophrenia affects 1% to 2% of the general population.

Schizophrenia is generally diagnosed in early adulthood, usually before age 45 (see Figure 16.4). The incidence has been found to vary with socioeconomic status (SES). In particular, members of the low-

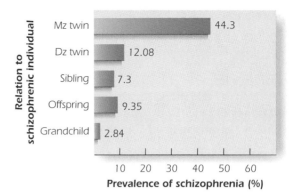

FIGURE 16.3
Vulnerability to Schizophrenia. The rates of overlap in the occurrence of schizophrenia increase in relation to the closeness of the hereditary link among individuals. (After data from Gottesman, 1991; Gottesman, McGuffin, & Farmer, 1987)

est SES group are roughly eight times more likely to suffer from schizophrenia than members of the middle and upper SES groups (B. S. Dohrenwend & Dohrenwend, 1974; Strauss, Kokes, Ritzler, Harder, & Van Ord, 1978). The difference may reflect differ-

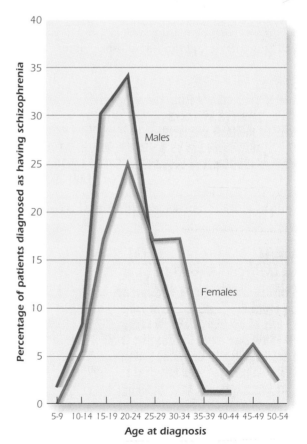

FIGURE 16.4
Diagnosis of Schizophrenia. According to A. W. Loranger, schizophrenia is usually diagnosed in males at younger ages than in females. (After Loranger, 1984)

ent prevalences across SES groups, different rates of diagnosis of existing conditions, or both. Different diagnostic rates might result, for example, if therapists were more likely to assign a label of "schizophrenia" to individuals from lower SES levels than upper ones. However, stress also increases the likelihood of display of schizophrenia (B. P. Dohrenwend, 2000), and stress may be greater in lower SES than in higher SES groups.

TYPES OF SCHIZOPHRENIA

DSM-IV recognizes five main types of schizophrenia: disorganized, catatonic, paranoid, undifferentiated, and residual schizophrenia.

DISORGANIZED SCHIZOPHRENIA

Disorganized schizophrenia is characterized by profound psychological disorganization. Sufferers may experience hallucinations and delusions, and their speech is often incoherent. When a 23-year-old person with schizophrenia was asked, "How have you been feeling?" he answered flatly, "I'm as sure as you can help me as I have ice cubes in my ears" (R. L. Spitzer, Skodol, Gibbon, & Williams, 1983, p. 156). People with disorganized schizophrenia show flat affect and may grimace or smile fatuously for no particular reason. They may giggle in a childish manner, invent words, and experience rapid mood swings.

CATATONIC SCHIZOPHRENIA

People with *catatonic schizophrenia* experience predominantly negative symptoms, often exhibiting stupor and immobility for long periods of time. Affected individuals often stare into space, seemingly completely detached from the rest of the world. Because catatonics move so little, their limbs may become stiff and swollen. This form of schizophrenia is less common today than it was in the past, although no one knows why for sure.

PARANOID SCHIZOPHRENIA

People with *paranoid schizophrenia* may have delusions of persecution, hearing voices criticizing or threatening them. Or they may have delusions of grandeur, hearing voices telling them how wonderful they are. The people do not show disorganized speech or behavior, or flat or inappropriate affect. Consider this example:

> A 26-year-old woman was referred to a psychiatric hospital after attempting suicide by drug overdose. Her father had been diagnosed as having schizophrenia and died when she was 13 by committing suicide. She was hospitalized twice in the past year for various psychotic episodes. For the previous few weeks, she had been convinced that the Devil was persecuting her. She would lay awake at night fanta-

People with catatonic schizophrenia may assume odd positions and hold them for a long time, a condition called waxy flexibility. If this woman's arm were manipulated into a different position she would hold the new pose indefinitely.

sizing that the Devil was tapping on her window. She believed that other individuals were talking to her and could read her mind. Many times she felt she was under the Devil's control. He would talk through her and had the power to inflict pain. She believed the only way to avoid the Devil was to kill herself. Her mother found her on the floor and called the ambulance. At the hospital, she said that she still heard voices talking to her and that they had the power to control her thinking. (After Fottrell, 1983, p. 128)

A person who suffers from paranoid schizophrenia may retreat into isolation and self-protectiveness.

People with paranoid schizophrenia are particularly susceptible to delusions of reference; that is, they take an insignificant event and interpret it as though it has great personal meaning.

UNDIFFERENTIATED SCHIZOPHRENIA

Undifferentiated schizophrenia is a catchall category for schizophrenic symptoms either that do not quite fit any of the other patterns or that fit more than one pattern.

RESIDUAL SCHIZOPHRENIA

Residual schizophrenia is a diagnosis applied to people who have had at least one schizophrenic episode and who currently show some mild symptoms but do not exhibit profoundly disturbed behavior.

STRESSORS THAT CONTRIBUTE TO SCHIZOPHRENIA

Why is there such a pronounced difference among people with schizophrenia across the SES groups? According to the *social-drift hypothesis* (Myerson, 1940), people who suffer from schizophrenia tend to drift downward in SES. Their inability to earn a living, relate to other people, and function effectively leads them to successively lower SES levels until they bottom out. Evidence shows that people with schizophrenia are much more likely than are others to drift downward in SES (R. J. Turner & Wagonfeld, 1967).

An alternative explanation is that the social and economic conditions a person faces in the lowest SES groups are so stressful that they tend to precipitate schizophrenia, at least more so than higher SES groups. According to the diathesis-stress theory discussed earlier (see p. 572), people with a genetic susceptibility to schizophrenia are more likely to develop the disorder when they are subjected to life stresses. Recent data suggest that members of groups experiencing discrimination and the stress that results from it are more prone to schizophrenia, regardless of social class (B. P. Dohrenwend, 2000; B. P. Dohrenwend et al., 1992).

Still another explanation is that people of lower SES are more likely to be diagnosed as having schizophrenia because people of higher SES may be able to hide their symptoms better. It appears that the lower-SES individual is more likely to be diagnosed as having schizophrenia even when the symptoms are the same as those of someone of higher SES (Hollingshead & Redlich, 1958; M. A. Kramer, 1957). Why do people of any SES develop schizophrenia?

EXPLANATIONS OF SCHIZOPHRENIA

The many explanations of schizophrenia are not necessarily mutually exclusive. They may simply apply to different kinds or levels of severity of schizophrenia.

At present, none of the existing theories seems to account for all aspects of every schizophrenic disorder.

PSYCHODYNAMIC EXPLANATIONS

The psychodynamic paradigm has offered some explanations for schizophrenia that currently do not receive much support. The classic Freudian explanation focuses on *primary narcissism*; that is, the person who has schizophrenia regresses to the oral stage of psychological development, which occurs before the ego has differentiated itself from the id. Persons with schizophrenia are securely wrapped up in themselves but out of touch with the world (Arieti, 1974). Even Freud, though, felt that his theory did not adequately explain schizophrenia or offer a means to treat it.

HUMANISTIC EXPLANATIONS

Humanistic psychologists usually deal with disorders that are less seriously disruptive than schizophrenia. However, two humanistic psychologists have unorthodox views on the subject. Thomas Szasz (1961) argued that schizophrenia and other so-called mental illnesses are merely alternative ways of experiencing the world. In a related vein, therapist R. D. Laing (1964) suggested that schizophrenia is not an illness but merely a label that society applies to behavior it finds problematic. According to Laing, people acquire schizophrenic tendencies when they live in situations that are simply not livable. No matter what they do, nothing seems to work and they feel in checkmate. Today the theories of Szasz and Laing generally are given little credence.

BEHAVIORAL EXPLANATIONS

A prominent behavioral theory, *labeling theory* (Scheff, 1966), holds that once people are labeled as having schizophrenia, they are more likely to appear to exhibit symptoms of the disorder. In part this is because they come to feel rewarded for their behavior. For one thing, people who have been labeled as having schizophrenia may feel free (or even expected) to engage in antisocial behavior that would not be tolerated in so-called normal people. Also, once they begin to act abnormally, more of their behavior is likely to be interpreted as abnormal. David Rosenhan (1973) observed that the behavior of patients in psychiatric wards is likely to be viewed as abnormal even when the supposed patients are mentally healthy. According to this theory, someone who is labeled as having schizophrenia is susceptible to becoming schizophrenic merely because of the label. The label itself may create a self-fulfilling prophecy.

Most evidence does not favor labeling theory, however, at least to the extent one attempts to explain a disorder solely on the basis of labeling. If the theory were correct, one might expect that in other cultures schizophrenic behavior would be viewed as normal. But in both the Eskimo and Yoruba cultures, for example, the behavior labeled in our society as schizophrenic is also viewed as "crazy" (Murphy, 1976). Thus, there is at least some agreement about what is nonadaptive across societies.

COGNITIVE EXPLANATIONS

Cognitive explanations of schizophrenia suggest that people with schizophrenia have sensory experiences that differ from those of normal individuals. From this perspective, many symptoms of schizophrenia may be construed as attempts by the sufferers to explain their sensory experiences to others. Unlike the other explanations of schizophrenia we have considered, cognitive explanations interpret the bizarre sensory experiences of schizophrenics as genuine and as causing the disorder. According to this view, breakdowns in communication with people who have schizophrenia often result from their attempt to explain what is happening to them. People with schizophrenia are particularly susceptible to stimulus overload, which leads them to function in a maladaptive manner. It may be that they lack a filtering mechanism that allows most people to screen out irrelevant stimuli (Payne, Matussek, & George, 1959).

BIOLOGICAL EXPLANATIONS

Biological explanations of schizophrenia emphasize neurochemical imbalances. Some of the most promising theories today focus on biology. One view holds that schizophrenia results from an excess of the neurotransmitter dopamine (Seidman, 1990; Wong et al., 1986; see Chapter 3), although the evidence is mixed (Heinrichs, 1993, 2001). Another view sug-

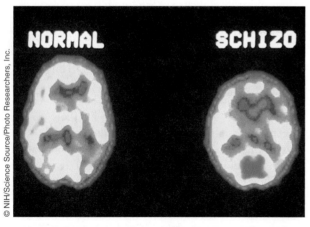

Contemporary imaging techniques offer insight into some of the cerebral processes that underlie psychological disorders. These images show the differences in the patterns of activity in a normal brain compared with the brain of a schizophrenic.

gests the possibility of structural abnormalities in the brain as the cause (Heinrichs & Zakzanis, 1998; Seidman, 1983). Some evidence indicates that people with schizophrenia have enlarged *ventricles*—the canals through which cerebrospinal fluid (CSF) flows—in the brain (Andreasen et al., 1994; Andreasen et al., 1990; Andreasen, Olsen, Dennert, & Smith, 1982a, 1982b; DeGreef et al., 1992). The ventricles generally appear enlarged when the surrounding tissue has atrophied, and evidence documents atrophy in portions of the brains of people with schizophrenia. Another intriguing finding is that people with schizophrenia show less use of the prefrontal region of the brain than do nonschizophrenics (Berman, Torrey, Daniel, & Weinberger, 1992; Weinberger, Wagner, & Wyatt, 1983). The prefrontal cortex is generally smaller and shows less activation in people who have schizophrenia (Andreasen, Flaum, Schultz, Duzyurek, & Miller, 1997; Buchsbaum, Haier, Potkin, & Nuechterlein, 1992).

One biological explanation of schizophrenia, or at least of certain variants, is that it is primarily caused by a virus contracted by the mother during the prenatal period (usually the second trimester, when the brain is developing most rapidly) (Conejero-Goldberg, Torrey, & Yolken, 2003; Torrey, 1988; Torrey, Bowler, Taylor, & Gottesman, 1994). This explanation might account for why mothers exposed to the influenza or other serious respiratory viruses during the second trimester of pregnancy have a somewhat greater tendency to have children who later develop schizophrenia (Barr, Mednick, & Munk-Jorgensen, 1990; Brown & Susser, 2002; Mednick, Hutunen, & Machon, 1994). At the present time, though, this explanation must be viewed as speculative. A second and even more speculative viral explanation is that schizophrenia is itself caused by a slow-acting virus (see Gottesman, 1991).

Although schizophrenia is usually maladaptive, some psychologists have argued that it may, in certain forms, have some evolutionary value. For example, people who do not have schizophrenia but have some tendencies like those associated with the personality of someone with schizophrenia may be predisposed toward creativity. They exhibit what Eysenck (1997) calls *psychoticism* (see Chapter 15). And full-blown schizophrenia is sometimes associated with the ability to generate novel relationships with new kinds of problems (Palmer & Palmer, 2002). In extreme circumstances, and at certain points in history, such people have been seen as divinely inspired leaders (Palmer & Palmer, 2002).

Nonpsychologists often confuse schizophrenia with what is popularly called "multiple personality," formally known as dissociative identity disorder.

IN THE LAB OF ELAINE WALKER

SEARCHING FOR THE PRECURSORS OF SCHIZOPHRENIA

Schizophrenia is the most devastating of all mental disorders. It usually strikes in late adolescence or adulthood, and it often has a chronic course. The illness can deprive the patient of attaining adult milestones such as occupational satisfaction, marriage, and children.

My first exposure to schizophrenia was during college, when I worked at a psychiatric hospital. Like others, I felt deep compassion for the patients, and I was saddened to see the pervasive negative impact of the illness on their lives. In reviewing patients' medical records, I was also amazed by the abrupt behavioral changes they manifested with the transition into adolescence. The parents of many patients did not notice any abnormalities before late adolescence. Yet it seemed implausible that an illness like schizophrenia could be preceded by a completely normal developmental course. Had earlier signs been missed?

At the time I began my career, only a few facts about schizophrenia were widely accepted by researchers. A pivotal assumption was that vulnerability to the disorder involved a biological abnormality that often had a genetic basis and was thus inborn. I became interested in identifying the earliest signs of this vulnerability. What, if any, were the signs of risk during infancy and early childhood? With this question as the impetus, I pursued

Elaine Walker is the Samuel Candler Dobbs Professor of Psychology and Neuroscience at Emory University. She is the recipient of the Zubin Award from the New York Psychiatric Institute, the Gralnick Award from the American Psychological Foundation, Career Development Awards from the National Institute of Mental Health, and an Established Investigator Award from the National Alliance for Research on Schizophrenia and Depression.

research on schizophrenia during graduate school, and I have continued to study the disorder as a professional psychologist.

Of course, researching a mental disorder is not easy, especially when the goal is to identify its precursors. If we ask friends or family members to describe the patient's childhood, we may get biased information because the informants are aware that the person has been diagnosed with schizophrenia. In order to avoid this "retrospective bias," we could look at the patient's childhood school or medical records (the "follow-back" approach). This offers the advantage of avoiding retrospective bias, but it may fail to tell us about subtle behavioral characteristics.

As I considered strategies for obtaining more detailed information about patients' early development, it occurred to me that one promising approach might be home movies. The National Alliance for the Mentally Ill is an organization

whose membership includes many parents of children diagnosed with schizophrenia. With its support, we surveyed members to determine how many had films of a child who was later diagnosed with schizophrenia. We obtained childhood films of enough patients to conduct a controlled study. With grant support form the National Institute of Mental Health and the National Alliance for Research on Schizophrenia and Depression, I launched the research project.

We obtained childhood movies of patients with schizophrenia, of patients suffering from major depression or bipolar disorder, and of a group of individuals with no mental illness. The healthy siblings who also appeared in the films served as another comparison group. The home movies covered the patients' first 3 years of life, and many extended through adolescence. We also collected data on development, medical history,

continued

neuropsychological functions, and, for some, MRI brain scans.

In one of the first studies from the project, we coded the children's facial expressions of emotion on a frame-by-frame basis. (The raters, of course, did not know which research participants had been diagnosed with schizophrenia.) We found that the preschizophrenic children showed more negative emotion than did children in the comparison groups (Walker, Grimes, Davis, & Smith, 1993). Also, the preschizophrenic females showed fewer expressions of positive emotion than did their sisters who did not have mental illness. These differences were stable across childhood. Overall, the findings indicated that at least some people who later develop schizophrenia manifest subtle signs of vulnerability in their emotional behavior from a very young age. Because some differences were apparent during the first year of life, the results were consistent with the idea that vulnerability can be present at birth.

We had specialists in neuromotor development code delays and abnormalities in the children's motor functions. Their results showed that those who later developed schizophrenia manifested significant delays and abnormalities in motor behavior (Walker, Savoie,

& Davis, 1994). In learning to crawl and walk, they were less coordinated than their siblings with healthy adult outcomes. They also showed more abnormalities in limb posture and movements. A child with abnormal posture and movement of the left hand is shown in the photo below. Again, group differences were detected as early as infancy. It is worth noting that in most cases the parents had not noticed the subtle abnormalities we observed in their children. This is not surprising because even normal children vary in their developmental pace.

Having established that schizophrenia is predicted by abnormalities in infant emotional expressions and motor behavior, we next focused on the origins of these signs. Deficits in motor functions often reflect abnormalities in the brain. We therefore

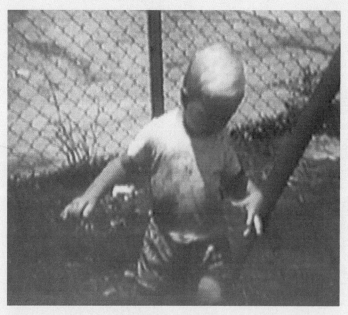

This 4-year-old boy habitually held his left hand in an abnormal position. He later developed schizophrenia.

wanted to determine whether this is true in schizophrenia. Our analysis of the data confirmed the relation: Among the patients we studied, early childhood neuromotor deficits and negative affect were linked with greater brain ventricular enlargement in adulthood (Walker, Lewine, & Neumann, 1996). This led us to conclude that early signs of vulnerability stem from brain abnormalities that are present at birth.

The findings from our study of home videos provided important information about precursors, but also raised intriguing questions. Given that the vulnerability is present at birth, why does the onset of clinical schizophrenia typically occur in late adolescence or early adulthood? To address this question, we have shifted our focus to study the biological and psychological development of adolescents who are at risk for schizophrenia (Walker, 2002). The participants in these studies are adolescents who show a syndrome called schizotypal personality disorder, which involves signs of schizophrenia that are below the clinical threshold. Preliminary findings indicate that maturational changes in the biological response to stress may play a role in triggering the expression of schizophrenia (Walker, Walder, & Reynolds, 2001).

1. People who giggle in a childish manner or invent words are most likely to suffer from _____ schizophrenia.
   a. disorganized
   b. catatonic
   c. paranoid
   d. residual
2. People who exhibit immobility for long periods of time most likely suffer from _____ schizophrenia.
   a. disorganized
   b. catatonic
   c. undifferentiated
   d. residual
3. People who have delusions of persecution most likely suffer from _____ schizophrenia.
   a. disorganized
   b. catatonic
   c. paranoid
   d. residual

DISSOCIATIVE DISORDERS

What are dissociative disorders? What are their symptoms?

Dissociative disorders involve an alteration in the normally integrative functions of consciousness or identity, whereby an individual's present conscious awareness becomes separated (dissociated) from previous thoughts and feelings. These disorders tend to be severe but rare. The three main *dissociative disorders* are dissociative amnesia, dissociative fugue, and dissociative identity disorder (also termed *multiple personality disorder*). For some of the dissociative disorders, environmental traumas have been more strongly implicated than hereditary factors.

DISSOCIATIVE AMNESIA

Dissociative amnesia is characterized by sudden memory loss of declarative knowledge (facts and ideas) and usually impairs the recollection of events that took place during and immediately after a stressful event. In addition, the affected person has difficulty remembering most important personal details, such as name, address, and family members. The amnesic is able to function relatively normally, though. The duration of the amnesia may be from several hours to several years. Recovery of the lost information is usually as rapid as the loss was, after which the episode ends and memory loss does not recur.

DISSOCIATIVE FUGUE

A person who suffers from **dissociative fugue** responds to severe stress by experiencing total amnesia about the past and embarking upon a whole new life. He or she assumes a new identity, may take a new job, and behaves like totally different person, perhaps even with a new personality. Recovery time is variable. When a person does recover, he or she may or may not remember anything that took place during the fugue.

DISSOCIATIVE IDENTITY DISORDER

Dissociative identity disorder (DID) typically arises as a result of extreme early trauma—usually severe child abuse—and is characterized by the appearance of two or more identities (*alters*) within the same individual. Each identity is relatively independent of the others, has a stable life of its own, and occasionally takes full control of the person's behavior. One personality may know about the others. This disorder may begin early, when the child first experiences the serious emotional trauma (Bliss, 1980). It is more common in women than in men, perhaps because girls are more likely to be subjected to sexual abuse than boys (Boon & Draijer, 1993). Individuals with DID tend to have a rich fantasy life and are susceptible to self-hypnosis (see Chapter 5). Once they unconsciously discover that they can create another identity through self-hypnosis, the primary identity is partly relieved of some of the emotional burden. Later, when the existing identities cannot readily handle an emotional trauma, they create another to deal with it. People who develop multiple personalities in childhood may not know about the other personalities until adulthood. Recovery requires extensive therapy.

One of the most famous cases of dissociative identities is Chris Sizemore, whose story was popularized in the movie *The Three Faces of Eve* (see also Thigpen & Cleckley, 1957). One face was "Eve White," a quiet, proper, relatively inhibited young woman. Eve White sought psychotherapy to treat headaches and blackouts. One day, in the presence of her physician, she suddenly grasped her head as though seized by a sudden and violent headache. She soon seemed to recover, but then she was not the same person who had had the headache. She identified herself as "Eve Black." Eve Black's personality

Chris Sizemore was diagnosed as suffering from multiple personality disorder. She became famous after serving as the subject of the book and the movie The Three Faces of Eve.

was wild, promiscuous, and reckless—almost the opposite of Eve White's. Eve Black was aware of Eve White, but the reverse was not true. The third personality, Jane, was the most stable of the three and seemed to be the most well integrated. Jane was aware of both of the other two personalities and had a higher regard for Eve Black than for Eve White. Sizemore later wrote a book in which she claimed to have had as many as 21 separate personalities (Sizemore & Pittillo, 1977). Contrary to the claims of C. Thigpen and H. Cleckley (1957), who popularized her story, Sizemore says that the therapy she received did not cure her.

There is hot controversy today over whether dissociative identity disorder really exists (S. D. Miller & Triggiano, 1992; Spanos, 1994). Almost certainly, some cases that have been described as presenting this disorder have been misdiagnosed, especially in highly suggestible people (American Psychiatric Association, 1994). It has been proposed, for example, that some clients may wish to believe they suffer from the disorder. It also has been hypothesized that some therapists may inadvertently implant the idea of the disorder in clients in order to confirm their prior hypotheses about the clients' problems. At present, we cannot say for sure whether or not the disorder is genuine.

✓ CONCEPT CHECK 6

1. Dissociative amnesia is characterized by sudden loss of _____ knowledge.
   a. procedural
   b. declarative
   c. secret
   d. semantic

2. A person who starts a whole new life and experiences total amnesia about the past exhibits dissociative
   a. identity disorder.
   b. fugue.
   c. amnesia.
   d. sonata.
3. Dissociative identity order is a condition that _____ psychologists accept as real.
   a. no
   b. only a handful of
   c. some but far from all
   d. all

DISORDERS USUALLY DIAGNOSED IN INFANCY, CHILDHOOD, OR ADOLESCENCE

Can children have mental disorders? Are they the same as those seen in adults?

Depression and anxiety disorders unfortunately affect children as well as adults. Some disorders, however, characteristically appear first in infancy, childhood, or adolescence.

ATTENTION-DEFICIT HYPERACTIVITY DISORDER (ADHD)

Attention-deficit hyperactivity disorder (ADHD) is characterized by inattention, impulsiveness, and hyperactivity that are inappropriate for the age of the child. The three subtypes are hyperactive/impulsive, inattentive, and combined. Many children with this disorder tend to be impulsive and disruptive in social settings. They are often unable to sit still, and they constantly seek attention. This disorder is diagnosed more often in boys than in girls and appears before age 7. Indeed, it is likely that the child will exhibit symptoms by age 4, although they may not be recognized as the disorder until the child enters school. Psychologists do not know what causes ADHD, but it is generally believed to reflect an organic brain dysfunction. It is often treated with a stimulant, such as Ritalin. Because the prevalence of this disorder has risen over the last decade, some believe that the diagnosis is being abused by educators and parents who simply wish to make normally energetic and at times unruly children less troublesome. In such cases, children may be medicated who do not need medication. As many as 3% to 5% of children may have this disorder (American Psychiatric Association, 1987).

An inability to sit still, a tendency to behave inappropriately, and disregard of others are characteristic of attention-deficit hyperactivity disorder (ADHD).

The disorder tends to run in families (Faraone, Biederman, Feighner, & Monuteaux, 2000). Although there is probably a genetic predisposition, environmental factors such as marital unhappiness or alcoholism of parents can increase the chances of the disorder's manifesting itself. This fact is consistent with the diathesis-stress model discussed earlier. Morever, there is a high level of comorbidity with other problems, such as learning disabilities, conduct disorders, and substance abuse.

ADHD appears to be a lifelong condition. Thus, individuals diagnosed with ADHD in childhood may need psychological counseling throughout their lives, not just in their early years. ADHD may manifest itself in different ways at different points in the life span (Biederman, Mick, & Faraone, 2000). Adults, for example, generally do not have to sit still for long periods of time in classrooms, and hence they may find coping easier in adulthood than in childhood. But adults still may be fidgety, have trouble focusing on tasks, and find their attention wandering despite efforts to pay attention.

CONDUCT DISORDERS

Conduct disorders are characterized by habitual misbehavior, such as stealing, skipping school, destroying property, fighting, being cruel to animals and to other people, and lying. Children who have this disorder may misbehave independently or in groups or gangs. Conduct disorder is often a precursor to antisocial personality disorder.

PERVASIVE DEVELOPMENTAL DISORDER (PDD)

Pervasive developmental disorder (PDD) is characterized by three main symptoms: (1) minimal or no responsiveness to others or to the surrounding world;

(2) impairment in verbal and nonverbal communication; and (3) highly restricted range of interest, sitting alone for hours, immobility, rocking back and forth, and staring off into space. Infants who have PDD do not cry when left alone and do not smile back. Even by age 5, many children with PDD are unable to use language. *Autism* is one form of pervasive developmental disorder. Some believe that it is caused by the lack of *theory of mind;* that is, the children do not understand their own minds (Baron-Cohen, Leslie, & Frith, 1985; Leslie, 1999). They fail to comprehend their feelings, their perceptions, and their thoughts, as well as what kinds of behavior they might predict. PDD occurs in only about 0.04% of the population and is four times more likely to occur in boys than in girls.

> Five-year-old Jimmy Patterson was brought to the inpatient child psychiatric unit at a large city hospital. His parents complained that he was impossible to manage, was not toilet trained, and screamed or gestured whenever he became frustrated or wanted to be noticed. He was allowed a free-play period and an interaction period involving a cooperative task with his mother. He wandered about the playroom and played by himself with a number of toys. His mother then tried to involve him in some cooperative play with wooden blocks. She spoke to Jimmy in a cheerful tone, but he seemed not to notice her and moved to an opposite part of the room. Mrs. Patterson made several comments to Jimmy, but he remained oblivious to her encouragements. She then tried to begin a jigsaw puzzle with Jimmy. She led him over to a chair, but as soon as he sat down, he got up again and continued to wander about the room. His mother then firmly, although not harshly, took Jimmy by the arm and led him over to a chair. Jimmy began to whine and scream and flail his arms about, and eventually wiggled out of his mother's grasp. (After G. R. Leon, 1974, p. 9)

Clinicians originally believed that PDD might be a childhood form of schizophrenia. They now believe that the two disorders are different (American Psychiatric Association, 1994). Children with schizophrenia often have a family history of the disorder, but those with PDD do not. Also, the drugs that alleviate symptoms of schizophrenia are not effective with PDD (see Chapter 17).

✓ CONCEPT CHECK 7

1. Children with ADHD _____ their attention.
   a. are completely unable to focus
   b. have difficulty focusing
   c. always can focus
   d. do not want to focus

2. A youth who steals, skips school, lies, fights, and is cruel to animals most likely suffers from _____ disorder.
   a. attention-deficit hyperactivity
   b. pervasive developmental
   c. conduct
   d. posttraumatic stress
3. Which of the following is *not* a typical symptom of autism?
   a. minimal responsiveness to others
   b. impairment in communication
   c. highly restricted range of interest
   d. an IQ of less than 30

PERSONALITY DISORDERS

What are personality disorders? What are their symptoms?

Personality disorders involve exaggerated and maladaptive characteristics that persist over a long period of time and that interfere with a person's adjustment to everyday situations. DSM-IV places personality disorders on their own axis. As difficult as it may be to categorize various types of schizophrenia, it is even more difficult to differentiate the many personality disorders in DSM-IV.

Although it may be possible to detect some features of personality disorders during childhood or adolescence, they are not generally diagnosed until early adulthood.

PARANOID PERSONALITY DISORDER

In *paranoid personality disorder*, individuals are suspicious of others, expect to be poorly treated, and blame others for things that happen to them.

SCHIZOID PERSONALITY DISORDER

In *schizoid personality disorder*, individuals have difficulty forming relationships with other people and tend to be indifferent to what others think, say, or feel about them.

SCHIZOTYPAL PERSONALITY DISORDER

Individuals with *schizotypal personality disorder* have serious problems with other people and show eccentric or bizarre behavior. They are susceptible to illusions and may engage in magical thinking, believing that they have contact with the supernatural. This disorder may be a mild form of schizophrenia.

BORDERLINE PERSONALITY DISORDER

Individuals with *borderline personality disorder* show extreme instability in moods, self-image, and relationships with other people.

NARCISSISTIC PERSONALITY DISORDER

Individuals with *narcissistic personality disorder* have an inflated view of themselves and are intensely self-centered and selfish in their personal relationships. They lack empathy for others and often use others for their own ends. They often spend time fantasizing about past and future successes.

HISTRIONIC PERSONALITY DISORDER

Individuals with *histrionic personality disorder* generally act as though they are on stage, are very dramatic, and continually try to draw attention to themselves. They are lavish in their emotional displays, but shallow in the depth of their emotions. They often have trouble in relationships and tend to be manipulative and demanding. This case of histrionic personality disorder probably includes complicating factors:

> A 58-year-old woman recently was brought to the hospital after police picked her up off the street where she had been shouting, crying, and banging her head against a wall. During the initial interview she recalled that, "I had my first breakdown when I learned of my husband's illness." Since then she has had 16 admissions to the hospital for a variety of reasons. She indicated that her present illness began when she was discharged to an apartment she did not like, and was upset with her son because she did not approve of the woman he had chosen to marry. During the next few days, she became depressed and began to behave in a boisterous, attention-seeking manner. She created various disturbances in her neighborhood and subsequently was brought to the hospital by police. In the hospital, she was extremely uncooperative. She kept eyes firmly shut and refused to open them. She would sit up on her bed only when told, and then immediately fall back under the covers. (After Fottrell, 1983, p. 122)

AVOIDANT PERSONALITY DISORDER

Individuals with *avoidant personality disorder* are reluctant to enter into close personal relationships. They may wish for intimacy but be so sensitive to rejection that they are afraid to be close to others. These individuals often have very low self-esteem and devalue much of what they do.

DEPENDENT PERSONALITY DISORDER

Individuals with *dependent personality disorder* lack self-confidence and have difficulty taking personal responsibility. They subordinate their needs to those of loved ones, partly in fear of losing the loved ones if they express their own needs. They are extremely sensitive to criticism. This disorder is more common in women than in men.

OBSESSIVE–COMPULSIVE PERSONALITY DISORDER

Individuals who suffer from *obsessive–compulsive personality disorder* display excessive concern with details, rules, and codes of behavior; they tend to be perfectionists and require that everything be done just so; they further tend to be highly work-oriented. They often have trouble relating to other people and may be cold and distant in interpersonal relationships. The disorder is more common in men than in women. This disorder differs from obsessive–compulsive anxiety disorder (see p. 579), in which the person experiences feelings of dread if the compulsive behaviors are not performed.

ANTISOCIAL PERSONALITY DISORDER

Individuals with *antisocial personality disorder* have a tendency to be superficially charming and appear to be sincere. In fact, they are insincere, untruthful, and unreliable in their relations with others. They have virtually no sense of responsibility and feel no shame or remorse when they hurt others. They tend to process information in a way that views many acts toward them as aggressively motivated and in need of an aggressive response (Crick & Dodge, 1994). They are extremely self-centered and incapable of genuine love or affection. Typically, people with this disorder are poised and verbally facile. They often fool people into believing they care for them, when, in fact, they care for no one except themselves. The evidence shows both genetic and environmental contributory factors. This disorder can run in families. People with this disorder may have low baseline levels of arousal and may seek stimulation through antisocial means in order to arouse themselves and thus make their lives less seemingly dull (Morey, 1993). This disorder is more common in men than in women. It is very difficult to treat.

People with antisocial personality disorder are likely to run into trouble with the law. Indeed, it is hard to discuss abnormal behavior without discussing legal issues.

✓ CONCEPT CHECK 8

1. Someone who has difficulty forming relationships and tends to be indifferent to what others think of him or her is most likely to suffer from _____ personality disorder.
   a. schizoid
   b. obsessive–compulsive
   c. dependent personality
   d. histrionic
2. Someone who has a highly inflated self-image and who is extremely self-centered most likely suffers from _____ personality disorder.
   a. histrionic
   b. narcissistic
   c. borderline personality
   d. schizotypal
3. Someone who is superficially charming and seems sincere but who is in fact insincere, untruthful, and unreliable in relationships with others most likely suffers from _____ personality disorder.
   a. histrionic
   b. avoidant
   c. schizotypal
   d. antisocial

LEGAL ISSUES

How do clinical psychologists become involved in legal issues?

The DSM-IV descriptions of abnormal behavior are designed to help clinicians diagnose their patients and to aid psychologists in understanding their behavior. Although the descriptions are imperfect, often permitting ambiguous diagnoses and flawed understandings, they generally serve the purpose for which psychiatrists and psychologists intended them. Nonpsychologists, however, may have different requirements, which may lead to different definitions.

For example, *sanity* is a legal term for describing behavior, not a psychological term. Perhaps the best-known construction of the insanity defense is the *M'Naghten Rule*, formulated as the result of a murder trial in 1843 in England. This rule holds that "to establish a defense on the ground of insanity, it must be clearly proved that, at the time of committing the act, the party accused was laboring under such a defect of reasoning, from disease of the mind, as not to know the nature and quality of the act he [or she] was doing, or if he [or she] did know it, that he [or she] did not know he [or she] was doing what was wrong" (*Stedman's Medical Dictionary*, 25th edition, 1990, p. 1374; see also *Stedman's Medical Dictionary*, 27th edition, 2000).

In 1962, the American Law Institute provided a set of guidelines intended to reflect the current state of the insanity defense and its legal and psychological

Mark David Chapman, who murdered John Lennon, initially pleaded insanity in court but later changed his plea to guilty.

ramifications. These guidelines state that people cannot be held responsible for criminal conduct if, as a consequence of a mental disease or defect, they lack the capacity either to appreciate the wrongness of their conduct or to conform to the requirements of the law. The guidelines exclude, however, repeated criminal actions or antisocial conduct. In other words, the intent of the guidelines is to exonerate extraordinary acts, not habitual criminal behavior.

The topic of insanity remains controversial, and some psychiatrists, such as Thomas Szasz and R. D. Laing, have argued that mental illness should not be considered in the courtroom at all. According to Szasz, acts of violence are as rational and goal directed as any other acts, and perpetrators should be treated accordingly.

In 1981, John Hinckley, Jr., in an attempt to impress actress Jodie Foster, tried to assassinate President Ronald Reagan. Hinckley was found not guilty by reason of insanity. This verdict is scarcely a "free ride" because life imprisonment in a mental facility usually follows. But as a result of this case and the subsequent outrage, a number of states have introduced a new verdict, "guilty but mentally ill." Federal courts have also tightened guidelines for finding a defendant not guilty by reason of insanity. The Insanity Defense Reform Act, passed by the U.S. Congress in October 1984, makes it much more difficult for a defendant to escape the punishment of the law, regardless of the defendant's mental state.

Psychology and the law are also interrelated in noncriminal matters. For example, do the mentally ill have a right to treatment? In the case of *Wyatt* v. *Stickney*, decided in Alabama in 1971, the court ruled that they do. This ruling has generally held up. There is always latitude in interpreting who is mentally ill and really needs treatment, however. In recent years, federal spending on mental institutions has decreased, so many patients who were formerly in psychiatric

hospitals have been released. These people sometimes join the ranks of the homeless and now wander the streets instead of the halls of mental hospitals.

People who suffer from mental illnesses today are recognized as having a right to refuse treatment unless their behavior is potentially dangerous to others. In deciding whether to require treatment or confinement, we need to consider not only the rights of the potential patient but also the rights of persons they might harm. Once again, we face a dilemma: trying to find a balance between the rights of the prospective patient to refuse treatment or hospitalization and the rights of other persons to be protected from any harm that the prospective patient might cause.

We consider treatment in the next chapter.

✓ **CONCEPT CHECK 9**

1. Insanity is a _____ concept.
   a. psychological
   b. psychiatric
   c. legal
   d. illegal
2. A rule for understanding insanity that resulted from an 1843 murder trial in England is the _____ Rule.
   a. O'Brien
   b. McCormick
   c. M'Naghten
   d. O'Leary
3. Antisocial conduct and repeated criminal actions _____ satisfy an insanity defense.
   a. never
   b. occasionally
   c. usually
   d. always

SNIPERS: THE CRIMINAL MIND

In October 2002, the public watched in horror as 13 people in the Washington, DC, area were randomly gunned down while they shopped or pumped gas, going about their everyday lives. In the end, ten people died and three more were critically wounded, including a 13-year-old who was shot as he entered his school. This reign of terror lasted more than three weeks. Two snipers were finally captured as they slept in their car at a rest stop on an interstate highway.

People who watched the news on television heard commentaries from several different kinds of psychologists while the snipers were on the loose. **Social psychologist** Jack Levin, a professor of psychology at Northeastern University, studies such topics as hate crimes and serial murder. When asked to speculate about the psychological profile of the sniper (before the capture there was assumed to be only one), Levin and other psychologists who were interviewed predicted that a white, middle-aged man who had recently suffered a devastating divorce and severe financial loss was carrying out a plan developed by a team of killers.

Some **forensic psychologists** are trained to do psychological profiling of criminal suspects, although most are not (Holloway, 2003). Police psychologist Scott Allen of the Miami Dade Police Department believed that there was not enough evidence to construct a professional psychological profile in this case. Other forensic psychologists maintained that no professional psychologist should discuss a suspect with the media, and that profiling should be done only behind the scenes, well out of the public eye (Holloway, 2003).

The alleged snipers turned out to be a 41-year-old black man, John Allen Muhammed, and his 17-year-old stepson, John Lee Malvo. Muhammed had recently been through a traumatic divorce and had been denied visiting privileges with his children. However, many predictions about the snipers proved to be wrong. How could the profilers have been so mistaken?

Forensic psychologists who do psychological profiling conduct painstaking statistical analyses of the behaviors common to people who commit a certain type of crime. Unfortunately, the results of these analyses are rarely shared publicly. In one of the few published studies, forensic psychologist Richard Kocsis and his colleagues analyzed the behavior patterns of 85 men who were convicted of murder and sexual molestation of the murder victim. They found four distinct patterns: predation, fury, perversion, and rape (Kocsis, Cooksey, & Irwin, 2002). For each pattern, specific characteristics were observed in the offender. In the case of the DC snipers, sexual molestation of the murder victims did not occur, and no obvious pattern of murder was detected. The victims appeared to be randomly targeted, and their ages and ethnic backgrounds were diverse.

You learned in Chapter 14 that social learning plays an important role in the development of violent behavior. Research into the nature of serial killers indicates that social learning in the military, particularly in boot camp, may be responsible for their violent behavior (Castle & Hensley, 2002). John Allen Muhammed served in the military before embarking on his deadly shooting spree.

Muhammed's alleged accomplice was an adolescent boy. Adolescents commit 50% of all crimes in the United States (van Dalen, 2001). **Clinical psychologists** and social workers who study youthful offenders have found that their criminality is related to at least one of several factors, including drug addiction, family violence, mental retardation, or a behavioral disorder. **Developmental psychologists,** too, have determined that exposure to family and community violence during critical periods of development can encourage children to glamorize violence (McLaughlin, Yelon, Ivatury, & Sugarman, 2000). John Lee Malvo had a history of family violence.

Political psychologist Ervin Staub (2003) has studied the importance of universal psychological needs (for love, for example, or freedom from fear), and how they are fulfilled by family and society. Staub's cross-cultural research has revealed that when their basic needs are met, children learn to be caring and peaceful and to perceive themselves as good. When these needs are not met, children can develop hostile, aggressive, even violent behaviors.

Research by **personality psychologists** is beginning to help us understand the minds of violent adolescents. In a recent study of 72 male adolescents, Karen Salekin and her colleagues administered the Minnesota Multiphasic Personality Inventory (MMPI) and compared the hostility scores of 18 adolescent murderers, 18 violent youthful offenders with no history of murder, 18 nonviolent youthful offenders, and 18 adolescent nonoffenders. Adolescent murderers were found to have the highest levels of hostility (Salekin, Ogloff, Ley, & Salekin, 2002).

Our understanding of the criminal mind is far from complete. Research by social, forensic, clinical, political, developmental, and personality psychologists will ultimately assist clinical psychologists in the development of assessment and treatment protocols to be used with violent criminals.

SUMMARY

WHAT BEHAVIOR IS ABNORMAL? 570
How do we distinguish abnormal from normal behavior?

1. An individual exhibits a *psychological disorder* if (a) the individual shows a clinically significant behavior or psychological syndrome that is associated with present distress or disability or with an increased risk of suffering death, pain, disability, or an important loss of freedom; (b) the syndrome is not merely an expectable and culturally sanctioned response to a particular event, such as the death of a loved one; and (c) the syndrome is not a deliberate response to particular conditions, such as poverty, conflicts with society, or prejudice.

2. Early explanations of abnormal behavior focused on witchcraft and spiritual possession by demons. More contemporary perspectives on abnormal behavior include the psychodynamic, humanistic, behavioral (learning), cognitive, and biological approaches.

CLASSIFYING AND DIAGNOSING ABNORMAL BEHAVIOR 573
What criteria do clinicians use to classify and diagnose various mental disorders?

3. In the middle of the 20th century, clinicians began to reach formalized consensus regarding the diagnosis of mental disorders. Subsequently, clinicians have continued to refine these consensual agreements, reported both in the United States (DSM-IV) and in the world community (ICD-10).

ANXIETY DISORDERS 576
When does anxiety become a disorder? What different kinds of anxiety disorders do people experience?

4. *Anxiety disorders* encompass the individual's feelings of anxiety—tension, nervousness, distress, or uncomfortable arousal. DSM-IV divides anxiety disorders into five main categories: *phobias*, including *specific phobias*, *social phobias*, and *agoraphobia*; *panic disorder*; *generalized anxiety disorder*; *stress disorders*, including *posttraumatic stress disorder* and *acute stress disorder*; and *obsessive–compulsive anxiety disorder*. Anxiety disorders involve mood, cognitive, somatic, and motor symptoms.

5. There are various explanations of the disorders and the symptoms they cause. For example, psy-chodynamic explanations emphasize childhood events, whereas biological explanations emphasize links to neurotransmitters.

MOOD DISORDERS 582
How do mood disorders differ from the highs and lows we all experience?

6. The two major *mood disorders* (extreme disturbances in a person's emotional state) are major depression and bipolar disorder. *Major depression* is relatively common and is generally believed to be influenced by situational factors. *Bipolar disorder* is much rarer and runs in families, which suggests a possible genetic, biological component.

7. Both mood disorders probably are influenced by biological factors and situational factors. For example, bipolar disorder may be biologically rooted, but some environments may lead to more intense expression of the disorder than do other environments.

8. Cultures vary widely in their rates of suicide.

9. Many myths surround suicide. Perhaps the most important caution is that any person, of any background or set of characteristics, may decide to commit suicide, and any threats of suicide should be considered serious.

SCHIZOPHRENIC DISORDERS 588
What are the main symptoms of schizophrenia? What causes it?

10. *Schizophrenia* is a set of disorders encompassing a variety of symptoms, including hallucinations, *delusions*, disturbed thought processes, and disturbed emotional responses.

11. Types of schizophrenia include disorganized schizophrenia, catatonic schizophrenia, paranoid schizophrenia, undifferentiated schizophrenia, and residual schizophrenia.

12. Of the various explanations for schizophrenia, biological explanations seem particularly interesting because they may explain the familial trends in the development of schizophrenia (as well as the positive outcomes associated with antipsychotic drugs). The specific biological causes remain unknown, however. Other explanations have different emphases. For example, a psychodynamic explanation emphasizes the role of primary narcissism—a return to a very early stage of psychological development.

DISSOCIATIVE DISORDERS 595

What are dissociative disorders? What are their symptoms?

13. Environmental traumas have been implicated more strongly in *dissociative disorders* than have hereditary or biological factors.
14. The three main dissociative disorders are *dissociative amnesia* (sudden memory loss, usually after a highly stressful life experience), *dissociative fugue* (amnesia about a past identity and assumption of an entirely new identity), and *dissociative identity disorder* (the occurrence of two or more distinct, independent identities within the same individual). All of these disorders involve an alteration in the normally integrative functions of consciousness, identity, or motor behavior.

DISORDERS USUALLY DIAGNOSED IN INFANCY, CHILDHOOD, OR ADOLESCENCE 596

Can children have mental disorders? Are they the same as those seen in adults?

15. Three major disorders usually are diagnosed first in infancy, childhood, or adolescence: *attention-deficit hyperactivity disorder (ADHD)*, *conduct disorder*, and *pervasive developmental disorder (PDD)*.

PERSONALITY DISORDERS 598

What are personality disorders? What are their symptoms?

16. *Personality disorders* are consistent, long-term, extreme personality characteristics that cause great unhappiness or that seriously impair a person's ability to adjust to the demands of everyday living or to function well in her or his environment.
17. The major personality disorders are paranoid, schizoid, schizotypal, borderline, narcissistic, histrionic, avoidant, dependent, obsessive–compulsive, and antisocial disorders.

LEGAL ISSUES 599

How do clinical psychologists become involved in legal issues?

18. *Sanity* is a legal term for describing behavior, not a psychological term. At present, a person's sanity is an important factor in determining the adjudication of the person's criminal behavior. Just how sanity is determined and how it is considered in making legal judgments are still being evaluated in the courts.

KEY TERMS

acute stress disorder 578
agoraphobia 577
anxiety disorders 572
attention-deficit hyperactivity disorder (ADHD) 596
bipolar disorder 584
compulsion 579
conduct disorders 597
delusions 584
diathesis-stress theory 572
dissociative amnesia 595
dissociative disorders 595

dissociative fugue 595
dissociative identity disorder 595
etiology 572
generalized anxiety disorder 578
major depression 582
mania 584
mood disorders 582
obsession 579
obsessive–compulsive anxiety disorder 579
panic disorder 578
personality disorders 598

pervasive developmental disorder 597
phobias 577
posttraumatic stress disorder (PTSD) 578
psychological disorder 570
schizophrenia 588
seasonal affective disorder (SAD) 583
social phobias 577
specific phobias 577
stress disorder 578

ANSWERS TO CONCEPT CHECKS

Concept Check 1

1. d   2. a   3. d

Concept Check 2

1. a   2. a   3. d

Concept Check 3

1. b   2. c   3. c

Concept Check 4

1. c   2. d   3. b

Concept Check 5

1. a   2. b   3. c

Concept Check 6

1. b   2. b   3. c

Concept Check 7

1. b   2. c   3. d

Concept Check 8

1. a   2. b   3. d

Concept Check 9

1. c   2. c   3. a

KNOWLEDGE CHECK

1. Which of the following is *not* one of the four humors posited by Hippocrates?
   a. black bile
   b. yellow bile
   c. phlegm
   d. bilious humor
2. The view that abnormal behavior derives from oversensitivity to others' judgments or a failure of self-acceptance is associated with the _____ approach.
   a. psychodynamic
   b. humanistic
   c. behavioral
   d. biopsychosocial
3. Physical disorders are shown on Axis _____ of DSM-IV.
   a. I
   b. II
   c. III
   d. IV
4. DSM-IV is based on _____ theory.
   a. no
   b. psychoanalytic
   c. behavioral
   d. cognitive
5. Comorbidity refers to the extent to which symptoms of multiple disorders are
   a. independent.
   b. exactly the same.
   c. different.
   d. overlapping.
6. Brief, abrupt, and unprovoked but recurrent episodes of intense and uncontrollable anxiety are referred to as _____ disorder.
   a. stress
   b. panic

   c. mood
   d. anxiety
7. Flashbacks to painful memories, recurring nightmares, and/or unpleasant recurring memories of an event are characteristic of _____ disorder.
   a. generalized anxiety
   b. panic
   c. posttraumatic stress
   d. bipolar
8. Automatic self-defeating thoughts are the basis for the _____ account of anxiety disorders.
   a. psychodynamic
   b. behavioral
   c. cognitive
   d. biological
9. Which of the following is true of potential victims of suicide?
   a. People who commit suicide are always depressed beforehand.
   b. Suicide can be a way of manipulating others.
   c. The risk of suicide ends when a person's mood improves.
   d. People who commit suicide are crazy.
10. Schizophrenia is usually first diagnosed in
    a. early childhood.
    b. later childhood.
    c. early adolescence.
    d. early adulthood.

Answers
1. d   2. b   3. c   4. a   5. d   6. b   7. c   8. c
9. b   10. d

THINK ABOUT IT

1. Why does science as a whole benefit when researchers base their studies on explicit rather than implicit underlying assumptions about their theoretical perspectives?
2. Choose the psychological perspectives you find most suitable to your own beliefs about psychological disorders. Compare your preferred perspective with the others, showing why yours makes better sense.
3. Suppose you are assigned to choose exactly one personality disorder to be allowed as a legal defense for a not-guilty-by-reason-of-insanity plea. Which disorder would you choose and why? If you would not be willing to make such a choice, explain why.

4. Suppose your English teacher assigns you the task of creating a believable literary character who is schizophrenic. Briefly describe that person as others view the person; then describe how that person sees the world, including other persons.
5. Suppose you are volunteering to answer telephone calls on a suicide hotline. What kinds of strategies would you use—and what might you actually say—to try to prevent someone from committing suicide?
6. Sometimes it is tempting to analyze people you know in terms of the disorders they seem to show. What are the risks of assuming the role of an amateur psychologist?

WEB RESOURCES

For a chapter tutorial quiz, direct links to Internet sites, and other useful features, visit the book-specific website at http://psychology.wadsworth.com/sternberg4e. You can also connect directly to the following sites:

The Anxiety Panic Internet Resource
http://www.algy.com/anxiety/index.shtml
This is site contains much information about many anxiety disorders.

National Alliance for the Mentally Ill (NAMI)
http://www.nami.org/
NAMI describes itself as "a grassroots, self-help support and advocacy organization of families and friends of people with serious mental illness, and those persons themselves." Its online site meets their need for

extensive current information about schizophrenia, bipolar disorder, and other severe disorders.

Dr. Ivan's Depression Central
http://www.psycom.net/depression.central.html
You might think this site would be better titled "Everything You Ever Wanted to Know About Depression . . ." Psychiatrist Ivan Goldberg offers a great range of resources regarding depression and mood disorders.

For additional readings on many of the topics covered in this chapter, check out InfoTrac College Edition at **www.infotrac-college.com/ wadsworth.**

CD-ROM: UNIFYING PSYCHOLOGY

Disk Two
Classifying and Diagnosing Abnormal Behavior
Mood Disorders
Schizophrenic Disorders
Chapter Quiz
Critical Thinking Questions

CHAPTER 17

THERAPY

Your therapist matters more than your choice of therapeutic system. Someone to whom you connect profoundly can probably help you a lot just by chatting with you in an unstructured environment; someone to whom you do not connect will not really help you no matter how sophisticated his technique or how numerous his qualifications. The key things are intelligence and insight: the format in which that insight is communicated, and the type of insight that is used, are really secondary.

—Andrew Solomon, *The Noonday Sun: An Atlas of Depression*

Therapy uses the principles of psychology to treat mental disorders and improve the life of an unhappy or disturbed person. Therapy has many forms. There is little disagreement that working on problems with a trained therapist can make one's life better.

HISTORY OF THERAPY

How were people who behaved abnormally treated before the development of modern therapy?

In ancient times, people thought abnormal behavior was caused by demons (see Chapter 16). To some extent, this belief persists among some groups today. The treatment of those suspected of being possessed (demoniacs) has ranged from the innocuous to the brutally homicidal. Harsher forms of exorcism included flogging, drowning, and starving the suspected demoniac in an attempt to drive out evil spirits.

As the Middle Ages came to an end, so did the treatment of the mentally ill with exorcism (at least in most cases). During the 15th and 16th centuries, commitment to **asylums**—hospitals for the mentally ill—became the standard means of housing and possibly rehabilitating people who suffered from mental disorders. At that time, the definition of what constituted a disorder was flexible, and asylums housed a diverse assortment of people, including those who were viewed as socially undesirable for one reason or another, whether or not they had true disorders.

In 1547, King Henry VIII donated a 300-year-old hospital, St. Mary of Bethlehem (commonly known as "Bedlam"), to the city of London. Bedlam became the first hospital devoted exclusively to the mentally ill. The term *bedlam* became synonymous with uproar or confusion. Many inmates were chained to the walls of cramped quarters, often in positions that prohibited proper sleep. Others were chained to large iron balls, which they had to drag with them whenever they moved.

Such conditions appalled Philippe Pinel (1745–1826), the first chief physician at the Paris men's asylum, La Bicêtre, and then director of the women's asylum, Salpêtrière. Pinel removed the shackles and other instruments of confinement. Much to everyone's surprise, the crazed inmates became much calmer and more manageable.

By the beginning of the 19th century, clinicians were attempting to treat the psychological bases of abnormal behavior. For example, neurologist Jean Martin Charcot used hypnosis

During earlier eras, people whose behavior did not conform to societal expectations might be subjected to repeated "dunking" to make them confess that they practiced witchcraft. The longer it took the person to die, the more fervently the accusers asserted that devilish powers were prolonging survival.

© Bettmann/Corbis

to cure hysteria (see Chapter 16) and other mental illnesses. Later, a Viennese physician, Josef Breuer (1842–1925), found that if he could get hypnotized patients to talk about their problems, they seemed to improve. His method became known as the **cathartic method,** in which discussing the painful origins of a psychological problem helps resolve it. After Sigmund Freud worked with Breuer, the modern history of therapy began.

Many kinds of therapy are available today. In most cases, the therapist begins by trying to define the problem. The process of diagnosis and assessment may be brief, as in the case of someone who fears heights. Or it may be lengthier, as for a child who is afraid to go to school: Is the core issue separation from the parents? The behavior of schoolmates? A reaction to something going on at home? Or an earlier trauma that the child may or may not remember? Whatever the process and approach of therapy, the initial stage is to pinpoint the problem.

The need for therapy is as strong as it ever has been. E. Fuller Torrey and Judy Miller (2002) have examined records of mental illness in England, Ireland, Canada, and the United States over a 250-year period. They concluded that mental illness has been, and continues to be, an unrecognized modern-day plague.

✓CONCEPT CHECK 1

1. In ancient times, abnormal behavior was viewed as being caused by
   a. God.
   b. wild animals.
   c. demons.
   d. pride.
2. The conditions in 16th-century asylums were generally
   a. humane but sparse.
   b. rather luxurious compared with modern institutions.
   c. indicative of benign neglect.
   d. horrible and inhumane.
3. The idea of Breuer's cathartic method was for patients to
   a. reveal problems in order to rid themselves of them.
   b. hide problems in the hope they would go away.
   c. be physically tortured to extract confessions.
   d. be given the "silent treatment" in the hope it would make them talk.

DIAGNOSING AND ASSESSING ABNORMAL BEHAVIOR

How do therapists diagnose the people who come to them for treatment?

Given both clinical expertise and diagnostic tools such as the DSM-IV (see Chapter 16), a clinician must answer three questions when deciding how to respond to a new client: (1) Are there one or more problems? (2) What are the problems? (3) How should they be treated? Clinicians use a variety of techniques to answer these questions, such as clinical interviews, psychological tests, neuropsychological tests, and biological measurements. The terms *client* and *patient* are often used interchangeably.

CLINICAL INTERVIEWS

In the *clinical interview*, the therapist asks the client questions about his or her condition and surrounding circumstances. The clinical interview is by far the most widely used clinical assessment technique. It may be structured, unstructured, or both.

In a *structured interview*, the therapist rarely departs from a formal sequence of questions. The advantage of a structured interview is that the clinician can obtain a relatively large amount of information in a short period of time. Moreover, by asking prepared questions, clinicians ensure that they will not miss information that later might be important in making a diagnosis. The main disadvantage of the structured interview is that it lacks flexibility, tending to emphasize breadth at the expense of depth.

In contrast, an *unstructured interview* does not involve a list of questions. The interviewer follows rather than leads the client. Because people differ in the kinds of issues that bring them to therapy, an unstructured interview has the advantage of focusing on those that are particularly important to the client. The unstructured interview has two key potential disadvantages. First, the clinician might not ask the important questions. Second, he or she cannot obtain comparable data from one interview to the next. Unstructured interviews tend to emphasize depth at the expense of breadth. The ideal is to combine the techniques of structured and unstructured interviews. The therapist asks standard questions, yet freely pursues particular issues that appear to be important to the client.

In a clinical interview, *how* clients say something may be more important than *what* they say. Suppose a male client repeatedly emphasizes his success with women and goes to great pains to underscore that he can have any woman he wants. The therapist would almost certainly be suspicious. Other behavior, such as crying while saying something or suddenly having memory lapses or becoming fatigued while talking about a particular topic, is also important to understanding the meaning of what is being said. In each instance, the words are less important than the way they are being delivered.

In addition to being sensitive to what clients say and to how they say it, clinicians note how their clients' relationship with them may affect the content of the interview. Clinicians must remember that diagnosis is not the same as explanation (Carson, 1996). The interviewer may reach a diagnosis without being able to explain why the client has problems. Clients react differently to different interviewers. An interviewer's age, gender, ethnic group, way of thinking, and even manner of dress can affect the outcome of a clinical interview.

When clients are members of another culture, clinicians have to be especially careful both to recognize and to appreciate cultural differences and to avoid attributing genuinely abnormal behavior to them (Lopez & Nuñez, 1987). For example, persistent fears of spirits might be viewed as abnormal in one culture but as perfectly normal in another. But killing someone out of fear that the person is harboring such a spirit is abnormal, regardless of culture.

PSYCHOLOGICAL TESTS

Some clinicians regularly use psychological tests, others never do, and the rest use them sometimes. Many who use these tests swear by their diagnostic utility. Most who do not are confident that psychological tests are not useful.

Personality tests are either projective, such as the TAT and Rorschach tests, or objective, like the MMPI (see Chapter 15). Clinicians sometimes use intelligence tests (see Chapter 9) both to assess various cognitive disorders and to observe an individual's approach to solving problems. Neuropsychological and psychophysiological tests also are used in formulating a diagnosis that is a basis for treatment.

NEUROPSYCHOLOGICAL TESTS

Clinicians use neuropsychological tests when they suspect organic brain damage and are making other assessments on Axis III (physical disorders and conditions) of the DSM-IV. The two most widely used neuropsychological tests are the *Halstead–Reitan Battery* (see Boll, 1978) and the *Luria–Nebraska Battery* (see Golden,

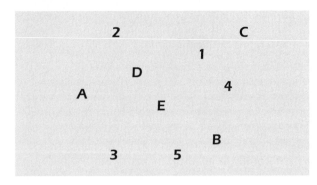

FIGURE 17.1

Trail-Making Test of the Halstead–Reitan Battery. In the Trail-Making test, you are shown a page like this, speckled with numerals and letters. You are asked to start with 1, then go to A, then to 2, then to B, and so on, alternating between numerals and letters. This test measures frontal-lobe function.

Hammecke, & Purisch, 1978). In fact, often the Halstead–Reitan Battery (a series of tests given sequentially over a period of hours or days) is administered along with the *Wechsler Adult Intelligence Scale, 3rd ed.* (WAIS-III) and the *Minnesota Multiphasic Personality Inventory—Revised* (MMPI-R). Thus, in applied (practical) settings, clinicians integrate information obtained with several types of diagnostic tools.

Suppose that a client is given two tests from the Halstead–Reitan Battery. On the Tactual Performance test, the client is blindfolded and asked to place blocks of various shapes into a board that has corresponding spaces. Because he cannot see the board, the client has to use tactile cues to determine which blocks go into which spaces. After completing the task to the best of his ability, the client is asked to draw what he believes the board looks like, showing the spaces and the blocks that fill them in their proper locations. A second test is Trail-Making. To find out how you might perform, see Figure 17.1.

The scoring of the Tactual Performance test reflects the relationship between performance and localization of function in different parts of the brain. The test draws largely on right-hemisphere functioning. The idea is to relate brain function to behavior and to infer neurological impairments from the behavior.

BIOLOGICAL MEASUREMENTS

Clinicians also assess reflex functions and sensory function. Your physician has probably tested your knee-jerk reflex (in response to a tap with a rubber mallet) and your pupillary reflex (in response to a bright light).

Biologically based measurement indices include heart rate, muscle tension, blood flow to various parts

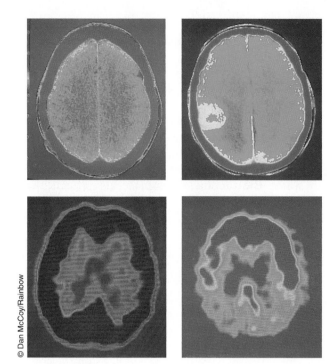

FIGURE 17.2

Psychophysiological Indications of Disorder. Compare the CAT-scan images at top left and right, both showing a horizontal slice through the brain. The brain on the left is normal, and the brain on the right shows a tumor. The bottom images are from PET scans. The one on the left shows a normal brain, and the one on the right shows the brain of a patient with senile dementia.

© Dan McCoy/Rainbow

of the body, galvanic skin response (GSR), evoked potentials (series of electroencephalograph recordings that minimize electrical interference), CAT and PET scans, and other measurements of biological functioning (see Chapters 3 and 12). Clinicians have found, nevertheless, that PET scans of people with bipolar disorder show higher levels of glucose metabolism in the cerebrum during manic phases than during depressive phases; see Figure 17.2 (Baxter et al., 1985).

No single form of assessment gives a complete picture, but used together, the assessments produce sufficient information for clinicians to integrate and interpret. Once a patient's problem is diagnosed, the next step is to treat it.

✓CONCEPT CHECK 2

1. The most widely used clinical assessment technique is the
   a. Rorschach Test.
   b. Thematic Apperception Test.
   c. Minnesota Multiphasic Inventory.
   d. clinical interview.

2. The _____ is a projective test.
   a. TAT
   b. SAT
   c. MMPI
   d. ACT
3. The Halstead–Reitan Battery is a(n) _____ test.
   a. projective
   b. personality
   c. achievement
   d. neuropsychological

APPROACHES TO THERAPY

How do the various theoretical perspectives on personality and abnormal behavior relate to therapy?

Therapy is practiced by clinical psychologists (who usually possess a doctor of philosophy, doctor of psychology, or doctor of education degree), psychiatrists (who possess a doctor of medicine degree), social workers (who usually have a master of social work degree), and others. Each of the many approaches to therapy has advantages and disadvantages. Many therapies overlap, but it is still useful to consider the distinctions among the five main approaches: psychodynamic, humanistic, behavioral, cognitive, and biological. Cultural influences should be taken into consideration as well.

ASSUMPTIONS ABOUT PSYCHOLOGICAL DISORDERS

Various kinds of therapists make different assumptions about the nature of psychological disorders and the optimal ways to treat them. It seems that they cannot all be right, but at some levels the approaches to therapy may be more complementary than they initially appear.

Consider, for example, the issue of what causes mental disorders. Part of the difference in treatment procedures derives from different views of causation. Psychodynamic theories tend to focus on repressed early childhood experiences as the cause of mental disorders. Humanistic theories consider the primary cause of these disorders to be deficits either in feelings of self-worth or in feelings of unconditional acceptance by others. Behavior therapies look to faulty con-

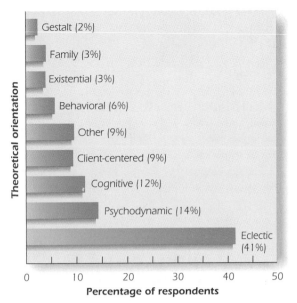

FIGURE 17.3

Orientation of Therapists. Out of 415 clinical psychologists surveyed, almost half indicated that they followed an eclectic approach. (After D. Smith, 1982)

ditioning. Cognitive theories emphasize maladaptive thoughts or schemas. Biological therapies look to psychophysiological causes of distress, such as depletion of neurotransmitters. To what extent are these causal explanations mutually exclusive?

To see how the various approaches are complementary, we can view mental disorders as having causes at different levels of analysis. For example, traumatic experiences in early childhood may lead to or even be viewed as inappropriate forms of behavioral conditioning. Imbalances in or lack of neurotransmitter substances may lead to maladaptive thoughts, or maladaptive thoughts may lead to low self-esteem, which may in turn affect neurotransmitter levels. Often, the causal direction of these various levels of analysis is not clear.

Some therapists synthesize several therapies into a single approach. The term *eclectic therapy* describes a therapeutic strategy that integrates several approaches. Indeed, many therapists today take an eclectic approach (see Figure 17.3).

WHO USES THERAPY?

Not everyone who needs therapy seeks it out (Pekarik, 1993). Indeed, it is estimated that more than half of those who need therapy do not get it (Torrey, 1997). Those who do find a therapist are likely to be the more educated among the population and also those who have health insurance (Olfson & Pincus, 1996). Women use therapy more than men. Some who do not initiate therapy are unable to simply because the areas in which they live have no facilities for

therapy, or because they lack the economic resources to use the help that is available (*Mental Health, United States,* 1997). There are, as discussed in a later section, alternatives to individual therapy, many offered in areas that may be underserved in terms of individual therapy. The people who do seek help may be suffering from a particular identifiable set of symptoms or may simply be uncomfortable with the way their life is going (Strupp, 1996). The culture of the therapist and the person seeking therapy as well as that in which the therapy takes place also affects the approach used.

ⓒ CROSS-CULTURAL PERSPECTIVES ON THERAPY

Across such diverse therapists as U.S. and European clinical psychologists, psychiatrists, Native-American *shamans,* Latin-American *curanderos* (or *curanderas,* in Mexico and elsewhere), and Yoruban *babalawo* (in Nigeria), therapy appears to have five basic components (Torrey, 1986): (1) an emphasis on the construction of a shared worldview between client and therapist, including a common language and similar conceptions of causes and effects; (2) therapist characteristics such as warmth, genuineness, and empathy; (3) patient expectations that reflect the culturally relevant beliefs of the patient and the therapist; (4) a set of specific techniques employed by the therapist; and (5) a process by which the therapist enables or empowers the client to gain increased knowledge, awareness, and mastery, thereby gaining hope. According to E. Fuller Torrey (1986), therapists perform essentially the same function regardless of culture. Both Western and non-Western therapists treat patients using similar techniques and results.

The Native American shaman and Latin American curandero *or* curandera *share with Western therapists an emphasis on empathy, warmth, and genuineness; specialized techniques; and the goal of empowering the person seeking help to gain increased knowledge and mastery.*

There are not only many commonalities but also many differences among cultures. As nations become more diverse, it is increasingly necessary for counselors and therapists to develop competence in dealing with clients who are culturally different from themselves. It is not unusual for counselors to encounter clients from diverse ethnic groups or even recent immigrants from other countries. Asian-American and Hispanic-American therapists may well confront Haitian, Ukrainian, or Turkish clients. Therapists need to consider the backgrounds of their clients, which may influence the process of therapy. When clients and therapists come from radically different places, in which they were socialized to have sharply different beliefs, values, expectations, or conceptions of self, significant problems can arise. These problems may lead to distrust, disappointment, or failed interventions.

The need for guidance in cross-cultural therapy has spawned numerous books and articles dealing with various key issues in the field (e.g., Axelson, 1993; Chung, Bemak, & Kilinc, 2002; Erim & Senf, 2002; Ivey, Ivey, & Simek-Morgan, 1993). Many college professors and administrators are becoming aware of the need to provide courses and lectures on cross-cultural psychology. Among the many issues in cross-cultural therapy, these questions frequently arise: Are certain types of therapy more appropriate for particular ethnic groups? How can mental-health programs reach out to the members of ethnic groups who typically underuse available resources? How can a therapist communicate empathically with clients who have worldviews that differ from the therapist's?

PSYCHODYNAMIC METHODS

Psychodynamic therapies have in common their emphasis on gaining *insight* as the key to improvement. The basic assumption is that when patients have insight into the source or sources of their problems, they will be largely freed of their problems. Psychoanalytic therapy is a major type of psychodynamic therapy, although there are many offshoots.

CLASSIC PSYCHOANALYSIS

Psychoanalytic therapists assume that disorders result from people's lack of awareness of their own underlying thoughts, feelings, and especially motivations. According to this view, patients need to gain insight into the childhood roots of their problematic feelings and patterns in relationships. Patients will improve when they become conscious of ego-threatening material that they have repressed. Thus, treatment focuses on breaking through defense mechanisms in an attempt to discover

the underlying truth. If a patient enters therapy to conquer anxiety, for example, the therapist would be foolish to treat the anxiety directly because, according to this view, the anxiety is only a symptom of unconscious repressed feelings, thoughts, and motives. The therapy is nondirective, and often the psychoanalytic

© Rhoda F. Sidney/Picture Person Plus

The goal of psychoanalytic therapy is to help patients gain insight into their defenses. The therapist sits out of sight to avoid influencing the client's thought process.

therapist sits out of sight of the patient in order to avoid influencing the patient's stream of thought.

How does the therapist actually go about eliciting the unconscious conflicts that underlie an observable disorder? Psychoanalysts use several techniques.

FREE ASSOCIATION. In **free association,** the patient freely says whatever comes to mind, not censoring or otherwise editing the free flow of words before reporting them. At first, the patient may find the unedited reporting of free associations difficult. After gaining practice and familiarity with the analyst and the process, however, the patient usually improves. According to the psychoanalytic view, it is critical not to edit anything out. Chances are good that the most interesting and important details will be those that the patient reveals unconsciously. The therapist acts only as a guide. He or she does not try to direct the course of the associations. Typically, the patient seeks to enter a relaxed state of mind in a comfortable setting, with only the therapist present.

RESISTANCE. If patients could make free associations that immediately led them to repressed material, then psychoanalysis would be over in short order. The actual course of therapy rarely works that way. Resistances are attempts by the client to block therapeutic progress in psychodynamic treatment, usually as a result of unconscious conflicts. Why would rational patients want to block progress, especially when they are paying for therapy? Dealing with the contents of the unconscious is often painful and possibly even devastating. So patients unconsciously attempt to divert the therapy from doing so. Resistances can take a variety of forms, such as remaining silent, trying to digress from unpleasant topics, making jokes, and even not attending sessions. Psychoanalysts identify and deal with resistances when they arise.

DREAMS. According to Freud (see Chapters 5 and 15), the *manifest content* of dreams—the actual occurrences that take place within the dreams—is symbolic of the underlying *latent content*. Thus, the job of the analyst is to penetrate the manifest content in order to understand what lies beneath it. For example, a male patient's dream of sticking an old man with a pencil might represent an unresolved Oedipal conflict in which the dreamer is battling with his father for possession of his mother. Psychoanalysts believe that the dream sufficiently disguises these symbolic elements to avoid causing extreme discomfort to the dreamer.

After the patient has been in therapy for a while, the psychoanalyst increasingly interprets the content of what the patient says. Often, patients are unhappy with and may not believe what they hear. Freud believed that such attempts at denial were ways in which patients could resist learning the truth about themselves. From the psychoanalytic standpoint, the more vigorously a patient denies a particular interpretation, the more the therapist needs seriously to consider whether it is true.

TRANSFERENCE. Psychoanalytic therapists remain relatively detached from their patients and avoid overt emotional signs. The therapist seems almost like a shadowy parent figure who tries to help the patient without becoming too involved. Patients often become quite involved, however, imbuing the therapist with qualities and thoughts that the therapist may not actually have. Indeed, patients may start to view the therapist as the source of, or at least an active contributor to, their problems. This involvement is referred to as transference. In transference, the patient projects her or his feelings and internal conflicts onto the therapist, often including aspects of the patient's early childhood relationships. If the patient's parents were extremely concerned with school performance, for example, then the patient may assume that the analyst is similarly judging the patient's performance in therapy. By staying neutral and seemingly detached, therapists actually encourage transference because patients can

project whatever conflicts or fantasies arise. The detached therapist is like a blank screen onto which patients can project their past relationships. According to Freud, such transference is a positive rather than a negative phenomenon. It helps the patient bring out into the open conflicts that have been suppressed in the past.

All psychoanalysts must themselves be psychoanalyzed during their training to understand better their own conflicts and sources of psychological distress. In countertransference, the therapist projects feelings onto the patient that can cause the therapy to go seriously awry. Thus, it is important that psychoanalytic therapists recognize their own problems and fantasies, so they can deal with their issues as they arise and avoid projecting them onto the patient.

MODERN PSYCHOANALYSIS

Psychoanalytic therapy has generated a variety of offshoots. Many developed from the theories of personality offered by Freud's followers, neo-Freudians such as Carl Jung, Erik Erikson, and Karen Horney (described in Chapter 15). The various forms of neo-Freudian therapy are sometimes termed *ego analysis* because of their common view that the ego is at least as important as is the id. In other words, conscious processing is just as important as—and possibly more important than—unconscious processing. People have purposes and goals, and to a large extent, they act to meet those goals. To understand the patient fully, the therapist needs to understand not only the patient's past but also where the patient sees himself or herself heading.

Classical psychoanalysis can be a long process, continuing over years, during which the patient and the therapist may meet as often as three to five times per week. Psychodynamic therapists, however, have placed increasing emphasis on *time-limited psychotherapy* (Bein et al., 2000; H. Levenson & Strupp, 1999; Mann, 1973; Strupp, 1981). The idea is to apply the principles of psychoanalysis but to effect improvement in a relatively short time. To this end, the therapist is somewhat more directive—pointing out, for example, the patient's defenses and conflicts more readily than an analyst would.

HUMANISTIC THERAPIES

Humanistic therapy emphasizes insight. Beyond this similarity, however, there are salient differences that are not merely semantic. Psychodynamic therapy is based on a model of disorder that is much closer to a medical model (recall Freud's medical training), according to which an underlying disease process is the source of the patient's troubles. In contrast, the humanistic model eschews the medical model. It views each person as an individual with feelings and thoughts that may come into conflict with society or with each other, thereby causing problems in living.

For psychodynamic therapists, understanding behavior is extremely difficult for all but the most skilled psychoanalyst (much like a physician's expertise). For humanistic therapists, understanding is not so elusive. The therapist is not an authority who dictates the correct perceptions to the passive patient. Rather, the therapist is a facilitator who helps the client gain insights.

In the psychodynamic view, we are deterministically ruled by unconscious forces. In the humanistic view, we have free will and are ruled by our own conscious decisions. Humanistic therapists assume that people who are mentally well understand their own behavior. Those people can thus change their behavior at will. Because people are free to make choices, a goal of therapy is to help people *feel* completely free in the choices they make. Of the various forms of humanistic therapies, some are briefly described here.

All humanistic therapy focuses on the client because, according to this view, it is in the client's experience of his or her deepest needs that the power to make fulfilling choices lies. Carl Rogers (1961a) used **client-centered therapy,** which assumes that the client's construction of reality provides the basis for understanding the client. Thus, client-centered therapy is *nondirective*, in that the therapist is not supposed to guide the course of therapy in any particular direction. What matters are not the events that occur in people's lives, but rather the way people construe these events. Thus, client-centered therapists make little effort to impose a theoretical system on the client. Instead, they try to understand their client's view of the world.

Carl Rogers was a leading humanistic psychologist of the 20th century.

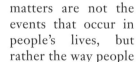

Rogers believed that people are basically good and adaptive both in what they do and in the goals they set for themselves. When they act otherwise, it is because of flaws that have taken place in their socialization processes. As a result, they are not fully functioning. For example, the clients may receive inadequate socialization or may have inappropriate role models. The goal of client-centered therapy is to help people realize their full potential.

Rogers believed that three keys can unlock the doors that bar clients from realizing their potential.

The first key is *genuineness* on the part of the therapist. Client-centered therapists need to be totally honest, both with themselves and with their clients. Whereas psychoanalysts might be viewed as having a detached objectivity, Rogerian therapists must present no detachment whatsoever. They should be as open and genuine in expressing their feelings as they want their clients to be. In effect, they become models for their clients. They show their clients how to be open and self-disclosing in a world that often seems not to value the qualities of openness and self-disclosure.

The second key is for the therapist to give the client *unconditional positive regard.* Rogers believed that growing up receiving only conditional positive regard causes many of our problems. We were given approval only when we behaved in socially acceptable ways. It was withdrawn when we behaved in less accepted ways. The result, according to Rogers, is that we develop a conditional sense of self-worth. We feel that we will be loved or appreciated only if we do those things that others have deemed acceptable. To be psychologically whole, however, we must achieve a sense of unconditional self-worth. The Rogerian therapist's unconditional positive regard helps the client achieve this state.

The third key is for the therapist to experience *accurate empathic understanding* of the client. A good therapist needs to be able to see the world in the same way that the client sees it. Without such empathy, the therapist does not truly understand the client's point of view. The result will be miscommunication, which limits the client's ability to profit from the therapy.

In client-centered, nondirective therapy, the therapist follows the client's lead. In contrast, in psychodynamic therapy, the therapist has a particular direction in mind while leading the patient—namely, toward the uncovering of unconscious conflicts. Thus, the course of client-centered therapy is likely to be quite different from the course of psychodynamic therapy. Nondirective, client-centered therapists listen empathically to clients and help clients to clarify and explore their feelings. The clients then should feel free to live as they choose. Behavior therapists use different means to achieve the same ends.

BEHAVIOR THERAPY

Behavior therapy techniques are based primarily on the principles of classical or operant conditioning as well as on observational learning from models (see Chapter 6). Behavior therapy differs in several fundamental ways from all the other kinds of therapies considered up to this point. First, behavior therapy is deliberately short term. Thus, whereas psychoanalysis may go on for years, behavior therapy typically lasts only months or even less.

Second, whereas psychoanalysis shuns the treatment of symptoms, behavior therapy deliberately intervenes to alleviate symptoms. To the behavior therapist, the symptom *is* the problem. If a person is experiencing anxiety, then the person needs to reduce that anxiety in order to function effectively. If a person is depressed, then the goal is to relieve the depression. In the behaviorists' view, chasing after deep-seated causes in the murky past is essentially a waste of time. The original causes of the maladaptive behavior may have nothing to do with the factors that currently maintain the behavior.

Third, although the behavior therapist collaborates with the client, it is the therapist who formulates an explicit treatment plan. The client follows the therapist's treatment plan, and when the plan has been implemented, the therapy ends.

Fourth, as its name implies, behavior therapy concentrates on behavior, such as quitting smoking or overcoming a fear of public speaking. Whereas other techniques of therapy seek to obtain behavioral change through psychological insights and changes, behavior therapy seeks to obtain psychological changes through behavioral changes. Indeed, some behavior therapists do not even particularly concern themselves with the psychological changes. What they seek is modification of maladaptive behavior.

Finally, behavior therapists try to follow more closely the classic scientific model than do some other types of therapists. Behavior therapists are very concerned with taking a scientific, objective approach, both to the therapy and to the evaluation of the outcomes of the therapy. Many behaviorists have said that the precepts of psychoanalysis cannot be disconfirmed by scientific investigation. Probably no one says the same of behavior therapy.

COUNTERCONDITIONING

In *counterconditioning*, a particular response to a given stimulus is replaced by an alternative response to that same stimulus. The alternative response is incompatible with the unwanted initial response. Suppose that before counterconditioning, a person enjoys positive feelings toward the stimulus of smoking cigarettes. Through counterconditioning, the person would learn to feel negatively about cigarettes. In contrast, if a person became anxious when taking tests, counterconditioning would replace the negative anxiety response with a positive relaxation response that would permit the person to take tests without feeling nervous. Two of the main techniques used to achieve counterconditioning are aversion therapy and systematic desensitization.

AVERSION THERAPY

In **aversion therapy,** the client is taught to experience negative feelings in the presence of a stimulus that is considered inappropriately attractive, with the aim of eventually learning to feel repelled by the stimulus. For example, a *pedophiliac* (an adult who is sexually attracted to children) might seek aversion therapy to learn not to respond with sexual interest when presented with the stimulus of a little child. The client's exposure to the inappropriately attractive stimulus would be accompanied by an aversive unconditioned stimulus, such as a painful electric shock. The pedophiliac might be exposed to a picture of an attractive child at the exact moment or immediately before being shocked. Similarly, an alcoholic might seek aversion therapy. Problem drinkers sometimes are given a drug that causes them to feel nauseated immediately after they have consumed any alcohol (see Chapter 6). Aversion therapy seeks to foster avoidance learning. It is generally used in combination with other techniques. It is often useful to substitute some other more socially desirable interest for the one that is being replaced.

SYSTEMATIC DESENSITIZATION

In **systematic desensitization,** the therapist teaches the client a set of relaxation techniques to combat a problem, such as a phobia. Joseph Wolpe (1958) introduced the technique as a way of combating particular psychological problems—most notably, anxiety. Wolpe's basic idea involves replacing one response with another—typically, a response of anxiety with one of relaxation. In all cases, systematic desensitization involves engaging in a response that is incompatible with the initial unwanted response.

Suppose that your extreme anxiety about standardized admissions tests threatened your ability to compete successfully for admission to graduate school. The therapist would create with you a *desensitization hierarchy*, which is a series of imagined scenes, each one more anxiety-provoking than the previous one. Next, you would learn a set of techniques to achieve deep relaxation. These techniques would involve relaxing individual muscle groups, picturing pleasant scenes, and other similar activities. Once you had learned how to relax deeply, the actual systematic desensitization process would begin. You would first imagine the least anxiety-provoking scene. If you were feeling anxious, you would be reminded immediately to relax deeply. After several efforts, you would find yourself able to handle the first step of your hierarchy without feeling anxious. After you were sure of your ability to deal with that initial stimulus, you would proceed to the next step. You would continue in this manner until you had mastered each step in your hierarchy. Many studies (see Cottraux, 1993; Cottraux et al., 2000) indicate that variants of behavior therapy are highly effective in helping clients who have simple phobias and many other anxiety disorders.

EXTINCTION PROCEDURES

Extinction procedures weaken maladaptive responses with flooding and implosion therapy. **Flooding** lessens anxiety by exposing a client to a carefully controlled environment in which an anxiety-provoking stimulus is presented harmlessly. The client is placed in a situation that causes anxiety and is not instructed in how to use relaxation techniques. The idea underlying this technique is that clients who have been forced to remain in the anxiety-provoking situation will realize that nothing horrible has happened to them. As a result, they are able to cope when they face the same situation in the future. For instance, a person with a phobia of snakes would be forced to confront snakes. A person who is afraid of heights would be taken to the top of a tall building.

Implosion is an intermediate form of therapy that includes elements of both flooding and systematic desensitization. **Implosion therapy** weakens anxiety by having clients imagine as vividly as possible the unpleasant events that cause it. Suppose that you once almost drowned and you now fear swimming. Your implosion therapist might ask you to imagine stepping into a bottomless bathtub and then to imagine yourself starting to slip beneath the water. Of course, this scene would cause you intense anxiety. Soon, however, you would realize that nothing has happened to you. You would then be asked to imagine this scene more and more frequently. Eventually, the scene would lose its ability to cause you anxiety. You would stop feeling afraid.

This visualization technique is similar to systematic desensitization in that the client imagines but does not actually experience the anxiety-producing scenes. It differs from systematic desensitization in the method of relieving anxiety. Of the two techniques, systematic desensitization has proven to be demonstrably superior to implosion therapy (see M. L. Smith & Glass, 1977).

The techniques described up to this point have basically made use of the classical-conditioning model. However, operant conditioning has also been used for achieving behavioral change. A simple example of operant conditioning, often used by parents, is to reward children with, say, candy or money for good grades or for going to bed early. Several methods of using operant conditioning are relevant, including the use of token economies (introduced in Chapter 6) and behavioral contracting.

TOKEN ECONOMIES

In a **token economy,** tangible objects that have no intrinsic worth are used to reinforce various operant behaviors. The tokens can later be exchanged for goods or services that the individuals desire. The clients are generally in an institutional setting, which allows the therapist to control the distribution of the tokens and other

reinforcers. This technique has been used primarily with children who have PDD (pervasive developmental disorder, or autism), although it has been employed with other populations as well (see Figure 17.4).

The use of tokens has several attractive features. First, the number of tokens can be linked directly to whether the client exhibits the desired behavior. Second, there is very little ambiguity about the nature of the reward. Third, the therapist can tailor the goods or services that can be purchased to the client's needs and wants. As time goes on, the nature of the things that can be purchased with the tokens can be changed to suit the client's current desires. Fourth, the tokens can be distributed immediately as a reward for desirable behavior. Fifth, the client can choose the reward, rather than having to accept whatever is given. Finally, there is a touch of realism in the token economy because it resembles what happens in the world outside the institution (Carson, 1996; G. L. Paul & Lentz, 1977; G. L. Paul & Menditto, 1992).

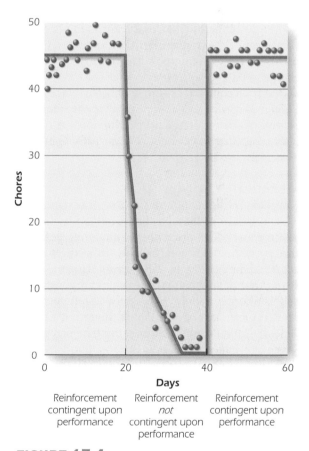

FIGURE 17.4

Results of a Token Economy. A token economy can be highly effective in modifying the behavior of confined individuals. Positive behaviors that may be reinforced include self-help (e.g., grooming) and chores. The results show that reinforcement contingent upon performance increases the frequency with which chores are done.

For noninstitutionalized populations, some researchers have expressed concern that these *extrinsic reinforcers* (external, material rewards, as opposed to intrinsic rewards such as self-esteem and achievement motivation) may undermine children's natural interest in performing the behaviors that are being rewarded (Deci & Ryan, 1985, 2002a, 2002b; Henderlong & Lepper, 2002; Iyengar & Lepper, 2000; Lepper et al., 1973). Therapists and other clinicians must often choose from among imperfect alternatives, balancing desired benefits against possible risks.

BEHAVIORAL CONTRACTING

In **behavioral contracting,** the therapist and the client draw up a contract that clearly specifies their responsibilities and behavioral expectations. The contract requires the client to exhibit specific behaviors that are sought as part of the therapy. In return, the therapist will give the client particular rewards that the client may want. Behavioral contracting has two key advantages: (1) The responsibilities of both the therapist and the patient are clear, and (2) the criteria for success in meeting the goals of the therapy are concretely defined. Behavioral contracting is not itself a form of therapy, rather it is a supplement that can be used in conjunction with virtually any type of therapy.

Part of a contract, or simply of behavioral therapy in general, may be self-administered rewards for self-control. In other words, a client who achieves certain clearly specified goals chooses rewards for achieving these goals.

MODELING

In **modeling,** the client observes people coping effectively in situations that the client responds to in maladaptive ways. The principles of modeling derive in large part, though not exclusively, from the work of Albert Bandura (1969; see Chapter 6). Bandura's basic idea is that people can change simply by watching models of other people successfully coping with the problems they face. For example, Bandura, Edward Blanchard, and Brunhilde Ritter (1969) helped people overcome snake phobias by having phobic adults watch other people confront snakes, preferably in live situations but also on film. The clients watched as the models moved closer and closer to the snakes. With time, the phobias subsided.

Modeling has been used in a variety of other kinds of therapy, including the treatment of sexual disorders. The therapeutic effects of many interventions may stem in part from modeling (Braswell & Kendall, 1988). Modeling appears to be effective compared with other forms of therapy, especially if it is live modeling, involving the actual confrontation of the phobia (see Figure 17.5).

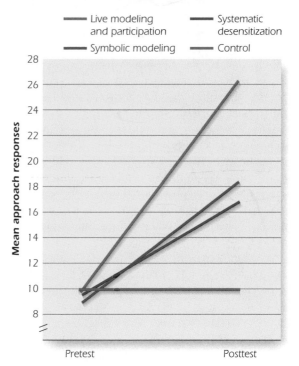

FIGURE 17.5

Effectiveness of Various Behavior Therapies. Approach responses increased in the treatment groups but not the control group. Live modeling and participation appear to be much more potent in effecting behavioral changes than symbolic modeling and systematic desensitization. (From "Effectiveness of Various Therapies," Bandura et al., *Journal of Personality and Social Psychology,* Vol. 13, 1968, pp. 173-199. Copyright © 1969 by the American Psychological Association. Reprinted with permission.)

COGNITIVE THERAPIES

The modeling approach provides the transition between behaviorally and cognitively oriented approaches to therapy. The thought processes that the observer uses for imitating the model are certainly cognitive ones (Bandura, 1986).

Cognitive therapists believe that clients change their behaviors by changing their thinking. If people can be made to think differently about themselves and about the phenomena they experience, then they can feel and act differently. The two most well-known cognitive approaches are probably Albert Ellis's rational-emotive therapy and Aaron Beck's cognitive therapy (see Chapter 15).

ALBERT ELLIS: RATIONAL-EMOTIVE THERAPY (RET)

Albert Ellis (1962, 1973, 1989, 2002; Ellis & Dryden, 1997; Ellis, Shaughnessy, & Mahan, 2002) formulated **rational-emotive therapy (RET)** (sometimes referred to as *rational emotive behavior therapy*), according to which emotional reactions occur because people internally recite sentences that express incorrect or maladaptive thoughts. They must change the thoughts in order to correct the reactions. For example, Ellis believes that cognition precedes emotion (in agreement with Richard Lazarus; see Chapter 12). According to Ellis, our emotions are caused by our thoughts. We can change our emotions only by changing our thoughts. The goal of Ellis's therapy, therefore, is to help people control their emotional reactions by helping them correct their thoughts. Ellis's RET and other forms of cognitive-behavioral therapy have been particularly effective in treating anxious patients who abuse antianxiety medications (Perris & Herlofson, 1993). We may presume that this form of therapy will also be effective in persons at risk for such abuse.

Albert Ellis founded rational-emotive therapy.

Ellis (1970) has given a number of examples of the incorrect beliefs that have led people to maladjustment. Some are listed in Table 17.1. Ellis believes that the best technique for dealing with these beliefs is to confront the client directly. In other words, the therapist actually attempts to show the client that these false, futile beliefs are causing the client to be unhappy and dysfunctional in everyday life. Thus, Ellis's techniques are quite different from those of humanistic therapy, in which a therapist almost never directly confronts a client. Although the method is different, the goals are similar to those of humanistic therapy: to increase a client's sense of self-worth and to facilitate the client's ability to grow and to make choices by recognizing all of the available options.

AARON BECK: COGNITIVE THERAPY

Aaron Beck's (1976, 1986, 1997, 2002a; Young, Weinberger, & Beck, 2001) **cognitive therapy** focuses on developing adaptive, rather than maladaptive, thoughts and thought processes. Beck views people as being maladjusted as a result of cognitive distortion (see Chapter 16). Beck has concentrated particularly on depression, and a World Health Organization

Aaron Beck's (1991) cognitive therapy focuses on getting people to change maladaptive cognitive schemas that lead them to believe they are incompetent or worthless.

TABLE 17.1

Ellis's List of Common Irrational Beliefs. Ellis believes that false ideas, such as those listed, lead to maladjustment in peoples' lives.

1. It is a dire necessity for an adult to be loved or approved by virtually every other significant person in his or her community.

2. One should be thoroughly competent, adequate, and achieving in all possible respects if one is to consider oneself worthwhile.

3. Certain people are bad, wicked, or villainous and should be severely blamed and punished for their villainy.

4. It is awful and catastrophic when things are not the way one would very much like them to be.

5. Human unhappiness is externally caused and people have little or no ability to control their sorrows and disturbances.

6. If something is or may be dangerous or fearsome, one should be terribly concerned about it and should keep dwelling on the possibility of its occurring.

7. It is easier to avoid than to face certain life difficulties and self-responsibilities.

8. One should be dependent on others and need someone stronger than oneself on whom to rely.

9. One's past history is an all-important determiner of one's present behavior, and because something once strongly affected one's life, it should indefinitely have a similar effect.

10. One should become quite upset over other people's problems and disturbances.

11. There is invariably a right, precise, and perfect solution to human problems and it is catastrophic if this perfect solution is not found.

Source: "List of Common Irrational Beliefs." Reprinted by permission of Albert Ellis, Institute of Rational Emotive Behavior Therapy.

report (Perris & Herlofson, 1993) on therapy has indicated that the demonstrated efficacy of cognitive therapy may be somewhat higher for depressive disorders than for other disorders. (See in Chapter 16 Beck's list of some of the cognitive distortions that frequently underlie depression.) Cognitive therapy also seems to work quite well with anxiety disorders (Hollon & Beck, 1994; Sanderson, Beck, & McGinn, 2002). Beck particularly emphasizes the importance of maladaptive schemas, such as feeling unattractive or incompetent, that lead us to feel distress (see also Sookman, Pinard, & Beck, 2001; Young, 1990; Young & Klosko, 1993).

BIOLOGICAL THERAPIES

Biological therapies treat psychological disorders through medical or quasi-medical intervention. These therapies differ from all those we have considered up to this point because the client–therapist discourse plays no real role, or at least no greater role than would be the case for any patient–doctor discourse. Biological therapies can be used in conjunction with more psychologically oriented ones, of course, and they often are.

HISTORY OF BIOLOGICAL THERAPIES

Biological therapies date back at least to ancient Rome, where particular psychological disorders were viewed as being caused by poisons or other undesirable substances that had entered the body. As a result, laxatives and emetics were used to purge the body of these foreign substances. Such treatment continued into the 18th century (Agnew, 1985). Another way of ridding the body of unwanted substances was through selective bleeding, which also was used as recently as the 18th century. The idea was that undesirable substances were mixed with the blood. As the blood left the body, so would the undesirable substances. New blood created to replace the old would be free of the contamination.

PSYCHOSURGERY

In the 20th century, another treatment proved to be among the most disastrous attempts of the psychiatric profession to achieve biological cures. *Prefrontal lobotomy*, a form of psychosurgery, is a procedure intended to alleviate mental disorders by probing, slicing, dissecting, or removing some part of the brain. The procedure severed the frontal lobes from the posterior portions of the brain, thereby cutting off all communication between them. It left many patients vegetative, incapable of functioning independently in any meaningful way. Even operations that were less disastrously tragic could not be considered successful in terms of restoring mental health and normal cognitive function. Between 1935 (when the operation was introduced) and 1955 (when antipsychotic drugs became the method of choice for treating schizophrenia and other disorders), tens of thousands of patients are estimated to have undergone prefrontal lobotomy, primarily in mental institutions (Freeman, 1959). The inventor of the operation received the Nobel Prize in medicine for his contribution, which at the time seemed to revolutionize treatment in a positive way.

How could such a disaster have taken place? Elliot Valenstein (1986) has suggested several explanations. For one thing, the treatment came into prominence at a time when psychiatry was trying to gain respectability as a medical science. Psychosurgery seemed to offer such respectability because it was a medical procedure. Psychosurgery also allowed those in charge of mental hospitals to maintain control; the patients who received the operation stopped being disorderly and disruptive to the institutional regimen. Psychosurgery was not only a societal disaster. It also had pervasive negative effects on the brains of those who received it (Arai et al., 2001).

When we analyze the failure of early psychosurgery, we should view it in the broader context of many other failed medical and psychological treatments. For example, one drug company sold heroin as an analgesic. Countless other harmful and addictive drugs have been given to patients in the mistaken belief that they would be beneficial. Interventions designed to help people can end up causing more harm than good in the long run. We must pay more attention to the long-term consequences of the interventions we practice. Today, some modern forms of psychosurgery are used in extreme cases, but rarely. Therapy has moved on.

ELECTROCONVULSIVE THERAPY (ECT)

In **electroconvulsive therapy** (ECT), a brief but severe electric shock to the brain is used to treat severe, unremitting depression that does not respond to therapy or drugs (Bolwig, 1993; Grunhaus, Schreiber, Dolberg, Polak, & Dannon, 2003). In one form of ECT, a current of about 150 volts is passed from one side of the patient's head to the other for approximately $1\frac{1}{2}$ seconds.

ECT seems to be effective for some patients (Abrams, 1988; Grunhaus et al., 2003; Scovern & Kilmann, 1980; Vangu, Esser, Boyd, & Berk, 2003), but it does not work for others (Scott, 1989). Keep in mind that ECT's success rate may appear somewhat lower because those individuals to whom it is administered are almost always ones for whom other treatments have not succeeded. ECT thus is sensibly recommended when other treatments fail. Today it can be administered safely and with efficacy. In the majority of cases, depression can be treated with therapy, perhaps combined with antidepressant drugs, thus rendering ECT unnecessary.

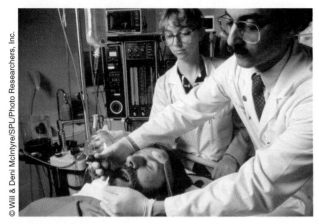

Depression is sometimes treated with electroconvulsive therapy when drug treatments are not successful.

The four main classes are antipsychotic drugs, antidepressant drugs, antianxiety drugs, and lithium.

ANTIPSYCHOTIC DRUGS. Antipsychotic drugs were a breakthrough in the treatment of psychotic patients. Prior to the introduction of these drugs, the wards of mental hospitals resembled many of our worst stereotypes. They were characterized by wild screaming and the constant threat of violence. The administration of antipsychotic drugs completely changed the atmosphere in many of these wards.

Antipsychotic drugs called phenothiazines were introduced in the early 1950s. The best known of these is also the first that was introduced: chlorpromazine, usually sold under the trade name Thorazine. Another common antipsychotic drug is haloperidol (Haldol). These antipsychotic drugs alleviate the symptoms of schizophrenia by blocking the dopamine receptors in the schizophrenic brain (see Chapter 3). Although these drugs are quite successful in treating the positive symptoms of schizophrenia (see Figure 17.6), they are less successful in treating the negative symptoms (see Chapter 16).

The traditional antipsychotic drugs also have serious side effects, including dryness of the mouth, tremors, stiffness, and involuntary jerking movements. Patients differ in the severity of their symptoms and in the length of time until symptom onset. Severe side effects can appear after prolonged use of these drugs.

DRUG THERAPIES

During the second half of the 20th century, the introduction of drug therapies has unquestionably been the major advance in the biological approach to the treatment of mental disorders. When many drugs currently in use were first introduced, scientists and practitioners had only the foggiest notion of how they worked at a biological level. Today we have more understanding, but it is far from complete. Disorders that formerly were resistant to treatment now have become treatable, at least to some degree. **Psychotropic drugs** affect psychological processes or state of mind.

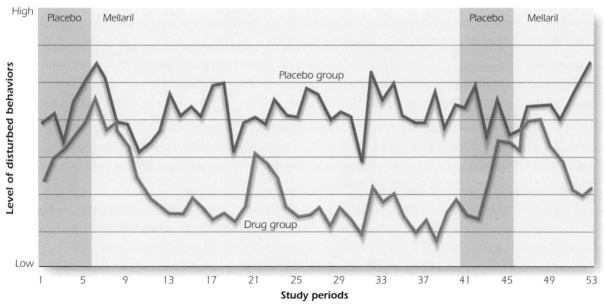

FIGURE 17.6

Antipsychotic Medication versus Placebo. The rates of symptomatic behavior are much higher for people in the placebo-control group than for those in the treatment group (who received Mellaril, a brand name of phenothiazine). In addition, the rate of symptomatic behavior for the treatment group temporarily rose during a brief trial (observations 41–45) of placebo substitution, and declined again after the drug was reinstated.

Another problem with traditional antipsychotic drugs is that not all psychotic patients respond to the traditional antipsychotic medications. Occasionally, another drug, such as clozapine, may be successful when the traditional drugs have failed. The overall success rate for treating patients who do not respond to other antipsychotic medications is about 30% (Kane et al., 1988). Clozapine can occasionally cause side effects (e.g., immune-system deficiencies), although the effects differ from those of the traditional antipsychotic drugs. Clearly, we are far from finding any panaceas in the biological treatment of psychoses. At the same time, the benefits of these drugs appear far to outweigh their costs. The potential costs pertain not only to the patient but also to the world around the patient.

A new generation of antipsychotic drugs, called *atypicals*, is becoming increasingly widely used for the treatment of schizophrenia. These drugs, such as clozapine (Clozaril), olanzapine (Zyprexa), risperidone (Risperdal), ziprasidone (Zeldox), and quetiapine (Seroquel), appear to be efficacious and to be less likely than traditional medications to lead to side effects such as depression and tardive dyskinesia. These medications simultaneously affect both dopamine receptors and other neurotransmitters that are implicated in schizophrenia. They seem to improve negative as well as positive symptoms, and may result in some improvement in mental functioning (What are, 2003). There remains some debate, however, over just how much more effective the newer drugs are than the older ones (Schizophrenia, 2000).

Social issues are involved in the use of antipsychotic drugs. The clinician is duty-bound to obtain informed consent from those who are to receive the drugs. One could easily argue that people who are suffering from psychotic episodes are in no position to give true informed consent, however. Nor is it clear that a patient's relatives can give true informed consent. There is no easy answer.

ANTIDEPRESSANT DRUGS. The three main kinds of antidepressant drugs are *tricyclics, monoamine oxidase (MAO) inhibitors,* and *selective serotonin reuptake inhibitors (SSRI)*. MAO inhibitors are used least frequently because they are more toxic and require adherence to a special diet. MAO inhibitors thus tend to be used for those patients who do not respond to other drugs. The MAO inhibitors include isocarboxazid (Marplan) and phenelzine (Nardil). Examples of the tricyclics are imipramine (Tofranil) and amitriptyline (Elavil).

Both tricyclics and MAO inhibitors increase concentrations of two neurotransmitters, serotonin and norepinephrine, at particular synapses in the brain (see Chapter 3). Concentrations of these neurotransmitters begin to increase almost immediately after patients start taking the drugs. However, the antidepressant effect does not begin immediately. It can take several weeks, and sometimes longer, before the patient starts to feel the effects.

The SSRIs have been introduced more recently. They work by inhibiting the reuptake of serotonin during transmission between neurons. This inhibition effectively increases the concentrations of the neurotransmitter, but it does so less directly than do the other two types of antidepressant drugs. One of the best known of these new drugs is fluoxetine (Prozac). Other such drugs are paroxetine (Paxil) and sertraline (Zoloft), fluvoxamine (Luvox), and venlafaxine (Effexor). Depressed patients typically start to show improvement after they have taken the drug for about three weeks. The SSRIs seem to work for a wide variety of patients, but some of them may have side effects, such as nausea, nervousness, and dysfunction in sexual performance. These drugs even have been shown to work for persons who have obsessive-compulsive disorder, although at this point it appears that a particular tricyclic drug, Anafranil, is more effective in this case (Greist, Jefferson, Koback, Katzelnick, & Serline, 1995).

From one point of view, drug treatment of depression has been considerably more successful than drug treatment of schizophrenia. Whereas antipsychotic drugs only suppress symptoms, antidepressant drugs seem to cause more lasting change. Patients who stop taking antipsychotic drugs typically return to their earlier psychotic state, whereas patients who stop taking antidepressant drugs often remain symptom free for quite some time, and possibly indefinitely.

Spontaneous recovery is the unprompted and unaided (untreated) disappearance of maladaptive symptoms over the course of time. Spontaneous recovery is very powerful. Many people get better over time without any particular intervention at all. But others do not, and for them, therapy is highly desirable. When we consider the difference in the longer term effectiveness of antipsychotic versus antidepressant drugs, we must also consider the rates of spontaneous recovery. The rate for depression is much higher than for schizophrenia and other psychoses. So an unknown proportion of the depressed patients who become better through the use of drugs or therapy might have become better even if they had received no treatment at all. In addition, researchers and clinicians must consider the effects of placebos. Patients may improve simply because they believe that they are being helped, even if the treatment they receive actually has no direct effect. Researchers need to rule out the effects of both spontaneous recovery and placebos. Hence, they often study the effects of drugs using both control groups that take placebos and control groups that are simply put on a waiting list for subsequent treatment. The control group taking placebos also may be studied using a *double-blind technique*, in which both the experimenter administering the

IN THE LAB OF DAVID H. BARLOW

EFFECTIVELY TREATING PANIC DISORDER

Panic disorder is a devastating emotional condition characterized by enormous surges of fear. Symptoms include rapidly increasing heart rate and respiration, dizziness, and sometimes a sense of unreality. People in the grip of a "panic attack" may feel that the world is collapsing in on them, that they are losing control of their bodies, and that they may be at death's door. The most puzzling feature of this phenomenon is that there seems to be no reason for it. Because people with panic disorder feel very vulnerable to attacks, they may refuse to leave a safe place or let go of a person who represents safety. What they fear is the possibility that they might have an attack where help is not available or escape is impossible. This kind of avoidance behavior is called *agoraphobia*.

We have recently discovered two successful treatments for panic disorder: drugs and brief psychological treatments. Which one works better? Is there any advantage to combining them? We evaluated these questions in a large clinical trial (in which the effectiveness of various treatments is evaluated by testing them on real patients) (Barlow, Gorman, Shear, & Woods, 2000).

In the study, 312 carefully screened patients with panic disorder were treated at three clinics in addition to our own. Two are known for their expertise with medication and two (including ours) for their expertise with psychological treatments. The purpose of this arrangement was to control for any bias that might affect the results—that is, if investigators at one site were committed to one particular type of treatment. Patients were randomly

David H. Barlow received his PhD from the University of Vermont in 1969. He has published more than 450 articles and chapters and more than 20 books, mostly in the areas of anxiety disorders, sexual problems, and clinical research methodology. Dr. Barlow is the recipient of the 2000 American Psychological Association (APA) Distinguished Scientific Award for the Applications of Psychology. He has also received the First Annual Science Dissemination Award from the Society for a Science of Clinical Psychology of the APA, and the 2000 Distinguished Scientific Contribution Award from the Society of Clinical Psychology of the APA.

assigned to five different treatment conditions: (1) psychological treatment alone (cognitive behavioral treatment, or CBT); (2) drug treatment alone (using imipramine, or IMI, a tricyclic antidepressant); (3) a combined treatment condition (CBT + IMI); (4) placebo alone (PBO); and (5) placebo + CBT. We wanted to determine the extent to which any advantage for the combined treatment was due to a placebo contribution. The participants in the study were initially treated for three months. The results indicated that members of all treatment groups improved significantly more than those on placebo, and approximately the same number of patients responded to each treatment. Treatments that combined two approaches were generally no more effective than treatments that used only one.

After six more months of maintenance treatment, during which each patient was seen once a month, the results looked very much as they did after the initial treatment, although there was now a slight advantage for combined treatment. The number of people responding to placebo had diminished. Six months after treat-

ment was discontinued (15 months after it was initiated), patients who were on medication, alone or combined with CBT, had deteriorated somewhat, and those who received CBT alone or combined with placebo had retained most of their gains. For example, 14 of 29 (48%) of the patients who began the six-month follow-up phase using medication along with CBT had relapsed, and so had 10 of 25 (40%) of the patients who were taking the drug alone. CBT alone (or with placebo) was associated with a lower relapse rate, between 16% and 18%. Thus, treatments that used CBT and no medication appeared to be superior at this point.

Conclusions from this large and important study suggest that there is no worthwhile incremental effect of combining treatments. Furthermore, the psychological treatments were more durable as measured (six months after treatment stopped). Adhering to the principle of using the least intrusive treatment first, the public health recommendation emanating from this study is that psychological treatment should be offered initially, followed by drug

continued

treatment for patients who do not respond adequately or for whom psychological treatment is not available. Because this was such a large study, involving so many different research centers, it is likely to have a substantial impact on national health-care policy.

One of the sites where this study was conducted is the Center for Anxiety and Related Disorders at Boston University, a large clinic under my direction that is devoted to the study and treatment of patients with anxiety disorders. We assess and treat approximately 500 new patients each year. Research into other types of psychological disorders is also ongoing. We study the nature and causes of anxiety, depression, and other emotional disorders, and try to determine how best to organize or classify them. The clinic also serves as a teaching facility for doctoral students in clinical psychology, and for psychiatric residents who, under supervision, learn how to diagnose and treat patients who have emotional disorders. Clinical psychology doctoral students carry out important research of their own that fulfills requirements for the master's thesis and doctoral dissertation. Undergraduate majors in psychology often participate in many aspects of the research.

treatment and the patient do not know whether a particular patient is receiving a placebo or an active drug.

ANTIANXIETY DRUGS. Clinicians prescribe antianxiety drugs (also called anxiolytics or tranquilizers) to alleviate their patients' feelings of tension and anxiety, to increase patients' feelings of well-being, and to counteract symptoms of insomnia. The earliest antianxiety drugs, the *barbiturates*, are rarely used today because they are highly addictive and potentially dangerous (see Chapter 5). More commonly used are two classes of antianxiety drugs: muscle relaxants and benzodiazepines. Muscle relaxants, such as cyclobenzaprine (Flexoril) and methocarbamol (Robaxin), cause feelings of tranquility.

Benzodiazepines also cause muscle relaxation and have an additional notable tranquilizing effect. Two of the most widely used of these drugs are chlordiazepoxide (Librium) and diazepam (Valium). Two more recent such drugs are Xanax and Klonopine. Clinicians have commonly prescribed these drugs without sufficient concern for their possible consequences. The drugs can be habit-forming, and their tranquilizing effect can impair attention and alertness while driving and engaging in similarly complex activities (Ramaekers, 2003; Schweizer, Rickels, Case, & Greenblatt, 1990), where their effects are comparable to those of moderate to high doses of alcohol. The SSRI drugs appear to work not only for depression but for anxiety as well (Lydiard, Brawman, & Ballenger, 1996).

MOOD STABILIZERS. In 1949, lithium was found to be effective in treating manic–depressive disorders, and it remains a drug of choice for these cases. It is very effective, almost immediately alleviating symptoms in roughly three-fourths of cases. It alleviates only depressive symptoms in manic–depressives (persons with bipolar disorder), however, which adds credence to the notion that bipolar disorder differs qualitatively from major (unipolar) depression (M. Baron, Gershon, Rudy, Jonas, & Buchsbaum, 1975). We still do not know why lithium has the effect it does (Manji et al., 1991). The drug must be used with care because overdoses can lead to convulsions and even to death. Another drug, Valproate, is also used to treat cases of bipolar disorder where there is rapid cycling of mood. Caramazepine has been used to treat acute manic episodes and other symptoms of bipolar disorder. It has been associated with potentially severe side effects.

A 1993 World Health Organization report (Sartorius, de Girolano, Andrews, German, & Eisenberg, 1993a) indicated that the main breakthroughs in pharmacotherapy (represented by the preceding four classes of psychotropic drugs) have revolutionized the psychiatric treatment of mental illness. Subsequent developments have offered refinements that enhance the applicability of these treatments, but they have not offered additional breakthroughs. In other cultures, very different drugs, as well as other forms of therapy, may be used more generally.

✓ CONCEPT CHECK 3

1. Free association is most characteristic of _____ therapy.
   a. psychodynamic
   b. behavioral
   c. cognitive
   d. biological
2. _____ is designed to lessen anxiety by having clients imagine as vividly as possible whatever causes them anxiety.
   a. Systematic desensitization
   b. Token economy
   c. Hypnotherapy
   d. Implosion therapy

3. A therapist points out that a client becomes irrationally upset about other people's problems and disturbances. The therapist is most likely a follower of
   a. B. F. Skinner.
   b. Sigmund Freud.
   c. Albert Ellis.
   d. Henry Murray.

ALTERNATIVES TO INDIVIDUAL THERAPY

Are there alternatives to individual therapy?

We have described drug therapies and the other forms of therapy in terms of one therapist administering treatment to one client. In some circumstances, however, various alternatives to one-on-one therapy may be more helpful. These options include group therapy, couples and family therapy, community psychology, and self-help. A 1993 World Health Organization report (Langsley, Hodes, & Grimson, 1993) indicated that these alternatives to individual therapy have been widely available in many non-Western cultures.

GROUP THERAPY

Therapy can be administered either individually or in groups. Group therapy offers several distinct advantages over individual therapy. First, it is almost always

The advantages of being in a large therapeutic group include reduced cost, social pressure to effect positive changes, and greater diversity of people who may offer fresh perspectives on a troubling situation. The disadvantages of group therapy include the potential dilution of treatment, and group dynamics may take precedence over solving the presenting problems that brought individual members to therapy.

less expensive than individual therapy. Second, it may offer greater support because groups are usually made up of individuals who have similar problems. Third, it offers the potential value of social pressure to change, which may supplement (or even supplant) the therapist's authoritative pressure to change. Fourth and finally, the very dynamic of group interaction may lead to therapeutic change, especially for people who have problems with interpersonal interactions.

Group therapy also has several potential disadvantages. First, the treatment effect may be diluted by the presence of others who require the attention of the therapist. Second, group therapy may embroil the clients in so many issues related to the group interactions that the clients no longer focus on resolving the problems that prompted them to seek therapy in the first place. Third, the content of the group process may move away from the dynamics of therapy, so that group members start to deal with problems that are interesting but irrelevant to the issues for which the group was formed. Group therapy thus has both advantages and disadvantages over individual therapy (M. Galanter, 2002).

Group therapy should be distinguished from "encounter groups" or "T-groups," which are formed in order to help individuals grow psychologically and sometimes to achieve spiritual fulfillment. Some of these groups subject individuals to fairly harsh psychological and even physical rigors. Although these groups may help some people, they seem to take a heavy toll in terms of the psychological harm they can cause (M. Galanter, 1989; Mithers, 1994), as in the case of cults.

M. Galanter (2000) has investigated religious cults and other charismatic groups, to which some people turn when they have psychological disorders. He refers to these groups as "charismatic" because the members typically commit themselves to a fervently espoused, transcendent goal that is frequently and passionately propounded by a charismatic leader. Galanter has proposed that such groups, along with zealous self-help movements, typically have three characteristics: a high level of social cohesiveness, an intensely held belief system, and a profound influence on members' behavior. Galanter has suggested that such groups can either help or hurt people who have mental disorders. In some cases, they precipitate disorders that did not previously exist.

Twelve-step groups are very popular for the treatment of addictions. Such groups typically do not use a professionally trained therapist or other leader. The first such group was Alcoholics Anonymous (AA), founded in the mid-1930s. Twelve-step groups are based on developing the addicts' relationship to a "higher power" as well as to self and others (see Table 17.2). When fighting addiction, members typically attend three to five meetings each week. At each meeting, members are free to discuss their dif-

TABLE 17.2

The 12 Steps of Alcoholics Anonymous. These 12 steps are well known around the world to the many members of Alcoholics Anonymous.

1. We admitted we were powerless over alcohol—that our lives had become unmanageable.

2. Came to believe that a power greater than ourselves could restore us to sanity.

3. Made a decision to turn our will and our lives over to the care of God *as we understood Him.*

4. Made a searching and fearless moral inventory of ourselves.

5. Admitted to God, to ourselves, and to another human being the exact nature of our wrongs.

6. Were entirely ready to have God remove all these defects of character.

7. Humbly asked Him to remove our shortcomings.

8. Made a list of all persons we had harmed, and became willing to make amends to them all.

9. Made direct amends to such people wherever possible, except when to do so would injure them or others.

10. Continued to take personal inventory and, when we were wrong, promptly admitted it.

11. Sought through prayer and meditation to improve our conscious contact with God *as we understood Him*, praying only for knowledge of His will for us and the power to carry that out.

12. Having had a spiritual awakening as the result of these steps, we tried to carry this message to alcoholics and to practice these principles in all our affairs.

Source: The Twelve Steps are reprinted with permission of Alcoholics Anonymous World Services, Inc. (A.A.W.S.). Permission to reprint the Twelve Steps does not mean that A.A.W.S. has reviewed or approved the contents of this publication, or that A.A.W.S. necessarily agrees with the view expressed herein. A.A. is a program of recovery from alcoholism only—use of the Twelve Steps in Connection with programs and activities which are patterned after A.A., but which address other problems, or in any other non-A.A. context, does not imply otherwise.

ficulties in overcoming their addiction. The support of other members is viewed as key to overcoming the addictions. Today, the 12-step approach has gained popularity not only for fighting substance abuse but for other kinds of group therapy as well.

The philosophy of AA is that alcoholism is a disease that can be managed but never completely cured. AA members who are in *recovery* have acknowledged that they have the disease, that there is no cure for it, and that alcohol therefore can never again play a part in their lives. Related groups include Al-Anon (for the spouses and adult children of alcoholics), Alateen (for the adolescent children of alcoholics), and Overeaters Anonymous (for those who feel unable to control how much or what they eat). Attendance at programs such as these goes beyond mere participation in therapy. It is more of a *conversion experience*, in which a person adopts a totally new way of living. People attempt to move beyond the addiction that has ruled their lives, and they do so by participating in a group that can itself become a way of life.

The effectiveness of AA and similar programs is not thoroughly documented (see D. C. Walsh et al., 1991), but there is some evidence for their potential success. In general, positive correlations have been identified between AA involvement and superior alcohol-related outcomes. But there has been some question whether these outcomes reflect AA involvement. McKellar, Stewart, and Humphreys (2003)

studied this issue in a sample of 2,319 alcohol-dependent men. They found that attending AA meetings for 1 year after treatment predicted lower alcohol-related problems at the 2-year follow-up, but that alcohol-related problems at 1 year did not predict AA affiliation at the 2-year follow-up. In other words, AA affiliation appears to have caused improvement in alcohol-related outcomes. The authors also ruled out motivation as a factor in the results. Their findings are consistent with the general view that participation in AA has some positive effect, at least for men, on alcohol-related outcomes.

Behavior therapy also can be done in groups. A. A. Lazarus (1961, 1968, 1989) has used behavioral techniques in a group setting. Phobias are especially treatable in this way. In group desensitization, a single psychotherapist can teach many people at once how to relax deeply, and then can develop a common desensitization hierarchy to alleviate various kinds of phobias, such as fear of snakes, heights, and so on. Various behavioral techniques also have been used in other group treatment programs, such as programs to lose weight (Wollersheim, 1970).

COUPLES AND FAMILY THERAPY

Family systems therapy treats a couple or family unit as a whole, which involves complex interactions more than the discrete problems of individual members.

Couples therapy can be highly effective in helping partners resolve interpersonal conflict and enhance communication.

The identified problem may be centered on the family unit, such as troubled communication among family members, or it may focus on the problem of one member. The underlying notion in family therapy is that individual problems often have roots in the family system, and that to treat the problem, the whole family should be part of the solution (see Langsley et al., 1993). For example, a child's disorderly conduct almost inevitably affects the whole family.

In cases of marital conflict, couples therapy may be more successful in some instances than individual therapy both in holding couples together and in bringing them back together (Gurman, Kniskern, & Pinsoff, 1986). Couples therapy tends to be particularly successful for people who have had problems for only a short time before they seek therapy and when they have not yet initiated action toward divorce. One reason for the greater success of couples therapy is that the therapist can hear about the reality expressed by both members of the couple. Hearing both points of view enables the therapist to mediate more effectively than does hearing just a single point of view.

Couples therapy emphasizes communication and mutual empathy. Partners are trained to listen carefully and empathically to each other. They learn to restate what the partner is saying, thereby confirming that they accurately understood the partner's point of view. Couples are also taught how to make requests of each other in constructive but direct ways, rather than to make indirect requests that can be confusing and at times harmful to the relationship. Erving Goffman (1967) found that partners in unsuccessful relationships often fail to hear even the positive things that they say about each other.

Aaron Beck (1988) has emphasized the importance of having each partner understand the perspective of the other. He urges partners to clarify the differences in what they seek for the relationship, not-ing that partners often have secret "shoulds": things that each of us believes our partner ought to do, but that our partner may not believe to be important or worth doing. Beck believes many problems in a relationship can be attributed to the *automatic thoughts* that can rise into our consciousness and that we believe to be self-evident, whether they are or not. For example, one might think that a recent failure is so important that it will destroy the rest of one's life, no matter what one does.

Arnold Lazarus (2000) has suggested that temperamental compatibility may be more important to a lasting marriage than compatibility of interests. He has found that both happy and unhappy couples have heated disagreements from time to time, but that successful couples tend to resolve them quickly and then drop the matter. He has found, as a result, that it is often possible after very few sessions, sometimes even one, to predict the likely outcome of marital therapy. Couples who can resolve problems quickly and let go of them have the best prognosis.

COMMUNITY PSYCHOLOGY

Community psychology views people not only as a part of a couple or a family system but also as part of the larger system of the community. The community psychologist may intervene at any level, ranging from the individual to the community, depending on what will most effectively help clients.

Mental disorders are common both in the United States and internationally. An estimated 22.1% of Americans aged 18 and older—slightly more than 1 in 5 adults—suffer from a diagnosable mental disorder in a given year. When applied to the 1998 U.S. Census residential population estimate, this figure translates to 44.3 million people. Moreover, 4 of the 10 leading sources of disability in the United States and other developed countries are mental disorders: major depression, bipolar disorder, schizophrenia, and obsessive-compulsive disorder. Large numbers of people suffer from more than one mental disorder at any given time ("Mental Disorders in America," http://www.nimh.nih.gov/publicat/numbers.cfm, 2003). The best course of action, certainly, is to treat people before they even begin to show impairment—in other words, to focus on prevention.

The emphasis in community psychology is at least as much on prevention as it is on treatment. With so many people at risk for psychological distress, it makes sense to try to prevent problems before they happen. Community psychologists may intervene at one or more of three levels of prevention. *Primary prevention* is aimed at preventing disorders before they happen. *Secondary prevention* is targeted at detecting disorders

Therapy for individuals, couples, families, and communities involves personal interactions between therapists and the clients they serve. There is yet another alternative for people seeking therapeutic assistance: self-help. Your bookstore probably features a generously stocked self-help section, with books suggesting how to help yourself resolve almost any problem you could imagine: how to treat addiction, how to improve your love life, how to become more assertive, how to overcome various forms of self-defeating behavior, and more. Thousands of such books are published every year, some making outrageous claims (Rosen, 1987, 1993) but others offering reasonable advice. Moreover, as many as 15 million people may be involved in self-help groups (Christensen & Jacobson, 1994).

Does any of this advice actually work? This is a hard question to answer because no one is monitoring the effectiveness of the various programs. There are relatively few classics in the field—books that continue to be printed long after the initial burst of sales—which suggests that the large majority of these books are not so helpful that purchasers recommend them to an ever-widening circle of buyers. Perhaps the most appropriate comment about such books is: Let the buyer beware! Some books may be helpful, others not. Users need to judge each on its own merit and realize that for serious problems, no self-help book is likely to suffice. Those in need of therapy might do better to choose the most appropriate professionally administered treatment.

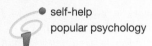

self-help
popular psychology

early, before they become major problems. *Tertiary prevention* treats disorders once they have developed fully.

Whereas most traditional therapists wait for clients to come to them, community psychologists often actively seek out people who have problems or who are likely to have them in the future. Moreover, community psychologists often perceive themselves as part of the communities they serve rather than as detached, outside experts. That is, community psychologists may become actively involved in the lives of people in the community.

One of the means by which community psychologists offer appropriate services to members of the community is through outpatient *community mental-health centers.* Costs are generally lower than for individual therapy, and many centers offer 24-hour walk-in crisis services.

Hotlines serve people, usually 24 hours a day, who are desperate for assistance. The most well-known hotlines deal with suicide prevention and domestic violence. There are also hotlines for potential child abusers and for people with other problems as well. People who answer the phones are taught procedures to defuse the immediate problem. For example, a person who answers a suicide-prevention hotline is taught to communicate empathy to the caller, show understanding of the problem, provide information about sources of help, and obtain the caller's verbal agreement to take actions that will lead away from suicide (Speer, 1972).

Many mentally ill people who might have remained hospitalized in the past have been *deinstitutionalized* (re-leased from health-care institutions and onto the streets). The reasons for this include lack of funding, concerns about whether institutions served the purpose they were supposed to serve, and issues regarding whether mental patients could give informed consent. Although community-based outpatient treatment may be as effective as—or more effective than—inpatient treatment for many disorders, many deinstitutionalized patients receive little or no treatment whatsoever. As a result, they are left homeless with no appropriate treatment. It is often very difficult to reach people in need once they are out on the streets. And, even when contact has been made, keeping patients on the therapy and

Some homeless people are mentally ill but do not seek or receive proper treatment.

medication they may need is very difficult. The deinstitutionalization of the mentally ill in many countries has created problems when there has been an accompanying failure to deliver appropriate community-based mental-health care (Burti & Yastrebov, 1993). Moreover, Beadle-Brown and Forrester-Jones (2003) found that, after deinstitutionalization, released individuals showed a significant decrease in conversation and social mixing, nonverbal communication, and initiation of conversation and social interaction.

The cost of professional treatment is one reason many people try to improve their mental health on their own, as discussed in the Psychology in Everyday Life box, "Self Help."

✓ CONCEPT CHECK 4

1. Which of the following is *not* a reason to use group as opposed to individual therapy?
   a. It is usually less expensive.
   b. One can help others, even if one is not particularly helped oneself.
   c. It may offer greater support.
   d. The dynamics of group interaction may help achieve change.
2. Twelve-step groups are most often used to treat
   a. addictions.
   b. phobias.
   c. depression.
   d. psychosis.
3. Community psychologists differ from most other psychologists in
   a. the number of years of training they require.
   b. that they have an MD rather than a PhD degree.
   c. actively seeking out clients in community settings rather than waiting for clients to come to them.
   d. using psychoactive drugs as a first rather than as a last resort.

EFFECTIVENESS OF THERAPY

How effective is therapy in permanently solving psychological problems?

Does therapy work? A great deal of research attempts to answer this question. Perhaps the most striking finding is that, on average, therapy seems to work (Lambert & Bergin, 1994; Lipsey & Wilson, 1993; Maling & Howard, 1994; Overholser, 2002; Seligman, 1995; van Schaik et al., 2002).

In evaluating the effectiveness of therapy, researchers must compare a given treatment not only with alternative treatments but also with no therapy at all. Over time, some people show spontaneous remission: They simply get better of their own accord. Humans, like members of other species, have evolved in ways that equip them to fight off a variety of threats to their existence, ranging from large-animal predators to parasitic infections to the kinds of problems in living that therapy is meant to address. Thus, we can expect that some people will improve without any active intervention. The success of therapy needs always to be measured against this baseline rate of improvement. At the same time, there can be ethical problems with giving a person in need no therapy at all. It is also important to remember that a label does not always adequately describe exactly what happens in therapy sessions. For example, Malik, Beutler, Alimohamed, Gallagher-Thompson, and Thompson (2003) found that what is called "cognitive therapy" can mean very different things to different practitioners.

Other factors also should be considered in an ideal research program; for example, the length of treatment dramatically affects therapeutic outcomes. One *meta-analytic study* (i.e., a study that analyzes a large number of other studies; K. I. Howard, Kopta, Krause, & Orlinsky, 1986) showed that when the effects of dropping out of treatment are statistically controlled, 29%–38% of therapy clients improve by the first 3 sessions, 48%–58% improve by the first 4 to 7 sessions, 56%–68% improve by the first 8 to 16 sessions, 74%–81% by the first 17 to 52 sessions, and 85% by the first 53 to 100 sessions. Clearly, studies that failed to consider treatment length would obtain inconclusive results.

THE IMPACT OF MANAGED CARE

Under the general label of *managed care*, insurance companies often control both the initiation and the duration of therapy. The problem is that sometimes the management emphasizes cost cutting more than high-quality service. Access to therapy may be restricted or its duration may be curtailed. Managed-care companies may prefer insufficiently trained practitioners over better trained practitioners, in part because their services cost less. The issues surrounding the attainment of good therapeutic care at what managed-care companies consider to be a reasonable cost are far from being resolved. The increased decision making by insurance companies is likely to increase the importance of evaluation in therapy because evaluations provide a basis for managed-care companies to decide whether or how much therapy is called for (Beutler, Kim, Davison, Karno, & Fisher, 1996).

ISSUES IN THERAPY RESEARCH

Researchers should consider the length of treatment for specific disorders. Figure 17.7 shows the results of the meta-analytic study by Kenneth Howard and his colleagues (1986). If researchers were to determine the effectiveness of therapy for borderline psychotic patients in terms of therapist ratings at the conclusion of eight sessions, the results would be profoundly discouraging; yet if the researchers were to assess therapist ratings in these same patients at the conclusion of 104 sessions, the studies would be extremely encouraging. For depressed and anxious patients, however, therapy results would be much more positive after shorter durations of therapy.

Additional factors to consider might be whether individual, family, couple, or group therapy would be most helpful; the relevant type of setting (e.g., inpatient or outpatient); additional characteristics of the client and of the therapist (e.g., cultural background, personality variables such as extroversion/introversion, attitudes, and values); and the therapeutic technique (e.g., how closely the therapist followed the approach prescribed by a particular theoretical paradigm). Al-

though the call for this kind of research first went out decades ago (e.g., Kiesler, 1966; G. L. Paul, 1967), it has yet to materialize. Given complexity of the issue, this is not surprising.

Although the ideal research that would allow therapy to be perfectly tailored to client diagnosis has not yet been done, meta-analytic and other research clearly shows that therapy produces significant improvement in clients, above and beyond any spontaneous recovery that might have occurred (e.g., Andrews, 1993; Overholser, 2002; M. L. Smith & Glass, 1977; Stiles, Shapiro, & Elliott, 1986). In particular, clients who receive therapy, on average, are better off than 75% or more of research control participants who did not receive therapy. Therapy is especially helpful (better than for 82%–83% of untreated controls) in improving clients' self-esteem and in reducing their anxiety. However, therapy was less helpful (better than for only 71% of untreated controls) in increasing the level of adjustment in persons institutionalized for psychotic, alcoholic, or criminal behaviors. It was even less helpful (better than for only 62% of untreated controls) in increasing clients' grade-point averages or otherwise enhancing their work or school achievements (M. L. Smith & Glass, 1977). In general, therapy is more effective for those with less serious, rather than with more serious,

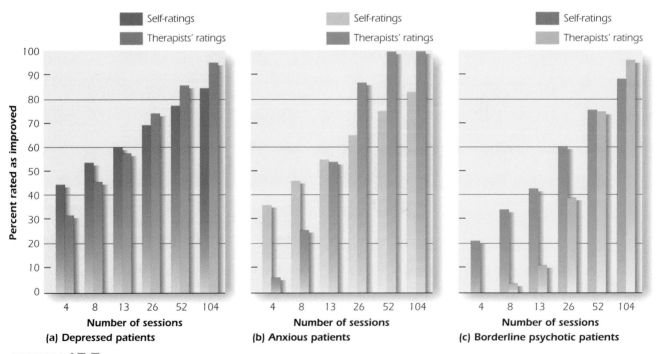

FIGURE 17.7

Meta-Analysis of the Course of Therapy. Although self-ratings and therapist ratings differed, as did the degree of improvement across various diagnoses, the data seem to show that therapy is a highly effective way to help people who have psychological problems. Note, however, that these results reflect ratings of improvement and not necessarily objective changes in behavior. (After Howard et al., 1986)

psychological problems (Kopta, Howard, Lowry, & Beutler, 1994) and for people who really want to improve (Orlinsky & Howard, 1994). There is even evidence that therapy can result in improved health and recovery from illness (Bennett, 1996). It may thereby reduce the cost of health care (Gabbard, Lazar, Hornberger, & Spiegel, 1997). Therapy also is perceived as playing a positive role in the lives of those who receive it (Shadish et al., 1997). The ideal form of therapy may depend, to some extent, on the patient. For example, Karno, Beutler, and Harwood (2002) found that patients with high emotional distress did best when the therapy they received addressed emotional experiences. The opposite was found for patients with low emotional distress.

LONG-TERM VERSUS SHORT-TERM TREATMENT

A study published in *Consumer Reports* (1995), directed in large part by psychologist Martin Seligman, suggested the efficacy of therapy. In particular, Seligman (1995; Seligman & Levant, 1998) has reported that patients who received long-term treatment did substantially better than those who received only short-term treatment. No specific type of therapy was, on average, better than any other for any disorder. Psychologists, psychiatrists, and social workers did not differ, on average, in effectiveness, although all were more effective than marriage counselors and family doctors. Patients whose length of therapy or whose choice of therapist was dictated by an insurance company or a managed-care program did worse than those who had freedom of choice.

It is important in evaluating these results to take into account that the *Consumer Reports* survey was based on users' subjective impressions of the effectiveness of the therapy rather than on any objective measures of therapeutic outcomes. The response rate for surveys was very low, which further leaves one somewhat skeptical of the validity of the results. The responses also were from the standpoint of the clients. It would be interesting to compare their views with those of the therapists (Brock, Green, & Reich, 1998).

Moreover, not all research suggests that all therapies are equally effective. Many studies have reported that, on average, behavior therapies and cognitive therapies may be more effective than psychodynamic therapy or no therapy at all (Chambless, 1995, 1999; Chambless & Ollendick, 2000; Lambert & Bergin, 1994; A. A. Lazarus, 1990; Weisz, Weiss, Hun, Granger, & Morton, 1995). Some research suggests that particular techniques may work especially well for particular disorders. For example, fears and phobias seem best to be treated behaviorally by exposing clients to the source of their fears (S. L. Kaplan, Randolph, & Lemli, 1991).

Cognitive therapies appear to be effective in treating depression (Beck, 2002; Robinson, Berman, & Neimeyer, 1990). There is room for improvement in all techniques.

Not everyone is as positive about the value of therapy as Seligman (1995). A carefully controlled study, the Fort Bragg Demonstration Project, also set out to test the value of therapy (Bickman, 1996; Bickman et al., 1995). The study involved a unit that served more than 42,000 children and adolescent dependents for more than 5 years, from June 1990 to September 1995. This study, unlike Seligman's, evaluated treatment effectiveness rather than relying only on reports of satisfaction from clients. It looked at whether there were actual improvements in functioning. The results suggested that therapy was not particularly useful and that a longer time in therapy often did not improve outcomes (see also Dineen, 1998; Hoagwood, 1997). At the very least, the study suggested the need to know better under what kinds of circumstances therapy is more or less effective.

In sum, therapy is often, though certainly not always, beneficial. Somewhat surprising is the finding in some studies that the positive outcomes of therapy seem to occur regardless of type. That is, when the researchers' allegiance to a particular therapy is ruled out, each type of therapy seems to be just about as effective as the next. When the researchers' allegiance is not ruled out, whatever therapy program the researcher prefers seems to fare better in comparisons.

ELEMENTS OF EFFECTIVE THERAPY

CHARACTERISTICS ACROSS THERAPISTS

Despite the variety of therapeutic approaches, all therapists seek to communicate to their clients a new perspective on the client and his or her situation. Perhaps these attributes account for the primary effects of therapy of all sorts.

Several meta-analytic studies have shown that despite widely divergent therapeutic techniques and approaches, two global characteristics of therapists appear across theoretical orientations: (1) their "warm involvement with the client" and (2) their "communication of a new perspective on the client's person and situation" (Stiles et al., 1986, p. 172). Thus, regardless of the therapist's theoretical orientation, all therapists try to establish *rapport* with clients, which means that they try to convey feelings of trust and to establish ease of communication. Furthermore, the client needs to feel that the therapist genuinely cares about the outcome, or else therapeutic change is much less likely to occur.

CHARACTERISTICS ACROSS CLIENTS

An interesting counterpart to the hypothesized crucial importance of the role of the therapist is that the role of the client in a therapeutic relationship also affects the results. The client's style of communication in a therapeutic context is distinctively self-disclosing, which may in itself promote improvement. The client's desire to improve and belief in the efficacy of therapy may also facilitate the therapeutic process.

THE THERAPEUTIC ALLIANCE

The client and the therapist form a distinctive *therapeutic alliance*, in which they join in the effort to help the client improve through the process of therapy. William Stiles and his colleagues (1986) evaluated dozens of studies and found that the available research supported the importance of this alliance to therapeutic outcomes. Also important for success is scrupulously ethical behavior on the part of the therapist.

✓ **CONCEPT CHECK 5**

1. Spontaneous remission refers to people getting better
   a. without therapy.
   b. after brief treatment.
   c. after prolonged treatment.
   d. during therapy but then reverting back to their original state.
2. A meta-analytic study
   a. analyzes a large number of other studies.
   b. is a study within a study.
   c. is qualitative rather than quantitative.
   d. is humanistic in design.
3. Managed care has tended to _____ the amount of therapy clients are able to receive.
   a. decrease
   b. leave the same
   c. increase
   d. decrease for neurotic patients but increase for psychotic patients

ETHICAL ISSUES IN THERAPY

What ethical obligations must therapists fulfill?

In the fall of 1992, the late Ann Landers devoted her entire advice column to exposing a world-renowned psychiatrist who had held various prestigious positions in psychiatric associations. The disgraced psychiatrist was forced to resign from the American Psychiatric Association after losing a lawsuit brought by former patients who claimed he had abused them sexually and in other ways. This type of case is not unique, although it is rare. Therapists are in a position to cause enormous harm to patients by virtue of their status and their position as dispensers of treatment; a few of them do so. Inevitably, they hurt not only their clients and themselves but also the entire profession through their unethical behavior.

Perhaps even more than many other professionals, therapists are expected to behave ethically toward clients. Therapists are expected to refrain from becoming sexually involved with clients, for example. Moreover, therapists are expected to maintain the confidentiality of communications between themselves and their clients. Only in rare cases can they be required to divulge the contents of these communications. Such cases occur primarily when the therapist determines that clients may be dangerous to themselves or to others. In addition, in some states, therapists must breach confidentiality when a client has been accused of a crime and the records of the therapist might be relevant to determining the client's sanity, when the therapist has been accused of malpractice, when a client has sought therapy with the goal of evading the law, or when a child under age 16 has been a victim of child abuse. In most states, in cases of child abuse or of potential danger to others, therapists are legally required to take action. In other words, they cannot expose a child or other person to great risk simply to keep their communications confidential. As of April 14, 2003, new U.S. (HIPAA—Health Insurance Portability and Accountability Act) regulations have been put into effect that carefully protect patient privacy.

Sometimes therapy poses risks that spring from good but misdirected intentions. In May 1994, a civil court awarded half a million dollars to a man whose adult daughter had accused him of sexually abusing her during her childhood (Berkman, 1994; LaGanga, 1994; Shuit, 1994). The award followed a verdict asserting that the daughter's therapists negligently had reinforced false memories of sexual abuse (see Chapter 7). The man's 23-year-old daughter had accused him of sexually abusing her after she underwent treatment that her therapists asserted was designed to "recover suppressed memories." After the daughter made those accusations, her father lost his $400,000-a-year job as a vice president of marketing for a major company and her mother divorced him.

In this case, the therapists used questionable therapeutic techniques to elicit the daughter's horrifying recollections. The daughter remains entirely sure of her memories. Many other people, including the jurors in her father's civil case, question the accuracy of the memories. Whatever the verdict in cases such as this one, it is clear that both the parent and the child suffer greatly. One source (described in Geyelin, 1994) estimates that thousands of parents and their adult children are confronting the heart-wrenching problems posed by trying to determine whether disturbing memories arise from accurate recollection. Are memories elicited by techniques that facilitate their recovery, or are they inaccurate distortions introduced by techniques that lead to their creation? Professional organizations of clinical therapists are grappling with the need to guide therapists in the treatment of people who appear to be suffering ill effects from suppressed or repressed memories of painful events.

Another ethical protection is the demand that before clients participate in experimental treatments, they must give their informed consent, which is based on being fully informed of the nature of the procedure and of all possible harmful side effects or consequences, as well as of the likelihood of such consequences occurring. Throughout the experiment, the therapist is expected to preserve the well-being of the participants to the fullest extent possible.

Although we would like to believe that ethical issues could be viewed in black and white, they often come in shades of gray. For example, in the past, homosexuality was treated as a disorder. It was thought that people with homosexual preferences needed to change their sexual orientation to be restored to full mental health. Today, treatment is recommended only if homosexuals either want to feel satisfied with this preference or want to try to change it. The gray area becomes visible when we ask: To what extent should the therapist encourage the client either to accept a homosexual preference or to try to change it? Different therapists approach this question with different points of view. On the one hand, it is important for therapists to respect the values of their clients; on the other hand, some view therapy partly as a tool for the therapist to transmit a value system to the client.

The important point is that therapists need to consider ethics in their treatment of clients. They need to take into account not only their own ethical standards but also those of the field and of the society in which it is embedded.

When therapy is implemented appropriately, another benefit appears to be a reduction in overall health-care costs. Thus, when companies provide mental-health counseling for their employees, they obtain not only increases in productivity and decreases in employee absenteeism and turnover, but also savings in the overall cost of health care (Docherty, 1993).

✓**CONCEPT CHECK 6**

1. High ethical standards are very important
   a. in neither psychological research nor practice.
   b. in psychological research but not in practice.
   c. in psychological practice but not in research.
   d. in both psychological research and practice.
2. In general, informed consent is _____ in psychological research.
   a. almost never required
   b. sometimes required
   c. often required
   d. almost always required
3. Today, homosexuality is regarded as needing treatment
   a. only if the individual is dissatisfied with her or his sexual preference.
   b. if the individual or the family is dissatisfied with her or his sexual preference.
   c. under no circumstances.
   d. under essentially all circumstances.

TREATMENTS FOR OBESITY

In 2000, newspapers throughout the United States reported that the New Mexico state child-welfare department had removed a 3-year-old girl from her parents' home because she was grossly overweight. At only 42 inches tall, this little girl weighed 120 pounds. (The average weight for a 3-year-old is 33 pounds.) The girl's parents were cited for maintaining an unhealthy environment and for not providing their daughter with necessary medical attention. The mother maintained that she tried to control her daughter's eating and to get help for her, but that the weight problem was out of control. In a 2003 case in Michigan, a 3-year-old boy who weighed 120 pounds was removed from his home and placed in foster care. He was so obese that he could barely move.

Certainly we all know at least one person who struggles with a weight problem. As the parents of the morbidly obese 3-year-olds learned, appetite control is extremely difficult for some people. Behavioral neuroscientists, psychopharmacologists, health psychologists, applied behavioral psychologists, and clinical and counseling psychologists are working together to develop successful treatments for obesity.

Behavioral neuroscientists study the role of brain processes in the development and maintenance of obesity. For example, Gene-Jack Wang and his colleagues (Wang, Volkow, Thanos, & Fowler, 2003) compared PET scans of obese and non-obese people. The scans revealed that obese people had fewer dopamine receptors than people of normal weight. Lower dopamine function makes them less sensitive to reward, which in turn makes them eat more in order to compensate for reduced pleasure levels. These findings suggest that successful

treatment for obesity probably should address reduced dopamine function. Wang's team also discovered that the brain regions that process taste are overactive in obese subjects.

Psychopharmacologists study brain processes in order to develop drugs that can be used to treat obesity. For decades, drugs that increase norepinephrine and dopamine activity in the brain have been used to suppress appetite and therefore to promote weight loss. Unfortunately, these drugs either are very addictive or damage vital organs. The search is on for a drug that will help reduce food intake without adversely affecting the patient's health. Some psychopharmacologists are trying to develop a drug that will control the growth of fat cells (Hofbauer, 2002). Medications such as SSRIs that increase the activity of serotonin have been found to control overeating in obese binge eaters, but they don't work for obese people who do not binge eat (Malhotra, King, Welge, Brunsman-Lovins, & McElroy, 2002).

Research by sports and health psychologists has shown that exercising as well as dieting is important in the treatment of obesity. In a study by **sports psychologists** of 108 obese women in an 18-month weight-loss program, those who both dieted and exercised 2 to 4 hours per week lost more weight than those who either dieted or exercised alone (Jakicic, Wing, & Winters-Hart, 2002). Drug therapy also appears to work best when used in conjunction with exercise and dieting (Jakicic, Coleman, Donnelly, Foreyt, Melanson, Volek, & Volpe, 2001).

Health psychologists study the impact of lifestyle changes on weight loss. Lifestyle clinics require obese patients to change their dietary intake,

increase their physical activity, and take medication. Patients in one lifestyle clinic lost an average of 17.2 pounds over a 6-month period, compared to a loss of 3.7 pounds in patients who dieted only (Frost, Lyons, Bovill-Taylor, Carter, Stuttard, & Dornhorst, 2002).

Applied behavioral psychologists use learning principles to fight obesity. Behavior modification programs, which involve rewarding patients for weight loss, have been successful in helping patients lose weight and keep it off (Latner, Wilson, Stunkard, & Jackson, 2002). One behavioral technique that is especially effective is self-monitoring, in which the individual keeps a list of everything he or she eats. When patients engage in self-monitoring, their food intake (especially binge eating) goes down (Latner & Wilson, 2002). Cognitive-behavioral therapy, also widely used with obese individuals, combines behavioral principles with cognitive techniques to give them more control over the thoughts and emotional reactions that may lead to overeating (Cooper & Fairburn, 2002).

Clinical psychologists are involved in the day-to-day treatment of obesity. They use cognitive-behavioral and other forms of therapy to treat people who want to lose weight. Issues such as poor body image, depression, and low self-esteem must be addressed in the therapy sessions (Faith, Matz, & Jorge, 2002; Wolff & Clark, 2001). In treating eating disorders, clinical psychologists make use of research by behavioral neuroscientists, psychopharmocologists, and sports and health psychologists in helping obese individuals who want to change their lives.

SUMMARY

HISTORY OF THERAPY 603

How were people who behaved abnormally treated before the development of modern therapy?

1. Early views of therapy reflected the prevalent idea that persons afflicted with mental illness were possessed by demons. Subsequent treatment in *asylums* was essentially a way to warehouse mentally ill persons to keep them off the streets, with little thought given to humane treatment, let alone therapy. By the 19th century, Josef Breuer proposed the *cathartic method*, which became the basis for Freud's psychoanalytic methods.

DIAGNOSING AND ASSESSING ABNORMAL BEHAVIOR 609

How do therapists diagnose the people who come to them for treatment?

2. The DSM-IV and ICD systems of diagnostic classification have helped clinicians make appropriate and consensually understood diagnoses as a basis for treatment.
3. Clinical assessment procedures include clinical interviews, which may be structured or unstructured, and psychological tests.
4. Psychological tests include personality tests (both objective and projective measures), intelligence tests, neuropsychological tests, and biological measurements.

APPROACHES TO THERAPY 611

How do the various theoretical perspectives on personality and abnormal behavior relate to therapy?

5. The five main approaches to therapy are psychodynamic, humanistic, behavioral, cognitive, and biological. The cultural approach can be viewed as an additional tool.
6. More than half the people who need therapy probably do not seek it out.
7. Psychodynamic therapies emphasize insight into underlying unconscious processes as the key to the therapeutic process. Freudian psychoanalytic therapy and neo-Freudian ego-analysis therapies are the two major types of psychodynamic therapies. In *free association*, the patient freely says whatever comes to mind, not censoring or other-

wise editing the free flow of words before reporting them. *Resistances* are attempts by the client to block therapeutic progress in psychodynamic treatment, usually as a result of unconscious conflicts. Dreams have both manifest content and latent content. In *transference*, the patient projects her or his feelings and internal conflicts onto the therapist, often including aspects of the patient's early childhood relationships.

8. Humanistic therapies emphasize the therapeutic effects of the therapist's unconditional positive regard for the client, as exemplified by Carl Rogers's *client-centered therapy*.
9. *Behavior therapies* emphasize techniques based on principles of operant and classical conditioning. Techniques include counterconditioning, *aversion therapy*, *systematic desensitization*, and *extinction procedures* such as *flooding* and *implosion therapy*. Additional techniques include the use of *token economies* and *behavioral contracting*. *Modeling* bridges the gap between behavioral and cognitive therapies.
10. Cognitive therapies encourage patients to change their cognitions in order to achieve therapeutic changes in behavior and other desired outcomes. Albert Ellis's *rational-emotive therapy* and Aaron Beck's *cognitive therapy* are two of the main schools of cognitive therapy.
11. Historically, biological treatments of mental illness have included a wide array of treatments. *Psychosurgery* proved to be, for the most part, a disaster in the history of therapy. A more recent and successful treatment is *electroconvulsive therapy (ECT)*.
12. Modern biological treatments, such as effective *psychotropic drugs*, have revolutionized biological treatments. Today, the four key classes of psychotropic drugs are antipsychotics, antidepressants, antianxiety drugs, and lithium. Although these drugs are certainly not cure-alls, they are a welcome asset in the clinician's armamentarium. A cultural perspective provides an additional approach.

ALTERNATIVES TO INDIVIDUAL THERAPY 625

Are there alternatives to individual therapy?

13. Alternatives to individual therapy include group therapy, couples and family therapy, community psychology, and self-help. Group therapy, couples therapy, and family therapy often address prob-

lems specific to interpersonal relationships, and they deal with these problems through the dynamic interplay that occurs in the group, the couple, or the family. Community psychology focuses primarily on preventive mental health; community psychologists may use several strategies, including education of all members of a community, outreach to persons experiencing stress, and treatment of persons in distress. In self-help therapies, individuals seek guidance in handling stressful situations or minor psychological difficulties through books and other informational media.

14. No single approach to therapy is ideal for all persons, or in all situations or cultural settings. Rather, the various approaches to therapy may be viewed as complementary alternatives for aiding persons in need of therapeutic assistance. For example, drug therapy often may be combined with verbal forms of therapy to achieve results neither form of therapy would yield alone.

EFFECTIVENESS OF THERAPY 629

How effective is therapy in permanently solving psychological problems?

15. In some studies, the different forms of therapy have proven to be about equally effective. Several possible explanations for this paradox (i.e., differ-

ent forms but similar outcomes) have been proposed. Other studies, however, have shown differential effectiveness of various kinds of therapy. The success of any therapy has to be evaluated against rates of *spontaneous recovery*—that is, recovery without treatment.

16. The length of treatment and other factors not specific to a particular approach may play a role in the relative effectiveness of therapy.

17. Each approach to therapy has distinctive advantages and disadvantages, and it may be best to view the approaches as complementary rather than competing. We have not yet achieved the ability to prescribe a particular form of therapy for a given type of psychological problem. Effective therapy generally requires warm involvement of the therapist with the patient and good communications. In particular, the therapist and the client need to feel that they are allies in trying to overcome the client's difficulties.

ETHICAL ISSUES IN THERAPY 632

What ethical obligations must therapists fulfill?

18. Because therapists have the potential to influence clients profoundly, they must be especially mindful of ethical considerations.

KEY TERMS

ANSWERS TO CONCEPT CHECKS

Concept Check 1

1. c   2. d   3. a

Concept Check 2

1. d   2. a   3. d

Concept Check 3

1. a   2. d   3. c

Concept Check 4

1. b   2. a   3. c

Concept Check 5

1. a   2. a   3. a

Concept Check 6

1. d   2. d   3. a

KNOWLEDGE CHECK

1. When Philippe Pinel removed the shackles and other instruments of confinement from patients in an asylum, the patients' behavior
   a. got worse.
   b. got better.
   c. stayed the same.
   d. first got better and then got worse.
2. Which of the following is *not* one of the questions therapists using DSM-IV must answer?
   a. Does the client have one or more problems?
   b. What are the problems a client has, if any?
   c. Why does the client have the problem(s) he or she has?
   d. Once diagnosed, how should the problem(s) be treated?
3. A disadvantage of the unstructured clinical interview is that
   a. the client rather than the therapist asks the questions.
   b. the interview is usually very long.
   c. the interview can be used only with adults.
   d. the therapist cannot obtain strictly comparable data across different interviews.
4. In the Halstead–Reitan Battery, trail-making involves drawing lines from
   a. numbers to numbers.
   b. letters to letters.
   c. numbers to letters.
   d. numbers to geometric shapes.
5. According to psychoanalytic theory, resistances are set up by
   a. patients.
   b. therapists.
   c. both patients and therapists.
   d. neither patients nor therapists.

6. Ego analysis refers to _____ therapy.
   a. humanistic
   b. neo-Freudian
   c. behavior
   d. cognitive
7. Unconditional positive regard is an essential aspect of _____ therapy.
   a. humanistic
   b. neo-Freudian
   c. behavior
   d. cognitive
8. A particular response to a given stimulus is replaced by an alternative response to that same stimulus in _____ conditioning.
   a. positive
   b. negative
   c. total
   d. counter
9. Thorazine is most likely to be used to treat
   a. depression.
   b. bipolar disorder.
   c. schizophrenia.
   d. post-traumatic stress disorder.
10. Lithium is most likely to be used to treat
    a. depression.
    b. bipolar disorder.
    c. schizophrenia.
    d. post-traumatic stress disorder.

Answers

1. b   2. c   3. d   4. c   5. a   6. b   7. a   8. d
9. c   10. b

THINK ABOUT IT

1. Cognitive and behavioral therapies often are paired. What does each technique have to offer that complements the other?
2. If you were a marriage and family therapist, which two therapeutic approaches might you be most likely to use? Why would you choose those two methods?
3. Suppose you were a biochemist concocting the next big breakthrough drug that would minimize the problems caused by a particular psychological disorder. If you could choose any disorder to attack and any negative side effects to tolerate, which disorder—and which symptoms of the disorder—would you wish that your drug could minimize? What modest negative side effects would you find least offensive in your new wonder drug?

4. What would you view as an ideal treatment for depression, one that perhaps combines elements of the therapies about which you have read?
5. How might a therapist who has doubts about the ethics of a new treatment program go about resolving his or her doubts prior to administering the treatment?
6. If you had a need for therapy, which method of therapy would you choose? If you were to decide to become a therapist, would your choice be the same? Analyze the benefits and drawbacks of the method you would prefer in each role.

WEB RESOURCES

For a chapter tutorial quiz, direct links to Internet sites, and other useful features, visit the book-specific website at http://psychology.wadsworth.com/sternberg4e. You can also connect directly to the following sites:

National Psychological Association for Psychoanalysis
www.npap.org
This site provides copious information about therapy in general and psychoanalysis in particular. A very useful feature called FAQ (frequently asked questions) addresses issues such as the time and money required by therapy, and the differences among psychiatrists, psychologists, and social workers.

Medscape
http://www.medscape.com/psychiatryhome
Psychiatry and mental health resources can be found here, including psychiatry news articles, case studies, and quizzes.

Online Dictionary of Mental Health
http://www.shef.ac.uk/~psysc/psychotherapy/index.html
This thematically arranged "dictionary" from the University of Sheffield (UK) Medical School comprises diverse links to many sites about therapy, the treatment of psychological disorders, and general issues of mental health.

For additional readings on many of the topics covered in this chapter, check out InfoTrac College Edition at **www.infotrac-college.com/wadsworth**.

Disk Two
Psychotherapies
Drug Therapies
Chapter Quiz
Critical Thinking Questions

CHAPTER 18

HEALTH, STRESS, AND COPING

If you don't mind, it doesn't matter.

PSYCHOLOGY AND HEALTH

What is the relationship between our mental and physical health? What does it mean for psychology?

To what extent is it true that mind over matter means that "If you don't mind, it doesn't matter"? Does our feeling bothered or stressed out truly affect our physical as well as our mental health?

As we have seen, the body and the mind—the physical and the mental—are intimately connected. It is therefore no surprise that an entire area of psychology is devoted to the ways in which our mental state affects our physical health, and vice versa. It's no surprise either that part of what health psychology has discovered is, to some degree, that if you don't mind, it doesn't matter.

Health psychology is the study of the interaction between psychological processes and physical conditions. Particular psychological processes can lead to better or worse health, which in turn can trigger particular psychological processes. For example, research has shown that people under stress are more susceptible to catching colds (S. Cohen, Tyrrell, & Smith, 1993) and, of course, having a cold can be stressful.

Health psychologists are interested in the psychological antecedents and consequences of physical states, how we maintain good health or become ill, and how we respond to illness. Health psychologists delve into many aspects of the mind–body connection.

A primary goal of health psychology is to promote good health and health-enhancing behavior. Of course, health psychologists recognize that serious disorders affect health. Nonetheless, they assume that we can influence our own health by regulating our behavior. For example, we can significantly reduce our risk of dying at any age by following seven positive practices (Belloc & Breslow, 1972; Breslow, 1983):

1. Sleeping 7 to 8 hours a day
2. Eating breakfast almost every day
3. Rarely eating between meals
4. Being at an appropriate weight in relation to height
5. Not smoking
6. Drinking alcohol only in moderation, if at all
7. Exercising regularly

Note that we support good health by *not* engaging in compromising behavior. Health psychology is a wide field. Indeed, some of the topics frequently addressed by health psychologists have been covered elsewhere in this book, so this chapter covers only those that have not been discussed before. First, we examine the models of health and illness throughout the history of health psychology.

THE MIND–BODY CONNECTION

Hippocrates (ca. 430 B.C.) revolutionized ancient Greek medicine with the notion that disease had specific physical origins and was not punishment inflicted by the gods (S. E. Taylor, 2002; see Chapter 1). Centuries after Hippocrates described his iconoclastic views of health and well-being, Galen, who practiced medicine in Rome (ca. A.D. 129–199), suggested that illnesses are attributable to **pathogens,** which are specific disease-causing agents (Stone, 1979). Subsequent medical practitioners eventually agreed with him, and Galen's views became the basis of medical treatment for centuries. Today, of course, we have identified many more of these pathogens than Galen imagined possible.

The pathogenic view of illness gave rise to the **biomedical model,** according to which disease is caused by pathogens that have invaded the body and must be eliminated. This model has served people's needs relatively successfully for almost 2,000 years. Nonetheless, it has not been universally accepted. Some consider it too mechanistic and narrow in scope. Although the model centers on treatment and allows for some attention to prevention, it does little to promote wellness. It also ignores both the psychological factors that contribute to various diseases and the psychological processes that promote healing and well-being. Today, we seek a broader model that incorporates the biomedical perspective as one part of our total understanding of health.

The **biopsychosocial model** seeks an understanding of the psychological, social, and biological factors that contribute to illness, to the prevention of illness, to recovery from illness, and to the promotion of wellness (Dodge & Pettit, 2003; G. L. Engel, 1977, 1980; Kotsiubinskii, 2002; G. E. Schwartz, 1982). In health psychology, the biopsychosocial model has largely replaced the biomedical model. Most of us em-

Frequent vigorous exercise contributes to good health.

© Ken Redding/Corbis

brace this model intuitively. For example, most people believe that changes in weather, poor diet, lack of sleep, and stress can contribute to a cold (Lau & Hartman, 1983). Although a virus may be the direct cause of a cold, other factors make us susceptible to it. When we refer to someone as "worried sick" or as having a "tension headache," we imply that psychological and social factors contribute to physiological states. History shows that people have long recognized these connections.

HISTORICAL TRENDS IN PREVENTION AND TREATMENT

People have been trying to understand health and illness for centuries. During some eras, the mind was seen as relevant; in others, neither the mind nor the body was considered of primary importance. People believed that illness was sent by divine beings as a punishment for misbehavior or disbelief. Ancient literature and legends contain many instances of a punitive god causing illness or injury to those who mistreated believers, disobeyed divine commandments, or otherwise showed a lack of respect or belief. In the 21st century, it is widely accepted that the mind is influential in both health and illness.

For much of the 20th century, researchers in the field of **psychosomatic medicine** studied the psychological roots of such physical illnesses as ulcers, asthma, and migraine headaches. Whether or not psychological factors actually *cause* diseases, they are known to exacerbate symptoms.

In the 1970s, behavioral approaches to psychology became more popular than psychodynamic ones. Originally, **behavioral medicine** focused on techniques to help people modify health-related activities, such as smoking or overeating (see Chapter 17). As the cognitive revolution began to affect all aspects of psychology, health psychologists embraced a cognitive orientation, emphasizing how thought processes influence good health and the progression of illnesses. As the biopsychosocial model suggests, the fairly simplistic view that psychological factors "cause" disease has been replaced by one that recognizes the complex psychological, physical, and environmental factors that interact in both illness and health.

Initially, health practitioners focused exclusively on helping people respond to illness or injury. The illnesses that received the most attention were brief, like influenza. A patient who survived required no further care from health professionals. Much less attention was given to enduring illnesses, like diabetes. In most cases, only discrete episodes or symptoms were treated.

This early emphasis on treatment was entirely appropriate, given the leading causes of death. Antibiotics and other medical treatments later nearly wiped out major diseases such as smallpox, which had devas-

| TABLE 18.1 |
| Ten Leading Causes of Death in 1900 and 1999 |

1900
1. Influenza and pneumonia
2. Tuberculosis
3. Gastritis, duodenitis, enteritis, etc.
4. Diseases of the heart
5. Vascular lesions affecting the central nervous system
6. Chronic nephritis (kidney failure)
7. Accidents
8. Cancer
9. Certain diseases of early infancy
10. Diphtheria

1999
1. Diseases of the heart
2. Cancer
3. Cerebrovascular diseases
4. Chronic lower respiratory diseases
5. Accidents
6. Diabetes mellitus
7. Influenza and pneumonia
8. Alzheimer's disease
9. Nephritis and related diseases
10. Septicemia

Source: U.S. Bureau of the Census (1975); Hoyert et al. (2001); based on Corr, Nabe, & Corr (2003).

tated huge proportions of the world's population. Diseases such as influenza, diphtheria, and tuberculosis became far less deadly (see Table 18.1).

As medical tools for conquering illnesses, particularly acute ones, have become more powerful, health-care professionals have turned their attention to preventing illness. They encourage people to watch for early symptoms, to seek medical care, to avoid behaviors that compromise health, to take appropriate preventive steps, and to engage in appropriate hygiene and safety practices. Health psychologists and other health practitioners have now turned their attention to promoting overall health and well-being.

EMOTIONAL LONGEVITY

Research in health psychology now can help us understand the psychological factors that contribute to good health and long life, what N. Anderson (2003) refers to as "emotional longevity." One factor is optimism (Seligman, 1991). For example, women who are optimists are less likely to develop symptoms of postpartum depression (N. Anderson, 1998). A second factor is the way we interpret the past—whether we interpet it positively or negatively (Peterson, Seligman, & Vaillant, 1998). A third factor is communicating our problems to others. Even writing about our problems relieves us of stress and makes us feel better (Pennebaker, 1990; Pennebaker & Graybeal, 2001). Thus, ways we feel and things we do can increase our psychological well-being and even our likelihood of long life.

✓ CONCEPT CHECK 1

1. Health psychologists assume that
   a. people have relatively little control over their own health.
   b. people can influence their own health through psychological regulation of their behavior.
   c. health affects psychological state but not vice versa.
   d. psychological state affects health but not vice versa.
2. Risk of death at an early age does *not* appear to be significantly reduced by
   a. eating breakfast almost every day.
   b. rarely eating between meals.
   c. smoking in moderation
   d. sleeping 7 to 8 hours per day.
3. The most widely accepted model in health psychology is the _____ model.
   a. biomedical
   b. psychosocial
   c. biopsychological
   d. biopsychosocial

STRESS AND COPING

What is stress? Is it the same for everyone? Why do some people seem to handle stress better than others?

"I'm totally stressed out" is a sentence most of us have muttered at one time or another. What this means is the subject of inquiry by health and behavioral psychologists and other scientists. Some work in the field of psychoneuroimmunology, examining the effects of stress at the cellular level, particularly in our immune systems.

STRESS AND STRESSORS

We usually think of stress as feeling mentally and perhaps physically distressed due to something external, such as time, work, or family pressures. That implicit definition works pretty well, but it is only part of the picture. When researchers investigate stress, they define the term in a slightly different way. **Stress** is a response to something challenging in the environment. A **stress response** is the internal and external adaptation by an individual. Sometimes, for example, the little hassles of everyday life may accumulate and lead to considerable stress (Pearlstone, Russell, & Wells, 1994), which may reduce our resistance to infection (Brosschot, Benschop, Godaert, & Olf, 1994) and other physical ailments (P. M. Kohn, Gurevich, Pickering, & MacDonald, 1994). Sometimes, one major stressful event gives rise to a multitude of minor ones. A divorce often leads to the need for an attorney, a new house, a new perspective on economic affairs, and so forth. It thereby increases stress in many ways (Greene, Anderson, Hetherington, Forgatch, & DeGarmo, 2003; Pillow, Zautra, & Sandler, 1996). A major move can also involve many stressors.

Chronic or accumulated stress can be detrimental to health and well-being (House & Smith, 1985) and can result in psychological dysfunction (Eckenrode, 1984; Eckenrode & Gore, 1990). For example, among women who have compromised immune systems as a result of HIV infection, higher levels of stress are predictive of recurrences of genital herpes outbreaks (Pereira et al., 2003). Students of nursing and physiotherapy also showed increased antibodies to cytomegalovirus (CMV), which indicates greater activity of the virus in the body, when they were experiencing increased levels of stress (Sarid, Anson, Yaari, & Margalith, 2003). In fact, stress can lead to worsening of a wide variety of physical conditions, including cardiovascular disease, osteoporosis, arthritis, Type-2 diabetes, certain cancers, Alzheimer's disease, and gum disease, among other conditions (Kiecolt-Glaser, McGuire, Robles, & Glaser, 2002). Stress encountered on the job may ultimately lead to *burnout*—a feeling of emotional exhaustion and distance from colleagues and the sense that one is no longer accomplishing anything meaningful.

Surprisingly, stressors do not necessarily have to be things we perceive as negative. For example, having a new baby, getting married, and moving to a new home are all stressors because they require the new parent, spouse, or resident to adapt in many ways. Most of us would welcome such stressors as outstanding personal achievement or marriage. Most stressors are indeed negative events, though.

Stressors vary in their intensity. Unhappiness in marriage and divorce are both major stressors (Kiecolt-Glaser et al., 1993; Kiecolt-Glaser et al.,

Crowding can cause negative stress, whereas a wedding may cause stress, but of a positive kind.

1996). Kiecolt-Glaser, Bane, Glaser, and Malarkey (2003) have found that stress-related hormones actually can predict marital adjustment. In one study, levels of stress hormones were measured in 90 couples during their first year of marriage. Couples who later divorced had higher levels of epinephrine, norepinephrine, and acetylcholine (see Chapter 3) at times of marital conflict during the first year of marriage than did couples who did not later divorce. These findings suggest that it may not be the number of conflicts but rather the stress couples experience during those conflicts that predicts later marital problems. Another source of stress is feeling imposed upon by others (Evans & Lepore, 1993). Pleasant changes are potential stressors because they require you to adapt in some way: In the middle of the night in a strange hotel, you must find your way to the bathroom; or while your best friend is visiting, you must cope with demands on your time and space. Stressors even can be routine annoyances or challenges to your ability to cope, such as dealing with traffic hassles, disagreeing with an acquaintance, having disputes with a bureaucratic functionary, getting accustomed to new equipment or appliances, or arranging for car repairs.

Thomas Holmes and Richard Rahe (1967) designed a test to measure the amount of accumulated stress a person is experiencing. In the Social Readjustment Rating Scale (SRRS), various stressors are rank-ordered (see Table 18.2). The test has been revised and rescaled several times. The most recent version is the SRRS-R (C. J. Hobson et al., 1998). Norms are available for as recently as 2001. These researchers then correlated the stressors with the likelihood of becoming ill. They found that vulnerability to illness was positively correlated with increasing weighted values of the stressors. (Recall, however, the difficulties in determining causality based on correlational evidence alone; see Chapter 2.)

Shortly after the SRRS was introduced in 1967, it was adopted in other countries, either in its original form or adjusted (see, e.g., Yahiro, Inoue, & Nozawa, 1993). Research suggests that the scale has wide cross-cultural applicability but that some descriptions, weightings, and rankings should be adapted to suit different cultural contexts. An early study illustrates both the usefulness of the scale and the need to adapt it across cultures. The responses of 266 Malaysian medical students were compared with a matched sample in Seattle, Washington, where the SRRS was created. Although the responses showed many similarities, there were also significant differences, particularly on items involving romantic love and illegal behavior (Woon, Masuda, Wagner, & Holmes, 1971). In a later study of Chinese citizens, events related to family and career were rated as more stressful than those related to personal activities and living conditions (Hwang, 1981).

Although the SRRS is widely used, it has been criticized on several grounds (Rabkin, 1993). First, some of the terms can be viewed as vague (S. E. Taylor, 2002). Second, what is stressful for one person may be less stressful for another (Schroeder & Costa, 1984). Third, whether an event is stressful, or how stressful it is, may depend on how well it is resolved (Thoits, 1994). For example, one person may cope well with retirement, pursuing many relaxing and enjoyable activities, while another person may feel frustrated and unable to cope. Finally, although the SRRS includes both positive and negative events, research suggests that negative events cause considerably more stress (J. C. Smith, 1993; Turner & Wheaton, 1995).

A major stressor not included in the SRRS is the adjustment associated with adapting to a new culture. The technical term for stress of this kind is *acculturative stress* (J. W. Berry, 1989; Nwadiora & McAdoo, 1996). Acculturative stress can range from relatively minor (e.g., voluntary migration to be with loved ones or to seek out desired lifestyles) to catastrophic (e.g., involuntary uprooting as the result of religious or ethnic persecution or the threat of genocide). Such stress

TABLE 18.2

Social Readjustment Rating Scale. Thomas Holmes and Richard Rahe analyzed the life events that lead to stress and assigned various weights to each of these potential stressors. (After Hobson & Delunas, 2001, pp. 311–312)

Life Event (Rank-ordered from most to least stressful)

1. Death of close family member
2. Major injury/illness to close family member
3. Experiencing financial problems/difficulties
4. Major injury/illness to self
5. Being fired/laid off/unemployed
6. Death of a close friend
7. Being a victim of crime
8. Employer reorganization/downsizing
9. Separation or reconciliation with spouse/mate
10. Assuming responsibility for sick or elderly loved one
11. Changing employers/careers
12. Experiencing/involved in auto accident
13. Attempting to modify addictive behavior of self
14. Loss of or major reduction in health insurance/benefits
15. Change in residence
16. Changing work responsibilities
17. Major disagreement with boss/coworker
18. Discovering/attempting to modify addictive behavior of close family member
19. Divorce
20. Death of spouse/mate
21. Surviving a disaster
22. Major disagreement over child support/custody/visitation
23. Detention in jail or other institution
24. Infidelity
25. Change in employment position
26. Self/close family member being arrested for violating the law
27. Gaining a new family member
28. Foreclosure on loan/mortgage
29. Child develops behavior or learning problems
30. Experiencing domestic violence/sexual abuse
31. Becoming a single parent
32. Spouse/mate begins/ceases work outside the home
33. Adult child moving in with parent/parent moving in with adult child
34. Being the victim of police brutality
35. Receiving a ticket for violating the law
36. Obtaining a major loan other than home mortgage
37. Obtaining a home mortgage
38. Pregnancy of spouse/mate/self
39. Experiencing employment discrimination/sexual harassment
40. Finding appropriate child care/daycare
41. Child leaving home
42. Being disciplined at work/demoted
43. Failure to obtain/qualify for mortgage
44. Getting married/remarried
45. Experiencing discrimination/harassment outside the workplace
46. Dealing with unwanted pregnancy
47. Dealing with infertility/miscarriage
48. Beginning/ceasing formal education
49. Experiencing a large unexpected monetary gain
50. Retirement
51. Release from jail

has particularly interested cross-cultural psychologists who live in pluralistic societies that are especially attractive to immigrants (see Ataca & J. W. Berry, 2002; J. W. Berry, 1994, 2000).

One of the worst stressors is torture, which is widely practiced in many parts of the world (Basoglu, 1997; Holmboe, Wang, & Brass, 2002). A study of victims of torture found that nearly half still suffered many years later from nightmares and other symptoms, such as anxiety, depression, and social withdrawal (Basoglu et al., 1994). The effects can last throughout a victim's life span (Huggins, Haritos-Fatouros, & Zimbardo, 2002). Treating victims of torture is a major challenge for psychologists.

PHYSICAL RESPONSES TO STRESS

Environmental events alone do not create stress; the individual must *perceive* the stressor and must respond to it in some way. Often—initially, at least—the primary response of the individual is physiological. When we feel challenged by the need to adapt or threatened by some menace, our bodies physiologically prepare us to confront the challenge ("fight") or to escape from the threatening situation ("flight") (see Chapter 3). This fight-or-flight response probably has its origins in evolutionary adaptation. Those who reacted too slowly or inappropriately to mortal threats in the distant past died on the spot.

The physiological fight-or-flight response was discovered by accident. Hans Selye was looking for a new sex hormone when he happened across a surprising phenomenon: When the body is attacked or is damaged, it seems to respond in the same general way regardless of the nature of the assault (e.g., shock, extreme temperatures, or fatigue) or the target of the damage (e.g., the whole body or only a particular body part or organ). Selye soon saw the potential ramifications of this discovery. He then shifted his research to focus on this puzzling physiological response. Selye and other researchers have noted some patterns in our physiological response to relatively extreme levels of stress, which Selye (e.g., 1976) termed the **general adaptation syndrome (GAS),** in which the body initially exerts maximal effort to adapt through three phases of response: alarm, resistance, and exhaustion (see Figure 18.1).

ALARM

The body immediately is aroused, and the sympathetic nervous system triggers the release of hormones from the adrenal glands—corticosteroids, epinephrine (adrenaline), and norepinephrine (noradrenaline). These hormones increase heart and respiration rate; slow down or stop the activity of the digestive tract, making more blood available to other organs; trigger biochemical reactions that create tension in the muscles; increase energy consumption, which produces heat; increase perspiration, which helps cool the body; and increase the release of clotting factors into the bloodstream, to minimize blood loss in case of injury. All these responses go on automatically. The state of alarm drops to the extent that we can predict or control potential stressors in our environment. Stressors may be particular to the individual, or they may affect a whole group, such as racism and sexism.

RESISTANCE

The alarm state cannot continue indefinitely; the body imposes a counterbalance to the sympathetic nervous system's plundering of energy stores. Quite soon, the parasympathetic nervous system (which is involved in anabolic, energy-storing processes) calls for a more prudent use of reserves. For example, the demands on the heart and lungs decline. Physiological stress responses generally decrease in intensity, although they do not return to normal if the perceived stress continues.

EXHAUSTION

Eventually, even at the reduced rates associated with the resistance phase, the body's reserves are exhausted, and its ability to restore damaged or worn-out tissues is diminished. The individual becomes more susceptible to many health problems, including heart disease. Another outcome is that resistance decreases to *opportunistic infections* (those that take advantage of a weakened

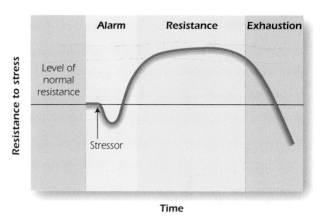

FIGURE 18.1

General Adaptation Syndrome (GAS). According to Hans Selye, we undergo three phases in responding to stressors. In the alarm phase we shift into high gear, using up our bodily resources at a rapid rate; in the resistance phase we conserve our resources; and in the exhaustion phase our bodily resources are depleted. Source: *General Adaptations Syndrome from Stress Without Distress,* by Hans Selye, M.D. Copyright © 1974 by Hans Seyle, M.D. Reprinted by permission of HarperColllins Publishers, Inc.

immune system or other vulnerability). Stress has been linked now to a large number of infectious diseases, including various types of herpes virus infections such as cold sores, chicken pox, mononucleosis, and genital lesions (S. Cohen, Kaplan, Cunnick, Manuck, & Rabin, 1992; S. Cohen, Tyrrell, & Smith, 1991; S. Cohen & Williamson, 1991; van der Ven et al., 2003). *Chronic fatigue syndrome (CFS)*, an ailment in which a person feels tired much of the time and has trouble meeting the demands of daily life, tends to be aggravated by stress. The cause of this illness is unknown, and it may be a collection of illnesses that have similar symptoms.

Even the anticipation of stress can suppress the functioning of the immune system (Kemeny, Cohen, Zegans, & Conant, 1989). Researchers in the cross-disciplinary field of psychoneuroimmunology revel in their almost daily discoveries about how our psychological processes, neural physiology, and immune systems interact in ways we never imagined—let alone understood.

Although Selye's model has helped elucidate the effects of stress, it also has been criticized. For example, it assumes greater uniformity in response to stress than there probably is (Hobfoll, 1989), and it underestimates the role of psychological factors in responding to stress (R. S. Lazarus & Folkman, 1984).

PERCEIVING STRESS

It is not a given set of events, per se, that compromises our immune system, but rather the resulting subjectively experienced stress that is significant. For example, one individual might feel that dealing with an extremely dependent friend is highly stressful. Another individual might perceive the same experience as an interesting challenge. Also, each of us perceives some stressors as more distressing than others. Suppose that you hate confrontation of any kind and find conflict extremely stressful. Someone else might feel little distress in confrontational situations or might even relish conflict. Both you and your adversarial counterpart may experience the physiological alarm phase of the stress response and even the resistance phase. Because you fret about the confrontation for a while afterward, however, you may reach the stage of exhaustion. Possibly, your antagonist may forget quickly about the conflict and avoid the exhaustion phase. In general, long-term stressors associated with negative events (e.g., problems resulting from war, great financial distress, or long-term care of a partner who is very ill) are those that have the most detrimental outcomes on health.

Each of us also experiences different degrees of internal conflict in response to external demands (work versus family, partner versus friend, etc.). Moreover, the very same environment can be experienced as quite different depending on personality variables. An extrovert who works in a library that serves a remote community of nonreaders might be about as distressed as an introvert who leads all the recreational activities for a cruise ship. Each, however, would consider the other's job perfect.

Susan Folkman and Richard Lazarus (Folkman & Lazarus, 1988; Folkman, Lazarus, Gruen, & DeLongis, 1986) proposed a model for the way personality factors, stressful circumstances, and health interact. According to Folkman and Lazarus, when confronted with a potentially stressful situation, we go first through a two-step appraisal process and then a two-dimensional coping process, both of which interact with our distinctive personalities and the situation at hand (see Figure 18.2).

Primary appraisal involves determining whether it is important even to address a stressful situation, based on its significance and the possible outcomes of dealing or not dealing with the situation. Suppose that, at the end of the term, a professor unexpectedly assigns a long paper. Some students might perform a primary appraisal and immediately feel their stress

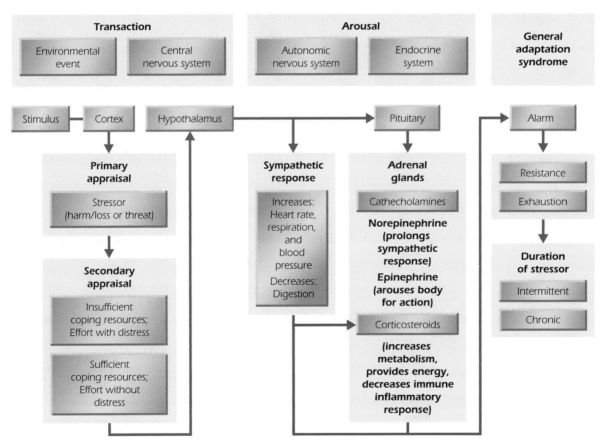

FIGURE 18.2

An Integrated Model of Stress. The biopsychosocial model of stress incorporates psychological and physiological mechanisms in responding to stress.

COPING STRATEGIES AND THE ISSUE OF CONTROL

Both primary and secondary appraisals originate at a cognitive level, where you have yet to crack a book or jot down a note. Once these appraisals are complete, you are ready to begin **coping,** the process of trying to manage the internal and external challenges posed by a troublesome situation. The two dimensions of coping serve different functions. **Problem-focused coping** involves specific strategies for confronting and resolving the problematic situation. For example, you might study the textbook, attend study sessions, and review your lecture notes. **Emotion-focused coping** involves handling internal emotional reactions to the situation. An example is trying to suppress your anxiety about an exam. Just before taking it, you might use some relaxation techniques to reduce your anxiety.

In circumstances over which we have more control (e.g., being graded), problem-focused coping strategies are most likely to yield satisfactory outcomes. In circumstances when we have less control (e.g., having to answer unforeseen questions), emotion-focused coping is most likely to yield satisfactory outcomes. Myriad interactions are possible, depending on the individual's primary appraisal of what is at stake, the secondary appraisal of what coping options are available, and the implementation of those coping options. The net interaction determines the degree of stress that the individual experiences. According to Folkman and Lazarus, detrimental health consequences are associated with experiencing greatest stress, particularly if the person feels that his or her options for coping are inadequate to the situation at hand. Low self-esteem and lack of social support can also contribute to a sense of having inadequate options for coping (DeLongis, Folkman, & Lazarus, 1988).

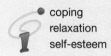

coping
relaxation
self-esteem

level skyrocket. Few things in their everyday world stress them out more than writing a paper, especially one assigned at the end of the term. Other students, for whom writing a paper even at the last moment is no big deal, may hardly react. They view the assignment as just another one in a long list of things to do.

Secondary appraisal involves assessing strategies for making a beneficial outcome more likely and a harmful outcome less likely. In thinking about final exams, you would probably try to assess how you could increase the probability of scoring well and decrease the possibility of scoring poorly. Reading textbooks and studying lecture notes might figure prominently in your secondary appraisal.

INTERNAL VARIABLES: TYPE-A VERSUS TYPE-B BEHAVIOR PATTERNS

Like Selye's discovery of the physiological response to stress, a set of personality variables linked to health was discovered quite by accident. Meyer Friedman and Ray Rosenman (1974) were studying the differences in dietary cholesterol levels in male victims of heart disease and their wives, when one woman commented, "If you really want to know what is giving our husbands heart attacks, I'll tell you. It's stress, the stress they receive in their work, that's what's doing it" (p. 56). This comment led the researchers to look at differences not only in levels of stress experienced by the victims of heart disease, but also in how they responded to stress.

Eventually, Friedman and Rosenman formulated the notion of the **Type-A behavior pattern,** characterized by: (1) a competitive orientation toward achievement, (2) a sense of urgency about time, and (3) a strong tendency to feel anger and hostility. Type As tend to strive very hard and competitively toward their goals, often without much enjoyment in the process; they tend constantly to be racing against the clock; and they tend to feel anger and hostility toward other people.

In contrast, the **Type-B behavior pattern** is characterized by relatively low levels of competitiveness, urgency about time, and hostility. Type Bs tend to be more easygoing, relaxed, and willing to enjoy life. Before you read on, stop for a moment to reflect on which pattern describes your own behavior. (*Clue:* If you felt angry at the suggestion to stop working toward your goal of finishing this chapter as quickly as possible, perhaps you do not need to think too much about which pattern best describes you.) If you are unsure which pattern fits you, think about how a family member or a close friend might describe your behavior.

A variety of methods have sprung up for measuring Type-A behavior. They include both structured interviews, which ask a more or less fixed set of questions, and paper-and-pencil questionnaires. The *Jenkins*

Someone with a Type-A personality is likely to take office work on vacation. A Type B is likely to escape mentally as well as physically.

Activity Survey (JAS; Jenkins, Zyzanski, & Rosenman, 1979), a self-report questionnaire, asks questions such as these: When you listen to other people talking, do you sometimes wish that they would hurry up and say what they have to say? Do you tend to set deadlines or quotas for getting work done? Would people you know agree that you tend to be easily irritated? Do you find that you are often doing things in a hurry? In essence, Type-A people create their own stress.

DIFFERENTIAL REACTIONS TO STRESS

Type-A individuals tend to react differently to stress than do Type-B individuals. Type As generally respond more quickly and forcefully and tend to view sources of stress as threats to their personal self-control (Carver, Diamond, & Humphries, 1985; Glass, 1977). Type-A people also act in ways that increase the likelihood that they will encounter stress. In other words, they create some of the stress by seeking out demanding, competitive situations and by creating artificial deadlines for themselves (D. G. Byrne & Rosenman, 1986; T. W. Smith & Anderson, 1986). Although most people profit from exercise, Type-A people seem to show mood enhancement more for noncompetitive than for competitive exercise. Beneficial effects of the exercise on their mood are pretty much wiped out by their attention to the competitive aspects (Masters, Lacaille, & Shearer, 2003).

The critical question from the standpoint of this chapter is whether Type As are more susceptible to health problems than Type Bs. A number of studies have found a link between Type-A behavior and coronary heart disease (Booth-Kewley & Friedman, 1987; Haynes & Matthews, 1988; Sehgal, 2000). Other studies have not confirmed the link (e.g., Shekelle et al., 1985). It appears that merely linking Type-A behavior to coronary heart disease is too simplistic. For example, Suzanne Haynes and Karen Matthews (1988) found that Type-A behavior leads to increased risk of coronary heart disease for men with white-collar jobs but not for those with blue-collar jobs.

The three components of Type-A behavior may not contribute equally to heart attack, although each may be related to generally poorer health outcomes (Adler & Matthews, 1994). Redford Williams (1986) argued that the component of anger and hostility is the most lethal (see also Ewart & Kolodner, 1994; Lassner, Matthews, & Stony, 1994; T. W. Smith, 1992; S. E. Taylor, 2002). Cynical distrust of people, which is related to hostility, is especially associated with negative health outcomes. Hostility can be subdivided by type. People who are chronic complainers or who tend to be irritable much of the time are sometimes said to show *neurotic hostility*. In contrast, those who seek out confrontations and conflicts with others are said to show *antagonistic hostility*, the kind that appears to be related to heart attacks (Dembroski & Costa, 1988; Helmers & Krantz, 1996; G. N. Marshall, Wortman, Vickers, Kusulas, & Hewig, 1994). Other studies have supported this position (e.g., Barefoot, Dahlstrom, & Williams, 1983). Anger and hostility directed against the self may be especially damaging to health (Dembroski, MacDougall, Williams, Haney, & Blumenthal, 1985; Nakano & Kitamura, 2001; R. Williams, 1986). Also, hostility characterized by suspiciousness, resentment, frequent anger, and antagonism toward others (sometimes referred to as *cynical hostility*) seems to be especially deleterious to health (Barefoot, Dodge, Peterson, Dahlstrom, & Williams, 1989; Dembroski & Costa, 1988; T. W. Smith, 1992; R. B. Williams & Barefoot, 1988). People who are cynically hostile are likely to have difficulty getting social support from others (Benotsch, Christensen, & McKelvey, 1997) and they may fail to use what supports are available (Lepore, 1995). It also appears that the overt expression of cynical hostility toward others, rather than merely feeling such hostility, may be most associated with adverse cardiovascular outcomes (Siegman & Snow, 1997).

Some people who appear to be Type Bs are so only on the surface. These *phony Type Bs* (M. I. Friedman, 1991) or *defensive deniers* (Shedler, Mayman, & Manis, 1993) seem relaxed, unaggressive, and unresponsive to pressure. Deep down, however, they are tense, hostile, and troubled. These individuals appear to be more at risk for illness than are even hostile Type As. Once they become ill, they show greater than average rates of mortality from the illness (Burgess, Morris, & Pettingale, 1988).

POSSIBLE PHYSIOLOGICAL MECHANISMS OF TYPE-A ILLNESS

Researchers agree that Type-A individuals, especially hostile ones, experience more stress than true Type-B individuals, and greater levels of stress are linked to coronary heart disease. Although scientists are not certain of the exact physiological mechanisms that link stress to coronary heart disease, they are likely to espouse one of three major theories. One theory suggests that perceived stress causes the blood vessels to constrict while the heart rate increases. In effect, when people feel stress, their bodies try to pump larger volumes of blood through narrower vessels. This process may wear out the coronary arteries and lead to lesions (areas of injury or disease). Eventually they may produce a heart attack (Eliot & Buell, 1983). Another theory suggests that hormones activated by stress may cause rapid and continual changes in blood pressure, undermining the resilience of blood vessels (Glass, 1977; Haft, 1974; Herd, 1978). A third possibility is that stress may cause lipids to be released into the bloodstream. This release contributes to *atherosclerosis*, a disease in which fatty deposits constrict the blood vessels, making them rigid and hampering circulation. Of course, these three possibilities are not mutually exclusive. Each may contribute to the net detrimental effect (Laragh, 1988; Parfyonova, Korichneva, Suvorov, & Krasnikova, 1988). When there is a problem, intervention is called for.

POSSIBLE OPTIONS FOR INTERVENTION

Type-A behavior appears to be at least somewhat modifiable (Levenkron & Moore, 1988). A variety of techniques have been used, including relaxation (Roskies, Spevack, Surkis, Cohen, & Gilman, 1978), aerobic exercise, weight training, and cognitive-behavioral stress management (Blumenthal et al., 1988; Roskies et al., 1986). To a certain extent, as we have seen, we can influence our perceptions by changing our cognitions. Thus, interventions to increase the functioning of the immune system tend to be oriented toward improving our reactions to events so that we feel less distressed in the face of life's challenges. In addition, lifestyle changes might be appropriate interventions. Type-A individuals tend to live very differently from Type-B individuals. It may be as much the lifestyle as the personality itself that leads to coronary heart disease.

Stress can affect the *immune system*, the body's major means for combating infections, including bacterial, viral, fungal, and other illnesses. White blood cells, called *lympohocytes*, help the immune system in this important task. These cells circulate throughout the body, searching for and destroying elements that they recognize as foreign to the body.

There are two types of specialized white blood cells that are especially important: *B cells*, which mature in bone marrow, and *T cells*, which mature in the thymus, an organ that is in the area of the chest. A type of T cell is a *natural killer (NK) cell*, which detects and then destroys cells that have been damaged. For example, an important role of NK cells is to dispense with precancerous cells in the body before they turn cancerous. When there are not enough NK cells to do the job, or the precancerous cells are too numerous to be fended off, the affected individual becomes susceptible to developing cancer. Another important fighter of disease is the *macrophage*, which, in effect, eats and thereby destroys foreign material. Indeed, "macrophage" means "big eater."

The immune system is constantly replenishing itself so that it can be ready to fight off new invaders. Diseases that attack the immune system, however (such as AIDS, discussed later), may eventually impair and even destroy the ability of the body to defend itself against attack. When people's immune systems are compromised, they become more susceptible to opportunistic infections, such as various forms of herpes virus and cytomegalovirus, as noted earlier.

Autoimmune diseases develop when the immune system becomes, in effect, too powerful and begins to overreact, mistakenly recognizing as foreign cells that actually are integral parts of the body. Diseases such as lupus and multiple sclerosis result from such overactivity of the immune system. Allergies also represent auto-immune responses.

Stress can compromise the functioning of the immune system. For example, animals that are exposed to stressors such as noise, crowding, or shocks that cannot be escaped show reductions in immune-system function (Coe, 1993; Moynihan & Ader, 1996). In humans, even such common activities as taking examinations can harm the functioning of the immune system (Kiecolt-Glaser, Garner, Speicher, Penn, Holliday, & Glaser, 1984; Stone, Nele, Cox, Napoli, Valdimarsdottir, & Kennedy-Moore, 1994). Natural disasters, such as hurricanes, can also result in stress that impairs the human immune system (Ironson, Wynings, Schneiderman, Baum, Rodriguez, Greenwood, Benight, Antoni, LaPerriere, Huang, Klimas, & Fletcher, 1997). Moreover, as noted in the "In the Lab of Sheldon Cohen" box (p. 655), stress can increase the probability of contracting a common cold.

Stress can even affect the development of cancerous tumors. When the immune system is suppressed, such as by stress, the functioning of NK cells is decreased, and as a result, tumor cells are more susceptible to spreading. Stress can even increase the growth of tumors by facilitating the growth of capillaries that make blood available to and hence nourish tumors.

✓ CONCEPT CHECK 2

1. Which of the following is *not* a phase of the general adaptation syndrome?
   a. alarm
   b. adaptation
   c. resistance
   d. exhaustion
2. When a person determines whether a situation is important to deal with, he or she is engaging in _____ appraisal.
   a. psychic
   b. primary
   c. secondary
   d. tertiary
3. A person who is highly competitive and has a sense of urgency about time is likely to be Type
   a. A.
   b. B.
   c. C.
   d. D.

THE PSYCHOLOGY OF HEALTH CARE

What does the relationship between mental and physical health imply for the field of health care?

Health care can be improved if both providers and patients recognize the importance of psychology to health-care outcomes.

RECOGNIZING AND INTERPRETING SYMPTOMS

The first step in obtaining medical treatment is to recognize and interpret symptoms. **Symptoms** are any unusual sensations or features that a patient thinks indicate some kind of pathology. Symptoms are, by definition, from the patient's point of view. **Signs** are any unusual features observed by the physician. For the most part, people seek health services only when they think they have symptoms.

When clinicians make diagnoses based on reported symptoms and observed signs, they use *explicit theories* to mentally represent various illnesses. Non-clinicians are not without mental models, however. Most have *implicit theories*—commonsense schemas—of illnesses and of the symptoms they comprise. These schemas help us organize information about various diseases. This information includes the symptoms, probable consequences, relative seriousness, and probable duration of an illness.

We use schemas to recognize and interpret our symptoms, matching the sensations or observations we perceive with our existing schemas for illness and wellness. If the sensations or observations seem to match our schemas for illness more closely than our schemas for wellness, we are more likely to attribute them to being sick (or injured). Then we think of them as symptoms. If the sensations and observations more closely match our schemas for wellness, we are less likely to view them as symptoms of illness. Health psychologists have observed that our reactions to illness are usually different when we face what we believe is a **chronic illness**—recurrent, constant, or very long in duration, like migraine headaches or hypertension—than when we suffer from one we believe is an **acute illness**—brief, usually characterized by sudden onset and intense symptomatology, but in any case not recurrent and not long in duration, such as a cold or flu (Nerenz & Leventhal, 1983). It appears that we are more likely to seek medical help if we have clear labels to attach to our symptoms and if we believe that they are treatable (Lau, Bernard, & Hartman, 1989).

Once we recognize that we have symptoms, our next decision is whether or not to seek medical attention. This decision can be affected by factors other than our schemas for illness and wellness.

MANAGED CARE

One of the main challenges to health is the growing influence of managed care. Because of the skyrocketing costs of health care and insurance, many people have joined health maintenance organizations (HMOs) and other plans that, for a fixed cost, provide reimbursement for health care as well as insurance in the case of major medical or psychological problems. Often, individuals are forced to join HMOs as a result of employers' health-care plans. These plans have the advantage of protecting people from health costs that could bankrupt them. But the drawback to the plans is that they make money the way any insurance company does—by seeking policy holders who do *not* file claims and by minimizing the payouts on claims. Many of these organizations have been quite aggressive in restricting the amount of care they allow. Moreover, health providers, including psychotherapists, who are not willing to agree to these terms may be declared ineligible to be involved in the plans and thus suffer a loss of patients. Typically, health providers also receive less money per patient visit when the patient is sponsored by a managed-care organization than when the patient has traditional insurance. Not only doctors but also patients have expressed widespread dissatisfaction with HMOs (Freudenheim, 1993; http://members.aol.com/jasonwolff/hmomain.htm, 2003).

As a result of the spread of managed care, many people are less concerned about doctors who provide unnecessary services in order to increase their income than about doctors who may be unable to provide all the services that are needed because of restrictions by managed-care companies. As the years go on, we can hope that a system will be worked out whereby patients can receive the services they need at reasonable prices.

What happens when a medical practitioner and a patient finally do get together?

THE PATIENT-DOCTOR RELATIONSHIP

The conversation between a doctor and a patient is at once professional and personal. The two people may be strangers, but they need to communicate clearly in short order. A good deal of work among health psychologists has focused on answering questions such as: Which factors affect this communication? and How can it be improved?

PATIENT STYLES. Medical schools gradually have come to appreciate a problem that patients have long recognized: The physician who received the highest grades in medical school or who is most technically competent does not necessarily interact best with patients. To be highly effective, a medical practitioner needs to take into account not only the medical condition but also the distinctive psychological needs of the patient. Researchers have found that patients are more satisfied with their treatment if they are able to participate in a way that matches their own preferences (Auerbach, Martelli, & Mercuri, 1983; Martelli, Auerbach, Alexander, & Mercuri, 1987). Those wishes, based on a health-opinion survey (Krantz, Baum, & Wideman, 1980), include (1) preference for information about health care, (2) preference for self-care, and (3) preference for involvement in health care. People vary in how much they need of each of these factors—information, self-sufficiency, and involvement with their practitioner.

PHYSICIAN STYLES. The regard the physician shows toward patients can substantially affect how the patient reacts not only toward the physician but also to the entire health-care experience (J. A. Hall, Epstein, DeCiantis, & McNeil, 1993). Physicians, like patients, have distinctive interaction styles. P. Byrne and B. Long (1976) ana-

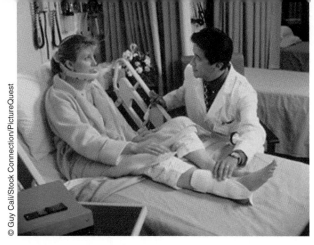

Patients tend to prefer and fare better with doctors who have a patient-centered rather than a doctor-centered style.

lyzed 2,500 tape-recorded medical consultations in various countries. They found that physicians interacted with their patients in one of two styles. A doctor-centered style involves a highly directive interaction pattern, in which a physician narrowly focuses on presenting the problem for which the patient has made the appointment, uses highly convergent questioning to elicit brief and targeted responses from the patient, and then formulates a diagnosis and a treatment regimen. If the patient diverges from the narrow, focused response and mentions other problems or other symptoms, the doctor tends to ignore the extra information. A patient-centered style is characterized by a relatively nondirective pattern of interaction, in which the physician asks divergent questions and allows the patient to take part in guiding the course of the interview, the diagnosis of the presenting problem, and the decision regarding the optimal treatment. Patients prefer a patient-centered style to a doctor-centered one, particularly when their prognosis is poor (Dowsett et al., 2000).

Patient-centered doctors are less likely to use medical jargon than doctor-centered ones. Medical jargon can seriously impede communication between doctors and patients. Indeed, a number of studies have found that most patients do not understand many of the terms that physicians use (DiMatteo & DiNicola, 1982; McKinlay, 1975). The result of using such jargon is that a patient may not really understand the information the physician is providing.

HOSPITAL CARE

In 2001, there were 5,801 registered hospitals in the United States. Among them, they had 987,440 beds. The number of hospital admissions was 35,644,400. The expenses of the hospitals totaled $426,849,488,000 (http://www.hospitalconnect.com/aha/resource_center/fastfacts/fast_facts_US_hospitals.html, 2003). Why are people admitted to hospitals? The ten leading causes of admissions, in order, are (1) pneumonia, (2) congestive heart failure, (3) hardening of the arteries of the heart, (4) heart attack, (5) stroke, (6) nonspecific chest pain, (7) chronic obstructive lung disease, (8) irregular heartbeat, (9) asthma, and (10) blood infection (http://www.ahcpr.gov/data/hcup/factbk1/, 2003). Physical problems such as these interact with psychological factors in greater or lesser degrees. For example, asthma attacks can be worsened or even be brought on by stress, and, as we have seen, heart-related ailments are also affected by psychological factors.

CHARACTERIZING HOSPITALIZED PATIENTS

Although most patients feel anxious, confused, and perhaps even depressed when they are admitted to the hospital, staffers tend to categorize them as either "good" or "bad." "Good" patients are fully compliant with hospital procedures and regimens; "bad" patients are more likely to complain, to demand attention, and to engage in behavior that is contrary to hospital policies. Staff members tend to react negatively to "bad" patients and want to have as little to do with them as possible. Ironically, assertive patients may be at greater risk at the hands of health professionals than are less assertive patients (Lorber, 1975). Hospital staff members are more likely to deal with assertive patients by medicating them, ignoring them, referring them to psychiatric care, or discharging them before they are ready.

When you think about the kinds of behavior that are fostered in hospitals, you may realize that the setting actually encourages patients to think and act in a manner that we described in Chapter 6 as demonstrating *learned helplessness* (Raps, Peterson, Jonas, & Seligman, 1982; S. E. Taylor, 1979). Learned helplessness discourages patients from actively participating in their own recovery (E. Brown, 1963; S. E. Taylor, 1979). Unfortunately, although it is adaptive for getting help from hospital staff members, this behavior can be detrimental to recovery, both in the hospital and at home. Once patients leave the hospital setting, they are expected to take full responsibility for their own recovery, despite having adaptively learned not to take any responsibility whatsoever in the hospital recovery.

INCREASING PATIENTS' SENSE OF CONTROL

If hospitals tend to discourage a sense of control in patients, and if a sense of control is important for patients' well-being and recovery, what can be done? A number of researchers have sought to figure out what hospitals could do to increase patients' psychological as well as physical well-being. Methods for increasing patients' sense of control are control-enhancing interventions, which increase patients' abilities to respond appropriately to illness and eventually to cope effectively with it. In a classic, trailblazing study by Irving Janis (1958), postoperative recovery was compared in three groups: one group with a low level of

fear about an impending operation, a second group with a moderate level of fear, and a third group with a high level of fear. Janis also looked at how well patients in each of the three groups understood and were able to use the information given them in the hospital about probable aftereffects of the surgery. Janis found that patients in the moderate-fear group had the best postoperative recovery.

Subsequent research has shown that what is most important is the extent to which patients process the advance information about the effects of the surgery, rather than their level of fear per se (K. O. Anderson & Masur, 1983; J. E. Johnson, Lauver, & Nail, 1989). Patients who know better what to expect are less upset after surgery and are able to leave the hospital more quickly than less informed patients (J. E. Johnson, 1984). Other investigators have extended this work to suggest that patients who are prepared in advance may feel a stronger sense of personal control and self-efficacy in mastering their reactions (S. E. Taylor, 2002), which results in more positive outcomes.

Research further suggests that it is important to teach patients not only *what* will happen during and after surgery, but also *how* they should respond to what happens. One study showed that if patients are instructed to distract themselves from those aspects of surgery that are unpleasant, and to concentrate instead on the benefits they will receive from the surgery, they will need fewer *analgesics* (pain-relieving drugs) after the surgery (Langer, Janis, & Wolfer, 1975). Other effective control-enhancing interventions include learning relaxation responses and cognitive-behavioral interventions to overcome anxiety and to adapt to the situation more effectively (Ludwick-Rosenthal & Neufeld, 1988).

Even children can benefit from the control that increased information provides. In some ways, hospitalization is most difficult on children because they have little idea of what is going on or what to expect. Research suggests that giving children information before hospitalization or at least before they undergo surgical procedures, and even showing them films of children undergoing a similar procedure, can help them adjust to the hospital and the surgical procedures they are about to experience (Melamed & Siegel, 1975; Pinto & Hollandsworth, 1989). Thus, we should not assume that children should be kept entirely uninformed. On the contrary, they need to be given appropriate information.

The preceding studies have shown the benefits of control-enhancing procedures. As we might expect, given the interactive dialectical evolution of scientific research, subsequent studies have shown that there are limitations on what control-enhancing procedures can provide. For one thing, people differ in their desire for control, just as they differ in most other personal attributes (Burger & Cooper, 1979). Patients who are low in their desire for control may become anxious if they

IN THE LAB OF SHELDON COHEN

ENDURING STRESS AND FIGHTING INFECTION

The belief that when we are under stress we are more susceptible to the common cold, influenza, and other infectious diseases is widely accepted in our culture. It is endorsed in newspaper and magazine articles. It is also supported by the fact that 60% of the volunteers in our studies report that they are more likely to catch a cold during stressful than nonstressful periods.

For the last 18 years, my colleagues and I have studied the effects of psychological stress on the immune system and, consequently, its relation to infectious diseases. The questions we have posed include: Does stress impede the body's ability to fight infections? If so, what kinds of stressful events have the most influence? How could a psychological state influence the immune system?

We developed a unique experimental design for studying the effects of stress on our susceptibility to infectious diseases. First, we use questionnaires or interviews to measure psychological stress in healthy volunteers. After our subjects complete the stress assessments, we intentionally expose them to a common cold virus by putting drops containing the virus into their nostrils. The volunteers are then quarantined. We follow them closely for five to seven days to see who develops a cold. Approximately 40% of them do. Then we ask whether the stress levels we assessed earlier predicted who would resist infection.

Numerous studies have led us to conclude that people who report high levels of psychological stress are most likely to be infected when exposed to a cold virus. This association is confirmed no matter which virus we use. (We have used seven so far out of as many as 200.) The greater the stress that subjects report, the greater their susceptibility to illness, and the longer the stress lasts, the greater the probability that it will contribute to ill health. Stress that lasted at least a month was

Sheldon Cohen is the Carnegie Professor of Psychology at Carnegie Mellon University. He has received the APS James McKeen Cattell Fellow Award for outstanding contributions to research in applied psychology; the APA Award for Outstanding Contributions to Health Psychology; and the NIMH Research Scientist Development Award and Senior Scientist Award. He was an APA Distinguished Lecturer and a British Psychological Association Senior Fellow Lecturer. Dr. Cohen's research focuses on stress, affect, and social support in relation to health. He also studies the effects of psychosocial factors on asthma, and of social support on psychological adjustment in women with breast cancer.

most toxic in its effects. Stressful events that involved conflicts with others were more powerful predictors of illness than other sources of stress.

How could a stressful experience like failing an important exam, getting divorced, or enduring the death of someone close to us hamper our ability to fight infection? When we face demands that we feel unable to cope with, we label ourselves "stressed." We experience such emotions as anxiety, anger, and depression, which, in turn, set into motion a series of biological and behavioral changes that alter our immune function. As a consequence, we may be at higher risk than usual for developing an infectious illness when exposed to a virus. The effects of stress on immunity are probably attributable to direct (through nerves) communication between the brain and immune cells, to destructive behaviors that often accompany stress (e.g., smoking, drinking too much alcohol, eating poorly), and to the effects of stress-related hormones on immune cell functioning.

In our research we attempt to identify the pathways that are responsible for the associations between stress and illness. Unfortunately, in human studies we cannot directly assess the importance of the nerve fibers that connect the brain and immune system. We have, however, studied the roles of stress-elicited behaviors and hormones. On the one hand, we have found that stress-induced increases in self-destructive behaviors are not responsible for increased susceptibility to illness. On the other hand, initial evidence suggests that the activation of the sympathetic nervous system, as indicated by stress-induced increases in the hormones epinephrine and norepinephrine, may contribute to low resistance to infection.

We are extending our work in two directions. First, we are studying the possibility that positive social relations decrease our susceptibility to disease. What are the effects on our ability to fight off infection of being contentedly married, having close friends and relatives, or belonging to enjoyable social groups? Second, we are concentrating on identifying the pathways through which stress influences immune function. That is, what specific changes in the stressed immune system account for the association between stress and increased susceptibility to colds and influenza? We are excited about initial evidence that symptoms of illness occur in people under stress because a group of molecules known as pro-inflammatory cytokines cannot be regulated effectively. These molecules,

continued

which are responsible for triggering symptoms of respiratory diseases, may be under the control of stress hormones such as epinephrine and cortisol. We hope that our work will definitively establish that stress influences the release of the hormones

that alter the release of cytokines and, consequently, produce cold symptoms.

Our work is an example of a growing area of psychology in which researchers investigate how thoughts and emotions are associated with changes in the brain and body. As we

learn more about these relationships, we will come closer to understanding both the importance of psychological phenomena for health and how we can intervene at a psychological level to improve our physical health.

are given more control than they would like. Such patients may feel a burden of responsibility or self-blame when asked to make decisions that they do not want to make in a stressful situation, such as the context surrounding surgery (Burger, 1989; S. C. Thompson, Cheek, & Graham, 1988). Moreover, giving patients too much information to absorb about operative procedures and about postoperative recovery may make them feel even more distressed than they ordinarily would feel. Attempts to enhance patients' sense of control may boomerang and actually overwhelm them and make them feel powerless (Mills & Krantz, 1979; S. C. Thompson et al., 1988). Although a greater sense of control is probably good for most patients in most surgical situations, patients do best when the style of the medical worker matches their own.

THE PSYCHOLOGICAL PROCESSES OF HEALING

As we saw earlier, we are beginning to understand some of the ways our personalities may affect our physical health and well-being. In addition, we are beginning to recognize some of the ways psychological processes can influence physiological healing. For example, both hypnosis and meditation are used to influence health-related behaviors.

Emotions may play a role in healing. Some people have suggested that laughter has a restorative effect (Restak, 1988), and others posit that expressing sadness may have recuperative properties (Moyers, 1993). Even physicians generally acknowledge the power of a positive attitude to effect recovery.

Medical-care providers can influence patients' attitudes toward recovery through their interactions. For example, it has been found that children adjust better to hospitalization when they have a warm and nurturing relationship with someone such as a nurse (Branstetter, 1969). Indeed, all patients benefit from warm relationships while they are confined in a hospital. Such associations may help mitigate some of the negative aspects of hospitalization and of the illness itself.

Psychological processes even affect our perception and ability to manage pain, as discussed next.

PAIN MANAGEMENT

Pain is the intense sensory discomfort and emotional suffering associated with actual, imagined, or threatened damage to or irritation of body tissues (Merskey, 2000; Sanders, 1985). It has psychological, physiological, and behavioral components (Kroner-Herwig et al., 1996). We discussed the sensory aspects of pain in Chapter 4. Here, we discuss the adaptive value of pain, its cognitive and emotional aspects, different kinds of pain, the relationship of pain and personality, and what can be done to alleviate pain.

Few people enjoy pain. Indeed, inadequate pain relief is the most common reason patients request euthanasia or commit suicide (Cherny, 1996). Yet, from an evolutionary standpoint, pain has tremendous adaptive value. Why? Because it alerts us to the fact that tissue damage has been or may be taking place. Those rare individuals who do not feel pain are at great risk. By the time they discover that tissue damage has taken place, as in the case of burns, it may be too late for them even to save their own lives.

Many psychologists conceptualize pain in a way very similar to the popular notion. It has both a *sensory* component (the sensations at the site where the pain originates, such as throbbing, aching, or stinging pain) and an *affective* component (the emotions that accompany the pain, such as fear, anger, or sadness). These two components are highly interactive, each profoundly affecting the other, but it is possible to distinguish the contribution of each (Dar, Leventhal, & Leventhal, 1993; Fernandez & Turk, 1992; Turk & Okifuji, 2002, 2003).

Our perceptions of pain interact with our cognitions regarding it. Based on our experiences, we form schemas about pain as well as beliefs about our ability to control it. The interaction goes both ways. Just as our cognitions are affected by our experiences, our cognitions affect our perceptions. For example, if we believe that we will be able to overcome pain, we may be more effective in doing so than if we believe that we will be defeated by our sensations. This is described as *catastrophizing* and is sometimes a result of learned helplessness. In fact, self-efficacy beliefs may play an important role in pain control (Turk & Rudy, 1992).

Pain can be acute, lasting no longer than 6 months, or chronic, long-term and recurrent. Those with chronic pain are at greater risk for depression, which may be a result rather than a cause of pain.

KINDS OF PAIN

A distinction is sometimes made between organic pain and psychogenic pain. **Organic pain** is characterized by sensations of extreme discomfort and suffering caused by damage to bodily tissue. **Psychogenic pain** is an intense sensory emotional suffering for which physiological origins cannot be found. We need to be careful in labeling pain "psychogenic" because even if the medical profession has been unable to find the source, it does not mean that the pain does not exist or even that it has no organic cause. The current tools for diagnosing the sources of pain are still imprecise (Turk & Okifuji, 2002; Turk & Rudy, 1992). A cause may exist but may simply not have been found. In most cases, the experience of pain represents an interaction between physiological and psychological factors.

The three most common kinds of psychogenic pain are neuralgia, causalgia, and phantom-limb pains. *Neuralgia* is a syndrome in which a person experiences recurrent episodes of intense shooting pain along a nerve (C. R. Chapman, 1984; Melzack & Wall, 1982). The cause of this pattern of pain remains a mystery. *Causalgia* is characterized by recurrent episodes of severe burning pain (Melzack & Wall, 1982). People experiencing causalgia may suddenly feel as though a body part or region is on fire or is being pressed against a hot oven. Often, patients who have this syndrome once suffered a serious wound in the place where they feel the burning pain. *Phantom-limb pain* is felt in a limb that either has been amputated or no longer has functioning nerves (C. R. Chapman, 1984; Melzack &

Wall, 1982). Many patients report feeling phantom-limb pain even though they lost the limb years earlier.

The phenomenon of psychogenic pain shows that the perception of pain and the presence of a known pathology or injury are not inevitably linked. Additional evidence for the weakness of the link is the phenomenon in which the experience of pain is delayed for a while after serious injury or is altogether absent despite extreme pathology (Melzack, Wall, & Ty, 1982; see also Fernandez & Turk, 1992).

Whether pain is organic or psychogenic, it can be classified as either acute or chronic. **Acute pain** is brief, intense, uncomfortable stimulation usually associated with internal or external tissue damage. Some researchers (e.g., Turk, Meichenbaum, & Genest, 1983) have used 6 months as a somewhat arbitrary cutoff. **Chronic pain** is recurrent or constant long-term discomfort, usually associated with tissue damage, and lasting at least 6 months. On average, patients endure chronic pain for 7 years before seeking treatment (Turk & Rudy, 1992).

PERSONALITY AND PAIN

Given the wide differences in people's thresholds and limits for pain, some investigators have sought to discover whether there is a relationship between personality attributes and the experience of pain. Such research might sound relatively easy to do. You just think of a few traits that you believe might be associated with pain perceptions (e.g., perfectionism or emotional sensitivity), and then test to see whether they match up with measurements of people's perceptions of pain. The problem with this research is the same one that arises with most correlational studies. Finding a correlation between a personality attribute and the experience of pain may indicate a relationship between the two, but it does not indicate the direction or the cause of the relationship. Someone may be susceptible to experiencing pain because of particular personality attributes. However, an equally plausible explanation is that the person acquired those attributes from having experienced the pain. For example, if we were to find a correlation between anxiety or depression and scores on a scale measuring chronic pain, we would scarcely be surprised to learn that the anxiety or depression was caused by the pain, rather than vice versa. It is also possible that both the personality attribute and the experiencing of pain may depend on some higher-order third factor.

Some research has found that scales of the Minnesota Multiphasic Personality Inventory (MMPI; see Chapter 15) can help identify patients who are particularly susceptible to pain. Michael Bond (1979) has found that patients who experience *acute pain* tend to score especially high on the hypochondriasis and hysteria scales of the MMPI. People high in hysteria tend to show extreme emotional behavior and also tend to exaggerate the level and seriousness of their symp-

TABLE 18.3

Methods of Pain Control. Using various methods of pain control increases the likelihood that both chronic and acute pain can be brought under control with a minimum of undesirable side effects. Medical investigators constantly develop new pharmacological, technological, and psychological methods of controlling pain.

Method	How It Controls Pain	Drawbacks
Pharmacological control	The administration of drugs	Some drugs are addictive, so their use must be controlled carefully; even mild drugs can have negative consequences if used in excess or over long periods of time
Patient-controlled analgesia	Intravenous infusion of medications: the patient pushes a button that triggers a pump to release analgesic from a computer-regulated reservoir; generally used in a hospital or hospice when patients suffer from extreme pain	Some risks exist, but specially selecting patient populations usually minimizes the likelihood of addiction
Surgical control	Surgical incisions create lesions in the fibers that carry the sensation of pain; intended to prevent or at least diminish the transmission of pain sensations	The risks associated with surgery, possible side effects, cost, and short-lived positive outcomes have made this technique less preferable
Acupuncture	Originated in Asia; involves using needles on particular points on the body; Western adaptation is transcutaneous (under the skin) electrical nerve stimulation (TENS)	May not be as effective in minimizing chronic pain as acute pain
Biofeedback	Biofeedback is an operant-learning procedure (see Chapter 6): a machine translates the body's responses into a form that the patient observes on a screen and can bring under conscious control	Because the equipment is expensive and cumbersome, and the technique provides results no better than relaxation training, it may not be the treatment of choice
Hypnosis	The patient receives a subliminal suggestion that he or she is not feeling pain	Requires that the patient be susceptible to hypnosis or to self-hypnosis
Relaxation techniques	The patient enters a state of low arousal, controls breathing, and relaxes muscles; meditation (see Chapter 5) also can induce a state of relaxation	An inexpensive strategy that often proves effective; requires a modest amount of training as well as full patient participation
Guided imagery	Similar to and often used as an adjunct to deep relaxation; when people experience pain, they imagine scenes that help them cope with the pain; in one form, visualization, patients imagine actively confronting the pain, as a soldier or other fighter who ultimately conquers the pain	An inexpensive strategy that often proves effective; may require some additional training of the patient; requires full patient participation, and effectiveness depends in part on the patient's ability to visualize
Sensory control through counterirritation	Involves stimulating or mildly irritating a different part of the body than the one experiencing pain; effective in reducing the original pain, perhaps because the patient starts to concentrate on the area that is being irritated	Does not work in all cases or at all times, particularly in cases of severe pain
Distraction	Patients shift their attention away from the pain to focus on something else; the technique has been used successfully for thousands of years	Does not work in all cases or at all times, particularly in cases of severe pain

toms. Similarly, Bond found that *chronic-pain* patients tend to score high on hypochondriasis and hysteria as well as on depression. As it happens, this grouping of three attributes is sometimes referred to as the "neurotic triad" because elevated scores on these three scales are frequently associated with various types of neurotic disorders.

The fact that greater indications of depression are seen in chronic-pain than in acute-pain patients suggests that the depression is a result, rather than a cause, of the pain. However, Thomas Rudy, Robert Kerns, and Dennis Turk (1988) have found that the development of depression may be related not just to the experience of pain itself, but also to its concomitants, such as a reduced level of activity and a diminished sense of personal control.

PAIN CONTROL

A wide variety of techniques have been used to control pain (S. E. Taylor, 2002). Some of the major methods, described in Table 18.3, are pharmacological control (including patient-controlled analgesia), surgical control, acupuncture, biofeedback, hypnosis, relaxation techniques, guided imagery, sensory control, and distraction. Pain-treatment centers use a variety of techniques for helping patients cope with pain. In many cases, these techniques have been quite successful, and they are particularly important in cases of chronic pain related to serious illness.

LIVING WITH SERIOUS HEALTH PROBLEMS

We often do not truly value our health until we no longer have it. When we recover from acute illnesses, we sometimes briefly cherish our health, only to take it for granted again soon. People with chronic illnesses do not have this luxury. The most dramatic chronic illnesses of our time are AIDS and SARS.

AIDS

Acquired immune deficiency syndrome, or AIDS, is caused by the human immunodeficiency virus (HIV). HIV attacks the immune system and especially the *T-cells*, which, as mentioned before, are specialized, relatively long-living white blood cells that protect the body at the cellular level (G. F. Solomon & Temoshok, 1987). The virus is transmitted by the exchange of bodily fluids, most notably blood and semen. Tests can detect HIV antibodies in the body, indicating whether a person has been infected.

Being *HIV-positive* (having HIV in the blood) does not mean that the person already has developed AIDS. Individuals differ widely in the time it takes them to develop AIDS after they contract the virus; the latency period can be as long as 8 to 10 years or, with the use of modern drugs, even longer. Even with full-blown AIDS, it is not the AIDS virus itself that kills people, but rather opportunistic infections that thrive in the person's impaired immune system. Common infections of this type are rare forms of pneumonia and cancer.

Despite its rapid spread, AIDS can be controlled and, in principle, avoided through behavioral interventions. For example, people who engage in sexual relations outside of marriage should always use condoms during intercourse and restrict their number of sexual contacts. People who inject themselves with drugs should not share needles. Prevention is especially important for this disease because there is no known cure. Moreover, as far as we know, the overwhelming majority of those worldwide who contract HIV eventually will develop AIDS. Particular drugs seem to postpone the development of the disease but do not head it off entirely. Of course, the most difficult psychological phenomenon associated with AIDS is living your life as HIV-positive, knowing that you are likely to develop a disease that causes intense pain and suffering and is almost always fatal. Triple-drug therapies (combinations of drugs that together are more effective than any are alone) may reduce what has been an extremely high mortality rate. Coping mechanisms are extremely important.

Health psychologists can play and have played several roles in controlling the AIDS epidemic. One is research on understanding why people engage in risky behavior that can lead to HIV infection. A second is devising ways of using the knowledge gained in such research to discourage people from indulging in risky behavior and encourage them instead to engage in safer behavior. A third is in devising ways of helping people who are HIV positive or who have AIDS to cope with their health status.

SARS

In April 2003, a new disease became prominent, SARS (severe acute respiratory syndrome). As of June 21, 2003, the worldwide death toll from SARS is 801 persons (Bradsher & Altman, 2003). This disease has had major effects not only on the physical health but also on the psychological health of many tens of thousands of people. The cause of the disease is believed to be a mutation of a coronavirus, a virus that in the past typically was associated with colds. The illness is highly contagious and superspreaders can pass the disease to hundreds of people. Many people in China, Taiwan, Singapore, and elsewhere stopped going outside their homes to avoid contracting the illness, which is fatal in more than 5% of cases. People who come from infected areas are often viewed with suspicion. The disease has already had a major economic impact on Asia, Canada, and other parts of the world. The impact is likely to be due as much to fear as to actual danger of getting the disease.

As of the end of June 2003, there has been great progress in controlling the spread of the disease. Health psy-

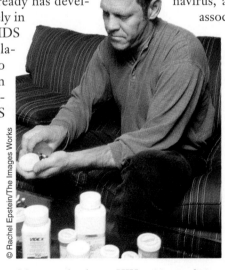

Many people who are HIV-positive are living satisfying and fulfilling lives.

© Rachel Epstein/The Images Works

chologists can play a role in controlling this spread by helping people understand the realistic risks of going into areas affected by SARS or similar ailments. In some cases, the risks are greater than perceived. But in others, they are much less. For example, many people avoided areas that had been SARS-affected even after no new cases had been reported in these areas for prolonged periods of time.

PSYCHOLOGICAL MODELS FOR COPING WITH CHRONIC ILLNESS

People who have chronic illnesses encounter a variety of psychological challenges usually only secondarily related to the physical cause of the illness, such as depression and anxiety. Therefore, part of the mission of health psychology is to help people deal with their psychological reactions to serious illness, particularly if it has long-term repercussions.

Franklin C. Shontz (1975) proposed a stage model of how people react when they realize that they have a chronic and possibly life-threatening disease. The first stage is *shock*. People are stunned, bewildered, and often feel detached from the situation: How can this be happening to *me?* The second stage is *encounter*. The person gives way to feelings of despair, loss, grief, and hopelessness. During this stage, people are often unable to function effectively. They do not think well, they have difficulty planning, and they are ineffective in solving problems. During *retreat*, the third stage, individuals often try to deny the existence of the problem or at least the implications of what the problem means for them. Eventually, however, people reach a fourth stage, *adjustment*, during which they do whatever is necessary to live with the disease.

It is important in evaluating a stage model to keep in mind that not everyone is likely to go through all the stages in the exact order specified, or to do so in a strictly linear fashion. People may enter a stage, leave it, and then return to it. Thus, stage models are useful for a general understanding of coping, but only if viewed flexibly (Silver & Wortman, 1980).

Shelley Taylor (1983; Taylor & Aspinwall, 1990) proposed an alternative model that highlights the ways people adapt cognitively to serious chronic illness. Taylor's model specifies aspects of cognitive adaptation. According to Taylor, patients try to *find meaning* in the experience of the illness. They may try to figure out what they were doing wrong that led to the illness—and start doing whatever it is right—or they may simply rethink their own attitudes and priorities. Patients further try to *gain a sense of control* over the illness and over the rest of their lives. They may seek as much information as possible about their illness and its treatment. Or they may undertake activities that they believe will help restore function and well-being or will at least inhibit the degenerative progress of their illness. Finally, patients try to *restore their self-esteem*, despite the offense of being struck by such an illness. They may compare their situations with others', in ways that shed a favorable light on their own.

Individuals differ in their effectiveness in coping. Rudolf Moos (1982, 1988; 1995; Moos & Schaefer, 1986) has described a *crisis theory* that characterizes individual differences in people's abilities to cope with serious health problems (see Figure 18.3). According to this model, how well we cope depends on three sets of factors:

1. *Background and personal factors*, such as emotional maturity, self-esteem, religion, and age. Men are more likely to respond negatively to diseases that compromise their ability to work; older people

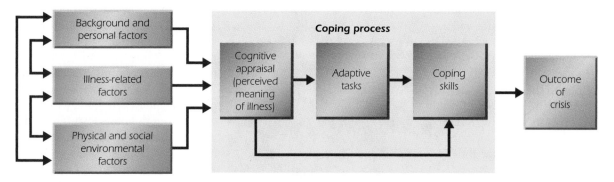

FIGURE 18.3

Three Sets of Factors in Coping. In his crisis theory, Rudolf Moos emphasizes individual differences in coping with serious illness. Personal and background factors affect the coping process, which in turn affects the outcome. He has identified three sets of factors influencing each individual's response and three main components of adjusting to serious illness. It is the interaction of individual differences and the coping process that influences the outcome of the crisis.

have fewer years to live with a chronic illness than younger ones and thus may be better able to cope with the prospects.

2. *Illness-related factors*, such as how disabling, painful, or life-threatening the disease is. It is not surprising that the greater the disability, pain, or threat, the more difficulty people have in coping with the illness.

3. *Environmental factors*, such as social supports, financial situation, and living conditions. Some factors may diminish the ability to cope, whereas others may enhance it.

According to Moos, the coping process has three main components: cognitive appraisal, the decision to adapt, and the development of coping skills. In *cognitive appraisal*, the individual assesses the personal meaning and significance of the health problem. (Note that this kind of cognitive appraisal is similar to the primary and secondary appraisals described by Folkman and Lazarus in the perception of stress, and it is somewhat related to the appraisals involved in symptom recognition and interpretation.) As a result of cognitive appraisal, the person decides how to perform tasks in a way that is *adaptive*, given the illness. In this way, the person *develops coping skills* for living with the illness. The outcome of the coping process will, in turn, affect the outcome of the crisis in general—how well the person is able to live with the disabling illness.

Ultimately, the key to coping with serious chronic illness is *adaptation*. The individual has to make changes and adjustments to live happily and effectively. On the one hand, people who have serious chronic illnesses need to make more effort than practically anyone else to adapt to the environment. On the other hand, each of us confronts situations that require us to adapt in varying ways and to varying degrees. We constantly need to regulate our fit to the environment. But whether we are healthy or ill, young or old, lucky or not, we can *shape* our environment, too. If there is a key to psychological adjustment, perhaps it is in the balance between adaptation to and shaping of the environment, with the added option of *selection*. When we find that a particular environment simply cannot be shaped to fit us, and we cannot adapt ourselves to fit it, we can seek a more suitable environment. It is my hope that you can adapt to your environment, find what you want in life, reach for it, and obtain it.

Be careful in choosing what you want in life, for it shall be yours.—Proverb

✓ CONCEPT CHECK 3

1. A doctor who is highly directive in interactions with a patient shows a _____ style.
   a. patient-centered
   b. allopathic
   c. homeopathic
   d. doctor-centered

2. Control-enhancing interventions generally _____ patient recovery.
   a. have no effect on
   b. prolong
   c. enhance
   d. first enhance and then interfere with

3. Which of the following is *not* a stage in Shontz's model of coping with chronic disease?
   a. shock
   b. encounter
   c. review
   d. retreat

THE MANY FACES OF PAIN RESEARCH

Her clothes on fire, Marlena rushed back into the thick smoke and flames to find her child in the burning house. Firefighters pulled her back and tried to extinguish the flames that engulfed her. Marlena appeared to feel no pain, even though more than 50% of her body was burned. She paced the driveway, begging the firefighters to save her baby.

The perception of pain has intrigued psychologists for more than a century. **Health psychologists** study the origins and management of pain, as you are learning in this chapter. However, other kinds of psychologists also conduct research about pain. Psychologists who study sensation and perception, motivation, personality, cultural differences, psychopharmacology, and genetics all contribute to our understanding. For example, **psychopharmacology** refers to the study of psychoactive drugs, which you learned about in Chapter 5. The research of **psychopharmocologists** has led to the development of new drugs for pain control, including some that target receptors that bind with endorphins: norepinephrine, serotonin, and glutamate.

Have you ever noticed that some people tolerate pain very well and others complain at the tiniest twinge of discomfort? Or that at certain times people can simply ignore pain, especially when, like Marlena, they are focusing hard on something else? Although pain messages travel to the brain along discrete pathways, research by **psychologists who study sensation and perception** has demonstrated that overstimulating any sensory modality (such as the visual, auditory, olfactory, and skin

senses) can produce pain. Very bright light or very loud sounds can leave us wincing. **Sensory psychologists** study these aspects of pain.

The experience of pain depends on motivational level. **Psychologists who study motivation and emotion** have observed that a person feels pain more intensely when he or she is tired, hungry, or thirsty. Emotional states, such as frustration and sadness, can also intensify one's experience of pain. **Personality psychologists** have examined the relationship between pain and certain personality traits. For example, James Wade and his colleagues examined the association between pain sensation and personality variables such as extroversion and neuroticism (a measure of anxiety) in 205 patients being treated for chronic pain (Wade, Dougherty, Hart, & Rafii, 1992). They found no relationship between these personality variables and the ability to sense pain. People who are highly anxious are more likely to rate pain as very unpleasant, however, which suggests that personality traits can affect how we think about pain and how much we suffer.

Psychologists who study cultural differences have reported that people in different cultures vary in their responses to pain but not in their ability to detect it (Chapman, 1982; Clark & Clark, 1980; Lau, Egger, Coggon, & Cooper, 1995; Zatzick & Dimsdale, 1990). For example, people from different parts of Asia (Hong Kong, Japan, Nepal) appear to have higher tolerance for pain and are less likely to complain than people from Great Britain and the United States.

Within a culture, people also differ in their responses to pain. **Neuroscien-**

tists who investigate the physiology of pain have recently discovered a gene that may account for why some people tolerate pain better than others. This gene controls the amount of endorphins produced by the nervous system. (Recall that endorphins are the body's natural painkillers.) The gene has two forms: one that contains an amino acid called methionine, and one that contains an amino acid called valine. As a recent study by Jon-Kar Zubieta and his colleagues has demonstrated, people who have the gene that contains valine can tolerate more pain than people who don't. Zubieta injected saltwater into the jaws of healthy college students, which caused intense pain. Those students who had the gene that contains valine were able to tolerate significantly more injections than those who possessed the same gene with methionine (Zubieta et al., 2003).

Our current understanding of pain is the result of research conducted by many different kinds of psychologists. A recent review of articles published between 1939 and 1999 revealed that pain research falls into several categories: case studies conducted by clinical psychologists; studies of personality differences; psychophysiological studies; studies of the effects of cultural, race, and ethnic differences; studies of the effects of sex differences; and studies testing treatments for pain (Keefe et al., 2002). Thus, clinical psychologists, personality psychologists, psychophysiologists, social psychologists, ethnopsychologists, and health psychologists are all contributing to our understanding of pain.

SUMMARY

PSYCHOLOGY AND HEALTH 642

What is the relationship between our mental and physical health? What does it mean for psychology?

1. *Health psychology* is the study of the interaction between mental processes and physiological health.
2. Galen is credited with being the first to suggest a *biomedical model* of illness. According to this model, disease results when disease-causing agents *(pathogens)* invade the body, and we can eliminate disease if we eliminate the causative pathogens.
3. Almost all health psychologists now embrace a more contemporary alternative model, the *biopsychosocial model*, which proposes that psychological, social, and biological factors can influence health.
4. As one of the newest fields in psychology, health psychology has roots in *psychosomatic medicine* and in *behavioral medicine.*

STRESS AND COPING 644

What is stress? Is it the same for everyone? Why do some people seem to handle stress better than others?

5. *Stress* is the response when environmental factors cause a person to feel threatened or challenged in some way.
6. Stressors (situations or events that create the stress) are environmental changes that cause the person to have to adapt to or cope with the situation. These adaptations are *stress responses.*
7. The initial stress response is adaptive in helping the person to prepare to flee from or fight in the threatening situation. After the initial alarm phase of stress, if the perceived stressor continues to confront the individual, the body shifts down to a resistance phase and finally to an exhaustion phase.
8. Stress has been linked to many diseases, and its direct effect on the immune system is now being explored.
9. In *primary appraisal*, we analyze our stake in the outcome of handling a particular situation.
10. In *secondary appraisal*, we assess what we can do to maximize the likelihood of potentially beneficial outcomes and to minimize the likelihood of potentially harmful outcomes of a situation.
11. *Problem-focused coping* is directed at solving a problem. *Emotion-focused coping* is directed at handling the emotions you experience as a result of the problem.
12. Several personality factors influence health, particularly the personality characteristics related to competitiveness, a sense of urgency, and the tendency to feel anger and hostility. Persons who rate high on these three characteristics have a *Type-A behavior pattern;* persons who rate low on these characteristics have a *Type-B behavior pattern.* Of the three characteristics, feelings of anger and hostility seem most clearly threatening to health, particularly in terms of coronary heart disease and other stress-related illnesses. Lifestyle differences also may contribute to these effects.

THE PSYCHOLOGY OF HEALTH CARE 652

What does the relationship between mental and physical health imply for the field of health care?

13. People generally seek health services only after they notice *symptoms* of ill health. Whereas doctors use explicit theories to make diagnoses, most laypersons have an implicit theory (based on commonsense schemas) to explain their symptoms and what might be the probable course of their illness.
14. We classify illnesses according to their duration: *acute illnesses* are relatively brief; *chronic illnesses* last for a long time, often throughout the entire life span.
15. Patient styles differ in how much they wish to participate in their own medical care. Physician styles also differ; they may be *doctor centered* (focused on the single problem that prompted the visit) or *patient centered* (focused on serving the patients' needs even when they go beyond the identified problem). Using medical jargon (more common in doctor-centered physicians) may hinder communication with some patients.
16. Patient characteristics affect the treatment patients receive. More compliant, passive, unquestioning, and unassertive patients generally receive better treatment in the hospital, although their passivity and lack of awareness about the treatment may impede their recovery outside the hospital setting.
17. *Organic pain* is caused by damage to bodily tissue. *Psychogenic pain* is the discomfort felt when there appears to be no physical cause of the pain. Examples are neuralgia (involving recurrent pain along a nerve), causalgia (involving burning pain), and phantom-limb pain (occurring in the absence

of a neurological connection to the perceived source of the pain). What may appear to be psychogenic pain, however, may be caused by unidentified organic pathology.

18. Pain may be *acute* (lasting less than 6 months) or *chronic* (lasting 6 months or longer).

19. Although several personality traits have been associated with pain, it has proven difficult to determine the direction of causality for these correlations.

20. Methods for controlling pain include pharmacological control (via drugs, including patient-controlled analgesia), surgical control, sensory control (e.g., counterirritation), biofeedback, relaxation techniques, distraction, guided imagery, hypnosis, and acupuncture.

21. AIDS (acquired immune deficiency syndrome) is usually a terminal illness caused by the human immunodeficiency virus (HIV). AIDS is contracted largely through contact with the semen or blood of those who carry HIV.

22. Severe acute respiratory syndrome, or SARS, has become a potential serious health hazard.

23. When people recognize that they have a serious, chronic health problem, they may experience shock (stunned detachment), encounter (grief and despair), and retreat (withdrawal from the problem) before they finally make the needed adjustment. An alternative model describes cognitive adaptations to chronic illness, such as the needs to find meaning, to gain control, and to restore self-esteem. Factors that influence these reactions include characteristics of the individual (including experiences and background), the illness, and the environment.

24. Three adaptive ways to respond to chronic illness are to change the individual (and his or her lifestyle), to change the environment (making it fit the individual's different needs and abilities), and to select a different environment.

KEY TERMS

acute illness 652
acute pain 657
behavioral medicine 643
biomedical model 642
biopsychosocial model 642
chronic illness 652
chronic pain 657
control-enhancing interventions 654
coping 649
doctor-centered style 653

emotion-focused coping 649
general adaptation syndrome (GAS) 647
health psychology 642
organic pain 657
pain 656
pathogens 642
patient-centered style 653
primary appraisal 648
problem-focused coping 649

psychogenic pain 657
psychosomatic medicine 643
secondary appraisal 649
signs 652
stress 644
stress response 644
symptoms 652
Type-A behavior pattern 649
Type-B behavior pattern 649

ANSWERS TO CONCEPT CHECKS

Concept Check 1

1. b   2. c   3. d

Concept Check 2

1. b   2. b   3. a

Concept Check 3

1. d   2. c   3. c

KNOWLEDGE CHECK

1. The use of behavioral techniques to help people modify health-related problems is
   a. behavioral pharmacology.
   b. behavioral medicine.
   c. psychobiosocial intervention.
   d. secondary appraisal.

2. A feeling of emotional exhaustion and distance from people you work with along with the sense that you are no longer accomplishing anything meaningful is called
   a. stress response.
   b. social readjustment.
   c. anomie.
   d. burnout.

3. A person's assessment of coping strategies to make a beneficial outcome more likely is called _____ appraisal.
   a. psychic
   b. primary
   c. secondary
   d. tertiary

4. Individuals who are easygoing, relaxed, and willing to enjoy the process of life are referred to as Type
   a. A.
   b. B.
   c. C.
   d. D.

5. A recurrent, constant disease is referred to as
   a. acute.
   b. primary.
   c. chronic.
   d. secondary.

6. Pain has
   a. a sensory but not an affective component.
   b. an affective but not a sensory component.
   c. both an affective and a sensory component.
   d. neither an affective nor a sensory component.

7. Which of the following is a drawback of hypnosis as a technique for controlling pain?
   a. It requires the patient to be susceptible to hypnosis.
   b. It is extremely costly.
   c. It almost never works.
   d. It violates the tenets of many religions.

8. According to Rudolph Moos, how well a person copes with serious health problems does *not* depend on _____ factors.
   a. background and personal
   b. illness-related
   c. environmental
   d. inheritance of biological pain-control

9. According to Shelley Taylor, patients try to _____ the experience of illness.
   a. find meaning in
   b. reject
   c. enjoy
   d. repress

10. At the present time, AIDS is
    a. neither treatable nor curable.
    b. treatable but not curable.
    c. curable but not treatable.
    d. both treatable and curable.

Answers
1. b   2. d   3. c   4. b   5. c   6. c   7. a   8. d
9. a   10. b

THINK ABOUT IT

1. Suppose that an instructor of student nurses invites you to discuss the patient's view of hospital care. What are the key points you would try to communicate? How would you communicate those points so that the nurses would really understand you and would not feel threatened by what you say?

2. This chapter included health recommendations regarding several aspects of lifestyle. Which recommendation do you consider the most important of these? Why?

3. What advice would you give doctors, based on your knowledge of psychology, to help them communicate with patients who have to be told that they have a life-threatening illness?

4. Choose the pain-relief or pain-control method you consider most likely to be effective in a variety of situations. Describe a situation in which pain relief or pain control would be needed and in which this technique might be effective. State how you would use it.

5. What decision criteria should you use to decide when you need to consult a physician?
6. What are some realistic things that you can do to minimize feelings of stress in your life?

WEB RESOURCES

For a chapter tutorial quiz, direct links to Internet sites, and other useful features, visit the book-specific website at http://psychology.wadsworth.com/sternberg4e. You can also connect directly to the following sites:

American Institute of Stress
www.stress.org
This site provides very useful information about stress: how to avoid it, how to cope with it, and how it can affect your life. It presents some surprising statistics— 75 to 90% of visits to primary care physicians are for stress-related problems, 78% of Americans describe their jobs as stressful, and a majority claim that this has worsened in the last 10 years.

Health News Network
http://healthnewsnet.com/index.html
This is a large site on the interactions of the mind, body, stress, and disease. There are links to information on psychoneuroimmunology, the placebo effect, and health states, among many others.

National Center for PTSD
http://www.ncptsd.org/
This site offers numerous resources devoted to posttraumatic stress disorder (PTSD). Browsers also have access to the PILOTS database, a free searchable guide to the worldwide literature on traumatic stress.

Exercise and Sport Psychology
http://www.psyc.unt.edu/apadiv47/
If you wonder about how psychological science deals with sports and athletics, this site, maintained by Division 47 of the American Psychological Association, is an excellent starting point, especially for those interested in career information.

For additional readings on many of the topics covered in this chapter, check out InfoTrac College Edition at **www.infotrac-college.com/ wadsworth.**

CD-ROM: UNIFYING PSYCHOLOGY

Disk Two
Stress and Coping
Chapter Quiz
Critical Thinking Questions

Do you ever wonder whether some groups of people are smarter, or more assertive, or more honest than others? Or whether students who earn better grades actually work more, on average, than do students who earn lower grades? Or whether, in close relationships, women feel more intimacy toward men, or men toward women? These are all questions that can be addressed by using statistics.

Although statistics can help us answer questions, they cannot themselves provide definitive answers. The answers lie not in the statistics themselves, but in how the statistics are interpreted. Statistics provide people with tools—with information to explore issues, answer questions, solve problems, and make decisions. Statistics do not actually do the exploration, question answering, problem solving, or decision making. People do.

A **statistic** is a numerical value obtained by analyzing numerical data about a representative sample of a population. For example, if you want to know how satisfied people are in their close relationships, you might give people a scale that measures relationship satisfaction and then compute various numbers summarizing their level of satisfaction. Statistics as a field of study involves the analysis of numerical data about representative samples of populations.

Statistics are often used in psychology, and they can also be applied to other aspects of our lives. Consider this example. Suppose you are interested in qualities of love and how they relate to satisfaction in close relationships. In particular, you decide to explore the three aspects of love incorporated in the triangular theory of love (R. J. Sternberg, 1986b, 1988c, 1998c): *intimacy* (feelings of warmth, closeness, communication, and support), *passion* (feelings of intense longing and desire), and *commitment* (desire to remain in the relationship; see Chapter 12). You might be interested in the relation of these aspects to each other; or of each of the aspects to overall satisfaction; or of the relative levels of each of these aspects people experience in different close relationships—for example, with lovers, friends, or parents.

In order to use statistics to assess these issues, you would first need a scale to measure them. *The Triangular Love Scale*, a version of which is shown in Table A.1, is such a scale (R. J. Sternberg, 1988c). If you wish, you can compare your data with those from a sample of 84 adults whose summary data will be presented later (R. J. Sternberg, 1997a).

Note that this version of the scale has a total of 36 items, 12 of which measure intimacy; 12, passion; and 12, commitment. Each item consists of a statement rated on a 1-to-9 scale, where 1 means that the statement does not characterize the person at all, 5 means that it is moderately characteristic of the person, and 9 means that it is extremely characteristic. Intermediate points represent intermediate levels of feelings. The final score on each of the three subscales is the average of the numbers assigned to each of the statements in that subscale (i.e., the sum of the numbers divided by 12, the number of items).

In research that uses statistics, we are interested in two kinds of variables: *independent* and *dependent* (see Chapter 2). **Independent variables** are attributes that are individually manipulated by the experimenter while other aspects of the investigation are held constant; **dependent variables** are outcome responses or attributes that vary as a consequence of variation in one or more independent variables. In an experiment, some of the independent variables are usually manipulated, and the dependent variable may change in value as a function of the manipulations. Other independent variables may be predictors but not be manipulated variables. For example, the sex of the participants may be an independent variable that predicts various aspects of love, but it is not manipulated by the experimenter. Rather, data may be separated by sex of participants if the data are expected to show different patterns for males versus females.

DESCRIPTIVE STATISTICS

Descriptive statistics are numerical analyses that summarize quantitative information about a population. They reduce a larger mass of information down to a smaller and more useful base of information.

MEASURES OF CENTRAL TENDENCY

In studying love, you might be interested in typical levels of intimacy, passion, and commitment for different relationships—say, for a lover and a sibling. There are several ways in which you might characterize the typical value, or **central tendency**, of a set of data.

Triangular Love Scale. The blanks represent a person with whom you are in a close relationship. Rate on a scale of 1–9 the extent to which each statement characterizes your feelings, where 1 = not at all, 5 = moderately, 9 = extremely, and other numerals indicate levels in between.

Intimacy

1. I have a warm and comfortable relationship with _____.
2. I experience intimate communication with _____.
3. I strongly desire to promote the well-being of _____.
4. I have a relationship of mutual understanding with _____.
5. I receive considerable emotional support from _____.
6. I am able to count on _____ in times of need.
7. _____ is able to count on me in times of need.
8. I value _____ greatly in my life.
9. I am willing to share myself and my possessions with _____.
10. I experience great happiness with _____.
11. I feel emotionally close to _____.
12. I give considerable emotional support to _____.

Passion

1. I cannot imagine another person making me as happy as _____ does.
2. There is nothing more important to me than my relationship with _____.
3. My relationship with _____ is very romantic.
4. I cannot imagine life without _____.
5. I adore _____.
6. I find myself thinking about _____ frequently during the day.
7. Just seeing _____ is exciting for me.
8. I find _____ very attractive physically.
9. I idealize _____.
10. There is something almost "magical" about my relationship with _____.
11. My relationship with _____ is very "alive."
12. I especially like giving presents to _____.

Commitment

1. I will always feel a strong responsibility for _____.
2. I expect my love for _____ to last for the rest of my life.
3. I can't imagine ending my relationship with _____.
4. I view my relationship with _____ as permanent.
5. I would stay with _____ through the most difficult times.
6. I view my commitment to _____ as a matter of principle.
7. I am certain of my love for _____.
8. I have decided that I love _____.
9. I am committed to maintaining my relationship with _____.
10. I view my relationship with _____ as, in part, a thought-out decision.
11. I could not let anything get in the way of my commitment to _____.
12. I have confidence in the stability of my relationship with _____.

Note: Scores are obtained by adding scale values (from 1 = low to 9 = high) for each item in each subscale, and then dividing by 12 (the number of items per subscale), yielding a score for each subscale of between 1 and 9.

The **mean** is the average score within a distribution of values, computed by adding all the scores and then dividing by the number of scores.

Another measure of central tendency is the **median,** which is the middle score or other measurement value within a distribution of values. With an odd number of values, the median is the number right in the middle. For example, if you have seven values ranked from lowest to highest, the median will be the fourth (middle) value. With an even number of values, there is no one middle value. For example, if you have eight values ranked from lowest to highest, the median will be the number halfway between (the average) the fourth and fifth values—again, the middle.

A third measure of central tendency is the **mode,** or the most frequent score or other measurement value within a distribution of values. Obviously, the mode is useful only when there are at least some repeated values.

Consider, for example, the scores of eight individuals on the intimacy subscale, rounded to the nearest whole number and ranked from lowest to highest: 3, 4, 4, 4, 5, 5, 6, 7. In this set of numbers, the mean is 4.75, or $(3 + 4 + 4 + 4 + 5 + 5 + 6 + 7)/8$; the median is 4.5, or the middle value between the fourth and fifth values above (4 and 5); and the mode is 4, the value that occurs most frequently.

The advantage of the mean as a measure of central tendency is that it fully takes into account the information in each data point. Because of this fact, the mean is generally the preferred measure of central tendency. However, the mean is also sensitive to extremes. If just a few numbers in a distribution are extreme, the mean will be greatly affected by them. For example, if five people took the passion subscale to indicate their feelings toward their pet gerbils, and their scores were 1, 1, 1, 1, and 8, the mean of 3 would reflect a number that is higher than the rating given by four of the five people surveyed.

The advantage of the median is that it is less sensitive to extremes. In the distribution of passion scores for pet gerbils, the median is 1, better reflecting the distribution than does the mean. The median does not take into account all the information given, however. For example, the median would have been the same if the fifth score were 2 rather than 8.

The advantage of the mode is that it provides a quick index of central tendency. It is rough, though. Sometimes no number in a distribution appears more than once, and hence there is no mode. Other times, several numbers appear most often, so that the distribution is **multimodal** (characteristic of a nonnormal distribution of values, in which the distribution comprises more than one mode). The mode takes into account the least information in the distribution. For

these reasons, the mode is the least used of the three measures of central tendency.

Sometimes, it is useful to show values obtained via a **frequency distribution,** which shows the dispersion of values in a set of values, represented as the number, proportion, or percentage of instances of each value. We can distinguish between two kinds of numbers at each score level. The **relative frequency** is the number of cases that received a given score or range of scores. The **cumulative frequency** is the total number of instances of values up to a given level—that is, of that level or lower. In the case of the two distributions of numbers mentioned previously for two sets of participants in connection with the Triangular Love Scale, the frequency distributions are as follows:

	Intimacy Subscale			**Passion Subscale**	
Value	Relative frequency	Cumulative frequency	Value	Relative frequency	Cumulative frequency
3	1	1	1	4	4
4	3	4	8	1	5
5	2	6			
6	1	7			
7	1	8			

In these frequency distributions, relative and cumulative frequencies are represented by numbers of cases at each level. An alternative would have been to represent them by proportions or percentages. For example, expressed as a proportion, the relative frequency at score value 3 on the intimacy subscale is .125 (1/8).

Scatter plots also can be represented graphically in various ways. Two of the main kinds of graphic representations are a **bar graph,** in which items reflecting larger numeric values are represented as longer bars on the graph, and a **line graph,** in which quantities (e.g., amounts or scores) are associated with linear information (e.g., time or age) and this association is represented by changing heights of a broken line. Both are shown in Figure A.1 for the simple frequency distribution of intimacy scores expressed above numerically. People use graphs to help readers visualize the relations among numbers and to help the readers clarify just what these relations are.

MEASURES OF DISPERSION

You now know three ways to assess the central tendency of a distribution of numbers. Another question you might have about the distribution concerns *dispersion* of the distribution. How much do scores vary? You might assess dispersion in several different ways.

A first measure of dispersion is the **range,** which is the full expanse of a distribution of values, from

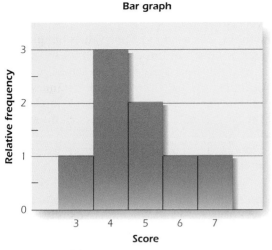

Bar graph

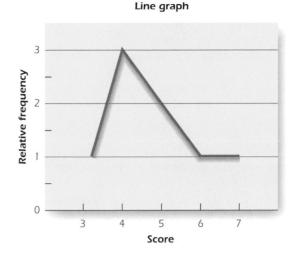

Line graph

FIGURE A.1

Graphing Frequency Distributions. Frequency distributions may be represented graphically either as bar graphs, showing discontinuous levels of a variable, or as line graphs, showing continuous levels of a variable.

the lowest to the highest value. For example, the range of intimacy scores represented previously is 4 (i.e., 7 − 3). But the range is a rough measure. For example, consider two distributions of intimacy scores: 3, 4, 5, 6, 7, and 3, 3, 3, 3, 7. Although the range is the same, the dispersions of scores seem different. Other measures take more information into account.

A second measure of variability is the **standard deviation,** which is a statistical measurement of dispersion, indicating the degree to which a set of values typically deviates from the mean value for the set. The advantage of the standard deviation over the range is that the standard deviation takes into account the full information in the distribution of scores. Researchers care about the standard deviation because it indicates how much scores group together, on the one hand, or are more dispersed, on the other. The standard deviation also is used in statistical significance testing, as discussed later.

To compute the standard deviation, you must:

1. Compute the difference between each value and the mean.
2. Square the difference between each value and the mean (to get rid of negative signs).
3. Sum the squared differences.
4. Take the average of the sum of squared differences.
5. Take the square root of this average, in order to bring the final value back to the original scale.

Let us take the two distributions above to see whether their standard deviations are indeed different. The mean of 3, 4, 5, 6, 7 is 5. So the squared dif-

ferences of each value from the mean are 4, 1, 0, 1, and 4. The sum of the squared differences is 10, and the average, 2. The square root of 2 is about 1.41, which is the standard deviation. In contrast, the mean of 3, 3, 3, 3, 7 is 3.80. So the squared differences of each value from the mean are 0.64, 0.64, 0.64, 0.64, and 10.24. The sum of the squared differences is 12.80, and the average, 2.56. The square root of 2.56 is 1.60. Thus, the second distribution has a higher standard deviation, 1.60, than the first distribution, 1.41.

What does a standard deviation tell us? As a measure of variability, it tells us how much scores depart from the mean. At the extreme, if all values were equal to the mean, the standard deviation would be 0. At the opposite extreme, the maximum value of the standard deviation is half the value of the range (for numerical values that are very spread apart).

For typical (but not all) distributions of values, about 68% of the values fall between the mean and plus or minus one standard deviation from that mean; about 95% of the values fall between the mean and plus or minus two standard deviations from that mean. And well over 99% of the values fall between the mean and plus or minus three standard deviations. For example, the mean of the scale for intelligence quotients (IQs) is 100, and the standard deviation is typically 15 (see Chapter 9). Thus, roughly two-thirds of IQs fall between 85 and 115 (plus or minus one standard deviation from the mean), and about 19 out of 20 IQs fall between 70 and 130 (plus or minus two standard deviations from the mean).

A third measure of variability is the **variance,** which is the degree to which a set of values varies from the mean of the set of values. Thus, the variances of

Basic Statistics for the Triangular Love Scale. The relative extent to which individuals indicate feelings of intimacy, passion, and commitment differ across various kinds of relationships.

	Intimacy		Passion		Commitment	
	Mean	*SD*	*Mean*	*SD*	*Mean*	*SD*
Mother	6.49	1.74	4.98	1.90	6.83	1.57
Father	5.17	2.10	3.99	1.84	5.82	2.22
Sibling	5.92	1.67	4.51	1.71	6.60	1.67
Lover	7.55	1.49	6.91	1.65	7.06	1.49
Friend	6.78	1.67	4.90	1.71	6.06	1.63

Note: "Friend" refers to a close friend of the same sex; "SD" refers to standard deviation. Statistics are based on a sample of 84 adults from southern Connecticut.

the distributions of intimacy scores above are 2 and 2.56 (which were the values obtained before taking square roots). The variance of IQ scores is 15 squared, or 225. Variances are useful in many statistical calculations, but are not as readily interpretable as are standard deviations.

Now that you have read about measures of central tendency and dispersion, you can appreciate two of these measures—the mean and standard deviation— for the Triangular Love Scale. Table A.2 shows means and standard deviations of intimacy, passion, and commitment scores for various relationships computed from a sample of 84 adults. If you took the scale yourself, you can compare your own scores to that of our normative sample.

THE NORMAL DISTRIBUTION

In the previous discussion of the percentages of values between the mean and various numbers of standard deviations from the mean, we have been making an assumption without making that assumption explicit. The assumption is that the distribution of values is a **normal distribution**—that is, a distribution of scores or other measurement values in which most values congregate around the median, and the measurement values rapidly decline in number on either side of the median, tailing off more slowly as scores get more extreme. The shape of the normal distribution is shown in Figure A.2. Notice that the distribution of scores is symmetrical and that indeed the large majority of scores fall close to the center of the distribution.

Nature seems to favor normal distributions, because the distributions of an amazing variety of attributes prove to be roughly normal. For example, heights are roughly distributed around the average, as are intelligence quotients. In a *completely normal distribution*, the mean, the median, and the mode are all exactly equal.

Not all distributions are normal. Distributions can be nonnormal in a variety of ways, but one of the most common is in terms of **skewness,** or lopsidedness, which indicates the degree to which the modal value is shifted above or below the mean and median values. Figure A.3 shows both a *negatively skewed distribution*, in which the values on the lower (left) side of the mode tail off more slowly than do the values on the right; and a *positively skewed distribution*, in which values on the upper (right) side of the mode tail off more slowly than do the values on the left.

Notice that the respective values of the mean, median, and mode are displaced in these two kinds of distributions. Why? Consider as an example a distribution that is almost always positively skewed:

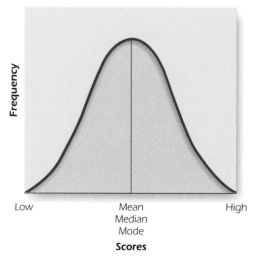

FIGURE A.2

Normal Distribution. In a normal distribution, the median (the middle value in the distribution), the mean (the average value in the distribution), and the mode (the most frequent value in the distribution) are the same.

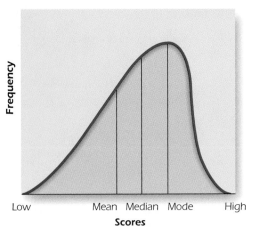

(a) Negatively skewed distribution

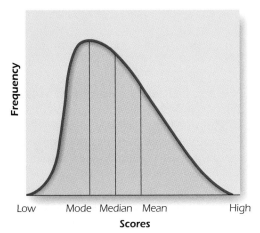

(b) Positively skewed distribution

Skewed Distribution. In a skewed distribution, the mean, the median, and the mode differ. In a negatively skewed distribution (a), the values of the median and the mode are greater than the value of the mean. In a positively skewed distribution (b), the value of the mean is greater than the values of the mode and the median.

personal incomes. The distribution tends to rise quickly up to the mode and then trail off. The existence of a small number of very high-income earners creates the positive skew. What will be the effect of the small number of very high-income earners? They will tend to displace the mean upward because, as we have seen, the mean is especially sensitive to extreme values. The median is less affected by the extreme values, and the mode is not affected at all. Thus, in this positively skewed distribution, the mean will be the highest, followed by the median and then the mode. In a negatively skewed distribution, the opposite ordering will tend to occur.

As we have seen, one way to obtain skewness is to have a distribution with a natural "tail," as is the case with high incomes. Another way to obtain such a dis-

tribution is the way something is measured. Suppose a professor gave a very easy test, with an average score of 90% correct and a range of scores from 60% to 100%. This distribution would be negatively skewed because of a ceiling effect: Many people received very high scores because the easiness of the test placed an artificial limit, or ceiling, on how well they could do on the test.

Suppose, instead, that the professor gave a very difficult test, with an average score of just 10% correct and a range of scores from 0% to 40%. This distribution would be positively skewed because of a floor effect: Many people received very low scores because the difficulty of the test placed an artificial limit, or floor, on how poorly they could do on the test.

Fortunately, most distributions are approximately normal. The advantage of such distributions is that many of the statistics used in psychology, only a few of which are discussed here, assume a normal distribution. Other statistics do not assume a normal distribution, but are more interpretable when we have such a distribution.

TYPES OF SCORES

One such statistic is the *standard score*. The standard score is one that can be used for any distribution to equate the scores for that distribution to scores for other distributions. Standard scores, also called *z-scores*, are arbitrarily defined to have a mean of 0 and a standard deviation of 1. If the distribution of scores is normal, therefore, roughly 68% of the scores will be between −1 and 1, and roughly 95% of scores will be between −2 and 2.

Why bother to have standard scores? The advantage of standard scores is that they render comparable scores that are initially on different scales. For example, suppose two professors teaching the same course to two comparable classes of students differ in the difficulty of the tests they give. Professor A tends to give relatively difficult tests, and the mean score on his tests is 65%. Professor B, on the other hand, tends to give very easy tests, and the mean score on his tests is 80%. Yet, the difference in these two means reflects not a difference in achievement, but a difference in the difficulty of the tests the professors give. If we convert scores separately in each class to standard scores, the mean and standard deviation will be the same in the two classes (that is, a mean of 0 and a standard deviation of 1), so that it will be possible to compare achievement in the two classes in a way that corrects for the differential difficulty of the professors' tests.

Standard scores also can be applied to the distributions of love-scale scores described earlier. People who feel more intimacy, passion, or commitment toward a partner will have a higher standard score relative to the mean, and people who feel less intimacy, passion, or commitment will have a lower standard score.

The computation of standard scores is simple. Start with a **raw score,** which is simply the actual total sum of points obtained by a given test-taker for a given test, which often equals the actual number of items answered correctly on the test. Then convert the raw score to a standard score following these steps:

1. Subtract the mean raw score from the raw score of interest.
2. Divide the difference by the standard deviation of the distribution of raw scores.

You can now see why standard scores always have a mean of 0 and a standard deviation of 1. Suppose that a given raw score equals the mean. If the raw score equals the mean, when the mean is subtracted from that score, the number will be subtracted from itself, yielding a difference in the numerator (see step 1 above) of 0. Of course, 0 divided by anything equals 0. Suppose now that the score is 1 standard deviation above the mean. When the mean is subtracted from that score, the difference will be the value of the standard deviation. When this value (the standard deviation) is divided by the standard deviation (in step 2 above), the result is a value of 1 because any value divided by itself equals 1.

Thus, if we take our distribution of intimacy scores of 3, 4, 5, 6, 7, with a mean of 5 and a standard deviation of 1.41, the standard score for a raw score of 6 will be (6 − 5)/1.41, or .71. The standard score for a raw score of 5, which is the mean, will be (5 − 5)/1.41, or 0. The standard score for a raw score of 4 will be (4 − 5)/1.41, or −.71.

Many kinds of scores are variants of standard scores. For example, an IQ of 115, which is one standard deviation above the mean, corresponds to a z-score (standard score) of 1. An IQ of 85 corresponds to a z-score of −1, and so on. The SAT uses scores set to have a mean of 500 and a standard deviation of 100. In the verbal and mathematical parts, therefore, a score of 600 represents a score of 1 standard deviation above the mean (i.e., a z-score of 1), whereas a score of 400 represents a score of 1 standard deviation below the mean (i.e., a z-score of −1).

Another convenient kind of score is called the **percentile,** which is the proportion of persons whose scores fall below a given score, multiplied by 100. Thus, if, on a test, your score is higher than that of half (50%) of the students who have taken the test (and lower than that of the other half), your percentile will be 50. If your score is higher than everyone else's (and lower than no one else's), your percentile will be 100. In the distribution 3, 4, 5, 6, 7, the score corresponding to the 50th percentile is 5 (the median) because it is higher than half the other scores and lower than half the other scores. The 100th percentile is 7 because it is higher than all the other scores and lower than none of them.

CORRELATION AND REGRESSION

So now you know something about central tendency and dispersion, as well as about the kinds of scores that can contribute to central tendency and dispersion. You also may be interested in a different question: How are scores on one kind of measure related to scores on another kind of measure? For example, how do people's scores on the intimacy subscale relate to their scores on the passion subscale, or to their scores on the commitment subscale? The question here would be whether people who feel more intimacy toward someone also tend to feel more passion or commitment toward that person.

The measure of statistical association, called the **correlation coefficient,** ranges from −1 (perfect inverse relation) to 0 (no relation) to +1 (perfect positive relation) and addresses the question of the degree of relation between two arrays of values. Basically, correlation expresses the degree of relation between two variables. A correlation of 0 indicates no relation at all between two variables; a correlation of 1 indicates a perfect (positive) relation between the two variables; a correlation of −1 indicates a perfect inverse relation between the two variables. Figure A.4 shows hypothetical distributions with correlations of 0, 1, and −1.

Most frequently, people use a measure of linear relation called the **Pearson product-moment correlation coefficient.** There are other correlation coefficients as well, but they go beyond the scope of this text, as do the mathematical formulas for the coefficients of correlation. The Pearson product-moment correlation coefficient expresses only the degree of **linear relation,** meaning that it considers only the association between two quantities that takes the form of a straight line, or $Y' = a + bX$, as shown in the second and third graphs of Figure A.4. What this means is that you can have a perfect correlation between two variables without regard to their scale as long as they are linearly related.

Suppose that in a hypothetical group of participants, the scores of five participants on the intimacy subscale were 4, 5, 6, 6, and 7, and the scores of the same participants on the passion subscale were also 4, 5, 6, 6, and 7. In other words, each participant received the same score on the passion subscale as on the intimacy scale. The correlation between the two sets of scores is 1. Now suppose that you add a constant (of 1) to the passion scores, so that instead of being 4, 5, 6, 6, and 7, they are 5, 6, 7, 7, and 8. Because correlations

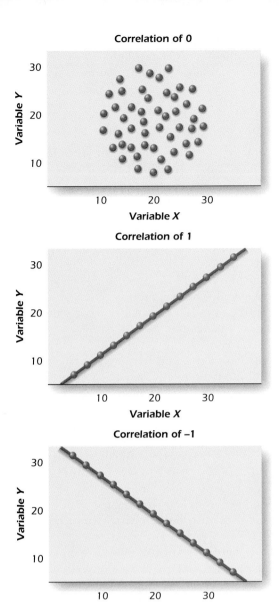

FIGURE A.4

Correlation Coefficient. When two variables show a correlation of 0, increases or decreases in the value of one variable (variable X) bear no relation to increases or decreases in the value of the other variable (variable Y). When variable X and variable Y are positively correlated, increases in X are related to increases in Y, and decreases in X are related to decreases in Y. When variable X and variable Y are negatively (inversely) correlated, increases in X are related to decreases in Y, and decreases in X are related to increases in Y.

do not change with the addition or subtraction of a constant, the correlation would still be 1. And if, instead of adding a constant, you multiplied by a constant, the correlation would still be 1. Remember, then, correlation looks at degree of linear relation, regardless of the scale on which the numbers are expressed. There are other kinds of relations—quadratic, cubic,

and so on—but the Pearson coefficient does not take them into account.

The prediction of one quantified variable from one or more others, in which the two sets of variables are assumed to have a relation that takes the form of a straight line, is called **linear regression.** If the correlation is perfect, the prediction will be perfect. For example, if you predict people's height in inches from their height in centimeters, the prediction will be perfect, yielding a correlation of 1.

The predictive equation specifying the relation between predicted values of a dependent variable (Y') and one or more independent variables (X) is called a **regression equation.** In the equation $Y' = a + bX$, a is called the *regression constant* and b is called the *regression coefficient*. Note that the regression constant is additive, whereas the regression coefficient is multiplicative. The formula, which is that of a straight line, is what relates the Y' (predicted) values to the X (predictor) values.

Well, what are the correlations among the various subscales of the Triangular Love Scale? For love of a lover, the correlations are very high: .88 between intimacy and passion, .84 between intimacy and commitment, and .85 between passion and commitment. These data suggest that if you feel high (or low) levels of one of these aspects of love toward a lover, you are likely also to feel high (or low) levels of the other two of the aspects toward your lover. However, the correlations vary somewhat with the relationship. For example, the comparable correlations for a sibling are .79, .77, and .76. Incidentally, in close relationships with a lover, the correlations between satisfaction and each of the subscales are .86 for intimacy, .77 for passion, and .75 for commitment.

So now you know that there is a strong relation between intimacy, passion, and commitment in feelings toward a lover, as well as between each of these aspects of love and satisfaction in the relationship with the lover. Can you infer anything about the causal relations from these correlations? For example, might you be able to conclude that intimacy leads to commitment? Unfortunately, you cannot infer anything for sure. Consider three alternative interpretations of the correlation between intimacy and commitment.

One possibility is that intimacy produces commitment. This interpretation makes sense. As you develop more trust, communication, and support in a relationship, you are likely to feel more committed to that relationship. However, there is a second possibility—namely, that commitment leads to intimacy. This interpretation also makes sense. You may feel that until you really commit yourself to a relationship, you do not want to trust your partner with the more intimate secrets of your life, or to communicate some of your deepest feelings about things. A third possibility exists as well—that both intimacy and commitment depend on some third factor. In this view, neither causes the other, but both are dependent on some third variable. For example, it may be that intimacy and commitment both depend on a shared sense of values. Without such shared values, it may be difficult to build a relationship based on either intimacy or commitment.

The point is simple: As is often said in statistics, *correlation does not imply causation*. You cannot infer the direction of causality without further information. Correlation indicates only that there is a relation, not how the relation came to be. You can make a guess about the direction of causal relationship, but to be certain, you would need additional data.

In the example of the correlation between intimacy and commitment, you have a problem in addition to direction of causality. How much of a correlation do you need in order to characterize a relationship between two variables as statistically meaningful? In other words, at what level is a correlation strong enough to take it as indicating a true relationship between two variables, rather than a relationship that might have occurred by chance—by a fluke? Fortunately, there are statistics that can tell us when correlations, and other indices, are statistically meaningful. These statistics are called inferential statistics.

INFERENTIAL STATISTICS

Inferential statistics are one of two key ways in which statistics are used, in which a researcher analyzes numerical data in order to determine the likelihood that the given findings are a result of systematic, rather than random, fluctuations or events. In order to understand how inferential statistics are used, you need to understand the concepts of a population and a sample.

POPULATIONS AND SAMPLES

A **population** is the entire set of individuals to which a generalization is to be made. Suppose a psychologist does an experiment involving feelings of love in close relationships. She tests a group of college students on the Triangular Love Scale. The psychologist is probably not interested in drawing conclusions only about the students she happened to test in a given place on a given day. Rather, she is more likely to be interested in generalizing the results obtained to college students in general, or perhaps even to adults in general. If so, then college students (or adults) in general constitute the population of interest, and the college students actually tested constitute the **sample**—that is, the subset of individuals actually tested.

In order to generalize results from the sample to college students (or adults) in general, the sample must be **representative**—that is, a subset of the population, carefully chosen to represent the proportionate diversity of the population as a whole. The less representative of the population the sample is, the harder it will be to generalize. For example, it probably would be safer to generalize the results the psychologist obtained to all college students than to all adults. However, even this generalization would be suspect because college students differ from one college to another, and even from year to year within the same college.

Occasionally, you work with populations rather than with samples. Suppose that you are interested only in the people you have tested and no others. Then you are dealing with the population of interest, and inferential statistics do not apply. The values you obtain are for the population rather than just for a sample of the population. There is no need to generalize from sample to population because you have the population. If, however, you view these students as only a sample of all college students, then you are working with a sample, and inferential statistics do apply.

In particular, inferential statistics indicate the probability that you can reject the **null hypothesis**—that is, a proposed expectation of no difference or relation in the population from which the tested sample or samples were drawn. Typically, the question you are asking when you use inferential statistics is whether the results you have obtained for your sample can be generalized to a population. For example, suppose you find a difference in intimacy scores between men and women in your sample. The null hypothesis would be that the difference you obtained in your sample is a result of chance variation in the data, and would not generalize to the population of all college men and women. The alternative hypothesis would be that the difference is statistically meaningful and generalizes to the population.

STATISTICAL SIGNIFICANCE

When we speak of the meaningfulness of statistical results, we often use something called a test of *statistical significance*. Such a test tells us the probability that a given result would be obtained if only chance were at work. A result, therefore, is statistically significant when the result is ascribed as most likely due to systematic rather than to chance factors. It is important to realize that a statistical test can show only the probability that one group differs from another in some respect. For example, you can compute the probability that a mean or a correlation is different from zero, or the probability that one mean differs meaningfully from another mean. You cannot use statistics to estimate the probability that two samples are the same in any respect.

The distinction is an important one. Suppose you have two hypothetical individuals who are identical twins and who have always scored exactly the same on every test they have ever been given. There is no statistical way of estimating the probability that they truly are the same on every test. Some future test might always distinguish them.

Psychologists need to pay particular attention to two types of error in research. One type concerns drawing a conclusion when you should not, and the other not drawing a conclusion when you should.

The first is called **Type I error** and refers to the belief that a finding has appeared due to systematic changes, when in fact the finding is a result of random fluctuation. In signal-detection theory (considered in Chapter 4), this probability corresponds to the probability of a false alarm. Suppose you compare mean intimacy scores that individuals express toward mothers and fathers. The two values shown in Table A.2 are 6.49 and 5.17 for the mother and father, respectively. You find that the score for the mother is higher than that for the father. A Type I error would occur if you believed that the difference was meaningful when in fact it was due just to random error of measurement.

The second type, **Type II error**, refers to the belief that a finding has appeared due to random fluctuations, when in fact the finding is a result of systematic changes. In signal-detection theory, this kind of error is called a miss. For example, if you conclude that the difference between mothers and fathers is due to chance, when in fact the difference exists in the population, you would be committing a Type II error.

Most researchers pay more attention to Type I than to Type II errors, although both are important. The reason for the greater attention to Type I errors is probably conservatism: Type I error deals with making a claim for a finding when there is none, whereas Type II error deals with failing to make a claim when there might be one to make. Researchers tend to be more concerned about investigators who make false claims than about those who fail to make claims that they might be entitled to make.

When we do psychological research, we usually compute inferential statistics that allow us to calculate the probability of a Type I error. Typically, re-searchers are allowed to report a result as "statistically significant" if the probability of a Type I error is less than .05. This probability is referred to as a **p-value,** the statistical quantity indicating the probability (p) that a particular outcome as extreme as that observed would have occurred as a result of random variation when the null hypothesis is true. In other words, we allow just 1 chance in 20 that we are claiming a finding when we do not have one. Investigators often report p-values as being either less than .05 or less than .01. A decision made with just a .01 chance of being erroneous generally is considered a very strong decision indeed. We can have a lot of confidence in that decision, although we cannot be certain of it.

The chances of finding a statistically significant result generally increase as more participants are tested, because with greater numbers of participants, random errors tend to average out. Thus, if you tested only 10 male participants and 10 female participants for their feelings of intimacy toward their partners, you probably would hesitate to draw any conclusions from this sample about whether there is a difference between men and women in general in their experiencing of intimacy toward their partners. However, if you tested 10,000 men and 10,000 women, you probably would have considerable confidence in your results, so long as your sample was representative of the population of interest.

It is important to distinguish between statistical significance and practical significance, which refers to whether a result is of any practical or everyday import. Suppose, for example, you find that the difference between the men and the women in intimacy feelings is 0.07 point on a 1 to 9 scale. With a large enough sample, the result may reach statistical significance. But is this result of practical significance? Perhaps not. Remember, an inferential statistical test can merely tell you the probability that a result would occur if only chance were at work. It does not tell you how large the difference is, nor whether the difference is great enough really to matter for whatever practical purposes you might wish to use the information. In research, investigators often pay primary attention to statistical significance. However, as a consumer of research, you need to pay attention to practical significance as well, whether the researchers do or not. Ultimately, in psychology, we need to concentrate on results that make a difference to us as we go about living our lives.

THINK ABOUT IT SAMPLE RESPONSES

CHAPTER 1

1.   If you were to accept Thales's invitation to participate in the critical tradition, what perspectives and ideas in this chapter would you criticize? Critique at least one of the views that has been described in this chapter.

You might critique any point of view. Perhaps the most important thing is to learn to critique not only the points of view with which you tend to disagree, but also the points of view with which you tend to agree. As the author of this book, I have tended to favor the cognitivist perspective in much of my work, but I realize that the perspective has limitations. Often cognitivists fail adequately to take into account individual differences, treating individual differences merely as sources of error rather than as important in their own right. Cognitivists also sometimes fail to take into account cultural differences, assuming that a finding that emerges in one culture automatically applies to all others. The important thing is to be as skeptical of your own preferred beliefs as you are of the beliefs of others.

2.   Choose an early school of thought and a current one. In what ways did the older one pave the way for the newer one? (List both similarities and differences.)

British empiricism paved the way for behaviorism. Empiricism, like behaviorism, emphasized the importance of experience in determining behavior and placed little or no emphasis on innate dispositions. Indeed, Locke referred to the baby's mind as a blank slate. Empiricism also stressed the importance of observation for acquiring knowledge, as did behaviorism. Both schools of thought also emphasized the malleability of human behavior: People's destinies are not predetermined. Rather, people can shape their own destiny, or their destiny can be shaped for them.

3.   Quickly jot down a description of your sensations as you believe a structuralist would describe them introspectively.

Right now I am looking at a solid white, rectangular structure that is longer than it is wide and that is supported by metallic objects fastened to the structure and connected to another structure. The structure at which I am peering can swing back and forth toward or away from me. (It is what we call a "door.")

4.   In *Walden Two*, B. F. Skinner (1948) describes a utopia in which behaviorist principles are applied to all aspects of life for people of all ages. Choose one of the schools of thought described in this chapter and

briefly describe a utopian community being governed by psychologists with that viewpoint.

In a Gestaltist utopia, people might be judged only as a whole in terms of their global contribution to the society. People might not much care whether they did one particular kind of thing or another, and they might not make distinctions according to single features like religion, ethnic group, a score on a test, or a grade-point average in a school. Rather, people might see others as wholes, and value them for their total personhood.

5.   In your everyday life you confront many new situations. Describe a situation in which your theory of the nature of the situation (which may be entirely idiosyncratic) largely guided your responses.

When I went on college-admissions interviews, as many students do, I went to one college expecting not to like it. I had heard some very mixed reviews of the place and was almost convinced it was not the place for me. My expectations were fulfilled, perhaps because I was seeking confirmation of my prior beliefs. I was dissatisfied with the people I met and with the physical layout of the place, and the weather was terrible to boot. I left the place and remember saying to myself, "Thank goodness I'll never have to visit that dump again." As it turned out, I went to college there and have been teaching there for over a quarter of a century. For the most part, I have been very satisfied. Sometimes life takes unexpected twists.

6.   What is one thing that your psychology professor—or the author of this book—could do to apply the notion of the dialectic to your current psychology course? Give a specific example of how you might apply this notion.

When I took tests in my introductory psychology course, I was dissatisfied with them. The multiple-choice questions were objective but often seemed to measure picky facts that seemed to me of little interest or importance to anyone. The essay questions on the tests, although dealing with larger questions, seemed to lend themselves only to very subjective grading. So I thought both means of assessment were inadequate. In a sense, then, I found both the thesis of multiple-choice questions and the antithesis of essay questions unsatisfactory. Then I realized that the professor of the course used both kinds of assessments precisely because he thought each, in itself, was inadequate. His synthesis was to combine them so that the strengths of each would compensate for the weaknesses of the other.

1.   For what kinds of psychological phenomena is *control* a suitable goal? What kinds of psychological phenomena should be off-limits in terms of control? (If you answer "none" to any question, tell why you say so.)

Control is a suitable goal for those thoughts, feelings, and patterns of behavior an individual wishes to change. The individual may wish to change these behaviors through expanded self-control or through control established in collaboration with others, such as a psychotherapist. Control is not a suitable goal for behavior that an individual does not wish to change, unless the individual is a danger to him- or herself or to others.

2.   If you were in charge of an institutional review board deciding which experiments should be permitted, what questions about the experiments would you ask the researcher?

You would wish to know the costs and benefits of the experiments. You should be particularly concerned with deceptions, breaches of confidentiality, and risks to potential participants' physical or psychological well-being. You would also wish to be assured that participants will give full, informed consent. You also may seek assurance that potential participants will be adequately debriefed about the experiments after they have completed their assigned tasks.

3.   Describe the steps you would take if you were systematically to observe members of an unfamiliar culture with the goal of learning what their customs are and why they have those customs.

You would first wish to have local informants who are familiar with the culture and speak the language of the culture. These informants would need to orient you to the culture and, ideally, teach you the language and as many of the customs as possible. It is important that you understand the culture from its own point of view and not just your own point of view as an outsider. You also would wish to observe the behavior of people in many different roles and in many different stations in life. It would be important that you not "take sides" but rather try to be as objective as possible. You would need to seek multiple points of view on your observations in order to sort out how different people in the culture themselves understand what is going on.

4.   If psychologists from a distant planet were to observe television programs, what conclusions would they draw about our culture?

The psychologists likely would view our planet as preoccupied by sex and violence. The psychologists also would be likely to view men as being assigned dominant roles. The psychologists further would be likely to conclude that a major goal of television, as important as or more important than entertainment, is to persuade people to buy products

or services they do not need or even initially have no desire for. The psychologists might further conclude that the media seek to entertain people by appealing to a "lowest common denominator" in terms of people's intellectual sophistication.

5.   What is a challenging problem you have solved in your personal life? Compare the steps you took in solving your problem with the steps of the problem-solving process described in this chapter.

One problem that many people have confronted or will confront is the choice of a college major. They need first to identify the problem—namely, their need before some deadline to decide in what area of academic endeavor they wish to specialize. Then they need to define the problem. On what bases should they decide on a major? In terms of interest to them? Future income possibilities? Desire to please parents? Social prestige? Meaningfulness of the work? Or what? Next they need to formulate hypotheses about what might be good potential majors for them. Perhaps they will decide on one of the social sciences, such as psychology, anthropology, or sociology. Then they need to construct a strategy to make their decision. Perhaps they will decide to take at least two courses in each area in which they are potentially interested. Perhaps they will talk to faculty who teach in the department of interest, or students who currently are pursuing a major in which they are interested. Finally, they will want to monitor and evaluate their judgment. If they start majoring in something and then come to regret their decision, they may wish to switch as soon as possible to an alternative major.

6.   Why should all psychological interventions in schools and communities have control groups of some kind?

Without a control group, it is difficult to draw meaningful conclusions about interventions. Suppose that a group of students receives a special educational program designed to improve their school achievement. The group that receives the intervention does, in fact, improve. Can one conclude that the intervention caused the improvement? No, because the improvement may have resulted simply because of the passage of time between pretest and posttest. Or it may have resulted from instruction students would have received anyway, whether or not they had the intervention. In order to rule out alternative hypotheses, a control group is necessary for the experimental design to yield valid conclusions.

7.   Why do researchers and psychotherapists both need to think scientifically?

Researchers think scientifically in order to discover and explain new findings. Psychotherapists use scientific thinking to understand their clients' problems and to decide among alternative explanations for these problems.

1. What ethical issues would be involved in tinkering with humans' genetic material?

A number of issues are involved. One issue is whether humans—any humans—have the right to tinker with the genetic material of other humans. A second issue is how one can possibly know, in a complex system such as the genetic one, whether the costs may be greater than the benefits. For example, certain desirable traits may be obtained at the cost of other negative ones. A third issue is what even constitutes a "positive" change. A change that one individual might view as positive, another might view as negative. A fourth issue is whether changes might be made for nefarious purposes, such as to breed assassins or warriors without a conscience.

2. Compare and contrast the ways in which people you know respond to new information that casts doubt onto existing beliefs. How might people improve their ways of responding?

Some people respond to such new information defensively. They seek to maintain their prior beliefs at any cost. The cost of such an attitude is that they tend to maintain old beliefs even in the face of evidence that contradicts these beliefs. People can improve their responding by pledging to themselves that they will be ever-vigilant regarding their beliefs and open to changing these beliefs as new information arrives. In this way, they can continue to grow intellectually, and not just during the years when they are students, but during all the years of their lives.

3. If you were designing the human brain, what, if anything, would you do differently to render humans more adaptive to their environments?

It is always hard to know whether the changes one would make actually would improve functioning or degrade it. But one change that some people might view as desirable would be a lesser tendency for people to form stereotypes about or prejudices against other people. Stereotypes and especially prejudices bias our thinking about others and lead us to see flaws where they may not exist as well as to refuse to see strengths that may be staring us in the face.

4. Imagine beings who evolved on another planet and who differed from humans in ways that led them never to have wars. What differences in brain structure might be associated with such a course of evolution?

Such individuals might have amygdalas that are less susceptible to certain kinds of negative emotions, particularly emotions related to anger.

5. Karl Spencer Lashley, a pioneering neuropsychologist in the study of brain localization, suffered from migraine headaches, the specific nature of which still puzzles neuropsychologists. Many scientists have personal reasons for their intense curiosity about particular psychological phenomena or special fields of study. What aspect of human behavior particularly puzzles you? Which area or areas of the brain might you wish to study to find out about that behavior? Why?

Everyone has to answer this question for himself or herself, of course. In my own case, I started studying intelligence because, as a child, I performed poorly on IQ tests. For much of my career, I have tried to figure out why! A wonderful feature of psychology is that it can enable us to answer questions we always have had about ourselves and others.

6. What is a circumstance in which you find it particularly difficult to think as clearly or as insightfully as you would like? If you were a biological psychologist trying to determine the physiological factors that contribute to this circumstance, how might you investigate these factors?

People often find it difficult to think clearly when they are under great stress. A biological psychologist might seek to relate quantities of stress-related hormones in the body to the quality of thinking people show when they solve insightful-thinking problems, such as crossword puzzles or brain-teasers.

CHAPTER 4

1. What are the main limitations of template-matching theories of visual perception?

These theories do not deal well with the fact that symbols such as letters or numbers can come in various forms and still be recognized. For example, two letters in different fonts (f, f) are both recognizable as the same letter even though their appearances are different. These theories also do not well explain context effects—that is, effects of the surrounding context on perception, as illustrated by the word-superiority effect.

2. Why are objects closer than they visually appear on a foggy day?

On a foggy day, many particles of moisture are suspended in the air. The amount of intervening particulate matter in the air is usually a cue to distance: The hazier objects appear, the more distant they are. We do not automatically adjust to the greater amount of particulate material in the foggy air. Hence we tend to believe the objects are at a distance that would be appropriate for a less foggy day—that is, farther away.

3. Hubel and Wiesel noted that their discoveries and their research were possible because of the technologies available to them. What current technology do you find not only pleasant but also even important to your ability to perform a task you do often? How would your life be different without that technology? (It does not have to be a complex or "high-tech" item.)

There are many examples of technologies that make our lives easier. One is the use of computers in word processing. With computers, it is possible to erase unwanted letters, words, paragraphs, or even pages at the click of a button or two. This process greatly speeds up writing. When I was young, for example, every typewriting mistake would have to be erased, with an eraser, by hand, consuming enormous amounts of time. For most writers, such time-consuming erasures are a relic of the past.

4. Try eating your next meal (or a snack) with your eyes closed. Briefly describe how the other senses work together to help you prevent yourself from ingesting bad food.

You generally see the food, which helps you decide whether it is fresh and whether it has an appealing appearance. Then you insert it in your mouth and immediately begin to taste and smell it. If either the taste or smell is "off," you may stop eating the food and even spit it out. In this way, you protect yourself from poisons. You can also feel its texture, and if the texture is different from what it is supposed to be (e.g., crunchy food that is softened), you may decide that the food is old and should not be eaten. You also even can hear yourself consuming the food, and again the process of eating a food that is crunchy should produce a certain sound. If it does not, something may be wrong with the food.

5. In what ways have you noticed that smells affect the way you feel about particular people, particular kinds of food, and particular situations or settings?

The multimillion dollar perfume industry is so successful because people are attracted to certain kinds of personal smells. The deodorant industry succeeds because people find other kinds of personal smells unappealing. Similarly, going into a town that has a bad smell (as from an industrial complex) can predispose people not to like the town.

6. If you had to memorize a long list of terms and definitions, would you be better off trying to remember them by seeing them (e.g., reading printed flashcards) or by hearing them (e.g., having someone drill you by saying the words aloud)? Do you seem to be able to remember material better if it is presented visually (e.g., in a book) or vocally (e.g., in a lecture)? How do you tailor your studying to your sensory preferences?

Each individual has to answer this question for him- or herself. Many people find that they have distinct sensory preferences. I would rather read something than hear it, but I know many people who would rather hear it than read it. Some people profit from engaging with learning material kinesthetically: they seek some kind of bodily movement. We maximize our learning when we come to understand how we learn best.

CHAPTER 5

1. What are your normal sleep patterns? How do you react when your normal patterns are interrupted?

Most people sleep about 8 hours a day in the evening. College students often sleep somewhat less because of pressures on their time. Minor interruptions have little effect, but more persistent interruptions can produce crankiness and irritability and lead to mental confusion. Severe interruptions, as noted in the chapter, can lead to hallucinations and delusions.

2. Why might meditation improve psychological well-being in some people?

Meditation can lower blood pressure and lead to relaxation and a state of inner peace. There may be an additional placebo effect: The very fact that people think meditation helps them feel better may in and of itself help them feel better.

3. What effect does divided attention have on your work, for example, if you listen to music and work at the same time?

Many people find that music facilitates or at least does not interfere with tasks that require light to moderate levels of concentration. People are more likely to find interference for tasks that require very high levels of concentration.

4. Why is hypnosis used in some psychotherapeutic contexts?

Hypnosis is used for a variety of reasons, such as to help people stop smoking or to reduce pain. It can also be used to help people dredge up memories, although this use of hypnosis has been widely criticized with respect to the accuracy of the memories it produces.

5. How should society regulate the sale, purchase, possession, and use of psychoactive drugs? How should society respond to individuals who abuse such drugs but who do not directly harm others with their drug use?

Opinions on this question vary from ones in favor of legalization to those in favor of strict criminal penalties for people who use such drugs. Some people argue that if drug use does not hurt others, then it should not be regulated by the legal system. The issue is complex, however, given that there is no guarantee that drug use might not hurt others, such as future children who may risk potential genetic damage. The complexities of the issues are part of the reason that it is unlikely any consensus will develop in the near future regarding what consists of an equitable system of regulation.

6. What factors do you believe lead people to abuse psychoactive drugs? What do you believe can be done to help people to avoid becoming involved in the abuse of these drugs?

Abuse of psychoactive drugs may stem from high levels of stress, desire to conform to the behavior of others, or simple desire to escape. Drug-education programs have proved to have mixed effectiveness. Perhaps the best way to help people avoid becoming involved in abuse is to educate them about the potential costs but also help them prevent or deal with the problems that lead to drug abuse in the first place.

CHAPTER 6

1. In what kinds of situations does learning tend to be advantageous? In what kinds of situations might learning be disadvantageous?

Learning tends to be advantageous in situations in which we use experience to figure out how to deal with a relatively novel task or situation. Learning can be disadvantageous if we apply it in situations in which it turns out not to apply—for example, when we behave toward a teacher in a way that we have learned is appropriate for our peers but that is not in fact appropriate in interactions with a teacher. It also can be disadvantageous in situations where an extremely rapid response is necessary—for example, when one is burned by touching an extremely hot object. In this case, a reflex reaction likely will be more adaptive than a reaction processed by the brain.

2. What are the main similarities and differences between classical and operant conditioning?

In classical conditioning, behavior is elicited. The organism has little or no control over the learning situation. In operant conditioning, the behavior is emitted, with the organism typically having more control over the learning situation. In classical conditioning, the sequence of events typically begins with the initiation of a conditioned stimulus. In operant conditioning, the sequence of events typically begins with the initiation of an operant response, which either is or is not reinforced (or punished). Extinction of classical conditioning occurs when the CS is uncoupled from the US, which can occur by repeatedly presenting the CS in the absence of the US. Extinction of operant conditioning occurs when the operant behavior is uncoupled from the reinforcer or punishment.

3. Prescribe a counterconditioning program for a specific phobia or addiction.

Counterconditioning to alcohol is sometimes achieved by prescribing a drug that produces extreme distress in the individual if that individual consumes alcohol. The idea is that the alcohol then becomes associated with an adverse experience.

4. Suppose you worked for a company and wanted people to buy a particular product you believe they need. How could you use some of the principles of conditioning to encourage people to buy this product?

You might believe that couples should purchase condoms to reduce the risks of unwanted pregnancies or to prevent the spread of venereal disease. Thus, you would want to provide some kind of reward to people who buy condoms. One kind of reward might be to design condoms that enhance the pleasure of sexual experience (e.g., condoms of unusual colors or shapes). Another kind of reward might be a money-back offer or the assurance of sex without undue risk.

5. What is something (a skill, a task, or an achievement) that you think is worthwhile but that you feel a sense of learned helplessness about successfully accomplishing? How could you design a conditioning program for yourself to overcome your learned helplessness?

Each person needs to answer this question for himself or herself. In my own case, I wanted to lose weight at various points in my life but had not had much success. I decided that the reason was that I was setting unrealistic goals. I wanted to lose a lot of weight fast, and when I did not succeed in doing so, I viewed myself as having failed. I then decided I needed to work out a reinforcement schedule whereby I would reward myself for small weight losses. I did just that. I allowed myself to engage in an activity I looked forward to when I lost small amounts of weight (2 pounds). This reinforcement schedule enabled me to attain realistic goals and to lose weight slowly but surely.

6. Given the powerful effects of social learning, how might the medium of television be used as a medium for *lowering* the rate of violent crimes in our society?

Television shows might provide nonviolent rather than violent role models. At the very least, the proportion of nonviolent to violent shows could be greatly increased. Shows could be constructed so that nonviolence led to more positive results, violence to less positive or negative ones.

CHAPTER 7

1. How did the Atkinson–Shiffrin model shape both the questions asked about memory and the methods used to find answers to those questions?

This model assumed that memories are stored in relatively static receptacles. Thus, the goal of research became to understand how these static receptacles are used in the encoding, storage, and retrieval of information. Later theorists began to question whether memory storage truly is so static and whether the model of "receptacles" accurately captures the nature of memory storage.

2. It is often said that Alzheimer's patients eventually lose their personalities and their distinctive identities when they lose their memories. How does your memory serve as the basis for your unique personality and identity?

Through our memory, we remember the experiences that have made us who we are. In making decisions in life, we also think back to past experiences and events and use them as a guide. We may think about not only our own past experiences but those of others. Without memory, we would not have our unique knowledge base on which to draw. And it is this knowledge base, as it guides our actions, that is part of what makes us who we are.

3.   Why might people sometimes think they remember events that in fact never have happened?

Research shows that people often have difficulty distinguishing between events they have imagined and events that actually have happened to them. Moreover, even when people remember events, they often remember them incorrectly, despite their belief they remember them correctly. If people are interrogated, leading questions can result in the people thinking they remember things that never happened. It is for this reason that interrogations to be used for legal purposes must be scrupulously fair in avoiding questions asked in a way that might lead people to believe things happened that, in fact, never occurred.

4.   Describe one means by which a researcher could study the relationship between perception and memory.

There are many means by which this relationship could be studied. One means would be to have people either form strong images of pictures they perceive or not form strong images. One would then compare people's recall under the two conditions to investigate the extent to which actively forming strong images of what is perceived influences later recall.

5.   Cognitive psychologists frequently study patterns of errors when they investigate how a particular cognitive process works. What is a pattern of errors in memory tasks that you have performed?

In short-term memory tasks, people tend to show a primacy effect and a recency effect. For example, if you try to remember a phone number that you look up in the phone book or hear from telephone directory assistance, you are more likely to remember the first few digits and the last few digits than all the rest of the digits.

6.   What have you learned that has led to both positive transfer and negative transfer when you were learning something else? Explain the effects of each.

Often people show both positive and negative transfer when they are learning a second language. On the one hand, the first language often helps them learn the second language. For example, knowing the English word maternal *may help a person learn the word* madre *(mother)* in Spanish. But knowing the English word* deception *may actually hurt a person in learning that the word* decepcionado *in Spanish means* disappointed. *The words are so-called*

false cognates: They look like they should mean roughly the same thing, but they do not.

CHAPTER 8

1.   Many language lovers enjoy the dynamic quality of language and relish each new nuance of meaning and change of form that arises. In contrast, others believe that to cherish a language is to preserve it exactly as it is at present—or even exactly as it was at some time in the past. Give the pros and cons of both welcoming and resisting change in language.

An advantage of preserving a language in all its features is that people can better continue to understand and appreciate records from the past and literature that has been preserved over time. A disadvantage is the loss of flexibility. Often new words and expressions are needed to keep up with changes in the world. For example, a word such as Internet *may not have been useful 100 years ago, but it certainly is useful now.*

2.   If we assume that some animals can be taught rudimentary language or language-like skills, what distinguishes humans from other animals?

What most distinguishes humans from animals appears to be complexity of thinking. Research suggests that humans are capable of solving problems and making decisions that are considerably more complex than the problems solved or decisions made by other animals.

3.   What steps can nonnatives take when studying another culture to understand the breadth and depth of that culture with minimal distortion from their own biases?

It is important when learning about a culture to learn the language of that culture, if possible. First, this enables one to communicate firsthand with people of that culture. This is especially important because translations can distort what people say. Second, it may enable one to read the literature without translation. Third, informants often will reveal things to people who speak their language that they will not reveal to those who do not speak it. Fourth, the people will appreciate your attempt to learn their language and may return the "favor" by telling you more.

4.   How do advertisers (and other propagandists) use invalid reasoning to influence people? Give some specific examples of ads you have seen or experiences you have had with salespersons or other persuaders.

Advertisers frequently try to associate products with certain states people would like to enjoy. For example, advertisers for cigarettes are likely to show young, happy, apparently healthy, "with it" people enjoying smoking. The idea is to get you to believe that you, too, will share these attributes if you smoke. Needless to say, the inductive inference the advertisers want you to make is invalid.

5. If you were the head of a problem-solving team and your team members seemed to be running into a block in their approach to the problem being addressed, what would you have the team members do to get around the block?

One of the best things you can encourage them to do is to incubate. They might put the problem aside for a few days, and then come back to it with a new perspective or from a fresh angle.

6. What is a particularly challenging ill-structured problem that you now face (or have recently faced)? What strategies do you find (or did you find) most helpful in confronting this problem?

Obviously, everyone has to answer this question for himself or herself. But an example of an ill-structured problem is studying for an exam. One of the best strategies is to start studying well in advance because we know (see Chapter 7) that distributed learning results in better retention than does massed learning.

CHAPTER 9

1. Does it make sense to speak of "overachievers"? Why or why not?

It really does not make sense to speak of "overachievers" because someone cannot achieve at a level that is higher than his or her capabilities. If the person seems to be achieving at a higher level, it is because the predictive assessment of capabilities missed some capabilities that are instrumental to success. There are abilities besides those measured by conventional tests that are very important to success in school and in life.

2. To what extent are people's achievements—including your own—an accurate reflection of their aptitudes? What factors beside aptitudes affect achievement?

Other factors that affect achievement include luck, determination, willingness to work hard, belief in one's ability to succeed, willingness to surmount obstacles, and willingness to take sensible risks.

3. Create a test question that assesses a particular skill or topic of knowledge. Tailor that question to the following persons: (a) a 9-year-old homeless boy who supports himself by whatever means he finds available, (b) a 20-year-old college student, and (c) a 70-year-old retired plumber.

(a) Where can you find food for free without stealing it? (b) What is the difference between studying for a multiple-choice test and studying for an essay test? (c) How long does a Social Security pension last?

4. Many museums now include child-oriented experiences and exhibits. Think of an exhibit you have vis-

ited or heard about. How might you enhance the learning experience of a 10-year-old to help the child profit from the exhibit?

One of the best things an exhibit can do is not only provide information but also show the children why they should care about the information. Exhibits tend to be more informative when people can relate them to their lives.

5. Are there things you could do to increase your own abilities? If so, what?

Research suggests that schooling in itself increases abilities. So just by being in and profiting from school, you are increasing your abilities. Another thing you can do is to adopt an attitude that learning is a lifelong endeavor. You should view learning as something you do inside and outside of school, for the duration of your life span.

6. Are there aspects of your abilities that you could use better? If so, how might you better use them?

Many people fail to use their abilities fully because they doubt they have them. For example, they are convinced that they cannot write well, so they do not try. Or they are convinced that they cannot succeed in physical activities (such as jogging or tennis), so they never try to develop expertise. The first step to using abilities better is to accept that abilities can be best used when one believes one has them.

CHAPTER 10

1. What steps should researchers take to avoid confusing their own limitations as investigators with the cognitive limitations of children?

It is important to word questions to children in a variety of ways, to make sure that children's answers reflect their inability to answer, not their failure to understand what is being asked. It is also important to have the questions asked by a variety of examiners to make sure that failures to respond to wrong answers truly reflect lack of knowledge or skill rather than poor rapport with an examiner.

2. How does Piaget's notion of equilibration through assimilation and accommodation compare with Vygotsky's concept of the zone of proximal development?

Equilibration can tell us about the level of cognitive development a child has achieved. The zone of proximal development can tell us about the level of cognitive development a child is just about ready to achieve but has not yet quite achieved. It is important to know both where the child is in terms of cognitive development and where the child is ready to go.

3. What might you suggest as a possible fifth stage of cognitive development?

Possible fifth stages might be finding important problems to solve, having wisdom, thinking dialectically, and under-

standing how to achieve one's goals in a way that helps others in addition to oneself.

4. What skills might a child in a remote village in Kenya have that a child in a city in a highly developed country might not have?

The child in Kenya might have skills pertaining to agriculture and fishing that the urban child would not have. The Kenyan child would also be likely to know a number of herbal remedies for illnesses that the urban child in the developed world would not know.

5. How have you developed cognitively in the past 3 years? In what ways do you think differently?

Some theorists believe that students in college, particularly, gain sophisticated skills in their ability to see issues from a multitude of perspectives. Indeed, one of the main purposes of a college education is to develop these skills. Hence, you might be substantially better at understanding multiple points of view now than you were a few years ago.

6. What principal aspects of your parents' or your teachers' behavior have you internalized over the years?

Answers will be different for different people. Students often internalize codes of moral and ethical behavior, ways of behaving toward other people, and attitudes toward intellectual tasks.

CHAPTER 11

1. Describe a moral dilemma and tell how someone at Kohlberg's postconventional level of morality might respond to the dilemma. Give the rationale for the individual's response.

An example of a moral dilemma is a bribe a government official receives to award a government contract to a particular firm. The individual offering the bribe points out that his company will do just as good a job as any other contractor, and quite possibly a better job. Thus, only good ends will come out of awarding the contract to his firm. He points out that no one will be hurt because the job will get done, it will get done well, and you, as the government official, will benefit at no one's expense. Should you accept the bribe and award the contract to the company whose official is attempting to bribe you? Someone at the postconventional stage of morality would certainly recognize that the bribe should not be accepted. First, it is not true that no one is hurt. Honest companies that don't offer bribes are being hurt if their honesty causes them to lose business. Eventually, they may go out of business or conclude that they need to offer bribes. Second, the taxpayers get hurt. The money for the bribe has to come from somewhere. Most likely it will be factored into the cost of the contract, and ultimately taxpayers will pay. Third, accepting the bribe is dishonest, regardless of who gains and who loses.

2. How do the development of the self-concept and interpersonal development interact?

Your self-concept will affect the way you interact with other people. If you think poorly of yourself, you are likely to show this to others, who will then respond to your poor self-concept. They may agree or disagree, but the way they treat you will be affected by your own opinion of yourself. If you think well of yourself (but not unreasonably so), people may accept your positive view. Often they can then move on to the more important aspects of interpersonal interactions rather than concentrating on dealing with your opinion of yourself.

3. Design an experience that would help children broaden their views about the range of behaviors that are appropriate for boys and for girls, helping them avoid being narrowly constrained by rigid sex-role stereotypes.

Many boys believe that being sensitive to people's feelings is a "feminine" activity. Yet it is important for everyone to be sensitive to the feelings of others as well as of themselves. An activity children can do is to relate an event in their lives that left a strong emotional impression on them, positive or negative. The event, but not the feelings of the moment, should be described orally. Children in the classroom, including boys, then will be invited to comment on how the child must have felt when he experienced the event he describes.

4. Suggest some criteria to be used in assessing the quality of child care for children less than 5 years of age.

The criteria to be used might include (a) number of caretakers, (b) past experience of the caretakers, (c) caretakers' training in working with children, (d) average longevity on the job of the caretaking staff, (e) number of toys and books available for children to use, and (f) quality of nutrition offered in the program.

5. How do your emotions influence your behavior?

Emotions influence everyone's behavior. For example, when they are angry, people often look for outlets through which to express their anger. When they are happy, they do the same. When people are sad, sometimes they become withdrawn or they may seek the comfort others have to provide.

6. Give examples of your own sex-role development. In what ways do you conform to traditional gender roles, and in what ways have you departed from traditional gender roles?

Everyone must answer this question for himself or herself. If you conform very strongly to your traditional gender role, you might consider trying out some activities that would render you more androgynous—that is, more flexible in the role you carry out.

CHAPTER 12

1. Why is disgust a key emotion from an evolutionary standpoint?

We tend to be disgusted by substances that are poisonous. This can be very important because it tends to prevent us from ingesting poisons.

2. Why are negative-feedback loops important to the homeostatic regulation of temperature in the body?

Negative-feedback loops tell the body when temperature has gone under or over the acceptable range. The body then takes steps to restore its temperature to an acceptable level.

3. What strategies could you use to help a child increase his or her motivation to do homework?

One strategy is to try to turn the homework into a game or otherwise render it fun. A related strategy is to try to make it more interesting in some other way. Another strategy is to emphasize the importance of the homework to the child's understanding of the material he or she is learning. A strategy that is risky is to offer an extrinsic reward: The child may then become dependent on extrinsic rewards, or find his or her interest in the homework activity undermined by the reward.

4. How might you expect people's motivation to succeed economically to vary across cultures?

In some cultures, monetary success is viewed as very important. The United States tends to be that way. In other cultures, enjoyment of life or personal fulfillment may be viewed as far more important. Many people in developing cultures (and developed ones as well) are skeptical of those who place a great emphasis on monetary success. Because money is a secondary reinforcer, people have no innate desire for it. The desire is learned, and that learning takes place in a cultural context.

5. What goal can you set for yourself that would satisfy your need for achievement and that would enhance your sense of competence, autonomy, and self-efficacy? Devise a specific plan for reaching your goal, including the specific subtasks and subgoals you would need to accomplish it.

Everyone must answer this for himself or herself. In my own case, I quit playing the cello when I was in college. In recent years, I began seriously to regret this decision and became more and more motivated to return to playing the cello. I finally decided that I was not too old to restart, and so I did. I set as a goal having a weekly lesson and practicing at least a half-hour a day. Now I play the cello regularly and hope soon to join an amateur orchestra.

6. When advertisers want you to buy their products or services, they seek to tap into some of the fundamental human emotions. Describe a recent advertisement you have seen or heard and explain how the advertiser was trying to manipulate your fundamental emotions to persuade you to buy the advertised product or service.

Advertisements for luxury products often emphasize how happy these products will make you. You are encouraged to buy these products to achieve happiness. It is a safe bet that none of these products will truly bring you happiness!

CHAPTER 13

1. Many advertisers spend a lot of money to get celebrity endorsements of their products. Do you think that the advertisers' money is well spent? Why or why not?

From the standpoint of selling products, celebrity endorsements often are successful. People come to associate the products with the celebrities and may use the products in order to be more like the celebrities. People also may assign greater credibility to celebrities than to other people, even though the celebrities may have no expertise in the area for which they endorse products and almost always are paid to endorse the products. At the same time, it is perhaps unfortunate that advertisers take advantage of people's gullibility through celebrity endorsements.

2. Some investigators, such as Deborah Tannen, believe that men place more emphasis on social hierarchies than women do. Do you agree? Why or why not?

Tannen may be correct, although her evidence lacks the controls for extraneous variables or even scientific evidence that most social psychologists expect. At this time, Tannen's idea remains more a hypothesis than a well-demonstrated phenomenon.

3. Describe a particular conflict you have observed, first from the perspective of one participant and then from the perspective of the other. Which heuristics and biases affected the views of each participant?

George W. Bush and John McCain slugged it out for the Republican presidential nomination for the 2000 election. Bush and his camp seemed to view themselves as representing the true Republican mainstream and the traditional values of Republicans. They therefore believed that Bush should be nominated. McCain and his camp seemed to view themselves as representing a reform movement that would dispense with patronage politics as usual. They believed that their reforms were necessary to straighten out the government. Each side believed that what they had to offer was what the country needed. Republicans chose Bush.

4. How would you create an advertisement for a product using the principles discussed in this chapter?

There are many principles you might use to create your advertisement. One is the foot-in-the-door technique. You might advertise a magazine with a low introductory rate for subscriptions. Often these introductory rates are way below the rates for resubscriptions. The reason is that the hardest thing is to get people interested in the first place. Once people have initiated a subscription, they may continue it because they like the magazine or simply because of inertia.

5. How could you use one or more principles of persuasion, as described in this chapter, to help elect a candidate for a student-government position?

In such an election, you might decide to use the central route to persuasion, figuring that the election is important to students and that they will be at least somewhat informed about their options. In this case, you would want to give strong, solid reasons to elect your candidate. You would also want to respond to and discount arguments against your candidate.

6. Give an example of a self-handicapping behavior (e.g., drug abuse). Why and how does this example show self-handicapping?

Sometimes students are convinced that they cannot do well in a course, no matter how hard they try. They therefore do not try very hard. They then can conclude that they did not do well because they did not try to do well. But their self-handicapping may be the main reason behind their failure to do well. If they had tried harder, they might indeed have succeeded.

CHAPTER 14
1. What criteria would you propose for determining whether behavior derives from motives that are truly altruistic?

An action is altruistic when it helps one or more persons but does not necessarily benefit the person who has engaged in the action. One could argue that no actions are 100% altruistic because people can gain a sense of pleasure by helping others and therefore benefit indirectly from their actions that apparently help only others. In order to circumvent this problem, altruistic actions can be characterized in terms of material benefits. But there are clear benefits to actors that go beyond the materialistic.

2. Some developmental psychologists have noticed that people who demonstrate a high degree of conformity to their peers during adolescence are more likely to have shown a high degree of obedience to their parents during childhood. What do you believe is the relationship between conformity and obedience, if any?

Obedience requires conformity to the implicit or explicit desires of others. It therefore may in general promote a mind-set toward conformity. When a child obeys his or her parents, the child is conforming to the parents' wishes. The stage therefore may be set for other types of conformity.

3. How might a working group avoid the ill effects of groupthink?

A working group should be aware of what it is and constantly monitor its own behavior in terms of whether it is showing any signs of groupthink. Ideally, an outside consultant would also monitor the group because those within the group may not be fully sensitive to the signs of groupthink.

4. How might you help people avoid falling prey to some of the strategies for gaining compliance described in this chapter?

One way to help people is to point out what the strategies are, give examples, and ask learners to generate their own examples and to tell how they might resist these techniques. It is important for the learners to be involved in generating both examples and counterstrategies so that their knowledge becomes useful, not just "book" knowledge that they are unable to translate into practice.

5. Imagine that you wished to reduce the likelihood of your own aggression or the aggression of another person. What would you do?

Aggression is most likely to occur when the only point of view you see or appreciate is your own. One way to reduce aggression, therefore, is to try to understand the other person's point of view.

6. Which compliance-seeking strategy is the most likely to be effective in gaining your own compliance? Why?

Everyone must answer this question for himself or herself. Often people find reciprocity to be particularly effective. It is the only technique that involves someone first doing something explicitly for you. You are then likely to wish to repay the favor.

CHAPTER 15
1. Of the various theories of personality proposed in this chapter, which seems to you to be most reasonable; that is, which explains personality most effectively? Why?

Everyone must answer this question for himself or herself, of course. Many trait theorists today accept five-factor theory because it seems to capture in a parsimonious fashion many of the major aspects of personality. Some researchers find other approaches to personality more useful. There is no one "right" approach to personality, and at present, no one theory of personality dominates others the way Freud's theory once did.

2. In what ways do both humanistic and cognitive-behavioral theories view personality similarly to the psychodynamic perspective? How do these two theories differ from the psychodynamic perspective?

The humanistic and cognitive-behavioral perspectives share with the psychodynamic perspective an emphasis on how personality develops, in contrast, say, to trait theory. The humanistic and cognitive-behavioral approaches place much less emphasis on early experience than does the psychodynamic approach, and they also are much less deterministic.

3.   Picture yourself as a medically trained neurologist living in Victorian Vienna. Many of your patients are women, and a number of them come to ask you to relieve their hysterical symptoms (i.e., physical complaints for which you can find no medical explanations). How might you help your patients and what theory might you propose to explain the underlying cause of their ailments?

If you were a Freudian, you might try to discover some early traumatic but repressed experience that is responsible for the symptoms. You might use extensive psychoanalysis to try to uncover the experience and help the patient understand its significance for her life.

4.   What are several ways in which you can ensure that your significant other or your child (hypothetical or real) feels sure of your unconditional positive regard?

When you criticize, be sure to criticize actions rather than the person. You can also emphasize, even when you criticize the person, the unconditional positive regard you have for the person.

5.   What do you consider to be the essential personality characteristics, based on yourself and on the people you know?

Everyone must answer this question for himself or herself. Many people generate theories related to the five-factor theory. This is because that theory is based largely on analyses of people's implicit theories (conceptions) of personality.

6.   In what ways might your self-schemas be limiting your flexibility? What can you do to increase your flexibility?

People all have certain ways of conceiving of themselves. They may think of themselves as introverts, for example, and then avoid people because they believe they are the kinds of people who avoid others. Or they may conceive of themselves as extroverts and be afraid to spend much time alone because they believe that they need others. People need constantly to be aware of the self-schemas that limit their flexibility.

CHAPTER 16

1.   Why does science as a whole benefit when researchers base their studies on explicit rather than implicit underlying assumptions about their theoretical perspectives?

The problem with implicit underlying assumptions is that, because the researchers are unaware of their own assumptions, they also are unaware of how these assumptions affect their scientific work. The researchers may ask only certain questions but not others, or do only certain experiments but not others that are more important, because they are restricted by these underlying assumptions.

2.   Choose the psychological perspective you find most suitable to your own beliefs about psychological disorders. Compare your preferred perspective with the others, showing why yours makes better sense.

Everyone must choose a perspective that makes particular sense to him or her. Some people might, for example, choose the cognitive perspective. An advantage of this perspective is that it recognizes that much of the reaction people have to situations is not determined by the situations, per se, but by the cognitive interpretations people give to these situations. One person might interpret as depressing a certain event that another person would interpret as cheerful, such as spending a day helping people who live in very poor conditions. Each perspective has its own advantages and, of course, disadvantages. The cognitive perspective at times may overemphasize the role of thought in psychological disorders.

3.   Suppose you are assigned to choose exactly one personality disorder to be allowed as a legal defense for a not-guilty-by-reason-of-insanity plea. Which disorder would you choose and why? If you would not be willing to make such a choice, explain why.

Almost certainly your choice would depend not only on the disorder but also on the severity of the disorder experienced. One disorder for which such a defense might be considered is disorganized schizophrenia, which can be particularly severe. Persons with severe disorganized schizophrenia may cause harm without necessarily realizing what they are doing.

4.   Suppose your English teacher assigns you the task of creating a believable literary character who is schizophrenic. Briefly describe that person as others view the person; then describe how that person sees the world, including other persons.

The way the character perceives the world will depend in part upon the type of schizophrenia from which the person suffers. For example, a paranoid schizophrenic may imagine being attacked by another person, whereas a catatonic schizophrenic may be oblivious to the other person.

5.   Suppose you are volunteering to answer telephone calls on a suicide hotline. What kinds of strategies would you use—and what might you actu-

ally say—to try to prevent someone from committing suicide?

Your goal is to stop the person from committing suicide and to get the person to find help. One strategy is to point out that everyone goes through bad periods but generally the periods do not last forever. Often people find that things not only get better, but even that they get much better. A second thing you might point out is how much other people depend on him or her and wish to have his or her presence in their lives. A third thing you might point out is that suicide is a final decision and that it certainly is not a decision to be made in a time of great distress. The person should wait. You can add that you personally care about the outcome and will do everything you can to make sure the person gets help.

6.　Sometimes it is tempting to analyze people you know in terms of the disorders they seem to show. What are the risks of assuming the role of an amateur psychologist?

This kind of behavior is very risky because you are likely to make a diagnosis for which there really is no justification and then to treat the people as though the diagnosis were true. If you truly believe that someone you know needs help, you should encourage the person to seek professional help rather than giving the person amateur help that may hurt rather than help.

CHAPTER 17

1.　Cognitive and behavioral therapies often are paired. What does each technique have to offer that complements the other?

Cognitive therapy focuses on how people think and behavior therapy on how people behave. The combination is often viewed as particularly useful because both thought and action are critical to psychological disorders and to curing them or at least lessening their severity.

2.　If you were a marriage and family therapist, which two psychotherapeutic approaches might you be most likely to use? Why would you choose those two methods?

Each individual must answer this question for himself or herself. Some people might find cognitive and behavioral techniques particularly useful because they focus on both thought and action. Other people might prefer other combinations.

3.　Suppose you were a biochemist concocting the next big breakthrough drug that would minimize the problems caused by a particular psychological disorder. If you could choose any disorder to attack and any negative side effects to tolerate, which disorder—and which symptoms of the disorder—would you wish that your drug could minimize? What modest

negative side effects would you find least offensive in your new wonder drug?

Each individual must answer for himself or herself. For example, schizophrenia can severely disrupt people's lives. But depression can be very disruptive too and is far more likely to lead to suicidal behavior. Depression is also far more prevalent. Many antidepressants have side effects, but they are usually relatively mild, such as dry mouth.

4.　What would you view as an ideal treatment for depression, one that perhaps combines elements of the therapies about which you have read?

An ideal treatment for some would be a combination of cognitive-behavioral therapy and drug treatment. But the ideal treatment must depend on the particular symptoms, their severity, and a constant monitoring of treatment to evaluate how it is working.

5.　How might a psychotherapist who has doubts about the ethics of a new treatment program go about resolving his or her doubts prior to administering the treatment?

The psychotherapist might talk to colleagues in order to get their advice. He or she might consult the American Psychological Association for guidelines. He or she also might talk to someone who specializes in ethics.

6.　If you had a need for psychotherapy, which method of therapy would you choose? If you were to decide to become a psychotherapist, would your choice be the same? Analyze the benefits and drawbacks of the method you would prefer in each role.

Each individual must decide for himself or herself. I would prefer an eclectic approach, trying to deal with each problem in the way that has proven most effective in the past and that works best with each client.

CHAPTER 18

1.　Suppose that an instructor of student nurses invites you to discuss the patient's view of hospital care. What are the key points you would try to communicate? How would you communicate those points so that the nurses would really understand you and would not feel threatened by what you say?

A patient will generally want to be treated with courtesy and respect. The patient also will wish to understand both the nature of the illness confronting him or her and the treatment options available. Patients often will have better medical outcomes if they have a feeling of some control over their treatment options.

2.　This chapter included health recommendations regarding several aspects of lifestyle. Which recommendation do you consider the most important of these? Why?

Everyone must answer this question for himself or herself. Important things one can do to improve one's health are to eat well, exercise, stop smoking, and avoid the use of harmful drugs.

3. What advice would you give doctors, based on your knowledge of psychology, to help them communicate with patients who have to be told that they have a life-threatening illness?

Doctors should treat patients with dignity and emphasize their compassion for their patients. They should also emphasize their own professionalism and their commitment to doing the best they can to provide optimal patient care. Where possible, they should allow patients to have some control over the situation and to participate in important treatment decisions.

4. Choose the pain-relief or pain-control method you consider most likely to be effective in a variety of situations. Describe a situation in which pain relief or pain control would be needed and in which this technique might be effective. State how you would use it.

What method of pain relief works best depends on the person, the cause of the pain, and the particular situation in which pain relief is to be administered. One particularly effective method for some people in some situations is relaxation. People can make pain worse by becoming tense. The pain causes tension, which in turn may worsen the pain, which may in turn lead to more tension, and so on. Relaxation can help break this cycle and help the individual focus to the extent possible on positive aspects of his or her life.

5. What decision criteria should you use to decide when you need to consult a physician?

You should consult a doctor if you have a fever, if you are ill for several days without signs of getting better, or if your illness notably impairs your ability to function in daily life. In cases of doubt, it is better to consult a physician than to hope that you will somehow get better.

6. What are some realistic things that you can do to minimize feelings of stress in your life?

You can ask yourself how many of the things causing you stress really will matter in the long run. Often things are stressful at the moment but are of little long-term consequence. You can also exercise as a form of stress relief. A third thing you can do is practice guided relaxation or meditation.

absolute refractory phase. A time following the firing of a *neuron* during which the neuron cannot fire again regardless of the strength of the *stimulus* that reaches it (cf. *relative refractory phase*)

absolute threshold. The hypothetical construct of a minimum amount of a particular form of physical energy (e.g., mechanical pressure of sounds, electrochemical scents or tastes) that reaches a sensory receptor that is sufficient for the individual to detect that energy (*stimulus*); hypothetically, a person will be able to sense any stimuli that are at or above the absolute threshold, and unable to detect stimuli that are below that threshold

accessibility. The ease of gaining access to information that has been stored in long-term memory (cf. *availability, long-term store*)

accommodation (as a cognitive process). The process of responding to cognitively disequilibrating information about the environment by modifying relevant *schemas*, thereby adapting the schemas to fit the new information and thus reestablishing cognitive equilibrium (cf. *assimilation*; see also *equilibration*)

accommodation (as a means of adjusting the focus of the eye). The process by which curvature of the *lens* changes in order to focus on objects at different distances

acetylcholine (Ach). A *neurotransmitter* synthesized from choline in the diet; present in both the *central nervous system* and the *peripheral nervous system*; may affect memory function as well as other neural processes in the brain; is involved in muscle contraction in the body and affects the muscles of the heart (see *neurotransmitter*; cf. *dopamine, serotonin*)

achievement. An accomplishment, an attained level of expertise on performance of a task, or an acquired base of knowledge (cf. *aptitude*)

acquisition. The phase of *classical conditioning* during which a *conditioned response* strengthens and the occurrence of the response increases in likelihood

acronyms. See *mnemonic devices*

acrostics. See *mnemonic devices*

action potential. When an action potential occurs, the *neuron* is said to "fire"; a change in the electrochemical balance inside and outside a neuron that occurs when positively and negatively charged ions quickly flood across the neuronal membrane; occurs when electrochemical stimulation of the neuron reaches or exceeds the neuronal *threshold of excitation*

activation–synthesis hypothesis. A proposed perspective on dreaming that considers dreams to be the result of subjective organization and interpretation (synthesis) of neural activity (activation) that takes place during sleep; contrasting views include the Freudian view of dreams as a symbolic manifestation of wishes and the view of dreams as mental housekeeping

actor-observer effect. A psychological phenomenon in which people attribute the actions of others to the stable dispositional characteristics of those persons, but they attribute their own actions to the momentary characteristics of the situation (see also *fundamental attribution error, self-handicapping*)

acuity. The keenness (sharpness) of *sensation* in a sensory mode

acute (symptom or illness). Brief, usually characterized by sudden onset and intense symptomatology, but in any case not recurrent and not long in duration (cf. *chronic*)

acute pain. Brief (lasting no longer than 6 months), intense, uncomfortable stimulation usually associated with internal or external damage of tissue (cf. *chronic pain*)

acute stress disorder. A brief mental illness (lasting fewer than 4 months) that arises in response to a traumatic event; characterized by perceptual distortions, memory disturbances, and/or physical or social detachment (cf. *posttraumatic stress disorder*; see *anxiety disorders*)

adaptation level. The existing level of sensory stimulation (e.g., brightness or sound intensity) that an individual uses as a reference level for sensing new *stimuli* or changes in existing stimuli

addiction. A persistent, habitual, or compulsive physiological, or at least psychological, dependency on one or more *psychoactive* drugs (see also *tolerance, withdrawal*, as well as specific psychoactive drugs)

additive color mixture. The blending of various *wavelengths* of light (such as in spotlights) that add together to produce a summative effect of the combined wavelengths that is perceived as a different color from the original lights (cf. *subtractive color mixture*)

adrenal cortex. The outer part of the adrenal *glands*; produces more than 50 *hormones*, many of which are vital to physiological survival, sexual differentiation, and reproductive functions

adrenal medulla. One of the two adrenal (*a-*, "near" or "toward"; *renal*, "kidney" [Latin]) *glands*, which are located above the kidneys; secretes epinephrine (*epi-*, "on"; *nephron*, "kidney" [Greek]) and norepinephrine, which act as *neurotransmitters* in the *brain* and as *hormones* elsewhere in the body, particularly aiding in *stress*-related responses, such as sudden *arousal*

aerial perspective. See *monocular depth cues*

afferent. A *neuron* that brings information into a structure (see also *sensory neuron*)

aggression. A form of *antisocial behavior* that is directed against another person or persons, intended to cause harm or injury to the recipient of the aggression (see *hostile aggression, instrumental aggression*)

agnosia. A severe deficit in the ability to perceive sensory information, usually related to the visual sensory modality; oddly, agnosics have normal sensations but lack the ability to interpret and recognize what they sense, usually as a result of lesions in the *brain* (*a-*, "lack"; *gnosis-*, "knowledge" [Greek])

agoraphobia. An *anxiety disorder* characterized by an intense fear (*phobia*) of open spaces or of being in public places from which it might be difficult to escape in the event of a panic attack; usually associated with panic attacks or with a fear of losing control or of some other dreaded but indistinct consequence that might occur outside the home (cf. *social phobia*)

agreeableness. See *Big Five*

algorithm. A means of solving a problem that—if implemented correctly and appropriately—guarantees an accurate solution; generally involves successive, somewhat mechanical, repetitions of a particular strategy until the correct solution is reached; in many situations, implementation of an algorithm is either impossible or impractical as a means for solving problems (cf. *heuristics*)

alienated achievement. An alternative to the four main types of identity (cf. *foreclosure, identity achievement, identity diffusion, moratorium*), in which the individual considers the values of mainstream society to be inappropriate, or even bankrupt, and rejects identification with that society

altruism. Selfless behavior focused on helping another person or persons, or at least behavior performed out of concern for another person or persons, regardless of whether the action has positive or negative consequences for the altruist (see also *prosocial behavior*)

amacrine cells. One of three kinds of *interneuron* cells in the middle of three layers of cells in the *retina*; the amacrine cells and the *horizontal cells* provide lateral connections, which permit lateral communication with adjacent areas of the retina in the middle layer of cells (cf. *bipolar cells*; see *ganglion cells, photoreceptors*)

amnesia. Severe loss of memory, usually affecting primarily *episodic memory* (see also *dissociative amnesia*); *anterograde amnesia*—inability to recall events that occur *after* whatever trauma caused the memory loss (affects the acquisition of episodic memory but apparently not the acquisition of *procedural memory*); *infantile amnesia*—the inability to recall events that happened during early development of the *brain* (usually the first 3 to 5 years); *retrograde amnesia*—inability to recall events that occurred *before* the trauma that caused the memory loss (often, the amnesic gradually begins to recall earlier events, starting with the earliest experiences and gradually recalling events that occurred closer to the time of the trauma, perhaps eventually even recalling the traumatic episode)

amphetamine. A type of synthetic *central nervous system (CNS) stimulant* that is usually either ingested orally or injected; short-term effects include increased body temperature, heart rate, and endurance, as well as reduced appetite; psychological effects include stimulation of the release of *neurotransmitters*, such as norepinephrine and *dopamine* into brain *synapses*, as well as inhibition of *reuptake* of neurotransmitters, leading to a sense of euphoria and increased alertness, *arousal*, and motor activity; long-term effects are a reduction of *serotonin* and other neurotransmitters in the brain, thereby impairing neural communication within the brain; long-term use also leads to *tolerance* and intermittent use may lead to *sensitization*

amplitude. The objective physical *intensity* of sound or light; when sound or light energy is displayed on an oscilloscope, higher waves correspond to greater intensity; in terms of subjective *perception*, greater amplitude of light is perceived as increased *brightness* and greater amplitude of sound is perceived as increased loudness

amygdala. The portion of the *brain* that plays a role in anger and *aggression*

anal stage. A stage of *psychosexual development* that typically occurs between the ages of 2 and 4 years, during which time the child learns to derive gratification from the control over urination and especially defecation

angiograms. Essentially X-ray pictures for which the visual contrast has been enhanced by injecting special dyes into the blood vessels of the head; primarily used clinically to assess vascular diseases (diseases of the blood vessels, which may lead to strokes) and to locate particular kinds of *brain* tumors; also used experimentally as a means of determining which parts of the brain are active when people perform different kinds of listening, speaking, or movement tasks

anorexia nervosa. A pathological mental disorder in which an individual does not eat enough to avoid starvation, despite the availability of food

anterograde amnesia. See *amnesia*

antisocial behavior. Behavior that is harmful to a society or to its members

antithesis. A statement of opinion presenting an alternative view that differs from the opinion stated originally and may seem to contradict it (cf. *thesis*; see *dialectic*; see also *synthesis*)

anxiety. A generalized, diffused feeling of being threatened, despite the inability to pinpoint the source of the threat; tends to be more pervasive and long-lasting than fear; characterized by tension, nervousness, distress, or uncomfortable *arousal*

anxiety disorders. A category of psychological disorders (e.g., *generalized anxiety disorder, obsessive-compulsive disorder, panic disorder, phobia*, and *stress* disorders such as *acute stress disorder* and *posttraumatic stress disorder*) characterized primarily by feelings of *anxiety* (a mood symptom) of varying levels of intensity, excessive worry and a concentration of thoughts on worrisome phenomena (cognitive symptoms), many purposeless movements (e.g., fidgeting, pacing, motor tics, and other *motor* symptoms), and somatic symptoms associated with high *arousal* of the *autonomic nervous system* (e.g., sweating, muscle tension, high pulse and respiration rates, and high blood pressure)

aptitude. A potential ability to accomplish something, to attain a level of expertise in the performance of a task or a set of tasks, or to acquire knowledge in a given domain or set of domains

archetype. A universal, inherited human tendency to perceive and act on things in particular ways, as evidenced by the similarities among various myths, legends, religions, and even customs across cultures; the most common Jungian archetypes are *anima*—the feminine side of a man's personality, which shows tenderness, caring, compassion, and warmth toward others yet is more irrational and based on *emotions*; *animus*—the masculine side of a woman's personality, the more rational and logical side of the woman; *persona*—the part of the personality that a person shows the world and that the person is willing to share with other persons; *shadow*—the part of the personality that is viewed as frightening, hateful, or even evil, and that the individual therefore hides not only from others but also from herself or himself

arousal. A hypothetical construct representing alertness, wakefulness, and activation, caused by the activity of the *central nervous system (CNS)*

assimilation (as a cognitive process). The process of adapting to new information that conflicts with existing *schemas* by changing the new information to fit the existing schemas, thereby reestablishing cognitive equilibrium (cf. *accommodation;* see also *equilibration*)

association areas. Regions of the cerebral lobes that are not part of the sensory (visual, auditory, somatosensory) or motor cortices, believed to connect (associate) the activity of the sensory and motor cortices

associationism. A school of psychological thought that examines how events or ideas can become associated with one another in the mind, thereby resulting in a form of *learning*

asylum. Institution intended for housing mentally ill persons, sometimes also involving some form of rehabilitative treatment for the residents

asymptote. The most stable level of *response* associated with a psychological phenomenon, usually graphed as a curve on which the maximum level of stability can be observed as the region of response that shows the least variation; for learning curves, the most stable level of response appears at the high point of the curve; for habituation, the asymptote appears at a low point on the curve; for other psychological phenomena, the most stable level of response may appear at other locations of the curve

attachment. A strong and relatively long-lasting emotional tie between two humans

attention. The active cognitive processing of a limited amount of information from the vast amount of information available through the senses, in memory and through cognitive processes; focus on a small subset of available *stimuli*

attention-deficit hyperactivity disorder (ADHD). A condition characterized by inattention, impulsiveness, and hyperactivity that are inappropriate for the age of the child

attitude. A learned (not inherited), stable (not volatile), and relatively enduring (not transitory) evaluation (positive or negative judgment) of a person, object, or idea that can affect an individual's behavior

attribution. An explanation that points to the cause of a person's behavior, including the behavior of the individual devising the explanation (see *personal attribution, situational attribution*)

attribution theory. A theory regarding the way in which people point to the causes of a person's behavior, including the behavior of the individual devising the explanation (see *attribution;* see also *actor–observer effect, fundamental attribution error, self-handicapping*)

authoritarian parents. Mothers and fathers who exhibit a style of parenting in which they tend to be firm, punitive, and generally unsympathetic to their children, who highlight their own authority, who hold exacting standards for and prize obedience in their children, and who show little praise toward and attachment to their children (cf. *permissive parents, authoritative parents*)

authoritative parents. Mothers and fathers who exhibit a style of parenting in which they tend to encourage and support responsibility and reasoning in their children, explain their reasoning for what they do, and establish firm limits within which they encourage children to be independent and which they enforce firmly but with understanding (cf. *authoritarian parents, permissive parents*)

autonomic nervous system. The part of the *peripheral nervous system* that controls movement of nonskeletal muscles (the heart muscle and the smooth muscles), over which people have little or no voluntary control or even conscious awareness (*autonomic* means "self-regulating"; cf. *somatic nervous system*)

availability. The existing storage of given information in long-term memory, without which it would be impossible to retrieve the information, and with which it is possible to retrieve the information if appropriate *retrieval* strategies can be implemented (cf. *accessibility*)

availability heuristic. An intuitive strategy for making judgments or inferences, or for solving problems, on the basis of the ease with which particular examples or ideas may be called to mind, without necessarily considering the degree to which the particular examples or ideas are relevant to or suitable for the given context (see *heuristic*)

aversion therapy. A behavioristic *counterconditioning* technique in which the client learns to experience negative feelings in the presence of a *stimulus* that is considered inappropriately attractive, with the aim that the client will eventually learn to feel repelled by the stimulus

aversive conditioning. A form of *operant conditioning* in which the subject is encouraged to avoid a particular behavior or setting as a consequence of *punishment* in association with the given behavior or setting (see *avoidance learning*)

avoidance learning. A form of *operant conditioning* in which the subject learns to refrain from a particular behavior or to keep away from a particular *stimulus* as a result of *aversive conditioning*

avoidant attachment pattern. Pattern in which a child generally ignores the mother while she is present and shows minimal distress when the mother leaves; one of three major attachment patterns observed in the *strange situation* (cf. *resistant attachment pattern, secure attachment pattern*)

axon. The long, thin, tubular part of the *neuron* that responds to information received by the *dendrites* and some of the neuron, either ignoring or transmitting the information through the neuron until it can be transmitted to other neurons through the release of chemical substances by the *axon's* terminal buttons

babbling. A preferential production of distinct phonemes characteristic of the babbler's own *language* (cf. *cooing*)

balance theory. A proposed means of attaining *cognitive consistency* regarding friendships, in which it is suggested that people attempt to maintain a sense of give and take (reciprocity) in a relationship, and that people tend to be drawn to friends whose attitudes toward other people are similar to their own (similarity)

bar graph. One of many types of graphic displays of numerical information, in which items that reflect larger numerical values are represented as longer bars on the graph (cf. *line graph*)

barbiturate. An antianxiety drug prescribed to reduce *anxiety* through physiological inhibition of *arousal* (high dosages can even induce sleep); may lead to grogginess that may impair functioning in situations requiring alertness; chronic use leads to *tolerance* and to physiological *addiction*, and high doses can lead to respiratory failure (see also *central nervous system (CNS) depressant*)

basal ganglia. A set of structures close to the *thalamus* and *hypothalamus*; involved in control of movements as well as in judgments and decisions that require minimal thought

base rate. The prevalence of an event or characteristic within its population of events or characteristics (cf. *representativeness heuristic*)

basic anxiety. A feeling of isolation and helplessness in a world conceived as being potentially hostile, due to the competitiveness of modern culture

basilar membrane. One of the membranes that separates the fluid-filled canals of the *cochlea*; the physiological structure on which the *hair cells* (auditory receptors) are arranged; vibrations from the *stapes* stimulate the hair cells on the membrane in various locations in association with differing sound frequencies

behavior therapy. A collection of techniques (see *counterconditioning, extinction procedure, modeling*) that are based at least partly on the principles of *classical conditioning* or *operant conditioning*, or on observational learning; usually involves short-term treatment in which the therapist directs the patient in techniques that focus exclusively on relieving *symptoms* and on changes in behavior, unconcerned with whether patients may gain *insights* or other nonbehavioral benefits of treatment

behavioral contracting. A behavioristic psychotherapeutic technique in which the therapist and the client draw up a contract that clearly specifies the responsibilities and behavioral expectations of each party, and that obligates both parties to live up to the terms of the contract

behavioral genetics. A branch of psychology that attempts to account for behavior (and often particular psychological characteristics and phenomena, such as *intelligence*) by attributing behavior in part to the influence of particular combinations of *genes*; often viewed as a marriage of psychology and genetics (see *genetics*)

behavioral medicine. A psychological approach to medicine that focuses on the use of behavioral techniques to help people modify health-related problems, such as heavy smoking or overeating

behaviorism. A school of psychology that focuses entirely on the association between an observed *stimulus* and an observed *response* and therefore may be viewed as an extreme extension of *associationism*

Big Five. The five key characteristics that are often described by various theorists as a useful way to organize and describe individual differences in *personality*: *agreeableness*—characterized by a pleasant disposition, a charitable nature, empathy toward others, and friendliness; *conscientiousness*—characterized by reliability, hard work, punctuality, and a concern with doing things right; *extroversion*—characterized by sociability, expansiveness, liveliness, an orientation toward having fun, and an interest in interacting with other people; *neuroticism*—characterized by nervousness, emotional instability, moodiness, tension, irritability, and frequent tendency to worry (cf. *psychoticism*); *openness*—characterized by imagination, intelligence, curiosity, and aesthetic sensitivity

binocular convergence. Use of two eyes in coordination to perceive *depth*

binocular depth cues. One of the two chief means of judging the distances of visible objects, based on the two different angles from which each eye views a scene, which leads to a disparity of viewing angles that provides information about *depth* (*bi-*, "two"; *ocular*, pertaining to the eye; see *binocular disparity*; cf. *monocular depth cues*)

binocular disparity. The modest discrepancy in the viewpoint of each eye due to the slightly different positions of each eye, which leads to slightly different sets of sensory information going to the *brain* from each of the two optic nerves; in the brain, the information is integrated in order to make determinations about *depth* as well as height and width (see *binocular depth cues*)

biological psychology. A branch of psychology that attempts to understand behavior through the careful study of anatomy and physiology, especially of the *brain* (often considered synonymous with *physiological psychology* and *neuropsychology*)

biological traits. See *central traits*

biomedical model. A *paradigm* for health care in which the focus is on the elimination of *pathogens* that cause diseases; serves as a basis for treating and often for curing illnesses, with little concern for preventive health practices, for health practices that promote wellness, or for psychological factors that may contribute to illness, recovery, or wellness

biopsychosocial model. A *paradigm* for health care in which the focus is on an understanding of the various psychological, social, and biological factors that contribute to illness, prevention of illness, recovery from illness, and promotion of wellness

bipolar cells. One of three kinds of *interneuron* cells in the middle of three layers of cells in the *retina*; provide vertical connections that permit communication between the *ganglion cells* in the first (outermost) layer of the retina and the *photoreceptors* in the third (innermost) of the three layers of retinal cells (cf. *amacrine cells, horizontal cells*)

bipolar disorder. A mental illness characterized by alternating extremes of depression and *mania* (also termed *manic-depressive disorder*)

bisexual. A person whose sexual orientation may be both heterosexual and homosexual (see *homosexuality*)

blind spot. The small area on the *retina* where the optic nerve leaves the eye, pushing aside *photoreceptors* to exit the eye

blindsight. A phenomenon in which individuals can see something but are not aware of what they are seeing

blocking effect. The failure of a second *unconditioned stimulus* to become *classically conditioned* because the first unconditioned stimulus blocks the effectiveness of the second one in eliciting a *conditioned response* (see *classical conditioning*)

bottom-up approach. The view of *perception* or other cognitive processes as originating with simple or low-level processes

bounded rationality. The limits within which humans demonstrate reasoned behavior (see also *satisficing*)

brain. The organ of the body encased in the skull that most directly controls thoughts, *emotions*, and *motivations*, as well as *motor* responses, and that responds to information it receives from elsewhere in the body, such as through sensory *receptors*

brain stem. The portion of the *brain* that comprises the *thalamus* and *hypothal-*

amus, the *midbrain*, and the *hindbrain*, and that connects the rest of the brain to the *spinal cord;* essential to the independent functioning of fundamental physiological processes (without which a physician will certify that the individual is brain dead)

brightness. The psychological *perception* of light *intensity*, rather than the actual physical quantity of light intensity, based on light wave *amplitude*

Broca's area. A structure in the left *frontal lobe* of the *brain;* involved in the movements of the mouth needed for speech and the ability to speak grammatically

bystander effect. A decreased likelihood that an individual will help a person or persons in distress, due to the actual or implied presence of other potential helpers (see *prosocial behavior*)

caffeine. A mild *central nervous system (CNS) stimulant*

cardinal trait. A single personality *trait* that is so salient in an individual's personality and so dominant in the person's behavior that almost everything the person does somehow relates back to this trait; although many people do not have cardinal traits, all people do have *central traits* and *secondary traits*

case study. Intensive investigation of a single individual or set of individuals that is used as a basis for drawing general conclusions about the behavior of the individual and perhaps about other persons as well (cf. *experiment, naturalistic observation, survey, test*)

categorical clustering. See *mnemonic devices*

cathartic method. A psychotherapeutic technique associated with psychodynamic treatments, in which the patient is encouraged to reveal and discuss the painful origins of a psychological problem as a means of purging the problem from the patient's mental life

causal inference. A conclusion regarding one or more antecedents that are believed to have led to a given consequence; although a goal of science is to draw conclusions about causality, the complex interactions of multiple variables impinging on a particular phenomenon make it difficult to assert such conclusions with certainty, so scientists generally infer causality in terms of the relative likeli-

hood that a particular variable was crucial in causing a particular phenomenon to occur (see also *inductive reasoning*)

central nervous system (CNS). The *brain* (encased in the skull) and the *spinal cord* (encased in the spinal column), including all of the *neurons*

central nervous system (CNS) depressant. A drug (e.g., alcohol and *sedatives*) that slows the operation of the *CNS* and is often prescribed in low doses to reduce *anxiety* and in relatively higher doses to combat *insomnia* (see *barbiturate, tranquilizer;* cf. *narcotic;* see also *central nervous system (CNS) stimulant*)

central nervous system (CNS) stimulant. A drug (e.g., *caffeine, amphetamines, cocaine,* and nicotine—found in tobacco) that arouses and excites the *CNS,* either by stimulating the heart or by inhibiting the actions of natural compounds that depress brain activity (in other words, it acts as a "double-negative" on brain stimulation); short-term effects of relatively low doses include increased stamina and alertness, reduced appetite, and exuberant euphoria; higher doses may cause anxiety and irritability; problems with *tolerance* and *addiction* are linked with long-term use, and problems with *sensitization* are tied to intermittent use (cf. *central nervous system (CNS) depressant*)

central route to persuasion. One of two routes to persuasion (cf. *peripheral route to persuasion*), which emphasizes thoughtful arguments related to the issue about which an *attitude* is being formed; most effective when the recipient is both motivated to think about the issue and able to do so

central tendency. The value (or values) that most commonly typifies an entire set of values (see *mean, median, mode*)

central traits of personality. The 5 to 10 most salient traits in a person's disposition, affecting much of the person's behavior (cf. *cardinal trait, secondary traits*)

cerebellum. The part of the *brain* (*cerebellum,* "little brain" [Latin]) that controls bodily coordination, balance, and muscle tone; when damaged, subsequent movement becomes jerky and disjointed; located in the *hindbrain*

cerebral cortex. (plural: *cortices*) A highly convoluted 2-millimeter layer (give or take a millimeter) on the surface

of the *brain* that forms part of the *forebrain;* responsible for most high-level cognitive processes, such as planning and using *language*

cerebral hemispheres. The two rounded halves of the *brain*, on the surface of which is the *cerebral cortex* and inside which are the other structures of the brain (*hemi-,* "half"; *spherical,* "globe-shaped")

cerebrospinal fluid. The clear, colorless fluid that circulates constantly throughout the *brain* and *spinal cord,* buffering them from shocks and minor traumas (injuries) and possibly helping in the elimination of waste products from the *central nervous system*

cerebrum. The largest part of the *brain,* comprising 85% of its total weight; the unmyelinated outer part gives the cerebrum its gray color

characteristic features. The qualities that describe a prototypical model of a word (or concept) and thereby serve as the basis for the meaning of the word, according to *prototype theory;* these qualities would characterize many or most of the instances of the word but not necessarily all instances (cf. *defining features*)

child-directed speech. The characteristic form of speech that adults tend to use when speaking with infants and young children; usually involves a higher pitch, exaggerated vocal inflections (i.e., more extreme raising and lowering of pitch and volume), and simpler sentence constructions; generally more effective than normal speech in gaining and keeping the attention of infants and young children (formerly termed *motherese*)

chromosome. Each of a pair of rod-shaped bodies that contain innumerable *genes,* composed largely of *deoxyribonucleic acid (DNA);* humans have 23 chromosomal pairs

chronic (symptom or illness). Recurrent, constant, or very long in duration (cf. *acute*)

chronic pain. Recurrent or constant long-term (lasting at least 6 months or longer) discomfort (of any level of intensity), usually associated with tissue damage (cf. *acute pain*)

chunk. A collection of separate items into a single clump that can be more readily stored in *memory* and recalled later than is likely to occur if the various discrete items are stored and later retrieved as separate entities

circadian rhythm. The usual sleeping–waking pattern that corresponds roughly to the cycle of darkness and light associated with a single day (*circa*, "around"; *dies*, "day" [Latin]); many physiological changes (e.g., body temperature and hormone levels) are associated with this daily rhythmic pattern

classical conditioning. A *learning* process whereby an originally neutral *stimulus* (see *conditioned stimulus, CS*) comes to be associated with a stimulus (see *unconditioned stimulus, US*) that already produces a particular physiological or emotional *response* (see *unconditioned response, UR*), such that once the conditioning takes place, the physiological or emotional response (see *conditioned response, CR*) occurs as a direct result of the stimulus that was originally neutral (the CS), even in the absence of the other stimulus (the US); also termed *classically conditioned learning* (see *delay conditioning, temporal conditioning, trace conditioning*)

classically conditioned learning. See *classical conditioning*

client-centered therapy. A form of humanistic therapy that assumes that the client's construction of reality provides the basis for understanding the client; characterized by nondirective interactions (thereby allowing the client to direct the course of therapy), genuineness (thereby offering honest communication with the client, rather than communications calculated to create a particular effect in the client), unconditional positive regard for the client (thereby encouraging the client to discontinue self-imposed conditions for positive self-regard), and accurate empathic understanding of the client (thereby helping the client to explore and to clarify her or his own worldview)

clinical. Describing a branch of psychology oriented toward the treatment of clients who require therapeutic guidance by psychologists and psychiatrists

clinical interview. The most widely used clinical assessment technique; involves a meeting between the person who is seeking psychological assistance and a clinician who tries to obtain information from the client in order to diagnose the client's need for psychotherapeutic treatment (cf. *naturalistic observation, objective personality test, projective test*)

cocaine. A powerful *central nervous system (CNS) stimulant*

cochlea. The coiled and channeled main structure of the inner ear, which contains three fluid-filled canals that run along its entire convoluted length; the fluid-filled canals are separated by membranes, one of which is the *basilar membrane*, on which thousands of *hair cells* (auditory *receptors*) are arranged and are stimulated by the vibration of the *stapes*

cocktail party phenomenon. The process of tracking one conversation in the face of the distraction of other conversations; a phenomenon often experienced at cocktail parties

cognitive consistency. A match between the cognitions (thoughts) and the behaviors of a person, as perceived by the person who is thinking and behaving (cf. *cognitive dissonance;* see *self-perception theory*)

cognitive development. The study of how mental skills build and change with increasing physiological maturity and experience

cognitive dissonance. A person's disquieting perception of a mismatch between her or his attitudes (cognitions) and her or his behavior (cf. *cognitive consistency, self-perception theory*)

cognitive-evolutionary theory. The theory that *emotions* help an organism adapt to its own changing needs in changing circumstances

cognitive map. An internal mental representation of a pattern (e.g., a maze or a hierarchy) or an abstraction (e.g., a concept)

cognitive theorists. Scientists who seek to understand how individuals perform mental tasks, particularly as they solve challenging problems

cognitive therapy. *Psychotherapy* involving a cognitivistic approach to psychological problems, such as a focus on developing adaptive, rather than maladaptive, thoughts and thought processes

cognitivism. A school of psychology that underscores the importance of cognition as a basis for understanding much of human behavior

cohort effects. The distinctive effects of a particular group of participants who have lived through a particular time in history, in which they experienced particular educational systems, opportunities, and values, which may affect

findings based on *cross-sectional studies* (cf. *longitudinal study*)

cold fibers. Bundles of *neurons* that respond to cooling of the skin by increasing their rate of firing relative to the rate at which they fire when at rest (cf. *warm fibers*)

collective unconscious. A Jungian construct involving an aspect of the unconscious that contains memories and behavioral predispositions that all people have inherited from common ancestors in the distant human past (cf. *personal unconscious*)

commitment. One of three basic components of love, according to the *triangular theory of love* (cf. *intimacy, passion*); the decision to maintain a relationship over the long term

complex cells. One of the key physiological structures described by the *feature-detector approach* to form *perception*, according to which any members of a given group of *simple cells* may prompt the complex cell to fire in response to lines of particular orientations anywhere in the receptive field for the given complex cell; the particular type of light–dark contrasts of a line segment appear not to affect the firing of the complex cell as long as the line segment demonstrates the appropriate orientation; however, for some complex cells, the length of the line segments may also play a role in whether the cells fire

complexes. Clusters of independently functioning, emotionally tinged unconscious thoughts that may be found within the Jungian construct of the *personal unconscious*

compliance. The modification of behavior as a result of a request by another person or by other persons, which may involve taking an action, refraining from an action, or tailoring an action to suit another person or persons (cf. *conformity, obedience*); several techniques are often used: *door in the face*—the compliance-seeker makes an outlandishly large request that is almost certain to be rejected, in the hope of getting the "target" (person whose compliance is being sought) of such efforts to accede to a more reasonable but perhaps still quite large request; *foot in the door*—the compliance-seeker asks for compliance with a relatively small request, which is designed to "soften up" the target for a big request; *hard to get*—the compliance-seeker convinces the target that whatever the compliance-seeker is offering (or trying to get rid of) is very difficult to obtain; *justification*—the compliance-seeker justifies the request for compliance (often effective even when the justification is astonishingly weak); *low-balling*—the compliance-seeker gets the target to comply and to commit to a deal under misleadingly favorable circumstances, and then adds hidden costs or reveals hidden drawbacks only after obtaining a commitment to comply; *reciprocity*—the compliance-seeker appears to be giving something to the target, thereby obligating the target to give something in return, based on the notion that people should not receive things without giving things of comparable value in return; *that's not all*—the compliance-seeker offers something at a high price and then, before the target has a chance to respond, throws in something else to sweeten the deal (or offers a discounted price on the product or service), thereby enticing the target to buy the offered product or service

componental theory.   One of two primary theories of *semantics*, which claims that the meaning of a word (or concept) can be understood by disassembling the word into a set of *defining features*, which are essential elements of meaning that are singly necessary and jointly sufficient to define the word; that is, each defining feature is an essential element of the meaning of a concept, and the combination of those defining features uniquely defines the concept (also termed *definitional theory*; cf. *prototype theory, characteristic features*)

compulsion.   An irresistible impulse to perform a relatively meaningless act repeatedly and in a stereotypical fashion; associated with feelings of *anxiety*, not joy, and often associated with *obsessions* (see also *obsessive–compulsive anxiety disorder*)

computerized axial tomogram (CAT).   A highly sophisticated X ray-based technique that produces pictures (*-gram*, "drawing" or "recording") of cross-sectional slices (*tomo-*, "slice" or "cut" [Greek]) of the living brain, derived from computer analysis of X rays that pass through the brain at various angles around a central axis in the brain (often termed *CAT scan*); usually used clinically to detect blood clots, tumors, or brain diseases, but also used experimentally to study how particular types and locations

of brain damage (lesions) affect people's behavior

concentrative meditation.   A form of contemplation in which the meditator focuses on an object or thought and attempts to remove all else from *consciousness* (see *meditation*)

concept.   Idea to which various characteristics may be attached and to which other ideas may be connected; may be used to describe a highly abstract idea or a concrete one

concrete operations.   A stage of *cognitive development* in Piaget's theory of development, in which the individual can engage in mental manipulations of internal representations of tangible (concrete) objects (cf. *formal–operational stage, preoperational stage, sensorimotor stage*)

condition (as an aspect of experimental design).   A situation in an *experiment* in which a group of participants experience a carefully prescribed set of circumstances (see *control condition, experiment, experimental condition*)

conditioned emotional responses. *Classically conditioned* feelings (*emotions*) that an individual experiences in association with particular *stimulus* events

conditioned response (CR).   A learned (*classically conditioned*) pattern of behavior that occurs in association with a *stimulus* that was not associated with this pattern of behavior prior to *learning*

conditioned stimulus (CS).   A *stimulus* that initially does not lead to a particular physiological or emotional *response*, but that eventually does lead to the particular response, as a result of *classical conditioning*

conduct disorders.   Conditions characterized by habitual misbehavior, such as stealing, skipping school, destroying property, fighting, being cruel to animals and to other people, and lying

cones.   One of the two kinds of *photoreceptors* in the eye; less numerous, shorter, thicker, and more highly concentrated in the foveal region of the *retina* than in the periphery of the retina than are *rods* (the other type of photoreceptor); virtually nonfunctional in dim light, but highly effective in bright light, and essential to color vision (see *fovea*)

confirmation bias.   The human tendency to seek ways in which to confirm rather than to refute existing beliefs

conformity.   The modification of behavior in order to bring it in line with the norms of the social group; may involve taking an action, refraining from an action, or tailoring an action to suit the social group (cf. *compliance, obedience*); also, the tendency to give up personal individuality and independent decision making in order to become like others and to share in the power of a collectivity

conscientiousness.   See *Big Five*

consciousness.   The complex phenomenon of evaluating the environment and then filtering that information through the mind, with awareness of doing so; may be viewed as the mental reality created in order to adapt to the world

constructive memory.   The psychological phenomenon in which an individual actually builds memories, based on prior experience and expectations, such that existing *schemas* may affect the way in which new information is stored in *memory* (cf. *reconstructive memory*)

contact hypothesis.   The unsubstantiated assumption that *prejudice* will be reduced simply as a result of direct contact between social groups that have prejudicial attitudes toward each other, without any regard to the context in which such contact occurs

context effects.   The influences of the surrounding environment on cognition, particularly as applied to the visual *perception* of forms

contextualist.   A psychologist who theorizes about a psychological phenomenon (e.g., *intelligence*) strictly in terms of the context in which an individual is observed, and who suggests that the phenomenon cannot be understood—let alone measured—outside the real-world context of the individual; particularly, a theorist who studies how intelligence relates to the external world

contingency.   The dependent relationship between the occurrence of an *unconditioned stimulus* and the occurrence of a *conditioned stimulus* (cf. *temporal contiguity*)

continuous reinforcement.   A pattern of *operant conditioning* in which reinforcement always and invariably follows a particular *operant* behavior (cf. *partial reinforcement*)

contour.   The features of a surface that permit differentiation of one surface from another (e.g., convexity or concavity)

contralateral. Occurring or appearing on the opposite side (*contra-*, "opposite"; *lateral*, "side"); often used for describing the crossed pattern of sensory and motor connections between the physiological structures of the body and those of the brain (cf. *ipsilateral*)

control. Power or authority over something; the ability to manage or manipulate; one of four goals of psychological research (the other three are *description*, *explanation*, and *prediction*)

control condition. A situation in which a group of experimental participants experience a carefully prescribed set of circumstances that are almost identical to the *experimental condition* but that do not involve the *independent variable* being manipulated in the experimental treatment condition

control-enhancing interventions. Methods for increasing patients' sense of control, thereby enhancing their ability to respond appropriately to illness and eventually to cope effectively with illness; such methods may include informing patients about the origins of their illness, the symptoms and other consequences of their illness, and the strategies they may use for promoting their recovery from illness or at least for minimizing the negative consequences of their illness

controlled experimental design. A plan for conducting a study in which the experimenter carefully manipulates or controls one or more *independent variables* in order to see the effect on the *dependent variable* or variables; although experimental control is usually the ideal means by which to study cause-and-effect relationships, for many phenomena, such control is either impossible or highly impractical, so other means of study must be used instead (cf. *correlational design*, *quasi-experimental design*)

controlling. The individual plans what to do, based on the information received from the monitoring process; one of the two main purposes of *consciousness* (cf. *monitoring*)

conventional morality. A phase of moral development in which moral reasoning is guided by mutual interpersonal expectations (e.g., to be good and to show good motives) and by interpersonal conformity (e.g., obeying rules and showing respect for authority); societal rules have become internalized, and the individual conforms because it is the right thing to do

convergent thinking. A form of *critical thinking* that involves focusing in (converging toward) on one idea from an assortment of possible ideas (cf. *divergent thinking*)

cooing. Oral expression that explores the production of all the phones that humans can possibly produce; precedes *babbling*, which precedes language articulation

coping. The process of trying to manage the internal and external challenges posed by a troublesome situation; sometimes conceptualized in terms of emotion-focused coping, which involves handling internal emotional reactions to the situation, and problem-focused coping, which involves the specific strategies used for confronting and resolving the problematic situation

cornea. On the eye, the clear dome-shaped window that forms a specialized region of the sclera (the external rubbery layer that holds in the gelatinous substance of the eye), through which light passes and which serves primarily as a curved exterior surface that gathers and focuses the entering light, making gross adjustments of the curvature in order to focus the image relatively well (cf. *lens*)

corpus callosum. A dense aggregate of nerve fibers (*corpus*, "body"; *callosum*, "dense") that connects the two cerebral hemispheres, thereby allowing easy transmission of information between the two hemispheres

correct rejection. One of the four possible combinations of *stimulus* and *response*, according to *signal-detection theory (SDT)* (cf. *false alarm*, *hit*, *miss*); the accurate recognition that a signal stimulus was not detected

correlation. The statistical relationship between two attributes (characteristics of the subjects, of a setting, or of a situation), expressed as a number on a scale that ranges from −1 (a *negative correlation*) to 0 (no correlation) to +1 (a *positive correlation*) (see also *correlational design*)

correlation coefficient. A measure of statistical association that ranges from −1 (perfect inverse relationship) to 0 (no relation) to +1 (perfect positive relationship)

correlational design. A plan for conducting a study in which the researchers merely observe the degree of association between two (or more) attributes that already occur naturally in the group(s) under study, and researchers do not directly manipulate the variables (cf. *controlled experimental design*, *quasi-experimental design*)

correlational methods. Methods to assess the degree of relationship between two or more variables or attributes

counterconditioning. A technique of *behavioral therapy* (or experimentation) in which the positive association between a given *unconditioned stimulus (US)* and a given *conditioned stimulus (CS)* is replaced with a negative association by substituting a new US that has a different (and negative) *unconditioned response (UR)*, and in which the alternative response is incompatible with the initial response (see *classical conditioning*; see also *aversion therapy*, *systematic desensitization*)

countertransference. An unwanted phenomenon sometimes arising during psychodynamic therapy, in which the therapist projects onto the patient the therapist's own feelings (cf. *transference*)

CR. See *conditioned response*

creativity. The process of producing something that is both original and valuable; one of the fundamental processes of *thinking* (cf. *judgment and decision making*, *problem solving*, *reasoning*)

credibility. Believability

critical period. A brief period of rapid development, during which the organism is preprogrammed for *learning* to take place, given adequate environmental support for the learning, and after which learning is less likely to occur

critical thinking. The conscious direction of mental processes toward representing and processing information, usually in order to find thoughtful solutions to problems (see *thinking*; see also *convergent thinking*, *divergent thinking*, *synthesis*)

cross-sectional study. Research that investigates a diverse sampling of persons of various ages at a given time (cf. *longitudinal study*; see also *cohort effects*)

crystallized intelligence. One of two major subfactors of general *intelligence*; represents the accumulation of knowledge over the life span of the individual;

may be measured by tests in areas such as vocabulary, general information, and achievement (cf. *fluid intelligence*)

CS. See *conditioned stimulus*

cued recall. Recall for which a cue, prompt, or other reminder is provided

culture-fair test. Assessment that is equally appropriate for members of all cultures and that comprises items that are equally fair to members of all cultures; it is difficult, if not impossible, to attain (cf. *culture-relevant test*)

culture-relevant test. Assessment that employs skills and knowledge that relate to the cultural experiences of the test-takers by using content and procedures that are relatively appropriate to the cultural context of the test-takers, although the test-makers' definitions of competent performance that demonstrates the hypothetical construct (e.g., intelligence) may differ from the definitions of the test-takers (cf. *culture-fair test*)

cumulative frequency. The total number of instances of values up to a given level (i.e., at or below a given level)

dark adaptation. The unconscious physiological response to a reduction of light intensity in the environment, characterized by an increase in *pupil* area by a factor of about 16, and an increase in visual sensitivity to light by a factor of as much as 100,000; usually takes about 30–40 minutes for full dark adaptation to occur (cf. *light adaptation*)

daydreaming. A state of consciousness somewhere between waking and sleeping that permits a shift in the focus of conscious processing toward internal thoughts and images and away from external events; useful in cognitive processes that involve the generation of creative ideas, but disruptive in cognitive processes that require focused attention on environmental events

decay. The phenomenon of *memory* by which simply the passage of time leads to forgetting

decay theory. The assertion that information is forgotten because it gradually disappears over time, rather than because the information is displaced by other information (cf. *interference theory*)

declarative memory. A recognition and understanding of factual information ("knowing that" *not* "knowing how"; cf. *procedural memory*)

deductive reasoning. The process of drawing conclusions from evidence involving one or more general *premises* regarding what is known, to reach a logically certain specific conclusion (see *reasoning, syllogism*; cf. *inductive reasoning*)

deep-structure level. A level of syntactical analysis at which the underlying meanings (*deep structures*) of a sentence may be derived from a given surface structure and from which a given deep structure may be viewed as providing the basis for deriving various surface structures; a given deep structure may be expressed in more than one surface structure, and a given surface structure may serve as the basis for deriving more than one deep structure; takes into account the meanings derived from sentence structure (see *transformational grammar*)

defense mechanisms. Methods for protecting the *ego* from *anxiety* associated with the conflicting urges and prohibitions of the *id* and the *superego*; eight main defense mechanisms are denial, displacement, projection, rationalization, reaction formation, regression, repression, and sublimation

defining features. A set of component characteristics, each of which is an essential element of a given *concept*, and which together compose the properties that uniquely define the concept, according to *componential theory* (cf. *characteristic features, prototype theory*)

deindividuation. A loss of a sense of individual identity, associated with a reduction of internal constraints against socially unacceptable behavior

delay conditioning. A *paradigm* for *classical conditioning*, in which there is a long delay between the onset of the CS and the onset of the US (cf. *trace conditioning*)

delusion. Distorted thought process characterized by an erroneous belief that persists despite strong evidence to the contrary (e.g., *delusions of persecution* involve the belief that others are scheming to harm the person in some manner; *delusions of reference* involve the belief that particular chance events or appearances have special significance; *delusions of identity* involve the person's belief that she or he is somebody else, usually someone famous; other delusions involve the belief that persons can insert thoughts into the minds of others or can transmit their thoughts nonverbally) (cf. *illusion*)

dendrites. Parts of the *neuron* at the end of the *soma*; primary structures for receiving communications from other cells via distinctive *receptors* on their external membranes, although some communications are also received by the soma (from the Greek word for "trees," which the multibranched dendrites resemble)

deoxyribonucleic acid (DNA). The physiological material that provides the mechanism for transmission of genetic information (see also *chromosomes, genes*)

dependent variable. The outcome response or attribute that varies as a consequence of variation in one or more independent variables (cf. *independent variable*)

depth. As applied to *perception*: the perceived distance of something from the body of the perceiver (see *monocular depth cues, binocular depth cues*)

description. A goal of science in which the scientist characterizes what and how people think, feel, or act in response to various kinds of situations (other goals are *explanation, prediction,* and perhaps even *control* of phenomena)

descriptive grammar. See *grammar*

descriptive statistic. Numerical analysis that summarizes quantitative information about a *population*

design (of experiments). A way in which a given set of experimental variables are chosen and interrelated, as well as a plan for selecting and assigning participants to experimental and control conditions

detection. Active, usually conscious, sensing of a *stimulus*, influenced by an individual's threshold for a given sense and by confounding sensory stimuli in the surrounding environment

determinism. The belief that people's behavior is ruled by forces over which we have little or no control

development. Qualitative changes in complexity, often accompanied by quantitative increases in size or amount (cf. *growth*)

developmental psychologists. Psychologists who study the differences and similarities among people of different ages, as well as the qualitative and quantitative psychological changes that occur across the life span

deviation IQs. A means of determining intelligence-test scores, based on deviations from an average score, calculated such that the normative equivalent for the *median* score is 100, about 68% of the scores are computed to fall between 85 and 115, and about 95% of the scores fall between 70 and 130; not, strictly speaking, IQs, because no quotient is involved (cf. *mental age, ratio IQ*)

dialectic. A continuing intellectual dialogue in which thinkers strive for increased understanding, first by formulating an initial *thesis*, then by considering an *antithesis* to the initial view, and finally by integrating the most insightful and well-founded aspects of each view to form a *synthesis*; because ultimate truth and understanding are elusive, the dialogue never ends, and the synthesis view then serves as a new thesis for which a new antithesis may be posited, and so on

dialectical thinking. A form of *thinking* that characterizes a stage of mental operations hypothesized to follow the Piagetian stage of *formal operations*; such thinking recognizes that humans seldom find final, correct answers to the important questions in life, but rather pass through a progression of beliefs comprising some kind of *thesis*, a subsequent *antithesis*, and then a *synthesis*, which then serves as the new thesis for the continuing evolution of thought (see *dialectic;* cf. *postformal thinking*)

diathesis-stress theory. According to this theory, people have differential genetic vulnerability to particular psychological disorders. The likelihood that people will develop these disorders increases as they are exposed to increasing amounts of *stress*. The disorder to which the person is vulnerable then develops if the person experiences so much stress that he or she is unable to cope with the environment.

difference threshold. See *just noticeable difference*

differentiation theory. A theory of emotional development that asserts that humans are born in a generalized state of *arousal* that becomes differentiated into many *emotions*

diffusion of responsibility. An implied reduction of personal responsibility to take action due to the presence of other persons, particularly in considering how to respond to a crisis (see also *bystander effect*)

disconfirm. Show that a particular *hypothesis* is not supported by data

discourse. The most comprehensive level of linguistic analysis, which encompasses *language* use at the level beyond the sentence, such as in conversation, in paragraphs, articles, and chapters, and entire books (cf. *semantics, syntax*)

discrete-emotions theory. A theory of emotional development that asserts that the human neural system is innately predisposed to feel various discrete *emotions*, given the appropriate situation in which to express those emotions

discrimination. The ability to ascertain the difference between one *stimulus* and another (see *stimulus discrimination;* cf. *stimulus generalization*)

dissociative amnesia. A *dissociative disorder* characterized by a sudden loss of *declarative memory* (e.g, difficulty or inability in recalling important personal details) and usually affecting the recollection of the events that took place during and immediately after the stressful event (see also *acute stress disorder*), but usually not affecting *procedural memory;* duration of the *amnesia* is variable (anywhere from several hours to several years), although recovery of the lost information is usually as rapid as was the loss of the information, after which the episode typically ends and the memory loss is not repeated

dissociative disorder. Disorder characterized by an alteration in the normally integrative functions of consciousness and identity, usually in response to a highly stressful life experience (see *dissociative amnesia, dissociative fugue, dissociative identity disorder*)

dissociative fugue. A *dissociative disorder* in which a person responds to severe *stress* by starting a whole new life and experiencing total *amnesia* about the past; the person moves to a new place, assumes a new identity, takes a new job, and behaves as though she or he were a completely new person, perhaps even with a new *personality;* duration of the fugue state is variable, but when recovery occurs it is usually total, and the individual fully remembers her or his life prior to the fugue state but completely forgets the events that took place during the fugue state

dissociative identity disorder. (Formerly termed *multiple personality disorder*) A *dissociative disorder* that typically arises as a result of extreme early trauma—usually, severe child abuse—and that is

characterized by the occurrence of two or more individual identities (*personalities*) within the same individual, in which each identity is relatively independent of any others, has a stable life of its own, and occasionally takes full control of the person's behavior (some psychologists question whether this disorder actually exists)

distraction–conflict theory. A view of *social facilitation* and social interference in which it is held that the effect of the presence of others is due not to their mere presence, or even to evaluation apprehension, but rather to the distracting effect of having other people around

distributed learning. An apportionment of time spent learning a body of information by spacing the total time over various sessions, rather than consolidating the total time in a single session; generally leads to more learning than does *massed learning*

divergent production. Generation of a diverse assortment of appropriate responses to a problem, question, or task; often considered an aspect of *creativity* (see also *divergent thinking*)

divergent thinking. A form of *critical thinking* that involves generating many ideas, and that may be considered to complement *convergent thinking*

doctor-centered style (of physician interactions). One of two basic patterns for physician–patient interactions (cf. *patient-centered style*); characterized by a highly directive interaction pattern, in which a physician narrowly focuses on the presenting medical problem, uses highly convergent questioning to elicit brief and targeted responses from the patient, and then formulates a diagnosis and a treatment regimen that is prescribed to the patient

dominant trait. The stronger genetic trait that appears in the *phenotype* of an organism when the *genotype* comprises a dominant trait and a *recessive trait*

dopamine. A *neurotransmitter* that seems to influence several important activities, including movement, *attention*, and *learning*; deficits of the substance are linked with Parkinson's disease, but surpluses may be linked to symptoms of *schizophrenia* (cf. *acetylcholine, serotonin*)

drive. A hypothesized composite source of energy related to physiological needs, which impels people to behave in ways that reduce the given source of energy and thereby to satisfy the physiological needs

duplicity theory. A currently accepted view of the way in which humans sense *pitch*; gives some credence to both *place theory* and *frequency theory* but has yet to provide a full explanation of the specific mechanisms and their interactions

dynamic assessment environment. A context for measurement of cognitive abilities, in which the interaction between the test-taker and the examiner does not end when the test-taker gives an incorrect response; rather, the examiner offers the test-taker a sequence of guided and graded hints designed to facilitate problem solving; this kind of assessment environment is oriented toward determining the test-taker's ability to use hints and to profit from opportunities to learn, not toward determining the fixed state of existing knowledge in the test-taker (cf. *static assessment environment*; see also *zone of proximal development*)

eardrum. An anatomical structure of the outer ear that vibrates in response to sound waves that have moved through the auditory canal from the *pinna*; its vibrations are passed to the middle ear, where its vibrations are transferred to a series of ossicles (see *incus, malleus, stapes*) such that higher *frequencies* of sound cause more rapid vibrations (also termed *tympanum*)

echoic store. A hypothesized sensory register for fleeting storage of auditory stimuli; evidence of such a register has been insubstantial to date

efferents. The *neurons* and *nerves* that transmit motor information (e.g., movements of the large and small muscles) either from the *brain* through the spinal cord to the muscles (for voluntary muscle movements) or directly from the *spinal cord* to the muscles (in the case of *reflexes*), thus controlling bodily responses (cf. *receptors*; see *motor neuron*)

ego. One of three psychodynamic concepts (cf. *id, superego*); responds to the real world as it is perceived to be, rather than as the person may want it to be or may believe that it should be; more broadly, an individual's unique sense of herself or himself, which embraces the person's wishes and urges but tempers them with a realization of how the world works (see *reality principle*)

egocentrism. A cognitive characteristic (not a personality trait) in which mental representations are focused on the point of view and experiences of the individual thinker and the individual finds it difficult to grasp the viewpoint of others

Electra conflict. A conflict believed by Freudians to be characteristically experienced by girls during the *phallic stage* of *psychosexual development*; named for the Greek myth in which Electra despised her mother for having cheated on and killed her husband, Electra's father; often considered the female equivalent of the *Oedipal conflict*

electroconvulsive therapy (ECT). A psychophysiological treatment for severe, unremitting depression, in which electric shocks are passed through the head of a patient, causing the patient to experience convulsive muscular seizures and temporary loss of consciousness; this treatment is largely used as a last resort

electroencephalogram (EEG). A recording (*-gram*) of the electrical activity of the living brain, as detected by various electrodes (*en-*, "in", *cephalo-*, "head" [Greek])

electromagnetic spectrum. A range of energy of varying *wavelengths*, a narrow band of which is visible to the human eye

emotion. A feeling that comprises physiological and behavioral (and possibly cognitive) reactions to internal (e.g., thoughts, memories) and external events

emotion-focused coping. See *coping*

emotional intelligence. The ability to perceive and express *emotion*, assimilate emotion in thought, understand and reason with emotion, and regulate emotion in the self and others

empirical method. Means of obtaining information and understanding through experience, observation, and experimentation

empiricist. A person who believes that knowledge is most effectively acquired through *empirical methods* (cf. *rationalist*)

empty-nest syndrome. Transitional period in adult social development during which parents adjust to having their children grow up and move out of the family home

encoding. Process by which a physical, sensory input is transformed into a representation that can be stored in memory (see also *memory, rehearsal*)

encoding specificity. Phenomenon of *memory* in which the specific way of representing information as it is placed into memory affects the specific way in which the information may be recalled later

endocrine system. A physiological communication network that complements the *nervous system*; operates via *glands* that secrete *hormones* directly into the bloodstream; regulates the levels of hormones in the bloodstream via *negative-feedback loops* (*endo-*, "inside"; *-crine*, related to secretion [Greek])

episodic buffer. A limited-capacity system that is capable of binding information from the subsidiary systems and from long-term memory into a unitary episodic representation; that is, this component integrates information from different parts of *working memory* so that they make sense to us

episodic memory. *Encoding, storage, and retrieval* of events or episodes that the rememberer experienced personally at a particular time and place (cf. *semantic memory*)

equilibration. A process of *cognitive development* in which thinkers seek a balance (equilibrium) between the information and experiences they encounter in their environments and the cognitive processes and structures they bring to the encounter, as well as among the cognitive capabilities themselves; comprises three processes: the use of existing modes of thought and existing *schemas*, the process of *assimilation*, and the process of *accommodation*

equity theory. A theory of interpersonal attraction that holds that individuals will be attracted to persons with whom they have an equitable give-and-take relationship

ethologist. A scientist who studies the way in which different species of animals behave and how behavior has evolved within differing species

etiology. All of the causes of an abnormal condition

event-related potentials (ERPs). *Electroencephalogram (EEG)* recordings in response to a *stimulus* in which at least some of the electrical interference has been averaged out of the data by means of averaging the EEG wave forms on successive EEG recordings; experimental uses in mapping the electrical activity of various parts of the brain during various cognitive tasks or in response to various kinds of stimuli

evolutionary psychology. The branch of psychology whose goal is to explain behavior in terms of organisms' evolved adaptations to a constantly changing environment

exemplar. One of several typical representatives of a particular *concept* or of a class of objects; sometimes several exemplars are used as a set of alternatives to a single prototype for deriving the meaning of a concept (see *prototype theory*)

experiment. An investigation of cause-and-effect relationships through the control of variables and the careful manipulation of one or more particular variables, to note their outcome effects on other variables (see *control condition, experimental condition; cf. case study, naturalistic observation, survey, test*)

experimental analysis of behavior. An extreme behavioristic view that all behavior should be studied and analyzed in terms of specific behavior emitted as a result of environmental *contingencies*

experimental condition. A situation in which a group of experimental participants experience a carefully prescribed set of circumstances that are almost identical to the *control condition* but also include the treatment involving the *independent variable* that is being manipulated in the *experiment* (also termed *treatment condition*)

experimental methods. Methods that permit researchers to investigate cause-and-effect relationships by controlling or carefully manipulating particular variables to assess their effects on other variables

explanation. Addresses why people think, feel, or act as they do. One of four goals of psychological research (the other three are *control, description,* and *prediction*)

explicit memory. A form of memory *retrieval* in which an individual consciously acts to recall or recognize particular information (cf. *implicit memory*)

external locus of control. Characterized by the tendency to believe that the causes of behavioral consequences originate in the environment, sometimes involving an extreme view in which the individual consistently misattributes

causality to external rather than to internal causes (cf. *internal locus of control*)

extinction (as a phase of learning). A period of time during which the probability of the occurrence of a *CR* decreases, eventually approaching zero, due to the unlinking of the *CS* with the *US*; the individual still retains some memory of the *learning*; however, the *CR* can be relearned very quickly if the *CS* and the *US* become paired again

extinction procedure. A *behavior therapy* technique (e.g., *flooding, implosion therapy*) that is designed to weaken maladaptive responses

extrinsic motivators. One of the two primary types of sources of *motivation* (cf. *intrinsic motivators*); motivating forces that come from *outside* the motivated individual, which encourage the person to engage in behavior because the person either is rewarded for doing so or is threatened with *punishment* for not doing so; often decrease intrinsic motivation to engage in behavior, such that the individual discontinues the behavior when extrinsic motivators are removed, even though the individual may have been intrinsically motivated to engage in the behavior prior to the introduction of extrinsic motivators; decrements in intrinsic motivation are particularly likely if extrinsic motivators are expected, are perceived as relevant and important to the individual, and are tangible

extroversion. See *Big Five*

facial-feedback hypothesis. An assumption suggesting that the cognitive feedback going to the *brain* as a result of the stimulation of particular facial muscles associated with particular emotional expressions (e.g., a smile or a frown) causes a person to infer that she or he is feeling a particular *emotion*

factor analysis. A method of statistical decomposition that allows an investigator to infer distinct hypothetical constructs, elements, or structures that underlie a phenomenon

false alarm. A response in which an individual inaccurately asserts that a signal *stimulus* has been observed; in *signal-detection theory (SDT)*, the inaccurate belief that a signal stimulus was detected when it was actually absent (cf. *correct rejection, hit, miss*); in memory tasks, a response in which subjects indicate that

they have previously seen an item in a list, even though the item was not shown previously

family systems therapy. The treatment of the couple or the family unit as a whole, which involves complex internal interactions, rather than in terms of the discrete problems of distinct members of the unit

feature-detector approach. A psychophysiological approach to form *perception* that attempts to link the psychological perception of form to the functioning of *neurons* in the *brain*, based on single-cell (neuronal) recording techniques for tracing the route of the neurons from the *receptors* within the *retina*, through the *ganglion cells*, then the thalamic nucleus cells, to the visual cortex; these psychophysiological studies indicate that specific neurons of the visual cortex respond to various stimuli that are presented to the specific retinal regions connected to these neurons; apparently, each individual cortical neuron can be mapped to a specific receptive field on the retina (see *complex cells, simple cells*)

feature hypothesis. A view regarding the means by which children make *overextension errors:* Children form definitions that include too few features, and they therefore overextend the use of given words because they lack one or more defining features that would more narrowly constrain the application of a given word (cf. *functional hypothesis*)

feature-matching theories. Theories of form perception according to which people attempt to match the features of an observed pattern to features stored in *memory*, without considering the prior experience of the perceiver or what the perceiver already knows about the context in which the form is presented

fetal alcohol syndrome. An assemblage of disorders, chiefly permanent and irreparable mental retardation and facial deformities, that may result when pregnant mothers consume alcohol during the fetal development of their infants

field. A domain of study centered on a set of topics that have a common sphere of related interests or a common core of related phenomena (cf. *perspective*)

figure. See *figure–ground*; cf. *ground*

figure–ground. A Gestalt principle of form *perception* (see *Gestalt approach*); the tendency to perceive that an object in or an aspect of a perceptual field seems prominent (termed the *figure*), while other aspects or objects recede into the background (termed the *ground*)

first-order conditioning. A *classical-conditioning* procedure whereby a *CS* is linked directly with a *US* (cf. *higher-order conditioning*)

fixated. A phenomenon of *psychosexual development* in which an individual is unable to resolve the relevant issues of the current stage and therefore is unable to progress to the next stage (see also *defense mechanisms*)

fixed-interval reinforcement. A schedule of *operant conditioning* in which reinforcement always occurs after a certain amount of time has passed, as long as the *operant* response has occurred at least once during the particular period of time (see *partial reinforcement*; cf. *fixed-ratio reinforcement, variable-interval reinforcement, variable-ratio reinforcement*)

fixed-ratio reinforcement. An *operant-conditioning* schedule in which reinforcement always occurs after a certain number of operant responses, regardless of the amount of time it takes to produce that number of responses (see *partial reinforcement*; cf. *fixed-interval reinforcement, variable-ratio reinforcement, variable-interval reinforcement*)

flashbulb memory. Recollection of an event that is so emotionally powerful that the recollection is highly vivid and richly detailed, as if it were indelibly preserved on film, although the true accuracy of such recall is not as great as the rememberer might believe it to be

flooding. *Extinction procedures* designed to lessen *anxiety* by exposing a client to a carefully controlled environment in which an anxiety-provoking *stimulus* is presented, but the client experiences no harm from the stimulus, so the client is expected to cease to feel anxiety in response to the stimulus (cf. *implosion therapy*)

fluid intelligence. One of two major subfactors of general *intelligence*; represents the acquisition of new information or the grasping of new relationships and abstractions about known information (may be measured, for example, by timed tests involving analogies, series completions, or inductive reasoning; cf. *crystallized intelligence*)

forebrain. The farthest forward (toward the face) of the three major regions of the *brain* (cf. *midbrain, hindbrain*; names correspond roughly to the front-to-back arrangement of these parts in the developing embryo); the region located toward the top and front of the brain in adults; comprises the *cerebral cortex*, the *limbic system*, the *thalamus*, and the *hypothalamus*

foreclosure. One of four main types of identity (cf. *identity achievement, identity diffusion, moratorium*; cf. also *alienated achievement*), in which an individual makes a *commitment* to beliefs without ever having considered various alternatives to those beliefs

formal-operational stage. A stage of *cognitive development* in Piaget's theory in which the individual can engage in mental manipulations of internal representations of abstract symbols that (1) may not have specific concrete equivalents, and (2) may relate to experiences the individual may not have encountered personally (cf. *concrete operations, preoperational stage, sensorimotor stage*)

fovea. A small, central, thin region of the *retina* that has a high concentration of *cones*, each of which has its own *ganglion cell* leading to the optic nerve, thereby increasing the visual *acuity* in bright light of images within the visual field of the foveal region (in contrast, the periphery of the retina has relatively fewer cones and more *rods*, which have to share ganglion cells with other rods, thereby reducing visual acuity in the peripheral visual field and in dim light)

free association. A phenomenon of psychodynamic therapy in which the patient freely says whatever comes to mind, not censoring or otherwise editing the free flow of words before reporting them

free nerve endings. Sensory *receptors* in the skin that lack the globular swellings that characterize some other somatosensory receptors

free recall. A type of *memory* task in which a participant is presented with a list of items and is asked to repeat the items in any order the participant prefers (cf. *paired-associates recall, serial recall*)

frequency distribution. The dispersion of values in a set of values, represented as the number, proportion, or percentage (i.e., the frequency) of instances of each value

frequency theory. One of two views of the way in which humans sense *pitch* (cf. *place theory*); the *basilar membrane* reproduces the vibrations that enter the ear, triggering neural impulses at the same *frequency* as the original sound wave, so that the frequency of the impulses that enter the auditory nerve determines the number of electrical responses per second in the auditory nerve; these responses are then sensed as a given pitch by the brain (see also *duplicity theory, volley principle*)

frontal lobe. One of the four major regions of the *cerebral cortex* (cf. *occipital lobe, parietal lobe, temporal lobe*); generally responsible for motor processing and for higher thought processes, such as abstract reasoning

functional fixedness. A particular type of *mental set* in which the problem solver is unable to recognize that something that is known to be used in one way, for one purpose, may also be used for performing other functions, perhaps even through use in another way

functional hypothesis. A view regarding the means by which children make *overextension errors* (cf. *feature hypothesis*); children base their initial use of words on the important purposes (functions) of the *concepts* represented by the words, and children then make overextension errors because of their confusion about the functions of the objects being identified

functionalism. A school of psychology that focuses on active psychological processes rather than on passive psychological structures or elements; for example, functionalists were more interested in how people think than in what they think, in how people perceive rather than in what they perceive, and in how and why organisms evolve as they do rather than what particular outcomes are produced by the evolutionary process (cf. *structuralism*)

fundamental attribution error. A bias of *attribution* in which an individual tends to overemphasize internal causes and personal responsibility and to deemphasize external causes and situational influences when observing the behavior of other people (see also *actor–observer effect, self-handicapping*)

fundamental frequency. The single tone produced by a note played on a musical instrument, which may also produce a series of *harmonic* tones at various multiples of the fundamental frequency (see *harmonics*)

gambler's fallacy. An intuitive and fallacious inference that when a sequence of coincidental events appears to be occurring in a nonrandom pattern (e.g., a protracted series of heads in a coin toss), subsequent events are more likely to deviate from the apparent pattern (e.g., the appearance of a tail) than to continue in the apparent pattern (e.g., the appearance of another head), when actually the probability of each event continues to have the same random probability at each occurrence (see *heuristic*)

ganglion cells. Cells that form the first of three layers of cells in the *retina*; the *axons* of these cells form the optic nerve and communicate with the *photoreceptors* (in the third layer) via the middle layer of cells in the retina (cf. *amacrine cells, bipolar cells, horizontal cells*)

gender constancy. The realization that a person's gender is stable and cannot be changed by changing superficial characteristics (e.g., hair length) or behaviors (e.g., carrying a purse) (see *gender typing*)

gender typing. The process of acquiring the roles and associations related to the social and psychological distinction of being masculine or feminine

gene. Each of the basic physiological building blocks for the hereditary transmission of *traits* in all life forms (see *chromosomes, deoxyribonucleic acid [DNA]*)

general adaptation syndrome (GAS). A physiological response to stress in which the body initially exerts maximal effort to adapt; if the stressor continues to prompt a response, however, the body reduces exertion in order to conserve physiological resources until eventually the body exhausts those resources

generalized anxiety disorder. An *anxiety disorder* characterized by general, persistent, constant, and often debilitating high levels of anxiety, which are accompanied by psychophysiological symptoms typical of a hyperactive *autonomic nervous system*, and which can last any length of time, from a month to years; such anxiety is often described as "free floating" because a cause or source is not readily available

genes. The basic building blocks of hereditary transmission of *traits* in all life forms

genetics. The study of *genes* and heredity and variations among individuals as well as their expression in the environment (see *behavioral genetics*)

genital stage. A stage of *psychosexual development*; typically starts in adolescence, continues through adulthood, and involves normal adult sexuality, as Freud defined it—i.e., the adoption of traditional sex roles and of a heterosexual orientation

genotype. The pair of *genes* on a given *chromosome* pair that is inherited from each parent and *not* subject to environmental influence (except in cases of genetic mutation); possibilities include both *dominant traits* and *recessive traits*, either of which may be passed on to biological offspring (cf. *phenotype*)

Gestalt approach. A way of studying form *perception*, based on the notion that the whole of the form is different from the sum of its individual parts (*Gestalt*, "form" or "shape" [German]) (see also *Gestalt psychology*)

Gestalt psychology. A school of psychological thought that holds that psychological phenomena are best understood when viewed as organized, structured wholes, not analyzed into myriad component elements (*Gestalt*, "form" or "shape" [German]) (see also *Gestalt approach*)

gland. A group of cells that secretes chemical substances; in the *endocrine system*, glands secrete *hormones* directly into the bloodstream; in the exocrine system, glands secrete fluids (e.g., tears, sweat) into ducts that channel the fluids out of the body

glial cell. A type of structure (also termed *neuroglia*) that nourishes, supports, and positions *neurons* within the *central nervous system (CNS)*, functioning as a kind of glue holding the CNS together, and keeping the neurons at optimal distances from one another and from other structures in the body, thereby helping to minimize miscommunication problems among neurons; also assists in forming the *myelin sheath*, such that the gaps between glial cells form the nodes in the sheath (see *nodes of Ranvier*)

glucostatic hypothesis. One of two major alternative assumptions about how the body signals hunger versus satiety (cf. *lipostatic hypothesis*); suggests that the levels of glucose (a simple body sugar) in the bloodstream signal the body regarding the need for food; *glucostatic*: maintaining the stability (-*static*) of glucose (*gluco-*) levels in the body and in the brain

gradient of reinforcement. An important consideration in establishing, maintaining, or extinguishing *operant conditioning*, in which the length of time that elapses between the operant *response* and the reinforcing *stimulus* affects the strength of the conditioning; the longer the interval of time, the weaker the effect of the reinforcer

grammar. The study of *language* in terms of regular patterns that relate to the functions and relationships of words in a sentence—extending as broadly as the level of discourse and as narrowly as the pronunciation and meaning of individual words; *descriptive grammar*—the description of language patterns that relate to the structures, functions, and relationships of words in a sentence (see *phrase-structure grammar; transformational grammar*); *prescriptive grammar*—the formulation of various rules that dictate the preferred use of written and spoken language, such as the functions, structures, and relationships of words in a sentence

ground. See *figure–ground*

group. A collection of individuals who interact with one another, often for a common purpose or activity

group polarization. Exaggeration of the initial views of members of a group through the dynamic processes of group interaction

groupthink. The dynamics of group interactions in which group members focus on the goal of unanimity of opinion more than they focus on the achievement of other goals, such as the purpose for which the group may have been designed in the first place; such a process is characterized by six symptoms: (1) close-mindedness to alternative conceptualizations; (2) rationalization of both the processes and the products of group decision making; (3) the squelching of dissent through ostracism, criticism, or ignoring; (4) the inclusion of a self-appointed mindguard, who diligently upholds the group norm; (5) the feeling of invulnerability, due to special knowledge or expertise; and (6) the feeling of unanimity; the net result of this process is defective decision making

growth. Quantitative linear increases in size or amount (cf. *development*)

hair cells. The thousands of specialized hairlike appendages on the *basilar membrane* that function as auditory *receptors*, transducing mechanical energy from the vibration of the *stapes* into electrochemical energy that goes to the sensory *neurons*, which carry the auditory information to the *brain* (see *transduce*; see also *cochlea*)

hallucinations. *Perceptions* of sensory stimulation (e.g., sounds, the most common hallucinated sensations; sights; smells; or tactile sensations) in the absence of any actual corresponding external sensory input from the physical world

hallucinogenic. A type of *psychoactive* drug (e.g., mescaline, LSD, and marijuana) that alters *consciousness* by inducing *hallucinations* and affecting the way the drug-takers perceive both their inner worlds and their external environments; often termed *psychotomimetics* (also known as "psychedelics") because some clinicians believe that these drugs mimic the effects produced by psychosis

haptic. Characterized by sensitivity to pressure, temperature, and *pain* stimulation directly on the skin

harmonics. Distinctive tones that musical instruments generate, along with the *fundamental frequency* of the note being played, which are higher multiples of the fundamental frequency (cf. *noise*); different musical instruments yield distinctive multiples of the fundamental frequencies, resulting in the distinctive tonal qualities of the instruments

health psychology. The study of the reciprocal interaction between the psychological processes of the mind and the physical health of the body

heritability. The proportion of variation among individuals that is due to genetic causes

heritability coefficient. The degree to which heredity contributes to *intelligence*, expressed in terms of a number on a scale from 0 to 1, such that a coefficient of 0 means that heredity has no influence on variation among people, whereas a coefficient of 1 means that heredity is the only influence on such variation

heuristic. An informal, intuitive, speculative strategy (e.g., a trial-and-error heuristic) that sometimes works effectively for solving problems (cf. *algorithm*; see *availability heuristic, gambler's fallacy, illusory correlation, representativeness heuristic*)

higher-order conditioning. A *classical-conditioning* procedure (e.g., *first-order conditioning*) whereby a *CS* is not linked directly with a *US* but rather with an established CS, thereby producing a weaker (more volatile and more susceptible to *extinction*) form of classical conditioning

hindbrain. The farthest back of the three major regions of the *brain* (cf. *forebrain, midbrain*), located near the back of the neck in adults; comprises the *medulla oblongata*, the *pons*, and the *cerebellum*

hippocampus. A portion of the *limbic system* (*hippocampus* is Greek for "seahorse," its approximate shape); plays an essential role in the formation of new memories

hit. One of the four possible combinations of *stimulus* and *response* described in *signal-detection theory (SDT)* (cf. *correct rejection, false alarm, miss*); the accurate recognition that a signal stimulus was detected that was truly present

homeostatic regulation. Process by which the body maintains a state of equilibrium, such that when the body lacks something, it sends signals that prompt the individual to seek the missing resource, whereas when the body is satiated, it sends signals to stop obtaining that resource

homosexuality. A tendency to direct sexual desire toward another person of the same sex (*homo-*, "same" [Greek]); often termed *lesbianism* in women (cf. *bisexual*)

horizontal cells. One of three kinds of *interneuron* cells in the middle of three layers of cells in the *retina*; the *amacrine cells* and the horizontal cells provide lateral connections that permit lateral communication with adjacent areas of the retina in the middle layer of cells (cf. *bipolar cells*; see *ganglion cells, photoreceptors*)

hormone. A chemical substance, secreted by one or more *glands*, that regulates many physiological processes through specific actions on cells, fosters the growth and proliferation of cells, and may affect the way a receptive cell goes about its activities (see *endocrine system*)

hostile aggression. An emotional and usually impulsive action intended to cause harm or injury to another person or persons, often provoked by feelings of *pain* or distress, not by a desire to gain something through the aggressive act; in fact, valuable relationships and objects may be harmed or put at risk of harm through hostile aggression (see *aggression*, cf. *instrumental aggression*)

hue. Physical properties of light waves that correspond closely to the psychological properties of color, which is the subjective interpretation of the physiological processing of various *wavelengths* of the narrow band of visible light within the electromagnetic spectrum

humanism. A philosophical approach that centers on the unique character of humans and their relationship to the natural world, on human interactions, on human concerns, and on secular human values, including the need for humans to treat one another humanely; arose during the Renaissance, in contrast to the prevailing philosophy, which emphasized divinely determined values and divine explanations for human behavior

humanistic psychology. A school of psychological thought that emphasizes (1) conscious experience in personal development rather than unconscious experience, (2) free will and the importance of human potential rather than *determinism*, and (3) holistic approaches to psychological phenomena rather than analytic approaches

hypnosis. An altered state of *consciousness* that usually involves deep relaxation and extreme sensitivity to suggestion and appears to bear some resemblance to sleep (see *posthypnotic suggestion*)

hypothalamus. Located at the base of the *forebrain*, beneath the *thalamus* (*hypo-*, "under" [Greek]); controls water balance in the tissues and bloodstream; regulates internal temperature, appetite, and thirst, as well as many other functions of the *autonomic nervous system*; plays a key role in controlling the *endocrine system*; interacts with the *limbic system* for regulating behavior related to species survival (fighting, feeding, fleeing, and mating); in conjunction with the *reticular activating system*, plays a role in controlling *consciousness*; involved in regulating *emotions*, pleasure, *pain*, and *stress* reactions

hypotheses. Tentative proposals regarding expected consequences, such as the outcomes of research (singular: *hypothesis*)

hypothesis testing. A view of *language* acquisition that asserts that children acquire language by mentally forming tentative *hypotheses* about language and then testing these hypotheses in the environment, using several operating principles for generating and testing their hypotheses; also more broadly applies to testing of scientific and other hypotheses

hypothetical construct. An abstract *concept* (e.g., beauty, truth, or intelligence) that is not itself directly measurable or observable but that can be presumed to give rise to responses and attributes that can be observed and measured

iconic store. A sensory register for the fleeting storage of discrete visual images in the form of icons (visual images that represent something, usually resembling whatever is being represented)

id. The most primitive of three psychodynamic concepts (cf. *ego*, *superego*): the unconscious, instinctual source of impulsive urges, such as sexual and aggressive impulses, as well as the source of the wishes and fantasies that derive from these impulses, without consideration for rationality or for external reality

ideal self. A person's view of the personal characteristics that he or she would like to embody (cf. *self-concept*)

idealistic principle. The operating principle of the *superego*, which guides a person's actions in terms of what she or he should do, as dictated by internalized authority figures, without regard for rationality or even for external reality (cf. *pleasure principle*, *reality principle*)

identity achievement. One of four main types of identity (cf. *foreclosure*, *identity diffusion*, *moratorium*; cf. also *alienated achievement*), in which the individual establishes a firm and secure sense of self, following a period of questioning her or his personal values and beliefs

identity diffusion. One of four main types of identity (cf. *foreclosure*, *identity achievement*, *moratorium*; cf. also *alienated achievement*), in which the individual cannot establish a firm and secure sense of self and therefore lacks direction and *commitment*

ill-structured problem. A type of problem for which a clear path to a solution is not known (cf. *well-structured problem*)

illusion. A distorted *perception* of objects and other external *stimuli* that may be due to misleading cues in the objects themselves or to distortions of the perceptual process, such as distortions caused by altered states of consciousness or psychological disorder (see *optical illusion*; cf. *delusion*)

illusory correlation. An inferred perception of a relationship between unrelated variables, usually arising because the instances in which the variables coincide seem more noticeable than the instances in which the variables do not coincide; as applied to *prejudice*, people are more likely to notice instances of unusual behavior in a minority population than to notice common behaviors in members of a minority population or unusual behaviors in members of a majority population (see *heuristic*)

imaginary audience. A form of adolescent *egocentrism*, in which the adolescent believes that other people are constantly watching and judging his or her behavior

implicit memory. A form of memory *retrieval* in which an individual uses recalled or recognized information without consciously being aware of doing so (cf. *explicit memory*)

implosion therapy. A set of *extinction procedures* designed to weaken *anxiety* by having clients imagine as vividly as possible the unpleasant events that are causing them anxiety; clients repeat the procedure as often as necessary to extinguish their anxiety (cf. *flooding*)

impression formation. The process by which individuals form intuitive concepts about other people, based on inferences from information obtained both directly and indirectly (see *confirmation bias*, *person-positivity bias*, *primacy effect*, *self-fulfilling prophecy*)

incubation. A process in which a problem solver discontinues intensive work on solving a problem, stops focusing conscious attention on solving the problem for a while, and permits problem solving to occur at a subconscious level for a period of time; believed to be particularly helpful in solving some *insight* problems

incus. One of the three bones of the middle ear (cf. *malleus*, *stapes*) that normally receive and amplify the vibrations transmitted by the tympanum (*eardrum*) and then transmit those vibrations to the *cochlea*

independent variable. An attribute that is individually manipulated by the experimenter, while other aspects of the investigation are held constant—that is, not subject to variation (cf. *dependent variable*)

induced movement. The perceptual phenomenon in which individuals who are moving and are observing other objects within a stable perceptual frame (such as the side window of a car or train) perceive that the fixed objects are moving rather than that they (the observers) are moving

inductive reasoning. The process of drawing general explanatory conclusions based on evidence involving specific facts or observations; permits the reasoner to draw well-founded or probable conclusions but not logically certain conclusions (see *reasoning*; cf. *deductive reasoning*)

infantile amnesia. See *amnesia*

inferential statistics. One of two key ways in which statistics are used (cf. *descriptive statistic*), in which a researcher analyzes numerical data in order to determine the likelihood that the obtained findings would have occurred solely by chance

inferiority complex. A means by which people organize their thoughts, emotions, and behavior based on their perceived mistakes and feelings of inferiority

information processing. The operations by which people mentally manipulate what they learn and know about the world

informed consent. An ethical procedure of experimentation; experimental participants are briefed prior to the implementation of the experiment and are fully informed of the nature of the treatment procedure and any possible harmful side effects or consequences of the treatment, as well as the likelihood that these consequences may take place

insight. A distinctive and apparently sudden understanding of a problem or a sudden realization of a strategy that aids in solving a problem, which is usually preceded by a great deal of prior thought and hard work; often involves reconceptualizing a problem or a strategy for its solution in a totally new way; frequently emerges by detecting and combining relevant old and new information to gain a novel view of the problem or of its solution; often associated with finding solutions to *ill-structured problems*

insomnia. Any of various disturbances of sleep, including difficulty falling asleep, waking up during the night and being unable to go back to sleep, or waking up too early in the morning, and which may vary in intensity and duration

instinct. An inherited, species-specific, stereotyped pattern of preprogrammed behavior that involves a relatively complex pattern of response (cf. *reflex*); generally characterized by less flexibility in adaptability to changes in an environment but greater assurance that a complex pattern of behavior will occur as it is preprogrammed to occur without variation

instrumental aggression. A form of *antisocial behavior* that the aggressor realizes may result in harm or injury to the recipient(s) of the *aggression* but that the aggressor pursues anyway in order to gain something of value; generally not as impulsive or emotional as *hostile aggression* and often implemented without particularly malicious intentions toward the recipients of the aggression; that is, the recipients of the aggression were not seen as targets but rather were viewed as obstacles in the way of obtaining something valuable to the aggressor

intelligence. Goal-directed adaptive behavior

intensity. The amount of physical energy that is *transduced* by a sensory *receptor* and then sensed in the *brain* (cf. *quality*)

interactionist approach. A theoretical approach that emphasizes the interaction between characteristics of the person and characteristics of the situation

interactive images. See *mnemonic devices*

interference. Information that competes with the information that the individual is trying to store in *memory*, thereby causing the individual to forget that information (cf. *decay;* see also *interference theory*)

interference theory. The assertion that information is forgotten because it is displaced by interfering information that disrupts and displaces the information that the individual had tried to store in *memory* originally, rather than because the information gradually disappears over time (cf. *decay theory*)

internal locus of control. Characterized by an individual's tendency to believe that the causes of behavioral consequences originate within the individual; sometimes involves an extreme view in which the individual misattributes causality to internal rather than to external causes (cf. *external locus of control*)

internalization. A process of *cognitive development* in which an individual absorbs knowledge from an external environmental context

interneuron. The most numerous of the three main types of *neurons* in humans (cf. *motor neuron, sensory neuron*); intermediate between (*inter-,* "between") sensory and motor neurons, receiving signals from either sensory neurons or other interneurons, and then sending signals either to other interneurons or to motor neurons

interposition. See *monocular depth cues*

interval schedule. See *fixed-interval reinforcement, variable-interval reinforcement;* see also *partial reinforcement*

intimacy. One of three basic components of love, according to the *triangular theory of love* (cf. *commitment, passion*); feelings that promote closeness and connection

intoxicated. Characterized by stupefaction due to the effects of toxins such as alcohol or *sedatives*

intrinsic motivators. One of the two primary sources of *motivation* (cf. *extrinsic motivators*); motivating forces that come from within a motivated individual, which are at work when the person engages in behavior because the person enjoys doing so

introspection. Self-examination of inner ideas and experiences; used by early psychologists as a method of studying psychological phenomena (*intro-,* "inward, within"; *-spect,* "look")

invincibility fallacy. A form of adolescent *egocentrism,* in which the adolescent believes that he or she is invulnerable to harm or ill fortune

ipsilateral. Characterized as occurring or appearing on the same side (*ipsi-,* "self"; *lateral,* "side"); often used in describing physiological structures (cf. *contralateral*)

iris. A circular membrane that reflects light beams outward and away from the eye; surrounds the *pupil,* which is essentially a hole in the center of the iris

judgment and decision making. One of the fundamental kinds of *thinking* (cf. *creativity, problem solving, reasoning*), in which the goal is to evaluate various opportunities or to choose from among various options (see *heuristic*)

just noticeable difference (jnd). The minimum amount of difference between two sensory *stimuli* that a given individual can detect at a particular time and place, subject to variations that may cause measurement error, for which psychophysical psychologists often compensate by averaging data from multiple trials; operationally defined as the difference between two stimuli that can be detected 50% of the time (sometimes termed the *difference threshold;* cf. *absolute threshold*)

justification of effort. A means by which an individual rationalizes the expenditure of energy

keyword system. See *mnemonic devices*

kinesthesis. The sense that helps in ascertaining skeletal movements and positioning via *receptors* in the muscles, tendons, joints, and skin; changes in position are detected by kinesthetic receptors that *transduce* the mechanical energy caused by pressure into electrochemical neural energy, which codes information about the speed of the change, the angle of the bones, and the tension of the muscles, and then sends this information through the *spinal cord* to the *contralateral* region of the somatosensory cortex and to the *cerebellum*

language. An organized means of combining words in order to communicate

language-acquisition device (LAD). The hypothetical construct of an innate human predisposition to acquire *language;* not yet found as a specific physiological structure or function

latency. An interim period that occurs during *psychosexual development,* between the *phallic stage* and the *genital stage,* in which children repress their sexual feelings toward their parents and sublimate their sexual energy into productive fields of endeavor

latent content. The repressed impulses and other unconscious material expressed in dreams or in other *primary-process thoughts,* which give rise to the *manifest content* of such processes, as these processes are understood by psychodynamic psychologists

latent learning. Conditioning or acquired knowledge that is not presently reflected in performance; the learned information or response may be elicited when the individual believes that it may be rewarding to demonstrate the learning

law of effect. A behavioristic principle used for explaining *operant conditioning*, which states that over time, actions ("the effect") for which an organism is rewarded ("the satisfaction") are strengthened and are therefore more likely to occur again in the future, whereas actions that are followed by *punishment* tend to be weakened and are thus less likely to occur in the future

learned helplessness. A negative consequence of conditioning, particularly of *punishment*, in which an individual is conditioned to make no response, including no attempt to escape aversive conditions (e.g., after repeated trials in which the individual is unable to escape an aversive condition, the individual has so effectively learned not to attempt escape that the individual continues not to attempt escape even when a means becomes available)

learning. Any relatively permanent change in the behavior, thoughts, or feelings of an organism as a consequence of prior experience (cf. *maturation*)

lens. The curved interior surface of the eye that bends (refracts) light into the eye and complements the *cornea's* gross adjustments in curvature by making fine adjustments in the amount of curvature in order to focus the image as clearly as possible (cf. *cornea*)

lesbianism. See *homosexuality*

lexicon. The entire set of *morphemes* in a given language or in a given person's linguistic repertoire (cf. *vocabulary*)

life-span development. The changes in characteristics that occur over the course of a lifetime

light adaptation. The unconscious physiological response to an increase in light *intensity* in the environment, characterized by a decrease in pupillary area (cf. *dark adaptation*)

lightness constancy. A form of *perceptual constancy* in which an individual continues to perceive a constant degree of illumination of an object, even when the actual amount of light that reaches the *retina* differs for different parts of the object

likability effect. Tendency for the recipient of a message to be persuaded more easily by messages from people the message recipient likes than by messages from people the recipient does not like

Likert scale. A type of *self-report measure* (also termed *summated rating scale*) in which a participant first is asked to review statements about his or her feelings, thoughts, attitudes, or behaviors, worded from the person's point of view (e.g., "I love psychology," "I plan to buy 10 more copies of my psychology textbook"); the participant is then asked to rate each of the statements on a numerical scale, such as from 0 (which means that the statement is not at all accurate) to the highest value on the scale (which means that the statement is very accurate); the person's responses are then averaged (or summed) to determine an overall rating

limbic system. Comprises the *hippocampus*, the *amygdala*, and the *septum* and forms part of the *forebrain*, as does the *cerebral cortex*; important to *emotion*, *motivation*, and *learning*, as well as the suppression of instinctive responses, thereby enabling humans to adapt behaviors more flexibly in response to a changing environment

line graph. One of many types of graphic displays of numerical information, in which quantities (e.g., amounts or scores) are associated with linear information (e.g., time or age), and this association is represented by changing heights of a horizontal line (cf. *bar graph*)

linear perspective. See *monocular depth cues*; see also *vanishing point*

linear regression. Prediction of one quantified variable from one or more others, in which the two sets of variables are assumed to have a relationship that takes the form of a straight line

linear relation. An association between two quantities that takes the form of a straight line

linguistic relativity. One of two interrelated propositions regarding the relationship between thought and language that asserts that the speakers of different languages have differing cognitive systems, based on the languages they use, and that these different cognitive systems influence the ways in which people who speak the various languages think about the world

linguistic universals. Characteristic patterns of language that apply across all of the languages of various cultures

linguistics. The study of language structure and change

lipostatic hypothesis. One of two major alternative assumptions about how the body signals hunger versus satiety (cf. *glucostatic hypothesis*); suggests that the levels of lipids (fats) in the blood signal the body regarding the need for food; *lipostatic:* maintaining the stability (-*static*) of lipid (*lipo-*) levels in the body

location in the picture plane. See *monocular depth cues*

long-term store. According to a three-stores theory of memory, the hypothetical construct of a long-term store has a greater capacity than both the *sensory store* and the *short-term store*, and it can store information for very long periods of time, perhaps even indefinitely

longitudinal study. Research that follows a particular group of individuals (usually selected as a *sample* representing a *population* as a whole) over the course of time, often over many years (cf. *cross-sectional study*)

magnetic resonance imaging (MRI). A sophisticated technique for revealing high-resolution images of the structure of the living *brain* by computing and analyzing magnetic changes in the energy of the orbits of nuclear particles in the molecules of the body (sometimes termed *NMR*, for *nuclear magnetic resonance*); produces clearer and more detailed images than *computerized axial tomography (CAT)* scans and uses no X radiation

major depression. A *mood disorder* characterized by feeling down, discouraged, and hopeless. Typical cognitive symptoms of depression are low self-esteem, loss of *motivation*, and pessimism. A depressed person may also experience a very low energy level, slow body movements and speech, and difficulty sleeping and waking up

malleus. One of the three bones of the middle ear that normally receive and amplify the vibrations transmitted by the *eardrum* and then transmit those vibrations to the *cochlea* (cf. *incus, stapes*)

mania. A mood of unrestrained euphoria involving high excitement, expansiveness, and often hyperactivity;

often accompanied by an overinflated sense of *self-esteem*, grandiose illusions with regard to what the manic person can accomplish, difficulty in focusing attention on one activity, and a tendency to flit from one activity to another in rapid succession (see *bipolar disorder*)

manifest content. The stream of events that pass through the mind of an individual during dreams or other *primary-process thoughts*, as these processes are understood by psychodynamic psychologists (cf. *latent content*)

massed learning. *Learning* a body of knowledge or a task all at one time rather than spaced out over time; generally does not lead to as much learning as does *distributed learning*

maturation. One of the two key processes by which *cognitive development* occurs (cf. *learning*); any relatively permanent change in thought or behavior that occurs as a result of the internally (biologically) prompted processes of aging, without regard to personal experiences and subject to little environmental influence

mean. The average score within a distribution of values, computed by adding all the scores and then dividing the sum by the number of scores (cf. *median, mode*)

median. The middle score (half of the scores fall above and half the scores fall below) or other measurement value within a distribution of values (cf. *mean, mode*)

meditation. A set of techniques used for altering *consciousness* through focused contemplation (see *concentrative meditation, opening-up meditation*)

medulla oblongata. An elongated interior structure of the *brain*, located at the point where the *spinal cord* enters the skull and joins with the brain; forms part of the *reticular activating system* and thereby helps to sustain life by controlling the heartbeat and helping to control breathing, swallowing, and digestion; the location in the brain where *nerves* from the right side of the body cross over to the left side of the brain, and nerves from the left side of the body cross over to the right side of the brain (see *contralateral*)

memory. The means by which individuals draw on past knowledge in order to use such knowledge in the present; the dynamic mechanisms associated with the retention and *retrieval* of information; the three operations through which information is processed by and for the memory are *encoding* (translating sensory information into a form that can be represented and stored in memory), *storage* (moving encoded information into a memory store and maintaining the information in storage), and *retrieval* (recovering stored information from a memory store and moving the information into *consciousness* for use in active cognitive processing)

memory scanning. A phenomenon of memory in which an individual checks what is contained in memory, usually in short-term memory

menarche. The onset of menstruation

menopause. The end of a woman's menstrual cycle

mental age. A means of indicating a person's level of *intelligence* (generally in reference to a child), based on the individual's performance on tests of intelligence, by indicating the chronological age of persons who typically perform at the same level of intelligence as the test-taker (used less frequently today than in the past) (cf. *deviation IQs, intelligence, ratio IQ*)

mental retardation. Low level of *intelligence*, usually reflected by both poor performance on tests of intelligence and poor adaptive competence (the degree to which a person functions effectively within a normal situational context)

mental set. A frame of mind in which a problem-solver is predisposed to think of a problem or a situation in a particular way (sometimes termed *entrenchment*), often leading the problem-solver to fixate on a strategy that normally works in solving some (or perhaps even most) problems, but that does not work in solving this particular problem (see also *negative transfer*; cf. *positive transfer*)

mere exposure effect. The positive effect on attitudes that results from repeated exposure to a message that supports the attitude or even just exposure to the *stimulus* about which the attitude is being formed or modified

metamemory. An aspect of metacognition that involves knowledge and understanding of memory abilities and ways to enhance memory abilities, such as through the use of *mnemonic devices*

method of loci. See *mnemonic devices*

method of successive approximations. The sequence of *operant* behaviors reinforced during the *shaping* of a desired behavior

midbrain. Located between the *forebrain* and the *hindbrain*; comprises several cerebral structures, including the *reticular activating system (RAS)*, which also extends into the hindbrain

mind–body dualism. A philosophical belief that the body is separate from the mind; the body is composed of physical substance, whereas the mind is ephemeral and is not composed of physical substance (cf. *monism*)

miss. One of the four possible combinations of *stimulus* and *response* described in *signal-detection theory (SDT)* (cf. *correct rejection, false alarm, hit*); the state in which the individual did not detect a signal stimulus even though the stimulus was actually present

mnemonic devices. Specific techniques for aiding in the memorization of isolated items, thereby adding meaning or imagery to an otherwise arbitrary listing of isolated items that may be difficult to remember; for example, *acronym*—a set of letters that forms a word or phrase, in which each letter stands for a certain other word or concept (e.g., USA, IQ, and laser) and which thereby may aid in recalling the words or concepts that the letters represent; *acrostics*—the initial letters of a series of items are used in forming a sentence, such that the sentence prompts recall of the initial letters, and the letters prompt recall of each of the items; *categorical clustering*—various items are grouped into categories in order to facilitate recall; *interactive images*—a means of linking a set of isolated words by creating visual representations for the words and then picturing interactions among the items (e.g., causing one item to act on or with another); *keywords*—a mnemonic strategy for learning isolated words in a foreign language by forming an interactive image that links the sound and meaning of a foreign word with the sound and meaning of a familiar word; *method of loci*—visualization of a familiar area with distinctive landmarks that can be linked (via interactive images) to specific items to be remembered; *pegword system*—memorization of a familiar list of items (e.g., in a nursery rhyme) that can then be linked (via interactive images) with unfamiliar items on a new list

mnemonist. A person who uses memory-enhancing techniques to greatly improve his or her memory or who has a distinctive sensory or cognitive ability to remember information, particularly information that is highly concrete or can be visualized readily

mode. The most frequent score or other measurement value within a distribution of values (cf. *mean, median*)

modeling. A situation in which an individual observes another person and acts in kind; also a form of *behavior therapy* in which clients are asked to observe persons coping effectively in situations that the clients find *anxiety* provoking or that the clients respond to in other maladaptive ways

monism. A philosophical belief that the body and mind are unified, based on the belief that reality is a unified whole, existing in a single plane, rather than separated in terms of physical substance versus nonphysical mind (*mon[o]-*, "one"; *-ism*, set of beliefs, school of thought, or dogma [Greek]) (cf. *mind–body dualism*)

monitoring. One of the two main purposes of *consciousness* (cf. *controlling*); the individual keeps track of internal mental processes, of personal behavior, and of the environment, in order to maintain self-awareness in relation to the surrounding environment

monocular depth cues. One of the two chief means of judging the distances of visible objects (cf. *binocular depth cues*), based on sensed information that can be represented in just two dimensions and observed with just one (*mono-*) eye (*ocular*): *aerial perspective*—nearer objects appear to be more highly resolved and more clearly distinct than farther objects, which appear to be hazier (occurs because farther objects are observed through more moisture and dust particles, whereas closer objects are observed through fewer such particles); *interposition*—an object that appears to block or partially obstruct the view of another object is perceived as being nearer, whereas the blocked object is perceived to be farther away, such that the blocking object is perceived to be closer to the observer and in front of the blocked object; *linear perspective*—parallel lines seem to converge as they move farther into the distance; *location in the picture plane*—objects that are higher in the picture plane but are below the horizon, or

at least extend below it, are perceived as being farther from the viewer, whereas objects that are entirely above the horizon and higher in the picture plane are perceived as being closer to the viewer than are objects that are lower in the picture plane (i.e., as objects converge toward the horizon line, they are perceived as being farther from the viewer); *motion parallax*—the perception of stationary objects from a moving viewpoint, such that if an observer visually fixates on a single point in the scene, the objects that are closer to the observer than is the fixation point will appear to be moving in the direction opposite to the direction in which the observer is moving, whereas objects farther from the observer than is the fixation point will appear to be moving in the same direction as the observer (also, objects closer to the observer appear to be moving faster than objects farther from the observer); *relative size*—objects that are farther away appear to be smaller in the *retina*, and the farther away the object, the smaller is its image on the retina; *texture gradient*—the relative sizes of objects decrease and the densities of the distribution of objects increase as objects appear farther from the observer

mood disorders. Extreme disturbances in a person's emotional state, which may involve either unipolar disorder (also termed *depression*) or *bipolar disorder* (also termed *manic-depressive disorder*)

moratorium. One of four main types of identity (cf. *foreclosure, identity achievement, identity diffusion*; cf. also *alienated achievement*), in which the individual is questioning her or his values and beliefs prior to establishing a firm and secure sense of *self*

morpheme. The smallest unit of sound that denotes meaning within a particular *language*

motion parallax. See *monocular depth cues*

motivation. Processes that give behavior its energy and direction

motive. An intended goal that prompts a person to act in a particular way

motor. Characterized by the movement of muscles (related to *psychomotor*—motor skills associated with psychological processes)

motor efferents. See *efferents*

motor neuron. One of the three main types of *neurons* (cf. *interneuron, sensory neuron*); carries information away from the *spinal cord* and the *brain* and toward the body parts that are supposed to respond to the information in some way (see *efferents*)

Müller–Lyer illusion. An *optical illusion* in which two equally long line segments are perceived to differ in length because one of the line segments is braced by inward-facing, arrowhead-shaped diagonal lines and the other line segment is braced by outward-facing, arrowhead-shaped diagonal lines; an optical illusion that causes the observer to perceive that two equally long line segments differ in length; may be an artifact of some of the *monocular depth cues* with which perceivers are familiar (cf. *Ponzo illusion*)

multimodal. Characteristic of a non-normal distribution of values, in which the distribution comprises more than one *mode* (cf. *normal distribution*)

mutation. A sudden structural change in a hereditary characteristic; serves as a mechanism for changes in inheritance from one generation to the next and thereby permits evolutionary changes to occur (see also *behavioral genetics, genes, genetics*)

myelin sheath. A protective, insulating layer of myelin that coats the *axons* of some *neurons*, thereby speeding up neuronal conduction and insulating and protecting the axons from electrochemical interference by nearby neurons (see *nodes of Ranvier*)

N-REM sleep. The four stages of sleep that are not characterized by rapid eye movements (hence, the acronym for **n**on-**r**apid **e**ye **m**ovement) and that are less frequently associated with dreaming (cf. *REM sleep*)

narcolepsy. A disturbance of the pattern of wakefulness and sleep, in which the narcoleptic person experiences an uncontrollable urge to fall asleep periodically during the day and as a result loses *consciousness* for brief periods of time (usually 10 to 15 minutes), thereby putting the narcoleptic in grave danger if the attacks occur when the person is driving or otherwise engaged in activities for which sudden sleep might be hazardous

narcotic. Any drug in a class of drugs derived from opium (*opiates* such as heroin, morphine, or codeine) or synthetically produced to create the numbing, stuporous effects of opium (*opioids* such as meperidine or methadone) and that lead to addiction; lead to a reduction in pain and an overall sense of well-being (from the Greek term for "numbness") (see also *central nervous system (CNS) depressant*)

natural selection. Evolutionary principle describing a mechanism by which organisms have developed and changed, based on what is commonly called the "survival of the fittest," in that those organisms that are best suited for adapting to a given environment are the ones most likely to reach sexual maturity and to produce offspring; that is, the organisms that are best suited for adapting to a given environment are then selected by nature for survival and ultimately the birth of descendants

naturalistic observation. A method of scientific study in which the researcher goes out into the field (settings in the community) to record the behavior of people engaged in the normal activities of their daily lives (also termed *field study*; cf. *case study, experiment, survey, test*); occasionally used as a clinical assessment technique (cf. *clinical interview*)

near-death experience. An experience in which an individual either comes extremely close to dying or is actually believed to be dead and is then revived before permanent brain death occurs; the unusual psychological phenomena associated with such experiences are believed to be linked to the oxygen deprivation that occurs during such experiences

negative acceleration. Gradual reduction in the amount of increase that occurs in successive conditioning trials; that is, as the strength of the conditioned association increases, subsequent conditioning trials provide smaller increases in the strength of the association

negative (inverse) correlation. A relationship between two attributes, in which an increase in either one of the attributes is associated with a decrease in the other attribute; a perfect negative correlation is indicated by −1 (also termed *inverse correlation*; see *correlation*; cf. *positive correlation*)

negative-feedback loop. A physiological mechanism whereby the body monitors a particular resource (e.g., *hormones,* glucose, or lipids in the blood), signaling to find a way to increase the levels of the resource when levels are low, and then signaling to find a way to decrease the levels of the resource when levels are high—for example, by discontinuing the release of hormones or refraining from eating or drinking (see also *homeostatic regulation*)

negative punishment. The removal of a pleasant *stimulus,* intended to decrease the probability of a response (also called *penalty*)

negative reinforcement. The process of removing an unpleasant *stimulus* that results in an increased probability of a *response* (see *negative reinforcer*)

negative reinforcer. An unpleasant *stimulus* (e.g., physical or psychological *pain* or discomfort) whose removal is welcome following an *operant* response; its removal strengthens the operant response (see *negative reinforcement*)

negative transfer. A situation in which prior *learning* may lead to greater difficulty in learning and remembering new material (see *mental set*; cf. *positive transfer*)

neodissociative theory. A view of hypnosis in which it is asserted that some individuals are capable of separating one part of their conscious minds from another part; in one part, the individual responds to the hypnotist's commands, while in the other part, the individual observes and monitors the events and actions taking place, including some of the actions that the hypnotized individual appears not to be processing in the part of the conscious mind that is engaging in the actions

neo-Freudians. The psychodynamically oriented theorists who followed Freud and who differed from Freud in some ways but still clung to many Freudian principles regarding human personality development

neonate. Newborn (*neo-,* "new"; *-nate,* "born")

nerve. Bundle of *neurons;* many neurons can be observed as fibers extending from the *brain* down through the center of the back (in the *central nervous system*) and then out to various parts of the body (in the *peripheral nervous system*)

nervous system. Physiological network of *nerves* that form the basis of the ability to perceive, adapt to, and interact with the world; the means by which humans and other vertebrates receive, process, and then respond to messages from the environment and from inside our bodies (see *central nervous system, peripheral nervous system*; cf. *endocrine system*; see also *autonomic nervous system, parasympathetic nervous system, somatic nervous system, sympathetic nervous system*)

neuromodulator. Chemical substance released by the *terminal buttons* of some *neurons;* serves to enhance or to diminish the responsivity of postsynaptic neurons, either by directly affecting the axons or by affecting the sensitivity of the *receptor* sites (cf. *neurotransmitter*)

neuron. *Nerve* cell, involved in neural communication within the *nervous system* (see also *interneuron, motor neuron, sensory neuron*; cf. *glial cell*)

neuroticism. See *Big Five*

neurotransmitter. A chemical messenger that is released by the *terminal buttons* on the *axon* of a presynaptic *neuron* and then carries the chemical messages across the *synapse* to *receptor* sites on the receiving *dendrites* or *soma* of the postsynaptic neuron (cf. *neuromodulator*; see also *acetylcholine, dopamine, serotonin*)

nodes of Ranvier. Small gaps in the myelin coating along the *axons* of myelinated *neurons* (see *glial cell, myelin sheath*)

noise. Confusing, nonsensical, and often unpleasant sound that results when the note of a *fundamental frequency* is accompanied by irregular and unrelated sound waves, rather than by multiples of the fundamental frequency (cf. *harmonics*)

normal distribution. A distribution of scores or other measurement values in which most values congregate around the *median,* and the measurement values rapidly decline in number on either side of the median, tailing off more slowly as scores get more extreme; in such a distribution, the median is approximately the same as both the *mean* and the *mode*

normative scores. The set of normative equivalents for a range of raw *test* scores that represent the *normal distribution* of scores obtained by giving a test to a huge number of individuals; once a set of normative scores (also termed *norm*; for standardized tests, also termed *standard scores*) are established for a given test, the normative scores for subsequent test-takers represent a translation of *raw scores* into scaled equivalents that reflect the relative levels of performance of the various test-takers within the normal distribution of scores

null hypothesis. A proposed expectation of no difference or relationship between levels of performance; may be assessed in terms of likelihood but not in terms of absolute certainty

obedience. Modification of behavior in response to the command of an actual or perceived authority; may involve taking an action, refraining from an action, or tailoring an action to suit another person or persons (cf. *compliance, conformity*)

object permanence. A cognitive realization that objects continue to exist even when the objects are not immediately perceptible

object-relations theory. A contemporary extension of Freudian theory; primarily concerned with how people relate to one another and how people conceptualize these relationships largely in terms of their investment of libidinal energy in other persons or objects

objective personality test. A means of assessing *personality* by using a standardized and uniform procedure for scoring the assessment instrument; not necessarily characterized by objective means of determining what to test, how to interpret test scores, or the theory on which to base the test (cf. *projective test*)

obsession. An unwanted, persistent thought, image, or impulse that cannot be suppressed; obsessions may focus on persistent doubts regarding task completion, persistent thoughts about something like a person or a relationship, persistent impulses to engage in undesired behavior, persistent fears, or persistent images

obsessive–compulsive anxiety disorder. Characterized by unwanted, persistent thoughts and irresistible impulses to perform a ritual to relieve those thoughts

occipital lobe. Located at the back of the *brain*, chiefly responsible for visual processing; one of the four major regions of the *cerebral cortex* (cf. *frontal lobe, parietal lobe, temporal lobe*)

Oedipal conflict. A central issue of the *phallic stage* of *psychosexual development*, in which boys feel sexual desires toward their mothers but fear the powerful wrath of their fathers; named for the Greek myth in which Oedipus, who had long been separated from his par-

ents and therefore did not recognize them, killed his father and married his mother; sometimes also used as a generic term to encompass both the Oedipal conflict and the analogous *Electra conflict* in girls

olfaction. Sense of smell, which is chemically activated by airborne molecules that can dissolve in either water or fat

olfactory bulb. The location, just below the *frontal lobes*, where sensory *receptors* receive chemical inputs and send them on to the *temporal lobe* or to the *limbic system* (especially the *hypothalamus*)

olfactory epithelium. The "smell skin" in the nasal membranes, where airborne scent molecules contact the olfactory *receptor* cells that detect the scent molecules and then initiate the transduction of the chemical energy of the odors into the electrochemical energy of neural transmission

opening-up meditation. One of the two main forms of contemplation, in which the meditator integrates *meditation* with the events of everyday life, seeking to expand awareness of everyday events, rather than to separate meditation from mundane existence; often involves an attempt to focus on becoming one with an ordinary activity, and on putting all other interfering thoughts out of *consciousness* (cf. *concentrative meditation*)

openness. See *Big Five*

operant. Active behavioral response during interactions with the environment, which may be strengthened by positive or negative reinforcement or may be weakened either by a lack of reinforcement or by *punishment* during interactions with the environment

operant conditioning. *Learning* that occurs as a result of *stimuli* that either strengthen (through reinforcement) or weaken (through *punishment* or through lack of reinforcement) the likelihood of a given behavioral response (an *operant*) (also termed *instrumental conditioning*)

operational definition. A specific description of one or more precise elements and procedures involved in solving a given research problem, which allows researchers to communicate clearly the means by which they conducted an experiment and reached their conclusions

opiate. A *narcotic* that is derived from the opium poppy bulb; may be injected

intravenously, smoked, ingested orally, or inhaled (cf. *opioid*)

opioid. A *narcotic* that has a similar chemical structure and set of effects to those of an *opiate* but that is made synthetically through combinations of chemicals

opponent-process theory (of addiction and motivation). In regard to emotions, the theory posits the existence of a process whereby the body seeks to ensure motivational neutrality, such that when one process or motivational source impels the person to feel positive or negative motivations, an opposing motivational force (an opponent process) acts to bring the person back to the neutral baseline; in the case of positive motivations, the opponent process will involve negative movement back down to the baseline; in the case of negative motivations, the opponent process will involve positive movement back up to the baseline; in regard to addictions to *psychoactive* drugs, opponent processes counteract the effects of consuming the addictive substance, thus leading to or at least exacerbating the effects of *addiction, tolerance,* and *withdrawal*

opponent-process theory (of color vision). One of the two major theories of color vision (cf. *trichromatic theory of color vision*); based on the notion of three opposing processes in human vision, two of which contrast each of two colors with another (yielding four fundamental colors—red/green and yellow/blue) and one of which contrasts black and white as a third opposing set of achromatic primaries that are perceived in much the same way as are the other opposing pairs

optic chiasma. The place in the *occipital lobe* of the *brain* where neural fibers carrying visual information cross over from one side of the body to the *contralateral* hemisphere of the brain (*chiasma,* "X-shaped or crossed configuration")

optic nerve. *Axons* of *ganglion cells* in the first (outer) layer of the *retina*

optical illusion. A visual *stimulus* that leads to distortion in visual *perception* (see *Müller–Lyer illusion, Ponzo illusion*)

oral stage. A Freudian stage of *psychosexual development;* typically occurs during the first 2 years, when an infant explores sucking and other oral activity, learning that such activity provides not only nourishment but also gratification

organic pain.   Sensations of extreme discomfort and suffering caused by damage to bodily tissue (cf. *psychogenic pain;* see also *pain*)

orienting reflex.   A series of preprogrammed responses that are prompted by a sudden change in the environment (e.g., a flash of light or an abrupt loud noise); included among the specific preprogrammed responses are a generalized reflexive orientation toward the origin of the change, changes in brain-wave patterns (see *electroencephalogram*), dilation of the pupils, and some other physiological changes associated with *stress* (see also *instinct, reflex*)

outgroup homogeneity bias.   Tendency to view the members of an outgroup (of which the individual is not a member) as all being alike, often in contrast to a tendency to view members of an ingroup (of which the individual is a member) as distinct individuals who have dissimilar characteristics, thus facilitating the ease of forming *stereotypes* of outgroups but not of ingroups

oval window.   The first part of the inner ear, at one end of which is the *cochlea* and at the other end of which is the spot where the *stapes* either rests or vibrates in response to sounds; when the stapes vibrates, the mechanical vibration is transmitted to the cochlea via the oval window

overconfidence.   Excessively high evaluation of skills, knowledge, or judgment, usually applied to a person's valuation of her or his own abilities

overdose.   Ingestion of a life-threatening or lethal dose of drugs, often associated with the use of *psychoactive* drugs, such as *narcotics, amphetamines,* or *sedatives;* though often linked to intentional suicide, overdoses commonly occur due to *tolerance* or *sensitization,* particularly when the users are also using street drugs, which contain many impurities and are not reliably controlled with regard to the concentrations of psychoactive elements in the drug compounds

overextension error.   Overapplication (usually by children or other persons acquiring a language) of the meaning of a given word to more things, ideas, and situations than is appropriate for the denotation and the defining features of the word; generally no longer typifies

language once the vocabulary of the language user has expanded to include enough words to describe the meanings the individual intends to convey (see also *feature hypothesis, functional hypothesis*)

overregularization.   An error that commonly occurs during language acquisition, in which the novice language user has gained an understanding of how a language usually works and then over-applies the general rules of the language to the exceptions in which the rule does not apply

p-value.   A statistical quantity that indicates the probability (*p*) that a particular outcome may have occurred as a result of chance

pain.   Intense sensory discomfort and emotional suffering associated with actual, imagined, or threatened damage to or irritation of body tissues (see *organic pain, psychogenic pain*)

paired-associates recall.   A memory task in which the individual is presented with a list of paired (and often related) items, which the individual is asked to store in memory, and then the individual is presented with one item in each pair and asked to provide the mate of each given item (cf. *free recall, serial recall*)

panic disorder.   An *anxiety disorder* characterized by brief (usually only a few minutes), abrupt, and unprovoked, but recurrent episodes during which a person experiences intense and uncontrollable anxiety; during the episodes (termed *panic attacks*), the panicked individual feels terrified and exhibits psychophysiological symptoms of heightened *arousal,* such as difficulty in breathing, heart palpitations, dizziness, sweating, and trembling; often associated with *agoraphobia* and sometimes associated with feelings of depersonalization (the feeling of being outside of the body looking in rather than on the inside looking out)

papillae.   Small visible protrusions on the tongue that contain thousands of taste-receptor cells (see *taste buds*)

paradigm.   A theoretical system that provides an overarching model for organizing related theories for understanding a particular phenomenon such as *intelligence, learning, personality,* or psychological development; also used to describe a model or framework for conducting a particular type of experiment (e.g., *simulating paradigm*)

parallel processing.   Cognitive manipulation of multiple operations simultaneously; as applied to short-term memory, the items stored in short-term memory would be retrieved all at once, not one at a time (cf. *serial processing*)

parasympathetic nervous system.   The part of the *autonomic nervous system* that is concerned primarily with anabolism (cf. *sympathetic nervous system*)

parietal lobe.   One of the four major regions of the *cerebral cortex* (cf. *frontal lobe, occipital lobe, temporal lobe*); chiefly responsible for processing the somatosensory sensations that come from the skin and muscles of the body

partial reinforcement.   An *operant-conditioning* schedule (also termed *intermittent reinforcement*) in which a given *operant* response is rewarded some of the time but not all of the time; comprises two types of reinforcement schedules: *ratio schedules* (see *fixed-ratio reinforcement, variable-ratio reinforcement*) and *interval schedules* (see *fixed-interval reinforcement, variable-interval reinforcement*); such schedules are more resistant to *extinction* than are *continuous reinforcement* schedules

passion.   The intense desire for union with another person; one of three basic components of love, according to the *triangular theory of love* (cf. *commitment, intimacy*)

pathogen.   A specific disease-causing agent (*patho-,* "suffering" or "disease"; *-gen,* "producer")

patient-centered style (of physician interactions).   One of two basic patterns for physician–patient interactions (cf. *doctor-centered style*); characterized by a relatively nondirective style of interaction, in which the physician asks divergent questions and allows the patient to take part in guiding the course of the interview, the diagnosis of the presenting problem, and the decision regarding the optimal treatment for the problem

Pearson product-moment correlation coefficient.   A measure of linear relation, ranging from −1 (perfect inverse relation) to 0 (no relation) to +1 (perfect positive relation)

pegword system.   See *mnemonic devices*

perception.   The set of psychological processes by which people recognize, organize, synthesize, and give meaning (in the *brain*) to the *sensations* received from environmental *stimuli* by the sense organs; (cf. *sensation*)

perceptual constancy. The perception that a given object remains the same even when the immediate *sensation* of the object changes (see *lightness constancy*, *shape constancy*, *size constancy*)

peripheral nervous system (PNS). One of the two main parts of the *nervous system* (cf. *central nervous system [CNS]*); comprises all of the *nerve* cells, including the nerves of the face and head, except the *neurons* of the *brain* and the *spinal cord* (the CNS); primarily relays information between the CNS and the rest of the body (including the face and the internal organs other than the brain); connects the CNS with sensory *receptors* in both external sensory organs (e.g., skin, ears, eyes) and internal body parts (e.g., stomach, muscles) and connects the CNS with motor effectors in parts of the body that produce movement, speech, and so on (*peripheral* means both "auxiliary," for the PNS assists the CNS, and "away from the center," for the peripheral nerves are external to the CNS)

peripheral route to persuasion. One of two routes to persuasion (cf. *central route to persuasion*); emphasizes tangential, situational features of the persuasive message, such as the appeal of the message sender, the attractiveness of the message's presentation, or rewarding features of the message or its source; most effective when the recipient is not strongly interested in the issue or is unable to consider the issue carefully

permissive parents. Mothers and fathers who exhibit a style of parenting in which they tend to give their children a great deal of freedom, possibly more than the children can handle, and who tend to be lax in discipline and to let children make their own decisions about many things that other parents might find questionably appropriate (cf. *authoritarian parents*, *authoritative parents*)

person-centered approach. A humanistic approach to personality theory, which strongly emphasizes the *self* and each person's perception of self

person–environment interaction. The individual fit between a particular person and the environment in which the individual develops and interacts with others

person-positivity bias. A bias of *impression formation* that involves the tendency for people to evaluate individuals more positively than they evaluate groups, including the groups to which those individuals belong

personal attribution. One of two fundamental types of *attributions* (cf. *situational attribution*); the causes of human behavior are attributed to the internal factors in the person who is engaging in the given behavior (also termed *dispositional attribution*)

personal dispositions. Personality *traits* that are unique to each individual and therefore may be difficult to assess via interpersonal correlational studies or standardized personality inventories

personal fable. A form of adolescent *egocentrism*, in which the adolescent believes that he or she is somehow unique and destined for fame and fortune

personal unconscious. One of two Jungian parts of the unconscious mind (cf. *collective unconscious*), in which is stored each person's unique personal experiences and repressed memories (see also *complexes*)

personality. The enduring characteristics and dispositions of a person that provide some degree of coherence across the various ways in which the person behaves

personality disorders. Psychological disorders involving a pattern of consistent, long-term, extreme personality characteristics that cause the person great unhappiness or that seriously impair the person's ability to adjust to the demands of everyday living or to function well in her or his environment, such as the following: *antisocial personality disorder*—characterized by at least average intelligence and the tendency to appear superficially charming, sincere, poised, calm, and verbally facile as a strategy for winning the trust and cooperation of other persons despite actually being insincere, untruthful, self-centered, ungrateful, and unreliable in interpersonal relations (formerly termed *psychopathy* or *sociopathy*); *avoidant personality disorder*—characterized by reluctance to enter into close personal relationships due to an intense fear of rejection, often accompanied by self-devaluation, very low *self-esteem*, and a wish for unattainable closeness; *borderline personality disorder*—characterized by extreme volatility and instability in mood, self-image, and interpersonal relationships; *dependent personality disorder*—characterized by little self-confidence, extreme sensitivity to criticism, difficulty in taking personal responsibility for self-care; *histrionic personality disorder*—characterized by highly dramatic behavior and continual attempts to attract attention, such as lavish displays of emotionality and affection (despite actual shallowness of feeling), extreme volatility, great vanity, and manipulative interpersonal relationships (formerly called "hysterical personality"); *narcissistic personality disorder*—characterized by an inflated self-image, intense self-centeredness and selfishness in interpersonal relationships, lack of empathy for others, and strong feelings of entitlement from others without concern for reciprocating to others; *obsessive–compulsive personality disorder*—characterized by having *obsessions* or *compulsions* or both; *paranoid personality disorder*—characterized by suspiciousness of others and a tendency to suspect that others are plotting against the paranoid individual, to view other people's innocuous behavior as directed against the individual (cf. *schizophrenia* [paranoid]); *schizoid personality disorder*—characterized by difficulty in forming relationships with other people, a tendency to prefer solitude over companionship, and apparent indifference to what others think, say, or even feel about the disordered individual; *schizotypal personality disorder*—characterized by major problems in interpersonal interactions and by other attributes that tend to cause these persons to be viewed as eccentric or even bizarre, such as susceptibility to *illusions* and to magical thinking (e.g., believing in extrasensory perceptive powers or other supernatural phenomena for which there is little supporting evidence)

perspective. A view of psychological phenomena that centers on a particular set of theories and beliefs (cf. *field*)

pervasive developmental disorder (PDD). A condition, of which autism is one type, characterized by three main symptoms: (1) minimal or no responsiveness to others or to the surrounding world; (2) impaired verbal and nonverbal communication; and (3) having a highly restricted range of interest, sitting alone for hours, being immobile, rocking back and forth, and staring off into space

phallic stage. A Freudian stage of *psychosexual development*; typically begins at about 4 years of age and continues until about 6 years of age; during this stage, children discover that stimulation of the genitals can be pleasurable, and they first experience either the *Oedipal conflict* (in boys) or the *Electra conflict* (in girls)

phenotype. Expression of an inherited *trait*, based on the dominant trait in the *genotype* and also subject to environmental influence; *dominant traits* prevail over *recessive traits* in determining whether genotypic traits are expressed in the phenotype

pheromones. Chemical substances secreted by animals that trigger specific kinds of reactions (largely related to reproduction, territory, or aggression) in other animals, usually of the same species

philosophy. A system of ideas or a set of fundamental beliefs; a means of seeking to explore and understand the general nature of many aspects of the world

phobia. One of five main categories of *anxiety disorders*, characterized by an exaggerated, persistent, irrational, and disruptive fear of a particular object, a particular event, or a particular setting, or a fear of a general kind of object, event, or setting (see also *agoraphobia*, *social phobia*)

phoneme. The particular speech sounds the users of a specific *language* can identify

photopigments. Chemical substances that absorb light, thereby starting the complex transduction process that transforms physical electromagnetic energy into an electrochemical neural impulse; the *rods* and the *cones* contain different types of photopigments; different types of photopigments absorb differing amounts of light, and some detect different *hues* (see *photoreceptors*)

photoreceptors. The physiological structures in the *retina* of the eye that *transduce* light energy into electrochemical energy, thus enabling the eye to see; located in the innermost layer of the retina, farthest from the light source; the two kinds of photoreceptors are the *rods* and the *cones* (see also *photopigments*)

phrase-structure grammar. A form of syntactical analysis that analyzes sentences in terms of the superficial sequence of words in sentences, regardless of differences or similarities of meaning; analysis often centers on the analysis of noun phrases and verb phrases; also termed *surface-structure grammars* because analysis centers on *syntax* at a surface level of

analysis (cf. *deep-structure level*, *transformational grammar*)

physiology. Scientific study of living organisms and of life-sustaining functions and processes (in contrast to *anatomy*, which studies the structures of living organisms)

pinna. Visible outer part of the ear that collects sound waves

pitch. *Sensation* of how high or low a tone sounds, based on the frequency of the sound wave that reaches the auditory *receptors*

pituitary gland. An endocrine *gland* located above the mouth and underneath the *hypothalamus* (in the *forebrain*), to which it is attached and by which it is controlled; sometimes considered the master gland of the body because of its central importance to the *endocrine system*; provides a direct link from the endocrine system to the *nervous system* via the hypothalamus; secretes *hormones* that directly affect other physiological functions and that indirectly affect other functions through the release of pituitary hormones that control many other endocrine glands, stimulating those glands to release hormones that produce specific physiological effects; in particular, when stimulated by the hypothalamus, the pituitary gland plays an important role in the response to *stress*, secreting adrenocorticotropic hormone (ACTH), which is carried by the bloodstream to other organs, most notably the adrenal glands, which then release epinephrine and norepinephrine

place theory. One of the two alternative views of the way humans sense *pitch* (cf. *frequency theory*; see also *duplicity theory*); suggests that the sensation of pitch is determined by the location on the *basilar membrane* where the sound wave vibrates the *hair cells*; thus, hair cells located at various places on the basilar membrane vibrate in response to sounds of different frequencies and then stimulate different sensory neurons, which then determine the pitch that is perceived

plasticity. Modifiable, subject to being changed

pleasure principle. The operating principle by which the *id* irrationally pursues immediate gratification of libidinal urges, regardless of the external realities that might impinge on those urges (cf. *idealistic principle*, *reality principle*)

polygraph. (Referred to as a *lie detector*.) A device for evaluating the truthfulness of *self-report measures*, by assessing the psychophysiological reactivity of various physiological processes, such as heart rate, galvanic skin response (GSR), and respiration; such measurements assess *arousal*, usually associated with emotional *stress*; thus, for persons who feel stressful arousal in association with lying, such measures indicate instances of lying; however, for persons who feel stressful arousal in association with other situations, such measures also indicate those sources of arousal; and for persons who feel no stressful arousal in association with lying, such measures do not indicate instances of lying

pons. A structure in the *hindbrain* that contains nerve cells that pass signals from one part of the *brain* to another, thereby serving as a kind of relay station or bridge (*pons*, "bridge" [Latin]); also contains a portion of the *reticular activating system* and *nerves* that serve parts of the head and face

Ponzo illusion. An *optical illusion* in which two equally long horizontal line segments, which are framed by diagonally converging line segments, are perceived to differ in length; may be an artifact of some of the *monocular depth cues* with which perceivers are familiar (cf. *Müller–Lyer illusion*)

population. The entire set of individuals to which a generalization is to be made

population parameters. The set of numerical values that characterizes all persons in a *population* under investigation; under most circumstances, it is impossible or impractical to determine population parameters, so *sample statistics* are used as an indication of the population parameters (see also *representative sample*)

positive correlation. A relationship between two attributes in which an increase in either one of the attributes is associated with an increase in the other attribute, and a decrease in either one of the attributes is associated with a decrease in the other attribute; a perfect positive correlation is indicated by +1 (see *correlation*; cf. *negative correlation*)

positive punishment. The application of an unpleasant *stimulus*, intended to decrease the probability of a *response*

positive reinforcement. The pairing of a given *operant* behavior with a *stimulus* that is rewarding to the organism engaged in the operant, which thereby strengthens the likelihood that the organism will produce the operant again (see *operant conditioning, positive reinforcer*; cf. *negative reinforcement*)

positive reinforcer. A reward (pleasant *stimulus*) that follows an *operant* and strengthens the associated *response* (see *operant conditioning, positive reinforcement*; cf. *negative reinforcer*; cf. also *punishment*)

positive transfer. A situation in which prior *learning* may lead to greater ease of learning and remembering new material (cf. *negative transfer*)

positron emission tomography (PET). A technique for creating dynamic images of the *brain* in action (thus revealing physiological processes, not just anatomical structures); involves injecting into a patient a mildly radioactive form of glucose, which is absorbed by cells of the body including the brain; the amount of glucose absorption in the brain indicates the level of metabolic activity of the cells; computer analysis of the glucose absorption thereby indicates the locations of high rates of metabolic activity during various cognitive tasks (e.g., playing computer games, speaking, moving parts of the body); largely used as a research tool, but clinical applications are forthcoming

postconventional (principled) morality. A phase of moral development in which the individual recognizes the importance of (1) social contracts (the importance of societal rules as a basis for behavior) and (2) individual rights (internal moral rights and principles that may outweigh societal rules in some situations—for example, rights to life and liberty)

postformal thinking. A stage of *cognitive development* that may follow the stage of *formal operations*, in which individuals recognize the constant unfolding and evolution of thought (see *dialectical thinking*), and they can manipulate mentally various options for decisions and diverse alternative answers to questions, recognizing that a single ideal option or a simple unambiguous answer may not be available

posthypnotic suggestion. An instruction given to an individual during *hypnosis*, which the individual is to implement

after having wakened from the hypnotic state; subjects often have no recollection of having been given the instructions or even of having been hypnotized

posttraumatic stress disorder. A stress disorder (a form of *anxiety disorder*; cf. also *acute stress disorder*) characterized by the intrusive psychological reenactment of a past traumatic event, such as recurring nightmares or repeated wakeful resurfacing of painful memories of the event while consciously engaged in unrelated activities; often accompanied by difficulties in sleeping or in concentrating while awake; sometimes accompanied by an uncomfortable feeling of experiencing life in ways that other people do not, as well as by feelings of apathy and detachment

pragmatics. The study of how people use *language*, emphasizing the social contexts in which language is used as well as the nonverbal communication that augments verbal communication

preconscious. A part of *consciousness* that comprises information that could become conscious readily but that is not continuously available in awareness

preconventional morality. A phase of moral development in which moral reasoning is guided by *punishments* and rewards; initially, individual moral reasoners focus on the avoidance of *punishment* and on *obedience* to authority, without concern for the interests or feelings of other persons, except as those interests or feelings may affect the likelihood of punishment; later in this phase, moral reasoners recognize the interests of others, but strictly in terms of how to strike deals in order to gain self-interested advantages (rewards)

prediction. One of the four goals of psychological research (the other three are *control, description*, and *explanation*); a declaration or indication about the future in advance, based on observation, experience, or reasoning

predictive validity. An aspect of criterion-related *validity* that assesses the extent to which a test or other measurement (the predictor) predicts some kind of performance outcome (the criterion), which is to be measured well after the test or other measurement has been taken

prejudice. A form of thinking in which an individual forms an unfavor-

able attitude toward groups of people (usually outgroups, of which they are not members) based on insufficient or incorrect evidence about these groups (see *realistic-conflict theory, social-identity theory*)

Premack principle. An axiom of *operant conditioning* that asserts that (1) more preferred activities reinforce less preferred ones, and (2) the specific degree of preference is determined by the individual who holds the preference; to apply this principle, a person's *operant* behavior can be reinforced by offering as a reward something the person prefers more than the behavior being reinforced

premise. Statement of fact or assertion of belief, on which a deductively reasoned argument may be based (see *deductive reasoning*)

preoperational stage. Second stage of *cognitive development*, according to Piaget, which is characterized by the development of internal mental representations (the precursors of which actually arose at the end of the previous [sensorimotor] stage) and verbal communication (cf. *concrete operations, formal-operational stage, sensorimotor stage*)

prescriptive grammar. Rules that specify the correct ways to structure the use of written or spoken *language*

primacy effect. Tendency to show superior recall of words that occur at and near the beginning of a list of words (cf. *recency effect*); affects *impression formation*, such that first impressions can influence subsequent ones

primary appraisal. The first step in a two-step process of appraising a potentially stressful situation (cf. *secondary appraisal*); involves a person's determination of whether it is important to deal with the situation, based on the significance of the situation for the person and its possible outcomes for the person as a result of dealing with versus not dealing with the situation

primary colors. The three colors (red, green, and blue) that can be combined additively to form all other colors (see also *additive mixture, trichromatic theory of color vision*)

primary motor cortex. The portion of the *frontal lobe* that plans, controls, and executes movements, particularly movements that involve any kind of delayed response; this portion of the *cere-*

bral cortex can be mapped to show the places in the *brain* that control specific groups of muscles in the body

primary-process thought. A form of thought that is irrational, instinct driven, and out of touch with reality, often thought to be a wellspring of creativity and of dreams, as well as of symbolic expressions of sexual and aggressive urges (cf. *secondary-process thought*)

primary reinforcer. A rewarding *stimulus* used in *operant conditioning* that provides immediate satisfaction to the learner (cf. *secondary reinforcer*)

primary somatosensory cortex. The portion of the *parietal lobe* (located directly behind the *primary motor cortex* in the *frontal lobe*) that receives information from the senses about pressure, texture, temperature, and *pain*; this portion of the *cerebral cortex* can be mapped to show the places in the brain that receive sensory information from precise locations on the surface of the body

priming. The activation of a node by a *prime* (activating node) to which the node is connected in a network, in the process of spreading activation, according to the network view of *memory* processes

proactive interference. A type of memory disruption that occurs when interfering information is presented before, rather than after, the information that is to be remembered (also termed *proactive inhibition*; cf. *retroactive interference*)

problem-focused coping. See *coping*

problem solving. One of the fundamental kinds of *thinking* that involves resolving a difficulty, overcoming obstacles, answering a question, or achieving a goal (see *problem-solving cycle*; cf. *creativity, judgment and decision making, reasoning*)

procedural memory. A recognition and awareness of how to perform particular tasks, skills, or procedures ("knowing how," not "knowing that"; cf. *declarative memory*)

productive thinking. A form of *critical thinking* that involves *insight* that goes beyond the bounds of the existing associations identified by the thinker (cf. *reproductive thinking*)

projection areas. The areas in the cortical lobes where sensory and motor processing occurs; sensory projection areas are the locations in the *cerebral cor-*

tex to which *sensory neurons* are projected via the *thalamus* from elsewhere in the body; motor projection areas are the regions that project *motor neurons* downward through the *spinal cord*, via the *peripheral nervous system*, to control desired movement of the appropriate muscles

projective test. A psychological assessment based on *psychodynamic theory*, in which it is held that the individual's unconscious conflicts may be projected into responses to the assessment (cf. *objective personality test*)

prosocial behavior. Societally approved actions that are seen as furthering the common good, that are at least consistent with the interests of the social group, or that help one or more other persons (cf. *antisocial behavior*)

prototype theory. One of two primary theories of *semantics* (cf. *componential theory*), which claims that the meaning of a word (or *concept*) can be understood by describing the concept in terms of a *prototype* (see also *exemplar*) that best represents a given concept and comprises a set of *characteristic features* that tend to be typical of most examples of the concept (cf. *defining features*)

proximity (as an aspect of interpersonal attraction). The geographical nearness of people toward whom an individual might feel attracted; a factor increasing the likelihood that a person may be attracted to another person, perhaps by also enhancing the probability of familiarity with or *arousal* by the other person

psychoactive. Characteristic of drugs that produce a *psychopharmacological* effect, thereby affecting behavior, mood, and consciousness; can be classified into four basic categories: *central nervous system (CNS) depressant, central nervous system (CNS) stimulant, hallucinogenic,* and *narcotic*

psychoanalysis. A form of psychological treatment based on *psychodynamic theory*

psychodynamic theory. A theory of human *motivations* and behavior that emphasizes the importance of conflicting unconscious mental processes and early childhood experiences in affecting adult *personality*

psychogenic pain. Intense sensory discomfort and emotional suffering for which physiological origins (due to in-

jury of body tissues) cannot be found (cf. *organic pain*); three common types are: *causalgia*—characterized by recurrent episodes of severe burning pain in a body part or region (often in a location where tissue has been damaged due to a serious wound); *neuralgia*—characterized by recurrent episodes of intense shooting pain along a nerve; and *phantom-limb pain*—characterized by pain sensations in a limb that no longer has functioning nerves (e.g., due to amputation)

psychological disorder. A condition exhibited by an individual if (1) the individual shows a clinically significant behavior or psychological syndrome that is associated with present distress or disability or with an increased risk of suffering death, *pain*, disability, or an important loss of freedom; (2) the syndrome is not merely an expected and culturally sanctioned response to a particular event, such as the death of a loved one; and (3) the syndrome is not a deliberate response to particular conditions, such as poverty, conflicts with society, or *prejudice*

psychology. The study of the mind and of the behavior of people and other organisms

psychometric. Characterized by psychological measurement (*psycho-*, pertaining to the mind or mental processes, *-metric*, "measurement")

psychopharmacological. An outcome that affects behavior, mood, and consciousness, produced by drugs (see *psychoactive*)

psychophysics. The study and measurement of the functioning of the senses, which involve the attempt to measure the relationship between a form of physical stimulation and the psychological sensations produced as a consequence

psychosexual development. An aspect of *personality* development that refers to the increasing self-identification with a particular gender and changing self-perception about sexuality

psychosocial theory (of personality development). A theory of *personality* development that deals with how social factors interact with personality throughout the entire life span

psychosomatic medicine. A psychodynamic view of illness that studied the psychological roots of physical illnesses (e.g., ulcers, asthma, migraine headaches)

psychosurgery. A surgical procedure intended to alleviate mental disorders by probing, slicing, dissecting, or removing some part of the *brain*

psychotherapy. An intervention that uses the principles of *psychology* to treat mental or emotional disorders or otherwise to improve the adjustment and well-being of the person who receives the intervention

psychoticism. A personality attribute characterized by solitariness, detached interpersonal relationships, and a lack of feelings, especially a lack of caring, empathy, and sensitivity (cf. *Big Five*)

psychotropic drugs. Drugs that affect the individual's psychological processes or state of mind; four main classes of psychotropic drugs are *antipsychotics, antidepressants*, antianxiety drugs, and lithium (see also *psychoactive*)

puberty. The stage of development at which humans become capable of reproduction

punishment. A process used in *operant conditioning* that *decreases* the probability of an operant response through either the application of an unpleasant *stimulus* or the removal of a pleasant one; an ineffective means of reducing *aggression* if physical *punishment* (rather than penalty) is used as a means of operant conditioning (cf. *negative reinforcer, positive reinforcer*)

pupil. The hole in the *iris* (roughly in its center) through which light gains access to the interior of the eye, particularly the *retina*; in dim light, the pupil reflexively expands, permitting more light to enter, but in bright light, it reflexively contracts, limiting the amount of light that can enter the eye

purity (as related to color). The extent to which a *hue* cannot be analyzed in terms of a combination of other hues (see also *additive mixture, subtractive mixture*)

quality. The nature of a *stimulus* that reaches a sensory *receptor* and is then sensed in the *brain* (cf. *intensity*)

quasi-experimental design. A plan for conducting a study that has many of the features of a *controlled experimental design* but that does not ensure the random assignment of participants to the treatment and the control groups (cf. *controlled experimental design, correlational design*)

questionnaire. A set of questions used by social-science researchers for conducting a *survey* (cf. *test*; cf. also *case study, experiment, naturalistic observation*)

random sample. A *sample* in which every person in a *population* has an equal chance of being selected

range. The full expanse of a distribution of values, from the lowest to the highest value

ratio IQ. A means of indicating performance on intelligence tests, based on a quotient of *mental age* divided by chronological age, times 100 (cf. *deviation IQs*)

ratio schedule. A schedule of reinforcement in *operant conditioning*, in which a proportion (ratio) of *operant* responses are reinforced, regardless of the amount of time that has passed (see *fixed-ratio reinforcement, variable-ratio reinforcement*; cf. *fixed-interval reinforcement, variable-interval reinforcement*; see also *partial reinforcement, positive reinforcement*)

rational-emotive therapy (RET). A form of cognitive therapy designed to help people with their emotional reactions by helping them to rectify their incorrect or maladaptive thoughts (see *cognitivism*)

rationalist. Person who believes that knowledge is most effectively acquired through rational methods (cf. *empiricist*)

raw score. The actual total sum of points obtained by a given test-taker on a given test; often equals the actual number of items answered correctly on the test

reaction range. The broad limits within which a particular attribute (e.g., *intelligence*) may be expressed in various possible ways, given the inherited potential for expression of the attribute in the particular individual

realistic-conflict theory. A theory about *prejudice* that argues that competition among groups for valuable but scarce resources leads to prejudice

reality principle. The operating principle by which the *ego* responds as rationally as possible to the real world as it is consciously perceived to be, rather than as the person desires the world to be (cf. *pleasure principle*) or as the person believes that the world should be (cf. *idealistic principle*); mediates among the urges of the *id*, the prohibitions of the *superego*, and the realities of the external world

reasoning. One of the fundamental processes of *thinking* that involves drawing conclusions from evidence; often classified as involving either *deductive reasoning* or *inductive reasoning* (cf. *creativity, judgment and decision making, problem solving*)

recall memory. A process of memory often used in memory tasks, in which the individual is asked to produce (not just to recognize as correct) a fact, a word, or another item from memory (see also *free recall, paired-associates recall, serial recall*; cf. *recognition memory*)

recency effect. Tendency to show superior recall of words that occur at and near the end of a list of words (cf. *primacy effect*)

receptors. Physiological structures designed to receive something (e.g., a given substance or a particular kind of information), which may refer either to (1) the structures that receive external stimulation and *transduce* it into electrochemical sensory information, or to (2) the structures that receive electrochemical sensory information; sensory receptors are physiological structures that provide a mechanism for receiving external stimulation (from outside the body), which can then be transduced into sensation as electrochemical sensory information within the body; receptor *nerves* and *neurons* receive electrochemical sensory information (e.g., sensations in the eyes, ears, and skin) from sensory receptors or from other *sensory neurons* and then transmit that information back up through the *spinal cord* to the *brain* (cf. *interneuron, motor neuron*)

recessive trait. The weaker genetic trait in a pair of *traits*; does not appear in the *phenotype* of an organism when the *genotype* comprises a *dominant trait* and a recessive trait

reciprocal determinism. A principle of a *personality* theory that attributes human functioning to an interaction among behavior, personal variables, and the environment

recognition memory. A process of memory often used in memory tasks, in which the individual is asked just to recognize as correct (not to produce) a fact, a word, or another item from memory (cf. *recall memory*)

reconstructive memory. A psychological phenomenon in which an individual stores and then retrieves from memory some information about events or facts, almost exactly as the events or facts took place (cf. *constructive memory*)

reflex. An automatic physiological response to an external *stimulus*; the *spinal cord* transmits a message directly from receptor nerves to effector nerves, without routing the message through the *brain* prior to the bodily response to the sensory information (cf. *instinct, learning*)

refraction. The degree to which light waves are bent, usually by curvature of the surface of the medium (e.g., a lens) through which the light waves are passing

regression equation. A predictive equation that specifies the relationship between a *dependent variable* and one or more *independent variables*

rehearsal. A strategy for keeping information in short-term memory or for moving information into long–term memory by repeating the information over and over

reinforcer. A *stimulus* used in *operant conditioning* that increases the probability that a given *operant* behavior associated with the stimulus (which usually has occurred immediately or almost immediately before the reinforcing stimulus) will be repeated (see *positive reinforcers, negative reinforcers*)

relative frequency. The number of cases that received a given score or range of scores (see *frequency distribution*; cf. *cumulative frequency*)

relative refractory phase. A time following the firing of a *neuron*, during which the neuron can fire again, but only in response to a much stronger *stimulus* than is normally required (cf. *absolute refractory phase*)

relative size. See *monocular depth cues*

reliability. The dependability of an experimental procedure, indicating that the procedure consistently yields the same results as long as it is administered in the same way each time; the dependability of a measurement instrument (e.g., a *test*), indicating that the instrument consistently measures the outcome being measured

reliable. See *reliability*

REM sleep. The distinctive kind of sleep that is characterized by r**a**pid **e**ye **m**ovements (REMs) and frequently—though not exclusively—associated with dreaming (cf. *N-REM sleep*)

replicate. Repeat the methods used in a previous experiment in order to observe whether the same methods will yield the same results; also used to refer to success in repeating results

representational thought. Cognitive processes that involve internal representations of external *stimuli*

representative (as a characteristic of a sample). See *representative sample*

representative sample. A subset of the *population* carefully chosen to represent the proportionate diversity of the population as a whole; well-chosen representative samples permit inferences regarding the probability that a given set of *sample statistics* accurately reflects a comparable set of *population parameters*

representativeness heuristic. A judgment regarding the probability of an uncertain event according to (1) how obviously the event is similar to or representative of the *population* from which it is derived, and (2) the degree to which the event reflects the salient features, such as randomness, of the process by which it is generated (see *heuristic*)

reproductive thinking. A form of *thinking* in which the thinker makes use of existing associations involving what the thinker already knows (cf. *productive thinking*)

resilience. An individual's ability to function in the face of adversity by adapting and changing

resistance. An attempt to block therapeutic progress in psychodynamic treatment, usually as a result of unconscious conflicts

resistant attachment pattern. One of three attachment patterns observed in the *strange situation* (cf. *avoidant attachment pattern, secure attachment pattern*); a child generally shows ambivalence toward the mother while she is present, seeking both to gain and to resist physical contact with her when the mother returns after being gone a short time

response. An action or reaction that is linked to a *stimulus*

reticular activating system (RAS). A network of *neurons* (located primarily in the *midbrain* and extending into the *hindbrain*) that is essential to the regulation of *consciousness* (sleep, wakefulness, *arousal*, and even attention, to some ex-

tent) as well as to such vital functions as heartbeat and breathing

retina. A network of *neurons* that extends over most of the posterior surface of the interior of the eye, containing the *photoreceptors* responsible for transducing electromagnetic light energy into neural electrochemical impulses (see *amacrine cells, bipolar cells, ganglion cells, horizontal cells*; see also *cones, photopigments, rods*)

retrieval. See *memory*

retroactive interference. A type of memory disruption that occurs when interfering information is presented after, rather than before, the information that is to be remembered (also termed *retroactive inhibition*; cf. *proactive interference*)

retrograde amnesia. See *amnesia*

reuptake. The more common of two mechanisms by which *neurotransmitters* are removed from the synaptic cleft; the *terminal buttons* of an *axon* reabsorb (take up again) any remaining neurotransmitter or *neuromodulator* substances that had been released into the *synapse*, thereby conserving these substances and sparing the surrounding *neurons* from excessive stimulation

reversible figures. Displayed images in which each of a given pair of adjacent or even interconnecting figures can be seen as either *figure* or *ground*, although both cannot be the focus of *perception* simultaneously (see *figure–ground*)

rods. One of the two kinds of *photoreceptors* in the eye; more numerous, longer, thinner, and more highly concentrated in the periphery of the *retina* than in the foveal region of the retina than are *cones*, the other type of photoreceptor; function more effectively in dim light than in bright light, but incapable of color vision (see *fovea*)

sample. See *representative sample* and *sample statistics*

sample statistics. The set of numerical values that (1) characterize the sample of persons who have been measured in regard to the attributes under investigation and (2) are presumed to give some indication of the *population parameters* (see also *representative sample*)

satisficing. A strategy for making decisions in which the decision maker considers options one by one, immediately selecting the first option that appears to be satisfactory (just good enough), rather than considering all of the possible options and then carefully computing which of the entire universe of options will maximize gains and minimize losses; that is, decision makers consider only the minimum possible number of options that are believed necessary to achieve a satisfactory decision (see *judgment and decision making*)

saturation. One of three properties of color (cf. *hue, brightness*); the vividness, vibrancy, or richness of the hue

savings. A phenomenon of *classical conditioning* in which there is a period of time during which the *CS* and the *US* are not linked, and then the CS is presented again in the presence of the US; even when the CS is paired with the US only briefly, the CR returns to levels approaching those at the *asymptote* of the *acquisition* phase of conditioning (cf. *spontaneous recovery*)

schedules of reinforcement. Patterns of *operant conditioning* that determine the timing of reinforcement following the *operant* behavior (see *continuous reinforcement, fixed-interval reinforcement, fixed-ratio reinforcement, partial reinforcement, variable-interval reinforcement, variable-ratio reinforcement*)

schema. A cognitive framework for organizing associated *concepts*, based on previous experiences

schema theory. A cognitively based theory of sex-role development, which is based on the view that organized mental systems of information (i.e., *schemas*) help people both to make sense of their experiences and to shape their interactions, particularly in terms of their gender-relevant schemes for how males and females demonstrate differing sex-role–relevant behaviors and attitudes

schizophrenia. A set of disorders that encompasses a variety of *symptoms*, including disturbances of *perception*, cognition, emotion, and even motor behavior (see *delusions, hallucinations*): *catatonic schizophrenia*—characterized by stupor, apparently complete detachment from the rest of the world, and long periods of immobility and of staring into space; *disorganized schizophrenia*—characterized by profound psychological disorganization, including cognitive symptoms (e.g., hallucinations, delusions, and incoherent speech such as meaningless neologisms), apparent disturbances of mood (e.g., rapid mood swings and either flat affect

or inappropriate affect), and extreme neglect of self-care and self-grooming; *paranoid schizophrenia*—characterized by delusions of persecution or of grandeur, which may be accompanied by auditory hallucinations of voices telling the people either of plots against them (persecution) or of their own magnificence (grandeur), as well as by particular susceptibility to delusions of reference; *residual schizophrenia*—characterized by some mild symptoms of schizophrenia that seem to linger after the individual has experienced one or more severe episodes of one of the other forms of schizophrenia; *undifferentiated schizophrenia*—characterized by symptoms of schizophrenia that do not seem to fit neatly into one of the other patterns of schizophrenia (cf. *personality disorder* [schizoid and schizotypal personality disorders])

script(s). A shared understanding about the characteristic actors, objects, and sequence of actions in a situation being described; facilitates interactions and conversational communication about the situation

seasonal affective disorder (SAD). A form of depression that typically occurs during the winter months or the months surrounding them

secondary appraisal. The second step in a two-step process of appraising a potentially stressful situation (cf. *primary appraisal*); involves a person's assessment of strategies she or he can use to maximize the likelihood of potentially beneficial outcomes and to minimize the likelihood of potentially harmful outcomes of the stressful situation

secondary-process thought. A form of thought that is basically rational and based on reality, helping the thinker to make sense of the world and to act in ways that make sense both to the thinker and to observers of the thinker's actions (cf. *primary-process thought*)

secondary reinforcer(s). Rewarding *stimuli* that are less immediately satisfying and perhaps also less tangible than *primary reinforcers*, but that may gain reinforcing value through association with primary reinforcers; often used during *operant conditioning* when a primary reinforcer is not immediately available or is inconvenient to administer, such that the secondary reinforcers provide sufficient reinforcement until primary reinforcers can be administered; greatly

enhances the flexibility of applying *operant* conditioning because so many stimuli can be used as secondary reinforcers (see also *token economy*); a behavioristic theory of interpersonal attraction suggests that persons who are present in rewarding situations may acquire some of the properties of secondary reinforcers

secondary traits. Personality *traits* that have some bearing on a person's behavior but that are not particularly central to what the person does (cf. *cardinal trait, central traits of personality*)

secure attachment pattern. One of three attachment patterns observed in the *strange situation* (cf. *avoidant attachment pattern, resistant attachment pattern*); a child generally shows preferential interest in—but not excessive dependence on—the attention of the mother while she is present, and the child shows some distress when the mother leaves but can be calmed and reassured by her when she returns

sedative. One type of *central nervous system (CNS) depressant*, used for calming *anxiety* and relieving *insomnia* (e.g., *barbiturate, tranquilizer*, methequalone, and chloral hydrate)

selective attention. A process by which an individual attempts to track one *stimulus* or one type of stimulus and to ignore another

self. The whole of the *personality*, including both conscious and unconscious elements, which is posited to strive for unity among often opposing parts of the personality (see also *ideal self, self-concept, self-esteem, self-understanding*)

self-concept. An individual's view of herself or himself (cf. *ideal self*), which may or may not be realistic or even perceived similarly by other persons; often believed to involve both *self-understanding* (cognitions regarding the self) and *self-esteem* (emotions and valuations regarding the self)

self-determination theory. A theory of *motivation* that posits that people need to feel competent, autonomous, and securely and satisfyingly connected to other people

self-efficacy theory. A theory of *motivation* that considers goal-related behavior in terms of the importance of people's belief in their ability to reach their goal

self-esteem. The degree to which a person values himself or herself (cf. *self-understanding*; see *self-concept*)

self-fulfilling prophecy. A psychological phenomenon whereby what is believed to be true becomes true or at least is perceived to have become true

self-handicapping. An *attribution* bias in which people take actions to sabotage their own performance so that they will have excuses in case they fail to perform satisfactorily (see also *actor–observer effect, fundamental attribution error*)

self-monitoring (in regard to personality theory). The degree to which people monitor and change their behavior in response to situational demands, from the perspective of the degree to which individuals show consistency across various situations

self-perception theory. A theory regarding *cognitive consistency*, which suggests that when people are not sure of what they believe, they infer their beliefs from their behavior, perceiving their own actions much as an outside observer would and thereby drawing conclusions about themselves based on their actions (cf. *cognitive dissonance*)

self-report measures. Measures of psychological attitudes, feelings, opinions, or behaviors that are obtained simply by asking people to state their responses to questions regarding those psychological processes and products (see also *Likert scale*)

self-understanding. The way individuals comprehend themselves, including the various roles and characteristics that form a part of the individual's identity (cf. *self-esteem*; see *self-concept*)

semantic memory. *Encoding, storage,* and *retrieval* of facts (e.g., *declarative knowledge* about the world) that do not describe the unique experiences of the individual recalling the facts, and that are not characterized by any particular temporal context in which the individual acquired the facts (cf. *episodic memory*)

semantics. The study of the meanings of words

sensation. The neural information that the *brain* receives from the sensory *receptors* (cf. *perception*)

sense. A physiological system that collects information from *receptors* regarding various forms of energy that are

received from within the body and from the external world and that then translates the collected information into an electrochemical form that can be comprehended by the *nervous system*, particularly the *brain*

sensitization. A paradoxical phenomenon in which an intermittent user of a drug actually demonstrates heightened sensitivity to low doses of the drug

sensorimotor stage. The first stage of *cognitive development* in Piaget's theory, in which individuals largely develop in terms of sensory (input) and *motor* (output) abilities, beginning with reflexive responses and gradually expanding in complexity to modify reflexive *schemas* toward purposeful actions that are environmentally adaptive (cf. *concrete operations, formal-operational stage, preoperational stage*)

sensory adaptation. A temporary physiological response to a sensed change in the environment that is generally not subject to conscious manipulation or control

sensory afferents. See *afferents*

sensory coding. The way in which sensory *receptors* transform a range of information about various *stimuli*, which arrives in a variety of forms of energy, changing that information into electrochemical representations that signify the various kinds of information

sensory neurons. *Nerve* cells that receive information from the environment through sensory *receptors* and then carry that information away from the sensory receptors and toward the *central nervous system* (see *neuron*; cf. *interneuron, motor neuron*)

sensory store. According to a three-stores theory of memory (cf. *long-term store, short-term store*), the hypothetical construct of a sensory store that stores relatively limited amounts of information for very brief periods of time

separation anxiety. A generalized fear of being separated from a primary caregiver (e.g., a parent) or other familiar adult

septum. The portion of the *brain* that is involved in anger and fear

serial-position curve. A graphic display that represents the probability that each of a series of given items will be recalled, given the order in which the items were presented in a list

serial processing. The cognitive manipulation of operations in which each operation is executed one at a time, in a series; as applied to short-term memory, the items stored in short-term memory would be retrieved one at a time, not all at once (cf. *parallel processing*)

serial recall. A type of *memory* task in which the participant is presented with a list of items and is asked to repeat the items in the exact order in which they were presented (cf. *free recall*)

serotonin. A *neurotransmitter* synthesized from tryptophan in the diet; appears to be related to *arousal*, sleep, and dreams as well as to regulation of mood, appetite, and sensitivity to *pain* (cf. *acetylcholine, dopamine*)

set-point theory. A theory about hunger, linked to the *lipostatic hypothesis*, according to which each person has a preset body weight that is biologically determined either at birth or within the first few years following birth, based on the fat cells in the body, which may increase but not decrease in number over the life span; that is, although the size of the cells may fluctuate in relation to the amount of food consumed, the number may never decrease, regardless of how little food is consumed; according to this view, people with more fat cells tend to have greater body weight, although the size of their fat cells may be the same as the fat cells in persons who are lighter in body weight

shape constancy. A form of *perceptual constancy* in which an individual continues to perceive that an observed object retains its shape, even though the actual retinal *sensations* of the shape of the object change

shaping. A means of *operant conditioning* for behavior that is unlikely to be generated spontaneously by the organism; accomplished using a method of successive approximations, by which crude approximations of the desired behavior are rewarded, then when the initial approximations are fully conditioned, closer approximations are conditioned, and this process of reinforcing successive approximations continues until full performance of the desired behavior is being reinforced (see *positive reinforcement*)

short-term store. According to a three-stores theory of memory (cf. *long-term store, sensory store*), the hypothetical construct of a short-term store has the capacity to store information longer than the sensory store but is still relatively limited

sign. In medicine, any unusual feature observed by the physician (cf. *symptom*)

signal-detection theory (SDT). A psychophysical theory that posits four possible stimulus–response pairs: a *hit*, a *miss*, a *false alarm*, or a *correct rejection*

simple cells. One of the key physiological structures described by the *feature-detector approach* to form *perception* according to which primitive cortical cells provide information to adjacent simple cells regarding the features of objects in the receptive field for each simple cell; the simple cells then fire in response to lines with particular features, such as particular angular orientations, particular light/dark boundaries and contrasts, and particular locations in the receptive field of the cell, with the specifically stimulating features differing from one simple cell to another (see also *complex cells*)

simulating paradigm. A research technique for determining the true effects of a psychological treatment (e.g., *hypnosis*), in which one group of participants is subjected to the treatment and another group (a control group) is not, but the control participants are asked to behave as though they had received the treatment; people must then try to distinguish between the behavior of the treatment group and the behavior of the control group (most effective if the persons who make the distinction are blind about which participants are in the treatment group and which are in the control group)

single-cell recording. A technique for detecting the firing patterns of individual *neurons* in response to *stimuli;* used on monkeys and other animals

situational attribution. One of two fundamental types of *attributions* (cf. *personal attribution*); the causes of human behavior are attributed to external factors such as the settings, events, or other people in the environment of the person engaging in the given behavior

size constancy. A form of *perceptual constancy* in which an individual continues to perceive that an object remains the same size despite changes in the size of the object in the *retina*

skewness. A characteristic of a distribution of values, indicating the degree to which the *mode* is shifted above or below the *mean* and the *median* values; when the distribution is plotted graphically, skewness appears as a lopsidedness toward the left or the right of the middle value

Skinner box. A container in which an animal undergoes conditioning experiments, named after behaviorist B. F. Skinner

sleep apnea. A breathing disorder that occurs during sleep, in which the sleeper repeatedly (perhaps hundreds of times per night) stops breathing

slips of the tongue. Inadvertent *semantic* or articulatory (related to the production of language sounds) errors in what is said (e.g., *spoonerism*)

social categorization. The normal human tendency to sort things and people into groups, based on perceived common attributes; often leads to the formation of *stereotypes*

social cognition. The thought processes through which people perceive and interpret information from and about themselves (intrapersonal world) and other persons (interpersonal world) (see *cognitive consistency, impression formation, social-comparison theory*)

social-comparison theory. A *social-cognition* theory, which suggests that people evaluate their own abilities and accomplishments largely by comparing these abilities and accomplishments with the abilities and accomplishments of others, particularly in novel, uncertain, or ambiguous settings for which internal standards are not yet established

social development. The process by which people learn to interact with other people and learn about themselves as human beings

social facilitation. The beneficial effect on performance that results from the perceived presence of other persons

social-identity theory. A theory regarding *prejudice* that suggests that people are motivated to protect their *self-esteem* and that they have prejudices in order to increase their self-esteem by believing that outgroups (of which they are not members) have less status than ingroups (of which they are members)

social inhibition. The detrimental effect on performance that results from the perceived presence of other persons

social learning. A form of vicarious (rather than direct) learning that occurs as a result of observing both the behavior of others and the environmental outcomes of the behavior observed

social-learning theory. The view that attributes *psychosexual development* to role *modeling* and the expectation of external rewards

social loafing. The phenomenon by which the average amount of effort exerted by each individual in a group decreases in association with increases in the number of people participating in a joint effort

social phobia. An *anxiety disorder* characterized by extreme fear of being criticized by others, which leads to the avoidance of groups of people and the avoidance of any situations that may lead to the possibility of being criticized, embarrassed, or otherwise subject to ridicule (see *phobia*)

social psychology. The study of the ways in which human thoughts, emotions, and behavior are affected by other people, whose presence may be actual, imagined, or implied

sociolinguistics. The study of how people use *language* in the context of social interaction

soma. The part of the *neuron* that contains the nucleus (center portion, which performs metabolic and reproductive functions for the cell) and that is responsible for the life of the neuron

somatic nervous system. The portion of the *peripheral nervous system* that is in charge of quick and conscious movement of skeletal muscles, which are attached directly to bones, thereby permitting movements such as walking or typing (cf. *autonomic nervous system*)

somnambulism. Sleepwalking, which combines aspects of waking and sleeping, with the sleepwalker able to see, walk, and perhaps even talk, but usually unable to remember the sleepwalking episodes; rarely accompanied by dreaming

specific phobias. Characterized by marked, persistent, irrational fears of objects, such as spiders, snakes, rats, high places, and darkness

spinal cord.   A slender, roughly cylindrical bundle of interconnected *nerves*, which is enclosed within the spinal column and which extends through the center of the back, starting at the *brain* and ending at the branches of the *peripheral nervous system* that go to each of the two legs

spontaneous recovery.   A phenomenon of *classical conditioning* in which a *CR* reappears without any environmental prompting; the unprompted reappearance of the CR occurs after a conditioned behavior has been established and then extinguished and then the organism is allowed to rest; that is, the organism appears spontaneously to recover a modest level of response during the rest period, although the response disappears again if the *CS* is not paired with the *US* again (cf. *savings*)

spontaneous recovery (from mental illness).   The unprompted and unaided (i.e., untreated) disappearance of maladaptive symptomatology over the course of time

spoonerism.   A *slip of the tongue*, in which a reversal of the initial sounds of two words produces two entirely different words, usually yielding a humorous outcome (named after the Reverend William Spooner, who was famous for producing humorous instances of such reversals)

standard deviation.   A statistical measurement of dispersion, indicating the degree to which a set of values typically deviates from the *mean* value for the set; calculated by determining the square root of the *variance* for the distribution of values

standardization.   The administration of a test in a way that ensures that the conditions for taking the test are the same for all test-takers; also, the administration of an experimental procedure in a way that ensures that the experimental conditions are the same for all participants

stapes.   The last in the series of three bones in the middle ear (cf. *incus*, *malleus*), which normally receive and amplify the vibrations transmitted by the tympanum (*eardrum*) and then transmit those vibrations to the *cochlea*

state-dependent memory.   The tendency for a person to recall learned information more easily when in the same emotional state as the state in which the information was learned

static assessment environment.   A context for testing in which an examiner asks a series of questions, offering no hints or guidance if the test-taker makes incorrect responses, and usually not even signaling whether the test-taker has answered correctly or incorrectly (cf. *dynamic assessment environment*)

statistic.   A numerical value obtained by analyzing numerical data about a *representative sample* of a *population* (see *sample statistics*; cf. *population parameters*)

statistical significance.   A degree of numerically analyzed probability suggesting the likelihood that a particular outcome may have occurred as a result of systematic factors rather than by chance

statistics.   A field of study involving the analysis of numerical data about *representative samples* of *populations*

stereopsis.   Three-dimensional *perception* of the world through the cognitive fusion of the visual fields seen by each of the two eyes (see *binocular depth cues*, *binocular disparity*)

stereotype.   A *schema* about groups of persons, in which it is held that members of a group tend more or less uniformly to have particular types of characteristics (see also *outgroup homogeneity*, *prejudice*, *social categorization*)

stimulus.   Something that prompts action (plural: *stimuli; stimulus* is Latin for the sharpened stick used by Romans for goading sluggish animals into action)

stimulus discrimination.   The ability to ascertain the difference between one stimulus and another; often used in *psychophysics* experiments and assessments as well as in behavioral experiments (cf. *stimulus generalization*)

stimulus generalization (in classical conditioning).   A broadening of the *conditioned response*, such that stimuli that resemble a specifically *conditioned stimulus* also elicit the conditioned response (cf. *stimulus discrimination*)

storage.   See *memory*

strange situation.   An experimental technique for observing attachment in young children, conducted in a laboratory room that contains various toys and some chairs; in the room is a one-way mirror, behind which an observer watches and records the behavior of the subject (usually a toddler, age 12–18 months); for the procedure, the toddler and her or his mother enter the room and the mother sits in one of the chairs; a few minutes later, an unfamiliar woman enters the room, talks to the mother, and then tries to play with the child; while the stranger is trying to play with the child, the mother quietly walks out of the room, leaving her purse on the chair to indicate that she will return; later the mother returns, and soon after, the stranger leaves; still later, the mother leaves the child alone in the room; soon after, she returns and sits in the chair again; finally, the toddler and mother leave the room, thus ending the experimental procedure

stress.   A phenomenon in which some factor (or factors) in the environment causes a person to feel threatened or challenged in some way; usually involves some kind of environmental change that requires the person to make some kind of adaptive or *coping* response

stress disorder.   An *anxiety disorder* (see *acute stress disorder* and *posttraumatic stress disorder*)

stress response.   A reaction to some kind of *stressor*, involving internal and external adaptation by an individual (see *stress*)

stressor.   A situation or event that leads to *stress* (see *stress response*)

stroboscopic motion.   The *perception* of movement that is produced when a stroboscope (*strobo-*, "whirling"; *-scope*, "device or means of viewing") intermittently flashes an alternating pair of lights against a dark background at appropriate distances and appropriately timed intervals (within milliseconds), such that it appears that a single light has moved forward and backward across the visual field

Stroop effect.   Difficulty in selectively attending to the colors of inks and ignoring words written in those colors (e.g., the word *green* printed in red letters)

structuralism.   The first major school of thought in *psychology*, which focused on analyzing the distinctive configuration of component elements of the mind, such as particular *sensations* or thoughts; for example, structuralists would be more interested in what people think than in how they think, in what people perceive, rather than how they perceive (cf. *functionalism*)

subconscious.   A level of *consciousness* that involves less awareness than full consciousness and either is synonymous with the *unconscious* level (according to many theorists) or is slightly more accessible to consciousness than is the unconscious level (according to a few theorists)

subtractive color mixture. The remaining combined *wavelengths* of light that are reflected from an object after other wavelengths of light have been absorbed (subtracted from the reflected light) by the object; darker objects absorb more wavelengths of light and reflect fewer wavelengths than do brighter objects (cf. *additive color mixture*)

superego. One of three psychodynamic concepts (cf. *ego*, *id*), which comprises all the internalized representations of the norms and values of society acquired during early *psychosexual development*, through interactions with the parents as figures of societal authority (see *idealistic principle*)

survey. A method of social-science research in which the researcher records people's responses to questions about their beliefs and opinions; rarely involves answers that are scored as either right or wrong (see, e.g., *questionnaire*; cf. *test*; cf. also *case study*, *experiment*, *naturalistic observation*)

syllogism. A deductive argument that permits a conclusion to be drawn based on two *premises*, in which each premise contains two terms, at least one term of which is common to both premises

sympathetic nervous system. The portion of the *autonomic nervous system* that is concerned primarily with catabolism (cf. *parasympathetic nervous system*)

symptom. Any unusual *sensation* in or feature on the body, and which is believed to indicate some kind of pathology (cf. *sign*)

synapse. The point of communication between two *neurons*; the area comprising the interneuronal gap between the *terminal buttons* of one neuron's *axon* and the *dendrites* (or sometimes the *soma*) of the next *neuron*; the cleft into which the terminal buttons of the presynaptic neuron may release a chemical *neurotransmitter* or *neuromodulator* for receipt by the postsynaptic neuron

syntax. A level of linguistic analysis that centers on the patterns by which users of a particular *language* put words together at the level of the sentence; systematic structure through which words can be combined and sequenced to make

meaningful phrases and sentences (see also *grammar*)

synthesis. As an aspect of a *dialectic*: a statement of opinion that integrates some aspects of a *thesis* and some aspects of an *antithesis*, usually based on evidence or logic that supports the aspects that have been integrated; as a process of *critical thinking*: a process that involves integrating component parts into wholes and that may be viewed as a process that complements analysis

systematic desensitization. A *counterconditioning* technique of behavioral therapy (cf. *aversion therapy*) in which the therapist seeks to help the client combat *anxiety* and other troublesome responses by teaching the client a set of relaxation techniques so that the client can effectively replace the troublesome responses with relaxation responses, usually in association with a *desensitization hierarchy* of stimuli that previously induced the troublesome responses

taste bud. A cluster of taste-receptor cells located inside the *papillae* of the tongue; in the center of each cluster are pores into which the molecules from foods and beverages may fall, and when moistened chemicals contact the receptor cells, the cells *transduce* the chemical energy of the tastes into the electrochemical energy of neural transmission, which involves encoding of the tastes to distinguish among particular kinds of chemicals (e.g., salts, acids, or alkalies)

telegraphic speech. Rudimentary syntactical communications of two words or more, which are characteristic of very early language acquisition and which seem more like telegrams than like conversation because articles, prepositions, and other function *morphemes* are usually omitted

temperament. Individual differences in the intensity and duration of *emotions*, as well as the individual's characteristic disposition

template-matching theory. The view that we have prototypes (templates) stored in the mind and that our *perception* of a pattern depends on matching the prototype

temporal conditioning. A *classical conditioning* procedure in which the *CS* is a fixed interval of time between presentations of the *US*, so that the learner learns that the US will occur at a given, fixed time

temporal contiguity. The *proximity* in time between two events or *stimuli*; without *contingency* between the two events or stimuli, conditioning does not take place (see also *classical conditioning*, *operant conditioning*)

temporal lobe. On the lower portion of the sides of the *brain*, chiefly responsible for auditory processing; one of the four major regions of the *cerebral cortex* (cf. *frontal lobe*, *occipital lobe*, *parietal lobe*)

terminal buttons. Small knobby structures located at the tips of the branches of *axons*, which release *neurotransmitters* or *neuromodulators* into a *synapse*, which borders on the *dendrites* or *somas* of nearby *neurons*

test. A research method used for measuring a given ability or attribute in a particular individual or set of individuals at a particular time and in a particular place; almost invariably involves keying the test-takers' responses as either right or wrong or at least as being better (more accurate, more appropriate, more creative, etc.) or worse; (cf. *survey*; cf. also *case study*, *experiment*, *naturalistic observation*)

texture gradient. See *monocular depth cues*

thalamus. A two-lobed structure, located in about the center of the *brain*, at about the level of the eyes, which helps in the control of sleep and waking and seems to serve as a relay for sensory information; contains various nuclei (groups of *neurons* with a similar function) that receive assorted types of sensory input entering the brain and then transmit that input via projection fibers to the appropriate sensory regions of the *cerebral cortex*

Thematic Apperception Test (TAT). A psychodynamic personality assessment tool in which the examiner presents a series of ambiguous but representationally realistic pictures; test-takers are believed to project their feelings into their descriptions of the pictures

theory. A statement of some general principles that explains a psychological phenomenon or set of phenomena

theory of multiple intelligences. A theory of suggesting that intelligence comprises eight distinct constructs that function somewhat independently but may interact to produce intelligent behavior: bodily–kinesthetic intelligence,

interpersonal intelligence, intrapersonal intelligence, linguistic intelligence, mathematical–logical intelligence, musical intelligence, naturalist intelligence, and **spatial intelligence**

thesis. A statement of an opinion or of a perspective (cf. *antithesis, synthesis;* see *dialectic*)

thinking. A psychological function that involves the representation and processing of information in the mind (also termed *cognition;* see *critical thinking, creativity, judgment and decision making, problem solving, reasoning*)

threshold of excitation. The level of electrochemical stimulation at or above which an *action potential* may be generated but below which an action potential cannot be generated; the specific threshold required for a given neuron's action potential differs for the various neurons and depends on whether the neuron is in the midst of a refractory period (see *absolute refractory phase, relative refractory phase*)

thyroid gland. An endocrine *gland* located at the front of the throat, which regulates the metabolic rate of cells, thereby influencing weight gain or loss, blood pressure, muscular strength, and level of activity

timbre. A psychological quality of sound that permits detection of the difference between a note (e.g., B-flat) played on a piano and the same note played on a harmonica, based on the distinctive *harmonics* produced by each instrument rather than the *fundamental frequency* of the note

tobacco. A plant product that contains nicotine, a *central nervous system (CNS) stimulant*

token economy. A system of *operant conditioning* in which tokens are used as a means of reinforcing various *operant* behaviors; most frequently used in controlled environments such as residential institutions for persons who are psychologically impaired, in order to encourage adaptive behavior and discourage maladaptive behavior; generally not used with persons for whom their natural interest in performing the operant behavior would be reduced as a result of the use of extrinsic reinforcers (see *extrinsic motivators*)

tolerance. A consequence of prolonged use of *psychoactive* drugs, in which the drug user stops feeling the *psychotropic* effects of a given drug at one dose and must take increasing amounts of the drug in order to achieve the effects, eventually reaching a level of nonresponse at which the current level no longer produces the desired effects, but higher levels will cause overdose; the person generally still continues to take the drugs, despite the lack of psychotropic effects, simply to avoid experiencing the unpleasant feelings associated with drug *withdrawal* (see *addiction;* see also specific drugs, e.g., *amphetamine* and *barbiturate*)

top-down approach. The view of *perception* or other cognitive processes as originating with complex cognitive processes and problem solving

total-time hypothesis. A widely accepted assumption about memory that holds that the degree to which a person is able to learn information by storing it in memory depends on the total amount of time spent studying the material in a given session, rather than on the way in which the time is apportioned within a given session

trace conditioning. A form of *classical conditioning* in which the *CS* is terminated for a while before the *US* begins (cf. *delay conditioning*)

trait. May refer either to a personality trait or to a genetic trait; personality traits are stable sources of individual differences that characterize a person and that may originate in the person's nature (heredity) or the person's nurture (environment); genetic traits are distinctive characteristics or behavior patterns that are genetically determined

tranquilizer. A *sedative* used for combating *anxiety;* considered to be safer than *barbiturates* because of the lower dosages required and the reduced likelihood of drowsiness and respiratory difficulties, although the potential for *addiction* remains a problem (see *central nervous system (CNS) depressants*)

transduce. Convert energy from one form into another, such as the process that occurs in a sensory *receptor,* which converts a form of energy (mechanical, chemical, etc.) received from the environment into the electrochemical form of energy that is meaningful to the *nervous system*

transfer. Prior *learning* that may help or hinder future learning or *problem solving*

transference. A phenomenon of psychodynamic therapy whereby the patient projects her or his feelings and internal conflicts onto the therapist, often also projecting onto the therapist–patient relationship many aspects of the patient's early childhood relationships, such as with parents; deemed to be an important means by which the patient can resolve some of the conflicts that characterized these early relationships (cf. *countertransference*)

transformational grammar. A form of syntactical analysis that centers on the transformational operations used for generating surface structures from deep structures (cf. *phrase-structure grammars;* see also *deep-structure level*)

triangular theory of love. A theory of love according to which love has three basic components: *commitment, intimacy,* and *passion;* different combinations of the components yield different kinds of love

triarchic theory of human intelligence. A theory of intelligence that asserts that intelligence comprises three aspects, which deal with the relationship of intelligence to the internal world, to experience, and to the external world

trichromatic theory of color vision. One of two proposed mechanisms for explaining how color vision occurs (also termed *Young–Helmholtz theory;* cf. *opponent-process theory*); draws on the notion of *primary colors,* which can combine additively to form all other colors; according to this view, various photoreceptive *cones* are somehow attuned to each of the primary colors, such that some cones are sensitive to red (and are therefore activated in response to the sight of red), others to green, and others to blue, and the full range of colors may be seen when various combinations of these three primary colors are sensed

two-component theory of emotion. A view that *emotions* comprise two elements: a state of physiological *arousal* and a cognitive label identifying the aroused state as signifying a particular emotion

Type-A behavior pattern. A characteristic pattern of *personality* and behavior in which the individual demonstrates a competitive orientation toward achievement, a sense of urgency about time, and a strong tendency to feel anger and hostility (cf. *Type-B behavior pattern*)

Type-B behavior pattern. A characteristic pattern of *personality* and behavior in which the individual demonstrates relatively low levels of competitiveness, urgency about time, and hostility (cf. *Type-A behavior pattern*)

Type I error. An error in interpreting research that is the belief that a finding has appeared due to systematic changes, when in fact the finding is a result of random fluctuation

Type II error. An error in interpreting research that is the belief that a finding has appeared due to random fluctuations, when in fact the finding is a result of systematic changes

unconditioned response (UR). Automatic, unlearned physiological *response* to a *stimulus* (the *unconditioned stimulus*), used in *classical conditioning* as a means of eventually teaching the learner to produce a *conditioned response*

unconditioned stimulus (US). A *stimulus* that automatically, without prior learning, elicits a given physiological or emotional *response*, used in *classical conditioning* as a means of eventually teaching the learner to respond to a *conditioned stimulus* (see also *unconditioned response*)

unconscious. A level of *consciousness* at which thoughts, wishes, and feelings are not accessible to conscious awareness (often considered synonymous with *subconscious*); an important construct of *psychodynamic theory*

UR. See *unconditioned response*

US. See *unconditioned stimulus*

valid. See *validity*

validity. The extent to which a given form of measurement assesses what it is supposed to measure; the extent to which a set of experimental procedures reveals what it is purported to reveal (cf. *reliability*)

vanishing point. A phenomenon of visual perception in which parallel lines seem to converge as they move farther into the distance and eventually to converge entirely, to become indistinguishable, and then to disappear entirely at the horizon (see *monocular depth cues, linear perspective*)

variable. An attribute or characteristic of a situation, a person, or a phenomenon that may differ or fluctuate across situations, across persons, or across phe-

nomena (see also *dependent variable, independent variable*)

variable-interval reinforcement. A schedule for implementing *operant conditioning* in which reinforcement occurs, on average, after a certain period of time, assuming that the *operant* behavior has occurred at least once during that time period, but in which the specific amount of time preceding reinforcement changes from one reinforcement to the next (see *partial reinforcement, schedules of reinforcement*; cf. *fixed-interval reinforcement, variable-ratio reinforcement*)

variable-ratio reinforcement. A schedule for implementing *operant conditioning* in which reinforcement occurs, on average, after a certain number of operant responses, but in which the specific number of responses preceding reinforcement changes from one reinforcement to the next (see *partial reinforcement, schedules of reinforcement*; cf. *fixed-ratio reinforcement, variable-interval reinforcement*)

variance. A statistical measurement that indicates the degree to which a set of values varies from the *mean* of the set of values; the basis for determining a *standard deviation*, which is more commonly used in psychological research

verifiable. Characteristic of scientific findings, by which there is some means of confirming the results

vertebrae. The protective backbones that encase the *spinal cord* and that form the spinal column of vertebrates

vestibular system. The sensory system that comprises the vestibular sacs and semicircular canals in the inner ear, which contains *receptors* for the *sensations* associated with equilibrium; operates via movement of the head, which causes movement of fluid in the sacs and canals, which bends hairlike cells that *transduce* the mechanical energy of the various movements into the electrochemical energy of neural transmission; this energy travels via the auditory nerve to the *cerebellum* and to the *cerebral cortex* and is encoded as information about the direction of movement, relative orientation, and rate of acceleration of the head

vocabulary. A repertoire of words, formed by combining *morphemes*

volley principle. A hypothesis supportive of the *frequency theory* of hearing, which suggests that auditory *neurons* fire cooperatively in alternating groups, such

that while some neurons are resting, neighboring neurons are firing, thereby yielding a combined pattern of neural firing that can indicate high-frequency vibrations of sound (cf. *place theory*; see also *duplicity theory*)

warm fibers. Bundles of *neurons* that respond to warming of the skin (in the range of 95–115° Fahrenheit [35–4° centigrade]; cf. *cold fibers*)

wavelength. The distance from the crest of one wave to the crest of the next wave (e.g., sound waves or light waves), often used as a means of measuring a quality of sound or light; for light waves, the objective wavelength of a light wave is associated with *hue*, and for sound waves, the objective wavelength is associated with the sensation of *pitch* (actually, for sound, frequency is the more common measurement)

Weber fraction. The value that indicates the relationship between the intensity of a standard stimulus and the intensity of a stimulus required to produce a *just noticeable difference (jnd)*; this value varies for different types of sensory experiences, and smaller fractions are required for sensory modalities to which humans experience greater sensitivity (e.g., the painful sensation of electric shock), whereas larger fractions are required for less sensitive modalities (e.g., the sensation of taste)

Weber's law. Broadly interpreted, the law suggests that the greater the magnitude of the *stimulus*, the larger the distance must be in order to be detectable as a difference; a principle relating the intensity of a standard stimulus to the intensity of a stimulus required to produce a *just noticeable difference (jnd)*, often expressed as an equation: $\Delta I = KI$, where K is a constant (a numerical value that does not vary, such as π), I is the intensity of the standard stimulus, and ΔI is the increase in intensity needed to produce a jnd

well-structured problem. A type of problem for which a clear path to the solution is known, although it may still be very difficult to implement (cf. *ill-structured problem*)

Wernicke's area. An area in the left hemisphere of the *brain* involved in *language* comprehension

withdrawal. The temporary discomfort (which may be extremely negative, much like a severe case of intestinal flu, accompanied by extreme depression or *anxiety*) associated with a decrease in dosage or a discontinuation altogether of a *psychoactive* drug, during which the drug user's physiology and mental processes must adjust to an absence of the drug; during withdrawal from some drugs (e.g., some stimulants and some *sedatives*), the user should obtain medical supervision to avoid life-threatening complications that may arise during the readjustment to normal physiological and mental functioning

word-superiority effect. A phenomenon of form *perception* in which an individual can more readily identify (discriminate) letters when they are presented in the context of words than when they are presented as solitary letters

working memory. A portion of memory that may be viewed as a specialized part of long-term memory that holds only the most recently activated portion of long-term memory, and that moves these activated elements into and out of short-term memory (which may be viewed as the narrow portion of working memory that enters immediate awareness); some psychologists consider working memory to be a hypothetical construct, in opposition to the three-stores view, but others consider it a complement to the three-stores view

zone of proximal development (ZPD). The range of ability between a person's observable level of ability and the person's latent capacity, which is not directly observable but may be detected by providing a context in which the latent capacity may be revealed and expressed (sometimes termed the *zone of potential development*)

Abrams, D., Wetherell, M., Cochrane, S., Hogg, M. A., & Turner, J. C. (2001). Knowing what to think by knowing who you are: Self-categorization and the nature of norm formation, conformity and group polarization. In M. A. Hogg & D. Abrams (Eds.), *Intergroup relations: Essential readings. Key readings in social psychology* (pp. 270–288). Philadelphia: Psychology Press.

Abrams, R. (1988). *Electroconvulsive treatment: It apparently works, but how and at what risks are not yet clear.* New York: Oxford University Press.

Abramson, L. Y., Metalsky, G. I., & Alloy, L. B. (1989). Hopelessness depression: A theory-based subtype of depression. *Psychological Review, 96,* 358–372.

Ackerman, P. L. (1996). A theory of adult intellectual development: Process, personality, interests, and knowledge. *Intelligence, 22,* 227–257.

Ackil, J. K., & Zaragoza, M. S. (1998). Memorial consequences of forced confabulation: Age differences in susceptibility to false memories. *Developmental Psychology, 34,* 1358–1372.

Acredolo, L. P., & Goodwyn, S. W. (1998). *Baby signs: How to talk with your baby before your baby can talk.* Chicago: NTB/Contemporary Publishers.

Adams, M. (1990). *Beginning to read: Thinking and learning about print.* Cambridge, MA: MIT Press.

Adams, M. (1999). Reading. In R. A. Wilson & F. C. Keil (Eds.), *The MIT encyclopedia of the cognitive sciences* (pp. 705–707). Cambridge, MA: MIT Press.

Adams, M. J. (Ed.). (1986). *Odyssey: A curriculum for thinking* (Vols. 1–6). Watertown, MA: Charlesbridge.

Adams, M. J., Treiman, R., & Pressley, M. (1997). Reading, writing and literacy. In I. Sigel & A. Renninger (Eds.), *Handbook of child psychology* (5th ed., Vol. 4). *Child psychology in practice* (pp. 275–357). New York: Wiley.

Adler, N., & Matthews, K. A. (1994). Health and psychology: Why do some people get sick and some stay well? *Annual Review of Psychology, 45,* 229–259.

Adolphs, R., Tranel, D., Damasio, H., & Damasio, A. (1994). Impaired recognition of emotion in facial expressions following bilateral damage to the human amygdala. *Nature, 372,* 669–672.

Agnew, J. (1985). Man's purgative passion. *American Journal of Psychotherapy, 39*(2), 236–246.

Aguilar, C. M., & Medin, D. L. (1999). Asymmetries of comparison. *Psychonomic Bulletin & Review,6*(2), 328–337.

Ahn, W.-K., Kalish, C. W., Medin, D. L., & Gelman, S. A. (1995). The role of covariation versus mechanism information in causal attribution. *Cognition, 54,* 299–352.

Ainsworth, M.D.S. (1973). The development of infant–mother attachment. In B. M. Caldwell & H. M. Ricciuti (Eds.), *Review of child development research* (Vol. 3). Chicago: University of Chicago Press.

Ainsworth, M.D.S. (1989). Attachments beyond infancy. *American Psychologist, 44,* 709–716.

Ainsworth, M.D.S., Bell, S. M., & Stayton, D. J. (1971). Individual differences in strange-situation behavior in one-year-olds. In H. R. Schaffer (Ed.), *The origins of human social relations.* London: Academic Press.

Ainsworth, M.D.S., Blehar, M., Waters, E., & Wall, S. (1978). *Patterns of attachment.* Hillsdale, NJ: Erlbaum.

Akhtar, N., & Montague, L. (1999). Early lexical acquisition: The role of cross-situational learning. *First Language, 19,* 347–358.

Albano, A. M., Chorpita, B. F., & Barlow, D. H. (2003). Childhood anxiety disorders. In E. J. Mash & R. A. Barkley (Eds.), *Child psychopathology* (2nd ed., pp. 279–329). New York: Guilford.

Albert, D. J., Jonik, R. H., & Walsh, M. L. (1991). Hormone-dependent aggression in the female rat: Testosterone plus estradiol implants prevent the decline in aggression following ovariectomy. *Physiology & Behavior, 49,* 673–677.

Albright, T. D., Kandel, E. R., & Posner, M. I. (2000). Cognitive neuroscience. *Current Opinion in Neurobiology, 10,* 612–624.

Alcock, K. J., & Bundy, D. A. (2001). The impact of infectious disease on cognitive development. In R. J. Sternberg & E. L. Grigorenko (Eds.), *Environmental effects on cognitive abilities* (pp. 221–254). Mahwah, NJ: Erlbaum.

Alexander, J. M., & Schwanenflugel, P. J. (1994). Strategy regulation: The role of intelligence, metacognitive attributions, and knowledge base. *Developmental Psychology, 30,* 709–723.

Alicke, M. D., LoSchiavo, F. M., Zerbst, J., & Zhang, S. (1997). The person who outperforms me is a genius: Maintaining perceived competence in upward social comparison. *Journal of Personality and Social Psychology, 73,* 781–789.

Alkire, M. T., Haier, R. J., & Fallon, J. H. (2000). Toward a unified theory of narcosis: Brain imaging evidence for a thalamocortical switch as the neurophysiologic basis of anesthetic-induced unconsciousness. *Consciousness and Cognition, 9 (3),* 370-386.

Alkire, M. T., Haier, R. J., Fallon, J., & Barker, S. J. (1996). PET imaging of conscious and unconscious memory. *Journal of Consciousness Studies, 3(5-6),* 448-462.

Allison, T., & Cicchetti, D. V. (1976). Sleep in mammals: Ecological and constitutional correlates. *Science, 194,* 732–734.

Allport, G. W. (1935). Attitudes. In C. M. Murchison (Ed.), *Handbook of social psychology.* Worcester, MA: Clark University Press.

Allport, G. W. (1937). *Personality: A psychological interpretation.* New York: Holt, Rinehart & Winston.

Allport, G. W. (1954). *The nature of prejudice.* Reading, MA: Addison-Wesley.

Allport, G. W. (1961). *Pattern and growth in personality.* New York: Holt, Rinehart & Winston.

Allum, P. (2002). CALL and the classroom: The case for comparative research. *ReCALL: Journal of Eurocall, 14,* 146–166.

Amabile, T. M. (1983). *The social psychology of creativity.* New York: Springer Verlag.

Amabile, T. M. (1985). Motivation and creativity: Effects of motivational orientation on creative writers. *Journal of Personality and Social Psychology, 48,* 393–399.

Amabile, T. M. (1996). *The context of creativity.* Boulder, CO: Westview.

Amabile, T. M. (2001). Beyond talent: John Irving and the passionate craft of creativity. *American Psychologist, 56,* 333–336.

American Association of University Women Educational Foundation and the Wellesley College Center for Research on Women. (1992). *The AAUW Report: How schools shortchange girls—A study of major findings on girls and education.* Washington, DC: Author.

American Association on Mental Retardation. (1992). *Mental retardation: Definition, classification, and systems of supports.* Washington, DC: Author.

American Psychiatric Association. (1987). *Diagnostic and statistical manual of mental disorders* (3rd ed.-Rev.). Washington, DC: Author.

American Psychiatric Association. (1994). *Diagnostic and statistical manual of mental disorders* (4th ed.). Washington, DC: Author.

American Psychiatric Association. (1994). *Diagnostic and statistical manual of mental disorders* (4th ed.). Washington, DC: Author.

Ames, C. (1992). Classrooms: Goals, structures, and student motivation. *Journal of Educational Psychology, 84,* 261–271.

Amsel, E., & Renninger, A. K. (Eds.). (1997). *Change and development: Issues of theory, method and application.* Mahwah, NJ: Erlbaum.

Anand, B. K., & Brobeck, J. R. (1951). Hypothalamic control of food intake in rats and cats. *Yale Journal of Biology and Medicine, 24,* 123–140.

Anastasi, A., & Urbina, S. (1997). *Psychological testing* (7th ed.). Upper Saddle River, NJ: Prentice-Hall.

Anderson, C. A. (1987). Temperature and aggression: Effects on quarterly, yearly, and city rates of violent and nonviolent crime. *Journal of Personality and Social Psychology, 52*, 1161–1173.

Anderson, C. A. (1989). Temperature and aggression: Ubiquitous effects of heat on occurrence of human violence. *Psychological Bulletin, 106*(1), 74–96.

Anderson, J. R. (1983). Retrieval of information from long-term memory. *Science, 220*, 25–30.

Anderson, J. R. (1993). Problem solving and learning. *American Psychologist, 48*, 35–44.

Anderson, J. R. (2002). Spanning seven orders of magnitude: A challenge for cognitive modeling. *Cognitive Science, 26*, 85–112.

Anderson, J. R., & Betz, J. (2001). A hybrid model of categorization. *Psychonomic Bulletin & Review, 8*, 629–647.

Anderson, J. R., & Bower, G. H. (1973). *Human associative memory.* New York: Wiley.

Anderson, J. R., Budiu, R., & Reder, L. M. (2001). A theory of sentence memory as part of a general theory of memory. *Journal of Memory and Language, 45*, 337–367.

Anderson, K. O., & Masur, F. T. III. (1983). Psychological preparation for invasive medical and dental procedures. *Journal of Behavioral Medicine, 6*, 1–40.

Anderson, N. B. (2003). *Emotional longevity: What really determines how long you live.* New York: Viking.

Andersson, B. E. (1989). Effects of public daycare: A longitudinal study. *Child Development, 60*, 857–866.

Andreasen, N. C. (2001). *Brave new brain: Conquering mental illness in the era of the genome.* London: Oxford University Press.

Andreasen, N. C., & Black, D. W. (1991). *Introductory text of psychiatry.* Washington, DC: American Psychiatric Press.

Andreasen, N. C., Arndt, S., Swayze, V., & Cizadlo, T., et al. (1994). Thalamic abnormalities in schizophrenia visualized through magnetic resonance image averaging. *Science, 266*, 294–298.

Andreasen, N. C., Ehrhardt, J., Swayze, V., Alliger, R., Yuh, T., Cohen, G., & Ziebell, S. (1990). Magnetic resonance imaging of the brain in schizophrenia. *Archives of General Psychiatry, 47*, 35–44.

Andreasen, N. C., Flaum, M., Schultz, S., Duzyurek, S., & Miller, D. (1997). Diagnosis, methodology and subtypes of schizophrenia. *Neuropsychobiology, 35*, 61–63.

Andreasen, N. C., Olsen, S. A., Dennert, J. W., & Smith, M. R. (1982a). Ventricular enlargement in schizophrenia: Definition and prevalence. *American Journal of Psychiatry, 139*, 292–296.

Andreasen, N. C., Olsen, S. A., Dennert, J. W., & Smith, M. R. (1982b). Ventricular enlargement in schizophrenia: Relationship to positive and negative symptoms. *American Journal of Psychiatry, 139*, 297–302.

Andrews, G. (1993). The benefits of psychotherapy. In N. Sartorius, G. de Girolano, G. Andrews, G. A. German, & L. Eisenberg (Eds.), *Treatment of mental disorders: A review of effectiveness.* Geneva, Switzerland, and Washington, DC: World Health Organization and American Psychiatric Press.

Andrews, G., Creamer, M., Crino, R., Hunt, C., Lampe, L., & Page, A. (2003). *The treatment of anxiety disorders: Clinican guides and patient manuals* (2nd ed.). New York: Cambridge University Press.

Angier, N. (1993, April 25). "Stop it!" she said. "No more!" [Review of the book *Genie: An abused child's flight from silence*]. *New York Times Book Review*, p. 12.

Anglin, J. M. (1993). Vocabulary development: A morphological analysis. *Monographs of the Society for Research in Child Development, 58* (No. 10).

Antony, M. M., & Swinson, R. P. (2000a). Social phobia. In M. M. Antony & R. P. Swinson, *Phobic disorders and panic in adults: A guide to assessment and treatment* (pp. 49–77). Washington, DC: American Psychological Association.

Antony, M. M., & Swinson, R. P. (2000b). Specific phobia. In M. M. Antony & R. P. Swinson, *Phobic disorders and panic in adults: A guide to assessment and treatment* (pp. 79–104). Washington, DC: American Psychological Association.

Antrobus, J. (1991). Dreaming: Cognitive processes during cortical activation and high afferent thresholds. *Psychological Review, 98*, 69–121.

Antrobus, J. (2001). Rethinking the fundamental processes of dream and sleep mentation production: Defining new questions that avoid the distraction of REM versus NREM comparisons. *Sleep & Hypnosis, 3*, 1–8.

Antrobus, J., & Conroy, D. (1999). Dissociated neurocognitive processes in dreaming sleep. *Sleep & Hypnosis, 1*, 105–111.

Arai, Y., Tsutsui, Y., Shinmura, Y., Kosugi, T., Nishikage, H., & Yamamoto, J. (2001). An autopsy case of the schizophrenic 32 years after lobotomy. *Neuropathology, 21*, 53–60.

Archer, J. (1991). Human sociobiology: Basic concepts and limitations. *Journal of Social Issues, 47*(3), 11–26.

Archer, J., & Lloyd, B. B. (1985). *Sex and gender.* New York: Cambridge University Press.

Arendt, J., Aldhous, M., & Wright, J. (1988, April 2). Synchronization of a disturbed sleep-wake cycle in a blind man by melatonin treatment. *Lancet, 1*(8588), 772–773.

Arieti, S. (1974). An overview of schizophrenia from a predominantly psychological approach. *American Journal of Psychiatry, 131*(3), 241–249.

Arkes, H. R., Boehm, L. E., & Xu, G. (1991). The determinants of judged validity. *Journal of Experimental Social Psychology, 27*, 576–605.

Arnold, M. B. (1960). *Emotion and personality* (Vols. 1–2). New York: Columbia University Press.

Arnold, M. B. (1970). Perennial problems in the field of emotion. In M. B. Arnold (Ed.), *Feelings and emotions* (pp. 169–185). New York: Academic Press.

Aron, A., & Westbay, L. (1996). Dimensions of the prototype of love. *Journal of Personality and Social Psychology, 70*, 535–551.

Aron, L. (1996). *A meeting of minds: Mutuality in psychoanalysis.* Hillsdale, NJ: Analytic Press.

Aronson, J. (2002). Stereotype threat: Contending and coping with unnerving expectations. In J. Aronson (Ed.), *Improving academic achievement: Impact of psychological factors on education.* San Diego: Academic Press.

Aronson, J., Lustina, M. J., Good, C., Keough, K., Steele, C. M., & Brown, J. (1999). When white men can't do math: Necessary and sufficient factors in stereotype threat. *Journal of Experimental Social Psychology, 35*, 29–46.

Asch, S. E. (1946). Forming impressions of personality. *Journal of Abnormal and Social Psychology, 41*, 258–290.

Asch, S. E. (1951). Effects of group pressure upon the modification and distortion of judgments. In H. Guetzkow (Ed.), *Groups, leadership, and men.* Pittsburgh: Carnegie.

Asch, S. E. (1952). *Social psychology.* New York: Prentice-Hall.

Asch, S. E. (1955). Opinions and social pressure. *Scientific American, 193*, 31–35.

Asch, S. E. (1956). Studies of independence and conformity: A minority of one against a unanimous majority. *Psychological Monographs, 70*, 416.

Astatke, H., & Serpell, R. (2000). Testing the application of a Western scientific theory of AIDS risk behavior among adolescents in Ethiopia. *Journal of Pediatric Psychology, 25*, 367–379.

Astington, J. W. (1993). *The child's discovery of the mind.* Cambridge, MA: Harvard University Press.

Ataca, B., & Berry, J. W. (2002). Psychological, sociocultural, and marital adaptation of Turkish immigrant couples in Canada. *International Journal of Psychology, 37*, 13–26.

Atkinson, J. W. (Ed.). (1958). *Motives in fantasy, action, and society.* Princeton, NJ: Van Nostrand.

Atkinson, R. C., & Shiffrin, R. M. (1968). Human memory: A proposed system and its control processes. In K. W. Spence & J. T. Spence (Eds.), *The psychology of learning and motivation: Advances in research and theory* (Vol. 2). New York: Academic Press.

Atkinson, R. C., & Shiffrin, R. M. (1971). The control of short-term memory. *Scientific American, 225*, 82–90.

Atkinson, R. L., Atkinson, R. C., Smith, E. E., & Bem, D. J. (1993). *Introduction to psychology* (11th ed.). Fort Worth, TX: Harcourt Brace Jovanovich.

Atran, S. (1999). Itzaj Maya folkbiological taxonomy: Cognitive universals and cultural particulars. In D. L. Medin & S. Atran (Eds.), *Folkbiology* (pp. 119–213). Cambridge, MA: MIT Press.

Auerbach, S. M., Martelli, M. F., & Mercuri, L. G. (1983). Anxiety, information, interpersonal impacts, and adjustment to a stressful health care situation. *Journal of Personality and Social Psychology, 44*, 1284–1296.

Austin, S. B. (2001). Population-based prevention of eating disorders: An application of the Rose Prevention Model. *Preventive Medicine: An International Journal Devoted to Practice & Theory, 32*, 268–283.

Averill, J. R. (1980). A constructionist view of emotion. In R. Plutchik & H. Kellerman (Eds.), *Emotion: Theory, research, and experience.* Vol. 1: *Theories of emotion* (pp. 305–339). New York: Academic Press.

Averill, J. R. (1983). Studies on anger and aggression: Implications for theories of emotions? *American Psychologist, 38*, 1145–1160.

Averill, J. R. (1993). Putting the social in social cognition, with special reference to emotion. In R. S. Wyer & T. K. Srull (Eds.), *Toward a general theory of anger and emotional aggression.* Vol. 6: *Advances in social cognition.* Hillsdale, NJ: Erlbaum.

Axelson, J. A. (1993). *Counseling and development in a multicultural society* (2nd ed.). Pacific Grove, CA: Brooks/Cole.

Ayers, M. S., & Reder, L. M. (1998). A theoretical review of the misinformation effect: Predictions from an activation-based memory model. *Psychonomic Bulletin & Review, 5*, 1–21.

Azrin, N. H. (1967, May). Pain and aggression. *Psychology Today,* pp. 27–33.

Azuma, H. (1986). Why study child development in Japan? In H. Stevenson, H. Azuma, & K. Hakuta (Eds.), *Child development and education in Japan* (pp. 3–12). New York: Freeman.

Baddeley, A. D. (1966). Short-term memory for word sequences as a function of acoustic, semantic, and formal similarity. *Quarterly Journal of Experimental Psychology, 18*, 362–365.

Baddeley, A. D. (1989). The psychology of remembering and forgetting. In T. Butler (Ed.), *Memory: History, culture and the mind.* London: Basil Blackwell.

Baddeley, A. D. (1990a). *Human memory.* Hove, UK: Erlbaum.

Baddeley, A. D. (1990b). *Human memory: Theory and practice.* Needham Heights, MA: Allyn & Bacon.

Baddeley, A. D. (1992). Working memory. *Science, 255*, 356–559.

Baddeley, A. R. (2000a). The episodic buffer: A new component of working memory. *Trends in Cognitive Sciences, 4*, 417–423.

Baddeley, A. R. (2000b). Short-term and working memory. In E. Tulving & F. I. M. Craik (Eds.), *The Oxford handbook of memory* (pp. 77–92). New York: Oxford University Press.

Baddeley, A., & Hitch, G. J. (1994). Developments in the concept of working memory. *Neuropsychology, 8*, 485–493.

Bahrick, H. P. (2000). Long-term maintenance of knowledge. In E. Tulving & F. I. M. Craik (Eds.), *The Oxford handbook of memory* (pp. 347–362). New York: Oxford University Press.

Bahrick, H. P., & Phelps, E. (1987). Retention of Spanish vocabulary over eight years. *Journal of Experimental Psychology: Learning Memory and Cognition, 13*, 344–349.

Bahrick, H. P., Bahrick, P. O., & Wittlinger, R. P. (1975). Fifty years of memory for names and faces: A cross-sectional approach. *Journal of Experimental Psychology: General, 104*, 54–75.

Bailey, C. (1991). *The new fit or fat* (Rev. ed.). Boston: Houghton Mifflin.

Bailey, C. H., Alberini, C., Ghirardi, M., & Kandel, E. R. (1994). Molecular and structural changes underlying long-term memory storage in Aplysia. *Advances in Second Messenger and Phosphoprotein Research, 29*, 529–544.

Bailey, J. M., & Pillard, R. C. (1991). A genetic study of male sexual orientation. *Archives of General Psychiatry, 48*(N12), 1089–1096.

Baillargeon, R. (1987). Object permanence in 3- and 4-month-old infants. *Developmental Psychology, 23*, 655–664.

Baillargeon, R. (2002). The acquisition of physical knowledge in infancy: A summary in eight lessons. In U. Goswami (Ed.), *Blackwell handbook of childhood cognitive development* (pp. 47–83). Malden, MA: Blackwell.

Baillargeon, R., & DeVos, J. (1991). Object permanence in young infants: Further evidence. *Child Development, 62*, 1227–1246.

Bakshi, V. P., & Kalin, N. H. (2000). Corticotropin-releasing hormone and animal models of anxiety: Gene-environment interactions. *Biological Psychiatry, 48*, 1175–1198.

Bales, R. F. (1958). Task roles and social roles in problem-solving groups. In E. E. Maccoby, T. M. Newcomb, & E. L. Hartley (Eds.), *Readings in social psychology.* New York: Holt, Rinehart & Winston.

Bales, R. F. (1999). *Social interaction systems: Theory and measurement.* Somerset, NJ: Transaction Books.

Balkin, J. (1988). Why policemen don't like policewomen. *Journal of Police Science and Administration, 16*(1), 29–38.

Balota, D. A., Cortese, M. J., Duchek, J. M., Adams, D., Roediger, H. L., McDermott, K. B., & Yerys, B. E. (1999). Veridical and false memories in healthy older adults and in dementia and Alzheimer's types. *Cognitive Neuropsychology, 16*, 361–384.

Baltes, P. B. (1997). On the incomplete architecture of human ontogeny: Selection, optimization, and compensation as foundations of developmental theory. *American Psychologist, 52*, 366–380.

Baltes, P. B., & Staudinger, U. M. (2000). Wisdom: A metaheuristic (pragmatic) to orchestrate mind and virtue toward excellence. *American Psychologist, 55*, 122–135.

Baltes, P. B., & Willis, S. L. (1979). Toward psychological theories of aging and development. In J. E. Birren & K. W. Schaie (Eds.), *Handbook of the psychology of aging.* New York: Van Nostrand Reinhold.

Baltes, P. B., Lindenberger, U., & Staudinger, U. M. (1998). Lifespan theory in developmental psychology. In W. Damon (Series Ed.) and R. M. Lerner (Vol. Ed.), *Handbook of child psychology* (Vol. 1, pp. 1029–1143). New York: Wiley.

Banaji, M. R., & Hardin, C. D. (1996). Automatic stereotyping. *Psychological Science, 7*, 136–141.

Bandler, R., & Shipley, M. T. (1994). Columnar organization in the midbrain periaqueductal gray: Modules for emotional expression? *Trends in Neuroscience, 17*, 379–389.

Bandura, A. (1965). Influence of models' reinforcement contingencies on the acquisition of imitative responses. *Journal of Personality and Social Psychology, 1*, 589–595.

Bandura, A. (1969). *Principles of behavior modification.* New York: Holt, Rinehart & Winston.

Bandura, A. (1973). *Aggression: A social learning analysis.* Englewood Cliffs, NJ: Prentice-Hall.

Bandura, A. (1977a). Self-efficacy: Toward a unifying theory of behavioral change. *Psychological Review, 84*, 181–215.

Bandura, A. (1977b). *Social learning theory.* Englewood Cliffs, NJ: Prentice-Hall.

Bandura, A. (1983). Psychological mechanisms of aggression. In R. G. Geen & E. I. Donnerstein (Eds.), *Aggression: Theoretical and empirical reviews.* Vol. I: *Theoretical and methodological issues* (pp. 1–40). New York: Academic Press.

Bandura, A. (1986). *Social foundations of thought and action: A social cognitive theory.* Englewood Cliffs, NJ: Prentice-Hall.

Bandura, A. (1995). *Self-efficacy in changing societies.* New York: Cambridge University Press.

Bandura, A. (1996). *Self-efficacy: The exercise of control.* New York: Freeman.

Bandura, A. (1999). Moral disengagement in the perpetration of inhumanities. *Personality and Social Psychology Review, 3*, 193–209.

Bandura, A. (2001). Social cognitive theory: An agentic perspective. *Annual Review of Psychology, 52*, 1–26.

Bandura, A. (2002). Social cognitive theory in cultural context. *Applied Psychology, 51*, 269–290.

Bandura, A., & Rosenthal, T. (1966). Vicarious classical conditioning as a function of arousal level. *Journal of Personality and Social Psychology, 3*, 54–62.

Bandura, A., Barbaranelli, C., Caprara, G. V., & Pastorelli, C. (1996). Multifaceted impact of self-efficacy beliefs on academic functioning. *Child Development, 67*, 1206–1222.

Bandura, A., Blanchard, E. B., & Ritter, B. (1969). Relative efficacy of desensitization and modelling approaches for inducing behavioral, affective, and attitudinal changes. *Journal of Personality and Social Psychology, 13*, 173–199.

Bandura, A., Ross, D., & Ross, S. (1963). Imitation of film-mediated aggressive models. *Journal of Abnormal and Social Psychology, 66*, 3–11.

Bandura, A., Underwood, B., & Fromson, M. E. (1975). Disinhibition of aggression through diffusion of responsibility and dehumanization of victims. *Journal of Research in Personality, 9*, 253–269.

Banks, M. S., & Salapatek, P. (1983). Infant visual perception. In M. M. Haith & J. J. Campos (Eds.), *Handbook of child psychology: Infancy and developmental psychobiology* (4th ed., Vol. 2). New York: Wiley.

Bao, J. X., Kandel, E. R., & Hawkins, R. D. (1998). Involvement of presynaptic and postsynaptic mechanisms in a cellular analog of classical conditioning at Aplysia sensory-motor neuron synapses in isolated cell culture. *Journal of Neuroscience, 18*, 458–466.

Barber, T. X. (1979). Suggested ("hypnotic") behavior: The trance paradigm versus an alternative paradigm. In E. Fromm, & R. E. Shor (Eds.), *Hypnosis: Developments in research and new perspectives.* New York: Aldine.

Barber, T. X. (1986). Realities of stage hypnosis. In B. Zilbergeld, M. G. Edelstein, & D. L. Araoz (Eds.), *Hypnosis: Questions and answers.* New York: Norton.

Barber, T. X. (1999a). The essence and mechanism of superb hypnotic performances. *Contemporary Hypnosis, 16*, 192–208.

Barber, T. X. (1999b). Hypnosis: A mature view. *Contemporary Hypnosis, 16*, 123–127.

Barber, T. X. (2000). A deeper understanding of hypnosis: Its secrets, its nature, its essence. *American Journal of Clinical Hypnosis, 42*, 208–272.

Bard, P. (1934). On emotional experience after decortication with some remarks on theoretical views. *Psychological Review, 41*, 309–329.

Barefoot, J. C., Dodge, K. A., Peterson, B. L., Dahlstrom, W. G., & Williams, R. B. (1989). The Cook-Medley hostility scale: Item content and ability to predict survival. *Psychosomatic Medicine, 51*, 46–57.

Bargh, J. A. (1997). The automaticity of everyday life. In R. S. Wyer (Ed.), *The automaticity of everyday life: Advances in social cognition* (Vol. 10, pp. 1–61). Mahwah, NJ: Erlbaum.

Barker, R. G., Dembo, T., & Lewin, K. (1941). Frustration and regression: An experiment with young children. *University of Iowa Studies in Child Welfare, 18*(1).

Barlow, D. H. (1988). *Anxiety and its disorders.* New York: Guilford.

Barlow, D. H., Gorman, J. M., Shear, M. K., & Woods, S. W. (2000). Cognitive-behavioral therapy, imipramine, or their combination for panic disorder: A randomized controlled trial. *JAMA, 283*, 2529–2536.

Barlow, D. H., Raffa, S. D., & Cohen, E. M. (2002). Psychosocial treatments for panic disorders, phobias, and generalized anxiety disorder. In P. E. Nathan & J. M. Gorman (Eds.), *A guide to treatments that work* (2nd ed., pp. 301–335). London: Oxford University Press.

Barnes, M. L., & Sternberg, R. J. (1997). A hierarchical model of love and its prediction of satisfaction in close relationships. In R. J. Sternberg & M. Hojjat (Eds.), *Satisfaction in close relationships.* New York: Guilford.

Barnes, R. C., & Earnshaw, S. M. (1995). Problems with the savant syndrome: A brief case study. *British Journal of Learning Disabilities, 23*,124–126.

Baron, M., Gershon, E. S., Rudy, V., Jonas, W. Z., & Buchsbaum, M. (1975). Lithium carbonate response in depression. *Archives of General Psychiatry, 32*, 1107–1111.

Baron, R. A. (1977). *Human aggression.* New York: Plenum.

Baron, R. A., & Bell, P. A. (1975). Aggression and heat: Mediating effects of prior provocation and exposure to an aggressive model. *Journal of Personality and Social Psychology, 31*, 825–832.

Baron, R. A., & Richardson, D. R. (1992). *Human aggression* (2nd ed.). New York: Plenum.

Baron, R. A., Neuman, J. H., & Geddes, D. (1999). Social and personal determinants of workplace aggression: Evidence for the impact of perceived injustice and the Type A behavior pattern. *Aggressive Behavior, 25*, 281–296.

Baron, R. S. (1986). Distraction-conflict theory: Progress and problems. In L. Berkowitz (Ed.), *Advances in experimental social psychology.* Orlando, FL: Academic Press.

Baron, R. S., Moore, D., & Sanders, G. S. (1978). Distraction as a source of drive social facilitation. *Journal of Personality and Social Psychology, 36*, 816–824.

Baron-Cohen, S., Leslie, A. M., & Frith, U. (1985). Does the autistic child have a "theory of mind"? *Cognition, 21*, 37–46.

Barr, C. E., Mednick, S. A., & Munk-Jorgensen, P. (1990). Exposure to influenza epidemics during gestation and adult schizophrenia: A 40-year study. *Archives of General Psychiatry, 47*, 869–874.

Barrett, P. T., & Eysenck, H. J. (1992). Brain evoked potentials and intelligence: The Hendrickson paradigm. *Intelligence, 16*(3–4), 361–381.

Barsalou, L. W. (2000). Concepts: Structure. In A. E. Kazdin (Ed.), *Encyclopedia of psychology* (Vol. 2, pp. 245–248). New York: Oxford University Press (American Psychological Association).

Bartlett, F. C. (1932). *Remembering: A study in experimental and social psychology.* Cambridge, UK: Cambridge University Press.

Bartoshuk, L. M. (1988). Taste. In R. C. Atkinson, R. J. Herrnstein, G. Lindzey, & R. D. Luce (Eds.), *Stevens handbook of experimental psychology: Perception and motivation* (Vol. 1). New York: Wiley.

Bartoshuk, L. M. (1993). The biological basis of food perception and acceptance. *Food Quality and Preference, 4*, 21–32.

Bashore, T. R., & Rapp, P. E. (1993). Are there alternatives to traditional polygraph procedures? *Psychological Bulletin, 113*(1), 3–22.

Bashore, T. R., Osman, A., & Hefley, E. F. (1989). Mental slowing in elderly persons: A cognitive psychophysiological analysis. *Psychology and Aging, 4*, 235–244.

Basoglu, M. (1997). Torture as a stressful life event: A review of the current status of knowledge. In T. W. Miller (Ed.), *Clinical disorders and stressful life events* (pp. 45–70). Madison, CT: International Universities Press.

Basoglu, M., Paker, O., Pozmen, E., Marks, I., Sahin, D., & Sarimurat, N. (1994). Psychological effects of torture: A comparison of tortured with nontortured political activists in Turkey. *American Journal of Psychiatry, 11*, 6–81.

Basow, S. A. (1986). *Gender stereotypes: Traditions and alternatives* (2nd ed.). Belmont, CA: Brooks/Cole.

Basow, S. A. (1992). *Gender: Stereotypes and roles* (3rd ed.). Belmont, CA: Wadsworth.

Basow, S. A., & Willis, J. (2001). Perceptions of body hair on White women: Effects of labeling. *Psychological Reports, 89*, 571–576.

Bassok, M., Wu, L., & Olseth, K. L. (1995). Judging a book by its cover: Interpretative effects of content on problem solving transfer. *Memory and Cognition, 23*, 354–367.

Bastik, T. (1982). *Intuition: How we think and act.* Chichester, UK: Wiley.

Bates, E., & Goodman, J. (1999). On the emergence of grammar from the lexicon. In B. MacWhinney (Ed.), *The emergence of language* (pp. 29–80). Mahwah, NJ: Erlbaum.

Batson, C. D. (1997). Self-other merging and the empathy-altruism hypothesis: Reply to Neuberg et al. (1997). *Journal of Personality and Social Psychology, 73*, 517–522.

Batson, C. D., Batson, J. G., Griffitt, C. A., Barrientos, S., Brandt, J. R., Sprengelmeyer, P., & Bayly, M. J. (1989). Negative-state relief and the empathy–altruism hypothesis. *Journal of Personality and Social Psychology, 56*, 922–933.

Batson, C. D., Dyck, J. L., Brandt, J. R., Batson, J. G., Powell, A. L., McMaster, R. M., & Griffit, C. A. (1988). Five studies testing two new egoistic alternatives to the empathy–altruism hypothesis. *Journal of Personality and Social Psychology, 55*, 52–77.

Bauer, P. J. (2002). Early memory development. In U. Goswami (Ed.), *Blackwell handbook of childhood cognitive development* (pp. 127–146). Malden, MA: Blackwell.

Baumeister, R. F. (1996). *Evil: Inside human violence and cruelty.* New York: Freeman.

Baumeister, R. F., & Campbell, W. K. (1999). The intrinsic appeal of evil: Sadism, sensational thrills, and threatened egotism. *Personality and Social Psychology Review, 3*, 210–221.

Baumeister, R. F., Stillwell, A. M., & Wotman, S. R. (1990). Victim and perpetrator accounts of interpersonal conflict: Autobiographical narratives about anger. *Journal of Personality and Social Psychology, 59*, 994–1005.

Baumrind, D. (1971). Current patterns of parental authority. *Developmental Psychology Monograph, 4*(1, Pt. 2), 79–103.

Baumrind, D. (1978). Parental disciplinary patterns and social competence in children. *Youth and Society, 9*, 239–276.

Baumrind, D. (1986). Sex differences in moral reasoning: Response to Walker's (1984) conclusion that there are none. *Child Development, 57*, 511–521.

Baumrind, D. (1991). Effective parenting during the early adolescent transition. In P. A. Cowan & E. M. Hetherington (Eds.), *Family transitions* (pp. 111–164). Hillsdale, NJ: Erlbaum.

Baxter, L. R., Phelps, M. E., Mazziotta, J. C., Schwartz, J. M., Gerner, R. H., Selin, C. E., & Sumida, R. M. (1985). Cerebral metabolic rates for glucose in mood disorders. *Archives of General Psychiatry, 42*, 441–447.

Bayley, N. (1993). *The Bayley Scales of Mental and Motor Development* (Revised). New York: Psychological Corporation.

Bayley, N., & Oden, M. H. (1955). The maintenance of intellectual ability in gifted adults. *Journal of Gerontology, 10*, 91–107.

Beadle-Brown, J., & Forrester-Jones, R. (2003). Social impairment in the "Care in the Community" cohort: The effect of deinstitutionalization and changes over time in the community. *Research in Developmental Disabilities, 24*, 33–43.

Beall, A., & Sternberg, R. J. (1995). The social construction of love. *Journal of Personal and Social Relationships, 2*(3), 417–438.

Beall, A., & Sternberg, R. J. (Eds.). (1993). *Perspectives on the psychology of gender.* New York: Guilford.

Bear, M. E., Connors, B. W., & Paradiso, M. A. (1996). *Neuroscience: Exploring the brain.* Baltimore, MD: Williams & Wilkins.

Beck, A. T. (1967). *Depression: Causes and treatment.* Philadelphia: University of Pennsylvania Press.

Beck, A. T. (1976). *Cognitive therapy and the emotional disorders.* New York: International Universities Press.

Beck, A. T. (1985). Theoretical perspectives on clinical anxiety. In A. H. Tuma & J. D. Maser (Eds.), *Anxiety and the anxiety disorder* (pp. 183–198). Hillsdale, NJ: Erlbaum.

Beck, A. T. (1986). Cognitive therapy: A sign of retrogression of progress. *The Behavior Therapist, 9*, 2–3.

Beck, A. T. (1988). Cognitive approaches to panic disorder: Theory and therapy. In S. Rachman & J. D. Maser (Eds.), *Panic: Psychological perspectives.* Hillsdale, NJ: Erlbaum.

Beck, A. T. (1991). Cognitive therapy: A thirty-year retrospective. *American Psychologist, 46*, 368–375.

Beck, A. T. (1997). Interview. *Cognitive Therapy Today, 2*, 1–3.

Beck, A. T. (2002a). Cognitive models of depression. In R. Leahy & E. T. Dowd (Eds.), *Clinical advances in cognitive psychotherapy: Theory and application* (pp. 29–61). New York: Springer.

Beck, A. T. (2002b). Cognitive patterns in dreams and daydreams. *Journal of Cognitive Psychotherapy, 16*, 23–28.

Beck, A. T., & Emery, G., (with) Greenberg, R. L. (1985). *Anxiety disorders and phobias: A cognitive perspective.* New York: Basic Books.

Beeri, R., Le Novere, N., Mervis, R., Huberman, T., Grauer, E., Changeux, J. P., & Soreq, H. (1997). Enhanced hemicholinium binding and attenuated dendrite branching in cognitively impaired acetylcholinesterase-transgenic mice. *Journal of Neurochemistry, 69*, 2441–2451.

Beilin, H. (1971). The training and acquisition of logical operation. In M. Rosskopf, L. Steffe, & S. Taback (Eds.), *Piagetian cognitive development research and mathematical education.* Washington, DC: National Council of Teachers of Mathematics.

Beilin, H. (1994). Mechanisms in the explanation of developmental change. *Advances in Child Development and Behavior, 25*, 327–352.

Beilin, H., & Fireman, G. (2000). The foundation of Piaget's theories: Mental and physical action. *Advances in Child Development and Behavior, 27*, 221–246.

Bein, E., Anderson, T., Strupp, H. H., Henry, W. P., Schacht, T. E., Binder, J. L., & Butler, S. F. (2000). The effects of training in time-limited dynamic psychotherapy: Changes in therapeutic outcome. *Psychotherapy Research, 10*, 119–132.

Bekerian, D. A. (1993). In search of the typical eyewitness. *American Psychologist, 48*(5), 574–576.

Békésy, G. von. (1960). *Experiments in hearing.* New York: McGraw-Hill.

Bell, P. A., & Baron, R. A. (1976). Aggression and heat: The mediating role of negative affect. *Journal of Applied Social Psychology, 6*, 18–30.

Bellinger, D. C., & Adams, H. F. (2001). Environmental pollutant exposures and children's cognitive abilities. In R. J. Sternberg & E. L. Grigorenko (Eds.), *Environmental effects on cognitive abilities* (pp. 157–188). Mahwah, NJ: Erlbaum.

Belloc, N. D., & Breslow, L. (1972). Relationship of physical health status and family practices. *Preventive Medicine, 1*, 409–421.

Belsky, J. (1990). Parental and nonparental child care and children's socioemotional development: A decade in review. *Journal of Marriage and the Family, 52*, 885–903.

Belsky, J., & Rovine, M. (1988). Nonmaternal care in the first year of life and the security of infant–parent attachment. *Child Development, 59*, 157–167.

Bem, D. J. (1967). Self-perception: An alternative interpretation of cognitive dissonance phenomena. *Psychological Review, 74*, 183–200.

Bem, D. J. (1972). Self-perception theory. In L. Berkowitz (Ed.), *Advances in experimental social psychology* (Vol. 6). New York: Academic Press.

Bem, D. J. (1996). Exotic becomes erotic: A developmental theory of sexual orientation. *Psychological Review, 103*, 320–323.

Bem, D. J. (2000a). Exotic becomes erotic: Interpreting the biological correlates of sexual orientation. *Archives of Sexual Behavior, 29*, 531–548.

Bem, D. J. (2000b). The exotic-becomes-erotic theory of sexual orientation. In J. Bancroft (Ed.), *The role of theory in sex research. The Kinsey Institute series* (Vol. 6, pp. 67–81). Bloomington: Indiana University Press.

Bem, D. J. (2000c). Writing an empirical article. In R. J. Sternberg (Ed.), *Guide to publishing in psychology journals* (pp. 3–16). New York: Cambridge University Press.

Bem, S. (1993). *The lenses of gender: Transforming the debate on sexual inequality.* New Haven, CT: Yale University Press.

Bem, S. L. (1981). Gender schema theory: A cognitive account of sex typing. *Psychological Review, 88*, 354–364.

Benbow, C. P., & Stanley, J. C. (1980). Sex differences in mathematical ability: Fact or artifact? *Science, 210*, 1262–1264.

Benjamin, L. T. Jr. (1986). Why don't they understand us? A history of psychology's public image. *American Psychologist, 41*, 941–946.

Benjamin, L. T. Jr., & Baker, D. B. (2004). *From séance to science: A history of the profession of psychology in America.* Belmont, CA: Wadsworth.

Benjamin, L. T. Jr., & Bryant, W. H. M. (1997). A history of popular psychology magazines in America. In W. G. Bringmann, et al., (Eds.), *A pictorial history of psychology* (pp. 585–593). Carol Stream, IL: Quintessence.

Benjamin, L. T. Jr., & Nielsen-Gammon, E. (1999). B. F. Skinner and psychotechnology: The case of the heir conditioner. *Review of General Psychology, 3*, 155–167.

Benjamin, L. T. Jr., Bryant, W. H. M., Campbell, C., Luttrell, J., & Holtz, C. (1997). Between psoriasis and ptarmigan: American encyclopedias portray psychology, 1880-1940. *Review of General Psychology, 1*, 5–18.

Bennett, M. (1999). Introduction. In M. Bennett (Ed.), *Developmental psychology* (pp. 1–12). Philadelphia: Psychology Press.

Bennett, M. J. (1996). Is psychotherapy ever medically necessary? *Psychiatric Services, 47*, 966–970.

Benotsch, E. G., Christensen, A. J., & McKelvey, L. (1997). Hostility, social support, and ambulatory cardiovascular activity. *Journal of Behavioral Medicine, 20*, 163–182.

Ben-Shakhar, G., & Furedy, J. J. (1990). *Theories and applications in the detection of deception: A psychophysiological and international perspective.* New York: Springer Verlag.

Benson, A. J. (1984) Motion Sickness. In M. R. Dix & J. D. Hood, *Vertigo.* New York: John Wiley & Sons, Ltd.

Benson, A. J. (1984). Motion sickness. In M. R. Dix & J. D. Hood (Eds.), *Vertigo.* New York: Wiley.

Benson, H. (1977). Systemic hypertension and the relaxation response. *New England Journal of Medicine, 296*, 1152–1156.

Ben-Zeev, T. (1996). When erroneous mathematical thinking is just as "correct": The oxymoron of rational errors. In R. J. Sternberg & T. Ben-Zeev (Eds.), *The nature of mathematical thinking* (pp. 55–79). Mahwah, NJ: Erlbaum.

Bereiter, C. (2002). *Education and mind in the Knowledge Age.* Mahwah, NJ: Erlbaum.

Berg, C. A. (2000). Intellectual development in adulthood. In R. J. Sternberg (Ed.), *Handbook of intelligence* (pp. 117–137). New York: Cambridge University Press.

Berg, C. A., & Klaczynski, P. (2002). Contextual variability in the expression and meaning of intelligence. In R. J. Sternberg & E. L. Grigorenko (Eds.), *The general factor of intelligence: How general is it?* (pp. 381–412). Mahwah, NJ: Erlbaum.

Berg, C. A., & Sternberg, R. J. (1992). Adults' conceptions of intelligence across the adult life span. *Psychology and Aging, 7*(2), 221–231.

Berg, C. A., Meegan, S. P., & Deviney, F. P. (1998). A social contextual model of coping with everyday problems across the lifespan. *International Journal of Behavioral Development, 22,* 239–261.

Berg, C. A., Strough, J., Calderone, K. S., Sansone, C., & Weir, C. (1998). The role of problem definitions in understanding age and context effects on strategies for solving everyday problems. *Psychology and Aging, 13,* 29–44.

Berger, K. S. (1980). *The developing person.* New York: Worth.

Berglas, S., & Jones, E. E. (1978). Drug choice as a self-handicapping strategy in response to noncontingent success. *Journal of Personality and Social Psychology, 36,* 405–417.

Bergman, E. T., & Roediger, H. L. (1999). Can Bartlett's repeated reproduction experiments be replicated? *Memory & Cognition, 27,* 937–947.

Berkman, L. (1994, May 22). "I really was hurt by the verdict." (Holly Ramona says jury's decision will undermine her attempt to recover damages from her father, Gary Ramona, who she alleges molested her.) *Los Angeles Times,* p. A3.

Berkowitz, L. (1993). *Aggression: Its causes, consequences, and control.* New York: McGraw-Hill.

Berkowitz, L. (1994). On the escalation of aggression. In M. Potegal & J. F. Knutson (Eds.), *The dynamics of aggression: Biological and social processes in dyads and groups* (pp. 33–41). Hillsdale, NJ: Erlbaum.

Berkowitz, L. (1999). Evil is more than banal: Situationism and the concept of evil. *Personality and Social Psychology Review, 3,* 246–253.

Berkowitz, L., Cochran, S., & Embree, M. (1981). Physical pain and the goal of aversively stimulated aggression. *Journal of Personality and Social Psychology, 40,* 687–700.

Berlin, B., & Kay, P. (1969). *Basic color terms: Their universality and evolution.* Los Angeles: University of California Press.

Berlyne, D. E. (1960). *Conflict, arousal, and curiosity.* New York: McGraw-Hill.

Berlyne, D. E. (1967). Arousal reinforcement. In D. Levine (Ed.), *Nebraska symposium on motivation* (pp. 1–110). Lincoln: University of Nebraska Press.

Berman, K. F., Torrey, E. F., Daniel, D. G., & Weinberger, D. R. (1992). Regional cerebral blood flow in monozygotic twins discordant and concordant for schizophrenia. *Archives for General Psychiatry, 49,* 927–934.

Berman, M., Gladue, B., & Taylor, S. (1993). The effects of hormones, Type A behavior pattern, and provocation on aggression in men. *Motivation and Emotion, 17,* 125–148.

Bernard, L. L. (1924). *Instinct.* New York: Holt, Rinehart & Winston.

Berndt, T. J. (1982). The features and effects of friendship in early adolescence. *Child Development, 53*(6), 1447–1460.

Berndt, T. J. (1986). Children's comments about their friendships. In M. Perlmutter (Ed.), *Cognitive perspectives on children's social and behavioral development: The Minnesota symposia on child psychology* (Vol. 18, pp. 189–212). Hillsdale, NJ: Erlbaum.

Bernichon, T., Cook, K. E., & Brown, J. D. (2003). Seeking self-evaluative feedback: The interactive role of global self-esteem and specific self-views. *Journal of Personality and Social Psychology, 84,* 194–204.

Berry, J. W. (1974). Radical cultural relativism and the concept of intelligence. In J. W. Berry & P. R. Dasen (Eds.), *Culture and cognition: Readings in cross-cultural psychology* (pp. 225–229). London: Methuen.

Berry, J. W. (1989). Psychology of acculturation. In J. Berman (Ed.), *Nebraska Symposium on Motivation* (Vol. 37, pp. 201–234). Lincoln: University of Nebraska Press.

Berry, J. W. (1994). Acculturative stress. In W. J. Lonner & R. W. Malpass (Eds.), *Psychology and culture.* Boston: Allyn & Bacon.

Berry, J. W. (2000). Cross-cultural psychology: A symbiosis of cultural and comparative approaches. *Asian Journal of Social Psychology, 3,* 197–205.

Berry, J. W., Poortinga, Y. H., Segall, M. H., & Dasen, P. R. (1992). *Cross-cultural psychology: Research and applications.* New York: Cambridge University Press.

Berry, S. L., Beatty, W. W., & Klesges, R. C. (1985). Sensory and social influences on ice cream consumption by males and females in a laboratory setting. *Appetite, 6,* 41–45.

Berscheid, E. (1999). The greening of relationship science. *American Psychologist, 54,* 260–266.

Berscheid, E., & Collins, W. A. (2000). Who cares? For whom and when, how, and why? *Psychological Inquiry, 11,* 107–109.

Berscheid, E., & Reis, H. T. (1998). Attraction and close relationships. In D. Gilbert, S. Fiske, & G. Lindzey (Eds.), *Handbook of social psychology* (4th ed.). New York: Oxford University Press.

Berscheid, E., & Walster, E. (1974). A little bit about love. In T. L. Huston (Ed.), *Foundations of interpersonal attraction.* New York: Academic Press.

Bersoff, D. M., & Miller, J. (1993). Culture, context, and the development of moral accountability judgments. *Developmental Psychology, 29,* 664–676.

Bertenthal, B. I., & Fischer, K. W. (1978). Development of self-recognition in the infant. *Developmental Psychology, 14,* 44–50.

Bertilsson, L. (1978). Mechanism of action of benzodiazepines: The GABA hypothesis. *Acta Psychiatrica Scandinavica, 274,* 19–26.

Bertoncini, J. (1993). Infants' perception of speech units: Primary representation capacities. In B. B. De Boysson-Bardies, S. DeSchonen, P. Jusczyk, P. MacNeilage, & J. Morton (Eds.), *Developmental neurocognition: Speech and face processing in the first year of life.* Dordrecht: Kluwer.

Beutler, L. E., Kim, E. J., Davison, E., Karno, M., & Fisher, D. (1996). Research contributions to improving managed health care outcomes. *Psychotherapy, 33,* 197–206.

Bexton, W. H., Heron, W., & Scott, T. H. (1954). Effects of decreased variation in the sensory environment. *Canadian Journal of Psychology, 8,* 70–76.

Bezooijen, R. V., Otto, S. A., & Heenan, T. A. (1983). Recognition of vocal expressions of emotion: A three nation study to identify universal characteristics. *Journal of Cross-Cultural Psychology, 14,* 387–406.

Bhatia, T. T., & Ritchie, W. C. (1999). The bilingual child: Some issues and perspectives. In W. C. Ritchie & T. K. Bhatia (Eds.), *Handbook of child language acquisition* (pp. 569–646). San Diego, CA: Academic Press.

Bianchin, M., Mello E., Souza, T., Medina, J. H., & Izquierdo, I. (1999). The amygdala is involved in the modulation of long-term memory, but not in working or short-term memory. *Neurobiology of Learning & Memory, 71,* 127–131.

Bickman, L. (1996). A continuum of care: More is not always better. *American Psychologist, 51.*

Bickman, L., Guthrie, P. R., Foster, E. M., Lambert, E. W., Summerfelt, W. T., Breda, C. S., & Heflinger, C. A. (1995). *Evaluating managed mental health services: The Fort Bragg Experiment.* New York: Plenum.

Biederman, I. (1987). Recognition-by-components: A theory of human image understanding. *Psychological Review, 94,* 115–147.

Biederman, J., Mick, E., & Faraone, S. V. (2000). Age-dependent decline of symptoms of attention deficit hyperactivity disorder: Impact of remission definition and symptom type. *American Journal of Psychiatry, 157,* 816–818.

Biery, R. E. (1990). *Understanding homosexuality: The pride and the prejudice.* Austin, TX: Edward-William.

Bilotta, J., Saszik, S., Givin, C. J., Hardesty, H. R., & Sutherland, S. E. (2002). Effects of embryonic exposure to ethanol on zebrafish visual function. *Neurotoxiocology & Teratology, 24,* 759–766.

Binet, A., & Simon, T. (1916). *The development of intelligence in children* (E. S. Kite, Trans.). Baltimore, MD: Williams & Wilkins.

Bingham, C. R., Bennion, L. D., Openshaw, D. K., & Adams, G. R. (1994). An analysis of age, gender, and racial differences in recent national trends of youth suicide. *Journal of Adolescence, 17,* 53–71.

Birdsong, D. (1999). Introduction: Whys and why nots of the critical period hypothesis for second language acquisition. In D. Birdsong (Ed.), *Second language acquisition and the critical period hypothesis* (pp. 1–22). Mahwah, NJ: Erlbaum.

Birenbaum, M., and Kraemer, R. (1995). Gender and ethnic group differences in causal attributions for success and failure in mathematics and language examinations. *Journal of Cross-Cultural Psychology, 26*(4), 342–359.

Bisanz, J., Bisanz, G. L., & Korpan, C. A. (1994). Inductive reasoning. In R. J. Sternberg (Ed.), *Thinking and problem solving* (pp. 181–213). San Diego, CA: Academic Press.

Biswas-Diener, R., & Diener, E. (2001). Making the best of a bad situation: Satisfaction in the slums of Calcutta. *Social Indicators Research, 55,* 329–352.

Bizer, G. Y., & Krosnick, J. A. (2001). Exploring the structure of strength-related attitude features: The relation between attitude importance and attitude accessibility. *Journal of Personality & Social Psychology, 81,* 566–586.

Bjorklund, D. F. (2000). *Children's thinking: Developmental function and individual differences.* Belmont, CA: Wadsworth.

Bjorklund, D. F., & Kipp, K. (2002). Social cognition, inhibition, and theory of mind: The evolution of human intelligence. In R. J. Sternberg & J. C. Kaufman (Eds.), *The evolution of intelligence* (pp. 27–54). Mahwah, NJ: Erlbaum.

Blackmore, S. (1999). Tunnel vision and tunnel experiences. *Journal of Near-Death Studies, 17,* 271–272.

Blackmore, S. J. (1993). *Dying to live: Science and the near-death experience.* London: Grafton.

Blake, R. (2000). Vision and sight: Structure and function. In A. E. Kazdin (Ed.), *Encyclopedia of psychology* (pp. 177–178). Washington, DC: American Psychological Association.

Blakemore, S. J., Wolpert, D., & Frith, C. (2000). Why can't you tickle yourself? *Neuroreport, 3,* R11-116.

Blasi, A. (1980). Bridging moral cognition and moral action: A critical review of the literature. *Psychological Bulletin, 88,* 1–45.

Blass, E. M. (1990). Suckling: Determinants, changes, mechanisms, and lasting impressions. *Developmental Psychology, 26,* 520–533.

Blass, T. (1993). Psychological perspectives on the perpetrators of the Holocaust: The role of situational pressures, personal dispositions, and their interactions. *Holocaust and Genocide Studies, 7,* 30–50.

Blatt, S. J., Auerbach, J. S., & Levy, K. N. (1997). Mental representations in personality development, psychopathology, and the psychotherapeutic process. *Review of General Psychology, 1,* 351–374.

Blessing, S. B., & Ross, B. H. (1996). Content effects in problem categorization and problem solving. *Journal of Experimental Psychology: Learning, Memory, and Cognition, 22,* 792–810.

Bliss, E. L. (1980). Multiple personality. *Archives of General Psychiatry, 37,* 1388–1397.

Block, J. (1983). Differential premises arising from differential socialization of the sexes: Some conjectures. *Child Development, 54,* 1335–1354.

Block, J. (1995). A contrarian view of the five-factor approach to personality description. *Psychological Bulletin, 117,* 187–215.

Block, J. H. (1980). From infancy to adulthood: A clarification. *Child Development, 51*(2), 622–623.

Bloom, B. S. (1964). *Stability and change in human characteristics.* New York: Wiley.

Bloom, B. S., & Broder, L. J. (1950). *Problem-solving processes of college students.* Chicago: University of Chicago Press.

Bloom, P. (2000). *How children learn the meanings of words.* Cambridge, MA: MIT Press.

Blume, A. W., Marlatt, G. A., & Schmaling, K. B. (2000). Executive cognitive function and heavy drinking behavior among college students. *Psychology of Addictive Behaviors, 14,* 299–302.

Blumenthal, J. A., Emery, C. F., Walsh, M. A., Cox, D. R., Kuhn, C. M., Williams, R. B., & Williams, R. S. (1988). Exercise training in healthy Type A middle-aged men: Effects to behavioral and cardiovascular responses. *Psychosomatic Medicine, 50,* 418–433.

Bock, K., Loebell, H., & Morey, R. (1992). From conceptual roles to structural relations: Bridging the syntactic cleft. *Psychological Review, 99*(1), 150–171.

Boden, M. A. (1999). Computer models of creativity. In R. J. Sternberg (Ed.), *Handbook of creativity* (pp. 351–372). New York: Cambridge University Press.

Bodenhausen, G. V., & Moreno, K. N. (2000). How do I feel about them? The role of affective reactions in intergroup perception. In H. Bless & J. P. Forgas (Eds.), *The message within: The role of subjective experience in social cognition and behavior* (pp. 283–303). Philadelphia: Psychology Press.

Bolger, N. (1990). Coping as a personality process: A prospective study. *Journal of Personality and Social Psychology, 59*(3), 531.

Boll, T. J. (1978). Diagnosing brain impairment. In B. B. Wolman (Ed.), *Clinical diagnosis of mental disorders: A handbook.* New York: Plenum.

Bolwig, T. G. (1993). Biological treatments other than drugs (electroconvulsive therapy, brain surgery, insulin therapy, and photo therapy). In N. Sartorius, G. de Girolano, G. Andrews, G. A. German, & L. Eisenberg (Eds.), *Treatment of mental disorders: A review of effectiveness.* Geneva, Switzerland, and Washington, DC: World Health Organization and American Psychiatric Press.

Bond, C. F. Jr., & Kenny, D. A. (2002). The triangle of interpersonal models. *Journal of Personality and Social Psychology, 83,* 355–366.

Bond, C. F. Jr., Atoum, A. O., & VanLeeuwen, M. D. (1996). Social impairment of complex learning in the wake of public embarrassment. *Basic & Applied Social Psychology, 18,* 31–44.

Bond, C. F., & Titus, L. J. (1983). Social facilitation: A meta-analysis of 241 studies. *Psychological Bulletin, 94,* 265–292.

Bond, M. H. (1986). *The psychology of the Chinese people.* Hong Kong: Oxford University Press.

Bond, M. H. (Ed.). (1988). *Cross-cultural research and methodology series.* Vol. 11: *The cross-cultural challenge to social psychology.* Newbury Park, CA: Sage.

Bond, M. R. (1979). *Pain: Its nature, analysis and treatment.* New York: Longman.

Bongiovanni, A. (1977). *A review of research on the effects of punishment in the schools.* Paper presented at the Conference on Child Abuse, Children's Hospital National Medical Center, Washington, DC.

Boon, S., & Draijer, N. (1993). Multiple personality disorder in the Netherlands: A clinical investigation of 71 patients. *American Journal of Psychiatry, 150,* 489–494.

Booth-Kewley, S., & Friedman, H. S. (1987). Psychological predictors of heart disease: A quantitative review. *Psychological Bulletin, 101,* 343–362.

Bootzin, R. R., Manger, R., Perlis, M. L., Salvio, M. A., & Wyatt, J. K. (1993). Sleep disorders. In P. B. Sutker & H. E. Adams (Eds.), *Comprehensive handbook of psychopathology* (2nd ed.). New York: Plenum.

Borbely, A. (1986). *Secrets of sleep.* New York: Basic Books.

Borbely, A. A., & Tononi, G. (2001). The quest for the essence of sleep. In G. M. Edelman & J.-P. Changeux (Eds.), *The brain* (pp. 167–196). New Brunswick, NJ: Transaction Publishers.

Borden, R. J., Bowen, R., & Taylor, S. P. (1971). School setting as a function of physical attack and extrinsic reward. *Perceptual and Motor Skills, 33,* 563–568.

Boring, E. G. (1923, June 6). Intelligence as the tests test it. *New Republic,* 35–37.

Borkovec, T., Stöber, J., & Ray, W. (1998). The nature, functions, and origins of worry. NIMH workshop on Cognition and Anxiety, *Cognitive Therapy and Research, 22,* 561-576.

Bornstein, M. H. (1989). Information processing (habituation) in infancy and stability in cognitive development. *Human Development, 32*(3–4), 129–136.

Bornstein, M. H. (1999). Human infancy: Past, present, and future. In M. Bennett (Ed.), *Developmental psychology* (pp. 35). Philadelphia: Psychology Press.

Bornstein, M. H., & Krinsky, S. J. (1985). Perception of symmetry in infancy: The salience of vertical symmetry and the perception of pattern wholes. *Journal of Experimental Child Psychology, 39,* 1–19.

Bornstein, M. H., & Sigman, M. D. (1986). Continuity in mental development from infancy. *Child Development, 57,* 251–274.

Bornstein, M. H., Tal, J., & Tamis-LeMonda, C. S. (1991). Parenting in crosscultural perspective: The United States, France, and Japan. In M. H. Bornstein (Ed.), *Cultural approaches to parenting* (pp. 69–90). Hillsdale, NJ: Erlbaum.

Bornstein, M. H., Toda, S., Azuma, H., Tamis-LeMonda, C. S., & Ogino, M. (1990). Mother and infant activity and interaction in Japan and in the United States: Pt. II. A comparative microanalysis of naturalistic exchanges focused on the organization of infant attention. *International Journal of Behavioral Development, 13,* 289–308.

Bothwell, R. K., Brigham, J. C., & Malpass, R. S. (1989). Cross-racial identification. *Personality & Social Psychology Bulletin, 15,* 19–25.

Bouchard, T. J. (1997). IQ similarity in twins reared apart: Findings and responses to critics. In R. J. Sternberg & E. L. Grigorenko

(Eds.), *Intelligence, heredity, and environment* (pp. 126–160). New York: Cambridge University Press.

Bouchard, T. J. Jr., & Loehlin, J. C. (2001). Genes, evolution, and personality. *Behavior Genetics, 31*, 243–273.

Bouchard, T. J., & McGue, M. (1981). Familial studies of intelligence: A review. *Science, 212*, 1055–1059.

Bouchard, T. J., Lykken, D. T., McGue, M., Segal, N. L., & Tellegen, A. (1990). Sources of human psychological differences. The Minnesota study of twins reared apart. *Science, 250*, 223–228.

Bousfield, W. A. (1953). The occurrence of clustering in the recall of randomly arranged associates. *Journal of General Psychology, 49*, 229–240.

Bouton, M. E. (1991). Context and retrieval in extinction and in other examples of interference in simple associative learning. In L. Dachowski & C. F. Flaherty (Eds.), *Current topics in animal learning* (pp. 25–53). Hillsdale, NJ: Erlbaum.

Bouton, M. E. (1993). Context, time, and memory retrieval in the interference paradigms of Pavlovian learning. *Psychological Bulletin, 114*, 80–99.

Bowden, C. L. (1993). The clinical approach to the differential diagnosis of bipolar disorder. *Psychiatric Annals, 23*, 57–63.

Bower, B. (1993). A child's theory of mind. *Science News, 144*, 40–42.

Bower, G. H. (1983). Affect and cognition. *Philosophical Transaction: Royal Society of London, 302* (Series B), 387–402.

Bower, G. H., Black, J. B., & Turner, T. J. (1979). Scripts in memory for texts. *Cognitive Psychology, 11*, 177–220.

Bower, T.G.R. (1989). *The rational infant: Learning in infancy.* New York: Freeman.

Bowers, K. S. (1973). Situationism in psychology: An analysis and critique. *Psychological Review, 80*, 307–336.

Bowers, K. S. (1976). *Hypnosis for the seriously curious.* New York: Norton.

Bowers, K. S. (1998). Waterloo-Stanford Group Scale of Hypnotic Susceptibility, Form C: Manual and response booklet. *International Journal of Clinical & Experimental Hypnosis, 46*, 250–268.

Bowers, K. S., & Farvolden, P. (1996). Revisiting a century-old Freudian slip: From suggestion disavowed to the truth repressed. *Psychological Bulletin, 119*, 355–380.

Bowlby, J. (1951). *Maternal care and mental health* (World Health Organization Monograph Series No. 2). Schocken Books, 1966. Geneva, Switzerland: World Health Organization.

Bowlby, J. (1958). The nature of the child's tie to his mother. *International Journal of Psycho-Analysis, 39*, 350–373.

Bowlby, J. (1969). *Attachment: Vol. 1. Attachment and loss.* New York: Basic Books.

Boyce, W. T., Essex, M. J., Alkon, A., Smider, N. A., Pickrell, T., & Kagan, J. (2002). Temperament, tympanum and temperature: Four provisional studies of the biobehavioral correlates of tympanic membrane temperature asymmetries. *Child Development, 73*, 718–733.

Bradburn, N. M. (1969). *The structure of psychological well-being.* Chicago: Aldine.

Bradburn, N. M., & Capovitz, D. (1965). *Reports on happiness.* Chicago: Aldine.

Bradley, R. H., & Caldwell, B. M. (1984). 174 Children: A study of the relationship between home environment and cognitive development during the first 5 years. In A. W. Gottfried (Ed.), *Home environment and early cognitive development: Longitudinal research.* San Diego, CA: Academic Press.

Bradshaw, J. L. (2002). The evolution of intellect: Cognitive, neurological, and primatological aspects and hominid culture. In R. J. Sternberg & J. C. Kaufman (Eds.), *The evolution of intelligence* (pp. 55–78). Mahwah, NJ: Erlbaum.

Bradsher, K., with Altman, L. K. (2003). Isolation, an old medical tool, has SARS fading. (2003, June 21). *The New York Times on the Web.* Retrieved June 21, 2003 from http://www.nytimes.com/2003/06/21/science/sciencespecial/21INFE.html.

Brainerd, C. J. (1978). The stage question in cognitive-developmental theory. *Behavioral and Brain Sciences, 1*, 173–182.

Brandon, S. E., Vogel, E. H., & Wagner, A R. (2000). A componential view of configural cues in generalization and discrimination in Pavlovian conditioning. *Behavioural Brain Research, 110*, 67–72.

Bransford, J. D. (1979). *Human cognition: Learning, understanding, and remembering.* Belmont, CA: Wadsworth.

Bransford, J. D., & Johnson, M. K. (1972). Contextual prerequisites for understanding: Some investigations of comprehension and recall. *Journal of Verbal Learning and Verbal Behavior, 11*, 717–726.

Bransford, J. D., Brophy, S., & Williams, S. (2000). When computer technologies meet the learning sciences: Issues and opportunities. *Journal of Appied Developmental Psychology, 21*, 59–84.

Bransford, J. D., Brown, A. L., & Cocking, R. (Eds.). (1999). *How people learn: Brain, mind, experience, and school.* Washington, DC: National Academy Press.

Bransford, J. D., Zech, L., Schwartz, D., Barron, B., & Vye, N. (2000). Designs for environments that invite and sustain mathematical thinking. In P. Cobb, E. Yackel, et al. (Eds.), *Symbolizing and communicating in mathematics classrooms: Perspectives on discourse, tools, and instructional design* (pp. 275–324). Mahwah, NJ: Erlbaum.

Branstetter, E. (1969). The young child's response to hospitalization: Separation anxiety or lack of mothering care? *American Journal of Public Health, 59*, 92–97.

Braswell, L., & Kendall, P. C. (1988). Cognitive-behavioral methods with children. In K. S. Dobson (Ed.), *Handbook of cognitive-behavioral therapies.* New York: Guilford.

Brazelton, T. B. (1983). Precursors for the development of emotions in early infancy. In R. Plutchik & H. Kellerman (Eds.), *Emotion: Theory, research, and experience* (Vol. 2). New York: Academic Press.

Brehm, S. S., & Kassin, S. M. (1990). *Social psychology.* Boston: Houghton Mifflin.

Breslow, L. (1983). The potential of health promotion. In D. Mechanic (Ed.), *Handbook of health, health care, and the health professions.* New York: Free Press.

Bretherton, I., & Waters, E. (Eds.). (1985). Growing points of attachment theory research. *Monographs of the Society for Research in Child Development, 50*(1–2, Serial No. 209).

Brewer, W. F. (1999). Scientific theories and naive theories as forms of mental representation: Psychologism revived. *Science and Education, 8*, 489–505.

Bridges, L. J., Connell, J. P., & Belsky, J. (1988). Similarities and differences in infant–mother and infant–father interaction in the strange situation: A component process analysis. *Developmental Psychology, 24*, 92–100.

Brigham, J. C., & Malpass, R. S. (1985). The role of experience and contact in the recognition of faces of own and other-race persons. *Journal of Social Issues, 41*, 139–155.

Broadbent, D. (1958). *Perception and communication.* Oxford, UK: Pergamon.

Broadhurst, P. L. (1957). Emotionality and the Yerkes–Dodson law. *Journal of Experimental Psychology, 54*, 345–352.

Brock, T. C., Green, M. C., & Reich, D. A. (1998). New evidence in the *Consumer Reports* study of psychotherapy. *American Psychologist, 53*, 62–63.

Brody, L. R. (1996). Gender, emotional expression, and parent-child boundaries. In R. D. Kavanaugh, B. Zimmerberg, & S. Fein (Eds.), *Emotion: Interdisciplinary perspectives.* Hillsdale, NJ: Erlbaum.

Brody, N. (2000). History of theories and measurements of intelligence. In R. J. Sternberg (Ed.), *Handbook of intelligence.* New York: Cambridge University Press.

Bronfenbrenner, U., & Morris, P. A. (1998). The ecology of developmental processes. In R.M. Lerner (Ed.), *Handbook of child psychology* (5th ed., Vol. 1): *Theory* (pp. 993–1028). New York: Wiley.

Brosschot, J. F., Benschop, R. J., Godaert, G.L.R., & Olf, M. (1994). Influence of life stress on immunological reactivity to mild psychological stress. *Psychosomatic Medicine, 56*(3), 216–224.

Brown, A. L., & French, A. L. (1979). The zone of potential development: Implications for intelligence testing in the year 2000. In R. J. Sternberg & D. K. Detterman (Eds.), *Human intelligence: Perspectives on its theory and measurement* (pp. 217–235). Norwood, NJ: Ablex.

Brown, A. L., Campione, J. C., Bray, N. W., & Wilcox, B. L. (1973). Keeping track of changing variables: Effects of rehearsal training and rehearsal prevention in normal and retarded adolescents. *Journal of Experimental Psychology, 101*, 123–131.

Brown, A. S., & Susser, E. S. (2002). In utero infection and adult schizophrenia. *Mental Retardation & Developmental Disabilities Research Reviews, 8*, 51–57.

Brown, E. (1963). Meeting patients' psychosocial needs in the general hospital. *Annals of the American Academy of Political and Social Science, 346,* 117–122.

Brown, G. P., & Beck, A. T. (2002). Dysfunctional attitudes, perfectionism, and models of vulnerability to depression. In G. L. Flett & P. L. Hewitt (Eds.), *Perfectionism: Theory, research, and treatment* (pp. 231–251). Washington, DC: American Psychological Association.

Brown, J. A. (1958). Some tests of the decay theory of immediate memory. *Quarterly Journal of Experimental Psychology, 10,* 12–21.

Brown, J. D., Dutton, K. A., & Cook, K. E. (2001). From the top down: Self-esteem and self-evaluation. *Cognition & Emotion, 15,* 615–631.

Brown, R. (1965). *Social psychology.* New York: Free Press.

Brown, R. (1973). *A first language: The early stages.* Cambridge, MA: Harvard University Press.

Brown, R., & Kulik, J. (1977). Flashbulb memories. *Cognition, 5,* 73–99.

Brown, R., Cazden, C. B., & Bellugi, U. (1969). The child's grammar from 1 to 3. In J. P. Hill (Ed.), *Minnesota symposium on child psychology* (Vol. 2). Minneapolis: University of Minnesota Press.

Brown, S. C., & Craik, F. I. M. (2000). Encoding and retrieval of information. In E. Tulving & F. I. M. Craik (Eds.), *The Oxford handbook of memory* (pp. 93–108). New York: Oxford University Press.

Brown, W. J., & Basil, M. D. (1995). Media celebrities and public health: Responses to "Magic" Johnson's HIV disclosure and its impact on AIDS risk and high-risk behaviors. *Health Communication, 7,* 345–370.

Brownell, K. D., & Rodin, J. (1994). The dieting maelstrom: Is it possible and advisable to lose weight? *American Psychologist, 49,* 781–791.

Brownell, K. D., & Wadden, T. A. (1992). Etiology and treatment of obesity: Understanding a serious, prevalent, and refractory disorder. *Journal of Consulting and Clinical Psychology, 60,* 505–517.

Bruch, H. (1973). *Eating disorders: Obesity, anorexia nervosa, and the person within.* New York: Basic Books.

Bruer, J. T. (1993). *Schools for thought.* Cambridge, MA: MIT Press.

Bruner, J. S., Goodnow, J. J., & Austin, G. A. (1956). *A study of thinking.* Cambridge, MA: Harvard University Press.

Brunner, D., Buhot, M. C., Hen, R., & Hofer, M. (1999). Anxiety, motor activation, and maternal-infant interactions in $5HT_{1B}$ knockout mice. *Behavioral Neuroscience, 113,* 587–601.

Bryant, P., & Nuñes, T. (2002). Children's understanding of mathematics. In U. Goswami (Ed.), *Blackwell handbook of childhood cognitive development* (pp. 412–439). Malden, MA: Blackwell.

Bryant, R. A., & Harvey, A. G. (2000). *Acute stress disorder: A handbook of theory, assessment, and treatment.* Washington, DC: American Psychological Association.

Bryson, M., Bereiter, C., Scardamalia, M., & Joram, E. (1991). Going beyond the problem as given: Problem solving in expert and novice writers. In R. J. Sternberg & P. A. Frensch (Eds.), *Complex problem solving: Principles and mechanisms* (pp. 61–84). Hillsdale, NJ: Erlbaum.

Buchsbaum, M. S., Haier, R. J., Potkin, S. G., & Nuechterlein, K. (1992). Frontostriatal disorder of cerebral metabolism in never-medicated schizophrenics. *Archives of General Psychiatry, 49,* 935–942.

Buckner, R. (2000a). Brain imaging techniques. In A. E. Kazdin (Ed.), *Encyclopedia of psychology* (Vol. 1, pp. 457–459). Washington, DC: American Psychological Association.

Buckner, R. L. (2000b). Neuroimaging of memory. In M. S. Gazzaniga (Ed.), *The new cognitive neurosciences* (2nd ed., pp. 817–828). Cambridge, MA: MIT Press.

Buckner, R. L., Bandettini, P. A., O'Craven, K. M., Savoy, R. L., Petersen, E., Raichle, M. E., & Rosen, B. R. (1996). Detection of cortical activation during averaged single trials of a cognitive task using functional magnetic resonance imaging. *Proceedings of the National Academy of Sciences, 93,* 14878–14883.

Budwig, N. (1995). *A developmental-functionalist approach to child language.* Mahwah, NJ: Erlbaum.

Bunge, S. A., Ochsner, K. N., Desmond, J. E., Glover, G. H., & Gabrieli, J.D.E. (2001). Prefrontal regions involved in keeping information in and out of mind. *Brain, 124,* 2074–2086.

Bunney, W. E., Goodwin, F. K., & Murphy, D. L. (1972). The "switch process" in manic–depressive illness. *Archives in General Psychiatry, 27,* 312–317.

Bunney, W. E., Murphy, D. L., Goodwin, F. K., & Borge, G. F. (1970). The switch process from depression to mania: Relationship to drugs which alter brain amines. *Lancet, 1*(1022).

Burger, J. M. (1989). Negative reactions to increases in perceived personal control. *Journal of Personality and Social Psychology, 56,* 246–256.

Burger, J. M. (1992). *Desire for control: Personality, social, and clinical perspectives.* New York: Plenum.

Burger, J. M., & Cooper, H. M. (1979). The desirability of control. *Motivation and Emotion, 3,* 381–393.

Burgess, C., Morris, T., & Pettingale, K. W. (1988). Psychological response to cancer diagnosis—II. Evidence for coping styles. *Journal of Psychosomatic Research, 32,* 263–272.

Burgess, E. W., & Wallin, P. (1953). *Engagement and marriage.* Philadelphia: Lippincott.

Burleson, B. R., & Denton, W. H. (1992). A new look at similarity and attraction in marriage: Similarities in social-cognitive and communication skills as predictors of attraction and satisfaction. *Communication Monographs, 59*(3), 268–287.

Burnstein, E., & Vinokur, A. (1973). Testing two classes of theories about group-induced shifts in individual choice. *Journal of Experimental Social Psychology, 9,* 123–137.

Burnstein, E., & Vinokur, A. (1977). Persuasive arguments and social comparison as determinates of attitude polarization. *Journal of Experimental Social Psychology, 13,* 315–332.

Burti, L., & Yastrebov, V. S. (1993). Procedures used in rehabilitation. In N. Sartorius, G. de Girolano, G. Andrews, G. A. German, & L. Eisenberg (Eds.), *Treatment of mental disorders: A review of effectiveness.* Geneva, Switzerland, and Washington, DC: World Health Organization and American Psychiatric Press.

Buschke, H., Kulansky, G., Katz, M., Stewart, W. F., Sliwinski, M. J., Eckholdt, H. M., & Lipton, R. B. (1999). Screening for dementia with the Memory Impairment Screen. *Neurology, 52,* 231–238.

Bushman, B. J. (1996). Individual differences in the extent and development of aggressive cognitive-associative networks. *Personality and Social Psychology Bulletin, 22,* 811–819.

Buss, D. M. (1988a). The evolution of human intrasexual competition: Tactics of mate attraction. *Journal of Personality and Social Psychology, 54,* 616–628.

Buss, D. M. (1988b). Love acts: The evolutionary biology of love. In R. J. Sternberg & M. L. Barnes (Eds.), *The psychology of love* (pp. 100–118). New Haven, CT: Yale University Press.

Buss, D. M. (1994). *The evolution of desire.* New York: Basic Books.

Buss, D. M. (1995). Evolutionary psychology: A new paradigm for psychological science. *Psychological Inquiry, 6,* 1–30.

Buss, D. M. (1996). The evolutionary psychology of human social strategies. In E. T. Higgins & A. W. Kruglanski (Eds.), *Social psychology: Handbook of basic principles.* New York: Guilford.

Buss, D. M. (2000). The evolution of happiness. *American Psychologist, 55*(1), 15–23.

Buss, D. M. (2001a). Cognitive biases and emotional wisdom in the evolution of conflict between the sexes. *Current Directions in Psychological Science, 10,* 219–223.

Buss, D. M. (2001b). The design of the human mind. *Psychologist, 14,* 425–426.

Buss, D. M. (2001c). Human nature and culture: An evolutionary psychological perspective. *Journal of Personality, 69,* 955–978.

Buss, D. M. (2003). The dangerous passion: Why jealousy is as necessary as love and sex. *Archives of Sexual Behavior, 32,* 79–80.

Buss, D. M., & Kenrick, D. T. (1998). Evolutionary social psychology. In D. T. Gilbert, S. T. Fiske, & G. Lindzey (Eds.), *The handbook of social psychology* (4th ed., Vol. 2, pp. 982–1026). New York: McGraw-Hill.

Buss, D. M., & Schmitt, D. P. (1993). Sexual strategies theory: A contextual evolutionary analysis of human mating. *Psychological Review, 100,* 204–232.

Buss, K. A., Schumacher, J. R., Dolski, I., Kalin, N. H., Goldsmith, H. H., & Davidson, R. J. (2003). Right frontal brain activity, cortisol, and withdrawal behavior in 6-month-old infants. *Behavioral Neuroscience, 117,* 11–20.

Butcher, J. N., & Pancheri, P. (1976). *A handbook of cross-national MMPI research.* Minneapolis: University of Minnesota Press.

Butcher, J. N., & Williams, C. L. (1992). *Essentials of MMPI-2 and MMPI-A interpretation.* Minneapolis: University of Minnesota Press.

Butcher, J. N., Dahlström, W. G., Graham, J. R., Tellegen, A., & Kaemmer, B. (1989). *Minnesota Multiphasic Personality Inventory (MMPI-2): Manual for administration and scoring.* Minneapolis: University of Minnesota Press.

Butler, J., & Rovee-Collier, C. (1989). Contextual gating of memory retrieval. *Developmental Psychobiology, 22,* 533–552.

Buunk, B. P., & Mussweiler, T. (2001). New directions in social comparison research. *European Journal of Social Psychology, 31,* 467–475.

Bylin, S., & Christianson, S.-A. (2002). Characteristics of malingered amnesia: Consequences of withholding vs. distorting information on later memory of a crime event. *Legal & Criminological Psychology, 7,* 45–61.

Byrne, D. (1961). Anxiety and the experimental arousal of affiliation need. *Journal of Abnormal and Social Psychology, 63,* 660–662.

Byrne, D. (1971). *The attraction paradigm.* New York: Academic Press.

Byrne, D. G., & Rosenman, R. H. (1986). The Type A behaviour pattern as a precursor to stressful life-events: A confluence of coronary risks. *British Journal of Medical Psychology, 59,* 75–82.

Byrne, P. S., & Long, B.E.L. (1976). *Doctors talking to patients.* London: Her Majesty's Stationery Office.

Byrne, R. (1995). *The thinking ape: Evolutionary origins of intelligence.* Oxford, UK: Oxford University Press.

Byrne, R. W. (2002). The primate origins of human intelligence. In R. J. Sternberg & J. C. Kaufman (Eds.), *The evolution of intelligence* (pp. 79–96). Mahwah, NJ: Erlbaum.

Byrnes, J. P. (1988). Formal operations: A systematic reformulation. *Developmental Review, 8,* 66–87.

Cabeza, R., & Nyberg, L. (1997). Imaging cognition: An empirical review of PET studies with normal subjects. *Journal of Cognitive Neuroscience, 9,* 1–26.

Cacioppo, J. T., & Berntson, G. G. (1999). The affect system: Architecture and operating characteristics. *Current Directions in Psychological Science, 8,* 133–137.

Cacioppo, J. T., & Gardner, W. L. (1999). Emotions. *Annual Review of Psychology. 50,* 191–214.

Cacioppo, J. T., & Petty, R. E. (1979). Effects of message repetition and position on cognitive responses, recall, and persuasion. *Journal of Personality and Social Psychology, 37,* 97–109.

Cacioppo, J. T., & Petty, R. E. (1980). Persuasiveness of commercials is affected by exposure frequency and communicator cogency: A theoretical and empirical analysis. In J. H. Leigh & C. R. Martin (Eds.), *Current issues and research in advertising.* Ann Arbor: University of Michigan Press.

Cacioppo, J. T., & Petty, R. E. (1983). *Social psychophysiology: A sourcebook.* New York: Guilford.

Cacioppo, J. T., & Petty, R. E. (1986). Social processes. In M.G.H. Coles, E. Donehin, & S. W. Porges (Eds.), *Psychophysiology.* New York: Guilford.

Cahill, L., & McGaugh, J. L. (1996). Modulation of memory storage. *Current Opinion in Neurobiology, 6,* 237–242.

Cahill, L., Babinsky, R., Markowitsch, H. J., & McGaugh, J. L. (1995). The amygdala and emotional memory. *Nature, 377,* 295–296.

Cain, W. S. (1977). Differential sensitivity for smell: "Noise" at the nose. *Science, 195,* 796–798.

Calkins, S. D., & Fox, N. A. (1994). Individual differences in the biological aspects of temperament. In J. E. Bates & T. D. Wachs (Eds.), *Temperament: Individual differences at the interface of biology and behavior* (pp. 199–217). Washington, DC: American Psychological Association.

Calkins, S. D., & Fox, N. A. (2002). Self-regulatory processes in early personality development: A multilevel approach to the study of childhood social withdrawal and aggression. *Development & Psychopathology, 14,* 77–498.

Callahan, C. (2000). Intelligence and giftedness. In R. J. Sternberg (Ed.), *Handbook of intelligence.* New York: Cambridge University Press.

Cameron, J., & Pierce, W. D. (1994). Reinforcement, reward and intrinsic motivation: A meta-analysis. *Review of Educational Research, 64,* 363–423.

Cameron, J., & Pierce, W. D. (2002). *Rewards and intrinsic motivation: Resolving the controversy.* Westport, CT: Bergin & Garvey.

Cameron, J., Banko, K. M., & Pierce, W. D. (2001, Spring). Pervasive negative effects of rewards on intrinsic motivation: The myth continues. *Behavior Analyst, 24,* 1–44.

Camp, M. M. (2001). The use of service dogs as an adaptive strategy: A qualitative study. *American Journal of Occupational Therapy, 55,* 509–517.

Campbell, D. (1960). Blind variation and selective retention in creative thought as in other knowledge processes. *Psychological Review, 67,* 380–400.

Campbell, D. A. (1960). Blind variation and selective retention in creative thought as in other knowledge processes. *Psychological Review, 67,* 380–400.

Campione, J. C. (1989). Assisted assessments: A taxonomy of approaches and an outline of strengths and weaknesses. *Journal of Learning Disabilities, 22,* 151–165.

Campione, J. C., & Brown, A. L. (1990). Guided learning and transfer: Implications for approaches to assessment. In N. Frederiksen, R. Glaser, A. Lesgold, & M. Shafto (Eds.), *Diagnostic monitoring of skill and knowledge acquisition* (pp. 141–172). Hillsdale, NJ: Erlbaum.

Campione, J. C., Brown, A. L., & Ferrara, R. (1982). Mental retardation and intelligence. In R. J. Sternberg (Ed.), *Handbook of human intelligence* (pp. 392–490). New York: Cambridge University Press.

Campos, J. J., Barrett, K. C., Lamb, M. E., Goldsmith, H. H., & Stenberg, C. (1983). Socioemotional development. In P. H. Mussen (Ed.), *Handbook of child psychology* (4th ed., Vol. 2, pp. 783–915). New York: Wiley.

Canli, T., Sivers, H., Whitfield, S. L., Gotlib, I. H., & Gabrieli, J.D.E. (2002). Amygdala response to happy faces as a function of extraversion. *Science, 296,* 2191.

Cannon, W. B. (1929). *Bodily changes in pain, hunger, fear, and rage, on account of recent researches into the function of emotional excitement* (2nd ed.). New York: Appleton.

Cannon, W. B., & Washburn, A. L. (1912). An explanation of hunger. *American Journal of Psychology, 29,* 444–454.

Cantor, J., & Engle, R. W. (1993). Working memory capacity as long-term memory activation: An individual differences approach. *Journal of Experimental Psychology: Learning, Memory, and Cognition, 19,* 1101–1114.

Cantor, N., & Kihlstrom, J. F. (1987a). Social intelligence: The cognitive basis of personality. In P. Shaver (Ed.), *Review of personality and social psychology* (Vol. 6, pp. 15–34). Beverly Hills, CA: Sage.

Cantor, N., & Kihlstrom. J. F. (1987b). *Personality and social intelligence.* Englewood Cliffs, NJ: Prentice-Hall.

Capaldi, E. J. (2000). Learning: Cognitive approach for animals. In A. E. Kazdin (Ed.), *Encyclopedia of psychology* (Vol. 5, pp. 11–13). Washington, DC: American Psychological Association.

Caporael, L. (1976). Ergotism: The satan loosed in Salem? *Science, 192,* 21–26.

Caporael, L. (2003). Interview retrieved May 14, 2003, at http://www.pbs.org/wnet/secrets/case_salem/interview.html.

Cappa, S. F., Perani, D., Grassli, F., Bressi, S., et al. (1997). A PET follow-up study of recovery after stroke in acute aphasics. *Brain and Language, 56,* 55–67.

Caramazza, A., & Shelton, J. R. (1998). Domain-specific knowledge systems in the brain: The animate-inanimate distinction. *Journal of Cognitive Neuroscience, 10,* 1–34.

Carey, S. (1994). Does learning a language require the child to reconceptualize the world? In L. Gleitman & B. Landau (Eds.), *The acquisition of the lexicon* (pp. 143–168). Cambridge, MA: Elsevier/MIT Press.

Carlson, E. R. (1995). Evaluating the credibility of sources: A missing link in the teaching of critical thinking. *Teaching of Psychology, 22,* 39–41.

Carlson, G., & Goodwin, F. K. (1973). The stages of mania: A longitudinal analysis of the manic episode. *Archives of General Psychiatry, 28*(2), 221–228.

Carlson, J. G., & Hatfield, E. (1992). *Psychology of emotion.* New York: Harcourt Brace Jovanovich.

Carlson, N. (2000a). Neuron. In A. E. Kazdin (Ed.), *Encyclopedia of psychology* (Vol. 5, pp. 418–420). Washington, DC: American Psychological Association.

Carlson, N. (2000b). Synapse. In A. E. Kazdin (Ed.), *Encyclopedia of psychology* (Vol. 7, pp. 531–533). Washington, DC: American Psychological Association.

Carpenter, M., Nagell, K., & Tomasello, M. (1998). Social cognition, joint attention, and communicative competence from 9 to 15 months of age. *Monographs of the Society for Research in Child Development, 63* (4, Serial No. 255).

Carraher, T. N., Carraher, D., & Schliemann, A. D. (1985). Mathematics in the streets and in the schools. *British Journal of Developmental Psychology, 3,* 21–29.

Carraher, T. N., Schliemann, A. D., & Carraher, D. W. (1988). Mathematical concepts in everyday life. *New Directions in Child Development, 41,* 71–87.

Carroll, J. B. (1993). *Human cognitive abilities: A survey of factor-analytic studies.* New York: Cambridge University Press.

Carson, R. C. (1996). Aristotle, Galileo, and the DSM taxonomy: The case of schizophrenia. *Journal of Consulting and Clinical Psychology, 64,* 1133–1139.

Carson, R. C., & Butcher, J. N. (1992). *Abnormal psychology and modern life* (9th ed.). New York: HarperCollins.

Cartwright, R. D. (1977). *Night life: Explorations in dreaming.* Englewood Cliffs, NJ: Prentice-Hall.

Cartwright, R. D. (1991). Dreams that work: The relation of dream incorporation to adaptation to stressful events. *Dreaming, 1,* 3–9.

Cartwright, R. D. (1993). Who needs their dreams? The usefulness of dreams in psychotherapy. *Journal of the American Academy of Psychoanalysis, 21,* 539–547.

Cartwright, R. D., & Lamberg, L. (1992). *Crisis dreaming.* New York: HarperCollins.

Cartwright, R., Newell, P., & Mercer, P. (2001). Dream incorporation of a sentinel life event and its relation to waking adaptation. *Sleep & Hypnosis, 3,* 25–32.

Carver, C. S., Diamond, E. L., & Humphries, C. (1985). Coronary prone behavior. In N. Schneiderman & J. T. Tapp (Eds.), *Behavioral medicine: The biopsychosocial approach.* Hillsdale, NJ: Erlbaum.

Caryl, P. G. (1994). Early event-related potentials correlate with inspection time and intelligence. *Intelligence, 18,* 15–46.

Case, R. (1992a). Neo-Piagetian theories of child development. In R. J. Sternberg & C. A. Berg (Eds.), *Intellectual development* (pp. 161–196). New York: Cambridge University Press.

Case, R. (1992b). The role of the frontal lobes in the regulation of cognitive development. *Brain and Cognition, 20,* 51–73.

Case, R. (1999). Conceptual development. In M. Bennett (Ed.), *Developmental psychology: Achievements and prospects* (pp. 36–54). Philadelphia: Psychology Press.

Case, R., & Okamoto, Y. (1996). The role of central conceptual structures in the development of scientific and social thought. In C. A. Hauert (Ed.), *Developmental psychology: Cognitive, perceptuo-motor and neuropsychological perspectives.* Amsterdam: North-Holland.

Casey, B. J., Giedd, J. N., & Thomas, K. M. (2000). Structural and functional brain development and its relation to cognitive development. *Biological Psychology, 54,* 241–257.

Caspi, A. (1998). Personality development across the life course. In W. Damon (Gen. Ed.) & N. Eisenberg (Vol. Ed.), *Handbook of child psychology.* Vol. 3: *Social, emotional, and personality development* (pp. 311–388). New York: Wiley.

Caspi, A., & Moffitt, T. E. (1991). Individual differences are accentuated during periods of social change: The sample case of girls at puberty. *Journal of Personality and Social Psychology, 61,* 157–168.

Caspi, A., Elder, G. E., & Herbener, E. (1990). Childhood personality and the prediction of life-course patterns. In L. N. Robins & M. Rutter (Eds.), *Straight and devious pathways from childhood to adulthood* (pp. 13–35). New York: Cambridge University Press.

Cassidy, J., & Shaver, P. (Eds.). (1999). *Handbook of attachment.* New York: Guilford.

Castle, T., & Hensley, C. (2002). Serial killers with military experience: Applying learning theory to serial murder. *International Journal of Offender Therapy & Comparative Criminology, 46,* 453–465.

Cattell, J. M. (1886). The influence of the intensity of the stimulus on the length of the reaction time. *Brain, 9,* 512–514.

Cattell, J. M. (1890). Mental tests and measurements. *Mind, 15,* 373–380.

Cattell, R. B. (1971). *Abilities: Their structure, growth, and action.* Boston: Houghton Mifflin.

Ceci, S. J. (1996). *On intelligence.* Cambridge, MA: Cambridge University Press.

Ceci, S. J., & Bronfenbrenner, U. (1985). Don't forget to take the cupcakes out of the oven: Strategic time-monitoring, prospective memory and context. *Child Development, 56,* 175–190.

Ceci, S. J., & Bruck, M. (1993). Suggestibility of the child witness: A historical review and synthesis. *Psychological Bulletin, 113*(3), 403–439.

Ceci, S. J., & Bruck, M. (1995). *Jeopardy in the courtroom.* Washington, DC: APA Books.

Ceci, S. J., & Loftus, E. F. (1994). "Memory work": A royal road to false memories? *Applied Cognitive Psychology, 8,* 351–364.

Ceci, S. J., & Roazzi, A. (1994). The effects of context on cognition: Postcards from Brazil. In R. J. Sternberg & R. K. Wagner (Eds.), *Minds in context: Interactionist perspectives on human intelligence.* New York: Cambridge University Press.

Cellucci, T., & Heffer, R. W. (2002). The psychology training clinic: Arena for ethics training. *Behavior Therapist, 25,* 127–130.

Cerella, J. (1985). Information processing rates in the elderly. *Psychological Bulletin, 98,* 67–83.

Cernoch, J. M., & Porter, R. H. (1985). Recognition of maternal axillary odors by infants. *Child Development, 56,* 1593–1598.

Chaiken, S., & Eagly, A. (1983). Communication modality as a determinant of persuasion: The role of communicator salience. *Journal of Personality and Social Psychology, 45,* 241–256.

Chambless, D. L. (1995). Training in and dissemination of empirically validated psychological treatments: Report and recommendations. *The Clinical Psychologist, 48,* 3–24.

Chambless, D. L. (1999). Empirically validated treatments? What now? *Applied & Preventive Psychology, 8,* 281–284.

Chambless, D. L., & Ollendick, T. H. (2000). Empirically supported psychological interventions: Controversies and evidence. *Annual Review of Psychology, 52,* 685–716.

Chandrashekaran, M., Walker, B. A., Ward, J. C., & Reingen, P. H. (1996). Modeling individual preference evolution and choice in a dynamic group setting. *Journal of Marketing Research, 33,* 211–223.

Chapman, C. R. (1982). Comparative effects of acupuncture in Japan and the United States on dental pain perception. *Pain, 12,* 319–328.

Chapman, C. R. (1984). New directions in the understanding and management of pain. *Social Science and Medicine, 19,* 1262–1277.

Chapman, L. J., & Chapman, J. P. (1969). Illusory correlation as an obstacle to the use of valid psycho-diagnostic signs. *Journal of Abnormal Psychology, 74,* 271–280.

Chase, W. G., & Simon, H. A. (1973). The mind's eye in chess. In W. G. Chase (Ed.), *Visual information processing* (pp. 215–281). New York: Academic Press.

Chavira, D. A., Stein, M. B., & Malcarne, V. L. (2002). Scrutinizing the relationship between shyness and social phobia. *Journal of Anxiety Disorders, 16,* 585–598.

Chen, M., & Bargh, J. A. (1997). Nonconscious behavioral confirmation processes: The self-fulfilling consequences of automatic stereotype activation. *Journal of Experimental Social Psychology, 33,* 541–560.

Chen, N. Y., Shaffer, D. R., & Wu, C. (1997). On physical attractiveness stereotyping in Taiwan: A revised sociocultural perspective. *Journal of Social Psychology, 137,* 117–124.

Chen, Z., & Siegler, R. S. (2000). Intellectual development in childhood. In R. J. Sternberg (Ed.), *Handbook of intelligence* (pp. 92–116). New York: Cambridge University Press.

Cheng, P. (1999). Causal reasoning. In R. A. Wilson & F. C. Keil (Eds.), *The MIT encyclopedia of the cognitive sciences* (pp. 106–108). Cambridge, MA: MIT Press.

Cheng, P. W. (1997). From covariation to causation: A causal power theory. *Psychological Review, 104*(2), 367–405.

Cheng, P., & Holyoak, K. (1995). Complex adaptive systems as intuitive statisticians: Causality, contingency, and prediction. In H. L. Roitblat & J.-A. Meyer (Eds.), *Comparative approaches to cognitive science* (pp. 271–302). Cambridge, MA: MIT Press.

Cherny, N. I. (1996). The problem of inadequately relieved suffering. *Journal of Social Issues, 52*, 13–30.

Cherry, E. C. (1953). Some experiments on the recognition of speech with one and two ears. *Journal of the Acoustical Society of America, 25*, 975–979.

Chi, M.T.H. (1978). Knowledge structures and memory development. In R. S. Siegler (Ed.), *Children's thinking: What develops?* Hillsdale, NJ: Erlbaum.

Chi, M.T.H., Feltovich, P., & Glaser, R. (1981). Categorization and representation of physics problems by experts and novices. *Cognitive Science, 5*, 121–152.

Chi, M.T.H., Glaser, R., & Farr, M. (Eds.). (1988). *The nature of expertise*. Hillsdale, NJ: Erlbaum.

Chisholm, K. M., Carter, M., et al. (1995). Attachment security and indiscriminately friendly behavior in children adopted from Romanian orphanages. *Development and Psychopathology, 7*, 283–294.

Chodorow, N. (1978). *The reproduction of mothering*. Berkeley: University of California Press.

Chodorow, N. (1992). *Feminism and psychoanalytic theory*. New Haven, CT: Yale University Press.

Choi, I., Nisbett, R. E., & Norenzayan, A. (1999). Causal attribution across cultures: Variation and universality. Psychological Bulletin, 125, 47–63.

Chomsky, N. (1957). *Syntactic structures*. The Hague, Netherlands: Mouton.

Chomsky, N. (1965). *Aspects of the theory of syntax*. Cambridge, MA: MIT Press.

Chomsky, N. (1972). *Language and mind* (2nd ed.). New York: Harcourt Brace Jovanovich.

Chomsky, N. (1980). *Rules and representations*. New York: Columbia University Press.

Chomsky, N. (1991, March). [Quoted in] *Discover, 12*(3), 20.

Christensen, A., & Jacobson, N. S. (1994). Who (or what) can do psychotherapy: The status and challenge of nonprofessional therapies. *Psychological Science, 5*, 8–14.

Christian, K., Bachnan, H. J., & Morrison, F. J. (2001). Schooling and cognitive development. In R. J. Sternberg & E. L. Grigorenko (Eds.), *Environmental effects on cognitive abilities* (pp. 287–336). Mahwah, NJ: Erlbaum.

Christie, D. J., Winter, D.D.N., & Wagner, R. V. (2000). *Peace, conflict, and violence: Peace psychology for the 21st century*. Englewood Cliffs, NJ: Prentice-Hall.

Christophersen, E. R., & Mortweet, S. L. (2001). Diagnosis and management of anxiety disorders. In E. R. Christophersen & S. L. Mortweet (Eds.), *Treatments that work with children: Empirically supported strategies for managing childhood problems* (pp. 49–78). Washington, DC: American Psychological Association.

Chung, R.C.-Y., Bemak, F., & Kilinc, A. (2002). Culture and empathy: Case studies in cross-cultural counseling. In P. R. Breggin & G. Breggin (Eds.), *Dimensions of empathic therapy* (pp. 119–128). New York: Springer.

Cialdini, R. B. (1993). *Influence: Science and practice* (3rd ed.). New York: HarperCollins.

Cialdini, R. B., Brown, S. L., Lewis, B. P., Luce, C., & Neuberg, S. L. (1997). Reinterpreting the empathy-altruism relationship: When one into one equals oneness. *Journal of Personality and Social Psychology, 73*, 481–494.

Cialdini, R. B., Brown, S. L., Lewis, B. P., Luce, C., et al. (1997). Reinterpreting the empathy-altruism relationship: When one into one equals oneness. *Journal of Personality and Social Psychology, 73*(3), 481–494.

Cialdini, R. B., Petty, R. E., & Cacioppo, J. T. (1981). Attitude and attitude change. *Annual Review of Psychology, 32*, 357–404.

Cialdini, R. B., Schaller, M., Houlihan, D., Arps, K., Fultz, J., & Beaman, A. L. (1987). Empathy-based helping: Is it selflessly or selfishly motivated? *Journal of Personality and Social Psychology, 52*, 599–604.

Ciarrochi, J., Forgas, J. P., & Mayer, J. D. (Eds.). (2001). *Emotional intelligence in everyday life: A scientific inquiry*. Philadelphia: Psychology Press.

Cima, M., Merckelbach, H., Nijman, H., Knauer, E., & Hollnack, S. (2002). I can't remember, your Honor: Offenders who claim amnesia. *German Journal of Psychiatry, 5*, 24–34.

Clark, E. V. (1973). What's in a word? On the child's acquisition of semantics in his first language. In T. E. Moore (Ed.), *Cognitive development and the acquisition of language*. New York: Academic Press.

Clark, E. V. (1993). *The lexicon in acquisition*. Cambridge, UK: Cambridge University Press.

Clark, E. V. (1995). Later lexical development and word formation. In P. Fletcher & B. MacWhinney (Eds.), *The handbook of child language* (pp. 393–412). Oxford, UK: Blackwell.

Clark, H. H., & Chase, W. G. (1972). On the process of comparing sentences against pictures. *Cognitive Psychology, 3*, 472–517.

Clark, H. H., & Clark, E. V. (1977). *Psychology and language: An introduction to psycholinguistics*. New York: Harcourt Brace Jovanovich.

Clark, K. B. (1988). *Prejudice and your child* (2nd ed.). Middletown, CT: Wesleyan University Press. [First edition published 1955]

Clark, K. B. (1992). Infecting our children with hostility. In G. W. Albee, L. A. Bond, et al. (Eds.), *Improving children's lives: Global perspectives on prevention. Primary prevention of psychopathology* (Vol. 14, pp. 330–333). Thousand Oaks, CA: Sage.

Clark, W. C., & Clark, S. B. (1980). Pain responses in Nepalese porters. *Science, 209*, 410–411.

Clarke-Stewart, K. A. (1978). And daddy makes three: The father's impact on mother and young child. *Child Development, 49*, 466–478.

Clarke-Stewart, K. A. (1989). Infant day care: Maligned or malignant? *American Psychologist, 44*, 266–273.

Clarke-Stewart, K. A. (1993). *Daycare* (Rev. ed.). Cambridge, MA: Harvard University Press.

Clarke-Stewart, K. A., Perlmutter, M., & Friedman, S. (1988). *Lifelong human development*. New York: Wiley.

Clarren, S. K., & Smith, D. W. (1978). The fetal alcohol syndrome. *New England Journal of Medicine, 298*, 1063–1067.

Clayton, I. C., Richards, J. C., & Edwards, C. J. (1999). Selective attention in obsessive-compulsive disorder. *Journal of Abnormal Psychology, 108*, 171–175.

Clore, G. L., & Byrne, D. (1974). A reinforcement-affect model of attraction. In T. L. Huston (Ed.), *Foundations of interpersonal attraction* (pp. 143–170). New York: Academic Press.

Coe, C. L. (1993). Psychosocial factors and immunity in nonhuman primates: A review. *Psychosomatic Medicine, 55*, 298–308.

Cohen, D., Nisbett, R. E., Bowdle, B. F., & Schwarz, N. (1996). Insult, aggression, and the southern culture of honor: An "experimental ethnography." *Journal of Personality and Social Psychology, 70*, 945–960.

Cohen, J. (1981). Can human irrationality be experimentally demonstrated? *Behavioral and Brain Sciences, 4*, 317–331.

Cohen, J. D., Forman, S. D., Braver, T. S., Casey, B. J., Servan-Schreiber, D., & Noll, D. C. (1994). Activation of prefrontal cortex in a non-spatial working memory task with functional MRI. *Human Brain Mapping, 1*, 293–304.

Cohen, J. D., Romero, R. D., Servan-Schreiber, D., & Farah, M. J. (1994). Mechanisms of spatial attention: The relation of macrostructure to microstructure in parietal neglect. *Journal of Cognitive Neuroscience, 6*, 377–387.

Cohen, N. J., & Eichenbaum, H. (1993). *Memory, amnesia, and the hippocampal system*. Cambridge, MA: MIT Press.

Cohen, S., & Williamson, G. (1991). Stress and infectious disease. *Psychological Bulletin, 109*, 5–24.

Cohen, S., Kaplan, J. R., Cunnick, J. E., Manuck, S. B., & Rabin, B. S. (1992). Chronic social stress, affiliation, and cellular immune response in nonhuman primates. *Psychological Science, 3*, 301–304.

Cohen, S., Tyrrell, D., & Smith, A. (1991). Psychological stress and susceptibility to the common cold. *The New England Journal of Medicine, 235*, 606–612.

Cohen, S., Tyrrell, D.A.J., & Smith, A. P. (1993). Negative life events, perceived stress, negative affect, and susceptibility to the common cold. *Journal of Personality and Social Psychology, 64*, 131–140.

Colby, A., Kohlberg, L., Gibbs, J., & Lieberman, M. (1983). A longitudinal study of moral judgment. *Monographs of the Society for Research in Child Development, 48*(1–2), 124.

Cole, J. (2001). Empathy needs a face. *Journal of Consciousness Studies, 8,* 51–68.

Cole, M. (1999). Culture in development. In M. H. Bornstein & M. E. Lamb (Eds.), *Developmental psychology: An advanced textbook* (4th ed., pp. 73–123). Mahwah, NJ: Erlbaum.

Cole, M., & Scribner, S. (1974). *Culture and thought: A psychological introduction.* New York: Wiley.

Cole, M., Gay, J., Glick, J., & Sharp, D. W. (1971). *The cultural context of learning and thinking.* New York: Basic Books.

Coleman, P. D., & Flood, D. G. (1986). Dendritic proliferation in the aging brain as a compensatory repair mechanism. In D. F. Swaab, E. Fliers, M. Mirmiram, W. A. Van Gool, & F. Van Haaren (Eds.), *Progress in brain research* (Vol. 20). New York: Elsevier.

Coley, J. D., Medin, D. L., Proffitt, J. B., Lynch, E., & Atran, S. (1999). Inductive reasoning in folkbiological thought. In Douglas L. Medin & Scott Atran (Eds.), *Folkbiology* (pp. 205–232). Cambridge, MA: MIT Press.

Coley, R. L. (2001). Emerging research on low-income, unmarried, and minority fathers. *American Psychologist, 56,* 743–753.

Colin, V. L. (1996). *Human attachment.* New York: McGraw-Hill.

Collins, M. A., & Amabile, T. M. (1999). Motivation and creativity. In R. J. Sternberg (Ed.), *Handbook of creativity* (pp. 297–312). New York: Cambridge University Press.

Colman, A. M. (2001). *Oxford dictionary of psychology.* Oxford, UK: Oxford University Press.

Colombo, J. (1993). *Infant cognition: Predicting childhood intellectual function.* Newbury Park, CA: Sage.

Colonia-Willner, R. (1998). Practical intelligence at work: Relationship between aging and cognitive efficiency among managers in a bank environment. *Psychology and Aging, 13,* 45–57.

Colwill, R. M., & Delamater, B. A. (1995). An associative analysis of instrumental biconditional discrimination learning. *Animal Learning & Behavior, 22,* 384–394.

Comer, R. J. (2002). *Fundamentals of abnormal psychology* (3rd ed.). New York: Worth.

Commissioner's Office of Research and Evaluation, Head Start Bureau, Administration on Children, Youth, and Families, & Department of Health and Human Services. (2001a, December–June). *Building their futures: How Early Head Start programs are enhancing the lives of infants and toddlers in low-income families. Vol. 1. Technical report.* Washington, DC: U.S. Department of Health and Human Services.

Commissioner's Office of Research and Evaluation, Head Start Bureau, Administration on Children, Youth, and Families, & Department of Health and Human Services. (2001b, December–June). *Building their futures: How Early Head Start programs are enhancing the lives of infants and toddlers in low-income families. Vol. 1. Technical report appendices.* Washington, DC: U.S. Department of Health and Human Services.

Commissioner's Office of Research and Evaluation, Head Start Bureau, Administration on Children, Youth, and Families, & Department of Health and Human Services. (2001c, December–June). *Building their futures: How Early Head Start programs are enhancing the lives of infants and toddlers in low-income families. Vol. 1. Summary report.* Washington, DC: U.S. Department of Health and Human Services.

Conejero-Goldberg, C., Torrey, E. F., & Yolken, R. H. (2003). Herpesviruses and Toxoplasma gondii in orbital frontal cortex of psychiatric patients. *Schizophrenia Research, 60,* 65–69.

Conrad, R. (1964). Acoustic confusions in immediate memory. *British Journal of Psychology, 55,* 75–84.

Cook, B. H., Stein, M. A., Krasowski, M. D., Cox, N. J., Olkon, D. M., Keiffer, J. E., & Leventhal, B. L. (1995). Association of attention-deficit disorder and the dopamine transporter gene. *American Journal of Human Genetics, 86,* 993–998.

Cook, H. B. K. (1992). Matrilocality and female aggression in Margariteño society. In K. Björkqvist & P. Niemelä (Eds.), *Of mice and women: Aspects of female aggression* (pp. 149–162). San Diego, CA: Harcourt Brace.

Cook, M., & Mineka, S. (1990). Selective associations in the observational conditioning of fear in rhesus monkeys. *Journal of Experimental Psychology: Animal Behavior Processes, 16,* 372–389.

Cooley, C. H. (1982). *Human nature and the social order.* New York: Scribners. (Original work published 1902)

Cooper, J. R., Bloom, F. E., & Roth, R. H. (1996). *The biochemical basis of neuropharmacology* (7th ed.). New Haven, CT: Yale University Press.

Cooper, J., Zanna, M. P., & Taves, P. A. (1978). Arousal as a necessary condition for attitude change following induced compliance. *Journal of Personality and Social Psychology, 36,* 1101–1106.

Cooper, Z., & Fairburn, C. G. (2002). Cognitive-behavioral treatment of obesity. In T. A. Wadden & A. J. Stunkard (Eds.), *Handbook of obesity treatment* (pp. 465–479). New York: Guilford.

Corballis, M. C. (2002). Evolution of the generative mind. In R. J. Sternberg & J. C. Kaufman (Eds.), *The evolution of intelligence* (pp. 117–144). Mahwah, NJ: Erlbaum.

Corbetta, M., Miezin, F. M., Dobmeyer, S., Shulman, G. L., & Petersen, S. E. (1991). Selective and divided attention during visual discriminations of shape, color and speed: Functional anatomy by positron emission tomography. *Journal of Neuroscience, 11,* 2383–2402.

Corbetta, M., Miezin, F. M., Shulman, G. L., & Petersen, S. E. (1993). A PET study of visuospatial attention. *Journal of Neuroscience, 13,* 1202–1226.

Coren, S. (1994). *Intelligence in dogs.* New York: Macmillan.

Coren, S., & Girgus, J. S. (1978). *Seeing is deceiving: The psychology of visual illusions.* Hillsdale, NJ: Erlbaum.

Coren, S., Ward, L. M., & Enns, J. T. (1994). *Sensation and perception* (4th ed.). Orlando, FL: Harcourt Brace.

Corr, C. A., Nabe, C. M., & Corr, D. M. (2003). *Death, dying, life, and living.* Belmont, CA: Wadsworth.

Cosmides, L. (1989). The logic of social exchange: Has natural selection shaped how humans reason? Studies with the selection task. *Cognition, 31,* 187–276.

Cosmides, L., & Tooby, J. (1987). From evolution to behavior: Evolutionary psychology as the missing link. In J. Dupre (Ed.), *The latest on the best: Essays on evolution and optimality* (pp. 277–306). Cambridge, MA: MIT Press.

Cosmides, L., & Tooby, J. (1992). Cognitive adaptations for social exchange. In J. H. Barkow, L. Cosmides, & J. Tooby (Eds.), *The adapted mind: Evolutionary psychology and the generation of culture.* Oxford, UK: Oxford University Press.

Cosmides, L., & Tooby, J. (1996). Are humans good intuitive statisticians after all? Rethinking some conclusions from the literature on judgment under uncertainty. *Cognition, 58,* 1–73.

Cosmides, L., & Tooby, J. (2002). Unraveling the enigma of human intelligence: Evolutionary psychology and the multimodular mind. In R. J. Sternberg & J. C. Kaufman (Eds.), *The evolution of intelligence* (pp. 145–198). Mahwah, NJ: Erlbaum.

Costa, A. L. (2000). Mediative environments: Creating conditions for intellectual growth. In A. Kozulin & Y. Rand (Eds.), *Experience of mediated learning: An impact of Feuerstein's theory in education and psychology* (pp. 34–44). Elmsford, NY: Pergamon.

Costa, P. T. Jr. & Widiger, T. A. (Eds.). (2002b). *Personality disorders and the five-factor model of personality* (2nd ed.). Washington, DC: American Psychological Association.

Costa, P. T. Jr., & McCrae, R. (1985). *NEO Personality Inventory.* Odessa, FL: Psychological Assessment Resources.

Costa, P. T. Jr., & McCrae, R. (1992c). Normal personality assessment in clinical practice: The NEO Personality Inventory. *Psychological Assessment: A Journal of Consulting and Clinical Psychology, 4,* 5–13.

Costa, P. T. Jr., & Widiger, T. A. (2002a). Introduction: Personality disorders and the five-factor model of personality. In P. T. Costa Jr. & T. A. Widiger (Eds.), *Personality disorders and the five-factor model of personality* (2nd ed., pp. 3–14). Washington, DC: American Psychological Association.

Costa, P. T. Jr., & McCrae, R. R. (1988). Personality in adulthood: A six-year longitudinal study of self-reports and spouse ratings on the NEO personality inventory. *Journal of Personality and Social Psychology, 54,* 853–863.

Costa, P. T. Jr., & McCrae, R. R. (1992a). "Four ways five factors are not basic": Reply. *Personality & Individual Differences, 13*(8), 861–865.

Costa, P. T. Jr., & McCrae, R. R. (1992b). Four ways five factors are basic. *Personality & Individual Differences, 13*(6), 653–665.

Costa, P. T. Jr., & McCrae, R. R. (1995). Domains and facets: Hierarchical personality assessment using the revised NEO personality inventory. *Journal of Personality Assessment, 64*, 21–50.

Cotman, C. W., & McGaugh, J. L. (1980). *Behavioral neuroscience: An introduction.* New York: Academic Press.

Cottraux, J. (1993). Behavior therapy. In N. Sartorius, G. de Girolano, G. Andrews, G. A. German, & L. Eisenberg (Eds.), *Treatment of mental disorders: A review of effectiveness.* Geneva, Switzerland, and Washington, DC: World Health Organization and American Psychiatric Press.

Cottraux, J., Note, I., Albuisson, E., Yao, S. N., Note, B., Mollard, E., Bonasse, F., Jalenques, I., Guerin, J., & Coudert, A. J. (2000). Cognitive behavior therapy versus supportive therapy in social phobia: A randomized controlled trial. *Psychotherapy & Psychosomatics, 69*, 137–146.

Court, J. H. (1984). Sex and violence: A ripple effect. In N. M. Malamuth & E. Donnerstein (Eds.), *Pornography and social aggression.* Orlando, FL: Academic Press.

Cowan, N. (2001). The magical number 4 in short-term memory: A reconsideration of mental storage capacity. *Behavioral and Brain Sciences, 24*, 87–114.

Cowan, R., O'Connor, N., & Samella, K. (2003). The skills and methods of calendrical savants. *Intelligence, 31*, 51–65.

Coyne, J. C. (1976a). Depression and the response of others. *Journal of Abnormal Psychology, 55*(2), 186–193.

Coyne, J. C. (1976b). Toward an interactional description of depression. *Psychiatry, 39*, 14–27.

Craik, F. I. M., & Brown, S. C. (2000). Memory: Coding processes. In A. E. Kazdin (Ed.), *Encyclopedia of psychology* (Vol. 5, pp. 162–166). Washington, DC: American Psychological Association.

Craik, F. I. M., & Lockhart, R. S. (1972). Levels of processing: A framework for memory research. *Journal of Verbal Learning and Verbal Behavior, 11*, 671–684.

Crandall, C. S. (1988). Social contagion of binge eating. *Journal of Personality and Social Psychology, 55*, 588–598.

Crawford Solberg, E., Diener, E., Wirtz, D., Lucas, R. E., & Oishi, S. (2002). Wanting, having, and satisfaction: Examining the role of desire discrepancies in satisfaction with income. *Journal of Personality and Social Psychology, 83*, 725–734.

Cremer, D. de, Snyder, M., & Dewitte, S. (2001). 'The less I trust, the less I contribute (or not)?' The effects of trust, accountability and self-monitoring in social dilemmas. *European Journal of Social Psychology, 31*, 93–107.

Crick, F., & Mitchison, G. (1983). The function of dream sleep. *Nature, 304*, 111–114.

Crick, F., & Mitchison, G. (1995). REM sleep and neural nets. *Behavioural Brain Research, 69*, 147–155.

Crick, N. R., & Dodge, K. A. (1994). A review and reformulation of social information-processing mechanisms in children's social adjustment. *Psychological Bulletin, 115*, 74–101.

Croizet, J. C., & Claire, T. (1998). Extending the concept of stereotype threat to social class: The intellectual underperformance of students from low socioeconomic backgrounds. *Personality and Social Psychology Bulletin, 24*, 588–594.

Cross-National Collaborative Group. (1992). The changing rate of major depression. *Journal of the American Medical Association, 268*(21), 3098–3105.

Crowder, R. G., & Green, R. L. (2000). Serial learning: Cognition and behavior. In E. Tulving & F. I. M. Craik (Eds.), *The Oxford handbook of memory* (pp. 125–136). New York: Oxford University Press.

Crystal, D. S., Watanabe, H., & Chen, R. S. (2000). Reactions to morphological deviance: A comparison of Japanese and American children and adolescents. *Social Development, 9*, 40–61.

Csikszentmihalyi, M. (1988). Society, culture, and person: A systems view of creativity. In R. J. Sternberg (Ed.), *The nature of creativity* (pp. 325–339). New York: Cambridge University Press.

Csikszentmihalyi, M. (1996). *Creativity: Flow and the psychology of discovery and invention.* New York: HarperCollins.

Csikszentmihalyi, M. (1999). Creativity. In R. A. Wilson & F. C. Keil (Eds.), *The MIT encyclopedia of the cognitive sciences* (pp. 205–206). Cambridge, MA: MIT Press.

Csikszentmihalyi, M. (1999b). Implications of a systems perspective for the study of creativity. In R. J. Sternberg (Ed.), *Handbook of creativity* (pp. 313–335). New York: Cambridge University Press.

Csikszentmihalyi, M. (2000). Creativity: An overview. In A. E. Kazdin (Ed.), *Encyclopedia of psychology* (Vol. 2, p. 342). Washington, DC: American Psychological Association.

Cuellar, I., & Paniagua, F. A. (Eds.). (2000). *Handbook of multicultural mental health: Assessment and treatment of diverse populations.* San Diego, CA: Academic Press.

Cummings, E. M., Braungart-Rieker, J. M., & Du Rocher-Schudlich, T. (2003). Emotion and personality development. In R. M. Lerner, M. A. Easterbrooks, & J. Mistry (Vol. Eds.) and I. B. Weiner (Ed.-in-Chief), *Handbook of psychology.* Vol. 6: *Developmental psychology* (pp. 211–239). New York: Wiley.

Cummings, J. L. (1993). The neuroanatomy of depression. *Journal of Clinical Psychiatry, 54*(Suppl. 11), 14–20.

Curtiss, S. (1977). *Genie: A linguistic study of a modern-day wild child.* New York: Academic Press.

Cutler, B. L., & Penrod, S. D. (1995). *Mistaken identification: The eyewitness, psychology, and the law.* New York: Cambridge University Press.

Cutler, W. B., Preti, G., Krieger, A., Huggins, G. R., Garcia, C. R., & Lawley, H. J. (1986). Human axillary secretions influence women's menstrual cycles: The role of donor extract from men. *Hormones and Behavior, 20*, 463–473.

Cutting, J. E., Proffitt, D. R., & Kozlowski, L. T. (1978). A biomechanical invariant for gait perception. *Journal of Experimental Psychology: Human Perception and Performance, 4*, 357–372.

Cziko, G. A. (1998). From blind to creative: In defense of Donald Campbell's selectionist theory of human creativity. *Journal of Creative Behavior, 32*, 192–208.

Dabbs, J. M. Jr., Karpas, A. E., Dyomina, N., Juechter, J., & Roberts, A. (2002). Experimental raising or lowering of testosterone level affects mood in normal men and women. *Social Behavior & Personality, 30*, 795–806.

Dadds, M. R. (2002). Learning and intimacy in the families of anxious children. In R. J. McMahon & R. D. Peters (Eds.), *The effects of parental dysfunction on children* (pp. 87–104). New York: Kluwer Academic/Plenum Publishers.

Dalton, P., & Wysocki, C. J. (1996). The nature and duration of adaptation following long-term odor exposure. *Perception and Psychophysics, 58*, 781–792.

Daly, M., & Wilson, M. I. (1991). A reply to Gelles: Stepchildren are disproportionately abused, and diverse forms of violence can share causal factors. *Human Nature, 2*, 419–426.

Daly, M., & Wilson, M. I. (1996). Violence against stepchildren. *Current Directions in Psychological Science, 5*, 77–81.

Damasio, H., Grabowski, T., Frank, R., Galaburda, A. M., & Damasio, A. M. (1994). The return of Phineas Gage: Clues about the brain from the skull of a famous patient. *Science, 264*, 1102–1105.

Damon, W., & Hart, D. (1982). The development of self-understanding from childhood to adolescence. *Child Development, 53*, 841–864.

Damon, W., & Hart, D. (1992). Self-understanding and its role in social and moral development. In M. H. Bornstein & M. E. Lamb (Eds.), *Developmental psychology: An advanced textbook* (3rd ed., pp. 421–464). Hillsdale, NJ: Erlbaum.

Daneman, M., & Carpenter, P. A. (1983). Individual differences in integrating information between and within sentences. *Journal of Experimental Psychology: Learning, Memory, and Cognition, 9*, 561–583.

Daneman, M., & Tardif, T. (1987). Working memory and reading skill re-examined. In M. Coltheart (Ed.), *Attention and performance.* Vol. 12: *The psychology of reading* (pp. 491–508). Hove, UK: Erlbaum.

Daniel, M. (1997). Intelligence testing: Status and trends. *American Psychologist, 52*, 1038–1045.

Daniel, M. (2000). Interpretation of intelligence test scores. In R. J. Sternberg (Ed.), *Handbook of intelligence* (pp. 477–491). New York: Cambridge University Press.

Dar, R., Leventhal, E. A., & Leventhal, H. (1993). Schematic processes in pain perception. *Cognitive Therapy and Research, 17*, 341–357.

Darley, C. F., Tinklenberg, J. R., Roth, W. T., Hollister, L. E., & Atkinson, R. C. (1973). Influence of marijuana on storage and retrieval processes in memory. *Memory & Cognition, 1*, 196–200.

Darley, J. M. (1992). Social organization for the production of evil. *Psychological Inquiry, 3*, 199–218.

Darley, J. M. (1998). Methods for the study of evil-doing actions. *Personality and Social Psychology Review, 3*, 269–275.

Darley, J. M., & Batson, C. D. (1973). From Jerusalem to Jericho: A study of situational and dispositional variables in helping behavior. *Journal of Personality and Social Psychology, 27*, 100–108.

Darwin, C. (1859). *Origin of species.* London: John Murray.

Darwin, C. (1965). *The expression of the emotions in man and animals.* Chicago: University of Chicago Press. (Original work published 1872)

Dasen, P. R., & Heron, A. (1981). Cross-cultural tests of Piaget's theory. In H. C. Triandis & A. Heron (Eds.), *Handbook of cross-cultural psychology* (Vol. 4). Boston: Allyn & Bacon.

Davidson, J. E. (1995). The suddenness of insight. In R. J. Sternberg & J. E. Davidson (Eds.), *The nature of insight* (pp.125–155). Cambridge, MA: MIT Press.

Davidson, J. E., & Downing, C. L. (2000). Contemporary models of intelligence. In R. J. Sternberg (Ed.), *Handbook of intelligence.* New York: Cambridge University Press.

Davidson, J. W., & Lytle, M. H. (1986). *After the fact: The art of historical detection* (2nd ed.). New York: Knopf.

Davidson, R. J. (1994). The role of prefrontal activation in the inhibition of negative affect. *Psychophysiology, 31*, S7.

Davidson, R. J. (1994a). Asymmetric brain function, affective style, and psychopathology: The role of early experience and plasticity. *Development and Psychopathology, 6*, 741–758.

Davidson, R. J., & Hugdahl, K. (Eds.). (1995). *Cerebral asymmetry.* Cambridge, MA: MIT Press.

Davidson, R. J., & Slagter, A. (2000). Probing emotion in the developing brain: Functional neuroimaging in the assessment of the neural substrates of emotion in normal and disordered children and adolescents. *Mental Retardation and Developmental Disabilities Research Reviews, 6*(30), 166–170.

Davidson, R. J., & Sutton, S. K. (1995). Affective neuroscience: The emergence of a discipline. *Current Opinion in Neurobiology, 5*, 217–224.

Davies, I. (1998). A study of colour grouping in three languages: A test of the linguistic relativity hypothesis. *British Journal of Psychology, 89*, 433–452.

Davies, I., & Corbett, G. G. (1997). A cross-cultural study of colour grouping: Evidence for a weak linguistic relativity. *British Journal of Psychology, 88*, 493–517.

Davies, M., Stankov, L., & Roberts, R. D. (1998). Emotional intelligence: In search of an elusive construct. *Journal of Personality and Social Psychology, 75*, 985–1015.

Davis, G. A., & Rimm, S. (1977). Characteristics of creatively gifted children. *Gifted Child Quarterly, 21*, 546–551.

Davis, K., & Jones, E. E. (1960). Changes in interpersonal perception as a means of reducing cognitive dissonance. *Journal of Abnormal and Social Psychology, 61*, 402–410.

Davison, G. C., & Neale, J. (2001). *Abnormal psychology* (8th ed.). New York: Wiley.

Dawes, R. (2000). Tversky, Amos. In A. Kazdin (Ed.), *Encyclopedia of psychology* (Vol. 8, pp. 127–128). Washington, DC: American Psychological Association.

Dawes, R. M. (1994). *House of cards.* New York: Free Press.

Dawes, R. M., & Mulford, M. (1996). The false consensus effect and overconfidence: Flaws in judgment or flaws in how we study judgment? *Organizational Behavior & Human Decision Processes, 65*(3), 201–211.

Dawkins, R. (1989). *The selfish gene* (New ed.). New York: Oxford University Press.

Dawson, B., & Ashman, S. B. (2000). On the origins of a vulnerability to depression: The influence of early social environment on the development of psychobiological systems related to risk for affective disorder. In C. A. Nelson (Ed.), *The Minnesota Symposia on Child Development. Vol. 31: The effects of early adversity on neurobehavioral development* (pp. 245–279). Mahwah, NJ: Erlbaum.

Dawson, D., Lack, L., & Morris, M. (1993). Phase resetting of the human circadian pacemaker with use of a single use of bright light. *Chronobiology International, 10*, 94–102.

Day, N. L., Leech, S. L., Richardson, G. A., Cornelius, M. D., Robles, N., & Larkby, C. (2002). Prenatal alcohol exposure predicts continued deficits in offspring size at 14 years of age. *Alcoholism: Clinical & Experimental Research, 26*, 1584–1591.

de Groot, A. D. (1965). *Thought and choice in chess.* The Hague, Netherlands: Mouton.

De Houwer, A. (1995). Bilingual language acquisition. In P. Fletcher & B. MacWhinney (Eds.), *The handbook of child language* (pp. 219–250). Oxford: Blackwell.

De Houwer, A. (1998). Comparing error frequencies in monolingual and bilingual acquisition. *Bilingualism, 1*(3), 173–174.

de Wilde, E. J., Kienhorst, I. C. W. M., & Diekstra, R. F. W. (2001). Suicidal behaviour in adolescents. In I. M. Goodyer (Ed.), *The depressed child and adolescent* (2nd ed., pp. 267–291). New York: Cambridge University Press.

De Yoe, E. A., & Van Essen, D. C. (1988). Concurrent processing streams in monkey visual cortex. *Trends in Neurosciences, 11*, 219–226.

DeAngelis, T. (1992, May). Senate seeks answers to rising tide of violence. *APA Monitor,* p. 11.

Deary, I. (2000). Simple information processing and intelligence. In R. J. Sternberg (Ed.), *Handbook of intelligence.* New York: Cambridge University Press.

Deary, I. J., & Stough, L. (1996). Intelligence and inspection time: Achievements, prospects, and problems. *American Psychologist, 51*, 599–608.

DeCasper, A. J., & Fifer, W. P. (1980). Of human bonding: Newborns prefer their mothers' voices. *Science, 208*, 1174–1176.

DeCasper, A. J., & Spence, M. J. (1986). Prenatal maternal speech influences newborns' perception of speech sounds. *Infant Behavior and Development, 9*, 133–150.

deCastro, J. M., & Brewer, E. M. (1992). The amount eaten in meals by humans is a power function of the number of people present. *Physiology and Behavior, 51*, 121–125.

deCharms, R. (1968). *Personal causation: The internal affective determinants of behavior.* New York: Academic Press.

Deci, E. L. (1971). Effects of externally mediated rewards on intrinsic motivation. *Journal of Personality and Social Psychology, 18*, 105–115.

Deci, E. L. (1972). Intrinsic motivation, extrinsic reinforcement, and inequity. *Journal of Personality and Social Psychology, 22*, 113–120.

Deci, E. L., & Ryan, R. M. (1985). *Intrinsic motivation and self-determination in human behavior.* New York: Plenum.

Deci, E. L., & Ryan, R. M. (1995). Human autonomy: The basis for true self-esteem. In M. Kernis (Ed.), *Efficacy, agency, and self-esteem* (pp. 31–49). New York: Plenum.

Deci, E. L., & Ryan, R. M. (2002a). The paradox of achievement: The harder you push, the worse it gets. In J. Aronson (Ed.), *Improving academic achievement: Impact of psychological factors on education* (pp. 61–87). San Diego, CA: Academic Press.

Deci, E. L., & Ryan, R. M. (2002b). Self-determination research: Reflections and future directions. In E. L. Deci & R. M. Ryan (Eds.), *Handbook of self-determination research* (pp. 431–441). Rochester, NY: University of Rochester Press.

Deci, E. L., Connell, J. P., & Ryan, R. M. (1989). Self-determination in a work organization. *Journal of Applied Psychology, 74*, 580–590.

Deci, E. L., Koestner, R., & Ryan, R. M. (1999a). A meta-analytic review of experiments examining the effects of extrinsic rewards on intrinsic motivation. *Psychological Bulletin, 125*, 627–668.

Deci, E. L., Koestner, R., & Ryan, R. M. (1999b). The undermining effect is a reality after all—extrinsic rewards, task interest, and self-determination: Reply to Eisenberger, Pierce, and Cameron (1999) and Lepper, Henderlong, and Gingras (1999). *Psychological Bulletin, 125*, 692–700.

Deci, E. L., Schwartz, A. J., Sheinman, L., & Ryan, R. M. (1981). An instrument to assess adults' orientations toward control versus autonomy with children: Reflections on intrinsic motivation and perceived competence. *Journal of Educational Psychology, 73*, 642–650.

Deci, E. L., Vallerand, R. J., Pelletier, L. G., & Ryan, R. M. (1991). Motivation and education: The self-determination perspective. *Educational Psychologist, 26*(3–4), 325–346.

Deese, J. (1959). On the prediction of occurrence of particular verbal intrusions in immediate recall. *Journal of Experimental Psychology, 58*, 17–22.

Deffenbacher, J. L. (1994, August). *Anger and diagnosis: Where has all the anger gone?* Paper presented at the meeting of the American Psychological Association, Los Angeles, CA.

DeGreef, G., Ashari, M., Bogerts, B., Bilder, R. M., Jody, D. N., Alvir, J. M. J., & Lieberman, J. A. (1992). Volumes of ventricular system subdivisions measured from magnetic resonance images in first-episode schizophrenic patients. *Archives of General Psychiatry, 49,* 531–537.

Dehue, F. M., McClintock, C. G., & Liebrand, W. B. (1993). Social value related response latencies: Unobtrusive evidence for individual differences in information processing. *European Journal of Social Psychology, 23,* 273–293.

Dekkers, T., Wessel, I., & Roefs, A. (2003). Dissociative symptoms and amnesia in Dutch concentration camp survivors. *Comprehensive Psychiatry, 44,* 65–69.

Delgado, J. M. R. (1969). *Physical control of the mind: Toward a psychocivilized society.* New York: Harper & Row.

Delgado, J. M. R., Roberts, W. W., & Miller, N. E. (1954). Learning motivated by electrical stimulation of the brain. *American Journal of Physiology, 179,* 587–593.

DeLoache, J. S. (1987). Rapid change in the symbolic functioning of young children. *Science, 9238,* 1556–1557.

DeLoache, J. S. (1991). Symbolic functioning in very young children: Understanding of pictures and models. *Child Development, 62,* 736–752.

DeLoache, J. S. (1995). Early understanding and use of symbols: The model model. *Current Directions in Psychological Science, 4,* 109–113.

DeLoache, J. S. (2002). Early development of the understanding and use of symbolic artifacts. In U. Goswami (Ed.), *Blackwell handbook of childhood cognitive development* (pp. 206–226). Malden, MA: Blackwell.

DeLoache, J. S., Kolstad, V., & Anderson, K. N. (1991). Physical similarity and young children's understanding of scale models. *Child Development, 62,* 111–126.

DeLongis, A., Folkman, S., & Lazarus, R. S. (1988). The impact of daily stress on health and mood: Psychological and social resources as mediators. *Journal of Personality and Social Psychology, 54*(3), 486–495.

Dembroski, T. M., & Costa, P. T. (1988). Assessment of coronary-prone behavior: A current overview. *Annals of Behavioral Medicine, 10,* 60–63.

Dembroski, T. M., MacDougall, J. M., Williams, R. B., Haney, T. L., & Blumenthal, J. A. (1985). Components of Type A, hostility, and anger in relationship to angiographic findings. *Psychosomatic Medicine, 47,* 219–233.

Dement, W. C. (1976). *Some must watch while some must sleep.* New York: Norton.

Dement, W. C., & Kleitman, N. (1957). The relation of eye movements during sleep to dream activity: An objective method for the study of dreaming. *Journal of Experimental Psychology, 55,* 543–553.

Dement, W. C., & Vaughan, C. (1999). *The promise of sleep: A pioneer in sleep medicine explores the vital connection between health, happiness, and a good night's sleep.* New York: Dell.

Demetriou, A. (2002). Tracing psychology's invisible g$_{iant}$ and its visible guards. In R. J. Sternberg & E. L. Grigorenko (Eds.), *The general factor of intelligence: How general is it?* (pp. 3–18). Mahwah, NJ: Erlbaum.

Demetriou, A., & Papadopoulos, T. C. (in press). Human intelligence: From local models to universal theory. In R. Sternberg (Ed.), *International handbook of the psychology of human intelligence.* New York: Cambridge University Press.

Demetriou, A., Efklides, A., & Platsidou, M. (1993). The architecture and dynamics of developing mind. *Monographs of the Society for Research in Child Development, 58*(5–6), Serial No. 234.

Dennett, D. (2001). Are we explaining consciousness yet? *Cognition, 79,* 221–237.

Dennett, D. C. (1995). *Darwin's dangerous idea.* New York: Simon & Schuster.

Dennett, D. C. (1997). Consciousness in human and robot minds. In M. Ito, Y. Miyashita, et al. (Eds.), *Cognition, computation, and consciousness* (pp. 17–29). New York: Oxford University Press.

Denny, N. W. (1980). Task demands and problem-solving strategies in middle-age and older adults. *Journal of Gerontology, 35,* 559–564.

Descartes, R. (1972). *The treatise of man.* Cambridge, MA: Harvard University Press. (Original work published 1662)

DeSteno, D., Bartlett, M.Y., Braverman, J., & Salovey, P. (2002). Sex differences in jealousy: Evolutionary mechanism or artifact of measurement? *Journal of Personality and Social Psychology, 83,* 1103–1116.

Detterman, D. K. (2002). General intelligence: Cognitive and biological explanations. In R. J. Sternberg & E. L. Grigorenko (Eds.), *The general factor of intelligence: How general is it?* (pp. 223–244). Mahwah, NJ: Erlbaum.

Detterman, D. K., & Sternberg, R. J. (Eds.). (1982). *How and how much can intelligence be increased?* Norwood, NJ: Ablex.

Detterman, D. K., & Sternberg, R. J. (Eds.). (1993). *Transfer on trial: Intelligence, cognition, and instruction.* Norwood, NJ: Ablex.

Detterman, D. K., & Thompson, L. A. (1997). What is so special about special education? *American Psychologist, 52,* 1082–1090.

Detterman, D. K., Gabriel, L., & Ruthsatz, J. (2000). Intelligence and mental retardation. In R. J. Sternberg (Ed.), *Handbook of intelligence.* New York: Cambridge University Press.

Detweiler-Bedell, B., & Salovey, P. (2002). A second-generation psychology of emotion. *Psychological Inquiry, 13,* 45–48.

Deutsch, J. A., & Deutsch, D. (1963). Attention: Some theoretical considerations. *Psychological Review, 70,* 80–90.

Devine, P. G., Evett, S. R., & Vasquez-Suson, K. A. (1995). Exploring the interpersonal dynamics of intergroup contact. In R. Sorrentino & E. T. Higgins (Eds.), *Handbook of motivation and cognition: The interpersonal context* (Vol. 3). New York: Guilford.

Devine, P. G., Monteith, M. J., Zuwerink, J. R., & Elliot, A. J. (1991). Prejudice with and without compunction. *Journal of Personality and Social Psychology, 60*(6), 817–830.

Devine, P. G., Plant, E. A., Amodio, D. M, Harmon-Jones, E., & Vance, S. L. (2002). The regulation of explicit and implicit race bias: The role of motivations to respond without prejudice. *Journal of Personality and Social Psychology, 82,* 835–848.

Devos-Comby, L., & Salovey, P. (2002). Applying persuasion strategies to alter HIV-relevant thoughts and behavior. *Review of General Psychology, 6,* 287–304.

Diamond, I. T. (1979). The subdivisions of neocortex: A proposal to revise the traditional view of sensory, motor, and association areas. *Progress in Psychobiology and Physiological Psychology, 8,* 1–43.

Diamond, I. T. (1983). Parallel pathways in the auditory, visual, and somatic systems. In G. Macchi, R. Rustioni, & R. Spreafico (Eds.), *Somatosensory integration in the thalamus* (pp. 251–272). Amsterdam: Elsevier.

Dichgans, J., & Brandt, T. (1973). Optokinetic motion sickness and pseudo-Coriolis effects induced by moving visual stimuli. *Acta Otolaryngology – Stockholm, 76*(5), 339–348.

Diekstra, R. F. W. (1996). The epidemiology of suicide and parasuicide. *Archives of Suicide Research, 2,* 1–29.

Diener, E., & Biswas-Diener, R. (2002). Will money increase subjective well-being? *Social Indicators Research, 57,* 119–169.

Diener, E., Lucas, R. E., & Oishi, S. (2002). Sujective well-being: The science of happiness and life satisfaction. In C. R. Snyder & S. J. Lopez (Eds.), *Handbook of positive psychology* (pp. 463–73). London: Oxford University Press.

DiMatteo, M. R., & DiNicola, D. D. (1982). *Achieving patient compliance: The psychology of the medical practitioner's role.* New York: Pergamon.

Dineen, T. (1998). Psychotherapy: The snake oil of the 90s? *Skeptic, 6*(3), 54–63.

Dinnerstein, D. (1976). *The mermaid and the minotaur: Sexual arrangements and human malaise.* New York: Harper & Row.

Dion, K. K., Berscheid, E., & Walster, E. (1972). What is beautiful is good. *Journal of Personality and Social Psychology, 24,* 285–290.

DiPietro, J. A., Costigan, K. A., Shupe, A. K., Pressman, E. K., & Johnson, T. R. (1999). Fetal neurobehavioral development associated with social class and fetal sex. *Developmental Psychology, 33,* 79–81.

DiTomasso, R. A., & Gosch, E. A. (2002). Anxiety disorders: An overview. In R. A. DiTomasso & E. A. Gosch (Eds.), *Comparative treatments for anxiety disorders* (pp. 1–31). New York: Springer.

Dittes, J. E., & Kelley, H. H. (1956). Effects of different conditions of acceptance upon conformity to group norms. *Journal of Abnormal and Social Psychology, 53,* 100–107.

Dixon, L. B., Lehman, A. F., & Levine, J. (1995). Conventional antipsychotic medications for schizophrenia. *Schizophrenia Bulletin, 21,* 567–577.

Dixon, R. A., & Baltes, P. B. (1986). Toward life-span research on the functions and pragmatics of intelligence. In R. J. Sternberg & R. K. Wagner (Eds.), *Practical intelligence: Nature and origins of competence in the everyday world* (pp. 203–235). New York: Cambridge University Press.

Docherty, J. (1993, May 23). Pay for mental health care—and save. *New York Times,* Sect. 3, p. 13.

Docherty, N. M., & Gottesman, I. I. (2000). A twin study of communication disturbances in schizophrenia. *Journal of Nervous & Mental Disease, 188,* 395–401.

Dodge, K. A., & Pettit, G. S. (2003). A biopsychosocial model of the development of chronic conduct problems in adolescence. *Developmental Psychology, 39,* 349–371.

Dohrenwend, B. P. (2000). The role of adversity and stress in psychopathology: Some evidence and its implications for theory and research. *Journal of Health & Social Behavior, 41,* 1–19.

Dohrenwend, B. P., Levav, I., Schwartz, S., Naveh, G., Link, B. G., Skodol, A. G., & Stueve, A. (1992). Socioeconomic status and psychiatric disorders: The causation–selection issue. *Science, 255,* 946–952.

Dohrenwend, B. S., & Dohrenwend, B. P. (1974). *Stressful life events.* New York: Wiley.

Dolan, M. (1995, February 11). When the mind's eye blinks. *Los Angeles Times,* pp. A1, A24, A25.

Dolinski, D. (2000). On inferring one's beliefs from one's attempt and consequences for subsequent compliance. *Journal of Personality and Social Psychology, 78,* 260–272.

Dollard, J., Miller, N., Doob, L., Mowrer, O. H., & Sears, R. R. (1939). *Frustration and aggression.* New Haven, CT: Institute of Human Relations, Yale University Press.

Domjan, M. (1997). Behavior systems and the demise of equipotentiality: Historical antecedents and evidence from sexual conditioning. In M. E. Bouton & M. S. Fanselow (Eds.), *Learning, motivation, and cognition* (pp. 31–51). Washington, DC: American Psychological Association.

Domjan, M. (2000a). General process learning theory: Challenges from response and stimulus factors. *International Journal of Comparative Psychology, 13,* 101–118.

Domjan, M. (2000b). Learning: An overview. In A. E. Kazdin (Ed.), *Encyclopedia of psychology* (Vol. 5, pp. 1–3). Washington, DC: American Psychological Association.

Domjan, M., & Krause, M. A. (2002). Research productivity in animal learning from 1953 to 2000. *Animal Learning & Behavior, 30,* 282–285.

Donnerstein, E., & Berkowitz, L. (1981). Victim reaction in aggressive erotic films as a factor in violence against women. *Journal of Personality and Social Psychology, 41,* 710–724.

Doty, R. L. (2000). Smell. In A. E. Kazdin (Ed.), *Encyclopedia of psychology* (Vol. 7, pp. 313–320). Washington, DC: American Psychological Association.

Douvan, E., & Adelson, J. (1966). *The adolescent experience.* New York: Wiley.

Dowsett, S. M., Saul, J. L., Butow, P. N., Dunn, S. M., Boyer, M. J., Findlow, R., & Dunsmore, J. (2000). Communication styles in the cancer consultation: Preferences for a patient-centered approach. *Psycho-Oncology, 9,* 147–156.

Dozier, M., & Kobak, R. R. (1992). Psychophysiology in attachment interviews: Converging evidence for deactivating strategies. *Child Development, 63,* 1473–1480.

Draycock, S. G., & Kline, R. P. (1995). The Big Three or the Big Five—the EPQ-R vs. the NEO-PI: A research note, replication and elaboration. *Personality and Individual Differences, 18,* 801–804.

Dubnau, J., & Tully, T. (1998). Gene discovery in *Drosophila*: New insights for learning and memory. *Annual Review of Neuroscience, 21,* 407–444.

Duckworth, K. L., Bargh, J. A., Garcia, M., & Chaiken, S. (2002). The automatic evaluation of novel stimuli. *Psychological Science, 13,* 513–519.

Duncan, G. J., & Brooks-Gunn, J. (Eds.). (1997). *Consequences of growing up poor.* New York: Russell Sage.

Dunkley, T. L., Wertheim, E. H., & Paxton, S. J. (2001). Examination of a model of multiple sociocultural influences on adolescent girls' body dissatisfaction and dietary restraint. *Adolescence, 36,* 265–279.

Dunn, J., & Plomin, R. (1990). *Separate lives: Why siblings are so different.* New York: Basic Books.

Dupuy, J.-P. (1998). Rationality and self-deception. In J.-P. Dupuy (Ed.), *Self-deception and paradoxes of rationality* (pp. 113–150). Stanford, CA: CSLI Publications.

Dupuy, J.-P. (1999). Rational choice theory. In R. A. Wilson & F. C. Keil (Eds.), *The MIT encyclopedia of the cognitive sciences* (pp. 699–701). Cambridge, MA: MIT Press.

Durgin, F. H. (2000). Visual adaptation. In A. E. Kazdin (Ed.), *Encyclopedia of psychology* (Vol. 8, pp. 183–187). Washington, DC: American Psychological Association.

Durlach, N. I., & Colburn, H. S. (1978). Binaural phenomenon. In E. C. Carterette & M. P. Friedman (Eds.), *Handbook of perception* (Vol. 4). New York: Academic Press.

Dusek, J. A., & Eichenbaum, H. (1997). The hippocampus and memory for orderly stimulus relations. *Proceedings of the National Academy of Sciences, USA, 94,* 7109–7114.

Dutton, D. G., & Aron, A. P. (1974). Some evidence for heightened sexual attraction under conditions of high anxiety. *Journal of Personality and Social Psychology, 30,* 510–517.

Dweck, C. S. (1992). The study of goals in human behavior. *Psychological Science, 3,* 165–167.

Dweck, C. S. (1999). *Self-theories: Their role in motivation, personality, and development.* Philadelphia: Psychology Press.

Dweck, C. S. (2002). The development of ability conceptions. In A. Wigfield & J. S. Eccles (Eds.), *Development of achievement motivation* (pp. 57–88). San Diego, CA: Academic Press.

Dyal, J. A. (1984). Cross-cultural research with the locus of control concept. In H. Lefcourt (Ed.), *Research with the locus of control construct. Vol. 3: Extensions and limitations.* San Diego, CA: Academic Press.

Eagly, A. H. (1987). *Sex differences and social behavior: A social-role interpretation.* Hillsdale, NJ: Erlbaum.

Eagly, A. H., & Chaiken, S. (1975). An attribution analysis of communicator attractiveness. *Journal of Personality and Social Psychology, 32,* 136–144.

Eagly, A. H., & Chaiken, S. (1992). *The psychology of attitudes.* San Diego: Harcourt Brace.

Eagly, A. H., & Chaiken, S. (1998). Attitude structure and function. In D. Gilbert, S. Fiske, & G. Lindzey (Eds.), *The handbook of social psychology* (4th ed.). New York: McGraw-Hill.

Eagly, A. H., & Johannesen-Schmidt, M. C. (2001). The leadership styles of women and men. *Journal of Social Issues, 57,* 781–797.

Eagly, A. H., & Karau, S. J. (2002). Role congruity theory of prejudice toward female leaders. *Psychological Review, 109,* 573–598.

Eagly, A. H., Chen, S., Chaiken, S., & Shaw-Barnes, K. (1999). The impact of attitudes on memory: An affair to remember. *Psychological Bulletin, 125,* 64–89.

Eagly, A. H., Makhijani, M. G., & Klonsky, B. G. (1992). Gender and the evaluation of leaders: A meta-analysis. *Psychological Bulletin, 111*(1), 3–22.

Eagly, A., Beall, A. E., & Sternberg, R. J. (in press). *The psychology of gender* (2nd ed.). New York: Guilford.

Early, P. C. (1989). Social loafing and collectivism: A comparison of the United States and the People's Republic of China. *Administrative Science Quarterly, 34,* 565–581.

Ebbinghaus, H. E. (1902). *Grundzuge der psychologie.* Leipzig, Germany: Von Veit.

Ebbinghaus, H. E. (1964). *Memory: A contribution to experimental psychology.* New York: Dover. (Original work published 1885)

Ebenholtz, S. M., Cohen, M. M., & Linder, B. J. (1994). The possible role of nystagmus in motion sickness: A hypothesis. *Aviation, Space and Environmental Medicine, 65*(11), 1032–1035.

Ebstein, R. P., Novick, O., Umansky, R., Priel, B., Osher, Y., Blaine, D., Bennett, E. R., Nemanov, L., Katz, M., & Belmaker, R. H. (1996). Dopamine D4 receptor (D4DR) exon III polymorphism associated with human personality trait of novelty seeking. *Nature Genetics, 12,* 78–80.

Eccles, J. S., Wigfield, A., & Schiefele, U. (1998). Motivation to succeed. In W. Damon (Gen. Ed.) & N. Eisenberg (Vol. Ed.), *Handbook of child psychology.* Vol. 3: *Social, emotional, and personality development.* New York: Wiley.

Eccles, J. S., Wigfield, A., Harold, R. D., & Blumenfeld, P. (1993). Age and gender differences in children's self- and task perceptions during elementary school. *Child Development, 64,* 830–847.

Eckenrode, J. (1984). Impact of chronic and acute stressors on daily reports of mood. *Journal of Personality and Social Psychology, 46,* 907–918.

Eckenrode, J., & Gore, S. (Eds.). (1990). *Stress between work and family.* New York: Plenum Press.

Edgerton, R. (1967). *The cloak of competence.* Berkeley: University of California Press.

Edmonston, W. E. Jr. (1981). *Hypnosis and relaxation.* New York: Wiley.

Edmonston, W. E. Jr. (1991). Anesis. In S. J. Lynn & J. W. Rhue (Eds.), *Theories of hypnosis: Current models and perspectives. The Guilford clinical and experimental hypnosis series* (pp. 197–237). New York: Guilford.

Edwards, J. C., McKinley, W., & Moon, G. (2002). The enactment of organizational decline: The self-fulfilling prophecy. *The International Journal of Organizational Analysis, 10,* 55–75

Edwards, K., & Smith, E. E. (1996). A disconfirmation bias in the evaluation of arguments. *Journal of Personality and Social Psychology, 71,* 5–24.

Egeland, B., & Sroufe, L. A. (1981). Attachment and early maltreatment. *Child Development, 52,* 44–52.

Egeth, H. E. (1993). What do we not know about eyewitness identification? *American Psychologist, 48*(5), 577–580.

Ehret, G., & Romand, R. (Eds.). (1997). *The central auditory system.* New York: Oxford University Press.

Eichenbaum, H. (1997). Declarative memory: Insights from cognitive neurobiology. *Annual Review of Psychology, 48,* 547–572.

Eichenbaum, H. (1999). Hippocampus. In R. A. Wilson & F. C. Keil (Eds.), *The MIT encyclopedia of the cognitive sciences* (pp. 377–378). Cambridge, MA: MIT Press.

Eimas, P. D. (1985). The perception of speech in early infancy. *Scientific American, 252,* 46–52.

Eisenberg, N. (2000). Writing a literature review. In R. J. Sternberg (Ed.), *Guide to publishing in psychology journals* (pp. 17–34). New York: Cambridge University Press.

Eisenberg, N., & Fabes, R. A. (1998). Prosocial development. In W. Damon (Gen. Ed.) & N. Eisenberg (Vol. Ed.), *Handbook of child psychology.* Vol. 3: *Social, emotional, and personality development* (pp. 701–778). New York: Wiley.

Eisenberger, R., & Armeli, S. (1997). Can salient reward increase creative performance without reducing intrinsic creative interest? *Journal of Personality and Social Psychology, 72,* 652–663.

Eisenberger, R., & Cameron, J. (1996). Detrimental effects of reward: Reality or myth? *American Psychologist, 51,* 1153–1166.

Eisenberger, R., & Rhoades, L. (2001). Incremental effects of reward on creativity. *Journal of Personality and Social Psychology, 81,* 728–741.

Eisenberger, R., Haskins, F., & Gambleton, P. (1999). Promised reward and creativity: Effects of prior experience. *Journal of Experimental Social Psychology, 35,* 308–325.

Eisenstock, B. (1984). Sex-role differences in children's identification with counterstereotypical televised portrayals. *Sex Roles, 10*(5–6), 417–430.

Ekman, P. (1971). Universals and cultural differences in the facial expression of emotion. In J. Cole (Ed.), *Nebraska Symposium on Motivation* (Vol. 19, pp. 207–284). Lincoln: University of Nebraska Press.

Ekman, P. (1984). Expression and the nature of emotion. In P. Ekman & K. Scherer (Eds.), *Approaches to emotion* (pp. 319–343). Hillsdale, NJ: Erlbaum.

Ekman, P. (1992a). *Telling lies.* New York: Norton.

Ekman, P. (1992b). Facial expressions of emotion: New findings, new questions. *Psychological Science, 3,* 34–38.

Ekman, P. (1993). Facial expression and emotion. *American Psychologist, 48,* 384–392.

Ekman, P. (1994). Strong evidence of universals in facial expressions: A reply to Russell's mistaken critique. *Psychological Bulletin, 115,* 268–287.

Ekman, P. (2001). *Telling lies: Clues to deceit in the marketplace, politics, and marriage.* New York: Norton.

Ekman, P., & Davidson, R. J. (Eds.). (1994). *The nature of emotion: Fundamental questions.* New York: Oxford University Press.

Ekman, P., & Friesen, W. V. (1975). *Unmasking the face.* Englewood Cliffs, NJ: Prentice-Hall.

Ekman, P., & Friesen, W. V. (1984). *Unmasking the face* (2nd ed.). Palo Alto, CA: Consulting Psychologists Press.

Ekman, P., & Oster, H. (1979). Facial expression of emotion. *Annual Review of Psychology, 30,* 527–554.

Ekman, P., Friesen, W. V., & O'Sullivan, M. (1988). Smiles when lying. *Journal of Personality and Social Psychology, 54,* 414–420.

Ekman, P., Levenson, R. W., & Friesen, W. V. (1983). Autonomic nervous system activity distinguishes among emotions. *Science, 221,* 1208–1210.

Ekman, P., O'Sullivan, M., & Frank, M. G. (1999). A few can catch a liar. *Psychological Science, 10,* 263–266.

Elashoff, J. R., & Snow, R. E. (1971). *Pygmalion reconsidered.* Worthington, OH: Charles A. Jones.

Elbert, T., Ray, W., Kowalik, Z., Skinner, S., Graf, K., & Birbaumer, N., (1994). Chaos and Physiology, *Physiological Reviews, 74,* 1–47.

Elfenbein, H. A., March, A. A., & Ambady, N. (2002). Emotional intelligence and the recognition of emotion from facial expressions. In L. F. Barrett & P. Salovey (Eds.), *The wisdom in feeling: Psychological processes in emotional intelligence* (pp. 37–59). New York: Guilford.

Eliot, R. S., & Buell, J. C. (1983). The role of the central nervous system in sudden cardiac death. In T. M. Dembroski, T. Schmidt, & G. Blunchen (Eds.), *Biobehavioral bases of coronary-prone behavior.* New York: Plenum.

Elkind, D. (1967). Egocentrism in adolescence. *Child Development, 38,* 1025–1034.

Elkind, D. (1985). Egocentrism redux. *Developmental Review, 5,* 218–226.

Ellis, A. (1962). *Reason and emotion in psychotherapy.* Secaucus, NJ: Lyle Stuart.

Ellis, A. (1970). *Reason and emotion in psychotherapy.* New York: Lyle Stuart.

Ellis, A. (1973). Rational-emotive therapy. In R. J. Corsini (Ed.), *Current psychotherapies.* Itasca, IL: Peacock.

Ellis, A. (1989). The history of cognition in psychotherapy. In A. Freeman, K. M. Simon, L. E. Beutler, & H. Arkowitz (Eds.), *Comprehensive handbook of cognitive therapy* (pp. 5–19). New York: Plenum.

Ellis, A. (2002). *Overcoming resistance: A rational emotive behavior therapy integrated approach* (2nd ed.). New York: Springer.

Ellis, A., & Dryden, W. (1997). *The practice of rational-emotive behavior therapy* (2nd ed.). New York: Springer.

Ellis, A., Shaughnessy, M. F., & Mahan, V. (2002). An interview with Albert Ellis about rational emotive behavior therapy. *North American Journal of Psychology, 4,* 355–366.

Elman, J. L., Bates, E. A., Johnson, M. H., Karmiloff-Smith, A., Parisi, D., & Plunkett, K. (1996). *Rethinking innateness: A connectionist perspective on development.* Cambridge, MA: MIT Press.

Embretson, S., & McCollam, K. (2000). Psychometric approaches to the understanding of intelligence. In R. J. Sternberg (Ed.), *Handbook of intelligence.* New York: Cambridge University Press.

Endler, N. S., & Magnusson, D. (1976). Toward an interactional psychology of personality. *Psychological Bulletin, 83,* 956–974.

Engel, A. S., Rumelhart, D. E., Wandell, B. A., Lee A. T., Gover, G. H., Chichilisky, E. J., & Shadlen, M. S. (1994). MRI measurement of language lateralization in Wada-tested patients. *Brain, 118,* 1411–1419.

Engel, G. L. (1977). The need for a new medical model: A challenge for biomedicine. *Science, 196,* 129–136.

Engel, G. L. (1980). The clincial application of the biopsychosocial model. *American Journal of Psychiatry, 137,* 535–544.

Engle, R. W. (1994). Memory. In R. J. Sternberg (Ed.), *Encyclopedia of intelligence* (Vol. 2, pp. 700–704). New York: Macmillan.

Enna, S. J., & DeFranz, J. F. (1980). Glycine, GABA and benzodiazepine receptors. In S. J. Enna & H. I. Yamamura (Eds.), *Neurotransmitter receptors* (Part 1). London: Chapman & Hall.

Ennis, R. H. (1987). A taxonomy of critical thinking dispositions and abilities. In J. B. Baron & R. J. Sternberg (Eds.), *Teaching thinking skills: Theory and practice (A series of books in psychology)* (pp. 9–26). New York: Freeman.

Entwistle, D. R., & Baker, D. P. (1983). Gender and young children's expectations for performance in arithmetic. *Developmental Psychology, 19,* 200–209.

Epstein, R. (1997). Folk wisdom. *Psychology Today, 30,* 46–50.

Epstein, S. (1992). Coping ability, negative self-evaluation, and overgeneralization: Experiment and theory. *Journal of Personality and Social Psychology, 62,* 826–836.

Erdberg, P. (1990). Rorschach assessment. In G. Goldstein & M. Hersen (Eds.), *Psychological assessment* (2nd ed.). New York: Pergamon.

Erickson, M. A., & Kruschke, J. K. (1998). Rules and exemplars in category learning. *Journal of Experimental Psychology: General, 127*(2), 107–140.

Erickson, M. A., & Kruschke, J. K. (1998). Rules and exemplars in category learning. *Journal of Experimental Psychology: General, 127,* 107–140.

Ericsson, K. A. (1996). *The road to excellence.* Mahwah, NJ: Erlbaum.

Ericsson, K. A. (1999). Expertise. In R. A. Wilson & F. C. Keil (Eds.), *The MIT encyclopedia of the cognitive sciences* (pp. 298–300). Cambridge, MA: MIT Press.

Ericsson, K. A. (2000). How experts attain and maintain superior performance: Implications for the enhancement of skilled performance in older individuals. *Journal of Aging & Physical Activity, 8,* 366–372.

Ericsson, K. A. (2002). Attaining excellence through deliberate practice: Insights from the study of expert performance. In M. Ferrari (Ed.), *The pursuit of excellence through education.* Mahwah, NJ: Erlbaum.

Ericsson, K. A., Chase, W. G., & Faloon, S. (1980). Acquisition of a memory skill. *Science, 208,* 1181–1182.

Ericsson, K. A., Krampe, R. T., & Tesch-Römer, C. (1993). The role of deliberate practice in the acquisition of expert performance. *Psychological Review, 100,* 363–406.

Erikson, E. H. (1950). *Childhood and society.* New York: Norton.

Erikson, E. H. (1968). *Identity, youth, and crisis.* New York: Norton.

Erim, Y., & Senf, W. (2002). Psychotherapy for minority patients: Cross cultural affairs in psychotherapy. *Psychotherapeut., 47,* 336–346.

Eron, L., Huesmann, R., Spindler, A., Guerra, N., Henry, D., & Tolan, P. (2002). A cognitive-ecological approach to preventing aggression in urban settings: Initial outcomes for high-risk children. *Journal of Consulting & Clinical Psychology, 70,* 179–194.

Estes, W. K. (1982). Learning, memory, and intelligence. In R. J. Sternberg (Ed.), *Handbook of intelligence* (pp. 170–224). New York: Cambridge University Press.

Estes, W. K. (1994). *Classification and cognition.* Oxford, UK: Oxford University Press.

Estrada, M., Brown, J., & Lee, F. (1995). Who gets the credit? Perceptions of idiosyncrasy credit in work groups. *Small Group Research, 26,* 56–76.

Etcoff, N. L., Ekman, P., Magee, J. J., & Frank, M. G. (2000). Lie detection and language comprehension. *Nature, 405*(6783), 139.

Evans, G. W., & Lepore, S. J. (1993). Household crowding and social support: A quasiexperimental analysis. *Journal of Personality and Social Psychology, 65,* 308–316.

Evans, J. St. B. T., & Over, D. E. (1996). Rationality in the selection task: Epistemic utility versus uncertainty reduction. *Psychological Review, 103,* 356–363.

Ewart, C. K., & Kolodner, K. B. (1994). Negative affect, gender, and expressive style predict elevated ambulatory blood pressure in adolescents. *Journal of Personality and Social Psychology, 66,* 596–605.

Exline, R. V. (1962). Need affiliation and initial communication behavior in problem solving groups characterized by low interpersonal visibility. *Psychological Reports, 10,* 405–411.

Exner, J. E. Jr. (1974). *The Rorschach: A comprehensive system* (Vol. 1). New York: Wiley.

Exner, J. E. Jr. (1978). *The Rorschach: A comprehensive system* (Vol. 2). *Current research and advanced interpretation.* New York: Wiley.

Exner, J. E. Jr. (1985). *The Rorschach: A comprehensive system* (Vol. 1, 2nd ed.). New York: Wiley.

Exner, J. E. Jr. (1999). The Rorschach: Measurement concepts and issues of validity. In S. E. Embretson & S. L. Hershberger (Eds.), *The new rules of measurement: What every psychologist and educator should know* (pp. 159–183). Mahwah, NJ: Erlbaum.

Eyferth, K. (1961). Leistungen verschiedener Gruppen von Besatzungskindern in Hamburg—Weschler Intelligenztest für kinder (HAWIK). *Archiv für die gesamte Psychologie, 113,* 222–241.

Eysenck, H. (1975). *The inequality of man.* San Diego: EdITS/Educational & Industrial Testing Service.

Eysenck, H. J. (1952). *The scientific study of personality.* London: Routledge & Kegan Paul.

Eysenck, H. J. (1997). Addiction, personality and motivation. *Human Psychopharmacology, Clinical and Experimental, 12*(Suppl. 2), 79–87.

Eysenck, H. J. (Ed.). (1981). *A model for personality.* New York: Springer.

Eysenck, H. J., & Kamin, L. (1981). *The intelligence controversy: H. J. Eysenck vs. Leon Kamin.* New York: Wiley.

Fabrigar, L. R., & Petty, R. E. (1999). The role of the affective and cognitive bases of attitudes in susceptibility to affectively and cognitively based persuasion. *Personality & Social Psychology Bulletin, 25,* 363–381.

Fagan, J. F. (1984). The intelligent infant: Theoretical implications. *Intelligence, 8,* 1–9.

Fagan, J. F. (1985). A new look at infant intelligence. In D. K. Detterman (Ed.), *Current topics in human intelligence.* Vol. 1: *Research methodology.* Norwood, NJ: Ablex.

Fagan, J. F. III, & Montie, J. E. (1988). Behavioral assessment of cognitive well-being in the infant. In J. Kavanagh (Ed.), *Understanding mental retardation: Research accomplishments and new frontiers.* Baltimore: Brookes.

Faith, M. S., Matz, P. E., & Jorge, M. A. (2002). Obesity-depression associations in the population. *Journal of Psychosomatic Research, 53,* 935–942.

Fan, J., McCandliss, B. D., Sommer, T., Raz, A., & Posner, M. I. (2002). Testing the efficiency and independence of attentional networks. *Journal of Cognitive Neuroscience, 14,* 340–347.

Fanselow, M., & Lester, L. (1988). A functional behavioristic approach to aversively motivated behavior: Predatory imminence as a determinant of the topography of defensive behavior. In R. C. Bolles & M. D. Beecher (Eds.), *Evolution and learning* (pp. 185–212). Hillsdale, NJ: Erlbaum.

Fantz, R. L. (1958). Pattern vision in young infants. *Psychological Record, 8,* 43–47.

Fantz, R. L. (1961). The origin of form perception. *Scientific American, 204,* 66–72.

Farah, M. J. (1988a). Is visual imagery really visual? Overlooked evidence from neuropsychology. *Psychological Review, 95*(3), 307–317.

Farah, M. J. (1988b). The neuropsychology of mental imagery: Converging evidence from brain-damaged and normal subjects. In J. Stiles-Davis, M. Kritchevsky, & U. Bellugi (Eds.), *Spatial cognition: Brain bases and development* (pp. 33–56). Hillsdale, NJ: Erlbaum.

Farah, M. J. (1994). Neuropsychological inference with an interactive brain: A critique of the "locality" assumption. *Behavioral and Brain Sciences, 17,* 43–104.

Farah, M. J. (2001). Consciousness. In B. Rapp (Ed.), *The handbook of cognitive neuropsychology: What deficits reveal about the human mind* (pp. 159–182). Philadelphia: Psychology Press/Taylor & Francis.

Farah, M. J., Levinson, K. L., & Klein, K. L. (1995). Face perception and within category discrimination in prosopagnosia. *Neuropsychologia, 33,* 661–674.

Farah, M. J., Wilson, K. D., Drain, H. M., & Tanaka, J. R. (1995). The inverted face inversion effect in prosopagnosia: Evidence for mandatory, face-specific, perceptual mechanisms. *Vision Research, 35,* 2089–2093.

Faraone, S. V., Biederman, J., Feighner, J. A., & Monuteaux, M. C. (2000). Assessing symptoms of attention deficit hyperactivity disorder in children and adults: Which is more valid? *Journal of Consulting and Clinical Psychology, 678,* 830–842.

Fassino, S., Abbate-Daga, G., Amianto, F., Leombruni, P., Boggio, S., & Rovera, G. G. (2002). Temperament and character profile of eating disorders: A controlled study with the Temperament and Character Inventory. *International Journal of Eating Disorders, 32,* 412–425.

Faubert, J. (2002). Visual perception and aging. *Canadian Journal of Experimental Psychology, 56,* 164–176.

Faust, I. M., Johnson, P. R., & Hirsch, J. (1977a). Adipose tissue regeneration following lipectomy. *Science, 197,* 391–393.

Faust, I. M., Johnson, P. R., & Hirsch, J. (1977b). Surgical removal of adipose tissue alters feeding behavior and the development of obesity in rats. *Science, 197,* 393–396.

Fay, R. E., Turner, C. F., Klassen, A. D., & Gagnon, J. H. (1989). Prevalence and patterns of same-gender sexual contact among men. *Science, 243,* 338–348.

Fazio, R. H., & Olson, M. A. (2003). Implicit measures in social cognition research: Their meaning and uses. *Annual Review of Psychology, 54,* 297–327.

Fazio, R. H., Zanna, M. P., & Cooper, J. (1977). Dissonance and self perception: An integrative view of each theory's proper domain of application. *Journal of Experimental Social Psychology, 13,* 464–479.

Feeney, J. A., & Noller, P. (1990). Attachment style as a predictor of adult romantic relationships. *Journal of Personality and Social Psychology, 58,* 284–291.

Fein, S., Goethals, G. R., & Kassin, S. M. (1998). *Social influence and presidential debates.* Manuscript submitted for publication.

Feingold, A. (1988). Cognitive gender differences are disappearing. *American Psychologist, 43,* 95–103.

Feingold, A. (1992). Good-looking people are not what we think. *Psychological Bulletin, 111*(2), 304–341.

Feingold, R. (1988). Cognitive gender differences are disappearing. *American Psychologist, 43,* 95–103.

Feldman, D. H. (1999). The development of creativity. In R. J. Sternberg (Ed.), *Handbook of creativity* (pp. 169–186). New York: Cambridge University Press.

Fenichel, E., & Mann, T. L. (2001). Early Head Start for low-income families with infants and toddlers. *The Future of Children, 11,* 135–141.

Fenwick, P. (1987). Meditation and the EEG. In M. A. West (Ed.), *The psychology of meditation.* Oxford, UK: Clarendon Press.

Ferguson, M. J., & Bargh, J. A. (2002). Sensitivity and flexibility: Exploring the knowledge function of automatic attitudes. In L. F. Barrett & P. Salovey (Eds.), *The wisdom in feeling: Psychological processes in emotional intelligence. Emotions and social behavior* (pp. 383–405). New York: Guilford.

Fernald, A. (1985). Four-month-old infants prefer to listen to motherese. *Infant Behavior and Development, 8,* 118–195.

Fernald, A., Taeschner, T., Dunn, J., Papousek, M., De Boysson-Bardies, B., & Fukui, I. (1989). A cross-cultural study of prosodic modification in mothers' and fathers' speech to preverbal infants. *Journal of Child Language, 16,* 477–501.

Fernandez, E., & Turk, D. C. (1992). Sensory and affective components of pain: Separation and synthesis. *Psychological Bulletin, 112*(2), 205–217.

Fernandez-Ballesteros, R., Diez-Nicolas, J., Caprara, G. V., Barbaranelli, C., & Bandura, A. (2002). Determinants and structural relation of personal efficacy to collective efficacy. *Applied Psychology, 51,* 107–125.

Ferster, C. B. (1973). A functional analysis of depression. *American Psychology, 28*(110), 857–870.

Feshbach, S. (1970). Aggression. In P. H. Mussen (Ed.), *Carmichael's manual of child psychology.* New York: Wiley.

Festinger, L. (1954). A theory of social comparison processes. *Human Relations, 7,* 117–140.

Festinger, L., & Carlsmith, J. M. (1959). Cognitive consequences of forced compliance. *Journal of Abnormal and Social Psychology, 58,* 203–210.

Festinger, L., Schachter, S., & Back, K. (1950). *Social pressures in informal groups: A study of human factors in housing.* New York: Harper & Brothers.

Feuerstein, R. (1979). *The dynamic assessment of retarded performers: The learning potential assessment device, theory, instruments, and techniques.* Baltimore, MD: University Park Press.

Field, T. M. (1978). Interaction behaviors of primary versus secondary caregiver fathers. *Developmental Psychology, 14,* 183–184.

Field, T. M. (1989). Individual and maturational differences in infant expressivity. In N. Eisenberg (Ed.), *Empathy and related responses.* San Francisco: Jossey-Bass.

Field, T. M. (1990). *Infant daycare has positive effects on grade school behavior and performance.* Unpublished manuscript. University of Miami, Coral Gables, FL.

Fiese, B. H. (2001). Family matters: A systems view of family effects on children's cognitive health. In R. J. Sternberg & E. L. Grigorenko (Eds.), *Environmental effects on cognitive abilities* (pp. 39–58). Mahwah, NJ: Erlbaum.

Figlewicz, D. P., Schwartz, M. W., Seeley, R. J., Chavez, M., Baskin, D. G., Woods, S. C., & Porte, D. (1996). Endocrine regulation of food intake and body weight. *Journal of Laboratory and Clinical Medicine, 127,* 328–332.

Finger, W. J., Borduin, C. M., & Baumstark, K. E. (1992). Correlates of moral judgment development in college students. *Journal of Genetic Psychology, 153*(2), 221–223.

Fink, B., & Penton-Voak, I. (2002). Evolutionary psychology of facial attractiveness. *Current Directions in Psychological Science, 11,* 154–158.

Fiore, E. (1989). *Encounters: A psychologist reveals case studies of abductions by extraterrestrials.* New York: Doubleday.

Fiore, N. A., & Sedlacek, W. E. (1972). An empirical description of university student subcultures. *College Student Journal, 6,* 142–149.

Fischer, C. S., Hout, M., Jankowski, M. S., Lucas, S. R., Swidler, A., & Voss, K. (1996). *Inequality by design.* Princeton: Princeton University Press.

Fischer, C. T. (2002). Introduction to special issue on humanistic approaches to psychological assessment. Part II: Philosophical and theoretical approaches to humanistic psychological assessment. *Humanistic Psychologist, 30,* 178–179.

Fischer, K. W., & Grannott, N. (1995). Beyond one-dimensional change: Parallel, concurrent, socially distributed processes in learning and development. *Human Development, 38,* 302–314.

Fischetti, M., Curran, S. P., & Wessberg, H. W. (1977). Sense of timing. *Behavior Modification, 1,* 179–194.

Fischhoff, B. (1988). Judgment and decision making. In R. J. Sternberg & E. E. Smith (Eds.), *The psychology of human thought* (pp. 153–187). New York: Cambridge University Press.

Fischhoff, B. (1999). Judgment heuristics. In R. A. Wilson & F. C. Keil (Eds.), *The MIT encyclopedia of the cognitive sciences* (pp. 423–425). Cambridge, MA: MIT Press.

Fischhoff, B., Slovic, P., & Lichtenstein, S. (1977). Knowing with certainty: The appropriateness of extreme confidence. *Journal of Experimental Psychology: Human Perception and Performance, 3,* 552–564.

Fiske, S. (1995). Social cognition. In A. Tesser (Ed.), *Constructing social psychology.* New York: McGraw Hill.

Fiske, S., & Taylor, S. E. (1991). *Social cognition.* New York: McGraw-Hill.

Fitzgerald, H. E., Johnson, R. B., Van Eqeren, L. A., Castellino, D. R., Johnson, C. B., & Judge-Hawton, M. (1999). *Infancy and culture: An international review and source book.* New York: Falmer Press.

Fitzgerald, H. E., Mann, T., Cabrera, N., & Wong, M. M. (2003). Diversity in caregiving contexts. In R. M. Lerner, A. M. Easterbrooks, et al. (Eds.), *Handbook of psychology: Developmental psychology,* Vol. 6. (pp. 135-167). New York: John Wiley & Sons, Inc.

Fitzgerald, H. E., Zucker, R. A., & Yang, H.-Y. (1995). Developmental systems theory and alcoholism: Analyzing patterns of variation in high risk families. *Psychology of Addictive Behaviors, 11,* 49–58.

Fivush, R., & Hamond, N. R. (1991). Autobiographical memory across the preschool years: Toward reconceptualizing childhood memory. In R. Fivush & N. R. Hamond (Eds.), *Knowing and remembering in young children.* New York: Cambridge University Press.

Flanagan, M. B., May, J. G., & Dobie, T. G. (in press). The role of vection, eye movements and postural stability in the etiology of motion sickness. *Aviation, Space, and Environmental Medicine.*

Flanagan, M. B., May, J. G., & Dobie, T. G. (2002). Optokinetic nystagmus, vection, and motion sickness. *Aviation, Space, and Environmental Medicine, 73*(11), 1067-1073.

Flanagan, O., Hardcastle, V. G., & Nahmias, E. (2002). Is human intelligence an adaptation? Cautionary observations of biology. In R. J. Sternberg & J. C. Kaufman (Eds.), *The evolution of intelligence* (pp. 199–222). Mahwah, NJ: Erlbaum.

Flavell, J. H. (1971). Stage-related properties of cognitive development. *Cognitive Psychology, 2*, 421–453.

Flavell, J. H. (1976). Metacognitive aspects of problem solving. In L. Resnick (Ed.), *The nature of intelligence.* Hillsdale, NJ: Erlbaum.

Flavell, J. H. (1981). Cognitive monitoring. In W. P. Dickson (Ed.), *Children's oral communication skills* (pp. 35–60). New York: Academic Press.

Flavell, J. H. (1985). *Cognitive development* (2nd ed.). Englewood Cliffs, NJ: Prentice-Hall.

Flavell, J. H. (1999). Cognitive development: Children's knowledge about the mind. *Annual Review of Psychology, 50*, 21–45.

Flavell, J. H., & Wellman, H. M. (1977). Metamemory. In R. V. Kail Jr. & J. W. Hagen (Eds.), *Perspectives on the development of memory and cognition* (pp. 3–33). Hillsdale, NJ: Erlbaum.

Flavell, J. H., Flavell, E. R., & Green, F. L. (1983). Development of the appearance–reality distinction. *Cognitive Psychology, 15*, 95–120.

Flavell, J. H., Green, F. L., & Flavell, E. R. (1995). Young children's knowledge about thinking. *Monographs of the Society for Research in Child Development, 60* (1, Serial No. 243).

Flavell, J. H., Green, F. L., & Flavell, E. R. (2000). Development of children's awareness of their own thoughts. *Journal of Cognition & Development, 1*, 97–112.

Floody, O. R. (1983). Hormones and aggression in female mammals. In B. B. Svare (Ed.), *Hormones and aggressive behavior* (pp. 39–89). New York: Plenum.

Flynn, J. R. (1987). Massive IQ gains in 14 nations: What IQ tests really measure. *Psychological Bulletin, 95*, 29–51.

Fodor, J. (1994). Concepts: A potboiler. *Cognition, 50*(1–3), 95–113.

Fodor, J. A. (1975). *The language of thought.* New York: Crowell.

Fodor, J. A. (1997, May 16). Do we have it in us? (Review of Elman et al., *Rethinking innateness).* *Times Literary Supplement,* pp. 3–4.

Fogel, A. (1992). Movement and communication in human infancy: The social dynamics of development. *Human Movement Science, 11*(4), 387–423.

Folkman, S., & Lazarus, R. S. (1988). *Manual for the ways of coping questionnaire.* Palo Alto, CA: Consulting Psychologists Press.

Folkman, S., Lazarus, R. S., Gruen, R. J., & DeLongis, A. (1986). Appraisal, coping, health status, and psychological symptoms. *Journal of Personality and Social Psychology, 50*(3), 571–579.

Follett, K., & Hess, T. M. (2002). Aging, cognitive complexity, and the fundamental attribution error. *Journals of Gerontology Series B—Psychological Sciences & Social Sciences, 57B,* P312–P323.

Fontaine, K. R. (1994). Personality correlates of sexual risk-taking among men. *Personality and Individual Differences, 17*, 693–694.

Forbes, M. S. (1990). *Women who made a difference.* New York: Simon & Schuster.

Ford, C. S., & Beach, F. A. (1951). *Patterns of sexual behavior.* New York: Harper & Row.

Ford, M. E. (1994). Social intelligence. In R. J. Sternberg (Ed.), *Encyclopedia of human intelligence* (Vol. 2, pp. 974–978). New York: Macmillan.

Forgas, J. P. (1998). On being happy and mistaken: Mood effects on the fundamental attribution error. *Journal of Personality and Social Psychology, 75*, 318–331.

Forsyth, D. R. (1990). *An introduction to group dynamics.* Pacific Grove, CA: Brooks/Cole.

Forsyth, D. R. (2000). One hundred years of group research: Introduction to the special issue. *Group Dynamics: Theory, Research, & Practice, 4*, 3–6.

Forsyth, D. R., Zyzniewski, L. E., & Giammanco, C. A. (2002). Responsibility diffusion in cooperative collectives. *Personality & Social Psychology Bulletin, 28*, 54–65.

Fosse, R., Stickgold, R., & Hobson, J. A. (2001). The mind in REM sleep: Reports of emotional experience. *Sleep: Journal of Sleep & Sleep Disorders Research, 24*, 947–955.

Fottrell, E. (1983). *Case histories in psychiatry.* New York: Churchill Livingstone.

Foulkes, D. (1990). Dreaming and consciousness. *European Journal of Cognitive Psychology, 2*, 39–55.

Foulkes, D. (1996). Dream research: 1953–1993. *Sleep, 19*, 609–624.

Foulkes, D. (1999). *Children's dreaming and the development of consciousness.* Cambridge, MA: Harvard University Press.

Fox, N. A. (1989). Heart-rate variability and behavioral reactivity: Individual differences in autonomic patterning and their relation to infant and child temperament. In S. J. Reznick & J. Steven (Eds.), *Perspectives on behavioral inhibition* (pp. 177–195). Chicago: University of Chicago Press.

Frackowiak, R. S. J., Friston, C. J., Frith, C. D., Dolan, R., & Mazziotta, J. C. (Eds.). (1997). *Human brain function.* San Diego, CA: Academic Press.

Frankl, V. (1959). *From death camp to existentialism.* Boston: Beacon.

Fraser, S. (Ed.). (1995). *The bell curve wars: Race, intelligence, and the future of America.* New York: Basic Books.

Freeman, A. W., & Badcock, D. R. (1999). Visual sensitivity in the presence of a patterned background. *Journal of the Optical Society of America, 16*, 979–986.

Freeman, W. (1959). Psychosurgery. In S. Arieti (Ed.), *American handbook of psychiatry* (Vol. 2, pp. 1521–1540). New York: Basic Books.

Frei, R. L., Racicot, B., & Travagline, A. (1999). The impact of monochronic and Type A behavior patterns on research productivity and stress. *Journal of Managerial Psychology, 14*, 374–387.

Fremouw, W. J., Perczel, W. J., & Ellis, T. E. (1990). *Suicide risk: Assessment and response guidelines.* Elmsford, NY: Pergamon.

French, S. A., & Jeffery, R. W. (1994). Consequences of dieting to lose weight: Effects on physical and mental health. *Health Psychology, 13*, 195–212.

Frensch, P. A., & Buchner, A. (1999). Domain-generality versus domain-specificity in cognition. In R. J. Sternberg (Ed.), *The nature of cognition* (pp. 137–172). Cambridge, MA: MIT Press.

Freud, A. (1946). *The ego and the mechanisms of defense.* New York: International Universities Press.

Freud, S. (1949). *A general introduction to psychoanalysis.* New York: Penguin.

Freud, S. (1954). *Interpretation of dreams.* London: Allen & Unwin. (Original work published 1900)

Freud, S. (1957). Mourning and melancholia. In *Standard edition of the complete psychological works of Sigmund Freud* (Vol. 14). London: Hogarth. (Original work published 1917)

Freud, S. (1963a). *Dora: An analysis of a case of hysteria.* New York: Macmillan. (Original work published 1905)

Freud, S. (1963b). Introductory lectures on psychoanalysis. In *Standard edition of the complete psychological works of Sigmund Freud* (Vols. 15, 16). (Original work published 1917)

Freud, S. (1964a). New introductory lectures. In *Standard edition of the complete psychological works of Sigmund Freud* (Vol. 21). London: Hogarth. (Original work published 1933)

Freud, S. (1964b). Three essays on the theory of sexuality. In *Standard edition of the complete psychological works of Sigmund Freud* (Vol. 7). London: Hogarth Press—Institute of Psychological Analysis. (Original work published 1905)

Freudenheim, M. (1993, August 18). Many patients unhappy with H.M.O.'s. *New York Times,* pp. 5,16.

Frey, D., & Schulz-Hardt, S. (2001). Confirmation bias in group information seeking and its implications for decision making in administration, business and politics. In F. Butera & G. Mugny (Eds.), *Social influence in social reality: Promoting individual and social change* (pp. 53–73). Ashland, OH: Hogrefe & Huber.

Frey, K. S., & Ruble, D. N. (1987). Social comparison and self-evaluation in the classroom: Developmental changes in knowledge and function. In J. C. Masters & W. S. Smith (Eds.), *Social comparisons, social justice, and relative deprivation* (pp. 81–104). Hillsdale, NJ: Erlbaum.

Friedman, M. I. (1991). Metabolic control of calorie intake. In M. I. Friedman, M. G. Tordoff, & M. R. Kare (Eds.), *Chemical senses.* Vol. 4: *Appetite and nutrition* (pp. 19–38). New York: Marcel Dekker.

Friedman, M. I., & Stricker, E. M. (1976). The physiological psychology of hunger: A physiological perspective. *Psychological Review, 83*, 409–431.

Friedman, M., & Rosenman, R. H. (1974). *Type A behavior and your heart.* New York: Knopf.

Friedrich-Cofer, L., & Huston, A. C. (1986). Television violence and aggression: The debate continues. *Psychological Bulletin, 100*(3), 364–371.

Frost, G., Lyons, F., Bovill-Taylor, C., Carter, L., Stuttard, J., & Dornhorst, A. (2002). Intensive lifestyle intervention combined with the choice of pharmacotherapy improves weight loss and cardiac risk factors in the obese. *Journal of Human Nutrition & Dietetics, 15*, 287–295.

Frost, N. (1972). Encoding and retrieval in visual memory tasks. *Journal of Experimental Psychology, 95*, 317–326.

Fuchs, J., Levinson, R., Stoddard, R., Mullet, M., & Jones, D. (1990). Health risk factors among the Amish: Results of a survey. *Health Education Quarterly, 17*, 197–211.

Funder, D. C. (2000). Personality. *Annual Review of Psychology, 52*, 197–221.

Funder, D. C. (2001). The really, really fundamental attribution error. *Psychological Inquiry, 12*, 21–23.

Funder, D. C., & Ozer, D. J. (1983). Behavior as a function of the situation. *Journal of Personality and Social Psychology, 44*(1), 107–112.

Funder, D. C., Kolar, D. C., & Blackman, M. C. (1995). Agreement among judges of personality: Interpersonal relations, similarity, and acquaintanceship. *Journal of Personality and Social Psychology, 69*, 656–672.

Furnham, A., & Budhani, S. (2002). Sex differences in the estimated intelligence of school children. *European Journal of Personality, 16*, 201–220.

Furnham, A., & Medhurst, S. (1995). Personality correlates of academic seminar behaviour: A study of four instruments. *Personality and Individual Differences, 19*, 197–208.

Furnham, A., & Skae, E. (1997). Changes in the stereotypical portrayal of men and women in British television advertisements. *European Psychologist, 2*, 44–51.

Furumoto, L. (1980). Mary Whiton Calkins (1863–1930). *Psychology of Women Quarterly, 5*, 55–68.

Furumoto, L., & Scarborough, E. (1986). Placing women in the history of psychology: The first American women psychologists. *American Psychologist, 41*(1), 35–42.

Gabbard, G. O., Lazar, S. G., Hornberger, J., & Spiegel, D. (1997). The economic impact of psychotherapy: A review. *American Journal of Psychiatry, 154*, 147–155.

Gabrenya, W. K., Latané, B., & Wang, Y. E. (1983). Social loafing in cross-cultural perspective: Chinese in Taiwan. *Journal of Cross-Cultural Psychology, 14*, 368–384.

Gabrenya, W. K., Wang, Y. E., & Latané, B. (1985). Social loafing on an optimizing task: Cross-cultural differences among Chinese and Americans. *Journal of Cross-Cultural Psychology, 16*, 223–242.

Gabrieli, J.D.E., Desmond, J. E., Demb, J. B., Wagner, A. D., Stone, M. V., Vaidya, C. J., & Glover, G. H. (1996). Functional magnetic resonance imaging of semantic memory processes in the frontal lobes. *Psychological Science, 7*, 278–283.

Gagnon, J. H. (1973). Scripts and the coordination of sexual conduct. In J. K. Cole & R. Riensteiber (Eds.), *Nebraska Symposium on Motivation* (Vol. 21, pp. 27–59). Lincoln: University of Nebraska Press.

Gagnon, J. H., Giami, A., Michaels, S., & Colomby, P. (2001). A comparative study of the couple in the social organization of sexuality in France and the United States. *Journal of Sex Research, 38*, 24–34.

Galaburda, A. M. (1999). Dyslexia. In R. A. Wilson & F. C. Keil (Eds.), *The MIT encyclopedia of the cognitive sciences* (pp. 249–251). Cambridge, MA: MIT Press.

Galambos, N. L., & Costigan, C. L. (2003). Emotional and personality development in adolescence. In R. M. Lerner, M. A. Easterbrooks, & J. Mistry (Vol. Eds.) and I. B. Weiner (Ed.-in-Chief), *Handbook of psychology.* Vol. 6: *Developmental psychology* (pp. 351–372). New York: Wiley.

Galanter, E. (1962). Contemporary psychophysics. In R. Brown et al. (Eds.), *New directions in psychology* (Vol. 1). New York: Holt, Rinehart & Winston.

Galanter, E. (2000). Psychophysics. In A. E. Kazdin (Ed.), *Encyclopedia of psychology* (Vol. 6, pp. 443–450). Washington, DC: American Psychological Association.

Galanter, M. (1989). *Cults: Faith, healing, and coercion.* New York: Oxford University Press.

Galanter, M. (2000). A psychological perspective on cults. In J. K. Boehnlein (Ed.), *Psychiatry and religion: The convergence of mind and spirit. Issues in psychiatry* (pp. 71–83). Washington, DC: American Psychiatric Publishing.

Galanter, M. (2002). Healing through social and spiritual affiliation. *Psychiatric Services, 53*, 1072–1074.

Galef, B. G. Jr., & Whiskin, E. E. (1998). Limits on social influence on food choices of Norway rats. *Animal Behavior, 56*, 1015–1020.

Galef, B. G. Jr., Whiskin, E. E., & Bielavska, E. (1997). Interaction with demonstrator rats changes observer rats' affective responses to flavors. *Journal of Comparative Psychology, 111*, 393–398.

Galotti, K. M. (2002). *Making decisions that matter: How people face important life choices.* Mahwah, NJ : Erlbaum.

Galton, F. (1883). *Inquiry into human faculty and its development.* London: Macmillan.

Gan, S., Zillmann, D., & Mitrook, M. (1997). Stereotyping effect of Black women's sexual rap on White audiences. *Basic and Applied Social Psychology, 19*, 381–399.

Gandevia, S. C. (1996). Kinesthesia: Roles for afferent signals and motor commands. In L. B. Rowell & J. T. Shepherd (Eds.), *Handbook of physiology: Section 12. Exercise regulation and integration of multiple systems* (pp. 128–172). New York: Oxford University Press.

Gangestad, S. W., & Snyder, M. (2000). Self-monitoring: Appraisal and reappraisal. *Psychological Bulletin, 126*, 530–555.

Gangestad, S. W., & Thornhill, R. (1998). Menstrual cycle variation in women's preferences for the scent of symmetrical men. *Proceedings of the Royal Society of London, 265*, 927–933.

Gangestad, S. W., Thornhill, R., & Yeo, R. A. (1994). Facial attractiveness, developmental stability, and fluctuating asymmetry. *Ethology & Sociobiology, 15*, 73–85.

Garcia, J., & Garcia y Robertson, R. (1985). Evolution of learning mechanisms. In B. L. Hammonds (Ed.), *The master lecture series* (Vol. 4). Washington, DC: American Psychological Association.

Garcia, J., & Koelling, R. A. (1966). The relation of cue to consequence in avoidance learning. *Psychonomic Science, 4*, 123–124.

Garcia, L. D., & Khersonsky, D. (1997). "They are a lovely couple": Further examination of perceptions of couple attractiveness. *Journal of Social Behavior and Personality, 12*, 367–380.

Garcia-Madruga, J. A., Moreno, S., Carriedo, N., & Gutierrez, F. (2000). Task, premise order, and strategies in Rips's conjunction-disjunction and conditionals problems. In W. Schaeken & G. De Vooght (Eds.), *Deductive reasoning and strategies* (pp. 49–71). Mahwah, NJ: Erlbaum.

Gardner, H. (1983). *Frames of mind: The theory of multiple intelligences.* New York: Basic Books.

Gardner, H. (1993a). Intelligence and intelligences: Universal principles and differences. *Archives de Psychologie, 61*(238), 169–172.

Gardner, H. (1993b). *Multiple intelligences: The theory in practice.* New York: Basic Books.

Gardner, H. (1999). Are there additional intelligences? The case for naturalist, spiritual, and existential intelligences. In J. Kane (Ed.), *Education, information, and transformation* (pp. 111–131). Upper Saddle River, NJ: Prentice-Hall.

Garland, A. F., & Zigler, E. (1994). Adolescent suicide prevention: Current research and social policy implications. *American Psychologist, 48*, 169–182.

Garn, S. M. (1980). Human growth. *Annual Review of Anthropology, 9*, 275–292.

Garrett, M. F. (1992). Disorders of lexical selection. *Cognition, 42*, 143–180.

Garry, M., Manning, C. G., Loftus, E. F., & Sherman, S. J. (1996). Imagination inflation: Imaging a childhood event inflates confidence that it occurred. *Psychonomic Bulletin & Review, 3*, 208–214.

Gatchel, R. J., & Turk, D. C. (Eds.). (1996). *Psychological approaches to pain management: A practitioner's handbook.* New York: Guilford.

Gayan, J., & Olson, R. K. (2001). Genetic and environmental influences on orthographic and phonological skills in children with reading disabilities. *Developmental Neuropsychology, 20*, 483–507.

Gazzaniga, M. (1995). Principles of human brain organization derived from split-brain studies. *Neuron, 14*, 217–228.

Gazzaniga, M. (Ed.). (2000). *The new cognitive neurosciences* (2nd ed.). Cambridge, MA: MIT Press.

Gazzaniga, M. S. (1970). *The bisected brain.* New York: Appleton-Century-Crofts.

Gazzaniga, M. S. (1985). *The social brain: Discovering the networks of the mind*. New York: Basic Books.

Gazzaniga, M. S., & Hutsler, J. J. (1999). Hemispheric specialization. In R. A. Wilson & F. C. Keil (Eds.), *The MIT encyclopedia of the cognitive sciences* (pp. 369–372). Cambridge, MA: MIT Press.

Gazzaniga, M. S., & LeDoux, J. E. (1978). *The integrated mind*. New York: Plenum.

Gazzaniga, M. S., Ivry, R. B., & Mangun, G. R. (1998). *Cognitive neuroscience: The biology of the mind*. New York: Norton.

Ge, X., Conger, R. D., & Elder, G. H. (2001). Pubertal transition, stressful life events, and the emergence of gender differences in adolescent depressive symptoms. *Developmental Psychology, 37,* 404–417.

Geen, R. G. (1990). *Human aggression*. Stony Stratford, UK: Open University Press.

Gegenfurtner, K. R., Mayser, H., & Sharpe, L. T. (1999). Seeing movement in the dark. *Nature, 398,* 475–476.

Geiselman, R. E., Fisher, R. P., MacKinnon, P. P., & Holland, H. L. (1985). Eyewitness memory enhancement in the police interview: Cognitive retrieval mnemonics versus hypnosis. *Journal of Applied Psychology, 70,* 401–412.

Gelman, R., & Baillargeon, R. (1983). A review of some Piagetian concepts. In P. H. Mussen (Series Ed.), J. Flavell & E. Markman (Vol. Eds.), *Handbook of child psychology*. Vol. 3: *Cognitive development* (4th ed., pp. 167–230). New York: Wiley.

Gelman, R., & Gallistel, C. R. (1978). *The child's understanding of number*. Cambridge, MA: Harvard University Press.

Gelman, S. A. (1985). Children's inductive inferences from natural kind and artifact categories (Doctoral dissertation, Stanford University, 1984). *Dissertation Abstracts International, 45*(10–B), 3351–3352.

Gelman, S. A., & Kremer, K. E. (1991). Understanding natural causes: Children's explanations of how objects and their properties originate. *Child Development, 62*(2), 396–414.

Gelman, S. A., & Markman, E. M. (1987). Young children's inductions from natural kinds: The role of categories and appearances. *Child Development, 58*(6), 1532–1541.

Gelman, S. A., & Opfer, J. E. (2002). Development of the animate-inanimate distinction. In U. Goswami (Ed.), *Blackwell handbook of childhood cognitive development* (pp. 151–166). Malden, MA: Blackwell.

Gelman, S. A., & Wellman, H. M. (1991). Insides and essence: Early understandings of the non-obvious. *Cognition, 38,* 213–244.

Gentile, J. R. (2000). Learning, transfer of. In A. E. Kazdin (Ed.), *Encyclopedia of psychology* (Vol. 5, pp. 13–16). Washington, DC: American Psychological Association.

Gentner, D. (2000). Analogy. In R. A. Wilson & F. C. Keil (Eds.), *The MIT encyclopedia of the cognitive sciences* (pp. 17–20). Cambridge, MA: MIT Press.

Gentner, D., & Markman, A. B. (1997). Structure-mapping in analogy and similarity. *American Psychologist, 52,* 45–56.

George, M. S., Ring, H. A., & Costa, D. C. (1991). *Neuroactivation and neuroimaging with SPECT*. London: Springer-Verlag.

Gerrig, R. J., & Banaji, M. R. (1994). Language and thought. In R. J. Sternberg (Ed.), *Handbook of perception and cognition: Thinking and problem solving*. New York: Academic Press.

Gershon, E. S., & Nurnberger, J. I. Jr. (1995). Bipolar illness. *American Psychiatric Press Review of Psychiatry, 14,* 405–424.

Gescheider, G. A. (1997). *Psychophysics: The fundamentals* (3rd ed.). Mahwah, NJ: Erlbaum.

Gesell, A. L. (1928). *Infancy and human growth*. New York: Macmillan.

Gesell, A. L., & Ilg, F. L. (1949). *Child development*. New York: Harper.

Geyelin, M. (1994, May 15). Lawsuits over false memories face hurdles. *Wall Street Journal*, p. 10(N).

Ghirlanda, S., Jansson, L., & Enquist, M. (2002). Chickens prefer beautiful humans. *Human Nature, 13,* 383–389.

Gibbons, F. X., Benhow, C. P., & Gerrard, M. (1994). From top dog to bottom half: Social comparison strategies in response to poor performance. *Journal of Personality and Social Psychology, 67,* 638–652.

Gibbons, F. X., Lane, D. J., Gerrard, M., Reis-Bergan, M., Lautrup, C. L., Pexa, N. A., & Blanton, H. (2002). Comparison-level preferences after performance: Is downward comparison theory still useful? *Journal of Personality and Social Psychology, 83,* 865–880.

Gibbs, J. C., Arnold, K. D., Ahlborn, H. H., & Cheesman, F. L. (1984). Facilitation of sociomoral reasoning in delinquents. *Journal of Consulting and Clinical Psychology, 52,* 37–45.

Gibson, J. J. (1950). *The perception of the visual world*. Boston: Houghton Mifflin.

Gick, M. L., & Holyoak, K. J. (1980). Analogical problem solving. *Cognitive Psychology, 12,* 306–355.

Gick, M. L., & Holyoak, K. J. (1983). Schema induction and analogical transfer. *Cognitive Psychology, 15,* 1–38.

Gifford, R., & Hine, D. W. (1997). "I'm cooperative, but you're greedy": Some cognitive tendencies in a common dilemma. *Canadian Journal of Behavioural Science, 29,* 257–265.

Gigerenzer, G. (1996). On narrow norms and vague heuristics: A reply to Kahneman and Tversky. *Psychological Review, 103,* 592–596.

Gigerenzer, G. (2000). *Adaptive thinking: Rationality in the real world*. London: Oxford University Press.

Gigerenzer, G., & Goldstein, D. G. (1996). Reasoning the fast and frugal way: Models of bounded rationality. *Psychological Review, 103,* 650–669.

Gigerenzer, G., & Selten, R. (2003). Bounded rationality: The adaptive toolbox. *Psychology & Marketing, 20,* 87–92.

Gigerenzer, G., Todd, P. M., & the ABC Research Group. (1999). *Simple heuristics that make us smart*. New York: Oxford University Press.

Gilbert, E., & DeBlassie, R. (1984). Anorexia nervosa: Adolescent starvation by choice. *Adolescence, 19,* 840–846.

Gilbert, P. (2002). Evolutionary approaches to psychopathology and cognitive therapy. *Journal of Cognitive Psychotherapy, 16,* 263–294.

Gilger, J. W. (1996). How can behavioral genetic research help us understand language development and disorders? In M. L. Rice (Ed.), *Toward a genetics of language* (pp. 77–110). Mahwah, NJ: Erlbaum.

Gillam, B. (2000). Perceptual constancies. In A. E. Kazdin (Ed.), *Encyclopedia of psychology* (Vol. 6, pp. 89–93). Washington, DC: American Psychological Association.

Gillham, J. E. (Ed.). (2000). *The science of optimism and hope: Research essays in honor of Martin E. P. Seligman*. Philadelphia: Templeton Foundation Press.

Gilligan, C. (1982). *In a different voice: Psychological theory and women's development*. Cambridge, MA: Harvard University Press.

Gilligan, C., & Attanucci, J. (1988). Two moral orientations: Gender differences and similarities. *Merrill-Palmer Quarterly, 34,* 223–237.

Gilligan, C., Hamner, T., & Lyons, N. (1990). *Making connections*. Cambridge, MA: Harvard University Press.

Gilly, M. C. (1988). Sex roles in advertising: A comparison of television advertisements in Australia, Mexico, and the United States. *Journal of Marketing, 52*(2), 75–85.

Gladwin, T. (1970). *East is a big bird*. Cambridge, MA: Belknap Press.

Glass, D. C. (1977). *Behavior patterns, stress, and coronary heart disease*. Hillsdale, NJ: Erlbaum.

Glick, J. (1975). Cognitive development in cross-cultural perspective. In T. D. Horowitz (Ed.), *Review of child development research*. Chicago: University of Chicago Press.

Gloor, P. (1997). *The temporal lobe and limbic system*. New York: Oxford University Press.

Gluck, M. A. (Ed.). (1996). Computational models of hippocampal function in memory. Special issue of *Hippocampus, 6*(6).

Glucksberg, S., & Danks, J. H. (1975). *Experimental psycholinguistics*. Hillsdale, NJ: Erlbaum.

Glueck, B. C., & Stroebel, C. F. (1975). Biofeedback and meditation in the treatment of psychiatric illness. *Comprehensive Psychiatry, 16,* 302–321.

Goddard, H. H. (1917). Mental tests and immigrants. *Journal of Delinquency, 2,* 243–277.

Godden, D. R., & Baddeley, A. D. (1975). Context-dependent memory in two natural environments: On land and underwater. *British Journal of Psychology, 66,* 325–331.

Goethals, G. R., & Darley, J. M. (1977). Social comparison theory: An attributional approach. In J. M. Suls & R. L. Miller (Eds.), *Social comparison processes: Theoretical and empirical perspectives* (pp. 259–278). Washington, DC: Hemisphere.

Goff, L. M., & Roediger, H. L. (1998). Imagination inflation for action events: Repeated imaginings lead to illusory recollections. *Memory & Cognition, 26,* 20–33.

Goff, L. M., & Roediger, H. L. (1998). Imagination inflation for action events: Repeated imaginings lead to illusory recollections. *Memory & Cognition, 26,* 20–33.

Goffman, E. (1967). *Interaction ritual.* New York: Doubleday.

Golby, A. J., Gabrieli, J. D. E., Chiao, J. R., & Eberhardt, J. L. (2001). Differential responses in the fusiform region to same-race and other-race faces. *Nature Neuroscience, 4,* 845–850.

Golby, A. J., Poldrack, R. A., Brewer, J. B., Spencer, D., Desmond, J. E., Aron, A. P., & Gabrieli, J. D. E. (2001). Material-specific lateralization in the medial temporal lobe and prefrontal cortex during memory encoding. *Brain, 124,* 1841–1854.

Goldberg, L. R., & Rosolack, T. K. (1994). The Big Five factor structure as an integrative framework: An empirical comparison with Eysenck's P-E-N model. In C. F. Halverson, Jr., G. A. Kohnstamm, & R. P. Martin (Eds.), *The developing structure of temperament and personality from infancy to adulthood.* Hillsdale, NJ: Erlbaum.

Goldberg, L. R., & Saucier, G. (1995). So what do you propose we use instead? A reply to Block. *Psychological Bulletin, 117,* 221–225.

Golden, C. J., Hammecke, T., & Purisch, A. (1978). Diagnostic validity of a standardized neuropsychological battery derived from Luria's neuropsychological test. *Journal of Consulting and Clinical Psychology, 46,* 1258–1265.

Goldstein, D. G., & Gigerenzer, G. (2002). Models of ecological rationality: The recognition heuristic. *Psychological Review, 109,* 75–90.

Goldstein, W. N. (2001). Contemporary influences in psychoanalytic thinking: An overview. *Journal of Clinical Psychoanalysis, 10,* 281–292.

Goleman, D. (1995). *Emotional intelligence.* New York: Bantam.

Goleman, D. (1998). *Working with emotional intelligence.* New York: Bantam.

Gomez, T. H., Roache, J. D., & Meisch, R. A. (2002). Relative reinforcing effects of different benzodiazepine doses for rhesus monkeys. *Drug & Alcohol Dependence, 68,* 275–283.

Goodale, M. A. (2000). Perception and action. In A. E. Kazdin (Ed.), *Encyclopedia of psychology* (Vol. 6, pp. 86–89). Washington, DC: American Psychological Association.

Goodnow, J. J. (1999). Families and development. In M. Bennett (Ed.), *Developmental psychology: Achievements and prospects* (pp. 72–88). Philadelphia: Psychology Press.

Gopnik, A., & Choi, S. (1995). Names, relational words, and cognitive development in English and Korean speakers: Nouns are not always learned before verbs. In M. Tomasello & W. E. Merriman (Eds.), *Beyond names for things: Young children's acquisition of verbs* (pp. 83–90). Mahwah, NJ: Erlbaum.

Gopnik, A., Choi, S., & Baumberger, T. (1996). Cross-linguistic differences in early semantic and cognitive development. *Cognitive Development, 11,* 197–227.

Gorman, M. E. (1992). *Simulating science: Heuristics, mental models, and technoscientific thinking.* Bloomington: Indiana University Press.

Gormezano, I. (2000). Learning: Conditioning approach. In A. E. Kazdin (Ed.), *Encyclopedia of psychology* (Vol. 5, pp. 5–8). Washington, DC: American Psychological Association.

Gosselin, P., Perron, M., Legault, M., & Campanella, P. (2002). Children's and adults' knowledge of the distinction between enjoyment and nonenjoyment smiles. *Journal of Nonverbal Behavior, 26,* 83–108.

Goswami, U. (2002). Inductive and deductive reasoning. In U. Goswami (Ed.), *Blackwell handbook of childhood cognitive development* (pp. 282–302). Malden, MA: Blackwell.

Gotlib, I. H., & Robinson, L. A. (1982). Responses to depressed individuals: Discrepancies between self-report and observer-rated behavior. *Journal of Abnormal Psychology, 91,* 231–240.

Gottesman, I. I. (1991). *Schizophrenia genesis: The origins of madness.* New York: Freeman.

Gottesman, I. I. (1994). *Perils and pleasures of genetic psychopathology.* Distinguished Scientist Award address presented at the annual meeting of the American Psychological Association, Los Angeles.

Gottesman, I. I., & Reilly, J. L. (2003). Strengthening the evidence for genetic factors in schizophrenia (without abetting genetic discrimination). In M. F. Lenzenweger & J. M. Hooley (Eds.), *Principles of experimental psychopathology: Essays in honor of Brendan A. Maher* (pp. 31–44). Washington, DC: American Psychological Association.

Gottesman, I. I., McGuffin, P., & Farmer, A. E. (1987). Clinical genetics as clues to the "real" genetics of schizophrenia. *Schizophrenia Bulletin, 13,* 23–47.

Gottfried, A. E., & Gottfried, A. W. (Eds.). (1988). *Maternal employment and children's development.* New York: Plenum.

Gottman, J. M. (1979). *Marital interaction.* New York: Academic Press.

Gottman, J. M. (1983). How children become friends. *Monographs of the Society for Research in Child Development, 48*(Serial No. 201).

Gottman, J. M. (1986). The world of coordinated play: Same- and cross-sex friendship in young children. In J. M. Gottman & J. G. Parker (Eds.), *Conversations of friends: Speculations on affective development* (pp. 139–191). Cambridge, UK: Cambridge University Press.

Gottman, J. M. (1994). *Why marriages succeed or fail.* New York: Simon & Schuster.

Gottman, J. M., & Levenson, R. W. (1992). Marital processes predictive of later dissolution: Behavior, physiology, and health. *Journal of Personality and Social Psychology, 63,* 221–233.

Gottman, J. M., & Notarius, C. I. (2002). Marital research in the 20th century and a research agenda for the 21st century. *Family Process, 41,* 159–197.

Gottman, J. M., Notarius, C., Gonso, J., & Markman, H. J. (1976). *A couple's guide to communication.* Champaign, IL: Research Press.

Gottman, J., Swanson, C., & Swanson, K. (2002). A general systems theory of marriage: Nonlinear difference equation modeling of marital interaction. *Personality & Social Psychology Review, 6,* 326–340.

Gottschalk, L. A., Buchsbaum, M. S., Gillin, J. C., Wu, J. C., et al. (1991). Anxiety levels in dreams: Relation to localized cerebral glucose metabolic rate. *Brain Research, 538*(1), 107–110.

Gould, S. J. (1981). *The mismeasure of man.* New York: Norton.

Gould, S. J. (2002a). *I have landed: The end of a beginning in natural history.* New York: Harmony Books.

Gould, S. J. (2002b). *The structure of evolutionary theory.* Cambridge, MA: Harvard University Press.

Govern, J. M., & Greco, M (2002). Evidence for the "guilt by familial association" effect: Evil twins excepted. *Current Psychology: Developmental, Learning, Personality, Social, 21,* 213–219.

Graf, P. (1990). Life-span changes in implicit and explicit memory. *Bulletin of the Psychonomic Society, 28,* 353–358.

Graf, P., & Schacter, D. L. (1985). Implicit and explicit memory for new associations in normal and amnesic subjects. *Journal of Experimental Psychology: Learning, Memory, and Cognition, 11,* 501–518.

Graham, C. H., & Hsia, Y. (1954). Luminosity curves for normal and dichromatic subjects including a case of unilateral color blindness. *Science, 120,* 780.

Graham, J. R. (1990). *MMPI-2: Assessing personality and psychopathology.* New York: Oxford University Press.

Grant, E. R., & Ceci, S. J. (2000). Memory: Constructive processes. In A. E. Kazdin (Ed.), *Encyclopedia of psychology* (Vol. 5, pp. 166–169). Washington, DC: American Psychological Association.

Grant, H., & Dweck, C. S. (2001). Cross-cultural response to failure: Considering outcome attributions with different goals. In F. Salili, C.-Y. Chiu, et al. (Eds.), *Student motivation: The culture and context of learning* (pp. 203–219). New York: Plenum.

Grantham-McGregor, S., Ani, C., & Fernald, L. (2001). The role of nutrition in intellectual development. In R. J. Sternberg & E. L. Grigorenko (Eds.), *Environmental effects on cognitive abilities* (pp. 119–156). Mahwah, NJ: Erlbaum.

Gray, A. L., Bowers, K. S., & Fenz, W. D. (1970). Heart rate in anticipation of and during a negative visual hallucination. *International Journal of Clinical and Experimental Hypnosis, 18,* 41–51.

Green, D. M., & Swets, J. A. (1966). *Signal detection theory and psychophysics.* Reprint. New York: Krieger.

Greenberg, G., & Haraway, M. M. (2002). *Principles of comparative psychology.* Boston: Allyn & Bacon.

Greenberg, M., Szmukler, G., & Tantam, D. (1986). *Making sense of psychiatric cases.* New York: Oxford University Press.

Greene, J., Sommerville, R. B., Nystrom, L. E., Darley, J. M., & Cohen, J. D. (2001). An fMRI investigation of emotional engagement in moral judgment. *Science, 293,* 2105–2108.

Greene, R. L. (1987). Ethnicity and MMPI performance: A review. *Journal of Consulting and Clinical Psychology, 55,* 497–512.

Greene, S. M., Anderson, E. R., Hetherington, E. M., Forgatch, M. S., & DeGarmo, D. S. (2003). Risk and resilience after divorce. In F. Walsh (Ed.), *Normal family processes: Growing diversity and complexity* (3rd ed., pp. 96–120). New York: Guilford.

Greenfield, P. M. (1997). You can't take it with you: Why ability assessments don't cross cultures. *American Psychologist, 52,* 1115–1124.

Greenfield, P. M., & Savage-Rumbaugh, S. (1990). Grammatical combination in Pan paniscus: Processes of learning and invention in the evolution and development of language. In S. Parker & K. Gibson (Eds.), *"Language" and intelligence in monkeys and apes: Comparative developmental perspectives.* New York: Cambridge University Press.

Greenough, W. T., & Black, J. E. (2000). Learning: Molecular and cellular aspects. In A. E. Kazdin (Ed.), *Encyclopedia of psychology* (Vol. 5, pp. 3–5). Washington, DC: American Psychological Association.

Greenwald, A. G., & Banaji, M. R. (1995). Implicit social cognition: Attitudes, self-esteem, and stereotypes. *Psychological Review, 102,* 4–27.

Greenwald, A. G., Banaji, M. R., Rudman, L. A., Farnham, S. D., Nosek, B. A., & Mellott, D. S. (2002). A unified theory of implicit attitudes, stereotypes, self-esteem, and self-concept. *Psychological Review, 109,* 3–25.

Greenwald, A. G., Spangenberg, E. R., Pratkanis, A. R., & Eskenazi, J. (1991). Double-blind tests of subliminal self-help audiotapes. *Psychological Science, 2,* 119–122.

Greer, D. L. (1983). Spectator booing and the home advantage: A study of social influence in the basketball arena. *Social Psychology Quarterly, 46,* 252–261.

Gregory, R. L. (1966). *Eye and brain.* New York: World University Library.

Gregory, R. L. (1998). *Eye and brain* (5th ed.). Oxford, UK: Oxford University Press.

Gregory, R. L. (2000). Visual illusions. In A. E. Kazdin (Ed.), *Encyclopedia of psychology* (Vol. 8, pp. 193–200). Washington, DC: American Psychological Association.

Greisberg, S., & McKay, D. (2003). Neuropsychology of obsessive-compulsive disorder: A review and treatment implications. *Clinical Psychology Review, 23,* 95–117.

Greist, J. H., Jefferson, J. W., Kobak, K. A., Katzelnick, D. J., & Serline, R. C. (1995). Efficacy and tolerability of serotonin transport inhibitors in obsessive–compulsive disorder: A meta-analysis. *Archives of General Psychiatry, 21,* 53–60.

Griffin, D., & Tversky, A. (1992). The weighing of evidence and the determinants of confidence. *Cognitive Psychology, 24,* 411–435.

Griffith, D. R., Azuma, S. D., & Chasnoff, I. J. (1994). Three-year outcome of children exposed prenatally to drugs. Special section: Cocaine babies. *Journal of the American Academy of Child and Adolescent Psychiatry, 33,* 20–27.

Grigorenko, E. L. & Sternberg, R. J. (1998). Dynamic testing. *Psychological Bulletin, 24,* 75–111.

Grigorenko, E. L. (1999). Heredity versus environment as the basis of cognitive abilities. In R. J. Sternberg (Ed.), *The nature of cognition* (pp. 665–696). Cambridge, MA: MIT Press.

Grigorenko, E. L. (2000). Genes, environment, and intelligence. In R. J. Sternberg (Ed.), *Handbook of intelligence.* New York: Cambridge University Press.

Grigorenko, E. L. (2000a). Doing data analyses and writing up their results: Selected tricks and artifices. In R. J. Sternberg (Ed.), *Guide to publishing in psychology journals* (pp. 98–120). New York: Cambridge University Press.

Grigorenko, E. L. (2000b). Heritability and intelligence. In R. J. Sternberg (Ed.), *Handbook of intelligence* (pp. 53–91). New York: Cambridge University Press.

Grigorenko, E. L. (2001a). Developmental dyslexia: An update on genes, brains, and environments. *Journal of Child Psychology and Psychiatry, 42,* 91–125.

Grigorenko, E. L. (2001b). The invisible danger: The impact of ionizing radiation on cognitive development and functioning. In R. J. Sternberg & E. L. Grigorenko (Eds.), *Environmental effects on cognitive abilities* (pp. 255–283). Mahwah, NJ: Erlbaum.

Grigorenko, E. L. (2002). Other than g: The value of persistence. In R. J. Sternberg & E. L. Grigorenko (Eds.), *The general factor of intelligence: How general is it?* (pp. 299–327). Mahwah, NJ: Erlbaum.

Grigorenko, E. L., Geissler, P. W., Prince, R., Okatcha, F., Nokes, C., Kenny, D. A., Bundy, D. A., & Sternberg, R. J. (2001). The organization of Luo conceptions of intelligence: A study of implicit theories in a Kenyan village. *International Journal of Behavioral Development, 25,* 367–378.

Grigorenko, E. L., Jarvin, L., & Sternberg, R. J. (2002). School-based tests of the triarchic theory of intelligence: Three settings, three samples, three syllabi. *Contemporary Educational Psychology, 27,* 167–208.

Grigorenko, E. L., Wood, F. B., Meyer, M. D., Hart, L. A., Speed, W. C., Shuster, A., & Pauls, D. L. (1997). Susceptibility loci for distinct components of developmental dyslexia on chromosomes 6 and 15. *American Journal of Human Genetics, 60,* 27–39.

Grilo, C. M., & Pogue-Geile, M. F. (1991). The nature of environmental influences on weight and obesity: A behavior genetic analysis. *Psychological Bulletin, 110,* 520–537.

Grossman, J. B., & Kaufman, J. C. (2002). Evolutionary psychology: Promise and perils. In R. J. Sternberg & J. C. Kaufman (Eds.), *The evolution of intelligence* (pp. 9–26). Mahwah, NJ: Erlbaum.

Grossman, M. I., & Stein, I. F. (1948). Vagotomy and the hunger producing action of insulin in man. *Journal of Applied Physiology, 1,* 263–269.

Grotzer, T., & Perkins, D. (2000). Teaching intelligence. In R. J. Sternberg (Ed.), *Handbook of intelligence* (pp. 492–515). New York: Cambridge University Press.

Groves, P. M., & Rebec, G. V. (1988). *Introduction to biological psychology* (3rd ed.). Dubuque, IA: William C. Brown.

Grunhaus, L., Schreiber, S., Dolberg, O. T., Polak, D., & Dannon, P. N. (2003). A randomized controlled comparison of electroconvulsive therapy and repetitive transcranial magnetic stimulation in severe and resistant nonpsychotic major depression. *Biological Psychiatry, 53,* 324–331.

Gudjonsson, G. H., Hannesdottir, K., & Petursson, H. (1999). The relationship between amnesia and crime: The role of personality. *Personality & Individual Differences, 26,* 505–510.

Guidubaldi, J., & Duckworth, J. (2001). Divorce and children's cognitive ability. In E. L. Grigorenko & R. J. Sternberg (Eds.), *Family environment and intellectual functioning* (pp. 97–118). Mahwah, NJ: Erlbaum.

Guilford, J. P. (1950). Creativity. *American Psychologist, 5*(9), 444–454.

Gunderson, E. W., Vosburg, S. K., & Hart, C. L. (2002). Does marijuana use cause long-term cognitive deficit? *JAMA: Journal of the American Medical Association, 287,* 2652.

Gunnar, M. R. (2000). Early adversity and the development of stress reactivity and regulation. In C. A. Nelson (Ed.), *Minnesota Symposia on Child Psychology.* Vol. 31: *The effects of early adversity on neurobehavioral development* (pp. 163–200).

Gunnar, M. R., & Davis, E. P. (2003). Stress and emotion in early childhood. In R. M. Lerner, M. A. Easterbrooks, & J. Mistry (Vol. Eds.) and I. B. Weiner (Ed.-in-Chief), *Handbook of psychology.* Vol. 6: *Developmental psychology* (pp. 113–134). New York: Wiley.

Gurman, A. S., Kniskern, D. P., & Pinsoff, W. M. (1986). Research on the process and outcome of marital and family therapy. In S. L. Garfield & A. E. Bergin (Eds.), *Handbook of psychotherapy and behavior change* (3rd ed.). New York: Wiley.

Gustavson, C. R., Kelly, D. J., Sweeny, M., & Garcia. J. (1976). Prey-lithium aversions: I: Coyotes and wolves. *Behavioral Biology, 17,* 61–72.

Guttmacher Institute. (2000). *Fulfilling the promise: Public policy and U.S. family planning clinics.* New York: Author.

Guzman, A. (1971). *Analysis of curved line drawings using context and global information. Machine intelligence* (Vol. 6, pp. 325–375). Edinburgh, Scotland: Edinburgh University Press.

Gwirtsman, H. E., & Germer, R. H. (1981). Abnormalities of dexamethasone suppression test and urinary MHPG in anorexia nervosa. *American Journal of Psychiatry, 138,* 650–653.

Haefely, W. E. (1977). Synaptic pharmacology of barbiturates and benzodiazepines. *Agents and Actions, 713*, 353–359.

Haft, J. I. (1974). Cardiovascular injury induced by sympathetic catecholamines. *Progress in Cardiovascular Disease, 17*, 73.

Haier, R. J., Siegel, B., Tang, C., Abel, L., & Buchsbaum, M. S. (1992). Intelligence and changes in regional cerebral glucose metabolic rate following learning. *Intelligence, 16*(3–4), 415–426.

Haier, R. J., Chueh, D., Touchette, P., Lott, I., MacMillan, D., Sandman, C., Lacasse, L., & Sosa, E. (1995). Brain size and glucose metabolic rate in mental retardation and down syndrome. *Intelligence, 20*, 191–210.

Haier, R. J., Siegel, B. V. Jr., Nuechterlein, K. H., Hazlett, E., Wu, J. C., Paek, J., Browning, H. L., & Buchsbaum, M. S. (1988). Cortical glucose metabolic rate correlates of abstract reasoning and attention studied with positron emission tomography. *Intelligence, 12*, 199–217.

Haier, R. J., Siegel, B. V., MacLachlan, A., Soderling, E., Lottenberg, S., & Buchsbaum, M. S. (1992). Regional glucose metabolic changes after learning a complex visuospatial/motor task: A positron emission tomographic study. *Brain Research, 570*, 134–143.

Haier, R. J., Siegel, B. V., Tang, C., Abel, L., & Buchsbaum, M. S. (1992). Intelligence and changes in regional cerebral glucose metabolic rate following learning. *Intelligence, 16*, 415–426.

Haier, R. J., White, N. S., & Alkire, M. T. (in press). Individual differences in general intelligence correlate to brain function during non-reasoning tasks, *Intelligence*.

Haith, M. M. (1979). Visual cognition in early infancy. In R. B. Kearsley & I. E. Sigel (Eds.), *Infants at risk: Assessment of cognitive functioning*. Hillsdale, NJ: Erlbaum.

Haith, M. M. (1994). Visual expectations as the first step toward the development of future-oriented processes. In M. M. Haith, J. B. Benseon, R. J. Roberts, Jr., & B. F. Pennington (Eds.), *The development of future-oriented processes*. Chicago: University of Chicago Press.

Halford, G. S. (1995). Learning processes in cognitive development: A reassessment with some unexpected implications. *Child Development, 38*, 295–301.

Halford, G. S. (2002). Information-processing models of cognitive development. In U. Goswami (Ed.), *Blackwell handbook of childhood cognitive development* (pp. 555–574). Malden, MA: Blackwell.

Hall, E. T. (1966). *The hidden dimension*. New York: Doubleday.

Hall, J. A., Epstein, A. M., DeCiantis, M. L., & McNeil, B. (1993). Physician's liking for their patients: More evidence for the role of affect in medical care. *Health Psychology, 12*, 140–146.

Halpern, A. R. (1986). Memory for tune titles after organized or unorganized presentation. *American Journal of Psychology, 49*, 57–70.

Halpern, A. R. (1989). Disappearance of cognitive gender differences: What you see depends on where you look. *American Psychologist, 44*, 1156–1158.

Halpern, D. F. (1995). *Thought and knowledge: An introduction to critical thinking* (3rd ed.). Hillsdale, NJ: Erlbaum.

Halpern, D. F. (1996). *Thinking critically about critical thinking*. Mahwah, NJ: Erlbaum.

Halpern, D. F. (1997). Sex differences in intelligence. *American Psychologist, 52*, 1091–1102.

Halpern, D. F. (2000). *Sex differences in cognitive abilities* (3rd ed.). Mahwah, NJ: Erlbaum.

Hameroff, S. R. (1994). Quantum coherence in microtubules: A neural basis for emergent consciousness. *Journal of Consciousness Studies, 1*, 91–118.

Hameroff, S., & Penrose, R. (1995). Orchestrated reduction of quantum coherence in brain microtubules: A model for consciousness. In J. King & K. H. Pribram (Eds.), *Scale in conscious experience: Is the brain too important to be left to specialists to study?* (pp. 243–274). Mahwah, NJ: Erlbaum.

Hamilton, D. L., & Gifford, R. K. (1976). Illusory correlation in interpersonal perception: A cognitive basis of stereotypic judgments. *Journal of Experimental Social Psychology, 12*, 392–407.

Hamilton, D. L., & Sherman, S. J. (1996). Perceiving persons and groups. *Psychological Review, 103*, 336–355.

Hampton, J. A. (1997a). Conceptual combination: Conjunction and negation of natural concepts. *Memory & Cognition, 25*(6), 888–909.

Hampton, J. A. (1997b). Psychological representation of concepts. In M. A. Conway (Ed.), *Cognitive models of memory: Studies in cognition* (pp. 81–110). Cambridge, MA: MIT Press.

Hampton, J. A. (1999). Conceptions of concepts. In B. Kokinov (Ed.), *Perspectives in Cognitive Science, 4*, 27–38. Sofia: New Bulgarian University Press.

Han, S., & Shavitt, S. (1994). Persuasion and culture: Advertising appeals in individualistic and collectivistic societies. *Journal of Experimental Social Psychology, 30*, 326–350.

Hann, D. M., Huffman, L. C., Lederhendler, I. I., & Meinecke, D. (Eds.). (1998). *Advancing research on developmental plasticity: Integrating the behavioral science and neuroscience of mental health* (Vol. 98). Washington, DC: National Institutes of Health.

Harding, C. M., Zubin, J., & Strauss, J. S. (1992). Chronicity in schizophrenia: Revisited. *British Journal of Psychiatry, 161*(Suppl. 18), 27–37.

Harkins, S. G. (1987). Social loafing and social facilitation. *Journal of Experimental Social Psychology, 23*, 1–18.

Harkins, S. G., & Szymanski, K. (1987). Social loafing and social facilitation: New wine in old bottles. In C. Hendrick (Ed.), *Review of personality and social psychology: Group processes and intergroup relations* (Vol. 9, pp. 167–188). Beverly Hills, CA: Sage.

Harlow, H. F. (1958). The nature of love. *American Psychologist, 13*, 673–685.

Harlow, H. F. (1962). Heterosexual affectional system in monkeys. *American Psychologist, 17*, 1–9.

Harlow, H. F., & Harlow, M. K. (1965). The affectional systems. In A. M. Schrier, H. F. Harlow, & F. Stollnitz (Eds.), *Behavior of nonhuman primates* (Vol. 2, pp. 287–334). New York: Academic Press.

Harlow, H. F., & Harlow, M. K. (1966). Learning to love. *American Scientist, 54*, 244–272.

Harlow, H. F., Harlow, M. K., & Meyer, D. R. (1950). Learning motivated by a manipulation drive. *Journal of Experimental Psychology, 40*, 228–234.

Harman, G. (1995). Rationality. In E. E. Smith & D. N. Osherson (Eds.), *An invitation to cognitive science. Vol. 3: Thinking* (pp. 175–211). Cambridge, MA: MIT Press.

Harris, J. R. (1995). Where's the child's environment? A group socialization theory of development. *Psychological Review, 102*, 458–489.

Harris, M. J., Millich, R., Corbitt, E. M., Hoover, D. W., & Brady, M. (1992). Self-fulfilling effects of stigmatizing information on children's social interactions. *Journal of Personality and Social Psychology, 63*, 41–50.

Harris, T. O. (1992). Social support and unsupportive behaviors. In H. O. F. Veiel & U. Baumann (Eds.), *The meaning and measurement of social support* (pp. 171–192). New York: Hemisphere.

Harter, S. (1983). Developmental perspectives on the self-system. In P. H. Mussen (Ed.), *Handbook of child psychology* (4th ed., Vol. 4, pp. 275–385). New York: Wiley.

Harter, S. (1985). Competence as a dimension of self-evaluation: Toward a comprehensive model of self-worth. In R. Leahy (Ed.), *The development of the self* (pp. 55–118). New York: Academic Press.

Harter, S. (1990). Causes, correlates, and the functional role of global self-worth: A life-span perspective. In R. J. Sternberg & J. Kolligian, Jr. (Eds.), *Competence considered* (pp. 67–97). New Haven, CT: Yale University Press.

Harter, S. (1998). The development of self-representations. In W. Damon (Gen. Ed.) & N. Eisenberg (Vol. Ed.), *Handbook of child psychology. Vol. 3: Social, emotional, and personality development* (pp. 553–618). New York: Wiley.

Harter, S., & Pike, R. (1984). The pictorial perceived competence scale for young children. *Child Development, 55*, 1969–1982.

Hartmann, E. (1968). The 90-minute sleep–dream cycle. *Archives of General Psychiatry, 18*(3), 280–286.

Hartup, W. W. (1996). The company they keep: Friendships and their developmental significance. *Child Development, 67*, 1–13.

Hartup, W. W., & Stevens, N. (1999). Friendships and adaptation across the life span. *Current Directions in Psychological Science, 8*, 76–79.

Harwood, R. L., Scholmerich, A., & Schulze, P. A. (2000). Homogeneity and heterogeneity in cultural belief systems. In S. Harkness, C. Raeff, & C. M. Super (Eds.), *Variability in the social construction of the child* (pp. 41–58). San Francisco: Jossey-Bass.

Hasselhorn, M. (1990). The emergence of strategic knowledge activation in categorical clustering during retrieval. *Journal of Experimental Child Psychology, 50*, 59–80.

Hastings, E. H., & Hastings, P. K. (Eds.). (1982). *Index to international public opinion, 1980–81.* Westport, CT: Greenwood Press.

Hatfield, E., & Rapson, R. L. (1992). Similarity and attraction in close relationships. *Communication Monographs, 59*(2), 209–212.

Hatfield, E., & Sprecher, S. (1986). Measuring passionate love in intimate relationships. *Journal of Adolescence, 9,* 383–410.

Hatfield, E., & Walster, G. W. (1981). *A new look at love.* Reading, MA: Addison-Wesley.

Hathaway, S. R., & McKinley, J. C. (1943). *Manual for the Minnesota Multiphasic Personality Inventory.* New York: Psychological Corporation.

Hathaway, S. R., & McKinley, J. C. (1951). *The Minnesota Multiphasic Personality Inventory* (Rev. ed.). New York: Psychological Corporation.

Hathaway, S. R., & McKinley, J. C. (1983). *Minnesota Multiphasic Personality Inventory: Manual for administration and scoring.* New York: Psychological Corporation.

Hauri, P. (1994). Primary insomnia. In M. H. Kryger, T. Roth, & W. C. Dement (Eds.), *Principles and practice of sleep medicine* (2nd ed.). Philadelphia: Saunders.

Hawkins, R. D., Greene, W., & Kandel, E. R. (1998). Classical conditioning, differential conditioning, and second-order conditioning of the Aplysia gill-withdrawal reflex in a simplified mantle organ preparation. *Behavioral Neuroscience, 112,* 636–645.

Haxby, J. V., Ungerleider, L. G., Horwitz, B., Maisog, J. M., Rappaport, S. L., & Grady, C. L. (1995). Hemispheric differences in neural systems for face working memory: A PET-rCBF study. *Human Brain Mapping, 3,* 68–82.

Haxby, J. V., Ungerleider, L. G., Horwitz, B., Maisog, J. M., Rappaport, W. L., & Grady, C. L. (1996). Face encoding and recognition in the human brain. *Proceedings of the National Academy of Sciences USA, 98,* 922–927.

Haynes, S. G., & Matthews, K. A. (1988). Review and methodological critique of recent studies on Type A behavior and cardiovascular disease. *Annals of Behavioral Medicine, 10,* 47–59.

Hazan, C., & Shaver, P. (1987). Romantic love conceptualized as an attachment process. *Journal of Personality and Social Psychology, 52,* 511–524.

Hazan, C., & Shaver, P. (1994). Attachment as an organizational framework for research or close relationship. *Psychological Inquiry, 5,* 1–22.

Heaps, C., & Nash, M. (1999). Individual differences in imagination inflation. *Psychonomic Bulletin & Review, 6,* 313–318.

Heath, S. B., & McLaughlin, M. W. (Eds.). (1993). *Identity and inner-city youth.* New York: Teachers College Press.

Heesacker, M., Samson, A. W., & Shir, J. L. (2000). Assessment of disordered eating by Israeli and American college women. *College Student Journal, 34,* 572–584.

Hegel, G.W.F. (1931). *The phenomenology of mind* (2nd ed., J. B. Baillie, Trans.). London: Allen & Unwin. (Original work published 1807)

Heider, F. (1958). *The psychology of interpersonal relations.* New York: Wiley.

Heilbrun, A. B., & Witt, N. (1990). Distorted body image as a risk factor in anorexia nervosa: Replication and clarification. *Psychological Reports, 66,* 407–416.

Heimpel, S. A., Wood, J. V., Marshall, M. A., & Brown, J. D. (2002). Do people with low self-esteem really want to feel better? Self-esteem differences in motivation to repair negative moods. *Journal of Personality and Social Psychology, 82,* 128–147.

Heine, S. J., Kitayama, S., Lehman, D. R., Takata, T., Ide, E., Leung, C., & Matsumoto, H. (2001). Divergent consequences of success and failure in Japan and North America: An investigation of self-improving motivations and malleable selves. *Journal of Personality and Social Psychology, 81,* 599–615.

Heinrichs, R. W. (1993). Schizophrenia and the brain: Conditions for a neuropsychology of madness. *American Psychologist, 48,* 221–233.

Heinrichs, R. W. (2001). *In search of madness: Schizophrenia and neuroscience.* New York: Oxford University Press.

Heinrichs, R. W., & Zakzanis, K. K. (1998). Neurocognitive deficit in schizophrenia: A quantitative review of the evidence. *Neuropsychology, 12,* 426–445.

Hellige, J. B. (1993). *Hemispheric asymmetry.* Cambridge, MA: Harvard University Press.

Hellige, J. B. (1995). Hemispheric asymmetry for components of visual information processing. In R. J. Davidson & K. Hugdahl (Eds.), *Brain asymmetry.* Cambridge, MA: MIT Press.

Helmers, K. F., & Krantz, D. S. (1996). Defensive hostility, gender and cardiovascular levels and responses to stress. *Annals of Behavioral Medicine, 18,* 246–254.

Helmes, E., & Reddon, J. R. (1993). A perspective on developments in assessing psychopathology: A critical review of the MMPI and MMPI-2. *Psychological Bulletin, 113*(3), 453–471.

Helmholtz, H. L. F. von. (1930). *The sensations of tone* (A. J. Ellis, Trans.). New York: Longmans, Green. (Original work published 1863)

Helmholtz, H. L. F. von. (1962). *Treatise on physiological optics* (3rd ed., J. P. C. Southall, Ed. and Trans.). New York: Dover. (Original work published 1909)

Helson, H. (1964). *Adaptation level theory: An experimental and systematic approach to behavior.* New York: Harper.

Helwig, C. C. (1995). Adolescents' and young adults' conceptions of civil liberties: Freedom of speech and religion. *Child Development, 66,* 152–166.

Henderlong, J., & Lepper, M. R. (2002). The effects of praise on children's intrinsic motivation: A review and synthesis. *Psychological Bulletin, 128,* 774–795.

Henderson, A. S. (1992). Social support and depression. In H. O. F. Veiel & U. Baumann (Eds.), *The meaning and measurement of social support* (pp. 85–92). New York: Hemisphere.

Hendrick, C., & Hendrick, S. (1986). A theory and method of love. *Journal of Personality and Social Psychology, 50,* 392–402.

Hendrick, S. S., & Hendrick, C. (1992). *Romantic love.* Newbury Park, CA: Sage.

Hendrick, S. S., & Hendrick, C. (1997). Love and satisfaction. In R. J. Sternberg & M. Hojjat (Eds.), *Satisfaction in close relationships* (pp. 56–78). New York: Guilford.

Hendrick, S., & Hendrick, C. (2002). Love. In C. R. Snyder & S. J. Lopez (Eds.), *Handbook of positive psychology* (pp. 472–484). London: Oxford University Press.

Hennessey, B. A., & Amabile, T. M. (1988). The conditions of creativity. In R. J. Sternberg (Ed.), *The nature of creativity* (pp. 11–38). New York: Cambridge University Press.

Henning, F. (1915). *Die Grundlagen, Methoden und Ergebnisse der Temperaturmessung.* Braunschweig, Germany: Vieweg und Sohn.

Henry, D., Guerra, N., Huesmann, R., Tolan, P., VanAcker, R., & Eron, L. (2000). Normative influences on aggression in urban elementary school classrooms. *American Journal of Community Psychology, 28,* 59–81.

Henry, J. P., & Stephens, P. M. (1977). *Stress, health, and the social environment: A sociobiologic approach to medicine.* New York: Springer-Verlag.

Hensel, H. (1981). *Thermoreception and temperature regulation.* London: Academic Press.

Herbert, A. M., Overbury, O., Singh, J., & Faubert, J. (2002). Aging and bilateral symmetry detection. *Journals of Gerontology: Series B: Psychological Sciences & Social Sciences, 57,* 241–245.

Herd, J. A. (1978). Physiological correlates of coronary-prone behavior. In T. Dembroski, S. Weiss, J. Shields, S. Haynes, & M. Feinleib (Eds.), *Coronary-prone behavior.* New York: Springer.

Hergovich, A., Monshi, B., Semmler, G., & Zieglmayer, V. (2002). The effects of the presence of a dog in the classroom. *Anthrozoos, 15,* 37–50.

Hering, E. (1964). *Outlines of a theory of the light sense* (L. M. Hurvich & D. Jameson, Trans.). Cambridge, MA: Harvard University Press. (Original work published in 1878)

Herity, B., Moriarty, M., Daly, L., Dunn, J., & Bourke, G. J. (1982). The role of tobacco and alcohol in the aetiology of lung and larynx cancer. *British Journal of Cancer, 46,* 961–964.

Herman, J. L., Perry, J. C., & Van der Kolk, B. A. (1989). Childhood trauma in borderline personality disorder. *American Journal of Psychiatry, 146*(4), 490–495.

Hermelin, B., Pring, L., Buhler, M., Wolff, S., & Heaton, P. (1999). A visually impaired savant artist: Interacting perceptual and memory representations. *Journal of Child Psychology & Psychiatry & Allied Disciplines, 40,* 1129–1139.

Herrnstein, R. J, & Murray, C. (1994). *The bell curve.* New York: The Free Press.

Hetherington, A. W., & Ranson, S. W. (1940). Hypothalamic lesions and adiposity in the rat. *Anatomical Record, 78,* 149–172.

Heuch, I., Kvale, G., Jacobsen, B. K., & Bjelke, E. (1983). Use of alcohol, tobacco and coffee, and risk of pancreatic cancer. *British Journal of Cancer, 48,* 637–643.

Hewitt, C. (1998). Homosexual demography: Implications for the spread of AIDS. *Journal of Sex Research, 35,* 390–397.

Heyduk, R. G., & Bahrick, L. E. (1977). Complexity, response competition, and preference implications for affective consequences of repeated exposure. *Motivation and Emotion, 1,* 249–259.

Higgins, S. T., Wong, C. J., Badger, G. J., Ogden, D. E., & Dantona, R. L. (2000). Contingent reinforcement increases cocaine abstinence during outpatient treatment and 1 year of follow-up. *Journal of Consulting & Clinical Psychology, 68,* 64–72.

Hilgard, E. R. (1965). *Hypnotic susceptibility.* New York: Harcourt, Brace & World.

Hilgard, E. R. (1977). *Divided consciousness: Multiple controls in human thought and action.* New York: Wiley.

Hilgard, E. R. (1987). *Psychology in America.* Orlando, FL: Harcourt Brace Jovanovich.

Hilgard, E. R. (1992a). Dissociation and theories of hypnosis. In E. Fromm & M. R. Nash (Eds.), *Contemporary hypnosis research* (pp. 69–101). New York: Guilford.

Hilgard, E. R. (1992b). Divided consciousness and dissociation. *Consciousness & Cognition, 1,* 16–31.

Hilgard, E. R. (1994). Neodissociation theory. In S. J. Lynn & J. W. Rhue (Eds.), *Dissociation: Clinical and theoretical perspectives* (pp. 32–51). New York: Guilford.

Hinton, G. E., & Shallice, T. (1991). Lesioning an attractor network: Investigations of acquired dyslexia. *Psychological Review, 98*(1), 74–95.

Hinton, G. E., Plaut, D. C., & Shallice, T. (2000). Simulating brain damage. In G. Cohen, R. A. Johnston, et al. (Eds.), *Exploring cognition: Damaged brains and neural networks: Readings in cognitive neuropsychology and connectionist modelling* (pp. 409–421). Philadelphia: Psychology Press.

Hintzman, D. L. (1978). *The psychology of learning and memory.* San Francisco: Freeman.

Hirschfield, R. A., & Cross, C. K. (1982). Epidemiology of affective disorders. *Archives of General Psychiatry, 39,* 35–46.

Hittner, J. B. (1997). Alcohol-related outcome expectancies: Construct overview and implications for primary and secondary prevention. *Journal of Primary Prevention, 17,* 297–314.

Ho, D. Y. F. (1986). Chinese patterns of socialization. In M. H. Bond (Ed.), *The psychology of the Chinese people.* Hong Kong: Oxford University Press.

Hoagwood, K. (1997). Interpreting nullity: The Fort Bragg Experiment—a comparative success or failure? *American Psychologist, 52,* 548.

Hobfoll, S. E. (1989). Conservation of resources: A new attempt at conceptualizing stress. *American Psychologist, 44,* 513–524.

Hobson, C. J., & Delunas, L. (2001). National norms and life-event frequencies for the revised Social Readjustment Rating Scale. *International Journal of Stress Management, 8,* 299–314.

Hobson, C. J., Kamen, J., Szostek, J., Neithercut, C. M., Tiedmann, J. W., & Wojnarowicz, S. (1998). Stressful life events: A revision and update of the Social Readustment Rating Scale. *International Journal of Stress Management, 5,* 1–23.

Hobson, J. A. (1989). *Sleep.* New York: Scientific American Library.

Hobson, J. A. (2001). *The dream drugstore: Chemically altered states of consciousness.* Cambridge, MA: MIT Press.

Hobson, J. A., Pace-Schott, E. F., & Stickgold, R. (2000). Dreaming and the brain: Toward a cognitive neuroscience of conscious states. *Behavioral & Brain Sciences, 23,* 793–842, 904–1018, 1083–1121.

Hodapp, R. N. (1994). Mental retardation: Cultural-familial. In R. J. Sternberg (Ed.), *Encyclopedia of human intelligence* (Vol. 2, pp. 711–717). New York: Macmillan.

Hoebel, B. G., & Teitelbaum, G. (1966). Weight regulation in normal and hypothalamic hyperphagic rats. *Journal of Comparative and Physiological Psychology, 61,* 189–193.

Hofbauer, K. G. (2002). Molecular pathways to obesity. *International Journal of Obesity & Related Metabolic Disorders, 26*(Suppl. 2), S18–S27.

Hoff, E., & Naigles, L. (1999, July). *Fast mapping is only the beginning: Complete word learning requires multiple exposures.* Paper presented at the VIIIth International Congress for the Study of Child Language, San Sebastian, Spain.

Hoffman, C., Lau, I., & Johnson, D. R. (1986). The linguistic relativity of person cognition: An English–Chinese comparison. *Journal of Personality and Social Psychology, 51,* 1097–1105.

Hoffman, L. W. (1989). Effects of maternal employment in the two-parent family. *American Psychologist, 44,* 283–292.

Hofling, C. K., Brotzman, E., Dalrymple, S., Graves, N., & Pierce, C. (1966). An experimental study of nurse–physician relations. *Journal of Nervous and Mental Disease, 143,* 171–180.

Hogan, R. (1996). A socioanalytic perspective on the five-factor model. In J. S. Wiggins (Ed.), *The five-factor model of personality: Theoretical perspectives* (pp. 163–179). New York: Guilford.

Hogg, M. A., & Reid, S. A. (2001). Social identity, leadership, and power. In A. Y. Lee-Chai & J. A. Bargh (Eds.), *The use and abuse of power: Multiple perspectives on the causes of corruption* (pp. 159–180). Philadelphia: Psychology Press.

Holland, P. C. (1992). Occasion setting in Pavlovian conditioning. In D. L. Medin (Ed.), *The psychology of learning and motivation* (Vol. 28, pp. 69–125). San Diego, CA: Academic Press.

Hollander, E. P. (1958). Conformity, status, and idiosyncrasy credit. *Psychological Review, 65,* 117–127.

Hollander, E. P. (1985). Leadership and power. In G. Lindzey & E. Aronson (Eds.), *Handbook of social psychology* (3rd ed., Vol. 2, pp. 485–537). New York: Random House.

Hollander, E., Simeon, D., & Aronson, J. M. (1994). Anxiety disorders. In R. E. Hales, S. C. Yudofsky, & J. A. Talbott (Eds.), *The American Psychiatric Press textbook of psychiatry* (2nd ed.). Washington, DC: American Psychiatric Press.

Hollingshead, A. B., & Redlich, F. C. (1958). *Social class and mental illness.* New York: Wiley.

Hollon, S. D., & Beck, A. T. (1994). Cognitive and cognitive-behavioral therapies. In A. E. Bergin & S. L. Garfield (Eds.), *Handbook of psychotherapy and behavior change* (4th ed., pp. 428–466). New York: Wiley.

Holloway, J. D. (2003). The perils of profiling for the media. *APA Monitor, 34,* 30.

Holmboe, E. S., Wang, Y., & Brass, L. M. (2002). Long-term consequences of upper extremity peripheral neuropathy in former Vietnam prisoners of war. *Military Medicine, 167,* 736–741.

Holmes, T. H., & Rahe, R. H. (1967). The social readjustment rating scale. *Journal of Psychosomatic Research, 11,* 213–218.

Holmes, T., & Rahe, R. (1967). The social readjustment rating scale. *Journal of Psychosomatic Research, 11,* 213–218.

Holstein, C. B. (1976). Irreversible, stepwise sequence in the development of moral judgment: A longitudinal study of males and females. *Child Development, 47,* 51–61.

Holyoak, K. J. (1990). Problem solving. In D. N. Osherson & E. E. Smith (Eds.), *Thinking: An invitation to cognitive science, 3,* 117–146. Cambridge, MA: MIT Press.

Holyoak, K. J. (1995). Problem solving. In E. E. Smith & D. N. Osherson (Eds.), *An invitation to cognitive science. Vol. 3: Thinking* (pp. 267–296). Cambridge, MA: MIT Press.

Holyoak, K. J., & Thagard, P. (1995). *Mental leaps.* Cambridge, MA: MIT Press.

Honsberger, R. W., & Wilson, A. F. (1973). Transcendental meditation in treating asthma. *Respiratory Therapy: The Journal of Inhalation Technology, 3,* 79–80.

Hooker, E. (1993). Reflections of a 40-year exploration: A scientific view on homosexuality. *American Psychologist, 48*(4), 450–453.

Hoosain, R., & Salili, F. (1987). Language differences in pronunciation speed for numbers, digit span, and mathematics ability. *Psychologia: An International Journal of Psychology in the Orient, 30*(1), 34–38.

Horn, J. L. (1994). Theory of fluid and crystallized intelligence. In R. J. Sternberg (Ed.), *The encyclopedia of human intelligence* (Vol. 1, pp. 443–451). New York: Macmillan.

Horn, J. L., & Cattell, R. B. (1966). Refinement and test of the theory of fluid and crystallized ability intelligences. *Journal of Educational Psychology, 57,* 253–270.

Horn, J. L., & Hofer, S. M. (1992). Major abilities and development in the adult period. In R. J. Sternberg and C. A. Berg (Eds.), *Intellectual development* (pp. 44–99). New York: Cambridge University Press.

Horner, A. J. (1991). *Psychoanalytic object relations therapy*. New York: Jason Aronson.

Horney, K. (1937). *The neurotic personality of our time*. New York: Norton.

Horney, K. (1939). *New ways in psychoanalysis*. New York: Norton.

Horney, K. (1950). *Neurosis and human growth: The struggle toward self-realization*. New York: Norton.

Horvath, P., & Zuckerman, M. (1993). Sensation seeking, risk appraisal, and risky behavior. *Personality and Individual Differences, 14,* 41–52.

Hou, C., Miller, B. L., Cummings, J. L., Goldberg, M., Mychack, P., Bottino, V., & Benson, D. F. (2000). Artistic savants. *Neuropsychiatry, Neuropsychology, & Behavioral Neurology, 13,* 29–38.

Houpt, T. A., Boulos, Z., & Moore-Ede, M. C. (1996). Midnight-Sun: Software for determining light exposure and phase-shifting schedules during global travel. *Physiology & Behavior, 59,* 561–568.

House, J. S., & Smith, D. A. (1985). Evaluating the health effects of demanding work on and off the job. In T. F. Drury (Ed.), *Assessing physical fitness and physical activity in population-base surveys* (pp. 481–508). Hyattsville, MD: National Center for Health Statistics.

Houston, J. P. (1985). *Motivation*. New York: Macmillan.

Houston, V., & Bull, R. (1994). Do people avoid sitting next to someone who is facially disfigured? *European Journal of Social Psychology, 24,* 279–284.

Hovland, C. I., & Weiss, W. (1951). The influences of source credibility on communication effectiveness. *Public Opinion Quarterly, 15,* 635–650.

Hovland, C. I., Janis, I. L., & Kelley, H. H. (1953). *Communication and persuasion: Psychological studies of opinion change*. New Haven, CT: Yale University Press.

Howard, K. I., Kopta, S. M., Krause, M. S., & Orlinsky, D. E. (1986). The dose–effect relationship in psychotherapy. *American Psychologist, 41*(2), 159–164.

Howe, M. J. (1999). *The psychology of high abilities*. New York: New York University Press.

Howe, M. J. (2001). Why I study geniuses. *Psychologist, 14,* 294–295.

Howe, M. J., Davidson, J. W., & Sloboda, J. A. (1999). Innate talents: Reality or myth? In S. J. Ceci & W. M. Williams (Eds.), *The nature–nurture debate: The essential readings* (pp. 257–289). Malden, MA: Blackwell.

Howes, C. (1988). Peer interaction of young children. *Monographs of the Society for Research in Child Development, 53*(1, Serial No. 217).

Howes, C. (1990). Can the age of entry into childcare and the quality of childcare predict adjustment in kindergarten? *Developmental Psychology, 26,* 292–303.

Howes, C. (1999). Attachment relationships in the context of multiple caregivers. In J. Cassidy & P. R. Shaver (Eds.), *Handbook of attachment* (pp. 671–687). New York: Guilford.

Hoyert, D. L., Arias, E., Smith, B. L., Murphy, S. F., & Kochanek, K. D. (2001). Deaths: Final data for 1999. *National Vital Statistics Reports, 49*(8). Hyattsville, MD: National Center for Health Statistics.

Hubel, D. H., & Wiesel, T. N. (1979). Brain mechanisms of vision. *Scientific American, 241,* 150–162.

Huebner, R. R., & Izard, C. E. (1988). Mothers' responses to infants' facial expressions of sadness, anger, and physical distress. *Motivation and Emotion, 12,* 185–196.

Huesmann, L. R., & Miller, L. S. (1994). Long-term effects of repeated exposure to media violence in childhood. In L. R Huesmann (Ed.), *Aggressive behavior: Current perspectives* (pp. 153–186). New York: Plenum.

Huesmann, L. R., Lagerspetz, K., & Eron, L. D. (1984). Intervening variable in the TV violence-aggression relation: Evidence from two countries. *Developmental Psychology, 20,* 746–775.

Huggins, M. K., Haritos-Fatouros, M., & Zimbardo, P. G. (2002). *Violence workers: Police torturers and murderers reconstruct Brazilian atrocities*. Berkeley: University of California Press.

Hughes, J. M. (1989). *Reshaping the psychoanalytic domain: The work of Melanie Klein, W. R. D. Fairburn, and D. W. Winnicott*. Berkeley: University of California Press.

Huizink, A. C., de Medina, P. G. R., Mulder, E. J. H., Visser, G. H. A., & Buitelaar, J. K. (2000). Prenatal psychosocial and endocrinologic predictors of infant temperament. In A. C. Huizink (Ed.), *Prenatal stress and its effects on infant development* (pp. 171–200). Hoorn, Netherlands: Drukkerij van Vliet.

Hull, C. L. (1943). *Principles of behavior*. New York: Appleton-Century-Crofts.

Hull, C. L. (1952). *A behavior system: An introduction to behavior theory concerning the individual organism*. New Haven, CT: Yale University Press.

Hultsch, D. F., & Dixon, R. A. (1990). Learning and memory in aging. In J. E. Birren & K. W. Schaie (Eds.), *Handbook of the psychology of aging: The handbooks of aging* (3rd ed.). San Diego, CA: Academic Press.

Humphreys, L. G., & Stark, S. (2002). General intelligence: Measurement, correlates, and interpretations of the cultural-genetic construct. In R. J. Sternberg & E. L. Grigorenko (Eds.), *The general factor of intelligence: How general is it?* (pp. 87–116). Mahwah, NJ: Erlbaum.

Humphreys, T. P. (2001). Sexual consent in heterosexual dating relationships: Attitudes and behaviours of university students. *Dissertation Abstracts International: Section B: The Sciences & Engineering, 61*(12-B), 6760. University Microfilms International.

Hunt, E. (1999). What is a theory of thought? In R. J. Sternberg (Ed.), *The nature of cognition* (pp. 3–49). Cambridge, MA: MIT Press.

Hunt, E. B., Lunneberg, C., & Lewis, J. (1975). What does it mean to be high verbal? *Cognitive Psychology, 7,* 194–227.

Hunt, E. B., Streissguth, A. P., Kerr, B., & Olsen, H. C. (1995). Mothers' alcohol consumption during pregnancy: Effects on spatial-visual reasoning in 14-year-old children. *Psychological Science, 6,* 339–342.

Hurvich, L. M. (1981). *Color vision*. Sunderland, MA: Sinnauer Associates.

Hurvich, L., & Jameson, D. (1957). An opponent-process theory of color vision. *Psychological Review, 64,* 384–404.

Huston, A. C. (1983). Sex-typing. In P. H. Mussen (Series Ed.) & E. M. Hetherington (Vol. Ed.), *Handbook of child psychology*. Vol. 4: *Socialization, personality, and social development* (4th ed., pp. 387–467). New York: Wiley.

Huston, A. C., Carpenter, C. J., Atwater, J. B., & Johnson, L. M. (1986). Gender, adult structuring of activities, and social behavior in middle childhood. *Child Development, 57*(5), 1200–1209.

Huston, T. L., & Levinger, G. (1978). Interpersonal attraction and relationships. *Annual Review of Psychology, 29,* 115–156.

Huttenlocher, J., Newcombe, N., & Sandberg, E. H. (1994). The coding of spatial location in young children. *Cognitive Psychology, 27,* 115–147.

Hwang, K. K. (1981). Perception of life events: The application of nonmetric multidimensional scaling. *Acta Psychologica Taiwanica, 22,* 22–32.

Ingram, D. (1999). Phonological acquisition. In M. Barrett (Ed.), *The development of language* (pp. 73–98). East Sussex, UK: Psychology Press.

Inhelder, B., & Piaget, J. (1958). *The growth of logical thinking from childhood to adolescence*. New York: Basic Books.

Innes, F. K. (2000). The influence of an animal on normally developing children's ideas about helping children with disabilities. *Dissertation Abstracts International Section A: Humanities & Social Sciences, 60*(11-A), 3897.

Inoue, S., Uchizono, K., & Nagasaki, H. (1982). Endogenous sleep-promoting factors. *Trends in Neurosciences, 5,* 218–220.

Insell, T. R. (1986). The neurobiology of anxiety. In B. F. Shaw, Z. V. Segal, T. M. Wallis, & F. E. Cashman (Eds.), *Anxiety disorders*. New York: Plenum.

Insko, C. A. (1965). Verbal reinforcement of attitude. *Journal of Personality and Social Psychology, 21,* 621–623.

Intelligence and its measurement: A symposium. (1921). *Journal of Educational Psychology, 12,* 123–147, 195–216, 271–275.

Ironson, G., Synings, C., Schneiderman, N., Baum, A., Rodriguez, M., Greenwood, D., et al. (1997). Posttraumatic stress symptoms, intrusive thoughts, loss, and immune function after Hurricane Andrew. *Psychosomatic Medicine, 59,* 128–141.

Islam, M. R., & Hewstone, M. (1993). Intergroup attributions and affective consequences in majority and minority groups. *Journal of Personality and Social Psychology, 64,* 936–950.

Iverson, P., Kuhl, P. K., Akahane-Yamada, R., Diesch, E., Tohkura, Y., Kettermann, A., Siebert, C., & Iverson, P. (2003). A perceptual interference account of acquisition difficulties for non-native phonemes. *Cognition, 87*, B47–B57.

Ivey, A. E., Ivey, M. B., & Simek-Morgan, L. (1993). *Counseling and psychotherapy: A multicultural perspective.* Boston: Allyn & Bacon.

Iwanaga, S., & Namatame, A. (2002). The complexity of collective decision. *Nonlinear Dynamics, Psychology, & Life Sciences, 6*, 137–158.

Iyengar, S. S., & Lepper, M. R. (2000). When choice is demotivating: Can one desire too much of a good thing? *Journal of Personality and Social Psychology, 79*, 995–1006.

Izard, C. E. (1977). *Human emotions.* New York: Plenum.

Izard, C. E. (1989). The structure and functions of emotions: Implications for cognition, motivation, and personality. In I. S. Cohen (Ed.), *The G. Stanley Hall lecture series* (Vol. 9, pp. 39–73). Washington, DC: American Psychological Association.

Izard, C. E. (1991). *The psychology of emotions.* New York: Plenum.

Izard, C. E. (1993). Four systems for emotional activation: Cognitive and noncognitive development. *Psychological Review, 100*, 69–90.

Izard, C. E. (1994). Innate and universal facial expressions: Evidence from developmental and cross-cultural research. *Psychological Bulletin, 115*, 288–299.

Izard, C. E., Fantauzzo, C. A., Castle, J. M., Haynes, O. M., & Slomine, B. S. (1995). *The morphological stability and social validity of infants' facial expression.* Unpublished manuscript, University of Delaware.

Izard, C. E., Kagan, J., & Zajonc, R. B. (1984). *Emotions, cognition, and behavior.* New York: Cambridge University Press.

Jackendoff, R. (1991). Parts and boundaries. *Cognition, 41*, 9–45.

Jacob, T., Krahn, G. L., & Leonard, K. (1991). Parent-child interactions in families with alcoholic fathers. *Journal of Consulting & Clinical Psychology, 59*, 176–181.

Jacobs, B. L. (1987). How hallucinogenic drugs work. *American Scientist, 75*, 386–392.

Jacobs, B. L., & Trulson, M. E. (1979). Mechanisms of action of LSD. *American Scientist, 67*, 396–404.

Jacobson, J. L., Jacobson, S. W., & Humphrey, H. E. (1990). Effects of exposure to PCBs and related compounds on growth and activity in children. *Neurotoxicology & Teratology, 12*(4), 319–326.

Jacobson, J. L., Jacobson, S. W., Padgett, R. J., Brunitt, G. A., & Billings, R. L. (1992). Effects of prenatal PCB exposure on cognitive processing efficiency and sustained attention. *Developmental Psychology, 28*(2), 297–306.

Jacoby, R., & Glauberman, N. (1995). *The bell curve debate: History, documents, opinions.* New York: Times Books.

Jakicic, J. M., Clark, K., Coleman, E., Donnelly, J. E., Foreyt, J., Melanson, E., Volek, J., & Volpe, S. L. (2001). Appropriate intervention strategies for weight loss and prevention of weight regain for adults. *Medicine & Science in Sports & Exercise, 33*, 2145–2156.

Jakicic, J. M., Wing, R. R., & Winters-Hart, C. (2002). Relationship of physical activity to eating behaviors and weight loss in women. *Medicine & Science in Sports & Exercise, 34*, 1653–1659.

James, W. (1890a). *Psychology.* New York: Holt.

James, W. (1890b). *Principles of psychology* (Vol. 1). New York: Holt. (Reprinted 1983, Cambridge, MA: Harvard University Press)

Jamison, K. R. (2000). Suicide and bipolar disorder. *Journal of Clinical Psychiatry, 61*(Suppl. 9), 47–51.

Janis, I. L. (1958). *Psychological stress.* New York: Wiley.

Janis, I. L. (1972). *Victims of groupthink.* Boston: Houghton Mifflin.

Janis, I. L., Kaye, D., & Kirschner, P. (1965). Facilitating effects of "eating while reading" on responsiveness to persuasive communications. *Journal of Personality and Social Psychology, 1*, 17–27.

Janowitz, H. D. (1967). Role of gastrointestinal tract in the regulation of food intake. In C. F. Code (Ed.), *Handbook of physiology: Alimentary canal 1.* Washington, DC: American Physiological Society.

Jenkins, C. D., Zyzanski, S. J., & Rosenman, R. H. (1979). *Jenkins Activity Survey.* Cleveland, OH: Psychological Corporation.

Jensen, A. R. (1997). The puzzle of nongenetic variance. In R. J. Sternberg & E. L. Grigorenko (Eds.), *Intelligence, heredity, and*

environment (pp. 42–88.) New York: Cambridge University Press.

Jensen, A. R. (1998). *The g factor.* Westport, CT: Praeger.

Jensen, A. R. (2002). Psychometric g: Definition and substantiation. In R. J. Sternberg & E. L. Grigorenko (Eds.), *The general factor of intelligence: How general is it?* (pp. 39–54). Mahwah, NJ: Erlbaum.

Jerald, J. (2000). Early Head Start. *National Head Start Bulletin, 69*, 1–3.

Jerison, H. (2000). The evolution of intelligence. In R. J. Sternberg (Ed.), *Handbook of intelligence* (pp. 216–244). New York: Cambridge University Press.

Jerison, H. J. (2002). On theory in comparative psychology. In R. J. Sternberg & J. C. Kaufman (Eds.), *The evolution of intelligence* (pp. 251–288). Mahwah, NJ: Erlbaum.

Jha, A. P., Kroll, N. E. A., Baynes, K., & Gazzaniga, M. S. (1997). Memory encoding following complete callostomy. *Journal of Cognitive Neuroscience, 9*, 143–159.

Ji, L.-J., Nisbett, R. E., & Su, Y. (2001). Culture, change, and prediction. *Psychological Science, 12*, 450–456.

Jia, G., & Aaronson, D. (1999). Age differences in second language acquisition: The dominant language switch and maintenance hypothesis. In A. Greenhill, H. Littlefield, & C. Tano (Eds.), *Proceedings of the 23rd Annual Boston University Conference on Language Development* (pp. 301–312). Somerville, MA: Cascadilla Press.

Johanssen, G. (1975, June). Visual motion perception. *Scientific American*, 76–87.

Johnson, J. A., & Osterdorf, F. (1993). Clarification of the five-factor model with the abridged Big Five dimensional circumflex. *Journal of Personality and Social Psychology, 65*, 563–576.

Johnson, J. E. (1984). Psychological interventions and coping with surgery. In A. Baum, S. E. Taylor, & J. E. Singer (Eds.), *Handbook of psychology and health* (Vol. 4, pp. 167–188). Hillsdale, NJ: Erlbaum.

Johnson, J. E., Lauver, D. R., & Nail, L. M. (1989). Process of coping with radiation therapy. *Journal of Consulting and Clinical Psychology, 57*, 358–364.

Johnson, M. H. (1997). *Developmental cognitive neuroscience: An introduction.* Oxford, UK: Oxford University Press.

Johnson, M. H. (1999). Developmental cognitive neuroscience. In M. Bennett (Ed.), *Developmental psychology* (pp. 147–164). Philadelphia: Psychology Press.

Johnson, M. K. (1996). Fact, fantasy, and public policy. In D. J. Herrmann, C. McEvoy, C. Hertzog, P. Hertel, & M. K. Johnson (Eds.), *Basic and applied memory research: Theory in context* (Vol. 1). Mahwah, NJ: Erlbaum.

Johnson, M. K., & Raye, C. L. (1998). False memories and confabulation. *Trends in Cognitive Sciences, 2*, 137–145.

Johnson, M. K., Hashtroudi, S., & Lindsay, D. S. (1993). Source monitoring. *Psychological Bulletin, 114*, 3–28.

Johnson-Laird, P. N. (1988). Freedom and constraint in creativity. In R. J. Sternberg (Ed.), *The nature of creativity* (pp. 202–219). New York: Cambridge University Press.

Johnson-Laird, P. N. (1997). Rules and illusions: A critical study of Rips's *The psychology of proof. Minds and Machines, 7*, 387–407.

Johnson-Laird, P. N. (1999). Formal rules versus mental models in reasoning. In R. J. Sternberg (Ed.), *The nature of cognition* (pp. 587–624). Cambridge, MA: MIT Press.

Johnson-Laird, P. N. (2000). Thinking: Reasoning. In A. Kazdin (Ed.), *Encyclopedia of psychology* (Vol. 8, pp. 75–79). Washington, DC: American Psychological Association.

Johnson-Laird, P. N., & Byrne, R. M. J. (1991). *Deduction.* Hillsdale, NJ: Erlbaum.

Johnson-Laird, P. N., & Savary, F. (1999). Illusory inference: A novel class of erroneous deductions. *Cognition, 71*, 191–229.

Johnson-Laird, P. N., & Steedman, M. (1978). The psychology of syllogisms. *Cognitive Psychology, 10*, 64–99.

Johnson-Laird, P. N., Legrenzi, P., Girotto, V., Legrenzi, M. S., & Caverni, J. P. (1999). Naïve probability: A model theory of extensional reasoning. *Psychological Review, 106*, 62–88.

Johnston, T. D., & Pietrewica, A. T. (Eds.). (1985). *Issues in the ecological study of learning.* Hillsdale, NJ: Erlbaum.

Jonas, E., Schulz-Hardt, S., Frey, D., & Thelen, N. (2001). Confirmation bias in sequential information search after preliminary decisions: An expansion of dissonance theoretical research on selective exposure to information. *Journal of Personality and Social Psychology, 80,* 557–571.

Jones, B. E. (1994). Basic mechanisms of sleep-wake states. In M. H. Kryger, T. Roth, & W. C. Dement (Eds.), *Principles and practice of sleep medicine* (2nd ed.). Philadelphia: Saunders.

Jones, E. E., & Davis, K. E. (1965). From acts to dispositions: The attribution process in person perception. In L. Berkowitz (Ed.), *Advances in experimental social psychology* (Vol. 2). New York: Academic Press.

Jones, E. E., & Nisbett, R. (1971). *The actor and the observer: Divergent perceptions of the causes of behavior.* Morristown, NJ: General Learning Press.

Jones, L. A. (2000). Kinesthesis. In A. E. Kazdin (Ed.), *Encyclopedia of psychology* (Vol. 4, pp. 441–443). Washington, DC: American Psychological Association.

Joslyn, S., Loftus, E., McNoughton, A., & Powers, J. (2001). Memory for memory. *Memory & Cognition, 29,* 789–797.

Jost, J. T., & Banaji, M. R. (1994). The role of stereotyping in system justification and the production of false consciousness. *British Journal of Social Psychology, 33,* 1–27.

Judd, C. M., & Park, B. (1993). Definition and assessment of accuracy in social stereotypes. *Psychological Review, 100,* 109–128.

Judd, C. M., Park, B., Brauer, M., Ryan, C. S., & Kraus, S. (1995). Stereotypes and ethnocentrism: Diverging interethnic perceptions of African American and White American youth. *Journal of Personality and Social Psychology, 69,* 460–481.

Juel-Nielsen, N. (1965). Individual and environment: A psychiatric-psychological investigation of monozygous twins reared apart. *Acta Psychiatrica et Neurologica Scandinavica* (Monograph Supplement, 183).

Julien, R. M. (1995). *A primer of drug action.* New York: Freeman.

Jurkovac, T. (1985). *Collegiate basketball players' perceptions of the home advantage.* Unpublished master's thesis, Bowling Green State University, Bowling Green, OH.

Jusczyk, P. W. (1997). *The discovery of spoken language.* Cambridge, MA: MIT Press.

Kaemingk, K. L., Mulvaney, S., & Halverson, P. T. (2003). Learning following prenatal alcohol exposure: Performance on verbal and visual multitrial tasks. *Archives of Clinical Neuropsychology, 18,* 33–47.

Kagan, J. (1981). *The second year: The emergence of self-awareness.* Cambridge, MA: Harvard University Press.

Kagan, J. (1982). *Psychological research on the infant: An evaluative summary.* New York: W. T. Grant Foundation.

Kagan, J. (1984). *The nature of the child.* New York: Basic Books.

Kagan, J. (1986). *Psychological research on the human infant: An evaluative summary.* New York: W. T. Grant Foundation.

Kagan, J. (1994). *Galen's prophecy: Temperament in human nature.* New York: Basic Books.

Kagan, J. (1998). Biology and the child. In W. Damon (Series Ed.) and N. Eisenberg (Vol. Ed.), *Handbook of child psychology.* Vol. 3: *Social, emotional, and personality development* (5th ed., pp. 177–235). New York: Wiley.

Kagan, J. (2001). Temperamental contributions to affective and behavioral profiles in childhood. In S. G. Hoffman & P. Di Bartolo (Eds.), *Social phobia and social anxiety: An integration.* Boston: Allyn & Bacon.

Kagan, J. (2003). Biology, context and developmental inquiry. *Annual Review of Psychology, 54,* 1–23.

Kagan, J., & Moss, H. A. (1962). *From birth to maturity.* New York: Wiley.

Kagan, J., Kearsley, R., & Zelazo P. (1978). *Infancy: Its place in human development.* Cambridge, MA: Harvard University Press.

Kagan, J., Reznick, R. J., Clarke, C., Snidman, N., & Garcia-Coll, C. (1984). Behavioral inhibition to the unfamiliar. *Child Development, 55,* 2212–2225.

Kagan, J., Snidman, N., & Arcus, D. (1998). Childhood derivatives of high and low reactivity in infancy. *Child Development, 69,* 1483–1493.

Kahneman, D. (1973). *Attention and effort.* Englewood Cliffs, NJ: Prentice-Hall.

Kahneman, D., & Tversky, A. (1971). Subjective probability: A judgment of representativeness. *Cognitive Psychology, 3,* 430–454.

Kahneman, D., & Tversky, A. (1979). Intuitive prediction: Biases and corrective procedures. *Management Science, 12,* 313–327.

Kahneman, D., & Tversky, A. (1996). On the reality of cognitive illusions. *Psychological Review, 103,* 582–591.

Kail, R. V. (1990). *The development of memory in children* (3rd ed.). New York: Freeman.

Kaiser, P. K., & Boynton, R. M. (1996). *Human color vision* (2nd ed.). Washington, DC: Optical Society of America.

Kalin, N. H. (1993, May). The neurobiology of fear. *Scientific American,* 94–101.

Kalin, N. H., & Shelton, S. E. (1989). Defensive behaviors in infant rhesus monkeys: Environmental cues and neurochemical regulation. *Science, 243,* 1718–1721.

Kalin, N. H., Shelton, S. E., Davidson, R. J., & Kelley, A. E. (2001). The primate amygdala mediates acute fear but not the behavioral and physiological components of anxious temperament. *Journal of Neuroscience, 21,* 2067–2074.

Kalmar, D. A., & Sternberg, R. J. (1988). Theory knitting: An integrative approach to theory development. *Philosophical Psychology, 1,* 153–170.

Kalsner, S. (1990). Heteroreceptors, autoreceptors, and other terminal sites. *Annals of the New York Academy of Sciences, 604,* 1–6.

Kamin, L. J. (1969). Predictability, surprise, attention, and conditioning. In B. A. Campbell & R. M. Church (Eds.), *Punishment and aversive behavior* (pp. 279–296). New York: Appleton-Century-Crofts.

Kamins, M., & Dweck, C. S. (1999). Person vs. process praise and criticism: Implications for contingent self-worth and coping. *Developmental Psychology, 35,* 835–847.

Kandel, E. (1991). Cellular mechanisms of learning and the biological basis of individuality. In E. R. Kandel, J. H. Schwartz, & T. M. Jessell (Eds.), *Principles of neural science* (3rd ed.). New York: Elsevier.

Kane, J., Honigfeld, G., Singer, J., Meltzer, H., et al. (1988). Clozapine for treatment of resistant schizophrenics. *Archives of General Psychiatry, 45,* 789–796.

Kant, I. (1987). The critique of pure reason. In *Great books of the Western world: Vol. 42. Kant.* Chicago: Encyclopaedia Britannica.

Kaplan, S. L., Randolph, S. W., & Lemli, J. M. (1991). *Treatment outcomes in the reduction of fear: A meta-analysis.* Paper presented at the annual meeting of the American Psychological Association, San Francisco.

Karau, S. J., & Williams, K. D. (1993). Social loafing: A meta-analytic review and theoretical integration. *Journal of Personality and Social Psychology, 65,* 681–706.

Karau, S. J., & Williams, K. D. (1997). The effects of group cohesiveness on social loafing and social compensation. *Group Dynamics, 1,* 156–168.

Karlin, R. A., & Orne, M. T. (1997). Hypnosis and the iatrogenic creation of memory: On the need for a per se exclusion of testimony based on hypnotically influenced recall. *Cultic Studies Journal, 14,* 172–206.

Karno, M. P., Beutler, L. E., & Harwood, T. M. (2002). Interactions between psychotherapy procedures and patient attributes that predict alcohol treatment effectiveness: A preliminary report. *Addictive Behaviors, 27,* 779–797.

Kasper, S., & Resinger, E. (2003). Cognitive effects and antipsychotic treatment. *Psychoneuroendocrinology, 28* (Suppl. 1), 27–38.

Katz, D. (1960). The functional approach to the study of attitudes. *Public Opinion Quarterly, 24,* 163–204.

Katz, D., & Stotland, E. (1959). A preliminary statement to a theory of attitude structure and change. In S. Koch (Ed.), *Psychology: A study of a science* (Vol. 3, pp. 423–475). New York: McGraw-Hill.

Katz, J. J. (1972). *Semantic theory.* New York: Harper & Row.

Katz, J. J., & Fodor, J. A. (1963). The structure of a semantic theory. *Language, 39,* 170–210.

Kaufman, A. S. (2000). Tests of intelligence. In R. J. Sternberg (Ed.), *Handbook of intelligence* (pp. 445–476). New York: Cambridge University Press.

Kaufman, A. S., & Lichtenberger, E. O. (1998). Intellectual assessment. In C. R. Reynolds (Ed.), *Comprehensive clinical psychology.* Vol. 4: *Assessment* (pp. 203–238). Tarrytown, NY : Elsevier Science.

Kaufman-Scarborough, C., & Lindquist, J. D. (1999). Time management and polychronicity: Comparisons, contrasts, and insights for the workplace. *Journal of Managerial Psychology, 14,* 288–312.

Kay, P. (1975). Synchronic variability and diachronic changes in basic color terms. *Language in Society, 4,* 257–270.

Kearins, J. M. (1981). Visual spatial memory in Australian aboriginal children of desert regions. *Cognitive Psychology, 13*(3), 434–460.

Keating, D. P., & Bobbitt, B. L. (1978). Individual and developmental differences in cognitive-processing components of mental ability. *Child Development, 49,* 155–167.

Keefe, F. J., Lumley, M. A., Buffington, A. L. H., Carson, J. W., Studts, J. L., Edwards, C. L., Macklem, D. J., Aspnes, A. K., Fox, L., & Steffey, D. (2002). Changing face of pain: Evolution of pain research in psychosomatic medicine. *Psychosomatic Medicine, 64,* 921–938.

Keefer, L., & Blanchard, E. B. (2002). A one-year follow-up of relaxation response meditation as a treatment for irritable bowel syndrome. *Behaviour Research & Therapy, 40,* 541–546.

Keesey, R. E. (1980). A set point analysis of the regulation of body weight. In A. J. Stunkard (Ed.), *Obesity.* Philadelphia: Saunders.

Keesey, R. E., & Powley, T. L. (1975). Hypothalamic regulation of body weight. *American Scientist, 63,* 558–565.

Keesey, R. E., & Powley, T. L. (1986). The regulation of body weight. *Annual Review of Psychology, 37,* 109–133.

Keesey, R. E., Boyle, P. C., Kemnitz, J. W., & Mitchell, J. J. (1976). The role of the lateral hypothalamus in determining the body weight set point. In D. Novin, W. Wyrwicka, & G. A. Bray (Eds.), *Hunger: Basic mechanisms and clinical implications.* New York: Raven Press.

Keil, F. C. (1989). *Concepts, kinds, and cognitive development.* Cambridge, MA: MIT Press.

Keil, F. C. (1999). Cognition, content, and development. In M. Bennett (Ed.), *Developmental psychology* (pp. 165–184). Philadelphia: Psychology Press.

Keith, K. W. (2000). Helson, Harry. In A. E. Kazdin (Ed.), *Encyclopedia of psychology* (Vol. 4, pp. 111–113). Washington, DC: American Psychological Association.

Keller, J. (2002). Blatant stereotype threat and women's math performance: Self-handicapping as a strategic means to cope with obtrusive negative performance expectations. *Sex Roles, 47,* 193–198.

Keller, M., Eckensberger, L. H., & von Rosen, K. (1989). A critical note on the conception of preconventional morality: The case of stage 2 in Kohlberg's theory. *International Journal of Behavioral Development, 12*(1), 57–69.

Kellman, P. J. (1995). Ontogenesis of space and motion perception. In W. Epstein & S. Rogers (Eds.), *Perception of space and motion* (pp. 327–364). San Diego, CA: Academic Press.

Kelly, A. E. (1999). Revealing personal secrets. *Current Directions in Psychological Science, 8*(4), 105–108.

Kelly, S. J., Day, N., & Streissguth, A. P. (2000). Effects of prenatal alcohol exposure on social behavior in humans and other species. *Neurotoxicology & Teratology, 22,* 143–149.

Kelsoe, J. R. (2003). Arguments for the genetic basis of the bipolar spectrum. *Journal of Affective Disorders, 73,* 183–197.

Keltner, D., & Ekman, P. (2000). Emotion: An overview. In A. E. Kazdin (Ed.), *Encyclopedia of psychology* (Vol. 3, pp. 162–167). Washington, DC: American Psychological Association.

Kemeny, M. E., Cohen, R., Zegans, L. S., & Conant, M. A. (1989). Psychological and immunological predictors of genital herpes recurrence. *Psychosomatic Medicine, 51,* 195–208.

Kennedy, R. S., Lanham, D. S., Drexler, J. M., & Massey, C. J. (1997). A comparison of cybersickness incidences, symptom profiles, measurement technique, and suggestions for further research. *Presence, 6,* 638–644.

Kenny, D. (1994). *Interpersonal perception: A social relations analysis.* New York: Guilford.

Kenny, D., & DePaulo, B. M. (1993). Do people know how others view them? An empirical and theoretical account. *Psychological Bulletin, 114,* 145–161.

Kenrick, D. T., & Keefe, R. C. (1992). Age preferences in mates reflect sex differences in human reproductive strategies. *Behavioral and Brain Sciences, 15,* 75–133.

Kenrick, D. T., & Trost, M. R. (1993). The evolutionary perspective. In A. Beall & R. J. Sternberg (Eds.), *Perspectives on the psychology of gender.* New York: Guilford.

Kenrick, D. T., Groth, G. E., Trost, M. R., & Sadalla, E. K. (1993). Integrating evolutionary and social exchange perspective on relationships: Effects of gender, self-appraisal, and involvement level on mate selection criteria. *Journal of Personality and Social Psychology, 64,* 951–969.

Kenrick, D. T., Li, N. P., & Butner, J (2003). Dynamical evolutionary psychology: Individual decision rules and emergent social norms. *Psychological Review, 110,* 3–28.

Kenshalo, D. R., Nafe, J. P., & Brooks, B. (1961). Variations in thermal sensitivity. *Science, 134,* 104–105.

Kent, G. (2000). Understanding the experiences of people with disfigurements: An integration of four models of social and psychological functioning. *Psychology, Health & Medicine, 5,* 117–129.

Kent, G., & Keohane, S. (2001). Social anxiety and disfigurement: The moderating effects of fear of negative evaluation and past experience. *British Journal of Clinical Psychology, 40,* 23–34.

Keppel, G., & Underwood, B. J. (1962). Proactive inhibition in short-term retention of single items. *Journal of Verbal Learning and Verbal Behavior, 1,* 153–161.

Kernberg, O. F. (1975). Transference and countertransference in the treatment of borderline patients. *Journal of the National Association of Private Psychiatric Hospitals, 7*(2), 14–24.

Kessler Shaw, L. (1999). *Acquiring the meaning of* know *and* think. Unpublished doctoral dissertation, City University of New York Graduate Center.

Kessler, J., Markowitsch, H. J., Huber, M., Kalbe, E., Weber-Luxenburger, G., & Kock, P. (1997). Anterograde psychogenic amnesia or gross reduction in sustained effort? *Journal of Clinical & Experimental Neuropsychology, 19,* 604–614.

Kessler, R. C. (1995). Epidemiology of psychiatric comorbidity. In M. T. Tsuang, M. Tohen, & G. E. P. Zahner (Eds.), *Textbook in psychiatric epidemiology.* New York: Wiley.

Khubchandani, L. M. (1997). Bilingual education for indigenous groups in India. In J. Cummins & D. Corson (Eds.), *Encyclopedia of language and education.* Vol. 5: *Bilingual education* (pp. 67–76). Dordrecht, Netherlands: Kluwer.

Kiang, N. Y. (2000). Hearing: Behavioral and functional aspects. In A. E. Kazdin (Ed.), *Encyclopedia of psychology* (Vol. 4, pp. 101–105). Washington, DC: American Psychological Association.

Kiecolt-Glaser, J. K., Bane, C., Glaser, R., & Malarkey, W. B. (2003). Love, marriage, and divorce: Newlyweds' stress hormones foreshadow relationship changes. *Journal of Consulting & Clinical Psychology, 71,* 176–188.

Kiecolt-Glaser, J. K., Garner, W., Speicher, C., Penn. G. M., Holliday, J., & Glaser, R. (1984). Psychosocial modifiers of immunocompetence in medical students. *Psychosomatic Medicine, 46,* 17.

Kiecolt-Glaser, J. K., Malarkey, W. B., Chee, M., Newton, T., et al. (1993). Negative behavior during marital conflict is associated with immunological down-regulation. *Psychosomatic Medicine, 55,* 395–404.

Kiecolt-Glaser, J. K., McGuire, L., Robles, T. F., & Glaser, R. (2002a). Psychoneuroimmunology: Psychological influences on immune function and health. *Journal of Consulting and Clinical Psychology, 70,* 537–547.

Kiecolt-Glaser, J. K., McGuire, L., Robles, T. F., & Glaser, R. (2002b). Psychoneuroimmunology and psychosomatic medicine: Back to the future. *Psychosomatic Medicine, 64,* 15–28.

Kiecolt-Glaser, J. K., McGuire, L., Robles, T. F., & Glaser, R. (2002c). Emotions, morbidity, and mortality: New perspectives from psychoneuroimmunology. *Annual Review of Psychology, 53,* 83–107.

Kiecolt-Glaser, J. K., Newton, T., Cacioppo, J. T., MacCallum, R. C., Glaser, R., & Malarkey, W. B. (1996). Marital conflict and endocrine function: Are men really more psychologically affected than women? *Journal of Consulting and Clinical Psychology, 64,* 324–332.

Kierein, N. M., & Gold, M. A. (2000). Pygmalion in work organizations: A meta-analysis. *Journal of Organizational Behavior, 21,* 913–928.

Kiesler, D. J. (1966). Some myths of psychotherapy research and the search for a paradigm. *Psychological Bulletin, 65,* 110–136.

Kihlstrom, J. F. (1984). Conscious, subconscious, unconscious: A cognitive view. In K. S. Bowers & D. Meichenbaum (Eds.), *The unconscious: Reconsidered.* New York: Wiley.

Kihlstrom, J. F. (1985). Hypnosis. *Annual Review of Psychology, 36,* 385–418.

Kihlstrom, J. F., Mulvaney, S., Tobias, B. A., & Tobias, I. P. (2000). The emotional unconscious. In E. Eich, J. F. Kohlstrom, et al. (Eds.), *Cognition and emotion* (pp. 30–86). New York: Oxford University Press.

Kihlstrom, J., & Cantor, N. (2000). Social intelligence. In R. J. Sternberg (Ed.), *Handbook of intelligence.* New York: Cambridge University Press.

Killen, M., Crystal, D. S., & Watanabe, H. (2002). Japanese and American children's evaluations of peer exclusion, tolerance of differences, and prescriptions for conformity. *Child Development, 73,* 1788–1802.

Kim, S. G., Ashe, J., Hendrick, K., Ellermann, J. M., Merkle, H., Ugurbil, K., & Georgopolus, A. P. (1993). Functional magnetic resonance imaging of motor cortex: Hemispheric asymmetry and handedness. *Science, 161,* 615–617.

Kim, U., Triandis, H. C., & Kagitcibasi, C. (Eds.). (1994). *Individualism and collectivism: Theory and applications.* Newbury Park, CA: Sage.

Kimura, D. (1987). Are men's and women's brains really different? *Canadian Psychology, 28*(2), 133–147.

King, L. A. (2001). The health benefits of writing about life goals. *Personality and Social Psychology Bulletin, 27,* 798–807.

King, L. A., & Emmons, R. A. (2000). Motivation: Assessment. In A. E. Kazdin (Ed.), *Encyclopedia of psychology* (Vol. 5, pp. 320–324). Washington, DC: American Psychological Association.

King, L. A., & Miner, K. N. (2000). Writing about the perceived benefits of traumatic life events: Implications for physical health. *Personality and Social Psychology Bulletin, 26,* 220–230.

Kinnunen, T., Zamansky, H. B., & Block, M. L. (1994). Is the hypnotized subject lying? *Journal of Abnormal Psychology, 103,* 184–191.

Kirmayer, L. (1991). The place of culture in psychiatric nosology: Taijin-kyofusho and the DSM-III-R. *Journal of Nervous and Mental Disease, 179,* 19–28.

Klahr, D., & MacWhinney, B. (1998). Information processing. In W. Damon (Series Ed.) and D. Kuhn & R. S. Siegler (Vol. Eds.), *Handbook of child psychology* (Vol. 2, pp. 631–678). New York: Wiley.

Klahr, D., Fay, A. L., & Dunbar, K. (1993). Heuristics for scientific experimentation: A developmental study. *Cognitive Psychology, 25,* 111–145.

Klein, M. (1975). *The writings of Melanie Klein* (Vol. 3). London: Hogarth Press.

Klein, S. B., Loftus, J., & Kihlstrom, J. F. (2002). Memory and temporal experience: The effects of episodic memory loss on an amnesic patient's ability to remember the past and imagine the future. *Social Cognition, 20,* 353–379.

Kleinknecht, R. A., Dinnel, D. L., Tanouye, S., & Lonner, W. (1993). *The relationship between symptoms of taijin-kyofusho and social phobia among Japanese-Americans in Hawaii.* Manuscript submitted for publication, Department of Psychology, Western Washington University, Bellingham, WA.

Kleinmuntz, B., & Szucko, J. J. (1984). A field study of the fallibility of polygraphic lie detection. *Nature, 308,* 449–450.

Kleitman, N. (1963). *Sleep and wakefulness* (2nd ed.). Chicago: University of Chicago Press.

Klineberg, O., Clark, K. B., Clark, M. P., & Samelson, F. (1997). American psychology's social agenda: The issue of race. In L. T. Benjamin, Jr. (Ed.), *A history of psychology: Original sources and contemporary research* (2nd ed., pp. 607–645). New York: McGraw-Hill.

Kluger, A. N., & DeNisi, A. (1996). The effects of feedback interventions on performance: A historical review, a meta-analysis, and a preliminary feedback intervention theory. *Psychological Bulletin, 119,* 254–284.

Knauth, P. (1996). Designing better shift systems. *Applied Ergonomics, 27,* 39–44.

Knox, V. J., Crutchfield, L., & Hilgard, E. R. (1975). The nature of task interference in hypnotic dissociation: An investigation of hypnotic behavior. *International Journal of Clinical and Experimental Hypnosis, 23,* 305–323.

Kocsis, R. N., Cooksey, R. W., & Irwin, H. J. (2002). Psychological profiling of sexual murders: An empirical model. *International Journal of Offender Therapy & Comparative Criminology, 46,* 532–554.

Koda, N. (2001). Inappropriate behavior of potential guide dogs for the blind and coping behavior of human raisers. *Applied Animal Behaviour Science, 72,* 79–87.

Koehler, J. J. (1996). The base rate fallacy reconsidered: Descriptive, normative, and methodological challenges. *Behavioral and Brain Sciences, 19,* 1–53.

Koehler, N., Rhodes, G., & Simmons, L. W. (2002). Are human female preferences for symmetrical male faces enhanced when conception is likely? *Animal Behaviour, 64,* 233–238.

Kohlberg, L. (1963). The development of children's orientations toward a moral order: Pt. 1. Sequence in the development of moral thought. *Vita Humana, 6,* 11–33.

Kohlberg, L. (1984). The psychology of moral development: The nature and validity of moral stages. In *Essays on moral development* (Vol. 2). New York: Harper & Row.

Kohlberg, L., & Kramer, R. (1969). Continuities and discontinuities in childhood and adult moral development. *Human Development, 12,* 93–120.

Köhler, W. (1927). *The mentality of apes.* New York: Harcourt Brace.

Köhler, W., Kapur, S., Moscovitch, M., Winocur, G., & Houle, S. (1995). Dissociation of pathways for object and spatial vision in the intact human brain. *Neuroreport, 6,* 1865–1868.

Kohn, M. L. (1976). Social class and parental values: Another confirmation of the relationship. *American Sociological Review, 41,* 538–545.

Kohn, P. M., Gurevich, M., Pickering, D. I., & MacDonald, J. E. (1994). Alexithymia, reactivity, and the adverse impact of hassles-based stress. *Personality and Individual Differences, 16*(6), 805–812.

Kohnstamm, G. A. (1989). Temperament in childhood: Cross-cultural and sex differences. In G. A. Kohnstamm, J. E. Bates, & M. K. Rothbart (Eds.), *Temperament in childhood* (pp. 483–508). West Sussex, UK: Wiley.

Kohut, H. (1984). Selected problems of self-psychological theory. In J. D. Lichtenberg & S. Kaplan (Eds.), *Reflection on self psychology* (pp. 387–416). Hillsdale, NJ: Erlbaum.

Kolb, B., & Whishaw, I. Q. (1990). *Fundamentals of human neuropsychology* (3rd ed.). New York: Freeman.

Kolb, B., & Whishaw, I. Q. (2001). *Introduction to brain and behavior.* New York: Freeman.

Kolotkin, R. L., Revis, E. S., Kirkley, B. G., & Janick, L. (1987). Binge eating and obesity: Associated with MMPI characteristics. *Journal of Consulting and Clinical Psychology, 55,* 872–876.

Koob, G. F. & Bloom, F. E. (1988). Cellular and molecular mechanisms of drug dependence. *Science, 242,* 715–723.

Kopta, S. M., Howard, K. I., Lowry, J. L., & Beutler, L. E. (1994). Patterns of symptomatic recovery in psychotherapy. *Journal of Consulting and Clinical Psychology, 62,* 1009–1016.

Korf, R. (1999). Heuristic search. In R. A. Wilson & F. C. Keil (Eds.), *The MIT encyclopedia of the cognitive sciences* (pp. 372–373). Cambridge, MA: MIT Press.

Koriat, A., & Goldsmith, M. (1996). Monitoring and control processes in the strategic regulation of memory accuracy. *Psychological Review, 103,* 490–517.

Koslowski, B. (1996). *Theory and evidence: The development of scientific reasoning.* Cambridge, MA: MIT Press.

Kosslyn, S. M. (1988). Aspects of a cognitive neuroscience of mental imagery. *Science, 240,* 1621–1626.

Kosslyn, S. M., & Koenig, O. (1992). *Wet mind: The new cognitive neuroscience.* New York: Free Press.

Kosslyn, S. M., & Koenig, O. (1995). *Wet mind: The new cognitive neuroscience.* (Paperback). New York: Free Press.

Kosslyn, S. M., & Plomin, R. (2001). Toward a neurocognitive genetics: Goals and issues. In D. D. Doughterty & S. L. Rauch (Eds.), *Psychiatric neuroimaging research: Contemporary strategies* (pp. 383–402). Washington, DC: American Psychiatric Publishing.

Kosslyn, S. M., Ball, T. M., & Reiser, B. J. (1978). Visual images preserve metric spatial information: Evidence from studies of image scanning. *Journal of Experimental Psychology: Human Perception and Performance, 4,* 47–60.

Kotsiubinskii, A. P. (2002). A biopsychosocial model of schizophrenia. *International Journal of Mental Health, 31,* 51–60.

Kowert, P. A. (2002). *Groupthink or deadlock: When do leaders learn from their advisors?* Albany: State University of New York Press.

Kozulin, A., & Rand, Y. (Eds.). (2000). *Experience of mediated learning: An impact of Feuerstein's theory in education and psychology.* Elmsford, NY: Pergamon.

Krafka, C., Linz, D., Donnerstein, E., & Penrod, S. (1997). Women's reactions to sexually aggressive mass media depictions. *Violence Against Women, 3,* 149–181.

Kramer, D. A. (1990). Conceptualizing wisdom: The primacy of affect-cognition relations. In R. J. Sternberg (Ed.), *Wisdom: Its nature, origins, and development* (pp. 279–313). New York: Cambridge University Press.

Kramer, M. A. (1957). A discussion of the concepts of incidence and prevalence as related to epidemiologic studies of mental disorders. *American Journal of Public Health, 47,* 826–840.

Krantz, D. S., Baum, A., & Wideman, M. V. (1980). Assessment for preferences for self-treatment and information in health care. *Journal of Personality and Social Psychology, 39,* 977–990.

Krantz, L. (1992). *What the odds are: A-to-Z odds on everything you hoped or feared could happen.* New York: Harper Perennial.

Krauthammer, C., & Klerman, G. L. (1979). The epidemiology of mania. In B. Shopsin (Ed.), *Manic illness* (pp. 11–28). New York: Raven Press.

Krefetz, D. G., Steer, R. A., Gulab, N. A., & Beck, A. T. (2002). Convergent validity of the Beck Depression Inventory–II with the Reynolds Adolescent Depression Scale in psychiatric inpatients. *Journal of Personality Assessment, 78,* 451–460.

Kries, J. A. von (1895). Ueber die Natur gewisser mit den psychischen Vorgangen verknupfter Gehirnzustande. *Zeitschrift fur Psychologie, 8,* 1–33.

Kroner-Herwig, B., Jakle, C., Frettloh, J., Peters, K., Seemann, H., Franz, C., & Basler, H. D. (1996). Predicting subjective disability in chronic pain patients. *International Journal of Behavioral Medicine, 3,* 30–41.

Krosnick, J. A., Betz, A. I., Jussim, L. J., & Lynn, A. R. (1992). Subliminal conditioning of atttitudes. *Personality and Social Psychology Bulletin, 18,* 152–162.

Krueger, J. (1998). Enhancement bias in descriptions of self and others. *Personality & Social Psychology Bulletin, 24*(5), 505–516.

Kübler-Ross, E. (1969). *On death and dying.* New York: Macmillan.

Kubovy, M. (2000). Visual and design arts. In A. E. Kazdin (Ed.), *Encyclopedia of psychology* (Vol. 8, pp. 188–193). Washington, DC: American Psychological Association.

Kuhl, P. K., & Meltzoff, A. N. (1997). Evolution, nativism, and learning in the development of language and speech. In M. Gopnik (Ed.), *The inheritance and innateness of grammars* (pp. 7–44). New York: Oxford University Press.

Kuhlman, D. M., & Marshello, A. F. J. (1975). Individual differences in game motivation as moderators of pre-programmed strategy effects in prisoner's dilemma. *Journal of Personality and Social Psychology, 32,* 922–931.

Kuhn, D. (2002). What is scientific thinking and how does it develop? In U. Goswami (Ed.), *Blackwell handbook of childhood cognitive development* (pp. 371–393). Malden, MA: Blackwell.

Kuhn, D., Garcia-Mila, M., Zohar, A., & Andersen, C. (1995). Strategies of knowledge acquisition. *Monographs of the Society for Research in Child Development, 60,* Serial No. 245.

Kuhn, D., Schauble, L., & Garcia-Mila, M. (1992). Cross-domain development of scientific reasoning. *Cognition and Instruction, 9,* 285–327.

Kuhn, T. S. (1970). *The structure of scientific revolutions* (2nd ed.). Chicago: University of Chicago Press.

Kujala, T., & Naeaetaenen, R. (2001). The mismatch negativity in evaluating central auditory dysfunction in dyslexia. *Neuroscience & Biobehavioral Reviews, 25,* 535–543.

Kulik, J. A., & Gump, B. B. (1997). Affective reactions to social comparison: The effects of relative performance and related attributes information about another person. *Personality & Social Psychology Bulletin, 23*(5), 452–468.

Kulik, L. (2002). Marital equality and the quality of long-term marriage in later life. *Ageing & Society, 22,* 459–481.

Kuo, Z. Y. (1921). Giving up instincts in psychology. *Journal of Philosophy, 17,* 645–664.

Kurtines, W., & Greif, E. B. (1974). The development of moral thought: Review and evaluation of Kohlberg's approach. *Psychological Bulletin, 81,* 453–470.

Kurtzberg, T. R., & Amabile, T. M. (2001). From Guilford to creative synergy: Opening the black box of team-level creativity. *Creativity Research Journal, 13*(3–4), 285–294.

Kyllonen, P. C. (2002). g: Knowledge, speed, strategies, or working-memory capacity? A systems perspective. In R. J. Sternberg & E. L. Grigorenko (Eds.), *The general factor of intelligence: How general is it?* (pp. 415–446). Mahwah, NJ: Erlbaum.

Kyllonen, P. C., & Christal, R. E. (1990). Reasoning ability is (little more than) working-memory capacity?! *Intelligence, 14,* 389–433.

Labouvie-Vief, G. (1980). Beyond formal operations: Uses and limits of pure logic in life span development. *Human Development, 23,* 141–161.

Labouvie-Vief, G. (1990). Wisdom as integrated thought: Historical and developmental perspectives. In R. J. Sternberg (Ed.), *Wisdom: Its nature, origins, and development* (pp. 52–83). New York: Cambridge University Press.

Labouvie-Vief, G., & Schell, D. A. (1982). Learning and memory in later life. In B. B. Wolman (Ed.), *Handbook of developmental psychology.* Englewood Cliffs, NJ: Prentice-Hall.

Ladd, G. W. (1999). Peer relationships and social competence during early and middle childhood. *Annual Review of Psychology, 50,* 333–359.

Ladefoged, P., & Maddieson, I. (1996). *The sounds of the world's languages.* Cambridge: Blackwell.

LaFraniere, S. (1992, August 27). Identifying 'Ivan': Does memory mislead? *Washington Post,* p. A29.

LaGanga, M. L. (1994, May 14). Father wins in "false memory" case. *Los Angeles Times,* p. A1.

Laing, R. D. (1964). Is schizophrenia a disease? *International Journal of Social Psychiatry, 10,* 184–193.

Lamb, M. E. (1977a). The development of mother–infant and father–infant attachments in the second year of life. *Developmental Psychology, 13,* 637–648.

Lamb, M. E. (1977b). Father–infant and mother–infant interactions in the first year of life. *Child Development, 48,* 167–181.

Lamb, M. E. (1979). Separation and reunion behaviors as criteria of attachment to mothers and fathers. *Early Human Development, 3/4,* 329–339.

Lamb, M. E. (1996). *The role of the father in child development* (3rd ed.). New York: Wiley.

Lambert, M. J., & Bergin, A. E. (1994). The effectiveness of psychotherapy. In A. E. Bergin and S. L. Garfield (Eds.), *Handbook of psychotherapy and behavior change* (4th ed.), pp. 143–189. New York: Wiley.

Lambie, J. A., & Marcel, A. J. (2002). Consciousness and the varieties of emotion experience: A theoretical framework. *Psychological Review, 109,* 219–259.

Landolt, H.-P., & Borbely, A. A. (2001). Age-dependent changes in sleep EEG topography. *Clinical Neurophysiology, 112,* 369–377.

Lane, J. D., & Williams, R. B. (1987). Cardiovascular effects of caffeine and stress in regular coffee drinkers. *Psychophysiology, 24,* 157–164.

Lange, R. D., & James, W. (1922). *The emotions.* Baltimore, MD: Williams & Wilkins.

Langer, E. (1989). *Mindfulness.* Reading, MA: Addison Wesley.

Langer, E. (1997). *The power of mindful learning.* New York: Perseus.

Langer, E. (2002). Well-being: Mindfulness versus positive evaluation. In C. R. Snyder & S. J. Lopez (Eds.), *Handbook of positive psychology* (pp. 214–230). London: Oxford University Press.

Langer, E. (2003). *Mindful creativity.* To be published by Ballantine.

Langer, E. J. (1989). *Mindfulness.* New York: Addison-Wesley.

Langer, E. J. (1997). *The power of mindful learning.* Needham Heights, MA: Addison-Wesley.

Langer, E. J. (2000). Mindful learning. *Current Directions in Psychological Science, 9,* 220–223.

Langer, E. J., Janis, I. L., & Wolfer, J. A. (1975). Reduction of psychological stress in surgical patients. *Journal of Experimental Social Psychology, 11,* 155–165.

Langfeldt, H.-P. (1992). Teachers' perceptions of problem behaviour: A cross-cultural study between Germany and South Korea. *British Journal of Educational Psychology, 62,* 217–224.

Langlois, J. H., Ritter, J. M., Casey, R. J., & Savin, D. B. (1995). Infant attractiveness predicts maternal behaviors and attitudes. *Developmental Psychology, 31,* 164–472.

Langsley, D. G., Hodes, M., & Grimson, W. R. (1993). In N. Sartorius, G. de Girolano, G. Andrews, G. A. German, & L. Eisenberg (Eds.), *Treatment of mental disorders: A review of effectiveness.* Geneva, Switzerland, and Washington, DC: World Health Organization and American Psychiatric Press.

Laragh, J. H. (1988). Pathophysiology of diastolic hypertension. *Health Psychology, 7*(Suppl.), 15–31.

Large, M.-E., McMullen, P. A., & Hamm, J. P. (2003). The role of axes of elongation and symmetry in rotated object naming. *Perception & Psychophysics, 65,* 1–19.

Larimer, M. E., Anderson, B. K., Baer, J. S., & Marlatt, G. A. (2000). An individual in context: Predictors of alcohol use and drinking problems among Greek and residence hall students. *Journal of Substance Abuse, 11*(1), 53–68.

Larkin, J. H., McDermott, J., Simon, D. P., & Simon, H. A. (1980). Expert and novice performance in solving physics problems. *Science, 208,* 1335–1342.

Lassner, J. B., Matthews, K. A., & Stony, C. M. (1994). Are cardiovascular reactors to asocial stress also reactors to social stress? *Journal of Personality and Social Psychology, 66,* 69–77.

Latané, B. (1981). The psychology of social impact. *American Psychologist, 36,* 343–356.

Latané, B., & Darley, J. M. (1968). Group inhibition of bystander intervention. *Journal of Personality and Social Psychology, 10,* 215–221.

Latané, B., & Darley, J. M. (1970). *The unresponsive bystander: Why doesn't he help?* New York: Appleton-Century-Crofts.

Latané, B., Nida, S. A., & Wilson, D. W. (1981). The effects of a group size on helping behavior. In J. P. Rushton & R. M. Sorrentino (Eds.), *Altruism and helping behavior: Social, personality, and developmental perspectives.* Hillsdale, NJ: Erlbaum.

Latané, B., Williams, K., & Harkins, S. (1979). Many hands make light the work: The causes and consequences of social loafing. *Journal of Personality and Social Psychology, 37,* 822–832.

Latner, J. D., & Wilson, G. T. (2002). Self-monitoring and the assessment of binge eating. *Behavior Therapy, 33,* 465–477.

Latner, J. D., Wilson, G. T., Stunkard, A. J., & Jackson, M. L. (2002). Self-help and long-term behavior therapy for obesity. *Behaviour Research & Therapy, 40,* 804–812.

Lau, E.M.C., Egger, P., Coggon, D., & Cooper, C. (1995). Low back pain in Hong Kong: Prevalence and characteristics compared with Britain. *Journal of Epidemiology & Community Health, 49,* 492–494.

Lau, R. R., & Hartman, K. A. (1983). Commonsense representations of common illnesses. *Health Psychology, 2,* 167–185.

Lau, R. R., Bernard, T. M., & Hartman, K. A. (1989). Further explorations of commonsense representations of common illness. *Health Psychology, 8,* 195–219.

Lazar, I., & Darlington, R. (1982). Lasting effects of early education: A report from the consortium for longitudinal studies. *Monographs of the Society for Research in Child Development, 47*(2–3, Serial No. 195).

Lazarus, A. A. (1961). Group therapy of phobic disorders by systematic desensitization. *Journal of Abnormal and Social Psychology, 63,* 504–510.

Lazarus, A. A. (1968). Learning theory and the treatment of depression. *Behaviour Research and Therapy, 6,* 83–89.

Lazarus, A. A. (1989). *The practice of multimodal therapy.* Baltimore, MD: Johns Hopkins University Press.

Lazarus, A. A. (1990). If this be research... . *American Psychologist, 58,* 670–671.

Lazarus, A. A. (2000). Working effectively and efficiently with couples. *Family Journal: Counseling & Therapy for Couples & Families, 8,* 222–228.

Lazarus, R. S. (1977). A cognitive analysis of biofeedback control. In G. E. Schwartz & J. Beatty (Eds.), *Biofeedback: Theory and research* (pp. 69–71). New York: Academic Press.

Lazarus, R. S. (1984). On the primacy of cognition. *American Psychologist, 39,* 124–129.

Lazarus, R. S. (1991). *Emotion and adaptation.* New York: Oxford University Press.

Lazarus, R. S. (1993). From psychological stress to the emotions: A history of changing outlooks. *Annual Review of Psychology, 44,* 1–21.

Lazarus, R. S. (2000). How emotions influence performance in competitive sports. *Sport Psychologist, 14,* 229–252.

Lazarus, R. S. (2001). Relational meaning and discrete emotions. In K. R. Scherer, A. Schorr, & T. Johnstone (Eds.), *Appraisal processes in emotion: Theory, methods, research. Series in affective science* (pp. 37–67). New York: Oxford University Press.

Lazarus, R. S. (in press). Does the positive psychology movement have legs? *Psychological Inquiry.*

Lazarus, R. S., & Folkman, S. (1984). *Stress, appraisal, and coping.* New York: Springer.

Lazarus, R. S., Kanner, A., & Folkman, F. (1980). Emotions: A cognitive-phenomenological analysis. In R. Plutchik & H. Kellerman (Eds.), *Emotion: Theory, research and experience:* Vol. 1. *Theories of emotion.* New York: Academic Press.

Le Bon, G. (1896). *The crowd: A study of the popular mind.* New York: Macmillan.

Lederer, R. (1987). *Anguished English.* New York: Pocket Books.

LeDoux, J. E. (1986). The neurobiology of emotion. In J. E. LeDoux & W. Hirst (Eds.), *Mind and brain: Dialogues in cognitive neuroscience* (pp. 301–354). Cambridge, UK: Cambridge University Press.

LeDoux, J. E. (1992). Emotional memory systems in the brain. *Behavioural Brain Research, 58,* 69–79.

LeDoux, J. E. (1993). Emotional networks in the brain. In M. Lewis & J. M. Haviland (Eds.), *Handbook of emotions.* New York: Guilford.

LeDoux, J. E. (1995). Emotion: Clues from the brain. *Annual Review of Psychology, 46,* 209–235.

LeDoux, J. E. (1996). *The emotional brain.* New York: Simon & Schuster.

LeDoux, J. E., Romanski, L., & Xagoraris, A. (1989). Indelibility of subcortical emotional memories. *Journal of Cognitive Neuroscience, 1,* 238–243.

Lee, J. A. (1977). A typology of styles of loving. *Personality and Social Psychology Bulletin, 3,* 173–182.

Lee, J. A. (1988). Love-styles. In R. J. Sternberg & M. L. Barnes (Eds.), *The psychology of love* (pp. 38–67). New Haven, CT: Yale University Press.

Lee, T. F. (1993). *Gene future: The promise and perils of the new biology.* New York; Plenum.

Leitschuh, C. A., & Dunn, J. M. (2001). Prediction of the gross motor development quotient in young children prenatally exposed to cocaine/polydrugs. *Adapted Physical Activity Quarterly, 18,* 240–256.

Leon, G. R. (1974). *Case histories of deviant behavior: A social learning analysis.* Boston: Holbrook Press.

Lepore, S. J. (1995). Cynicism, social support, and cardiovascular reactivity. *Health Psychology, 14,* 210–216.

Leppaenen, P. H. T., Richardson, U., Pihko, E., Eklund, K. M., Guttorm, T. K., Aro, M., & Lyytinen, H. (2002). Brain responses to changes in speech sound durations differ between infants with and without familial risk for dyslexia. *Developmental Neuropsychology, 22,* 407–422.

Lepper, M. R. (1998). A whole much less than the sum of its parts. *American Psychologist, 53,* 675–676.

Lepper, M. R., & Henderlong, J. (2000). Turning "play" into "work" and "work" into "play": 25 years of research on intrinsic versus extrinsic motivation. In C. Sansone & J. M. Harackiewicz (Eds.), *Intrinsic and extrinsic motivation: The search for optimal motivation and performance* (pp. 257–307). New York: Academic Press.

Lepper, M. R., Greene, D., & Nisbett, R. E. (1973). Undermining children's intrinsic interest with extrinsic rewards: A test of the "overjustification" hypothesis. *Journal of Personality and Social Psychology, 28,* 129–137.

Lepper, M. R., Henderlong, J., & Gingras, I. (1999). Understanding the effects of extrinsic rewards on intrinsic motivation—Uses and abuses of meta-analysis: Comment on Deci, Koestner, and Ryan (1999). *Psychological Bulletin, 125,* 669–676.

Lerner, R. M. (2002). *Concepts and theories of human development* (3rd ed.). Mahwah, NJ: Erlbaum.

Lerner, R. M., Freund, A. M., DeStefanis, I., & Habermas, T. (2001). Understanding developmental regulation in adolescence: The use of the Selection, Optimization and Compensation Model. *Human Development, 44,* 29–50.

Lerner, R. M., & Castellin, D. R. (2002). Contemporary developmental theory and adolescence: Developmental systems and applied developmental sciences. *Journal of Adolescent Health, 31,* 122–135.

Lesch, K. P., Bengel, D., Heils, A., Sabol, S. Z., Greenberg, B. D., Petri, S., Benjamin, J., Muelller, C. R., Hamer, D. H., & Murphy, D. (1996). Association of anxiety-related traits with a polymorphism in the serotonin transporter gene regulatory region. *Science, 274,* 1527–1531.

Lesgold, A. M. (1988). Problem solving. In R. J. Sternberg & E. E. Smith (Eds.), *The psychology of human thought* (pp. 188–213). New York: Cambridge University Press.

Lesgold, A. M., Rubinson, H., Feltovich, P., Glaser, R., Klopfer, D., & Wang, Y. (1988). Expertise in a complex skill: Diagnosing X-ray pictures. In M. T. H. Chi, R. Glaser, & M. Farr (Eds.), *The nature of expertise.* Hillsdale, NJ: Erlbaum.

Leslie, A. M. (1999). Competence and performance in false belief understanding: A comparison of autistic and three-year-old children. *British Journal of Developmental Psychology, 14,* 131–153.

Lester, B. M., Corwin, M. J., Sepkoski, C., Seifer, R., et al. (1991). Neurobehavioral syndromes in cocaine-exposed newborn infants. *Child Development, 62,* 694–705.

Lester, D. (1979). Food fads and psychological health. *Psychological Reports, 44,* 222.

LeVay, S. (1991). A difference in hypothalamic structure between heterosexual and homosexual men. *Science, 253,* 1034–1037.

Levenkron, J. C., & Moore, L. G. (1988). The Type A behavior pattern: Issues for intervention research. *Annals of Behavioral Medicine, 10,* 78–83.

Levenson, H., & Strupp, H. H. (1999). Recommendations for the future of training in brief dynamic psychotherapy. *Journal of Clinical Psychology, 55,* 385–391.

Levenson, R. W., Ekman, P., & Friesen, W. V. (1990). Voluntary facial action generates emotion-specific autonomic nervous system activity. *Psychophysiology, 27*(4), 363–384.

Leventhal, H., & Tomarken, A. J. (1986). Emotion: Today's problems. *Annual Review of Psychology, 37,* 565–610.

Levine, L. E. (1983). Mine: Self-definition in 2-year-old boys. *Developmental Psychology, 19,* 544–549.

Levine, R. A., & Campbell, D. T. (1972). *Ethnocentrism: Theories of conflict, ethnic attitudes, and group behavior.* New York: Wiley.

Levine, R. V., & Bartlett, K. (1984). Pace of life, punctuality, and coronary heart disease in six countries. *Journal of Cross-Cultural Psychology, 15*(2), 233–255.

Levine, R. V., Martinez, T. S., Brase, G., & Sorenson, K. (1994). Helping in 36 U.S. cities. *Journal of Personality and Social Psychology, 67,* 69–82.

Levi-Strauss, C. (1966). *The savage mind.* Chicago: University of Chicago Press.

Levy, J. (1974). Cerebral asymmetries as manifested in split-brain man. In M. Kinsbourne & W. L. Smith (Eds.), *Hemispheric disconnection and cerebral function.* Springfield, IL: Charles C. Thomas.

Levy, J. (2000). Hemispheric functions. In A. E. Kazdin (Ed.), *Encyclopedia of psychology* (Vol. 4, pp. 113–115). Washington, DC: American Psychological Association.

Levy, J., Trevarthen, C., & Sperry, R. W. (1972). Perception of bilateral chimeric figures following hemispheric deconnexion. *Brain, 95*(1), 61–78.

Lewinsohn, P. M. (1974). A behavioral approach to depression. In R. J. Friedman & M. M. Katz (Eds.), *The psychology of depression: Contemporary theory and research.* New York: Halstead Press.

Lewis, C. A., & Maltby, J. (1995). Religiosity and personality among U.S. adults. *Personality and Individual Differences, 18,* 293–295.

Lewis, C., & Carpendale, J. (2002). Social cognition. In P. K. Smith & C. H. Hart (Eds.), *Blackwell handbook of childhood social development* (pp. 376–393). Malden, MA: Blackwell.

Lewis, M. (1989). Culture and biology: The role of temperament. In P. R. Zelazo & R. G. Barr (Eds.), *Challenges to developmental paradigms: Implications for theory, assessment and treatment* (pp. 203–223). Hillsdale, NJ: Erlbaum.

Lewis, M., & Brooks-Gunn, J. (1981). Visual attention at three months as a predictor of cognitive functioning at two years of age. *Intelligence, 5,* 131–140.

Lewontin, R. C. (1975). Genetic aspects of intelligence. *Annual Review of Genetics, 9,* 387–405.

Lewy, A. J., Ahmed, S., Jackson, J. L., & Sack, R. L. (1992). Melatonin shifts human circadian ryhthms according to a phase-response curve. *Chronobiology International, 9,* 380–392.

Lewy, A., Sack, L., Miller, S., & Hoban, T. M. (1987). Antidepressant and circadian-phase shifting effects of light. *Science, 235,* 352–367.

Li, P. (1975). *Path analysis: A primer.* Pacific Grove, CA: Boxwood Press.

Liben, L. S. (2002). Spatial development in childhood. In U. Goswami (Ed.), *Blackwell handbook of childhood cognitive development* (pp. 326–348). Malden, MA: Blackwell.

Liebert, R. M., & Baron, R. A. (1972). Some immediate effects of televised violence on children's behavior. *Developmental Psychology, 6,* 469–475.

Liebert, R. M., & Liebert, L. L. (1998). *Liebert & Spiegler's Personality: Strategies and issues* (8th ed.). Pacific Grove, CA: Brooks/Cole.

Lindemann, E. (1991). The symptomatology and management of acute grief. *American Journal of Psychiatry, 144,* 141–148.

Lindsay, D. S., & Johnson, M. K. (1991). Recognition memory and source monitoring. *Bulletin of the Psychonomic Society, 29,* 203–205.

Lindsay, D. S., & Read, J. D. (1994). Psychotherapy and memories of childhood sexual abuse: A cognitive perspective. *Applied Cognitive Psychology, 8,* 281–338.

Lindskold, S. (1978). Trust development, the GRIT proposal, and the effects of conciliatory acts on conflict and cooperation. *Psychological Bulletin, 85,* 772–793.

Lindskold, S. (1986). GRIT: Reducing distrust through carefully introduced conciliation. In S. Worchel & W. G. Austin (Eds.), *Psychology of intergroup relations* (2nd ed.). Chicago: Nelson-Hall.

Linton, M. (1982). Transformations of memory in everyday life. In U. Neisser (Ed.), *Memory observed: Remembering in natural contexts.* San Francisco: Freeman.

Linville, P. (1998). The heterogeneity of homogeneity. In J. Cooper & J. Darley (Eds.), *Attribution processes, person perception, and social interaction: The legacy of Ned Jones.* Washington, DC: American Psychological Association.

Linville, P. W., Brewer, M. B., & Mackie, D. M. (1998). The heterogeneity of homogeneity. In J. M. Darley & J. Cooper (Eds.), *Attribution and social interaction: The legacy of Edward E. Jones* (pp. 423–487). Washington, DC: American Psychological Association.

Linz, D., Donnerstein, E., & Penrod, S. (1984). The effects of multiple exposures to filmed violence against women. *Journal of Communication, 43,* 130–147.

Lipsey, M. W., & Wilson, D. B. (1993). The efficacy of psychological, educational, and behavioral treatment: Confirmation from meta-analysis. *American Psychologist, 48,* 1181–1209.

Lissner, L., Odell, P. M., D'Agostino, R. B., Stokes, J., Kreger, B. E., Belanger, A. J., & Brownell, K. D. (1991). Variability of body weight and health outcomes in the Framingham population. *New England Journal of Medicine, 324,* 1839–1844.

Lloyd, G. K., Fletcher, A., & Minchin, M. C. W. (1992). GABA agonists as potential anxiolytics. In G. D. Burrows, S .G. M. Roth, & R. Noyes, Jr. (Eds.), *Handbook of anxiety* (Vol. 5). Oxford, UK: Elsevier.

Lobitz, W. C., & Post, R. D. (1979). Parameters of self-reinforcement and depression. *Journal of Abnormal Psychology, 88,* 33–41.

Locke, E. A., & Latham, G. P. (1985). The application of goal setting to sports. *Journal of Sport Psychology, 7,* 205–222.

Locke, E. A., & Latham, G. P. (1990). *A theory of goal-setting and task perfomance.* Englewood Cliffs, NJ: Prentice-Hall.

Locke, J. (1961). An essay concerning human understanding. In *Great books of the Western world: Vol. 35. Locke, Berkeley, Hume.* Chicago: Encyclopaedia Britannica. (Original work published 1690)

Locke, J. L. (1994). Phases in the child's development of language. *American Scientist, 82,* 436–445.

Lockhart, R. S. (2000). Methods of memory research. In E. Tulving & F. I. M. Craik (Eds.), *The Oxford handbook of memory* (pp. 45–58). New York: Oxford University Press.

Loehlin, J. C. (1992a). *Genes and environment in personality development*. Newbury Park, CA: Sage.

Loehlin, J. C. (1992b). Using EQs for a simple analysis of the Colorado Adoption Project data on height and intelligence. *Behavior Genetics, 22,* 234–245.

Loehlin, J. C. (2000). Group differences in intelligence. In R. J. Sternberg (Ed.), *Handbook of intelligence.* New York: Cambridge University Press.

Loehlin, J. C., Horn, J. M., & Willerman, L. (1997). Heredity, environment, and IQ in the Texas Adoption Project. In R. J. Sternberg & E. L. Grigorenko (Eds.), *Intelligence, heredity, and environment* (pp. 105–125). New York: Cambridge University Press.

Loehlin, J. C., McCrae, R. R., Costa, P. T. Jr., & John, O. P. (1998). Heritabilities of common and measure-specific components of the Big Five personality factors. *Journal of Research in Personality, 32,* 431–453.

Loewenstein, G. (1994). The psychology of curiosity: A review and reinterpretation. *Psychological Bulletin, 116,* 75–98.

Loftus, E. F. (1975). Leading questions and the eyewitness report. *Cognitive Psychology, 7,* 560–572.

Loftus, E. F. (1977). Shifting human color memory. *Memory & Cognition, 5,* 696–699.

Loftus, E. F. (1993a). Psychologists in the eyewitness world. *American Psychologist, 48*(5), 550–552.

Loftus, E. F. (1993b). The reality of repressed memories. *American Psychologist, 48*(5), 518–537.

Loftus, E. F. (1998). Imaginary memories. In M. A. Conway, S. E. Gathercole, & C. Cornoldi (Eds.), *Theory of memory II* (pp. 135–145). Hove, UK: Psychology Press.

Loftus, E. F., & Ketcham, K. (1991). *Witness for the defense: The accused, the eyewitness, and the expert who puts memory on trial.* New York: St. Martin's Press.

Loftus, E. F., Miller, D. G., & Burns, H. J. (1978). Semantic integration of verbal information into a visual memory. *Journal of Experimental Psychology: Human Learning and Memory, 4,* 19–31.

Loftus, E. G. (2001). Imagining the past. *Psychologist, 14,* 854–857.

Lohman, D. (2000). Complex information processing and intelligence. In R. J. Sternberg (Ed.), *Handbook of intelligence.* New York: Cambridge University Press.

Long, D., & DeVault, S. (1990). Disfigurement and adolescent development: Exacerbating factors in personal injury. *American Journal of Forensic Psychology, 8,* 3–14.

Lonner, W. J. (1989). The introductory psychology text: Beyond Ekman, Whorf, and biased IQ tests. In D. M. Keats, D. Munro, & L. Mann (Eds.), *Heterogeneity in cross-cultural psychology.* Amsterdam: Swets & Zeitlinger.

Lonner, W. J. (1990). An overview of cross-cultural testing and assessment. In R. W. Brislin (Ed.), *Applied cross-cultural psychology.* Newbury Park, CA: Sage.

Lonner, W. J., & Berry, J. W. (1986). Sampling and surveying. In W. J. Lonner & J. W. Berry (Eds.), *Field methods in cross-cultural research:* Vol. 8. *Cross-cultural research and methodology series.* Beverly Hills, CA: Sage.

Lopez, S., & Nuñez, J. A. (1987). Cultural factors considered in selected diagnostic criteria and interview schedules. *Journal of Abnormal Psychology, 96,* 270–272.

Loranger, A. W. (1984). Sex differences in age of onset of schizophrenia. *Archives of General Psychiatry, 41,* 157–161.

Lorber, J. (1975). Good patients and problem patients: Conformity and deviance in a general hospital. *Journal of Health and Social Behavior, 16,* 213–225.

Lore, R., & Schultz, L. A. (1993). Control of human aggression: A comparative perspective. *American Psychologist, 48,* 16–25.

Lott, A., & Lott, B. (1968). A learning theory approach to interpersonal attitudes. In A. G. Greenwald, T. C. Brock, & T. M.Ostrom (Eds.), *Psychological foundations of attitude.* New York: Academic Press.

Louis Steel, A. (2002). Music therapy with offenders in a substance abuse/mental illness treatment program. *Music Therapy Perspectives, 20,* 117–122.

Lovaas, O. I. (1968). Learning theory approach to the treatment of childhood schizophrenia. In *California Mental Health Research Symposium:* No. 2. *Behavior theory and therapy.* Sacramento: California Department of Mental Hygiene.

Lovaas, O. I. (1977). *The autistic child.* New York: Wiley.

Luchins, A. S. (1942). Mechanization in problem solving. *Psychological Monographs, 54*(6, Whole No. 248).

Lucy, J. A. (1997). Linguistic relativity. *Annual Review of Anthropology, 26,* 291–312.

Ludwick-Rosenthal, R., & Neufeld, R.W.J. (1988). Stress management during noxious medical procedures: An evaluative review of outcome studies. *Psychological Bulletin, 104,* 326–342.

Lugo, J. N. Jr., Marino, M. D., Cronise, K., & Kelly, S. J. (2003). Effects of alcohol exposure during development on social behavior in rats. *Physiology & Behavior, 78,* 185–194.

Lumsdaine, A. A., & Janis, I. L. (1953). Resistance to "counterpropaganda" produced by one-sided and two-sided "propaganda" presentation. *Public Opinion Quarterly, 17,* 311–318.

Lumsden, C. J. (1998). Evolving creative minds: Stories and mechanisms. In R. J. Sternberg (Ed.), *Handbook of creativity* (pp. 153–168). New York: Cambridge University Press.

Lundberg, I. (2002). Second language learning and reading with the additional load of dyslexia. *Annals of Dyslexia, 52,* 165–187.

Luria, A. R. (1968). *The mind of a mnemonist.* New York: Basic Books.

Luria, A. R. (1973). *The working brain.* London: Penguin.

Luria, A. R. (1976). *Cognitive development: Its cultural and social foundations.* Cambridge, MA: Harvard University Press.

Luthar, S. S., & Cushing, G. (1999). Measurement issues in the empirical study of resiliency: An overview. In M. D. Glantz & J. L. Johnson (Eds.), *Resiliency and development: Positive life adaptations* (pp. 129–160). New York: Kluwer.

Luthar, S. S., Cicchetti, D., & Becker, B. (2000). The construct of resilience: A critical evaluation and guidelines for future work. *Child Development, 71,* 543–562.

Lutz, D., & Sternberg, R. J. (1999). Cognitive development. In M. H. Bornstein & M. E. Lamb (Eds.), *Developmental psychology: An advanced textbook* (4th ed., pp. 275–311). Mahwah, NJ: Erlbaum.

Lydiard, L. R., Brawman, M. O., & Ballenger, J. C. (1996). Recent developments in the psychopharmacology of anxiety disorders. *Journal of Consulting and Clinical Psychology, 64,* 660–668.

Lykken, D. (1998). *A tremor in the blood.* New York: Plenum.

Lyon, J., & Gorner, P. (1995). *Altered fates: Gene therapy and the retooling of human life.* New York: Norton.

Maass, W., & Markram, H. (2002). Synapses as dynamic memory buffers. *Neural Networks, 15,* 155–161.

MacDonald, D. J., & Standing, L. G. (2002). Does self-serving bias cancel the Barnum effect? *Social Behavior & Personality, 30,* 625–630.

MacKinnon, D., Jamison, R., & DePaulo, J. R. (1997). Genetics of manic depressive illness. *Annual Review of Neuroscience, 20,* 355–373.

Mackintosh, N. (1998). *IQ and intelligence.* New York: Oxford University Press.

MacLeod, C. (1991). Half a century of research on the Stroop effect: An integrative review. *Psychological Bulletin, 109,* 163–203.

MacLeod, C. M. (1996). How priming affects two speeded implicit tests of remembering: Naming colors versus reading words. *Consciousness and Cognition: An International Journal, 5,* 73–90.

MacLeod, C. M., Hunt, E. B., & Mathews, N. N. (1978). Individual differences in the verification of sentence-picture relationships. *Journal of Verbal Learning and Verbal Behavior, 17,* 493–507.

Macrae, C. N., Bodenhausen, G. V., Milne, A. B., Thorn, T., & Castelli, L. (1997). On the activation of social stereotypes: The moderating role of processing *x* objectives. *Journal of Experimental Social Psychology, 33,* 471–489.

MacWhinney, B. (1999). *The emergence of language.* Mahwah, NJ: Erlbaum.

Mader, B., Hart, L. A., & Bergin, B. (1989). Social acknowledgments for children with disabilities: Effects of service dogs. *Child Development, 60,* 1529–1534.

Maehr, M., & Nicholls, J. (1980). Culture and achievement motivation: A second look. In N. Warren (Ed.), *Studies in cross-cultural psychology* (Vol. 2). London: Academic Press.

Magnus, K., Diener, E., Fujita, F., & Pavot, W. (1993). Extraversion and neuroticism as predictors of objective life events: A longitudinal analysis. *Journal of Personality and Social Psychology, 65*, 1046–1053.

Main, M., & Solomon, J. (1990). Procedures for identifying infants as disorganized/disoriented during the Ainsworth strange situation. In M. Greenberg, D. Cicchetti, & E. M. Cummings (Eds.), *Attachment in the preschool years: Theory, research and intervention* (pp. 121–160). Chicago: University of Chicago Press.

Main, M., Kaplan, N., & Cassidy, J. (1985). Security in infancy, childhood, and adulthood: A move to the level of representation. In I. Bretherton and E. Waters (Eds.), *Growing points of attachment theory and research: Monographs of the Society for Research in Child Development, 50* (Nos. 1–2), 67–104.

Maj, M., Gaebel, W., Lopez-Ibor, J., & Sartorius, N. (2002). Psychiatric diagnosis and classification. *Psychotherapy & Psychosomatics, 71*, 363.

Malhotra, S., King, K. H., Welge, J. A., Brusman-Lovins, L., & McElroy, S. L. (2002). Venlafaxine treatment of binge-eating disorder associated with obesity: A series of 35 patients. *Journal of Clinical Psychiatry, 63*(9), 802–806.

Malik, M. L., Beutler, L. E., Alimohamed, S., Gallagher-Thompson, D., & Thompson, L. (2003). Are all cognitive therapies alike? A comparison of cognitive and noncognitive therapy process and implications for the application of empirically supported treatments. *Journal of Consulting & Clinical Psychology, 71*, 150–158.

Maling, M. S., & Howard, K. I. (1994). From research to practice to research to . . . . In P. F. Talley, H. H. Strupp, & S. F. Butler (Eds.), *Psychotherapy research and practice: Bridging the gap.* New York: Basic Books.

Malone, K. Y., & Mann, J. J. (1993). Serotonin and major depression. In J. J. Mann & D. J. Kupfer (Eds.), *Biology of depressive disorders: Part A. A systems perspective* (pp. 29–49). New York: Plenum.

Malonek, D., & Grinvald, A. (1996). Interactions between electrical activity and cortical microcirculation revealed by imaging spectroscopy: Implication for functional brain mapping. *Science, 272*, 551–554.

Maltby, J. (1995). Personality, prayer, and church attendance among U.S. female adults. *Journal of Social Psychology, 135*, 529–531.

Maner, J. K., Luce, C. L., Neuberg, S. L., Cialdini, R. B., Brown, S., & Sagarin, B. J. (2002). The effects of perspective taking on motivations for helping: Still no evidence for altruism. *Personality & Social Psychology Bulletin, 28*, 1601–1610.

Mangelsdorf, S. C., Shapiro, J. R., & Marzolf, D. (1995). Developmental and temperamental differences in emotion regulation in infancy. *Child Development, 66*, 1817–1828.

Mangun, G. R., Plager, R., Loftus, W., Hillyard, S. A., Luck, S. J., Clark, V., Handy, T., & Gazzaniga, M. S. (1994). Monitoring the visual world: Hemispheric asymmetries and subcortical processes in attention. *Journal of Cognitive Neuroscience, 6*, 265–273.

Manji, H. K., Hsiao, J. K., Risby, E. D., et al. (1991). The mechanisms of action of lithium: I. Effects on serotonergic and noradrenergic systems in normal subjects. *Archives of General Psychiatry, 48*, 505–512.

Mann, J. (1973). *Time-dated psychotherapy.* Cambridge, MA: Harvard University Press.

Mantyla, T. (1986). Optimizing cue effectiveness: Recall of 500 and 600 incidentally learned words. *Journal of Experimental Psychology: Learning, Memory, and Cognition, 12*, 66–71.

Maqsud, M., & Rouhani, S. (1990). Self-concept and moral reasoning among Batswana adolescents. *Journal of Social Psychology, 130*(6), 829–830.

Maratsos, M. (1998). The acquisition of grammar. In D. Kuhn & R. S. Siegler (Eds.), *Handbook of child psychology. Vol. 2: Cognition, perception, and language* (5th ed., pp. 421–466). New York: Wiley.

Marcel, A. J. (1983). Conscious and unconscious perception: An approach to the relations between phenomenal experience and perceptual processes. *Cognitive Psychology, 15*, 238–300.

Marcia, J. E. (1966). Development and validation of ego identity status. *Journal of Personality and Social Psychology, 3*(5), 551–558.

Marcia, J. E. (1980). Identity in adolescence. In J. Adelson (Ed.), *Handbook of adolescent psychology* (pp. 159–187). New York: Wiley.

Marcus, G. F. (1998). Rethinking eliminative connectionism. *Cognitive Psychology, 37*, 243–282.

Marcus, G. F., Vijayan, S., Bandi Rao, S., & Vishton, P. M. (1999). Rule learning by seven-month-old infants. *Science, 283*, 77–80.

Marie, A., Gabrieli, J. D. E., Vaidya, C., Brown, B., Pratto, F., Zajonc, R. B., & Shaw, R. J. (2001). The mere exposure effect in patients with schizophrenia. *Schizophrenia Bulletin, 27*, 297–303.

Markman, E. M. (1977). Realizing that you don't understand: A preliminary investigation. *Child Development, 48*, 986–992.

Markman, E. M. (1979). Realizing that you don't understand: Elementary school children's awareness of inconsistencies. *Child Development, 50*, 643–655.

Markman, E. M. (1992). Constraints on word learning: Speculation about their nature, origins and domain specificity. In M. R. Gunner & M. P. Maratsos (Eds.), *Modularity and constraints in language and cognition: The Minnesota symposium on child psychology.* Hillsdale, NJ: Erlbaum.

Markowitsch, H. J. (2000). Neuroanatomy of memory. In E. Tulving & F. I. M. Craik (Eds.), *The Oxford handbook of memory* (pp. 465–484). New York: Oxford University Press.

Markowitsch, H. J., Calabrese, P., Fink, G. R., Durwen, H. F., et al. (1997). Impaired episodic memory retrieval in a case of probable psychogenic amnesia. *Psychiatry Research: Neuroimaging, 74*(2), 119–126.

Markus, H. R., & Kitayama, S. (1994). The cultural construction of self and emotion: Implications for social behavior. In S. Kitayama & H. R. Markus (Eds.), *Emotions and culture: Empirical studies of mutual influence.* Washington, DC: American Psychological Association.

Markus, H. R., Kitayama, S., & Heiman, R. J. (1996). Culture and "basic" psychological principles. In E. T. Higgins & A. W. Kruglanski (Eds.), *Social psychology: Handbook of basic principles* (pp. 857–913). New York: Guilford.

Markus, H., & Kitayama, S. (1991). Culture and the self: Implications for cognition, emotion, and motivation. *Psychological Review, 98*(2), 224–253.

Marlatt, G. A. (2002). Buddhist philosophy and the treatment of addictive behavior. *Cognitive & Behavioral Practice, 9*, 44–49.

Marr, D. (1982). *Vision.* San Francisco: Freeman.

Marshall, G. D., & Zimbardo, P. G. (1979). Affective consequences of inadequately explained arousal. *Journal of Personality and Social Psychology, 37*, 970–985.

Marshall, G. N., Wortman, C. B., Vickers, R. R., Kusulas, J. W., & Hewig, L. K. (1994). The five-factor model of personality as a framework for personality-health research. *Journal of Personality and Social Psychology, 48*, 278–286.

Martelli, M. F., Auerbach, S. M., Alexander, J., & Mercuri, L. G. (1987). Stress management in the health care setting: Matching interventions with patient coping styles. *Journal of Consulting and Clinical Psychology, 55*, 201–207.

Martin, C. L., Ruble, D. N., & Szkrybalo, J. (2002). Cognitive theories of early gender development. *Psychological Bulletin, 128*, 903–933.

Martin, F. E. (1985). The treatment and outcome of anorexia nervosa in adolescents: A prospective study and five year follow-up. *Journal of Psychiatric Research, 19*, 509–514.

Martin, J. A. (1981). A longitudinal study of the consequences of early mother–infant interaction: A microanalytic approach. *Monographs of the Society for Research in Child Development, 46*(203, Serial No. 190).

Martin, L. (1986). Eskimo words for snow: A case study in the genesis and decay of an anthropological example. *American Psychologist, 88*, 418–423.

Martindale, C. (1981). *Cognition and consciousness.* Homewood, IL: Dorsey Press.

Martorell, R. (1998). Nutrition and the worldwide rise in IQ scores. In U. Neisser (Ed.), *The rising curve: Long-term gains in IQ and related measures* (pp. 183–206). Washington, DC: American Psychological Association.

Marusic, A., Gudjonsson, G. H., Eysenck, H. J., & Starc, R. (1999). Biological and psychosocial risk factors in ischaemic heart disease: Empirical findings and a biopsychosocial model. *Personality & Individual Differences, 26*, 285–304.

Maslow, A. H. (1943). A theory of human motivation. *Psychological Review, 50*, 370–396.

Maslow, A. H. (1954). *Motivation and personality*. New York: Harper & Row.

Maslow, A. H. (1970). *Motivation and personality* (2nd ed.). New York: Harper.

Masten, A. S. (1999). Resilience comes of age: Reflections on the past and outlook for the next generation of research. In M. D. Glantz & J. L. Johnson (Eds.), *Resiliency and development: Possible life adaptations* (pp. 281–295). New York: Kluwer.

Masten, A. S. (2001). Ordinary magic: Resilience processes in development. *American Psychologist, 56,* 227–238.

Masten, A. S., & Coatsworth, J. D. (1998). The development of competence in favorable and noncompetitive environments: Lessons from research on successful children. *American Psychologist, 53,* 205–220.

Masters, K. S., Lacaille, R. A., & Shearer, D. S. (2003). The acute affective response of Type A behaviour pattern individuals to competitive and noncompetitive exercise. *Canadian Journal of Behavioural Science, 35,* 25–34.

Matarazzo, J. D. (1992). Biological and physiological correlates of intelligence. *Intelligence, 16*(3–4), 257–258.

Matas, L., Arend, R., & Sroufe, L. A. (1978). Continuity of adaptation in the second year: The relationship between quality of attachment and later competence. *Child Development, 49,* 547–556.

Mathur, M., & Chattopadhyay, A. (1991). The impact of moods generated by TV programs on responses to advertising. *Psychology and Marketing, 8,* 59–77.

Matlin, M. (1993). *The psychology of women* (2nd ed.). Fort Worth, TX: Harcourt Brace Jovanovich.

Matsumoto, D. (1994). *People: Psychology from a cross-cultural perspective.* Belmont, CA: Brooks/Cole.

Matsumoto, D. (1996). *Culture and psychology.* Belmont, CA: Brooks/Cole.

Matsumoto, D. R. (Ed.). (2001). *Handbook of culture and psychology.* New York: Oxford University Press.

Maurer, K. L., Park, B., & Judd, C. M. (1996). Stereotypes, prejudice, and judgments of group members: The mediating role of public policy decisions. *Journal of Experimental Social Psychology, 32,* 411–436.

Mayer, J. D., & Gehr, G. (1996). Emotional intelligence and the identification of emotion. *Intelligence, 22,* 89–114.

Mayer, J. D., & Salovey, P. (1993). The intelligence of emotional intelligence. *Intelligence, 197,* 433–442.

Mayer, J. D., & Salovey, P. (1995). Emotional intelligence and the construction and regulation of feelings. *Applied and Preventive Psychology, 4,* 197–208.

Mayer, J. D., & Salovey, P. (1997). What is emotional intelligence? In P. Salovey & D. Sluyter (Eds.), *Emotional development and emotional intelligence*: *Implications for educators* (pp. 3–31). New York: Basic Books.

Mayer, J. D., Salovey, P., & Caruso, D. (2000). Models of emotional intelligence. In R. J. Sternberg (Ed.), *Handbook of intelligence* (pp. 396–420). New York: Cambridge University Press.

Mayer, R. E. (2000). Intelligence and education. In R. J. Sternberg (Ed.), *Handbook of intelligence* (pp. 519–533). New York: Cambridge University Press.

Mayes, L. C., & Fahy, T. (2001). Prenatal drug exposure and cognitive development. In R. J. Sternberg & E. L. Grigorenko (Eds.), *Environmental effects on cognitive abilities* (pp. 189–220). Mahwah, NJ: Erlbaum.

McAdams, D. P. (1993). *The stories we live by: Personal myths and the making of the self.* New York: Morrow.

McBride, P., Brown, R. P., Demeo, M., & Keilp, J. (1994). The relationship of platelet 5-HT-sub-2 receptor indices to major depressive disorder, personality traits, and suicidal behavior. *Biological Psychiatry, 35,* 295–308.

McCall, R. B., & Carriger, M. S. (1993). A meta-analysis of infant habituation and recognition memory performance as predictors of later IQ. *Child Development, 64,* 57–79.

McCall, R. B., Kennedy, C. B., & Appelbaum, M. I. (1977). Magnitude of discrepancy and the distribution of attention in infants. *Child Development, 48,* 772–786.

McCarley, R. W., & Hobson, J. A. (1981). REM sleep dreams and the activation-synthesis hypothesis. *American Journal of Psychiatry, 138,* 904–912.

McCarthy, G., Blamire, A. M., Puce, A., Nobe, A. C., Bloch, G., Hyder, F., Goldman-Rakic, P., & Shulman, R. G. (1994). Functional magnetic resonance imaging of human prefrontal cortex activation during a spatial working memory task. *Proceedings of the National Academy of Sciences, USA, 91,* 8690–8694.

McCarthy, G., Blamire, A. M., Rothman, D. L., Gruetter, R., & Shulman, R. G. (1993). Echo-planar magnetic resonance imaging studies of frontal cortex activation during word generation in humans. *Proceedings of the National Academy of Sciences, USA, 90,* 4952–4956.

McClelland, D. C. (1961). *The achieving society.* Princeton, NJ: Van Nostrand.

McClelland, D. C. (1985). *Human motivation.* New York: Scott, Foresman.

McClelland, D. C., & Franz, C. E. (1992). Motivational and other sources of work accomplishments in mid-life: A longitudinal study. *Journey of Personality, 60,* 679–707.

McClelland, D. C., & Koestner, R. (1992). The achievement motive. In C. P. Smith (Ed.), *Motivation and personality: Handbook of thematic content analysis.* New York: Cambridge University Press.

McClelland, D. C., & Teague, G. (1975). Predicting risk preferences among power-related tasks. *Journal of Personality, 43,* 266–285.

McClelland, D. C., & Winter, D. G. (1969). *Motivating economic achievement.* New York: Free Press.

McClelland, D. C., Atkinson, J. W., Clark, R. A., & Lowell, E. L. (1953). *The achievement motive.* New York: Appleton-Century-Crofts.

McClelland, D. C., Koestner, R., & Weinberger, J. (1992). How do self-attributed and implicit motives differ? In C. P. Smith (Ed.), *Motivation and personality: Handbook of thematic content analysis.* New York: Cambridge University Press.

McClelland, J. L. (2000). Connectionist models of memory. In E. Tulving & F. I. M. Craik (Eds.), *The Oxford handbook of memory* (pp. 583–596). New York: Oxford University Press.

McClelland, J. L. (2001). Failures to learn and their remediation: A Hebbian account. In J. L. McClelland & R. S. Siegler (Eds.), *Mechanisms of cognitive development: Behavioral and neural perspectives: Carnegie Mellon symposia on cognition* (pp. 97–121). Mahwah, NJ: Erlbaum.

McClelland, J. L., McNaughton, B. L., & O'Reilly, R. C. (1995). Why there are complementary learning systems in the hippocampus and neocortex: Insights from the successes and failures of connectionist models of learning and memory. *Psychological Review, 102*(3), 419–457.

McClintock, C. G., & Liebrand, W. B. G. (1988). Role of interdependence structure, individual value orientation, and another's strategy in social decision making: A transformational analysis. *Journal of Personality and Social Psychology, 55*(3), 396–409.

McConkey, K. M. (1992). The effects of hypnotic procedures on remembering: The experimental findings and their implications for forensic hypnosis. In E. Fromm & M. R. Nash (Eds.), *Contemporary hypnosis research* (pp. 405–426). New York: Guilford.

McCord, D. M. (1995). Toward a typology of wilderness-based residential treatment program participants. *Residential Treatment for Children & Youth, 12*(4), 51–60.

McCormick, D. A., & Thompson, R. F. (1984). Cerebellum: Essential involvement in the classically conditioned eyelid response. *Science, 223,* 296–299.

McCrae, R. R. (1996). Social consequences of experiential openness. *Psychological Bulletin, 120,* 323–337.

McCrae, R. R., & Costa, P. T. (1991). Adding Liebe und Arbeit: The full five-factor model and well-being. *Personality and Social Psychology Bulletin, 17,* 227–232.

McCrae, R. R., & Costa, P. T. (1997). Personality trait structure as a human universal. *American Psychologist, 5,* 509–516.

McCrae, R. R., Costa, P. T. Jr., & Yik, M. S. M. (1996). Universal aspects of Chinese personality structure. In M. H. Bond (Ed.), *The handbook of Chinese psychology* (pp. 189–207). Hong Kong: Oxford University Press.

McDermott, K. B. (1996). The persistence of false memories in list recall. *Journal of Memory and Language, 35,* 212–230.

McDermut, W., Zimmerman, M., & Chelminski, I. (2003). The construct validity of depressive personality disorder. *Journal of Abnormal Psychology, 112,* 49–60.

McDougall, W. (1908). *An introduction to social psychology*. London: Methuen.

McGarry-Roberts, P. A., Stelmack, R. M., & Campbell, K. B. (1992). Intelligence, reaction time, and event-related potentials. *Intelligence, 16*(3–4), 289–313.

McGaugh, J. L. (1999). Memory storage, modulation of. In R. A. Wilson & F. C. Keil (Eds.), *The MIT encyclopedia of the cognitive sciences* (pp. 522–524). Cambridge, MA: MIT Press.

McGaugh, J. L., Cahill, L., & Roozendaal, B. (1996). Involvement of the amygdala in memory storage: Interaction with other brain systems. *Proceedings of the National Academy of Sciences, USA, 93*, 13508–13514.

McGinn, L. K., & Sanderson, W. C. (1995). The nature of panic disorder. *In Session: Psychotherapy in Practice, 1*, 7–19.

McGue, M., Bouchard, T. J. Jr., Iacono, W. G., & Lykken, D. T. (1993). Behavioral genetics of cognitive ability: A life-span perspective. In R. Plomin & & G. E. McClearn (Eds.), *Nature, nurture, and psychology* (pp. 59–76). Washington, DC: American Psychological Association.

McGuire, L., Kiecolt-Glaser, J. K., & Glaser, R. (2002). Depressive symptoms and lymphocyte proliferation in older adults. *Journal of Abnormal Psychology, 111*, 192–197.

McHale, S. M., Dariotis, J. K., & Kauh, T. J. (2003). Social development and social relationships in middle childhood. In R. M. Lerner, M. A. Easterbrooks, & J. Mistry (Vol. Eds.) and I. B. Weiner (Ed.-in-Chief), *Handbook of psychology. Vol. 6: Developmental psychology* (pp. 241–265). New York: Wiley.

McHugh, P. R., & Moran, T. H. (1985). The stomach: A conception of its dynamic role in satiety. In J. M. Sprague & A. N. Epstein (Eds.), *Progress in psychobiology and physiological psychology* (Vol. 11, pp. 197–232). Orlando, FL: Academic Press.

McKellar, J., Stewart, E., & Humphreys, K. (2003). Alcoholics Anonymous involvement and positive alcohol-related outcomes: Cause, consequence, or just a correlate? A prospective 2-year study of 2,319 alcohol-dependent men. *Journal of Consulting & Clinical Psychology, 71*, 302–308.

McKenna, J., Treadway, M., & McCloskey, M. E. (1992). Expert psychological testimony on eyewitness reliability: Selling psychology before its time. In P. Suedfeld & P. E. Tetlock (Eds.), *Psychology and social policy* (pp. 283–293). New York: Hemisphere.

McKinlay, J. B. (1975). Who is really ignorant—Physician or patient? *Journal of Health and Social Behavior, 16*, 3–11.

McLaughlin, C. R., Yelon, J. A., Ivatury, R., & Sugerman, H. J. (2000). Youth violence: A tripartite examination of putative causes, consequences, and correlates. *Trauma Violence & Abuse, 1*, 115–127.

McLeod, P., Plunkett, K., & Rolls, E. T. (1998). *Introduction to connectionist modelling of cognitive processes*. Oxford, UK: Oxford University Press.

McLeod, P., Shallice, T., & Plaut, D. C. (2000). Attractor dynamics in word recognition: Converging evidence from errors by normal subjects, dyslexic patients and a connectionist model. *Cognition, 74*, 91–113.

McNicholas, J., & Collis, G. M. (2000). Dogs as catalysts for social interaction: Robustness of the effect. *British Journal of Psychology, 91*, 61–70.

Meacham, A. (1982). A note on remembering to execute planned actions. *Journal of Applied Developmental Psychology, 3*, 121–133.

Meacham, J. A., & Singer, J. (1977). Incentive in prospective remembering. *Journal of Psychology, 97*, 191–197.

Mednick, S. A., Hutunen, M. O., & Machon, R. (1994). Prenatal influenza infections and adult schizophrenia. *Schizophrenia Bulletin, 20*, 263–267.

Meeus, W. H. J., & Raaijmakers, Q. A. W. (1995). Obedience in modern society: The Utrecht studies. *Journal of Social Issues, 51*, 155–175.

Mehler, J., Dupoux, E., Nazzi, T., & Dehaene-Lambertz, G. (1996). Coping with linguistic diversity: The infant's viewpoint. In J. L. Morgan & K. Demuth (Eds.), *Signal to syntax: Bootstrapping from speech to grammar in early acquisition* (pp. 101–116). Mahwah, NJ: Erlbaum.

Meier, R. P. (1991). Language acquisition by deaf children. *American Scientist, 79*, 60–76.

Melamed, B. G., & Siegel, L. (1975). Reduction of anxiety in children facing hospitalization and surgery by use of filmed modeling. *Journal of Consulting and Clinical Psychology, 43*, 511–521.

Melfse, S., & Florin, I. (2002). Do socially anxious children show deficits in classifying facial expressions of emotions? *Journal of Nonverbal Behavior, 26*(2), 109–126.

Mellgren, R. L. (1998). Foraging. In G. Greenberg & M. M. Haraway (Eds.), *Comparative psychology: A handbook* (pp. 666–673). New York: Garland.

Mellinger, G. D., Balter, M. B., & Uhlenhuth, E. H. (1985). Insomnia and its treatment: Prevalence and correlations. *Archives of General Psychiatry, 42*, 225–232.

Meltzoff, A. N., & Moore, M. K. (1989). Imitation in newborn infants: Exploring the range of gestures imitated and the underlying mechanisms. *Developmental Psychology, 25*(6), 954–962.

Melzack, R., & Wall, P. D. (1982). *The challenge of pain*. New York: Basic Books.

Melzack, R., Wall, P. D., & Ty, T. C. (1982). Acute pain in an emergency clinic: Latency of onset and descriptor patterns related to different injuries. *Pain, 14*(1), 33–43.

Mental Health, United States, 1996–1997. (1997). Washington, DC: Substance Abuse and Mental Health Services Administration.

Merskey, H. (2000). Pain, psychogenesis, and psychiatric diagnosis. *International Review of Psychiatry, 12*, 99–102.

Mesquita, B., & Frijda, N. H. (1992). Cultural variations in emotions: A review. *Psychological Bulletin, 112*(3), 179–204.

Messer, B., & Harter, S. (1985). *The self-perception scale for adults*. Unpublished manuscript, University of Denver.

Messick, S. (1995). Validity of psychological assessment: Validation of inferences from persons' responses and performances as scientific inquiry into score meaning. *American Psychologist, 50*, 741–749.

Metcalfe, J. (2000). Metamemory: Theory and data. In E. Tulving & F. I. M. Craik (Eds.), *The Oxford handbook of memory* (pp. 197–211). New York: Oxford University Press.

Meyer, G. J., Hilsenroth, M. J., Baxter, D., Exner, J. E. Jr., Fowler, J. C., Piers, C. C., & Resnick, J. (2002). An examination of interrater reliability for scoring the Rorschach comprehensive system in eight data sets. *Journal of Personality Assessment, 78*, 219–274.

Meyers, S. A., & Berscheid, E. (1997). The language of love: The difference a preposition makes. *Personality and Social Psychology Bulletin, 23*, 347–362.

Michael, R. T., Gagnon, J. H., Laumann, E. O., & Kolatu, G. (1994). *Sex in America: A definitive survey*. Boston: Little, Brown.

Michinov, E., & Monteil, J.-M. (2002). The similarity-attraction relationship revisited: Divergence between the affective and behavioral facets of attraction. *European Journal of Social Psychology, 32*, 485–500.

Mickelson, K. D., Kessler, R. C., & Shaver, P. R. (1997). Adult attachment in a nationally representative sample. *Journal of Personality and Social Psychology, 73*, 1092–1106.

Mikula, G., Athenstaedt, U., Heschgl, S., & Heimgartner, A. (1998). Does it only depend on the point of view? Perspective-related differences in justice evaluations of negative incidents in personal relationships. *European Journal of Social Psychology, 28*, 931–962.

Miles, D. R., & Carey, G. (1997). Genetic and environmental architecture of human aggression. *Journal of Personality and Social Psychology, 72*, 207–217.

Milgram, S. (1963). Behavioral study of obedience. *Journal of Abnormal and Social Psychology, 67*, 371–378.

Milgram, S. (1965). Some conditions of obedience and disobedience to authority. *Human Relations, 18*, 57–76.

Milgram, S. (1974). *Obedience to authority: An experimental view*. New York: Harper & Row.

Miller, A. G. (1999). Harming other people: Perspectives on evil and violence. *Personality and Social Psychology Review, 3*, 176–178.

Miller, D. T., & McFarland, C. (1987). Pluralistic ignorance: When similarity is interpreted as dissimilarity. *Journal of Personality and Social Psychology, 53*, 298–305.

Miller, G. A. (1956). The magical number seven, plus or minus two: Some limits on our capacity for processing information. *Psychological Review, 63*, 81–97.

Miller, G. A. (1990). *The science of words*. New York: Scientific American Library.

Miller, G. A., Galanter, E. H., & Pribram, K. H. (1960). *Plans and the structure of behavior*. New York: Holt, Rinehart & Winston.

Miller, J. G. (1984). Culture and the development of everyday social explanation. *Journal of Personality and Social Psychology, 46*, 961–978.

Miller, L. K. (1999). The savant syndrome: Intellectual impairment and exceptional skill. *Psychological Bulletin, 125*(1), 331–346.

Miller, N., & Brewer, M. B. (Eds.). (1984). *Groups in contact: The psychology of desegregation*. New York: Academic Press.

Miller, S. D., & Triggiano, P. J. (1992). The psychophysiological investigation of multiple personality disorder: Review and update. *American Journal of Clinical Hypnosis, 35*, 47–61.

Mills, D. L., Coffey-Corina, S., & Neville, H. J. (1997). Language comprehension and cerebral specialization from 13 to 20 months. *Developmental Neuropsychology, 13*(3), 397–445.

Mills, J. S., Polivy, J., Herman, C. P., & Tiggeman, M. (2002). Effects of exposure to thin media images: Evidence of self-enhancement among restrained eaters. *Personality & Social Psychology Bulletin, 28*, 1687–1699.

Mills, R. T., & Krantz, D. S. (1979). Information, choice, and reactions to stress: A field experiment in a blood bank with laboratory analogue. *Journal of Personality and Social Psychology, 4*, 608–620.

Millsap, R. E. (1994). Psychometrics. In R. J. Sternberg (Ed.), *Encyclopedia of human intelligence* (Vol. 2, pp. 866–868). New York: Macmillan.

Milner, B., Corkin, S., & Teuber, H. L. (1968). Further analysis of the hippocampal amnesic syndrome: 14-year follow-up study of H. M. *Neuropsychologia, 6*, 215–234.

Mischel, W. (1968). *Personality and assessment*. New York: Wiley.

Mischel, W. (1977). On the future of personality measurement. *American Psychologist, 32*, 246–254.

Mischel, W. (1986). *Introduction to personality* (4th ed.). New York: Holt, Rinehart & Winston.

Mischel, W., & Peake, P. K. (1983). Some facets of consistency: Replies to Epstein, Funder, and Bem. *Psychological Review, 90*, 394–402.

Mishkin, M., & Petri, H. L. (1984). Memories and habits: Some implications for the analysis of learning and retention. In L. R. Squire & N. Butters (Eds.), *Neurophysiology of memory* (pp. 287–296). New York: Guilford.

Mistlberger, R. E., & Rusak, B. (1999). Circadian rhythms in mammmals: Formal properties and environmental influences. In M. H. Kryger, T. Roth, & W. C. Dement (Eds.), *Principles and practice of sleep medicine* (2nd ed.). Philadelphia: Saunders.

Mistry, J., & Saraswathi, T. S. (2003). The cultural context of child development. In R. M. Lerner, M. A. Easterbrooks, & J. Mistry (Vol. Eds.) and I. B. Weiner (Ed.-in-Chief), *Handbook of psychology*. Vol. 6: *Developmental psychology* (pp. 267–291). New York: Wiley.

Mitchell, K. J., & Johnson, M. K. (2000). Source monitoring: Attributing mental experiences. In E. Tulving & F. I. M. Craik (Eds.), *The Oxford handbook of memory* (pp. 179–195). New York: Oxford University Press.

Mithers, C. L. (1994). *Reasonable insanity: A true story of the seventies*. Reading, MA: Addison-Wesley.

Mitroff, S. R., Simons, D. J., & Franconeri, S. L. (2002). The siren song of implicit change detection. *Journal of Experimental Psychology: Human Perception & Performance, 28*, 798–815.

Miyake, K., Chen, S., & Campos, J. J. (1985). Infant temperament, mother's mode of interaction, and attachment in Japan: An interim report. In I. Bretherton & E. Waters (Eds.), *Growing points of attachment in theory and research*. Chicago: University of Chicago Press. (Reprinted from *Monographs of the Society for Research in Child Development 50*, 1–2, Serial No. 209)

Moghaddam, F. M., Taylor, D. M., & Wright, S. C. (1993). *Social psychology in cross-cultural perspective*. New York: Freeman.

Mogil, J. (2000). Pain: Mechanisms. In A. E. Kazdin (Ed.), *Encyclopedia of psychology* (Vol. 6, pp. 23–24). Washington, DC: American Psychological Association.

Mohamed, A. A., & Wiebe, F. A. (1996). Toward a process theory of groupthink. *Small Group Research, 27*, 416–430.

Moldoveanu, M., & Langer, E. (2002). When "stupid" is smarter than we are: Mindlessness and the attribution of stupidity. In R. J. Sternberg (Ed.), *Why smart people can be so stupid* (pp. 212–231). New Haven, CT: Yale University Press.

Monahan, J. L., Murphy, S. T., & Zajonc, R. B. (2000). Subliminal mere exposure: Specific, general, and diffuse effects. *Psychological Science, 11*, 462–466.

Money, J., Wiedeking, C., Walker, P. A., & Gain, D. (1976). Combined antiandrogenic and counseling program for treatment of 46 XY and 47 XYY sex offenders. *Hormones, behavior, and psychopathology, 66*, 105–109.

Montag, I., & Levin, J. (1994). The five-factor personality model in applied settings. *European Journal of Personality, 8*, 1–11.

Montagu, A. (1976). *The nature of human aggression*. New York: Oxford University Press.

Monteith, M. J., Devine, P. G., & Zuwerink, J. R. (1993). Self-directed versus other-directed affect as a consequence of prejudice-related discrepancies. *Journal of Personality and Social Psychology, 64*, 198–210.

Moore, E. G. J. (1986). Family socialization and the IQ test performance of traditionally and transracially adopted black children. *Developmental Psychology, 22*, 317–326.

Moore, J. T., & Brylinsky, J. (1993). Spectator effect on team performance in college basketball. *Journal of Sport Behavior, 16*, 77–84.

Moos, R. H. (1982). Coping with acute health crises. In T. Millon, C. Green, & R. Meagher (Eds.), *Handbook of clinical health psychology*. New York: Plenum.

Moos, R. H. (1988). Life stressors and coping resources influence health and well-being. *Psychological Assessment, 4*, 133–158.

Moos, R. H. (1995). Development and applications of new measures of life stressors, social resources, and coping responses. *European Journal of Psychological Assessment, 11*, 1–13.

Moos, R. H., & Schaefer, J. A. (1986). Life transitions and crises: A conceptual overview. In R. H. Moos (Ed.), *Coping with life crises: An integrated approach*. New York: Plenum.

Moray, N. (1959). Attention in dichotic listening: Affective cues and the influence of instructions. *Quarterly Journal of Experimental Psychology, 11*, 56–60.

Morelli, G. A., & Tronick, E. Z. (1991). Parenting and child development in the Efe foragers and Lese farmers of Zaire. In Marc H. Bornstein (Ed.), *Cultural approaches to parenting. Crosscurrents in contemporary psychology* (pp. 91–113). Mahwah, NJ: Erlbaum.

Morelli, G. A., Rogoff, B., Oppenheim, D., & Goldsmith, D. (1992). Cultural variations in infants' sleeping arrangements: Questions of independence. *Developmental Psychology, 28*, 604–613.

Morey, L. C. (1993). Psychological correlates of personality disorder. *Journal of Personality Disorders* (Suppl.), 149–166.

Morgan, C. D., & Murray, H. A. (1935). A method for investigating fantasy: The Thematic Apperception Test. *Archives of Neurology and Psychiatry, 34*, 289–306.

Morgan, C. T., & Morgan, J. T. (1940). Studies in hunger II: The relation of gastric denervation and dietary sugar to the effect of insulin upon food-intake in the rat. *Journal of Genetic Psychology, 57*, 153–163.

Morris, M. W., & Larrick, R. P. (1995). When one cause casts doubt on another: A normative analysis of discounting in causal attribution. *Psychological Review, 102*, 331–355.

Morris, M. W., & Peng, K. (1994). Culture and cause: American and Chinese attributions for social and physical events. *Journal of Personality and Social Psychology, 67*, 949–971.

Moscovici, S. (1976). *Social influence and social change*. London: Academic Press.

Moscovici, S. (1980). Toward a theory of conversion behavior. In L. Berkowitz (Ed.), *Advances in Experimental Social Psychology, 6*, 149–202.

Moscovici, S., & Zavalloni, M. (1969). The group as a polarizer of attitudes. *Journal of Personality and Social Psychology, 12*, 125–135.

Moshman, D. (2001). Conceptual constraints on thinking about genocide. *Journal of Genocide Research, 3*, 431–450.

Moshman, D. (in press). Theories of self and theories as selves: Identity in Rwanda. In M. Chandler, C. Lalonde, & C. Lightfoot (Eds.), *Changing conceptions of psychological life*. Mahwah, NJ: Erlbaum.

Moss, P. A. (1994). Validity. In R. J. Sternberg (Ed.), *Encyclopedia of human intelligence* (Vol. 2, pp. 1101–1106). New York: Macmillan.

Moyers, B. D. (1993). *Healing and the mind*. New York: Doubleday.

Moynihan, J. A., & Ader, R. (1996). Psychoneuroimmunology: Animal models of disease. *Psychosomatic Medicine, 58*, 546–558.

Muehlenhard, C. L., & Kimes, L. A. (1999). The social construction of violence: The case of sexual and domestic violence. *Personality & Social Psychology Review, 3,* 234–245.

Mueller, C. M., & Dweck, C. S. (1998). Intelligence praise can undermine motivation and performance. *Journal of Personality and Social Psychology, 75,* 33–52.

Murnen, S. K., Peroit, A., & Byrne, D. (1989). Coping with unwanted sexual activity: Normative responses, situational determinants, and individual differences. *Journal of Sex Research, 26,* 85–106.

Murphy, G. L. (1993). A rational theory of concepts. In G. V. Nakamura, D. L. Medin, et al. (Eds.), *Categorization by humans and machines. The psychology of learning and motivation: Advances in research and theory* (Vol. 29, pp. 327–359). San Diego: Academic Press.

Murphy, J. (1976). Psychiatric labeling in cross-cultural perspective. *Science, 191,* 1019–1028.

Murray, C. D. (2001). The experience of body boundaries by Siamese twins. *New Ideas in Psychology, 19,* 117–130.

Murray, D. J. (2000). Weber, Ernst Heinrich. In A. E. Kazdin (Ed.), *Encyclopedia of psychology* (Vol. 8, pp. 236–238). Washington, DC: American Psychological Association.

Murray, H. A. (1938). *Explorations in personality.* New York: Oxford University Press.

Murray, H. A. (1943a). *Explorations in personality.* New York: Oxford University Press.

Murray, H. A. (1943b). *Thematic apperception test.* Cambridge, MA: Harvard University Press.

Murray, H. A. (1943c). *The Thematic Apperception Test: Manual.* Cambridge, MA: Harvard University Press.

Murstein, B. I., & Brust, R. G. (1985). Humor and interpersonal attraction. *Journal of Personality Assessment, 49*(6), 637–640.

Mustonen, A. (1997). Nature of screen violence and its relation to program popularity. *Aggressive Behavior, 23,* 281–292.

Muzur, A., Fabbro, F., Clarici, A., Braun, S., & Bava, A. (1998). Encoding and recall of parsed stories in hypnosis. *Perceptual & Motor Skills, 87,* 963–971.

Mwangi, M. W. (1996). Gender roles portrayed in Kenyan television commericals. *Sex Roles, 34,* 205–214.

Myers, D. G., & Lamm, H. (1976). The group polarization phenomenon. *Psychological Bulletin, 83,* 602–627.

Myers, D., & Diener, E. (1995). Who is happy? *Psychological Science, 6,* 10–19.

Myers, J. K., Weissman, M. M., Tischler, G. L., Holzer, C. E., Leaf, P. J., & Stoltzman, R. (1984). Six-month prevalence of psychiatric disorders in three communities: 1980 to 1982. *Archives of General Psychiatry, 41,* 959–967.

Myers, K. M., Vogel, E. H., Shin, J., & Wagner, A. R. (2001). A comparison of the Rescorla–Wagner and Pearce models in a negative patterning and a summation problem. *Animal Learning & Behavior, 29,* 36–45.

Myerson, A. (1940). Review of mental disorders in urban areas: An ecological study of schizophrenia and other psychoses. *American Journal of Psychiatry, 96,* 995–997.

Naglieri, J. A., & Das. J. P. (2002). Practical implications of general intelligence and PASS cognitive processes. In R. J. Sternberg & E. L. Grigorenko (Eds.), *The general factor of intelligence: How general is it?* (pp. 55–84). Mahwah, NJ: Erlbaum.

Nakamura, M. (2002). Relationship between anxiety and physical traits of facial expressions. *Japanese Journal of Psychology, 73,* 140–147.

Nakano, K., & Kitamura, T. (2001). The relation of the anger subcomponent of Type A behavior to psychological symptoms in Japanese and foreign students. *Japanese Psychological Research, 43,* 50–54.

Nathans, J., Thomas, D., & Hogness, D. S. (1986). Molecular genetics of human color vision: The genes encoding blue, green, and red pigments. *Science, 232*(47), 193–202.

National Institute of Child Health and Human Development (1996), Early Child Care Research Network. (1996, Spring). Child care and the family: An opportunity to study development in context. *Society for Research in Child Development Newsletter.* Ann Arbor, MI: SRCD.

National Institute of Child Health and Human Development Early Child Care Research Network. (1994). Child care and child development: The NICHD study of early child care. In S. L. Friedman & H. C. Haywood (Eds.), *Developmental follow-up: Concepts, domains and methods* (pp. 377–396). New York: Academic Press.

National Institute of Child Health and Human Development Early Child Care Research Network. (1996). Characteristics of infant child care: Factors contributing to positive caregiving. *Early Childhood Research Quarterly, 11,* 269–306.

National Institute of Child Health and Human Development Early Child Care Research Network. (1997). Familial factors associated with the characteristics of nonmaternal care of infants. *Journal of Marriage and the Family, 59,* 389–408.

National Institute of Child Health and Human Development Early Child Care Research Network. (2000). Characteristics and quality of child care for toddlers and preschoolers. *Applied Developmental Science, 4,* 116–135.

National Research Council. (1998). *Preventing reading difficulties in young children.* Washington, DC: National Academy Press.

Neisser, U. (1967). *Cognitive psychology.* New York: Appleton-Century-Crofts.

Neisser, U. (1982). Snapshots or benchmarks? In U. Neisser (Ed.), *Memory observed: Remembering in natural contexts.* San Francisco: Freeman.

Neisser, U. (Ed.). (1998). *The rising curve.* Washington, DC: American Psychological Association.

Nelson, C. (1990). *Gender and the social studies: Training preservice secondary social studies teachers.* Doctoral dissertation, University of Minnesota.

Nelson, C. A., & Bloom, F. E. (1997). Child development and neuroscience. *Child Development, 68,* 970–987.

Nelson, K. (1973). Structure and strategy in learning to talk. *Monograph of the Society for Research in Child Development, 38*(149).

Nelson, K. (1999). The developmental psychology of language and thought. In M. Bennett (Ed.), *Developmental psychology* (pp. 185–204). Philadelphia: Psychology Press.

Nelson, R. E., & Craighead, W. E. (1977). Selective recall of positive and negative feedback, self-control behaviors and depression. *Journal of Abnormal Psychology, 86,* 379–388.

Nelson, R. E., & Craighead, W. E. (1981). Tests of a self-control model of depression. *Behavior Therapy, 12,* 123–129.

Nelson, T. O. (1996). Consciousness and metacognition. *American Psychologist, 51,* 102–116.

Nelson, T. O. (1999). Cognition versus metacognition. In R. J. Sternberg (Ed.), *The nature of cognition* (pp. 625–641). Cambridge, MA: MIT Press.

Nelson, T. O., & Narens, L. (1994). Why investigate metacognition? In J. Metcalfe & A. P. Shimamura (Eds.), *Metacognition: Knowing about knowing* (pp. 1–26). Cambridge, MA: MIT Press.

Nelson, T. O., & Rothbart, R. (1972). Acoustic savings for items forgotten from long-term memory. *Journal of Experimental Psychology, 93,* 357–360.

Nerenz, D. R., & Leventhal, H. (1983). Self-regulation theory in chronic illness. In T. G. Burish & L. A. Bradley (Eds.), *Coping with chronic disease: Research and applications* (pp. 13–38). New York: Academic Press.

Neto, F., Williams, J. E., & Widner, S. C. (1991). Portuguese children's knowledge of sex stereotypes: Effects of age, gender, and socioeconomic status. *Journal of Cross-Cultural Psychology, 22*(3), 376–388.

Neuberg, S. L., Cialdini, R. B., Brown, S. L., Luce, C., Sagarin, B. J., & Lewis, B. P. (1997). Does empathy lead to anything more than superficial helping? Comment on Batson et al., (1997). *Journal of Personality and Social Psychology, 73,* 510–516.

Neville, H. J. (1995). Developmental specificity in neurocognitive development in humans. In M. S. Gazzaniga (Ed.), *The cognitive neurosciences* (pp. 219–231). Cambridge, MA: MIT Press.

Neville, H. J. (1998). An interview with Helen J. Neville, Ph.D. In M. S. Gazzaniga, R. B. Ivry, & G. R. Mangun (Eds.), *Cognitive neuroscience* (pp. 492–493). New York: Norton.

Newcomb, A. F., & Bagwell, C. (1995). Children's friendship relations: A meta-analytic review. *Psychological Bulletin, 117,* 306–347.

Newcomb, A. F., Bukowski, W. M., & Pattee, L. (1993). Children's peer relations: A meta-analytic review of popular, rejected, neglected, controversial, and average sociometric status. *Psychological Bulletin, 113,* 99–128.

Newcomb, T. M. (1943). *Personality and social change.* New York: Dryden.

Newell, A. (1990). *Unified theories of cognition.* Cambridge, MA: Harvard University Press.

Newell, A., & Simon, H. A. (1972). *Human problem solving.* Englewood Cliffs, NJ: Prentice-Hall.

Newman, H. H., Freeman, F. N., & Holzinger, K. J. (1937). *Twins: A study of heredity and environment.* Chicago: University of Chicago Press.

Newman, L. S., & Baumeister, R. F. (1994, August). *"Who would wish for the trauma?" Explaining UFO abductions.* Paper presented at the meeting of the American Psychological Association, Los Angeles, CA.

Newport, E. L. (1990). Maturational constraints on language learning. *Cognitive Science, 14,* 11–28.

Newport, E. L. (1991). Constraining concepts of the critical period of language. In S. Carey & R. Gelman (Eds.), *The epigenesis of mind: Essays on biology and cognition* (pp. 111–130). Mahwah, NJ: Erlbaum.

Nicholls, J. G., Martin, A. R., Wallace, B. G., & Kuffler, S. W. (1992). *From neuron to brain* (3rd ed.). Sunderland, MA: Sinauer.

Nielsen, K. H., & Hynd, G. W. (2000). Dyslexia. In A. E. Kazdin (Ed.), *Encyclopedia of psychology* (Vol. 3, pp. 108–110). Washington, DC: American Psychological Association.

Nielsen, S. (1990). Epidemiology of anorexia nervosa in Denmark from 1983–1987: A nationwide register study of psychiatric admission. *Acta Psychiatrica Scandinavica, 81,* 507–514.

Niemczynski, A., Czyzowska, D., Pourkos, M., & Mirski, A. (1988). The Cracow study with Kohlberg's Moral Judgment Interview: Data pertaining to the assumption of cross-cultural validity. *Polish Psychological Bulletin, 19*(1), 43–53.

Nisan, M., & Kohlberg, L. (1982). Universality and variation in moral judgment: A longitudinal and cross-sectional study in Turkey. *Child Development, 53,* 865–876.

Nisbett, R. E. & Cohen, D. (1996). *Culture of honor: The psychology of violence in the South.* Boulder, CO: Westview Press.

Nisbett, R. E. (1995). Dangerous, but important. In R. Jacoby & N. Glauberman (Eds.), *The bell curve debate.* New York: Times Books.

Nisbett, R. E. (2003). *The geography of thought: How Asians and Westerners think differently…and why.* New York: Free Press.

Nisbett, R. E. (Ed.). (1993). *Rules for reasoning.* Hillsdale, NJ: Erlbaum.

Nisbett, R. E., & Norenzayan, A. (2002). Culture and cognition. In H. Pashler & D. Medin (Eds.), *Steven's handbook of experimental psychology* (3rd ed.). *Vol. 2: Memory and cognitive processes* (pp. 561–597).

Nisbett, R. E., Peng, K., Choi, I., & Norenzayan, A. (2001). Culture and systems of thought: Holistic versus analytic cognition. *Psychological Review, 108,* 291–310.

Nishino, S., Mignot, E., & Dement, W. C. (2001). Sedative-hypnotics. In A. F. Schatzberg & C. B. Nemeroff (Eds.), *Essentials of clinical psychopharmacology* (pp. 283–301). Washington, DC: American Psychiatric Association.

Noctor, S. C., Flint, C., Weissman, T. A., Wong, W. S., Clinton, B. K., & Kriegstein, A. R. (2002). Dividing precursor cells of the embryonic cortical ventricular zone have morphological and molecular characteristics of radial glia. *Journal of Neuroscience, 22,* 3161–3173.

Nolen-Hoeksema, S. (1990). *Sex differences in depression.* Stanford, CA: Stanford University Press.

Nolen-Hoeksema, S. (2002). Gender differences in depression. In I. H. Gotlib & C. L. Hammen (Eds.), *Handbook of depression* (pp. 492–509). New York: Guilford.

Nolen-Hoeksema, S., & Girgus, J. S. (1994). The emergence of gender differences in depression during adolescence. *Psychological Bulletin, 115,* 424–443.

Nolen-Hoeksema, S., & Jackson, B. (2001). Mediators of the gender difference in rumination. *Psychology of Women Quarterly, 25,* 37–47.

Noller, P., Law, H., & Comrey, A. L. (1987). Cattell, Comrey, and Eysenck personality factors compared: More evidence for the five robust factors? *Journal of Personality and Social Psychology, 53,* 775–782.

Norenzayan, A. C., & Nisbett, R. E. (2002). Cultural similarities and differences in social inference: Evidence from behavioral predictions and lay theories of behavior. *Personality & Social Psychology Bulletin, 28,* 109–120.

Norman, D. A. (1968). Toward a theory of memory and attention. *Psychological Review, 75,* 522–536.

Norman, K. A., & Schacter, D. L. (1997). False recognition in younger and older adults: Exploring the characteristics of illusory memories. *Memory & Cognition, 25,* 838–848.

Norman, W. T. (1963). Toward an adequate taxonomy of personality attributes: Replicated factor structure in peer nomination personality ratings. *Journal of Abnormal and Social Psychology, 66,* 574–583.

North, A. C., Linley, A., & Hargreaves, D. (2000). Social loafing in a co-operative classroom task. *Educational Psychology, 20,* 389–392.

Notarius, C., & Markman, H. (1993). *We can work it out.* New York: Putnam.

Nucci, L. P., & Weber, E. (1995). Social interactions in the home and the development of young children's conceptions of the personal. *Child Development, 66,* 1438–1452.

Nuñes, T. (1994). Street intelligence. In R. J. Sternberg (Ed.), *Encyclopedia of human intelligence* (pp. 1045–1049). New York: Macmillan.

Nuñes, T., Schliemann, A. D., & Carraher, D. W. (1993). *Street mathematics and school mathematics.* New York: Cambridge University Press.

Nwadiora, E., & McAdoo, H. (1996). Acculturative stress among Amerasian refugees: Gender and racial differences. *Adolescence, 31,* 477–487.

Nyberg, L., & Cabeza, R. (2000). Brain imaging of memory. In E. Tulving & F. I. M. Craik (Eds.), *The Oxford handbook of memory* (pp. 501–520). New York: Oxford University Press.

O'Connor, M. J., Kogan, N., & Findlay, R. (2002). Prenatal alcohol exposure and attachment behavior in children. *Alcoholism: Clinical & Experimental Research, 26,* 1592–1602.

O'Connor, M. J., Shah, B., Whaley, S., Cronin, P., Gunderson, B., & Graham, J. (2002). Psychiatric illness in a clinical sample of children with prenatal alcohol exposure. *American Journal of Drug & Alcohol Abuse, 28,* 743–754.

O'Doherty, J., Winston, J., Critchley, H., Perrett, D., Burt, D. M., & Dolan, R. J. (2003). Beauty in a smile: The role of medial orbitofrontal cortex in facial attractiveness. *Neuropsychologia, 41,* 147–155.

Oakes, L. M., & Cohen, L. B. (1995). Infant causal perception. In C. Rovee-Collier & L. P. Lipsitt (Eds.), *Advances in infancy research* (Vol. 9). Norwood, NJ: Ablex.

Oakhill, J., & Garnham, A. (1993). On theories of belief bias in syllogistic reasoning. *Cognition, 46,* 87–92.

Oakman, J. M., Woody, E. Z., & Bowers, K. S. (1996). Contextual influences on the relationship between absorption and hypnotic ability. *Contemporary Hypnosis, 13,* 19–28.

Oatley, K. (1993). Those to whom evil is done. In R. S. Wyer & T. K. Srull (Eds.), *Perspectives on anger and emotion: Advances in social cognition* (Vol. 6, pp. 159–165). Hillsdale, NJ: Erlbaum.

Oatley, K. (2000). Emotion: Theories. In A. E. Kazdin (Ed.), *Encyclopedia of psychology* (Vol. 3, pp. 167–170). Washington, DC: American Psychological Association.

Oberlechner, T. (2002). Fairbairn's theory of object relations. *Journal for the Psychoanalysis of Culture & Society, 7,* 298–304.

Ogawa, S., Lee, T. M., Nayak, A. S., & Glynn, P. (1990). Oxygenation-sensitive contrast in magnetic resonance image of rodent brain at high magnetic fields. *Magnetic Resonance in Medicine, 14,* 68–78.

Ogbu, J. U., & Stern, P. (2001). Caste status and intellectual development. In R. J. Sternberg & E. L. Grigorenko (Eds.), *Environmental effects on cognitive abilities* (pp. 3–38). Mahwah, NJ: Erlbaum.

Ohbuchi, K., & Kambara, T. (1985). Attacker's intent and awareness of outcome, impression management, and retaliation. *Journal of Experimental Social Psychology, 2,* 321–330.

Ohtsubo, Y., Masuchi, A., & Nakanishi, D. (2002). Majority influence process in group judgment: Test of the social judgment scheme model in a group polarization context. *Group Processes & Intergroup Relations, 5,* 249–261.

Ojemann, G. A. (1982). Models of the brain organization for higher integrative functions derived with electrical stimulation techniques. *Human Neurobiology, 1,* 243–250.

Ojemann, G. A., & Mateer, C. (1979). Human language cortex: Localization of memory, syntax, and sequential motor–phoneme identification systems. *Science, 205,* 1401–1403.

Okagaki, L., & Sternberg, R. J. (1993). Parental beliefs and children's school performance. *Child Development, 64,* 36–56.

Olds, J., & Milner, P. (1954). Positive reinforcement produced by electrical stimulation of septal area and other regions of the rat brain. *Journal of Comparative and Physiological Psychology, 47,* 419–427.

Olfson, M., & Pincus, H. J. A. (1996). Outpatient mental health care in nonhospital settings: Distribution of patients across provider groups. *American Journal of Psychiatry, 153,* 1353–1356.

Oliner, S. P., & Oliner, P. M. (1988). *The altruistic personality: Rescuers of Jews in Nazi Europe.* New York: Free Press.

Olson, H. C. (1994). Fetal alcohol syndrome. In R. J. Sternberg (Ed.), *Encyclopedia of human intelligence* (Vol. 1, pp. 439–443). New York: Macmillan.

Öngel, U., & Smith, P. B. (1994). Who are we and where are we going? JCCP approaches its 100th issue. *Journal of Cross-Cultural Psychology, 25*(1), 25–54.

Operario, D., & Fiske, S. (1998). Power plus prejudice: Sociocultural and psychological foundations of racial oppression. In J. L. Eberhardt & S. T. Fiske (Eds.), *Racism: The problem and the response.* Thousand Oaks, CA: Sage.

Operario, D., & Fiske, S. T. (1999). Social cognition permeates social psychology: Motivated mental processes guide the study of human social behavior. *Asian Journal of Social Psychology, 2,* 63–78.

Opotow, S. (1990). Moral exclusion and injustice: An introduction. *Journal of Social Issues, 46,* 1–20.

Orengo, C. A., Kunik, M. E., Ghusn, H., & Yudofsky, S. C. (1997). Correlation of testosterone with aggression in demented elderly men. *Journal of Nervous and Mental Disease, 185,* 349–351.

Orlinsky, D. E., & Howard, K. I. (1994). Unity and diversity among psychotherapies: A comparative perspective. In B. Bonger & L. E. Beutler (Eds.), *Foundations of psychotherapy: Theory, research, and practice.* New York: Basic Books.

Ormel, J., & Wohlfarth, T. (1991). How neuroticism, long-term difficulties, and life situation change influence psychological distress: A longitudinal model. *Journal of Personality and Social Psychology, 60,* 744–755.

Orne, M. T. (1959). Hypnosis: Artifact and essence. *Journal of Abnormal Psychology, 58,* 277–299.

Ornstein, R. (1977). *The psychology of consciousness* (2nd ed.). New York: Harcourt Brace Jovanovich.

Ornstein, R. (1986). *The psychology of consciousness* (2nd rev. ed.). New York: Pelican Books.

Osgood, C. E. (1962). *An alternative to war or surrender.* Urabana: University of Illinois Press.

Osgood, C. E. (1980). *GRIT: A strategy for survival in mankind's nuclear age?* Paper presented at the Pugwash Conference on New Directions in Disarmament.

Osherson, D. N. (1995). Probability judgment. In E. E. Smith & D. N. Osherson (Eds.), *An invitation to cognitive science: Vol. 3. Thinking* (pp. 35–75). Cambridge, MA: MIT Press.

Ostendorf, F., & Angleitner, A. (1994, July). *Psychometric properties of the German translation of the NEO Personality Inventory (NEO-PI-R).* Poster session presented at the Seventh Conference of the European Association for Personality Psychology, Madrid, Spain.

Ott, E. M. (1989). Effects of male–female ratio at work: Policewomen and male nurses. *Psychology of Women Quarterly, 13*(1), 41–57.

Overholser, J. C. (2002). Contemporary psychotherapy: Gold mines and land mines. *Journal of Contemporary Psychotherapy, 32,* 249–258.

Packard, M. G., Cahill, L., & McGaugh, J. L. (1994). Amygdala modulation of hippocampal-dependent and caudate nucleus-dependent memory processes. *Proceedings of the National Academy of Sciences, USA, 91,* 8477–8481.

Paivio, A. (1971). *Imagery and verbal processes.* New York: Holt, Rinehart & Winston.

Paivio, A. (1986). *Mental representations: A dual coding approach.* New York: Oxford University Press.

Palmer, J. A., & Palmer, L. K. (2002). *Evolutionary psychology: The ultimate origins of human behavior.* Boston: Allyn & Bacon.

Palmer, S. E. (1975). The effects of contextual scenes on the identification of objects. *Memory & Cognition, 3,* 519–526.

Palmer, S. E. (1992). Modern theories of Gestalt perception. In G. W. Humphreys (Ed.), *Understanding vision: An interdisciplinary perspective—Readings in mind and language* (pp. 39–72). Oxford, UK: Blackwell.

Palmer, S. E. (2000). Perceptual organization. In A. E. Kazdin (Ed.), *Encyclopedia of psychology* (Vol. 6, pp. 93–97). Washington, DC: American Psychological Association.

Pappenheimer, J. R., Koski, G., Fencl, V., Karnovsky, M. L., & Krueger, J. (1975). Extraction of sleep-promoting factors from cerebrospinal fluid and from brains of sleep-deprived animals. *Journal of Neurophysiology, 38,* 1299–1311.

Parfyonova, G. V., Korichneva, I. L., Suvorov, Y. I., & Krasnikova, T. L. (1988). Characteristics of lymphocyte b-adrenoreceptors in essential hypertension: Effects of propranolol treatment and dynamic exercise. *Health Psychology, 7*(Suppl.), 33–52.

Parke, R. D. (1981). *Fathers.* Cambridge, MA: Harvard University Press.

Parke, R. D. (1996). *Fatherhood.* Cambridge, MA: Harvard University Press.

Parke, R. D., & Asher, S. R. (1983). Social and personality development. In M. R. Rosenzweig & L. W. Porter (Eds.), *Annual Review of Psychology, 34,* 465–509.

Parke, R. D., & O'Neil, R. (1997). The influence of significant others on learning about relationships. In S. Duck (Ed.), *Handbook of personal relationships* (2nd ed., pp. 29–60). New York: Wiley.

Parke, R. D., & O'Neil, R. (1998). Social relationships across contexts: Family-peer linkages. In W. A. Collins & B. Laursen (Eds.), *Minnesota symposium on child psychology* (Vol. 3). Mahwah, NJ: Erlbaum.

Parke, R. D., & Sawin, D. B. (1980). The family in early infancy: Social interaction and attitudinal analyses. In F. A. Pederson (Ed.), *The father–infant relationship: Observational studies in a family context.* New York: Praeger.

Parke, R. D., & Tinsley, B. J. (1987). Family interaction in infancy. In J. D. Osofsky (Ed.), *Handbook of infant development* (pp. 579–641). New York: Wiley.

Parke, R. D., & Walters, R. H. (1967). Some factors influencing the efficacy of punishment training for inducing response inhibition. *Monographs of the Society for Research in Child Development, 32*(1, Whole No. 109).

Parke, R. D., Berkowitz, L., Leyens, J. P., West, S. G., & Sebastian, R. J. (1977). Some effects of violent and nonviolent movies on the behavior of juvenile delinquents. In L. Berkowitz (Ed.), *Advances in experimental social psychology* (Vol. 10). New York: Academic Press.

Parks, G. A., Marlatt, G. A., & Anderson, B. K. (2001). Cognitive-behavioral alcohol treatment: In N. Heather & T. J. Peters (Eds.), *International handbook of alcohol dependence and problems* (pp. 557–573). New York: Wiley.

Parovel, G., & Vezzani, S. (2002). Mirror symmetry opposes splitting of chromatically homogeneous surfaces. *Perception, 31,* 693–709.

Pascual-Leone, J. (1984). Attentional, dialectic, and mental effort. In M. L. Commons, F. A. Richards, & C. Armon (Eds.), *Beyond formal operations.* New York: Plenum.

Pascual-Leone, J. (1990). An essay on wisdom: Toward organismic processes that make it possible. In R. J. Sternberg (Ed.), *Wisdom: Its nature, origins, and development* (pp. 244–278). New York: Cambridge University Press.

Pashler, H. (1998). *The psychology of attention.* Cambridge, MA: MIT Press.

Paul, G. L. (1967). Strategy of outcome research in psychotherapy. *Journal of Consulting Psychology, 31,* 109–118.

Paul, G. L., & Lentz, R. J. (1977). *Psychosocial treatment of chronic mental patients: Milieu versus social learning programs.* Cambridge, MA: Harvard University Press.

Paul, G. L., & Menditto, A. A. (1992). Effectiveness of inpatient treatment programs for mentally ill adults in public psychiatric facilities. *Applied and Preventive Psychology: Current Scientific Perspectives, 1,* 41–63.

Pavlov, I. P. (1928). *Lectures on conditioned reflexes: The higher nervous activity of animals* (Vol. 1, H. Gantt, Trans.). London: Lawrence & Wishart.

Pavlov, I. P. (1955). *Selected works.* Moscow: Foreign Languages Publishing House.

Paykel, E. S. (1991). Depression in women. *British Journal of Psychiatry, 158,* 22–29.

Payne, R. W., Matussek, P., & George, E. I. (1959). An experimental study of schizophrenic thought disorder. *Journal of Mental Science, 105,* 627–652.

Pearce, J. M. (1997). *Animal learning and cognition: An introduction* (2nd ed.). East Sussex, UK: Psychology Press.

Pearlstone, A., Russell, R.J.H., & Wells, P. A. (1994). A re-examination of the stress/illness relationship: How useful is the concept of stress? *Personality and Individual Differences, 17*(4), 577–580.

Pearson, B. Z., Fernandez, S. C., Lewedeg, V., & Oller, K. (1997). The relation of input factors to lexical learning by bilingual infants. *Applied Psycholinguistics, 18*(1), 41–58.

Pekarik, G. (1993). Beyond effectiveness: Uses of consumer-oriented criteria in defining treatment success. In T. R. Giles (Ed.), *Handbook of effective psychotherapy.* New York: Plenum.

Pellegrino, J. W., & Glaser, R. (1980). Components of inductive reasoning. In R. E. Snow, P.-A. Federico, & W. E. Montague (Eds.), *Aptitude, learning, and instruction: Vol 1. Cognitive process analyses of aptitude.* Hillsdale, NJ: Erlbaum.

Penfield, W., & Roberts, L. (1959). *Speech and brain mechanisms.* Princeton, NJ: Princeton University Press.

Peng, K., & Nisbett, R. E. (1999). Culture, dialectics, and reasoning about contradiction. *American Psychologist, 54,* 741–754.

Peng, K., & Nisbett, R. E. (2000). Dialectical responses to questions about dialectical thinking. *American Psychologist, 55,* 1067–1068.

Pennebaker, J. W. (1990). *Opening up: The healing power of confiding in others.* New York: Morrow.

Pennebaker, J. W. (1997). *Opening up: The healing power of expressing emotions* (rev. ed.). New York: Guilford.

Pennebaker, J. W. (1997). Writing about emotional experiences as a therapeutic process. *Psychological Science, 8,* 162–166.

Pennebaker, J. W., & Graybeal, A. (2001). Patterns of natural language use: Disclosure, personality, and social integration. *Current Directions in Psychological Science, 10,* 90–93.

Pennebaker, J. W., & Memon, A. (1996). Recovered memories in context: Thoughts and elaborations on Bowers and Farvolden (1996). *Psychological Bulletin, 119,* 381–385.

Penrose, R. (1994). *Shadows of the mind: A search for the missing science of consciousness.* Oxford: Oxford University Press.

Penton-Voak, I. E., Perrett, D. I., Castles, D. L., Kobayashi, T., Burt, D. M., Murray, L. K., & Minamisawa, R. (1999). Menstrual cycle alters face preference. *Nature, 399,* 741–742.

Peplau, L. A. (1983). Roles and gender. In H. H. Kelley (Ed.), *Close relationships.* New York: Freeman.

Pereira, D. B., Antoni, M. H., Danielson, A., Simon, T., Efantis-Potter, J., Carver, C. S., Duran, R. E. F., Ironson, G., Klimas, N., Fletcher, M. A., & O'Sullivan, M. J. (2003). Stress as a predictor of symptomatic genital herpes virus recurrence in women with human immunodeficiency virus. *Journal of Psychosomatic Research, 54,* 237–244.

Perkins, D. F., & Borden, L. M. (2003). Positive behaviors, problem behaviors, and resiliency in adolescence. In R. M. Lerner, M. A. Easterbrooks, & J. Mistry (Vol. Eds.) and I. B. Weiner (Ed.-in-Chief), *Handbook of psychology. Vol. 6: Developmental psychology* (pp. 373–394). New York: Wiley.

Perkins, D. N. (1981). *The mind's best work.* Cambridge, MA: Harvard University Press.

Perkins, D. N. (1995a). *Outsmarting IQ.* New York: Free Press.

Perkins, D. N. (1995b). Insight in minds and genes. In R. J. Sternberg & J. E. Davidson (Eds.), *The nature of insight* (pp. 495–533). Cambridge, MA: MIT Press.

Perkins, D. N. (2002). The engine of folly. In R. J. Sternberg (Ed.), *Why smart people can be so stupid* (pp. 64–85). New Haven, CT: Yale University Press.

Perkins, D. N., & Grotzer, T. A. (1997). Teaching intelligence. *American Psychologist, 52,* 1125–1133.

Perlmutter, M. (1983). Learning and memory through adulthood. In M. W. Riley, B. B. Hess, & K. Bond (Eds.), *Aging in society: Selected reviews of recent research.* Hillsdale, NJ: Erlbaum.

Perner, J. (1998). The meta-intentional nature of executive functions and theory of mind. In P. Carruthers & J. Boucher (Eds.), *Language and thought* (pp. 270–283). Cambridge, UK: Cambridge University Press.

Perner, J. (1999). Theory of mind. In M. Bennett (Ed.), *Developmental psychology* (pp. 205–230). Philadelphia: Psychology Press.

Perris, C., & Herlofson, J. (1993). Cognitive therapy. In N. Sartorius, G. de Girolano, G. Andrews, G. A. German, & L. Eisenberg (Eds.), *Treatment of mental disorders: A review of effectiveness.* Geneva, Switzerland, and Washington, DC: World Health Organization and American Psychiatric Press.

Persinger, M. A. (1999). Near-death experiences and ecstasy: A product of the organization of the human brain? In S. Della Salla (Ed.), *Mind myths: Exploring popular assumptions about the mind and brain* (pp. 85–99). New York: Wiley.

Persinger, M. A. (2001). The neuropsychiatry of paranormal experiences. *Journal of Neuropsychiatry & Clinical Neurosciences, 13,* 515–523.

Persinger, M. A., & Richards, P. M. (1995). Vestibular experiences during brief periods of partial sensory deprivation are enhanced when daily geomagnetic activity exceeds 15–20 nT. *Neuroscience Letters, 194,* 169–172.

Persky, V. M., Kempthorne-Rawson, J., & Shekele, R. B. (1987). Personality and the risk of cancer: 20-year follow-up of the Western Electric Study. *Psychosomatic Medicine, 49,* 435–449.

Pervin, L. A. (2003). *The science of personality* (2nd ed.). New York: Oxford University Press.

Petersen, S., Fox, P. T., Posner, M. I., Mintun, M., & Raichle, M. E. (1988). Positron-emission tomographic studies of the cortical anatomy of single-word processing. *Nature, 331*(6157), 585–589.

Peterson, C., Maier, S. F., & Seligman, M. E. P. (1993). *Learned helplessness: A theory for the age of personal control.* New York: Oxford University Press.

Peterson, C., Seligman, M. E. P., & Vaillant, G. E. (1988). Pessimistic explanatory style is a risk factor for physical illness: A thirty-five-year longitudinal study. *Journal of Personality and Social Psychology, 55,* 23-27.

Peterson, L. R., & Peterson, M. J. (1959). Short-term retention of individual verbal items. *Journal of Experimental Psychology, 58,* 193–198.

Petitto, L., & Marentette, P. F. (1991). Babbling in the manual mode: Evidence for the ontogeny of language. *Science, 251,* 1493–1499.

Petrill, S. A. (2002). The case for general intelligence: A behavioral genetic perspective. In R. J. Sternberg & E. L. Grigorenko (Eds.), *The general factor of intelligence: How general is it?* (pp. 281–298). Mahwah, NJ: Erlbaum.

Pettigrew, T. (1998). Intergroup contact theory. *Annual Review of Psychology, 49,* 65–85.

Petty, R. E., & Cacioppo, J. T. (1981). *Attitudes and persuasion: Classic and contemporary approaches.* Dubuque, IA: William C. Brown.

Petty, R. E., & Wegener, D. T. (1998). Attitude change: Multiple roles for persuasion variables. In D. Gilbert, S. Fiske, & G. Lindzey (Eds.), *The handbook of social psychology* (4th ed., pp. 323–390). New York: McGraw-Hill.

Petty, R. E., Brinol, P., & Tormala, Z. L. (2002). Thought confidence as a determinant of persuasion: The self-validation hypothesis. *Journal of Personality & Social Psychology, 82,* 722–741.

Petty, R. E., DeSteno, D., & Rucker, D. D. (2001). The role of affect in attitude change. In J. P. Forgas (Ed.), *Handbook of affect and social cognition* (pp. 212–233). Mahwah, NJ: Erlbaum.

Petty, R. E., Priester, J. R., & Brinol, P. (2002). Mass media attitude change: Implications of the elaboration likelihood model of persuasion. In J. Bryant & D. Zillmann (Eds.), *Media effects: Advances in theory and research* (2nd ed., pp. 155–198). Mahwah, NJ: Erlbaum.

Pfaffman, C. (1974). Specificity of the sweet receptors of the squirrel monkey. *Chemical Senses and Flavor, 1,* 61–67.

Pfaffman, C. (1978). The vertebrate phylogeny, neural code, and integrative process of taste. In E. Carterette & M. P. Friedman (Eds.), *Handbook of perception* (Vol. 6A). San Diego: Academic Press.

Pfeiffer, W. M. (1982). Culture-bound syndromes. In I. Al-Issa (Ed.), *Culture and psychopathology.* Baltimore, MD: University Park Press.

Phillips, D. A. (1984). The illusion of incompetence among academically competent children. *Child Development, 55,* 2000–2016.

Phillips, D. A. (1987). Socialization of perceived academic competence among highly competent children. *Child Development, 58,* 1308–1320.

Phillips, D. A., & Zimmerman, M. (1990). The developmental course of perceived competence and incompetence among competent children. In R. J. Sternberg & J. Kolligian, Jr. (Eds.), *Competence considered* (pp. 41–66). New Haven, CT: Yale University Press.

Phillips, M. R., Liu, H., & Zhang, Y. (1999). Suicide and social change in China. *Cultural Medical Psychiatry, 23,* 25–50.

Piaget, J. (1952). *The origins of intelligence in children.* New York: International Universities Press.

Piaget, J. (1954). *The construction of reality in the child.* New York: Basic Books.

Piaget, J. (1969). *The child's conception of physical causality.* Totowa, NJ: Littlefield, Adams.

Piaget, J. (1972). *The psychology of intelligence.* Totowa, NJ: Littlefield, Adams.

Pickren, W. E., & Tomes, H. (2002). The legacy of Kenneth B. Clark to the APA: The Board of Social and Ethical Responsibility for Psychology. *American Psychologist, 57,* 51–59.

Piedmont, R. L., & Chae, J. H. (1997). Cross-cultural generalizability of the Five-Factor Model of personality: Development and validation of the NEO-PI-R for Koreans. *Journal of Cross-Cultural Psychology, 28,* 131–155.

Pillow, D. R., Zautra, A. J., & Sandler, I. (1996). Major life events and minor stressors: Identifying mediational links in the stress process. *Journal of Personality and Social Psychology, 70,* 381–394.

Pinker, S. (1994) *The language instinct.* New York: William Morrow.

Pinker, S. (1997). Letter to the editor. *Science, 276,* 1177–1178.

Pinker, S. (1998). *How the mind works.* New York: Norton.

Pinker, S. (1999). *How the mind works.* New York: Norton.

Pinker, S. (1999). *Words and rules.* New York: Basic Books.

Pinker, S. (2002). *The blank slate: The modern denial of human nature.* New York: Viking.

Pinto, R. P., & Hollandsworth, J. G. Jr. (1989). Using videotape modeling to prepare children psychologically for surgery: Influence of parents and costs versus benefits of providing preparation services. *Health Psychology, 8,* 79–95.

Pizzagalli, D., Koenig, T., Regard, M., & Lehmann, D. (1999). Affective attitudes to face images associated with intracerebral EEG source location before face viewing. *Cognitive Brain Research, 7,* 371–377.

Plaut, D. C. (2001). A connectionist approach to word reading and acquired dyslexia: Extension to sequential processing. In M. H. Christiansen & N. Chater (Eds.), *Connectionist psycholinguistics* (pp. 244–278). Westport, CT: Ablex.

Plaut, D. C., & Gonnerman, L. M. (2000). Are non-semantic morphological effects incompatible with a distributed connectionist approach to lexical processing? *Language & Cognitive Processes, 15,* 445–487.

Plaut, D. C., & Shallice, T. (1994). *Connectionist modelling in cognitive neuropsychology: A case study.* Mahwah, NJ: Erlbaum.

Plaut, D. C., McClelland, J. L., Seidenberg, M. S., & Patterson, K. (1996). Understanding normal and impaired word reading: Computational principles in quasi-regular domains. *Psychological Review, 103,* 56–115.

Plomin, R. (1994). *Genetics and experience: The interplay between nature and nurture.* Thousand Oaks, CA: Sage.

Plomin, R. (1995). Molecular genetics and psychology. *Current Directions in Psychological Science, 4,* 114–177.

Plomin, R. (1997). Identifying genes for cognitive abilities and disabilities. In R. J. Sternberg & E. L. Grigorenko (Eds.), *Intelligence, heredity and environment* (pp. 89–104). New York: Cambridge University Press.

Plomin, R. (1999). Behavioral genetics. In M. Bennett (Ed.), *Developmental psychology* (pp. 231–252). Philadelphia: Psychology Press.

Plomin, R. (2001a). Genetic factors contributing to learning and language delays and disabilities. *Child & Adolescent Psychiatry Clinics of North America, 10,* 259–277.

Plomin, R. (2001b). Genetics and behaviour. *Psychologist, 14,* 134–139.

Plomin, R. (2002). Quantitative trait loci and general cognitive ability. In J. Benjamin & R. P. Ebstein (Eds.), *Molecular genetics and the human personality* (pp. 211–230). Washington, DC: American Psychiatric Publishing.

Plomin, R., & Colledge, E. (2001). Genetics and psychology: Beyond heritability. *European Psychologist, 6,* 229–240.

Plomin, R., & Crabbe, J. (2000). DNA. *Psychological Bulletin, 126,* 806–828.

Plomin, R., & McGuffin, P. (2003). Psychopathology in the postgenomic era. *Annual Review of Psychology, 54,* 205–228.

Plomin, R., & Rutter, M. (1998). Child development, molecular genetics, and what to do with genes once they are found. *Child Development, 69,* 1223–1242.

Plomin, R., DeFries, J. C., Craig, I. W., & McGuffin, P. (2003a). Behavioral genetics. In R. Plomin, J. C. DeFries, I. W. Craig, & P. McGuffin (Eds.), *Behavioral genetics in the postgenomic era* (pp. 3–15). Washington, DC: American Psychological Association.

Plomin, R., DeFries, J. C., Craig, I. W., & McGuffin, P. (Eds.). (2003b). *Behavioral genetics in the postgenomic era.* Washington, DC: American Psychological Association.

Plomin, R., DeFries, J. C., McClearn, G. E., & Rutter, M. (1997). *Behavioral genetics* (3rd ed.). New York: Freeman.

Plomin, R., Fulker, D. W., Corley, R., & DeFries, J. C. (1997). Nature, nurture and cognitive development from 1 to 16 years: A parent-offspring adoption study. *Psychological Science, 8,* 442–447.

Plomin, R., Owen, M. J., & McGuffin, P. (1994). The genetic basis of complex human behaviors. *Science, 264,* 1733–1739.

Plunkett, K. (1998). Language acquisition and connectionism. *Language and Cognitive Processes, 13,* 97–104.

Plutchik, R. (1980). *Emotion: A psychoevolutionary analysis.* New York: Harper & Row.

Plutchik, R. (1983). Emotions in early development: A psychoevolutionary approach. In R. Plutchik & H. Kellerman (Eds.), *Emotion: Theory, research, and experience:* Vol. 2. *Emotions in early development.* New York: Academic Press.

Plutchik, R. (2003). *Emotions and life: Perspectives from psychology, biology, and evolution.* Washington, DC: American Psychological Association.

Pokorny, A. D. (1968). Myths about suicide. In H. Resnik (Ed.), *Suicidal behaviors.* Boston: Little, Brown.

Policastro, E., & Gardner, H. (1999). From case studies to robust generalizations: An approach to the study of creativity. In R. J. Sternberg (Ed.), *Handbook of creativity* (pp. 213–225). New York: Cambridge University Press.

Policastro, E., & Gardner, H. (1999). From case studies to robust generalizations: An approach to the study of creativity. In R. J. Sternberg (Ed.), *Handbook of creativity* (pp. 213–225). New York: Cambridge University Press.

Polivy, J., & Herman, C. P. (1983). *Breaking the diet habit.* New York: Basic Books.

Polivy, J., & Herman, C. P. (1985). Dieting and binging. *American Psychologist, 40,* 193–201.

Polivy, J., & Herman, C. P. (1993). Etiology of binge eating: Psychological mechanisms. In C. E. Fairburn & G. T. Wilson (Eds.), *Binge eating: Nature, assessment, and treatment.* New York: Guilford.

Polivy, J., & Herman, C. P. (2002a). Causes of eating disorders. *Annual Review of Psychology, 53,* 187–213.

Polivy, J., & Herman, C. P. (2002b). If at first you don't succeed: False hopes of self-change. *American Psychologist, 57,* 677–689.

Polivy, J., Herman, C. P., & McFarlane, T. (1994). Effects of anxiety on eating: Does palatability moderate distress-induced overeating in dieters? *Journal of Abnormal Psychology, 103,* 505–510.

Polk, T. A., & Farah, M. J. (2002). Functional MRI evidence for an abstract, not perceptual, word-form area. *Journal of Experimental Psychology: General, 131,* 65–72.

Polk, T. A., Stallcup, M., Aguirre, G. K., Alsop, D. C., D'Esposito, M., Detre, J. A., & Farah, M. J. (2002). Neural specialization for letter recognition. *Journal of Cognitive Neuroscience, 14,* 145–159.

Pollatsek, A., & Rayner, K. (1989). *Reading.* In M. I. Posner (Ed.), *Foundations of cognitive science* (pp. 401–436). Cambridge, MA: MIT Press.

Poon, L. W. (1987). *Myths and truisms: Beyond extant analyses of speed of behavior and age.* Address to the Eastern Psychological Association Convention.

Poortinga, Y. H., Kop, P. F. M., & van de Vijver, F. J. R. (1990). Differences between psychological domains in the range of cross-cultural variation. In P. J. D. Drenth, J. A. Sergeant, & R. J. Takens (Eds.), *European perspectives in psychology:* Vol. 3. *Work and organizational, social and economic, cross-cultural* (pp. 355–376). Chichester, UK: Wiley.

Pope, H. G., & Katz, D. L. (1988). Affective and psychotic symptoms associated with anabolic steroid use. *American Journal of Psychiatry, 145*(4), 487–490.

Popper, K. R. (1959). *The logic of scientific discovery.* London: Hutchinson.

Posner, M. I. (1995). Attention in cognitive neuroscience: An overview. In M. Gazzaniga (Ed.), *The cognitive neurosciences* (pp. 615–624). Cambridge, MA: MIT Press.

Posner, M. I. (2000). Exploiting cognitive brain maps. *Brain & Cognition, 42*(1), 64–67.

Posner, M. I. (2001a). Cognitive neuroscience: The synthesis of mind and brain. In E. Dupoux (Ed.), *Language, brain, and cognitive development: Essays in honor of Jacques Mehler* (pp. 403–416). Cambridge, MA: MIT Press.

Posner, M. I. (2001b). The developing human brain. *Developmental Science, 4,* 253–387.

Posner, M. I. (2002). Convergence of psychological and biological development. *Developmental Psychobiology, 40*(3), 339–343.

Posner, M. I., & Raichle, M. E. (1994). *Images of mind.* New York: Freeman.

Pratto, F., Stallworth, L. M., Sidanius, J., & Siers, B. (1997). The gender gap in occupational attainment: A social dominance approach. *Journal of Personality and Social Psychology, 72,* 37–53.

Premack, D. (1959). Toward empirical behavior laws: I. Positive reinforcement. *Psychological Review, 66,* 219–233.

Premack, D. (1971). Language in chimpanzees? *Science, 172,* 808–822.

Prentice, D. A., & Miller, D. T. (1996). Pluralistic ignorance and the perpetuation of social norms by unwitting actors. *Advances in Experimental Social Psychology, 28,* 161–209.

Preston, G. A. N. (1986). Dementia in elderly adults: Prevalence and institutionalization. *Journal of Gerontology, 41,* 261–267.

Pretzer, J. L., Beck, A., & Newman, C. F. (2002). Stress and stress management: A cognitive view. In R. L. Leahy & E. T. Dowd (Eds.), *Clinical advances in cognitive psychotherapy: Theory and application* (pp. 345–360). New York: Springer.

Pring, L., & Hermelin, B. (2002). Numbers and letters: Exploring an autistic savant's unpracticed ability. *Neurocase, 8,* 330–337.

Prochazka, A. (1996). Proprioceptive feedback and movement regulation. In L. B. Rowell & J. T. Shepherd (Eds.), *Handbook of physiology: Section 12. Exercise regulation and integration of multiple systems* (pp. 89–127). New York: Oxford University Press.

Pullum, G. K. (1991). *The great Eskimo vocabulary hoax and other irreverent essays on the study of language.* Chicago: University of Chicago Press.

Purdy, M., Jacobs, A., & Jones, R. L. (2003, January 12). Life behind basement doors: Family and system fail boys. *New York Times,* pp. 1, 25.

Quadagno, D. M. (1987). Pheromones and human sexuality. *Medical Aspects of Human Sexuality, 21,* 149–154.

Quinn, P. C. (2002). Early categorization: A new synthesis. In U. Goswami (Ed.), *Blackwell handbook of childhood cognitive development* (pp. 84–101). Malden, MA: Blackwell.

Rabkin, J. G. (1993). Stress and psychiatric disorders. In L. Goldberger & S. Breznitz (Eds.), *Handbook of stress: Theoretical and clinical aspects* (2nd ed.). New York: Free Press.

Raichle, M. (1999). Positron emission tomography. In R. A. Wilson & F. C. Keil (Eds.), *The MIT encyclopedia of the cognitive sciences* (pp. 656–659). Cambridge, MA: MIT Press.

Raichle, M. E. (1998). Behind the scenes of function brain imaging: A historical and physiological perspective. *Proceedings of the National Academy of Sciences, 95,* 765–772.

Raikes, H. H., & Love, J. M. (2002). History and purpose of Early Head Start. *Infant Mental Health Journal, 23,* 1–13.

Ralph, M. R., Foster, R. G., Davis, F. C., & Menaker, M. (1990). Transplanted suprachiasmatic nucleus determines circadian period. *Science, 247,* 975–978.

Ramaekers, J. G. (2003). Antidepressants and driver impairment: Empirical evidence from a standard on-the-road test. *Journal of Clinical Psychiatry, 64,* 20–29.

Ramey, C. T., & Ramey, S. L. (2000). Intelligence and public policy. In R. J. Sternberg (Ed.), *Handbook of intelligence* (pp. 534–548). New York: Cambridge University Press.

Ramey, C. T., Ramey, S. L., & Lanzi, R. G. (2001). Intelligence and experience. In R. J. Sternberg & E. L. Grigorenko (Eds.), *Environmental effects on cognitive abilities* (pp. 83–115). Mahwah, NJ: Erlbaum.

Rapaport, A. (1960). *Fights, games, and debates.* Ann Arbor: University of Michigan Press.

Rapaport, D., Gill, M. M., & Schafer, R. (1968). *Diagnostic psychological testing.* New York: International Universities Press.

Raps, C. S., Peterson, C., Jonas, M., & Seligman, M. E. P. (1982). Patient behavior in hospitals: Helplessness, reactance, or both? *Journal of Personality and Social Psychology, 42,* 1036–1041.

Ray, O., & Ksir, C. (1990). *Drugs, society, & human behavior.* St. Louis, MO: Times Mirror/Mosby.

Ray, W. (1996). Dissociation in Normal Populations. In L. Michelson & W. Ray (Eds.) *Handbook of dissociation: Theoretical, empirical, and clinical perspectives.* New York: Plenum Publishing.

Ray, W. J. (2003). *Methods toward a science of behavior and experience, 7th Edition.* Belmont, CA: Wadsworth Publishing.

Ray, W. J., & Cole, H. W. (1985). EEG alpha reflects attentional demands, Beta reflects emotional and cognitive processes. *Science, 228,* 750–752.

Ray, W. J., Keil, A., Mikuteit, A., Bongartz, W. & Elbert, T. (2002). High resolution EEG indicators of pain responses in relation to hypnotic susceptibility and suggestion. *Biological Psychology, 60,* 17–36.

Ray, W., Slobounow, S., & Simon, R. (2000). Rate of force development and the lateralized readiness potential. *Psychophysiology, 37,* 757–765.

Rayner, K., & Pollatsek, A. (2000). Reading. In A. E. Kazdin (Ed.), *Encyclopedia of psychology* (Vol. 7, pp. 14–18). Washington, DC: American Psychological Association.

Reed, S. K. (2000). Thinking: Problem solving. In A. E. Kazdin (Ed.), *Encyclopedia of psychology* (Vol. 8, pp. 71–75). Washington, DC: American Psychological Association.

Reed, T. E., & Jensen, A. R. (1992). Conduction velocity in a brain nerve pathway of normal adults correlates with intelligence level. *Intelligence, 16*(3–4), 259–272.

Reep, D. C., & Dambrot, F. H. (1988). In the eye of the beholder: Viewer perceptions of TV's male/female working partners. *Communication Research, 15*(1), 51–69.

Reeve, J., & Deci, E. L. (1996). Elements of the competitive situation that affect intrinsic motivation. *Personality and Social Psychology Bulletin, 22,* 24–33.

Regier, D. A., First, M., Marshall, T., & Narrow, W. E. (2002). The American Psychiatric Association (APA) classification of mental disorders: Strengths, limitations and future perspectives. In M. Maj & W. Gaebel, et al. (Eds.), *Psychiatric diagnosis and classification* (pp. 47–77). New York: Wiley.

Regier, D. A., Narrow, W. E., First, M. B., & Marshall, T. (2002). The APA classification of mental disorders: Future perspectives. *Psychopathology, 35,* 166–170.

Rehm, L. P. (1977). A self-control model of depression. *Behavior Therapy, 8,* 787–804.

Reicher, G. M. (1969). Perceptual recognition as a function of meaningfulness of stimulus material. *Journal of Experimental Psychology, 81,* 275–280.

Reid, R. C. (2000). Sensory systems. In A. E. Kazdin (Ed.), *Handbook of psychology* (Vol. 7, pp. 229–232). Washington, DC: American Psychological Association.

Reifman, A. (1998). Social psychology of false confessions: Bem's early contribution. *American Psychologist, 53,* 320.

Reinisch, J. M., Ziemba-Davis, M., & Sanders, S. A. (1991). Hormonal contributions to sexually dimorphic behavioral development in humans: Neuroendocrine effects on brain development and cognition [Special issue]. *Psychoneuroendocrinology, 16*(1–3), 213–278.

Reis, H. T. (2000). Writing effectively about design. In R. J. Sternberg (Ed.), *Guide to publishing in psychology journals* (pp. 81–97). New York: Cambridge University Press.

Reis, H. T., Collins, W. A., & Berscheid, E. (2000). The relationship context of human behavior and development. *Psychological Bulletin, 126,* 844–872.

Reissland, N. (1988). Neonatal imitation in the first hour of life: Observations in rural Nepal. *Developmental Psychology, 24,* 464–469.

Reitman, J. S. (1971). Mechanisms of forgetting in short-term memory. *Cognitive Psychology, 2,* 185–195.

Reitman, J. S. (1974). Without surreptitious rehearsal, information in short-term memory decays. *Journal of Verbal Learning and Verbal Behavior, 13,* 365–377.

Rempel-Clower, N., Zola, S. M., Squire, L. R., & Amaral, D. G. (1996). Three cases of enduring memory impairment following bilateral damage limited to the hippocampal formation. *Journal of Neuroscience, 16,* 5233–5255.

Renfrew, J. W. (1997). *Aggression and its causes: A biopsychosocial approach.* New York: Oxford University Press.

Renzulli, J. S. (1986). The three ring conception of giftedness: A developmental model for creative productivity. In R. J. Sternberg & J. E. Davidson (Eds.), *Conceptions of giftedness* (pp. 53–92). New York: Cambridge University Press.

Reppert, S. M., Weaver, D. R., Rivkees, S. A., & Stopa, E. G. (1988). Putative melatonin receptors in a human biological clock. *Science, 242,* 78–81.

Rescorla, R. A. (1967). Pavlovian conditioning and its proper control procedures. *Psychological Review, 74,* 71–80.

Rescorla, R. A. (1985). Conditioned inhibition and facilitation. In R. R. Miller & N. E. Spear (Eds.), *Information processing in animals: Conditioned inhibition* (pp. 299–326). Hillsdale, NJ; Erlbaum.

Rescorla, R. A. (1988). Pavlovian conditioning: It's not what you think it is. *American Psychologist, 43,* 151–160.

Rescorla, R. A. (2001). Are associative changes in acquisition and extinction negatively accelerated? *Journal of Experimental Psychology: Animal Behavior Processes, 27,* 307–315.

Rescorla, R. A. (2002a). Comparison of the rates of associative change during acquisition and extinction. *Journal of Experimental Psychology: Animal Behavior Processes, 28,* 406–415.

Rescorla, R. A. (2002b). Savings tests: Separating differences in rate of learning from differences in initial levels. *Journal of Experimental Psychology: Animal Behavior Processes, 28,* 369–377.

Rescorla, R. A., & Wagner, A. R. (1972). A theory of Pavlovian conditioning: Variations in the effectiveness of reinforcement and non-reinforcement. In A. H. Black & W. F. Prokasy (Eds.), *Classical conditioning*: Vol. 2. *Current research and theory.* New York: Appleton-Century-Crofts.

Resing, W. C., & Nijland, M. I. (2002). Are children becoming more intelligent? Twenty-five years' research using the Leiden Diagnostic Test. *Kind en Adolescent, 23,* 42–49.

Rest, J. R. (1983). Moral development. In P. H. Mussen (Ed.), *Handbook of child psychology* (4th ed., Vol. 3, pp. 556–629). New York: Wiley.

Rest, J. R. (1986). *Moral development: advances in research and theory.* New York: Praeger.

Rest, J. R., & Thoma, S. J. (1985). Relation of moral judgment development to formal education. *Developmental Psychology, 21*(4), 709–714.

Restak, R. (1988). *The mind.* New York: Bantam.

Rhodes, G., Geddes, K., Jeffery, L., Dziurawiec,S., & Clark, A. (2002). Are average and symmetric faces attractive to infants? Discrimination and looking preferences. *Perception, 31,* 315–321.

Rholes, W. S., Jones, M., & Wade, C. (1980). A developmental study of learned helplessness. *Developmental Psychology, 16,* 616–624.

Richard, H. L., Fortune, D. G., Griffiths, C.E.M., & Main, C. J. (2001). The contribution of perceptions of stigmatization to disability in patients with psoriasis. *Journal of Psychosomatic Research, 50,* 11–15.

Richards, D. D., & Siegler, R. S. (1984). The effects of task requirements on children's life judgments. *Child Development, 55,* 1687–1696.

Ricks, S. S. (1985). Father–infant interaction: A review of empirical research. *Family Relations, 34,* 505–511.

Rieder, R. O., Kaufmann, C. A., & Knowles, J. A. (1994). Genetics. In R. E. Hales, S. C. Yudofsky, & J. A. Talbott (Eds.), *The American Psychiatric Press textbook of psychiatry* (2nd ed.). Washington, DC: American Psychiatric Press.

Riegel, K. F. (1973). Dialectical operations: The final period of cognitive development. *Human Development, 16,* 346–370.

Rigby, C. S., Deci, E. L., Patrick, B. P., & Ryan, R. M. (1992). Beyond the intrinsic-extrinsic dichotomy: Self-determination in motivation and learning. *Motivation and Emotion, 16,* 165–185.

Ringelmann, M. (1913). Recherches sur les moteurs animés: Travail de l'homme. *Annales de l'Institut National Agronomique,* 2s série, tom XII, 1–40.

Rips, L. J. (1994). Deduction and its cognitive basis. In R. J. Sternberg (Ed.), *Thinking and problem solving* (pp. 150–178). San Diego, CA: Academic Press.

Rips, L. J. (1995). Deduction and cognition. In E. E. Smith & D. N. Osherson (Eds.), *An invitation to cognitive science:* Vol. 3. *Thinking* (pp. 297–343). Cambridge, MA: MIT Press.

Rips, L. J. (1999). Deductive reasoning. In R. A. Wilson & F. C. Keil (Eds.), *The MIT encyclopedia of the cognitive sciences* (pp. 225–226). Cambridge, MA: MIT Press.

Risk factors for suicide: Summary of a workshop. (2001). Washington, DC: National Academies Press.

Ritchhart, R., & Perkins, D. N. (2000). Life in the mindful classroom: Nurturing the disposition of mindfulness. *Journal of Social Issues, 56,* 27–47.

Roach, A. A., Wyman, L. T., Brookes, H., Chavez, C., Heath, S. B., & Valdes, G. (1999). Leadership giftedness: Models revisited. *Gifted Child Quarterly, 43*(1), 13–25.

Roberts, A. C., Robbins, T. W., & Weiskrantz, L. (1996). Executive and cognitive functions of the pre-frontal cortex. *Philosophical Transactions of the Royal Society (London), B, 351,* 1346.

Roberts, W. A. (1998). *Principles of animal cognition.* Boston: McGraw-Hill.

Robertson, D. A., Gernsbacher, M. A., Guidotti, S. J., Robertson, R. W. R., Irwin, W., Mock, B. J., & Campana, M. E. (2000). FMRI investigation of the cognitive process of mapping during discourse comprehension. *Psychological Science, 11,* 1-8.

Robins, L. N., & Regier, D. A. (1991). *Psychiatric disorders in America: The epidemiological catchment area.* New York: Free Press.

Robins, L. N., Helzer, J. E., Weissman, M. M., Orvaschel, H., Gruenberg, E., Burke, J. D., & Regier, D. (1984). Lifetime prevalence of specific psychiatric disorders in three sites. *Archives of General Psychiatry, 41,* 949–958.

Robinson, L. A., Berman, J. S., & Neimeyer, R. A. (1990). Psychotherapy for the treatment of depression: A comprehensive review of controlled outcome research. *Psychological Bulletin, 108*(1), 30–49.

Rockland, K. S. (2000). Brain. In A. E. Kazdin (Ed.), *Encyclopedia of psychology* (Vol. 1, pp. 447–455). Washington, DC: American Psychological Association.

Roebuck, T. M., Mattson, S. N., & Riley, E. P. (2002). Interhemispheric transfer in children with heavy prenatal alcohol exposure. *Alcoholism: Clinical & Experimental Research, 26,* 1863–1871.

Roediger, H. L. III, & McDermott, K. B. (1995). Creating false memories: Remembering words not presented in lists. *Journal of Experimental Psychology: Learning, Memory, and Cognition, 21,* 803–814.

Roediger, H. L. III, & Meade, M. L. (2000). Learning: Cognitive approach for humans. In A. E. Kazdin (Ed.), *Encyclopedia of psychology* (Vol. 5, pp. 8–11). Washington, DC: American Psychological Association.

Roediger, H. L. III. (1980). Memory metaphors in cognitive psychology. *Memory & Cognition, 8*(3), 231–246.

Roediger, H. L. III, & McDermott, K. B. (2000). Distortions of memory. In E. Tulving & F. I. M. Craik (Eds.), *The Oxford handbook of memory* (pp. 149–162). New York: Oxford University Press.

Roediger, H. L. III, & Gallo, D. A. Associative memory illusions. In R.F. Pohl (Ed). *Cognitive illusions: Fallacies and biases in thinking, judgment and memory*. Oxford: Oxford University Press.

Roediger, H. L. III, & McDermott, K. B. (2000). Tricks of memory. *Current Directions in Psychological Science, 9,* 123-127.

Roediger, H. L. III, & McDermott, K. B. (1995). Creating false memories: Remembering words that were not presented in lists. *Journal of Experimental Psychology: Learning, Memory and Cognition, 21,* 803-814.

Roger, D., & Morris, J. (1991). The internal structure of the EPQ scales. *Personality and Individual Differences, 12,* 759–764.

Rogers, A., & Gilligan, C. (1988). *Translating girls' voices: Two languages of development* (pp. 42–43). Harvard University Graduate School of Education, Harvard Project on the Psychology of Women and the Development of Girls.

Rogers, C. R. (1959). A theory of therapy, personality, and interpersonal relationships, as developed in the client-centered framework. In S. Koch (Ed.), *Psychology: A study of a science* (Vol. 3). New York: McGraw-Hill.

Rogers, C. R. (1961a). *On becoming a person: A client's view of psychotherapy.* Boston: Houghton Mifflin.

Rogers, C. R. (1961b). *On becoming a person: A therapist's view of psychotherapy.* Boston: Houghton Mifflin.

Rogers, C. R. (1978). The formative tendency. *Journal of Humanistic Psychology, 18*(1), 23–26.

Rogers, C. R. (1980). *A way of being.* Boston: Houghton Mifflin.

Rogers, C. R., & Russell, D. E. (2002). *Carl Rogers: The quiet revolutionary, an oral history.* Roseville, CA: Penmarin Books.

Rogers, S. M., & Turner, C. F. (1991). Male–male sexual contact in the U.S.A.: Findings from five sample surveys, 1970–1990. *Journal of Sex Research, 28*(4), 491–519.

Rogoff, B. (1986). The development of strategic use of context in spatial memory. In M. Perlmutter (Ed.), *Perspectives on intellectual development.* Hillsdale, NJ: Erlbaum.

Rogoff, B. (1990). *Apprenticeship in thinking.* New York: Oxford University Press.

Rogoff, B. (1998). Cognition as a collaborative process. In W. Damon (Series Ed.) and D. Kuhn & R. S. Siegler (Vol. Eds.), *Handbook of child psychology* (Vol. 2, pp. 371–420). New York: Wiley.

Rogoff, B., Mistry, J., Goncu, A., & Mosler, C. (1993). Guided participation in cultural activity by toddlers and caregivers. *Monographs of the Society for Research in Child Development, 58*(8, Serial No. 236).

Rohan, K. J., Sigmon, S. T., & Dorhofer, D. M. (2003). Cognitive-behavioral factors in seasonal affective disorder. *Journal of Consulting & Clinical Psychology, 71,* 22–30.

Rohde, D. L. T., & Plaut, D. (1999). Language acquisition in the absence of explicit negative evidence: How important is starting small? *Cognition, 72,* 67–109.

Rohner, R. P., & Rohner, E. C. (1981). Assessing interrater influence in holocultural research: A methodological note. *Behavior Science Research, 16*(3–4), 341–351.

Rohner-Jeanrenaud, F., Cusin, I., Sainsbury, A., Zahrzewska, K. E., & Jeanrenaud, B. (1996). The loop system between neuropeptide Y and leptin in normal and obese rodents. *Hormone and Metabolic Research, 28,* 642–648.

Roitblat, H. L., & von Fersen, L. (1992). Comparative cognition: Representations and processes in learning and memory. *Annual Review of Psychology, 43,* 671–710.

Rojahn, K., & Pettigrew, T. F. (1992). Memory for schema-relevant information: A meta-analytic resolution. *British Journal of Social Psychology, 31*(2), 81–109.

Rolls, B. J. (1979). How variety and palatability can stimulate appetite. *Nutrition Bulletin, 5,* 78–86.

Rolls, B. J., Rowe, E. T., & Rolls, E. T. (1982). How sensory properties of food affect human feeding behavior. *Physiology and Behavior, 29,* 409–417.

Rolls, E. T. (1997). Taste and olfactory processing in the brain and its relation to the control of eating. *Critical Reviews in Neurobiology, 11,* 263–287.

Rosch, E. (1978). Principles of categorization. In E. Rosch & B. B. Lloyd (Eds.), *Cognition and categorization* (pp. 27–48). Hillsdale, N.J.: Erlbaum.

Rosch, E. H., & Mervis, C. B. (1975). Family resemblances: Studies in the internal structure of categories. *Cognitive Psychology, 7,* 573–605.

Rose, S. A, & Feldman, J. F. (1995). Prediction of IQ and specific cognitive abilities at 11 years from infancy measures. *Developmental Psychology, 31,* 685–696.

Rosen, B. R., Buckner, R. L., & Dale, A. M. (1998). Event-related fMRI: Past, present, and future. *Proceedings of the National Academy of Sciences, USA, 95,* 773–780.

Rosen, G. M. (1987). Self-help treatment books and the commercialization of psychotherapy. *American Psychologist, 42*(1), 46–51.

Rosen, G. M. (1993). Self-help or hype? Comments on psychology's failure to advance self-care. *Professional Psychology: Research and Practice, 24,* 340–345.

Rosenberg, E. L., & Ekman, P. (2000). Emotion: Methods of study. In A. E. Kazdin (Ed.), *Encyclopedia of psychology* (Vol. 3, pp. 171–175). Washington, DC: American Psychological Association.

Rosenhan, D. L. (1973). On being sane in insane places. *Science, 179,* 250–258.

Rosenthal, R., & Jacobson, L. (1968). *Pygmalion in the classroom: Teacher expectation and pupils' intellectual development.* New York: Holt, Rinehart & Winston.

Rosenzweig, M. R., Leiman, A. L., & Breedlove, S. M. (1999). *Biological psychology: An introduction to behavioral, cognitive and clinical neuroscience.* Sunderland, MA: Sinauer.

Roskies, E., Seraganian, R., Hanley, J. A., Collu, R., Martin, N., & Smilga, C. (1986). The Montreal Type A intervention project: Major findings. *Health Psychology, 5,* 45–69.

Roskies, E., Spevack, M., Surkis, A., Cohen, C., & Gilman, S. (1978). Changing the coronary-prone (Type A) behavior pattern in a nonclinical population. *Journal of Behavioral Medicine, 1,* 201–216.

Ross, B. H. (2000). The effects of category use on learned categories. *Memory & Cognition, 28*(1), 51–63.

Ross, B. H., & Makin, V. S. (1999). Prototype versus exemplar models in cognition. In R. J. Sternberg (Ed.), *The nature of cognition* (pp. 205–241). Cambridge, MA: MIT Press.

Ross, B. H., & Spalding, T. L. (1994). Concepts and categories. In R. J. Sternberg (Ed.), *Handbook of perception and cognition: Thinking and problem solving* (pp. 119–148). San Francisco: Academic Press.

Ross, L. (1977). The intuitive psychologist and his shortcomings: Distortions in the attribution process. In L. Berkowitz (Ed.), *Advances in experimental social psychology* (Vol. 10). New York: Academic Press.

Ross, L., Greene, D., & House, P. (1977). The false consensus effect: An egocentric bias in social perception and attribution processes. *Journal of Experimental Social Psychology, 13*(3), 279–301.

Ross, R. (1975). Salience of reward and intrinsic motivation. *Journal of Personality and Social Psychology, 32,* 245–254.

Ross, R. T. (1983). Relationships between the determinants of performance in serial feature-positive discriminations. *Journal of Experimental Psychology: Animal Behavior Processes, 9,* 349–373.

Ross, R. T., & Holland, P. C. (1981). Conditioning of simultaneous and serial feature-positive discriminations. *Animal Learning & Behavior, 9,* 293–303.

Rothbart, M. K., & Bates, J. E. (1998). Temperament. In W. Damon (Gen. Ed.) & N. Eisenberg (Vol. Ed.), *Handbook of child psychology.* Vol. 3: *Social, emotional, and personality development* (pp. 37–86). New York: Wiley.

Rotter, J. B. (1966). Generalized expectancies for internal versus external control of reinforcement. *Psychological Monographs, 80*(1, Whole No. 609).

Rotter, J. B. (1990). Internal versus external control of reinforcement: A case history of a variable. *American Psychologist, 45,* 489–493.

Rotter, J. B., & Hochreich, D. J. (1975). *Personality.* Glenview, IL: Scott, Foresman.

Rotton, J., & Frey, J. (1985). Air pollution, weather, and violent crimes: Concomitant time-series analysis of archival data. *Journal of Personality and Social Psychology, 49*(5), 1207–1220.

Rotton, J., Barry, T., Frey, J., & Soler, E. (1978). Air pollution and interpersonal attraction. *Journal of Applied Social Psychology, 8,* 57–71.

Rovee-Collier, C., Borza, M. A., Adler, S. A., & Boller, K. (1993). Infants' eyewitness testimony: Effects of postevent information on a prior memory representation. *Memory & Cognition, 21,* 267–279.

Rovee-Collier, C., Evancio, S., & Earley, L. A. (1995). The time window hypothesis: Spacing effects. *Infant Behavior & Development, 18,* 69–78.

Rowe, S. M., & Wertsch, J. V. (2002). Vygotsky's model of cognitive development. In U. Goswami (Ed.), *Blackwell handbook of childhood cognitive development* (pp. 538–554). Malden, MA: Blackwell.

Rozin, P. (1996). Towards a psychology of food and eating: From motivation to module to model to marker, morality, meaning, and metaphor. *Current Directions in Psychological Science, 5,* 18–24.

Rozin, P., & Fallon, A. (1987). A perspective on disgust. *Psychological Review, 94,* 23–41.

Rozin, P., Haidt, J., McCauley, C., Dunlop, L., & Ashmore, M. (1999). Individual differences in disgust sensitivity: Comparisons and evaluations of paper-and-pencil versus behavioral measures. *Journal of Research in Personality, 33,* 330–351.

Rozin, P., Millman, L., & Nemeroff, C. (1986). Operation of the laws of sympathetic magic in disgust and other domains. *Journal of Personality and Social Psychology, 50,* 703–712.

Rubin, D. C. (1982). On the retention function for autobiographical memory. *Journal of Verbal Learning and Verbal Behavior, 19,* 21–38.

Rubin, D. C. (Ed.). (1996). *Remembering our past: Studies in autobiographical memory.* New York: Cambridge University Press.

Rubin, G. S. (2000). Visual impairment: Physical causes. In A. E. Kazdin (Ed.), *Encyclopedia of psychology* (Vol. 8, pp. 200–204). Washington, DC: American Psychological Association.

Rubin, G., West, S., Muñoz, B., Bandeen-Roche, K., Zeger, S., Fried, L., & See Project Team. (1997). A comprehensive assessment of visual impairment in an older American population: SEE study. *Investigative Ophthalmology and Visual Science, 38,* 557–568.

Rubin, K. H. (1980). Fantasy play: Its role in the development of social skills and social cognition. In K. H. Rubin (Ed.), *Children's play: New directions for child development.* San Francisco: Jossey-Bass.

Rubin, K. H., Bukowski, W., & Parker, J. (1998). Peer interactions, relationships, and groups. In W. Damon (Gen. Ed.) & N. Eisenberg (Vol. Ed.), *Handbook of child psychology. Vol. 3: Social, emotional, and personality development* (pp. 619–700). New York: Wiley.

Rubin, K. H., Burgess, K. B., Kennedy, A. E., & Stewart, S. L. (2003). Social withdrawal in childhood. In E. J. Mash & R. A. Barkley (Eds.), *Child psychopathology* (pp. 372–406). New York: Guilford.

Rubin, K. H., Coplan, R. J., Nelson, L. J., Cheah, C. S. L., & Lagace-Seguin, D. G. (1999). Peer relationships in childhood. In M. H. Bornstein & M. E. Lamb (Eds.), *Developmental psychology: An advanced textbook* (4th ed., pp. 451–501). Mahwah, NJ: Erlbaum.

Rubin, V., & Comitas, L. (1974). *Ganja in Jamaica: A medical anthropological study of chronic marijuana use.* The Hague, Netherlands: Mouton.

Rubinstein, G. (2001). Sex-role reversal and clinical judgment of mental health. *Journal of Sex & Marital Therapy, 27,* 9–19.

Ruble, D. N., & Martin, C. L. (1998). Gender development. In W. Damon (Gen. Ed.) & N. Eisenberg (Vol. Ed.), *Handbook of child psychology* (Vol. 3, pp. 933–1016). New York: Wiley.

Ruch, J. C. (1975). Self-hypnosis: The result of heterohypnosis or vice versa? *International Journal of Clinical and Experimental Hypnosis, 23,* 282–304.

Rudy, T. E., Kerns, R. D., & Turk, D. C. (1988). Chronic pain and depression: Toward a cognitive-behavioral mediation model. *Pain, 35,* 129–140.

Ruffman, T., Perner, J., Naito, M., Parkin, L., & Clements, W. A. (1998). Older (but not younger) siblings facilitate false belief understanding. *Developmental Psychology, 34,* 161–174.

Rugg, M. D. (Ed.). (1997). *Cognitive neuroscience.* Hove, UK: Psychology Press.

Rule, S. R., & Ferguson, T. J. (1986). The effects of media violence on attitudes, emotions, and cognitions. *Journal of Social Issues, 42*(3), 29–50.

Rumsey, N. (2001). Visible disfigurement. In D. Johnston & M. Johnston (Eds.), *Health psychology. Vol. 8: Comprehensive clinical psychology* (pp. 575–593). Washington, DC: American Psychological Association.

Runco, M. A. (2000). Creativity: Research on the process of creativity. In A. E. Kazdin (Ed.), *Encyclopedia of psychology* (Vol. 2, pp. 342–346).

Runeson, S., & Frykholm, G. (1986). Kinematic specification of gender and gender expression. In V. McCabe and G. J. Balzano (Eds.), *Event cognition: An ecological perspective.* Hillsdale, NJ: Erlbaum.

Russell, J. A. (1991). Culture and categorization of emotions. *Psychological Bulletin, 110*(3), 426–450.

Russell, J. A. (1994). Is there universal recognition of emotion from facial expression? A review of the cross-cultural studies. *Psychological Bulletin, 115,* 102–141.

Russell, W. R., & Nathan, P. W. (1946). Traumatic amnesia. *Brain, 69,* 280–300.

Ryan, C., Willford, J., Day, N. L., & Goldschmidt, L. (2002). Prenatal alcohol and marijuana exposure: Effects on neuropsychological outcomes at 10 years. *Neurotoxicology & Teratology, 24,* 311–320.

Ryan, R. M., Mims, V., & Koestner, R. (1983). Relation of reward contingency and interpersonal context to intrinsic motivation: A review and test using cognitive evaluation theory. *Journal of Personality and Social Psychology, 45,* 736–750.

Rymer, R. (1993). *Genie: An abused child's flight from silence.* New York: HarperCollins.

Rypma, B., Prabhakaran, V., Desmond, J. E., & Gabrieli, J. D. (2001). Age differences in prefrontal cortical activity in working memory. *Psychology & Aging, 16*(3), 371–384.

Sackett, G., & Korner, A. (1993). Organization of sleep-waking states in conjoined twin neonates. *Sleep: Journal of Sleep Research & Sleep Medicine, 16,* 414–427.

Sadeh, A., Gruber, R., & Raviv, A. (2002). Sleep, neurobehavioral functioning, and behavior problems in school-age children. *Child Development, 73,* 405–441.

Sadker, M., & Sadker, D. (1984). *Year three: Final report, promoting effectiveness in classroom instruction.* Washington, DC: National Institute of Education.

Safer, D. J. (1991). Diet, behavior modification, and exercise: A review of obesity treatments from a long-term perspective. *Southern Medical Journal, 84,* 1470–1474.

Sagan, E. (1988). *Freud, women, and morality: The psychology of good and evil.* New York: Basic Books.

Sahraie, A., Weiskrantz, L., Barbur, J. L., Simmons, A., Williams, S. C., & Brammer, M. (1997). Pattern of neuronal activity associated with conscious and unconscious processing of visual signals. *Proceedings of the National Academy of Sciences, USA, 94,* 9406–9411.

Salekin, K. L., Ogloff, J. R. P., Ley, R. G., & Salekin, R. T. (2002). The overcontrolled hostility scale: An evaluation of its applicability with an adolescent population. *Criminal Justice & Behavior, 29,* 718–733.

Salili, F. (1994). Age, sex, and cultural differences in the meaning and dimensions of achievement. *Personality & Social Psychology Bulletin, 20,* 635–648.

Salovey, P. (2000). Results that get results: Telling a good story. In R. J. Sternberg (Ed.), *Guide to publishing in psychology journals* (pp. 121–132). New York: Cambridge University Press.

Salovey, P. (2001). Applied emotional intelligence: Regulating emotions to become healthy, wealthy, and wise. In J. Ciarrochi & J. P. Forgas (Eds.), *Emotional intelligence in everyday life: A scientific inquiry* (pp. 168–184). Philadelphia: Psychology Press.

Salovey, P., & Mayer, J. D. (1990). Emotional intelligence. *Imagination, Cognition, and Personality, 9,* 185–211.

Salovey, P., & Pizarro, D. A. (2003). The value of emotional intelligence. In R. J. Sternberg, J. Lautrey, & T. I. Lubart (Eds.), *Models of intelligence: International perspectives* (pp. 263–278). Washington, DC: American Psychological Association.

Salovey, P., & Sluyter, D. J. (1997). *Emotional development and emotional intelligence: Implications for educators.* New York: Basic Books.

Salovey, P., Mayer, J. D., & Caruso, D. (2002). The positive psychology of emotional intelligence. In C. R. Snyder & S. J. Lopez (Eds.), *Handbook of positive psychology* (pp. 159–171). London: Oxford University Press.

Salthouse, T. A. (1992). The information-processing perspective on cognitive aging. In R. J. Sternberg & C. A. Berg (Eds.), *Intellectual development* (pp. 261–277). New York: Cambridge University Press.

Salthouse, T. A. (1996). The processing-speed theory of adult age differences in cognition. *Psychological Review, 103,* 403–428.

Salthouse, T. A., & Somberg, B. L. (1982). Skilled performance: Effects of adult age and experience on elementary processes. *Journal of Experimental Psychology: General, 111*(2), 176–207.

Sameroff, A. J. (2000). Ecological perspectives on developmental risk. In J. D. Osofsky & H. E. Fitzgerald (Eds.), *WAIMH handbook of infant mental health.* Vol. 4: *Infant mental health in groups at high risk* (pp. 1–34). New York: Wiley.

Sandell, J. (2000). Vision and sight: Behavioral and functional aspects. In A. E. Kazdin (Ed.), *Encyclopedia of psychology* (Vol. 8, pp. 178–180). Washington, DC: American Psychological Association.

Sanders, S. H. (1985). Chronic pain: Conceptualization and epidemiology. *Annals of Behavioral Medicine, 7*(3), 3–5.

Sanderson, C. A., Darley, J. M., & Messinger, C. S. (2002). "I'm not as thin as you think I am": The development and consequences of feeling discrepant from the thinness norm. *Personality & Social Psychology Bulletin, 28,* 172–183.

Sanderson, W. C., Beck, A. T., & McGinn, L. K. (2002). Cognitive therapy for generalized anxiety disorder: Significance of comorbid personality disorders. In R. L. Leahy & E. T. Dowd (Eds.), *Clinical advances in cognitive psychotherapy: Theory and application* (pp. 287–293). New York: Springer.

Sapir, E. (1964). *Culture, language and personality.* Berkeley: University of California Press. (Original work published 1941)

Sarason, S. B., & Doris, J. (1979). *Educational handicap, public policy, and social history.* New York: Free Press.

Sarid, O., Anson, O., Yaari, A., & Margalith, M. (2003). Are coping resources related to humoral reaction induced by academic stress? An analysis of specific salivary antibodies to Epstein-Barr virus and cytomegalovirus. *Psychology Health & Medicine, 8,* 105–117.

Sartorius, N., de Girolano, G., Andrews, G., German, G. A., & Eisenberg, L. (Eds.). (1993a). *Treatment of mental disorders: A review of effectiveness.* Geneva, Switzerland, and Washington, DC: World Health Organization and American Psychiatric Press.

Sartorius, N., Kaelber, C., Cooper, J. E., Roper, M. T., et al. (1993b). Progress toward achieving a common language in psychiatry: Results from the field trial of the clinical guidelines accompanying the WHO classification of mental and behavioral disorders in ICD-10. *Archives of General Psychiatry, 50*(2), 115–124.

Sartorius, N., Shapiro, R., & Jablonsky, A. (1974). The international pilot study of schizophrenia. *Schizophrenia Bulletin, 2,* 21–35.

Saucier, G., & Goldberg, L. R. (1998). What is beyond the Big Five? *Journal of Personality, 66,* 495–524.

Saucier, G., & Goldberg, L. R. (2002). Assessing the big five: Applications of 10 psychometric criteria to the development of marker scales. In B. de Raad (Ed.), *Big five assessment* (pp. 30–54). Ashland, OH: Hogrefe & Huber.

Savage, D. D., Becher, M., de la Torre, A. J., & Sutherland, R. J. (2002). Dose-dependent effects of prenatal ethanol exposure on synaptic plasticity and learning in mature offspring. *Alcoholism: Clinical & Experimental Research, 26,* 1752–1758.

Savage-Rumbaugh, S., McDonald, K., Sevcik, R. A., Hopkins, W. D., & Rubert, E. (1986). Spontaneous symbol acquisition and communicative use by pygmy chimpanzees (*Pan paniscus*). *Journal of Experimental Psychology: General, 112,* 211–235.

Savage-Rumbaugh, S., Murphy, J., Sevcik, R., Brakke, K., Williams, S., & Rumbaugh, D. M. (1993). Language comprehension in ape and child. *Monographs of the Society for Research in Child Development, 58*(3–4, Serial No. 233).

Saxe, L., Dougherty, D., & Cross, T. (1985). The validity of polygraph testing: Scientific analysis and public controversy. *American Psychologist, 40,* 355–366.

Scarr, H. A. (1994). United States population: A typical American as seen through the eyes of the Census Bureau. In *The World Almanac and Book of Facts, 1994.* Mahwah, NJ: Funk & Wagnalls.

Scarr, S. (1997). Behavior-genetic and socialization theories of intelligence: Truce and reconciliation. In R. J. Sternberg & E. L. Grigorenko (Eds.), *Intelligence, heredity, and environment* (pp. 3–41). New York: Cambridge University Press.

Scarr, S., & Weinberg, R. A. (1976). I.Q. test performance of black children adopted by white families. *American Psychologist, 31,* 726–739.

Scarr, S., & Weinberg, R. A., & Waldman, I. D. (1993). IQ correlations in transracial adoptive families. *Intelligence, 17,* 541–555.

Scarr, S., Phillips, D., & McCartney, K. (1990). Facts, fantasies, and the future of child care in the United States. *Psychological Science, 1,* 26–35.

Schachter, S. (1951). Deviation, rejection, and communication. *Journal of Abnormal Social Psychology, 46,* 190–207.

Schachter, S., & Singer, J. (1962). Cognitive, social, and physiological determinants of emotional state. *Psychological Review, 69,* 379–399.

Schacter, D. L. (1995). Memory distortion: History and current status. In D. L. Schacter, J. T. Coyle, G. D. Fischbach, M. M. Mesulam, & L. E. Sullivan (Eds.), *Memory distortions* (pp. 1–43). Cambridge, MA: Harvard University Press.

Schacter, D. L. (1996). *Searching for memory: The brain, the mind, and the past.* New York: Basic Books.

Schacter, D. L. (2000). Memory: Memory systems. In A. E. Kazdin (Ed.) *Encyclopedia of psychology* (Vol. 5, pp. 169–172). Washington, DC: American Psychological Association.

Schacter, D. L. (2001). *The seven sins of memory: How the mind forgets and remembers.* Boston: Houghton Mifflin.

Schacter, D. L., & Curran, T. (2000). Memory without remembering and remembering without memory: Implicit and false memories. In M. S. Gazzaniga (Ed.), *The new cognitive neurosciences* (2nd ed., pp. 829–840). Cambridge, MA: MIT Press.

Schacter, D. L., & Tulving, E. (Eds.). (1994). *Memory systems 1994.* Cambridge, MA: MIT Press.

Schacter, D. L., Chiu, C.Y.P., & Ochsner, K. N. (1993). Implicit memory: A selective review. *Annual Review of Neuroscience, 16,* 159–182.

Schacter, D. L., Verfaellie, M., & Pradere, D. (1996). The neuropsychology of memory illusions: False recall and recognition in amnesic patients. *Journal of Memory and Language, 35,* 319–334.

Schaffer, H. R. (1977). *Mothering.* Cambridge, MA: Harvard University Press.

Schaie, K. W. (1974). Translations in gerontology—from lab to life. *American Psychologist, 29,* 802–807.

Schaie, K. W. (1989). Perceptual speed in adulthood: Cross-sectional and longitudinal studies. *Psychology and Aging, 4,* 443–453.

Schaie, K. W. (1995). *Intellectual development in adulthood.* New York: Cambridge University Press.

Schaie, K. W. (1996). *Intellectual development in adulthood: The Seattle Longitudinal Study.* New York: Cambridge University Press.

Schaie, K. W., & Willis, S. L. (1986). Can decline in intellectual functioning in the elderly be reversed? *Developmental Psychology, 22,* 223–232.

Schank, R. C., & Abelson, R. P. (1977). *Scripts, plans, goals, and understanding.* Hillsdale. NJ: Erlbaum.

Schank, R. C., & Towle, B. (2000). Artificial intelligence. In R. J. Sternberg (Ed.), *Handbook of intelligence* (pp. 341–356). New York: Cambridge University Press.

Scharfe, E., & Bartholomew, K. (1994). Reliability and stability of adult attachment patterns. *Personal Relationships, 1,* 23–43.

Scharli, H., Harman, A. M., & Hogben, J. H. (1999). Blindsight in subjects with homonymous visual field defects. *Journal of Cognitive Neuroscience, 11,* 52–66.

Scheff, T. J. (1966). *Being mentally ill: A sociological theory.* Chicago: Aldine.

Scheier, M. F., & Carver, C. S. (1985). Optimism, coping, and health: Assessment and implications of generalized outcome expectancies. *Health Psychology, 4,* 219–247.

Schiffer, F., Zaidel, E., Bogen, J., & Chasan-Taber, S. (1998). Different psychological status in the two hemispheres of two split-brain patients. *Neuropsychiatry, Neuropsychology, & Behavioral Neurology, 11*(3), 151–156.

Schiffman, S. (2000). Taste: Biological organization. In A. E. Kazdin (Ed.), *Encyclopedia of psychology* (Vol. 8, pp. 6–8). Washington, DC: American Psychological Association.

Schildkraut, J. J. (1965). The catecholamine hypothesis of affective disorders: A review of supporting evidence. *American Journal of Psychiatry, 122,* 509–522.

Schizophrenia drug dispute intensifies, BBC News Online (2000, Dec. 3). retrieved June 20, 2003 from http://news.bbc.co.uk/1/hi/health/1049798.stm.

Schliemann, A. D., & Magalhües, V. P. (1990). *Proportional reasoning: From shops, to kitchens, laboratories, and, hopefully, schools.* Proceedings of the Fourteenth International Conference for the Psychology of Mathematics Education, Oaxtepec, Mexico.

Schmidt, F. L., Ones, D. S., & Hunter, J. E. (1992). Personnel selection. *Annual Review of Psychology, 43,* 627–670.

Schmitt, B. H., Gilovich, T., Goore, N., & Joseph, L. (1986). Mere exposure and social facilitation: One more time. *Journal of Experimental and Social Psychology, 22,* 242–248.

Schnall, S., Abrahamson, A., & Laird, J. D. (2002). Premenstrual syndrome and misattribution: A self-perception, individual differences perspective. *Basic & Applied Social Psychology, 24,* 215–228.

Schneider, A., & Domhoff, G. W. (2003). The quantitative study of dreams. Retrieved June 14, 2003 from http://www.dreamresearch.net/.

Schneider, M. L., Moore, C. F., & Becker, E. F. (2001). Timing of moderate alcohol exposure during pregnancy and neonatal outcome in rhesus monkeys *(Macaca mulatta). Alcoholism: Clinical & Experimental Research, 25,* 1238–1246.

Schneider, W. (2002). Memory development in childhood. In U. Goswami (Ed.), *Blackwell handbook of childhood cognitive development* (pp. 236–256). Malden, MA: Blackwell.

Schonfield, D., & Robertson, D. A. (1966). Memory storage and aging. *Canadian Journal of Psychology, 20,* 228–236.

Schroeder, D. H., & Costa, P. T. Jr. (1984). Influence of life event stress on physical illness: Substantive effects or methodological flaws? *Journal of Personality and Social Psychology, 46,* 853–863.

Schroeder-Helmert, D. (1985). Clinical evaluation of DSIP. In A. Wauquier, J. M. Gaillard, J. M. Monti, & M. Radulovacki (Eds.), *Sleep: Neurotransmitters and neuromodulators* (pp. 279–291). New York: Raven Press.

Schroth, M. L. (1991). Dyadic adjustment and sensation seeking compatibility. *Personality and Individual Differences, 12,* 467–471.

Schulz, S. C. (1995). Schizophrenia: Somatic treatment. In H. I. Kaplan & B. J. Sadock (Eds.), *Comprehensive textbook of psychiatry* (6th ed., pp. 987–998). Baltimore, MD: Williams & Wilkins.

Schwartz, B. (1989). *Psychology of learning and behavior* (3rd ed.). New York: Norton.

Schwartz, B. L., & Metcalfe, J. (1994). Methodological problems and pitfalls in the study of human metacognition. In J. Metcalfe & A. P. Shimamura (Eds.), *Metacognition: Knowing about knowing* (pp. 93–114). Cambridge, MA: MIT Press.

Schwartz, G. E. (1982). Testing the biopsychosocial model: The ultimate challenge facing behavioral medicine. *Journal of Consulting and Clinical Psychology, 50,* 1040–1053.

Schweizer, E., Rickels, K., Case, G., & Greenblatt, D. J. (1990). Long-term therapeutic use of benzodiazepines: II. Effects of gradual taper. *Archives of General Psychiatry, 47*(10), 908–915.

Scott, A. I. F. (1989). Which depressed patients will respond to electroconvulsive therapy? The search for biological predictors of recovery. *British Journal of Psychiatry, 154,* 8–17.

Scott, T. R. (2000). Taste: Behavioral and functional aspects. In A. E. Kazdin (Ed.), *Encyclopedia of psychology* (pp. 8–100). Washington, DC: American Psychological Association.

Scovern, A. W., & Kilmann, P. R. (1980). Status of electroconvulsive therapy: Review of the outcome literature. *Psychological Bulletin, 87,* 260–303.

Scoville, W. B., & Milner, B. (1957). Loss of recent memory after bilateral hippocampal lesions. *Journal of Neurology, Neurosurgery, and Psychiatry, 20,* 11–19.

Sears, D. O. (1983). The person-positivity bias. *Journal of Personality and Social Psychology, 44,* 233–250.

Sedlacek, W. E., Walters, P., & Valente, J. (1985). Differences between counseling clients and nonclients on Clark-Trow subcultures. *Journal of College Student Personnel, 26,* 319–322.

Segal, B. (1988). *Drugs and behavior.* New York: Gardner Press.

Segal, N. L. & Roy, A. (2001). Suicidal attempts and ideation in twins whose co-twins' deaths were non-suicides: Replication and elaboration. *Personality & Individual Differences, 31*(3), 445–452.

Segal, N. L. (1999). *Entwined lives: Twins and what they tell us about human behavior.* New York: Dutton.

Sehgal, M. (2000). Anger, anxiety and type A behaviour as determinants of essential hypertension and coronary heart disease. *Journal of the Indian Academy of Applied Psychology, 26*(1–2), 33–39.

Sehulster, J. R. (1989). Content and temporal structure of autobiographical knowledge: Remembering twenty-five seasons at the Metropolitan Opera. *Memory & Cognition, 17,* 290–606.

Seidenberg, M. S. (1993). Connectionist models and cognitive theory. *Psychological Science, 4,* 228–235.

Seidman, L. J. (1983). Schizophrenia and brain dysfunction: An integration of recent neurodiagnostic findings. *Psychological Bulletin, 94,* 195–238.

Seidman, L. J. (1990). The neuropsychology of schizophrenia: A neurodevelopmental and case study approach. *Journal of Neuropsychiatry and Clinical Neuroscience, 2,* 301–312.

Seifer, R. (2001). Socioeconomic status, multiple risks, and development of intelligence. In R. J. Sternberg & E. L. Grigorenko (Eds.), *Environmental effects on cognitive abilities* (pp. 59–82). Mahwah, NJ: Erlbaum.

Seifert, C. M., Meyer, D. E., Davidson, N., Palatano, A. L., & Yaniv, I. (1995). Demystification of cognitive insight: Opportunistic assimilation and the prepare-mind perspective. In R. J. Sternberg & J. E. Davidson (Eds.), *The nature of insight* (pp. 65–124). Cambridge, MA: MIT Press.

Seifert, C. M., Meyer, D. E., Davidson, N., Patalano, A. L., & Yaniv, I. (1995). Demystification of cognitive insight: Opportunistic assimilation and the prepared-mind perspective. In R. J. Sternberg & J. E. Davidson (Eds.), *The nature of insight* (pp. 65–124). Cambridge, MA: MIT Press.

Sekuler, R., & Sekuler, A. B. (2000). In A. E. Kazdin (Ed.), *Handbook of psychology* (Vol. 8, pp. 180–183). Washington, DC: American Psychological Association.

Selfridge, O. G. (1959). Pandemonium: A paradigm for learning. In D. V. Blake & A. M. Uttley (Eds.), *Proceedings of the symposium on the mechanization of thought processes* (pp. 511–529). London: Her Majesty's Stationery Office.

Selfridge, O. G., & Neisser, U. (1960). Pattern recognition by machine. *Scientific American, 203,* 60–68.

Seligman, M.E.P. (1971). Phobias and preparedness. *Behavior Therapy, 193,* 323–325.

Seligman, M. E. P. (1974). Depression and learned helplessness. In R. J. Friedman & M. M. Katz (Eds.), *The psychology of depression: Contemporary theory and research.* Washington, DC: Winston-Wiley.

Seligman, M. E. P. (1975). *Helplessness.* San Francisco: Freeman.

Seligman, M. E. P. (1991). *Learned optimism.* New York: Norton.

Seligman, M. E. P. (1995). The effectiveness of psychotherapy: The *Consumer Reports* study. *American Psychologist, 50*(12), 965–983.

Seligman, M. E. P. (2002a). *Authentic happiness.* New York: Free Press.

Seligman, M. E. P. (2002b). Positive psychology, positive prevention, and positive therapy. In C. R. Snyder & S. Lopez (Eds.), *Handbook of positive psychology* (pp. 3–9). London: Oxford University Press.

Seligman, M. E. P., & Csikszentmihalyi, M. (2000). Positive psychology: An introduction. *American Psychologist, 55,* 5–14.

Seligman, M. E. P., & Levant, R. F. (1998). Managed care policies rely on inadequate science. *Professional Psychology Research & Practice, 29,* 211–212.

Seligman, M. E. P., & Maier, S. F. (1967). Failure to escape traumatic shock. *Journal of Experimental Psychology, 74,* 1–9.

Sell, R. L., Wells, J. A., & Wypij, D. (1995). The prevalence of homosexual behavior and attraction in the United States, the United Kingdom and France: Results of national population-based samples. *Archives of Sexual Behavior, 24,* 235–248.

Selye, H. (1976). *The stress of life* (Rev. ed.). New York: McGraw-Hill.

Sepple, C. P., & Read, N. W. (1989). Gastrointestinal correlates of the development of hunger in man. *Appetite, 13,* 183–191.

Sera, M. D. (1992). To be or not to be: Use and acquisition of the Spanish copulas. *Journal of Memory and Language, 31,* 408–427.

Seraganian, P. (Ed.). (1993). *Exercise psychology: The influence of physical exercise on psychological processes.* New York: Wiley.

Serdahely, W. J. (1990). Pediatric near-death experiences. *Journal of Near-Death Studies, 9,* 33–39.

Serpell, R. (1993). The *significance of schooling: Life journeys in an African society.* Cambridge, UK: University of Cambridge Press.

Serpell, R. (1994). The cultural construction of intelligence. In W. J. Lonner & R. S. Malpass (Eds.), *Psychology and culture.* Boston: Allyn & Bacon.

Serpell, R. (2000). Intelligence and culture. In R. J. Sternberg (Ed.), *Handbook of intelligence* (pp. 549–577). New York: Cambridge University Press.

Serpell, R. (2002). The embeddedness of human development within sociocultural context: Pedagogical and political implications. *Social Development, 11,* 290–295.

Seymour, R. B., & Smith, D. E. (1987). *Guide to psychoactive drugs: An up-to-the-minute reference to mind-altering substances.* New York: Harrington Park Press.

Shackelford, T. K., Buss, D. M., & Bennett, K. (2002). Forgiveness or breakup: Sex differences in responses to a partner's infidelity. *Cognition & Emotion, 16(2),* 299–307.

Shadish, W. R., Navarro, A. M., Crits-Cristoph, P., Jorm, A. F., Nietzel, M. T., Robinson, L., Svartberg, M., Matt, G. E., Siegle, G., Hazelrigg, M. D. Lyons, L. C., Prout, H. T., Smith, M. L., & Weiss, B. (1997). Evidence that therapy works in clinically representative conditions. *Journal of Consulting and Clinical Psychology, 65,* 355–365.

Shafir, E., & Tversky, A. (1995). Decision making. In E. E. Smith & D. N. Osherson (Eds.), *An invitation to cognitive science:* Vol. 3. *Thinking* (pp. 77–100). Cambridge, MA: MIT Press.

Shanab, M. E., & Yahya, K. A. (1977). A behavioral study of obedience in children. *Journal of Personality and Social Psychology, 35,* 530–536.

Shanab, M. E., & Yahya, K. A. (1978). A cross-cultural study of obedience. *Bulletin of the Psychonomic Society, 11,* 267–269.

Shapiro, D. H., & Giber, D. (1978). Meditation and psychotherapeutic effects: Self-regulation strategy and altered states of consciousness. *Archives of General Psychiatry, 35,* 294–302.

Shapiro, D., Lane, J. D., & Henry, J. P. (1986). Caffeine, cardiovascular reactivity, and cardiovascular disease. In K. A. Matthews, S. M. Weiss, T. Detre, T. M. Dembroski, B. Falkner, S. B. Manuck, & R. B. Williams (Eds.), *Handbook of stress, reactivity, and cardiovascular disease.* New York: Wiley.

Shapiro, P., & Penrod, S. (1986). Meta-analysis of facial identification studies. *Psychological Bulletin, 100,* 139–156.

Shaver, P. R., & Mikulincer, M. (2002a). Attachment-related psychodynamics. *Attachment & Human Development, 4,* 133–161.

Shaver, P. R., & Mikulincer, M. (2002b). Dialogue on adult attachment: Diversity and integration. *Attachment & Human Development, 4,* 243–257.

Shaver, P. R., Collins, N., & Clark, C. (1996). Attachment styles and internal working models of self and relationship partners. In G. J. O. Fletcher & J. Fitness (Eds.), *Knowledge structures in close relationships: A social psychological approach.* Mahwah, NJ: Erlbaum.

Shaver, P., Schwartz, J., Krison, D., & O'Connor, C. (1987). Emotion knowledge: Further exploration of a prototype approach. *Journal of Personality and Social Psychology, 52,* 1061–1086.

Shaver, P., Wu, S., & Schwartz, J. (1992). Cross-cultural similarities and differences in emotion and its representation: A prototype approach. In M. S. Clark (Ed.), *Review of personality and social psychology* (Vol. 13). Newbury Park, CA: Sage.

Shaywitz, B. A., Pugh, K. R., Constable, R. T., Skudlarski, P., Fulbright, R. K., Bronen, R. A., Fletcher, J. M., Shankweiler, P., Katz, L., & Gore, J. L. (1995). Sex differences in the functional organization of the brain for language. *Nature, 373,* 607–609.

Shaywitz, B. A., Shaywitz, S. E., Sebrechts, M. M., Anderson, G. M., et al. (1990). Growth hormone and prolactin response to methylphenidate in children with attention deficit disorder. *Life Sciences, 46,* 625–633.

Shear, M. K., Cassano, G. B., Frank, E., Paola, R., Rotondo, A., & Fagiolini, A. (2002). The panic-agoraphobic spectrum: Development, description, and clinical significance. *Psychiatric Clinics of North America, 25,* 739–756.

Shedler, J., Mayman, M., & Manis, M. (1993). The illusion of mental health. *American Psychologist, 48,* 1117–1131.

Shekelle, R. B., Hulley, S. B., Neaton, J. D., Billings, J. H., Borhani, N. O., Gerace, T. A., Jacobs, D. R., Lasser, N. L., Mittelmark, M. B., & Stamler, J. (1985). The MRFIT behavior pattern study: II. Type A behavior and incidence of coronary heart disease. *American Journal of Epidemiology, 122,* 559–570.

Shepherd, G. (1991). *Foundations of the neuron doctrine.* New York: Oxford University Press.

Shepherd, G. (1999). Neuron. In R. A. Wilson & F. C. Keil (Eds.), *The MIT encyclopedia of the cognitive sciences* (pp. 603–605). Cambridge, MA: MIT Press.

Shepherd, G. (Ed.). (1998). *The synaptic organization of the brain.* New York: Oxford University Press.

Sheppard, J. A. (1993). Productivity loss in performance groups: A motivation analysis. *Psychological Bulletin, 114,* 67–81.

Sherif, M., Harvey, L. J., White, B. J., Hood, W. R., & Sherif, C. W. (1988). *The Robber's Cave experiment: Intergroup conflict and cooperation.* Middletown, CT: Wesleyan University Press. (Original work published 1961)

Sherman, S. J., Judd, C. M., & Park, B. (1989). Social cognition. *Annual Review of Psychology, 40,* 281–326.

Shevell, S. K. (2000a). Color vision. In A. E. Kazdin (Ed.), *Encyclopedia of psychology* (Vol. 2, pp. 182–186). Washington, DC: American Psychological Association.

Shevell, S. K. (2000b). *The science of color* (2nd ed.). New York: Wiley

Shibazaki, M. (1983). Development of hemispheric function in hiragana, kanji, and figure processing for normal children and mentally retarded children. *Japanese Journal of Special Education, 21(3),* 1–9.

Shields, J. (1962). *Monozygotic twins brought up apart and brought up together.* London: Oxford University Press.

Shiffrin, R. M. (1996). Laboratory experimentation on the genesis of expertise. In K. A. Ericsson (Ed.), *The road to excellence* (pp. 337–347). Mahwah, NJ: Erlbaum.

Shimada, M., & Otsuka, A. (1981). Functional hemispheric differences in kanji processing in Japanese. *Japanese Psychological Review, 24(4),* 472–489.

Shipster, C., Hearst, D., Dockrell, J. E., Kilby, E., & Hayward, R. (2002). Speech and language skills and cognitive functioning in children with Apert syndrome: A pilot study. *International Journal of Language & Communication Disorders, 37,* 325–343.

Shneidman, E. S. (1973). Suicide. In *Encyclopedia Britannica.* Chicago: Encyclopedia Britannica.

Shneidman, E. S. (2001). *Comprehending suicide: Landmarks in 20th-century suicidology.* Washington, DC: American Psychological Association.

Shonkoff, J., & Phillips, D. (Eds.). (2000). *From neurons to neighborhoods: The science of early childhood development.* Washington, DC: National Academy Press.

Shontz, F. C. (1975). *The psychological aspects of physical illness and disability.* New York: Macmillan.

Shook, M. D., & Shook, R. L. (1991). *The book of odds.* New York: Penguin.

Shuit, D. P. (1994, May 22). Verdict heats up memory debate. *Los Angeles Times,* p. A3.

Shulman, H. G. (1970). Encoding and retention of semantic and phonemic information in short-term memory. *Journal of Verbal Learning and Verbal Behavior, 9,* 499–508.

Shulman, R. (1967). A survey of vitamin B12 deficiency in an elderly psychiatric population. *British Journal of Psychiatry, 113,* 241–251.

Shumaker, S. A., & Hill, D. R. (1991). Gender differences in social support and physical health. *Health Psychology, 10,* 102–111.

Sibitani, A. (1980). The Japanese brain. *Science, 80,* 22–26.

Siegler, R. S. (1976). Three aspects of cognitive development. *Cognitive Psychology, 8,* 481–520.

Siegler, R. S. (1978). The origins of scientific reasoning. In R. S. Siegler (Ed.), *Children's thinking: What develops?* (pp. 109–149). Hillsdale, NJ: Erlbaum.

Siegler, R. S. (1986). *Children's thinking.* Englewood Cliffs, NJ: Prentice-Hall.

Siegler, R. S. (1996). *Emerging minds: The process of change in children's thinking.* New York: Oxford University Press.

Siegler, R. S. (1998). *Children's thinking* (3rd ed.). Upper Saddle River, NJ: Prentice-Hall.

Siegler, R. S., & Chen, Z. (1998). Developmental differences in rule learning: A microgenetic analysis. *Cognitive Psychology, 36,* 273–310.

Siegman, A. W., & Snow, S. C. (1997). The outward expression of anger, the inward experience of anger, and CVR: The role of vocal expression. *Journal of Behavioral Medicine, 20,* 29–46.

Signorielli, N., McLeod, D., & Healy, E. (1994). Gender stereotypes in MTV commercials: The beat goes on. *Journal of Broadcasting and Electronic Media, 38,* 91–101.

Silver, R. L., & Wortman, C. B. (1980). Coping with undesirable life events. In J. Garber & M. E. P. Seligman (Eds.), *Human helplessness: Theory and applications.* New York: Academic Press.

Silverman, I., & Eals, M. (1992). Sex differences in spatial abilities: Evolutionary theory and data. In J. Barkow, L. Cosmides, & J. Tooby (Eds.), *The adapted mind* (pp. 533–549). New York: Oxford University Press.

Silverstein, B., Peterson, B., & Perdue, L. (1986). Some correlates of the thin standard of bodily attractiveness in women. *International Journal of Eating Disorders, 5,* 145–155.

Simon, H. A. (1957). *Administrative behavior* (2nd ed.). Totowa, NJ: Littlefield, Adams.

Simon, H. A. (1999). Problem solving. In R. A. Wilson & F. C. Keil (Eds.), *The MIT encyclopedia of the cognitive sciences* (pp. 674–676). Cambridge, MA: MIT Press.

Simon, W. H., & Gagnon, J. H. (1986). Sexual scripts: Permanence and change. *Archives of Sexual Behavior, 15*(2), 97–120.

Simons, D. J., & Levin, D. T. (1998). Failure to detect changes to people during a real-world interaction. *Psychonomic Bulletin & Review, 5,* 644–649.

Simons, D. J., Chabris, C. F., Schnur, T., & Levin, D. T. (2002). Evidence for preserved representations in change blindness. *Consciousness and Cognition, 11,* 78–97.

Simonton, D. K. (1975). Age and literary creativity: A cross-cultural and transhistorical survey. *Journal of Cross-Cultural Psychology, 6*(3), 259–277.

Simonton, D. K. (1988). Creativity, leadership, and chance. In R. J. Sternberg (Ed.), *The nature of creativity* (pp. 386–426). New York: Cambridge University Press.

Simonton, D. K. (1995). Foresight in insight: A Darwinian answer. In R. J. Sternberg & J. E. Davidson (Eds.), *The nature of insight* (pp. 495–534). Cambridge, MA: MIT Press.

Simonton, D. K. (1998). Donald Campbell's model of the creative process: Creativity as blind variation and selective retention. *Journal of Creative Behavior, 32,* 153–158.

Simonton, D. K. (1999). Creativity from a historiometric perspective. In R. J. Sternberg (Ed.), *Handbook of creativity* (pp. 116–133). New York: Cambridge University Press.

Simonton, D. K. (1999). Creativity from a historiometric perspective. In R. J. Sternberg (Ed.), *Handbook of creativity* (pp. 116–133). New York: Cambridge University Press.

Simpson, J. A., Rholes, W. S., & Nelligan. J. S. (1992). Support-seeking and support-giving within couple members in an anxiety-provoking situation: The role of attachment styles. *Journal of Personality and Social Psychology, 62,* 434–446.

Simpson, S. G., & Jamison, K. R. (1999). The risk of suicide in patients with bipolar disorders. *Journal of Clinical Psychiatry, 60* (Suppl. 2), 53–56.

Sincoff, J. B., & Sternberg, R. J. (1988). The development of verbal fluency abilities and strategies in elementary-school-aged children. *Developmental Psychology, 24,* 646–653.

Singer, D. G., & Singer, J. L. (2001). *Make-believe: Games and activities for imaginative play: A book for parents, teachers, and the young children in their lives.* Washington, DC: Magination Press/American Psychological Association.

Singer, J. A., Singer, J. L., & Zittel, C. (2000). Personality variations in autobiographical memories, self-representations, and daydreaming. In R. G. Kunzendorf & B. Wallace (Eds.), *Individual differences in conscious experience. Advances in consciousness research* (Vol. 20, pp. 351–373). Amsterdam: John Benjamins.

Singer, J. L. (1998). Daydreams, the stream of consciousness, and self-representations. In R. F. Bornstein & J. M. Masling (Eds.), *Empirical perspectives on the psychoanalytic unconscious: Empirical studies of psychoanalytic theories* (Vol. 7, pp. 141–186). Washington, DC: American Psychological Association.

Singh, R. (1998). Causal analyses in interpersonal relations: On importance of the control condition. *Asian Journal of Social Psychology, 1,* 33–50.

Sizemore, C. C., & Pittillo, E. S. (1977). *I'm Eve.* Garden City, NY: Doubleday.

Skinner, B. F. (1948). *Walden II.* New York: Macmillan.

Skinner, B. F. (1953). *Science and human behavior.* New York: Macmillan.

Skinner, B. F. (1974). *About behaviorism.* New York: Knopf.

Skoric, M., & Furnham, A. (2002). Gender role stereotyping in television advertisements: A comparative study of British and Serbian television. In S. P. Shohov (Ed.), *Advances in psychology research* (Vol. 10, pp. 123–142). Huntington, NY: Nova Science Publishers.

Slobin, D. I. (1971). Cognitive prerequisites for the acquisition of grammar. In C. A. Ferguson & D. I. Slobin (Eds.), *Studies of child language development.* New York: Holt, Rinehart & Winston.

Slobin, D. I. (Ed.). (1985). *The cross-linguistic study of language acquisition.* Hillsdale, NJ: Erlbaum.

Sloboda, J. A., Davidson, J. W., Howe, M. J. A., & Moore, D. G. (1996). The role of practice in the development of performing musicians. *British Journal of Psychology, 87,* 287–309.

Sloman, S. A. (1996). The empirical case for two systems of reasoning. *Psychological Bulletin, 199,* 3–22.

Sloman, S. A. (1999). Rational versus arational models of thought. In R. J. Sternberg (Ed.), *The nature of cognition* (pp. 557–585). Cambridge, MA: MIT Press.

Smetana, J. G. (1995). Morality in context: Abstractions, ambiguities, and applications. In R. Vasta (Ed.), *Annals of child development* (Vol. 10, pp. 83–130). London: Jessica Kingsley.

Smetana, J. G. (1997). Parenting and the development of social knowledge reconceptualized: A social domain analysis. In J. E. Grusec & L. Kuczynski (Eds.), *Parenting and children's internalization of values* (pp. 162–192). New York: Wiley.

Smetana, J. G., & Asquith, P. (1994). Adolescents' and parents' conceptions of parental authority and adolescent autonomy. *Child Development, 65,* 1147–1162.

Smith, B. N., Kerr, N. A., Markus, M. J., & Stasson, M. F. (2001). Individual differences in social loafing: Need for cognition as a motivator in collective performance. *Group Dynamics: Theory, Research, & Practice, 5,* 150–158.

Smith, D. (1982). Trends in counseling and psychotherapy. *American Psychologist, 37*(7), 802–809.

Smith, D. E., & Muenchen, R. A. (1995). Gender and age variations in the self-image of Jamaican adolescents. *Adolescence, 30*(119), 643–654.

Smith, E. E. (1995). Concepts and categorization. In E. E. Smith & Daniel N. Osherson (Eds.), *Thinking: An invitation to cognitive science* (Vol. 3, 2nd ed., pp. 3–33). Cambridge, MA: MIT Press.

Smith, E. E., & Jonides, J. (1995). Working memory in humans: Neuropsychological evidence. In M. Gazzaniga (Ed.), *The cognitive neurosciences* (pp. 1009–1020). Cambridge, MA: MIT Press.

Smith, E. E., & Medin, D. L. (1981). *Categories and concepts.* Cambridge, MA: Harvard University Press.

Smith, E. E., Osherson, D., Rips L., & Keane, M. (1988). Combining prototypes: A selective modification model. *Cognitive Science, 12,* 485–527. [Reprinted in E. Margolis & S. Laurence (Eds.), *Concepts: Core readings,* Cambridge, MA: MIT Press, 1999.]

Smith, E. E., Patalano, A. L., & Jonides, J. (1998). Alternative strategies of categorization. *Cognition, 65,* 167–196.

Smith, J. C. (1993). *Understanding stress and coping.* New York: Macmillan.

Smith, J. D. (1988). *Psychological profiles of conjoined twins: Heredity, environment, and identity.* New York: Praeger

Smith, L. (2002). Piaget's model. In U. Goswami (Ed.), *Blackwell handbook of childhood cognitive development* (pp. 515–537). Malden, MA: Blackwell.

Smith, M. E., McEvoy, L. K., & Gevins, A. (1999). Neurophysiological indices of strategy development and skill acquisition. *Cognitive Brain Research, 7,* 389–404.

Smith, M. L., & Glass, G. V. (1977, November). Meta-analysis of psychotherapy outcome studies. *American Psychologist,* pp. 752–760.

Smith, N. K., Cacioppo, J. T., Larsen, J. T., & Chartrand, T. L. (2003). May I have your attention, please: Electrocortical responses to positive and negative stimuli. *Neuropsychologia, 41,* 171–183.

Smith, P. B., & Bond, M. H. (1994). *Social psychology across cultures: Analysis and perspectives.* Boston: Allyn & Bacon.

Smith, R. A. (2000). Documenting your scholarship: Citations and references. In R. J. Sternberg (Ed.), *Guide to publishing in psychology journals* (pp. 146–157). New York: Cambridge University Press.

Smith, T. W. (1992). Hostility and health: Current status of a psychosomatic hypothesis. *Health Psychology, 11,* 139–150.

Smith, T. W., & Anderson, N. B. (1986). Models of personality and disease: An interactional approach to Type A behavior and cardiovascular risk. *Journal of Personality and Social Psychology, 50*(6), 1166–1173.

Smolensky, P. (1999). Grammar-based connectionist approaches to language. *Cognitive Science, 23*(4), 589–613.

Snarey, J. R. (1985). Cross-cultural universality of social-moral development: A critical review of Kohlbergian research. *Psychological Bulletin, 97,* 202–232.

Snarey, J. R., Reimer, J., & Kohlberg, L. (1985a). Development of social-moral reasoning among kibbutz adolescents: A longitudinal cross-cultural study. *Developmental Psychology, 21,* 3–17.

Snarey, J. R., Reimer, J., & Kohlberg, L. (1985b). The kibbutz as a model for moral education: A longitudinal cross-cultural study. *Journal of Applied Developmental Psychology, 6,* 151–172.

Sneed, C. D., McCrae, R. R., & Funder, D. C. (1998). Lay conceptions of the Five-Factor Model and its indicators. *Personality and Social Psychology Bulletin, 24,* 115–126.

Snow, C. (1999). Social perspectives on the emergence of language. In B. MacWhinney (Ed.), *The emergence of language* (pp. 257–276). Mahwah, NJ: Erlbaum.

Snow, C. E. (1977). The development of conversation between mothers and babies. *Journal of Child Language, 4,* 1–22.

Snow, R. E. (1980). Aptitude processes. In R. E. Snow, P.-A. Federico, & W. E. Montague (Eds.), *Aptitude, learning, and instruction: Cognitive process analyses* (Vol. 1). Hillsdale, NJ: Erlbaum.

Snow, R. E. (1995). Pygmalion and intelligence? *Current Directions in Psychological Science, 4,* 169–171.

Snyder, C. R., & Lopez, S. J. (Eds.). (2002). *Handbook of positive psychology.* London: Oxford University Press.

Snyder, M. (1979). Self-monitoring processes. In L. Berkowitz (Ed.), *Advances in experimental social psychology* (Vol. 12). New York: Academic Press.

Snyder, M. (1983). The influence of individuals on situations: Implications for understanding the links between personality and social behavior. *Journal of Personality, 51,* 497–516.

Sohn, M.-H., & Anderson, J. R. (2001). Task preparation and task repetition: Two-component model of task switching. *Journal of Experimental Psychology: General, 130,* 764–778.

Solomon, G. F., & Temoshok, L. (1987). A psychoneuroimmunologic perspective on AIDS research: Questions, preliminary findings, and suggestions. *Journal of Applied Social Psychology, 17,* 286–308.

Solomon, R. L. (1980). The opponent-process theory of motivation: The costs of pleasure and the benefits of pain. *American Psychologist, 35,* 681–712.

Solomon, R. L., & Corbit, J. D. (1974). An opponent-process theory of motivation: I. Temporal dynamics of affect. *Psychological Review, 81,* 119–145.

Sookman, D., Pinard, G., & Beck, A. T. (2001). Vulnerability schemas in obsessive-compulsive disorder. *Journal of Cognitive Psychotherapy, 15,* 109–130.

Spangler, W. (1992). Validity of questionnaire and TAT measures of need for achievement: Two meta-analyses. *Psychological Bulletin, 112,* 140–154.

Spanos, N. P, DuBreuil, S. C., & Gabora, N. J. (1991). Four-month follow-up of skill training induced enhancements in hypnotizability. *Contemporary Hypnosis, 8,* 25–32.

Spanos, N. P. (1986). Hypnotic behavior: A social-psychological interpretation of amnesia, analgesia, and "trance logic." *Behavioral and Brain Sciences, 9,* 449–467.

Spanos, N. P. (1994). Multiple identity enactments and multiple personality disorder: A socio-cognitive perspective. *Psychological Bulletin, 116,* 143–165.

Spanos, N. P., & Coe, W. C. (1992). A social-psychological approach to hypnosis. In E. Fromm & M. R. Nash (Eds.), *Contemporary hypnosis research.* New York: Guilford.

Spanos, N. P., Burgess, C. A., Roncon, V., Wallace-Capretta, S., & Cross, P. (1993). Surreptitiously observed hypnotic responding in simulators and in skill-trained and untrained high hypnotizables. *Journal of Personality and Social Psychology, 65,* 391–398.

Spanos, N. P., Burgess, C. A., Wallace-Capretta, S., & Ouaida, N. (1996). Simulation, surreptitious observation and the modification of hypnotizability: Two tests of the compliance hypothesis. *Contemporary Hypnosis, 13,* 161–176.

Spearman, C. (1927). *The abilities of man.* New York: Macmillan.

Spear-Swerling, L., & Sternberg, R. J. (1996). *Off-track: When poor readers become learning disabled.* Boulder, CO: Westview.

Speer, D. C. (1972). Inventory commitment: Some considerations for crisis intervention outreach workers. *Crisis Intervention, 4*(4), 112–116.

Spelke, E. (1976). Infant's intermodal perception of events. *Cognitive Psychology, 8,* 553–560.

Spellman, B. A. (1997). Crediting causality. *Journal of Experimental Psychology: General, 126,* 1–26.

Spence, J. T., & Helmreich, R. L. (1983). Achievement-related motives and behavior. In J. T. Spence (Ed.), *Achievement and achievement motives: Psychological and sociological approaches.* New York: Freeman.

Sperling, G. (1960). The information available in brief visual presentations. *Psychological Monographs: General and Applied, 74,* 1–28.

Sperry, R. W. (1964a). The great cerebral commissure. *Scientific American, 210*(1), 42–52.

Sperry, R. W. (1964b). *Problems outstanding in the evolution of brain function.* New York: American Museum of Natural History.

Spielberger, C. D., Gorsuch, R. L., & Lushene, R. E. (1983). *Manual for the State-Trait Anxiety Inventory (STAI).* Palo Alto, CA: Consulting Psychologists Press.

Spitzer, L., & Rodin, J. (1981). Human eating behavior: A critical review of studies in normal weight and overweight individuals. *Appetite, 2,* 293–329.

Spitzer, R. L., Skodol, A. E., Gibbon, M., & Williams, J.B.W. (1983). *Psychopathology: A case book.* New York: McGraw-Hill.

Sporakowski, M. J. (1988). A therapist's views on the consequences of change for the contemporary family. *Family Relations, 37,* 373–378.

Springer, S. P., & Deutsch, G. (1985). *Left brain, right brain.* New York: Freeman.

Squire, L. (1999). Memory, human neuropsychology. In R. A. Wilson & F. C. Keil (Eds.), *The MIT encyclopedia of the cognitive sciences* (pp. 521–522). Cambridge, MA: MIT Press.

Squire, L. R. (1987). *Memory and the brain.* New York: Oxford University Press.

Squire, L. R. (1992). Memory and the hippocampus: A synthesis of findings with rats, monkeys, and humans. *Psychological Review, 99,* 195–231.

Squire, L. R., & Knowlton, B. J. (2000). The medial temporal lobe, the hippocampus, and the memory systems of the brain. In M. Gazzaniga (Ed.), *The new cognitive neurosciences* (2nd ed., pp. 765–780). Cambridge, MA: MIT Press.

Squire, L. R., Cohen, N. J., & Nadel, L. (1984). The medial temporal region and memory consolidations: A new hypothesis. In H. Weingardner & E. Parker (Eds.), *Memory consolidation.* Hillsdale, NJ: Erlbaum.

Squire, L. R., Knowlton, B. J., & Musen, G. (1993). The structure and organization of memory. *Annual Review of Psychology, 44,* 453–495.

Squire, L. R., Ojeman, J. G., Miezin, F. M., Petersen, S. E., Videen, T. O., & Raichle, M. E., (1992). Activation of the hippocampus in normal humans: A functional neuroanatomical study of memory. *Proceedings of the National Academy of Sciences, USA, 89,* 1837–1841.

Sroufe, L. A. (1979). Socioemotional development. In J. D. Osofsky (Ed.), *Handbook of infant development.* New York: Wiley.

Sroufe, L. A. (1996). *Emotional development: The organization of emotional life in the early years.* New York: Cambridge University Press.

Srull, T. K., & Wyer, R. S. Jr. (1989). Person memory and judgment. *Psychological Review, 96*(1), 58–83.

Staats, A. W., & Staats, C. K. (1958). Attitudes established by classical conditioning. *Journal of Abnormal and Social Psychology, 57,* 37–40.

Stacy, A. W., Widaman, K. F., & Marlatt, G. A. (1990). Expectancy models of alcohol use. *Journal of Personality and Social Psychology, 58,* 918–928.

Standing, L., Conezio, J., & Haber, R. N. (1970). Perception and memory for pictures: Single-trial learning of 2500 visual stimuli. *Psychonomic Science, 19,* 73–74.

Stankov, L. (2002). *g:* A diminutive general. In R. J. Sternberg & E. L. Grigorenko (Eds.), *The general factor of intelligence: How general is it?* (pp. 19–38). Mahwah, NJ: Erlbaum.

Stanovich, K. E. (1994). Reconceptualizing intelligence: Dysrationalia as an intuition pump. *Educational Researcher, 23*(4), 11–22.

Stanovich, K. E. (1996). *How to think straight about psychology* (4th ed.). New York: HarperCollins.

Stanovich, K. E. (2002). Rationality, intelligence, and levels of analysis in cognitive science: Is dysrationalia possible? In R. J. Sternberg (Ed.), *Why smart people can be so stupid* (pp. 124–158). New Haven: Yale University Press.

Stanovich, K. E., & West, R. F. (2000). Individual differences in reasoning: Implications for the rationality debate? *Behavioral and Brain Sciences, 23,* 645–726.

Starr, R. H., Dietrich, K. N., Fischoff, J., Ceresnie, S., & Zweier, D. (1984). The contribution of handicapping conditions to child abuse. *Topics in Early Childhood Special Education, 4*(1), 59–69.

Stastny, J., Konstantinidis, A., Schwarz, M. J., Rosenthal, N. E., Vitouch, O., Kasper, S., & Neumeister, A. (2003). Effects of tryptophan depletion and catecholamine depletion on immune parameters in patients with seasonal affective disorder in remission with light therapy. *Biological Psychiatry, 53,* 332–337.

Stattin, H., & Magnusson, E. (1990). *Pubertal maturation in female development.* Hillsdale, NJ: Erlbaum.

Staub, E. (1989). *The roots of evil: The origins of genocide and other group violence.* New York: Cambridge University Press.

Staub, E. (1995). Torture: Psychological and cultural origins. In R. D. Crelinsten, A. P. Schmid, et al. (Eds.), *The politics of pain: Torturers and their masters. Series on state violence, state terrorism, and human rights* (pp. 99–111). Boulder, CO: Westview.

Staub, E. (1996a). Cultural-societal roots of violence: The examples of genocidal violence and of contemporary youth violence in the United States. *American Psychologist, 51,* 117–132.

Staub, E. (1996b). Responsibility, helping, aggression, and evil. *Psychological Inquiry, 7,* 252–254.

Staub, E. (1999b). The origins and prevention of genocide, mass killing, and other collective violence. *Peace and Conflict: Journal of Peace Psychology, 5,* 303–336.

Staub, E. (1999c). The roots of evil: Social conditions, culture, personality, and basic human needs. *Personality & Social Psychology Review, 3,* 179–192.

Staub, E. (2000). Genocide and mass killing: Origins, prevention, healing, and reconciliation. *Political Psychology, 21,* 367–382.

Staub, E. (2003). *A brighter future: Raising caring and nonviolent children.* Manuscript in preparation.

Staub, E. (2003). Notes on cultures of violence, cultures of caring and peace, and the fulfillment of basic human needs. *Political Psychology, 24,* 1–21.

Staw, B. M., & Epstein, L. D. (2000). What bandwagons bring: Effects of popular management techniques on corporate performance, reputation, and CEO pay. *Administrative Science Quarterly, 45,* 523–556.

Stebbins, G. T., Carrillo, M. C., Dorfman, J., Dirksen, C., Desmond, J. E., Turner, D. A., et al. (2002). Aging effects on memory encoding in the frontal lobes. *Psychology & Aging, 17,* 44–55.

Stedman's medical dictionary (25th ed.). (1990). Philadelphia: Lippincott Williams & Wilkins.

Stedman's medical dictionary (27th ed.). (2000). Philadelphia: Lippincott Williams & Wilkins.

Steele, C. M. (1997). A threat in the air: How stereotypes shape intellectual identity and performance. *American Psychologist, 52,* 613–629.

Steele, C. M., & Aronson, J. (1995). Stereotype threat and the intellectual test performance of African-Americans. *Journal of Personality and Social Psychology, 69*(5), 797–811.

Steele, C. M., & Aronson, J. (1995). Stereotype threats and the intellectual test performance of African Americans. *Journal of Personality and Social Psychology, 69,* 797–811.

Steele, R. L. (1992). Dying, death, and bereavement among the Maya Indians of Mesoamerica: A study in anthropological psychology. In L. A. Platt & V. R. Persico, Jr. (Eds.), *Grief in cross-cultural perspective: A casebook* (pp. 399–424). New York: Garland.

Steenland, K., & Deddens, J. A. (1997). Effects of travel and rest on performance of professional basketball players. *Sleep, 20,* 366–369.

Steffanaci, L. (1999). Amygdala, primate. In R. A. Wilson & F. C. Keil (Eds.), *The MIT encyclopedia of the cognitive sciences* (pp. 15–17). Cambridge, MA: MIT Press.

Stein, M. B., & Uhde, T. W. (1995). Biology of anxiety disorders. In A. F. Schatzberg & C. B. Nemeroff (Eds.), *The American Psychiatric Press textbook of psychopharmacology.* Washington, DC: American Psychiatric Press.

Steiner, M., Eriksson, E., & Yonkers, K. A. (Eds.). (2000). *Mood disorders in women.* Boston: Blackwell.

Stemberger, R. T., Turner, S. M., Beidel, D. C., & Calhoun, K. S. (1995). Social phobia: An analysis of possible developmental factors. *Journal of Abnormal Psychology, 104,* 526–531.

Steriade, M., Jones, E. G., & McCormick, D. A. (1997). *Thalamus, organization and function* (Vol. 1). New York: Elsevier.

Stern, R. M., Ray, W. J., & Quigley, K. (2000). *Psychophysiological recording, 2nd edition.* New York: Oxford University Press.

Stern, W. (1912). *Psychologische Methoden der Intelligenz-Prüfung.* Leipzig, Germany: Barth.

Sternbach, R. A. (1963). Congenital insensitivity to pain: A review. *Psychological Bulletin, 60,* 252–264.

Sternberg, R. J. (1977). *Intelligence, information processing, and analogical reasoning: The componential analysis of human abilities.* Hillsdale, NJ: Erlbaum.

Sternberg, R. J. (1981a). Intelligence and nonentrenchment. *Journal of Educational Psychology, 73,* 1–16.

Sternberg, R. J. (1981b). Novelty-seeking, novelty-finding, and the developmental continuity of intelligence. *Intelligence, 5,* 149–155.

Sternberg, R. J. (Ed.). (1982). *Handbook of human intelligence.* New York: Cambridge University Press.

Sternberg, R. J. (Ed.). (1984). *Human abilities: An information-processing approach.* San Francisco, CA: Freeman.

Sternberg, R. J. (1985a). *Beyond IQ: A triarchic theory of human intelligence.* New York: Cambridge University Press.

Sternberg, R. J. (1985b). Implicit theories of intelligence, creativity, and wisdom. *Journal of Personality and Social Psychology, 49,* 607–627.

Sternberg, R. J. (1986a). *Intelligence applied: Understanding and increasing your intellectual skills.* San Diego, CA: Harcourt Brace Jovanovich.

Sternberg, R. J. (1986b). A triangular theory of love. *Psychological Review, 93,* 119–135.

Sternberg, R. J. (Ed.). (1988a). *The nature of creativity.* New York: Cambridge University Press.

Sternberg, R. J. (1988b). A three-facet model of creativity. In R. J. Sternberg (Ed.), *The nature of creativity* (pp. 125–147). New York: Cambridge University Press.

Sternberg, R. J. (1988c). Triangulating love. In R. J. Sternberg & M. L. Barnes (Eds.), *The psychology of love* (pp. 119–138). New Haven, CT: Yale University Press.

Sternberg, R. J. (1990a). *Metaphors of mind.* New York: Cambridge University Press.

Sternberg, R. J. (Ed.). (1990b). *Wisdom: Its nature, origins, and development.* New York: Cambridge University Press.

Sternberg, R. J. (1995a). Love as a story. *Journal of Social and Personal Relationships, 12*(4), 541–546.

Sternberg, R. J. (1995b). Theory and measurement of tacit knowledge as a part of practical intelligence. *Zeitschrift fur Psychologie, 203,* 319–334.

Sternberg, R. J. (1995c). What it means to be intelligent: The triarchic theory of human intelligence. In W. Tomic (Ed.), *Textbook for undergraduate intelligence course.* The Netherlands: The Open University.

Sternberg, R. J. (1996a). Love stories. *Personal Relationships, 3,* 1359–1379.

Sternberg, R. J. (1996b). *Successful intelligence*. New York: Simon & Schuster.

Sternberg, R. J. (Ed.). (1997a). *Career paths in psychology*. Washington, DC: APA Books.

Sternberg, R. J. (1997b). What does it mean to be smart? *Educational Leadership, 54*, 20–24.

Sternberg, R. J. (1998a). A balance theory of wisdom. *Review of General Psychology, 2*, 347–365.

Sternberg, R. J. (1998b). *Cupid's arrow*. New York: Cambridge University Press.

Sternberg, R. J. (1998c). *Love is a story*. New York: Oxford University Press.

Sternberg, R. J. (1999a). A dialectical basis for understanding the study of cognition. In R. J. Sternberg (Ed.), *The nature of cognition* (pp. 51–78). Cambridge, MA: MIT Press.

Sternberg, R. J. (1999b). A propulsion model of types of creative contributions. *Review of General Psychology, 3*, 83–100.

Sternberg, R. J. (1999c). Successful intelligence: Finding a balance. *Trends in Cognitive Sciences, 3*, 436–442.

Sternberg, R. J. (1999d). The theory of successful intelligence. *Review of General Intelligence, 3*, 292–316.

Sternberg, R. J. (2000a). The concept of intelligence. In R. J. Sternberg (Ed.), *Handbook of intelligence*. New York: Cambridge University Press.

Sternberg, R. J. (Ed.). (2000b). *Guide to publishing in psychology journals*. New York: Cambridge University Press.

Sternberg, R. J. (2000c). Thinking: An overview. In A. Kazdin (Ed.), *Encyclopedia of psychology* (Vol. 8, pp. 68–71). Washington, DC: American Psychological Association.

Sternberg, R. J. (2002a). Beyond g: The theory of successful intelligence. In R. J. Sternberg & E. L. Grigorenko (Eds.), *The general factor of intelligence: How general is it?* (pp. 447–479). Mahwah, NJ: Erlbaum.

Sternberg, R. J. (2002b). Smart people are not stupid, but they sure can be foolish: The imbalance theory of foolishness. In R. J. Sternberg (Ed.), *Why smart people can be so stupid* (pp. 232–242). New Haven, CT: Yale University Press.

Sternberg, R. J. (Ed.). (2003a). *The anatomy of impact: What has made the great works of psychology great?* Washington, DC: American Psychological Association.

Sternberg, R. J. (Ed.). (2003b). *Psychologists defying the crowd: Stories of those who battled the establishment and won*. Washington, DC: American Psychological Association.

Sternberg, R. J. (in press-a). *The psychologist's companion* (4th ed.). New York: Cambridge University Press.

Sternberg, R. J. (in press-b). Understanding hate. *Psychology Today*.

Sternberg, R. J. (in press-c). A duplex theory of hate and its development and its application to terrorism, massacres, and genocide. *Review of General Psychology*.

Sternberg, R. J., & Barnes, M. L. (1985). Real and ideal others in romantic relationships: Is four a crowd? *Journal of Personality and Social Psychology, 49*, 1586–1608.

Sternberg, R. J., & Ben-Zeev, T. (2001). *Complex cognition*. New York: Oxford University Press.

Sternberg, R. J., & Clinkenbeard, P. R. (1995). A triarchic view of identifying, teaching, and assessing gifted children. *Roeper Review, 17*(4), 255–260.

Sternberg, R. J., & Davidson, J. E. (Eds.). (1986). *Conceptions of giftedness*. New York: Cambridge University Press.

Sternberg, R. J., & Detterman, D. K. (Eds.). (1986). *What is intelligence? Contemporary viewpoints on its nature and definition*. Norwood, NJ: Ablex.

Sternberg, R. J., & Frensch, P. A. (Eds.). (1991). *Complex problem solving: Principles and mechanisms*. Hillsdale, NJ: Erlbaum.

Sternberg, R. J., & Grigorenko, E. L. (1999). Myths in psychology and education regarding the gene environment debate. *Teachers College Record, 100*, 536–553.

Sternberg, R. J., & Grigorenko, E. L. (1999). *Our labeled children: What every parent and teacher needs to know about learning disabilities*. Reading, MA: Perseus.

Sternberg, R. J., & Grigorenko, E. L. (Eds.). (1997). *Intelligence, heredity, and environment*. New York: Cambridge University Press.

Sternberg, R. J., & Grigorenko, E. L. (Eds.). (2002). *The general factor of intelligence: How general is it?* Mahwah, NJ: Erlbaum.

Sternberg, R. J., & Grigorenko, E. L. (in press). *Intelligence applied* (2nd ed.). New York: Oxford University Press.

Sternberg, R. J., & Kaufman, J. C. (1998). Human abilities. *Annual Review of Psychology, 49*, 479–502.

Sternberg, R. J., & Kaufman, J. C. (Eds.). (2002). *The evolution of intelligence*. Mahwah, NJ: Erlbaum.

Sternberg, R. J., & Lubart, T. I. (1995). *Defying the crowd: Cultivating creativity in a culture of conformity*. New York: Free Press.

Sternberg, R. J., & Lubart, T. I. (1996). Investing in creativity. *American Psychologist, 51*(7), 677–688.

Sternberg, R. J., & Lubart, T. I. (1999). The concept of creativity: Prospects and paradigms. In R. J. Sternberg (Ed.), *Handbook of creativity* (pp. 3–15). New York: Cambridge University Press.

Sternberg, R. J., & Okagaki, L. (1989). Continuity and discontinuity in intellectual development are not a matter of "either–or." *Human Development, 32*, 158–166.

Sternberg, R. J., & Powell, J. S. (1983). Comprehending verbal comprehension. *American Psychologist, 38*, 878–893.

Sternberg, R. J., & Spear-Swerling, L. (Eds.). (1999). *Perspectives on learning disabilities: Biological, cognitive, contextual*. Boulder, CO: Westview.

Sternberg, R. J., & Williams, W. (1997). Does the Graduate Record Examination predict meaningful success in the graduate training of psychologists? A case study. *American Psychologist, 52*, 630–641.

Sternberg, R. J., Castejón, J. L., Prieto, M. D., Hautamäki, J., & Grigorenko, E. L. (2001). Confirmatory factor analysis of the Sternberg triarchic abilities test in three international samples: An empirical test of the triarchic theory of intelligence. *European Journal of Psychological Assessment, 17*, 1–16.

Sternberg, R. J., Ferrari, M., Clinkenbeard, P. R., & Grigorenko, E. L. (1996). Identification, instruction, and assessment of gifted children: A construct validation of a triarchic model. *Gifted Child Quarterly, 40*(3), 129–137.

Sternberg, R. J., Forsythe, G. B., Hedlund, J., Horvath, J., Snook, S., Williiams, W. M., Wagner, R. K., & Grigorenko, E. L. (2000). *Practical intelligence in everyday life*. New York: Cambridge University Press.

Sternberg, R. J., Grigorenko, E. L., & Oh, S. (2001). The development of intelligence at midlife. In M. E. Lachman (Ed.), *Handbook of midlife development* (pp. 217–247). New York: Wiley.

Sternberg, R. J., Grigorenko, E. L., Ferrari, M., & Clinkenbeard, P. (1999). A triarchic analysis of an aptitude-treatment interaction. *European Journal of Psychological Assessment, 15*, 1–11.

Sternberg, R. J., Kaufman, J. C., & Pretz, J. E. (2001). The propulsion model of creative contributions applied to the arts and letters. *Journal of Creative Behavior, 35*(2), 75–101.

Sternberg, R. J., Kaufman, J. C., & Pretz, J. E. (2002). *The creativity conundrum: A propulsion model of kinds of creative contributions*. New York: Psychology Press.

Sternberg, R. J., Nokes, K., Geissler, P. W., Price, R., Okatcha, F., Bundy, D. A., & Grigorenko, E. L. (2002). The relationship between academic and practical intelligence: A case study in Kenya. *Intelligence, 29*, 1–18.

Sternberg, R. J., Torff, B., & Grigorenko, E. L. (1998). Teaching triarchically improves school achievement. *Journal of Educational Psychology, 90*, 374–384.

Sternberg, S. (1966). High-speed memory scanning in human memory. *Science, 153*, 652–654.

Stevenage, S. V., & McKay, Y. (1999). Model applicants: The effect of facial appearance on recruitment decisions. *British Journal of Psychology, 90*, 221–234.

Stevens, A., & Coupe, P. (1978). Distortions in judged spatial relations. *Cognitive Psychology, 10*, 422–437.

Stewart, A. J. (1982). The course of individual adaptation to life changes. *Journal of Personality and Social Psychology, 42*, 1100–1113.

Stewart, A. J., & Healy, J. M. (1989). Linking individual development and social changes. *American Psychologist, 44*(1), 30–42.

Stewart, A. J., & Healy, J. M. Jr. (1985). Personality and adaptation to change. In R. Hogan & W. H. Jones (Eds.), *Perspectives in personality* (Vol. 1, pp. 117–144). Greenwich, CT: JAI Press.

Stewart, A. J., Sokol, M., Healy, J. M., & Chester, N. L. (1986). Longitudinal studies of psychological consequences of life changes in children and adults. *Journal of Personality and Social Psychology, 50*, 143–151.

Stewart, S. M., Bond, M. H., Ho, L. M., Zaman, R. M., Dar, R., & Anwar, M. (2000). Perceptions of parents and adolescent outcomes in Pakistan. *British Journal of Developmental Psychology, 18*, 335–352.

Stewart, S. M., Bond, M. H., Kennard, B. D., Ho, L. M, & Zaman, R. M. (2002). Does the Chinese construct of guan export to the West? *International Journal of Psychology, 37*, 74–82.

Stiles, J., Bates, E. A., Thal, D., Trauner, D., & Reilly, J. (1998). Linguistic, cognitive, and affective development in children with pre- and perinatal focal brain injury: A ten-year overview from the San Diego longitudinal proejct. In C. Rovee-Collier, L. Lipsitt, & H. Hayne (Eds.), *Advances in infancy research* (Vol. 12, pp. 131–164). Stamford, CT: Ablex.

Stiles, W. B., Shapiro, D. A., & Elliott, R. (1986). Are all psychotherapies equivalent? *American Psychologist, 41*(2), 165–180.

Stiles, W. B., Walz, N. C., Schroeder, M.A.B., Williams, L. L., & Ickes, W. (1996). Attractiveness and disclosure in initial encounters of mixed-sex dyads. *Journal of Social and Personal Relationships, 13*, 303–312.

Stipek, D. J. (1984). Young children's performance expectations: Logical analysis or wishful thinking? In J. G. Nicholls (Ed.), *Advances in motivation and achievement:* Vol 3. *The development of achievement motivation* (pp. 33–56). Greenwich, CT: JAI Press.

Stoffregan, T. A., & Smart, J. Jr. Postural instability precedes motion sickness. *Brain Research Bulletin, 1998, 47*, 437–448.

Stone, A. A., Neale, J. M., Cox, D. S., Napoli, A., Valdimarsdottir, H., & Kennedy-Moore, E. (1994). Daily events are associated with a secretory immune response to an oral antigen in men. *Health Psychology, 13*, 400–446.

Stone, G. C. (1979). Health and the health system: A historical overview and conceptual framework. In G. C. Stone, F. Cohen, & N. E. Adler (Eds.), *Health psychology–A handbook* (pp. 1–17). San Francisco: Jossey-Bass.

Stone, J., Lynch, C. I., Sjomeling, M., & Darley, J. M. (1999). Stereotype threat effects on Black and White athletic performance. *Journal of Personality and Social Psychology, 77*, 1213–1227.

Stoohs, R. A., Guilleminault, C., Itoi, A., & Dement, W. C. (1994). Traffic accidents in commercial long-haul truck drivers: The influence of sleep-disordered breathing and obesity. *Sleep, 17*, 619–623.

Stowell, J. R., Kiecolt-Glaser, J. K., & Glaser, R. (2001). Perceived stress and cellular immunity: When coping counts. *Journal of Behavioral Medicine, 24*, 323–339.

Strauss, B. (2002a). The impact of supportive sports spectators on performance in team sports. *International Journal of Sport Psychology, 33*, 372–390.

Strauss, B. (2002b). Social facilitation in motor tasks. *Psychology of Sport and Exercise, 3*, 237–256.

Strauss, J. S., Kokes, F. R., Ritzler, B. A., Harder, D. W., & Van Ord, A. (1978). Patterns of disorder in first admission psychiatric patients. *Journal of Nervous and Mental Disease, 166*, 611–623.

Street, M. D. (1997). Groupthink: An examination of theoretical issues, implications, and future research suggestions. *Small Group Research, 28*, 72–93.

Streissguth, A. P., Martin, D. C., Barr, H. M., Sandman, B. M., Kirchner, G. L., & Darby, B. L. (1984). Intrauterine alcohol and nicotine exposure. Attention and reaction time in 4-year-old children. *Developmental Psychology, 20*, 533–541.

Streissguth, A. P., Sampson, P. D., & Barr, H. M. (1989). Neurobehavioral dose-response effects of prenatal alcohol exposure in humans from infancy to adulthood. Conference of the Behavioral Teratology Society, the National Institute on Drug Abuse, and the New York Academy of Sciences: Prenatal abuse of licit and illicit drugs (1988, Bethesda, Maryland). *Annals of the New York Academy of Sciences, 562*, 145–158.

Stricker, E. M. (2000). Motivation: Physiological aspects. In A. E. Kazdin (Ed.), *Encyclopedia of psychology* (Vol. 5, pp. 317–320). Washington, DC: American Psychological Association.

Strickland, B. (1992). Women and depression. *Current Directions in Psychological Science, 1*, 132–135.

Striegel-Moore, R. H., Silberstein, L. R., & Rodin, J. (1993). The social self in bulimia nervosa: Public self-consciousness, social anxiety, and perceived fraudulence. *Journal of Abnormal Psychology, 102*, 297–303.

Stromswold, K. (1998). The genetics of spoken language disorders. *Human Biology, 70*, 297–324.

Stromswold, K. (2000). The cognitive neuroscience of language acquisition. In M. Gazzaniga (Ed.), *The new cognitive neurosciences* (2nd ed., pp. 909–932). Cambridge, MA: MIT Press.

Stroop, J. (1935). Studies of interference in serial verbal reactions. *Journal of Experimental Psychology, 18*, 624–643.

Strupp, H. H. (1981). Toward a refinement of time-limited dynamic psychotherapy. In S. H. Budman (Ed.), *Forms of brief therapy.* New York: Guilford.

Strupp, H. H. (1996). The tripartite model and the *Consumer Reports* study. *American Psychologist, 51*, 1017–1024.

Suematsu, H., Ishikawa, H., Kuboki, T., & Ito, T. (1985). Statistical studies on anorexia nervosa in Japan: Detailed clinical data on 1,011 patients. *Psychotherapy and Psychosomatics, 43*, 96–103.

Sullivan, H. S. (1953). *The interpersonal theory of psychiatry.* New York: Norton.

Sullivan, J. M. (2000). Cellular and molecular mechanisms underlying learning and memory impairments produced by cannabinoids. *Learning & Memory, 7*, 132–139.

Suls, J. M., & Miller, R. L. (Eds.). (1977). *Social comparison processes: Theoretical and empirical perspectives.* Washington, DC: Hemisphere.

Suls, J., & Fletcher, R. L. (1983). Social comparison in the social and physical sciences: An archival study. *Journal of Personality and Social Psychology, 44*, 575–580.

Super, D. E. (1985). Career and life development. In D. Brown & L. Brooks (Eds.), *Career choice and development.* San Francisco: Jossey-Bass.

Sutton, S. K., & Davidson, R. J. (1997). Prefrontal brain asymmetry: A biological substrate of the behavioral approach and inhibition systems. *Psychological Science, 8*, 204–210.

Suzuki, L. A., & Valencia, R. R. (1997). Race-ethnicity and measured intelligence: Educational implications. *American Psychologist, 52*, 1103–1114.

Suzuki, L. A., Meller, P. J., & Ponterotto, J. G. (Eds.). (1996). *Handbook of multicultural assessment: Clinical, psychological, and educational applications.* San Francisco: Jossey-Bass.

Swann, W. B. Jr., & Pittman, T. S. (1977). Initiating play activity in children: The moderating influence of verbal cues on intrinsic motivation. *Child Development, 48*, 1125–1132.

Swets, J. A., Tanner, W. P. Jr., & Birdsall, T. G. (1961). Decision processes in perception. *Psychological Review, 68*, 301–340.

Szasz, T. S. (1961). *The myth of mental illness.* New York: Harper & Row.

Szmukler, G. I., & Russell, G. F. M. (1986). Outcome and prognosis of anorexia nervosa. In K. D. Brownell & J. P. Foreyt (Eds.), *Handbook of eating disorders.* New York: Basic Books.

Szymanski, K., & Harkins, S. G. (1993). The effect of experimenter evaluation on self-evaluation within the social loafing paradigm. *Journal of Experimental Social Psychology, 29*, 268–286.

Tajfel, H. (Ed.). (1982). *Social identity and intergroup relations.* London: Cambridge University Press.

Tajfel, H., & Turner, J. C. (1986). The social identity theory of intergroup behavior. In S. Worchel & W. G. Austin (Eds.), *The psychology of intergroup relations* (2nd ed., pp. 7–24). Chicago: Nelson Hall.

Tandon, R., & Jibson, M. D. (2003). Efficacy of newer generation antipsychotics in the treatment of schizophrenia. *Psychoneuroendocrinology, 28* (Suppl. 1), 9–26.

Tanford, S., & Penrod, S. (1984). Social influence model: A formal integration of research on majority and minority influence processes. *Psychological Bulletin, 95*, 189–225.

Tardif, T. (1996). Nouns are not always learned before verbs: Evidence from Mandarin speakers' early vocabularies. *Developmental Psychology, 32*, 492–504.

Tardif, T., Shatz, M., & Naigles, L. (1997). Caregiver speech and children's use of nouns versus verbs: A comparison of English, Italian, and Mandarin. *Journal of Child Language, 24*, 535–565.

Tauber, R. T. (1997). *Self-fulfilling prophecy: A practical guide to its use in education.* Westport, CT: Praeger.

Tavris, C. (1989) *Anger: The misunderstood emotion* (2nd ed.). New York: Simon & Schuster/Touchstone.

Taylor, J. A., & Sanderson, M. (1995). A reexamination of the risk factors for the sudden infant death syndrome. *Journal of Pediatrics, 126*(6), 887–891.

Taylor, M. E. (2002). Meditation as treatment for performance anxiety in singers. *Dissertation Abstracts International, 62*(9-A), 2925. Ann Arbor, MI: University Microfilms International.

Taylor, S. E. (1979). Hospital patient behavior: Reactance, helplessness, or control? *Journal of Social Issues, 35,* 156–184.

Taylor, S. E. (1983). Adjustment to threatening events: A theory of cognitive adaptation. *American Psychologist, 38,* 1161–1173.

Taylor, S. E. (2002). *Health psychology* (5th ed.). New York: McGraw-Hill.

Taylor, S. E., & Aspinwall, L. G. (1990). Psychological aspects of chronic illness. In G. R. Van den Bos & P. T. Costa, Jr. (Eds.), *Psychological apects of serious illness.* Washington, DC: American Psychological Association.

Taylor, S. E., & Brown, J. D. (1988). Illusion and well-being: A social psychological perspective on mental health. *Psychological Bulletin, 103*(2), 193–210.

Taylor, S. E., Pham, L. B., Rivkin, I. D., & Armor, D. A. (1998). Harnessing the imagination: Mental stimulation, self-regulation, and coping. *American Psychologist, 53*(4), 429–439.

Teghtsoonian, R. (1971). On the exponents in Stevens' law and the constant in Ekman's law. *Psychological Review, 78*(1), 71–80.

Teitelbaum, P. (1961). Disturbances in feeding and drinking behavior after hypothalamic lesions. In M. R. Jones (Ed.), *Nebraska Symposium on Motivation.* Lincoln: University of Nebraska Press.

Teller, D. Y., & Movshon, J. A. (1986). Visual development. *Vision Research, 26,* 1483–1506.

Terhune, K. W. (1968). Studies of motives, cooperation, and conflict within laboratory microcosms. In G. H. Snyder (Ed.), *Studies in international conflict* (Vol. 4, pp. 29–58). Buffalo: State University of New York at Buffalo, Council on International Studies.

Terman, L. M. (1925). *Genetic studies of genius: Mental and physical traits of a thousand gifted children* (Vol. 1). Stanford, CA: Stanford University Press.

Terman, L. M., & Merrill, M. A. (1937). *Measuring intelligence.* Boston: Houghton Mifflin.

Terman, L. M., & Merrill, M. A. (1973). *Stanford-Binet Intelligence Scale: Manual for the third revision.* Boston: Houghton Mifflin.

Terman, L. M., & Oden, M. H. (1959). *Genetic studies of genius: The gifted group at midlife* (Vol. 4). Stanford, CA: Stanford University Press.

Terrace, H. S. (1979). *Nim.* New York: Knopf.

Tesser, A. (2000). Theories and hypotheses. In R. J. Sternberg (Ed.), *Guide to publishing in psychology journals* (pp. 58–80). New York: Cambridge University Press.

Tetlock, P. E. (1998). Social psychology and world politics. In D. T. Gilbert, S. T. Fiske, & G. Lindzey (Eds.), *The handbook of social psychology* (4th ed., Vol. 2, pp. 868–912). New York: McGraw-Hill.

Thagard, P. (1999). Induction. In R. A. Wilson & F. C. Keil (Eds.), *The MIT encyclopedia of the cognitive sciences* (pp. 399–400). Cambridge, MA: MIT Press

Thatcher, R. W. (1992). Development as a dynamic system. *Current Directions in Psychological Science, 1,* 189–193.

Thatcher, R. W., Walker, R. A., & Giudice, S. (1987). Human cerebral hemispheres develop at different rates and ages. *Science, 236,* 1110–1113.

Thelen, E. (1995). Motor development: A new synthesis. *American Psychologist, 50,* 79–95.

Thigpen, C. H., & Cleckley, H. M. (1957). *The three faces of Eve.* New York: Fawcett.

Thoits, P. A. (1994). Stressors and problem solving: The individual as psychological activist. *Journal of Health and Social Behavior, 35,* 143–159.

Thomas, A. K., & Loftus, E. F. (2002). Creating bizarre false memories through imagination. *Memory & Cognition, 30,* 423–431.

Thomas, A., & Chess, S. (1977). *Temperament and development.* New York: Brunner/Mazel.

Thomas, A., & Chess, S. (1987). Commentary. In H. Goldsmith, A. Buss, R. Plomin, M. Rothbart, A. Thomas, S. Chess, R. Hinde, & R. McCall, Roundtable: What is temperament? Four approaches. *Child Development, 58,* 505–529.

Thomas, A., Chess, S., & Birch, H. G. (1970). The origin of personality. *Scientific American, 223*(2).

Thomas, R. M. (2000). *Comparing theories of child development* (5th ed.). Belmont, CA: Wadsworth.

Thomas, V. J., & Rose, F. D. (1991). Ethnic differences in the experience of pain. *Social Science and Medicine, 32,* 1063–1066.

Thompson, A., & Kent, G. (2001). Adjusting to disfigurement: Processes involved in dealing with being visibly different. *Clinical Psychology Review, 21,* 663–682.

Thompson, R. A. (1998). Early sociopersonality development. In W. Damon (Gen. Ed.) & N. Eisenberg (Vol. Ed.), *Handbook of child psychology.* Vol. 3: *Social, emotional, and personality development* (pp. 25–104). New York: Wiley.

Thompson, R. A. (1999). The individual child: Temperament, emotion, self, and personality. In M. H. Bornstein & M. E. Lamb (Eds.), *Developmental psychology: An advanced textbook* (pp. 377–409). Mahwah, NJ: Erlbaum.

Thompson, R. A. (2002). *Early brain development, the media, and public policy.* In preparation (cited in Thompson, Easterbrooks, & Padilla-Walker, 2003).

Thompson, R. A., & Nelson, C. E. (2001). Developmental science and the media: Early brain development. *American Psychologist, 56,* 5–15.

Thompson, R. A., Easterbrooks, M. A., & Padilla-Walker, L. M. (2003). Social and emotional development in infancy. In R. M. Lerner, M. A. Easterbrooks, & J. Mistry (Vol. Eds.) and I. B. Weiner (Ed.-in-Chief), *Handbook of psychology.* Vol. 6: *Developmental psychology* (pp. 91–112). New York: Wiley.

Thompson, R. A., Lamb, M. E., & Estes, D. (1982). Stability of infant–mother attachment and its relationship to changing life circumstances in an unselected middle class sample. *Child Development, 53,* 144–148.

Thompson, R. F. (1975). *Introduction to physiological psychology.* New York: Harper & Row.

Thompson, R. F. (1987). The cerebellum and memory storage: A response to Bloedel. *Science, 238,* 1729–1730.

Thompson, R. F. (2000). Memory: Brain systems. In A. E. Kazdin (Ed.), *Encyclopedia of psychology* (Vol. 5, pp. 175–178). Washington, DC: American Psychological Association.

Thompson, R. F., & Krupa, D. J. (1994). Organization of memory traces in the mammalian brain. *Annual Review of Neuroscience, 17,* 519–549.

Thompson, S. C., Cheek, P. R., & Graham, M. A. (1988). The other side of perceived control: Disadvantages and negative effects. In S. Spacapan & S. Oskamp (Eds.), *The social psychology of health: The Claremont Applied Social Psychology Conference* (Vol. 2, pp. 69–94). Beverly Hills, CA: Sage.

Thompson, S. K. (1975). Gender labels and early sex role development. *Child Development, 46,* 339–347.

Thompson, W. R. (1954). The inheritance and development of intelligence. *Proceedings of the Association for Research on Nervous and Mental Disease, 33,* 209–231.

Thorndike, E. L. (1898). Animal intelligence: An experimental study of the associative processes in animals. *Psychological Monographs, 2*(Whole No. 8).

Thorndike, E. L. (1905). *The elements of psychology.* New York: Seiler.

Thorndike, E. L. (1911). *Animal intelligence: Experimental studies.* New York: Macmillan.

Thorndike, R. L., Hagen, E. P., & Sattler, J. M. (1986). *Stanford-Binet Intelligence Scale: Guide for administering and scoring the fourth edition.* Chicago: Riverside.

Thurstone, L. L. (1938). *Primary mental abilities.* Chicago: University of Chicago Press.

Timberlake, W. T. (1993). Behavior systems and reinforcement: An integrative approach. *Journal of the Experimental Analysis of Behavior, 60,* 105–128.

Timko, C., Moos, R. H., Finney, J. W., & Moos, B. S. (1994). Outcome of treatment for alcohol abuse and involvement in Alcoholics Anonymous among previously untreated problem drinkers. *Journal of Mental Health Administration, 21,* 145–160.

Tinsley, H. E., Hinson, J. A., Tinsley, D. J., & Holt, M. S. (1993). Attributes of leisure and work experiences. *Journal of Counseling Psychology, 40,* 447–455.

Titchener, E. B. (1910). *A textbook of psychology.* New York: Macmillan.

Todd, P. M., & Gigerenzer, G. (2001). Putting naturalistic decision making into the adaptive toolbox. *Journal of Behavioral Decision Making, 14*, 381–383.

Tolman, E. C. (1932). *Purposive behavior in animals and men.* New York: Appleton-Century-Crofts.

Tolman, E. C. (1959). Principles of purposive behavior. In S. Koch (Ed.), *Psychology: A study of science* (Vol. 2, pp. 92–157). New York: McGraw-Hill.

Tolman, E. C., & Honzik, C. H. (1930). "Insight" in rats. *University of California Publications in Psychology, 4*, 215–232.

Tomasello, M. (1999). *The cultural origins of human cognition.* Cambridge, MA: Harvard University Press.

Tomaszuk, A., Simpson, C., & Williams, G. (1996). Neuropeptide Y, the hypothalamus and the regulation of energy homeostasis. *Hormone Research, 46*, 53–58.

Tomkins, S. S. (1962). *Affect, imagery, and consciousness:* Vol. 1. *The positive affects.* New York: Springer.

Tomkins, S. S. (1963). *Affect, imagery, and consciousness:* Vol. 2. *The negative affects.* New York: Springer.

Torff, B., & Sternberg, R. J. (2001). Intuitive conceptions among learners and teachers. In B. Torff & R. J. Sternberg (Eds.), *Understanding and teaching the intuitive mind: Student and teacher learning* (pp. 3–26). Mahwah, NJ: Erlbaum.

Torgesen, J. K. (1997). The prevention and remediation of reading disabilities: Evaluating what we know from research. *Journal of Academic Language Therapy, 1*, 11–47.

Torgesen, J. K. (2002). The prevention of reading difficulties. *Journal of School Psychology, 40*, 7–26.

Tormala, Z. L., & Petty, R. E. (2002). What doesn't kill me makes me stronger: The effects of resisting persuasion on attitude certainty. *Journal of Personality and Social Psychology, 83*, 1298–1313.

Torrey, E. F. (1986). *Witchdoctors and psychiatrists: The common roots of psychotherapy and its future.* New York: Harper & Row.

Torrey, E. F. (1988). Stalking the schizovirus. *Schizophrenia Bulletin, 14*, 223–229.

Torrey, E. F. (1997). *Out of the shadows: Confronting America's mental illness crisis.* New York: Wiley.

Torrey, E. F., & Miller, J. (2002). *The invisible plague: The rise of mental illness from 1750 to the present.* New Brunswick, NJ: Rutgers University Press.

Torrey, E. F., Bowler, A. E., Taylor, E. H., & Gottesman, I. I. (1994). *Schizophrenia and manic–depressive disorder.* New York: Basic Books.

Torsvall, L., Akerstedt, T., & Lindbeck, G. (1984). Effects on sleep stages and EEG power density of different degrees of exercise in fit subjects. *Electroencephalography & Clinical Neurophysiology, 57*, 347–353.

Tourangeau, R., & Ellsworth, P. C. (1979). The role of facial response in the experience of emotion. *Journal of Personality and Social Psychology, 37*, 1519–1531.

Townsend, J. T. (1971). A note on the identifiability of parallel and serial processes. *Perception and Psychophysics, 10*, 161–163.

Treisman, A. M. (1964a). Monitoring and storage of irrelevant messages in selective attention. *Journal of Verbal Learning and Verbal Behavior, 3*, 449–459.

Treisman, A. M. (1964b). Selective attention in man. *British Medical Bulletin, 20*, 12–16.

Treisman, M. (1977). Motion sickness: an evolutionary hypothesis. *Science, 1977, 197*: 493-495.

Triandis, H. (1990). Cross-cultural studies of individualism and collectivism. In J. Berman (Ed.), *Nebraska Symposium on Motivation, 1989* (pp. 41–133). Lincoln: University of Nebraska Press.

Triandis, H. C. (1994). Culture and social behavior. In W. J. Lonner & R. S. Malpass (Eds.), *Psychology and culture.* Boston: Allyn & Bacon.

Tripathi, A. N. (1979). Memory for meaning and grammatical structure: An experiment on retention of a story. *Psychological Studies, 24*(2), 136–145.

Triplett, N. (1898). The dynamogenic factors in pacemaking and competition. *American Journal of Psychology, 9*, 507–533.

Trivers, R. L. (1971). The evolution of reciprocal altruism. *Quarterly Review of Biology, 46*, 35–57.

Truscott, S. D., & Frank, A. J. (2001). Does the Flynn effect affect IQ scores of students classified as LD? *Journal of School Psychology, 39*, 319–334.

Tryon, R. (1940). Genetic differences in maze-learning ability in rats. In the *39th yearbook of the National Society for the Study of Education.* Chicago: University of Chicago Press.

Tsunoda, T. (1979). Difference in the mechanism of emotion in Japanese and Westerner. *Psychotherapy and Psychosomatics, 31*(1–4), 367–372.

Tulving, E. (1966). Subjective organization and effects of repetition in multi-trial free-recall learning. *Journal of Verbal Learning and Verbal Behavior, 5*, 193–197.

Tulving, E. (1972). Episodic and semantic memory. In E. Tulving & W. Donaldson (Eds.), *Organization of memory.* New York: Academic Press.

Tulving, E. (2000a). Concepts of memory. In E. Tulving & F. I. M. Craik (Eds.), *The Oxford handbook of memory* (pp. 33–44). New York: Oxford University Press.

Tulving, E. (2000b). Memory: An overview. In A. E. Kazdin (Ed.), *Encyclopedia of psychology* (Vol. 5, pp. 161–162). Washington, DC: American Psychological Association.

Tulving, E., & Craik, F. I. M. (Eds.). (2000). *The Oxford handbook of memory.* New York: Oxford University Press.

Tulving, E., & Thomson, D. M. (1973). Encoding specificity and retrieval processes in episodic memory. *Psychological Review, 80*, 352–373.

Tulving, E., Kapur, S., Markowitsch, H. J., Craik, F.I.M., Habib, R., & Houle, S. (1994). Neuroanatomical correlates of retrieval in episodic memory: Auditory sentence recognition. *Proceedings of the National Academy of Sciences, USA, 91*, 2012–2015.

Turiel, E. (1998). The development of morality. In W. Damon (Gen. Ed.) & N. Eisenberg (Vol. Ed.), *Handbook of child psychology: Social, emotional, and personality development* (Vol. 3, pp. 863–932). New York: Wiley.

Turk, D. C., & Okifuji, A. (2000). Pain: Models and management. In A. E. Kazdin (Ed.), *Encyclopedia of psychology* (Vol. 6, pp. 24–27). Washington, DC: American Psychological Association.

Turk, D. C., & Okifuji, A. (2002). Chronic pain. In A. J. Christensen & M. H. Antoni (Eds.), *Chronic physical disorders: Behavioral medicine's perspective* (pp. 165–190). Malden, MA: Blackwell.

Turk, D. C., & Okifuji, A. (2003). Pain management. In A. M. Nezu, C. M. Nezu, et al. (Eds.), *Handbook of psychology: Health psychology* (Vol. 9, pp. 293–315). New York: Wiley.

Turk, D. C., & Rudy, T. E. (1992). Cognitive factors and persistent pain: A glimpse into Pandora's box. *Cognitive Therapy and Research, 16*(2), 99–122.

Turk, D. C., Meichenbaum, D., & Genest, M. (1983). *Pain and behavioral medicine: A cognitive behavioral perspective.* New York: Guilford.

Turnbull, C. (1961). *The forest people: A study of pygmies of the Congo.* New York: Simon & Schuster.

Turner, J. C. (1987). *Rediscovering the social group: A self-categorization theory.* Oxford, UK: Basil Blackwell.

Turner, J. R., & Wheaton, B. (1995). Checklist measurement of stressful life events. In S. Cohen, R. C. Kessler, & L. U. Gordon (Eds.), *Measuring stress: A guide for health and social scientists.* New York: Oxford University Press.

Turner, M. E., Pratkanis, A. R., Probasco, P., & Leve, C. (1992). Threat, cohesion, and group effectiveness: Testing a social identity maintenance perspective on groupthink. *Journal of Personality and Social Psychology, 63*, 781–796.

Turner, M. L., & Engle, R. W. (1989). Is working-memory capacity task dependent? *Journal of Memory and Language, 28*, 127–154.

Turner, R. J., & Wagonfeld, M. O. (1967). Occupational mobility and schizophrenia: An assessment of the social causation and the social selection hypothesis. *American Sociological Review, 32*, 104–113.

Turner, R. S. (2000a). Helmholtz, Hermann von. In A. E. Kazdin (Ed.), *Encyclopedia of psychology* (Vol. 4, pp. 109–111). Washington, DC: American Psychological Association.

Turner, R. S. (2000b). Hering, Ewald. In A. E. Kazdin (Ed.), *Encyclopedia of psychology* (Vol. 4, pp. 117–119). Washington, DC: American Psychological Association.

Tversky, A., & Kahneman, D. (1973). Availability: A heuristic for judging frequency and probability. *Cognitive Psychology, 5*, 207–232.

Twamley, E. W., & Davis, M. C. (1999). The sociocultural model of eating disturbance in young women: The effects of personal attributes and family environment. *Journal of Social & Clinical Psychology, 18*, 467–489.

Tyrka, A. R., Graber, J. A., & Brooks-Gunn, J. (2000). The development of disordered eating: Correlates and predictors of eating problems in the context of adolescence. In A. J. Sameroff, M. Lewis, & S. M. Miller (Eds.), *Handbook of developmental psychopathology* (pp. 607–624). New York: Kluwer Academic.

Tzischinsky, O., Pal, I., Epstein, R., Dagan, Y., & Lavie, P. (1992). The importance of timing in melatonin administration in a blind man. *Journal of Pineal Research, 12*, 105–108.

Ugurbil, K. (1999). Magnetic resonance imaging. In R. A. Wilson & F. C. Keil (Eds.), *The MIT encyclopedia of the cognitive sciences* (pp. 505–507). Cambridge, MA: MIT Press.

Ulrich, R., & Azrin, N. H. (1962). Reflexive fighting in response to aversive stimulation. *Journal of the Experimental Analysis of Behavior, 5*, 511–520.

Ungerleider, L. G. (1995). Functional brain imaging studies of cortical mechanisms for memory. *Science, 270*, 760–775.

Urbszat, D., Herman, C. P., & Polivy, J. (2002). Eat, drink, and be merry, for tomorrow we diet: Effects of anticipated deprivation on food intake in restrained and unrestrained eaters. *Journal of Abnormal Psychology, 111*, 396–401.

Uylings, H. B. M. (2002). About assumptions in estimation of density of neurons and glial cells. *Biological Psychiatry, 51*, 840–842.

Valdes, G. (2002). *Expanding definitions of giftedness: The case of young interpreters from immigrant communities.* Mahwah, NJ: Erlbaum.

Valenstein, E. S. (1973). *Brain control.* New York: Wiley.

Valenstein, E. S. (1986). *Great and desperate cures.* New York: Basic Books.

Vallerand, R. J., Fortier, M. S., & Guay, F. (1997). Self-determination and persistence in a real-life setting: Toward a motivational model of high school dropout. *Journal of Personality and Social Psychology, 72*, 1161–1176.

Van Dalen, A. (2001). Juvenile violence and addiction: Tangled roots in childhood trauma. *Journal of Social Work Practice, 1*, 25–40.

van der Ven, A., van Diest, R., Hamulyak, K., Maes, M., Bruggeman, C., & Appels, A. (2003). Herpes viruses, cytokines, and altered hemostasis in vital exhaustion. *Psychosomatic Medicine, 65*, 194–200.

Van Hoesen, G. W. (1993). The modern concept of association cortex. *Current Opinion in Neurobiology, 3*, 150–154.

van Schaik, D. J. F., van Marwijk, H. W. J., van der Windt, A. W. M., Beekman, A. T. F., de Haan, M., & van Dyck, R. (2002). Effectiveness of psychotherapy for depressive disorder in primary care. A systematic review. *Tijdschrift voor Psychiatrie, 44*, 609–619.

Van Tonder, G. J., Lyons, M., & Ejima, Y. (2002). Visual structure of a Japanese Zen garden: The mysterious appeal of a simple and ancient composition of rocks is unveiled. *Nature, 419*, 359–360.

Van Wieringen, J. C. (1978). Secular growth changes. In F. Falkner & J. M. Tanner (Eds.), *Human growth* (Vol. 2). New York: Plenum.

Vandell, D., & Mueller, E. C. (1980). Peer play and friendships during the first two years. In H. C. Foot, A. J. Chapman, & J. R. Smith (Eds.), *Friendship and social relations in children.* New York: Wiley.

Vangu, M. Di T., Esser, J. D., Boyd, I. H., & Berk, M. (2003). Effects of electroconvulsive therapy on regional cerebral blood flow measured by -super(99m) technetium HMPAO SPECT. *Progress in Neuro-Psychopharmacology & Biological Psychiatry, 27*, 15–19.

Vaughn, B. E., Gove, F. L., & Egeland, B. (1980). The relationship between out-of-home care and the quality of infant–mother attachment in an economically disadvantaged population. *Child Development, 51*, 1203–1214.

Velting, D. M., & Liebert, R. M. (1997). Predicting three mood phenomena from factors and facets of the NEO-PI. *Journal of Personaltiy Assessment, 68*, 164–171.

Vernon, P. A., & Mori, M. (1992). Intelligence, reaction times, and peripheral nerve conduction velocity. *Intelligence, 16*(3–4), 273–288.

Vernon, P. A., Wickett. J. C., Bazana, P. G., & Stelmack, R. M. (2000). The neuropsychology and psychophysiology of intelligence. In R. J. Sternberg (Ed.), *Handbook of intelligence* (pp. 245–264). New York: Cambridge University Press.

Veroff, J. (1957). Development and validation of a projective measure of power motivation. *Journal of Abnormal and Social Psychology, 54*, 1–8.

Vertue, F. M. (2003). From adaptive emotion to dysfunction: An attachment perspective on social anxiety disorder. *Personality & Social Psychology Review, 7*, 170–191.

Viglione, D. J., & Exner, J. E. (1983). Current research in the comprehensive Rorschach system. In J. N. Butcher & C. D. Spielberger (Eds.), *Advances in personality assessment* (Vol. 2, pp. 13–40). Hillsdale, NJ: Erlbaum.

Vincent, M. A., & McCabe, M. P. (2000). Gender differences among adolescents in family, and peer influences on body dissatisfaction, weight loss, and binge eating behaviors. *Journal of Youth & Adolescence, 29*, 205–221.

Viney, W. (1993). *A history of psychology: Ideas and context.* Needham Heights, MA: Allyn & Bacon.

Vonk, R., & van Knippenberg, A. (1995). Processing attitude statements from in-group and out-group members: Effects of within-group and within-person inconsistencies on reading times. *Journal of Personality and Social Psychology, 68*, 215–227.

Vygotsky, L. S. (1962). *Thought and language.* Cambridge, MA: MIT Press. (Original work published 1934)

Vygotsky, L. S. (1978). *Mind in society: The development of higher psychological processes.* Cambridge, MA: Harvard University Press.

Wade, C., & Cirese, S. (1991). *Human sexuality* (2nd ed.). New York: Harcourt Brace Jovanovich.

Wade, J. B., & Price, D. D. (2000). Nonpathological factors in chronic pain: Implications for assessment and treatment. In R. J. Gatchel & J. N. Weisberg (Eds.), *Personality characteristics of patients with pain* (pp. 89–107). Washington, DC: American Psychological Association.

Wade, J. B., Dougherty, L. M., Hart, R. P., & Rafil, A. (1992). A canonical correlation analysis of the influence of neuroticism and extraversion on chronic pain, suffering, and pain behavior. *Pain, 51*, 67–73.

Wadhwa, P. D., Sandman, C. A., & Garite, T. J. (2001). The neurobiology of stress in human pregnancy: Implications for prematurity and development of the fetal central nervous system. *Progress in Brain Research, 133*, 131–142.

Wagenaar, W. (1986). My memory: A study of autobiographic memory over the past six years. *Cognitive Psychology, 18*, 225–252.

Wagner, A. R., & Brandon, S. E. (2001). A componential theory of Pavlovian conditioning. In R. R. Mowrer & S. B. Klein (Eds.), *Handbook of contemporary learning theories* (pp. 23–64). Mahwah, NJ: Erlbaum.

Wagner, A. R., & Rescorla, R. A. (1972). Inhibition in Pavlovian conditioning: Application of a theory. In R. A. Boakes & M. S. Halliday (Eds.), *Inhibition and learning.* New York: Academic Press.

Wagner, R. K. (1997). Intelligence, training, and employment. *American Psychologist, 52*, 1059–1069.

Wagner, R. K. (2000). Practical intelligence. In R. J. Sternberg (Ed.), *Handbook of intelligence.* New York: Cambridge University Press.

Wagner, R. K., & Stanovich, K. E. (1996). Expertise in reading. In K. A. Ericsson (Eds.), *The road to excellence* (pp. 159–227). Mahwah, NJ: Erlbaum.

Wahl, H.-W. (2000). Visual impairment: Psychological implications. In A. E. Kazdin (Ed.), *Encyclopedia of psychology* (Vol. 8, pp. 204–207). Washington, DC: American Psychological Association.

Wahl, H.-W., Schilling, O., Oswald, F., & Heyl, V. (1999). Psychosocial consequences of age-related visual impairment: Comparison with mobility-impaired older adults and long-term outcome. *Journal of Gerontology: Psychological Sciences, 54B*, 304–316.

Wahlsten, D. (2002). The theory of biological intelligence: History and a critical appraisal. In R. J. Sternberg & E. L. Grigorenko

(Eds.), *The general factor of intelligence: How general is it?* (pp. 245–277). Mahwah, NJ: Erlbaum.

Wahlsten, D., & Gottlieb, G. (1997). The invalid separation of effects of nature and nurture: Lessons from animal experimentation. In R. J. Sternberg & E. L. Grigorenko (Eds.), *Intelligence, heredity, and environment* (pp. 163–192). New York: Cambridge University Press.

Wald, G., & Brown, P. K. (1965). Human color vision and color blindness. *Cold Spring Harbor Symposia on Quantitative Biology, 30,* 345–359.

Walker, E. F. (2002). Adolescent neurodevelopment and psychopathology. *Current Directions in Psychological Science, 11*(1), 24–28.

Walker, E. F., Grimes, K. E., Davis, D. M., & Smith, A. J. (1993). Childhood precursors of schizophrenia: Facial expressions of emotion. *American Journal of Psychiatry, 150*(11), 1654–1660.

Walker, E. F., Lewine, R. R. J., & Neumann, C. (1996). Childhood behavioral characteristics and adult brain morphology in schizophrenia. *Schizophrenia Research, 22*(2), 93–101.

Walker, E. F., Savoie, T., & Davis, D. (1994). Neuromotor precursors of schizophrenia. *Schizophrenia Bulletin, 20*(3), 441–451.

Walker, E. F., Walder, D. J., & Reynolds, F. (2001). Developmental changes in cortisol secretion in normal and at-risk youth. *Development & Psychopathology, 13*(3), 721–732.

Walker, L. J. (1984). Sex differences in the development of moral reasoning: A critical review. *Child Development, 55,* 677–691.

Walker, L. J. (1989). A longitudinal study of moral reasoning. *Child Development, 60,* 157–166.

Wall, P. D., & Melzack, R. (Eds.). (1999). *Textbook of pain* (4th ed.). Edinburgh, Scotland: Livingstone.

Wallace, B. (1993). Day persons, night persons, and variability in hypnotic susceptibility. *Journal of Personality and Social Psychology, 64,* 827–833.

Wallace, R. K., & Benson, H. (1972). The physiology of meditation. *Scientific American,* 84–90.

Waller, M. J., Giambatista, R. C., & Zellmer-Bruhn, M. E. (1999). The effects of individual time urgency on group polychronicity. *Journal of Managerial Psychology, 14,* 244–256.

Walsh, D. C., Hingson, R. W., Merrigan, D. M., Levenson, S. M., et al. (1991). A randomized trial of treatment for alcohol abusing workers. *New England Journal of Medicine, 325,* 775–782.

Walsh, W. (1997). *When stereotypes get applied to the self: The role of perceived ingroup variability in self-stereotyping.* Unpublished doctoral dissertation, Yale University, New Haven, CT.

Walster, E., Walster, G. W., & Berscheid, E. (1978). *Equity: Theory and research.* Boston: Allyn & Bacon.

Walters, G. C., & Grusec, J. F. (1977). *Punishment.* San Francisco: Freeman.

Wang, G.-J., Volkkow, N. D., Thanos, P. K., & Fowler, J. S. (2003). Positron emission tomographic evidence of similarity between obesity and drug addiction. *Psychiatric Annals, 33,* 104–111.

Wangensteen, O. H., & Carlson, A. J. (1931). Hunger sensation after total gastrectomy. *Proceedings of the Society for Experimental Biology, 28,* 545–547.

Ward, T. B., Smith, S. M., & Finke, R. A. (1999). Creative cognition. In R. J. Sternberg (Ed.), *Handbook of creativity* (pp. 189–225). New York: Cambridge University Press.

Washburn, D., & Humphrey, D. (2001). Symmetries in the mind: Production, perception, and preference for seven one-dimensional patterns. *Visual Arts Research, 27,* 57–68.

Wason, P. C., & Johnson-Laird, P. N. (1972). *Psychology of reasoning: Structure and content.* London: B. T. Batsford.

Wass, T. S., Simmons, R. W., Thomas, J. D., & Riley, E. P. (2002). Timing accuracy and variability in children with prenatal exposure to alcohol. *Alcoholism: Clinical & Experimental Research, 26,* 1887–1896.

Wasserman, R., DiBasio, C. M., Bond, L. A., Young P., & Collett, R. (1990). Infant temperament and school age behavior: A pediatric practice. *Pediatrics, 85,* 801–807.

Watanabe, S., Sakamoto, J., & Wakita, M. (1995). Pigeons' discrimination of painting by Monet and Picasso. *Journal of the Experimental Analysis of Behavior, 63,* 165–174.

Waters, E., Wippman, J., & Sroufe, L. A. (1979). Attachment, positive affect, and competence in the peer group: Two studies in construct validation. *Child Development, 50,* 821–829.

Watson, J. B. (1930). *Behaviorism* (Rev. ed.). New York: Norton.

Watson, J. B., & McDougall, W. (1929). *The battle of behaviorism.* New York: Norton.

Watson, J. B., & Rayner, R. (1920). Conditioned emotional reactions. *Journal of Experimental Psychology, 3,* 1–14.

Waxman, S. R. (2002). Early word-learning and conceptual development: Everything had a name, and each name gave birth to a new thought. In U. Goswami (Ed.), *Blackwell handbook of childhood cognitive development* (pp. 102–126). Malden, MA: Blackwell.

Webb, W. B. (1982). Some theories about sleep and their clinical applications. *Psychiatric Annals, 11,* 415–422.

Wechsler, D. (1974). *The measurement and appraisal of adult intelligence.* Baltimore, MD: Williams & Wilkins.

Weiller, C., Isansee, C., Rijntgis, M., Huber, W., et al., (1996). Recovery from Wernicke's aphasia: A positron emission tomography study. *Annals of Neurology, 37,* 723–732.

Weinberg, M. K. (1992). *Boys and girls: Sex differences in emotional expressivity and self-regulation during early infancy.* Paper presented in L. J. Bridges (Chair), Early emotional self-regulation: New approaches to understanding developmental change and individual differences. Symposium presented at the International Conference on Infant Studies (ICIS), Miami, Florida.

Weinberg, R. A., Scarr, S., & Waldman, I. D. (1992). The Minnesota transracial adoption study: A follow-up of IQ test performance at adolescence. *Intelligence, 16,* 117–135.

Weinberger, D. R., Wagner, R. L., & Wyatt, R. J. (1983). Neuropathological studies of schizophrenia: A selective review. *Schizophrenia Bulletin, 9,* 193–212.

Weinberger, J., & Westen, D. (2001). Science and psychodynamics: From Arguments about Freud to data. *Psychological Inquiry, 12,* 129–132.

Weiner, B. (2000). Motivation: An overview. In A. E. Kazdin (Ed.), *Encyclopedia of psychology* (Vol. 5, pp. 314–317). Washington, DC: American Psychological Association.

Weingartner, H., Rudorfer, M. V., Buchsbaum, M. S., & Linnoila, M. (1983). Effects of serotonin on memory impairments produced by ethanol. *Science, 221,* 442–473.

Weinstein, R. (2002). *Reviews of reaching higher: The power of expectations in schooling.* Cambridge, MA: Harvard University Press.

Weinstein, S. (1968). Intensive and extensive aspects of tactile sensitivity as a function of body part, sex, and laterality. In D. R. Renshalo (Ed.), *The skin senses* (pp. 195–218). Springfield, IL: Thomas.

Weisberg, R. W. (1992). *Creativity: Beyond the myth of genius.* New York: Freeman.

Weisberg, R. W. (1999). Creativity and knowledge: A challenge to theories. In R. J. Sternberg (Ed.), *Handbook of creativity* (pp. 226–250). New York: Cambridge University Press.

Weiskrantz, L., Warrington, E., Sanders, M. D., & Marshall, J. (1974). Visual capacity in the hemianopic field following a restricted occipital ablation. *Brain, 97,* 709–728.

Weiss, R. S. (1975). *Marital separation.* New York: Basic Books.

Weiss, R. S. (1982). Attachment in adult life. In C. M. Parkes & J. Stevenson-Hinde (Eds.), *The place of attachment in human behavior.* New York: Basic Books.

Weisz, J. R., Weiss, B., Hun, S. S., Granger D. A., & Morton, T. (1995). Effects of psychotherapy with children and adolescents revisited: A meta-analysis of treatment outcome studies. *Psychological Bulletin, 117,* 450–468.

Welch, S. S. (2001). A review of the literature on the epidemiology of parasuicide in the general population. *Psychiatric Services, 52,* 368–375.

Wellman, H. M. (2002). Understanding the psychological world: Developing a theory of mind. In U. Goswami (Ed.), *Blackwell handbook of childhood cognitive development* (pp. 167–187). Malden, MA: Blackwell.

Wells, G. L. (1993). What do we know about eyewitness identification? *American Psychologist, 48*(5), 553–571.

Wells, G. L., & Loftus, E. G. (1984). *Eyewitness testimony: Psychological perspectives.* New York: Cambridge University Press.

Wells, G. L., Luus, C. A. E., & Windschitl, P. D. (1994). Maximizing the utility of eyewitness identification evidence. *Current Directions in Psychological Science, 6,* 194–197.

Welsh, D. K. (1993). Timing of sleep and wakefulness. In M. A. Carskadon (Ed.), *Encyclopedia of sleep and dreaming.* New York: Macmillan.

Wertheimer, M. (1912). Experimentelle Studien uber das Sehen von Bewegung. *Zeitschrift fur Psychologie, 61,* 161–165.

Wertheimer, M. (1959). *Productive thinking* (Rev. ed.). New York: Harper & Row. (Original work published 1945)

Wesman, A. E., & Ricks, D. F. (1966). *Mood and personality.* New York: Holt, Rinehart & Winston.

West, R. L. (1986). Everyday memory and aging. *Developmental Neuropsychology, 2*(4), 323–344.

Westen, D. (1992). The cognitive self and the psychoanalytic self: Can we put ourselves together? *Psychological Inquiry, 3,* 1–13.

Westen, D. (1995). A clinical-empirical model of personality: Life after the Mischellian Ice Age and the NEO-Lithic Era. *Journal of Personality, 63,* 495–524.

Westen, D. (1998). The scientific legacy of Sigmund Freud: Toward a psychodynamically informed psychological science. *Psychological Bulletin, 124,* 333–371.

Westen, D., & Gabbard, G. (1999). Psychoanalytic approaches to personality. In L. Pervin & O. John (Eds.), *Handbook of personality: Theory and research* (2nd ed., pp. 57–101). New York: Guilford.

Westen, D., & Gabbard, G. O. (2002a). Developments in cognitive neuroscience: I. Conflict, compromise, and connectionism. *Journal of the American Psychoanalytic Association, 50,* 53–98.

Westen, D., & Gabbard, G. O. (2002b). Developments in cognitive neuroscience: II. Implications for theories of transference. *Journal of the American Psychoanalytic Association, 50,* 99–134.

Wever, E. G. (1970). *Theory of hearing.* New York: Wiley.

Wever, R. A. (1979). *The circadian system of man.* Heidelberg, Germany: Springer Verlag.

Wexler, K. (1996). The development of inflection in a biologically based theory of language acquisition. In M. L. Rice (Ed.), *Toward a genetics of language* (pp. 113–144). Mahwah, NJ: Erlbaum.

What are the specific drug treatments for schizophrenia? Retrieved June 20, 2003 from http://www.ucdmc.ucdavis.edu/ucdhs/health/a-z/47Schizophrenia/doc47specificdrugs.html.

Wheeler, D. D. (1970). Processes in word recognition. *Cognitive Psychology, 1,* 59–85.

Wheeler, L., & Kim. Y. (1997). What is beautiful is culturally good: The physical attractiveness stereotype has different content in collectivist cultures. *Personality and Social Psychology Bulletin, 23,* 795–800.

White, B. W., & Martin, R. J. (1997). Evidence for a central mechanism of obesity in the Zucker rat: Role of neuropeptide Y and leptin. *Proceedings of the Society for Experimental Biology and Medicine, 214,* 222–232.

White, J., Joseph, S., & Neil, A. (1993). Religiosity, psychoticism, and schizotypal traits. *Personality and Individual Differences, 19,* 847–851.

White, R. W. (1959). Motivation reconsidered: The concept of competence. *Psychological Review, 66,* 297–333.

White, T., Andreasen, N. C., & Nopoulos, P. (2002). Brain volumes and surface morphology in monozygotic twins. *Cerebral Cortex, 12,* 486–493.

Whitley, B. E. Jr., & Frieze, I. H. (1985). Children's causal attributions for success and failure in achievement settings: A meta-analysis. *Journal of Educational Psychology, 77,* 608–616.

Whittaker, D. (1971). The psychological adjustment of intellectual, nonconformist, collegiate dropouts. Adolescence, 6, 415–424.

Whittaker, D., & Watts, W. A. (1969). Personality characteristics of a nonconformist youth subculture: A study of the Berkeley non-student. *Journal of Social Issues, 25,* 65–89.

Whorf, B. L. (1956). In J. B. Carroll (Ed.), *Language, thought and reality: Selected writings of Benjamin Lee Whorf.* Cambridge, MA: MIT Press.

Wickesberg, R. E. (2000). Hearing. In A. E. Kazdin (Ed.), *Encyclopedia of psychology* (Vol. 4, pp. 97–101). Washington, DC: American Psychological Association.

Wiggins, J. S. (Ed.). (1996). *The Five-Factor Model of personality: Theoretical perspectives.* New York: Guilford.

Wiggins, J. S., & Trapnell, P. D. (1997). Personality structure: The return of the big five. In R. Hogan, J. Johnson, & S. R. Briggs (Eds.), *Handbook of personality psychology* (pp. 737–765). San Diego, CA: Academic Press.

Wilder, D. A., & Allen, V. L. (1978). Group membership and preference for information about others. *Personality and Social Psychology Bulletin, 4*(1), 106–110.

Wilder, D. H., McKeegan, H. F., & Midkiff, R. M. Jr. (2000). A factor-analytic reinterpretation of the Clark-Trow " educational philosophies." *Journal of College Student Development, 41,* 513–528.

Wilkening, F., & Huber, S. (2002). Children's intuitive physics. In U. Goswami (Ed.), *Blackwell handbook of childhood cognitive development* (pp. 349–370). Malden, MA: Blackwell.

Willcutt, E. G., & Pennington, B. F. (2000). Comorbidity of reading disability and attention-deficit hyperactivity disorder: Differences by gender and subtype. *Journal of Learning Disabilities, 33,* 179–191.

Williams, G. C. (1966). *Adaptation and natural selection.* Princeton, NJ: Princeton University Press.

Williams, J. M., & Dunlop, L. C. (1999). Pubertal timing and self-reported delinquency among male adolescents. *Journal of Adolescence, 22,* 157–171.

Williams, R. (1986). An untrusting heart. In M. G. Walraven & H. E. Fitzgerald (Eds.), *Annuals editions: Human development 86/87.* Guilford, CT: Dushkin.

Williams, R. B. Jr. (1989). *The trusting heart.* New York: Random House.

Williams, R. B. Jr., & Barefoot, J. C. (1988). Coronary-prone behavior: The emerging role of the hostility complex. In B. K. Houston & C. R. Snyder (Eds.), *Type A behavior pattern: Current trends and future directions* (pp. 189–211). New York: Wiley.

Williams, W. M. (1998). Are we raising smarter children today? School- and home-related influences on IQ. In U. Neisser (Ed.), *The rising curve: Long-term gains in IQ and related measures* (pp. 125–154). Washington, DC: American Psychological Association.

Williams, W., Blythe, T., White, N., Li, J., Sternberg, R. J., & Gardner, H. (1996). *Practical intelligence for school.* New York: HarperCollins.

Willis, S. L. (1985). Towards an educational psychology of the older adult learner: Intellectual and cognitive bases. In J. E. Birren & K. W. Schaie (Eds.), *Handbook of the psychology of aging* (2nd ed.). New York: Van Nostrand Reinhold.

Wills, T. A. (1987). Downward comparison as a coping mechanism. In C. R. Snyder & C. E. Ford (Eds.), *Coping with negative life events: Clinical and social psychological perspectives* (pp. 243–268). New York: Plenum Press.

Wilson, D. W. (1981). Is helping a laughing matter? *Psychology, 18,* 6–9.

Wingert, P., & Kantrowitz, B. (1990). The day care generation. *Newsweek special edition: The 21st century family,* 86–92.

Winner, E. (1996). *Gifted children.* New York: Basic Books.

Winner, E. (1997). Exceptionally high intelligence and schooling. *American Psychologist, 52,* 1070–1081.

Winokur, G., Coryll, W., Keller, M., Endicott, J., & Leon, A. (1995). A family study of manic-depressive (Bipolar I) disease. *Archives of General Psychiatry, 52,* 367–373.

Winter, D. G. (1973). *The power motive.* New York: Free Press.

Winter, D. G. (1992). Content analysis of archival materials, personal documents, and everyday verbal productions. In C. P. Smith (Ed.), *Motivation and personality: Handbook of thematic content analysis.* New York: Cambridge University Press.

Winter, D. G. (1993). Power, affiliation, and war: Three tests of a motivational model. *Journal of Personality and Social Psychology, 65,* 532–545.

Winter, D. G. (1998). A motivational analysis of the Clinton first term and the 1996 presidential campaign. *Leadership Quarterly, 9,* 367–376.

Winter, D. G. (2002). The motivational dimensions of leadership: Power, achievement, and affiliation. In R. Riggio, S. E. Murphy, & F. J. Pirozzolo (Eds.), *Multiple intelligences and leadership* (pp. 119–138). Mahwah, NJ: Erlbaum.

Winter, D. G., & Stewart, A. J. (1978). Power motivation. In H. London & J. Exner (Eds.), *Dimensions of personality.* New York: Wiley.

Wisniewski, E. J. (1997). When concepts combine. *Psychonomic Bulletin & Review, 4*(2), 167–183.

Wisniewski, E. J. (2000). The copying machine metaphor. In D. L. Medin (Ed.), *The psychology of learning and motivation: Advances in research and theory* (Vol. 39, pp. 129–162). San Diego, CA: Academic Press.

Wittchen, H. U., Zhao, S., Kessler, R. C., & Eaton, W. W. (1994). DSM-III-R generalized anxiety disorder in the National Co-morbidity Survey. *Archives of General Psychiatry, 51,* 355–364.

Wiztum, E., Maragalit, H., & van der Hart, O. (2002). Combat-induced dissociative amnesia: Review and case example of gen-eralized dissociative amnesia. *Journal of Trauma & Dissociation, 3,* 35–55.

Wolff, G. E., & Clark, M. M. (2001). Changes in eating self-efficacy and body image following cognitive-behavioral group therapy for binge eating disorder: A clinical study. *Eating Behaviors, 2,* 97–104.

Wolfson, S. (1997). Actor–observer bias and perceived sensitivity to internal and external factors in competitive swimmers. *Journal of Sport Behavior, 20,* 477–484.

Wollersheim, J. P. (1970). Effectiveness of group therapy based upon learning principles in the treatment of overweight women. *Journal of Abnormal Psychology, 76*(3, Pt. 1), 462–474.

Wolpe, J. (1958). *Psychotherapy by reciprocal inhibition.* Stanford, CA: Stanford University Press.

Wong, C. J., Badger, G. J., Sigmon, S. C., & Higgins, S. T. (2002). Examining possible gender differences among cocaine-dependent outpatients. *Experimental & Clinical Psychophar-macology, 10,* 316–323.

Wong, D. F., Wagner, H. N., Tune, L. E., Dannals, R. F., Pearlson, G. D., Links, J. M., Tamminga, C. A., Broussolle, E. P., Ravert, H. T., Wilson, A. A., Toung, J. K. T., Malat, J., Williams, J. A., O'Tuma, L. A., Snyder, S. H., Kuhar, M. J., & Gjedde, A. (1986). Positron emission tomography reveals elevated D2 dopamine receptors in drug-naive schizophrenics. *Science, 234,* 1558–1563.

Wood, W., & Eagly, A. H. (2002). A cross-cultural analysis of the behavior of women and men: Implications for the origins of sex differences. *Psychological Bulletin, 128,* 699–727.

Wood, W., Jones, M., & Benjamin, Jr., L. T. (1986). Surveying psychology's public image. *American Psychologist, 41,* 947-953.

Woodward, A. L., & Markman, E. M. (1998). Early word learning. In D. Kuhn & R. S. Siegler (Eds.), *Handbook of child psychology. Vol. 2: Cognition, perception, and language* (5th ed., pp. 371–420). New York: Wiley.

Woodward, A. L., & Somerville, J. A. (2000). Twelve-month-old infants interpret action in context. *Psychological Science, 11,* 73-76.

Woodworth, R. S. (1918). *Dynamic psychology.* New York: Columbia University Press.

Woolf, N. J. (1998). A structural basis for memory storage in mam-mals. *Progress in Neurobiology, 55,* 59–77.

Woolfolk, R. L., Carr-Kaffashan, K., McNulty, T. F., & Lehrer P. M. (1976). Meditation training as a treatment for insomnia. *Behavior Therapy, 7,* 359–365.

Woon, T., Masuda, M., Wagner, N. N., & Holmes, T. H. (1971). The Social Readjustment Rating Scale: A cross-cultural study of Malaysians and Americans. *Journal of Cross-Cultural Psychol-ogy, 2,* 373–386.

World Health Organization. (1992). *International classification of diseases* (10th ed.). Geneva: Author.

Wright, R. (1994). *The moral animal.* New York: Vintage.

Wurtman, R. J. (1999). Neurotransmitters. In R. A. Wilson & F. C. Keil (Eds.), *The MIT encyclopedia of the cognitive sciences* (pp. 605–607). Cambridge, MA: MIT Press.

Wynn, K. (1995). Infants possess a system of numerical knowledge. *Current Directions in Psychological Science, 4,* 172–177.

Xu, F., & Carey, S. (1995). Do children's first object kind names map onto adult-like conceptual representations? In D. MacLaughlin & S. McEwen (Eds.), *Proceedings of the 19th Annual Boston University Conference on Language Development* (pp. 679–688). Somerville, MA: Cascadilla Press.

Xu, F., & Carey, S. (1996). Infants' metaphysics: The case of numeri-cal identity. *Cognitive Psychology, 30,* 111–153.

Yahiro, K., Inoue, M., & Nozawa, Y. (1993). An examination on the Social Readjustment Rating Scale (Holmes et al.) by Japanese subjects. *Japanese Journal of Health Psychology, 6*(1), 18–32.

Yang, J., Dai, X., Yao, S., Cai, T., Gao, B., McCrae, R. R., & Costa, P. T. Jr. (2002). Personality disorders and the five-factor model of personality in Chinese psychiatric patients. In P. T. Costa & T. A. Widiger (Eds.), *Personality disorders and the five-factor model of personality* (2nd ed., pp. 215–221). Washington, DC: Ameri-can Psychological Association.

Yang, S.-Y., & Sternberg, R. J. (1997). Taiwanese Chinese people's conceptions of intelligence. *Intelligence, 25,* 21–36.

Yaniv, I., & Meyer, D. E. (1987). Activation and metacognition of inaccessible stored information: Potential bases of incubation effects in problem solving. *Journal of Experimental Psychology: Learning, Memory, and Cognition, 13,* 187–205.

Yerkes, R. M., & Dodson, J. B. (1908). The relation of strength of stimulus to rapidity of habit formation. *Journal of Comparative Neurology and Psychology, 18,* 459–482.

Yonkers, K. A., & Kidner, C. L. (2002). Sex differences in anxiety disorders. In F. Lewis-Hall & T. S. Williams, et al. (Eds.), *Psy-chiatric illness in women: Emerging treatments and research* (pp. 5–30). Washington, DC: American Psychiatric Publishing.

Yonkers, K. A., Warshaw, M. G., Massion, A. O., & Keller, M. B. (1996). Phenomenology and course of generalized anxiety dis-order. *British Journal of Psychiatry, 168,* 308–313.

Yoshida, T. (1995). The effect of distraction-conflict on task per-formance: Reexamination on the energizing effect of cognitive dissonance. *Japanese Journal of Experimental Social Psychology, 35,* 80–86.

Young, E. A., McFatter, R., & Clopton, J. R. (2001). Family func-tioning, peer influence, and media influence as predictors of bulimic behavior. *Eating Behaviors, 2,* 323–337.

Young, J. E. (1990). *Cognitive therapy for personality disorders: A schema-focused approach.* Sarasota, FL: Professional Resource Exchange.

Young, J. E., Weinberger, A. D., & Beck, A. T. (2001). Cognitive therapy for depression. In D. H. Barlow (Ed.), *Clinical handbook of psychological disorders: A step-by-step treatment manual* (3rd ed., pp. 264–308). New York: Guilford.

Young, J., & Klosko, J. (1993). *Reinventing your life.* New York: St. Martin's Press.

Young, T. (1948). Observations on vision. In W. Dennis (Ed.), *Readings in the history of psychology* (pp. 96–101). New York: Appleton-Century-Crofts. (Original work published 1901)

Yuille, J. C. (1993). We must study forensic eyewitnesses to know about them. *American Psychologist, 48*(5), 572–573.

Yussen, S. R. (1977). Characteristics of moral dilemmas written by adolescents. *Developmental Psychology, 13,* 162–163.

Yzerbyt, V. Y., Rocher, S., & Schadron, G. (1996). Stereotypes as explanations: A subjective essentialistic view of group percep-tion. In R. Spears, P. J. Oakes, N. Ellemers, & S. A. Haslam (Eds.), *The social psychology of stereotyping and group life.* Cam-bridge: Blackwell.

Zaidel, E. (1983). A response to Gazzaniga: Language in the right hemisphere, convergent perspectives. *American Psychologist, 38*(5), 542–546.

Zajonc, R. B. (1965). Social facilitation. *Science, 149,* 269–274.

Zajonc, R. B. (1968). Attitudinal effects of mere exposure. *Journal of Personality and Social Psychology Monograph Supplement, 9*(2), 1–27.

Zajonc, R. B. (1980). Compliance. In P. B. Paulus (Ed.), *Psychology of group influence* (pp. 35–60). Hillsdale, NJ: Erlbaum.

Zajonc, R. B. (1984). On the primacy of affect. *American Psycholo-gist, 39,* 117–129.

Zajonc, R. B. (1998). Emotions. In D. T. Gilbert, S. T. Fiske, & G. Lindzey (Eds.), *The handbook of social psychology* (4th ed., Vol. 2, pp. 591–632). New York: McGraw-Hill.

Zajonc, R. B. (2001). Mere exposure: A gateway to the subliminal. *Current Directions in Psychological Science, 10,* 224–228.

Zajonc, R. B. (2002). Feeling and thinking: Closing the debate over the independence of affect. In J. P. Forgas (Ed.), *Feeling and thinking: The role of affect in social cognition. Studies in emotion and social interaction* (Second series, pp. 31–58). New York: Cam-bridge University Press.

Zajonc, R. B., Heingartner, A., & Herman, E. M. (1969). Social enhancement and impairment of performance in the cockroach. *Journal of Personality and Social Psychology, 22,* 242–248.

Zajonc, R. B., Pietromonaco, P., & Bargh, J. (1982). Independence and interaction of affect and cognition. In M. S. Clark & S. T.

Fiske (Eds.), *Affect and cognition* (pp. 211–227). Hillsdale, NJ: LEA Publications.

Zaleski, C. G. (1987). Evaluating near-death testimony: A challenge for theology. *Anabiosis, 5*(2), 17–52.

Zamansky, H. S., & Bartis, S. P. (1985). The dissociation of an experience: The hidden observer observed. *Journal of Abnormal Psychology, 94,* 243–248.

Zanna, M. P., & Hamilton, D. L. (1972). Attribute dimension and patterns of trait inferences. *Psychonomic Science, 27,* 353–354.

Zaragoza, M. S., McCloskey, M., & Jamis, M. (1987). Misleading postevent information and recall of the original event: Further evidence against the memory impairment hypothesis. *Journal of Experimental Psychology: Learning, Memory, and Cognition, 13,* 36–44.

Zatzick, D. F., & Dimsdale, J. E. (1990). Cultural variations in response to painful stimuli. *Psychosomatic Medicine, 52,* 544–557.

Zentall, T. (2000). Animal intelligence. In R. J. Sternberg (Ed.), *Handbook of intelligence.* New York: Cambridge University Press.

Zentall, T. R. (2000). Animal intelligence. In R. J. Sternberg (Ed.), *Handbook of intelligence* (pp. 197–215). New York: Cambridge University Press.

Zigler, E. (1982). Development versus difference theories of mental retardation and the problem of motivation. In E. Zigler & D. Balla (Eds.), *Mental retardation: The developmental-difference controversy.* Hillsdale, NJ: Erlbaum.

Zigler, E., & Berman, W. (1983). Discerning the future of early childhood intervention. *American Psychologist, 38,* 894–906.

Zillmer, E. A., & Spiers, M. V. (2001). *Principles of neuropsychology.* Belmont, CA: Wadsworth.

Zimbardo, P. G. (1972, April). Psychology of imprisonment. *Transition/Society,* pp. 4–8.

Zimmerman, B. J., Bandura, A., & Martinez-Pons, M. (1992). Self-motivation for academic attainment: The role of self-efficacy beliefs and personal goal setting. *American Educational Research Journal, 29,* 663–676.

Zola, S. M., & Squire, L. R. (2000). The medial temporal lobe and the hippocampus. In E. Tulving & F. I. M. Craik (Eds.), *The Oxford handbook of memory* (pp. 485–500). New York: Oxford University Press.

Zola-Morgan, S. M., & Squire, L. R. (1990). The primate hippocampal formation: Evidence for a time-limited role in memory storage. *Science, 250,* 228–290.

Zubenko, G. S., Hughes, H. B., Stiffler, J. S., Zubenko, W. N., & Kaplan, B. B. (2002). D2S2944 identifies a likely susceptibility locus for recurrent, early-onset, major depression in women. *Molecular Psychiatry, 7,* 460–467.

Zubin, J., & Spring, B. (1977). Vulnerability—a new view of schizophrenia. *Journal of Abnormal Psychology, 86,* 103–126.

Zubin, J., Magaziner, J., & Steinhauer, S. R. (1983). The metamorphosis of schizophrenia: From chronicity to vulnerability. *Psychological Medicine, 13,* 551–571.

Zucker, R. A., Fitzgerald, H. E., Refior, S. K., Puttler, L. I., Pallas, D. M., & Ellis, D. A. (2000). The clinical and social ecology of children of alcoholics: Description of a study and implications for a differentiated social policy. In H. E. Fitzgerald, B. M. Lester, & B. S. Zuckerman (Eds.), *Children of addiction: Research, health and policy issues* (pp. 109–141). New York: Garland Press.

Zuckerman, H. (1983). The scientific elite: Nobel laureates' mutual influences. In R. S. Albert (Ed.), *Genius and eminence: The social psychology of creativity and exceptional achievement* (Vol. 5, pp. 241–252). New York: Pergamon.

Zuckerman, M. (1998). Psychobiological theories of personality. In D. F. Barone, M. Hersen, & V. B. Van Hasselt (Eds.), *Advanced personality* (pp. 123–154). New York: Plenum Press.

Zuckerman, M. (2002). Genetics of sensation seeking. In J. Benjamin & R P. Ebstein (Eds.), *Molecular genetics and the human personality* (pp. 193–210). Washington, DC: American Psychiatric Publishing.

Zuckerman, M., & Kuhlman, D. M. (2000). Personality and risk-taking: Common biosocial factors. *Journal of Personality, 68,* 999–1029.

Zuckerman, M., Klorman, R., Larrance, D. T., & Speigel, N. H. (1981). Facial, autonomic, and subjective components of emotion: The facial feedback hypothesis versus the externalizer-internalizer distinction. *Journal of Personality and Social Psychology, 41,* 929–944.

Zurif, E. B. (1995). Brain regions of relevance to syntactic processing. In L. R. Gleitman & M. Liberman (Eds.), *Language: An invitation to cognitive science* (Vol. 1, 2nd ed., pp. 381–398). Cambridge, MA: MIT Press

Zwaan, R. A., & Radvansky, G. A. (1998). Situation models in language comprehension and memory. *Psychological Bulletin, 123,* 62–185.

CREDITS

ILLUSTRATION AND LITERARY

CHAPTER 3
63: Oliver Sacks, The Man Who Mistook His Wife for a Hat. Reprinted with permission of Simon & Schuster. Copyright © 1990, 1981, 1983, 1984, 1985 by Oliver Sacks.

CHAPTER 4
118: From Galanter, Eugene (1962). Contemporary psychophysics. In R. Brown, et al. (Eds.), New Directions in Psychology, New York: Holt, Rinehart & Winston, p. 97. Reprinted by permission. **137:** From James J. Gibson, "Shape Constancy Illusion—Door from The Ecological Approach to Visual Perception. Copyright © 1979 James J. Gibson. Reprinted by permission. **146:** From "Diederman's Geons" in "Geons" by I. Biederman from Computer Vision, Graphics, and Image Processing, 1985, No. 32. Copyright © 1985 Academic Press, Inc. Reprinted by permission. **161:** From "Average Absolute Thresholds for Different Regions of the Female and Male Skin" from Weinstein and Kenshalo, The Skin Senses, Copyright © 1968. Reprinted courtesy of Charles C. Thomas, Publishers, Ltd., Springfield, IL. **189:** From Hartman, The Biology of Dreaming, 1967. Courtesy Charles C. Thomas, Publishers, Ltd., Springfield, IL.

CHAPTER 5
175: Reprinted by permission of International Creative Management, Inc. Copyright © 1977 Alfred A. Knopf, Inc.

CHAPTER 7
247: Reprinted by permission of the publishers and the Trustees of Amherst College from The Poems of Emily Dickinson, Ralph W. Franklin, ed., Cambridge, Mass.:The Belknap Press of Harvard University Press, Copyright © 1998 by the President and Fellows of Harvard College. Copyright © 1951, 1955, 1979 by the President and Fellows of Harvard College. **251:** From "The Control of Short-term Memory" by Atkinson & Shiffrin, August 1971, Scientific American. **257:** From "Visual Images Preserve Metric Spatial Information" by Kosslyn, et al., Journal of Experimental Psychology, No.4, p. 47-60, 1978. Copyright © 1978 by the American Psychological Association. Reprinted with permission. **263:** From Bartlett, Sir Frederic C., "The War of the Ghosts" from Remembering, p. 65. Copyright Cambridge University Press. Reprinted by permission of the publisher.

CHAPTER 8
306: From Luchins, A. S., "Water Jar Problems" from "Mechanization in Problem Solving: The Effect of Einsetellung," Psychological Monographs, Vol. 54, No. 6, 1942, p. 1. Reprinted by permission of the author.

CHAPTER 12
437: From "Acquired Motivation" by R. Solomon & Corbitt, Psychological Review, No. 81, p. 119-145, 1974. Copyright © 1974 by the American Psychological Association. Reprinted by permission. **452:** From R. Plutchik, "A Language for the Emotions," Psychology Today, February 1980. Reprinted by permission from Psychology Today Magazine. Copyright © 1980 Sussex Publishers, Inc. **457:** From Unmasking the Face, 2nd Edition, by Ekman & Friesen. Copyright © 1984. Reprinted by permission of the author.

CHAPTER 13
469: Oliver Sacks, The Man Who Mistook His Wife for a Hat. Reprinted with permission of Simon & Schuster. Copyright © 1990, 1981, 1983, 1984, 1985 by Oliver Sacks. **478:** From "Qualifying Conditions for Cognitive Dissonance" from Introduction to Social Psychology, R. A. Lippa. Copyright © 1980, 1994. Reprinted by permission. **484:** From "Trait Data/Impression Formation," S. E. Asch, Journal of Abnormal and Social Psychology, Vol. 41, 1946, p. 258-290. Reprinted by permission of the author.

CHAPTER 14
504: From "Social Loafing," Latane, et al., Journal of Personality and Social Psychology, Vol. 37, 1979, p. 822-832. Copyright © 1979 by the American Psychological Association. Reprinted with permission. **509:** Reprinted by permission of Solomon Asch. **514:** From "Milgram's Results on Voltage Levels," from Obedience to Authority by Stanley Milgram. Copyright © 1974 by Stanley Milgram. Reprinted by permission of HarperCollins Publishers, Inc. **525:** From C. A. Anderson, "Temperature and Aggression," Psychological Bulletin, Vol. 106, 1989, p. 74-96. Reprinted by permission of the author.

CHAPTER 16
561: From Minnesota Multiphasic Personality Inventory [MMPI]. Copyright © The University of Minnesota 1943 (renewed 1970). This report 1983. Reprinted by permission of the University of Minnesota Press. **573:** DSM-IV Axes reprinted with permission from the Diagnostic and Statistical Manual of Mental Disorders, Fourth Edition. Copyright © 1994 American Psychiatric Association. **580:** From "Anxiety and Exams" by N. Bolger, Journal of Personality and Social Psychology, Vol. 59, No. 3, p. 531, 1990. Copyright © 1990 by the American Psychological Association. Reprinted with permission.

CHAPTER 17
618: "Effectiveness of Various Behavior Therapies," Bandura, et al., Journal of Personality and Social Psychology, Vol. 13, 1968, p. 173-199. Copyright © 1969 by the American Psychological Association. Reprinted with permission. **619:** "List of Common Irrational Beliefs." Reprinted by permission of Albert Ellis, Institute of Rational Emotive Behavior Therapy. **626:** The Twelve Steps are reprinted with permission of Alcoholics Anonymous World Services, Inc. (A.A.W.S.) Permission to reprint the Twelve Steps does not mean that A.A.W.S. has reviewed or approved the contents of this publication, or that A.A.W.S. necessarily agrees with the new expressed herein. A.A. is a program of recovery from alcoholism only-use of the Twelve Steps in connection with programs and activities which are patterned after A.A., but which address other problems, or in any other non-A.A. context, does not imply otherwise.

ca. 1664, Widener Collection, #1942.9.97 (693)Photograph © 2001 Board of Trustees, National Gallery of Art, Washington, D.C. **138:** left, The Granger Collection, New York. **142:** Kaiser Porcelain Ltd., London, England. **148:** Dr. J. E. Hawkins, Kresge Hearing Research Institute. **149:** © Ted Streshinsky/Corbis. **151:** center left, © Biophotos Associates/Science Source/Photo Researchers. **160:** © Ed Reschke/Peter Arnold, Inc. **161:** © Claus Meyer/Black Star. **163:** top left, © Dimitri Lundt/Corbis. **165:** © Biophoto Associates/Science Source/Photo Researchers.

CHAPTER 5
176: © image100/Alamy Images. **177:** © Paul Barton/Corbis. **184:** © Phyllis Picardi/Stock, Boston. **185:** Michel Siffre, © National Geographic Society-Getty Images. **186:** © Getty Images, Getty Images AsiaPac. **188:** © Philippe Plailly/SPL/Photo Researchers, Inc. **189:** © Mark Richards/PhotoEdit. **192:** © Will & Demi McIntyre/Photo Researchers, Inc. **193:** © National Library of Medicine/Peter Arnold, Inc. **194:** Stanford News Service. **196:** right, © Big Shots/Getty Images. **196:** left, © Marc Grimberg/The Image Bank-Getty Images. **199:** © Robert E. Daemmrich/Stone-Getty Images. **202:** © Norris Blake/Visuals Unlimited. **203:** right, © David Cummings, Eye Ubiquitous/Corbis. **203:** left, © Jeremy Horner/Corbis. **205:** © William Weber/Visuals Unlimited.

CHAPTER 6
215: center, © Bettmann/Corbis. **223:** Archives of History of American Psychology, University of Akron, Akron, Ohio. **224:** Courtesy of John Garcia. **225:** © Deb Cram/Portsmouth Herald. **228:** Photo by Larry Hamill. Courtesy of Kenyon College. **230:** right, © Bill Aron/PhotoEdit. **230:** left, © John Henley/Corbis. **233:** © Bill Greene/Liaison-Getty Images. **234:** © David Young-Wolff/PhotoEdit. **239:** © Dr. Albert Bandura.

CHAPTER 7
250: © Rich Beauchesne/Portsmouth Herald. **251:** © Patti Murray/Animals Animals/Earth Science. **252:** © M. Douglas/The Image Works. **253:** © Lee Snider/The Images Works. **259:** © Gale Zucker/Stock, Boston. **261:** © Michael Newman/PhotoEdit. **262:** left, © 2001 AP/Wide World Photos. **262:** right, © 2003 AP/Wide World Photos. **265:** © Owen Franken/Corbis. **268:** © Darama/Corbis. **274:** left, © Biophoto Associates/Photo Researchers, Inc. **274:** right, © Cecil Fox/Science Source/Photo Researchers, Inc.

CHAPTER 8
285: © Wellcome Department of Cognitive Neurology/SPL/Photo Researchers, Inc. **286:** © Shaywitz, et al., 1995, Nature, 373, 607-609. Courtesy of NMR Research/Yale Medical School. **290:** right, © D. Robert & Lorri Franz/Corbis. **290:** left, © Heather Angel/Natural Visions. **291:** Donna Coveny/MIT. **295:** © David Young-Wolff/PhotoEdit. **296:** ©David Young-Wolff/PhotoEdit. **298:** top, © Bonnie Kamin/PhotoEdit. **298:** left, © Will & Deni McIntyre/Photo Researchers, Inc. **300:** right, © Michael Nichols/Magnum Photos. **300:** left, © Steve Bloom Images/Alamy Images. **305:** left, © SuperStock. **305:** center, © SuperStock. **305:** right, © SuperStock. **306:** right, Cesanne, Paul, Mont Saint-Victorie, 1902-04. Philadelphia Museum of Art, George W. Elkins Collection, # E1936-1-1. **306:** left, © Scala/Art Resource, NY. **307:** © Toni Michaels/The Image Works. **310:** right, © David G Curran/Rainbow. **310:** left, © Michael Grecco/Stock, Boston. **313:** © Christiana Dittmann/Rainbow. **315:** left, Renoir, Auguste Le Moulin de la Galette, 1876, Musee d'Orsay, Paris. © Giraudon/Art Resource, NY. **315:** right, Rijks Museum Kroller-Muller, Otterlo, Netherlands/A.K.G., Berlin/SuperStock.

CHAPTER 9
327: left, © Bettmann/Corbis. **327:** top, © Bettmann/Corbis. **327:** bottom, © Rollie McKenna/Photo Researchers, Inc. **329:** left,

© Mimi Forsyth. **329:** right, © Bob Daemmrich/The Image Works. **338:** Photo by David Hines, courtesy of Sharon L. Cummings, Ph.D., University of California, Davis. **339:** Courtesy of Dr. Michael Cole. **341:** right, © 2002 AP/Wide World Photos. **341:** left, © Erika McConnell/Taxi-Getty Images. **345:** © AP/Wide World Photos. **346:** © AP/Wide World Photos. **348:** © Laura Dwight. **350:** bottom right, © Laura Dwight. **350:** bottom left, © Roy Morsch/Corbis. **350:** top left, © Thomas K. Wanstal/The Image Works.

CHAPTER 10
360: ©Sean Sprague/The Image Works. **362:** left, © Laura Dwight. **362:** right, © Laura Dwight. **362:** center, © Laura Dwight. **366:** © Claude Edelmann/Photo Researchers, Inc. **367:** © Publiphoto/Explorer/Photo Researchers, Inc. **372:** ©Bill Anderson/Photo Researchers, Inc. **373:** left, © Doug Goodman/Photo Reseachers, Inc. **373:** right, © Doug Goodman/Photo Reseachers, Inc. **374:** top, © Tony Freeman/PhotoEdit. **374:** bottom, © Tony Freeman/PhotoEdit. **374:** center, © Tony Freeman/PhotoEdit. **378:** Archives of the History of American Psychology, University of Akron, Akron, Ohio. **380:** © Laura Dwight. **382:** © Laura Dwight. **386:** left, © AP/Wide World Photos. **386:** right, © Reuters NewMedia, Inc./Corbis. **387:** © Reuters NewMedia, Inc./Corbis.

CHAPTER 11
395: bottom left, © Bill Aron/PhotoEdit. **395:** top right, © Brand X/Alamy Images. **395:** center left, © Ellen B. Senisi/The Image Works. **395:** top left, © George Chan/Photo Researchers, Inc. **396:** © Laura Dwight. **398:** © AP/Wide World Photos. **401:** © Chris Rogers/Rainbow. **404:** center, © Doug Crouch/Corbis. **404:** top left, © Laura Dwight. **404:** top right, © Laura Dwight. **406:** top left, © Brand X/Alamy Images. **406:** top right, © Donna Disario/Corbis. **406:** center left, © Michael Keller/Corbis. **406:** center right, © Norbert Schaefer/Corbis. **408:** Courtesy of Dr. Mary Strange. **409:** © Roy McMahon/Corbis. **410:** © Bill Lai/Rainbow. **411:** left, Courtesy Harlow Primate Lab, University of Wisconsin. **411:** right, Courtesy Harlow Primate Lab, University of Wisconsin. **413:** left, © David Hoffman Photo Library/Alamy Images. **413:** right, © Laura Dwight. **415:** © 2001 Becky Ah You.

CHAPTER 12
436: © Bob Krist/Corbis. **438:** © 2002 AP/Wide World Photos. **439:** © 2002 AP/Wide World Photos. **441:** © Jeff Zaruba/Corbis. **443:** right, © Brooklyn Production/Corbis. **443:** left, © Don Mason/Corbis. **445:** © Richard Howard. **448:** left, © William Thompson/Index Stock Imagery. **448:** right, © William Thompson/Index Stock Imagery. **449:** © Gianni Muratore/Alamy Images. **450:** © Bob Jones/Alamy Images. **453:** © Robbie Jack/Corbis. **454:** © Nita Winter/The Image Works. **455:** © Tom Walker/Stock, Boston. **458:** Ekman, P., Friesen, W. V., & O'Sullivan, M. (1988). Smiles: "Genuine" and "Fake" Journal of Personality and Social Psychology, 54, 414-420. Reprinted by permission of Paul Ekman. **460:** © Jerry Millevoi/Stock, Boston.

CHAPTER 13
470: © ePhoto/Alamy. **472:** © Hugo Philpott/Getty Images. **473:** © Bettmann/Corbis. **475:** left, © Michael Goldman/Photis/PictureQuest. **475:** right, © Sergio Pitamitz/Corbis. **477:** © Mark Peterson/Corbis Saba. **483:** © Michael Newman/PhotoEdit. **486:** © Bob Daemmrich/Stock, Boston. **489:** left, © AP/Wide World Photos. **489:** right, © Alexandre Luis Serra/The Image Bank-Getty Images. **491:** right, © Kavaler/Art Resource, NY. **491:** left, © Martha Cooper/Peter Arnold, Inc.

CHAPTER 14
503: © PhotoNetwork/Alamy Images. **505:** © 2003 AP/Wide World Photos. **509:** (all) Dr. Solomon Asch, courtesy of Florence

NAME INDEX

Names are located in both the main text and the captions of the figures.

Aaronson, D., 298
AAUW Education Foundation, 403
Abbate-Daga, G., 494
ABC Research Group, 311, 484
Abel, L., 336
Abelson, R., 291
Abrahamson, A., 479
Abrams, D., 504
Abrams, R., 620
Abramson, L. Y., 586
Ackerman, P. L., 341
Ackil, J. K., 264
Acredolo, L. P., 296
Acton, G. S., 567
Adams, G. R., 587
Adams, H. F., 348
Adams, M. J., 296, 351
Adelson, J., 414
Adler, A., 541-542, 545, 556, 580
Adler, N., 650
Adler, S. A., 265
Adolphs, R., 81
Agnew, J., 620
Aguilar, C. M., 289
Ahlborn, H. H., 420
Ahmed, S., 186
Ahn, W.-K., 375
Ainsworth, M. D. S., 407, 423, 491, 544
Akahane-Yamada, R., 317
Akerstedt, T., 206
Akhtar, N., 296
Albano, A. M., 462, 581
Alberini, C., 226
Albert, D. J., 523
Albright, T. D., 176
Alcock, K. J., 348
Aldhous, M., 186
Alexander, J., 653
Alexander, J. M., 380
Alicke, M. D., 486
Alimohamed, S., 629
Alkire, M., 337-338
Allen, R., 300
Allen, S., 601
Allen, V. L., 520
Allison, T., 184
Alloy, L. B., 586
Allport, G. W., 471, 522, 550
Allum, P., 318
Alvarez, M. de J., 387
Alvarez, M. T., 387
Amabile, T. M., 314, 315, 440
Amaral, D. G., 249

Ambady, N., 167
American Assocation of University Women (AAUW) Education Foundation, 403
American Association on Mental Retardation, 347
American Psychiatric Association, 573-574, 596, 597, 632
Ames, C., 444
Amianto, F., 494
Amodio, D. M., 521
Amsel, E., 362
Anand, B. K., 445
Anastasi, A., 332
Anderson, B. K., 200, 201
Anderson, C., 375, 381
Anderson, C. A., 525
Anderson, E. R., 644
Anderson, J. R., 17, 257, 301
Anderson, K. N., 373
Anderson, K. O., 654
Anderson, N. B., 650
Andersson, B. E., 413
Andreasen, N. C., 581, 592
Andrew, 353
Andrews, G., 578, 624, 630
Angelou, M., 315
Angier, N., 410
Angleitner, A., 551
Anglin, J. M., 296
Ani, C., 348
Anson, O., 644
Antony, M. M., 577
Antrobus, J., 184, 188, 191
Appelbaum, M. I., 370
Arai, Y., 620
Archer, J., 405, 523
Arcus, D., 404
Arend, R., 40
Arendt, H., 526
Arendt, J., 186
Arieti, S., 591
Aristotle, 6-7
Arkes, H. R., 474
Armeli, S., 441
Armour, D. A., 32
Arnold, K. D., 420
Arnold, M. B., 460
Aro, M., 318
Aron, A., 492
Aron, A. P., 488
Aron, L., 544
Aronson, J., 46, 507-508
Asakura, 494
Asch, S. E., 483-484, 508-511
Asher, S. R., 410
Ashman, S. B., 409
Ashmore, M., 454
Aspinwall, L. G., 660

Asquith, P., 416
Astatke, H., 502
Astington, J. W., 380
Ataca, B., 646
Athenstaedt, U., 527
Atkinson, J. W., 438, 558
Atkinson, R. C., 189, 205, 250-251
Atkinson, R. L., 189
Atoum, A. O., 503
Atran, S., 289, 382
Attanucci, J., 420
Atwater, J. B., 405
Auerbach, J. S., 544
Auerbach, S. M., 653
Austin, G. A., 289
Averill, J. R., 453, 524
Axelson, J. A., 613
Ayers, M. S., 264
Azrin, N. H., 525
Azuma, H., 412
Azuma, S. D., 366

Babinsky, R., 274
Bachnan, H. J., 348
Back, K., 489
Badcock, D. R., 123
Baddeley, A., 253, 261, 269, 270, 271
Badger, G. J., 240-241
Baer, J. S., 200
Bagwell, C., 414
Bahrick, H. P., 251, 259, 260, 384
Bahrick, L. E., 441
Bahrick, P. O., 260, 384
Bailey, C., 369
Bailey, C. H., 226
Bailey, J. M., 451
Baillargeon, R., 370, 375
Baker, D. B., 9, 10
Baker, D. P., 403
Bakshi, V. P., 462
Bales, R. F., 502
Balkin, J., 522
Ball, T. M., 257
Ballenger, J. C., 624
Balota, D. A., 264
Baltes, P. B., 384-385
Banaji, M. R., 292, 520, 521, 527
Bandi Rao, S., 294
Bandler, R., 80
Bandura, A., 238-239, 405, 443-444, 524, 527, 549, 555, 556, 581, 618
Bane, C., 654
Banko, K. M., 441
Banks, M. S., 366
Bao, J. X., 226
Barbaranelli, C., 443-444, 527
Barber, T. X., 194, 195

Bard, P., 459
Barefoot, J. C., 650
Bargh, J., 461, 520, 521
Barker, R. G., 525
Barlow, D. H., 462, 581, 623-624
Barnes, M. L., 31, 492, 543
Barnes, R. C., 353
Baron, R. A., 523, 524, 525
Baron, R. S., 503
Baron-Cohen, S., 353, 382, 597
Barr, C. E., 592
Barr, H. M., 366
Barrett, K. C., 397
Barrett, P. T., 336
Barron, B., 42
Barry, T., 525
Barsalou, L. W., 289
Bartholomew, K., 410
Bartis, S. P., 195
Bartlett, F. C., 261-263
Bartlett, K., 476
Bartlett, M. Y., 449
Bartoshuk, L. M., 154, 155
Bashore, T. R., 384, 456
Basil, M. D., 20
Basoglu, M., 646
Basow, S. A., 472, 563
Bassok, M., 312
Bastik, T., 308
Bates, E., 298
Bates, E. A., 286
Bates, J. E., 403
Batler, M. B., 189
Batson, C. D., 517-518
Batson, J. G., 518
Bauer, P. J., 380
Baum, A., 653
Baumberger, T., 293
Baumeister, R. F., 38, 195, 526-527
Baumrind, D., 412, 420
Baumstark, K. E., 419
Bava, A., 195
Baxter, L. R., 611
Bayley, N., 364, 365, 368
Baynes, K., 82
Bazana, P. G., 336
Beach, F. A., 490
Beadle-Brown, J., 629
Beall, A. E., 407
Bear, M. E., 65
Beatty, W. W., 447
Becher, M., 107
Beck, A. T., 17, 581, 586, 618, 619-620, 627, 631
Becker, B., 414
Becker, E. F., 107
Beeri, R., 275
Beidel, D. C., 581
Beilin, H., 363

Joseph, L., 503
Joseph, S., 552
Joslyn, S., 260
Jost, J. T., 521, 527
Judd, C. M., 520, 527
Juechter, J., 523
Juel-Nielsen, N., 350
Julien, R. M., 366
Jung, C., 192, 542-543, 545, 556, 614
Jurkovac, T., 487
Jusczyk, P. W., 299
Jussim, L. J., 182

Kaemingk, K. L., 107
Kaemmer, B., 558
Kagan, 401, 403, 404, 405, 409
Kagan, J., 396, 397, 404, 554
Kagitcibasi, C., 510
Kahlo, F., 315
Kahneman, D. D., 181, 309-310, 311
Kail, R. V., 378
Kaiser, P. K., 132
Kalbe, E., 277
Kalin, N. H., 106, 462
Kalish, C. W., 375
Kalmar, D. A., 153
Kalsner, S., 76
Kambara, T., 525
Kamin, L., 218, 340
Kamins, M., 402
Kandel, E., 13, 57, 176, 226
Kane, J., 622
Kanner, A., 460
Kant, I., 4, 7-8, 214
Kantrowitz, B., 413
Kaplan, B. B., 586
Kaplan, J. R., 647
Kaplan, N., 410
Kaplan, S. L., 631
Kapur, S., 147
Karau, S. J., 504, 520
Karlin, R. A., 195
Karno, M. P., 630, 631
Karnovsky, M. L., 185
Karpas, A. E., 523
Karwautz, 494
Kasper, S., 589
Kassin, S. M., 475, 509, 520
Katz, D., 471-472
Katz, D. L., 98, 524
Katz, I., 508
Katz, J. J., 290
Katzelnick, D. J., 62
Kaufman, A. S., 326, 328
Kaufman, J. C., 18, 314, 338-340
Kaufmann, C. A., 586
Kaufman-Scarborough, C., 475
Kauh, T. J., 398
Kay, P., 294
Kaye, D., 472
Keane, M., 290
Kearins, J. M., 380
Kearsley, R., 396, 397
Keating, D. P., 380
Keefe, F. J., 662

Keefe, R. C., 491
Keefer, L., 196
Keesey, R. E., 446
Keil, A., 37
Keil, F. C., 363, 382
Keilp, J., 586
Keith, K. W., 122
Keller, H., 327, 328
Keller, J., 483
Keller, M., 420, 576, 582
Kelley, A. E., 462
Kelley, H. H., 476, 510
Kellman, P. J., 362
Kelly, A. E., 34
Kelly, D. J., 224
Kelly, S. J., 107
Kelsoe, J. R., 586
Keltner, D., 452
Kemeny, M. E., 647
Kemnitz, J. W., 446
Kempthorne-Rawson, J., 562
Kendall, P. C., 618
Kennard, B. D., 502
Kennedy, A. E., 462
Kennedy, C. B., 370
Kennedy, J. F., 262
Kennedy, R. S., 164
Kenny, D. A., 470
Kenrick, D. T., 18, 405, 491
Kenshalo, D. R., 161, 162
Kent, G., 426
Keohane, S., 426
Keppel, G., 254
Kernberg, O. F., 544
Kerns, R., 658
Kerr, B., 366
Kerr, N. A., 503
Kessler, J., 277
Kessler, R. C., 491, 576
Kessler Shaw, L., 382
Ketcham, K., 260, 265
Kettermann, A., 317
Khersonsky, R. A., 490
Khubchandani, L. M., 293
Kiang, N. Y., 150
Kidner, C. L., 577
Kiecolt-Glaser, J. K., 3, 644, 645
Kienhorst, J. C. W. M., 586-587
Kierein, N. M., 485
Kiesler, D. J., 630
Kihlstrom, J. F., 181, 195, 276, 341
Kilby, E., 425
Kilinc, A., 613
Killen, M., 510-511
Kilmann, P. R., 620
Kim, E. J., 630
Kim, S. G., 96
Kim, U., 510
Kim, Y., 490
Kimes, L. A., 38
Kimura, D., 286-287
King, K. H., 634
King, L. A., 434, 559-560
Kinnunen, T., 194
Kinsey Institute, 450
Kipp, K., 338
Kirkley, B. G., 562

Kirmayer, L., 580
Kirschner, P., 472
Kitagawa, 494
Kitamura, T., 650
Kitayama, S., 400, 439, 482
Klaczynski, P., 335
Klahr, D., 378, 381
Klassen, A. D., 450
Klein, K. L., 147
Klein, M., 544
Klein, S. B., 276
Kleinknecht, R. A., 580
Kleinmuntz, B., 456
Kleitman, N., 188
Klerman, G. L., 582
Klesges, R. C., 447
Kline, R. P., 551
Klineberg, O., 38
Klonsky, B. G., 520
Klorman, R., 458
Klosko, J., 620
Kluger, A. N., 487
Knauer, E., 276
Knauth, P., 34
Kniskern, D. P., 627
Knowles, J. A., 586
Knowlton, B. J., 249, 269
Knox, V. J., 195
Koback, K. A., 62
Kobak, R. R., 410
Kock, P., 277
Kocsis, R., 601
Koda, N., 57
Koehler, J. J., 310
Koehler, N., 166
Koelling, R., 223-224
Koenig, O., 257, 274
Koenig, T., 92
Koestner, R., 438, 440, 441, 442
Koffka, K., 13, 15
Kogan, N., 107
Kohlberg, L., 25, 417-420, 423-425
Köhler, W., 13, 15, 147, 304, 305
Kohn, M. L., 412
Kohn, P. M., 644
Kohnstamm, G. A., 396
Kohut, H., 544
Kokes, F. R., 589
Kolar, D. C., 552
Kolatu, G., 448
Kolb, B., 226, 274, 285, 286
Kolodner, K. B., 650
Kolotkin, R. L., 562
Kolstad, V., 373
Koob, G. F., 198
Koopmans, M., 93
Kop, P. F. M., 116
Kopta, S. M., 629, 630
Korf, R., 303
Koriat, A., 253
Korichneva, I. L., 651
Korner, A., 387
Korpan, C. A., 313
Koski, G., 185
Koslowski, B., 312

Kosslyn, S. M., 17, 92, 257-258, 274
Kotsiubinskii, A. P., 642
Kowert, P. A., 505
Koyama, 494
Kozlowski, L. T., 146
Kozulin, A., 42
Kraemer, R., 510
Krafka, C., 524
Krahn, G. L., 55
Kramer, D., 375
Kramer, M. A., 591
Kramer, R., 419
Krampe, R. T., 308
Krantz, D. S., 650, 653, 656
Krantz, L., 310
Krasnikova, T. L., 651
Kraus, S., 527
Krause, M. A., 214
Krause, M. S., 629
Krauthammer, C., 582
Krefetz, D. G., 17
Kremer, K. E., 382
Kries, J. A. von, 126
Krinsky, S., 167
Krison, D., 454
Kroll, N. E. A., 82
Kroner-Herwig, B., 656
Krosnick, J. A., 182
Krueger, J., 185, 312
Krupa, D. J., 274
Kruschke, J. K., 290
Ksir, C., 198, 202
Kübler-Ross, E., 421
Kuboki, T., 448
Kubovy, M., 137, 166
Kuffler, S. W., 70
Kuhl, P. K., 294, 317
Kuhlman, D. M., 505, 555
Kuhn, D., 375, 381
Kuhn, T. S., 34, 314
Kujala, T., 318
Kulik, J. A., 262, 486
Kulik, L., 490
Kunda, Z., 482
Kunik, M. E., 523
Kuo, Z. Y., 434
Kurtines, W., 363, 419
Kurtzberg, T. R., 440
Kusulas, J. W., 650
Kusumi, 494
Kvale, G., 200
Kyllonen, P. C., 335, 336

Labouvie-Vief, G., 375, 384
Lacaille, R. A., 650
Lack, L., 186
Ladefoged, P., 287
LaFraniere, S., 268
Lagace-Seguin, D. G., 414
LaGanga, M. L., 632
Lagerspetz, K., 239, 524
Laing, R. D., 591, 600
Laird, J. D., 479
Lamb, M. E., 397, 408, 409
Lamberg, L., 192
Lambert, M. J., 629, 631

Rothman, D. L., 96
Rotter, J. B., 548, 555, 556
Rotton, J., 525
Rouhani, S., 420
Rousseau, J.-J., 366
Rovee-Collier, C., 261, 265, 372
Rovera, G. G., 494
Rovine, M., 408, 413
Rowe, E. T., 447
Rowe, S. M., 375
Rozin, P., 454
Rubenstein, G. 563
Rubert, E., 300-301
Rubin, D., 263
Rubin, G. S., 124
Rubin, K. H., 414, 462
Rubin, V., 205
Ruble, D. N., 403, 439
Ruch, J. C., 193
Rucker, D. D., 471
Rudorfer, M. V., 275
Rudy, T. E., 656, 657, 658
Rudy, V., 624
Ruffman, T., 382
Rugg, M. D., 64
Rule, S. R., 524
Runco, M. A., 314
Runeson, S., 146
Rusak, B., 186
Russell, D. E., 546-547
Russell, J., 456, 461
Russell, R. J. H., 644
Russell, W. R., 271
Ruthsatz, J., 347
Rutter, M., 104, 106, 362, 553
Ryan, C. S., 527
Ryan, R. M., 440, 441, 442-443, 618
Ryder, W., 264
Rymer, R., 298, 410
Rypma, B., 17

Sack, L., 583
Sack, R. L., 186
Sackett, G., 387
Sacks, O., 63, 64, 276-277, 469, 470
Sadalla, E. K., 491
Sadeh, A., 206-207
Sadker, D., 403
Sadker, M., 403
Safer, D. J., 446
Sagan, E., 545
Sahraie, A., 182
Sainsbury, A., 446
Sakamoto, J., 232
Salapatek, P., 366
Salekin, K., 601
Salekin, R. T., 601
Salili, F., 255, 536
Salovey, P., 17, 20, 33, 341, 449, 455
Salthouse, T. A., 385
Salvio, M. A., 189
Samella, K., 353
Samelson, F., 38
Sameroff, A. J., 409

Sampson, P. D., 366
Samson, A. W., 529
Sandberg, E. H., 375
Sandell, J., 126
Sanders, G. S., 503
Sanders, M. D., 182
Sanders, S. A., 524
Sanders, S. H., 656
Sanderson, C. A., 528
Sanderson, M., 190
Sanderson, W. C., 17, 578, 581, 620
Sandler, I., 644
Sandman, C. A., 413
Sanford, E., 191
Sansone, C., 384
Sapir, E., 293
Sarason, S., 340
Saraswathi, T. S., 394
Sargent, 494
Sarid, O., 644
Sartorius, N., 576, 589, 624
Saszik, S., 107
Sattler, J. M., 328
Saucier, G., 551
Savage, D., 107
Savage-Rumbaugh, S., 300-301
Savary, F., 312
Savin, D. B., 490
Savoie, T., 594
Sawin, D. B., 408
Saxe, L., 456
Scarborough, E., 38
Scardamalia, M., 40
Scarr, H. A., 361, 411
Scarr, S., 345, 413
Schachter, S., 460, 489, 509
Schacter, D. L., 81, 249, 262, 264, 265, 271, 276
Schadron, G., 485
Schafer, R., 557
Schaffer, H. R., 294
Schaie, K. W., 384
Schaller, M., 517
Schank, R., 291, 340
Schapiro, S., 75
Schappell, L., 387
Schappell, R., 387
Scharfe, E., 410
Scharli, H., 182
Schauble, L., 381
Scheff, T. J., 591
Scheibel, A., 75
Scheier, M. F., 535
Schell, D. A., 384
Schiefele, U., 403
Schiffer, F., 86
Schiffman, S., 154
Schildkraut, J. J., 586
Schilling, O., 124
Schliemann, A. D., 340, 381
Schmaling, K. B., 200
Schmidt, F. L., 329
Schmitt, B. H., 503
Schmitt, D. P., 18, 491
Schnall, S., 479
Schneider, M. L., 107

Schneider, W., 378
Schnur, T., 46
Scholmerich, A., 412
Schonfield, D. H., 384
Schreiber, S., 620
Schroeder, D. H., 645
Schroeder, M. A. B., 490
Schroeder-Helmert, D., 185
Schroth, M. L., 557
Schultz, L. A., 523
Schultz, S., 592
Schulz, S. C., 589
Schulze, P. A., 412
Schulz-Hardt, S., 485, 505
Schumacher, J. R., 462
Schwanenflugel, P. J., 380
Schwartz, A. J., 443
Schwartz, B., 226
Schwartz, B. L., 253
Schwartz, D., 42
Schwartz, G. E., 642
Schwartz, J., 454
Schwarz, N., 481
Schweizer, E., 624
Scott, A. I. F., 620
Scott, T. H., 435
Scott, T. R., 154
Scovern, A. W., 620
Scoville, W., 271
Scribner, S., 307
Sears, D. O., 485
Sears, R. R., 525
Sebastian, R. J., 239
Sedlacek, W. E., 563
Segal, B., 200
Segal, N., 386
Segal, N. L., 553
Segall, M. H., 106
Sehgal, M., 650
Sehulster, J. R., 264
Seidenberg, M. S., 17, 301
Seidman, L. J., 592
Seifer, R., 348
Seifert, C. M., 308
Sekuler, A. B., 123
Sekuler, R., 123
Selfridge, O., 144, 145
Seligman, M. E. P., 23, 48, 223, 236, 441, 585, 629, 631, 654
Sell, R. L., 450
Selten, R., 484
Selye, H., 647, 649
Semmler, G., 57
Senf, W., 613
Sepple, C. P., 445
Sera, M. D., 293
Seraganian, P., 446
Serdahely, W. J., 183
Serline, R. C., 62
Serpell, R., 339, 502
Servan-Schreiber, D., 176
Seurat, G., 16
Seuss, Dr., 367, 377
Sevcik, R. A., 300-301
Seymour, R. B., 197, 201, 202, 204, 206
Shackelford, T. K., 18, 449, 491

Shadish, W. R., 631
Shaefer, J. A., 660
Shaffer, D. R., 490
Shaffer, L., 9
Shafir, E., 309
Shakespeare, W., 284
Shallice, T., 17, 301
Shanab, M. E., 514
Shapiro, D., 202
Shapiro, D. A., 630
Shapiro, D. H., 196
Shapiro, J. R., 396
Shapiro, P., 265
Shapiro, R., 589
Sharp, D. W., 313, 339
Sharpe, L. T., 146
Shatz, M., 293
Shaughnessy, M. F., 618
Shaver, P., 159, 410, 454, 491-492
Shavitt, S., 510
Shaw-Barnes, K., 475
Shaywitz, B. A., 51, 287
Shear, M. K., 578, 623
Shearer, D. S., 650
Shedler, J., 651
Sheinman, L., 443
Shekelle, R. B., 562, 650
Shelton, J. R., 382
Shelton, S. E., 462
Shepherd, G., 64, 65
Sheppard, J. A., 504
Sherif, C. W., 521
Sherif, M., 521
Sherman, S. J., 264, 483, 520
Shevell, S. K., 132
Shibazaki, M., 87
Shields, J., 350
Shiffrin, R. M., 250-251, 308
Shimada, M., 87
Shin, J., 220
Shipley, M. T., 80
Shipster, C., 425
Shir, J. L., 529
Shneidman, E. S., 586, 588
Shonkoff, J., 394
Shontz, F. C., 660
Shook, M. D., 310
Shook, R. L., 310
Shuit, D. P., 632
Shulman, G. L., 97
Shulman, H. G., 253
Shulman, R., 494
Shulman, R. G., 96
Shumaker, S. A., 582
Shupe, A. K., 409
Sibitani, A., 87
Sidanius, J., 521
Siebert, C., 317
Siegel, B. V., 336
Siegel, L., 654
Siegler, R. S., 295, 364, 365, 374, 378, 380, 381
Siegman, A. W., 650
Siers, B., 521
Siffre, M., 185
Sigman, M. D., 370
Sigmon, S. C., 240

Sigmon, S. T., 583
Signorielli, N., 472
Silberstein, L. R., 448
Silver, R. L., 660
Silverman, I., 41
Silverstein, B., 447
Simek-Morgan, L., 613
Simeon, D., 578
Simmons, L. W., 166
Simmons, R. W., 107
Simon, D. P., 39, 336
Simon, H., 13, 16, 38, 308, 309
Simon, H. A., 39, 301, 336, 363
Simon, R., 36
Simon, T., 327-328
Simon, W. H., 449
Simons, D. J., 46
Simonton, D. K., 102, 157, 315, 316
Simpson, C., 446
Simpson, J. A., 492
Simpson, O. J., 20
Simpson, S. G., 584
Sincoff, J. B., 380
Singer, D., 17, 192
Singer, J., 272, 460
Singer, J. A., 192
Singer, J. L., 17, 192
Singh, J., 167
Singh, R., 485
Sivers, H., 17, 81
Sizemore, C., 595-596
Skae, E., 472
Skinner, B. F., 4, 13, 15, 25, 228, 548
Skodol, A. E., 590
Skoric, M., 472
Slagter, A., 395
Slobin, D., 299
Sloboda, J. A., 39, 308
Slobounow, S., 36
Sloman, S. A., 312
Slomine, B. S., 397
Slovic, P., 311
Sluyter, D. J., 341
Smart, J. Jr., 164
Smetana, J. G., 416
Smith, A., 642, 647
Smith, A. J., 594
Smith, B. N., 503
Smith, D., 612
Smith, D. A., 644
Smith, D. E., 197, 201, 202, 204, 206, 510
Smith, D. W., 107
Smith, E. E., 189, 269, 290, 485
Smith, J. C., 645
Smith, J. D., 387
Smith, L., 371
Smith, M. E., 92
Smith, M. L., 617, 630
Smith, M. R., 592
Smith, N. K., 460
Smith, P. B., 502, 510
Smith, R. A., 33
Smith, S. M., 314
Smith, T. W., 650

Smolensky, P., 301
Snarey, J. R., 419, 420
Sneed, C. D., 552
Snidman, N., 404
Snow, C., 294, 299
Snow, R. E., 42, 336
Snow, S. C., 650
Snyder, C. R., 23
Snyder, M., 555
Sohn, M.-H., 17
Sokol, M., 558
Soler, E., 525
Solomon, A., 607
Solomon, G. F., 659
Solomon, J., 408
Solomon, R., 435-437, 438
Somberg, B. L., 385
Somerville, J. A., 382
Sommer, T., 176
Sommerville, R. B., 25
Sookman, D., 581, 620
Sorenson, K., 516
Souza, T., 81
Spalding, T. L., 290
Spangenberg, E. R., 182
Spangler, W., 558
Spanos, N. P., 194, 195, 596
Spearman, C., 334-335
Spear-Swerling, L., 45, 296
Speer, D. C., 628
Speigel, N. H., 458
Spelke, E., 378
Spellman, B. A., 312
Spence, J., 439, 440-441
Spence, M. J., 294, 367
Spencer, S., 507
Sperling, G., 252
Sperry, R., 13, 17, 84-86
Spevack, M., 651
Spiegel, D., 631
Spielberger, C. D., 455
Spiers, M. V., 89
Spitzer, L., 437
Spitzer, R. L., 590
Spooner, W., 292
Sporakowski, M. J., 415
Sprecher, S., 490
Spring, B., 572
Springer, S. P., 92
Squire, L. R., 76, 81, 96, 249, 269, 271, 274, 275
Sroufe, L. A., 396, 397, 409, 410, 423-424
Srull, T. K., 520
Staats, A. W., 472
Staats, C. K., 472
Stacy, A. W., 200
Stallworth, L. M., 521
Standing, L., 249
Standing, L. G., 482
Stankov, L., 335, 341, 455
Stanley, J. C., 405
Stanovich, K. E., 40, 52, 308
Starc, R., 550
Stark, S., 335
Starr, R. H., 405
Stasson, M. F., 503

Stastny, J., 583
Stattin, H., 369
Staub, E., 38, 526-527, 601
Staudinger, U. M., 385
Staw, B., 494
Stayton, D. J., 407
Stebbins, G. T., 17
Steedman, M., 312
Steele, A., 241
Steele, C., 46, 344
Steele, C. M., 507-508
Steele, R. L., 421
Steenland, K., 186
Steer, R. A., 17
Stefannaci, L., 81
Stein, B. S., 38, 351
Stein, G., 315
Stein, I. F., 445
Stein, M. B., 462, 581
Steiner, M., 576-577
Steinhauer, S. R., 572
Stelmack, R. M., 336
Stemberger, R. T., 581
Stenberg, C., 397
Stephens, P. M., 460
Steriade, M., 82
Stern, P., 348
Stern, R. M., 36
Stern, W., 328
Sternbach, R. A., 162
Sternberg, R. J., 10, 17, 18, 23, 33, 34, 38, 39, 42, 45, 53, 104, 106, 153, 292, 296, 301, 303, 307, 308, 311, 314, 316, 326, 333, 334, 335, 336, 339, 340, 341-343, 344, 345, 346, 348, 349, 351, 361, 377, 380, 384, 385, 407, 440, 488, 492-493, 502, 528, 541, 543, 667
Sternberg, S., 255-256
Stevenage, S. V., 426
Stevens, A., 258
Stevens, N., 414
Stewart, A. J., 438, 558
Stewart, E., 626
Stewart, S. L., 462
Stickgold, R., 188
Stiffler, J. S., 586
Stiles, J., 286
Stiles, W., 490, 630, 631, 632
Stillwell, A. M., 527
Stipek, D. J., 403
Stöber, J., 36
Stoffregan, T. A., 164
Stone, G. C., 642
Stony, C. M., 650
Stoohs, R. A., 190
Stopa, E. G., 186
Stotland, E., 471
Stough, L., 335
Stowell, J. R., 3
Strauss, B., 487-488
Strauss, J. S., 572, 589
Street, M. D., 505
Streissguth, A. P., 107, 366
Stricker, E. M., 434, 446
Strickland, B., 586

Striegel-Moore, R. H., 448
Stroebel, C. F., 196
Stromswold, K., 297
Stroop, J. R., 177
Strough, J., 384
Strupp, H. H., 612, 614
Stunkard, A. J., 634
Stuttard, J., 634
Styron, W., 582
Su, Y., 116
Suematsu, H., 448
Sugarman, H. J., 601
Sullivan, H. S., 541
Sullivan, J. M., 205
Suls, J. M., 486
Super, D., 416
Surkis, A., 651
Susser, E. S., 592
Sutherland, R. J., 107
Sutherland, S. E., 107
Sutton, S. K., 554
Suvorov, Y. I., 651
Suzuki, L. A., 339, 570
Swann, W. B. Jr., 441
Swanson, C., 492
Swanson, K., 492
Sweeny, M., 224
Swets, J. A., 119
Swinson, R. P., 577
Szasz, T., 591, 600
Szkrybalo, J., 403
Szmukler, G., 578
Szucko, J. J., 456
Szymanski, K., 504

Tajfel, H., 521
Tal, J., 412
Tamis-LeMonda, C. S., 412
Tanaka, J. R., 147
Tandon, R., 589
Tanford, S., 510
Tang, C., 336
Tanner, W. P. Jr., 119
Tanouye, S., 580
Tantam, D., 578
Tardif, T., 269, 270, 293
Tauber, R. T., 42
Taussig, H., 316
Taves, P. A., 479
Tavris, C., 453
Taylor, D. M., 502
Taylor, E. H., 592
Taylor, J. A., 190
Taylor, M. E., 196
Taylor, S., 35, 523, 570
Taylor, S. E., 32, 470, 642, 645, 650, 654, 659, 660
Taylor, S. P., 525
Teague, G., 438
Teghtsoonian, R., 120
Teitelbaum, G., 446
Teitelbaum, P., 445
Tellegen, A., 553, 558
Teller, D. Y., 367
Temoshok, L., 659
Terhune, K. W., 438
Terman, L. M., 328, 329, 346

Terrace, H., 300
Tesch-Römer, C., 308
Tesser, A., 33
Tetlock, P. E., 505
Teuber, H. L., 271
Thagard, P., 312, 313
Thal, D., 286
Thales, 4, 25
Thanos, P. K., 634
Thatcher, R. W., 370
Thelen, E., 361
Thelen, N., 485
Theroux, P., 292
Thigpen, C., 595, 596
Thoits, P. A., 645
Thoma, S. J., 419
Thomas, A., 404-405
Thomas, A. K., 260
Thomas, D., 133
Thomas, J. D., 107
Thomas, K. M., 365
Thomas, R. M., 374
Thomas, V. J., 162
Thompson, A., 426
Thompson, L., 629
Thompson, L. A., 347
Thompson, R. A., 299, 394, 404, 409
Thompson, R. F., 274, 405
Thompson, S. C., 656
Thompson, S. K., 239
Thompson, W. R., 105
Thomson, D., 261
Thorn, T., 527
Thorndike, E. L., 10, 12, 14, 15, 227
Thorndike, R. L., 328
Thornhill, R., 157, 166
Thurstone, L. L., 334, 335
Tiggeman, M., 447
Timberlake, W. T., 239
Timko, C., 241
Tinklenberg, J. R., 205
Tinsley, B. J., 408
Tinsley, D. J., 34
Tinsley, H. E., 34
Titchener, E., 10, 11
Titus, L. J., 487
Tobias, B. A., 181
Tobias, I. P., 181
Toda, S., 412
Todd, P. M., 311, 484
Tohkura, Y., 317
Tolman, E. C., 237-238, 444
Tomarken, A. J., 460
Tomasello, M., 299
Tomaszuk, A., 446
Tomes, H., 38
Tomkins, S., 454, 456
Tononi, G., 184
Tooby, J., 18, 312, 338
Torff, B., 343, 384
Torgesen, J. K., 45, 296
Tormala, Z. L., 471, 473
Torrey, E. F., 592, 609, 612
Torsvall, L., 206
Tourangeau, R., 456

Towle, B., 340
Townsend, J. T., 256
Tranel, D., 81
Trapnell, P. D., 551
Trauner, D., 286
Travagline, A., 476
Treadway, M., 265
Treasure, 494
Treiman, R., 296
Treisman, A., 177, 180
Treisman, M., 164
Trevarthen, C., 84-86
Triandis, H., 439, 502, 510
Triggiano, P. J., 596
Tripathi, A. N., 262
Triplett, N., 502
Trivers, R., 405, 518
Tronick, E. Z., 394
Troop, 494
Trost, M. R., 405, 491
Trow, 563
Trulson, M. E., 205
Truscott, S. D., 7
Truth, S., 316
Tryon, R., 105
Tsunoda, T., 87
Tuchman, B. W., 219-220
Tully, T., 226
Tulving, E., 17, 81, 96, 248, 249, 251, 253, 259, 261
Turiel, E., 416, 417
Turk, D. C., 162, 656, 657, 658
Turnbull, C., 134-135
Turner, C. F., 450
Turner, J. C., 504, 521
Turner, J. R., 645
Turner, M. E., 505
Turner, M. L., 336
Turner, R. J., 591
Turner, R. S., 132, 133
Turner, S. M., 581
Turner, T., 292
Tversky, A., 309-310, 311
Twamley, E. W., 529
Ty, T. C., 657
Tyrka, A. R., 529
Tyrrell, D., 642, 647
Tyson, M., 523
Tzischinsky, O., 186

Uchizono, K., 185
Ugurbil, K., 96
Uhde, T. W., 581
Uhlenhuth, E. H., 189
Ulla, 318
Ulrich, R., 525
Underwood, B., 254, 527
U.S. Bureau of the Census, 643
Urbina, S., 332
Urbszat, D., 447
Uylings, H. B. M., 65, 72

Valdes, G., 43
Valencia, R. R., 339
Valenstein, E., 445, 620
Valente, J., 563
Vallerand, R. J., 441

Valois, 494
Van Dalen, A., 601
Van der Hart, O., 276
Van der Kolk, B. A., 544
Van der Ven, 647
Van Essen, D. C., 147
Van Gogh, V., 315
Van Hoesen, G. W., 88
Van Knippenberg, A., 520
Van Ord, A., 589
Van Schaik, D. J. F., 629
Van Tonder, G. J., 167
Van Wieringen, J. C., 349
Vance, S. L., 521
Vandell, D., 414, 423
Vangu, M. di T., 620
VanLeeuwen, M. D., 503
Vasquez-Suson, K. A., 521
Vaughan, C., 184, 191
Vaughn, B. E., 409
Velting, D. M., 551
Verfaellie, M., 265
Vermeer, J., 136-137
Vernon, P. A., 336, 338
Veroff, J., 558
Vertue, F., 462
Vezzani, S., 167
Vickers, R. R., 650
Vigée-Lebrun, M., 491
Viglione, D. J., 557
Vijayan, S., 294
Vincent, M. A., 529
Viney, W., 15
Vinokur, A., 504
Vishton, P. M., 294
Visser, G. H. A., 413
Vogel, E. H., 220
Volek, J., 634
Volkow, N. D., 634
Volpe, S. L., 634
Von Bekesy, G., 57
Von Fersen, L., 218
Von Rosen, K., 420
Vonk, R., 520
Vosburg, S. K., 205
Vvan de Vijver, F. J. R., 116
Vye, N., 42
Vygotsky, L. S., 365, 371, 375-378, 383, 401

Wadden, T. A., 447
Wade, C., 203, 403, 451
Wade, J. B., 662
Wadhwa, P. D., 413
Wagenaar, W., 264
Wagner, A. R., 42, 220-221
Wagner, N. N., 645
Wagner, R. K., 308, 329, 341
Wagner, R. L., 594
Wagner, R. V., 518
Wagonfeld, M. O., 591
Wahl, H.-W., 124
Wahlsten, D., 104, 335, 349
Wakita, M., 232
Wald, G., 133
Walder, D. J., 594
Waldman, I. D., 345

Walker, A., 315
Walker, B. A., 504
Walker, E. F., 593-594
Walker, L., 420
Walker, P. A., 449
Walker, R. A., 370
Wall, P. D., 162, 657
Wall, W., 407
Wallace, B., 185
Wallace, B. G., 70
Wallace, M., 582
Wallace, R. K., 196
Wallace-Capretta, S., 194
Waller, M. J., 475
Wallin, P., 490
Walsh, D. C., 626
Walsh, M. L., 523
Walsh, W., 46
Walster, E., 489, 490, 492
Walster, G. W., 490, 492
Walters, G. C., 229
Walters, P., 563
Walters, R. H., 229
Walz, N. C., 490
Wang, G.-J., 634
Wang, Y., 646
Wang, Y. E., 504
Wangensteen, O. H., 445
Ward, J. C., 504
Ward, L. M., 118
Ward, T. B., 314
Warrington, E., 182
Warshaw, M. G., 576
Washburn, A. L., 445
Washburn, D., 167
Washburn, M. F., 38
Wason, P. C., 34, 312
Wass, T. S., 107
Wasserman, R., 405
Watanabe, H., 425, 510-511
Watanabe, S., 232
Waters, E., 407, 409, 410
Watson, J. B., 13, 14-15, 34, 222-223, 572
Watts, W. A., 563
Waxman, S. R., 363
Weaver, D. R., 186
Webb, W. B., 184
Weber, E., 120, 416
Weber-Luxenberger, G., 277
Wechsler, D., 329
Wegener, D. T., 473
Weiller, C., 286
Weinberg, M. K., 396
Weinberg, R. A., 345, 413
Weinberger, A. D., 619
Weinberger, D. R., 592
Weinberger, J., 19, 438
Weiner, B., 434
Weingartner, H., 275
Weinstein, R., 42
Weinstein, S., 161
Weir, C., 384
Weisberg, R. W., 305, 314
Weiskrantz, L., 182, 269
Weiss, B., 631
Weiss, R., 44, 410

savings and, 221, 222
spontaneous recovery in, 221, 222
stimulus discrimination, 223
stimulus generalization, 222-223
Web resources, 245
Classical neurotransmitters, 76
Classically conditioned learning, 14
Client-centered therapy, 615
Clinical, 43-44
Clinical interviews, 609-610
Clinical psychology. *See also* Therapy
  autistic savant syndrome, 353
  bulimia, 529
  drug addiction treatment, 241
  ethical dilemmas, 25
  facial disfigurement, 426
  fads, 494
  fetal alcohol syndrome (FAS), 107
  motivation, 437-440
  nonconformists, 563
  obesity, 634
  overview of, 22
  psychogenic amnesia, 276
  shyness, 462
  sleep deprivation, 206
  snipers, 601
  training and job description for, 24
Closure, 142, 143
Clozapine, 622
CNS. *See* Central nervous system (CNS)
CNS depressant. *See* Central nervous system (CNS) depressant
CNS stimulant. *See* Central nervous system (CNS) stimulant
Cocaine, 203, 204, 240-241
Cochlea, 150
Cocktail party phenomenon, 177
Codeine, 198
Cognitive-behavioral approach
  antecedents of, 548
  Bandura's social-cognitive theory, 549
  evaluation of, 549-550
  Rotter's social-learning theory, 548
Cognitive consistency, 476-477
Cognitive development. *See also* Cognitive psychology; Intelligence; Thinking
  in adulthood, 384-385
  continuity versus discontinuity in, 362-363
  definition of, **360**
  domain generality and domain specificity in, 363-364
  of inductive reasoning, 381-382
  internalization and, 377
  maturation and learning in, 361-362
  of memory, 378-380
  milestones in, 363-364, 365
  moderate-discrepancy hypothesis of, 370
  of perceptual understanding, 378
  Piaget's theory of, 365, 371-375, 375, 383
  of problem solving, 381
  of quantitative skills, 381
  questions in study of, 361-365
  research methods on, 364-365
  theory of mind and, 382-383
  of verbal comprehension and fluency, 380-381
  Vygotsky's theory of, 365, 375-378

Web resources, 391
  zone of proximal development, 377-378
Cognitive dissonance, 477-478, 479
Cognitive-evolutionary theory, 397-398
Cognitive map, 237-238
Cognitive neuroscience, 25
Cognitive psychology. *See also* Cognitive development; Intelligence; Thinking
  of anxiety disorders, 581
  of autistic savant syndrome, 353
  definition of, 16
  of emotions, 460-461
  of ethical dilemmas, 25
  of fads, 494
  of mood disorders, 586
  of motivation, 440-444
  overview of, 21
  of psychological disorders, 572
  of schizophrenia, 592
  of second-language learning, 317, 318
  of sleep deprivation, 206
  of symmetry, 167
Cognitive theorists, 378, 383
Cognitive therapies, 618-620
Cognitive therapy (Beck), **619**-620
Cognitivism, 13, **16**-17
Cohort effects, 364
Cold fibers, 161-162
Collective, 502
Collective unconscious, 542-543
Collectivism, 439, 489-490, 504, 510, 525
Color-blindness, 130
Color vision, 130-134
Columbia Space Shuttle, 505
Commitment, 492-493
Common movement, 142
Communication. *See also* Language
  compared with language, 299-300
  in groups, 502
  in marriage, 492-493
Community mental-health centers, 628
Community psychology, 627-629
Comorbidity, 576
Complexes, 542
Compliance, 508, 511-512
Componential theory, 290
Composition fallacy, 53
Comprehension monitoring, 380
Compulsion, 579
Computer-assisted language learning (CALL), 318
Computerized axial tomogram (CAT), 94, 95, 611
Concentrative meditation, 195-196
Concept (unit of symbolic knowledge), **289**
Concepts (semantic memory), **259**
Concordance, 576
Concrete operations, 373-373
Condensation, 538
Conditioned emotional responses, 225-226
Conditioned response (CR), 216-217, 223-224, 237
Conditioned stimulus (CS), 216-218, 227-228, 237
Conditioning. *See* Classical conditioning; Learning; Operant conditioning
Conduct disorders, 597

Cones, **125**-126, 128
Confidentiality, 55, 632
Confirmation bias, 34, 485, 486
Conflict-avoiding marriage, 415
Conflict resolution, 505
Conformity, 508-511
Conjoined twins, 386-387
Conscience, 417, 418, 538
Conscientiousness, 551, 554
Conscious versus unconscious, 18
Consciousness
  altered states of, 183-184
  attention, 176-181
  controlling and, 181
  definition of, **176**
  dreams, 188, 191-192, 538, 614
  hypnosis, 193-95
  intelligence and, 337-338
  levels of, 181-184
  meditation, 195-196
  monitoring and, 181
  near-death experience, 183
  preconscious level, 182, 538
  psychoactive drugs, 197-206
  sleep, 184-190, 206-207
  subconscious level, 182-183
  unconscious versus conscious, 18, 183, 537, 545
  Web resources, 211
Conservation of liquid quantity, 373, 374
Constructive memory, 261-268
Consulting psychologists, 20, 24
Consumer psychologists, 24
Contact hypothesis, 522
Context effects, 145-146
Contextualist, 339
Contingency, 217-218
Continuous reinforcement, 234
Contralateral transmission in brain, 82
Contrast principle, 289-290
Control, 42
Control condition, 46
Control-enhancing interventions, 654-655
Control group, 46-47
Controlled experimental design, 49-50
Controlling, 181
Conventional morality, 417-419
Conventionality principle, 289
Convergent thinking, 301, 302
Cooing, 295
Coping, 649
Cornea, 123, 125
Coronary heart disease, 651
Corpus callosum, 78, **82,** 84
Correlation, 51-52, 673-675
Correlation coefficient, 673
Correlational design, 50, 51-52
Correlational methods, 51-52
Counseling psychology, 24, 241, 529
Counterconditioning, 226, 616
Countertransference, 614
Crack cocaine, 203, 204
Creativity, 302, 314-317, 440
Credibility, 474
Critical period, 297-299
Critical thinking, 52-54, **301**-302
Cross-complain, 492

Eclectic therapy, 612
Ecstasy (MDMA), 205
ECT (electroconvulsive therapy), 620
Educational psychology. *See also* Learning
  autistic savant syndrome, 353
  nonconformists, 563
  overview of, 22
  second-language learning, 317-318
Educational Testing Service (ETS), 357
EEG, 92-93, 187-188, 194, 196, 370
Effexor, 622
Ego, 18, **538**, 539, 571
Ego analysis, 614
Ego ideal, 539
Egocentrism, 54, 362, **373**
Elaborative rehearsal, 253
Elavil, 622
Elderly. *See also* Adulthood
  ageism against, 369
  Alzheimer's disease and, 76, 274, 275, 384,
    644
  cognitive development and, 384-385
  personality development of, 399
  physical development and, 384
  summary on social development during, 425
  Web resources, 391
  wisdom and, 385
Electra conflict, 540
Electroconvulsive therapy (ECT), 620
Electroencephalogram (EEG), 92-93,
  187-188, 194, 196, 370
Electromagnetic spectrum, 123, 124
Embryonic stage, 365
Emetic, 221
Emotion-focused coping, 649
Emotional development, 395-398. *See also*
  Emotions
Emotional intelligence, 341, 455
Emotions. *See also* Motivation
  anger, 397, 452, 453
  basic emotions, 454
  central nervous system and, 460
  classical conditioning of, 222-223, 224-226
  cognitive approaches to, 460-461
  cognitive-evolutionary theory of, 397-398
  cultural approaches to, 453, 454, 456, 457,
    461
  definition of, **395**, 452
  differentiation theory of, 396
  discrete-emotions theory, 397
  disgust, 452, 454
  endocrine system and, 460
  evolutionary value of, 454-455
  facial-feedback hypothesis of, 456-458
  fear and anxiety, 222-223, 225, 398, 452,
    453, 462
  flashbulb memories and, 262
  happiness, 397, 452, 453
  measurement of, 455-458
  physical appearance of, 456
  Plutchik's emotion wheel, 452
  psychophysiological approaches to, 458,
    460
  sadness and grief, 397, 421-422, 452, 454
  temporal-sequence theories of, 460-461
  two-component theory of, 460
  Web resources, 466

Empirical methods, 6
Empiricist, 6
Employment, 416
Empty-nest syndrome, 415
Encoding, 251-252, 253, 256-257, 260-261
Encoding specificity, 261
Endocrine system, 97-100, 460
Endogenous morphines, 198
Endorphins, 198, 662
Engineering psychology, 23, 24, 117
England. *See* United Kingdom
Entrenchment, 305
Enzymatic deactivation, 74, 76
Enzymes, 76
Epinephrine, 460, 645, 656
Epiphenomenon, 194
Episodic buffer, 269
Episodic memory, 259
Equilibration, 371
Equity theory, 490
Erikson's theory of psychosocial development,
  398-400
Eros, 492
ERP (event-related potential), 92-93
Estradiol, 523
Estrogen, 449
Ethical dilemmas, 25
Ethics
  in animal research, 55-56
  confidentiality, 55, 632
  debriefing of research subjects, 55
  deception of research subjects, 54-55
  informed consent, 55, 633
  institutional review boards (IRBs), 56
  pain administered to research subjects, 55
  in research, 54-56
  in therapy, 632-633
Ethnic/racial groups. *See* African Americans;
  Asian Americans; Latino Americans;
  Socially defined racial/ethnic groups
Ethological psychology, 166
Etiology, 572
ETS (Educational Testing Service), 357
Eugenics, 327
Event-related potential (ERP), 92-93
Evil, 526-528
Evolution of ideas, 101-102, 157
Evolutionary psychology
  aggression and, 523
  creativity and, 316-317
  definition of, **18**, 101
  emotions and, 454-455, 462
  evolutionary theory and, 100-102, 117, 157
  evolution of ideas and, 101-102, 157
  fear and shyness and, 462
  intelligence and, 338-339
  language and, 299
  love and, 491
  overview of, 13, 18
  perception and, 137-138
  personality and, 554
  sexual desire and, 449
  symmetry and, 166
Exchange, 417, 418
Exemplars, 290
Exercise, 642, 666
Exhaustive serial processing, 256

Exocrine system, 97
Exorcism, 571, 608
Expectations for the future, 542
Experiment
  control condition, 46
  controlled and quasi-experimental designs,
    49-51
  definition of, **45**
  experimental and control groups in, 46-47
  experimental condition, 46
  variables in, 46, 667
Experimental analysis of behavior, 228-230
Experimental condition, 46
Experimental group, 46-47
Experimental methods, 45-47
Experimental neurosis, 225-226
Experimental psychology, 240-241, 276. *See
  also* Experiment; Research and research
  methods
Expertise and problem solving, 308
Explanation, 41-42
Explanatory style, 441
Explicit memory, 249
Explicit theories, 652
External locus of control, 548
Exteroceptive systems, 159
Extinction, 221, 222, **233**-234, 237
Extinction procedures, 617
Extrinsic motivators, 315, 416, **440**-441, 444
Extrinsic reinforcers, 618
Extroversion, 550, 551, 554
Eye. *See also* Vision
  deteriorating functioning of, with age,
    123-124
  diagram of, 125
  functional organization of, 123-126
  neural pathways to brain from, 126, 127
  rods and cones in, 126-128
Eye movement hypothesis, 164
Eyewitness accounts, 264-265, 267, 268
Eysenck's three dimensions of personality,
  550-551

Facial disfigurement, 425-426
Facial expressions, 166-167, 456-458
Facial-feedback hypothesis, 456-458
Factor analysis, 334-335
Fads, 494
Fallacies in logic, 53-54
False cause fallacy, 53
False-consensus effect, 312
False memory, 266-267, 632
Family, 394, 415-416. *See also* Adolescence;
  Children; Parenting
Family systems therapy, 626-627
FAS. *See* Fetal alcohol syndrome (FAS)
Fathers. *See* Males
Fear. *See also* Phobia
  classical conditioning of, 222-223, 225, 581
  distinguished from phobia, 580
  emotion of, 398, 452, 453
  shyness and, 462
Feature-detector approach, 142, 144
Feature hypothesis of language acquisition,
  295
Feature-matching theories, 144
Feelings. *See* Emotions

historical trends in prevention and treatment, 643
hospital care, 653-656
leading causes of death, 643
living with serious health problems, 659-661
mind-body connection, 642-643
obesity, 445, 446-447, 466, 634
overview of, 22
pain management, 654, 659
patient-doctor relationship, 653
recognizing and interpreting symptoms, 652
SARS, 421, 659-660
sleep deprivation, 206
stress, 644-652
Type-A versus Type-B behavior patterns, 649-651
Web resources, 665-666
Hearing
absolute threshold for, 118
brain and, 150, 152
duplicity theory of, 153
frequency theory of, 152-153
functional organization of ear, 149-150
of infants, 366-367
locating sounds, 153
place theory of, 151-152
sound waves, 147-149
theories of, 150-153
Heart disease, 651
Heaven's Gate cult, 506
Heinz's dilemma, 417-419
Helping behavior. See Prosocial behavior
Hemispheres of brain, 82-87, 286, 289, 370
Heritability. See also Genetics
adoption studies and, 352
of aggression, 523
chromosomes, 104-105
definition of, **104**
of handedness, 104, 106
of intelligence, 104, 106, 349-352
mental retardation, 348
nature and nurture, 106
of personality, 553-554
of schizophrenia, 589
selective breeding, 105
twin studies and, 349-351, 386, 523, 553
Heritability coefficient, 349
Hertz (Hz), 148-149
Heuristics
attribution heuristics, 480-482
availability heuristic, 310-311
decision making and judgment, 309-311
definition of, **303**, 480
impression formation, 484-486
problem solving, 303
representativeness heuristic, 310
take the best heuristic, 311
Hierarchical learning, 240
Hierarchical log linear analysis, 487
Hierarchy of needs, 439-440
Higher-order conditioning, 222
Hindbrain, 78-79, 80
Hippocampus, 78, **81**, 274, 275
Hispanics. See Latino Americans
Histrionic personality disorder, 598

HIV-positive, 644, 659
HMOs (health maintenance organizations), 652
Holophrases, 295
Homeostatic regulation, 437, 438
Homework versus testing, 219-220
Homosexuality, 450-452, 633
Homunculus, 87, 88, 89
Hong Kong, 255, 662
Honor, culture of, 481, 525
Hopelessness depression, 586
Horizontal cells, 125
Hormones, 97, 98, 446, 449, 460, 523-524, 645, 656
Horney's psychoanalytic theory, 543-544
Hospital care, 653-656
Hostile aggression, 523, 525
Hotlines, 628
Hue, 130-132
Human factors psychology, 117
Human Genome Project, 17, 104
Humanism, 546
Humanistic psychology
of anxiety disorders, 581
definition of, **19**
evaluation of, 547
of Maslow, 19, 439-440, 546
of mood disorders, 585
overview of, 13, 19
of psychological disorders, 572
of Rogers, 19, 546-547
of schizophrenia, 591
Humanistic therapies, 614-615
Hunger, 445-448
Hunger regulation theories, 445-446
Hybrids, 102-103
Hyperthyroidism, 98
Hypnosis, 193-95, 608-609, 659
Hypothalamus, 58, 78, 80, **82**, 99, 185, 445, 449, 462, 586, 623
Hypothesis
null hypothesis, 48, 675
in research, 39
Hypothesis testing, 299
Hypothetical construct, 38
Hypothyroidism, 98
Hysterical symptoms, 541

ICD (International Classification of Diseases), 573
Iconic store, 252
Icons, 252
Id, 18, **538**, 539, 571
Ideal self, 546
Idealistic principle, 539
Ideas, evolution of, 101-102, 157
Identity achievement, 400
Idiosyncrasy credits, 511
Illness. See Health psychology; and specific illnesses
Ill-structured problems, 303-305
Illusions, 187
Illusory correlation, 520
Image-based encoding, 257-258
Imaginary audience, 415
Imipramine (Tofranil), 622
Imitation, 296-297

Implicit memory, 249-250
Implicit theories, 652
Implosion therapy, 617
Impression formation, 483-486
Impression of light intensity, 128
In vivo study, 93
Incentive-motivation theory of attitude change, 476-477
Incest, 450
Incidence, 576
Incubation, 307-308
Incus, 150
Independence, 400
Independent variables, 46, 667
India, 262-263, 439
Individual rights, 418, 419
Individualism, 417, 418, 439, 504, 510, 525
Inductive reasoning, 312, 314-315
Industrial psychology, 24, 494
Infantile amnesia, 271
Infants. See also Children
attachment and, 159, 407-410
capabilities of, 366-369
cognitive development of, 370-371, 372-373
difficult babies, 404-405
easy babies, 404-405
extinction and, 234
fear and shyness of, 462
motor development of, 368-369
perceptual abilities of, 366-367
personality development of, 398, 399
psychological disorder of, 597
reflexes of, 367
separation anxiety and, 396, 407
sleep apnea and, 190
slow-to-warm-up babies, 404
stranger anxiety and, 396
sudden infant death syndrome (SIDS), 190
summary on social development of, 423
symmetry perception of, 167
temperament of, 404, 554
Infectious disease, 647, 655-656
Inferential statistics, 48, 675-676
Inferiority complex, 542
Information processing, 335-336
Informed consent, 55, 633
Ingroups, 520
Insanity defense, 599-600
Insanity Defense Reform Act, 600
Insight, 304-305, 613
Insomnia, 188-189
Instinct theory, 434
Institutional review boards (IRBs), 56
Instrumental aggression, 523
Intelligence. See also Cognitive development; Thinking
adoption studies of, 352
in adulthood, 384-385
aptitude and achievement tests, 329, 331
assessment issues, 332-333
autistic savant syndrome, 352-353
biological models of, 336-338
brain size and, 338
computational models of, 335-336
consciousness and, 337-338
crystallized intelligence, 335, 385

cultural and contextual models of, 339-340
definitions of, **326-332**
deviation IQs, 332
electrophysiological evidence on, 336
emotional intelligence, 341, 455
environmental differences in, 345
evolutionary theory of, 338-339
fluid intelligence, 335, 384, 385
g factor, 334-335
giftedness in, 346-347
group differences in, 344-345
heritability of, 104, 106, 349-352
hierarchical model of, 335
historical perspectives on, 326-328
improvement of, 351
as information processing, 335-336
mental age and intelligence quotient, 328
mental retardation, 347-348
metabolic evidence on, 336, 338
multiple intelligences (Gardner), 340-342
practical intelligence, 342
praising children's intelligence, 402
psychometric models of, 334-335
ratio IQ, 328
sex differences in, 344
social intelligence, 341
socially defined racial/ethnic group
    differences in, 344-345
systems models of, 340-343
tests of, 328-329, 331-333
Thurstone's primary mental abilities, 335
triarchic theory of, 341-343
twin studies of, 349-351, 386
Web resources, 357
Intelligence tests, 328-329, 331-332
Intensity-difference method of locating
    sounds, 153
Intensity of sensory stimulus, 121
Interactionist perspective on personality, 555,
    557
Interactive images, 273
Interdependence, 400
Interest, 398
Interference, 253-254, 259-260
Interference theory, 254
Intermittent reinforcement, 234
Internal-External (I-E) Control Scale, 548
Internal locus of control, 548
Internalization, 377
International Classification of Diseases (ICD),
    573
Interneurons, 70, 124-125
Interoceptive systems, 159
Interpersonal conformity, 417, 418
Interpersonal development
    attachment, 407-411
    child care and children's development,
        411-414
    marriage and family, 415-416
    parenting styles, 412
    peer interactions, 414-415
    work world, 416
Interposition, 139
Interval schedule of reinforcement,
    234-235
Intimacy, 492-493
Intoxicated, 200

Intrapersonal development, 407
Intrinsic motivators, 315, 416, **440**-443, 444
Introspection, 10-11
Investment theory of creativity, 316
Invincibility fallacy, 415
Invulnerability trap, 54
Ions, 72
Ipsilateral transmission in brain, 82
IQ, 328, 331-333, 340, 344-347, 350-352. *See
    also* Intelligence
IRBs (institutional review boards), 56
Iris, 123, 125
Irrelevant conclusion fallacy, 53
Islam, 580
Isocarboxazid (Marplan), 622
Israel, 409, 529
Italian Americans, 340
Italian language, 293, 317

James-Lange theory, 459
Japan
    anxiety disorders, 580
    attachment, 409
    conformity, 510-511
    dementia in, 384
    emotions and facial expressions, 456, 457
    language processing, 86-87
    motivation, 439
    pain perception, 662
    parenting styles, 412
    self-concept, 400
    in World War II, 473
JAS (Jenkins Activity Survey), 649-650
Jenkins Activity Survey (JAS), 649-650
Jet lag, 186
Jnd (just noticeable difference), 120
Joy, 397. *See also* Happiness
Judgment and decision making, 302,
    309-311, 322
Jung's analytical psychology, 542-543
Jury selection, 20
Just noticeable difference (jnd), 120
Justice, universal principles of, 418, 419
Justification of effort, 477

K-complexes, 187
Keyword system, 273
Kinesthesis, 162
Kinsey Institute, 450
Klonopine, 624
Koan, 196
Kohlberg's model of moral development,
    417-420
Korea, 490, 519, 563
Korean language, 293
Korsakoff's syndrome, 201
Kosovars, 525
Kosovo, 514
Kpelle tribe, 339

Labeling emotions, 460
Labeling theory, 591-592
LAD (language-acquisition device), 297
Lamictal, 586
Language
    acquisition of, 294-299
    animals and, 299-301

aspects of, 287, 289-294
brain and, 83-84, 86-87, 285-289, 317
characteristics of, 284-285
conditioning in acquisition of, 297
cooing and babbling, 295
critical periods for acquisition of, 297-299
definition of, **284**
evolutionary processes in acquisition of,
    299
explanations of language acquisition,
    296-299
hemispheres of brain and, 83-84, 86-87,
    286, 289
holophrastic speech, 295
imitation in acquisition of, 296-297
linguistic relativity, 292-293
linguistic universals, 294
pragmatics, 291-292
prenatal influences on, 294
second-language learning, 298, 317-318
semantics, 289-290
sex differences in, 286-287, 344
stages of language acquisition, 294-296
syntax, 291
telegraphic speech, 295-296
thought and, 292-294
Web resources, 322
Language-acquisition device (LAD), 297
Latency, 540, 541
Latent content, 538, 614
Latent learning, 237
Latino Americans, 340, 344
Law of effect, 12, 227-228
Learned helplessness, 236, 585-586, 654
Learning. *See also* Classical conditioning;
        Operant conditioning
    avoidance learning, 229-230
    classical conditioning, 214-226, 236-238
    definition of, **214, 361**
    direct instruction for, 378
    distributed learning, 259
    hierarchical learning, 240
    language acquisition, 296-299
    latent learning, 237
    massed learning, 259
    maturation and, 361-362
    mediated learning experiences, 378
    operant conditioning, 227-238
    preparedness for, 223
    second-language learning, 298, 317-318
    social learning, 238-239, 405-406, 472-473,
        524, 548-549
    synaptic bases for, 75
    systems view of, 239-240
    Web resources, 245
Learning Potential Assessment Device, 377
Learning psychology, 462. *See also*
        Educational psychology; Learning
Left hemisphere. *See* Cerebral hemispheres
        (left and right)
Legal issues on psychological disorders,
    599-600
Lens, of eye, **123,** 125
Leptin, 446
Levels-of-processing model of memory, 269
Lexicon, 287
Liars' facial expressions, 458

Phantom-limb pain, 657
Phencyclidine (PCP), 205
Phenelzine (Nardil), 622
Phenothiazines, 621
Phenotype, 102, 103
Phenylketonuria (PKU), 348
Pheromones, 157-158
Philosophy, 5
Phobias, 577-578, 580. *See also* Fear
Phoneme, 287
Phonological loop, 269
Phony Type Bs, 651
Photopigments, 126
Photoreceptors, 125
Phrase-structure grammars, 291
Physical anthropology, 3
Physical attractiveness, 489-490
Physical development
   in adolescence and adulthood, 369-370
   of brain, 369-370
   continuity versus discontinuity in, 362-363
   domain generality and domain specificity
      in, 363-364
   of infants and children, 366-369
   maturation and learning, 361-362
   neural development, 369-370
   in prenatal period, 365-366
   questions in study of, 361-365
   research methods on, 364-365
Physical self, 401
Physiological needs, 440
Physiological psychology, 25, 57, 435-437,
   438
Physiology, 2, 5
Piaget's theory of cognitive development, 365,
   371-375, 375, 383
Piece-work wages, 234
Pilot studies, 40
Pinna, 150
Pitch, 148
Pituitary gland, 78, **99**
PKU (phenylketonuria), 348
Place theory, 151-152
Placebo effect, 182
Plasticity, 75, 385
Play, 414-415
Pleasure principle, 538
PNS. *See* Peripheral nervous system (PNS)
Political psychology, 23, 601
Polychronic cultures, 475-476
Polygraph, 44-45, 456
Pons, 78, 79, 80
Ponzo illusion, 135, 136
Population, 675
Population parameters, 47
Pornography, 524
Positive correlation, 51, 52
Positive psychology, 23
Positive punishment, 229, 231
Positive reinforcement, 228, 231
Positive reinforcer, 228
Positive transfer, 259
Positively skewed distribution, 671-672
Positron emission tomography (PET), 95,
   96-97, 269, 337-338, 611
Postconventional morality, 418, 419
Postformal thinking, 375, 385

Posthypnotic suggestion, 193
Posttest, 50
**Posttraumatic stress disorder (PTSD),
   578**, 666
Postural instability theory, 164
Potentiation, 226
Practical intelligence, 342
Pragma, 492
Pragmatics, 291-292
Pragmatism, 11
Preconscious, 182, 538
Preconventional morality, 417, 418
Prediction, 42
Predictive validity, 332-333
Prefrontal lobotomy, 620
Prejudice
   definition of, **519**
   ingroups and outgroups, 520
   reduction of, 522
   Robber's Cave study of, 521
   social categorization and stereotypes,
      519-520
   theories of, 521
Premack principle, 230-231
Premises, 312
Prenatal development
   of brain, 79, 365-366
   fetal alcohol syndrome (FAS), 107, 201,
      366
   intelligence and, 345
   language acquisition and, 294
   mental retardation and, 348
   schizophrenia and, 592
   stages of prenatal period, 365
   tobacco use by mothers, 204
Preoperational stage, 373
Preparedness to learn, 223
Prescriptive grammar, 291
Pressure, skin sense of, 159
Pretest, 50
Prevalence, 576
Prevention
   historical trends in, 643
   of psychological disorders, 627-628
Primacy effect, 255, 484-485, 486
Primary appraisal, 460, 648-649
Primary colors, 132-133
Primary motor cortex, 87, 88
Primary narcissism, 591
Primary prevention, 627
Primary-process thought, 538
Primary reinforcers, 231
Primary sex characteristics, 369
Primary smells, 156-157
Primary somatosensory cortex, 87, 89
Priming, 250
Principle of contrast, 289-290
Principle of conventionality, 289
Prison experiment (Zimbardo), 526
Proactive interference, 254, 259
Problem-focused coping, 649
Problem solving
   in adulthood, 384
   in children, 381
   definition of, **301-302**
   dreams and, 191-192
   expertise and, 308

   functional fixedness as hindrance to, 307
   heuristics and algorithms for, 303
   hindrances to, 305-308
   ill-structured problems, 303-305
   incubation and, 307-308
   insight and, 304-305
   mental sets and fixation as hindrance to,
      305-307
   transfer and, 307
   well-structured problems, 303
Procedural memory, 249, 250, 271, 274
Productive thinking, 304
Projection, 540
Projection areas, 87
Projection fibers, 81
Projective tests, 557-558
Propaganda, 473
Proprioception, 159
Prosocial behavior
   altruism, 517-519
   bystander intervention, 515-517
   definition of, **515**
   peacemaking, 518-519
Prosopagnosia, 147
Prospective memory, 272
Prototype theory, 290
Proverbs, 34, 222, 229, 238, 434
Proxemics, 291
Proximity, 141, 143, 489
Prozac, 622
Psychedelics, 204-206
Psychoactive drugs
   alcohol abuse and treatment, 200-201
   amphetamines, 202-203
   barbiturates, 201-202
   caffeine, 202
   central nervous system (CNS) depressants,
      197, 199-202
   central nervous system (CNS) stimulants,
      197, 202-204
   cocaine, 203, 204, 240-241
   definition of, **197**
   hallucinogens, 197, 204-206
   LSD, 77, 205, 571
   marijuana, 205
   MDMA (ecstasy), 205
   narcotics, 197, 198-199
   phencyclidine (PCP), 205
   tobacco, 203-204
   tolerance and dependency, 198
   tranquilizers, 201-202
   treatment for addicted women, 240-241
Psychoanalysis, 18, 19, 292, 537-541,
   613-614, 638. *See also* Freudian theories;
   Psychodynamic theory
Psychobiology, 17, 21, 166
Psychodynamic methods of therapy, 613-614
Psychodynamic theory. *See also* Freudian
   theories
   Adler's individual psychology, 541-542
   of anxiety disorders, 580
   biology and adaptation and, 537
   common components of, 537
   conflict and, 537
   defense mechanisms, 539
   definition of, **18**
   dreams, 191, 192, 538, 614

Serotonin, 76, **77**, 204, 275, 586, 662
Sertraline (Zoloft), 622
Service dogs, 57
SES. *See* Socioeconomic status (SES)
Set-point theory, 446
Sex and sexuality, 448-452, 466, 540, 541
Sex/gender differences
  conformity, 510
  creativity, 315-316
  friendships, 414-415
  intelligence, 344
  language, 286-287, 344
  major depression, 582, 585-586
  motivation, 439
  perception of date rape, 449-450
  self-esteem, 403
  spatial ability, 41-42, 344
  suicide, 587
Sex hormones, 449, 523-524
Sex-role stereotypes, 472-473
Sexual abuse
  by therapists, 632
  of children, 260
  false memories of, 632-633
Sexual disorders, 574
Sexual scripts, 449
Shadow, 543
Shadowing, 177
Shape constancy, 135-136
Shaping, 233
Short-term memory, 252-256, 269-270
Short-term store, 250-251
Shyness, 462
SIDS (sudden infant death syndrome), 190
Sight. *See* Vision
Sign language, 298, 300-301
Signal-detection analysis, 117-118
Signal-detection theory (SDT), 117-118
Signs, 652
Similarity, 141, 143, 490
Simulating paradigm, 193-194
Simultaneous conditioning, 217
Singapore, 659
Single-cell recording, 121
Situational attribution, 480
Size constancy, 134-135
Skeletal muscles, 68
Skin senses, 118, 159-162
Skinner boxes, 228
Sleep
  circadian rhythms and, 185-186
  daylight's effect on sleep cycles, 185-186
  deprivation in, 187, 206-207
  disorders in, 188-190
  dreams and, 188, 191-192, 538, 614
  microsleep, 187
  neurochemical influences on sleep cycles, 86
  N-REM sleep, 188, 189
  reasons for and benefits of, 184-185
  recommendations for getting good night's sleep, 189
  REM sleep, 188, 189, 206
  stages of, 187-188
Sleep apnea, 190
Sleep deprivation, 187, 206-207
Sleep disorders, 188-190

Sleep spindles, 187
Sleep state misperception, 189-190
Sleeping pills, 189
Sleepwalking, 190
Slips of the tongue, 292
Slow-to-warm-up babies, 404
Smell, 118, 156-158, 523
Smiling, 166, 490
Smooth muscles, 68
Snipers, 601
Social action and, 20
Social categorization, 519-520
Social cognition
  attitudes, 471-480
  attraction, 488-491
  attributions, 481-483
  culture of honor, 481, 525
  definition of, **470**
  fads, 494
  impressions, 483-488
  liking, 490-491
  love, 491-493
  social comparison, 486
  spectators at athletic events, 487-488
Social-comparison theory, 486
Social contracts, 418, 419
Social desirability and attribution, 481, 482
Social development
  attachment, 407-411
  child care and children's development, 411-414
  death and dying, 421-422
  definition of, **394**
  emotional development, 395-398
  Erikson's psychosocial development theory, 398-400
  facial disfigurement and, 425-426
  interpersonal development, 407-416
  Marcia's achievement of personal identity, 400
  marriage and family, 415-416
  moral development, 416-420
  parenting styles, 412
  peer interactions, 414-415
  personality development, 398-407
  psychosexual development and gender typing, 405-407
  self-concept, 400-403
  self-esteem, 401, 403
  self-understanding, 401
  summary chart on, 423-425
  temperament, 403-405, 553-554
  Web resources, 430
  work world, 416
Social-drift hypothesis, 591
Social facilitation, 502-503
Social-identity theory, 521
Social inhibition, 503
Social intelligence, 341
Social learning
  of aggression, 524
  of anxiety disorders, 581
  of attitudes, 472-473
  definition of, **238**
  gender typing and, 405-406
  motivation and attention and, 238-239
  Rotter's social-learning theory, 548

Social-learning theory, 405-406, 548
Social loafing, 503-504
Social phobias, 577
Social psychology
  aggression, 523-526
  altruism, 517-519
  antisocial behavior, 519-528
  attitudes, 471-480
  attraction, 488-491
  attributions, 481-483
  bulimia and, 528-529
  bystander intervention, 515-517
  compliance, 511-512
  conformity, 508-511
  culture of honor, 481, 525
  definition of, **470**
  ethical dilemmas and, 25
  evil and hatred, 526-528
  facial disfigurement and, 425-426
  fads, 494
  groups, 502-506
  impressions, 483-488
  liking, 490-491
  love, 491-493
  nonconformists, 563
  obedience, 512-514
  overview and nature of, 22, 470-471
  peacemaking, 518-519
  prejudice, 519-522
  prosocial behavior, 515-519
  snipers and, 601
  social comparison, 486
  spectators at athletic events, 487-488
  symmetry and, 166, 166-167
  Web resources, 498, 532
Social Readjustment Rating Scale (SRRS), 645, 646
Social-roles theory of gender, 510
Social self, 401
Social status and conformity, 510
Social system, 417, 418
Socialization, 405
Socially defined racial/ethnic groups. *See also* African Americans; Asian Americans; Latino Americans
  academic performance of, 507-508
  intelligence and, 344-345
Socioeconomic status (SES)
  attachment and, 409
  depression and, 582
  schizophrenia and, 589-590, 591
Sociolinguistics, 291
Sociology, 2-3
Soma, 70
Somatic nervous system, 68
Somatoform disorders, 574
Somatosensory processing, 87
Somnambulism, 190
Sound waves, 147-149
Source monitoring, 267
Source-monitoring error, 267
South Korea, 490
Space program, 505
Spanish language, 293
Spatial ability, 41-42, 344
Specific phobias, 577
Spectators at athletic events, 487-488

TO THE OWNER OF THIS BOOK:

I hope that you have found *Psychology,* Fourth Edition, useful. So that this book can be improved in a future edition, would you take the time to complete this sheet and return it? Thank you.

School and department: _____

Address: _____

Instructor's name: _____

1. What I found most informative about this book is: _____

   _____

   _____

2. What I found problematic about this book is: _____

   _____

   _____

3. What was your impression of the CD? _____

   _____

   _____

4. How often did you use the CD? _____

5. Did you use the book companion Web site? If you did, what features did you use? _____

   _____

6. Were all of the chapters of the book assigned for you to read? _____

   If not, which ones weren't? _____

7. Did you buy this book new or used? _____ Will you keep it or resell it? _____

8. In the space below, or on a separate sheet of paper, please write specific suggestions for improving

   this book and anything else you'd care to share about your experience in using this book.

   _____

   _____

   _____

   _____

   _____

THE COMPANION WEBSITE FOR STERNBERG'S PSYCHOLOGY

COMMAND POWERFUL LEARNING AIDS
WITH A SINGLE CLICK OF THE MOUSE

You now have unlimited free access to cutting-edge learning tools—helping you master the concepts covered in this text easily *and* efficiently! This site includes such time-saving resources as:

- **Self-Study Assessments** for each chapter, featuring:
  - a *Pre-Test* that you can complete after you read the chapter to determine what you know
  - a *Post-Test* that lets you see what you've learned after further study
  - *Study Plans*—automatically generated based on your responses to the Pre-Test and Post-Test—that prioritize your studies
- **Chapter Outlines** that clearly map out the topics that Sternberg covers
- **Learning Objectives** that provide straightforward guidance on what you'll need to know
- **MediaWorks** demonstrations and simulations (with **Critical Thinking Questions**) that walk you through key psychological concepts
- **Flash Cards** that can be used for quick review sessions
- **Crossword Puzzles** that offer another fun way to test your knowledge
- **Quizzing** that prepares you for the kinds of questions you may encounter on course quizzes, mid-terms, and finals
- A **Glossary** that provides quick reference to key terms
- **InfoTrac College Edition** search terms, as well as **InfoWrite**, featuring research and writing guides (with tips on APA style)
- A **Careers in Psychology** area that lets you explore what you can accomplish with a degree in psychology
- **Links** to the best psychology resources on the Internet

And because the site does not require a username and password, it's easy to access—anytime, from any computer with Internet access.

Pictorial Dictionary
of
British 18th Century
FURNITURE DESIGN
The Printed Sources

Pictorial Dictionary
of
British 18th Century
FURNITURE DESIGN

The Printed Sources

Compiled by Elizabeth White

Antique Collectors' Club

Designed by John and Griselda Lewis

Printed in England by the Antique Collectors' Club,
Woodbridge, Suffolk IP12 1DS

Antique Collectors' Club

The Antique Collectors' Club was formed in 1966 and quickly grew to a five figure membership spread throughout the world. It publishes the only independently run monthly antiques magazine, *Antique Collecting*, which caters for those collectors who are interested in widening their knowledge of antiques, both by greater awareness of quality and by discussion of the factors which influence the price that is likely to be asked. The Antique Collectors' Club pioneered the provision of information on prices for collectors and the magazine still leads in the provision of detailed articles on a variety of subjects.

It was in response to the enormous demand for information on 'what to pay' that the price guide series was introduced in 1968 with the first edition of *The Price Guide to Antique Furniture* (completely revised 1978 and 1989), a book which broke new ground by illustrating the more common types of antique furniture, the sort that collectors could buy in shops and at auctions rather than the rare museum pieces which had previously been used (and still to a large extent are used) to make up the limited amount of illustrations in books published by commercial publishers. Many other price guides have followed, all copiously illustrated, and greatly appreciated by collectors for the valuable information they contain, quite apart from prices. The Price Guide Series heralded the publication of many standard works of reference on art and antiques. *The Dictionary of British Art* (now in six volumes), *The Pictorial Dictionary of British 19th Century Furniture Design, Oak Furniture* and *Early English Clocks* were followed by many deeply researched reference works such as *The Directory of Gold and Silversmiths*, providing new information. Many of these books are now accepted as the standard work of reference on their subject.

The Antique Collectors' Club has widened its list to include books on gardens and architecture. All the Club's publications are available through bookshops world wide and a full catalogue of all these titles is available free of charge from the addresses below.

Club membership, open to all collectors, costs little. Members receive free of charge *Antique Collecting*, the Club's magazine (published ten times a year), which contains well-illustrated articles dealing with the practical aspects of collecting not normally dealt with by magazines. Prices, features of value, investment potential, fakes and forgeries are all given prominence in the magazine.

Among other facilities available to members are private buying and selling facilities and the opportunity to meet other collectors at their local antique collectors' clubs. There are over eighty in Britain and more than a dozen overseas. Members may also buy the Club's publications at special pre-publication prices.

As its motto implies, the Club is an organisation designed to help collectors get the most out of their hobby: it is informal and friendly and gives enormous enjoyment to all concerned.

For Collectors — By Collectors — About Collecting

ANTIQUE COLLECTORS' CLUB
5 Church Street, Woodbridge Suffolk IP12 1DS, UK
Tel: 01394 385501 Fax: 01394 384434
Email: sales@antique-acc.com
Website: www.antique-acc.com
——— or ———
Market Street Industrial Park, Wappingers' Falls, NY 12590, USA
Tel: 914 297 0003 Fax: 914 297 0068
Email: info@antiquecc.com
Website: www.antiquecc.com

For my son, Philip

Contents

Acknowledgements

I am deeply indebted to the following people who have helped, encouraged and endured the preparation of this work:

Simon Jervis, F.S.A., and Dr. Clive Wainwright, F.S.A., of the Department of Furniture and Interior Design at the Victoria and Albert Museum, who first encouraged me to undertake this task and who have assisted me throughout; Peter Thornton, F.S.A., Director of Sir John Soane's Museum, who guided and taught me with great enthusiasm during my years in the Furniture Department at the Victoria and Albert Museum; Desmond Fitzgerald, F.S.A., the Knight of Glin, of Christie's, who gave me my first research work at the Victoria and Albert Museum on background material to the Rococo period; John Hardy, F.S.A., also now of Christie's, who introduced me to the wealth of archive material in the Department of Furniture and Woodwork and the Department of Prints and Drawings at the Victoria and Albert Museum; and other colleagues at the Victoria and Albert Museum including Frances Collard, Michael Snodin, and the staff of the Print Room and the National Art Library and the Picture Library, and to the staff of the British Library, the Guildhall Library, and the Metropolitan Museum of Art, Department of Western Art; Dr. Christopher Gilbert, F.S.A., Director of Leeds City Art Galleries; Helena Hayward, F.S.A., Dr. Geoffrey Beard, F.S.A., and Eileen Harris, all of whose knowledge of eighteenth century English design has been of great help; Christopher Monkhouse of the Museum of Art, Rhode Island School of Design, who kindly discussed with me the pattern books from the Redwood Library.

John Bedford, of William Bedford p.l.c., Islington, London, has been of the greatest assistance in allowing me access to his extensive library and archive and I am particularly grateful to him for allowing photography of so many rare and delicate volumes.

I am very grateful to John Steel of the Antique Collectors' Club Ltd. for commissioning me to undertake this project, and for carrying such a mammoth exercise into print.

Finally I would like to thank my long-suffering family which has endured years of having the floor covered by heaps of photographs, books and papers, but has encouraged me none the less: my husband George, who has read the text and advised on the arrangement of the plates, and has helped me in particular with the designs for clock and watch-cases; my dear good friends Rosalind Savill, F.S.A., Lucy Knox, Dr. Ian Bristow, Dr. Richard Mones, Suzette Cole; and Heather Jeffery, whose loving care of our daughter for nearly three years gave me the chance to carry out the research for this book.

Preface

The purpose of this book is to provide the student, collector, dealer and general reader with as comprehensive a reference as possible to the printed furniture designs published in England during the eighteenth century. Some of these pattern books are very rare, and are not easily available to the public. Others are well known and have been reprinted many times during the last hundred years, although some plates from earlier or later editions have been forgotten. This volume is intended to extend the coverage of printed designs which was so admirably undertaken by Peter Ward-Jackson in *English Furniture Designs of the Eighteenth Century,* first published in 1958, to act as the companion to the *Pictorial Dictionary of British Nineteenth Century Furniture Design* published by the Antique Collectors' Club in 1976, edited by the late Edward Joy, and to be used in conjunction with the relevant entries in Macquoid and Edwards' *Dictionary of English Furniture,* first published by Country Life Books in 1924, and currently re-issued by the Antique Collectors' Club, and with the *Dictionary of English Furniture Makers 1660-1840* edited by Geoffrey Beard and Christopher Gilbert and published by The Furniture History Society in 1986. The essays, biographies and notes to the sections in this book have been kept as short as possible, in order to leave space for the numerous illustrations, and are intended primarily as introductions to the subject for the newcomer. A list of books for further reading and study has been included at the end of the book. Illustrated title pages and relevant original text accompanying the plates have been included where possible, as have the miscellaneous plates of ornament that are often found in the furniture pattern books. The arrangement of the designs and their history are discussed in the accompanying Introduction.

Elizabeth White, M.A., F.R.S.A.
September 1990

Introduction

This book contains only those engraved designs for furniture published in England during the eighteenth century. It does not, therefore, include the work of many eminent eighteenth century designers and craftsmen who did not publish their designs, such as John Vardy, John Linnell, John Yenn and Henry Holland, nor the prodigious output of the firm of Gillows[1]. It contains only part of the *oeuvre* of such towering figures as William Kent, Matthias Lock, Thomas Chippendale and the brothers Robert and James Adam, but it does include virtually all the known designs of less prominent men like Robert Manwaring, John Crunden and George Hepplewhite. As such it is an unbalanced book, and its user should bear this in mind and consult other sources for unpublished material such as original sketches, working drawings and watercolours[2]. On the other hand, by restricting its contents to printed designs only, it has been possible to include a very large number (approximately 3,000), and to present the reader with nearly all the printed English patterns for furniture available to the eighteenth century customer. It must not be forgotten that many French, Italian and German pattern books were also for sale in England at the time, and that English pattern books were sold abroad. The scrapbook compiled by the mid-eighteenth century carver and gilder Gideon Saint illustrates the variety of sources from which craftsmen could draw inspiration: among the 290 prints and 162 drawings pasted into the book were designs by and drawings after Jean Bérain, Francois Roumier, André Charles Boulle, Jean Mariette and Nicholas Pineau, as well as Matthias Lock and Thomas Johnson[3] (Figure I).

The relationship between cabinet-maker, upholsterer and interior designer was a close one in the eighteenth century, and furniture occupied a well-defined place in overall schemes of interior decoration[4]. The upholsterer, according to Campbell in 1747, came next in importance after the architect and was the 'Chief Agent' in the fitting up of a house: 'He employs journeymen to his own proper calling, Cabinet-Makers, Glass-Grinders,

---

1. For coverage of some of the work of these designers, see:-

Lever, J., *Architects' Designs for Furniture,* R.I.B.A. Drawing Series, London, 1982.

Hayward, H., and Kirkham, P., *William and John Linnell,* London, 1980.

Stroud, D., *Henry Holland, His Life and Architecture,* London, 1986.

Ward-Jackson, P., *English Furniture Designs of the Eighteenth Century,* London, 1958, republished 1984.

2. For instance, in the collections of the Department of Prints and Drawings, The Victoria and Albert Museum, London; the Department of Prints and Drawings, The British Museum, London; The Royal Institute of British Architects Drawings Collection, London; Sir John Soane's Museum, London; The Metropolitan Museum of Art, New York and The Cooper Hewitt-Museum of Decorative Arts and Design, New York.

3. Heckscher, M., 'Gideon Saint, An Eighteenth-Century Carver and his Scrapbook', *Bulletin of the Metropolitan Museum of Art,* Vol.XXVII, 1969, pp.299-310.

Freidman, T., 'Two Eighteenth Century Catalogues of Ornamental Pattern Books', *Furniture History,* Vol.XI, 1975, pp.66-75.

Hardy, J., 'Rococo Furniture and Carving', *Rococo: Art and Design in Hogarth's England,* Victoria and Albert Museum, London, 1984, p.155.

4. Fowler, J. and Cornforth, J., *English Decoration in the Eighteenth Century,* London, 1974, p.56, pp.71-4.

I. Page showing engraved designs and a drawing for girandoles, from the scrapbook of the carver and gilder Gideon Saint, who worked in London in the 1760s and 1770s. Two of the engravings are extracted from Thomas Johnson's designs published in 1758; the drawing may be by Saint himself. *Metropolitan Museum of Art, New York.*

Look-Glass Frame Carvers, Carvers for Chairs, Testers, and Posts of Bed, the Woolen-Draper, the Mercer, the Linen-Draper, several Species of Smiths, and a vast many Tradesmen of the other mechanic Branches'[5]. It is not surprising therefore to find that some of the furniture pattern books contained designs for the sides of rooms, usually showing the correct formal arrangement of the furniture around the walls[6].

Printed designs for carved ornament proliferated rapidly during the century, and it is impossible, for reasons of space, to include them all in this book, so they have been confined to those showing specific items of furniture, such as frames, chimney-pieces with carved overmantels, stands, brackets, and patterns for fretwork and borders, although some more general designs have been inserted in the accompanying biographies of the designers.

---

5. Campbell, R., *The London Tradesman*, 1747.
6. See the Section on Interiors, below, p.473.

i. The Purpose of the Designs

Most of the eighteenth century furniture pattern books were intended mainly for the use of practising craftsmen, although the larger and more famous were directed towards the customer as well: — Chippendale's list of subscribers in 1754 included fellow cabinet-makers, upholsterers, carvers and architects as well as members of the nobility and gentry[7]. The designs were intended to guide the craftsman, to extend his repertoire and to introduce new and fashionable shapes and motifs. They were not intended to be copied slavishly. Many of their titles bear out this intention, using the descriptions 'Guide', 'Companion', 'Bench-Mate', 'Instructor', 'Assistant' and so on. One of the most charming titles was that used by John Crunden for his 'Joyner and Cabinet-Maker's Darling, or Pocket Director', of 1765. Contemporary newspaper advertisements reinforce this, for many of them praise a publication's usefulness to a wide range of designers and craftsmen. Ince and Mayhew in 1762 recommended their *Universal System's* utility 'as well in assisting the Nobility and Gentry, as in improving the young Artist in his Ideas of Designing...'[8].

To the newcomer to the subject, some of the plates reproduced here may seem very confusing, as they are crowded with ornament and are sometimes wildly asymmetrical, even by mid-eighteenth century standards. Few objects were intended to be so fully decorated, or so irregular in their execution but, in order to save space and maximise the use of an expensive copper plate, designer and engraver packed in as much ornament as possible (Figure II). The experienced craftsman could then make his choice, and compose scaled working drawings and templates from which he and his assistants would work. Quite often there is an accompanying note in the text suggesting that part or most of the decoration may be left out, according to the taste and pocket of the client[9]. This general purpose of guidance explains why so few pieces of executed furniture correspond exactly to Hepplewhite's eminently practical designs, even though virtually all elements of his patterns can be found in pieces made in the 1790s[10].

Occasionally authors stated in their accompanying texts that a particular piece of furniture had been executed from a design. Chippendale, for instance, published a design for a bed 'made for the Earl of Dumfries and Morton' (*The*

---

7. Chippendale, T., *The Gentleman and Cabinet-Maker's Director,* 1st Edition, 1754. Of the 308 subscribers, twenty-eight noble and gentlemen subscribed, including the Dukes of Beaufort and Portland, the Earls of Northumberland and Morton, and the Countess of Shaftesbury. See Gilbert, C., *The Life and Work of Thomas Chippendale,* London, 1978, Vol.I, p.70.

8. Advertisement accompanying the first part of Ince and Mayhew's *Universal System of Houshold Furniture,* 1759, Print Department, Metropolitan Museum of Art, New York. See Heckscher, M., 'Ince and Mayhew, Biographical Notes from New York', *Furniture History,* Vol.X, 1974, pp.61-7.

9. For example, Manwaring, R. *The Cabinet and Chair Maker's Real Friend and Companion,* 1975, the Preface: 'the Author has the Boldness to assert, that should the ornamental Parts be left out, there will still remain Grandeur and Magnificence behind, and the Design will appear open and genteel'.

10. Musgrave, C., *Adam, Hepplewhite and other Neo-Classical Furniture,* London, 1966, pp.105-6.

II. Designs for ribbon-back chairs, c.1760, published by A Society of Upholsterers in *Houshold Furniture in the Genteel Taste* (Plate 7). Each design shows as many variations and as much ornament as possible, from which the craftsman could select when preparing his working drawings.

Director, 3rd Edition, 1763, Plate XXXIX), (page 155) and Robert Manwaring refers to his Gothic and Chinese chairs, 'some of them I have executed in Mahogany and some in Pear Tree for Japanning' (*The Cabinet and Chair-Maker's Real Friend and Companion,* 1765, Plates 10-15) (see page 78).

The published furniture designs of Robert and James Adam fall into a slightly different category as they illustrated many examples executed specifically for their clients[11], as do Isaac Ware's plates of furniture designed by William Kent and executed for Houghton Hall, Norfolk[12], and William Thomas' designs in his publication of 1783. However, these books also helped to disseminate ideas about current fashions to other designers, craftsmen and clients.

Sir William Chambers' illustrations in his *Designs of Chinese Buildings* of 1757 were also somewhat different. They were indeed taken from existing oriental examples sketched by him during his travels in the Far East, and were published with the intention of 'putting a stop to the extravagances that daily appear under the name of Chinese, though most of them are mere inventions, the rest copies from the lame representations found on porcelain and paper hangings.' His plates of Chinese furniture 'were taken from such models as appeared to me to be the most beautiful and reasonable; some of them are pretty, and may be useful to our cabinet-makers'. Other designers jumped on Chambers' bandwagon of authenticity, and advertised their chinoiserie designs of the mid-century as taken 'from real Designs, drawn in China, adapted to this Climate' (Decker, *Chinese Architecture, Civil and Ornamental,*

11. Harris, E., *The Furniture of Robert Adam,* London, 1963.

12. Ware, I., *Designs of Inigo Jones and Others,* 1733.

Whoever makes a DESIGN, *without the Knowledge of* PERSPECTIVE *will be liable to such . Absurdities as are shewn in this* Frontispiece.

III. Frontispiece of J.J. Kirby, *Dr. Brook Taylor's Perspective Made Easy,* 1754. It was vital for the furniture designer to be able to draw well in perspective, without which, according to Thomas Chippendale, he 'cannot make the Designs of his Work intelligible, nor show, in a little Compass, the whole Conduct and Effect of the Piece . . .' *Victoria and Albert Museum, London.*

1759). The results were not always so convincing[13].

Another category of printed furniture designs in the eighteenth century was that shown in books on perspective, such as Thomas Malton's *Compleat Treatise on Perspective* (1775 and later editions). The main purpose of these plates was to teach the correct method of drawing in perspective, but they often showed quite typical and contemporary pieces of furniture, and these books were used

---

13. Satirical comment on the lack of authenticity in English chinoiserie design of the mid-eighteenth century was widespread: see Honour, H., *Chinoiserie: The Vision of Cathay,* London, 1973, pp.129-132. See also notes on Robert Morris (p.41).

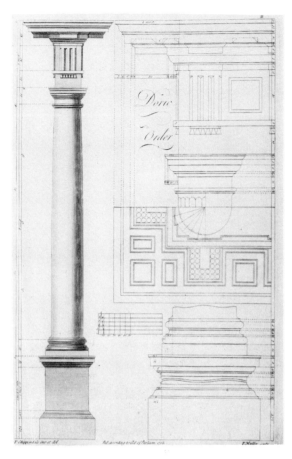

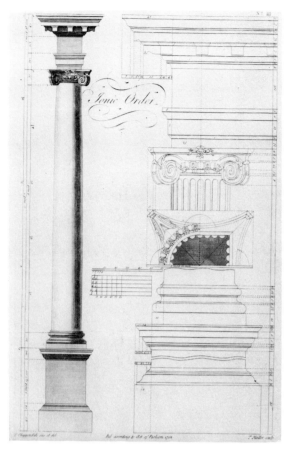

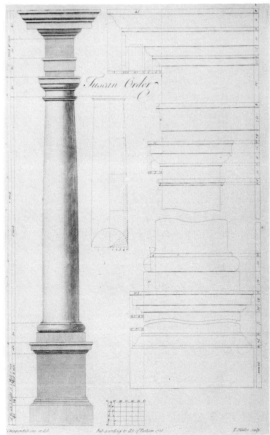

16

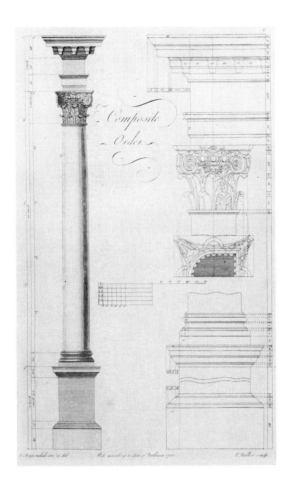

IV. The Five Orders of classical architecture, printed at the beginning of Thomas Chippendale's *The Gentleman and Cabinet-Maker's Director,* first edition, 1754. The plates were taken from James Gibbs' *Rules for Drawing the Several Parts of Architecture,* 1732. Knowledge of the rules and proportions of classical architecture was essential to the 18th century designer, and Chippendale wrote in his Preface, 'Of all the Arts which are either improved or ornamented by Architecture, that of Cabinet-Making is not only the most useful and ornamental, but capable of receiving as great Assistance from it as any whatever.'

extensively by furniture craftsmen and designers (Figure III). In the sixteenth and seventeenth centuries they had constituted one of the few printed sources of furniture design, and were still valued in the eighteenth century. Indeed, as Chippendale pointed out in his preface to *The Director* (1754), knowledge of the basic rules of classical architecture embodied in the Five Orders, and of drawing in perspective, were essential to the cabinet-maker, and without them 'he cannot make the designs of his work intelligible, nor show, in a little compass, the whole conduct and effect of the piece' (Figure IV). Thomas Sheraton also emphasised the necessity for furniture designers and makers to make correct use of perspective drawing (which he himself taught), and devoted a whole section to the subject in *The Cabinet-Maker and Upholsterer's Drawing Book* in 1793[14].

---

14. Sheraton, T., *The Cabinet-Maker and Upholsterer's Drawing-Book,* 1st Edition, 1793, Part II, with three plates showing furniture in perspective (included in the designs illustrated in this work).

ii. The Development of Furniture Design Books in Eighteenth Century England

Very few printed English furniture designs were available at the end of the seventeenth and the beginning of the eighteenth centuries, judging by later standards. The plates on perspective, mentioned above, gave some ideas for the furniture makers, but provided little detail. One example of such a work was Joseph Moxon's *Practical Perspective, or Perspective made easie,* published in London in 1670, which included various plates for chairs, tables and a linen press. Another was the Jesuit P. Jean de Breuil's *The Practice of Perspective,* translated from the French and published in London first by Robert Pricke and later by E. Chambers (1726). Another source were the sheets of flat ornament which were widely available on the continent and were intended for use by many designers and craftsmen, from watch-case engravers to plasterers[15]. They were for sale in London, and furniture-makers took from them ideas for carved and inlaid ornament. Examples of such sheets were those published in Paris by the architect, designer and engraver Jean Bérain (1637-1711). A third source of inspiration were the architectural pattern books, from which furniture designers could extract shapes and motifs and adapt them to suit their smaller objects. All these ingredients were used by Daniel Marot in the series of books published in Amsterdam and The Hague in 1703 and 1713 respectively, which were available in England and which had very considerable influence on English furniture design in the first quarter of the century. Here were specific designs for chairs, tables, mirror frames and candle stands, as well as designs for full schemes of interior decoration and the arrangement of furniture, which could be understood by craftsman and customer alike[16].

It was not until the middle years of the eighteenth century that English furniture designers started to publish such comprehensive books. During the 1720s and 1730s most furniture designs were tucked into books on architecture, and the pieces shown were nearly always of an architectural nature: — carved overmantels for chimney-pieces, pier tables (which were often fixed permanently to the wall), and mirror frames with classical pediments, such as those in William Jones' *Gentleman or Builder's Companion* of 1739. Occasional designs for pieces of furniture could also be found in books of ornament, such as Gaetano Brunetti's *Sixty Different Sorts of Ornament,* published in London in 1736, which included designs for frames and armchairs.

During the 1740s more books devoted solely to designs for carved furniture and carvers' ornaments began to appear, undoubtedly encouraged by the passing of the Engravers' Copyright Act (known as 'Hogarth's Act') in 1735. For the first time, the designer was protected by law from copying. At first the period extended for fourteen years from the date on the print, and from 1767 the length of copyright was extended to twenty-eight years[17]. The brilliant

---

15. Ed. Lambert, S., *Pattern and Design: Designs for the Decorative Arts,* London, Victoria and Albert Museum, 1983, Section 2, pp.40-68.

16. Jessen, P., *Das Ornamentwerk des Daniel Marot,* Amsterdam, 1892.

17. Paulson, R., *Hogarth's Graphic Works,* Newhaven and London, 1965, p.9. I am indebted to John Fisher of the Guildhall Library, London, for this reference.

carver and designer Matthias Lock, the engravers H. Copland and Matthias Darly all published small furniture and ornamental design books between 1744 and 1752. By the mid-1750s an average of two or three furniture pattern books appeared in print nearly every year, and this output continued fairly evenly until the end of the century. The size and complexity of the books also changed, and among them Chippendale's *Gentleman and Cabinet-Maker's Director* (1754) stands out as the first, and possibly the finest book devoted entirely to furniture design, with a huge range of pieces, measurements and accompanying text. Its success was immediate, and a second edition was needed within twelve months[18].

From the 1760s onwards a wide range of recently published pattern books was nearly always available, from the large, comprehensive and fashionable examples, such as Chippendale's third edition of his *Director* (1763), and Ince and Mayhew's *Universal System of Houshold Furniture* (1762), to lesser volumes devoted only to chairs, frames or even patterns for frets and borders (John Crunden's *Joyner and Cabinet-Maker's Darling,* 1765). Many designs were issued first in single sheets, or *cahiers* of about six sheets, or 'Parts', all of which could subsequently be bound into single volumes: Chippendale's third edition of *The Director,* for instance, appeared in sets between 1760 and 1762, with a complete volume appearing in 1763. This sometimes meant that different plates occasionally appeared in copies of the same edition[19]. Many books went into further editions, or their plates were re-issued under different titles at later dates, for instance by the publisher and bookseller Robert Sayer at the Golden Buck in Fleet Street[20]. Authors and publishers advertised extensively in contemporary newspapers, and the books were distributed to many provincial bookshops and printsellers[21]. The standard for furniture pattern books had been set by Thomas Chippendale for the rest of the century; his format was copied by Hepplewhite in 1788 and by many early nineteenth century designers[22].

In the 1830s fresh interest arose in the styles of the mid-eighteenth century and many designs by Chippendale, Lock and Johnson were republished by John Weale, not necessarily with the correct designer's name on the plate[23]. Further republications of eighteenth century books occurred in the 1880s and 1890s, particularly of the neo-classical designs by Adam, Hepplewhite and Sheraton, and most of the more famous publications have been available during the present century[24].

Coloured engravings were extremely rare in eighteenth century English pattern books. Some of the plates for Robert and James Adam's *Designs in Architecture* were coloured, as was Carter's design for a statuary marble table in 1777. Otherwise nearly all prints were black line engravings.

---

18. Gilbert, C., *op. cit.,* Vol.I, p.74.

19. For example, Plate 27 (candlestands) varies in two copies of Edwards' and Darly's *New Book of Chinese Designs,* 1754. See Gilbert, C., 'The Early Furniture of Matthias Darly', *Furniture History,* Vol.XI, 1975, pp.33-9.

20. See biographical notes on Matthias Lock and Robert Manwaring, below.

21. Clinton, L. (now Elizabeth White): Collection of Newspaper Entries relating to artists and craftsmen in England, 1735-55: extracts from the Burney Collection of Newspapers, The British Library. Typescript, Department of Furniture and Interior Design, Victoria and Albert Museum.

22. For example, Smith, G., *A Collection of Designs for Household Furniture,* 1808. It became customary to deal with upholstered furniture and drapery first, followed by cabinet work and carved work: the order in which the designs are shown in this book.

23. See Appendix.

24. See book list at the end of the book.

iii. English Furniture Design in the Eighteenth Century: a Brief Outline

Throughout the eighteenth century English furniture design was influenced by ideas from continental Europe, particularly France and Italy, and in its turn influenced developments in design and decoration in both Europe and the American colonies. The leading English patrons of the arts and manufactures were continually crossing and re-crossing Europe in their searches for classical antiquities, Renaissance paintings, sculptures, and contemporary works of art with which to furnish their houses at home. While abroad, they saw, admired (and sometimes ridiculed) contemporary styles of decoration, brought back such items as Italian *pietra dura* and scagliola table tops, ordered commodes and chairs in Paris from leading ébénistes and menuisiers, bought furnishing and costume fabrics, and all the little tourists' souvenirs such as paper fans depicting the eruption of Vesuvius or the fireworks celebrating the Treaty of Aix-la-Chapelle[25].

Architects, artists and designers went too, sometimes with the assistance of a noble patron (as did William Kent with the 3rd Earl of Burlington[26]), or by working their passage, dealing in works of art, selling their sketches, portraits and engravings, and working up larger volumes for publication on their return (as did the brothers Adam after their journeys to Italy and Dalmatia)[27].

Continental craftsmen and designers flowed in the opposite direction as well, and many settled in London for part or all of their lives. The exodus of Huguenots from France and the Low Countries continued from the Revocation of the Edict of Nantes in 1685 until well into the eighteenth century, and a group of them played a particularly significant role in the development of the Rococo style in London in the 1740s and 1750s[28]. Italian designers and craftsmen also found patrons in England — for instance Giovanni Battista Borra for Lord Temple at Stowe, and for the Duke of Norfolk at Norfolk House in London[29]. The Swedish cabinet-makers Christopher Fürlohg and George Haupt found patrons in England in the later 1760s, and perhaps best known are Robert and James Adam's team of decorative craftsmen which included Antonio Zucchi and Michelangelo Pergolesi[30].

In addition, London booksellers and printsellers stocked sheets of engraved ornament, published in France, Italy and Germany, from which native designers and craftsmen could take ideas, or even, in some cases, could simply

---

25. Trease, G., *The Grand Tour,* London, 1967.

26. Wilson, M.I., *William Kent, Architect, Painter, Designer, Gardener, 1685-1748,* London, 1984, pp.24-38.

27. Fleming, J., 'Robert Adam, the Grand Tourist', *Cornhill Magazine,* 1004 (1955), pp.118-37.

28. Murdoch, T., 'The Huguenots and English Rococo', *The Rococo in England — A Symposium,* edited by Charles Hind, London, 1986, pp.60-81.

29. Fitzgerald, D., *The Norfolk House Music Room,* London, H.M.S.O., 1973.

30. Hayward, J., 'Christopher Fürlohg, an Anglo-Swedish Cabinet-Maker', *Burlington Magazine,* CXI, 1969, 648-55.
Lagerquist, H., *Georg Haupt, Ébéniste du Roi,* Nordiska Museet, Stockholm, 1979.
Croft Murray, E., *Decorative Painting in England, 1537-1837,* Vol.II, London, 1970.

pirate a complete pattern[31]. It is impossible, therefore, to study the design of English furniture in the eighteenth century in isolation, and although this book illustrates only the work of designers publishing in England, their European connections must not be forgotten.

At the start of the century English furniture design was dominated by the French style of decoration developed under the patronage of Louis XIV and disseminated widely through Europe by French craftsmen, designers and publications (Figure V). Its chief exponent in England between c.1689 and 1702 was William III's architect and designer Daniel Marot, who used a full vocabulary of what is known as the 'baroque' style of ornament in his numerous decorative schemes. These were all forms drawn from classical architecture and interpretations of it during the Renaissance, and included acanthus leaves, shells, masks, caryatids and other supporting figures, fruit, flowers, foliage, and heavy scrolls in C- and S-shapes[32]. They were arranged in vigorous patterns to produce ornamental objects of great splendour, movement and richness (Figure VI).

31. As, for example, Batty Langley did with published designs by Nicholas Pineau and J.F. Lauch: see biography of Langley, p.35.

32. Ward-Jackson, P., *Some Mainstreams and Tributaries in European Ornament from 1500 to 1750,* London, H.M.S.O., 1958.

V. Jean Le Pautre (1618-82): Design for a table, mirror and stands. Engraving. *Victoria and Albert Museum.*

VI. Daniel Marot (c.1663-1752): Design for grotesque ornament. Engraving. *Victoria and Albert Museum.*

In furniture design the key features of the baroque style were elaborate and deep carving of woodwork, plenty of gilding, the use of colourful and intricate marquetry on cabinet work, exaggerated height in chair backs, beds and mirror frames, and extremely rich furnishing fabrics for upholstery[33]. Among the pieces made in England which correspond most closely to Marot's published designs were some of the magnificent state beds executed for William III, Queen Anne, their courtiers and ministers[34]. Although Marot's designs were not published in England, they were available and were very influential at a time when English designers and engravers were not producing designs for furniture in any quantity; the designs have been included here for that reason.

After about 1710 the style became somewhat less exuberant; patterns became more abstract, for instance in delicate 'arabesque' designs for marquetry, but still retained their sinuous lines (Figure VI). Another feature of Marot's decorative schemes was his use of oriental materials such as lacquer, porcelain and embroideries, and chinoiserie motifs, all of which were to become part of mid-eighteenth century designers' repertoires.

During the 1720s changes in English furniture design were prompted by the 3rd Earl of Burlington's campaign to observe more closely the rules of classical architecture as laid down by the Italian Renaissance architect Andrea Palladio (1508-1580), and exemplified in England by Inigo Jones (1573-1652)[35]. Furniture, as part of the 'Palladian' interior, was expected to complement the architectural style. But this presented problems, for although plenty of examples of classical Roman architecture survived for study and emulation, little was known about classical Roman domestic furnishing. William Kent, the chief exponent of Lord Burlington's style, and other contemporary designers, were obliged to adapt classical architectural shapes and features to furniture: columns, capitals, friezes, pediments, Vitruvian scrolls, Greek-key frets, paterae, and the symbols and images of classical mythology all made their appearance on English furniture in an ordered fashion, and with slightly less exuberance than the decoration of the previous decades (Figure VII). However, Kent and his contemporaries were also influenced by their French and Italian baroque inheritance and borrowed freely from the work of Jean Le Pautre, Daniel Marot and Jean Berain[36]. Some of Kent's own designs were engraved and published by John Vardy and Isaac Ware. Other architects issued printed designs for Palladian furniture: they included William Jones, Robert Morris, Batty Langley and Abraham Swan, but before 1744 no pattern books were published that were devoted solely to furniture.

At the same time, much more advanced ideas of modern decorative design were coming into England from France, and were being developed in London.

---

33. Jackson-Stops, G., 'Daniel Marot and the Court Style of William and Mary', *Antiques,* CXXXIV No.6, December 1988, pp.1321-31.
Jackson-Stops, G., 'Courtiers and Craftsmen: The William and Mary Style', *Country Life,* CLXXXII, No.41, 13 October, 1988, pp.200-9.
White, L., 'The Furnishing of Interiors during the Time of William and Mary', *Antiques,* CXXIV, No.6, December 1988, pp.1362-9.

34. Clinton, L., *The State Bed from Melville House,* Victoria and Albert Museum Masterpieces Sheet No.21, 1979.
White, L., 'Two English State Beds in the Metropolitan Museum of Art', *Apollo,* Vol.116, August 1982, pp.84-8.
Wingfield-Digby, G., 'Damasks and Velvets at Hampton Court', *Connoisseur,* Vol.103, January 1939, p.248.

35. Wittkower, R., *Palladio and English Palladianism,* (The Collected Essays), London, 1974, Chapters 4-5.

36. Wilson, M.I., *op. cit.,* p.105.

VII. Anon., c.1740: Design for a pier table, mirror and girandoles. Pen, ink and wash. *Victoria and Albert Museum.*

VIII. J.B. Guélard after J. de la Joue: *Fontaine Glacée — Livre Nouveau de Douze Morceaux de Fantasie 1736. Victoria and Albert Museum.*

These were the ideas associated with what is now called the 'Rococo' style — a description taken from the French word 'rocaille', for rockwork, which for a time was used in a derogatory sense[37]. The style certainly utilised many features of sixteenth century Italian *grotesque* design, such as shells, jagged rocks and stones, dripping water, ferns, mosses and leaves, and combined them in fanciful decorative patterns[38] (Figure VIII). Above all, it made use of naturalistic ornament, apparently unrestricted by classical structural form, such as trees, stems, leaves, flowers, animals, birds, fish and insects, with a generous dose of exotic 'fantasies' such as Chinese buildings, bridges and gates. The sinuous C-shaped or S-shaped curve, admired by Hogarth as 'the serpentine line of beauty'[39], was used as the framework for many of these

---

37. 'Rococo, or rocaille. . . a style of architectural and mobiliary decoration popular throughout the greater part of Europe during the first half of the eighteenth century. . . A debased style at the best, essentially fantastic and bizarre, it ended in extravagance and decadence. . . England did not escape the infection, and Chippendale and his school produced examples of rocaille work and *coquillage* which were quite foreign to their own sentiment, and rarely rose above respectable mediocrity.' *Encyclopaedia Britannica,* 11th Edition, 1911. The word 'rococo' was not used to describe the style in the eighteenth century; instead it was referred to as 'modern' or 'French'.

39. Hogarth, W., *The Analysis of Beauty,* 1753.

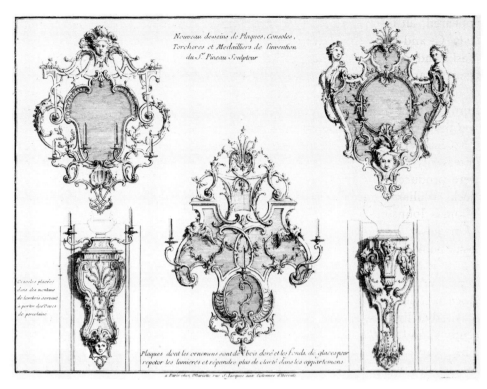

IX. Nicholas Pineau (1684-1754): Designs for girandoles. Engraving. *Victoria and Albert Museum.*

complex designs, and the straight line was virtually eliminated from most Rococo ornament (Figure IX).

French designers and engravers working in London were the first to publish designs in Rococo style, in sheets of 'flat' engraved ornament which were for use mainly by metalworkers, but soon extended to almost every area of the decorative arts. From 1732 to 1745 the French designer Hubert Gravelot (1699-1773) was working in London, publishing a wide variety of illustrations and patterns[40], and involved in teaching at the St. Martin's Lane Academy which became the source of early English Rococo design. The Academy included in its membership such luminaries as Hogarth, Hayman, and Roubiliac, who collaborated over the decoration of the supper boxes at Vauxhall Gardens in the 1740s[41].

St. Martin's Lane was also becoming the centre of London's fashionable furniture industry, and leading cabinet-makers and upholsterers were working within a short distance of the Academy — Thomas Chippendale, William Vile and John Cobb, and John Channon in the Lane, and Matthias Lock not far away in Nottingham Court, off the Strand. It was also close to the offices of the Board of Works, from which tenders were sought and commissions given for the building, decorating and furnishing of the royal palaces and government offices.

Specific designs for Rococo furniture appeared in London from about 1740. Batty Langley's *Treasury of Designs* included a number for side tables plagiarised from Pineau and others. After c.1744 more and more printed furniture designs

40. Fitzgerald, D., 'Gravelot and his Influence on English Furniture', *Apollo,* August 1969, pp.140-7.
41. Girouard, M., 'Coffee at Slaughter's', *Country Life,* 13 January, 1966, pp.58-61.
Girouard, M., 'Hogarth and his Friends', *Country Life,* 27 January, 1966, pp.188-90.
Girouard, M., 'The Two Worlds of St. Martin's Lane', *Country Life,* 3 February, 1966, pp.224-7.

appeared, all inspired by the naturalistic and fanciful features of the French style. C- and S-scrolls, twisting stems, leaves, flowers, ribbons, shells, puckish masks and alert creatures made their appearance in carved mirror and table-frames, candle stands, bedsteads and girandoles (Figure X). A popular source of inspiration was Barlow's illustrations of *Aesop's Fables,* and the creatures from the tales — the fox, the monkey, the goat, the deer, the lion, the dove and the crow — can be found on chimney-pieces, sconces and stands. On the other hand, some designs were composed simply of sinuous lines and were not necessarily crowded with ornament. Beautiful, elegant and inspired designs were produced in the period 1755-1768 by Thomas Chippendale, Matthias Lock, William Ince and John Mayhew. The curious, spiky style used by Thomas Johnson was unusual, and some of the designs published by Robert Manwaring were little more than mundane. The style began to wane in fashionable circles after 1763, although the publisher Robert Sayer re-issued many of Matthias Lock's and Matthias Darly's designs in 1766, and lesser designers like Robert Manwaring issued further editions of their work in the Rococo style up to 1770.

Another light-hearted style popular in England in the middle years of the century, and which was closely associated with the Rococo, was the Chinese. The sources for these designs were much the same as those used at the end of the seventeenth century and were taken mainly from oriental objects — porcelain, lacquer, textiles and painted papers — and from European interpretations of those designs such as Stalker and Parker's *Treatise of Japanning and Varnishing,* 1688[42].

Favourite motifs were Chinese flowers such as prunus or peonies, willow trees, Chinese figures, dragons, landscapes and exotic birds. 'Chinese' patterns for garden railing, gates and bridges, summer houses, 'palaces' and 'retreats for angling' were suitable ornaments for outside, complemented by chairs with Chinese lattice backs and other Chinese motifs (Figure XI).

X. Matthias Lock (d.1765): Design for a girandole, c.1746. Drawing. *Victoria and Albert Museum.*

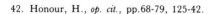

42. Honour, H., *op. cit.,* pp.68-79, 125-42.

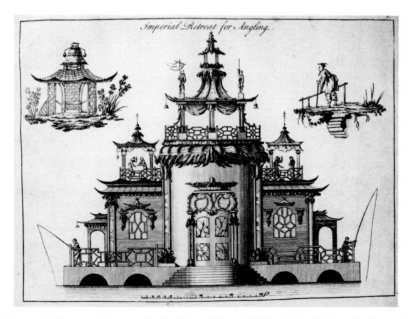

XI. 'Imperial Retreat for Angling', Plate I from P. Decker's *Chinese Architecture, Civil and Ornamental,* 1759.

Among early publications of chinoiserie designs were William Halfpenny's *New Designs for Chinese Temples* of 1750, and Matthias Darly's little *New Book of Chinese, Gothic and Modern Chairs* of 1751. Indoors the style was particularly popular for bedrooms and closets (or boudoirs) and smaller drawing rooms. One of the first whole chinoiserie interiors executed at this time was the bedchamber at Badminton House for the 4th Duke of Beaufort in 1752-3, carried out by William and John Linnell of Berkeley Square[43].

The style remained popular for garden ornament more or less for the rest of the century. The wilder types of chinoiserie furniture for indoors died away after c.1770, although painted or japanned chinoiserie decoration was applied to furniture of neo-classical outline by Thomas Chippendale to the designs of Robert Adam[44].

Mid-eighteenth century furniture design was also affected by a revival of interest in Gothic architecture, demonstrated by Batty Langley's publications of 1741 and 1747, and Horace Walpole's transformation of his villa at Twickenham between 1747 and 1764[45]. By 1751 Matthias Darly included designs for Gothic chairs in his *New Book...*, and in 1754 and 1760-62 Chippendale included designs with Gothic ornament for chairs, beds, sideboards, desks and bookcases (Figure XII). Gothic furniture was considered especially suited to the decoration of libraries, where it was thought to enhance the atmosphere of scholarship imparted by ancient volumes and busts of Homer and Vergil. The designers used Gothic ornament freely, and often in conjunction with other elements of mid-eighteenth century designs, on pieces of standard eighteenth century shape and form: they did not intend to create faithful representations of true mediaeval furniture[46]. Few Gothic designs were published after c.1768, although N. Wallis included patterns for Gothic rails in *The Carpenter's Treasure* of 1773.

While Rococo furniture was still popular in England in the early 1760s, avant-garde designers were already aware of the changes of direction that had commenced in France in the 1750s. These involved renewed study and use of classical architectural form and decoration, inspired by the work of French scholars at the French Academy in Rome, by Piranesi's engravings of classical Roman architecture, by Winckelmann's and Le Roy's praise of ancient Greek art, and by fresh excavations of classical buildings at Herculaneum and Pompeii from c.1740 onwards[47]. It also involved a reaction against the excesses of the Rococo style, and found fertile ground in England where the Palladian tradition of the 1720s and 1730s had never been entirely usurped[48]. Among the first architects and interior designers to practise in what came to be known as the Neo-Classical style were William Chambers at Osterley Park,

43. Hayward, H., 'Chinoiserie at Badminton: the furniture of John and William Linnell', *Apollo*, August 1969, pp.134-9.

44. For the furniture of David Garrick's villa at Hampton, see Tomlin, M., *Catalogue of Adam Period Furniture*, London, Victoria and Albert Museum, 1972, pp.119-24, Museum Nos. W.21-1917 to W.32-1917. See also:
Gilbert, C., *The Life and Work of Thomas Chippendale*, London, 1978, pp.115-6, 171.
Symonds, R.W., 'Chippendale Furniture at Nostell Priory', *Country Life*, 3 October, 1952, pp.1028-30.

45. Wainwright, C., *The Romantic Interior, The British Collector at Home, 1750-1850*, London, 1989, pp.84-108.

46. Though see Wainwright, *op. cit.*, p.85 for Walpole's statement that the chairs made by Hallett for the Great Parlour at Strawberry Hill were inspired by mediaeval lancet windows, and pp.86-7 for Walpole's views on Langley's 'rules' for Gothic architecture.

47. Honour, H., 'Neo-Classicism', Catalogue of the Exhibition, *The Age of Neo-Classicism*, Arts Council of Great Britain, London, 1972, pp.xxi-xxix.

48. Udy, D., 'New Light on the Sources of English Neo-Classical Design', *Apollo*, March 1976, pp.202-7.

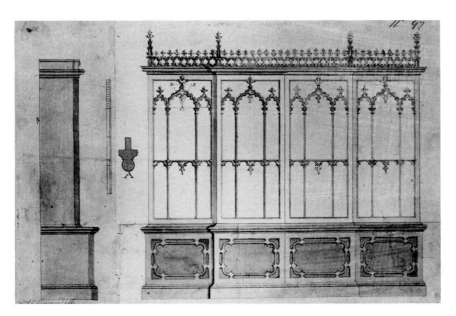

XII. Thomas Chippendale: manuscript design for a Gothic library bookcase, published as Plate XCVII in *The Gentleman and Cabinet-Maker's Director,* third edition, 1763. *The Cooper-Hewitt Museum, New York.*

XIII. Robert Adam (1728-92): Design for a girandole for Osterley Park House, c.1773. Pen, ink and wash. *Victoria and Albert Museum.*

and James 'Athenian' Stuart, who executed the drawing room at Spencer House, London in 1758 and published the first volume of his *Antiquities of Athens* in 1762[49]. However, the leading exponent from c.1765 onwards was the architect and designer Robert Adam (1728-1792) who, with his family firm and team of craftsmen, soon developed a light, pleasant, neo-classical style for all decorative schemes. In contrast to the somewhat ponderous work of Kent and his contempories, Adam's new style used more delicate, small-scale ornament, lighter colours and simpler shapes. Many of the same decorative elements were used, such as vine, palm, acanthus and laurel leaves, wheat husks, honeysuckle, classical deities and mythical beasts, Vitruvian scrolls and Greek-key patterns, but with a new lightness and delicacy (Figure XIII). Early neo-classical designers continued to make use of some Rococo elements, particularly in the use of serpentine shapes and, in furniture design, the cabriole leg for gilded drawing-room furniture.

Adam's designs for furniture for his numerous country — and town — house commissions were executed by the leading makers in London in the period 1770-85, including Thomas Chippendale (and his son), John Linnell, Ince and Mayhew, Vile and Cobb, William Gordon and Samuel Gordon[50] (Figure XIV). These craftsmen readily adapted themselves to the new style, and designs were soon published which reflected the move away from Rococo. Chippendale's third edition of *The Director,* published from 1760-62, excluded some of the more excessive Rococo designs of the earlier editions, and introduced a few more delicately classical designs for pedestals and clock cases, a pier table with caryatids and two chimney-pieces. It was not until c.1769-70

49. Watkin, D., *Athenian Stuart, Pioneer of the Greek Revival,* London, 1982, pp.35-40.
50. Harris, E., *The Furniture of Robert Adam,* London, 1973, pp.25-30.

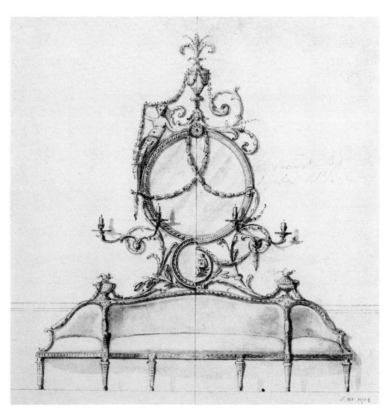

XIV. John Linnell (1729-96): Design for a sofa and glass, c.1770. Drawing. *Victoria and Albert Museum.*

that designs for furniture in the neo-classical style began to be published on a regular basis; examples were Lock's *New Book of Pier Frames...* (1769), and Darly's *Architectural Designs and Ornaments* (1769). The first part of Robert Adam's own designs (Part I of *Works in Architecture*) was published in parts from 1773-78 and had a significant effect in spreading knowledge of the style.

From c.1775 a wide variety of neo-classical furniture designs and books of ornament were available, largely inspired by Adam's work. They included volumes by Columbani, Pastorini, Pergolesi, Begbie and Chippendale the Younger. The antiquarian draughtsman John Carter published some curious and highly individualistic designs in the *Builder's Magazine* (1774-78), and the young John Soane produced some designs for garden seats in a small architectural work (1778) which he later tried to suppress. Other architects and craftsmen who executed designs in the neo-classical style at this time, but who did not publish them, included John Linnell, John Yenn, and the firm of Gillows (figure XV)[51].

By the 1780s Adam-inspired neo-classical style was well established in English furniture. It received a further boost in 1788 with the publication by George Hepplewhite's widow of the latter's designs in *The Cabinet-Maker and Upholsterer's Guide*. This work was effectively a compendium of designs reflecting the general current taste, and certainly did not show any knowledge of the more avant-garde ideas being developed by the architect Henry Holland for the Prince of Wales at Carlton House, or of new developments in French

51. Ward-Jackson, P., *English Furniture Designs of the Eighteenth Century,* London, 1958, pp.54, 59-61.
Hall, I., 'Patterns of Elegance: The Gillows' Furniture Designs I', *Country Life,* Vol.CXLIII, No.42222, 8 June, 1978, pp.1612-15.
Hall, I., 'Models with a Choice of Leg: The Gillows' Furniture Designs, II', *Country Life,* CLXIII, No.4223, 15 June, 1978, pp.1740-42.

design[52]. These gradually began to appear in the 1790s, starting in Thomas Sheraton's *Drawing Book* of 1793, where his accusation that Hepplewhite's designs had already 'caught the decline' prompted the appearance of a third edition of *The Guide* with more up-to-date designs for seat furniture. In both these publications, the sinuous shapes that were a legacy of the Rococo were abandoned in favour of more rectilinear shapes and decorative ornament was considerably reduced to produce an effect of 'taste and propriety', as Horace Walpole described it. This formed the basis of the style which came to dominate English furniture design in the early years of the nineteenth century and which is usually referred to as the 'Regency' style[53].

52. Stroud, D., *Henry Holland, His Life and Architecture,* London, 1966.
Watson, J.F.B., 'Holland and Daguerre: French Undercurrents in English Neo-Classical Furniture Design', *Apollo,* XCVI, No.128, October 1972, pp.282-7.
de Bellaigue, G., 'The Furnishings of the Chinese Drawing Room, Carlton House', *Burlington Magazine,* CIX, No.774, September 1987, pp.518-528.
53. Collard, F., *Regency Furniture,* Woodbridge, 1985, Chapters 1-2.

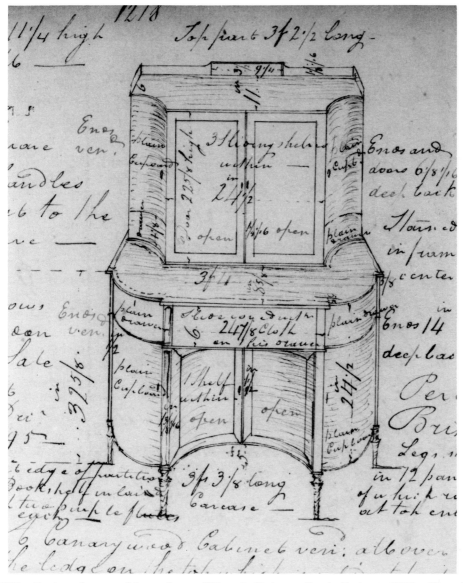

XV. Design for a cabinet, from Gillows' *Estimate Sketch Books,* c.1793. *City of Westminster Archives Department.*

iv. Books from which plates are reproduced in this work

(in chronological order)

Short titles only are given here; longer titles, and dates of subsequent editions, are given in the notes on the designers.

The dates given refer to first editions, except where a later edition is specifically mentioned.

All books were published in London, unless specified otherwise.

1703 & 1713	Marot, D.	*Oeuvres Du Sr. D. Marot...* (The Hague, 1703; Amsterdam, 1713)
1728	Gibbs, J.	*A Book of Architecture*
1731	Ware, I.	*Designs of Inigo Jones and Others*
1733	Price, F.	*Treatise on Carpentry* (re-named *The British Carpenter* 1735)
1736	Brunetti, G.	*Sixty Different Sorts of Ornament*
1736	Salmon, W.	*The Builder's Guide*
1737	Hoppus, E.	*The Gentleman and Builder's Repository*
1739	Jones, W.	*The Gentleman or Builder's Companion*
1740	Langley, B.	*The City and Country Builder's and Workman's Treasury of Designs*
1741	Langley, B.	*The Builder's Jewell, or Youth's Instructor*
1741	De la Cour, W.	*First Book of Ornament*
1742	Langley, B.	*Ancient Architecture* (reissued as *Gothic Architecture Improv'd by Rules and Proportions...* 1747)
1744	Vardy, J.	*Some Designs of Mr. Inigo Jones and Mr. William Kent*
1744	Lock, M.	*Six Sconces*
1745	Swan, A.	*The British Architect*
1745	Toro, B.	*Masks and other Ornaments*
1746		*Gentleman's Magazine* (April)
1746	Lock, M.	*Six Tables*
1746	Copland, H.	*A New Book of Ornaments*
1750	Halfpenny, W.	*Twenty New Designs of Chinese Lattice*
1750-52	Halfpenny, W.	*New Designs for Chinese Temples*
1751	Darly, M.	*A New Book of Chinese, Gothic and Modern Chairs*
c.1751	Darly, M.	*A Second Book of Chairs*
1751	Morris, R.	*The Architectural Remembrancer*
1752	Halfpenny, W.	*Rural Architecture in the Chinese Taste*
1752	Lock, M. & Copland, H.	*A New Book of Ornaments*
1752	Babel, P.	*A New Book of Ornaments*
1752	Salmon, W.	*Palladio Londoniensis* (4th edition)
1754	Edwards & Darly	*A New Book of Chinese Designs*
1754	Chippendale, T.	*The Gentleman and Cabinet-Maker's Director*
1755	Johnson, T.	*Twelve Girandoles*
1755	Pillement, J.	*A New Book of Chinese Ornaments*

1756	Ware, I.	*A Complete Body of Architecture*
1756 on	Vivares, F.	*Various designs* (unbound)
1757	Halfpenny, W.	*The Modern Builder's Assistant*
1757	Chambers, W.	*Designs of Chinese Buildings*
1757	Morris, R.	*Architecture Improv'd in a Collection of Modern, Useful and Elegant Designs*
1758	Johnson, T.	*Collection of Designs*
1758	Over, C.	*Ornamental Architecture in the Gothic, Chinese and Modern Taste*
1758	Major, T.	*Designs for frets* (unbound)
1758	Pain, W.	*The Builder's Companion and Workman's General Assistant*
1759	Decker, P.	*Chinese Architecture, Civil and Ornamental*
1759	Decker, P.	*Gothic Architecture, Decorated*
1760-62	Chippendale, T.	*The Gentleman and Cabinet-Maker's Director* (3rd edition, in sheets)
1761	Johnson, T.	*One Hundred and Fifty New Designs*
1762	Ince, W., and Mayhew, J.	*The Universal System of Houshold Furniture*
1762	Baretti, P.	*A New Book of Ornaments for the Year 1762*
1763	Chippendale, T.	*The Gentleman and Cabinet-Maker's Director* (complete 3rd edition)
c.1765	A Society of Upholsterers	*Genteel Houshold Furniture in the Present Taste* (2nd edition)
1765	Crunden, J.	*The Joyner and Cabinet-Maker's Darling*
1765	Crunden, J. and Morris, J.	*The Carpenter's Companion for Chinese Railing and Gates*
1765	Manwaring, R.	*The Cabinet and Chair-Maker's Real Friend and Companion*
1765	Manwaring, R.	*The Carpenter's Compleat Guide to the Whole System of Gothic Railing*
1766	Manwaring, R. and others	*The Chair-Maker's Guide*
1766	Crunden, Milton & Columbani	*The Chimney-Piece Maker's Daily Assistant*
1766	pub. Sayer, R.	*The Ladies' Amusement, or whole Art of Japanning made Easy*
1766	Willson, A.	*The Antique and Modern Embellisher*
1767	Wrighte, W.	*Grotesque Architecture, or Rural Amusement*
1768	Lock, M. and Copland, H.	*A New Book of Ornaments* (2nd edition)
1768	Swan, A.	*One Hundred and Fifty New Designs for Chimney Pieces etc.*
1769	Lock, M.	*A New Book of Ornaments for Looking Glass Frames*

1769	Lock, M.	*A New Book of Pier-Frames*
1769-70	Darly, M.	*Architectural Designs and Ornaments*
1770	Crunden, J.	*Convenient and Ornamental Architecture*
1773	Wallis, N.	*The Carpenter's Treasure*
1773	Pether, T.	*A Book of Ornaments*
1773-8	Adam, R. & J.	*Works in Architecture, Part I*
1774-8	Carter, J.	*The Builder's Magazine*
1775	Columbani, P.	*A New Book of Ornaments*
1775	Malton, T.	*Compleat Treatise on Perspective*
1775	Pastorini, B.	*A New Book of Designs for Girandoles and Glass Frames in the present Taste*
1775	Johnson, T.	*Designs for Three Mirrors* (unbound)
c.1777	Anon.	*Brass Ornaments for Furniture*
1777-1801	Pergolesi, M.A.	*Designs for Various Ornaments*
1778	Soane, J.	*Designs in Architecture*
1779	Adam, R. & J.	*Works in Architecture, Part II*
1779	Begbie, P.	*Vases after the Manner of the Antique*
1779	'S.H.'	*Twelve New Designs of Frames*
1783	Thomas, W.	*Original Designs in Architecture*
1788	Hepplewhite, A. & Co.	*The Cabinet-Maker and Upholsterer's Guide*
1788	Pain, W. & J.	*Pain's British Palladio*
c.1788 or before	Pain, W.	*The Practical House Carpenter*
1788		*The Cabinet-Maker's London Book of Prices*
1789	Hepplewhite, A. & Co.	*The Cabinet-Maker and Upholsterer's Guide* (2nd edition)
c.1790	Anon.	*Ideas for Rustic Furniture*
1793	Richardson, G.	*New Designs for Vases and Tripods*
1793		*The Cabinet-Maker's London Book of Prices* (2nd edition)
1793	Sheraton, T.	*The Cabinet-Maker and Upholsterer's Drawing Book*
1794	Hepplewhite, A. & Co.	*The Cabinet-Maker and Upholsterer's Guide* (3rd edition)
1795	Middleton, C.	*Picturesque and Architectural Views for Cottages, Farmhouses and Country Villas*
1799	Middleton, C.	*The Architect and Builder's Miscellany*

v. Notes on the Designers whose work is reproduced in this book

Daniel Marot c.1663-1752

Architect, designer, ornamentalist and engraver. Marot was born in Paris, the son of the architect and designer Jean Marot and nephew of the royal cabinet-maker Pierre Golle. He had begun a successful career as a designer in the French capital before the Revocation of the Edict of Nantes, in 1685, forced him as a Protestant to leave France and seek the patronage of Prince William of Orange, who became William III of England in 1688. He styled himself 'Architect to William III, King of Great Britain'. Between 1689 and 1706 Marot spent periods in England, working at Hampton Court, Petworth and Montagu House. He published many designs for gardens and garden buildings, for interior decoration, for furniture, metalwork, textiles and ceramics; these were issued in sets of six sheets at a time, as for instance in the *Nouveaux Livre d'Apartements* or the *Nouveaux Livre de Boites de Pendules*. Collected editions of the designs were published in The Hague in 1703 in 108 plates, and in Amsterdam in 1713 in 126 plates, with a further undated Dutch edition containing 237 plates. There is no doubt that these designs were available in England, at a time when such printed material by English designers was virtually non-

existent, and their influence here was very considerable, for instance in the magnificently upholstered beds of the late seventeenth and early eighteenth centuries, and in the design of English clock cases. This is why they are reproduced here, although they were not published in England. Daniel Marot settled permanently in The Hague in 1713, and died there at a ripe old age in 1752.

James Gibbs 1682-1754

Architect. Gibbs' outstanding achievements as an architect are well documented and many of his original drawings survive (Victoria and Albert Museum, Royal Institute of British Architects, the Bodleian Library, Oxford, and Sir John Soane's Museum, London). His publications included *A Book of Architecture* (1728), *Rules for Drawing the Several Parts of Architecture* (1732), *Bibliotheca Redcliviana* (1747). In his introduction to *A Book of Architecture* he expressed the hope that it 'would be of use to such Gentlemen as might be concerned in Building, especially in the remote parts of this Country, where little or no assistance for Designs can be

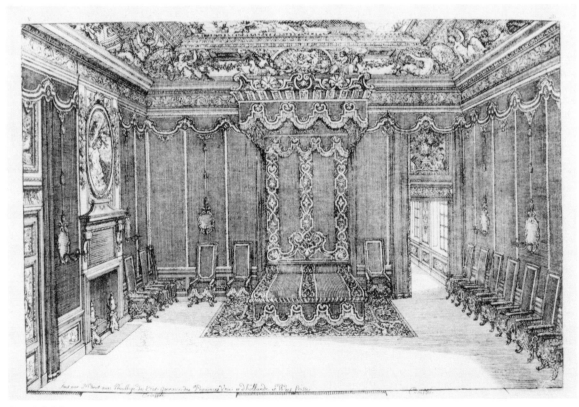

Daniel Marot
Engraved design for a bedchamber from *Nouveaux Livre d'Apartements,* 1703.

procured' — a frequent purpose for publication during the eighteenth century. Among the architectural designs are some for chimney-pieces, marble or stone tables 'for Gardens or Summer Houses', and pedestals for sundials and classical busts, which are included here.

Francis Price 1704-1753

Architect and Clerk of Works of Salisbury Cathedral 1737-53. (c.f. his obituary, 29 March, 1753, *The Public Advertiser*.) A monument to his memory is in the cloisters of Salisbury Cathedral; a portrait of him by George Bear, 1747, is in the National Portrait Gallery.

In 1733 he first published *The British Carpenter, or a Treatise on British Carpentry* (further editions 1735, 1753, 1759, 1765, 1768). It was advertised in *The Craftsman* 12 April 1735 with recommendations from Nicholas Hawksmoor, John James and James Gibbs, and has been described by Colvin as 'long regarded as one of the best [books] of its kind.' It included Palladio's Orders of Architecture, and the 1735 edition included designs for doors, windows, picture or glass frames and chimney-pieces.

Isaac Ware d.1766

Architect with a successful career in the Board of Works from 1728 for over thirty years; an apocryphal story relates that as a child chimney-sweep, he was 'discovered' by Lord Burlington sketching the elevation of Inigo Jones' Banqueting House in Whitehall. Certainly he was closely associated with Burlington's circle, and may have been able to travel to Italy with the Earl's assistance. By 1733 he had published *Designs of Inigo Jones and Others,* which included engravings of chimney-pieces by Jones, Burlington and Kent. Later editions were published in 1743 and 1756. Other published works by him were *The Plans, Elevations and Sections of Houghton in Norfolk,* 1735, the translation of Palladio's *Four Books of Architecture,* 1738, and *A Complete Body of Architecture,* 1756 and several later editions, which Colvin described as 'a comprehensive statement of Georgian architectural theory and practice which held the field until superseded by Chambers' *Treatise*'.

Ware was also associated with the emergent Rococo movement in London in the 1740s and belonged to the St. Martin's Lane Academy with Hogarth, Hayman, Roubiliac and Gravelot.

Gaetano Brunetti fl.c.1731, d.1758

Designer and ornamentalist from Bologna. He worked as a decorative painter in England during the 1730s, for instance with Amigoni at Chandos House, Cavendish Square, and for the Earl of Tankerville in St. James's Square, London. By 1739 he had gone to Paris where he continued to work as a decorative painter with his son.

In 1736 he published *Sixty Different Sorts of Ornament* 'in the Italian Taste', which, according to an advertisement in the *Daily Gazetteer* (28 June, 1736), would be 'of the utmost advantage to Painters, Sculptors, Stone Carvers, Wood Carvers, Silversmiths &c...'. Among the plates are six for furniture — chairs, frames, tables and brackets, all executed in a vigorous early Rococo style. Peter Ward-Jackson has suggested that these designs 'played some part in

Gaetano Brunetti
Engraved design for a cartouche. 1736.

introducing the Rococo style to English designers', and rank among the earliest in that style to be published in England.

Edward Hoppus d.1739

Architect and surveyor, and best known for his publication of *Practical Measuring,* which remained in print from 1736 until 1973 when metrication made it obsolete. In 1737 he published a collection of designs (largely second-hand), entitled *The Gentleman and Builder's Repository, or Architecture Display'd,* of which there were further editions in 1738, 1748 and 1760. The plates illustrated the contemporary Palladian style for architectural features and decoration.

William Salmon c.1703-1799

Carpenter of Colchester, who published a number of architectural books which ran to many editions between 1737 and 1773. Among these were *The Builder's Guide, and Gentleman and Trader's Assistant,* and *The Country Builder's Estimator, or Architect's Companion,* both of which were advertised in the *Daily Post,* 3 June, 1736, and the *London Evening Post,* 8-10 February, 1737. In 1734 he had published

Palladio Londoniensis, or the London Art of Building, with a second edition, by E. Hoppus, 'very much enlarged' and costing 7s.6d., in July 1738, a fourth edition in 1752 and an eighth edition in 1773. Among the plates were some designs for classical overmantels of a fairly standard type.

William Jones
Design for frames from *Designs for Frontispieces etc.* 1736.

William Jones fl. from 1737, d.1757

Architect of the Rotunda in Ranelagh gardens, Chelsea (opened 1742) and appointed Surveyor to the East India Company in 1752. In 1736 his *Designs for Frontispieces &c.* were appended to James Smith's *Specimens of Ancient Carpentry,* and were republished in 1739 as a separate book entitled *The Gentleman or Builder's Companion, containing Variety of usefull Designs for Doors, Gateways, Peers, Pavilions, Temples, Chimney-Pieces &c...'.* His address was given as near the Chapel in King Street, Golden Square. The *Companion* included designs for chimney-pieces, pier tables and glass frames, mostly in the prevailing Palladian style, but some, like Langley's, plagiarised from Pineau and in a lighter Rococo style. Simon Jervis classified them as 'the earliest published group of furniture designs by an English designer.'

Batty Langley 1696-1751

Described in his obituary (*General Advertiser,* 6 March, 1751) as 'that eminent Surveyor and Architect', Langley was the son of a Twickenham gardener who had come to London and made a living by teaching drawing and architecture, and publishing numerous works on the latter (a full list may be found in *Colvin*). By 1743 he was living in York Street, near Covent Garden (*London Evening Post,* 29 January to 1 February, 1743), and he died at his house in Dean Street, Soho in 1751. His earliest works included instruction on

Geometry (1726), the Five Orders of Architecture (1727), and gardening 'or the laying out and planting Parterres, Groves, Wildernesses, Labyrinths, Avenues, Parks &c.', (1728). Included in his architectural publications are various designs for furniture, particularly in *The City and Country Builder's and Workman's Treasury of Designs* (1740, with further editions in 1745, '50, '56 and '70); these consisted of patterns for marquetry and parquetry for cabinet work and floors, borders and frames, chests of drawers and bookcases and a medal cabinet, all in a fairly typical Palladian style. In contrast to these Langley added various designs pirated from continental publications in the Rococo style — two timepieces from J.F. Lauch, and pier table frames from Nicholas Pineau; these plates undoubtedly played a part in disseminating Rococo design to English woodcarvers.

Langley also espoused the cause of Gothic architecture, and published one of the earliest studies of the subject in 1741 — 2, which was re-issued in 1747 as *Gothic Architecture,*

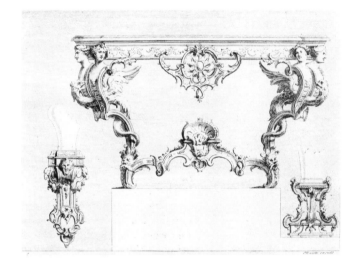

Nicholas Pineau
Design for a table issued in Mariette's *Architecture à la Mode.* (Below) Plagiarised by Batty Langley (Plate CXLIII *The City and Country Builder's and Workman's Treasury of Designs*). c.1731.

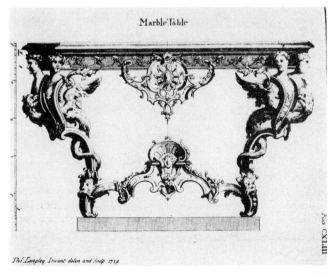

Improved by Rules and Proportions in many Grand Designs of Columns, Doors, Windows, Chimney Pieces.. Temples and Pavillions &c...'. The designs for Gothic chimney-pieces are included here.

On a lighter note he advertised in 1743 the publication of 'A Set of Fruit and Flowers done from Nature... making the most beautiful furniture for Dining-Rooms, Banquetting-Rooms, Closets &c as also the most useful for Ladies delighting in Embroidery, Painting, Japanning &c' (*London Evening Post*, 26-28 May). His books were available throughout the English provinces and the American colonies and in addition he seems to have had a good reputation in London, according to his obituary, 'for his great Integrity... in reducing the exhorbitant Bills of such Workmen who endeavoured to impose upon their Employers.' (*London Advertiser and Literary Gazette*, 6 March, 1751.)

William de la Cour
Engraved title-page for *First Book of Ornament.* 1741. *Victoria and Albert Museum.*

William de la Cour fl.1740s, d.1767

Ornamental designer, theatrical scenery painter and teacher of painting and drawing, he is presumed to have been of French origin and worked in London in the 1740s and '50s before settling in Edinburgh in 1757. In the *Daily Advertiser* of 13 February, 1745 he gave his address as Coventry-Court, The Haymarket, St. James's, where he taught 'Gentlemen and Ladies to draw and paint in Crayons and Watercolours', and sold artists' materials, old prints and drawings, and monochrome landscapes and watercolours for colouring.

In 1741 he began publication of eight *Books of Ornament*, issued annually, 'all in a new taste', i.e. in the Rococo style. The plates, which include some designs for chairs, were engraved by Vivares and various others including Jacob Bonneau, another drawing master practising in London. De la Cour was familiar, presumably through Vivares, with other members of the avant-garde group of artists in the St. Martin's Lane Academy who were so active in establishing the Rococo style in London in the 1740s.

The only complete set of the *Books of Ornament* is at the Cooper-Hewitt Museum, New York (1962-126-1 (1-56)).

William Kent c.1685-1748

Decorative painter, designer, architect and gardener whose style and career is well documented elsewhere. Peter Ward-Jackson stated that he was 'the first English architect to take a serious interest in furniture and, like Robert Adam later in the century, he sought to establish a harmonious relation between the architecture of a room and its furniture'. Despite his many commissions for designs of furniture for the houses in which he worked (including Houghton and Holkham in Norfolk, Chiswick House, Sherborne House, and Badminton, Gloucestershire), very few drawings or engravings survive. Some were published by John Vardy in 1744 in *Some Designs of Mr. Inigo Jones and Mr. William Kent*, which included 'Garden Seats, Chimney Pieces, Tables,

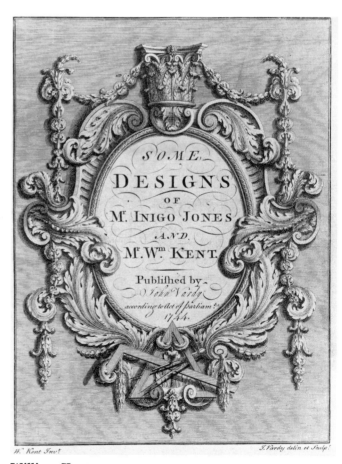

William Kent
Title-page of John Vardy's *Some Designs of Mr. Inigo Jones and Mr. Wm. Kent.* 1744.

William Kent
Drawing for a table for Sir Robert Walpole at Houghton Hall, Norfolk. 1731. *Victoria and Albert Museum.*

Chairs, Vauses, Candlesticks, Chandeliers and several useful Ornaments... To be sold at Mr. Sissons, Mathematical Instrument Maker to His Royal Highness the Prince of Wales, in the Strand; Mr. Loggins, Fan-Painter, in Albemarle Street... and at Mr. Vardy's at Hampton Court, at 16s. each book.' (*London Evening Post,* 30 April to 2 May, 1745). The designs for tables are in his characteristic classical style with many elements of Italian Baroque architecture and decoration (with which he was so familiar), while his design for the interior of Merlin's Cave at Richmond for the Queen (1735) contained light-hearted 'rustic' bookcases which anticipated the work of various later eighteenth century designers.

Abraham Swan fl.1745-68

Carpenter and joiner, active in London. He stated in his *Designs in Architecture* (1757) that he had 'more than thirty years application and experience in the Theory and Practice of Architecture'. Despite work at Blair Castle for the Duke of Atholl and for Lord Scarsdale at Kedleston, Stratton suggested that most of his clientele came from the middle classes rather than the nobility. In 1745 he first published *The British Architect; or The Builder's Treasury of Staircases,* of which further editions were printed in London in 1750 and 1758, in Philadelphia in 1775 and Boston in 1794. Apart from the Five Orders and architectural features such as doorcases, windows and staircases, it contained 'a great Variety of new and curious Chimney Pieces, in the most elegant and modern Taste', and 'Four different sorts of Corbels or Consoles, for setting Statues or Busts upon.' These latter were in quite an advanced Rococo style and clearly illustrate Swan's self-stated intention to 'communicate for the benefit of his brother Artificers' the elements of fashionable decoration. In 1757 he published *A Collection of Designs in Architecture,* and in 1758 *One Hundred and Fifty New Designs for Chimney Pieces,* of which six are reproduced here. Other publications were *Designs in Carpentry,* 1759, and *The Carpenter's Complete Instructor,* 1758.

Abraham Swan
Engraved design for a chimney-piece from *The British Architect; or The Builder's Treasury of Staircases.* 1745.

J.B.H. Toro 1672-1731

Carver and designer who was born and worked in Toulon, and who published many suites of ornament in Paris and a set in London in 1744 which included a design for a carved bracket with a grotesque mask. An advertisement for this work appeared in the *Daily Advertiser* on Saturday 10 November, 1744: 'A Book of Masks, and other Ornaments, design'd by B. Toro, engraved on nine Copper Plates, for the use of Coach-Painters &c, Watch-Engravers &c, Chasers and Carvers in Wood, Stone and Metals. Also proper for Youth to draw after. Sold by F. Noble at Otway's Head in St. Martin's Court near Leicester Fields.' These, and the designs published in Paris, were well known to such English Rococo designers as Matthias Lock and Thomas Johnson, who borrowed freely from them.

For illustration see overleaf.

J.B.H. Toro
Title-page for *A Compleat Book of Ornaments*. 1728. *Victoria and Albert Museum.*

Matthias Lock
Design for a table for the Tapestry Room, Hinton House, Dorset. 1745. Victoria and Albert Museum.

Matthias Lock c.1710-1765

One of the outstanding English carvers and designers in the Rococo style. He lived at 9, Nottingham Court, Castle Street, Long Acre, in the Tottenham Court Road, and was buried at St. Paul's, Covent Garden. In addition to designing and making some superb pieces of carved furniture for, among others, Earl Paulet of Hinton House, Dorset (which are now in the Victoria and Albert Museum), he was, according to the upholder James Cullen, 'reputed the best draftsman in that way that had ever been in England.' Many of his original drawings are preserved in the Victoria and Albert Museum and the Metropolitan Museum, New York. His first published work appeared in 1740 entitled *A New Drawing Book of Ornaments, Shields, Compartments, Masks &c.* His suites of designs for *Six Sconces* (1744), and *Six Tables* (1746), epitomise the advanced early Rococo style in English furniture, roughly a decade before Chippendale's first publication, while his designs in the 1750s show that he had advanced again to a lighter style and had introduced more chinoiserie elements. He collaborated with H. Copland (q.v.) in the publication of *A New Book of Ornaments* in 1752, in which the quality of engraving is

Matthias Lock
Title-page for *Six Tables*. 1746.

38

outstanding. In addition to his partnership with Copland, there appears to have been a working relationship with Thomas Chippendale (q.v.). In 1768 Robert Sayer republished Lock's *Six Sconces, Six Tables, Book of Shields, New Drawing Book of Ornaments,* and *A New Book of Ornaments for Looking Glass Frames, Chimney Pieces &c in the Chinese Taste...,* suggesting that these designs were still in popular demand in London. Many of Lock's designs were among the first eighteenth century Rococo furniture plates to be republished by Weale in 1831 and 1834, and accelerated the development of a Rococo, or Louis XV revival in the 1830s.

In 1769 *A New Book of Pier Frames* and *A New Drawing Book* by 'M. Lock' were published in London, with designs in the neo-classical style. There is some doubt as to whether these are by the same Matthias Lock, or one recorded at Clerkenwell Green by 1788. Heckscher believes this must be Lock's son. In this work therefore, the designs published between 1744 and 1768 are designated as by Matthias Lock, and those of 1769 by M. Lock.

H. Copland
Title-page for *A New Book of Ornaments*. 1746.

H. Copland fl.c.1738 on, d.1753

Designer and engraver, at Gutter Lane, Cheapside, with Bucksher in 1746. He engraved many trade cards for London and some provincial tradesmen, and in 1746 published *A New Book of Ornaments* in a bold Rococo style. In 1752 he collaborated with Matthias Lock (q.v.) in the publication of *A New Book of Ornaments of Twelve Leaves...* After c.1761 Sayer published *A New Book of Ornaments... Very Necessary for Those Unacquainted with that Useful Part of Drawing. By Copland and Others...,* the six plates of which were mainly devoted to instruction on drawing and shading, although Plate 6 included a design for the top part of a frame and a bracket (included here). Six designs for Hall chairs, signed 'Copland fecit', were included in Sayer's publication of Robert Manwaring's *Chair-Maker's Guide,* 1766. Very little else is known about him.

William Halfpenny fl. from c.1722, d.1755

Described himself as 'Architect and Carpenter' and occasionally 'Surveyor'; sometimes used the alias 'Michael Hoare, Carpenter'. Batty Langley referred to him in 1736 as 'Mr. William Halfpeny, *alias* Hoare, lately of Richmond in Surrey, Carpenter'; he may have been living in Bristol in the 1740s, and by 1752 was living in Greek Street, Soho. Various architectural commissions survive including Redland Chapel, Bristol, Stouts Hill, Gloucestershire, and the Orangery at Frampton Court, Gloucestershire. From 1722 onwards he published numerous architectural works, many of which went into subsequent editions, and his son John assisted him in many of the later works. While most of his designs were in the standard Palladian style, he also produced some imaginative essays in the Gothic and Chinese, in particular for garden buildings, for instance in his 1750 publication *New Designs for Chinese Temples, Triumphal Arches, Garden Seats, Palings &c... small but exceedingly beautiful Plans and Elevations in the Chinese Taste, elegantly decorated in the Indian Manner, yet suitably adapted to these Climates...'.* Halfpenny advertised his books extensively in the London newspapers and it appears that his work was being copied, for one advertisement stated that 'the true designs of Mr. Halfpenny have his name fix'd to each of them.' (*General Advertiser,* 15 December, 1750.) As well as designs for garden buildings, ornaments and furniture he published designs for parsonages, farmhouses, bridges,

William Halfpenny
Engraved design for a garden seat. c.1752.

39

Chinese and Gothic railing for fences and staircases, and a series of designs for chimney-pieces and the sides of rooms in a charming Rococo style by the ornamental carver Timothy Lightoler in *The Modern Builder's Assistant* (1757). His books were available in the American colonies, and Weinreb comments that Halfpenny's *Rural Architecture in the Chinese Taste* 'occupies an important place in the history of Chinese influence on 18th Century European Architecture' (it was well known in Germany and North America as well as in Britain).

Matthew (or Matthias) Darly fl.1741-1773

Engraver, designer, caricaturist and publisher. By 1754 he was living in Northumberland Court, The Strand, sharing premises with Thomas Chippendale (q.v.). In 1751 he issued his first pattern book, *A New Book of Chinese, Gothic and Modern Chairs* — objects primarily designed for the light-

Matthew Darly
Engraving from *A New Book of Chinese Designs*, 1754, Plate 32.

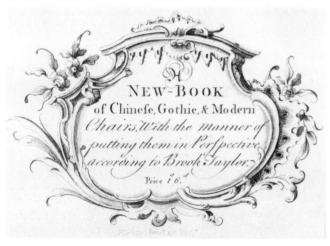

Matthew Darly
Title-page for *A New Book of Chinese, Gothic and Modern Chairs*. 1751.

hearted summer houses and garden pavilions popularised by William Halfpenny and others, although full chinoiserie schemes of decoration were soon to appear in English houses — for example, in the Chinese bedchamber at Badminton by 1753. This little book also includes, in Plate 7, the earliest eighteenth century designs for Gothic chairs. Darly's designs are curious as there is no attempt to depict the seats and legs of the chairs in proportion to their backs, and many variations for the carved work are shown, giving the illustrations an ungainly, misshapen character at first sight. At about the same time, Gilbert suggests, Darly issued a 'Second Book of Chairs', five plates of which were republished by Sayer in Manwaring's *Chair-Maker's Guide* of 1766, along with all the plates of the 1751 book. In 1753-4 Darly engraved many of the plates for Thomas Chippendale's first edition of *The Gentleman and Cabinet-Maker's Director* (q.v.). In 1754 he issued, with George Edwards, a collection of 120 designs in *A New Book of Chinese Designs calculated to improve the Present Taste, consisting of Figures,*

Buildings and Furniture, Lanskips, Birds, Beasts, Flowers and Ornaments &c...'; it represented the contemporary craze for chinoiserie ornament in all areas of the decorative arts — furniture, porcelain, wallpapers, textiles and metalwork — and its influence was very extensive. Some of the designs for tables and seats have a fairly authentic Chinese character, while others, (for example, the 'Grand Bed', Plate 10) are a mixture of French Rococo and European chinoiserie elements. Some of the plates were used by Sayer in *The Ladies' Amusement*, 1766. In 1762 Darly engraved plates for *The Universal System of Houshold Furniture* by Ince and Mayhew (q.v.). By 1770, in *The Ornamental Architect, or young Artist's Instructor* he was producing competent designs for tripods and frames in the neo-classical style, or 'Antique Taste'; his last work appears to have been *A New Book of Ornaments in the Present (Antique) Taste*, in 1772 in which he praised 'the light and airy ornaments... now practiz'd by our best modern Architects...'.

Robert Morris, c.1702-1754

Architect and surveyor, chiefly known for his publications devoted to the exposition of Palladio's rules of classical architecture from 1728. In 1750 he published *Rural Architecture*, republished as *Select Architecture* in 1755, which contained designs for garden buildings such as Plate IV, 'A Seat for a Garden purposed for Retirement, Where purling Rills, and Aromatick Sweets / In unfrequented Gloom, diffusive spread...' etc. In 1751 he published *The Architectural Remembrancer, being a Collection of New and useful Designs of Ornamental Buildings and Decorations for Parks, Gardens, Woods etc, to which are added, A Variety of Chimney-Pieces, after the Manner of Inigo Jones and Mr. Kent:* this was re-issued as *Architecture Improv'd, in a Collection of Modern, Useful and Elegant Designs* in 1752. However an advertisement in the *General Advertiser* for Wednesday, 22 April of that year still referred to the first title of the *Architectural Remembrancer*, 'designed by Robert Morris, Surveyor, printed for the Author and sold by Mr. Owen at Temple-Bar, where may be had... *Rural Architecture;* consisting of regular designs of Plans, Decorations etc. not in the Modern, Gothic or

Chinese Taste, exemplified with Dragons, Monkeys and other ridiculous Decorations; but with the pure Greek and Roman Orders, whose Beauty and Antiquity can never be eradicated by Modern Follies'. Notwithstanding, he included a 'Chimerical Seat for a Garden' in the Chinese style (Plate 26 of *Architecture Improv'd*): 'I have placed it here, to keep in countenance all true Lovers of the Oriental Taste, and to show how trifles may be esteemed, when it is the Fashion to be ridiculous.' Best of all is his postscript in *The Architectural Remembrancer,* with its spoof advertisement for more Chinoiserie designs, and which is worth quoting in full:

'I beg leave to make an Observation or two on the peculiar Fondness of Novelty, which reigns at present: I mean the Affectation of the (improperly called) Chinese Taste; as it consists in mere Whim and Chimera, without Rules or Order, it requires no Fertility of Genius to put in Execution; the Principals are a good Choice of Chains and Bells, and different Colours of Paint. — As to the Serpents, Dragons and Monkeys &c., they, like the Rest of the Beauties, may be cut in Paper, and pasted on any where, or in any Manner: A few Laths nailed across each other, and made Black, Red, Blue, Yellow, or any other Colour, or mix'd with any sort of Chequer-Work, or Impropriety of Ornament, completes the Whole. But as this far-fetch'd Fashion has lately been introduced, I am prevailed on by a Friend to give him a Place for the following Advertisement:- There is now in the Press, and speedily will be published, *A Treatise on Country Five-Barr'd Gates, Stiles and Wickets, elegant Pig-Styes, beautiful Hen-Houses, and delightful Cow-Cribs, superb Cart-Houses, magnificent Barn-Doors, variegated Barn-Racks and admirable Sheep-Folds, according to the Turkish and Persian Manner* a Work never (till now) attempted, To which are added, *Some Designs of Fly-Traps, Bees' Palaces, and Emmet Houses, in the Muscovite and Arabian Architecture,* all adapted to the Latitude and Genius of England. The Whole entirely new, and inimitably designed in Two Parts, on Forty Pewter Plates, under the immediate Inspection of Don Gulielmus de Demi Je ne Sçai Quoi, Chief Advisor to the Grand Signor, originally printed in the Grand Seraglio at Constantinople, and now translated into English by Jemmy Gymp. To be sold (only by Ebenezer Sly) at the Brazen Head near Temple-Bar'.

After his death his house, coach-house and stables in Hyde Park Street, Grosvenor Square were sold for the benefit of his orphans, together with 'his Household Furniture, Plate, China and Wearing Apparel. A small but well-chosen collection of Books, in History, Architecture, and most Branches of Polite Literature, some MSS., the Copies of his Books of Architecture with the Copper-Plates, printed in his Lifetime, and two new Books of Drawings intended to be printed this Summer, with several other Sketches and Designs' (*Public Advertiser* 8 April, 1755). According to another advertisement for his books by Robert Sayer, Morris' work 'always exhibited the nicest judgement and most refined selection' (*Public Advertiser,* 6 June, 1755). Morris himself stated in the Preface to *The Architectural Remembrancer* that 'The chiefest Skill required in the Designer, is Proportion and proper Bearings, that the Ornaments are not inconsistent, too petite, or gross and luxuriant, illy appropriated or unnecessary.'

Babel of Paris
Title-page for *A New Book of Ornaments.* 1752.

Babel 1720-1770

Both Dr. Geoffrey Beard and Simon Jervis query whether this is Peter Babel, mentioned in Mortimer's *Universal Director,* London, 1763, as 'Designer and Modeller, Long Acre, near James Street — one of the first Importers of Papier-Mache Ornaments for Ceilings, Chimney-Pieces, Picture-Frames &c...', or whether it is Pierre-Edmé Babel, a woodcarver and designer working in Paris from c.1736 who published a number of designs for carved ornament. Michael Snodin states that it is more likely to have been the latter who issued in 1752 *A New Book of Ornaments for Glasses, Chairs, Tables, Sconces &c., with Trophies in ye Chinese Way, drawn for ye Use of Artificers in General,* by Babel of Paris 'and engraved by George Bickham Junior (1706?-1771). The plates are crowded with wildly asymmetrical ornament and obviously were intended for 'artificers' to extract whichever elements they might choose — a system common among eighteenth century designers which made maximum use of fairly expensive copper-plates.

Thomas Chippendale c.1718-1779

Cabinet-maker, upholsterer and designer, whose name has been virtually synonymous with the English Rococo style in furniture. By 1748 he had come to London from his native Yorkshire and in 1753 was sharing premises with Matthias Darly (q.v.) in Northumberland Court, The Strand. In that year he moved to St. Martin's Lane with his partner James Rannie (d.1776) and from c.1771 until his death was in partnership with Thomas Haig. His career has been documented fully and with great scholarship in recent years by Christopher Gilbert. His reputation as a fine cabinet-maker and upholsterer, an astute businessman and a remarkable designer has remained consistently high

Thomas Chippendale
Original design for a toilet table. Engraved as Plate CXVIII from *The Director* 3rd ed. 1763. *Victoria and Albert Museum.*

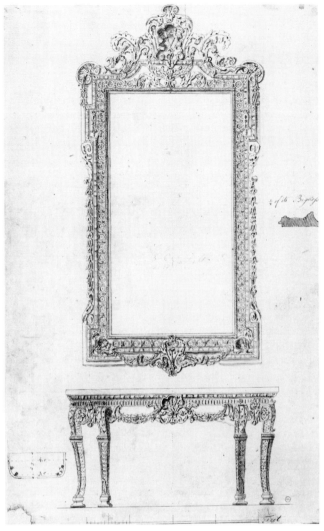

Thomas Chippendale
Original design for mirror and table, c.1760. *Victoria and Albert Museum.*

virtually since his own time, and today he is still the best known of all English furniture makers and designers.

In 1753 he published advertisements for his famous work, *The Gentleman and Cabinet-Maker's Director,* 'Being a new Book of Designs of Household Furniture in the Gothic, Chinese and Modern Taste, as improved by the politest and most able Artists... A Work long wish'd for, of universal Utility, and accomodated to the Fancy and Circumstance of Persons in every Degree of Life...'. *(Public Advertiser,* 7 June, 1753). It was published in April 1754 and was available immediately in London, York and Edinburgh. It was a *tour de force*:- the largest pattern book ever devoted solely to furniture designs, comprehending all branches of the business, giving measurements, full instructions for the finish and even the intended location of individual pieces.

Chippendale attracted 308 subscribers before publication, including nobility and gentry and many cabinet-makers, upholsterers, carvers, joiners, carpenters, frame makers,

engravers, enamellers, other craftsmen and a number of booksellers, thus ensuring the book's wide popularity. The one hundred and sixty plates were finely engraved by Matthias Darly, J.S. Muller and others. It sold out rapidly and a second edition, with the same plates and a few minor alterations, was issued in 1755.

By 1759 he was working on a third edition which was first issued in loose sheets from 1760-62, and finally in a complete volume in 1763, with 104 plates from the first edition (some modified) and 106 new plates by a total of nine engravers. The notes to the plates show greater attention to the details of finishes, upholstery materials, locations for various pieces and more elements of interior decoration — for example, chimney-pieces and gilt borders for damask wall hangings and papers. The more naïve of the Rococo designs of the first edition were omitted and new plates revealed a move towards classicism that characterised most of Chippendale's executed work in the 1760s and 1770s. A French edition

THE
GENTLEMAN
AND
CABINET-MAKER's
DIRECTOR.

BEING A LARGE
COLLECTION
OF THE MOST
Elegant and Useful Designs of Houshold Furniture
IN THE
GOTHIC, CHINESE and MODERN TASTE:

Including a great VARIETY of

BOOK-CASES for LIBRARIES or Private ROOMS. COMMODES, LIBRARY and WRITING-TABLES, BUROES, BREAKFAST-TABLES, DRESSING and CHINA-TABLES, CHINA-CASES, HANGING-SHELVES,	TEA-CHESTS, TRAYS, FIRE-SCREENS, CHAIRS, SETTEES, SOPHA'S, BEDS, PRESSES and CLOATHS-CHESTS, PIER-GLASS SCONCES, SLAB FRAMES, BRACKETS, CANDLE-STANDS, CLOCK-CASES, FRETS,

AND OTHER
ORNAMENTS.

TO WHICH IS PREFIXED,
A Short EXPLANATION of the Five ORDERS of ARCHITECTURE, and RULES of PERSPECTIVE;
WITH
Proper DIRECTIONS for executing the most difficult Pieces, the Mouldings being exhibited at large, and the Dimensions of each DESIGN specified:

THE WHOLE COMPREHENDED IN
One Hundred and Sixty COPPER-PLATES, neatly Engraved,

Calculated to improve and refine the present TASTE, and suited to the Fancy and Circumstances of Persons in all Degrees of Life.

Dulcique animos novitate tenebo. OVID.
Ludentis speciem dabit & torquebitur. HOR.

BY
THOMAS CHIPPENDALE,
Of St. *MARTIN's-LANE*, CABINET-MAKER.

LONDON,

Printed for the AUTHOR, and sold at his House in St. MARTIN's-LANE. MDCCLIV.
Also by T. OSBORNE, Bookseller, in Gray's-Inn; H. PIERS, Bookseller, in Holborn; R. SAYER, Print-seller, in Fleetstreet; J. SWAN, near Northumberland-House, in the Strand. At EDINBURGH, by Messrs. HAMILTON and BALFOUR: And at DUBLIN, by Mr. JOHN SMITH, on the Blind-Quay.

Thomas Chippendale
Title-page from *The Director,* 1st ed. 1754

Thomas Chippendale
Drawing for a bookcase, c.1760.
Victoria and Albert Museum.

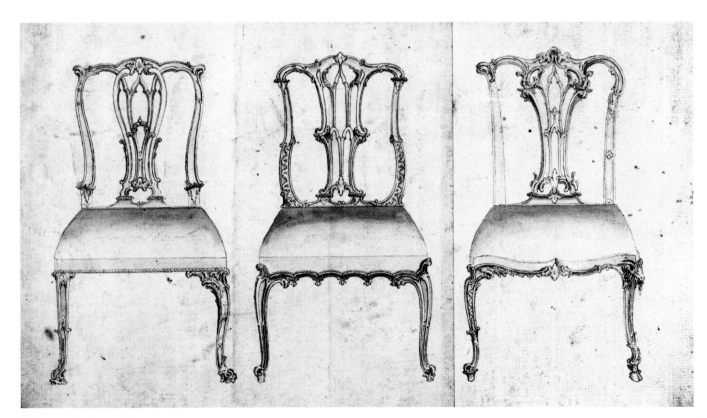

Thomas Chippendale
Drawing for chairs. Engraved as Plate XIV from *The Director*, 3rd ed. 1763. *Victoria and Albert Museum.*

appeared at the same time, and copies were in the libraries of the Empress Catherine the Great and Louis XVI. At least nine copies are known to have been in America before 1786.

Many of Chippendale's original designs for *The Director* survive (mainly in the collections of the Victoria and Albert Museum and the Metropolitan Museum of Art, New York), and according to Christopher Gilbert 'reveal myriad subtleties which the engraver's burin failed to capture and unquestionably rank as one of the finest collections of English Rococo ornament. Chippendale's linear expression ranges from dynamic exuberance, through rhythmic animation to delicate static patterns.' It is generally accepted that the three editions of *The Director* made his name and brought him such commercial success that further publications of designs were unnecessary, although he contributed at least six plates to the Society of Upholsterers' *Houshold Furniture in the Genteel Taste,* published by Sayer in 1760 (q.v.). Modern reprints of the 3rd edition have been available since 1900.

several other Pieces.' He lived at various addresses in Soho. Johnson's career as a carver and designer has been researched with great scholarship, and he ranks with Matthias Lock and Thomas Chippendale as one of the great interpreters of English Rococo. In 1755 he issued a set of *Twelve Girandoles,* engraved by William Austin, composed of fanciful ornament incorporating animals and birds from Barlow's illustrations of Aesop's Fables. From 1756-58 he published more designs in four parts on a total of fifty-two plates engraved by Butler Clowes and James Kirk. This was re-issued, with one extra plate in 1761 as *One Hundred and Fifty New Designs.* The patterns are for carved work only (Johnson's own skill) and include mirror and picture frames, candle stands, pier tables, chimney-pieces and overmantels, brackets, clock cases, watch cases, girandoles and candle-sticks. There is one design for an elaborately decorated wall of a room, and one plate of ceiling patterns. All of them are in a vigorous, fanciful style, again taking images from Aesop's Fables and using 'rustic' touches with imitation moss, twigs and bark, as well as marine and land creatures, leaves, flowers and birds. Some of these designs were republished by Weale in 1834 in *Chippendale's Designs for Sconces... in the Old French Style* and *Chippendale's Ornaments and Interior Decoration in the Old French Style:* on some of the plates Johnson's name was erased and that of Chippendale inserted. Johnson also published a design for a girandole representing Earth in 1760, *A New Book of Ornaments* in 1762, with details of friezes and tablets for chimney-pieces 'Useful for Youth to draw after', and in 1775 a sheet of designs for neo-classical oval mirrors appeared, inscribed 'Plate 5... Tho. Johnson fecit'. There is no documentary evidence concerning his executed carved work, although various pieces survive that relate directly to his designs.

Thomas Johnson
Dedication page to Lord Blakeney from *One Hundred and Fifty New Designs.* 1761.

Thomas Johnson 1714-c.1778

Described in Mortimer's *Universal Director,* 1763, as 'Carver, Teacher of Drawings and Modelling and Author of a Book of Designs for Chimney Pieces and other ornaments, and of

Jean Pillement
Engraving from *A New Book of Chinese Ornaments.* 1755.

Jean Pillement 1728-1808

Painter and designer. Born in Lyon, he worked as a designer at the Gobelins Tapestry Manufactory in Paris between 1750 and 1763, and published sheets of ornament in a light Rococo and chinoiserie style. In 1755 he issued in London *A New Book of Chinese Ornaments* which added to the repertoire of chinoiserie ornament used by a wide range of English craftsmen, if not specifically furniture makers. In 1766 his engravings were included in Robert Sayer's *The Ladies' Amusement,* together with some by Decker (q.v.): these included designs for garden pavilions, temples, and seats in the rustic, chinoiserie and Gothic styles.

François Vivares.
Engraved design for a cartouche, c.1750.

François Vivares 1709-1780

An engraver and designer of French origin who came to England in 1727 and spent the rest of his life in this country, engraving a wide range of subjects from landscapes after Claude to decorative details, borders, and cartouches. In 1755 he was living in Newport Street, London. Various loose sheets of ornamental designs for brackets, frames and borders are reproduced here.

Sir William Chambers 1723-1796

An outstanding British architect and designer, whose best known works include Somerset House, London, and the decorative buildings in Kew Gardens. He was the son of a Scottish merchant and born in Gothenburg, Sweden. As an employee of the Swedish East India Company he made three voyages to China before studying in Paris and Italy between 1749 and 1755. In 1757 he was living in Russell Street, Covent Garden, and in that year he published *Designs of Chinese Buildings, Furniture, Dresses, Machines and Utensils... from the Originals drawn in China.* The purpose of the book was to put 'a stop to the extravagancies that daily appear under the name of Chinese, though most of them are mere inventions, the rest copies from the lame representations found on porcelain and paper hangings.' The plates illustrating authentic Chinese furniture 'were taken from such models as appeared to me the most beautiful, and reasonable; some of them are pretty, and may be useful to our cabinetmakers.'

His subscribers included royalty, nobility and cognoscenti, as well as the decorative painter Cipriani, the plasterer Joseph Rose, the chaser George Michael Moser and the cabinet-maker Sefferin Alken. In his introduction he denied that he wished to promote Chinese architecture in preference to the Antique, 'at least the knowledge is curious, and on particular occasions may likewise be useful... For though, generally speaking, Chinese Architecture does not suit European purposes, yet in extensive parks and gardens, where a great variety of scenes are required, or in immense palaces, containing a numerous series of apartments, I do not see the impropriety of furnishing some of the inferior ones in the Chinese taste. Variety is always delightful, and novelty, attended with nothing inconsistent or disagreeable, sometimes takes place of beauty.' Chambers failed to put an end to the 'extragavancies' of European chinoiserie, and his more characteristic work in the classical style was undoubtedly of greater importance. In 1759 he published the first part of his *Treatise on Civil Architecture* which became one of the standard English works on classical building: further editions were printed in 1768 and 1791, 1825, and 1826. He paid great attention to the details of interior decoration and furnishing, and claimed that he was 'really a very pretty Connoisseur in furniture.' The most important collections of his drawings are in the R.I.B.A. Drawings Collection, Sir John Soane's Museum, The Victoria and Albert Museum and the Royal Library at Windsor. He is buried in Westminster Abbey.

Thomas Major 1720-1799

Engraver and designer, who in 1754 lived at The Golden Head, Chandos Street near St. Martin's Lane. From 1756 he was Seal Engraver to the King, and the first engraver appointed to serve the Royal Academy. He published many engravings after well-known paintings, for example Watteau's *Fêtes Venitiennes,* and various sheets of ornamental borders for frames, panelling etc., reproduced here.

Charles Over fl.1755-60

Nothing is known about this man except for his own description of himself as an architect and his publication in 1758 of *Ornamental Architecture in the Gothic, Chinese and Modern Taste, being above fifty intire new Designs of Plans, Sections, Elevations &c, (many of which may be executed with Roots of Trees), for Gardens, Parks, Forests, Woods, Canals &c.'* This little book has been described as 'the most elegant, the most inventive (in a true Rococo way) and in many ways the most influential of the "Chinese" pattern books before Chambers' (Weinreb, Catalogue 17, 1966, No.111). The designs for garden seats with their descriptions are included in this work. The other designs were for grottoes, hermitages, temples, ice-houses, banqueting-houses, bridges, Chinese boats, cascades and obelisks.

Paul Decker
'An Honorary Pagoda'; engraving from *Chinese Architecture, Civil and Ornamental*. 1759.

Paul Decker fl.1759

Nothing is known about this man except that he described himself as an architect in the title-pages of two design books published in 1759. Michael Snodin suggests that Decker may be a pseudonym, for many of the plates in the first work to bear this name, entitled *Chinese Architecture, Civil and Ornamental,* were originally published in Darly and Edwards' *New Book of Chinese Designs*, 1754. The plates were claimed to be 'from real designs, drawn in China, adapted to this climate', showing an awareness of the impact of Chambers' work published in 1757. Many of the plates were republished in Sayer's *The Ladies' Amusement* in 1766. They included designs for garden seats, Chinese paling and fencing and windows in the Chinese taste, as well as fanciful buildings. The second volume was *Gothic Architecture, Decorated, consisting of a large Collection of Temples, Banquetting, Summer and Green Houses, Gazebos, Alcoves, Faced, Garden and Umbrello'd Seats, Rustic Garden Seats, Root Houses and Hermitages*

for Summer and Winter, Obelisks, Pyramids &c. Many of which may be executed with Pollards, Rude Branches and Roots of Trees, being a Taste entirely new...'. Included here are the designs for garden seats, Gothic railing and fencing (as easily used for staircases and fretwork indoors as in the garden), frets and Gothic windows. Two of the plates were republished in Sayer's *The Ladies' Amusement*, 1766. The fashion for root and twig furniture can also be seen in Robert Manwaring's designs a few years later (q.v.).

A Society of Upholsterers fl.1760

No firm documentary evidence survives about the identity of this 'Society', but it appears to have been a group of the most fashionable furniture makers and designers in London who provided the publisher Robert Sayer with patterns for a volume of sixty plates entitled *Household Furniture in the Genteel Taste for the Year 1760... Consisting of China, Breakfast, Sideboard, Dressing, Toilet, Card, Writing, Claw, Library, Slab and Night Tables, Chairs, Couches, French Stools, Cabinets, Commodes, China Shelves and Cases, Trays, Chests, Stands for Candles, Tea-Kettles, Pedestals, Stair-Case Lights, Screens, Desks, Book and Clock-Cases, Frames for Glasses, Sconce and Chimney Pieces, Girandoles, Lanthorns, Chandalaers [sic] &c &c.* Among

Plate from the Society of Upholsterers' *Houshold Furniture in the Genteel Taste...*, 1760-65. This may have been contributed by Matthias Lock and is one of the higher quality patterns.

those involved were Thomas Chippendale, William Ince and John Mayhew, Thomas Johnson, Robert Manwaring, Matthias Darly and possibly Matthias Lock (q.v.). There was no accompanying text. A second edition was published by Sayer in 1762 with 100 plates and was reissued in 1763 with only the date altered. In 1764 or 1765 Sayer issued a fourth and final version of the second edition, entitled *Genteel Houshold Furniture in the present Taste,* which was republished in facsimile in 1978 with an introduction by Christopher Gilbert. As the title shows, the designs were for all types of domestic furniture, including firegrates and irons. Robert Manwaring may have contributed most of the designs for chairs, which were republished by Sayer in 1766 in *The Chair Maker's Guide;* three plates of seat furniture have been attributed to Ince and Mayhew. Some of the tables and pieces of cabinet furniture have been attributed to Chippendale (e.g. Plate 30, for which an original drawing by him survives in the Metropolitan Museum of Art, New York), while some of the beds, pedestals and firescreens have been attributed to Ince and Mayhew, and some carved frames and stands to Thomas Johnson. Peter Ward-Jackson has criticised these designs as 'mostly for rather plain and modest-looking furniture, and they are somewhat dull and lacking in originality', and Christopher Gilbert suggests that their publication may have been directed at practising craftsmen rather than prospective clients. A copy in the Victoria and Albert Museum, however, contains Horace Walpole's bookplate.

Ince and Mayhew

William Ince (active 1758-1803) and John Mayhew (active c.1755-1811)

Cabinet-makers and upholsterers in partnership in Broad Street, Carnaby Market, London, from 1758/9 to 1804. Their reputation has hung largely on their publication, at the very beginning of their long business partnership, of Rococo designs for furniture in 1759-60, whereas in fact the greater part of their business career was spent in the manufacture of high quality furniture in the neo-classical style, often to the designs of Robert Adam. The publication of their only book, *The Universal System of Houshold Furniture,*

Ince and Mayhew
Title-page for *The Universal System of Houshold Furniture.* 1762.

Ince and Mayhew
Original watercolour for a State Bed, engraved as Plate XXXII of *The Universal System,* 1762, 'which has been executed, and may be esteemed among the best in England; the Furniture was blue Damask, and all the Ornaments in burnish'd Gold...'. *Victoria and Albert Museum.*

was first advertised in July 1759 and the sheets were issued at one shilling each over the next twelve months. A complete volume was available in 1762. The work was intended to have one hundred and sixty plates (in fact it had one hundred and one) comprising about three hundred designs, intended 'to render the Work of the greatest Utility, as well as in assisting the Fancy of the Nobility and Gentry, as in improving the young Artist in his Ideas of Designing...'. In their introduction they acknowledged the example set by Chippendale's *Director*, and although their work was modelled on that format and content, it was no slavish copy.

Ince contributed all but seven of the designs and also provided plates for the various editions of the Society of Upholsterers' *Houshold Furniture in the Genteel Taste...* between 1760 and 1765. John Mayhew contributed some of the designs for seat furniture. Their notes to the plates, in French and English, give brief directions for the finish of some of the pieces, for instance the Hall Chairs (Plate IV), 'the ornaments of which, if thought too expensive, may be painted' (rather than carved), 'and have a very good Effect,' and Chinese Dressing Chairs (Plate XXXV) 'very proper for a Lady's Dressing Room, especially if it is hung with India Paper...'. They stated that some of the pieces illustrated had been executed by them 'and much admired', and in Plate LXV illustrated a design for a whole side of a dressing room, with an alcove containing a Turkish Sofa, dedicated to Lady Fludyer. This, and the final two plates for stove grates, show that the partners, like Chippendale, were aiming to provide a complete interior furnishing service. The careers of Ince and Mayhew have been researched by Hugh Roberts and Charles Cator. *The Universal System* was reissued in facsimile by Alec Tiranti in 1960.

P. Baretti
Title-page from *A New Book of Ornaments*. 1762.

P. Baretti fl.c.1762-66

Ornamental designer about whom nothing is known beyond the publication of a slim volume entitled *A New Book of Ornaments on Sixteen Leaves for the year 1762, very useful for Cabinet Makers, Carvers, Painters, Engravers &c*. These are outline drawings and shaded plates depicting carved

ornament including two cornices and ornamental cresting. All the designs are in a competent Rococo style. Another volume, for the year 1766, was advertised in Webley's catalogue bound into John Crunden's *Chimney-Piece Maker's Daily Assistant*, but no extant copy of this edition has been found.

John Crunden
'Two New Frets for Cabinet-Makers &c'. Engraving from *The Joyner and Cabinet-Maker's Darling*. 1765.

John Crunden 1745-1835

Architect and surveyor in London who published various design books, mainly in the Rococo style, both on his own and in collaboration with others between 1765 and 1770. He did not publish designs for actual pieces of furniture, but for decorative carved fretwork and railing for use on such pieces. Examples can be seen in his first work, *The Joyner and Cabinet-Maker's Darling, or Pocket-Book... containing Sixty different Designs, Forty of which are Gothic, Chinese, Mosaic and Ornamental Frets, Proper for Friezes, Book-Cases, Tea Tables, Tea Stands, Trays...'* (1765). Other designs were for ornamental door-tops. Also in 1765 he published *Designs for Ornamental Ceilings* and contributed two plates of designs for railings to Robert Manwaring's *The Carpenter's Compleat Guide to the Whole System of Gothic Railing* (Plates 15 and 16). In 1766 he collaborated with Thomas Milton and Placido Columbani to issue *The Chimney-Piece Maker's Daily Assistant, or a Treasury of New Designs for Chimney-Pieces,... in the Antique, Modern, Ornamental and Gothic Taste...* In 1770 he published *Convenient and Ornamental Architecture... calculated both for Town and Country and to suit all Persons in every Station in Life...'*, which contained designs for interiors decorated with Rococo plasterwork. In 1770 he also issued, with J.H. Morris, *The Carpenter's Companion for Chinese Railing and Gates... being a Work of Universal Use to Carpenters, Joyners &c., and intended to furnish the Nobility and Gentry with Variety of Choice...* Once again these designs were adaptable to furniture and interior woodwork, and are included here.

Robert Manwaring fl.1760-66

He described himself as a cabinet-maker, with premises in the Haymarket, London, but nothing is known about his practice of the trade. His reputation exists on the publication of a number of design books in a fairly standard Rococo style between 1760 and 1766, although it is worth noticing that in one of them he claims that 'there are very few designs advanced, but what he has either executed himself, or seen completely finished by others'. He contributed most of the plates 1-28 for seat furniture to the Society of Upholsterers' *Household Furniture in the Genteel Taste for the Year 1760* (q.v.). These were republished by Sayer in 1766 as part of *The Chair-Maker's Guide; being upwards of two Hundred new and genteel Designs... for Gothic, Chinese, Ribbon and other Chairs, Couches, Settees, Burjairs, French, Dressing and Corner Stools... many of the rural Kind may be executed with rude Branches, or Limbs of Trees &c...'*. Other plates in the book (33-4, 37, 39-45) for hall and parlour chairs were by Matthias Darly (q.v.) and had already been published in the latter's *New Book of Chinese, Gothic and Modern Chairs*, 1751 and his *Second Book of Chairs* of about the same date. Three plates were signed by Ince and Mayhew (q.v.) and others by Copland (q.v.). It is impossible to tell whether Manwaring was behind this compilation or whether (which is more likely) it was the publisher and print seller Robert Sayer making a living out of re-issuing so many of the furniture designs of the 1750s.

In 1765 Manwaring issued *The Carpenter's Compleat Guide to the whole System of Gothic Railing...* A further edition was published in 1775, two plates of which were contributed by J.H. Muntz, 'one of the most ingenious gentlemen that ever was in England', and two plates by John Crunden (q.v.). These designs were intended primarily for ornamental garden fences and gates, but were adaptable for interior staircases and dados and are included here.

In 1765 Manwaring also issued his best known work, *The Cabinet and Chair-Maker's Real Friend and Companion, or the whole System of Chair Making made Plain and Easy; containing upwards of one Hundred new and useful Designs for all Sorts of Chairs, and adapted to be made for Halls, Lobbies, Parlours, State, Dining, Ball and Drawing Rooms, amongst which are some very elegant in the Chinese and Gothic Taste, Ladies Dressing Chairs and Stools, Grand French Settees and Elbows, Back Stools, very rich and elegant rural Chairs for Summer Houses finely ornamented with Carvings, Fountains and beautiful Landscapes... Also some very beautiful Designs, supposed to be executed with the Limbs of Yew, Apple or Pear Trees, ornamented with Leaves and Blossoms, which if properly painted will appear like Nature; these are the only Designs of the Kind that ever were published...* In his Preface he stated that 'the Designs are calculated for all People in different Stations of Life, that they are actually Originals, and not pirated or copied from the Designs and Inventions of Others, which of late hath been much practised.'. He gives suggestions for the use of different sorts of woods, for painted finishes, loose cushions, and careful instructions for making the twig or root chairs in Plates 26 and 27. He stated that he had executed chairs to some of the designs, and some which are similar to the plates do exist.

Alexander Willson fl.1766

Described himself as 'Architect and Professor of Ornament', but nothing is known about him beyond the publication in 1766 of *The Antique and Modern Embellisher, or young Architect's Assistant... collected from Antique Reliques, Ancient Authors, Original Drawings from the best Italian, French and English*

Alexander Willson
Title-page for *The Antique and Modern Embellisher*. 1766.

Architects. Willson stated that 'This Work is absolutely necessary for the Study and Instruction of the following Professions, viz. Architects, Painters, Joiners, Carpenters, Upholsterers, Goldsmiths, Cabinet and Chair Makers, Stucco Workers, Carvers, Engravers, Chasers, Smiths, Japanners, Enamellers, Tin-Workers, Founders, Gunsmiths, Coachmakers, Coach-Harness Makers, Buckle-Makers, Confectioners, Pattern-Drawers and Stove-Grate Makers.' Most of the fifty plates were classical borders, but some were Persian, Indian and Moresque border patterns for 'Japanners, Porcelain Painters &c.'.

William Wrighte fl.1767

Architect and author of *Grotesque Architecture, or Rural Amusement, consisting of Plans, Elevations and Sections for Huts, Retreats, Summer and Winter Hermitages, Terminaries, Chinese, Gothic and Natural Grottos, Cascades, Mosques, Moresque Pavilions, Grotesque and Rustic Seats, Green houses &c, many of which may be executed with Flints, irregular Stones, rude Branches and Roots of Trees*, 1767 (second edition, 1790). Wrighte gave full desciptions of the 28 plates, which, although they do not include individual designs for furniture, nevertheless give an excellent idea of the variety and originality of mid-eighteenth century buildings. In Plate 6, for instance, the floor of a Summer Hermitage 'should be paved with Sheep's Marrow Bones placed upright, or any other pretty Device intermixed with them'. The seats in Plate 4 were rustic, and intended to be made 'of large irregular Stones, Roots of Pollard Trees cemented together.'

N. Wallis fl.1771-3

Described himself as an architect, although nothing is known about him apart from his publication of three books of designs in the early 1770s. The first of these was *A Book of Ornaments in the Palmyrene Taste*, 1771; it contained designs for ceilings, panels and mouldings. The second was *The Complete Modern Joiner, or a Collection of Designs in the present Taste for Chimney Pieces and Door Cases...*, 1772. In 1773 he published *The Carpenter's Treasure, A Collection of Designs for*

William Wrighte
Plate 19 from *Grotesque Architecture*, 1767.

Temples, Gates, Doors and Bridges in the Gothic Taste. . . and some Specimens of Rails in the Chinese Taste. The designs for rails are reproduced here. Colvin assessed the standard of Wallis' designs as 'not high, and they were not among the more influential pattern books of their time.'.

Thomas Pether
Title-page for *A Book of Ornaments*. 1773.

Thomas Pether fl.1773

Described himself as a carver but nothing is known about him apart from his publication in January 1773 of *A Book of Ornaments, suitable for Beginners: by Tho⁵ Pether, Carver. . . and sold at his Print Shop in Berwick Street, Soho, London. Price One Shilling.* The six plates were for carved ribbons, husks, acanthus, volutes and foliage in the neo-classical style, intended for use on the tablets of chimney-pieces. The book was listed in I. and J. Taylor's Architectural Library, c.1780, and was republished by John Weale in *Old English and French Ornaments. . .* 1858-9, and again with a text by Dick Reid in *Furniture History*, Vol.XI, 1975.

Robert Adam 1728-1792

Arguably the most famous eighteenth century British architect and designer, whose remarkable career in partnership with his brothers James and William has been thoroughly documented elsewhere and whose major commissions can still be seen at Harewood House, Kedleston Hall, Kenwood, Syon House and Osterley Park. He established a business in London after a study tour in Paris and Italy from 1754-58, and in 1761 was appointed Architect of the King's Works, with Sir William Chambers (q.v.). He achieved early success with his designs for interiors in a light classical style that was based on fresh study of Roman domestic, rather than public, decoration, and Raphael's interpretations of it in the sixteenth century. Adam referred to the style as 'by far the most perfect that has ever appeared for inside decorations', and through it he aimed to achieve complete harmony by including in its scope all aspects of furnishings, from the decoration of walls to tables, frames, and the finer details of door furniture, lighting and, very importantly, the position of objects within a room. Nearly 9,000 original drawings by him are preserved in Sir John Soane's Museum, London, and others in the collections of the Victoria and Albert Museum, the R.I.B.A. and the National Gallery of Scotland.

Robert Adam's first publication was an illustrated treatise on *The Ruins of the Palace of the Emperor Diocletian at Spalatro in Dalmatia*, 1764 — a result of his visit in 1757. From 1773-78 Robert and James issued in sets Part I of *Works in Architecture* which proudly publicised their own achievements:- 'We have not trod in the path of others, nor derived aid from their labours. In the works which we have had the honour to execute, we have. . . in some measure. . . brought about in this country a kind of revolution in the whole system of this useful and elegant art.' Part II was published in 1779, and Part III posthumously in 1822 by Priestley and Weale. The text and titles are given throughout in French as well as English, and this accounts in part for Adam's influence on contemporary French decoration. The plates were engraved by a number of artists including Pastorini, Zucchi, Vivares and Begbie, and illustrated designs executed for specific patrons as well as for the Adam brothers' own building venture, the Adelphi, London. The published *Works*, therefore, only represent a fragment of the firm's vast output of designs and executed work. There are quite a number of designs for furniture, either shown as part of whole schemes of decoration, or singly, and they concentrate mainly on items that formed part of the architectural entity of a room

Robert Adam
Engraving of a chimney-piece for Derby House, Grosvenor Square, Vol.II *Works in Architecture*, No. I, Plate V, dated 1777.

Robert Adam
'Design of a Bookcase for Lady Wynn's Dressing Room'. Dated 'Adelphi 9th February', 1776. Pen, ink and watercolour. (For 20 St. James's Square, built for Sir Watkin Williams Wynn, 1772-4). *By courtesy of the Trustees of Sir John Soane's Museum.*

— pier tables, mirror frames, sideboards and pedestals, and lighting equipment. There are hardly any designs for seat furniture, no beds, only one design for a commode, but some designs for rather splendid individual pieces such as the harpsichord for the Empress of Russia, and a Sedan chair for the Queen. Two plates in Part III include designs for clocks, intended to be executed in gilt metal or wood. Thus the published designs give only a slight idea of the enormous variety of pieces of furniture which Adam designed and which were executed by the leading craftsmen of the time, including John Linnell, Chippendale, Ince and Mayhew, Vile and Cobb, and Samuel Norman.

John Carter 1748-1817

The son of a mason and monumental sculptor in London, Carter received training as an architect but devoted most of his life to recording and illustrating mediaeval antiquities, for example in Gough's *Sepulchral Monuments*, 1786, and his own *Specimens of Ancient Sculpture and Paintings*, 1780-94, and *Views of Ancient Buildings of England*, 1786-93. He was a determined opponent of James Wyatt's 'improvements' to ancient buildings. Between 1774 and 1786 he contributed 185 plates to the monthly *Builder's Magazine*, mainly of architectural designs but also some for furniture in an individual, neo-classical style which he referred to as 'the present reigning taste', and a few in fanciful Gothic style. These range from door-cases, 'with the strictest adherence to the Rules of Palladio', to chairs, mirrors, lights, cabinets, tables, a clock case, locks, escutcheons and door knockers, and, for the garden, a Gothic pigeon house on a pole. Many of his antiquarian drawings are preserved in the British Museum, Bodleian Library, the R.I.B.A. Drawings Collection and the Victoria and Albert Museum.

Placido Columbani
Engraving of a chimney panel from *A New Book of Ornaments*.
1775.

Placido Columbani c.1744-c.1801

Architect and designer who was a native of Milan but spent
most of his life in England, executing various commissions
for both exterior work and interior decoration. His first
designs to be published were included in *The Chimney-Piece
Maker's Daily Assistant,* 1766, with other drawings by
Thomas Milton and John Crunden (q.v.). He published
Vases and Tripods in 1770, and *A New Book of Ornaments,
containing a Variety of Elegant Designs for Modern Panels,
commonly executed in Stucco, Wood or Painting, and used in
decorating Principal Rooms* in 1775. *A Variety of Capitals, Friezes
and Cornices...* appeared in 1776. All these designs, as
Colvin has pointed out, served to popularise the neo-
classical style expressed by the brothers Adam, and a few of
them are reproduced here.

Thomas Malton
Illustration from *Compleat Treatise on Perspective*. 1775.

Thomas Malton 1726-1801

Malton was recorded as 'for several years a cabinet maker,
having a large shop in the Strand' (probably until c.1761),
but he is better known for his work as an architectural
draughtsman and teacher and writer on geometry and
perspective. In 1775 he published *Compleat Treatise on
Perspective* which he dedicated to the President and Members
of the Royal Academy. Among the subscribers were
architects and twenty-five cabinet-makers and upholsterers
including Bradshaw, Saunders, Fell, Chipchase, Belcher,
Chippendale, Linnell and Ince and Mayhew. There is some
doubt as to whether the two relevant plates can be classified
as furniture designs *per se,* as the perspective content is their
key feature and the furniture shown quite out of date, but
there can be no doubt that Malton intended the work to be
used by cabinet-makers, as the subscribers' list proves. A
second edition in 1778 contained an additional plate with
eleven pieces much more representative of the prevailing
neo-classical style.

B. Pastorini
Title-page from *A New Book of Designs for Girandoles and Glass
Frames*. 1775.

B. Pastorini fl.1775

A designer about whom nothing is known beyond the
existence of a slim volume published in March 1775 by I.
Taylor, entitled *A New Book of Designs for Girandoles and Glass
Frames in the present Taste,* drawn and engraved by B. Pastorini on
Ten Plates Price 4ˢ. Each of the well-executed plates gives
two designs for oval or rectangular frames very close in style
to those of the brothers Adam. Only one copy of this rare
book has been located so far.

Michelangelo Pergolesi fl.c.1760-1801

An Italian decorative painter, designer and engraver who probably came to England with the encouragement of Robert Adam, for whom he decorated various interiors including the pilasters of the long gallery at Syon House in 1768. Between 1777 and 1801 he published *Designs for Various Ornaments* in numbers, engraved by Bartolozzi, and dedicated to the Duke of Northumberland (his patron at Syon). Pergolesi stated that he had 'long applied his attention to the ornaments of the Ancients, and has had the honour of designing and painting Rooms, Ceilings, Staircases and Ornaments for many of the Nobility and Gentry in England, and other Countries.' His designs were intended to be 'of great Utility to the Architect, Painter, Sculptor, Modeller, Carver &c'. Most of them are for decorative panels, but there are some for the sides of rooms which show pier tables, frames, lights, seats and curtains, and others for carvers' work such as frames, girandoles and stands. One plate was published posthumously in 1801 by 'M. Dulouchamp, Bookseller, Successor to the late Signor Pergolesi.'. Over the long perod of publication, Pergolesi's designs became considerably more complex, but still reflect the prevailing influence of Robert Adam's classicism.

Sir John Soane 1753-1837

One of the outstanding architects of the period, whose best known works are the Bank of England and Dulwich College Picture Gallery and Mausoleum, and whose career is excellently documented elsewhere. He designed a considerable amount of furniture, including ivory and ebonised furniture in the Gothic style for the Library at Stowe in 1805, and some for his own house in Lincoln's Inn Fields, now Sir John Soane's Museum. The only furniture designs to be published, however, were some in a youthful work of Soane's entitled *Designs in Architecture*, 1778, which he apparently later tried to suppress by buying up all the copies he could find. They were designs for garden seats and arbours, mostly in the neo-classical style but also in the Gothic style, and are reproduced here.

'S.H.' 1779

Probably Solomon Hudson of 16, Great Titchfield Street, London, a carver and gilder, upholsterer and cabinet maker working from c.1780-93. He executed work in the London house of Sir John Griffin Griffin of Audley End, Essex, to designs by Robert Adam, and also for the Earl of Buckinghamshire at Blickling Hall, Norfolk. He is the most likely author of a small book published in 1779 entitled *Twelve New Designs of Frames for Looking Glasses, Pictures &c.*, by S.H. Carver and published by I. Taylor. The six plates each contain two half-designs for oval or rectangular frames in the neo-classical style. Other possibilities for authorship of these designs are Simon Henekin and Samuel Hayworth (see Geoffrey Wills, 'Twelve New Designs of Frames by S.H., 1779', *Furniture History*, Vol.XI, 1975, pp.53-55).

William Thomas d.1800

Architect, from Pembrokeshire, and described in his obituary as 'architect to His Royal Highness the Duke of

Clarence'. In 1783 he published *Original Designs in Architecture,* which included schemes for villas, a temple, a grotto, and some furniture for William Dymock Esq., and Jnº Harris Esq., in an elegant neo-classical style inspired by Robert Adam. He exhibited original designs at the Royal Academy for Eaton Hall, Cheshire, and for various other houses and monuments, few of which were executed.

P. Begbie fl.1779

Designer and engraver who engraved plates for Robert and James Adam's *Works in Architecture,* and who published under his own name three small suites entitled *Vases after the Manner of the Antique* in 1779. The designs include girandoles in a confident Adam-inspired neo-classical style.

George Hepplewhite d.1786

Cabinet-maker and designer in London, about whom very little is actually known, although his name is famous now for the publication of *The Cabinet-Maker and Upholsterer's Guide* by I. and J. Taylor for his widow Anne in 1788. The first edition contained 126 unsigned plates of designs 'for every Article of Household Furniture, in the newest and most approved taste...' and intended 'to unite elegance and utility, and blend the useful with the agreeable.'. In fact the designs were very much in the neo-classical style used by Robert Adam during the 1780s, though without much of Adam's inventiveness or use of classical animals and figures and were by no means avant-garde: some of the heavier pieces of cabinet furniture such as clothes presses hardly varied from mid-eighteenth century designs, and curvilinear shapes dominated the designs for chairs, sofas and tables. The accompanying text gave measurements and suggestions for upholstery materials, painted and carved decoration, and the fitting out of useful pieces such as sideboards and

'S.H.'
Title-page for *Twelve New Designs of Frames.* 1779.

54

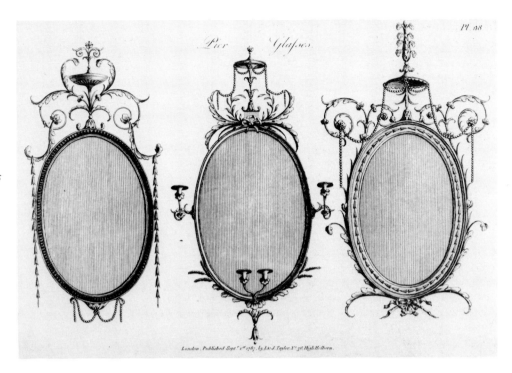

George Hepplewhite
Engraving of pier glasses from
*The Cabinet-Maker and Upholsterer's
Guide.* 1st ed. 1788.

dressing tables. Plate 10 illustrated a chair which had 'been executed with good effect for His Royal Highness the Prince of Wales', but no documentary evidence has come to light about this commission. The last plate showed 'at one view, the necessary and proper Furniture for a Drawing Room, and also for a Dining-Room or Parlour'; the text gave the necessary variations of pieces of furniture to suit each room, and the plan gave the correct positions of each piece in the conventional manner that had prevailed throughout the eighteenth century, but was shortly to change.

A second edition of *The Guide* was published in 1789; the introduction, text and most of the plates were the same as the first edition except for Plate 5, where two side chairs of almost mid-eighteenth century style were replaced with shield-back types; Plate 9, where the left-hand design for a shield-back chair was replaced by a square-backed example, Plate 11 where another square-backed chair was introduced, and Plate 25 where a square-backed sofa replaced a curvaceous one, and which was referred to in the text as 'of the newest fashion: the frame should be japanned, with green on a white ground, and the edges gilt, the covering of red Morocco leather.' These minor changes anticipated the more substantial changes made to the third edition, published in 1794, probably in response to Sheraton's criticism in his *Drawing Book* of 1791 (q.v.) that Hepplewhite's designs 'had already caught the decline'. Plates 1, 3, 5, 6, 8-13, 21, 23, 25, 39, 40 and 118 were all new, and reflected a change in taste in the late 1780s and early 1790s influenced by the Louis XVI style in France. Backs and seats were much squarer in shape, and the designs for rectangular mirror frames superseded the earlier oval examples. The designs for cabinet work, beds, cornices and smaller items remained the same as in the first edition.

Six more plates (Nos. 21-25, and No. 29) bearing Hepplewhite's name and dated 1792 and 1793 appear in *The Cabinet-Maker's London Book of Prices,* issued by the London Society of Cabinet Makers (q.v.) in 1793. The rest of the plates were contributed by Thomas Shearer and William Casement. Hepplewhite's designs included some quite innovative pieces such as a 'Carlton House' desk (Plate 21), and the final plate (No. 29), a series of quite plain designs for legs and feet for stands, tripod tables and firescreens, for which the prices were listed in the text.

William Pain fl.c.1758-c.1793

Pain referred to himself as an architect and carpenter or joiner in the many architectural pattern books he published during a long career:- books which, as Colvin pointed out, 'were as successful in popularizing the "Adam style" as the earlier books of William Halfpenny had been in disseminating Palladian and rococo motifs.' Most of them went into several editions, with such titles as *The Builder's Companion and Workman's General Assistant* (1758), *The Carpenter and Joiner's Repository* (1778) and *The Builder's Sketch Book* (1793). *The Practical House Carpenter* which must have been first published before 1788 (the exact date is uncertain) had reached an eighth edition by 1815, and by 1791 included some designs for a library and a dining room, which are included here. As well as the fitted bookcases and niches, the plates also show pier and chimney glasses in a typical Adam style. Very little is known about Pain's career apart from the publications, but many of his grandsons pursued well-known architectural careers in the nineteenth century both in England and Ireland.

Thomas Shearer fl.c.1788-90

Christopher Gilbert suggests that he may have been a journeyman cabinet-maker rather than a professional designer, although he is known principally for his authorship

Thomas Shearer
Frontispiece from *The Cabinet-Maker's London Book of Prices.*
c.1788.

of seventeen of the twenty plates in *The Cabinet-Maker's London Book of Prices,* (first edition 1788, second edition 1793 and subsequent editions). This and other similar *Books of Prices* for cabinet work, chairs and dining tables in the first decades of the nineteenth century were primarily intended as price guides to working cabinet-makers for the various types of manufactures and finishes, with extensive texts and price tables, rather than as pattern books of avant-garde fashionable furniture. Shearer's designs are similar to Hepplewhite's of the same date (and the three other plates were contributed by the Hepplewhite firm). The designs were only for cabinet work:- secretaires, sideboards, chests of drawers, dressing tables and wash-stands, all showing quite complicated arrangements of small drawers and compartments for the benefit of the pricing tables included in the text. The second edition of 1793 had six additional plates by Hepplewhite and three by Casement.

Anonymous: Ideas for Rustic Furniture c.1790-95

A slim volume of twenty-five plates, entitled *Ideas for Rustic Furniture, proper for Garden Seats, Summer Houses, Hermitages, Cottages &c...* was published by I. and J. Taylor, The Architectural Library, London, between about 1790 and 1795. The date of publication cannot be much later as some of the plates were pirated for a German publication of 1797. Morrison Heckscher ('Eighteenth Century Rustic Furniture

Designs', *Furniture History,* Vol. XI, 1975) discounts previous attributions for authorship to Wrighte, and suggests an unknown designer who would have been commissioned by the Taylors. The designs are charming essays in the use of imitation twigs and branches to form chairs, stools, settees, tables, frames, basin stands, chimney-pieces and, on the title-page, a rustic doorway. Inspiration for this type of furniture dates back to designs by Robert Manwaring in the 1760s, although the new designs of the 1790s were for lighter pieces with some contemporary neo-classical ornaments, such as wheat-husks, paterae, urns and simple ribbon bows. The looking glass in Plate 20, right, may have been inspired by a design published in Hepplewhite's second edition of *The Guide* in 1789 (Plate 118, left).

Anonymous
Frontispiece for *Ideas for Rustic Furniture.* c.1790-5.

George Richardson fl.c.1760-d.1813

Designer, engraver and drawing master who accompanied James Adam (q.v.) to Italy 1760-63 and had worked as a designer and draughtsman for the Adam firm for 'upwards of eighteen years' by 1774. Among his executed designs was that of the ceiling of the Great Hall at Kedleston for Lord Scarsdale. His published books of designs were mainly for architectural ornament (e.g. *Capitals of Columns and Friezes measured from the Antique,* 1793), but also in that year he published with his son *New Designs for Vases and Tripods decorated in the antique taste:* the twelve designs for tripods or stands are reproduced here, though whether they were intended to be executed in wood or metal is not certain.

Charles Middleton 1756-c.1818

Architect and pupil of James Paine, who practised in London (later in partnership with James Bailey) from c.1780 to c.1816. He appears to have had some connection with Henry Holland's work at Carlton House and may have worked in Holland's office. He published various architectural design books, including *Picturesque and Architectural Views for Cottages, Farmhouses and Country Villas* (1793 and 1795), *The Architect and Builder's Miscellany or Pocket Library* (1799), *Designs for Gates and Rails suitable to Parks, Pleasure Grounds, Balconys &c* (n.d.). The second of these works listed included among its sixty plates one for garden seats in a variety of styles, and is included here.

Thomas Sheraton
Trade Card, c.1796. *British Museum, Heal Collection.*

Thomas Sheraton 1751-1806

One of the most famous names in the history of English furniture, although no furniture exists that is known to have been made by him. He came from Co. Durham to London in about 1790, having received training as a cabinet-maker and draughtsman. A trade card of c.1796 records that he taught perspective, architecture and ornament, made designs for cabinet-makers and sold drawings and books. His obituary (*Gentleman's Magazine,* November 1806) stated that from about 1793 he had 'supported himself, a wife and two children, by his exertions as an author.' In 1800 he returned to Co. Durham and later was ordained a Baptist minister there, although he was buried in London in the churchyard of St. James's Piccadilly in 1806.

His reputation exists entirely on the publication of three books of furniture designs, the first of which was *The Cabinet-Maker and Upholsterer's Drawing Book,* which was published in fortnightly numbers between 1791 and 1793. A second edition with seven new plates came out in 1794, and a German edition appeared with a preface of the same date. A third edition appeared in 1802. The list of subscribers included cabinet-makers and upholsterers in London and all over the provinces as well as Scotland: among the most noted subscribers were the cabinet-makers Thomas Seddon and William France, Eckhardt, proprietor of the Printed Silk Manufactory in Chelsea, and the draughtsman Peter Nicholson. Parts I and II of the *Drawing Book* were devoted to extensive dissertations on geometry and perspective, while Part III was intended 'to exhibit the present taste for furniture, and at the same time give the workman some assistance in the manufacturing part of it.'. Both this part of the book and his next publication, the *Cabinet Dictionary* of 1803, concentrated on designs for cabinet makers' and upholsterers' work, with very few carvers' pieces (there are, for instance, no carved mirror or picture frames). Sheraton's text to the plates gave detailed instructions, especially for complicated constructions used in such items as a cylinder desk and bookcase (Plate XLVII). He recommended various woods for particular use — mahogany, rosewood

Thomas Sheraton
Frontispiece to *The Cabinet Maker and Upholsterer's Drawing Book,* 1793.

and satinwood for example, as well as fashionable painted finishes, and showed a considerable knowledge of contemporary French furniture and design. In Plates 60 and 61 he illustrated the dining room and drawing room of the Prince of Wales' Carlton House, where the architect and designer Henry Holland had been employed in the redecoration and refurnishing since 1783 and whose style Sheraton admired greatly.

Many of Sheraton's designs in the *Drawing Book* show an advance in design from Hepplewhite's publication of a few years earlier: straight legs and square backs supersede more rounded shapes for seat furniture and such items as the lady's cabinet in Plate XVI were inspired by French examples. The window curtains in Plate LI illustrate the contemporary change to draw-curtains from festoons. His designs were influential in both Europe and America. Hepplewhite's reaction was to update some of his designs for chairs and sofas in the third edition of 1794. In many respects Sheraton's work in the 1790s anticipated styles which came into popular use in the first decade of the nineteenth century, and to which he made further contributions in his *Cabinet Dictionary*, 1803, and *Encyclopaedia* in 1804-7. (See *Pictorial Dictionary of British 19th Century Furniture Design.*)

The Arrangement of the Plates

The plates that follow have been arranged in sections in chronological order. The order of the sections follows, as far as possible, the way in which they were arranged in the original versions of the eighteenth century. This was not an alphabetical arrangement, but one divided roughly thus:

Part I. UPHOLSTERY WORK: mainly the province of the upholsterer or upholder (with the initial work of the carver and joiner), and consisting of chairs, settees and sofas, stools, beds and window curtains. Non-upholstered seat furniture such as hall seats and garden seats have also been included here.

Part II. CABINET WORK: consisting of commodes, chests of drawers, cabinets, desks, bookcases, cupboards and the smaller items of carcase furniture such as pot cupboards and washstands.

Part III. CARVERS' WORK: including tables, stands, picture and mirror frames, chandeliers and girandoles, overmantels for chimney-pieces, brackets, shelves, and the detailed work of frets, borders and rails.

Part IV. MISCELLANEOUS items which appear in the furniture pattern books and do not fit easily into any of the previous sections: including clock cases, trays, pulpits, steps, carved door tops, chimney furniture, locks and handles, and general designs for ornament.

Part V. INTERIOR DECORATION. During the course of the eighteenth century the leading cabinet-makers, upholsterers and designers became more involved in the overall designs of fashionable interiors, in conjunction with architects and clients, and some of the pattern books included room plans and elevations of rooms.

Part I. Upholstery Work and other Seat Furniture

Section I. CHAIRS. Carved backs, upholstered seats

Eighteenth century chairs with carved backs and upholstered seats were intended for use in parlours (smaller sitting rooms), dining rooms, libraries, less grand drawing rooms and bedrooms. They were designed to stand against the walls of the rooms when not in use and were finished quite plainly at the back. Early eighteenth century examples were made of walnut, japanned or painted beech, and ebonised fruitwood. After c.1740 most were made of mahogany, carved and polished, although some continued to be made of walnut and fruit woods, or japanned beech. In the last quarter of the century paler mahogany and satinwood were more widely used, in conjunction with painted panels, roundels, flowers and leaves. Mahogany however gave the carver the greatest opportunity for elaborately pierced and fretted chair backs, well carved knees and feet, and most of the designs in the following pages were intended to be executed in that wood. Gilding was occasionally used to highlight carving in some of the more elaborate and expensive examples. Most of the designs are for side chairs (i.e. without arms), but some are shown with arms, and with a great variety of different ornament from which client and carver could choose. Many executed examples had considerably less ornament than shown on the designs, depending on the amount any customer wished to spend: — as Manwaring suggested in the *Cabinet and Chair-Maker's Real Friend and Companion* (1765), 'the Author has the boldness to assert, that should the ornamental Parts be left out, there will still remain Grandeur and Magnificence behind, and the design will appear open and genteel.'

The seats were to be stuffed with horsehair (without springs) and covered in various fabrics: — woven horsehair was usual for dining room chairs (being durable and easy to clean), leather for library chairs, tapestry, needlework or patterned woollen plush for parlour chairs, silk damask or velvet, tapestry or needlework for drawing room chairs and embroideries, silk or cottons for bedroom chairs — in many cases, as Chippendale directed, 'the same Stuff as the Window Curtains'. In 1793 Sheraton illustrated a drawing room chair with a seat cover of printed chintz, 'which now may be had on purpose for chair seats, together with borders to suit them' (Appendix, Plate VI). The fixed covers were secured with brass or gilt brass nails in decorative patterns, many of which are shown in the designs. Chairs with cane seats had loose cushions or 'squabs' covered with a matching material, and upholstered chairs were often provided with loose linen or cotton check or plain covers or 'cases' for everyday use and protection.

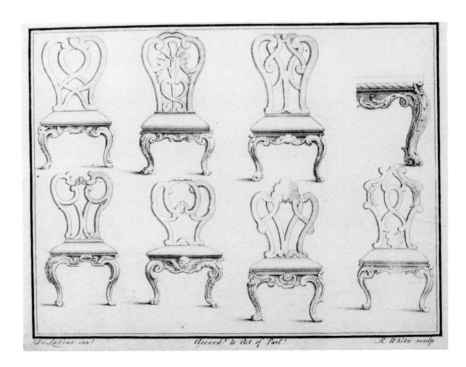

William de la Cour
'First Book of Ornament', 1741.

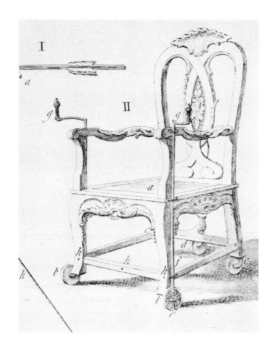

'Gentleman's Magazine', April 1746
Wheel-chair 'in which a person may move himself about a room, or garden, without any assistance; very convenient for those who are lame, or gouty'.

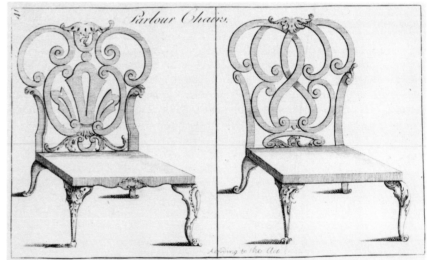

Probably Matthias Darly
'Second Book of Chairs', c.1751. Plate 2.
Re-issued in *The Chair-Maker's Guide*. 1766.
Plate 41. Parlour Chairs.

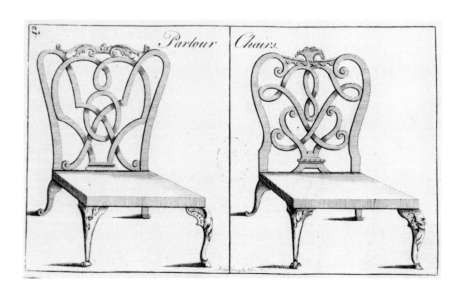

Probably Matthias Darly
'Second Book of Chairs', c.1751. Plate 14.
Re-issued in *The Chair-Maker's Guide*. 1766.
Plate 42. Parlour Chairs.

Probably Matthias Darly
'Second Book of Chairs', c.1751. Plate 1.
Re-issued in *The Chair-Maker's Guide*. 1766.
Plate 44. Parlour Chairs.

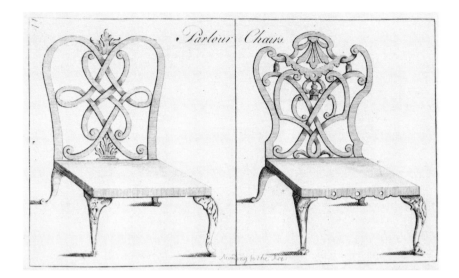

See also *Hall Chairs* — Matthias Darly.
1751, 1766.

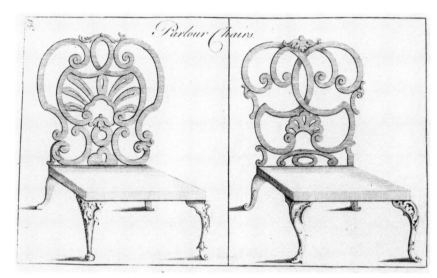

Probably Matthias Darly
'Second Book of Chairs', c.1751.
Re-issued in *The Chair-Maker's Guide*. 1766.
Plate 54. Parlour Chairs.

P. Babel
'A New Book of Ornaments', 1752.
Plate 3.

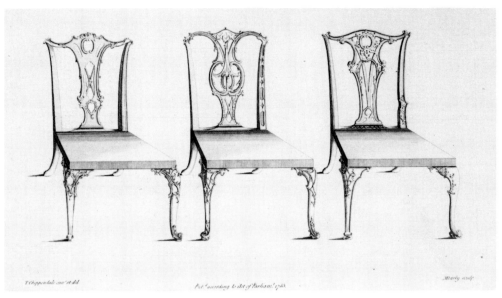

Thomas Chippendale 'The Gentleman and Cabinet-Maker's Director', 1st Edition. 1754.

Plate XII. 'A variety of new-pattern chairs... the Fore Feet are different for your better choice... proper Dimensions 1′ 10″ in the front, 1′ 5½″ behind, 1′ 5″ from the front of the back foot to the front rail; the back 1′ 10″ high, the seat 1′ 5″ high, but that is made lower according as the seat is to be stuffed'. Not in 3rd Edition, 1763.

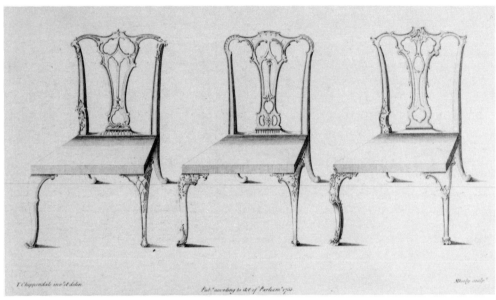

Plate XIII. 1st Edition, 1754.
Plate X in 3rd Edition, 1763.

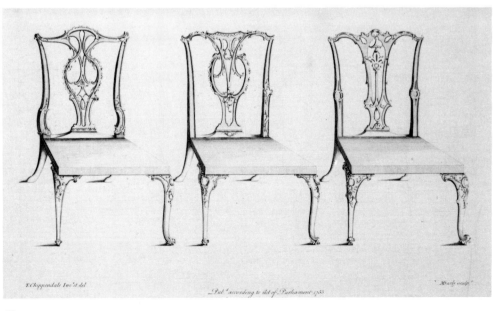

Plate 14. 1st Edition, 1754.
Plate XI in 3rd Edition, 1763.

Plate 15. 1st Edition, 1754. Not in 3rd Edition, 1763.

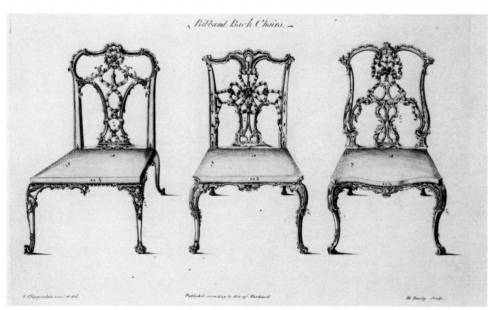

Plate XVI. 1st Edition. 1754. 'Ribband Back chairs... which, if I may speak without vanity, are the best I have ever seen (or perhaps have ever been made)'. Reprinted in 3rd Edition, 1763, Plate XV, with some alteration.

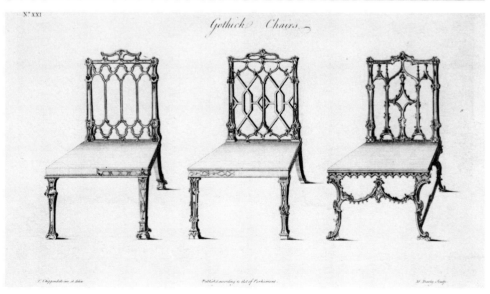

Plate XXI. Gothick chairs. 1st Edition, 1754. Not in 3rd Edition, 1763. 'Most of the ornaments may be left out if required'.

Plate XXII. Gothick Chairs. Plate 25a
in 3rd Edition, 1763.

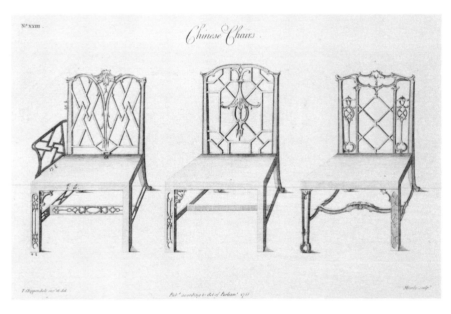

Plate XXIII. Chinese Chairs. 1st Edition,
1754. Plate 27 in 3rd Edition, 1763.

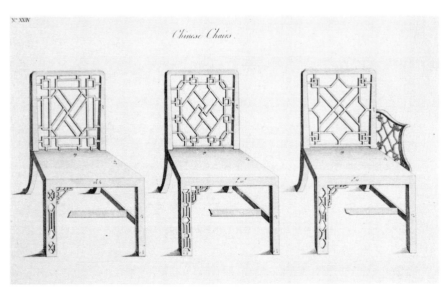

Plate XXIV. Chinese Chairs. 1st Edition,
1754. Plate 26 in 3rd Edition, 1763.
Chairs 'in the present Chinese Manner,
which I hope will improve that Taste, or
Manner of work, it never having yet
arrived to any Perfection...' (1754
Edition.)

**Thomas Chippendale
'The Gentleman and Cabinet-Maker's
Director', 1st Edition, 1754.**

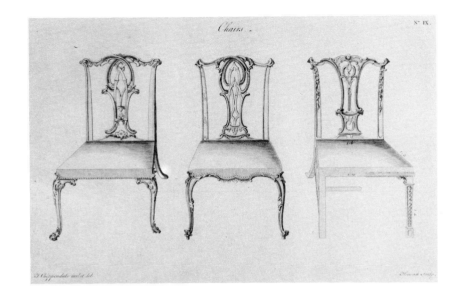

Plate IX. Chairs. 3rd Edition, 1763. 'The
seats look best when stuffed over the rails,
and have a brass Border neatly chased; but
are most commonly done with brass nails, in
one or two rows, and sometimes the Nails
are done to imitate Fretwork. They are
usually covered with the same Stuff as the
Window Curtains. The Height of the back
seldom exceeds 22 Inches above the
Seats... sometimes the Dimensions are less,
to suit the Chairs to the Rooms.'

Plate 12. Chairs. 1st Edition. 1754. Plate
12 in 3rd Edition, 1763.

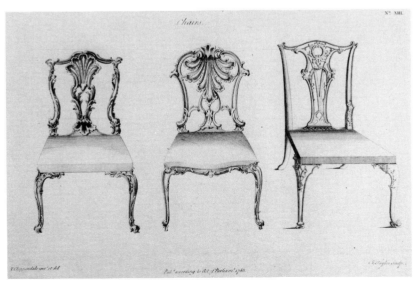

Plate XIII. Chairs. 1st Edition. 1754. Plate
XIII in 3rd Edition, 1763.

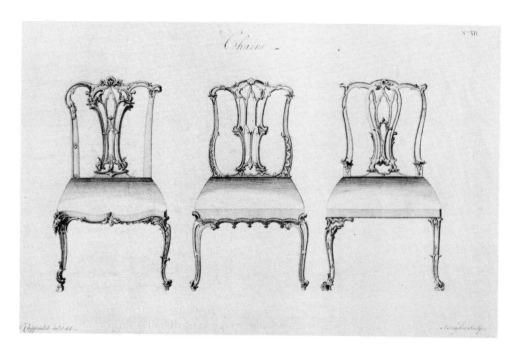

**Thomas Chippendale
'The Gentleman and Cabinet-
Maker's Director', 3rd Edition,
1763.**

Plate XIV.

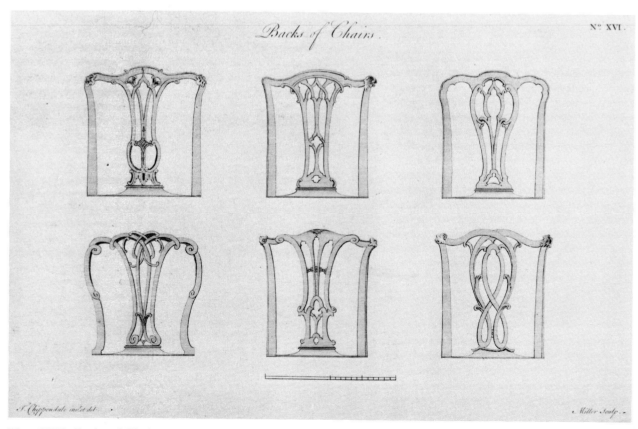

Plate XVI. Backs of Chairs. 3rd Edition, 1763.

66

Thomas Chippendale
'The Gentleman and Cabinet-Maker's Director', 3rd Edition, 1763.

Plate XXV. Gothick Chairs. 3rd Edition, 1763. 'That in the middle is proper for a library; the two others are Gothick, and fit for Eating Parlours.' Engraving dated 1761.

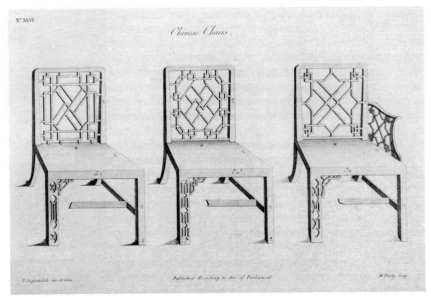

Plate XXVI. Chinese Chairs. 3rd Edition, 1763. Chairs 'after the Chinese manner, and are very proper for a Lady's Dressing Room, especially if it is hung with India Paper. They will likewise suit Chinese Temples. They have commonly cane-bottoms, with loose cushions, but, if required, may have stuffed seats and brass nails'.

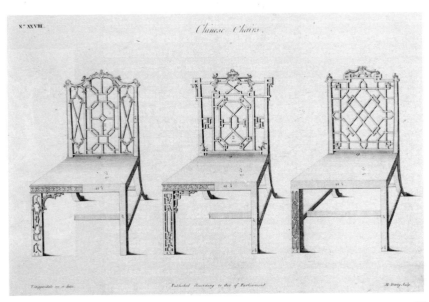

Plate XXVIII. Chinese Chairs. 3rd Edition, 1763.

William Ince and John Mayhew
The Universal System of Houshold Furniture, 1762.

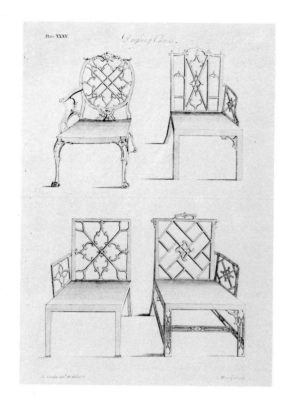

Plate XXXV. Dressing chairs, 1762.

Plates IX, X. Designs for Parlour Chairs.

A Society of Upholsterers
'Genteel Houshold Furniture in the Present Taste. 2nd Edition, c.1765.
Plates 1, 2, and 3. Parlour Chairs. Probably designed by Manwaring. Re-issued by Sayer in *The Chair-Maker's Guide,* 1766.

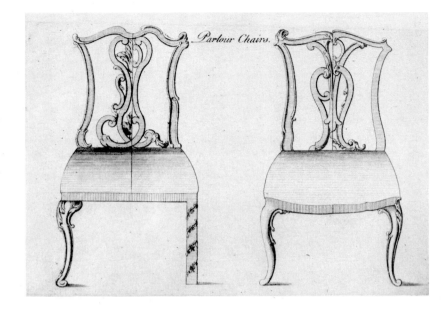

Plate 1. Parlour Chairs.

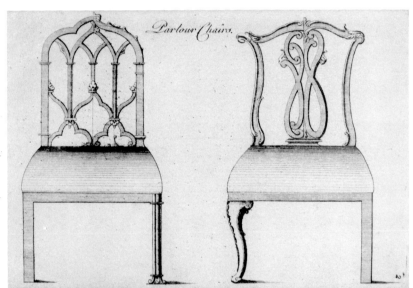

Plate 2. Parlour Chairs.

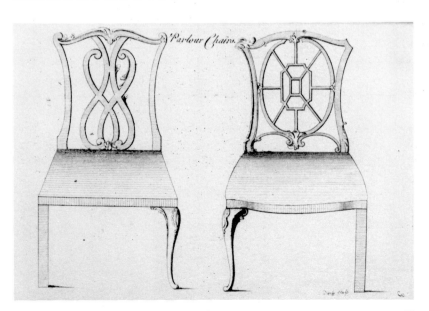

Plate 3. Parlour Chairs.

A Society of Upholsterers
'Genteel Houshold Furniture in the Present Taste'. 2nd Edition, c.1765.
Plates 4, 5 and 6. Parlour Chairs. Probably designed by Robert Manwaring. These plates were re-issued by Sayer in *The Chair-Maker's Guide*, 1766.

Plate 4. Parlour Chairs.

Plate 5. Parlour Chairs.

Plate 6. Parlour Chairs.

A Society of Upholsterers
'Genteel Houshold Furniture in the
Present Taste'. 2nd Edition, c.1765.
Plates 7, 8 and 9. Parlour Chairs. Probably
designed by Manwaring. Re-issued by Sayer
in *The Chair-Maker's Guide*, 1766.

Plate 7. Ribbon Back Chairs.

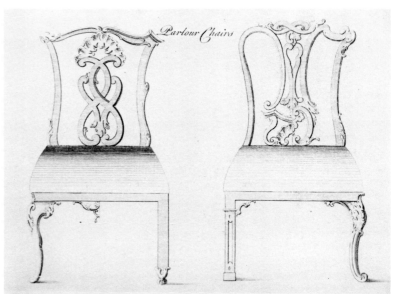

Plate 8. Parlour Chairs.

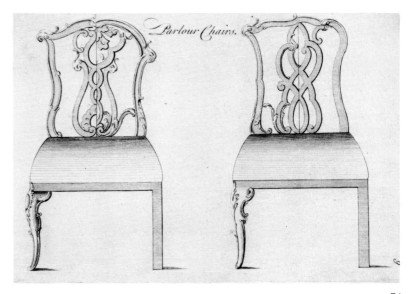

Plate 9. Parlour Chairs.

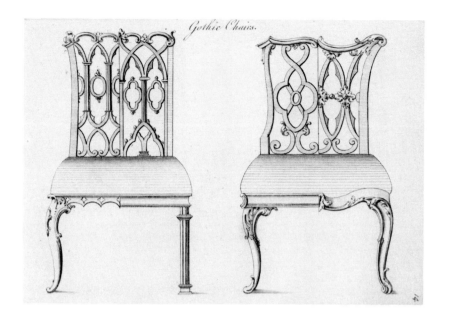

A Society of Upholsterers
'Genteel Houshold Furniture in the
Present Taste. 2nd Edition, c.1765.
Probably designed by Manwaring. Re-
issued by Sayer in *The Chair-Maker's Guide*,
1766.

Plate 14. Gothic Chairs.

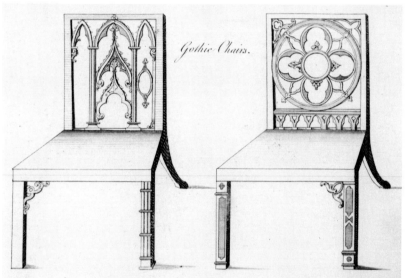

Plate 15. Gothic Chairs.

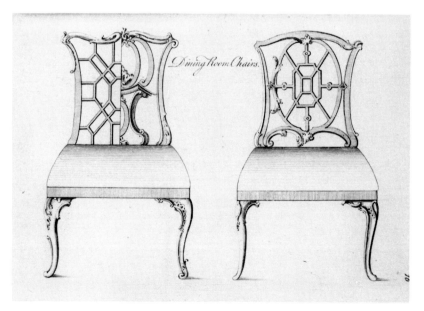

Plate 16. Dining Room Chairs

A Society of Upholsterers
'Genteel Houshold Furniture in the
Present Taste'. 2nd Edition, c.1765.

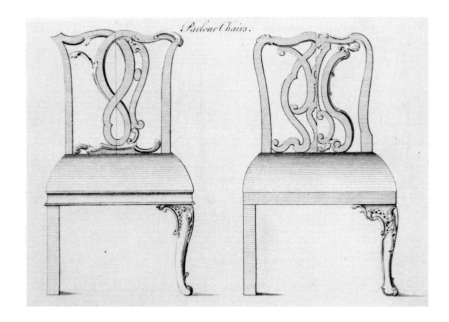

Plate 17. Parlour Chairs.

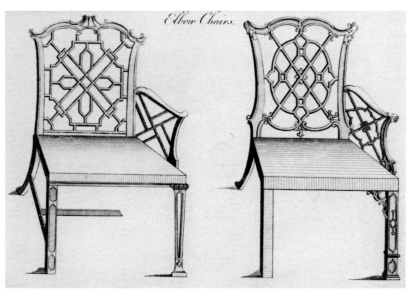

Plate 21. Elbow Chairs.

Plate 23. Chair with a Frett Back.
Plate 24. Gothic Chair.

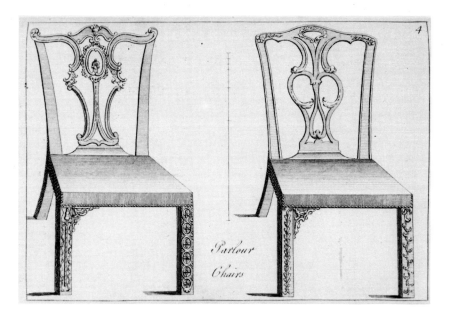

Robert Manwaring
'The Cabinet and Chair-Maker's Real
Friend and Companion', 1765.

Plate 4. Parlour Chairs.

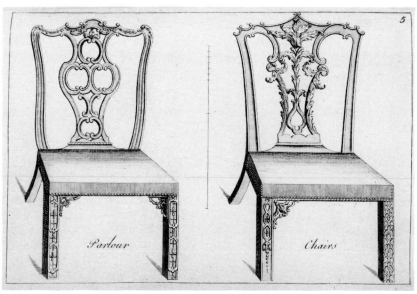

Plate 5. Parlour Chairs.

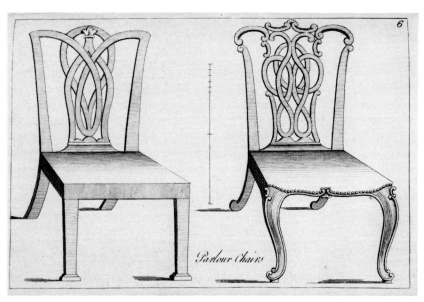

Plate 6. Parlour Chairs.

Robert Manwaring
'The Cabinet and Chair-Maker's Real
Friend and Companion', 1765.

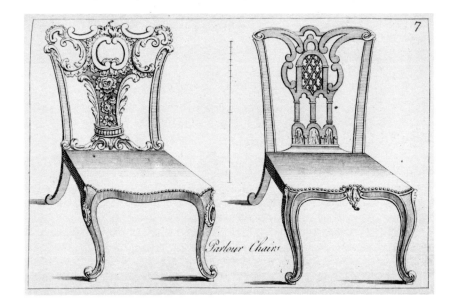

Plate 7. Parlour Chairs.

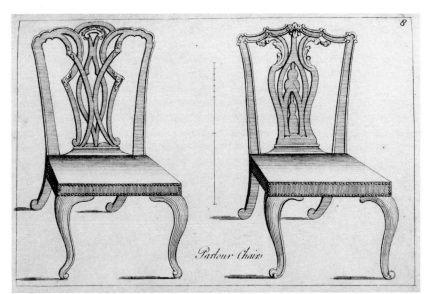

Plate 8. Parlour Chairs.

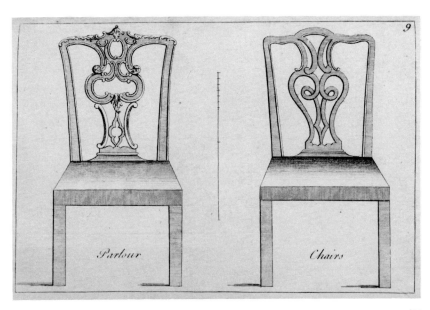

Plate 9. Parlour Chairs.

Plate 33. Parlour Chair Backs and
Brackets for Chairs.

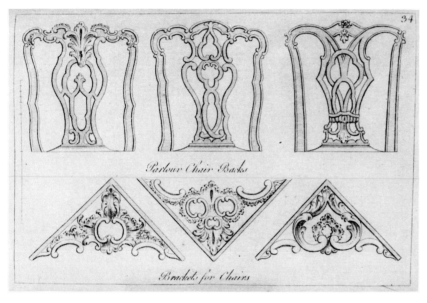

Plate 34. Parlour Chair Backs and
Brackets for Chairs.

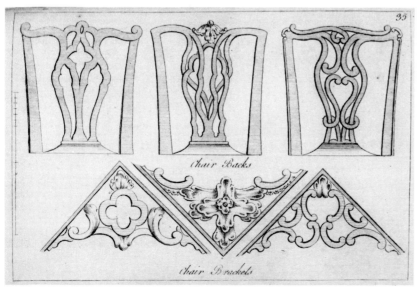

Plate 35. Chair Backs and Chair
Brackets.

76

**Robert Manwaring
'The Cabinet and Chair-Maker's Real
Friend and Companion', 1765.**

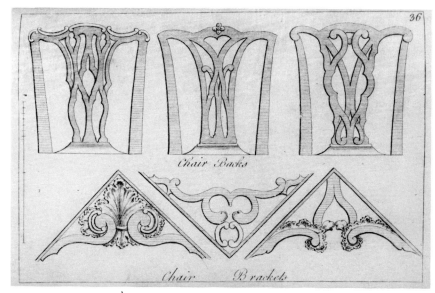

Plate 36. Chair Backs and Chair
Brackets.

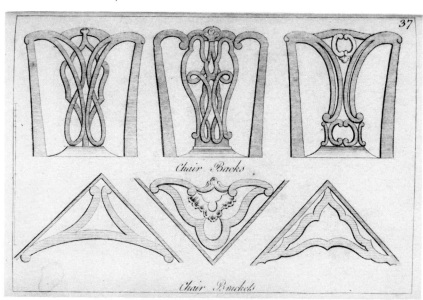

Plate 37. Chair Backs and Chair
Brackets.

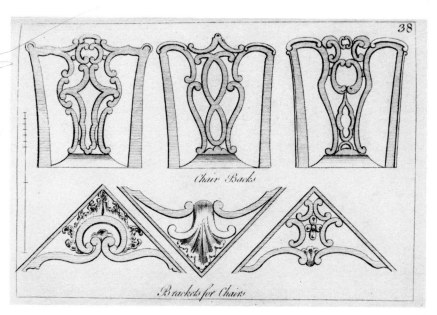

Plate 38. Chair Backs and Brackets
for Chairs.

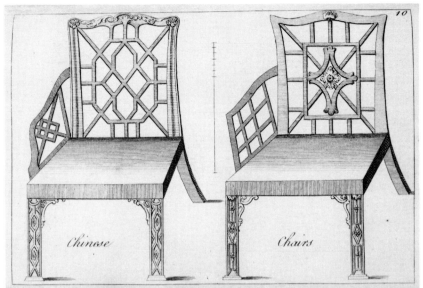

**Robert Manwaring
'The Cabinet and Chair-Maker's Real Friend and Companion', 1765.**
'The Hall, Gothic and Chinese Chairs, though they appear so very elegant and superb, are upon a simple construction, and may be very easily executed...'
Plates 10, 11, 12, 13, 14 and 15, 'are very magnificent and beautiful Designs for Chinese and Gothic Chairs... some of them I have executed in Mahogany and some in Pear Tree for Japanning.'

Plate 10. Chinese Chairs.

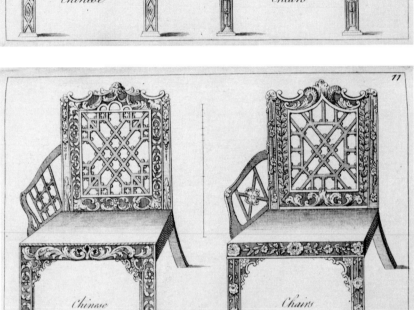

Plate 11. Chinese Chairs.

Plate 12. Chinese Chairs.

Robert Manwaring
'The Cabinet and Chair-Maker's Real
Friend and Companion', 1765.

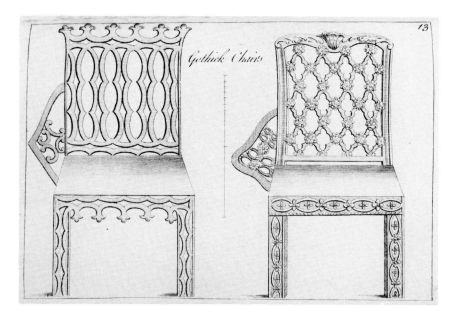

Plate 13. Gothick Chairs.

Plate 14. Gothick Chairs.

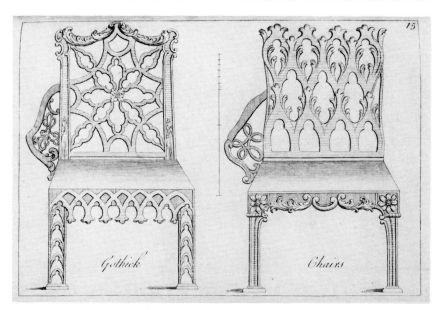

Plate 15. Gothick Chairs.

Robert Manwaring
'The Chair-Maker's Guide', 1766.

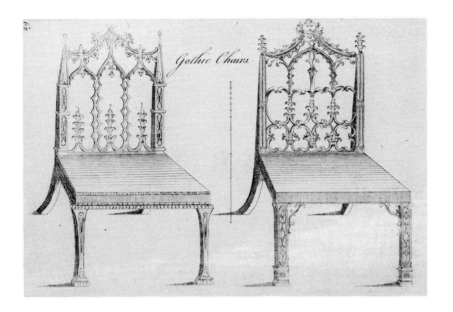

Plate 29. Gothic Chairs.

Plate 30. Ladies' Dressing Chairs.

Plate 31. Gothic Chairs.

Robert Manwaring
'The Chair-Maker's Guide', 1766.

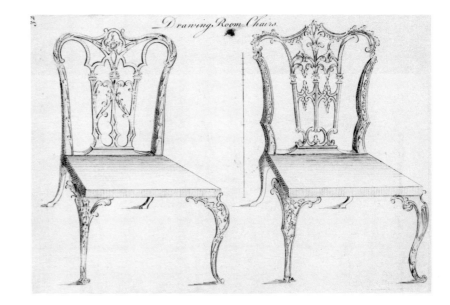

Plate 32. Drawing Room Chairs.

Plate 35. Parlour Chairs.

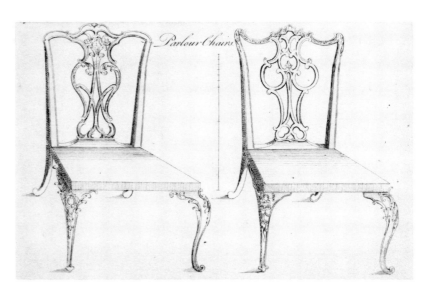

Plate 36. Parlour Chairs.

Plate 38. Parlour Chairs.

Plate 43. Parlour Chairs. Reprinted from Matthias Darly's *A New Book of Chinese, Gothic and Modern Chairs,* 1751, with new titles.

Robert Manwaring
'The Chair-Maker's Guide', 1766.
Plates 49-54, 59 and 74. Chairs for Bed Chambers.

Plates 49 and 50.

Plates 51, 52 and 53.

Plates 54, 59 and 74.

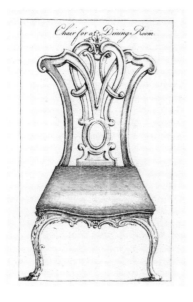

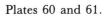

**Robert Manwaring
'The Chair-Maker's Guide', 1766.**
Plates 60-65. Chairs for Dining Rooms. Possibly by Copland.

Plates 60 and 61.

Plates 62 and 63.

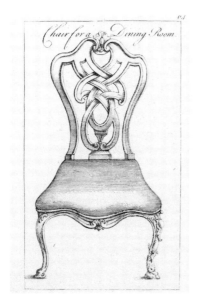
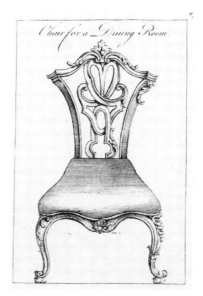

Plates 64 and 65.

Thomas Malton
'Compleat Treatise on Perspective', 1775.

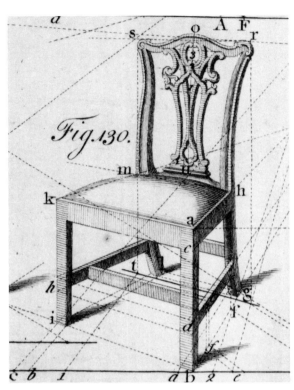

Plate XXXIII. Fig. 130. Chair.

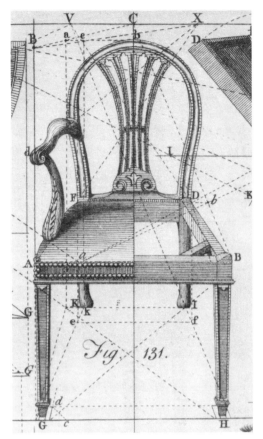

Plate XXXIV. Fig. 131. Chair.

J. Carter
'The Builder's Magazine', 1774-8.

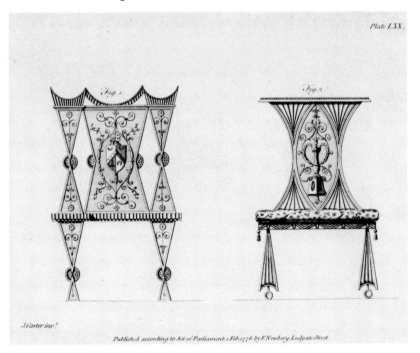

Plate LXX. Fig. 1. Design for a Hall Chair and Fig. 2 Design for a Dressing Room Chair with squab, 1776.

Plate CXXIII. Design for a Chair, 1777.

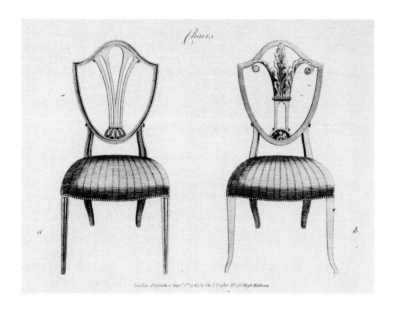

A. Hepplewhite & Co.
'The Cabinet-Maker and Upholsterer's Guide',
1st Edition, 1788. 2nd Edition, 1789. 3rd Edition,
1794.
Plates 1-4. Chairs 'in general, are made of Mahogany... should have seats of horse hair, plain, striped, chequered etc at pleasure'. 'This kind of Chair in general is called Banister back chair'.

Plate 1. Chair 'b' not in 3rd Edition, 1794.

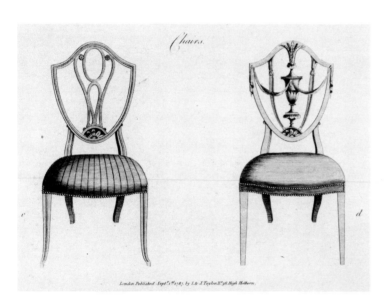

Plate 2.

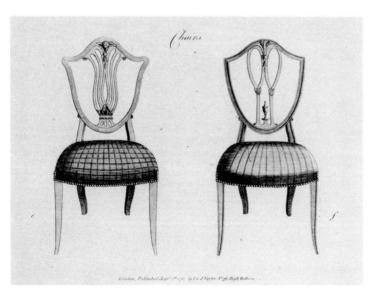

Plate 3.

86

A. Hepplewhite & Co.
'The Cabinet-Maker and Upholsterer's Guide',
1st Edition, 1788. 2nd Edition, 1789. 3rd Edition,
1794.

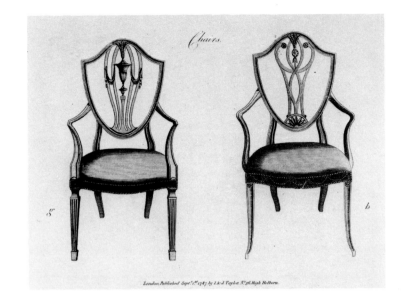

Plate 4.

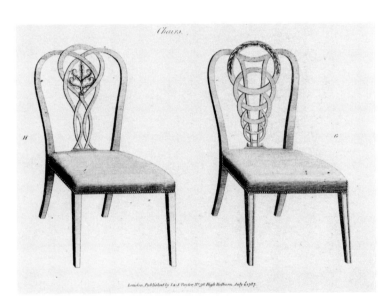

Plate 5. Not in 3rd Edition, 1794.

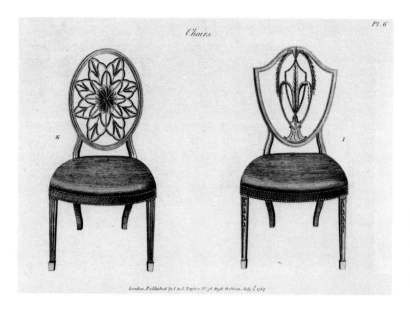

A. Hepplewhite & Co.
'The Cabinet-Maker and Upholsterer's Guide',
1st Edition, 1788. 2nd Edition, 1789. 3rd Edition,
1794.

Plates 6, 7 and 8. Japanned Chairs. 'a new and very elegant fashion has arisen within these few years, of finishing them with painted or japanned work, which gives a rich and splendid appearance to the minutest parts of the Ornaments'; see 'K', Plate 6 (chair 'K' is not in 3rd Edition, 1794), 'Q', Plate 7, 'R' and 'S', Plate 8: 'which allows a framework less massy than is requisite for Mahogany; and by assorting the prevailing colour to the furniture and light of the room, affords opportunity, by the variety of grounds which may be introduced, to make the whole accord in harmony, with a pleasing and striking effect to the eye. Japanned chairs should always have linen or cotton cases to accord with the general hue of the chair'.

Plate 6.

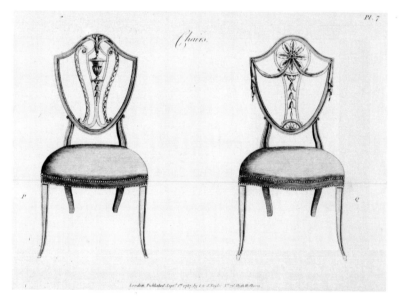

Plate 7.

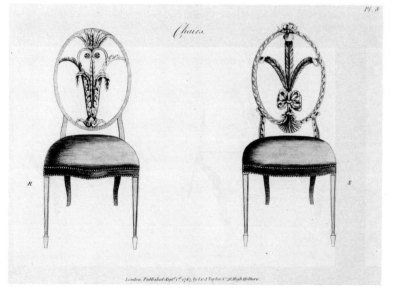

Plate 8.

A. Hepplewhite & Co.
'The Cabinet-Maker and Upholsterer's Guide', 1st Edition, 1788. 2nd
Edition, 1789. 3rd Edition, 1794.

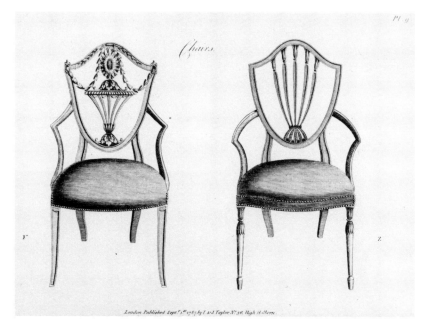

Plate 9. 1st Edition, 1788. Chair Y is not in 2nd or 3rd Editions. Chair
Z in all three Editions.

Plate 9. 2nd Edition, 1789. 3rd Edition,
1794.

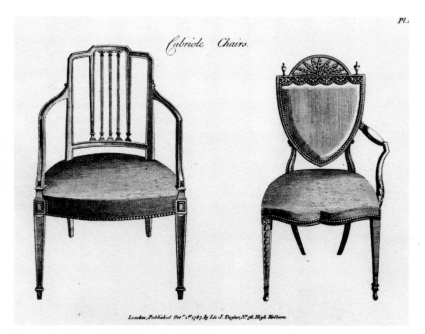

Plate 11. Cabriole Chairs. 2nd Edition, 1789, and 3rd Edition, 1794.

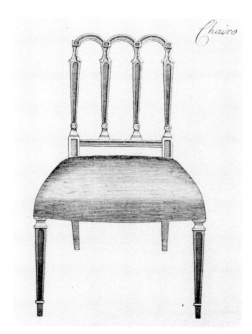

Plate 3. 3rd Edition, 1794.

Plate 5. Chairs. Not in 1st Edition.

Plate 1. Chair. Not in 1st Edition.

Plate 6. Left-hand chair not in 1st Edition.

Plate 8. Both chairs not in 1st Edition.

A. Hepplewhite & Co.
'The Cabinet-Maker and Upholsterer's Guide',
1st Edition, 1788. 2nd Edition, 1789. 3rd
Edition, 1794.

Plate 9 (b) Both chairs not in 1st Edition. 'Two
designs of chairs with cane bottoms; these may be
of mahogany or japanned, and should have cushions
of linen, leather etc.'

Plate 12.

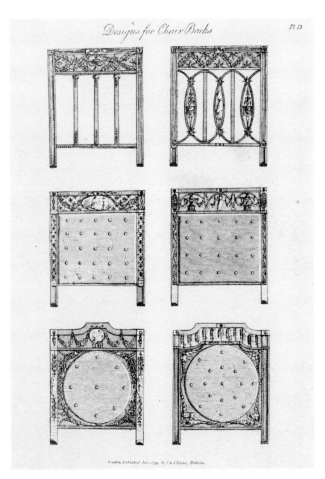

Plate 13.

Plates 12 and 13. 'twelve designs for chair backs, proper to
be executed in mahogany or japan; some of them applicable
to the more elegant kind of chairs with backs and seats of red
or blue morocco leather, in these backs which are sometimes
made a little circular, are frequently inserted medallions,
printed or painted on silk of the natural colours; when the
backs and seats are of leather they should be tied down with
tassels of silk or thread as shewn in several of the preceding
designs.' 3rd Edition only.

Thomas Sheraton
'The Cabinet-Maker and Upholsterer's Drawing Book',
1st Edition, 1793.

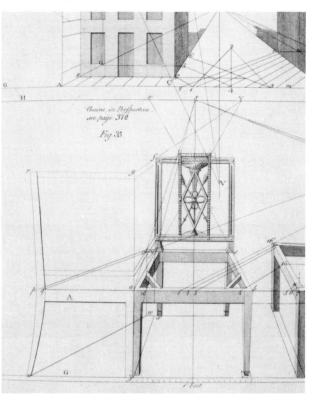

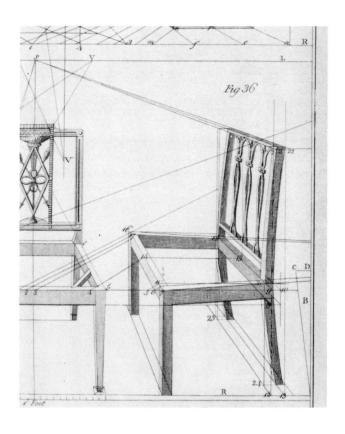

Part II, Plate 24, Figs. 35 and 36 'How to represent a chair...'

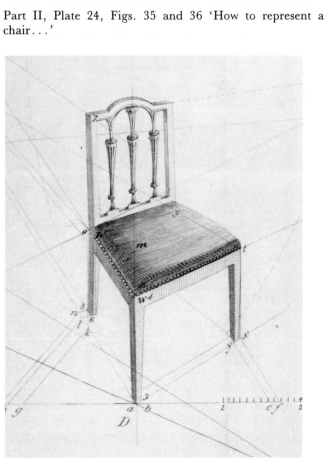

Part II, Plate XXVI. Parlour Chair in perspective.

92

Thomas Sheraton
'The Cabinet-Maker and Upholsterer's Drawing Book', 1st Edition, 1793.

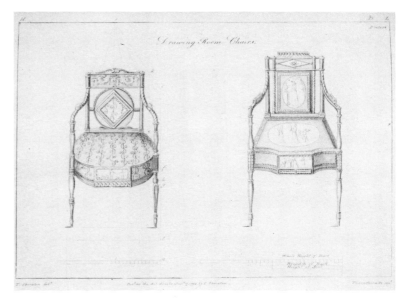

Part III, Plates XXXII, XXXIV. Drawing Room Chairs. 'These chairs are finished in white and gold, or the ornaments may be japanned; but the French finish them in mahogany, with gilt mouldings. The figures in the tables above the front rails are on French printed silk or satin, sewed on to the stuffing, with borders around them... Chairs of this kind have an effect which far exceeds any conception we can have of them from an uncoloured engraving, or even of a coloured one.'

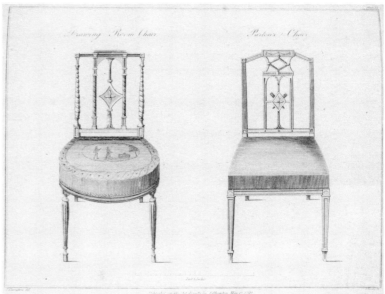

Part III, Plate XXXIII. Parlour Chairs 'need no explanation, as every one must easily see how they are to be finished.'.

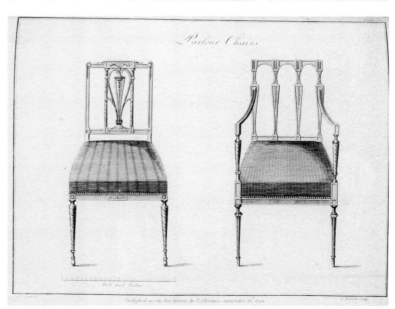

Part III, Plate XXXIV. Parlour and Drawing Room Chairs.

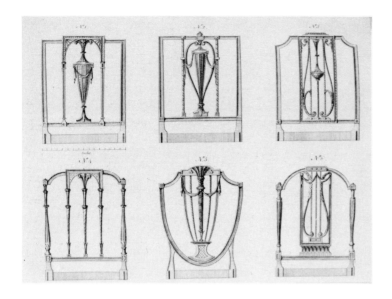

Thomas Sheraton
'The Cabinet-Maker and Upholsterer's Drawing
Book'. 1st Edition, 1793. 2nd Edition, 1794. 3rd
Edition, 1802.

Plate XXXVI. Chair Backs.

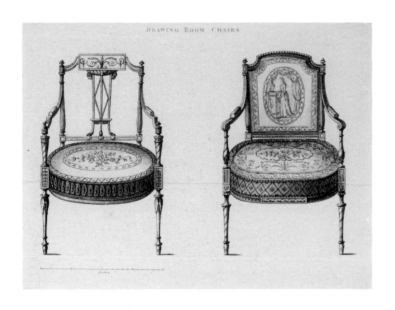

Appendix, Plate VI. Drawing Room Chairs. 'The frame of the right-hand chair is intended to be finished in burnished gold, and the seat and back covered with printed silk... The chair on the left may be finished in japan painting, interspersed with a little gilding in different parts of the banister, which has a lively effect. The covering of the seat is of printed chintz, which may now be had of various patterns on purpose for chair seats, together with borders to suit them.'

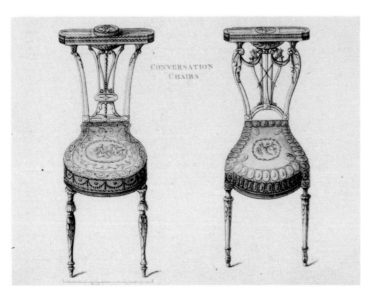

Appendix, Plate X. Conversation Chairs. 'The conversation chairs are used in library or drawing rooms. The parties who converse with each other sit with their legs across the seat, and rest their arms on the top rail, which, for this purpose, is made about three inches and a half wide, stuffed and covered...'

Thomas Sheraton
'The Cabinet-Maker and Upholsterer's Drawing
Book'. 1st Edition, 1793. 2nd Edition, 1794. 3rd
Edition, 1802.

Appendix, Plate XXV. Backs for Parlour Chairs.

Appendix, Plate XXVIII. Backs for Parlour Chairs.

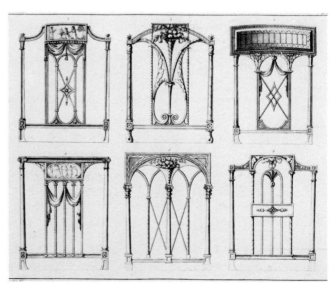

Appendix, Plate XLIX. New Designs of Chair
Backs.

Thomas Sheraton
'The Cabinet-Maker and Upholsterer's Drawing Book', 1793.
Accompaniment to the *Drawing Book*.

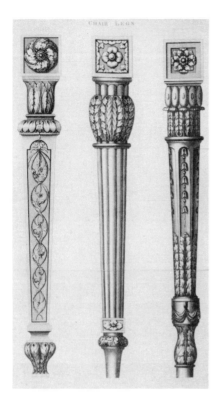

Plate 2. Chair Legs.

Plate 2. Detail. Chair Legs.

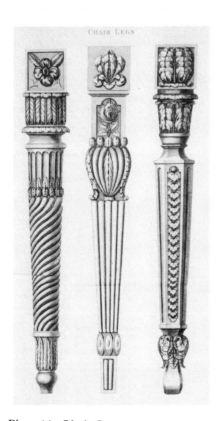

Plate 14. Chair Legs.

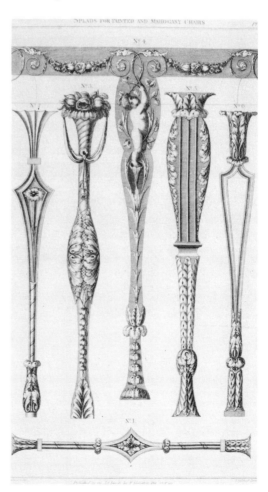

Plate 8. Chair Splats. 'No. 1, 2, 3 and 6 are intended for Parlour Chairs, carved in mahogany. No.1 and 3 are for painted chairs.

Thomas Sheraton
'The Cabinet-Maker and Upholsterer's Drawing Book, 1793.
Accompaniment to the *Drawing Book.*

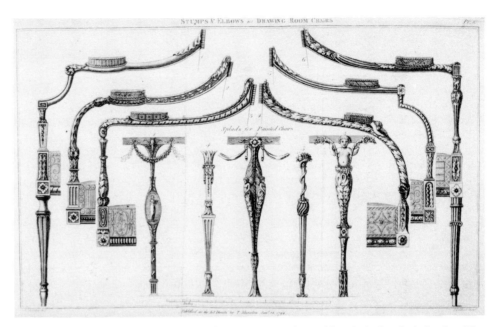

Plate 10. 'Chair Elbows, with part of the seat, together with splads for chair backs. The splads are all intended for japanning, except No. 4 which may be worked in mahogany. The elbows are meant chiefly to be carved and gilt; but the mere outlines of any of them will serve as patterns either for painted or mahogany chairs, by leaving out the ornaments for the mahogany, and retaining some of them, or even all of them may be adapted for painting.'

'The Cabinet-Maker's London Book of Prices', 2nd Edition, 1793.

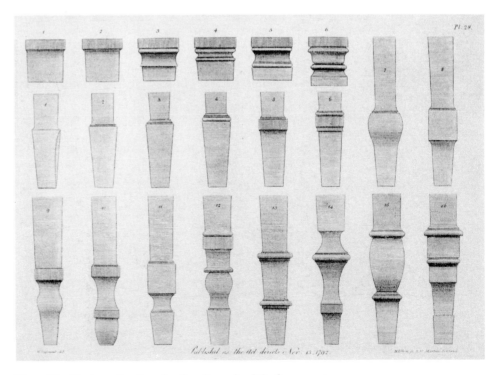

Plate 28. Designs for feet for furniture by W. Casement.

Section 2. CHAIRS. Upholstered armchairs and side chairs

These chairs were usually intended for Drawing Rooms and the rooms of grand apartments in large houses. They were often referred to by the designers as 'French Chairs', although in 1788 Hepplewhite referred to them as 'Cabriole Chairs'. They could be made in pairs or multiples in large sets. Their frames were made either of mahogany and polished, or lime or beechwood and gilded. In 1754 Chippendale issued designs for 'French Chairs' with an open space between the back and seat, 'which greatly lightens them, and has no ill Effect': this pattern was used by most subsequent designers.

The seats, backs and arms were stuffed with horsehair (without springs) and covered with fabrics such as leather, tapestries, embroideries, patterned silk damasks or velvets, and fixed by gilt brass nails in decorative patterns, or gilt brass borders on straight edges. The stuffing was held in place on the back and seat by stitches and 'tufts' of silk or buttons which pulled the fabric down slightly, but not as severely as mid-nineteenth century buttoning. As they were intended to stand against the walls of a room when not in use, the backs were covered in a plain material, usually a woollen cloth called Moreen, and linen or cotton 'cases' or loose covers provided for protection.

Chairs with upholstered backs and seats, but without arms, were often still referred to by designers as 'Back Stools' (their seventeenth century name), and were designed either as part of a larger suite with arm chairs, or as dressing chairs for bedrooms, where their covers would be made en suite with the bed hangings and window curtains.

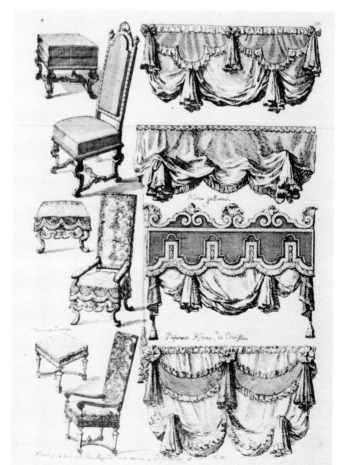

Daniel Marot
'Nouveaux Livres de Licts de differentes pensseez',
c.1703 and 1713.
Plate VII. Nouveaux Fauteuils.

'Seconde Livre d'Apartements', c.1703 and 1713.
Plate V.

Gaetano Brunetti
'Sixty Different Sorts of Ornament', 1736.

Brunetti: Side Chairs. 1736.

William Kent

Brunetti: Armchair. 1736.

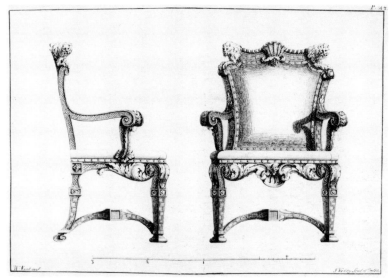

Plate 43 from J. Vardy's *Some Designs of Mr. Inigo Jones & Mr. William Kent*, 1744.

Brunetti: Armchair. 1736.

Kent: Plate 42. Chairs. 1744.

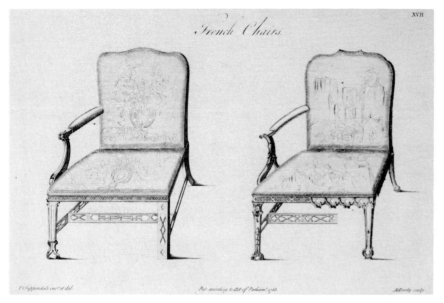

Thomas Chippendale
'The Gentleman and Cabinet-Maker's Director', 1st Edition, 1754.

Plate XVII. French Chairs, 'some designed to be open below at the seat, which greatly lightens them, and has no ill Effect.' Not in 3rd Edition, 1763.

Plate XVIII. French Chairs. 1st Edition, 1754. Not in 3rd Edition, 1763.

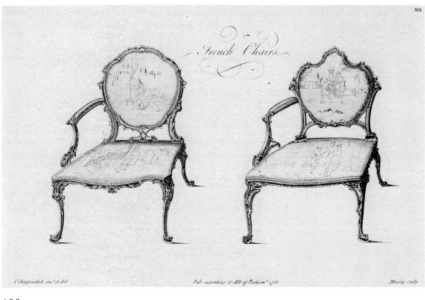

Plate XIX. French Chairs. 1st Edition, 1754. Not in 3rd Edition, 1763.

Thomas Chippendale
'The Gentleman and Cabinet-Maker's Director', 3rd Edition, 1763.

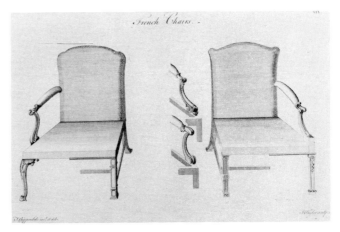

Plate XIX. French Chairs. 3rd Edition, 1763.

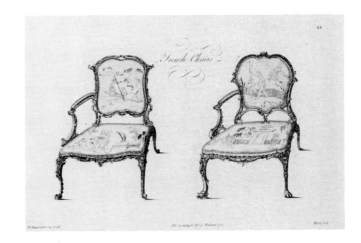

Plate XX. French Chairs. 'Dimensions for French Chairs: 2′ 3″ wide at front, 1′ 11″ at back of seat rail, 1′ 10″ front of back to front of seat rail. Seat 1′ 2½″ high. Back 2′ 3″ high.'

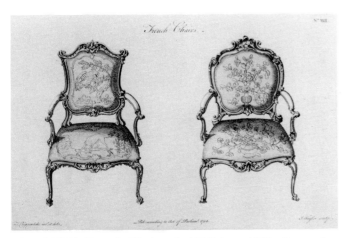

Plate XXII. French Chairs. 3rd Edition, 1763. Engraving dated 1759. 'Both the Backs and the Seats must be covered with Tapestry, or other sort of needlework.'

Plate XXIII. French Chairs. 3rd Edition. Engraving dated 1759.

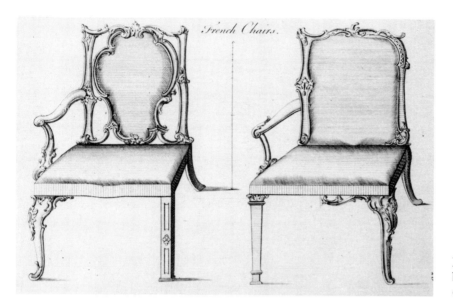

A Society of Upholsterers
'Genteel Houshold Furniture in the Present Taste'. 2nd Edition, c.1765.

Plate 26. French Chairs. Probably designed by Manwaring. Re-issued by Sayer in *The Chair-Maker's Guide,* 1766.

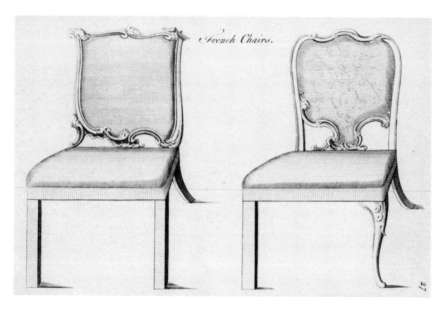

Plate 27. French Chairs. Probably designed by Manwaring.

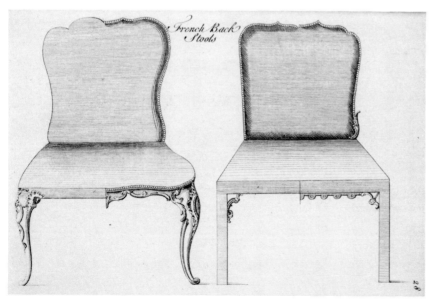

Plate 28. French Back Stools. Probably designed by Manwaring.

William Ince and John Mayhew
'The Universal System of Houshold Furniture', 1762.

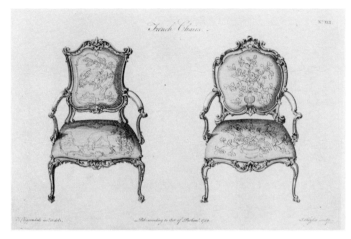

Plate LVIII. French Elbow Chairs.

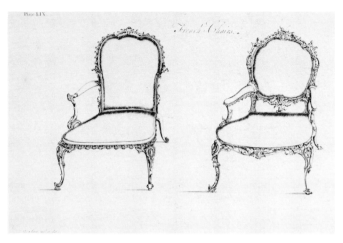

Plate LIX. French Elbow Chairs.

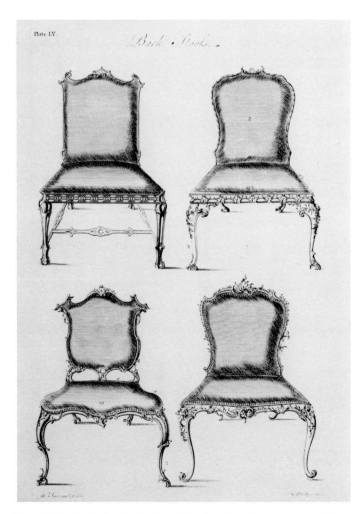

Plate LV. Back Stool Chairs. 'The last has been executed in burnish'd Gold, from the Plate, and covered with blue Damask.'

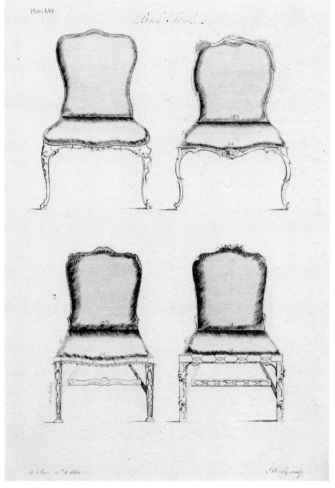

Plate LVI. Back Stools.

Robert Manwaring
'The Cabinet and Chair-Maker's Real Friend and Companion', 1765.

Plate 16. Dressing Chairs.

Plate 17. Ladies Dressing Chairs. 'four genteel Designs for Ladies Dressing Chairs, and may be executed either in Mahogany or Lime Tree.'

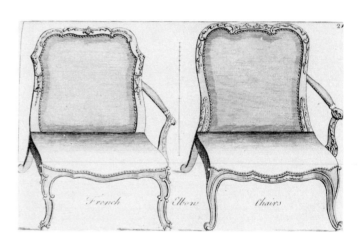

Plate 21. French Elbow Chairs.

Plate 22. Back Stools.

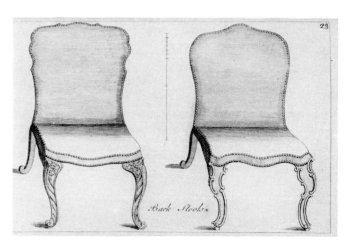

Plate 23. Back Stools.

104

Thomas Malton
'Compleat Treatise on Perspective', 1775.

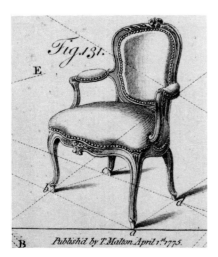

Plate XXXIII. Fig. 131. 'Modern Chair now in use.'

A. Hepplewhite & Co.
'The Cabinet Maker and Upholsterer's Guide',
1788. 2nd Edition, 1789. 3rd Edition, 1794.

Plate 11. Hepplewhite Cabriole Chairs. Left-hand chair not in 3rd Edition, 1794.

Plates 10-12. Chairs with stuffed backs 'are called cabriole chairs, The Designs E and F (Plate 10) are of the newest fashion. The arms to F though much higher than usual, have been executed with a good effect for His Royal Highness the Prince of Wales. The Designs, Plate 11, are also quite new. To the design X, Plate 12, we have given a French foot, the enrichments of which may be either carved, carved and gilt, or japanned.'

Plate 12. Chairs. Not in 3rd Edition, 1794.

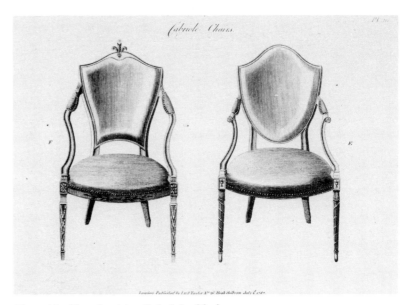

Plate 10. Hepplewhite Cabriole Chairs.

A. Hepplewhite & Co.
'The Cabinet Maker and Upholsterer's Guide',
1st Edition, 1788. 2nd Edition, 1789.

Plate 13. 'Two Designs for State Chairs, the form of which is properly adapted to receive that grandeur of ornament and gravity of appearance which is required in this article of furniture. The ornaments may be carved, carved and gilt, or japanned. The design U is proper for burnished gold on the ornaments, with the groundwork painted of a dark colour, which will give this design an appearance of stately grandeur, yet avoiding a disagreeable and heavy appearance. The covering to this kind of chair may be of red morocco...'
Not in 3rd Edition, 1794.

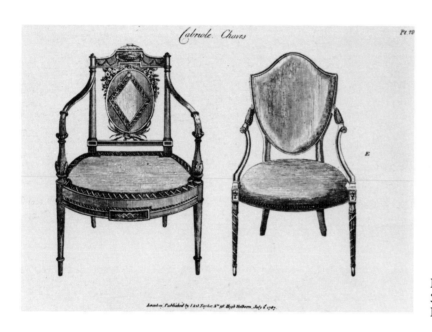

Plate 10. Cabriole Chairs. 2nd Edition, 1789. 3rd Edition, 1794. Left-hand chair not in 1st Edition.

A Society of Upholsterers
'Genteel Houshold Furniture in the Present Taste'.
2nd Edition, c.1765.

Reclining and Easy Chairs

Reclining and easy chairs were intended primarily for bedchambers and smaller private sitting rooms where their owners and guests were able to relax in comfort. They had been in use from the late seventeenth century. A typical example was the Bergère, an upholstered chair with arms, elongated seat, raked and often adjustable back, and thick comfortable cushions stuffed with wool and down. A variation on the theme was a linked chair and stool which Chippendale referred to as 'what the French called *Pêché-Mortel'* (1754), or two chairs and a stool which Hepplewhite called a Duchesse (1788). By 1793 Sheraton used the description *'Chaise Longue'*, and 'their use is to rest or loll upon after dinner.'

Fabrics used to cover these chairs would usually correspond to those used for other upholstery and hangings in the room. Some were 'stuffed over', (that is, had fixed upholstery), others had cane seats and backs, a mattress and loose cushions.

Hepplewhite's design for a wing chair exemplified a standard eighteenth century pattern for the use of invalids and the elderly, derived from late seventeenth century models. The frames were usually made fairly plainly and stoutly of mahogany, often with stretchers between the legs for extra support, and sometimes with castors. The seats often had squab or loose cushions stuffed with wool, and the inner faces of the 'wings' were also stuffed with wool for greater comfort and warmth. Coverings ranged from horsehair or leather to woollen embroideries and most had loose linen cases.

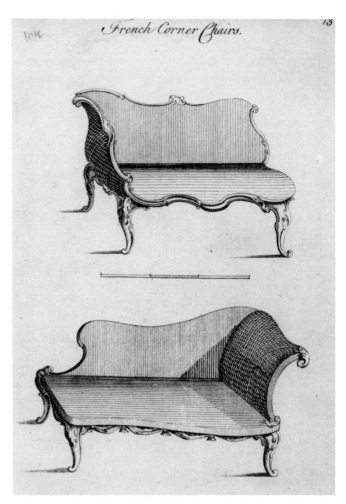

Plate 13. French Corner Chairs. Adapted from Ince and Mayhew *The Universal System of Houshold Furniture,* Plate LVII, 1762.

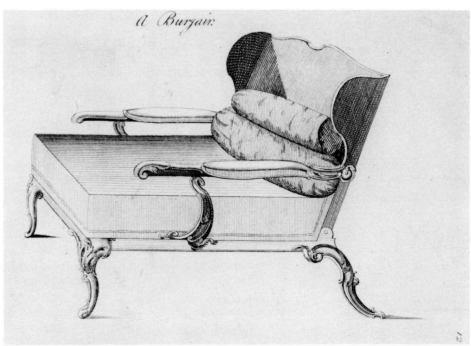

Plate 12. Bergère. Adapted from Ince and Mayhew, *The Universal System of Houshold Furniture,* Plate LX, 1762.

William Ince and John Mayhew
'The Universal System of Houshold Furniture', 1762.

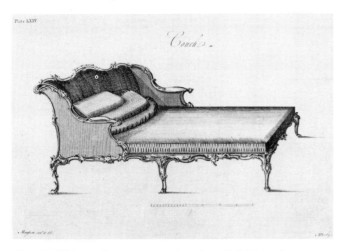

Plate LXIV. 'A single headed Couch, which if the Ornaments of the Frame are well carved will be very handsome.'

Plate LX (right) 'Birjairs, or half couches, the Back of the Lower one, is made to fall down at pleasure...'

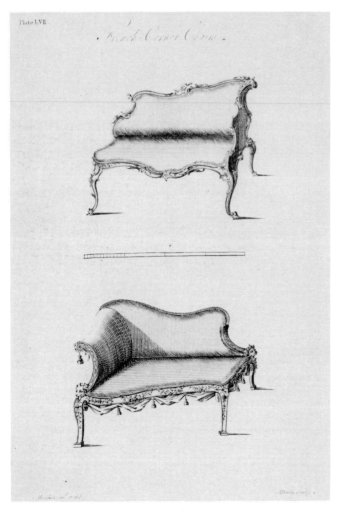

Plate LVII. Corner Chairs or Settees.

Thomas Chippendale
'The Gentleman and Cabinet-Maker's Director', 3rd Edition, 1763.

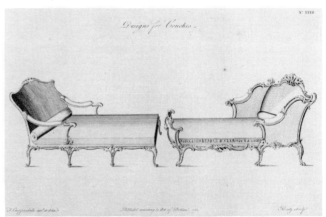

Plate XXXII (above) 'What the French call *Pêché-Mortel*. They are sometimes made to take asunder in the middle; one part makes a large Easy-Chair, and the other a Stool, and the feet join in the middle, which looks badly. Therefore I would recommend their being made as in these designs, with a pretty thick mattrass.' Engraving dated 1761.

A. Hepplewhite & Co.
'The Cabinet-Maker and Upholsterer's Guide', 1st Edition 1788. 2nd Edition, 1789. 3rd Edition, 1794.
Plate 28. Duchesse. 'also derived from the French. Two Barjier chairs, of proper construction, with a stool in the middle, form the duchesse, which is alotted to large and spacious anti-rooms' 6ft.-8ft. long.
'The stuffing may be of the round manner as shown in the drawing or low-stuffed, with a loose squab or bordered cushion fitted to each part; with a duplicate linen cover to cover the whole, or each part separately.'

Plate 15. 'a saddle check, or easy chair: the construction and use of which is very apparent, they may be covered with leather, horsehair, or have a linen case to fit over the canvas stuffing.'

Thomas Sheraton
'The Cabinet-Maker and Upholsterer's Drawing Book', 1793.

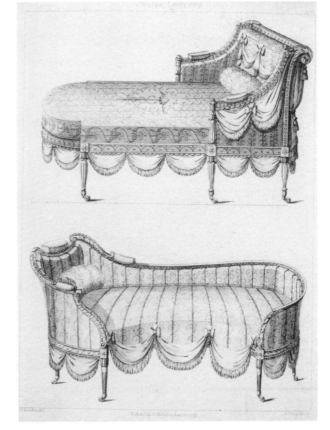

Appendix, Plate XVIII. Chaises Longues.
'These have their name from the French, which imports a long chair. Their use is to rest or loll upon after dinner, and in some cases the lower one will serve for a sofa...'

Section 3. SETTEES and SOFAS

The word 'settee' was generally used throughout the eighteenth century for seats with both carved and upholstered backs, although 'sopha' or 'sofa' came into use for fully upholstered examples, and more precisely for those following Bailey's description in *Dictionarium Britannicum,* 'A sort of Alcove much used in Asia; it is an Apartment of State, raised from about half a foot, to two feet higher than the floor, and furnished with rich carpets and cushions, where honourable personages are entertained' (2nd Edition, 1736). Designs in the Society of Upholsterers' *Genteel Houshold Furniture* (1765) used the words 'Couch's' and 'Settee Couches', and Hepplewhite produced a variation called a 'Confidante', with additional seats at each end

(Plate 27, 1788). As most settees formed part of suites of furniture their carved decoration usually followed the patterns of the corresponding chair legs and, like the chairs, they were placed against the walls of the rooms, so their backs were finished plainly. The frames, as for the chairs, were either of polished walnut, mahogany and satinwood, or gilded beech, limewood or pine. They were upholstered and covered in the same manner as armchairs (see Section 2) and often provided with extra bolsters. Loose back cushions only appear in Sheraton's Plate XXXV, 1793. Seats and stuffed backs were often 'tufted', as can be seen in Manwaring's designs of 1765 and Hepplewhite's of 1794.

Probably Matthias Darly
Plate 58. Settee. Attributed by Gilbert to Darly, *A Second Book of Chairs,* 1751. Re-issued in *The Chair-Maker's Guide,* 1766 with original plate number erased, title inserted.

William Kent
Plate 42 from J. Vardy's *Some Designs of Mr. Inigo Jones & Mr. William Kent,* 1744.

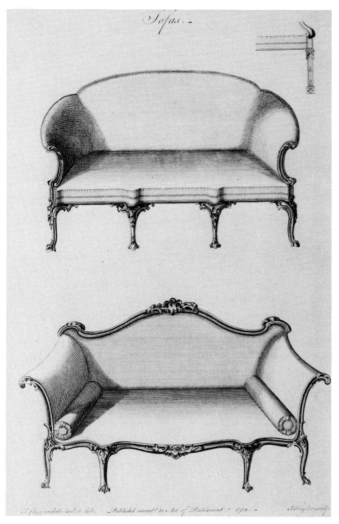

Thomas Chippendale
'The Gentleman and Cabinet-Maker's Director', 3rd
Edition, 1763.
Plate XXIX. Sofas, 'commonly 6′ 9″ or 10′ long, 2′ 3″ – 3′
front to back of seat, 1′ 2″ height of back. Engraving dated
1759.

Plate XXX. Sofas. Engraving dated 1759.

Plate XXXI. A Sofa, 'a sofa for a Grand
Apartment, . . . and will require great
Care in the Execution. Embossments . . .
to be gilt with burnish'd Gold . . . I
would advise the workman to make a
Model of it at large, before he begins to
execute it.' Engraving dated 1760.

111

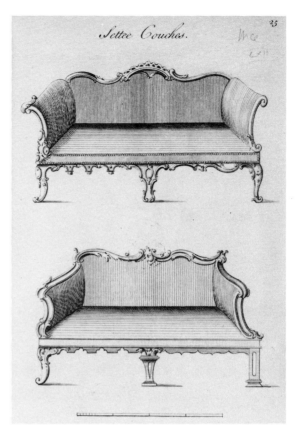

A Society of Upholsterers
'Genteel Houshold Furniture in the Present Taste', 2nd Edition, c.1765.
Plate 20. Couches, probably designed by Manwaring, and re-issed in *The Chair-Maker's Guide,* 1766.

Plate 25. Settee Couches, possibly adapted from Ince and Mayhew, *The Universal System of Houshold Furniture,* 1762. Plate LXII. (Upper design.)

William Ince and John Mayhew
'The Universal System of Houshold Furniture', 1762.

Plate LXIII (above). 'An Alcove ornamented in the Gothic Taste; with a Soffa adapted to the whole Side of a Room.'

Plate LXII (left). Sofas.

William Ince and John Mayhew
'The Universal System of Houshold Furniture', 1762.

Plate LXV. 'An Alcove with the whole Side of a Room described, fitted up compleat with cushions in form of a Turkish Soffa, a Drapery Curtain in Front, and Girandoles on each Side.'

Robert Manwaring
'The Cabinet and Chair-Maker's Real Friend and Companion', 1765.

Plates 19 and 20. Grand French Settee Chairs.
'Two very magnificent and superb Designs for French Settee Chairs; they may be executed either in Lime Tree or Yellow Deal.'

Plate 20.

113

A. Hepplewhite & Co.
'The Cabinet-Maker and Upholsterer's Guide', 1st Edition 1788.
Plate 26. Bar-back sofa 'this kind of sofa is of modern invention; and the lightness of its appearance has procured it a favourable reception in the first circles of fashion. The pattern of the back must match the chairs; these will also regulate the sort of framework and covering.'
Also in 3rd Edition, 1794.

R. & J. Adam
'Works in Architecture', Vol.I, No.II, 1778.
Plate V. Detail from the Library at Kenwood, Settee and Glass in recess.

A. Hepplewhite & Co.
'The Cabinet-Maker and Upholsterer's Guide', 1st Edition, 1788. 2nd Edition, 1789.
Plates 21-4. Sofas. General sizes: 6ft.-7ft. long, 30ins. deep, 14in. high to seat, 3ft. total height of back. 'the woodwork of which should be either mahogany or japanned, in accordance to the chairs; the covering must also be of the same.'

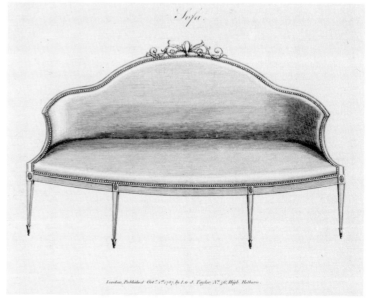

Plate 21. Sofa. 1st Edition, 1788. 2nd Edition, 1789. 3rd Edition, 1794.

A. Hepplewhite & Co.
'The Cabinet-Maker and Upholsterer's Guide',
1st Edition, 1788. 2nd Edition, 1789.
Plates 21-4. Sofas. General sizes: 6ft.-7ft. long, 30ins. deep, 14in. high to seat, 3ft. total height of back. 'the woodwork of which should be either mahogany or japanned, in accordance to the chairs; the covering must also be of the same.'

Plate 22. Sofa. 1st Edition, 1788. 2nd Edition, 1789. 3rd Edition, 1794.

Plate 23. Sofa. 1st Edition, 1788. 2nd Edition, 1789. Not in 3rd Edition.

Plate 24. Sofa. 1st Edition, 1788. 2nd Edition, 1789. Not in 3rd Edition.

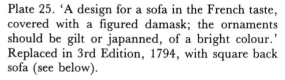

A. Hepplewhite & Co.
'The Cabinet-Maker and Upholsterer's Guide',
1st Edition, 1788. 2nd Edition, 1789. 3rd Edition, 1794.

Plate 25. 'A design for a sofa in the French taste, covered with a figured damask; the ornaments should be gilt or japanned, of a bright colour.' Replaced in 3rd Edition, 1794, with square back sofa (see below).

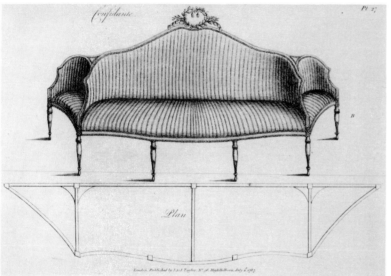

Plate 27. Confidante. 'This piece of furniture is of French origin, and is in pretty general request for large and spacious suits of apartments. An elegant drawing-room, with modern furniture, is scarce complete without a confidant.' Length — approx. 9ft. 'This piece of furniture is sometimes so constructed, that the ends take away and leave a regular sofa, the ends may be used as Barjier chairs.'
Also in 3rd Edition, 1794.

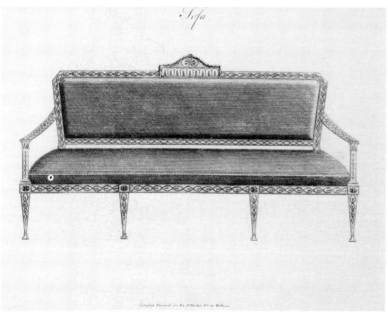

Plate 25. Sofa 'of the newest fashion; the frame should be japanned, with green on a white ground, and the edges gilt; the covering of red morocco leather.
In 2nd Edition, 1789, and 3rd Edition, 1794.

A. Hepplewhite & Co.
'The Cabinet-Maker and Upholsterer's Guide',
3rd Edition, 1794.

Plate 21. Sofa 'the woodwork of which should be either mahogany or japanned, in accordance to the chairs; the covering also must be of the same.'

Plate 23. Sofa 'the woodwork of which should be either mahogany or japanned, in accordance to the chairs; the covering also must be of the same.'

Thomas Sheraton
'The Cabinet-Maker and Upholsterer's Drawing Book', 1793.
Part III. Plate XXXV. Sofa. 'These are done in white and gold, or japanned. The loose cushions at the back are generally made to fill the whole length, which would have taken four; but I could not make the design so striking with four... The seat is stuffed up in front about three inches high above the rail, denoted by the figure of the sprig running longways; all above that is a squab, which may be taken off occasionally...'

Thomas Sheraton
'The Cabinet-Maker and Upholsterer's Drawing Book',
2nd Edition, 1794.

Plate 52. A Turkey Sofa.

'These are genteel seats introduced in the most fashionable houses, and are an imitation of the Turkish mode of fitting. They are therefore made very low, scarcely exceeding a foot to the upper side of the cushion.

The frame may be made of beech, and must be webbed and strained with canvas to support the cushions.

The back cushions in this design have spaces between them, with drapery inserted, but they are generally made to fill close up without leaving any intervals. In rooms where there are no columns nor architrave suitable for such a seat, these may easily be put up in a temporary way, so that, if requisite, they may be taken down without any injury to the room. The back of the sofa, by which I mean the whole height of the wall, from surbase to cornice, must have a deal frame fixed to it, against which the canvas, drapery at the top, and the fluting, must be tacked.'

See also Part V. Interiors. Section 7E Sofa Beds.

Section 4. STOOLS

Many eighteenth century stools were part of larger suites of seat furniture and their designs were adapted from chair patterns. Some designs were also produced for 'Dressing Stools', to accompany ladies' dressing tables, and 'French Stools' which were intended to be placed in window recesses and sometimes had low backs. Hepplewhite directed that 'the size of window stools must be regulated by the size of the place where they are to stand; their heights must not exceed the seats of the chairs.' Quite a few designs show patterns for 'tufting' on the seats. Hepplewhite and Sheraton included designs for 'Gouty Stools', on which the unfortunate sufferer could rest an afflicted foot or leg. Sheraton also gave a design for a 'Chamber Horse', on which the rider could sit astride and exercise — an early 'keep-fit' device, and one of the few pieces of eighteenth century furniture to make use of coiled springs.

Edwards and Darly
'A New Book of Chinese Designs', 1754.
'Idol' stool.

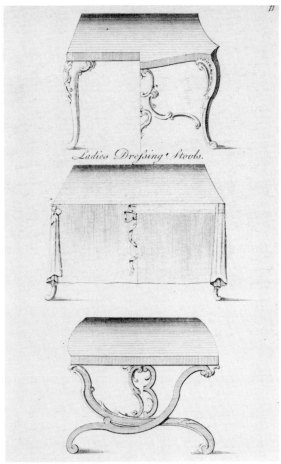

A Society of Upholsterers
'Genteel Houshold Furniture in the Present Taste', 2nd Edition, c.1765.
Plate 11 (above). Ladies' Dressing Stools. Probably designed by Manwaring. Re-issued by Sayer in *The Chair-Maker's Guide,* 1766.

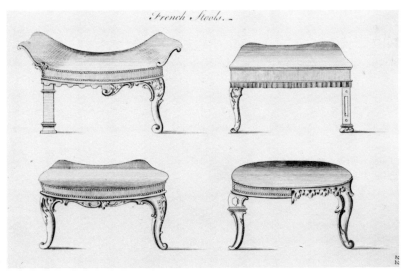

Plate 22 (left). French Stools. Probably designed by Manwaring. Re-issued by Sayer in *The Chair-Maker's Guide,* 1766.

119

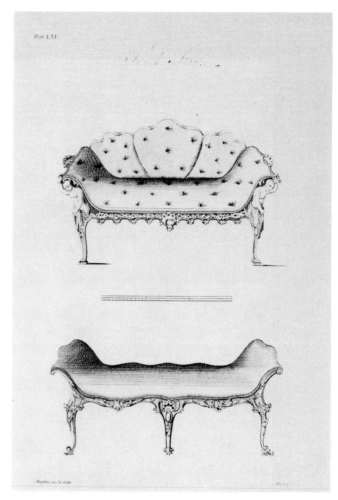

A Society of Upholsterers
'Genteel Houshold Furniture in the Present Taste', 2nd
Edition, c.1765.
Plate 10. French Stools. Probably designed by Manwaring.
Re-issued by Sayer in *The Chair-Maker's Guide,* 1766.

William Ince and John Mayhew
'The Universal System of Houshold Furniture', 1762.
Plate LXI. Designs of Stools for recesses of Windows.

William Ince and John Mayhew
'The Universal System of Houshold
Furniture', 1762.
Plate XXXIV. Dressing Stools.

Robert Manwaring
'The Cabinet and Chair-Maker's Real Friend and Companion', 1765.

Plate 18. Lady's Dressing Stools.

A. Hepplewhite & Co.
'The Cabinet-Maker and Upholsterer's Guide', 1788.
Plates 16 and 17. Stools. 'the framework for which may be of mahogany, or japanned, as most agreeable, or to match the suit of chairs, and of consequence should have the same sort of covering. The design O, Plate 17, is proper for a dressing or music stool.' Also in 3rd Edition, 1794.

Plate 17.

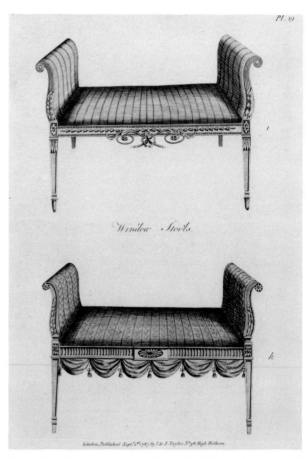

A. Hepplewhite & Co.
'The Cabinet Maker and Upholsterer's Guide', 1788.
2nd Edition, 1789. 3rd Edition, 1794.

Plates 18 and 19. Window Stools. Plate 18. 'proper for mahogany or japan, covered with linen or cotton to match the chairs.'

Plate 19. 'the upper one is applicable to japan-work, with striped furniture; the under one of mahogany carved, with furniture of an elegant pattern festooned in front, will produce a very pleasing effect.'

Plate 20. Window stools. 'These two designs are peculiarly adapted for an elegant drawing room of japanned furniture; the covering should be of taberray or morine of a pea green or other light colour.' 'The size of window stools must be regulated by the size of the place where they are to stand; their heights should not exceed the seats of the chairs.'

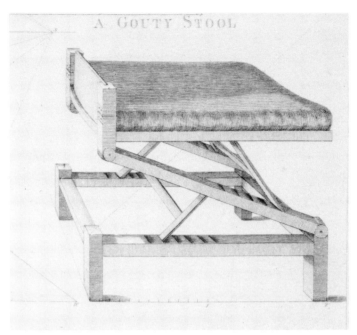

Thomas Sheraton
'The Cabinet-Maker and Upholsterer's Drawing Book',
1793.
Appendix. Also Plate 30. Gouty Stool.

A. Hepplewhite & Co.
'The Cabinet-Maker and Upholsterer's Guide', 1788.
2nd Edition, 1789. 3rd Edition, 1794.
Plate 15. Gouty Stool 'particularly useful for the afflicted.'

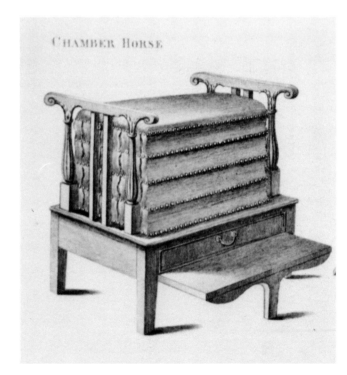

Thomas Sheraton
'The Cabinet-Maker and Upholsterer's Drawing Book',
1793.
Appendix, Plate XXII. Chamber Horse.

Section 5. HALL SEATS

Described by Sheraton as 'such as are placed in Halls, for the use of servants or strangers waiting on business. — They are generally made all of mahogany, with turned seats, and the crest or arms of the family painted on the centre of the back.' (*The Cabinet Dictionary,* 1803). Eighteenth century designs for them were sometimes quite fanciful and were intended not only for the hall, but also for passages and garden buildings, where delicate or upholstered chairs were unsuitable. Settees and stools, with either plain wooden or leather seats, were also used in halls.

Matthias Darly
'A New Book of Chinese, Gothic and Modern Chairs',
1751.

Plate 2. Reprinted in *The Chair-Maker's Guide,* 1766, Plate 33, with slight alterations to legs, titled Hall Chairs.

Plate 3. Reprinted in *The Chair-Maker's Guide,* 1766, Plate 39, with alterations to legs, titled Hall Chairs.

Plate 4. Reprinted in *The Chair-Maker's Guide,* 1766, Plate 37, with alterations to legs, titled Hall Chairs.

Plate 5. Reprinted in *The Chair-Maker's Guide,* 1766, Plate 40, with alterations to legs, titled Hall Chairs.

Matthias Darly
'A New Book of Chinese, Gothic and Modern Chairs',
1751.
Plate 6. Re-issued by Sayer in Manwaring's *The Chair-Maker's Guide,* 1766, Plate 43, with alterations.

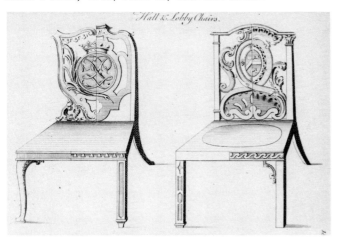

A Society of Upholsterers
'Genteel Houshold Furniture in the Present Taste', 2nd
Edition, c.1765.
Plate 18. Hall and Lobby Chairs; probably designed by Manwaring; re-issued by Sayer in *The Chair-Maker's Guide,* 1766.

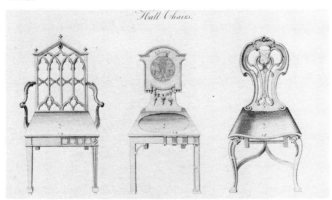

Thomas Chippendale
'The Gentleman and Cabinet-Maker's Director', 3rd
Edition, 1763.
Plate XVII. 'Chairs for Halls, Passages or Summer Houses.' Engraving dated 1759.

Plate 7. Reprinted in *The Chair-Maker's Guide,* 1766, Plate 34, with alterations to left chair, titled Hall Chairs.

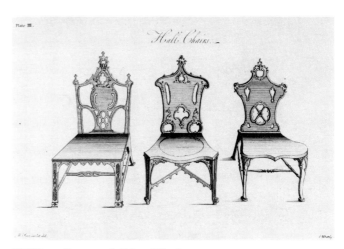

William Ince and John Mayhew
'The Universal System of Houshold Furniture', 1762.
Plate IV. 'Hall Chairs in The Gothic Taste, the Ornaments of which, if thought too expensive, may be painted, and have a very good effect.'

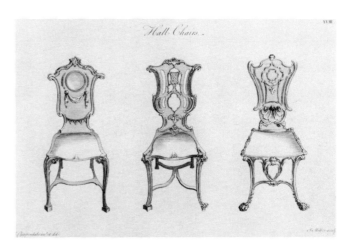

Thomas Chippendale
'The Gentleman and Cabinet-Maker's Director', 3rd
Edition, 1763.
Plate XVIII. Hall Chairs.

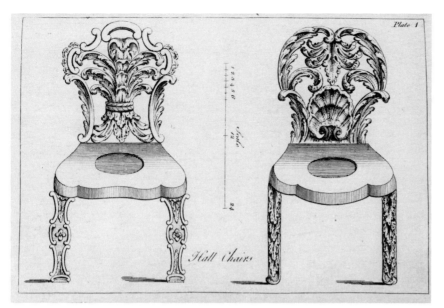

Plate 1. Hall Chairs.

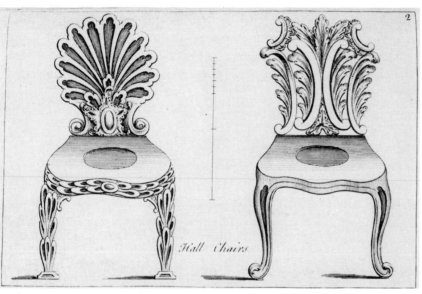

Plate 2. Hall Chairs. 'six Different and beautiful Designs for Hall Chairs, and may be executed either in Mahogany, Walnut, Pear or Lime Tree.'

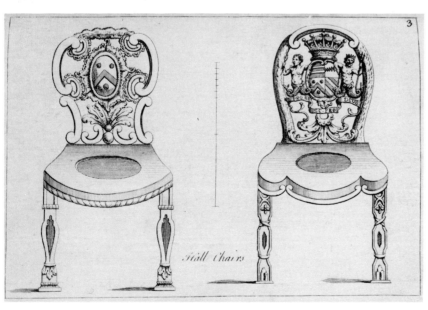

Plate 3. Hall Chairs.

'The Chair-Maker's Guide', 1766.
Plate 55. Hall Chair, signed Copland.

Plate 56. Hall Chair. Attributed to Copland.

Plate 57. Hall Chair. Attributed to Copland.

Plate 66. Hall Chair. Attributed to Copland.

Plate 67. Hall Chair. Attributed to Copland.

Plate 68. Hall Chair. Attributed to Copland.

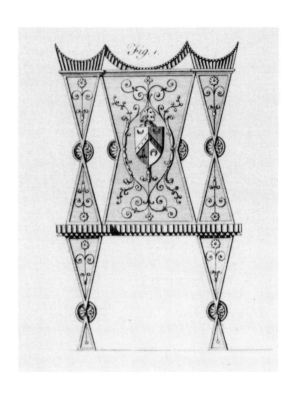

J. Carter
'The Builder's Magazine', 1774-8.

Plate LXX. Hall Chair.

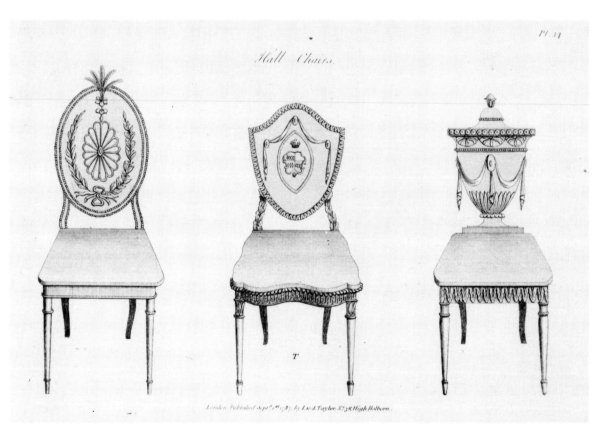

A. Hepplewhite & Co.
'The Cabinet-Maker and Upholsterer's Guide', 1788.
2nd Edition, 1789. 3rd Edition, 1794.
Plate 14. Hall Chairs 'all of wood, either carved or painted.
The designs with vase backs are new and have been much
approved.'

128

Section 6. GARDEN SEATS

Some of the most imaginative of all eighteenth century furniture designs were published for garden seats, and as very few executed examples survive, they are an invaluable source of information. The designs covered the whole range of styles used during the century, but perhaps the most entertaining were those for rustic furniture, intended to resemble the roots, branches and twigs of trees, 'which, if properly painted, will appear like Nature' (Manwaring, *The Cabinet and Chair-Maker's Real Friend and Companion*, 1765). Most garden chairs and benches were designed to be painted, usually green or white, for weather protection; the wooden seats often had little tufted squabs or cushions tied on when the chairs were in regular use.

Daniel Marot
'Nouveaux Fauteuils', c.1703.

Plate 25. Garden Seat.

Plate 28. Garden Seats.

Plate 29. Garden Seat.

Plate 30. Garden Seat.

129

William Halfpenny
'New Designs for Chinese Temples', 1750.

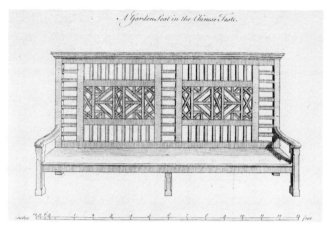

Plate 38. A Garden Seat in the Chinese Taste.

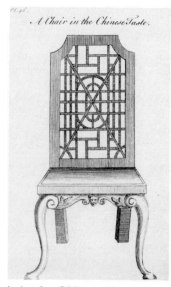

Plate 46. A Chair in the Chinese Taste.

Plate 39. A Garden Seat in the Chinese Taste.

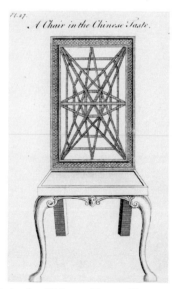

Plate 47. A Chair in the Chinese Taste. 'Perspective Designs for Chairs, partly in the Chinese Manner, most suitable for Banquetting Houses, Rural Buildings etc.'

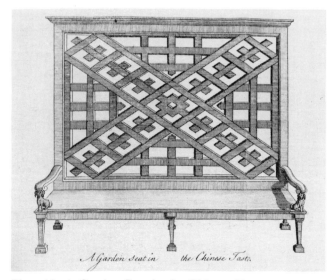

Plate 40. A Garden Seat in the Chinese Taste.

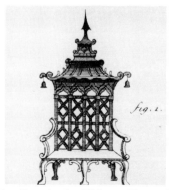

Plate 48. A Garden Seat in the Chinese Taste, 'cover'd with a Chinese cov'd Canopy.'

Edwards & Darly
'A New Book of Chinese Designs', 1754.

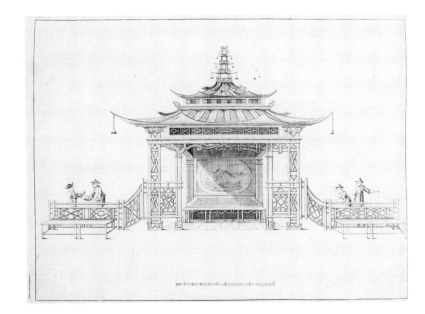

Alcove Summer House with Benches.

Alcove Summer House with Benches.

Alcove Summer House with Bench.

Plate 66. Armchair.

Plate 86. Garden Chair.

Plate 117. Garden Chairs.

William Chambers
'Designs of Chinese Buildings', 1757.

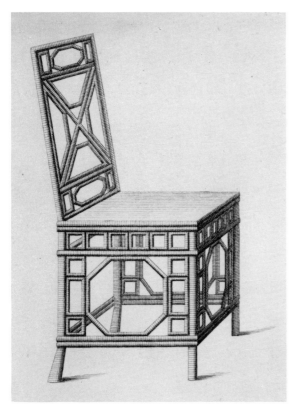

Garden Chair.

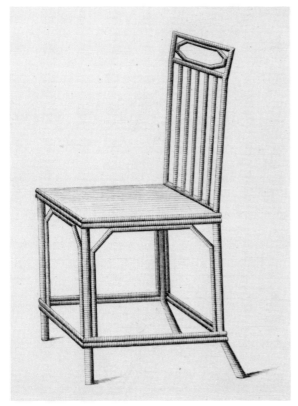

Garden Chair.

'The moveables of the Saloon consist of Chairs, Stools and Tables, made sometimes of rose-wood, ebony, or lacquered work, and sometimes of Bamboo only, which is cheap, and nevertheless very neat.'

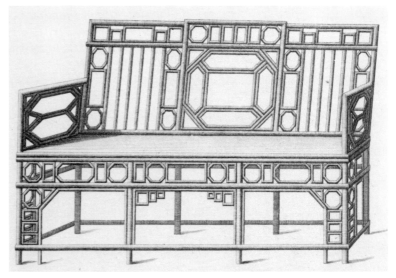

Garden Seat.

Robert Morris
'Architecture Improv'd in a Collection of Modern, Useful and Elegant Designs', 1757.
Design for a Chimerical Seat. First published in the *Architectural Remembrancer*, 1751. 'I have placed it here to keep in countenance all true lovers of the Oriental Taste, and to show how Trifles may be esteemed, when it is the Fashion to be ridiculous.'

133

Charles Over
'Ornamental Architecture in the Gothic, Chinese and Modern Taste',
1758.

Plate 7. A Covered Garden Seat.

Plates 5 and 6. Garden Seats.
'Two Designs for Garden Seats in the Chinese Taste, of small Expence, Genteel and Durable'.

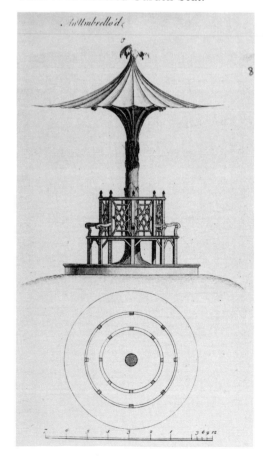

Plate 8. 'An Umbrello'd Garden Seat'. 'An Umbrello Seat after the Indian Manner, being one of the most agreeable Decorations yet known, from its affording a Shade when extended, and being on Occasion easily contracted or removed'.

134

Charles Over
'Ornamental
Architecture in the
Gothic, Chinese and
Modern Taste',
1758.

Plate 9. A Cover'd Seat or Alcove, proper to terminate Avenues.

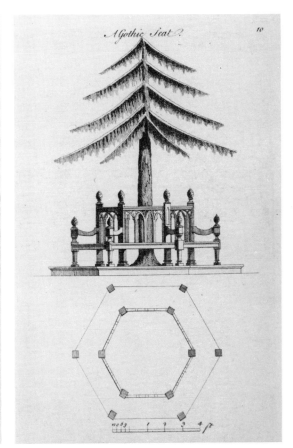

Plate 10. 'A Gothic Seat, fit to place round a Tree etc., to take the Advantage of Shade, or an Eminence to command a general Prospect'.

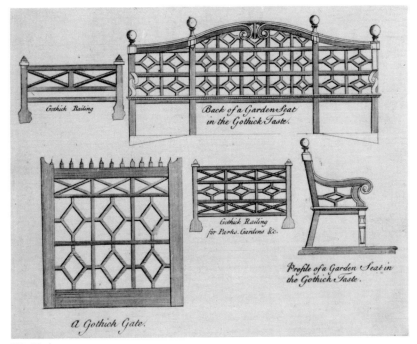

W. Pain
'The Builder's Companion and Workman's General Assistant',
1758.
Page 89 (above). Gothick seats, gate and railings.
Page 90 (right). Gothick Garden seat.

135

W. Pain
'The Builder's Companion and Workman's General Assistant', 1758.

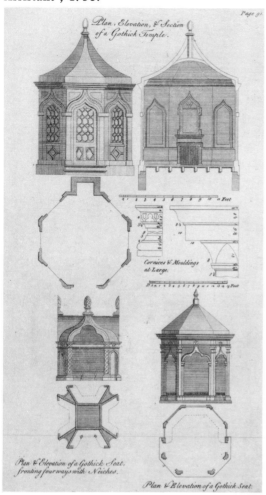

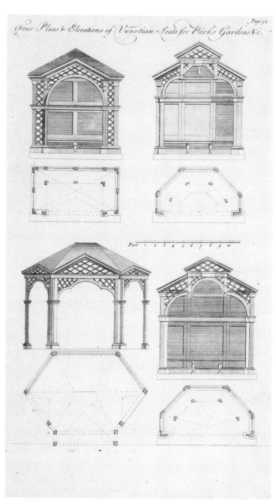

Page 91. Designs for a Gothick Temple.

Page 92. Designs for Venetian Seats.

Paul Decker
'Chinese Architecture, Civil and Ornamental', 1759.

Plate 2. 'Royal Garden Seat'. Re-issued by Sayer in *The Ladies' Amusement,* 1766. Plate 180.

Plate 4. 'Alcove and Gallery in the Front of a Banquetting House'. Re-issued by Sayer, 1766. Plate 185.

Paul Decker
'Chinese Architecture, Civil and Ornamental', 1759.

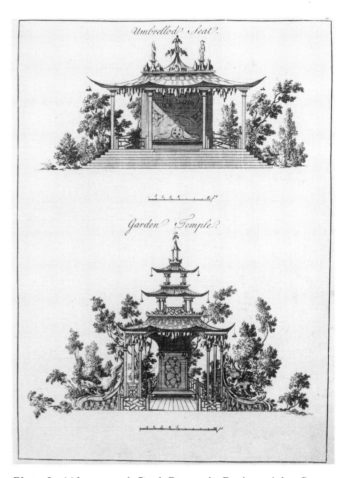

Plate 8. 'Umbrello'd Seat and Garden Temple'. Re-issued by Sayer, 1766. Plate 187.

Plate 9. 'Alcove and Cool Retreat'. Re-issued by Sayer, 1766. Plate 45.

Plate 10. 'Summer Dwelling of a Chief Bonzee or Priest'.

Paul Decker
'Gothic Architecture, Decorated', 1759.

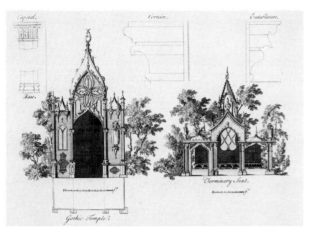

Plate 1. 'A Gothic Temple with Fassedde Seats attach'd'.

Plate 7. Alcove Seat.

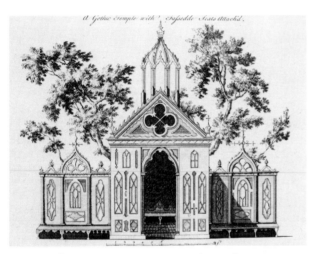

Plate 5. Gothic Temple and Terminary Seat.

Plate 8. Thatch'd Seat, Obelisk and Look-Out.

Plate 6. Garden Seat, Gazebo, Alcove and Summer House.
Re-issued by Sayer, 1766. Plate 188.

Plate 9. Rustic Garden Seat and Alcove Seat. Re-issued by
Sayer, 1766. Plate 189.

138

**Thomas Chippendale
'The Gentleman and Cabinet
Maker's Director', 3rd Edition,
1763.**

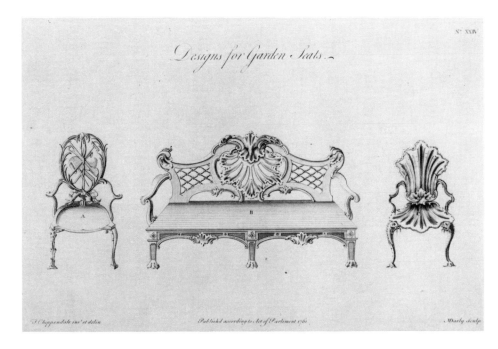

Plate XXIV. Garden Seats.
A. 'Proper for Arbours and
Summer Houses'. B. 'May be
placed in Walks or the Ends of
Avenues'. C. 'Proper for Grottos'.
Engraving dated 1761.

**A Society of Upholsterers
'Genteel Houshold Furniture in the Present Taste', 3rd
Edition, c.1765.**
Plate 19. Garden Seats.

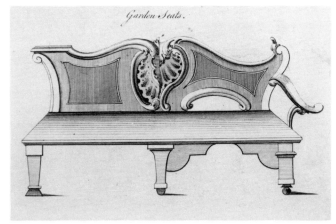

**Robert Manwaring
'The Cabinet and Chair-Maker's Real Friend and
Companion', 1765.**

Plates 29 and 30. 'are two very superb and grand Designs
for Rural Garden Seats, the ornamental Parts should be
painted green, and shaded as expressed in the Plate, which
will appear extremely beautiful.'

Robert Manwaring
'The Cabinet and Chair-Maker's Real Friend and
Companion', 1765.

Plates 31 and 32. 'are two very good Designs for Garden
Seats in the Gothic Taste; they will look very genteel painted
white intermixed with green...'

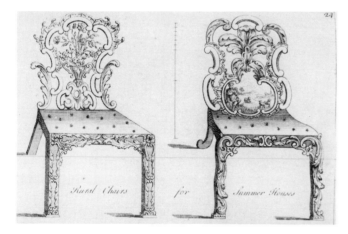

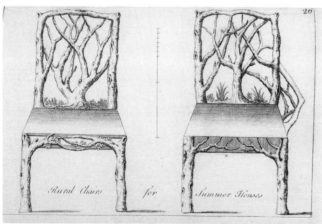

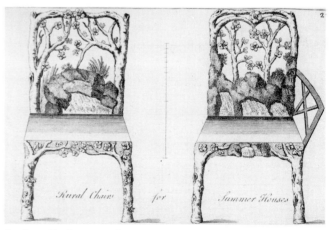

Plates 24-28. 'are ten very curious and beautiful Designs of
Rural Chairs, intended to be placed in Summer Houses,
Temples &c., and are the only ones of this kind that ever
were published; the Backs may be executed in the same
manner as the Hall Chairs with Regard to the Wood and
Carvings; there are Landscapes introduced in some of them,
which are intended to be painted... The Seats in Plates 24,
25 and 28 are represented to have loose quilted cushions and

the Seat Rails are to be executed the same as in the Gothic
Chairs; the Ornaments may be painted green, and will look
very genteel. Plates 26, 27, may be made with the Limbs of
Yew or Apple Trees, as Nature produces them, but the Stuff
should be very dry and well seasoned; after the bark is
peeled clean off, Chuse for your Pitches the nearest Pieces
you can match for the Shape of the Back, Fore Feet and
Elbows... they are generally painted in various Colours...'

140

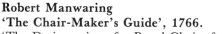

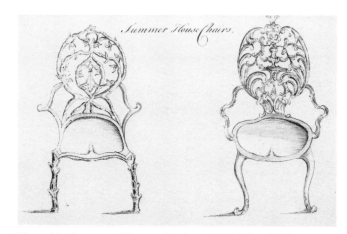

Plate 28. Rural Chairs for Summer Houses. (**'Companion'**, 1765)

Plate 46. Summer House Chairs. (**'Guide', 1766**)

Robert Manwaring
'The Chair-Maker's Guide', 1766.
'The Designs given for Rural Chairs for Summer-Houses,

Gardens and Parks, are entirely new, and are the only ones that were ever published... I hope they will give general Satisfaction with respect to their Grandeur, Variety, Novelty and Usefulness'.

Plates 69, 70 and 71. Summer House Chairs.

Plates 72, 73 and 75. Summer House Chairs.

Robert Manwaring
'The Chair-Maker's Guide', 1766.

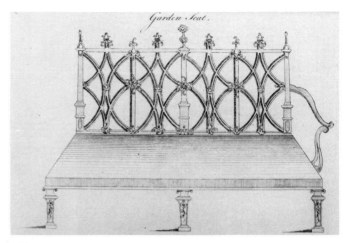

Plate 47. Garden Seat.

Plate 48. Garden Seat.

William Wrighte
'Grotesque Architecture, or Rural Amusement', 1767.

Plate 3. 'Hermit's Cell, with Rustic Seats attached' 'to be built partly of large stones and Trunks of Trees, set round with ivy and lined with Rushes &c. The Roof should be covered with Thatch, and the Floor paved with small Pebble Stones or Cockle Shells. The Seats attached are intended to be composed of large irregular Stones, Roots of Trees &c.'.

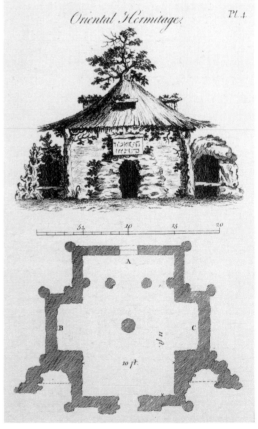

Plate 4. Oriental Hermitage 'in the Eastern Stile, supposed to be built round a Tree which supports its Roof "Thatch" in the Chinese Taste "The inside to be lined with Billet Wood and Moss". The Rustic Seats on the Side are intended to be composed of large rough Stones and Roots of Pollard Trees cemented together'.

John Soane
'Designs in Architecture', 1778.

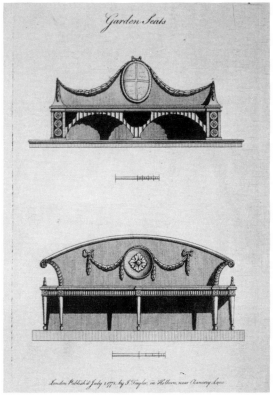

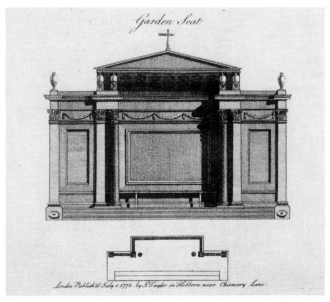

Plate I. Garden Seats.

Plate II. Garden Seats.

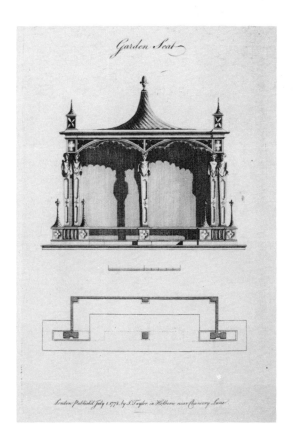

Plate IV. Garden Seat.

Plate V. Garden Seat.

Anon 1790-97
'Ideas for Rustic Furniture'
Plates 2 to 8. Garden Chairs.

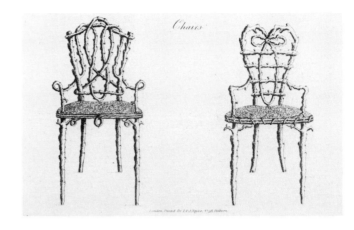

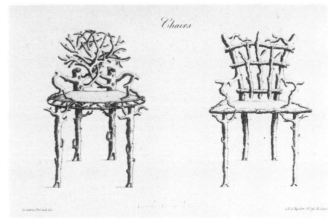

Plate 9. Stools.

Plate 10. Stools.

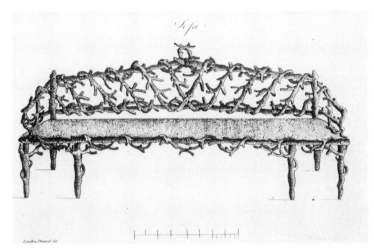

Plate 11. Sofa.

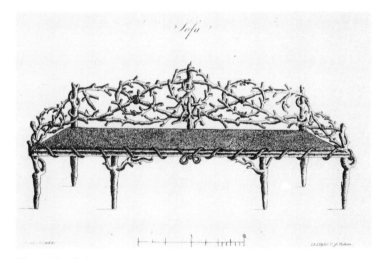

Plate 12. Sofa.

Anon 1790-97
'Ideas for Rustic Furniture.'

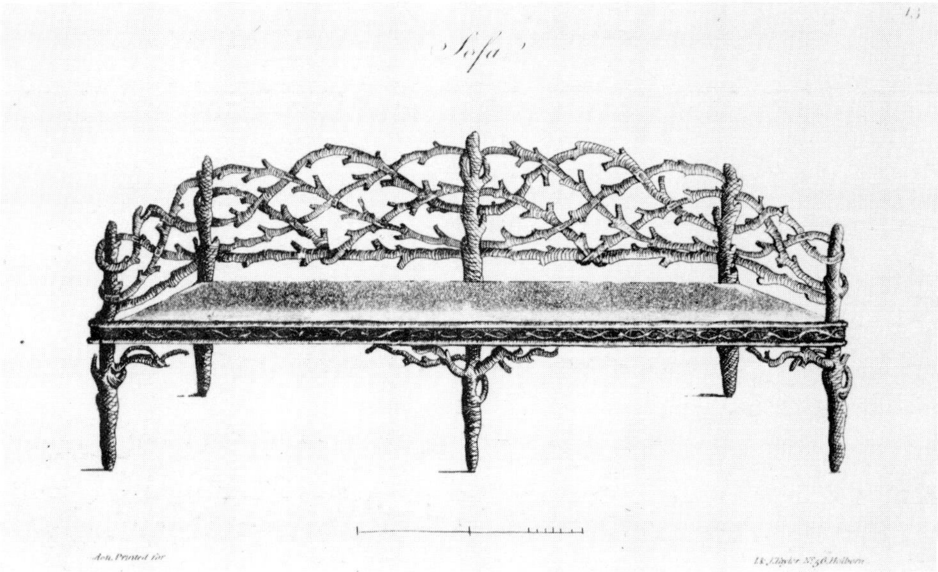

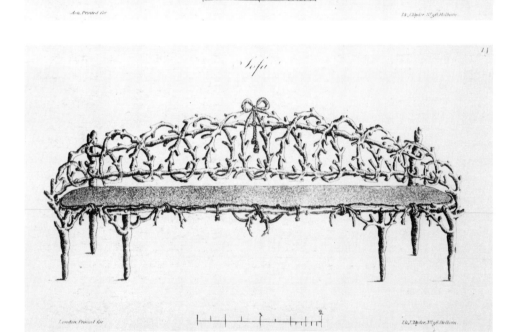

Plate 13. Sofa.

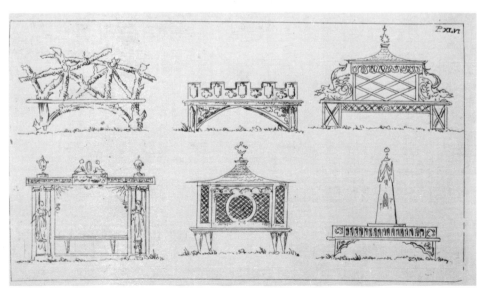

Plate 14. Sofa.

C. Middleton
'The Architect and Builder's Miscellany', 1799.
Plate XLVI. Garden Seats.

Section 7. BEDS

Beds, according to Hepplewhite, 'are an article of much importance, as well on account of the great expence attending them, as the variety of shapes, and the high degree of elegance which may be shewn in them.' (*The Cabinet-Maker and Upholsterer's Guide,* 1788.) In the first half of the century beds continued to be made after the designs of Daniel Marot, either with flying testers or (more usually in England) with four posts supporting the roof. The slightly archaic nature of these designs was disregarded in favour of their overwhelming importance as status symbols. New designs published from the middle years of the century onwards continued with highly elaborate state beds, which nearly always had gilded woodwork, while simpler styles with mahogany and satinwood or painted or japanned beech and pine frames were used for ordinary bedrooms. Four-post bedsteads seem to have been the most popular, with four or six curtains enclosing the bed completely when drawn; however the full set of curtains was rarely included in the designs, enabling the designer to show instead the carved details of the bed-posts. The curtains, upper and lower valances, insides of the roofs and counterpanes could be made of 'almost every stuff which the loom produces' (Hepplewhite, *Guide,* 1788): — silk damask and velvet on the grandest beds (crimson being the most favoured colour), Chinese embroidered silks, printed Indian calicoes or European cottons, 'the elegance and variety of patterns of which, afford as much scope for taste, elegance and simplicity, as the most lively fancy can wish' (Hepplewhite, *Guide,* 1788), woollens for winter hangings and white dimity and muslin for summer beds. Braids, fringes and tassels completed these elaborate constructions.

Smaller beds with canopies were designed for use in closets, dressing rooms and smaller bedrooms, as day or night beds: these were usually called 'French Beds' or 'Field Beds' and had sloping canopies with 'reefed' curtains; some were designed to fold up. Designs for other, more practical folding beds were also published, including a camp bed, and a 'Press bed' which folded away inside a clothes press.

Designs for sofa beds appeared in the eighteenth century pattern books: as today, the sofas could have bases which folded out to form a bed, and were surmounted by elaborate and very beautiful canopies with reefed and tied curtains. The grander versions were intended to fit into alcoves or recesses 'as are often seen in large Apartments', or 'may also be placed at the end of a Long Gallery'. (Chippendale, *Director,* 3rd Edition, 1763, Plate L.)

A. BEDS WITH FLYING TESTERS.

Daniel Marot
'Seconde Livre d'Apartements', c.1703.

Plate 33. Angel Bed.

Plate 34. Angel Bed.

Plate 35. Angel Bed.

Plates 19 and 20. Angel Beds from Marot's *Nouveaux Livre Licts,* c.1703.

Daniel Marot
'Nouveaux Livre Licts', c.1703.

Plate 21. Angel Bed.

Plate 22. Angel Bed.

Plate 23. Angel Bed.

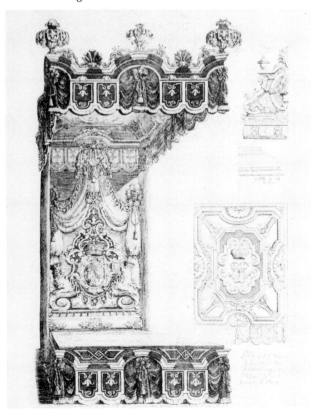

Plate 24. Angel Bed.

Daniel Marot
'Nouveaux Livre Licts', c.1703.

Plate 25. Angel Bed.

Plate 26. Angel Bed.

Plate 27. Angel Bed.

**'Daniel Marot
Nouveaux Livre de Licts de Differentes Pensseez', c.1703.**

**Daniel Marot
'Nouveaux Livre da Partements', c.1703.**

Plate 28. 'Nouveaux Ciel, de Lict Gallonée et Brodée' (Roofs of Testers).

**Daniel Marot
'Nouveaux Livre da Partements', c.1703.**

Plate 29. Headboards.

Plate 30. Counterpanes. 'Imperialle de Lict en Gallons'.

**Daniel Marot
'Nouveaux Livre de Licts de Differentes Pensseez', c.1703.**

Plate 29. Counterpanes.

B. FOUR POST BEDS.

**Daniel Marot
'Seconde Livre
Dappartements', c.1703.**

Plate 31. Bedchamber with
Four Post Bed.

Plate 32. Four Post Bed.

152

Thomas Chippendale
'The Gentleman and Cabinet-Maker's
Director', 1st Edition, 1754. 3rd Edition,
1763.

Plate XXVII. Four Post Bed. Plate XLI in
3rd Edition, 1763.

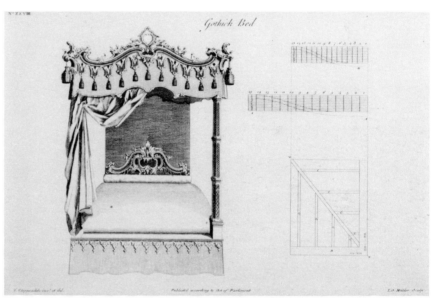

Plate XXVIII. Gothick Bed. Plate XLVIII
in 3rd Edition, 1763.

Plate XXIX. Gothick Bed. Plate XLIV in
3rd Edition, 1763.

Thomas Chippendale
'The Gentleman and Cabinet-Maker's Director', 1st Edition, 1754, 3rd Edition, 1763.

Plate XXX. Canopy Bed. Plate XLII in 3rd Edition, 1763.

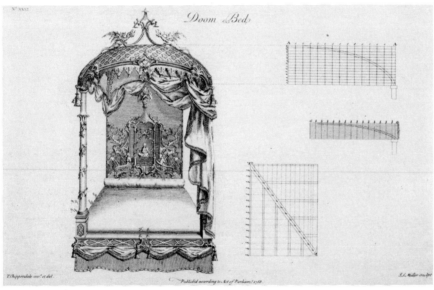

Plate XXXI. Dome Bed. 'the outside of the dome is intended to be japann'd and mosaic work drawn upon it; the other ornaments to be gilt. The headboard has a small Chinese Temple, with a Joss or Chinese God, on each side is a Chinese man at worship...'. Plate XLIII 'Dome Bed' in 3rd Edition, 1763.

Plate XXXII. Chinese Bed. Plate XLV in 3rd Edition, 1763.

Edwards & Darly
'A New Book of Chinese Designs', 1754.

Plate 10. 'Grand Bed'.

Plate 76. Bed.

Thomas Chippendale
'The Gentleman and Cabinet-Maker's Director', 3rd Edition, 1763.

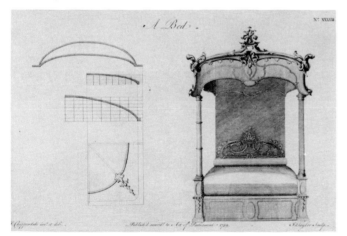

Plate XXXVIII. A Bed. Engraving dated 1759.

Plate XXXIX. Bed, 'made for the Earl of Dumfries and Morton, one of the Pillars composed of Reeds with a Palm-Branch twisting round...' Engraving dated 1759.

Thomas Chippendale
'The Gentleman and Cabinet-Maker's Director', 3rd Edition, 1763.

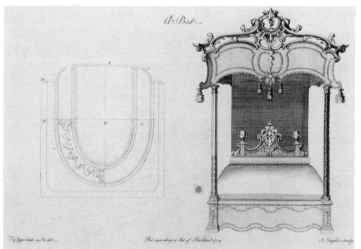

Plate XL. A Bed. Engraving dated 1759.

Plate XLIV. Cornices 'may be gilt, or covered with the same stuff as the curtains.'

Plate XLV. A Design for a Bed. Engraving dated 1760. 'There are found Magnificence, Proportion and Harmony' '6ft.-7ft. wide, 7ft.-8ft. long, 14ft.-15ft. high. All carved work to be gilded.'

Plate XLVII. A Design for a State Bed. Engraving dated 1761.

Plate XXIX. A Bed.

Plate XXXII. 'A State Bed, with a Dome Tester, which has been executed, and may be esteemed amongst the best in England: the Furniture was Blue Damask, and all the Ornaments in burnish'd gold, and richly fringed...'

Plate XXX. 'A Bed proper for an Alcove; the Ornaments may be either gilt or cover'd with Damask...'.

A Society of Upholsterers
'Houshold Furniture in Genteel Taste', 2nd Edition, c.1765.

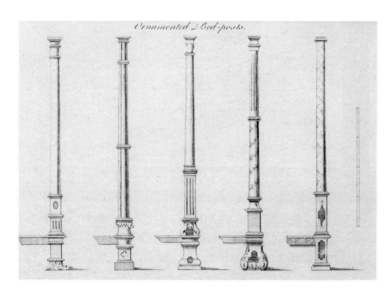

Plate 81 from Part III. Bed Posts, designer unidentified.

Plate 82 from Part III. Bed, attributed to Ince and Mayhew.

For Chippendale Bed Pillars see page 178.

Plate 102 from Part III. Ornamental Beds, designer unidentified.

Thomas Malton
'Compleat Treatise on Perspective', 1778, 2nd Edition.

Plate XXXIV, Figure 134. Bed with Canopy-Tester.

A. Hepplewhite & Co.
'The Cabinet-Maker and Upholsterer's Guide', 1788.
2nd Edition, 1789. 3rd Edition, 1794.

Plate 95.

'Beds are an article of much importance, as well on account of the great expence attending them, as the variety of shapes, and the high degree of elegance which may be shewn in them.

They may be executed of almost every stuff which the loom produces. White dimity, plain or corded, is peculiarly applicable for the furniture, which, with a fringe with a gymp head, produces an effect of elegance and neatness truly agreeable.

The Manchester stuffs have been wrought into Bed-furniture with good success. Printed cottons and linens are also very suitable; the elegance and variety of patterns of which, afford as much scope for taste, elegance, and simplicity, as the most lively fancy can wish. In general, the lining to these kinds of furniture is a plain white cotton. To furniture of a dark pattern, a green silk lining may be used with a good effect. From the designs, Plates 98, we have been informed, a bed, with little variation, has been made of dove-coloured satin curtains, with a lining of green silk.

In state-rooms, where a high degree of elegance and grandeur are wanted, beds are frequently made of silk or satin, figured or plain, also of velvet, with gold fringe, &c.

The *Vallance* to elegant beds should always be gathered full, which is called a *Petticoat Vallance*. The *Cornices* may be either of mahogany carved, carved and gilt, or painted and japanned. The *Ornaments* over the cornices may be in the same manner; carved and gilt, or japanned, will produce the most lively effect.

Arms, or other ornaments to *Stuffed Head Boards,* should be carved in small relief, gilt and burnished. The *Pillars* should be of mahogany, with the enrichments carved.'

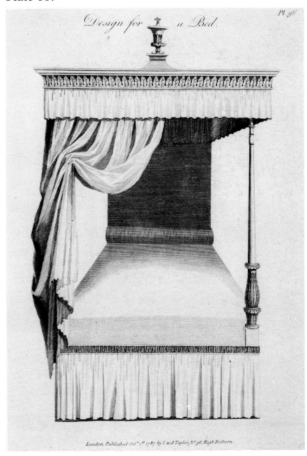

Plate 95. Design for a Bed. 'The vallance to this bed is tied up in festoons. The Cornice of mahogany, may come so low as to hide the curtain-roods.'

Plate 96. Design for a Bed. 'To this design the cornice will look well japanned. The curtain to this bed is drawn up and fastened by lines at the head, or with a loop and button.'

A. Hepplewhite & Co.
'The Cabinet-Maker and Upholsterer's Guide', 1788.
2nd Edition, 1789. 3rd Edition, 1794.

Plate 97. Design for a Bed. 'This design has a sweep top; the ornaments and cornice may be of mahogany, or gilt. To this bed is added a stuffed headboard, with ornaments and drapery over it. The drapery may be the same as the furniture or the lining; the ornaments gilt; the headboard is stuffed, and projects like as the back of a sofa. The addition of stuffed headboards gives an elegant and high finish to the appearance of beds. The curtains here are drawn up in double drapery, and fastened by lines at the head.'

Plate 98. Design for a Bed. 'This design has a Venetian or waggon top; the ornaments on which, with the cornice, may be japanned; the pending ornaments under the cornice are intended to act and serve as a Vallance: may be either gilt or japanned. The bases are enriched with festooned drapery.'

160

A. Hepplewhite & Co.
'The Cabinet-Maker and Upholsterer's Guide', 1788. 2nd Edition, 1789. 3rd Edition, 1794.

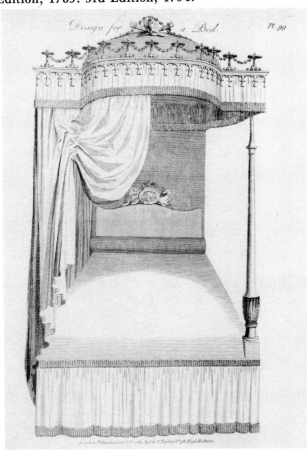

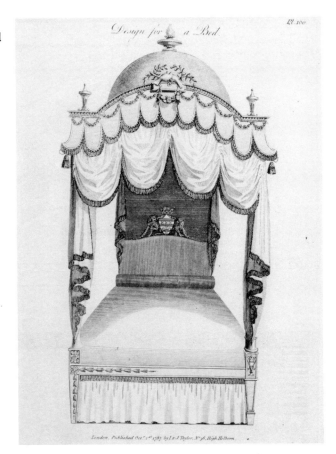

Plate 99. Design for a Bed. 'Design for a Bed, with a low dome-top, and projecting front. The cornice and ornaments to this design should be gilt. The arms to the head-board, if cut in low relief by a skilful workman, and gilt, will have a lively effect.'

Plate 100.

Plate 100. Design for a Bed. 'To this design a dome-top is given; the inner part of which may be in the same form; the cornice and enrichments of gold burnished in parts. The curtains to this bed are festooned by lines which draw at the head. The design is proper for satin or velvet furniture.'

Plate 101. Design for a Bed. 'Design for a bed with a square dome-top. The inner part in the same manner. The cornice will look well japanned or gilt. The vallance to this bed is enriched with festooned drapery. In this design the effect of a stuffed headboard and drapery are completely shewn.'

A. Hepplewhite & Co.
'The Cabinet-Maker and Upholsterer's Guide', 1788. 2nd Edition, 1789. 3rd Edition, 1794.

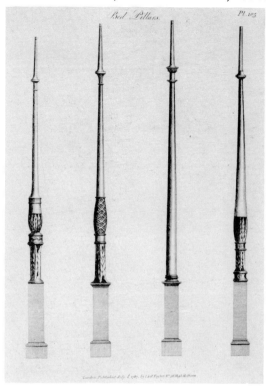

Plate 105. Bed Pillars.

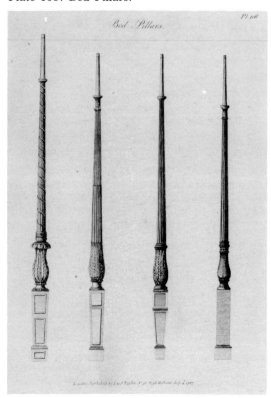

Plate 106. Bed Pillars. 'The feet to three designs, on Plate 106 are called Term feet, and are intended to be shewn when the bed is complete, as in Plate 100 etc.'

Thomas Sheraton
'The Cabinet-Maker and Upholsterer's Drawing Book', 1793.

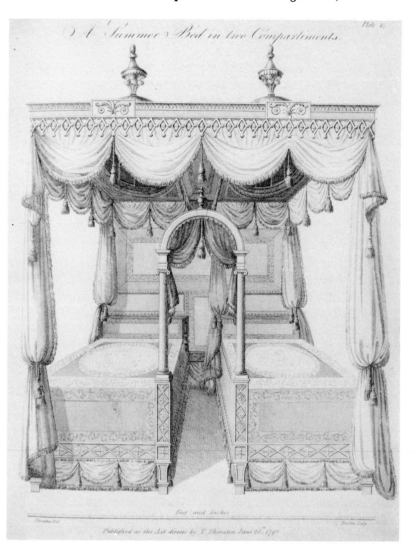

Plate XLI from Part III. Summer Bed in two Compartments. 'The beds are intended for a nobleman or gentleman and his lady to sleep in separately in hot weather... the passage up the middle, which is about twenty-two inches in width, gives room for the circulation of air, and likewise affords an easy access to the servants when they make the beds. Secondly, the passage gives opportunity for curtains to enclose each compartment, if necessary, on account of any sudden change of weather. Thirdly, it makes the whole considerably more ornamental, uniform, and light. The first idea of this bed was communicated to me by Mr. Thompson, groom of the household furniture to the Duke of York, which, I presume, is now improved, as it appears in this design.'

Plate XLV, Part III. French State Bed. 'Beds of this kind have been introduced of late with great success in England... The head-boards of these beds are framed and stuffed, and covered to suit the hangings, and the frame is white and gold, if the pillars and cornice are. The bed-frame is sometimes ornamented, and has drapery valances below... Square bolsters are now often introduced, with margins of various colours stitched all round. The counterpane has also these margins: they are also fringed at bottom, and have sometimes a drapery tied up in cords and tassels on the side.'

Plate I. Appendix. Elliptic Bed. 'As fancifulness seems most peculiar to the taste of females, I have therefore assigned the use of this bed for a single lady, though it will equally accommodate a single gentleman.

...The circular part of the top is intended to be panelled out in gilt mouldings, which cannot fail of producing a fine effect, particularly so if the furniture and covering of the dome be light blue...'.

Plate I. Appendix. Elliptic Bed.

Plate IX. Appendix. Design for a Bed. '...The Pillars are to be japanned...'

163

Thomas Sheraton
'The Cabinet-Maker and Upholsterer's Drawing Book',
1793.

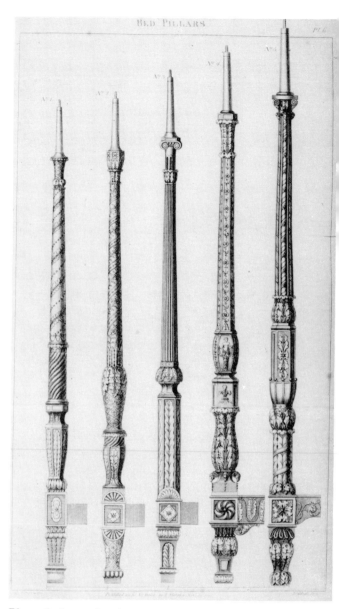

Plate 19 from the Appendix. Design for an English State Bed. 'For ornament to a bed of this kind, it struck me that nothing could be more suitable and characteristic than such as expressed symbolically the different parts of our government, together with those virtues and principles which ought to be the support of regal authority, and the ruling maxims of every good government of whatever kind, whether monarchical, aristocratical, or democratical. Emblems of war have been avoided as much as possible, being inconsistent ornaments for a bed, and because good kings ought not to delight in war, but in peace, unity, and the love of men and their subjects.'

'. . . Upon the whole, though a bed of this kind is not likely to be executed according to this design, except under the munificence of a royal order, yet I am not without hopes that useful ideas may be gathered from it, and applied to beds of a more general kind.'.

Plate 6 from the Accompaniment to the *Drawing Book*. Designs for Bed Pillars. 'No.1 and 2 are to be painted, No.3 carved in mahogany, and No.4 and 5 are intended for rich state beds, carved in white and gold.'

C. FRENCH BED AND FIELD BEDS.
Thomas Chippendale
'The Gentleman and Cabinet-Maker's Director', 3rd Edition, 1763.

Plate XLIX. Designs for Field Beds. Engraving dated 1762.

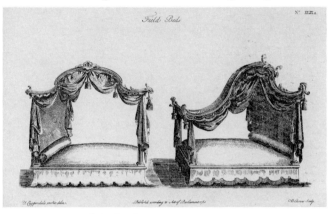

Plate XLIXa. Field Beds.

William Ince and John Mayhew
'The Universal System of Houshold Furniture', 1762.

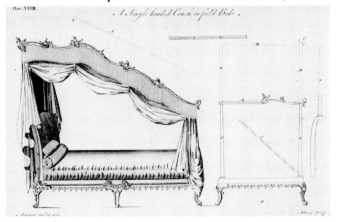

Plate XXVIII. 'A Couch or Bed occasionally: the Tester being to take off, and conceal'd in the Recess under the Seat.'

William Ince and John Mayhew
'The Universal System of Houshold Furniture', 1762.

Plate XXXI. 'A French Bed, with Fronts each way...'.

A Society of Upholsterers
'Genteel Houshold Furniture in the Present Taste', 2nd Edition, c.1765.

Plate 83 from Part III. Design for a Field Bed. Attributed to Ince and Mayhew.

A. Hepplewhite & Co.
'The Cabinet-Maker and Upholsterer's Guide',
1788. 2nd Edition, 1789. 3rd Edition, 1794.

Plates 102 and 103. Field Beds. 'two designs are here given, which shew the manner of hanging the furniture and placing the ornaments.'

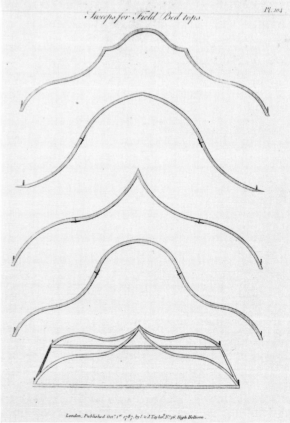

Plate 104. Sweeps for Field Bed Tops.

166

D. PRESS BEDSTEADS.

A. Hepplewhite & Co.
'The Cabinet-Maker and Upholsterer's Guide',
1st Edition, 1788. 2nd Edition, 1789. 3rd Edition,
1794.

Plate 85. The Wardrobe 'has all the appearance of a Press-bed; in which case the upper drawers would be only sham, and form part of the door which may be made to turn up all in one piece, and form a tester; or may open in the middle, and swing on each side; the under-drawer is useful to hold parts of the bed-furniture; may be 5 feet 6 inches high, and 4 feet wide.'

From the Introduction to the 3rd Edition. 'Of these we have purposely omitted to give any designs: their general appearance varying so little from wardrobes, which piece of furniture they are intended to represent, that designs for them were not necessary.'

E. SOFA BEDS AND CANOPIES. (See also Settees and Sofas.)

Thomas Chippendale
'The Gentleman and Cabinet-Maker's Director',
1754, 3rd Edition, 1763.

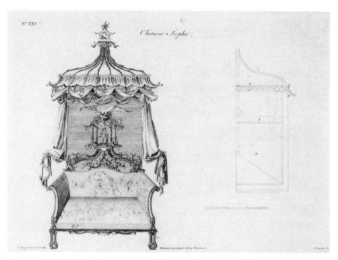

Plate XXV. Design for a Chinese Sopha. 'This design may be converted into a Bed... and look very grand.' The ornaments to be burnished gold. Plate XXXIII in 3rd Edition, 1763.

Plate XXVI. Design for a Chinese Sopha. Not in 3rd Edition, 1763.

Edwards & Darly
'A New Book of Chinese Designs', 1754.

Plate 85. Design for a Canopy.

Plate 88. Design for a Canopy.

168

**Thomas Chippendale
'The Gentleman and Cabinet-
Maker's Director', 3rd Edition,
1763.**

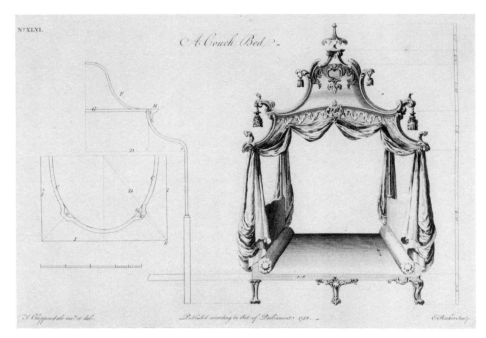

Plate XLVI. Couch Bed, with a
Canopy. 'This couch was made for
an Alcove in Lord Pembroke's House
at Whitehall.' Engraving dated 1759.

Plate L. Couch Bed 'very fit for Alcoves, or such deep
recesses as are often seen in large Apartments. It may also
be placed at the end of a long Gallery.' The crane is 'the
Emblem of Care and Watchfulness which, I think, is not
unbecoming in a place of rest.' Engraving dated 1760.

William Ince and John Mayhew
'The Universal System of Houshold Furniture', 1762.

Thomas Sheraton
'The Cabinet-Maker and Upholsterer's Drawing Book', 1793.

Plate XXVII. Design for a Sofa Bed.

Plate XXXI. Sofa Bed from Part III of the *Drawing Book*. 'The frames of these beds are sometimes painted in ornaments to suit the furniture. But when the furniture is of rich silk, they are done in white and gold, and the ornaments carved... The drapery under the cornice is of the French kind; it is fringed all round, and laps onto each other like unto waves. The valance serves as a ground, and is also fringed. The roses which tuck up the curtains are formed by silk cord etc, on the wall, to suit the hangings... the curtains will come forward and entirely enclose the bed.

The sofa part is sometimes made without any back, in the manner of a couch. It must also be observed, that the best kinds of these beds have behind them what the upholsterers call a fluting, which is done by a slight frame of wood fastened to the wall, on which is strained, in straight puckers, some of the same stuff of which the curtains are made.'

Plate XL. Alcove Bed from Part III of the *Drawing Book*. '..The learned inform us, that the word alcove is from the Arabic *elcauf*, which means a cabinet or sleeping-place. This design is represented standing on a plinth, covered with carpet, and having a border round it supposed to be on the floor of the room. The steps are introduced to shew that beds of this sort are raised high, and require something to step on before they can be got into. The steps are generally covered with carpet and framed in mahogany...'

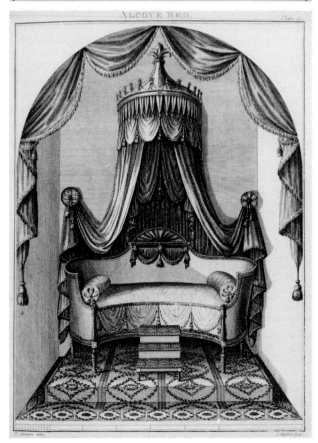

170

Section 8. CURTAINS and CORNICES

During the eighteenth century the standard type of window curtain used was the single festoon curtain fixed above the window below a wooden or fabric cornice and let up and down on lines. An alternative type was drawn diagonally up to one side or both sides, rather like a theatre curtain. Both types left the window surrounds revealed, thus complementing the architraves around the doors and chimney-pieces. The relatively simple styles for festoons published by Marot at the beginning of the century continued in use for many years, until new designs appeared in the 1750s and 1760s for more elaborate carved wooden cornices in the Rococo style. These were made either of beech or pine and gilded, or of mahogany and polished, and were equally usable for the cornices of four-post bedsteads. In the 1770s and 1780s designs for wooden cornices in the neo-classical style were published, intended to be gilded, japanned or painted: according to Hepplewhite, 'a mixture of these two manners produces an elegant and grand effect' (*Guide,* 1788). The curtains themselves were made of light materials such as silk taffeta, lutestring or cotton chintz, although some heavier velvet ones are known. Roller blinds, fitted close to the window, gave protection from excessive sunlight.

The use of drapery at the sides of windows was revived in France in the 1770s, and gradually made an appearance in fashionable English houses during the 1780s. A new feature was the use of 'French rods' which allowed a pair of curtains to draw together and overlap, a system which Sheraton described carefully in 1793 as they were still fairly unfamiliar to most English clients (*Drawing Book* Plate LI). By 1803 he was able to announce that festoon curtains 'are still in use in bedrooms, notwithstanding the general introduction of French-rod curtains in most genteel houses.' (*Cabinet Dictionary.*)

Daniel Marot
'Seconde Livre Da Partements', 1703.
Plate 36. Various designs for festoon curtains.

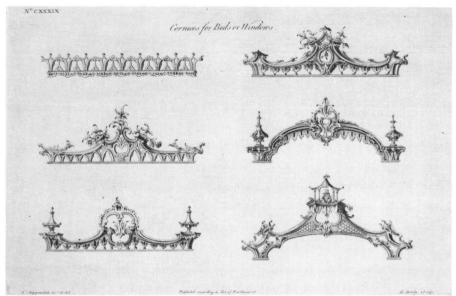

**Thomas Chippendale
'The Gentleman and Cabinet-
Maker's Director', 3rd Edition,
1763.**

Plate CXXXIX. Designs for Cornices
for Beds or Windows. 1st Edition, 1754.
Not in 3rd Edition, 1763.

Plate XXXVI. A design for a Cornice
for a Venetian Window. Engraving
dated 1762.

Plate XXXVII. Designs for Cornices
for Beds or Windows. Engraving dated
1759.

Thomas Chippendale
'The Gentleman and Cabinet-
Maker's Director', 3rd Edition, 1763.

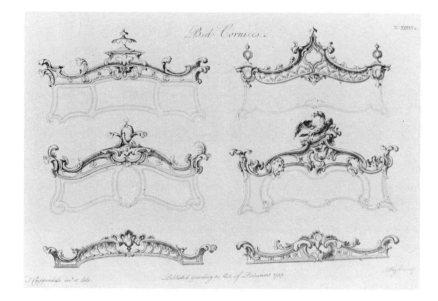

Plate XXXVIa. Bed Cornices. Engraving
dated 1759.

A Society of Upholsterers
'Genteel Houshold Furniture in the Present
Taste', 2nd Edition, c.1765.

Plate 80.

P. Baretti
'A New Book of Ornaments', 1762.

Plate 6. Designs for two Cornices. *Courtesy*
British Museum.

173

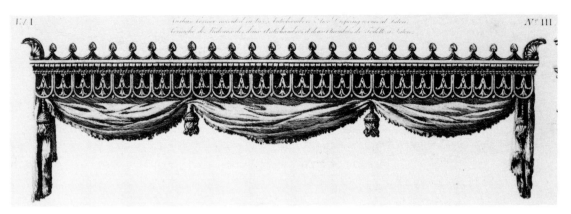

Plate VIII from Vol.I, No.III. Cornices for the Withdrawing Room at Luton Park House.

Plate VIII from Vol.I, No.III. Cornices for the two Antechambers and two Dressing Rooms at Luton Park House.

Plate VIII from Vol.I, No.III. Cornices for the Saloon at Luton Park House.

R. & J. Adam
'Works in Architecture', 1777.

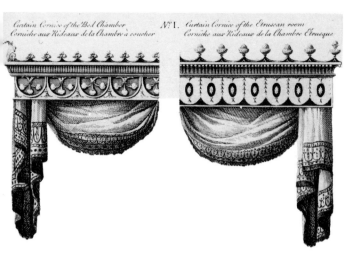

Plate VIII, Vol. II, No.I. Designs for the Earl of Derby's House, Grosvenor Square. Cornices for the Bed Chamber and the Etruscan Dressing Room.

M.A. Pergolesi
'Designs for Various Ornaments', 1784.

R. & J. Adam
'Works in Architecture', 1778.

Plate VIII, Vol.II, No.IV. Designs for various pieces of furniture 'which were invented for particular persons, but are since brought into general use.' Design for a Curtain Cornice over a window.

R. & J. Adam
'Works in Architecture', 1822.

Plate IX, Vol.III. Furniture at Syon House. Curtain cornice.

A. Hepplewhite & Co.
'The Cabinet-Maker and Upholsterer's Guide', 1788.
Plates 107-109. Cornices for Beds or Windows. Also in 3rd Edition, 1794. 'These may be executed in wood painted and japanned, or in gold. A mixture of these two manners produces an elegant and grand effect. The foliage may be gilt, and the groundwork painted; or the reverse, the designs marked C F G are intended to be all gilt — with parts matted and burnished.'

**A. Hepplewhite & Co.
'The Cabinet-Maker
and Upholsterer's Guide',
1788.**

Plate 108.   Plate 109.

**Thomas Sheraton
'The Cabinet-Maker and Upholsterer's Drawing Book',
1793.**

Plate 12. From the Accompaniment to the *Drawing Book*.
Cornices for windows. 'The one across the plate is intended
for japanning, the upper one for carving and gilding, and
the two under ones may be either carved or japanned.'

Plate LI. Drapery Design from Part III of the *Drawing Book*.
'. . . the French strapping and tassels in the right-hand
design is no part of the cornice, as some cabinet-makers have
already mistaken it to be. It is the upholsterers work, and is
sewed on within the valance or ground of the drapery. These
curtains are drawn on French rods. When the cords are
drawn the curtains meet in the center at the same time, but
are no way raised from the floor. . .'

Thomas Sheraton
'The Cabinet-Maker and Upholsterer's Drawing Book',
1793.

Plate 31. From the Accompaniment to the *Drawing Book*. A view of the South End of the Prince of Wales' Chinese Drawing Room.

Plate 32. From the Accompaniment to the *Drawing Book*.

For Sheraton's Turkey sofa see page 118.

Dulouchamp
'Successor to the late Signor Pergolesi', 1801.

Plate 64 (variant).

Thomas Chippendale
'The Gentleman and Cabinet-Maker's Director', 3rd Edition, 1763.

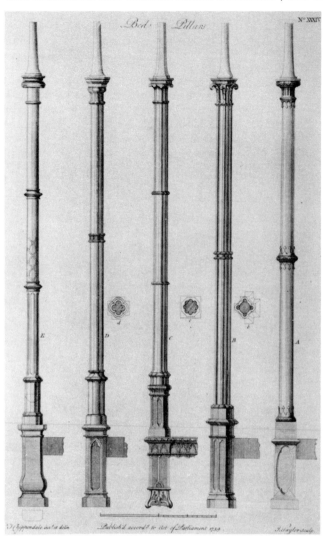

Plate XXXIV. Bed Pillars. Engraving dated 1759.

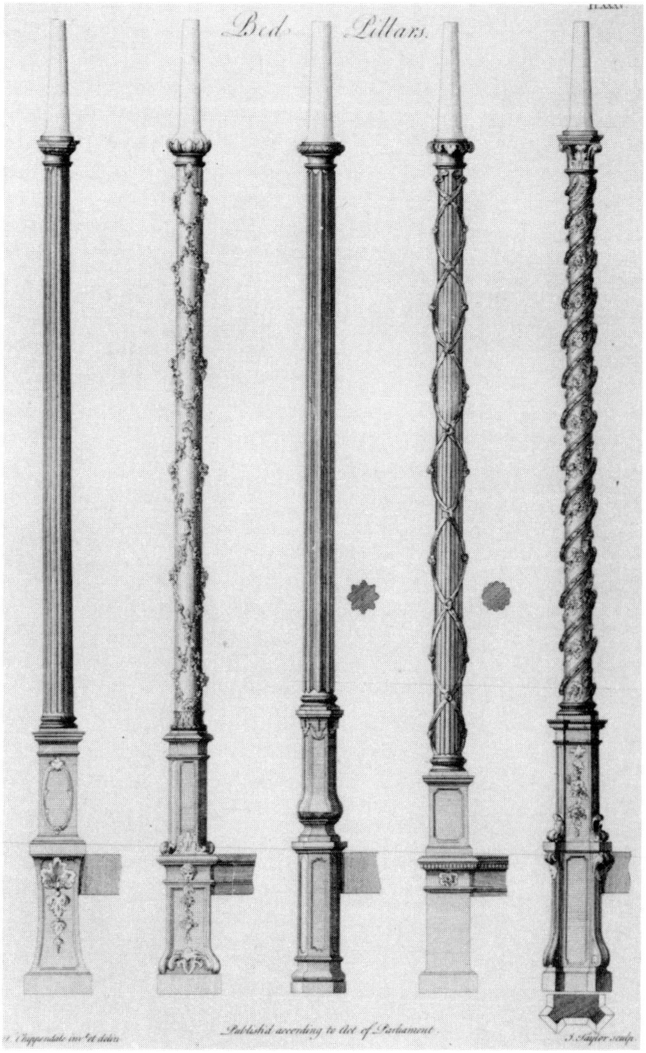

Plate XXXV. Bed Pillars.

Bed Pillars. 'They are all designed with pedestals which must certainly look better than Bases of Stuff round the Bed, and the Pillars to be unsupported.' Height depends on height of room.

See Section 7, page 158, for context.

Part II. Cabinet Work
Section 1. COMMODES and CHESTS OF DRAWERS (Low)

During the eighteenth century the term 'commode' was used in England in its correct French form to define a low chest of drawers, and not a night table as in the nineteenth century. Chippendale referred to them as 'Commode Tables' and 'French Commode Tables'. Eighteenth century designs for commodes either had drawers showing at the front or had doors which enclosed drawers or shelves. The finest ones made in the Rococo style in the middle years of the century demonstrated some of the best cabinet work made in England, combining fine carving, beautiful serpentine shapes, lacquer or japanned work, delicate marquetry and magnificent metal mounts. The grandest versions were intended for drawing rooms, where they were

placed on the pier between windows, beneath a mirror, as an alternative to a table: in such a situation they were almost entirely reserved for show rather than use. Otherwise they were for use in bedrooms and dressing rooms, along with plainer chests of drawers made of mahogany or satinwood. Some of the latter were fitted with 'dressing slides': — either a flat board which pulled out just underneath the top of the chest, on which brushes, powder boxes and other necessities could be placed, or a top drawer containing a series of boxes and compartments for such equipment. Sheraton, in the *Drawing Book*, added a writing table flap to the dressing drawer for additional use.

(See also Dressing Tables.)

Thomas Chippendale
'The Gentleman and Cabinet-Maker's Director', 1st Edition, 1754. 3rd Edition, 1763.

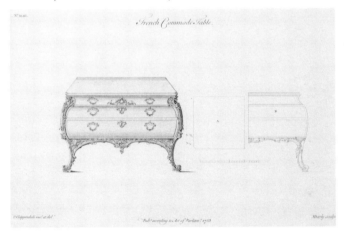

Plate XLIII. French Commode Table. Plate LXIV, 3rd Edition, 1763.

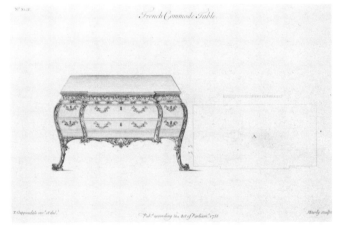

Plate XLIV. French Commode Table. Plate LXV, 3rd Edition, 1763.

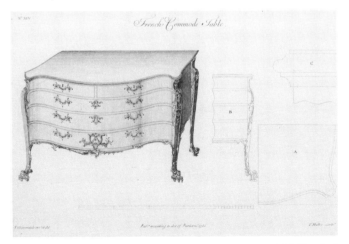

Plate XLV. French Commode Table. Plate LXVI, 3rd Edition, 1763.

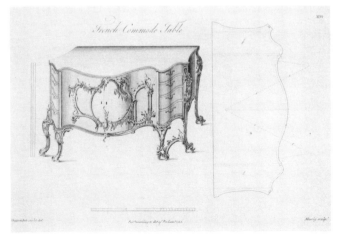

Plate XLVI. French Commode Table. Not in 3rd Edition, 1763.

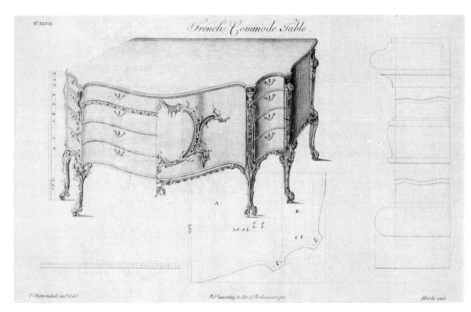

**Thomas Chippendale
'The Gentleman and Cabinet-Maker's Director', 1st Edition, 1754. 3rd Edition, 1763.**

Plate XLVII. French Commode Table. Plate LXVIIIa in 3rd Edition, 1763.

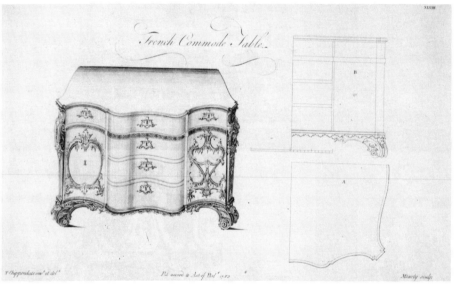

XLVIII. French Commode Table. Plate LXIX in 3rd Edition.

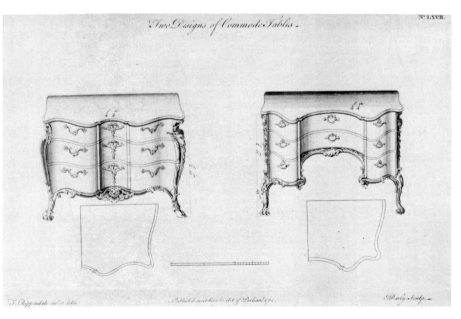

Plate LXVII. 3rd Edition. Two Designs of Commode Tables. Engraving dated 1762.

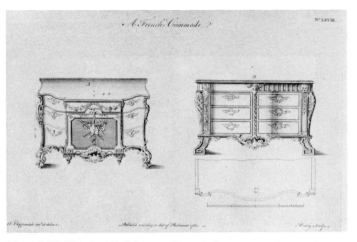

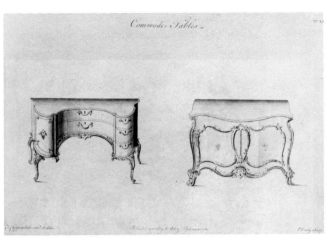

Plate LXVIII. 3rd Edition. A French Commode. Engraving dated 1762.

Plate LXX. 3rd Edition. Commode Tables. Engraving dated 1760.

Plate LXVIIa. 3rd Edition. Commode Tables. Engraving dated 1760.

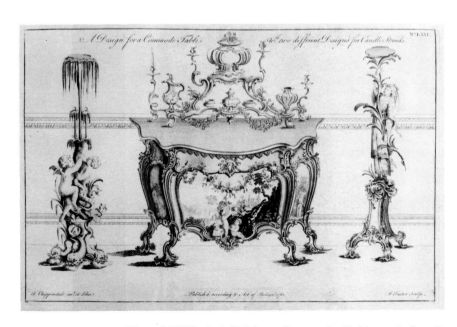

Plate LXXI. 3rd Edition. Commode Table and Candle Stands. 'The Bass Relief in the middle may be carved in wood, or cast in Brass, or painted on wood or copper.'

181

A Society of Upholsterers
'Genteel Houshold Furniture in the Present Taste',
2nd Edition, c.1765.

R. & J. Adam
'Works in Architecture', 1777.

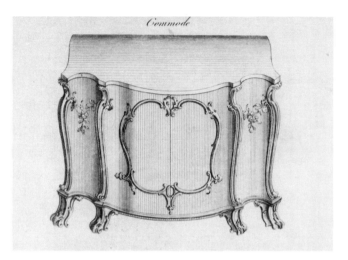

Plate 100 from Part III. Commode. Designer unidentified.

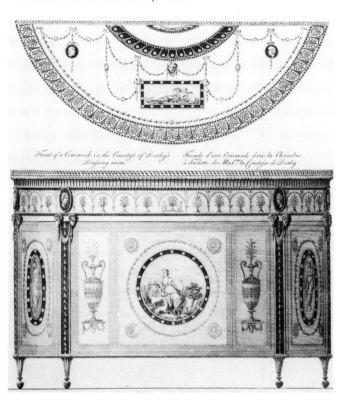

Plate VIII from Vol. II, No. I. Top and Front of a Commode for the Countess of Derby's Dressing Room (Derby House, Grosvenor Square.) (Original drawing (1774) shows a colour scheme of terracotta and black on a pale blue ground, with gilt metal mounts.)

William Ince and John Mayhew
'The Universal System of Houshold Furniture',
1762.

J. Carter
'The Builder's Magazine', 1778.

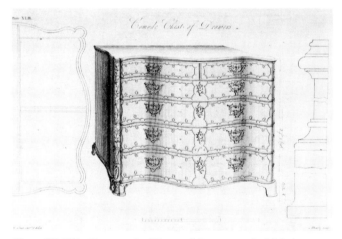

Plate XLIII. Commode Chest of Drawers, 'which has been executed from the Plate, and much admired.'

Plate CLXI. Design for a Commode for a 'Ladies Dressing Room'.

A. Hepplewhite
'The Cabinet-Maker and Upholsterer's Guide', 1st Edition, 1788. 2nd Edition, 1789. 3rd Edition, 1794.

Plate 52. Chests of Drawers. 'Two designs are here shown for this article, which admits of little variation or ornament; general dimensions 3 feet 6 inches long, by 20 inches deep.'

Plate 74. 'Dressing Drawers'. 'The top drawer in which contains the necessary dressing equipage; the others are applicable to common uses.'

Plate 74.

Plate 75. 'Dressing Drawers'.

A. Hepplewhite & Co.
'The Cabinet-Maker and Upholsterer's Guide', 1st Edition, 1788. 2nd Edition, 1789. 3rd Edition, 1794.

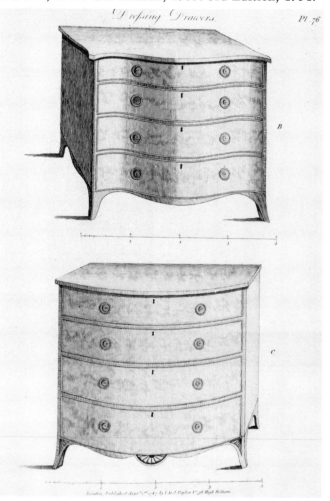

Plate 76. 'Dressing Drawers'.

Plate 77. Commode Dressing Table. 'a design for one with a serpentine front; the drawers to which are elegantly ornamented with inlaid or painted work, which is applied with great beauty and elegance to this piece of furniture. Some made of satinwood with the ornaments of suitable colours, have produced a most pleasing and agreeable effect.'

Plate 78. Commode. 'enriched with painted or inlaid work. This piece of furniture is adapted for a drawing-room; within are shelves which answer the use of a closet or cupboard... may have one principal door in the front, or one at each end; are made of various shapes; and being used in principal rooms, require considerable elegance, The pannels may be of satin wood, plain, or inlaid: the top and also the border round the front, should be inlaid.'

184

A. Hepplewhite
'The Cabinet-Maker and Upholsterer's Guide', 1st Edition, 1788. 2nd Edition, 1789. 3rd Edition, 1794.

'The Cabinet-Maker's London Book of Prices', 1st Edition, 1788.
2nd Edition 1793. 3rd Edition 1803.

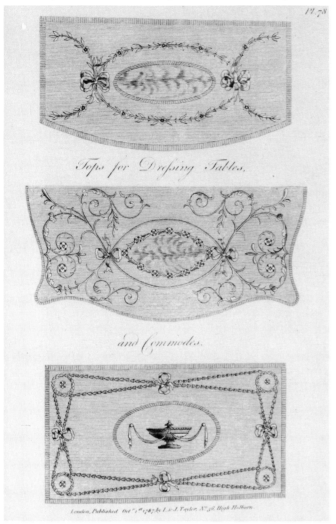

Plate 78. Tops for Dressing Tables and Commodes (see Plates 76 and 77). 'inriched with inlaid or painted work.'

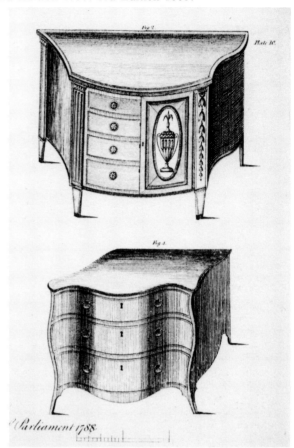

Plate 10, Figure 4. French Commode Dressing Chest. 3ft. long. French feet. Basic cost £3.10.0.

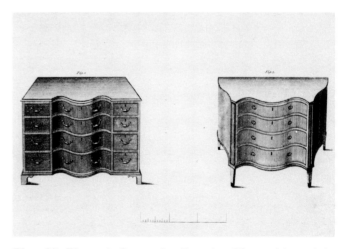

Plate 20, Figure 1. Serpentine Dressing Chest with straight wings. 4ft. long 'common bracket' feet. Basic cost £3.11.0. Figure 2. Serpentine Dressing Chest, with ogee ends. 3ft. long at front, 5ft. at back, 'taper stump' feet. Basic cost £4.10.0. Designed by Shearer.

185

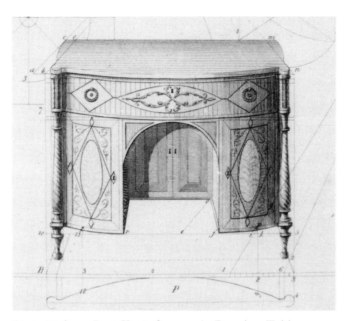

Plate 25 from Part II. A Commode Dressing Table.

Plate 66 from 2nd Edition, 1794. Commode with white marble top 'ornaments painted on satinwood or other ground. The internal part is merely plain shelves, as these pieces are never intended for use but for ornament.'

Plate XV from The Appendix to the *Drawing Book*. Dressing Chest of Drawers. 'These chests are also in a new plan, particularly as the common slider for merely writing on is turned into a shallow drawer, which contains a little writing flap which rises behind by a horse, and places for ink, sand and pens, and also dressing boxes... The height of these chests are always governed by the slider, which runs thirty-two or thirty-three inches from the floor... and their breadth is twenty-two or twenty-three inches.'

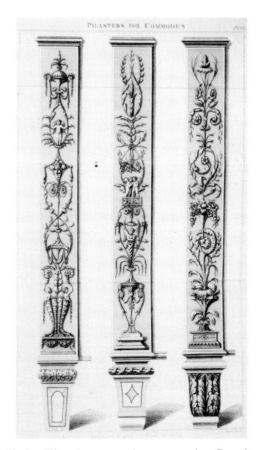

Plate 13 in The Accompaniment to the *Drawing Book*. Pilasters for Commodes. 'These may be painted, inlaid, or gilt in gold behind glass, and the glass being then beded in the pilaster, it is secure, and has a good effect.'

Section 2. CLOTHES and LINEN CHESTS

Eighteenth century designers produced a variety of patterns for low chests intended to contain clothes and linen which were usually stored flat; fewer items of clothing hung in cupboards than today, and designs for freestanding wardrobes only appeared in the later eighteenth century

Thomas Chippendale
'The Gentleman and Cabinet-Maker's Director', 1st Edition, 1754. 3rd Edition, 1763.

books (see section below). Low 'Clothes Presses' had doors which opened to reveal sliding shelves, whereas 'Clothes Chests' and 'Linen Chests' had rising lids like blanket chests. Some were raised on short legs. They were made in almost every way: of oak veneered with walnut, of mahogany or satinwood, or were japanned or painted. They usually stood on landings outside bedchambers for everyday use.

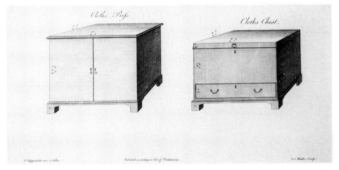

Plate XCVI. Clothes Press and Low Clothes Chest. Not in 3rd Edition, 1763.

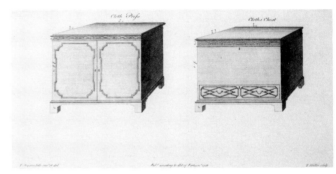

Plate XCVII. Clothes Press and Low Clothes Chest. Plate CXXVI in 3rd Edition, 1763.

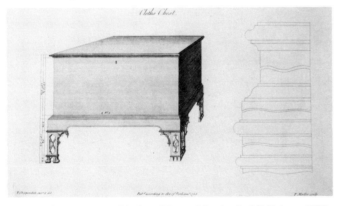

Plate XCVIII. Low Clothes Chest. Not in 3rd Edition, 1763.

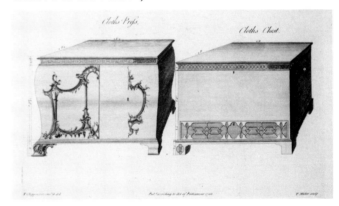

Plate XCIX. Clothes Press and Low Clothes Chest. Not in 3rd Edition, 1763.

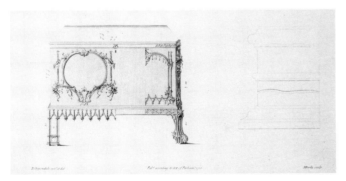

Plate C. Gothic Clothes Chest. Plate CXXVII in 3rd Edition, 1763.

Plate CI. Two Designs of Clothes Chest. Plate CXXVIII in 3rd Edition, 1763.

A Society of Upholsterers
'Genteel Houshold Furniture in the Present Taste',
c.1765.

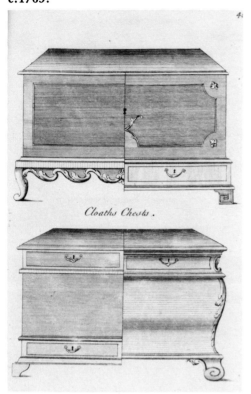

Plate 45 of Part II. Clothes Chests. Attributed to Chippendale.

Plate 46 of Part II. Linen Chests. Attributed to Chippendale.

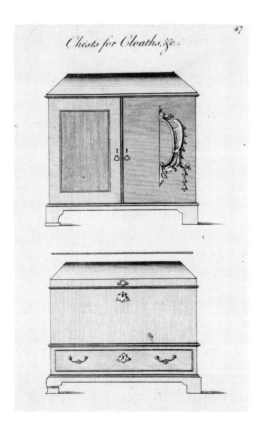

William Ince and John Mayhew
'The Universal System of Houshold Furniture', 1762.

Plate 47 of Part II. Clothes Chests. Attributed to Chippendale.

Plate XLIV. Clothes Chests.

Section 3. TEA CHESTS and TEA CADDIES

These small boxes containing tea were usually referred to in the eighteenth century as Tea Chests rather than Tea caddies, although if made entirely of metal the name 'Tea Canister' might be used. They were made of various woods — mahogany, rosewood, satinwood, or japanned or decorated with veneers of tortoiseshell, mother-of-pearl, straw-work, shell-work and Tunbridge Ware, and had pretty metal mounts. Their interiors were usually divided into two compartments for black and green tea which could be mixed to taste at the table. Most had locks, reflecting the high prices paid for tea in the early years of the century.

Thomas Chippendale
'The Gentleman and Cabinet-Maker's Director', 1st Edition, 1754. 3rd Edition, 1763.

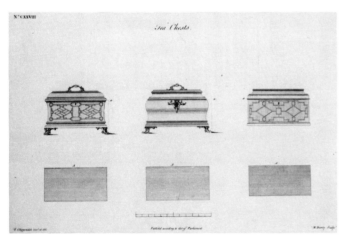

Plate CXXVIII. Tea Chests. Not in 3rd Edition, 1763.

Plate CLIX. Tea Chests. 3rd Edition, 1763. Engraving dated 1762.

Plates 57 and 58. Tea Chests and Caddies. 'The ornaments may be inlaid with various coloured woods or painted or varnished.'

Plate CXXIX. Tea Chests. Plate CLIXa in 3rd Edition, 1763.

A. Hepplewhite & Co.
'The Cabinet-Maker and Upholsterer's Guide', 1788. 2nd Edition, 1789. 3rd Edition, 1794.

Plate 57.

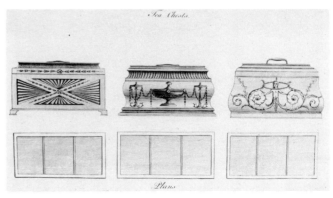

189

Section 4. TALL CHESTS OF DRAWERS and CLOTHES PRESSES

A wide range of tall pieces of furniture was available during the eighteenth century for the storage of clothes and household items in bedchambers and dressing rooms. Some were simple 'double chests' of drawers which were usually made in two sections and are referred to today as 'Tallboys'. Others consisted of a chest of drawers above a lower section with one or two drawers raised on legs, which are often described in America as 'Highboys'. There were also 'Clothes Presses' in two sections, with drawers in the lower part and doors enclosing sliding shelves above; these are described as 'Wardrobes' by Hepplewhite although they do not have hanging space. A 'Wardrobe' in Sheraton's *Drawing Book,* however, had wings with 'arms, to hang clothes on, made of beech, with a swivel in their centre, which slips on to an iron rod...' — clothes hangers. These pieces of cabinet work were made of all the usual woods available in the eighteenth century — walnut, mahogany, oak, painted and japanned beech and pine, and satinwood. Some were made *en suite* with other bedroom furniture.

Batty Langley
'City and Country Builder's and Workman's Treasury of Designs', 1740.

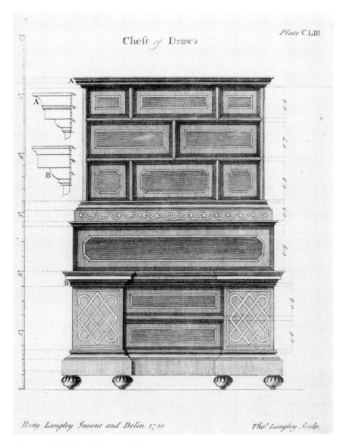

Plate CLIII. Chest of Drawers.

Plate CLIV. Medal Case.

**Thomas Chippendale
'The Gentleman and Cabinet-Maker's
Director', 1st Edition, 1754. 3rd Edition,
1763.**

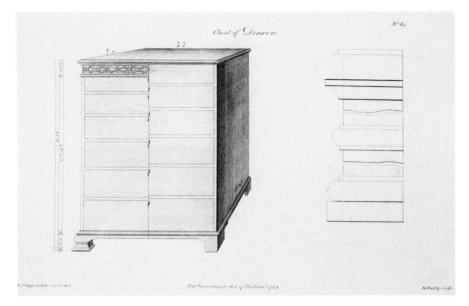

Plate 85. Chest of Drawers. Not in 3rd
Edition.

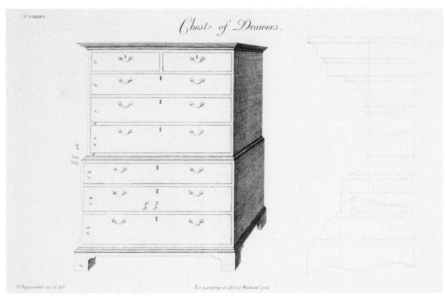

Plate LXXXVI. Chest of Drawers. Not
in 3rd Edition, 1763.

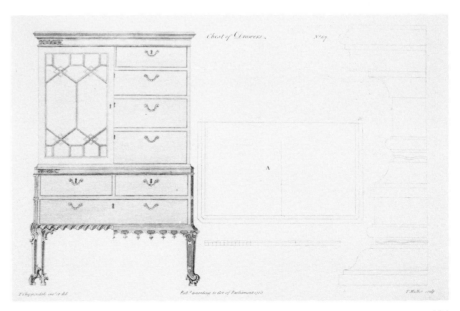

Plate 87. Chest of Drawers. Not in 3rd
Edition, 1763.

**Thomas Chippendale
'The Gentleman and Cabinet-Maker's
Director', 1st Edition, 1754. 3rd
Edition, 1763.**

Plate LXXXVIII. Chest of Drawers.
Plate CXIII in 3rd Edition, 1763.

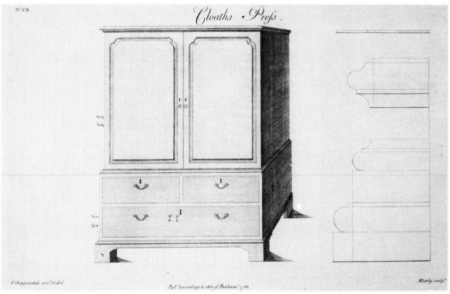

Plate CII. Clothes Press. Plate CXXIX
in 3rd Edition, 1763.

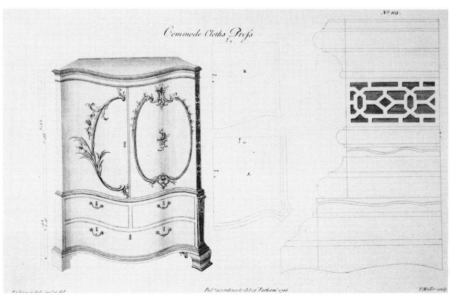

Plate 103. Commode Clothes Press.
Plate CXXX in 3rd Edition, 1763.

Thomas Chippendale
'The Gentleman and Cabinet-
Maker's Director', 1st Edition,
1754. 3rd Edition, 1763.

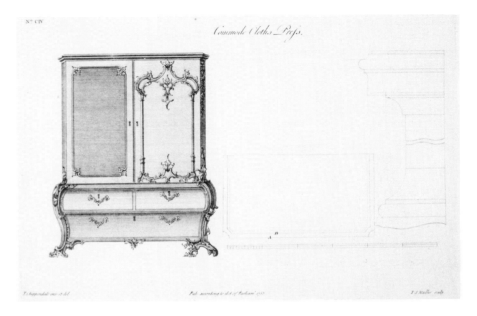

Plate CIV. Commode Clothes Press.
Plate CXXXI in 3rd Edition, 1763.

A Society of Upholsterers
'Genteel Houshold Furniture in the Present Taste', 2nd
Edition, 1765.

Plate 44 from Part II. Commode Clothes Press: designer unidentified.

Plate 50 from Part II. Chest of Drawers: designer unidentified.

Plates 53 and 54. Double Chests of Drawers. 'Two designs for these are here shewn; to the latter one is given fluted pilasters at the angles; these may have the same depth as the former ones, and height 5 feet 6 inches'.

Plate 54.

Plates 85 to 88. Wardrobes. 'An article of considerable consequence... they are usually made plain, but of the best

mahogany... The dimensions may be 4 feet long, 22 inches deep, 5 feet 6 inches high or more.'

Plate 87. Wardrobe.

Plate 88. Wardrobe.

'The Cabinet-Maker's London Book of Prices', 1st Edition, 1788. 2nd Edition 1793, 3rd Edition 1803.

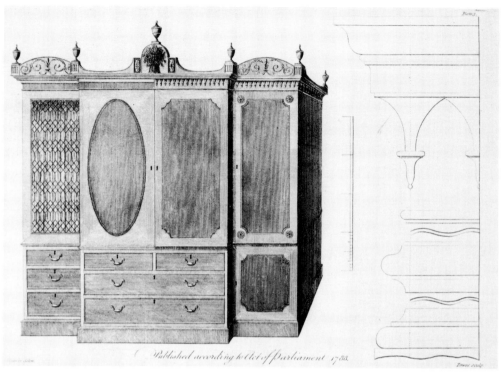

Plate 3. A Wing Clothes Press, designed by Shearer. 6ft. 8in. long, 6ft. 9in. high. Basic cost £5.16.0.

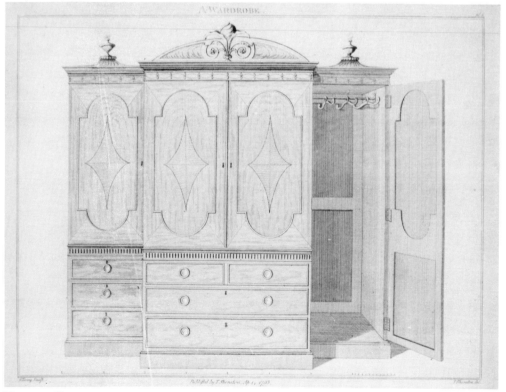

Thomas Sheraton
'The Cabinet-Maker and Upholsterer's Drawing Book', 1793.

Plate 8 from the Appendix. Wardrobe '... the wings have each of them arms, to hang clothes on, made of beech, with a swivel in their center, which slips on to an iron rod...'.

Section 5. CABINETS ON STANDS

Cabinets on carved stands were less widely used than they had been during the last years of the seventeenth century, but a variety of designs was published, from simple sets of drawers to elaborate pieces for drawing rooms. They were often intended more for show than for use, although Sheraton described them as 'those curious and neat pieces of furniture, used by ladies in which to preserve their trinkets, and other curious matters. The cabinets of gentlemen consist in ancient medals, manuscripts and drawings &c., with places fitted up for some natural curiosities.' (*Cabinet Dictionary*, 1803.) Some were intended for japanning, while others were made of mahogany, rosewood or satinwood with fine metal mounts.

Batty Langley
'City and Country Builder's and Workman's Treasury of Designs', 1740.

Plate CLV. Chest on Stand.

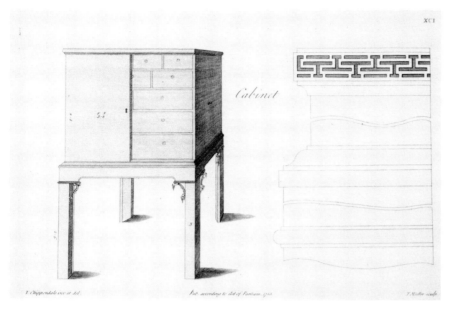

**Thomas Chippendale
'The Gentleman and Cabinet-Maker's
Director', 1st Edition, 1754. 2nd
Edition, 1763.**

Plate XCI. Cabinet. 'Intended for Japan'. Plate CXX in 3rd Edition, 1763.

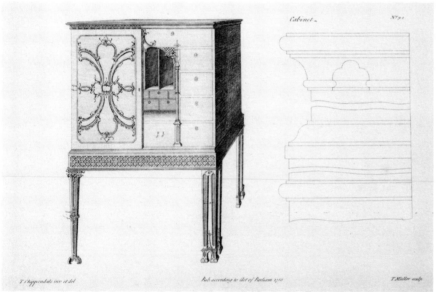

Plate 92. Cabinet on Stand. Plate CXXI in 3rd Edition, 1763.

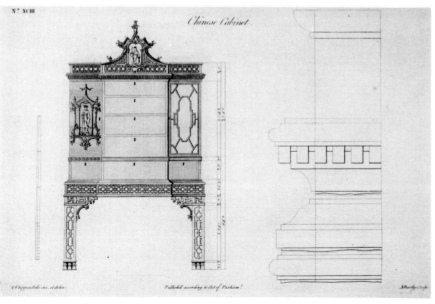

Plate XCIII. Chinese Cabinet. Plate CXXIII in 3rd Edition, 1763.

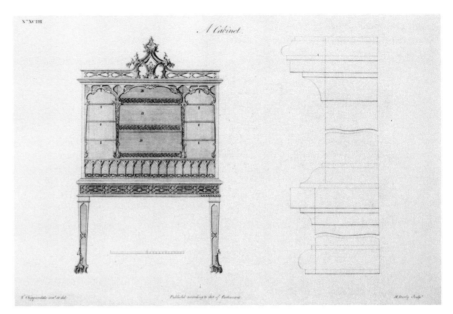

Plate XCIIII. Cabinet on Stand. Plate
CXXIV in 3rd Edition, 1763.

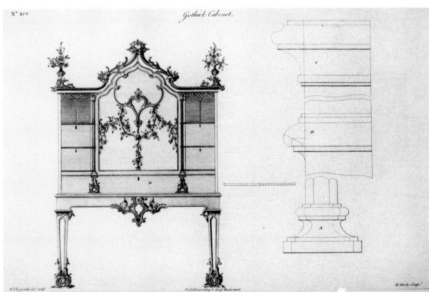

Plate XCV. Gothic Cabinet on Stand.
Plate CXXV in 3rd Edition, 1763.

**Thomas Chippendale
'The Gentleman and Cabinet-
Maker's Director', 3rd Edition,
1763.**

Plate CXXII. Designs for Cabinets.
'Ornaments may be Brass or Silver,
finely chased and put on; or they may
be cut in Filigree-Work, in Wood,
Brass or Silver.' Engraving dated
1762.

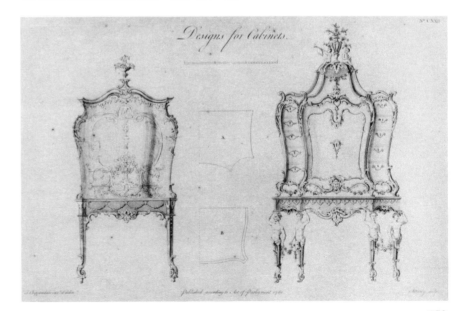

A Society of Upholsterers
'Genteel Houshold Furniture in the Present Taste', 2nd Edition, c.1765.

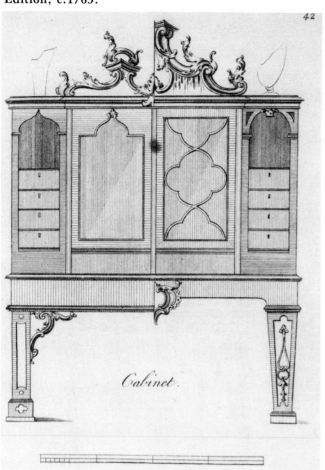

Plate 42 from Part II. Designer unidentified.

Plate 43 from Part II. Cabinet with Shelves. Designer unidentified.

J. Carter
'The Builder's Magazine', 1776.

Plate LXXVII. Cabinet on Stand. Design for furnishing the Pier of a Lady's Dressing Room.

Plate XIV from the Appendix. Cabinet (fallfront writing desk) '... The flower pot at the top is supposed to be real, not carved, but that on the stretcher is carved...'.

Plate XLVIII, Part III. Cabinet. 'The use of this piece is to accommodate a lady with conveniences for writing, reading, and holding her trinkets, and other articles of that kind. The style of finishing them is elegant, being often richly japanned, and veneered with the finest satin-wood...'.

Thomas Sheraton
'The Cabinet-Maker and Upholsterer's Drawing Book', 1793.

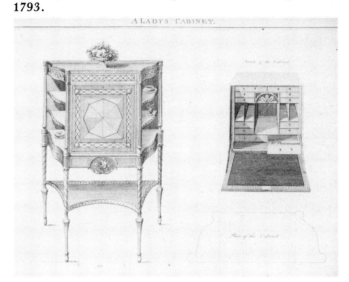

Plate XVI from the Appendix. Lady's Cabinet. '... the marble shelves, with frets at each end, are for a tea equipage...'

'The Cabinet-Maker's London Book of Prices', 2nd Edition, 1793.

Plate 24. A Serpentine Front Cabinet. Designed by Hepplewhite. 4ft. long, 5ft. high. Basic cost £4.16.0.

Section 6. CHINA CABINETS

Some designs were published during the middle decades of the eighteenth century for 'China Cases', which were glazed cabinets on stands intended for the display of oriental porcelain in drawing rooms, boudoirs and dressing rooms. Some of the woodwork was intended to be japanned with chinoiserie decoration in keeping with the contents, and designs by Ince and Mayhew showed mirror glass at the backs of the cases. These objects appear to have gone out of fashion after c.1770.

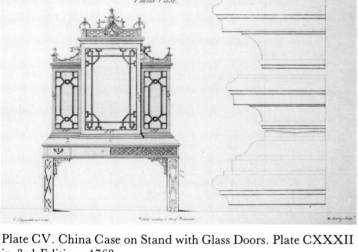

Plate CV. China Case on Stand with Glass Doors. Plate CXXXII in 3rd Edition, 1763.

Thomas Chippendale
'The Gentleman and Cabinet-Maker's Director', 1st Edition, 1754. 3rd Edition, 1763.

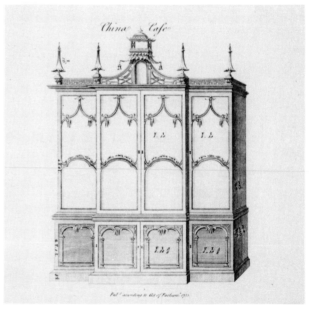

Plate 106. China Case with Glass Doors... 'I have executed this design, and it looks much better than in the drawing.' Not in 3rd Edition, 1763.

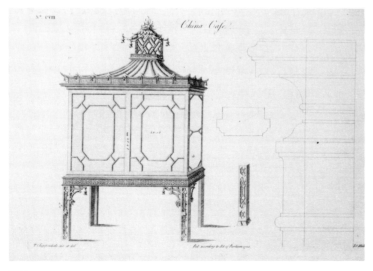

Plate CVIII. Cabinet on Stand with Glass Doors. Plate CXXXIII in 3rd Edition, 1763. 'This design I have executed with great satisfaction to the purchaser.'

Plate CIX. China Case on Stand with Glass Doors. Plate CXXXIV in 3rd Edition, 1763. Intended to be japanned.

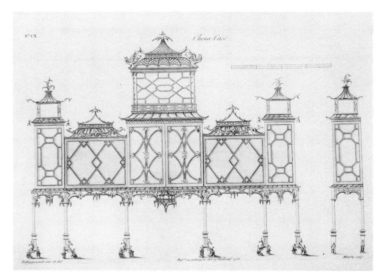

Plate CX. China Case on Stand with Glass Doors. Plate CXXXV in 3rd Edition, 1763. 'This Design is calculated purely for holding China, or for some Apartment where it is frequently put.'

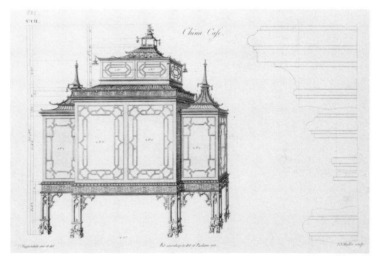

Plate CXI. China Case on Stand with Glass Doors. Plate CXXXVII in 3rd Edition, 1763. 'Not only the richest and most magnificent in the whole (of England) but perhaps in all Europe.'

3rd Edition, 1763.
Plate CXXXVI. China Case on Stand with Glass Doors. 'Very proper for a lady's Dressing Room. It may be made of any soft wood, and japanned any colour.' Engraving dated 1760.

William Ince and John Mayhew
'The Universal System of Houshold Furniture', 1762.

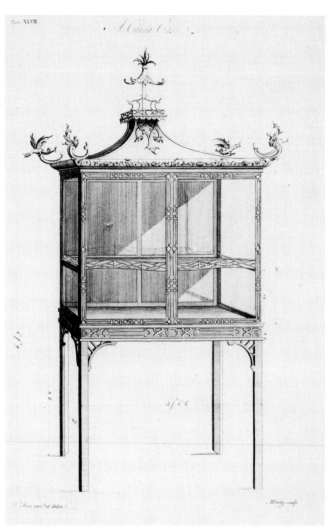

Plate XLVIII. 'A China Case for japanning, the inside all of looking-glass, in that manner it has been executed and has a very elegant effect.'

Plate XLIX. 'Another China Case for Japaning'.

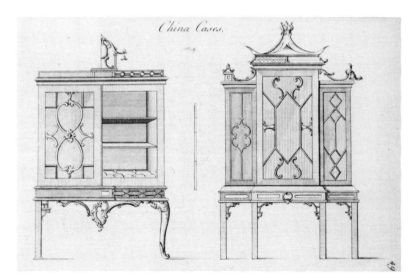

A Society of Upholsterers
'Genteel Houshold Furniture in the Present Taste', 2nd Edition, c.1765.

Plate 49 from Part II. China Cases on Stands with Glass Doors. Designer unidentified.

Section 7. ORGAN and HARPSICHORD CASES

The eighteenth century cabinet-maker's repertoire extended to cases for both church and chamber organs, and some fine designs were published in the pattern-books, particularly those in the Rococo style, although Chippendale included a design for a Gothic one with the comment that 'As most of the Cathedral Churches are of Gothick Architecture, it is a Pity that the Organs are not better adapted.' Mahogany, or painted pine or limewood, were the usual materials, with fine gilt embellishments. Most harpsichord cases were fairly plain rectangular boxes with some painted or inlaid decoration, and no published designs have yet been found, except for Adam's extremely grand design for a harpsichord for the Empress of Russia.

J. Vardy
'Some Designs of Mr. Inigo Jones and Mr. William Kent', 1744.

Thomas Johnson
'Collection of Designs', 1758, 'One Hundred and Fifty New Designs', 1761.

Plate 47. Organ Case by Kent.

Plate 16. Organ Case.

Thomas Chippendale
'The Gentleman and Cabinet-Maker's Director', 3rd
Edition, 1763.

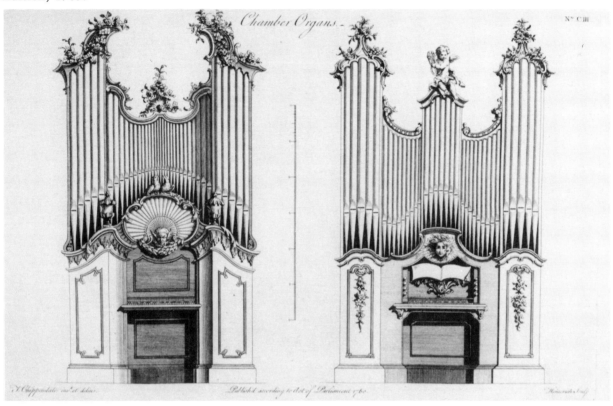

Plate CIII. Organ Case. Engraving dated 1760.

Plate CIV. Organ Case. Engraving dated 1760.

Plate CV. Organ Case, 'Fit for a small Church.'
Engraving dated 1760.

Plate CVI. Organ Case 'In Gothic taste as most
of the Cathedral Churches are of Gothick
Architecture, it is a pity that the organs are not
better adapted.' Engraving dated 1761.

**William Ince and John Mayhew
'The Universal Systems of Houshold Furniture',
1762.**

Plate LIV. Organ Case.

Thomas Malton
'Compleat Treatise on Perspective', 1775.

R. & J. Adam
'Works in Architecture', 1777.

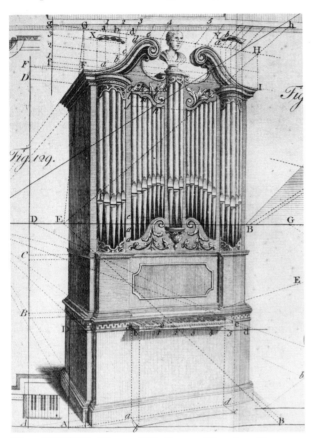

Plate XXXIII, Figure 129. Large Chamber Organ.

Plate VIII. No.II, Vol.II. Organ in the Music Room, Sir Watkin Williams Wynn's House, St. James's Square.

Plate VIII. No.V, Vol.I, 1778. 'Design of a Harpsichord, inlaid with various coloured woods, executed in London for the Empress of Russia. This design was considerably altered by the person who executed the work.'

Section 8. DESKS and WRITING TABLES

Many designs for flat-topped writing desks were published in the eighteenth century. The largest type was the 'Library Table' (now usually referred to as a pedestal desk) which stood in the centre of the room and had doors and/or drawers on both sides. It was the only piece of eighteenth century furniture intended to stand on its own in such a way, and the grandest versions were magnificently decorated. Mahogany was the most favoured wood for such pieces: Sheraton suggested that 'japanned ornaments are not suitable, as these tables frequently meet with a little harsh usage.'

A second type of flat-topped desk was the 'Buroe Table', often referred to now as a knee-hole desk. These were designed to stand against the wall of a room and had pedestals beneath a flat top, with a solid board across the

back. Sheraton's 'Kidney Table' was a derivation from this type.

From 1750 to 1800 many designs were published for desks or writing tables with low superstructures to contain small books and papers in drawers and pigeon-holes. By the 1780s these started to have 'roll-tops' or 'tambour' tops to protect them. Gillows had sketches, and Hepplewhite and Sheraton published designs, for writing tables with drawers arranged in a curve which are now described as 'Carlton House Desks'.

Designs for small travelling desks were published which show neatly arranged compartments for pens, paper, ink and other necessities as well as a flat slide for writing. The exteriors provided surfaces for inlaid work and cross-banding; carved work was avoided because of the hard wear these items had to face.

A. LIBRARY TABLES

Thomas Chippendale
'The Gentleman and Cabinet-Maker's Director',
1st Edition, 1754. 3rd Edition, 1763.

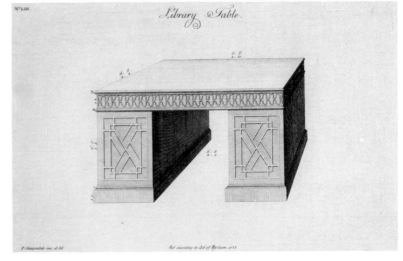

Plate LIII. Library Table. Plate LXXVIII in 3rd Edition, 1763.

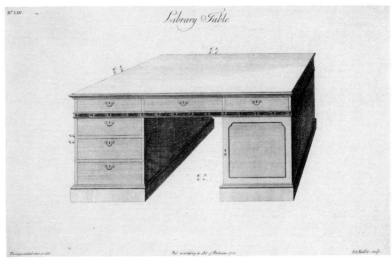

Plate LIV. Library Table. Plate LXXIX in 3rd Edition, 1763.

Thomas Chippendale
'The Gentleman and Cabinet-Maker's Director', 1st Edition, 1754. 3rd Edition, 1763.

Plate LV. Library Table. Plate LXXXI in 3rd Edition, 1763.

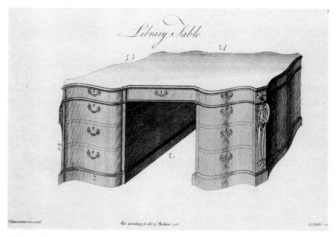

Plate LVI. Library Table. Not in 3rd Edition, 1763.

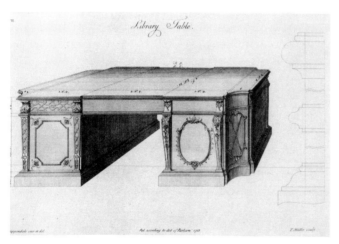

Plate LVII. Library Table. Plate LXXXIII in 3rd Edition, 1763.

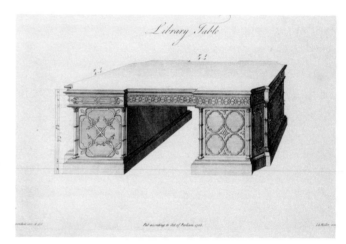

Plate LVIII. Library Table. Plate LXXXV in 3rd Edition, 1763.

Thomas Chippendale
'The Gentleman and Cabinet-Maker's Director', 3rd Edition, 1763.

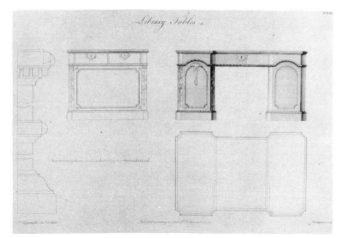

Plate LXXVII. Library Table. Engraving dated 1759.

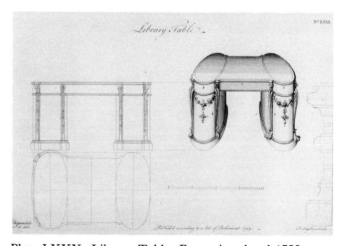

Plate LXXX. Library Table. Engraving dated 1759.

210

Thomas Chippendale
'The Gentleman and Cabinet-Maker's Director', 3rd Edition, 1763.

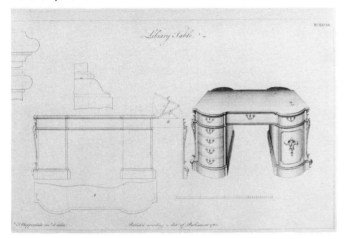

Plate LXXXII. Library Table. Engraving dated 1760.

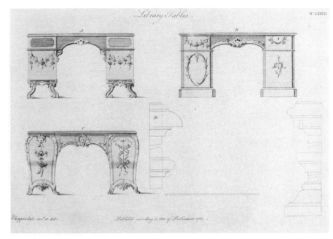

Plate LXXXIV. Library Table. Engraving dated 1760.

A Society of Upholsterers
'Genteel Houshold Furniture in the Present Taste', 2nd Edition, c.1765.

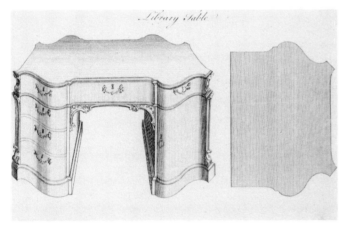

Plate 32, Part II. Library Table, attributed to Chippendale.

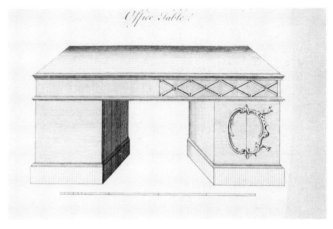

33, Part II. Office Table, attributed to Chippendale.

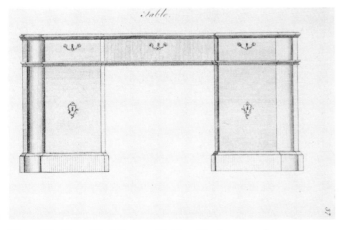

Plate 37, Part II. Library Table. Designer unknown.

Plate 63, Part II. Library Table, attributed to Chippendale.

211

William Ince and John Mayhew
'The Universal System of Houshold Furniture', 1762.

Plate XXIII. Library Table.

A. Hepplewhite & Co.
'The Cabinet-Maker and Upholsterer's Guide', 1st Edition, 1788. 2nd Edition, 1789. 3rd Edition, 1794.

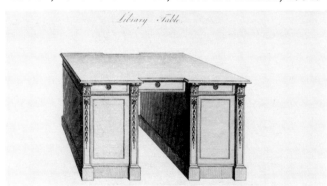

Plates 49 and 50. Library Tables.
'Three designs are given on Plates 49, 50, for Library Tables, which are generally made of mahogany, covered on the top with leather or green cloth. Plate 49 shews a front with cupboards for books, papers, &c; the other side has drawers which run half-way back; the dimensions in use are from 3 to 4 feet long, by 3 feet deep.'

Thomas Malton
'Compleat Treatise on Perspective', 1775.

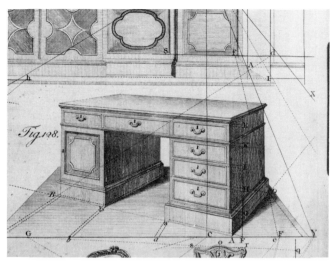

Plate XXXIII, Figure 128. Library Table.

Plate 50.

'The Cabinet-Maker's London Book of Prices', 2nd Edition, 1793.

Plate 2, Figure 1. Library Desk. Designed by Shearer.
Figure 2. Round front cellaret sideboard.

Thomas Sheraton
**'The Cabinet-Maker's and Upholsterers Drawing Book',
1793.**

Plate XXX from Part III. A Library Table.
'This piece is intended for a gentleman to write on, or to stand or sit to read at, having desk-drawers at each end, and is generally employed in studies or library-rooms. It has already been executed for the Duke of York, excepting the desk-drawers, which are here added as an improvement.
'... Mahogany is the most suitable wood, and the ornaments should be carved or inlaid, what little there is: japanned ornaments are not suitable, as these tables frequently meet with a little harsh usage.
'The strength, solidity and effect of brass mouldings are very suitable to such a design, when expense is no object...'

Thomas Sheraton
**'The Cabinet-Maker and Upholsterer's Drawing Book',
1793.**

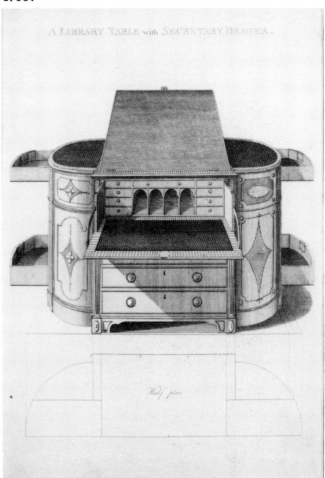

Plate XII from the Appendix. Library Table with a Writing Drawer.
'This table is intended either to sit or stand and write at. The height of the secretary-drawer is adjusted for sitting, and the top of the table is high enough to stand and write on... This table will also prove very useful to draw on... The drawers under the secretary will hold the large sheets of drawing-paper, together with the tee-squares...'

**Thomas Chippendale
'The Gentleman and Cabinet-
Maker's Director', 1st Edition,
1754. 3rd Edition, 1763.**

Plate XLI. 'Buroe Tables'. Not in 3rd
Edition, 1763.

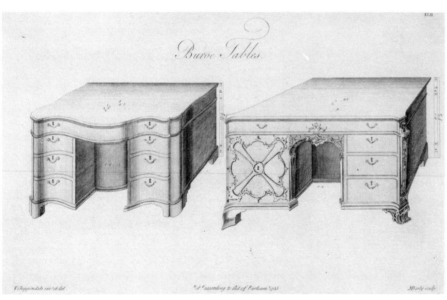

Plate XLII. 'Buroe Tables'. Not in 3rd
Edition, 1763.

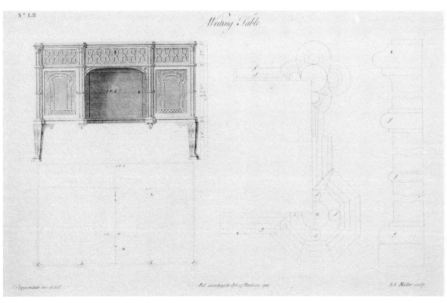

Plate LII. Writing Table. Plate LXXVI
in 3rd Edition, 1763.

A Society of Upholsterers
'Genteel Houshold Furniture in the Present Taste', 2nd Edition, c.1765.

Plate 39 from Part II. Writing Table. Designer unknown.

William Ince and John Mayhew
'The Universal System of Houshold Furniture', 1762.

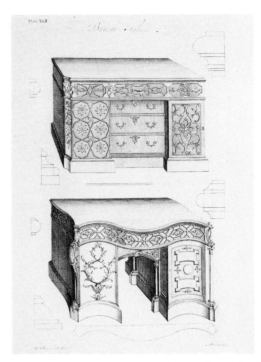

Plate XLII. Bureau Tables '... either of which if well executed must be very elegant'.

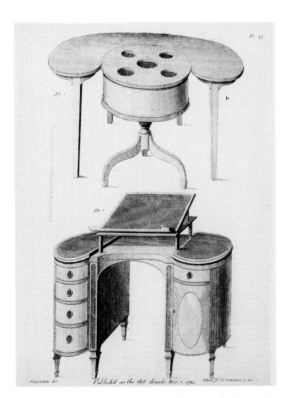

'The Cabinet-Maker's London Book of Prices', 2nd Edition, 1793.
Plate 22. Figure 1. A Gentleman's Social Table, designed by Hepplewhite. Basic cost £1.8.0.
Figure 2. A Kneehole Kidney Writing Table, taper stump feet, designed by Hepplewhite. Basic cost £5.2.0.

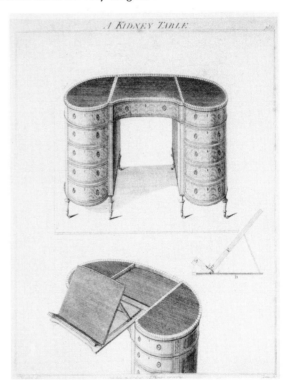

Thomas Sheraton
'The Cabinet-Maker and Upholsterer's Drawing Book', 1793.
Plate LVIII from Part III. Kidney Library Table. 'This piece is termed a Kidney Table, on account of the resemblance to that intestine part of animals so called...'

C. WRITING DESKS AND TABLES WITH SUPERSTRUCTURE.

Thomas Chippendale
'The Gentleman and Cabinet-Maker's Director', 3rd Edition, 1763.

Plate LXXII. A Writing Table. Engraving dated 1760.

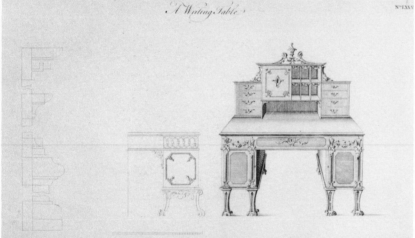

Plate LXXV. A Writing Table. Engraving dated 1760.

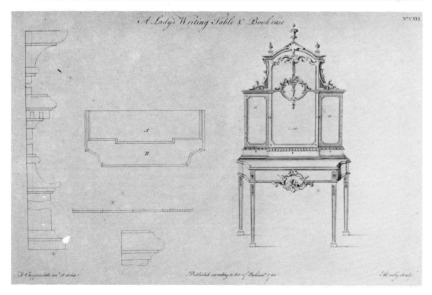

Plate CXVI. A Lady's Writing Table and Bookcase. Engraving dated 1760.

Thomas Chippendale
'The Gentleman and Cabinet-Maker's Director', 3rd Edition, 1763.

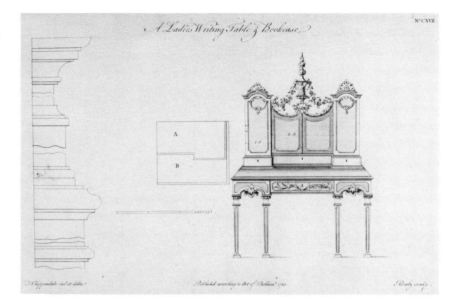

Plate CXVII. A Lady's Writing Table and Bookcase. Engraving dated 1760.

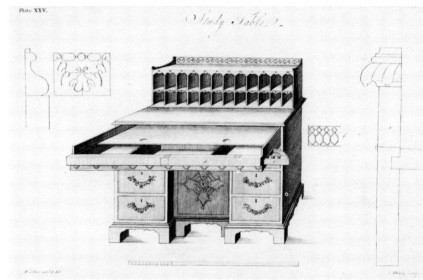

William Ince and John Mayhew
'The Universal System of Houshold Furniture', 1762.

Plate XXV. A Study or Writing Table.

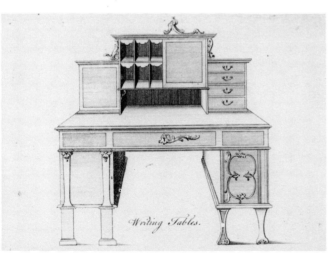

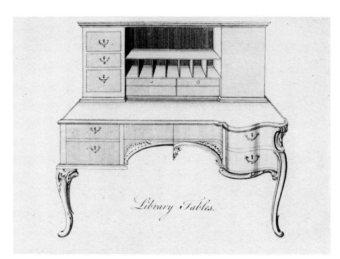

A Society of Upholsterers
'Genteel Houshold Furniture in the Present Taste', 2nd Edition, 1765.

Plate 61. Writing Table. Designer unidentified.   Plate 62. Library Table. Designer unidentified.

A. Hepplewhite & Co.
'The Cabinet-Maker and Upholsterer's Guide', 1st Edition, 1788. 2nd Edition, 1789. 3rd Edition, 1794.

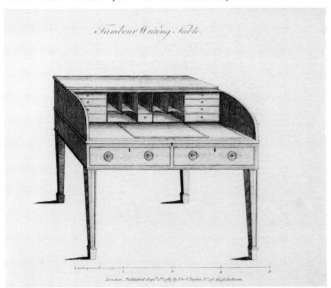

Plate 67. Tambour Writing Table. 'A very convenient piece of furniture, answering all the uses of a desk, with a much lighter appearance.'

Plate 68. Tambour Writing Table.

'The Cabinet-Maker's London Book of Prices', 1st Edition, 1788. 2nd Edition 1793, 3rd Edition, 1803.

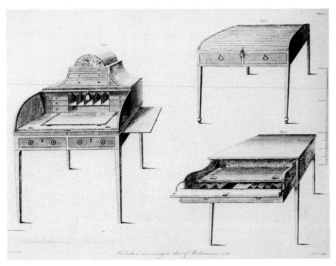

Plate 13. Writing Tables, designed by Shearer.
Figure 1. Tambour Writing Table.
Figure 2. The same, closed.
Figure 3. Writing Table 3ft. long, 2ft. wide. 'The drawer front to represent two, the top one to turn down, supported by quadrants, a case and six drawers in the upper part of the inside to slide as a clothes press shelf, the space below empty, plain taper legs, and an astragal round the bottom of the frame...' £2.4.0.

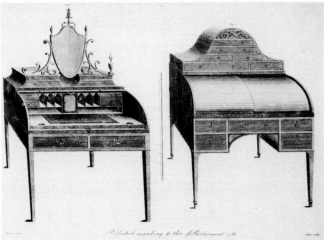

Plate 14. Tambour Writing Tables, designed by Shearer.

'The Cabinet-Maker's London Book of Prices', 1st Edition, 1788. 2nd Edition 1793, 3rd Edition, 1803.

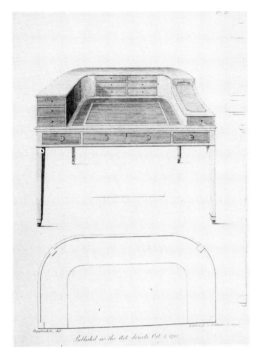

Plate 21. A Gentleman's Writing Table, designed by Hepplewhite. Basic cost £8.0.0.

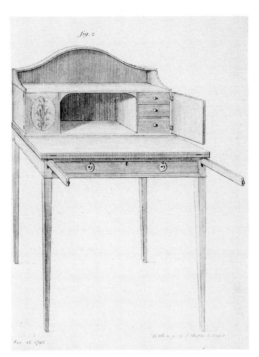

Plate 23, Figure 2. A Lady's Cabinet-Writing Table, designed by Hepplewhite.

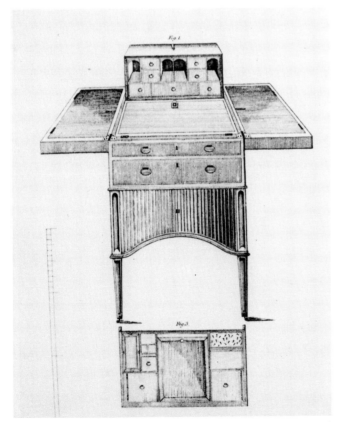

Plate 10, Figure 1. Harlequin Table. 2ft. 2in. long, 3ft. high. Basic cost £3.6.0.

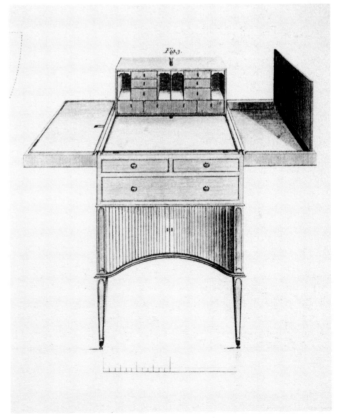

Plate 19, Figure 3. Harlequin Table, designed by Shearer.

Thomas Sheraton
'The Cabinet-Maker and Upholsterer's Drawing Book', 1793.

Plate XXXVII from Part III. Lady's Writing Table.
'The convenience of this table is, that a lady, when writing at it, may both receive the benefit of the fire, and have her face screened from its scorching heat.

'The style of finishing them is neat, and rather elegant. They are frequently made of satin-wood, cross-banded, japanned, and the top lined with green leather...'

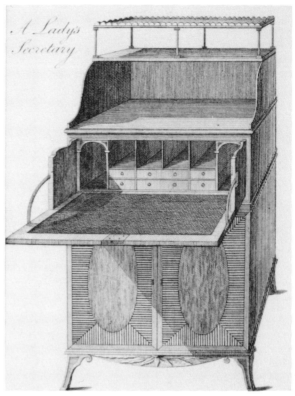

Plate XLIII from Part III. Lady's Secretary.
'These are sometimes finished in black rose-wood and tulip cross-banding together with brass mouldings, which produce a fine effect. The upper shelf is intended to be marble, supported with brass pillars, and a brass ornamented rim round the top. The lower part may be fitted up in drawers on one side, and the other with a shelf to hold a lady's hat, or the like.'

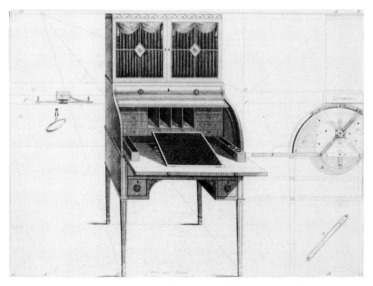

Plate XLVII from Part III. Cylinder Desk and Bookcase.
'The use of this piece is plain, both from the title and design. The style of finishing them is somewhat elegant, being made of satin-wood, cross-banded, and varnished. This design shews green silk fluting behind the glass, and drapery put on at top before the fluting is tacked to, which has a good look when properly managed. The square figure of the door is much in fashion now. The ornament in the diamond part is meant to be carved and gilt, laid on to some sort of silk ground. The rim round the top is intended to be brass, it may, however, be done in wood.'

220

Thomas Sheraton
'The Cabinet-Maker and Upholsterer's Drawing Book', 1793.

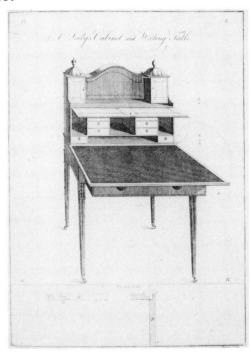

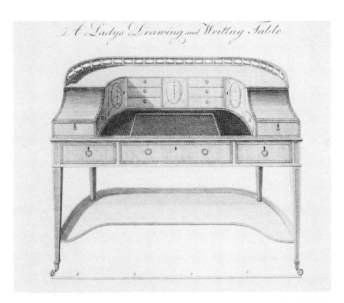

Plate LX from Part III. Lady's Drawing and Writing Table.
'These tables are finished neat, either in mahogany or satinwood, with a brass rim round the top part... The drawer in the middle of the front serves to put the drawings in.'

Plate L from Part III. Lady's Cabinet and Writing Table.
'This table is intended for writing on, and to hold a few small books in the back of the upper part...'

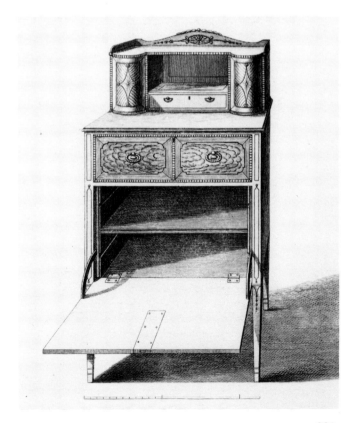

Thomas Sheraton
'The Cabinet-Maker and Upholsterer's Drawing Book', 2nd Edition 1794.

Plate 64. A Lady's Secretary and Cabinet.

D. TRAVELLING DESKS.

'The Cabinet-Maker's London Book of Prices', 1st Edition, 1788. 2nd Edition 1793, 3rd Edition 1803.

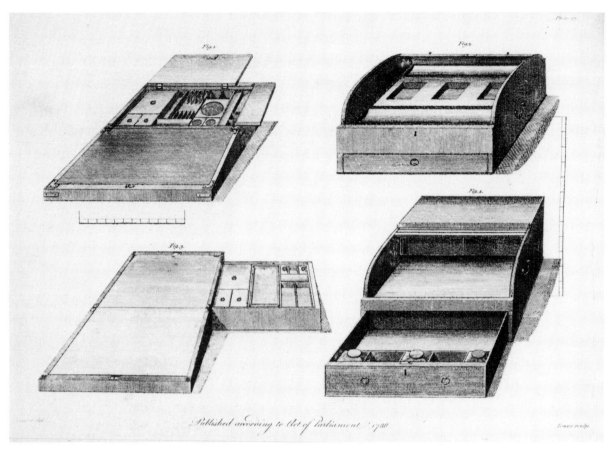

Plate 17. Portable Desks and Ink Stands. Designed by Shearer. Figure 1. A Gentleman's Portable Desk. Basic cost £1.10.0. Figure 2. A Black Tambour Ink Stand (7½ in. long) 7/- or 9/-. Figure 3. Portable Writing Desk. Figure 4. Black Cylinder Ink Stand.

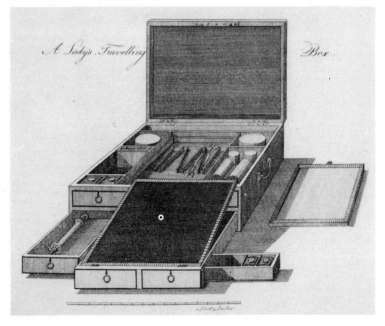

Thomas Sheraton
'The Cabinet-Maker and Upholsterer's Drawing Book', 2nd Edition, 1793.

Plate XXXIX from Part III. Lady's Travelling Desk. '... is intended to accommodate her in her travels with conveniences for writing, dressing and working...'

Section 9. BUREAU BOOKCASES

The description 'Bureau and Bookcase' and 'Desk and Bookcase' applied in the eighteenth century to those pieces with drawers or doors enclosing shelves at the bottom, a desk section with a sloping front in the middle, and a glazed bookcase at the top. Sheraton stated that 'the use of this piece is to hold books in the upper part, and in the lower it contains a writing-drawer and clothes-press shelves.' They were usually made in two sections, dividing between the desk and bookcase, although some early eighteenth century examples divided between the desk and drawer sections as well, and carrying handles were still sometimes fixed to the lower sides. A variation on the theme was the 'Secretaire and Bookcase' or Secretary which had a sham drawer front to the desk section instead of a slope: this let down on brass quadrants to provide a writing surface. They were, according to Hepplewhite, 'usually made of good mahogany', though walnut and burr-yew veneers were used widely in the earlier part of the century and satinwood in later years, and simpler country examples were made of oak and elm. They were originally intended for use in bedchambers, but their use in other parts of the house may have become more regular during the century.

Thomas Chippendale
'The Gentleman and Cabinet-Maker's Director', 1754.
3rd Edition, 1763.

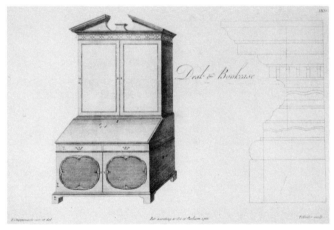

Plate LXXVII. Bureau Bookcase. Not in 3rd Edition, 1763.

Plate LXXVIII. Bureau Bookcase. Plate CVIII in 3rd Edition, 1763.

Thomas Chippendale
'The Gentleman and Cabinet-Maker's Director', 1st
Edition, 1754. 3rd Edition, 1763.

Plate LXXX. Bureau Bookcase. Plate CIX in 3rd Edition, 1763.

Plate LXXXII. Bureau Bookcase. Plate CX in 3rd Edition, 1763.

Plate LXXXIII. Bureau Bookcase. Plate CXI in 3rd Edition, 1763.

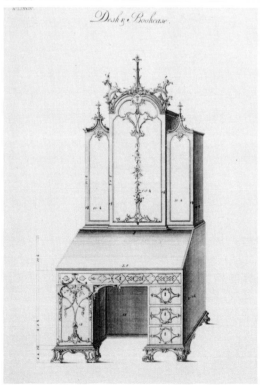

Plate LXXXIV. Bureau Bookcase. Not in 3rd Edition, 1763.

Thomas Chippendale
'The Gentleman and Cabinet-Maker's Director', 3rd Edition, 1763.

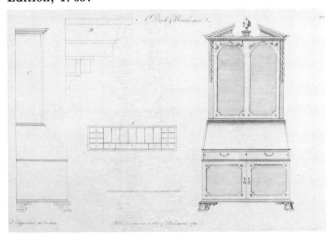

Plate CVII. Bureau Bookcase. Engraving dated 1760.

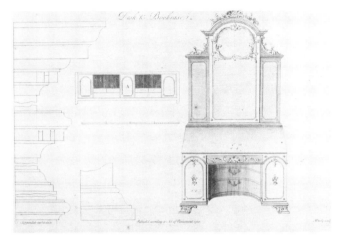

Plate CXII. Bureau Bookcase. Engraving dated 1760.

William Ince and John Mayhew
'The Universal System of Houshold Furniture', 1762.

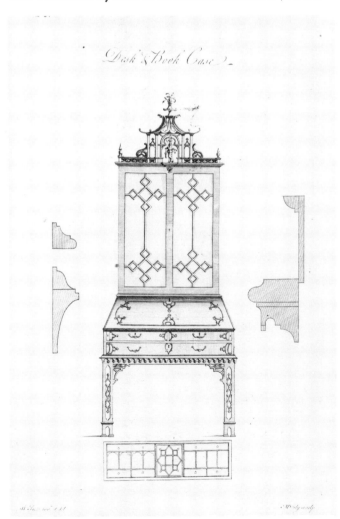

Plate XVI. Desk and Bookcase '. . . on a Frame, the Doors for Glass, the Legs to be cut through.'

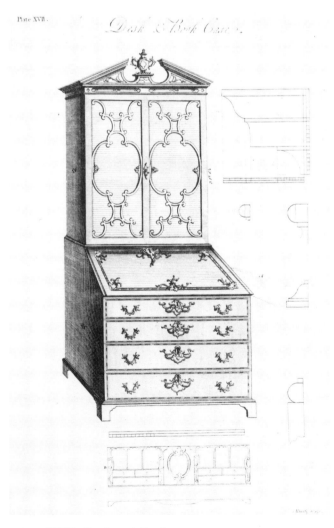

Plate XVII. Desk and Bookcase.

William Ince and John Mayhew
'The Universal System of Houshold Furniture', 1762.

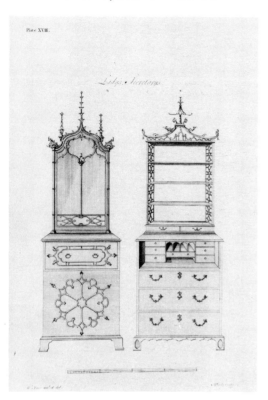

Plate XVIII. 'Two Ladies Secretaires; the first is in the Gothic Taste, with Glass Doors; the other is intended to be open, and may have a green Silk Curtain; the Desk Part draws out, and when up, shews Draws to the Top.'

A Society of Upholsterers
'Genteel Houshold Furniture in the Present Taste', 2nd Edition, c.1765.

Plate XXI. Gentleman's Repository. 'the upper Part or Middle is a Bookcase; on each side is Draws; the Top of the under Part or Middle, is a Desk Drawer; under that either Draws or Cloaths Press, as shewn by two Designs; on each Side Cupboards.'

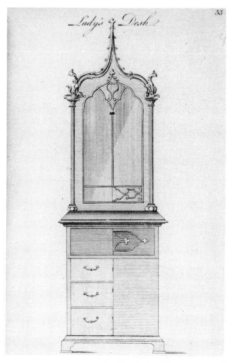

Plate 51, Part II. Writing Table and Bookcase, attributed to Chippendale.

Plate 53, Part II. Lady's Desk, attributed to Ince and Mayhew.

226

Plate 54, Part II. Lady's Bookcase, attributed to Chippendale.

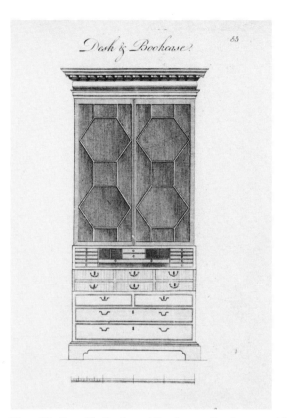

Plate 55, Part II. Desk and Bookcase. Designer unidentified.

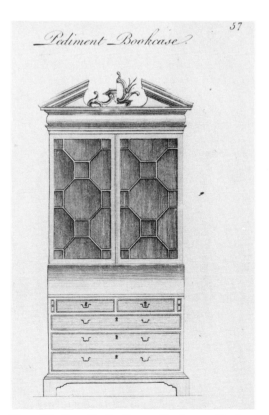

Plate 57, Part II. Pediment Bookcase. Designer unidentified.

Plate 70, Part II. Bureau Bookcase. Designer unidentified.

Thomas Malton
'Compleat Treatise on Perspective', 2nd Edition, 1778.

Plate XXXIV, Figure 133. Lady's Secretary and Library.

Plate 41. Desk and Bureau. (Hepplewhite)

228

A. Hepplewhite & Co.
'The Cabinet-Maker and Upholsterer's Guide', 1st Edition, 1788. 2nd Edition, 1789. 3rd Edition, 1794.

Plate 40. Desk and Bookcase.

'This article of furniture affords a great variety of patterns. The three designs here given [Plates 40, 41 and 42] will shew their general appearance.

Desks and bookcases are usually made of good mahogany; the drawers and internal conveniences admit of much variation. The designs shew three different ways of making them: the patterns of the bookcase doors may also be very much varied. On plate 40* are shewn four designs for doors, which will apply to any of the following designs. On the top, when ornamented, is placed between a scroll of foliage, a vase, bust, or other ornament, which may be of mahogany, or gilt, or of light-coloured wood.

The dimensions of this article, will in general, be regulated by the height of the room, the place where it must stand, or the particular to which it is destined. The following are the general proportions; length 3 feet 6 inches, depth 22 inches, height of desk 3 feet 2 inches, including 10 inches for the inside of the desk; total height about six feet; depth of Book-case about 12 inches.'

[see page 245 for Plate 40*]

A. Hepplewhite & Co.
'The Cabinet-Maker and Upholsterer's Guide', 1st Edition, 1788. 2nd Edition, 1789. 3rd Edition, 1794.

Plate 42. Desk and Bookcase.

Plate 43. Secretary and Bookcase.

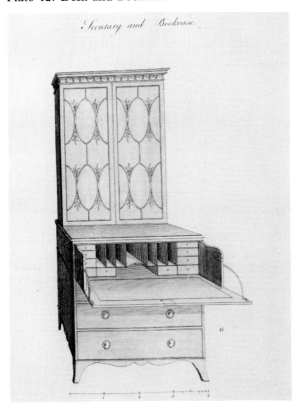

Plate 44. Secretary and Bookcase.

[Secretary and Book-cases] 'Have the same general use as the former article; they differ in not being sloped in front. The accommodations therefore for writing are produced by the face of the upper drawer falling down by means of a spring and quadrant, which produces the same usefulness as the flap to a desk. To one design are drawers — the other has doors, within which are sliding shelves for clothes, &c. like a wardrobe.'

A. Hepplewhite & Co.
'The Cabinet-Maker and Upholsterer's Guide', 1st Edition, 1778. 2nd Edition, 1789. 3rd Edition, 1794.

'The Cabinet-Maker's London Book of Prices', 1st Edition, 1788. 2nd Edition, 1792. 3rd Edition, 1803.

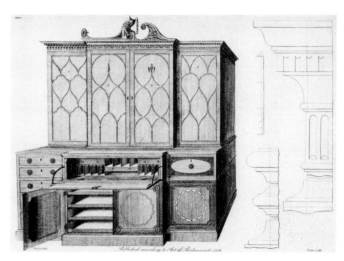

Plate 1. Bookcase. Design contributed by Shearer. A Library Bookcase 6ft. long, 8ft. high to the top of cornice. Basic cost £5.15.0.

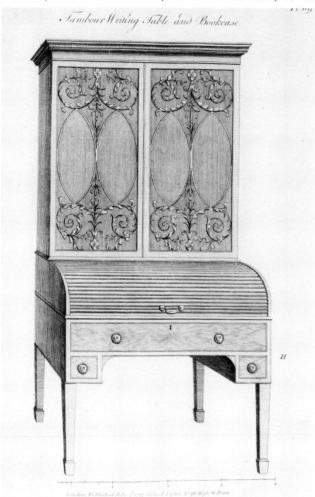

Plate 69. Tambour Writing Table and Bookcase 'the doors to which are intended to be made of, and ornamented with, metal frames; these painted of a light, or various colours, produce a lively and pleasing effect.'

Plate 7. Secretaries. Designed by Shearer. Basic cost 2gns.

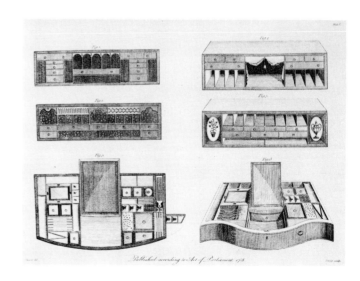

Plate 8. Drawers for Secretaries and Dressing Tables. Designed by Shearer. 3ft. 6in. long. Basic cost £1.0.0.

230

Thomas Sheraton
'The Cabinet-Maker and Upholsterer's Drawing Book',
1793.

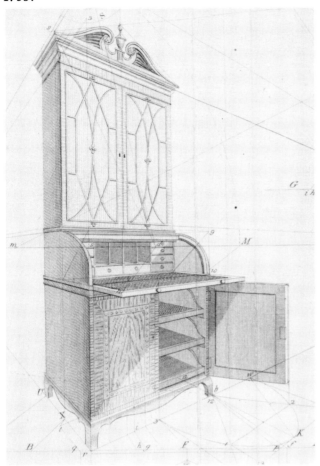

Plate XXVI. Bureau Bookcase in Perspective.

Plate XXVIII. Secretary and Bookcase. 'The use of this piece is to hold books in the upper part, and in the lower it contains a writing-drawer and clothes-press-shelves. The design is intended to be executed in satinwood and the ornaments japanned. It may, however, be done in mahogany; and in place of the ornaments in the friezes, flutes may be substituted...'

Thomas Sheraton
'The Cabinet-Maker and Upholsterer's Drawing Book', 1793.

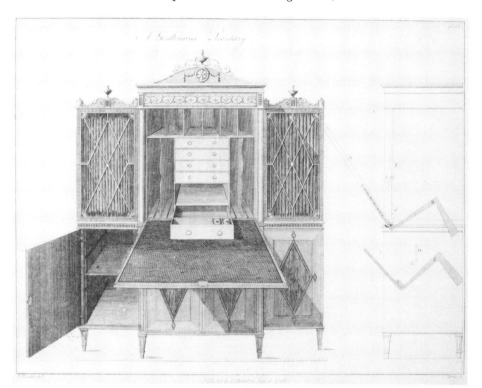

Plate LII from Part III. Gentleman's Secretary.
'This piece is intended for a gentleman to write at, to keep his own accounts, and serve as a library. The style of finishing it is neat, and sometimes approaching to elegance, being at times made of satin-wood, with japanned ornaments.'

(See also Bookcases and Dressing Tables.)

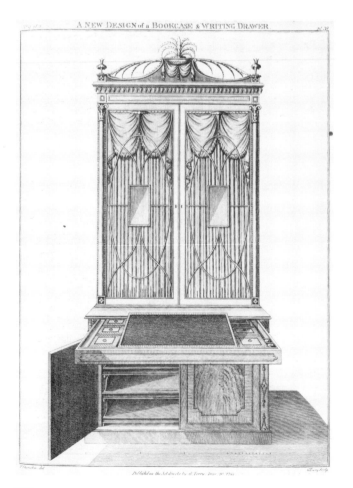

Additional Plate No.39, 2nd Edition, 1794. A New design of a Bookcase and Writing Drawer with looking-glass panels and green silk drapery.

Section 10. BOOKCASES

Free-standing library bookcases, according to Hepplewhite, 'are usually made of the finest mahogany; the doors of fine waved or curled wood . . .'. The upper sections had glazed doors, the lower sections had drawers or doors enclosing sliding shelves or spaces for folios. Pediments, glazing bars and door panels all provided the cabinetmaker and carver with areas for decoration of these otherwise sober and massive pieces of furniture, and some designers included additional patterns for glazed doors for use either on these bookcases or on bureau bookcases.

(See also Interiors for fitted bookcases.
See also Bureau Bookcases.)

**Batty Langley
'City and Country Builder's and Workman's Treasury of Designs', 1740.**

Plate CLVIII. Tuscan Bookcase.

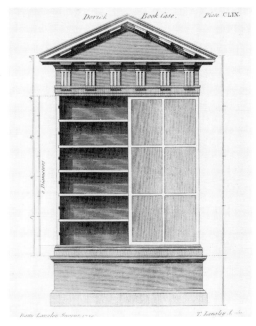

Plate CLVII. Tuscan Bookcase.

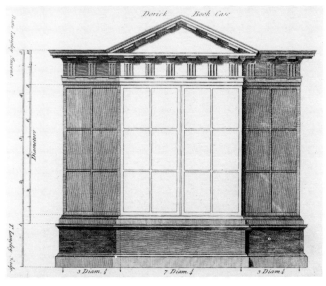

Plate CLIX. 'Dorick' Bookcase.

Plate CLX. 'Dorick' Bookcase.

Batty Langley
'City and Country Builder's and Workman's Treasury of Designs, 1740.

Plate CLXI. 'Ionick' Bookcase.

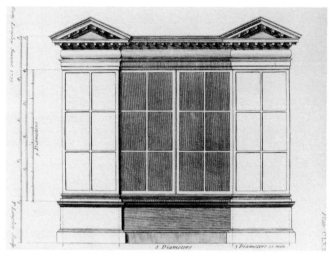

Plate CLXII. Bookcase.

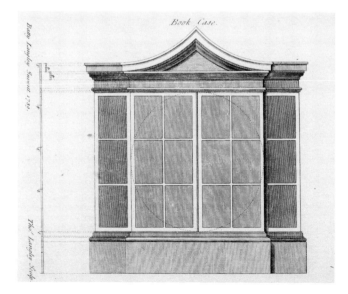

Plate CLXIII. Bookcase.

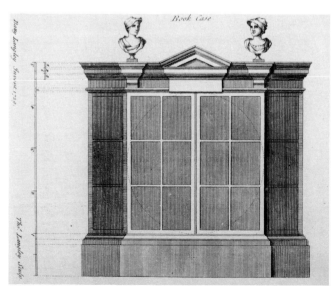

Plate CLXIV. Bookcase.

Thomas Chippendale
'The Gentleman and Cabinet-Maker's Director', 1st Edition, 1754. 3rd Edition, 1763.

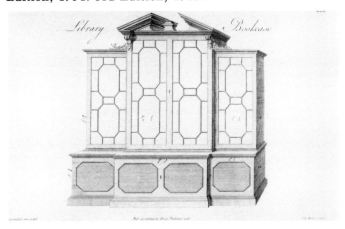

Plate LXIX. Library Bookcase. Not in 3rd Edition, 1763.

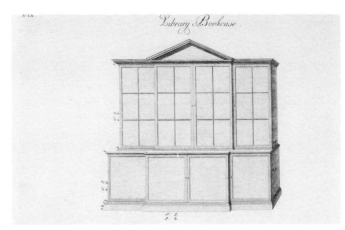

Plate LX. Library Bookcase. Not in 3rd Edition, 1763.

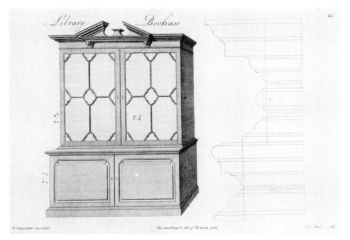

Plate LXI. Library Bookcase. Not in 3rd Edition, 1763.

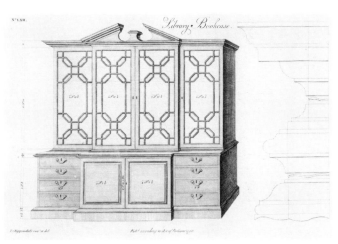

Plate LXII. Library Bookcase. Plate XC in 3rd Edition, 1763.

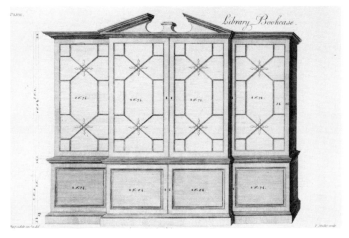

Plate LXIII. Library Bookcase. Plate XCI in 3rd Edition, 1763.

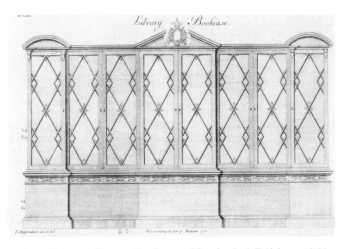

Plate LXV. Library Bookcase. Not in 3rd Edition, 1763.

Thomas Chippendale
'The Gentleman and Cabinet-Maker's Director', 1st Edition, 1754. 3rd Edition, 1763.

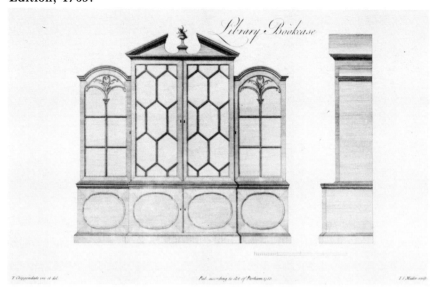

Plate LXVII. Library Bookcase. Plate XCIII in 3rd Edition, 1763.

Plate LXIX. Library Bookcase. Plate XCV in 3rd Edition, 1763.

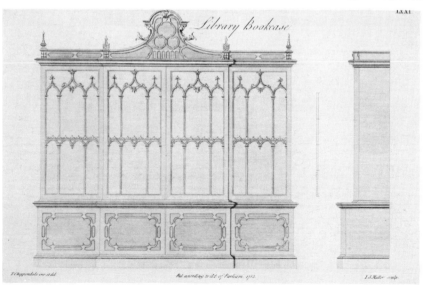

Plate LXXI. Library Bookcase. Not in 3rd Edition, 1763.

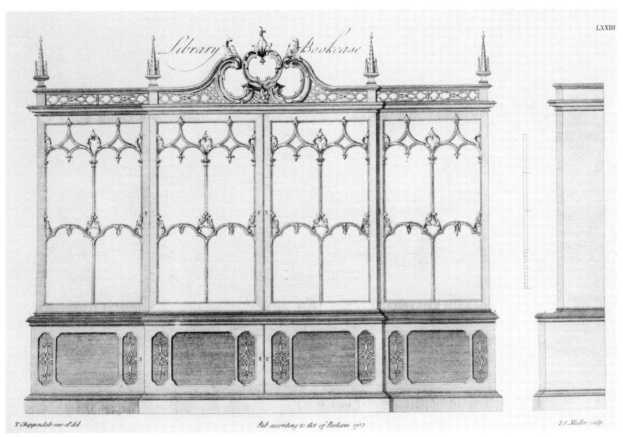

Plate LXXIII. Library Bookcase. Plate XCVIII in 3rd Edition, 1763.

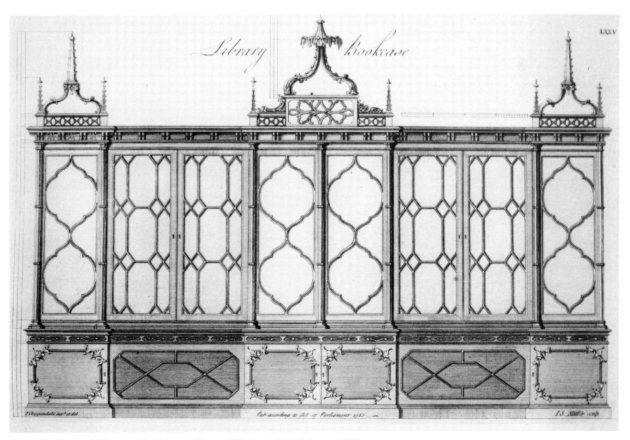

Plate LXXV. Library Bookcase. Plate CI in 3rd Edition, 1763.

Thomas Chippendale
'The Gentleman and Cabinet-Maker's Director', 3rd
Edition, 1763.

Plate LXXXVII. Two Bookcases. Engraving dated 1759.

Plate LXXXVIII. Two Library Bookcases. Engraving dated 1760.

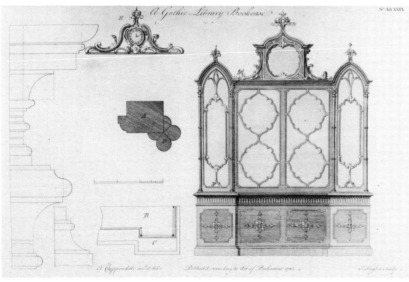

Plate LXXXIX. A Gothic Library Bookcase. Engraving dated 1760.

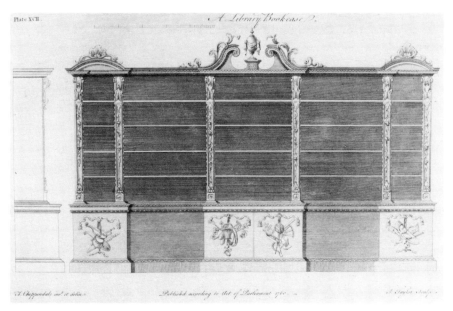

Plate XCII. Library Bookcase.
Engraving dated 1760.

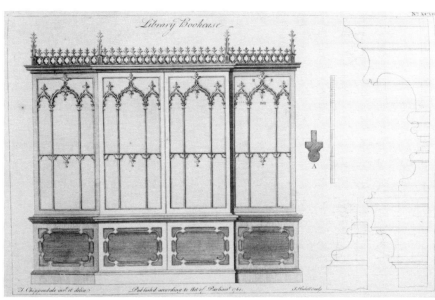

Plate XCVII. Library Bookcase.
Engraving dated 1761.

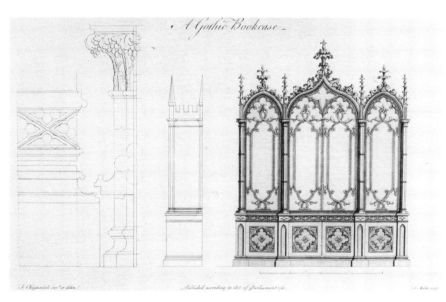

Plate C. A Gothic Bookcase.
Engraving dated 1761.

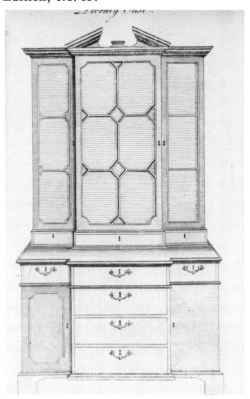

Plate 52 from Part II. Library Bookcase
attributed to Chippendale.

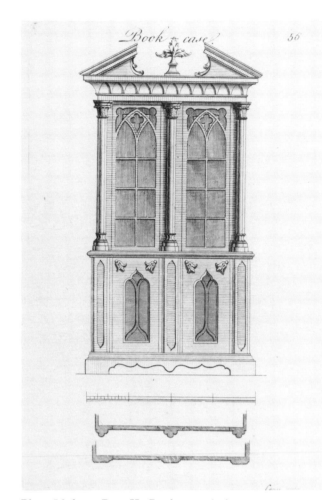

Plate 56 from Part II. Bookcase, designer
unidentified.

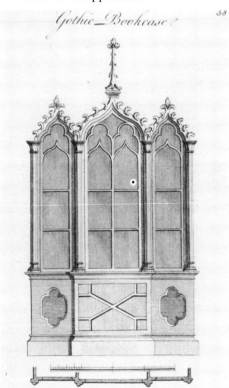

Plate 58 from Part II. Gothic Bookcase,
designer unidentified.

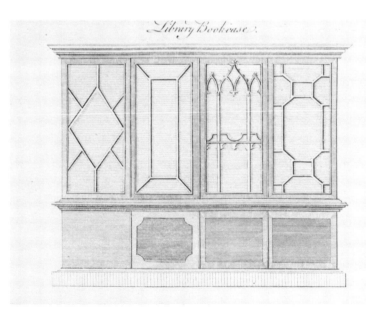

Plate 65 from Part II. Library Bookcase, designer unidentified.

Plate 66 from Part II. Gothic Bookcase, designer unidentified.

Plate 67 from Part II. Pediment Bookcase, designer unidentified.

Plate 68 from Part II. Gothic Bookcase, designer unidentified.

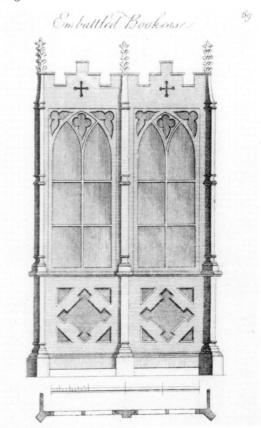

Plate 69 from Part II. Embattled Bookcase, designer unidentified.

241

William Ince and John Mayhew
'The Universal System of Houshold
Furniture', 1762.

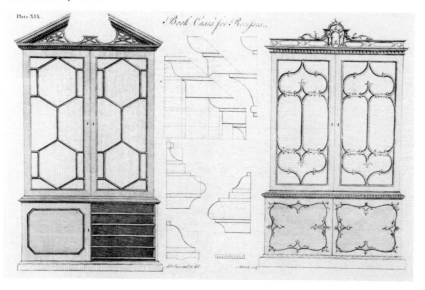

Plate XIX. Bookcases for Recesses.

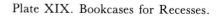

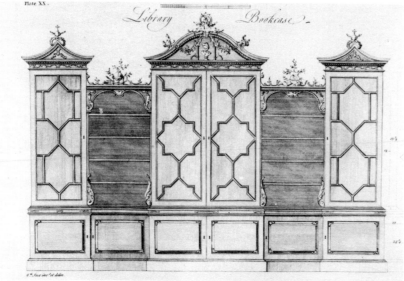

Plate XX. 'A Large Bookcase for a
Library or Side of a Room...'

Thomas Malton
'Compleat Treatise on Perspective',
1775.

Plate XXXIII, Figure 127. Large Library
Bookcase.

242

J. Carter
'The Builder's Magazine', 1774.

Plate XLV. Section of the Side of a Library (opposite the Windows) in Plate 39. Design for a Gentleman's Villa.

A. Hepplewhite & Co.
'The Cabinet-Maker and Upholsterer's Guide', 1st Edition, 1788. 2nd Edition, 1789. 3rd Edition, 1794.

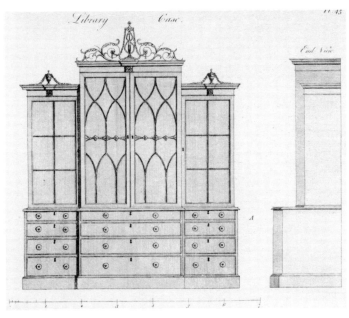

Plates 45-48. Library Bookcases. 'usually made of the finest mahogany; the doors of fine waved or curled wood, may be inlaid on the pannels etc. with various coloured woods. The ornamented sash bars are intended to be of metal which, painted of a light colour or gilt, will produce a pleasing and lively effect.'

Plate 45. Library case.

A. Hepplewhite & Co.
'The Cabinet-Maker and Upholsterer's Guide', 1st Edition,
1788. 2nd Edition, 1789. 3rd Edition, 1794.

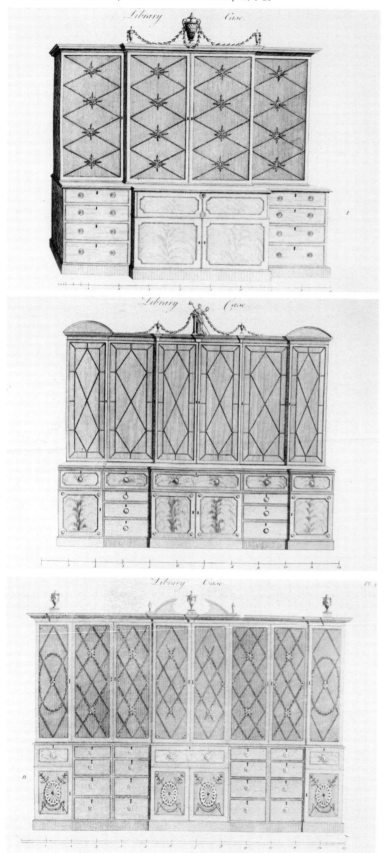

Plate 46. Library case.

Plate 47. Library case.

Plate 48. Library case.

A. Hepplewhite & Co.
'The Cabinet-Maker and Upholsterer's Guide', 1st Edition, 1788.
2nd Edition, 1789. 3rd Edition, 1794.

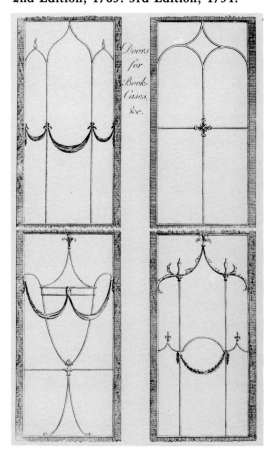

Plate 40*. Doors for Bookcases etc. from 3rd Edition, 1794.

(*See page 228.)

Thomas Sheraton
'The Cabinet-Maker and Upholsterer's Drawing Book', 1793.

Plate 41. Library Bookcase, with looking-glass door panels and green drapery.

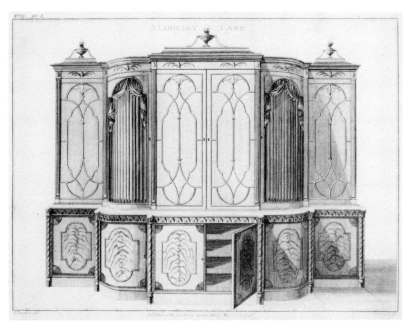

Plate III from the Appendix. Library Bookcase. 'The doors in the upper part are intended to have fluted green silk behind, and a drapery at top.

. . . The lower middle part contains clothes-press shelves, and every other part may be fitted up for books . . .'

A. Hepplewhite & Co.
'The Cabinet-Maker and Upholsterer's Guide', 1st Edition, 1788. 2nd Edition,
1789. 3rd Edition, 1794.

Plate 121. Cornice Mouldings for Bookcases,
Wardrobes, etc.

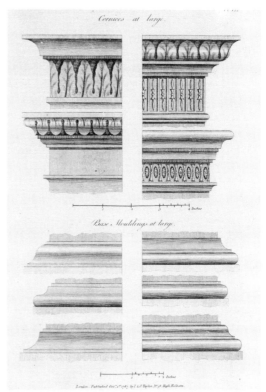

Plate 122. Cornice and Base Mouldings.

Thomas Sheraton
'The Cabinet-Maker and Upholsterer's Drawing Book', 1793.

Plate 123. Surbase Mouldings.

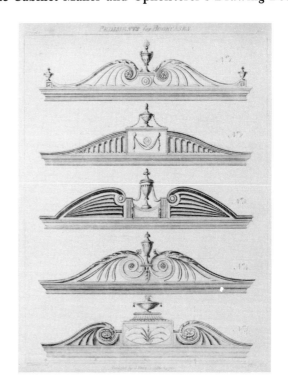

Plate LVII from Part III. Pediments for Bookcases.

246

Thomas Sheraton
'The Cabinet-Maker and Upholsterer's Drawing Book', 1793.

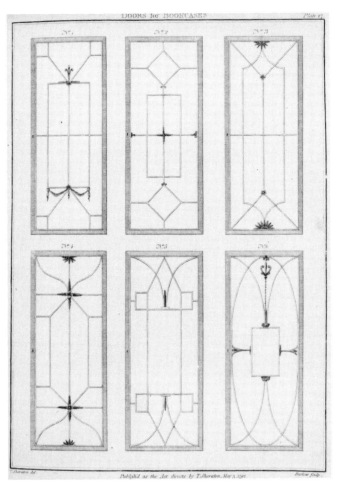

Plate XXVII from Part III. Bookcase Doors.

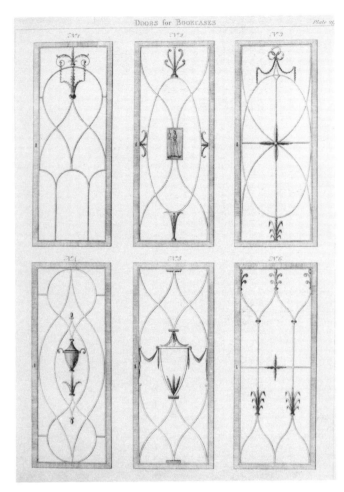

Plate XXIX.

Plate XXIX from Part III. Bookcase Doors.
'In the execution of these doors, the candid and ingenious workman may exercise his judgement, both by varying some parts of the figure, and taking other parts entirely away, when the door is thought to have too much work.'

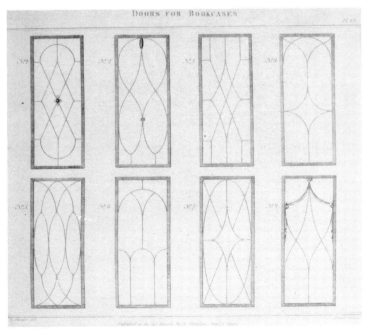

Plate XXVII from the Appendix. Bookcase Doors.

'The Cabinet-Maker's London Book of Prices', 2nd Edition, 1793. 3rd Edition, 1803.

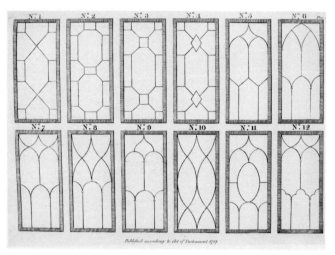

Plate 15. Bookcase Doors, glazing patterns. Designer unknown.

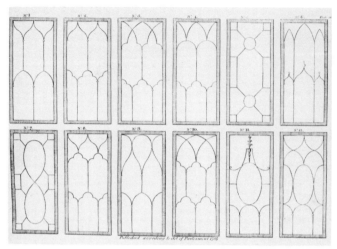

Plate 16. Bookcase Doors, glazing patterns. Designer unknown.

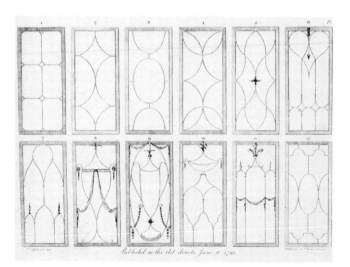

Plate 26. Patterns for glazing bars for Bookcases, Cabinets, etc. Designed by W. Casement.

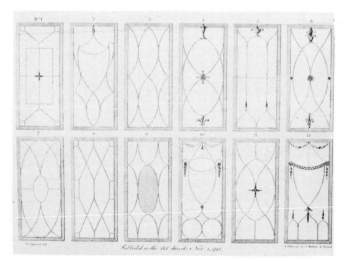

Plate 27. Patterns for glazing bars for Bookcases, Cabinets, etc. Designed by W. Casement.

(See also Bureau Bookcases and Dressing Tables.)

248

Section 11. DRESSING TABLES

Eighteenth century dressing tables could be very elaborate constructions: for ladies, these pieces could have drapery around the dressing mirror and over the table, and for both ladies and gentlemen tables or 'buroe dressing tables' could be fitted up with 'Apparatus' consisting of drawers, boxes, compartments and folding mirrors to assist the complex art of dressing. Where textiles were used they would be such delicate stuffs as silk lutestrings, taffetas and damasks, or fine lace, with silk ribbons. The tables themselves were of the usual woods such as walnut, mahogany and satinwood, or japanned softwoods. Most of the larger 'tables' resembled knee-hole desks with drawers below the dressing drawer, though many smaller, simpler examples were also designed with a single dressing drawer, or with rising lids. Hepplewhite and Sheraton published designs for extremely complex tables with swinging mirrors, washbasins and 'every requisite' for a lady's or gentleman's toilette.

A. DRESSING TABLES WITH DRAPERY.

Batty Langley
'City and Country Builder's and Workman's Treasury of Designs', 1740.

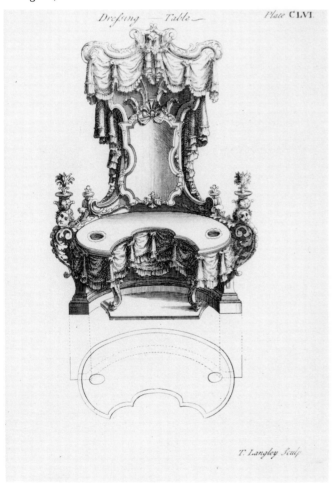

Plate CLVI. Dressing Table with Drapery '...enriched after the French Manner.' After Schübler.

Thomas Chippendale
'The Gentleman and Cabinet-Maker's Director', 3rd Edition, 1763.

Plate CXVIII. Toilet or Dressing Table for a Lady. 'The ornaments should be gilt in burnish'd gold; or the whole work may be japanned, and the drapery may be silk damask, with Gold Fringes and Tassels.' Engraving dated 1761.

**Thomas Chippendale
'The Gentleman and Cabinet-Maker's Director', 3rd
Edition, 1763.**

Plate LII. A Lady's Dressing Table. The middle drawer
intended for 'conveniences for Dressing'. Top 'at' each side,
'a Cupboard with Glass Doors which may be either
transparent or silvered; and the inside Drawers or Pigeon
Holes... Two Dressing Tables have been made of
Rosewood from this Design...' Engraving dated 1761.

Plate CXIX. 'A Toilet Table'. Engraving dated 1760.

**A Society of Upholsterers
'Genteel Houshold Furniture in the Present Taste', 2nd
Edition, c.1765.**

**William Ince and John Mayhew
'The Universal System of Houshold Furniture', 1762.**

Plate XXXVI. 'Lady's Toilettas'.

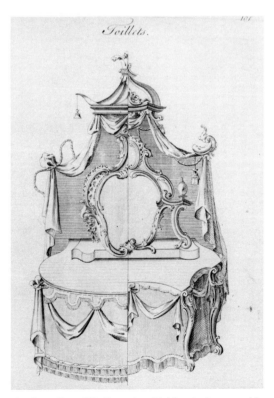

Plate 101 from Part III. Dressing Table, designer unidentified,
possibly Chippendale.

Plate XXXVII. A Lady's 'Toiletta', 'with Drawers under
the Glass, intended either for Japan or Burnish'd Gold.'

B. BUREAU DRESSING TABLES

Thomas Chippendale
'The Gentleman and Cabinet-Maker's Director', 1754.

'Buroe Dressing Tables. The Ornamental Parts are intended for Brass-Work, which, I would advise, should be modelled in Wax, and then cast from these models.'

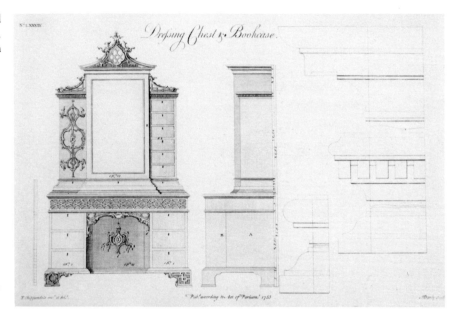

Plate LXXIX. Dressing Chest and Bookcase. Plate CXIV in 3rd Edition, 1763.

Thomas Chippendale
'The Gentleman and Cabinet-Maker's Director', 1st Edition, 1754. 3rd Edition, 1763.

Plate XC. Dressing Chest and Bookcase. Plate CXV in 3rd Edition, 1763.

Thomas Chippendale
'The Gentleman and Cabinet-Maker's Director', 3rd Edition, 1763.

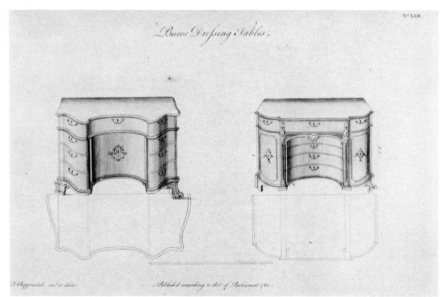

Plate LXII. Bureau Dressing Tables. Engraving dated 1760.

Thomas Chippendale
'The Gentleman and Cabinet-Maker's Director', 3rd Edition, 1763.

Plate LXIII. Bureau Dressing Tables. Engraving dated 1760.

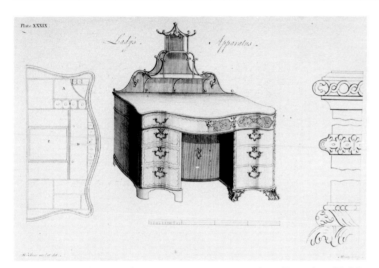

Plate XXXIX. Lady's Apparatus '... another Dressing Table and contrived for Writing also...'

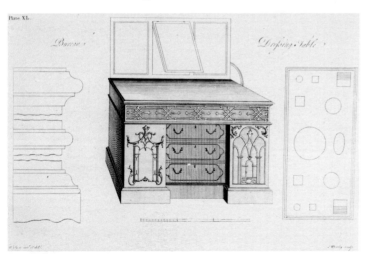

Plate XL. Gentleman's Bureau Dressing Table.

William Ince and John Mayhew
'The Universal System of Houshold Furniture', 1762.

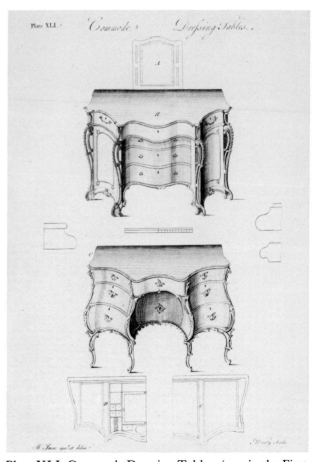

Plate XLI. Commode Dressing Tables. '... in the First at A the top lifts up and has the Dressing Glass in it.' 2nd Design '... the ornaments of which may be either Brass or Wood gilt...'

252

A Society of Upholsterers
'Genteel Houshold Furniture in the Present Taste',
2nd Edition, c.1765.

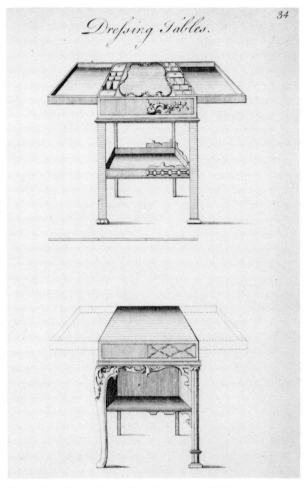

Plate 34 from Part II. Dressing Tables, designer unidentified.

Thomas Malton
'Compleat Treatise on Perspective', 2nd Edition,
1778.

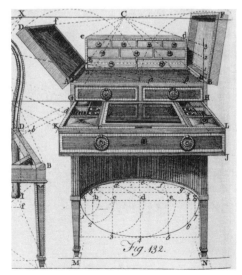

Plate XXXIV, Figure 132. Lady's Dressing Table.

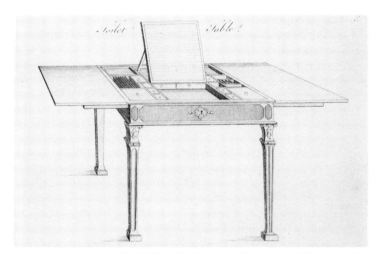

Plate 35 from Part II. Toilet Tables, attributed to Chippendale.

William Ince and John Mayhew
'The Universal System of Houshold Furniture', 1762.

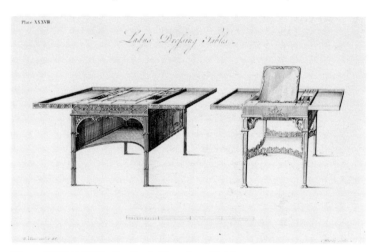

Plate XXXVIIII. Ladies' Dressing Tables.

A. Hepplewhite & Co.
'The Cabinet-Maker and Upholsterer's Guide', 1st Edition,
1788. 2nd Edition, 1789. 3rd Edition, 1794.

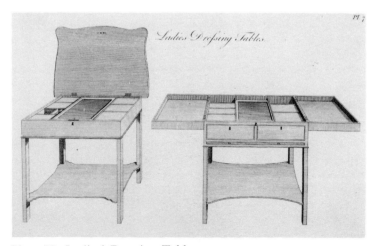

Plate 72. Ladies' Dressing Tables.

A. Hepplewhite & Co.
'The Cabinet-Maker and Upholsterer's Guide', 1st Edition, 1788. 2nd Edition, 1789. 3rd Edition, 1794.

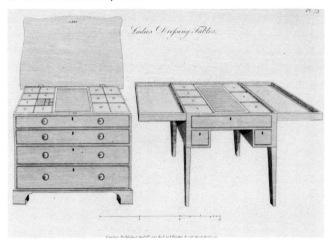

Plate 73. Ladies' Dressing Tables.

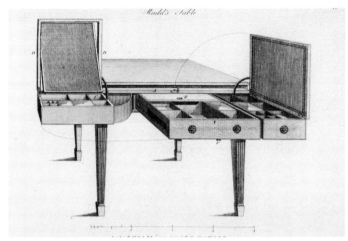

Plate 79. Rudd's Table 'or reflecting dressing table'. 'This is the most complete dressing table made, possessing every convenience which can be wanted, or mechanism and ingenuity supply. It derives its name from a once popular character, for whom it is reported it was first invented.'

'The Cabinet-Maker's London Book of Prices', 1st Edition, 1788. 2nd Edition, 1793. 3rd Edition, 1803.

Plate 4. Figure 2. A Rudd, or Lady's Dressing Table, designed by Shearer. 3ft. 4in. long, 2ft. wide. Plain Marlborough Legs. Basic cost 3gns.

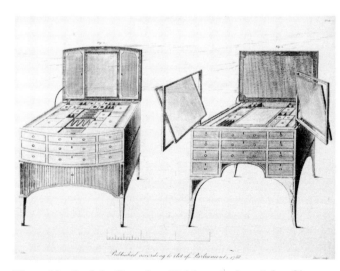

Plate 11. Lady's Dressing Tables, designed by Shearer. Basic cost 3gns.

Thomas Sheraton
'The Cabinet-Maker and Upholsterer's Drawing Book', 1793.

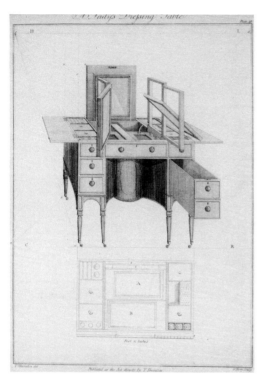

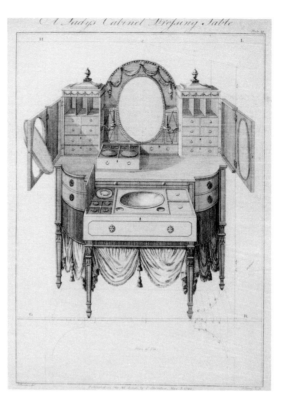

Plate XLVI from Part III. Lady's Dressing Table. 'The style of finishing these tables is neat. They are often made of satin-wood, and banded; but sometimes they are made of mahogany... These side-glasses are an addition of my own, which I take to be an improvement: judging that, when they are finished in this manner, they will answer the end of a Rudd's table, at a less expence...'

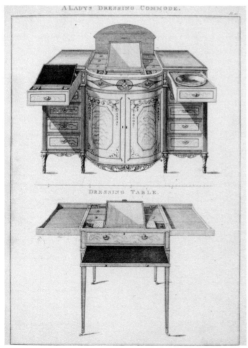

Plate XX from the Appendix. Dressing Commode and Dressing Table.

Plate XLIX, from Part III. Lady's Cabinet Dressing Table. 'This table contains every requisite for a lady to dress at. The style of finishing them is neat and somewhat elegant... ...Behind the drapery, which is tacked to a rabbet, and fringed or gimped, is a shelf, on which may stand any vessel to receive the dirty water... The drawers in the cabinet part are intended to hold all the ornaments of dress, as rings, drops etc. Behind the center glass is drapery: it may be real to suit that below, or it may only be painted in imitation of it...'

(See also Dressing Glasses (Frames))

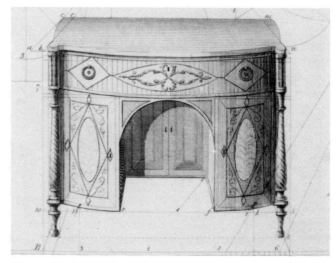

Plate 25 from Part II. Commode Dressing Table in Perspective.

Section 12. WASH-STANDS, BASIN-STANDS and SHAVING-TABLES

Wash-stands, basin-stands and shaving-tables were all equipped with removable bowls for water and soap, and ranged from the simplest type to quite complicated pieces with adjustable mirrors and small cisterns. Designers were concerned to produce functional objects which 'may stand in a genteel room without giving offence to the eye.' (Sheraton, *Drawing Book,* 1793.)

(See also Part III, Carvers' Work, II Stands.)

Thomas Chippendale
'The Gentleman and Cabinet-Maker's Director', 3rd Edition, 1763.

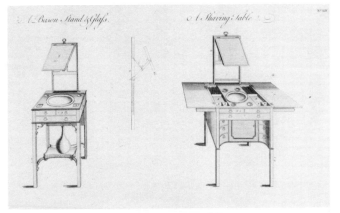

Plate LIV. A Basin-Stand and a Shaving Table. Engraving dated 1761.

A. Hepplewhite & Co.
'The Cabinet-Maker and Upholsterer's Guide', 1st Edition, 1788. 2nd Edition, 1789. 3rd Edition, 1794.

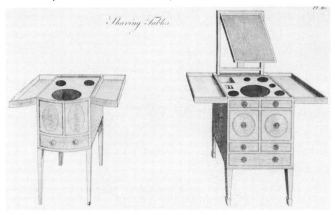

Plate 80. Shaving Tables. 'the tops of which turn over on each side; the glas to each draws up the back, and is supported by a spring stop... within the doors is a place for water bottles, etc. The drawer is designed to hold napkins etc; are made of mahogany.'

'The Cabinet-Maker's London Book of Prices', 1st Edition, 1788. 2nd Edition, 1793. 3rd Edition, 1803.

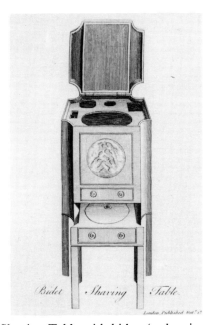

Plate 81. Shaving Table with bidet. 'a dressing or shaving table, with the usual conveniences; and also a bidet, which draws out and is supported by half legs; this is on a new construction, and has been much approved for its use and conveniences.'

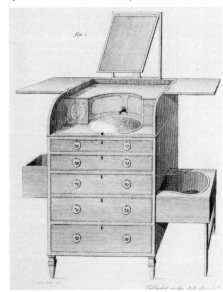

Plate 23, Figure 1. A Cylinder-Fall Wash-Hand Table, designed by Hepplewhite.

'The Cabinet-Maker's London Book of Prices', 1st Edition, 1788. 2nd Edition, 1793. 3rd Edition, 1803.

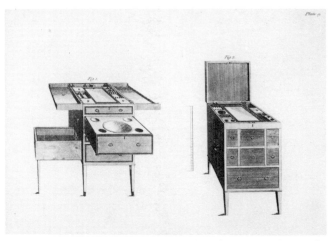

Plate 9, Figure 1. Lady's Dressing Stand, designed by Shearer. 1ft. 8in. square. Basic cost £1.12.0.
Figure 2. Gentleman's Dressing Stand, including night stool bidet etc., designed by Shearer.

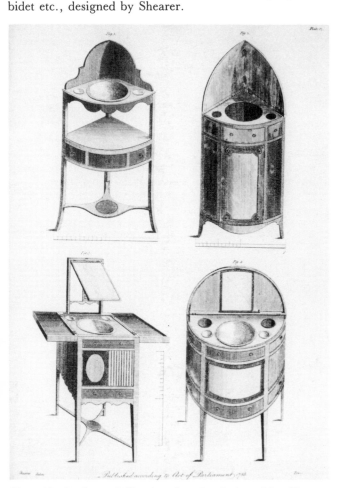

Plate 12. Basin and Shaving Stands, designed by Shearer.
Figure 1. 'A Corner Bason Stand'. Basic cost 13s.
Figure 2. 'A Corner inclos'd bason Stand'. Basic cost £1.10.0.
Figure 3. Shaving Stand. Basic cost £1.1.0.
Figure 4. Half round Shaving Stand. Basic cost £2.5.0.

A. Hepplewhite & Co.
'The Cabinet-Maker and Upholsterer's Guide', 1st Edition, 1788. 2nd Edition, 1789. 3rd Edition, 1794.

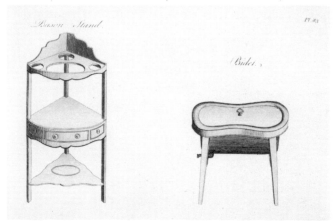

Plates 83, 84. Basin stands. 'A design for a new one, Plate 83, on a triangular plan. This is a very useful shape, as it stands in a corner out of the way.'

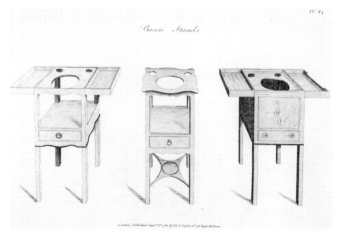

Plate 84.

Anon
'Ideas for Rustic Furniture', 1790-95.

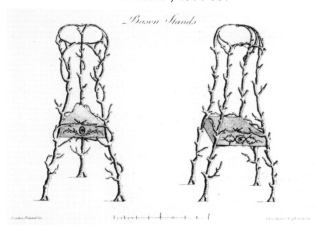

Figure 18. Basin Stands.

Thomas Sheraton
'The Cabinet-Maker and Upholsterer's Drawing Book',
1793.

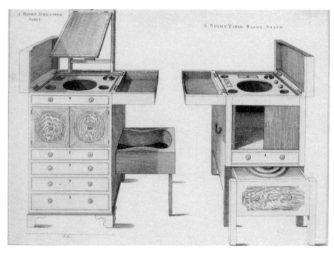

Plate XLII from Part III. Corner Basin Stands.
Left-hand type: 'The advantage of this kind of bason-stand is, that it may stand in a genteel room without giving offence to the eye, their appearance being somewhat like a cabinet.'

Plate VII from the Appendix. Bidet Dressing Table and Night Table Basin Stand.

'The Cabinet-Maker's London Book of Prices', 1st Edition, 1788. 2nd Edition, 1793. 3rd Edition, 1803.

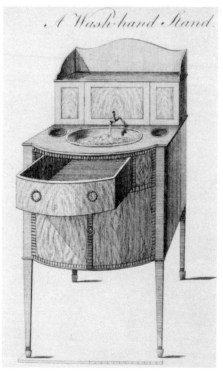

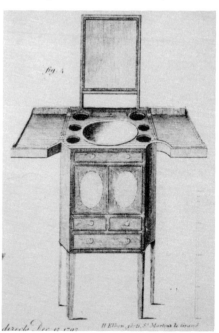

Plate LIII from Part III. Cylinder Wash-Hand Table: 'These are always made of mahogany, and having a cylinder to rise up to hide the washing apparatus, they look neat in any genteel dressing room.

Plate XLIII from Part III. Wash-Hand Stand. 'The drawer in this wash-hand stand is lined with lead, into which the bason is emptied. The upper part which contains the cistern takes off occasionally.'

Plate 25, Figure 4. Shaving Stand, Marlborough legs. Designed by Hepplewhite.

258

Section 13. NIGHT TABLES and POT CUPBOARDS

Night tables and pot cupboards were designed to be smart, serviceable and discreet: the grander sorts were intended to stand beside a bed with a flat top on which candles could be placed; plainer, smaller types could be used, according to Hepplewhite, in 'bed-chambers, counting-houses, offices etc.'. The description 'commode' for this piece of furniture was not generally used in the eighteenth century.

William Ince and John Mayhew
'The Universal System of Houshold Furniture', 1762.

Plate XXXIII. Night Tables. 'The Middle one is intended to be lined with silk, to shew the Frets; the other has its top to rise for reading.'

A Society of Upholsterers
'Genteel Houshold Furniture in the Present Taste', 2nd Edition, c.1765.

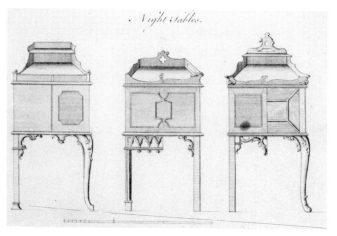

Plate 41 from Part II. Night Tables, designer unidentified.

A. Hepplewhite & Co.
'The Cabinet-Maker and Upholsterer's Guide', 1st Edition, 1788. 2nd Edition, 1789. 3rd Edition, 1794.

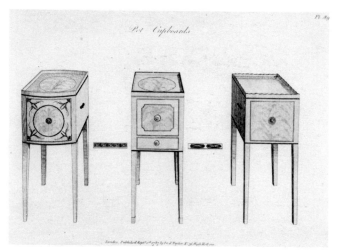

Plate 89. Pot Cupboards. 'An article of much use in bed-chambers, counting houses, offices, etc.'

A. Hepplewhite & Co.
'The Cabinet-Maker and Upholsterer's Guide', 1st Edition, 1788. 2nd Edition, 1789. 3rd Edition, 1794.

Plate 81. Night Table.

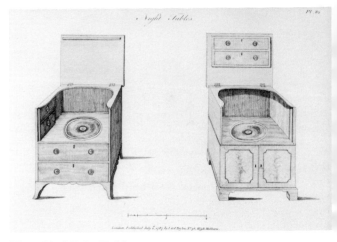

Plate 82. Night Tables.

Thomas Sheraton
'The Cabinet-Maker and Upholsterer's Drawing Book', 1793.

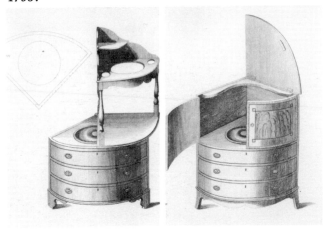

Plate XXIII from Appendix. Corner Night Table.

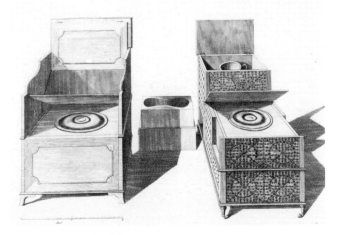

Plate 77. New Bed Steps.

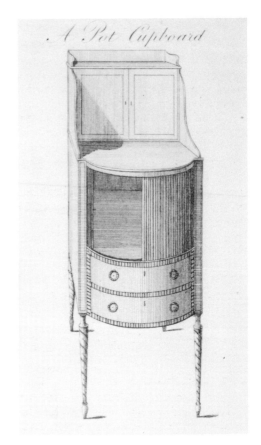

Plate XLIII from Part III. Pot Cupboard. 'These are used in genteel bedrooms, and are sometimes finished in satinwood, and in a style a little elevated above their use... Sometimes there are folding doors to the cupboard part, and sometimes a curtain of green silk, fixed on a brass wire at top and bottom; but in this design a tambour door is used, as preferable. The upper cupboard contains shelves, and is intended to keep medicines to be taken in the night, or to hold other little articles which servants are not permitted to overlook.'

260

Part III. Carver's Work

I. TABLES. Section 1. PIER TABLES

By far the largest number of eighteenth century published designs for tables were those for pier tables — pieces of furniture which were placed between the windows, against the 'pier' of the wall, and usually had an accompanying mirror or 'pier glass' fixed to the wall above them. Apart from their decorative function, which was most important, they also served to support candelabra which, when their candles were lit, threw their own and reflected light from the mirror above into a room, thus providing a night-time source of light from the same side of a room as daylight: this was an important facility in the arrangement of pictures. In larger rooms, candelabra were placed on pairs of carved stands placed on either side of the pier table and the table top left clear. This arrangement, or 'triad', of pier table, glass and stands was brought into England from Paris in the second half of the seventeenth century, and remained a standard feature in eighteenth century interior decoration. In 1788 Hepplewhite referred to the pier table as an article 'of much fashion; and not being applied to as much use as other tables, admit, with great propriety, of much elegance and orament... The height of Pier Tables varies from the general rule, as they are now made universally to fit the pier, and rise level with or above the dado of the room, nearly touching the ornaments of the glass; if the latter, the top fits close to the wall.' (See also *Interiors*.)

Pier tables were intended for most of the main rooms of a smart house, especially drawing rooms, saloons, galleries and dining rooms as well as grand bedchambers if a commode (q.v.) did not fill the position. In the earlier and middle years of the century most were intended to be elaborately carved and gilded, often 'after the French manner' according to Batty Langley, who published designs for them after Pineau in 1739. They afforded a perfect opportunity for the virtuoso designers and carvers of the mid-eighteenth century working in the Rococo style — Matthias Lock, Thomas Johnson and Thomas Chippendale — who incorporated fantasy, fable and humour into these decorative objects. Most were made of soft woods, carved and gilded, with marble 'slab' tops: scagliola, mosaic and gilt gesso tops were also used. Some were made with four legs and were free standing against the wall; others had only front legs or a single support and were fixed at the back with brackets — usually called console tables. When new they were usually supplied with leather covers to protect the tops when not on show.

Later in the eighteenth century, when the Neo-classical style dominated English furniture, pier table designs became more delicate and although gilt examples were still intended for the grandest drawing-rooms, ones made of mahogany and satinwood with decorative marquetry also became fashionable: more designs for these were published by Hepplewhite and Sheraton. The latter also introduced designs for pier tables with mirror glass below the top and stretcher rails, which 'afforded an opportunity of fixing a vase or basket of flowers, which, with their reflection... produce a brilliant appearance' — a style that was developed during the early decades of the nineteenth century.

Daniel Marot
'Nouveaux Livre d'Orfeuverie', c.1703.

Daniel Marot
'Nouveaux Livre d'Orfeuverie', c.1703.

Plate 8. Design for a Pier Table, frame and stand.

Gaetano Brunetti
'Sixty Different Sorts of Ornament', 1736.

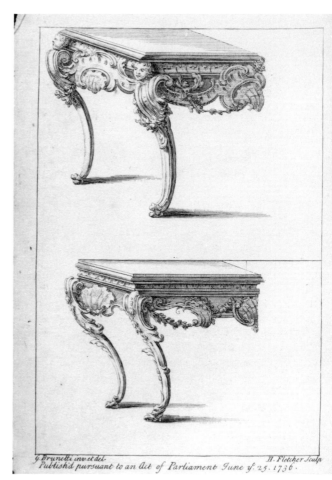

Pier Tables.

William Jones
'The Gentleman or Builder's Companion', 1739.

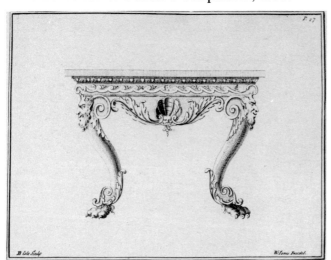

Plate 27. Pier Table.

Plate 28. Pier Table.

William Jones
'The Gentleman or Builder's Companion', 1739.

Plate 29. Pier Table.

Plate 30. Pier Table.

Plate 31. Pier Table.

Batty Langley (after Pineau)
'The City and Country Builder's and Workman's Treasury of Designs', 1740.

Plate 32. Pier Table.

'Frames for marble tables in Rooms of State, etc. Ten designs for the feet and frames of marble tables, after the French Manner.'

Plate CXLI. Marble Table.

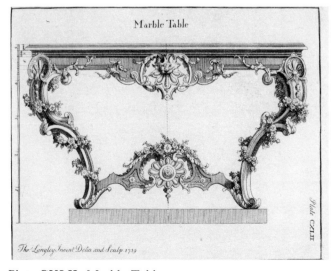

Plate CXLII. Marble Table.

Batty Langley
'The City and Country Builder's and Workman's Treasury of Designs', 1740.

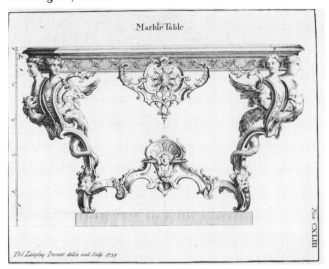

Plate CXLIII. Marble Table (after Pineau).

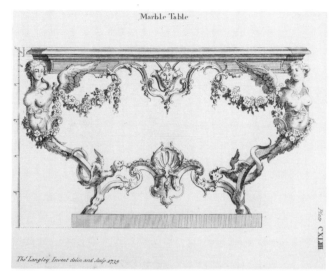

Plate CXLIV. Marble Table.

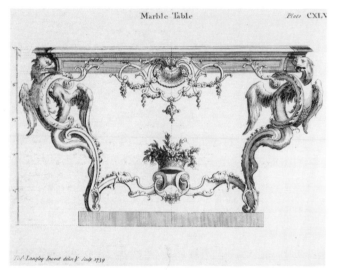

Plate CXLV. Marble Table.

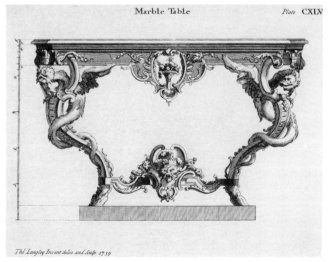

Plate CXLVI. Marble Table.

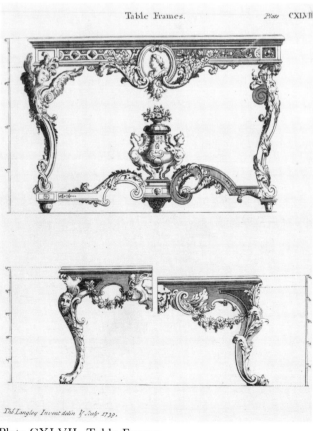

Plate CXLVII. Table Frames.

264

J. Vardy
'Some Designs of Mr. Inigo Jones and Mr. William Kent',
1744.

Plate 41. Table design for Lord Orford.

Plate 40. Table designed for Lord
Burlington at Chiswick.

Matthias Lock
'Six Tables', 1746.

Plate 2. Pier Table.

Plate 3. Pier Table.

Plate 4. Pier Table.

**Matthias Lock
'Six Tables', 1746.**

**M. Lock and H. Copland
'A New Book of Ornaments', 1752, re-issued by Sayer,
1768.**

Plate 5. Pier Tables.

Title-page from *A New Book of Ornaments.*

Plate 6. Pier Table and details of ornament.

Plate 2. Pier Table

266

Paul Babel
'A New Book of Ornaments', 1752.

Plate 4. Pier Table.

Thomas Chippendale
'The Gentleman and Cabinet-Maker's Director', 3rd Edition, 1763.

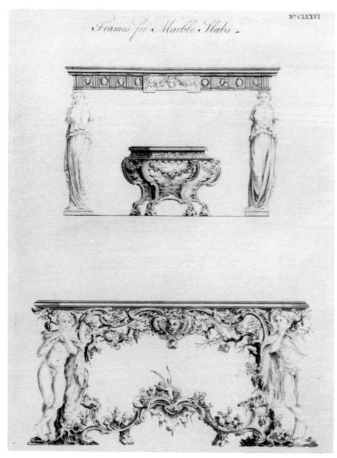

Plate CLXXVI. Frames for marble slabs. Engraving dated 1760.

Thomas Chippendale
'The Gentleman and Cabinet-Maker's Director', 1754.

Plate CXLVIII. Frames for marble slabs.

Plate CLXXV. Frames for marble slabs. Engraving dated 1760.

Thomas Chippendale
'The Gentleman and Cabinet-Maker's Director', 3rd Edition, 1763.

A Society of Upholsterers
'Genteel Household Furniture in the Present Taste', 2nd Edition, 1765.

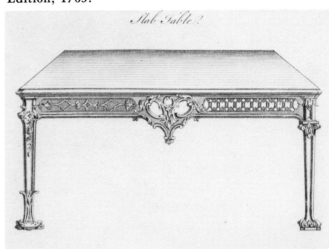

Plate 29 from Part II. Slab Table (attributed to Chippendale).

Plate CLXX. A Pier Glass Table. Engraving dated 1760.

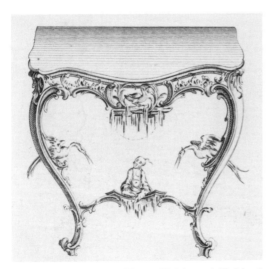

Plate 30 from Part II. A Sideboard Table (possibly contributed by Chippendale).

Plate 60 from Part II. Pier Tables (attributed to Thomas Johnson).

268

Thomas Johnson
'Collection of Designs', 1758, 'One Hundred and
Fifty New Designs', 1761.

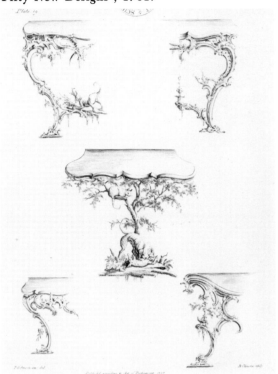

Plate 19 (1758), Plate 40 (1761). Designs for Pier
Tables.

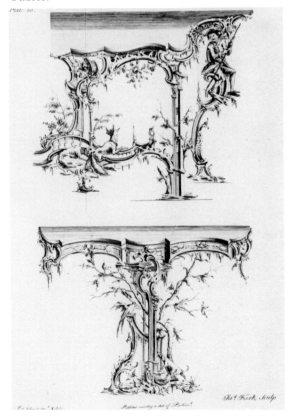

Plate 20 (1758), Plate 26 (1761). Designs for Pier
Tables.

Plate 18 (1758), Plate 54 (1761). Designs for Pier
Tables.

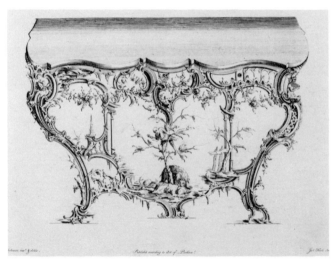

Plate 21 (1758), Plate 37 (1761). Designs for Pier
Tables.

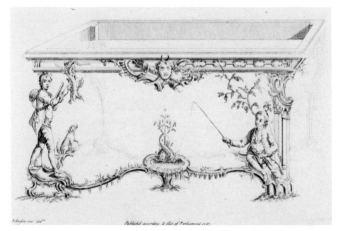

Plate 23 (1758), Plate 44 (1761). Designs for Pier
Tables.

Thomas Johnson
'Collection of Designs', 1758, 'One Hundred and Fifty New Designs', 1761.

Plate 22 (1758), Plate 12 (1761). Designs for Pier Tables.

William Ince and John Mayhew
'The Universal System of Houshold Furniture', 1762.

Plate LXXIII. Two Designs for Slab Frames, 'in Piers under Glasses'.

Plate 24 (1758), Plate 41 (1761). Designs for Pier Tables.

Plate LXXIV. Slab Frames.

270

William Ince and John Mayhew
'The Universal System of Houshold Furniture', 1762.

Plate LXXV. Slab Frames 'both of which must bè very elegant and grand, work'd by the hand of an ingenious Carver'.

Plate LXXXII. 'An elegant Pier Glass Frame, with Borders, a Slab Table under ditto'.

M. Lock
'A New Book of Pier Frames', 1769.

Plate 2.

Plate 3.

J. Carter
'The Builder's Magazine', 1776-7.

Plate CV. 'Table Frame, to be fixed to a Pier in a Dressing Room'. Engraving dated 1776.

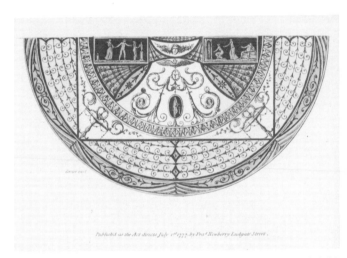

Plate CXXXII. Design for a Statuary Marble Table inlaid with Japan Paintings. Coloured engraving dated 1777.

R. & J. Adam
'Works in Architecture', Vol.II, 1777.

Plate IV from Vol.II No.IV. Pier Table in the Ante Room, Syon House.

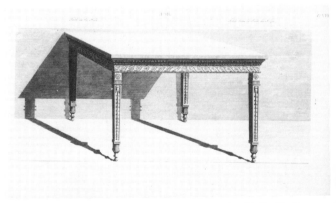

Plate VIII from Vol. II No.III. Table in the Hall, Shelburne House, Berkeley Square.

272

R. & J. Adam
'Works in Architecture', Vol.III, 1822.

Plate IX from Vol.III. Pier tables from Syon House.

Plate XI from Vol.III. Drawing Room Glass and Table, assigned for the Earl of Bute.

Plate VIII from Vol.I No.I, 1773. Table 'executed for us in Wood Gilt for Adelphi'.

Thomas Malton
'Compleat Treatise on Perspective', 2nd Edition, 1778.

A. Hepplewhite & Co.
'The Cabinet-Maker and Upholsterer's Guide', 1st Edition, 1788. 2nd Edition, 1789. 3rd Edition, 1794.

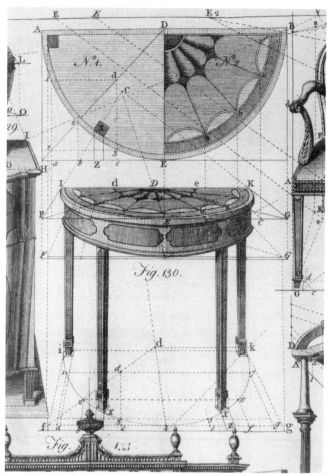

Plate XXXIV. Figure 130. Side Table 'according to the present taste'.

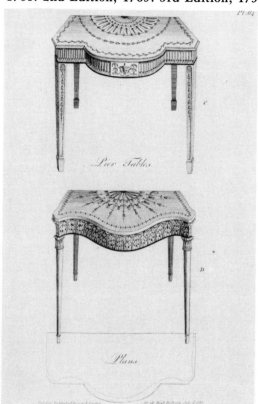

Plate 64.

Plate 65.

Plates 64 and 65. Pier Tables.
'Pier Tables are become an article of much fashion; and not being applied to such general use as other Tables, admit, with great propriety, of much elegance and ornament... The height of Pier Tables varies from the general rule, as they are now universally made to fit the pier, and rise level with or above the dado of the room, nearly touching the ornaments of the glass; if the latter, the top fits close to the wall.'

A. Hepplewhite & Co.
'The Cabinet-Maker and Upholsterer's Guide', 1st Edition, 1788. 2nd Edition, 1789. 3rd Edition, 1794.

Plate 66. Tops of Pier Table.

Thomas Sheraton
'The Cabinet-Maker and Upholsterer's Drawing Book', 1793.

Thomas Sheraton
'The Cabinet-Maker and Upholsterer's Drawing Book', 1793.

Plate IV from the Appendix. Pier Tables.
'As pier tables are merely for ornament under a glass, they are generally made very light, and the style of finishing them is rich and elegant. Sometimes the tops are solid marble, but most commonly veneered in rich satin, or other valuable wood, with a cross-band on the outside, a border about two inches richly japanned, and a narrow cross-band beyond it, to go all round. The frames are commonly gold, or white and burnished gold. Stretching-rails have of late been introduced to these tables, and it must be owned that it is with good effect, as they take off the long appearance of the legs, and make the under part appear more furnished; besides they afford an opportunity of fixing a vase or basket of flowers, which, with their reflection when there is a glass behind, produced a brilliant appearance.

Some, in place of a stretcher, have a thin marble shelf, with a brass rim round it, supported by a light frame; in which case the top ought to be of marble also.'

Plate 3 from the Accompaniment to the Drawing Book. Borders for Pier Tables, 'for japanning or inlaying'.

Thomas Sheraton
'The Cabinet-Maker and Upholsterer's Drawing Book',
1793.

Plate 7 from the Accompaniment to the Drawing Book.
Ornaments for the centre of a Pembroke and a Pier Table.

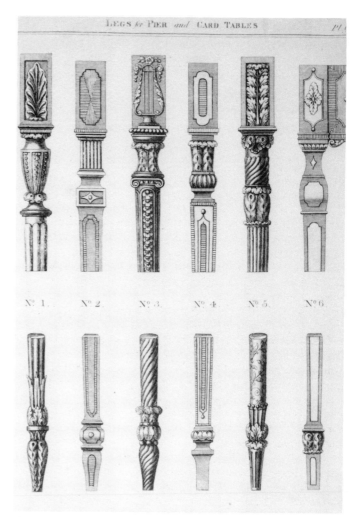

Plate 9 from the Accompaniment to the Drawing Book 'Toes
and knees for pier and card tables. No. 1, 3, 5 are meant for
pier tables, the ornaments of which are intended to be
carved and gilt. No. 2, 4, 6 are for card tables, with stringing
and pannels let in'.

Plate XXXI from the Appendix. A View of
the South End of the Prince of Wales'
Chinese Drawing Room '. . .the pier table
under the glass is richly ornamented in gold.
The top is marble, and also the shelf at each
end; the back of it is composed of three
pannels of glass, the Chinese figure sitting
on a cushion is metal and painted. The
candle branches are gilt metal, the pannels
painted in the style of the Chinese; the whole
producing a brilliant effect.'

Section 2. SIDEBOARD TABLES and SIDEBOARDS

For the greater part of the eighteenth century the term 'sideboard table' was used to refer to the tables, without drawers, which were placed against the walls of a dining room on which to display silver and gold plate, wine decanters and knife cases. They were similar in design to pier tables (q.v.) and frequently had marble, scagliola or mosaic 'slabs' or tops. Their carving and decoration tended to be more substantial and masculine in character, befitting the general decoration of dining rooms, and the emblems of Bacchus and Ceres were often present. Some frames were made of soft woods and gilded, but more often, from c.1740 onwards, they were made of mahogany and polished. Some designed by Robert Adam were executed in softwood and painted, for example at Osterley Park and Saltram House. They were intended to stand at the far end of a dining room where the plate could be shown to its best advantage, but pairs of such tables could also fill the piers. After c.1770 designs were published for accompanying sideboard pedestals and urns which contained water cisterns, knife cases, heated boxes and other necessities; these appear regularly in Adam's designs and were well described by Hepplewhite (Plates 35, 36 of the *Guide*). Beneath the table itself stood a wine cistern, usually decorated *en suite* with the table and pedestals. This ensemble remained a standard feature of the large dining room until the end of the century.

In smaller dining rooms of the later eighteenth century, a new type of 'sideboard' was introduced which incorporated the facilities of the pedestals in cupboards and drawers beneath the top: Hepplewhite commented that 'the great utility of this piece of furniture has procured it a very general

reception, and the conveniences it affords renders a dining-room incomplete without a sideboard.' They were usually made of mahogany, and had partitions for bottles and napkins, a tin-lined cupboard for warming plates, a basin for washing glasses and even a pot cupboard. These were referred to in the *Cabinet-Maker's London Book of Prices* as 'celleret sideboards', and Sheraton published designs for ones with brass rods above the top at the back, against which to rest the plate on display. The tops themselves tended to be of mahogany rather than marble. Knife cases were also displayed on the top, either in the shapes of urns with rising tops, or squarer boxes with sloping lids, both of which had green baize linings and compartments for the knives.

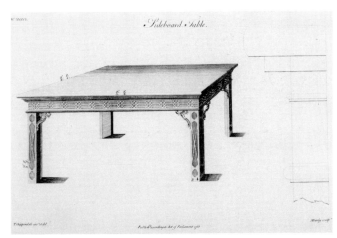

Plate XXXVI. Sideboard Table. Plate LVII, 3rd Edition, 1763.

Thomas Chippendale
'The Gentleman and Cabinet-Maker's Director', 1754.

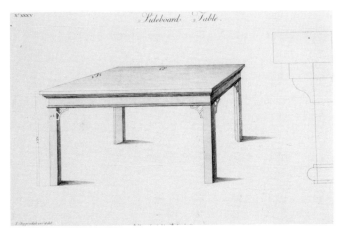

Plate XXXV. Sideboard Table. Plate LVI, 3rd Edition, 1763.

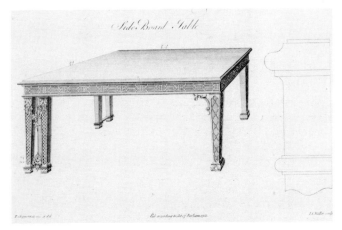

Plate XXXVII. Sideboard Table. Plate LVIII, 3rd Edition, 1763.

277

Thomas Chippendale
'The Gentleman and Cabinet-Maker's Director', 1754.

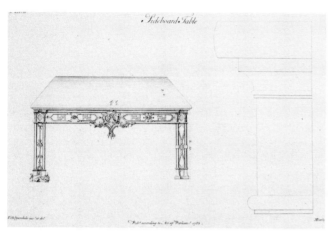

Plate XXXVIII. Sideboard Table. Plate LIX, 3rd Edition, 1763. 'The feet and rails... are cut through; which gives it an airy look, but will be too slight for marble tops, therefore the tops will be better made of wood.'

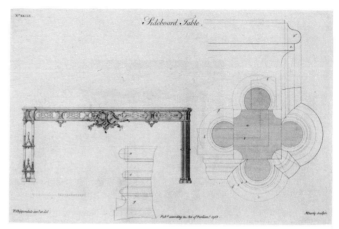

Plate XXXIX. Sideboard Table. Plate LX, 3rd Edition, 1763.

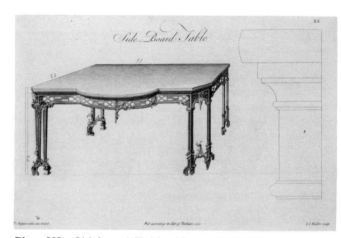

Plate XL. Sideboard Table. Not in 3rd Edition.

Thomas Chippendale
'The Gentleman and Cabinet-Maker's Director', 3rd Edition, 1763.

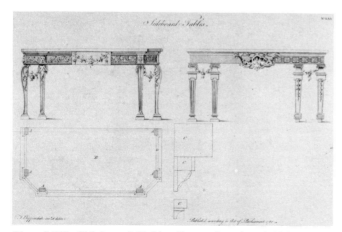

Plate LXI. Sideboard Table. Engraving dated 1760.

A Society of Upholsterers
'Genteel Houshold Furniture in the Present Taste', 2nd Edition, 1765.

William Ince and John Mayhew
'The Universal System of Houshold Furniture', 1762.

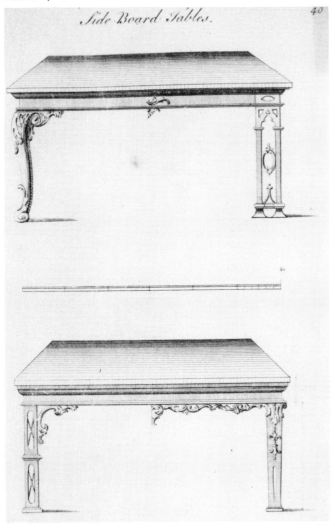

Plate 40 from Part II. Sideboard Tables. Designer unidentified.

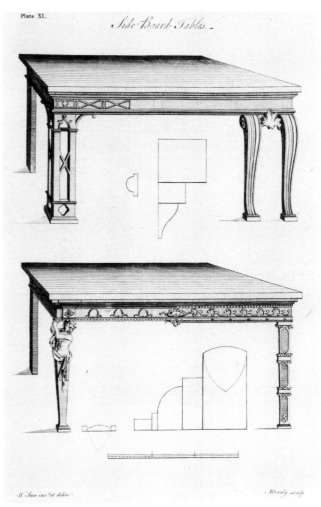

Plate XI. Sideboard Tables.

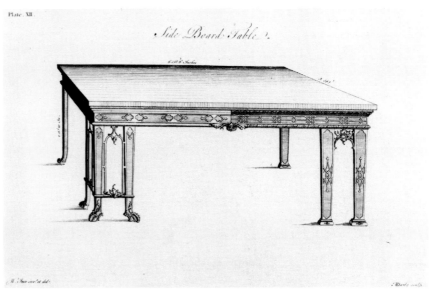

Plate XII. Sideboard Tables.

Plate VIII from Vol.I No.II. Dining Room Sideboard and
Pedestals, designed for Kenwood.

Plate VIII from Vol.III, 1822. Sideboard and Wine Cooler,
designed for Syon House, and to the right and above details
of Sideboard Pedestals.

J. Carter
'The Builder's Magazine', 1776.

Thomas Malton
'Compleat Treatise on Perspective', 2nd Edition, 1788.

Plate CVI. Design for a Sideboard.

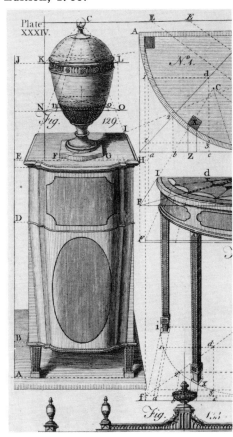

Plate XXXIV. Figure 129. Pedestal and Vase.

W. Thomas
'Original Designs in Architecture', 1783.

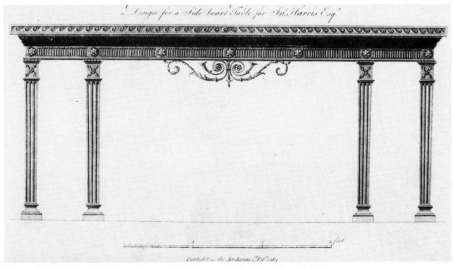

Plate XXVII. Design for a Sideboard Table, for John Harris Esquire.

A. Hepplewhite & Co.
'The Cabinet-Maker and Upholsterer's Guide', 1st Edition, 1788. 2nd Edition, 1789. 3rd Edition, 1794.

Plate 29. Sideboard. 'The great utility of this piece of furniture has procured it a very general reception, and the conveniences it affords renders a dining room incomplete without a sideboard.'

'The right hand drawer has partitions for nine bottles; behind this is a place for cloths or napkins.' Left hand drawer with 2 divisions, 'the hinder one lined with green cloth to hold plate etc under a cover; the front one is lined with lead for the convenience of holding water to wash glasses etc, — there must be a valve-cock or plug at the bottom, to let off the dirty water.' Table linen to go in centre drawer.

Measurements: generally 5-7ft. long, 3ft. high, 28-32ins. wide.

Plate 30. Sideboard.

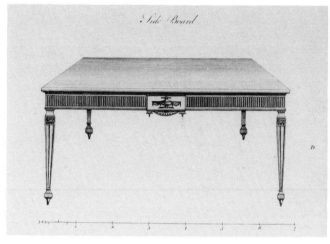

Plates 31-34. Sideboard Tables. 'The ornaments to the fronts of which may be carved, painted, or inlaid with various coloured woods.'

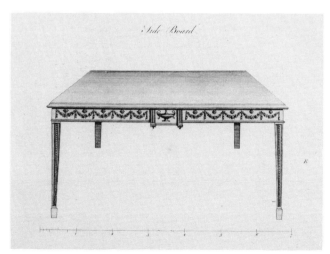

Plate 32. Sideboard.

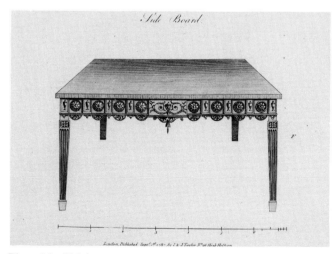

Plate 33. Sideboard.

282

A. Hepplewhite & Co.
'The Cabinet-Maker and Upholsterer's Guide', 1st
Edition, 1788. 2nd Edition, 1789. 3rd Edition, 1794.

Plate 34. Sideboard.

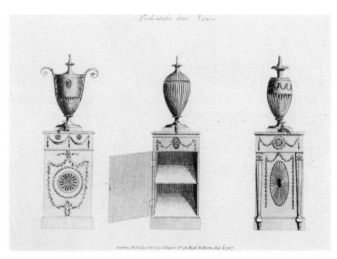

Plates 35 and 36. Pedestals and vases. 'much used in
spacious dining-rooms' (on either side of sideboard tables).
'One pedestal serves as a plate-warmer, being provided with
racks and a stand for a heater, and is lined with strong tin;
the other pedestal is used as a pot cupboard.

'The vases may be used to hold water for the use of the
butler, or iced water for drinking, which is enclosed in an
inner partition, the ice surrounding it; or may be used as
knife-cases, in which case they are made of wood, carved,
painted, or inlaid; if used for water may be made of wood
or of copper japanned. The height of the pedestal is the same
as the sideboard, and 16 or 18 inches square; the height of
the vase about 2 feet 3 inches.'

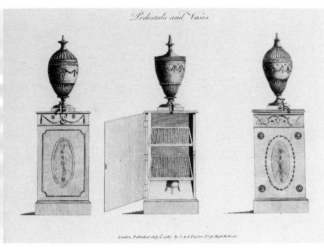

Plate 36.

'The Cabinet-Maker's London Book of Prices', 1788.
2nd Edition, 1793. 3rd Edition, 1803.

Plate 1. Figure 2. A Round-Front Celleret Sideboard.
Designed by Shearer, with 'a deep drawer at one end
prepared for the plumber'. 5ft. long, 2ft. 6in. wide. Plain
Marlborough legs. Basic cost £2.2.0.

Plate 4. Figure 1. A Serpentine Front Celleret Sideboard.
Designed by Shearer. 5ft. long, 2ft. 6in. wide. Basic cost
£3.3.0.

Plate 5. Figure 1. Circular Celleret Sideboard. Designed by Shearer. 5ft. long. Plain Marlborough legs. Basic cost £2.16.0.

Figure 2. A Celleret Sideboard, with Eliptic Middle, and Eliptic Hollow on each side (r.h. end) an ogee on each side (l.h. end). Designed by Shearer. Basic cost £3.6.0.

Plate 6. Sideboard with cellerets and urns. Designed by Shearer. 2nd Edition, 1793.

Thomas Sheraton
'The Cabinet-Maker and Upholsterer's Drawing Book',
1793.

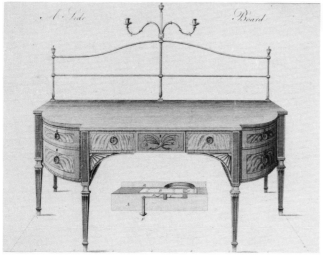

Plate 26 from Part III. A Sideboard 'has a brass rod to it, which is used to set large dishes against, and to support a couple of candle or lamp branches in the middle which, when lighted, give a very brilliant effect to the silver ware...

These rods have sometimes returns at each end of the sideboard; and sometimes they are made straight, the whole length of the sideboard, and have a narrow shelf in the middle, made of full half-inch mahogany, for the purpose of setting smaller dishes on, and sometimes small silver ware.

The right-hand drawer, as in common, contains the celleret... partitioned and lined with lead, to hold nine or ten wine bottles...

The drawer on the left is generally plain, but sometimes divided into two; the back division being lined with baize to hold plates, having a cover hinged to enclose the whole. The front division is lined with lead, so that it may hold water to wash glasses; which may be made to take out, or have a plug-hole to let off the dirty water' (or a pot cupboard at the very back in a little cupboard behind the drawer).

'In spacious dining-rooms the sideboards are often made without drawers of any sort, having simply a rail a little ornamented, and pedestals with bases at each end, which produce a grand effect. One pedestal is used as a plate-warmer, and is lined with tin; the other as a pot-cupboard, and sometimes it contains a celleret for wine. The vases are used for water for the use of the butler, and sometimes as knife-cases. They are sometimes made of copper japanned, but generally of mahogany.'

284

Thomas Sheraton
'The Cabinet-Maker and Upholsterer's Drawing Book',
1793.

Plate 29 from Part III. Sideboard Table: design at left end 'is intended to have four marble shelves at each end, inclosed by two backs, and open in front. These shelves are used in grand sideboards to place the small silver ware on...

'It is not usual to make sideboards hollow in front, but in some circumstances it is evident that advantages will arise from it. If a sideboard be required nine or ten feet long, as in some noblemen's houses, and if the breadth be in proportion to the length, it will not be easy for a butler to reach across it.... a hollow front would obviate this difficulty, and at the same time have a very good effect, by taking off part of the appearance of the great length of such a sideboard. Besides, if the sideboard be near the entering-door of the dining-room, the hollow front will sometimes secure the butler from the jostles of the other servants.'

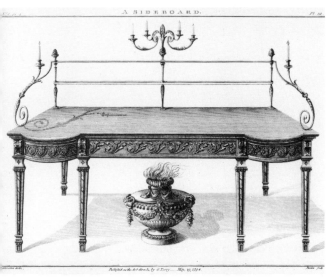

Plate 21 from the Appendix. Sideboard with Vase Knife Cases... 'the pedestal parts of this Sideboard may be made separate, and then screwed to the Sideboard...'. Engraving dated 1793.

Plate 31. A Sideboard, with mahogany wine box or 'merely ornamented vase'. This was an additional new plate for the 1794 2nd Edition. Engraving dated 1793.

Thomas Chippendale
'The Gentleman and Cabinet-Maker's Director', 1762.
3rd Edition.

Plate CLI. Cisterns or Wine Coolers.

285

A. Hepplewhite & Co.
'The Cabinet-Maker and Upholsterer's Guide', 1st Edition,
1788. 2nd Edition, 1789. 3rd Edition, 1794.

Plate 37. Cellerets.
'Called also *gardes de vin*, are generally made of mahogany
and hooped with brass hoops lacquered; the inner part i
divided with partitions, and lined with lead for bottles; may
be made of any shape. These are of general use where
sideboards are without drawers; the proportion may be
known by applying the scale.'

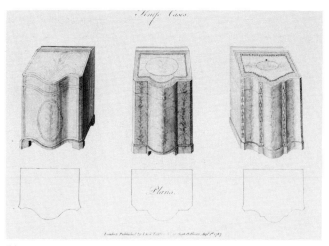

Plates 38 and 39. Knife Cases.
'The universal utility of this piece of furniture renders a
particular description not necessary. Those on plate 38 may
be made of mahogany inlaid, or of satin, or other wood at
pleasure.

'Four designs for *Vase knife-cases* are given on plate 39; they
are usually made of satin or other light-coloured wood, and
may be placed at each end on the sideboards, or on a
pedestal; the knives, &c. fall into the body of the vase, the
top of which is kept up by a small spring which is fixed to
the stem which supports the top; may be made of copper,
painted and japanned.'

Thomas Sheraton
'The Cabinet-Maker and Upholsterer's Drawing Book',
1793.

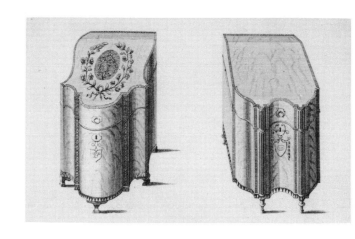

Plate XXXIX from Part III. Knife Cases. 'Little need be
said respecting these... the top is sometimes japanned, and
sometimes has only an inlaid patera... The feet may be
turned and twisted, which will have a good effect.'

'As these cases are not made in regular cabinet shops, it
may be of service to mention where they are executed in the
best taste, by one who makes it his main business; i.e. John
Lane, No.44, St. Martin's Le Grand, London.'

Section 3. BREAKFAST, TEA, SUPPER and DINING TABLES

A variety of small tables were made in the eighteenth century on which food and drink were placed, and a few designs for them were published. They were intended for use in parlours, sitting rooms and bedrooms for light meals taken privately, in contrast to the tables regularly placed in dining rooms for the main meal of the day, which was a more formal and public occasion. In the early and middle years of the century a standard type was the 'claw table', with a small-diameter hinged top raised above a carved single pillar and tripod base, which could be used for breakfast or tea, and when not in use could be stored in the corner of a room or passage with the top tilted up. Another type was the breakfast table, illustrated by Chippendale, with hinged flaps to the top and a 'cage' enclosed by wire netting below, where a tray might be stored after use; some of these tables were provided with a drawer equipped for writing as well, and are occasionally referred to (erroneously) as 'hound tables'. Chippendale also published designs for 'China Tables' with galleried edges, intended to hold the equipage of delicate Oriental porcelain tea cups, while the tea kettle or urn stood on a small stand nearby (see *Stands*).

A more standard type of breakfast table in the second half of the century was the 'Pembroke' table, also with hinged flaps and a single drawer beneath the top, suitable, according to Sheraton, 'for a lady or gentleman to breakfast on', and which could be elegantly decorated with marquetry, painted designs, stringing and finely chased brass mounts. A variation on the Pembroke table was the 'Harlequin Table', which included a box of small pigeon-holes and drawers which rose through the top on a system of springs or weights — a device much liked by Sheraton, who also developed the theme with his 'Universal Table', intended for breakfast, tea and dining for up to eight people.

Designs for the standard types of dining tables were not included in the pattern books — neither gate-leg tables, nor extending tables with D-shaped ends and straight boards supported on pillars or gate-legs, with the exception of Sheraton's illustration of the dining room 'in imitation of the Prince of Wales's' at Carlton House. Designs by Shearer for a 'Horsehoe Dining Table', appeared in *The Cabinet-Maker's London Book of Prices* in 1788.

A Society of Upholsterers
'Genteel Houshold Furniture in the Present Taste', 2nd Edition, c.1765.

Plate 38 from Part II. Claw Tables, possibly by Ince and Mayhew.

William Ince and John Mayhew
'The Universal System of Houshold Furniture', 1762.

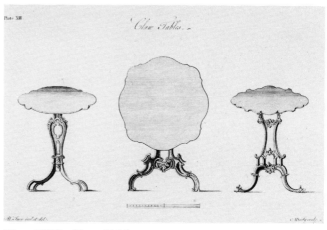

Plate XIII. Claw Tables.

Thomas Malton
'Compleat Treatise on Perspective', 1775.

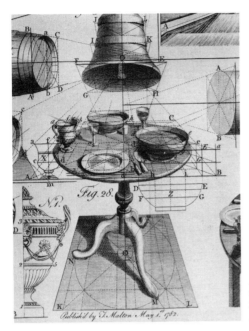

Plate IV. Figure 28 from the Appendix. Supper Tables.

Thomas Chippendale
'The Gentleman and Cabinet-Maker's Director', 1754. 3rd Edition, 1763.

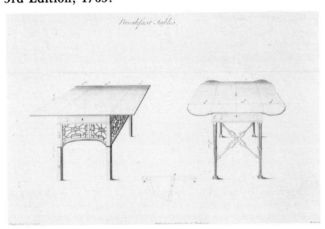

Plate XXXIII. Breakfast Tables.

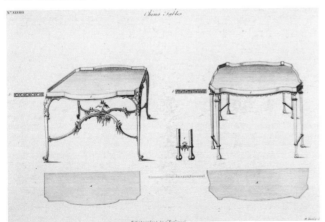

Plate XXXIV. China Tables.

Thomas Sheraton
'The Cabinet-Maker and Upholsterer's Drawing Book', 1793.

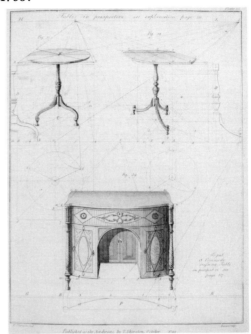

Plate 25 from Part II. Tables in Perspective and Commode Dressing Table in Perspective.

A. Hepplewhite & Co.
'The Cabinet-Maker and Upholsterer's Guide', 1st Edition, 1788. 2nd Edition, 1789. 3rd Edition, 1794.

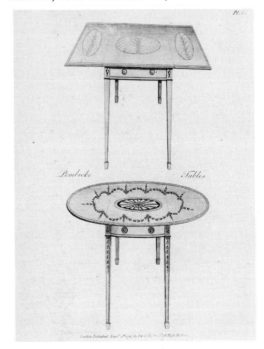

Plate 62. Pembroke Tables. 'Pembroke Tables are the most useful of this species of furniture: they may be of various shapes. The long square and oval are the most fashionable. These articles admit of considerable elegance in the workmanship and ornaments.

A. Hepplewhite & Co.
'The Cabinet-Maker and Upholsterer's Guide', 1st Edition, 1788. 2nd Edition, 1789. 3rd Edition, 1794.

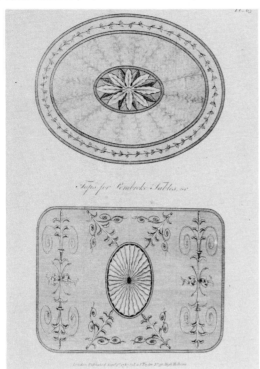

Plate 63. Tops for Pembroke Tables. 'Proper for tops, inlaid, or painted and varnished.'

Thomas Sheraton
'The Cabinet-Maker and Upholsterer's Drawing Book', 1793.

Thomas Sheraton
'The Cabinet-Maker and Upholsterer's Drawing Book', 1793.

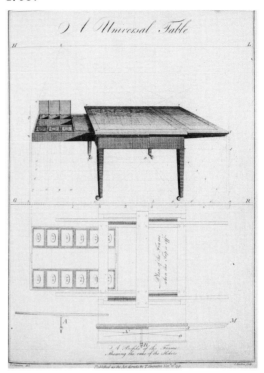

Plate XXV from Part II. A Universal Table.
'The use of this piece is both to answer the purpose of a breakfast and dining-table. When both the leaves are slipped under the bed, it will then serve as a breakfast-table; when one leaf is out, as in this view, it will accommodate five persons as a dining-table; and if both are out, it will admit of eight, being near seven feet long, and three feet six inches in width.

'The drawer is divided into six boxes at each side, as in the plan, and are found useful for different sorts of tea and sugar, and sometimes for notes, and the like. In this drawer is a slider lined with green cloth to write on. The style of finishing them is plain and simple, with straight tapered legs, socket castors, and an astragel around the frame.

'This table should be made of particularly good and well-seasoned mahogany, as a great deal depends upon its not being liable to cast...'.

'... The covers of each box before mentioned, may have an oval of dark wood, and the alphabet cut out of ivory or white wood let into them, as in the plan; or they may be white ovals and black letters; the use of which is to distinguish the contents of each box.'

Plate LIV from Part III. Pembroke Table. 'The use of this piece is for a gentleman or lady to breakfast on. The style of finishing these tables is very neat, sometimes bordering upon elegance, being at times made of satin-wood, and having richly japanned borders around their tops, with ornamented drawer-fronts.

Thomas Sheraton
'The Cabinet-Maker and Upholsterer's Drawing Book', 1793.

The Cabinet-Maker's London Book of Prices', 1788. 2nd Edition 1793, 3rd Edition 1803.

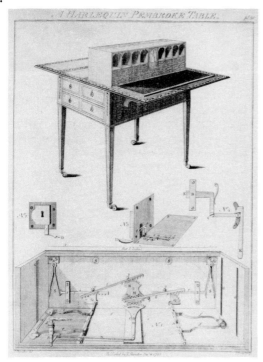

Plate LVI from Part III. Harlequin Pembroke Table. 'This piece serves not only as a breakfast, but also as a writing-table, very suitable for a lady. It is termed a Harlequin Table, for no other reason but because, in exhibitions of that sort, there is generally a great deal of machinery introduced into the scenery.

Tables like this have already been made, but not according to the improved plan of the machinery here proposed.'

Plate 19, Figure 1. Horseshoe Dining Table, designed by Shearer. '7ft. long, 2ft. 6in. wide...'. Basic cost £2.5.0.

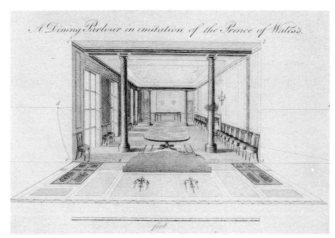

Plate LX from Part III. 'Dining Parlour in imitation of the Prince of Wales's.'

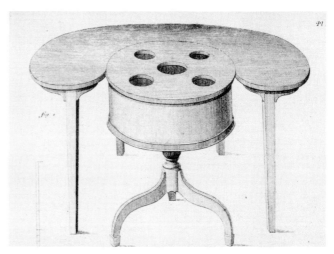

Plate 22, Figure 1. A Gentleman's Social Table, designed by Hepplewhite. Basic cost £1.8.0. In 2nd Edition, 1793.

Section 4. WRITING, DRAWING and WORK TABLES
(with rising tops)

Various designers published patterns for tables with rising hinged tops which are sometimes referred to as 'Architects' Tables'. They were probably intended to be placed in gentlemen's libraries and could take the largest sheets of paper available. Designs were also produced for other smaller tables for reading, writing and working at, especially towards the end of the century, replacing the standard type of multi-purpose claw table of earlier decades, and their decoration could be quite elaborate, with silk drapery and delicate inlays and brass mounts.

Thomas Chippendale
'The Gentleman and Cabinet-Maker's Director', 1754.

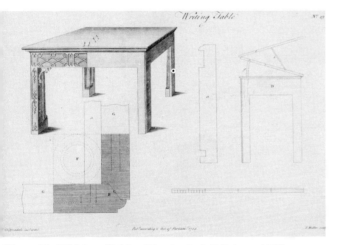

Plate 49. Writing Table. Not in 3rd Edition, 1763.

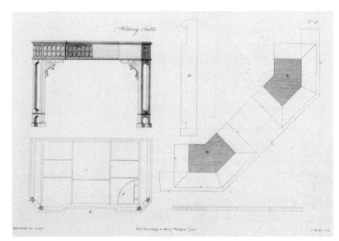

Plate 50. Writing Table. Plate LXXIII in 3rd Edition, 1763.

A Society of Upholsterers
'Genteel Household Furniture in the Present Taste', 2nd Edition, c.1765.

Plate 51. Writing Table. Plate LXXIV in 3rd Edition, 1763.

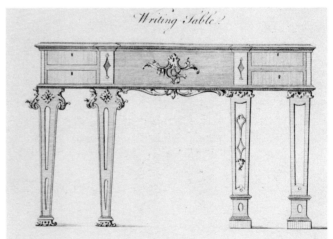

Plate 31 from Part II. Writing Table, attributed to Chippendale.

William Ince and John Mayhew
'The Universal System of Houshold Furniture', 1762.

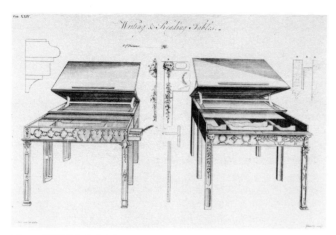

Plate XXIV. Writing and Reading Tables.

Thomas Sheraton
'The Cabinet-Maker and Upholsterer's Drawing Book',
1793.

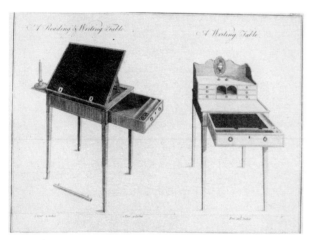

Plate XLIV from Part III. Writing and Reading Tables. Right hand table '... being made for the convenience of moving from one room to another, there is a handle fixed on to the upper shelf, as the drawing shews...'.

Plate XXVI from Appendix. Ladies' Work Tables.

Thomas Sheraton
'The Cabinet-Maker and Upholsterer's Drawing Book',
1793.

Plate XLIII from Part III. Screen Table. 'This Table is intended for a lady to write or work at near the fire; the screen part behind securing her face from its injuries...'.

Plate LIV from Part III. Work table or 'French Work Table'. 'The style of finishing them is neat, being commonly made of satinwood, with a brass moulding round the edge of the rim.'

Plate XXX from Appendix. Drawing Table. '... as it is sometimes necessary to copy from models or flower-pots etc., a small flap may be made to draw out of the top...'.

Section 5. CARD TABLES

Card tables were usually made with folding tops and, according to Hepplewhite, 'may be either square, circular or oval; the inner part is lined with green cloth; the fronts may be enriched with inlaid or painted ornaments; the tops also admit of great elegance in the same styles'. As they were intended for use in drawing rooms during the evening, their decoration was to be suitable to other furniture in those rooms, and when not in use they could be folded up and stored at the sides of the room or in the passage outside. Ince and Mayhew included a design for a triangular tilt-top card table in a pillar support, for use in three-handed games. Some were fitted with concave 'dishes' for coins or counters, and plain wooden circles on which to place candlesticks. Early in the century they were made of walnut, then after c.1740 of rich coloured mahogany. After c.1760 a variety of woods were used, both for structure and decoration, including lighter Honduras mahogany, satinwood, rosewood and harewood. Some were fitted with two hinged flaps, one lined with baize, the other with a wooden surface.

A Society of Upholsterers
'Genteel Household Furniture in the Present Taste', 2nd Edition, c.1765.

William Ince and John Mayhew
'The Universal System of Houshold Furniture', 1762.

Plate 36 from Part II. Card Tables. Designer unknown.

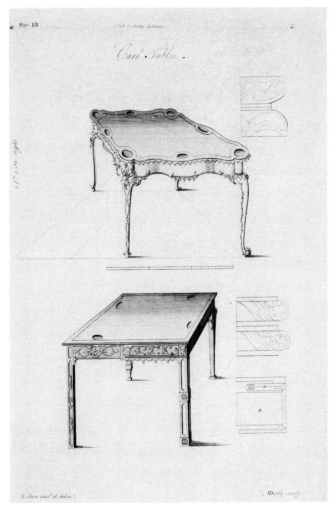

Plate LII. Card Tables.

William Ince and John Mayhew
'The Universal System of Houshold Furniture', 1762.

Plate LIII. Card Tables.

A. Hepplewhite & Co.
'The Cabinet-Maker and Upholsterer's Guide', 1st Edition,
1788. 2nd Edition, 1789. 3rd Edition, 1794.

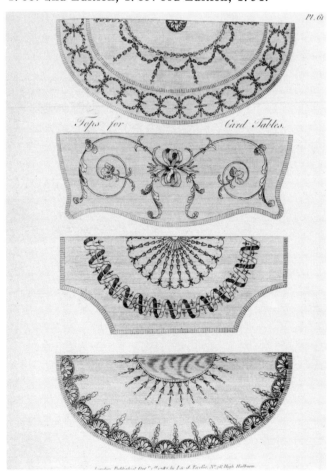

Plate 61. Tops for Card Tables. '... four designs proper for inlaid or painted tops for Card Tables.'

A. Hepplewhite & Co.
'The Cabinet-Maker and Upholsterer's Guide', 1st Edition,
1788. 2nd Edition, 1789. 3rd Edition, 1794.

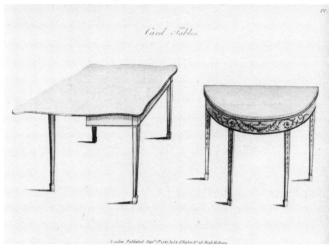

Plate 60. Card Tables.
'... in general, Tables are made of the best mahogany. Their size very various, but their height should not exceed 28 inches.'
Card Tables 'may be either square, circular or oval; the inner part is lined with green cloth; the fronts may be enriched with inlaid or painted ornaments; the tops also admit of great elegance in the same styles.'

Thomas Sheraton
'The Cabinet-Maker and Upholsterer's Drawing Book',
1793.

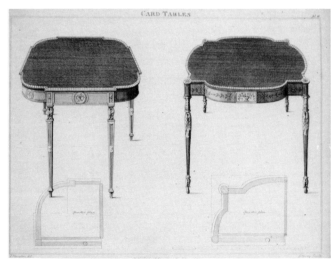

Plate XI from the Appendix. Card Tables. '... the ornaments may be japanned on the frames and carved in the legs...'.

Section 6. TABLES for SUMMER HOUSES, GARDENS, GROTTOS and MISCELLANEOUS

Some eighteenth century publications included designs for tables for gardens, summer houses, hermitages and grottoes and which reflected contemporary taste in such structures: some were classical, others inspired by Chinese examples such as those illustrated by Chambers (1757) which he claimed 'are pretty, and may be useful to our cabinet-makers', and some were considerably more bizarre, like Edwards' and Darly's 'root-table', or those designs published anonymously in about 1790, which, with the corresponding chairs, were intended for hermitages or root-houses.

James Gibbs
'Book of Architecture', 1728.

Plate 147. Designs for marble or stone tables for gardens or summer houses.

Batty Langley
'The City and Country Builder's and Workman's Treasury of Designs', 1740.

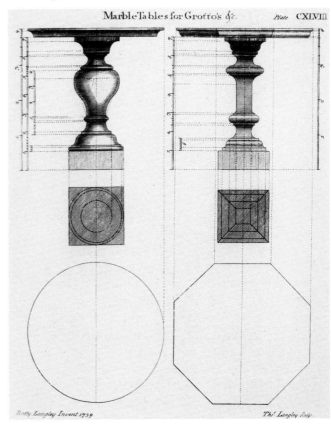

Plate CXLVIII. Marble Tables for Grottos, etc.

Edwards & Darly
'A New Book of Chinese Designs', 1754.

'Conversation'.

'Conversation'.

'Trade'.

Edwards & Darly
'A New Book of Chinese Designs',
1754.

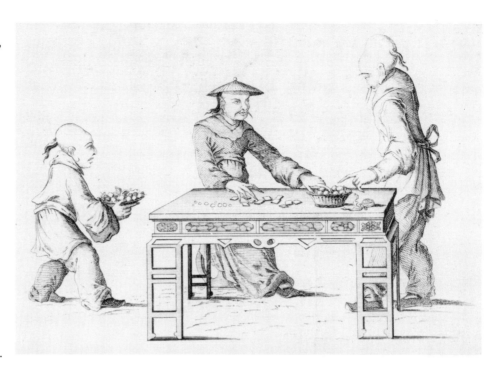

'Trade'.

William Chambers
'Designs of Chinese Buildings', 1757.

Edwards & Darly
'A New Book of Chinese Designs',
1754.

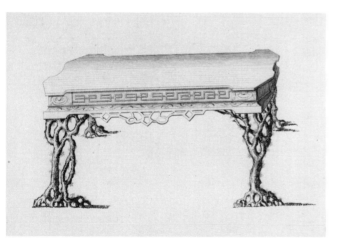

Plate 37. Table.

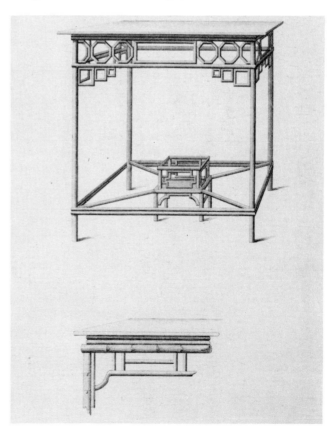

One of the three designs for tables.
'Those of the furniture were taken from such models as appeared to me the most beautiful and reasonable; some of them are pretty, and may be useful to our Cabinet-Makers.'

William Chambers
'Designs of Chinese Buildings', 1757.

Two more designs for tables.

Anon
'Ideas for Rustic Furniture', c.1790.

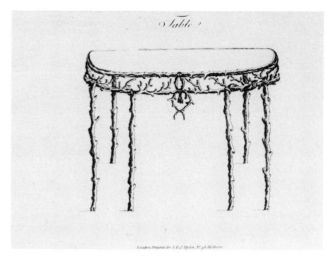

Plate 15. Table.

Plate 16. Table.

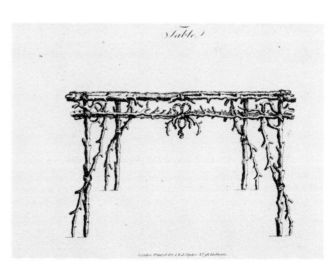

Plate 17. Table.

298

II. STANDS

Numerous designs for various types of stands filled the pages of eighteenth century furniture pattern books, and provided a fine opportunity, particularly in the middle of the century, for virtuoso carving. The more solid pedestals were intended to carry marble busts or urns, and, according to Hepplewhite, 'their height must be regulated by the subject they are intended to support. The height, for a bust as large as life, is between three and four feet.'

Candlestands were much more elaborately carved, and because they needed to support only a little weight, they could be pierced through to an almost extreme degree. Here, the Rococo designers and carvers had the greatest freedom of fancy, and their patterns included Chinese temples and figures, rustic dwellings, fabled creatures, and naturalistic ornament such as trees, water, leaves and flowers. Some were intended to be gilded, or part gilded and part painted white, while others were decorated in more naturalistic colours. Sometimes the candle branches and holders were made of gesso-covered and gilded wire. The simpler stands composed of carved C- and S-scrolls and acanthus leaves were made of plain polished mahogany. They were usually made in pairs and designed to stand on either side of a pier table: the light from their candelabra, reflected in a pier glass, would thus be thrown into a room from the same position as daylight, an important consideration for the hanging of pictures. Some stands were also intended to be placed in the inner corners of rooms to provide additional night light, or, as Hepplewhite wrote, 'may be placed in any part at pleasure — in drawing rooms, halls, or on staircases, they are frequently used.'

A few simple designs for music or reading stands were published: these had pillars which could be adjusted in height and sloping desks to hold music pages or books. Various designs were also included in the pattern books for stands supporting Oriental porcelain jars, classical urns and figures, most of which were of fairly solid construction in order to carry considerable weights.

More delicate were the designs for small tea-kettle stands: these were either circular, with tripod bases, or square, and had a raised or galleried edge to the small top to prevent a silver kettle and spirit burner sliding off, or water spilling over. They were intended to stand next to the tea table in a drawing room or parlour and were stored in a corner or passage when not in use.

Many designs for fire-screens were published, usually of two types — a pole screen, standing on a tripod base with sliding panel on the pole, or a 'Horse Fire Screen' or cheval screen with a rectangular panel supported on legs at either side. The panels were intended to take painted designs, embroideries, japanning, lacquer, straw-work, cut-paperwork or almost any other fanciful decoration and were often the work of gifted amateurs.

Some designs for stands or bases for garden sundials were also published and, although intended to be made of stone and not strictly wood-carvers' work, they are included here.

Section 1.
PEDESTALS FOR BUSTS

James Gibbs
'Book of Architecture', 1728. 2nd Edition, 1739.

Plate 150. Fifteen pedestals for busts.

Thomas Chippendale
'The Gentleman and Cabinet-Maker's
Director', 3rd Edition, 1763.

Plate CXLVII. Terms for Busts etc.
Engraving dated 1760.

A Society of Upholsterers
'Genteel Houshold Furniture in The Present Taste', 2nd
Edition, c.1765.

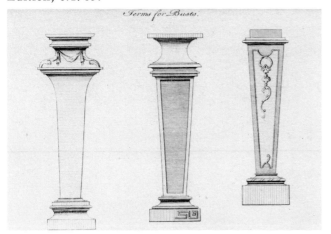

Plate 86 from Part III. Stands, attributed to Ince and Mayhew.

Plate 87 from Part III. Stands, attributed to Ince and Mayhew.

William Ince and John Mayhew
'The Universal System of Houshold
Furniture', 1762.

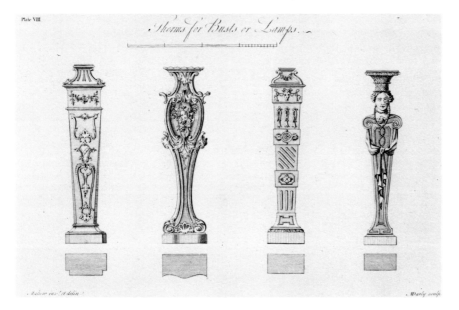

Plate VIII. Terms for Busts or Lamps.

300

J. Carter
'The Builder's Magazine', 1778.

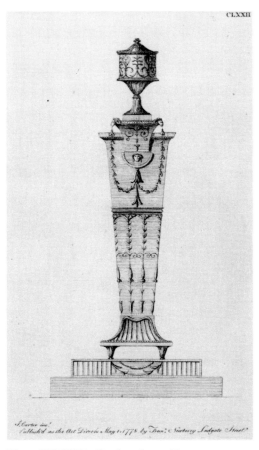

Plate CLXXII. Design for a Term.

A. Hepplewhite & Co.
'The Cabinet-Maker and Upholsterer's Guide', 1st Edition, 1788. 2nd Edition, 1789. 3rd Edition, 1794.

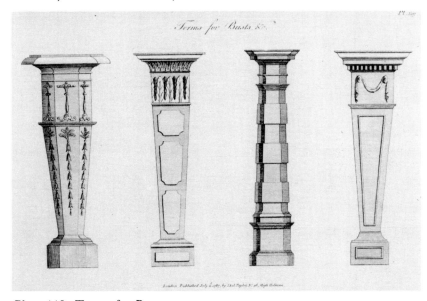

Plate 119. Terms for Busts, etc.

'. . . they are generally made of mahogany, with the ornaments carved; their height must be regulated by the subject they are intended to support. The height for a bust as large as life is between 3 and 4 feet. . . .'.

Plate 120. Terms for Busts, etc.

Section 2. CANDLE STANDS

Daniel Marot
'Nouveaux Livre d'Orfeuverie', 1703, 1713.

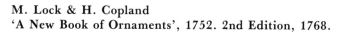

Plate 3. Candle Stands.

Plate 8. Table, Frame and Candle Stands.

M. Lock & H. Copland
'A New Book of Ornaments', 1752. 2nd Edition, 1768.

Plate 8. Candle Stand.
1st Edition.

Plate 9. Candle Stand. Re-issued by
Sayer, 1768, with alterations.

Edwards & Darly
'A New Book of Chinese Designs', 1754.

Plate 24. Candelabra Stands.

Plate 27. Candelabra Stands.

Plate 27. Candelabra Stands, from another copy of the same book.

Thomas Chippendale
'The Gentleman and Cabinet-Maker's Director', 1754.

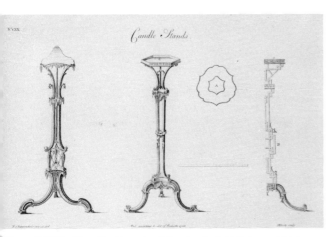

Plate CXX. Candle Stands. Not in 3rd Edition, 1763.

Plate CXXI. Candle Stands. Not in 3rd Edition, 1763.

Thomas Chippendale
'The Gentleman and Cabinet-Maker's Director', 1754.

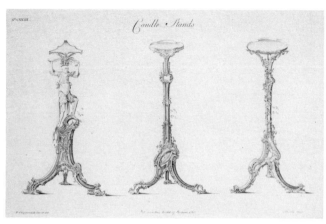

Plate CXXII. Candle Stands. Plate CXLVI in 3rd Edition, 1763.

Plate CXXIII. Candle Stands. Not in 3rd Edition, 1763.

Thomas Johnson
'Collection of Designs', 1758, 'One Hundred and Fifty New Designs', 1761.

Plate 13 (1758), Plate 39 (1761). Candle Stands.

Plate 14 (1758), Plate 56 (1761). Candle Stands.

Plate 15 (1758), Plate 25 (1761). Candle Stands.

Thomas Chippendale
'The Gentleman and Cabinet-Maker's Director', 3rd Edition, 1763.

Plate LXXI. Two different designs for Candle Stands. Engraving dated 1761.

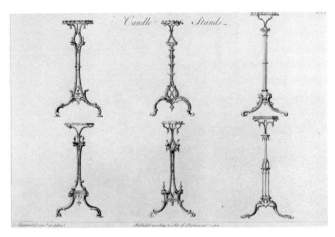

Plate CXLIV. Candle Stands. Engraving dated 1760.

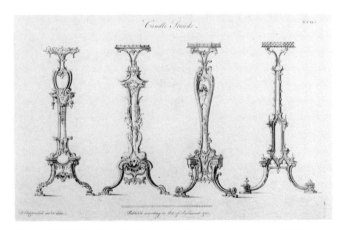

Plate CXLV. Candle Stands. Engraving dated 1760.

Plate CXLVII. Candle Stands. Engraving dated 1760.

A Society of Upholsterers
'Genteel Houshold Furniture in the Present Taste', 2nd Edition, c.1765.

William Ince and John Mayhew
'The Universal System of Houshold Furniture', 1762.

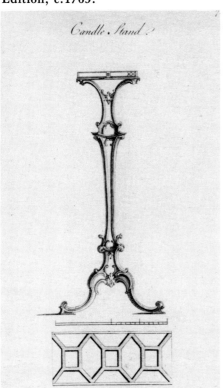

Plate 72 from Part III. Candle Stand. Attributed to Chippendale.

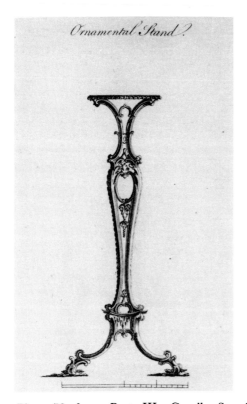

Plate 73 from Part III. Candle Stand. Attributed to Chippendale.

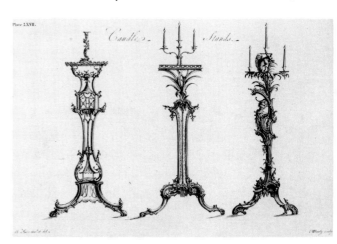

Plate LXVII. Candle Stands, '... the first of which is intended for White and Gold, or Japan; the others for Gilding.'

Plate LXVIII. Candle Stands '... the first has been executed in Japan, the second likewise in burnish'd Gold, and has very good Effects.'

Plate LXIX. Candle Stands '... the third of which has gained great Applause in the execution; the last would certainly have as good an appearance in work.'

R. & J. Adam
'Works in Architecture', 1773.

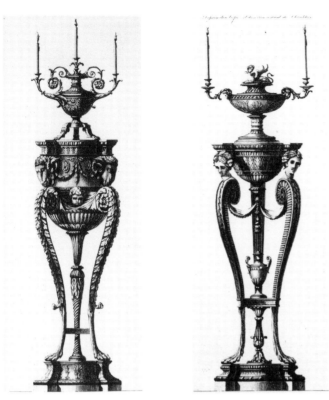

Plate VIII from Vol.I No.1. 'Design of a Tripod and Vase for Candles', for the Earl of Coventry.

Plate VIII from Vol.I No.I. 'Design of a Tripod with a Vase and Branches for three Candles'. 'Tripod for the Earl of Coventry executed in Ormolu for Sir Lawrence Dundas, and afterwards for the Duke of Bolton'.

Plate V from Vol.II No.I, 1777. Designs for the Earl of Derby's house, Grosvenor Square. Inside view of the third and great withdrawing room. 'The ornaments of the ceiling and entablature are chiefly of stucco gilt, with a mixture of paintings. The grounds are coloured with various tints. The frames for glasses, the pedestals and vases in the niches, and the girandoles on the piers, are of wood gilt. This room is hung with satin, and is undoubtedly one of the most elegant in Europe, whether we consider the variety or the richness of its decoration.'

Plate VIII from Vol.I No.III. Candle Stands designed for Luton Park House.

A. Hepplewhite & Co.
'The Cabinet-Maker and Upholsterer's Guide', 1st Edition,
1788. 2nd Edition, 1789. 3rd Edition, 1794.

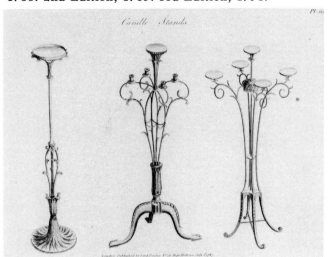

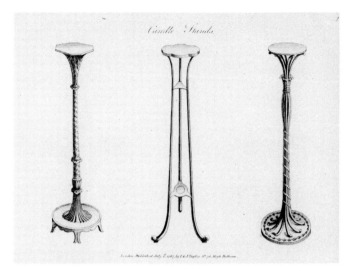

Plates 110 and 111. Candle Stands.
'These are very useful in large suits of apartments, as the light may be placed in any part at pleasure — in drawing-rooms, halls and on large staircases, they are frequently

used. These designs may be executed in mahogany or wood japanned. The branches to the designs, Plate 110, should be of lacquered brass.'

M.A. Pergolesi
'Designs for Various Ornaments', 1777-1801.

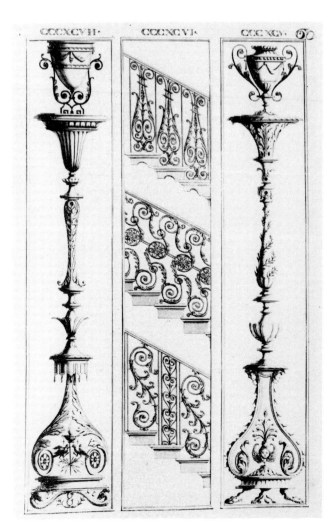

Plate 60. Stands, dated 1792.

Thomas Sheraton
'The Cabinet-Maker and Upholsterer's Drawing Book',
1793.

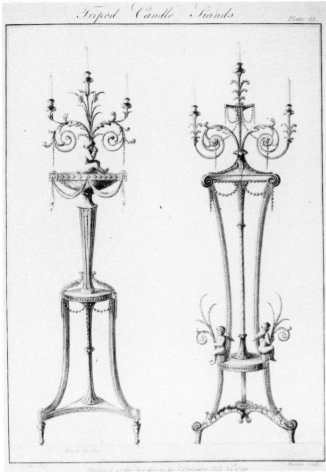

Plate LV from Part III. Candle Stands. 'These are used in drawing-rooms, for the convenience of affording additional light to such parts of the room where it would be neither ornamental nor easy to introduce in any other kind.

'The style of finishing these for noblemen's drawing rooms is exceedingly rich. Sometimes they are finished in white and gold, and sometimes all gold, to suit the other furniture. In inferior drawing-rooms they are japanned answerable to the furniture.

'Persons unacquainted with the manufacturing part of these stands may apprehend them to be slight and easily broken; but this objection vanishes, when it is considered that the scrolls are made of strong wire, and the ornament cemented to them...'.

G. Richardson
'New Designs for Vases and Tripods', 1793.

Plate 3.

Plate 5.

Plate 7.

Plate 9.

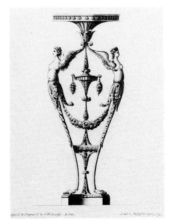

Plate 11.

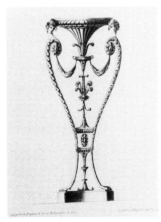

Plate 13.

309

G. Richardson
'New Designs for Vases and Tripods', 1793.

Plate 15.

Plate 17.

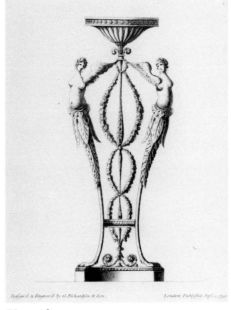

Plate 19.

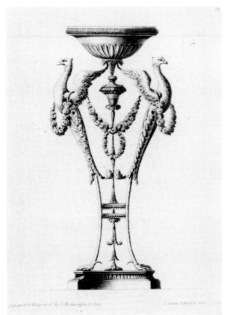

Plate 21.

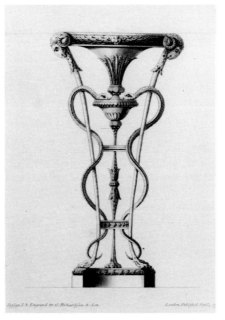

Plate 23.

Plate 25.

Section 3. READING and MUSIC STANDS

William Ince and John Mayhew
'The Universal System of Houshold Furniture', 1762.

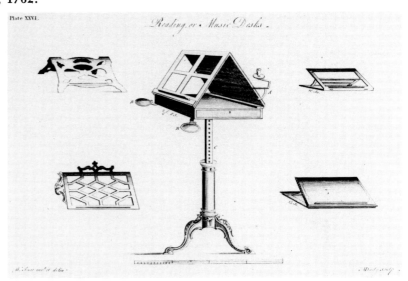

Plate XXVI. Reading or Music Desks.

'The Cabinet-Maker's London Book of Prices',
2nd Edition, 1793.

A. Hepplewhite & Co.
'The Cabinet-Maker and Upholsterer's Guide', 1st Edition, 1788.
2nd Edition, 1789. 3rd Edition, 1794.

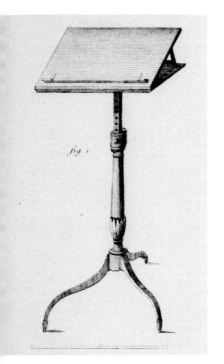

Plate 25, Figure 1. Music or Reading Stand.
Basic cost 11/-. 4/- extra for rising rack.

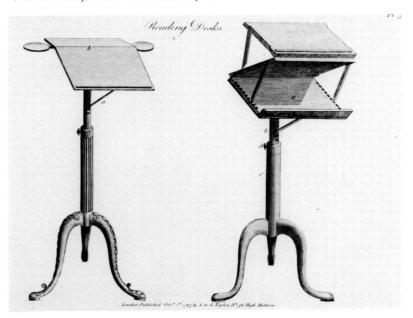

Plate 51. Reading Desks. Also in 3rd Edition, 1794.
'... shews two different kinds of Reading Desks; the mechanism and use of which are clearly shewn in the drawings. The desk may be raised by means of the staff which slides in the stem, and is fixed by the screw at the top.'

Section 4. STANDS for JARS, URNS, SCULPTURE, etc.

William Chambers
'Designs of Chinese Buildings', 1757.

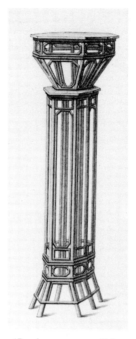
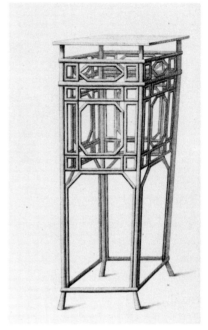

'In the corners of the rooms are stands, four or five feet high, on which they set plates of citrons, and other fragrant fruits, or branches of coral in vases of porcelain, and glass globes containing goldfish, together with a certain weed somewhat resembling fennel.'

Thomas Chippendale
'The Gentleman and Cabinet-Maker's Director', 3rd Edition, 1763.

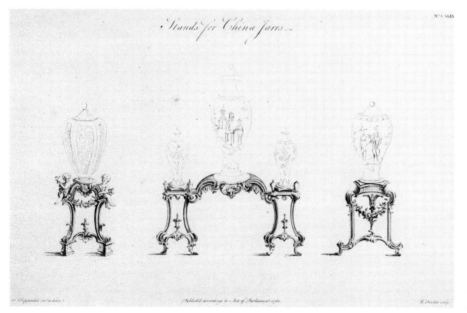

Plate CXLIX. Stands for China Jars. Engraving dated 1760.

Thomas Chippendale
'The Gentleman and Cabinet-Maker's Director', 3rd Edition, 1763.

Plate CL. Designs for Stands. Engraving dated 1761.

William Ince and John Mayhew
'The Universal System of Houshold Furniture', 1762.

Plate LI. Stands for Figures and China Jars '. . . the upper one has been executed to hold a Jar and two Beakers.'

A Society of Upholsterers
'Genteel Houshold Furniture in the Present Taste', 2nd Edition, c.1765.

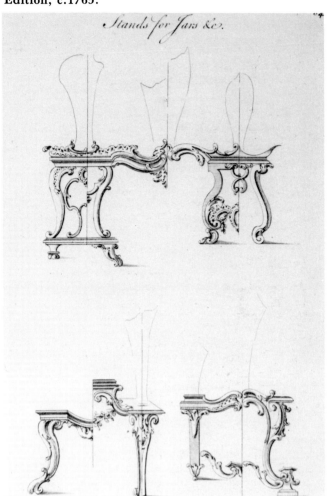

Plate 84 from Part III. Stands for Jars etc. Attributed to Ince & Mayhew.

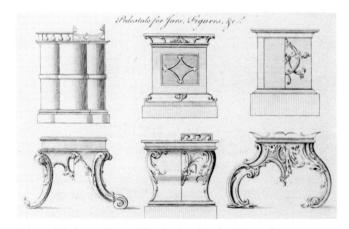

Plate 88 from Part III. Pedestals for Jars, Figures, etc. Designer unidentified.

313

R. & J. Adam
'Works in Architecture', 1778.

Plate II from Vol.II No.IV. Pedestal in the Great Circular Niche, in the Hall, Syon House.

Plate II from Vol.II No.IV. Pedestal between the doors and windows in the Hall, Syon House.

Section 5. TEA KETTLE STANDS

Thomas Johnson
'Collection of Designs', 1758, 'One Hundred and Fifty New Designs', 1761.

Plate 14 (1758), Plate 56 (1761) (detail). Tea Kettle Stand.

William Ince and John Mayhew
'The Universal System of Houshold Furniture',
1762.

Plate XIV. Tea Kettle Stands.

A Society of Upholsterers
'Genteel Houshold Furniture in the Present Taste', 2nd Edition, c.1765.

Plate 85 from Part III. Stands for Tea Kettles, etc. Attributed to Ince and Mayhew.

Plate 93 (wrongly printed 42) from Part III. Tea Kettle Stands. Designer unidentified.

**Thomas Chippendale
'The Gentleman and Cabinet-Maker's Director',
3rd Edition, 1763.**

Plate LV. Designs for Tea Kettle Stands (below)
and Basin Stands. Engraving dated 1761.

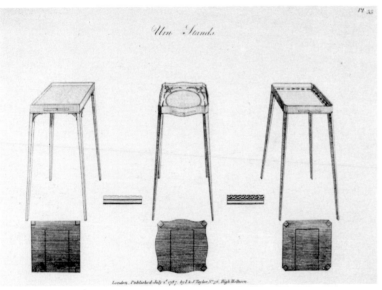

**A. Hepplewhite & Co.
'The Cabinet-Maker and Upholsterer's Guide',
1st Edition, 1788. 2nd Edition, 1789. 3rd Edition,
1794.**

Plates 55 and 56. Urn Stands '... may be of
various coloured woods, or painted and varnished.
The black line on the plan marks the slide, which
draws out to set the teapot on; that height may be
about 16 inches.'

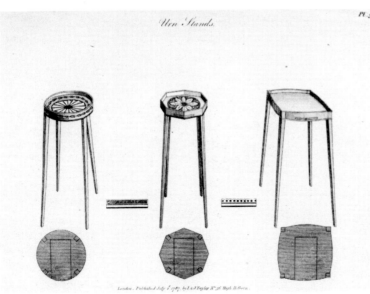

Section 6. FIRE SCREENS

William Ince and John Mayhew
'The Universal System of Houshold Furniture', 1762.

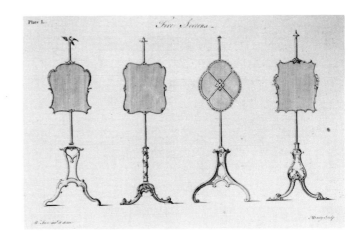

Plate L. Fire Screens.

Thomas Chippendale
'The Gentleman and Cabinet-Maker's Director', 1754.
3rd Edition, 1763.

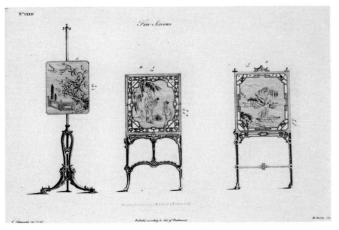

Plate CXXIV. Fire Screens. Plate CLVI in 3rd Edition.

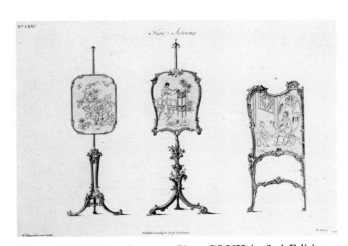

Plate CXXV. Fire Screens. Plate CLVII in 3rd Edition.

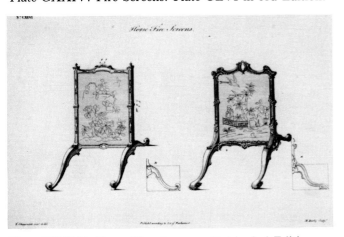

Plate CXXVI. Horse Fire Screens. Not in 3rd Edition.

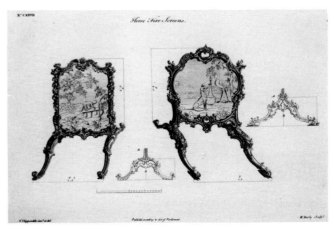

Plate CXXVII. Horse Fire Screens. Not in 3rd Edition.

Thomas Chippendale
'The Gentleman and Cabinet-Maker's Director', 3rd Edition, 1763.

Plate CLVIII. Designs for Fire Screens. Engraving dated 1761.

A Society of Upholsterers
'Genteel Houshold Furniture in the Present Taste', 2nd Edition, c.1765.

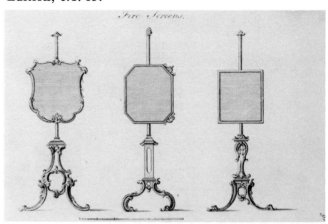

Plate 91 from Part III. Fire Screens, attributed to Ince and Mayhew.

A. Hepplewhite & Co.
'The Cabinet-Maker and Upholsterer's Guide', 1st Edition, 1788. 2nd Edition, 1789. 3rd Edition, 1794.

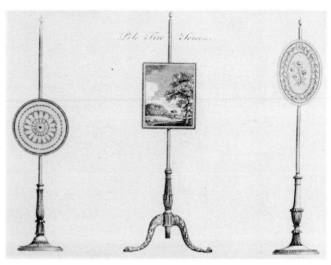

Plate 93. Pole Fire Screens '... the screens may be ornamented variously, with maps, Chinese figures, needlework, etc... may be made of mahogany, but more frequently of wood japanned.'

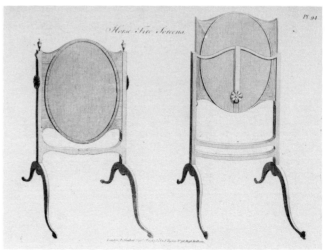

Plate 94. Horse Fire Screens '... the framework to these should be of mahogany; the screen may be covered with green silk, needlework, etc. at pleasure.'

318

Thomas Sheraton
'The Cabinet-Maker and Upholsterer's Drawing Book', 1793.

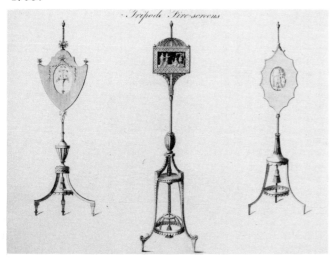

Plate XXXVIII from Part III. Tripod Fire Screens. '... the middle screen may be finished in white and gold, or japanned; the other two of mahogany, or japanned... such screens as have very fine prints, or worked satin, commonly have a glass before them...'

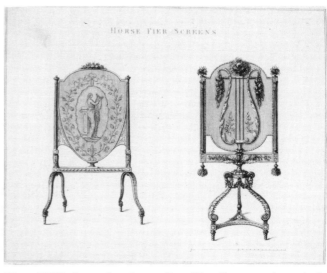

Plate XIII from the Appendix. Fire Screens. '... it is intended that the lyre ornament be carved in bas relief, gilt and burnished; which, when planted onto a blue silk or satin ground, cannot fail to produce a fine effect...'.

'The Cabinet-Maker's London Book of Prices', 1788. 2nd Edition 1793, 3rd Edition 1803.

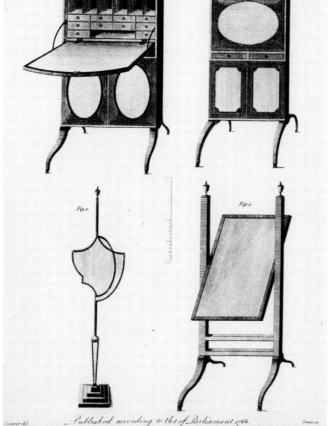

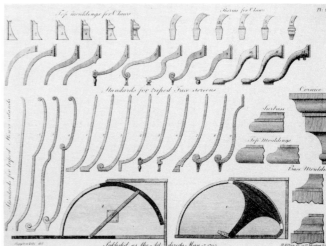

Plate 29. Legs for Claw Tables, Fire Screens, Flower Stands etc., designed by Hepplewhite. 2nd Edition, 1793.

Plate 18, Figures 1 and 2. Ladies' Writing Screens, designed by Shearer. Figure 3. Pole Screen. Figure 4. A Screen Dressing Glass Frame, designed by Shearer.

Section 7. STANDS for SUNDIALS

James Gibbs
'Book of Architecture', 1728. 2nd Edition, 1739.

Plate 148. Pedestals for Sundials.

Plate 149. Pedestals for Sundials.

J. Carter
'The Builder's Magazine', 1777.

Plate CXI. Term to support a Sundial.

III. MIRROR and PICTURE FRAMES and DRESSING GLASSES

Many pages of eighteenth century furniture pattern books were devoted to designs for looking-glass and picture frames. With pier tables they were among the earliest designs to be published in England and by English artists, and throughout the century they provided magnificent opportunities for carvers and gilders to produce some of their finest work. There were various types: frames for looking-glasses to fit above chimney pieces (and often an integral part of the chimney piece below), which were usually wider than they were tall; frames for pier glasses, which were fixed between the windows of a room, usually above a pier table (q.v.), and which were either rectangular or oval, and taller than they were wide; frames for paintings, whose ornament could be adapted to suit a wide range of sizes; tall, thin frames for mirror glasses to fit the spaces in bow-windows, which became fashionable during the middle of the century; and 'dressing glasses' which swung on posts, either above a small set of drawers, or the larger type of cheval glass mounted on castors which became popular at the end of the century. With the exception of the latter, nearly all frames were intended to be carved in soft woods (preferably limewood), covered in gesso and gilded, though some were carved in walut or mahogany and either left plain or partly gilded. The shapes and sizes of eighteenth century looking-glasses were affected by taxation and technology: in 1740 a duty was re-imposed, making glass an expensive item, so pieces were carefully preserved from old frames and incorporated in the side panels of new ones. Until the 1770s very large plates of glass could not be made in England, so additional 'slips' were added at the sides, cleverly disguised by carved woodwork, to increase the height and width, particularly of pier glasses. Most of the finest and largest glass plates were imported from France at enormous cost. After 1773 new casting processes enabled larger single plates to be used, and their frames consequently became somewhat thinner. The use of coloured glass in side panels also re-appeared around this time.

Designs for frames followed the prevailing tastes, from fairly severe classical architectural forms in the 1730s to some of the finest early Rococo shapes of the 1740s in the work of Matthias Lock. The most spirited and fanciful designs of the Rococo style were published in the 1750s and early 1760s by Lock, Chippendale, Johnson, and Ince and Mayhew: thereafter Neo-Classical patterns predominated, with some beautiful examples published by the brothers Adam, Pastorini, a carver known only by his initials 'S.H.', and by Hepplewhite.

Designs for whole single frames are shown in this section, with some part-pieces such as corners of picture frames. Designs for overmantels which form part of whole chimney pieces appear on page 356. Smaller designs for borders are found on page 411 and designs for girandoles, small frames with mirror glass and candle-branches, on page 381. See also Pier Tables, page 261.

Daniel Marot
'Nouveaux Livre d'Orfeuverie', 1703, 1713.

Plate 4. Mirrors and Frames.

See also Plate 8 from *Nouveaux Livre d'Orfeuverie* on page 262 in Section 1, under Pier Tables.

Daniel Marot
'Nouveaux Livre d'Ornements', 1703, 1713.

Plate 7. Title-page.

Plate 9. Frames.

Gaetano Brunetti
'Sixty Different Sorts of Ornament', 1736.

Plate 10. Frames and Mouldings.

Frames.

William Jones
'The Gentleman or Builder's Companion', 1739.

Plate 41.

Plate 42.

Plate 43.

Plate 45.

Plate 44.

William Jones
'The Gentleman or Builder's Companion', 1739.

Plate 46.

Plate 47.

Plate 48.

Plate 49.

Batty Langley
'The Builder's Jewell, or Youth's Instructor', 1741.

Matthias Lock
'Six Sconces', 1744. 2nd Edition, 1768.

Plate 78. Mouldings for Tabernacle Frames.

Plate 1. Title-page.

Plate 2.

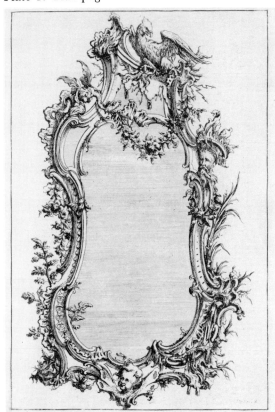

Plate 3.

Matthias Lock
'Six Sconces', 1744. 2nd Edition, 1768.

Plate 4.

Plate 5.

Matthias Lock
'A Book of Ornaments', n.d.

Plate 6.

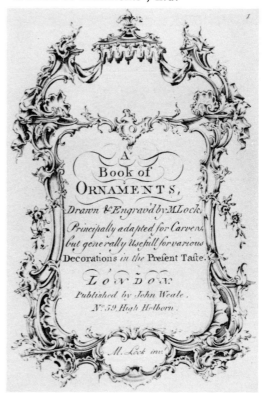

Title-page.

Matthias Lock & Henry Copland
'A New Book of Ornaments', 1752.

Plate 2. Design for a Frame. Reissued by Sayer in 1768 with some alterations.

Plate 1. Title-page.

Plate 3. Dated 1752, reissued by Sayer in 1768.

Plate 4. Dated 1752, reissued by Sayer in 1768 as Plate 2 with some alterations.

Matthias Lock & Henry Copland
'A New Book of Ornaments', 1752.

Plate 5. Dated 1752, reissued by Sayer in 1768 as Plate 4, with slight alterations.

Plate 6. Dated 1752, reissued by Sayer in 1768 as Plate 5.

Plate 8. Reissued by Sayer in 1768 with alterations as Plate 7.

Plate 11. Dated 1752, reissued by Sayer in 1768 with slight alterations.

Plate 12. Detail from Plate dated 1752 showing corner of a frame, reissued by Sayer in 1768 with slight alterations.

328

P. Babel
'A New Book of Ornaments', 1752.

Edwards & Darly
'A New Book of Chinese Designs', 1754.

Plate 5. Mirror Frame.

Plate 61. Glass Frame.

Plate 68. Glass Frame.

Thomas Chippendale
'The Gentleman and Cabinet-Maker's Director', 1754.

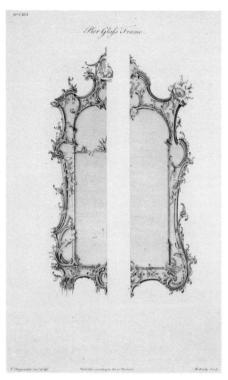

Plate CXLI. Pier Glass Frames. Not in 3rd Edition, 1763.

Plate CXLII. Pier Glass Frames. Not in 3rd Edition, 1763.

Plate CXLIII. Pier Glass Frames. Not in 3rd Edition, 1763.

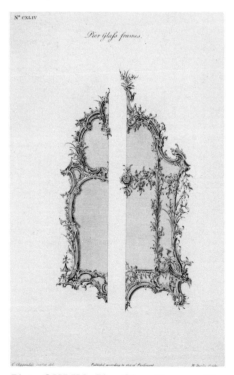

Plate CXLIV. Pier Glass Frames. Not in 3rd Edition, 1763.

Plate CXLV. Pier Glass Frames. Not in 3rd Edition, 1763.

Plate CXLVI. Pier Glass Frames. Not in 3rd Edition, 1763.

Thomas Chippendale
'The Gentleman and Cabinet-Maker's Director',
1754.

Plate CXLVII. Pier Glass Frames.
Plate CLXXIV in 3rd Edition, 1763.

Thomas Johnson
'Collection of Designs', 1758, 'One Hundred and Fifty New Designs',
1761.

Plate 1 (1758), Plate 34 (1761). Mirror Frames.

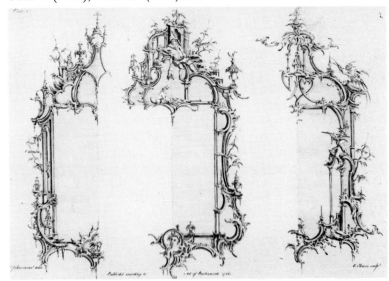

Plate 2 (1758), Plate 53 (1761). Mirror Frames.

Plate 3 (1758), Plate 7 (1761). Mirror Frames.

Thomas Johnson
'Collection of Designs', 1758, 'One Hundred and Fifty New Designs',
1761.

Plate 4 (1758), Plate 22 (1761). Mirror Frame.

Plate 5 (1758), Plate 31 (1761). Mirror Frame.

Plate 6 (1758), Plate 21 (1761). Mirror Frame.

Plate 7 (1758), Plate 8 (1761). Mirror Frame.

Thomas Johnson
'Collection of Designs', 1758, 'One Hundred and Fifty New Designs',
1761.

Plate 8 (1758), Plate 23 (1761). Mirror Frames.

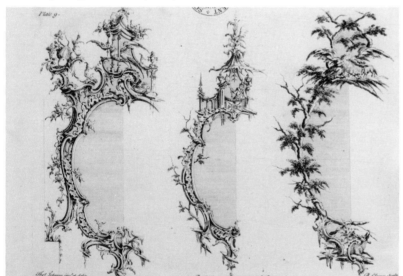

Plate 9 (1758), Plate 33 (1761). Mirror Frames.

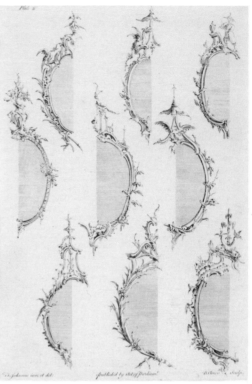

Plate 11 (1758), Plate 9 (1761). Mirror Frames.

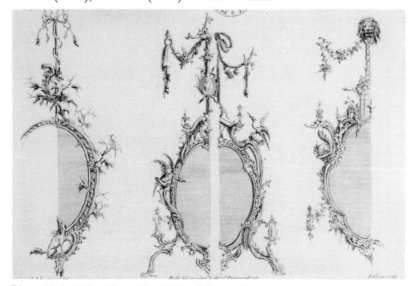

Plate 10 (1758), Plate 55 (1761). Mirror Frames.

Plate 12 (1758), Plate 43 (1761). Mirror Frames.

Thomas Johnson
'Collection of Designs', 1758, 'One Hundred
and Fifty New Designs', 1761.

Plate 17 (1758), Plate 35 (1761). Picture Frames.

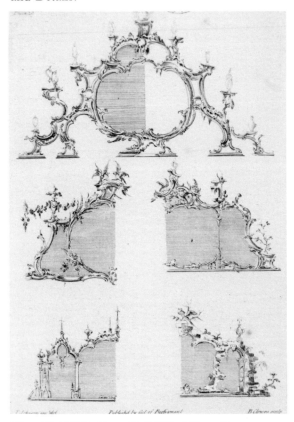

Plate 16 (1758), Plate 2 (1761). Picture Frame
and Details.

Plate 29 (1758), Plate 32 (1761). Mirror Frames.

Plate 30 (1758), Plate 5 (1761). Mirror Frames.

Thomas Johnson
'Collection of Designs', 1758, 'One Hundred and Fifty New Designs', 1761.

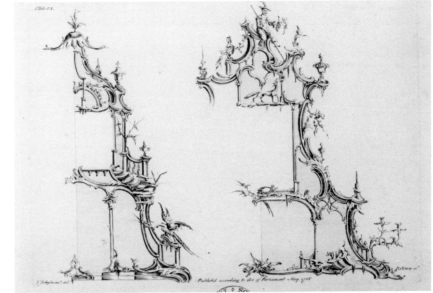

Plate 32 (1758), Plate 16 (1761). Mirror Frames.

Thomas Chippendale
'The Gentleman and Cabinet-Maker's Director', 3rd Edition, 1763.

Plate CLXVII. Designs for Glass Frames. Engraving dated 1762.

Plate CLXVIIa. Pier Glasses. Engraving dated 1760.

Thomas Chippendale
'The Gentleman and Cabinet-Maker's Director', 3rd Edition, 1763.

Plate CLXVIII. Oval Glass Frames. Engraving dated 1760.

Plate CLXIX. Pier Glass Frame.

Plate CLXX. A Pier Glass and Table. Engraving dated 1760.

Plate CLXXI. Glass Frames. Engraving dated 1762.

336

Thomas Chippendale
'The Gentleman and Cabinet-Maker's Director', 3rd
Edition, 1763.

Plate CLXXII. Glass Frames. Engraving dated 1760.

Plate CLXXIa. Pier Glass Frame. Engraving
dated 1760.

Plate CLXXIII. Designs for Pier Glasses.
Engraving dated 1761.

Thomas Chippendale
'The Gentleman and Cabinet-Maker's Director, 3rd Edition, 1763.

Plate CLXXXV. Picture Frame. Engraving dated 1761.

Plate CLXXXVI. Picture Frame. Engraving dated 1761.

Plate CLXXXVII. A Picture Frame. Engraving dated 1762.

Plate CLXXXVIIa. Glass Frames. Engraving dated 1760.

Plate CLXXXVIII. Tabernacle Frames. Engraving dated 1760.

William Ince and John Mayhew
'The Universal System of Houshold Furniture', 1762.

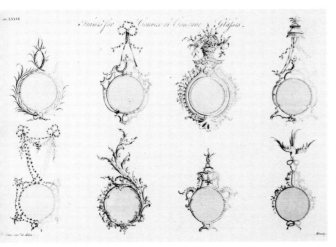

Plate LXXVII. 'Frames for Convex or Concave Glasses, which have a very pretty Effect in a well-furnish'd Room.'

Plate LXXIX. Architectural Frames.

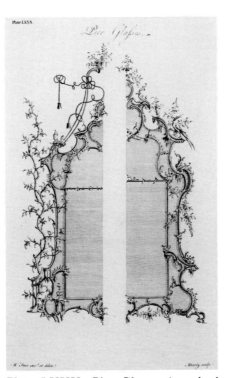

Plate LXXVIII. Oval Glass Frames.

Plate LXXX. Pier Glasses ' ... both which have been executed from the Plate in burnish'd Gold, and make a handsome appearance.'

Plate LXXXI. Architectural Pier Glasses 'with Glass Borders'.

William Ince and John Mayhew
'The Universal System of Houshold Furniture', 1762.

Plate LXXXII. 'An elegant Pier Glass Frame, with Borders; a Slab Table under ditto.'

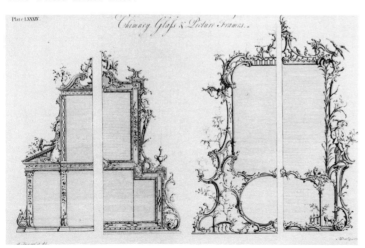

Plate LXXXVIII. Picture Frames '. . . the Ornaments of which may be executed to suit any siz'd Picture.'

Plate LXXXIV. Chimney Glasses and Pictures over them.

340

A Society of Upholsterers
'Genteel Houshold Furniture in the Present Taste', 2nd
Edition, c.1765.

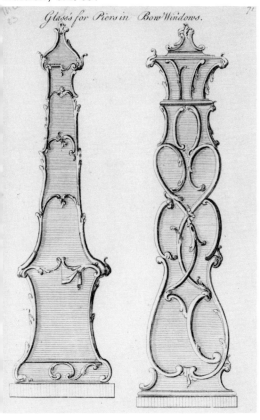

Plate 71 from Part II. Pier Glasses. Attributed to Ince and Mayhew.

Plate 97 from Part III. Frames. Attributed to Johnson.

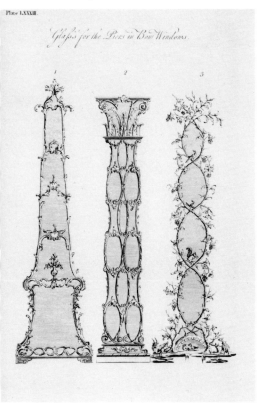

Ince and Mayhew
'The Universal System of Houshold Furniture', 1762.

Plate LXXXIII. 'Three Designs of Glasses to line the Piers of Bow-Windows.'

P. Baretti
'A New Book of Ornaments for the Year 1762'.

Plate 4. Foliate canopy, possibly a design for the top of a frame.

Plate 16. Ornamental Cresting.

Matthias Lock
'A New Book of Ornaments for Looking Glass Frames', 1769. Reissue by Sayer of 1st Edition, c.1752.
(Metropolitan Museum of Art, Harris Brisbane Dick Fund, 1928.)

Title-page.

Plate 2. Looking Glass Frame.

342

Matthias Lock
'A New Book of Ornaments for Looking Glass Frames',
1769. Reissue by Sayer of 1st Edition, c.1752.

Plate 4. Looking Glass Frame.

Plate 6. Looking Glass Frame.

M. Lock
'A New Book of Pier-Frames',
1769.

Title-page.

Plate 4. Girandole Frames.

343

M. Lock
'A New Book of Pier-Frames', 1769.

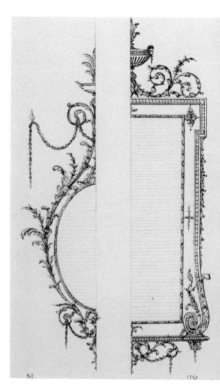

Plate 5. Pier Glass Frames.

Plate 6. Pier Glass Frames.

Plate 7. Pier Glass Frames.

Matthias Darly
'Architectural Designs and Ornaments', 1769-70.

Plate LXXIX. Frames for Pictures, Glass, etc. Engraving dated 1770.

Picture Frames. Engraving dated 1771.

F. Vivares
Unbound Engravings, 1773.

R. & J. Adam
'Works in Architecture', 1773.

Frame for a Looking Glass.

Plate VIII from Vol.I No.I. Frame 'executed for us in wood gilt' for the Adelphi. Original design dated 1772.

R. & J. Adam
'Works in Architecture', 1774.

Plate V from Vol.I No.II. Detail: Frame over Chimney-piece in the Library at Kenwood.

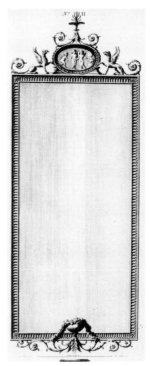

Plate VIII from Vol.I No.II. Design for the Pier Glasses in the Great Room at Kenwood, 1774.

R. & J. Adam
'Works in Architecture', 1774.

Thomas Johnson
'A Set of Engravings', 1775.
(Metropolitan Museum of Art, the Elisha Whittelsey Collection, 1956.)

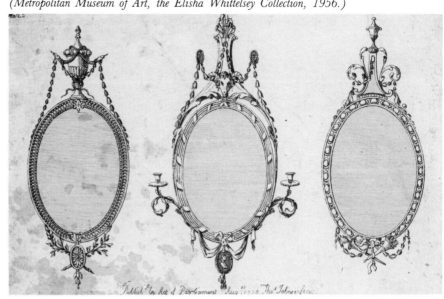

Plate 5.

Plate VIII from Vol.I No.II. Pier
Glass in the Parlour, Kenwood.

B. Pastorini
'A New Book of Designs for Girandoles and Glass Frames', 1775.

Plate VIII from Vol.I No.II. Pier
Glass in the Dining Room, Kenwood.

Title-page.

B. Pastorini
'A New Book of Designs for Girandoles and Glass Frames',
1775.

Plate II. Design for Girandole.

Plate III. Design for a Glass Frame.

Plate IV. Design for a Glass Frame.

Plate V. Design for a Glass Frame.

Plate VI. Design for a Glass Frame.

Plate VII. Design for a Glass Frame.

347

B. Pastorini
**'A New Book of Designs for Girandoles and Glass Frames',
1775.**

Plate VIII. Design for a Girandole.

Plate IX. Design for a Glass Frame.

Plate X. Design for a Glass Frame.

J. Carter
'The Builder's Magazine', 1776-78.

Plate LXXXII. Design for a Looking Glass.
Engraving dated 1776.

Plate CLVII. Design for a Looking
Glass. Engraving dated 1778

Plate CLXXIX. Design for a
Panel with a Frame. Engraving
dated 1778.

R. & J. Adam
'Works in Architecture', 1777, 1822.

Plate IV from Vol.II No.I. Side of the Second Drawing Room in the Earl of Derby's House in Grosvenor Square. 'The magnificent Glass Frame in the Recess is finely executed in wood and gilt.'

Plate III from Vol.III 1822. Detail of a Pier Glass from the Library of Syon House.

Plate IX from Vol.III 1822. Pier Glass at Syon House.

Plate XI from Vol.III 1822. Drawing Room Glass and Table assigned for the Earl of Bute.

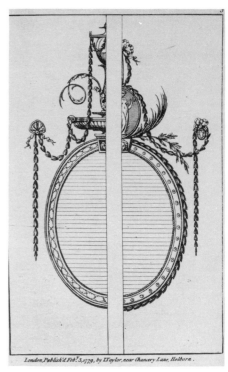

Title-page.

Plate 2. Designs for Frames.

Plate 3. Designs for Frames.

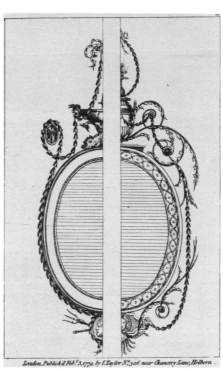

Plate 4. Designs for Frames.

Plate 5. Designs for Frames.

Plate 6. Designs for Frames.

William Thomas
'Original Designs in Architecture', 1783.

Plate XXVII. Design for the Pier Glass in the Drawing Room of Jno. Harris Esqr.

Plate XXVII. Design for the Pier Glass in the Drawing Room of Wm. Dymock Esqr.

A. Hepplewhite & Co.
'The Cabinet-Maker and Upholsterer's Guide', 1788.
2nd Edition, 1789.

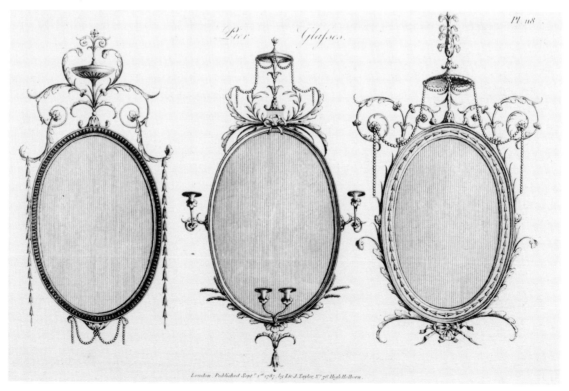

Plate 118. Pier Glasses. Not in 3rd Edition, 1794.

A. Hepplewhite & Co.
'The Cabinet-Maker and Upholsterer's Guide', 1st Edition, 1788.
2nd Edition, 1789. 3rd Edition, 1794.

Plates 116, 117 Pier Glasses. 'For Glasses, a great variety of patterns may be invented. The frames to glasses are almost invariably of good carved work, gilt and burnished. Six designs for square glasses are here shewn, which is the shape most in fashion at this time; they should be made to nearly fill the pier.'

Plate 118 in 2nd Edition, 1789, and 3rd Edition, 1794. '... two designs for Glasses of the newest fashion, proper to be placed over Chimney-Pieces, Sofas etc; they must be fixed very low. The pannels of the sides are frequently made of various coloured glass.'

Anon
'Ideas for Rustic Furniture', c.1790.

Plate 19. Looking Glasses.

Plate 20. Looking Glasses.

Plate 21. Looking Glasses.

M.A. Pergolesi
'Designs for Various Ornaments', 1777-1801

Plate 56. Frame; design dated 1792.

Plate 62. Frame; design dated 1791.

A. Hepplewhite & Co.
'The Cabinet-Maker and Upholsterer's Guide', 1st Edition, 1788. 2nd Edition, 1789. 3rd Edition, 1794.

DRESSING GLASSES

See also Dressing Tables, pages 249-255.

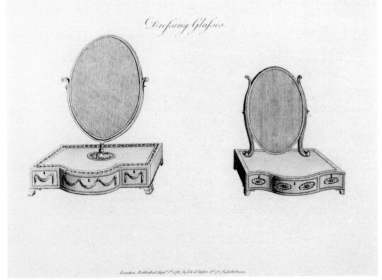

Plate 70. Dressing Glasses.

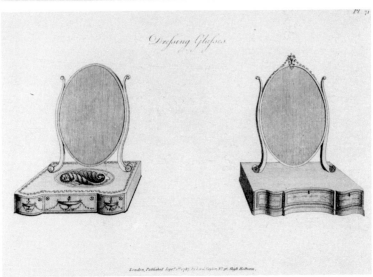

Plate 71. Dressing Glasses '. . . the ornaments. . . may be inlaid with various coloured woods, or painted and varnished.'

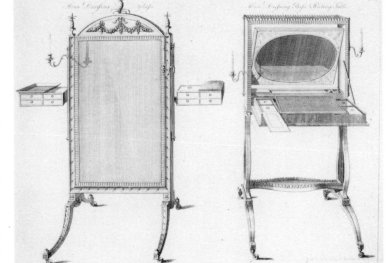

Thomas Sheraton
'The Cabinet-Maker and Upholsterer's Drawing Book', 1793.

Plate XVII from the Appendix. Horse Dressing Glasses. Left-hand design: '. . . The boxes on each side are intended to hold conveniences for dressing. On these, there is a comb-tray on the leftside, and a pin-cushion on the right. When the dressing boxes are not in use, they are intended to turn behind the glass. . . The other dressing glass has a convenience for writing as well as dressing. . .'.

IV. CHIMNEY-PIECES with OVERMANTELS

Hundreds of designs for chimney-pieces were published during the eighteenth century, in architectural pattern books, in books of furniture designs, and even in books to themselves, such as Crunden, Milton and Columbani's *Chimney-Piece Maker's Daily Assistant* of 1766. Of these, a large percentage were intended to be executed by the woodcarver, particularly those with carved overmantels, while the rest were to be carved in statuary marble or stone. To include them all would have created a serious imbalance in this book, so only those with carved overmantels have been reproduced here, as they relate most closely to the rest of the eighteenth century English carver's repertoire. Throughout the century, wooden chimney-pieces were carved in a variety of soft and hard woods, and were finished in a variety of ways: many, particularly for drawing rooms and state apartments in great houses, were gilded. Others were painted, or part painted and gilded, or grained and varnished. Overmantels often held mirror glass, and had candle branches attached, made of gilt gesso-covered wire with metal holders; like pier-glasses, this arrangement had the advantage of throwing additional reflected light into a room at night. Some had little shelves on which candlesticks could stand, or (particularly in some of the designs of the 1760s) where small Oriental porcelain bowls could be displayed. Other overmantel frames were designed to hold paintings, or a combination of mirror-glass and a small central picture. The fireplaces themselves were designed to contain metal baskets or grates for coal; these were usually free-standing, but some fitted grates were made and designs for both types, as well as fire dogs on which to burn logs, were included in the furniture pattern books (see Part IV, Section 7, Chimney Furniture). The back of the aperture might be straight, or curved to reflect heat more efficiently.

Chimney-piece designs reflected the general style in furniture and interior decoration during the period, ranging from relatively sober classical forms in the 1720s and 1730s, through the wildest extravagancies of Rococo fancy in the 1750s and 1760s, to renewed classical simplicity in the 1770s and 1780s. As with other carver's work, fantasy, fable and humour appear in many of the designs: Lock and Johnson made extensive use of the creatures in Aesop's Fables, and nearly all the mid-century designs used Chinese Ho-Ho birds, figures and dragons. The designs for rustic chimney-pieces of c.1790 were intended for a small garden building such as a root-house or hermitage, and had chairs, tables and mirror frames *en suite*. Robert Manwaring gave detailed instructions in his *Cabinet and Chair-Maker's Real Friend and Companion*, 1765, as to how these pieces were made to imitate twigs and branches of trees (See Part I, Section 6, Garden Seats).

James Gibbs
'Book of Architecture', 1728. 2nd Edition, 1739.

Plate 91. Frames over fireplaces.

Plate 92. Fireplaces.

356

James Gibbs
'Book of Architecture', 1728. 2nd Edition,
1739.

Plate 93. Chimney-piece designs.

Plate 95. Chimney-piece designs.

Plate 96. Chimney-piece designs.

Plate 97. Chimney-piece designs.

Isaac Ware
'Designs of Inigo Jones and others', 1733.

Plate 2. Chimney-piece design.

Plate 3. Chimney-piece design.

Plate 4. Chimney-piece design.

Plate 5. Chimney-piece design.

Plate 33. Chimney-piece design.

Plate 34. Chimney-piece design.

358

Isaac Ware
'Designs of Inigo Jones and others', 1731.

Plate 37. Chimney-piece design.

Plate 38. Interior design including chimney-piece.

Plate 42. Interior design including chimney-piece.

Plate 39. Chimney-piece design.

Plate 40. Chimney-piece design.

Plate 41. Chimney-piece design.

Isaac Ware
'Designs of Inigo Jones and others', 1731.

Plate 53. Chimney-piece design.

E. Hoppus
'The Gentleman and Builder's Repository', 1737.

Plate XLVII. Chimney-piece with overmantel.

E. Hoppus
'The Gentleman and Builder's Repository', 1737.

Plate XLVIII. Chimney-piece with overmantel.

Plate XLIX. Chimney-piece with overmantel.

Plate L. Chimney-piece with overmantel.

Plate LII. Chimney-piece with overmantel.

Plate LV. Chimney-piece with overmantel.

Plate LIII. Chimney-piece with overmantel.

Plate LIV. Chimney-piece with overmantel.

Plate LVI. Chimney-piece with overmantel.

361

Plate 22. Chimney-piece with over-mantel.

Plate 23. Chimney-piece with over-mantel.

Plate 24. Chimney-piece with over-mantel.

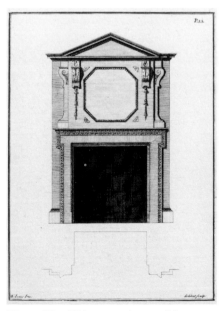

Plate 25. Chimney-piece with over-mantel.

Plate 26. Chimney-piece with over-mantel.

Plate 33. Chimney-piece with over-mantel.

W. Jones
'The Gentleman or Builder's Companion', 1739.

Plate 34. Chimney-piece with over-mantel.

Plate 35. Chimney-piece with over-mantel.

Plate 36. Chimney-piece with over-mantel.

Batty Langley
'Gothic Architecture Improv'd by Rules and Proportions', 1742.

Plate XLVII. Chimney Piece.

Plate LXVIII. Chimney Piece.

Plate XLVIII. Chimney-piece and frame.

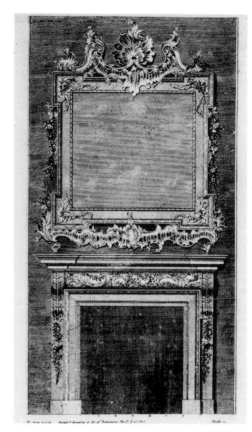

Plate XLIX. Chimney-piece and frame.

Plate L. Chimney-piece and frame.

Plate LI. Chimney-piece with overmantel.

A. Swan
'The British Architect', 1745.

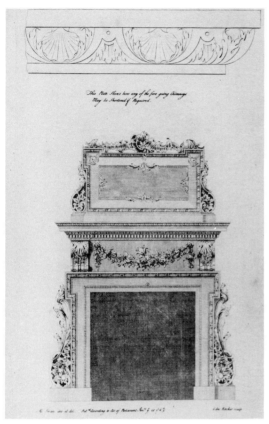

Plate LII. Chimney-piece with overmantel.

Plate LIII. Chimney-pieces, one with overmantel.

W. Halfpenny
'New Designs for Chinese Temples', 1750.

Plate 56. A Chimney-piece in the Chinese Taste.

Plate 57. A Chimney-piece in the Chinese Taste.

Plate 58. A Chimney-piece in the Chinese Taste.

W. Salmon
'Palladio Londoniensis'. 4th Edition, 1752.

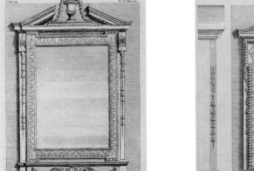

Plate H. Two designs for chimney-pieces with frame and overmantel.

Plate I. Chimney-piece with overmantel.

Isaac Ware
'A Complete Body of Architecture', 1756.

For Rococo chimney-pieces designed by Lock and Copland, 1752, see section on Frames, pages 327-328.

Plate 85. Chimney-piece with over-mantel.

Plate 92. Chimney-piece with over-mantel.

Plate 93. Chimney-piece with over-mantel.

Isaac Ware
'A Complete Body of Architecture', 1756.

W. Halfpenny
'The Modern Builder's Assistant', 1757.

Plate 96. Chimney-piece with over-mantel.

R. Morris
'Architecture Improv'd in a Collection of Modern, Useful and Elegant Designs', 1757.

Plate LXVIII, designed by Lightoler.

Plate 35. Chimney-piece with over-mantel.

Plate 36. Chimney-piece with over-mantel.

Plate 37. Chimney-piece with over-mantel.

R. Morris
**'Architecture Improv'd in a Collection of Modern, Useful
and Elegant Designs', 1757.**

Plate 38. Chimney-piece with over-
mantel.

Plate 39. Chimney-piece with over-
mantel.

Plate 40. Chimney-piece with over-
mantel.

Plate 41. Chimney-piece with over-
mantel.

Plate 42. Chimney-piece with over-
mantel.

Plate 43. Chimney-piece with over-
mantel.

368

R. Morris
'Architecture Improv'd in a Collection of Modern, Useful and Elegant Designs', 1757.

Plate 44. Chimney-piece with over-mantel.

Plate 45. Chimney-piece with over-mantel.

Plate 46. Chimney-piece with over-mantel.

Plate 47. Chimney-piece with over-mantel.

Plate 48. Chimney-piece with over-mantel.

Plate 49. Chimney-piece with over-mantel.

R. Morris
'Architecture Improv'd in a Collection of Modern, Useful and Elegant Designs', 1757.

Plate 50. Chimney-piece with overmantel.

W. Pain
'The Builder's Companion and Workman's General Assistant', 1758.

Page 61. Six Designs for Chimney Pieces.

Page 62. Three Chimney Pieces.

Page 85. Gothick Chimneys.

A. Swan
'One Hundred and Fifty New Designs for Chimney-Pieces', 1768.

Plate 8. Design for Upper Parts of Chimney Pieces.

Plate 10. Design for Upper Part of Chimneys.

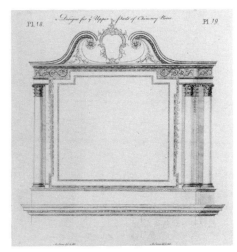

Plate 12. Different Designs for Chimney Pieces.

Plate 13. Different Designs for Chimney Pieces.

Plates 18/19. Design for Upper Parts of Chimney Pieces.

Thomas Johnson
'Collection of Designs', 1758, 'One Hundred and Fifty
New Designs', 1761.

Plate 31 (1758), Plate 24, (1761). Chimney Pieces.

Plate 33 (1758), Plate 29 (1761). Chimney Piece.

Plate 34 (1758), Plate 3 (1761). Chimney Piece.

Plate 35 (1758), Plate 45 (1761). Chimney Piece.

Thomas Johnson
'Collection of Designs', 1758, 'One Hundred and Fifty
New Designs', 1761.

Plate 36 (1758), Plate 19 (1761). Chimney Piece.

Plate 37 (1758), Plate 49 (1761). Chimney Piece.

Plate 38 (1758), Plate 30 (1761).
Chimney Piece.

Plate 39 (1758), Plate 20 (1761).
Chimney Piece.

Plate 40 (1758), Plate 4 (1761).
Chimney Piece.

Thomas Chippendale
'The Gentleman and Cabinet-Maker's Director', 3rd Edition, 1763.

Plate CLXXIX. Chimney Pieces. Engraving dated 1760.

Plate CLXXIXa. A Design for a Chimney Piece. Engraving dated 1762.

Plate CLXXXI. Two Designs for Chimney Pieces. Engraving dated 1761.

374

Thomas Chippendale
'The Gentleman and Cabinet-Maker's Director', 3rd Edition, 1763.

Plate CLXXXII. Chimney Piece. Engraving dated 1761.

Plate CLXXXIII. Chimney Piece. Engraving dated 1761.

Plate CLXXXIV. A Design for a Chimney Piece. Engraving dated 1761.

A Society of Upholsterers
'Genteel Houshold Furniture in the Present Taste', 2nd Edition, c.1765.

William Ince and John Mayhew
'The Universal System of Houshold Furniture', 1762.

Plate 93, from Part III. Chimney-piece Glass and Picture, attributed to Thomas Johnson.

Plate 94, from Part III. Chimney Glass, attributed to Thomas Johnson.

Plate LXXXV. Chimney Pieces &c.

William Ince and John Mayhew
'The Universal System of Houshold Furniture', 1762.

Plate LXXXVI. Gothic Chimney Pieces.

Plate LXXXVII. Chimney Piece &c.

Crunden, Milton & Columbani
'The Chimney-Piece Maker's Daily Assistant', 1766.

Plate 27. Chimney-piece designed by Crunden.

Plate 28. Chimney-piece designed by Crunden.

Plate 29. Chimney-piece designed by Crunden.

Crunden, Milton & Columbani
'The Chimney-Piece Maker's Daily Assistant', 1766.

Plate 30. Chimney-piece designed by Crunden.

Plate 31. Chimney-piece designed by Crunden.

Plate 32. Chimney-piece designed by Crunden.

Matthias Lock
'A New Book of Ornaments for Looking Glass Frames, Chimney Pieces &c &c in the Chinese Taste', 1768, reissue by Sayer of 1st Edition, c.1752. *(Metropolitan Museum of Art, Harris Brisbane Dick Fund, 1928.)*

Plate 3. Chimney-piece.

Plate 5. Chimney-piece.

R. & J. Adam
'Works in Architecture', 1777.

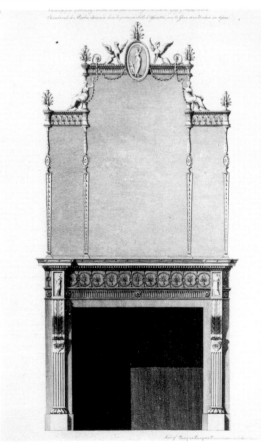

Plate II No.I from Vol.II. (To the left). Designs for the Earl of Derby's house in Grosvenor Square. 'Section of the Chimney-side of the Anti-Room in the principal Story. The ornaments are all in stucco; and the grounds, both of the ceiling and side walls, are all picked in, with different tints of green, which has a simple and elegant effect. The chimney-piece is of statuary marble, and the girandoles are painted.'

Plate III from Vol.II No.I. (Bottom left and above). Designs for the Earl of Derby's house in Grosvenor Square. Chimney-pieces for the first and second Withdrawing Rooms. 'These chimney-pieces are of statuary marble, and the frames for the glasses are carved in wood and gilt. The figure in the oval at the top of the first frame is painted; and the whole is beautifully executed, and has been allowed to have an elegant effect.'

Plate VI from Vol. II No. I. Designs for the Earl of Derby's house, Grosvenor Square. 'Two chimney-pieces in the Great Withdrawing Room, and the Countess of Derby's Dressing Room. The former is finely executed, in statuary marble, inlaid with various coloured *scagliola* and brass ornaments, gilt in *ormoulu*. The glass frame over it is carved in wood and gilt. The latter is likewise executed in statuary marble, inlaid with scagliola, in the Etruscan style, both with regard to the form of the ornament, and the peculiarity of the colouring. The glass frame over it is of wood, carved and coloured in the same manner.'

W. Thomas
'Original Designs in Architecture', 1783.

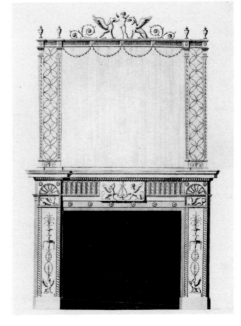

Plate VI. Chimney Piece and Glass Frame for the Music Room.

Anon
'Ideas for Rustic Furniture', c.1790.

Plate 22. Chimney-piece.

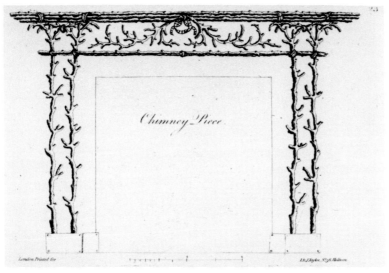

Plate 23. Chimney-piece.

Plate 24. Chimney-piece.

V. LIGHTING

Lighting equipment was made by eighteenth century English woodcarvers, and designs for wall-lights, chandeliers, lanterns and staircase lights appear in the furniture pattern books. The usual type of wall-light was the girandole, a term taken from the French to describe a carved wooden frame holding mirror glass and candle branches. Girandoles were often made in pairs and were smaller than pier glasses, but served a similar purpose in reflecting candlelight into a room, and could be fixed on the inner walls (See Part V, Interiors). Between 1752 and 1765 some particularly delightful designs were published for them, with asymmetrical outlines, naturalistic candle branches in imitation of twigs, *chinoiseries* and creatures from Aesop's Fables. Some, like overmantels, had little shelves on which to place small porcelain bowls and jars. Later eighteenth century Neo-Classical designs for

them were less extravagant, but according to Hepplewhite, allowed 'great variety in pattern and elegance; they are usually executed of the best carved work — gilt and burnished in parts. They may be carved and coloured suitable to the room.' (*Guide,* 1788, Plates 113-115).

Chandeliers, according to Chippendale, 'are generally made of Glass, and sometimes of Brass; But if neatly done in Wood, and gilt in burnish'd Gold, would look better, and come much cheaper.' (*Director,* 3rd Edition, 1762, Plates CLIV, CLV.) A few designs for them were included in the furniture pattern books, along with ideas for hall lanterns and staircase lights. Most of the later eighteenth century designs for hanging lamps were probably intended to be executed in metalwork.

Section 1. GIRANDOLES

M. Lock & H. Copland
'A New Book of Ornaments', 1752. 2nd Edition, 1768.

See also Plate 10 from the same book, showing a girandole with a chandelier on page 391.

Plate 8. Detail showing girandole. This plate was reissued by Sayer in 1768 with alterations.

Plate 9. Detail showing girandole. This plate was reissued by Sayer in 1768 with alterations.

P. Babel
'A New Book of Ornaments', 1752.

Edwards & Darly
'A New Book of Chinese Designs', 1754.

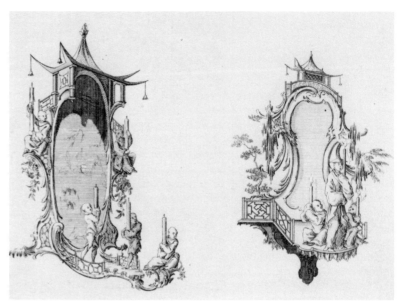

Plate 13. Girandoles.

Plate 6. Girandole.

Thomas Chippendale
'The Gentleman and Cabinet-Maker's
Director', 1754.

Plate CXL. Girandoles. (See also Plates CXLII
and CXLIII on page 330, in section on Frames.)

Thomas Johnson
'Twelve Girandoles', 1755.

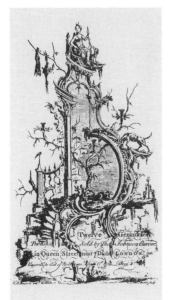

Plate 1. Title page.

Plate 2. A design for a
Girandole.

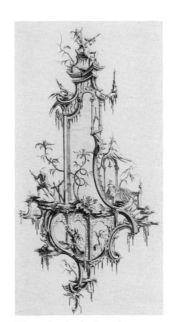

Plate 3. A design for a
Girandole.

Plate 4. A design for a
Girandole.

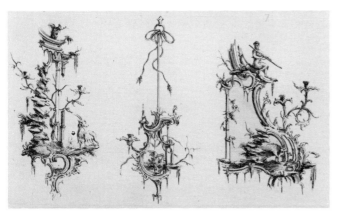

Plates 5, 6, 7. Three
Girandoles.

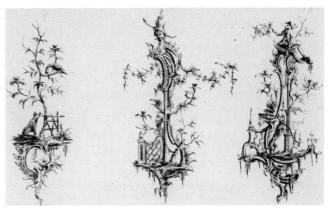

Plate 8, 9, 10. Three
Girandoles.

Plate 11. A design for a
Girandole.

Plate 12. A design for
a Girandole.

Thomas Johnson
'An Emblemetical Girandole, EARTH', 1760.

'Inscribed, 'T. Johnson Inv^t Sculp^t. Publish'd by Act of Parli^{mt} Dec y^e 6th 1760 & sold pr 1s. by y^e Proprietor at the Golden Boy in Grafton Street, St. Ann's, Soho, London, where this and all other ornaments are carv'd and gilt.'
(Trustees of the British Museum.)

For another girandole by Johnson see Plate 37 in the section on Chimney-pieces, page 373.

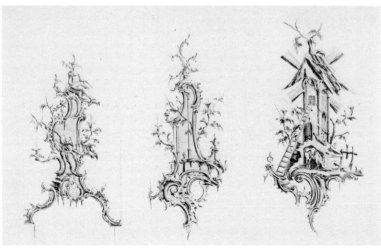

Thomas Johnson
'Collection of Designs', 1758, 'One Hundred and Fifty New Designs', 1761.

Plate 41 (1758), Plate 51 (1761). Three girandoles.

384

Thomas Johnson
'Collection of Designs', 1758, 'One Hundred and Fifty
New Designs', 1761.

Plate 49 (1758), Plate 46 (1761). Girandoles.

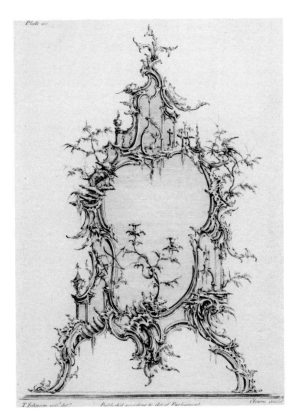

Plate 50 (1758), Plate 47 (1761). Girandoles.

Plate 51 (1758), Plate 14 (1761). Five girandoles.

Plate 52 (1758), Plate 17 (1761). Girandoles.

385

A Society of Upholsterers
'Genteel Houshold Furniture in the Present Taste', 2nd
Edition, c.1765.

Plate 95 from Part III. Girandoles, attributed to Johnson.

Plate 98 from Part III. Frame, attributed to Johnson.

William Ince and John Mayhew
'The Universal System of Houshold Furniture', 1762.

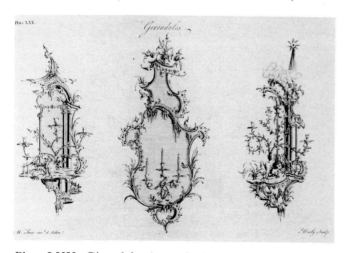

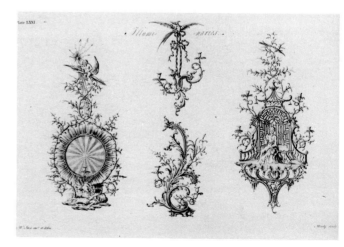

Plate LXX. Girandoles 'two of which have been executed from this Plate since engraved.'

Plate LXXI. Girandoles. '. . .that of the Story of Phaeton is meant to have Glass cut in the Manner it is engraved, the several Rays of which will reflect the Candles in so many different Colours as to render it very beautiful.'

Plate CLXXVII. Girandoles.

Plate CLXXVIII. Girandoles.

An additional Girandole by Chippendale, Plate CLXIX, is shown on page 336.

Plate VIII from Vol. II No. I. Girandole in the niche of the Etruscan Room at Derby House.

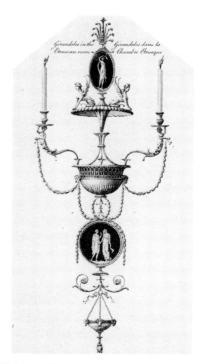

Plate VIII from Vol. II. No. I. Girandoles in the Etruscan Room at Derby House.

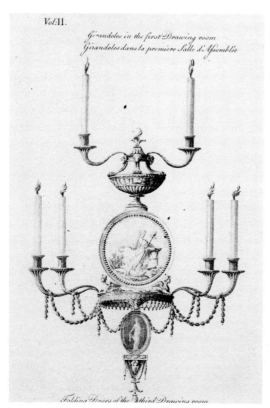

Plate VIII from Vol. II No. I. Designs for the Earl of Derby's house, Grosvenor Square. Girandoles in the First Drawing Room.

Plate II in Vol. II No. I. Designs for the Earl of Derby's house in Grosvenor Square. 'Section of the Chimney-side of the Anti-Room in the principal Story. The ornaments are all in stucco; and the grounds, both of the ceiling and side walls, are all picked in, with different tints of green, which has a simple and elegant effect. The chimney-piece is of statuary marble, and the girandoles are painted.'

W. Thomas
'Original Designs in Architecture', 1783.

A. Hepplewhite & Co.
'The Cabinet-Maker and Upholsterer's Guide', 1788,
2nd Edition, 1789, 3rd Edition, 1794.

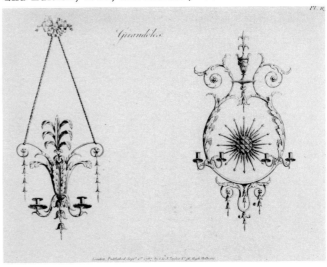

Plate 113.

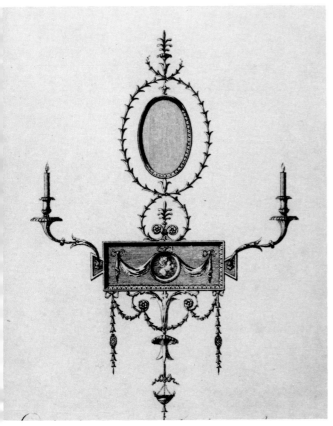

Plate XXVII. Design for the Girandole in the Drawing Room of Wm. Dymock Esq[r].

Plate 114.

Plates 113-115 Girandoles. 'This kind of ornament admits a great variety in pattern and in elegance; they are usually executed of the best carved work — gilt and burnished in parts. They may be carved, and coloured suitable to the room. The star in the design, Plate 113, is intended to be of cut glass, either white or coloured.'

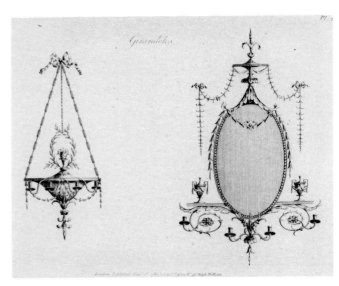

Plate 115.

M.A. Pergolesi
'Designs for Various Ornaments',
1777-1801.

Plate 59. A Girandole.

Thomas Sheraton
'The Cabinet-Maker and Upholsterer's Drawing Book', 1793.

Plate 4 from the Accompaniment. Ornaments for panels, with lights.

Section 2. CHANDELIERS

Daniel Marot
'Nouveaux Livre d'Orfeuverie', 1703, 1713.

Plate VI. Designs for chandeliers.

M. Lock & H. Copland
'A New Book of Ornaments', 1752.

Plate 10. Design for a chandelier. Reissued 1768 by Sayer.

Thomas Chippendale
'The Gentleman and Cabinet-Maker's Director', 3rd Edition, 1763.

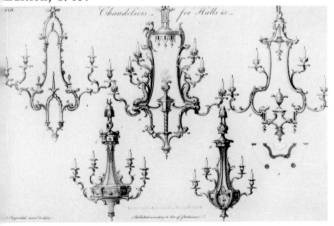

Plate CLIV. Chandeliers for Halls etc.

Plate CLV. Chandeliers for Halls etc. '... they are generally made of Glass, and sometimes of Brass: But if neatly done in Wood, and gilt in burnish'd Gold, would look better and come much cheaper.' Engraving dated 1760.

William Ince and John Mayhew
'The Universal System of Houshold Furniture', 1762.

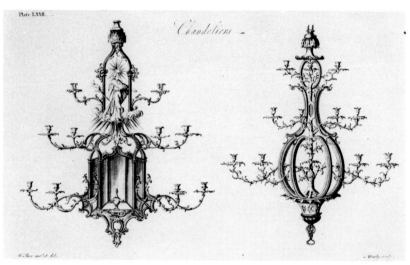

Plate LXXII. Chandeliers. '. . . the first is meant to represent a Temple, and each lined with Glass, and may be executed in Wood and burnish'd Gold; the last has been worked, and looks very grand.'

J. Carter
'The Builder's Magazine', 1774-8.

Plate CXVIII. Design for a chandelier, 1777.

392

A Society of Upholsterers
'Genteel Houshold Furniture in the Present Taste', 2nd Edition, c.1765.

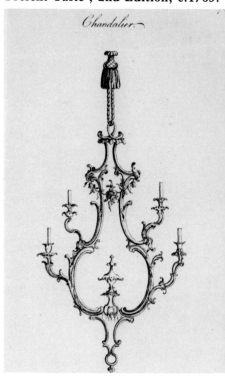

Plate 74 from Part III. Chandelier, attributed to Chippendale.

P. Begbie
'Vases after the Manner of the Antique', 1779.

Design for a chandelier.

Section 3. LANTERNS and STAIRCASE LIGHTS

Thomas Johnson
'Collection of Designs', 1758, 'One Hundred and Fifty New Designs', 1761.

Plate 28 (1758), Plate 28 (1761). Three Lantern designs.

Thomas Chippendale
'The Gentleman and Cabinet-Maker's Director', 3rd Edition, 1763.

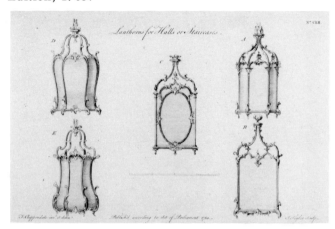

Plate CLII. Lanthorns for Halls or Staircases. Engraving dated 1760.

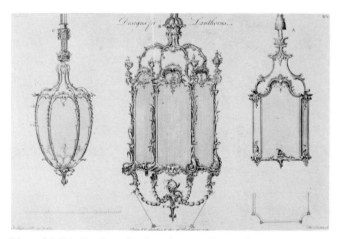

Plate CLIII. Designs for Lanthorns. Engraving dated 1761.

A Society of Upholsterers
'Genteel Houshold Furniture in the Present Taste', 2nd Edition, c.1765.

Plate 75 from Part III. Hall Lanthorn, designer unidentified.

Plate CLIIIa. Lanthorns for Halls or Staircases. Engraving dated 1760.

A Society of Upholsterers
'Genteel Houshold Furniture in the Present Taste', 2nd Edition, c.1765.

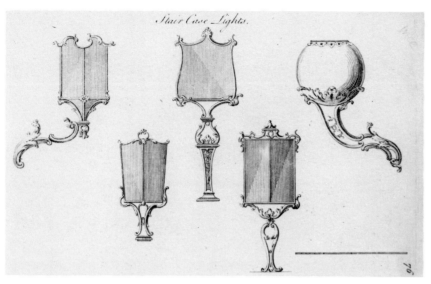

Plate 76 from Part III. Staircase Lights, attributed to Ince and Mayhew.

Plate 77 from Part III. Lanthorn, designer unidentified.

Plate 78 from Part III. Chinese Hall Lanthorn, designer unidentified.

Plate 79. Hall Lanthorns, designer unidentified.

394

William Ince and John Mayhew
'The Universal System of Houshold Furniture', 1762.

Plate V. Hall Lanthorns '... the first is an hexagon in the Gothic Taste, and would have a very good effect: the other square, with French Ornaments.'

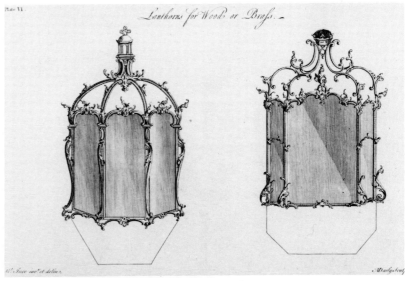

Plate VI. Lanthorns for Wood or Brass '... calculated for being made in Brass or Wood; of the latter we have executed some which are much admired, and at a much less Expence than Brass.'

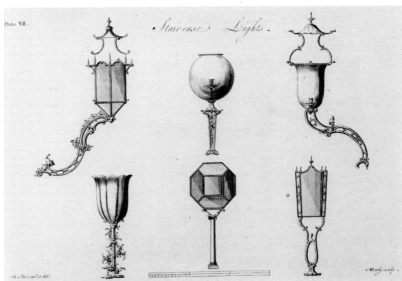

Plate VII. Staircase Lights '... mostly designed to fix on the Hand Rail.'

J. & R. Adam
'Works in Architecture', 1776.

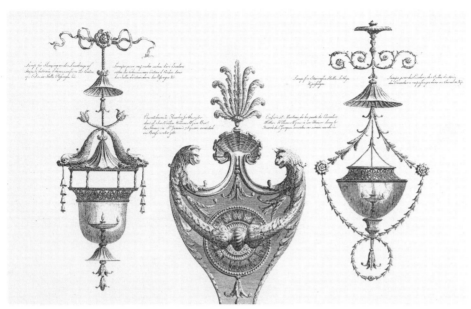

Plate VIII from Vol.I No.IV. Left: 'Lamp for Hanging under Landings of Stairs & between Columns or from the centres of Arches in Halls, Passages, &c.' Right: 'Lamp for Hanging in Halls, Lobbys & Passages.'

J. Carter
'The Builder's Magazine', 1776-78.

Plate XCVII. Design for a Lamp.
Engraving dated 1776.

Plate CLXV. Design for a Hall Lamp.
Engraving dated 1778.

396

A. Hepplewhite & Co.
'The Cabinet-Maker and Upholsterer's Guide', 1788, 2nd Edition, 1789, 3rd Edition, 1794.

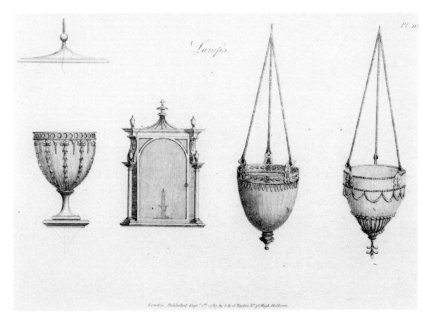

Plate 112. Lamps. 'The ornaments are of brass-work; the square one may be wrought in mahogany.'

R. & J. Adam
'Works in Architecture', 1822.

Plate VIII from Vol. III. Furniture at Syon House. Three
Hanging Lamps.

VI. BRACKETS and SHELVES, FRETS, BORDERS and FENCES

Brackets and sets of shelves were made to a considerable variety of patterns and were used for many purposes. Brackets could support plaster busts, candlesticks, clocks or porcelain urns and bowls. Sets of hanging shelves, according to Hepplewhite, 'are often wanted as Book-Shelves in Closets or Ladies' rooms; they are also adapted to place china on; should be made of mahogany'. Some of the chinoiserie designs with fretted sides remained popular for over thirty years, and some of the patterns shown for them in Chippendale's first edition (1754) and Hepplewhite's first edition (1788) are very similar. Standing shelves for china seem to have been popular only in the middle years of the century, when the craze for chinoiserie was at its height; they do not appear in the later pattern books.

Section 1. BRACKETS

Gaetano Brunetti
'Sixty Different Sorts of Ornament', 1736.

Six designs for brackets or consoles.

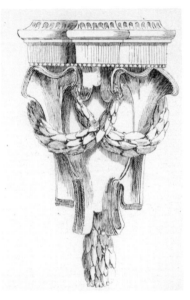

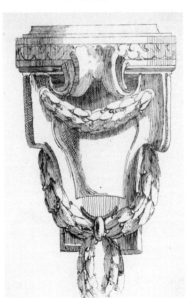

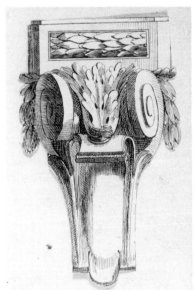

B. Toro
'Masks and other Ornaments', 1745.

Plate 5. Detail from plate showing bracket.

A. Swan
'The British Architect', 1745.

'Four different sorts of corbels, or consoles, for setting Statues or Busts upon'.

Lock & Copland
'A New Book of Ornaments', 1752.

Plate 12. Detail showing brackets. Re-issued by Sayer, 1768.

Edwards & Darly
'A New Book of Chinese Designs', 1754.

Plate 67. Girandoles.

Plate 79. Brackets.

Thomas Chippendale
'The Gentleman and Cabinet-Maker's Director', 1754.

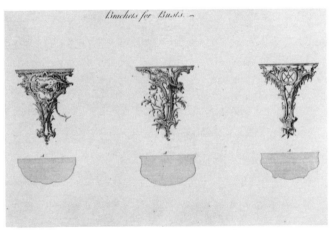

Plate CXXXI. Brackets for Busts. Plate CLX, 3rd Edition, 1763.

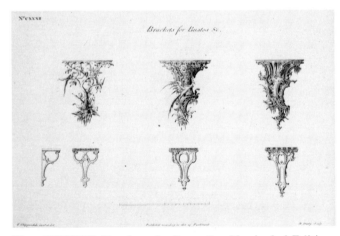

Plate CXXXII. Brackets for Busts &c. Not in 3rd Edition.

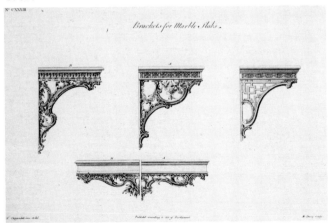

Plate CXXXIII. Brackets for Marble Slabs. Not in 3rd Edition.

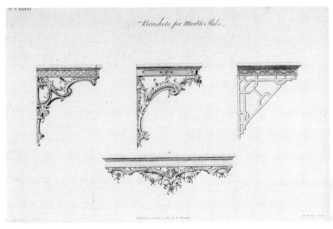

Plate CXXXIV. Brackets for Marble Slabs. Plate CLXII, 3rd Edition, 1763.

400

F. Vivares
'Various Designs', unbound, 1759.

Thomas Johnson
'Collection of Designs', 1758, 'One Hundred and Fifty New Designs', 1761.

Bracketts No. 1.

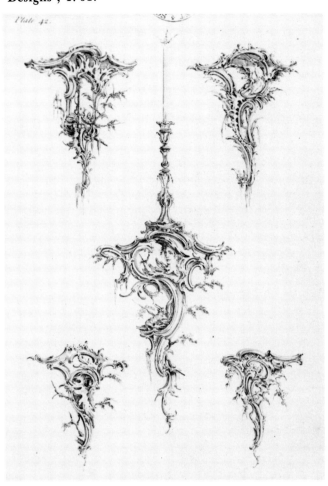

Plate 42 (1758), Plate 27 (1761). Five brackets.

Plate 41 (1758), Plate 51 (1761). Detail showing bracket.

Plate 43 (1758), Plate 38 (1761). Six brackets.

401

Copland and others
'A New Book of Ornaments', 2nd Edition,
post 1761. *(Metropolitan Museum of Art, Harris Brisbane Dick Fund, 1934.)*

Plate 48. Carved Bracket, surrounded by other ornamental details.

Thomas Chippendale
'The Gentleman and Cabinet-Maker's Director',
3rd Edition, 1763.

Plate CLXI. Brackets for Bustos. Engraving dated 1760.

William Ince and John Mayhew
'The Universal System of Houshold Furniture', 1762.

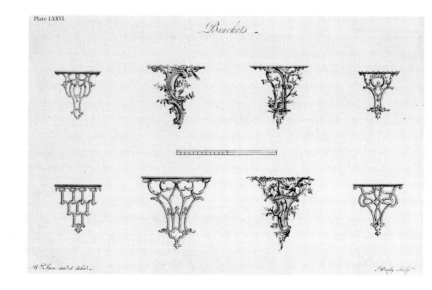

Plate LXXVI. Brackets 'for Candles or Busts'.

402

F. Vivares
'Various Designs' (unbound) c.1763.

A Society of Upholsterers
'Genteel Houshold Furniture in the Present Taste', 2nd Edition, c.1765.

Plate 2. Bracket.

Plate 90 from Part III. Brackets, attributed to Ince and Mayhew.

Matthias Darly
'Architectural Designs and Ornaments', 1769-70.

Design for a bracket.

Plate VIII from Vol.I, No.I. Bracket and Vase executed in wood gilt for James Bourdieu.

Plate VIII from Vol.II, No.IV, 1778. Design of a Bracket with a Vase for Candles.

Plate VIII from Vol.I., No.IV, 1778. Design of a Vase for Candles to be fixed to the Wainscotting of a Room.

Plate VIII from Vol.I, No.I. Bracket and Vase executed in wood gilt for George Keate.

A. Hepplewhite & Co.
'The Cabinet-Maker and Upholsterer's Guide',
1788, 2nd Edition, 1789, 3rd Edition, 1794.

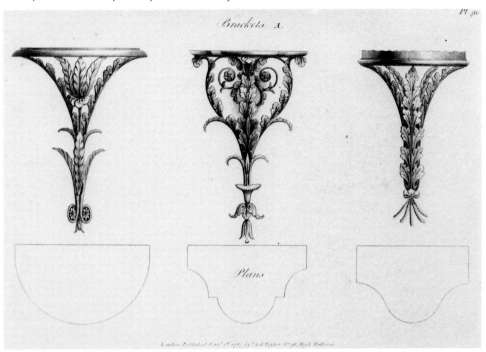

Plates 90 and 91. 'The open form of the three first, marked A, is particularly applicable to place lights on. Some of very large dimensions (6 or 7ft. high) have been made in this manner, for placing patent lamps on in the large Subscription Room at Newmarket; these should be of burnished gold. The three on Plate 91 are better calculated for clocks, busts etc. These may be of mahogany or gilt'.

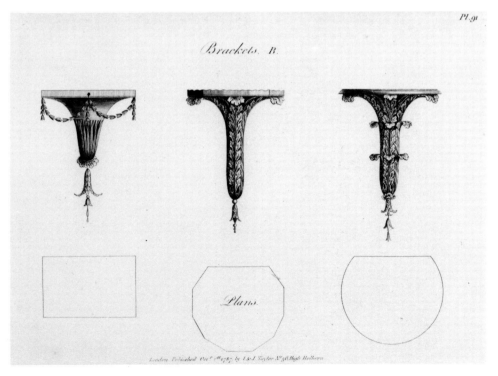

Plate 91.

Section 2. HANGING SHELVES

Thomas Chippendale
'The Gentleman and Cabinet-Maker's Director', 1754.
3rd Edition, 1763.

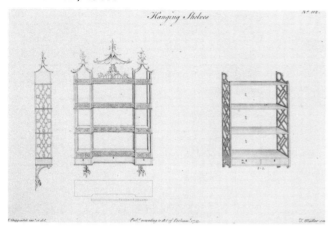

Plate 112. Hanging Shelves. Not in 3rd Edition.

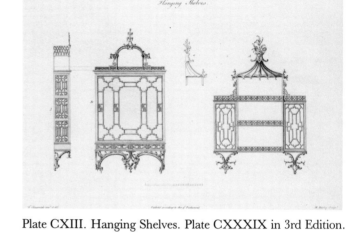

Plate CXIII. Hanging Shelves. Plate CXXXIX in 3rd Edition.

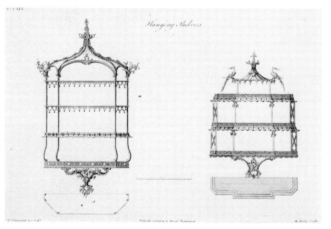

Plate CXIV. Hanging Shelves. Plate CXL in 3rd Edition.

A Society of Upholsterers
'Genteel Houshold Furniture in the Present Taste', 2nd
Edition, c.1765.

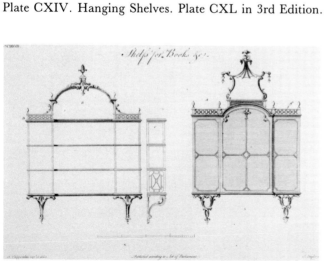

Plate CXXXVIII. Shelfs for Books &c. in 3rd Edition, 1763.

Plate 48 from Part II. China Shelves; designer unidentified.

A Society of Upholsterers
'Genteel Houshold Furniture in the Present Taste', 2nd Edition, c.1765.

William Ince and John Mayhew
'The Universal System of Houshold Furniture', 1762.

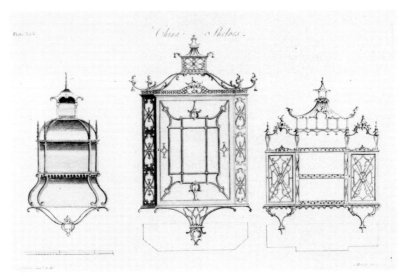

Plate XLV. Book or China Shelves... 'the middle one intended for Glass.'

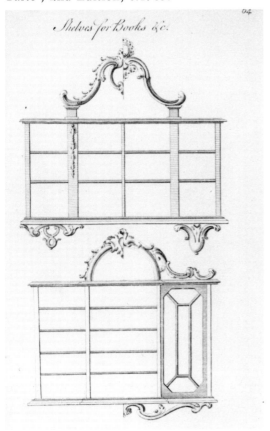

Plate 64 from Part III. Shelves for Books &c. Designer unidentified.

A. Hepplewhite & Co.
'The Gentleman and Cabinet-Maker's Guide', 1788, 2nd Edition, 1789, 3rd Edition, 1794.

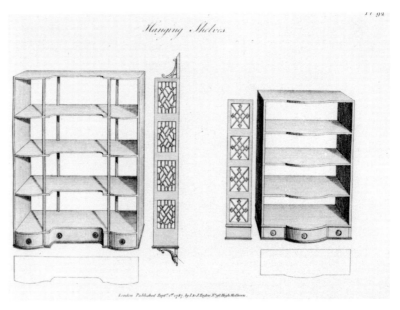

Plate 92. Hanging Shelves. 'These are often wanted as Book-shelves in closets or Ladies' rooms; they are also adapted to place china on; should be made of mahogany.

Section 3. STANDING SHELVES

Thomas Chippendale
'The Gentleman and Cabinet-Maker's Director', 1754. 3rd Edition, 1763.

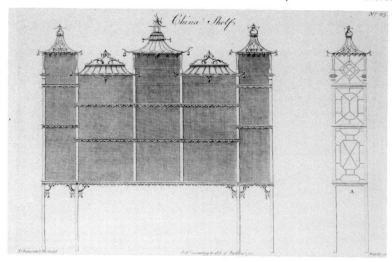

Plate 115. China Shelf. Not in 3rd Edition.

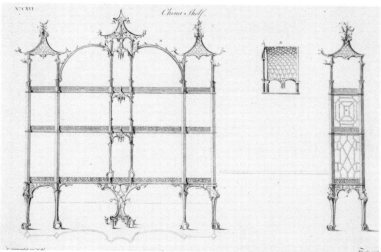

Plate CXVI. China Shelf. Not in 3rd Edition.

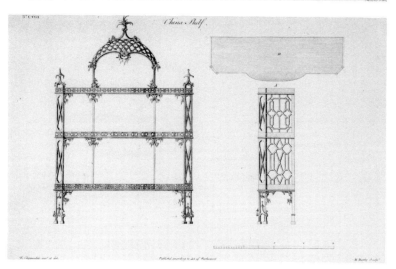

Plate CXVII. China Shelf. Plate CXLI in 3rd Edition. (See page 409.)

Thomas Chippendale
'The Gentleman and Cabinet-Maker's Director', 1754. 3rd Edition, 1763.

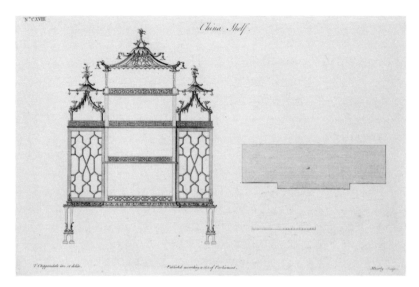

Plate CXVIII. China Shelf. Plate CXLII in 3rd Edition.

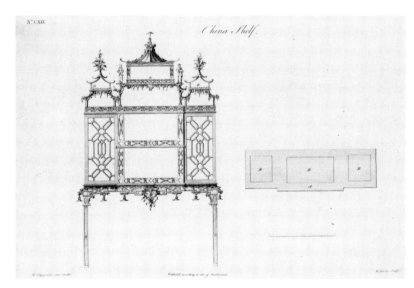

Plate CXIX. China Shelf. Plate CXLIII in 3rd Edition. Re-engraved by M. Darly in 1761 with minor alterations.

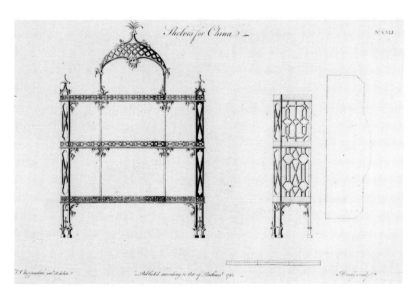

Plate CXLI. Shelves for China. 3rd Edition, 1762. Altered and re-engraved by M. Darly, 1761.

William Ince and John Mayhew
'The Universal System of Houshold Furniture', 1762.

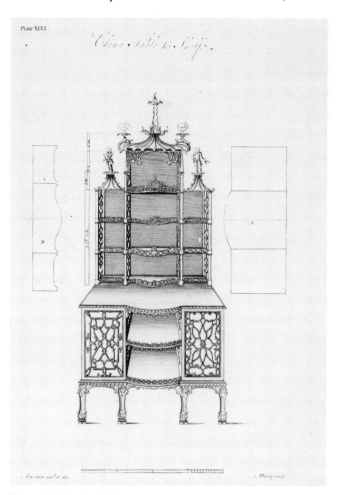

Plate XLVI. 'A China Table and Shelf over it for Books or China...'.

Plate XLVII. 'Two corner Shelves, the second of which has been executed from the Plate; the Sides or back Part to the Shelves were lined with Glass silver'd.'

Section 4. FRETS and BORDERS

Hundreds of designs for frets and borders were published during the eighteenth century; many were included in the furniture pattern books, and some filled books by themselves, such as John Crunden's *Joyner and Cabinet-Maker's Darling, or Pocket-Book* of 1765. They could be applied to almost any piece of furniture, and when executed in mahogany could be fretted out to a remarkable extent, and used for instance on the galleries of tea-kettle stands, trays, candle stands and brackets. Others were carved as blind frets for the decoration of seat rails and legs of chairs, the friezes of tables and cabinet work such as bureaux, bookcases, and double chests of drawers, and mirror and picture frames, the latter often referred to in the plates as 'Tabernacle Frames'. The designs could also be used for

inlaid work in a variety of coloured woods for the borders of table tops and for ornamental friezes on most pieces of furniture. Other designs were published for the use of japanners and painters, and although many of these were probably intended for smaller items such as porcelain, they too could be used on smaller items of furniture. Thomas Chippendale included designs for borders to fix around wallpaper and damask hangings, to be made of papier-mâché and gilded.

The full range of eighteenth century styles can be seen in these designs:- sober Greek key-patterns and Vitruvian scrolls, Chinese lattice, Gothic tracery, sinuous bands of vine leaves and honeysuckle, swags of flowers and classical masks and creatures.

E. Hoppus
'The Gentleman and Builder's Repository', 1737.

Four plates of designs for borders and mouldings.

Plate LVII.

Plate LVIII.

Plate LXIII.

Plate LXIV.

Batty Langley
'The City and Country Builder's and Workman's Treasury
of Designs', 1740.

Plate XCVI.

Plate XCVII.

Plate XCVIII.

Plate XCIX.

Plate C.

Plate CI.

Plate CII.

Plate CIII.

Plate CIV.

412

Batty Langley
'The City and Country Builder's and Workman's Treasury of Designs, 1740.

Plate CV. Guilochi's for Decorations according to the Ancients.

Opposite: a selection of plates from the above book, the engravings all dated 1739. They are decorations for cabinet work, floors, looking glasses and picture frames.

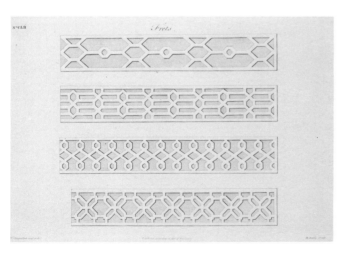

Plate CLII. Frets. Plate CXCIII in 3rd Edition.

Thomas Chippendale
'The Gentleman and Cabinet-Maker's Director', 1754. 3rd Edition, 1763.

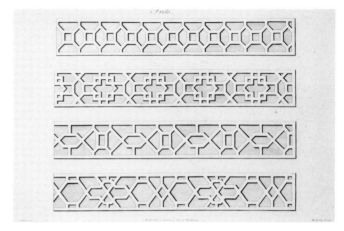

Plate CL. Frets. Not in 3rd Edition.

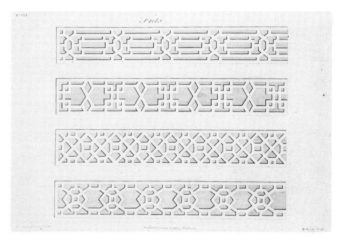

Plate CLI. Frets. Plate CXCII in 3rd Edition.

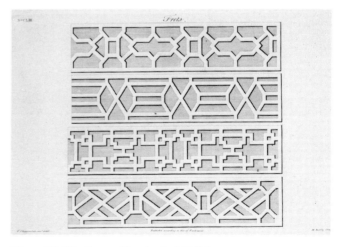

Plate CLIII. Frets. Not in 3rd Edition.

413

Thomas Chippendale
'The Gentleman and Cabinet-Maker's Director', 1754,
3rd Edition, 1763.

Plate CLVI. Gothick frets. Plate CXCVI in 3rd Edition.

F. Vivares
'Various Designs' (unbound), 1758.

Plate 13. Border design.

Plate 21. Designs for a border with details.

T. Major
'Designs for Frets' (unbound), 1758.

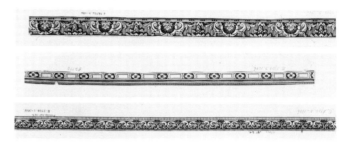

Plate 24. Border Designs.

P. Decker
'Gothic Architecture, Decorated', 1759, Part II.

Plate 7. Frets for Friezes or Smiths Work.

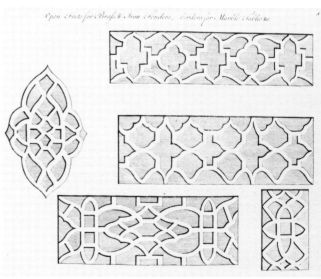

Plate 8. Open Frets for Brass and Iron Fenders, borders for Marble Tables &c.

414

P. Decker
'Gothic Architecture, Decorated', 1759, Part II.

Plate 9. Frets for Joyners, Cabinet Makers and Smiths &c.

Thomas Chippendale
'The Gentleman and Cabinet-Maker's Director', 1763.
3rd Edition.

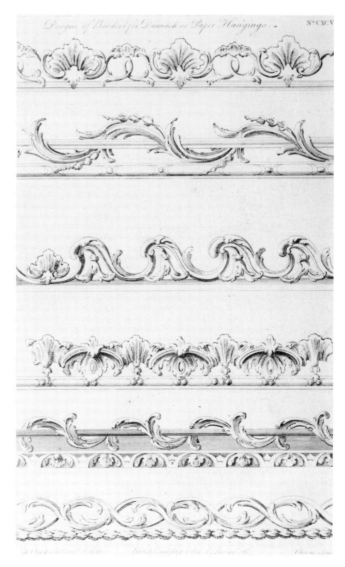

Plate CXCIV. Designs of Borders for Paper Hangings &c. Engraving dated 1761.

Plate CXCV. Designs of Borders for Damask or Paper Hangings. Engraving dated 1761.

A Society of Upholsterers
'Genteel Houshold Furniture in the Present Taste', 2nd Edition, c.1765.

Plate 106 from Part III. Frets for Friezes &c., possibly designed by Chippendale.

J. Crunden
'The Joyner and Cabinet-Maker's Darling', 1765.

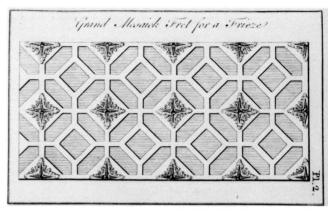

Plate 2. Grand Mosaick Fret for a Frieze.

J. Crunden
'The Joyner and Cabinet-Maker's Darling', 1765.

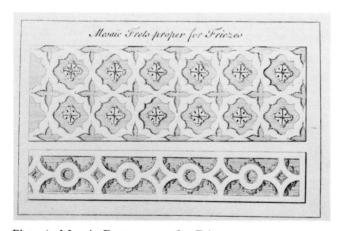

Plate 1. Mosaic Frets proper for Friezes.

Plate 3. Ornamental Frets for Friezes.

Plate 4. A Grand Gothic Fret.

J. Crunden
'The Joyner and Cabinet-Maker's Darling', 1765.

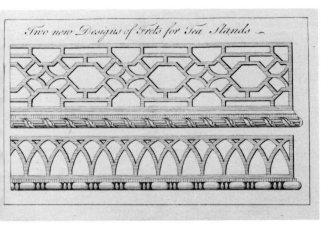

Plate 5. Two new Designs of Frets for Tea Stands.

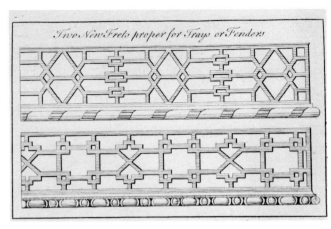

Plate 6. Two New Frets proper for Trays or Fenders.

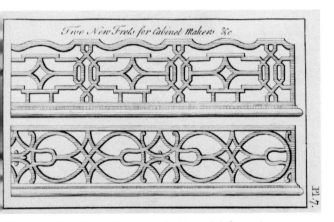

Plate 7. Two New Frets for Cabinet Makers &c.

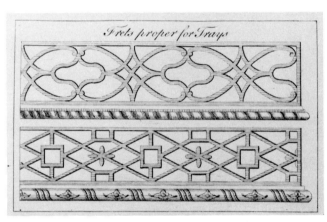

Plate 8. Frets proper for Trays.

Plate 9. Frets proper for Tea Stands, Trays and Fenders.

Plate 10. Frets proper for Tabernacle Frames.

J. Crunden
'The Joyner and Cabinet-Maker's Darling', 1765.

Plate 11. A Gothic Fret for Friezes &c. and A Chinese Fret proper for Cabinet Makers &c.

Plate 12. Gothic Frets proper for Tabernacle Frames &c

Plate 13. Two New Designs of Gothic Frets for Friezes.

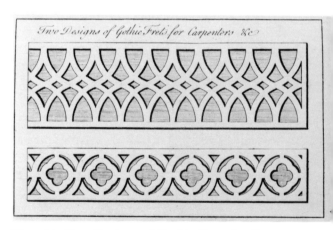

Plate 14. Two Designs of Gothic Frets for Carpenters &c

Plate 15. Gothic Frets proper for Imposts or Architraves.

Plate 16. Two Chinese Frets proper for Tabernacle Frames

J. Crunden
'The Joyner and Cabinet-Maker's Darling', 1765.

Plate 17. Two Designs of Chinese Frets for Architraves &c.

Plate 18. Two New Designs of Frets proper for Imposts.

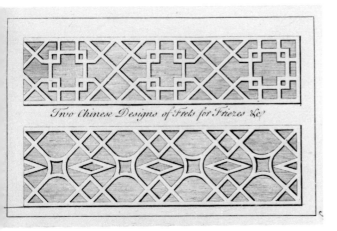

Plate 19. Two Chinese Designs of Frets for Friezes &c.

Plate 20. A New Design for a Greek Fret and a New Gothic Design for a Fret.

Plate 21. Two Chinese Frets for Friezes &c.

A. Willson
'The Antique and Modern Embellisher', 1766.

Plate 1. Greek Frets.

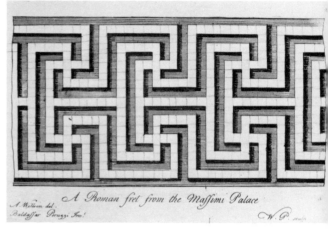

Plate 2. A Roman fret from the Massimi Palace.

Plate 6. Italian Frets.

Plate 8. Italian Frets.

Plate 11. Greek Frets.

Plate 12. Roman Frets.

A. Willson
The Antique and Modern Embellisher', 1766.

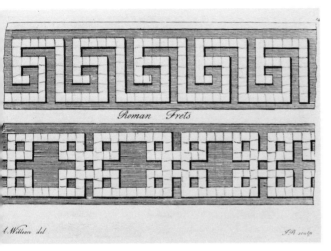

Plate 14. Roman Frets.

Plate 15. A Greek Fret.

Plate 16. A Greek Fret.

Plate 18. Greek Frets and Chinese Frets.

Plate 19. Greek Frets.

Plate 22. Greek Frets.

A. Willson
'The Antique and Modern Embellisher', 1766.

Plate 32. A Greek Fret and a Roman Ornamental Torus.

Plate 42. An Ornament for a Fascia and Antique Torus.

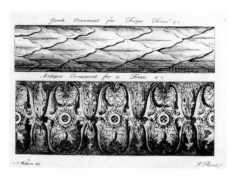

Plate 5. Greek Ornament for Frizes, Torus &c., and an Antique Ornament for a Freze &c.

Plate 7. A Grecian Ornamental Border.

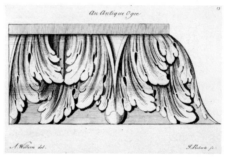

Plate 13. An Antique Ogee.

Plate 17. Antique Ornamented Cyma.

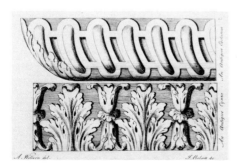

Plate 20. An Antique Cyma and An Antique Eschinus.

Plate 37. Part of an Antique frize.

422

A. Willson
'The Antique and Modern Embellisher', 1766.

Plate 10. Borders for Jappaners China Painters &c.

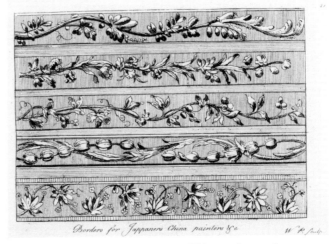

Plate 21. Borders for Jappaners China painters &c.

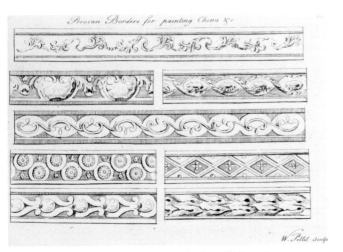

Plate 24. Persian Borders for painting China &c.

Plate 29. Persian Borders for painting &c.

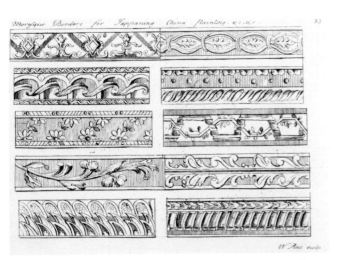

Plate 33. Moresque Borders for Jappanning China Painting &c., &c

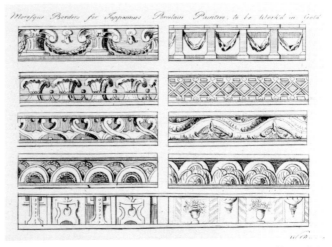

Plate 34. Moresque Borders for Jappanners Porcelain Painters to be Work'd in Gold.

A. Willson
'The Antique and Modern Embellisher', 1766.

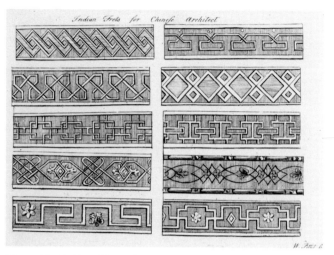

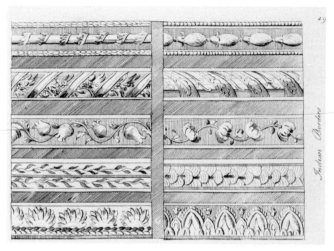

Plate 41. Indian Frets for Chinese Architect.

Plate 49. Indian Borders.

M.A. Pergolesi
'Designs for Various Ornaments', 1777-1801

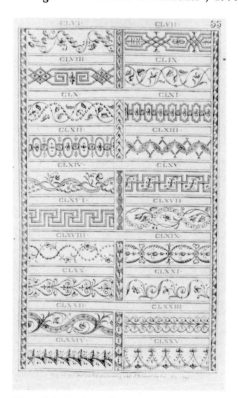

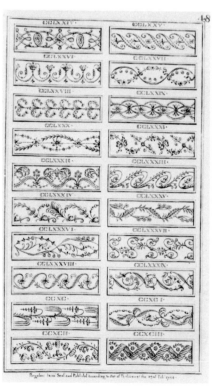

Plate 33. Designs for decorative borders, dated 1781.

Plate 48. Designs for decorative borders, dated 1784.

Plate 58. Designs for decorative borders, dated 1791.

W. Pain
'The Practical House Carpenter', c.1788.

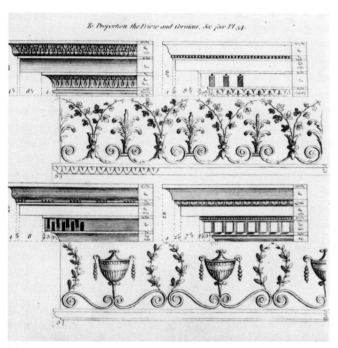

Plate 59. Designs for Friezes and Cornices.

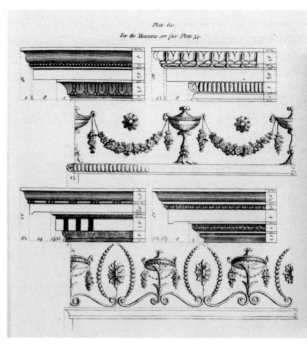

Plate 60. Three Designs for Friezes and Cornices.

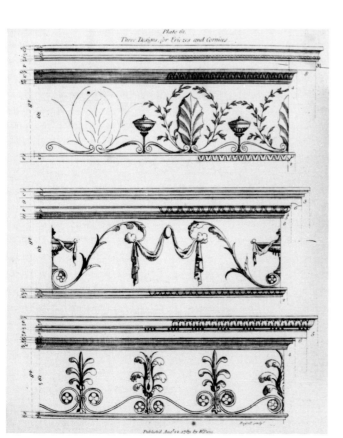

Plate 61. Three Designs for Friezes and Cornices.
Engraving dated 1789.

Plate 62. Four Designs for Friezes.

Thomas Sheraton
'The Cabinet-Maker and Upholsterer's Drawing Book',
1793.

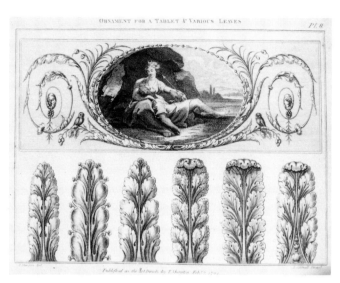

Plate 5 from the Accompaniment. 'Ornament for a tablet, intended for painting on a grey or blue ground, as best calculated 'to throw forward the figure and fruit.'

Plate 11 from the Accompaniment. 'Ornament for a tablet intended for painting. .'.

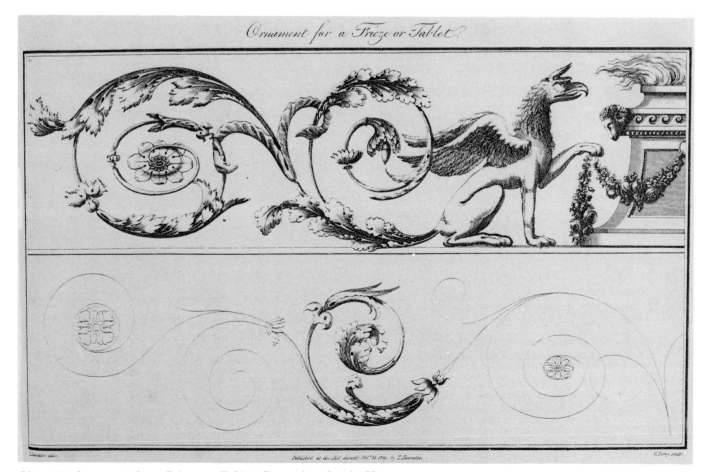

Plate 56. Ornament for a Frieze or Tablet. Engraving dated 1791.

Section 5. FENCING and GATES

A number of the furniture pattern books, and other publications by designers of furniture, included designs for decorative garden fencing and gates, particularly during the middle years of the century when Gothic and Chinese styles were much used for garden ornament. Some of these designs are reproduced here as they too formed part of the eighteenth century carver's work, and many of the patterns could be adapted for use in furniture (for instance in carved chair backs, frets and friezes), and for interior woodwork such as staircases and galleries.

W. Halfpenny
'Twenty New Designs of Chinese Lattice', 1750.

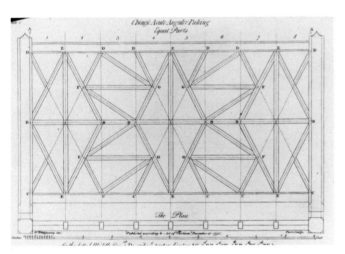

Plate 1. Chinese Acute Anguler Paleing.

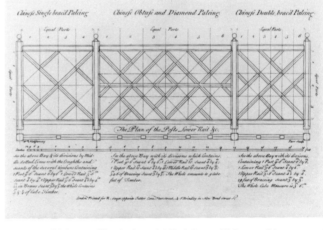

Plate 2. Chinese Single brac'd Paleing. Chinese Obtuse and Diamond Paleing, Chinese Double brac'd Paleing.

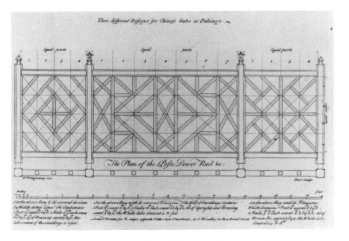

Three different Designs for Chinese Gates and Paleing.

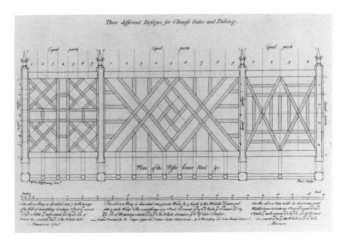

Three different Designs for Chinese Gates or Paleings.

427

W. Halfpenny
'Twenty New Designs of Chinese Lattice', 1750.

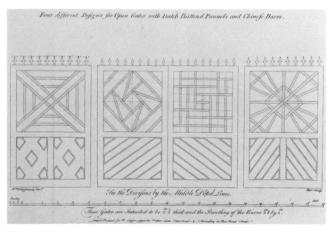

Four different Designs for Open Gates with Dutch Battend Pannels and Chinese Barrs.

P. Decker
'Chinese Architecture, Civil and Ornamental', 1758.

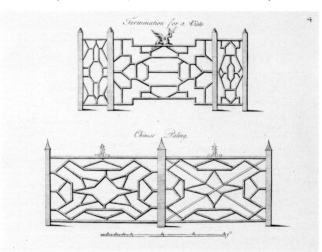

Plate 4 from Part 2. Termination for a Visto and Chinese Paling.

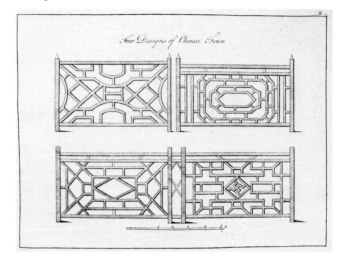

Plate 8 from Part 2. Four Designs of Chinese Fence.

P. Decker
'Chinese Architecture, Civil and Ornamental', 1759.

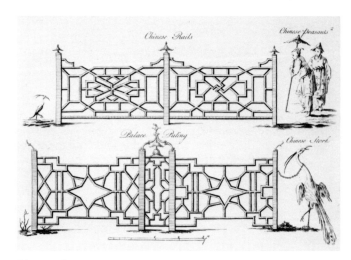

Plate 2 from Part 2. Chinese Rails and Palace Paling.

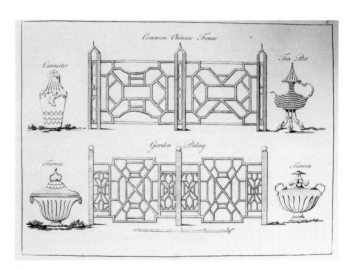

Plate 5 from Part 2. Common Chinese Fence and Garden Paling.

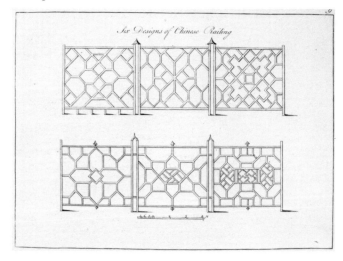

Plate 9 from Part 2. Six Designs of Chinese Railing.

P. Decker
'Chinese Architecture, Civil and Ornamental', 1759.

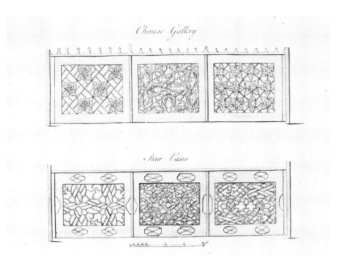

Plate 11 from Part 2. Chinese Gallery and Stair Cases.

P. Decker
'Gothic Architecture, Decorated', 1759.

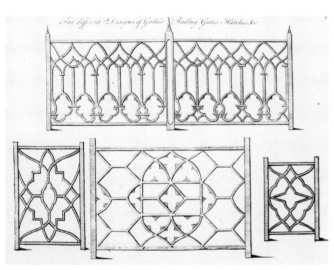

Plate 1 from Part II. Five different Designs of Gothic Railing Gates, Hatches &c.

Plate 2 from Part II. Four Designs of Gothic Gates and Paleing.

Plate 3 from Part II. Four Designs of Gothic Railing.

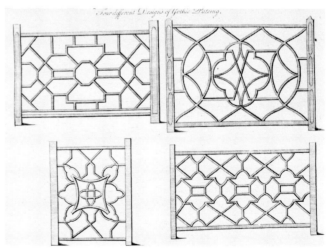

Plate 4 from Part II. Four different Designs of Gothic Paleing.

429

P. Decker
'Gothic Architecture, Decorated', 1759.

Plate 5 from Part II. Three Designs of Gothic Rails.

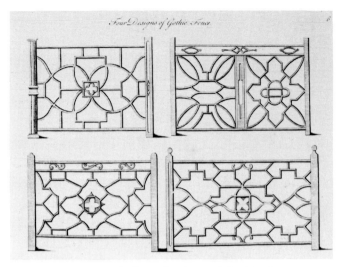

Plate 6 from Part II. Four Designs of Gothic Fence.

E. Hoppus
'The Gentleman and Builder's Repository', 4th Edition,
1760.

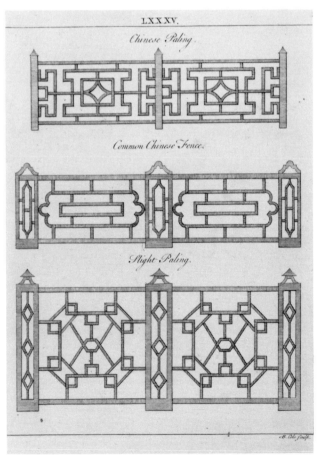

Plate LXXXV. Chinese Paling, Common Chinese Fence
and Slight Paling.

Plate LXXXVI. Garden Paling, Close Garden Paling and
Open Paling.

E. Hoppus
'The Gentleman and Builder's Repository', 4th Edition, 1760.

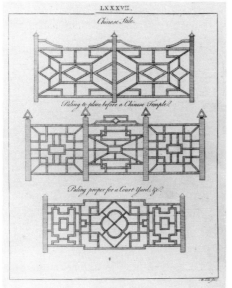

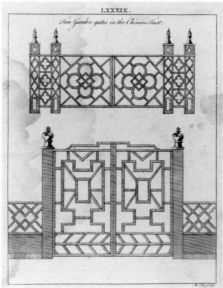

Plate LXXXVII. Chinese Stile, Paling to place before a Chinese Temple and Paling proper for a Court Yard &c.

Plate LXXXIX. Two Garden-gates in the Chinese Tast.

Plate XC. Two Stair Cases in the Chinese Taste.

Thomas Chippendale
'The Gentleman and Cabinet-Maker's Director', 3rd Edition, 1763.

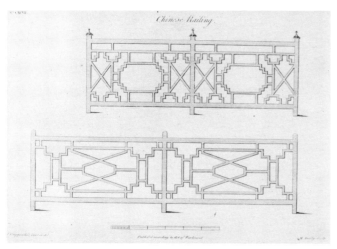

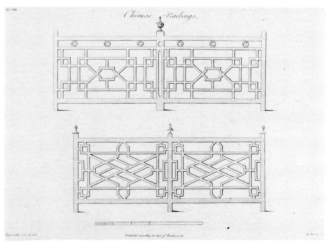

Plate CXCVII. Chinese Railing.

Plate CXCVIII. Chinese Railings.

J. Crunden and J. Morris
'The Carpenter's Companion for Chinese Railing and Gates', 1765.

Plates 1-8. Designs for Chinese and Gothic Gates and Railings.

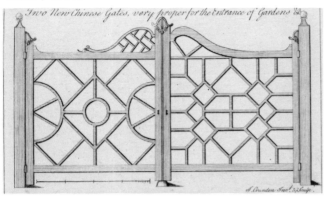

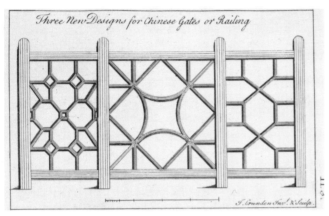

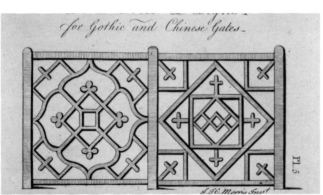

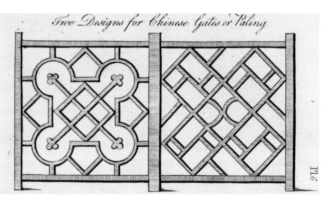

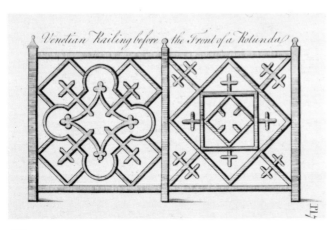

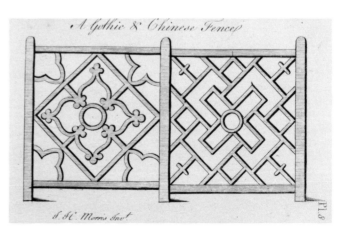

432

J. Crunden and J. Morris
'The Carpenter's Companion for Chinese Railing and Gates', 1765.

Plates 9-16.

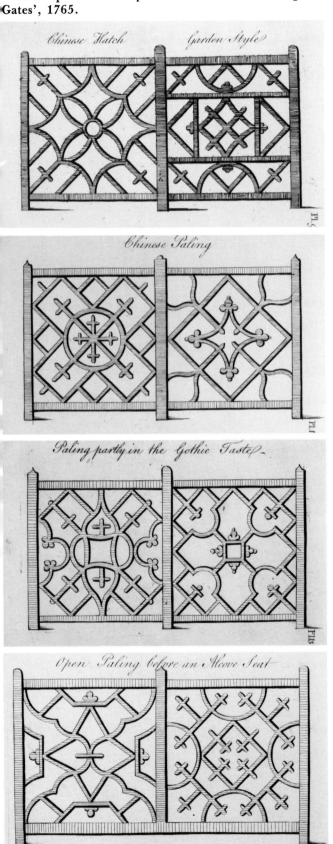

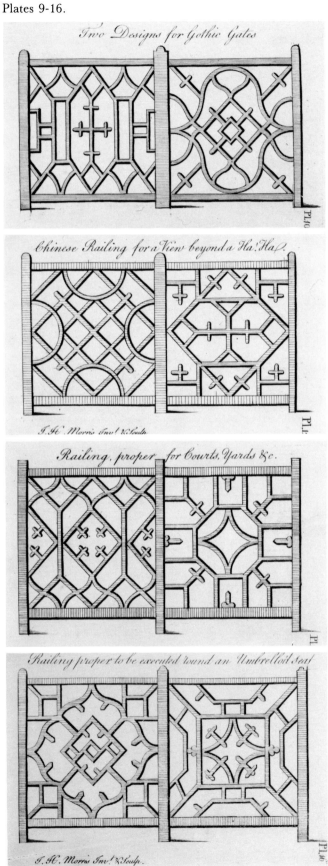

R. Manwaring
'The Carpenter's Compleat Guide to the Whole System of Gothic Railing', 1765.

Plates 1-8. Gothick Gates, Railings, Fences and Hatches.

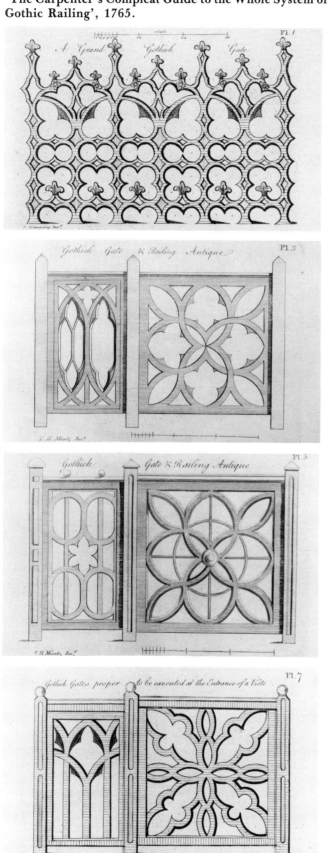

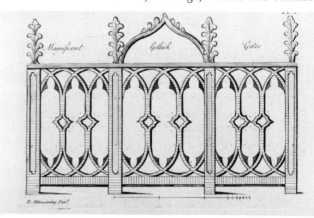

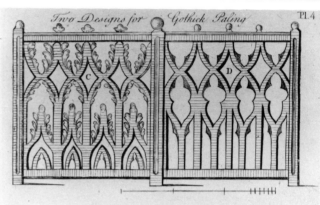

R. Manwaring
'The Carpenter's Compleat Guide to the Whole System of Gothic Railing', 1765.

Plates 9-16. Gothick Gates, Fencing, Palings and Stiles. Plates 3 and 5 designed by J.H. Muntz, Plates 15 and 16 by J. Crunden.

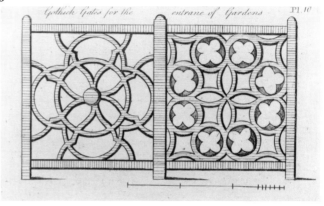

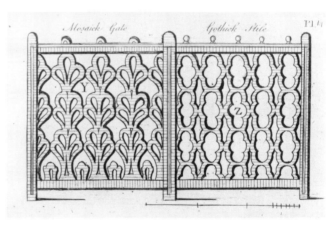

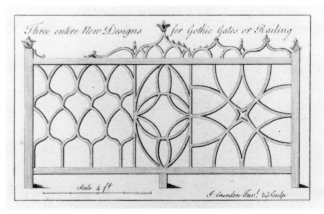

435

N. Wallis
'The Carpenter's Treasure', 1773.

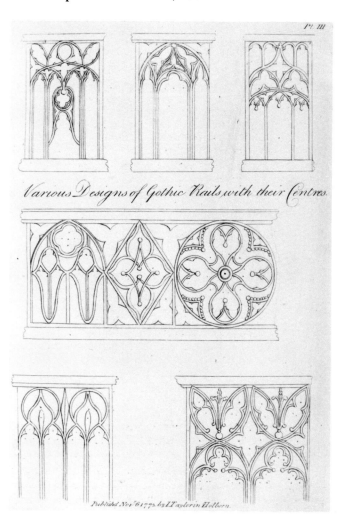

Plate III. Various Designs for Gothic Rails with their Centres.

Plate XVI. Chinese Rails with a detail of Moulding for the top Rail.

436

Part IV. Miscellaneous Items

Many eighteenth century pattern books included in their last pages designs for miscellaneous items of furniture and woodwork which do not fit into the previous categories, such as clock cases, trays, library steps, church fittings, chimney furniture, handles and escutcheons for cabinet work, and internal architectural features such as doors, doorcases and overdoors. Many more designs for handles, lock plates and so on can be found in the numerous metalwork pattern books of the eighteenth century (see Nicholas Goodison, 'The Victoria and Albert Museum's Collection of Metal-Work Pattern Books', *Furniture History,* Volume XI, 1975, pages 1-29).

Section 1. CLOCK CASES

Designs for clock cases appeared only occasionally in English eighteenth century furniture pattern books, despite the high reputation held by English clockmakers from the seventeenth to the nineteenth centuries, and their considerable output both for the domestic and foreign markets. This may have been due, in part, to the existence of specialised bracket, table and longcase makers in London, who developed and maintained standard types and styles during the eighteenth century. Provincial customers, if they did not buy from London, relied on their local cabinet-makers who did resort to the published designs for inspiration, such as Penny of Wells, Veitch of Haddington and Rayment of Stamford, who all produced longcase clocks inspired by Chippendale's plates in the *Director.*

Daniel Marot's designs, published early in the century, reflected many aspects of late seventeenth century English, French and Dutch clockmaking; Marot-esque features may be found on many fine cases with movements by Thomas Tompion (1638-1713) and Daniel Quare (1647-1724), although the elaborate shapes shown in Marot's designs were more in tune with Parisian styles and were not widely adopted in England. The plates are interesting for their variety and amount of detail, for they include not only designs for clock cases, but also barometers, seals and all sorts of watch parts such as cases, pillars, keys, hands and cocks.

The designs published by Batty Langley also reflected Continental clockmaking, as they were taken directly from the designs published in Leipzig by Johann Friedrich Lauch (active 1724-57), and were inspired by the work of Jean Berain. Matthias Lock's and Thomas Johnson's designs for watch and clock cases were again inspired by Continental styles and were extremely fanciful: it is difficult to tell if they were intended to be made of gilt metal or gilt wood, and their scale is occasionally confusing. Only Chippendale's more sober designs approach a reflection of standard mid-eighteenth century English taste for table, bracket and long-case clocks, and even these are too elaborate: most executed examples were made of well-figured mahogany, with some fairly restrained carved ornament and gilt metal mounts.

The Adam brothers' and John Carter's neo-classical designs for table and mantel clocks and watch cases were intended for execution either in wood or gilt brass with marble: many examples inspired by these designs were produced through the co-operation in business of the brass founder Matthew Boulton and the clockmaker Benjamin Vulliamy in the 1770s and 1780s.

A number of designs were published for elaborately carved wall or 'cartel' clocks between c.1750 and c.1775, some of which were intended for public spaces and were quite large. The dials were usually silvered and the surrounding carved foliage would have been gilded to complement mirror and picture frames and chandeliers, and would have been executed by the same craftsmen.

By the last quarter of the century, standard longcase clocks had virtually ceased to be fashionable in London, although cases for domestic regulators continued to be made to a high standard. As a result, few longcase designs appeared: Hepplewhite did not publish any in the *Guide,* although Sheraton did include two designs in the *Drawing Book* in 1793 for elaborately decorated cases in fashionable woods.

Plate 13.

Plate 14.

Plate 15.

Plate 16.

Plate 17.

Plate 18.

TABLE OR BRACKET CLOCKS
Matthias Lock
'Six Tables', 1746.

Thomas Chippendale
'The Gentleman and Cabinet-Maker's Director',
1754. 3rd Edition, 1763.

Plate 5. Table or Bracket Clock.

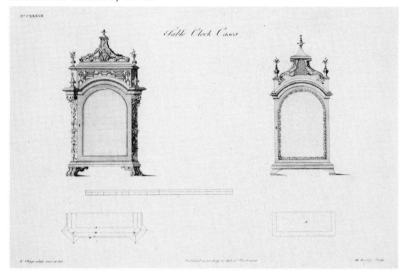

Plate CXXXVII. Table Clock Cases. Not in 3rd
Edition.

Plate CXXXVIII. Table Clock Cases. Plate CLXV
in 3rd Edition.

Thomas Johnson
**'Collection of Designs', 1758, 'One Hundred
and Fifty New Designs', 1761.**

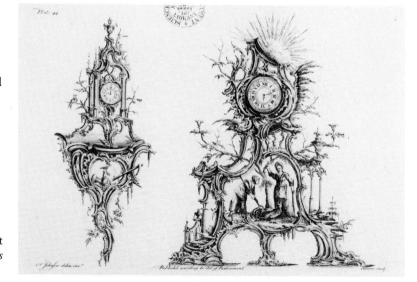

Plate 44 (1758), Plate 13 (1761). Table or Bracket
Clocks. Re-issued by Weale, *Chippendale's Ornaments
and Interior Decoration in the old French style*, 1834.

Thomas Johnson
'Collection of Designs', 1758, 'One Hundred and Fifty New Designs', 1761.

A Society of Upholsterers
'Genteel Houshold Furniture in the Present Taste', 2nd Edition, c.1765.

Plate 46 (1758), Plate 16 (1761).

Plate 53 (1758), Plate 36 (1761). Reissued by Weale, 1834.

Plate 99 from Part III. Stands for Table Clocks, attributed to Johnson.

Thomas Chippendale
'The Gentleman and Cabinet-Maker's Director', 1754. 3rd Edition, 1763.

TABLE OR BRACKET CLOCKS

Plate CLXVI. 'That in the Middle is very large, and fit for a Public Hall, or an Assembly-Room, The others are for Spring Clocks.' Engraving dated 1761.

J. Carter
'The Builder's Magazine', c.1775.

Plate CXLIX. Clock Case.

R. & J. Adam
'Works in Architecture', 1776.

Plate VIII from Vol.I, No.IV. Watch Case executed for
Lady Apsley's Dressing Room.

R. & J. Adam
'Works in Architecture', 1776.

Plate VIII from Vol.I, No.IV. Case for a Watch to Stand
on a Table, Commode or Chimney.

Plate VIII from Vol.I, No.IV. Case for a Watch proposed
to be placed upon a Table or Chimney piece & may be
executed in Metals or in Wood gilt.

Batty Langley
'The City and Country Builder's and Workman's Treasury of Designs', 1740.

Plate CXXXIX. Timepiece 'for the inside of a Church or against a gallery etc.' (after Lauch).

Plate CXL. Timepiece 'for the inside of a Church or against a gallery etc.' (after Lauch).

For a Chippendale Hanging Wall Clock, Plate CLXVI, see page 440.

Matthias Darly
'Architectural Designs and Ornaments', 1771.

Lock & Copland
'A New Book of Ornaments', 1752, 1768.

Plate 12. Two Wall Clocks.

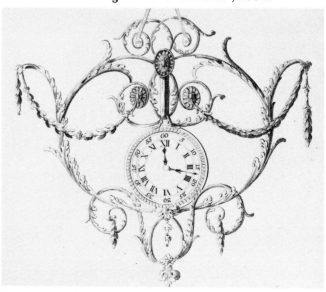

Design for a hanging clock.

Plate 19. Three Long Case Clocks and a barometer.

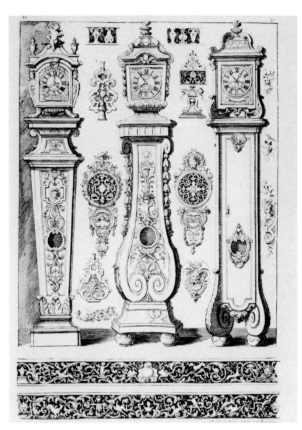

Plate 20. Three Long Case Clocks, watch keys, frets and seals.

Plate 21. Three Long Case Clocks, watch cases, etc.

Thomas Chippendale
'The Gentleman and Cabinet-Maker's Director', 1754.
3rd Edition, 1763.

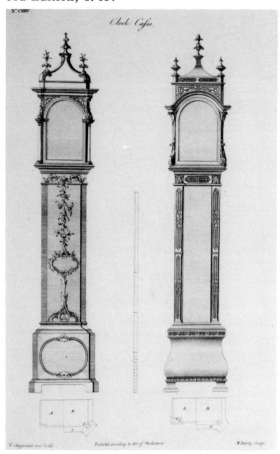

Plate CXXXV. Clock Cases. Not in 3rd Edition.

Plate CXXXVI. Clock Cases. Plate CLXIII in 3rd Edition.

Thomas Johnson
'A Collection of Designs', 1758, 'One Hundred and Fifty New Designs', 1761.

Plate 45 (1758), Plate 50 (1761). Two Long Case Clocks.

Thomas Chippendale
'The Gentleman and Cabinet-Maker's Director', 3rd Edition, 1763.

Plate CLXIV. Three Designs for Clock Cases. Engraving dated 1761.

Plate CLXIII. Two Clock Cases.

Thomas Sheraton
'The Cabinet-Maker and Upholsterer's Drawing Book',
1793.

Plate XXIX from the Appendix. Two Clock Cases.

Section 2. TRAYS

Thomas Chippendale
'The Gentleman and Cabinet-Maker's Director', 1754.

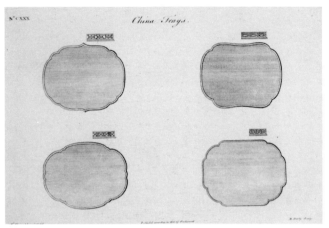

Plate CXXX. Four China Trays. Not in 3rd Edition.

William Ince and John Mayhew
'The Universal System of Houshold Furniture', 1762.

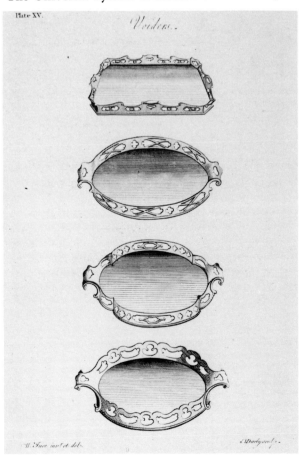

Plate XV. Four Trays, 'Voiders'.

A Society of Upholsterers
'Genteel Houshold Furniture in the Present Taste', 2nd Edition, c.1765.

Plate 89 from Part III. Four trays, attributed to Ince and Mayhew.

A. Hepplewhite & Co.
'The Cabinet-Maker and Upholsterer's Guide', 1788, 2nd Edition, 1789, 3rd Edition, 1794.

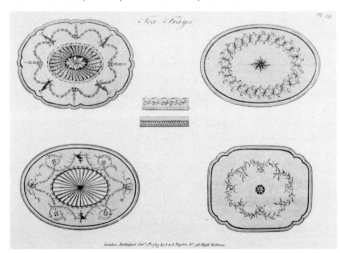

Plate 59. Four Tea Trays. 'For Tea Trays a very great variety of patterns may be invented; almost any kind of ornament may be introduced. Several very good and proper designs may be chosen from the various kinds of inlaid table tops which are given in this book. Four designs for this article are here shewn with the inner borders. Tea Trays may be inlaid of various coloured woods, or painted and varnished. This is an article where much taste and fancy may be shewn.'

Section 3. STEPS

William Ince and John Mayhew
'The Universal System of Houshold Furniture', 1762.

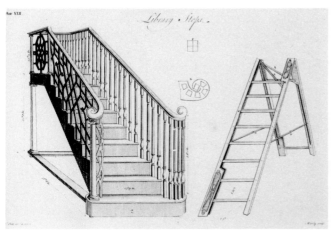

Plate XXII. Library Steps '. . . the First intended for a large Room . . . the other contrived (for little Room) to fold up.'

Plate XXII from the Appendix. Library Steps '. . . vastly cheaper than those in Plate V.'

Thomas Sheraton
'The Cabinet-Maker and Upholsterer's Drawing Book', 1793.

Plate V from the Appendix. Library Steps and Table.

'This design was taken from steps that have been made by Mr. Campbell, Upholsterer to the Prince of Wales. They were first made for the King, and highly approved of by him, as every way answering the intended purpose. . . The steps may be put half in half a minute, and the whole may be taken down and enclosed within the table frame in about the same time . . .'.

Section 4. PULPITS

J. Carter
'The Builder's Magazine', 1776.

Thomas Sheraton
'The Cabinet-Maker and Upholsterer's Drawing Book', 1793.

Plate CIV. Gothic Pulpit.

Plate XXIV from the Appendix.

'The design of introducing a pulpit into this work was to afford some assistance to the cabinetmaker, who in the country is generally employed on such occasions.'

Section 5. ARCHITECTURAL FEATURES

P. Decker
'Chinese Architecture, Civil and Ornamental',
1759.

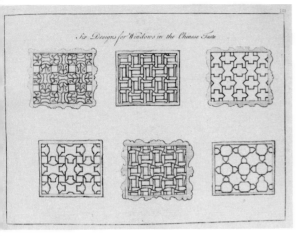

Plate 10 from Part II. Six Designs for Windows in the
Chinese Taste.

DESIGNS FOR WINDOWS

E. Hoppus
'The Gentleman and Builder's Repository', 4th
Edition, 1760.

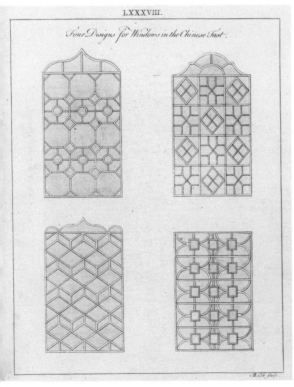

Plate LXXXVIII. Four Designs for Windows in the
Chinese Taste.

P. Decker
'Gothic Architecture, Decorated', 1759.

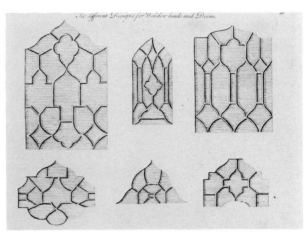

Plate 10 from Part II. Six different Designs for
Window-heads and Doors.

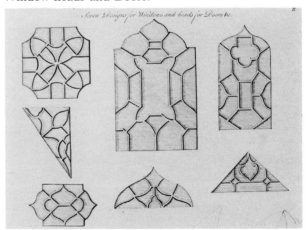

Plate 11 from Part II. Seven Designs for Windows
and heads for Doors &c.

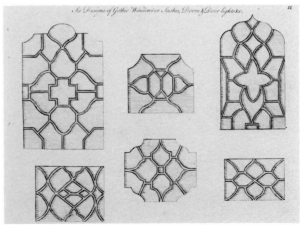

Plate 12 from Part II. Six Designs of Gothic
Windows or Sashes, Doors & Door lights &c.

Thomas Chippendale
'The Gentleman and Cabinet-Maker's Director', 1754.
3rd Edition, 1763.

SHIELDS FOR PEDIMENTS

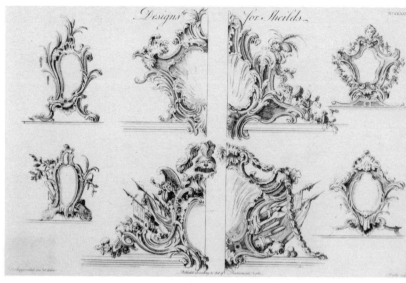

Plate CLXXXIX. Designs for Sheilds. 3rd Edition. Engraving dated 1761.

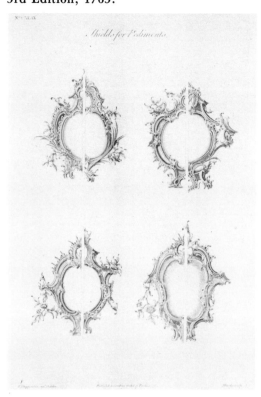

Plate CXLIX. Shields for Pediments. Not in 3rd Edition.

J. Crunden
'The Joyner and Cabinet-Maker's Darling', 1765.

DESIGNS FOR WINDOWS OVER DOORS

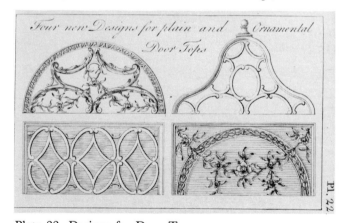

Plate 22. Designs for Door Tops.

Plate 23. Designs for Door Tops.

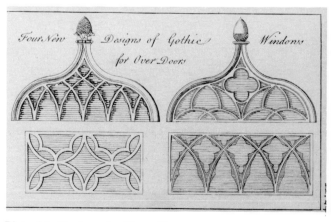

Plate 24. Designs for Door Tops.

J. Crunden
'The Joyner and Cabinet-Maker's Darling', 1765.

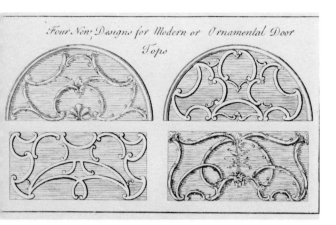

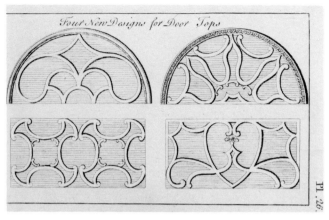

Plate 25. Designs for Door Tops.

Plate 26. Designs for Door Tops.

Batty Langley
'The Builder's Jewell, or Youth's Instructor', 1741.

DESIGNS FOR PEDIMENTS

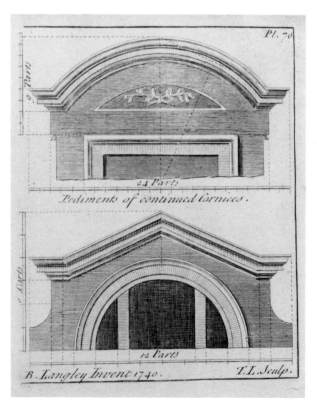

Plate 69. Designs for Pediments.

Plate 70. Designs for Pediments.

451

Batty Langley
'The Builder's Jewell, or Youth's Instructor', 1741.

DESIGNS FOR PEDIMENTS

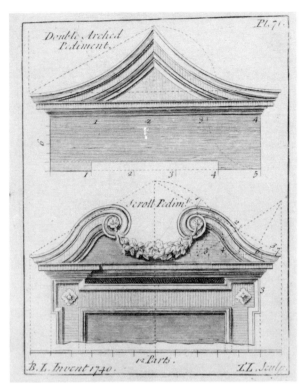

Plate 71. Designs for Pediments.

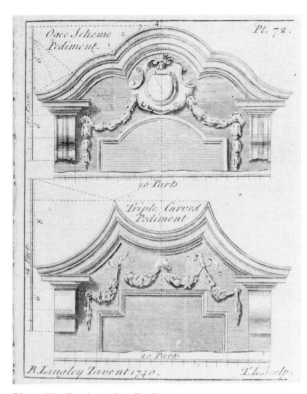

Plate 72. Designs for Pediments.

Plate 73. Designs for Pediments.

Plate 74. Designs for Pediments.

452

Edwards & Darly
'A New Book of Chinese Designs', 1754.

Door Cases.

Door Cases.

A Society of Upholsterers
'Genteel Houshold Furniture in the Present Taste', 2nd Edition, c.1765.

J. Crunden
'Convenient and Ornamental Architecture', 1770.

Plate 68-9. Designs for Doors.

Plate 59 from Part II. Gothic Door, designer unidentified.

J. Carter
'The Builder's Magazine', 1774.

Plate V. Door for a Room of State, '... with the Strictest Adherence to the Rules of Palladio'.

M.A. Pergolesi
'Designs for Various Ornaments', 1777-1801.

R. & J. Adam
'Works in Architecture', 1777.

Plate VIII from Vol.II, No.I. Folding Doors for the Third Drawing Room and the Etruscan Dressing Room for the Earl of Derby's House, Grosvenor Square.

Plate 22. Door Case, dated 1780.

M.A. Pergolesi
'Designs for Various Ornaments', 1777-1801

Plate 32. Door Case, dated 1781.

Plate 61. Grand Door Case, dated 1792.

Section 6. FURNITURE HANDLES and ESCUTCHEONS

Thomas Chippendale
'The Gentleman and Cabinet-Maker's Director', 3rd Edition, 1763.

Plate CXCIX. Designs of Handles for Brass Work. Engraving dated 1761.

Plate CC. Designs of Handles & Escutcheons for Brass Work. Engraving dated 1761.

J. Carter
'The Builder's Magazine', 1777-78.

Plate CXV. Designs for lock furniture, 1777.

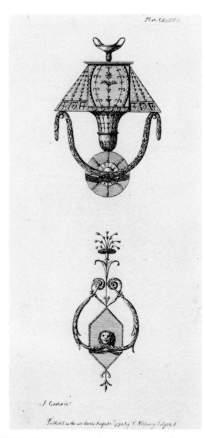

Plate CLXXXII. Designs for door knockers, 1778.

Anon
'Brass Ornaments for Furniture', c.1777.

Items 321, 322. Urn designs for Brass Work.

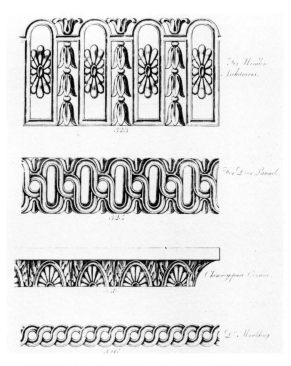

Items 323-326. Border designs for Brass Work.

Anon
'Brass Ornaments for Furniture', c.1777.

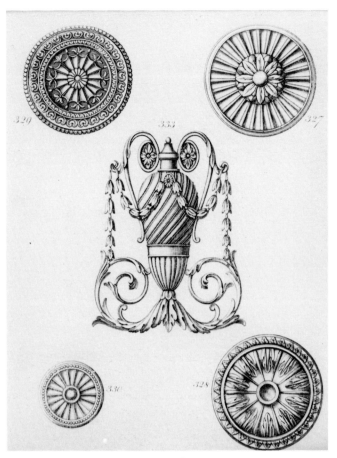

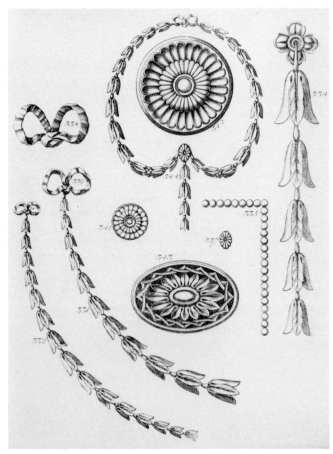

Items 327-330 and 333. Brass Ornaments.

Items 331-332, 334-335, 337-344. Brass Ornaments.

R. & J. Adam
'Works in Architecture', 1778.

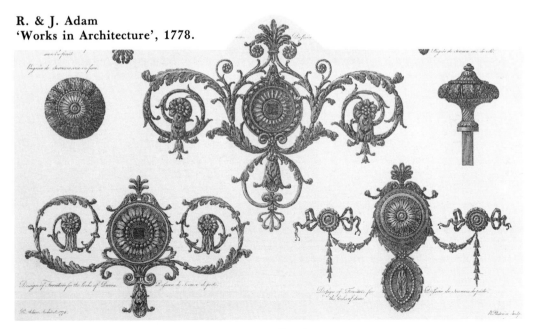

Plate VIII in Vol.II, No.IV. Designs for Brass Furniture.

Section 7. CHIMNEY FURNITURE and other METALWORK FITTINGS

Edwards & Darly
'A New Book of Chinese Designs', 1754.

Plate 64. Chimney Furniture.

J. Carter
'The Builder's Magazine', 1778.

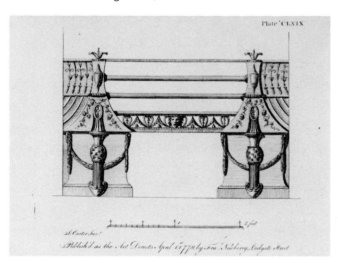

Plate CLXIX. Fire Grate.

A Society of Upholsterers
'Genteel Houshold Furniture in the Present Taste', 2nd Edition, c.1765.

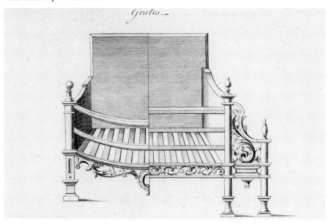

Plate 103 from Part III. Grates. Attributed to Ince and Mayhew.

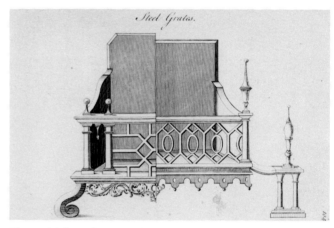

Plate 104 from Part III. Steel Grates. Attributed to Ince and Mayhew.

Plate 105 from Part III. Ornaments to Grates for Burning Wood &c. Designer unidentified.

A Society of Upholsterers
'Genteel Houshold Furniture in the Present Taste', 2nd
Edition, c.1765.

Plate 107 from Part III. Fenders.

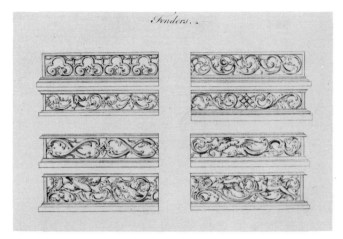

Plate 108 from Part III. Fenders.

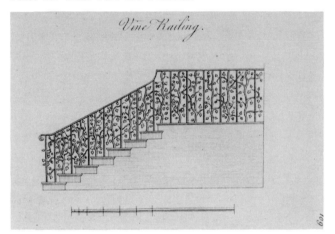

Plate 109 from Part III. Vine Railing.

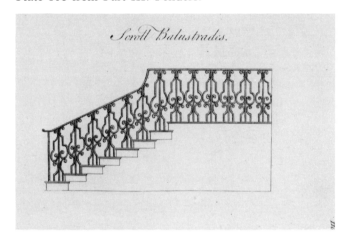

Plate 110 from Part III. Scroll Balustrades.

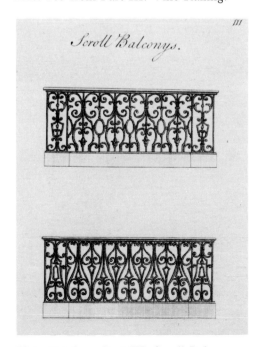

Plate 111 from Part III. Scroll Balconys.

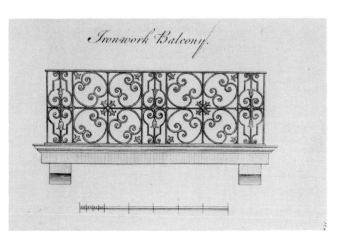

Plate 112 from Part III. Iron-work Balcony.

A Society of Upholsterers
'Genteel Houshold Furniture in the Present Taste', 2nd
Edition, c.1765.

Plate 113 from Part III. Iron Railing.

Plate 114 from Part III. Door Tops.

Thomas Chippendale
'The Gentleman and Cabinet-Maker's Director', 3rd
Edition, 1763.

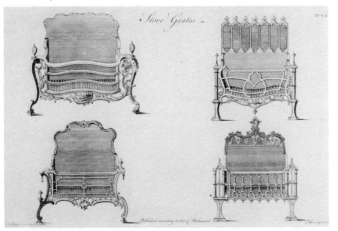

Plate CXC. Stove Grates.

Plate CXCI. Stove Grates.

William Ince and John Mayhew
'The Universal System of Houshold Furniture', 1762.

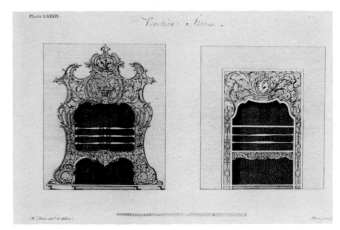

Plate LXXXIX. Venetian Stoves.

William Ince and John Mayhew
'The Universal System of Houshold Furniture', 1762.

Plates 90 and 91. Stove Grates.

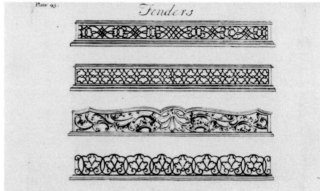

Plates 92 and 93. Stove Grates and Fenders.

Plates 94 and 95. Bracketts for Marble Slabs and Hand rail for a Balcony.

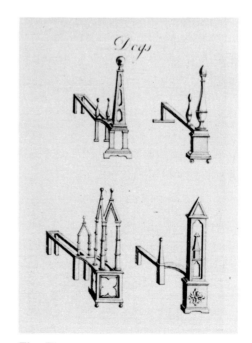

Fire Dogs.

462

William Ince and John Mayhew
'The Universal System of Houshold Furniture', 1762.

Stair Case Railing.

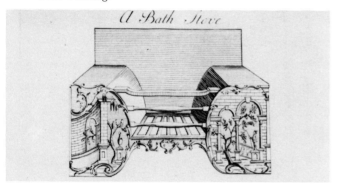

A Bath Stove.

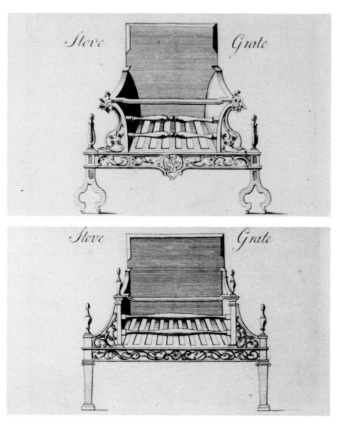

Stove Grates.

Brackets for Lanthorns.

A Society of Upholsterers
'Genteel Houshold Furniture in the Present Taste', 2nd Edition, c.1765.

Plate 118. Obelisks for Lamps &c.

Section 8. MISCELLANEOUS ORNAMENTS FOR CARVERS etc.

H. Copland
'A New Book of Ornaments', 1746.

Plate 2.

Plate 3.

J. Pillement
'A New Book of Chinese Ornaments', 1755.

Title-page and Plates 1-5.

J. Pillement
'A New Book of Chinese Ornaments', 1755.

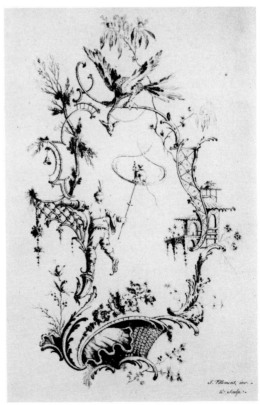

P. Baretti
'A New Book of Ornaments for the Year 1762.'

Plate 2. Ornamental Scroll.

Plate 8. Ornamental Cartouche.

Plate 10. Design for Foliage.

Plate 12. Design for Foliage.

Plate 13. Design for Foliage.

Plate 15. Design for Foliage.

Thomas Pether
'A Book of Ornaments', 1773.

The title-page and five of the etchings of ribbons, scrolls, swags and other ornaments.

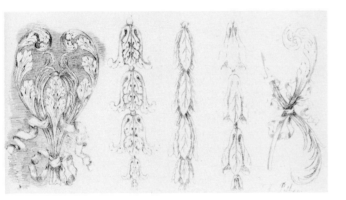

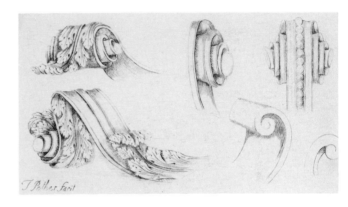

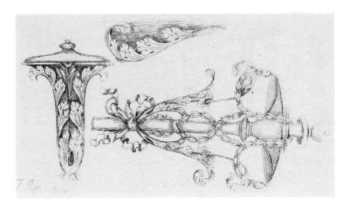

A. Willson
'The Antique and Modern Embellisher', 1766.

Plate 3. Sphinx.

Plate 28. Antique Sphinx.

Plate 4. An Antique Tablet.

A. Willson
The Antique and Modern Embellisher', 1766.

Plate 40. Water.

J. Carter
'The Builder's Magazine', 1774-78.

Plate CIX. Ornamental Panel, 1776.

Plate XIV. Designs for Panels 'in the present reigning taste', 1774.

469

P. Columbani
'A New Book of Ornaments', 1775.

Plate 3. Pannel over Chimney.

Pannel over Chimney.

Pannel over Chimney.

Plate 27. Design for an End Pannel.

Plate 28. Design for an End Pannel.

Plate 29. Design for an End Pannel.

Plate 30. Design for an End Pannel.

Anon, c.1777.

Plate 369. Design for a Gryphon.

Plate 376. Design for a Sphinx.

Thomas Sheraton
'The Cabinet-Maker and Upholsterer's Drawing Book',
1793.

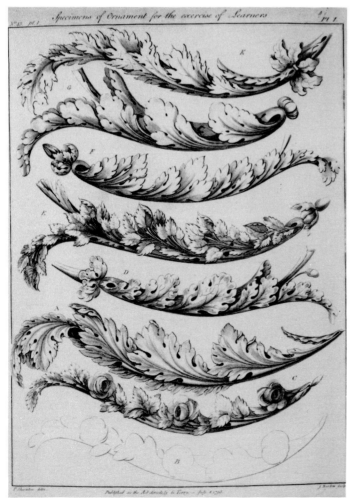

Accompaniment to the Drawing Book, Plate 1. 'Specimens of Ornament for the exercise of Learners'.

472

Part V.

INTERIOR ELEVATIONS and ROOM PLANS

Eighteenth century furniture pattern books and architectural design books contained plates illustrating interior elevations and room plans showing what Hepplewhite called 'the proper distribution of the furniture'. These have been studied and written about extensively in recent years by furniture historians and interior designers, and the reader of this work should certainly consult John Fowler and John Cornforth's *English Decoration in the Eighteenth Century* (1974) and Peter Thornton's *Authentic Decor* (1984).

During the greater part of the eighteenth century it was common practice for furniture to be arranged in a formal manner, so that chairs, tables, mirror frames and cabinet work formed part of the architectural entity of a room. The clearest expression of this discipline may be seen in the designs for window walls, where the pier glasses and table forms were fixed to the walls and literally formed part of the interior architecture in the same way as fireplaces. In drawing rooms, saloons and galleries, chairs, settees and tables were placed against the walls just in front of the dado rail (which protected expensive textiles, paintings or paper hangings from damage), and were brought out into the room for use, for instance around small card tables, supper tables, or in groups for conversation and musical entertainment. The English rarely seem to have taken the scheme as far as the wealthiest French, who arranged their rooms with two sets of chairs, the *chaises meublantes* which lined the walls and were purely for show, and the *chaises courantes* which were for use. Some of the designs reproduced here show elevations of walls complete with seats and tables; others show the decoration of the walls above the dado rail, but leave the area below the rail plain — this would have been 'decorated' by the furniture. Robert Adam took the idea of unity of architecture and furniture to its conclusion in applying the same ornament in both dado rail and seat rails in the Long Gallery at Osterley Park.

Dining rooms were also subject to this arrangement. As has been shown elsewhere in this book (see Tables), large dining tables were not frequently used in eighteenth century houses, but smaller gate-leg tables were set up in a dining room for meals, and stored either at the side of the room or in a passage outside; chairs were ranged round the walls in the same manner as in drawing rooms, and brought out when the dinner table was laid. A focal point in a grand dining room was the sideboard with its display of plate; once again, some of these tables were screwed to the walls and were thus permanent fixtures.

Libraries were slightly differently arranged, as massive library tables were permitted to stand in the centre of these rooms, almost as pieces of architecture in their own right, and were designed to be seen from all sides. Fitted bookcases appear in the design books as well as free-standing ones.

The formal arrangement of furniture extended to grand bedrooms as well, with the usual arrangement of chairs and a dressing table or commode filling the pier between the windows. In the smaller and more intimate rooms the rules were undoubtedly relaxed, but the published designs were not intended to show rooms with the usual clutter of family inhabitation.

After c.1785 a tendency towards less formal room arrangement began to appear in some more avant-garde houses, in imitation of French fashions, but Hepplewhite in 1788 and Sheraton in 1793 continued to show the usual formal arrangement of furniture. It was not until the very end of the eighteenth century, and the first decade of the nineteenth century, that furniture designers themselves began to assimilate the change and publish patterns for pieces that could stand freely and permanently in the centre of a room. The change can be seen quite clearly in the room plans produced by the firm of Gillows between c.1795 and c.1815.

One eighteenth century decorative scheme which somewhat contradicted the formal and, to twentieth century taste, uncomfortable arrangement of furniture, was the sofa in an alcove. Designs for these appear from the middle years of the century, either with fixed benches and squab cushions or with a free standing sofa, and with drapery around the arch. The word 'sofa' was used to convey the idea of Asian relaxation and comfort in contrast to the standard type of eighteenth century settee.

Finally, some of the designers devote quite an amount of the text accompanying their plates to the general style of decoration in rooms: Hepplewhite pointed out that the decoration for a dining room or parlour 'should be plain and neat', while that for a drawing room 'should possess all the elegance embellishments can give'. Both he and Sheraton directed that mahogany was best suited to dining-room furniture, while gilded and painted decoration and more decorative woods such as satinwood and rosewood were suitable for use in drawing rooms. Sheraton expanded on the theme in his *Cabinet Dictionary* of 1803 (page 216) in which he stated that 'The kitchen, the hall, the dining parlour, the anti-room, the drawing room, the library, the breakfast room, the music room, the gallery of paintings, the bedroom and dressing apartments, ought to have their proper suits of furniture, and to be finished in a style that will at once shew, to a competent judge, the place they are destined for.'

Daniel Marot
'Nouvelles Cheminées', 1703, 1713.

Plate 20. Cheminée.

Plate 22. Cheminée.

Daniel Marot
'Nouveaux Livre d'Apartements', 1703, 1713.

Plate 25. Dining Room.

Daniel Marot
'Nouveaux Livre d'Apartements', 1703, 1713.

For designs for Bed
Chambers, see pages 33
and 155.

Plate 27. Cabinet, showing Daybed, Stools, Triad and Festoons.

Plate 28. Library.

J. Vardy
'Some Designs of Mr. Inigo Jones & Mr. William Kent', 1744.

Plate 33. The Section of the Hermitage (Richmond), by William Kent.

W. Halfpenny
'The Modern Builder's Assistant', 1757.

Plate 73. Doorway and Picture Surrounds.

Plate 74. Section of a Room.

W. Halfpenny
'The Modern Builder's Assistant', 1757.

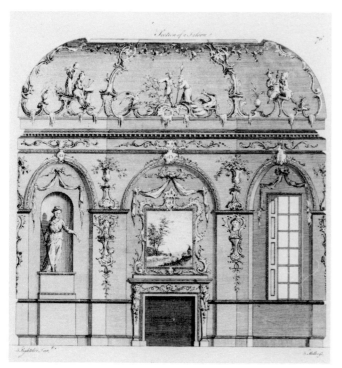

Plate 76. Section of a Saloon.

Plate 77. Section of a Saloon.

Thomas Johnson
'Collection of Designs', 1758, 'One Hundred and Fifty New Designs', 1761.

Plate 25 (1758), Plate 10 (1761). The Side of a Room.

For two furnished Alcoves by Ince and Mayhew see pages 112 and 113.

W. Wrighte
'Grotesque Architecture, or Rural Amusement', 1767.

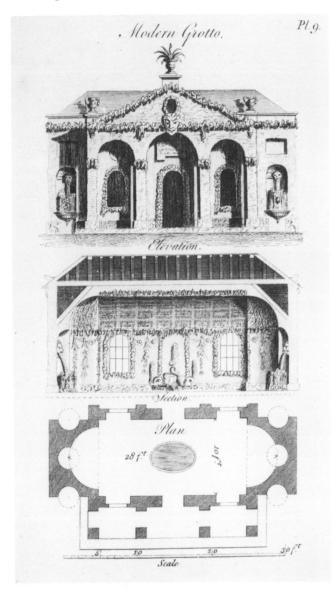

Plate 9. Modern Grotto; 'A modern Architectonic Stile, ornamented with jet d'eaux, Sea Weeds, Looking Glass, Fountains, and other Grotesque Decorations.'

Plate 23. Turkish Mosque with Minarets attached.

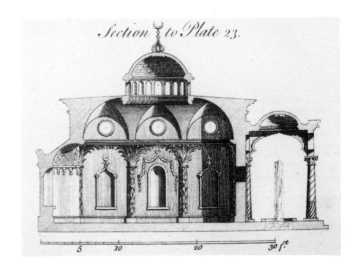

Plate 24. Section to Plate 23.

Matthias Darly
'Architectural Designs and Ornaments', 1769-70.

Section of a Room with Greek Ornaments.

Section of a Room with Two Chimney Pieces in the Antique Taste.

J. Crunden
'Convenient and Ornamental Architecture', 1770.

Plates 56 and 57. Four Sides of a Room ornamented with Stucco Work, proper for an Eating Parlour.

Plates 60 and 61. Four Sides of a Room, ornamented with Stucco Work.

479

Plate XIII. Section of a Banqueting Room '... as these kind of rooms are used for the Reception of Large Companies, for elegant Entertainments, and Variety of Diversions...'.

Plate XLIV. Interior.

Thomas Malton
'Compleat Treatise on Perspective', 1775.

Plate XXX. 'To represent an elegant Room, having a large, circular Bow-Window in the side, and a Cove-Ceiling.'

R. & J. Adam
'Works in Architecture', 1777.

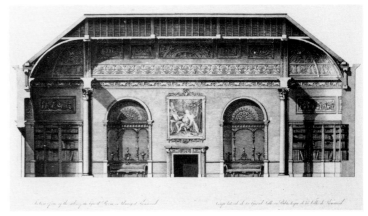

Plate II from Vol.II, No.I.

Designs for the Earl of Derby's House in Grosvenor Square. 'Section of the Chimney-side of the Anti-Room in the principal Story.
The ornaments are all in stucco; and the grounds, both of the ceiling and side walls, are all picked in, with different tints of green, which has a simple and elegant effect. The chimney-piece is of statuary marble; and the girándoles are painted.'

Plate V from Vol.II, No.II, 1778.
'Section of one of the sides of the Great Room, or Library at Kenwood.'
'The square recesses on this side are fitted up with glasses, which reflecting the objects which are seen from windows have a most singular and beautiful effect.'

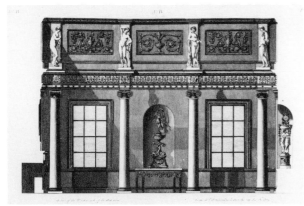

Section of the Window Side.

Plate IV from Vol.II, No.IV, 1778. The Anti Room, Syon House.

Plate III from Vol.III, 1822. The Library at Syon House.

Plate V from Vol.II, No.I, 1777. Designs for the Earl of Derby's House, Grosvenor Square. Inside view of the Third and Great Withdrawing Room.

'The ornaments of the ceiling and entablature are chiefly of stucco gilt, with a mixture of paintings. The grounds are coloured with various tints. The frames for glasses, the pedestals and vases in the niches, and the girandoles on the piers, are of wood gilt. This room is hung with satin, and is undoubtedly one of the most elegant in Europe, whether we consider the variety or the richness of its decoration.'

Plate IV from Vol.II, No.I, 1777. Designs for the Earl of Derby's House, Grosvenor Square.

Side of the second drawing room.
'The ornaments of the pilastres, arches, and pannels of the doors, are beautifully painted by Zucchi. Those in the freezes of the room and doors are of stucco, and of wood carved...'.

M.A. Pergolesi
'Designs for Various Ornaments', 1777-1801

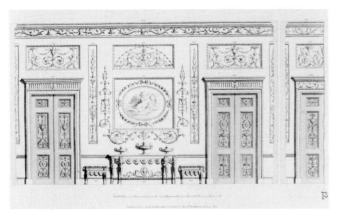

Plate 42. Design for the Side of a Room, 1782.

Plate 52. Design for the Side of a Room, 1784.

Plate 64. Design for the Side of a Room. Published by Dulouchamp 'successor to the late Signor Pergolesi', 1801.

W. & J. Pain
'Pain's British Palladio', 1788.

Plate 27.

A. Hepplewhite & Co.
'The Cabinet-Maker and Upholsterer's Guide', 1788.
2nd Edition 1789, 3rd Edition 1794.

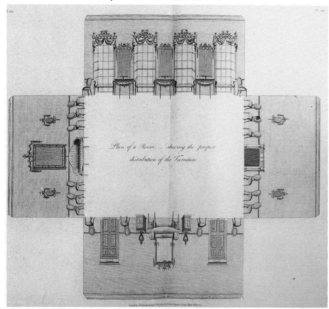

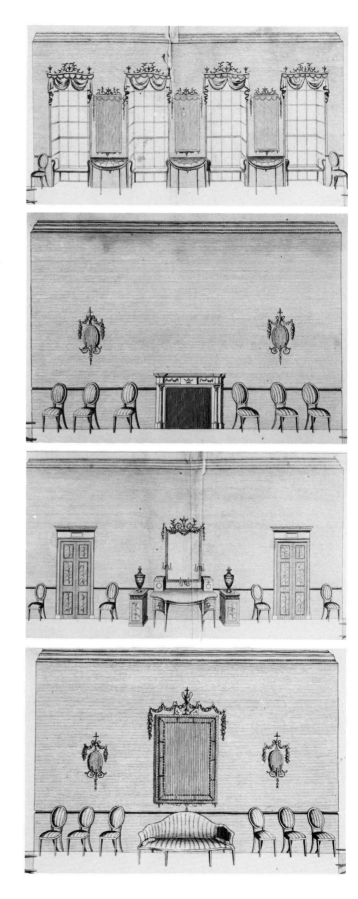

Plates 124 and 125. Plan of a Room showing the proper distribution of the Furniture.

'Here we shew, at one view, the necessary and proper furniture for a drawing-room, and also for a Dining-Room or Parlour, subject to the following variations.

If the object of this plan was a Drawing-Room only, on each side of the chimney-piece there should be a sofa, and on the opposite side, instead of a sofa, should be a confidante, the sideboard also should be removed and an elegant commode substituted in its place; the remaining space may be filled up with chairs.

For a Dining-room, instead of the per-tables, should be a set of Dining-tables; the rest of the furniture, and the general ordonnance of the room is equally proper, except the glass over the sofa, which might be omitted, but this is mere opinion, many of the Dining Parlours of our first Nobility having full as much glass as is here shewn.

The proper furniture for a Drawing-Room, and for a Dining-Room or Parlour being thus pointed out, it remains only to observe, that the general appearance of the latter should be plain and neat, while the former being considered as a State-Room, should possess all the elegance embellishments can give.'

Enlarged details from the plan shown in Plates 124-5.

W. Pain
'The Practical House Carpenter', 3rd Edition, 1791.

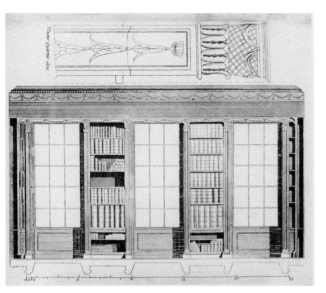

Plate 117.

Plate 118.

Plates 117-120. Sections of a Library, dated 1791.

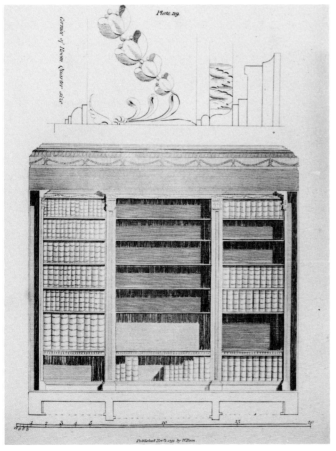

Plate 119.

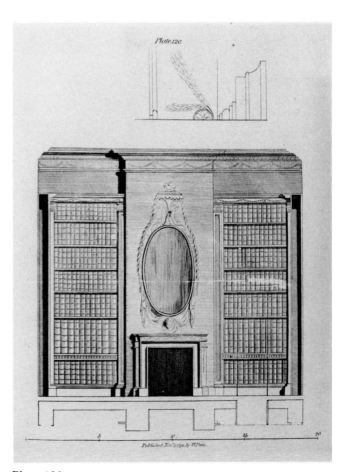

Plate 120.

W. Pain
'The Practical House Carpenter', 3rd Edition, 1791.

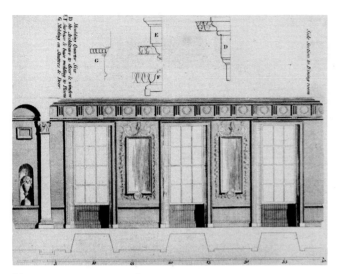

Plate 121.

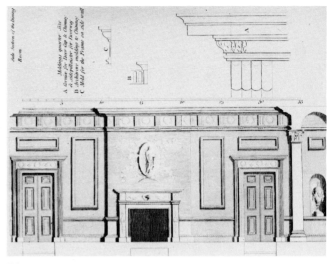

Plate 122.

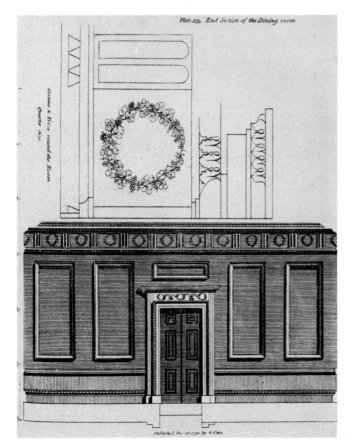

Plate 123.

Plates 121-124. Sections of a Dining Room, dated 1791.

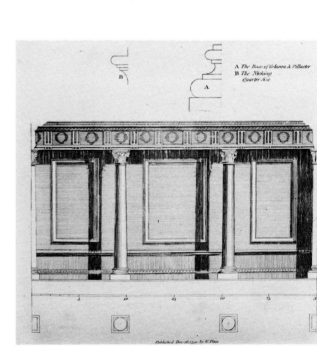

Plate 124.

486

Thomas Sheraton
'The Cabinet-Maker and Upholsterer's Drawing Book',
1793.

Plate XXXII from the Appendix. A View of the Prince of Wales' Chinese Drawing Room.

Plate XXXII from the Appendix. Another view of the Prince of Wales' Chinese Drawing Room, showing the ottoman.

'The view... contains an otoman, or long seat, extending the whole width of the room, and returning at each end about five feet. The Chinese columns are on the front of this seat, and mark out its boundaries. The upholstery work is very richly executed in figured satin, with extremely rich borders, all worked to suit the style of the room. Within this otoman are two grand tripod candle-stands with heating urns at the top, that the seat may be kept in a proper temperature in cold weather. On the front of the otoman before the columns are two censers containing perfumes, by which an agreeable smell may be diffused in every part of the room, preventing that of a contrary nature, which is the consequence of lighting a number of candles.

The chimneypiece is rich, adorned with a valuable timepiece, and two lights supported by two Chinese figures; on each side of the fireplace is also a Chinese figure, answerable to those which support a table on the opposite side, under which is seated a Chinese figure. Over each table, the fireplace, and in the center of the otoman, is a glass, which by their reflections greatly enliven the whole. The subjects painted on the pannels of each wall are Chinese views, and little scenes. The carpet is worked in one entire piece, with a border round it and the whole in effect, though it may appear extragavant to a vulgar eye, is but suitable to the dignity of the proprietor.'

487

Thomas Sheraton
'The Cabinet-Maker and Upholsterer's Drawing Book',
1793.

A Dining Parlour in imitation of the Prince of Wales's.

Plate LX from Part III. A Dining Parlour in imitation of the Prince of Wales'.

'This dining-parlour gives a general idea of the Prince of Wales' in Carlton-House; but in some particulars it will be a little varied, as I had but a very transient view of it.

The Prince's has five windows facing St. James's Park. This also has five, one of which is hid by the left column. His windows are made to come down to the floor, which open in two parts as a double door, leading to a large grass plat to walk in. If I remember right, there are pilasters between each window; but this is intended to have glass. In his is a large glass over the chimney piece, as this has. To these glass-frames are fixed candle branches. At each end of his is a large sideboard, nearly twelve feet in length, standing between a couple of ionic columns, worked in composition to imitate fine variegated marble, which have a most beautiful and magnificent effect. In the middle are placed a large range of dining tables, standing on pillars with four claws each, which is now the fashionable way of making these table. The chairs are of mahogany, made in the style of the French, with broad top-rails hanging over each back foot; the legs are turned, and the seats covered with red leather...

The general style of furnishing a dining-parlour should be in substantial and useful things, avoiding trifling ornaments and unnecessary decorations... The furniture, without exception, is of mahogany, as being the most suitable for such apartments.'

Thomas Sheraton
'The Cabinet-Maker and Upholsterer's Drawing Book',
1793.

Plate 61. Details from one of the Walls from the Plan Section of a Drawing Room.

Plate 61. The Fireplace Wall from the Plan Section of a Drawing Room.

Plate 61. Detail of one of the Walls, showing Door Case.

Plate LXI from Part III. Drawing Room. 'A Drawing Room is of that sort which admits of the highest taste and elegance; in furnishing of which, workmen in every nation exert the utmost efforts of their genius.

To assist me in what I have here shewn, I had the opportunity of seeing the Prince of Wales', the Duke of York's, and other noblemen's drawing-rooms.

... It may not be amiss to mention some particulars respecting the Prince's room, that the reader may form some idea of its taste and magnificence...

... In the drawing room which is here shewn... the pier tables have marble tops and gold frames, or white and gold. The glasses are often made to appear to come down to the stretcher of the table; that is, a piece of glass is fixed in behind the pier table, separate from the upper glass, which then appears to be the continuation of the same glass... this small piece of glass may be fixed either in the dado of the room, or in the frame of the table.

... The panelling of the walls are done in paper, with ornamented borders of various colours.

The figures above the glasses are paintings, in clare-obscure. The sofas are bordered off in three compartments, and covered with figured silk or satin. The ovals may be printed separately, and sewed on. These sofas may have cushions to fill their backs, together with bolsters at each end. In France, where their drawing-rooms are fitted up in the most splendid manner, they use a sett of small and plainer chairs, reserving the others merely for ornament.

The commode opposite the fireplace has four doors; its legs are intended to stand a little clear of the wings; and the top is marble, to match the pier-table. In the freeze part of the commode is a table in the center, made of an exquisite composition in imitation of statuary marble. These are to be had, of any figure, or on any subject, at Mr. Wedgwood's, near Soho square... The commode should be painted to suit the furniture, and the legs and other parts in gold to harmonize with the sofas, tables and chairs.'

489

C. Middleton
'Picturesque and Architectural Views for Cottages, Farmhouses and Country Villas', 1795.

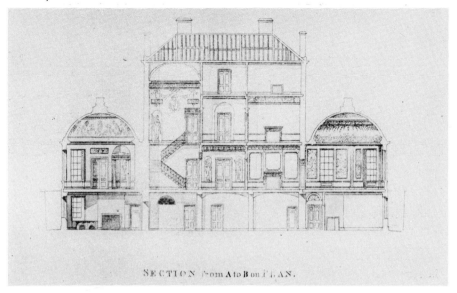

SECTION from A to B on PLAN.

Plate XV. Cross Section of a house.

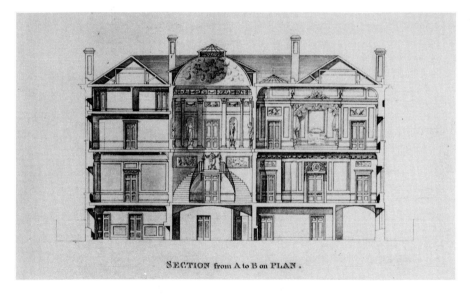

SECTION from A to B on PLAN.

Plate XVIII. Cross Section of a villa with raised alcove for the bed in the bedchamber.

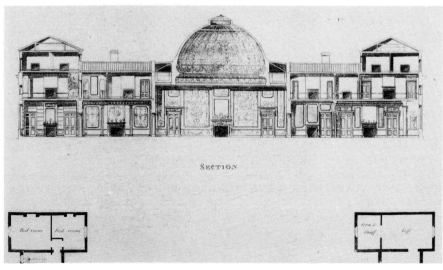

SECTION

Plate XX. Cross Section of a large villa.

490

Appendix

The Weale Re-Strikes, c.1833-1858

During the first two decades of the nineteenth century the 'French' or Rococo style of the mid-eighteenth century remained contemptuously out of fashion. However, in the later 1820s a revival of interest in the Louis Quatorze and Louis Quinze styles emerged in London, notably with the redecoration of Apsley House for the 1st Duke of Wellington from 1828. A London publisher soon capitalised on this interest; he was John Weale, of the 'Library of Architecture and Science', 59 High Holborn. Between about 1833 and 1858 he re-issued a considerable number of eighteenth century designs for furniture and interior decoration, but misrepresented their authorship by altering the signatures of many of the plates, particularly those by Thomas Johnson. Despite their titles, none of the publications included any plates from Chippendale's *Director.* They consisted of the following:-

c.1833. *Chippendale's Designs for Sconces, Chimney and Looking-Glass Frames in the Old French Style. Adapted for Carvers and Gilders, fashionable and ornamental Cabinet-Makers, Modellers &c. On eleven Plates. Prices 7s.* These were in fact plates 9, 12, 33, 34, and 36 from Thomas Johnson's *One Hundred and Fifty New Designs,* 1761, with Johnson's signature erased, and the plates from Lock's *Six Sconces* of 1744.

1834. *Chippendale's One Hundred and Thirty-Three Designs for Interior Decoration in the Old French and Antique Styles.* This comprised more of Thomas Johnson's plates from *One Hundred and Fifty New Designs,* again with Johnson's name erased, but now with that of Chippendale inserted.

1834. *Chippendale's Ornaments and Interior Decoration in the Old French Style, consisting of Hall, Glass and Picture Frames, Chimney-Pieces, Stands for China, Clock and Watch Cases, Girandoles, Brackets, Grates, Lanterns, Ornamental Furniture, and various Ornaments, for Carvers, Modellers &c &c &c.* This publication included plates for carver's work from Matthias Lock's *Six Sconces* (1744), Johnson's *One Hundred and Fifty New Designs* (again with Chippendale's name inserted) and various designs for chimney-pieces by Swan and Inigo Jones.

1835. *Old English and French Ornament, comprising 244 Designs on 105 Plates, of elaborate Engravings of Hall Glasses, Picture Frames, Chimney-Pieces, Stands for China, Clock and Watch-Cases, Girandoles, Brackets, Grates, Lanterns, Ornamental Furniture &c; by Chippendale, Inigo Jones, Lock and Pether.* A second edition was published in 1846 and a third, with additional plates, in 1858. The work included designs by Matthias Lock (*Six Sconces,* 1744, and *A New Book of Ornaments,* 1752), Thomas Johnson (*One Hundred and Fifty New Designs,* as used by Weale in previous publications, and *A New Book of Ornaments,* 1760), Abraham Swan and Inigo Jones (architectural designs), Thomas Pether (*A Book of Ornaments,* 1773), and

Matthias Darly (*Sixty Vases of English, French and Italian Masters,* 1767).

The original plates from Johnson's *New Book of Ornaments* of 1760 do not survive, with the exception of the title-page, but the Weale re-strikes have been included here for additional reference.

John Weale: Re-Strikes of Thomas Johnson, A Book of Ornaments, 1760.

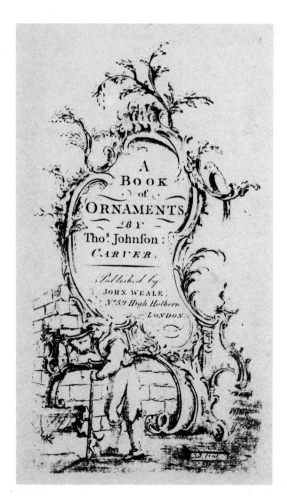

1. Title-page.

2. Mirror frame.

3. Chimney-piece.

5. Pier Tables.

4. Girandole.

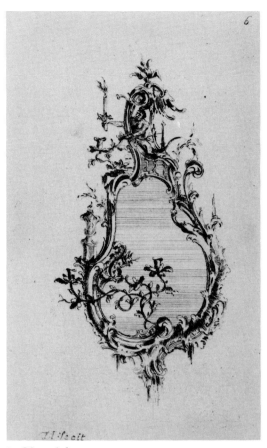

6. Girandole.

7. Mirror frame.

8. Candle stand.

Modern Reprints of Eighteenth Century Design Books

Adam, R. & J.	*The Works in Architecture,* Thézard, 1902, Tiranti 1929, 1939; (Edited with introduction by Robert Oresko), Academy Editions, London, and St. Martin's Press, New York, 1975.
Charles, R. (Comp.)	*The Compiler: Furniture and Decorations from the Best Authors,* London, 1878-9.
Chippendale, T.	*The Gentleman and Cabinet-Maker's Director,* 3rd Edition, 1763; Berlin 1900, New York, 1938, London, 1939, 1957, and New York, 1966.
Hepplewhite, A. & Co.	*The Cabinet-Maker and Upholsterer's Guide,* 3rd Edition, 1794; London (Batsford), 1897; New York (Dover Publications), 1969.
Ince, W., & Mayhew, J.	*The Universal System of Houshold Furniture,* 1762; London (Tiranti), 1960.
Sheraton, T.	*The Cabinet-Maker and Upholsterer's Drawing-Book,* 1793 with Appendix, Accompaniment and Additional Plates, London, (Batsford), 1895, New York (Dover Publications), 1972.
Society of Upholsterers	*Houshold Furniture in the Present Taste,* 2nd Edition, c.1765, Wakefield (EP Publishing), 1978.
The London Society of Cabinet Makers	*The Cabinet-Makers' London Book of Prices,* 2nd Edition, 1793, with Introductions by P. Kirkham and C. Gilbert, The Furniture History Society, Vol.XVIII, 1982.

Selective Bibliography of Modern Works

Barkley, H. (Ed.)	*Handbook to the Departments of Prints, Drawings, Photographs and Paintings,* Victoria and Albert Museum, London, 2nd Edition, 1982.
Beard, G.	*Decorative Plasterwork in Great Britain,* London, 1975.
Beard, G.	*The Work of Robert Adam,* Edinburgh, 1978.
Beard, G.	*Craftsmen and Interior Decoration in England 1660-1820,* Edinburgh, 1981.
Beard, G., & Gilbert, C. (Eds.)	*Dictionary of English Furniture Makers 1660-1840,* London, 1986.
Bell, J.M.	*Furniture Designs of George Hepplewhite,* London, 1910.
Bérard, A.	*Catalogue de Toutes les Estampes qui forment l'Oeuvre de Daniel Marot,* Brussels, 1865.
Bolton, T.	*The Architecture of Robert and James Adam,* 2 Vols., London, 1922.
Brackett, O.	*Thomas Chippendale: A Study of His Life, Work and Influence,* London, 1924.
Campbell, R.	*The London Tradesman,* 1747 (reprinted 1969).
Cescinsky, H.	*English Furniture of the Eighteenth Century,* 3 Vols., London, 1909-1911.
Coleridge, A.	*Chippendale Furniture,* London, 1968.
Collard, F.	*Regency Furniture,* Woodbridge, 1985.
Colvin, H.	*Biographical Dictionary of British Architects, 1600-1840.* London, 1978.

Edwards, R., & Macquoid, P.	*The Dictionary of English Furniture,* 3 Vols., Revised Edition, London, 1954, and reprinted Woodbridge, 1983.
Fastnedge, R.	*English Furniture Styles 1550-1830,* London, 1955.
Fastnedge, R.	*Shearer Furniture Designs,* London, 1962.
Fastnedge, R.	*Sheraton Furniture,* London, 1963.
Fitzgerald, D.	*The Norfolk House Music Room,* London, 1973.
Fleming, J.	*Robert Adam and His Circle,* London, 1962.
Fowler, J., & Cornforth, J.	*English Decoration in the Eighteenth Century,* London, 1974.
Gilbert, C.	*The Life and Work of Thomas Chippendale,* London, 1978.
Handford, S.A. (Transl.)	*The Fables of Aesop,* London, 1954.
Harris, E.	*The Furniture of Robert Adam,* London, 1963.
Harris, E.	*Thomas Wright's Arbours and Grottoes,* London, 1979.
Harris, E., & Savage, N.	*British Architectural Books and Writers 1556-1785,* Cambridge, 1990.
Harris, J.	*Sir William Chambers,* London, 1970.
Hayward, H.	*Thomas Johnson and the English Rococo,* London, 1964.
Hayward, H., & Kirkham, P.	*William and John Linnell,* London, 1980.
Hind, C. (Ed.)	*The Rococo in England: A Symposium,* London, 1986.
Jameson, C. (Comp.)	*The Potterton Pictorial Treasury of Drapery and Curtain Designs,* York, 1987.
Jervis, S.S.	*The Dictionary of Design and Designers,* London, 1984.
Jessen, P.	*Das Ornamentwerk des Daniel Marot,* Berlin, 1892.
Jourdain, M.	*The Work of William Kent,* London, 1948.
Jourdain, M.	*Regency Furniture,* London, 1949.
Jourdain, M., & Edwards, R.	*Georgian Cabinetmakers,* London, 1965.
Kimball, Fiske	*The Creation of the Rococo Style,* Philadelphia, 1943.
Lambert, S. (Ed.)	*Pattern and Design: Designs for the Decorative Arts 1480-1980,* London, 1983.
Lever, J.	*Architects' Designs for Furniture,* London, 1982.
Little, B.	*The Life and Work of James Gibbs,* London, 1955.
Monkhouse, C.P., & Michie, T.S.	*Furniture in Print: Pattern Books from the Redwood Library,* Rhode Island School of Design, 1989.
Musgrave, C.	*Adam, Hepplewhite and other Neo-Classical Furniture,* London, 1966.
Musgrave, C.	*Regency Furniture,* London, 1962.
Rykwert, J. & A.	*The Brothers Adam: The Men and the Style,* London, 1985.
Stratton, A.	*Interior Decoration of the XVIIIth Century from the Designs of Abraham Swan,* London, 1923.
Stroud, D.	*Henry Holland, His Life and Architecture,* London, 1966.
Taylor, L. (Intr.)	*The American Museum of Decorative Art and Design: Designs from the Cooper-Hewitt Collection, New York,* London, Victoria and Albert Museum, 1973.
Thornton, P.K.	*Seventeenth Century Interior Decoration in France, England and Holland,* London, 1978.
Thornton, P.K.	*Authentic Decor,* London, 1984.
Tomlin, M.	*Catalogue of Adam Period Furniture,* London, Victoria and Albert Museum, 1972.

Victoria & Albert Museum	*Rococo, Art and Design in Hogarth's England,* Catalogue of the Exhibition, London, 1984.
Ward-Jackson, P.	*English Furniture Designs of the Eighteenth Century,* London, 1958, republished 1984.
Ward-Jackson, P.	*Some Mainstreams and Tributaries in European Ornament from 1550 to 1750,* London, Victoria and Albert Museum, 1958.
Ward-Jackson, P.	*Rococo Ornament,* London, Victoria and Albert Museum, 1984.
Watkin, D.	*Athenian Stuart, Pioneer of the Greek Revival,* London, 1982.
Wilson, M.	*William Kent, Architect, Designer, Painter, Gardener,* London, 1984.

Articles

Beard, G.	'William Kent and the Cabinetmakers', *Burlington Magazine,* CXVII, 1975, p.867.
Beard, G.	'Babel's "A New Book of Ornaments", 1752', *Furniture History,* XI, 1975, pp.31-2.
de Bellaigue, G.	'The Furnishings of the Chinese Drawing Room, Carlton House', *Burlington Magazine,* CIX, No.774, September 1987, pp.518-28.
Fitz-Gerald, D.	'Chippendale's Place in the English Rococo', *Furniture History,* IV, 1968, pp.1-9.
Fitz-Gerald, D.	'Gravelot and his Influence on English Furniture', *Apollo,* August 1969, pp.140-7.
Friedman, T.F.	'James Gibbs' Designs for Domestic Furniture', *Leeds Art Calendar,* No.71, 1972, pp.19-25.
Friedman, T.F.	'Two Eighteenth-Century Catalogues of Ornamental Pattern-Books', *Furniture History,* Vol.XI, 1975, pp.66-75.
Gilbert, C.	'The Subscribers to Chippendale's *Director:* A Preliminary Analysis', *Furniture History,* X, 1974, pp.41-51.
Gilbert, C.	'The Early Furniture Designs of Matthias Darly', *Furniture History,* Vol.XI, 1975, pp.33-9.
Goodison, N.	'The Victoria and Albert Museum's Collection of Metal-Work Pattern Books', *Furniture History,* XI, 1975, pp.1-30.
Hall, I.	'Neo-Classical Elements in Chippendale's Designs for the *Director* of 1762', *Leeds Art Calendar,* 65, 1969, pp.14-19.
Hall, I.	'Some Sources of Chippendale's Inspiration', *Furniture History,* X, 1974, pp.38-40.
Hall, I.	'The Engravings of Thomas Chippendale, Jun. 1779', *Furniture History,* XI, 1975, pp.56-8.
Harris, E.	'The Architecture of Thomas Wright', *Country Life,* August 26, September 2 & 7, 1971.
Harris, E.	'Batty Langley; A Tutor to Freemasons, 1696-1751', *Burlington Magazine,* May 1977.
Hathaway, C.S.	'An Introduction to the Collection of Drawings', *Chronicle of the Museum for the Arts of Decoration of the Cooper-Union, II,* June 1952, 95-115.
Hayward, H.	'Thomas Johnson and Rococo Carving', *Connoisseur Year Book,* 1964, pp.94-100.

Hayward, H.	'Chinoiserie at Badminton: the Furniture of John and William Linnell', *Apollo*, August 1969, pp.134-9.
Hayward, H.	'The Drawings of John Linnell in the Victoria and Albert Museum', *Furniture History*, V, 1969, pp.1-118.
Hayward, H.	'A Unique Rococo Chair by Matthias Lock', *Apollo*, XCVII, October 1973, pp.268-71.
Hayward, H.	'Newly-discovered Designs by Thomas Johnson', *Furniture History*, XI, 1975, pp.40-2.
Hayward, H.	'Engraved Ornamental Designs after Francis Barlow', *Furniture History*, XI, 1975, pp.43-4.
Hayward, J.	'Furniture by Matthias Lock for Hinton House', *Connoisseur*, CXLVI, December 1960, pp.284-6.
Heckscher, M.	'Gideon Saint, An Eighteenth Century Carver and his Scrapbook', *Bulletin of the Metropolitan Museum of Art*, Vol.XXVII, 1969, pp.299-310.
Heckscher, M.	'Ince and Mayhew: Biographical Notes from New York', *Furniture History*, Vol.X, 1974, pp.61-7.
Heckscher, M.	'Eighteenth Century Rustic Furniture Designs', *Furniture History*, XI, 1975, pp.59-65.
Heckscher, M.	'Lock and Copland: A History of the Engraved Ornament', *Furniture History*, XV, 1979, pp.1-23.
Irvins, W.M.	'Eighteenth Century Furniture Drawings', *Bulletin of the Metropolitan Museum of Art*, XVI, Jan. 1921, pp.7-9.
Kimball, E., &	'The Creators of the Chippendale Style', *Metropolitan Museum Studies*, I, Part 2, 1929, pp.115-154, and II, Part 1, pp.41-59.
Kirkham, P.	'The Partnership of William Ince and John Mayhew', *Furniture History*, X, 1974, pp.56-60.
Redburn, S.	'The Furniture Designs of Thomas Malton 1775-9', *Furniture History*, XI, 1975, pp.48-52.
Reid, D.	'Thomas Pether's "Book of Ornaments"', *Furniture History*, XI, 1975, pp.46-7.
Rowan, A.	'Batty Langley's Gothic', *Studies in Memory of David Talbot Rice*, Edinburgh, 1975.
Smith, R.C.	'A Philadelphia Desk and Bookcase from Chippendale's *Director*', *Antiques*, CIII, no.1, pp.128-35.
Swain, M.	'Pictorial Chair Covers: Some Engraved Sources', *Furniture History*, XI, 1975, pp.76-82.
Udy, D.	'New Light on the Sources of English Neo-Classical Design', *Apollo*, March 1976, pp.202-7.
Watson, J.F.B.	'Holland and Daguerre: French Undercurrents in English Neo-Classical Furniture Design', *Apollo*, XCVI No.128, October 1972, pp.282-7
White, L.	'Furnishing your House and Garden in the 1760s', *Antique Collecting*, Vol.21, No.4, September 1986, pp.51-4.
White, L.	'The Furnishing of Interiors during the time of William and Mary', *Antiques*, CXXIV, No.6, December 1988, pp.1362-9.
Wills, G.	'Twelve New Designs of Frames by S.H., 1779', *Furniture History*, XI, 1975, pp.53-5.

Photographic Acknowledgements

The Antique Collectors' Club wishes to acknowledge the following for granting permission to reproduce material from their collections on the pages listed below:

Dr. Geoffrey Beard, FSA, pages 41, 61, 267, 329, 382; The British Library, 173, 303, 342, 427-8, 434-5, 466; The Trustees of the British Museum, 57, 434; City of Westminster Archives Dept., 29; The Cooper-Hewitt Museum, New York, 27; The Metropolitan Museum of Art, New York, 12, 342-3, 346, 377, 402; The Trustees of Sir John Soane's Museum, London, 52; The Trustees of the Victoria and Albert Museum, 15, 21, 23-5, 27-8, 36-8, 42, 44, 46, 48, 59, 99, 119, 130-1, 155, 168, 262, 265-6, 272, 302-3, 322, 325-8, 329, 343-5, 381-3, 391-2, 398-403, 414, 442, 453, 459, 464, 479; the remainder, private collections.

Index

Note: The titles of books from which plates are reproduced in this work are to be found on pages 30-32. Page numbers in bold type refer to biographical notes on designers.